CHARACTER ANALYSIS PAPERS

CULTURAL CONTEXT PAPERS

LITERARY ARGUMENT PAPERS

RESEARCH PAPERS

CRITICAL ANALYSIS PAPERS

Laurie G. Kirszner
University of the Sciences in Philadelphia

Stephen R. Mandell
Drexel University

Literature

READING ✱ REACTING ✱ WRITING

Seventh Edition

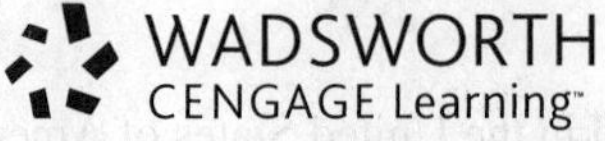

Australia • Brazil • Japan • Korea • Mexico • Singapore • Spain • United Kingdom • United States

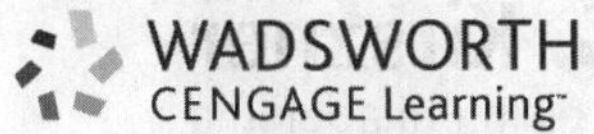

LITERATURE: Reading, Reacting, Writing, Seventh Edition
Kirszner/Mandell

Publisher: Michael Rosenberg

Development Editor: Karen Mauk

Assistant Editors: Rebekah Matthews and Megan Garvey

Marketing Manager: Christina Shea

Marketing Communications Manager: Elizabeth Rodio

Content Project Manager: Jessica Rasile

Senior Technology Project Manager: Cara Douglass-Graff

Senior Art Director: Cate Rickard Barr

Senior Print Buyer: Betsy Donaghey

Text Permissions Manager: Margaret Chamberlain-Gaston

Text Permissions Freelancer: Frederick T. Courtright

Image Manager: Don Schlotman

Image Researcher: Susan Van Etten

Production Service/Compositor/Text Designer: Nesbitt Graphics

Cover Designer: Cabbage Design Company

Cover Quilt Creator: Greta Vaught

Library of Congress Control Number: 2008938146

Student Edition:
ISBN-13: 978-0-495-90454-0
ISBN-10: 0-495-90454-6

Wadsworth
20 Channel Center Street
Boston, MA 02210
USA

Cengage Learning is a leading provider of customized learning solutions with office locations around the globe, including Singapore, the United Kingdom, Australia, Mexico, Brazil and Japan. Locate your local office at **international.cengage.com/region**

Cengage Learning products are represented in Canada by Nelson Education, Ltd.

For your course and learning solutions, visit **www.cengage.com.**

Purchase any of our products at your local college store or at our preferred online store **www.ichapters.com.**

Printed in the United States of America
1 2 3 4 5 6 13 12 11 10 09

3 Writing Special Kinds of Papers 43

Final panel from Lynda Barry's "Two Questions."

4 Thinking Critically about Your Writing 95

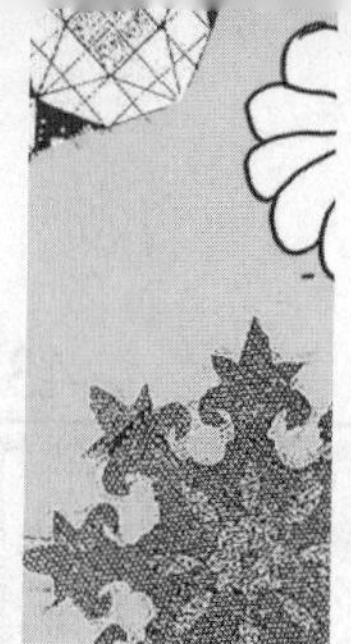

CONTENTS

Westminster Bridge, London (1886) by Claude Thomas Stanfield Moore.

Maya Angelou

PART 3 POETRY 793

PART 4 DRAMA 1233

BRIEF CONTENTS

Film still from the DVD version of Alice Walker's "Everyday Use."

Ernest Hemingway

ZZ Packer

Alberto Alvaro Ríos

12 Plot 219

Nadine Gordimer

13 Character 254

Jhumpa Lahiri

14 Setting 305

Sherman J. Alexie

15 Point of View 354

Edwidge Danticat

16 Style, Tone, and Language 417

Tim O'Brien

17 Symbol, Allegory, and Myth 487

Alice Walker

18 Theme 551

Michael Chabon

19 Joyce Carol Oates's "Where Are You Going, Where Have You Been?": A Casebook for Reading, Research, and Writing 614

Joyce Carol Oates

20 Fiction for Further Reading 660

Margaret Atwood

Online Novels, Novellas, and Stories

PART 3 POETRY 793

Nikki Giovanni

Robert Hayden

24 Voice 838

Janice Mirikitani

25 Word Choice, Word Order 875

Gwendolyn Brooks

26 Imagery 904

Octavio Paz

27 Figures of Speech 923

Martín Espada

Kay Ryan

Pat Mora

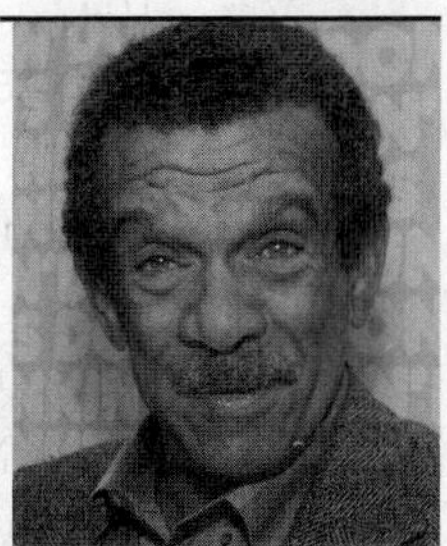
Derek Walcott

Judith Ortiz Cofer

Langston Hughes

Doris Lessing

Self Portrait with Monkey and Parrot (1938) by Frida Kahlo

Anton Chekhov

Zora Neale Hurston

Susan Glaspell

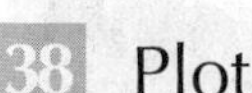

Lorraine Hansberry

39 Character 1457

David Auburn

40 Staging 1717

William Shakespeare

41 Theme 1849

42 Tennessee Williams's *The Glass Menagerie:* A Casebook for Reading, Research, and Writing 1957

A Using Literary Criticism in Your Writing 2045

AUTHORS REPRESENTED BY MULTIPLE WORKS

PREFACE

In Alice Walker's short story "Everyday Use" (p. 517), two sisters—one rural and traditional, one urban and modern—compete for possession of two quilts that have been in their family for years. At the end of the story, the narrator's description of the quilts suggests their significance—as a link between the old and the new, between what was and what is:

> One was in the Lone Star pattern. The other was Walk Around the Mountain. In both of them were scraps of dresses that Grandma Dee had worn fifty and more years ago. Bits and pieces of Grandpa Jarrell's Paisley shirts. And one teeny faded blue piece, about the size of a penny matchbox, that was from Great Grandpa Eza's uniform that he wore in the Civil War. (521–22)

In a sense, *Literature: Reading, Reacting, Writing* is a kind of literary quilt, one that places nontraditional works alongside classics, integrates the familiar with the unfamiliar, and invites students to see well-known works in new contexts. To convey this message, the publisher has commissioned a handmade quilt by textile artist Greta Vaught for each edition of the book. The quilt designed for this new edition uses contemporary as well as traditional quilting techniques to reflect our own increased focus on contemporary and emerging writers as well as on writers from diverse cultures and backgrounds.

The seventh edition of *Literature: Reading, Reacting, Writing,* like the previous editions, is designed to demystify the study of literature and to prepare students to explore the literary works collected here. Our goal in this edition remains what it has been from the start: to expand students' personal literary boundaries. To this end, we have fine-tuned the reading selections and expanded the pedagogical features that support the study of literature, acting in response to thoughtful comments from our reviewers and from our students. Having class-tested this book in our own literature classrooms, we have learned what kinds of selections and features best help our students to read, think about, understand, and write about literature in ways that make it meaningful to their lives in the twenty-first century.

To help instructors engage their students with literature and guide them in becoming better thinkers and writers, we have added new readings and enhanced key elements that have made *Literature: Reading, Reacting, Writing* a classroom success.

Unparalleled Writing Coverage

The first college literature anthology to address writing as a major component of the introductory literature course, *Literature: Reading, Reacting, Writing* begins with a comprehensive writing guide. **Part 1, "A Guide to Writing about Literature,"** consists of eight chapters that help students see writing about literature as a process of discovering, testing, and arguing ideas. In addition, comprehensive writing coverage is integrated throughout the book in the following features:

- **A general introduction to the writing process** Chapter 2, "Reading and Writing about Literature," explains and illustrates the process of planning, drafting, and revising essays about literary works, concluding with an exercise asking students to evaluate and compare two different student papers that examine the same three short stories.
- **Special treatment for writing about each genre** "Reading and Writing about Fiction" (Chapter 11), "Reading and Writing about Poetry" (Chapter 23), and "Reading and Writing about Drama" (Chapter 37) follow the writing process of students as they focus on works in each genre: Alberto Alvaro Ríos's short story "The Secret Lion" (p. 197); Seamus Heaney's poem "Digging" (p. 1040) and Robert Hayden's poem "Those Winter Sundays" (p. 1040); and Susan Glaspell's one-act play *Trifles* (p. 1319).
- **Two chapters on literary argument** Chapter 4, "Thinking Critically about Your Writing," and Chapter 5, "Writing Literary Arguments," help students to think critically about their writing and build cogent arguments about literary works. Chapter 5 takes students through the process of writing a literary argument and concludes with an annotated student paper.
- **Extensive research and documentation coverage** Tracing the research process of a student writing a short essay on Eudora Welty's "A Worn Path" (p. 568), Chapter 6, "Using Sources in Your Writing," includes extensive advice for conducting library and Internet research. Chapter 7, "Documenting Sources and Avoiding Plagiarism," includes strategies for avoiding plagiarism as well as the most up-to-date documentation and format guidelines from the Modern Language Association (including many examples of MLA-style citations for electronic sources).
- **Twenty model student papers** Because our own experience in the classroom has shown us that students often learn most easily from models, the text includes twenty model student papers (seven of which are new to the seventh edition) written in response to the kinds of topics that are frequently assigned in Introduction to Literature classes. Some of these model papers are source-based, and three are shown in multiple drafts, along with annotations and commentary. In addition, an annotated sample student answer to an essay exam appears in Chapter 8, "Writing Essay Exams about Literature."
- **New section on writing a response paper** Chapter 3, "Writing Special Kinds of Papers," includes a new section on writing a response paper. This important section contains two new student papers.
- **Casebooks for reading, research, and writing** Three casebooks—on Joyce Carol Oates, Langston Hughes, and Tennessee Williams—feature seminal works by each writer, accompanied by literary criticism, biographical essays, and other useful and interesting materials (interviews, photographs, popular magazine articles, and so on), including several visuals

that enhance each work's contextual coverage. The casebooks also include discussion questions as well as writing prompts for research papers. Students can use these casebooks to supplement their reading or as source material for a research project. (A model student paper in each casebook shows students how to use sources, including Internet sources, in their writing.) By gathering research materials in a convenient, accessible format, these casebooks offer students a controlled, self-contained introduction to source-based writing as well as all the materials they need to begin a research project.

- **Checklists** Most chapter introductions end with a checklist designed to help students measure their understanding of concepts introduced in the chapter. These checklists can also guide students as they generate, explore, focus, and organize ideas for writing about works of literature.
- **Writing suggestions** Imaginative suggestions for paper topics are included at the end of each chapter to spark students' interest and generate engaged writing.

 Fresh, Balanced Selections

The short stories, poems, and plays collected in this book represent a balance of old and new as well as a wide variety of nations and cultures and a full range of writing styles.

- **Extensive selection of fiction** The fiction selection includes not only perennial classics ("The Lottery," "A Rose for Emily," "The Cask of Amontillado") and stories we introduced to readers in the first edition, such as David Michael Kaplan's "Doe Season" and Charles Baxter's "Gryphon," but also a number of works never previously collected in a college literature anthology, such as Jonathan Safran Foer's "A Primer for the Punctuation of Heart Disease" and Amanda Holzer's "Love and Other Catastrophes: A Mix Tape." The twenty-seven new stories that appear in this edition include several popular contemporary works, such as Michael Chabon's "The Little Knife" and Louise Erdrich's "Sister Godzilla." In addition, a new **graphic fiction** selection begins each elements chapter, engaging students with contemporary, visual examples from the literary canon.
- **Blend of contemporary and classic poetry** The poetry section balances works by classic poets (such as Robert Frost, Emily Dickinson, and Langston Hughes) with works by more contemporary poets (such as Linda Pastan and Ted Kooser) and also introduces students to exciting twenty-first century works by poets such as A. E. Stallings, Kevin Young, and Kay Ryan. Now offering an even broader range of diverse works, the poetry section has been expanded with fifty-nine new works by poets such as Rhina Espaillat, Hart Crane, Richard Wilbur, Carmine Starnino, John Keats, Sor Juana Inés de la Cruz, Mary Jo Salter, Sharon Olds, Alan Shapiro, Walt Whitman, Edwin Muir, Julia Alvarez, John Ashbery, Elizabeth Bishop,

Thom Gunn, Doris Lessing, W. S. Merwin, Frank O'Hara, Dylan Thomas, Mona Van Duyn, and Charles Wright.

- **Varied selection of plays** The drama section juxtaposes classic selections—William Shakespeare's *Hamlet*, August Wilson's *Fences*, Milcha Sanchez-Scott's *The Cuban Swimmer*—with contemporary plays, such as David Auburn's *Proof* and David Ives's *Words, Words, Words*. Five plays are new to the seventh edition, including Wendy Wasserstein's *Workout* and Zora Neale Hurston's *Poker!*
- **Innovative "sampler" chapters** Chapter 10, "Fiction Sampler: The Short-Short"; an all-new Chapter 22, "Poetry Sampler: Song Lyrics," and the full-color "Poetry Sampler: Poetry and Art"; and Chapter 36, "Drama Sampler: Ten-Minute Plays," showcase representative selections from four popular literary subgenres, introducing students to the variety and diversity of literature with brief, accessible works.
- **Integrated fiction in film coverage** **"Fiction in Film"** sections throughout Part 2 help students to consider the challenges of adapting fiction to film. Appearing after five short stories in the text, this newly integrated material includes still photos taken from DVDs of the stories: John Updike's "A&P" (p. 259), Tillie Olsen's "I Stand Here Ironing" (p. 344), Alice Walker's "Everyday Use" (p. 517), Raymond Carver's "Cathedral" (p. 526), and Eudora Welty's "A Worn Path" (p. 568). The photos are followed by a series of questions that ask students to think critically about the decisions they would make if they were adapting each of the stories into a short film. (A marginal Film Series DVD icon highlights the "Fiction in Film" sections.)

Film Series DVD

- **Authors represented by multiple works** Many authors are represented in the book by more than one work, and in some cases, by more than one literary genre. A list of all such works follows the book's table of contents, giving students an opportunity to see at a glance how a particular writer explores different themes, styles, and genres.

Thorough Background Information

As we have learned in our classrooms over the years, part of helping students to demystify literature is helping them to understand the context in which the stories, poems, and plays were written. To achieve this goal, we continue to include contextual and background materials throughout the book in various forms:

- **Cultural context notes** A cultural context section follows each author headnote in fiction and drama, providing vital background about the social and historical climate in which the work was written.
- **Accessible discussion of literary history** "Origins of Modern Fiction" in Chapter 9, "Understanding Fiction"; "Origins of Modern Poetry" in Chapter 21, "Understanding Poetry"; and "Origins of Modern Drama" in Chapter 35, "Understanding Drama" are fully illustrated with visuals that trace each genre's development and bring the history of literature to life.

- **Literary history appendix** Appendix B, "Literary History: From Aristotle to the Present," gives students a brief historical overview of Western literary criticism.
- **Poets' biographies** Chapter 34, "Biographical Sketches of Selected Poets," includes biographical notes on sixty-five classic and contemporary poets whose work is featured in the text.

Other Pedagogical Features

A number of other pedagogical features appear throughout the text to prompt students to think critically about reading and to spark class discussions and energetic, thoughtful writing:

- **Introductory overview** Chapter 1, "Understanding Literature," presents an overview of some of the most important issues surrounding the study of literature, acquainting students with traditional literary themes as well as with the concept of the literary canon. The chapter also lays the groundwork for students' independent exploration of literary texts by discussing the processes of interpreting and evaluating literary texts, placing special emphasis on how readers' personal experiences affect meaning. Finally, the chapter examines the role of literary criticism and considers how critics' interpretations can help students expand their literary horizons.
- **Reading and Reacting questions** Reading and Reacting questions, including journal prompts, follow many selections throughout the text. These questions ask students to interpret and evaluate what they have read, sometimes encouraging them to make connections between the literary work being studied and other works in the text.
- **Critical Perspectives** Critical Perspective questions (included in most sets of Reading and Reacting questions) ask students to respond to analytical, interpretative, or evaluative comments that writers and critics have made about the work. This feature encourages students to apply their own critical thinking skills to literary criticism as well as to the work of literature itself.
- **Expanded literary criticism appendix** Appendix A, "Using Literary Criticism in Your Writing," explains and illustrates the key schools of literary criticism and shows how each can be applied to a typical student writing assignment inspired by a work in the text. This appendix now includes coverage of queer theory, postcolonial studies, and American multiculturalism.
- **Related Works** A Related Works section following the Reading and Reacting questions lists works linked (by theme, author, or genre) to the particular work under study. This feature encourages students to see connections between works by different writers, between works in different genres, or between two themes—connections they can explore in class discussion and in writing.

A Full Package of Supplementary Materials

To support students and instructors who use the seventh edition of *Literature: Reading, Reacting, Writing*, the following ancillary materials are available from Wadsworth:

- **Instructor's Resource Manual** A comprehensive instructor's manual provides all the materials necessary to support a variety of teaching styles. This resource includes discussion and activities for every short story, poem, and play in the anthology; a thematic table of contents; semester and quarter sample syllabi; and articles on the evolution of the literary canon and reader-response theory. In addition, many selections include a section called "Do Your Students Know?"—brief, entertaining notes that provide interesting, sometimes offbeat contextual information.
- **English21 for Literature: Literature in the Twenty-First Century** Now a fully online product (but also available in CD form), *English21 for Literature* has been thoroughly enhanced to provide students with a unique, interactive environment that can supplement the many aspects of the study of literature. In addition to sixty-eight stories, poems, and scenes from plays read aloud on the disk, *English21* offers thirty video clips of poetry readings, interviews, and selected scenes. Quizzes for every story, play, and element of literature help students review for class; they also complement the "brush-up" instruction on the elements of literature. Finally, Wadsworth's unique "explicator" technology actually guides students step by step through the process of close literary analysis while helping them prepare notes for an explication paper.
- **The Wadsworth Original Film Series in Literature** Original adaptations of Tillie Olsen's "I Stand Here Ironing," Alice Walker's "Everyday Use," Raymond Carver's "Cathedral," Eudora Welty's "A Worn Path," and John Updike's "A&P," accompanied by interviews with the authors, are available on DVD or VHS.
- **The Wadsworth Casebook Series for Reading, Research, and Writing** (previously titled *The Harcourt Brace Casebook Series in Literature*) Fourteen complete casebooks, each providing all the materials students need to jumpstart a literary research project, are available:

  Fiction

  Raymond Carver's "Cathedral"
  William Faulkner's "A Rose for Emily"
  Charlotte Perkins Gilman's "The Yellow Wallpaper"
  Flannery O'Connor's "A Good Man Is Hard to Find"
  Edgar Allan Poe's "The Cask of Amontillado"
  John Updike's "A&P"
  Eudora Welty's "A Worn Path"

  Poetry

  Emily Dickinson, A Collection of Poems

Robert Frost, A Collection of Poems
Langston Hughes, A Collection of Poems
Walt Whitman, A Collection of Poems

Drama

Athol Fugard's *Master Harold and the Boys*
Susan Glaspell's *Trifles*
William Shakespeare's *Hamlet*

- **Arden Shakespeare** Nine plays from the Arden Shakespeare Series can be packaged with *Literature: Reading, Reacting, Writing*, Seventh Edition, including *Hamlet, King Lear, A Midsummer Night's Dream, The Tempest, Othello*, and *Twelfth Night*.
- **Companion Website** This helpful companion site features author biographies for all of the authors represented in this volume, organized by chapter, and also alphabetically for the whole anthology. Each biography provides author birth and date dates, and also important contextual information about their lives.

Acknowledgments

From start to finish, this book has been a true collaboration, not only with each other, but also with our students and colleagues. We have worked hard on this book, and many people at Wadsworth have worked hard along with us.

We would like to begin by thanking our incredibly creative and talented Development Editor, Karen Mauk, who has always been there for us (and who we hope always will be there). She is one of a kind, and we are simply in awe of her abilities.

And we remain very grateful as well to our publisher, Michael Rosenberg, for coming back just in time.

Also at Wadsworth, we thank Jessica Rasile for guiding the manuscript through production, with skilled help from the team at Nesbitt Graphics, especially Susan McIntyre, copyeditor *extraordinaire*, Tom Conville, Project Manager, and Barbara Lipson, Production Coordinator.

We also very much appreciate the help we got on this project from William Coyle on the poetry selections and apparatus as well as the Instructor's Resource Manual; from Karen Mauk on updating the headnotes, footnotes, Cultural Contexts, and Critical Perspective questions; and from Jessie Swigger, Warren Hope, and John Hagen on the new student papers.

We would like to thank the following reviewers of the seventh edition: Walt Adams, Concordia Academy-Bloomington; Liz Ann Aguilar, San Antonio College; Nancy Alexander, Methodist University; Gwen Argersinger, Mesa Community College at Red Mountain; Gary Arms, Clarke College; Brenda Ayres, Liberty University; Clare Bannett, University of Alaska Southeast–Ketchikan; Richard Battaglia, California State-Northridge; Linda Belau, University of Texas-Pan American; Miriam Ben-Shalom, Milwaukee Area Technical College;

Dick Bentley, Western New England College; Mary Anne Bernal, San Antonio College; Susan Bernardin, State University of New York-Oneonta; Eric Birdsall, University of Akron; Sara Blake, El Camino College; Victor Bobb, Whitworth College; Robert Bonds, New England Institute of Art; Terri Bourus, Indiana University–Kokomo; Laura Brown, Central Alabama Community College; Rosemary Brown, Briarcliffe College; Thomas Cassidy, South Carolina University; Lisa Chong, Rider University; Howard Cox, Angelina College; Drucella Crutchfield, Southeastern University; Jenifer D'Elia, University of South Florida; Rebecca Daniel, Parkersburg South High School; Kristine Dassinger, Genesee Community College; Cynthia Denham, Snead State Community College; Joshua Dickinson, Jefferson Community College; Marcia Dinneen, Bridgewater State College; Reinhold Dooley, North Park University; Thomas Dow, Moraine Valley Community College; Douglas Dowland, The University of Iowa; Brenda Drewett, Columbia College; Kirk Duckers, Shawnee Heights High School; Stephanie Eason, Enterprise-Ozark Community College; Katherine Fargo, George Mason University; Lynn Fauth, Oxnard College; Gabrielle Fletcher, North Central Texas College; Joanne Gabel, Reading Area Community College; Joanne Galenski, Northwestern Regional School District No. 7; Corliss Gillman, Central Michigan University; Susan Goldstein, Mount Wachusett Community College; Angel Green, Universiity of Rhode Island; Audley Hall, NorthWest Arkansas Community College; Shirley Hanshaw, Mississippi State University; Kent Harrelson, Dalton State College; Jack Heller, Huntington University; Audrey Herbrich, Blinn College; Elizabeth Huergo, Montgomery College; Deborah Israel, University of Central Oklahoma; Suzi Jordan, Hillcrest High School; Douglas King, Gannon University; Elizabeth Kleinfeld, Red Rocks Community College; Susan M. Kornfeld, College of the Redwoods; Mark Kosinski, Gateway Community College; Joanne Krajeck, Canton South High School; Debbie LaCroix, Chemawa Indian High School; Mary Latela, Sacred Heart University; Cleve Latham, McCallie School; Jill Matthews, Pennsylvania Culinary Institute; Beatrice McKinsey, Grambling State University; Dani McLean, Fullerton College; David Merchant, Louisiana Tech University; James Merrill, Oxnard College; Tanya Millner-Harlee, Manchester Community College; Dorothy Minor, Tulsa Community College; Homer Mitchell, The State University of New York-Cortland; Deborah Montuori, Shippensburg University; Bryan Moore, Arkansas State University; Cleatta Morris, Louisiana State University-Shreveport; Sean Murphy, College of Lake County; Linda Nash, Dakota High School; Pam Nichols, Alma High School; Diana Nystedt, Palo Alto College; Karen O'Donnell, Finger Lakes Community College; James Papworth, Brigham Young University-Idaho; Robert Parker, Basic High School; Sarita Pereira, Heald College; Renee Pigeon, California State University-San Bernardino; David Rath, Biola University; Christina Rau, Briarcliffe College; Joan Reeves, Northeast Alabama Community College; Ruth Rhodes, College of the Redwoods; Shewanda Riley, Tarrant County College; Jill Rossiter, Lewis-Clark State College; Suzette Schlapkohl, Scottsdale Community College; Judith Schmitt, Macon State College; Patricia Sculley, Orange County Community College; Rick Seibert, Virginia College at Huntsville; Sue Serrano, Sierra College; Y. Sims, South Carolina State

University; Noel Sloboda, Penn State York; Michelle Somma, Westchester Community College; Ann Spurlock, Mississippi State University; Paul Stuewe, Green Mountain College; John Tagg, Palomar Community College; John Taylor, South Dakota State University; Patricia Teel, Victor Valley College; Pamela Turley, Community College of Allegheny County; Charles F. Warren, Salem State College; Frederick White, Slippery Rock University; Allison Whittenberg, Drexel University; Mary Wilcox, Notre Dame de Sion; Mike Williams, New Mexico Junior College; Rita Wisdom, Tarrant County College-Northeast; Randell Wolff, Bethel College; and Sarah Wood, Farmington High School.

We would also like to thank the following reviewers of the sixth edition: Joy L. Blom, Montclair State University; Terri Bourus, Indiana University–Kokomo; Jennifer Brown, University of Hartford; Sheryl Chisamore, State University of New York–Ulster; Wayne Christensen, Florida Memorial College; Kirk Colvin, American River College; Susan Cornett, St. Petersburg College; Joseph A. Correro Jr., Delta State University; Carl C. Curtis III, Liberty University; Patricia A. Daskivich, Los Angeles Harbor College; Tammy DiBenedetto, Riverside Community College; Josh Dickinson, Jefferson Community College (SUNY); Michael M. Dinielli, Chaffey College; Ellen Gross, Central Virginia Community College; Susan Isaac, Georgia Military College; Deborah Israel, University of Central Oklahoma; Susan A. Johnson, Sierra College; Jane Anderson Jones, Manatee Community College–Venice; Jason B. Jones, Central Connecticut State University; Kerrie Kawasaki-Hull, Ohlone College; Kevin Kelly, Andover College; James Kirkpatrick, Central Piedmont Community College; Judith Kleck, Central Washington University; Mark Kosinski, Manchester Community College; Mary Kramer, University of Massachusetts–Lowell; David Kucher, Westchester Community College; Carol Kushner, Dutchess Community College; Noreen Lace, California State University–Northridge; Paul Long, Baltimore City Community College; Martha B. Macdonald, York Technical College; Deanna Mascle, Morehead State University; Robert Mitchell, Ohlone College; Deborah Montuori, Shippensburg University; Robbi Muckenfuss, Durham Technical Community College; Michail W. Mulvey, Central Connecticut State University; L. J. Nutter, Liberty University; Nancy K. Pennell, McPherson College; Renee Pigeon, California State University–San Bernardino; David Schwankle, Riverside Community College–Norco; Shant Shahoian, Oxnard College; Andy Solomon, University of Tampa; Donald R. Stinson, Northern Oklahoma College; Carolyn Stonewell, Middlesex Community College; Gary Thomas, University of North Carolina–Charlotte; Regina Williams, Arkansas State University–Heber Springs; and David Winsper, Springfield Technical Community College.

We would also like to thank the following reviewers of the fifth edition: Jane Anderson Jones, Manatee Community College–Venice; Lee Barnes, Community College of Southern Nevada; Robin Calitri, Merced College; Janet Eber, County College of Morris; Charles Fisher, Aims Community College; Maryanne Garbowsky, County College of Morris; Clinton Gardner, Salt Lake City Community College; Diana Gatz, St. Petersburg College; Dawn Marie Hershberger, University of Indianapolis; Isara Kelley Tyson, Manatee Community College; Andrew Kozma, University of Florida; Bernard Morris, Modesto College; David Neff,

University of Alabama–Huntsville; Diana Nystedt, Palo Alto College; Roger Platizky, Austin College; Angela M. Rhoe, Prince George's Community College; Mark Rollins, University of Ohio; Christine Roth, University of Wisconsin; David A. Salomon, Black Hills State University; Ann Spurlock, Mississippi State University; and Pam Sutton, Union University.

We continue to be grateful to the reviewers of the fourth edition: Crystal V. Bacon, Glouchester County College; Gwen Barklay–Toy, North Carolina State University; Eric Birdsall, University of Akron; John Doyle, Quinnipiac College; David Fear, Valencia Community College; Elizabeth Keats Flores, College of Lake Country; Linda Gruber, Kishwaukee College; Lynn Hildenbrand, Chesapeake College; Teresa Kennedy, Mary Washington College; Michael Kraus, Marian College of Fond du Lac; Teri Maddox, Jackson State Community College; Judith P. Moray, Moraine Valley Community College; Mary Beth Namm, North Carolina State University; Rodney D. Newton, Central Texas College; Monte Prater, Tulsa Community College–Northeast; Gail Rung, Black Hawk College; Robert M. Temple, Manatee Community College; Maria W. Warren, University of West Florida; Donnie Yielding, Central Texas College; and Laura Mandell Zaidman, University of South Carolina–Sumter.

We would also like to thank all the reviewers who made valuable contributions to the third edition: Ben Accardi, University of Kansas; Thomas Bailey, Western Michigan University; John Bails, University of Sioux Falls; Leigh Boyd, Temple Junior College; Cathy Cowan, Cabrillo College; Pat Cowart, Frostburg State University; Kitty Dean, Nassau Community College; Jo Devine, University of Alaska–Southeast; Jack Doyle, University of South Carolina–Sumter; Lynn Fauth, Oxnard College; David Fear, Valencia Community College; Mary Fleming, Jackson State Community College; Ann Fogg, University of Maine; Wayne Gilbert, Community College of Aurora; Shain Graham, Orange Coast College; Linda Gruber, Kishwaukee College; Chris Hacskaylo, University of Alaska–Ketchikan; Richard Hascal, Contra Costa College; Gwen Hauk, Temple Junior College; Michael Herzog, Gonzaga University; Andrew Kelly, Jackson State Community College; Benna Kime, Jackson State Community College; Army Sparks Kolker, University of Kansas; Michael Kraus, Marian College of Fond du Lac; Heidi Ledett, Ulster County Community College; Teri Maddox, Jackson State Community College; Jeanne Mauzy, Valencia Community College; Fred Milley, Anderson University; Robert Milliken, University of Southern Maine; Andrew Moody, University of Kansas; Paul Perry, Palo Alto Community College; Angela Rapkin, Manatee Community College; Jean Reynolds, Polk Community College; Ellen Robbins, Ulster County Community College; Paul Rogauls, Plymouth State College; Neil Sebacher, Valencia Community College; Larry Severeid, College of Eastern Utah; Sharon Small, Des Moines Area Community College; Virginia Streamer, Dundalk Community College; Robert Temple, Manatee Community College; Margie Whelan, Mt. San Antonio College; Mike White, Odessa College; Rebecca Yancey, Jackson State Community College; Donnie Yielding, Central Texas College; and Martha Zamorano, Miami Dade–Kendall.

Reviewers of the second edition included Deborah Barberousse, Horry-Georgetown Technical College; Bob Mayberry, University of Nevada–Las Vegas; Shireen Carroll, University of Miami; Stephen Wright, Seminole Community College; Robert Dees, Orange Coast College; Larry Gray, Southeastern Louisiana University; Nancy Rayl, Cypress College; James Clemmer, Austin Peay State University; Roberta Kramer, Nassau Community College.

Reviewers of the first edition included Anne Agee, Anne Arundel Community College; Lucien Agosta, California State University–Sacramento; Diana Austin, University of New Brunswick; Judith Bechtel; Northern Kentucky University; Laureen Belmont, North Idaho College; Vivian Brown, Laredo Junior College; Rebecca Butler, Dalton Junior College; Susan Coffey, Central Virginia Community College; Douglas Crowell, Texas Tech University; Shirley Ann Curtis, Polk Community College; Kitty Dean, Nassau Community College; Robert Dees, Orange Coast College; Joyce Dempsey, Arkansas Tech University; Mindy Doyle, Orange County Community College; James Egan, University of Akron; Susan Fenyves, University of North Carolina–Charlotte; Marvin Garrett, University of Cincinnati; Ann Gebhard, State University of New York–Cortland; Emma Givaltney, Arkansas Tech University; Corrinne Hales, California State University–Fresno; Gary Hall, North Harris County College; Iris Hart, Santa Fe Community College; James Helvey, Davidson County Community College; Chris Henson, California State University–Fresno; Gloria Hochstein, University of Wisconsin–Eau Claire; Angela Ingram, Southwest Texas State University; John Iorio, University of South Florida; George Ives, North Idaho College; Lavinia Jennings, University of North Carolina–Chapel Hill; Judy Kidd, North Carolina State University; Leonard Leff, Oklahoma State University; Michael Matthews, Tarrant County Junior College–Northeast; Craig McLuckie, Okanagan College; Candy Meier, Des Moines Area Community College; Judith Michna, DeKalb College–North; Christopher O'Hearn, Los Angeles Harbor College; James O'Neil, Edison Community College; Melissa Pennell, University of Lowell; Sam Phillips, Gaston College; Robbie Pinter, Belmont College; Joseph Sternberg, Harper College; Kathleen Tickner, Brevard Community College; Betty Wells, Central Virginia Community College; Susan Yaeger, Monroe Business Institute.

We would also like to thank our families—Mark, Adam, and Rebecca Kirszner and Demi, David, and Sarah Mandell—for being there when we needed them. And finally, we each thank the person on the other side of the ampersand for making our collaboration work one more time.

1 A GUIDE TO WRITING ABOUT LITERATURE

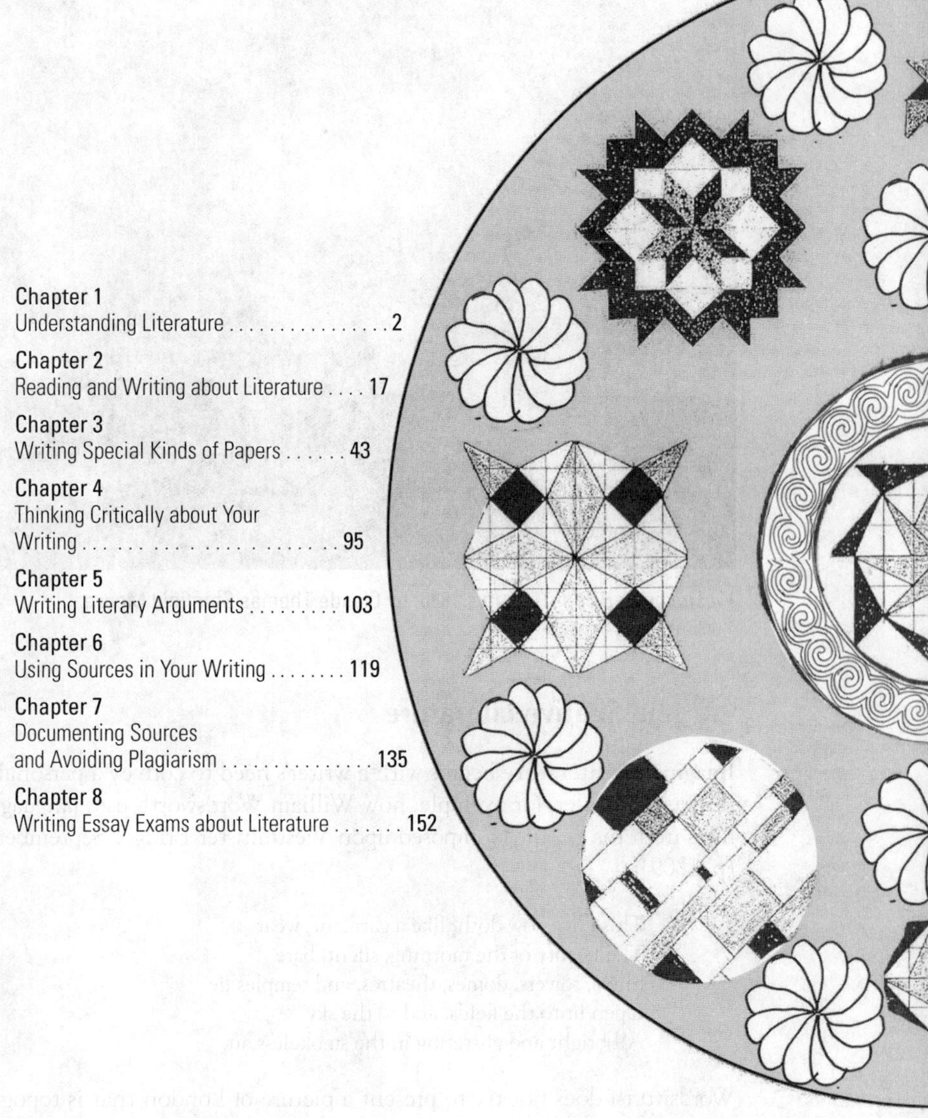

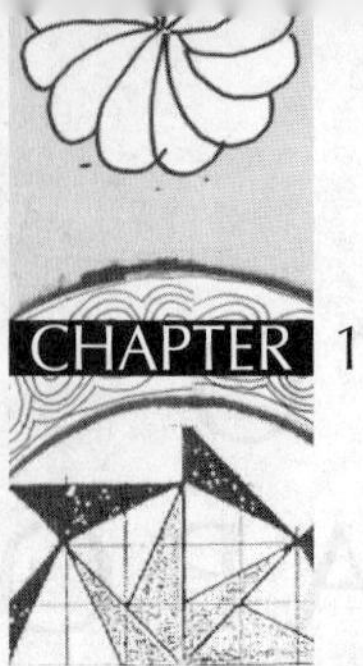

CHAPTER 1

UNDERSTANDING LITERATURE

Westminster Bridge, London (1886) by Claude Thomas Stanfield Moore.
Source: ©Fine Art Photographic Library/Corbis

Imaginative Literature

Imaginative literature begins with a writer's need to convey a personal vision to readers. Consider, for example, how William Wordsworth uses language in these lines from his poem "Composed upon Westminster Bridge, September 3, 1802" (p. 1209):

> This City now doth, like a garment, wear
> The beauty of the morning; silent, bare,
> Ships, towers, domes, theatres, and temples lie
> Open unto the fields, and to the sky;
> All bright and glittering in the smokeless air.

Wordsworth does not try to present a picture of London that is topographically or sociologically accurate. Instead, by comparing the city at dawn to a person wearing a beautiful garment, he creates a striking picture that has its own kind of truth. By using a vivid, original comparison, the poet is able to suggest the oneness of the city, nature, and himself.

Even when writers of imaginative literature use factual material—historical documents, newspaper stories, or personal experience, for example—their primary purpose is to present their unique view of experience, one that has significance beyond the moment. (As the poet Ezra Pound said, "Literature is the news that *stays* news.") To convey their views of experience, these writers often manipulate facts—changing dates, creating characters and events, and inventing dialogue. For example, when Herman Melville wrote his nineteenth-century novella *Benito Cereno,* he drew many of his facts from an account of an actual slave revolt. In his story, he reproduces court records and uses plot details from this primary source, but he leaves out some incidents, and he adds material of his own. The result is an original work of literature. Wanting to do more than retell the original story, Melville used the factual material as "a skeleton of actual reality" on which he built a story that attacks the institution of slavery and examines the nature of truth.

Imaginative literature is more likely than other types of writing to include words chosen not only because they communicate the writer's ideas, but also because they are memorable. Using vivid imagery and evocative comparisons, writers of imaginative literature often stretch language to its limits. By relying on the multiple connotations of words and images, a work of imaginative literature encourages readers to see the possibilities of language and to move beyond the factual details of an event.

Even though imaginative literature can be divided into types called **genres**—fiction, poetry, and drama—the nature of literary genres varies from culture to culture. In fact, some literary forms that Western readers take for granted are alien to other literary traditions. The sonnet, though fairly common in the West, is not a conventional literary form in Chinese or Arabic poetry. Similarly, the most popular theatrical entertainment in Japan since the mid-seventeenth century, the Kabuki play, has no counterpart in the West. (In a Kabuki play, which includes stories, scenes, dances, music, acrobatics, and elaborate costumes and stage settings, all of the actors are men, some of whom play the parts of females. Many Kabuki plays have little plot and seem to be primarily concerned with spectacle. One feature of this form of drama is a walkway that extends from the stage through the audience to the back of the theater.)

Conventions of narrative organization and character development can also vary considerably from culture to culture, especially in literature derived from oral traditions. For example, narrative organization in some Native American stories (and, even more commonly, in some African stories) can be very different from what contemporary Western readers are accustomed to. Events may be arranged spatially instead of chronologically: first a story presents all the events that happened in one place, then it presents everything that happened in another location, and so on. Character development is also much less important in some traditional African and Native American stories than it is in modern short fiction. In fact, a character's name, description, and personality can change dramatically (and without warning) during the course of a story.

Despite such differences, the imaginative literature of all cultures has similar effects on readers: memorable characters, vivid descriptions, imaginative use of language, and compelling plots can fascinate and delight. Literature can take readers where they have never been before and, in so doing, can create a sense of adventure and wonder.

At another level, however, readers can find more than just pleasure or escape in literature. Beyond transporting readers out of their lives and times, literature can enable readers to see their lives and times more clearly. Whether a work of imaginative literature depicts a young girl as she experiences the disillusionment of adulthood for the first time, as in David Michael Kaplan's "Doe Season" (p. 577), or examines the effect of discrimination on a black African who is looking for an apartment, as in Wole Soyinka's "Telephone Conversation" (p. 7), it can help readers to understand their own experiences and the experiences of others. In this sense, literature offers readers increased insight into the human condition. As the Chilean poet Pablo Neruda said, works of imaginative literature fulfill "the most ancient rites of our conscience in the awareness of being human and of believing in a common destiny."

Conventional Themes

The **theme** of a work of literature is its central or dominant idea. This idea is seldom stated explicitly. Instead, it is conveyed through the selection and arrangement of details; through the emphasis of certain words, events, or images; and through the actions and reactions of characters.

Although one central theme may dominate a literary work, many works explore a number of different themes or ideas. For example, the central theme of Mark Twain's *Adventures of Huckleberry Finn* might be the idea that an individual's innate sense of right and wrong is superior to society's artificial and sometimes unnatural values. The main character, Huck, gains a growing awareness of this idea by witnessing feuds, duels, and all manner of human folly. As a result, he makes a decision to help his friend Jim escape from slavery despite the fact that society, as well as his own conscience, condemns this action. However, *Huckleberry Finn* also examines other themes. Throughout his novel, Twain criticizes many of the ideas that prevailed in the pre–Civil War South, such as the racism and religious hypocrisy that pervaded the towns along the Mississippi.

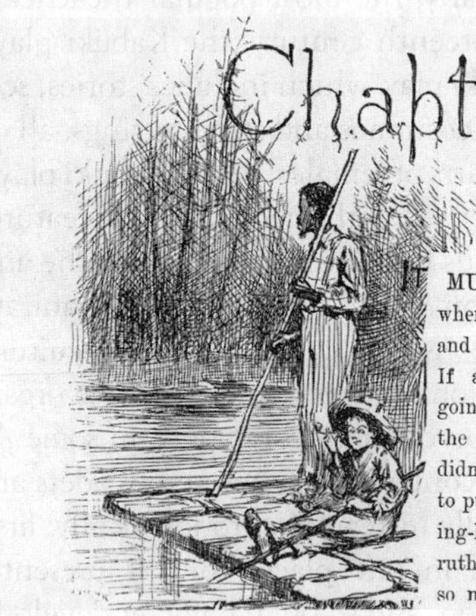

On the Raft, illustration from Mark Twain's *Adventures of Huckleberry Finn.*
Source: ©Corbis

Although a literary work can explore any theme, certain themes have recurred so frequently over the years that they have become **conventions.** One conventional theme—a character's loss of innocence—appears in the biblical story of Adam and Eve and later finds its way into works such as Nathaniel Hawthorne's 1835 short story "Young Goodman Brown" (p. 540) and James Joyce's 1914 short story "Araby" (p. 434). Another conventional theme—the conflict between an individual's values and the values of society—is examined in the ancient Greek play *Antigone* by Sophocles (p. 1863). Almost two thousand years later, Norwegian playwright Henrik Ibsen deals with the same theme in *A Doll House* (p. 1402).

Other conventional themes examined in literary works include the individual's quest for spiritual enlightenment, the *carpe diem* ("seize the day") philosophy, the making of the artist, the nostalgia for a vanished past, the disillusionment of adulthood, the pain of love, the struggle of women for equality, the conflict between parents and children, the clash between civilization and the wilderness, the evils of unchecked ambition, the inevitability of fate, the impact of the past on the present, the conflict between human beings and machines, and the tension between the ideal and the actual realms of experience.

Many cultures explore similar themes, but writers from different cultures may develop these themes differently. A culture's history, a particular region's geography, or a country's social structure can suggest unique ways of developing conventional themes. In addition, the assumptions, concerns, values, ideals, and beliefs of a particular country or society—or of a particular group within that society—can help to determine the themes writers choose to explore and the manner in which they do so.

In American literature, for instance, familiar themes include the loss of innocence, rites of passage, childhood epiphanies, and the ability (or inability) to form relationships. American writers of color may use these themes to express their frustration with racism or to celebrate their cultural identities. For example, the theme of loss of innocence may be presented as a first encounter with racial prejudice; a conflict between the individual and society may be presented as a conflict between a minority view and the values of the dominant group; and the theme of failure or aborted relationships may be explored in a work about cultural misunderstandings.

Finally, modern works of literature sometimes treat conventional themes in new ways. For example, in *1984* George Orwell explores the negative consequences of unchecked power by creating a nightmare world in which the government controls and dehumanizes a population. Even though Orwell's novel is set in an imaginary future (it was written in 1948), its theme echoes ideas frequently examined in the plays of both Sophocles and Shakespeare.

The Literary Canon

Originally, the term **canon** referred to the accepted list of books that made up the Christian Bible. More recently, the term **literary canon** has come to denote a group of works generally agreed upon by writers, teachers, and critics to be worth reading and studying. Over the years, as standards have changed, the definition of "good" literature has also changed, and the literary canon has been modified accordingly. For example, at various times, critics have characterized Shakespeare's plays as mundane, immoral, commonplace, and brilliant. The eighteenth-century critic Samuel Johnson said of Shakespeare that "in his comick scenes he is seldom very successful" and in tragedy "his performance seems constantly to be worse, as his labor is more." Many people find it difficult to believe that a writer whose name today is synonymous with great literature could ever have been judged so harshly. Like all aesthetic works, however, the plays of Shakespeare affect individuals in different periods of history and in different societies in different ways.

Some educators and literary scholars believe that the traditional literary canon, like a restricted club, arbitrarily admits some authors and excludes others. This fact is borne out, they say, by an examination of the literature curriculum that until recently was standard at many North American universities. This curriculum typically began with Homer, Plato, Dante, and Chaucer, progressed to Shakespeare, Milton, the eighteenth-century novel, the Romantics, and the Victorians, and ended with some of the "classics" of modern British and American literature. Most of the authors of these works are white and male, and their writing for the most part reflects Western values.

Missing from the literature courses in North American universities for many years were South American, African, and Asian writers. Students of American literature were not encouraged to consider the perspectives of women, of gay and lesbian writers, or of Latinos, Native Americans, or other ethnic or racial groups. During the past four decades, however, most universities have expanded the traditional canon by including more works by women, people of color, and writers from a variety of cultures. These additional works, studied alongside those representing the traditional canon, have opened up the curriculum and redefined the standards by which literature is judged.

One example of a literary work that challenged the traditional canon is "All about Suicide" by Luisa Valenzuela, an Argentinean writer. Currently, she is one of the most widely translated South American writers. This brief, shocking story is part of a large and growing body of literature from around the world that purposely violates our standard literary expectations to make its point—in this case, a point about the political realities of Argentina in the 1960s.

LUISA VALENZUELA (1938–)

All about Suicide (1967)

Translated by Helen Lane

Ismael grabbed the gun and slowly rubbed it across his face. Then he pulled the trigger and there was a shot. Bang. One more person dead in the city. It's getting to be a vice. First he grabbed the revolver that was in a desk drawer, rubbed it gently across his face, put it to his temple, and pulled the trigger. Without saying a word. Bang. Dead.

Let's recapitulate: the office is grand, fit for a minister. The desk is ministerial too, and covered with a glass that must have reflected the scene, the shock. Ismael knew where the gun was, he'd hidden it there himself. So he didn't lose any time, all he had to do was open the right-hand drawer and stick his hand in. Then he got a good hold on it and rubbed it over his face with a certain pleasure before putting it to his temple and pulling the trigger. It was something almost sensual and quite unexpected. He hadn't even had time to think about it. A trivial gesture, and the gun had fired.

There's something missing: Ismael in the bar with a glass in his hand thinking over his future act and its possible consequences.

We must go back farther if we want to get at the truth: Ismael in the cradle crying because his diapers are dirty and nobody is changing him.

Not that far.

Ismael in the first grade fighting with a classmate who'll one day become a minister, his friend, a traitor.

No, Ismael in the ministry without being able to tell what he knew, forced to be silent. Ismael in the bar with the glass (his third) in his hand, and the irrevocable decision: better death.

Ismael pushing the revolving door at the entrance to the building, pushing the swinging door leading to the office section, saying good morning to the guard, opening the door of his office. Once in his office, seven steps to his desk. Terror, the act of opening the drawer, taking out the revolver, and rubbing it across his face, almost a single gesture and very quick. The act of putting it to his temple and pulling the trigger—another act, immediately following the previous one. Bang. Dead. And Ismael coming out of his office (the other man's office, the minister's) almost relieved, even though he can predict what awaits him.

* * *

The Nigerian poet and playwright Wole Soyinka is another writer whose works were not part of the traditional Western canon—until, in 1986, he won the Nobel Prize in Literature. The subject of the following poem may not seem "relevant" to European audiences, and the language ("pillar-box," "omnibus") may not be familiar to Americans. Still, as a reading of the poem demonstrates, Soyinka's work makes a compelling plea for individual rights and self-determination—a theme that transcends the boundaries of time and place.

WOLE SOYINKA (1934–)

Telephone Conversation (1962)

The price seemed reasonable, location
Indifferent. The landlady swore she lived
Off premises. Nothing remained
But self-confession. "Madam," I warned
"I hate a wasted journey—I am—African."
Silence. Silenced transmission of

Pressurized good-breeding. Voice, when it came,
Lip-stick coated, long gold-rolled
Cigarette-holder pipped. Caught I was, foully.
"HOW DARK?" . . . I had not misheard . . .
"ARE YOU LIGHT
OR VERY DARK?" Button B. Button A. Stench
Of rancid breath of public-hide-and-speak.
Red booth. Red pillar-box. Red double-tiered
Omnibus squelching tar. It *was* real! Shamed
By ill-mannered silence, surrender
Pushed dumbfoundment to beg simplification.
Considerate she was, varying the emphasis—
"ARE YOU DARK? OR VERY LIGHT?" Revelation came.
"You mean—like plain or milk chocolate?"
Her assent was clinical, crushing in its light,
Impersonality. Rapidly, wave-length adjusted,
I chose, "West African sepia"—and as an afterthought,
"Down in my passport." Silence for spectroscopic
Flight of fancy, till truthfulness clanged her accent
Hard on the mouthpiece. "WHAT'S THAT?" conceding
"DON'T KNOW WHAT THAT IS." "Like brunette."
"THAT'S DARK, ISN'T IT?" "Not altogether.
Facially, I am brunette, but madam, you should see
The rest of me. Palm of my hand, soles of my feet
Are a peroxide blond. Friction, caused—
Foolishly madam—by sitting down, has turned
My bottom raven black—One moment madam!"—sensing
Her receiver rearing on the thunder clap
About my ears—"Madam," I pleaded, "Wouldn't you rather
See for yourself?"

* * *

Certainly canon revision is not without problems—for example, the possibility of including a work more for political or sociological reasons than for its literary merit. Nevertheless, if the debate about the literary canon has accomplished anything, it has revealed that the canon is not fixed and that many works formerly excluded—African-American slave narratives and eighteenth-century women's diaries, for example—deserve to be read.

Interpreting Literature

When you **interpret** a literary work, you explore its possible meanings. One commonly held idea about reading a literary work is that its meaning lies buried somewhere within it, waiting to be unearthed. This reasoning suggests that a clever reader has only to discover the author's intent to find out what a story or poem means, and that the one actual meaning of a work is hidden "between the lines," unaffected by a reader's experiences or interpretations. More recently, however, a different model of the reading process—one that takes into consideration the reader as well as the work he or she is interpreting—has emerged.

Many contemporary critics see the reading process as **interactive.** In other words, meaning is created through the reader's interaction with a text. Thus, the meaning of a particular work comes alive in the imagination of an individual reader, and no reader can determine a work's meaning without considering his or her own reaction to the text. Meaning, therefore, is created partly by what is supplied by a work and partly by what is supplied by the reader.

The most obvious thing a work supplies is **facts,** the information that enables a reader to follow the plot of a story, the action of a play, or the development of a poem. The work itself will provide factual details about the setting; about the characters' names, ages, and appearances; about the sequence of events; and about the emotions and attitudes of a poem's speaker, a story's narrator, or the characters in a play or story. This factual information cannot be ignored: if a play's stage directions identify its setting as nineteenth-century Norway or the forest of Arden, that is where the play is set.

In addition to facts, a work also conveys the social, political, class, and gender **attitudes** of the writer. Thus, a work may have an overt feminist or working-class bias or a subtle (or obvious) political agenda; it may confirm or challenge contemporary attitudes; it may communicate a writer's nostalgia for a vanished past or outrage at a corrupt present; it may take an elitist, distant view of characters and events or present a sympathetic perspective. A reader's understanding of these attitudes will contribute to his or her interpretation of the work.

Finally, a work also includes **assumptions** about literary conventions. A poet, for example, may have definite ideas about whether a poem should be rhymed or unrhymed or about whether a particular subject is appropriate or inappropriate for poetic treatment. Therefore, a knowledge of the literary conventions of a particular period or the preferences of a particular writer can provide a starting point for your interpretation of literature.

As a reader, you bring to a work your own **personal perspectives.** Your experiences, your beliefs, your ideas about the issues discussed in the work, and your assumptions about literature color your interpretations. In fact, nearly every literary work has somewhat different meanings for different people, depending on their age, gender, nationality, political and religious beliefs, ethnic background, social and economic class, education, knowledge, and personal experiences. Depending on your religious beliefs, for instance, you can react to a passage from the Old Testament as literal truth, symbolic truth, or fiction. Depending on your race, where you live, your biases, and the nature of your experience, a story about racial discrimination can strike you as accurate and realistic, exaggerated and unrealistic, or understated and restrained.

In a sense, then, the process of determining meaning is like a conversation, one in which both you and the text have a voice. Sometimes, by clearly dictating the terms of the discussion, the text determines the direction of the conversation;

at other times, by using your knowledge and experience to interpret the text, you dominate. Thus, because every reading of a literary work is actually an interpretation, it is a mistake to look for a single "correct" reading.

The 1923 poem "Stopping by Woods on a Snowy Evening" (p. 1159), by the American poet Robert Frost, illustrates how a single work can have more than one interpretation. Readers may interpret the poem as being about the inevitability of death, as suggesting that the poet is tired or world weary, or as making a comment about duty and the need to persevere or about the conflicting pulls of life and art. Beyond these possibilities, readers' own associations of snow with quiet and sadness

Whose woods these are I think I know.

Opening pages from Susan Jeffers's illustrated children's book *Stopping by Woods on a Snowy Evening* (1978).

Source: Courtesy, Susan Van Etten

could lead them to define the mood of the poem as sorrowful or melancholy. Information about Robert Frost's life or his ideas about poetry could add to readers' understanding of the poem, and they might even develop ideas about the poem that are quite different from the poet's. In fact, on several occasions, Frost himself gave strikingly different—even contradictory—interpretations of "Stopping by Woods on a Snowy Evening," sometimes insisting that the poem had no hidden meaning and at other times saying that it required a good deal of explication. (Literary critics also disagree about its meaning.) When reading a work of literature, then, keep in mind that the meaning of the text is not fixed. Your best strategy is to open yourself up to the text's many possibilities and explore the full range of your responses.

Although no single reading of a literary work is "correct," some readings are more defensible than others. Like a scientific theory, a literary interpretation must have a basis in fact, and the text supplies the facts against which your interpretation should be judged. For example, after you read Shirley Jackson's "The Lottery" (p. 509), a 1948 short story in which a randomly chosen victim is stoned to death by her neighbors, it would be reasonable to conclude that the ceremonial aspects of the lottery suggest a pagan ritual. Your understanding of what a pagan ritual is, combined with your observation that a number of details in the text suggest ancient fertility rites, might lead you to this conclusion. Another possibility is that "The Lottery" provides a commentary on mob psychology. The way characters reinforce one another's violent tendencies lends support to this interpretation. However, the interpretation that the ritual of the lottery is a thinly veiled attack on the death penalty would be difficult to support. Certainly a character in the story is killed, but she is not accused of a crime, nor is she tried or convicted; in fact, the killing is random and seemingly without motivation. Still, although seeing "The Lottery" as a comment on the death penalty may be far-fetched, this interpretation could be a starting point. A second, closer reading of the story would allow you to explore other, more plausible, interpretations.

As you read, do not be afraid to develop unusual or creative interpretations. A **safe reading** of a work is likely to result in a dull paper that simply states the obvious, but an aggressive or **strong reading** of a work— one that challenges generally held assumptions—can lead to interesting and intellectually challenging conclusions. Even if your reading differs from established critics' interpretations, you should not automatically assume it has no merit. Your own special knowledge of the material discussed in the text—a regional practice, an ethnic custom, a personal experience—may give you a unique perspective from which to view the work. Whatever interpretation you make, be sure that you support it with specific references to the text. If your interpretation is based on your own experiences, explain those experiences and relate them clearly to the work you are discussing. As long as you can make a reasonable case, you have the right (and perhaps the obligation) to present your ideas. By doing so, you may give your fellow students and your instructor new insight into the work.

NOTE: Keep in mind that some interpretations are *not* reasonable. You may contribute ideas based on your own perspectives, but you cannot ignore or contradict evidence in the text to suit your own biases. As you read and reread a text, continue to question and reexamine your judgments. The conversation between you and the text should be a dialogue, not a monologue or a shouting match.

Evaluating Literature

When you **evaluate** a work of literature, you do more than interpret it; you make a judgment about it. You reach conclusions not simply about whether the work is "good" or "bad," but also about how effectively the work presents itself to you, the reader. To evaluate a work, you **analyze** it, breaking it apart and considering its individual elements. As you evaluate a work of literature, remember that different works are designed to fulfill different needs—entertainment, education, or enlightenment, for example. Before you begin to evaluate a work, be sure you understand its purpose; then, follow these guidelines:

- ***Begin your evaluation by considering how various literary elements function within a work.*** Fiction may be divided into chapters and use flashbacks and foreshadowing; plays may be divided into scenes and acts and include dialogue and special staging techniques; poems may be arranged in regularly ordered groups of lines and use poetic devices such as rhyme and meter. Understanding the choices writers make about these and other literary elements can help you form judgments about a work. For example, why does Alberto Alvaro Ríos use a first-person narrator in his story "The Secret Lion" (p. 197)? Would the story have been different had it been told in the third person by a narrator who was not a character in the story? How does unusual staging contribute to the effect Milcha Sanchez-Scott achieves in her play *The Cuban Swimmer* (p. 1732)? How would a more realistic setting change the play? Naturally, you cannot focus on every element of a particular story, poem, or play. But you can and should focus on those aspects that determine your responses to a work. For this reason, elements such as the unusual stanzaic form in E. E. Cummings's poem "Buffalo Bill's" (p. 1140) and the very specific stage directions in Arthur Miller's play *Death of a Salesman* (p.1531) should be of special interest to you.

  As you read, then, you should ask questions. Do the characters in a short story seem real, or do they seem like cardboard cutouts? Are the images in a poem original and thought provoking, or are they clichéd? Are the stage directions of a play minimal or very detailed? The answers to these and other questions will help you to shape your evaluation.
- ***As you continue your evaluation, decide whether the literary elements of a work interact to achieve a common goal.*** Good writers are like master cabinetmakers: their skill disguises the actual work that has gone into the process of creation. Thus, the elements of a well-crafted literary work often fit together in a way that conceals the craft of the writer. Consider the subtlety of the following stanza from the 1862 poem "Echo" by Christina Rossetti:

  Come to me in the silence of the night;
      Come to me in the speaking silence of a dream;
  Come with soft round cheeks and eyes as bright
      As sunlight on a stream;
          Come back in tears,
  O memory, hope, love of finished years.

  Throughout this stanza, Rossetti repeats words ("Come to me . . . / Come with soft . . . / Come back . . .") and initial consonants ("speaking silence"; "sunlight on a stream"), using sound to create an almost hypnotic mood. The rhyme scheme (*night/bright*, *dream/stream*, and *tears/years*) reinforces the mood by establishing a musical undercurrent that extends throughout the poem. Thus, this stanza is effective because its repeated words and sounds work together to create a single lyrical effect.

  The chorus in *Antigone* by Sophocles (p. 1863) also illustrates how the elements of a well-crafted work of literature function together. In ancient

Greece, plays were performed by masked male actors who played both male and female roles. A chorus of fifteen men remained in a central circle called the *orchestra* and commented on and reacted to the action taking place around them. The chorus expresses the judgment of the community and acts as a moral guide for the audience. Once modern audiences grow accustomed to the presence of the chorus, it becomes an important part of the play. It neither distracts the audience nor intrudes on the action. In fact, eliminating the chorus would diminish the impact of the play.

- ***Next, consider whether a work reinforces or calls into question your ideas about the world.*** Works of **popular fiction**—those aimed at a mass audience—usually do little more than reassure readers that what they believe is correct. Catering to people's desires (for wealth or success, for example), to their prejudices, or to their fears, these works serve as escapes from life. More serious fiction, however, often goes against the grain, challenging cherished beliefs and leading readers to reexamine long-held assumptions. For instance, in the 1957 short story "Big Black Good Man" (p. 374), Richard Wright's protagonist, a night porter at a hotel, struggles with his consuming yet irrational fear of a "big black" sailor and with his inability to see beyond the sailor's size and color. Only at the end of the story do many readers see that they, like the night porter, have stereotyped and dehumanized the sailor.
- ***Now, consider whether a work is intellectually challenging.*** The extended comparison between the legs of a compass and two people in love in "A Valediction: Forbidding Mourning" by the seventeenth-century English poet John Donne (p. 933) illustrates how effectively an image can communicate complex ideas to readers. Compressed into this comparison are ideas about the perfection of love, the pain of enforced separation, and the difference between sexual and spiritual love. As intellectually challenging as the extended comparison is, it is nonetheless accessible to the careful reader. After all, many people have used a compass to draw a circle and, therefore, are able to understand the relationship between the two legs of the compass (and the two lovers).

  A fine line exists, however, between works that are intellectually challenging and those that are simply obscure. An **intellectually challenging** work requires effort from readers to unlock ideas that enrich and expand their understanding of themselves and the world. Although complex, the work gives readers a sense that they have gained something by putting forth the effort to interpret it. An **obscure** work exists solely to display a writer's erudition or intellectual idiosyncrasies. Allusions to other works and events are so numerous and confusing that the work may seem more like a private code than an effort to enlighten readers. Consider the following excerpt from "Canto LXXVI" by the twentieth-century American poet Ezra Pound:

> Le Paradis n'est pas artificiel
>   States of mind are inexplicable to us.
>   δακρύων   δακρύων   δακρύων
> L.   P. gli onesti
>   J'ai eu pitié des autres

probablement pas assez, and at moments that suited my own
convenience
Le paradis n'est pas artificiel,
l'enfer non plus.
Came Eurus as comforter
and at sunset la pastorella dei suini
driving the pigs home, benecomata dea
under the two-winged cloud
as of less and more than a day

This passage contains lines in French, Greek, and Italian, as well as a reference to Eurus, the ancient Greek personification of the east wind, and the initials L. P. (Loomis Pound?). It demands a lot from readers; the question is whether or not the reward is worth the effort.

No hard-and-fast rule exists for determining whether a work is intellectually challenging or simply obscure. Just as a poem has no fixed meaning, it also has no fixed value. Some readers would say that the passage from "Canto LXXVI" is good, even great, poetry. Others would argue that those lines do not yield enough pleasure and insight to justify the effort needed to analyze them. As a reader, you must draw your own conclusions and justify them in a clear and reasonable way. Do not assume that just because a work is difficult, it is obscure. (Nor should you assume that all difficult works are great literature or that all accessible literature is trivial.) Some of the most beautiful and inspiring literary works demand a great deal of effort. Most readers would agree, however, that the time spent exploring such works yields tremendous rewards.

- ***Consider whether a work gives you pleasure.*** One of the primary reasons literature endures is that it gives readers enjoyment. As subjective as this assessment is, it is a starting point for critical judgment. When readers ask themselves what they liked about a work, why they liked it, or what they learned, they begin the process of evaluation. Although this process is largely uncritical, it can lead to an involvement with the work and to a valid critical response. When you encounter great literature, with all its complexities, you may lose sight of the idea of literature as a source of pleasure. But literature should touch you on a deep emotional or intellectual level. If it does not—despite its technical perfection—it fails to achieve one of its primary aims.

(For a model student paper, that **evaluates** several literary works, see "The Rhythms of African-American Life: Langston Hughes and the Poetics of Blues and Jazz" on p. 1112.)

The Function of Literary Criticism

Sometimes your personal reactions and knowledge cannot give you enough insight into a literary work. For example, archaic language, references to mythology, historical allusions, and textual inconsistencies can make reading a work difficult. Similarly, an intellectual or philosophical movement such as Darwinism, Marxism, naturalism, structuralism, or feminism may influence a work, and if this is the case, you need some knowledge of the movement before you can interpret the work. In addition, you may not have the background to appreciate the technical or historical dimensions of a work. To increase your understanding, you may choose to read **literary criticism**—books and journal articles written by experts who describe, analyze, interpret, or evaluate a work of literature (see Appendix A: "Using Literary Criticism in Your Writing"). Reading literary criticism enables you to expand your knowledge of a particular work and to participate in ongoing critical discussions about literature. In a sense, when you read literary criticism, you become part of a community of scholars who share their ideas and who are connected to one another through their writing.

Literary criticism is written by experts, but this does not mean you must always agree with it. You have to evaluate literary criticism just as you would any new opinion that you encounter. Not all criticism is sound, timely, or responsible (and not all literary criticism is pertinent to your assignment or useful for your purposes). Some critical comments will strike you as plausible; others will seem unfounded or biased.

Quite often, two critics will reach strikingly different conclusions about the quality or significance of the same work or writer, or they will interpret a character, a symbol, or even the entire work quite differently. The Fiction Casebook that begins on page 614 includes articles in which critics disagree in just this way. In "In Fairyland, without a Map: Connie's Exploration Inward in Joyce Carol Oates's 'Where Are You Going, Where Have You Been?'" Gretchen Schulz and R. J. R. Rockwood examine the parallels between a character, Arnold Friend, and a real-life psychopathic killer. They see Arnold in mythological terms and conclude that he is the "exact transpositional counterpart of the real-life Pied Piper of Tucson." In Mike Tierce and John Michael Crafton's "Connie's Tambourine Man: A New Reading of Arnold Friend," however, the authors explicitly reject this suggestion as well as other critical interpretations, concluding instead that "The key question . . . is who is this musical messiah, and the key to the answer is the dedication 'For Bob Dylan.'"

Although critics may disagree, even conflicting ideas can help you reach your own conclusions about a work. It is up to you to sort out the various opinions and decide which have merit and which do not.

✔ CHECKLIST Evaluating Literary Criticism

- ☐ What is the main point of the book or article you are reading?
- ☐ Does the critic supply enough examples to support his or her conclusions?
- ☐ Does the critic acknowledge and refute the most obvious arguments against his or her position?

continued on next page

- Does the critic ignore any information in the text that might call his or her conclusions into question?
- Does the critic present historical information? Biographical information? Literary information? How does this information shed light on the work or works being discussed?
- Does the critic hold any beliefs that might interfere with his or her critical judgment?
- Does the critic slant the facts, or does he or she approach the text critically and objectively?
- Does the critic support conclusions with references to other sources? Does the critic provide documentation and a list of works cited?
- Does the critic take into consideration the most important critical books and articles on his or her subject? Are there works that should have been mentioned but were not?
- Do other critics mention the source you are reading? Do they agree or disagree with its conclusions?
- Is the critic identified with a particular critical school of thought—deconstruction or Marxism, for example? What perspective does this school of thought provide?
- Is the critic well known and respected?
- Is the critical work's publication date of any significance?

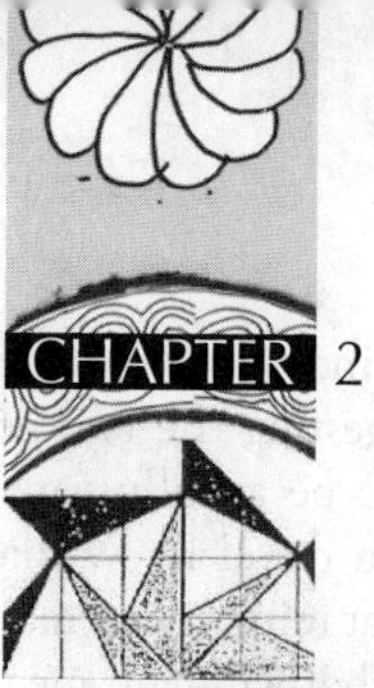

CHAPTER 2

READING AND WRITING ABOUT LITERATURE

 Reading Literature

Much of the time, readers are passive; they expect the text to give them everything they need, and they do not expect to contribute much to the reading process. In contrast, **active reading** means participating in the reading process: thinking about what you read, asking questions, and challenging ideas. Active reading is excellent preparation for the discussion and writing you will do in college literature classes. And, because it helps you understand and appreciate the works you read, active reading will continue to be of value to you long after your formal classroom study of literature has ended.

Previewing

You begin active reading by **previewing** a work to get a general idea of what to look for later, when you read it more carefully.

Start your prewriting with the work's most obvious physical characteristics. How long is a short story? How many acts and scenes does a play have? Is a poem divided into stanzas? The answers to these and similar questions will help you begin to notice more subtle aspects of the work's form. For example, previewing may reveal that a contemporary short story is presented entirely in a question-and-answer format, that it is organized as diary entries, or that it is divided into sections by headings. Previewing may identify poems that seem to lack formal structure, such as E. E. Cummings's unconventional "l(a" (p. 803); poems written in traditional forms (such as **sonnets**) or in experimental forms, such as the numbered list of questions and answers in Denise Levertov's "What Were They Like?" (p. 1066); or **concrete poems,** such as George Herbert's "Easter Wings" (p. 1008). Your awareness of these and other distinctive features at this point may help you gain insight into a work later on.

Perhaps the most physically distinctive element of a work is its title. Not only can the title give you a general idea of what the work is about, as straightforward titles like "Miss Brill" and "The Cask of Amontillado" do, but it can also isolate (and thus call attention to) a word or phrase that emphasizes an important idea. For example, the title of Amy Tan's short story "Two Kinds" (p. 777) refers to two kinds of daughters—Chinese and American—suggesting the two perspectives that create the story's conflict. A title can also be an allusion to another work. Thus, *The Sound and the Fury*, the title of a novel by William Faulkner, alludes to a speech from Shakespeare's *Macbeth* that reinforces a major theme of the novel. Finally, a title can introduce a symbol that will gain meaning in the course of a work—as the quilt does in Alice Walker's "Everyday Use" (p. 517).

Other physical elements—such as paragraphing, capitalization, italics, and punctuation—can also provide clues about how to read a work. In William Faulkner's short story "Barn Burning" (p. 391), for instance, previewing would help you to notice passages in italic type, indicating the protagonist's thoughts, which occasionally interrupt the narrator's story. In Jonathan Safran Foer's "A Primer for the Punctuation of Heart Disease" (p. 440), previewing would draw your attention to the writer's unconventional use of punctuation marks and other symbols.

Finally, previewing can enable you to see some of the more obvious stylistic and structural features of a work— the point of view used in a story, how many characters a play has and where it is set, or the repetition of certain words or lines in a poem, for example. Such features may or may not be important; at this stage, your goal is to observe, not to analyze or evaluate.

Previewing is a useful strategy not because it provides answers but because it suggests questions to ask later, as you read more closely. For instance, *why* does Faulkner use italics in "Barn Burning," and *why* does Herbert shape his poem like a pair of wings? Elements such as those described above will gain significance as you read more carefully.

Highlighting

When you read a work closely, you will notice additional, more subtle, elements that you may want to examine further. At this point, you should begin **highlighting**—physically marking the text to identify key words or details and to note relationships among ideas.

For example, you might notice that particular words or phrases are repeated, as in Tim O'Brien's short story "The Things They Carried" (p. 473), in which the word *carried* appears again and again. Because this word appears so frequently, and because it appears at key points in the story, it helps to reinforce a key theme: the burdens and responsibilities soldiers carry in wartime. Repeated words and phrases are particularly important in poetry. In Dylan Thomas's "Do not go gentle into that good night" (p. 1046), for example, the repetition of two of the poem's nineteen lines four times each enhances the poem's rhythmic, almost monotonous, cadence. As you read, highlight your text to identify such repeated words and phrases. Later, you can consider *why* these elements are repeated.

During the highlighting stage, you might also pay particular attention to **patterns of imagery** that can help you to interpret the work. When highlighting Robert Frost's "Stopping by Woods on a Snowy Evening" (p. 1159), for instance, you might identify the related images of silence, cold, and darkness. Later, you can consider their significance.

✔ CHECKLIST Using Highlighting Symbols

Here are some other ways to use highlighting:

- ☐ Underline important ideas.
- ☐ Box or circle words, phrases, or images that you want to think more about.
- ☐ Put question marks beside confusing passages, unfamiliar references, or words that need to be defined.
- ☐ Circle related words, ideas, or images and draw lines or arrows to connect them.
- ☐ Number incidents that occur in sequence.
- ☐ Identify a key portion of the text with a vertical line in the margin.
- ☐ Place stars beside particularly important ideas.

The following poem by Maya Angelou has been highlighted by a student preparing to write about it. Notice how the student uses highlighting symbols to help him identify stylistic features, key ideas, and patterns of repetition that he plans to examine later.

MAYA ANGELOU (1928–)

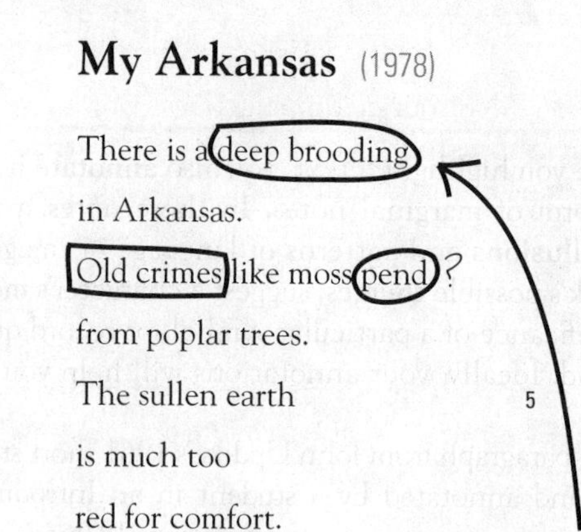

My Arkansas (1978)

There is a deep brooding
in Arkansas.
Old crimes like moss pend ?
from poplar trees.
The sullen earth
is much too
red for comfort.

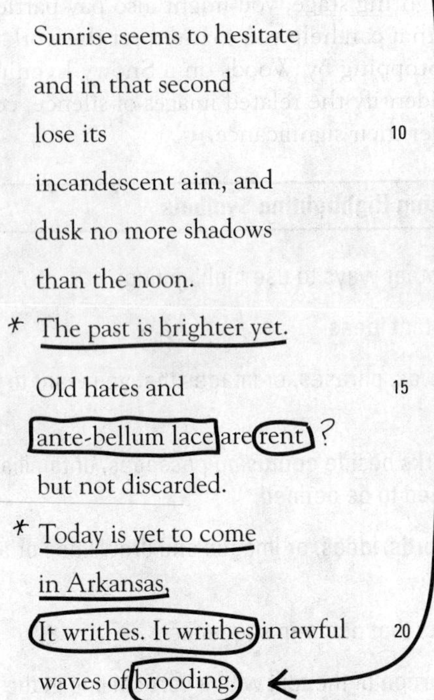

Sunrise seems to hesitate
and in that second
lose its
incandescent aim, and
dusk no more shadows
than the noon.
The past is brighter yet.
Old hates and
ante-bellum lace are rent
but not discarded.
Today is yet to come
in Arkansas,
It writhes. It writhes in awful
waves of brooding.

This student identifies repeated words and phases ("brooding"; "It writhes") and places question marks beside the two words ("pend" and "rent") whose meanings he needs to check. He also boxes two phrases—"Old crimes" and "ante-bellum lace"—that he needs to think more about. Finally, he stars what he tentatively identifies as the poem's key ideas. When he rereads the poem, his highlighting will make it easier for him to react to and interpret the writer's ideas.

Annotating

At the same time you highlight a text, you also **annotate** it, recording your reactions in the form of marginal notes. In these notes, you may define new words, identify **allusions** and patterns of language or imagery, summarize key events, list a work's possible themes, suggest a character's motivation, examine the possible significance of a particular symbol, or record questions that occur to you as you read. Ideally, your annotations will help you find ideas to write about.

The following paragraph from John Updike's 1961 short story "A&P" (p. 259) was highlighted and annotated by a student in an Introduction to Literature course who was writing in response to the question, "Why does Sammy really quit his job?"

Action isn't the result of thought.

Lengel sighs and begins to look very patient and old and gray. He's been a friend of my parents for years. "Sammy, you don't want to do this to your Mom and Dad," he tells me. It's true, I don't. But it seems to me that once you begin a gesture it's fatal not to go through with it. I fold the apron, "Sammy" stitched in red on the pocket, and put it on the counter, and drop the bow tie on top of it. The bow tie is theirs, if you've ever wondered. "You'll feel this for the rest of your life," Lengel says, and I know that's true, too, but remembering how he made the pretty girl blush makes me so scrunchy inside I punch the No Sale tab and the machine whirs "pee-pul" and the drawer splats out. One advantage to this scene taking place in summer, I can follow this up with a clean exit, there's no fumbling around getting your coat and galoshes, I just saunter into the electric eye in my white shirt that my mother ironed the night before, and the door heaves itself open, and outside the sunshine is skating around on the asphalt.

Sammy reacts to the girl's embarrassment. *

Need for a clean exit—romantic idea.

Romantic cowboy, but his mother irons his shirt (irony).

Because the instructor had discussed the story in class and given the class a specific assignment, the student's annotations are quite focused. In addition to highlighting important information, she notes her reactions to the story and tries to interpret the main character's actions.

Sometimes, however, you annotate a work before you have decided on a topic. In fact, the process of reading and responding to the text can help you find a topic to write about. If you don't yet have a topic, your annotations are likely to be somewhat unfocused, so you will probably need to annotate again when your paper's direction is clearer.

Writing about Literature

Writing about literature—or about anything else—is an idiosyncratic process during which many activities occur at once: as you write, you think of ideas; as you think of ideas, you clarify the focus of your essay; and as you clarify your focus, you reshape your paragraphs and sentences and refine your word choice. Even though this process may sound disorganized, it has three distinct stages: *planning*, *drafting*, and *revising and editing*.

Planning an Essay

Considering Your Audience

Sometimes you write primarily for yourself—for example, when you write a journal entry. At other times, you write for others. As you write an essay, consider the special requirements of your **audience.** Is your audience your classmates or your instructor? Can you assume your readers are familiar with your paper's topic and with any technical terms you will use, or should you include brief plot summaries or definitions of key terms? If your audience is your instructor, remember that he or she is a representative of a larger academic audience and therefore expects accurate information, logical arguments, and a certain degree of stylistic fluency—as well as standard English and correct grammar, mechanics, and spelling. In addition, your instructor expects you to support your statements with specific information, to express yourself clearly and unambiguously, and to document your sources. In short, your instructor wants to see how clearly you think and whether you are able to arrange your ideas into a well-organized, coherent essay.

In addition to being a member of a general academic audience, your instructor is also a member of a particular community of scholars—in this case, those who study literature. By writing about literature, you engage in a dialogue with this community. For this reason, you need to follow certain specific **conventions**—procedures that by habitual use have become accepted practice. Many of the conventions that apply specifically to writing about literature—matters of style, format, and the like—are discussed in this book. (The checklist on page 35 addresses some of these conventions.)

Understanding Your Purpose

Sometimes you write with a single **purpose** in mind. At other times, you may have more than one purpose. In general terms, you may write for any of the following three reasons:

1. ***Writing to respond*** When you write to **respond,** your goal is to discover and express your reactions to a work. To record your responses, you engage in relatively informal activities, such as brainstorming, listing, and journal writing (see pp. 24–25). As you write, you explore your own ideas, forming and re-forming your impressions of the work.
2. ***Writing to interpret*** When you write to **interpret,** your aim is to explain a work's possible meanings. As you interpret a work of literature, you may summarize, give examples, or compare and contrast the work to other works or to your own experiences. Then, you may go on to analyze the work: as you discuss each of its elements, you put complex statements into your own words, define difficult concepts, and place ideas in context.
3. ***Writing to evaluate*** When you write to **evaluate,** your purpose is to assess a work's literary merits. You may consider not only its aesthetic appeal but also its ability to retain that appeal over time and across national or cultural

boundaries. As you write, you use your own critical sense and the opinions of experts to help you make judgments about the work.

NOTE: When you write a **literary argument,** your purpose is to **persuade.** See Chapter 5.

Choosing a Topic

When you write an essay about literature, you develop and support an idea about one or more literary works. Before you begin writing, you should make certain that you understand your assignment. Do you know how much time you have to complete your essay? Are you expected to rely on your own ideas, or are you able to consult outside sources? Is your essay to focus on a specific work or on a particular element of literature? Do you have to write on an assigned topic, or are you free to choose a topic? About how long should your essay be? Do you understand exactly what the assignment is asking you to do?

Sometimes your assignment limits your options by telling you what you should discuss:

- Write an essay analyzing Thomas Hardy's use of irony in his poem "The Man He Killed."
- Discuss Hawthorne's use of allegory in his short story "Young Goodman Brown."
- Write a short essay explaining Nora's actions at the end of Ibsen's *A Doll House*.

At other times, your instructor may give you few guidelines other than a paper's required length and format. In such situations, when you must choose a topic on your own, you can often find a topic by brainstorming or by writing journal entries. As you engage in these activities, keep in mind that you have many options to choose from:

- You can **explicate** a poem or a passage of a play or short story, doing a close reading and analyzing the text.
- You can **compare two works** of literature. (The Related Works list at the end of each "Reading and Reacting" section in this book suggests possible connections.)
- You can **compare two characters** or discuss some trait those characters share.
- You can **trace a common theme**—jealousy, revenge, power, coming of age—in two or more works.
- You can **discuss a common subject**—war, love, nature—in two or more works.
- You can **analyze a single literary element** in one or more works—for instance, plot, point of view, or character development.

- You can **focus on a single aspect** of a literary element, such as the use of flashbacks, the effect of a shifting narrative perspective, or the role of a minor character.
- You can **apply a critical theory** to a work of literature—for instance, a feminist perspective to Tillie Olsen's "I Stand Here Ironing" (p. 344).
- You can **consider a work's cultural context,** examining connections between an issue treated in a work of literature—for instance, racism in Ralph Ellison's "Battle Royal" (p. 332) or postpartum psychosis in Charlotte Perkins Gilman's "The Yellow Wallpaper" (p. 459)—and that same issue as it is treated in a professional journal or in the popular press.
- You can **examine some aspect of history or biography** and consider its relationship to a literary work—for instance, the influence of World War I on Wilfred Owen's poems.
- You can **explore a problem within a work and propose a possible solution**—for example, consider Montresor's possible motives for killing Fortunato in Edgar Allan Poe's "The Cask of Amontillado" and suggest the most likely one.
- You can **compare fiction and film,** exploring similarities and differences between a literary work and a film version of the work—for example, the different endings in Joyce Carol Oates's short story "Where Are You Going, Where Have You Been?" (p. 617) and *Smooth Talk,* the film version of the story.

Finding Something to Say

Once you have a topic, you have to find something to say about it. The ideas you came up with as you highlighted and annotated will help you formulate a statement that will be the central idea of your essay and will help you find material that can support that statement.

You can use a variety of strategies to find supporting material:

- You can discuss ideas with others—friends, classmates, instructors, parents, and so on.
- You can ask questions.
- You can do research, either in the library or on the Internet.
- You can **freewrite**—that is, write on a topic for a given period of time without pausing to consider style, structure, or content.

Two additional strategies—*brainstorming* and *keeping a journal*—are especially helpful at this stage of the writing process.

Brainstorming When you **brainstorm,** you record ideas—single words, phrases, or sentences (in the form of statements or questions)—as they occur to you, moving as quickly as possible. Your starting point may be a general assignment, a particular work (or works) of literature, or a specific topic. You can brainstorm at any stage of the writing process—alone or in a group—and you can repeat this activity as often as you like.

A student preparing to write a paper on the relationships between children and parents in four poems brainstormed about each poem. The following excerpt from her notes shows her preliminary reactions to one of the four poems Adrienne Rich's "A Woman Mourned by Daughters" (p. 1045):

```
Memory: then and now
    Then: leaf, straw, dead insect (= light);
        ignored
    Now: swollen, puffed up, weight (= heavy);
        focus of attention controls their
        movements.
* Kitchen = a "universe"
    Teaspoons, goblets, etc. = concrete
        representations of mother; also =
        obligations, responsibilities (like
        plants and father)
    (weigh on them, keep them under her spell)
Milestones of past: weddings, being fed as
children, "You breathe upon us now"
    PARADOX? (Dead, she breathes, has weight,
    fills house and sky. Alive, she was a dead
    insect, no one paid attention to her.)
```

Keeping a Journal You can record ideas in a journal (a notebook, a small notepad, or a computer file)—and, later, you can use these ideas in your paper. In a **journal,** you expand your marginal annotations, recording your responses to works you have read, noting questions, exploring emerging ideas, experimenting with possible paper topics, trying to paraphrase or summarize difficult concepts, or speculating about a work's ambiguities. A journal is the place to take chances, to try out ideas that may initially seem frivolous or irrelevant; here you can think on paper (or on your computer) until connections become clear or ideas crystallize. You can also use your journal as a convenient place to collect your brainstorming notes.

As he prepared to write a paper analyzing the role of Jim, the "gentleman caller" in Tennessee Williams's play *The Glass Menagerie* (p. 1961), a student explored ideas in the following journal entry.

```
    When he tells Laura that being disappointed is not the
same as being discouraged, and that he's disappointed but not
discouraged, Jim reveals his role as a symbol of the power of
newness and change—a "bulldozer" that will clear out whatever
is in its path, even delicate people like Laura. But the fact
that he is disappointed shows Jim's human side. He has run
into problems since high school, and these problems have blocked
his progress toward a successful future. Working at the
warehouse, Jim needs Tom's friendship to remind him of what
he used to be (and what he still can be?), and this shows his
insecurity. He isn't as sure of himself as he seems to be.
```

Seeing Connections

As you review your notes, you try to discover patterns—to see repeated images, similar characters, recurring words and phrases, and interrelated themes or ideas. Identifying these patterns can help you to decide which points to make in your paper and what information you will use to support these points.

A student preparing a paper about D. H. Lawrence's short story "The Rocking-Horse Winner" (p. 589) made the following list of related ideas:

```
Secrets
   Mother can't feel love
   Paul gambles
   Paul gives mother money
   Family lives beyond means
   Paul gets information from horse
Religion
   Gambling becomes like a religion
   They all worship money
   Specific references: "serious as a church"; "It's as if
   he had it from heaven"; "secret, religious voice"
Luck
   Father is unlucky
   Mother is desperate for luck
   Paul is lucky (ironic)
```

Deciding on a Thesis

Whenever you are ready, you should try to express the main idea of your emerging essay in a **thesis statement**—an idea, usually expressed in a single sentence, that the rest of your essay will support. This idea should emerge logically out of your highlighting, annotating, brainstorming notes, journal entries, and lists of related ideas. Eventually, you will write a **thesis-and-support paper:** stating your thesis in your introduction, supporting the thesis in the body paragraphs of your essay, and reinforcing the thesis or summarizing your paper's key points in your conclusion.

An effective thesis statement tells readers what your essay will discuss and how you will approach your material. For this reason, it should be precisely worded, making its point clear to your readers, and it should contain no vague words or imprecise phrases that will make it difficult for readers to follow your discussion.

In addition to being specific, your thesis statement should give your readers an accurate sense of the scope and direction of your essay. It should not make promises that you do not intend to fulfill or include extraneous details that might confuse your readers. If, for example, you are going to write a paper about the dominant image in a poem, your thesis should not imply that you will focus on the poem's setting or tone.

Remember that as you organize your ideas and as you write, you will probably modify and sharpen your thesis. Sometimes you will even begin planning your essay with one thesis in mind and end up with an entirely different one. If this happens, be sure to revise your body paragraphs so that they support your new thesis. If you find that your ideas about your topic are changing, don't be concerned; this is how the writing process works.

Preparing an Outline

Once you have decided on a thesis and have some idea how you will support it, you can begin to plan your essay's structure. At this stage of the writing process, an **outline** can help you to clarify your ideas and show how these ideas relate to one another.

A **scratch outline** is perhaps the most useful kind of outline for a short paper. An informal list of the main points you will discuss in your essay, a scratch outline is more focused than a simple list of related ideas because it presents ideas in the order in which they will be introduced. As its name implies, however, a scratch outline lacks the detail and the degree of organization of a more formal outline. The main purpose of a scratch outline is to give you a sense of the shape and order of your paper and thus enable you to begin writing.

A student writing a short essay on Edwin Arlington Robinson's use of irony in his poem "Miniver Cheevy" (p. 1191) used the following scratch outline as a guide.

```
Speaker's Attitude
    Ironic
    Cynical
    Critical
Use of Diction
    Formal
    Detached
Use of Allusions
    Thebes
    Camelot
    Priam
    Medici
Use of Repetition
    "Miniver"
    "thought"
Regular Rhyme Scheme
```

Once this outline was complete, the student was ready to write a first draft.

Drafting an Essay

A first draft is a preliminary version of your paper, something to react to and revise. Even before you actually begin drafting your paper, however, you should review the material you have collected. To make sure you are ready to begin drafting, take the following three steps:

1. ***Make sure you have collected enough information to support your thesis.*** The points you make are only as convincing as the evidence you present to support them. As you read and take notes, you collect supporting examples from the work or works about which you are writing. How many of these examples you need to use in your draft depends on the scope of your thesis. In general, the broader your thesis, the more material you need to support it. For example, if you were supporting the rather narrow thesis that the speech of a certain character in one scene of a play reveals important information about his motivation, only a few examples would be needed. However, if you wanted to support the broader thesis that Nora and Torvald Helmer in Henrik Ibsen's *A Doll House* (p. 1402) are trapped in their roles, you would need to present a wide range of examples.

2. ***See if the work includes any details that contradict your thesis.*** Before you begin writing, test the validity of your thesis by looking for details that contradict it. For example, if you plan to support the thesis that in *A Doll House*, Ibsen makes a strong case for the rights of women, you should look for counterexamples. Can you find subtle hints in the play that suggest women should remain locked in their traditional roles and continue to defer to their fathers and husbands? If so, you will want to modify your thesis accordingly.

3. ***Consider whether you need to use outside sources to help you support your thesis.*** You could, for example, strengthen the thesis that *A Doll House* challenged contemporary attitudes about marriage by including the information that when the play first opened, Ibsen was convinced by an apprehensive theater manager to write an alternative ending. In this new ending, Ibsen had Nora decide, after she stopped briefly to look in at her sleeping children, that she could not leave her family. Sometimes information from another source can even lead you to change your thesis. For example, after reading *A Doll House*, you might have decided that Ibsen's purpose was to make a strong case for the rights of women. In class, however, you might learn that Ibsen repeatedly said that his play was about the rights of all human beings, not just of women. This information could lead you to a thesis that suggests Torvald is just as trapped in his role as Nora is in hers. Naturally, Ibsen's interpretation of his own work does not invalidate your first judgment, but it does suggest another conclusion that is worth investigating.

After carefully evaluating the completeness, relevance, and validity of your supporting material, you can begin drafting your essay, using your scratch outline as a guide. In this first draft, your focus should be on the body of your essay; this is not the time to worry about constructing the "perfect" introduction and conclusion. (In fact, many writers, knowing that their ideas will change as they write, postpone writing these paragraphs until a later draft, preferring instead to begin simply by stating their thesis.) As you write, remember that your first draft is going to be rough and will probably not be as clear as you would like it to be; still, it will enable you to see your ideas begin to take shape.

Revising and Editing an Essay

Revision

When you **revise,** you literally "re-see" your draft; in many cases, you go on to reorder and rewrite substantial portions of your essay. Before you are satisfied with your essay, you will probably write several drafts, each more closely focused and more coherent than the previous one.

Strategies for Revision

Two strategies can help you to revise your drafts: *peer review* and *a dialogue with your instructor*:

1. **Peer review** is a process in which students assess each other's work-in-progress. This activity may be carried out in informal sessions during which one student comments on another's draft, or it may be a formal process in which students respond to specific questions on a form supplied by the instructor or participate in an electronic exchange. In either case, one student's reactions can help another student revise.
2. **A dialogue with your instructor**—in conference or by email— can give you a sense of how to proceed with your revision. Establishing such an oral or written dialogue can help you learn how to respond critically to your own writing, and your reactions to your instructor's comments on any draft can help you to clarify your essay's goals and write drafts that are increasingly consistent with these goals. (If your instructor is not available, try to schedule a conference with a writing center tutor.)

As you move through successive drafts, the task of revising your essay will be easier if you follow a systematic process. As you read and react to your essay, begin by assessing the effectiveness of the larger elements—for example, your thesis statement and your key supporting ideas—and then move on to examine increasingly smaller elements.

Thesis Statement First, reconsider your **thesis statement.** Is it carefully and precisely worded? Does it provide a realistic idea of what your essay will cover? Does it make a point that is worth supporting?

Vague: Many important reasons exist to explain why Margot Macomber's shooting of her husband was probably intentional.

Revised: Although Hemingway's text states that Margot Macomber "shot at the buffalo," a careful analysis of her relationship with her husband suggests that in fact she intended to kill him.

Vague: Dickens's characters are a lot like those of Addison and Steele.

Revised: With their familiar physical and moral traits, Charles Dickens's minor characters are similar to the "characters" created by the eighteenth-century essayists Joseph Addison and Richard Steele for the newspaper the *Spectator*.

Supporting Ideas Next, assess the appropriateness of your **supporting ideas,** considering whether you present enough support for your thesis and whether all the details you include are relevant to that thesis. Make sure you have supported your key points with specific, concrete examples from the work or works you are discussing, briefly summarizing key events, quoting dialogue or description, and describing characters or settings. Make certain, however, that your own ideas are central to the essay and that you have not substituted plot summary for analysis and interpretation. Your goal is to draw a conclusion about one or more works and to support that conclusion with pertinent details. If an event in a story you are analyzing supports a point you wish to make, include a *brief* summary; then, explain its relevance to the point you are making.

In the following excerpt from a paper on a short story by James Joyce, the first sentence briefly summarizes a key event, and the second sentence explains its significance.

> At the end of James Joyce's "Counterparts," when Farrington returns home after a day of frustration and abuse at work, his reaction is to strike out at his son Tom. This act shows that although he and his son are similarly victimized, Farrington is also the counterpart of his tyrannical boss.

Topic Sentences Now, turn your attention to the **topic sentences** that present the main ideas of your body paragraphs. Make sure that each topic sentence is clearly worded and that it signals the direction of your discussion.

Be especially careful to avoid abstractions and vague generalities in topic sentences. Also avoid words and phrases like *involves*, *deals with*, *concerns*, and *pertains to*, which are likely to make your topic sentences wordy and imprecise.

Vague: `One similarity involves the dominance of the men by women.` (What is the similarity?)

Revised: `In both stories, a man is dominated by a woman.`

Vague: `There is one reason for the fact that Jay Gatsby remains a mystery.` (What is the reason?)

Revised: Because *The Great Gatsby* is narrated by the outsider Nick Carraway, Jay Gatsby himself remains a mystery.

When revising topic sentences that are intended to move readers from one point (or one section of your paper) to another, be sure the relationship between the ideas they link is clear. A topic sentence should include transitions that look back at the previous paragraphs as well as ahead to the paragraph it introduces.

Unclear: Now, the poem's imagery will be discussed.

Revised: <u>Another reason</u> for the poem's effectiveness is its unusual imagery.

Unclear: The sheriff's wife is another interesting character.

Revised: <u>Like her friend Mrs. Hale,</u> the sheriff's wife also has mixed feelings about what Mrs. Wright has done.

Introduction and Conclusion When you are satisfied with the body of your essay, you can turn your attention to your paper's *introduction* and *conclusion*.

The **introduction** of an essay about literature should identify the works to be discussed and their authors and indicate the emphasis of the discussion to follow. Depending on your purpose and on your paper's topic, you may want to provide some historical background or biographical information or to briefly discuss the work in relation to similar works. Like all introductions, the one you write for an essay about literature should create interest in your topic and should include a clear thesis statement.

The following introduction, though acceptable for a first draft, is in need of revision.

Draft: *Revenge*, which is defined as "the chance to retaliate, get satisfaction, take vengeance, or inflict damage or injury in return for an injury, insult, etc.," is a major theme in many of the stories we have read. The stories that will be discussed here deal with a variety of ways to seek revenge. In my essay, I will consider some of these differences.

Although the student clearly identifies her paper's topic, she does not identify the works she will discuss or the particular point she will make about revenge. Her tired opening strategy, a dictionary definition, is not likely to create interest in her topic, and her announcement of her intention in the last sentence is awkward and unnecessary. The following revision is much more effective.

Revised: In Edgar Allan Poe's "The Cask of Amontillado," Montresor vows revenge on Fortunato for an unspecified "insult" (p.385); in Ring Lardner's "Haircut," Paul, a young retarded man, gets even with a cruel practical joker who has taunted him for years. Both of these stories present characters who seek revenge, and both stories end in murder. However, the murderers' motivations are presented very differently. In "Haircut," the narrator is unaware of the significance of many events, and his ignorance helps to create sympathy for the murderer; in "The Cask of Amontillado," where the narrator is the murderer himself, Montresor's inability to offer a convincing motive turns the reader against him.

In your **conclusion,** you restate your thesis and perhaps sum up your essay's main points; then, you make a graceful exit.

The concluding paragraph that follows is acceptable for a first draft, but it needs further development.

Draft: Although the characters of Montresor and Paul were created by different authors at different times, they do have similar motives and goals. However, they are portrayed very differently.

The following revision reinforces the essay's main point, effectively incorporating a brief quotation from "The Cask of Amontillado" (p. 385):

Revised: What is significant is not whether each murderer's act is justified, but rather how each murderer, and each victim, is portrayed by the narrator. Montresor—driven by a thirst to avenge a "thousand injuries" (p.385) as well as a final insult—is shown to be sadistic and unrepentant; in "Haircut," it is Jim, the victim, whose sadism and lack of remorse are revealed to the reader.

Sentences and Words Now, focus on the individual sentences and words of your essay. Begin by evaluating your **transitions,** the words and phrases that link sentences and paragraphs. Be sure that every necessary transitional element has been supplied and that each word or phrase you have selected accurately conveys the exact relationship (sequence, contradiction, and so on) between ideas.

When you are satisfied with the clarity and appropriateness of your paper's transitions, consider sentence variety and word choice:

- Be sure you have varied your sentence structure. You will bore your readers if all your sentences begin with the subject ("He. . . . He. . . ."; "The story. . . . The story. . . .").
- Make sure that all the words you have selected communicate your ideas accurately and that you have not used vague, inexact diction. For example, saying that a character is *bad* is a lot less helpful than describing him or her as *ruthless*, *conniving*, or *malicious*.
- Eliminate subjective expressions, such as *I think*, *in my opinion*, *I believe*, *it seems to me*, and *I feel*. These phrases weaken your essay by suggesting that its ideas are "only" your opinions and have no objective validity.

Using and Documenting Sources Make certain that all references to sources are integrated smoothly into your sentences and that all information that is not your own is documented appropriately. For specific information on documenting sources, see Chapter 7.

✔ CHECKLIST Using Sources

- ☐ Acknowledge all material from sources, including the literary work or works under discussion, using the documentation style of the Modern Language Association (MLA).
- ☐ Combine paraphrases, summaries, and quotations with your own interpretations, weaving quotations smoothly into your paper. Introduce the words or ideas of others with a phrase that identifies their source (`According to Richard Wright's biographer, . . .`), and end with appropriate parenthetical documentation.
- ☐ Use quotations *only* when something vital would be lost if you did not reproduce the author's exact words.
- ☐ Integrate short quotations (four lines or fewer of prose or three lines or fewer of poetry) smoothly into your paper. Use a slash (/) with one space on either side to separate lines of poetry. Be sure to enclose quotations in quotation marks.

continued on next page

- Set off quotations of more than four lines of prose or more than three lines of poetry by indenting one inch from the left-hand margin. Double-space, and do not use quotation marks. If you are quoting just one paragraph, do not indent the first line.
- Use ellipses — three spaced periods — to indicate that you have omitted material within a quotation (but never use ellipses at the beginning of a quoted passage).
- Use brackets to indicate that you have added words to a quotation: `As Earl notes, "[Willie] is a modern-day Everyman" (201).` Use brackets to alter a quotation so that it fits grammatically into your sentence: `Wilson says that Miller "offer[s] audiences a dark view of the present" (74).`
- Place commas and periods *inside* quotation marks: `According to Robert Coles, the child could "make others smile."`
- Place punctuation marks other than commas and periods *outside* quotation marks: `What does Frost mean when he says, "a poem must ride on its own melting"?` If the punctuation mark is part of the quoted material, place it *inside* the quotation marks: `In "Mending Wall," Frost asks, "Why do they make good neighbors?"`
- When citing part of a short story or novel, supply the page number `(143)`. For a poem, supply line numbers `(3-5)`, including the word *line* or *lines* just in the first reference. For a play, supply act, scene, and line numbers `(2.2.17-22)`.
- Include a works-cited list (unless your instructor tells you not to).

Editing and Proofreading

Once you have finished revising, you **edit**— that is, you make certain that your paper's grammar, punctuation, spelling, and mechanics are correct. Always run a spell check, but remember that you still have to **proofread**—look carefully for errors that the spell checker will not identify. These include homophones (*brake* incorrectly used instead of *break*), typos that create correctly spelled words (*work* instead of *word*), and words (such as a technical or foreign term or a writer's name) that may not be in your computer's dictionary. If you use a grammar checker, remember that although grammar programs may identify potential problems— long sentences, for example— they may not be able to determine whether a particular long sentence is grammatically correct (let alone stylistically pleasing). Always keep a style handbook nearby so that you can double-check any problems a spell checker or grammar checker highlights in your writing.

As you edit, pay particular attention to the special conventions of literary essays, some of which are addressed in the checklist below. When your editing is complete, give your essay a descriptive title. Before you print your final copy, be sure that its format conforms to your instructor's requirements.

✔ CHECKLIST Conventions of Writing about Literature

- Use present-tense verbs when discussing works of literature: `The character of Mrs. Mallard's husband is not developed. . . .`
- Use past-tense verbs only when discussing historical events (`Owen's poem conveys the destructiveness of World War I, which at the time the poem was written was considered to be . . .`); when presenting historical or biographical data (`Her first novel, which was published in 1811 when Austen was thirty-six, . . .`); or when identifying events that occurred prior to the time of the story's main action (`"Miss Emily is a recluse; since her father's death she has lived alone except for a servant"`).
- Avoid unnecessary plot summary. Your goal is to draw a conclusion about one or more works and to support that conclusion with pertinent details. If a plot detail supports a point you wish to make, a *brief* summary is acceptable. But remember, plot summary is no substitute for analysis.
- Use literary terms accurately. For example, be careful not to confuse *narrator* or *speaker* with *author;* feelings or opinions expressed by a narrator or character do not necessarily represent those of the author. You should not say, `"In the poem's last stanza, Frost expresses his indecision"` when you mean that the poem's *speaker* is indecisive.
- Underline titles of novels and plays; place titles of short stories and poems within quotation marks.
- Refer to authors of literary works by their full names (*Edgar Allan Poe*) in your first reference to them and by their last names (*Poe*) in subsequent references. Never refer to authors by their first names, and never use titles that indicate marital status (*Flannery O'Connor* or *O'Connor*, never *Flannery* or *Miss O'Connor*).

Exercise: Two Student Papers

The following student papers, "Initiation into Adulthood" and "Hard Choices," were written for the same Introduction to Literature class. Both consider the initiation theme in the same three short stories: James Joyce's "Eveline" (p. 719), John Updike's "A&P" (p. 259), and William Faulkner's "Barn Burning" (p. 391). "Hard Choices" conforms to the conventions of writing about literature discussed in this chapter. "Initiation into Adulthood" does not.

Read the two essays. Then, guided by this chapter's discussion of writing about literature and by the checklists on pages 33–34 and 35, identify the features that make "Hard Choices" the more effective essay, and decide where "Initiation into Adulthood" needs further revision. Finally, suggest some possible revisions for "Hard Choices."

Initiation into Adulthood

Introduction

At an early age, the main focus in a child's life is his parents. But as this child grows, he begins to get his own view of life, which may be, and usually is, different from that of his parents. Sooner or later, there will come a time in this child's life when he must stand up for what he truly believes in. At this point in his life, he can no longer be called a child, and he becomes part of the adult world. In literature, many stories—such as James Joyce's "Eveline," John Updike's "A&P," and William Faulkner's "Barn Burning"—focus on this initiation into adulthood.

Thesis statement

Discussion of first story: "Eveline"

James Joyce's "Eveline" is a story that describes a major turning point in a woman's life. At home, Eveline's life was very hard. She was responsible for keeping the house together and caring for the younger children after her mother's death. Unfortunately, the only thoughts that ran through her mind were thoughts of escape, of leaving her unhappy life and beginning a new life of her own. The night before she was to secretly leave with Frank on a boat to Buenos Ayres, a street organ playing reminded her of her promise to her dying mother to keep the home together as long as she could. She was now forced to make a decision between life with Frank and her present life, which didn't look wholly undesirable now that she was about to leave. The next night, just as she was about to step on the boat, she realized she could not leave. The making of this decision was in essence Eveline's initiation into adulthood.

Discussion of second story: "A&P"

John Updike's "A&P" presents the brief infatuation of a young boy, Sammy, and the consequences that follow. Sammy's home was a small quiet town a few miles from the shore. He worked in the local A&P as a cashier, a job his father had gotten for him. One day, three girls in nothing but bathing suits walked through the front door. Immediately they caught Sammy's eye, especially the leader, the one he nicknamed "Queenie." After prancing through the store, they eventually came to Sammy's checkout with an unusual purchase. It was not long before they caught the attention of Mr. Lengel, the manager. Unpleasant words were exchanged between the manager and Queenie pertaining to their inappropriate shopping attire. Before the girls left the store, Sammy told Lengel that he quit, hoping they would stop and watch him, their unsuspected hero. But they kept walking, and Sammy was faced with the decision of whether or not to follow through with his gesture. Knowing that it is "fatal" not to follow through with a gesture once you've started, he removed his apron and bow tie and walked out the door, realizing how hard the world was going to be to him hereafter. The making of this decision, to leave the mundane life of the A&P and enter the harsh world, was in essence Sammy's initiation into adulthood.

Discussion of third story: "Barn Burning"

William Faulkner's "Barn Burning" is a story about Sarty Snopes, an innocent young boy who must make a decision between his family and his honor. Because Abner Snopes, Sarty's father, had so little, he tried to hurt those who had more than he had—often by burning down their barns. These acts forced the Snopes family to move around quite a bit. The last time Snopes burned a barn, he did it without warning his victim, making Sarty realize how cruel and dishonest his father really was. Because of this realization, Sarty decided to leave his family. This decision of Sarty's not to stick to his own blood was his initiation into adulthood.

Conclusion

"Eveline," "A&P," and "Barn Burning" all deal with a youth maturing to adulthood in the process of deciding whether to stay unhappy or to go and seek a better life. Sammy and Sarty leave their unpleasant situations because of something done unfairly. Eveline, on the other hand, decides to stay, remembering a promise to her mother. The decisions of these characters presented in their respective stories are focal points in the literary works and pertain to initiation into adulthood.

Hard Choices

Introduction

Although William Faulkner's "Barn Burning" focuses on a young boy in the American South, John Updike's "A&P" on a teenager in a town north of Boston, and James Joyce's "Eveline" on a young woman in Dublin, each of the three stories revolves around a decision the central character must make. These decisions are not easy ones; in all three cases, family loyalty competes with a desire for individual freedom.

Thesis statement

However, the difficult decision-making process helps each character to mature, and in this sense, all three works are initiation stories.

Discussion of first story: "Barn Burning"

For Sarty Snopes in "Barn Burning," initiation into adulthood means coming to terms with his father's concept of revenge. Mr. Snopes believes that a person should take revenge himself if he cannot get justice in court. Revenge, for this bitter man, means burning down barns. Sarty knows that his father is doing wrong, but Mr. Snopes drills into his son's mind the idea that "You got to learn to stick to your own blood or you ain't going to have any blood to stick to you" (Faulkner 394), and for a long time Sarty believes him. Naturally, this blood tie makes Sarty's decision to leave his family extremely difficult. In the end, though, Sarty decides to reject his father's values and remain behind when his family moves.

Discussion of second story: "A&P"

Like Sarty, Sammy must choose between his values and his parents' values (reflected in his job at the supermarket). While Sammy is working in the A&P, he notices how much like sheep people are. Most customers have a routine life that they never consider changing, and Sammy does not want to end up like them. When three seemingly carefree girls enter the store and exhibit nonconformist behavior—such as going against the flow of people in the aisles, not having a grocery list, and wearing bathing suits—Sammy sees them as rebels, and he longs to escape through them from his humdrum world. In the end, he chooses to defend the girls and quit the job his parents helped him to get.

Discussion of third story: "Eveline"

Likewise, Eveline has to decide between a new life with her boyfriend, Frank, in South America and her dull, hard life at home with her father. The new life offers change and freedom, while her life at home is spent working and keeping house. Still, when given the chance to leave, she declines because she promised her dying mother to "keep the home together as long as she could" (722).

Comparative analysis of the three stories

All three characters enter adulthood by making difficult decisions. Sarty realizes that in order to grow, he must repudiate his father's wrongdoings. He stands up for his values and rejects his "blood." Sammy makes the same decision although with less extreme consequences: knowing that he will have to confront his parents, he still defends the three girls and stands up to his boss, rejecting a life of conformity and security. Unlike the other two, Eveline does not reject her parents' values. Instead, she decides to sacrifice her own future by remaining with her father. She keeps her promise to her mother and puts her father before herself because she believes that caring for him is her duty.

Further analysis of the three stories

Each of the three characters confronts a challenging future. Sarty must support himself and make a new life. Because he is very young and because he has no one to help him, his future is the most uncertain of the three. Unlike Sammy and Eveline, who still have homes, Sarty has only his judgment and his values to guide him. Sammy's future is less bleak but still unpredictable: he knows that the world will be a harder place for him from now on (Updike 259) because now he is a man of principle. Unlike the other two, Eveline knows exactly what her future holds: work, pain, and boredom. She has no fear or uncertainty—but no hope for a better tomorrow either.

Conclusion

"Barn Burning," "A&P," and "Eveline" are stories of initiation in which the main characters struggle with decisions that help them to grow up. All three consider giving up the known for the unknown, challenging their parents and becoming truly themselves, but only Sarty and Sammy actually do so. Both boys defy their parents and thus trade difficult lives for uncertain ones. Eveline, however, decides to stay on in her familiar life, choosing the known—however deadening—over the unknown. Still, all three, in confronting hard choices and deciding to do what their values tell them they must do, experience an initiation into adulthood.

WRITING SPECIAL KINDS OF PAPERS

When you write a paper about literature, you have many options (some of these are listed in Chapter 2, p. 22). Often, however, you will be asked to respond to one of five special assignments: to write a *response paper*, to write a *comparison-contrast*, to write an *explication*, to write a *character analysis*, or to write about a work's *cultural context*. The pages that follow offer guidelines for responding to each of these assignments as well as annotated model student papers.

Writing a Response Paper

When you write a **response paper,** you explore and explain your reactions to a short story, poem, or play by focusing on one or more of the work's elements. This kind of assignment can help you to discover how a work's elements contribute to its overall effectiveness, meaning, and impact. For example, a controversial theme in a particular work may elicit a strong response, or a character's actions might amuse, enrage, or enlighten you. Probing your own personal reactions to various elements can help you begin to understand the work as a whole and bring the work to life in a meaningful way. Writing a response paper allows you to shape and reshape your impressions of a story, poem, or play. As you consider how a particular literary work relates to others you have read and to your own experiences, you create your own interpretation of the work. (See also Reader-Response Criticism in Appendix A, p. 2047.)

Eventually, you may develop a response paper into a longer, more formal paper. In fact, a response paper is often assigned as an initial step toward formulating a thesis statement for a more complex assignment. A response paper, sometimes written as a **journal entry** (see p. 25), is generally less formal than other types of writing about literature, and it can incorporate freewriting, brainstorming, and informal outlining techniques. Remember, however, that although your response paper may use an informal—even personal—style and tone, it cannot be based solely on your personal opinions. You must always include examples and details from the work to support your reactions to it.

✔ **CHECKLIST Writing a Response Paper**

- ☐ Have you focused your responses in an interesting and meaningful way?
- ☐ Have you clearly explained how one or more of the work's elements relate to the overall effectiveness of the work?
- ☐ If your response paper analyzes more than one literary element, have you paid enough attention to each element in your response?
- ☐ Do you use examples and details—including paraphrases and quotations—from the work to illustrate your points and to support your reactions?
- ☐ Have you followed your instructor's format and documentation guidelines?

Responding to a Short Story

The following student paper is a response to questions about Tim O'Brien's story "The Things They Carried" (p. 473).

> At the end of the story, what has Lieutenant Cross learned? What more do you think he still has to learn?

Note that this paper does not include a works-cited list because the instructor did not require one for this informal assignment.

Russell 1

Brad Russell

Professor Chu

English 102

12 February 2009

Response to Tim O'Brien's "The Things They Carried"

Tim O'Brien's "The Things They Carried" is a coming-of-age story, and Lieutenant Cross, a young soldier, learns the hard way that war can have serious consequences. Throughout the story, the narrator

Russell 2

lists all the weapons and tools and mementos that the soldiers carry, and having to read about all the technical specifications of guns, ammunition, and other machinery that the men carry got to be really boring after a while. I actually felt like I was carrying these things as I read about them, but I couldn't figure out why all this information was in the story. I looked forward to the short paragraphs where the narrator describes the men's emotions and the deeper impact of the war.

It didn't occur to me until I read the story a second time that what I was experiencing as a reader is similar to what Lieutenant Cross experiences. He feels the burden of all the monotonous details, and they prevent him from seeing the big picture. Some details show how dull and uneventful war can be, like when the narrator describes "moving on to the next village, then other villages, where it would always be the same" (480). Other details are shocking; for example, the narrator describes in a flat, detached way how Norman Bowker carries around a dead Vietcong soldier's severed thumb that is "dark brown, rubbery to the touch," (479) and how Ted Lavender gets shot and "[t]he cheekbone was gone" (478). I understand that all these details are supposed to show readers the heavy burden war places on the soldiers, but I wanted to get past the details. I wanted to know what these things and events mean to the men, and especially to Lieutenant Cross.

For a long time, Lieutenant Cross relies on the details of his job—and on his memories of home—to help him survive. He is unable to focus on the

Russell 3

brutal reality of war, and he slips into daydreams about Martha and the New Jersey shore when he and his men are on long missions, or when they face danger (like when one of them gets picked to search out a tunnel they're about to destroy). Lieutenant Cross blames himself for Lavender's death because he was unable to focus on his men's safety and on the dangers all around them, but eventually he learns that blaming himself will not make the situation better or bring Ted Lavender back. What he needs to do now is stop focusing on the endless burdens he and his men carry, or on the monotony and pointlessness of the daily struggle to survive, or on "all the emotional baggage of men who might die" (482). Now, he has to focus on being a leader.

Lieutenant Cross finally realizes that war "was another world, where there were no pretty poems or midterm exams, a place where men died because of carelessness and gross stupidity" (484). He learns that he has to "dispense with love; it was not now a factor" (485). But I think Lieutenant Cross still has more to learn. What I learned while reading the story is that we *need* the "pretty poems" and "midterm exams" and especially the "love" that make us human; we need to carry these things with us to survive in times, such as wartime, when these things are absent. Although Lieutenant Cross doesn't realize it by the end of the story, he still must carry these memories with him in order to "[c]arry on" and to get back to a place where people are allowed to dream and love (485).

Responding to a Poem

The following student paper is a response to questions about John Donne's poem "Death Be Not Proud" (p. 1148).

> The speaker implies that he is not afraid of death. Why not? Do you believe him?

Note that this paper does not include a works-cited list because the instructor did not require one for this informal assignment.

Hollingsworth 1

Rebecca Hollingsworth

Professor Owens

English 102

9 February 2009

Response to John Donne's "Death Be Not Proud"

In John Donne's poem "Death Be Not Proud," the speaker implies that he is not afraid of death. At first, I admired the speaker for being so confident as he confronts death. The speaker personifies and addresses death directly in the first line ("Death be not proud"). He suggests that he doesn't think that death is actually "Mighty and dreadful," as "some" people think (lines 1-2). The speaker even seems to suggest in lines 3-4 that death can't kill him or anyone else. In line 5, he compares death to "rest and sleep," which seems like a way of saying that death is not horrible, but in fact can offer some sort of renewal. Later on, the speaker takes this sleep idea a step further by suggesting that "poppy, or charms" actually offer "better" sleep than death (11-12). Again, I'm not really sure what the speaker means here, but I think he's trying to downplay death's power by comparing death to other states of unconsciousness and suggesting that death is inferior.

Hollingsworth 2

Toward the end of the poem, the speaker becomes even more critical of death when he says that death is a "slave to fate, chance, kings, and desperate men" (9). In addition, the speaker points out that death is linked "with poison, war, and sickness" (10). In the last two lines of the poem, the speaker again suggests that death won't succeed in killing people. At least, I think that's what he means by "we wake eternally" (13). He even says in the last line that death itself will die. Here, I think he's suggesting that after death, people will live in the afterlife, where death does not exist.

As I reread the poem, I realized that the speaker must understand how powerful death really is even though he is trying to deny its power. After all, death is not the same as "rest and sleep," and no one can truly overcome death. Maybe the speaker is about to die and is trying to comfort himself by suggesting that death is not something to be afraid of. It almost seems as if the speaker is deluded when he says at the end, "death, thou shalt die" (14). Also, when I looked back at the line breaks in the poem, I noticed that certain words, like "Mighty and dreadful" (2) and "Die not" (4), stand out. I wonder if these words actually reveal the speaker's fear of dying.

This poem can be read in several ways. On the surface, the speaker seems not to be afraid of death. But when reading the poem more closely, I realized that the speaker isn't believable; he must know that death can't be overcome. It seems as if the speaker is trying to convince himself that death is really not so horrible, but he's resisting death rather than

Hollingsworth 3

accepting it. I wonder, though, about the meaning of lines 7-8, where the speaker says, "And soonest our best men with thee do go, / Rest of their bones, and soul's delivery." Could these lines suggest that the speaker is beginning to find some peace at the thought of dying? "Death Be Not Proud" is a complex poem, and there are no easy answers to the questions it raises.

 Writing a Comparison-Contrast

Writing a **comparison-contrast,** one of the most common assignments in literature classes, offers many possibilities. For example, you can compare two stories, two poems, or two plays—or you can cross genres, comparing a story with a poem or a play on a similar topic. Alternatively, you can compare two characters, two works by the same author, a poem to a work of fine art, a conventional print story to a graphic story, or a literary work to a film.

When you write a comparison-contrast, you look first for significant similarities between your two subjects. For example, two characters may have a similar motivation or similar goals or flaws; two stories may have similar settings; two plays may have similar plots; and two poems may have parallels in their use of sound or imagery. Once you have identified the key similarities, you can consider why these similarities are important and what they reveal about the works.

There are two ways to arrange material in a comparison-contrast essay. When you write a **point-by-point comparison,** you discuss one point of similarity at a time, alternating between subjects. When you write a **subject-by-subject comparison,** you approach each subject separately, discussing all your points first for one subject and then for the other. The outlines that follow illustrate how you could use either a point-by-point or a subject-by-subject strategy to support the same thesis statement.

Thesis Statement: Both David Michael Kaplan's "Doe Season" and Alice Munro's "Boys and Girls" focus on a young girl who learns that her gender limits her and comes to accept that such limitations are inevitable.

Point-by-Point Comparison

First point: In both stories, the girls are tomboys who like being with their fathers.

"Doe Season": Andy goes hunting with her father.

"Boys and Girls": The narrator does farm chores with her father.

Second point: In both stories, the girls struggle against the expectations of others.

"Doe Season": Mac and Charlie challenge Andy's right to hunt.

"Boys and Girls": Narrator's mother expects her to do household chores.

Third point: In both stories, the girls learn that they are limited by their gender.

"Doe Season": Andy shoots the deer but runs away, thinking of her mother.

"Boys and Girls": The narrator fails to save the horse and realizes she is "only a girl."

Subject-by-Subject Comparison

First subject: "Doe Season"

First point: Andy is a tomboy who is excited about going hunting with her father.

Second point: Charlie and Mac challenge her right to hunt.

Third point: Through her encounter with the deer, she learns that she is not as brave as she thought she was.

Second subject: "Boys and Girls"

First point: Like Andy, the narrator likes being with her father and is glad not to be in the house with her mother.

Second point: Like Andy, she is criticized by others.

Third point: Like Andy, she learns through her encounter with an animal—in her case, the horse whose life she cannot save—that she is limited by her gender.

✔ CHECKLIST Writing a Comparison-Contrast

- ☐ Have you chosen two subjects that have significant similarities?
- ☐ Does your thesis statement identify the two subjects you are comparing and tell why they are alike (and perhaps also briefly acknowledge their differences)?
- ☐ Does your paper's structure follow either a point-by-point or a subject-by-subject pattern?
- ☐ Does each of your topic sentences identify the subject you are discussing and the point you are focusing on in the paragraph?
- ☐ Do transitional words and phrases clearly lead readers from subject to subject and from point to point?
- ☐ Have you followed your instructor's format and documentation guidelines?

Comparing Two Fictional Characters

The following student paper, "The Dangerous Consequences of Societal Limbo," is a point-by-point comparison of two characters created by William Faulkner: Emily Grierson in "A Rose for Emily" (p. 243) and Abner (Ab) Snopes in "Barn Burning" (p. 391).

Quinn 1

David Quinn

Professor Warren

Literature 1120

27 February 2009

The Dangerous Consequences of Societal Limbo

In his many works of fiction, William Faulkner explores the lives of characters who live in the closed society of the American South, a society rooted in traditional values. In the stories "Barn Burning" and "A Rose for Emily," Faulkner explores what happens when individuals lose their connection to this society and its values. Both Abner Snopes, a rebellious sharecropper, and Emily Grierson, an unmarried woman from a prominent family, are isolated from their respective communities, and both find themselves in a kind of societal limbo. Once in that limbo, they no longer feel the need to adhere to the values of their society and, as a result, they are free to violate both traditional and moral rules.

Introduction

Thesis statement

Initially, Emily's isolation is not voluntary; it is thrust upon her. From childhood on, Emily is never really allowed to be part of Jefferson society; she is seen as having a "high and mighty" attitude (Faulkner, "Rose" 245). Her father stands between her and the rest of the town, refusing to allow her to date

Emily's isolation

Quinn 2

the young men who pursue her, whom he sees as somehow not good enough for her. As a result, her only close relationship is with her father, who essentially becomes her whole world. Recalling father and daughter, the narrator depicts them as static and alone, trapped in a living portrait, "Miss Emily a slender figure in white in the background, her father a spraddled silhouette in the foreground, his back to her and clutching a horsewhip" (Faulkner, "Rose" 246), framed by the archway of the entrance to their house. When Emily's father dies, and the townspeople insist on removing his body from her home, the only world she knows is physically taken from her, and she has nothing to take its place. Without her father, without friends, without a husband, she withdraws from her community—and, thus, is free to defy its rules with a shocking act of violence.

Ab's isolation

While Emily's removal from society is forced upon her, Abner Snopes voluntarily rejects his society's values. During the Civil War, he does not fight alongside the Confederate army; instead, he adopts an aggressive neutrality, stealing from both sides for his own personal gain. He is finally caught by the side he betrays when a Confederate policeman shoots him in the heel as Abner tries to escape on a stolen horse. Unable to see that he did something wrong, Abner uses his injury as an excuse for a personal vendetta against society. However, because he has a wife and three children whom he must feed and provide for, Ab must constantly return to the society that he turned his back on.

Quinn 3

This conflict between his rebellious nature and his need to work as a sharecropper makes him unstable. Like Emily, he does not see himself as part of the community, and therefore he feels free to violate its rules.

Once Emily and Abner are estranged from their respective communities, they no longer feel bound by society's laws and rules. This makes it possible for Abner to burn barns and for Emily to commit murder.

Transitional paragraph

Emily's courting and capturing of Homer Barron fills the void left by her father's death; for her, the act of poisoning Homer is a perverse method of regaining control. With this act, she takes away the very life that attracted her to him, but she is able to hold on to him as a physical entity. As an exile from society, Emily can rationalize this antisocial act: in her eyes, murder is no longer wrong; it is merely a method of preservation, a means to an end that ensures that Homer will remain with her until her death. Once Emily has completed the gruesome task of poisoning her "husband," she further withdraws from her community, and her neighbors (the narrator included) never suspect her secret. Without suspicion from the townspeople, Emily is left alone, free to live as she chooses.

Emily's antisocial act

Abner's impotent rage and search for vengeance push him to lash out violently at almost anyone with whom he comes in contact. His method of destruction comes in the primitive form of fire, which he uses not

Ab's anti-social acts

to kill but simply to threaten. In the two barn burnings of the story, Abner incites confrontations and then uses the burnings as a way of getting even for imagined offenses. In one incident, for example, Mr. Harris, a landowner, finds that Abner's hog ate a section of his corn crop. When Harris demands a dollar pound fee for the return of the hog, Abner sends him a threatening message: "Wood and hay kin burn" (Faulkner, "Barn" 392). Despite Harris's efforts to resolve their dispute, Abner is determined to carry out his threat. Ultimately, the barn burnings further alienate Ab from the society whose laws he is defying.

Emily's punishment

Like Ab Snopes, Emily makes her own rules and develops her own twisted concepts of justice and revenge. Although she is not directly punished by the community for her crime, Emily suffers terribly. She may possess the body of Homer Barron, but his death renders her incapable of holding onto him as a person and as a husband. The result of her gradual estrangement from society—involuntary at first but eventually confirmed by her willing violent act—is complete isolation from the real world and withdrawal into an empty world of her own.

Ab's punishment

Although Ab operates from within a similar societal limbo, he is unable to escape society's punishment. Sarty Snopes, Abner's son, is a firsthand witness to his father's second barn burning. Sarty is caught in a moral dilemma, pulled between the values of his community and the selfish motives of his father.

Quinn 5

Rather than remain in the alienated condition that his father has created for his family, Sarty renounces his loyalty to Abner and turns his father in to plantation owner Major De Spain.

Conclusion

Despite their estrangement from society, then, neither Emily nor Ab is ultimately able to escape its influence. In withdrawing from their respective communities, Emily Grierson and Abner Snopes are able to defy society's traditions and break its rules, but they also create empty lives for themselves and tragedy for those closest to them.

Quinn 6

Works Cited

Faulkner, William. "Barn Burning." Kirszner and Mandell 391-404.

---. "A Rose for Emily." Kirszner and Mandell 243-50.

Kirszner, Laurie G., and Stephen R. Mandell, eds. *Literature: Reading, Reacting, Writing.* 7th ed. Boston: Wadsworth, 2010. Print.

Comparing a Short Story and a Film

The following student paper, "Two Cathedrals," is a point-by-point comparison of Raymond Carver's short story "Cathedral" (p. 526) and a film version of the story.

Townsend 1

Jason Townsend

Professor Blair

English 102

8 February 2009

Two Cathedrals

Thesis statement

In many ways, the movie of Raymond Carver's "Cathedral" is very similar to the short story on which it is based. The plots are the same, the characters are the same, and much of the movie's dialogue is taken directly from the story. Still, there are a number of differences in how the characters' relationships, and other important information, are presented, and these differences help to explain the very different impacts of the endings.

First point of contrast: importance of past relationships

Early in the story, the first-person narrator tells about his wife's first marriage. The subject comes up as part of his explanation of how his wife came to work for Robert, the blind man who is about to visit. But the narrator describes her first marriage in a way that raises questions about the strength of their current marriage, saying, "she was in love with the guy, and he was in love with her, etc." (527). In the movie, on the other hand, the wife's first husband is not mentioned until after Robert's arrival. Here, the first husband is brought up to explain the wife's suicide attempt rather than to explain how she met Robert.

Townsend 2

As a result, the importance of the wife's first marriage is diminished in the movie, and the possibility of her romantic connection with Robert is heightened. This relationship is reinforced in the movie when Robert reminisces about how they sometimes drank Scotch together at the end of the workday—a memory that does not exist in the story.

Throughout the story, the narrator has no name. In addition, he refuses to use the name of his wife's first husband, asking, "why should he have a name? he was the childhood sweetheart, and what more does he want?"(528). The wife is also unnamed. Only Robert has a name and, thus, only he has an identity, a distinctive self. However, in the movie the wife calls the narrator Ed on one occasion; only she herself remains nameless. As a result, any notion that the story is about namelessness or identity is lost. Moreover, the wife's use of her husband's name in the film makes Robert's tendency to call him "Bub" hard to understand. In the story, this familiar usage makes sense, following logically from Robert's statement when they first meet: "'I feel like we've already met'" (529).

Second point of contrast: use of names

For years, Robert and the wife have stayed in touch through an exchange of audio tapes, and these tapes have different purposes in the story and the film. In the story, this exchange of tapes is used to emphasize the relationship, or potential relationship, between Robert and the husband. The narrator concludes his discussion of the tapes with a memory of his wife and himself listening to a tape from Robert. The narrator says they were interrupted just as Robert was about to say what he thought of

Third point of contrast: role of audio tapes

Townsend 3

the husband: "'From what you've said about him, I can only conclude —.'" The husband never listened to Robert's conclusion; he admits, "I'd heard all I wanted to" (528). In the movie, however, the tapes are used to emphasize the relationship between the husband and the wife. In a flashback in which the husband listens alone to a tape his wife had made for Robert, she tells Robert why she will probably remarry. The husband turns the recorder off in anger at the thought that he had been "settled for."

Fourth point of contrast: treatment of Robert's marriage

Robert's own marriage is also treated differently in the story and the film. In the story, the wife has two reasons for telling her husband about the death of Robert's wife. First, she uses it in connection with her attempt to make the husband's reaction to Robert a kind of test of their own relationship: "'If you love me,'" she tells him, "'you can do this for me'" (528). Second, she tells the story of Robert's wife dying as Robert held her hand to increase the husband's sympathy for Robert. In the movie, however, Robert himself tells the husband and the wife about his wife's death, and he presents information that does not exist in the story at all. Robert says that at the end his wife "lost her voice" and could only communicate by squeezing his hand, one squeeze for "yes" and two for "no." This discussion of touch as a means of communication, absent in the story, tends to decrease the surprise (and, therefore, diminish the power) of the joined hands that draw the cathedral at the story's end.

Fifth point of contrast: showing vs. suggesting

Similarly, Robert's touching of the wife's face with his hands on her last day of work is merely described by the narrator of the story. The narrator

Townsend 4

reports that his wife wrote a poem about this experience that he did not think much of, although he admits, "Maybe I just don't understand poetry" (527). A flashback in the movie actually shows Robert's hands feeling the features of the wife's face while the wife's voice reads the poem aloud. In short, what the reader of the story is encouraged to imagine is actually depicted in visual and audio images for a viewer of the movie. The film's ability to show rather than suggesting is one of the things that makes the endings of the story and the film so different.

Sixth point of contrast: staging of drawing scene

In the story, the narrator seeks out some ballpoint pens and a brown paper shopping bag in preparation for drawing a cathedral as Robert has suggested. When the narrator returns to the living room, he puts the paper bag on the coffee table and sits on the floor. At this point, the narrator says, "The blind man got down from the sofa and sat next to me on the carpet" (536). The description of the two men sitting together on the floor to draw almost suggests boys at play, childlike innocents who are more or less equals. In the movie, however, the husband returns to the dining room and sits in a chair to work at the table. Robert stands behind him, blind but still "looking" over his shoulder, suggesting a teacher and a student or a parent and a child—people who are unequal.

Last (and most important) point of contrast: treatment of cathedral picture

The greatest single difference between the story and the movie is the treatment of the actual picture of a cathedral that the men draw. Viewers of the movie see it being drawn and see it in its finished state. When the husband—with his eyes still closed—judges the work he has done with Robert and says, "'It's really

Townsend 5

something,'" viewers know exactly what the picture looks like. Readers of the story, on the other hand, must imagine the picture and the experience of creating the drawing—an experience that is, the narrator says, "like nothing else in my life up to now" (537). Their own inability to see the finished product makes it possible for readers to understand both the limitations and the power of Robert's blindness.

Conclusion

Because the story is about blindness and sight, the visual capabilities of the movie are important. However, rather than strengthening the story, the film's visual images are to some extent intrusive. The substitution of an actual visual image of the cathedral for readers' own imagined image changes everything. In fact, those who read the story are more likely to understand Robert's perspective, and to sense what the narrator experienced, than those who see the movie are.

Townsend 6

Works Cited

Carver, Raymond. "Cathedral." *Literature: Reading, Reacting, Writing*. Ed. Laurie G. Kirszner and Stephen R. Mandell. 7th ed. Boston: Wadsworth, 2010. 526-37. Print.

The Heinle Original Film Series in Literature: Raymond Carver's "Cathedral." Dir. Bruce R. Schwartz. Wadsworth, 2003. DVD.

NOTE:

- For a model student paper that compares two stories, see "Mesmerizing Men and Vulnerable Teens. . . ." (p. 654).
- For a model student paper that compares two poems, see "Digging for Memories" (p. 833).
- For possible topics for comparing a poem and a work of art, see Chapter 23.
- For additional possibilities for comparison-contrast papers, see the "Related Works" lists that follow many of the selections in this book.

Writing an Explication

When you write an **explication** (of a poem, a short story, or a scene in a play), you do a close reading of a work or a portion of a work, carefully analyzing one or more of its elements. For example, you might decide to analyze a story's characters, symbols, or setting; a poem's language, rhyme scheme, meter, or form; or a play's dialogue or staging. One way to approach a work you wish to explicate is to apply the guidelines for reading fiction (pp. 195–96), poetry (pp. 817–20), or drama (pp. 1287-89) in a systematic way. Another way is to use the Explicator mark-up tool on *English21*.

When you organize your material in an explication, you should proceed systematically. If you are focusing on a single element, analyze its importance in one section of the work at a time. If you are analyzing several elements, consider each—plot, setting, point of view, and so on—in turn. You will probably choose to group the less significant elements together in a single paragraph or section of your paper and then devote several paragraphs to one particularly important element, carefully considering how symbols, for example, shed light on the work. For each element you discuss, you will give examples from the work you are explicating, quoting words, phrases, lines, and passages that illustrate each point you are making.

✔ CHECKLIST Writing an Explication

- ☐ Is the work you have chosen sufficiently rich to support an explication?
- ☐ Do topic sentences make clear which element (or elements) you are focusing on in each paragraph?
- ☐ Do you use quotations from the work to illustrate your points?
- ☐ Does your thesis state the central point about the work that your explication supports?
- ☐ Have you followed your instructor's format and documentation guidelines?

Explicating a Poem

The following student paper, "A Lingering Doubt," is an explication of Robert Frost's poem "The Road Not Taken" (p. 1159).

Craff 1

Jeanette Craff

Professor Rosenberg

English 102

13 February 2009

A Lingering Doubt

Introduction

Sometimes it is tempting to look back on a lifetime of choices and decisions and to think, "What if? What if I had made a different choice? Would my life be better? Worse? More interesting?" In Robert Frost's poem "The Road Not Taken," the speaker does just this: he looks back at a time in his life when he came to a fork in the road and chose one path over another. He tells readers that he "took the one less traveled by, /And that has made all the difference" (lines 19-20). At first, this statement seems to suggest that the speaker is satisfied with the decision he made long ago. However, certain elements in the poem—its structure, its language, and even its title—suggest that the speaker is regretting his decision, not celebrating it.

Thesis statement

Overview of poem's language and theme

The title of the poem, "The Road Not Taken," immediately suggests that the speaker is focusing not on the choice he *did* make long ago but on the road he chose *not* to take. The poem's language supports this interpretation. Frost begins his poem with the speaker recalling that "Two roads diverged in a yellow wood" and saying that he is "sorry [he] could not

Craff 2

travel both" (1-2). The image Frost uses of the two roads diverging is an obvious metaphor for the choices a person has to make in the course of a lifetime. As a young man, the speaker was not aware of any major difference between the two roads. He says that he saw one as "just as fair" (6) as the other, and he uses words and phrases such as "equally" (11) and "really about the same" (10). However, in the third stanza of the poem, the older and wiser speaker, looking back on that period of his life, says that he still might take the other road "another day" (13). That the mature speaker still continues to examine a decision he made earlier in life suggests that he may not be completely satisfied with that decision.

Analysis of poem's structure and meter

A close look at the poem suggests that it is the departures from the expected structure and meter that make its meaning clear. The poem is divided into four stanzas, each made up of five lines. The regular meter of these four stanzas conveys a sense of tranquillity and certainty. The regularity of the poem's rhyme scheme (a, b, a, a, b) also contributes to the poem's natural fluidity. This fluidity is evident, for example, in the first stanza:

> Two roads diverged in a yellow wood,
> And sorry I could not travel both
> And be one traveler, long I stood
> And looked down one as far as I could
> To where it bent in the undergrowth; (1-5)

Here, the end rhyme of lines 1, 3, and 4 and of lines 2 and 5, as well as the even line lengths (each line contains nine syllables), make the poem flow smoothly.

Craff 3

Further analysis of poem's structure and meter

However, the poem does not maintain this fluidity. In other stanzas, lines range from eight to ten syllables, and the important final stanza ends with a line that is an awkward metrical departure from the rest of the poem:

I shall be telling this with a sigh
Somewhere ages and ages hence:
Two roads diverged in a wood, and I—
I took the one less traveled by, And
that has made all the difference. (16-20)

In this stanza, line 20 has nine syllables as lines 16 and 18 do, but unlike them, it also has an irregular meter ("And that has made all the difference"), which forces readers to hesitate on the word "all" before landing on "difference." This hesitation, coupled with the hesitation signaled by the dash that ends line 18, suggests the speaker's doubts about his decision. When the speaker was young, he did not notice any significant difference between the two roads, or the two life choices, presented to him. Now, looking back, he believes that there was a difference, and he may be lamenting the fact that he will never know where life would have taken him had he chosen differently.

Analysis of poem's language

Departure from expected meter is not the only strategy Frost uses to convey a sense of hesitation and an air of regret. Frost's choice of words also plays an important part in helping readers understand the poem's theme. In the first stanza, for example, the speaker thinks back to the period of his life in

Craff 4

which he had to choose between two separate paths, and he says that he was "sorry [he] could not travel both" (2). The word "sorry" helps to establish the tone of regret that pervades the poem.

In the second stanza, Frost begins to use words and phrases to convey indecision and doubt in the speaker's voice. The speaker attempts to pacify himself by saying that the road he chose had "perhaps the better claim" (7), but then he is quick to say that the passage of time has worn both roads "really about the same" (10). The words "perhaps" and "really" suggest indecision, and Frost's choice of these words helps to convey the doubt in the speaker's mind.

The speaker's sense of regret deepens in the third stanza as he continues to think back on his decision. When the speaker says, "Oh, I kept the first for another day!" (13), the word "Oh" expresses his regret. The exclamation point at the end of the statement helps reinforce the finality of his decision. When the speaker continues, "Yet knowing how way leads on to way, / I doubted if I should ever come back" (14-15), the word "Yet" is filled with uncertainty.

In the poem's final stanza, the speaker suddenly leaves his thoughts of the past and speaks in the future tense: "I shall be telling this [story] with a sigh" (16). Frost's use of the word "sigh" here is very revealing because it connotes resignation or

Craff 5

regret. The speaker concludes, "Two roads diverged in a wood, and I— / I took the one less traveled by, / And that has made all the difference" (18-20). Both the dash and the repetition of the word "I" convey hesitation and thus communicate his lingering doubts over the decision he made long ago.

Conclusion

Although this doubt is evident throughout the poem, "The Road Not Taken" has frequently been interpreted as optimistic because of the speaker's final statement that the choice he made "has made all the difference" (20). However, "made all the difference" can be interpreted as neutral (or even negative) as well as positive, and so the speaker's statement at the end of the poem may actually be a statement of regret, not celebration. The "difference" mentioned in the final line has left a doubt in the speaker's mind, and, as Frost suggests in the title of his poem, the speaker is left thinking about the road he did not take—and will never be able to take.

Craff 6

Work Cited

Frost, Robert. "The Road Not Taken." *Literature: Reading, Reacting, Writing*. Ed. Laurie G. Kirszner and Stephen R. Mandell. 7th ed. Boston: Wadsworth, 2010. 1159. Print.

Explicating a Graphic Story

The following student paper, "Tough Questions," is an explication of Lynda Barry's graphic story "Two Questions" (p. 556).

Frederick 1

Jay Frederick

Professor Barlow

English 102

10 February 2009

Tough Questions

Lynda Barry's graphic story "Two Questions" focuses on a writer's thirty-year career "making pictures and stories." Barry's illustrations work together with her words not only to tell a story but also to give advice to other aspiring writers and artists: "Both self-doubt and criticism from others will eventually stifle inherent creativity. Don't let it. Ignore these two questions: 'Is this good?' and 'Does this suck?'" In this graphic story, both words and illustrations convey the idea that creative self-expression requires letting go of the need for approval.

Thesis statement

Using words, the first-person narrator describes a "floating feeling" that would arise when, as a child, she made lines on paper, making her feel "like I was both there and not there" (557). "The lines made a picture and the picture made a story," she remembers (557). In "Two Questions," the story's words convey both the fun and excitement of a child freely experimenting with imaginative thoughts and the frustration of an adult whose writing and drawing must serve a particular purpose. Key words used to

Analysis of story's words

Frederick 2

describe the innocent child and her creative process include "spontaneity," "genius," "enjoyment," "talent," "brilliant," "fun," and "surprise" (562-565). In contrast, the jaded adult who still draws or writes is described as experiencing "doubt," "worry," "regrets," and "dread" and as feeling "stupid" and under "extreme pressure" (562,564). Still, even after most of her classmates "quit drawing and never drew again," the adult narrator confesses that she kept drawing because she had "figured out how to make the good kind"—drawings that drew praise from adults (560). (Of course, these drawings were devoid of originality.)

The story's two questions—"Is this good?" and "Does this suck?"—do not even occur to a child. The adult narrator suggests, however, that as these questions came to dominate her thoughts about her work, she "stopped enjoying it and instead began to dread it" (556). Ignoring the two questions "long enough to let something alive take shape" is the only way to restore the writer's spontaneous creativity and thus enable her to create more compelling work (567).

Analysis of story's graphics

The story's graphics, like its words, reveal both the child's and the adult's perspectives (as well as the conflict between the two). The illustrations show some of the "many ways for a picture to be bad" in the eyes of critics (561) by including abstract, scatological, and sexual images. Children are more likely to be amused than embarrassed or ashamed upon witnessing images of nudity, defecation, or sex. Eventually, however, innocence and creativity are lost when children are taught that such images are "bad" and they

Frederick 3

learn to work not for their own joy but for someone else's approval. Only when the narrator realizes that "so much is possible" (567) without the two questions can she regain the creativity of her childhood.

"Bad" images

The abstract images in "Two Questions" include amoeba-like images that haunt and taunt with facial expressions. Humans and animals (including cats, dogs, birds, and various sea creatures) are often barely recognizable. Abstract depictions of reality are often regarded as inferior to more realistic images, and as children grow older they learn that unless their drawings clearly resemble reality, they are considered "bad." The story suggests that negative reinforcement causes many children, no matter how much talent they have, to give up their drawing—and writing—as they get older. Those who do not give up are the few who are able to produce "good" work according to either critics or their own self-judgment. Unfortunately, however, this "good" work often lacks creativity.

Scatological images also appear throughout the story—for example, in the third panel of the story, where a cat is depicted making rude noises ("sssuck!" and "rawk") while defecating (558). The scene is repeated five times on succeeding pages until the final panel (see fig. 1), where the cat, smiling and standing on two feet, has finally stopped the offensive behavior. This final scene suggests that writers and illustrators of all ages who have refused to contemplate the "two questions"—that is, refused to judge their own work—have had their creativity restored.

Frederick 4

Fig. 1. Final panel from Lynda Barry's "Two Questions"; Lynda Barry, "Two Questions," *Literature: Reading, Reacting, Writing*, ed. Laurie G. Kirszner and Stephen R. Mandell, 7th ed. (Boston: Wadsworth, 2010; print; 567).

Other images in "Two Questions" might also be seen as "bad." One is a drawing of a pair of topless bathing beauties posing on a sunny beach, described by the innocent six-year-old creator as "very pretty" (559). The other image, packed into a panel crowded with both graphics and words, is a pair of copulating figures, presumably non-human (562). (Species and gender are both unclear; if the image were more "realistic," it might be offensive.)

Images that reveal writer's fears and doubts

Like recurring dreams, graphic images dramatize the self-doubt and fear that accompany a writer who is

Frederick 5

facing judgment and deadlines. The first such image to appear in "Two Questions" is a scissors-wielding, topsy-turvy editor demanding "Let's see that picture-story!!" (558). The editor represents deadline pressure and literary judgment (approval or disapproval) in the same persona. Another image is Miss Astringent, the first-grade teacher who used the innocently conceived drawing of the pair of semi-naked beach girls as evidence that the youthful artist was "dirty, stupid or lame" (560), suggesting "You'll never amount to anything." Impending doom is represented by images of the narrator in a tiny boat fighting a tide and about to plunge over a waterfall. These images appear when "bad" drawings carry enough stigma to make their creators quit drawing and never draw again. Finally, Octopus, the only symbol appearing prominently on each page of "Two Questions," suggests the dominant inner voice, which in the end (see fig. 1) guides and nurtures the narrator's creative nature as she regains the "strange floating feeling" (567) that she experienced as a child.

Conclusion

In "Two Questions," Lynda Barry describes the inevitable decline of creativity in aspiring writers and artists. Her narrator expresses both the euphoria and satisfaction of creativity ("good" work) and the gloom and doom that come with self-doubt and disapproval (the fear of producing "bad" work). In "Two Questions," the complementary use of narrative and images encourages aspiring writers and illustrators to work for themselves—and let the critics be damned.

Frederick 6

Work Cited

Barry, Lynda. "Two Questions." *Literature: Reading, Reacting, Writing*. Ed. Laurie G. Kirszner and Stephen R. Mandell. 7th ed. Boston: Wadsworth, 2010. 556-6. Print.

NOTE: For model student papers that explicate short stories, see "'The Secret Lion': Everything Changes" (p. 215) and "And Again She Makes the Journey: Character and Act in Eudora Welty's 'A Worn Path'" (p. 129).

Writing a Character Analysis

When you write a **character analysis** of a character in a short story or play, you can focus on a major or a minor character, examining the character's language, behavior, background, interaction with other characters, and reaction to his or her environment. Everything you are told about a character—and everything you can reasonably infer about him or her from words, actions, or appearance—can help you to understand the character. In your analysis, you can focus on the influences that shaped the character, the character's effect on others, how the character changes during the course of the story or play, or what motivates him or her to act (or not to act).

✔ CHECKLIST Writing a Character Analysis

- ☐ Have you chosen a character who is interesting enough to serve as the focus of your paper?
- ☐ Have you considered the character's words, actions, appearance, and interactions with others?
- ☐ Have you considered how and why the character changes—or why he or she fails to change?
- ☐ Have you considered how the work would be different if the character had made different choices?
- ☐ Have you considered how the work would be different without the character?
- ☐ Have you considered what motivates the character to act (or not to act)?
- ☐ Have you followed your instructor's format and documentation guidelines?

Analyzing a Character in a Play

The following student paper, "Linda Loman: Breaking the Mold," analyzes a character in Arthur Miller's play *Death of a Salesman* (p. 1531).

Dube 1

Caroline Dube
Professor Nelson
English 1302
14 February 2009

Linda Loman: Breaking the Mold

In many ways, Linda Loman appears to play the part of the stereotypical dutiful and loving wife in Arthur Miller's *Death of a Salesman*. She eagerly greets her husband, ignores his shortcomings, and maintains an upbeat attitude, all while managing the bills, waxing the floors, and mending the clothes. Her kindness and infinite patience seem to establish her as a foil for Willy, with his turbulent temperament. In addition, most of her actions seem to be only reactions to the other characters in the play. However, a closer look at Linda reveals a more complex woman: a fully developed character with dreams, insights, and flashes of defiance.

Thesis statement

Unlike stock characters, whose motivations seem transparent and obvious, Linda has dreams that are both complex and realistically human. The stage directions that introduce Linda describe her as sharing Willy's "turbulent longings" but lacking the temperament to pursue them (1532). It seems she has applied the wisdom she shares with Willy, that "life is a casting off," to her own cast-away dreams (1533). Linda's hopes seem more realistic than Willy's. She wants Biff to settle down, the mortgage to be paid off, and the members of her

Linda's hopes and dreams

Dube 2

family to coexist happily. These modest aspirations are the product of Linda's long experience. The fact that Linda does not pursue unrealistic goals, as Willy does, does not make her a flat character (or even a less interesting one); instead, her weaknesses give her character a degree of depth and human realism.

Linda's actions

At times, Linda takes on the role of family peacemaker—a role we would expect her to play consistently throughout the play if she were simply a stock character. But Linda breaks out of the obedient wife mode on several occasions. When Willy insists that she stop mending her stockings, Linda quietly puts them into her pocket to resume her mending later. When Biff and Happy show they are ashamed of their father, Linda fiercely lashes out at them in his defense, calling Happy a "philandering bum" and threatening to kick Biff out of the house for good (1557). Although at first she cannot bring herself to remove the rubber pipe that Willy used to commit suicide, Linda says she had finally decided to destroy the pipe when Biff removed it. She does not always have an opportunity to follow through on her threats, but Linda demonstrates clearly that she will not always follow orders—especially when she is protecting Willy.

Linda's awareness of family problems

Linda seems to be the cheerful voice of the family, but beneath the surface, she is keenly aware of the ongoing problems. She knows that Charley has been giving money to Willy every week, but she says

Dube 3

nothing for fear of embarrassing Willy. She senses Willy's suicidal tendencies and even finds physical evidence of his plans. Linda is the first to raise doubts about Biff's plans to ask Mr. Oliver for money, suggesting that he may not remember Biff. Above all, Linda understands human nature and how the minds of those around her work. She gives an honest description of her husband and his situation:

> I don't say he's a great man. Willy Loman never made a lot of money. His name was never in the paper. He's not the finest character that ever lived. But he's a human being, and a terrible thing is happening to him. So attention must be paid. (1556)

Linda sees past her sons' exaggerated lies and is not afraid to criticize them for their selfish choices. She pretends to be unaware of their shortcomings, but her feigned obliviousness is simply another layer in her multifaceted personality.

Linda appears to be the steadiest character in the play, providing stability for the other characters, but her constant brushing aside of problems actually makes her the most responsible for the ultimate tragedy of the play. She lies to Willy in order to soothe him, telling him he has "too much on the ball to worry about" (1535) and is "the handsomest man in the world" (1546). In the process, she allows him to continue believing in the unattainable dreams that ultimately lead him to self-destruct. She also

Linda's failure to confront family problems

Dube 4

makes exceptions for her sons, suggesting Willy can simply talk to Biff's teacher to change his grade and encouraging Biff's business plans even when she knows he will not succeed. As a result, failure hits Biff hard because he has not been forced to think realistically.

Conclusion

In the end, Linda goes beyond the stereotypical boundaries of her role as ever-supportive wife and mother. There are many layers to her character: beneath her simple goals of owning her home and living happily with her family lie years of disappointments and failed dreams. Hidden beneath her eagerness to please is her willingness to defy orders to defend her husband. And, although she seems not to notice what is going on, she is perceptive about the family's problems long before others show awareness. Her actions clearly show that she is more than a minor supporting character. Linda is deeply involved in the actions and impulses of the other characters in the play. As a fully developed character, she has complex motivations and human qualities (including faults) that set her apart from stock characters. As her son Happy notes, "They broke the mold when they made her" (1561).

Dube 5

Work Cited

Miller, Arthur. *Death of a Salesman. Literature: Reading, Reacting, Writing*. Ed. Laurie G. Kirszner and Stephen R. Mandell. 7th ed. Boston: Wadsworth, 2010. 1534-602. Print.

Analyzing a Character in a Short Story

The following student paper, "A Change of Seasons," analyzes the main character in Katherine Mansfield's classic short story "Miss Brill" (p. 266).

Mohan 1

Elizabeth Mohan

Professor Hope

English 202

22 February 2009

A Change of Seasons

The title character in Katherine Mansfield's "Miss Brill" seems at first to be a familiar static character, following a predictable, unchanging routine. She spends every Sunday afternoon at a park, attending a band concert. While in the park, she is in the habit of observing other people and listening in on their conversations. In fact, she thinks of herself as "really quite expert . . . at listening as though she didn't listen, at sitting in other people's lives just for a minute while they talked round her" (267). Every Sunday, after she leaves the park, she stops at a bakery for a piece of cake. Her routine never varies, and she seems to be in complete control of her orderly life. However, this control turns out to be an illusion. On one particular Sunday afternoon, Miss Brill experiences a series of small changes as she sits on her park bench, and with these changes she becomes a dynamic character who is transformed when she finally understands her limited role in life.

Thesis statement

Miss Brill is cut off from friends and family. Whether by choice or chance, she lives in a seaside town in France, a country other than her own.

Miss Brill's character: Background

Mohan 2

She is also completely cut off from her own past. Her thoughts never drift further back in time than to a conversation she overheard in the park the previous week. Miss Brill seems to work hard to maintain a public persona in front of strangers and to keep her thoughts firmly in the present. For years, her struggle for control has been successful. Now, however, everything is about to change.

Changes foreshadowed

The changes in Miss Brill are foreshadowed by a change in the weather. The story's action unfolds on the first Sunday of the new "Season," a time of year when tourists come to the town where Miss Brill lives. This period coincides with a shift in the weather, the beginning of autumn, and there is a chill in the air as well as an occasional falling leaf. It is this change in the weather that makes Miss Brill decide to bring out her fur and wear it around her neck.

The fur—the skin of a small animal shaped so that its teeth are biting its tail—was perhaps once elegant and fashionable, but it is now the worse for wear. Miss Brill does the best she can to revive it—she "rubbed the life back into the dim little eyes" (266)—and make it presentable. Her failure to replace or properly repair the fur suggests that Miss Brill has limited economic resources. Her emotional resources are also limited, and the fur comforts her and serves as a companion for her—as a replacement for a pet, or a child, or a lover. She calls it "little rogue" and feels the urge to place it in her lap and stroke it (266). At the sight of a falling leaf, Miss Brill touches the fur for reassurance.

Mohan 3

At first, as she sits on her bench, Miss Brill is content to be an observer, a member of the audience both for the band concert and for the life around her. She watches, she listens, and she judges—sometimes harshly. But an unusual observation leads her to discover something new about her public role, leading her to elevate herself from a member of the audience to an actress, from an observer to a participant: Changes begin

> But it wasn't till a little brown dog trotted on solemn and then slowly trotted off, like a little "theatre" dog, a little dog that had been drugged, that Miss Brill discovered what it was that made it so exciting. They were all on the stage. (268)

This discovery allows Miss Brill for the first time to explain elements of her own behavior that had puzzled her. She has always taken care to leave her room for the park at precisely the same time every Sunday. Now she thinks she knows why: to play her part in the performance. She also now feels able to explain why she "had quite a queer, shy feeling" when she told her "English pupils"—no doubt French children to whom she taught English—how she spends her Sunday afternoons (268).

Now that she sees herself as part of the drama taking place around her, Miss Brill feels the urge to sing and imagines all of the people in the park breaking into song. She now has a new feeling of sympathy with the other people sitting on the benches—people she had previously thought of as odd,

Mohan 4

old, and solitary: "Miss Brill's eyes filled with tears and she looked smiling at all the other members of the company. Yes, we understand, we understand, she thought—though what they understood she didn't know" (269).

Epiphany occurs

This sense of belonging is quickly shown to be false when two lovers sit near her. Miss Brill recognizes them immediately as the "hero and heroine" of the play taking place in the park. When she listens to their conversation, she hears them brutally describe her as an unwanted obstacle to their desires. Worse, the girl describes Miss Brill's beloved fur as "funny" and says, "It's exactly like a fried whiting" (269). Stunned by the revelation of how she appears to strangers and how they think of her, Miss Brill leaves the park and goes home.

Negative changes

The last two brief paragraphs of the story make clear for the first time the extent to which Miss Brill's Sunday ritual has always kept her going, revived her spirit. The trip to the park is always followed by the purchase of a slice of cake at a bakery. She thinks of the slice of cake as "her Sunday treat" (269), and this treat has a magical element. The slice of cake sometimes has an almond in it, and whether an almond was present or absent "made a great difference" (269) to her. The presence of an almond meant spiritual renewal, a heightening of her morale. The narrator explains, "She hurried on the almond Sundays and struck the match for the kettle in quite a dashing way" (269). After overhearing the young lovers mock her, however,

Mohan 5

Miss Brill goes home without stopping to buy a piece of cake, as if she has lost faith in the chance for renewal.

Once home, Miss Brill returns her fur to the box without looking at it. She is still unable to face directly the fact that she is in pain, but clearly she is suffering. The story ends with Miss Brill thinking that "she heard something crying," as if trying to attribute her own feelings to the fur (269).

"Miss Brill" is the story of an isolated, friendless woman who is growing older and who, at the end, finally realizes her limitations. She has limited options, limited funds, and a limited social range. She is not really a participant in the life around her but, after all, just an observer. Although for years she was able to maintain a routine that allowed her to ignore her life's shortcomings and keep going, when her world begins to change, the routine is no longer enough.

Conclusion

Mohan 6

Work Cited

Mansfield, Katherine. "Miss Brill." *Literature: Reading, Reacting, Writing*. Ed. Laurie G. Kirszner and Stephen R. Mandell. 7th ed. Boston: Wadsworth, 2010. 266-69. Print.

NOTE:

- For a model student paper analyzing a major character in a short story, see "And Again She Makes the Journey: Character and Act in Eudora Welty's 'A Worn Path'" (p. 129).
- For two model student papers analyzing characters in plays, see "Laura's Gentleman Caller" (p. 2039) and "Desperate Measures: Acts of Defiance in *Trifles*" (p. 1301).

Writing about a Work's Cultural Context

When you explore the **cultural context** of a short story, poem, or play, you set the work in a particular time and place. Acknowledging that literary works do not exist in a vacuum, you consider factors such as the characters' social class and cultural or racial background as well as specific events that occurred at the time in which the story is set or written. You can also consider practices and situations that were characteristic of the time—for example, the wife's subservient role in Arthur Miller's *Death of a Salesman* (p. 1531) or racial discrimination in Richard Wright's "Big Black Good Man" (p. 374).

When you write your paper, you examine the connections between the work's cultural setting and the work itself, considering how particular situations and events influence the characters' actions. For example, you might see that a character in a story or play is limited— or inspired to act—by his or her race or class or gender, or by a social movement, such as feminism, or a particular event, such as a war. To set the work in context, you will probably need to do some research—perhaps reading contemporary newspapers, diaries, and letters as well as current critical interpretations of the cultural period on which you are focusing. You might even want to interview someone who lived through the events that influenced the work—for example, someone who lived through the Great Depression, which has a great impact on the lives of the characters in "I Stand Here Ironing" (p. 344).

It usually makes sense to begin your paper with an overview to help orient readers who are not familiar with the work's background. You might also **explicate** the work (see p. 61), systematically exploring specific parallels between the historical setting and the work. Alternatively, you might focus on one character in a story or play, examining how that character is shaped by the events or conventions of a particular cultural time—for example, how Ab Snopes in William Faulkner's "Barn Burning" (p. 391) has been affected by the Civil War—and by his inferior station in life.

✔ **CHECKLIST Writing about a Work's Cultural Context**

- ☐ Is a particular figure or event an important influence on the work?
- ☐ Is a cultural movement an important influence on the work?

- Do you summarize and explain the relevant cultural background?
- Do you clearly explain the relationship between the cultural background and the literary work?
- Do you use examples and quotations from the literary work to illustrate specific parallels between the work of literature and its cultural context?
- Have you followed your instructor's format and documentation guidelines?

Writing about a Poem's Cultural Context

The following student paper, "Dreaming of Home," sets Louise Erdrich's poem "Indian Boarding School: The Runaways" (p. 1155) in the context of the events that inspired it.

Monteleone 1

Matt Monteleone
Professor Kennedy
Composition 101
11 February 2009

Dreaming of Home

Louise Erdrich's poem "Indian Boarding School: The Runaways" describes the experiences of Native American children who have been sent to a US-government-sponsored boarding school. Although the experiences themselves are traumatic and heart wrenching, the full impact of the poem comes only with an understanding of the United States government's motivation for creating these schools and of their treatment of the Native American children who lived there during the late nineteenth and early twentieth centuries. With this background, Erdrich's work becomes not only a moving description of the painful experience of Native American children at federal boarding schools, but also a political statement about the treatment of Native Americans in the United States—and, perhaps, a statement about the pain of forced cultural assimilation.

Introduction

Thesis statement

Monteleone 2

Explication of poem's theme

"Indian Boarding School: The Runaways" relates the experience of Indian children struggling to maintain their cultural identities and preserve their cherished memories of home despite a series of efforts to purge them of their Indian heritage. Erdrich uses haunting language to explain that, for these children, the world they once knew has changed to such an extent that it exists only in their imaginations. Therefore, the children can escape to their home only when they go to sleep, and dream. In the first stanza, the narrator conveys her longing when she says, "Home's the place we head for in our sleep. / Boxcars stumbling north in dreams / don't wait for us. We catch them on the run" (lines 1-3). At night, the children dream of making their way home. In the daytime, they are "cold in regulation clothes" (11), forced to wear "dresses, long green ones" (17) and to engage in "shameful" manual labor (19). To fight the assimilation being forced upon them, the children have only their memories.

Transitional paragraph

By relating the experiences of these "runaways" and their dreams of home, Erdrich recreates the emotional experience of Native American children sent to the US government's boarding schools. The history of these Indian schools further explains the experience described in the poem and sheds light on the consequences of America's policy of forced assimilation.

Background: Rationalization for US government's Indian boarding schools

During the late 1800s and early 1900s, the United States government sponsored a variety of initiatives aimed at assimilating Native Americans into white culture. Although some government officials genuinely believed that assimilation was the best way for Native Americans to live better, happier lives, this policy was grounded in the assumption that white

Monteleone 3

culture is superior to Indian culture. As a result, government officials used a variety of methods to encourage assimilation, and the establishment of the non-reservation boarding school was one of them. According to the *Modern American Poetry* Web site, the Carlisle Indian Industrial School, established in 1879 with 139 students from the Rosebud and Pine Ridge nations, was one of the first of these schools. A description of the Carlisle Indian Industrial School reveals that Erdrich's poem is rooted in actual events.

Background: History of Indian boarding schools

According to the Cumberland County Historical Society in Pennsylvania, where the Carlisle Industrial School was located, in 1879 General Richard Henry Pratt received permission from the United States government to use a former military base as the site of the first Indian boarding school. Although the school closed in 1918, Carlisle served as a model for many of the other Indian boarding schools around the United States. Consequently, an examination of its policies and practices will explain how most Indian boarding schools operated.

After receiving permission from the government, Pratt traveled to the Rosebud and Pine Ridge reservations to recruit students. According to the *Carlisle Indian Industrial School,* the chief of the Rosebud reservation, although initially reluctant, eventually agreed to send some children from the reservation to the school. Pratt soon convinced other Indian nations, including the Cheyenne, Kiowa, and Lakota, to send their children to the school as well. At the Carlisle school, the teachers used a variety of methods to "civilize" the Native American students.

Monteleone 4

For example, as the *Modern American Poetry* Web site explains, students were given new names, their hair was cut, and they were forced to speak English instead of their tribal languages. (The *Carlisle Indian Industrial School* notes that members of the Lakota nation cut hair to symbolize mourning, so this practice was particularly upsetting to the Lakota children.) The photo in fig. 1 shows a group of Indian children at the Carlisle school. Like the girls being forced to wear long green dresses in Erdrich's poem, these Indian students are dressed in school uniforms, not in their native clothing.

Source: Photograph by U.S. Army Signal Corps, Courtesy of the Arizona Historical Foundation

Fig. 1. Apache children four months after arriving at the Carlisle Indian Industrial School in Pennsylvania; Owen Lindauer, "Archaeology of the Phoenix Indian School," *Archaeology* (Archaeological Inst. of Amer., 27 Mar. 1998; Web; 10 Jan. 2009).

Monteleone 5

Parents did not always send their children to Carlisle willingly. The *Carlisle Indian Industrial School* explains that when Geronimo, chief of the Apache nation, was arrested, Pratt traveled to Fort Mario prison, where the Apache children were being held. Pratt then picked sixty-two of the children to be sent to Carlisle, despite pleas from their parents. In an effort to prevent them from leaving, several of the parents hid the children, but Pratt eventually found them, and the children were sent to the school.

Erdrich closes her poem by explaining how the children try to remember their cultural heritage even as they are being forced to adopt the customs of white America:

> Our brushes cut the stone in watered arcs
> and in the soak frail outlines shiver clear
> a moment, things us kids pressed on the dark
> face before it hardened, pale, remembering
> delicate old injuries, the spines of names
> and leaves. (20-24)

The history of the Indian boarding schools, and how they worked to rid children of their Native American identities, clearly informs this poem. In this sense, Erdrich's work is not only literary; it is also political. By invoking an emotional response in her readers, Erdrich is able to expose a dark side of United States history and its treatment of Native Americans.

Monteleone 6

Works Cited

"Carlisle Indian Industrial School." *Cumberland County Historical Society*. PaDotNet, n.d. Web. 11 Jan. 2009

Erdrich, Louise. "Indian Boarding School: The Runaways." *Literature: Reading, Reacting, Writing*. Ed. Laurie G. Kirszner and Stephen R. Mandell. 7th ed. Boston: Wadsworth, 2010. 1155. Print.

Landis, Barbara. "History." *Carlisle Indian Industrial School*. N.p., 1996. Web. 10 Jan. 2009.

Nelson, Cary, comp. "About Indian Boarding Schools: Key Issues and Challenges." *Modern American Poetry*. Dept. of English, U of Illinois, Urbana-Champaign, 2002. Web. 10 Jan. 2009.

Writing about a Story's Cultural Context

The following student paper, "'A&P': A Class Act," explores class conflict in John Updike's short story "A&P" (p. 259).

NOTE: For additional possibilities for writing about a work's cultural context, see the **cultural context** paragraphs that precede many of the selections in this text.

Westmoreland 1

Tim Westmoreland

Professor Adkins

Literature 2101

25 February 2009

"A&P": A Class Act

John Updike's "A&P," like many of his other works, is a "profoundly American" story about social inequality and an attempt to bridge the gap between social classes (Steiner). The story is told by an eighteen-year-old boy who is working as a checkout clerk in an A&P in a small New England town five miles from the beach. The narrative is delivered in a slangy, colloquial voice that tells of a brief but powerful encounter with a "beautiful but inaccessible girl" from another social and economic level (Wells 128). Sammy, the narrator, is working his cash register on a slow Thursday afternoon when, as he says, "In walks these three girls in nothing but bathing suits" (Updike, "A&P" 259). Lengel, the store's manager—a Sunday school teacher and "self-appointed moral policeman"—confronts the girls, telling them that they should be decently dressed (Wells 131). It is a moment of embarrassment and insight for all parties concerned, and in an apparently impulsive act, Sammy quits his job. Although the plot is simple, what is at the heart of the story is complex: a noble gesture that serves as a futile attempt to cross social and economic boundaries.

Thesis statement

Through Sammy's eyes, we see the class conflict that defines the story. The privileged young girls in bathing suits are very different from the few

Sammy's view of Queenie

Westmoreland 2

customers who are shopping in the store. Sammy refers to the customers as "sheep" (Updike, "A&P" 261) and describes one of them as "a witch about fifty with rouge on her cheekbones and no eyebrows" (Updike, "A&P" 259). Other customers are characterized in equally negative terms—for example, "houseslaves in pin curlers" (Updike, "A&P" 261) and "an old party in baggy gray pants" (Updike, "A&P" 262). Unlike the other customers, the leader of the three girls is described as a "queen":

> She came down a little hard on her heels, as if she didn't walk in her bare feet that much, putting down her heels and then letting the weight move along to her toes as if she was testing the floor with every step, putting a little deliberate extra action into it. (Updike, "A&P" 260)

It seems clear that Sammy realizes that Queenie and her friends come from farther away than just the beach. They have come to "test the floors" of a store patronized by the less well-off and do it openly, in defiance of social rules. In a sense, they are "slumming."

Queenie's class status

Queenie, whose name suggests her superior status, understands her position in social as well as sexual terms. Sammy has to spend the summer working, but she has come to the A&P just to purchase "Kingfish Fancy Herring Snacks in Pure Sour Cream" for her parents. (The exotic and expensive herring snacks hints at their different backgrounds.) Regardless, the two act in ways that are not all that different. Both are self-consciously trying out new roles, with

Westmoreland 3

Sammy trying to rise above his station in life and Queenie trying to move below hers. As Queenie arrives at the register, Sammy observes, "Now her hands are empty, not a ring or a bracelet, . . . and I wonder where the money's coming from. Still with that prim look she lifts a folded dollar bill out of the hollow at the center of her nubbled pink top" (Updike, "A&P" 262). With this gesture, she not only tests her own sexual powers but also sinks to the level of the supermarket. Despite her act, though, Sammy knows how different Queenie's world is from his:

> I slid right down her voice into her living room. Her father and the other men were standing around in ice-cream coats and bow ties and the women were in sandals picking up herring snacks on toothpicks off a big plate and they were all holding drinks the color of water with olives and sprigs of mint in them. When my parents have somebody over they get lemonade and if it's a real racy affair Schlitz in tall glasses with "They'll Do It Every Time" cartoons stencilled on. (Updike, "A&P" 262)

As Updike says in an interview with writer Donald Murray, "[Sammy] is a blue-collar kid longing for a white-collar girl."

Lengel's role as catalyst

At this point in the story, as Sammy says, "everybody's luck begins to run out" (Updike, "A&P" 262). Lengel, the store manager, who represents "the cruel and unethical" rules that govern matters of social etiquette (Updike, interview), confronts the girls, telling them that they are indecently dressed. "'We

Westmoreland 4

are decent,' Queenie says suddenly, her lower lip pushing, getting sore now that she remembers her place, a place from which the crowd that runs the A&P must look pretty crummy" (Updike, "A&P" 262). Suddenly, Sammy can no longer be a detached observer and, in a gesture of defiance, he quits. The real question here is *why* he quits. In fact, Updike himself wonders "to what extent his gesture of quitting has to do with the fact that she is rich and he is poor" (Interview).

Sammy's motives for quitting his job

By quitting, Sammy challenges social inequality, but is his response really just heroic posturing—or simply an expression of his long-standing frustration? In other words, does Sammy quit because of what Updike calls a "misunderstanding of how the world is put together" (Interview) or because he is "a boy who's tried to reach out of his immediate environment towards something bigger and better" ("Still Afraid")? Although Sammy's action may be simply impulsive—Sammy even states it would be "fatal" (Updike, "A&P" 263) not to go through with his initial gesture—it seems likely that he is taking a deliberate stand against what he sees as social injustice. Unlike Queenie's act of defiance, Sammy's gesture will have long-term consequences (Oates). As Updike points out, in Sammy's small town everyone will find out what he has done, and he may be "known . . . as a quitter" (Interview). Sammy's understanding and acceptance of these consequences ("'You'll feel

Westmoreland 5

this for the rest of your life.' Lengel says, and I know that's true, . . . "), and of the limitations his social class imposes upon him, constitute his initiation into adulthood (Updike, "A&P" 263). Whether quitting is Sammy's first step toward overcoming these limitations or a romantic gesture he will live to regret remains to be seen. As Updike says, "How blind we are, as we awkwardly push outward into the world!" ("Still Afraid").

Conclusion

Although it is true that both Queenie and Sammy attempt to cross social boundaries, the reasons for their actions are different. Queenie's provocative gesture is well thought out: she deliberately relinquishes her trappings, her clothes and jewelry. If only for a few minutes, she sheds her dignity and her wealth in order to flaunt her sexuality and her power. In contrast, Sammy chooses impulsively, in what Updike calls a "hot flash," a "moment of manly decisiveness," to take action and, ultimately, gives up both his dignity and his power (Interview). He gains only a brief moment of glory before he finds himself alone in the parking lot. In this instant, he confronts the social inequality and the unspeakable frustration it represents. According to Updike, Sammy cannot win—even though in a "noble surrender of his position," he gains an understanding of the weight he must bear (Interview).

Westmoreland 6

Works Cited

Oates, Joyce Carol. "John Updike's American Comedies." *Joyce Carol Oates on John Updike*. U of San Francisco, 5 Apr. 1998. Web. 15 Jan. 2009.

Steiner, George. "Supreme Fiction: America Is in the Details." *The New Yorker*. Condé Nast, 11 Mar. 1996. Web. 20 Jan. 2009.

Updike, John. "A&P." *Literature: Reading, Reacting, Writing*. Ed. Laurie G. Kirszner and Stephen R. Mandell. 7th ed. Boston: Wadsworth, 2010. 259-64. Print.

---. Interview by Donald Murray. *The Heinle Original Film Series in Literature*. Dir. Bruce Schwartz. Wadsworth, 2003. DVD.

---. "Still Afraid of Being Caught." *New York Times*. New York Times, 8 Oct. 1995. Web. 16 Jan. 2009.

Wells, Walter. "John Updike's 'A&P': A Return Visit to Araby." *Studies in Short Fiction* 30.2 (1993): 127-33. *Magazine Index Plus*. Web. 15 Jan. 2009.

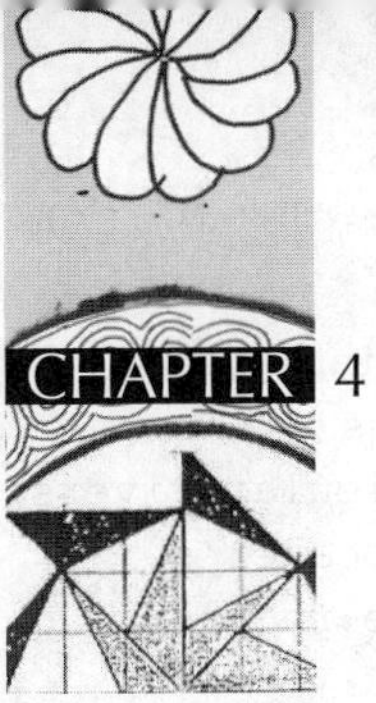

THINKING CRITICALLY ABOUT YOUR WRITING

As you write about literature, you should carefully assess the strength of the ideas you present to readers. This is especially true in **literary arguments,** essays in which you take a stand on a debatable topic and try to convince readers to accept your position (see Chapter 5). If you learn to **think critically** about your writing, you will be able to distinguish fact from opinion, evaluate the usefulness and appropriateness of your supporting evidence, and keep any biases you have out of your writing. Then, guided by the basic principles of inductive and deductive reasoning, you will be able to structure your literary argument in a way that will encourage readers to accept (or at least acknowledge) the strengths of your ideas.

Distinguishing Fact from Opinion

A **fact** is a verifiable statement that something is true or that something occurred. An **opinion** is a personal judgment or belief that can never be substantiated beyond any doubt and is, therefore, debatable.

Fact: Langston Hughes mentions four rivers in his poem "The Negro Speaks of Rivers."

Opinion: Rivers have symbolic significance in Langston Hughes's poem "The Negro Speaks of Rivers."

An opinion may be *unsupported* or *supported*.

Unsupported Opinion: Rivers have symbolic significance in Langston Hughes's poem "The Negro Speaks of Rivers."

Supported Opinion: Rivers have symbolic significance in Langston Hughes's poem "The Negro Speaks of Rivers." In the poem, the speaker mentions four rivers—the Euphrates, the Congo, the Nile, and the Mississippi. According to the speaker, these rivers are as "ancient as the world and as old as the flow of human blood in human veins" (line 2). Through their associations with the black experience, these particular rivers are linked not only to the speaker's African roots but also to the racial situation in America at the time the poem was written.

As the above examples show, supported opinion is more convincing than unsupported opinion.

Supporting Your Opinions

Your opinions can be supported with **examples, quotations,** or **expert opinion.**

Examples:

In the play *The Glass Menagerie,* Jim's focus on the future challenges Amanda's unrealistic romantic dreams of the past. For example, when Jim comes to dinner, she dreams of entertaining him in the old Southern tradition, but he talks enthusiastically of the promise the future holds.

Quotations:

Although Gertrude is queen of Denmark, she is also a devoted mother. In her efforts to console her son, she speaks tenderly: "Good Hamlet, cast thy knighted color off" (1.2.68). She also conveys her wisdom about life: "Thou know'st 'tis common,—all that live must die, / Passing through nature to eternity" (1.2.72-73).

Expert Opinion (From Literary Criticism):

Throughout the short story "The Yellow Wallpaper," a number of clues suggest that the narrator has lost her hold on reality. According to Sandra Gilbert and Susan Gubar in *Madwoman in the Attic: The Woman Writer and the Nineteenth-Century Literary Imagination*, the extent of the narrator's dislike for the wallpaper should serve as an early warning that she is not responding well to her treatment and that she may in fact be losing her mind (464).

Evaluating Supporting Evidence

The examples, quotations, and opinions of literary critics that you use to support your statements constitute **evidence.** The more **reliable** your supporting evidence, the more willing your readers will be to accept a statement. Remember, though, that to be reliable the evidence you use must be *accurate, sufficient, representative*, and *relevant*.

For your evidence to be **accurate,** it must come from a trustworthy source. Such a source quotes *exactly* and does not present information out of context. It also presents examples, quotations, and expert opinion fairly, drawing them from other reliable sources.

For your evidence to be **sufficient,** you must present an adequate amount of evidence. It is not enough, for instance, to cite just one example from a Joyce Carol Oates short story in an attempt to demonstrate that her experiments with literary form and subject matter give her work universal appeal. Moreover, the opinions of a single literary critic, no matter how reputable, are not enough to support this position.

For your evidence to be **representative,** it must reflect a range of sources and viewpoints. You should not choose evidence that simply supports your thesis and ignore evidence that does not. For example, if you are making the point that the structure of Emily Dickinson's poems changed over the course of her career, you cannot disregard compelling evidence that, in fact, her poetic structure remained consistent over the years.

Finally, for your evidence to be **relevant,** it must apply to the case being discussed. For example, you cannot support the assertion that Arthur Miller's *Death of a Salesman* critiques post–World War II American society by citing examples from Miller's *The Crucible*.

Detecting Bias in Your Writing

A **bias** is an opinion, usually unfavorable, based on preconceived ideas rather than on evidence. As a critical thinker, you should be aware that your biases can sometimes lead you to see just what you want to see and to select evidence that is consistent with these biases.

Detecting Bias in Your Writing

When you write, be on the lookout for the following kinds of biases:

- **Slanted language:** Avoid slanted language—language that is inflammatory or confrontational. For example, do not say that a literary critic's article is stupid or that a character in a short story is immoral. Instead, use language that clearly and accurately conveys your ideas.
- **Biased tone:** Avoid using a tone that communicates bias toward your subject (for example, anger or sarcasm).

continued on next page

- **Stereotypes:** Avoid statements that perpetuate stereotypes. For example, be careful not to make unwarranted assumptions about gender roles or about a particular groups' attributes or shortcomings and then criticize characters on the basis of these generalizations. For example, saying that Andy in "Doe Season" gets what she deserves because a deer hunt is no place for girls stereotypes the character and reveals gender bias.
- **Preconceived ideas:** Don't let your own beliefs or attitudes prevent you from fairly evaluating a work of literature. For example, you may believe strongly that husbands and wives should be faithful to each other, but you should not let this belief prevent you from appreciating the literary strengths of Kate Chopin's "The Storm," a short story in which two characters commit adultery, apparently with no consequences.

✔ CHECKLIST Detecting Bias

- ☐ Have you chosen evidence that presents a balanced view of your topic?
- ☐ Have you cited experts? If so, do they represent a range of opinion?
- ☐ Have you avoided slanted language?
- ☐ Have you been careful not to convey your bias through your tone?
- ☐ Have you avoided statements that perpetuate stereotypes?

Understanding Logic

All argumentative essays, including literary arguments, rely on **logic**—inductive and deductive reasoning—to reach conclusions in a systematic way. If you understand the basic principles of inductive and deductive reasoning, you will be able to write clearer, more convincing essays.

Inductive Reasoning

Inductive reasoning is a process that moves from specific facts, observations, or experiences to a general conclusion. You use inductive reasoning in your writing when you want to lead readers from a series of specific observations to a general conclusion. You can see how inductive reasoning operates by studying the following list of statements about John Updike's short story "A&P":

- Sammy, the main character in "A&P," is nineteen and works as a cashier in a supermarket in a small New England town.
- Sammy sees the A&P's customers as sheep, with no individuality.
- Sammy's fellow workers include Stokesie, a married twenty-two-year-old with two children, and Lengel, the store manager.
- Stokesie and Lengel lead boring, predictable lives.
- On the day the story takes place, three girls in bathing suits walk into the store and change Sammy's life.
- Sammy fantasizes about the girls' lives and imagines what a party at one girl's home would be like.
- When Lengel scolds the girls for dressing inappropriately, Sammy abruptly quits his job.
- At the end of the story, Sammy realizes that although some people think he was foolish to quit his job, he did the right thing.

After reading the statements above, you can use inductive reasoning to reach a general conclusion about the theme of Updike's story: that someone who wants to escape a confining life must sometimes make a break with his community's values.

No matter how much evidence you present, an inductive conclusion is never certain, only probable. You arrive at an inductive conclusion by making an **inference,** a statement about the unknown based on the known. In order to bridge the gap that exists between your specific observations and your general conclusion, you have to make an **inductive leap.** If you have presented enough specific evidence, this gap will be relatively small and your readers will accept your conclusion. If the gap is too wide, your readers will accuse you of making a **hasty generalization**—a conclusion based on too little evidence.

Deductive Reasoning

Deductive reasoning is a process that moves from a general statement believed to be true or **self-evident** (so obvious that it needs no proof) to a specific conclusion. Writers use deductive reasoning when they think their audience is more likely to be influenced by logic than by evidence. The process of deduction has traditionally been illustrated by a **syllogism,** a three-part set of statements or propositions that includes a *major premise*, a *minor premise*, and a *conclusion*.

Major Premise: All tragic heroes have tragic flaws.

Minor Premise: Hamlet is a tragic hero.

Conclusion: Therefore, Hamlet has a tragic flaw.

The **major premise** of a syllogism makes a general statement that the writer believes to be true or self-evident. The **minor premise** presents a specific example of the belief that is stated in the major premise. If the reasoning is sound, the **conclusion** should follow from the two premises. (Note that the conclusion should introduce no terms that have not already appeared in the major and minor premises.) The advantage of a deductive argument is that if readers accept the premises, they usually grant the conclusion.

A syllogism is **valid** when its conclusion logically follows from its premises. A syllogism is **true** when the information it contains is consistent with the facts. To be **sound,** a syllogism must be *both* valid and true. However, a syllogism can be valid without being true or true without being valid. The following syllogism, for example, is valid but not true.

Major Premise: All poems contain rhymed lines.

Minor Premise: Walt Whitman's "Had I the Choice" is a poem.

Conclusion: Therefore, Walt Whitman's "Had I the Choice" contains rhymed lines.

This syllogism is valid. In the major premise, the phrase *all poems* establishes that the entire class *poems* contains rhymed lines. After Walt Whitman's "Had I the Choice" is identified as a poem, the conclusion that it contains rhymed lines logically follows. However, Whitman's poem, like many others, is unrhymed. Because the major premise of this syllogism is not true, no conclusion based on it can be true. For this reason, even though the logic of the syllogism is correct, its conclusion is not.

Toulmin Logic

Stephen Toulmin, a philosopher and rhetorician, has formulated another way to understand logical thinking. According to Toulmin, the traditional syllogism, while useful for identifying flaws in logic, is not useful for analyzing arguments that occur in the real world. To address this shortcoming, Toulmin divides arguments into three parts: the *claim*, the *grounds*, and the *warrant:*

- **The claim** is your thesis, the main point that you want to make in your essay.
- **The grounds** are the facts, examples, and opinions of experts that support your claim. In essays about literature, the grounds can come from a work of literature or from literary criticism.
- **The warrant** is an assumption that underlies both the claim and the grounds. Keep in mind that some warrants are explicitly stated while others may be simply implied.

In its simplest terms, an argument following Toulmin's structure would look like this:

- **The claim:** Phoenix Jackson, the main character in Eudora Welty's "A Worn Path," challenges the racial restrictions of her community.

- **The grounds:** Phoenix Jackson defies the man with the gun; she asks a white woman to tie her shoe; she steals a nickel; she gets free medicine from the doctor.
- **The warrant:** At the time "A Worn Path" takes place, racial segregation limited the actions of African Americans.

Notice that the claim presents a specific situation; the warrant, however, is a general principle that could apply to a number of situations. In a sense, the warrant is similar to the major premise of a syllogism, and the claim is similar to the conclusion. The grounds consist of the evidence that supports the claim.

Recognizing Logical Fallacies

Logical fallacies are flawed arguments. A writer who inadvertently uses such fallacies is not thinking clearly or logically; a writer who intentionally uses them is trying to deceive readers. Learn to recognize them so you can avoid them when you write.

Common Logical Fallacies

- **Hasty Generalization:** A form of induction that reaches a conclusion on the basis of too little evidence. For example, one appearance of a river in a poem is not enough to support the statement that it is an important symbol. Several mentions, however, might justify this conclusion.
- **Sweeping Generalization:** A generalization that cannot be supported no matter how much evidence is supplied. For example, the statement "All literary critics like August Wilson's plays" is a sweeping generalization. Certainly, many critics like Wilson's plays, but it is virtually impossible to prove that all do. To avoid making statements that cannot be supported, qualify your statements with words such as *some, many, often,* or *most.*
- ***Ad Hominem* (Argument to the Person):** A fallacy that occurs when you attack a person rather than the issue, as in the following argument: "Many critics see imagism as a very important literary movement. However, the fact that its founder, Ezra Pound, was a Nazi sympathizer challenges that assessment." Although you may find Pound's Nazi sympathies repugnant, his political ideas are not relevant to your evaluation of imagism.
- **Non Sequitur:** A conclusion that does not logically follow from what comes before it, as in the following statement: "John Updike writes critically acclaimed novels, so he must be a gifted poet." It does not logically follow that just because Updike can write good novels, he can also write good poetry.

continued on next page

- **Either/Or Fallacy:** A fallacy that occurs when a complex issue is presented as if it has only two sides. If you ask your readers to consider whether a character is good or evil, you commit this fallacy. In fact, a complex character may possess both positive and negative qualities.
- **Begging the Question:** A fallacy that occurs when you present a debatable premise as if it were true, as in the following statement: "Hemingway's negative portrayals of women have caused his popularity to decline in recent years." Hemingway's portrayals of women may be negative, but readers do not have to accept this statement as fact just because you say it is true. Before you can make a judgment based on this assertion, you must support it with examples from Hemingway's work as well as with statements from a fair range of literary critics.
- **Bandwagon:** A fallacy that occurs when you try to establish that something is true just because everyone believes it is. You commit this fallacy when you say, for example, that a certain literary work must be good because it is so popular.

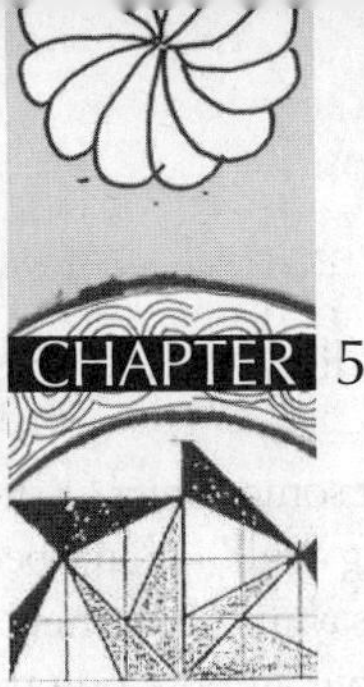

CHAPTER 5

WRITING LITERARY ARGUMENTS

Many of the essays you write about literature are **expository**—that is, you write to give information to readers. For example, you might discuss the rhyme or meter of a poem or examine the interaction of two characters in a play. Other essays you write, however, may be **literary arguments**—that is, you take a position on a debatable topic and attempt to change readers' minds about it. For example, you might argue that the boy's quest in James Joyce's short story "Araby" (p. 434) has symbolic meaning or that Sammy, the main character in John Updike's short story "A&P" (p. 259) is sexist.

When you write a literary argument, you follow the same process you do when you write any essay about a literary topic. However, because the purpose of an argument is to convince readers, you need to use some additional strategies to present your ideas.

 Planning a Literary Argument

Choosing a Topic

Your first step in writing a literary argument will be to decide on a specific topic to write about. Because an argumentative essay attempts to change the way readers think, it must focus on a **topic,** one about which reasonable people may disagree. **Factual statements**—statements about which reasonable people do *not* disagree—are therefore inappropriate as topics for argument.

Factual Statement: Linda Loman is Willy Loman's long-suffering wife in Arthur Miller's play *Death of a Salesman.*

Debatable Topic: More than a stereotype of the long-suffering wife, Linda Loman in Arthur Miller's play *Death of a Salesman* is a complex character.

Your topic should also be narrow enough for you to develop within your page limit. After all, in an argumentative essay, you will have to present your own ideas and supply convincing support while possibly also addressing opposing arguments. If your topic is too broad, you will not be able to discuss it in enough detail.

Finally, your topic should be interesting. Keep in mind that some topics—such as the significance of the wall in Robert Frost's poem "Mending Wall"—have been written about so often that you will probably not be able to say anything new or interesting about them. Instead of relying on an overused topic, choose one that allows you to write something original.

Developing an Argumentative Thesis

After you have chosen your topic, your next step is to develop an **argumentative thesis**—one that takes a strong stand. An argumentative thesis must be debatable; that is, it must have at least two sides. Properly worded, this thesis statement will state your position and lay the foundation for the rest of your argument.

One way to make sure that your thesis actually does take a stand is to try to formulate an **antithesis**—a statement that takes an arguable position opposite from yours. If you can construct an antithesis, you can be certain that your thesis statement is debatable. If you cannot, your thesis statement needs further revision.

Thesis Statement: The last line of Richard Wright's short story "Big Black Good Man" indicates that Jim was fully aware all along of Olaf's deep-seated racial prejudice.

Antithesis: The last line of Richard Wright's short story "Big Black Good Man" indicates that Jim remained unaware of Olaf's feelings toward him.

NOTE: Your thesis statement is an assertion that your entire essay supports. Keep in mind, however, that you can never prove your thesis conclusively—if you could, there would be no argument. The best you can do is provide enough evidence to establish a high probability that your thesis is reasonable.

✔ CHECKLIST Developing an Argumentative Thesis

- ☐ Can you formulate an antithesis?
- ☐ Does your thesis statement make clear to readers what position you are taking?
- ☐ Can you support your thesis with evidence from the text and from research?

Defining Your Terms

You should always define the key terms you use in your argument. For example, if you are using the term *narrator* in an essay, make sure that readers know whether you are referring to a first-person or a third-person narrator. In addition, you may need to clarify the difference between an **unreliable narrator**—someone who misrepresents or misinterprets events—and a **reliable narrator**—someone who accurately describes events. Without a clear definition of the terms you are using, readers may have a difficult time understanding the point you are making.

Defining Your Terms

Be especially careful to use precise terms in your thesis statement. Avoid vague and judgmental words, such as *wrong, bad, good, right,* and *immoral.*

Vague: The poem "Birmingham Sunday (September 15, 1963)" by Langston Hughes shows how bad racism can be.

Clearer: The poem "Birmingham Sunday (September 15, 1963)" by Langston Hughes makes a moving statement about how destructive racism can be.

Considering Your Audience

As you plan your essay, keep your audience in mind. For example, if you are writing about a work that has been discussed in class, you can assume that your readers are familiar with it; include plot summary only when it is needed to explain a point you are making. Keep in mind that you will be addressing an academic audience—your instructor and possibly some students. For this reason, you should be sure to follow the conventions of writing about literature as well as the conventions of standard written English. (For information on the conventions of writing about literature, see the checklist in Chapter 2, p. 35.)

When you write an argumentative essay, assume that you are addressing a skeptical audience. Remember, your thesis is debatable, so not everyone will agree with you—and even if your readers are sympathetic to your position, you cannot assume that they will accept your ideas without question.

The strategies you use to convince your readers will vary according to your relationship with them. Somewhat skeptical readers may need to see only that your argument is logical and that your evidence is solid. More skeptical readers, however, may need to see that you understand their reservations and that you concede some of their points. Of course, you may never be able to convince hostile readers that your conclusions are legitimate. The best you can hope for is that these readers will acknowledge the strengths of your argument even if they do not accept your conclusion.

Refuting Opposing Arguments

As you develop your literary argument, you may need to **refute**—that is, to disprove—opposing arguments by demonstrating that they are false, misguided, or illogical. By summarizing and refuting opposing views, you make opposing arguments seem less credible to readers; thus, you strengthen your case. When an opposing argument is so strong that it cannot be easily dismissed, however, you should **concede** (admit the strength of) the argument and then point out its limitations.

Notice in the following paragraph how a student refutes the argument that Homer Barron, a character in William Faulkner's short story "A Rose for Emily," is gay.

Opposing argument

A number of critics have suggested that Homer Barron, Miss Emily's suitor, is gay. Actually, there is some evidence in the story to support this

Concession

interpretation. For example, the narrator points out that Homer "liked men" (Faulkner 247) and that he was not "a marrying man" (Faulkner 247). In addition, the narrator describes Homer as wearing yellow gloves when he took Emily for drives. According to the critic William Greenslade, in the 1890s yellow was associated

Refutation

with homosexuality (24). This evidence does not prove that Homer is gay, however. During the nineteenth century, many men preferred the company of other men (as many do today). This, in itself, did not mean they were gay. Neither does the fact that Homer wore yellow gloves. According to the narrator, Homer was a man who liked to dress well. It is certainly possible that he wore these gloves to impress Miss Emily, a woman he was trying to attract.

 Using Evidence Effectively

Supporting Your Literary Argument

Many literary arguments are built on **assertions**—statements made about a debatable topic—backed by **evidence**—supporting examples in the form of references to the text, quotations, and the opinions of literary critics. For example, if you stated that Torvald Helmer, Nora's husband in Henrik Ibsen's play *A Doll House*, is as much a victim of society as his wife is, you could support this assertion with relevant quotations and examples from the play. You could also paraphrase, summarize, or quote the ideas of literary critics who also hold this opinion. Remember, only assertions that are **self-evident** (All plays include characters and dialogue) or **factual** (*A Doll House* was published in 1879) need no supporting evidence. All other kinds of assertions require support.

Establishing Credibility

Some people bring **credibility** with them whenever they write. When a well-known literary critic evaluates the contributions of a particular writer, you can assume that he or she speaks with authority. (Although you might question the critic's opinions, you do not question his or her expertise.) But most people do not have this kind of credibility. When you write a literary argument, you must constantly work to establish credibility. You do this by *demonstrating knowledge*, *maintaining a reasonable tone*, and *presenting yourself as someone worth listening to*.

Demonstrating Knowledge One way to establish credibility is by presenting your own carefully considered ideas about a subject. A clear argument and compelling support can demonstrate to readers that you know what you are talking about.

You can also show readers that you have thoroughly researched your subject. By referring to important sources and by providing accurate documentation for your information, you present evidence that you have done the necessary background reading. Including a range of sources—not just one or two—suggests that you are well acquainted with your subject. Remember, however, that questionable sources, inaccurate (or missing) documentation, and factual errors can undermine your credibility. For many readers, an undocumented quotation or even an incorrect date can call an entire argument into question.

Maintaining a Reasonable Tone Your **tone**—your attitude toward your readers or subject—is almost as important as the information you convey. Talk *to* your readers, not *at* them. If you lecture your readers or appear to talk down to them, you will alienate them. Generally speaking, readers are more likely to respond to a writer who seems balanced and respectful than one who seems strident or condescending.

As you write your essay, use moderate language, and qualify your statements so that they seem reasonable. Try to avoid words and phrases such as *all, never, always*, and *in every case*, which can make your points seem simplistic, exaggerated, or unrealistic. Also, avoid absolute statements. For example, the statement, In "Doe Season," the ocean symbolizes Andy's attachment to her mother, leaves no room for other possible interpretations. A more measured and accurate statement might be, In "Doe Season," the use of the ocean as a symbol suggests Andy's identification with her mother and her realization that she is becoming a woman.

Presenting Yourself as Someone Worth Listening To When you write a literary argument, you should present yourself as someone your readers will want to listen to. Make your argument confidently, and don't apologize for your views. For example, do not use phrases such as "In my opinion" and "It seems to me," which undercut your credibility. Be consistent, and be careful not to contradict yourself. Finally, avoid the use of *I* (unless you are asked to give your opinion or to write a response paper), and avoid slang and colloquialisms.

Being Fair

Argument promotes one point of view over all others, so it is seldom objective. However, college writing requires that you stay within the bounds of fairness and that you avoid **bias**— opinions based on preconceived ideas rather than on evidence (see pp. 97–98). To make sure that the support for your argument is not misleading or distorted, follow these guidelines:

- ***Avoid misrepresenting evidence.*** Be careful not to misrepresent the extent to which critical opinion supports your thesis. For example, don't try to make a weak case stronger than it actually is by saying that "many critics" think that something is so when only one or two do.
- ***Avoid quoting out of context.*** When you take words from their original setting and use them in another, you run the risk of quoting out of context. When you quote a source's words out of context, you can change the meaning of what someone has said or suggested. For example, you are quoting out of context if you say, `Emily Dickinson's poems are so idiosyncratic that they do not appeal to readers` when your source says, "Emily Dickinson's poems are so idiosyncratic that they do not appeal to readers *who are accustomed to safe, conventional subjects*." By eliminating a key portion of the sentence, you alter the meaning of the original.
- ***Avoid slanting.*** When you select only information that supports your case and ignore information that does not, you are guilty of slanting. You can eliminate this problem by including a full range of examples, not just examples that support your thesis. Be sure to consult books and articles that represent a cross-section of critical opinion about your subject.
- ***Avoid using unfair appeals.*** Traditionally, writers of arguments use three types of appeals to influence readers: **logical appeals,** which address a reader's sense of reason, **emotional appeals,** which play on a reader's emotions, and **ethical appeals,** which emphasize the credibility of the writer. Problems arise, however, when these appeals are used unfairly. For example, writers can use **logical fallacies**—flawed arguments—to fool readers into thinking a conclusion is logical when it is not (see Chapter 4 for a discussion of logical fallacies). Writers can also use inappropriate emotional appeals—appeals to prejudice, for example—to influence readers. And finally, writers can undercut their credibility if they use questionable support—books and articles written by people who have little or

no expertise on the topic. This is especially true when information is obtained from the Internet, where the credentials of the writer may be difficult or impossible to assess. If you want your readers to accept your position, you must be careful to avoid logical fallacies and unfair appeals.

✔ **CHECKLIST Being Fair**

- ☐ Have you distorted evidence?
- ☐ Have you quoted material out of context, changing the meaning of a statement by focusing on certain words and ignoring others?
- ☐ Have you slanted information, selecting material that supports your points and ignoring information that does not?
- ☐ Have you used any unfair appeals?

Using Visuals as Evidence

Visuals—pictures, drawings, diagrams, and the like—can add a persuasive dimension to your essay. Because visual images have an immediate impact, they can sometimes make a strong literary argument even stronger. In a sense, visuals are another type of evidence that can support your thesis. For example, suppose you are writing an essay about the play *Trifles* in which you argue that Mrs. Wright's quilt is an important symbol in the play. In fact, your research leads you to conclude that the process of creating the quilt by piecing together its log cabin pattern parallels the process by which the two female characters in the play determine why Mrs. Wright murdered her husband. The addition of a photograph of a quilt with a log cabin pattern could not only eliminate several paragraphs of description but also help support your conclusion.

Of course, not all visuals will be appropriate or effective for a literary argument. Before using a visual, make certain it actually supports the point you want to make. If it does not, it will distract readers and undercut your argument. To ensure that readers understand the purpose of the visual, introduce it with a sentence that establishes its context; then, discuss its significance, paying particular attention to how it helps you make your point. Finally, be sure to include full documentation for any visual that is not your original creation. (See pages 86 and 112 for examples of visuals used as evidence in a student paper.)

Organizing a Literary Argument

In its simplest form, a literary argument—like any argumentative essay—consists of a thesis statement and supporting evidence. Literary arguments, however, frequently use additional strategies to win audience approval and to overcome potential opposition.

Elements of Literary Arguments

- **Introduction:** The introduction should orient readers to the subject of your essay, presenting the issue you will discuss and explaining its significance.
- **Thesis statement:** In most literary arguments, you will present your thesis statement in your introduction. However, if you think your readers may not be familiar with the issue you are discussing (or if it is very controversial), you may want to postpone stating your thesis until later in the essay.
- **Background:** In this section, you can survey critical opinion about your topic, perhaps pointing out the shortcomings of these opinions. You can also define key terms, review basic facts, or briefly summarize the plot of the work or works you will discuss.
- **Arguments in support of your thesis:** Here you present your arguments and the evidence to support them. It makes sense to move from the least controversial to the most controversial point or from the most familiar to the least familiar idea. In other words, you should begin with arguments that your readers are most likely to accept and then deal with those that require more discussion and more evidence.
- **Refutation of opposing arguments:** In a literary argument, you should summarize and refute the most obvious arguments against your thesis. If you do not address these opposing arguments, doubts about your position will remain in your readers' minds. If the opposing arguments are relatively weak, refute them after you have presented your own arguments. However, if the opposing arguments are strong, you may want to concede their strengths and discuss their limitations *before* you present your own arguments.
- **Conclusion:** Your conclusion will often restate your thesis as well as the major arguments you have made in support of it. Your conclusion can also summarize key points, remind readers of the weaknesses of opposing arguments, or underscore the logic of your position. Many writers like to end their essays with a strong last line—for example, a quotation or a memorable statement that they hope will stay with readers after they finish the essay.

Writing a Literary Argument

The following student paper presents a literary argument about Dee, a character in Alice Walker's short story "Everyday Use." The student author supports her thesis with ideas she developed as she read the story as well as with information she found when she did research. She also includes two visuals from a DVD of the story.

Chase 1

Margaret Chase

Professor Sierra

English 1001

6 February 2009

The Politics of "Everyday Use"

Introduction

Alice Walker's "Everyday Use" focuses on a mother, Mrs. Johnson, and her two daughters, Maggie and Dee, and how they view their heritage. The story's climax comes when Mrs. Johnson rejects Dee's request to take a hand-stitched quilt with her so that she can hang it on her wall. Knowing that Maggie will put the quilt to "everyday use," Dee is horrified, and she tells her mother and Maggie that they do not understand their heritage. Although many literary critics see Dee's desire for the quilt as materialistic and shallow, a closer examination of this story, written in 1973, suggests a more positive interpretation of Dee's character.

Thesis statement

Background

On the surface, "Everyday Use" is a story about two sisters, Dee and Maggie, and Mrs. Johnson, their mother. Mrs. Johnson tells the reader that "Dee, . . . would always look anyone in the eye. Hesitation was no part of her nature" (518). Unlike her sister, Maggie is shy and introverted. She is described as looking like a lame animal that has been run over by a car. According to the narrator, "She has been like this, chin on chest, eyes on ground, feet in shuffle" (518) ever since she was burned in a fire.

Unlike Dee, Mrs. Johnson never got an education. After second grade, she explains, the school closed down. She says, "Don't ask me why: in 1927 colored asked fewer questions than they do now" (518). Mrs. Johnson admits that she accepts the status quo even though she knows that it is unjust. This admission further establishes the difference between Mrs. Johnson and Dee: Mrs. Johnson has accepted her circumstances, while Dee has worked to change hers. Their differences are illustrated in a film version of the story by their contrasting dress. As shown in fig. 1, Dee and her boyfriend

Source: ©Denna Bendall / Worn Path Productions

Fig. 1. Dee and Hakim-a-barber arrive at the family home; *The Wadsworth Original Film Series in Literature: "Everyday Use,"* dir. Bruce R. Schwartz; Wadsworth, 2005; DVD.

Chase 3

Hakim-a-barber dress in a style that celebrates their African heritage; Mrs. Johnson and Maggie dress in plain, conservative clothing.

When Dee arrives home with her new boyfriend, other differences soon become obvious. As she eyes her mother's belongings and asks Mrs. Johnson if she can take the top of the butter churn home with her, it is clear that she is very materialistic. However, her years away from home have also politicized her. Dee now wants to be called "Wangero" because she believes (although mistakenly) that her given name comes from whites who owned her ancestors. In addition, she talks about how a new day is dawning for African Americans.

Background continued

The meaning and political importance of Dee's decision to adopt an African name and wear African clothing cannot be fully understood without a knowledge of the social and political context in which Walker wrote this story. Walker's own comments about this time period explain Dee's behavior and add meaning to it. In her interview with White, Walker explains that the late 1960s was a time of cultural and intellectual awakening for African Americans. Many turned ideologically and culturally to Africa, adopting the dress, hairstyles, and even the names of their African ancestors. Walker admits that as a young woman she too became interested in discovering her African heritage. (In fact, she herself was given

Social and historical context used as evidence to support thesis

Chase 4

the name *Wangero* during a visit to Kenya in the late 1960s.) Walker tells White that she considered keeping this new name, but eventually realized that to do so would be to "dismiss" her family and her American heritage. When she researched her American family, she found that her great-great-grandmother had walked from Virginia to Georgia carrying two children. "If that's not a Walker," she says, "I don't know what is." Thus, Walker realized that, over time, African Americans had actually transformed the names they had originally taken from their enslavers. To respect the ancestors she knew, Walker says, she decided it was important to keep her name.

Along with adopting symbols of their African heritage, many African Americans also elevated these symbols, such as the quilt shown in fig. 2, to the status of art. According to Salaam, one way of doing this was to put these objects in museums; another was to hang them on the walls of their homes. Such acts were aimed at convincing whites that African Americans had an old and rich culture and that, consequently, they deserved not only basic civil rights but also respect. These gestures were also meant to improve self-esteem and pride within black communities (Salaam 42-43).

Acknowledgment of opposing argument

Admittedly, as some critics have pointed out, Dee is more materialistic than political. For example, although Mrs. Johnson makes several

Chase 5

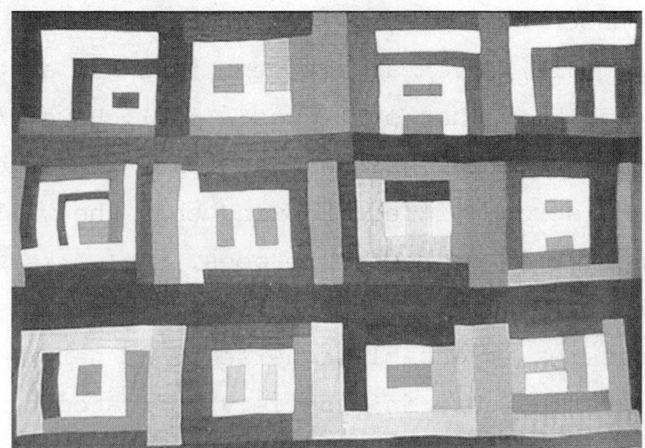

Source: ©Suzanne English / Worn Path Productions

Fig. 2. Traditional hand-stitched quilt; Evelyn C. White, "Alice Walker: Stitches in Time," interview, *The Wadsworth Original Film Series in Literature: "Everyday Use,"* dir. Bruce R. Schwartz; Wadsworth, 2005; DVD.

statements throughout the story that suggest her admiration of Dee's defiant character, she also identifies incidents that highlight Dee's materialism and selfishness. When their first house burned down, Dee watched it burn while she stood under a tree with "a look of concentration" (518) rather than remorse. Mrs. Johnson knows that Dee hated their small, dingy house, and she knows too that Dee was glad to see it destroyed. Furthermore, Walker acknowledges in an interview with her biographer, Evelyn C. White, that as she was writing the story, she imagined that Dee might even have set the fire that destroyed the house and scarred her sister. Even now, Dee is ashamed of the tin-roofed house her family lives in, and she has said that she would never bring her friends there.

Chase 6

Refutation of opposing argument

Mrs. Johnson has always known that Dee wanted "nice things" (518); even at sixteen, "she had a style of her own: and knew what style was" (518). However, although Dee is materialistic and self-serving, she is also proud and strong willed. Knowing that she will encounter opposition wherever she goes, she works to establish power. Thus, her desire for the quilt can be seen as an attempt to establish herself and her African-American culture in a society dominated by whites.

Analysis of Mrs. Johnson's final act

Even though Mrs. Johnson knows Dee wants the quilt, she gives it to Maggie. According to literary critics Houston Baker and Charlotte Pierce-Baker, when Mrs. Johnson decides to give the quilt to Maggie, she is challenging Dee's understanding of her heritage. Unlike Dee, Mrs. Johnson recognizes that quilts signify "sacred generations of women who have made their own special kind of beauty separate from the traditional artistic world" (qtd. in Piedmont-Marton 45). According to Baker and Pierce-Baker, Mrs. Johnson realizes that her daughter Maggie, whom she has long dismissed because of her quiet nature and shyness, understands the true meaning of the quilt in a way that Dee never will (Piedmont-Marton 45).

Unlike Dee, Maggie has paid close attention to the traditions and skills of her mother and grandmother: she has actually learned to quilt. More important, by staying with her mother instead of going to school, she has gotten to know her family. She

Chase 7

underscores this fact when she tells her mother that Dee can have the quilt because she does not need it to remember her grandmother. Even though Maggie's and Mrs. Johnson's understanding of heritage may be more emotionally profound than Dee's, it is important not to dismiss Dee's interest in elevating the quilt to the level of high art. The political stakes of defining an object as art in the late 1960s and early 1970s were high, and the fight for equality went beyond basic civil rights.

Although there is much in the story that indicates Dee's materialism, her desire to hang the quilt should not be dismissed as a selfish act. Like Mrs. Johnson and Maggie, Dee is a complicated character. In 1973, when "Everyday Use" was written, displaying the quilt would have been not only a personal act, but also a political act—an act with important implications. The final message of "Everyday Use" may just be that an accurate understanding of the quilt (and, by extension, of African-American culture) requires both views—Maggie's and Mrs. Johnson's "everyday use" and Dee's elevation of the quilt to art.

Conclusion (restating thesis)

Chase 8

Works Cited

Piedmont-Marton, Elisabeth. "An Overview of 'Everyday Use.'" *Short Stories for Students* 2 (1997): 42-45. *Literature Resource Center*. Web. 20 Jan. 2009.

Salaam, Kalamu Ya. "A Primer of the Black Arts Movement: Excerpts from *The Magic of Juju: An Appreciation of the Black Arts Movement*." *Black Renaissance/Renaissance Noire* (2002): 40-59. *Expanded Academic ASAP*. Web. 21 Jan. 2009.

Walker, Alice. "Alice Walker: Stitches in Time." Interview by Evelyn C. White. *The Wadsworth Original Film Series in Literature: "Everyday Use."* Dir. Bruce R. Schwartz. Wadsworth, 2005. DVD.

---. "Everyday Use." *Literature: Reading, Reacting, Writing*. Ed. Laurie G. Kirszner and Stephen R. Mandell. 7th ed. Boston: Wadsworth, 2010. 517-23. Print.

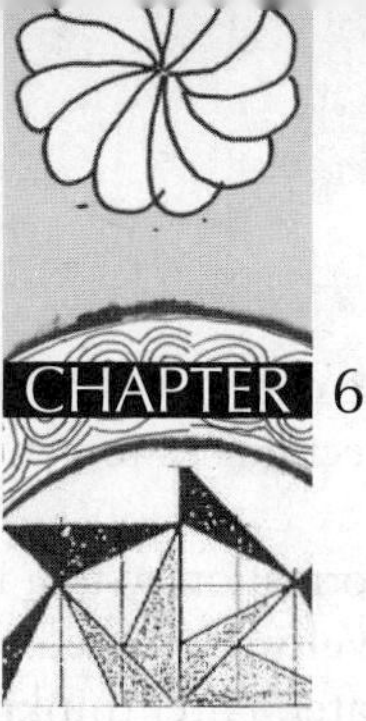

CHAPTER 6

USING SOURCES IN YOUR WRITING

When you write a paper about a literary topic, you often do **research,** supplementing your own interpretations with information from other sources. These sources may include works of literature as well as books and journal articles by literary critics (see p. 14). You may get this information from print sources, from electronic databases in the library, or from the Internet. When you write a literary research paper, follow the process discussed in this chapter.

Choosing a Topic

Your instructor may assign a topic or allow you to choose one. If you choose a topic, make sure it is narrow enough for your paper's length, the amount of time you have for writing, and the number of sources your instructor expects you to use.

Daniel Collins, a student in an Introduction to Literature course, was given three weeks to write a four- to six-page research paper on one of the short stories the class had read. Daniel chose to write about Eudora Welty's short story "A Worn Path" because the main character, Phoenix Jackson, interested him. He knew, however, that he would have to narrow his topic before he could begin. In class, Daniel's instructor had asked some provocative questions about the significance of Phoenix Jackson's journey. Daniel thought that this topic might work well because he could explore it in a short paper and could complete the paper within the three-week time limit.

Doing Exploratory Research

To see whether you will be able to find enough material about your topic, you should do some **exploratory research** by taking a quick survey of your library's resources. Your goal at this stage is to formulate a **research question,** the question that you want your research to answer. This question will help you decide which sources to look for, which to examine first, and which to skip entirely.

Begin your exploratory research by consulting your library's **online central information system.** This system usually includes the library's **catalog** as well as a number of **bibliographic databases,** such as *Readers' Guide to Periodical Literature* and

Humanities Index. Then, consult **general reference works** like encyclopedias and specialized dictionaries and browse your search engine's subject guides to get an overview of your subject.

A quick look showed Daniel that his library's central information system included several books and a number of articles on Eudora Welty. He noted the titles of the most promising sources so he could find them later. After thinking more about his topic, Daniel came up with the following research question: `What enabled Phoenix Jackson to continue her journey despite the many obstacles she faced?`

Narrowing Your Topic

As you survey your library's resources, the titles of books and articles as well as the subject headings of the catalog should help you to narrow your topic.

Daniel found two critical articles that discussed the significance of Phoenix Jackson's journey, and he hoped they would help him to understand why this character continued her journey despite all the hardships she encountered. However, Daniel knew that he would have to do more than just summarize his sources; he would have to make a point about the journey, one that he could support with examples from the story as well as from his research.

Doing Focused Research

Once you have completed your exploratory research and formulated your research question, you are ready to begin **focused research**—the process of looking in the library and on the Internet for the specific information you need.

Library Research

Using the Library

The first step is to go back to the library and check out any books that you think will be useful. Then, consult **specialized reference works**—indexes, bibliographies, and specialized encyclopedias, for example—to find relevant articles. If you find print articles, photocopy them (and make sure to copy all the publication information you will need to document these sources).

Your library's **periodical indexes** (usually accessed through your library's Web site) will also help you find information. A **periodical** is a newspaper, magazine, or scholarly journal published at regular intervals. **Periodical indexes** are databases that list articles from a selected group of periodicals. Although you may occasionally find scholarly articles on the free Internet, the easiest (and most reliable) way to access scholarly journals is through the databases to which your college library subscribes. These **subscription databases** are updated frequently, and the articles they include usually provide current, reliable information.

Choosing the right periodical index for your research is important. Each database has a different focus and lists different magazines or journals. In addition, some indexes include just citations while others contain the full text of articles. Using the wrong database can lead to wasted time and frustration. For example, searching a database that focuses on business will not help you much if you are looking for information on a literary topic. Be sure to ask a reference librarian which database will be most helpful.

Frequently Used Subscription Databases

The following databases are useful for literary research.

EBSCOhost	Includes thousands of periodical articles on many subjects
Expanded Academic ASAP	Largely full-text database covering all subjects in thousands of magazines and journals
FirstSearch	Full-text articles in many popular and scholarly periodicals

Evaluating Library Sources

Whenever you find a library source (print or electronic), take the time to **evaluate** it—to assess its usefulness and reliability.

✔ CHECKLIST Evaluating Library Sources

- ☐ *Does the source treat your topic in enough detail?* To be of real help, a book should include a section or a chapter on your topic. An article should have your topic as its central subject or at least one of its main concerns.
- ☐ *Is the source current?* Although currency is not as important for literary research as it is in the sciences, it should still be a consideration. Check the date of publication to see whether the information in a book or article is up to date.
- ☐ *Is the source respected?* A contemporary review of a source can help you make this assessment. You can find reviews in *Book Review Digest,* available in print and online.

continued on next page

- *Is the source reliable?* Does the author support his or her opinions? Does the author include documentation? Does the author have a particular agenda to advance? Compare a few statements with a more neutral source—an encyclopedia or a textbook, for example—to see whether the author seems to be slanting facts. If you have difficulty making this assessment, ask your instructor or a reference librarian for help.

Internet Research

Using the Internet

As you can imagine, the Internet has revolutionized the way scholars conduct research, offering instant access to a host of useful sources. Keep in mind, however, that the Internet does not give you access to the large number of high-quality print and electronic sources that you find in your college library.

Locating Sources

You can locate sources on the Internet in three ways:

1. The most direct way to locate an Internet source is to enter a **URL (uniform resource locator)**—a source's electronic address. Once you type in the URL, hit *Enter,* and you will be connected to the Web site you want. Make sure that you type in the URL exactly as it appears. A missed letter or an extra space or punctuation mark will send you to the wrong site—or to no site at all.
2. Another way to locate Internet sources is to use **subject guides**—the lists of general subject areas provided by search engines such as *Yahoo!, About.com,* and *LookSmart.* Each of these subject areas will lead you to a more specific list until, eventually, you get to the topic you want.
3. A third way to locate Internet sources is to enter a **keyword** (or words) into your search engine's search field. The search engine will identify any site in its database on which the keyword (or words) you have typed appears.

Some search engines are more user friendly than others, some allow for more sophisticated searching, and some are more comprehensive. As you try out various search engines, you will eventually settle on one that you will turn to when you need to find information.

Some General-Purpose Search Engines	
AllTheWeb	An excellent, comprehensive search engine that enables you to search for news stories, pictures, video, and audio. Many users think it is as good as *Google*.
AltaVista	A good, precise search engine for focused searches.
Excite	Searches more than 250 million Web sites.
Google	Considered by many to be the best search engine available. Accesses a large database that enables you to search for Web sites, images, discussion groups, and news stories.
Google Scholar	A new member of the Google family; enables you to search a broad range of scholarly literature, including peer-reviewed papers, books, abstracts, and technical reports as well as scholarly articles.
Yahoo!	A search tool that allows you to use either subject headings or keywords. Searches its own indexes as well as the Web.
Dogpile	A **metasearch engine** that searches several search engines simultaneously.

In addition to the general-purpose search engines listed above, you can use **specialized search engines**—search sites that are especially useful during focused research when you are looking for in-depth information about a specific topic.

Some Specialized Search Engines	
Librarians' Index <www.lii.org>	A high-quality, reliable site designed for librarians
Litengine.com <www.litengine.com>	A highly selective search engine for information about authors
Literary Criticism <www.accd.edu/pac/lrc/litcriticism.htm>	An alphabetical list of links to literary criticism on the Web
Thinkers.net <www.thinkers.net>	Discussions on literature and information about the publishing world
Voice of the Shuttle <www.vos.ucsb.edu>	Reliable in-depth research in the humanities

Evaluating Web Sites

Anyone can operate a Web site and thereby publish anything. For this reason, it is important to determine the quality of a Web site before you use it as a source. Asking the questions below will help you evaluate Web sites and the information they contain.

✔ CHECKLIST Evaluating Web Sites

- ☐ *How credible is the person or organization responsible for the site?* Does the site list an author? Can you determine the author's expertise?
- ☐ *How accurate is the information on the Web site?* Is it free of factual and grammatical errors? Can you verify the information by checking other sources?
- ☐ *How balanced does the information on the Web site seem?* Does a business, political organization, or special interest group sponsor the site? Does the site express only one viewpoint?
- ☐ *How comprehensive is the Web site?* Does the site provide in-depth coverage, or is the information largely common knowledge?
- ☐ *How well maintained is the Web site?* Has it been active for a long period of time? Has the site been updated recently?

Daniel Collins, the student writing about Phoenix Jackson's journey, was lucky enough to find everything he needed in his college library. He found two print articles about the Welty story, and he found two more articles in the *Humanities Index* database. Finally, a search of his library's online central information system revealed that among the library's holdings was a DVD of "A Worn Path" that included an interview with the author.

Taking Notes

Once you have located your sources, you should record information that you think will be useful. There is no single correct way to take notes. Some writers store information in a computer file; others keep their notes on index cards. Whatever system you use, be sure to record the author's full name as well as *complete* publication information. You will need this information later on to compile your works-cited list (see p. 142).

When you take notes from a source, you have three options: you can *paraphrase*, *summarize*, or *quote*.

When you **paraphrase**, you put the author's points into your own words, keeping the order and emphasis of the original. You paraphrase when you want to make a difficult or complex discussion accessible to readers so that you can comment on it or use it to support your own points. Here is a passage from a critical article, followed by Daniel's paraphrase.

Original

> The assumption that the grandson is dead helps explain Phoenix Jackson's stoical behavior in the doctor's office. She displays a "ceremonial stiffness" as she sits "bolt upright" staring "straight ahead, her face solemn and withdrawn into rigidity." This passiveness suggests her psychological dilemma — she cannot explain why she made the journey. Her attempt to blame the lapse of memory on her illiteracy is unconvincing. Her lack of education is hardly an excuse for forgetting her grandson, but it goes a long way toward explaining her inability to articulate her subconscious motives for her journey. (Bartel, Roland. "Life and Death in Eudora Welty's 'A Worn Path.'" *Studies in Short Fiction* 14 (1977): 288-90)

Paraphrase

As Roland Bartel points out in "Life and Death in Eudora Welty's 'A Worn Path,'" Phoenix Jackson's "stoical behavior" at the doctor's office makes sense if her grandson is actually dead. Although she says that her forgetfulness is due to her lack of education, Bartel does not accept this excuse. According to him, the fact that Phoenix is uneducated cannot fully explain her forgetting about her grandson—although it might explain why she cannot communicate her reasons for her trip (289).

When you write a **summary,** you also put an author's ideas into your own words, but you present just the main idea of a passage. For this reason, a summary is always much shorter than the original. Here is Daniel's summary of the passage from Bartel's article.

Summary

As Roland Bartel points out in "Life and Death in Eudora Welty's 'A Worn Path,'" Phoenix Jackson's behavior at the doctor's office makes sense if we assume that her grandson is dead and that she does not have the skill to explain her reasons for making her trip (289).

When you **quote,** you reproduce a passage exactly, word for word and punctuation mark for punctuation mark, enclosing the entire passage in quotation marks. Because a large number of quotations will distract readers, use a quotation only when you think that the author's words will add something—memorable wording, for example — to your paper.

Integrating Sources

To integrate a paraphrase, summary, or quotation smoothly into your paper, use a phrase that introduces your source and its author—*Bartel points out, according to Bartel, Bartel claims,* or *Bartel says,* for example. You can place this identifying phrase at various points in a sentence.

According to Roland Bartel, "The assumption that the grandson is dead helps explain Phoenix Jackson's stoical behavior in the doctor's office" (289).

"The assumption that the grandson is dead helps explain Phoenix Jackson's stoical behavior in the doctor's office," observes Roland Bartel in his article "Life and Death in Eudora Welty's 'A Worn Path'" (289).

"The assumption that the grandson is dead," notes the literary critic Roland Bartel, "helps explain Phoenix Jackson's stoical behavior in the doctor's office" (289).

NOTE: Remember to document all paraphrases, summaries, and quotations that you use in your essays. (See Chapter 7, Documenting Sources and Avoiding Plagiarism.)

Exercise: Integrating Quotations

For each of the quotations below, write three sentences: one that integrates the complete quotation into your sentence, one that integrates part of the quotation into your sentence, and one that quotes just a distinctive word or phrase.

Example

- **Original quotation:** "But it seems to me that once you begin a gesture it's fatal not to go through with it" (Updike 223).
- **Sentence integrating complete quotation:** Readers understand Sammy's determination to stand up to Lengel when he says, "But it seems to me that once you begin a gesture it's fatal not to go through with it" (Updike 223).
- **Sentence integrating part of the quotation:** Sammy has mixed feelings about quitting his job but feels that "once you begin a gesture it's fatal not to go through with it" (Updike 223).

- **Sentence quoting one distinctive word:** Sammy considers changing his mind but decides that to do so would be "fatal" (Updike 223).

Quotations

1. "We all remembered all the young men her father had driven away, and we knew that with nothing left she would have to cling to that which had robbed her, as people will" (Faulkner 208).
2. "And so the house came to be haunted by the unspoken phrase: *There must be more money! There must be more money*!" (Lawrence 470).
3. "That moment she was mine, mine, fair" (Browning, line 36)
4. "But I have promises to keep, / And miles to go before I sleep / and miles to go before I sleep" (Frost, lines 14–16).
5. "We live close together and we live far apart. We all go through the same things—it's just a different kind of the same thing" (Glaspell 1119).

Drafting a Thesis Statement

After you have taken notes, review the information you have gathered, and use it to help you draft a **thesis statement**—a single sentence that states the main idea of your paper. You will support this thesis with a combination of your own ideas and the ideas you have drawn from your research.

After reviewing his notes, Daniel developed the following thesis statement about Eudora Welty's "A Worn Path."

Thesis Statement: `What is most important in the story is the spiritual and emotional strength of Phoenix Jackson and how this strength enables her to continue her journey.`

As you draft and revise your paper, your thesis statement will probably change. At this point in the writing process, however, it gives your ideas focus and enables you to organize them into an outline.

Making a Formal Outline

Once you have drafted a thesis statement, you can construct a formal outline from your notes. Begin by writing your thesis statement at the top of the page. Then, review your notes, and arrange them in the order in which you plan to use them. As you construct your outline, group these points under appropriate headings.

When it is completed, your outline will show you how much support you have for each of your points, and it will guide you as you write a draft of your paper. Your outline, which covers the body paragraphs of your essay, can be a **sentence outline,** in which each idea is expressed as a sentence, or a **topic outline,** in which each idea is expressed in a word or a short phrase.

After reviewing his notes, Daniel constructed the following topic outline. Notice that he uses roman numerals for first-level headings, capital letters for second-level headings, and arabic numerals for third-level headings. Notice too that all points in the outline are expressed in parallel terms.

```
Thesis Statement: What is most important in the story is the
spiritual and emotional strength of Phoenix Jackson and how
this strength enables her to continue her journey.

  I. Critical interpretations of "A Worn Path"
     A. Heroic act of sacrifice
     B. Journey of life
     C. Religious pilgrimage
 II. Focus on journey
     A. Jackson and her grandson
     B. Nurse's question
     C. Jackson's reply
III. Jackson's character
     A. Interaction between Jackson's character and journey
        1. Significance of Jackson's first name
        2. Jackson as a complex character
     B. Jackson's physical problems
        1. Failing eyesight
        2. Difficulty walking
 IV. Jackson's spiritual strength
     A. Belief in God
     B. Child of nature
  V. Jackson's emotional strength
     A. Love for grandson
     B. Fearlessness and selflessness
     C. Determination
```

Drafting Your Paper

Once you have constructed your outline, you can draft your paper. Follow your outline as you write, using your notes as the need arises.

Your paper's **introduction** will usually be a single paragraph. In addition to identifying the work (or works) you are writing about and stating your thesis, the introduction to a literary research paper may present an overview of your topic or necessary background information.

The **body** of your paper supports your thesis statement, with each of your paragraphs developing a single point. Support your points with examples from the literary work you are discussing or with summaries, paraphrases, and quotations from your sources. In addition, be sure to include your own observations and inferences.

Your paper's **conclusion,** usually a single paragraph (but sometimes more), restates your main points and reinforces your thesis statement.

Remember, the purpose of your first draft is to get ideas down on paper so that you can react to them. You should expect to revise, possibly writing several drafts.

The final draft of Daniel Collins's paper on Eudora Welty's "A Worn Path" appears on the pages that follow.

 Model Literature Paper with MLA Documentation

Collins 1

Daniel Collins
Professor Smith
English 201
28 February 2009

And Again She Makes the Journey: Character and Act in Eudora Welty's "A Worn Path"

Over the past fifty years, Eudora Welty's "A Worn Path," the tale of an elderly black woman, Phoenix Jackson, traveling to the city to obtain medicine for her sick grandson, has been the subject of much critical interpretation. Critics have wondered about the meaning of the many death and rebirth symbols, including the scarecrow, which the old woman believes is a ghost; the buzzard who watches her travel; the skeleton-like branches that reach out to slow her; and her first name, Phoenix. Various critics have concluded that "A Worn Path" is

Collins 2

either a "heroic act of sacrifice," "a parable for the journey of life," or "a religious pilgrimage" (Piwinski 40). It is certainly true that Phoenix Jackson's journey has symbolic significance. However, what is most important in the story is the spiritual and emotional strength of Phoenix Jackson and how this strength enables her to continue her journey.

Eudora Welty discusses Phoenix Jackson in a DVD interview with Beth Henley. Welty points out that Jackson's first name refers to a mythical bird that dies and is reborn every five hundred years. She explains, however, that despite her symbolic name, Phoenix Jackson is more than a symbol: she is a complex character with human frailties and emotions.

Phoenix Jackson has a number of physical problems that make it difficult for her to perform daily tasks. Because of her age, she has failing eyesight, which distorts her perception of the objects she encounters during her journey. For example, Phoenix mistakes a patch of thorns for "a pretty little *green* bush" (569), and she believes a scarecrow is the ghost of a man. She also has difficulty walking, so she must use a cane; at one point, she is unable to bend and tie her own shoes. Because of these physical problems, readers might expect her to fail in her attempt to reach town; as the narrator points out, the journey is long and difficult. So what gives Phoenix Jackson the energy and endurance for the journey?

Although Phoenix Jackson's body is weak, she has great spiritual and emotional strength. According to

Collins 3

James Saunders, her oneness with nature helps her overcome the challenges that she encounters (67). Because Phoenix Jackson is "a child of nature," her impaired vision, although it slows her journey, does not stop it. As Saunders explains, "mere human vision would not have been sufficient for the journey" (67). Instead, Phoenix Jackson relies on her spiritual connection with nature; thus, she warns various animals to "Keep out from under these feet . . ." (569). Her spiritual strength also comes from her belief in God—a quality seen when she refers to God watching her steal the hunter's nickel.

Phoenix Jackson's spiritual strength is matched by her emotional strength. Her love for her grandson compels her to endure any difficulty and to defy any danger. Therefore, throughout her journey, she demonstrates fearlessness and selflessness. For example, when the hunter threatens her with his gun, she tells him that she has faced worse dangers. And, despite her need for new shoes, she buys a paper windmill for her grandson instead.

In her interview with Beth Henley, Eudora Welty explains how she created Phoenix Jackson—outwardly frail and inwardly strong. Welty tells how she noticed an "old lady" slowly making her way across a "silent horizon,"[1] driven by an overwhelming need to reach her destination; as Welty says, "she had a purpose." Welty created Phoenix Jackson in the image of this determined woman. In order to emphasize the character's strength, Welty had her make the journey to Natchez to get medication for her grandson.

Because the act had to be performed repeatedly, the journey became a ritual that had to be completed at all costs. Thus, as Welty explains in the interview, the act of making the journey—not the journey itself—is the most important element in the story.

In order to emphasize the importance of the journey, Welty gives little information about the daily life of the boy and his grandmother or about the illness for which the boy is being treated. Regardless of the boy's condition—or even whether he is alive or dead—Jackson must complete her journey. The nurse's statement—"The doctor said as long as you came to get it [the medicine], you could have it" (573)—reinforces the ritualistic nature of Jackson's journey, a journey that Bartel suggests is a "subconscious" act (289). Thus, Phoenix Jackson cannot answer the nurse's questions because she does not consciously know what forces her to make the journey. Nevertheless, next Saturday, Phoenix Jackson will again walk, and "will continue to do so, regardless of the difficulties facing her, along the worn path that leads through the wilderness of the Natchez Trace, cheerfully performing her labor of love" (Howard 84).

Clearly, the interaction of character (Phoenix Jackson) and act (the ritual journey in search of medication) is the most important element of Welty's story. By describing Phoenix Jackson's difficult

Collins 5

encounters during her ritual journey to town, Welty emphasizes how spiritual and emotional strength can overcome physical frailty and how determination and fearlessness can overcome any danger (Bethea 37). These moral messages become clear by the time Jackson reaches the doctor's office. The image of the elderly woman determinedly walking across the horizon, the image that prompted Welty to write the story, remains in the minds of readers.

Collins 6

Note

1. Unlike the written version of "A Worn Path," the DVD version of the short story ends not at the doctor's office but with a vision similar to the one that inspired Welty to write the story—the elderly African-American woman silently walking along the horizon at dusk.

Collins 7

Works Cited

Bartel, Roland. "Life and Death in Eudora Welty's 'A Worn Path.'" *Studies in Short Fiction* 14.1 (1977): 288-90. Print.

Bethea, Dean. "Phoenix Has No Coat: Historicity, Eschatology, and Sins of Omission in Eudora Welty's 'A Worn Path.'" *International Fiction Review* 27.5 (2001): 32-38. *Expanded Academic ASAP*. Web. 19 Jan. 2009.

Howard, Zelma Turner. *The Rhetoric of Eudora Welty's Short Stories*. Jackson: UP of Mississippi, 1973. Print.

Piwinski, David J. "Mistletoe in Eudora Welty's 'A Worn Path.'" *ANQ* 16.1 (2003): 40-43. *Expanded Academic ASAP*. Web. 19 Jan. 2009.

Saunders, James Robert. "'A Worn Path': The Eternal Quest of Welty's Phoenix Jackson." *Southern Literary Journal* 25.1 (1992): 62-73. Print.

Welty, Eudora. Interview by Beth Henley. *The Heinle Original Film Series in Literature: Eudora Welty's "A Worn Path."* Dir. Bruce R. Schwartz. Wadsworth, 2003. DVD.

---. "A Worn Path." *Literature: Reading, Reacting, Writing*. Ed. Laurie G. Kirszner and Stephen R. Mandell. 7th ed. Boston: Wadsworth, 2010. 568-74. Print.

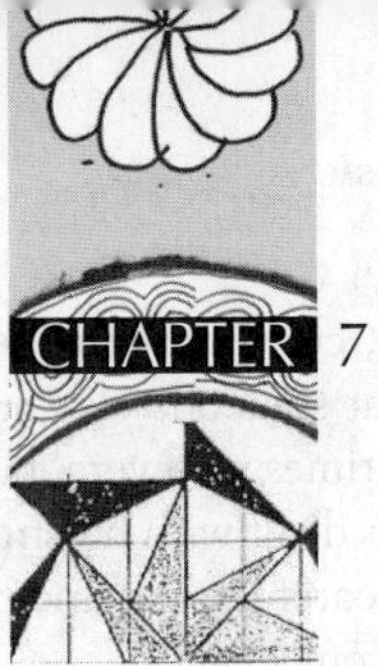

CHAPTER 7

DOCUMENTING SOURCES AND AVOIDING PLAGIARISM

Documentation is the formal acknowledgment of the sources in a research paper. This chapter explains and illustrates the documentation style recommended by the Modern Language Association (MLA), the style used by students of literature.

What to Document

In general, you must document the following types of information from a source (print or electronic):

- ***All word-for-word quotations from a source.*** Whenever you use a writer's exact words, you must document them. Even if you quote only a word or two within a paraphrase or summary, you must document the quoted words separately, after the final quotation marks.
- ***All ideas from a source that you put into your own words.*** Be sure to document all paraphrases or summaries of a source's ideas, including the author's judgments, conclusions, and debatable assertions.
- ***All visuals—tables, charts, and photographs—from a source.*** Because visuals are almost always someone's original creation, they must be documented.

NOTE: Certain items do not require documentation: **common knowledge** (information most readers probably know), facts available from a variety of reference sources, familiar sayings and well-known quotations, and your own ideas and conclusions.

Avoiding Plagiarism

Plagiarism is the presentation of another person's words or ideas as if they were your own. Most plagiarism is **unintentional plagiarism**—for example, pasting a passage from a downloaded document directly into your paper and forgetting to include quotation marks and documentation. However, there is a difference between an honest mistake and **intentional plagiarism**—for example, copying sentences from a journal article or submitting as your own an essay that someone else has written. The penalties for unintentional plagiarism may sometimes be severe, but intentional plagiarism is intellectual theft and is almost always dealt with harshly.

The best way to avoid unintentional plagiarism is to keep careful notes and to make sure you differentiate your words and ideas from those of your sources.

The guidelines that follow can help you avoid mistakes that lead to unintentional plagiarism.

Document All Material That Requires Documentation

Original: In Oates's stories there are no safe relationships, but the most perilous of all possibilities is sex. Sex is always destructive. (Tierce, Mike, and John Michael Crafton. "Connie's Tambourine Man: A New Reading of Arnold Friend." *Studies in Short Fiction* 22.2 (1985): 219–24. Print.)

Plagiarism: In many of Oates's stories, relationships—especially sexual relationships—are dangerous.

In the example above, the writer uses an idea from a source but does not include documentation. As a result, she gives readers the mistaken impression that the source's idea is actually her own.

Correct: Tierce and Crafton point out that in many of Oates's stories, relationships—especially sexual relationships—are dangerous (220).

Enclose Borrowed Words in Quotation Marks

Original: "The Yellow Wallpaper," which Gilman herself called "a description of a case of nervous breakdown," recalls in the first person the experiences of a woman who is evidently suffering from postpartum psychosis. (Gilbert, Sandra M., and Susan Gubar. *The Madwoman in the Attic: The Woman Writer and the Nineteenth-Century Literary Imagination*. New Haven: Yale UP, 1984. Print.)

Plagiarism: As Gilbert and Gubar point out, the narrator in "The Yellow Wallpaper" is evidently suffering from postpartum psychosis (212).

Even though the writer documents the passage, he uses the source's exact words without putting them in quotation marks.

Correct: As Gilbert and Gubar point out, the narrator in "The Yellow Wallpaper" is "evidently suffering from postpartum psychosis" (212).

Do Not Imitate a Source's Syntax and Phrasing

Original: Tennessee Williams's *The Glass Menagerie*, though it has achieved a firmly established position in the canon of American plays, is often distorted, if not misunderstood, by readers, directors, and audiences. (King, Thomas. "Irony and Distance in *The Glass Menagerie*." *Educational Theatre Journal* 31 (1992): 123–34. Print.)

Plagiarism: Although *The Glass Menagerie* has a well-established place in the American theater, it is frequently misinterpreted by those who read it, direct it, and see it (King 125).

Although the student does not use the exact words of the source, he closely follows the sentence structure of the original and simply substitutes synonyms for the writer's key words. Remember, acceptable paraphrases and summaries do more than change words; they use original phrasing and syntax to convey the source's meaning.

Correct: According to Thomas King, although *The Glass Menagerie* has become an American classic, it is still not fully appreciated (125).

Differentiate Your Words from Those of Your Source

Original: At some colleges and universities, traditional survey courses of world and English literature . . . have been scrapped or diluted. . . . What replaces them is sometimes a mere option of electives, sometimes "multicultural" courses introducing material from Third World cultures and thinning out an already thin sampling of Western writings, and sometimes courses geared especially to issues of class, race, and gender. (Howe, Irving. "The Value of the Canon." *New Republic* 2 Feb. 1991: 40–47. Print.)

Plagiarism: At many universities, the Western literature survey courses have been edged out by courses that emphasize minority concerns. These courses are "thinning an already thin sampling of Western writings" in favor of courses geared especially to issues of "class, race, and gender" (Howe 40).

Because the student writer does not differentiate his ideas from those of his source, it appears that only the two quotations in the last sentence are borrowed when, in fact, the first sentence also borrows ideas from the original. The student should have identified the boundaries of the borrowed material by introducing it with an identifying phrase and ending with documentation. (Note that a quotation always requires its own documentation.)

Correct: According to Irving Howe, at many universities the Western literature survey courses have been edged

> out by courses that emphasize minority concerns (41). These courses, says Howe, are "thinning an already thin sampling of Western writings" in favor of courses geared especially to issues of "class, race, and gender" (40).

✔ CHECKLIST Plagiarism and Internet Sources

Because it is so simple to download and manipulate documents from the Internet, you can easily lose track of where you found this material. As a result, you can confuse your ideas with those of your sources and commit unintentional plagiarism. You can effectively manage downloaded material by following these guidelines:

- Download material into individual files so you can easily keep track of your sources.
- Do not cut and paste blocks of downloaded text directly into your paper. Summarize or paraphrase this material first.
- If you use the exact words of a source, enclose them in boldface quotation marks. If you do this, you will know that you need to document this material.
- Record full documentation information for emails, Web sites, and online postings.

Documenting Sources

MLA documentation has three parts: *parenthetical references in the body of the paper* (also known as *in-text citations*), a *works-cited list*, and *content notes.**

Parenthetical References in the Text

MLA documentation style uses parenthetical references within the text to refer to an alphabetical works-cited list at the end of the paper. A parenthetical reference should contain just enough information to guide readers to the appropriate entry on your works-cited list.

A typical parenthetical reference consists of the author's last name and a page number.

> Gwendolyn Brooks uses the sonnet form to create poems that have a wide social and aesthetic range (Williams 972).

*For more information, see the *MLA Handbook for Writers of Research Papers*, 7th ed. (New York: MLA, 2009). You can also consult the MLA Web site at <http://www.mlahandbook.org>.

✔ CHECKLIST Guidelines for Punctuating Parenthetical References

Paraphrases and Summaries

Place the parenthetical reference *after* the last word of the sentence and before the final punctuation.

```
In her poems, Brooks combines the pessimism of
modernist poetry with the optimism of the Harlem
Renaissance (Smith 978).
```

Direct Quotations Run in with the Text

Place the parenthetical reference *after* the quotation marks and *before* the final punctuation.

According to Gary Smith, Brooks's *A Street in Bronzeville* "conveys the primacy of suffering in the lives of poor Black women" (980).

According to Gary Smith, the poems in *A Street in Bronzeville* "served notice that Brooks had learned her craft..." (978).

Along with Thompson, we must ask, "Why did it take so long for critics to acknowledge that Gwendolyn Brooks is an important voice in twentieth-century American poetry" (123)?

Quotations Set Off from the Text

Omit the quotation marks, and place the parenthetical reference one space *after* the final punctuation. (For guidelines for setting off long quotations, see pp. 33–34.)

For Gary Smith, the identity of Brooks's African-American women is inextricably linked with their sense of race and poverty:

> For Brooks, unlike the Renaissance poets, the victimization of poor Black women becomes not simply a minor chord but a predominant theme of *A Street in Bronzeville*. Few, if any, of her female characters are able to free themselves from a web of poverty that threatens to strangle their lives.(980)

If you mention the author's name or the title of the work in your paper, only a page reference is needed.

According to Gladys Margaret Williams in "Gwendolyn Brooks's Way with the Sonnet," Brooks combines a sensitivity to poetic forms with a depth of emotion appropriate for her subject matter (972-73).

If you use more than one source by the same author, include a shortened title in the parenthetical reference.

Brooks knows not only Shakespeare, Spenser, and Milton, but also the full range of African-American poetry (Williams, "Brooks's Way" 972).

SAMPLE PARENTHETICAL REFERENCES

An entire work

When citing an entire work, state the name of the author in your paper instead of in a parenthetical reference.

August Wilson's play *Fences* treats many themes frequently expressed in modern drama.

A work by two or three authors

Myths cut across boundaries and cultural spheres and reappear in strikingly similar forms from country to country (Feldman and Richardson 124).

The effect of a work of literature depends on the audience's predispositions that derive from membership in various social groups (Hovland, Janis, and Kelley 87).

A work by more than three authors

State the last name of the first author, and use the abbreviation *et al.* (Latin for "and others") for the rest.

Hawthorne's short stories frequently use a combination of allegorical and symbolic methods (Guerin et al. 91).

A work in an anthology

In his essay "Flat and Round Characters," E. M. Forster distinguishes between one-dimensional characters and those that are well developed (Stevick 223-31).

Note that the parenthetical reference cites the anthology (edited by Stevick) that contains Forster's essay; full information about the anthology appears in the works-cited list.

A work with volume and page numbers

Critics consider *The Zoo Story* to be one of Albee's best plays (Eagleton 2: 17).

An indirect source

Use the abbreviation qtd. in ("quoted in") to indicate that the quoted material was not taken directly from the original source.

Wagner observed that myth and history stood before him "with opposing claims" (qtd. in Winkler 10).

A play with numbered lines

The parenthetical reference should contain the act, scene, and line numbers (in arabic numerals), separated by periods. When included in parenthetical references, titles of the books of the Bible and well-known literary works are often abbreviated—Gen. for Genesis and *Ham.* for *Hamlet*, for example.

"Give thy thoughts no tongue," says Polonius, "Nor any unproportioned thought his act" (*Ham.* 1.3.64-65).

A poem

Use a slash (/) to separate lines of poetry run in with the text. (The slash is preceded and followed by one space.) The parenthetical reference should cite the lines quoted. Include the word line or lines in the first reference but just the numbers in subsequent references.

"I muse my life-long hate, and without flinch / I bear it nobly as I live my part," says the speaker in Claude McKay's bitterly ironic poem "The White City" (lines 3-4).

An electronic source

If you are citing a source from the Internet or from an online database, remember that these sources frequently do not contain page numbers. If the source uses paragraph, section, or screen numbers, use the abbreviation par. or sec. or the full word screen.

The earliest type of movie censoring came in the form of licensing fees, and in Deer River, Minnesota, "a licensing fee of $200 was deemed not excessive for a town of 1000" (Ernst, par. 20).

If an Internet source has no page numbers or markers of any kind, cite the entire work. (When readers consult your works-cited list, they will be able to determine the nature of the source.)

In her article "Limited Horizons," Lynne Cheney says that schools do best when students read literature not for practical information but for its insights into the human condition.

```
Because of its parody of communism, the film Antz is actually
an adult film masquerading as a child's tale (Clemin).
```

The Works-Cited List

Parenthetical references refer to a **works-cited list** that includes all the sources you refer to in your paper:

- Begin the works-cited list on a new page, continuing the page numbers of the paper. For example, if the text of the paper ends on page 6, the works-cited list will begin on page 7.
- Center the title `Works Cited` one inch from the top of the page.
- Arrange entries alphabetically, according to the last name of each author. Use the first word of the title if the author is unknown (articles—*a, an,* and *the*—at the beginning of a title are not considered first words).
- Double-space the entire works-cited list between and within entries.
- Begin typing each entry at the left margin, and indent subsequent lines one-half inch.
- Each works-cited entry has three divisions—*author, title,* and *publishing information*—separated by periods. The *MLA Handbook for Writers of Research Papers* shows a single space after all end punctuation.

Below is a directory listing the sample MLA works-cited list entries that begin on page 144.

DIRECTORY OF MLA WORKS-CITED LIST ENTRIES

Print Sources: Entries for Books

1. A book by a single author
2. A book by two or three authors
3. A book by more than three authors
4. Two or more works by the same author
5. An edited book
6. A book with a volume number
7. A short story, poem, or play in a collection of the author's work
8. A short story in an anthology
9. A poem in an anthology
10. A play in an anthology
11. An article in an anthology
12. More than one selection from the same anthology
13. A translation

Print Sources: Entries for Articles

14. An article in a journal
15. An article in a magazine

16. An article in a daily newspaper
17. An article in a reference book

Entries for Other Sources

18. A film, videocassette, DVD, or CD-ROM
19. An interview
20. A lecture or an address

Electronic Sources: Entries from Internet Sites

21. A scholarly project or information database on the Internet
22. A document within a scholarly project or information database on the Internet
23. A personal site on the Internet
24. A book on the Internet
25. An article in a scholarly journal on the Internet
26. An article in an encyclopedia on the Internet
27. An article in a newspaper on the Internet
28. An article in a magazine on the Internet
29. A painting or photograph on the Internet
30. An email
31. An online posting

Electronic Sources: Entries from Online Databases

32. A scholarly journal article from an online database
33. A monthly magazine article from an online database
34. A newspaper article from an online database
35. A reference book article from an online database
36. A dictionary definition from an online database

Entries for Other Electronic Sources

37. A nonperiodical publication on DVD-ROM or CD-ROM
38. A periodical publication on DVD-ROM or CD-ROM

MLA • Print Sources: Entries for Books

Book citations include the author's name; book title (italicized); and publication information (place, publisher, date, publication medium). Capitalize all major words in the title except articles, prepositions, and the *to* of an infinitive (unless it is the first or last word of the title or subtitle). MLA requires that you abbreviate publishers' names—for example, *Basic* for Basic Books and *Oxford UP* for Oxford University Press.

1. A book by a single author

Kingston, Maxine Hong. *The Woman Warrior: Memoirs of a Girlhood among Ghosts*. New York: Knopf, 1976. Print.

2. A book by two or three authors

Feldman, Burton, and Robert D. Richardson. *The Rise of Modern Mythology*. Bloomington: Indiana UP, 1972. Print.

Note that only the *first* author's name is in reverse order.

3. A book by more than three authors

Guerin, Wilfred, et al., eds. *A Handbook of Critical Approaches to Literature*. 5th ed. New York: Harper, 2004. Print.

Note that instead of using `et al.`, you may list all the authors' names in the order in which they appear on the title page.

4. Two or more works by the same author

List two or more works by the same author in alphabetical order by *title*. Include the author's full name in the first entry; use three unspaced hyphens followed by a period to take the place of the author's name in second and subsequent entries.

Novoa, Juan-Bruce. *Chicano Authors: Inquiry by Interview*. Austin: U of Texas P, 1980. Print.

---. "Themes in Rudolfo Anaya's Work." Literature Colloquium. New Mexico State U, Las Cruces. 11 Apr. 2002. Address.

5. An edited book

Oosthuizen, Ann, ed. *Sometimes When It Rains: Writings by South African Women*. New York: Pandora, 1987. Print.

Note that here the abbreviation *ed.* stands for *editor*.

6. A book with a volume number

When all the volumes of a multivolume work have the same title, list the number of the volume you used.

Eagleton, T. Allston. *A History of the New York Stage*. Vol. 2. Englewood Cliffs: Prentice, 1987. Print.

When each volume of a multivolume work has a separate title, list the title of the volume you used.

Durant, Will, and Ariel Durant. *The Age of Napoleon: A History of European Civilization from 1789 to 1815*. New York: Simon, 1975. Print.

(*The Age of Napoleon* is volume 2 of *The Story of Civilization*. You need not provide documentation for the entire multivolume work.)

7. A short story, poem, or play in a collection of the author's work

Gordimer, Nadine. "Once upon a Time." *"Jump" and Other Stories*. New York: Farrar, 1991. 23-30. Print.

8. A short story in an anthology

Salinas, Marta. "The Scholarship Jacket." *Nosotros: Latina Literature Today*. Ed. Maria del Carmen Boza, Beverly Silva, and Carmen Valle. Binghamton: Bilingual, 1986. 68-70. Print.

Note that here the abbreviation *Ed.* stands for *Edited by*. The inclusive page numbers follow the year of publication.

9. A poem in an anthology

Simmerman, Jim. "Child's Grave, Hale County, Alabama." *The Pushcart Prize, X: Best of the Small Presses*. Ed. Bill Henderson. New York: Penguin, 1986. 198-99. Print.

10. A play in an anthology

Hughes, Langston. *Mother and Child*. *Black Drama Anthology*. Ed. Woodie King and Ron Miller. New York: NAL, 1986. 399-406. Print.

11. An article in an anthology

Forster, E. M. "Flat and Round Characters." *The Theory of the Novel*. Ed. Philip Stevick. New York: Free, 1980. 223-31. Print.

12. More than one selection from the same anthology

If you are using more than one selection from an anthology, cite the anthology in a separate entry. Then, list each individual selection separately, including the author and title of the selection, the anthology editor's last name, and the inclusive page numbers.

Baxter, Charles. "Gryphon." Kirszner and Mandell 277-89.

Kirszner, Laurie G., and Stephen R. Mandell, eds. *Literature: Reading, Reacting, Writing*. 7th ed. Boston: Wadsworth, 2010. Print.

Rich, Adrienne. "Diving into the Wreck." Kirszner and Mandell 1020-22.

13. A translation

Carpentier, Alejo. *Reasons of State*. Trans. Francis Partridge. New York: Norton, 1976. Print.

MLA • Print Sources: Entries for Articles

Article citations include the author's name; the title of the article (in quotation marks); the name of the periodical (italicized); the volume and issue numbers (if applicable; see below); the month, if applicable (abbreviated, except for May, June, and July), and the year; the pages on which the full article appears (without the abbreviations *p.* or *pp.*); and the publication medium.

14. An article in a journal

Grossman, Robert. "The Grotesque in Faulkner's 'A Rose for Emily.'" *Mosaic* 20.3 (1987): 40-55. Print.

Note that *20.3* signifies volume 20, issue 3.

15. An article in a magazine

Milosz, Czeslaw. "A Lecture." *New Yorker* 22 June 1992: 32. Print.

An article with no listed author is entered by title on the works-cited list.

"Solzhenitsyn: An Artist Becomes an Exile." *Time* 25 Feb. 1974: 34+. Print.

Note that *34+* indicates that the article appears on pages that are not consecutive; in this case, the article begins on page 34 and continues on page 37.

16. An article in a daily newspaper

Omit the article *the* from the title of a newspaper even if the newspaper's actual title includes the article.

Oates, Joyce Carol. "When Characters from the Page Are Made Flesh on the Screen." *New York Times* 23 Mar. 1986, late ed.: C1+. Print.

Note that *C1+* indicates that the article begins on page 1 of Section C and continues on a subsequent page.

17. An article in a reference book

Do not include full publication information for well-known reference books.

"Dance Theatre of Harlem." *The New Encyclopaedia Britannica: Micropaedia*. 2007 ed. Print.

Include full publication information when citing reference books that are not well known.

Grimstead, David. "Fuller, Margaret Sarah." *Encyclopedia of American Biography*. Ed. John A. Garraty. New York: Harper, 1996. Print.

Entries for Other Sources

18. A film, videocassette, DVD, or CD-ROM

The Heinle Original Film Series in Literature: Eudora Welty's "A Worn Path." Dir. Bruce R. Schwartz. Wadsworth, 2003. DVD.

19. An interview

Brooks, Gwendolyn. "An Interview with Gwendolyn Brooks." *Triquarterly* 60 (1984): 405-10. Print.

20. A lecture or an address

Novoa, Juan-Bruce. "Themes in Rudolfo Anaya's Work." Literature Colloquium. New Mexico State U, Las Cruces. 11 Apr. 2002. Address.

MLA • Electronic Sources: Entries from Internet Sites

MLA style recognizes that full publication information is not always available for electronic sources. Include in your citation whatever information you can reasonably obtain: the author or editor of the site (if available); the title of the Internet site (italicized); the version number of the source (if applicable); the name of any sponsoring institution (if unavailable, include the abbreviation `N.p.` for "no publisher"); the date of electronic publication or update (if unavailable, include the abbreviation `n.d.` for "no date of publication"); the publication medium (`Web`); and the date of access. MLA recommends omitting the URL from the citation unless it is necessary to find the source. If a URL is necessary, MLA requires that you enclose it within angle brackets. If you have to carry the URL over to the next line, divide it after a slash.

21. A scholarly project or information database on the Internet

Nelson, Cary, ed. *Modern American Poetry*. Dept. of English, U of Illinois, Urbana-Champaign, 2002. Web. 26 May 2008.

22. A document within a scholarly project or information database on the Internet

"D-Day: June 6th, 1944." *History.com.* History Channel, 1999. Web. 7 June 2003.

23. A personal site on the Internet

Yerkes, James. *The Centaurian: John Updike Home Page.* Prexar, 15 June 2009. Web. 19 June 2009. <http://userpages.prexar.com/joyerkes/>.

24. A book on the Internet

Douglass, Frederick. *My Bondage and My Freedom.* Boston, 1855. *Google Book Search.* Web. 8 June 2007.

25. An article in a scholarly journal on the Internet

DeKoven, Marianne. "Utopias Limited: Post-Sixties and Postmodern American Fiction." *Modern Fiction Studies* 41.1 (1995): 75-97. Web. 17 Mar. 2005.

When you cite information from the print version of an electronic source, include the publication information for the printed source, the inclusive page numbers (if available), the publication medium, and the date of access.

26. An article in an encyclopedia on the Internet

"Hawthorne, Nathaniel." *Encyclopaedia Britannica Online.* Encyclopaedia Britannica, 2007. Web. 16 May 2007.

27. An article in a newspaper on the Internet

Cave, Damien. "Election Day May Look Familiar." *New York Times.* New York Times, 28 Apr. 2008. Web. 29 Apr. 2008.

28. An article in a magazine on the Internet

Weiser, Jay. "The Tyranny of Informality." *Time.* Time, 26 Feb. 1996. Web. 1 Mar. 2003.

29. A painting or photograph on the Internet

Lange, Dorothea. *Looking at Pictures.* 1936. Museum of Mod. Art, New York. *MoMA.org.* Web. 17 July 2007.

30. An email

Mauk, Karen. Message to the author. 28 June 2007. E-mail.

31. An online posting

Berg, Kirsten. "Bright Angel." Online posting. *PowellsBooks.Blog*. Powells, 17 June 2009. Web. 18 June 2009.

MLA • Electronic Sources: Entries from Online Databases

To cite information from an online database, supply the publication information (including page numbers, if available; if unavailable, use n. pag.) followed by the italicized name of the database, the publication medium (Web), and the date of access.

Luckenbill, Trent. "Environmental Litigation: Down the Endless Corridor." *Environment* 17 July 2001: 34-42. *ABI/INFORM GLOBAL*. Web. 12 Oct. 2005.

32. A scholarly journal article from an online database

Schaefer, Richard J. "Editing Strategies in Television News Documentaries." *Journal of Communication* 47.4 (1997): 69-89. *InfoTrac OneFile Plus*. Web. 2 Oct. 2005.

33. A monthly magazine article from an online database

Livermore, Beth. "Meteorites on Ice." *Astronomy* July 1993: 54-58. *Expanded Academic ASAP Plus*. Web. 2 Oct. 2005.

34. A newspaper article from an online database

Meyer, Greg. "Answering Questions about the West Nile Virus." *Dayton Daily News* 11 July 2002: Z3-7. *LexisNexis*. Web. 2 Oct. 2006.

35. A reference book article from an online database

Laird, Judith. "Geoffrey Chaucer." *Cyclopedia of World Authors*. 1997. *MagillOnLiterature*. Web. 2 Oct. 2005.

36. A dictionary definition from an online database

"Migraine." *Mosby's Medical, Nursing, and Allied Health Dictionary*. 1998 ed. *Health Reference Center*. Web. 2 Oct. 2005.

MLA • Electronic Sources: Entries for Other Electronic Sources

37. A nonperiodical publication on DVD-ROM or CD-ROM

"Windhover." *Concise Oxford English Dictionary*. 11th ed. Oxford: Oxford UP, 2006. CD-ROM.

38. A periodical publication on DVD-ROM or CD-ROM

Zurbach, Kate. "The Linguistic Roots of Three Terms." *Linguistic Quarterly* 37 (1994): 12-47. CD-ROM. *InfoTrac: Magazine Index Plus*. Information Access. Jan. 2005.

> **WARNING:** Using information from an Internet source can be risky. Contributors are not necessarily experts. Unless you can be certain that the information you are obtaining from these sources is reliable, do not use it. You can check the reliability of an Internet source by asking your instructor or librarian for guidance.

Content Notes

Use **content notes,** indicated by a superscript (a raised number) in the text, to cite several sources at once or to provide commentary or explanations that do not fit smoothly into your paper. The full text of these notes appears on the first numbered page following the last page of the paper. (If your paper has no content notes, the works-cited page follows the last page of the paper.) Like works-cited entries, content notes are double-spaced within and between entries. However, the first line of each explanatory note is indented one-half inch, and subsequent lines are flush with the left-hand margin.

To Cite Several Sources

In the paper

Surprising as it may seem, there have been many attempts to define literature.[1]

In the note

1. For an overview of critical opinion, see Arnold 72; Eagleton 1-2; Howe 43-44; and Abrams 232-34.

To Provide Explanations

In the paper

In recent years, gothic novels have achieved great popularity.[3]

In the note

3. Gothic novels, works written in imitation of medieval romances, originally relied on supernatural occurrences. They flourished in the late eighteenth and early nineteenth centuries.

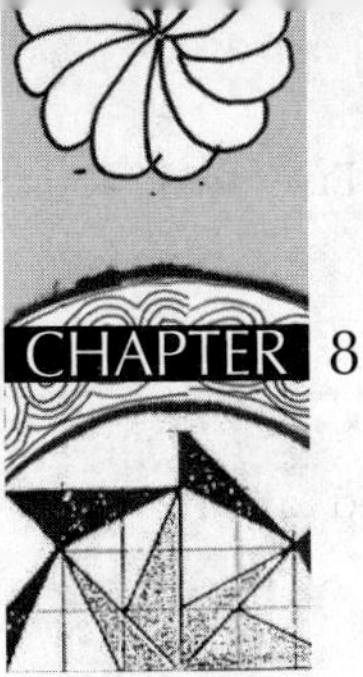

CHAPTER 8

WRITING ESSAY EXAMS ABOUT LITERATURE

Taking exams is a skill that you have been developing throughout your career as a student. Both short-answer exams and essay exams require you to study, to recall what you know, and to budget your time carefully as you write your answers. Only essay questions, however, ask you to synthesize information and to arrange ideas in a series of clear, logically connected sentences and paragraphs. For this reason, taking essay exams requires writing skills. To write an essay exam—or even a paragraph-length response—you must do more than memorize facts; you must identify the relationships among them. In other words, you must **think critically** about your subject, and you must plan, shape, draft, and revise an essay that clearly communicates your ideas to your audience.

Planning an Essay Exam Answer

Because you are under pressure during an exam and tend to write quickly, you may be tempted to skip the planning and revision stages of the writing process. But if you write in a frenzy and hand in your exam without a second glance, you are likely to produce a disorganized (or even incoherent) answer. With careful planning and editing, you can write an essay that demonstrates your understanding of the material.

Review Your Material

Be sure you know beforehand the scope and format of the exam. How much of your textbook and class notes will the exam cover—the entire semester's work or only the material covered since the last test? Will you have to answer every question, or will you be able to choose among alternatives? Will the exam test your ability to recall specific facts, or will it require you to demonstrate your understanding of the course material by drawing original conclusions?

Exams challenge you to recall and express in writing what you already know—what you have read, what you have heard in class, what you have reviewed in your notes. Before you even begin an exam, you must study: reread your textbook and class notes, highlight key points, and perhaps outline particularly important sections of your notes. When you prepare for a short-answer exam, you may memorize facts without analyzing their relationship to one another or their relationship to a body of knowledge as a whole: the definition of romanticism, the date of Queen Victoria's death, two examples of irony, four characteristics of a villanelle. When you prepare for an essay exam, however, you must do more than remember bits of information; you must also make connections among ideas.

When you are sure you know what to expect, try to anticipate the essay questions your instructor might ask. Try out likely questions on classmates, and see whether you can do some collaborative brainstorming to outline answers to possible questions. If you have time, you might even practice answering one or two in writing.

Consider Your Audience and Purpose

The audience for any exam is the instructor who prepared it. As you read the questions, think about what your instructor has emphasized in class. Although you may certainly arrange material in a new way or use it to make an original point, keep in mind that your purpose is to demonstrate that you understand the material, not to make clever remarks or introduce irrelevant information. In addition, you should make every effort to use the vocabulary of the discipline for which you are writing and to follow the specific **conventions** for writing about literature (p. 35).

Read Through the Entire Exam

Your time is usually limited when you take an exam, so plan carefully. How long should a "one-paragraph" or "essay-length" answer be? How much time should you devote to answering each question? The exam question itself may specify the time allotted for each answer, so look for that information. More often, the point value of each question or the number of questions on the exam indicates how much time to spend on each answer. If an essay question is worth 50 out of 100 points, for example, you will probably have to spend at least half of your time planning, writing, and revising your answer.

Before you begin to write, read the entire exam carefully to determine your priorities and your strategy. First, be sure that your copy of the test is complete and that you understand exactly what each question requires. If you need clarification, ask your instructor or proctor for help. Then, decide where to start. If there is more than one question on the exam, responding first to the one you feel most confident about is usually a good strategy. This approach ensures that you will not become bogged down responding to a question that baffles you and have too little time to write a strong answer to a question that you understand well.

Read Each Question Carefully

To write an effective answer, you need to understand the question. As you read any essay question, you may find it helpful to underline key words and important terms.

<u>Summarize in detail</u> the contributions of American <u>writers</u> of the <u>Harlem Renaissance</u>, <u>briefly outlining</u> the contributions of <u>artists and musicians.</u>

Look carefully at the question's wording. If the question calls for a comparison and contrast of two works of literature, a description or analysis of *one* work, no matter how comprehensive, will not be acceptable. If a question asks for causes *and* effects, a discussion of causes alone will be insufficient.

Key Words in Exam Questions

Analyze	Describe	Interpret
Clarify	Discuss	Justify
Classify	Evaluate	Relate
Compare	Explain	Summarize
Contrast	Identify	Support
Define	Illustrate	Trace

As its key words indicate, the following question calls for a very specific kind of response.

Question

Identify three differences between the hard-boiled detective story and the classical detective story.

The following response to the question simply *identifies* three characteristics of *one* kind of detective story and is therefore not acceptable.

Unacceptable Answer

The hard-boiled detective story, popularized in *Black Mask* magazine in the 1930s and 1940s, is very different from the classical detective stories of Edgar Allan Poe or Agatha Christie. The hard-boiled stories feature a down-on-his-luck detective who is constantly tempted and betrayed. His world is dark and chaotic, and the crimes he tries to solve are not out-of-the-ordinary occurrences; they are the norm. These stories have no happy endings; even when the crime is solved, the world is still corrupt.

The answer below, which *contrasts* the two kinds of detective stories, is acceptable.

Acceptable Answer

The hard-boiled detective story differs from the classical detective story in its characters, its setting, and its plot. The classical detective is usually well educated and well off; he is aloof from the other characters and therefore can remain in total control of the situation. The hard-boiled detective, on the other hand, is typically a decent but down-on-his-luck man who is drawn into the chaos around him, constantly tempted and betrayed. In the orderly world of the classical detective, the crime is a temporary disruption. In the hard-boiled detective's dark and chaotic world, the crimes he tries to solve are the norm. In the classical detective story, order is restored at the end. Hard-boiled stories have no happy endings; even when the crime is solved, the world is still a corrupt and dangerous place.

Brainstorm to Find Ideas

Once you understand the question, you need to find something to say. Begin by **brainstorming**—quickly listing all of the relevant ideas you can remember about a topic. Then, identify the most important points on your list, and delete the others. A quick review of the exam question and your supporting ideas should lead you toward a workable thesis for your essay.

 Shaping an Essay Exam Answer

State Your Thesis

Often, you can rephrase the exam question as a **thesis statement.** For example, the question "Discuss in detail the contributions of American writers of the Harlem Renaissance, briefly outlining the contributions of artists and musicians" suggests the following thesis statement.

Effective Thesis Statement

Writers of the Harlem Renaissance—notably Richard Wright, Gwendolyn Brooks, Zora Neale Hurston, and Langston Hughes—made significant contributions to American literature; artists and musicians of the movement also left an important legacy.

An effective thesis statement addresses all aspects of the exam question but highlights only relevant concerns. The following thesis statements are not effective.

Vague Thesis Statement

The Harlem Renaissance produced many important writers, artists, and musicians.

Incomplete Thesis Statement

The writers of the Harlem Renaissance, such as Richard Wright, Gwendolyn Brooks, Zora Neale Hurston, and Langston Hughes, made significant contributions to American literature.

Irrelevant Thesis Statement

The writers of the Harlem Renaissance had a greater impact on American literature than the writers of the Beat generation, such as Jack Kerouac.

Make a Scratch Outline

Because time is limited, you should plan your answer before you write it. Therefore, once you have decided on a suitable thesis, you should make a **scratch outline** that lists the points you will use to support your thesis.

On the inside cover of your exam book, arrange your supporting points in the order in which you plan to discuss them. Once you have completed your outline, check it against the exam question to make certain it covers everything the question calls for—and *only* what the question calls for.

A scratch outline for an answer to the question "Discuss in detail the contributions of American writers of the Harlem Renaissance, briefly outlining the contributions of artists and musicians" might look like this.

Thesis statement: Writers of the Harlem Renaissance—notably Richard Wright, Gwendolyn Brooks, Zora Neale Hurston, and Langston Hughes—made significant contributions to American literature; artists and musicians of the movement also left an important legacy.

Writers

Wright—*Uncle Tom's Children*, *Black Boy*, *Native Son*

Brooks—poetry (classical forms; social issues)

Hurston—*Their Eyes Were Watching God*, essays, autobiography

Hughes—poetry (ballads, blues); "Simple" stories

Artists and Musicians

Henry Tanner

Duke Ellington

Drafting and Revising an Essay Exam Answer

Referring to your outline, you can now begin to draft your answer. Don't bother crafting an elaborate or unusual **introduction;** your time is precious, and so is your reader's. A simple statement of your thesis that summarizes your answer is your best introductory strategy. This approach is efficient, and it reminds you to address the question directly.

To develop the **body** of the essay, follow your outline point by point, using specifically worded topic sentences to introduce your supporting points and clear transitions to indicate your progression from point to point (and to help your instructor see that you are answering the question in full). Such signals, along with parallel sentence structure and repeated words, will make your essay easy to follow.

The most effective **conclusion** for an essay exam is a clear, simple restatement of the thesis or a summary of the essay's main points.

Essay answers should be complete and detailed, but they should not contain irrelevant material. Every unnecessary fact or opinion increases your chance of error, so don't repeat yourself or volunteer unrequested information, and don't express your own feelings or opinions unless such information is specifically called for. Finally, be sure to support all your general statements with specific examples.

Don't forget to leave enough time to reread and revise what you have written. When you reread, try to view your answer from a fresh perspective. Is your thesis statement clearly worded? Does your essay support your thesis and answer the question? Are your facts correct, and are your ideas presented in a logical order? Review your topic sentences and transitions, and check sentence structure and word choice, spelling and punctuation. If a sentence—or even a whole paragraph—seems irrelevant, cross it out. If you suddenly remember something you want to add, you can insert a few additional words with a caret (^). Neatly insert a longer addition at the end of your answer, box it, and label it so your instructor will know where it belongs. Finally, be sure that you have written legibly and that you have not inadvertently left out any words.

Model Student Essay Exam Answer

The essay exam answer on pages 158–160 was written in response to the following question.

Question

> Fictional characters (like real people) do not always behave as others want them to. Sometimes they rebel against the expectations of their family or their society. In a clearly written and supported essay, explain how the specific actions of any three characters in works we have read this semester defy the expectations of those around them. Then, briefly consider the consequences of each character's decision to rebel.

As you read the following response to the question, notice that the student writer does not include any irrelevant information. She does not, for example, provide unnecessary plot summary or discuss more than three characters; she covers only what the question asks for. Guided by the question's key words—*explain* and *briefly consider*—she describes how each character's actions are defiant and outlines the consequences of those actions.

Introduction echoes wording of exam question and introduces three characters to be discussed

Thesis statement

Many characters we have read about this semester do not behave as others believe they should behave. This is apparent in the actions of Connie in Joyce Carol Oates's short story "Where Are You Going, Where Have You Been?," Nora in Henrik Ibsen's play *A Doll House*, and Marty in Paddy Chayefsky's play *Marty*. For each of these characters, rebellion comes with a significant sacrifice.

First character's actions explained

Consequences of actions

Connie's rebellion is somewhat typical for a teenager: she rebels against the constraints her parents put on her to be a "good girl" by being a "bad girl" (at least in their terms). The makeup and style of clothing that Connie wears when she is away from home reinforce this "bad girl" image. Her behavior—staying out late, lying about where she is going, having "trashy daydreams"—creates a problem for her parents because she is not conforming to their standards and because she is not conducting herself in a manner they consider appropriate. Her actions also put a strain on the relationship between her and her sister, who is the perfect example of a "good girl." Her determination to rebel ultimately makes her stay home from the family outing, and this in turn leaves her alone and vulnerable to Arnold's advances. Thus, her rebellious actions lead to probable violence (she goes with Arnold, who we know has frightening plans for her). The ending of the story is ambiguous. We do not know if she ever comes back; possibly, her innocent rebellion leads to her death.

Second character's actions explained

Nora in *A Doll House* rebels only after she understands the conflict between her duty to herself to be a "real" person and her duty to her husband and children. Throughout the play, we see this conflict escalating until Nora has no choice but to act to resolve it, choosing to go against the norms of society and against how others think she should act. This behavior creates a problem for Torvald because of the image it presents to others. Torvald's greatest fear is that society will not accept him, and when Nora admits what she has done, he panics. At the end of the play, Nora chooses to be true to herself even though the person closest to her does not approve—and even though she will lose her children. She will be a stronger person because she has found the courage to stand up for herself.

Consequences of actions

Marty's rebellious act is simply his decision to call Clara even though his friends and his mother do not approve. Although Marty is an adult, he is very much still an adolescent in some ways. He has not yet broken away from his mother, and he continues to seek approval from her (and from his friends). He struggles to please his mother—by going to the dance, by allowing Aunt Catherine to move in with them—even when her desires are in conflict with his own. Marty's action at the play's end—calling Clara—will create a problem for his mother and for his friends, who fear his growing independence and fight his decision to pursue a relationship with Clara. But Marty, like Nora, chooses to be true to himself and to do what he thinks is the right thing for him, rather than what others force upon him. He risks hurting his mother, alienating his friends, and losing the only life he

Third character's actions explained

Consequences of actions

knows. But for Marty, the potential gains seem worth the risk.

Conclusion

Connie, Nora, and Marty all break with family and society; all struggle to be independent. For all three, this independence has a cost. Connie may lose her life, Nora gives up her marriage and her children, and Marty leaves behind the comforting, secure existence he has known. Although each character deals with conflict and rebellion in a different way, all three struggle within themselves when decisions they must make are in conflict with the norms and expectations of society. For all three, rebellion leads to sacrifice.

2 | FICTION

UNDERSTANDING FICTION

A **narrative** tells a story by presenting events in some logical or orderly way. A work of **fiction** is a narrative that originates in the imagination of the author rather than in history or fact. Certainly some fiction—historical or autobiographical fiction, for example—focuses on real people and is grounded in actual events, but the way the characters interact, what they say, and how the plot unfolds are largely the author's invention.

Even before they know how to read, most people have learned how narratives are structured. As children learn how to tell a story, they start to experiment with its form, learning the value of exaggerating, adding or deleting details, rearranging events, and bending facts. In other words, they learn how to *fictionalize* a narrative to achieve a desired effect. This kind of informal personal narrative is similar in many respects to more structured literary narratives.

Origins of Modern Fiction

The earliest examples of narrative fiction are linked with our understanding of stories in general. People have always had stories to tell, and as we evolved, so did our means of self-expression. Our early ancestors depicted the stories of their daily lives and beliefs in primitive drawings that used pictures as symbols. As language evolved, so too did our means of communicating—and our need to preserve what we understood to be our past.

Stories and songs emerged as an oral means of communicating and preserving the past: tales of heroic battles or struggles, myths, or religious beliefs. In a society that was not literate, and in a time before mass communication, the oral tradition enabled people to pass down these stories, usually in the form of long rhyming poems. These poems used various literary devices—including **rhyme** and **alliteration** as well as **anaphora** (the repetition of key words or phrases)—to make them easier to remember. Thus, the earliest works of fiction were in fact poetry.

Eventually written down, these extended narratives developed into **epics**—long narrative poems about heroic figures whose actions determine the fate of a nation or of an entire race. Homer's *Iliad* and *Odyssey*, the ancient Babylonian *Epic of Gilgamesh*, the Hindu *Bhagavad Gita*, and the Anglo-Saxon *Beowulf* are examples of epics. Many of the tales of the Old Testament also came out of this tradition. The setting of an epic is vast—sometimes worldwide or cosmic, including heaven

Engraving of Ulysses slaying Penelope's suitors, from Homer's *Odyssey*.
Source: ©Bettmann/Corbis

Engraving of the Trojan horse from Homer's *Iliad*.
Source: ©Bettmann/Corbis

and hell—and the action commonly involves a battle or a perilous journey. Quite often, divine beings participate in the action and influence the outcome of events, as they do in the Trojan War in the *Iliad* and in the founding of Rome in Virgil's *Aeneid*.

During the Middle Ages, these early epics were supplanted by the **romance.** Written initially in verse and later in prose, the romance replaced the gods, goddesses, and central heroic characters of the epic with knights, kings, and damsels in distress. Events were controlled by enchantments rather than by the will of divine beings. The anonymously written *Sir Gawain and the Green Knight* and Thomas Malory's *Le Morte d'Arthur* are romances based on the legend of King Arthur and the Knights of the Round Table.

Other significant texts of the Middle Ages are Geoffrey Chaucer's *The Canterbury Tales* and Giovanni Boccaccio's *The Decameron*, both written in the fourteenth century. These works are made up of poems and stories, respectively, which (although integrated into a larger narrative framework), have much in common with today's collections of short stories.

The History of the Novel

The evolution of the **novel** has been a gradual but steady process. Early forms of literature share many of the characteristics of the novel (although not necessarily sharing its recognizable form). Epics and romances, for instance, often had unified plots, developed characters, and complex themes, and in this way, they were precursors of what today we call the novel.

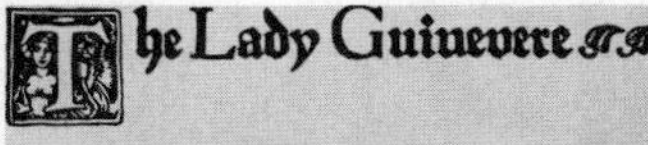

Portrait of Queen Guinevere, King Arthur's wife and Sir Lancelot's mistress.
Source: ©Bettmann/Corbis

Perhaps the most notable event in the development of the novel, and of literature as a whole, was the invention of the printing press by Johannes Gutenberg in 1440. Before this milestone, printing was a costly and impractical process that was largely reserved for medical books and sacred texts. In fact, this invention made the production and distribution of longer works a practical possibility and forever expanded the scope of what we consider literature to be—and how we access it. In fact, the printing press was one of the factors that made the Renaissance possible. During this period, philosophy, science, literature, and the arts flowered. The **pastoral romance,** a prose tale set in an idealized rural world, and the **character,** a brief satirical sketch illustrating a type of personality, both became popular in Renaissance England. The **picaresque novel,** an episodic, often satirical work about a rogue or rascal (such as Miguel de Cervantes' *Don Quixote*), emerged in seventeenth-century Spain. Other notable Renaissance-era texts included Sir Philip Sidney's *Arcadia*, Edmund Spenser's *The Faerie Queen*, and John Bunyan's *The Pilgrim's Progress*. Each of these texts included features now associated with the novel—longer narratives, extended plots, the development of characters over time, and a hero/protagonist—and the form continued to evolve.

An 1863 engraving by Gustave Doré depicting a scene from Miguel de Cervantes' *Don Quixote*.
Source: ©Susan Van Etten

The English writer Daniel Defoe is commonly given credit for writing the first novel. His *Robinson Crusoe* (1719) is an episodic narrative similar to a picaresque but unified by a single setting as well as by a central character. Another early novel, Jonathan Swift's *Gulliver's Travels* (1726), is a satirical commentary on the undesirable outcomes of science. During this time, the **epistolary novel** also flourished. This kind of novel told a story in letters, or included letters as a means of disseminating information. Samuel Richardson's *Clarissa* (1748) is an example from the eighteenth century; a contemporary example is Alice Walker's *The Color Purple*.

By the nineteenth century, the novel had reached a high point in its development, and its influence and importance were widespread. During the Victorian era in England (1837–1901), many novels reflected the era's preoccupation with propriety and manners. The most notable examples of these **novels of manners** were Jane Austen's *Sense and Sensibility* and *Pride and Prejudice*. Beyond the world of the aristocracy, members of the middle class clamored for novels that mirrored their own experiences, and writers such as George Eliot, Charles Dickens, William Thackeray, and Charlotte and Emily Brontë appealed to this desire by creating large fictional worlds populated by many different characters who reflected the complexity—and at times the melodrama—of Victorian society. Other writers addressed the dire consequences of science and ambition, as Mary Wollstonecraft Shelley did in her Gothic tale *Frankenstein* (1817).

Nineteenth-century woodcut by J. Mahoney depicting a scene from Charles Dickens's *Oliver Twist*.
Source: ©Bettmann/Corbis

In the United States, the early nineteenth century was marked by novels that reflected the concerns of a growing country with burgeoning interests. James Fenimore Cooper (*Last of the Mohicans*) and Nathaniel Hawthorne (*The Scarlet Letter*) wrote historical fiction, while Herman Melville (*Moby-Dick*) examined good and evil, madness and sanity. **Realism,** which strove to portray everyday

Scene from the 1931 film *Frankenstein.*
Source: Bettmann/Coribis

events and people in a realistic fashion, began in France with Honoré de Balzac and Gustav Flaubert and spread to the United States, influencing writers such as Henry James, Stephen Crane, and Mark Twain. Other nineteenth-century writers addressed social and even feminist themes in their work. In the United States, writers who addressed such concerns included Harriet Beecher Stowe (*Uncle Tom's Cabin*) and Kate Chopin (*The Awakening*). Meanwhile, in Russia, novelists such as Fyodor Dostoyevsky (*Crime and Punishment*) and Leo Tolstoy (*War and Peace*) examined the everyday lives, as well as the larger political struggles and triumphs, of their people.

The early twentieth century marked the beginning of a literary movement known as **modernism,** in which writers reacted to the increasing complexity of a changing world and mourned the passing of old ways under the pressures of modernity. World War I, urbanization, and the rise of industrialism all contributed to a sense that new ideas needed to be expressed in new ways, and writers such as James Joyce (*Ulysses*), Virginia Woolf (*To the Lighthouse*), and D. H. Lawrence (*Sons and Lovers*) experimented with both form and content.

In the United States, the Roaring Twenties and the Great Depression inspired numerous novelists who set out to write the "Great American Novel" and capture the culture and concerns of the times, often in very gritty and realistic ways. These authors included F. Scott Fitzgerald (*The Great Gatsby*), Ernest Hemingway (*The Sun Also Rises*), William Faulkner (*The Sound and the Fury*), and John Steinbeck (*The Grapes of Wrath*). A little later, novelists such as Richard Wright (*Native Son*) and Ralph Ellison (*Invisible Man*) made important literary contributions by addressing the sociopolitical climate for African Americans in a segregated society.

In the aftermath of modernism, a movement called **postmodernism** emerged. Postmodern artists reacted to the confines and limitations placed on form and meaning. For them, the search for meaning in a text often became more important than the meaning itself. With these experimental techniques, postmodern novelists, such as Donald Barthelme, Margaret Atwood, Thomas Pynchon, Salman Rushdie, and Kurt Vonnegut, confronted the changing society and the future.

Contemporary fiction has been marked and influenced by the developments of the latter part of the twentieth century, including globalization, the rise of technology, and the advent of the Internet and the Age of Communication. As our ability to interact and communicate with other

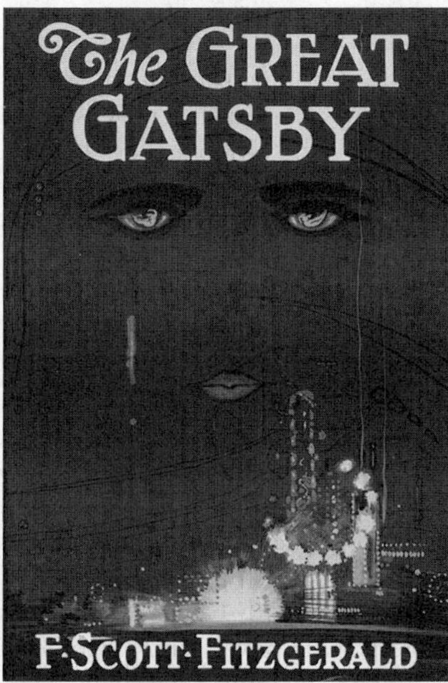

Source: Courtesy, Charles Scribner's Sons

Cover images of *The Great Gatsby, The Sun Also Rises,* and *The Sound and the Fury.*
Source: Courtesy, Charles Scribner's Sons

Source: Courtesy, Royal Books, Inc.

societies has increased exponentially, so too has our access to the literature of other cultures. Contemporary fiction is a world that mirrors the diversity of its participants in terms of form, content, themes, styles, and language. There are many writers worthy of mention, as each culture makes its own invaluable contributions. Some particularly noteworthy contemporary writers include the Nobel Prize–winning novelists Orhan Pamuk, José Saramago, Doris Lessing, Gabriel García Márquez, Nadine Gordimer, Saul Bellow, Toni Morrison, and V. S. Naipul. As we continue into the twenty-first century, the only thing that remains certain about the future of the novel, and of fiction in general, is its past.

The History of the Graphic Novel

The term ***graphic novel*** can be applied to a wide range of visual material, including individual and collected comics and cartoons. As graphic novelist Ivan Brunetti explains, when creating graphic fiction, "The cartoonist uses his own particular set of marks (or 'visual handwriting') to establish a consistent visual vocabulary in which to communicate experience, memory, and imagination—in short, the stuff of narratives."

Like the **short-short story** (see p. 176), graphic novels pack ideas into small spaces (in this case, the "cells" or "panels" on a page). While many graphic novels, as their name would suggest, are fictional narratives, others—such as graphic essays, biographies, autobiographies, historical accounts, and journalistic pieces—actually qualify as nonfiction. Graphic novels appear in printed books, magazines, newspapers, and pamphlets, and many are published online as **Web comics.** Two of today's most popular kinds of graphic novels are **manga** (Japanese comics translated into English) and **superhero comic books.** In the genre's volatile history, graphic novels have taken various forms, appealing to popular and literary audiences alike. In fact, the genre is constantly being redefined. As graphic novelist Eddie Campbell argues, the graphic novel genre "signifies a movement rather than a form" as it strives "to take the form of the comic book, which has become an embarrassment, and raise it to a more ambitious and meaningful level."

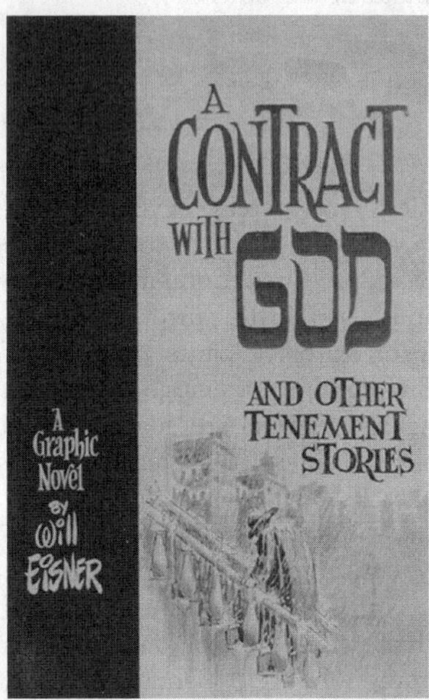

Cover image of the first graphic novel, Eisner's *A Contract with God* (1978).
Source: © Baronet Books

The graphic novel had its origins in comic strips. In the late nineteenth and early twentieth centuries, American newspapers started to feature comic strips that ranged in variety from popular, slapstick, and sci-fi (*The Yellow Kid*, 1895; *Happy Hooligan*, 1900; *Thimble Theatre* [later renamed *Popeye*], 1929; *Flash Gordon*, 1934) to literary and artistic (*Little Nemo*, 1905; *Krazy Kat*, 1913). Comic books, or collections of previously published comic strips, appeared in the mid 1930s, and shortly thereafter the superhero comic emerged and exploded. Comic book characters like Superman, Batman, Wonder Woman, and Captain Marvel began to dominate the genre in the 1940s, and contemporary superhero comics such as *Spider-Man* (1962) and *X-Men* (1963) have achieved international fame both in traditional print formats and in major motion pictures.

In response to the superhero subgenre, **underground** or **alternative comics** appeared in the 1960s, challenging the status quo and depicting taboo topics such as drugs and sex. These unconventional comics, created by artists such as Robert Crumb (1943–) and S. Clay Wilson (1941–), have experienced ups and downs throughout their sales history, unlike their consistently best-selling superhero counterparts. Alternative comics helped usher in the more acclaimed literary graphic novels of the 1980s and 1990s, including Art Spiegelman's Pulitzer Prize–winning *Maus* (1986) and Daniel Clowes's *Ghost World* (1993).

Will Eisner's *A Contract with God* (1978) is widely acknowledged as the first graphic novel. Actually a collection of four short stories, the book displayed the label "graphic novel" on its cover, establishing this new genre as a literary form fundamentally different from mainstream comics. The graphic novel continues to evolve today in its attempt to contribute in fresh, new ways to the changing literary canon.

The History of the Short Story

Early precursors of the short story include **anecdotes, parables, fables, folk tales**, and **fairy tales.** What all of these forms have in common is brevity and a moral. The ones that have survived, such as "Cinderella" and Aesop's *Fables*, are contemporary versions of old, even ancient, tales that can be traced back centuries through many different cultures.

Folktales and fairy tales share many characteristics. First, they feature simple characters who illustrate a quality or trait that can be summed up in a few words. Much of the appeal of "Cinderella," for example, depends on the contrast between the selfish, sadistic stepsisters and the poor, gentle, victimized Cinderella. In addition, the folktale or fairy tale has an obvious theme or **moral**—good triumphing over evil, for instance. The stories move directly to their conclusions, never interrupted by ingenious or unexpected plot twists. (Love is temporarily thwarted, but the prince eventually finds Cinderella and marries her.) Finally, these tales are anchored not in specific times or places but in "Once upon a time" settings, green worlds of prehistory filled with royalty, talking animals, and magic.

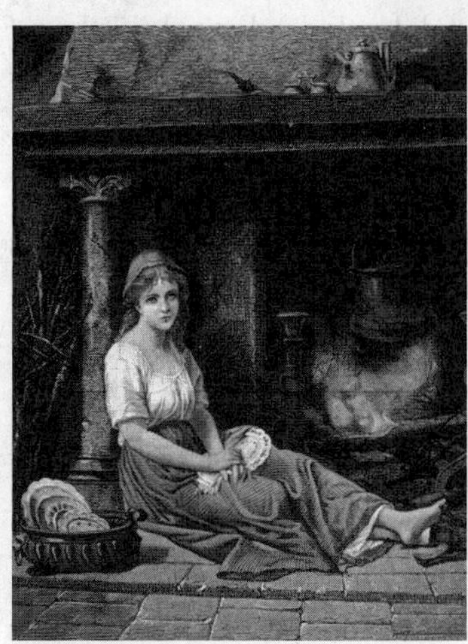

Undated woodcut of Cinderella.
Source: ©Bettmann/Corbis

The thematically linked stories in Giovanni Boccaccio's *The Decameron* and Geoffrey Chaucer's *The Canterbury Tales*, both written in the fourteenth century, were precursors of the modern short story. *Grimm's Fairy Tales* (1824–1826), an early collection of short narratives and folk stories, also helped to pave the way for the development of the genre, but it was not until the nineteenth century that the contemporary version of the short story emerged.

During the last quarter of the nineteenth century, a proliferation of literary and popular magazines and journals created a demand for short fiction (between 3,000 and 15,000 words) that could be published in their entirety rather than in serial installments, as most novels at the time were. Nathaniel Hawthorne's *Twice Told Tales* (1842) and Edgar Allan Poe's *Tales of the Grotesque and Arabesque* (1836) were early collections of short stories. Americans in particular hungrily consumed the written word, and short stories soared in popularity. In fact, because the short story was embraced so readily and developed so quickly in the United States, it is commonly (although not quite accurately) thought of as an American literary form.

Defining the Short Story

Like the novel, the short story evolved from various forms of narrative and has its roots in an oral tradition. However, whereas the novel is an extended piece of narrative fiction, the **short story** is distinguished by its relative brevity, which creates a specific set of expectations and possibilities as well as certain limitations. Unlike the novelist, the short story writer cannot devote a great deal of space to developing a highly complex plot or a large number of characters. As a result, the short story often begins close to or at the height of action and develops a limited number of characters. Usually focusing on a single incident, the writer develops one or more characters by showing their reactions to events. This attention to character development, as well as its detailed description of setting, is what distinguishes the short story from earlier short narrative forms.

In many contemporary short stories, a character experiences an **epiphany,** a moment of illumination in which something hidden or not understood becomes immediately clear. In other short stories, the thematic significance, or meaning, is communicated through the way in which the characters develop, or react. Regardless of the specifics of its format or its theme, a short story offers readers an open window to a world that they can enter—if only briefly.

The short story that follows, Ernest Hemingway's "Hills Like White Elephants" (1927), illustrates many of the characteristics of the modern **short story.** Although it is so brief that it might be more accurately called a **short-short story,** it uses its limited space to establish a distinct setting and develop two characters. From the story's first paragraph, readers know where the story takes place and whom it is about: "The American and the girl with him sat at a table in the shade, outside the building. It was very hot and the express from Barcelona would come in forty minutes." As time elapses and the man and woman wait for the train to Madrid, their strained dialogue reveals the tension between them and hints at the serious conflict they must resolve.

Source: ©AP Photo

ERNEST HEMINGWAY (1898–1961) grew up in Oak Park, Illinois, and after high school graduation began his writing career as a reporter on the *Kansas City Star.* While working as a volunteer ambulance driver in World War I, eighteen-year-old Hemingway was wounded. As Hemingway himself told the story, he was hit by machine-gun fire while carrying an Italian soldier to safety. (Hemingway biographer Michael Reynolds, however, reports that Hemingway was wounded when a mortar shell fell and killed the man next to him.)

Success for Hemingway came early, with publication of the short story collection *In Our Time* (1925) and his first and most acclaimed novel, *The Sun Also Rises* (1926), a portrait of a postwar "lost generation" of Americans adrift in Europe. This group was based on his own circle of friends and their experiences, and thus the novel established Hemingway's ability to create fiction out of the reality of his own life. *A Farewell to Arms* (1929) harks back to his war experiences; *For Whom the Bell Tolls* (1940) emerged out of his experiences as a journalist in Spain during the Spanish Civil War. Later in life, he made his home in Key West, Florida, and then in Cuba, where he wrote *The Old Man and the Sea* (1952). In 1954, he won the Nobel Prize in Literature. In 1961, plagued by poor health and mental illness—and perhaps also by the difficulty of living up to his own image—Hemingway took his own life.

Cultural Context At the time this story was written, Ernest Hemingway was part of a group of American expatriates living in Paris. Disillusioned by World War I and seeking a more bohemian lifestyle, free from the concerns of American materialism, this group of artists, intellectuals, poets, and writers were known as the "Lost Generation." Some of the group's most famous members included F. Scott Fitzgerald, Gertrude Stein, and John Dos Passos. The literary legacy they left behind is arguably one of the greatest of the twentieth century.

Hills Like White Elephants (1927)

The hills across the valley of the Ebro° were long and white. On this side there was no shade and no trees and the station was between two lines of rails in the sun. Close against the side of the station there was the warm shadow of the building and a curtain, made of strings of bamboo beads, hung across the open door into the bar, to keep out flies. The American and the girl with him sat at a table in the shade, outside the building. It was very hot and the express from Barcelona would come in forty minutes. It stopped at this junction for two minutes and went on to Madrid.

"What should we drink?" the girl asked. She had taken off her hat and put it on the table.

"It's pretty hot," the man said.

"Let's drink beer."

"Dos cervezas," the man said into the curtain. 5

Ebro: A river in northern Spain.

"Big ones?" a woman asked from the doorway.

"Yes. Two big ones."

The woman brought two glasses of beer and two felt pads. She put the felt pads and the beer glasses on the table and looked at the man and the girl. The girl was looking off at the line of hills. They were white in the sun and the country was brown and dry.

"They look like white elephants," she said.

"I've never seen one," the man drank his beer.

"No, you wouldn't have."

"I might have," the man said. "Just because you say I wouldn't have doesn't prove anything."

The girl looked at the bead curtain. "They've painted something on it," she said. "What does it say?"

"Anis del Toro.° It's a drink."

"Could we try it?"

The man called "Listen" through the curtain. The woman came out from the bar.

"Four reales."°

"We want two Anis del Toro."

"With water?"

"Do you want it with water?"

"I don't know," the girl said. "Is it good with water?"

"It's all right."

"You want them with water?" asked the woman.

"Yes, with water."

"It tastes like licorice," the girl said and put the glass down.

"That's the way with everything."

"Yes," said the girl. "Everything tastes of licorice. Especially all the things you've waited so long for, like absinthe."

"Oh, cut it out."

"You started it," the girl said. "I was being amused. I was having a fine time."

"Well, let's try and have a fine time."

"All right I was trying. I said the mountains looked like white elephants. Wasn't that bright?"

"That was bright."

"I wanted to try this new drink. That's all we do, isn't it—look at things and try new drinks?"

"I guess so."

The girl looked across at the hills.

"They're lovely hills," she said. "They don't really look like white elephants. I just meant the coloring of their skin through the trees."

"Should we have another drink?"

"All right."

Anis del Toro: A dark alcoholic drink made from anise, an herb that tastes like licorice.

reales: Spanish coins.

The warm wind blew the bead curtain against the table.

"The beer's nice and cool," the man said.

"It's lovely," the girl said.

"It's really an awfully simple operation, Jig," the man said. "It's not really an operation at all."

The girl looked at the ground the table legs rested on.

"I know you wouldn't mind it, Jig. It's really not anything. It's just to let the air in."

The girl did not say anything.

"I'll go with you and I'll stay with you all the time. They just let the air in and then it's all perfectly natural."

"Then what will we do afterward?"

"We'll be fine afterward. Just like we were before."

"What makes you think so?"

"That's the only thing that bothers us. It's the only thing that's made us unhappy."

The girl looked at the bead curtain, put her hand out and took hold of two of the strings of beads.

"And you think then we'll be all right and be happy."

"I know we will. You don't have to be afraid. I've known lots of people that have done it."

"So have I," said the girl. "And afterward they were all so happy."

"Well," the man said, "if you don't want to you don't have to. I wouldn't have you do it if you didn't want to. But I know it's perfectly simple."

"And you really want to?"

"I think it's the best thing to do. But I don't want you to do it if you don't really want to."

"And if I do it you'll be happy and things will be like they were and you'll love me?"

"I love you now. You know I love you."

"I know. But if I do it, then it will be nice again if I say things are like white elephants, and you'll like it?"

"I'll love it. I love it now but I just can't think about it. You know how I get when I worry."

"If I do it you won't ever worry?"

"I won't worry about that because it's perfectly simple."

"Then I'll do it. Because I don't care about me."

"What do you mean?"

"I don't care about me."

"Well, I care about you."

"Oh, yes. But I don't care about me. And I'll do it and then everything will be fine."

"I don't want you to do it if you feel that way."

The girl stood up and walked to the end of the station. Across, on the other side, were fields of grain and trees along the banks of the Ebro. Far away beyond the river, were mountains. The shadow of a cloud moved across the field of grain and she saw the river through the trees.

"And we could have all this," she said. "And we could have everything and every day we make it more impossible."

"What did you say?"

"I said we could have everything."

"We can have everything."

"No, we can't."

"We can have the whole world."

"No, we can't."

"We can go everywhere."

"No, we can't. It isn't ours any more."

"It's ours."

"No, it isn't. And once they take it away, you never get it back."

"But they haven't taken it away."

"We'll wait and see."

"Come on back in the shade," he said. "You mustn't feel that way."

"I don't feel any way," the girl said. "I just know things."

"I don't want you to do anything that you don't want to do—."

"Nor that isn't good for me," she said. "I know. Could we have another beer?"

"All right. But you've got to realize—"

"I realize," the girl said. "Can't we maybe stop talking?"

They sat down at the table and the girl looked across at the hills on the dry side of the valley and the man looked at her and at the table.

"You've got to realize," he said, "that I don't want you to do it if you don't want to. I'm perfectly willing to go through with it if it means anything to you."

"Doesn't it mean anything to you? We could get along."

"Of course it does. But I don't want anybody but you. I don't want any one else. And I know it's perfectly simple."

"Yes, you know it's perfectly simple."

"It's all right for you to say that, but I do know it."

"Would you do something for me now?"

"I'd do anything for you."

"Would you please please please please please please please stop talking?"

He did not say anything but looked at the bags against the wall of the station. There were labels on them from all the hotels where they had spent nights.

"But I don't want you to," he said, "I don't care anything about it."

"I'll scream," the girl said.

The woman came out through the curtains with two glasses of beer and put them down on the damp felt pads. "The train comes in five minutes," she said.

"What did she say?" asked the girl.

"That the train is coming in five minutes."

The girl smiled brightly at the woman, to thank her.

"I'd better take the bags over to the other side of the station," the man said. She smiled at him.

"All right. Then come back and we'll finish the beer."

He picked up the two heavy bags and carried them around the station to the other tracks. He looked up the tracks but could not see the train. Coming back, he walked through the barroom, where people waiting for the train were drinking. He drank an Anis at the bar and looked at the people. They were all waiting reasonably for the train. He went out through the bead curtain. She was sitting at the table and smiled at him.

"Do you feel better?" he asked.

"I feel fine," she said. "There's nothing wrong with me. I feel fine."

* * *

 The Boundaries of Fiction

As noted earlier, a **short story** is a work of fiction that is marked by its brevity, its relatively limited number of characters, its short time frame, and its ability to achieve thematic significance in a relatively short space. A **novella** (such as Franz Kafka's "The Metamorphosis" and Herman Melville's "Bartleby, the Scrivener") is an extended short story that shares some characteristics (for example, concentrated action) with a short story while retaining some qualities of a novel, including greater character development. At the other end of the spectrum are **short-short stories,** which are under 1,500 words (about five pages) in length. (Examples of those very brief stories are included in the Fiction Sampler, Chapter 10.) **Prose poems,** such as Carolyn Forché's, "The Colonel" (p. 1004), are hybrid versions of literature that have characteristics of both prose (being written in paragraphs) and poetry (being written in verse form, often using imagery, meter, and rhyme to convey lyrical beauty). In addition, **graphic stories** —sometimes complete in themselves, sometimes part of **graphic novels** — have proliferated in recent years. Finally, the Internet offers endless possibilities for arranging, presenting, and disseminating text.

There are, it seems, as many different ways to tell a story as there are stories to be told. A short story may be comic or tragic; its subject may be growing up, marriage, crime and punishment, war, sexual awakening, death, or any number of other human concerns. The setting can be an imaginary world, the old West, rural America, the jungles of Uruguay, nineteenth-century Russia, precommunist China, or modern Egypt. The story may have a conventional form, with a definite beginning, middle, and end, or it may be structured as a letter, as a diary entry, or even as a collection of random notes. The story may use just words, or it may juxtapose conventional text with symbols, pictures, or empty space. The narrator of a story may be trustworthy or unreliable, involved in the action or a disinterested observer, sympathetic or deserving of scorn, extremely ignorant or highly insightful, limited in vision or able to see inside the minds of all the characters. As the selections in this anthology show, the possibilities of the short story are almost infinite.

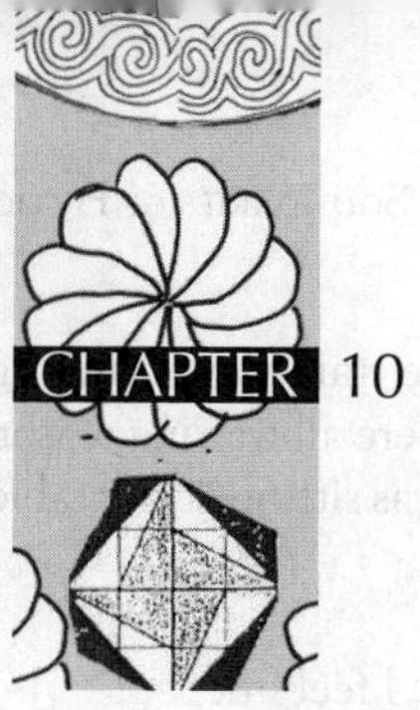

CHAPTER 10

FICTION SAMPLER: THE SHORT-SHORT

This chapter focuses on the **short-short story,** a short story that is fewer than 1,500 words in length. Short-shorts are often classified according to their overall length. For example, **micro fiction,** at approximately 250 words or fewer, is one of the shortest kinds of short-short fiction, followed by **flash fiction** (fewer than approximately 1,000 words) and then by **sudden fiction** (fewer than approximately 1,500 words). Short-shorts are sometimes also categorized according to how long they take to read or how long they take to write. Regardless of their individual characteristics, all short-shorts compress ideas into a small package and, to varying degrees, test the limits of the short story genre. Some short-shorts are quite conventional (that is, they include recognizable characters and have an identifiable beginning, middle, and end); others are experimental, perhaps lacking a definite setting or a clear plot. As defined by Robert Shapard (who, along with James Thomas, edited the short-short story collections *Sudden Fiction* and *New Sudden Fiction*), short-shorts are "Highly compressed, highly charged, insidious, protean, sudden, alarming, tantalizing"; they can "confer form on small corners of chaos, can do in a page what a novel does in two hundred." One of the most extreme examples is Ernest Hemingway's famous six-word story: "For sale: baby shoes, never worn."

The stories in this chapter represent a wide range of short-short fiction. Of the eleven stories collected here, Julia Alvarez's "Snow," Alice Munro's "Prue," ZZ Packer's "Buffalo Soldiers," and John Updike's "Oliver's Evolution" most resemble traditional short stories in that they develop a main character and place that character in a distinct setting. Aimee Bender's "Jinx" also focuses on familiar characters in a recognizable setting, capturing the style, tone, and language of its adolescent protagonists in a vivid snapshot.

Other stories in this chapter are more experimental. For example, Annie Proulx's "55 Miles to the Gas Pump" presents a stunning vignette, in a mere three sentences, of a married Wyoming couple, and David Foster Wallace tells his unnamed characters' horrifying story in a single extended paragraph in "Incarnations of Burned Children." Jamaica Kincaid's "Girl," a **stream-of-consciousness** monologue, is also unusual in its style and form (the entire story is a single sentence), as is Amanda Holzer's "Love and Other Catastrophes: A Mix Tape," consisting entirely of a list of song titles. An example of **metafiction,** Jorge Luis Borges's "The Plot" explores the function of plot in certain literary works.

Finally, Dave Eggers's "Accident" maintains narrative distance with an unusual point of view.

Despite their brevity, the stories in this chapter have much in common with the stories that appear elsewhere in this book. Each, in its own distinctive way, "tells a story."

The following short-shorts are included in this sampler:

Source: ©AP Photo/Ramon Espinosa

JULIA ALVAREZ (1950–) was born in New York City. Soon after her birth, Alvarez's family relocated to the Dominican Republic, where they lived for ten years until they emigrated back to New York. Alvarez describes herself as "a Dominican, hyphen, American. . . . As a fiction writer, I find that the most exciting things happen in the realm of that hyphen—the place where two worlds collide or blend together." Alvarez's works explore the experiences and emotions of immigrants, particularly female Hispanic immigrants, as they struggle to redefine themselves in the context of a new culture. She has published many highly regarded works of fiction and poetry, including *How the García Girls Lost Their Accents* (1991); *In the Time of Butterflies* (1995); and, most recently, *Once Upon a Quinceañera* (2007). Alvarez currently teaches English at Middlebury College in Vermont.

Snow (1984)

Our first year in New York we rented a small apartment with a Catholic school nearby, taught by the Sisters of Charity, hefty women in long black gowns and bonnets that made them look peculiar, like dolls in mourning. I liked them a lot, especially my grandmotherly fourth grade teacher, Sister Zoe. I had a lovely name, she said, and she had me teach the whole class how to pronounce it. *Yo-lan-da.* As the only immigrant in my class. I was put in a special seat in the first row by the window, apart from the other children so that Sister Zoe could tutor me without distributing them. Slowly, she enunciated the new words I was to repeat: *laundromat, cornflakes, subway, snow*.

Soon I picked up enough English to understand holocaust was in the air. Sister Zoe explained to a wide-eyed classroom what was happening in Cuba. Russian missiles were being assembled, trained supposedly on New York City. President

Kennedy, looking worried too, was on the television at home, explaining we might have to go to war against the Communists. At school, we had air-raid drills: an ominous bell would go off and we'd file into the hall, fall to the floor, cover our heads with our coats, and imagine our hair falling out, the bones in our arms going soft. At home, Mami and my sisters and I said a rosary for world peace. I heard new vocabulary: *nuclear bomb*, *radioactive fallout*, *bomb shelter*. Sister Zoe explained how it would happen. She drew a picture of a mushroom on the blackboard and dotted a flurry of chalkmarks for the dusty fallout that would kill us all.

The months grew cold, November, December. It was dark when I got up in the morning, frosty when I followed my breath to school. One morning as I sat at my desk daydreaming out the window, I saw dots in the air like the ones Sister Zoe had drawn—random at first, then lots and lots. I shrieked, "Bomb Bomb!" Sister Zoe jerked around, her full black skirt ballooning as she hurried to my side. A few girls began to cry.

But then Sister Zoe's shocked look faded. "Why, Yolanda dear, that's snow!" She laughed. "Snow."

5 "Snow," I repeated. I looked out the window warily. All my life I had heard about the white crystals that fell out of American skies in the winter. From my desk I watched the fine powder dust the sidewalk and parked cars below. Each flake was different, Sister Zoe said, like a person, irreplaceable and beautiful.

Source: ©Marion Ettinger/Corbis

AIMEE BENDER (1971–), a native of Los Angeles, teaches creative writing at the University of Southern California. Praised for her playful use of language and nonconformist style, Bender has published numerous short stories as well as the novel *An Invisible Sign of My Own* (2000), a *Los Angeles Times* pick of the year in 2000. Collections of her work include the *New York Times* Notable Book *The Girl in the Flammable Skirt* (1998), *Willful Creatures* (2005), and the anonymous story collection *The Secret Society of Demolition Writers* (2005). Bender has won two Pushcart prizes and is currently writing her second novel.

Jinx (2003)

Two teenagers were standing on a street corner. They were both wearing the hot new pants and both had great new butts, discovered on their bodies, a gift from the god of time, boom, a butt. Shiny and nice.

They did not like their butts.

One was complaining to the other that she thought her butt was more heart than bubble and that she wanted bubble and her friend said she thought heart was the best and they stood there on the street corner pressing the little silver nub that changed the mean red hand to the friendly walking man and the light did not change.

One friend had breasts, the other was waiting.

5 When the light changed, they both walked to the poster store where the cute boy worked. He was growing so fast he slept fourteen hours a day and when he came to work he had a stooped look like he'd been lifting large objects for hours and in fact there was

some truth in that, he'd been unfurling his body up through his spine, up through itself. Each day people looked shorter and today these two cute girls—the one he liked with the ponytail bobbing, the other one that touched his elbow which he liked too—they were there again looking in the glass case at the skull rings and joking.

The boy showed them a new poster of a rock-and-roll star in a ripped shirt on a stage with a big wide open mouth that you could fall into. The girls, at the same time, said they thought it was gross. Jinx! They laughed endlessly. Too much tonsil, said one and she grunted in such a way that made them laugh for another ten minutes. It was that sixteen year old laugh that is like a stream of bubbles but makes everyone else feel stupid and left out. Which is part of its point. The boy got a break halfway through the time they were there and one girl said she wanted to look at the posters one by one, flipping those big plastic lined poster holders, because she liked to stare at her own pace, and the other girl, ponytail, went out back with the growing boy, rapidly notching out another vertebrae right as they spoke, straightening higher like a snake head rising from an egg. They went out back so he could smoke a cigarette and she smoked it with him and when touchy girl finished flipping through the leather pants women and the leather pants men and looked for her friend, she couldn't find her and wandered out of the store by herself.

Ponytail girl leaned over and she and the tall boy kissed and it was carcinogen gums and magical.

She liked to kiss in public, so that if someone had a movie camera she could show people. See.

The other girl, now called Cathy, was on the street alone, looking for her friend who was out back with ash on her lips pushing lips against ash, using her tongue in all the different interesting ways she could think of, her breasts rising.

Cathy, teenager, out on the street alone. 10

This is so rare. This moment is rare. This teenage girl out on the shopping street alone: rare. She walked by herself, eyes swooping side to side, looking for the bobbing blur of her friend, Tina's, ponytail, but Tina was not to be seen, not even in the dressing room of the cute clothes store next door where they'd recently tried on skirts made of almost plastic that were so short they reminded you of wrist bands.

Tina now had his hands on her waist, thinking of that exact skirt right as Cathy walked by it, thinking how it had held in her butt and if she was wearing that plastic skirt now, and he held her butt, it would remind him of a bubble, not a heart. I do not want guys to feel my butt and think of hearts, she said to herself, that is too weird.

Cathy walked to the corner. She thought did Tina leave? She thought she'd head back to the poster store but she sat down on a bench instead and when the bus came she just took it. She looked at the people on the bus and no one was looking at her except some creepy old man at the front with those weird deep cuffs on his pants and the seat was cold and Tina was somewhere left out in the stores and would they miss each other? Did she miss Tina? Oh, she thought, probably not. And this was her stop and she got off and walked home, and it was hours too early, they were supposed to be at a movie and when she went inside her mother was sitting there on the couch looking at the backyard. It was like the whole afternoon had got a haircut that was too short. She sat with her mom, making sure the backyard stayed put, which it did, and when her mom fell asleep it all seemed disgusting and this was what happened in that afternoon and she went and looked at herself in the mirror for an hour and felt terrible even though she liked the pose of her left profile best.

And Tina, done with kissing, done with skull rings—the boy settled back behind the counter after waiting two minutes, counting, to tame his erection—Tina was walking the streets and asking people if they'd seen a girl with a great yellow shirt on. No one had, they though she meant some older woman but Tina said no no, and she started to cry on the street because she thought the worst thing, but when she called on the phone just to see, just in case, the most familiar numbers in the world, Cathy answered. Hello? Tina forgot how to talk for a second, she was so surprised, and then she just said Oh. Oh? Hi. Cathy? Tina? Hi? The two girls bumped around the conversation for a few minutes, but for the first time in life, they didn't know what to say to each other. After awhile they just said goodbye and hung up. From then on at school they tended to be friendly but distant and awkwardly found other people to sit with at lunch. By graduation day, three years later, they had forgotten each other's phone numbers completely, even though they hugged in their caps and gowns and tassels for old times sake and said good luck, keep in touch, have a hot summer, later.

Source: ©Charles H. Phillips/Time Life Pictures/Getty Images

JORGE LUIS BORGES (1899–1986) was born in Buenos Aires, Argentina. Widely regarded as one of the most influential modernist and symbolist writers of his time, Borges wrote challenging and deeply metaphysical poetry and fiction. *Ficciones,* published in 1945, is perhaps his most famous collection of short stories. Borges also wrote essays, several screenplays, and a considerable volume of literary criticism, prologues, and reviews. In addition, he edited numerous anthologies and was a prominent translator of English, French, and German literature into Spanish.

The Plot (1949)

To make his horror perfect, Caesar,° hemmed about at the foot of a statue by his friends' impatient knives, discovers among the faces and the blades the face of Marcus Junius Brutus,° his ward, perhaps his very son—and so Caesar stops defending himself, and cries out *Et tu, Brute?*° Shakespeare and Quevedo° record that pathetic cry.

Fate is partial to repetitions, variations symmetries. Nineteen centuries later, in the southern part of the province of Buenos Aires, a gaucho° is set upon by other gauchos, and as he falls he recognizes a godson of his, and says to him in gentle remonstrance and slow surprise (these words must be heard, not read): *Pero, che!*° He dies, but he does not know that he has died so that a scene can be played out again.

Caesar: Julius Caesar (100 B.C.–44 B.C.), Roman dictator assassinated by a band of conspirators.
Marcus Junius Brutus: Roman politician (85 B.C.–42 B.C.) and the lead conspirator who assassinated Julius Caesar.
Et tu. Brute?: Latin for "*You too, Brutus?*"
Quevedo: Francisco Gómez de Quevedo y Villegas (1580–1645), Spanish poet and satirist.
gaucho: South American cowboy.
Pero, che!: Spanish expression expressing surprise.

Source: ©David Levenson/Getty Images

DAVE EGGERS (1970–) grew up near Chicago. In addition to many short stories, he has also published the memoir *A Heartbreaking Work of Staggering Genius* (2000), a finalist for the Pulitzer Prize, as well as two novels, *You Shall Know Our Velocity!* (2002) and *What Is the What* (2006). As the founder of McSweeney's (a literary group that publishes the journal *McSweeney's,* the magazine *The Believer,* and the DVD magazine *Wholphin*) and as editor of *The Best American Nonrequired Reading 2002* and *2003,* Eggers has helped to popularize experimental, irreverent literature in print and electronic formats.

Accident (2005)

You all get out of your cars. You are alone in yours, and there are three teenagers in theirs, an older Camaro in new condition. The accident was your fault, and you walk over to tell them this.

Walking over to their car, which you have ruined, it occurs to you that if the three teenagers are angry teenagers, this encounter could be very unpleasant. You pulled into an intersection, obstructing them, and their car hit yours. They have every right to be upset, or livid, or even violence-contemplating.

As you approach, you see that their driver's side door won't open. The driver pushes against it, and you are reminded of scenes where drivers are stuck in submerged cars. Soon they all exit through the passenger side door and walk around the Camaro, inspecting the damage. None of them is hurt, but the car is wrecked. "Just bought this today," the driver says. He is 18, blond, average in all ways. "Today?" you ask.

You are a bad person, you think. You also think: what a dorky car for a teenager to buy in 2005. "Yeah, today," he says, then sighs. You tell him that you are sorry. That you are so, so sorry. That it was your fault and that you will cover all costs.

You exchange insurance information, and you find yourself, minute by minute, ever 5
more thankful that none of these teenagers has punched you, or even made a remark about your being drunk, which you are not, or being stupid, which you are, often. You become more friendly with all of them, and you realize that you are much more connected to them, particularly to the driver, than possible in perhaps any other way.

You have done him and his friends harm, in a way, and you jeopardized their health, and now you are so close you feel like you share a heart. He knows your name and you know his, and you almost killed him and, because you got so close to doing so but didn't, you want to fall on him, weeping, because you are so lonely, so lonely always, and all contact is contact, and all contact makes us so grateful we want to cry and dance and cry and cry.

In a moment of clarity, you finally understand why boxers, who want so badly to hurt each other, can rest their heads on the shoulders of their opponents, can lean against one another like tired lovers, so thankful for a moment of peace.

AMANDA HOLZER (1981–), a graduate of Emerson College, co-owns the independent record label Not Not Fun. "Love and Other Catastrophes" was first published in 2002 in *Story Quarterly* and was reprinted in *Best American Nonrequired Reading 2003*.

Love and Other Catastrophes: A Mix Tape (2002)

"All By Myself" (Eric Carmen). "Looking for Love" (Lou Reed). "I Wanna Dance With Somebody" (Whitney Houston). "Let's Dance" (David Bowie). "Let's Kiss" (Beat Happening). "Let's Talk About Sex" (Salt N' Pepa). "Like A Virgin" (Madonna). "We've Only Just Begun" (The Carpenters). "I Wanna Be Your Boyfriend" (The Ramones). "I'll Tumble 4 Ya" (Culture Club). "Head Over Heels" (The Go-Go's). "Nothing Compares To You" (Sinéad O'Connor). "My Girl" (The Temptations). "Could This Be Love?" (Bob Marley). "Love and Marriage" (Frank Sinatra). "White Wedding" (Billy Idol). "Stuck in the Middle with You" (Steelers Wheel). "Tempted" (The Squeeze). "There Goes My Baby" (The Drifters). "What's Going On?" (Marvin Gaye). "Where Did You Sleep Last Night?" (Leadbelly). "Whose Bed Have Your Boots Been Under?" (Shania Twain). "Jealous Guy" (John Lennon). "Your Cheatin' Heart" (Tammy Wynette). "Shot Through the Heart" (Bon Jovi). "Don't Go Breaking My Heart" (Elton John and Kiki Dee). "My Achy Breaky Heart" (Billy Ray Cyrus). "Heartbreak Hotel" (Elvis Presley), "Stop, In the Name of Love" (The Supremes). "Try a Little Tenderness" (Otis Redding). "Try (Just a Little Bit Harder)" (Janis Joplin). "All Apologies" (Nirvana). "Hanging on the Telephone" (Blondie). "I Just Called to Say I Love You" (Stevie Wonder). "Love Will Keep Us Together" (Captain and Tennille). "Let's Stay Together" (Al Green). "It Ain't Over 'Till It's Over" (Lenny Kravitz). "What's Love Got To Do With It? (Tina Turner). "You Don't Bring Me Flowers Anymore" (Barbara Streisand and Neil Diamond). "I Wish You Wouldn't Say That" (Talking Heads). "You're So Vain" (Carly Simon). "Love Is a Battlefield" (Pat Benatar). "Heaven Knows I'm Miserable Now" (The Smiths). "(Can't Get No) Satisfaction" (Rolling Stones). "Must Have Been Love (But It's Over Now)" (Roxette). "Breaking Up is Hard to Do" (Neil Sedaka). "I Will Survive" (Gloria Gaynor). "Hit the Road, Jack" (Mary McCaslin and Jim Ringer). "These Boots Were Made for Walking" (Nancy Sinatra). "All Out of Love" (Air Supply). "All By Myself" (Eric Carmen).

* * *

Source: ©Time & Life Pictures/Getty Images

JAMAICA KINCAID (1949–) was born Elaine Potter Richardson on the island of Antigua, where she received a British education and was often at the top of her class. In early childhood, she was very close to her mother, but when her mother gave birth to three sons in quick succession, it altered their relationship forever. According to Kincaid, she was treated badly and neglected, and she left Antigua in 1965 to work as an au pair in Westchester county, near New York City. She went on to study photography at the New School for Social Research and attended Franconia College in New Hampshire for a year. In 1973, after having begun her writing career, she changed her name to Jamaica Kincaid because her family disapproved of her writing. She soon began writing a regular column for the *New Yorker*. Her best-known works include the novel *Annie John* (1986) and the nonfiction book *A Small Place* (1988), which criticizes British Colonialism in Antigua. Her most recent books include *Talk Stories* (2001) and *My Favorite Tool* (2005).

Girl (1984)

Wash the white clothes on Monday and put them on the stone heap; wash the color clothes on Tuesday and put them on the clothesline to dry; don't walk barehead in the hot sun; cook pumpkin fritters in very hot sweet oil; soak your little clothes right after you take them off; when buying cotton to make yourself a nice blouse, be sure that it doesn't have gum on it, because that way it won't hold up well after a wash; soak salt fish overnight before you cook it; is it true that you sing benna° in Sunday School?; always eat your food in such a way that it won't turn someone else's stomach; on Sundays try to walk like a lady and not like the slut you are so bent on becoming; don't sing benna in Sunday School; you mustn't speak to wharf-rat boys, not even to give directions; don't eat fruits on the street—flies will follow you; *but I don't sing benna on Sundays at all and never in Sunday school;* this is how to sew on a button; this is how to make a buttonhole for the button you have just sewed on; this is how to hem a dress when you see the hem coming down and so to prevent yourself from looking like the slut I know you are so bent on becoming; this is how you iron your father's khaki shirt so that it doesn't have a crease; this is how you iron your father's khaki pants so that they don't have a crease; this is how you grow okra—far from the house, because okra tree harbors red ants; when you are growing dasheen, make sure it gets plenty of water or else it makes your throat itch when you are eating it; this is how you sweep a corner; this is how you sweep a whole house; this is how you sweep a yard; this is how you smile to someone you don't like too much; this is how you smile to someone you don't like at all; this is how you smile to someone you like completely; this is how you set a table for tea; this is how you set a table for dinner; this is how you set a table for dinner with an important guest; this is how you set a table for lunch; this is how you set a table for breakfast; this is how to behave in the presence of men who don't know you very well, and this way they won't recognize immediately the slut I have warned you against becoming; be sure to wash every day, even if it is with your own spit; don't squat down to play marbles—you are not a boy, you know; don't pick people's flowers—you might catch something; don't throw stones at blackbirds, because it might not be a blackbird at all; this is how to make a bread pudding; this is how to make doukona;° this is how to make pepper pot; this is how to make a good medicine for a cold; this is how to make a good medicine to throw away a child before it even becomes a child; this is how to catch a fish; this is how to throw back a fish you don't like, and that way something bad won't fall on you; this is how to bully a man; this is how a man bullies you; this is how to love a man, and if this doesn't work there are other ways, and if they don't work don't feel too bad about giving up; this is how to spit up in the air if you feel like it, and this is how to move quick so that it doesn't fall on you; this is how to make ends meet; always squeeze bread to make sure it's fresh; *but what if the baker won't let me feel the bread?*; you mean to say that after all you are really going to be the kind of woman who the baker won't let near the bread?

---

benna: Calypso music.
doukona: Spicy plantain pudding.

Source: Alice Munro

ALICE MUNRO (1931–), one of Canada's foremost contemporary authors, was born in Wingham, Ontario. Over the last few decades, she has published one novel, *Lives of Girls and Women* (1971), and several collections of short stories, including *Friend of My Youth* (1990); *Open Secrets* (1994); *Selected Stories* (1996); *Hateship, Friendship, Courtship, Loveship, Marriage* (2001); *Runaway* (2004); *Something I've Been Meaning to Tell You* (2004); *Carried Away* (2006); and *The View from Castle Rock* (2006). The feature film *Away from Her* (2006), which was nominated for two Academy Awards, is based on Munro's story "The Bear Came over the Mountain." She is a three-time winner of the Governor General's Award, one of the most prestigious literary awards in Canada, and many other awards. Nearly all of her fiction is set in southwestern Ontario, but her writing has captured the imagination of readers worldwide. Often focusing on the lives and loves of women, Munro's stories reflect the various rites of passage and the joys and pains inherent in coming of age. She has explained in various interviews that, while her work is not necessarily autobiographical, it does reflect an "emotional reality" that is drawn from her own life.

Prue (1982)

Prue used to live with Gordon. This was after Gordon had left his wife and before he went back to her—a year and four months in all. Some time later, he and his wife were divorced. After that came a period of indecision, of living together off and on; then the wife went away to New Zealand, most likely for good.

Prue did not go back to Vancouver Island, where Gordon had met her when she was working as a dining-room hostess in a resort hotel. She got a job in Toronto, working in a plant shop. She had many friends in Toronto by that time, most of them Gordon's friends and his wife's friends. They liked Prue and were ready to feel sorry for her, but she laughed them out of it. She is very likable. She has what eastern Canadians call an English accent, though she was born in Canada—in Duncan, on Vancouver Island. This accent helps her to say the most cynical things in a winning and lighthearted way. She presents her life in anecdotes, and though it is the point of most of her anecdotes that hopes are dashed, dreams ridiculed, things never turn out as expected, everything is altered in a bizarre way and there is no explanation ever, people always feel cheered up after listening to her; they say of her that it is a relief to meet somebody who doesn't take herself too seriously, who is so unintense, and civilized, and never makes any real demands or complaints.

The only thing she complains about readily is her name. Prue is a schoolgirl, she says, and Prudence is an old virgin; the parents who gave her that name must have been too shortsighted even to take account of puberty. What if she had grown a great bosom, she says, or developed a sultry look? Or was the name itself a guarantee that she wouldn't? in her late forties now, slight and fair, attending to customers with a dutiful vivacity, giving pleasure to dinner guests, she might not be far from what those parents had in mind: bright and thoughtful, a cheerful spectator. It is hard to grant her maturity, maternity, real troubles.

Her grownup children, the products of an early Vancouver Island marriage she calls a cosmic disaster, come to see her, and instead of wanting money, like other people's children, they bring presents, try to do her accounts, arrange to have her house insulated. She is delighted with their presents, listens to their advice, and, like a flighty daughter, neglects to answer their letters.

Her children hope she is not staying on in Toronto because of Gordon. Everybody hopes that. She would laugh at the idea. She gives parties and goes to parties: she goes out sometimes with other men. Her attitude toward sex is very comforting to those of her friends who get into terrible states of passion and jealousy, and feel cut loose from their moorings. She seems to regard sex as a wholesome, slightly silly indulgence, like dancing and nice dinners—something that shouldn't interfere with people's being kind and cheerful to each other.

Now that his wife is gone for good. Gordon comes to see Prue occasionally, and sometimes asks her out for dinner. They may not go to a restaurant; they may go to his house. Gordon is a good cook. When Prue or his wife lived with him he couldn't cook at all, but as soon as he put his mind to it he became—he says truthfully—better than either of them.

Recently he and Prue were having dinner at his house. He had made Chicken Kiev, and crème brûlée for dessert. Like most new, serious cooks, he talked about food.

Gordon is rich, by Prue's—and most people's—standards. He is a neurologist. His house is new, built on a hillside north of the city, where there used to be picturesque, unprofitable farms. Now there are one-of-a-kind, architect-designed, very expensive houses on half-acre lots. Prue, describing Gordon's house, will say. "Do you know there are four bathrooms? So that if four people want to have baths at the same time there's no problem. It seems a bit much, but it's very nice, really, and you'd never have to go through the hall."

Gordon's house has a raised dining area—a sort of platform, surrounded by a conversation pit, a music pit, and a bank of heavy greenery under sloping glass. You can't see the entrance area form the dining area, but there are no intervening walls, so that from one area you can hear something of what is going on in the other.

During dinner the doorbell range. Gordon excused himself and went down the steps. Prue heard a female voice. The person it belonged to was still outside, so she could not hear the words. She heard Gordon's voice, pitched low, cautioning. The door didn't close—it seemed the person had not been invited in—but the voices went on, muted and angry. Suddenly there was a cry from Gordon, and he appeared halfway up the steps, waving his arms.

"The crème brûlée," he said. "Could you?" He ran back down as Prue got up and went into the kitchen to save the dessert. When she returned he was climbing the stairs more slowly, looking both agitated and tired.

"A friend," he said gloomily. "Was it all right?"

Prue realized he was speaking of the crème brûlée, and she said yes, it was perfect, she had got it just in time. He thanked her but did not cheer up. It seemed it was not the dessert he was troubled over but whatever had happened at the door. To take his mind off if, Prue started asking him professional questions about the plants.

"I don't know a thing about them," he said. "You know that."

"I thought you might have picked it up. Like the cooking."

"She takes care of them."

"Mrs. Carr?" said Prue, naming his housekeeper.

"Who did you think?"

Prue blushed. She hated to be thought suspicious.

"The problem is that I think I would like to marry you," said Gordon, with no noticeable lightening of his spirits. Gordon is a large man, with heavy features. He likes to wear thick clothing, bulky sweaters. His blue eyes are often bloodshot, and their expression indicates that there is a helpless, baffled soul squirming around inside this doughty fortress.

"What a problem," said Prue lightly, though she knew Gordon well enough to know that it was.

The doorbell rang again, rang twice, three times, before Gordon could get to it. This time there was a crash, as of something flung and landing hard. The door slammed and Gordon was immediately back in view. He staggered on the steps and held his hand to his head, meanwhile making a gesture with the other hand to signify that nothing serious had happened, Prue was to sit down.

"Bloody overnight bag," he said. "She threw it at me."

"Did it hit you?"

"Glancing."

"It made a hard sound for an overnight bag. Were there rocks in it?"

"Probably cans. Her deodorant and so forth."

"Oh."

Prue watched him pour himself a drink. "I'd like some coffee, if I might," she said. She went to the kitchen to put the water on, and Gordon followed her.

"I think I'm in love with this person," he said.

"Who is she?"

"You don't know her. She's quite young."

"Oh."

"But I do think I want to marry you, in a few years' time."

"After you get over being in love?"

"Yes."

"Well. I guess nobody knows what can happen in a few years' time."

When Prue tells about this, she says, "I think he was afraid I was going to laugh. He doesn't know why people laugh or throw their overnight bags at him, but he's noticed they do. He's such a proper person, really. The lovely dinner. Then she comes and throws her overnight bag. And it's quite reasonable to think of marrying me in a few years' time, when he gets over being in love. I think he first thought of telling me to sort of put my mind at rest."

She doesn't mention that the next morning she picked up one of Gordon's cufflinks from his dresser. The cufflinks are made of amber and he bought them in Russia, on the holiday he and wife took when they got back together again. They look like squares of candy, golden, translucent, and this one warms quickly in her hand. She drops it into the pocket of her jacket. Taking one is not a real theft. It could be a reminder, an intimate prank, a piece of nonsense.

She is alone in Gordon's house; he has gone off early, as he always does. The housekeeper does not come till nine. Prue doesn't have to be at the shop until ten; she could make herself breakfast, stay and have coffee with the housekeeper, who is her friend from olden times. But once she has the cufflink in her pocket she doesn't linger. The house seems too bleak a place to spend an extra moment in. It was Prue, actually, who helped choose the building lot. But she's not responsible for approving the plans—the wife was back by that time.

When she gets home she puts the cufflink in an old tobacco tin. The children bought this tobacco tin in a junk shop years ago, and gave it to her for a present. She used to smoke, in those days, and the children were worried about her, so they gave her this tin full of toffees, jelly beans, and gumdrops, with a note saying, "Please get fat instead." That was for her birthday. Now the tin has in it several things besides the cufflink—all small things, not of great value but not worthless, either. A little enameled dish, a sterling-silver spoon for salt, a crystal fish. These are not sentimental keepsakes. She never looks at them, and often forgets what she has there. They are not booty, they don't have ritualistic significance. She does not take something every time she goes to Gordon's house, or every time she stays over, or to mark what she might call memorable visits. She doesn't do it in a daze and she doesn't seem to be under a compulsion. She just takes something, every now and then, and puts it away in the dark of the old tobacco tin, and more or less forgets about it.

Source: ©Marc Brasz/Corbis

ZZ PACKER (1973–) was born in Chicago and raised in Atlanta and Louisville, Kentucky. Her stories have appeared in the *New Yorker, Harper's,* and *Zoetrope.* She has also published a collection of stories entitled *Drinking Coffee Elsewhere* (2003), a *New York Times* Notable Book and a PEN/Faulkner Award finalist. Packer's work, which focuses largely on the lives of young African-American girls, also explores universal themes of acceptance, belonging, and loss. "I like to discover things that I'm writing," Packer explains, "and I like to explore what I've seen in the world, through writing. And it doesn't have to be autobiographical or verbatim, but the sort of essential truth that I see in the world." Packer is currently at work on her first novel, *The Thousands,* from which the following story is excerpted.

Buffalo Soldiers° (2007)

It had seemed that just riding at a walk was difficult enough, but heading into the mountains meant slight drifts of fear at every incline, every pass. It was enough to make Lazarus realize that whatever little hillocks they'd encountered on their march from San Antonio to their headquarters at Fort Stockton were nothing. They tried to file two by two, but there were some places the scouts had led them where the men had to go through one at a time, and it was then that Lazarus feared that the horse in front of him would lose its footing and fall, smacking him with the might of an avalanche of horseflesh, or that Grey Bat, his own horse—who was a little too fond of leaping up or rushing down a slope—would miscalculate, and that would be the end of them both.

Buffalo soldiers: African-American cavalry regiments of the United States Army stationed in the west from 1867–1896.

No one spoke. All that could be heard were the horses negotiating the passes with grunts and whinnies and the razor sharp zips of passing mosquitoes and horseflies, locusts bouncing at crazy angles as the horses crushed their hiding places. Lazarus had never heard the men so quiet, and still the scout Liege seemed quieter than the rest, separate from the other scouts, looking around occasionally as if he were the colonel himself, surveying his men.

They stood at the next pass, waiting—for what, Lazarus did not know. All he could think upon seeing the land was that it was somehow ugly and strangely beautiful at the same time. Then without so much as a word from Lieutenant Heyl, they were ascending again, and with each ascent, a shoulder of rock on his near side or far side would bring blessed shade and calm, so different from anything he'd seen in Mississippi or Louisiana that he sometimes forgot that it was home he wanted to be going towards. He could not make out the expressions on the faces of the scouts up ahead, but they were pacing back and forth on their horses, as if in confusion, and when he went to look at Liege, Liege looked worried.

"I think they want you to get on up there, Mr. Indian," Redbone said, but Liege didn't pay Redbone and mind. He just started sniffing and rolling his eyes up to the ceiling of the sky, figuring.

Then came the sound of shots, and the horses started, and the men up front with Lieutenant Heyl fought to keep them under control. Along with shots came Indian whoops and cries, sounding like they were calling for the end of the world to commence.

"This is it, Niggers," Heyl called out, "This is it."

The men in front bounded forward, while Lazarus and the rest of the advance party manoeuvred behind. He could hear the front men returning fire but a blizzard of dust from the pounding of horse hooves made it impossible to see.

"Spread out you fucking niggers!" Heyl yelled, as if unaware that the men had already surged forward. Lazarus was deep in the middle of the men, and saw men in the very front line falling to an invisible enemy—all he saw were clouds of dust, and when the dust cleared just the sheer facing of rocks. He had to push his way against other men coming forward, the horses jostling each other, their flanks briefly caroming off one another while Lazarus sought partial protection by lying flush against Grey Bat's bristly mane.

The bullets came in little pings. One man was down already, his horse hit, whinnying and rearing before it fell on to the ground in a crash of meat, pinning his rider while everyone still upright sidestepped fallen horse and rider as if they were prickly cactus.

Heyl yelled out another command, and once again, the men shuffled into a loose formation—not nearly as tight as before. He didn't know if the formation had loosened because all was just complete chaos and men simply couldn't hear, but he knew there would be hell to pay from Heyl later. Lazarus wanted to shoehorn everyone into place just so he wouldn't have to hear Heyl yelling everyday for the next week, and he even tried lining up behind the horse in front of him, but Liege reined his horse sideways so that his flanks pushed at Grey Bat's. "Don't fall into no formation!" Liege yelled at him, then yelled it again, his toad's voice shouting.

"We got to follow orders!" Lazarus shouted to him over the din. Insubordination. The word he'd heard Hatch hissing over and over again to his officers, and the officers to any of the soldiers who dated complain.

"Don't fall into no goddamned formation," Liege said again, and though he didn't yell it, it had more force somehow, and all the men around him seemed to understand. His horse kept skittering sideways into Grey Bat, trying poor Grey Bat's patience. "I been fighting with Indians my whole life. Ain't no way to fight 'em by standing in line, clear and plain for them to see, waiting for them to kill us off. That ain't no Indian way of fighting."

Lazarus didn't know what Liege had in mind, but Liege kept his arm braced just inches in front of Lazarus, as if in ready to knock the carbine° out of his hand if need be. It was as if Liege knew that it would take these few but vital moments before Lazarus understood what was happening. Lazarus now saw the limited use of the formation point, advance party, support and reserve, if only because the Kickapoos° were not coming from some designated place the Ninth could see, but from all around, and there was no way of knowing how many were in front or back of them, due of their stealth. Instead of one army meeting another, Lazarus now saw their situation was more like a spider lured into an anthill, and he had no way of knowing how Liege proposed to get them out, if retreat had already been struck as an option.

Heyl was busy yelling again, but this time, only a few scampered into formation while the rest were all scattered and shooting, advancing towards the rocks whichever way they could get there while the Indians kept up fire, and in the few beats it took Lazarus to understand what was happening—that Leige was taking over and giving the commands instead of Heyl—Lazarus and the wave of men who'd listened to Liege were swept up into the advance from behind. Suddenly, all was clear to see, and Heyl came crashing down in the volley of fire coming from the rocks.

"Man down!" came the call, and though all was chaos at first, with Heyl screaming for his life in one moment, and then in another—Lazarus charging forwards towards the rocks, and for the first time, sighting Indians. Not the roadside stumps he'd seen coming through San Antonio, drowsily biding their time with corn husks while their lethargic children wove baskets—and putted their leather balls about, but blurs of brown, a flash of some sort of animal pelt covering their loins, and streaming hair, straight as a horse's mane.

He had finally managed to unleash his carbine and cock it, but hadn't the chance to use it for fear of shooting one of his own in the back while they had still been prisoners to the dust cloud.

For a time, he hid his face behind Grey Bat's mane. Then, as the wave of men cleared and without the least bit of pressure on the reigns, Grey Bat took off with even greater speed straight towards the whoops and ululations of Indians. He could not believe it; he was heading into fire, headed straight towards the bullets, and so he aimed his carbine where the dust cloud had cleared before him—a straight shot with none of his own impeding the way—but when he went to shoot, there was nothing, nothing at all.

No bullet, no recoil, no shot.

---

carbine: A short-barreled lightweight rifle.

Kickapoos: Native American tribe living in Kansas, Oklahoma, Texas, and northern Mexico.

They'd never used bullets for target practice, as the Army rationed out its ammunition with the coloured regiments. They'd all gotten their share of ammunition before heading out, and Lazarus had dutifully loaded his carbine as demonstrated, and yet, it did not fire.

20 He pumped his carbine furiously, and found to his surprise that this was the first time since the skirmish began that he began to fear for his life. "Lord Jesus," he said, or thought he said, and looked round for Liege, but could not find him. The fear that pulsed through his body kept him moving and dodging, but he had no gun that worked, and he could not turn Grey Bat around lest he be stampeded, and even if no one blocked his path, he knew he could never retreat, or he'd get branded as yellow, and furthermore a traitor, and would have proven all the East Texas papers right: the Negro was not ready for battle.

Source: ©AP Photo/Daniel Ochoa de Olza

ANNIE PROULX (1935–) lives in Wyoming, where most of her short stories are set. Many of Proulx's works reveal the ways in which geography and landscape influence a character's language, thoughts, and development. Her story collections include *Heart Songs and Other Stories* (1988), *Close Range: Wyoming Stories* (1999), and *Bad Dirt: Wyoming Stories 2* (2004). Proulx has also published four novels, including the PEN/Faulkner Award winner *Postcards* (1992) and the Pulitzer Prize and National Book Award winner *The Shipping News* (1993). The critically acclaimed feature films *The Shipping News* (2001) and *Brokeback Mountain* (2005) are based on her novel and story of the same names.

55 Miles to the Gas Pump (1999)

Rancher Croom in handmade boots and filthy hat, that walleyed cattleman, stray hairs like curling fiddle string ends, that warm-handed, quick-foot dancer on splintery boards or down the cellar stairs to a rack of bottles of his own strange beer, yeasty, cloudy, bursting out in garlands of foam, Rancher Croom at night galloping drunk over the dark plain, turning off at a place he knows to arrive at a canyon brink where he dismounts and looks down on tumbled rock, waits, then steps out, parting the air with his last roar, sleeves surging up windmill arms, jeans riding over boot tops, but before he hits he rises again to the top of the cliff like a cork in a bucket of milk.

Mrs. Croom on the roof with a saw cutting a hole into the attic where she has not been for twelve years thanks to old Croom's padlocks and warnings, whets to her desire, and the sweat flies as she exchanges the saw for a chisel and hammer until a ragged slab of peak is free and she can see inside: just as she thought: the corpses of Mr. Croom's paramours°— she recognizes them from their photographs in the paper: MISSING WOMAN— some desiccated as jerky and much the same color, some moldy from lying beneath roof leaks, and all of them used hard, covered with tarry handprints, the marks of boot heels, some bright blue with the remnants of paint used on the shutters years ago, one wrapped in newspaper nipple to knee.

When you live a long way out you make your own fun.

---

paramours: Secret lovers.

John Updike (1932–)

(See this writer's biography and photo on p. 259)

Oliver's Evolution (2000)

His parents had not meant to abuse him; they had meant to love him, and did love him. But Oliver had come late in their little pack of offspring, at a time when the challenge of childrearing was wearing thin, and he proved susceptible to mishaps. A big fetus, cramped in his mother's womb, he was born with inturned feet, and learned to crawl with corrective casts up to his ankles. When they were at last removed, he cried in terror, because he thought those heavy plaster boots scraping and bumping along the floor had been part of himself.

One day in his infancy they found him on their dressing-room floor with a box of mothballs, some of which were wet with saliva; in retrospect they wondered if there had really been a need to rush him to the hospital and have his poor little stomach pumped. His face was gray-green afterwards. The following summer, when he had learned to walk, his parents had unthinkingly swum away off the beach together, striving for romantic harmony the morning after a late party and an alcoholic quarrel, and were quite unaware, until they saw the lifeguard racing along the beach, that Oliver had toddled after them and had been floating on his face for what might have been, given a less alert lifeguard, a fatal couple of minutes. This time, his face was blue, and he coughed for hours.

He was the least complaining of their children. He did not blame his parents when neither they nor the school authorities detected his "sleepy" right eye in time for therapy, with the result that when he closed that eye everything looked intractably fuzzy. Just the sight of the boy holding a schoolbook at a curious angle to the light made his father want to weep, impotently.

And it happened that he was just the wrong, vulnerable age when his parents went through their separation and divorce. His older brothers were off in boarding school and college, embarked on manhood, free of family. His younger sister was small enough to find the new arrangements—the meals in restaurants with her father, the friendly men who appeared to take her mother out—exciting. But Oliver, at thirteen, felt the weight of the household descend on him; he made his mother's sense of abandonment his own. Again, his father impotently grieved. It was he, and not the boy, who was at fault, really, when the bad grades began to come in from day school, and then from college, and Oliver broke his arm falling down the frat stairs, or leaping, by another account of the confused incident, from a girl's dormitory window. Not one but several family automobiles met a ruinous end with him at the wheel, though with no more injury, as it happened, than contused knees and loosened front teeth. The teeth grew firm again, thank God, for his innocent smile, slowly spreading across his face as the full humor of his newest misadventure dawned, was one of his best features. His teeth were small and round and widely spaced—baby teeth.

Then he married, which seemed yet another mishap, to go with the late 5
nights, abandoned jobs, and fallen-through opportunities of his life as a young adult. The girl, Alicia, was as accident-prone as he, given to substance abuse and unwanted pregnancies. Her emotional disturbances left herself and others

bruised. By comparison, Oliver was solid and surefooted, and she looked up to him. This was the key. What we expect of others, they endeavor to provide. He held on to a job, and she held on to her pregnancies. You should see him now, with their two children, a fair little girl and a dark-haired boy. Oliver has grown broad, and holds the two of them at once. They are birds in a nest. He is a tree, a sheltering boulder. He is a protector of the weak.

Source: ©Keith Bedford/Getty Images

DAVID FOSTER WALLACE (1962–2008) was the author of the short-story collections *Girl with Curious Hair* (1989), *Brief Interviews with Hideous Men* (1999), and *Oblivion* (2004). His novels include *The Broom of the System* (1987) and *Infinite Jest* (1996). In addition to writing award-winning fiction, Wallace was an acclaimed author of nonfiction on a variety of subjects, combining an almost journalistic style with an acute attention to detail.

Incarnations of Burned Children (2004)

The Daddy was around the side of the house hanging a door for the tenant when he heard the child's screams and the Mommy's voice gone high between them. He could move fast, and the back porch gave onto the kitchen, and before the screen door had banged shut behind him the Daddy had taken the scene in whole, the overturned pot on the floortile before the stove and the burner's blue jet and the floor's pool of water still steaming as its many arms extended, the toddler in his baggy diaper standing rigid with steam coming off his hair and his chest and shoulders scarlet and his eyes rolled up and mouth open very wide and seeming somehow separate from the sounds that issued, the Mommy down on one knee with the dishrag dabbing pointlessly at him and matching the screams with cries of her own, hysterical so she was almost frozen. Her one knee and the bare little soft feet were still in the steaming pool and the Daddy's first act was to take the child under the arms and lift him away from it and take him to the sink, where he threw out plates and struck the tap to let cold well water run over the boy's feet while with his cupped hand he gathered and poured or flung cold water over his head and shoulders and chest, wanting first to see the steam stop coming off him, the Mommy over his shoulder invoking God until he sent her for towels and gauze if they had it, the Daddy moving quickly and well and his man's mind empty of everything but purpose, not yet aware of how smoothly he moved or that he'd ceased to hear the high screams because to hear them would freeze him and make impossible what had to be done help his child, whose screams were regular as breath and went on so long they'd become already a thing in the kitchen, something else to move quickly around. The tenant side's door outside hung half off its top hinge and moved slightly in the wind, and a bird in the oak across the driveway appeared to observe the door with a cocked head as the cries still came from inside. The worst scalds seemed to be the right arm and shoulder, the chest and stomach's red was fading to pink under the cold water and his feet's soft soles weren't blistered that the Daddy could see, but the toddler still made little fists and screamed except now merely on reflex from fear, the Daddy would know he thought possible later, small face distended and thready veins standing out at the temples and the Daddy kept saying he was here he was here, adrenaline ebbing and an anger at the Mommy for allowing this thing to happen just starting to gather in wisps at his mind's extreme rear still hours from expression. When the Mommy returned he wasn't sure whether to wrap the child in a towel or not but he wet the towel down and did, swaddled him tight and lifted his baby out of the sink and set him on the kitchen table's edge to soothe him while the Mommy tried to check the feet's soles with one hand waving around in the area of her mouth and uttering objectless words while the Daddy bent in and was face to face with the child on the table's checked edge repeating the fact that he was here and trying to calm the toddler's cries but still the child breathlessly screamed, a high pure shining sound that could stop his heart and his bitty lips and gums now tinged with the light blue of a low flame the Daddy thought, screaming as if almost still under the tilted pot in pain. A minute, two like this that seemed much longer, with the Mommy at the Daddy's side talking sing-song at the child's face and the lark on the limb with its head to the side and the hinge going white in a line from the weight of the canted door until the first wisp of steam came lazy from under the wrapped towel's hem and the parents' eyes met and widened—the diaper, which when they opened the towel and leaned their little boy back on the checkered cloth and unfastened the softened tabs and tried to remove it resisted slightly with new high cries and was hot, their baby's diaper burned their hand and they saw where the real water'd fallen and pooled and been burning their baby all this time while he screamed for them to help him and they hadn't, hadn't thought and when they got it off and saw the state of what was there the Mommy said their God's first name and grabbed the table to keep her feet while the father turned away and threw a haymaker° at the air of the kitchen and cursed both himself and the world for not the last time while his child might now have been sleeping if not for the rate of his breathing and the tiny stricken motions of his hands in the air above where he lay, hands the size of a grown man's thumb that had clutched the Daddy's thumb in the crib while he'd watched the Daddy's mouth move in song, his head cocked and seeming to see way past him into something his eyes made the Daddy lonesome for in a sideways way. If you've never wept and want to, have a child. Break your heart inside and something will a child is the twangy song the Daddy hears again as if the radio's lady was almost there with him looking down at what they've done, though hours later what the Daddy won't most forgive is how badly he wanted a cigarette right then as they diapered the child as best they could in gauze and two crossed handtowels and the Daddy lifted him like a newborn with his skull in one palm and ran him out to the hot truck and burned custom rubber all the way to town and the clinic's ER with the tenant's door hanging open like that all day until the hinge gave but by then it was too late, when it wouldn't stop and they couldn't make it the child had learned to leave himself and watch the whole rest unfold from a point overhead, and whatever was lost never thenceforth mattered, and the child's body expanded and walked about and drew pay and lived its life untenanted, a thing among things, its self's soul so much vapor aloft, falling as rain and then rising, the sun up and down like a yoyo.

---

haymaker: A forceful punch.

Reading and Reacting

1. Which of the stories in this chapter do you see as most conventional? Which seems *least* conventional? Why?
2. Does every story seem complete? What, if anything, seems to be missing from each story that might be present in a longer story?
3. If you were going to add material to "Snow," what would you add? Why?
4. How would "Accident" be different if the writer had used *I* instead of *you* to express the narrator's point of view?
5. In "Incarnations of Burned Children," the writer calls his characters "the Daddy," "the Mommy," and "the child" instead of naming them. Why do you think he does this?
6. Some stories in this chapter—such as "Prue" and "Buffalo Soldiers"—include dialogue; others include none (or very little). How would these stories—for example, "Girl" or "Oliver's Evolution"—be different if dialogue (or more dialogue) were added? What kind of dialogue would be useful?
7. **CRITICAL PERSPECTIVE** Writing for *Studies in Short Fiction*, William C. Hamlin describes the essential characteristics of the short-short.

> Perhaps in no kind of fiction other than the short-short can Poe's "rules" for the "tale" be so fully adapted and realized. He wrote about organic unity and singleness of effect and the totality of that effect. In the short-short there is simply no room for sub-plotting, for Jamesian penetration, for slowly developing tensions, for any kind of byplay. The writer is trying to go from A to B in the shortest time consistent with purpose and reason. If he or she is successful, then the reader is richer by a minor masterpiece.

Do you think all the stories in this sampler meet Hamlin's criteria for success? Why or why not?

WRITING SUGGESTIONS: The Short-Short

1. Write a **response paper** (see Chapter 3) expressing your reactions to the ending of "Buffalo Soldiers" or "55 Miles to the Gas Pump."
2. Write an **explication** (see Chapter 3) of "Incarnations of Burned Children" or of a short-short story located elsewhere in this book—for example, Kate Chopin's "Story of an Hour" (p. 226) or Larry Fondation's "Deportation at Breakfast" (p. 229).
3. Write a **comparison-contrast** (see Chapter 3) comparing "Love and Other Catastrophes: A Mix Tape" with one of the love poems in Chapter 31.
4. Write a **comparison-contrast** comparing "Jinx" to Joyce Carol Oates's "Where Are You Going, Where Have You Been?" (p. 617)—or to another story about adolescence. (Or, compare the two girls in "Jinx.")
5. Write a **character analysis** (see Chapter 3) of Prue ("Prue") or Oliver ("Oliver's Evolution").
6. Write an essay about the **cultural context** (see Chapter 3) of "Buffalo Soldiers."
7. Write a "mix tape" story about an experience in your own life.

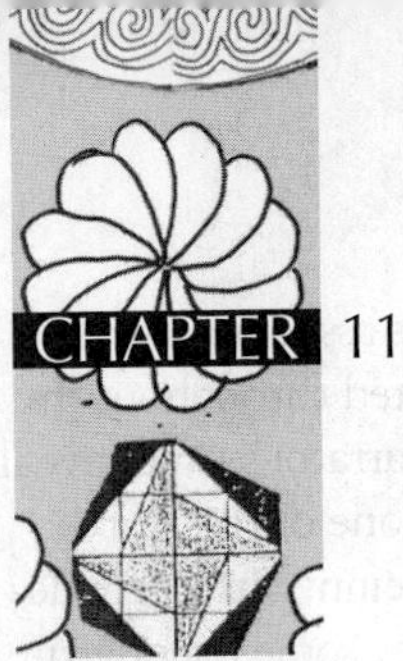

CHAPTER 11

READING AND WRITING ABOUT FICTION

Reading Fiction

As you read works of short fiction, you should pay careful attention to elements such as plot; character; setting; point of view; style, tone, and language; symbol, allegory, and myth; and theme. By looking at these elements you will be able to understand and appreciate the story more fully. The following guidelines, designed to help you explore works of fiction, focus on issues that are examined in depth in chapters to come:

- *Look at the **plot** of the story.* How do the events in the story relate to one another, and how do they relate to the story as a whole? What conflicts occur in the story, and how are these conflicts developed or resolved? Does the story include any noteworthy plot devices, such as flashbacks or foreshadowing? (See Chapter 12.)
- *Analyze the **characters** in the story.* What are their most striking traits? How do these individuals interact with one another? What motivates them? Are the characters fully developed, or are they stereotypes whose sole purpose is to express a single trait (innocence, evil, generosity, and so on) or to move the plot along? (See Chapter 13.)
- *Identify the **setting** of the story.* During what time period, and in what geographic location, does the action of the story occur? How does the setting affect the characters' lives? How does it affect their relationships? Does the setting create a mood for the story? How does the setting reinforce the central ideas that the story examines? (See Chapter 14.)
- *Examine the narrative **point of view** of the story.* Who is telling the story? Is the story told by an outside narrator? Is the story told from the perspective of a character? If so, is the narrator a major character telling his or her own story or a minor character who witnesses events? How much does this narrator know about the events in the story? Does the narrator present an accurate picture of events? Does the narrator understand the full significance of the story he or she is telling? (See Chapter 15.)
- *Analyze the **style, tone,** and **language** of the story.* Does the writer make any unusual use of diction or syntax? Does the writer use imaginative figures

of speech? Patterns of imagery? What level of diction is associated with particular characters? What words or phrases are repeated throughout the work? Is the story's style plain or elaborate? Does the narrator's tone reveal his or her attitude toward characters or events? Is the tone of the story playful, humorous, ironic, satirical, serious, somber, solemn, bitter, condescending, formal, or informal—or does the tone convey some other attitude? (See Chapter 16.)

- *Focus on* ***symbol, allegory, and myth.*** Does the author use any objects or ideas symbolically? Are characters or objects in the story part of an allegorical framework? How does an object establish its symbolic or allegorical significance in the story? Are the symbols or allegorical figures conventional or unusual? At what points in the story do symbols or allegorical figures appear? Does the story allude to a myth? (See Chapter 17.)
- *Identify the* ***themes*** *of the story.* What is the central theme? How is this idea or concept expressed in the work? What elements of the story develop the central theme? How do character, plot, setting, point of view, and symbols reinforce the central theme? How does the title of the story contribute to readers' understanding of the central theme? What other themes are explored? (See Chapter 18.)

Active Reading

John Frei, a student in an Introduction to Literature course, was assigned to write a three- to four-page essay on a topic of his choice, focusing on any short story in this literature anthology, without consulting outside sources. After considering a number of possible choices, John selected Alberto Alvaro Ríos's "The Secret Lion."

Source: Courtesy of Alberto Avaro Rios

ALBERTO ALVARO RÍOS (1952–) was born and raised in the border town of Nogales, Arizona, the son of a Mexican father and an English mother. He is the author of twelve books and chapbooks of poetry, including *The Theater of Night* (2005), *The Smallest Muscle in the Human Body* (2002), *Teodoro Luna's Two Kisses* (1990), and *Whispering to Fool the Wind* (1982), which won the American Academy of Poets Walt Whitman Award. His collections of short stories include *The Curtain of Trees* (1999), *Pig Cookies and Other Stories* (1995), and *The Iguana Killer: Twelve Stories of the Heart* (1984), in which "The Secret Lion" appeared. *Capirotada,* which was published in 1999, is a memoir about growing up on the Mexican border. Ríos is presently Regents' Professor of English at Arizona State University.

Reviewer Mary Logue, writing in the *Village Voice Literary Supplement,* observes that Ríos's writings "carry the feel of another world. . . . Ríos's tongue is both foreign and familiar," reflecting an upbringing "where one is neither in this country nor the other." In many of his stories, Ríos expresses the seeming "other-ness" of Anglo culture as seen through the eyes of Chicano children: a little boy frightened by the sight of his first snowfall or (as in "The Secret Lion") boys amazed by the otherworldly sight of "heaven." Through Ríos's children, we see our own world with new eyes.

Cultural Context With their rolling hills, freshwater ponds, lush greens, and fastidiously trimmed turf, golf courses are designed to convey a sense of wealth and comfort, typically providing recreation for the middle and upper classes. In a dry region—or even in a densely populated city—an irrigated, sculpted golf course may look like an oasis in the desert. The golf course that plays a role in this story is probably (like many others) part of a privately owned, exclusive country club.

The Secret Lion (1984)

I was twelve and in junior high school and something happened that we didn't have a name for, but it was there nonetheless like a lion, and roaring, roaring that way the biggest things do. Everything changed. Just that. Like the rug, the one that gets pulled—or better, like the tablecloth those magicians pull where the stuff on the table stays the same but the gasp! from the audience makes the staying-the-same part not matter. Like that.

What happened was there were teachers now, not just one teacher, teach-erz, and we felt personally abandoned somehow. When a person had all these teachers now, he didn't get taken care of the same way, even though six was more than one. Arithmetic went out the door when we walked in. And we saw girls now, but they weren't the same girls we used to know because we couldn't talk to them anymore, not the same way we used to, certainly not to Sandy, even though she was my neighbor, too. Not even to her. She just played the piano all the time. And there were words, oh there were words in junior high school, and we wanted to know what they were, and how a person did them—that's what school was supposed to be for. Only, in junior high school, school wasn't school, everything was backward-like. If you went up to a teacher and said the word to try and find out what it meant you got in trouble for saying it. So we didn't. And we figured it must have been that way about other stuff, too, so we never said anything about anything—we weren't stupid.

But my friend Sergio and I, we solved junior high school. We would come home from school on the bus, put our books away, change shoes, and go across the highway to the arroyo. It was the one place we were not supposed to go. So we did. This was, after all, what junior high had at least shown us. It was our river, though, our personal Mississippi, our friend from long back, and it was full of stories and all the branch forts we had built in it when we were still the Vikings of America, with our own symbol, which we had carved everywhere, even in the sand, which let the water take it. That was good, we had decided; whoever was at the end of this river would know about us.

At the very very top of our growing lungs, what we would do down there was shout every dirty word we could think of, in every combination we could come up with, and we would yell about girls, and all the things we wanted to do with them, as loud as we could—we didn't know what we wanted to do with them, just things—and we would yell about teachers, and how we loved some of them, like Miss Crevelone, and how we wanted to dissect some of them, making signs of the cross, like priests, and we would yell this stuff over and over because it felt good, we couldn't explain why, it just felt good and for the first time in our lives there was nobody to tell us we couldn't. So we did.

5 One Thursday we were walking along shouting this way, and the railroad, the Southern Pacific, which ran above and along the far side of the arroyo, had dropped a grinding ball down there, which was, we found out later, a cannonball thing used in mining. A bunch of them were put in a big vat which turned around and crushed the ore. One had been dropped, or thrown—what do caboose men do when they get bored—but it got down there regardless and as we were walking along yelling about one girl or another, a particular Claudia, we found it, one of these things, looked at it, picked it up, and got very very excited, and held it and passed it back and forth, and we were saying "Guythisis, this is, geeGuythis . . .": we had this perception about nature then, that nature is imperfect and that round things are perfect: we said "Guy-Godthis is perfect, thisisthis is perfect, it's round, round and heavy, it'sit's the best thing we'veeverseen. Whatisit?" We didn't know. We just knew it was great. We just, whatever, we played with it, held it some more.

And then we had to decide what to do with it. We knew, because of a lot of things, that if we were going to take this and show it to anybody, this discovery, this best thing, was going to be taken away from us. That's the way it works with little kids, like all the polished quartz, the tons of it we had collected piece by piece over the years. Junior high kids too. If we took it home, my mother, we knew, was going to look at it and say "throw that dirty thing in the, get rid of it." Simple like, like that. "But ma it's the best thing I" "Getridofit." Simple.

So we didn't. Take it home. Instead, we came up with the answer. We dug a hole and buried it. And we marked it secretly. Lots of secret signs. And came back the next week to dig it up and, we didn't know, pass it around some more or something, but we didn't find it. We dug up that whole bank, and we never found it again. We tried.

Sergio and I talked about that ball or whatever it was when we couldn't find it. All we used were small words, neat, good. Kid words. What we were really saying, but didn't know the words, was how much that ball was like that place, that whole arroyo: couldn't tell anybody about it, didn't understand what it was, didn't have a name for it. It just felt good. It was just perfect in the way it was that place, that whole going to that place, that whole junior high school lion. It was just iron-heavy, it had no name, it felt good or not, we couldn't take it home to show our mothers, and once we buried it, it was gone forever.

The ball was gone, like the first reasons we had come to that arroyo years earlier, like the first time we had seen the arroyo, it was gone like everything else that had been taken away. This was not our first lesson. We stopped going to the arroyo after not finding the thing, the same way we had stopped going there years earlier and headed for the mountains. Nature seemed to keep pushing us around one way or another, teaching us the same thing every place we ended up. Nature's gang was tough that way, teaching us stuff.

10 When we were young we moved away from town, me and my family. Sergio's was already out there. Out in the wilds. Or at least the new place seemed like the wilds since everything looks bigger the smaller a man is. I was five, I guess, and we had moved three miles north of Nogales where we had lived, three miles north of the Mexican border. We looked across the highway in one direction and there was the arroyo; hills stood up in the other direction. Mountains, for a small man.

When the first summer came the very first place we went to was of course the one place we weren't supposed to go, the arroyo. We went down in there and found water running, summer rain water mostly, and we went swimming. But every third or fourth or fifth day, the sewage treatment plant that was, we found out, upstream, would release whatever it was that it released, and we would never know exactly what day that was, and a person really couldn't tell right off by looking at the water, not every time, not so a person could get out in time. So, we went swimming that summer and some days we had a lot of fun. Some days we didn't. We found a thousand ways to explain what happened on those other days, constructing elaborate stories about the neighborhood dogs, and hadn't she, my mother, miscalculated her step before, too? But she knew something was up because we'd come running into the house those days, wanting to take a shower, even—if this can be imagined—in the middle of the day.

That was the first time we stopped going to the arroyo. It taught us to look the other way. We decided, as the second side of summer came, we wanted to go into the mountains. They were still mountains then. We went running in one summer Thursday morning, my friend Sergio and I, into my mother's kitchen, and said, well, what'zin, what'zin those hills over there—we used her word so she'd understand us—and she said nothingdon'tworryaboutit. So we went out, and we weren't dumb, we thought with our eyes to each other, ohhoshe'stryingtokeepsomethingfromus. We knew adults.

We had read the books, after all; we knew about bridges and castles and wildtreacherousraging alligatormouth rivers. We wanted them. So we were going to go out and get them. We went back that morning into that kitchen and we said, "We're going out there, we're going into the hills, we're going away for three days, don't worry." She said, "All right."

"You know," I said to Sergio, "if we're going to go away for three days, well, we ought to at least pack a lunch."

But we were two young boys with no patience for what we thought at the 15
time was mom-stuff: making sa-and-wiches. My mother didn't offer. So we got out little kid knapsacks that my mother had sewn for us, and into them we put the jar of mustard. A loaf of bread. Knivesforksplates, bottles of Coke, a can opener. This was lunch for the two of us. And we were weighed down, humped over to be strong enough to carry this stuff. But we started walking anyway, into the hills. We were going to eat berries and stuff otherwise. "Goodbye." My mom said that.

After the first hill we were dead. But we walked. My mother could still see us. And we kept walking. We walked until we got to where the sun is straight overhead, noon. That place. Where that is doesn't matter; it's time to eat. The truth is we weren't anywhere close to that place. We just agreed that the sun was overhead and that it was time to eat, and by tilting our heads a little we could make that the truth.

"We really ought to start looking for a place to eat."

"Yeah. Let's look for a good place to eat." We went back and forth saying that for fifteen minutes, making it lunchtime because that's what we always said back and forth before lunchtimes at home. "Yeah, I'm hungry all right." I nodded my head. "Yeah, I'm hungry all right too. I'm hungry." He nodded his head. I nodded my head back. After a good deal more nodding, we were ready, just as we came over a little hill. We hadn't found the mountains yet. This was a little hill.

And on the other side of this hill we found heaven.

20 It was just what we thought it would be.

Perfect. Heaven was green, like nothing else in Arizona. And it wasn't a cemetery or like that because we had seen cemeteries and they had gravestones and stuff and this didn't. This was perfect, had trees, lots of trees, had birds, like we had never seen before. It was like "The Wizard of Oz," like when they got to Oz and everything was so green, so emerald, they had to wear those glasses, and we ran just like them, laughing, laughing that way we did that moment, and we went running down to this clearing in it all, hitting each other that good way we did.

We got down there, we kept laughing, we kept hitting each other, we unpacked our stuff, and we started acting "rich." We knew all about how to do that, like blowing on our nails, then rubbing them on our chests for the shine. We made our sandwiches, opened our Cokes, got out the rest of the stuff, the salt and pepper shakers. I found this particular hole and I put my Coke right into it, a perfect fit, and I called it my Coke-holder. I got down next to it on my back, because everyone knows that rich people eat lying down, and I got my sandwich in one hand and put my other arm around the Coke in its holder. When I wanted a drink, I lifted my neck a little, put out my lips, and tipped my Coke a little with the crook of my elbow. Ah.

We were there, lying down, eating our sandwiches, laughing, throwing bread at each other and out for the birds. This was heaven. We were laughing and we couldn't believe it. My mother was keeping something from us, ah ha, but we had found her out. We even found water over at the side of the clearing to wash our plates with—we had brought plates. Sergio started washing his plates when he was done, and I was being rich with my Coke, and this day in summer was right.

When suddenly these two men came, from around a corner of trees and the tallest grass we had ever seen. They had bags on their backs, leather bags, bags and sticks.

25 We didn't know what clubs were, but I learned later, like I learned about the grinding balls. The two men yelled at us. Most specifically, one wanted me to take my Coke out of my Coke-holder so he could sink his golf ball into it.

Something got taken away from us that moment. Heaven. We grew up a little bit, and couldn't go backward. We learned. No one had ever told us about golf. They had told us about heaven. And it went away. We got golf in exchange.

We went back to the arroyo for the rest of that summer, and tried to have fun the best we could. We learned to be ready for finding the grinding ball. We loved it, and when we buried it we knew what would happen. The truth is, we didn't look so hard for it. We were two boys and twelve summers then, and not stupid. Things get taken away.

We buried it because it was perfect. We didn't tell my mother, but together it was all we talked about, till we forgot. It was the lion.

* * *

Previewing

Student John Frei began the reading process by previewing his text. A quick glance at the story showed him that it was quite short (under five pages), that it was written in the first person ("I was twelve"), that it included dialogue as well as narrative, and that it had an interesting title.

Highlighting and Annotating

As he reread the story, John highlighted words and ideas that he thought might be useful to him, indicated possible connections among ideas, and wrote down questions and comments as they occurred to him. During this process, he considered the meaning of the term *secret lion*, and he paid close attention to the narrator's voice. The highlighted and annotated passage that follows illustrates his responses to the last five paragraphs of the story.

When suddenly these two men came, from around a corner of trees and the tallest grass we had ever seen. They had bags on their backs, leather bags, bags and sticks.

pt. of view

We didn't know what clubs were, but I learned later, like I learned about the grinding balls. The two men yelled at us. Most specifically, one wanted me to take my Coke out of my Coke-holder so he could sink his golf ball into it. Something got taken away from us that moment. Heaven. We grew up a little bit, and couldn't go backward. We learned. No one had ever told us about golf. They had told us about heaven. And it went away. We got golf in exchange.

Heaven = innocence

Golf = adulthood

We went back to the arroyo for the rest of that summer, and tried to have fun the best we could. We learned to be ready for finding the grinding ball. We loved it, and when we buried it we knew what would happen. The truth is, we didn't look so hard for it. We were two boys and twelve summers then, and not stupid. Things get taken away.

Things lose their magic + specialness.

Loss of innocence, trust, belief in perfection.

We buried it because it was perfect. We didn't tell my mother but together it was all we talked about, till we forgot. It was the lion.

ball?

Lion=knowledge that growing up=loss? or is lion growing up itself?

John's highlighting and annotation of the entire story suggested a number of interesting possibilities for his paper. First, he noticed that the story contrasts the narrator's childhood innocence with his adult knowledge. John's highlighting also identified some unusual stylistic features, such as words run together ("Getridofit") and the repetition of words like *neat* and *perfect*. Finally, he noticed that four items—the arroyo, the grinding ball, the golf course, and the lion—are mentioned again and again. This observation led him to suspect that one or more of these items—particularly the secret lion, prominently mentioned in the story's title—might have symbolic significance.

 Writing about Fiction

Planning an Essay

At this stage, John had not yet decided on a topic; however, his previewing, highlighting, and annotations had revealed some interesting ideas about style and point of view—and, possibly, about symbolism. Now, because his paper was to be no more than four pages long, he needed to select one element on which to concentrate.

Choosing a Topic

John decided to explore possible topics in his journal. Here are his journal entries on the story's style and point of view.

Style—Style is informal, with lots of contractions and slang terms like "neat." Words are run together. Most of the time, the boys combine words to indicate something unimportant to them. When they're packing the lunch, they include "knivesforksplates." They're not interested in packing the lunch—they just want to get to the "mountains." Packing lunch is very important to the mother, so she does the opposite of combining words: she breaks them down ("sa-and-wiches"). This style can get pretty annoying.

Point of view—We see the story through the eyes of the narrator, who is a character in the story. Sergio is developed along with the narrator as part of a "we." The characters are not really individuals—they function as "we" for most of the story. We don't see into the minds of the boys to any great extent. The narrator has a double perspective: he takes readers back to his childhood, and this helps us understand the boys' excitement and disappointment, but he also shows us how much more he knows now, so we know that, too.

John had no trouble writing paragraphs on style and point of view in his journal, but he ran out of ideas quickly; he knew that he did not have enough material for a paper about either of these two topics. However, when he started to write a journal entry about the symbolic significance of certain elements in the story, he found that he had a lot more to say. As a result, he chose "Symbols in 'The Secret Lion'" as his paper's topic. Here is his journal entry on symbolism.

Symbolism—The arroyo, the grinding ball, the golf course, and of course the secret lion all seem to mean something beyond their literal meanings as objects and places. (Maybe the "mountains" do too.) For one thing, they're all repeated over and over again. Also, they all seem to be related somehow to magic and perfection and surprise and expectation and idealism (and, later, to disillusionment and disappointment). If this is a story about growing up, these things could be related to that theme.

Finding Something to Say

Brainstorming Once he decided to write about symbolism, John moved on to brainstorm about his topic, focusing on what he considered the story's most important—and most obvious—symbol: the secret lion itself.

Lion = "roaring, roaring that way the biggest things do"

EVERYTHING CHANGED (= secret because it's something they have to find out on their own, not from adults?)

Tablecloth-rug (= magic). "Staying-the-same part" is most important—why?

Arroyo: not supposed to go (= rebellion)—Mississippi, "friend from long back"; freedom. Place that doesn't change.

Grinding ball—Perfection in imperfect world,

innocence in adult world. "Nature = imperfect," but "round things = "perfect"—"the best thing." ("That ball was like that place, that whole arroyo")

Buried and "gone forever"—"taken away" (like arroyo)

Mountains: "everything looks bigger the smaller a man is"; hills = "Mountains for a small man." (Mother calls them hills)

Arroyo = polluted with sewage (never know when it's coming)—went to mts. On other side of hills = golf course (= heaven) "perfect"

"perfect" x3

*Like Oz—green, emerald

*Place to act "rich"

*Men with clubs = reality, future (= end of innocence)

"Things get taken away": heaven, ball (something buried and lost), arroyo

"We buried it because it was "perfect." ... It was the lion."

Lion = secret place inside us that still craves childhood (as adults, we learn we have to keep it buried, like ball). *How can a "roaring" lion be secret?

Seeing Connections

When John looked over his brainstorming notes in search of an organizing scheme for his paper, he saw that he had plenty of information about the secret lion, the arroyo, the grinding ball, and the golf course. His most obvious option was to discuss one item at a time, but he knew that he needed to find something that would tie the four separate items together. When he noticed that each item seemed to have different meanings at different periods of the boys' lives, he realized that his essay could discuss how these meanings change as the boys move from childhood to adolescence to adulthood. He experimented with this possibility as he grouped related details in the following lists.

```
The secret lion
Beginning: "raging beast" inside of them (6th grade class) =
   frustration, puberty
Beginning: "roaring, roaring that way the biggest things
   do"
Middle: "that whole junior high school lion"
End: Lion = greatness, something important (also =
   puberty?)
Also = great discoveries they expect to make in their
   lives.
End: "It was the lion."

Arroyo
Place that doesn't change (= childhood); constant in
   their changing lives. (But it changes too)
Mississippi—horizons
Freedom of childhood
Waste dump

Grinding ball
Perfection (in imperfect world)
Childhood innocence (in adult world)
Undiscovered knowledge?
Secrets of childhood (buried)
Something lost: "Things get taken away"

Golf course
Heaven—knowledge that there is no heaven, that it's a
   fraud, like the Wizard of Oz.
Adulthood—men with clubs
Scene of remembered humiliation
End of innocence (realization that it's just a golf
   course)
```

John's lists confirmed that the meanings of the four items did seem to change as the boys grew up. To the boys, the arroyo, the grinding ball, and the golf course are magical, but when they grow up, all three items lose their magic and became ordinary. The secret lion, however, seemed more complex than the other three items, and John knew that he would have to develop his ideas further before he could show how the lion's meaning changes and what these changes contribute to the story as a whole.

Deciding on a Thesis

With his ideas organized into lists that clarified some possible relationships among them, John began to see a central idea for his essay. He expressed this idea in a tentative **thesis statement,** a sentence that he could use to guide his essay's first draft.

```
The meanings of the story's key symbols change as the boys
move from childhood to adolescence to adulthood, and these
changes reveal corresponding changes in the boys' view of
the world as they move from idealism to frustration to
resignation.
```

Preparing an Outline

Even though his essay was to be short, John prepared a scratch outline that mapped out an arrangement for his ideas. He decided to discuss the four key symbols one by one, tracing each through the boys' childhood, adolescence, and adulthood. He planned to discuss the lion last because he saw it as the story's most important symbol. Looking back over all his notes, and paying close attention to his tentative thesis statement, John constructed this scratch outline.

```
Arroyo
    Mississippi
    Rebellion
    Waste dump

Grinding ball
    [Not yet discovered]
    Lost perfection
    "Things get taken away."

Golf course
    "Heaven"
    Humiliation
    Golf course

Lion
    [Not yet discovered]
    "roaring"; "raging beast"
    Just the lion
```

Drafting an Essay

Guided by his scratch outline, his tentative thesis statement, and his notes, John wrote the following first draft.

first draft

Symbols in "The Secret Lion"

"The Secret Lion" is a story that is rich in symbols. It is also a story about change. The meanings of the story's key symbols change as the boys move from childhood to adolescence to adulthood, and these changes reveal corresponding changes in the boys' view of the world as they move from idealism to frustration to resignation.

The arroyo, a dry gulch that can fill up with water, is special to the narrator and his friend Sergio when they are boys. Literally, it is a place to play. Symbolically, it is a place to rebel (they're not supposed to be there; they yell forbidden words). It could also symbolize all the discoveries they will make before they are completely grown up. To the young boys, the arroyo symbolizes a retreat from the disappointment of the golf course; it is their second choice. Later, it represents adventure, the uncertainty and unpredictability of adolescence, as illustrated by the fact that they cannot tell just by looking at it from the riverside whether the river was going to be tainted with sewage. When they are children, it is their Mississippi. When they are adolescents, it is a place to hang out and a symbol of adolescent rebellion; as an adult, the narrator looks back at it for what it was: an ordinary river polluted by sewage. The arroyo doesn't change, but the boys' view of it changes as they change.

At first, when they find the grinding ball, it stands for everything that is perfect and fascinating (and therefore forbidden and unattainable) in life. Like a child's life, it is perfect. They knew they couldn't keep it forever, just as they couldn't be children forever, so they buried it. When they tried to look for it again, they couldn't find it. They admit later that they don't look very hard. (People always wish they can find youth again, but they can't.) The ball represents perfection in an imperfect world, childhood innocence in an adult world. They hide it from their mother because they know she won't see it as perfect; she'll make them "getridofit" (198). They hide it because they want to retain the excitement of the undiscovered, but once they've used it and seen it and buried it, it's not new anymore. Even if they'd been able to find it, it would still be lost. To the adult narrator, it's just an ordinary object used in mining.

The golf course, which they wander into at age five, is, for a short period of time, "heaven" (200). It is lush and green and carefully cared for, and it is the opposite of the polluted arroyo. It is also another world, as mysterious as the Land of Oz. With the realization that it is not heaven to the golfers, the boys see what outsiders they really are. They may start "acting 'rich'" (200), but it will be just an act. There are no Coke-holders, no Oz, no heaven. The adolescents see the golf course as a scene of defeat and embarrassment, the setting for the confrontation that sent them back to the arroyo. To the adult, the golf course is just a golf course.

The secret lion is the most complex symbol in the story. In a sense it stands for the innocence of childhood, something we lose when we learn more. The lion symbolizes a great "roaring" disturbance (197). It is a change that unsettles everything for a brief time and then passes, leaving everything changed in irrevocable, indescribable ways. It symbolizes the boys' growing up: they are changed, but still the same people. The "secret lion" is that thing that changes little boys into men. It is secret because no one notices it happening; by the time it is noticed, the change has already occurred, and the little boy is gone forever. It is a lion because it "roars" through the boy like a storm and causes all of the growing-up changes, which can be "the biggest things" (197). In a more specific sense, the lion stands for puberty, reflected in their rage and frustration when they shout profanity. In the beginning of the story, the lion is rage (puberty, adolescence); in the middle, it suggests greatness (passing through adolescence into manhood); at the end, it's just the lion—"It was the lion" (200)—without any symbolic significance.

By the time they bury the ball, they have already learned one lesson, and the force of adulthood is pushing childhood aside. The golf course changes from heaven to shame to golf course; the ball changes from a special, perfect thing to something ordinary; the arroyo changes from grand river to polluted stream. Maybe it is the knowledge that life is not perfect, the knowledge that comes from growing up, that is the secret lion.

First Draft: Commentary

Discussions with other students in a peer-review session helped to guide John's revision of his first draft. The students' major criticism was that John's thesis seemed to make a complicated claim he could not support: that the development of all four symbols follows the three stages of the boys' lives. One student pointed out that two of the four symbols (the grinding ball and the secret lion) do not even enter the boys' lives until adolescence and that John's treatment of the story's most prominent symbol—the lion—does not show it changing in any significant way. The group agreed that he should simplify his thesis, focusing on the way the four symbols all reflect the story's theme about the inevitability of change.

John also met with his instructor, who suggested that he discuss the golf course first because it is the setting for the event that occurs first in time and because the disillusionment associated with it influences subsequent events. His instructor then expressed his concern about John's tendency to engage in "symbol hunting." He suggested that rather than focusing on finding equivalents for each of the four items ("the ball represents perfection," "the lion stands for puberty," and so on), John should consider how these symbols work together to communicate the story's theme. His instructor pointed out that in looking for neat equivalent values for each symbol, John was oversimplifying very complex ideas.

After discussing his first draft with his classmates and his instructor, John made changes in his essay's content and organization. In his next draft, he also planned to delete wordiness and repetition; revise inconsistent verb tenses; add more specific references, including quotations, from the story; sharpen transitions and add clearer topic sentences; and reorganize paragraphs to make logical and causal connections more obvious.

Revising and Editing an Essay

The revisions John decided to make are reflected in his second draft.

second draft

Symbols in "The Secret Lion"

"The Secret Lion" is a story about change. The first paragraph of the story gives a twelve-year-old's view of growing up: everything changes. When the child watches the magician, he is amazed at the "staying-the-same part" (197); adults focus on the tablecloth. As adults, we lose the ability to see the world through innocent eyes. We have the benefit of experience, confident the trick will work as long as the magician pulls the tablecloth in the proper way. The "staying-the-same part" is less important than the technique. In a story full of prominent symbols, the magician's trick does not seem very important, but all the key symbols, like the magician's trick, are about change. In fact, each of the story's key symbols highlights the theme of the inevitability of change that permeates the lives of the narrator and his friend Sergio.

The golf course is one such symbol. When the boys first see it, it is "heaven" (200). Lush and green and carefully cared for, it is completely different from the dry brown Arizona countryside and the polluted arroyo. In fact, to the boys it is another world, as mysterious as Oz—and just as unreal. Almost at once, the Emerald City becomes black and white again, the "Coke—holders" disappear, and the boys stop "acting 'rich'" (200). Heaven becomes a golf course, and the boys are changed forever.

The arroyo, a dry gulch that can fill up with water, is another symbol that reinforces the theme of the inevitability of change. It is a special place for the boys—a place to rebel, to shout forbidden words, to swim in waters polluted by a sewage treatment plant. Although it represents a retreat from the disillusionment of the golf course, clearly second choice, it is the boys' "personal Mississippi" (197), full of possibilities. Eventually, though, the arroyo too disappoints the boys, and they stop going there. "Nature seemed to keep pushing us around one way or another, teaching us the same thing every place we ended up" (198). The lesson they keep learning is that nothing is permanent.

The grinding ball, round and perfect, seems to suggest permanence and stability. But when the boys find it, they realize at once that they cannot keep it forever, just as they cannot remain children forever. Like a child's life, it is perfect but temporary. Burying it is their futile attempt to make time stand still, to preserve perfection in an imperfect world, innocence in an adult world, and they have already learned Nature's lesson well enough to know that this is not possible. They do not look very hard for the ball, but even if they'd been able to find it, the perfection and the innocence it represents would still be unattainable.

The secret lion, the most complex symbol, suggests the most profound kind of change: moving from innocence to experience, from childhood to adulthood. When the narrator is twelve, he says, "something happened that we didn't have a name for, but it was there nonetheless like a lion, and roaring, roaring that way the biggest things do. Everything changed" (197). School is different, girls are different, language is different. Innocence has been lost. The lion is associated with a great "roaring" disturbance, a change that unsettles everything for a brief time and then passes, leaving everything changed in irrevocable, indescribable ways. The secret lion is the thing that changes little boys into men. It is a lion because it "roars" through the boys like a storm; everything changes.

In an attempt to make things stay the same, to make time stand still, the boys bury the grinding ball "because it was perfect. . . . It was the lion" (200200). The grinding ball is "like that place, that whole arroyo" (198): secret and perfect. In other words, the ball and the arroyo and the lion are all tightly connected. By the time the boys bury the ball, they have already learned one sad lesson and are on their way to adulthood. Heaven is just a golf course; the round, perfect object is only "a cannonball thing used in mining" (198); the arroyo is no Mississippi but only a polluted stream; and childhood does not last forever. "Things get taken away" (200), and this knowledge that things do not last is the secret lion.

Second Draft: Commentary

John felt satisfied with his second draft. His revised thesis statement was clearer and simpler than the one in his first draft; it was also convincingly supported, with clearly worded topic sentences introducing support paragraphs and connecting them to the thesis statement. The second draft was also a good deal less wordy and more focused than the first, notably in the paragraphs about the arroyo and the grinding ball, and the introduction and conclusion were more fully developed. Moreover, he had given up his search for the one true "meaning" of each symbol, focusing instead on the many possibilities of each.

Now, John felt ready to turn his attention to smaller items, such as grammar, mechanics, punctuation, and format. Specifically, he planned to eliminate contractions, to work quotations into his text more smoothly, to make his thesis statement more precise and his title more interesting, and to revise the language of his introduction and conclusion further.

Frei 1

John Frei

Professor Nyysola

English 102

14 April 2008

"The Secret Lion": Everything Changes

The first paragraph of Alberto Alvaro Ríos's "The Secret Lion" presents a twelve-year-old's view of growing up: everything changes. When the magician pulls a tablecloth out from under a pile of dishes, the child is amazed at the "staying-the-same part" (197); adults focus on the tablecloth. As adults, we have the benefit of experience; we know the trick will work as long as the technique is correct. We gain confidence, but we lose our innocence, and we lose our sense of wonder. The price we pay for knowledge is a permanent sense of loss, and this trade-off is central to "The Secret Lion," a story whose key symbols reinforce its central theme: that change is inevitable and that change is always accompanied by loss.

Opening paragraph identifies work and author. Parenthetical documentation identifies source of quotation.

Thesis statement

The golf course is one symbol that helps to convey this theme. When the boys first see the golf course, it is "heaven" (200). Lush and green and carefully tended, it is very different from the dry, brown Arizona landscape and the polluted arroyo. In fact, to the boys it is another world, as exotic as Oz and ultimately as unreal. Before long, the Emerald City becomes black and white again. They learn that there is no such thing as a "Coke-holder," that their "acting 'rich'" is just an act, and that their heaven is only a golf course (200). As the narrator acknowledges, "Something got taken away from us that moment. Heaven" (200).

Topic sentence identifies one key symbol.

Frei 2

Topic sentence identifies another key symbol.

The arroyo, a dry gulch that can fill up with water, is another symbol that reflects the idea of the inevitability of change and of the loss that accompanies change. It is a special, Edenlike place for the boys—a place where they can rebel by shouting forbidden words and by swimming in forbidden waters. Although it represents a retreat from the disillusionment of the golf course, and it is clearly second choice, it is still their "personal Mississippi" (197), full of possibilities. Eventually, though, the arroyo too disappoints the boys, and they stop going there. As the narrator says, "Nature seemed to keep pushing us around one way or another, teaching us the same thing every place we ended up" (198). The lesson they keep learning is that nothing is permanent.

Topic sentence identifies another key symbol.

The grinding ball, round and perfect, suggests permanence and stability. But when the boys find it, they realize at once that they cannot keep it forever, just as they cannot remain balanced forever between childhood and adulthood. Like a child's life, the ball is perfect but temporary. Burying it is their desperate attempt to stop time, to preserve perfection in an imperfect world, innocence in an adult world. But the boys are already twelve years old, and they have learned nature's lesson well enough to know that this action will not work. Even if they had been able to find the ball, the perfection and the innocence it suggests to them would still be unattainable. Perhaps that is why they do not try very hard to find it.

Frei 3

Like the story's other symbols, the secret lion itself suggests the most profound kind of change: the movement from innocence to experience, from childhood to adulthood, from expectation to disappointment to resignation. The narrator explains that when he was twelve, "something happened that we didn't have a name for, but it was there nonetheless like a lion, and roaring, roaring that way the biggest things do. Everything changed" (197). School was different, girls were different, language was different. Despite its loud roar, the lion remained paradoxically "secret," unnoticed until it passed. Like adolescence, the secret lion is a roaring disturbance that unsettles everything for a brief time and then passes, leaving everything changed.

Topic sentence identifies final (and most important) symbol.

In an attempt to make things stay the same, to make time stand still, the boys bury the grinding ball "because it was perfect. . . . It was the lion" (200). The grinding ball is "like that place, that whole arroyo" (198): secret and perfect. The ball and the arroyo and the lion are all perfect, but all, ironically, are temporary. The first paragraph of "The Secret Lion" tells us, "Everything changed" (197); by the last paragraph, we learn what this change means: "Things get taken away" (200). In other words, change implies loss. Heaven turns out to be just a golf course; the round, perfect object is only "a cannonball thing used in mining" (198); the arroyo is just a polluted stream; and childhood is just a phase. "Things get taken away," and this knowledge that things do not last is the lion, secret yet roaring.

Conclusion

Frei 4

Work Cited

Ríos, Alberto Alvaro. "The Secret Lion." *Literature: Reading, Reacting, Writing*. Ed. Laurie G. Kirszner and Stephen R. Mandell. 7th ed. Boston: Wadsworth, 2010. 197-200. Print.

Final Draft: Commentary

As John revised and edited his second draft, he made changes in word choice and sentence structure. He also changed his title and edited to eliminate errors in mechanics and punctuation. In this final draft, he made his thesis statement more precise than it was in the previous draft, to communicate the idea of the relationship between change and loss that is central to the essay. In addition, he worked all quoted material smoothly into his discussion, taking care to use quotations only when the author's words added something vital to the paper, and he added a works-cited page. Finally, John checked all his references to page numbers in the story so readers would be able to return to his source if necessary to check the accuracy and appropriateness of his quotations.

CHAPTER 12

PLOT

Alfred Hitchcock's 1951 film *Strangers on a Train*, based on a suspense novel by Patricia Highsmith, offers an intriguing premise: two men, strangers, each can murder someone the other wishes dead; because they have no apparent connection to their victims, both can escape suspicion. Many people would describe this ingenious scheme as the film's "plot," but in fact it is simply the gimmick around which the complex plot revolves. Certainly a clever twist can be an important ingredient of a story's plot, but **plot** is more than "what happens": it is how what happens is revealed, the way in which a story's events are arranged. Plot is shaped

Scene from Alfred Hitchcock's 1951 film *Strangers on a Train*.
Source: ©Warner Bros. / The Kobal Collection

by causal connections—historical, social, and personal—by the interaction between characters, and by the juxtaposition of events. In *Strangers on a Train*, the plot that unfolds is complex: one character directs the events and determines their order while the other character is drawn into the action against his will. The same elements that enrich the plot of the film—unexpected events, conflict, suspense, flashbacks, foreshadowing—can also enrich the plot of a work of short fiction.

Conflict

Readers' interest and involvement are heightened by a story's **conflict,** the struggle between opposing forces that emerges as the action develops. This conflict is a clash between the **protagonist,** a story's principal character, and an **antagonist,** someone or something presented in opposition to the protagonist. Sometimes the antagonist is a villain; more often, it is a character who represents a conflicting point of view or advocates a course of action different from the one the protagonist follows. Sometimes the antagonist is not a character at all but a situation (for instance, war or poverty) or an event (for example, a natural disaster, such as a flood or a storm) that challenges the protagonist. In other stories, the protagonist may struggle against a supernatural force, or the conflict may occur within a character's mind. It may, for example, be a struggle between two moral choices, such as whether to stay at home and care for an aging parent or to leave and make a new life.

Stages of Plot

A work's plot explores one or more conflicts, moving from *exposition* through a series of *complications* to a *climax* and, finally, to a *resolution*.

During a story's **exposition,** the writer presents the basic information readers need to understand the events that follow. Typically, the exposition sets the story in motion: it establishes the scene, introduces the major characters, and perhaps suggests the major events or conflicts to come.

Sometimes a single sentence can present a story's exposition clearly and economically, giving readers information vital to their understanding of the plot that will unfold. For example, the opening sentence of Amy Tan's "Two Kinds" (p. 777)—"My mother believed you could be anything you wanted to be in America"—reveals an important trait of a central character. Similarly, the opening sentence of Shirley Jackson's "The Lottery" (p. 509)—"The morning of June 27th was clear and sunny, with the fresh warmth of a full-summer day; the flowers were blossoming profusely and the grass was richly green"—introduces the picture-perfect setting that is essential to the story's irony. At other times, as in John Updike's "A&P" (p. 259), a more fully developed exposition section establishes the story's setting, introduces the main characters, and suggests possible conflicts. Finally, in some experimental stories, a distinct exposition component may be absent, as it is in Luisa Valenzuela's "All about Suicide" (p. 6) and Amanda Holzer's "Love and Other Catastrophes: A Mix Tape" (p. 182).

As the plot progresses, the story's conflict unfolds through a series of complications that eventually lead readers to the story's climax. As it develops, the story may include several crises. A **crisis** is a peak in the story's action, a moment of considerable tension or importance. The **climax** is the point of greatest tension or importance, the scene that presents a story's decisive action or event.

The final stage of plot, the **resolution,** or **denouement** (French for "untying of the knot"), draws the action to a close and accounts for all remaining loose ends.

Sometimes this resolution is achieved with the help of a **deus ex machina** (Latin for "a god from a machine"), an intervention of some force or agent previously extraneous to the story—for example, the sudden arrival of a long-lost relative or a fortuitous inheritance, the discovery of a character's true identity, or a last-minute rescue by a character not previously introduced. Usually, however, the resolution is more plausible: all the events lead logically and convincingly (though not necessarily predictably) to the resolution. Sometimes the ending of a story is indefinite—that is, readers are not quite sure what the protagonist will do or what will happen next. This kind of resolution, although it may leave some readers feeling cheated, has its advantages: it mirrors the complexity of life, where closure rarely occurs, and it can keep readers involved in the story as they try to understand the significance of its ending or to decide how conflicts should have been resolved.

Order and Sequence

A writer may present a story's events in strict chronological order, presenting each event in the sequence in which it actually takes place. More often, however, especially in relatively modern fiction, writers do not present events chronologically. Instead, they present incidents out of expected order, or in no apparent order. For example, a writer may choose to begin **in medias res** (Latin for "in the midst of things"), starting with a key event and later going back in time to explain events that preceded it, as Tillie Olsen does in "I Stand Here Ironing" (p. 344). Or, a writer can decide to begin a work of fiction at the end and then move back to reconstruct events that led up to the final outcome, as William Faulkner does in "A Rose for Emily" (p. 243). Many sequences are possible as the writer manipulates events to create interest, suspense, confusion, wonder, or some other effect.

Writers who wish to depart from strict chronological order use *flashbacks* and *foreshadowing*. A **flashback** moves out of sequence to examine an event or situation that occurred before the time in which the story's action takes place. A character can remember an earlier event, or a story's narrator can re-create an earlier situation. For example, in Alberto Alvaro Ríos's "The Secret Lion" (p. 197), the adult narrator looks back at events that occurred when he was twelve years old and then moves further back in time to consider related events that occurred when he was five. In Edgar Allan Poe's "The Cask of Amontillado" (p. 385), the entire story is told as a flashback. Flashbacks are valuable because they can substitute for or supplement formal exposition by presenting background readers need to understand a story's events. One disadvantage of flashbacks is that, because they interrupt the natural flow of events, they may be intrusive or distracting. Such distractions, however, can be an advantage if the writer wishes to reveal events gradually and subtly or to obscure causal links.

Foreshadowing is the introduction early in a story of situations, events, characters, or objects that hint at things to come. Typically, a seemingly simple element—a chance remark, a natural occurrence, a trivial event—is eventually revealed to have great significance. For example, a dark cloud passing across the sky during a wedding can foreshadow future problems for the marriage. Foreshadowing allows a writer to hint provocatively at what is to come, so that readers only gradually become aware of a particular detail's role in a story. Thus, foreshadowing helps readers sense what will occur and grow increasingly involved as they see the likelihood (or even the inevitability) of a particular outcome.

In addition to using conventional techniques like flashbacks and foreshadowing, writers may experiment with sequence by substantially tampering with—or even dispensing with—chronological order. (An example is the scrambled chronology of "A Rose for Emily.") In such instances, the experimental form enhances interest and encourages readers to become involved with the story as they work to untangle or reorder the events and determine their logical and causal connections.

Today, the computer has given a new fluidity to the nature of plot, with hypertext stories appearing on the Internet, where stories may be constructed to permit readers to actually participate in the creation of plot.

✔ CHECKLIST Writing about Plot

- ☐ What happens in the story?
- ☐ Where does the story's formal exposition section end? What do readers learn about characters in this section? What do readers learn about setting? What possible conflicts are suggested here?
- ☐ What is the story's central conflict? What other conflicts are presented? Who is the protagonist? Who (or what) serves as the antagonist?
- ☐ Identify the story's crisis or crises.
- ☐ Identify the story's climax.
- ☐ How is the story's central conflict resolved? Is this resolution plausible? Satisfying?
- ☐ Which part of the story constitutes the resolution? Do any problems remain unresolved? Does any uncertainty remain? If so, does this uncertainty strengthen or weaken the story? Would another ending be more effective?
- ☐ How are the story's events arranged? Are they presented in chronological order? What events are presented out of logical sequence? Does the story use foreshadowing? Flashbacks? Are the causal connections between events clear? Logical? If not, can you explain why?

Source: ©AP Photo/Tina Fineberg

BEN KATCHOR (1951–), born in Brooklyn, New York, has published numerous comics, or "picture-stories," in a range of publications, including the Jewish-American newspaper the *Forward* and the monthly magazine *Metropolis.* Much of his work focuses on the Jewish-American immigrant experience and the humor surrounding cultural assimilation. His graphic novels include *Cheap Novelties: The Pleasures of Urban Decay* (1991); *Julius Knipl, Real Estate Photographer: Stories* (1996); *The Jew of New York* (1998); and *Julius Knipl, Real Estate Photographer: The Beauty Supply District* (2000). A fifth graphic novel, *The Dairy Restaurant,* is forthcoming. Winner of a Guggenheim Memorial Foundation Fellowship and a MacArthur Foundation Fellowship, Katchor currently teaches visual narrative at the Parsons School of Design in New York City.

Cultural Context Before air-conditioning window units became widespread in the 1950s, residents of urban apartment houses often kept their windows open to get some relief from the sweltering city heat. Open windows provided opportunities for apartment dwellers to socialize with neighbors and observe neighborhood goings-on, as depicted in this graphic story. Between 1948 and 1953, sales in the United States of air-conditioning window units spiked from 74,000 to 1,045,000. As a result, more and more apartment dwellers began shutting their windows, bringing the era of "window gossip" to a close.

The Goner Pillow Company (2006)

This graphic story starts on the next page. →

Reading and Reacting

1. What actually happens during the course of "The Goner Pillow Company" (p. 224)? How much time do you think goes by from first panel to last?
2. In what sense does the first panel of the story provide exposition? Does the story include any foreshadowing? Does it include any flashbacks?
3. In panels 7–9, the narrator poses a series of questions. How do the illustrations answer these questions? How does panel 10 answer the questions?
4. **Journal Entry** How are the members of the Goner family different in terms of their attitude toward "the home entertainment industry"? Which family member's attitude is most like your own?
5. **Critical Perspective** Ben Katchor's illustrations have been praised for their depiction of an almost timeless urban landscape that seems at once both long gone and immediately present. Paul Buhle, a lecturer in American civilization at Brown University, notes how Katchor is particularly adept at "reconstructing the ancientness of a certain civilization and its odd but also eerily familiar habitants" and at capturing "a disappearing urban ambience." Katchor describes his inspiration for "Goner Pillow Company" by explaining, "I first saw a window pillow being used in the front room of my grandmother's apartment on Knickerbocker Avenue in Brooklyn, circa 1956."

   How do the words and images in this story work together to recreate a "disappearing urban ambience"?

Related Works: "A Primer for the Punctuation of Heart Disease" (p. 440), "The World Is Too Much with Us" (p. 855), "When I Heard the Learn'd Astronomer" (p. 877), "Ave Maria" (p. 1184), *Trifles* (p. 1319)

The Goner Pillow Company by Ben Katchor

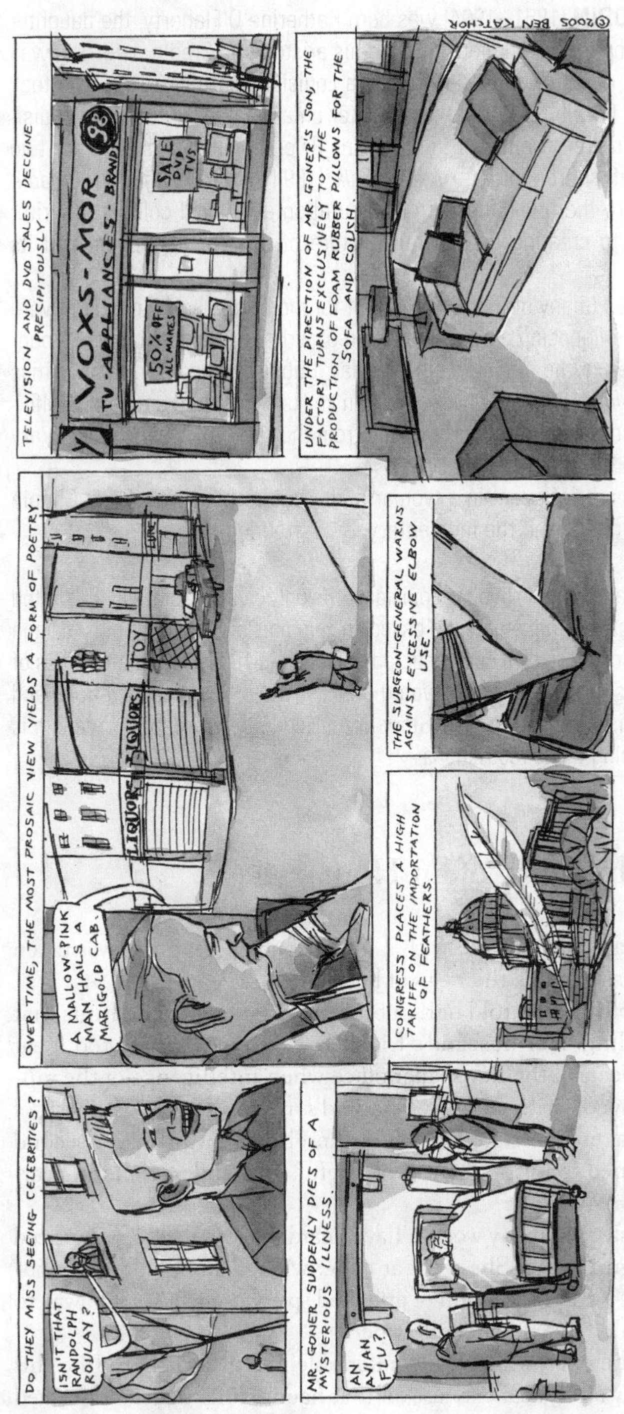
DO THEY MISS SEEING CELEBRITIES?
ISN'T THAT RANDOLPH ROULAY?
OVER TIME, THE MOST PROSAIC VIEW YIELDS A FORM OF POETRY.
A MALLOW-PINK MAN HAILS A MARIGOLD CAB.
LIQUORS
LIQUORS
TOY
TELEVISION AND DVD SALES DECLINE PRECIPITOUSLY.
VOXS-MOR
TV · APPLIANCES · BRAND
98
50% OFF ALL MAKES
SALE DVD TVS
MR. GONER SUDDENLY DIES OF A MYSTERIOUS ILLNESS.
AN AVIAN FLU?
CONGRESS PLACES A HIGH TARIFF ON THE IMPORTATION OF FEATHERS.
THE SURGEON-GENERAL WARNS AGAINST EXCESSIVE ELBOW USE.
UNDER THE DIRECTION OF MR. GONER'S SON, THE FACTORY TURNS EXCLUSIVELY TO THE PRODUCTION OF FOAM RUBBER PILLOWS FOR THE SOFA AND COUCH.
©2005 BEN KATCHOR

Source: Courtesy of Louisiana State University

KATE CHOPIN (1851–1904) was born Katherine O'Flaherty, the daughter of a wealthy Irish-born merchant and his aristocratic Creole wife. She was married at nineteen to Oscar Chopin, a Louisiana cotton broker, who took her to live first in New Orleans and later on a plantation in central Louisiana. Chopin's representations of the Cane River region and its people in two volumes of short stories—*Bayou Folk* (1894) and *A Night in Arcadie* (1897)—are the foundation of her reputation as a local colorist, a writer dedicated to creating an accurate picture of a particular region and its people.

Her honest, sexually frank stories (many of them out of print for more than half a century) were rediscovered in the 1960s and 1970s, influencing a new generation of writers. Though she was a popular contributor of stories and sketches to the magazines of her day, Chopin scandalized many critics with her outspoken novel *The Awakening* (1899), in which a woman seeks sexual and emotional fulfillment with a man who is not her husband. The book was removed from the shelves of the public library in St. Louis, where Chopin was born.

"The Story of an Hour" depicts a brief event in a woman's life, but in this single hour, Chopin reveals both a lifetime's emotional torment and the momentary joy of freedom.

Cultural Context During her marriage, Chopin lived in Louisiana, the only civil-law state in the United States. Whereas the legal systems of all other states are based on common law, the laws of Louisiana have their roots in the Napoleonic Code, the civil code enacted in France in 1804 to regulate issues of property, marriage, and divorce. This patriarchal code favored the husband in all domestic affairs and left women without many legal or fiscal rights. In "The Story of an Hour," the concept of freedom is closely tied to the prospect of escaping these restrictions.

The Story of an Hour (1894)

Knowing that Mrs. Mallard was afflicted with a heart trouble, great care was taken to break to her as gently as possible the news of her husband's death.

It was her sister Josephine who told her, in broken sentences, veiled hints that revealed in half concealing. Her husband's friend Richards was there, too, near her. It was he who had been in the newspaper office when intelligence of the railroad disaster was received, with Brently Mallard's name leading the list of "killed." He had only taken the time to assure himself of its truth by a second telegram, and had hastened to forestall any less careful, less tender friend in bearing the sad message.

She did not hear the story as many women have heard the same, with a paralyzed inability to accept its significance. She wept at once, with sudden, wild abandonment, in her sister's arms. When the storm of grief had spent itself she went away to her room alone. She would have no one follow her.

There stood, facing the open window, a comfortable, roomy armchair. Into this she sank, pressed down by a physical exhaustion that haunted her body and seemed to reach into her soul.

She could see in the open square before her house the tops of trees that were all 5
aquiver with the new spring life. The delicious breath of rain was in the air. In the street below a peddler was crying his wares. The notes of a distant song which some one was singing reached her faintly, and countless sparrows were twittering in the eaves.

There were patches of blue sky showing here and there through the clouds that had met and piled one above the other in the west facing her window.

She sat with her head thrown back upon the cushion of the chair, quite motionless, except when a sob came up into her throat and shook her, as a child who has cried itself to sleep continues to sob in its dreams.

She was young, with a fair, calm face, whose lines bespoke repression and even a certain strength. But now there was a dull stare in her eyes, whose gaze was fixed away off yonder on one of those patches of blue sky. It was not a glance of reflection, but rather indicated a suspension of intelligent thought.

There was something coming to her and she was waiting for it, fearfully. What was it? She did not know; it was too subtle and elusive to name. But she felt it, creeping out of the sky, reaching toward her through the sounds, the scents, the color that filled the air.

Now her bosom rose and fell tumultuously. She was beginning to recognize this 10
thing that was approaching to possess her, and she was striving to beat it back with her will—as powerless as her two white slender hands would have been.

When she abandoned herself a little whispered word escaped her slightly parted lips. She said it over and over under her breath: "Free, free, free!" The vacant stare and the look of terror that had followed it went from her eyes. They stayed keen and bright. Her pulses beat fast, and the coursing blood warmed and relaxed every inch of her body.

She did not stop to ask if it were not a monstrous joy that held her. A clear and exalted perception enabled her to dismiss the suggestion as trivial.

She knew that she would weep again when she saw the kind, tender hands folded in death; the face that had never looked save with love upon her, fixed and gray and dead. But she saw beyond that bitter moment a long procession of years to come that would belong to her absolutely. And she opened and spread her arms out to them in welcome.

There would be no one to live for during those coming years; she would live for herself. There would be no powerful will bending her in that blind persistence with which men and women believe they have a right to impose a private will upon a fellow creature. A kind intention or a cruel intention made the act seem no less a crime as she looked upon it in that brief moment of illumination.

And yet she had loved him—sometimes. Often she had not. What did it mat- 15
ter! What could love, the unsolved mystery, count for in face of this possession of self-assertion which she suddenly recognized as the strongest impulse of her being.

"Free! Body and soul free!" she kept whispering.

Josephine was kneeling before the closed door with her lips to the key-hole, imploring for admission. "Louise, open the door! I beg; open the door—you will make yourself ill. What are you doing, Louise? For heaven's sake open the door."

"Go away. I am not making myself ill." No; she was drinking in a very elixir of life through that open window.

Her fancy was running riot along those days ahead of her. Spring days, and summer days, and all sorts of days that would be her own. She breathed a quick prayer that life might be long. It was only yesterday she had thought with a shudder that life might be long.

She arose at length and opened the door to her sister's importunities. There was a feverish triumph in her eyes, and she carried herself unwittingly like a goddess of Victory. She clasped her sister's waist, and together they descended the stairs. Richards stood waiting for them at the bottom.

Some one was opening the front door with a latchkey. It was Brently Mallard who entered, a little travel-stained, composedly carrying his grip-sack and umbrella. He had been far from the scene of the accident, and did not even know there had been one. He stood amazed at Josephine's piercing cry; at Richards' quick motion to screen him from the view of his wife.

But Richards was too late.

When the doctors came they said she had died of heart disease—of joy that kills.

Reading and Reacting

1. The story's basic exposition is presented in its first two paragraphs. What additional information about character or setting would you like to know? Why do you suppose Chopin does not supply this information?
2. "The Story of an Hour" is a very economical story, with little action or dialogue. Do you see this economy as a strength or a weakness? Explain.
3. When "The Story of an Hour" was first published in *Vogue* magazine in 1894, the magazine's editors titled it "The Dream of an Hour." A film version, echoing the last words of the story, is called *The Joy That Kills*. Which of the three titles do you believe most accurately represents what happens in the story? Why?
4. Do you think Brently Mallard physically abused his wife? Did he love her? Did she love him? Exactly why was she so relieved to be rid of him? Can you answer any of these questions with certainty?
5. What is the nature of the conflict in this story? Who, or what, do you see as Mrs. Mallard's antagonist?
6. What emotions does Mrs. Mallard experience during the hour she spends alone in her room? What events do you imagine take place during this same period outside her room? Outside her house?
7. Do you find the story's ending satisfying? Believable? Contrived?
8. Was the story's ending unexpected, or were you prepared for it? What elements in the story foreshadow this ending?
9. **JOURNAL ENTRY** Rewrite the story's ending, substituting a few paragraphs of your own for the last three paragraphs.

10. **Critical Perspective** Kate Chopin is widely viewed today as an early feminist writer whose work often addressed the social injustices and inequalities that women faced during her time, the second half of the nineteenth century. According to literary critic Elaine Showalter, this story was written during a period in which women writers were able to "reject the accommodating postures of femininity and to use literature to dramatize the ordeals of wronged womanhood."

    Do you think this story rejects the "postures of femininity"? What "ordeals of wronged womanhood" are being dramatized here?

Related Works: "The Storm" (p. 313), "The Yellow Wallpaper" (p. 459), "The Disappearance" (p. 695), "Women" (p. 1007), *A Doll House* (p. 1402)

Source: ©Jessica Garrison

LARRY FONDATION (1957–) has lived in Los Angeles for two decades, gaining an intimate knowledge of the city that is the subject of much of his work. He has published three books in a projected five-book series exploring the "marginal" side of Los Angeles culture: a collection of stories entitled *Common Criminals* (2002) and the novels *Angry Nights* (1995) and *Fish, Soap and Bonds* (2007).

Cultural Context The all-American diner, the setting for this story, is an important cultural institution. In 1872, Providence, Rhode Island, native Walter Scott established the first American "diner" in the form of a horse-drawn wagon offering coffee, sandwiches, and other snacks to employees of the *Providence Journal* and other workers. Lunch wagons became widespread in urban centers of the Northeast throughout the latter part of the nineteenth century and into the early twentieth century, when vendors began moving their business from wagons to prefabricated buildings. Today's diners range from simple to elaborate, but all developed from modest roots.

Deportation at Breakfast (1991)

The signs on the windows lured me inside. For a dollar I could get two eggs, toast, and potatoes. The place looked better than most—family run and clean. The signs were hand-lettered and neat. The paper had yellowed some, but the black letters remained bold. A green-and-white awning was perched over the door, where the name "Clara's" was stenciled.

Inside, the place had an appealing and old-fashioned look. The air smelled fresh and homey, not greasy. The menu was printed on a chalkboard. It was short and to the point. It listed the kinds of toast you could choose from. One entry was erased from the middle of the list. By deduction, I figured it was rye. I didn't want rye toast anyway.

Because I was alone, I sat at the counter, leaving the empty tables free for other customers that might come in. At the time, business was quiet. Only two tables were occupied, and I was alone at the counter. But it was still early—not yet seven-thirty.

Behind the counter was a short man with dark black hair, a mustache, and a youthful beard, one that never grew much past stubble. He was dressed immaculately, all in chef's white—pants, shirt, and apron, but no hat. He had a thick accent. The name "Javier" was stitched on his shirt.

5 I ordered coffee, and asked for a minute to choose between the breakfast special for a dollar and the cheese omelette for $1.59. I selected the omelette.

The coffee was hot, strong, and fresh. I spread my newspaper on the counter and sipped at the mug as Javier went to the grill to cook my meal.

The eggs were spread out on the griddle, the bread plunged inside the toaster, when the authorities came in. They grabbed Javier quickly and without a word, forcing his hands behind his back. He, too, said nothing. He did not resist, and they shoved him out the door and into their waiting car.

On the grill, my eggs bubbled. I looked around for another employee—maybe out back somewhere, or in the washroom. I leaned over the counter and called for someone. No one answered. I looked behind me toward the tables. Two elderly men sat at one, two elderly women at the other. The two women were talking. The men were reading the paper. They seemed not to have noticed Javier's exit.

I could smell my eggs starting to burn. I wasn't quite sure what to do about it. I thought about Javier and stared at my eggs. After some hesitation, I got up from my red swivel stool and went behind the counter. I grabbed a spare apron, then picked up the spatula and turned my eggs. My toast had popped up, but it was not browned, so I put it down again.

10 While I was cooking, the two elderly women came to the counter and asked to pay. I asked what they had had. They seemed surprised that I didn't remember. I checked the prices on the chalkboard and rang up their order. They paid slowly, fishing through large purses, and went out, leaving me a dollar tip. I took my eggs off the grill and slid them onto a clean plate. My toast had come up. I buttered it and put it on my plate beside my eggs. I put the plate at my spot at the counter, right next to my newspaper.

As I began to come back from behind the counter to my stool, six new customers came through the door. "Can we pull some tables together?" they asked. "We're all one party." I told them yes. Then they ordered six coffees, two decaffeinated.

I thought of telling them I didn't work there. But perhaps they were hungry. I poured their coffee. Their order was simple: six breakfast specials, all with scrambled eggs and wheat toast. I got busy at the grill.

Then the elderly men came to pay. More new customers began arriving. By eight-thirty, I had my hands full. With this kind of business, I couldn't understand why Javier hadn't hired a waitress. Maybe I'd take out a help-wanted ad in the paper tomorrow. I had never been in the restaurant business. There was no way I could run this place alone.

Reading and Reacting

1. The story's first four paragraphs present its exposition. What information about characters and setting is revealed here? What information is *not* revealed?
2. Paragraph 4 gives readers a physical description of Javier, the only character who is given this kind of attention. What does this description tell you about Javier? What else would you like to know about him?
3. In paragraph 7, "the authorities" enter the diner and take the unresisting Javier to their car. Who are these "authorities"? How do you know?
4. In paragraph 9, after futile attempts to locate other employees, the narrator moves behind the counter and begins to cook. What do you think motivates him to take this action?
5. Throughout the story, the physical setting—the diner—is always in the forefront. What specific elements of this setting does the writer focus on? Why?
6. The story's last two lines illustrate its flat tone and understated style. Here, the narrator says, "I had never been in the restaurant business. There was no way I could run this place alone." What might the content and tone of these sentences suggest about the narrator's past—and about his future?
7. Does the story's resolution come as a surprise to you? Is the ending plausible? Does the writer foreshadow the ending in any way?
8. What would you expect to happen in the diner at lunchtime? At dinner? The next day? The next week?
9. **JOURNAL ENTRY** The story gives very little information about the narrator. What can you infer about him from his words, his observations, and his actions? For example, how old do you think he is? Do you think he has a job? A family?
10. **CRITICAL PERSPECTIVE** In *Review of Contemporary Fiction*, Michael Hemmingson characterizes Fondation's voice as "terse and directly to the point; he makes no judgments and does no editorializing, just tells it as he sees it. . . ."

    How does Fondation's terse and to-the-point style strengthen his story's plot? Do you see any drawbacks to this style?

Related Works: "A&P" (p. 259), "Bullet in the Brain" (p. 608), "The Unknown Citizen" (p. 864), *Nine Ten* (p. 1314), *The Cuban Swimmer* (p. 1732)

Source: ©AP Photo

NADINE GORDIMER (1923–), winner of the 1991 Nobel Prize in Literature, has been publishing short stories, essays, and novels about South Africa, her native country, since she was fifteen. Gordimer once explained that after growing up as a middle-class child of Jewish immigrants, becoming a politically aware writer in South Africa was like "peeling an onion. You're sloughing off all the conditioning that you've had since you were a child." The prevailing attitude of her extensive work evolved from cautious optimism to pessimism in accord with the changing nature of Africa. Under apartheid, Gordimer's work was often banned in her own country because of its condemnation of the political system, but she remained in Johannesburg.

Gordimer's fourteen novels include *Burger's Daughter* (1979), *July's People* (1981), *None to Accompany Me* (1994), and her most recent, *Get a Life*, published in 2005. Her twelve short story collections include *Jump and Other Stories* (1991), *Why Haven't You Written?* (1992), *Loot* (2003), and her most recent, *Beethoven Was One-Sixteenth Black* (2007). A founding member of the Congress of South African Writers, Gordimer has been awarded numerous prizes and honorary degrees, as well as France's prestigious *Commandeur de l'Ordre des Arts et des Lettres*.

Cultural Context Under South Africa's apartheid regime (1948–1991), race determined where citizens could live, what kind of work they could do, what kind of education they could receive, whom they could marry, and what political rights they had. Apartheid governed relations between South Africa's powerful white minority and its nonwhite majority and sanctioned racial segregation and political and economic discrimination against nonwhites. During this time, white South Africans separated themselves as much as possible, often living in gated communities or compounds, which exacerbated the hostility between the races. The fact that the family in "Once upon a Time" lives in such a compound is an important element of its plot.

Once upon a Time (1991)

Someone has written to ask me to contribute to an anthology of stories for children. I reply that I don't write children's stories; and he writes back that at a recent congress/book fair/seminar a certain novelist said every writer ought to write at least one story for children. I think of sending a postcard saying I don't accept that I "ought" to write anything.

And then last night I woke up—or rather was wakened without knowing what had roused me.

A voice in the echo-chamber of the subconscious?

A sound.

5 A creaking of the kind made by the weight carried by one foot after another along a wooden floor. I listened. I felt the apertures of my ears distend with concentration. Again: the creaking. I was waiting for it; waiting to hear if it indicated that feet were moving from room to room, coming up the passage—to my door. I have no burglar bars, no gun under the pillow, but I have the same fears as people who do take these precautions, and my windowpanes are thin as rime, could shatter like a wineglass. A woman was murdered (how do they put it) in broad daylight in a house two blocks away, last year, and the fierce dogs who guarded an old widower and his collection of antique clocks were strangled before he was knifed by a casual labourer he had dismissed without pay.

I was staring at the door, making it out in my mind rather than seeing it, in the dark. I lay quite still—a victim already—but the arrhythmia of my heart was fleeing, knocking this way and that against its body-cage. How finely tuned the senses are, just out of rest, sleep! I could never listen intently as that in the distractions of the day; I was reading every faintest sound, identifying and classifying its possible threat.

But I learned that I was to be neither threatened nor spared. There was no human weight pressing on the boards, the creaking was a buckling, an epicentre of stress. I was in it. The house that surrounds me while I sleep is built on undermined ground; far beneath my bed, the floor, the house's foundations, the stopes and passages of gold mines have hollowed the rock, and when some face trembles, detaches and falls, three thousand feet below, the whole house shifts slightly, bringing uneasy strain to the balance and counterbalance of brick, cement, wood and glass that hold it as a structure around me. The misbeats of my heart tailed off like the last muffled flourishes on one of the wooden xylophones made by the Chopi and Tsonga migrant miners who might have been down there, under me in the earth at that moment. The stope where the fall was could have been disused, dripping water from its ruptured veins; or men might now be interred there in the most profound of tombs.

I couldn't find a position in which my mind would let go of my body—release me to sleep again. So I began to tell myself a story; a bedtime story.

In a house, in a suburb, in a city, there were a man and his wife who loved each other very much and were living happily ever after. They had a little boy, and they loved him very much. They had a cat and a dog that the little boy loved very much. They had a car and a caravan trailer for holidays, and a swimming-pool which was fenced so that the little boy and his playmates would not fall in and drown. They had a housemaid who was absolutely trustworthy and an itinerant gardener who was highly recommended by the neighbours. For when they began to live happily ever after they were warned, by that wise old witch, the husband's mother, not to take on anyone off the street. They were inscribed in a medical benefit society, their pet dog was licensed, they were insured against fire, flood damage and theft, and subscribed to the local Neighbourhood Watch, which supplied them with a plaque for their gates lettered YOU HAVE BEEN WARNED over the silhouette of a would-be intruder. He was masked; it could not be said if he was black or white, and therefore proved the property owner was no racist.

It was not possible to insure the house, the swimming pool or the car against riot 10
damage. There were riots, but these were outside the city, where people of another colour were quartered. These people were not allowed into the suburb except as reliable housemaids and gardeners, so there was nothing to fear, the husband told the wife. Yet she was afraid that some day such people might come up the street and tear off the plaque YOU HAVE BEEN WARNED and open the gates and stream in . . . Nonsense, my dear, said the husband, there are police and soldiers and tear-gas and guns to keep them away. But to please her—for he loved her very much and buses were being burned, cars stoned, and schoolchildren shot by the police in those quarters out of sight and hearing of the suburb—he had electronically-controlled gates fitted. Anyone who pulled off the sign YOU HAVE BEEN WARNED and tried to open the gates would have to announce his intentions by pressing a button and speaking into a receiver relayed to the house. The little boy was fascinated by the device and used it as a walkie-talkie in cops and robbers play with his small friends.

The riots were suppressed, but there were many burglaries in the suburb and somebody's trusted housemaid was tied up and shut in a cupboard by thieves while she was in charge of her employers' house. The trusted housemaid of the man and wife and little boy was so upset by this misfortune befalling a friend left, as she herself often was, with responsibility for the possessions of the man and his wife and the little boy that she implored her employers to have burglar bars attached to the doors and windows of the house, and an alarm system installed. The wife said, She is right, let us take heed to her advice. So from every window and door in the house where they were living happily ever after they now saw the trees and sky through bars, and when the little boy's pet cat tried to climb in by the fanlight to keep him company in his little bed at night, as it customarily had done, it set off the alarm keening through the house.

The alarm was often answered—it seemed—by other burglar alarms, in other houses, that had been triggered by pet cats or nibbling mice. The alarms called to one another across the gardens in shrills and bleats and wails that everyone soon became accustomed to, so that the din roused the inhabitants of the suburb no more than the croak of frogs and musical grating of cicadas' legs. Under cover of the electronic harpies' discourse intruders sawed the iron bars and broke into homes, taking away hi-fi equipment, television sets, cassette players, cameras and radios, jewellery and clothing, and sometimes were hungry enough to devour everything in the refrigerator or paused audaciously to drink the whisky in the cabinets or patio bars. Insurance companies paid no compensation for single malt, a loss made keener by the property owner's knowledge that the thieves wouldn't even have been able to appreciate what it was they were drinking.

Then the time came when many of the people who were not trusted housemaids and gardeners hung about the suburb because they were unemployed. Some importuned for a job: weeding or painting a roof; anything, *baas*, madam. But the man and his wife remembered the warning about taking on anyone off the street. Some drank liquor and fouled the street with discarded bottles. Some begged, waiting for the man or his wife to drive the car out of the electronically-operated gates. They sat about with their feet in the gutters, under the jacaranda trees that made a green tunnel of the street—for it was a beautiful suburb, spoilt only by their presence—and sometimes they fell asleep lying right before the gates in the midday sun. The wife could never see anyone go hungry. She sent the trusted housemaid out with bread and tea, but the trusted housemaid said these were loafers and *tsotsis*,° who would come and tie her up and shut her in a cupboard. The husband said, She's right. Take heed of her advice. You only encourage them with your bread and tea. They are looking for their chance . . . And he brought the little boy's tricycle from the garden into the house every night, because if the house was surely secure, once locked and with the alarm set, someone might still be able to climb over the wall or the electronically-closed gates into the garden.

You are right, said the wife, then the wall should be higher. And the wise old witch, the husband's mother, paid for the extra bricks as her Christmas present to her son and his wife—the little boy got a Space Man outfit and a book of fairy tales.

But every week there were more reports of intrusion: in broad daylight and the dead of night, in the early hours of the morning, and even in the lovely summer twilight—a certain family was at dinner while the bedrooms were being ransacked upstairs. The man and his wife, talking of the latest armed robbery in the

---

tsotsis: Criminals.

suburb, were distracted by the sight of the little boy's pet cat effortlessly arriving over the seven-foot wall, descending first with a rapid bracing of extended forepaws down on the sheer vertical surface, and then a graceful launch, landing with swishing tail within the property. The whitewashed wall was marked with the cat's comings and goings; and on the street side of the wall there were larger red-earth smudges that could have been made by the kind of broken running shoes, seen on the feet of unemployed loiterers, that had no innocent destination.

When the man and wife and little boy took the pet dog for its walk round the neighbourhood streets they no longer paused to admire this show of roses or that perfect lawn; these were hidden behind an array of different varieties of security fences, walls and devices. The man, wife, little boy and dog passed a remarkable choice: there was the low-cost option of pieces of broken glass embedded in cement along the top of walls, there were iron grilles ending in lance-points, there were attempts at reconciling the aesthetics of prison architecture with the Spanish Villa style (spikes painted pink) and with the plaster urns of neoclassical façades (twelve-inch pikes finned like zigzags of lightning and painted pure white). Some walls had a small board affixed, giving the name and telephone number of the firm responsible for the installation of the devices. While the little boy and the pet dog raced ahead, the husband and wife found themselves comparing the possible effectiveness of each style against its appearance; and after several weeks when they paused before this barricade or that without needing to speak, both came out with the conclusion that only one was worth considering. It was the ugliest but the most honest in its suggestion of the pure concentration-camp style, no frills, all evident efficacy. Placed the length of walls, it consisted of a continuous coil of stiff and shining metal serrated into jagged blades, so that there would be no way of climbing over it and no way through its tunnel without getting entangled in its fangs. There would be no way out, only a struggle getting bloodier and bloodier, a deeper and sharper hooking and tearing of flesh. The wife shuddered to look at it. You're right, said the husband, anyone would think twice . . . And they took heed of the advice on a small board fixed to the wall: Consult DRAGON'S TEETH The People for Total Security.

Next day a gang of workmen came and stretched the razor-bladed coils all round the walls of the house where the husband and wife and little boy and pet dog and cat were living happily ever after. The sunlight flashed and slashed, off the serrations, the cornice of razor thorns encircled the home, shining. The husband said, Never mind. It will weather. The wife said, You're wrong. They guarantee it's rust-proof. And she waited until the little boy had run off to play before she said, I hope the cat will take heed . . . The husband said, Don't worry, my dear, cats always look before they leap. And it was true that from that day on the cat slept in the little boy's bed and kept to the garden, never risking a try at breaching security.

One evening, the mother read the little boy to sleep with a fairy story from the book the wise old witch had given him at Christmas. Next day he pretended to be the Prince who braves the terrible thicket of thorns to enter the palace and kiss the Sleeping Beauty back to life: he dragged a ladder to the wall, the shining coiled tunnel was just wide enough for his little body to creep in, and with the first fixing of its razor-teeth in his knees and hands and head he screamed and struggled deeper into its tangle. The trusted housemaid and the itinerant gardener, whose "day" it was, came running, the first to see and to scream with him, and the itinerant gardener tore his hands trying to get at the little boy. Then the man and his wife burst wildly into the garden and for some reason (the cat, probably) the alarm set up wailing against the screams while the bleeding mass of the little boy was hacked out of the security coil with saws, wire-cutters, choppers, and they carried it—the man, the wife, the hysterical trusted housemaid and the weeping gardener—into the house.

Reading and Reacting

1. How is the introduction—paragraphs 1 through 8—related thematically to the fairy tale the narrator tells?
2. In what respects is the story that begins with paragraph 9 of "Once upon a Time" similar to a fairy tale? In what respects is it different? Would the story be more or less effective without the narrator's introduction?
3. In paragraph 8, Gordimer characterizes the paragraphs that follow as a "bedtime story." How does her tale differ from your idea of a bedtime story?
4. The fairy tale's events are presented in strict chronological order. Give some examples of words and phrases that move readers from one time period to another. Why is chronological order so important?
5. Imagine Gordimer's fairy tale dramatized, perhaps as a television documentary. Where would you interrupt the story to provide commercial breaks or station identification? How would you present the introduction?
6. Throughout the fairy tale, various objects and events (and even specific warnings) foreshadow the grim ending. Give several examples of such hints, and explain how each anticipates the ending.
7. Which characters are in conflict in the fairy tale? Does the tale have a hero? A villain? What larger forces are in conflict? Are the conflicts between these forces resolved at the end? Explain.
8. What tendencies in her society do you think Gordimer means to criticize?
9. **JOURNAL ENTRY** "Once upon a Time" is set in South Africa. Could it have been set in the United States? Explain.
10. **CRITICAL PERSPECTIVE** In an interview conducted in the early 1980s, Gordimer spoke about her education and about the town in which she lived:

> When I got to university, it was through mixing with other people who were writing or painting that I got to know black people as equals. In a general and inclusive, nonracial way, I met people who lived in the world of ideas, in the world that interested me passionately.
>
> In the town where I lived, there was no mental food of this kind at all. I'm often amazed to think how they live, those people, and what an oppressed life it must be, because human beings must live in the world of ideas. This dimension in the human psyche is very important. It was there, but they didn't know how to express it. Conversation consisted of trivialities. For women, household matters, problems with children. The men would talk about golf or business or horseracing or whatever their practical interests were. Nobody ever talked about, or even around, the big things—life and death.

Focusing on Gordimer's characterization of the conversation in her town as consisting of "trivialities" rather than of "the big things," consider how her description of that town might apply to "Once upon a Time." How, for example, might the family's self-exclusion from what Gordimer calls "the world of ideas" have contributed to the story's tragic outcome?

Related Works: "The Rocking-Horse Winner" (p. 589), "Little Red Riding Hood" (p. 651), "Gretel in Darkness" (p. 839), "Cinderella" (p. 866), "The Chimney Sweeper" (p. 1127), *When I Was a Little Girl and My Mother Didn't Want Me* (p. 1266)

Source: ©Dorothy Alexander

STEPHEN DOBYNS (1941–) is a prolific writer in a variety of genres—poetry, novels, short stories, essays—whose work has been translated into ten languages. Dobyns was educated at Wayne State University, and he went on to earn an MFA from the University of Iowa. Of his twelve books of poetry and twenty novels, the most recent is *Mystery, So Long* (2005). His collection of short stories, *Eating Naked,* was published in 2000; his essays appear in *Best Words, Best Order* (1996). The recipient of numerous literary awards, Dobyns has taught at the University of Iowa, Boston University, Sarah Lawrence College, and Emerson College.

Cultural Context On "Black Tuesday"—October 29, 1929—the United States stock market crashed, triggering the Great Depression, the worst economic collapse in modern history. It is during this period that the key events in "Kansas" take place. With banks failing and businesses closing, more than fifteen million Americans (one-quarter of the workforce) were eventually unemployed. The economic disaster was soon paralleled by an agricultural one: attracted by the promise of rich, plentiful soil, thousands of farm families had moved from the North and East to Kansas as well as to Oklahoma, Texas, New Mexico, and Colorado. Farmers in this region plowed millions of acres of grassland; then, in the summer of 1931, the rains stopped. After a drought that lasted eight years, this area came to be called the "Dust Bowl."

Kansas (1999)

The boy hitchhiking on the back-country Kansas road was nineteen years old. He had been dropped there by a farmer in a Model T Ford who had turned off to the north. Then he waited for three hours. It was July and there were no clouds. The wheat fields were flat and went straight to the horizon. The boy had two plums and he ate them. A blue Plymouth coupe° went by with a man and a woman. They were laughing. The woman had blond hair and it was all loose and blew from the window. They didn't even see the boy. The strands of straw-colored hair seemed to be waving to him. Half an hour later a farmer stopped in a Ford pickup covered with a layer of

coupe: A two-door car, often one that seats only two people.

dust. The boy clambered into the front seat. The farmer took off again without glancing at him. A forty-five revolver lay next to the farmer's buttocks on the seat. Seeing it, the boy felt something electric go off inside of him. The revolver was old and there were rust spots on the barrel. Black electrician's tape was wrapped around the handle.

"You seen a woman and a man go by here in a Plymouth coupe?" asked the farmer. He pronounced it "koo-pay."

The boy said he had.

"How long ago?"

5 "About thirty minutes."

The farmer had light blue eyes and there was stubble on his chin. Perhaps he was forty, but to the boy he looked old. His skin was leather-colored from the sun. The farmer pressed his foot to the floor and the pickup roared. It was a dirt road and the boy had to hold his hands against the dashboard to keep from being bounced around. It was hot and both windows were open. There was grit in the boy's eyes and on his tongue. He kept glancing sideways at the revolver.

"They friends of yours?" asked the boy.

The farmer didn't look at him. "That's my wife," he said. "I'm going to put a bullet in her head." He put a hand to the revolver to make sure it was still there. "The man too," he added.

The boy didn't say anything. He was hitchhiking back to summer school from Oklahoma. He was the middle of three boys and the only one who had left home. He had already spent a year at the University of Oklahoma and was spending the summer at Lawrence. And there were other places, farther places. The boy played the piano. He intended to go to those farther places.

10 "What did they do?" the boy asked at last.

"You just guess," said the farmer.

The pickup was going about fifty miles per hour. The boy was afraid of seeing the dust cloud from the Plymouth up ahead, but there was only straight road. Then he was afraid that the Plymouth might have pulled off someplace. He touched his tongue to his upper lip but it was just one dry thing against another. Getting into the pickup, the boy had had a clear idea of the direction of his life. He meant to go to New York City at the end of summer. He meant to play the piano in Carnegie Hall.° The farmer and his forty-five seemed to stand between him and that future. They formed a wall that the boy was afraid to climb over.

"Do you have to kill them?" the boy asked. He didn't want to talk but he felt unable to remain silent.

The farmer had a red boil on the side of his neck and he kept touching it with two fingers. "When you have something wicked, what do you do?" asked the farmer.

15 The boy wanted to say he didn't know or he wanted to say he would call the police, but the farmer would have no patience with those answers. And the boy also wanted to say he would forgive the wickedness, but he was afraid of that answer as well. He was afraid of making the farmer angry and so he only shrugged.

"You stomp it out," said the farmer. "That's what you do — you stomp it out."

Carnegie Hall: A famous concert hall in New York City.

The boy stared straight ahead, searching for the dust cloud and hoping not to see it. The hot air seemed to bend in front of them. The boy was so frightened of seeing the dust cloud that he was sure he saw it. A little puff of gray getting closer. The pickup went straight down the middle of the road. There was no other traffic. Even if there had been other cars, the boy felt certain that the farmer wouldn't have moved out of the way. The wheat on either side of the road was coated with layers of dust, making it a reddish color, the color of dried blood.

"What about the police?" asked the boy.

"It's my wife," said the farmer. "It's my problem."

The boy never did see the dust cloud. They reached Lawrence and the boy got 20
out as soon as he could. His shirt was stuck to his back and he kept rubbing his palms on his dungarees. He thanked the farmer but the man didn't look at him, he just kept staring straight ahead.

"Don't tell the police," said the farmer. His hand rested lightly on the forty-five beside him on the seat.

"No," said the boy. "I promise." He slammed shut the dusty door of the pickup.

The boy didn't tell the police. For several days he didn't tell anyone at all. He looked at the newspapers twice a day for news of a killing, but he didn't find anything. More than the farmer's gun, he had been frightened by the strength of the farmer's resolve. It had been like a chunk of stone and compared to it the boy had felt as soft as a piece of white bread. The boy never knew what happened. Perhaps nothing had happened.

The summer wound to its conclusion. The boy went to New York. He never did play in Carnegie Hall. His piano playing never got good enough. The war came and went. He wasn't a boy any longer. He was a married man with two sons. The family moved to Michigan. The man was a teacher, then a minister. His own parents died. He told his sons the story about the farmer in the pickup. "What do you think happened?" they asked. Nobody knew. Perhaps the farmer caught up with them; perhaps he didn't. The man's sons went off to college and began their own lives. The man and his wife moved to New Hampshire. They grew old. Sixty years went by between that summer in Kansas and the present. The man entered his last illness. He stayed at home but he couldn't get out of bed. His wife gave him shots of morphine. He began to have dreams even when he was awake. The visiting nurse was always chipper. "Feeling better today?" she would ask. He tried to be polite, but he had no illusions. He went from one shot a day to two, and then three. The doctor said, "Give him as many as he needs." His wife started to ask about the danger of addiction, then she said nothing.

The man hardly knew when he was asleep or awake. He hardly knew if one day 25
had passed or many. He had oxygen. He didn't eat. The space between his eyes and the bedroom wall was always occupied with people of his invention, people of his past. He would lift his hand to wave them away, only to find his hand still lying motionless on the counterpane. Even music distracted him now. Always he was listening for something in the distance.

The boy was standing by the side of a dirt road. A Ford pickup stopped beside him and he got in. The farmer lifted a forty-five revolver. "I'm going to shoot my wife in the head."

"No," said the boy, "don't do it!"

The farmer drove fast. He had a red boil on the side of his neck and he kept touching it with two fingers. They found the Plymouth coupe pulled off into a hollow. There were shade trees and a brook. The farmer jammed down the brakes and the pickup slid sideways across the dirt. The man and woman were in the front seat of the Plymouth. Their clothes were half off. They jumped out of the car. The woman had big red breasts. The farmer jumped out with his forty-five. "No!" shouted the boy. The farmer shot the man in the head. His whole head exploded and he fell down in the dust. His head was just a broken thing on the ground. The woman covered her face and tried to cover her breasts as well. The farmer shot her as well. Bits of dust floated on the surface of her blood. "One last for me," said the farmer. He put the barrel of the gun in his mouth. "No, no!" cried the boy.

The boy was standing by the side of a dirt road. A Ford pickup stopped beside him and he got in. "I'm going to shoot my wife," said the farmer. He had a big revolver on the seat beside him.

30 "You can't," said the boy.

They talked all the way to Lawrence. The farmer was crying. "I've always been good to her," he said. He had a red boil on the side of his neck and he kept touching it.

"Give the gun to the police," said the boy.

"I'm afraid," said the farmer.

"You needn't be," said the boy. "The police won't hurt you."

35 They drove to the police station. The boy told the desk sergeant what had happened. The sergeant shook his head. He took the revolver away from the farmer. "We'll get her back, sir," he said. "Wife stealing's not permitted around here."

"I could have got in real trouble," said the farmer.

The boy was standing by the side of a dirt road. A pickup stopped beside him and he got in. The farmer said, "I'm going to kill my wife."

The boy was too frightened to say anything. He kept looking at the forty-five revolver. He was sure that he would be shot himself. He regretted not staying in Oklahoma, where he had friends and family. He couldn't imagine why he had moved away. The farmer drove straight to Lawrence. The boy was bounced all over the cab of the pickup but he didn't say anything. He was afraid that something would happen to his hands and he wouldn't be able to play the piano. It seemed to him that playing the piano was the only important thing in the entire world. The farmer had a red boil on the side of his neck and he kept touching it.

When they got to Lawrence, the boy jumped out of the pickup and ran. He saw a policeman and told him what had happened. An hour later he was getting a hamburger at a White Tower restaurant. He heard shooting. He ran out and saw the farmer's dusty pickup. There were police cars with their lights flashing. The boy pushed through the crowd. The farmer was hanging half out of the door of his pickup truck. There was blood all over the front of his workshirt. The forty-five revolver lay on the pavement. The policemen were clapping each other on the back. They had big grins. The boy began cracking his knuckles. They made snapping noises.

40 The boy was standing by the side of a dirt road. A pickup stopped beside him and he got in. The farmer pointed a forty-five revolver at his head. "Get in here," he said. They drove toward Lawrence.

"I'm going to shoot my wife for wickedness," said the farmer.

"No," said the boy, "you must forgive her."

"I'm going to kill her," said the farmer, "and her fancy man besides."

The boy said, "You can't take the law into your own hands."

The farmer raised his forty-five revolver. "They're as good as dead." He had a red boil on the side of his neck.

The boy was a college student. It was the Depression. He wanted to go to New York and become a classical pianist. He had already been accepted by Juilliard.° "Justice does not belong to you," said the boy.

"Wickedness must be punished," said the farmer.

They argued all the way to Lawrence. The boy stayed with the farmer. He could have jumped out of the pickup, but he didn't. The boy kept trying to convince him that he was wrong. The farmer drove to the train station.

The farmer's wife was in the waiting room with the man who had been driving the Plymouth coupe. She was very pretty, with blond hair and milky pink skin. She screamed when she saw the farmer. Her companion put his arms around her to protect her.

The boy hurried to stand between the woman and her husband. "Think of what you are doing," he said. "Think how you are throwing your life away." The first bullet struck him in the shoulder and whipped him around. He could see the woman open her mouth in a startled *Oh* of surprise. The second bullet caught him in the small of his back.

The man's family was with him in New Hampshire when he died: his wife and his two sons, neither of them young anymore. It was early evening in October at the very height of color. Even after sundown the maple trees seemed bright. The older son watched his father breathing. He kept twisting and trying to kick his feet. His face was very thin, his whole body was just a ridge under the middle of the sheet. He didn't talk anymore. He didn't want anyone to touch him. He seemed to be focusing his attention. He took a breath and they waited. He exhaled slowly. They continued to wait. He didn't breathe again. They waited several minutes. Then his wife removed the oxygen tubes from his nose, doing it quickly, as if afraid of doing something wrong.

The older son went back into the bedroom with the two men from the funeral home. They had a collapsible stretcher which they put next to the bed. They unrolled a dark blue body bag. They shifted the dead man onto the stretcher and wrestled him into the body bag, one at his feet, one at his head. The son stood in the doorway. The men from the funeral home muttered directions to each other. They were breathing heavily and their hair was mussed. At last they got him into the body bag. The son watched closely as the zipper was drawn up and across his father's face. It was a large silver zipper and the son watched it being pulled across his father's forehead. All the days after that he kept seeing its glittering progress, a picture repeating itself in his mind.

Juilliard: A highly respected school for the performing arts in New York City.

Reading and Reacting

1. Paragraph 1 presents the story's exposition. List the specific information this paragraph reveals. How will each detail be important later in the story? Are any details unnecessary? Are any important details *not* introduced in paragraph 1?
2. Summarize the story's plot in three sentences.
3. In paragraph 12, the narrator says, "Getting into the pickup, the boy had had a clear idea of the direction of his life. . . . The farmer and his forty-five seemed to stand between him and that future." What direction do you think the boy imagined his life would take? What direction did it actually take? Were "the farmer and his forty-five" in any way responsible for this change of direction? Explain.
4. How would the story be different without the presence of the revolver lying on the seat?
5. What specific information are readers told in the story's first twenty-five paragraphs about the boy? The farmer? The couple in the blue Plymouth? Is all this information essential to the story's plot? What additional information might you want to know? Why?
6. The first twenty-five paragraphs present the story's basic plot; then, this section of the story is followed by three alternate versions of the boy's experience, each beginning with the sentence "The boy was standing by the side of a dirt road." How are the three alternate versions of events similar to and different from the boy's story as it is first presented? Which version is most satisfying? Most logical? Most believable? Explain.
7. At the end of paragraph 25, as the boy (now a man) is dying, he is "listening for something in the distance." What do you suppose he might be listening for?
8. What does the last sentence add to the story?
9. **JOURNAL ENTRY** In paragraph 23, the narrator says, "The boy never knew what happened. Perhaps nothing had happened." What does he mean by this? What do you think really happened to the boy that day?
10. **CRITICAL PERSPECTIVE** In reviewing *Eating Naked*, the collection in which "Kansas" appeared, Roger Boylan says that Dobyns "almost gleefully imposes life's unpredictability on his characters." Boylan then goes on to give examples of the ways in which Dobyns "imposes life's unpredictability":

    > Cancer ends a life in one story; a car crash does so in another. A kidnapping goes ludicrously wrong. People betray each other. Lust overrides good sense. Absurdity rules. Marriages fall apart with depressing regularity—and if yours doesn't seem to be on the rocks, well, can you be sure you know what your better half's up to when you're away?

    Do you think "Kansas" fits the pattern Boylan has identified? Do you see it as a story in which "absurdity rules"?

Related Works: "I Stand Here Ironing" (p. 344), "A Good Man Is Hard to Find" (p. 447), "The Jilting of Granny Weatherall" (p. 763), "Do not go gentle into that good night" (p. 1046), "The Road Not Taken" (p. 1159), *Beauty* (p. 1270), *Tape* (p. 1275)

WILLIAM FAULKNER (1897–1962), winner of the 1949 Nobel Prize in Literature and the 1955 and 1963 Pulitzer Prizes for fiction, was a Southern writer whose work continues to transcend the regional label. His nineteen novels, notably *The Sound and the Fury* (1929), *As I Lay Dying* (1930), *Light in August* (1932), *Absalom, Absalom!* (1936), and *The Reivers* (1962), explore a wide range of human experience—from high comedy to tragedy—as seen in the life of one community, the fictional Yoknapatawpha County (modeled on the area around Faulkner's own hometown of Oxford, Mississippi). Faulkner's Yoknapatawpha stories—a fascinating blend of complex Latinate prose and primitive Southern dialect—paint an extraordinary portrait of a community bound together by ties of blood, by a shared belief in moral "verities," and by an old grief (the Civil War). Faulkner's grandfather raised "Billy" on Civil War tales and local legends, including many about the "Old Colonel," the writer's great-grandfather, who was a colorful Confederate officer. Although Faulkner's stories elegize the agrarian virtues of the Old South, they look unflinchingly at that world's tragic flaw: the "peculiar institution" of slavery.

Local legends and gossip frequently served as the spark for Faulkner's stories. As John B. Cullen, writing in *Old Times in Faulkner Country,* notes, "A Rose for Emily," Faulkner's first nationally published short story, was based on the tale of Oxford's aristocratic "Miss Mary" Neilson, who married Captain Jack Hume, the charming Yankee foreman of a street-paving crew, over her family's shocked protests. According to Cullen, one of Faulkner's neighbors said he created his story "out of fears and rumors"—the dire predictions of what *might* happen if Mary Neilson married her Yankee.

Cultural Context For many years, the pre–Civil War South was idealized as a land of prosperous plantations, large white houses, cultured and gracious people, and a stable economy based on farming. Central to the myth of the Old South was an adherence to the code of chivalry and a belief in the natural superiority of the white aristocracy, led by men who made their fortune by owning and running plantations that depended on slave labor. Once the South lost the Civil War, the idea of the Old South fell by the wayside, making room for the New South, which, like the North, was industrialized. In this story, Faulkner contrasts notions of the Old South and its decaying values with the newer ideas and innovations of the post-Reconstruction South.

A Rose for Emily (1930)

I

When Miss Emily Grierson died, our whole town went to her funeral: the men through a sort of respectful affection for a fallen monument, the women mostly out of curiosity to see the inside of her house, which no one save an old manservant—a combined gardener and cook—had seen in at least ten years.

It was a big, squarish frame house that had once been white, decorated with cupolas and spires and scrolled balconies in the heavily lightsome style of the seventies, set on what had once been our most select street. But garages and cotton gins had encroached and obliterated even the august names of that neighborhood; only Miss Emily's house was left, lifting its stubborn and coquettish decay above the cotton wagons and the gasoline pumps—an eyesore among eyesores. And now Miss Emily had gone to join the representatives of those august names where they lay in the cedar-bemused cemetery among the ranked and anonymous graves of Union and Confederate soldiers who fell at the battle of Jefferson.

Alive, Miss Emily had been a tradition, a duty, and a care; a sort of hereditary obligation upon the town, dating from that day in 1894 when Colonel Sartoris, the mayor—he who fathered the edict that no Negro woman should appear on the streets without an apron—remitted her taxes, the dispensation dating from the death of her father on into perpetuity. Not that Miss Emily would have accepted charity. Colonel Sartoris invented an involved tale to the effect that Miss Emily's father had loaned money to the town, which the town, as a matter of business, preferred this way of repaying. Only a man of Colonel Sartoris' generation and thought could have invented it, and only a woman could have believed it.

When the next generation, with its more modern ideas, became mayors and aldermen, this arrangement created some little dissatisfaction. On the first of the year they mailed her a tax notice. February came, and there was no reply. They wrote her a formal letter, asking her to call at the sheriff's office at her convenience. A week later the mayor wrote her himself, offering to call or to send his car for her, and received in reply a note on paper of an archaic shape, in a thin, flowing calligraphy in faded ink, to the effect that she no longer went out at all. The tax notice was also enclosed, without comment.

5 They called a special meeting of the Board of Aldermen. A deputation waited upon her, knocked at the door through which no visitor had passed since she ceased giving china-painting lessons eight or ten years earlier. They were admitted by the old Negro into a dim hall from which a stairway mounted into still more shadow. It smelled of dust and disuse—a close, dank smell. The Negro led them into the parlor. It was furnished in heavy, leather-covered furniture. When the Negro opened the blinds of one window, they could see that the leather was cracked; and when they sat down, a faint dust rose sluggishly about their thighs, spinning with slow motes in the single sun-ray. On a tarnished gilt easel before the fireplace stood a crayon portrait of Miss Emily's father.

They rose when she entered—a small, fat woman in black, with a thin gold chain descending to her waist and vanishing into her belt, leaning on an ebony cane with a tarnished gold head. Her skeleton was small and spare; perhaps that was why what would have been merely plumpness in another was obesity in her. She looked bloated, like a body long submerged in motionless water, and of that pallid hue. Her eyes, lost in the fatty ridges of her face, looked like two small pieces of coal pressed into a lump of dough as they moved from one face to another while the visitors stated their errand.

She did not ask them to sit. She just stood in the door and listened quietly until the spokesman came to a stumbling halt. Then they could hear the invisible watch ticking at the end of the gold chain.

Her voice was dry and cold. "I have no taxes in Jefferson. Colonel Sartoris explained it to me. Perhaps one of you can gain access to the city records and satisfy yourselves."

"But we have. We are the city authorities, Miss Emily. Didn't you get a notice from the sheriff, signed by him?"

"I received a paper, yes," Miss Emily said. "Perhaps he considers himself the 10
sheriff . . . I have no taxes in Jefferson."

"But there is nothing on the books to show that, you see. We must go by the—"

"See Colonel Sartoris. I have no taxes in Jefferson."

"But, Miss Emily—"

"See Colonel Sartoris." (Colonel Sartoris had been dead almost ten years.) "I have no taxes in Jefferson. Tobe!" The Negro appeared. "Show these gentlemen out."

II

So she vanquished them, horse and foot, just as she had vanquished their fathers 15
thirty years before about the smell. That was two years after her father's death and a short time after her sweetheart—the one we believed would marry her—had deserted her. After her father's death she went out very little; after her sweetheart went away, people hardly saw her at all. A few of the ladies had the temerity to call, but were not received, and the only sign of life about the place was the Negro man—a young man then—going in and out with a market basket.

"Just as if a man—any man—could keep a kitchen properly," the ladies said; so they were not surprised when the smell developed. It was another link between the gross, teeming world and the high and mighty Griersons.

A neighbor, a woman, complained to the mayor, Judge Stevens, eighty years old.

"But what will you have me do about it, madam?" he said.

"Why, send her word to stop it," the woman said. "Isn't there a law?"

"I'm sure that won't be necessary," Judge Stevens said. "It's probably just a snake 20
or a rat that nigger of hers killed in the yard. I'll speak to him about it."

The next day he received two more complaints, one from a man who came in diffident deprecation. "We really must do something about it, Judge. I'd be the last one in the world to bother Miss Emily, but we've got to do something." That night the Board of Aldermen met—three graybeards and one younger man, a member of the rising generation.

"It's simple enough," he said. "Send her word to have her place cleaned up. Give her a certain time to do it in, and if she don't . . ."

"Dammit, sir," Judge Stevens said, "will you accuse a lady to her face of smelling bad?"

So the next night, after midnight, four men crossed Miss Emily's lawn and slunk about the house like burglars, sniffing along the base of the brickwork and at the cellar openings while one of them performed a regular sowing motion with his hand out of a sack slung from his shoulder. They broke open the cellar door and sprinkled lime there, and in all the outbuildings. As they recrossed the lawn, a window that had been dark was lighted and Miss Emily sat in it, the light behind her, and her upright torso motionless as that of an idol. They crept quietly across the lawn and into the shadow of the locusts that lined the street. After a week or two the smell went away.

That was when people had begun to feel really sorry for her. People in our town, 25
remembering how old lady Wyatt, her great-aunt, had gone completely crazy at last, believed that the Griersons held themselves a little too high for what they really were.

None of the young men were quite good enough for Miss Emily and such. We had long thought of them as a tableau, Miss Emily a slender figure in white in the background, her father a spraddled silhouette in the foreground, his back to her and clutching a horsewhip, the two of them framed by the back-flung front door. So when she got to be thirty and was still single, we were not pleased exactly, but vindicated; even with insanity in the family she wouldn't have turned down all of her chances if they had really materialized.

When her father died, it got about that the house was all that was left to her; and in a way, people were glad. At last they could pity Miss Emily. Being left alone, and a pauper, she had become humanized. Now she too would know the old thrill and the old despair of a penny more or less.

The day after his death all the ladies prepared to call at the house and offer condolence and aid, as is our custom. Miss Emily met them at the door, dressed as usual and with no trace of grief on her face. She told them that her father was not dead. She did that for three days, with the ministers calling on her, and the doctors, trying to persuade her to let them dispose of the body. Just as they were about to resort to law and force, she broke down, and they buried her father quickly.

We did not say she was crazy then. We believed she had to do that. We remembered all the young men her father had driven away, and we knew that with nothing left, she would have to cling to that which had robbed her, as people will.

III

She was sick for a long time. When we saw her again, her hair was cut short, making her look like a girl, with a vague resemblance to those angels in colored church windows—sort of tragic and serene.

The town had just let the contracts for paving the sidewalks, and in the summer after her father's death they began the work. The construction company came with niggers and mules and machinery, and a foreman named Homer Barron, a Yankee—a big, dark, ready man, with a big voice and eyes lighter than his face. The little boys would follow in groups to hear him cuss the niggers, and the niggers singing in time to the rise and fall of picks. Pretty soon he knew everybody in town. Whenever you heard a lot of laughing anywhere about the square, Homer Barron would be in the center of the group. Presently we began to see him and Miss Emily on Sunday afternoons driving in the yellow-wheeled buggy and the matched team of bays from the livery stable.

At first we were glad that Miss Emily would have an interest, because the ladies all said, "Of course a Grierson would not think seriously of a Northerner, a day laborer." But there were still others, older people, who said that even grief could not cause a real lady to forget *noblesse oblige*°—without calling it *noblesse oblige*. They just said, "Poor Emily. Her kinsfolk should come to her." She had some kin in Alabama; but years ago her father had fallen out with them over the estate of old lady Wyatt, the crazy woman, and there was no communication between the two families. They had not even been represented at the funeral.

---

noblesse oblige: The obligation of those of high birth or rank to behave honorably.

And as soon as the old people said, "Poor Emily," the whispering began. "Do you suppose it's really so?" they said to one another. "Of course it is. What else could . . ." This behind their hands; rustling of craned silk and satin behind jalousies closed upon the sun of Sunday afternoon as the thin, swift clop-clop-clop of the matched team passed: "Poor Emily."

She carried her head high enough—even when we believed that she was fallen. It was as if she demanded more than ever the recognition of her dignity as the last Grierson; as if it had wanted that touch of earthiness to reaffirm her imperviousness. Like when she bought the rat poison, the arsenic. That was over a year after they had begun to say "Poor Emily," and while the two female cousins were visiting her.

"I want some poison," she said to the druggist. She was over thirty then, still a slight woman, though thinner than usual, with cold, haughty black eyes in a face the flesh of which was strained across the temples and about the eye-sockets as you imagine a lighthouse-keeper's face ought to look. "I want some poison," she said.

"Yes, Miss Emily. What kind? For rats and such? I'd recom—" 35

"I want the best you have. I don't care what kind."

The druggist named several. "They'll kill anything up to an elephant. But what you want is—"

"Arsenic," Miss Emily said. "Is that a good one?"

"Is . . . arsenic? Yes, ma'am. But what you want—"

"I want arsenic." 40

The druggist looked down at her. She looked back at him, erect, her face like a strained flag. "Why, of course," the druggist said. "If that's what you want. But the law requires you to tell what you are going to use it for."

Miss Emily just stared at him, her head tilted back in order to look him eye for eye, until he looked away and went and got the arsenic and wrapped it up. The Negro delivery boy brought her the package; the druggist didn't come back. When she opened the package at home there was written on the box, under the skull and bones: "For rats."

IV

So the next day we all said, "She will kill herself"; and we said it would be the best thing. When she had first begun to be seen with Homer Barron, we had said, "She will marry him." Then we said, "She will persuade him yet," because Homer himself had remarked—he liked men, and it was known that he drank with the younger men in the Elks' Club—that he was not a marrying man. Later we said, "Poor Emily" behind the jalousies as they passed on Sunday afternoon in the glittering buggy, Miss Emily with her head high and Homer Barron with his hat cocked and a cigar in his teeth, reins and whip in a yellow glove.

Then some of the ladies began to say that it was a disgrace to the town and a bad example to the young people. The men did not want to interfere, but at last the ladies forced the Baptist minister—Miss Emily's people were Episcopal—to call upon her. He would never divulge what happened during that interview, but he refused to go back again. The next Sunday they again drove about the streets, and the following day the minister's wife wrote to Miss Emily's relations in Alabama.

45 So she had blood-kin under her roof again and we sat back to watch developments. At first nothing happened. Then we were sure that they were to be married. We learned that Miss Emily had been to the jeweler's and ordered a man's toilet set in silver, with the letters H. B. on each piece. Two days later we learned that she had bought a complete outfit of men's clothing, including a nightshirt, and we said, "They are married." We were really glad. We were glad because the two female cousins were even more Grierson than Miss Emily had ever been.

So we were not surprised when Homer Barron—the streets had been finished some time since—was gone. We were a little disappointed that there was not a public blowing-off, but we believed that he had gone on to prepare for Miss Emily's coming, or to give her a chance to get rid of the cousins. (By that time it was a cabal, and we were all Miss Emily's allies to help circumvent the cousins.) Sure enough, after another week they departed. And, as we had expected all along, within three days Homer Barron was back in town. A neighbor saw the Negro man admit him at the kitchen door at dusk one evening.

And that was the last we saw of Homer Barron. And of Miss Emily for some time. The Negro man went in and out with the market basket, but the front door remained closed. Now and then we would see her at a window for a moment, as the men did that night when they sprinkled the lime, but for almost six months she did not appear on the streets. Then we knew that this was to be expected too; as if that quality of her father which had thwarted her woman's life so many times had been too virulent and too furious to die.

When we next saw Miss Emily, she had grown fat and her hair was turning gray. During the next few years it grew grayer and grayer until it attained an even pepper-and-salt iron-gray, when it ceased turning. Up to the day of her death at seventy-four it was still that vigorous iron-gray, like the hair of an active man.

From that time on her front door remained closed, save for a period of six or seven years, when she was about forty, during which she gave lessons in china-painting. She fitted up a studio in one of the downstairs rooms, where the daughters and granddaughters of Colonel Sartoris' contemporaries were sent to her with the same regularity and in the same spirit that they were sent to church on Sundays with a twenty-five-cent piece for the collection plate. Meanwhile her taxes had been remitted.

50 Then the newer generation became the backbone and the spirit of the town, and the painting pupils grew up and fell away and did not send their children to her with boxes of color and tedious brushes and pictures cut from the ladies' magazines. The front door closed upon the last one and remained closed for good. When the town got free postal delivery, Miss Emily alone refused to let them fasten the metal numbers above her door and attach a mailbox to it. She would not listen to them.

Daily, monthly, yearly we watched the Negro grow grayer and more stooped, going in and out with the market basket. Each December we sent her a tax notice, which would be returned by the post office a week later, unclaimed. Now and then we would see her in one of the downstairs windows—she had evidently shut up the top floor of the house—like the carven torso of an idol in a niche, looking or not looking at us, we could never tell which. Thus she passed from generation to generation—dear, inescapable, impervious, tranquil, and perverse.

And so she died. Fell ill in the house filled with dust and shadows, with only a doddering Negro man to wait on her. We did not even know she was sick; we had long since given up trying to get any information from the Negro. He talked to no one, probably not even to her, for his voice had grown harsh and rusty, as if from disuse.

She died in one of the downstairs rooms, in a heavy walnut bed with a curtain, her gray head propped on a pillow yellow and moldy with age and lack of sunlight.

V

The Negro met the first of the ladies at the front door and let them in, with their hushed, sibilant voices and their quick, curious glances, and then he disappeared. He walked right through the house and out the back and was not seen again.

The two female cousins came at once. They held the funeral on the second day, 55
with the town coming to look at Miss Emily beneath a mass of bought flowers, with the crayon face of her father musing profoundly above the bier and the ladies sibilant and macabre; and the very old men—some in their brushed Confederate uniforms—on the porch and the lawn, talking of Miss Emily as if she had been a contemporary of theirs, believing that they had danced with her and courted her perhaps, confusing time with its mathematical progression, as the old do, to whom all the past is not a diminishing road but, instead, a huge meadow which no winter ever quite touches, divided from them now by the narrow bottle-neck of the most recent decade of years.

Already we knew that there was one room in that region above stairs which no one had seen in forty years, and which would have to be forced. They waited until Miss Emily was decently in the ground before they opened it.

The violence of breaking down the door seemed to fill this room with pervading dust. A thin, acrid pall as of the tomb seemed to lie everywhere upon this room decked and furnished as for a bridal: upon the valance curtains of faded rose color, upon the rose-shaded lights, upon the dressing table, upon the delicate array of crystal and the man's toilet things backed with tarnished silver, silver so tarnished that the monogram was obscured. Among them lay collar and tie, as if they had just been removed, which, lifted, left upon the surface a pale crescent in the dust. Upon a chair hung the suit, carefully folded; beneath it the two mute shoes and the discarded socks.

The man himself lay in the bed.

For a long while we just stood there, looking down at the profound and fleshless grin. The body had apparently once lain in the attitude of an embrace, but now the long sleep that outlasts love, that conquers even the grimace of love, had cuckolded him. What was left of him, rotted beneath what was left of the nightshirt, had become inextricable from the bed in which he lay; and upon him and upon the pillow beside him lay that even coating of the patient and biding dust.

60 Then we noticed that in the second pillow was the indentation of a head. One of us lifted something from it, and leaning forward, that faint and invisible dust dry and acrid in the nostrils, we saw a long strand of iron-gray hair.

Reading and Reacting

1. Arrange these events in the sequence in which they actually occur: Homer's arrival in town, the aldermen's visit, Emily's purchase of poison, Colonel Sartoris's decision to remit Emily's taxes, the development of the odor around Emily's house, Emily's father's death, the arrival of Emily's relatives, Homer's disappearance. Then, list the events in the sequence in which they are introduced in the story. Why do you suppose Faulkner presents these events out of their actual chronological order?
2. Despite the story's confusing sequence, many events are foreshadowed. Give some examples of this technique. How does foreshadowing enrich the story?
3. Where does the exposition end and the movement toward the story's climax begin? Where does the resolution stage begin?
4. Emily is clearly the story's protagonist. In the sense that he opposes her wishes, Homer is the antagonist. What other characters—or what larger forces—are in conflict with Emily?
5. Explain how each of these phrases moves the story's plot along: "So she vanquished them, horse and foot . . ." (par. 15); "After a week or two the smell went away" (par. 24); "And that was the last we saw of Homer Barron" (par. 47); "And so she died" (par. 52); "The man himself lay in the bed" (par. 58).
6. The narrator of the story is an observer, not a participant. Who might this narrator be? Do you think the narrator is male or female? How do you suppose the narrator might know so much about Emily? Why do you think the narrator uses *we* instead of *I*?
7. The original version of "A Rose for Emily" included a two-page deathbed scene revealing that Tobe, Emily's servant, has shared her terrible secret all these years and that Emily has left her house to him. Why do you think Faulkner deleted this scene? Do you think he made the right decision?
8. Some critics have suggested that Miss Emily Grierson is a kind of symbol of the Old South, with its outdated ideas of chivalry, formal manners, and tradition. Do you see her also as a victim of those values? Explain.
9. **Journal Entry** When asked at a seminar at the University of Virginia about the meaning of the title "A Rose for Emily," Faulkner replied, "Oh, it's simply the poor woman had no life at all. Her father had kept her more or less locked up and then she had a lover who was about to quit her, she had to murder him. It was just 'A Rose for Emily'— that's all." In another interview, asked the same question, he replied, "I pitied her and this was a salute, just as if you were to make a gesture, a salute, to anyone; to a woman you would hand a rose, as you would lift a cup of *sake* to a man." What do you make of Faulkner's responses? What else might the title suggest?

10. **CRITICAL PERSPECTIVE** In his essay "William Faulkner: An American Dickens," literary critic Leslie A. Fiedler characterizes Faulkner as "primarily . . . a sentimental writer; not a writer with the occasional vice of sentimentality, but one whose basic mode of experience is sentimental." Fiedler continues, "In a writer whose very method is self-indulgence, that sentimentality becomes sometimes downright embarrassing." Fiedler also notes Faulkner's "excesses of maudlin feelings and absurd indulgences in overripe rhetoric."

    Do you think these criticisms apply to "A Rose for Emily"? If so, does the "vice of sentimentality" diminish the story, or do you agree with Fiedler—who calls Faulkner a "supereminently good 'bad' writer"—that the author is able to transcend these excesses?

Related Works: "Miss Brill" (p. 266), "Barn Burning" (p. 391), "Porphyria's Lover" (p. 860), "Richard Cory" (p. 1192), *Trifles* (p. 1319)

WRITING SUGGESTIONS: Plot

1. Write a sequel to "The Story of an Hour," telling the story in the voice of Brently Mallard. Use flashbacks to provide information about his view of the Mallards' marriage. Or, write a sequel to "Deportation at Breakfast," telling what happens in the days and weeks to come.
2. Locate a newspaper or magazine article that you find disturbing. Then, write a "once upon a time" story like Gordimer's in which you retell the story's events in a detached tone without adding analysis or commentary. Expand the original article by creating additional characters and adding invented settings.
3. "The Story of an Hour" includes a **deus ex machina,** an outside force or agent that suddenly appears to change the course of events. Consider the possible effects of a deus ex machina on the other stories in this chapter, including "Goner Pillow Company." What might this outside force be in each story? How might it change the story's action? How plausible would such a dramatic turn of events be in each case?
4. Both "Kansas" and Naguib Mahfouz's "Half a Day" (p. 733) manipulate time to create a dreamlike, disorienting atmosphere that affects both characters and readers. However, "Kansas" is essentially a realistic story while "Half a Day" is something quite different. Compare and contrast these two stories, focusing on how the passing of time affects the two protagonists and their perceptions of events.
5. Read the following article from the January 30, 1987, *Philadelphia Inquirer*. After listing some similarities and differences between the events in the article's story and those in "A Rose for Emily," write an essay in which you discuss how the presentation of events differs. Can you draw any conclusions about the differences between journalistic and fictional treatments of similar incidents?

DICK POTHIER AND THOMAS J. GIBBONS JR.

A Woman's Wintry Death Leads to a Long-Dead Friend

For more than two years, Frances Dawson Hamilton lived with the body of her long-time companion, draping his skeletonized remains with palm fronds and rosary beads.

Yesterday, the 70-year-old woman was found frozen to death in the home in the 4500 block of Higbee Street where she had lived all her life—the last year without heat or hot water. Her body was found by police accompanying a city social worker who came bearing an order to have her taken to a hospital.

Police investigators said the body of Bernard J. Kelly, 84, was found in an upstairs bedroom of the two-story brick home in the Wissinoming section, on the twin bed where he apparently died at least two years ago.

Two beds had been pushed together, and Hamilton apparently had been sleeping beside Kelly's remains since he died of unknown causes, police said.

Kelly's remains were clothed in long johns and socks, investigators said. The body was draped with rosary beads and palm fronds, and on the bed near his body were two boxes of Valentine's Day candy.

"It was basically a funeral—we've seen it before in such cases," said one investigator who was at the scene but declined to be identified.

Neighbors and investigators said Hamilton and Kelly had lived together in the house for at least 15 years. Several neighbors said Hamilton came from an affluent family, was educated in Europe, and lived on a trust fund until a year or so ago.

Last winter, said John Wasniewski, Hamilton's next-door neighbor, the basement of the home was flooded and the heater destroyed. "There was no heat in that house last winter or this winter," he said.

An autopsy will be performed on Hamilton today, but she apparently froze to death sometime since Monday, when a friend spoke to her on the telephone, investigators said.

Over the last two years, neighbors said, Hamilton had become increasingly reclusive and irrational. Just last week, a city social worker summoned by a friend arranged for a Philadelphia Gas Works team to visit the home and try to repair the furnace—but she refused to let them in.

The friend was James Phillips, 44, of Horsham, a salesman for Apex Electric in Souderton.

In October 1985, he said, Hamilton visited the Frankford Avenue electrical shop where he was then working, told him that she had an electrical problem in her house and had no lights, and asked whether he could help.

Phillips said he visited the house, fixed the problem and gave her some light bulbs.

"She was really paranoid," Phillips said. "She believed that all her problems were from people doing things to her. For some reason or other, she took to me."

Phillips said that he began visiting her, taking her shopping and doing some shopping for her. But, he said, he never saw the body on the second floor.

Hamilton told him there was a man up there. "I thought it was a story she was telling to protect herself," Phillips said.

He provided her with electric heaters and also contacted a caseworker with the city's Department of Human Services whom Phillips identified as Albert Zbik.

Between the two of them, he said, "we got her through last winter." Phillips said Zbik helped her obtain food stamps and Social Security assistance.

When the snowstorm hit last week, Phillips became concerned because he knew Hamilton would have trouble getting food. On Saturday, he took her a plate of hot food and bought more food from a local store.

On Monday, she telephoned him. "I didn't like the way she sounded," he said. He called Zbik and told him he felt it was time that they forced her to go to a hospital.

Phillips said Zbik went to her home yesterday, carrying a form authorizing an involuntary admission to a hospital for observation or required medical treatment.

Phillips told police that he was never allowed above the first floor and was often told by Hamilton that "Bernie is not feeling well today."

Neighbors and police investigators said Kelly was last seen alive about two years ago, and appeared to be quite ill at the time.

"As recently as last month, I asked Frances how Bernard was and whether she should get a doctor, and she said it wasn't necessary. She said 'He's sick, but I'm taking care of him—I'm feeding him with an eyedropper,'" Wasniewski said.

"I told her in December that if he was that sick, she should call a doctor, but she'd say she was taking care of him very well," Wasniewski said.

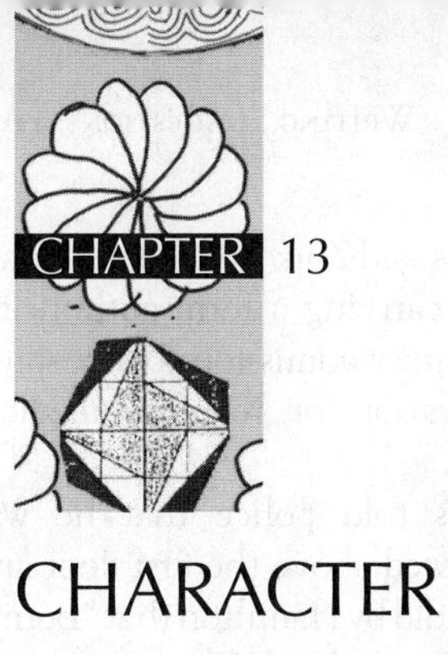

CHAPTER 13

CHARACTER

A **character** is a fictional representation of a person — usually (but not necessarily) a psychologically realistic depiction. Writers may develop characters through their actions, through their reactions to situations or to other characters, through their physical appearance, through their speech and gestures and expressions, and even through their names.

Generally speaking, characters' personality traits, as well as their appearances and their feelings and beliefs, are communicated to readers in two ways. First, readers can be *told* about characters. Third-person narrators can provide information about what characters are doing, saying, and thinking; what experiences they have had; what they look like; how they are dressed; and so on. Sometimes narrators also offer analysis of and judgments about a character's behavior or motivation. Similarly, first-person narrators can tell us about themselves or about other characters. Thus, Sammy in John Updike's "A&P" (p. 259) tells readers what he thinks about his job and about the girls who come into the supermarket where he works. He also tells us what various characters look like and describes their actions, attitudes, speech, and gestures. (For more information about first-person narrators, see Chapter 15, "Point of View.")

Alternatively, aspects of a character's personality and beliefs may be revealed through his or her actions, dialogue, or thoughts. For instance, Sammy's vivid fantasies and his disapproval of his customers' lives suggest to readers that he is something of a nonconformist; however, Sammy himself does not actually tell us this.

Round and Flat Characters

In his influential 1927 work *Aspects of the Novel,* English novelist E. M. Forster classifies characters as either **round** (well developed, closely involved in and responsive to the action) or **flat** (barely developed or stereotypical). To a great extent, these categories are still useful. In an effective story, the major characters are usually complex and fully developed; if they are not, readers will not care what happens to them. Sometimes readers are encouraged to become involved with the characters, even to identify with them, and this empathy is possible only when we know something about the characters — their strengths and weaknesses, their likes and dislikes. In some cases, of course, a story can be effective even when its central characters are not well developed. Sometimes, in fact, a story's effectiveness is enhanced by an *absence* of character development, as in Shirley Jackson's "The Lottery" (p. 509).

Readers often expect characters to behave as "real people" in their situation might behave. Real people are not perfect, and realistic characters cannot be perfect either. The flaws that are revealed as round characters are developed—greed, gullibility, naïveté, shyness, a quick temper, or a lack of insight or judgment or tolerance or even intelligence—make them believable. In modern fiction, the protagonist is seldom if ever the noble "hero"; more often, he or she is at least partly a victim, someone to whom unpleasant things happen and someone who is sometimes ill equipped to cope with events.

Unlike major characters, minor characters are frequently not well developed. Often they are flat, perhaps acting as *foils* for the protagonist. A **foil** is a supporting character whose role in the story is to highlight a major character by presenting a contrast with him or her. For instance, in "A&P," Stokesie, another young checkout clerk, is a foil for Sammy. Because he is a little older than Sammy and seems to have none of Sammy's imagination, restlessness, or nonconformity, Stokesie suggests what Sammy might become if he were to continue to work at the A&P. Some flat characters are **stock characters,** easily identifiable types who behave so predictably that readers can readily recognize them. The kindly old priest, the tough young bully, the ruthless business executive, and the reckless adventurer are all stock characters. Some flat characters can even be **caricatures,** characterized by a single dominant trait, such as miserliness, or even by one physical trait, such as nearsightedness.

 Dynamic and Static Characters

Characters may also be classified as either *dynamic* or *static*. A **dynamic character** grows and changes in the course of a story, developing as he or she reacts to events and to other characters. In "A&P," for instance, Sammy's decision to speak out in defense of the girls—as well as the events that lead him to do so—changes him. His view of the world has changed at the end of the story, and as a result his position in the world may change too. A **static character** may face the same challenges a dynamic character might face but will remain essentially unchanged: a static character who was selfish and arrogant will remain selfish and arrogant, regardless of the nature of the story's conflict. In the fairy tale "Cinderella," for example, the title character is as sweet and good-natured at the end of the story—despite her mistreatment by her family—as she is at the beginning. Her situation may have changed, but her character has not.

Whereas round characters tend to be dynamic, flat characters tend to be static. But even a very complex, well-developed major character may be static; sometimes, in fact, the point of a story may hinge on a character's inability to change. A familiar example is the title character in William Faulkner's "A Rose for Emily" (p. 243), who lives a wasted, empty life, at least in part because she is unwilling or unable to accept that the world around her and the people in it have changed.

A story's minor characters are often static; their growth is not usually relevant to the story's development. Moreover, we usually do not learn enough about a minor character's traits, thoughts, actions, or motivation to determine whether the character changes significantly.

Motivation

Because round characters are complex, they are not always easy to understand. They may act unpredictably, just as real people do. They wrestle with decisions, resist or succumb to temptation, make mistakes, ask questions, search for answers, hope and dream, rejoice and despair. What is important is not whether we approve of a character's actions but whether those actions are *plausible*—whether the actions make sense in light of what we know about the character. We need to understand a character's **motivation**— the reasons behind his or her behavior— or we will not believe or accept that behavior. For instance, given Sammy's age, his dissatisfaction with his job, and his desire to impress the young woman he calls Queenie, the decision he makes at the end of the story is perfectly plausible. Without having established his motivation, Updike could not have expected readers to accept Sammy's actions.

Of course, even when readers get to know a character, they still are not able to predict how a complex, round character will behave in a given situation; only a flat character is predictable. The tension that develops as readers wait to see how a character will act or react, and thus how a story's conflict will be resolved, is what holds readers' interest and keeps them involved as a story's action unfolds.

✔ CHECKLIST Writing about Character

- Who is the story's main character? Who are the other major characters?
- Who are the minor characters? What roles do they play in the story? How would the story be different without them?
- What do the major characters look like? Is their physical appearance important?
- What are the major characters' most notable? personality traits?
- What are the major characters' likes and dislikes? Their strengths and weaknesses?
- What are the main character's most strongly held feelings and beliefs?
- What are we told about the major characters' backgrounds and prior experiences? What can we infer?
- Are the characters round or flat?
- Are the characters dynamic or static?
- Does the story include any stock characters? Does any character serve as a foil?
- Do the characters act in a way that is consistent with how readers expect them to act?
- With which characters are readers likely to be most sympathetic? Least sympathetic?

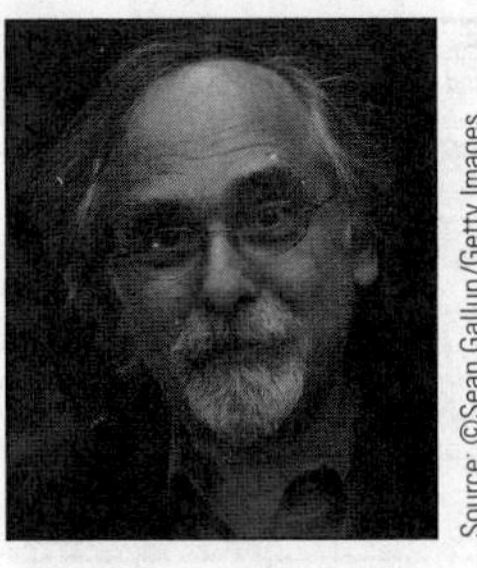
Source: ©Sean Gallup/Getty Images

ART SPIEGELMAN (1948–), born in Stockholm, Sweden, was raised in Queens, New York. He is arguably one of the most influential comic artists of the underground movement, which began (thanks in large part to R. Crumb) in the 1960s. In collaboration with his wife, Spiegelman founded the comics magazine *RAW* in 1980, and his comics have been featured in such publications as the *New Yorker,* the *New York Times,* and the *Village Voice.* His two-part masterpiece, the Pulitzer Prize–winning *Maus* (1986) and *Maus II* (1991), are based on his parents' struggle for survival during the Holocaust. Collections of his work include *In the Shadow of No Towers* (2004), one of the *New York Times Book Review*'s 100 Notable Books of 2004.

Cultural Context The young narrator of "Eye Ball" suffers from amblyopia, or "lazy eye," the most common cause of impaired vision in children. When one eye develops slowly or improperly, the stronger eye overcompensates, creating the kind of distorted vision depicted in this story. Amblyopia often develops in children before age seven, and early treatment (in the form of an eye patch or other device to help the brain relearn to use the weaker eye) is crucial to correct the problem.

Eye Ball (2006)

This graphic story starts on the next page.

Reading and Reacting

1. According to the narrator of "Eye Ball" (p. 258), what are the major traits cartoonists must possess? How are these traits in conflict with the characteristics of a typical "boy in 1950s America"?

2. This graphic story is limited to two settings, the ballfield and the library. Are these two settings sufficient to illustrate the narrator's major problem, or would other settings be helpful?

3. The last panel alludes to Franz Kafka's "The Metamorphosis," a novella in which an alienated office worker turns overnight into a large bug. What do you think the narrator means by his final comment?

4. **JOURNAL ENTRY** The action in this graphic story is largely propelled forward by narrative. Write a sentence or two of dialogue for each panel that lacks it.

5. **CRITICAL PERSPECTIVE** In a 2006 interview with the *Nation*, Art Spiegelman states:

> Cartoons have a kind of acidic potency for clarifying a situation because they're reductive. It also seems to me that cartoons are defamatory by nature. . . . If anything, I think the cartoons have gotten too damn polite in America over the last decades. The cartoons have to be gag cartoons instead of emblematizations and essentializations of situations, which is what they used to be. When one manages to do that, it usually gets someone upset.

Do you think "Eye Ball" is "too damn polite," or do you think it is "defamatory by nature"? Explain your answer.

Related Works: "A&P" (p. 259), "Cathedral" (p. 526), "Two Questions" (p. 556), "Teenage Wasteland" (p. 785)

EYE BALL
Forged in a crucible of humiliation and trauma, cartoonists are made, not born...
STRIKE ONE!
The young misfit must escape into fantasy and/or develop a rarefied sense of humor to survive.
For a boy in 1950s America, baseball was not optional...
STRIKE TWO!
YER OUT, FAGGOT!
...and to be inept assured a place in the social hierarchy even lower than a girl's.
I was inevitably relegated to right field, far out of harm's way.
Boredom undercut my anxiety that a ball might come at me...
So I often kept some comic book handy!
Any comic would do, except those 3-D comics,
WHAT'S SO GREAT ABOUT SEEING PANELS IN RED?!
...since I'm virtually blind in my left eye.
Amblyopia, a "lazy eye," made my whole world 2-D...
SPASTIC!
RETARD!
DOOFUS!
...so confusing 2-D comics with reality seems natural to me!
I started hiding in the library after school to avoid further ignominy...
JEEZ! HE TURNS INTO A GIANT BUG! THIS IS COOLER THAN THE TWILIGHT ZONE!
and learned that Kafka probably sucked at baseball too...
art spiegelman

Source: ©AP Photo/Reading Eagle/Times, Bill Uhrich

JOHN UPDIKE (1932–) is a prolific writer of novels, short stories, essays, poems, plays, and children's tales. Updike's earliest ambition was to be a cartoonist for the *New Yorker*. He attended Harvard hoping to draw cartoons for the *Harvard Lampoon*, studied drawing and fine art at Oxford, and in 1955 went to work for the *New Yorker*—not as a cartoonist but as a "Talk of the Town" reporter. Updike left the *New Yorker* after three years to write full-time but (over forty years later) is still contributing stories, reviews, and essays to the magazine. Among his novels are *Rabbit, Run* (1960), *The Centaur* (1963), *Rabbit Redux* (1971), *Rabbit Is Rich* (1981), *The Witches of Eastwick* (1985), and *Rabbit at Rest* (1990). His most recent novels are *Seek My Face* (2002), *Villages* (2004), *Of the Farm* (2004), and *Terrorist* (2006). Updike has also published *Collected Poems 1953–1993* (1993) and three collections of essays, including, most recently, *Due Considerations* (2007). In 1998, Updike received the National Book Foundation Medal for Distinguished Contribution to American Letters.

In early stories such as "A&P" (1961), Updike draws on memories of his childhood and teenage years for the sort of "small" scenes and stories for which he quickly became famous. "There is a great deal to be said about almost anything," Updike comments in an interview in *Contemporary Authors*. "All people can be equally interesting. . . . Now either nobody is a hero or everybody is. I vote for everybody. My subject is the American Protestant small-town middle class. I like middles. It is in middles that extremes clash."

Cultural Context The 1950s were a decade of prosperity for the United States. Soldiers returned from World War II, women who had worked in defense plants returned to their homes, and the population soared as a result of a "baby boom." Part of this prosperity manifested itself materially: Americans tried to keep up with one another in terms of their possessions, and manufacturers raced to produce the latest consumer goods. Conformity became the norm, with the advent of mass-produced suburban tract houses and a conservative code of dress and behavior that dictated what was appropriate. This atmosphere is the context for the manager's disapproval in "A&P"—and Sammy's reaction foreshadows the mood of the rebellious generation to come, which would refuse to conform.

A&P (1961)

In walks these three girls in nothing but bathing suits. I'm in the third check-out slot, with my back to the door, so I don't see them until they're over by the bread. The one that caught my eye first was the one in the plaid green two-piece. She was a chunky kid, with a good tan and a sweet broad soft-looking can with those two crescents of white just under it, where the sun never seems to hit, at the top of the backs of her legs. I stood there with my hand on a box of HiHo crackers trying to remember if I rang it up or not. I ring it up again and the customer starts giving me hell. She's one of these cash-register-watchers, a witch about fifty with rouge on her cheekbones and no eyebrows, and I know it made her day to trip me up. She'd been watching cash registers for fifty years and probably never seen a mistake before.

By the time I got her feathers smoothed and her goodies into a bag—she gives me a little snort in passing, if she'd been born at the right time they would have burned her over in Salem—by the time I get her on her way the girls had circled around the bread and were coming back, without a push-cart, back my way along the counters, in the aisle between the check-outs and the Special bins. They didn't even have shoes on. There was this chunky one, with the two-piece—it was bright green and the seams on the bra were still sharp and her belly was still pretty pale so I guessed she just got it (the suit)—there was this one, with one of those chubby berry-faces, the lips all bunched together under her nose, this one, and a tall one, with black hair that hadn't quite frizzed right, and one of these sunburns right across under the eyes, and a chin that was too long—you know, the kind of girl other girls think is very "striking" and "attractive" but never quite makes it, as they very well know, which is why they like her so much—and then the third one, that wasn't quite so tall. She was the queen. She kind of led them, the other two peeking around and making their shoulders round. She didn't look around, not this queen, she just walked straight on slowly, on these long white prima-donna legs. She came down a little hard on her heels, as if she didn't walk in her bare feet that much, putting down her heels and then letting the weight move along to her toes as if she was testing the floor with every step, putting a little deliberate extra action into it. You never know for sure how girls' minds work (do you really think it's a mind in there or just a little buzz like a bee in a glass jar?) but you got the idea she had talked the other two into coming in here with her, and now she was showing them how to do it, walk slow and hold yourself straight.

She had on a kind of dirty-pink—beige maybe, I don't know—bathing suit with a little nubble all over it and, what got me, the straps were down. They were off her shoulders looped loose around the cool tops of her arms, and I guess as a result the suit had slipped a little on her, so all around the top of the cloth there was this shining rim. If it hadn't been there you wouldn't have known there could have been anything whiter than those shoulders. With the straps pushed off, there was nothing between the top of the suit and the top of her head except just *her*, this clean bare plane of the top of her chest down from the shoulder bones like a dented sheet of metal tilted in the light. I mean, it was more than pretty.

She had sort of oaky hair that the sun and salt had bleached, done up in a bun that was unravelling, and a kind of prim face. Walking into the A&P with your straps down, I suppose it's the only kind of face you *can* have. She held her head so high her neck, coming up out of those white shoulders, looked kind of stretched, but I didn't mind. The longer her neck was, the more of her there was.

5 She must have felt in the corner of her eye me and over my shoulder Stokesie in the second slot watching, but she didn't tip. Not this queen. She kept her eyes moving across the racks, and stopped, and turned so slow it made my stomach rub the inside of my apron, and buzzed to the other two, who kind of huddled against her for relief, and they all three of them went up the cat-and-dog-food-breakfast-cereal-macaroni-rice-raisins-seasonings-spreads-spaghetti-soft-drinks-crackers-and-cookies aisle. From the third slot I look straight up this aisle to the meat counter, and I watched them all the way. The fat one with the tan sort of fumbled with the cookies, but on

second thought she put the packages back. The sheep pushing their carts down the aisle — the girls were walking against the usual traffic (not that we have one-way signs or anything)— were pretty hilarious. You could see them, when Queenie's white shoulders dawned on them, kind of jerk, or hop, or hiccup, but their eyes snapped back to their own baskets and on they pushed. I bet you could set off dynamite in an A&P and the people would by and large keep reaching and checking oatmeal off their lists and muttering "Let me see, there was a third thing, began with A, asparagus, no, ah, yes, applesauce!" or whatever it is they do mutter. But there was no doubt, this jiggled them. A few houseslaves in pin curlers even looked around after pushing their carts past to make sure what they had seen was correct.

You know, it's one thing to have a girl in a bathing suit down on the beach, where what with the glare nobody can look at each other much anyway, and another thing in the cool of the A&P, under the fluorescent lights, against all those stacked packages, with her feet paddling along naked over our checkerboard green-and-cream rubber-tile floor.

"Oh Daddy," Stokesie said beside me. "I feel so faint."

"Darling," I said. "Hold me tight." Stokesie's married, with two babies chalked up on his fuselage already, but as far as I can tell that's the only difference. He's twenty-two, and I was nineteen this April.

"Is it done?" he asks, the responsible married man finding his voice. I forgot to say he thinks he's going to be manager some sunny day, maybe in 1990 when it's called the Great Alexandrov and Petrooshki Tea Company or something.

What he meant was, our town is five miles from a beach, with a big summer 10
colony out on the Point, but we're right in the middle of town, and the women generally put on a shirt or shorts or something before they get out of the car into the street. And anyway these are usually women with six children and varicose veins mapping their legs and nobody, including them, could care less. As I say, we're right in the middle of town, and if you stand at our front doors you can see two banks and the Congregational church and the newspaper store and three real-estate offices and about twenty-seven old freeloaders tearing up Central Street because the sewer broke again. It's not as if we're on the Cape; we're north of Boston and there's people in this town haven't seen the ocean for twenty years.

The girls had reached the meat counter and were asking McMahon something. He pointed, they pointed, and they shuffled out of sight behind a pyramid of Diet Delight peaches. All that was left for us to see was old McMahon patting his mouth and looking after them sizing up their joints. Poor kids, I began to feel sorry for them, they couldn't help it.

Now here comes the sad part of the story, at least my family says it's sad but I don't think it's sad myself. The store's pretty empty, it being Thursday afternoon, so there was nothing much to do except lean on the register and wait for the girls to show up again. The whole store was like a pinball machine and I didn't know which tunnel they'd come out of. After a while they come around out of the far aisle, around the light bulbs, records at discount of the Caribbean Six or Tony Martin Sings or some such gunk you wonder they waste the wax on, sixpacks of candy bars, and plastic toys done up in cellophane that fall apart when a kid looks at them anyway. Around they come, Queenie still leading the way, and holding a little gray jar in her hand. Slots Three through Seven are unmanned and I could see her wondering between Stokes and me, but Stokesie with his usual luck draws an old party in baggy gray pants who stumbles up with four giant cans of pineapple juice (what do these bums *do* with all that pineapple juice? I've often asked myself) so the girls come to me. Queenie puts down the jar and I take it into my fingers icy cold. Kingfish Fancy Herring Snacks in Pure Sour Cream: 49. Now her hands are empty, not a ring or a bracelet, bare as God made them, and I wonder where the money's coming from. Still with that prim look she lifts a folded dollar bill out of the hollow at the center of her nubbled pink top. The jar went heavy in my hand. Really, I thought that was so cute.

Then everybody's luck begins to run out. Lengel comes in from haggling with a truck full of cabbages on the lot and is about to scuttle into that door marked MANAGER behind which he hides all day when the girls touch his eye. Lengel's pretty dreary, teaches Sunday school and the rest, but he doesn't miss that much. He comes over and says, "Girls, this isn't the beach."

Queenie blushes, though maybe it's just a brush of sunburn I was noticing for the first time, now that she was so close. "My mother asked me to pick up a jar of herring snacks." Her voice kind of startled me, the way voices do when you see the people first, coming out so flat and dumb yet kind of tony, too, the way it ticked over "pick up" and "snacks." All of a sudden I slid right down her voice into her living room. Her father and the other men were standing around in ice-cream coats and bow ties and the women were in sandals picking up herring snacks on toothpicks off a big plate and they were all holding drinks the color of water with olives and sprigs of mint in them. When my parents have somebody over they get lemonade and if it's a real racy affair Schlitz in tall glasses with "They'll Do It Every Time" cartoons stencilled on.

15 "That's all right," Lengel said. "But this isn't the beach." His repeating this struck me as funny, as if it had just occurred to him, and he had been thinking all these years the A&P was a great big dune and he was the head lifeguard. He didn't like my smiling—as I say he doesn't miss much—but he concentrates on giving the girls that sad Sunday-school-superintendent stare.

Queenie's blush is no sunburn now, and the plump one in plaid, that I liked better from the back—a really sweet can—pipes up, "We weren't doing any shopping. We just came in for the one thing."

"That makes no difference," Lengel tells her, and I could see from the way his eyes went that he hadn't noticed she was wearing a two-piece before. "We want you decently dressed when you come in here."

"We *are* decent," Queenie says suddenly, her lower lip pushing, getting sore now that she remembers her place, a place from which the crowd that runs the A&P must look pretty crummy. Fancy Herring Snacks flashed in her very blue eyes.

"Girls, I don't want to argue with you. After this come in here with your shoulders covered. It's our policy." He turns his back. That's policy for you. Policy is what the kingpins want. What the others want is juvenile delinquency.

All this while, the customers had been showing up with their carts but, you know, sheep, seeing a scene, they had all bunched up on Stokesie, who shook open a paper bag as gently as peeling a peach, not wanting to miss a word. I could feel in the silence everybody getting nervous, most of all Lengel, who asks me, "Sammy, have you rung up this purchase?" 20

I thought and said "No" but it wasn't about that I was thinking. I go through the punches, 4, 9, GROC, TOT—it's more complicated than you think, and after you do it often enough, it begins to make a little song, that you hear words to, in my case "Hello *(bing)* there, you *(gung)* hap-py *pee*-pul *(splat)*!"—the *splat* being the drawer flying out. I uncrease the bill, tenderly as you may imagine, it just having come from between the two smoothest scoops of vanilla I had ever known were there, and pass a half and a penny into her narrow pink palm, and nestle the herrings in a bag and twist its neck and hand it over, all the time thinking.

The girls, and who'd blame them, are in a hurry to get out, so I say "I quit" to Lengel quick enough for them to hear, hoping they'll stop and watch me, their unsuspected hero. They keep right on going, into the electric eye; the door flies open and they flicker across the lot to their car, Queenie and Plaid and Big Tall Goony-Goony (not that as raw material she was so bad), leaving me with Lengel and a kink in his eyebrow.

"Did you say something, Sammy?"

"I said I quit."

"I thought you did." 25

"You didn't have to embarrass them."

"It was they who were embarrassing us."

I started to say something that came out "Fiddle-de-doo." It's a saying of my grandmother's, and I know she would have been pleased.

"I don't think you know what you're saying," Lengel said.

"I know you don't," I said. "But I do." I pull the bow at the back of my apron and 30 start shrugging it off my shoulders. A couple customers that had been heading for my slot begin to knock against each other, like scared pigs in a chute.

Lengel sighs and begins to look very patient and old and gray. He's been a friend of my parents for years. "Sammy, you don't want to do this to your Mom and Dad," he tells me. It's true, I don't. But it seems to me that once you begin a gesture it's fatal not to go through with it. I fold the apron, "Sammy" stitched in red on the pocket, and put it on the counter, and drop the bow tie on top of it. The bow tie is theirs, if you've ever wondered. "You'll feel this for the rest of your life," Lengel says, and I know that's true, too, but remembering how he made that pretty girl blush makes me so scrunchy inside I punch the No Sale tab and the machine whirs "pee-pul" and the drawer splats out. One advantage to this scene taking place in summer, I can follow this up with a clean exit, there's no fumbling around getting your coat and galoshes, I just saunter into the electric eye in my white shirt that my mother ironed the night before, and the door heaves itself open, and outside the sunshine is skating around the asphalt.

I look around for my girls, but they're gone, of course. There wasn't anybody but some young married screaming with her children about some candy they didn't get by the door of a powder-blue Falcon station wagon. Looking back in the big windows, over the bags of peat moss and aluminum lawn furniture stacked on the pavement, I could see Lengel in my place in the slot, checking the sheep through. His face was dark gray and his back stiff, as if he'd just had an injection of iron, and my stomach kind of fell as I felt how hard the world was going to be to me hereafter.

Reading and Reacting

1. Summarize the information Sammy gives readers about his tastes and background. Why is this exposition vital to the story's development?
2. List some of the most obvious physical characteristics of the A&P's customers. How do these characteristics make them foils for Queenie and her friends?
3. What is it about Queenie and her friends that appeals to Sammy?
4. Is Queenie a stock character? Explain.
5. What rules and conventions are customers expected to follow in a supermarket? How does the behavior of Queenie and her friends violate these rules?
6. Is the supermarket setting vital to the story? Could the story have been set in a car wash? In a fast-food restaurant? In a business office?
7. How accurate are Sammy's judgments about the other characters? How might the characters be portrayed if the story were told by Lengel?
8. Given what you learn about Sammy during the course of the story, what do you see as his *primary* motivation for quitting his job? What other factors motivate him?
9. **JOURNAL ENTRY** Where do you think Sammy will find himself in ten years? Why?
10. **CRITICAL PERSPECTIVE** In her 1976 book *The Necessary Blackness*, critic Mary Allen observes, "Updike's most tender reverence is reserved for women's bodies. The elegant style with which he describes female anatomy often becomes overwrought, as his descriptions do generally. But it always conveys wonder."

    In what passages in "A&P" does Updike (through Sammy) convey this sense of wonder? Do you think today's audience, reading the story nearly fifty years after Updike wrote it, and more than thirty years after Allen's essay was published, would still see such passages as conveying "tender reverence"? Or do you think readers might now see Sammy (and, indeed, Updike) as sexist? How do you react to these passages?

Related Works: "Deportation at Breakfast" (p. 229), "Araby" (p. 434), "Please Fire Me" (p. 858), "Ex-Basketball Player" (p. 930), "A Supermarket in California" (p. 952), "The Road Not Taken" (p. 1159), *The Glass Menagerie* (p. 1961)

Fiction in Film: John Updike's "A&P"

Character is central to "A&P," and the DVD version of the story characterizes Sammy, Stokesie, Lengel, and Queenie and her friends visually as well as through their dialogue and actions. The supermarket setting—so vividly described in the story—also comes to life on the screen. The stills included here depict scenes that appear on the DVD.

Sammy at the cash register with a customer.
Source: ©Steven Payne/Worn Path Productions

Queenie and her friends.
Source: ©Steven Payne/Worn Path Productions

Reading and Reacting

1. If you were making a film of "A&P," which scenes from the story would you consider essential? Which might you omit? Why?
2. Which minor characters would you include? Why?
3. Would you depict on screen any characters who are not described in the story—for example, Sammy's parents? If so, in what kind of scene would you introduce them?
4. How would you dramatize Sammy's fantasies about Queenie and her family?
5. Would you set the entire film inside the A&P, or would you create additional settings? For example, where might you set a scene designed to present background information about Sammy? A scene depicting events that might have followed the story?
6. If you were setting the film in the present (rather than in 1961), how would you depict Queenie and her friends? How would they look different from the girls in the photograph?
7. In a present-day film version of the story, which actor would you cast as Sammy? Queenie? Stokesie? Lengel?

Interior of the A&P.
Source: ©Steven Payne/Worn Path Productions

Mr. Lengel confronting the girls while Sammy watches.
Source: ©Steven Payne/Worn Path Productions

KATHERINE MANSFIELD (1888–1923), one of the pioneers of the modern short story, was born in New Zealand and educated in England. Very much a "modern young woman," she began living on her own in London at the age of nineteen, soon publishing stories and book reviews in many of the most influential literary magazines of the day.

A short story writer of great versatility, Mansfield produced sparkling social comedies as well as more intellectually and technically complex works intended for "perceptive readers." According to one critic, her best works "[w]ith delicate plainness . . . present elusive moments of decision, defeat, and small triumph." Her last two story collections—*Bliss and Other Stories* (1920) and *The Garden Party and Other Stories* (1922)—were met with immediate critical acclaim, but Mansfield's career was cut short in 1923 when she died of complications from tuberculosis at the age of thirty-five.

One notable theme in Mansfield's work is the *dame seule,* the "woman alone," which provides the basis for the poignant "Miss Brill."

Cultural Context During the nineteenth century, the task of spinning wool was typically given to unmarried women as a way for them to earn their keep in the home. Thus, the term *spinster* came into existence. Over time, the word acquired a negative stereotype, conjuring up the image of a lonely, childless, frumpy middle-aged woman who longs to be like other "normal" women—wives and mothers. Today, the word *spinster* is rarely used, reflecting the changed perception of unmarried women and the wider lifestyle choices open to them.

Miss Brill (1922)

Although it was so brilliantly fine—the blue sky powdered with gold and great spots of light like white wine splashed over the Jardins Publiques°—Miss Brill was glad that she had decided on her fur. The air was motionless, but when you opened your mouth there was just a faint chill, like a chill from a glass of iced water before you sip, and now and again a leaf came drifting—from nowhere, from the sky. Miss Brill put up her hand and touched her fur. Dear little thing! It was nice to feel it again. She had taken it out of its box that afternoon, shaken out the moth-powder, given it a good brush, and rubbed the life back into the dim little eyes. "What has been happening to me?" said the sad little eyes. Oh, how sweet it was to see them snap at her again from the red eiderdown! . . . But the nose, which was of some black composition, wasn't at all firm. It must have had a knock, somehow. Never mind—a little dab of black sealing-wax when the time came—when it was absolutely necessary. . . . Little rogue! Yes, she really felt like that about it. Little rogue biting its tail just by her left ear. She could have taken it off and laid it on her lap and stroked it. She felt a tingling in her hands and arms, but that came from walking, she supposed. And when

Jardins Publiques: "Public Gardens" (French).

she breathed, something light and sad—no, not sad, exactly—something gentle seemed to move in her bosom.

There were a number of people out this afternoon, far more than last Sunday. And the band sounded louder and gayer. That was because the Season had begun. For although the band played all year round on Sundays, out of season it was never the same. It was like some one playing with only the family to listen; it didn't care how it played if there weren't any strangers present. Wasn't the conductor wearing a new coat, too? She was sure it was new. He scraped with his foot and flapped his arms like a rooster about to crow, and the bandsmen sitting in the green rotunda blew out their cheeks and glared at the music. Now there came a little "flutey" bit—very pretty!—a little chain of bright drops. She was sure it would be repeated. It was; she lifted her head and smiled.

Only two people shared her "special" seat: a fine old man in a velvet coat, his hands clasped over a huge carved walking-stick, and a big old woman, sitting upright, with a roll of knitting on her embroidered apron. They did not speak. This was disappointing, for Miss Brill always looked forward to the conversation. She had become really quite expert, she thought, at listening as though she didn't listen, at sitting in other people's lives just for a minute while they talked round her.

She glanced, sideways, at the old couple. Perhaps they would go soon. Last Sunday, too, hadn't been as interesting as usual. An Englishman and his wife, he wearing a dreadful Panama hat and she button boots. And she'd gone on the whole time about how she ought to wear spectacles; she knew she needed them; but that it was no good getting any; they'd be sure to break and they'd never keep on. And he'd been so patient. He'd suggested everything—gold rims, the kind that curved round your ears, little pads inside the bridge. No, nothing would please her. "They'll always be sliding down my nose!" Miss Brill wanted to shake her.

The old people sat on the bench, still as statues. Never mind, there was always the 5
crowd to watch. To and fro, in front of the flower-beds and the band rotunda, the couples and groups paraded, stopped to talk, to greet, to buy a handful of flowers from the old beggar who had his tray fixed to the railings. Little children ran among them, swooping and laughing; little boys with big white silk bows under their chins, little girls, little French dolls, dressed up in velvet and lace. And sometimes a tiny staggerer came suddenly rocking into the open from under the trees, stopped, stared, as suddenly sat down "flop," until its small high-stepping mother, like a young hen, rushed scolding to its rescue. Other people sat on the benches and green chairs, but they were nearly always the same, Sunday after Sunday, and—Miss Brill had often noticed—there was something funny about nearly all of them. They were odd, silent, nearly all old, and from the way they stared they looked as though they'd just come from dark little rooms or even—even cupboards!

Behind the rotunda the slender trees with yellow leaves down drooping, and through them just a line of sea, and beyond the blue sky with gold-veined clouds.

Tum-tum-tum tiddle-um! tiddle-um! tum tiddley-um tum ta! blew the band.

Two young girls in red came by and two young soldiers in blue met them, and they laughed and paired and went off arm-in-arm. Two peasant women with funny straw hats passed, gravely, leading beautiful smoke-colored donkeys. A cold, pale nun hurried by. A beautiful woman came along and dropped her bunch of violets, and a little boy ran after to hand them to her, and she took them and threw them away as if they'd been poisoned. Dear me! Miss Brill didn't know whether to admire that or not! And now an ermine toque° and a gentleman in grey met just in front of her. He was tall, stiff, dignified, and she was wearing the ermine toque she'd bought when her hair was yellow. Now everything, her hair, her face, even her eyes, was the same color as the shabby ermine, and her hand, in its cleaned glove, lifted to dab her lips, was a tiny yellowish paw. Oh, she was so pleased to see him—delighted! She rather thought they were going to meet that afternoon. She described where she'd been—everywhere, here, there, along by the sea. The day was so charming—didn't he agree? And wouldn't he, perhaps? . . . But he shook his head, lighted a cigarette, slowly breathed a great deep puff into her face, and, even while she was still talking and laughing, flicked the match away and walked on. The ermine toque was alone; she smiled more brightly than ever. But even the band seemed to know what she was feeling and played more softly, played tenderly, and the drum beat, "The Brute! The Brute!" over and over. What would she do? What was going to happen now? But as Miss Brill wondered, the ermine toque turned, raised her hand as though she'd seen some one else, much nicer, just over there, and pattered away. And the band changed again and played more quickly, more gaily than ever, and the old couple on Miss Brill's seat got up and marched away, and such a funny old man with long whiskers hobbled along in time to the music and was nearly knocked over by four girls walking abreast.

Oh, how fascinating it was! How she enjoyed it! How she loved sitting here, watching it all! It was like a play. It was exactly like a play. Who could believe the sky at the back wasn't painted? But it wasn't till a little brown dog trotted on solemn and then slowly trotted off, like a little "theatre" dog, a little dog that had been drugged, that Miss Brill discovered what it was that made it so exciting. They were all on the stage. They weren't only the audience, not only looking on; they were acting. Even she had a part and came every Sunday. No doubt somebody would have noticed if she hadn't been there; she was part of the performance after all. How strange she'd never thought of it like that before! And yet it explained why she made such a point of starting from home at just the same time each week—so as not to be late for the performance—and it also explained why she had quite a queer, shy feeling at telling her English pupils how she spent her Sunday afternoons. No wonder! Miss Brill nearly laughed out loud. She was on the stage. She thought of the old invalid gentleman to whom she read the newspaper four afternoons a week while he slept in the garden. She had got quite used to the frail head on the cotton pillow, the hollowed eyes, the open mouth and the high pinched nose. If he'd been dead she mightn't have noticed for weeks; she wouldn't have minded. But suddenly he knew

---

toque: Small, close-fitting woman's hat.

he was having the paper read to him by an actress! "An actress!" The old head lifted; two points of light quivered in the old eyes. "An actress — are ye?" And Miss Brill smoothed the newspaper as though it were the manuscript of her part and said gently: "Yes, I have been an actress for a long time."

The band had been having a rest. Now they started again. And what they 10
played was warm, sunny, yet there was just a faint chill — a something, what was it? — not sadness — no, not sadness — a something that made you want to sing. The tune lifted, lifted, the light shone; and it seemed to Miss Brill that in another moment all of them, all the whole company, would begin singing. The young ones, the laughing ones who were moving together, they would begin, and the men's voices, very resolute and brave, would join them. And then she too, she too, and the others on the benches — they would come in with a kind of accompaniment — something low, that scarcely rose or fell, something so beautiful — moving. . . . And Miss Brill's eyes filled with tears and she looked smiling at all the other members of the company. Yes, we understand, we understand, she thought — though what they understood she didn't know.

Just at that moment a boy and a girl came and sat down where the old couple had been. They were beautifully dressed; they were in love. The hero and heroine, of course, just arrived from his father's yacht. And still soundlessly singing, still with that trembling smile, Miss Brill prepared to listen.

"No, not now," said the girl. "Not here, I can't."

"But why? Because of that stupid old thing at the end there?" asked the boy. "Why does she come here at all — who wants her? Why doesn't she keep her silly old mug at home?"

"It's her fu-fur which is so funny," giggled the girl. "It's exactly like a fried whiting."°

"Ah, be off with you!" said the boy in an angry whisper. Then: "Tell me, my 15
petite chérie —"°

"No, not here," said the girl. "Not *yet*."

On her way home she usually bought a slice of honeycake at the baker's. It was her Sunday treat. Sometimes there was an almond in her slice, sometimes not. It made a great difference. If there was an almond it was like carrying home a tiny present — a surprise — something that might very well not have been there. She hurried on the almond Sundays and struck the match for the kettle in quite a dashing way.

But to-day she passed the baker's by, climbed the stairs, went into the little dark room — her room like a cupboard — and sat down on the red eiderdown. She sat there for a long time. The box that the fur came out of was on the bed. She unclasped the necklet quickly; quickly, without looking, laid it inside. But when she put the lid on she thought she heard something crying.

---

whiting: Food fish related to the cod.

petite chérie: "Little darling" (French).

Reading and Reacting

1. What specific details can you infer about Miss Brill's character (and, perhaps, about her life) from this statement: "She had become really quite expert, she thought, at listening as though she didn't listen, at sitting in other people's lives just for a minute while they talked round her" (par. 3)?
2. How do Miss Brill's observations of the people around her give us insight into her own character? Why do you suppose she doesn't interact with any of the people she observes?
3. In paragraph 9, Miss Brill realizes that the scene she observes is "exactly like a play" and that "Even she had a part and came every Sunday." What part does Miss Brill play? Is she a stock character in this play, or is she a three-dimensional character? Does she play a lead role or a supporting role?
4. What do you think Miss Brill means when she says, "I have been an actress for a long time" (par. 9)? What does this comment reveal about how she sees herself? Is her view of herself similar to or different from the view the other characters have of her?
5. What role does Miss Brill's fur piece play in the story? In what sense, if any, does it function as a character?
6. What happens in paragraphs 11–16 to break Miss Brill's mood? Why is the scene she observes so upsetting to her?
7. At the end of the story, has Miss Brill changed as a result of what she has overheard, or is she the same person she was at the beginning? Do you think she will return to the park the following Sunday?
8. The story's last paragraph describes Miss Brill's room as being "like a cupboard." Where else has this image appeared in the story? What does its reappearance in the conclusion tell us?
9. **Journal Entry** Write a character sketch of Miss Brill, inventing a plausible family and personal history that might help to explain the character you see in the story.
10. **Critical Perspective** Critic Gillian Boddy, in *Katherine Mansfield: The Woman, The Writer,* offers the following analysis of Mansfield's fiction:

    > The story evolves through the characters' minds. The external narrator is almost eliminated. As so often in her work, the reader is dropped into the story and simply confronted by a particular situation. There is no preliminary establishing and identification of time and place. The reader is immediately involved; it is assumed that he or she has any necessary prerequisite knowledge and is, in a sense, part of the story too.

    Do you see this absence of conventional exposition as a problem in "Miss Brill"? Do you think the story would be more effective if Mansfield had supplied more preliminary information about setting and character? Or do you believe that what Boddy calls Mansfield's "concentration on a moment or episode" is a satisfactory substitute for the missing exposition, effectively shifting interest from "*what* happens" to "*why* it happens"?

Related Works: "Prue" (p. 184), "Eveline" (p. 719), "Rooming houses are old women" (p. 926), "Aunt Jennifer's Tigers" (p. 963), "After great pain, a formal feeling comes—" (p. 1141), "Acquainted with the Night" (p. 1156), *The Stronger* (p. 1470)

ZADIE SMITH (1975–), born in London as Sadie Smith, changed her name at a young age "because," she said in an interview, "it seemed right, exotic, different." The author of three novels, she has published short stories in such publications as the *New Yorker, McSweeney's,* and *Granta.* Her highly praised first novel, *White Teeth* (2000), winner of numerous awards, was followed by *The Autograph Man* (2002) and *On Beauty,* winner of the 2006 Orange Prize for Fiction. Smith wrote "The Girl with Bangs" in response to the song "Bangs" by They Might Be Giants.

Cultural Context As a cultural trend, bangs have come and gone and come again with American women throughout the latter part of the twentieth century and into the twenty-first century. The hairstyle has evolved from the long "mall bangs" of the 1960s, bangs that start at the crown of the head, to a range of subtler styles used to frame the face with hair. Today, popular styles of bangs among twenty- and thirty-something women include side-swept bangs, angled bangs, short choppy bangs, classic blunt bangs, straight bangs, super-short bangs, curly bangs, and eyebrow-skimming bangs. Celebrities helping to repopularize the look include Jessica Simpson, Lara Flynn Boyle, Kim Cattrall, Ashlee Simpson, Jennifer Lopez, Paris Hilton, and Nicole Richie.

The Girl with Bangs (2001)

I fell in love with a girl once. Some time ago, now. She had bangs. I was twenty years old at the time and prey to the usual rag-bag of foolish ideas. I believed, for example, that one might meet some sweet kid and like them a lot—maybe even marry them—while all the time allowing that kid to sleep with other kids, and that this could be done with no fuss at all, just a chuck under the chin, and no tears. I believed the majority of people to be bores, however you cut them; that the mark of their dullness was easy to spot (clothes, hair) and impossible to avoid, running right through them like a watermark. I had made mental notes, too, on other empty notions—the death of certain things (socialism, certain types of music, old people), the future of others (film, footwear, poetry)—but no one need be bored with those now. The only significant bit of nonsense I carried around in those days, the only one that came from the gut, if you like, was this feeling that a girl with soft black bangs falling into eyes the color of a Perrier bottle must be good news. Look at her palming the bangs away from her face, pressing them back along her hairline, only to have them fall forward again! I found this combination to be good, *intrinsically* good in both form and content, the same way you think of cherries (life is a bowl of; she was a real sweet) until the very center of one becomes lodged in your windpipe. I believed Charlotte Greaves and her bangs to be good news. But Charlotte was emphatically bad news, requiring only eight months to take me entirely apart; the kind of clinically efficient dismembering you see when a bright child gets his hand on some toy he assembled in the first place. I'd never dated a girl before, and she was bad news the way boys can never be, because with boys it's always possible to draw up a list of pros and cons, and see the matter rationally, from either side. But you could make a list of cons on Charlotte stretching to Azerbaijan,° and "her bangs" sitting solitary in the pros column would outweigh all objections. Boys are just boys after all, but sometimes girls *really seem to be* the turn of a pale wrist, or the sudden jut of a hip, or a clutch of very dark hair falling across a freckled forehead. I'm not saying that's what they really are. I'm just saying sometimes it seems that way, and that those details (a thigh mole, a full face flush, a scar the precise shape and size of a cashew nut) are so many hooks waiting to land you. In this case, it was those bangs, plush and dramatic, curtains opening on to a face one would queue up to see. All women have a backstage, of course, of course. Labyrinthine, many-roomed, no doubt, no doubt. But you come to see the show, that's all I'm saying.

I first set eyes on Charlotte when she was seeing a Belgian who lived across the hall from me in college. I'd see her first thing, shuffling around the communal bathroom looking a mess—undone, always, in every sense—with her T-shirt tucked in her knickers, a fag° hanging out of her mouth, some kind of toothpaste or maybe mouthwash residue by her lips and those bangs in her eyes. It was hard to understand why this Belgian, Maurice, had chosen to date her. He had this great accent, Maurice, *elaborately* French, like you couldn't *be* more French, and a jaw line that seemed in fashion at the time, and you could tick all the boxes vis-à-vis personal charms; Maurice was an impressive kind of a guy. Charlotte was the kind of woman who has only two bras, both of them gray. But after a while, if you paid attention, you came to realize that she had a look about her like she just got out of a bed, no matter what time of day you collided with her (she had a stalk of a walk, never looked where she was going, so you had no choice) and this tendency, if put under the heading "Qualities That Girls Sometimes Have," was a kind of poor relation of "Bedroom Eyes" or "Looks Like She's Thinking about Sex All the Time"—and it worked. She seemed always to be stumbling away from someone else, toward you. A limping figure smiling widely, arms outstretched, dressed in rags, a smouldering city as backdrop. I had watched too many films, possibly. But still: a bundle of precious things thrown at you from a third-floor European window, wrapped loosely in a blanket, chosen frantically and at random by the well-meaning owner slung haphazardly from a burning building; launched at you; it could hurt, this bundle, but look! You have caught it! A little chipped, but otherwise fine. Look what you have saved! (You understand me, I know. This is how it feels. What is the purpose of metaphor, anyway, if not to describe women?)

Now, it came to pass that this Maurice was offered a well-paid TV job in Thailand as a newscaster, and he agonized, and weighed Charlotte in one hand and the money in the other and found he could not leave without the promise that she would wait

---

Azerbaijan: Country on the coast of the Caspian Sea, bordered by Russia, Armenia, and Iran.
fag: Cigarette.

for him. This promise she gave him, but he was still gone, and gone is gone, and that's where I came in. Not immediately—I am no thief—but by degrees, studying near her in the library, watching her hair make reading difficult. Sitting next to her at lunch watching the bangs go hither, and, I suppose, thither, as people swished by with their food trays. Befriending her friends and then her; making as many nice noises about Maurice as I could. I became a boy for the duration. I stood under the window with my open arms. I did all the old boy tricks. These tricks are not as difficult as some boys will have you believe, but they are indeed slow, and work only by a very gradual process of accumulation. You have sad moments when you wonder if there will ever be an end to it. But then, usually without warning, the hard work pays off. With Charlotte it went like this: she came by for a herbal tea one day, and I rolled a joint and then another and soon enough she was lying across my lap, spineless as a mollusk, and I had my fingers in those bangs—teasing them, as the hairdressers say—and we had begun.

Most of the time we spent together was in her room. At the beginning of an affair you've no need to be outside. And it was like a filthy cocoon, her room, ankle deep in rubbish; it was the kind of room that took you in and held you close. With no clocks and my watch lost and buried, we passed time by the degeneration of things, the rotting of fruit, the accumulation of bacteria, the rising-tideline of cigarettes in the vase we used to put them out. It was a quarter past this apple. The third Saturday in the month of that stain. These things were unpleasant and tiresome. And she was no intellectual; any book I gave her she treated like a kid treats a Christmas present—fascination for a day and then the quick pall of boredom; by the end of the week it was flung across the room and submerged; weeks later when we made love I'd find the spine of the novel sticking into the small of my back, paper cuts on my toes. There was no bed to speak of. There was just a bit of the floor that was marginally clearer than the rest of it. (But wait! Here she comes, falling in an impossible arc, and here I am by careful design in just the right spot, under the window, and here she is, landing and nothing is broken, and I cannot believe my luck. You understand me. Every time I looked at the bangs, the bad stuff went away.)

5 Again: I know it doesn't sound great, but let's not forget the bangs. Let us not forget that after a stand-up row, a real screaming match, she could look at me from underneath the distinct hairs, separated by sweat, and I had no more resistance. *Yes, you can leave the overturned plant pot where it is. Yes, Rousseau is an idiot if you say so.* So this is what it's like being a boy. The cobbled street, the hopeful arms hugging air. There is nothing you won't do.

Charlotte's exams were coming up. I begged her to look through her reading list once more, and plan some strategic line of attack, but she wanted to do it her way. Her way meant reading the same two books—Rousseau's *Social Contract* and Plato's *Republic* (her paper was to be on people, and the way they organize their lives, or the way they did, or the way they should, I don't remember; it had a technical title, I don't remember that either)—again and again, in the study room that sat in a quiet corner of the college. The study room was meant to be for everyone but since Charlotte had moved in, all others had gradually moved out. I recall one German graduate who stood his ground for a month or so, who cleared his throat regularly and pointedly picked up things that she had dropped—but she got to him, finally. Charlotte's papers all over the floor, Charlotte's old lunches on every table, Charlottes clothes and my clothes (now indistinguishable) thrown over every chair. People would come up to me in the bar and say, "Look, Charlotte did X. Could you please, for the love of God, stop Charlotte doing X, *please*?" and I would try, but Charlotte's bangs kept Charlotte in the world of Charlotte and she barely heard me. And now, please, before we go any further: tell me. Tell me if you've ever stood under a window and caught an unworthy bundle of chintz.° Gold plating that came off with one rub; faked signatures, worthless trinkets. Have you? Maybe the bait was different—not bangs, but deep pockets either side of the smile or unusually vivid eye pigmentation. Or some other bodily attribute (hair, skin, curves) that recalled in you some natural phenomenon (wheat, sea, cream). Some difference. So: have you? Have you ever been out with a girl like this?

Some time after Charlotte's exams, after the 2.2 that had been stalking her for so long finally pounced, there was a knock on the door. *My* door—I recall now that we were in my room that morning. I hauled on a dressing-gown and went to answer it. It was Maurice, tanned and dressed like one of the Beatles when they went to see the Maharashi,° a white suit with a Nehru collar, his own bangs and tousled hair, slightly long at the back. He looked terrific. He said, "Someone in ze bar says you might have an idea where Charlotte is. I need to see 'er—it is very urgent. Have you seen 'er?" I had seen her. She was in my bed, about five feet from where Maurice stood, but obscured by a partition wall. "No . . ." I said. "No, not this morning. She'll probably be in the hall for breakfast though, she usually is. So, Maurice! When did you get back?" He said, "All zat must come later. I 'ave to find Charlotte. I sink I am going to marry 'er." And I thought, *Christ, which bad movie am I in?*

I got Charlotte up, shook her, poured her into some clothes, and told her to run around the back of the college and get to the dining hall before Maurice. I saw her in my head, the moment the door closed—no great feat of imagination, I had seen her run before, like a naturally uncoordinated animal (a panda?) that somebody has just shot—I saw her dashing incompetently past the ancient walls, catching herself on ivy, tripping up steps, and finally falling through the swing doors, looking wildly round the dining hall like those movie time-travellers who know not in which period they have just landed. But still she managed it, apparently she got there in time, though as the whole world now knows, Maurice took one look at her strands matted against her forehead, running in line with the ridge-ways of sleep left by the pillows, and said, "You're sleeping with her?" (Or maybe, "You're sleeping with *her?*"—I don't know; this is all reported speech) and Charlotte, who, like a lot of low-maintenance women, cannot tell a lie, said "Er . . . yes. Yes" and then made that signal of feminine relief; bottom lip out, air blown upward; bangs all of a flutter.

Later that afternoon, Maurice came back round to my room, looking all the more noble, and seemingly determined to have a calm man-to-man "you see, I have

---

chintz: A usually brightly printed and glazed cotton fabric.

Maharashi: Maharishi Mahesh Yogi (1911?–2008), Hindu religious leader revered by the British rock group the Beatles.

returned to marry her / I will not stand in your way" type of a chat, which was very reasonable and English of him. I let him have it alone. I nodded when it seemed appropriate; sometimes I lifted my hands in protest but soon let them fall again. You can't fight it when you've been replaced: a simple side-step and here is some old/new Belgian guy standing in the cobbled street with his face upturned, and his arms wide open, judging the angles. I thought of this girl he wanted back, who had taken me apart piece by piece, causing me nothing but trouble, with her bangs and her antisocial behaviour. I was all (un)done, I realized. I sort of marvelled at the devotion he felt for her. From a thousand miles away, with a smoldering city as a backdrop, I watched him beg me to leave them both alone; tears in his eyes, the works. I agreed it was the best thing, all round. I had the impression that here was a girl who would be thrown from person to person over years, and each would think they had saved her by some miracle when in actual fact she was in no danger at all. Never even for a second.

He said, "Let us go, zen, and tell 'er the decision we have come to," and I said yes, 10
let's, but when we got to Charlotte's room, someone else was putting his fingers through her curls. Charlotte was always one of those people for whom sex is available at all times—it just happens to her, quickly, and with a minimum of conversation. This guy was some other guy that she'd been sleeping with on the days when she wasn't with me. It had been going on for four months. This all came out later, naturally.

Would you believe he married her anyway? And not only that, he married her after she'd shaved her head that afternoon just to spite us. All of us—even the other guy no one had seen before. Maurice took a bald English woman with a strange lopsided walk and a temper like a gorgon back to Thailand and married her despite friends' complaints and the voluble protest of Aneepa Kapoor, who was the woman he read the news with. The anchorwoman, who had that Hitchcock style: hair tied back tight in a bun, a spiky nose and a vicious red mouth. The kind of woman who doesn't need catching. "Maurice," she said, "you *owe* me. You can't just throw four months away like it wasn't worth a bloody thing!" He emailed me about it. He admitted that he'd been stringing Aneepa along for a while, and she'd been expecting something at the end of it. For in the real world, or so it seems to me, it is almost always women and not men who are waiting under windows, and they are almost always disappointed. In this matter, Charlotte was unusual.

Reading and Reacting

1. At what point did you realize that the narrator was female? Do you think her feelings and behavior would have been any different if she were male?
2. What exactly is it about Charlotte that fascinates the narrator? Do you share this fascination?
3. What do we learn in paragraph 1 about the narrator's tastes, feelings, and beliefs? Is this information enough to explain her obsession with Charlotte?
4. Why do you think the narrator focuses on Charlotte's bangs? What other physical traits does Charlotte have?

5. In paragraph 2, the narrator characterizes Charlotte as "the kind of woman who has only two bras, both of them gray." What does this tell readers about Charlotte? What does the description of Charlotte's room in paragraph 4 reveal about her?
6. What role does Maurice play in the story? What do we know about him? Is he a flat or a round character? Is he essential to the story?
7. At the end of paragraph 4, the narrator tells us, "Every time I looked at the bangs, the bad stuff went away." What do you think this "bad stuff" is?
8. In the story's last lines, the narrator explains that "in the real world, or so it seems to me, it is almost always women and not men who are waiting under windows, and they are almost always disappointed. In this matter, Charlotte was unusual." What does the narrator mean? How do these words help to explain her infatuation with Charlotte?
9. **JOURNAL ENTRY** Write a farewell email to the narrator from Charlotte. Try to explain her feelings for the narrator as well as her motivation for shaving her head and for marrying Maurice.
10. **CRITICAL PERSPECTIVE** Writing about Zadie Smith's novel *On Beauty*, Max Watman makes the following comments:

> Smith's characters are expertly portrayed. . . . She can blow them up in all their chalky whites and lively pinks. She is one of the best character writers working. . . . *On Beauty* is one of the few contemporary novels that feels as if it is stuffed with fully formed people rather than tics and mannerisms.

Do you think Charlotte in "The Girl with Bangs" is depicted as a "fully formed" person? Or, do you think she is really just "tics and mannerisms"?

Related Works: "Love and Other Catastrophes: A Mix Tape" (p. 182), "Araby" (p. 434), "My mistress' eyes are nothing like the sun" (p. 917), "General Review of the Sex Situation" (p. 1056), "She Walks in Beauty" (p. 1133), *Beauty* (p. 1270)

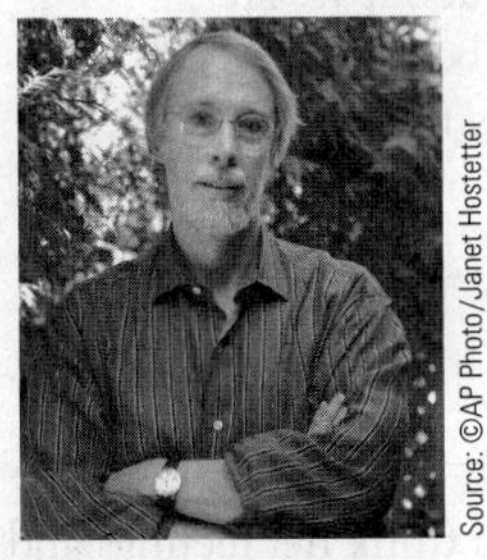
Source: ©AP Photo/Janet Hostetter

CHARLES BAXTER (1947–) was born in Minneapolis and educated at Macalester College and at the State University of New York, Buffalo. Currently teaching in the creative writing program at the University of Minnesota, Baxter is the author of four critically praised collections of short stories: *Harmony of the World* (1984), *Through the Safety Net* (1985), *A Relative Stranger: Stories* (1990), and *Believers: A Novella and Stories* (1997). He is also the author of five novels, *First Light* (1987), *Shadow Play* (1993), *The Feast of Love* (2002), *Saul and Patsy* (2003), and *The Soul Thief* (2008), and one book of poetry, *Imaginary Paintings and Other Poems* (1989). Baxter has also written *Burning Down the House* (1997), a collection of essays on fiction.

Baxter's critics often mention the compassion he shows in writing about his fictional characters: a couple who lose their child, a hospital worker who wants to be famous, a tired businessman who really wants to paint. In many of his short stories in *Through the Safety Net* (in which "Gryphon" appeared), unexpected events jar Baxter's characters out of their routines, forcing them to consider different choices, to call on inner strength, or to swim against the tide of "middle America's" conventions.

Cultural Context One of the key elements of this story is a character's use of a deck of tarot cards to predict the future. Originating more than 500 years ago in northern Italy in a game called "Triumphs," the Tarot was quickly adopted as a tool for divining the future. With deep roots in the symbolism of medieval and Renaissance Europe, the Tarot is today the singular most popular tool for spiritual introspection and prophesy. While the death card in particular is often feared, many interpreters argue that it hardly ever points to literal death but rather symbolizes the ending of something significant and the beginning of something new. In "Gryphon," the accuracy of the Tarot's prediction is less important than various characters' reactions to it.

Gryphon (1985)

On Wednesday afternoon, between the geography lesson on ancient Egypt's hand-operated irrigation system and an art project that involved drawing a model city next to a mountain, our fourth-grade teacher, Mr. Hibler, developed a cough. This cough began with a series of muffled throat clearings and progressed to propulsive noises contained within Mr. Hibler's closed mouth. "Listen to him," Carol Peterson whispered to me. "He's gonna blow up." Mr. Hibler's laughter—dazed and infrequent—sounded a bit like his cough, but as we worked on our model cities we would look up, thinking he was enjoying a joke, and see Mr. Hibler's face turning red, his cheeks puffed out. This was not laughter. Twice he bent over, and his loose tie, like a plumb line, hung down straight from his neck as he exploded himself into a Kleenex. He would excuse himself, then go on coughing. "I'll bet you a dime," Carol Peterson whispered, "we get a substitute tomorrow."

Carol sat at the desk in front of mine and was a bad person—when she thought no one was looking she would blow her nose on notebook paper, then crumble it up and throw it into the wastebasket—but at times of crisis she spoke the truth. I knew I'd lose the dime.

"No deal," I said.

When Mr. Hibler stood us up in formation at the door just prior to the final bell, he was almost incapable of speech. "I'm sorry, boys and girls," he said. "I seem to be coming down with something."

5 "I hope you feel better tomorrow, Mr. Hibler," Bobby Kryzanowicz, the faultless brown-noser said, and I heard Carol Peterson's evil giggle. Then Mr. Hibler opened the door and we walked out to the buses, a clique of us starting noisily to hawk and cough as soon as we thought we were a few feet beyond Mr. Hibler's earshot.

Five Oaks being a rural community, and in Michigan, the supply of substitute teachers was limited to the town's unemployed community college graduates, a pool of about four mothers. These ladies fluttered, provided easeful class days, and nervously covered material we had mastered weeks earlier. Therefore it was a surprise when a woman we had never seen came into the class the next day, carrying a purple purse, a checkerboard lunchbox, and a few books. She put the books on one side of Mr. Hibler's desk and the lunchbox on the other, next to the Voice of Music phonograph. Three of us in the back of the room were playing with Heever, the chameleon that lived in the terrarium and on one of the plastic drapes, when she walked in.

She clapped her hands at us. “Little boys,” she said, “why are you bent over together like that?” She didn’t wait for us to answer. “Are you tormenting an animal? Put it back. Please sit down at your desks. I want no cabals this time of the day.” We just stared at her. “Boys,” she repeated, “I asked you to sit down.”

I put the chameleon in his terrarium and felt my way to my desk, never taking my eyes off the woman. With white and green chalk, she had started to draw a tree on the left side of the blackboard. She didn’t look usual. Furthermore, her tree was outsized, disproportionate, for some reason.

“This room needs a tree,” she said, with one line drawing the suggestion of a leaf. “A large, leafy, shady, deciduous . . . oak.”

10 Her fine, light hair had been done up in what I would learn years later was called a chignon, and she wore gold-rimmed glasses whose lenses seemed to have the faintest blue tint. Harold Knardahl, who sat across from me, whispered “Mars,” and I nodded slowly, savoring the imminent weirdness of the day. The substitute drew another branch with an extravagant arm gesture, then turned around and said, “Good morning. I don’t believe I said good morning to all of you yet.”

Facing us, she was no special age—an adult is an adult—but her face had two prominent lines, descending vertically from the sides of her mouth to her chin. I knew where I had seen those lines before: *Pinocchio*. They were marionette lines. “You may stare at me,” she said to us, as a few more kids from the last bus came into the room, their eyes fixed on her, “for a few more seconds, until the bell rings. Then I will permit no more staring. Looking I will permit. Staring, no. It is impolite to stare, and a sign of bad breeding. You cannot make a social effort while staring.”

Harold Knardahl did not glance at me, or nudge, but I heard him whisper “Mars” again, trying to get more mileage out of his single joke with the kids who had just come in.

When everyone was seated, the substitute teacher finished her tree, put down her chalk fastidiously on the phonograph, brushed her hands, and faced us. “Good morning,” she said. “I am Miss Ferenczi, your teacher for the day. I am fairly new to your community, and I don’t believe any of you know me. I will therefore start by telling you a story about myself.”

While we settled back, she launched into her tale. She said her grandfather had been a Hungarian prince; her mother had been born in some place called Flanders, had been a pianist, and had played concerts for people Miss Ferenczi referred to as “crowned heads.” She gave us a knowing look. “Grieg,” she said, “the Norwegian master, wrote a concerto for piano that was,” she paused, “my mother’s triumph at her debut concert in London.” Her eyes searched the ceiling. Our eyes followed. Nothing up there but ceiling tile. “For reasons that I shall not go into, my family’s fortunes took us to Detroit, then north to dreadful Saginaw, and now here I am in Five Oaks, as your substitute teacher, for today, Thursday, October the eleventh. I believe it will be a good day: All the forecasts coincide. We shall start with your reading lesson. Take out your reading book. I believe it is called *Broad Horizons*, or something along those lines.”

15 Jeannie Vermeesch raised her hand. Miss Ferenczi nodded at her. “Mr. Hibler always starts the day with the Pledge of Allegiance,” Jeannie whined.

“Oh, does he? In that case,” Miss Ferenczi said, “you must know it *very* well by now, and we certainly need not spend our time on it. No, no allegiance pledging on the premises today, by my reckoning. Not with so much sunlight coming into the room. A pledge does not suit my mood." She glanced at her watch. "Time *is* flying. Take out *Broad Horizons*."

She disappointed us by giving us an ordinary lesson, complete with vocabulary word drills, comprehension questions, and recitation. She didn't seem to care for the material, however. She sighed every few minutes and rubbed her glasses with a frilly perfumed handkerchief that she withdrew, magician style, from her left sleeve.

After reading we moved on to arithmetic. It was my favorite time of the morning, when the lazy autumn sunlight dazzled its way through ribbons of clouds past the windows on the east side of the classroom, and crept across the linoleum floor. On the playground the first group of children, the kindergartners, were running on the quack grass just beyond the monkey bars. We were doing multiplication tables. Miss Ferenczi had made John Wazny stand up at his desk in the front row. He was supposed to go through the tables of six. From where I was sitting, I could smell the Vitalis soaked into John's plastered hair. He was doing fine until he came to six times eleven and six times twelve. "Six times eleven," he said, "is sixty-eight. Six times twelve is . . ." He put his fingers to his head, quickly and secretly sniffed his fingertips, and said, "seventy-two." Then he sat down.

"Fine," Miss Ferenczi said. "Well now. That was very good."

"Miss Ferenczi!" One of the Eddy twins was waving her hand desperately in the air. "Miss Ferenczi! Miss Ferenczi!"

"Yes?"

"John said that six times eleven is sixty-eight and you said he was right!"

"*Did* I?" She gazed at the class with a jolly look breaking across her marionette's face. "Did I say that? Well, what *is* six times eleven?"

"It's sixty-six!"

She nodded. "Yes. So it is. But, and I know some people will not entirely agree with me, at some times it is sixty-eight."

"When? When is it sixty-eight?"

We were all waiting.

"In higher mathematics, which you children do not yet understand, six times eleven can be considered to be sixty-eight." She laughed through her nose. "In higher mathematics numbers are . . . more fluid. The only thing a number does is contain a certain amount of something. Think of water. A cup is not the only way to measure a certain amount of water, is it?" We were staring, shaking our heads. "You could use saucepans or thimbles. In either case, the water *would be the same*. Perhaps," she started again, "it would be better for you to think that six times eleven is sixty-eight only when I am in the room."

"Why is it sixty-eight," Mark Poole asked, "when you're in the room?"

"Because it's more interesting that way," she said, smiling very rapidly behind her blue-tinted glasses. "Besides, I'm your substitute teacher, am I not?" We all nodded. "Well, then, think of six times eleven equals sixty-eight as a substitute fact."

"A substitute fact?"

"Yes." Then she looked at us carefully. "Do you think," she asked, "that anyone is going to be hurt by a substitute fact?"

We looked back at her.

"Will the plants on the windowsill be hurt?" We glanced at them. There were sensitive plants thriving in a green plastic tray, and several wilted ferns in small clay pots. "Your dogs and cats, or your moms and dads?" She waited. "So," she concluded, "what's the problem?"

"But it's wrong," Janice Weber said, "isn't it?"

"What's your name, young lady?"

"Janice Weber."

"And you think it's wrong, Janice?"

"I was just asking."

"Well, all right. You were just asking. I think we've spent enough time on this matter by now, don't you, class? You are free to think what you like. When your teacher, Mr. Hibler, returns, six times eleven will be sixty-six again, you can rest assured. And it will be that for the rest of your lives in Five Oaks. Too bad, eh?" She raised her eyebrows and glinted herself at us. "But for now, it wasn't. So much for that. Let us go to your assigned problems for today, as painstakingly outlined, I see, in Mr. Hibler's lesson plan. Take out a sheet of paper and write your names in the upper left-hand corner."

For the next half hour we did the rest of our arithmetic problems. We handed them in and went on to spelling, my worst subject. Spelling always came before lunch. We were taking spelling dictation and looking at the clock. "Thorough," Miss Ferenczi said. "Boundary." She walked in the aisles between the desks, holding the spelling book open and looking down at our papers. "Balcony." I clutched my pencil. Somehow, the way she said those words, they seemed foreign, Hungarian, mis-voweled and mis-consonanted. I stared down at what I had spelled. *Balconie*. I turned my pencil upside down and erased my mistake. *Balconey*. That looked better, but still incorrect. I cursed the world of spelling and tried erasing it again and saw the paper beginning to wear away. *Balkony*. Suddenly I felt a hand on my shoulder.

"I don't like that word either," Miss Ferenczi whispered, bent over, her mouth near my ear. "It's ugly. My feeling is, if you don't like a word, you don't have to use it." She straightened up, leaving behind a slight odor of Clorets.

At lunchtime we went out to get our trays of sloppy joes, peaches in heavy syrup, coconut cookies, and milk, and brought them back to the classroom, where Miss Ferenczi was sitting at the desk, eating a brown sticky thing she had unwrapped from tightly rubber-banded wax paper. "Miss Ferenczi," I said, raising my hand. "You don't have to eat with us. You can eat with the other teachers. There's a teachers' lounge," I ended up, "next to the principal's office."

"No, thank you," she said. "I prefer it here."

"We've got a room monitor," I said. "Mrs. Eddy." I pointed to where Mrs. Eddy, Joyce and Judy's mother, sat silently at the back of the room, doing her knitting.

"That's fine," Miss Ferenczi said. "But I shall continue to eat here, with you children. I prefer it," she repeated.

"How come?" Wayne Razmer asked without raising his hand.

"I talked with the other teachers before class this morning," Miss Ferenczi said, biting into her brown food. "There was a great rattling of the words for the fewness of ideas. I didn't care for their brand of hilarity. I don't like ditto machine jokes."

"Oh," Wayne said.

"What's that you're eating?" Maxine Sylvester asked, twitching her nose. "Is it food?"

"It most certainly *is* food. It's a stuffed fig. I had to drive almost down to Detroit to get it. I also bought some smoked sturgeon. And this," she said, lifting some green leaves out of her lunchbox, "is raw spinach, cleaned this morning before I came out here to the Garfield-Murry school."

"Why're you eating raw spinach?" Maxine asked.

"It's good for you," Miss Ferenczi said. "More stimulating than soda pop or smelling salts." I bit into my sloppy joe and stared blankly out the window. An almost invisible moon was faintly silvered in the daytime autumn sky. "As far as food is concerned," Miss Ferenczi was saying, "you have to shuffle the pack. Mix it up. Too many people eat . . . well, never mind."

"Miss Ferenczi," Carol Peterson said, "what are we going to do this afternoon?"

"Well," she said, looking down at Mr. Hibler's lesson plan, "I see that your teacher, Mr. Hibler, has you scheduled for a unit on the Egyptians." Carol groaned. "Yessss," Miss Ferenczi continued, "that is what we will do: the Egyptians. A remarkable people. Almost as remarkable as the Americans. But not quite." She lowered her head, did her quick smile, and went back to eating her spinach.

After noon recess we came back into the classroom and saw that Miss Ferenczi had drawn a pyramid on the blackboard, close to her oak tree. Some of us who had been playing baseball were messing around in the back of the room, dropping the bats and the gloves into the playground box, and I think that Ray Schontzeler had just slugged me when I heard Miss Ferenczi's high-pitched voice quavering with emotion. "Boys," she said, "come to order right this minute and take your seats. I do not wish to waste a minute of class time. Take out your geography books." We trudged to our desks and, still sweating, pulled out *Distant Lands and Their People*. "Turn to page forty-two." She waited for thirty seconds, then looked over at Kelly Munger. "Young man," she said, "why are you still fossicking in your desk?"

Kelly looked as if his foot had been stepped on. "Why am I what?"

"Why are you . . . burrowing in your desk like that?"

"I'm lookin' for the book, Miss Ferenczi."

Bobby Kryzanowicz, the faultless brown-noser who sat in the first row by choice, softly said, "His name is Kelly Munger. He can't ever find his stuff. He always does that."

"I don't care what his name is, especially after lunch," Miss Ferenczi said. "*Where is your book?*"

"I just found it." Kelly was peering into his desk and with both hands pulled at the book, shoveling along in front of it several pencils and crayons, which fell into his lap and then to the floor.

"I hate a mess," Miss Ferenczi said. "I hate a mess in a desk or a mind. It's . . . unsanitary. You wouldn't want your house at home to look like your desk at school, now, would you?" She didn't wait for an answer. "I should think not. A house at home should be as neat as human hands can make it. What were we talking about? Egypt. Page forty-two. I note from Mr. Hibler's lesson plan that you have been discussing the modes of Egyptian irrigation. Interesting, in my view, but not so interesting as what we are about to cover. The pyramids and Egyptian slave labor. A plus on one side, a minus on the other." We had our books open to page forty-two, where there was a picture of a pyramid, but Miss Ferenczi wasn't looking at the book. Instead, she was staring at some object just outside the window.

"Pyramids," Miss Ferenczi said, still looking past the window. "I want you to think about the pyramids. And what was inside. The bodies of the pharaohs, of course, and their attendant treasures. Scrolls. Perhaps," Miss Ferenczi said, with something gleeful but unsmiling in her face, "these scrolls were novels for the pharaohs, helping them to pass the time in their long voyage through the centuries. But then, I am joking." I was looking at the lines on Miss Ferenczi's face. "Pyramids," Miss Ferenczi went on, "were the repositories of special cosmic powers. The nature of a pyramid is to guide cosmic energy forces into a concentrated point. The Egyptians knew that; we have generally forgotten it. Did you know," she asked, walking to the side of the room so that she was standing by the coat closet, "that George Washington had Egyptian blood, from his grandmother? Certain features of the Constitution of the United States are notable for their Egyptian ideas."

Without glancing down at the book, she began to talk about the movement of souls in Egyptian religion. She said that when people die, their souls return to Earth in the form of carpenter ants or walnut trees, depending on how they behaved—"well or ill"—in life. She said that the Egyptians believed that people act the way they do because of magnetism produced by tidal forces in the solar system, forces produced by the sun and by its "planetary ally," Jupiter. Jupiter, she said, was a planet, as we had been told, but had "certain properties of stars." She was speaking very fast. She said that the Egyptians were great explorers and conquerors. She said that the greatest of all the conquerors, Genghis Khan, had had forty horses and forty young women killed on the site of his grave. We listened. No one tried to stop her. "I myself have been in Egypt," she said, "and have witnessed much dust and many brutalities." She said that an old man in Egypt who worked for a circus had personally shown her an animal in a cage, a monster, half bird and half lion. She said that this monster was called a gryphon and that she had heard about them but never seen them until she traveled to the outskirts of Cairo. She said that Egyptian astronomers had discovered the planet Saturn, but had not seen its rings. She said that the Egyptians were the first to discover that dogs, when they are ill, will not drink from rivers, but wait for rain, and hold their jaws open to catch it.

* * *

"She lies."

We were on the school bus home. I was sitting next to Carl Whiteside, who had bad breath and a huge collection of marbles. We were arguing. Carl thought she was lying. I said she wasn't, probably.

"I didn't believe that stuff about the bird," Carl said, "and what she told us about the pyramids? I didn't believe that either. She didn't know what she was talking about."

"Oh yeah?" I had liked her. She was strange. I thought I could nail him. "If she was lying," I said, "what'd she say that was a lie?"

"Six times eleven isn't sixty-eight. It isn't ever. It's sixty-six, I know for a fact." 70

"She said so. She admitted it. What else did she lie about?"

"I don't know," he said. "Stuff."

"What stuff?"

"Well." He swung his legs back and forth. "You ever see an animal that was half lion and half bird?" He crossed his arms. "It sounded real fakey to me."

"It could happen," I said. I had to improvise, to outrage him. "I read in this news- 75
paper my mom bought in the IGA about this scientist, this mad scientist in the Swiss Alps, and he's been putting genes and chromosomes and stuff together in test tubes, and he combined a human being and a hamster." I waited, for effect. "It's called a humster."

"You never." Carl was staring at me, his mouth open, his terrible bad breath making its way toward me. "What newspaper was it?"

"The *National Enquirer*," I said, "that they sell next to the cash registers." When I saw his look of recognition, I knew I had bested him. "And this mad scientist," I said, "his name was, um, Dr. Frankenbush." I realized belatedly that this name was a mistake and waited for Carl to notice its resemblance to the name of the other famous mad master of permutations, but he only sat there.

"A man and a hamster?" He was staring at me, squinting, his mouth opening in distaste. "Jeez. What'd it look like?"

When the bus reached my stop, I took off down our dirt road and ran up through the back yard, kicking the tire swing for good luck. I dropped my books on the back steps so I could hug and kiss our dog, Mr. Selby. Then I hurried inside. I could smell Brussels sprouts cooking, my unfavorite vegetable. My mother was washing other vegetables in the kitchen sink, and my baby brother was hollering in his yellow playpen on the kitchen floor.

"Hi, Mom," I said, hopping around the playpen to kiss her, "Guess what?" 80

"I have no idea."

"We had this substitute today, Miss Ferenczi, and I'd never seen her before, and she had all these stories and ideas and stuff."

"Well. That's good." My mother looked out the window behind the sink, her eyes on the pine woods west of our house. Her face and hairstyle always reminded other people of Betty Crocker, whose picture was framed inside a gigantic spoon on the side of the Bisquick box; to me, though, my mother's face just looked white. "Listen, Tommy," she said, "go upstairs and pick your clothes off the bathroom floor, then go outside to the shed and put the shovel and ax away that your father left outside this morning."

"She said that six times eleven was sometimes sixty-eight!" I said. "And she said she once saw a monster that was half lion and half bird." I waited. "In Egypt, she said."

"Did you hear me?" my mother asked, raising her arm to wipe her forehead with 85
the back of her hand. "You have chores to do."

"I know," I said. "I was just telling you about the substitute."

"It's very interesting," my mother said, quickly glancing down at me, "and we can talk about it later when your father gets home. But right now you have some work to do."

"Okay, Mom." I took a cookie out of the jar on the counter and was about to go outside when I had a thought. I ran into the living room, pulled out a dictionary next to the TV stand, and opened it to the G's. *Gryphon:* "variant of griffin." *Griffin:* "a fabulous beast with the head and wings of an eagle and the body of a lion." Fabulous was right. I shouted with triumph and ran outside to put my father's tools back in their place.

Miss Ferenczi was back the next day, slightly altered. She had pulled her hair down and twisted it into pigtails, with red rubber bands holding them tight one inch from the ends. She was wearing a green blouse and pink scarf, making her difficult to look at for a full class day. This time there was no pretense of doing a reading lesson or moving on to arithmetic. As soon as the bell rang, she simply began to talk.

She talked for forty minutes straight. There seemed to be less connection between her ideas, but the ideas themselves were, as the dictionary would say, fabulous. She said she had heard of a huge jewel, in what she called the Antipodes, that was so brilliant that when the light shone into it at a certain angle it would blind whoever was looking at its center. She said that the biggest diamond in the world was cursed and had killed everyone who owned it, and that by a trick of fate it was called the Hope diamond. Diamonds are magic, she said, and this is why women wear them on their fingers, as a sign of the magic of womanhood. Men have strength, Miss Ferenczi said, but no true magic. That is why men fall in love with women but women do not fall in love with men; they just love being loved. George Washington had died because of a mistake he made about a diamond. Washington was not the first *true* President, but she did not say who was. In some places in the world, she said, men and women still live in the trees and eat monkeys for breakfast. Their doctors are magicians. At the bottom of the sea are creatures thin as pancakes which have never been studied by scientists because when you take them up to the air, the fish explode.

There was not a sound in the classroom, except for Miss Ferenczi's voice, and Donna DeShano's coughing. No one even went to the bathroom.

Beethoven, she said, had not been deaf; it was a trick to make himself famous, and it worked. As she talked, Miss Ferenczi's pigtails swung back and forth. There are trees in the world, she said, that eat meat: their leaves are sticky and close up on bugs like hands. She lifted her hands and brought them together, palm to palm. Venus, which most people think is the next closest planet to the sun, is not always closer, and, besides, it is the planet of greatest mystery because of its thick cloud cover. "I know what lies underneath those clouds," Miss Ferenczi said, and waited. After the silence, she said, "Angels. Angels live under those clouds." She said that angels were not invisible to everyone and were in fact smarter than most people. They did not dress in robes as was often claimed but instead wore formal evening clothes, as if they were about to attend a concert. Often angels *do* attend concerts and sit in the aisles where, she said, most people pay no attention to them. She said the most terrible angel had the shape of the Sphinx. "There is no running away from that one," she said. She said that unquenchable fires burn just under the surface of the earth in Ohio, and that the baby Mozart fainted dead away in his cradle when he first heard the sound of a trumpet. She said that someone named Narzim al Harrardim was the greatest writer who ever lived. She said that planets control behavior, and anyone conceived during a solar eclipse would be born with webbed feet.

"I know you children like to hear these things," she said, "these secrets, and that is why I am telling you all this." We nodded. It was better than doing comprehension questions for the readings in *Broad Horizons*.

"I will tell you one more story," she said, "and then we will have to do arithmetic." She leaned over, and her voice grew soft. "There is no death," she said. "You must never be afraid. Never. That which is, cannot die. It will change into different earthly and unearthly elements, but I know this as sure as I stand here in front of you, and I swear it: you must not be afraid. I have seen this truth with these eyes. I know it because in a dream God kissed me. Here." And she pointed with her right index finger to the side of her head, below the mouth, where the vertical lines were carved into her skin.

Absent-mindedly we all did our arithmetic problems. At recess the class was out 95
on the playground, but no one was playing. We were all standing in small groups, talking about Miss Ferenczi. We didn't know if she was crazy, or what. I looked out beyond the playground, at the rusted cars piled in a small heap behind a clump of sumac, and I wanted to see shapes there, approaching me.

On the way home, Carl sat next to me again. He didn't say much, and I didn't either. At last he turned to me. "You know what she said about the leaves that close up on bugs?"

"Huh?"

"The leaves," Carl insisted. "The meat-eating plants. I know it's true. I saw it on television. The leaves have this icky glue that the plants have got smeared all over them and the insects can't get off, 'cause they're stuck. I saw it." He seemed demoralized. "She's tellin' the truth."

"Yeah."

"You think she's seen all those angels?" 100

I shrugged.

"I don't think she has," Carl informed me. "I think she made that part up."

"There's a tree," I suddenly said. I was looking out the window at the farms along County Road H. I knew every barn, every broken windmill, every fence, every anhydrous ammonia tank, by heart. "There's a tree that's . . . that I've seen . . ."

"Don't you try to do it," Carl said. "You'll just sound like a jerk."

I kissed my mother. She was standing in front of the stove. "How was your day?" 105
she asked.

"Fine."

"Did you have Miss Ferenczi again?"

"Yeah."

"Well?"

110 "She was fine. Mom," I asked, "can I go to my room?"

"No," she said, "not until you've gone out to the vegetable garden and picked me a few tomatoes." She glanced at the sky. "I think it's going to rain. Skedaddle and do it now. Then you come back inside and watch your brother for a few minutes while I go upstairs. I need to clean up before dinner." She looked down at me. "You're looking a little pale, Tommy." She touched the back of her hand to my forehead and I felt her diamond ring against my skin. "Do you feel all right?"

"I'm fine," I said, and went out to pick the tomatoes.

Coughing mutedly, Mr. Hibler was back the next day, slipping lozenges into his mouth when his back was turned at forty-five minute intervals and asking us how much of the prepared lesson plan Miss Ferenczi had followed. Edith Atwater took the responsibility for the class of explaining to Mr. Hibler that the substitute hadn't always done exactly what he would have done, but we had worked hard even though she talked a lot. About what? he asked. All kinds of things, Edith said. I sort of forgot. To our relief, Mr. Hibler seemed not at all interested in what Miss Ferenczi had said to fill the day. He probably thought it was woman's talk; unserious and not suited for school. It was enough that he had a pile of arithmetic problems from us to correct.

For the next month, the sumac turned a distracting red in the field, and the sun traveled toward the southern sky, so that its rays reached Mr. Hibler's Halloween display on the bulletin board in the back of the room, fading the scarecrow with a pumpkin head from orange to tan. Every three days I measured how much farther the sun had moved toward the southern horizon by making small marks with my black Crayola on the north wall, ant-sized marks only I knew were there, inching west.

115 And then in early December, four days after the first permanent snowfall, she appeared again in our classroom. The minute she came in the door, I felt my heart begin to pound. Once again, she was different: this time, her hair hung straight down and seemed hardly to have been combed. She hadn't brought her lunchbox with her, but she was carrying what seemed to be a small box. She greeted all of us and talked about the weather. Donna DeShano had to remind her to take her overcoat off.

When the bell to start the day finally rang, Miss Ferenczi looked out at all of us and said, "Children, I have enjoyed your company in the past, and today I am going to reward you." She held up the small box. "Do you know what this is?" She waited. "Of course you don't. It is a tarot pack."

Edith Atwater raised her hand. "What's a tarot pack, Miss Ferenczi?"

"It is used to tell fortunes," she said. "And that is what I shall do this morning. I shall tell your fortunes, as I have been taught to do."

"What's fortune?" Bobby Kryzanowicz asked.

120 "The future, young man. I shall tell you what your future will be. I can't do your whole future, of course. I shall have to limit myself to the five-card system, the wands, cups, swords, pentacles, and the higher arcanes. Now who wants to be first?"

There was a long silence. Then Carol Peterson raised her hand.

"All right," Miss Ferenczi said. She divided the pack into five smaller packs and walked back to Carol's desk, in front of mine. "Pick one card from each of these packs," she said. I saw that Carol had a four of cups, a six of swords, but I couldn't see the other cards. Miss Ferenczi studied the cards on Carol's desk for a minute. "Not bad," she said. "I do not see much higher education. Probably an early marriage. Many children. There's something bleak and dreary here, but I can't tell what. Perhaps just the tasks of a housewife life. I think you'll do very well, for the most part." She smiled at Carol, a smile with a certain lack of interest. "Who wants to be next?"

Carl Whiteside raised his hand slowly.

"Yes," Miss Ferenczi said, "let's do a boy." She walked over to where Carl sat. After he picked his five cards, she gazed at them for a long time. "Travel," she said. "Much distant travel. You might go into the Army. Not too much romantic interest here. A late marriage, if at all. Squabbles. But the Sun is in your major arcana, here, yes, that's a very good card." She giggled. "Maybe a good life."

Next I raised my hand, and she told me my future. She did the same with Bobby Kryzanowicz, Kelly Munger, Edith Atwater, and Kim Foor. Then she came to Wayne Razmer. He picked his five cards, and I could see that the Death card was one of them.

"What's your name?" Miss Ferenczi asked.

"Wayne."

"Well, Wayne," she said, you will undergo a *great* metamorphosis, the greatest, before you become an adult. Your earthly element will leap away, into thin air, you sweet boy. This card, this nine of swords here, tells of suffering and desolation. And this ten of wands, well, that's certainly a heavy load."

"What about this one?" Wayne pointed to the Death card.

"That one? That one means you will die soon, my dear." She gathered up the cards. We were all looking at Wayne. "But do not fear," she said. "It's not really death, so much as change." She put the cards on Mr. Hibler's desk. "And now, let's do some arithmetic."

At lunchtime Wayne went to Mr. Faegre, the principal, and told him what Miss Ferenczi had done. During the noon recess, we saw Miss Ferenczi drive out of the parking lot in her green Rambler. I stood under the slide, listening to the other kids coasting down and landing in the little depressive bowl at the bottom. I was kicking stones and tugging at my hair right up to the moment when I saw Wayne come out to the playground. He smiled, the dead fool, and with the fingers of his right hand he was showing everyone how he had told on Miss Ferenczi.

I made my way toward Wayne, pushing myself past two girls from another class. He was watching me with his little pinhead eyes.

"You told," I shouted at him. "She was just kidding."

"She shouldn't have," he shouted back. "We were supposed to be doing arithmetic."

"She just scared you," I said. "You're a chicken. You're a chicken, Wayne. You are. Scared of a little card," I singsonged.

Wayne fell at me, his two fists hammering down on my nose. I gave him a good one in the stomach and then I tried for his head. Aiming my fist, I saw that he was crying. I slugged him.

"She was right," I yelled. "She was always right! She told the truth!" Other kids were whooping. "You were just scared, that's all!"

And then large hands pulled at us, and it was my turn to speak to Mr. Faegre.

In the afternoon Miss Ferenczi was gone, and my nose was stuffed with cotton clotted with blood, and my lip had swelled, and our class had been combined with Mrs. Mantei's sixth-grade class for a crowded afternoon science unit on insect life in ditches and swamps. I knew where Mrs. Mantei lived: she had a new house trailer just down the road from us, at the Clearwater Park. She was no mystery. Somehow she and Mr. Bodine, the other fourth-grade teacher, had managed to fit forty-five desks into the room. Kelly Munger asked if Miss Ferenczi had been arrested, and Mrs. Mantei said no, of course not. All that afternoon, until the buses came to pick us up, we learned about field crickets and two-striped grasshoppers, water bugs, cicadas, mosquitoes, flies, and moths. We learned about insects' hard outer shell, the exoskeleton, and the usual parts of the mouth, including the labrum, mandible, maxilla, and glossa. We learned about compound eyes and the four-stage metamorphosis from egg to larva to pupa to adult. We learned something, but not much, about mating. Mrs. Mantei drew, very skillfully, the internal anatomy of the grasshopper on the blackboard. We learned about the dance of the honeybee, directing other bees in the hive to pollen. We found out about which insects were pests to man, and which were not. On lined white pieces of paper we made lists of insects we might actually see, then a list of insects too small to be clearly visible, such as fleas; Mrs. Mantei said that our assignment would be to memorize these lists for the next day, when Mr. Hibler would certainly return and test us on our knowledge.

Reading and Reacting

1. In classical mythology, a gryphon (also spelled *griffin*) is a monster that has the head and wings of an eagle and the body of a lion. Why is this story called "Gryphon"?
2. Describe Miss Ferenczi's physical appearance. Why is her appearance important to the story? How does it change as the story progresses?
3. How is Miss Ferenczi different from other teachers? From other substitute teachers? From other people in general? How is her differentness communicated to her pupils? To the story's readers?
4. What is the significance of the narrator's comment, in paragraph 11, that the lines on Miss Ferenczi's face remind him of Pinocchio?
5. Is Miss Ferenczi a round or a flat character? Explain.
6. In what sense is the narrator's mother a foil for Miss Ferenczi?
7. Why does the narrator defend Miss Ferenczi, first in his argument with Carl Whiteside and later on the playground? What does his attitude toward Miss Ferenczi reveal about his own character?

8. Are all of Miss Ferenczi's "substitute facts" lies, or is there some truth in what she says? Is she correct when she says that substitute facts cannot hurt anyone? Could it be argued that much of what is taught in schools today could be viewed as "substitute facts"?

9. Journal Entry Is Miss Ferenczi a good teacher? Why or why not?

10. Critical Perspective Writing in the *New York Times Book Review*, critic William Ferguson characterizes *A Relative Stranger*, a more recent collection of Baxter's short stories than the one in which "Gryphon" appeared, as follows:

> The thirteen stories in *A Relative Stranger*, in all quietly accomplished, suggest a mysterious yet fundamental marriage of despair and joy. Though in one way or another each story ends in disillusionment, the road that leads to that dismal state is so richly peopled, so finely drawn, that the effect is oddly reassuring.

Do you think this characterization of Baxter's work in A *Relative Stranger* applies to "Gryphon" as well? For example, do you see a "marriage of despair and joy"? Do you find the story reassuring in any way, or does it convey only a sense of disillusionment?

Related Works: "The Secret Lion" (p. 197), "A&P" (p. 259), "A Worn Path" (p. 568), "Sister Godzilla" (p. 700), "When I Heard the Learn'd Astronomer" (p. 877), "On First Looking into Chapman's Homer" (p. 984), *Proof* (p. 1476)

Source: ©AP Photo/Suzanne Plunkett

JHUMPA LAHIRI (1967–) was born in London to Indian parents and was raised in Rhode Island. She attended Barnard College, where she earned her BA, and Boston University, where she received four graduate degrees: an MA in English, an MA in creative writing, an MA in comparative literature and the arts, and a PhD in Renaissance studies. After completing her dissertation, Lahiri turned her attention solely to fiction. For her debut collection of stories, *The Interpreter of Maladies* (1999), Lahiri received the Pulitzer Prize for fiction (she was thirty-two years old), the PEN/Hemingway Award, The New Yorker Debut of the Year award, an American Academy of Arts and Letters Addison Metcalf Award, and a nomination for the *Los Angeles Times* Book Prize. Her first novel, *The Namesake*, was published in 2003, and her latest collection of stories, *Unaccustomed Earth,* was published in 2008.

Cultural Context In the 1950s, the United States and the Soviet Union were embroiled in the "Space Race," with each nation trying to be the first to reach and explore outer space. By the early 1960s, Russia was clearly ahead: both their satellite, *Sputnik,* and their cosmonaut, Yuri Gagarin, had already orbited the earth. But in 1969, America trumped these accomplishments by sending the first manned flight to the moon. On July 20, 1969, Neil Armstrong and Edwin "Buzz" Aldrin landed and walked on the moon, symbolizing a giant leap in progress for all of humanity. This historic event serves as a touchstone for the characters in "The Third and Final Continent."

The Third and Final Continent (2000)

I left India in 1964 with a certificate in commerce and the equivalent, in those days, of ten dollars to my name. For three weeks I sailed on the S.S. *Roma*, an Italian cargo vessel, in a cabin next to the ship's engine, across the Arabian Sea, the Red Sea, the Mediterranean, and finally to England. I lived in London, in Finsbury Park, in a house occupied entirely by penniless Bengali bachelors like myself, at least a dozen and sometimes more, all struggling to educate and establish ourselves abroad.

I attended lectures at LSE° and worked at the university library to get by. We lived three or four to a room, shared a single, icy toilet, and took turns cooking pots of egg curry, which we ate with our hands on a table covered with newspapers. Apart from our jobs we had few responsibilities. On weekends we lounged barefoot in drawstring pajamas, drinking tea and smoking Rothmans, or set out to watch cricket° at Lord's. Some weekends the house was crammed with still more Bengalis, to whom we had introduced ourselves at the greengrocer, or on the Tube,° and we made yet more egg curry, and played Mukesh° on a Grundig reel-to-reel,° and soaked our dirty dishes in the bathtub. Every now and then someone in the house moved out, to live with a woman whom his family back in Calcutta had determined he was to wed. In 1969, when I was thirty-six years old, my own marriage was arranged. Around the same time, I was offered a full-time job in America, in the processing department of a library at MIT. The salary was generous enough to support a wife, and I was honored to be hired by a world-famous university, and so I obtained a green card, and prepared to travel farther still.

By then I had enough money to go by plane. I flew first to Calcutta, to attend my wedding, and a week later to Boston, to begin my new job. During the flight I read "The Student Guide to North America," for although I was no longer a student, I was on a budget all the same. I learned that Americans drove on the right side of the road, not the left, and that they called a lift an elevator and an engaged phone busy. "The pace of life in North America is different from Britain, as you will soon discover," the guidebook informed me. "Everybody feels he must get to the top. Don't expect an English cup of tea." As the plane began its descent over Boston Harbor, the pilot announced the weather and the time, and that President Nixon had declared a national holiday: two American men had landed on the moon. Several passengers cheered. "God bless America!" one of them hollered. Across the aisle, I saw a woman praying.

I spent my first night at the YMCA in Central Square, Cambridge, an inexpensive accommodation recommended by my guidebook which was within walking distance of MIT. The room contained a cot, a desk, and a small wooden cross on one wall.

LSE: London School of Economics.

cricket: A game of English origin, a precursor to baseball, that features a batter, fielders, and a pitcher, called the hurler.

the Tube: The London Underground (subway).

Mukesh: Mukesh Sharma, an Indian musician.

Grundig reel-to-reel: high end audiotape player.

A sign on the door said that cooking was strictly forbidden. A bare window overlooked Massachusetts Avenue. Car horns, shrill and prolonged, blared one after another. Sirens and flashing lights heralded endless emergencies, and a succession of buses rumbled past, their doors opening and closing with a powerful hiss, throughout the night. The noise was constantly distracting, at times suffocating. I felt it deep in my ribs, just as I had felt the furious drone of the engine on the S.S. *Roma*. But there was no ship's deck to escape to, no glittering ocean to thrill my soul, no breeze to cool my face, no one to talk to. I was too tired to pace the gloomy corridors of the YMCA in my pajamas. Instead I sat at the desk and stared out the window. In the morning I reported to my job at the Dewey Library, a beige fortlike building by Memorial Drive. I also opened a bank account, rented a post office box, and bought a plastic bowl and a spoon. I went to a supermarket called Purity Supreme, wandering up and down the aisles, comparing prices with those in England. In the end I bought a carton of milk and a box of cornflakes. This was my first meal in America. Even the simple chore of buying milk was new to me; in London we'd had bottles delivered each morning to our door.

In a week I had adjusted, more or less. I ate cornflakes and milk morning and night, 5
and bought some bananas for variety, slicing them into the bowl with the edge of my spoon. I left my carton of milk on the shaded part of the windowsill, as I had seen other residents at the YMCA do. To pass the time in the evenings I read the *Boston Globe* downstairs, in a spacious room with stained-glass windows. I read every article and advertisement, so that I would grow familiar with things, and when my eyes grew tired I slept. Only I did not sleep well. Each night I had to keep the window wide open; it was the only source of air in the stifling room, and the noise was intolerable. I would lie on the cot with my fingers pressed into my ears, but when I drifted off to sleep my hands fell away, and the noise of the traffic would wake me up again. Pigeon feathers drifted onto the windowsill, and one evening, when I poured milk over my cornflakes, I saw that it had soured. Nevertheless I resolved to stay at the YMCA for six weeks, until my wife's passport and green card were ready. Once she arrived I would have to rent a proper apartment, and from time to time I studied the classified section of the newspaper, or stopped in at the housing office at MIT during my lunch break to see what was available. It was in this manner that I discovered a room for immediate occupancy, in a house on a quiet street, the listing said, for $8 per week. I dialed the number from a pay telephone, sorting through the coins, with which I was still unfamiliar, smaller and lighter than shillings, heavier and brighter than paisas.

"Who is speaking?" a woman demanded. Her voice was bold and clamorous.

"Yes, good afternoon, Madam. I am calling about the room for rent."

"Harvard or Tech?"

"I beg your pardon?"

"Are you from Harvard or Tech?" 10

Gathering that Tech referred to the Massachusetts Institute of Technology, I replied, "I work at Dewey Library," adding tentatively, "at Tech."

"I only rent rooms to boys from Harvard or Tech!"

"Yes, Madam."

I was given an address and an appointment for seven o'clock that evening. Thirty minutes before the hour I set out, my guidebook in my pocket, my breath fresh with Listerine. I turned down a street shaded with trees, perpendicular to Massachusetts Avenue. In spite of the heat I wore a coat and tie, regarding the event as I would any other interview; I had never lived in the home of a person who was not Indian. The house, surrounded by a chain-link fence was off-white with dark brown trim, with a tangle of forsythia bushes plastered against its front and sides. When I pressed the bell, the woman with whom I had spoken on the phone hollered from what seemed to be just the other side of the door, "One minute, please!"

15 Several minutes later the door was opened by a tiny, extremely old woman. A mass of snowy hair was arranged like a small sack on top of her head. As I stepped into the house she sat down on a wooden bench positioned at the bottom of a narrow carpeted staircase. Once she was settled on the bench, in a small pool of light, she peered up at me, giving me her undivided attention. She wore a long black skirt that spread like a stiff tent to the floor, and a starched white shirt edged with ruffles at the throat and cuffs. Her hands, folded together in her lap, had long pallid fingers, with swollen knuckles and tough yellow nails. Age had battered her features so that she almost resembled a man, with sharp, shrunken eyes and prominent creases on either side of her nose. Her lips, chapped and faded, had nearly disappeared, and her eyebrows were missing altogether. Nevertheless she looked fierce.

"Lock up!" she commanded. She shouted even though I stood only a few feet away. "Fasten the chain and firmly press that button on the knob! This is the first thing you shall do when you enter, is that clear?"

I locked the door as directed and examined the house. Next to the bench was a small round table, its legs fully concealed, much like the woman's, by a skirt of lace. The table held a lamp, a transistor radio, a leather change purse with a silver clasp, and a telephone. A thick wooden cane was propped against one side. There was a parlor to my right, lined with bookcases and filled with shabby claw-footed furniture. In the corner of the parlor I saw a grand piano with its top down, piled with papers. The piano's bench was missing; it seemed to be the one on which the woman was sitting. Somewhere in the house a clock chimed seven times.

"You're punctual!" the woman proclaimed. "I expect you shall be so with the rent!"

"I have a letter, Madam." In my jacket pocket was a letter from MIT confirming my employment, which I had brought along to prove that I was indeed from Tech.

20 She stared at the letter, then handed it back to me carefully, gripping it with her fingers as if it were a plate heaped with food. She did not wear glasses, and I wondered if she'd read a word of it. "The last boy was always late! Still owes me eight dollars! Harvard boys aren't what they used to be! Only Harvard and Tech in this house! How's Tech, boy?"

"It is very well."

"You checked the lock?"

"Yes, Madam."

She unclasped her fingers, slapped the space beside her on the bench with one hand, and told me to sit down. For a moment she was silent. Then she intoned, as if she alone possessed this knowledge:

25 "There is an American flag on the moon!"

"Yes, Madam." Until then I had not thought very much about the moon shot. It was in the newspaper, of course, article upon article. The astronauts had landed on the shores of the Sea of Tranquillity, I had read, traveling farther than anyone in the history of civilization. For a few hours they explored the moon's surface. They gathered rocks in their pockets, described their surroundings (a magnificent desolation, according to one astronaut), spoke by phone to the president, and planted a flag in lunar soil. The voyage was hailed as man's most awesome achievement.

The woman bellowed, "A flag on the moon, boy! I heard it on the radio! Isn't that splendid?"

"Yes, Madam."

But she was not satisfied with my reply. Instead she commanded, "Say 'Splendid!'"

I was both baffled and somewhat insulted by the request. It reminded me of the way I was taught multiplication tables as a child, repeating after the master, sitting cross-legged on the floor of my one-room Tollygunge school. It also reminded me of my wedding, when I had repeated endless Sanskrit verses after the priest, verses I barely understood, which joined me to my wife. I said nothing.

"Say 'Splendid!'" the woman bellowed once again.

"Splendid," I murmured. I had to repeat the word a second time at the top of my lungs, so she could hear. I was reluctant to raise my voice to an elderly woman, but she did not appear to be offended. If anything the reply pleased her, because her next command was:

"Go see the room!"

I rose from the bench and mounted the narrow staircase. There were five doors, two on either side of an equally narrow hallway, and one at the opposite end. Only one door was open. The room contained a twin bed under a sloping ceiling, a brown oval rug, a basin with an exposed pipe, and a chest of drawers. One door led to a closet, another to a toilet and a tub. The window was open; net curtains stirred in the breeze. I lifted them away and inspected the view: a small back yard, with a few fruit trees and an empty clothesline. I was satisfied.

When I returned to the foyer the woman picked up the leather change purse on the table, opened the clasp, fished about with her fingers, and produced a key on a thin wire hoop. She informed me that there was a kitchen at the back of the house, accessible through the parlor. I was welcome to use the stove as long as I left it as I found it. Sheets and towels were provided, but keeping them clean was my own responsibility. The rent was due Friday mornings on the ledge above the piano keys. "And no lady visitors!"

"I am a married man, Madam." It was the first time I had announced this fact to anyone.

But she had not heard. "No lady visitors!" she insisted. She introduced herself as Mrs. Croft.

My wife's name was Mala. The marriage had been arranged by my older brother and his wife. I regarded the proposition with neither objection nor enthusiasm. It was a duty expected of me, as it was expected of every man. She was the daughter of a schoolteacher in Beleghata. I was told that she could cook, knit, embroider, sketch landscapes, and recite poems by Tagore, but these talents could not make up for the fact that she did not possess a fair complexion, and so a string of men had rejected her to her face. She was twenty-seven, an age when her parents had begun to fear that she would never marry, and so they were willing to ship their only child halfway across the world in order to save her from spinsterhood.

For five nights we shared a bed. Each of those nights, after applying cold cream and braiding her hair, she turned from me and wept; she missed her parents. Although I would be leaving the country in a few days, custom dictated that she was now a part of my household, and for the next six weeks she was to live with my brother and his wife, cooking, cleaning, serving tea and sweets to guests. I did nothing to console her. I lay on my own side of the bed, reading my guidebook by flashlight. At times I thought of the tiny room on the other side of the wall which had belonged to my mother. Now the room was practically empty; the wooden pallet on which she'd once slept was piled with trunks and old bedding. Nearly six years ago, before leaving for London, I had watched her die on that bed, had found her playing with her excrement in her final days. Before we cremated her I had cleaned each of her fingernails with a hairpin, and then, because my brother could not bear it, I had assumed the role of eldest son, and had touched the flame to her temple, to release her tormented soul to heaven.

40 The next morning I moved into Mrs. Croft's house. When I unlocked the door I saw that she was sitting on the piano bench, on the same side as the previous evening. She wore the same black skirt, the same starched white blouse, and had her hands folded together the same way in her lap. She looked so much the same that I wondered if she'd spent the whole night on the bench. I put my suitcase upstairs and then headed off to work. That evening when I came home from the university, she was still there.

"Sit down, boy!" She slapped the space beside her.

I perched on the bench. I had a bag of groceries with me—more milk, more cornflakes, and more bananas, for my inspection of the kitchen earlier in the day had revealed no spare pots or pans. There were only two saucepans in the refrigerator, both containing some orange broth, and a copper kettle on the stove.

"Good evening, Madam."

She asked me if I had checked the lock. I told her I had.

45 For a moment she was silent. Then suddenly she declared, with the equal measures of disbelief and delight as the night before, "There's an American flag on the moon, boy!"

"Yes, Madam."

"A flag on the moon! Isn't that splendid?"

I nodded, dreading what I knew was coming. "Yes, Madam."

"Say 'Splendid!'"

50 This time I paused, looking to either side in case anyone was there to overhear me, though I knew perfectly well that the house was empty. I felt like an idiot. But it was a small enough thing to ask. "Splendid!" I cried out.

Within days it became our routine. In the mornings when I left for the library Mrs. Croft was either hidden away in her bedroom, on the other side of the staircase, or sitting on the bench, oblivious of my presence, listening to the news or classical music on the radio. But each evening when I returned the same thing happened: she slapped the bench, ordered me to sit down, declared that there was a flag on the moon, and declared that it was splendid. I said it was splendid, too, and then we sat in silence. As awkward as it was, and as endless as it felt to me then, the nightly encounter lasted only about ten minutes; inevitably she would drift off to sleep, her head falling abruptly toward her chest, leaving me free to retire to my room. By then, of course, there was no flag standing on the moon. The astronauts, I read in the paper, had seen it fall before they flew back to Earth. But I did not have the heart to tell her.

Friday morning, when my first week's rent was due, I went to the piano in the parlor to place my money on the ledge. The piano keys were dull and discolored. When I pressed one, it made no sound at all. I had put eight dollar bills in an envelope and written Mrs. Croft's name on the front of it. I was not in the habit of leaving money unmarked and unattended. From where I stood I could see the profile of her tent-shaped skirt in the hall. It seemed unnecessary to make her get up and walk all the way to the piano. I never saw her walking about, and assumed, from the cane propped against the round table, that she did so with difficulty. When I approached the bench she peered up at me and demanded:

"What is your business?"

"The rent, Madam."

"On the ledge above the piano keys!"

"I have it here." I extended the envelope toward her, but her fingers, folded together in her lap, did not budge. I bowed slightly and lowered the envelope; so that it hovered just above her hands. After a moment she accepted it, and nodded her head.

That night when I came home, she did not slap the bench, but out of habit I sat beside her as usual. She asked me if I had checked the lock, but she mentioned nothing about the flag on the moon. Instead she said:

"It was very kind of you!"

"I beg your pardon, Madam?"

"Very kind of you!"

She was still holding the envelope in her hands.

On Sunday there was a knock on my door. An elderly woman introduced herself: she was Mrs. Croft's daughter, Helen. She walked into the room and looked at each of the walls as if for signs of change, glancing at the shirts that hung in the closet, the neckties draped over the doorknob, the box of cornflakes on the chest of drawers, the dirty bowl and spoon in the basin. She was short and thick-waisted, with cropped silver hair and bright pink lipstick. She wore a sleeveless summer dress, a necklace of white plastic beads, and spectacles on a chain that hung like a swing against her chest. The backs of her legs were mapped with dark blue veins, and her upper arms sagged like the flesh of a roasted eggplant. She told me she lived in Arlington, a town farther up Massachusetts Avenue. "I come once a week to bring Mother groceries. Has she sent you packing yet?"

"It is very well, Madam."

"Some of the boys run screaming. But I think she likes you. You're the first boarder she's ever referred to as a gentleman."

She looked at me, noticing my bare feet. (I still felt strange wearing shoes indoors, and always removed them before entering my room.) "Are you new to Boston?"

"New to America, Madam."

"From?" She raised her eyebrows.

"I am from Calcutta, India."

"Is that right? We had a Brazilian fellow, about a year ago. You'll find Cambridge a very international city."

I nodded, and began to wonder how long our conversation would last. But at that moment we heard Mrs. Croft's electrifying voice rising up the stairs.

"You are to come downstairs immediately!"

"What is it?" Helen cried back.

"Immediately!"

I put on my shoes. Helen sighed.

I followed Helen down the staircase. She seemed to be in no hurry, and complained at one point that she had a bad knee. "Have you been walking without your cane?" Helen called out. "You know you're not supposed to walk without that cane." She paused, resting her hand on the banister, and looked back at me. "She slips sometimes."

For the first time Mrs. Croft seemed vulnerable. I pictured her on the floor in front of the bench, flat on her back, staring at the ceiling, her feet pointing in opposite directions. But when we reached the bottom of the staircase she was sitting there as usual, her hands folded together in her lap. Two grocery bags were at her feet. She did not slap the bench, or ask us to sit down. She glared.

"What is it, Mother?"

"It's improper!"

"What's improper?"

"It is improper for a lady and gentleman who are not married to one another to hold a private conversation without a chaperone!"

Helen said she was sixty-eight years old, old enough to be my mother, but Mrs. Croft insisted that Helen and I speak to each other downstairs, in the parlor. She added that it was also improper for a lady of Helen's station to reveal her age, and to wear a dress so high above the ankle.

"For your information, Mother, it's 1969. What would you do if you actually left the house one day and saw a girl in a miniskirt?"

Mrs. Croft sniffed. "I'd have her arrested."

Helen shook her head and picked up one of the grocery bags. I picked up the other one, and followed her through the parlor and into the kitchen. The bags were filled with cans of soup, which Helen opened up one by one with a few cranks of a can opener. She tossed the old soup into the sink, rinsed the saucepans under the tap, filled them with soup from the newly opened cans, and put them back in the refrigerator. "A few years ago she could still open the cans herself," Helen said. "She hates that I do it for her now. But the piano killed her hands." She put on her spectacles, glanced at the cupboards, and spotted my tea bags. "Shall we have a cup?"

I filled the kettle on the stove. "I beg your pardon, Madam. The piano?" 85

"She used to give lessons. For forty years. It was how she raised us after my father died." Helen put her hands on her hips, staring at the open refrigerator. She reached into the back, pulled out a wrapped stick of butter, frowned, and tossed it into the garbage. "That ought to do it," she said, and put the unopened cans of soup in the cupboard. I sat at the table and watched as Helen washed the dirty dishes, tied up the garbage bag, and poured boiling water into two cups. She handed one to me without milk, and sat down at the table.

"Excuse me, Madam, but is it enough?"

Helen took a sip of her tea. Her lipstick left a smiling pink stain on the rim of the cup. "Is what enough?"

"The soup in the pans. Is it enough food for Mrs. Croft?"

"She won't eat anything else. She stopped eating solids after she turned one hun- 90
dred. That was, let's see, three years ago.

I was mortified. I had assumed Mrs. Croft was in her eighties, perhaps as old as ninety. I had never known a person who had lived for over a century. That this person was a widow who lived alone mortified me further still. Widowhood had driven my own mother insane. My father, who worked as a clerk at the General Post office of Calcutta, died of encephalitis when I was sixteen. My mother refused to adjust to life without him; instead she sank deeper into a world of darkness from which neither I, nor my brother, nor concerned relatives, nor psychiatric clinics on Rash Behari Avenue could save her. What pained me most was to see her so unguarded, to hear her burp after meals or expel gas in front of company without the slightest embarrassment. After my father's death, my brother abandoned his schooling and began to work in the jute mill he would eventually manage, in order to keep the household running. And so it was my job to sit by my mother's feet and study for my exams as she counted and recounted the bracelets on her arm as if they were the beads of an abacus. We tried to keep an eye on her. Once she had wandered half-naked to the tram depot before we were able to bring her inside again.

"I am happy to warm Mrs. Croft's soup in the evenings," I suggested. "It is no trouble."

Helen looked at her watch, stood up, and poured the rest of her tea into the sink. "I wouldn't if I were you. That's the sort of thing that would kill her altogether."

That evening, when Helen had gone and Mrs. Croft and I were alone again, I began to worry. Now that I knew how very old she was, I worried that something would happen to her in the middle of the night, or when I was out during the day. As vigorous as her voice was, and as imperious as she seemed, I knew that even a scratch or a cough could kill a person that old; each day she lived, I knew, was something of a miracle. Helen didn't seem concerned. She came and went, bringing soup for Mrs. Croft, one Sunday after the next.

95 In this manner the six weeks of that summer passed. I came home each evening, after my hours at the library, and spent a few minutes on the piano bench with Mrs. Croft. Some evenings I sat beside her long after she had drifted off to sleep, still in awe of how many years she had spent on this earth. At times I tried to picture the world she had been born into, in 1866—a world, I imagined, filled with women in long black skirts, and chaste conversations in the parlor. Now, when I looked at her hands with their swollen knuckles folded together in her lap, I imagined them smooth and slim, striking the piano keys. At times I came downstairs before going to sleep, to make sure she was sitting upright on the bench, or was safe in her bedroom. On Fridays I put the rent in her hands. There was nothing I could do for her beyond these simple gestures. I was not her son, and, apart from those eight dollars, I owed her nothing.

At the end of August, Mala's passport and green card were ready. I received a telegram with her flight information; my brother's house in Calcutta had no telephone. Around that time I also received a letter from her, written only a few days after we had parted. There was no salutation; addressing me by name would have assumed an intimacy we had not yet discovered. It contained only a few lines. "I write in English in preparation for the journey. Here I am very much lonely. Is it very cold there. Is there snow. Yours, Mala."

I was not touched by her words. We had spent only a handful of days in each other's company. And yet we were bound together; for six weeks she had worn an iron bangle on her wrist, and applied vermilion powder to the part in her hair, to signify to the world that she was a bride. In those six weeks I regarded her arrival as I would the arrival of a coming month, or season—something inevitable, but meaningless at the time. So little did I know her that, while details of her face sometimes rose to my memory, I could not conjure up the whole of it.

A few days after receiving the letter, as I was walking to work in the morning, I saw an Indian woman on Massachusetts Avenue, wearing a sari with its free end nearly dragging on the footpath, and pushing a child in a stroller. An American woman with a small black dog on a leash was walking to one side of her. Suddenly the dog began barking. I watched as the Indian woman, startled, stopped in her path, at which point the dog leaped up and seized the end of the sari between its teeth. The American woman scolded the dog, appeared to apologize, and walked quickly away, leaving the Indian woman to fix her sari, and quiet her crying child. She did not see me standing there, and eventually she continued on her way. Such a mishap, I realized that morning, would soon be my concern. It was my duty to take care of Mala, to welcome her and protect her. I would have to buy her her first pair of snow boots, her first winter coat. I would have to tell her which streets to avoid, which way the traffic came, tell her to wear her sari so that the free end did not drag on the footpath. A five-mile separation from her parents, I recalled with some irritation, had caused her to weep.

Unlike Mala, I was used to it all by then: used to cornflakes and milk, used to Helen's visits, used to sitting on the bench with Mrs. Croft. The only thing I was not used to was Mala. Nevertheless, I did what I had to do. I went to the housing office at

MIT and found a furnished apartment a few blocks away, with a double bed and a private kitchen and bath, for $40 a week. One last Friday I handed Mrs. Croft eight dollar bills in an envelope, brought my suitcase downstairs, and informed her that I was moving. She put my key into her change purse. The last thing she asked me to do was hand her the cane propped against the table, so that she could walk to the door and lock it behind me. "Good-bye, then," she said, and retreated back into the house. I did not expect any display of emotion, but I was disappointed all the same. I was only a boarder, a man who paid her a bit of money and passed in and out of her home for six weeks. Compared with a century, it was no time at all.

At the airport I recognized Mala immediately. The free end of her sari did not drag 100
on the floor, but was draped in a sign of bridal modesty over her head, just as it had draped my mother until the day my father died. Her thin brown arms were stacked with gold bracelets, a small red circle was painted on her forehead, and the edges of her feet were tinted with a decorative red dye. I did not embrace her, or kiss her, or take her hand. Instead I asked her, speaking Bengali for the first time in America, if she was hungry.

She hesitated, then nodded yes.

I told her I had prepared some egg curry at home. "What did they give you to eat on the plane?"

"I didn't eat."

"All the way from Calcutta?"

"The menu said oxtail soup." 105

"But surely there were other items."

"The thought of eating an ox's tail made me lose my appetite."

When we arrived home, Mala opened up one of her suitcases, and presented me with two pullover sweaters, both made with bright blue wool, which she had knitted in the course of our separation, one with a V-neck, the other covered with cables. I tried them on; both were tight under the arms. She had also brought me two new pairs of drawstring pajamas, a letter from my brother, and a packet of loose Darjeeling tea. I had no present for her apart from the egg curry. We sat at a bare table, staring at our plates. We ate with our hands, another thing I had not yet done in America.

"The house is nice," she said. "Also the egg curry." With her left hand she held the end of her sari to her chest, so it would not slip off her head.

"I don't know many recipes." 110

She nodded, peeling the skin off each of her potatoes before eating them. At one point the sari slipped to her shoulders. She readjusted it at once.

"There is no need to cover your head," I said. "I don't mind. It doesn't matter here."

She kept it covered anyway.

I waited to get used to her, to her presence at my side, at my table and in my bed, but a week later we were still strangers. I still was not used to coming home to an apartment that smelled of steamed rice, and finding that the basin in the bathroom was always wiped clean, our two toothbrushes lying side by side, a cake of Pears soap residing in the soap dish. I was not used to the fragrance of the coconut oil she rubbed every other night into her scalp, or the delicate sound her bracelets made as she moved about the apartment. In the mornings she was always awake before I was. The first morning when I came into the kitchen she had heated up the leftovers and set a plate with a spoonful of salt on its edge, assuming I would eat rice for breakfast, as most Bengali husbands did. I told her cereal would do, and the next morning when I came into the kitchen she had already poured the cornflakes into my bowl. One morning she walked with me to MIT, where I gave her a short tour of the campus. The next morning before I left for work she asked me for a few dollars. I parted with them reluctantly, but I knew that this, too, was now normal. When I came home from work there was a potato peeler in the kitchen drawer, and a tablecloth on the table, and chicken curry made with fresh garlic and ginger on the stove. After dinner I read the newspaper, while Mala sat at the kitchen table, working on a cardigan for herself with more of the blue wool, or writing letters home.

On Friday, I suggested going out. Mala set down her knitting and disappeared into the bathroom. When she emerged I regretted the suggestion; she had put on a silk sari and extra bracelets, and coiled her hair with a flattering side part on top of her head. She was prepared as if for a party, or at the very least for the cinema, but I had no such destination in mind. The evening was balmy. We walked several blocks down Massachusetts Avenue, looking into the windows of restaurants and shops. Then, without thinking, I led her down the quiet street where for so many nights I had walked alone.

"This is where I lived before you came," I said, stopping at Mrs. Croft's chain-link fence.

"In such a big house?"

"I had a small room upstairs. At the back."

"Who else lives there?"

"A very old woman."

"With her family?"

"Alone."

"But who takes care of her?"

I opened the gate. "For the most part she takes care of herself."

I wondered if Mrs. Croft would remember me; I wondered if she had a new boarder to sit with her each evening. When I pressed the bell I expected the same long wait as that day of our first meeting, when I did not have a key. But this time the door was opened almost immediately, by Helen. Mrs. Croft was not sitting on the bench. The bench was gone.

"Hello there," Helen said, smiling with her bright pink lips at Mala. "Mother's in the parlor. Will you be visiting awhile?"

"As you wish, Madam."

"Then I think I'll run to the store, if you don't mind. She had a little accident. We can't leave her alone these days, not even for a minute."

I locked the door after Helen and walked into the parlor. Mrs. Croft was lying flat on her back, her head on a peach-colored cushion, a thin white quilt spread over her body. Her hands were folded together on her chest. When she saw me she pointed at the sofa, and told me to sit down. I took my place as directed, but Mala wandered over to the piano and sat on the bench, which was now positioned where it belonged.

"I broke my hip!" Mrs. Croft announced, as if no time had passed. 130

"Oh dear, Madam."

"I fell off the bench!"

"I am so sorry, Madam."

"It was the middle of the night! Do you know what I did, boy?"

I shook my head. 135

"I called the police!"

She stared up at the ceiling and grinned sedately, exposing a crowded row of long gray teeth. "What do you say to that, boy?"

As stunned as I was, I knew what I had to say. With no hesitation at all, I cried out, "Splendid!"

Mala laughed then. Her voice was full of kindness, her eyes bright with amusement. I had never heard her laugh before, and it was loud enough so that Mrs. Croft heard, too. She turned to Mala and glared.

"Who is she, boy?" 140

"She is my wife, Madam."

Mrs. Croft pressed her head at an angle against the cushion to get a better look. "Can you play the piano?"

"No, Madam," Mala replied.

"Then stand up!"

Mala rose to her feet, adjusting the end of her sari over her head and holding it to 145 her chest, and, for the first time since her arrival, I felt sympathy. I remembered my first days in London, learning how to take the Tube to Russell Square, riding an escalator for the first time, unable to understand that when the man cried "piper" it meant "paper," unable to decipher, for a whole year, that the conductor said "Mind the gap" as the train entered each station. Like me, Mala had traveled far from home, not knowing where she was going, or what she would find, for no reason other than to be my wife. As strange as it seemed, I knew in my heart that one day her death would affect me, and stranger still, that mine would affect her. I wanted somehow to explain this to Mrs. Croft, who was still scrutinizing Mala from top to toe with what seemed to be placid disdain. I wondered if Mrs. Croft had ever seen a woman in a sari, with a dot painted on her forehead and bracelets stacked on her wrists. I wondered what she would object to. I wondered if she could see the red dye still vivid on Mala's feet, all but obscured by the bottom edge of her sari. At last Mrs. Croft declared, with the equal measures of disbelief and delight I knew well:

"She is a perfect lady!"

Now it was I who laughed. I did so quietly, and Mrs. Croft did not hear me. But Mala had heard, and, for the first time, we looked at each other and smiled. I like to think of that moment in Mrs. Croft's parlor as the moment when the distance between Mala and me began to lessen. Although we were not yet fully in love, I like to think of the months that followed as a honeymoon of sorts. Together we explored the city and met other Bengalis, some of whom are still friends today. We discovered that a man named Bill sold fresh fish on Prospect Street, and that a shop in Harvard Square called Cardullo's sold bay leaves and cloves. In the evenings we walked to the Charles River to watch sailboats drift across the water, or had ice cream cones in Harvard Yard. We bought a camera with which to document our life together, and I took pictures of her posing in front of the Prudential building, so that she could send them to her parents. At night we kissed, shy at first but quickly bold, and discovered pleasure and solace in each other's arms. I told her about my voyage on the S.S. *Roma,* and about Finsbury Park and the YMCA, and my evenings on the bench with Mrs. Croft. When I told her stories about my mother, she wept. It was Mala who consoled me when, reading the *Globe* one evening, I came across Mrs. Croft's obituary. I had not thought of her in several months—by then those six weeks of the summer were already a remote interlude in my past—but when I learned of her death I was stricken, so much so that when Mala looked up from her knitting she found me staring at the wall, unable to speak. Mrs. Croft's was the first death I mourned in America, for hers was the first life I had admired; she had left this world at last, ancient and alone, never to return.

As for me, I have not strayed much farther. Mala and I live in a town about twenty miles from Boston, on a tree-lined street much like Mrs. Croft's, in a house we own, with room for guests, and a garden that saves us from buying tomatoes in summer. We are American citizens now, so that we can collect Social Security when it is time. Though we visit Calcutta every few years, we have decided to grow old here. I work in a small college library. We have a son who attends Harvard University. Mala no longer drapes the end of her sari over her head, or weeps at night for her parents, but occasionally she weeps for our son. So we drive to Cambridge to visit him, or bring him home for a weekend, so that he can eat rice with us with his hands, and speak in Bengali, things we sometimes worry he will no longer do after we die.

Whenever we make that drive, I always take Massachusetts Avenue, in spite of the traffic. I barely recognize the buildings now, but each time I am there I return instantly to those six weeks as if they were only the other day, and I slow down and point to Mrs. Croft's street, saying to my son, "Here was my first home in America, where I lived with a woman who was 103." "Remember?" Mala says, and smiles, amazed, as I am, that there was ever a time that we were strangers. My son always expresses his astonishment, not at Mrs. Croft's age but at how little I paid in rent, a fact nearly as inconceivable to him as a flag on the moon was to a woman born in 1866. In my son's eyes I see the ambition that had first hurled me across the world. In a few years he will graduate and pave his own way, alone and unprotected. But I remind myself that he has a father who is still living, a mother who is happy and strong. Whenever he is discouraged, I tell him that if I can survive on three continents, then there is no obstacle he cannot conquer. While the astronauts, heroes forever, spent mere hours on the moon, I have remained in this new world for nearly thirty years. I know that my achievement is quite ordinary. I am not the only man to seek his fortune far from home, and certainly I am not the first. Still, there are times I am bewildered by each mile I have traveled, each meal I have eaten, each person I have known, each room in which I have slept. As ordinary as it all appears, there are times when it is beyond my imagination.

Reading and Reacting

1. Mrs. Croft, who is 103 years old, is initially described as "a tiny, extremely old woman" (par. 15). Does she ever move beyond this stereotype to become a fully developed character, or does she remain a stereotype?
2. At the end of the story, the narrator says about Mrs. Croft, "hers was the first life I had admired" (par. 147). Exactly what do you think he admires about her life?
3. The narrator, having lived in India and in England, is now living in Boston, on his third continent. In what respects is he still tied to the other two continents? In what sense is the continent on which he is now living his "final continent"?
4. How does the narrator change during the course of the story? What causes these changes? In what respects is he still the same person he was when he arrived in Boston?
5. What is the significance of the piano? The piano bench? What do they tell readers about Mrs. Croft? About the narrator?
6. At one point in the story (par. 91), the narrator reveals information about his family in India, in particular about his mother's widowhood. Why does this information appear at this point in the story? What does it tell readers about the narrator's culture? About his marriage? About his reaction to Mrs. Croft?
7. Mala, the narrator's wife, does not really enter the story as a character until two-thirds of the way through, long after the narrator's relationship with Mrs. Croft has been established. How does his relationship with Mrs. Croft prepare readers for the relationship he will have with his wife? How does it prepare *him*?
8. The narrator arrives in the United States on the day American astronauts land on the moon, and the moon landing is mentioned throughout the story (for example, in paragraphs 3, 25–27, 45, 51, and the last paragraph). How does this historic event help to shed light on the narrator's life on his "third and final continent"?
9. **Journal Entry** In the last paragraphs, we learn that the narrator now has a son. How is the son's life different from the life his father led at the same age? How do you imagine the son's future life will be different from his parents' lives?
10. **Critical Perspective** While being interviewed about *The Interpreter of Maladies*, the collection in which this story appeared, Jhumpa Lahiri made the following comments:

    > For immigrants, the challenges of exile, the loneliness, the constant sense of alienation, the knowledge of and longing for a lost world, are more explicit and distressing than for their children. On the other hand, the problem for the children of immigrants, those with strong ties to their country of origin, is that they feel neither one thing nor the other.

    Do you think Lahiri's characterization of immigrants is an accurate description of the feelings experienced by the narrator of "The Third and Final Continent" and his wife? Are their concerns for their son related to the fact that he is in a sense caught between two cultures?

Related Works: "Telephone Conversation" (p. 7), "The Disappearance" (p. 695), "A Valediction: Forbidding Mourning" (p. 933), "Immigrants" (p. 1006). *The Cuban Swimmer* (p. 1732), *Trying to Find Chinatown* (p. 1856)

WRITING SUGGESTIONS: Character

1. In both "A&P," and "Gryphon," the main characters (Sammy and Tommy, respectively) struggle against rules, authority figures, and inflexible social systems. Compare and contrast the struggles in which these two characters are engaged.
2. Write an essay in which you contrast the character of Miss Brill (p. 266) with the character of Emily Grierson in "A Rose for Emily" (p. 243) or with Phoenix Jackson in "A Worn Path" (p. 568). Consider how each character interacts with those around her as well as how each seems to see her role or mission in the world.
3. Sammy, Miss Brill, and Miss Ferenczi all use their active imaginations to create scenarios that help get them through the day. None of them is able to sustain the illusion, however. As a result, all three find out how harsh reality can be. How are these scenarios alike, and how are they different? What steps could these three characters take to fit more comfortably into the worlds they inhabit? *Should* they take such steps? Are they able to do so?
4. Write an analysis of a minor character in one of this chapter's stories—for example, Mala or Mrs. Croft in "The Third and Final Continent" or Maurice in "The Girl with Bangs."
5. Several of the characters in this chapter's stories—for example, the narrator in "Eyeball," Tommy in "Gryphon," and the narrator in "The Third and Final Continent"—are presented as outsiders struggling to understand and adapt to the dominant culture. In what sense is each outside the mainstream? Which characters do you think have the best chance of surviving (and thriving) in the larger world? Why?

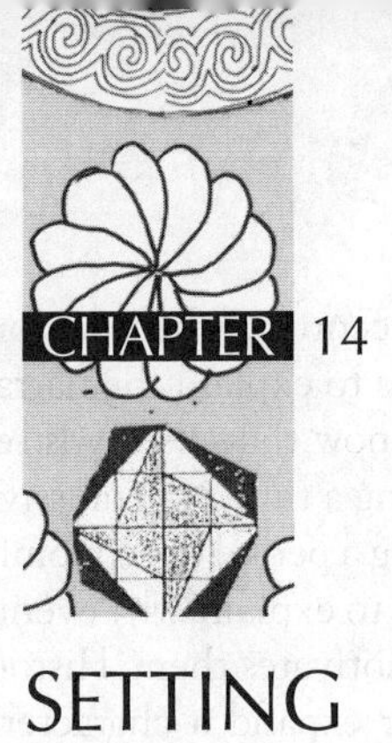

CHAPTER 14

SETTING

The **setting** of a work of fiction establishes its historical, geographical, and physical context. *Where* a work is set—on a tropical island, in a dungeon, at a crowded party, in the woods—influences our reactions to the story's events and characters. *When* a work takes place—during the French Revolution, during the Vietnam War, today, or in the future—is equally important. Setting, however, is more than just the approximate time and place in which a work is set; setting also encompasses a wide variety of physical and cultural elements.

Clearly, setting is more important in some works than in others. In some stories, no particular time or place is specified or even suggested, perhaps because the writer does not consider a specific setting to be important or because the writer wishes the story's events to seem timeless and universal. In Nadine Gordimer's "Once upon a Time" (p. 232), for example, the writer follows the conventions of fairy tales, which are set in unidentified faraway places. In other stories, a writer may provide only minimal information about setting, telling readers little more than where and when the action takes place. Sometimes, however, a particular setting may be vital to the story, perhaps influencing characters' feelings or behavior, as it does in the stories in this chapter.

Sometimes a story's central conflict is between the protagonist and the setting—for example, Alice in Wonderland, a northerner in the South, an unsophisticated American tourist in an old European city, a sane person in a psychiatric hospital, a moral person in a corrupt environment, an immigrant in a new world, or a city dweller in the country. Such a conflict may drive the story's plot and also help to define the characters. (A conflict between events and setting—for example, the arrival of a mysterious stranger in a typical suburban neighborhood, the intrusion of modern social ideas into an old-fashioned world, or the intrusion of a brutal murder into a peaceful village—can also enrich a story.)

Historical Setting

A particular historical period, and the events and customs associated with it, can be important to your understanding of a story; therefore, some knowledge of the period in which a story is set is useful (or even essential) for readers. The historical setting establishes a story's social, cultural, economic, and political environment. Knowing, for instance, that Charlotte Perkins Gilman's "The Yellow

Wallpaper" (p. 459) was written in the late nineteenth century, when doctors treated women as delicate and dependent creatures, helps to explain the narrator's emotional state. Likewise, it may be important to know that a story is set during a particularly volatile (or static) political era, during a time of permissive (or repressive) attitudes toward sex, during a war, or during a period of economic prosperity or recession. Any one of these factors may help to explain why events occur as well as why characters act as they do and what motivates them. Historical events or cultural norms may, for instance, limit or expand a character's options, and our knowledge of history may reveal to us a character's incompatibility with his or her milieu. For example, in F. Scott Fitzgerald's "Bernice Bobs Her Hair," set in the 1920s in a midwestern town, a young girl is goaded into cutting her long hair. To understand the significance of Bernice's act—and to understand the reactions of others to that act—readers must know that during that era only racy "society vampires," not nice girls from good families, bobbed their hair.

Knowing the approximate year or historical period during which a story takes place can help readers to better understand characters and events. This knowledge can explain forces that act on characters and account for their behavior, clarify circumstances that influence the story's action, and justify a writer's use of plot devices that might otherwise seem improbable. Thus, stories set before the development of modern transportation and communication systems may hinge on plot devices readers would not accept in a modern story. For example, in "Paul's Case," a 1904 story by Willa Cather, a young man who steals a large sum of money in Pittsburgh is able to spend several days enjoying it before the news of the theft reaches New York, where he has fled. In other stories, we see characters threatened by diseases that have now been eradicated (or subjected to outdated medical or psychiatric treatment) or constrained by social conventions very different from those that operate in our own society.

Geographical Setting

In addition to knowing *when* a work takes place, readers need to know *where* it takes place. Knowing whether a story is set in the United States, in Europe, or in a developing nation can help to explain anything from why language and customs are unfamiliar to us to why characters act in ways we find surprising. Even in stories set in our own country, regional differences may account for differences in plot development and characters' motivation. For example, knowing that William Faulkner's "A Rose for Emily" (p. 243) is set in the post–Civil War American South helps to explain why the townspeople are so chivalrously protective of Miss Emily. Similarly, the fact that Bret Harte's classic story "The Outcasts of Poker Flat" (1869) is set in a California mining camp accounts for its varied cast of characters—including a gambler, a prostitute, and a traveling salesman.

The size of the town or city in which a story takes place may also be important. In a small town, for example, a character's problems are more likely to be subject to intense scrutiny by other characters, as they are in stories of small-town life such as those in Sherwood Anderson's 1919 novel *Winesburg, Ohio*. In a large city, characters may be more likely to be isolated and anonymous, like Mrs. Miller in Truman Capote's gothic short story "Miriam" (1945), who is so lonely that she creates an imaginary companion. Characters may also be alienated by their big-city surroundings, as Gregor Samsa is in Franz Kafka's classic novella "The Metamorphosis" (1915).

Of course, a story may not have a recognizable geographical setting: its location may not be specified, or it may be set in a fantasy world. Choosing unusual settings may free writers from the constraints placed on them by familiar environments, allowing them to experiment with situations and characters, unaffected by readers' expectations or associations with familiar settings.

Physical Setting

Physical setting can influence a story's mood as well as its development. For example, *time of day* can be important. The gruesome murder described in Edgar Allan Poe's "The Cask of Amontillado" (p. 385) takes place in an appropriate setting: not just underground but in the darkness of night. Conversely, the horrifying events of Shirley Jackson's "The Lottery" (p. 509) take place in broad daylight, contrasting dramatically with the darkness of the society that permits—and even participates in—a shocking ritual. Many stories, of course, move through several time periods as the action unfolds, and changes in time may also be important. For instance, the approach of evening, or of dawn, can signal the end of a crisis in the plot.

Whether a story is set primarily *indoors* or *out-of-doors* may also be significant: characters may be physically constrained by a closed-in setting or liberated by an expansive landscape. Some interior settings may be psychologically limiting. For instance, the narrator in "The Yellow Wallpaper" feels suffocated by her room, whose ugly wallpaper comes to haunt her. In many of Poe's stories, the central character is trapped, physically or psychologically, in a confined, suffocating space. In other stories, an interior setting may have a symbolic function. For example, in "A Rose for Emily," the house is for Miss Emily a symbol of the South's past glory as well as a refuge, a fortress, and a hiding place. Similarly, a building or house may represent society, with its rules, norms, and limitations, as in John Updike's "A&P" (p. 259), where the supermarket establishes social as well as physical limits.

Conversely, an outdoor setting can free a character from social norms of behavior, as it does for Ernest Hemingway's Nick Adams, a war veteran who, in "Big Two-Hearted River" (1925), finds order, comfort, and peace only when he is away from civilization. An outdoor setting can also expose characters to physical dangers, such as untamed wilderness, uncharted seas, and frighteningly empty open spaces, as is the case in Stephen Crane's "The Open Boat" (1897).

Weather can be another important aspect of setting. A storm can threaten a character's life or just make the character—and readers—*think* danger is present, distracting us from other, more subtle threats. Extreme weather conditions can make characters act irrationally or uncharacteristically, as in Kate Chopin's "The Storm" (p. 313), where a storm provides the story's complication and determines the characters' actions. In numerous stories set in hostile landscapes, where extremes of heat and cold influence the action, weather may serve as a test for characters, as it does in Jack London's "To Build a Fire" (1908), in which the main character struggles unsuccessfully against the brutally cold, hostile environment of the Yukon.

The various physical attributes of setting combine to create a story's **atmosphere** or **mood.** In "The Cask of Amontillado," for example, several factors work together to create the story's eerie, intense atmosphere: it is nighttime; it is the hectic carnival season; and the catacombs are dark, damp, and filled with the bones of the narrator's ancestors. Sometimes the mood or atmosphere that is created helps to convey a story's central theme—as the ironic contrast between the pleasant atmosphere and the shocking events that unfold communicates the theme of "The Lottery." A story's atmosphere may also be linked to a character's mental state, perhaps reflecting his or her mood. For example, darkness and isolation can reflect a character's depression, whereas an idyllic, peaceful atmosphere can express a character's joy. And, of course, a story's atmosphere can also *influence* the characters' state of mind, causing them to react one way in a crowded, busy, urban atmosphere but to react very differently in a peaceful rural atmosphere.

✔ CHECKLIST Writing about Setting

- ☐ Is the setting specified or unspecified? Is it fully described or only suggested?
- ☐ Is the setting just background, or is it a key force in the story?
- ☐ Are any characters in conflict with their environment?
- ☐ How does the setting influence the story's plot? Does it cause characters to act?
- ☐ In what time period does the story take place? How can you tell? What social, political, or economic situations or events of the historical period might influence the story?
- ☐ In what geographical location is the story set? Is this location important to the story?
- ☐ At what time of day is the story set? Is time important to the development of the story?

continued on next page

- Is the story set primarily indoors or out-of-doors? What role does this aspect of the setting play in the story?
- What role do weather conditions play in the story?
- What kind of atmosphere or mood does the setting create?
- How does the setting influence the characters? Does it affect (or reflect) their emotional state? Does it help to explain their motivation?
- Does the atmosphere change as the story progresses? Is this change significant?

Source: ©AP Photo/Kirsty Wigglesworth

MARJANE SATRAPI (1969–), raised in Tehran, Iran, has published numerous graphic fiction books in both English and French, including the award-winning graphic memoir *Persepolis* (2003) and its sequel, *Persepolis 2* (2004). The *Persepolis* works, from which the following excerpt is taken, depict Satrapi's experiences growing up in Tehran during the Islamic Revolution and Iran's war with Iraq. Satrapi cowrote and codirected the animated feature film *Persepolis* (2007), which tied for a Special Jury Prize at the 2007 Cannes Film Festival and was nominated for an Academy Award for best animated feature film. Like *Persepolis,* Satrapi's latest graphic novel, *Embroideries* (2005), also portrays the female experience in modern-day Iran.

Cultural Context Persepolis is an ancient Persian city located in modern-day Iran. King of Persia from 522–486 B.C., Darius I named Persepolis the capital of Persia. The city is known for its monumental architecture, including several royal palaces and an audience hall, the ruins of which can still be seen today. Named after the ancient city, Satrapi's graphic novel, from which the following excerpt is taken, alludes to Iran's epic past and makes an ironic statement about the cultural climate of today.

Persepolis (2003)

This graphic story starts on the next page. →

Reading and Reacting

1. What specific visual elements establish the setting of "Persepolis" (p. 310) as harsh and restrictive for Marji?
2. Compare the facial expressions of the "guardians of the revolution" (especially in the final four panels) with Marji's. How are they different? In what other respects does Marji look different from these women?
3. The two panels that show Marji purchasing the tapes are the only ones that have a dark background. Do you think Satrapi should have used dark backgrounds in any other panels? Why or why not?
4. **Journal Entry** This story has a happy ending. Try writing (and perhaps drawing) a different ending to substitute for the story's last three panels.

Source: ©2003 Marjan Satrapi. Used courtesy of Pantheon Books at Random House.

THEIR JOB WAS TO PUT US BACK ON THE STRAIGHT AND NARROW BY EXPLAINING THE DUTIES OF MUSLIM WOMEN.
WHY ARE YOU WEARING THOSE "PUNK" SHOES?
WHAT PUNK SHOES?

THOSE!
BUT THESE ARE SNEAKERS!
SHUT UP! THEY'RE PUNK.
IT WAS OBVIOUS THAT SHE HAD NO IDEA WHAT PUNK WAS.

THERE WAS NO ALTERNATIVE. I HAD TO LIE.
I WEAR THESE BECAUSE I PLAY BASKETBALL.
I'M ON MY SCHOOL'S TEAM.
OH SURE. I CAN TELL BY YOUR HEIGHT!

AND YOU WEAR THIS JACKET FOR BASKETBALL TOO??

WHAT DO I SEE HERE? MICHAEL JACKSON! THAT SYMBOL OF DECADENCE?

NO, IT'S MALCOLM X, THE LEADER OF BLACK MUSLIMS IN AMERICA.
DON'T GIVE ME THAT! IT'S MICHAEL JACKSON!
WHO? I DON'T KNOW HIM.
BACK THEN, MICHAEL JACKSON WAS STILL BLACK.

LOWER YOUR SCARF, YOU LITTLE WHORE!

AREN'T YOU ASHAMED TO WEAR TIGHT JEANS LIKE THESE??
THEY SHRANK!!

GO ON, GET IN THE CAR. WE'RE TAKING YOU DOWN TO THE COMMITTEE.
THE COMMITTEE WAS THE HQ OF THE GUARDIANS OF THE REVOLUTION.

AT THE COMMITTEE, THEY DIDN'T HAVE TO INFORM MY PARENTS. THEY COULD DETAIN ME FOR HOURS, OR FOR DAYS. I COULD BE WHIPPED. IN SHORT, ANYTHING COULD HAPPEN TO ME. IT WAS TIME FOR ACTION.
I'M SORRY MA'AM! I'LL NEVER DO IT AGAIN...
GET IN THE CAR!

MA'AM, MY MOTHER'S DEAD. MY STEPMOTHER IS REALLY CRUEL AND IF I DON'T GO HOME RIGHT AWAY, SHE'LL KILL ME...

SHE'LL BURN ME WITH THE CLOTHES IRON!

SHE'LL MAKE MY FATHER PUT ME IN AN ORPHANAGE
MAYBE SHE BELIEVED ME, MAYBE SHE JUST PRETENDED TO. BUT, MIRACULOUSLY, SHE LET ME GO.

BACK HOME...
MARJI! WHAT HAPPENED? HAVE YOU BEEN CRYING?
NO MOM. I'M JUST TIRED. I'M GOING TO MY ROOM.
THERE WAS NO WAY I COULD TELL THE TRUTH. SHE NEVER WOULD HAVE LET ME GO OUT ALONE AGAIN.

I GOT OFF PRETTY EASY, CONSIDERING. THE GUARDIANS OF THE REVOLUTION DIDN'T FIND MY TAPES.

♫ WE'RE THE KIDS IN AMERICA WHOAO ♫
TO EACH HIS OWN WAY OF CALMING DOWN.

5. CRITICAL PERSPECTIVE In her discussion of a 2007 *Wall Street Journal* interview with Marjane Satrapi, editor Emily Parker describes what the graphic novel means to Satrapi:

> For Ms. Satrapi, graphic novels are not a "genre." Rather, they are just a way to tell a story. "If you consider it as a medium, then you can do anything with it," she says. "If you think that it is a genre, then you have to make superhero stories, or you have to make fairytales."

How does Satrapi convey the seriousness of her story in what traditionally has been seen as a genre of "superhero stories" and "fairytales"? What visual elements are most effective in creating a serious and realistic setting?

Related Works: "The Disappearance" (p. 695), "Saboteur" (p. 712), "Two Kinds" (p. 777), "Women" (p. 1007), *Antigone* (p. 1863)

KATE CHOPIN (1851–1904) (picture and biography on p. 226) wrote in a style that was realistic yet infused with a dense, sensual texture that was perhaps, in part, her artistic response to her memories of the exotic Louisiana bayou country. Like her contemporary Gustave Flaubert (Chopin's short novel *The Awakening* has often been called a "Creole *Bovary*"), Chopin used the physical world—as in the charged atmosphere of "The Storm"—to symbolize the inner truths of her characters' minds and hearts. Unlike Flaubert, however, she depicted sex not as a frantic and destructive force but as a joyous, elemental part of life. Apparently Kate Chopin knew how daring "The Storm" was: she never submitted it for publication.

Cultural Context In the following story, which presumably takes place in Louisiana, the character Calixta expresses fear that the powerful storm will break the levees, the raised embankments kept in place to prevent the river from overflowing. In August 2005, more than one hundred years after this story was written, the levees in New Orleans gave way to the sheer force of Hurricane Katrina, which flooded the city, destroyed the area's economic and cultural foundation, and displaced hundreds of thousands of residents.

The Storm (c. 1899)

I

The leaves were so still that even Bibi thought it was going to rain. Bobinôt, who was accustomed to converse on terms of perfect equality with his little son, called the child's attention to certain sombre clouds that were rolling with sinister intention from the west, accompanied by a sullen, threatening roar. They were at Friedheimer's store and decided to remain there till the storm had passed. They sat within the door on two empty kegs. Bibi was four years old and looked very wise.

"Mama'll be 'fraid, yes," he suggested with blinking eyes.

"She'll shut the house. Maybe she got Sylvie helpin' her this evenin'," Bobinôt responded reassuringly.

"No; she ent got Sylvie. Sylvie was helpin' her yistiday," piped Bibi.

5 Bobinôt arose and going across to the counter purchased a can of shrimps, of which Calixta was very fond. Then he returned to his perch on the keg and sat stolidly holding the can of shrimps while the storm burst. It shook the wooden store and seemed to be ripping great furrows in the distant field. Bibi laid his little hand on his father's knee and was not afraid.

II

Calixta, at home, felt no uneasiness for their safety. She sat at a side window sewing furiously on a sewing machine. She was greatly occupied and did not notice the approaching storm. But she felt very warm and often stopped to mop her face on which the perspiration gathered in beads. She unfastened her white sacque at the throat. It began to grow dark, and suddenly realizing the situation she got up hurriedly and went about closing windows and doors.

Out on the small front gallery she had hung Bobinôt's Sunday clothes to air and she hastened out to gather them before the rain fell. As she stepped outside, Alcée Laballière rode in at the gate. She had not seen him very often since her marriage, and never alone. She stood there with Bobinôt's coat in her hands, and the big rain drops began to fall. Alcée rode his horse under the shelter of a side projection where the chickens had huddled and there were plows and a harrow piled up in the corner.

"May I come and wait on your gallery till the storm is over, Calixta?" he asked.

"Come 'long in, M'sieur Alcée."

10 His voice and her own startled her as if from a trance, and she seized Bobinôt's vest. Alcée, mounting to the porch, grabbed the trousers and snatched Bibi's braided jacket that was about to be carried away by a sudden gust of wind. He expressed an intention to remain outside, but it was soon apparent that he might as well have been out in the open: the water beat in upon the boards in driving sheets, and he went inside, closing the door after him. It was even necessary to put something beneath the door to keep the water out.

"My! what a rain! It's good two years sence it rain' like that," exclaimed Calixta as she rolled up a piece of bagging and Alcée helped her to thrust it beneath the crack.

She was a little fuller of figure than five years before when she married; but she had lost nothing of her vivacity. Her blue eyes still retained their melting quality; and her yellow hair, dishevelled by the wind and rain, kinked more stubbornly than ever about her ears and temples.

The rain beat upon the low, shingled roof with a force and clatter that threatened to break an entrance and deluge them there. They were in the dining room — the sitting room — the general utility room. Adjoining was her bed room, with Bibi's couch along side her own. The door stood open, and the room with its white, monumental bed, its closed shutters, looked dim and mysterious.

Alcée flung himself into a rocker and Calixta nervously began to gather up from the floor the lengths of a cotton sheet which she had been sewing.

"If this keeps up, *Dieu sait*° if the levees° goin' to stan' it!" she exclaimed. 15

"What have you got to do with the levees?"

"I got enough to do! An' there's Bobinôt with Bibi out in that storm—if he only didn't left Friedheimer's!"

"Let us hope, Calixta, that Bobinôt's got sense enough to come in out of a cyclone."

She went and stood at the window with a greatly disturbed look on her face. She wiped the frame that was clouded with moisture. It was stiflingly hot. Alcée got up and joined her at the window, looking over her shoulder. The rain was coming down in sheets obscuring the view of far-off cabins and enveloping the distant wood in a gray mist. The playing of the lightning was incessant. A bolt struck a tall chinaberry tree at the edge of the field. It filled all visible space with a blinding glare and the crash seemed to invade the very boards they stood upon.

Calixta put her hands to her eyes, and with a cry, staggered backward. Alcée's arm 20
encircled her, and for an instant he drew her close and spasmodically to him.

"*Bonté!*"° she cried, releasing herself from his encircling arm and retreating from the window, "the house'll go next! If I only knew w'ere Bibi was!" She would not compose herself; she would not be seated. Alcée clasped her shoulders and looked into her face. The contact of her warm, palpitating body when he had unthinkingly drawn her into his arms, had aroused all the old-time infatuation and desire for her flesh.

"Calixta," he said, "don't be frightened. Nothing can happen. The house is too low to be struck, with so many tall trees standing about. There! aren't you going to be quiet? say, aren't you?" He pushed her hair back from her face that was warm and steaming. Her lips were as red and moist as pomegranate seed. Her white neck and a glimpse of her full, firm bosom disturbed him powerfully. As she glanced up at him the fear in her liquid blue eyes had given place to a drowsy gleam that unconsciously betrayed a sensuous desire. He looked down into her eyes and there was nothing for him to do but to gather her lips in a kiss. It reminded him of Assumption.

"Do you remember—in Assumption, Calixta?" he asked in a low voice broken by passion. Oh! she remembered; for in Assumption he had kissed her and kissed and kissed her; until his senses would well nigh fail, and to save her he would resort to a desperate flight. If she was not an immaculate dove in those days, she was still inviolate; a passionate creature whose very defenselessness had made her defense, against which his honor forbade him to prevail. Now—well, now—her lips seemed in a manner free to be tasted, as well as her round, white throat and her whiter breasts.

They did not heed the crashing torrents, and the roar of the elements made her laugh as she lay in his arms. She was a revelation in that dim, mysterious chamber; as white as the couch she lay upon. Her firm, elastic flesh that was knowing for the

Dieu sait: "God knows" (French).

levees: Raised embankments designed to keep a river from overflowing.

Bonté: "Goodness!" (French).

first time its birthright, was like a creamy lily that the sun invites to contribute its breath and perfume to the undying life of the world.

25 The generous abundance of her passion, without guile or trickery, was like a white flame which penetrated and found response in depths of his own sensuous nature that had never yet been reached.

When he touched her breasts they gave themselves up in quivering ecstasy, inviting his lips. Her mouth was a fountain of delight. And when he possessed her, they seemed to swoon together at the very borderland of life's mystery.

He stayed cushioned upon her, breathless, dazed, enervated, with his heart beating like a hammer upon her. With one hand she clasped his head, her lips lightly touching his forehead. The other hand stroked with a soothing rhythm his muscular shoulders.

The growl of the thunder was distant and passing away. The rain beat softly upon the shingles, inviting them to drowsiness and sleep. But they dared not yield.

The rain was over; and the sun was turning the glistening green world into a palace of gems. Calixta, on the gallery, watched Alcée ride away. He turned and smiled at her with a beaming face; and she lifted her pretty chin in the air and laughed aloud.

III

30 Bobinôt and Bibi, trudging home, stopped without at the cistern to make themselves presentable.

"My! Bibi, w'at will yo' mama say! You ought to be ashame'. You oughtn' put on those good pants. Look at 'em! An' that mud on yo' collar! How you got that mud on yo' collar, Bibi? I never saw such a boy!" Bibi was the picture of pathetic resignation. Bobinôt was the embodiment of serious solicitude as he strove to remove from his own person and his son's the signs of their tramp over heavy roads and through wet fields. He scraped the mud off Bibi's bare legs and feet with a stick and carefully removed all traces from his heavy brogans. Then, prepared for the worst — the meeting with an over-scrupulous housewife, they entered cautiously at the back door.

Calixta was preparing supper. She had set the table and was dripping coffee at the hearth. She sprang up as they came in.

"Oh, Bobinôt! You back! My! but I was uneasy. W'ere you been during the rain? An' Bibi? he ain't wet? he ain't hurt?" She had clasped Bibi and was kissing him effusively. Bobinôt's explanations and apologies which he had been composing all along the way, died on his lips as Calixta felt him to see if he were dry, and seemed to express nothing but satisfaction at their safe return.

"I brought you some shrimps, Calixta," offered Bobinôt, hauling the can from his ample side pocket and laying it on the table.

35 "Shrimps! Oh, Bobinôt! you too good fo' anything!" and she gave him a smacking kiss on the cheek that resounded. "*J'vous réponds,*° we'll have a feas' tonight! umph-umph!"

J'vous réponds: "I tell you" (French).

Bobinôt and Bibi began to relax and enjoy themselves, and when the three seated themselves at table they laughed much and so loud that anyone might have heard them as far away as Laballière's.

IV

Alcée Laballière wrote to his wife, Clarisse, that night. It was a loving letter, full of tender solicitude. He told her not to hurry back, but if she and the babies liked it at Biloxi, to stay a month longer. He was getting on nicely; and though he missed them, he was willing to bear the separation a while longer—realizing that their health and pleasure were the first things to be considered.

V

As for Clarisse, she was charmed upon receiving her husband's letter. She and the babies were doing well. The society was agreeable; many of her old friends and acquaintances were at the bay. And the first free breath since her marriage seemed to restore the pleasant liberty of her maiden days. Devoted as she was to her husband, their intimate conjugal life was something which she was more than willing to forego for a while.

So the storm passed and everyone was happy.

Reading and Reacting

1. Trace the progress of the storm through the five parts of the story. Then, trace the stages of the story's plot. How does the progress of the storm parallel the developing plot?
2. How does the weather help to create the story's atmosphere? How would you characterize this atmosphere?
3. In Part I, the "sombre clouds . . . rolling with sinister intention" introduce the storm. In what sense does this description introduce the story's action as well?
4. In what ways does the storm *cause* the events of the story? List specific events that occur because of the storm. Is the presence of the storm essential to the story?
5. In what sense does the storm act as a character in the story?
6. The weather is the most obvious element of the story's setting. What other aspects of setting are important to the story?
7. After Part II, the storm is not mentioned again until the last line of the story. What signs of the storm remain in Parts III, IV, and V?
8. Besides referring to the weather, what else might the title suggest?
9. **Journal Entry** The storm sets in motion the chain of events that leads to the characters' adultery. Do you think the storm excuses the characters in any way from responsibility for their actions?
10. **Critical Perspective** Kate Chopin is widely considered to be a regional, or "local color" writer. This term refers to writing in which descriptions of a particular geographic region are prominent. Local color writers strive to incorporate accurate speech patterns and dialects, as well as descriptions of local scenery, dress, and social customs, into their writing. A collection of source materials published by Prentice Hall notes the following:

Through her vivid descriptions and use of dialect, Chopin captured the local color of the region. In her stories, published in *Bayou Folk* (1894) and *Acadie* (1897), she exhibited her deep understanding of the different attitudes and concerns of the Louisiana natives. Yet her charming portraits of Louisiana life often obscured the fact that she explored the themes considered radical at the time: the nature of marriage, racial prejudice, and women's desire for social, economic, and political equality.

In what ways is "The Storm" an example of local color writing? In what ways is it more than just a "charming portrait of Louisiana life"?

Related Works: "Hills Like White Elephants" (p. 171), "The Girl with Bangs" (p. 271), "What Lips My Lips Have Kissed" (p. 1056), "General Review of the Sex Situation" (p. 1056), "Wild Nights—Wild Nights!" (p. 1148), *The Stronger* (p. 1470)

Source: ©AP Photo/Elise Amendola

LAN SAMANTHA CHANG (1965–) was born and raised in Appleton, Wisconsin, to parents who had emigrated from China during the Japanese occupation lasting from 1937 to 1945. She says that she "grew up feeling like an outsider. . . I cannot remember a time when I was not conscious of being different from the majority of people around me." Chang's work, which largely focuses on the complexities of being Chinese American, has been published in the *Atlantic Monthly, Story,* and *The Best American Short Stories 1994* and *1996.* She is the author of the award-winning story collection *Hunger* (1998) and the novel *Inheritance* (2004), winner of the 2005 PEN Beyond Margins Award. Chang has been awarded various fellowships, including one from the University of Iowa Writers' Workshop, where she currently serves as director of the creative writing program.

Cultural Context Chinese folktales, like the one told in this story, are central to Chinese culture and history. For thousands of years, Chinese elders have been telling stories to the young as part of a rich oral tradition. These stories teach valuable lessons and reinforce important cultural values, such as filial piety, loyalty, and duty. They feature a wide range of characters, including heroes, historical figures, animals, and everyday people. Over time, Chinese folktales have changed to reflect the prevailing cultural attitudes, beliefs, and behaviors of the current generation.

Water Names (1998)

Summertime at dusk we'd gather on the back porch, tired and sticky from another day of fierce encoded quarrels, nursing our mosquito bites and frail dignities, sisters in name only. At first we'd pinch and slap each other, fighting for the best—least ragged—folding chair. Then we'd argue over who would sit next to our grandmother. We were so close together on the tiny porch that we often pulled our own hair by mistake. Forbidden to bite, we planted silent toothmarks on each other's wrists. We ignored the bulk of house behind us, the yard, the fields, the darkening sky. We even forgot about our grandmother. Then suddenly we'd hear her old, dry voice, very close, almost on the backs of our necks.

"*Xiushila!* Shame on you. Fighting like a bunch of chickens."

And Ingrid, the oldest, would freeze with her thumb and forefinger right on the back of Lily's arm. I would slide my hand away from the end of Ingrid's braid. Ashamed, we would shuffle our feet while Waipuo calmly found her chair.

On some nights she sat with us in silence, the tip of her cigarette glowing red like a distant stoplight. But on some nights she told us stories, "just to keep up your Chinese," she said, and the red dot flickered and danced, making ghostly shapes as she moved her hands like a magician in the dark.

"In these prairie crickets I often hear the sound of rippling waters, of the Yangtze River," she said. "Granddaughters, you are descended on both sides from people of the water country, near the mouth of the great Chang Jiang, as it is called, where the river is so grand and broad that even on clear days you can scarcely see the other side.

5 "The Chang Jiang runs four thousand miles, originating in the Himalaya mountains where it crashes, flecked with gold dust, down steep cliffs so perilous and remote that few humans have ever seen them. In central China, the river squeezes through deep gorges, then widens in its last thousand miles to the sea. Our ancestors have lived near the mouth of this river, the ever-changing delta, near a city called Nanjing, for more than a thousand years."

"A thousand years," murmured Lily, who was only ten. When she was younger she had sometimes burst into nervous crying at the thought of so many years. Her small insistent fingers grabbed my fingers in the dark.

"Through your mother and I you are descended from a line of great men and women. We have survived countless floods and seasons of ill-fortune because we have the spirit of the river in us. Unlike mountains, we cannot be powdered down or broken apart. Instead, we run together, like raindrops. Our strength and spirit wear down mountains into sand. But even our people must respect the water."

She paused, and a bit of ash glowed briefly as it drifted to the floor.

"When I was young, my own grandmother once told me the story of Wen Zhiqing's daughter. Twelve hundred years ago the civilized parts of China still lay to the north, and the Yangtze valley lay unspoiled. In those days lived an ancestor named Wen Zhiqing, a resourceful man, and proud. He had been fishing for many years with trained cormorants, which you girls of course have never seen. Cormorants are sleek, black birds with long, bending necks which the fishermen fitted with metal rings so the fish they caught could not be swallowed. The birds would perch on the side of the old wooden boat and dive into the river." We had only known blue swimming pools, but we tried to imagine the sudden shock of cold and the plunge, deep into water.

10 "Now, Wen Zhiqing had a favorite daughter who was very beautiful and loved the river. She would beg to go out on the boat with him. This daughter was a restless one, never contented with their catch, and often she insisted they stay out until it was almost dark. Even then, she was not satisfied. She had been spoiled by her father, kept protected from the river, so she could not see its danger. To this young woman, the river was as familiar as the sky. It was a bright, broad road stretching out to curious lands. She did not fully understand the river's depths.

"One clear spring evening, as she watched the last bird dive off into the blackening waters, she said, 'If only this catch would bring back something more than another fish!'

"She leaned over the side of the boat and looked at the water. The stars and moon reflected back at her. And it is said that the spirits living underneath the water looked up at her as well. And the spirit of a young man who had drowned in the river many years before saw her lovely face."

We had heard about the ghosts of the drowned, who wait forever in the water for a living person to pull down instead. A faint breeze moved through the mosquito screens and we shivered.

"The cormorant was gone for a very long time," Waipuo said, "so long that the fisherman grew puzzled. Then, suddenly, the bird emerged from the waters, almost invisible in the night. Wen Zhiqing grasped his catch, a very large fish, and guided the boat back to shore. And when Wen reached home, he gutted the fish and discovered, in its stomach, a valuable pearl ring."

"From the man?" said Lily.

"Sshh, she'll tell you."

Waipuo ignored us. "His daughter was delighted that her wish had been fulfilled. What most excited her was the idea of an entire world like this, a world where such a beautiful ring would be only a bauble.° For part of her had always longed to see faraway things and places. The river had put a spell on her heart. In the evenings she began to sit on the bank, looking at her own reflection in the water. Sometimes she said she saw a handsome young man looking back at her. And her yearning for him filled her heart with sorrow and fear, for she knew that she would soon leave her beloved family.

"'It's just the moon,' said Wen Zhiqing, but his daughter shook her head. 'There's a kingdom under the water,' she said. 'The prince is asking me to marry him. He sent the ring as an offering to you.' 'Nonsense,' said her father, and he forbade her to sit by the water again.

"For a year things went as usual, but the next spring there came a terrible flood that swept away almost everything. In the middle of a torrential rain, the family noticed that the daughter was missing. She had taken advantage of the confusion to hurry to the river and visit her beloved. The family searched for days but they never found her."

Her smoky, rattling voice came to a stop.

"What happened to her?" Lily said.

"It's okay, stupid," I told her. "She was so beautiful that she went to join the kingdom of her beloved. Right?"

"Who knows?" Waipuo said. "They say she was seduced by a water ghost. Or perhaps she lost her mind to desiring."

"What do you mean?" asked Ingrid.

---

bauble: Trinket.

"I'm going inside," Waipuo said, and got out of her chair with a creak. A moment 25
later the light went on in her bedroom window. We knew she stood before the mirror, combing out her long, wavy silver-gray hair, and we imagined that in her youth she too had been beautiful.

We sat together without talking, breathing our dreams in the lingering smoke. We had gotten used to Waipuo's abruptness, her habit of creating a question and leaving without answering it, as if she were disappointed in the question itself. We tried to imagine Wen Zhiqing's daughter. What did she look like? How old was she? Why hadn't anyone remembered her name?

While we weren't watching, the stars had emerged. Their brilliant pinpoints mapped the heavens. They glittered over us, over Waipuo in her room, the house, and the small city we lived in, the great waves of grass that ran for miles around us, the ground beneath as dry and hard as bone.

Reading and Reacting

1. "Water Names" has two settings: one real and contemporary and one legendary and ancient. What specific details are readers told about each of these settings?
2. How are the story's two settings different? Do they have anything in common?
3. Which element of setting—historical, geographical, or physical—seems most important in the contemporary story? Which element of setting seems most important in the story of Wen Zhiqing's daughter?
4. What is the significance of water in the story of Wen Zhiqing's daughter? Does water have any significance to the three sisters who hear her story?
5. The sisters have clearly heard the grandmother's story before. How can you tell? What do you think motivates the grandmother to tell it again and again?
6. Reread the first three paragraphs and the last three paragraphs of the story. What has changed for the three girls by the end of the story?
7. What are the "water names" to which the title refers?
8. Does the grandmother's story have a moral or lesson for the sisters? How is it relevant to their lives?
9. **Journal Entry** Retell a story you remember being told in your childhood. Be sure to describe both the setting in which you heard the story and the setting of the story itself.
10. **Critical Perspective** In his article "History of a Hybrid," Martin E. Marty quotes Lan Samantha Chang as saying of her family, "Like the Pilgrims, we came to America from another country," and "like them, we have survived by adapting: both holding onto and letting go of our culture, our traditions and our past."

    How does this story both hold onto and let go of the cultural legacy represented by the grandmother's folktale?

Related Works: "Once upon a Time" (p. 232), "A Very Old Man with Enormous Wings" (p. 707), "Girl Powdering Her Neck" (p. PS5), "Sea Grapes" (p. 1031)

Source: ©Rex Rystedt

SHERMAN J. ALEXIE (1966–), a Spokane/Coeur d'Alene Indian, grew up on the Spokane Indian Reservation in Wellpinit, Washington, about fifty miles northwest of Spokane, where approximately 2,400 Spokane Tribal members live. Alexie has published short stories, novels, and poetry. He was named one of Granta's Best of Young American Novelists, and his first novel, *Reservation Blues* (1995), won the Before Columbus Foundation's American Book Award and the Murray Morgan Prize. His second novel, *Indian Killer* (1996), was named one of *People's* Best of Pages and was a *New York Times* Notable Book. "This Is What It Means to Say Phoenix, Arizona" (from his 1993 short story collection *The Lone Ranger and Tonto Fistfight in Heaven*) eventually became the movie *Smoke Signals*, which was released in 1998. To date, Alexie has written eighteen books, including poetry collections, novels, and short story collections. His most recent book is the young adult novel *The Absolutely True Story of a Part-Time Indian* (2007), for which he won the National Book Award for Young People's Literature.

Commenting on Native American culture, Alexie has said, "One of the biggest misconceptions about Indians is that we're stoic, but humor is an essential part of our culture." "This Is What It Means to Say Phoenix, Arizona" demonstrates this unique use of humor to transcend the harsh realities of life on the reservation and of the struggle to adapt to contemporary American life.

Cultural Context The United States policy of creating Native American reservations can be traced back to the administration of President Ulysses S. Grant, who determined that establishing such reservations was the best way to handle the "Indian problem" between white settlers and the Native Americans they encountered. (Even supporters of Native Americans believed that they were incapable of assimilating into the wider American society and that only on reservations would they be able to survive as a people.) Today, about half of America's 2.5 million Native Americans continue to live on reservations, where more than forty percent of the families live below the federal poverty line and the unemployment rate averages around seventy percent. At the same time, reservations are the one place where members of a tribe can live together and retain their culture, language, and heritage. The characters in "This Is What It Means to Say Phoenix, Arizona" experience both the positive and negative aspects of reservation life.

This Is What It Means to Say Phoenix, Arizona (1993)

Just after Victor lost his job at the Bureau of Indian Affairs,° he also found out that his father had died of a heart attack in Phoenix, Arizona. Victor hadn't seen his father in a few years, had only talked to him on the telephone once or twice, but there still was a genetic pain, which was as real and immediate as a broken bone. Victor didn't have any money. Who does have money on a reservation, except the cigarette and fireworks salespeople? His father had a savings account waiting to be

Bureau of Indian Affairs: The division of the U.S. Department of the Interior that manages Native American matters; the bureau is operated by government officials, not tribal leaders.

claimed, but Victor needed to find a way to get from Spokane to Phoenix. Victor's mother was just as poor as he was, and the rest of his family didn't have any use at all for him. So Victor called the tribal council.

"Listen," Victor said. "My father just died. I need some money to get to Phoenix to make arrangements."

"Now Victor," the council said, "you know we're having a difficult time financially."

"But I thought the council had special funds set aside for stuff like this."

"Now, Victor, we do have some money available for the proper return of tribal members' bodies. But I don't think we have enough to bring your father all the way back from Phoenix."

"Well," Victor said. "It ain't going to cost all that much. He had to be cremated. Things were kind of ugly. He died of a heart attack in his trailer and nobody found him for a week. It was really hot, too. You get the picture."

"Now, Victor, we're sorry for your loss and the circumstances. But we can really only afford to give you one hundred dollars."

"That's not even enough for a plane ticket."

"Well, you might consider driving down to Phoenix."

"I don't have a car. Besides, I was going to drive my father's pickup back up here."

"Now, Victor," the council said, "we're sure there is somebody who could drive you to Phoenix. Or could anybody lend you the rest of the money?"

"You know there ain't nobody around with that kind of money."

"Well, we're sorry, Victor, but that's the best we can do."

Victor accepted the tribal council's offer. What else could he do? So he signed the proper papers, picked up his check, and walked over to the Trading Post to cash it.

While Victor stood in line, he watched Thomas Builds-the-Fire standing near the magazine rack talking to himself. Like he always did. Thomas was a storyteller whom nobody wanted to listen to. That's like being a dentist in a town where everybody has false teeth.

Victor and Thomas Builds-the-Fire were the same age, had grown up and played in the dirt together. Ever since Victor could remember, it was Thomas who had always had something to say.

Once, when they were seven years old, when Victor's father still lived with the family, Thomas closed his eyes and told Victor this story: "Your father's heart is weak. He is afraid of his own family. He is afraid of you. Late at night, he sits in the dark. Watches the television until there's nothing but that white noise. Sometimes he feels like he wants to buy a motorcycle and ride away. He wants to run and hide. He doesn't want to be found."

Thomas Builds-the-Fire had known that Victor's father was going to leave, known it before anyone. Now Victor stood in the Trading Post with a one-hundred-dollar check in his hand, wondering if Thomas knew that Victor's father was dead, if he knew what was going to happen next.

Just then, Thomas looked at Victor, smiled, and walked over to him.

"Victor, I'm sorry about your father," Thomas said.

"How did you know about it?" Victor asked.

"I heard it on the wind. I heard it from the birds. I felt it in the sunlight. Also, your mother was just in here crying."

"Oh," Victor said and looked around the Trading Post. All the other Indians stared, surprised that Victor was even talking to Thomas. Nobody talked to Thomas anymore because he told the same damn stories over and over again. Victor was embarrassed, but he thought that Thomas might be able to help him. Victor felt a sudden need for tradition.

"I can lend you the money you need," Thomas said suddenly. "But you have to take me with you."

"I can't take your money," Victor said. "I mean, I haven't hardly talked to you in years. We're not really friends anymore."

"I didn't say we were friends. I said you had to take me with you."

"Let me think about it."

Victor went home with his one hundred dollars and sat at the kitchen table. He held his head in his hands and thought about Thomas Builds-the-Fire, remembered little details, tears and scars, the bicycle they shared for a summer, so many stories.

* * *

Thomas Builds-the-Fire sat on the bicycle, waiting in Victor's yard. He was ten years old and skinny. His hair was dirty because it was the Fourth of July.

"Victor," Thomas yelled. "Hurry up. We're going to miss the fireworks."

After a few minutes, Victor ran out of his family's house, vaulted over the porch railing, and landed gracefully on the sidewalk.

Thomas gave him the bike and they headed for the fireworks. It was nearly dark and the fireworks were about to start.

"You know," Thomas said, "it's strange how us Indians celebrate the Fourth of July. It ain't like it was our independence everybody was fighting for."

"You think about things too much," Victor said. "It's just supposed to be fun. Maybe Junior will be there."

"Which Junior? Everybody on this reservation is named Junior."

The fireworks were small, hardly more than a few bottle rockets and a fountain. But it was enough for two Indian boys. Years later, they would need much more.

Afterward, sitting in the dark, fighting off mosquitoes, Victor turned to Thomas Builds-the-Fire.

"Hey," Victor said. "Tell me a story."

Thomas closed his eyes and told this story: "There were these two Indian boys who wanted to be warriors. But it was too late to be warriors in the old way. All the horses were gone. So the two Indian boys stole a car and drove to the city. They parked the stolen car in the front of the police station and then hitchhiked back home to the reservation. When they got back, all their friends cheered and their parents' eyes shone with pride. 'You were very brave,' everybody said to the two Indian boys. 'Very brave.'"

"Ya-hey," Victor said. "That's a good one. I wish I could be a warrior."

"Me too," Thomas said.

Victor sat at his kitchen table. He counted his one hundred dollars again and again. He knew he needed more to make it to Phoenix and back. He knew he needed Thomas Builds-the-Fire. So he put his money in his wallet and opened the front door to find Thomas on the porch.

"Ya-hey, Victor," Thomas said. "I knew you'd call me."

Thomas walked into the living room and sat down in Victor's favorite chair.

"I've got some money saved up," Thomas said. "It's enough to get us down there, but you have to get us back."

"I've got this hundred dollars," Victor said. "And my dad had a savings account I'm going to claim."

"How much in your dad's account?"

"Enough. A few hundred."

"Sounds good. When we leaving?"

When they were fifteen and had long since stopped being friends, Victor and Thomas got into a fistfight. That is, Victor was really drunk and beat Thomas up for no reason at all. All the other Indian boys stood around and watched it happen. Junior was there and so were Lester, Seymour, and a lot of others.

The beating might have gone on until Thomas was dead if Norma Many Horses hadn't come along and stopped it.

"Hey, you boys," Norma yelled and jumped out of her car. "Leave him alone."

If it had been someone else, even another man, the Indian boys would've just ignored the warnings. But Norma was a warrior. She was powerful. She could have picked up any two of the boys and smashed their skulls together. But worse than that, she would have dragged them all over to some tepee and made them listen to some elder tell a dusty old story.

The Indian boys scattered, and Norma walked over to Thomas and picked him up.

"Hey, little man, are you O.K.?" she asked.

Thomas gave her a thumbs-up.

"Why they always picking on you?"

Thomas shook his head, closed his eyes, but no stories came to him, no words or music. He just wanted to go home, to lie in his bed and let his dreams tell the stories for him.

Thomas Builds-the-Fire and Victor sat next to each other in the airplane, coach section. A tiny white woman had the window seat. She was busy twisting her body into pretzels. She was flexible.

"I have to ask," Thomas said, and Victor closed his eyes in embarrassment.

"Don't," Victor said.

"Excuse me, miss," Thomas asked. "Are you a gymnast or something?"

"There's no something about it," she said. "I was first alternate on the 1980 Olympic team."

"Really?" Thomas asked.

"Really."

"I mean, you used to be a world-class athlete?" Thomas asked.

"My husband thinks I still am."

Thomas Builds-the-Fire smiled. She was a mental gymnast too. She pulled her leg straight up against her body so that she could've kissed her kneecap.

"I wish I could do that," Thomas said.

Victor was ready to jump out of the plane. Thomas, that crazy Indian storyteller with ratty old braids and broken teeth, was flirting with a beautiful Olympic gymnast. Nobody back home on the reservation would ever believe it.

"Well," the gymnast said. "It's easy. Try it."

Thomas grabbed at his leg and tried to pull it up into the same position as the gymnast's. He couldn't even come close, which made Victor and the gymnast laugh.

"Hey," she asked. "You two are Indian, right?"

"Full-blood," Victor said.

"Not me," Thomas said. "I'm half magician on my mother's side and half clown on my father's."

They all laughed.

"What are your names?" she asked.

"Victor and Thomas."

"Mine is Cathy. Pleased to meet you all."

The three of them talked for the duration of the flight. Cathy the gymnast complained about the government, how they screwed the 1980 Olympic team by boycotting the games.

"Sounds like you all got a lot in common with Indians," Thomas said.

Nobody laughed.

After the plane landed in Phoenix and they had all found their way to the terminal, Cathy the gymnast smiled and waved goodbye.

"She was really nice," Thomas said.

"Yeah, but everybody talks to everybody on airplanes," Victor said.

"You always used to tell me I think too much," Thomas said. "Now it sounds like you do."

"Maybe I caught it from you."

"Yeah."

Thomas and Victor rode in a taxi to the trailer where Victor's father had died.

"Listen," Victor said as they stopped in front of the trailer. "I never told you I was sorry for beating you up that time."

"Oh, it was nothing. We were just kids and you were drunk."

"Yeah, but I'm still sorry."

"That's all right."

Victor paid for the taxi, and the two of them stood in the hot Phoenix summer. They could smell the trailer.

"This ain't going to be nice," Victor said. "You don't have to go in."

"You're going to need help."

Victor walked to the front door and opened it. The stink rolled out and made them both gag. Victor's father had lain in that trailer for a week in hundred-degree temperatures before anyone had found him. And the only reason anyone found him was the smell. They needed dental records to identify him. That's exactly what the coroner said. They needed dental records.

"Oh, man," Victor said. "I don't know if I can do this."

"Well, then don't."

"But there might be something valuable in there." 100

"I thought his money was in the bank."

"It is: I was talking about pictures and letters and stuff like that."

"Oh," Thomas said as he held his breath and followed Victor into the trailer.

When Victor was twelve, he stepped into an underground wasps' nest. His foot was caught in the hole and no matter how hard he struggled, Victor couldn't pull free. He might have died there, stung a thousand times, if Thomas Builds-the-Fire had not come by.

"Run," Thomas yelled and pulled Victor's foot from the hole. They ran then, hard 105
as they ever had, faster than Billy Mills, faster than Jim Thorpe, faster than the wasps could fly.

Victor and Thomas ran until they couldn't breathe, ran until it was cold and dark outside, ran until they were lost and it took hours to find their way home. All the way back, Victor counted his stings.

"Seven," Victor said. "My lucky number."

* * *

Victor didn't find much to keep in the trailer. Only a photo album and a stereo. Everything else had that smell stuck in it or was useless anyway. "I guess this is all," Victor said. "It ain't much."

"Better than nothing," Thomas said.

"Yeah, and I do have the pickup." 110

"Yeah," Thomas said. "It's in good shape."

"Dad was good about that stuff."

"Yeah, I remember your dad."

"Really?" Victor asked. "What do you remember?"

Thomas Builds-the-Fire closed his eyes and told this story: "I remember when I 115
had this dream that told me to go to Spokane, to stand by the falls in the middle of the city and wait for a sign. I knew I had to go there but I didn't have a car. Didn't have a license. I was only thirteen. So I walked all the way, took me all day, and I finally made it to the falls. I stood there for an hour waiting. Then your dad came walking up. 'What the hell are you doing here?' he asked me. I said, 'Waiting for a vision.' Then your father said, 'All you're going to get here is mugged.' So he drove me over to Denny's, bought me dinner, and then drove me home to the reservation. For a long time, I was mad because I thought my dreams had lied to me. But they hadn't. Your dad was my vision. *Take care of each other* is what my dreams were saying. *Take care of each other*."

Victor was quiet for a long time. He searched his mind for memories of his father, found the good ones, found a few bad ones, added it all up, and smiled.

"My father never told me about finding you in Spokane," Victor said.

"He said he wouldn't tell anybody. Didn't want me to get in trouble. But he said I had to watch out for you as part of the deal."

"Really?"

"Really. Your father said you would need the help. He was right."

"That's why you came down here with me, isn't it?" Victor asked.

"I came because of your father."

Victor and Thomas climbed into the pickup, drove over to the bank, and claimed the three hundred dollars in the savings account.

Thomas Builds-the-Fire could fly.

Once, he jumped off the roof of the tribal school and flapped his arms like a crazy eagle. And he flew. For a second he hovered, suspended above all the other Indian boys, who were too smart or too scared to jump too.

"He's flying," Junior yelled, and Seymour was busy looking for the trick wires or mirrors. But it was real. As real as the dirt when Thomas lost altitude and crashed to the ground.

He broke his arm in two places.

"He broke his wing, he broke his wing, he broke his wing," all the Indian boys chanted as they ran off, flapping their wings, wishing they could fly too. They hated Thomas for his courage, his brief moment as a bird. Everybody has dreams about flying. Thomas flew.

One of his dreams came true for just a second, just enough to make it real.

* * *

Victor's father, his ashes, fit in one wooden box with enough left over to fill a cardboard box.

"He always was a big man," Thomas said.

Victor carried part of his father out to the pickup, and Thomas carried the rest. They set him down carefully behind the seats, put a cowboy hat on the wooden box and a Dodgers cap on the cardboard box. That was the way it was supposed to be.

"Ready to head back home?" Victor asked.

"It's going to be a long drive."

"Yeah, take a couple days, maybe."

"We can take turns," Thomas said.

"O.K.," Victor said, but they didn't take turns. Victor drove for sixteen hours straight north, made it halfway up Nevada toward home before he finally pulled over.

"Hey, Thomas," Victor said. "You got to drive for a while."

"O.K."

Thomas Builds-the-Fire slid behind the wheel and started off down the road. All through Nevada, Thomas and Victor had been amazed at the lack of animal life, at the absence of water, of movement.

"Where is everything?" Victor had asked more than once.

Now, when Thomas was finally driving, they saw the first animal, maybe the only animal in Nevada. It was a long-eared jackrabbit.

"Look," Victor yelled. "It's alive."

Thomas and Victor were busy congratulating themselves on their discovery when the jackrabbit darted out into the road and under the wheels of the pickup.

"Stop the goddamn car," Victor yelled, and Thomas did stop and backed the 145
pickup to the dead jackrabbit.

"Oh, man, he's dead," Victor said as he looked at the squashed animal.

"Really dead."

"The only thing alive in this whole state and we just killed it."

"I don't know," Thomas said. "I think it was suicide."

Victor looked around the desert, sniffed the air, felt the emptiness and loneliness, 150
and nodded his head.

"Yeah," Victor said. "It had to be suicide."

"I can't believe this," Thomas said. "You drive for a thousand miles and there ain't even any bugs smashed on the windshield. I drive for ten seconds and kill the only living thing in Nevada."

"Yeah," Victor said. "Maybe I should drive."

"Maybe you should."

Thomas Builds-the-Fire walked through the corridors of the tribal school by 155
himself. Nobody wanted to be anywhere near him because of all those stories. Story after story.

Thomas closed his eyes and this story came to him: "We are all given one thing by which our lives are measured, one determination. Mine are the stories that can change or not change the world. It doesn't matter which, as long as I continue to tell the stories. My father, he died on Okinawa° in World War II, died fighting for this country, which had tried to kill him for years. My mother, she died giving birth to me, died while I was still inside her. She pushed me out into the world with her last breath. I have no brothers or sisters. I have only my stories, which came to me before I even had the words to speak. I learned a thousand stories before I took my first thousand steps. They are all I have. It's all I can do."

Thomas Builds-the-Fire told his stories to all those who would stop and listen. He kept telling them long after people had stopped listening.

Victor and Thomas made it back to the reservation just as the sun was rising. It was the beginning of a new day on earth, but the same old shit on the reservation.

"Good morning," Thomas said.

"Good morning." 160

The tribe was waking up, ready for work, eating breakfast, reading the newspaper, just like everybody else does. Willene LeBret was out in her garden, wearing a bathrobe. She waved when Thomas and Victor drove by.

"Crazy Indians made it," she said to herself and went back to her roses.

Okinawa: Largest island of the Ryukyus, a chain of Japanese islands in the western Pacific Ocean.

Victor stopped the pickup in front of Thomas Builds-the-Fire's HUD° house. They both yawned, stretched a little, shook dust from their bodies.

"I'm tired," Victor said.

"Of everything," Thomas added.

They both searched for words to end the journey. Victor needed to thank Thomas for his help and for the money, and to make the promise to pay it all back.

"Don't worry about the money," Thomas said. "It don't make any difference anyhow."

"Probably not, enit?"

"Nope."

Victor knew that Thomas would remain the crazy storyteller who talked to dogs and cars, who listened to the wind and pine trees. Victor knew that he couldn't really be friends with Thomas, even after all that had happened. It was cruel but it was real. As real as the ash, as Victor's father, sitting behind the seats.

"I know how it is," Thomas said. "I know you ain't going to treat me any better than you did before. I know your friends would give you too much shit about it."

Victor was ashamed of himself. Whatever happened to the tribal ties, the sense of community? The only real thing he shared with anybody was a bottle and broken dreams. He owed Thomas something, anything.

"Listen," Victor said and handed Thomas the cardboard box that contained half of his father. "I want you to have this."

Thomas took the ashes and smiled, closed his eyes, and told this story: "I'm going to travel to Spokane Falls one last time and toss these ashes into the water. And your father will rise like a salmon, leap over the bridge, over me, and find his way home. It will be beautiful. His teeth will shine like silver, like a rainbow. He will rise, Victor, he will rise."

Victor smiled.

"I was planning on doing the same thing with my half," Victor said. "But I didn't imagine my father looking anything like a salmon. I thought it'd be like cleaning the attic or something. Like letting things go after they've stopped having any use."

"Nothing stops, cousin," Thomas said. "Nothing stops."

Thomas Builds-the-Fire got out of the pickup and walked up his driveway. Victor started the pickup and began the drive home.

"Wait," Thomas yelled suddenly from his porch. "I just got to ask one favor."

Victor stopped the pickup, leaned out the window, and shouted back.

"What do you want?" he asked.

"Just one time when I'm telling a story somewhere, why don't you stop and listen?" Thomas asked.

"Just once?"

"Just once."

Victor waved his arms to let Thomas know that the deal was good. It was a fair trade. That's all Thomas had ever wanted from his whole life. So Victor drove his father's pickup toward home while Thomas went into his house, closed the door behind him, and heard a new story come to him in the silence afterward.

HUD: The U.S. Department of Housing and Urban Development.

Reading and Reacting

1. In paragraph 1, readers are told that Victor lives on an Indian reservation. What details elsewhere in the story establish this setting? What associations does this setting have for you? Do you think the story could take place anywhere else?
2. In addition to various locations on the reservation, the story's settings include an airplane, a trailer in Phoenix, and a road through Nevada. What does each of these settings contribute to the story's plot?
3. Is the scene on the plane necessary? Intrusive? Distracting? Far-fetched?
4. How would you characterize the story's mood or atmosphere? How do Thomas's stories help to create this mood? How do they help to establish his character? Do you think Alexie should have included more of these stories?
5. Why do you suppose Victor and Thomas cannot be friends when they get back to the reservation? Why are they able to be friends when they are traveling to Phoenix?
6. Do the flashbacks to the two men's childhood add something vital to the story? What purpose do these flashbacks serve?
7. In Native American culture, the storyteller holds an important position, telling tales that transmit and preserve the tribe's basic beliefs. Do you think Thomas's stories serve such a function? Or, do you think that he is, as Victor characterizes him, simply "the crazy storyteller who talked to dogs and cars, who listened to the wind and pine trees" (par. 170)?
8. What do you think the story's title means?
9. **JOURNAL ENTRY** At the end of the story, when Thomas returns home, he hears "a new story come to him in the silence" after he closes the door. What kind of story do you think comes to him at this point?
10. **CRITICAL PERSPECTIVE** In the introduction to a collection of Native American literature, Clifford E. Trafzer, the collection's editor, discusses the unique characteristics of Native American writers:

    > Due to their grounding in the oral tradition of their people, Native American writers do not follow the literary canon of the dominant society in their approach to short stories. Rather than focusing on one theme or character in a brief time frame, or using one geographical area, they often use multiple themes and characters with few boundaries of time or place. Their stories do not always follow a linear and clear path, and frequently the past and present, real and mythic, and conscious and unconscious are not distinguishable. Multidimensional characters are common, and involved stories usually lack absolute conclusions. Native American writers may also play tricks with language, deliberately misusing grammar, syntax, and spelling—sometimes in defiance of the dominant culture—in order to make English reflect the language of their peoples.

    Do you think "This Is What It Means to Say Phoenix, Arizona" displays the characteristics Trafzer associates with Native American writers?

Related Works: "Sister Godzilla" (p. 700), "How to Write the Great American Indian Novel" (p. 871), "My Father's Song" (p. 1044), "Defending Walt Whitman" (p. 1117), "Indian Boarding School: The Runaways" (p. 1155), *The Glass Menagerie* (p. 1961)

Source: ©The Granger Collection, New York

RALPH ELLISON (1914–1994) was born in Oklahoma City, Oklahoma. After his father's death when Ellison was three, Ellison's mother took up work as a domestic servant to support herself and her son. Early on, Ellison developed an interest in literature and music. He enrolled as a musician at Tuskegee Institute in Alabama; then, in 1936, he moved to New York City, where he worked with the Federal Writer's Project. While there, Ellison met prominent African-American writers Langston Hughes and Richard Wright, who encouraged his literary ambitions. He began to publish stories in journals and became an editor of *Negro Quarterly*. After serving in the Merchant Marines during World War II, Ellison returned to New York and taught literature at New York University for many years.

Ellison's first novel, *Invisible Man* (1952), was an instant success. The book—a semiautobiographical chronicle of a young African-American man's search for intellectual identity—won the National Book Award for fiction and was listed in *Book Week* as the most distinguished American novel of the preceding twenty years. His short story "Battle Royal" was first published in 1948; it went on to become, in a slightly revised form, the opening chapter of *Invisible Man*. Ellison published two collections of essays, *Shadow and Act* (1964) and *Going to the Territories* (1986); his collected essays appeared in 1995. Ellison's second novel, *Juneteenth*, was planned as a trilogy, but after a large section of the novel burned in a fire in 1967, Ellison spent years reconstructing the text, only to leave it unfinished at his death. His manuscript, some two thousand pages, was edited by John Callahan and posthumously published in 1999.

Cultural Context The term *battle royal* was first coined by the ancient Romans to refer to a form of combat in which a number of gladiators, armed or unarmed, fought until only one remained standing or alive. Due to the random and chaotic nature of these contests, the winners were determined more by luck than by martial skill. In the period before the Civil War, these contests often involved slaves fighting bare-fisted at boxing matches. Today, this form of combat is a staple of professional wrestling, but at the time this story was written, the battle royal was relegated to back rooms and more clandestine functions and almost always involved African Americans.

Battle Royal (1952)

It goes a long way back, some twenty years. All my life I had been looking for something, and everywhere I turned someone tried to tell me what it was. I accepted their answers too, though they were often in contradiction and even self-contradictory. I was naïve. I was looking for myself and asking everyone except myself questions which I, and only I, could answer. It took me a long time and much painful boomeranging of my expectations to achieve a realization everyone else appears to have been born with: That I am nobody but myself. But first I had to discover that I am an invisible man!

And yet I am no freak of nature, nor of history. I was in the cards, other things having been equal (or unequal) eighty-five years ago. I am not ashamed of my grandparents for having been slaves. I am only ashamed of myself for having at one time been ashamed. About eighty-five years ago they were told that they were free, united with others of our country in everything pertaining to the common good, and, in everything social, separate like the fingers of the hand. And they believed it. They exulted in it. They stayed in their place, worked hard, and brought up my father to do the same. But my grandfather is the one. He was an odd old guy, my grandfather, and I am told I take after him. It was he who caused the trouble. On his deathbed he called my father to him and said, "Son, after I'm gone I want you to keep up the good fight. I never told you, but our life is a war and I have been a traitor all my born days, a spy in the enemy's country ever since I give up my gun back in the Reconstruction. Live with your head in the lion's mouth. I want you to overcome 'em with yeses, undermine 'em with grins, agree 'em to death and destruction, let 'em swoller you till they vomit or bust wide open." They thought the old man had gone out of his mind. He had been the meekest of men. The younger children were rushed from the room, the shades drawn and the flame of the lamp turned so low that it sputtered on the wick like the old man's breathing. "Learn it to the younguns," he whispered fiercely; then he died.

But my folks were more alarmed over his last words than over his dying. It was as though he had not died at all, his words caused so much anxiety. I was warned emphatically to forget what he had said and, indeed, this is the first time it has been mentioned outside the family circle. It had a tremendous effect upon me, however. I could never be sure of what he meant. Grandfather had been a quiet old man who never made any trouble, yet on his deathbed he had called himself a traitor and a spy, and he had spoken of his meekness as a dangerous activity. It became a constant puzzle which lay unanswered in the back of my mind. And whenever things went well for me I remembered my grandfather and felt guilty and uncomfortable. It was as though I was carrying out his advice in spite of myself. And to make it worse, everyone loved me for it. I was praised by the most lily-white men of the town. I was considered an example of desirable conduct—just as my grandfather had been. And what puzzled me was that the old man had defined it as *treachery*. When I was praised for my conduct I felt a guilt that in some way I was doing something that was really against the wishes of the white folks, that if they had understood they would have desired me to act just the opposite, that I should have been sulky and mean, and that that really would have been what they wanted, even though they were fooled and thought they wanted me to act as I did. It made me afraid that some day they would look upon me as a traitor and I would be lost. Still I was more afraid to act any other way because they didn't like that at all. The old man's words were like a curse. On my graduation day I delivered an oration in which I showed that humility was the secret, indeed, the very essence of progress. (Not that I believed this—how could I, remembering my grandfather?—I only believed that it worked.) It was a great success. Everyone praised me and I was invited to give the speech at a gathering of the town's leading white citizens. It was a triumph for our whole community.

It was in the main ballroom of the leading hotel. When I got there I discovered that it was on the occasion of a smoker° and I was told that since I was to be there anyway I might as well take part in the battle royal to be fought by some of my schoolmates as part of the entertainment. The battle royal came first.

All of the town's big shots were there in their tuxedoes, wolfing down the buffet 5
foods, drinking beer and whiskey and smoking black cigars. It was a large room with

smoker: Informal men-only social gathering.

a high ceiling. Chairs were arranged in neat rows around three sides of a portable boxing ring. The fourth side was clear, revealing a gleaming space of polished floor. I had some misgivings over the battle royal, by the way. Not from a distaste for fighting, but because I didn't care too much for the other fellows who were to take part. They were tough guys who seemed to have no grandfather's curse worrying their minds. No one could mistake their toughness. And besides, I suspected that fighting a battle royal might detract from the dignity of my speech. In those pre-invisible days I visualized myself as a potential Booker T. Washington.° But the other fellows didn't care too much for me either, and there were nine of them. I felt superior to them in my way, and I didn't like the manner in which we were all crowded together into the servants' elevator. Nor did they like my being there. In fact, as the warmly lighted floors flashed past the elevator we had words over the fact that I, by taking part in the fight, had knocked one of their friends out of a night's work.

We were led out of the elevator through a rococo hall into an anteroom and told to get into our fighting togs. Each of us was issued a pair of boxing gloves and ushered out into the big mirrored hall, which we entered looking cautiously about us and whispering, lest we might accidentally be heard above the noise of the room. It was foggy with cigar smoke. And already the whiskey was taking effect. I was shocked to see some of the most important men of the town quite tipsy. They were all there—bankers, lawyers, judges, doctors, fire chiefs, teachers, merchants. Even one of the more fashionable pastors. Something we could not see was going on up front. A clarinet was vibrating sensuously and the men were standing up and moving eagerly forward. We were a small tight group, clustered together, our bare upper bodies touching and shining with anticipatory sweat; while up front the big shots were becoming increasingly excited over something we still could not see. Suddenly I heard the school superintendent, who had told me to come, yell, "Bring up the shines° gentlemen! Bring up the little shines!"

We were rushed up to the front of the ballroom, where it smelled even more strongly of tobacco and whiskey. Then we were pushed into place. I almost wet my pants. A sea of faces, some hostile, some amused, ringed around us, and in the center, facing us, stood a magnificent blonde—stark naked. There was dead silence. I felt a blast of cold air chill me. I tried to back away, but they were behind me and around me. Some of the boys stood with lowered heads, trembling. I felt a wave of irrational guilt and fear. My teeth chattered, my skin turned to goose flesh, my knees knocked. Yet I was strongly attracted and looked in spite of myself. Had the price of looking been blindness, I would have looked. The hair was yellow like that of a circus kewpie doll, the face heavily powdered and rouged, as though to form an abstract mask, the eyes hollow and smeared a cool blue, the color of a baboon's butt. I felt a desire to spit upon her as my eyes brushed slowly over her body. Her breasts were firm and round as the domes of East Indian temples, and I stood so

---

Booker T. Washington: American educator (1856–1915), born into slavery, who gained an education after emancipation and in 1881 organized Tuskegee Institute, a vocational school for African-Americans.

shines: A racial slur for African Americans.

close as to see the fine skin texture and beads of pearly perspiration glistening like dew around the pink and erected buds of her nipples. I wanted at one and the same time to run from the room, to sink through the floor, or go to her and cover her from my eyes and the eyes of the others with my body; to feel the soft thighs, to caress her and destroy her, to love her and murder her, to hide from her, and yet to stroke where below the small American flag tattooed upon her belly her thighs formed a capital V. I had a notion that of all in the room she saw only me with her impersonal eyes.

And then she began to dance, a slow sensuous movement; the smoke of a hundred cigars clinging to her like the thinnest of veils. She seemed like a fair bird-girl girdled in veils calling to me from the angry surface of some gray and threatening sea. I was transported. Then I became aware of the clarinet playing and the big shots yelling at us. Some threatened us if we looked and others if we did not. On my right I saw one boy faint. And now a man grabbed a silver pitcher from a table and stepped close as he dashed ice water upon him and stood him up and forced two of us to support him as his head hung and moans issued from his thick bluish lips. Another boy began to plead to go home. He was the largest of the group, wearing dark red fighting trunks much too small to conceal the erection which projected from him as though in answer to the insinuating low-registered moaning of the clarinet. He tried to hide himself with his boxing gloves.

And all the while the blonde continued dancing, smiling faintly at the big shots who watched her with fascination, and faintly smiling at our fear. I noticed a certain merchant who followed her hungrily, his lips loose and drooling. He was a large man who wore diamond studs in a shirtfront which swelled with the ample paunch underneath, and each time the blonde swayed her undulating hips he ran his hand through the thin hair of his bald head and, with his arms upheld, his posture clumsy like that of an intoxicated panda, wound his belly in a slow and obscene grind. This creature was completely hypnotized. The music had quickened. As the dancer flung herself about with a detached expression on her face, the men began reaching out to touch her. I could see their beefy fingers sink into her soft flesh. Some of the others tried to stop them and she began to move around the floor in graceful circles, as they gave chase, slipping and sliding over the polished floor. It was mad. Chairs went crashing, drinks were spilt, as they ran laughing and howling after her. They caught her just as she reached a door, raised her from the floor, and tossed her as college boys are tossed at a hazing, and above her red, fixed-smiling lips I saw the terror and disgust in her eyes, almost like my own terror and that which I saw in some of the other boys. As I watched, they tossed her twice and her soft breasts seemed to flatten against the air and her legs flung wildly as she spun. Some of the more sober ones helped her to escape. And I started off the floor, heading for the anteroom with the rest of the boys.

Some were still crying and in hysteria. But as we tried to leave we were stopped 10
and ordered to get into the ring. There was nothing to do but what we were told. All ten of us climbed under the ropes and allowed ourselves to be blindfolded with broad bands of white cloth. One of the men seemed to feel a bit sympathetic and tried to cheer us up as we stood with our backs against the ropes. Some of us tried to

grin. "See that boy over there?" one of the men said. "I want you to run across at the bell and give it to him right in the belly. If you don't get him, I'm going to get you. I don't like his looks." Each of us was told the same. The blindfolds were put on. Yet even then I had been going over my speech. In my mind each word was as bright as flame. I felt the cloth pressed into place, and frowned so that it would be loosened when I relaxed.

But now I felt a sudden fit of blind terror. I was unused to darkness. It was as though I had suddenly found myself in a dark room filled with poisonous cottonmouths. I could hear the bleary voices yelling insistently for the battle royal to begin.

"Get going in there!"

"Let me at that big nigger!"

I strained to pick up the school superintendent's voice, as though to squeeze some security out of that slightly more familiar sound.

15 "Let me at those black sonsabitches!" someone yelled.

"No, Jackson, no!" another voice yelled. "Here, somebody, help me hold Jack."

"I want to get at that ginger-colored nigger. Tear him limb from limb," the first voice yelled.

I stood against the ropes trembling. For in those days I was what they called ginger-colored, and he sounded as though he might crunch me between his teeth like a crisp ginger cookie.

Quite a struggle was going on. Chairs were being kicked about and I could hear voices grunting as with a terrific effort. I wanted to see, to see more desperately than ever before. But the blindfold was as tight as a thick skin-puckering scab and when I raised my gloved hands to push the layers of white aside a voice yelled, "Oh, no you don't! black bastard! Leave that alone!"

20 "Ring the bell before Jackson kills him a coon!" someone boomed in the sudden silence. And I heard the bell clang and the sound of the feet scuffling forward.

A glove smacked against my head. I pivoted, striking out stiffly as someone went past, and felt the jar ripple along the length of my arm to my shoulder. Then it seemed as though all nine of the boys had turned upon me at once. Blows pounded me from all sides while I struck out as best I could. So many blows landed upon me that I wondered if I were not the only blindfolded fighter in the ring, or if the man called Jackson hadn't succeeded in getting me after all.

Blindfolded, I could no longer control my motions. I had no dignity. I stumbled about like a baby or a drunken man. The smoke had become thicker and with each new blow it seemed to sear and further restrict my lungs. My saliva became like hot bitter glue. A glove connected with my head, filling my mouth with warm blood. It was everywhere. I could not tell if the moisture I felt upon my body was sweat or blood. A blow landed hard against the nape of my neck. I felt myself going over, my head hitting the floor. Streaks of blue light filled the black world behind the blindfold. I lay prone, pretending that I was knocked out, but felt myself seized by hands and yanked to my feet. "Get going, black boy! Mix it up!" My arms were like lead, my head smarting from blows. I managed to feel my way to the ropes and held on, trying to catch my breath. A glove landed in my midsection and I went over again, feeling as though the smoke had become a knife jabbed into my guts. Pushed this way and that by the legs milling around me, I finally pulled erect and discovered that I could see the black, sweat-washed forms weaving in the smoky-blue atmosphere like drunken dancers weaving to the rapid drum-like thuds of blows.

Everyone fought hysterically. It was complete anarchy. Everybody fought everybody else. No group fought together for long. Two, three, four, fought one, then turned to fight each other, were themselves attacked. Blows landed below the belt and in the kidney, with the gloves open as well as closed, and with my eye partly opened now there was not so much terror. I moved carefully, avoiding blows, although not too many to attract attention, fighting from group to group. The boys groped about like blind, cautious crabs crouching to protect their midsections, their heads pulled in short against their shoulders, their arms stretched nervously before them, with their fists testing the smoke-filled air like the knobbed feelers of hypersensitive snails. In one corner I glimpsed a boy violently punching the air and heard him scream in pain as he smashed his hand against a ring post. For a second I saw him bent over holding his hand, then going down as a blow caught his unprotected head. I played one group against the other, slipping in and throwing a punch then stepping out of range while pushing the others into the melee to take the blows blindly aimed at me. The smoke was agonizing and there were no rounds, no bells at three minute intervals to relieve our exhaustion. The room spun round me, a swirl of lights, smoke, sweating bodies surrounded by tense white faces. I bled from both nose and mouth, the blood spattering upon my chest.

The men kept yelling, "Slug him, black boy! Knock his guts out!"

"Uppercut him! Kill him! Kill that big boy!" 25

Taking a fake fall, I saw a boy going down heavily beside me as though we were felled by a single blow, saw a sneaker-clad foot shoot into his groin as the two who had knocked him down stumbled upon him. I rolled out of range, feeling a twinge of nausea.

The harder we fought the more threatening the men became. And yet, I had begun to worry about my speech again. How would it go? Would they recognize my ability? What would they give me?

I was fighting automatically and suddenly I noticed that one after another of the boys was leaving the ring. I was surprised, filled with panic, as though I had been left alone with an unknown danger. Then I understood. The boys had arranged it among themselves. It was the custom for the two men left in the ring to slug it out for the winner's prize. I discovered this too late. When the bell sounded two men in tuxedoes leaped into the ring and removed the blindfold. I found myself facing Tatlock, the biggest of the gang. I felt sick at my stomach. Hardly had the bell stopped ringing in my ears than it clanged again and I saw him moving swiftly toward me. Thinking of nothing else to do I hit him smash on the nose. He kept coming, bringing the rank sharp violence of stale sweat. His face was a black blank of a face, only his eyes alive—with hate of me and aglow with a feverish terror from what had happened to us all. I became anxious. I wanted to deliver my speech and he came at me as though he meant to beat it out of me.

I smashed him again and again, taking his blows as they came. Then on a sudden impulse I struck him lightly and as we clinched, I whispered, "Fake like I knocked you out, you can have the prize."

"I'll break your behind," he whispered hoarsely.

30 "For *them?*"

"For *me,* sonofabitch!"

They were yelling for us to break it up and Tatlock spun me half around with a blow, and as a joggled camera sweeps in a reeling scene, I saw the howling red faces crouching tense beneath the cloud of blue-gray smoke. For a moment the world wavered, unraveled, flowed, then my head cleared and Tatlock bounced before me. That fluttering shadow before my eyes was his jabbing left hand. Then falling forward, my head against his damp shoulder, I whispered, "I'll make it five dollars more."

"Go to hell!"

But his muscles relaxed a trifle beneath my pressure and I breathed, "Seven!"

35 "Give it to your ma," he said, ripping me beneath the heart.

And while I still held him I butted him and moved away. I felt myself bombarded with punches. I fought back with hopeless desperation. I wanted to deliver my speech more than anything else in the world, because I felt that only these men could judge truly my ability, and now this stupid clown was ruining my chances. I began fighting carefully now, moving in to punch him and out again with my greater speed. A lucky blow to his chin and I had him going too — until I heard a loud voice yell, "I got my money on the big boy."

Hearing this, I almost dropped my guard. I was confused: Should I try to win against the voice out there? Would not this go against my speech, and was not this a moment for humility, for nonresistance? A blow to my head as I danced about sent my right eye popping like a jack-in-the-box and settled my dilemma. The room went red as I fell. It was a dream fall, my body languid and fastidious as to where to land, until the floor became impatient and smashed up to meet me. A moment later I came to. An hypnotic voice said FIVE emphatically. And I lay there, hazily watching a dark red spot of my own blood shaping itself into a butterfly, glistening and soaking into the soiled gray world of the canvas.

When the voice drawled TEN I was lifted up and dragged to a chair. I sat dazed. My eye pained and swelled with each throb of my pounding heart and I wondered if now I would be allowed to speak. I was wringing wet, my mouth still bleeding. We were grouped along the wall now. The other boys ignored me as they congratulated Tatlock and speculated as to how much they would be paid. One boy whimpered over his smashed hand. Looking up front, I saw attendants in white jackets rolling the portable ring away and placing a small square rug in the vacant space surrounded by chairs. Perhaps, I thought, I will stand on the rug to deliver my speech.

Then the M.C. called to us, "Come on up here boys and get your money."

40 We ran forward to where the men laughed and talked in their chairs, waiting. Everyone seemed friendly now.

"There it is on the rug," the man said. I saw the rug covered with coins of all dimensions and a few crumpled bills. But what excited me, scattered here and there, were the gold pieces.

"Boys, it's all yours," the man said. "You get all you grab."

"That's right, Sambo,"° a blond man said, winking at me confidentially.

I trembled with excitement, forgetting my pain. I would get the gold and the bills, I thought. I would use both hands. I would throw my body against the boys nearest me to block them from the gold.

"Get down around the rug now," the man commanded, "and don't anyone touch 45
it until I give the signal."

"This ought to be good," I heard.

As told, we got around the square rug on our knees. Slowly the man raised his freckled hand as we followed it upward with our eyes.

I heard, "These niggers look like they're about to pray!"

Then, "Ready," the man said. "Go!"

I lunged for a yellow coin lying on the blue design of the carpet, touching it and 50
sending a surprised shriek to join those rising around me. I tried frantically to remove my hand but could not let go. A hot, violent force tore through my body, shaking me like a wet rat. The rug was electrified. The hair bristled up on my head as I shook myself free. My muscles jumped, my nerves jangled, writhed. But I saw that this was not stopping the other boys. Laughing in fear and embarrassment, some were holding back and scooping up the coins knocked off by the painful contortions of the others. The men roared above us as we struggled.

"Pick it up, goddamnit, pick it up!" someone called like a bass-voiced parrot. "Go on, get it!"

I crawled rapidly around the floor, picking up the coins, trying to avoid the coppers and to get greenbacks and the gold. Ignoring the shock by laughing, as I brushed the coins off quickly, I discovered that I could contain the electricity — a contradiction, but it works. Then the men began to push us onto the rug. Laughing embarrassedly, we struggled out of their hands and kept after the coins. We were all wet and slippery and hard to hold. Suddenly I saw a boy lifted into the air, glistening with sweat like a circus seal, and dropped, his wet back landing flush upon the charged rug, heard him yell and saw him literally dance upon his back, his elbows beating a frenzied tattoo upon the floor, his muscles twitching like the flesh of a horse stung by many flies. When he finally rolled off, his face was gray and no one stopped him when he ran from the floor amid booming laughter.

"Get the money," the M.C. called. "That's good hard American cash!"

And we snatched and grabbed, snatched and grabbed. I was careful not to come too close to the rug now, and when I felt the hot whiskey breath descend upon me like a cloud of foul air I reached out and grabbed the leg of a chair. It was occupied and I held on desperately.

"Leggo, nigger! Leggo!" 55

The huge face wavered down to mine as he tried to push me free. But my body was slippery and he was too drunk. It was Mr. Colcord, who owned a chain of movie houses and "entertainment palaces." Each time he grabbed me I slipped out of his hands. It became a real struggle. I feared the rug more than I did the drunk, so I held

Sambo: A racial slur for blacks, referring to a character in a children's story.

on, surprising myself for a moment by trying to topple *him* upon the rug. It was such an enormous idea that I found myself actually carrying it out. I tried not to be obvious, yet when I grabbed his leg, trying to tumble him out of the chair, he raised up roaring with laughter, and, looking at me with soberness dead in the eye, kicked me viciously in the chest. The chair leg flew out of my hand. I felt myself going and rolled. It was as though I had rolled through a bed of hot coals. It seemed a whole century would pass before I would roll free, a century in which I was seared through the deepest levels of my body to the fearful breath within me and the breath seared and heated to the point of explosion. It'll all be over in a flash, I thought as I rolled clear. It'll all be over in a flash.

But not yet, the men on the other side were waiting, red faces swollen as though from apoplexy as they bent forward in their chairs. Seeing their fingers coming toward me I rolled away as a fumbled football rolls off the receiver's fingertips, back into the coals. That time I luckily sent the rug sliding out of place and heard the coins ringing against the floor and the boys scuffling to pick them up and the M.C. calling, "All right, boys, that's all. Go get dressed and get your money."

I was limp as a dish rag. My back felt as though it had been beaten with wires.

When we had dressed the M.C. came in and gave us each five dollars, except Tatlock, who got ten for being last in the ring. Then he told us to leave. I was not to get a chance to deliver my speech, I thought. I was going out into the dim alley in despair when I was stopped and told to go back. I returned to the ballroom, where the men were pushing back their chairs and gathering in groups to talk.

60 The M.C. knocked on a table for quiet. "Gentlemen," he said, "we almost forgot an important part of the program. A most serious part, gentlemen. This boy was brought here to deliver a speech which he made at his graduation yesterday. . . ."

"Bravo!"

"I'm told that he is the smartest boy we've got out there in Greenwood. I'm told that he knows more big words than a pocket-sized dictionary."

Much applause and laughter.

"So now, gentlemen, I want you to give him your attention."

65 There was still laughter as I faced them, my mouth dry, my eye throbbing. I began slowly, but evidently my throat was tense, because they began shouting, "Louder! Louder!"

"We of the younger generation extol the wisdom of that great leader and educator," I shouted, "who first spoke these flaming words of wisdom: 'A ship lost at sea for many days suddenly sighted a friendly vessel. From the mast of the unfortunate vessel was seen a signal: "Water, water; we die of thirst!" The answer from the friendly vessel came back: "Cast down your bucket where you are." The captain of the distressed vessel, at last heeding the injunction, cast down his bucket, and it came up full of fresh sparkling water from the mouth of the Amazon River.' And like him I say, and in his words, 'To those of my race who depend upon bettering their condition in a foreign land, or who underestimate the importance of cultivating friendly relations with the Southern white man, who is his next-door neighbor, I would say: "Cast down your bucket where you are"—cast it down in making friends in every manly way of the people of all races by whom we are surrounded. . . .'"

I spoke automatically and with such fervor that I did not realize that the men were still talking and laughing until my dry mouth, filling up with blood from the cut, almost strangled me. I coughed, wanting to stop and go to one of the tall brass, sand filled spittoons to relieve myself, but a few of the men, especially the superintendent, were listening and I was afraid. So I gulped it down, blood, saliva and all, and continued. (What powers of endurance I had during those days! What enthusiasm! What a belief in the rightness of things!) I spoke even louder in spite of the pain. But still they talked and still they laughed, as though deaf with cotton in dirty ears. So I spoke with greater emotional emphasis. I closed my ears and swallowed blood until I was nauseated. The speech seemed a hundred times as long as before, but I could not leave out a single word. All had to be said, each memorized nuance considered, rendered. Nor was that all. Whenever I uttered a word of three or more syllables a group of voices would yell for me to repeat it. I used the phrase "social responsibility" and they yelled:

"What's the word you say, boy?"

"Social responsibility," I said.

"What?"

"Social . . ."

"Louder."

". . . responsibility."

"More!"

"Respon —"

"Repeat!"

"— sibility."

The room filled with the uproar of laughter until, no doubt, distracted by having to gulp down my blood, I made a mistake and yelled a phrase I had often seen denounced in newspaper editorials, heard debated in private.

"Social . . ."

"What?" they yelled.

". . . equality —"

The laughter hung smokelike in the sudden stillness. I opened my eyes, puzzled. Sounds of displeasure filled the room. The M.C. rushed forward. They shouted hostile phrases at me. But I did not understand.

A small dry mustached man in the front row blared out, "Say that slowly, son!"

"What sir?"

"What you just said!"

"Social responsibility, sir," I said.

"You weren't being smart, were you, boy?" he said, not unkindly.

"No, sir!"

"You sure that about 'equality' was a mistake?"

"Oh, yes, sir," I said. "I was swallowing blood."

"Well, you had better speak more slowly so we can understand. We mean to do right by you, but you've got to know your place at all times. All right, now, go on with your speech."

I was afraid. I wanted to leave but I wanted also to speak and I was afraid they'd snatch me down.

"Thank you, sir," I said, beginning where I had left off, and having them ignore me as before.

Yet when I finished there was a thunderous applause. I was surprised to see the superintendent come forth with a package wrapped in white tissue paper, and, gesturing for quiet, address the men.

95 "Gentlemen, you see that I did not overpraise this boy. He makes a good speech and some day he'll lead his people in the proper paths. And I don't have to tell you that that is important in these days and times. This is a good, smart boy, and so to encourage him in the right direction, in the name of the Board of Education I wish to present him a prize in the form of this . . ."

He paused, removing the tissue paper and revealing a gleaming calfskin brief case.

". . . in the form of this first-class article from Shad Whitmore's shop."

"Boy," he said, addressing me, "take this prize and keep it well. Consider it a badge of office. Prize it. Keep developing as you are and some day it will be filled with important papers that will help shape the destiny of your people."

I was so moved that I could hardly express my thanks. A rope of bloody saliva forming a shape like an undiscovered continent drooled upon the leather and I wiped it quickly away. I felt an importance that I had never dreamed.

100 "Open it and see what's inside," I was told.

My fingers a-tremble, I complied, smelling the fresh leather and finding an official-looking document inside. It was a scholarship to the state college for Negroes. My eyes filled with tears and I ran awkwardly off the floor.

I was overjoyed; I did not even mind when I discovered that the gold pieces I had scrambled for were brass pocket tokens advertising a certain make of automobile.

When I reached home everyone was excited. Next day the neighbors came to congratulate me. I even felt safe from grandfather, whose deathbed curse usually spoiled my triumphs. I stood beneath his photograph with my brief case in hand and smiled triumphantly into his stolid black peasant's face. It was a face that fascinated me. The eyes seemed to follow everywhere I went.

That night I dreamed I was at a circus with him and that he refused to laugh at the clowns no matter what they did. Then later he told me to open my brief case and read what was inside and I did, finding an official envelope stamped with the state seal; and inside the envelope I found another and another, endlessly, and I thought I would fall of weariness. "Them's years," he said. "Now open that one." And I did and in it I found an engraved document containing a short message in letters of gold. "Read it," my grandfather said. "Out loud."

105 "To Whom It May Concern," I intoned. "Keep This Nigger-Boy Running."

I awoke with the old man's laughter ringing in my ears.

(It was a dream I was to remember and dream again for many years after. But at the time I had no insight into its meaning. First I had to attend college.)

Reading and Reacting

1. "Battle Royal," the first chapter of Ellison's *Invisible Man* (1952), takes place in the American South. How does the story's historical and geographical setting make possible the events that occur?
2. In paragraph 2, the narrator quotes his grandfather's deathbed statement. Why does the narrator think of his grandfather's words as a "curse" (par. 3)?
3. When the narrator is told he is expected to participate in the "battle royal," he feels that the battle will "detract from the dignity" of the speech he is to give (par. 5). Why, then, does he agree to take part in the fight? Why is he so intent on delivering his speech to the men assembled in the ballroom?
4. In his graduation speech, the narrator tells his audience that "humility [is] the secret, indeed, the very essence of progress" (par. 3). What do you suppose he means? How do you think his grandfather would feel about this statement?
5. Describe the physical setting (the sights, sounds, smells) of the ballroom. What is your emotional reaction to this setting?
6. Why is the narrator blindfolded before the fight? What effect does the blindfold have on him as a fighter? As a human being?
7. The superintendent tells the audience that the narrator will someday "lead his people in the proper paths" (par. 95). What "proper paths" do you think the superintendent has in mind?
8. Why do you think the narrator dreams about his grandfather after the fight? What do you think his dream means?
9. **JOURNAL ENTRY** Do you see the "battle royal" as simply a necessary evil, a hurdle the narrator has to leap over in order to win the college scholarship? Does the prize in any way make up for the humiliating ordeal? Do you think the narrator should (or even could) have turned down the scholarship?
10. **CRITICAL PERSPECTIVE** This story is set in the South in the 1940s, during a time of violent racism and "Jim Crow" laws that enforced legal segregation. Whites and blacks were not allowed equality on even the most fundamental levels, and this backdrop heightens the tension of the battle royal. Thomas F. Bertonneau offers this observation:

    > The atmosphere is gladiatorial and orgiastic. Before the fight, for example, the businessmen make the protagonist and his compeers watch a lewd performance by a blonde stripper, which shocks and humiliates them. In the perverse ethos of Jim Crow, it also sets them up, because it embroils them willy-nilly in a racial-sexual scenario in which they fill the role of lascivious onlookers. On the street, should any of them stare at a white woman, stripper or bourgeoisie, he would run the risk of accusation and be under the lethal threat of the outraged mob. It is a formula for lynching.

    In this scene in the story, what is the main attraction? Who is watching whom? In what ways is the scenario Bertonneau describes ironic? How does this irony contribute to the meaning of the story?

Related Works: "Buffalo Soldiers" (p. 187), "The secretary chant" (p. 932), "We Wear the Mask" (p. 1150), "If We Must Die" (p. 1179), *Fences* (p. 1902)

Source: ©AP Photo

TILLIE OLSEN (1912 or 1913–2007) is known for her works of fiction about working-class Americans. Her short stories and one novel are inhabited by those she called the "despised people"—coal miners, farm laborers, packinghouse butchers, and housewives. Olsen was born in Nebraska into a working-class family. According to an account in her nonfiction work *Silences* (1978), she was inspired at age fifteen to write about working-class people when she read Rebecca Harding Davis's *Life in the Iron Mills,* a tale of the effects of industrialization on workers, in an 1861 issue of *Atlantic Monthly* bought for ten cents in a junk shop.

Shortly after she left high school, Olsen was jailed for helping to organize packinghouse workers. Motivated by her experiences, she began to write a novel, *Yonnondio.* Under her maiden name, Tillie Lerner, she published two poems, a short story, and part of her novel during the 1930s. After her marriage, she did not publish again for twenty-two years, spending her time raising four children and working at a variety of jobs. The collection of short stories *Tell Me a Riddle* (1961), which includes "I Stand Here Ironing" (originally titled "Help Her to Believe"), was published when she was fifty. Her only other work of fiction is *Yonnondio* (1974), which she pieced together from drafts she wrote in the 1930s and edited for publication in 1974.

In 1984, she edited *Mother to Daughter, Daughter to Mother: Mothers on Mothering,* a collection of poems, letters, short fiction, and diary excerpts written by famous and not-so-famous women, and in 1987, she collaborated with photographer Estelle Jussim on *Mothers & Daughters: An Exploration in Photographs.*

Cultural Context During the Great Depression of the 1930s, jobs were scarce throughout the United States, and many people who managed to keep their jobs were forced to take pay cuts. At the height of the Depression in 1933, almost twenty-five percent of the total workforce—more than eleven million people—were unemployed. The displacement of the American worker and the destruction of farming communities caused families such as the one in this story to split up or migrate from their homes in search of work. In 1935, the Social Security Act established public assistance, unemployment insurance, and social security, which offered economic relief to American workers.

I Stand Here Ironing (1961)

Film Series

DVD

See p. 352 for film stills from the DVD version of this story.

I stand here ironing, and what you asked me moves tormented back and forth with the iron.

"I wish you would manage the time to come and talk with me about your daughter. I'm sure you can help me understand her. She's a youngster who needs help and whom I'm deeply interested in helping."

"Who needs help." . . . Even if I came, what good would it do? You think because I am her mother I have a key, or that in some way you could use me as a key? She has lived for nineteen years. There is all that life that has happened outside of me, beyond me.

And when is there time to remember, to sift, to weigh, to estimate, to total? I will start and there will be an interruption and I will have to gather it all together again. Or I will become engulfed with all I did or did not do, with what should have been and what cannot be helped.

She was a beautiful baby. The first and only one of our five that was beautiful at birth. You do not guess how new and uneasy her tenancy in her now-loveliness. You did not know her all those years she was thought homely, or see her poring over her baby pictures, making me tell her over and over how beautiful she had been—and would be, I would tell her—and was now, to the seeing eye. But the seeing eyes were few or nonexistent. Including mine. 5

I nursed her. They feel that's important nowadays. I nursed all the children, but with her, with all the fierce rigidity of first motherhood, I did like the books then said. Though her cries battered me to trembling and my breasts ached with swollenness, I waited till the clock decreed.

Why do I put that first? I do not even know if it matters, or if it explains anything.

She was a beautiful baby. She blew shining bubbles of sound. She loved motion, loved light, loved color and music and textures. She would lie on the floor in her blue overalls patting the surface so hard in ecstasy her hands and feet would blur. She was a miracle to me, but when she was eight months old I had to leave her daytimes with the woman downstairs to whom she was no miracle at all, for I worked or looked for work and for Emily's father, who "could no longer endure" (he wrote in his good-bye note) "sharing want with us."

I was nineteen. It was the pre-relief, pre-WPA° world of the depression. I would start running as soon as I got off the streetcar, running up the stairs, the place smelling sour, and awake or asleep to startle awake, when she saw me she would break into a clogged weeping that could not be comforted, a weeping I can hear yet.

After a while I found a job hashing at night so I could be with her days, and it 10
was better. But it came to where I had to bring her to his family and leave her.

It took a long time to raise the money for her fare back. Then she got chicken pox and I had to wait longer. When she finally came, I hardly knew her, walking quick and nervous like her father, looking like her father, thin, and dressed in a shoddy red that yellowed her skin and glared at the pockmarks. All the baby loveliness gone.

She was two. Old enough for nursery school they said, and I did not know then what I know now—the fatigue of the long day, and the lacerations of group life in the kinds of nurseries that are only parking places for children.

Except that it would have made no difference if I had known. It was the only place there was. It was the only way we could be together, the only way I could hold a job.

And even without knowing, I knew. I knew the teacher that was evil because all these years it has curdled into my memory, the little boy hunched in the corner, her rasp, "why aren't you outside, because Alvin hits you? that's no reason, go out, scaredy." I knew Emily hated it even if she did not clutch and implore "don't go Mommy" like the other children, mornings.

WPA: The Works Progress Administration, created in 1935 as part of President Franklin D. Roosevelt's New Deal program. The purpose of the WPA (renamed the Works Projects Administration in 1939) was to provide jobs for the unemployed during the Great Depression.

15 She always had a reason why we should stay home. Momma, you look sick. Momma, I feel sick. Momma, the teachers aren't there today, they're sick. Momma, we can't go, there was a fire there last night. Momma, it's a holiday today, no school, they told me.

But never a direct protest, never rebellion. I think of our others in their three-, four-year-oldness — the explosions, the tempers, the denunciations, the demands — and I feel suddenly ill. I put the iron down. What in me demanded that goodness in her? And what was the cost, the cost to her of such goodness?

The old man living in the back once said in his gentle way: "You should smile at Emily more when you look at her." What *was* in my face when I looked at her? I loved her. There were all the acts of love.

It was only with the others I remembered what he said, and it was the face of joy, and not of care or tightness or worry I turned to them — too late for Emily. She does not smile easily, let alone almost always as her brothers and sisters do. Her face is closed and sombre, but when she wants, how fluid. You must have seen it in her pantomimes, you spoke of her rare gift for comedy on the stage that rouses laughter out of the audience so dear they applaud and applaud and do not want to let her go.

Where does it come from, that comedy? There was none of it in her when she came back to me that second time, after I had had to send her away again. She had a new daddy now to learn to love, and I think perhaps it was a better time.

20 Except when we left her alone nights, telling ourselves she was old enough.

"Can't you go some other time, Mommy, like tomorrow?" she would ask. "Will it be just a little while you'll be gone? Do you promise?"

The time we came back, the front door open, the clock on the floor in the hall. She rigid awake. "It wasn't just a little while. I didn't cry. Three times I called you, just three times, and then I ran downstairs to open the door so you could come faster. The clock talked loud. I threw it away, it scared me what it talked."

She said the clock talked loud again that night I went to the hospital to have Susan. She was delirious with the fever that comes before red measles, but she was fully conscious all the week I was gone and the week after we were home when she could not come near the new baby or me.

She did not get well. She stayed skeleton thin, not wanting to eat, and night after night she had nightmares. She would call for me, and I would rouse from exhaustion to sleepily call back: "You're all right, darling, go to sleep, it's just a dream," and if she still called, in a sterner voice, "now go to sleep, Emily, there's nothing to hurt you." Twice, only twice, when I had to get up for Susan anyhow, I went in to sit with her.

25 Now when it is too late (as if she would let me hold and comfort her like I do the others) I get up and go to her at once at her moan or restless stirring. "Are you awake, Emily? Can I get you something?" And the answer is always the same: "No, I'm all right, go back to sleep, Mother."

They persuaded me at the clinic to send her away to a convalescent home in the country where "she can have the kind of food and care you can't manage for her, and you'll be free to concentrate on the new baby." They still send children to that place. I see pictures on the society page of sleek young women planning affairs to raise money for it, or dancing at the affairs, or decorating Easter eggs or filling Christmas stockings for the children.

They never have a picture of the children so I do not know if the girls still wear those gigantic red bows and the ravaged looks on the every other Sunday when parents can come to visit "unless otherwise notified"—as we were notified the first six weeks.

Oh it is a handsome place, green lawns and tall trees and fluted flower beds. High up on the balconies of each cottage the children stand, the girls in their red bows and white dresses, the boys in white suits and giant red ties. The parents stand below shrieking up to be heard and the children shriek down to be heard, and between them the invisible wall: "Not to Be Contaminated by Parental Germs or Physical Affection."

There was a tiny girl who always stood hand in hand with Emily. Her parents never came. One visit she was gone. "They moved her to Rose Cottage," Emily shouted in explanation. "They don't like you to love anybody here."

She wrote once a week, the labored writing of a seven-year-old. "I am fine. How 30
is the baby. If I write my leter nicly I will have a star. Love." There never was a star. We wrote every other day, letters she could never hold or keep but only hear read—once. "We simply do not have room for children to keep any personal possessions," they patiently explained when we pieced one Sunday's shrieking together to plead how much it would mean to Emily, who loved so to keep things, to be allowed to keep her letters and cards.

Each visit she looked frailer. "She isn't eating," they told us.

(They had runny eggs for breakfast or mush with lumps, Emily said later, I'd hold it in my mouth and not swallow. Nothing ever tasted good, just when they had chicken.)

It took us eight months to get her released home, and only the fact that she gained back so little of her seven lost pounds convinced the social worker.

I used to try to hold and love her after she came back, but her body would stay stiff, and after a while she'd push away. She ate little. Food sickened her, and I think much of life too. Oh she had physical lightness and brightness, twinkling by on skates, bouncing like a ball up and down up and down over the jump rope, skimming over the hill; but these were momentary.

She fretted about her appearance, thin and dark and foreign-looking at a time 35
when every little girl was supposed to look or thought she should look a chubby blonde replica of Shirley Temple. The doorbell sometimes rang for her, but no one seemed to come and play in the house or be a best friend. Maybe because we moved so much.

There was a boy she loved painfully through two school semesters. Months later she told me how she had taken pennies from my purse to buy him candy. "Licorice was his favorite and I brought him some every day, but he still liked Jennifer better'n me. Why, Mommy?" The kind of question for which there is no answer.

School was a worry to her. She was not glib or quick in a world where glibness and quickness were easily confused with ability to learn. To her overworked and exasperated teachers she was an overconscientious "slow learner" who kept trying to catch up and was absent entirely too often.

I let her be absent, though sometimes the illness was imaginary. How different from my now-strictness about attendance with the others. I wasn't working. We had a new baby, I was home anyhow. Sometimes, after Susan grew old enough, I would keep her home from school, too, to have them all together.

Mostly Emily had asthma, and her breathing, harsh and labored, would fill the house with a curiously tranquil sound. I would bring the two old dresser mirrors and her boxes of collections to her bed. She would select beads and single earrings, bottle tops and shells, dried flowers and pebbles, old postcards and scraps, all sorts of oddments; then she and Susan would play Kingdom, setting up landscapes and furniture, peopling them with action.

Those were the only times of peaceful companionship between her and Susan. I have edged away from it, that poisonous feeling between them, that terrible balancing of hurts and needs I had to do between the two, and did so badly, those earlier years.

Oh there are conflicts between the others too, each one human, needing, demanding, hurting, taking—but only between Emily and Susan, no, Emily toward Susan that corroding resentment. It seems so obvious on the surface, yet it is not obvious. Susan, the second child, Susan, golden- and curly-haired and chubby, quick and articulate and assured, everything in appearance and manner Emily was not; Susan, not able to resist Emily's precious things, losing or sometimes clumsily breaking them; Susan telling jokes and riddles to company for applause while Emily sat silent (to say to me later: that was *my* riddle, Mother, I told it to Susan); Susan, who for all the five years' difference in age was just a year behind Emily in developing physically.

I am glad for that slow physical development that widened the difference between her and her contemporaries, though she suffered over it. She was too vulnerable for that terrible world of youthful competition, of preening and parading, of constant measuring of yourself against every other, of envy, "If I had that copper hair," "If I had that skin. . . ." She tormented herself enough about not looking like the others, there was enough of the unsureness, the having to be conscious of words before you speak, the constant caring—what are they thinking of me? without having it all magnified by the merciless physical drives.

Ronnie is calling. He is wet and I change him. It is rare there is such a cry now. That time of motherhood is almost behind me when the ear is not one's own but must always be racked and listening for the child cry, the child call. We sit for a while and I hold him, looking out over the city spread in charcoal with its soft aisles of light. "*Shoogily,*" he breathes and curls closer. I carry him back to bed, asleep. *Shoogily*. A funny word, a family word, inherited from Emily, invented by her to say: *comfort*.

In this and other ways she leaves her seal, I say aloud. And startle at my saying it. What do I mean? What did I start to gather together, to try and make coherent? I was at the terrible, growing years. War years. I do not remember them well. I was working, there were four smaller ones now, there was not time for her. She had to help be a mother, and housekeeper, and shopper. She had to set her seal. Mornings of crisis and near hysteria trying to get lunches packed, hair combed, coats and shoes found, everyone to school or Child Care on time, the baby ready for transportation. And always the paper scribbled on by a smaller one, the book looked at by Susan then mislaid, the homework not done. Running out to that huge school where she was one, she was lost, she was a drop; suffering over the unpreparedness, stammering and unsure in her classes.

There was so little time left at night after the kids were bedded down. She would struggle over books, always eating (it was in those years she developed her enormous appetite that is legendary in our family) and I would be ironing, or preparing food for the next day, or writing V-mail° to Bill, or tending the baby. Sometimes, to make me laugh, or out of her despair, she would imitate happenings or types at school.

I think I said once: "Why don't you do something like this in the school amateur show?" One morning she phoned me at work, hardly understandable through the weeping: "Mother, I did it. I won, I won; they gave me first prize; they clapped and clapped and wouldn't let me go."

Now suddenly she was Somebody, and as imprisoned in her difference as she had been in anonymity.

She began to be asked to perform at other high schools, even in colleges, then at city and statewide affairs. The first one we went to, I only recognized her that first moment when thin, shy, she almost drowned herself into the curtains. Then: Was this Emily? The control, the command, the convulsing and deadly clowning, the spell, then the roaring, stamping audience, unwilling to let this rare and precious laughter out of their lives.

Afterwards: You ought to do something about her with a gift like that—but without money or knowing how, what does one do? We have left it all to her, and the gift has as often eddied inside, clogged and clotted, as been used and growing.

She is coming. She runs up the stairs two at a time with her light graceful step, and I know she is happy tonight. Whatever it was that occasioned your call did not happen today.

"Aren't you ever going to finish the ironing, Mother? Whistler painted his mother in a rocker. I'd have to paint mine standing over an ironing board." This is one of her communicative nights and she tells me everything and nothing as she fixes herself a plate of food out of the icebox.

She is so lovely. Why did you want me to come in at all? Why were you concerned? She will find her way.

She starts up the stairs to bed. "Don't get me up with the rest in the morning." "But I thought you were having midterms." "Oh, those," she comes back in, kisses me, and says quite lightly, "in a couple of years when we'll all be atom-dead they won't matter a bit."

She has said it before. She *believes* it. But because I have been dredging the past, and all that compounds a human being is so heavy and meaningful in me, I cannot endure it tonight.

V-mail: Mail sent to or from members of the armed forces during World War II. Letters were reduced onto microfilm and enlarged and printed out at their destination.

55 I will never total it all. I will never come in to say: She was a child seldom smiled at. Her father left me before she was a year old. I had to work her first six years when there was work, or I sent her home and to his relatives. There were years she had care she hated. She was dark and thin and foreign-looking in a world where the prestige went to blondeness and curly hair and dimples, she was slow where glibness was prized. She was a child of anxious, not proud, love. We were poor and could not afford for her the soil of easy growth. I was a young mother, I was a distracted mother. There were other children pushing up, demanding. Her younger sister seemed all that she was not. There were years she did not want me to touch her. She kept too much in herself, her life was such she had to keep too much in herself. My wisdom came too late. She has much to her and probably little will come of it. She is a child of her age, of depression, of war, of fear.

Let her be. So all that is in her will not bloom—but in how many does it? There is still enough left to live by. Only help her to know—help make it so there is cause for her to know—that she is more than this dress on the ironing board, helpless before the iron.

Reading and Reacting

1. "I Stand Here Ironing" focuses on incidents that took place in the "pre-relief, pre-WPA world" of the Depression (par. 9). In light of social, political, and economic changes that have occurred since the 1930s, do you think the events the story presents could occur today? Explain.
2. In what sense is the image of a mother at an ironing board appropriate for this story?
3. The narrator is overwhelmed by guilt. What does she believe she has done wrong? What, if anything, do *you* think she has done wrong? Do you think she has been a good mother? Why or why not?
4. Who, or what, do you blame for the narrator's problems? For example, do you blame Emily's father? The Depression? The social institutions and "experts" to which the narrator turns?
5. Do you see the narrator as a victim limited by the times in which she lives? Do you agree with the narrator that Emily is "a child of her age, of depression, of war, of fear" (par. 55)? Or do you believe both women have some control over their own destinies, regardless of the story's historical setting?
6. What do you think the narrator wants for her daughter? Do you think her goals for Emily are realistic? Why or why not?
7. Paragraph 28 describes the physical setting of the convalescent home to which Emily was sent. What does this description add to the story? Why do you suppose there is no physical description of the apartment in which Emily lived as a child? How do you picture this apartment?
8. To whom do you think the mother is speaking in this story?
9. **JOURNAL ENTRY** Put yourself in Emily's position. What do you think she would like to tell her mother?
10. **CRITICAL PERSPECTIVE** Writing in *The Red Wheelbarrow*, psychologist Robert Coles discusses the complex family relationships depicted in "I Stand Here Ironing" and reaches an optimistic conclusion:

> But the child did not grow to be a mere victim of the kind so many of us these days are rather eager to recognize—a hopeless tangle of psychopathology. The growing child, even in her troubled moments, revealed herself to be persistent, demanding, and observant. In the complaints we make, in the "symptoms" we develop, we reveal our strengths as well as our weaknesses. The hurt child could summon her intelligence, exercise her will, smile and make others smile.

Do you agree with Coles's psychological evaluation of Emily? Do you find the story's ending as essentially uplifting as he seems to? Why or why not?

Related Works: "Kansas" (p. 237), "A Primer for the Punctuation of Heart Disease" (p. 440), "Everyday Use" (p. 517), "Two Kinds" (p. 777), "Those Winter Sundays" (p. 1040), *When I Was a Little Girl and My Mother Didn't Want Me* (p. 1266), *The Glass Menagerie* (p. 1961)

Fiction in Film: Tillie Olsen's "I Stand Here Ironing"

Setting is very important in "I Stand Here Ironing," whose events and emotions are rooted in a particular historical time: the years of the Great Depression. In the DVD version of the story, that time and mood are conveyed through specific, vivid images of Depression-era street scenes. The film also establishes the family's economic status, a key factor in the story, by showing how they are dressed and what their apartment looks like. The stills included here depict scenes that appear on the DVD.

Narrator (as a young woman) at ironing board.
Source: ©Denna Bendall / Worn Path Productions

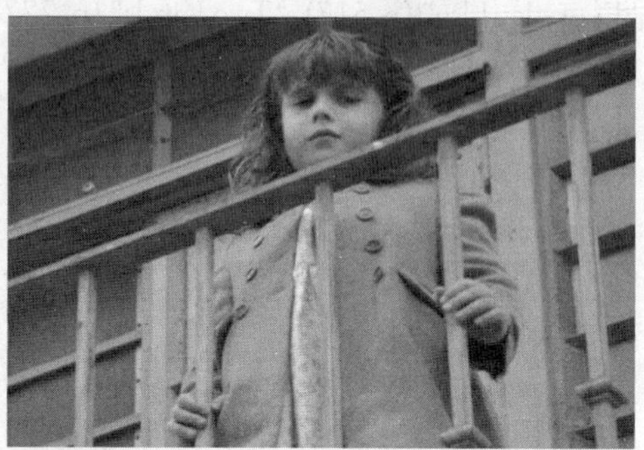

Emily as a child (in convalescent home).
Source: ©Denna Bendall / Worn Path Productions

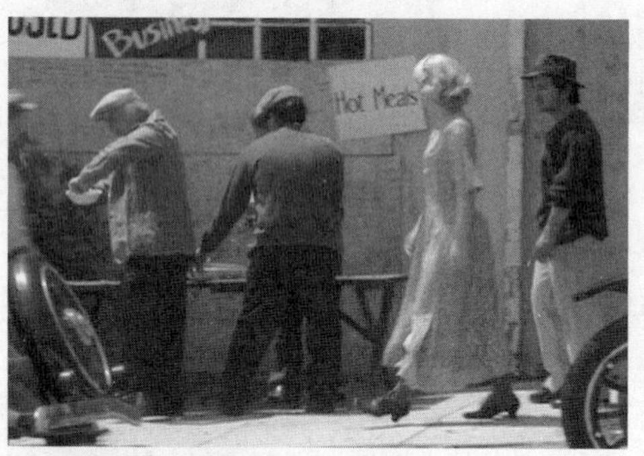

Street scene showing bread line.
Source: ©Denna Bendall / Worn Path Productions

Emily performing at her school's amateur show.
Source: ©Denna Bendall / Worn Path Productions

Reading and Reacting

1. The story does not describe the apartment in which Emily and her mother lived when she was a baby. How do you picture the apartment? If you were filming the story, how would you decorate and furnish it?
2. What other settings besides the apartment would you see as essential in a film version of the story? Why?
3. How would you convey the shifts in time presented in the story? For example, would you show the characters at different ages? Would you show certain scenes as flashbacks?

4. Would you include voice-over narration to reproduce the mother's voice, or would you have the story unfold without a narrator?
5. Where would you place the ironing board? Why? At what point (or points) in the story would you show the mother ironing?
6. The mother questions many of the decisions she made about Emily, and readers are left to decide if she is a good mother. What scenes could a film version include to portray her as a good mother? As a neglectful mother?
7. Would your film be in color or in black and white? Why?

WRITING SUGGESTIONS: Setting

1. Storytelling is important in both "Water Names" and "This Is What It Means to Say Phoenix, Arizona." Consider the stories told by the grandmother in "Water Names" and by Thomas Builds-the-Fire in "This Is What It Means to Say Phoenix, Arizona." What motivates the storytellers to tell their tales? How do they differ in the techniques they use to create compelling settings for the stories they tell?
2. In "The Storm," "I Stand Here Ironing," and "Persepolis," social constraints determined by the story's historical setting limit a woman's options. Explore the options each woman might reasonably exercise in order to break free of the limits that social institutions impose on her.
3. Write an essay in which you consider how "This Is What It Means to Say Phoenix, Arizona" would be different if its geographical and physical setting were changed to a setting of your choice. In your essay, examine the changes (in plot development as well as in the characters' conflicts, reactions, and motivation) that might occur as a result of the change in setting.
4. Select a story from another chapter, and write an essay in which you consider how setting affects its plot—for example, how it creates conflict or crisis, how it forces characters to act, or how it determines how the plot is resolved.
5. "The Storm," "Water Names," and "Battle Royal" all use rich descriptive language to create a mood that dominates the story. Analyze this use of language in one of these stories, or explicate and compare two short passages from different stories. How does language help to create and enrich each story's setting?

CHAPTER 15

POINT OF VIEW

One of the first choices writers make is who tells the story. This choice determines the story's **point of view**—the vantage point from which events are presented. The implications of this choice are far-reaching.

Consider the following scenario. Five people witness a crime and are questioned by the police. Their stories agree on certain points: a crime was committed, a body was found, and the crime occurred at noon. But in other ways their stories are different. The man who fled the scene was either tall or of average height; his hair was either dark or light; he either was carrying an object or was empty-handed. The events that led up to the crime and even the description of the crime itself are markedly different, depending on who tells the story. Thus, the **narrator**—the person telling the story—determines what details are included in the story and how they are arranged—in short, the plot. In addition, the perspective of the narrator affects the story's style, language, and themes.

The narrator of a work of fiction is not the same as the writer—even when a writer uses the first-person *I*. Writers create narrators to tell their stories. Often the personalities and opinions of narrators are far different from those of the author. The term **persona**—which literally means "mask"—is used for such narrators. By assuming this mask, a writer expands the creative possibilities of a work.

When deciding on a point of view for a work of fiction, a writer can choose to tell the story either in the **first person** or in the **third person.**

First-Person Narrators

Sometimes the narrator is a character who uses the **first person** (*I* or sometimes *we*) to tell the story. Often this narrator is a **major character**—Sammy in John Updike's "A&P" (p. 259) and the boy in James Joyce's "Araby" (p. 434), for example—who tells his or her own story and is the focus of that story. Sometimes, however, a first-person narrator tells a story that is primarily about someone else. Such a narrator may be a **minor character** who plays a relatively small part in the story or simply an **observer** who reports events experienced or related by others. The narrator of William Faulkner's "A Rose for Emily" (p. 243), for example, is an unidentified witness to the story's events. By using *we* instead of *I*, this narrator speaks on behalf of all the town's residents, expressing their shared views of their neighbor, Emily Grierson as the following excerpt illustrates:

> We did not say she was crazy then. We believed she had to do that. We remembered all the young men her father had driven away, and we knew that with nothing left, she would have to cling to that which had robbed her, as people will.

Writers gain a number of advantages when they use first-person narrators. First, they are able to present incidents convincingly. Readers are more willing to accept a statement like "My sister changed a lot after that day" than they are to accept the impersonal observations of a third-person narrator. The first-person narrator also simplifies a writer's task of selecting details. Only the events and details that the narrator could actually have observed or experienced can be introduced into the story.

Another major advantage of first-person narrators is that their restricted view can create **irony**—a discrepancy between what is said and what readers believe to be true. Irony may be *dramatic*, *situational*, or *verbal*. **Dramatic irony** occurs when a narrator (or a character) perceives less than readers do; **situational irony** occurs when what happens is at odds with what readers are led to expect; **verbal irony** occurs when the narrator says one thing but actually means another.

"Gryphon," by Charles Baxter (p. 277), illustrates all three kinds of irony. Baxter creates **dramatic irony** when he has his main character see less than readers do. For example, at the end of the story, the young boy does not yet realize what readers already know—that he has learned more from Miss Ferenczi's way of teaching than from Mr. Hibler's. The setting of the story—a conventional school—creates **situational irony** because it contrasts with the unexpected events that unfold there. In addition, many of the narrator's comments create **verbal irony** because they convey the opposite of their literal meaning. At the end of the story, for example, after the substitute, Miss Ferenczi, has been fired, the narrator relates another teacher's comment that life will now return to "normal" and that their regular teacher will soon return to test them on their "knowledge." This comment is ironic in light of all Miss Ferenczi has done to redefine the narrator's ideas about "normal" education and about "knowledge."

Unreliable Narrators

Sometimes first-person narrators are self-serving, mistaken, confused, unstable, or even insane. These **unreliable narrators,** whether intentionally or unintentionally, misrepresent events and misdirect readers. In Edgar Allan Poe's "The Cask of Amontillado" (p. 385), for example, the narrator, Montresor, tells his story to justify a crime he committed fifty years before. Montresor's version of what happened is not accurate, and perceptive readers know it: his obvious self-deception, his sadistic manipulation of Fortunato, his detached description of the cold-blooded murder, and his lack of remorse lead readers to question his sanity and, therefore, to distrust his version of events. This distrust creates an ironic distance between readers and narrator.

The narrator of Charlotte Perkins Gilman's "The Yellow Wallpaper" (p. 459) is also an unreliable narrator. Suffering from "nervous depression," she unintentionally distorts the facts when she says that the shapes in her bedroom wallpaper are changing and moving. Moreover, she does not realize what is wrong with her or why, or how her husband's "good intentions" are hurting her. Readers, however, see the disparity between the narrator's interpretation of events and their own, and this irony enriches their understanding of the story.

Some narrators are unreliable because they are naive. Because they are immature, sheltered, or innocent of evil, these narrators are not aware of the significance of the events they are relating. Having the benefit of experience, readers interpret events differently from the way these narrators do. When we read a passage by a child narrator—such as the following one from J. D. Salinger's classic 1951 novel *The Catcher in the Rye*—we are aware of the narrator's innocence, and we know his interpretation of events is flawed:

> Anyway, I keep picturing all these little kids playing some game in this big field of rye and all. Thousands of little kids, and nobody's around—nobody big, I mean—except me. And I'm standing on the edge of some crazy cliff. What I have to do, I have to catch everybody if they start to go over the cliff—I mean if they're running and they don't look where they're going I have to come out from somewhere and catch them. I'd just be the catcher in the rye. . . .

The irony in the preceding passage comes from our knowledge that the naive narrator, Holden Caulfield, cannot stop children from growing up. Ultimately, they all fall off the "crazy cliff" and mature into adults. Although Holden is not aware of the futility of trying to protect children from the dangers of adulthood, readers know that his efforts are doomed from the start.

A naive narrator's background can also limit his or her ability to understand a situation. The narrator in Sherwood Anderson's 1922 short story "I'm a Fool," for example, lies to impress a rich girl he meets at a racetrack. At the end of the story, the boy regrets the fact that he lied, believing that if he had told the truth, he could have seen the girl again. The reader knows, however, that the narrator (a laborer at the racetrack) is deceiving himself because the social gap that separates him and the girl could never be bridged.

Keep in mind that all first-person narrators are, in a sense, unreliable because they present a situation as only one person sees it. When you read, you should look for discrepancies between a narrator's view of events and your own. Discovering that a story has an unreliable narrator enables you not only to question the accuracy of the narrative but also to recognize the irony in the narrator's version of events. In this way, you gain insight into the story and learn something about the writer's purpose.

Third-Person Narrators

Sometimes a writer uses the **third person** (*he*, *she*, *they*) to tell the story from the point of view of a narrator who is not a character. Third-person narrators fall into three categories: **omniscient, limited omniscient,** and **objective.**

Omniscient Narrators

Some third-person narrators are **omniscient** (all-knowing) narrators, moving at will from one character's mind to another's. One advantage of omniscient narrators is that they have none of the naïveté, dishonesty, gullibility, or mental instability that can characterize first-person narrators. In addition, because omniscient narrators are not characters in the story, their perception is not limited to what any one character can observe or comprehend. As a result, they can present a more inclusive view of events and characters than first-person narrators can.

Omniscient narrators can also convey their attitude toward their subject matter. For example, the omniscient narrator in Nadine Gordimer's short story "Once upon a Time" (p. 232) uses sentence structure, word choice, and repetition to express distaste for the scene being described:

> In a house, in a suburb, in a city, there were a man and his wife who loved each other very much and were living happily ever after. They had a little boy, and they loved him very much. They had a cat and a dog that the little boy loved very much. They had a car and a caravan trailer for holidays, and a swimming-pool which was fenced so that the little boy and his playmates would not fall in and drown. They had a housemaid who was absolutely trustworthy and an itinerant gardener who was highly recommended by the neighbours. For when they began to live happily ever after they were warned, by that wise old witch, the husband's mother, not to take on anyone off the street.

Occasionally, omniscient narrators move not only in and out of the minds of the characters but also in and out of a **persona** (representing the voice of the author) who speaks directly to readers. This narrative technique was popular with writers during the eighteenth century, when the novel was a new literary form. It permitted writers to present themselves as masters of artifice, able to know and control all aspects of experience. Few contemporary writers would give themselves the license that Henry Fielding does in the following passage from *Tom Jones* (1749):

> And true it was that [Mr. Alworthy] did many of these things; but had he done nothing more I should have left him to have recorded his own merit on some fair freestone over the door of that hospital. Matters of a much more extraordinary kind are to be the subject of this history, or I should grossly misspend my time in writing so voluminous a work; and you my sagacious friend, might with equal profit and pleasure travel through some pages which certain droll authors have been facetiously pleased to call *The History of England*.

A contemporary example of this type of omniscient point of view occurs in Ursula K. LeGuin's "The Ones Who Walk Away from Omelas." This story presents a description of a city that in the narrator's words is "like a city in a fairy tale." As the story proceeds, however, the description of Omelas changes, and the narrator's tone changes as well: "Do you believe? Do you accept the festival, the city, the joy? No? Then let me describe one more thing." By undercutting her own narrative, the narrator underscores the ironic theme of the story, which suggests that it is impossible for human beings to ever achieve an ideal society.

Limited Omniscient Narrators

Third-person narrators can have **limited omniscience,** focusing on only what a single character experiences. In other words, nothing is revealed that the character does not see, hear, feel, or think.

Limited omniscient narrators, like all third-person narrators, have certain advantages over first-person narrators. When a writer uses a first-person narrator, the narrator's personality and speech color the story, creating a personal or even an idiosyncratic narrative. Also, the first-person narrator's character flaws or lack of knowledge may limit his or her awareness of the significance of events. Limited omniscient narrators are more flexible: they take readers into a particular character's mind just as a first-person narrator does, but without the first-person narrator's subjectivity, self-deception, or naïveté. In the following example from Anne Tyler's "Teenage Wasteland" (p. 785), the limited omniscient narrator presents the story from the point of view of a single character, Daisy:

> Daisy and Matt sat silent, shocked. Matt rubbed his forehead with his fingertips. Imagine, Daisy thought, how they must look to Mr. Lanham: an overweight housewife in a cotton dress and a too-tall, too-thin insurance agent in a baggy, frayed suit. Failures, both of them—the kind of people who are always hurrying to catch up, missing the point of things that everyone else grasps at once. She wished she'd worn nylons instead of knee socks.

Here the point of view gives readers the impression that they are standing off to the side watching Daisy and her husband Matt. However, at the same time that we have the advantage of this objective view, we are also able to see into the mind of one character.

Objective Narrators

Third-person **objective narrators,** who tell a story from an objective (or dramatic) point of view, remain entirely outside the characters' minds. With objective narrators, events unfold the way they would in a play or a movie: narrators tell the story only by presenting dialogue and recounting events; they do not reveal the characters' (or their own) thoughts or attitudes. Thus, they allow readers to interpret the actions of the characters without any interference. Ernest Hemingway uses the objective point of view in his short story "A Clean, Well-Lighted Place" (1933):

> The waiter took the brandy bottle and another saucer from the counter inside the café and marched out to the old man's table. He put down the saucer and poured the glass full of brandy.
>
> "You should have killed yourself last week," he said to the deaf man. The old man motioned with his finger. "A little more," he said. The waiter poured on into the glass so that the brandy slopped over and ran down the stem into the top saucer of the pile. "Thank you," the old man said. The waiter took the bottle back inside the café. He sat down at the table with his colleague again.

The story's narrator is distant, seemingly emotionless, and this perspective is consistent with the author's purpose: for Hemingway, the attitude of the narrator reflects the stunned, almost anesthetized condition of people in the post–World War I world.

Selecting an Appropriate Point of View

Writers of short stories often maintain a consistent point of view. The main criterion writers use when they decide on a point of view is how the point of view they select will affect their narrative. The passages that follow illustrate the options available to writers.

Limited Omniscient Point of View

In the following passage from the short story "Doe Season" (p. 577), David Michael Kaplan uses a third-person limited omniscient narrator to tell the story of Andy, a nine-year-old girl who is going hunting with her father for the first time:

> They were always the same woods, she thought sleepily as they drove through the early morning darkness—deep and immense, covered with yesterday's snowfall, which had frozen overnight. They were the same woods that lay behind her house, *and they stretch all the way to here*, she thought, *for miles and miles, longer than I could walk in a day, or a week even, but they are still the same woods*. The thought made her feel good: it was like thinking of God; it was like thinking of the space between here and the moon; it was like thinking of all the foreign countries from her geography book where even now, Andy knew, people were going to bed, while they—she and her father and Charlie Spoon and Mac, Charlie's eleven-year-old son—were driving deeper into the Pennsylvania countryside, to go hunting.
>
> They had risen long before dawn. Her mother, yawning and not trying to hide her sleepiness, cooked them eggs and French toast. Her father smoked a cigarette and flicked ashes into his saucer while Andy listened, wondering *Why doesn't he come?* and *Won't he ever come?* until at last a car pulled into the graveled drive and honked. "That will be Charlie Spoon," her father said; he always said "Charlie Spoon," even though his real name was Spreun, because Charlie was, in a sense, shaped like a spoon, with a large head and a narrow waist and chest.

Here the limited omniscient point of view has the advantage of allowing the narrator to focus on the thoughts, fears, and reactions of the child while at the same time giving readers information about Andy that she herself is too immature or unsophisticated to know. Rather than simply presenting the thoughts of the child (represented in the story by italics), the third-person narrator makes connections between ideas and displays a level of language and a degree of insight that readers would not accept from Andy as a first-person narrator. In addition, the limited omniscient perspective enables the narrator to maintain some distance.

First-Person Point of View (Child)

Consider how different the passage would be if it were narrated by nine-year-old Andy:

> "I like the woods," I thought. "They're big and scary. I wonder if they're the same woods that are behind my house. They go on for miles. They're bigger than I could walk in a day, or a week even." It was neat to think that while we were driving into the woods people were going to bed in other countries.

> When I woke up this morning, I couldn't wait to go hunting. My mother was cooking breakfast, but all I could think of was, "When will he come?" and "Won't he ever come?" Finally, I heard a car honk. "That will be Charlie Spoon," my father said. I think he called him "Charlie Spoon" because he thought Charlie was shaped like a big spoon.

As a first-person narrator, nine-year-old Andy must have the voice of a child; moreover, she is restricted to only those observations that a nine-year-old could reasonably make. Because of these limitations, the passage lacks the level of vocabulary, syntax, and insight necessary to develop the central character and the themes of the story. This point of view could succeed only if Andy's words established an ironic contrast between her naive sensibility and the reality of the situation.

First-Person Point of View (Adult)

The writer could have avoided these problems and still gained the advantages of using a first-person narrator by having Andy tell her story as an adult looking back on a childhood experience. (This technique is used by James Joyce in "Araby," p. 434; Charles Baxter in "Gryphon," p. 277; and Alberto Alvaro Ríos in "The Secret Lion," p. 197.)

> "They are always the same woods," I thought sleepily as we drove through the early morning darkness—deep and immense, covered with yesterday's snowfall, which had frozen overnight. "They're the same woods that lie behind my house, and they stretch all the way to here," I thought. I knew that they stretched for miles and miles, longer than I could walk in a day, or even in a week but that they were still the same woods. Knowing this made me feel good: I thought it was like thinking of God; it was like thinking of the space between that place and the moon; it was like thinking of all the foreign countries from my geography book where even then, I knew, people were going to bed, while we—my father and I and Charlie Spoon and Mac, Charlie's eleven-year-old son—were driving deeper into the Pennsylvania countryside, to go hunting.
>
> We had risen before dawn. My mother, who was yawning and not trying to hide her sleepiness, cooked us eggs and French toast. My father smoked a cigarette and flicked ashes into his saucer while I listened, wondering, "Why doesn't he come?" and "Won't he ever come?" until at last a car pulled into our driveway and honked. "That will be Charlie Spoon," my father said. He always said "Charlie Spoon," even though his real name was Spreun, because Charlie was, in a sense, shaped like a spoon, with a large head and a narrow waist and chest.

Although this passage presents the child's point of view, it does not use a child's voice; the language and scope of the passage are too sophisticated for a child. By using a mature style, the adult narrator considers ideas that a child could not possibly understand, such as the symbolic significance of the woods. In so doing, however, he sacrifices the degree of objectivity that characterizes the third-person limited omniscient narrator of the original story.

Omniscient Point of View

The writer could also have used an omniscient narrator to tell his story. In this case, the narrator would be free to reveal and comment not only on Andy's thoughts but also on those of her father, and possibly even on the thoughts of her mother and Charlie Spoon.

In the following passage, the omniscient narrator interprets the behavior of the characters and tells what each one is thinking.

> They were always the same woods, she thought sleepily as they drove through the early morning darkness—deep and immense, covered with yesterday's snowfall, which had frozen overnight. They were the same woods that lay behind her house, and they stretch all the way to here, she thought, for miles and miles, longer than I could walk in a day, or a week even, but they are still the same woods.
>
> They had risen before dawn. The mother, yawning and not trying to hide her sleepiness, cooked them eggs and French toast. She looked at her husband and her daughter and wondered if she was doing the right thing by allowing them to go hunting together. "After all," she thought, "he's not the most careful person. Will he watch her? Make sure that no harm comes to her?"
>
> The father smoked a cigarette and flicked ashes into his saucer. He was listening to the sounds of the early morning. "I know everything will be all right," he thought. "It's about time Andy went hunting. When I was her age. . . ." Andy listened, wondering Why doesn't he come? and Won't he ever come? until at last a car pulled into the graveled drive and honked. Suddenly the father cocked his head and said, "That will be Charlie Spoon."
>
> Andy thought it was funny that her father called Charlie "Spoon" even though his real name was Spreun, because Charlie was, in a sense, shaped like a spoon, with a large head and a narrow waist and chest.

Certainly this point of view has its advantages; for example, the wide scope of this perspective provides a great deal of information about the characters. However, the use of an omniscient point of view deprives the story of its focus on Andy.

Objective Point of View

Finally, the writer could have used an objective narrator. This point of view would eliminate all interpretation by the narrator and force readers to make judgments solely on the basis of what the characters say and do.

> Andy sat sleepily staring into her cereal. She played with the dry flakes of bran as they floated in the surface of the milk.
>
> Andy's mother, yawning, cooked them eggs and French toast. She looked at her husband and her daughter, paused for a second, and then went about what she was doing.
>
> Andy's father smoked a cigarette and flicked ashes into his saucer. He looked out the window and said, "I wonder where Charlie Spoon is?"
>
> Andy squirmed restlessly and repeatedly looked up at the clock that hung above the stove.

The disadvantage of this point of view is that it creates a great deal of distance between the characters and the readers. Instead of gaining the intimate knowledge of Andy that the limited omniscient point of view provides—knowledge even greater than she herself has—readers must infer what she thinks and feels without any help from the narrator.

✔ CHECKLIST Selecting an Appropriate Point of View: Review

First-Person Narrators (use *I* or *WE*)

- *Major character telling his or her own story* "Every morning I lay on the floor in the front parlour watching her door." (James Joyce, "Araby")
- *Minor character as witness* "And so she died. . . . We did not even know she was sick; we had long since given up trying to get information. . . ." (William Faulkner, "A Rose for Emily")

Third-Person Narrators (use *HE, SHE,* and *THEY*)

- *Omniscient — able to move at will from character to character and comment about them* "In a house, in a suburb, in a city, there were a man and his wife who loved each other very much. . . ." (Nadine Gordimer, "Once upon a Time")
- *Limited omniscient — restricts focus to a single character* "The wagon went on. He did not know where they were going." (William Faulkner, "Barn Burning")
- *Objective (dramatic) — simply reports the dialogue and the actions of characters* "'You'll be drunk,' the waiter said. The old man looked at him. The waiter went away." (Ernest Hemingway, "A Clean, Well-Lighted Place")

✔ CHECKLIST Writing about Point of View

- ☐ What is the dominant point of view from which the story is told?
- ☐ Is the narrator a character in the story? If so, is he or she a participant in the story's events or just a witness?
- ☐ Does the story's point of view create irony?
- ☐ If the story has a first-person narrator, is the narrator reliable or unreliable?
- ☐ If the story has a third-person narrator, is he or she omniscient? Does he or she have limited omniscience? Is the narrator objective?
- ☐ What are the advantages of the story's point of view? What are the disadvantages?
- ☐ Does the point of view remain consistent throughout the story, or does it shift?
- ☐ How might a different point of view change the story?

SHAUN TAN (1974–) was born in Perth, Western Australia, and as a teenager began drawing illustrations for science fiction and horror stories. He has since become a critically acclaimed illustrator. He has published the award-winning picture books *The Rabbits* (1999) and *The Arrival* (2006), from which the following excerpt is taken. Tan's work captures fundamental human desires, needs, and behaviors in a stunning visual format. According to Tan, he chose migration as the subject for *The Arrival* because "migration is a fundamental part of human history, both in the distant and recent past." Named Best Artist at the 2001 World Fantasy Awards in Montreal, Tan has also done illustration for film projects with Blue Sky and Pixar Studios.

Cultural Context Shaun Tan's graphic novel belongs to the rich literary tradition of the epic journey. In Western literature, this tradition is largely defined by Homer's *Odyssey,* the tale of Odysseus, the king of Ithaca, returning home from the Trojan War on an epic nine-year journey. Since Homer's time, countless other writers—from Dante in *The Divine Comedy* to Miguel de Cervantes in *Don Quixote*—have used the hero's journey as a central theme in their work. As mythologist Joseph Campbell notes in his book *The Hero with a Thousand Faces* (1949), the "hero's journey" is a universal experience, one that cuts across times and cultures. Shaun Tan's graphic novel embodies a number of elements of the epic journey. Using the universal language of pictures, Tan tells the story of an immigrant making a journey to a new and mysterious place where he faces and overcomes challenges that suggest the hero's journey that Campbell describes.

from The Arrival (2006)

This graphic story starts on the next page. ⟶

Reading and Reacting

1. "The Arrival" was published as a book for children ages ten and up. In what respects does this excerpt seem like a story for children? In what respects does it seem like a story for adults?
2. "The Arrival" has no written text. Do you see this absence of words as a strength or a weakness?
3. The excerpt printed here (like the entire book) mixes realistic elements with elements of fantasy. What do the fantasy elements represent? What do they contribute to the story?
4. **JOURNAL ENTRY** Write a brief summary telling what happens in this excerpt.
5. **CRITICAL PERSPECTIVE** Roger Sutton, editor of the *Horn Book Magazine*, a children's and young adults' literature journal, describes how Shaun Tan's graphic novel draws the reader in:

   > It's the triumph of this lavish yet somberly monochromatic wordless book that readers are put right into the refugee's shoes: we're as out of place as he, learning the customs of the country in step with the protagonist. With him, for example, we figure out how to use the transport system, and once aloft in the steam-driven air-ferry, we sit alongside him as another passenger tells her own story of imprisonment and escape.

   As you read this story, do you feel as if you are embarking on a trip with the protagonist? What visual effects does Tan use to enable the reader to experience the departing father's point of view?

Related Works: "Snow" (p. 177), "The Third and Final Continent" (p. 290), "The Disappearance" (p. 695), "The Emigrant Irish" (p. 1129), *Trying to Find Chinatown* (p. 1856)

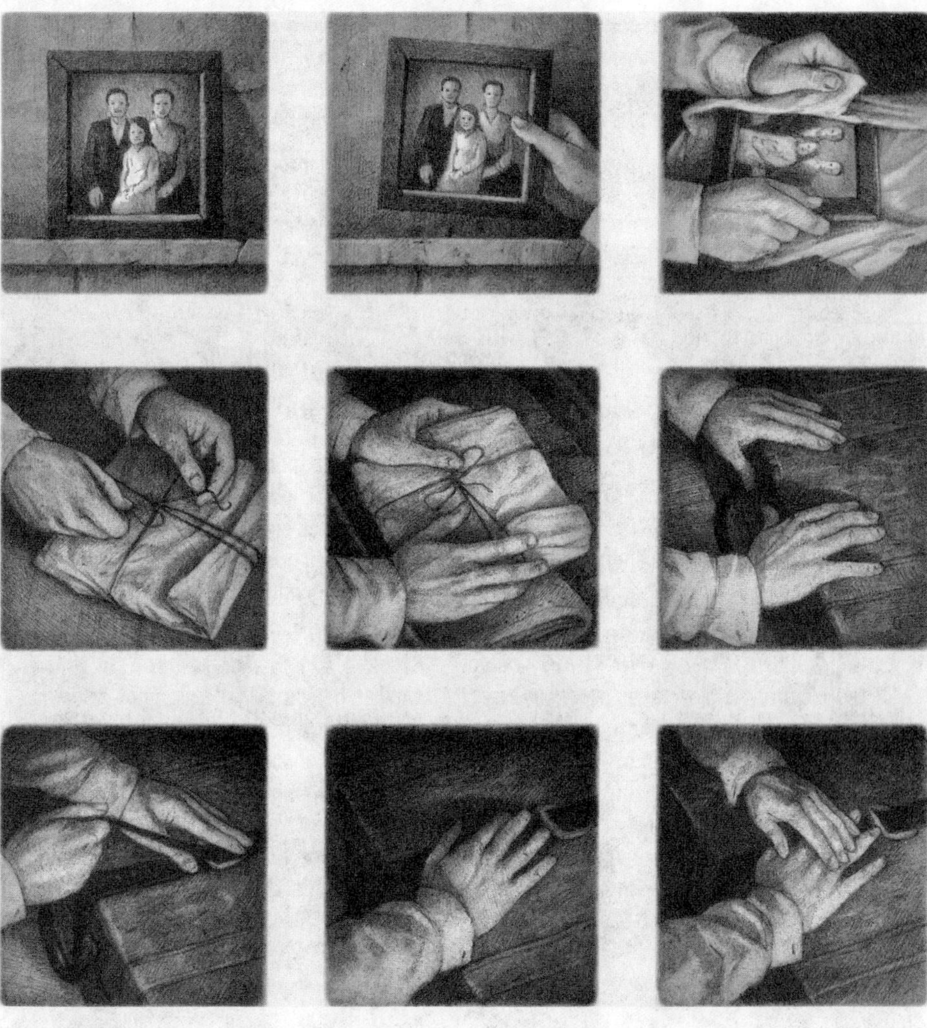

Source: ©AP Photo/Robert Kradin

RICHARD WRIGHT (1908–1960) was born near Natchez, Mississippi, the son of sharecroppers. He had little formal schooling but as a young man was a voracious reader, especially of naturalistic fiction. Relocating to Chicago in the late 1920s, Wright worked as a postal clerk until 1935, when he joined the Federal Writers' Project, an association that took him to New York City. Deeply troubled by the economic and social oppression of African Americans, Wright joined the Communist Party in 1932, and his early poems and stories reflect a distinctly Marxist perspective. In 1944, he broke with the party because of its stifling effect on his creativity.

Wright began to reach a mainstream audience when a group of four long stories on the theme of racial oppression and violence was judged best manuscript in a contest sponsored by *Story* magazine; these stories were published as *Uncle Tom's Children* in 1938. Two years later, Wright published his most famous work, *Native Son,* an angry and brutal novel exploring the moral devastation wrought by a racist society. The autobiographical *Black Boy* was published in 1945. Wright eventually left the United States for Paris in protest against the treatment of African Americans in his native country. His later work was concerned with national independence movements in Africa and elsewhere in the third world.

The following story, published in the posthumous collection *Eight Men* (1961), is uncharacteristic of Wright's work in a number of ways—not least of which is that it is told through the eyes of a white protagonist.

Cultural Context In 1957, the year "Big Black Good Man" was written, President Eisenhower sent paratroopers to Little Rock, Arkansas, to forestall violence over desegregation of the public schools. The crisis began on September 2, when Governor Orval Faubus ordered the Arkansas National Guard to blockade Central High School in Little Rock to prevent the entrance of nine black students. On September 20, NAACP lawyers Thurgood Marshall and Wiley Brandon obtained an injunction from the federal district court that ordered the troops removed. On September 25, the students entered the school, escorted by members of the 101st Airborne Division of the United States Army.

Big Black Good Man (1957)

Through the open window Olaf Jenson could smell the sea and hear the occasional foghorn of a freighter; outside, rain pelted down through an August night, drumming softly upon the pavements of Copenhagen,° inducing drowsiness, bringing dreamy memory, relaxing the tired muscles of his work-wracked body. He sat slumped in a swivel chair with his legs outstretched and his feet propped atop an edge of his desk. An inch of white ash tipped the end of his brown cigar and now and then he inserted the end of the stogie° into his mouth and drew gently upon it, letting wisps of blue smoke eddy from the corners of his wide, thin lips. The watery gray irises behind the thick lenses of his eyeglasses gave him a look of abstraction, of absentmindedness, of an almost genial idiocy. He sighed, reached for his half-empty bottle of beer, and drained it into his glass and downed it with a long slow gulp, then licked his lips. Replacing the cigar, he slapped his right palm against his thigh and said half aloud:

Copenhagen: The capital of Denmark.
stogie: A cheap cigar.

"Well, I'll be sixty tomorrow. I'm not rich, but I'm not poor either . . . Really, I can't complain. Got good health. Traveled all over the world and had my share of girls when I was young . . . And my Karen's a good wife. I own my home. Got no debts. And I love digging in my garden in the spring . . . Grew the biggest carrots of anybody last year. Ain't saved much money, but what the hell . . . Money ain't everything. Got a good job. Night portering ain't too bad." He shook his head and yawned. "Karen and I could of had some children, though. Would of been good company . . . 'Specially for Karen. And I could of taught 'em languages . . . English, French, German, Danish, Dutch, Swedish, Norwegian, and Spanish . . ." He took the cigar out of his mouth and eyed the white ash critically. "Hell of a lot of good language learning did me . . . Never got anything out of it. But those ten years in New York were fun . . . Maybe I could of got rich if I'd stayed in America . . . Maybe. But I'm satisfied. You can't have everything."

Behind him the office door opened and a young man, a medical student occupying room number nine, entered.

"Good evening," the student said.

"Good evening," Olaf said, turning. 5

The student went to the keyboard and took hold of the round, brown knob that anchored his key.

"Rain, rain, rain," the student said.

"That's Denmark for you," Olaf smiled at him.

"This dampness keeps me clogged up like a drainpipe," the student complained.

"That's Denmark for you," Olaf repeated with a smile. 10

"Good night," the student said.

"Good night, son," Olaf sighed, watching the door close.

Well, my tenants are my children, Olaf told himself. Almost all of his children were in their rooms now . . . Only seventy-two and forty-four were missing . . . Seventy-two might've gone to Sweden . . . And forty-four was maybe staying at his girl's place tonight, like he sometimes did . . . He studied the pear-shaped blobs of hard rubber, reddish brown like ripe fruit, that hung from the keyboard, then glanced at his watch. Only room thirty, eighty-one, and one hundred and one were empty . . . And it was almost midnight. In a few moments he could take a nap. Nobody hardly ever came looking for accommodations after midnight, unless a stray freighter came in, bringing thirsty, women-hungry sailors. Olaf chuckled softly. Why in hell was I ever a sailor? The whole time I was at sea I was thinking and dreaming about women. Then why didn't I stay on land where women could be had? Hunh? Sailors are crazy . . .

But he liked sailors. They reminded him of his youth, and there was something so direct, simple, and childlike about them. They always said straight out what they wanted, and what they wanted was almost always women and whisky . . . "Well, there's no harm in that . . . Nothing could be more natural," Olaf sighed, looking thirstily at his empty beer bottle. No; he'd not drink any more tonight; he'd had enough; he'd go to sleep . . .

He was bending forward and loosening his shoelaces when he heard the office 15 door crack open. He lifted his eyes, then sucked in his breath. He did not straighten;

he just stared up and around at the huge black thing that filled the doorway. His reflexes refused to function; it was not fear; it was just simple astonishment. He was staring at the biggest, strangest, and blackest man he'd ever seen in all his life.

"Good evening," the black giant said in a voice that filled the small office. "Say, you got a room?"

Olaf sat up slowly, not to answer but to look at this brooding black vision; it towered darkly some six and a half feet into the air, almost touching the ceiling, and its skin was so black that it had a bluish tint. And the sheer bulk of the man! . . . His chest bulged like a barrel; his rocklike and humped shoulders hinted of mountain ridges; the stomach ballooned like a threatening stone; and the legs were like telephone poles . . . The big black cloud of a man now lumbered into the office, bending to get its buffalolike head under the door frame, then advanced slowly upon Olaf, like a stormy sky descending.

"You got a room?" the big black man asked again in a resounding voice.

Olaf now noticed that the ebony giant was well dressed, carried a wonderful new suitcase, and wore black shoes that gleamed despite the raindrops that peppered their toes.

"You're American?" Olaf asked him.

"Yeah, man; sure," the black giant answered.

"Sailor?"

"Yeah. American Continental Lines."

Olaf had not answered the black man's question. It was not that the hotel did not admit men of color; Olaf took in all comers—blacks, yellows, whites, and browns . . . To Olaf, men were men, and, in his day, he'd worked and eaten and slept and fought with all kinds of men. But this particular black man . . . Well, he didn't seem human. Too big, too black, too loud, too direct, and probably too violent to boot . . . Olaf's five feet seven inches scarcely reached the black giant's shoulder and his frail body weighed less, perhaps, than one of the man's gigantic legs . . . There was something about the man's intense blackness and ungainly bigness that frightened and insulted Olaf; he felt as though this man had come here expressly to remind him how puny, how tiny, and how weak and how white he was. Olaf knew, while registering his reactions, that he was being irrational and foolish; yet, for the first time in his life, he was emotionally determined to refuse a man a room solely on the basis of the man's size and color . . . Olaf's lips parted as he groped for the right words in which to couch his refusal, but the black giant bent forward and boomed:

"I asked you if you got a room. I got to put up somewhere tonight, man."

"Yes, we got a room," Olaf murmured.

And at once he was ashamed and confused. Sheer fear had made him yield. And he seethed against himself for his involuntary weakness. Well, he'd look over his book and pretend that he'd made a mistake; he'd tell this hunk of blackness that there was really no free room in the hotel, and that he was so sorry . . . Then, just as he took out the hotel register to make believe that he was poring over it, a thick roll of American bank notes, crisp and green, was thrust under his nose.

"Keep this for me, will you?" the black giant commanded. "Cause I'm gonna get drunk tonight and I don't wanna lose it."

Olaf stared at the roll; it was huge, in denominations of fifties and hundreds. Olaf's eyes widened.

"How much is there?" he asked. 30

"Two thousand six hundred," the giant said. "Just put it into an envelope and write 'Jim' on it and lock it in your safe, hunh?"

The black mass of man had spoken in a manner that indicated that it was taking it for granted that Olaf would obey. Olaf was licked. Resentment clogged the pores of his wrinkled white skin. His hands trembled as he picked up the money. No; he couldn't refuse this man . . . The impulse to deny him was strong, but each time he was about to act upon it something thwarted him, made him shy off. He clutched about desperately for an idea. Oh yes, he could say that if he planned to stay for only one night, then he could not have the room, for it was against the policy of the hotel to rent rooms for only one night . . .

"How long are you staying? Just tonight?" Olaf asked.

"Naw. I'll be here for five or six days, I reckon," the giant answered off handedly.

"You take room number thirty," Olaf heard himself saying. "It's forty kroner 35
a day."

"That's all right with me," the giant said.

With slow, stiff movements, Olaf put the money in the safe and then turned and stared helplessly up into the living, breathing blackness looming above him. Suddenly he became conscious of the outstretched palm of the black giant; he was silently demanding the key to the room. His eyes downcast, Olaf surrendered the key, marveling at the black man's tremendous hands . . . He could kill me with one blow, Olaf told himself in fear.

Feeling himself beaten, Olaf reached for the suitcase, but the black hand of the giant whisked it out of his grasp.

"That's too heavy for you, big boy; I'll take it," the giant said.

Olaf let him. He thinks I'm nothing . . . He led the way down the corridor, sens- 40
ing the giant's lumbering presence behind him. Olaf opened the door of number thirty and stood politely to one side, allowing the black giant to enter. At once the room seemed like a doll's house, so dwarfed and filled and tiny it was with a great living blackness . . . Flinging his suitcase upon a chair, the giant turned. The two men looked directly at each other now. Olaf saw that the giant's eyes were tiny and red, buried, it seemed, in muscle and fat. Black cheeks spread, flat and broad, topping the wide and flaring nostrils. The mouth was the biggest that Olaf had ever seen on a human face; the lips were thick, pursed, parted, showing snow-white teeth. The black neck was like a bull's . . . The giant advanced upon Olaf and stood over him.

"I want a bottle of whiskey and a woman," he said. "Can you fix me up?"

"Yes," Olaf whispered, wild with anger and insult.

But what was he angry about? He'd had requests like this every night from all sorts of men and he was used to fulfilling them; he was a night porter in a cheap, water-front Copenhagen hotel that catered to sailors and students. Yes, men needed women, but this man, Olaf felt, ought to have a special sort of woman. He felt a deep and strange reluctance to phone any of the women whom he habitually sent to men. Yet he had promised. Could he lie and say that none was available? No. That sounded too fishy. The black giant sat upon the bed, staring straight before him. Olaf moved about quickly, pulling down the window shades, taking the pink coverlet off the bed, nudging the giant with his elbow to make him move as he did so . . . That's the way to treat 'im . . . Show 'im I ain't scared of 'im . . . But he was still seeking for an excuse to refuse. And he could think of nothing. He felt hypnotized, mentally immobilized. He stood hesitantly at the door.

"You send the whiskey and the woman quick, pal?" the black giant asked, rousing himself from a brooding stare.

"Yes," Olaf grunted, shutting the door.

Goddamn, Olaf sighed. He sat in his office at his desk before the phone. Why did *he* have to come here? . . . I'm not prejudiced . . . No, not at all . . . But . . . He couldn't think any more. God oughtn't make men as big and black as that . . . But what the hell was he worrying about? He'd sent women of all races to men of all colors . . . So why not a woman to the black giant? Oh, only if the man were small, brown, and intelligent-looking . . . Olaf felt trapped.

With a reflex movement of his hand, he picked up the phone and dialed Lena. She was big and strong and always cut him in for fifteen per cent instead of the usual ten per cent. Lena had four small children to feed and clothe. Lena was willing; she was, she said, coming over right now. She didn't give a good goddamn about how big and black the man was . . .

"Why you ask me that?" Lena wanted to know over the phone. "You never asked that before . . ."

"But this one is *big*," Olaf found himself saying.

"He's just a man," Lena told him, her voice singing stridently, laughingly over the wire. "You just leave that to me. You don't have to do anything. *I'll* handle 'im."

Lena had a key to the hotel door downstairs, but tonight Olaf stayed awake. He wanted to see her. Why? He didn't know. He stretched out on the sofa in his office, but sleep was far from him. When Lena arrived, he told her again how big and black the man was.

"You told me that over the phone," Lena reminded him.

Olaf said nothing. Lena flounced off on her errand of mercy. Olaf shut the office door, then opened it and left it ajar. But why? He didn't know. He lay upon the sofa and stared at the ceiling. He glanced at his watch; it was almost two o'clock . . . She's staying in there a long time . . . Ah, God, but he could do with a drink . . . Why was he so damned worked up and nervous about a nigger and a white whore? . . . He'd never been so upset in all his life. Before he knew it, he had drifted off to sleep. Then he heard the office door swinging creakingly open on its rusty hinges. Lena stood in it, grim and businesslike, her face scrubbed free of powder and rouge. Olaf scrambled to his feet, adjusting his eyeglasses, blinking.

"How was it?" he asked her in a confidential whisper.

Lena's eyes blazed.

"What the hell's that to you?" she snapped. "There's your cut," she said, flinging him his money, tossing it upon the covers of the sofa. "You're sure nosy tonight. You wanna take over my work?"

Olaf's pasty cheeks burned red.

"You go to hell," he said, slamming the door.

"I'll meet you there!" Lena's shouting voice reached him dimly.

He was being a fool; there was no doubt about it. But, try as he might, he could 60
not shake off a primitive hate for that black mountain of energy, of muscle, of bone; he envied the easy manner in which it moved with such a creeping and powerful motion; he winced at the booming and commanding voice that came to him when the tiny little eyes were not even looking at him; he shivered at the sight of those vast and clawlike hands that seemed always to hint of death . . .

Olaf kept his counsel. He never spoke to Karen about the sordid doings at the hotel. Such things were not for women like Karen. He knew instinctively that Karen would have been amazed had he told her that he was worried sick about a nigger and a blonde whore . . . No; he couldn't talk to anybody about it, not even the hard-bitten° old bitch who owned the hotel. She was concerned only about money; she didn't give a damn about how big and how black a client was as long as he paid his room rent.

Next evening, when Olaf arrived for duty, there was no sight or sound of the black giant. A little later after one o'clock in the morning he appeared, left his key, and went out wordlessly. A few moments past two the giant returned, took his key from the board, and paused.

"I want that Lena again tonight. And another bottle of whiskey," he said boomingly.

"I'll call her and see if she's in," Olaf said.

"Do that," the black giant said and was gone. 65

He thinks he's God, Olaf fumed. He picked up the phone and ordered Lena and a bottle of whiskey, and there was a taste of ashes in his mouth. On the third night came the same request: Lena and whiskey. When the black giant appeared on the fifth night, Olaf was about to make a sarcastic remark to the effect that maybe he ought to marry Lena, but he checked it in time . . . After all, he could kill me with one hand, he told himself.

Olaf was nervous and angry with himself for being nervous. Other black sailors came and asked for girls and Olaf sent them, but with none of the fear and loathing that he sent Lena and a bottle of whiskey to the giant . . . All right, the black giant's stay was almost up. He'd said that he was staying for five or six nights; tomorrow night was the sixth night and that ought to be the end of this nameless terror.

On the sixth night Olaf sat in his swivel chair with his bottle of beer and waited, his teeth on edge, his fingers drumming the desk. But what the hell am I fretting for? . . . The hell with 'im . . . Olaf sat and dozed. Occasionally he'd awaken and listen to the foghorns of freighters sounding as ships came and went in the misty Copenhagen harbor. He was half asleep when he felt a rough hand on his shoulder. He blinked his eyes open. The giant, black and vast and powerful, all but blotted out his vision.

"What I owe you, man?" the giant demanded. "And I want my money."

"Sure," Olaf said, relieved, but filled as always with fear of this living wall of black 70
flesh.

---

hard-bitten: Stubborn, tough.

With fumbling hands, he made out the bill and received payment, then gave the giant his roll of money, laying it on the desk so as not to let his hands touch the flesh of the black mountain. Well, his ordeal was over. It was past two o'clock in the morning. Olaf even managed a wry smile and muttered a guttural "Thanks" for the generous tip that the giant tossed him.

Then a strange tension entered the office. The office door was shut and Olaf was alone with the black mass of power, yearning for it to leave. But the black mass of power stood still, immobile, looking down at Olaf. And Olaf could not, for the life of him, guess at what was transpiring in that mysterious black mind. The two of them simply stared at each other for a full two minutes, the giant's tiny little beady eyes blinking slowly as they seemed to measure and search Olaf's face. Olaf's vision dimmed for a second as terror seized him and he could feel a flush of heat overspread his body. Then Olaf sucked in his breath as the devil of blackness commanded:

"Stand up!"

Olaf was paralyzed. Sweat broke on his face. His worst premonitions about this black beast were coming true. This evil blackness was about to attack him, maybe kill him . . . Slowly Olaf shook his head, his terror permitting him to breathe:

"What're you talking about?"

"Stand up, I say!" the black giant bellowed.

As though hypnotized, Olaf tried to rise; then he felt the black paw of the beast helping him roughly to his feet.

They stood an inch apart. Olaf's pasty-white features were glued to the giant's swollen black face. The ebony ensemble of eyes and nose and mouth and cheeks looked down at Olaf, silently; then, with a slow and deliberate movement of his gorillalike arms, he lifted his mammoth hands to Olaf's throat. Olaf had long known and felt that this dreadful moment was coming; he felt trapped in a nightmare. He could not move. He wanted to scream, but could find no words. His lips refused to open; his tongue felt icy and inert. Then he knew that his end had come when the giant's black fingers slowly, softly encircled his throat while a horrible grin of delight broke out on the sooty face . . . Olaf lost control of the reflexes of his body and he felt a hot stickiness flooding his underwear . . . He stared without breathing, gazing into the grinning blackness of the face that was bent over him, feeling the black fingers caressing his throat and waiting to feel the sharp, stinging ache and pain of the bones in his neck being snapped, crushed . . . He knew all along that I hated 'im . . . Yes, and now he's going to kill me for it, Olaf told himself with despair.

The black fingers still circled Olaf's neck, not closing, but gently massaging it, as it were, moving to and fro, while the obscene face grinned into his. Olaf could feel the giant's warm breath blowing on his eyelashes and he felt like a chicken about to have its neck wrung and its body tossed to flip and flap dyingly in the dust of the barnyard . . . Then suddenly the black giant withdrew his fingers from Olaf's neck and stepped back a pace, still grinning. Olaf sighed, trembling, his body seeming to shrink; he waited. Shame sheeted him for the hot wetness that was in his trousers. Oh, God, he's teasing me . . . He's showing me how easily he can kill me . . . He swallowed, waiting, his eyes stones of gray.

The giant's barrel-like chest gave forth a low, rumbling chuckle of delight.

"You laugh?" Olaf asked whimperingly.

"Sure I laugh," the giant shouted.

"Please don't hurt me," Olaf managed to say.

"I wouldn't hurt you, boy," the giant said in a tone of mockery. "So long."

And he was gone. Olaf fell limply into the swivel chair and fought off losing con- 85
sciousness. Then he wept. He was showing me how easily he could kill me . . . He made me shake with terror and then laughed and left . . . Slowly, Olaf recovered, stood, then gave vent to a string of curses:

"Goddamn 'im! My gun's right there in the desk drawer; I should of shot 'im. Jesus, I hope the ship he's on sinks . . . I hope he drowns and the sharks eat 'im . . ."

Later, he thought of going to the police, but sheer shame kept him back; and, anyway, the giant was probably on board his ship by now. And he had to get home and clean himself. Oh, Lord, what could he tell Karen? Yes, he would say that his stomach had been upset . . . He'd change clothes and return to work. He phoned the hotel owner that he was ill and wanted an hour off; the old bitch said that she was coming right over and that poor Olaf could have the evening off.

Olaf went home and lied to Karen. Then he lay awake the rest of the night dreaming of revenge. He saw that freighter on which the giant was sailing; he saw it springing a dangerous leak and saw a torrent of sea water flooding, gushing into all the compartments of the ship until it found the bunk in which the black giant slept. Ah, yes, the foamy, surging waters would surprise that sleeping black bastard of a giant and he would drown, gasping and choking like a trapped rat, his tiny eyes bulging until they glittered red, the bitter water of the sea pounding his lungs until they ached and finally burst . . . The ship would sink slowly to the bottom of the cold, black, silent depths of the sea and a shark, a *white* one, would glide aimlessly about the shut portholes until it found an open one and it would slither inside and nose about until it found that swollen, rotting, stinking carcass of the black beast and it would then begin to nibble at the decomposing mass of tarlike flesh, eating the bones clean . . . Olaf always pictured the giant's bones as being jet black and shining.

Once or twice, during these fantasies of cannibalistic revenge, Olaf felt a little guilty about all the many innocent people, women and children, all white and blonde, who would have to go down into watery graves in order that that white shark could devour the evil giant's black flesh . . . But, despite feelings of remorse, the fantasy lived persistently on, and when Olaf found himself alone, it would crowd and cloud his mind to the exclusion of all else, affording him the only revenge he knew. To make me suffer just for the pleasure of it, he fumed. Just to show me how strong he was . . . Olaf learned how to hate, and got pleasure out of it.

Summer fled on wings of rain. Autumn flooded Denmark with color. Winter 90
made rain and snow fall on Copenhagen. Finally spring came, bringing violets and roses. Olaf kept to his job. For many months he feared the return of the black giant. But when a year had passed and the giant had not put in an appearance, Olaf allowed his revenge fantasy to peter out, indulging in it only when recalling the shame that the black monster had made him feel.

Then one rainy August night, a year later, Olaf sat drowsing at his desk, his bottle of beer before him, tilting back in his swivel chair, his feet resting atop a corner of his desk, his mind mulling over the more pleasant aspects of his life. The office door cracked open. Olaf glanced boredly up and around. His heart jumped and skipped a beat. The black nightmare of terror and shame that he had hoped that he had lost forever was again upon him . . . Resplendently dressed, suitcase in hand, the black looming mountain filled the doorway. Olaf's thin lips parted and a silent moan, half a curse, escaped them.

"Hi," the black giant boomed from the doorway.

Olaf could not reply. But a sudden resolve swept him: this time he would even the score. If this black beast came within so much as three feet of him, he would snatch his gun out of the drawer and shoot him dead, so help him God . . .

"No rooms tonight," Olaf heard himself announcing in a determined voice.

The black giant grinned; it was the same infernal grimace of delight and triumph that he had had when his damnable black fingers had been around his throat . . .

"Don't want no room tonight," the giant announced.

"Then what are you doing here?" Olaf asked in a loud but tremulous voice.

The giant swept toward Olaf and stood over him; and Olaf could not move, despite his oath to kill him . . .

"What do you want then?" Olaf demanded once more, ashamed that he could not lift his voice above a whisper.

The giant still grinned, then tossed what seemed the same suitcase upon Olaf's sofa and bent over it; he zippered it open with a sweep of his clawlike hand and rummaged in it, drawing forth a flat, gleaming white object done up in glowing cellophane. Olaf watched with lowered lids, wondering what trick was now being played on him. Then, before he could defend himself, the giant had whirled and again long, black, snakelike fingers were encircling Olaf's throat . . . Olaf stiffened, his right hand clawing blindly for the drawer where the gun was kept. But the giant was quick.

"Wait," he bellowed, pushing Olaf back from the desk.

The giant turned quickly to the sofa and, still holding his fingers in a wide circle that seemed a noose for Olaf's neck, he inserted the rounded fingers into the top of the flat, gleaming object. Olaf had the drawer open and his sweaty fingers were now touching the gun, but something made him freeze. The flat, gleaming object was a shirt and the black giant's circled fingers were fitting themselves into its neck . . .

"A perfect fit!" the giant shouted.

Olaf stared, trying to understand. His fingers loosened about the gun. A mixture of a laugh and a curse struggled in him. He watched the giant plunge his hands into the suitcase and pull out other flat, gleaming shirts.

"One, two, three, four, five, six," the black giant intoned, his voice crisp and businesslike. "Six nylon shirts. And they're all yours. One shirt for each time Lena came . . . See, Daddy-O?"

The black, cupped hands, filled with billowing nylon whiteness, were extended under Olaf's nose. Olaf eased his damp fingers from his gun and pushed the drawer closed, staring at the shirts and then at the black giant's grinning face.

"Don't you like 'em?" the giant asked.

Olaf began to laugh hysterically, then suddenly he was crying, his eyes so flooded with tears that the pile of dazzling nylon looked like snow in the dead of winter.

Was this true? Could he believe it? Maybe this too was a trick? But, no. There were six shirts, all nylon, and the black giant had had Lena six nights.

"What's the matter with you, Daddy-O?" the giant asked. "You blowing your top? Laughing and crying . . ."

Olaf swallowed, dabbed his withered fists at his dimmed eyes; then he realized that he had his glasses on. He took them off and dried his eyes and sat up. He sighed, the tension and shame and fear and haunting dread of his fantasy went from him, and he leaned limply back in his chair . . .

"Try one on," the giant ordered.

Olaf fumbled with the buttons of his shirt, let down his suspenders, and pulled the shirt off. He donned a gleaming nylon one and the giant began buttoning it for him.

"Perfect, Daddy-O," the giant said.

His spectacled face framed in sparkling nylon, Olaf sat with trembling lips. So he'd not been trying to kill me after all.

"You want Lena, don't you?" he asked the giant in a soft whisper. "But I don't know where she is. She never came back here after you left—"

"I know where Lena is," the giant told him. "We been writing to each other. I'm going to her house. And, Daddy-O, I'm late." The giant zippered the suitcase shut and stood a moment gazing down at Olaf, his tiny little red eyes blinking slowly. Then Olaf realized that there was a compassion in that stare that he had never seen before.

"And I thought you wanted to kill me," Olaf told him. "I was scared of you . . ."

"Me? Kill you?" the giant blinked. "When?"

"That night when you put your fingers around my throat—"

"What?" the giant asked, then roared with laughter. "Daddy-O, you're a funny little man. I wouldn't hurt you. I like you. You a *good* man. You helped me."

Olaf smiled, clutching the pile of nylon shirts in his arms.

"You're a good man too," Olaf murmured. Then loudly, "You're a big black good man."

"Daddy-O, you're crazy," the giant said.

He swept his suitcase from the sofa, spun on his heel, and was at the door in one stride.

"Thanks!" Olaf cried after him.

The black giant paused, turned his vast black head, and flashed a grin.

"Daddy-O, drop dead," he said and was gone.

Reading and Reacting

1. Why do you suppose Wright presents events through Olaf's eyes? How would the story be different if Jim told it?
2. This story was published in 1957. What attitudes about race does Wright expect his American readers to have? Do these attitudes predispose readers to identify with Jim or with Olaf? Explain.

3. Why does Olaf dislike Jim? What does the narrator mean in paragraph 24 when he says that Jim's "intense blackness and ungainly bigness . . . frightened and insulted Olaf"?
4. In what ways do Jim's words and actions contribute to Olaf's fears? Do you think Olaf's reactions are reasonable, or do you believe he is overreacting?
5. The sailor's name is barely mentioned in the story. Why? List some words used to describe Jim. Why are these words used? How do they affect your reaction to him?
6. Do you think the story's title is ironic? In what other respects is the story ironic?
7. Why do you think Wright set the story in Copenhagen? Could it have been set in the United States in 1957?
8. What do you think Jim thinks of Olaf? Do you suppose he realizes the effect he has on him? How do you explain Jim's last comment?
9. **JOURNAL ENTRY** What point do you think the story makes about racial prejudice? Do you think Wright seems optimistic or pessimistic about race relations in the United States?
10. **CRITICAL PERSPECTIVE** In his 1982 article "The Short Stories: *Uncle Tom's Children, Eight Men*," Edward Margolies notes that "Big Black Good Man" was somewhat of a departure for Wright:

> "Big Black Good Man," which first appeared in *Esquire* in 1957, is the last short story Wright published in his lifetime. Possibly it is the last he ever wrote. In any event it represents a more traditional approach to storytelling in that Wright here avoids confining himself exclusively to dialogue. On the other hand, "Big Black Good Man" deviates from the usual Wright short story. For one thing, the narrative, by Wright's standards at least, is practically pointless. Scarcely anything "happens." There is no violence, practically no external narrative action, and no change of milieu.

Do you agree that the story is "practically pointless"? If not, what point do you think the story makes?

Related Works: "Buffalo Soldiers" (p. 187), "Battle Royal" (p. 332), "The Cask of Amontillado" (p. 385), "We Wear the Mask" (p. 1150), *The Stronger* (p. 1470)

Source: ©AP Photo

EDGAR ALLAN POE (1809–1849) profoundly influenced many writers all over the world. His tales of psychological terror and the macabre, his hauntingly musical lyric poems, and his writings on the craft of poetry and short story writing affected the development of symbolic fiction, the modern detective story, and the gothic horror tale. In most of Poe's horror tales (as in "The Cask of Amontillado"), readers vicariously "live" the story through the first-person narrator who tells the tale.

Poe was born in 1809, the son of a talented English-born actress who, deserted by her actor husband, died of tuberculosis before her son's third birthday. Although Poe was raised in material comfort by foster parents in Richmond, Virginia, his life was increasingly uncertain: his foster mother loved him, but her husband became antagonistic. He kept the young Poe so short of money at the University of Virginia (and later at West Point) that Poe resorted to gambling to raise money for food and clothing. Finally, disgraced and debt-ridden, he left school.

Poe found work as a magazine editor, gaining recognition as a literary critic. In 1836, he married his frail thirteen-year-old cousin, Virginia Clemm. Poe produced many of his most famous stories and poems in the next few years, working feverishly to support his tubercular wife, but although his stories were widely admired, he never achieved financial success. His wife died in 1847. Less than two years after her death, Poe was found barely conscious on a Baltimore street; three days later, he was dead at age forty.

Cultural Context Throughout antiquity, catacombs, such as those in Poe's story, were used to bury the dead. Catacombs are underground cemeteries composed of passages with recesses for tombs. The early Christian catacombs of Rome, consisting of approximately forty known chambers located in a rough circle about three miles from the center of the city, are the most extensive of all known catacombs. Funeral feasts were often celebrated in family vaults on the day of burial and on anniversary dates of the deaths of loved ones.

The Cask of Amontillado (1846)

The thousand injuries of Fortunato I had borne as I best could, but when he ventured upon insult I vowed revenge. You, who so well know the nature of my soul, will not suppose, however, that I gave utterance to a threat. *At length* I would be avenged; this was a point definitely settled—but the very definitiveness with which it was resolved precluded the idea of risk. I must not only punish but punish with impunity. A wrong is unredressed when retribution overtakes its redresser. It is equally unredressed when the avenger fails to make himself felt as such to him who has done the wrong.

It must be understood that neither by word nor deed had I given Fortunato cause to doubt my good will. I continued, as was my wont, to smile in his face, and he did not perceive that my smile *now* was at the thought of his immolation.

He had a weak point—this Fortunato—although in other regards he was a man to be respected and even feared. He prided himself on his connoisseurship in wine. Few Italians have the true virtuoso spirit. For the most part their enthusiasm is adopted to suit the time and opportunity, to practise imposture upon the British and Austrian *millionaires*. In painting and gemmary, Fortunato, like his countrymen, was a quack, but in the matter of old wines he was sincere. In this respect I did not differ from him materially;—I was skillful in the Italian vintages myself, and bought largely whenever I could.

It was about dusk, one evening during the supreme madness of the carnival season, that I encountered my friend. He accosted me with excessive warmth, for he had been drinking much. The man wore motley.° He had on a tight-fitting parti-striped dress, and his head was surmounted by the conical cap and bells. I was so pleased to see him that I thought I should never have done wringing his hand.

motley: The many-colored attire of a court jester.

5 I said to him—"My dear Fortunato, you are luckily met. How remarkably well you are looking to-day. But I have received a pipe° of what passes for Amontillado,° and I have my doubts."

"How?" said he. "Amontillado? A pipe? Impossible! And in the middle of the carnival!"

"I have my doubts," I replied; "and I was silly enough to pay the full Amontillado price without consulting you in the matter. You were not to be found, and I was fearful of losing a bargain."

"Amontillado!"

"I have my doubts."

10 "Amontillado!"

"And I must satisfy them."

"Amontillado!"

"As you are engaged, I am on my way to Luchresi. If any one has a critical turn it is he. He will tell me—"

"Luchresi cannot tell Amontillado from Sherry."

15 "And yet some fools will have it that his taste is a match for your own."

"Come, let us go."

"Whither?"

"To your vaults."

"My friend, no; I will not impose upon your good nature. I perceive you have an engagement. Luchresi—"

20 "I have no engagement;—come."

"My friend, no. It is not the engagement, but the severe cold with which I perceive you are afflicted. The vaults are insufferably damp. They are encrusted with nitre."°

"Let us go, nevertheless. The cold is merely nothing. Amontillado! You have been imposed upon. And as for Luchresi, he cannot distinguish Sherry from Amontillado."

Thus speaking, Fortunato possessed himself of my arm; and putting on a mask of black silk and drawing a *roquelaire*° closely about my person, I suffered him to hurry me to my palazzo.

There were no attendants at home; they had absconded to make merry in honor of the time. I had told them that I should not return until the morning, and had given them explicit orders not to stir from the house. These orders were sufficient, I well knew, to insure their immediate disappearance, one and all, as soon as my back was turned.

25 I took from their sconces two flambeaux, and giving one to Fortunato, bowed him through several suites of rooms to the archway that led into the vaults. I passed down

---

pipe: In the United States and England, a cask containing a volume equal to 126 gallons.

Amontillado: A pale, dry sherry; literally, a wine "from Montilla" (Spain).

nitre: Mineral deposits.

roquelaire: A short cloak.

a long and winding staircase, requesting him to be cautious as he followed. We came at length to the foot of the descent, and stood together upon the damp ground of the catacombs of the Montresors.

The gait of my friend was unsteady, and the bells upon his cap jingled as he strode.

"The pipe," he said.

"It is farther on," said I; "but observe the white web-work which gleams from these cavern walls."

He turned towards me, and looked into my eyes with two filmy orbs that distilled the rheum of intoxication.

"Nitre?" he asked at length.

"Nitre," I replied. "How long have you had that cough?"

"Ugh! ugh! ugh!—ugh! ugh! ugh!—ugh! ugh! ugh!—ugh! ugh! ugh!—ugh! ugh! ugh!"

My poor friend found it impossible to reply for many minutes.

"It is nothing," he said at last.

"Come," I said, with decision, "we will go back; your health is precious. You are rich, respected, admired, beloved; you are happy, as once I was. You are a man to be missed. For me it is no matter. We will go back; you will be ill, and I cannot be responsible. Besides, there is Luchresi—"

"Enough," he said; "the cough is a mere nothing; it will not kill me. I shall not die of a cough."

"True—true," I replied; "and, indeed, I had no intention of alarming you unnecessarily—but you should use all proper caution. A draught of this Médoc° will defend us from the damps."

Here I knocked off the neck of a bottle which I drew from a long row of its fellows that lay upon the mould.

"Drink," I said, presenting him the wine.

He raised it to his lips with a leer. He paused and nodded to me familiarly, while his bells jingled.

"I drink," he said, "to the buried that repose around us."

"And I to your long life."

He again took my arm, and we proceeded.

"These vaults," he said, "are extensive."

"The Montresors," I replied, "were a great and numerous family."

"I forget your arms."

"A huge human foot d'or, in a field azure; the foot crushes a serpent rampant whose fangs are imbedded in the heel."

"And the motto?"

"*Nemo me impune lacessit*."°

"Good!" he said.

Médoc: A red wine from the Médoc district, near Bordeaux, France.

Nemo me impune lacessit: "No one insults me with impunity" (Latin); this is the legend on the royal coat of arms of Scotland.

The wine sparkled in his eyes and the bells jingled. My own fancy grew warm with the Médoc. We had passed through long walls of piled skeletons, with casks and puncheons° intermingling, into the inmost recesses of the catacombs. I paused again, and this time I made bold to seize Fortunato by an arm above the elbow.

"The nitre!" I said; "see, it increases. It hangs like moss upon the vaults. We are below the river's bed. The drops of moisture trickle among the bones. Come, we will go back ere it is too late. Your cough—"

"It is nothing," he said; "let us go on. But first, another draught of the Médoc."

I broke and reached him a flagon of De Grâve.° He emptied it at a breath. His eyes flashed with a fierce light. He laughed and threw the bottle upwards with a gesticulation I did not understand.

I looked at him in surprise. He repeated the movement—a grotesque one.

"You do not comprehend?" he said.

"Not I," I replied.

"Then you are not of the brotherhood."

"How?"

"You are not of the masons."°

"Yes, yes," I said; "yes, yes."

"You? Impossible! A mason?"

"A mason," I replied.

"A sign," he said, "a sign."

"It is this," I answered, producing from beneath the folds of my *roquelaire* a trowel.

"You jest," he exclaimed, recoiling a few paces. "But let us proceed to the Amontillado."

"Be it so," I said, replacing the tool beneath the cloak and again offering him my arm. He leaned upon it heavily. We continued our route in search of the Amontillado. We passed through a range of low arches, descended, passed on, and descending again, arrived at a deep crypt, in which the foulness of the air caused our flambeaux rather to glow than flame.

At the most remote end of the crypt there appeared another less spacious. Its walls had been lined with human remains, piled to the vault overhead, in the fashion of the great catacombs of Paris. Three sides of this interior crypt were still ornamented in this manner. From the fourth side the bones had been thrown down, and lay promiscuously upon the earth, forming at one point a mound of some size. Within the wall thus exposed by the displacing of the bones, we perceived a still interior crypt or recess, in depth about four feet, in width three, in height six or seven. It seemed to have been constructed for no especial use within itself, but formed merely the interval between two of the colossal supports of the roof of the catacombs, and was backed by one of their circumscribing walls of solid granite.

---

puncheons: Barrels.

De Grâve: Correctly, "Graves," a light wine from the Bordeaux area.

masons: Freemasons (members of a secret fraternity). The trowel is a symbol of their alleged origin as a guild of stonemasons.

It was in vain that Fortunato, uplifting his dull torch, endeavored to pry into the depth of the recess. Its termination the feeble light did not enable us to see.

"Proceed," I said; "herein is the Amontillado. As for Luchresi—" 70

"He is an ignoramus," interrupted my friend, as he stepped unsteadily forward, while I followed immediately at his heels. In an instant he had reached the extremity of the niche, and finding his progress arrested by the rock, stood stupidly bewildered. A moment more and I had fettered him to the granite. In its surface were two iron staples, distant from each other about two feet, horizontally. From one of these depended a short chain, from the other a padlock. Throwing the links about his waist, it was but the work of a few seconds to secure it. He was too much astounded to resist. Withdrawing the key I stepped back from the recess.

"Pass your hand," I said, "over the wall; you cannot help feeling the nitre. Indeed, it is *very* damp. Once more let me *implore* you to return. No? Then I must positively leave you. But I must first render you all the little attentions in my power."

"The Amontillado!" ejaculated my friend, not yet recovered from his astonishment.

"True," I replied; "the Amontillado."

As I said these words I busied myself among the pile of bones of which I have 75
before spoken. Throwing them aside, I soon uncovered a quantity of building stone and mortar. With these materials and with the aid of my trowel, I began vigorously to wall up the entrance of the niche.

I had scarcely laid the first tier of the masonry when I discovered that the intoxication of Fortunato had in a great measure worn off. The earliest indication I had of this was a low moaning cry from the depth of the recess. It was *not* the cry of a drunken man. There was a long and obstinate silence. I laid the second tier, and the third, and the fourth; and then I heard the furious vibrations of the chain. The noise lasted for several minutes, during which, that I might hearken to it with the more satisfaction, I ceased my labors and sat down upon the bones. When at last the clanking subsided, I resumed the trowel, and finished without interruption the fifth, the sixth, and the seventh tier. The wall was now nearly upon a level with my breast. I again paused, and holding the flambeaux over the mason-work, threw a few feeble rays upon the figure within.

A succession of loud and shrill screams, bursting suddenly from the throat of the chained form, seemed to thrust me violently back. For a brief moment I hesitated, I trembled. Unsheathing my rapier, I began to grope with it about the recess; but the thought of an instant reassured me. I placed my hand upon the solid fabric of the catacombs, and felt satisfied. I reapproached the wall; I replied to the yells of him who clamoured. I re-echoed, I aided, I surpassed them in volume and in strength. I did this, and the clamourer grew still.

It was now midnight, and my task was drawing to a close. I had completed the eighth, the ninth and the tenth tier. I had finished a portion of the last and the eleventh; there remained but a single stone to be fitted and plastered in. I struggled with its weight; I placed it partially in its destined position. But now there came from out the niche a low laugh that erected the hairs upon my head. It was succeeded by a sad voice, which I had difficulty in recognizing as that of the noble Fortunato. The voice said—

"Ha! ha! ha!—he! he! he!—a very good joke, indeed—an excellent jest. We will have many a rich laugh about it at the palazzo—he! he! he!—over our wine—he! he! he!"

"The Amontillado!" I said.

"He! he! he!—he! he! he!—yes, the Amontillado. But is it not getting late? Will not they be awaiting us at the palazzo, the Lady Fortunato and the rest? Let us be gone."

"Yes," I said, "let us be gone."

"For the love of God, Montresor!"

"Yes," I said, "for the love of God."

But to these words I hearkened in vain for a reply. I grew impatient. I called aloud—

"Fortunato!"

No answer. I called again—

"Fortunato!"

No answer still. I thrust a torch through the remaining aperture and let it fall within. There came forth in return only a jingling of the bells. My heart grew sick; it was the dampness of the catacombs that made it so. I hastened to make an end of my labour. I forced the last stone into its position; I plastered it up. Against the new masonry I re-erected the old rampart of bones. For the half of a century no mortal has disturbed them. *In pace requiescat!* °

Reading and Reacting

1. Montresor cites a "thousand injuries" and an "insult" as his motivation for murdering Fortunato. Given what you learn about the two men during the course of the story, what do you suppose the "injuries" and "insult" might be?
2. Do you find Montresor to be a reliable narrator? If not, what makes you question his version of events?
3. What is Montresor's concept of personal honor? Is it consistent or inconsistent with the values of contemporary American society? How relevant are the story's ideas about revenge and guilt to present-day society? Explain.
4. Does Fortunato ever understand why Montresor hates him? What is Fortunato's attitude toward Montresor?
5. What is the significance of Montresor's family coat of arms and motto? What is the significance of Fortunato's costume?
6. In what ways does Montresor manipulate Fortunato? What weaknesses does Montresor exploit?
7. Why does Montresor wait fifty years to tell his story? How might the story be different if he had told it the morning after the murder?
8. Why does Montresor wait for a reply before he puts the last stone in position? What do you think he wants Fortunato to say?

---

pace requiescat: "May he rest in peace" (Latin).

9. JOURNAL ENTRY Do you think the use of a first-person point of view makes you more sympathetic toward Montresor than you would be if his story were told by a third-person narrator? Why or why not?

10. CRITICAL PERSPECTIVE In his discussion of this story in *Edgar Allan Poe: A Study of the Short Fiction*, Charles E. May says, "We can legitimately hypothesize that the listener is a priest and that Montresor is an old man who is dying and making final confession. . . ."

Do you agree or disagree with May's hypothesis? Do you think that Montresor has atoned for his sin? Who else could be listening to Montresor's story?

Related Works: "A Rose for Emily" (p. 243), "Half a Day" (p. 733), "Porphyria's Lover" (p. 860), *Tape* (p. 1275), *Trifles* (p. 1319)

WILLIAM FAULKNER (1897–1962) (picture and biography on p. 243) "Barn Burning" (1939) marks the first appearance of the Snopes clan in Faulkner's fiction. These ruthless, conniving, and unappealing poor white tenant farmers and traders run roughshod over the aristocratic families of Yoknapatawpha County in three Faulkner novels: *The Hamlet* (1940), *The Town* (1957), and *The Mansion* (1959). According to Ben Wasson in *Count No Count*, Faulkner once told a friend that "somebody said I was a genius writer. The only thing I'd claim genius for is thinking up that name *Snopes*." In Southern literary circles, at least, the name "Snopes" still serves as a shorthand term for the graceless and greedy (but frequently successful) opportunists of the "New South."

Cultural Context Tenant farming is a system of agriculture in which landowners contribute their land while tenants contribute labor. One form of tenant farming, known as sharecropping, required the landowner to furnish all the capital (and usually the food, clothing, and shelter) to the tenant in return for labor. Given the way the system worked, the sharecropper was lucky to end the year without owing money to the landowner. In "Barn Burning," Abner Snopes is a poor sharecropper who takes out his frustrations against the post–Civil War aristocracy of landowners.

Barn Burning (1939)

The store in which the Justice of the Peace's court was sitting smelled of cheese. The boy, crouched on his nail keg at the back of the crowded room, knew he smelled cheese, and more: from where he sat he could see the ranked shelves close-packed with the solid, squat, dynamic shapes of tin cans whose labels his stomach read, not from the lettering which meant nothing to his mind but from the scarlet devils and the silver curve of fish—this, the cheese which he knew he smelled and the hermetic° meat which his intestines believed he smelled coming in intermittent gusts momentary and brief between the other constant one, the smell and sense just a little of

---

hermetic: Canned.

fear because mostly of despair and grief, the old fierce pull of blood. He could not see the table where the Justice sat and before which his father and his father's enemy (*our enemy* he thought in that despair; *ourn! mine and hisn both! He's my father!*) stood, but he could hear them, the two of them that is, because his father had said no word yet:

"But what proof have you, Mr. Harris?"

"I told you. The hog got into my corn. I caught it up and sent it back to him. He had no fence that would hold it. I told him so, warned him. The next time I put the hog in my pen. When he came to get it I gave him enough wire to patch up his pen. The next time I put the hog up and kept it. I rode down to his house and saw the wire I gave him still rolled on to the spool in his yard. I told him he could have the hog when he paid me a dollar pound fee. That evening a nigger came with the dollar and got the hog. He was a strange nigger. He said, 'He say to tell you wood and hay kin burn.' I said, 'What?' 'That whut he say to tell you,' the nigger said. 'Wood and hay kin burn.' That night my barn burned. I got the stock out but I lost the barn."

"Where is the nigger? Have you got him?"

5 "He was a strange nigger, I tell you. I don't know what became of him."

"But that's not proof. Don't you see that's not proof?"

"Get that boy up here. He knows." For a moment the boy thought too that the man meant his older brother until Harris said, "Not him. The little one. The boy," and, crouching, small for his age, small and wiry like his father, in patched and faded jeans even too small for him, with straight, uncombed, brown hair and eyes gray and wild as storm scud, he saw the men between himself and the table part and become a lane of grim faces, at the end of which he saw the Justice, a shabby, collarless, graying man in spectacles, beckoning him. He felt no floor under his bare feet; he seemed to walk beneath the palpable weight of the grim turning faces. His father, stiff in his black Sunday coat donned not for the trial but for the moving, did not even look at him. *He aims for me to lie*, he thought, again with that frantic grief and despair. *And I will have to do hit*.

"What's your name, boy?" the Justice said.

"Colonel Sartoris Snopes," the boy whispered.

10 "Hey?" the Justice said. "Talk louder. Colonel Sartoris? I reckon anybody named for Colonel Sartoris in this country can't help but tell the truth, can they?" The boy said nothing. *Enemy! Enemy!* he thought; for a moment he could not even see, could not see that the Justice's face was kindly nor discern that his voice was troubled when he spoke to the man named Harris: "Do you want me to question this boy?" But he could hear, and during those subsequent long seconds while there was absolutely no sound in the crowded little room save that of quiet and intent breathing it was as if he had swung outward at the end of a grape vine, over a ravine, and at the top of the swing had been caught in a prolonged instant of mesmerized gravity, weightless in time.

"No!" Harris said violently, explosively. "Damnation! Send him out of here!" Now time, the fluid world, rushed beneath him again, the voices coming to him again through the smell of cheese and sealed meat, the fear and despair and the old grief of blood:

"This case is closed. I can't find against you, Snopes, but I can give you advice. Leave this country and don't come back to it."

His father spoke for the first time, his voice cold and harsh, level, without emphasis: "I aim to. I don't figure to stay in a country among people who . . ." he said something unprintable and vile, addressed to no one.

"That'll do," the Justice said. "Take your wagon and get out of this country before dark. Case dismissed."

His father turned, and he followed the stiff black coat, the wiry figure walking a 15
little stiffly from where a Confederate provost's man's° musket ball had taken him in the heel on a stolen horse thirty years ago, followed the two backs now, since his older brother had appeared from somewhere in the crowd, no taller than the father but thicker, chewing tobacco steadily, between the two lines of grim-faced men and out of the store and across the worn gallery and down the sagging steps and among the dogs and half-grown boys in the mild May dust, where as he passed a voice hissed:

"Barn burner!"

Again he could not see, whirling; there was a face in a red haze, moonlike, bigger than the full moon, the owner of it half again his size, he leaping in the red haze toward the face, feeling no blow, feeling no shock when his head struck the earth, scrabbling up and leaping again, feeling no blow this time either and tasting no blood, scrabbling up to see the other boy in full flight and himself already leaping into pursuit as his father's hand jerked him back, the harsh, cold voice speaking above him: "Go get in the wagon."

It stood in a grove of locusts and mulberries across the road. His two hulking sisters in their Sunday dresses and his mother and her sister in calico and sunbonnets were already in it, sitting on and among the sorry residue of the dozen and more movings which even the boy could remember—the battered stove, the broken beds and chairs, the clock inlaid with mother-of-pearl, which would not run, stopped at some fourteen minutes past two o'clock of a dead and forgotten day and time, which had been his mother's dowry. She was crying, though when she saw him she drew her sleeve across her face and began to descend from the wagon. "Get back," the father said.

"He's hurt. I got to get some water and wash his . . ."

"Get back in the wagon," his father said. He got in too, over the tail-gate. His 20
father mounted to the seat where the older brother already sat and struck the gaunt mules two savage blows with the peeled willow, but without heat. It was not even sadistic; it was exactly that same quality which in later years would cause his descendants to overrun the engine before putting a motor car into motion, striking and reining back in the same movement. The wagon went on, the store with its quiet crowd of grimly watching men dropped behind; a curve in the road hid it. *Forever* he thought. *Maybe he's done satisfied now, now that he has* . . . stopping himself, not to say it aloud even to himself. His mother's hand touched his shoulder.

"Does hit hurt?" she said.

---

provost's man's: Military policeman's.

"Naw," he said. "Hit don't hurt. Lemme be."

"Can't you wipe some of the blood off before hit dries?"

"I'll wash to-night," he said. "Lemme be, I tell you."

25 The wagon went on. He did not know where they were going. None of them ever did or ever asked, because it was always somewhere, always a house of sorts waiting for them a day or two days or even three days away. Likely his father had already arranged to make a crop on another farm before he . . . Again he had to stop himself. He (the father) always did. There was something about his wolf-like independence and even courage when the advantage was at least neutral which impressed strangers, as if they got from his latent ravening ferocity not so much a sense of dependability as a feeling that his ferocious conviction in the rightness of his own actions would be of advantage to all whose interest lay with his.

That night they camped, in a grove of oaks and beeches where a spring ran. The nights were still cool and they had a fire against it, of a rail lifted from a nearby fence and cut into lengths—a small fire, neat, niggard almost, a shrewd fire; such fires were his father's habit and custom always, even in freezing weather. Older, the boy might have remarked this and wondered why not a big one; why should not a man who had not only seen the waste and extravagance of war, but who had in his blood an inherent voracious prodigality with material not his own, have burned everything in sight? Then he might have gone a step farther and thought that that was the reason: that niggard blaze was the living fruit of nights passed during those four years in the woods hiding from all men, blue or gray, with his strings of horses (captured horses, he called them). And older still, he might have divined the true reason: that the element of fire spoke to some deep mainspring of his father's being, as the element of steel or of powder spoke to other men, as the one weapon for the preservation of integrity, else breath were not worth the breathing, and hence to be regarded with respect and used with discretion.

But he did not think this now and he had seen those same niggard blazes all his life. He merely ate his supper beside it and was already half asleep over his iron plate when his father called him, and once more he followed the stiff back, the stiff and ruthless limp, up the slope and on to the starlit road where, turning, he could see his father against the stars but without face or depth—a shape black, flat, and bloodless as though cut from tin in the iron folds of the frockcoat which had not been made for him, the voice harsh like tin and without heat like tin:

"You were fixing to tell them. You would have told him." He didn't answer. His father struck him with the flat of his hand on the side of the head, hard but without heat, exactly as he had struck the two mules at the store, exactly as he would strike either of them with any stick in order to kill a horse fly, his voice still without fear or anger: "You're getting to be a man. You got to learn. You got to learn to stick to your own blood or you ain't going to have any blood to stick to you. Do you think either of them, any man there this morning, would? Don't you know all they wanted was a chance to get at me because they knew I had them beat? Eh?" Later, twenty years later, he was to tell himself, "If I had said they wanted only truth, justice, he would have hit me again." But now he said nothing. He was not crying. He just stood there. "Answer me," his father said.

"Yes," he whispered. His father turned.

"Get on to bed. We'll be there tomorrow."

Tomorrow they were there. In the early afternoon the wagon stopped before a paintless two-room house identical almost with the dozen others it had stopped before even in the boy's ten years, and again, as on the other dozen occasions, his mother and aunt got down and began to unload the wagon, although his two sisters and his father and brother had not moved.

"Likely hit ain't fitten for hawgs," one of the sisters said.

"Nevertheless, fit it will and you'll hog it and like it," his father said. "Get out of them chairs and help your Ma unload."

The two sisters got down, big, bovine, in a flutter of cheap ribbons; one of them drew from the jumbled wagon bed a battered lantern, the other a worn broom. His father handed the reins to the older son and began to climb stiffly over the wheel. "When they get unloaded, take the team to the barn and feed them." Then he said, and at first the boy thought he was still speaking to his brother: "Come with me."

"Me?" he said.

"Yes," his father said. "You."

"Abner," his mother said. His father paused and looked back—the harsh level stare beneath the shaggy, graying, irascible brows.

"I reckon I'll have a word with the man that aims to begin tomorrow owning me body and soul for the next eight months."

They went back up the road. A week ago—or before last night, that is—he would have asked where they were going, but not now. His father had struck him before last night but never before had he paused afterward to explain why; it was as if the blow and the following calm, outrageous voice still rang, repercussed, divulging nothing to him save the terrible handicap of being young, the light weight of his few years, just heavy enough to prevent his soaring free of the world as it seemed to be ordered but not heavy enough to keep him footed solid in it, to resist it and try to change the course of its events.

Presently he could see the grove of oaks and cedars and the other flowering trees and shrubs, where the house would be, though not the house yet. They walked beside a fence massed with honeysuckle and Cherokee roses and came to a gate swinging open between two brick pillars, and now, beyond a sweep of drive, he saw the house for the first time and at that instant he forgot his father and the terror and despair both, and even when he remembered his father again (who had not stopped) the terror and despair did not return. Because, for all the twelve movings, they had sojourned until now in a poor country, a land of small farms and fields and houses, and he had never seen a house like this before. *Hit's big as a courthouse* he thought quietly, with a surge of peace and joy whose reason he could not have thought into words, being too young for that: *They are safe from him. People whose lives are a part of this peace and dignity are beyond his touch, he no more to them than a buzzing wasp: capable of stinging for a little moment but that's all; the spell of this peace and dignity rendering even the barns and stable and cribs which belong to it impervious to the puny flames he might contrive* . . . this, the peace and joy, ebbing for an instant as he looked again at the stiff black back, the stiff and implacable limp of the figure which was not dwarfed by the house, for the reason that it had never looked big anywhere and which now, against the serene columned backdrop, had more than ever that impervious quality of something cut ruthlessly from tin, depthless, as though, sidewise to the sun, it would cast no shadow. Watching him, the boy remarked the absolutely undeviating course which his father held and saw the stiff foot come squarely down in a pile of fresh droppings where a horse had stood in the drive and which his father could have avoided by a simple change of stride. But it ebbed only for a moment, though he could not have thought this into words either, walking on in the spell of the house, which he could even want but without envy, without sorrow, certainly never with that ravening and jealous rage which unknown to him walked in the ironlike black coat before him: *Maybe he will feel it too. Maybe it will even change him now from what maybe he couldn't help but be.*

They crossed the portico. Now he could hear his father's stiff foot as it came down on the boards with clocklike finality, a sound out of all proportion to the displacement of the body it bore and which was not dwarfed either by the white door before it, as though it had attained to a sort of vicious and ravening minimum not to be dwarfed by anything—the flat, wide, black hat, the formal coat of broadcloth which had once been black but which had now that friction-glazed greenish cast of the bodies of old house flies, the lifted sleeve which was too large, the lifted hand like a curled claw. The door opened so promptly that the boy knew the Negro must have been watching them all the time, an old man with neat grizzled hair, in a linen jacket, who stood barring the door with his body, saying, "Wipe yo foots, white man, fo you come in here. Major ain't home nohow."

"Get out of my way, nigger," his father said, without heat too, flinging the door back and the Negro also and entering, his hat still on his head. And now the boy saw the prints of the stiff foot on the doorjamb and saw them appear on the pale rug behind the machinelike deliberation of the foot which seemed to bear (or transmit) twice the weight which the body compassed. The Negro was shouting "Miss Lula! Miss Lula!" somewhere behind them, then the boy, deluged as though by a warm wave by a suave turn of carpeted stair and a pendant glitter of chandeliers and a mute gleam of gold frames, heard the swift feet and saw her too, a lady—perhaps he had never seen her like before either—in a gray, smooth gown with lace at the throat and an apron tied at the waist and the sleeves turned back, wiping cake or biscuit dough from her hands with a towel as she came up the hall, looking not at his father at all but at the tracks on the blond rug with an expression of incredulous amazement.

"I tried," the Negro cried, "I tole him to . . ."

"Will you please go away?" she said in a shaking voice. "Major de Spain is not at home. Will you please go away?"

45 His father had not spoken again. He did not speak again. He did not even look at her. He just stood stiff in the center of the rug, in his hat, the shaggy iron-gray brows twitching slightly above the pebble-colored eyes as he appeared to examine the house with brief deliberation. Then with the same deliberation he turned; the boy watched him pivot on the good leg and saw the stiff foot drag round the arc of the turning, leaving a final long and fading smear. His father never looked at it, he never once looked down at the rug. The Negro held the door. It closed behind them,

upon the hysteric and indistinguishable woman-wail. His father stopped at the top of the steps and scraped his boot clean on the edge of it. At the gate he stopped again. He stood for a moment, planted stiffly on the stiff foot, looking back at the house. "Pretty and white, ain't it?" he said. "That's sweat. Nigger sweat. Maybe it ain't white enough yet to suit him. Maybe he wants to mix some white sweat with it."

Two hours later the boy was chopping wood behind the house within which his mother and aunt and the two sisters (the mother and aunt, not the two girls, he knew that; even at this distance and muffled by walls the flat loud voices of the two girls emanated an incorrigible idle inertia) were setting up the stove to prepare a meal, when he heard the hooves and saw the linen-clad man on a fine sorrel mare, whom he recognized even before he saw the rolled rug in front of the Negro youth following on a fat bay carriage horse—a suffused, angry face vanishing, still at full gallop, beyond the corner of the house where his father and brother were sitting in the two tilted chairs; and a moment later, almost before he could have put the axe down, he heard the hooves again and watched the sorrel mare go back out of the yard, already galloping again. Then his father began to shout one of the sisters' names, who presently emerged backward from the kitchen door dragging the rolled rug along the ground by one end while the other sister walked behind it.

"If you ain't going to tote, go on and set up the wash pot," the first said.

"You, Sarty!" the second shouted. "Set up the wash pot!" His father appeared at the door, framed against that shabbiness, as he had been against that other bland perfection, impervious to either, the mother's anxious face at his shoulder.

"Go on," the father said. "Pick it up." The two sisters stooped, broad, lethargic; stooping, they presented an incredible expanse of pale cloth and a flutter of tawdry ribbons.

"If I thought enough of a rug to have to git hit all the way from France I 50
wouldn't keep hit where folks coming in would have to tromp on hit," the first said. They raised the rug.

"Abner," the mother said. "Let me do it."

"You go back and git dinner," his father said. "I'll tend to this."

From the woodpile through the rest of the afternoon the boy watched them, the rug spread flat in the dust beside the bubbling wash-pot, the two sisters stooping over it with that profound and lethargic reluctance, while the father stood over them in turn, implacable and grim, driving them though never raising his voice again. He could smell the harsh homemade lye° they were using; he saw his mother come to the door once and look toward them with an expression not anxious now but very like despair; he saw his father turn, and he fell to with the axe and saw from the corner of his eye his father raise from the ground a flattish fragment of field stone and examine it and return to the pot, and this time his mother actually spoke: "Abner. Abner. Please don't. Please, Abner."

Then he was done too. It was dusk; the whippoorwills had already begun. He could smell coffee from the room where they would presently eat the cold food

---

lye: A soap made from wood ashes and water, unsuitable for washing fine fabrics.

remaining from the mid-afternoon meal, though when he entered the house he realized they were having coffee again probably because there was a fire on the hearth, before which the rug now lay spread over the backs of the two chairs. The tracks of his father's foot were gone. Where they had been were now long, water-cloudy scoriations resembling the sporadic course of a Lilliputian mowing machine.

55 It still hung there while they ate the cold food and then went to bed, scattered without order or claim up and down the two rooms, his mother in one bed, where his father would later lie, the older brother in the other, himself, the aunt, and the two sisters on pallets on the floor. But his father was not in bed yet. The last thing the boy remembered was the depthless, harsh silhouette of the hat and coat bending over the rug and it seemed to him that he had not even closed his eyes when the silhouette was standing over him, the fire almost dead behind it, the stiff foot prodding him awake. "Catch up the mule," his father said.

When he returned with the mule his father was standing in the black door, the rolled rug over his shoulder. "Ain't you going to ride?" he said.

"No. Give me your foot."

He bent his knee into his father's hand, the wiry, surprising power flowed smoothly, rising, he rising with it, on to the mule's bare back (they had owned a saddle once; the boy could remember it though not when or where) and with the same effortlessness his father swung the rug up in front of him. Now in the starlight they retraced the afternoon's path, up the dusty road rife with honeysuckle, through the gate and up the black tunnel to the drive to the lightless house, where he sat on the mule and felt the rough warp of the rug drag across his thighs and vanish.

"Don't you want me to help?" he whispered. His father did not answer and now he heard again that stiff foot striking the hollow portico with that wooden and clocklike deliberation, that outrageous overstatement of the weight it carried. The rug, hunched, not flung (the boy could tell that even in the darkness) from his father's shoulder struck the angle of wall and floor with a sound unbelievably loud, thunderous, then the foot again, unhurried and enormous; a light came on in the house and the boy sat, tense, breathing steadily and quietly and just a little fast, though the foot itself did not increase its beat at all, descending the steps now; now the boy could see him.

60 "Don't you want to ride now?" he whispered. "We kin both ride now," the light within the house altering now, flaring up and sinking. *He's coming down the stairs now,* he thought. He had already ridden the mule up beside the horse block; presently his father was up behind him and he doubled the reins over and slashed the mule across the neck, but before the animal could begin to trot the hard, thin arm came round him, the hard, knotted hand jerking the mule back to a walk.

In the first red rays of the sun they were in the lot, putting plow gear on the mules. This time the sorrel mare was in the lot before he heard it at all, the rider collarless and even bareheaded, trembling, speaking in a shaking voice as the woman in the house had done, his father merely looking up once before stooping again to the hame° he was buckling, so that the man on the mare spoke to his stooping back:

---

hame: Harness.

"You must realize you have ruined that rug. Wasn't there anybody here, any of your women . . ." he ceased, shaking, the boy watching him, the older brother leaning now in the stable door, chewing, blinking slowly and steadily at nothing apparently. "It cost a hundred dollars. But you never had a hundred dollars. You never will. So I'm going to charge you twenty bushels of corn against your crop. I'll add it in your contract and when you come to the commissary you can sign it. That won't keep Mrs. de Spain quiet but maybe it will teach you to wipe your feet off before you enter her house again."

Then he was gone. The boy looked at his father, who still had not spoken or even looked up again, who was now adjusting the loggerhead in the hame.

"Pap," he said. His father looked at him — the inscrutable face, the shaggy brows beneath which the gray eyes glinted coldly. Suddenly the boy went toward him, fast, stopping as suddenly. "You done the best you could!" he cried. "If he wanted hit done different why didn't he wait and tell you how? He won't git no twenty bushels! He won't git none! We'll gether hit and hide hit! I kin watch . . ."

"Did you put the cutter back in that straight stock like I told you?" 65

"No, sir," he said.

"Then go do it."

That was Wednesday. During the rest of that week he worked steadily, at what was within his scope and some which was beyond it, with an industry that did not need to be driven nor even commanded twice; he had this from his mother, with the difference that some at least of what he did he liked to do, such as splitting wood with the half-size axe which his mother and aunt had earned, or saved money somehow, to present him with at Christmas. In company with the two older women (and on one afternoon, even one of the sisters), he built pens for the shoat and the cow which were a part of his father's contract with the landlord, and one afternoon, his father being absent, gone somewhere on one of the mules, he went to the field.

They were running a middle buster now, his brother holding the plow straight while he handled the reins, and walking beside the straining mule, the rich black soil shearing cool and damp against his bare ankles, he thought *Maybe this is the end of it. Maybe even that twenty bushels that seems hard to have to pay for just a rug will be a cheap price for him to stop forever and always from being what he used to be;* thinking, dreaming now, so that his brother had to speak sharply to him to mind the mule: *Maybe he even won't collect the twenty bushels. Maybe it will all add up and balance and vanish— corn, rug, fire; the terror and grief, the being pulled two ways like between two teams of horses—gone, done with for ever and ever.*

Then it was Saturday; he looked up from beneath the mule he was harnessing and 70 saw his father in the black coat and hat. "Not that," his father said. "The wagon gear." And then, two hours later, sitting in the wagon bed behind his father and brother on the seat, the wagon accomplished a final curve, and he saw the weathered paintless store with its tattered tobacco- and patent-medicine posters and the tethered wagons and saddle animals below the gallery. He mounted the gnawed steps behind his father and brother, and there again was the lane of quiet, watching faces for the three of them to walk through. He saw the man in spectacles sitting at the plank table and he did not need to be told this was a Justice of the Peace; he sent one glare of fierce, exultant, partisan defiance at the man in collar and cravat now, whom he had seen but twice before in his life, and that on a galloping horse, who now wore on his face an expression not of rage but of amazed unbelief which the boy could not have known was at the incredible circumstance of being sued by one of his own tenants, and came and stood against his father and cried at the Justice: "He ain't done it! He ain't burnt . . ."

"Go back to the wagon," his father said.

"Burnt?" the Justice said. "Do I understand this rug was burned too?"

"Does anybody here claim it was?" his father said. "Go back to the wagon." But he did not, he merely retreated to the rear of the room, crowded as that other had been, but not to sit down this time, instead, to stand pressing among the motionless bodies, listening to the voices:

"And you claim twenty bushels of corn is too high for the damage you did to the rug?"

"He brought the rug to me and said he wanted the tracks washed out of it. I washed the tracks out and took the rug back to him."

"But you didn't carry the rug back to him in the same condition it was in before you made the tracks on it."

His father did not answer, and now for perhaps half a minute there was no sound at all save that of breathing, the faint, steady suspiration of complete and intent listening.

"You decline to answer that, Mr. Snopes?" Again his father did not answer. "I'm going to find against you, Mr. Snopes. I'm going to find that you were responsible for the injury to Major de Spain's rug and hold you liable for it. But twenty bushels of corn seems a little high for a man in your circumstances to have to pay. Major de Spain claims it cost a hundred dollars. October corn will be worth about fifty cents. I figure that if Major de Spain can stand a ninety-five dollar loss on something he paid cash for, you can stand a five-dollar loss you haven't earned yet. I hold you in damages to Major de Spain to the amount of ten bushels of corn over and above your contract with him, to be paid to him out of your crop at gathering time. Court adjourned."

It had taken no time hardly, the morning was but half begun. He thought they would return home and perhaps back to the field, since they were late, far behind all other farmers. But instead his father passed on behind the wagon, merely indicating with his hand for the older brother to follow with it, and crossed the road toward the blacksmith shop opposite, pressing on after his father, overtaking him, speaking, whispering up at the harsh, calm face beneath the weathered hat: "He won't git no ten bushels neither. He won't git one. We'll . . ." until his father glanced for an instant down at him, the face absolutely calm, the grizzled eyebrows tangled above the cold eyes, the voice almost pleasant, almost gentle:

"You think so? Well, we'll wait till October anyway."

The matter of the wagon—the setting of a spoke or two and the tightening of the tires—did not take long either, the business of the tires accomplished by driving the wagon into the spring branch behind the shop and letting it stand there, the mules nuzzling into the water from time to time, and the boy on the seat with the idle reins, looking up the slope and through the sooty tunnel of the shed where the slow hammer rang and where his father sat on an upended cypress bolt, easily, either talking or listening, still sitting there when the boy brought the dripping wagon up out of the branch and halted it before the door.

"Take them on to the shade and hitch," his father said. He did so and returned. His father and the smith and a third man squatting on his heels inside the door were talking, about crops and animals; the boy, squatting too in the ammoniac dust and hoof-parings and scales of rust, heard his father tell a long and unhurried story out of the time before the birth of the older brother even when he had been a professional horsetrader. And then his father came up beside him where he stood before a tattered last year's circus poster on the other side of the store, gazing rapt and quiet at the scarlet horses, the incredible poisings and convolutions of tulle and tights and the painted leers of comedians, and said, "It's time to eat."

But not at home. Squatting beside his brother against the front wall, he watched his father emerge from the store and produce from a paper sack a segment of cheese and divide it carefully and deliberately into three with his pocket knife and produce crackers from the same sack. They all three squatted on the gallery and ate, slowly, without talking; then in the store again, they drank from a tin dipper tepid water smelling of the cedar bucket and of living beech trees. And still they did not go home. It was a horse lot this time, a tall rail fence upon and along which men stood and sat and out of which one by one horses were led, to be walked and trotted and then cantered back and forth along the road while the slow swapping and buying went on and the sun began to slant westward, they—the three of them—watching and listening, the older brother with his muddy eyes and his steady, inevitable tobacco, the father commenting now and then on certain of the animals, to no one in particular.

It was after sundown when they reached home. They ate supper by lamplight, then, sitting on the doorstep, the boy watched the night fully accomplish, listening to the whippoorwills and the frogs, when he heard his mother's voice: "Abner! No! No! Oh, God. Oh, God. Abner!" and he rose, whirled, and saw the altered light through the door where a candle stub now burned in a bottle neck on the table and his father, still in the hat and coat, at once formal and burlesque as though dressed carefully for some shabby and ceremonial violence, emptying the reservoir of the lamp back into the five-gallon kerosene can from which it had been filled, while the mother tugged at his arm until he shifted the lamp to the other hand and flung her back, not savagely or viciously, just hard, into the wall, her hands flung out against the wall for balance, her mouth open and in her face the same quality of hopeless despair as had been in her voice. Then his father saw him standing in the door.

"Go to the barn and get that can of oil we were oiling the wagon with," he said. 85
The boy did not move. Then he could speak.

"What . . ." he cried. "What are you . . ."

"Go get that oil," his father said. "Go."

Then he was moving, running, outside the house, toward the stable: this the old habit, the old blood which he had not been permitted to choose for himself, which had been bequeathed him willy nilly and which had run for so long (and who knew where, battening on what of outrage and savagery and lust) before it came to him. *I could keep on,* he thought. *I could run on and on and never look back, never need to see his face again. Only I can't. I can't,* the rusted can in his hand now, the liquid splashing in it as he ran back to the house and into it, into the sound of his mother's weeping in the next room, and handed the can to his father.

"Ain't you going to even send a nigger?" he cried. "At least you sent a nigger before!"

90 This time his father didn't strike him. The hand came even faster than the blow had, the same hand which had set the can on the table with almost excruciating care flashing from the can toward him too quick for him to follow it, gripping him by the back of his shirt and on to tiptoe before he had seen it quit the can, the face stooping at him in breathless and frozen ferocity, the cold, dead voice speaking over him to the older brother who leaned against the table, chewing with that steady, curious, sidewise motion of cows:

"Empty the can into the big one and go on. I'll catch up with you."

"Better tie him to the bedpost," the brother said.

"Do like I told you," the father said. Then the boy was moving, his bunched shirt and the hard, bony hand between his shoulderblades, his toes just touching the floor, across the room and into the other one, past the sisters sitting with spread heavy thighs in the two chairs over the cold hearth, and to where his mother and aunt sat side by side on the bed, the aunt's arms about his mother's shoulders.

"Hold him," the father said. The aunt made a startled movement. "Not you," the father said. "Lennie. Take hold of him. I want to see you do it." His mother took him by the wrist. "You'll hold him better than that. If he gets loose don't you know what he is going to do? He will go up yonder." He jerked his head toward the road. "Maybe I'd better tie him."

95 "I'll hold him," his mother whispered.

"See you do then." Then his father was gone, the stiff foot heavy and measured upon the boards, ceasing at last.

Then he began to struggle. His mother caught him in both arms, he jerking and wrenching at them. He would be stronger in the end, he knew that. But he had no time to wait for it. "Lemme go!" he cried. "I don't want to have to hit you!"

"Let him go!" the aunt said. "If he don't go, before God, I am going up there myself!"

"Don't you see I can't?" his mother cried. "Sarty! Sarty! No! No! Help me, Lizzie!"

100 Then he was free. His aunt grasped at him but it was too late. He whirled, running, his mother stumbled forward on to her knees behind him, crying to the nearest sister: "Catch him, Net! Catch him!" But that was too late too, the sister (the sisters were twins, born at the same time, yet either of them now gave the impression of being, encompassing as much living meat and volume and weight as any other two of the family) not yet having begun to rise from the chair, her head, face, alone merely turned, presenting to him in the flying instant an astonishing expanse of

young female features untroubled by any surprise even, wearing only an expression of bovine interest. Then he was out of the room, out of the house, in the mild dust of the starlit road and the heavy rifeness of honeysuckle, the pale ribbon unspooling with terrific slowness under his running feet, reaching the gate at last and turning in, running, his heart and lungs drumming, on up the drive toward the lighted house, the lighted door. He did not knock, he burst in, sobbing for breath, incapable for the moment of speech; he saw the astonished face of the Negro in the linen jacket without knowing when the Negro had appeared.

"De Spain!" he cried, panted. "Where's . . ." then he saw the white man too emerging from a white door down the hall. "Barn!" he cried. "Barn!"

"What?" the white man said. "Barn?"

"Yes!" the boy cried. "Barn!"

"Catch him!" the white man shouted.

But it was too late this time too. The Negro grasped his shirt, but the entire 105
sleeve, rotten with washing, carried away, and he was out that door too and in the drive again, and had actually never ceased to run even while he was screaming into the white man's face.

Behind him the white man was shouting, "My horse! Fetch my horse!" and he thought for an instant of cutting across the park and climbing the fence into the road, but he did not know the park nor how high the vine-massed fence might be and he dared not risk it. So he ran on down the drive, blood and breath roaring; presently he was in the road again though he could not see it. He could not hear either: the galloping mare was almost upon him before he heard her, and even then he held his course, as if the very urgency of his wild grief and need must in a moment more find him wings, waiting until the ultimate instant to hurl himself aside and into the weed-choked roadside ditch as the horse thundered past and on, for an instant in furious silhouette against the stars, the tranquil early summer night sky which, even before the shape of the horse and rider vanished, stained abruptly and violently upward: a long, swirling roar incredible and soundless, blotting the stars, and he springing up and into the road again, running again, knowing it was too late yet still running even after he heard the shot and, an instant later, two shots, pausing now without knowing he had ceased to run, crying "Pap! Pap!", running again before he knew he had begun to run, stumbling, tripping over something and scrabbling up again without ceasing to run, looking backward over his shoulder at the glare as he got up, running on among the invisible trees, panting, sobbing, "Father! Father!"

At midnight he was sitting on the crest of a hill. He did not know it was midnight and he did not know how far he had come. But there was no glare behind him now and he sat now, his back toward what he had called home for four days anyhow, his face toward the dark woods which he would enter when breath was strong again, small, shaking steadily in the chill darkness, hugging himself into the remainder of his thin, rotten shirt, the grief and despair now no longer terror and fear but just grief and despair. *Father. My father*, he thought. "He was brave!" he cried suddenly, aloud but not loud, no more than a whisper: "He was! He was in the war! He was in Colonel Sartoris' cav'ry!" not knowing that his father had gone to that war a private in the fine old European sense, wearing no uniform, admitting the authority of and giving fidelity to no man or army or flag, going to war as Malbrouck° himself did: for booty—it meant nothing and less than nothing to him if it were enemy booty or his own.

The slow constellations wheeled on. It would be dawn and then sunup after a while and he would be hungry. But that would be tomorrow and now he was only cold, and walking would cure that. His breathing was easier now and he decided to get up and go on, and then he found that he had been asleep because he knew it was almost dawn, the night almost over. He could tell that from the whippoorwills. They were everywhere now among the dark trees below him, constant and inflectioned and ceaseless, so that, as the instant for giving over to the day birds drew nearer and nearer, there was no interval at all between them. He got up. He was a little stiff, but walking would cure that too as it would the cold, and soon there would be the sun. He went on down the hill, toward the dark woods within which the liquid silver voices of the birds called unceasing—the rapid and urgent beating of the urgent and quiring heart of the late spring night. He did not look back.

Reading and Reacting

1. Is the third-person narrator of "Barn Burning" omniscient, or is his omniscience limited? Explain.
2. What is the point of view of the italicized passages? What do readers learn from them? Do they create irony? How would the story have been different without these passages?
3. "Barn Burning" includes a great deal of dialogue. How would you characterize the level of diction of this dialogue? What information about various characters does it provide?
4. What conflicts are presented in "Barn Burning"? Are any of these conflicts avoidable? Which, if any, are resolved in the story? Explain.
5. Why does Ab Snopes burn barns? Do you think his actions are justified? Explain your reasoning.
6. What role does the Civil War play in "Barn Burning"? What does Abner Snopes's behavior during the war tell readers about his character?
7. In the First and Second books of Samuel in the Old Testament, Abner was a relative of King Saul and commander in chief of his armies. Abner supported King Saul against David and was killed as a result of his own jealousy and rage. What, if any, significance is there in the fact that Faulkner names Ab Snopes—loyal to no man, fighter "for booty, and father of the Snopes clan"—after this mighty biblical leader?
8. Why does Sarty Snopes insist that his father was brave? How does your knowledge of events unknown to the boy create **irony**?

Malbrouck: A character in a popular eighteenth-century nursery rhyme about a famous warrior.

9. JOURNAL ENTRY How would the story be different if it were told from Ab's point of view? From Sarty's? From the point of view of Ab's wife? From the point of view of a member of a community in which the Snopeses have lived?

10. CRITICAL PERSPECTIVE Critic Edmond L. Volpe argues in his article "'Barn Burning': A Definition of Evil" that "Barn Burning" is not really about the class conflict between the sharecropping Snopeses and landowners like the de Spains but rather about Sarty:

> The story is centered upon Sarty's emotional dilemma. His conflict would not have been altered in any way if the person whose barn Ab burns had been a simple poor farmer, rather than an aristocratic plantation owner. . . . Sarty's struggle is against the repressive and divisive force his father represents. The boy's anxiety is created by his awakening sense of his own individuality. Torn between strong emotional attachment to the parent and his growing need to assert his own identity, Sarty's crisis is psychological and his battle is being waged far below the level of his intellectual and moral awareness.

Do you believe "Barn Burning" is, as Volpe suggests, essentially a coming-of-age story, or do you believe it is about something else—class conflict, for example?

Related Works: "A Primer for the Punctuation of Heart Disease" (p. 440), "A Worn Path" (p. 568), "Shiloh" (p. 735), "Baca Grande" (p. 889), "My Father as a Guitar" (p. 935), "Daddy" (p. 936), "For the Union Dead" (p. 1063), *Fences* (p. 1902)

Source: ©AP Photo/Laurent Rebours

EDWIDGE DANTICAT (1969–) was born in Port-au-Prince, Haiti, and immigrated as a child with her parents to New York. Her work focuses largely on Haitian culture and the immigrant experience. In an interview, Danticat explained her motivation for writing the story collection *Krik? Krak!* (1995), a finalist for the National Book Award: "I wanted to raise the voice of a lot of the people that I knew growing up, and this was, for the most part . . . poor people who had extraordinary dreams but also very amazing obstacles." Winner of the 1995 Pushcart Short Story Prize and other fiction awards, Danticat has recently published the novel *The Dew Breaker* (2004); the memoir *Brother, I'm Dying* (2007); and two young adult novels.

Cultural Context Haiti is a country that has been marked by authoritarian dictators, political unrest, and turbulent weather conditions, leading Haitian immigrants to seek refuge in the United States throughout the country's history. According to the 2000 United States Census, close to 420,000 Haitian immigrants live in the United States, primarily in Florida and New York. In recent years, Haitian asylum seekers have encountered increased difficulty upon entering the United States, due in large part to the United States government's efforts to monitor immigration more closely after the 9/11 terrorist attacks.

New York Day Women (1991)

Today, walking down the street, I see my mother. She is strolling with a happy gait, her body thrust toward the DON'T WALK sign and the yellow taxicabs that make forty-five-degree turns on the corner of Madison and Fifty-seventh Street.

I have never seen her in this kind of neighborhood, peering into Chanel and Tiffany's and gawking at the jewels glowing in the Bulgari windows. My mother never shops outside of Brooklyn. She has never seen the advertising office where I work. She is afraid to take the subway, where you may meet those young black militant street preachers who curse black women for straightening their hair.

Yet, here she is, my mother, who I left at home that morning in her bathrobe, with pieces of newspapers twisted like rollers in her hair. My mother, who accuses me of random offenses as I dash out of the house.

* * *

Would you get up and give an old lady like me your subway seat? In this state of mind, I bet you don't even give up your seat to a pregnant lady.

* * *

5 My mother, who is often right about that. Sometimes I get up and give my seat. Other times, I don't. It all depends on how pregnant the woman is and whether or not she is with her boyfriend or husband and whether or not *he* is sitting down.

As my mother stands in front of Carnegie Hall, one taxi driver yells to another, "What do you think this is, a dance floor?"

My mother waits patiently for this dispute to be settled before crossing the street.

* * *

In Haiti when you get hit by a car, the owner of the car gets out and kicks you for getting blood on his bumper.

* * *

My mother who laughs when she says this and shows a large gap in her mouth where she lost three more molars to the dentist last week. My mother, who at fifty-nine, says dentures are okay.

* * *

10 **You can take them out when they bother you. I'll like them. I'll like them fine.**

* * *

Will it feel empty when Papa kisses you?

* * *

Oh no, he doesn't kiss me that way anymore.

* * *

My mother, who watches the lottery drawing every night on channel 11 without ever having played the numbers.

* * *

A third of that money is all I would need. We would pay the mortgage, and your father could stop driving that taxicab all over Brooklyn.

* * *

I follow my mother, mesmerized by the many possibilities of her journey. Even in 15
a flowered dress, she is lost in a sea of pinstripes and gray suits, high heels and elegant short skirts, Reebok sneakers, dashing from building to building.

My mother, who won't go out to dinner with anyone.

* * *

If they want to eat with me, let them come to my house, even if I boil water and give it to them.

* * *

My mother, who talks to herself when she peels the skin off poultry.

* * *

Fat, you know, and cholesterol. Fat and cholesterol killed your aunt Hermine.

* * *

My mother, who makes jam with dried grapefruit peel and then puts in cinnamon 20
bark that I always think is cockroaches in the jam. My mother, whom I have always bought household appliances for, on her birthday. A nice rice cooker, a blender.

I trail the red orchids in her dress and the heavy faux leather bag on her shoulders. Realizing the ferocious pace of my pursuit, I stop against a wall to rest. My mother keeps on walking as though she owns the sidewalk under her feet.

As she heads toward the Plaza Hotel, a bicycle messenger swings so close to her that I want to dash forward and rescue her, but she stands dead in her tracks and lets him ride around her and then goes on.

My mother stops at a corner hot-dog stand and asks for something. The vendor hands her a can of soda that she slips into her bag. She stops by another vendor selling sundresses for seven dollars each. I can tell that she is looking at an African print dress, contemplating my size. I think to myself, Please Ma, don't buy it. It would be just another thing that I would bury in the garage or give to Goodwill.

* * *

Why should we give to Goodwill when there are so many people back home who need clothes? We save our clothes for the relatives in Haiti.

* * *

Twenty years we have been saving all kinds of things for the relatives in Haiti. I need the place in the garage for an exercise bike.

* * *

You are pretty enough to be a stewardess. Only dogs like bones.

* * *

This mother of mine, she stops at another hot-dog vendor's and buys a frankfurter that she eats on the street. I never knew that she ate frankfurters. With her blood pressure, she shouldn't eat anything with sodium. She has to be careful with her heart, this day woman.

* * *

I cannot just swallow salt. Salt is heavier than a hundred bags of shame.

* * *

She is slowing her pace, and now I am too close. If she turns around, she might see me. I let her walk into the park before I start to follow again.

My mother walks toward the sandbox in the middle of the park. There a woman is waiting with a child. The woman is wearing a leotard with biker's shorts and has small weights in her hands. The woman kisses the child good-bye and surrenders him to my mother; then she bolts off, running on the cemented stretches in the park.

The child given to my mother has frizzy blond hair. His hand slips into hers easily, like he's known her for a long time. When he raises his face to look at my mother, it is as though he is looking at the sky.

My mother gives this child the soda that she bought from the vendor on the street corner. The child's face lights up as she puts a straw in the can for him. This seems to be a conspiracy just between the two of them.

My mother and the child sit and watch the other children play in the sandbox. The child pulls out a comic book from a knapsack with Big Bird on the back. My mother peers into his comic book. My mother, who taught herself to read as a little girl in Haiti from the books that her brothers brought home from school.

My mother, who has now lost six of her seven sisters in Ville Rose° and has never had the strength to return for their funerals.

* * *

Ville Rose: Fictional Haitian town.

Many graves to kiss when I go back. Many graves to kiss. 35

* * *

She throws away the empty soda can when the child is done with it. I wait and watch from a corner until the woman in the leotard and biker's shorts returns, sweaty and breathless, an hour later. My mother gives the woman back her child and strolls farther into the park.

I turn around and start to walk out of the park before my mother can see me. My lunch hour is long since gone. I have to hurry back to work. I walk through a cluster of joggers, then race to a *Sweden Tours* bus. I stand behind the bus and take a peek at my mother in the park. She is standing in a circle, chatting with a group of women who are taking other people's children on an afternoon outing. They look like a Third World Parent-Teacher Association meeting.

I quickly jump into a cab heading back to the office. Would Ma have said hello had she been the one to see me first?

As the cab races away from the park, it occurs to me that perhaps one day I would chase an old woman down a street by mistake and that old woman would be somebody else's mother, who I would have mistaken for mine.

* * *

Day women come out when nobody expects them. 40

* * *

Tonight on the subway, I will get up and give my seat to a pregnant woman or a lady about Ma's age.

My mother, who stuffs thimbles in her mouth and then blows up her cheeks like Dizzy Gillespie° while sewing yet another Raggedy Ann doll that she names Suzette after me.

* * *

I will have all these little Suzettes in case you never have any babies, which looks more and more like it is going to happen.

* * *

My mother who had me when she was thirty-three—*l'âge du Christ*—at the age that Christ died on the cross.

* * *

That's a blessing, believe you me, even if American doctors say by that time you can make retarded babies. 45

* * *

Dizzy Gillespie: American jazz trumpeter (1917–1993).

My mother, who sews lace collars on my company softball T-shirts when she does my laundry.

* * *

Why can't you look like a lady playing softball?

* * *

My mother, who never went to any of my Parent-Teacher Association meetings when I was in school.

* * *

You're so good anyway. What are they going to tell me? I don't want to make you ashamed of this day woman. Shame is heavier than a hundred bags of salt.

Reading and Reacting

1. Who is the narrator of the story? How does the narrative point of view shape the story?
2. How is the narrator different from her mother? What details in the story lead you to your conclusion?
3. The story consists of alternating passages — one in standard type and then one in boldface type. How does the point of view of the story shift between these two kinds of passages?
4. The story begins when the narrator says, "Today, walking down the street, I see my mother." What motivates the narrator to follow her mother?
5. The narrator tells her story in the present tense. What would she have gained or lost by telling it in the past tense?
6. Why does the narrator hide from her mother? Why doesn't she greet her?
7. How would you characterize the relationship between the narrator and her mother?
8. In paragraph 28, the narrator's mother says, "Salt is heavier than a hundred bags of shame." However, the story ends with her saying, "Shame is heavier than a hundred bags of salt" (par. 49). What does she mean? What is the significance of this shift?
9. **JOURNAL ENTRY** Write a paragraph in which you define "day woman." Include some examples from the story to help you develop your definition.
10. **CRITICAL PERSPECTIVE** In a 2000 interview with the literary journal *Brick*, Edwidge Danticat explains how, as a Haitian immigrant living in the United States, she has a dualistic relationship with Haiti:

    > I have come to terms with the fact that my relationship with Haiti is different than someone who lives there . . . I love being there, there's a kind of peace about it that I can't explain. But I realize that I'm not living, I'm staying for a certain period of time, at the end of which I travel back. And so, it's a relationship of insider/outsider.

    How does "New York Day Women" convey the narrator's relationship of "insider/outsider" relationship with her mother and with Haiti?

Related Works: "Oliver's Evolution" (p. 191), "I Stand Here Ironing" (p. 344), "Fun Home" (p. 494), "Two Kinds" (p. 777), "Those Winter Sundays" (p. 1040), "The courage that my mother had" (p. 1042), *The Cuban Swimmer* (p. 1732)

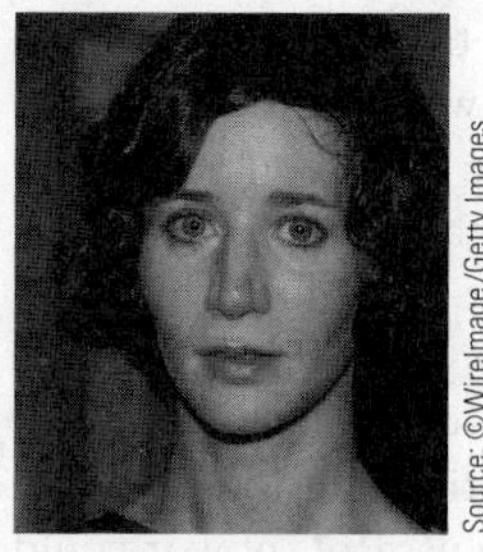
Source: ©WireImage/Getty Images

MIRANDA JULY (1974–) was born Miranda Jennifer Grossinger and raised in Berkeley, California. She is a fiction writer, filmmaker, and performance artist. Her work has appeared in such publications as the *New Yorker, Harper's, Zoetrope,* and the *Paris Review.* She is the author of the award-winning story collection *No One Belongs Here More Than You* (2007) and the director, writer, and star of the feature film *Me and You and Everyone We Know* (2005), which received a Special Jury Prize at the Sundance Film Festival and four prizes at the Cannes Film Festival. July is at work on her second feature film.

Cultural Context This story's title and plot allude to Nathaniel Hawthorne's classic short story "The Birthmark" (1843). In the story, a scientist marries a beautiful young woman who has a birthmark on her cheek in the shape of a small hand. The scientist becomes obsessed with the birthmark, thinking that it mars his wife's otherwise perfect beauty. Eventually, his wife also comes to hate the birthmark and agrees to drink a potion that will dissolve it. When the birthmark fades from the wife's face, however, she dies. Hawthorne's story critiques the unhealthy human drive toward an unreachable state of perfection, a theme that is revisited in the following story.

Birthmark (2003)

On a scale of one to ten, with ten being childbirth, this will be a three.

A three? Really?

Yes. That's what they say.

What other things are a three?

Well, five is supposed to be having your jaw reset.

So it's not as bad as that.

No.

What's two?

Having your foot run over by a car.

Wow, so it's worse than that?

But it's over quickly.

Okay, well, I'm ready. No—wait; let me adjust my sweater. Okay, I'm ready.

All right, then.

Here goes a three.

The laser, which had been described as pure white light, was more like a fist slammed against a countertop, and her body was a cup on the counter, jumping with each slam. It turned out three was just a number. It didn't describe the pain any more than money describes the thing it buys. Two thousand dollars for a port-wine stain removed. A kind of birthmark that seems messy and accidental, as if this red area covering one whole cheek were the careless result of too much fun. She spoke to her body like an animal at the vet, Shhh, it's okay, I'm sorry, I'm so sorry we have to do this to you. This is not unusual; most people feel that their bodies are innocent of their crimes, like animals or plants. Not that this was a crime. She had waited patiently from the time she was fourteen for aesthetic surgery to get cheap, like computers. Nineteen ninety-eight was the year lasers came to the people as good bread, eat and be full, be finally perfect. Oh yes, perfect. She didn't think she would have bothered if she hadn't been what people call "very beautiful except for." This is a special group of citizens living under special laws. Nobody knows what to do with them. We mostly want to stare at them like the optical illusion of a vase made out of the silhouette of two people kissing. Now it is a vase . . . now it could only be two people kissing . . . oh, but it is so completely a vase. It is both! Can the world sustain such a contradiction? And this was even better, because as the illusion of prettiness and horribleness flipped back and forth, we flipped with it. We were uglier than her, then suddenly we were lucky not to be her, but then again, at this angle she was too lovely to bear. She was both, we were both, and the world continued to spin.

Now began the part of her life where she was just very beautiful, except for nothing. Only winners will know what this feels like. Have you ever wanted something very badly and then gotten it? Then you know that winning is many things, but it is never the thing you thought it would be. Poor people who win the lottery do not become rich people. They become poor people who won the lottery. She was a very beautiful person who was missing something very ugly. Her winnings were the absence of something, and this quality hung around her. There was so much potential in the imagined removal of the birthmark; any fool on the bus could play the game of guessing how perfect she would look without it. Now there was not this game to play, there was just a spent feeling. And she was no idiot, she could sense it. In the first few months after the surgery, she received many compliments, but they were always coupled with a kind of disorientation.

Now you can wear your hair up and show off your face more.

Yeah, I'm going to try it that way.

Wait, say that again.

"I'm going to try it that way." What?

Your little accent is gone.

What accent?

You know, the little Norwegian thing.

Norwegian?

Isn't your mom Norwegian?

She's from Denver.

But you have that little bit of an accent, that little . . . way of saying things.

I do?

Well, not anymore, it's gone now.

And she felt a real sense of loss. Even though she knew she had never had an accent. It was the birthmark, which in its density had lent color even to her voice. She didn't miss the birthmark, but she missed her Norwegian heritage, like learning of new relatives, only to discover they have just died.

All in all, though, this was minor, less disruptive than insomnia (but more severe than déjà vu). Over time she knew more and more people who had never seen her with the birthmark. These people didn't feel any haunting absence, why should they? Her husband was one of these people. You could tell by looking at him. Not that he wouldn't have married a woman with a port-wine stain. But he probably wouldn't have. Most people don't and are none the worse for it. Of course, sometimes it would happen that she would see a couple and one of them would have a port-wine stain and the other would clearly be in love with this stained person and she would hate her husband a little. And he could feel it.

Are you being weird?

No.

You are.

Actually, I'm not. I'm just eating my salad.

I can see them, too, you know. I saw them come in.

Hers is worse than mine was. Mine didn't go down on my neck like that.

Do you want to try this soup?

I bet he's an environmentalist. Doesn't he look like one?

Maybe you should go sit with them.

Maybe I will.

I don't see you moving.

Did you just finish the soup? I thought we were splitting.

I offered it to you.

Well, you can't have any of this salad, then.

It was a small thing, but it was a thing, and things have a way of either dying or growing, and it wasn't dying. Years went by. This thing grew, like a child, microscopically, every day. And since they were a team, and all teams want to win, they continuously adjusted their vision to keep its growth invisible. They wordlessly excused each other for not loving each other as much as they had planned to. There were empty rooms in the house where they had meant to put their love, and they worked together to fill these rooms with midcentury modern furniture. Herman Miller, George Nelson, Charles and Ray Eames. They were never alone; it became crowded. The next sudden move would have to be through the wall. What happened was this. She was trying to get the lid off a new jar of jam, and she was banging it on the counter. This is a well-known tip, a kitchen trick, a bang to loosen the lid. It's not witchery or black magic, it's simply a way to release the pressure under the lid. She banged it too hard, and the jar broke. She screamed. Her husband came running when he heard the sound. There was red everywhere, and in that instant he saw blood. Hallucinatory clarity: you are certain of what you see. But in the next moment, your fear relinquishes control: it was jam. Everywhere. She was laughing, picking shards of glass out of the strawberry mash. She was laughing at the mess, and her face was down, looking at the floor, and her hair was around her face like a curtain, and then she looked up at him and said, Can you bring the trash can over here?

And it happened again. For a moment he thought he saw a port-wine stain on her cheek. It was fiercely red and bigger than he had ever imagined. It was bloodier than even blood, like sick blood, animal blood, the blood racist people think beats inside people of other races: blood that shouldn't touch my own. But the next moment it was just jam, and he laughed and rubbed the kitchen towel on her cheek. Her clean cheek. Her port-wine stain.

Honey

Can you get the trash can?

Honey.

What?

Go look in the mirror.

What?

Go look in the mirror.

Stop talking like that. Why are you talking like that?

What?

He was looking at her cheek. She instinctively put her hand on the mark and ran to the bathroom.

She was in there for a long time. Maybe thirty minutes. You've never had thirty minutes like these. She stared at the port-wine stain and she breathed in and she breathed out. It was like being twenty-three again, but she was thirty-eight now. Fifteen years without it, and now here it was. In the same exact place. She rubbed her finger around its edges. It came as high as her right eye, over to the edge of her right nostril, across her whole cheek to the ear, ending at her jawbone. In purplish-red. She wasn't thinking anything, she wasn't afraid or disappointed or worried. She was looking at the stain the way one would look at oneself fifteen years after one's own death. Oh, you again. Now it was obvious it had always been there; she had startled it back into sight. She looked into its redness and breathed in and breathed out and found herself in a kind of trance. She thought: I am in a kind of trance. She was just blowing around. It lasted about twenty-five minutes, a very, very long time to be just blowing around. Mostly, you waft for a second or two, a half second, maybe. And then you spend the rest of your life trying to describe it, to regain the perspective. You say, It was like I was just blowing around, and you wave your arms in the air. But there were no arms like that, and you know it. She came out of the trance like a plane taking off. Instead of being inside the stain, she was now looking down on it from above. Like a lake, it grew smaller and smaller until it was only a tiny region in a larger mass. One that this pilot favored, hovered over, but would not touch down on again. She pulled some toilet paper off the roll and blew her nose.

He found himself kneeling. He was waiting for her on his knees. He was worried she would not let him love her with the stain. He had already decided long ago, twenty or thirty minutes ago, that the stain was fine. He had only seen it for a moment, but he was already used to it. It was good. It somehow allowed them to have more. They could have a child now, he thought. There was a loose feeling in the air. The jam was still on the floor, and that was okay. He would just kneel here and wait for her to come out and hope he would be able to tell her about the looseness in a loose way. He wanted to keep the feeling. He hoped she wasn't removing it somehow, the stain. She should keep it, and they should have a kid. He could hear her blowing her nose; now she was opening the door. He would stay on his knees, just like this. She would see him this way and understand.

Reading and Reacting

1. This story alternates between sections of dialogue and long narrative passages. How is the point of view different in the dialogue and narrative passages?
2. Why does July shift the point of view the way she does? How does this shifting help her achieve her purpose?
3. Why does the main character have her birthmark removed?
4. What effect does removing the birthmark have on the main character? On her friends? On her husband?
5. Why does the main character feel "a real sense of loss" (par. 30) when someone tells her that her accent has gone? What else does the main character think she has lost?
6. In paragraph 46, the narrator says, "It was a small thing, but things have a way of either dying or growing, and it wasn't dying." To what is the narrator referring?
7. When the birthmark returns, is the main character happy or sad? What does the narrator mean when she says that the birthmark "had always been there" (par. 57)?
8. Why does the husband kneel at the end of the story? How does the birthmark allow the husband and wife "to have more" (par. 58)?
9. **JOURNAL ENTRY** Do you think the main character was right to have her birthmark removed? What point do you think July is trying to make?
10. **CRITICAL PERSPECTIVE** Novelist Helen Oyeyemi describes the importance of Miranda July's award-winning story collection *No One Belongs Here More Than You* (2007), from which "Birthmark" is taken: "One of the greatest strengths of the collection is the way it picks up on those behaviours suggestive of emotional realms that are under-explored in us, the behaviours that make an individual feel weird and completely alone."

    Which "under-explored" feelings and urges does "Birthmark" capture? How do these feelings and urges change throughout the story?

Related Works: "The Birthmark" (Web site), "Eye Ball" (p. 258), "The Girl with Bangs" (p. 271), "Everyday Use" (p. 517), "The Spray" (p. 729), "The World Is Too Much with Us" (p. 855), "Shall I compare thee to a summer's day?" (p. 923), *Beauty* (p. 1270)

WRITING SUGGESTIONS: Point of View

1. How would Poe's "The Cask of Amontillado" be different if it were told by a minor character who observed the events? Rewrite the story from this point of view—or tell the story that precedes the story, explaining the "thousand injuries" and the "insult."
2. Assume that you are Jim, the sailor in "Big Black Good Man," and that you are keeping a journal of your travels. Write the journal entries for the time you spent in Copenhagen. Include your impressions of Olaf, Lena, the hotel, and anything else that caught your attention. Make sure you present your version of the key events described in the story—especially Olaf's reaction to you.

3. Both "The Cask of Amontillado" and "Barn Burning" deal with crimes that essentially go unpunished and with the emotions that accompany these crimes. In what sense does each story's use of point of view shape its treatment of the crime in question? For instance, how does point of view determine how much readers know about the motives for the crime, the crime's basic circumstances, and the extent to which the crime is justified?
4. Write a story in which you retell "New York Day Women" from the mother's point of view. Be true to the original story. Be sure to reveal what she is thinking at various points in the story.
5. Write a letter from the wife in "The Birthmark" to the husband. Tell him why you are glad the birthmark has returned and how you want your relationship to be different.

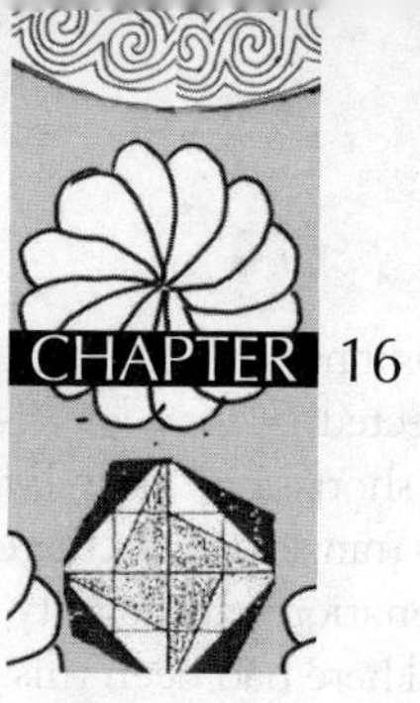

CHAPTER 16

STYLE, TONE, AND LANGUAGE

 Style and Tone

One of the qualities that gives a work of literature its individuality is its **style,** the way in which a writer uses language, selecting and arranging words to say what he or she wants to say. Style encompasses elements such as word choice; syntax; sentence length and structure; and the presence, frequency, and prominence of imagery and figures of speech.

Closely related to style is **tone,** the attitude of the narrator or author of a work toward the subject matter, characters, or audience. Word choice and sentence structure help to create a work's tone, which may be intimate or distant, bitter or affectionate, straightforward or cautious, supportive or critical, respectful or condescending. (Tone may also be **ironic;** see Chapter 15, "Point of View," for a discussion of irony.)

The Uses of Language

Language offers almost limitless possibilities to a writer. Creative use of language (such as unusual word choice, word order, or sentence structure) can enrich a story and add to its overall effect. Sometimes, in fact, a writer's use of language can expand a story's possibilities through its very inventiveness. For example, James Joyce's innovative **stream-of-consciousness** style mimics thought, allowing ideas to run into one another as random associations are made so that readers may follow and participate in the thought processes of the narrator. Here is a stream-of-consciousness passage from Joyce's experimental 1922 novel *Ulysses:*

> frseeeeeeeefronnnng train somewhere whistling the strength those engines have in them like big giants and the water rolling all over and out of them all sides like the end of Loves old sweet sonnnng the poor men that have to be out all the night from their wives and families in those roasting engines stifling it was today. . . .

Skillfully used, language can enhance a story's other elements. It may, for example, help to create an atmosphere that is important to the story's plot or theme, as Kate Chopin's lush, rhythmic sentences help to create the sexually charged atmosphere of "The Storm" (p. 313)—an atmosphere that overpowers the characters and thus drives the plot. Language may also help to delineate character, perhaps by conveying a character's mental state to readers. For instance, the breathless, disjointed style of Edgar Allan Poe's "The Tell-Tale Heart" (p. 760) suggests the narrator's increasing emotional instability: "Was it possible they heard not? Almighty God!—no, no! They heard!—they suspected!—they *knew!*—they were making a mockery of my horror!" In his 1925 short story "Big Two-Hearted River," Ernest Hemingway uses sentences without transitions to create a flat, emotionless prose style that reveals his character's alienation and fragility as he struggles to maintain control: "Now things were done. There had been this to do. Now it was done. It had been a hard trip. He was very tired. That was done. He had made his camp. He was settled. Nothing could touch him."

Language that places emphasis on the sounds and rhythm of words and sentences can also enrich a work of fiction. Consider the use of such language in the following sentence from James Joyce's "Araby" (p. 434):

> The light from the lamp opposite our door caught the white curve of her neck, lit up her hair that rested there and, falling, lit up the hand upon the railing.

Here the narrator is describing his first conversation with a girl who fascinates him, and the lyrical, almost musical language reflects his enchantment. Note in particular the **alliteration** (*l*ight/*l*amp; *c*aught/*c*urve; *h*air/*h*and), the repetition (lit up/lit up), and the rhyme (lit up her *hair*/that rested *there*) and **near rhyme** (falling/railing); these poetic devices connect the words of the sentence into a smooth, rhythmic whole.

Another example of this emphasis on sound may be found in the measured **parallelism** of this sentence from Nathaniel Hawthorne's 1843 story "The Birthmark":

> He had left his laboratory to the care of an assistant, cleared his fine countenance from the furnace smoke, washed the stain of acids from his fingers, and persuaded a beautiful woman to become his wife.

The style of this sentence, conveying methodical precision and order, reflects the compulsive personality of the character being described.

The following passage from Alberto Alvaro Ríos's story "The Secret Lion" (p. 197) illustrates the power of language to enrich a story:

> We had read the books, after all; we knew about bridges and castles and wildtreacherousraging alligatormouth rivers. We wanted them. So we were going to go out and get them. We went back that morning into that kitchen and we said, "We're going out there, we're going into the hills, we're going away for three days, don't worry." She said, "All right."
>
> "You know," I said to Sergio, "if we're going to go away for three days, well, we ought to at least pack a lunch."
>
> But we were two young boys with no patience for what we thought at the time was mom-stuff: making sa-and-wiches. My mother didn't offer. So we got out little kid knapsacks that my mother had sewn for us, and into them we put the jar of mustard. A loaf of bread. Knivesforksplates, bottles of Coke, a can opener. This was lunch for the two of us. And we were weighed down, humped over to be strong enough to carry this stuff. But we started walking anyway, into the hills. We were going to eat berries and stuff otherwise. "Goodbye." My mom said that.

Through language, the adult narrator of the preceding paragraphs recaptures the bravado of the boys in search of "wildtreacherousraging alligatormouth rivers" even as he suggests to readers that the boys are not going far. The story's use of language is original and inventive: words are blended together ("getridofit," "knivesforksplates"), linked to form new words ("mom-stuff"), and drawn out to mimic speech ("sa-and-wiches"). These experiments with language show the narrator's willingness to move back into a child's frame of reference while maintaining the advantage of distance. The adult narrator uses sentence fragments ("A loaf of bread."), colloquialisms ("kid," "mom," "stuff"), and contractions. He also includes conversational elements such as *you know* and *well* in the story's dialogue, accurately recreating the childhood scene even as he sees its folly and remains aware of the disillusionment that awaits him. Thus, the unique style permits the narrator to bring readers with him into the child's world while he maintains his adult stance: "But we were two young boys with no patience for what we thought at the time was mom-stuff. . . ."

Although many stylistic options are available to writers, a story's language must be consistent with the writer's purpose and with the effect he or she hopes to create. Just as writers may experiment with point of view or manipulate events to create a complex plot, so they can adjust language to suit a particular narrator or character or to convey a particular theme. In addition to the creative uses of language described above, writers also frequently experiment with *formal and informal diction*, *imagery*, and *figures of speech*.

 Formal and Informal Diction

The level of diction—how formal or informal a story's language is—can reveal a good deal about a story's narrator and characters.

Formal diction is characterized by elaborate, complex sentences; a learned vocabulary; and a serious, objective, detached tone. It does not generally include contractions, shortened word forms (like *phone*), regional expressions, or slang, and it may substitute *one* or *we* for *I*. At its most extreme, formal language is stiff and stilted, far removed from everyday speech.

When formal diction is used by a narrator or by a character, it may indicate erudition, a high educational level, a superior social or professional position, or emotional detachment. When one character's language is significantly more formal than others', he or she may seem old-fashioned or stuffy; when language is inappropriately elevated or complex, it may reveal the character to be pompous or ridiculous; when a narrator's language is noticeably more formal than that of the characters, the narrator may seem superior or even condescending. Thus, the choice of a particular level (or levels) of diction in a story can convey information about characters and about the narrator's attitude toward them.

The following passage from Hawthorne's "The Birthmark" illustrates formal style:

> In the latter part of the last century there lived a man of science, an eminent proficient in every branch of natural philosophy, who not long before our story opens had made experience of a spiritual affinity more attractive than any chemical one. He had left his laboratory to the care of an assistant, cleared his fine countenance from the furnace smoke, washed the stain of acids from his fingers, and persuaded a beautiful woman to become his wife. In those days when the comparatively recent discovery of electricity and other kindred mysteries of Nature seemed to open paths into the region of miracle, it was not unusual for the love of science to rival the love of woman in its depth and

> absorbing energy. The higher intellect, the imagination, the spirit, and even the heart might all find their congenial ailment in pursuits which, as some of their ardent votaries believed, would ascend from one step of powerful intelligence to another, until the philosopher should lay his hand on the secret of creative force and perhaps make new worlds for himself.

The long and complex sentences, learned vocabulary ("countenance," "ailment," "votaries"), and absence of colloquialisms suit Hawthorne's purpose well, recreating the formal language of the earlier era in which his story is set. The narrator is aloof and controlled, and his diction makes this clear to readers.

Informal diction, consistent with everyday speech, is characterized by slang, contractions, colloquial expressions like *you know* and *I mean*, shortened word forms, incomplete sentences, and a casual, conversational tone. A first-person narrator may use an informal style, or characters may speak informally; in either case, informal style tends to narrow the distance between readers and text.

Informal language can range from the straightforward contemporary style of Cal's speech in Anne Tyler's "Teenage Wasteland" ("'I think this kid is hurting. You know?'") to the regionalisms and dialect used in Flannery O'Connor's "A Good Man Is Hard to Find" ("aloose"; "you all"; "britches"). In "Teenage Wasteland" (p. 785), Cal's self-consciously slangy, conversational style tells readers a good deal about his motives and his method of operating; in "A Good Man Is Hard to Find" (p. 447), speech patterns and diction help to identify the region in which the characters live and their social class. Informal language may also include language readers find offensive. In this case, a character's use of obscenities may suggest his or her crudeness or adolescent bravado, and the use of racial or ethnic slurs indicates that a character is insensitive and bigoted.

The following passage from John Updike's "A&P" (p. 259) illustrates informal style:

> She had sort of oaky hair that the sun and salt had bleached, done up in a bun that was unravelling, and a kind of prim face. Walking into the A&P with your straps down, I suppose it's the only kind of face you *can* have. She held her head so high her neck, coming out of those white shoulders, looked kind of stretched, but I didn't mind. The longer her neck was, the more of her there was.

Here, the first-person narrator, a nineteen-year-old supermarket checkout clerk, uses a conversational style, including colloquialisms ("sort of," "I suppose," "kind of"), contractions ("it's," "didn't"), and the imprecise, informal *you* ("Walking into the A&P with *your* straps down. . . ."). The narrator uses neither elaborate syntax nor a learned vocabulary.

Imagery

Imagery—words and phrases that describe what is seen, heard, smelled, tasted, or touched—can have a significant impact in a story. A writer may use a pattern of repeated imagery to convey a particular impression about a character or situation or to communicate or reinforce a story's theme. For example, the theme of newly discovered sexuality can be conveyed through repeated use of words and phrases suggesting blooming or ripening.

In T. Coraghessan Boyle's "Greasy Lake" (p. 687), the narrator's vivid description of Greasy Lake uses rich visual imagery to evoke a scene:

> Through the center of town, up the strip, past the housing developments and shopping malls, street lights giving way to the thin streaming illumination of the headlights, trees crowding the asphalt in a black unbroken wall: that was the way out to Greasy Lake. The Indians had called it Wakan, a reference to the clarity of its waters. Now it was fetid and murky, the mud banks glittering with broken glass and strewn with beer cans and the charred remains of bonfires. There was a single ravaged island a hundred yards from shore, so stripped of vegetation it looked as if the air force had strafed it. We went up to the lake because everyone went there, because we wanted to snuff the rich scent of possibility on the breeze, watch a girl take off her clothes and plunge into the festering murk, drink beer, smoke pot, howl at the stars, savor the incongruous full-throated roar of rock and roll against the primeval susurrus of frogs and crickets. This was nature.

By characterizing a natural setting with surprising words like "fetid," "murky," and "greasy" and unpleasant images such as the "glittering of broken glass," the "ravaged island," and the "charred remains of bonfires," Boyle creates a picture that is completely at odds with the traditional view of nature. The incongruous images are nevertheless perfectly consistent with the sordid events that take place at Greasy Lake.

Figures of Speech

Figures of speech— such as *similes*, *metaphors*, and *personification*—can enrich a story, subtly revealing information about characters and themes.

By using **metaphors** and **similes**—figures of speech that compare two dissimilar items—writers can indicate a particular attitude toward characters and events. Thus, Flannery O'Connor's many grotesque similes in "A Good Man Is Hard to Find" help to dehumanize her characters; the children's mother, for instance, has a face "as broad and innocent as a cabbage." In Tillie Olsen's "I Stand Here Ironing" (p. 344), an extended metaphor in which a mother compares her daughter to a dress waiting to be ironed expresses the mother's attitude toward her child, effectively suggesting to readers the daughter's vulnerability. Similes and metaphors are used throughout in Kate Chopin's "The Storm" (p. 313). In a scene of sexual awakening, Calixta's skin is "like a creamy lily," her passion is "like a white flame," and her mouth is "a fountain of delight"; these figures of speech add a lushness and sensuality to the story.

Personification—a figure of speech, closely related to metaphor, that endows inanimate objects or abstract ideas with life or with human characteristics — is used in "Araby" (p. 434), where houses, "conscious of decent lives within them, gazed at one another with brown imperturbable faces." This use of figurative language expands readers' vision of the story's setting and gives a dreamlike quality to the passage. (Other figures of speech, such as **hyperbole** and **understatement,** can also enrich works of fiction. See Chapter 27, "Figures of Speech," for further information.)

Allusions—references to familiar historical, cultural, literary, or biblical texts, figures, or events—may also expand readers' understanding and appreciation of a work. An allusion widens a work's context by bringing it into the context of a related subject or idea. For instance, in Charles Baxter's short story "Gryphon" (p. 277), the narrator's allusions to Pinocchio and Betty Crocker enable readers who recognize the references to gain a deeper understanding of what certain characters are really like.

NOTE: In analyzing the use of language in a work of fiction, you may occasionally encounter obscure allusions (or foreign words and phrases or unfamiliar regional expressions), particularly in works treating cultures and historical periods other than your own. Frequently, such language will be clarified by the context, or by explanatory notes in your text. When it is not, you should consult a dictionary, encyclopedia, or other reference work.

✔ CHECKLIST Writing about Style, Tone, and Language

- Does the writer make any unusual creative use of word choice, word order, or sentence structure?
- Is the story's tone intimate? Distant? Ironic? How does the tone advance the writer's purpose?
- Does the style emphasize the sound and rhythm of language? For example, does the writer use alliteration and assonance? Repetition and parallelism? What do such techniques add to the story?
- Is the level of diction generally formal, informal, or somewhere in between?
- Is there a difference between the style of the narrator and the style of the characters' speech? If so, what is the effect of this difference?
- Do any of the story's characters use regionalisms, colloquial language, or nonstandard speech? If so, what effect does this language have?
- What do different characters' levels of diction reveal about them?
- What kind of imagery predominates? Where, and why, is imagery used?
- Does the story develop a pattern of imagery? How does this pattern of imagery help to convey the story's themes?
- Does the story use simile and metaphor? Personification? What is the effect of these figures of speech?
- Do figures of speech reinforce the story's themes? Reveal information about characters?

- Does the story make any historical, literary, or biblical allusions? What do these allusions contribute to the story?
- Are any unfamiliar, obscure, or foreign words, phrases, or images used in the story? What do these words or expressions contribute to the story?

Source: ©Oscar White/Corbis

R. CRUMB (1943–) is widely considered to be the founder of the underground or alternative comics movement, which emerged in the 1960s as a reaction against the popular superhero comics that had, until then, dominated and defined the comic book genre. Crumb and his underground contemporaries, including Art Spiegelman (p. 257), depicted taboo topics such as drugs and sex in a medium that had previously been perceived as a children's genre. He created the infamously risqué illustrated character Fritz the Cat, among others. With works such as *Introducing Kafka* (1993), in which he illustrates Franz Kafka's life and work and from which the following selection is excerpted, Crumb helped to raise the graphic novel to the level of high art. His work appears in numerous collections, including the *R. Crumb Sketchbook* volumes (1978, 1981, 2005) and *The Complete Crumb* (2005).

Cultural Context Throughout history, people have been fascinated with the effects of fasting on the human body and mind. In the early twentieth century, carnivals and freak shows throughout Europe featured "hunger artists," such as the one depicted in the following graphic story, who voluntarily starved themselves for the public's entertainment. Carnival goers would watch hunger artists, who were considered to be more oddities than "artists," while they would sit in a cage and do menial tasks, or nothing at all. Large crowds would often form when hunger artists, for whatever reason, decided to end their fast and finally eat.

A Hunger Artist (1993)

This graphic story starts on the next page. →

Reading and Reacting

1. How is the style—particularly the level of diction—used for the narrator's boxed comments different from the style used for dialogue?
2. How would you characterize this story's tone? What do the visual elements contribute to the tone?
3. Consider the story's visual style. How do visual elements—for example, the arrangement of images within panels, the relative size of the people depicted, and the use of white space—support the story's theme?
4. **JOURNAL ENTRY** Do you see the hunger artist as a mentally ill fanatic or as a man of high principles? In what sense, if any, do you see him as an "artist"? How is he different from the crowds that come to see him?
5. **CRITICAL PERSPECTIVE** Peter Poplaski, editor and designer of *The R. Crumb Coffee Table Art Book* (1997), describes the impact of R. Crumb's work in this way:

   Through the savage nervous energy of his pen lines, Crumb encourages his readers first to laugh, and then to take a good hard look at the unsavoury displays of their own quirky ids. It's not a pretty sight, but it is the reason Crumb is compared to artists such as Bruegel, Hogarth, Goya and Daumier. He is getting you to look at something you might not want to see.

What exactly is the "something you might not want to see" that Crumb "is getting you to look at" in "A Hunger Artist"?

Related Works: "Once upon a Time" (p. 232), "A Rose for Emily" (p. 243), "A Hunger Artist" (p. 723), "Not Waving but Drowning" (p. 1197)

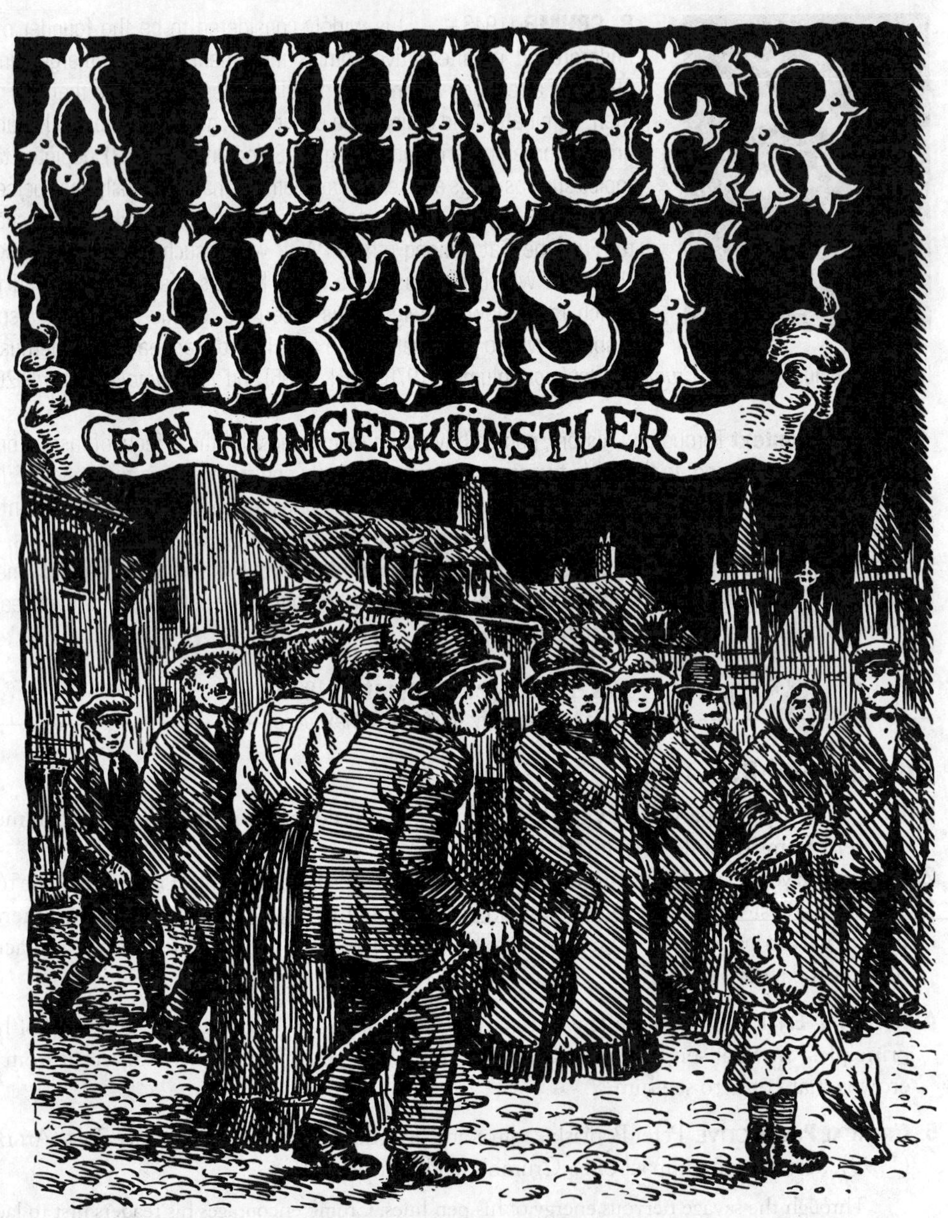

Source: ©1993 R. Crumb. Used by permission of Totem Books.

IN THE LAST FEW DECADES, THE INTEREST IN PROFESSIONAL HUNGER-ARTISTRY HAS GREATLY DIMINISHED. ONCE THE WHOLE TOWN CAME OUT TO SEE THE HUNGER-ARTIST. SOME EVEN BOUGHT SEASON TICKETS, AND AT NIGHT THE SCENE WAS BATHED IN THE LIGHT OF TORCHES.
GROUPS OF PROFESSIONAL WATCHERS, USUALLY BUTCHERS, WERE SENT TO WATCH HIM, IN CASE HE HAD SOME SECRET CACHE OF NOURISHMENT. BUT, DURING HIS FAST THE ARTISTE WOULD NEVER, EVEN UNDER COMPULSION, SWALLOW THE SMALLEST BIT OF FOOD; HIS PROFESSIONAL HONOR FORBADE IT. HE ALONE KNEW WHAT THE OTHERS DIDN'T: FASTING WAS THE EASIEST THING IN THE WORLD.
TICKETS
SEE THE HUNGER ARTIST

THE PERIOD OF FASTING WAS SET BY HIS IMPRESARIO AT FORTY DAYS MAXIMUM, BECAUSE AFTER THAT TIME THE PUBLIC BEGAN TO LOSE INTEREST. SO, ON THE FORTIETH DAY, WITH AN EXCITED CROWD FILLING THE ARENA AND A MILITARY BAND PLAYING, TWO YOUNG LADIES CAME TO LEAD THE HUNGER-ARTIST OUT OF HIS CAGE. WHEN THIS HAPPENED HE ALWAYS PUT UP SOME RESISTANCE...WHY STOP AFTER ONLY FORTY DAYS?!? WHY SHOULD THEY TAKE FROM HIM THE GLORY OF FASTING EVEN LONGER, OF SURPASSING EVEN HIMSELF TO REACH UNIMAGINABLE HEIGHTS, FOR HE SAW HIS ABILITY TO GO ON FASTING AS UNLIMITED!

THEN CAME THE FEAST, WITH THE IMPRESARIO TRYING TO SPOONFEED THE NEARLY COMATOSE HUNGER-ARTIST, ALL THE WHILE CHATTING CHEERFULLY IN ORDER TO DISTRACT ATTENTION FROM HIS CONDITION.
AFTER THAT THERE WAS EVEN A TOAST TO THE AUDIENCE, SUPPOSEDLY SUGGESTED BY THE HUNGER-ARTIST HIMSELF IN A WHISPER TO THE IMPRESARIO.

HE LIVED THIS WAY FOR MANY YEARS, HONORED BY ALL THE WORLD, YET TROUBLED IN HIS SOUL, DEEPLY FRUSTRATED THAT THEY WOULD NOT ALLOW HIS FASTING TO EXCEED FORTY DAYS. HE SPENT MOST OF HIS TIME IN A GLOOMY MOOD, AND WHEN SOME KIND-HEARTED PERSON WOULD TRY TO EXPLAIN THAT HIS DEPRES-SION WAS THE RESULT OF THE FAST-ING, HE WOULD SOMETIMES FLY IN-TO A RAGE AND BEGIN RATTLING THE BARS OF HIS CAGE LIKE AN ANIMAL.

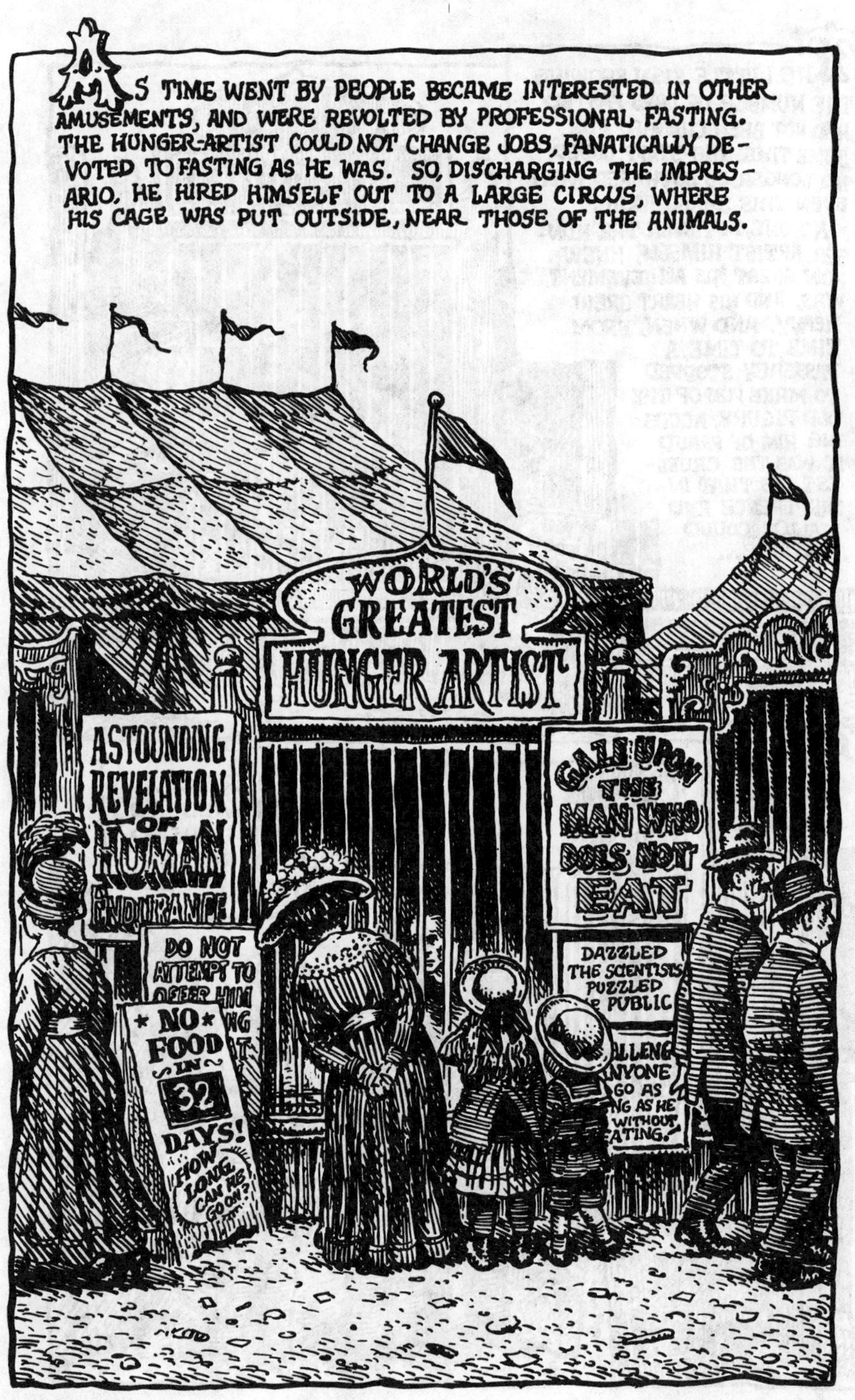
AS TIME WENT BY PEOPLE BECAME INTERESTED IN OTHER AMUSEMENTS, AND WERE REVOLTED BY PROFESSIONAL FASTING. THE HUNGER-ARTIST COULD NOT CHANGE JOBS, FANATICALLY DE-VOTED TO FASTING AS HE WAS. SO, DISCHARGING THE IMPRES-ARIO, HE HIRED HIMSELF OUT TO A LARGE CIRCUS, WHERE HIS CAGE WAS PUT OUTSIDE, NEAR THOSE OF THE ANIMALS.
WORLD'S GREATEST HUNGER ARTIST
ASTOUNDING REVELATION OF HUMAN ENDURANCE
GAZE UPON THE MAN WHO DOES NOT EAT
DO NOT ATTEMPT TO
DAZZLED THE SCIENTISTS PUZZLED
★NO★ FOOD IN 32 DAYS! HOW LONG CAN HE GO ON?

THE LITTLE SIGN SHOWING THE NUMBER OF DAYS FASTED HAD NOT BEEN CHANGED FOR SOME TIME. THE STAFF COULD NO LONGER BE BOTHERED WITH EVEN THIS SMALL TASK.
NO ONE, NOT EVEN THE HUNGER ARTIST HIMSELF, KNEW HOW GREAT HIS ACHIEVEMENT WAS, AND HIS HEART GREW HEAVY. AND WHEN, FROM TIME TO TIME, A PASSERBY STOPPED TO MAKE FUN OF THE OLD FIGURE, ACCUSING HIM OF FRAUD, IT WAS THE CRUELEST LIE THAT INDIFFERENCE AND MALICE COULD CONTRIVE...
WORLD'S GREATEST HUNGER ARTIST
NO FOOD IN
32
DAYS
THEN ONE DAY...
WHY IS THIS PERFECTLY GOOD CAGE ALLOWED TO STAND AROUND UNUSED, FULL OF ROTTEN STRAW ??
32

HE'S STILL IN THERE!
YOU STILL FASTING? AREN'T YOU EVER GOING TO STOP??
FORGIVE ME...
OF COURSE WE FORGIVE YOU!
I ALWAYS WANTED PEOPLE TO ADMIRE MY FASTING...
WE DO ADMIRE IT!
YOU SHOULDN'T...
WELL, ALRIGHT, WE DON'T ADMIRE IT, BUT WHY SHOULDN'T WE ADMIRE IT?
...BECAUSE I HAVE NO CHOICE... I HAVE TO FAST...
YOU HAVE NO CHOICE? WHY DON'T YOU HAVE ANY CHOICE?

BECAUSE ...BECAUSE I COULD NEVER FIND ANY FOOD I LIKED... IF I *HAD* FOUND ANY, BELIEVE ME, I WOULDN'T HAVE MADE ALL THIS FUSS! I'D HAVE STUFFED MYSELF THE SAME AS YOU OR ANYBODY ELSE!
THESE WERE HIS LAST WORDS, BUT IN HIS BROKEN EYES ONE COULD SEE THE FIRM, IF NO LONGER PROUD, CONVICTION THAT HE WAS FASTING STILL....
ALRIGHT, CLEAN UP THIS MESS...
THEY BURIED THE HUNGER-ARTIST TOGETHER WITH THE STRAW. INTO HIS CAGE THEY NOW PUT A YOUNG PANTHER...

EVEN THE MOST THICK-SKINNED PEOPLE WERE RELIEVED TO SEE THIS WILD CREATURE THROWING HIMSELF ABOUT IN THE CAGE THAT HAD SO LONG BEEN SO MISERABLE. WITHOUT ANY AFTERTHOUGHT HIS KEEPERS BROUGHT HIM ALL THE FOODS HE LIKED BEST.
HE SEEMED NOT EVEN TO MISS HIS FREEDOM, HIS NOBLE BODY, FILLED OUT TO BURSTING WITH ALL IT NEEDED, CARRIED FREEDOM AROUND WITH IT, AS IF HELD IN ITS JAWS, AND THE LIFE FORCE CAME SO PASSIONATELY FROM HIS THROAT THAT THE SPECTATORS COULD HARDLY BEAR THE SIGHT OF IT. BUT THEY BRACED THEMSELVES, CROWDED ROUND THE CAGE, AND DID NOT WANT TO MOVE AWAY.

Source: ©AP Photo

JAMES JOYCE (1882–1941) was born in Dublin but lived his entire adult life in self-imposed exile from his native Ireland. Though his parents sent him to schools that trained young men for the priesthood, Joyce saw himself as a religious and artistic rebel and fled to Paris soon after graduation in 1902. Recalled briefly to Dublin by his mother's fatal illness, Joyce returned to the Continent in 1904, taking with him an uneducated Irish country girl named Nora Barnacle, who became his wife in 1931. In dreary quarters in Trieste, Zurich, and Paris, Joyce struggled to support a growing family, sometimes teaching classes in Berlitz language schools.

Though Joyce never again lived in Ireland, he continued to write about Dublin. Publication of *Dubliners* (1914), a collection of short stories that included "Araby," was delayed for seven years because the Irish publisher feared libel suits from local citizens who were thinly disguised as characters in the stories. Joyce's autobiographical *Portrait of the Artist as a Young Man* (1916) tells of a young writer's rejection of family, church, and country. *Ulysses* (1922), the comic tale of eighteen hours in the life of a wandering Dublin advertising salesman, was banned when the United States Post Office brought charges of obscenity against the book, and it remained banned in the United States and England for more than a decade. With *Ulysses,* Joyce began a revolutionary journey away from traditional techniques of plot and characterization to the interior monologues and stream-of-consciousness style that mark his last great novel, *Finnegans Wake* (1939).

Cultural Context In the early twentieth century, as world travel and the shipment of goods around the world expanded at a dizzying pace, the West experienced a fascination with the "Orient." To peddle their wares, immigrants from the East established bazaars reminiscent of the ones in their homelands, displaying a dazzling array of spices, foods, and material goods. This exotic appeal to the senses, representing the allure of the distant and unknown, became a highlight of many towns and cities. In this story, the bazaar represents the allure of the strange and exotic for the young narrator.

Araby (1914)

North Richmond Street, being blind,° was a quiet street except at the hour when the Christian Brothers' School set the boys free. An uninhabited house of two storeys stood at the blind end, detached from its neighbours in a square ground. The other houses of the street, conscious of decent lives within them, gazed at one another with brown imperturbable faces.

The former tenant of our house, a priest, had died in the back drawing-room. Air, musty from having been long enclosed, hung in all the rooms, and the waste room behind the kitchen was littered with old useless papers. Among these I found a few paper-covered books, the pages of which were curled and damp: *The Abbot*,

blind: Dead-end.

by Walter Scott, *The Devout Communicant* and *The Memoirs of Vidocq*.° I liked the last best because its leaves were yellow. The wild garden behind the house contained a central apple-tree and a few straggling bushes under one of which I found the late tenant's rusty bicycle-pump. He had been a very charitable priest; in his will he had left all his money to institutions and the furniture of his house to his sister.

When the short days of winter came dusk fell before we had well eaten our dinners. When we met in the street the houses had grown sombre. The space of sky above us was the colour of ever-changing violet and towards it the lamps of the street lifted their feeble lanterns. The cold air stung us and we played till our bodies glowed. Our shouts echoed in the silent street. The career of our play brought us through the dark muddy lanes behind the houses where we ran the gauntlet of the rough tribes from the cottages, to the back doors of the dark dripping gardens where odours arose from the ashpits, to the dark odorous stables where a coach-man smoothed and combed the horse or shook music from the buckled harness. When we returned to the street light from the kitchen windows had filled the areas. If my uncle was seen turning the corner we hid in the shadow until we had seen him safely housed. Or if Mangan's sister came out on the doorstep to call her brother in to his tea we watched her from our shadow peer up and down the street. We waited to see whether she would remain or go in and, if she remained, we left our shadow and walked up to Mangan's steps resignedly. She was waiting for us, her figure defined by the light from the half-opened door. Her brother always teased her before he obeyed and I stood by the railings looking at her. Her dress swung as she moved her body and the soft rope of her hair tossed from side to side.

Every morning I lay on the floor in the front parlour watching her door. The blind was pulled down to within an inch of the sash so that I could not be seen. When she came out on the doorstep my heart leaped. I ran to the hall, seized my books and followed her. I kept her brown figure always in my eye and, when we came near the point at which our ways diverged, I quickened my pace and passed her. This happened morning after morning. I had never spoken to her, except for a few casual words, and yet her name was like a summons to all my foolish blood.

5 Her image accompanied me even in places the most hostile to romance. On Saturday evenings when my aunt went marketing I had to go to carry some of the parcels. We walked through the flaring streets, jostled by drunken men and bargaining women, amid the curses of labourers, the shrill litanies of shop-boys who stood on guard by the barrels of pigs' cheeks, the nasal chanting of street-singers, who sang a *come-all-you* about O'Donovan Rossa,° or a ballad about the troubles in our native

---

The Abbot . . . Vidocq: Sir Walter Scott (1771–1832)—an English Romantic novelist; *The Devout Communicant*—a variant title for *Pious Meditations,* written by an eighteenth-century English Franciscan friar, Pacifus Baker; *The Memoirs of Vidocq*—an autobiography of François-Jules Vidocq (1775–1857), a French criminal turned police agent.

O'Donovan Rossa: Any popular song beginning "Come all you gallant Irishmen . . ."; O'Donovan Rossa was an Irish nationalist who was banished in 1870 for advocating violent rebellion against the British.

land. These noises converged in a single sensation of life for me: I imagined that I bore my chalice safely through a throng of foes. Her name sprang to my lips at moments in strange prayers and praises which I myself did not understand. My eyes were often full of tears (I could not tell why) and at times a flood from my heart seemed to pour itself out into my bosom. I thought little of the future. I did not know whether I would ever speak to her or not or, if I spoke to her, how I could tell her of my confused adoration. But my body was like a harp and her words and gestures were like fingers running upon the wires.

One evening I went into the back drawing-room in which the priest had died. It was a dark rainy evening and there was no sound in the house. Through one of the broken panes I heard the rain impinge upon the earth, the fine incessant needles of water playing in the sodden beds. Some distant lamp or lighted window gleamed below me. I was thankful that I could see so little. All my senses seemed to desire to veil themselves and, feeling that I was about to slip from them, I pressed the palms of my hands together until they trembled, murmuring: "*O love! O love!*" many times.

At last she spoke to me. When she addressed the first words to me I was so confused that I did not know what to answer. She asked me was I going to *Araby*. I forgot whether I answered yes or no. It would be a splendid bazaar, she said she would love to go.

"And why can't you?" I asked.

While she spoke she turned a silver bracelet round and round her wrist. She could not go, she said, because there would be a retreat that week in her convent.° Her brother and two other boys were fighting for their caps and I was alone at the railings. She held one of the spikes, bowing her head towards me. The light from the lamp opposite our door caught the white curve of her neck, lit up her hair that rested there and, falling, lit up the hand upon the railing. It fell over one side of her dress and caught the white border of a petticoat, just visible as she stood at ease.

10 "It's well for you," she said.

"If I go," I said, "I will bring you something."

What innumerable follies laid waste my waking and sleeping thoughts after that evening! I wished to annihilate the tedious intervening days. I chafed against the work of school. At night in my bedroom and by day in the classroom her image came between me and the page I strove to read. The syllables of the word *Araby* were called to me through the silence in which my soul luxuriated and cast an Eastern enchantment over me. I asked for leave to go to the bazaar on Saturday night. My aunt was surprised and hoped it was not some Freemason° affair. I answered few questions in class. I watched my master's face pass from amiability to sternness; he hoped I was not beginning to idle. I could not call my wandering thoughts together. I had hardly any patience with the serious work of life which, now that it stood between me and my desire, seemed to me child's play, ugly monotonous child's play.

---

convent: Her convent school.

Freemason: At the time the story takes place, many Catholics in Ireland thought the Masonic Order was a threat to the church.

On Saturday morning I reminded my uncle that I wished to go to the bazaar in the evening. He was fussing at the hallstand, looking for the hatbrush, and answered me curtly:

"Yes, boy, I know."

As he was in the hall I could not go into the front parlour and lie at the window. I left the house in bad humour and walked slowly towards the school. The air was pitilessly raw and already my heart misgave me.

When I came home to dinner my uncle had not yet been home. Still it was early. I sat staring at the clock for some time and, when its ticking began to irritate me, I left the room. I mounted the staircase and gained the upper part of the house. The high cold empty gloomy rooms liberated me and I went from room to room singing. From the front window I saw my companions playing below in the street. Their cries reached me weakened and indistinct and, leaning my forehead against the cool glass, I looked over at the dark house where she lived. I may have stood there for an hour, seeing nothing but the brown-clad figure cast by my imagination, touched discreetly by the lamplight at the curved neck, at the hand upon the railings and at the border below the dress.

When I came downstairs again I found Mrs. Mercer sitting at the fire. She was an old garrulous woman, a pawnbroker's widow, who collected used stamps for some pious purpose. I had to endure the gossip of the tea-table. The meal was prolonged beyond an hour and still my uncle did not come. Mrs. Mercer stood up to go: she was sorry she couldn't wait any longer, but it was after eight o'clock and she did not like to be out late, as the night air was bad for her. When she had gone I began to walk up and down the room, clenching my fists. My aunt said:

"I'm afraid you may put off your bazaar for this night of Our Lord."

At nine o'clock I heard my uncle's latchkey in the halldoor. I heard him talking to himself and heard the hallstand rocking when it had received the weight of his overcoat. I could interpret these signs. When he was midway through his dinner I asked him to give me the money to go to the bazaar. He had forgotten.

"The people are in bed and after their first sleep now," he said.

I did not smile. My aunt said to him energetically:

"Can't you give him the money and let him go? You've kept him late enough as it is."

My uncle said he was very sorry he had forgotten. He said he believed in the old saying: "All work and no play makes Jack a dull boy." He asked me where I was going and, when I had told him a second time he asked me did I know *The Arab's Farewell to his Steed.*° When I left the kitchen he was about to recite the opening lines of the piece to my aunt.

I held a florin tightly in my hand as I strode down Buckingham Street towards the station. The sight of the streets thronged with buyers and glaring with gas recalled to me the purpose of my journey. I took my seat in a third-class carriage of

The Arab's Farewell to his Steed: A sentimental poem by Caroline Norton (1808–1877) that tells the story of a nomad's heartbreak after selling his much-loved horse.

a deserted train. After an intolerable delay the train moved out of the station slowly. It crept onward among ruinous houses and over the twinkling river. At Westland Row Station a crowd of people pressed to the carriage doors; but the porters moved them back, saying that it was a special train for the bazaar. I remained alone in the bare carriage. In a few minutes the train drew up beside an improvised wooden platform. I passed out on to the road and saw by the lighted dial of a clock that it was ten minutes to ten. In front of me was a large building which displayed the magical name.

I could not find any sixpenny entrance and, fearing that the bazaar would be closed, I passed in quickly through a turnstile, handing a shilling to a weary-looking man. I found myself in a big hall girdled at half its height by a gallery. Nearly all the stalls were closed and the greater part of the hall was in darkness. I recognised a silence like that which pervades a church after a service. I walked into the centre of the bazaar timidly. A few people were gathered about the stalls which were still open. Before a curtain, over which the words *Café Chantant*° were written in coloured lamps, two men were counting money on a salver. I listened to the fall of the coins.

Remembering with difficulty why I had come I went over to one of the stalls and examined porcelain vases and flowered tea-sets. At the door of the stall a young lady was talking and laughing with two young gentlemen. I remarked their English accents and listened vaguely to their conversation.

"O, I never said such a thing!"

"O, but you did!"

"O, but I didn't!"

"Didn't she say that?"

"Yes. I heard her."

"O, there's a . . . fib!"

Observing me the young lady came over and asked me did I wish to buy anything. The tone of her voice was not encouraging; she seemed to have spoken to me out of a sense of duty. I looked humbly at the great jars that stood like eastern guards at either side of the dark entrance to the stall and murmured:

"No, thank you."

The young lady changed the position of one of the vases and went back to the two young men. They began to talk of the same subject. Once or twice the young lady glanced at me over her shoulder.

I lingered before her stall, though I knew my stay was useless, to make my interest in her wares seem the more real. Then I turned away slowly and walked down the middle of the bazaar. I allowed the two pennies to fall against the sixpence in my pocket. I heard a voice call from one end of the gallery that the light was out. The upper part of the hall was now completely dark.

Gazing up into the darkness I saw myself as a creature driven and derided by vanity; and my eyes burned with anguish and anger.

Café Chantant: A Paris café featuring musical entertainment.

Reading and Reacting

1. How would you characterize the story's level of diction? Is this level appropriate for a story about a young boy's experiences? Explain.
2. Identify several figures of speech in the story. Where is Joyce most likely to use this kind of language? Why?
3. What words and phrases express the boy's extreme idealism and romantic view of the world? How does such language help to communicate the story's major theme?
4. In paragraph 4, the narrator says, "her name was like a summons to all my foolish blood." In the story's last sentence, he sees himself as "a creature driven and derided by vanity." What other expressions does the narrator use to describe his feelings? How would you characterize these feelings?
5. How does the narrator's choice of words illustrate the contrast between his day-to-day life and the exotic promise of the bazaar?
6. What does each of the italicized words suggest: "We walked through the *flaring* streets" (par. 5); "I heard the rain *impinge* upon the earth" (par. 6); "I *chafed* against the work of school" (par. 12); "I found myself in a big hall *girdled* at half its height by a gallery" (par. 25)? What other examples of unexpected word choice can you identify in the story?
7. What is it about the events in this story that causes the narrator to remember them years later?
8. Identify words and phrases in the story that are associated with religion. What purpose do these references to religion serve? Do you think this pattern of words and phrases is intentional?
9. **Journal Entry** Rewrite a brief passage from this story in the voice of the young boy. Use informal style, simple figures of speech, and vocabulary appropriate for a child.
10. **Critical Perspective** In *Notes on the American Short Story Today*, Richard Kostelanetz discusses the **epiphany,** one of Joyce's most significant contributions to literature:

> In Joyce's pervasively influential theory of the short story we remember, the fiction turned upon an epiphany, a moment of revelation in which, in [critic] Harry Levin's words, "amid the most encumbered circumstances it suddenly happens that the veil is lifted, the . . . mystery laid bare, and the ultimate secret of things made manifest." The epiphany, then, became a technique for jelling the narrative and locking the story's import into place. . . . What made this method revolutionary was the shifting of the focal point of the story from its end . . . to a spot within the body of the text, usually near (but not at) the end.

Where in "Araby" does the story's epiphany occur? Does it do all that Kostelanetz believes an epiphany should do? Or, do you think that—at least in the case of "Araby"—the epiphany may not be as significant a force as Kostelanetz suggests?

Related Works: "Snow" (p. 177), "The Secret Lion" (p. 197), "A&P" (p. 259), "Gryphon" (p. 277), "Doe Season" (p. 577), "Shall I compare thee to a summer's day?" (p. 923), *Beauty* (p. 1270)

Source: ©AP Photo/Jim Cooper

JONATHAN SAFRAN FOER (1977–) is an author, editor, and illustrator born in Washington, D.C. Winner of a Zoetrope Award for short fiction, Foer has had stories published in the *Paris Review*, *Conjunctions*, and *The New Yorker*. He edited the best-selling anthology *A Convergence of Birds: Original Fiction and Poetry Inspired by the Work of Joseph Cornell* (2001). For his first novel, *Everything Is Illuminated* (2002), Foer embarked on a journey to the Ukraine to research his grandfather's life. Among other things, the book concerns Foer's attempt to find out about the woman who may or may not have saved his grandfather from the Nazis. *Everything Is Illuminated* won The Guardian First Book Award and the National Jewish Book Award and was named Book of the Year by the *Los Angeles Times*. It was made into a movie in 2005. His second novel, *Extremely Loud and Incredibly Close*, released in 2005, relates the reactions of a nine-year-old boy to the events of 9/11.

Cultural Context The history of punctuation can be traced back to the ancient Greeks, who introduced marks into their language around 200 B.C. Serving primarily as pronunciation aids, punctuation marks evolved in the first century A.D. with new Latin translations of the Bible. Aldus Manutius, the Elder, an Italian printer living in the mid-second century, and his grandson are credited with developing a standardized system of punctuation that provides the basis for the marks used in the English language today.

A Primer for the Punctuation of Heart Disease (2002)

□ The "silence mark" signifies an absence of language, and there is at least one on every page of the story of my family life. Most often used in the conversations I have with my grandmother about her life in Europe during the war, and in conversations with my father about our family's history of heart disease—we have forty-one heart attacks between us, and counting—the silence mark is a staple of familial punctuation. Note the use of silence in the following brief exchange, when my father called me at college, the morning of his most recent angioplasty:

"Listen," he said, and then surrendered to a long pause, as if the pause were what I was supposed to listen to. "I'm sure everything's gonna be fine, but I just wanted to let you know—"

"I already know," I said.

"□"

5 "□"

"□"

"□"

"O.K.," he said.

"I'll talk to you tonight," I said, and I could hear, in the receiver, my own heartbeat.

10 He said, "Yup."

■ The "willed silence mark" signifies an intentional silence, the conversational equivalent of building a wall over which you can't climb, through which you can't see, against which you break the bones of your hands and wrists. I often inflict willed silences upon my mother when she asks about my relationships with girls. Perhaps this is because I never have *relationships* with girls—only *relations*. It depresses me to think that I've never had sex with anyone who really loved me. Sometimes I wonder if having sex with a girl who doesn't love me is like felling a tree, alone, in a forest: no one hears about it; it didn't happen.

?? The "insistent question mark" denotes one family member's refusal to yield to a willed silence, as in this conversation with my mother:

"Are you dating at all?"

"□"

"But you're seeing people, I'm sure. Right?"

"□"

"I don't get it. Are you ashamed of the girl? Are you ashamed of me?"

"■"

"??"

¡ As it visually suggests, the "unxclamation point" is the opposite of an exclamation point; it indicates a whisper.

The best example of this usage occurred when I was a boy. My grandmother was driving me to a piano lesson, and the Volvo's wipers only moved the rain around. She turned down the volume of the second side of the seventh tape of an audio version of "Shoah,"° put her hand on my cheek, and said, "I hope that you never love anyone as much as I love you¡"

Why was she whispering? We were the only ones who could hear.

¡¡ Theoretically, the "extraunxclamation points" would be used to denote twice an unxclamation point, but in practice any whisper that quiet would not be heard. I take comfort in believing that at least some of the silences in my life were really extraunxclamations.

!! The "extraexclamation points" are simply twice an exclamation point. I've never had a heated argument with any member of my family. We've never yelled at each other, or disagreed with any passion. In fact, I can't even remember a difference of opinion. There are those who would say that this is unhealthy. But, since it is the case, there exists only one instance of extraexclamation points in our family history, and they were uttered by a stranger who was vying with my father for a parking space in front of the National Zoo.

"Give it up, fucker!!" he hollered at my father, in front of my mother, my brothers, and me.

"Well, I'm sorry," my father said, pushing the bridge of his glasses up his nose, "but I think it's rather obvious that we arrived at this space first. You see, we were approaching from —"

"Give . . . it . . . up . . . fucker!!"

Shoah: A 1985 documentary about the Holocaust.

"Well, it's just that I think I'm in the right on this particu—"

"GIVE IT UP, FUCKER!!"

"Give it up, Dad¡" I said, suffering a minor coronary event as my fingers clenched his seat's headrest.

"Je-sus!" the man yelled, pounding his fist against the outside of his car door. "Giveitupfucker!!"

Ultimately, my father gave it up, and we found a spot several blocks away. Before we got out, he pushed in the cigarette lighter, and we waited, in silence, as it got hot. When it popped out, he pushed it back in. "It's never, ever worth it," he said, turning back to us, his hand against his heart.

~ Placed at the end of a sentence, the "pedal point" signifies a thought that dissolves into a suggestive silence. The pedal point is distinguished from the ellipsis and the dash in that the thought it follows is neither incomplete nor interrupted but an outstretched hand. My younger brother uses these a lot with me, probably because he, of all the members of my family, is the one most capable of telling me what he needs to tell me without having to say it. Or, rather, he's the one whose words I'm most convinced I don't need to hear. Very often he will say, "Jonathan~" and I will say, "I know."

A few weeks ago, he was having problems with his heart. A visit to his university's health center to check out some chest pains became a trip to the emergency room became a week in the intensive-care unit. As it turns out, he's been having one long heart attack for the last six years. "It's nowhere near as bad as it sounds," the doctor told my parents, "but it's definitely something we want to take care of."

I called my brother that night and told him that he shouldn't worry. He said, "I know. But that doesn't mean there's nothing to worry about~"

"I know~" I said.

"I know~" he said.

"I~"

"I~"

"□"

Does my little brother have relationships with girls? I don't know.

↓ Another commonly employed familial punctuation mark, the "low point," is used either in place—or for accentuation at the end—of such phrases as "This is terrible," "This is irremediable," "It couldn't possibly be worse."

"It's good to have somebody, Jonathan. It's necessary."

"□"

"It pains me to think of you alone."

"■↓"

"??↓"

Interestingly, low points always come in pairs in my family. That is, the acknowledgment of whatever is terrible and irremediable becomes itself something terrible and irremediable—and often worse than the original referent. For example, my sadness makes my mother sadder than the cause of my sadness does. Of course, her sadness then makes me sad. Thus is created a "low-point chain": ↓↓↓↓↓ . . . ∞.

❄ The “snowflake” is used at the end of a unique familial phrase — that is, any sequence of words that has never, in the history of our family life, been assembled as such. For example, “I didn’t die in the Holocaust, but all of my siblings did, so where does that leave me? ❄” Or, “My heart is no good, and I’m afraid of dying, and I’m also afraid of saying I love you.❄”

☺ The “corroboration mark” is more or less what it looks like. But it would be a mistake to think that it simply stands in place of “I agree,” or even “Yes.” Witness the subtle usage in this dialogue between my mother and my father:

“Could you add orange juice to the grocery list, but remember to get the kind with reduced acid. Also some cottage cheese. And that bacon-substitute stuff. And a few Yahrzeit candles.”

“☺”

“The car needs gas. I need tampons.”

“☺”

“Is Jonathan dating anyone? I’m not prying, but I’m very interested.”

“☺”

My father has suffered twenty-two heart attacks — more than the rest of us combined. Once, in a moment of frankness after his nineteenth, he told me that his marriage to my mother had been successful because he had become a yes-man early on.

“We’ve only had one fight,” he said. “It was in our first week of marriage. I realized that it’s never, ever worth it.”

My father and I were pulling weeds one afternoon a few weeks ago. He was disobeying his cardiologist’s order not to pull weeds. The problem, the doctor says, is not the physical exertion but the emotional stress that weeding inflicts on my father. He has dreams of weeds sprouting from his body, of having to pull them, at the roots, from his chest. He has also been told not to watch Orioles games and not to think about the current Administration.

As we weeded, my father made a joke about how my older brother, who, barring a fatal heart attack, was to get married in a few weeks, had already become a yes-man. Hearing this felt like having an elephant sit on my chest — my brother, whom I loved more than I loved myself, was surrendering.

“Your grandfather was a yes-man,” my father added, on his knees, his fingers pushing into the earth, “and your children will be yes-men.”

I’ve been thinking about that conversation ever since, and I’ve come to understand — with a straining heart — that I, too, am becoming a yes-man, and that, like my father’s and my brother’s, my surrender has little to do with the people I say yes to, or with the existence of questions at all. It has to do with a fear of dying, with rehearsal and preparation.

✂🕸 The “severed web” is a Barely Tolerable Substitute, whose meaning approximates “I love you,” and which can be used in place of “I love you.” Other Barely Tolerable Substitutes include, but are not limited to:

→|←, which approximates “I love you.”

👂□, which approximates “I love you.”

🔒, which approximates “I love you.”

✕✈, which approximates “I love you.”

I don't know how many Barely Tolerable Substitutes there are, but often it feels as if they were everywhere, as if everything that is spoken and done — every "Yup," "O.K.," and "I already know," every weed pulled from the lawn, every sexual act — were just Barely Tolerable.

∷ Unlike the colon, which is used to mark a major division in a sentence, and to indicate that what follows is an elaboration, summation, implication, etc., of what precedes, the "reversible colon" is used when what appears on either side elaborates, summates, implicates, etc., what's on the other side. In other words, the two halves of the sentence explain each other, as in the cases of "Mother::Me," and "Father::Death." Here are some examples of reversible sentences:

My eyes water when I speak about my family::I don't like to speak about my family.

I've never felt loved by anyone outside of my family::my persistent depression.

1938 to 1945::□.

Sex::yes.

My grandmother's sadness::my mother's sadness::my sadness::the sadness that will come after me.

To be Jewish::to be Jewish.

Heart disease::yes.

←Familial communication always has to do with failures to communicate. It is common that in the course of a conversation one of the participants will not hear something that the other has said. It is also quite common that one of the participants will not understand what the other has said. Somewhat less common is one participant's saying something whose words the other understands completely but whose meaning is not understood at all. This can happen with very simple sentences, like "I hope that you never love anyone as much as I love you¡"

But, in our best, least depressing moments, we *try* to understand what we have failed to understand. A "backup" is used: we start again at the beginning, we replay what was missed and make an effort to hear what was meant instead of what was said:

"It pains me to think of you alone."

"← It pains me to think of me without any grandchildren to love."

{} A related set of marks, the "should-have brackets," signify words that were not spoken but should have been, as in this dialogue with my father:

"Are you hearing static?"

"{I'm crying into the phone.}"

"Jonathan?"

"□"

"Jonathan~"

"■"

"??"

"I::not myself~"

"{A child's sadness is a parent's sadness.}"

"{A parent's sadness is a child's sadness.}"

"←"

"I'm probably just tired¡"

"{I never told you this, because I thought it might hurt you, but in my dreams it was *you*. Not me. *You* were pulling the weeds from my chest.}"

"{I want to love and be loved.}" 95

"☺"

"☺"

"↓"

"↓"

"🔒" 100

"☺"

"□↔□↔□"

"↓"

"↓"

"⏭○⏮" 105

"■+■→■"

"☺"

"👂□"

"⌦⌫"

"◎□❖⭘◆⭘○□⧫⊙●" 110

"■"

"{I love you.}"

"{I love you, too. So much.}"

Of course, my sense of the should-have is unlikely to be the same as my brothers', or my mother's, or my father's. Sometimes—when I'm in the car, or having sex, or talking to one of them on the phone—I imagine their should-have versions. I sew them together into a new life, leaving out everything that actually happened and was said.

Reading and Reacting

1. Explain how, despite its unusual appearance on the page, this story is in many respects a conventional work of fiction.
2. A **primer** is an elementary textbook used to teach children to read. In what sense is this story a primer? Who are the pupils?
3. What topics is the narrator's family unable to talk about? Why?
4. The narrator realizes that he is "becoming a yes-man" like his brother, grandfather, and father (par. 62). In what sense are all these family members "yes-men"? Given their family history and problems, do you think becoming a "yes-man" is a reasonable reaction?
5. In paragraph 77, the narrator explains, "Familial communication always has to do with failures to communicate." Do you think he is speaking here only of his own family, or of families in general? Explain.
6. After the confrontation in the parking space, the narrator's father says, "'It's never, ever worth it'" (par. 32). What does he mean?
7. Do you think the punctuation marks in this story are just visual gimmicks, or do you think that, taken together, they communicate something important?
8. Do you see the narrator's family as close or distant? Why?

9. **JOURNAL ENTRY** Devise a few symbols of your own, and explain how they might be used as substitutes for words and ideas in some of your family's difficult conversations.

10. **CRITICAL PERSPECTIVE** In a review of Jonathan Safran Foer's first novel, *Everything Is Illuminated* (2002), Lev Grossman makes the following comments:

> Foer spares no expense with his typographical special effects—italics, CAPITAL LETTERS, parentheses within parentheses, onomatopoeia, song lyrics and encyclopedia entries. . . . Under it all there's a funny, moving, unsteady, deeply felt novel about the dangers of confronting the past and the redemption that comes with laughing at it, even when that seems all but impossible.

Do you think this characterization also applies to "A Primer for the Punctuation of Heart Disease"? Explain.

Related Works: "I Stand Here Ironing" (p. 344), "The Rocking-Horse Winner" (p. 589), "The Little Knife" (p. 602), "The Disappearance" (p. 695), "My Papa's Waltz" (p. 1039), *Proof* (p. 1476), *The Glass Menagerie* (p. 1961)

Source: ©AP Photo

(MARY) FLANNERY O'CONNOR (1925–1964) was born to a prosperous Catholic family in Savannah, Georgia, and spent most of her adult life on a farm near the town of Milledgeville. She left the South to study writing at the University of Iowa, moving to New York to work on her first novel, *Wise Blood* (1952). On a train going south for Christmas, O'Connor became seriously ill; she was diagnosed as having lupus, the immune system disease that had killed her father and would cause O'Connor's death when she was only thirty-nine years old.

While her mother ran the farm, O'Connor spent mornings writing and afternoons wandering the fields with cane or crutches. Her short story collection *A Good Man Is Hard to Find* (1955) and an excellent French translation of *Wise Blood* established her international reputation, which was solidified with the publication of a second novel, *The Violent Bear It Away* (1960), and a posthumously published book of short stories, *Everything That Rises Must Converge* (1965).

O'Connor, said a friend, believed that an artist "should face all the truth down to the worst of it." Yet however dark, her stories are infused with grim humor and a fierce belief in the possibility of spiritual redemption, even for her most tortured characters. A line from her short story "A Good Man Is Hard to Find" says much about what O'Connor perceived about both natural things and her characters: "The trees were full of silver-white sunlight and the meanest of them sparkled." In O'Connor's work, the "meanest" things and people can sparkle, touched by a kind of holy madness and beauty.

Cultural Context Some readers consider O'Connor a Christian writer, and indeed the Christian concepts of free will, original sin, and the need for spiritual redemption appear throughout her work. According to Christian theology, humanity was created with free will — the freedom to choose to obey or to disobey God, the freedom to follow right or wrong. Human beings fell from their original state of innocence, however, and this fall allowed sin and corruption to enter the world. Thus, a "good man"—one who is perfectly upright—is not simply "hard to find" but *impossible* to find: *all* have sinned and fall short of the glory of God, says the Bible (Romans 3.23). Because of that first disobedience (original sin), humanity stands in need of redemption—a reuniting with God, which, according to Christian theology, comes through Jesus Christ.

A Good Man Is Hard to Find (1955)

The grandmother didn't want to go to Florida. She wanted to visit some of her connections in east Tennessee and she was seizing at every chance to change Bailey's mind. Bailey was the son she lived with, her only boy. He was sitting on the edge of his chair at the table, bent over the orange sports section of the *Journal*. "Now look here, Bailey," she said, "see here, read this," and she stood with one hand on her thin hip and the other rattling the newspaper at his bald head. "Here this fellow that calls himself The Misfit is aloose from the Federal Pen and headed toward Florida and you read here what it says he did to these people. Just you read it. I wouldn't take my children in any direction with a criminal like that aloose in it. I couldn't answer to my conscience if I did."

Bailey didn't look up from his reading so she wheeled around then and faced the children's mother, a young woman in slacks, whose face was as broad and innocent as a cabbage and was tied around with a green headkerchief that had two points on the top like a rabbit's ears. She was sitting on the sofa, feeding the baby his apricots out of a jar. "The children have been to Florida before," the old lady said. "You all ought to take them somewhere else for a change so they would see different parts of the world and be broad. They never have been to east Tennessee."

The children's mother didn't seem to hear her but the eight-year-old boy, John Wesley, a stocky child with glasses, said, "If you don't want to go to Florida, why dontcha stay at home?" He and the little girl, June Star, were reading the funny papers on the floor.

"She wouldn't stay at home to be queen for a day," June Star said without raising her yellow head.

"Yes and what would you do if this fellow, the Misfit, caught you?" the grand- 5
mother asked.

"I'd smack his face," John Wesley said.

"She wouldn't stay at home for a million bucks," June Star said. "Afraid she'd miss something. She has to go everywhere we go."

"All right, Miss," the grandmother said. "Just remember that the next time you want me to curl your hair."

June Star said her hair was naturally curly.

The next morning the grandmother was the first one in the car, ready to go. She 10
had her big black valise that looked like the head of a hippopotamus in one corner, and underneath it she was hiding a basket with Pitty Sing, the cat, in it. She didn't intend for the cat to be left alone in the house for three days because he would miss her too much and she was afraid he might brush against one of the gas burners and accidentally asphyxiate himself. Her son, Bailey, didn't like to arrive at a motel with a cat.

She sat in the middle of the back seat with John Wesley and June Star on either side of her. Bailey and the children's mother and the baby sat in front and they left Atlanta at eight forty-five with the mileage on the car at 55890. The grandmother wrote this down because she thought it would be interesting to say how many miles they had been when they got back. It took them twenty minutes to reach the outskirts of the city.

The old lady settled herself comfortably, removing her white cotton gloves and putting them up with her purse on the shelf in front of the back window. The children's mother still had on slacks and still had her head tied up in a green kerchief, but the grandmother had on a navy blue straw sailor hat with a bunch of white violets on the brim and a navy blue dress with a small white dot in the print. Her collars and cuffs were white organdy trimmed with lace and at her neckline she had pinned a purple spray of cloth violets containing a sachet. In case of an accident, anyone seeing her dead on the highway would know at once that she was a lady.

She said she thought it was going to be a good day for driving, neither too hot nor too cold, and she cautioned Bailey that the speed limit was fifty-five miles an hour and that the patrolmen hid themselves behind billboards and small clumps of trees and sped out after you before you had a chance to slow down. She pointed out interesting details of the scenery: Stone Mountain; the blue granite that in some places came up to both sides of the highway; the brilliant red clay banks slightly streaked with purple; and the various crops that made rows of green lace-work on the ground. The trees were full of silver-white sunlight and the meanest of them sparkled. The children were reading comic magazines and their mother had gone back to sleep.

"Let's go through Georgia fast so we won't have to look at it much," John Wesley said.

15 "If I were a little boy," said the grandmother, "I wouldn't talk about my native state that way. Tennessee has the mountains and Georgia has the hills."

"Tennessee is just a hillbilly dumping ground," John Wesley said, "and Georgia is a lousy state too."

"You said it," June Star said.

"In my time," said the grandmother, folding her thin veined fingers, "children were more respectful of their native states and their parents and everything else. People did right then. Oh look at the cute little pickaninny!" she said and pointed to a Negro child standing in the door of a shack. "Wouldn't that make a picture, now?" she asked and they all turned and looked at the little Negro out of the back window. He waved.

"He didn't have any britches on," June Star said.

20 "He probably didn't have any," the grandmother explained. "Little niggers in the country don't have things like we do. If I could paint, I'd paint that picture," she said.

The children exchanged comic books.

The grandmother offered to hold the baby and the children's mother passed him over the front seat to her. She set him on her knee and bounced him and told him about the things they were passing. She rolled her eyes and screwed up her mouth and stuck her leathery thin face into his smooth bland one. Occasionally he gave her a faraway smile. They passed a large cotton field with five or six graves fenced in the middle of it, like a small island. "Look at the graveyard!" the grandmother said, pointing it out. "That was the old family burying ground. That belonged to the plantation."

"Where's the plantation?" John Wesley asked.

"Gone With the Wind,"° said the grandmother. "Ha. Ha."

When the children finished all the comic books they had brought, they opened the 25
lunch and ate it. The grandmother ate a peanut butter sandwich and an olive and would not let the children throw the box and the paper napkins out the window. When there was nothing else to do they played a game by choosing a cloud and making the other two guess what shape it suggested. John Wesley took one the shape of a cow and June Star guessed a cow and John Wesley said, no, an automobile, and June Star said he didn't play fair, and they began to slap each other over the grandmother.

The grandmother said she would tell them a story if they would keep quiet. When she told a story, she rolled her eyes and waved her head and was very dramatic. She said once when she was a maiden lady she had been courted by a Mr. Edgar Atkins Teagarden from Jasper, Georgia. She said he was a very good-looking man and a gentleman and that he brought her a watermelon every Saturday afternoon with his initials cut in it, E. A. T. Well, one Saturday, she said, Mr. Teagarden brought the watermelon and there was nobody at home and he left it on the front porch and returned in his buggy to Jasper, but she never got the watermelon, she said, because a nigger boy ate it when he saw the initials, E. A. T.! This story tickled John Wesley's funny bone and he giggled and giggled but June Star didn't think it was any good. She said she wouldn't marry a man that just brought her a watermelon on Saturday. The grandmother said she would have done well to marry Mr. Teagarden because he was a gentleman and had bought Coca-Cola stock when it first came out and that he died only a few years ago, a very wealthy man.

They stopped at The Tower for barbecued sandwiches. The Tower was a part stucco and part wood filling station and dance hall set in a clearing outside of Timothy. A fat man named Red Sammy Butts ran it and there were signs stuck here and there on the building and for miles up and down the highway saying, TRY RED SAMMY'S FAMOUS BARBECUE. NONE LIKE FAMOUS RED SAMMY'S! RED SAM! THE FAT BOY WITH THE HAPPY LAUGH. A VETERAN! RED SAMMY'S YOUR MAN!

Red Sammy was lying on the bare ground outside The Tower with his head under a truck while a gray monkey about a foot high, chained to a small chinaberry tree, chattered nearby. The monkey sprang back into the tree and got on the highest limb as soon as he saw the children jump out of the car and run toward him.

Inside, The Tower was a long dark room with a counter at one end and tables at the other and dancing space in the middle. They all sat down at a board table next to the nickelodeon and Red Sam's wife, a tall burnt-brown woman with hair and eyes lighter than her skin, came and took their order. The children's mother put a dime in the machine and played "The Tennessee Waltz," and the grandmother said that tune always made her want to dance. She asked Bailey if he would like to dance but he only glared at her. He didn't have a naturally sweet disposition like she did and trips made him nervous. The grandmother's brown eyes were very bright. She

---

Gone with the Wind: A 1936 novel by Margaret Mitchell about the Civil War.

swayed her head from side to side and pretended she was dancing in her chair. June Star said play something she could tap to so the children's mother put in another dime and played a fast number and June Star stepped out onto the dance floor and did her tap routine.

30 "Ain't she cute?" Red Sam's wife said, leaning over the counter. "Would you like to come be my little girl?"

"No I certainly wouldn't," June Star said. "I wouldn't live in a broken-down place like this for a million bucks!" and she ran back to the table.

"Ain't she cute?" the woman repeated, stretching her mouth politely.

"Aren't you ashamed?" hissed the grandmother.

Red Sam came in and told his wife to quit lounging on the counter and hurry up with these people's order. His khaki trousers reached just to his hip bones and his stomach hung over them like a sack of meal swaying under his shirt. He came over and sat down at a table nearby and let out a combination sigh and yodel. "You can't win," he said. "You can't win," and he wiped his sweating red face off with a gray handkerchief. "These days you don't know who to trust," he said. "Ain't that the truth?"

35 "People are certainly not nice like they used to be," said the grandmother.

"Two fellers come in here last week," Red Sammy said, "driving a Chrysler. It was a old beat-up car but it was a good one and these boys looked all right to me. Said they worked at the mill and you know I let them fellers charge the gas they bought? Now why did I do that?"

"Because you're a good man!" the grandmother said at once.

"Yes'm, I suppose so," Red Sam said as if he were struck with this answer.

His wife brought the orders, carrying the five plates all at once without a tray, two in each hand and one balanced on her arm. "It isn't a soul in this green world of God's that you can trust," she said. "And I don't count nobody out of that, not nobody," she repeated, looking at Red Sammy.

40 "Did you read about that criminal, The Misfit, that's escaped?" asked the grandmother.

"I wouldn't be a bit surprised if he didn't attack this place right here," said the woman. "If he hears about it being here, I wouldn't be none surprised to see him. If he hears it's two cent in the cash register, I wouldn't be at all surprised if he . . ."

"That'll do," Red Sam said. "Go bring these people their Co'-Colas," and the woman went off to get the rest of the order.

"A good man is hard to find," Red Sammy said. "Everything is getting terrible. I remember the day you could go off and leave your screen door unlatched. Not no more."

He and the grandmother discussed better times. The old lady said that in her opinion Europe was entirely to blame for the way things were now. She said the way Europe acted you would think we were made of money and Red Sam said it was no use talking about it, she was exactly right. The children ran outside into the white sunlight and looked at the monkey in the lacy chinaberry tree. He was busy catching fleas on himself and biting each one carefully between his teeth as if it were a delicacy.

They drove off again into the hot afternoon. The grandmother took cat naps and 45
woke up every few minutes with her own snoring. Outside of Toombsboro she woke up and recalled an old plantation that she had visited in this neighborhood once when she was a young lady. She said the house had six white columns across the front and that there was an avenue of oaks leading up to it and two little wooden trellis arbors on either side in front where you sat down with your suitor after a stroll in the garden. She recalled exactly which road to turn off to get to it. She knew that Bailey would not be willing to lose any time looking at an old house, but the more she talked about it, the more she wanted to see it once again and find out if the little twin arbors were still standing. "There was a secret panel in this house," she said craftily, not telling the truth but wishing that she were, "and the story went that all the family silver was hidden in it when Sherman came through but it was never found . . ."

"Hey!" John Wesley said. "Let's go see it! We'll find it! We'll poke all the woodwork and find it! Who lives there? Where do you turn off at? Hey Pop, can't we turn off there?"

"We never have seen a house with a secret panel!" June Star shrieked. "Let's go to the house with the secret panel! Hey Pop, can't we go see the house with the secret panel!"

"It's not far from here, I know," the grandmother said. "It wouldn't take over twenty minutes."

Bailey was looking straight ahead. His jaw was as rigid as a horseshoe. "No," he said.

The children began to yell and scream that they wanted to see the house with the 50
secret panel. John Wesley kicked the back of the front seat and June Star hung over her mother's shoulder and whined desperately into her ear that they never had any fun even on their vacation, that they could never do what THEY wanted to do. The baby began to scream and John Wesley kicked the back of the seat so hard that his father could feel the blows in his kidney.

"All right!" he shouted and drew the car to a stop at the side of the road. "Will you all shut up? Will you all just shut up for one second? If you don't shut up, we won't go anywhere."

"It would be very educational for them," the grandmother murmured.

"All right," Bailey said, "but get this: this is the only time we're going to stop for anything like this. This is the one and only time."

"The dirt road that you have to turn down is about a mile back," the grandmother directed. "I marked it when we passed."

"A dirt road," Bailey groaned. 55

After they had turned around and were headed toward the dirt road, the grandmother recalled other points about the house, the beautiful glass over the front doorway and the candle-lamp in the hall. John Wesley said that the secret panel was probably in the fireplace.

"You can't go inside this house," Bailey said. "You don't know who lives there."

"While you all talk to the people in front, I'll run around behind and get in a window," John Wesley suggested.

"We'll all stay in the car," his mother said.

60 They turned onto the dirt road and the car raced roughly along in a swirl of pink dust. The grandmother recalled the times when there were no paved roads and thirty miles was a day's journey. The dirt road was hilly and there were sudden washes in it and sharp curves on dangerous embankments. All at once they would be on a hill, looking down over the blue tops of trees for miles around, then the next minute, they would be in a red depression with the dust-coated trees looking down on them.

"This place had better turn up in a minute," Bailey said, "or I'm going to turn around."

The road looked as if no one had traveled on it in months.

"It's not much farther," the grandmother said and just as she said it, a horrible thought came to her. The thought was so embarrassing that she turned red in the face and her eyes dilated and her feet jumped up, upsetting her valise in the corner. The instant the valise moved, the newspaper top she had over the basket under it rose with a snarl and Pitty Sing, the cat, sprang onto Bailey's shoulder.

The children were thrown to the floor and their mother, clutching the baby, was thrown out the door onto the ground; the old lady was thrown into the front seat. The car turned over once and landed right-side-up in a gulch off the side of the road. Bailey remained in the driver's seat with the cat—gray-striped with a broad white face and an orange nose—clinging to his neck like a caterpillar.

65 As soon as the children saw they could move their arms and legs, they scrambled out of the car, shouting, "We've had an ACCIDENT!" The grandmother was curled up under the dashboard, hoping she was injured so that Bailey's wrath would not come down on her all at once. The horrible thought she had had before the accident was that the house she had remembered so vividly was not in Georgia but in Tennessee.

Bailey removed the cat from his neck with both hands and flung it out the window against the side of a pine tree. Then he got out of the car and started looking for the children's mother. She was sitting against the side of the red gutted ditch, holding the screaming baby, but she only had a cut down her face and a broken shoulder. "We've had an ACCIDENT!" the children screamed in a frenzy of delight.

"But nobody's killed," June Star said with disappointment as the grandmother limped out of the car, her hat still pinned to her head but the broken front brim standing up at a jaunty angle and the violet spray hanging off the side. They all sat down in the ditch, except the children, to recover from the shock. They were all shaking.

"Maybe a car will come along," said the children's mother hoarsely.

"I believe I have injured an organ," said the grandmother, pressing her side, but no one answered her. Bailey's teeth were clattering. He had on a yellow sport shirt with bright blue parrots designed in it and his face was as yellow as the shirt. The grandmother decided that she would not mention that the house was in Tennessee.

70 The road was about ten feet above and they could see only the tops of the trees on the other side of it. Behind the ditch they were sitting in there were more woods, tall and dark and deep. In a few minutes they saw a car some distance away on top of a hill, coming slowly as if the occupants were watching them. The grandmother stood up and waved both arms dramatically to attract their attention. The car continued to

come on slowly, disappeared around a bend and appeared again, moving even slower, on top of the hill they had gone over. It was a big black battered hearse-like automobile. There were three men in it.

It came to a stop just over them and for some minutes, the driver looked down with a steady expressionless gaze to where they were sitting, and didn't speak. Then he turned his head and muttered something to the other two and they got out. One was a fat boy in black trousers and a red sweat shirt with a silver stallion embossed on the front of it. He moved around on the right side of them and stood staring, his mouth partly open in a kind of loose grin. The other had on khaki pants and a blue striped coat and a gray hat pulled down very low, hiding most of his face. He came around slowly on the left side. Neither spoke.

The driver got out of the car and stood by the side of it, looking down at them. He was an older man than the other two. His hair was just beginning to gray and he wore silver-rimmed spectacles that gave him a scholarly look. He had a long creased face and didn't have on any shirt or undershirt. He had on blue jeans that were too tight for him and was holding a black hat and a gun. The two boys also had guns.

"We've had an ACCIDENT!" the children screamed.

The grandmother had the peculiar feeling that the bespectacled man was someone she knew. His face was as familiar to her as if she had known him all her life but she could not recall who he was. He moved away from the car and began to come down the embankment, placing his feet carefully so that he wouldn't slip. He had on tan and white shoes and no socks, and his ankles were red and thin. "Good afternoon," he said. "I see you all had you a little spill."

"We turned over twice!" said the grandmother. 75

"Oncet," he corrected. "We seen it happen. Try their car and see will it run, Hiram," he said quietly to the boy with the gray hat.

"What you got that gun for?" John Wesley asked. "Watcha gonna do with that gun?"

"Lady," the man said to the children's mother, "would you mind calling them children to sit down by you? Children make me nervous. I want all you all to sit down right together there where you're at."

"What are you telling US what to do for?" June Star asked.

Behind them the line of woods gaped like a dark open mouth. "Come here," said 80
their mother.

"Look here now," Bailey began suddenly, "we're in a predicament! We're in . . ."

The grandmother shrieked. She scrambled to her feet and stood staring. "You're The Misfit!" she said. "I recognized you at once!"

"Yes'm," the man said, smiling slightly as if he were pleased in spite of himself to be known, "but it would have been better for all of you, lady, if you hadn't of reckernized me."

Bailey turned his head sharply and said something to his mother that shocked even the children. The old lady began to cry and The Misfit reddened.

"Lady," he said, "don't you get upset. Sometimes a man says things he don't mean. 85
I don't reckon he meant to talk to you thataway."

"You wouldn't shoot a lady, would you?" the grandmother said and removed a clean handkerchief from her cuff and began to slap at her eyes with it.

The Misfit pointed the toe of his shoe into the ground and made a little hole and then covered it up again. "I would hate to have to," he said.

"Listen," the grandmother almost screamed, "I know you're a good man. You don't look a bit like you have common blood. I know you must come from nice people!"

"Yes mam," he said, "finest people in the world." When he smiled he showed a row of strong white teeth. "God never made a finer woman than my mother and my daddy's heart was pure gold," he said. The boy with the red sweat shirt had come around behind them and was standing with his gun at his hip. The Misfit squatted down on the ground. "Watch them children, Bobby Lee," he said. "You know they make me nervous." He looked at the six of them huddled together in front of him and he seemed to be embarrassed as if he couldn't think of anything to say. "Ain't a cloud in the sky," he remarked, looking up at it. "Don't see no sun but don't see no cloud neither."

90 "Yes, it's a beautiful day," said the grandmother. "Listen," she said, "you shouldn't call yourself The Misfit because I know you're a good man at heart. I can just look at you and tell."

"Hush!" Bailey yelled. "Hush! Everybody shut up and let me handle this!" He was squatting in the position of a runner about to sprint forward but he didn't move.

"I pre-chate that, lady," The Misfit said and drew a little circle in the ground with the butt of his gun.

"It'll take a half a hour to fix this here car," Hiram called, looking over the raised hood of it.

"Well, first you and Bobby Lee get him and that little boy to step over yonder with you," The Misfit said, pointing to Bailey and John Wesley. "The boys want to ast you something," he said to Bailey. "Would you mind stepping back in them woods there with them?"

95 "Listen," Bailey began, "we're in a terrible predicament! Nobody realizes what this is," and his voice cracked. His eyes were as blue and intense as the parrots in his shirt and he remained perfectly still.

The grandmother reached up to adjust her hat brim as if she were going to the woods with him but it came off in her hand. She stood staring at it and after a second she let it fall on the ground. Hiram pulled Bailey up by the arm as if he were assisting an old man. John Wesley caught hold of his father's hand and Bobby Lee followed. They went off toward the woods and just as they reached the dark edge, Bailey turned and supporting himself against a gray naked pine trunk, he shouted, "I'll be back in a minute, Mamma, wait on me!"

"Come back this instant!" his mother shrilled but they all disappeared into the woods.

"Bailey Boy!" the grandmother called in a tragic voice but she found she was looking at The Misfit squatting on the ground in front of her. "I just know you're a good man," she said desperately. "You're not a bit common!"

"Nome, I ain't a good man," The Misfit said after a second as if he had considered her statement carefully, "but I ain't the worst in the world neither. My daddy said I was a different breed of dog from my brothers and sisters. 'You know,' Daddy said, 'it's some that can live their whole life out without asking about it and it's others has to know why it is, and this boy is one of the latters. He's going to be into everything!'" He put on his black hat and looked up suddenly and then away deep into the woods as if he were embarrassed again. "I'm sorry I don't have on a shirt before you ladies," he said, hunching his shoulders slightly. "We buried our clothes that we had on when we escaped and we're just making do until we can get better. We borrowed these from some folks we met," he explained.

"That's perfectly all right," the grandmother said. "Maybe Bailey has an extra 100
shirt in his suitcase."

"I'll look and see terrectly," The Misfit said.

"Where are they taking him?" the children's mother screamed.

"Daddy was a card himself," The Misfit said. "You couldn't put anything over on him. He never got in trouble with the Authorities though. Just had the knack of handling them."

"You could be honest too if you'd only try," said the grandmother. "Think how wonderful it would be to settle down and live a comfortable life and not have to think about somebody chasing you all the time."

The Misfit kept scratching in the ground with the butt of his gun as if he were 105
thinking about it. "Yes'm, somebody is always after you," he murmured.

The grandmother noticed how thin his shoulder blades were just behind his hat because she was standing up looking down on him. "Do you ever pray?" she asked.

He shook his head. All she saw was the black hat wiggle between his shoulder blades. "Nome," he said.

There was a pistol shot from the woods, followed closely by another. Then silence. The old lady's head jerked around. She could hear the wind move through the tree tops like a long satisfied insuck of breath. "Bailey Boy!" she called.

"I was a gospel singer for a while," The Misfit said. "I been most everything. Been in the arm service, both land and sea, at home and abroad, been twict married, been an undertaker, been with the railroads, plowed Mother Earth, been in a tornado, seen a man burnt alive oncet," and he looked up at the children's mother and the little girl who were sitting close together, their faces white and their eyes glassy; "I even seen a woman flogged," he said.

"Pray, pray," the grandmother began, "pray, pray . . ." 110

"I never was a bad boy that I remember of," The Misfit said in an almost dreamy voice, "but somewheres along the line I done something wrong and got sent to the penitentiary. I was buried alive," and he looked up and held her attention to him by a steady stare.

"That's when you should have started to pray," she said. "What did you do to get sent to the penitentiary that first time?"

"Turn to the right, it was a wall," The Misfit said, looking up again at the cloudless sky. "Turn to the left, it was a wall. Look up it was a ceiling, look down it was a floor. I forget what I done, lady. I set there and set there, trying to remember what it was I done and I ain't recalled it to this day. Oncet in a while, I would think it was coming to me, but it never come."

"Maybe they put you in by mistake," the old lady said vaguely.

"Nome," he said. "It wasn't no mistake. They had the papers on me."

"You must have stolen something," she said.

The Misfit sneered slightly. "Nobody had nothing I wanted," he said. "It was a head-doctor at the penitentiary said what I had done was kill my daddy but I known that for a lie. My daddy died in nineteen ought nineteen of the epidemic flu and I never had a thing to do with it. He was buried in the Mount Hopewell Baptist churchyard and you can go there and see for yourself."

"If you would pray," the old lady said, "Jesus would help you."

"That's right," The Misfit said.

"Well then, why don't you pray?" she asked trembling with delight suddenly.

"I don't want no hep," he said. "I'm doing all right by myself."

Bobby Lee and Hiram came ambling back from the woods. Bobby Lee was dragging a yellow shirt with bright blue parrots in it.

"Thow me that shirt, Bobby Lee," The Misfit said. The shirt came flying at him and landed on his shoulder and he put it on. The grandmother couldn't name what the shirt reminded her of. "No, lady," The Misfit said while he was buttoning it up, "I found out the crime don't matter. You can do one thing or you can do another, kill a man or take a tire off his car, because sooner or later you're going to forget what it was you done and just be punished for it."

The children's mother had begun to make heaving noises as if she couldn't get her breath. "Lady," he asked, "would you and that little girl like to step off yonder with Bobby Lee and Hiram and join your husband?"

"Yes, thank you," the mother said faintly. Her left arm dangled helplessly and she was holding the baby, who had gone to sleep, in the other. "Hep that lady up, Hiram," The Misfit said as she struggled to climb out of the ditch, "and Bobby Lee, you hold onto that little girl's hand."

"I don't want to hold hands with him," June Star said. "He reminds me of a pig."

The fat boy blushed and laughed and caught her by the arm and pulled her off into the woods after Hiram and her mother.

Alone with The Misfit, the grandmother found that she had lost her voice. There was not a cloud in the sky nor any sun. There was nothing around her but woods. She wanted to tell him that he must pray. She opened and closed her mouth several times before anything came out. Finally she found herself saying, "Jesus, Jesus," meaning, Jesus will help you, but the way she was saying it, it sounded as if she might be cursing.

"Yes'm," The Misfit said as if he agreed. "Jesus thown everything off balance. It was the same case with Him as with me except He hadn't committed any crime and they could prove I had committed one because they had the papers on me. Of course," he said, "they never shown me my papers. That's why I sign myself now. I said long ago, you get you a signature and sign everything you do and keep a copy of it. Then you'll know what you done and you can hold up the crime to the punishment and see do they match and in the end you'll have something to prove you ain't been treated right. I call myself The Misfit," he said, "because I can't make what all I done wrong fit what all I gone through in punishment."

130 There was a piercing scream from the woods, followed closely by a pistol report. "Does it seem right to you, lady, that one is punished a heap and another ain't punished at all?"

"Jesus!" the old lady cried. "You've got good blood! I know you wouldn't shoot a lady! I know you come from nice people! Pray! Jesus, you ought not to shoot a lady. I'll give you all the money I've got!"

"Lady," The Misfit said, looking beyond her far into the woods, "there never was a body that give the undertaker a tip."

There were two more pistol reports and the grandmother raised her head like a parched old turkey hen crying for water and called, "Bailey Boy, Bailey Boy!" as if her heart would break.

"Jesus was the only One that ever raised the dead," The Misfit continued, "and He shouldn't have done it. He thown everything off balance. If He did what He said, then it's nothing for you to do but thow away everything and follow Him, and if He didn't, then it's nothing for you to do but enjoy the few minutes you got left the best way you can—by killing somebody or burning down his house or doing some other meanness to him. No pleasure but meanness," he said and his voice became almost a snarl.

135 "Maybe He didn't raise the dead," the old lady mumbled, not knowing what she was saying and feeling so dizzy that she sank down in the ditch with her legs twisted under her.

"I wasn't there so I can't say He didn't," The Misfit said. "I wisht I had of been there," he said, hitting the ground with his fist. "It ain't right I wasn't there because if I had of been there I would of known. Listen, lady," he said in a high voice, "if I had of been there I would of known and I wouldn't be like I am now." His voice seemed about to crack and the grandmother's head cleared for an instant. She saw the man's face twisted close to her own as if he were going to cry and she murmured, "Why you're one of my babies. You're one of my own children!" She reached out and touched him on the shoulder. The Misfit sprang back as if a snake had bitten him and shot her three times through the chest. Then he put his gun down on the ground and took off his glasses and began to clean them.

Hiram and Bobby Lee returned from the woods and stood over the ditch, looking down at the grandmother who half sat and half lay in a puddle of blood with her legs crossed under her like a child's and her face smiling up at the cloudless sky.

Without his glasses, The Misfit's eyes were red-rimmed and pale and defenseless-looking. "Take her off and thow her where you thown the others," he said, picking up the cat that was rubbing itself against his leg.

"She was a talker, wasn't she?" Bobby Lee said, sliding down the ditch with a yodel.

140 "She would of been a good woman," The Misfit said, "if it had been somebody there to shoot her every minute of her life."

"Some fun!" Bobby Lee said.

"Shut up, Bobby Lee," The Misfit said. "It's no real pleasure in life."

Reading and Reacting

1. How are the style and tone of the narrator's voice different from those of the characters? What, if anything, is the significance of this difference?
2. The figures of speech used in this story sometimes create unflattering, even grotesque, pictures of the characters. Find several examples of such negative figures of speech. Why do you think O'Connor uses them?
3. What does the grandmother's use of the words *pickaninny* and *nigger* reveal about her? How are readers expected to reconcile this language with her very proper appearance and her preoccupation with manners? How does her use of these words affect your reaction to her?
4. Explain the **irony** in this statement: "In case of an accident, anyone seeing her dead on the highway would know at once that she was a lady" (par. 12).
5. How does The Misfit's dialect characterize him?
6. What does the **allusion** to *Gone with the Wind* (par. 24) contribute to the story?
7. How do the style and tone of the two-paragraph description of the three men in the car (pars. 71–72) help to prepare readers for the events that follow?
8. When The Misfit tells the grandmother about his life, his language takes on a measured, rhythmic quality: "Been in the arm service, both land and sea, at home and abroad, been twict married, been an undertaker, been with the railroads, plowed Mother Earth, been in a tornado, seen a man burnt alive oncet . . ." (par. 109). Find other examples of rhythmic repetition and parallelism in this character's speech. How does this style help to develop The Misfit's character?
9. **JOURNAL ENTRY** Why do you think the grandmother tells The Misfit that she recognizes him? Why does she fail to realize the danger of her remark?
10. **CRITICAL PERSPECTIVE** In his 2002 essay "Light and Shadow: Religious Grace in Two Stories by Flannery O'Connor," David Allen Cook writes:

> The literary works of Flannery O'Connor often contend that religious belief can only be consummated by direct confrontation with evil, and for those uncommitted and unprepared, tragedy seems inevitable. For O'Connor's religious "pretenders," a moment of religious grace—a revelation of Truth—often does come, but at a devastating price. In . . . "A Good Man Is Hard to Find," we are presented with main characters that experience a deep epiphany after being spiritually challenged by the darker side of human nature.

In this story, who are the religious "pretenders," and who has true faith? What is the price of achieving a moment of religious grace? What role does violence play in this equation?

Related Works: "Accident" (p. 181), "Incarnations of Burned Children" (p. 192), "The Lottery" (p. 509), "Where Are You Going, Where Have You Been?" (p. 617), "Everything That Rises Must Converge" (p. 749), "The Tell-Tale Heart" (p. 760), *The Glass Menagerie* (p. 1961)

Source: ©The Granger Collection, New York

CHARLOTTE PERKINS GILMAN (1860–1935) was a prominent feminist and social thinker at the turn of the century. Her essays, lectures, and nonfiction works—such as *Women and Economics* (1898), *Concerning Children* (1900), and *The Man-Made World* (1911)—are forceful statements of Gilman's opinions on women's need for economic independence and social equality. Gilman is probably best known for three utopian feminist novels: *Moving the Mountain* (1911), *Herland* (1915; unpublished until 1978), and *With Her in Ourland* (1916). Her works are full of humor and satire. In *Herland*, for instance, a male sociologist (wandering in by accident from the outside world) is chagrined to find that the women of "Herland" want him as a friend, not a lover.

Although "The Yellow Wallpaper" (1982) is not typical of Gilman's other fiction, it is considered her artistic masterpiece. The terse, clinical precision of the writing, conveying the tightly wound and distraught mental state of the narrator, is particularly chilling when it is read with a knowledge of Gilman's personal history. In the 1880s, she met and married a young artist, Charles Walter Stetson. Following the birth of their daughter, she grew increasingly depressed and turned to a noted Philadelphia neurologist for help. Following the traditions of the time, he prescribed complete bed rest and mental inactivity—a treatment that, Gilman said later, drove her "so near the borderline of utter mental ruin that I could see over." "The Yellow Wallpaper" is not simply a psychological study. Like most of Gilman's work, it makes a point—in this case, about the dangers of women's utter dependence on a male interpretation of their needs.

Cultural Context Recent research indicates that one out of every ten new mothers becomes seriously depressed within six months after childbirth. This condition is known as postpartum depression, and its symptoms include severe feelings of sadness or emptiness, withdrawal from family and friends, a strong sense of failure or inadequacy, intense concern (or lack of concern) about the baby, and, in more serious cases, thoughts about suicide or fears of harming the baby. Today's treatments include medication and psychotherapy, but at the time of this story, the standard treatment was a "rest cure," in which the patient was placed in isolation and kept from distractions that were believed to be dangerous. For many patients (as for the narrator of this story), this "cure" was worse than the disease itself.

The Yellow Wallpaper (1892)

It is very seldom that mere ordinary people like John and myself secure ancestral halls for the summer.

A colonial mansion, a hereditary estate, I would say a haunted house, and reach the height of romantic felicity—but that would be asking too much of fate!

Still I will proudly declare that there is something queer about it.

Else, why should it be let so cheaply? And why have stood so long untenanted?

John laughs at me, of course, but one expects that in marriage. 5

John is practical in the extreme. He has no patience with faith, an intense horror of superstition, and he scoffs openly at any talk of things not to be felt and seen and put down in figures.

John is a physician, and *perhaps*—(I would not say it to a living soul, of course, but this is dead paper and a great relief to my mind—) *perhaps* that is one reason I do not get well faster.

You see he does not believe I am sick!

And what can one do?

If a physician of high standing, and one's own husband, assures friends and relatives that there is really nothing the matter with one but temporary nervous depression—a slight hysterical tendency—what is one to do?

My brother is also a physician, and also of high standing, and he says the same thing.

So I take phosphates or phosphites°—whichever it is, and tonics, and journeys, and air, and exercise, and am absolutely forbidden to "work" until I am well again.

Personally, I disagree with their ideas.

Personally, I believe that congenial work, with excitement and change, would do me good.

But what is one to do?

I did write for a while in spite of them; but it *does* exhaust me a good deal—having to be so sly about it, or else meet with heavy opposition.

I sometimes fancy that in my condition if I had less opposition and more society and stimulus—but John says the very worst thing I can do is to think about my condition, and I confess it always makes me feel bad.

So I will let it alone and talk about the house.

The most beautiful place! It is quite alone, standing well back from the road, quite three miles from the village. It makes me think of English places that you read about, for there are hedges and walls and gates that lock, and lots of separate little houses for the gardeners and people.

There is a *delicious* garden! I never saw such a garden—large and shady, full of box-bordered paths, and lined with long grape-covered arbors with seats under them.

There were greenhouses, too, but they are all broken now.

There was some legal trouble, I believe, something about the heirs and co-heirs; anyhow, the place has been empty for years.

That spoils my ghostliness, I am afraid, but I don't care—there is something strange about the house—I can feel it.

I even said so to John one moonlight evening, but he said what I felt was a *draught*, and shut the window.

I get unreasonably angry with John sometimes. I'm sure I never used to be so sensitive. I think it is due to this nervous condition.

But John says if I feel so, I shall neglect proper self-control; so I take pains to control myself—before him, at least, and that makes me very tired.

I don't like our room a bit. I wanted one downstairs that opened on the piazza and had roses all over the window, and such pretty old-fashioned chintz hangings! But John would not hear of it.

He said there was only one window and not room for two beds, and no near room for him if he took another.

---

phosphates or phosphites: Both terms refer to salts of phosphorous acid. The narrator, however, means "phosphate," a carbonated beverage of water, flavoring, and a small amount of phosphoric acid.

He is very careful and loving, and hardly lets me stir without special direction.

I have a schedule prescription for each hour in the day; he takes all care from me, 30
and so I feel basely ungrateful not to value it more.

He said we came here solely on my account, that I was to have perfect rest and all the air I could get. "Your exercise depends on your strength, my dear," said he, "and your food somewhat on your appetite; but air you can absorb all the time." So we took the nursery at the top of the house.

It is a big, airy room, the whole floor nearly, with windows that look all ways, and air and sunshine galore. It was nursery first and then playroom and gymnasium, I should judge; for the windows are barred for little children, and there are rings and things in the walls.

The paint and paper look as if a boys' school had used it. It is stripped off—the paper—in great patches all around the head of my bed, about as far as I can reach, and in a great place on the other side of the room low down. I never saw a worse paper in my life.

One of those sprawling flamboyant patterns committing every artistic sin.

It is dull enough to confuse the eye in following, pronounced enough to con- 35
stantly irritate and provoke study, and when you follow the lame uncertain curves for a little distance they suddenly commit suicide—plunge off at outrageous angles, destroy themselves in unheard of contradictions.

The color is repellent, almost revolting; a smouldering unclean yellow, strangely faded by the slow-turning sunlight.

It is a dull yet lurid orange in some places, a sickly sulphur tint in others.

No wonder the children hated it! I should hate it myself if I had to live in this room long.

There comes John, and I must put this away,—he hates to have me write a word.

* * *

We have been here two weeks, and I haven't felt like writing before, since that 40
first day.

I am sitting by the window now, up in this atrocious nursery, and there is nothing to hinder my writing as much as I please, save lack of strength.

John is away all day, and even some nights when his cases are serious.

I am glad my case is not serious!

But these nervous troubles are dreadfully depressing.

John does not know how much I really suffer. He knows there is no *reason* to 45
suffer, and that satisfies him.

Of course it is only nervousness. It does weigh on me so not to do my duty in any way!

I meant to be such a help to John, such a real rest and comfort, and here I am a comparative burden already!

Nobody would believe what an effort it is to do what little I am able,— to dress and entertain, and order things.

It is fortunate Mary is so good with the baby. Such a dear baby!

And yet I *cannot* be with him, it makes me so nervous.

I suppose John never was nervous in his life. He laughs at me so about this wallpaper!

At first he meant to repaper the room, but afterwards he said that I was letting it get the better of me, and that nothing was worse for a nervous patient than to give way to such fancies.

He said that after the wallpaper was changed it would be the heavy bedstead, and then the barred windows, and then that gate at the head of the stairs, and so on.

"You know the place is doing you good," he said, "and really, dear, I don't care to renovate the house just for a three months' rental."

"Then do let us go downstairs," I said, "there are such pretty rooms there."

Then he took me in his arms and called me a blessed little goose, and said he would go down cellar, if I wished, and have it whitewashed into the bargain.

But he is right enough about the beds and windows and things.

It is an airy and comfortable room as any one need wish, and, of course, I would not be so silly as to make him uncomfortable just for a whim.

I'm really getting quite fond of the big room, all but that horrid paper.

Out of one window I can see the garden, those mysterious deep-shaded arbors, the riotous old-fashioned flowers, and bushes and gnarly trees.

Out of another I get a lovely view of the bay and a little private wharf belonging to the estate. There is a beautiful shaded lane that runs down there from the house. I always fancy I see people walking in these numerous paths and arbors, but John has cautioned me not to give way to fancy in the least. He says that with my imaginative power and habit of story-making, a nervous weakness like mine is sure to lead to all manner of excited fancies, and that I ought to use my will and good sense to check the tendency. So I try.

I think sometimes that if I were only well enough to write a little it would relieve the press of ideas and rest me.

But I find I get pretty tired when I try.

It is so discouraging not to have any advice and companionship about my work. When I get really well, John says we will ask Cousin Henry and Julia down for a long visit; but he says he would as soon put fireworks in my pillow-case as to let me have those stimulating people about now.

I wish I could get well faster.

But I must not think about that. This paper looks to me as if it *knew* what a vicious influence it had!

There is a recurrent spot where the pattern lolls like a broken neck and two bulbous eyes stare at you upside down.

I get positively angry with the impertinence of it and the everlastingness. Up and down and sideways they crawl, and those absurd, unblinking eyes are everywhere. There is one place where two breadths didn't match, and the eyes go all up and down the line, one a little higher than the other.

I never saw so much expression in an inanimate thing before, and we all know how much expression they have! I used to lie awake as a child and get more entertainment and terror out of blank walls and plain furniture than most children could find in a toy-store.

I remember what a kindly wink the knobs of our big, old bureau used to have, and there was one chair that always seemed like a strong friend.

I used to feel that if any of the other things looked too fierce I could always hop into that chair and be safe.

The furniture in this room is no worse than inharmonious, however, for we had to bring it all from downstairs. I suppose when this was used as a playroom they had to take the nursery things out, and no wonder! I never saw such ravages as the children have made here.

The wallpaper, as I said before, is torn off in spots, and it sticketh closer than a brother—they must have had perseverance as well as hatred.

Then the floor is scratched and gouged and splintered, the plaster itself is dug out here and there, and this great heavy bed which is all we found in the room, looks as if it had been through the wars.

But I don't mind it a bit—only the paper.

There comes John's sister. Such a dear girl as she is, and so careful of me! I must not let her find me writing.

She is a perfect and enthusiastic housekeeper, and hopes for no better profession. I verily believe she thinks it is the writing which made me sick!

But I can write when she is out, and see her a long way off from these windows.

There is one that commands the road, a lovely shaded winding road, and one that just looks off over the country. A lovely country, too, full of great elms and velvet meadows.

This wallpaper has a kind of sub-pattern in a different shade, a particularly irritating one, for you can only see it in certain lights, and not clearly then.

But in the places where it isn't faded and where the sun is just so—I can see a strange, provoking, formless sort of figure, that seems to skulk about behind that silly and conspicuous front design.

There's sister on the stairs!

* * *

Well, the Fourth of July is over! The people are all gone and I am tired out. John thought it might do me good to see a little company, so we just had mother and Nellie and the children down for a week.

Of course I didn't do a thing. Jennie sees to everything now.

But it tired me all the same.

John says if I don't pick up faster he shall send me to Weir Mitchell° in the fall.

But I don't want to go there at all. I had a friend who was in his hands once, and she says he is just like John and my brother, only more so!

Besides, it is such an undertaking to go so far.

Weir Mitchell: Silas Weir Mitchell (1829–1914), a Philadelphia neurologist-psychologist who introduced the "rest cure" for nervous diseases.

I don't feel as if it was worth while to turn my hand over for anything, and I'm getting dreadfully fretful and querulous.

I cry at nothing, and cry most of the time.

Of course I don't when John is here, or anybody else, but when I am alone.

And I am alone a good deal just now. John is kept in town very often by serious cases, and Jennie is good and lets me alone when I want her to.

So I walk a little in the garden or down that lovely lane, sit on the porch under the roses, and lie down up here a good deal.

I'm getting really fond of the room in spite of the wallpaper. Perhaps *because* of the wallpaper.

It dwells in my mind so!

I lie here on this great immovable bed—it is nailed down, I believe—and follow that pattern about by the hour. It is as good as gymnastics, I assure you. I start, we'll say, at the bottom, down in the corner over there where it has not been touched, and I determine for the thousandth time that I *will* follow that pointless pattern to some sort of a conclusion.

I know a little of the principle of design, and I know this thing was not arranged on any laws of radiation, or alternation, or repetition, or symmetry, or anything else that I ever heard of.

It is repeated, of course, by the breadths, but not otherwise.

Looked at in one way each breadth stands alone, the bloated curves and flourishes—a kind of "debased Romanesque" with *delirium tremens*° go waddling up and down in isolated columns of fatuity.

But, on the other hand, they connect diagonally, and the sprawling outlines run off in great slanting waves of optic horror, like a lot of wallowing seaweeds in full chase.

The whole thing goes horizontally, too, at least it seems so, and I exhaust myself in trying to distinguish the order of its going in that direction.

They have used a horizontal breadth for a frieze, and that adds wonderfully to the confusion.

There is one end of the room where it is almost intact, and there, when the crosslights fade and the low sun shines directly upon it, I can almost fancy radiation after all,—the interminable grotesques seems to form around a common center and rush off in headlong plunges of equal distraction.

It makes me tired to follow it. I will take a nap I guess.

I don't know why I should write this.

I don't want to.

I don't feel able.

And I know John would think it absurd. But I *must* say what I feel and think in some way—it is such a relief!

But the effort is getting to be greater than the relief.

Half the time now I am awfully lazy, and lie down ever so much.

---

delirium tremens: Mental confusion caused by alcohol poisoning and characterized by physical tremors and hallucinations.

John says I mustn't lose my strength, and has me take cod liver oil and lots of tonics and things, to say nothing of ale and wine and rare meat.

Dear John! He loves me very dearly, and hates to have me sick. I tried to have a real earnest reasonable talk with him the other day, and tell him how I wish he would let me go and make a visit to Cousin Henry and Julia.

But he said I wasn't able to go, nor able to stand it after I got there; and I did not make out a very good case for myself, for I was crying before I had finished.

It is getting to be a great effort for me to think straight. Just this nervous weakness I suppose.

And dear John gathered me up in his arms, and just carried me upstairs and laid 115
me on the bed, and sat by me and read to me till it tired my head.

He said I was his darling and his comfort and all he had, and that I must take care of myself for his sake, and keep well.

He says no one but myself can help me out of it, that I must use my will and self-control and not let any silly fancies run away with me.

There's one comfort, the baby is well and happy, and does not have to occupy this nursery with the horrid wallpaper.

If we had not used it, that blessed child would have! What a fortunate escape! Why, I wouldn't have a child of mine, an impressionable little thing, live in such a room for worlds.

I never thought of it before, but it is lucky that John kept me here after all, 120
I can stand it so much easier than a baby, you see.

Of course I never mention it to them any more—I am too wise,—but I keep watch of it all the same.

There are things in that paper that nobody knows but me, or ever will.

Behind that outside pattern the dim shapes get clearer every day.

It is always the same shape, only very numerous.

And it is like a woman stooping down and creeping about behind that pattern. I 125
don't like it a bit. I wonder—I begin to think—I wish John would take me away from here!

It is so hard to talk with John about my case, because he is so wise, and because he loves me so.

But I tried it last night.

It was moonlight. The moon shines in all around just as the sun does.

I hate to see it sometimes, it creeps so slowly, and always comes in by one window or another.

John was asleep and I hated to waken him, so I kept still and watched the moon- 130
light on that undulating wallpaper till I felt creepy.

The faint figure behind seemed to shake the pattern, just as if she wanted to get out.

I got up softly and went to feel and see if the paper *did* move, and when I came back John was awake.

"What is it, little girl?" he said. "Don't go walking about like that—you'll get cold."

I thought it was a good time to talk, so I told him that I really was not gaining here, and that I wished he would take me away.

135 "Why, darling!" said he, "our lease will be up in three weeks, and I can't see how to leave before.

"The repairs are not done at home, and I cannot possibly leave town just now. Of course if you were in any danger, I could and would, but you really are better, dear, whether you can see it or not. I am a doctor, dear, and I know. You are gaining flesh and color, your appetite is better, I feel really much easier about you."

"I don't weigh a bit more," said I, "nor as much; and my appetite may be better in the evening when you are here, but it is worse in the morning when you are away!"

"Bless her little heart!" said he with a big hug, "she shall be as sick as she pleases! But now let's improve the shining hours by going to sleep, and talk about it in the morning!"

"And you won't go away?" I asked gloomily.

140 "Why, how can I, dear? It is only three weeks more and then we will take a nice little trip of a few days while Jennie is getting the house ready. Really dear you are better!"

"Better in body perhaps—" I began, and stopped short, for he sat up straight and looked at me with such a stern, reproachful look that I could not say another word.

"My darling," said he, "I beg of you, for my sake and for our child's sake, as well as for your own, that you will never for one instant let that idea enter your mind! There is nothing so dangerous, so fascinating, to a temperament like yours. It is a false and foolish fancy. Can you not trust me as a physician when I tell you so?"

So of course I said no more on that score, and we went to sleep before long. He thought I was asleep first, but I wasn't, and lay there for hours trying to decide whether that front pattern and the back pattern really did move together or separately.

On a pattern like this, by daylight, there is a lack of sequence, a defiance of law, that is a constant irritant to a normal mind.

145 The color is hideous enough, and unreliable enough, and infuriating enough, but the pattern is torturing.

You think you have mastered it, but just as you get well underway in following, it turns back-somersault and there you are. It slaps you in the face, knocks you down, and tramples upon you. It is like a bad dream.

The outside pattern is a florid arabesque, reminding one of a fungus. If you can imagine a toadstool in joints, an interminable string of toadstools, budding and sprouting in endless convolutions—why, that is something like it.

That is, sometimes!

There is one marked peculiarity about this paper, a thing nobody seems to notice but myself, and that is that it changes as the light changes.

150 When the sun shoots in through the east window—I always watch for that first long, straight ray—it changes so quickly that I never can quite believe it.

That is why I watch it always.

By moonlight—the moon shines in all night when there is a moon—I wouldn't know it was the same paper.

At night in any kind of light, in twilight, candlelight, lamplight, and worst of all by moonlight, it becomes bars! The outside pattern I mean, and the woman behind it is as plain as can be.

I didn't realize for a long time what the thing was that showed behind, that dim sub-pattern, but now I am quite sure it is a woman.

155 By daylight she is subdued, quiet. I fancy it is the pattern that keeps her so still. It is so puzzling. It keeps me quiet by the hour.

I lie down ever so much now. John says it is good for me, and to sleep all I can.

Indeed he started the habit by making me lie down for an hour after each meal.

It is a very bad habit I am convinced, for you see I don't sleep.

And that cultivates deceit, for I don't tell them I'm awake—O no!

160 The fact is I am getting a little afraid of John.

He seems very queer sometimes, and even Jennie has an inexplicable look.

It strikes me occasionally, just as a scientific hypothesis,—that perhaps it is the paper!

I have watched John when he did not know I was looking, and come into the room suddenly on the most innocent excuses, and I've caught him several times *looking at the paper!* And Jennie too. I caught Jennie with her hand on it once.

She didn't know I was in the room, and when I asked her in a quiet, a very quiet voice, with the most restrained manner possible, what she was doing with the paper—she turned around as if she had been caught stealing, and looked quite angry—asked me why I should frighten her so!

165 Then she said that the paper stained everything it touched, that she had found yellow smooches on all my clothes and John's, and she wished we would be more careful!

Did not that sound innocent? But I know she was studying that pattern, and I am determined that nobody shall find it out but myself!

Life is very much more exciting now than it used to be. You see I have something more to expect, to look forward to, to watch. I really do eat better, and am more quiet than I was.

John is so pleased to see me improve! He laughed a little the other day, and said I seemed to be flourishing in spite of my wallpaper.

I turned it off with a laugh. I had no intention of telling him it was *because* of the wallpaper—he would make fun of me. He might even want to take me away.

170 I don't want to leave now until I have found it out. There is a week more, and I think that will be enough.

I'm feeling ever so much better! I don't sleep much at night, for it is so interesting to watch developments; but I sleep a good deal in the daytime.

In the daytime it is tiresome and perplexing.

There are always new shoots on the fungus, and new shades of yellow all over it. I cannot keep count of them, though I have tried conscientiously.

It is the strangest yellow, that wallpaper! It makes me think of all the yellow things I ever saw—not beautiful ones like buttercups, but old foul, bad yellow things.

But there is something else about that paper—the smell! I noticed it the moment we came into the room, but with so much air and sun it was not bad. Now we have had a week of fog and rain, and whether the windows are open or not, the smell is here.

It creeps all over the house.

I find it hovering in the dining-room, skulking in the parlor, hiding in the hall, lying in wait for me on the stairs.

It gets into my hair.

Even when I go to ride, if I turn my head suddenly and surprise it — there is that smell!

Such a peculiar odor, too! I have spent hours in trying to analyze it, to find what it smelled like.

It is not bad — at first, and very gentle, but quite the subtlest, most enduring odor I ever met.

In this damp weather it is awful, I wake up in the night and find it hanging over me.

It used to disturb me at first. I thought seriously of burning the house—to reach the smell.

But now I am used to it. The only thing I can think of that it is like is the *color* of the paper! A yellow smell.

There is a very funny mark on this wall, low down, near the mop-board. A streak that runs round the room. It goes behind every piece of furniture, except the bed, a long, straight, even *smooch,* as if it had been rubbed over and over.

I wonder how it was done and who did it, and what they did it for. Round and round and round—round and round and round!—it makes me dizzy!

I really have discovered something at last.

Through watching so much at night, when it changes so, I have finally found out.

The front pattern *does* move—and no wonder! The woman behind shakes it!

Sometimes I think there are a great many women behind, and sometimes only one, and she crawls around fast, and her crawling shakes it all over.

Then in the very bright spots she keeps still, and in the very shady spots she just takes hold of the bars and shakes them hard.

And she is all the time trying to climb through. But nobody could climb through that pattern—it strangles so; I think that is why it has so many heads.

They get through, and then the pattern strangles them off and turns them upside down, and makes their eyes white!

If those heads were covered or taken off it would not be half so bad.

I think that woman gets out in the daytime!

And I'll tell you why—privately—I've seen her!

I can see her out of every one of my windows!

It is the same woman, I know, for she is always creeping, and most women do not creep by daylight.

I see her in that long shaded lane, creeping up and down. I see her in those dark grape arbors, creeping all around the garden.

I see her on that long road under the trees, creeping along, and when a carriage comes she hides under the blackberry vines.

I don't blame her a bit. It must be very humiliating to be caught creeping by daylight!

I always lock the door when I creep by daylight. I can't do it at night, for I know John would suspect something at once.

And John is so queer now, that I don't want to irritate him. I wish he would take another room! Besides, I don't want anybody to get that woman out at night but myself.

I often wonder if I could see her out of all the windows at once.

But, turn as fast as I can, I can only see out of one at one time.

And though I always see her, she *may* be able to creep faster than I can turn!

I have watched her sometimes away off in the open country, creeping as fast as a cloud shadow in a high wind.

If only that top pattern could be gotten off from the under one! I mean to try it, little by little.

I have found out another funny thing, but I shan't tell it this time! It does not do to trust people too much.

There are only two more days to get this paper off, and I believe John is beginning to notice. I don't like the look in his eyes.

And I heard him ask Jennie a lot of professional questions about me. She had a very good report to give.

She said I slept a good deal in the daytime.

John knows I don't sleep very well at night, for all I'm so quiet!

He asked me all sorts of questions, too, and pretended to be very loving and kind.

As if I couldn't see through him!

Still, I don't wonder he acts so, sleeping under this paper for three months.

It only interests me, but I feel sure John and Jennie are secretly affected by it.

* * *

Hurrah! This is the last day, but it is enough. John is to stay in town over night, and won't be out until this evening.

Jennie wanted to sleep with me—the sly thing! But I told her I should undoubtedly rest better for a night all alone.

That was clever, for really I wasn't alone a bit! As soon as it was moon-light and that poor thing began to crawl and shake the pattern, I got up and ran to help her.

I pulled and she shook, I shook and she pulled, and before morning we had peeled off yards of that paper.

A strip about as high as my head and half around the room.

And then when the sun came and that awful pattern began to laugh at me, I declared I would finish it to-day!

We go away to-morrow, and they are moving all my furniture down again to leave things as they were before.

225 Jennie looked at the wall in amazement, but I told her merrily that I did it out of pure spite at the vicious thing.

She laughed and said she wouldn't mind doing it herself, but I must not get tired.

How she betrayed herself that time!

But I am here, and no person touches this paper but me,—not *alive!*

She tried to get me out of the room—it was too patent! But I said it was so quiet and empty and clean now that I believed I would lie down again and sleep all I could; and not to wake me even for dinner—I would call when I woke.

230 So now she is gone, and the servants are gone, and the things are gone, and there is nothing left but that great bedstead nailed down, with the canvas mattress we found on it.

We shall sleep downstairs to-night, and take the boat home tomorrow.

I quite enjoy the room, now it is bare again.

How those children did tear about here!

This bedstead is fairly gnawed!

235 But I must get to work.

I have locked the door and thrown the key down into the front path.

I don't want to go out, and I don't want to have anybody come in, till John comes.

I want to astonish him.

I've got a rope up here that even Jennie did not find. If that woman does get out, and tries to get away, I can tie her!

240 But I forgot I could not reach far without anything to stand on!

This bed will *not* move!

I tried to lift and push it until I was lame, and then I got so angry I bit off a little piece at one corner—but it hurt my teeth.

Then I peeled off all the paper I could reach standing on the floor. It sticks horribly and the pattern just enjoys it! All those strangled heads and bulbous eyes and waddling fungus growths just shriek with derision!

I am getting angry enough to do something desperate. To jump out of the window would be admirable exercise, but the bars are too strong even to try.

245 Besides I wouldn't do it. Of course not. I know well enough that a step like that is improper and might be misconstrued.

I don't like to *look* out of the windows even—there are so many of those creeping women, and they creep so fast.

I wonder if they come out of that wallpaper as I did?

But I am securely fastened now by my well-hidden rope—you don't get *me* out in the road there!

I suppose I shall have to get back behind the pattern when it comes night, and that is hard!

250 It is so pleasant to be out in this great room and creep around as I please!

I don't want to go outside. I won't, even if Jennie asks me to.

For outside you have to creep on the ground, and everything is green instead of yellow.

But here I can creep smoothly on the floor, and my shoulder just fits in that long smooch around the wall, so I cannot lose my way.

Why there's John at the door!

It is no use, young man, you can't open it! 255

How he does call and pound!

Now he's crying for an axe.

It would be a shame to break down that beautiful door!

"John dear!" said I in the gentlest voice, "the key is down by the front steps, under a plantain leaf!"

That silenced him for a few moments. 260

Then he said—very quietly indeed, "Open the door, my darling!"

"I can't," said I. "The key is down by the front door under a plantain leaf!"

And then I said it again, several times, very gently and slowly, and said it so often that he had to go and see, and he got it of course, and came in. He stopped short by the door.

"What is the matter?" he cried. "For God's sake, what are you doing!"

I kept on creeping just the same, but I looked at him over my shoulder. 265

"I've got out at last," said I, "in spite of you and Jane. And I've pulled off most of the paper, so you can't put me back!"

Now why should that man have fainted? But he did, and right across my path by the wall, so that I had to creep over him every time!

Reading and Reacting

1. The story's narrator, who has recently had a baby, is suffering from what her husband, a doctor, calls "temporary nervous depression—a slight hysterical tendency" (par. 10). How accurate is his diagnosis? Explain.
2. What do the following comments reveal about the narrator's situation: "John laughs at me, of course, but one expects that in marriage" (par. 5); "I must put this away,—he hates to have me write a word" (par. 39); "He laughs at me so about this wallpaper" (par. 51); "Then he took me in his arms and called me a blessed little goose" (par. 56)?
3. What is it about the house, the grounds, and her room that upsets the narrator?
4. What images and figures of speech does the narrator use to describe the wallpaper? To what extent do you think her descriptions are accurate? Which images do you think she sees, and which ones do you think she imagines?
5. How does the narrator's mood change as the story progresses? How does her language change?
6. How would you characterize the narrator's tone? Does she sound depressed? Delusional? Hysterical?

7. How do you explain the story's very short paragraphs? How do these short paragraphs help you to understand the narrator's mental state?
8. Study the story's punctuation—in particular, its use of dashes, question marks, and exclamation points. What does this use of punctuation contribute to the story?
9. **JOURNAL ENTRY** Do you think a present-day woman would respond differently to such advice from her husband or doctor? Explain.
10. **CRITICAL PERSPECTIVE** "The Yellow Wallpaper" was originally seen by some readers as a ghost story and was anthologized as such. More recently, critics have tended to interpret the story from a feminist perspective, focusing on the way in which the nameless narrator is victimized by the men around her and by the values of the Victorian society they uphold. In the essay "An Unnecessary Maze of Sign-Reading," Mary Jacobus concludes that the overwhelmingly feminist perspective of recent criticism, though certainly valuable and enlightening, has overlooked other promising critical possibilities—for example, "the Gothic and uncanny elements present in the text."

    If you were teaching "The Yellow Wallpaper," would you present it as a feminist story or as a chilling gothic ghost story? Do you think interpreting the story as a gothic horror tale precludes a feminist reading, or do you see the two interpretations as compatible?

Related Works: "The Story of an Hour" (p. 226), "The Disappearance" (p. 695), "Daddy" (p. 936), *Trifles* (p. 1319), *A Doll House* (p. 1402)

Source: ©AP Photo/David Pickoff

TIM O'BRIEN (1946–) is sometimes described as a writer whose books are on the short list of essential fiction about the Vietnam War. After graduating summa cum laude from Macalester College in 1968, O'Brien was immediately drafted into the United States Army and sent to Vietnam, where he served with the 198th Infantry Brigade. He was promoted to sergeant and awarded a Purple Heart after receiving a shrapnel wound in a battle near My Lai. In 1970, after his discharge from the army, he attended Harvard graduate school to study government. He worked as a reporter for the *Washington Post* before pursuing a full-time career as a writer.

O'Brien's plots focus on danger, violence, courage, endurance, despair, and other topics often associated with war fiction, but he treats these topics with an emphasis on the contemporary dilemmas faced by those who may be unwilling participants in an unpopular war. O'Brien calls *If I Die in a Combat Zone, Box Me Up and Ship Me Home* (1979) a memoir because it relates his war experiences as a naive young college graduate who suddenly finds himself facing bullets and land mines rather than sitting behind a desk. *Northern Lights* (1975) concentrates on the wilderness survival experiences of two brothers, one of whom has just returned from the Vietnam War. A fantastic daydream of an American soldier, *Going after Cacciato* (1978), won a National Book Award. *The Things They Carried* (1990) is a quasi-fictional collection of interrelated stories that deal with a single platoon. *The Vietnam in Me* (1994) emphasizes the destructive effects of war on a soldier, even after he has returned home, and *In the Lake of the Woods* (1994) tells a dramatic story of a couple missing in Minnesota. O'Brien's most recent books are *Tomcat in Love* (1998) and *July, July* (2002).

Cultural Context United States involvement in the Vietnam War lasted from the early 1960s until the mid 1970s. By the war's end, more than 47,000 Americans had been killed in action, nearly 11,000 had died of other causes, and more than 303,000 had been wounded. Estimates of South Vietnamese army casualties range from 185,000 to 225,000 killed and 500,000 to 570,000 wounded. The North Vietnamese and the Viet Cong, the guerrilla force that fought against South Vietnam and the United States, lost about 900,000 troops. In addition, more than 1 million North and South Vietnamese civilians were killed during the war. In 1976, North and South Vietnam reunified to form the Socialist Republic of Vietnam, which, due in large part to the Vietnamese occupation of Cambodia, continued to face domestic and international struggles through the late 1980s. Vietnamese troops finally withdrew from Cambodia in 1989.

The Things They Carried (1986)

First Lieutenant Jimmy Cross carried letters from a girl named Martha, a junior at Mount Sebastian College in New Jersey. They were not love letters, but Lieutenant Cross was hoping, so he kept them folded in plastic at the bottom of his rucksack. In the late afternoon, after a day's march, he would dig his foxhole, wash his hands under a canteen, unwrap the letters, hold them with the tips of his fingers, and spend the last hour of light pretending. He would imagine romantic camping trips into the White Mountains in New Hampshire. He would sometimes taste the envelope flaps, knowing her tongue had been there. More than anything, he wanted Martha to love him as he loved her, but the letters were mostly chatty, elusive on the matter of love. She was a virgin, he was almost sure. She was an English major at Mount Sebastian, and she wrote beautifully about her professors and roommates and midterm exams, about her respect for Chaucer and her great affection for Virginia Woolf. She often quoted lines of poetry; she never mentioned the war, except to say, Jimmy, take care of yourself. The letters weighed ten ounces. They were signed "Love, Martha," but Lieutenant Cross understood that "Love" was only a way of signing and did not mean what he sometimes pretended it meant. At dusk, he would carefully return the letters to his rucksack. Slowly, a bit distracted, he would get up and move among his men, checking the perimeter, then at full dark he would return to his hole and watch the night and wonder if Martha was a virgin.

The things they carried were largely determined by necessity. Among the necessities or near necessities were P-38 can openers, pocket knives, heat tabs, wrist watches, dog tags, mosquito repellent, chewing gum, candy, cigarettes, salt tablets, packets of Kool-Aid, lighters, matches, sewing kits, Military Payment Certificates, C rations, and two or three canteens of water. Together, these items weighed between fifteen and twenty pounds, depending upon a man's habits or rate of metabolism. Henry Dobbins, who was a big man, carried extra rations; he was especially fond of canned peaches in heavy syrup over pound cake. Dave Jensen, who practiced field hygiene, carried a toothbrush, dental floss, and several hotel-size bars of soap he'd stolen on R&R in Sydney, Australia. Ted Lavender, who was scared, carried tranquilizers until he was shot in the head outside the village of Than Khe in mid-April.

By necessity, and because it was SOP,° they all carried steel helmets that weighed five pounds including the liner and camouflage cover. They carried the standard fatigue jackets and trousers. Very few carried underwear. On their feet they carried jungle boots—2.1 pounds—and Dave Jensen carried three pairs of socks and a can of Dr. Scholl's foot powder as a precaution against trench foot. Until he was shot, Ted Lavender carried six or seven ounces of premium dope, which for him was a necessity. Mitchell Sanders, the RTO,° carried condoms. Norman Bowker carried a diary. Rat Kiley carried comic books. Kiowa, a devout Baptist, carried an illustrated New Testament that had been presented to him by his father, who taught Sunday school in Oklahoma City, Oklahoma. As a hedge against bad times, however, Kiowa also carried his grandmother's distrust of the white man, his grandfather's old hunting hatchet. Necessity dictated. Because the land was mined and booby-trapped, it was SOP for each man to carry a steel-centered, nylon-covered flak jacket, which weighed 6.7 pounds, but which on hot days seemed much heavier. Because you could die so quickly, each man carried at least one large compress bandage, usually in the helmet band for easy access. Because the nights were cold, and because the monsoons were wet, each carried a green plastic poncho that could be used as a raincoat or ground sheet or makeshift tent. With its quilted liner, the poncho weighed almost two pounds, but it was worth every ounce. In April, for instance, when Ted Lavender was shot, they used his poncho to wrap him up, then to carry him across the paddy, then to lift him into the chopper that took him away.

They were called legs or grunts.

To carry something was to "hump" it, as when Lieutenant Jimmy Cross humped his love for Martha up the hills and through the swamps. In its intransitive form, "to hump" meant "to walk," or "to march," but it implied burdens far beyond the intransitive.

5 Almost everyone humped photographs. In his wallet, Lieutenant Cross carried two photographs of Martha. The first was a Kodachrome snapshot signed "Love," though he knew better. She stood against a brick wall. Her eyes were gray and neutral, her lips slightly open as she stared straight-on at the camera. At night, sometimes, Lieutenant Cross wondered who had taken the picture, because he knew she had boyfriends, because he loved her so much, and because he could see the shadow of the picture taker spreading out against the brick wall. The second photograph had been clipped from the 1968 Mount Sebastian yearbook. It was an action shot—women's volleyball—and Martha was bent horizontal to the floor, reaching, the palms of her hands in sharp focus, the tongue taut, the expression frank and competitive. There was no visible sweat. She wore white gym shorts. Her legs, he thought, were almost certainly the legs of a virgin, dry and without hair, the left knee cocked and carrying her entire weight, which was just over one hundred pounds. Lieutenant Cross remembered touching that left knee. A dark theater, he remembered, and the movie was *Bonnie and Clyde*, and Martha wore a tweed skirt, and during the final scene, when he touched her knee, she turned and looked at him in a sad, sober way

SOP: Standard operating procedure.
RTO: Radio telephone operator.

that made him pull his hand back, but he would always remember the feel of the tweed skirt and the knee beneath it and the sound of the gunfire that killed Bonnie and Clyde, how embarrassing it was, how slow and oppressive. He remembered kissing her good night at the dorm door. Right then, he thought, he should've done something brave. He should've carried her up the stairs to her room and tied her to the bed and touched that left knee all night long. He should've risked it. Whenever he looked at the photographs, he thought of new things he should've done.

What they carried was partly a function of rank, partly of field specialty.

As a first lieutenant and platoon leader, Jimmy Cross carried a compass, maps, code books, binoculars, and a .45-caliber pistol that weighed 2.9 pounds fully loaded. He carried a strobe light and the responsibility for the lives of his men.

As an RTO, Mitchell Sanders carried the PRC-25 radio, a killer, twenty-six pounds with its battery.

As a medic, Rat Kiley carried a canvas satchel filled with morphine and plasma and malaria tablets and surgical tape and comic books and all the things a medic must carry, including M&M's for especially bad wounds, for a total weight of nearly twenty pounds.

As a big man, therefore a machine gunner, Henry Dobbins carried the M-60, 10
which weighed twenty-three pounds unloaded, but which was almost always loaded. In addition, Dobbins carried between ten and fifteen pounds of ammunition draped in belts across his chest and shoulders.

As PFCs or Spec 4s, most of them were common grunts and carried the standard M-16 gas-operated assault rifle. The weapon weighed 7.5 pounds unloaded, 8.2 pounds with its full twenty-round magazine. Depending on numerous factors, such as topography and psychology, the riflemen carried anywhere from twelve to twenty magazines, usually in cloth bandoliers, adding on another 8.4 pounds at minimum, fourteen pounds at maximum. When it was available, they also carried M-16 maintenance gear—rods and steel brushes and swabs and tubes of LSA oil—all of which weighed about a pound. Among the grunts, some carried the M-79 grenade launcher, 5.9 pounds unloaded, a reasonably light weapon except for the ammunition, which was heavy. A single round weighed ten ounces. The typical load was twenty-five rounds. But Ted Lavender, who was scared, carried thirty-four rounds when he was shot and killed outside Than Khe, and he went down under an exceptional burden, more than twenty pounds of ammunition, plus the flak jacket and helmet and rations and water and toilet paper and tranquilizers and all the rest, plus the unweighed fear. He was dead weight. There was no twitching or flopping. Kiowa, who saw it happen, said it was like watching a rock fall, or a big sandbag or something—just boom, then down—not like the movies where the dead guy rolls around and does fancy spins and goes ass over teakettle—not like that, Kiowa said, the poor bastard just flat-fuck fell. Boom. Down. Nothing else. It was a bright morning in mid-April. Lieutenant Cross felt the pain. He blamed himself. They stripped off Lavender's canteens and ammo, all the heavy things, and Rat Kiley said the obvious, the guy's dead, and Mitchell Sanders used his radio to report one U.S. KIA and to request a chopper. Then they wrapped Lavender in his poncho. They carried him out to a dry paddy, established security, and sat smoking the dead man's dope until the chopper came.

Lieutenant Cross kept to himself. He pictured Martha's smooth young face, thinking he loved her more than anything, more than his men, and now Ted Lavender was dead because he loved her so much and could not stop thinking about her. When the dust-off arrived, they carried Lavender aboard. Afterward they burned Than Khe. They marched until dusk, then dug their holes, and that night Kiowa kept explaining how you had to be there, how fast it was, how the poor guy just dropped like so much concrete. Boom-down, he said. Like cement.

* * *

In addition to the three standard weapons — the M-60, M-16, and M-79 — they carried whatever presented itself, or whatever seemed appropriate as a means of killing or staying alive. They carried catch-as-catch-can. At various times, in various situations, they carried M-14s and CAR-15s and Swedish Ks and grease guns and captured AK-47s and Chi-Coms and RPGs and Simonov carbines and black-market Uzis and .38-caliber Smith & Wesson handguns and 66 mm LAWs and shotguns and silencers and blackjacks and bayonets and C-4 plastic explosives. Lee Strunk carried a slingshot; a weapon of last resort, he called it. Mitchell Sanders carried brass knuckles. Kiowa carried his grandfather's feathered hatchet. Every third or fourth man carried a Claymore antipersonnel mine — 3.5 pounds with its firing device. They all carried fragmentation grenades — fourteen ounces each. They all carried at least one M-18 colored smoke grenade — twenty-four ounces. Some carried CS or tear-gas grenades. Some carried white-phosphorus grenades. They carried all they could bear, and then some, including a silent awe for the terrible power of the things they carried.

In the first week of April, before Lavender died, Lieutenant Jimmy Cross received a good-luck charm from Martha. It was a simple pebble, an ounce at most. Smooth to the touch, it was a milky-white color with flecks of orange and violet, oval-shaped, like a miniature egg. In the accompanying letter, Martha wrote that she had found the pebble on the Jersey shoreline, precisely where the land touched water at high tide, where things came together but also separated. It was this separate-but-together quality, she wrote, that had inspired her to pick up the pebble and to carry it in her breast pocket for several days, where it seemed weightless, and then to send it through the mail, by air, as a token of her truest feelings for him. Lieutenant Cross found this romantic. But he wondered what her truest feelings were, exactly, and what she meant by separate-but-together. He wondered how the tides and waves had come into play on that afternoon along the Jersey shoreline when Martha saw the pebble and bent down to rescue it from geology. He imagined bare feet. Martha was a poet, with the poet's sensibilities, and her feet would be brown and bare, the toenails unpainted, the eyes chilly and somber like the ocean in March, and though it was painful, he wondered who had been with her that afternoon. He imagined a pair of shadows moving along the strip of sand where things came together but also separated. It was phantom jealousy, he knew, but he couldn't help himself. He loved her so much. On the march, through the hot days of early April, he carried the pebble in his mouth, turning it with his tongue, tasting sea salts and moisture. His mind wandered. He had difficulty keeping his attention on the war. On occasion he would yell at his men to spread out the column, to keep their eyes open, but then he would slip away into daydreams, just pretending, walking barefoot along the Jersey shore, with Martha, carrying nothing. He would feel himself rising. Sun and waves and gentle winds, all love and lightness.

What they carried varied by mission.

When a mission took them to the mountains, they carried mosquito netting, 15
machetes, canvas tarps, and extra bug juice.

If a mission seemed especially hazardous, or if it involved a place they knew to be bad, they carried everything they could. In certain heavily mined AOs,° where the land was dense with Toe Poppers and Bouncing Betties, they took turns humping a twenty-eight-pound mine detector. With its headphones and big sensing plate, the equipment was a stress on the lower back and shoulders, awkward to handle, often useless because of the shrapnel in the earth, but they carried it anyway, partly for safety, partly for the illusion of safety.

On ambush, or other night missions, they carried peculiar little odds and ends. Kiowa always took along his New Testament and a pair of moccasins for silence. Dave Jensen carried night-sight vitamins high in carotin. Lee Strunk carried his slingshot; ammo, he claimed, would never be a problem. Rat Kiley carried brandy and M&M's. Until he was shot, Ted Lavender carried the starlight scope, which weighed 6.3 pounds with its aluminum carrying case. Henry Dobbins carried his girlfriend's panty-hose wrapped around his neck as a comforter. They all carried ghosts. When dark came, they would move out single file across the meadows and paddies to their ambush coordinates, where they would quietly set up the Claymores and lie down and spend the night waiting.

Other missions were more complicated and required special equipment. In mid-April, it was their mission to search out and destroy the elaborate tunnel complexes in the Than Khe area south of Chu Lai. To blow the tunnels, they carried one-pound blocks of pentrite high explosives, four blocks to a man, sixty-eight pounds in all. They carried wiring, detonators, and battery-powered clackers. Dave Jensen carried earplugs. Most often, before blowing the tunnels, they were ordered by higher command to search them, which was considered bad news, but by and large they just shrugged and carried out orders. Because he was a big man, Henry Dobbins was excused from tunnel duty. The others would draw numbers. Before Lavender died there were seventeen men in the platoon, and whoever drew the number seventeen would strip off his gear and crawl in head first with a flashlight and Lieutenant Cross's .45-caliber pistol. The rest of them would fan out as security. They would sit down or kneel, not facing the hole, listening to the ground beneath them, imagining cobwebs and ghosts, whatever was down there—the tunnel walls squeezing in—how the flashlight seemed impossibly heavy in the hand and how it was tunnel vision in the very strictest sense, compression in all ways, even time, and how you had to wiggle in—ass and elbows—a swallowed-up feeling—and how you found yourself worrying about odd things—will your flashlight go dead? Do rats carry rabies? If you screamed, how far would the sound carry? Would your buddies hear it? Would they have the courage to drag you out? In some respects, though not many, the waiting was worse than the tunnel itself. Imagination was a killer.

AOs: Areas of operation.

On April 16, when Lee Strunk drew the number seventeen, he laughed and muttered something and went down quickly. The morning was hot and very still. Not good, Kiowa said. He looked at the tunnel opening, then out across a dry paddy toward the village of Than Khe. Nothing moved. No clouds or birds or people. As they waited, the men smoked and drank Kool-Aid, not talking much, feeling sympathy for Lee Strunk but also feeling the luck of the draw. You win some, you lose some, said Mitchell Sanders, and sometimes you settle for a rain check. It was a tired line and no one laughed.

20 Henry Dobbins ate a tropical chocolate bar. Ted Lavender popped a tranquilizer and went off to pee.

After five minutes, Lieutenant Jimmy Cross moved to the tunnel, leaned down, and examined the darkness. Trouble, he thought—a cave-in maybe. And then suddenly, without willing it, he was thinking about Martha. The stresses and fractures, the quick collapse, the two of them buried alive under all that weight. Dense, crushing love. Kneeling, watching the hole, he tried to concentrate on Lee Strunk and the war, all the dangers, but his love was too much for him, he felt paralyzed, he wanted to sleep inside her lungs and breathe her blood and be smothered. He wanted her to be a virgin and not a virgin, all at once. He wanted to know her. Intimate secrets—why poetry? Why so sad? Why that grayness in her eyes? Why so alone? Not lonely, just alone—riding her bike across campus or sitting off by herself in the cafeteria. Even dancing, she danced alone—and it was the aloneness that filled him with love. He remembered telling her that one evening. How she nodded and looked away. And how, later, when he kissed her, she received the kiss without returning it, her eyes wide open, not afraid, not a virgin's eyes, just flat and uninvolved.

Lieutenant Cross gazed at the tunnel. But he was not there. He was buried with Martha under the white sand at the Jersey shore. They were pressed together, and the pebble in his mouth was her tongue. He was smiling. Vaguely, he was aware of how quiet the day was, the sullen paddies, yet he could not bring himself to worry about matters of security. He was beyond that. He was just a kid at war, in love. He was twenty-two years old. He couldn't help it.

A few moments later Lee Strunk crawled out of the tunnel. He came up grinning, filthy but alive. Lieutenant Cross nodded and closed his eyes while the others clapped Strunk on the back and made jokes about rising from the dead.

Worms, Rat Kiley said. Right out of the grave. Fuckin' zombie.

25 The men laughed. They all felt great relief.

Spook City, said Mitchell Sanders.

Lee Strunk made a funny ghost sound, a kind of moaning, yet very happy, and right then, when Strunk made that high happy moaning sound, when he went *Ahhooooo*, right then Ted Lavender was shot in the head on his way back from peeing. He lay with his mouth open. The teeth were broken. There was a swollen black bruise under his left eye. The cheekbone was gone. Oh shit, Rat Kiley said, the guy's dead. The guy's dead, he kept saying, which seemed profound—the guy's dead. I mean really.

The things they carried were determined to some extent by superstition. Lieutenant Cross carried his good-luck pebble. Dave Jensen carried a rabbit's foot. Norman Bowker, otherwise a very gentle person, carried a thumb that had been presented to him as a gift by Mitchell Sanders. The thumb was dark brown, rubbery to the touch, and weighed four ounces at most. It had been cut from a VC corpse, a boy of fifteen or sixteen. They'd found him at the bottom of an irrigation ditch, badly burned, flies in his mouth and eyes. The boy wore black shorts and sandals. At the time of his death he had been carrying a pouch of rice, a rifle, and three magazines of ammunition.

You want my opinion, Mitchell Sanders said, there's a definite moral here.

He put his hand on the dead boy's wrist. He was quiet for a time, as if counting a 30
pulse, then he patted the stomach, almost affectionately, and used Kiowa's hunting hatchet to remove the thumb.

Henry Dobbins asked what the moral was.

Moral?

You know. *Moral*.

Sanders wrapped the thumb in toilet paper and handed it across to Norman Bowker. There was no blood. Smiling, he kicked the boy's head, watched the flies scatter, and said, It's like with that old TV show—Paladin. Have gun, will travel.

Henry Dobbins thought about it. 35

Yeah, well, he finally said. I don't see no moral.

There it *is*, man.

Fuck off.

They carried USO stationery and pencils and pens. They carried Sterno, safety pins, trip flares, signal flares, spools of wire, razor blades, chewing tobacco, liberated joss sticks and statuettes of the smiling Buddha, candles, grease pencils, *The Stars and Stripes*, fingernail clippers, Psy Ops leaflets, bush hats, bolos, and much more. Twice a week, when the resupply choppers came in, they carried hot chow in green Mermite cans and large canvas bags filled with iced beer and soda pop. They carried plastic water containers, each with a two-gallon capacity. Mitchell Sanders carried a set of starched tiger fatigues for special occasions. Henry Dobbins carried Black Flag insecticide. Dave Jensen carried empty sandbags that could be filled at night for added protection. Lee Strunk carried tanning lotion. Some things they carried in common. Taking turns, they carried the big PRC-77 scrambler radio, which weighed thirty pounds with its battery. They shared the weight of memory. They took up what others could no longer bear. Often, they carried each other, the wounded or weak. They carried infections. They carried chess sets, basketballs, Vietnamese-English dictionaries, insignia of rank, Bronze Stars and Purple Hearts, plastic cards imprinted with the Code of Conduct. They carried diseases, among them malaria and dysentery. They carried lice and ringworm and leeches and paddy algae and various rots and molds. They carried the land itself—Vietnam, the place, the soil—a powdery orange-red dust that covered their boots and fatigues and faces. They carried the sky. The whole atmosphere, they carried it, the humidity, the monsoons, the stink of fungus and decay, all of it, they carried gravity. They moved like mules. By daylight they took sniper fire, at night they were mortared, but it was not battle, it was just the endless march, village to village, without purpose, nothing won or lost. They marched for the sake of the march. They plodded along slowly, dumbly, leaning forward against the heat, unthinking, all blood and bone, simple grunts, soldiering with their legs, toiling up the hills and down into the paddies and across the rivers and up again and down, just humping, one step and then the next and then another, but no volition, no will, because it was automatic, it was anatomy, and the war was entirely a matter of posture and carriage, the hump was everything, a kind of inertia, a kind of emptiness, a dullness of desire and intellect and conscience and hope and human sensibility. Their principles were in their feet. Their calculations were biological. They had no sense of strategy or mission. They searched the villages without knowing what to look for, not caring, kicking over jars of rice, frisking children and old men, blowing tunnels, sometimes setting fires and sometimes not, then forming up and moving on to the next village, then other villages, where it would always be the same. They carried their own lives. The pressures were enormous. In the heat of early afternoon, they would remove their helmets and flak jackets, walking bare, which was dangerous but which helped ease the strain. They would often discard things along the route of march. Purely for comfort, they would throw away rations, blow their Claymores and grenades, no matter, because by nightfall the resupply choppers would arrive with more of the same, then a day or two later still more, fresh watermelons and crates of ammunition and sunglasses and woolen sweaters—the resources were stunning—sparklers for the Fourth of July, colored eggs for Easter. It was the great American war chest—the fruits of science, the smokestacks, the canneries, the arsenals at Hartford, the Minnesota forests, the machine shops, the vast fields of corn and wheat—they carried like freight trains; they carried it on their backs and shoulders—and for all the ambiguities of Vietnam, all the mysteries and unknowns, there was at least the single abiding certainty that they would never be at a loss for things to carry.

* * *

After the chopper took Lavender away, Lieutenant Jimmy Cross led his men into the village of Than Khe. They burned everything. They shot chickens and dogs, they trashed the village well, they called in artillery and watched the wreckage, then they marched for several hours through the hot afternoon, and then at dusk, while Kiowa explained how Lavender died, Lieutenant Cross found himself trembling.

He tried not to cry. With his entrenching tool, which weighed five pounds, he began digging a hole in the earth.

He felt shame. He hated himself. He had loved Martha more than his men, and as a consequence Lavender was now dead, and this was something he would have to carry like a stone in his stomach for the rest of the war.

All he could do was dig. He used his entrenching tool like an ax, slashing, feeling both love and hate, and then later, when it was full dark, he sat at the bottom of his foxhole and wept. It went on for a long while. In part, he was grieving for Ted Lavender, but mostly it was for Martha, and for himself, because she belonged to another world, which was not quite real, and because she was a junior at Mount Sebastian College in New Jersey, a poet and a virgin and uninvolved, and because he realized she did not love him and never would.

Like cement, Kiowa whispered in the dark. I swear to God—boom-down. Not a word.

I've heard this, said Norman Bowker. 45

A pisser, you know? Still zipping himself up. Zapped while zipping.

All right, fine. That's enough.

Yeah, but you had to see it, the guy just—

I *heard,* man. Cement. So why not shut the fuck *up?*

Kiowa shook his head sadly and glanced over at the hole where Lieutenant 50
Jimmy Cross sat watching the night. The air was thick and wet. A warm, dense fog had settled over the paddies and there was the stillness that precedes rain.

After a time Kiowa sighed.

One thing for sure, he said. The Lieutenant's in some deep hurt. I mean that crying jag—the way he was carrying on—it wasn't fake or anything, it was real heavy-duty hurt. The man cares.

Sure, Norman Bowker said.

Say what you want, the man does care.

We all got problems. 55

Not Lavender.

No, I guess not, Bowker said. Do me a favor, though.

Shut up?

That's a smart Indian. Shut up.

Shrugging, Kiowa pulled off his boots. He wanted to say more, just to lighten up his 60
sleep, but instead he opened his New Testament and arranged it beneath his head as a pillow. The fog made things seem hollow and unattached. He tried not to think about Ted Lavender, but then he was thinking how fast it was, no drama, down and dead, and how it was hard to feel anything except surprise. It seemed un-Christian. He wished he could find some great sadness, or even anger, but the emotion wasn't there and he couldn't make it happen. Mostly he felt pleased to be alive. He liked the smell of the New Testament under his cheek, the leather and ink and paper and glue, whatever the chemicals were. He liked hearing the sounds of night. Even his fatigue, it felt fine, the stiff muscles and the prickly awareness of his own body, a floating feeling. He enjoyed not being dead. Lying there, Kiowa admired Lieutenant Jimmy Cross's capacity for grief. He wanted to share the man's pain, he wanted to care as Jimmy Cross cared. And yet when he closed his eyes, all he could think was Boom-down, and all he could feel was the pleasure of having his boots off and the fog curling in around him and the damp soil and the Bible smells and the plush comfort of night.

After a moment Norman Bowker sat up in the dark.

What the hell, he said. You want to talk, *talk*. Tell it to me.

Forget it.

No, man, go on. One thing I hate, it's a silent Indian.

For the most part they carried themselves with poise, a kind of dignity. Now and 65
then, however, there were times of panic, when they squealed or wanted to squeal but couldn't, when they twitched and made moaning sounds and covered their heads and said Dear Jesus and flopped around on the earth and fired their weapons blindly and cringed and sobbed and begged for the noise to stop and went wild and made stupid promises to themselves and to God and to their mothers and fathers, hoping not to die. In different ways, it happened to all of them. Afterward, when the firing ended,

they would blink and peek up. They would touch their bodies, feeling shame, then quickly hiding it. They would force themselves to stand. As if in slow motion, frame by frame, the world would take on the old logic—absolute silence, then the wind, then sunlight, then voices. It was the burden of being alive. Awkwardly, the men would reassemble themselves, first in private, then in groups, becoming soldiers again. They would repair the leaks in their eyes. They would check for casualties, call in dust-offs, light cigarettes, try to smile, clear their throats and spit and begin cleaning their weapons. After a time someone would shake his head and say, No lie, I almost shit my pants, and someone else would laugh, which meant it was bad, yes, but the guy had obviously not shit his pants, it wasn't that bad, and in any case nobody would ever do such a thing and then go ahead and talk about it. They would squint into the dense, oppressive sunlight. For a few moments, perhaps, they would fall silent, lighting a joint and tracking its passage from man to man, inhaling, holding in the humiliation. Scary stuff, one of them might say. But then someone else would grin or flick his eyebrows and say, Roger-dodger, almost cut me a new asshole, *almost*.

There were numerous such poses. Some carried themselves with a sort of wistful resignation, others with pride or stiff soldierly discipline or good humor or macho zeal. They were afraid of dying but they were even more afraid to show it.

They found jokes to tell.

They used a hard vocabulary to contain the terrible softness. *Greased*, they'd say. *Offed, lit up,*° *zapped while zipping.*° It wasn't cruelty, just stage presence. They were actors and the war came at them in 3-D. When someone died, it wasn't quite dying, because in a curious way it seemed scripted, and because they had their lines mostly memorized, irony mixed with tragedy, and because they called it by other names, as if to encyst and destroy the reality of death itself. They kicked corpses. They cut off thumbs. They talked grunt lingo. They told stories about Ted Lavender's supply of tranquilizers, how the poor guy didn't feel a thing, how incredibly tranquil he was.

There's a moral here, said Mitchell Sanders.

They were waiting for Lavender's chopper, smoking the dead man's dope.

The moral's pretty obvious, Sanders said, and winked. Stay away from drugs. No joke, they'll ruin your day every time.

Cute, said Henry Dobbins.

Mind-blower, get it? Talk about wiggy—nothing left, just blood and brains.

They made themselves laugh.

There it is, they'd say, over and over, as if the repetition itself were an act of poise, a balance between crazy and almost crazy, knowing without going. There it is, which meant be cool, let it ride, because oh yeah, man, you can't change what can't be changed, there it is, there it absolutely and positively and fucking well *is*.

They were tough.

They carried all the emotional baggage of men who might die. Grief, terror, love, longing—these were intangibles, but the intangibles had their own mass and specific gravity, they had tangible weight. They carried shameful memories. They

---

Offed, lit up: Killed.

zapped while zipping: Killed while urinating.

carried the common secret of cowardice barely restrained, the instinct to run or freeze or hide, and in many respects this was the heaviest burden of all, for it could never be put down, it required perfect balance and perfect posture. They carried their reputations. They carried the soldier's greatest fear, which was the fear of blushing. Men killed, and died, because they were embarrassed not to. It was what had brought them to the war in the first place, nothing positive, no dreams of glory or honor, just to avoid the blush of dishonor. They died so as not to die of embarrassment. They crawled into tunnels and walked point and advanced under fire. Each morning, despite the unknowns, they made their legs move. They endured. They kept humping. They did not submit to the obvious alternative, which was simply to close the eyes and fall. So easy, really. Go limp and tumble to the ground and let the muscles unwind and not speak and not budge until your buddies picked you up and lifted you into the chopper that would roar and dip its nose and carry you off to the world. A mere matter of falling, yet no one ever fell. It was not courage, exactly; the object was not valor. Rather, they were too frightened to be cowards.

By and large they carried these things inside, maintaining the masks of composure. They sneered at sick call. They spoke bitterly about guys who had found release by shooting off their own toes or fingers. Pussies, they'd say. Candyasses. It was fierce, mocking talk, with only a trace of envy or awe, but even so, the image played itself out behind their eyes.

They imagined the muzzle against flesh. They imagined the quick, sweet pain, then the evacuation to Japan, then a hospital with warm beds and cute geisha nurses.

They dreamed of freedom birds. 80

At night, on guard, staring into the dark, they were carried away by jumbo jets. They felt the rush of takeoff. *Gone!* they yelled. And then velocity, wings and engines, a smiling stewardess—but it was more than a plane, it was a real bird, a big sleek silver bird with feathers and talons and high screeching. They were flying. The weights fell off, there was nothing to bear. They laughed and held on tight, feeling the cold slap of wind and altitude, soaring, thinking *It's over, I'm gone!*— they were naked, they were light and free—it was all lightness, bright and fast and buoyant, light as light, a helium buzz in the brain, a giddy bubbling in the lungs as they were taken up over the clouds and the war, beyond duty, beyond gravity and mortification and global entanglements—*Sin loi!* they yelled, *I'm sorry, motherfuckers, but I'm out of it, I'm goofed, I'm on a space cruise, I'm gone!*—and it was a restful, disencumbered sensation, just riding the light waves, sailing that big silver freedom bird over the mountains and oceans, over America, over the farms and great sleeping cities and cemeteries and highways and the golden arches of McDonald's. It was flight, a kind of fleeing, a kind of falling, falling higher and higher, spinning off the edge of the earth and beyond the sun and through the vast, silent vacuum where there were no burdens and where everything weighed exactly nothing. *Gone!* they screamed, *I'm sorry but I'm gone!* And so at night, not quite dreaming, they gave themselves over to lightness, they were carried, they were purely borne.

On the morning after Ted Lavender died, First Lieutenant Jimmy Cross crouched at the bottom of his foxhole and burned Martha's letters. Then he burned the two photographs. There was a steady rain falling, which made it difficult, but he used heat tabs and Sterno to build a small fire, screening it with his body, holding the photographs over the tight blue flame with the tips of his fingers.

He realized it was only a gesture. Stupid, he thought. Sentimental, too, but mostly just stupid.

Lavender was dead. You couldn't burn the blame.

85 Besides, the letters were in his head. And even now, without photographs, Lieutenant Cross could see Martha playing volleyball in her white gym shorts and yellow T-shirt. He could see her moving in the rain.

When the fire died out, Lieutenant Cross pulled his poncho over his shoulders and ate breakfast from a can.

There was no great mystery, he decided.

In those burned letters Martha had never mentioned the war, except to say, Jimmy, take care of yourself. She wasn't involved. She signed the letters "Love," but it wasn't love, and all the fine lines and technicalities did not matter.

The morning came up wet and blurry. Everything seemed part of everything else, the fog and Martha and the deepening rain.

90 It was a war, after all.

Half smiling, Lieutenant Jimmy Cross took out his maps. He shook his head hard, as if to clear it, then bent forward and began planning the day's march. In ten minutes, or maybe twenty, he would rouse the men and they would pack up and head west, where the maps showed the country to be green and inviting. They would do what they had always done. The rain might add some weight, but otherwise it would be one more day layered upon all the other days.

He was realistic about it. There was that new hardness in his stomach.

No more fantasies, he told himself.

Henceforth, when he thought about Martha, it would be only to think that she belonged elsewhere. He would shut down the daydreams. This was not Mount Sebastian, it was another world, where there were no pretty poems or midterm exams, a place where men died because of carelessness and gross stupidity. Kiowa was right. Boom-down, and you were dead, never partly dead.

95 Briefly, in the rain, Lieutenant Cross saw Martha's gray eyes gazing back at him.

He understood.

It was very sad, he thought. The things men carried inside. The things men did or felt they had to do.

He almost nodded at her, but didn't.

Instead he went back to his maps. He was now determined to perform his duties firmly and without negligence. It wouldn't help Lavender, he knew that, but from this point on he would comport himself as a soldier. He would dispose of his good-luck pebble. Swallow it, maybe, or use Lee Strunk's slingshot, or just drop it along the trail. On the march he would impose strict field discipline. He would be careful to send out flank security, to prevent straggling or bunching up, to keep his troops moving at the proper pace and at the proper interval. He would insist on clean weapons. He would confiscate the remainder of Lavender's dope. Later in the day, perhaps, he would call the men together and speak to them plainly. He would accept the blame for what had happened to Ted Lavender. He would be a man about it. He would look them in the eyes, keeping his chin level, and he would issue the new

SOPs in a calm, impersonal tone of voice, an officer's voice, leaving no room for argument or discussion. Commencing immediately, he'd tell them, they would no longer abandon equipment along the route of march. They would police up their acts. They would get their shit together, and keep it together, and maintain it neatly and in good working order.

He would not tolerate laxity. He would show strength, distancing himself. 100

Among the men there would be grumbling, of course, and maybe worse, because their days would seem longer and their loads heavier, but Lieutenant Cross reminded himself that his obligation was not to be loved but to lead. He would dispense with love; it was not now a factor. And if anyone quarreled or complained, he would simply tighten his lips and arrange his shoulders in the correct command posture. He might give a curt little nod. Or he might not. He might just shrug and say Carry on, then they would saddle up and form into a column and move out toward the villages west of Than Khe.

Reading and Reacting

1. Although the setting and the events described in "The Things They Carried" are dramatic and moving, its tone is often flat and emotionless. Give some examples. Why do you think the narrator adopts this kind of tone?
2. Consider the different meanings of the word *carry*, which can refer to burdens abstract or concrete as well as to things carried physically or emotionally, actively or passively. Give one or two examples of each of the different senses in which O'Brien uses the word. How does his repeated use of the word enrich the story?
3. A striking characteristic of the story's style is its thorough catalogs of the concrete, tangible "things" the soldiers carry. Why do you suppose such detailed lists are included? What does what each man carries tell you about him? In a less literal, more abstract sense, what else do these men "carry"?
4. One stylistic technique O'Brien uses is intentional repetition — of phrases ("they carried"); people's names and identifying details (Martha's virginity, for example); and pieces of equipment. What effect do you think O'Brien hopes to achieve through such repetition? Is he successful?
5. Interspersed among long paragraphs crammed with detail are short one- or two-sentence paragraphs. What function do these brief paragraphs serve?
6. What role does Martha play in the story? Why does Lieutenant Cross burn her letters?
7. In paragraph 68, the narrator says of the soldiers, "They used a hard vocabulary to contain the terrible softness." What do you think he means by this? Do you think this "hard vocabulary" is necessary? How does it affect your reaction to the characters?
8. Describing Lieutenant Cross's new sense of purpose in the story's final paragraph, the narrator uses the phrase "Carry on." Do you think this phrase is linked in any way to the story's other uses of the word *carry*, or do you believe it is unrelated? Explain.
9. **JOURNAL ENTRY** "The Things They Carried" is a story about war. Do you think it is an antiwar story? Why or why not?
10. **CRITICAL PERSPECTIVE** In an essay about war memoirs, Clayton W. Lewis questions O'Brien's decision to present "the nightmare [he] faced in a Vietnam rice paddy" as fiction. Lewis believes that some of O'Brien's stories "dissolve into clever artifice" and, therefore,

are not as effective as actual memoirs of the Vietnam experience would be. He concludes that "for all its brilliance and emotional grounding, [the stories do not] satisfy one's appetite to hear what happened rendered as it was experienced and remembered."

Do you think Lewis has a point? Or do you think O'Brien's "artifice" communicates his emotions and experiences more effectively than a straightforward memoir could? Explain your position.

Related Works: "Dulce et Decorum Est" (p. 915), "The Soldier" (p. 1062), "Facing It" (p. 1067)

WRITING SUGGESTIONS: Style, Tone, and Language

1. In "The Things They Carried," Tim O'Brien considers his characters' emotional and psychological burdens as well as the physical "things they carry." Applying O'Brien's criteria to "The Yellow Wallpaper," write an essay in which you consider what the narrator "carries" (and what her husband "carries") and why.
2. In several of this chapter's stories—for example, "The Hunger Artist," "The Yellow Wallpaper," and "A Primer for the Punctuation of Heart Disease"—characters are trapped. Whether trapped by social roles, by circumstance, or by their own limitations, they are unable to escape their destinies. Choose two or three such stories, and explain what factors imprison each character; then, consider whether—and how—each might escape.
3. Although its form is experimental, "A Primer for the Punctuation of Heart Disease" is essentially a story about family members' struggles to communicate and to understand one another. Compare this story to another story or play about a dysfunctional family—for example, "Oliver's Evolution" (p. 191), "The Rocking-Horse Winner" (p. 589), or *When I Was a Little Girl and My Mother Didn't Want Me* (p. 1266).
4. Imagine The Misfit in a prison cell, relating the violent incident at the end of "A Good Man Is Hard to Find" to another prisoner—or to a member of the clergy. Would his tone be boastful? Regretful? Apologetic? Defiant? Would he use the elaborate poetic style he sometimes uses in the story or more straightforward language? Tell his version of the incident in his own words.
5. Both "Araby" and "The Things They Carried" deal, at least in part, with infatuation. Compare and contrast the infatuations described in the two stories. How does the language used by the narrators in the two stories communicate the two characters' fascination and subsequent disillusionment?

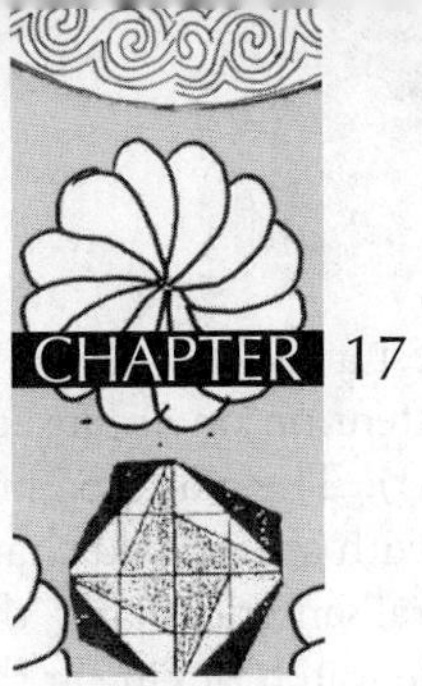

CHAPTER 17

SYMBOL, ALLEGORY, AND MYTH

Symbol

A **symbol** is a person, object, action, place, or event that, in addition to its literal meaning, suggests a more complex meaning or range of meanings. **Universal** or **archetypal symbols,** such as the Old Man, the Mother, or the Grim Reaper, are so much a part of human experience that they suggest the same thing to most people. **Conventional symbols** are also likely to suggest the same thing to most people (a rose suggests love, a skull and crossbones denotes poison), provided the people share cultural and social assumptions. For this reason, symbols are often used as a kind of shorthand in films, popular literature, and advertising, where they elicit predictable responses.

A conventional symbol, such as the stars and stripes of the American flag, can evoke powerful feelings of pride and patriotism in a group of people who share certain cultural assumptions, just as the maple leaf and the Union Jack can. Symbols used in works of literature can function in much the same way, enabling writers to convey particular emotions or messages with a high degree of predictability. Thus, spring can be expected to suggest rebirth and promise; autumn, declining years and powers; summer, youth and beauty. Because a writer expects a dark forest to evoke fear, or a rainbow to communicate hope, he or she can be quite confident in using such images to convey a particular idea or mood (provided the audience shares the writer's frame of reference).

Many symbols, however, suggest different things to different people, and different cultures may react differently to the same symbols. (In the United States, for example, an owl suggests wisdom; in India it suggests the opposite.) Thus, symbols enhance meaning, expanding the possibilities for interpretation and for readers' interaction with the text. Because they are so potentially rich, symbols have the power to open up a work of literature.

Literary Symbols

Both universal and conventional symbols can function as **literary symbols**—symbols that take on additional meanings in particular works. For instance, a watch or clock denotes time; as a conventional symbol, it suggests the passing of time; as a literary symbol in a particular work, it might also convey anything from a character's inability to recapture the past to the idea of time running out—or it might suggest something else.

Considering an object's symbolic significance can suggest a variety of ways to interpret a text. For instance, William Faulkner focuses attention on an unseen watch in a pivotal scene in "A Rose for Emily" (p. 243). The narrator first describes Emily Grierson as "a small, fat woman in black, with a thin gold chain descending to her waist and vanishing into her belt." Several sentences later, the narrator notes that Emily's visitors "could hear the invisible watch ticking at the end of the gold chain." Like these visitors, readers are drawn to the unseen watch as it ticks away. Because Emily is portrayed as a woman living in the past, readers can assume that the watch is intended to reinforce the impression that she cannot see that time (the watch) has moved on. The vivid picture of the pale, plump woman in the musty room with the watch invisibly ticking does indeed suggest both that she has been left back in time and that she remains unaware of the progress around her. Thus, the symbol of the watch enriches both the depiction of character and the story's theme.

In "Barn Burning" (p. 391), another Faulkner story, the clock is a more complex symbol. The itinerant Snopes family is without financial security and apparently without a future. The clock the mother carries from shack to shack—"The clock inlaid with mother-of-pearl, which would not run, stopped at some fourteen minutes past two o'clock of a dead and forgotten day and time, which had been [Sarty's] mother's dowry"—is their only possession of value. The fact that the clock no longer works seems at first to suggest that time has run out for the family. On another level, the clock stands in stark contrast to Major de Spain's grand home, with its gold and glitter and Oriental rugs. Knowing that the clock was part of the mother's dowry, and that a dowry suggests a promise, readers may decide that the broken clock symbolizes lost hope. The fact that the mother still clings to the clock, however, could suggest just the opposite: her refusal to give up.

As you read, you should not try to find one exact equivalent for each symbol; that kind of search is unproductive. Instead, consider the different meanings a symbol might suggest. Then, consider how these various interpretations enrich other elements of the story and the work as a whole.

Recognizing Symbols

When is a clock just a clock, and when is it also a symbol with a meaning (or meanings) beyond its literal significance? If a character waiting for a friend glances once at a watch to check the time, there is probably nothing symbolic about the watch or about the act of looking at it. If, however, the watch keeps appearing again and again in the story, at key moments; if the narrator devotes a good deal of time to describing it; if it is placed in a conspicuous physical location; if characters keep noticing it and commenting on its presence; if it is lost (or found) at a critical moment; if its function in some way parallels the development of plot or character (for instance, if it stops as a relationship ends or when a character dies); if the story's opening or closing paragraph focuses on the timepiece; or if the story is called "The Watch"—the watch most likely has symbolic significance. In other words, considering how an image is used, how often it is used, and when it appears will help you to determine whether or not it functions as a symbol.

Symbols expand the possible meanings of a story, thereby heightening interest and actively involving readers in the text. In "The Lottery" (p. 509), for example, the mysterious black box has symbolic significance. It is mentioned prominently and repeatedly, and it plays a pivotal role in the story's action. Of course, the black box is important on a purely literal level: it functions as a key component of the lottery. But the box has other associations as well, and it is these associations that suggest what its symbolic significance might be.

The black wooden box is very old, a relic of many past lotteries; the narrator observes that it represents tradition. It is also closed and closely guarded, suggesting mystery and uncertainty. It is shabby, "splintered badly along one side . . . and in places faded or stained," and this state of disrepair could suggest that the ritual it is part of has also deteriorated or that tradition itself has deteriorated. The box is also simple in construction and design, suggesting the primitive (and therefore perhaps outdated) nature of the ritual. Thus, this symbol encourages readers to probe the story for values and ideas, to consider and weigh the suitability of a variety of interpretations. It serves as a "hot spot" that invites questions, and the answers to these questions reinforce and enrich the story's theme.

Allegory

An **allegory** communicates a doctrine, message, or moral principle by making it into a narrative in which the characters personify ideas, concepts, qualities, or other abstractions. Thus, an allegory is a story with two parallel and consistent levels of meaning—one literal and one figurative. The figurative level, which offers some moral or political lesson, is the story's main concern.

Whereas a symbol has multiple symbolic associations as well as a literal meaning, an **allegorical figure**—a character, object, place, or event in the allegory—has just one meaning within an **allegorical framework,** the set of ideas that conveys the allegory's message. (At the simplest level, for instance, one character can stand for good and another can stand for evil.) For this reason, allegorical figures do not open up a text to various interpretations the way symbols do. The allegorical figures are significant only because they represent something beyond their literal meaning in a fixed system. Because the purpose of allegory is to communicate a particular lesson, readers are not encouraged to speculate about the allegory's possible meanings; each element has only one equivalent, which readers must discover if they are to make sense of the story.

Naturally, the better a reader understands the political, religious, and literary assumptions of a writer, the easier it will be to recognize the allegorical significance of his or her work. John Bunyan's *The Pilgrim's Progress*, for example, is a famous seventeenth-century allegory based on the Christian doctrine of salvation. In order to appreciate the complexity of Bunyan's work, readers would have to familiarize themselves with this doctrine.

One type of allegory, called a **beast fable,** is a short tale, usually including a moral, in which animals assume human characteristics. Aesop's fables are the best-known examples of beast fables. More recently, contemporary writers have used beast fables to satirize the political and social conditions of our time. In one such tale, "The Gentlemen of the Jungle" by the Kenyan writer Jomo Kenyatta, an elephant is allowed to put his trunk inside a man's hut during a rainstorm. Not content with keeping his trunk dry, the elephant pushes his entire body inside the hut, displacing the man. When the man protests, the elephant takes the matter to the lion, who appoints a Commission of Enquiry to settle the matter. Eventually, the man is forced not only to abandon his hut to the elephant but also to build new huts for all the animals on the Commission. Even so, the jealous animals occupy the man's new hut and begin fighting for space; while they are arguing, the man burns down the hut, animals and all. Like the tales told by Aesop, "The Gentlemen of the Jungle" has a moral: "Peace is costly," says the man as he walks away happily, "but it's worth the expense."

The following passage from Kenyatta's tale reveals how the allegorical figures work within the framework of the allegory:

> The elephant, obeying the command of his master (the lion), got busy with the other ministers to appoint a Commission of Enquiry. The following elders of the jungle were appointed to sit in the Commission: (1) Mr. Rhinoceros; (2) Mr. Buffalo; (3) Mr. Alligator; (4) The Rt. Hon. Mr. Fox to act as chairman; and (5) Mr. Leopard to act as Secretary of the Commission. On seeing the personnel, the man protested and asked if it was not necessary to include in this Commission a member from his side. But he was told that it was impossible, since no one from his side was well enough educated to understand the intricacy of jungle law.

From this excerpt, we can see that each character represents a particular idea. For example, the members of the Commission stand for bureaucratic smugness and inequity, and the man stands for the citizens who are victimized by the government. In order to fully understand the allegorical significance of each figure in this story, of course, readers would have to know something about government bureaucracies, colonialism in Africa, and possibly a specific historical event in Kenya.

Some works contain both symbolic elements *and* allegorical elements, as Nathaniel Hawthorne's "Young Goodman Brown" (p. 540) does. The names of the story's two main characters, "Goodman" and "Faith," suggest that they fit within an allegorical system of some sort: Young Goodman Brown represents a good person who, despite his best efforts, strays from the path of righteousness; his wife, Faith, represents the quality he must hold on to in order to avoid temptation. As characters, they have no significance outside of their allegorical functions. Other elements of the story, however, are not so clear-cut. The older man whom Young Goodman Brown meets in the woods carries a staff that has carved on it "the likeness of a great black snake, so curiously wrought, that it might almost be seen to twist and wriggle itself like a living serpent." This staff, carried by a Satanic figure who represents evil and temptation, suggests the snake in the Garden of Eden, an association that neatly fits into the allegorical framework of the story. Alternatively, however, the staff could suggest the "slippery," ever-changing nature of sin, the difficulty people have in perceiving sin, or even sexuality (which may explain Young Goodman Brown's susceptibility to temptation). This range of possible meanings suggests that the staff functions as a symbol (not an allegorical figure) that enriches Hawthorne's allegory.

Other stories work entirely on a symbolic level and contain no allegorical figures. "The Lottery," despite its moral overtones, is not an allegory because its characters, events, and objects are not arranged to serve one rigid, didactic purpose. In fact, many different interpretations have been suggested for this story. When it was first published in June 1948 in the *New Yorker*, some readers believed it to be a story about an actual custom or ritual. As author Shirley Jackson reports in her essay "Biography of a Story," even those who recognized it as fiction speculated about its meaning, seeing it as (among other things) an attack on prejudice, a criticism of society's need for a scapegoat, or a treatise on witchcraft, Christian martyrdom, or village gossip. The fact is that an allegorical interpretation will not account for every major character, object, and event in the story.

Myth

Throughout history, human beings have been makers of myths. For the purpose of this discussion, a **myth** is a story that is central to a culture; it embodies the values on which a culture or society is built. Thus, myths are not synonymous with falsehoods or fairy tales. Rather, they are stories that contain ideas that inform a culture and that give that culture meaning. In this sense, then, both an ancient epic and a contemporary religious text can be considered myths.

Although many myths have to do with religion, myths are not limited to the theological. Myths explain everything from natural phenomena—such as the creation of the world—to the existence of human beings and the beginnings of agriculture. The importance of myths rests on their ability to embody a set of beliefs that unifies both individuals and the society in which they live. By examining myths, we can learn much about our own origins and about our most deeply held beliefs.

One of the most prevalent types of myth is the **creation myth.** Almost every culture has an explanation for how the earth, sun, and stars—not to mention people—came into being. According to the ancient Greeks, for example, the world began as an empty void from which Nyx, a bird with black wings, emerged. She laid a golden egg, and out of it arose Eros, the god of love. The two halves of the eggshell became the earth and the sky, who fell in love with each other and had many children and grandchildren. These offspring became the gods of the Greek pantheon, who eventually created human beings in their own likeness. Each of these gods had a role to play in the creation and maintenance of the world, and their actions—in particular, their constant meddling in the lives of people—comprise the myths of ancient Greece.

In various cultures all over the world, creation myths take different forms. According to the ancient Japanese, for example, the world emerged from a single seed, which grew to form a god who, in turn, created other gods and eventually the islands of Japan and their inhabitants. Several Native American tribes share common beliefs about "sky ancestors," who created the people on the planet.

In Western culture, the most recognizable creation myth appears in Genesis, the first book of the Old Testament. According to Genesis, God created the heavens and the earth as well as all living creatures—including Adam and Eve. Other stories are part of the oral tradition of Judaism and do not appear in Genesis. An example of such a story is the tale of Lilith, which emerged sometime between the eighth and eleventh centuries. According to this Hebrew myth, Lilith, who was created before Eve, was Adam's first wife. However, she refused to be subservient to Adam, and so she left Eden, eventually to be replaced by Eve. Talmudic tradition holds that she later mated with demons and gave birth to a legion of demonic offspring who inhabit the dark places of the earth.

The influence of mythology on literature is profound, and our contemporary understanding of narrative fiction owes a great deal to mythology. In fact, many of the short stories in this anthology contain allusions to myth. Consider, for example, the role of myth in "The Lottery," "Young Goodman Brown," and Raymond Carver's "Cathedral" (p. 526). In each of these short stories, myth is central to the characters' behavior, sensibility, and understanding of the world in which they live.

✔ CHECKLIST Writing about Symbol, Allegory, and Myth

- ☐ Are any universal symbols used in the work? Any conventional symbols? What is their function?
- ☐ Is any character, place, action, event, or object given unusual prominence or emphasis in the story? If so, does this element seem to have symbolic as well as literal significance?
- ☐ What possible meanings does each symbol suggest?
- ☐ How do symbols help to depict the story's characters?
- ☐ How do symbols help to characterize the story's setting?
- ☐ How do symbols help to advance the story's plot?
- ☐ Does the story have a moral or didactic purpose? What is the message, idea, or moral principle the story seeks to convey? Is the story an allegory?
- ☐ What equivalent may be assigned to each allegorical figure in the story?
- ☐ What is the allegorical framework of the story?
- ☐ Does the story combine allegorical figures and symbols? How do they work together in the story?
- ☐ Does the story have any references to myth? If so, what do these references contribute to the story's plot or theme?

Source: Courtesy, Alison Bechdel

ALISON BECHDEL (1960–) was born in Loch Haven, Pennsylvania, where her parents, who were teachers, owned and operated a funeral home. After graduating from college, Bechdel created the comic strip *Dykes to Watch out For,* which appears on the author's Web site, <www.dykestowatchoutfor.com>, and in numerous award-winning collections. Her illustrations have appeared in the publications *Slate, Ms.,* and the *Advocate.* Her graphic memoir *Fun Home* (2006), from which the following excerpt is taken, has been hailed as the Best Book of the Year by numerous publications.

Cultural Context The following graphic story refers to the Greek myth of Icarus and Daedalus. According to the myth, Daedalus, a famous Greek architect, inventor, and craftsman, was imprisoned by King Minos of Crete. He devised an escape plan in which he and his son, Icarus, would fly to Sicily using wings he had made from feathers and wax. Daedalus warned Icarus not to fly too close to the hot sun, fearing that the wax would melt. The recklessly overconfident Icarus disobeyed his father, plummeting into the sea and drowning. This myth is often alluded to as a metaphor for the self-destructiveness caused by overly ambitious behavior.

from Fun Home (2006)

This graphic story starts on the next page. ⟶

Reading and Reacting

1. The title of this story, "Fun Home," is short for "funeral home," where the writer and her character grew up. In what sense is this title ironic?
2. Bechdel describes her father as a "Daedalus of décor." What does she mean?
3. Bechdel says that her father was both Icarus and Daedalus. What does this tell readers about her father?
4. **JOURNAL ENTRY** What do the visual images add to the story? What would be lost if you disregarded the pictures and read just the narrative at the top of each frame?
5. **CRITICAL PERSPECTIVE** In a review of *Fun Home,* poet, fiction writer, and lesbian-rights activist Merry Gangemi describes the relationship between the young Bechdel and her father, as depicted in the book:

> *Fun Home* is a tale of regeneration and mythic tragedy. Bechdel's close-to-the-bone-memoir of her relationship with her father successfully translates her gender-limited female self into an heir, into a visually gender-neutral woman, into a Spartan butch, into Daedalus's Icarus, into a postmodern, who accepts her lesbianism as normative and natural.

What visual elements in this graphic story help to establish the relationship between Bechdel and her father? How does the Daedalus/Icarus allusion help to clarify this relationship?

Related Works: "Oliver's Evolution" (p. 191), "Gryphon" (p. 277), "I'm nobody! Who are you?" (p. 838), "Those Winter Sundays" (p. 1040), "My Father's Song" (p. 1044), *Proof* (p. 1476)

LIKE MANY FATHERS, MINE COULD OCCASIONALLY BE PREVAILED ON FOR A SPOT OF "AIRPLANE."

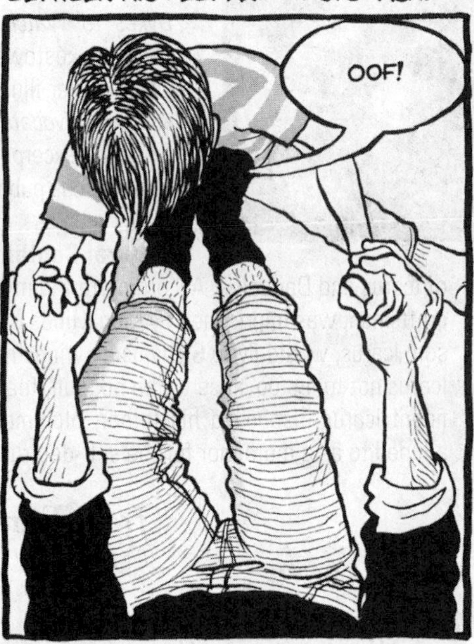

AS HE LAUNCHED ME, MY FULL WEIGHT WOULD FALL ON THE PIVOT POINT BETWEEN HIS FEET AND MY STOMACH.
OOF!

IT WAS A DISCOMFORT WELL WORTH THE RARE PHYSICAL CONTACT, AND CERTAINLY WORTH THE MOMENT OF PERFECT BALANCE WHEN I SOARED ABOVE HIM.
IN THE CIRCUS, ACROBATICS WHERE ONE PERSON LIES ON THE FLOOR BALANCING ANOTHER ARE CALLED "ICARIAN GAMES."
TOLSTOY
ANNA KARENINA

Source: ©Alison Bechdel. Used courtesy of Houghton Mifflin.

CONSIDERING THE FATE OF ICARUS AFTER HE FLOUTED HIS FATHER'S ADVICE AND FLEW SO CLOSE TO THE SUN HIS WINGS MELTED, PERHAPS SOME DARK HUMOR IS INTENDED.

UH-OH!
IN OUR PARTICULAR REENACTMENT OF THIS MYTHIC RELATIONSHIP, IT WAS NOT ME BUT MY FATHER WHO WAS TO PLUMMET FROM THE SKY.

BUT BEFORE HE DID SO, HE MANAGED TO GET QUITE A LOT DONE.

AGAIN!
THIS RUG IS FILTHY. GO GET THE VACUUM CLEANER.

HIS GREATEST ACHIEVEMENT, ARGUABLY, WAS HIS MONOMANIACAL RESTORATION OF OUR OLD HOUSE.

AND THEN GET ME MY TACK HAMMER. THAT STRIP OF MOLDING IS LOOSE.

WHEN OTHER CHILDREN CALLED OUR HOUSE A MANSION, I WOULD DEMUR. I RESENTED THE IMPLICATION THAT MY FAMILY WAS RICH, OR UNUSUAL IN ANY WAY.

IN FACT, WE WERE UNUSUAL, THOUGH I WOULDN'T APPRECIATE EXACTLY HOW UNUSUAL UNTIL MUCH LATER. BUT WE WERE NOT RICH.

THE GILT CORNICES, THE MARBLE FIREPLACE, THE CRYSTAL CHANDELIERS, THE SHELVES OF CALF-BOUND BOOKS--THESE WERE NOT SO MUCH BOUGHT AS PRODUCED FROM THIN AIR BY MY FATHER'S REMARKABLE LEGERDEMAIN.

MY FATHER COULD SPIN GARBAGE...

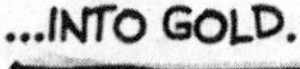

...INTO GOLD.

HE COULD TRANSFIGURE A ROOM WITH THE SMALLEST OFFHAND FLOURISH.

HE COULD CONJURE AN ENTIRE, FINISHED PERIOD INTERIOR FROM A PAINT CHIP.

HE WAS AN ALCHEMIST OF APPEARANCE, A SAVANT OF SURFACE, A DAEDALUS OF DECOR.

FOR IF MY FATHER WAS ICARUS, HE WAS ALSO DAEDALUS--THAT SKILLFUL ARTIFICER, THAT MAD SCIENTIST WHO BUILT THE WINGS FOR HIS SON AND DESIGNED THE FAMOUS LABYRINTH...
THIS IS THE WALLPAPER FOR MY ROOM?

...AND WHO ANSWERED NOT TO THE LAWS OF SOCIETY, BUT TO THOSE OF HIS CRAFT.
BUT I HATE PINK! I HATE FLOWERS!
TOUGH TITTY.

HISTORICAL RESTORATION WASN'T HIS JOB.
(TWELFTH-GRADE ENGLISH)
ARCHITECTURAL DIGEST

IT WAS HIS PASSION. AND I MEAN PASSION IN EVERY SENSE OF THE WORD.
LIBIDINAL. MANIC. MARTYRED.

Source: ©AP Photo/Patricia McDonnell

ALICE HOFFMAN (1952–) is a critically acclaimed fiction writer whose works have appeared in publications such as the *Kenyon Review* and *Ploughshares.* Writing on a range of subjects, Hoffman has published sixteen novels, two story collections, and eight books for children and young adults. Much of her work, including the following short story, focuses on the significance of magic and ritual. Her novel *Practical Magic* (1995) was adapted into an award-winning feature film, starring Sandra Bullock and Nicole Kidman. Her teen novel, *Aquamarine* (2006), has also been made into a film.

Cultural Context This story examines the effects of a car accident on the victim's friends and loved ones. Every year, thousands of teenagers die in car crashes caused by their own poor judgment, distraction, or intoxication. Of all the traffic-related deaths documented in the United States in 2006, more than forty percent involved alcohol. More than ten percent of the millions of intoxicated drivers documented in 2002 were eighteen to twenty years old. Currently, automobile accidents are the leading cause of death among teens between fifteen and nineteen years of age.

Saint Helene (2005)

In February, when the snow comes down hard, little globes of light are left along Route 23, not the side where the Arco station is, but on the other side, which slopes off when a driver least expects it. The lights are made out of paper bags and sand and candles, and they burn past midnight. They shouldn't burn for that amount of time; that's part of the miracle. Jack Harry from the Arco station has crept out at two in the morning to see if Helene's mother, Diana Boyd, goes along the road replacing each melting pool of white wax with a fresh candle. He used to want to reveal a con in process, although at this point he doesn't even want to catch Helene's mother at anything. Now he just sits there in his truck on the anniversary of the accident, wondering how many other strange things there are in this world that he has no hopes of ever understanding.

The light globes are made at the high school, Middleborough High, where Helene went until her junior year. People who never even knew her spend all afternoon in the cafeteria filling paper bags. One year, the art teacher, Rick DiCosmo, ordered special sand from Arizona, and the candles glowed with red light, but usually the sand is trucked in from Heyward's Gravel Pit, and it's white, pure white. It looks like diamonds when you run it through your fingers.

There are dozens of high school girls who lock themselves in their bedrooms on the anniversary night, their fingers dusted with sand. Everyone thanks her lucky stars she is not Helene. The fat, the unbeautiful, the lonely, the sorrowful, the lost, each is grateful to be who she is for that one evening. Even the most selfish girls — the ones who think nothing of snubbing their less attractive classmates — offer to collect the spent paper bags on their way to school on the morning after the anniversary. The wax will still be hot; the wick gives off smoke. Occasionally a candle will still be burning, so freshly it's as though it had just been lit. Then the girls gather round, even the ones who hate each other. They close their eyes and make a wish, the same one every time: *Let it never be me*.

The one person who is never included in the anniversary events, not the safe driving assembly at the school or the candle lighting ceremony, is Shelby Richmond. Not that she's a high school girl anymore; she graduated five years ago, when Helene would have, although Shelby didn't go off to college the way she and Helene had planned; she didn't even go to graduation. Both girls had applied to NYU, and they were both accepted, too late for Helene, though, and, as it turned out, too late for Shelby as well. Shelby's parents paid the first semester's tuition, but she didn't leave on the appointed day, or the day after, or the one after that. Her trunk sat in the front hall until her parents lost hope, until the leaves started changing; they waited so long to withdraw her, they lost all that tuition money for nothing.

5 Shelby has not done anything since the night when it happened. She sleepwalked through the rest of high school, and now she sleeps most of the day; she dreams of the way it used to be, back when she didn't think about anything, when the whole world was open and blue and shining, a globe no more complicated than a Christmas ball. Her diagnosis is major depression. She had a two-month stay in the hospital after the accident, when she stopped talking; then she wised up and started speaking again, enough to make them have no choice but to let her come home, finish up high school, then retreat to the basement, her lair, her den, the only place she wants—if that is not too strong a word—to be.

The doctors and her parents can call it whatever they like, Shelby is the only one who knows what's wrong with her. She is paying her penance. She is stopping her life, matching her breathing to be the counterpart of the slow intake of air of a girl in a coma. When it comes down to it, even though Shelby is the one person in town who has never been to a viewing, never stood over the hospital bed that has been set up in the sunroom of Helene's parents' house, in some sense she and Helene are still living identical lives, just as they had in high school. Shelby hasn't even bought new clothes since then, she still wears the same pair of boots, a wad of newspaper stuck inside the right boot because the heel is tearing away.

Of course there are differences. Helene's hair has not been cut since the accident, and now it reaches the floor of her parents' sunroom, while Shelby shaved her head in the hospital when they were still allowing her a razor for her legs. She's kept it that way, bald, so that when she does venture as far as the 7-Eleven for magazines and snacks, people treat her gently, as though she were a cancer patient. And then someone never fails to whisper, *That's the girl who was driving when Helene had the accident*, and it's even worse than if she'd had cancer. The way they look at her. Very bad. She tries to go out after dark, hat pulled down low, she wears gloves, scarves, a fat down jacket that makes her shapeless, anonymous. And still, everyone knows.

The other differences? Shelby's eyes register images; she eats, poorly, all junk food, but not the glucose drip Helene survives on; she walks, she talks, she also goes to Smithtown once or twice a month, on the bus, no more driving for her, that's for damned sure, to buy weed from a guy they knew in high school, Ben Mink, who has fallen upon hard times. They didn't run with the same crowd—Ben didn't have a crowd—yet they are comfortable with each other, if being comfortable is possible for either one. Shelby and Ben sit in the park on these occasions, mostly in silence, two losers who can barely make it through their own lives. When dusk falls they sometimes share a joint and talk about teachers they had. Whenever they do this, Shelby takes out her house key and digs it into her flesh until she bleeds. No miracle. That's Helene's business. Shelby's blood is strictly penance.

Once Ben Mink asked her if it was true that touching Helene's hand could cure an illness. That's what people said. They came from all over. Helene is famous; there are magazine articles about the miracle of the girl in the coma, and once a year Channel Four sends out a news team. Shelby had looked at Ben with horror when he asked her this, amazed he had the nerve to say Helene's name in her presence. Shelby had a tremor in her left hand; it was the left hand that was said to be the source of Helene's miracles.

"You don't believe in that shit, do you?" Ben had asked.

"Miracles?"

Shelby has sharp teeth, and a once beautiful smile. She made Ben Mink nervous. She tapped her foot constantly.

"I believe in tragedy," Shelby said.

"Yeah, right, that's what I thought." Ben seemed relieved.

"You thought something about me?" Shelby kept her good hand over her tremoring hand. She could actually feel her brain waves shift when he smoked pot. Pseudocoma. Drift of snow. "Let's not get too personal. I buy weed from you. Period."

On the bus, Shelby thought that in fact she had spoken to Ben Mink more in the past five years than she had to anyone else in her life. Count the words. They added up. Shrink. Parent. Clerk at the 7-Eleven. Her aunt Hillary who tried to talk sense into her. Ben Mink won by a long shot.

"I believe in tragedy, too," he told her, as if she cared what anyone else believed.

February was hard. Those globes of light. The ice on the street. High school girls crying. Shelby stayed in the basement; quieter, darker, she liked it there, if *like* was a word that could apply to anything. The couch folded into a bed, and the floor was linoleum, like a skating rink. She and Helene used to sneak down here and talk about true love. Sometimes, late, when Shelby has smoked more weed than she should, she thinks she sees Helene on the stairs. *Don't fall*, Helene says. *Just stay right where you are*. And then Helene is gone.

Shelby has never told anyone that she didn't want to go out that night. It sounds corny, a lame excuse; it feels like a lie, even to herself. By now, Shelby is so confused, all she can remember is stepping on the brake and the car spinning around and everything being blue, Christmas globe blue, and Helene laughing, like they were in a whirly car, and then metal. Bad bad sound. But before that, when they were still in the basement, lying on the couch, before they pulled on their coats and their boots, before they started laughing and talking about how cold it was, it was Helene saying, *Please please! Just drive me past his house, just once, that's all I'm asking*.

Helene and her boyfriend, Chris Wilson, had broken up, and she wanted to see if he was home or out with another girl. She wasn't all pure and good. She mistrusted people. She gossiped. She said she would kick that other girl's ass if she found her with Chris. Shelby can't even remember who that other girl was anymore. She has walked past Chris Wilson's house a few times since the accident. Chris himself went to Cornell, then moved to Boston but his mother still lives there. Once his mom came out on the porch and called to Shelby. She must have seen Shelby from the bay window in her living room; she must have had trouble sleeping, too. She was probably kind-hearted, worried about the crazy, stoned-out bald girl on the road, not even a girl anymore, a woman, but Shelby ran away, heart pounding. Off the road and into the woods. The crunch of twigs, of wood, reminded her of metal. She went right to bed and couldn't be woken, not for eighteen hours, not until her mother grew so worried she spilled a cup of cold water over Shelby.

Don't, was all Shelby said. She didn't even shift in her sopping, freezing bed. She didn't leap up and shout, *What have you done!*

One day Shelby's mother was driving home from the market when she made a right turn on Lewiston, something she always avoided, and there was Helene's house. Anyone would know which one it was because of the crowd outside, the line of people down the driveway, patient, quiet, most of them out-of-towners, some having driven from New Jersey or Pennsylvania or even Florida.

Sue Richmond had grocery sacks in the car, but she parked and got out, anyway. She felt something inside her cracking apart, and all of a sudden she felt vulnerable in some odd way. She stood in the street crying, watching the Boyds' yellow ranch house, the way the paint was peeling, the way there were all those bouquets of roses left on the porch. Lots of people were doing it, just standing there crying. Peacefully, though, like they were letting it all out, right here, right now. Sue noticed two of her neighbors, Pat Harrington and Martha Lee, and they waved to her. Sue wasn't particularly friendly, but she found herself walking over to them. They hugged her, maybe because she was crying, maybe because they pitied her for having a daughter like Shelby, or maybe because they remembered the scene Sue had made on the night of the accident, before they knew which girl was critically injured and which one had nothing more than a hairline fracture.

When she got home, Sue went downstairs to the basement, something she never did anymore. There was Shelby on the couch. The basement was smoky, and the odor was foul. Like old fruit, apple cores. A burning smell. If this had been years ago she would have called out, *Are you smoking down here?* Now she just came down the stairs and sat on the arm of the couch. Shelby was hunkered down under a blanket, staring at the TV. The light in the room was blue and wavery. It made Sue think of a night light. Shelby looked much the way she had as a baby, bald, those big dark eyes.

25 "Mom?" Shelby seemed confused. "What's up?"

It was a talent show on TV, *American Idol.* Everyone looked the same to Sue, hopeful and young.

"You like this show?" It didn't seem like something the old Shelby would have spent ten minutes on.

"It relaxes me," Shelby said.

Paralyzed her was more like it. Even while they were talking, she was still staring at the screen.

"I think something's happening at the Boyd's," Sue said.

"Watch this guy," Shelby said of the contestant taking the stage. "He's crap. I don't know how he made it through the first audition."

"Did you hear what I said?"

Shelby looked at her mother. "The Boyds."

"I think we should go. We should see her."

"You think so?" Shelby said. There was that sound in her voice, the one that was there before she stopped talking and went into the hospital, the thing Sue Richmond feared more than anything in the world. Almost more. "You think it's just fine that they prop her up in bed and have strangers come in there and kiss her hand and beg her for whatever they want? You think Helene would be happy with that? Helene wouldn't even sneeze in public. She'd rather have blown her brains out holding back a sneeze than embarrass herself, and now they have lines of people going into her bedroom where she shits into a bag. You think we should go to that? You think that would be what Helene wanted?"

Shelby threw herself sideways, deeper under the blanket, her back to her mother.

"Maybe she likes the fact that she's helping people," Sue said. "Maybe that's the miracle."

"Good Lord! Do you think I don't know what she would have liked?! I knew her better than anyone!"

"She's different," Sue said. "You don't know her anymore."

Shelby turned to glare at her mother.

"She wouldn't know you, either," Sue said. "You're nothing like you were."

Later in the month Shelby called Ben Mink to meet her in the park in Smithtown.

"No weed," he said. "There's some crackdown in the Bahamas or something, and it's filtering up to us. Call me back at the end of the week."

"How can you be out?" Shelby said. "I depend on you."

"That's a laugh."

"Don't make me sit through reality," Shelby said.

"Lie down, it's easier to get through that way."

"Do I seem different to you than I did in high school?"

"Sure," Ben said. "You're bald."

"I mean in some definitive way, asshole."

"That's definitive. You're completely different."

"I'm not." Shelby had a crack in her voice.

"You're like the weird fucked-up sister of yourself, Shelby. Whereas I'm just an extension of my loser self that anyone could have foreseen."

Without getting stoned, it was harder to sleep for more than fourteen hours at a time. Shelby went upstairs to look through her parents' medicine cabinet. Ativan. That might work. Her father was sitting in the living room. She usually managed to avoid him.

"I came to get some milk," Shelby said. She went to the fridge so he would believe her. "Where's Mom?"

"Nowhere," Dan Richmond said.

Shelby poured herself a glass of milk, then sat down on the couch to watch the talent show with her father.

"That guy's crap," she said of the contestant she despised.

"Yeah, well, he's there in Hollywood, and we're sitting here."

They watched for a while. Shelby was tapping her foot the way she did, and her father was trying his best not to mention it or even notice it. Thump against the floor. Against the couch. Like she was wound up.

"She went to the Boyd's," Shelby said finally. "Didn't she? I told her it was stupid and vile and disgusting."

"Maybe there's some truth in what people say. It doesn't hurt to see."

"Don't make me vomit."

"I wouldn't want to do that. You'd have to be alive to do that."

Shelby stared at her father. He looked old.

"If I wanted to be dead, I would be," Shelby said. "And what makes you think I want to talk about this?"

Shelby went back to the basement. She took two Ativan, then put on her coat and went out through the cellar door. She sat down on the picnic table, even though it was cold outside. The air was like crystals; it hurt just to breathe.

Her mother's car pulled up and parked. The headlights turned everything yellow, just as it had been that night, then they were cut off, and the night was pitch. All the same, Sue saw her daughter perched on the picnic table in the yard. She went round the back.

"It's freezing," Sue said.

"Stars," Shelby said. "I'm counting them. That should keep me busy."

Sue sat on the picnic table, and they both looked up.

"It's not the way you think it is," Sue said. "It's peaceful. She's peaceful. It wasn't anyone's fault."

Shelby made a sound she hadn't expected to be a sob.

"I think I lost my soul," she said.

"That can't happen," Sue said.

"You have no idea what can happen, Mom."

Shelby took out a cigarette and lit it. She used to be so against smoking she would go up to complete strangers to ask if they knew what they were doing to their lungs when they lit up. She had no shame back then.

Now she went back into the basement and phoned Ben Mink.

"I'm desperate," she said. "Beam me out of here."

He said he'd managed to score and he would meet her at the bus station at nine. His parents still lived a few blocks from the high school, and he would stay there overnight.

It was February, and Shelby hated to leave the house, but she put on extra socks and her old boots and gloves and a hat, then took off. Here parents were watching TV; the blue light from the window fell across the lawn and out into the road. Ice. Crystals. Real things. Shelby walked fast, along Main Street, toward the center of town. It was a small nothing town, and everything was closed but the Pizza Place, where a few high school kids were hanging out. Shelby wrapped her scarf around her head and looped it around her neck. Her boots made a crunching noise. She could hear herself breathing because the inhalations were sharp, soblike things. Like she couldn't catch her breath. All that smoking and the cold air and how fast she was walking. It all added up.

Ben Mink was standing outside the bus station, hands in his pockets, freezing.

"Damn, it's cold," he said. "That is you in there, right?"

He peered into Shelby's cloaked face. Hat, scarves, big eyes, bald. 85

"Who else would meet you, Ben?"

Shelby got her money from stealing from her parents; very grown-up to paw around in her mother's purse, her father's wallet. She knew they pretended not to know. Shelby gave Ben the cash, and he gave her a plastic bag, which she put in her pocket.

"I'm not going to be around much longer," Ben said.

"Really? Leaping from a bridge?"

"Don't laugh when I tell you," Ben said. "Promise." 90

Their breath came out like clouds, cold, cold. They were the only ones on the street. Ben was wearing old Doc Martin boots that crunched the snow, and the crunch echoed up and sounded like steel. Steel-toed boots.

"I'm going to pharmacy school."

Shelby bent over with laughter. Ben stopped and grinned himself. "That's perfect," Shelby said.

"Seriously, pharmacists can make a hundred grand a year."

"Oh, yeah, what are you going to do with all that money? Buy drugs?" 95

"Weren't you in the straight-and-narrow club at school?"

The anti-drug contingent that put up posters in the hallways and made a vow not to use drugs.

"Fuck you," Shelby said.

"I didn't mean it in a bad way. I just like you better now."

Shelby glanced at him through the slit between her scarf and her hat. 100

"Where do you think your soul goes when you lose it?"

"Around the corner and down the street."

They both laughed. They were turning the corner and going down the street. There was nothing there.

"I told you it was gone," Shelby said.

"So let's go find it," Ben said. 105

"Yeah, right."

They stopped so Ben could take a joint from his pocket. Shelby held her hands around it so the match wouldn't blow out.

"Let's just walk by."

"That's it? Just pass by it? Not stop or anything."

Ben offered her a hit. "I won't tell we did it if you don't." 110

They walked toward the Boyds' house. It was easy, really; Shelby had been there a thousand times before. She didn't even have to think about it. She remembered that once Ben had said something to her in high school and she had pretended not to hear him and walked right by. Now, she was curious as to what he had said. He swore he didn't remember, but there was a smirk on his face.

"You didn't like me in high school," Shelby said.

"Well, I didn't like anyone, so don't think you were special."

They laughed and leaned closer. Freezing cold. Shelby was shaking with it. There was no one at the Boyds', no lines in the driveway, just a darkened house with peeling paint.

"Come on," Ben said.

He grabbed Shelby by her sleeve, and they went on, across the yard, toward the house.

"Hey," Shelby said. "Wait a minute."

They were headed toward Helene's window.

"That's her room," Ben said. "I've been here before. I was kind of a peeping Tom back then."

"You are vile," Shelby said.

"I only saw her naked once."

"Only once? Like that's nothing? Once is a violation."

There was a rattle somewhere, a garbage can, perhaps, but unsettling. Ben pulled Shelby so that they were crouching down beside the house. Ben was actually crying now. He'd felt guilty all this time, and he hadn't even known how bad he felt. He'd been a pervert, and he had a pervert's remorse.

"I was only a kid," he said.

"Shit," Shelby said. "Pull yourself together. Okay, you spied on her."

"I was crazy about her."

"Helene?"

"Nuts, huh?"

They both started laughing, muffled, choked giggles.

"Insane," Shelby said.

"Did I ever have a chance?"

"Never. Not in a million years. She was in love with that guy Chris. Truthfully? It would have never been you."

It was kind of a relief to hear that, as though some cord had been cut.

"Do you want to look?" Ben asked.

They were leaning into each other, but they couldn't feel each other. Coats. Gloves. They had been whispering for some time.

"You."

Ben stepped onto a ledge Shelby hadn't known was there. A window well cover that allowed him to haul himself up and look into Helene's window. Shelby stayed where she was, knees pulled up, head spinning, her hands covering her eyes.

Ben stayed there for a while, then he got off the ledge and sunk back down next to Shelby. Close, so their shoulders touched. Shelby uncovered her eyes.

"How is she?"

Ben Mink's beard was patchy, and he smelled like smoke and dirty laundry.

"She looks like somebody in a fairy tale. Her hair reaches down past the bed and trails along the floor. There's white sheets and white blankets and a night light on. She looks peaceful."

"Really?"

"She was beautiful back then, too, but you had more personality. You had a great laugh. I could hear it down the hall in school and know it was you."

"I've become my own evil sister. You're right."

"I like you better this way. Really. But I'm freezing my ass off." 145

They were sitting in a frozen patch of ivy that had broken into shards under their weight.

"My ass is numb," Shelby said. But she didn't get up.

"When I get my first job, I'm getting a Volvo. Ever see their safety records? Man, nothing can hurt you in one of those. A truck can fucking hit you, and you walk out of there in one piece, every limb intact. You'd be safe with me."

"Are you coming on to me?" Shelby said suddenly. Here skull was so cold she felt it might shatter.

"I'm sitting in the fucking ivy with you," Ben Mink said. "It goes way beyond that." 150

Shelby moved still closer, her mouth to his ear, her breath damp and hot. "Should I look?"

"You can if you want to. I'll tell you one thing—that's not her in there."

Shelby thought that over. "How long did you stalk her?"

"It wasn't stalking. I told you, I was crazy about her."

"Did you stalk me?" 155

"What do you think I'm doing right now?"

Shelby started out laughing, and then it became something else. Ben covered her mouth with his gloved hand so Helene's parents wouldn't hear anything. When Shelby's shoulders stopped shaking, Ben said, "Okay?"

Shelby nodded, and he let go.

"I really am freezing," Shelby said.

Ben stood and helped her up. Shelby could have looked in the window. She could 160 have stepped onto the window well sill, held her gloved hand up to the glass, climbed into the room, gotten down on her knees, touched Helene's warm hand, and begged her for something, the way people did on a regular basis, greedy for a miracle. Instead, she followed Ben. They went back the way they'd come, conscious of the sound of their boots in the snow. The sky was black.

"I need something hot to drink," Shelby said.

"Being bald probably lowers your total body temperature," Ben Mink told her.

Shelby doubled her scarf around her head. "Being stupid probably lowers yours."

She smiled, or at least Ben thought she did.

"Probably," he agreed. "I bet it does." 165

But not so stupid that he'd actually opened his eyes when he leaned toward Helene's window. Some things were best remembered the way you wanted to remember them, like this road, these stars, this girl beside him walking into the center of the cold night, looking straight ahead.

Reading and Reacting

1. In paragraphs 1–3, the narrator describes a ritual that takes place each year. What are the elements of this ritual? Why does Hoffman begin her story in this way?
2. Why is Shelby Richmond different from the other people in the town? How did Helene's accident affect Shelby?

3. In paragraph 6, the narrator says, "Shelby is the only one who knows what's wrong with her." What do you think is wrong with Shelby?
4. In what ways are Helene and Shelby similar? In what ways are they different? What is the symbolic meaning of these similarities and differences?
5. Why do Shelby and Helene go out the night of the accident? What does Helene hope to find out about her boyfriend?
6. What significance does Helene have for the high school girls in the town? What significance does she have for the people who come from out of town?
7. Explain how each of the following people react to Helene:
    - Shelby Richmond
    - Shelby's mother
    - Ben Mink
    - The townspeople

   Do you think that their opinions of her are justified? How do you account for the differences in their reactions?
8. In paragraph 141, Ben Mink tells Shelby that Helene "looks like somebody in a fairy tale." In paragraph 166, however, the narrator says that Ben didn't actually open his eyes when he stood at Helene's window. Why does he lie to Shelby?
9. **JOURNAL ENTRY** What do you think will happen to Shelby? Will Ben Mink help her or hurt her? What effect will she have on him?
10. **CRITICAL PERSPECTIVE** Regarding her motivation for exploring magic and ritual in her fiction, Alice Hoffman says, "Magic in fiction is a long tradition. One of the reasons we like fables and fairy tales is that they're emotionally true, and page-turners at the same time."

    In what ways is "Saint Helene" "emotionally true"? What are the magical qualities of the story? Do you think these magical qualities make Shelby's emotions seem more or less real?

Related Works: "Jinx" (p. 178), "Accident" (p. 181), "Greasy Lake" (p. 687), "Teenage Wasteland" (p. 785), "Ex-Basketball Player" (p. 930), "The Road Not Taken" (p. 1159), *Tape* (p. 1275)

Source: ©AP Photo

SHIRLEY JACKSON (1916–1965) is best known for her restrained tales of horror and the supernatural, most notably her novel *The Haunting of Hill House* (1959) and the short story "The Lottery" (1948). Among her other works are two novels dealing with multiple personalities—*The Bird's Nest* (1954) and *We Have Always Lived in the Castle* (1962)—and two collections of comic tales about her children and family life, *Life among the Savages* (1953) and *Raising Demons* (1957). A posthumous collection of stories, *Just an Ordinary Day* (1997), was published after the discovery of a box of some of Jackson's unpublished papers in a Vermont barn and her heirs' subsequent search for her other uncollected works.

With her husband, literary critic Stanley Edgar Hyman, she settled in the small town of Bennington, Vermont, but was never accepted by the townspeople. "The Lottery" is set in much the same kind of small, parochial town. Despite the story's matter-of-fact tone and familiar setting, its publication in the *New*

Yorker provoked a torrent of letters from enraged and shocked readers. In her quiet way, Jackson presented the underside of village life and revealed to readers the dark side of human nature. Future writers of gothic tales recognized their great debt to Jackson. Horror master Stephen King dedicated his book *Firestarter* "to Shirley Jackson, who never had to raise her voice."

Cultural Context "The Lottery" is sometimes seen as a protest against totalitarianism, a form of authoritarian government that permits no individual freedom. In *Eichmann in Jerusalem* (1963), political scientist Hannah Arendt (1906–1975) wrote about totalitarianism as it pertained to Nazi Germany and the Holocaust. Here, she introduced the concept of "the banality of evil," the potential in ordinary people to do evil things. Americans of the post–World War II era saw themselves as "good guys" defending the world against foreign evils. Jackson's story, written scarcely three years after the liberation of Auschwitz, told Americans something they did not want to hear—that the face of human evil could look just like their next-door neighbor.

The Lottery (1948)

The morning of June 27th was clear and sunny, with the fresh warmth of a full-summer day; the flowers were blossoming profusely and the grass was richly green. The people of the village began to gather in the square, between the post office and the bank, around ten o'clock; in some towns there were so many people that the lottery took two days and had to be started on June 26th, but in this village, where there were only about three hundred people, the whole lottery took less than two hours, so it could begin at ten o'clock in the morning and still be through in time to allow the villagers to get home for noon dinner.

The children assembled first, of course. School was recently over for the summer, and the feeling of liberty sat uneasily on most of them; they tended to gather together quietly for a while before they broke into boisterous play, and their talk was still of the classroom and the teacher, of books and reprimands. Bobby Martin had already stuffed his pockets full of stones, and the other boys soon followed his example, selecting the smoothest and roundest stones; Bobby and Harry Jones and Dickie Delacroix—the villagers pronounced this name "Dellacroy"—eventually made a great pile of stones in one corner of the square and guarded it against the raids of the other boys. The girls stood aside, talking among themselves, looking over their shoulders at the boys, and the very small children rolled in the dust or clung to the hands of their older brothers or sisters.

Soon the men began to gather, surveying their own children, speaking of planting and rain, tractors and taxes. They stood together, away from the pile of stones in the corner, and their jokes were quiet and they smiled rather than laughed. The women, wearing faded house dresses and sweaters, came shortly after their menfolk. They greeted one another and exchanged bits of gossip as they went to join their husbands. Soon the women, standing by their husbands, began to call to their children, and the children came reluctantly, having to be called four or five times. Bobby Martin ducked under his mother's grasping hand and ran, laughing, back to the pile of stones. His father spoke up sharply, and Bobby came quickly and took his place between his father and his oldest brother.

The lottery was conducted — as were the square dances, the teen-age club, the Halloween program — by Mr. Summers, who had time and energy to devote to civic activities. He was a round-faced, jovial man and he ran the coal business, and people were sorry for him, because he had no children and his wife was a scold. When he arrived in the square, carrying the black wooden box, there was a murmur of conversation among the villagers, and he waved and called, "Little late today, folks." The postmaster, Mr. Graves, followed him, carrying a three-legged stool, and the stool was put in the center of the square and Mr. Summers set the black box down on it. The villagers kept their distance, leaving a space between themselves and the stool, and when Mr. Summers said, "Some of you fellows want to give me a hand?" there was a hesitation before two men, Mr. Martin and his oldest son, Baxter, came forward to hold the box steady on the stool while Mr. Summers stirred up the papers inside it.

5 The original paraphernalia for the lottery had been lost long ago, and the black box now resting on the stool had been put into use even before Old Man Warner, the oldest man in town, was born. Mr. Summers spoke frequently to the villagers about making a new box, but no one liked to upset even as much tradition as was represented by the black box. There was a story that the present box had been made with some pieces of the box that had preceded it, the one that had been constructed when the first people settled down to make a village here. Every year, after the lottery, Mr. Summers began talking again about a new box, but every year the subject was allowed to fade off without anything's being done. The black box grew shabbier each year; by now it was no longer completely black but splintered badly along one side to show the original wood color, and in some places faded or stained.

Mr. Martin and his oldest son, Baxter, held the black box securely on the stool until Mr. Summers had stirred the papers thoroughly with his hand. Because so much of the ritual had been forgotten or discarded, Mr. Summers had been successful in having slips of paper substituted for the chips of wood that had been used for generations. Chips of wood, Mr. Summers had argued, had been all very well when the village was tiny, but now that the population was more than three hundred and likely to keep on growing, it was necessary to use something that would fit more easily into the black box. The night before the lottery, Mr. Summers and Mr. Graves made up the slips of paper and put them in the box, and it was then taken to the safe of Mr. Summers's coal company and locked up until Mr. Summers was ready to take it to the square next morning. The rest of the year, the box was put away, sometimes one place, sometimes another; it had spent one year in Mr. Graves's barn and another year underfoot in the post office, and sometimes it was set on a shelf in the Martin grocery and left there.

There was a great deal of fussing to be done before Mr. Summers declared the lottery open. There were the lists to make up — of heads of families, heads of households in each family, members of each household in each family. There was the proper swearing-in of Mr. Summers by the postmaster, as the official of the lottery; at one time, some people remembered, there had been a recital of some sort, performed by the official of the lottery, a perfunctory, tuneless chant that had been rattled off duly each year; some people believed that the official of the lottery used to stand just so when he said or sang it, others believed that he was supposed to walk among the people, but years and years ago this part of the ritual had been allowed to lapse. There had been, also, a ritual salute, which the official of the lottery had had to use in addressing each person who came up to draw from the box, but this also had changed with time, until now it was felt necessary only for the official to speak to each person approaching. Mr. Summers was very good at all this; in his clean white shirt and blue jeans, with one hand resting carelessly on the black box, he seemed very proper and important as he talked interminably to Mr. Graves and the Martins.

Just as Mr. Summers finally left off talking and turned to the assembled villagers, Mrs. Hutchinson came hurriedly along the path to the square, her sweater thrown over her shoulders, and slid into place in the back of the crowd. "Clean forgot what day it was," she said to Mrs. Delacroix, who stood next to her, and they both laughed softly. "Thought my old man was out back stacking wood," Mrs. Hutchinson went on, "and then I looked out the window and the kids was gone, and then I remembered it was the twenty-seventh and came a-running." She dried her hands on her apron, and Mrs. Delacroix said, "You're in time, though. They're still talking away up there."

Mrs. Hutchinson craned her neck to see through the crowd and found her husband and children standing near the front. She tapped Mrs. Delacroix on the arm as a farewell and began to make her way through the crowd. The people separated good-humoredly to let her through; two or three people said, in voices just loud enough to be heard across the crowd, "Here comes your Missus, Hutchinson," and "Bill, she made it after all." Mrs. Hutchinson reached her husband, and Mr. Summers, who had been waiting, said cheerfully, "Thought we were going to have to get on without you, Tessie." Mrs. Hutchinson said, grinning, "Wouldn't have me leave m'dishes in the sink, now, would you, Joe?," and soft laughter ran through the crowd as the people stirred back into position after Mrs. Hutchinson's arrival.

"Well, now," Mr. Summers said soberly, "guess we better get started, get this over 10
with, so's we can go back to work. Anybody ain't here?"

"Dunbar," several people said. "Dunbar, Dunbar."

Mr. Summers consulted his list. "Clyde Dunbar," he said. "That's right. He's broke his leg, hasn't he? Who's drawing for him?"

"Me, I guess," a woman said, and Mr. Summers turned to look at her. "Wife draws for her husband," Mr. Summers said. "Don't you have a grown boy to do it for you, Janey?" Although Mr. Summers and everyone else in the village knew the answer perfectly well, it was the business of the official of the lottery to ask such questions formally. Mr. Summers waited with an expression of polite interest while Mrs. Dunbar answered.

"Horace's not but sixteen yet," Mrs. Dunbar said regretfully. "Guess I gotta fill in for the old man this year."

15 "Right," Mr. Summers said. He made a note on the list he was holding. Then he asked, "Watson boy drawing this year?"

A tall boy in the crowd raised his hand. "Here," he said. "I'm drawing for m'mother and me." He blinked his eyes nervously and ducked his head as several voices in the crowd said things like "Good fellow, Jack," and "Glad to see your mother's got a man to do it."

"Well," Mr. Summers said, "guess that's everyone. Old Man Warner make it?"

"Here," a voice said, and Mr. Summers nodded.

A sudden hush fell on the crowd as Mr. Summers cleared his throat and looked at the list. "All ready?" he called. "Now, I'll read the names—heads of families first — and the men come up and take a paper out of the box. Keep the paper folded in your hand without looking at it until everyone has had a turn. Everything clear?"

20 The people had done it so many times that they only half listened to the directions; most of them were quiet, wetting their lips, not looking around. Then Mr. Summers raised one hand high and said, "Adams." A man disengaged himself from the crowd and came forward. "Hi, Steve," Mr. Summers said, and Mr. Adams said, "Hi, Joe." They grinned at one another humorlessly and nervously. Then Mr. Adams reached into the black box and took out a folded paper. He held it firmly by one corner as he turned and went hastily back to his place in the crowd, where he stood a little apart from his family, not looking down at his hand.

"Allen," Mr. Summers said. "Anderson. . . . Bentham."

"Seems like there's no time at all between lotteries any more," Mrs. Delacroix said to Mrs. Graves in the back row. "Seems like we got through with the last one only last week."

"Time sure goes fast," Mrs. Graves said.

"Clark. . . . Delacroix."

25 "There goes my old man," Mrs. Delacroix said. She held her breath while her husband went forward.

"Dunbar," Mr. Summers said, and Mrs. Dunbar went steadily to the box while one of the women said, "Go on, Janey," and another said, "There she goes."

"We're next," Mrs. Graves said. She watched while Mr. Graves came around from the side of the box, greeted Mr. Summers gravely, and selected a slip of paper from the box. By now, all through the crowd there were men holding the small folded papers in their large hands, turning them over and over nervously. Mrs. Dunbar and her two sons stood together, Mrs. Dunbar holding the slip of paper.

"Harburt. . . . Hutchinson."

"Get up there, Bill," Mrs. Hutchinson said, and the people near her laughed.

30 "Jones."

"They do say," Mr. Adams said to Old Man Warner, who stood next to him, "that over in the north village they're talking of giving up the lottery."

Old Man Warner snorted. "Pack of crazy fools," he said. "Listening to the young folks, nothing's good enough for *them*. Next thing you know, they'll be wanting to go back to living in caves, nobody work any more, live *that* way for a while. Used to be a saying about 'Lottery in June, corn be heavy soon.' First thing you know, we'd all be eating stewed chickweed and acorns. There's *always* been a lottery," he added petulantly. "Bad enough to see young Joe Summers up there joking with everybody."

"Some places have already quit lotteries," Mrs. Adams said.

"Nothing but trouble in *that*," Old Man Warner said stoutly. "Pack of young fools."

"Martin." And Bobby Martin watched his father go forward. "Overdyke. . . . 35
Percy."

"I wish they'd hurry," Mrs. Dunbar said to her older son. "I wish they'd hurry."

"They're almost through," her son said.

"You get ready to run tell Dad," Mrs. Dunbar said.

Mr. Summers called his own name and then stepped forward precisely and selected a slip from the box. Then he called, "Warner."

"Seventy-seventh year I been in the lottery," Old Man Warner said as he went 40
through the crowd. "Seventy-seventh time."

"Watson." The tall boy came awkwardly through the crowd. Someone said, "Don't be nervous, Jack," and Mr. Summers said, "Take your time, son."

"Zanini."

After that, there was a long pause, a breathless pause, until Mr. Summers, holding his slip of paper in the air, said, "All right, fellows." For a minute, no one moved, and then all the slips of paper were opened. Suddenly, all the women began to speak at once, saying, "Who is it?," "Who's got it?," "Is it the Dunbars?," "Is it the Watsons?" Then the voices began to say, "It's Hutchinson. It's Bill," "Bill Hutchinson's got it."

"Go tell your father," Mrs. Dunbar said to her older son.

People began to look around to see the Hutchinsons. Bill Hutchinson was stand- 45
ing quiet, staring down at the paper in his hand. Suddenly, Tessie Hutchinson shouted to Mr. Summers, "You didn't give him time enough to take any paper he wanted. I saw you. It wasn't fair!"

"Be a good sport, Tessie," Mrs. Delacroix called, and Mrs. Graves said, "All of us took the same chance."

"Shut up, Tessie," Bill Hutchinson said.

"Well, everyone," Mr. Summers said, "that was done pretty fast, and now we've got to be hurrying a little more to get done in time." He consulted his next list. "Bill," he said, "you draw for the Hutchinson family. You got any other households in the Hutchinsons?"

"There's Don and Eva," Mrs. Hutchinson yelled, "Make *them* take their chance!"

"Daughters draw with their husbands' families, Tessie," Mr. Summers said gently. 50
"You know that as well as anyone else."

"It wasn't *fair*," Tessie said.

"I guess not, Joe," Bill Hutchinson said regretfully. "My daughter draws with her husband's family, that's only fair. And I've got no other family except the kids."

"Then, as far as drawing for families is concerned, it's you," Mr. Summers said in explanation, "and as far as drawing for households is concerned, that's you, too. Right?"

"Right," Bill Hutchinson said.

55 "How many kids, Bill?" Mr. Summers asked formally.

"Three," Bill Hutchinson said. "There's Bill, Jr., and Nancy, and little Dave. And Tessie and me."

"All right, then," Mr. Summers said. "Harry, you got their tickets back?"

Mr. Graves nodded and held up the slips of paper. "Put them in the box, then," Mr. Summers directed. "Take Bill's and put it in."

"I think we ought to start over," Mrs. Hutchinson said, as quietly as she could. "I tell you it wasn't *fair*. You didn't give him time enough to choose. *Every*body saw that."

60 Mr. Graves had selected the five slips and put them in the box, and he dropped all the papers but those onto the ground, where the breeze caught them and lifted them off.

"Listen, everybody," Mrs. Hutchinson was saying to the people around her.

"Ready, Bill?" Mr. Summers asked, and Bill Hutchinson, with one quick glance around at his wife and children, nodded.

"Remember," Mr. Summers said, "take the slips and keep them folded until each person has taken one. Harry, you help little Dave." Mr. Graves took the hand of the little boy, who came willingly with him up to the box. "Take a paper out of the box, Davy," Mr. Summers said. Davy put his hand into the box and laughed. "Take just *one* paper," Mr. Summers said. "Harry, you hold it for him." Mr. Graves took the child's hand and removed the folded paper from the tight fist and held it while little Dave stood next to him and looked at him wonderingly.

"Nancy next," Mr. Summers said. Nancy was twelve, and her school friends breathed heavily as she went forward, switching her skirt, and took a slip daintily from the box. "Bill, Jr.," Mr. Summers said, and Billy, his face red and his feet overlarge, nearly knocked the box over as he got a paper out. "Tessie," Mr. Summers said. She hesitated for a minute, looking around defiantly, and then set her lips and went up to the box. She snatched a paper out and held it behind her.

65 "Bill," Mr. Summers said, and Bill Hutchinson reached into the box and felt around, bringing his hand out at last with the slip of paper in it.

The crowd was quiet. A girl whispered, "I hope it's not Nancy," and the sound of the whisper reached the edges of the crowd.

"It's not the way it used to be," Old Man Warner said clearly. "People ain't the way they used to be."

"All right," Mr. Summers said. "Open the papers. Harry, you open little Dave's."

Mr. Graves opened the slip of paper and there was a general sigh through the crowd as he held it up and everyone could see that it was blank. Nancy and Bill, Jr., opened theirs at the same time, and both beamed and laughed, turning around to the crowd and holding their slips of paper above their heads.

70 "Tessie," Mr. Summers said. There was a pause, and then Mr. Summers looked at Bill Hutchinson, and Bill unfolded his paper and showed it. It was blank.

"It's Tessie," Mr. Summers said, and his voice was hushed. "Show us her paper, Bill."

Bill Hutchinson went over to his wife and forced the slip of paper out of her hand. It had a black spot on it, the black spot Mr. Summers had made the night before with the heavy pencil in the coal-company office. Bill Hutchinson held it up, and there was a stir in the crowd.

"All right, folks," Mr. Summers said. "Let's finish quickly."

Although the villagers had forgotten the ritual and lost the original black box, they still remembered to use stones. The pile of stones the boys had made earlier was ready; there were stones on the ground with the blowing scraps of paper that had come out of the box. Mrs. Delacroix selected a stone so large she had to pick it up with both hands and turned to Mrs. Dunbar. "Come on," she said. "Hurry up."

Mrs. Dunbar had small stones in both hands, and she said, gasping for breath, "I can't run at all. You'll have to go ahead and I'll catch up with you."

The children had stones already, and someone gave little Davy Hutchinson a few pebbles.

Tessie Hutchinson was in the center of a cleared space by now, and she held her hands out desperately as the villagers moved in on her. "It isn't fair," she said. A stone hit her on the side of the head.

Old Man Warner was saying, "Come on, come on, everyone." Steve Adams was in the front of the crowd of villagers, with Mrs. Graves beside him.

"It isn't fair, it isn't right," Mrs. Hutchinson screamed, and then they were upon her.

Reading and Reacting

1. What possible significance, beyond their literal meaning, might each of the following have:

- The village square
- Mrs. Hutchinson's apron
- Old Man Warner
- The slips of paper
- The black spot

2. "The Lottery" takes place in summer, a conventional symbol that has a positive connotation. What does this setting contribute to the story's plot? To its atmosphere?

3. What, if anything, might the names *Graves*, *Adams*, *Summers*, and *Delacroix* signify in the context of this story? Do you think these names are intended to have any special significance? Why or why not?

4. What role do the children play in the ritual? How can you explain their presence in the story? Do they have any symbolic role?

5. What symbolic significance might be found in the way the characters are dressed? In their conversation?

6. In what sense is the story's title ironic?

7. Throughout the story, there is a general atmosphere of excitement. What indication is there of nervousness or apprehension?

8. Early in the story, the boys stuff their pockets with stones, foreshadowing the attack in the story's conclusion. What other examples of foreshadowing can you identify?

9. **JOURNAL ENTRY** How can a ritual like the lottery continue to be held year after year? Why does no one move to end it? Can you think of a modern-day counterpart to this lottery—a situation in which people continue to act in ways they know to be wrong rather than challenge the status quo? How can you account for such behavior?

10. **CRITICAL PERSPECTIVE** When "The Lottery" was published in the June 26, 1948, issue of the *New Yorker*, its effect was immediate. The story, as the critic Judy Oppenheimer notes in her book *Private Demons: The Life of Shirley Jackson*, "provoked an unprecedented outpouring of fury, horror, rage, disgust, and intense fascination." As a result, Jackson received hundreds of letters, which included (among others) the following interpretations of the story:

    - The story is an attack on small-town America.
    - The story is a parable about the perversion of democracy.
    - The story is a criticism of prejudice, particularly anti-Semitism.
    - The story has no point at all.

    How plausible do you think each of these interpretations is? Which comes closest to your interpretation of the story? Why?

Related Works: "Young Goodman Brown" (p. 540), "Where Are You Going, Where Have You Been?" (p. 617), "Patterns" (p. 850), "How Did They Kill My Grandmother?" (p. 1065), *Nine Ten* (p. 1314)

ALICE WALKER (1944–) was the youngest of eight children born to Willie Lee and Minnie Tallulah Grant Walker, sharecroppers who raised cotton. She left the rural South to attend Spelman College in Atlanta (1961–1963) and Sarah Lawrence College in Bronxville, New York (1963–1965).

In 1967, Walker moved to Mississippi, where she was supported in the writing of her first novel, *The Third Life of Grange Copeland* (1970), by a National Endowment for the Arts grant. Her short story "Everyday Use" was included in *Best American Short Stories 1973* and has been widely anthologized and studied. Other novels and collections of short stories followed, including *In Love & Trouble: Stories of Black Women* (1973), *Meridian* (1976), *You Can't Keep a Good Woman Down* (1981), *The Temple of My Familiar* (1989), *Possessing the Secret of Joy* (1993), *The Complete Stories* (1994), *By the Light of My Father's Smile* (1998), and *Now Is the Time to Open Your Heart* (2004). Her latest book is a collection of essays, *We Are The Ones We Have Been Waiting For: Light in a Time of Darkness* (2006). Her third novel, *The Color Purple* (1982), won the American Book Award and a Pulitzer Prize and was made into an award-winning movie and a long-running Broadway play.

In the third year of her marriage, Walker took back her maiden name because she wanted to honor her great-great-great-grandmother who had walked, carrying her two children, from Virginia to Georgia.

Walker's renaming is consistent with one of her goals in writing, which is to further the process of reconnecting people to their ancestors. She has said that "it is fatal to see yourself as separate" and that if people can reaffirm the past, they can "make a different future."

Cultural Context Quilting attained the status of art in Europe in the fourteenth century but reached its fullest development later in North America. By the end of the eighteenth century, the American quilt had taken on unique and distinctive features that separated it from quilts made in other parts of the world. For African Americans, quilting has particular significance. Some scholars think that during slavery, members of the Underground Railroad used quilts to send messages. One design, the Log Cabin, was hung outside to mark a house of refuge for fugitive slaves. Other quilts mapped escape routes out of a plantation or county, often by marking the stars that would act as a guide to freedom for those escaping at night. After the emancipation of slaves, quilts retained their cultural and historical significance, as the quilt in this story does.

Everyday Use (1973)

For Your Grandmama

I will wait for her in the yard that Maggie and I made so clean and wavy yesterday afternoon. A yard like this is more comfortable than most people know. It is not just a yard. It is like an extended living room. When the hard clay is swept clean as a floor and the fine sand around the edges lined with tiny, irregular grooves, anyone can come and sit and look up into the elm tree and wait for the breezes that never come inside the house.

Film Series

DVD

See p. 525 for film stills from the DVD version of this story.

Maggie will be nervous until after her sister goes: she will stand hopelessly in corners, homely and ashamed of the burn scars down her arms and legs, eying her sister with a mixture of envy and awe. She thinks her sister has held life always in the palm of one hand, that "no" is a word the world never learned to say to her.

You've no doubt seen those TV shows where the child who has "made it" is confronted, as a surprise, by her own mother and father, tottering in weakly from backstage. (A pleasant surprise, of course: What would they do if parent and child came on the show only to curse out and insult each other?) On TV mother and child embrace and smile into each other's faces. Sometimes the mother and father weep, the child wraps them in her arms and leans across the table to tell how she would not have made it without their help. I have seen these programs.

Sometimes I dream a dream in which Dee and I are suddenly brought together on a TV program of this sort. Out of a dark and soft-seated limousine I am ushered into a bright room filled with many people. There I meet a smiling, gray, sporty man like Johnny Carson who shakes my hand and tells me what a fine girl I have. Then we are on the stage and Dee is embracing me with tears in her eyes. She pins on my dress a large orchid, even though she has told me once that she thinks orchids are tacky flowers.

5 In real life I am a large, big-boned woman with rough, man-working hands. In the winter I wear flannel nightgowns to bed and overalls during the day. I can kill and clean a hog as mercilessly as a man. My fat keeps me hot in zero weather. I can work outside all day, breaking ice to get water for washing; I can eat pork liver cooked over the open fire minutes after it comes steaming from the hog. One winter I knocked a bull calf straight in the brain between the eyes with a sledge hammer and had the meat hung up to chill before nightfall. But of course all this does not show on television. I am the way my daughter would want me to be: a hundred pounds lighter, my skin like an uncooked barley pancake. My hair glistens in the hot bright lights. Johnny Carson has much to do to keep up with my quick and witty tongue.

But that is a mistake. I know even before I wake up. Who ever knew a Johnson with a quick tongue? Who can even imagine me looking a strange white man in the eye? It seems to me I have talked to them always with one foot raised in flight, with my head turned in whichever way is farthest from them. Dee, though. She would always look anyone in the eye. Hesitation was no part of her nature.

"How do I look, Mama?" Maggie says, showing just enough of her thin body enveloped in pink skirt and red blouse for me to know she's there, almost hidden by the door.

"Come out into the yard," I say.

Have you ever seen a lame animal, perhaps a dog run over by some careless person rich enough to own a car, sidle up to someone who is ignorant enough to be kind to him? That is the way my Maggie walks. She has been like this, chin on chest, eyes on ground, feet in shuffle, ever since the fire that burned the other house to the ground.

10 Dee is lighter than Maggie, with nicer hair and a fuller figure. She's a woman now, though sometimes I forget. How long ago was it that the other house burned? Ten, twelve years? Sometimes I can still hear the flames and feel Maggie's arms sticking to me, her hair smoking and her dress falling off her in little black papery flakes. Her eyes seemed stretched open, blazed open by the flames reflected in them. And Dee. I see her standing off under the sweet gum tree she used to dig gum out of; a look of concentration on her face as she watched the last dingy gray board of the house fall in toward the red-hot brick chimney. Why don't you do a dance around the ashes? I'd wanted to ask her. She had hated the house that much.

I used to think she hated Maggie, too. But that was before we raised the money, the church and me, to send her to Augusta to school. She used to read to us without pity; forcing words, lies, other folks' habits, whole lives upon us two, sitting trapped and ignorant underneath her voice. She washed us in a river of make-believe, burned us with a lot of knowledge we didn't necessarily need to know. Pressed us to her with the serious way she read, to shove us away at just the moment, like dimwits, we seemed about to understand.

Dee wanted nice things. A yellow organdy dress to wear to her graduation from high school; black pumps to match a green suit she'd made from an old suit somebody gave me. She was determined to stare down any disaster in her efforts. Her eyelids would not flicker for minutes at a time. Often I fought off the temptation to shake her. At sixteen she had a style of her own, and knew what style was.

I never had an education myself. After second grade the school was closed down. Don't ask me why: in 1927 colored asked fewer questions than they do now. Sometimes Maggie reads to me. She stumbles along good-naturedly but can't see well. She knows she is not bright. Like good looks and money, quickness passed her by. She will marry John Thomas (who has mossy teeth in an earnest face) and then I'll be free to sit here and I guess just sing church songs to myself. Although I never was a good singer. Never could carry a tune. I was always better at a man's job. I used to love to milk till I was hooked in the side in '49. Cows are soothing and slow and don't bother you, unless you try to milk them the wrong way.

I have deliberately turned my back on the house. It is three rooms, just like the one that burned, except the roof is tin; they don't make shingle roofs any more. There are no real windows, just some holes cut in the sides, like the portholes in a ship, but not round and not square, with rawhide holding the shutters up on the outside. This house is in a pasture, too, like the other one. No doubt when Dee sees it she will want to tear it down. She wrote me once that no matter where we "choose" to live, she will manage to come see us. But she will never bring her friends. Maggie and I thought about this and Maggie asked me, "Mama, when did Dee ever *have* any friends?"

She had a few. Furtive boys in pink shirts hanging about on washday after school. 15
Nervous girls who never laughed. Impressed with her they worshiped the well-turned phrase, the cute shape, the scalding humor that erupted like bubbles in lye. She read to them.

When she was courting Jimmy T she didn't have much time to pay to us, but turned all her faultfinding power on him. He *flew* to marry a cheap city girl from a family of ignorant flashy people. She hardly had time to recompose herself.

When she comes I will meet—but there they are!

Maggie attempts to make a dash for the house, in her shuffling way, but I stay her with my hand. "Come back here," I say. And she stops and tries to dig a well in the sand with her toe.

It is hard to see them clearly through the strong sun. But even the first glimpse of leg out of the car tells me it is Dee. Her feet were always neat-looking, as if God himself had shaped them with a certain style. From the other side of the car comes a short, stocky man. Hair is all over his head a foot long and hanging from his chin like a kinky mule tail. I hear Maggie suck in her breath. "Uhnnnh," is what it sounds like. Like when you see the wriggling end of a snake just in front of your foot on the road. "Uhnnnh."

Dee next. A dress down to the ground, in this hot weather. A dress so loud it 20
hurts my eyes. There are yellows and oranges enough to throw back the light of the sun. I feel my whole face warming from the heat waves it throws out. Earrings gold,

too, and hanging down to her shoulders. Bracelets dangling and making noises when she moves her arm up to shake the folds of the dress out of her armpits. The dress is loose and flows, and as she walks closer, I like it. I hear Maggie go "Uhnnnh" again. It is her sister's hair. It stands straight up like the wool on a sheep. It is black as night and around the edges are two long pigtails that rope about like small lizards disappearing behind her ears.

"Wa-su-zo-Tean-o!"° she says, coming on in that gliding way the dress makes her move. The short stocky fellow with the hair to his navel is all grinning and he follows up with "Asalamalakim,° my mother and sister!" He moves to hug Maggie but she falls back, right up against the back of my chair. I feel her trembling there and when I look up I see the perspiration falling off her chin.

"Don't get up," says Dee. Since I am stout it takes something of a push. You can see me trying to move a second or two before I make it. She turns, showing white heels through her sandals, and goes back to the car. Out she peeks next with a Polaroid. She stoops down quickly and lines up picture after picture of me sitting there in front of the house with Maggie cowering behind me. She never takes a shot without making sure the house is included. When a cow comes nibbling around the edge of the yard she snaps it and me and Maggie *and* the house. Then she puts the Polaroid in the back seat of the car, and comes up and kisses me on the forehead.

Meanwhile Asalamalakim is going through motions with Maggie's hand. Maggie's hand is as limp as a fish, and probably as cold, despite the sweat, and she keeps trying to pull it back. It looks like Asalamalakim wants to shake hands but wants to do it fancy. Or maybe he don't know how people shake hands. Anyhow, he soon gives up on Maggie.

"Well," I say. "Dee."

25 "No, Mama," she says. "Not 'Dee,' Wangero Leewanika Kemanjo!"

"What happened to 'Dee'?" I wanted to know.

"She's dead," Wangero said. "I couldn't bear it any longer, being named after the people who oppress me."

"You know as well as me you was named after your aunt Dicie," I said. Dicie is my sister. She named Dee. We called her "Big Dee" after Dee was born.

"But who was *she* named after?" asked Wangero.

30 "I guess after Grandma Dee," I said.

"And who was she named after?" asked Wangero.

"Her mother," I said, and saw Wangero was getting tired. "That's about as far back as I can trace it," I said. Though, in fact, I probably could have carried it back beyond the Civil War through the branches.

"Well," said Asalamalakim, "there you are."

"Uhnnnh," I heard Maggie say.

Wa-su-zo-Tean-o: A greeting in Swahili; Dee sounds it out one syllable at a time.
Asalamalakim: A greeting in Arabic: "Peace be upon you."

"There I was not," I said, "before 'Dicie' cropped up in our family, so why should I try to trace it that far back?" 35

He just stood there grinning, looking down on me like somebody inspecting a Model A car. Every once in a while he and Wangero sent eye signals over my head.

"How do you pronounce this name?" I asked.

"You don't have to call me by it if you don't want to," said Wangero.

"Why shouldn't I?" I asked. "If that's what you want us to call you, we'll call you."

"I know it might sound awkward at first," said Wangero. 40

"I'll get used to it," I said. "Ream it out again."

Well, soon we got the name out of the way. Asalamalakim had a name twice as long and three times as hard. After I tripped over it two or three times he told me to just call him Hakim-a-barber. I wanted to ask him was he a barber, but I didn't really think he was, so I didn't ask.

"You must belong to those beef-cattle peoples down the road," I said. They said "Asalamalakim" when they met you, too, but they didn't shake hands. Always too busy: feeding the cattle, fixing the fences, putting up salt-lick shelters, throwing down hay. When the white folks poisoned some of the herd the men stayed up all night with rifles in their hands. I walked a mile and a half just to see the sight.

Hakim-a-barber said, "I accept some of their doctrines, but farming and raising cattle is not my style." (They didn't tell me, and I didn't ask, whether Wangero [Dee] had really gone and married him.)

We sat down to eat and right away he said he didn't eat collards and pork was 45
unclean. Wangero, though, went on through the chitlins and corn bread, the greens and everything else. She talked a blue streak over the sweet potatoes. Everything delighted her. Even the fact that we still used the benches her daddy made for the table when we couldn't afford to buy chairs.

"Oh, Mama!" she cried. Then turned to Hakim-a-barber. "I never knew how lovely these benches are. You can feel the rump prints," she said, running her hands underneath her and along the bench. Then she gave a sigh and her hand closed over Grandma Dee's butter dish. "That's it!" she said. "I knew there was something I wanted to ask you if I could have." She jumped up from the table and went over in the corner where the churn stood, the milk in it clabber by now. She looked at the churn and looked at it.

"This churn top is what I need," she said. "Didn't Uncle Buddy whittle it out of a tree you all used to have?"

"Yes," I said.

"Uh huh," she said happily. "And I want the dasher, too."

"Uncle Buddy whittle that, too?" asked the barber. 50

Dee (Wangero) looked up at me.

"Aunt Dee's first husband whittled the dash," said Maggie so low you almost couldn't hear her. "His name was Henry, but they called him Stash."

"Maggie's brain is like an elephant's," Wangero said, laughing. "I can use the churn top as a centerpiece for the alcove table," she said, sliding a plate over the churn, "and I'll think of something artistic to do with the dasher."

When she finished wrapping the dasher the handle stuck out. I took it for a moment in my hands. You didn't even have to look close to see where hands pushing the dasher up and down to make butter had left a kind of sink in the wood. In fact, there were a lot of small sinks; you could see where thumb and fingers had sunk into the wood. It was beautiful light yellow wood, from a tree that grew in the yard where Big Dee and Stash had lived.

55 After dinner Dee (Wangero) went to the trunk at the foot of my bed and started rifling through it. Maggie hung back in the kitchen over the dishpan. Out came Wangero with two quilts. They had been pieced by Grandma Dee and then Big Dee and me had hung them on the quilt frames on the front porch and quilted them. One was in the Lone Star pattern. The other was Walk Around the Mountain. In both of them were scraps of dresses Grandma Dee had worn fifty and more years ago. Bits and pieces of Grandpa Jarrell's Paisley shirts. And one teeny faded blue piece, about the size of a penny matchbox, that was from Great Grandpa Ezra's uniform that he wore in the Civil War.

"Mama," Wangero said sweet as a bird. "Can I have these old quilts?"

I heard something fall in the kitchen, and a minute later the kitchen door slammed.

"Why don't you take one or two of the others?" I asked. "These old things was just done by me and Big Dee from some tops your grandma pieced before she died."

"No," said Wangero. "I don't want those. They are stitched around the borders by machine."

60 "That'll make them last better," I said.

"That's not the point," said Wangero. "These are all pieces of dresses Grandma used to wear. She did all this stitching by hand. Imagine!" She held the quilts securely in her arms, stroking them.

"Some of the pieces, like those lavender ones, come from old clothes her mother handed down to her," I said, moving up to touch the quilts. Dee (Wangero) moved back just enough so that I couldn't reach the quilts. They already belonged to her.

"Imagine!" she breathed again, clutching them closely to her bosom.

"The truth is," I said, "I promised to give them quilts to Maggie, for when she marries John Thomas."

65 She gasped like a bee had stung her. "Maggie can't appreciate these quilts!" she said. "She'd probably be backward enough to put them to everyday use."

"I reckon she would," I said. "God knows I been saving 'em for long enough with nobody using 'em. I hope she will!" I didn't want to bring up how I had offered Dee (Wangero) a quilt when she went away to college. Then she had told me they were old-fashioned, out of style.

"But, they're *priceless!*" she was saying now, furiously; for she has a temper. "Maggie would put them on the bed and in five years they'd be in rags. Less than that!"

"She can always make some more," I said. "Maggie knows how to quilt."

Dee (Wangero) looked at me with hatred. "You just will not understand. The point is these quilts, *these* quilts!"

"Well," I said, stumped. "What would *you* do with them?" 70

"Hang them," she said. As if that was the only thing you *could* do with quilts.

Maggie by now was standing in the door. I could almost hear the sound her feet made as they scraped over each other.

"She can have them, Mama," she said, like somebody used to never winning anything, or having anything reserved for her. "I can 'member Grandma Dee without the quilts."

I looked at her hard. She had filled her bottom lip with checkerberry snuff and it gave her face a kind of dopey, hangdog look. It was Grandma Dee and Big Dee who taught her how to quilt herself. She stood there with her scarred hands hidden in the folds of her skirt. She looked at her sister with something like fear but she wasn't mad at her. This was Maggie's portion. This was the way she knew God to work.

When I looked at her like that something hit me in the top of my head and ran 75
down to the soles of my feet. Just like when I'm in church and the spirit of God touches me and I get happy and shout. I did something I never had done before: hugged Maggie to me, then dragged her on into the room, snatched the quilts out of Miss Wangero's hands and dumped them into Maggie's lap. Maggie just sat there on my bed with her mouth open.

"Take one or two of the others," I said to Dee.

But she turned without a word and went out to Hakim-a-barber.

"You just don't understand," she said, as Maggie and I came out to the car.

"What don't I understand?" I wanted to know.

"Your heritage," she said. And then she turned to Maggie, kissed her, and said, 80
"You ought to try to make something of yourself, too, Maggie. It's really a new day for us. But from the way you and Mama still live you'd never know it."

She put on some sunglasses that hid everything above the tip of her nose and her chin.

Maggie smiled; maybe at the sunglasses. But a real smile, not scared. After we watched the car dust settle I asked Maggie to bring me a dip of snuff. And then the two of us sat there just enjoying, until it was time to go in the house and go to bed.

Reading and Reacting

1. In American culture, what does a patchwork quilt symbolize?
2. What is the literal meaning of the two quilts to Maggie and her mother? To Dee? Beyond this literal meaning, what symbolic meaning, if any, do they have to Maggie and her mother? Do the quilts have any symbolic meaning to Dee?
3. How does the contrast between the two sisters' appearances, personalities, lifestyles, and feelings about the quilts help to convey the story's theme?

4. What does the name *Wangero* signify to Dee? To her mother and sister? Could the name be considered a symbol? Why or why not?
5. Why do you think Maggie gives the quilts to her sister?
6. What is Dee's opinion of her mother and sister? Do you agree with her assessment?
7. What does the story's title suggest to you? Is it ironic? What other titles would be effective?
8. Discuss the possible meanings, aside from their literal meanings, that each of the following suggest: the family's yard, Maggie's burn scars, the trunk in which the quilts are kept, Dee's Polaroid camera. What symbolic functions, if any, do these items serve in the story?
9. **JOURNAL ENTRY** What objects have the kind of symbolic value to you that the quilts have to Maggie? What gives these objects this value?
10. **CRITICAL PERSPECTIVE** In her article "The Black Woman Artist as Wayward," critic Barbara Christian characterizes "Everyday Use" as a story in which Alice Walker examines the "creative legacy" of ordinary African-American women. According to Christian, the story "is about the use and misuse of the concept of heritage. The mother of two daughters, one selfish and stylish, the other scarred and caring, passes on to us its true definition."

    What definition of *heritage* does the mother attempt to pass on to her children? How is this definition like or unlike Dee's definition?

Related Works: "Two Kinds" (p. 777), "My Grandmother Would Rock Quietly and Hum" (p. 840), "Aunt Jennifer's Tigers" (p. 963), "Digging" (p. 1040), *Trifles* (p. 1319), *Fences* (p. 1902)

Fiction in Film: Alice Walker's "Everyday Use"

At the heart of "Everyday Use" (p. 517) is the quilt, a symbol, among other things, of family unity, racial pride, and the strength of African-American women. The story is set in 1973, at a time when many African Americans asserted their racial pride and their connections with Africa. In the DVD version of the story, Dee and her friend Hakim-a-barber do this by sporting Afros and by wearing African clothing. In contrast, Maggie and Mrs. Johnson, who show little sympathy for Dee's cause, dress in a simple style associated with the rural American South. Central to the story are several symbols: the house, the bench, the churn, and of course, the quilt. The stills reproduced here depict scenes that appear on the DVD.

Reading and Reacting

1. When you read "Everyday Use," how did you picture the characters? How are the characters depicted below like or unlike those you imagined?
2. Mrs. Johnson, the narrator of "Everyday Use," not only tells the story but also adds her comments and insights. What aspects of her narrative could be dramatized in a film, and what parts would require a narrator's voice-over?
3. If you were making a film version of the story, how would you introduce the quilt? How would you emphasize its symbolic value?
4. How would you depict the house (inside and out)?
5. Would you use a flashback to show the fire? What would be gained and lost by actually showing—rather than telling about—this important event?
6. If you wanted to make a contemporary film of the story, what difficulties would you face? Which actor would you cast as Dee? Maggie? Hakim-a-barber? Mrs. Johnson?
7. In the story, Mrs. Johnson says that Dee is probably ashamed of her and Maggie as well as of their house. How would you make this apparent in a film version of the story?

Dee and Hakim-a-barber.
Source: ©Suzanne English / Worn Path Productions

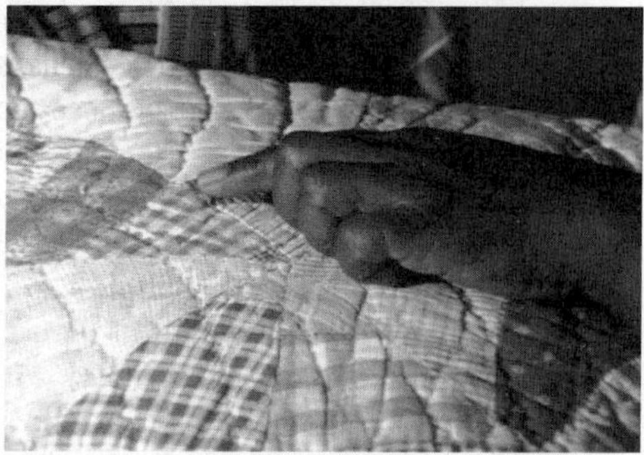

The quilt.
Source: ©Suzanne English / Worn Path Productions

Maggie and Mrs. Johnson in front of their house.
Source: ©Suzanne English / Worn Path Productions

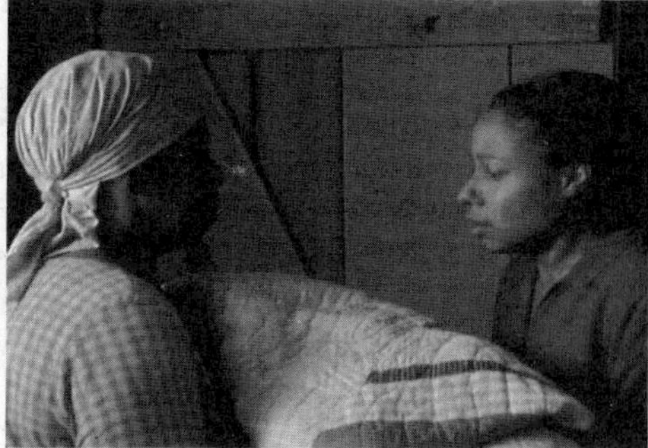

Mrs. Johnson giving the quilt to Maggie.
Source: ©Suzanne English / Worn Path Productions

Source: ©Marion Ettlinger

RAYMOND CARVER (1938–1988), one of the most influential and widely read writers of our time, fashioned his stories from the stuff of common life uncommonly perceived. He married at nineteen and fathered two children by the time he was twenty; during this period, he also began to write. He received a degree from Humboldt State University and later from the University of Iowa. His first collection of stories, *Will You Please Be Quiet, Please* (1976), was nominated for a National Book Award. Five more collections of stories followed, including *Cathedral* (1983)— nominated for both a Pulitzer Prize and a National Book Critics Circle Award — and *Where I'm Calling From: New and Selected Stories* (1988). Carver was also the author of five books of poetry. In his last years, Carver was praised as the best American short story writer since Ernest Hemingway; novelist Robert Stone called him "a hero of perception." He was made an Honorary Doctor of Letters at the University of Hartford and was inducted into the American Academy and Institute of Arts and Letters.

Cultural Context A cathedral is the principal church of a bishop's diocese. As centers of religious authority, civic pomp, and communal worship, cathedrals began to be built in Europe around the year 1000. They flourished throughout the Middle Ages as the power of the Catholic Church grew. The lavish decoration and dazzling design of these structures were meant not only to celebrate God but also to honor those secular and religious authorities who had financed the construction of the buildings. Cathedrals — especially those built in the Gothic period, between 1200 and 1500 — often featured pointed arches, flying buttresses, and high spires designed to lift worshipers' eyes toward heaven. The cathedral in this story serves a similar purpose on a symbolic level.

Cathedral (1983)

Film Series

DVD

See pp. 538–39 for film stills from the DVD version of this story.

This blind man, an old friend of my wife's, he was on his way to spend the night. His wife had died. So he was visiting the dead wife's relatives in Connecticut. He called my wife from his in-laws'. Arrangements were made. He would come by train, a five-hour trip, and my wife would meet him at the station. She hadn't seen him since she worked for him one summer in Seattle ten years ago. But she and the blind man had kept in touch. They made tapes and mailed them back and forth. I wasn't enthusiastic about his visit. He was no one I knew. And his being blind bothered me. My idea of blindness came from the movies. In the movies, the blind moved slowly and never laughed. Sometimes they were led by seeing-eye dogs. A blind man in my house was not something I looked forward to.

That summer in Seattle she had needed a job. She didn't have any money. The man she was going to marry at the end of the summer was in officers' training school.

He didn't have any money, either. But she was in love with the guy, and he was in love with her, etc. She'd seen something in the paper: HELP WANTED—*Reading to Blind Man,* and a telephone number. She phoned and went over, was hired on the spot. She'd worked with this blind man all summer. She read stuff to him, case studies, reports, that sort of thing. She helped him organize his little office in the county social-service department. They'd become good friends, my wife and the blind man. How do I know these things? She told me. And she told me something else. On her last day in the office, the blind man asked if he could touch her face. She agreed to this. She told me he touched his fingers to every part of her face, her nose—even her neck! She never forgot it. She even tried to write a poem about it. She was always trying to write a poem. She wrote a poem or two every year, usually after something really important had happened to her.

When we first started going out together, she showed me the poem. In the poem, she recalled his fingers and the way they had moved around over her face. In the poem, she talked about what she had felt at the time, about what went through her mind when the blind man touched her nose and lips. I can remember I didn't think much of the poem. Of course, I didn't tell her that. Maybe I just don't understand poetry. I admit it's not the first thing I reach for when I pick up something to read.

Anyway, this man who'd first enjoyed her favors, the officer-to-be, he'd been her childhood sweetheart. So okay. I'm saying that at the end of the summer she let the blind man run his hands over her face, said goodbye to him, married her childhood etc., who was now a commissioned officer, and she moved away from Seattle. But they'd kept in touch, she and the blind man. She made the first contact after a year or so. She called him up one night from an Air Force base in Alabama. She wanted to talk. They talked. He asked her to send a tape and tell him about her life. She did this. She sent the tape. On the tape, she told the blind man about her husband and about their life together in the military. She told the blind man she loved her husband but she didn't like it where they lived and she didn't like it that he was part of the military-industrial thing. She told the blind man she'd written a poem and he was in it. She told him that she was writing a poem about what it was like to be an Air Force officer's wife. The poem wasn't finished yet. She was still writing it. The blind man made a tape. He sent her the tape. She made a tape. This went on for years. My wife's officer was posted to one base and then another. She sent tapes from Moody AFB, McGuire, McConnell, and finally Travis,° near Sacramento, where one night she got to feeling lonely and cut off from people she kept losing in that moving-around life. She got to feeling she couldn't go it another step. She went in and swallowed all the pills and capsules in the medicine chest and washed them down with a bottle of gin. Then she got into a hot bath and passed out.

But instead of dying, she got sick. She threw up. Her officer—why should he 5
have a name? he was the childhood sweetheart, and what more does he want?—came home from somewhere, found her, and called the ambulance. In time, she put

Moody . . . Travis: United States Air Force bases.

it all on a tape and sent the tape to the blind man. Over the years, she put all kinds of stuff on tapes and sent the tapes off lickety-split. Next to writing a poem every year, I think it was her chief means of recreation. On one tape, she told the blind man she'd decided to live away from her officer for a time. On another tape, she told him about her divorce. She and I began going out, and of course she told her blind man about it. She told him everything, or so it seemed to me. Once she asked me if I'd like to hear the latest tape from the blind man. This was a year ago. I was on the tape, she said. So I said okay, I'd listen to it. I got us drinks and we settled down in the living room. We made ready to listen. First she inserted the tape into the player and adjusted a couple of dials. Then she pushed a lever. The tape squeaked and someone began to talk in this loud voice. She lowered the volume. After a few minutes of harmless chitchat, I heard my own name in the mouth of this stranger, this blind man I didn't even know! And then this: "From all you've said about him, I can only conclude—" But we were interrupted, a knock at the door, something, and we didn't ever get back to the tape. Maybe it was just as well. I'd heard all I wanted to.

Now this same blind man was coming to sleep in my house.

"Maybe I could take him bowling," I said to my wife. She was at the draining board doing scalloped potatoes. She put down the knife she was using and turned around.

"If you love me," she said, "you can do this for me. If you don't love me, okay. But if you had a friend, any friend, and the friend came to visit, I'd make him feel comfortable." She wiped her hands with the dish towel.

"I don't have any blind friends," I said.

10 "You don't have *any* friends," she said. "Period. Besides," she said, "goddamn it, his wife's just died! Don't you understand that? The man's lost his wife!"

I didn't answer. She'd told me a little about the blind man's wife. Her name was Beulah. Beulah! That's a name for a colored woman.

"Was his wife a Negro?" I asked.

"Are you crazy?" my wife said. "Have you just flipped or something?" She picked up a potato. I saw it hit the floor, then roll under the stove. "What's wrong with you?" she said. "Are you drunk?"

"I'm just asking," I said.

15 Right then my wife filled me in with more detail than I cared to know. I made a drink and sat at the kitchen table to listen. Pieces of the story began to fall into place.

Beulah had gone to work for the blind man the summer after my wife had stopped working for him. Pretty soon Beulah and the blind man had themselves a church wedding. It was a little wedding—who'd want to go to such a wedding in the first place?—just the two of them, plus the minister and the minister's wife. But it was a church wedding just the same. It was what Beulah had wanted, he'd said. But even then Beulah must have been carrying the cancer in her glands. After they had been inseparable for eight years—my wife's word, *inseparable*—Beulah's health went into a rapid decline. She died in a Seattle hospital room, the blind man sitting beside the bed and holding on to her hand. They'd married, lived and worked together, slept together—had sex, sure—and then the blind man had to bury her. All this without his having ever seen what the goddamned woman looked like. It was beyond my understanding. Hearing this, I felt sorry for the blind man for a little bit. And then I found myself thinking what a pitiful life this woman must have led. Imagine a woman who could never see herself as she was seen in the eyes of her loved one. A woman who could go on day after day and never receive the smallest compliment from her beloved. A woman whose husband could never read the expression on her face, be it misery or something better. Someone who could wear makeup or not—what difference to him? She could, if she wanted, wear green eye-shadow around one eye, a straight pin in her nostril, yellow slacks, and purple shoes, no matter. And then to slip off into death, the blind man's hand on her hand, his blind eyes streaming tears—I'm imagining now—her last thought maybe this: that he never even knew what she looked like, and she on an express to the grave. Robert was left with a small insurance policy and a half of a twenty-peso Mexican coin. The other half of the coin went into the box with her. Pathetic.

So when the time rolled around, my wife went to the depot to pick him up. With nothing to do but wait—sure, I blamed him for that—I was having a drink and watching the TV when I heard the car pull into the drive. I got up from the sofa with my drink and went to the window to have a look.

I saw my wife laughing as she parked the car. I saw her get out of the car and shut the door. She was still wearing a smile. Just amazing. She went around to the other side of the car to where the blind man was already starting to get out. This blind man, feature this, he was wearing a full beard! A beard on a blind man! Too much, I say. The blind man reached into the backseat and dragged out a suitcase. My wife took his arm, shut the car door, and, talking all the way, moved him down the drive and then up the steps to the front porch. I turned off the TV. I finished my drink, rinsed the glass, dried my hands. Then I went to the door.

My wife said, "I want you to meet Robert. Robert, this is my husband. I've told you all about him." She was beaming. She had this blind man by his coat sleeve.

The blind man let go of his suitcase and up came his hand. 20

I took it. He squeezed hard, held my hand, and then he let it go.

"I feel like we've already met," he boomed.

"Likewise," I said. I didn't know what else to say. Then I said, "Welcome. I've heard a lot about you." We began to move then, a little group, from the porch into the living room, my wife guiding him by the arm. The blind man was carrying his suitcase in his other hand. My wife said things like, "To your left here, Robert. That's right. Now watch it, there's a chair. That's it. Sit down right here. This is the sofa. We just bought this sofa two weeks ago."

I started to say something about the old sofa. I'd liked that old sofa. But I didn't say anything. Then I wanted to say something else, small-talk, about the scenic ride along the Hudson.° How going *to* New York, you should sit on the right-hand side of the train, and coming *from* New York, the left-hand side.

Hudson: A river in New York State.

25 "Did you have a good train ride?" I said. "Which side of the train did you sit on, by the way?"

"What a question, which side!" my wife said. "What's it matter which side?" she said.

"I just asked," I said.

"Right side," the blind man said. "I hadn't been on a train in nearly forty years. Not since I was a kid. With my folks. That's been a long time. I'd nearly forgotten the sensation. I have winter in my beard now," he said. "So I've been told, anyway. Do I look distinguished, my dear?" the blind man said to my wife.

"You look distinguished, Robert," she said. "Robert," she said. "Robert, it's just so good to see you."

30 My wife finally took her eyes off the blind man and looked at me. I had the feeling she didn't like what she saw. I shrugged.

I've never met, or personally known, anyone who was blind. This blind man was late forties, a heavy-set, balding man with stooped shoulders, as if he carried a great weight there. He wore brown slacks, brown shoes, a light-brown shirt, a tie, a sports coat. Spiffy. He also had this full beard. But he didn't use a cane and he didn't wear dark glasses. I'd always thought dark glasses were a must for the blind. Fact was, I wished he had a pair. At first glance, his eyes looked like anyone else's eyes. But if you looked close, there was something different about them. Too much white in the iris, for one thing, and the pupils seemed to move around in the sockets without his knowing it or being able to stop it. Creepy. As I stared at his face, I saw the left pupil turn in toward his nose while the other made an effort to keep in one place. But it was only an effort, for that eye was on the roam without his knowing it or wanting it to be.

I said, "Let me get you a drink. What's your pleasure? We have a little of everything. It's one of our pastimes."

"Bub, I'm a Scotch man myself," he said fast enough in this big voice.

"Right," I said. Bub! "Sure you are. I knew it."

35 He let his fingers touch his suitcase, which was sitting alongside the sofa. He was taking his bearings. I didn't blame him for that.

"I'll move that up to your room," my wife said.

"No, that's fine," the blind man said loudly. "It can go up when I go up."

"A little water with the Scotch?" I said.

"Very little," he said.

40 "I knew it," I said.

He said, "Just a tad. The Irish actor, Barry Fitzgerald? I'm like that fellow. When I drink water, Fitzgerald said, I drink water. When I drink whiskey, I drink whiskey." My wife laughed. The blind man brought his hand up under his beard. He lifted his beard slowly and let it drop.

I did the drinks, three big glasses of Scotch with a splash of water in each. Then we made ourselves comfortable and talked about Robert's travels. First the long flight from the West Coast to Connecticut, we covered that. Then from Connecticut up here by train. We had another drink concerning that leg of the trip.

I remembered having read somewhere that the blind didn't smoke because, as speculation had it, they couldn't see the smoke they exhaled. I thought I knew that much and that much only about blind people. But this blind man smoked his cigarette down to the nubbin and then lit another one. This blind man filled his ashtray and my wife emptied it.

When we sat down at the table for dinner, we had another drink. My wife heaped Robert's plate with cube steak, scalloped potatoes, green beans. I buttered him up two slices of bread. I said, "Here's bread and butter for you." I swallowed some of my drink. "Now let us pray," I said, and the blind man lowered his head. My wife looked at me, her mouth agape. "Pray the phone won't ring and the food doesn't get cold," I said.

45 We dug in. We ate everything there was to eat on the table. We ate like there was no tomorrow. We didn't talk. We ate. We scarfed. We grazed that table. We were into serious eating. The blind man had right away located his foods, he knew just where everything was on his plate. I watched with admiration as he used his knife and fork on the meat. He'd cut two pieces of meat, fork the meat into his mouth, and then go all out for the scalloped potatoes, the beans next, and then he'd tear off a hunk of buttered bread and eat that. He'd follow this up with a big drink of milk. It didn't seem to bother him to use his fingers once in a while, either.

We finished everything, including half a strawberry pie. For a few moments, we sat as if stunned. Sweat beaded on our faces. Finally, we got up from the table and left the dirty plates. We didn't look back. We took ourselves into the living room and sank into our places again. Robert and my wife sat on the sofa. I took the big chair. We had us two or three more drinks while they talked about the major things that had come to pass for them in the past ten years. For the most part, I just listened. Now and then I joined in. I didn't want him to think I'd left the room, and I didn't want her to think I was feeling left out. They talked of things that had happened to them — to them! — these past ten years. I waited in vain to hear my name on my wife's sweet lips: "And then my dear husband came into my life" — something like that. But I heard nothing of the sort. More talk of Robert. Robert had done a little of everything, it seemed, a regular blind jack-of-all-trades. But most recently he and his wife had had an Amway distributorship, from which, I gathered, they'd earned their living, such as it was. The blind man was also a ham radio operator.° He talked in his loud voice about conversations he'd had with fellow operators in Guam, in the Philippines, in Alaska, and even in Tahiti. He said he'd have a lot of friends there if he ever wanted to go visit those places. From time to time, he'd turn his blind face toward me, put his hand under his beard, ask me something. How long had I been in my present position? (Three years.) Did I like my work? (I didn't.) Was I going to stay with it? (What were the options?) Finally, when I thought he was beginning to run down, I got up and turned on the TV.

My wife looked at me with irritation. She was heading toward a boil. Then she looked at the blind man and said, "Robert, do you have a TV?"

The blind man said, "My dear, I have two TVs. I have a color set and a black-and-white thing, an old relic. It's funny, but if I turn the TV on, and I'm always turning it on, I turn on the color set. It's funny, don't you think?"

---

ham radio operator: A licensed amateur radio operator.

I didn't know what to say to that. I had absolutely nothing to say to that. No opinion. So I watched the news program and tried to listen to what the announcer was saying.

"This is a color TV," the blind man said. "Don't ask me how, but I can tell."

"We traded up a while ago," I said.

The blind man had another taste of his drink. He lifted his beard, sniffed it, and let it fall. He leaned forward on the sofa. He positioned his ashtray on the coffee table, then put the lighter to his cigarette. He leaned back on the sofa and crossed his legs at the ankles.

My wife covered her mouth, and then she yawned. She stretched. She said, "I think I'll go upstairs and put on my robe. I think I'll change into something else. Robert, you make yourself comfortable," she said.

"I'm comfortable," the blind man said.

"I want you to feel comfortable in this house," she said.

"I am comfortable," the blind man said.

After she'd left the room, he and I listened to the weather report and then to the sports roundup. By that time, she'd been gone so long I didn't know if she was going to come back. I thought she might have gone to bed. I wished she'd come back downstairs. I didn't want to be left alone with a blind man. I asked him if he wanted another drink, and he said sure. Then I asked if he wanted to smoke some dope with me. I said I'd just rolled a number. I hadn't, but I planned to do so in about two shakes.

"I'll try some with you," he said.

"Damn right," I said. "That's the stuff."

I got our drinks and sat down on the sofa with him. Then I rolled us two fat numbers. I lit one and passed it. I brought it to his fingers. He took it and inhaled.

"Hold it as long as you can," I said. I could tell he didn't know the first thing.

My wife came back downstairs wearing her pink robe and her pink slippers.

"What do I smell?" she said.

"We thought we'd have us some cannabis," I said.

My wife gave me a savage look. Then she looked at the blind man and said, "Robert, I didn't know you smoked."

He said, "I do now, my dear. There's a first time for everything. But I don't feel anything yet."

"This stuff is pretty mellow," I said. "This stuff is mild. It's dope you can reason with," I said. "It doesn't mess you up."

"Not much it doesn't, bub," he said, and laughed.

My wife sat on the sofa between the blind man and me. I passed her the number. She took it and toked° and then passed it back to me. "Which way is this going?" she said. Then she said, "I shouldn't be smoking this. I can hardly keep my eyes open as it is. That dinner did me in. I shouldn't have eaten so much."

"It was the strawberry pie," the blind man said. "That's what did it," he said, and he laughed his big laugh. Then he shook his head.

"There's more strawberry pie," I said.

---

toked: Inhaled.

"Do you want some more, Robert?" my wife said.

"Maybe in a little while," he said.

We gave our attention to the TV. My wife yawned again. She said, "Your bed is made up when you feel like going to bed, Robert. I know you must have had a long day. When you're ready to go to bed, say so." She pulled his arm. "Robert?"

He came to and said, "I've had a real nice time. This beats tapes, doesn't it?" 75

I said, "Coming at you," and I put the number between his fingers. He inhaled, held the smoke, and then let it go. It was like he'd been doing it since he was nine years old.

"Thanks, bub," he said. "But I think this is all for me. I think I'm beginning to feel it," he said. He held the burning roach out for my wife.

"Same here," she said. "Ditto. Me, too." She took the roach and passed it to me. "I may just sit here for a while between you two guys with my eyes closed. But don't let me bother you, okay? Either one of you. If it bothers you, say so. Otherwise, I may just sit here with my eyes closed until you're ready to go to bed," she said. "Your bed's made up, Robert, when you're ready. It's right next to our room at the top of the stairs. We'll show you up when you're ready. You wake me up now, you guys, if I fall asleep." She said that and then she closed her eyes and went to sleep.

The news program ended. I got up and changed the channel. I sat back down on the sofa. I wished my wife hadn't pooped out. Her head lay across the back of the sofa, her mouth open. She'd turned so that her robe slipped away from her legs, exposing a juicy thigh. I reached to draw her robe back over her, and it was then that I glanced at the blind man. What the hell! I flipped the robe open again.

"You say when you want some strawberry pie," I said. 80

"I will," he said.

I said, "Are you tired? Do you want me to take you up to your bed? Are you ready to hit the hay?"

"Not yet," he said. "No, I'll stay up with you, bub. If that's all right. I'll stay up until you're ready to turn in. We haven't had a chance to talk. Know what I mean? I feel like me and her monopolized the evening." He lifted his beard and he let it fall. He picked up his cigarettes and his lighter.

"That's all right," I said. Then I said, "I'm glad for the company."

And I guess I was. Every night I smoked dope and stayed up as long as I could 85
before I fell asleep. My wife and I hardly ever went to bed at the same time. When I did go to sleep, I had these dreams. Sometimes I'd wake up from one of them, my heart going crazy.

Something about the church and the Middle Ages was on the TV. Not your run-of-the-mill TV fare. I wanted to watch something else. I turned to the other channels. But there was nothing on them, either. So I turned back to the first channel and apologized.

"Bub, it's all right," the blind man said. "It's fine with me. Whatever you want to watch is okay. I'm always learning something. Learning never ends. It won't hurt me to learn something tonight. I got ears," he said.

We didn't say anything for a time. He was leaning forward with his head turned at me, his right ear aimed in the direction of the set. Very disconcerting. Now and then his eyelids drooped and then they snapped open again. Now and then he put his fingers into his beard and tugged, like he was thinking about something he was hearing on the television.

On the screen, a group of men wearing cowls was being set upon and tormented by men dressed in skeleton costumes and men dressed as devils. The men dressed as devils wore devil masks, horns, and long tails. This pageant was part of a procession. The Englishman who was narrating the thing said it took place in Spain once a year. I tried to explain to the blind man what was happening.

"Skeletons," he said. "I know about skeletons," he said, and nodded.

The TV showed this one cathedral. Then there was a long, slow look at another one. Finally, the picture switched to the famous one in Paris, with its flying buttresses and its spires reaching up to the clouds. The camera pulled away to show the whole of the cathedral rising above the skyline.

There were times when the Englishman who was telling the thing would shut up, would simply let the camera move around the cathedrals. Or else the camera would tour the countryside, men in fields walking behind oxen. I waited as long as I could. Then I felt I had to say something. I said, "They're showing the outside of this cathedral now. Gargoyles. Little statues carved to look like monsters. Now I guess they're in Italy. Yeah, they're in Italy. There's paintings on the walls of this one church."

"Are those fresco° paintings, bub?" he asked, and he sipped from his drink.

I reached for my glass. But it was empty. I tried to remember what I could remember. "You're asking me are those frescoes?" I said. "That's a good question. I don't know."

The camera moved to a cathedral outside Lisbon.° The differences in the Portuguese cathedral compared with the French and Italian were not that great. But they were there. Mostly the interior stuff. Then something occurred to me, and I said, "Something has occurred to me. Do you have any idea what a cathedral is? What they look like, that is? Do you follow me? If somebody says cathedral to you, do you have any notion what they're talking about? Do you know the difference between that and a Baptist church, say?"

He let the smoke dribble from his mouth. "I know they took hundreds of workers fifty or a hundred years to build," he said. "I just heard the man say that, of course. I know generations of the same families worked on a cathedral. I heard him say that, too. The men who began their life's work on them, they never lived to see the completion of their work. In that wise, bub, they're no different from the rest of us, right?" He laughed. Then his eyelids drooped again. His head nodded. He seemed to be snoozing. Maybe he was imagining himself in Portugal. The TV was showing another cathedral now. This one was in Germany. The Englishman's voice droned on. "Cathedrals," the blind man said. He sat up and rolled his head back and forth. "If you want the truth, bub, that's about all I know. What I just said. What I heard him say. But maybe you could describe one to me? I wish you'd do it. I'd like that. If you want to know, I really don't have a good idea."

---

fresco: Painted plaster.
Lisbon: The capital of Portugal.

I stared hard at the shot of the cathedral on the TV. How could I even begin to describe it? But say my life depended on it. Say my life was being threatened by an insane guy who said I had to do it or else.

I stared some more at the cathedral before the picture flipped off into the countryside. There was no use. I turned to the blind man and said, "To begin with, they're very tall." I was looking around the room for clues. "They reach way up. Up and up. Toward the sky. They're so big, some of them, they have to have these supports. To help hold them up, so to speak. These supports are called buttresses. They remind me of viaducts,° for some reason. But maybe you don't know viaducts, either? Sometimes the cathedrals have devils and such carved into the front. Sometimes lords and ladies. Don't ask me why this is," I said.

He was nodding. The whole upper part of his body seemed to be moving back and forth.

"I'm not doing so good, am I?" I said. 100

He stopped nodding and leaned forward on the edge of the sofa. As he listened to me, he was running his fingers through his beard. I wasn't getting through to him, I could see that. But he waited for me to go on just the same. He nodded, like he was trying to encourage me. I tried to think what else to say. "They're really big," I said. "They're massive. They're built of stone. Marble, too, sometimes. In those olden days, when they built cathedrals, men wanted to be close to God. In those olden days, God was an important part of everyone's life. You could tell this from their cathedral-building. I'm sorry," I said, "but it looks like that's the best I can do for you. I'm just no good at it."

"That's all right, bub," the blind man said. "Hey, listen. I hope you don't mind my asking you. Can I ask you something? Let me ask you a simple question, yes or no. I'm just curious and there's no offense. You're my host. But let me ask if you are in any way religious? You don't mind my asking?"

I shook my head. He couldn't see that, though. A wink is the same as a nod to a blind man. "I guess I don't believe in it. In anything. Sometimes it's hard. You know what I'm saying?"

"Sure, I do," he said.

"Right," I said. 105

The Englishman was still holding forth. My wife sighed in her sleep. She drew a long breath and went on with her sleeping.

"You'll have to forgive me," I said. "But I can't tell you what a cathedral looks like. It just isn't in me to do it. I can't do any more than I've done."

The blind man sat very still, his head down, as he listened to me.

I said, "The truth is, cathedrals don't mean anything special to me. Nothing. Cathedrals. They're something to look at on late-night TV. That's all they are."

It was then that the blind man cleared his throat. He brought something up. He 110
took a handkerchief from his back pocket. Then he said, "I get it, bub. It's okay. It happens. Don't worry about it," he said. "Hey, listen to me. Will you do me a favor?

---

viaducts: Long, elevated roadways.

I got an idea. Why don't you find us some heavy paper? And a pen. We'll do something. We'll draw one together. Get us a pen and some heavy paper. Go on, bub, get the stuff," he said.

So I went upstairs. My legs felt like they didn't have any strength in them. They felt like they did after I'd done some running. In my wife's room, I looked around. I found some ballpoints in a little basket on her table. And then I tried to think where to look for the kind of paper he was talking about.

Downstairs, in the kitchen, I found a shopping bag with onion skins in the bottom of the bag. I emptied the bag and shook it. I brought it into the living room and sat down with it near his legs. I moved some things, smoothed the wrinkles from the bag, spread it out on the coffee table.

The blind man got down from the sofa and sat next to me on the carpet.

He ran his fingers over the paper. He went up and down the sides of the paper. The edges, even the edges. He fingered the corners.

115 "All right," he said. "All right, let's do her."

He found my hand, the hand with the pen. He closed his hand over my hand. "Go ahead, bub, draw," he said. "Draw. You'll see. I'll follow along with you. It'll be okay. Just begin now like I'm telling you. You'll see. Draw," the blind man said.

So I began. First I drew a box that looked like a house. It could have been the house I lived in. Then I put a roof on it. At either end of the roof, I drew spires. Crazy.

"Swell," he said. "Terrific. You're doing fine," he said. "Never thought anything like this could happen in your lifetime, did you, bub? Well, it's a strange life, we all know that. Go on now. Keep it up."

I put in windows with arches. I drew flying buttresses. I hung great doors. I couldn't stop. The TV station went off the air. I put down the pen and closed and opened my fingers. The blind man felt around over the paper. He moved the tips of his fingers over the paper, all over what I had drawn, and he nodded.

120 "Doing fine," the blind man said.

I took up the pen again, and he found my hand. I kept at it. I'm no artist. But I kept drawing just the same.

My wife opened up her eyes and gazed at us. She sat up on the sofa, her robe hanging open. She said, "What are you doing? Tell me, I want to know."

I didn't answer her.

The blind man said, "We're drawing a cathedral. Me and him are working on it. Press hard," he said to me. "That's right. That's good," he said. "Sure. You got it, bub, I can tell. You didn't think you could. But you can, can't you? You're cooking with gas now. You know what I'm saying? We're going to really have us something here in a minute. How's the old arm?" he said. "Put some people in there now. What's a cathedral without people?"

125 My wife said, "What's going on? Robert, what are you doing? What's going on?"

"It's all right," he said to her. "Close your eyes now," the blind man said to me.

I did it. I closed them just like he said.

"Are they closed?" he said. "Don't fudge."

"They're closed," I said.

"Keep them that way," he said. He said, "Don't stop now. Draw." 130

So we kept on with it. His fingers rode my fingers as my hand went over the paper. It was like nothing else in my life up to now.

Then he said, "I think that's it. I think you got it," he said. "Take a look. What do you think?"

But I had my eyes closed. I thought I'd keep them that way for a little longer. I thought it was something I ought to do.

"Well?" he said. "Are you looking?"

My eyes were still closed. I was in my house. I knew that. But I didn't feel like I 135
was inside anything.

"It's really something," I said.

Reading and Reacting

1. Who is the narrator? What do we know about him? Why does the impending visit by the blind man disturb him?
2. At several points in the story, the narrator's wife loses patience with him. What causes her displeasure? What do her reactions reveal about the wife? About the narrator?
3. Why did the narrator's wife leave her first husband? What qualities in the narrator might have led his wife to marry him?
4. Why is the narrator's wife so devoted to the blind man? What does she gain from her relationship with him?
5. According to the narrator, his wife never forgot the blind man's running his fingers over her face. Why is this experience so important to her?
6. Toward the end of the story, the blind man asks the narrator to describe a cathedral. Why is the narrator unable to do so? What does his inability to do so reveal about him?
7. Why does the blind man tell the narrator to close his eyes while he is drawing? What does he hope to teach him? What is the narrator able to "see" with his eyes shut that he cannot see with them open?
8. In paragraph 96, the blind man observes that the men who began work on a cathedral never lived to see it completed. In this way, he says, "they're no different from the rest of us." What does the cathedral symbolize to the blind man? What does it come to symbolize to the narrator?

9. **JOURNAL ENTRY** The blind man is an old friend of the narrator's wife. Why then does he focus on the narrator? In what way is the narrator's spiritual development the blind man's gift to the narrator's wife?

10. **CRITICAL PERSPECTIVE** Critic Kirk Nesset, in his discussion of "Cathedral," notes that the narrator becomes more open as the story progresses, and that this coming out is mirrored by the rhetoric of the story. Early on in the story, the narrator feels momentarily "sorry for the blind man," his insulated hardness beginning to soften. As the walls of his resentment noticeably crack, he watches with "admiration" as Robert eats, recognizing Robert's handicap to be "no impairment to his performance at the dinner table. . . . Like Robert, who is

on a journey by train, dropping in on friends and relatives, trying to get over the loss of his wife, the narrator is also on a journey, one signaled by signposts in his language and played out by the events of the story he tells."

Do you agree that the narrator becomes more open? If so, can you cite any other instances where the words he chooses reflect this increasing openness?

Related Works: "Gryphon" (p. 277), "Doe Season" (p. 577), "When I Heard the Learn'd Astronomer" (p. 877), "The Value of Education" (p. 892), "On First Looking into Chapman's Homer" (p. 984), "Batter My Heart, Three-Personed God" (p. 1148), "God's Grandeur" (p. 1166), "The Gift" (p. 1174)

Fiction in Film: Raymond Carver's "Cathedral"

Symbolism is important in the story "Cathedral" (p. 526). In the DVD version of the story, the narrator's encounter with his wife's blind friend, Robert, culminates in a symbolic event — the drawing of a cathedral. In addition, blindness becomes symbolic not only of Robert's condition but also of the narrator's — and, by extension, symbolic of the condition of all of humanity. The film clearly portrays the narrator's spiritual quest as well as the blind man's ability to guide him to salvation. The stills included here depict scenes that appear on the DVD.

Reading and Reacting

1. The first part of the story gives background information about the wife's relationship with Robert. How would you present this information in a film? Would you show it in a series of flashbacks, or would you have a narrator or one of the characters tell about it?

Husband and wife on couch.
Source: ©Howard Ksia/Worn Path Productions

Husband drawing (with eyes open).
Source: ©Howard Ksia/Worn Path Productions

The three characters sitting and eating.
Source: ©Howard Ksia/Worn Path Productions

Husband drawing (with eyes shut) with wife and Robert beside him.
Source: ©Howard Ksia/Worn Path Productions

2. The husband has a number of preconceived ideas about blindness, and as a result, he does not look forward to having Robert visit him. How would you convey his discomfort in a film version of the story?

3. In the story, the wife is clearly uneasy about how her husband will react to Robert. How would you convey this emotion in the film?

4. Other than saying that Robert has a full beard, the narrator does not describe the characters in the story. If you were making a film, would the characters look different from the ones shown here?

5. What information from the story would you consider essential for a film version? What information could you do without?

6. What scene could you add to show what took place after the story was over? Which characters would be in this new scene? What would they be doing?

Source: ©AP Photo

NATHANIEL HAWTHORNE (1804–1864) was born in Salem, Massachusetts, the great-great-grandson of a judge who presided over the infamous Salem witch trials. After his sea captain father was killed on a voyage when Hawthorne was four years old, his childhood was one of genteel poverty. An uncle paid for his education at Bowdoin College in Maine, where Hawthorne's friends included a future president of the United States, Franklin Pierce, who in 1853 appointed him U.S. consul in Liverpool, England. Hawthorne published four novels—*The Scarlet Letter* (1850), *The House of the Seven Gables* (1851), *The Blithedale Romance* (1852), and *The Marble Faun* (1860)—and more than one hundred short stories and sketches.

Hawthorne referred to his own work as *romance.* He used this term to mean not an escape from reality but rather a method of confronting "the depths of our common nature" and "the truth of the heart." His stories probe the dark side of human nature and frequently paint a world that is virtuous on the surface but (as Young Goodman Brown comes to believe) "one stain of guilt, one mighty blood spot" beneath. Hawthorne's stories often emphasize the ambiguity of human experience. For example, the reader is left to wonder whether Goodman Brown actually saw a witch's coven or dreamed about the event. For Hawthorne, what is important is Brown's recognition that evil may be found everywhere. "Young Goodman Brown," as Hawthorne's neighbor and friend Herman Melville once said, is a tale "as deep as Dante."

Cultural Context During the five months of the Salem witch trials of 1692, nineteen women and men accused of being witches were put to death by hanging. The accusations began when a few young girls claimed they were possessed by the devil and accused three Salem women of witchcraft. As the hysteria grew throughout Massachusetts, the list of the accused grew as well. Eventually, 150 people were imprisoned before the governor dismissed the special witchcraft court and released the remaining prisoners. It is in this historical setting that "Young Goodman Brown" takes place.

Young Goodman° Brown (1835)

Young Goodman Brown came forth at sunset, into the street of Salem village, but put his head back, after crossing the threshold, to exchange a parting kiss with his young wife. And Faith, as the wife was aptly named, thrust her own pretty head into the street, letting the wind play with the pink ribbons of her cap, while she called to Goodman Brown.

"Dearest heart," whispered she, softly and rather sadly, when her lips were close to his ear, "prithee, put off your journey until sunrise, and sleep in your own bed to-night. A lone woman is troubled with such dreams and such thoughts, that she's afeard of herself, sometimes. Pray, tarry with me this night, dear husband, of all nights in the year!"

"My love and my Faith," replied young Goodman Brown, "of all nights in the year, this one night must I tarry away from thee. My journey, as thou callest it, forth and back again, must needs be done 'twixt now and sunrise. What, my sweet, pretty wife, dost thou doubt me already, and we but three months married!"

"Then God bless you!" said Faith with the pink ribbons, "and may you find all well, when you come back."

5 "Amen!" cried Goodman Brown. "Say thy prayers, dear Faith, and go to bed at dusk, and no harm will come to thee."

So they parted; and the young man pursued his way, until, being about to turn the corner by the meeting-house, he looked back and saw the head of Faith still peeping after him, with a melancholy air, in spite of her pink ribbons.

"Poor little Faith!" thought he, for his heart smote him. "What a wretch am I, to leave her on such an errand! She talks of dreams, too. Methought, as she spoke, there was trouble in her face, as if a dream had warned her what work is to be done to-night. But no, no! 't would kill her to think it. Well; she's a blessed angel on earth; and after this one night, I'll cling to her skirts and follow her to Heaven."

With this excellent resolve for the future, Goodman Brown felt himself justified in making more haste on his present evil purpose. He had taken a dreary road, darkened by all the gloomiest trees of the forest, which barely stood aside to let the narrow path creep through, and closed immediately behind. It was as lonely as could be; and

---

Goodman: A form of address, similar to *Mr.*, meaning "husband."

there is this peculiarity in such a solitude, that the traveller knows not who may be concealed by the innumerable trunks and the thick boughs overhead; so that, with lonely footsteps, he may yet be passing through an unseen multitude.

"There may be a devilish Indian behind every tree," said Goodman Brown to himself; and he glanced fearfully behind him, as he added, "What if the devil himself should be at my very elbow!"

10 His head being turned back, he passed a crook of the road, and looking forward again, beheld the figure of a man, in grave and decent attire, seated at the foot of an old tree. He arose at Goodman Brown's approach, and walked onward, side by side with him.

"You are late, Goodman Brown," said he. "The clock of the Old South° was striking, as I came through Boston; and that is full fifteen minutes agone."

"Faith kept me back awhile," replied the young man, with a tremor in his voice, caused by the sudden appearance of his companion, though not wholly unexpected.

It was now deep dusk in the forest, and deepest in that part of it where these two were journeying. As nearly as could be discerned, the second traveller was about fifty years old, apparently in the same rank of life as Goodman Brown, and bearing a considerable resemblance to him, though perhaps more in expression than features. Still, they might have been taken for father and son. And yet, though the elder person was as simply clad as the younger, and as simple in manner too, he had an indescribable air of one who knew the world, and would not have felt abashed at the governor's dinner-table, or in King William's court,° were it possible that his affairs should call him thither. But the only thing about him that could be fixed upon as remarkable, was his staff, which bore the likeness of a great black snake, so curiously wrought, that it might almost be seen to twist and wriggle itself like a living serpent. This, of course, must have been an ocular deception, assisted by the uncertain light.

"Come, Goodman Brown!" cried his fellow-traveller, "this is a dull pace for the beginning of a journey. Take my staff, if you are so soon weary."

15 "Friend," said the other, exchanging his slow pace for a full stop, "having kept covenant by meeting thee here, it is my purpose now to return whence I came. I have scruples, touching the matter thou wot'st° of."

"Sayest thou so?" replied he of the serpent, smiling apart. "Let us walk on, nevertheless, reasoning as we go, and if I convince thee not, thou shalt turn back. We are but a little way in the forest, yet."

"Too far, too far!" exclaimed the goodman, unconsciously resuming his walk. "My father never went into the woods on such an errand, nor his father before him. We have been a race of honest men and good Christians, since the days of the martyrs. And shall I be the first of the name of Brown that ever took this path and kept—"

"Such company, thou wouldst say," observed the elder person, interrupting his pause. "Well said, Goodman Brown! I have been as well acquainted with your family as with ever a one among the Puritans; and that's no trifle to say. I helped your

---

Old South: Old South Church in Boston, renowned meeting place for American patriots during the Revolution.

King William: William III, king of England from 1689 to 1702.

wot'st of: Know of.

grandfather, the constable, when he lashed the Quaker woman so smartly through the streets of Salem. And it was I that brought your father a pitch-pine knot, kindled at my own hearth, to set fire to an Indian village, in King Philip's war.° They were my good friends, both; and many a pleasant walk have we had along this path, and returned merrily after midnight. I would fain be friends with you, for their sake."

"If it be as thou sayest," replied Goodman Brown, "I marvel they never spoke of these matters. Or, verily, I marvel not, seeing that the least rumor of the sort would have driven them from New England. We are a people of prayer, and good works to boot, and abide no such wickedness."

20 "Wickedness or not," said the traveller with the twisted staff, "I have a very general acquaintance here in New England. The deacons of many a church have drunk the communion wine with me; the selectmen, of divers towns, make me their chairman; and a majority of the Great and General Court are firm supporters of my interest. The governor and I, too—but these are state secrets."

"Can this be so!" cried Goodman Brown, with a stare of amazement at his undisturbed companion. "Howbeit, I have nothing to do with the governor and council; they have their own ways, and are no rule for a simple husbandman like me. But, were I to go on with thee, how should I meet the eye of that good old man, our minister, at Salem village? Oh, his voice would make me tremble, both Sabbath-day and lecture-day!"°

Thus far, the elder traveller had listened with due gravity, but now burst into a fit of irrepressible mirth, shaking himself so violently, that his snakelike staff actually seemed to wriggle in sympathy.

"Ha, ha, ha!" shouted he, again and again; then composing himself, "Well, go on, Goodman Brown, go on; but, prithee, don't kill me with laughing!"

"Well, then, to end the matter at once," said Goodman Brown, considerably nettled, "there is my wife, Faith. It would break her dear little heart; and I'd rather break my own!"

25 "Nay, if that be the case," answered the other, "e'en go thy ways, Goodman Brown. I would not, for twenty old women like the one hobbling before us, that Faith should come to any harm."

As he spoke, he pointed his staff at a female figure on the path, in whom Goodman Brown recognized a very pious and exemplary dame, who had taught him his catechism in youth, and was still his moral and spiritual adviser, jointly with the minister and Deacon Gookin.

"A marvel, truly, that Goody° Cloyse should be so far in the wilderness, at nightfall!" said he. "But, with your leave, friend, I shall take a cut through the woods, until we have left this Christian woman behind. Being a stranger to you, she might ask whom I was consorting with, and whither I was going."

King Philip's war: A war of Indian resistance led by Metacomet of the Wampanoags, known to the English as "King Philip." The war, intended to halt expansion of English settlers in Massachusetts, collapsed after Metacomet's death in August 1676.

lecture-day: The day of the midweek sermon, usually Thursday.

Goody: A contraction of "Goodwife," a term of politeness used in addressing a woman of humble station. Goody Cloyse, like Goody Cory and Martha Carrier, who appear later in the story, was one of the Salem "witches" sentenced in 1692.

"Be it so," said his fellow-traveller. "Betake you to the woods, and let me keep the path."

Accordingly, the young man turned aside, but took care to watch his companion, who advanced softly along the road, until he had come within a staff's length of the old dame. She, meanwhile, was making the best of her way, with singular speed for so aged a woman, and mumbling some indistinct words, a prayer, doubtless, as she went. The traveller put forth his staff, and touched her withered neck with what seemed the serpent's tail.

"The devil!" screamed the pious old lady. 30

"Then Goody Cloyse knows her old friend?" observed the traveller, confronting her, and leaning on his writhing stick.

"Ah, forsooth, and is it your worship, indeed?" cried the good dame. "Yea, truly is it, and in the very image of my old gossip, Goodman Brown, the grandfather of the silly fellow that now is. But, would your worship believe it? my broomstick hath strangely disappeared, stolen, as I suspect, by that unhanged witch, Goody Cory, and that, too, when I was all anointed with the juice of smallage and cinque-foil and wolf's bane—"°

"Mingled with fine wheat and the fat of a new-born babe," said the shape of old Goodman Brown.

"Ah, your worship knows the recipe," cried the old lady, cackling aloud. "So, as I was saying, being all ready for the meeting, and no horse to ride on, I made up my mind to foot it; for they tell me there is a nice young man to be taken into communion to-night. But now your good worship will lend me your arm, and we shall be there in a twinkling."

"That can hardly be," answered her friend. "I may not spare you my arm, Goody 35
Cloyse, but here is my staff, if you will."

So saying, he threw it down at her feet, where, perhaps, it assumed life, being one of the rods which its owner had formerly lent to the Egyptian Magi. Of this fact, however, Goodman Brown could not take cognizance. He had cast his eyes in astonishment, and looking down again, beheld neither Goody Cloyse nor the serpentine staff, but his fellow-traveller alone, who waited for him as calmly as if nothing had happened.

"That old woman taught me my catechism!" said the young man; and there was a world of meaning in this simple comment.

They continued to walk onward, while the elder traveller exhorted his companion to make good speed and persevere in the path, discoursing so aptly, that his arguments seemed rather to spring up in the bosom of his auditor, than to be suggested by himself. As they went he plucked a branch of maple, to serve for a walking-stick, and began to strip it of the twigs and little boughs, which were wet with evening dew. The moment his fingers touched them, they became strangely withered and dried up, as with a week's sunshine. Thus the pair proceeded, at a good free pace, until suddenly, in a gloomy hollow of the road, Goodman Brown sat himself down on the stump of a tree, and refused to go any farther.

---

smallage . . . wolf's bane: Plants believed to have magical powers. Smallage is wild celery.

"Friend," said he, stubbornly, "my mind is made up. Not another step will I budge on this errand. What if a wretched old woman do choose to go to the devil, when I thought she was going to Heaven! Is that any reason why I should quit my dear Faith, and go after her?"

40 "You will think better of this by and by," said his acquaintance, composedly. "Sit here and rest yourself awhile; and when you feel like moving again, there is my staff to help you along."

Without more words, he threw his companion the maple stick, and was as speedily out of sight as if he had vanished into the deepening gloom. The young man sat a few moments by the roadside, applauding himself greatly, and thinking with how clear a conscience he should meet the minister, in his morning walk, nor shrink from the eye of good old Deacon Gookin. And what calm sleep would be his, that very night, which was to have been spent so wickedly, but purely and sweetly now, in the arms of Faith! Amidst these pleasant and praiseworthy meditations, Goodman Brown heard the tramp of horses along the road, and deemed it advisable to conceal himself within the verge of the forest, conscious of the guilty purpose that had brought him thither, though now so happily turned from it.

On came the hoof-tramps and the voices of the riders, two grave old voices, conversing soberly as they drew near. These mingled sounds appeared to pass along the road, within a few yards of the young man's hiding-place; but owing, doubtless, to the depth of the gloom, at that particular spot, neither the travellers nor their steeds were visible. Though their figures brushed the small boughs by the wayside, it could not be seen that they intercepted, even for a moment, the faint gleam from the strip of bright sky, athwart which they must have passed. Goodman Brown alternately crouched and stood on tiptoe, pulling aside the branches, and thrusting forth his head as far as he durst, without discerning so much as a shadow. It vexed him the more, because he could have sworn, were such a thing possible, that he recognized the voices of the minister and Deacon Gookin, jogging along quietly, as they were wont to do, when bound to some ordination or ecclesiastical council. While yet within hearing, one of the riders stopped to pluck a switch.

"Of the two, reverend Sir," said the voice like the deacon's, "I had rather miss an ordination dinner than to-night's meeting. They tell me that some of our community are to be here from Falmouth and beyond, and others from Connecticut and Rhode Island; besides several of the Indian powwows, who, after their fashion, know almost as much deviltry as the best of us. Moreover, there is a goodly young woman to be taken into communion."

"Mighty well, Deacon Gookin!" replied the solemn old tones of the minister. "Spur up, or we shall be late. Nothing can be done, you know, until I get on the ground."

45 The hoofs clattered again, and the voices, talking so strangely in the empty air, passed on through the forest, where no church had ever been gathered, nor solitary Christian prayed. Whither, then, could these holy men be journeying, so deep into the heathen wilderness? Young Goodman Brown caught hold of a tree, for support, being ready to sink down on the ground, faint and over-burthened with the heavy sickness of his heart. He looked up to the sky, doubting whether there really was a Heaven above him. Yet, there was the blue arch, and the stars brightening in it.

"With Heaven above, and Faith below, I will yet stand firm against the devil!" cried Goodman Brown.

While he still gazed upward, into the deep arch of the firmament, and had lifted his hands to pray, a cloud, though no wind was stirring, hurried across the zenith, and hid the brightening stars. The blue sky was still visible, except directly overhead, where this black mass of cloud was sweeping swiftly northward. Aloft in the air, as if from the depths of the cloud, came a confused and doubtful sound of voices. Once, the listener fancied that he could distinguish the accents of townspeople of his own, men and women, both pious and ungodly, many of whom he had met at the communion-table, and had seen others rioting at the tavern. The next moment, so indistinct were the sounds, he doubted whether he had heard aught but the murmur of the old forest, whispering without a wind. Then came a stronger swell of those familiar tones, heard daily in the sunshine, at Salem village, but never, until now, from a cloud at night. There was one voice, of a young woman, uttering lamentations, yet with an uncertain sorrow, and entreating for some favor, which, perhaps, it would grieve her to obtain. And all the unseen multitude, both saints and sinners, seemed to encourage her onward.

"Faith!" shouted Goodman Brown, in a voice of agony and desperation; and the echoes of the forest mocked him, crying—"Faith! Faith!" as if bewildered wretches were seeking her, all through the wilderness.

The cry of grief, rage, and terror was yet piercing the night, when the unhappy husband held his breath for a response. There was a scream, drowned immediately in a louder murmur of voices fading into far-off laughter, as the dark cloud swept away, leaving the clear and silent sky above Goodman Brown. But something fluttered lightly down through the air, and caught on the branch of a tree. The young man seized it and beheld a pink ribbon.

"My Faith is gone!" cried he, after one stupefied moment. "There is no good on 50
earth, and sin is but a name. Come, devil! for to thee is this world given."

And maddened with despair, so that he laughed loud and long, did Goodman Brown grasp his staff and set forth again, at such a rate, that he seemed to fly along the forest path, rather than to walk or run. The road grew wilder and drearier, and more faintly traced, and vanished at length, leaving him in the heart of the dark wilderness, still rushing onward, with the instinct that guides mortal man to evil. The whole forest was peopled with frightful sounds: the creaking of the trees, the howling of wild beasts, and the yell of Indians; while, sometimes, the wind tolled like a distant church bell, and sometimes gave a broad roar around the traveller, as if all Nature was laughing him to scorn. But he was himself the chief horror of the scene, and shrank not from its other horrors.

"Ha! ha! ha!" roared Goodman Brown, when the wind laughed at him. "Let us hear which will laugh loudest! Think not to frighten me with your deviltry! Come witch, come wizard, come Indian powwow, come devil himself! and here comes Goodman Brown. You may as well fear him as he fear you!"

In truth, all through the haunted forest, there could be nothing more frightful than the figure of Goodman Brown. On he flew, among the black pines, brandishing his staff with frenzied gestures, now giving vent to an inspiration of horrid blasphemy, and now shouting forth such laughter, as set all the echoes of the forest laughing like demons around him. The fiend in his own shape is less hideous, than when he rages in the breast of man. Thus sped the demoniac on his course, until, quivering among the trees, he saw a red light before him, as when the felled trunks and branches of a clearing have been set on fire, and throw up their lurid blaze against the sky, at the hour of midnight. He paused, in a lull of the tempest that had driven him onward, and heard the swell of what seemed a hymn, rolling solemnly from a distance, with the weight of many voices. He knew the tune. It was a familiar one in the choir of the village meeting-house. The verse died heavily away, and was lengthened by a chorus, not of human voices, but of all the sounds of the benighted wilderness, pealing in awful harmony together. Goodman Brown cried out; and his cry was lost to his own ear, by its unison with the cry of the desert.

In the interval of silence, he stole forward, until the light glared full upon his eyes. At one extremity of an open space, hemmed in by the dark wall of the forest, arose a rock, bearing some rude, natural resemblance either to an altar or a pulpit, and surrounded by four blazing pines, their tops aflame, their stems untouched, like candles at an evening meeting. The mass of foliage, that had overgrown the summit of the rock, was all on fire, blazing high into the night, and fitfully illuminating the whole field. Each pendent twig and leafy festoon was in a blaze. As the red light arose and fell, a numerous congregation alternately shone forth, then disappeared in shadow, and again grew, as it were, out of the darkness, peopling the heart of the solitary woods at once.

55 "A grave and dark-clad company!" quoth Goodman Brown.

In truth, they were such. Among them, quivering to-and-fro, between gloom and splendor, appeared faces that would be seen, next day, at the council-board of the province, and others which, Sabbath after Sabbath, looked devoutly heavenward, and benignantly over the crowded pews, from the holiest pulpits in the land. Some affirm, that the lady of the governor was there. At least, there were high dames well known to her, and wives of honored husbands, and widows a great multitude, and ancient maidens, all of excellent repute, and fair young girls, who trembled lest their mothers should espy them. Either the sudden gleams of light, flashing over the obscure field, bedazzled Goodman Brown, or he recognized a score of the church members of Salem village, famous for their especial sanctity. Good old Deacon Gookin had arrived, and waited at the skirts of that venerable saint, his reverend pastor. But, irreverently consorting with these grave, reputable, and pious people, these elders of the church, these chaste dames and dewy virgins, there were men of dissolute lives and women of spotted fame, wretches given over to all mean and filthy vice, and suspected even of horrid crimes. It was strange to see, that the good shrank not from the wicked, nor were the sinners abashed by the saints. Scattered, also, among their pale-faced enemies, were the Indian priests, or powwows, who had often scared their native forest with more hideous incantations than any known to English witchcraft.

"But, where is Faith?" thought Goodman Brown; and, as hope came into his heart, he trembled.

Another verse of the hymn arose, a slow and mournful strain, such as the pious love, but joined to words which expressed all that our nature can conceive of sin, and darkly hinted at far more. Unfathomable to mere mortals is the lore of fiends. Verse after verse was sung, and still the chorus of the desert swelled between, like the deepest tone of a mighty organ. And, with the final peal of that dreadful anthem, there came a sound, as if the roaring wind, the rushing streams, the howling beasts, and every other voice of the unconverted wilderness were mingling and according with the voice of guilty man, in homage to the prince of all. The four blazing pines threw up a loftier flame, and obscurely discovered shapes and visages of horror on the smoke-wreaths, above the impious assembly. At the same moment, the fire on the rock shot redly forth, and formed a glowing arch above its base, where now appeared a figure. With reverence be it spoken, the apparition bore no slight similitude, both in garb and manner, to some grave divine of the New England churches.

"Bring forth the converts!" cried a voice, that echoed through the field and rolled into the forest.

At the word, Goodman Brown stepped forth from the shadow of the trees, and 60
approached the congregation, with whom he felt a loathful brotherhood, by the sympathy of all that was wicked in his heart. He could have well-nigh sworn, that the shape of his own dead father beckoned him to advance, looking downward from a smoke-wreath, while a woman, with dim features of despair, threw out her hand to warn him back. Was it his mother? But he had no power to retreat one step, nor to resist, even in thought, when the minister and good old Deacon Gookin seized his arms, and led him to the blazing rock. Thither came also the slender form of a veiled female, led between Goody Cloyse, that pious teacher of the catechism, and Martha Carrier, who had received the devil's promise to be queen of hell. A rampant hag was she! And there stood the proselytes, beneath the canopy of fire.

"Welcome, my children," said the dark figure, "to the communion of your race! Ye have found, thus young, your nature and your destiny. My children, look behind you!"

They turned; and flashing forth, as it were, in a sheet of flame, the fiend-worshippers were seen; the smile of welcome gleamed darkly on every visage.

"There," resumed the sable form, "are all whom ye have reverenced from youth. Ye deemed them holier than yourselves, and shrank from your own sin, contrasting it with their lives of righteousness and prayerful aspirations heavenward. Yet, here are they all, in my worshipping assembly! This night it shall be granted you to know their secret deeds; how hoary-bearded elders of the church have whispered wanton words to the young maids of their households; how many a woman, eager for widow's weeds, has given her husband a drink at bedtime, and let him sleep his last sleep in her bosom; how beardless youths have made haste to inherit their father's wealth; and how fair damsels—blush not, sweet ones!—have dug little graves in the garden, and bidden me, the sole guest, to an infant's funeral. By the sympathy of your human hearts for sin, ye shall scent out all the places—whether in church, bedchamber, street, field, or forest—where crime has been committed, and shall exult to behold the whole earth one stain of guilt, one mighty blood-spot. Far more than this! It shall be yours to penetrate, in every bosom, the deep mystery of sin, the fountain of all wicked arts, and which inexhaustibly supplies more evil impulses than human power—than my power, at its utmost!—can make manifest in deeds. And now, my children, look upon each other."

They did so; and, by the blaze of the hell-kindled torches, the wretched man beheld his Faith, and the wife her husband, trembling before that unhallowed altar.

65 "Lo! there ye stand, my children," said the figure, in a deep and solemn tone, almost sad, with its despairing awfulness, as if his once angelic nature could yet mourn for our miserable race. "Depending upon one another's hearts, ye had still hoped that virtue were not all a dream! Now are ye undeceived!—Evil is the nature of mankind. Evil must be your only happiness. Welcome, again, my children, to the communion of your race!"

"Welcome!" repeated the fiend-worshippers, in one cry of despair and triumph.

And there they stood, the only pair, as it seemed, who were yet hesitating on the verge of wickedness, in this dark world. A basin was hollowed, naturally, in the rock. Did it contain water, reddened by the lurid light? or was it blood? or, perchance, a liquid flame? Herein did the Shape of Evil dip his hand, and prepare to lay the mark of baptism upon their foreheads, that they might be partakers of the mystery of sin, more conscious of the secret guilt of others, both in deed and thought, than they could now be of their own. The husband cast one look at his pale wife, and Faith at him. What polluted wretches would the next glance show them to each other, shuddering alike at what they disclosed and what they saw!

"Faith! Faith!" cried the husband. "Look up to Heaven, and resist the Wicked One!"

Whether Faith obeyed, he knew not. Hardly had he spoken, when he found himself amid calm night and solitude, listening to a roar of the wind, which died heavily away through the forest. He staggered against the rock, and felt it chill and damp, while a hanging twig, that had been all on fire, besprinkled his cheek with the coldest dew.

70 The next morning, young Goodman Brown came slowly into the street of Salem village staring around him like a bewildered man. The good old minister was taking a walk along the grave-yard, to get an appetite for breakfast and meditate his sermon, and bestowed a blessing, as he passed, on Goodman Brown. He shrank from the venerable saint, as if to avoid an anathema. Old Deacon Gookin was at domestic worship, and the holy words of his prayer were heard through the open window. "What God doth the wizard pray to?" quoth Goodman Brown. Goody Cloyse, that excellent old Christian, stood in the early sunshine, at her own lattice, catechising a little girl, who had brought her a pint of morning's milk. Goodman Brown snatched away the child, as from the grasp of the fiend himself. Turning the corner by the meeting-house, he spied the head of Faith, with the pink ribbons, gazing anxiously forth, and bursting into such joy at sight of him that she skipt along the street, and almost kissed her husband before the whole village. But Goodman Brown looked sternly and sadly into her face, and passed on without a greeting.

Had Goodman Brown fallen asleep in the forest, and only dreamed a wild dream of a witch-meeting?

Be it so, if you will. But, alas! it was a dream of evil omen for young Goodman Brown. A stern, a sad, a darkly meditative, a distrustful, if not a desperate man did he become, from the night of that fearful dream. On the Sabbath day, when the congregation were singing a holy psalm, he could not listen, because an anthem of sin rushed loudly upon his ear, and drowned all the blessed strain. When the minister spoke from the pulpit, with power and fervid eloquence, and with his hand on the open Bible, of the sacred truths of our religion, and of saint-like lives and triumphant deaths, and of future bliss or misery unutterable, then did Goodman Brown turn pale, dreading lest the roof should thunder down upon the gray blasphemer and his hearers. Often, awaking suddenly at midnight, he shrank from the bosom of Faith, and at morning or eventide, when the family knelt down at prayer, he scowled, and muttered to himself, and gazed sternly at his wife, and turned away. And when he had lived long, and was borne to his grave, a hoary corpse, followed by Faith, an aged woman, and children and grand-children, a goodly procession, besides neighbors not a few, they carved no hopeful verse upon his tombstone; for his dying hour was gloom.

Reading and Reacting

1. Who is the narrator of "Young Goodman Brown"? What advantages does the narrative point of view give the author?
2. What does young Goodman Brown mean when he says "of all nights in the year, this one night must I tarry away from thee" (par. 3)? What is important about *this* night, and why does Goodman Brown believe he must journey " 'twixt now and sunrise"?
3. Is Goodman Brown surprised to encounter the second traveler on the road, or does he seem to expect him? What is the significance of their encounter? What do you make of the fact that the stranger bears a strong resemblance to young Goodman Brown?
4. What sins are the various characters Goodman Brown meets in the woods guilty of committing?
5. "Young Goodman Brown" has two distinct settings: Salem and the woods. What are the differences between these settings? What significance does each setting have in the story?
6. Which figures in the story are allegorical, and which are symbols? On what evidence do you base your conclusions?
7. Why do the people gather in the woods? Why do they attend the ceremony?
8. Explain the change that takes place in young Goodman Brown at the end of the story. Why can he not listen to the singing of holy psalms or to the minister's sermons? What causes him to turn away from Faith and die in gloom?
9. **Journal Entry** At the end of the story, the narrator suggests that Goodman Brown might have fallen asleep and imagined his encounter with the witches. Do you think the events in the story are all a dream?
10. **Critical Perspective** In *The Power of Blackness*, his classic study of nineteenth-century American writers, Harry Levin observes that Hawthorne had doubts about conventional religion. This, Levin believes, is why all efforts to read an enlightening theological message into Hawthorne's works are "doomed to failure."

    What comment do you think Hawthorne is making in "Young Goodman Brown" about religious faith?

Related Works: "Once upon a Time" (p. 232), "Where Are You Going, Where Have You Been?" (p. 617), "Greasy Lake" (p. 687), "We Wear the Mask" (p. 1150), "La Belle Dame sans Merci: A Ballad" (p. 1169), *Nine Ten* (p. 1314)

WRITING SUGGESTIONS: Symbol, Allegory, and Myth

1. In "Saint Helene" and "Young Goodman Brown," minor characters offer the possibility of salvation or healing to the main characters. For example, in "Saint Helene," Helene holds out the possibility of healing to Shelby, and in "Young Goodman Brown," Faith offers her husband salvation from evil. Write an essay in which you examine the symbolic roles these minor characters play and explain why the central characters reject their offers.
2. Strangers figure prominently in "Young Goodman Brown" and "Cathedral." Write an essay in which you discuss the possible symbolic significance of strangers in each story. If you like, you may also discuss Arnold Friend in "Where Are You Going, Where Have You Been?" (p. 617) or The Misfit in "A Good Man Is Hard to Find" (p. 447).
3. Write an essay in which you discuss the use of myth in "Young Goodman Brown" or in "Fun Home."
4. If Shirley Jackson had wished to write "The Lottery" as an allegory whose purpose was to expose the evils of Nazi Germany, what revisions would she have had to make to convey the dangers of blind obedience to authority? Consider the story's symbols, the characters (and their names), and the setting.
5. In literary works, objects can function as symbols. In this chapter, for example, the quilt in "Everyday Use" and the box in "The Lottery" take on symbolic significance. Write an essay in which you analyze objects that have symbolic significance in two or three of the stories in this text and discuss how these objects help to convey the main themes of the stories in which they appear.

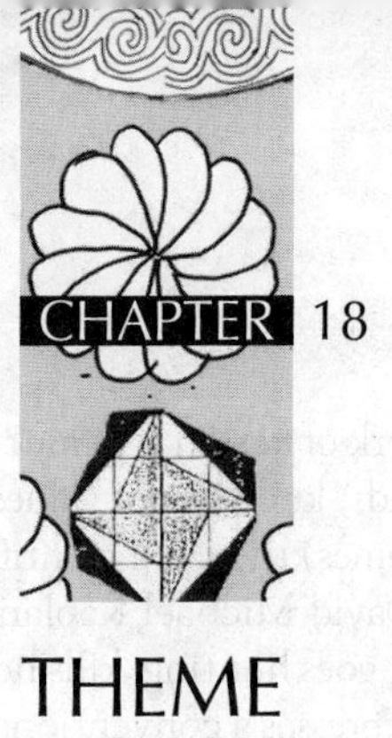

CHAPTER 18

THEME

The **theme** of a work of literature is its central or dominant idea. *Theme* is not the same as *plot* or *subject*, two terms with which it is sometimes confused. A summary of the **plot** of Tadeusz Borowski's "Silence," a story about survivors of the Holocaust, could be, "Prisoners are liberated from a concentration camp, and, despite the warnings of the American officer, they kill a captured German guard." The statement "'Silence' is about freed prisoners and a guard" could define the **subject** of the story. A statement of the **theme** of "Silence," however, has to do more than summarize its plot or define its subject; it has to convey the values and ideas expressed by the story.

Many effective stories are complex, expressing more than one theme, and "Silence" is no exception. You could say that "Silence" suggests that human beings have a need for vengeance. You could also say the story demonstrates that silence is sometimes the only response possible when people confront unspeakable horrors. Both these themes—and others—are expressed in the story, yet one theme seems to dominate: the idea that under extreme conditions the oppressed can have the same capacity for evil as their oppressors.

When you write about theme, you need to do more than tell what happens in the story. The theme you identify should be a general idea that extends beyond the story and applies to the world outside fiction. Compare these two statements that a student wrote about Edgar Allan Poe's "The Cask of Amontillado" (p. 385):

```
Poe's "The Cask of Amontillado" is about a man who has an
obsessive desire for revenge.

Poe's "The Cask of Amontillado" suggests that when the desire
for revenge becomes obsessive, it can deprive individuals of
all that makes them human.
```

The first statement merely tells what the story is about; the second statement identifies the story's theme, a general observation about humanity.

Granted, some short works (fairy tales or fables, for example) have themes that can only be expressed as **clichés**— overused phrases or expressions — or as **morals**— lessons dramatized by the work. The fairy tale "Cinderella," for example, expresses the clichéd theme that a virtuous girl who endures misfortune will eventually achieve her just reward; the fable "The Tortoise and the Hare" illustrates the moral "Slow and steady wins the race." Like "The Cask of Amontillado," however, the stories in this anthology have themes that are much more complex than clichés or morals.

Interpreting Themes

Contemporary critical theory holds that the theme of a work of fiction is as much a creation of readers as of the writer. Readers' backgrounds, knowledge, values, and beliefs all play a part in determining the theme (or themes) they will identify in a work. Many readers, for example, will realize that David Michael Kaplan's story "Doe Season" (p. 577)—in which the main character goes hunting, kills her first deer, and is forced to confront suffering and death—expresses a conventional **initiation theme**, revealing growing up to be a disillusioning and painful process. Still, different readers bring different perspectives to the story and, in some cases, see different themes.

During a classroom discussion of "Doe Season," a student familiar with hunting saw more than his classmates did in the story's conventional initiation theme. He knew that in many states there really is a doe season. Shorter than the ten-day buck season, it allows hunters to control the size of the deer herd by killing females. This knowledge enabled the student to conclude that by the end of the story the female child's innocence is destroyed, just as the doe is.

Another student pointed out that the participation of Andy—a female who uses a male name—in hunting, a traditional male rite of passage, leads to her killing the deer and to her subsequent disillusionment. It also leads to her decision to abandon her nickname. By contrasting "Andrea" with "Andy," the story reveals the conflict between her "female" nature (illustrated by her compassion) and her desire to emulate the men to whom killing is a sport. This interpretation led the student to conclude that the theme of "Doe Season" is that males and females have very different outlooks on life.

Other students rejected the negative portrayal of the story's male characters that the preceding interpretation implies. They pointed out that the father is a sympathetic figure who is extremely supportive; he encourages and defends his daughter. He takes her hunting because he loves her, not because he wants to initiate her into life or to hurt her. One student mentioned that Andy's reaction (called *buck fever*) when she sees the doe is common in children who kill their first deer. In light of this information, several students concluded that far from being about irreconcilable male and female differences, "Doe Season" makes a statement about a young girl who is hunting for her own identity and who in the process discovers her own mortality. Her father is therefore the agent who enables her to confront the inevitability of death, a fact she must accept if she is going to take her place in the adult world. In this sense, the theme of the story is the idea that in order to mature, a child must come to terms with the reality of death.

Different readers may see different themes in a story, but any interpretation of a theme must make sense in light of what is actually in the story. Evidence from the work, not just your own feelings or assumptions, must support your interpretation, and a single statement by a character is not enough in itself to reveal a story's theme. Therefore, you must present a cross-section of examples from the text to support your interpretation of the story's theme. If you say that the theme of James

Joyce's "Araby" (p. 434) is that an innocent idealist is inevitably doomed to disillusionment, you have to find examples from the text to support this statement. You could begin with the title, concluding that the word *Araby* suggests idealistic dreams of exotic beauty that the boy tries to find when he goes to the bazaar. You could reinforce your interpretation by pointing out that the unattainable woman is a symbol of all that the boy wants so desperately to find. Finally, you could show how idealism is ultimately crushed by society: at the end of the story, the boy stands alone in the darkness and realizes that his dreams are childish fantasies. Although other readers may have different responses to "Araby," they should find your interpretation reasonable if you support it with enough examples.

Identifying Themes

Every element of a story can shed light on its themes. As you analyze a short story, you should look for features that reveal and reinforce what you perceive to be the story's most important ideas.

- *The **title** can often provide insight into the theme or themes of a story*. The title of an F. Scott Fitzgerald story, "Babylon Revisited," emphasizes a major idea in the story—that Paris of the 1920s is like Babylon, the ancient city the Bible singles out as the epitome of evil and corruption. The story's protagonist, Charlie Wales, comes to realize that no matter how much money he lost after the 1929 stock market crash, he lost more—his wife and his daughter—during the boom, when he was in Paris. Charlie's search through his past—his return to "Babylon"—provides new meaning to his life and offers at least a small bit of hope for the future.
- *Sometimes a **narrator's or character's statement** can reveal a theme*. For example, at the beginning of Alberto Alvaro Ríos's "The Secret Lion" (p. 197), the first-person narrator says, "I was twelve and in junior high school and something happened that we didn't have a name for, but it was there nonetheless like a lion, and roaring, roaring that way the biggest things do. Everything changed." Although the narrator does not directly announce the story's theme, he suggests that the story will convey the idea that the price children pay for growing up is realizing that everything changes, that nothing stays the way it is.
- *The **arrangement of events** can suggest a story's theme*, as it does in an Ernest Hemingway story, "The Short Happy Life of Francis Macomber." At the beginning of the story, the title character is a coward who is stuck in an unhappy marriage. As the story progresses, he gradually learns the nature of courage and, finally, finds it in himself. At the moment of his triumph, however, Francis is shot by his wife; his "happy life" is short indeed. The way the events of the story are presented, through foreshadowing and flashbacks, reveals the connection between Macomber's marriage and his behavior as a hunter, and this connection in turn helps to reveal a possible theme: that sometimes courage can be more important than life itself.

- *A story's central* **conflict** *can offer clues to its theme*. For example, the main character in "The Yellow Wallpaper" (p. 459), a woman who has recently had a baby, is in conflict with the nineteenth-century society in which she lives. She is suffering from "temporary nervous depression," what doctors today recognize as postpartum depression. Following the practice of the time, her physician has ordered complete bed rest and has instructed her husband to deprive her of all mental and physical stimulation. This harsh treatment leads the narrator to lose her grasp on reality; eventually, she begins to hallucinate. The main conflict of the story is clearly between the woman and her society, controlled by men. This conflict communicates the central theme: that in nineteenth-century America, women are controlled not just by their husbands and the male medical establishment, but also by the society men have created.
- *The* **point of view** *of a story can shed light on its theme*. For instance, a writer's use of an unreliable first-person narrator can help to communicate the theme of a story. Thus, Montresor's self-serving first-person account of his crime in "The Cask of Amontillado"—along with his attempts to justify these actions—enables readers to understand the dangers of irrational anger and misplaced ideas about honor. The voice of a third-person narrator can also help to convey a story's theme. For example, the detachment of the narrator in Stephen Crane's Civil War novel *The Red Badge of Courage* reinforces the theme of the novel: that bravery, cowardice, war, and even life itself are insignificant when set beside the indifference of the universe.
- *Quite often a story's* **symbols**—*names, places, and objects—can suggest its theme*. For example, the rocking horse in D. H. Lawrence's "The Rocking-Horse Winner" (p. 589) can be seen as a symbol of the boy's desperate desire to remain a child. Interpreted in this way, it reinforces the theme that innocence cannot survive when it confronts adult greed and selfishness. Similarly, Hawthorne's "Young Goodman Brown" (p. 540) uses symbols such as the walking stick, the woods, sunset and night, and the vague shadows to develop one of its central themes: that once a person strays from the path of faith, evil is everywhere.
- *Finally,* **changes in a character** *can shed light on the theme or themes of the story*. The main character in Charles Baxter's "Gryphon" (p. 277), for example, eventually comes to realize that the "lies" his substitute teacher tells may be closer to the truth than the "facts" his other teachers present, and his changing attitude toward her helps to communicate the story's central theme about the nature of truth.

✔ CHECKLIST Writing about Theme

- ☐ What is the central theme of the story?
- ☐ What other themes can you identify?
- ☐ Does the title of the story suggest a theme?

continued on next page

- Does the narrator, or any character, make statements that express or imply a theme?
- In what way does the arrangement of events in the story suggest a theme?
- In what way does the central conflict of the story suggest a theme?
- How does the point of view shed light on the story's central theme?
- Do any symbols suggest a theme?
- Do any characters in the story change in any significant way? Do these changes convey a particular theme?

Source: ©Lynda Barry/Lewis & Clark College, Portland, OR

LYNDA BARRY (1956–) is a widely published comic artist whose strips have appeared in numerous newspapers, magazines, and collections. According to Barry, she began compulsively drawing comic strips in college when her boyfriend left her for another girl. Her schoolmate, Matt Groening, the creator of *The Simpsons,* saw her comics and published them in the school paper. Since then, her comic strips have appeared in over fifty papers. She has also published the illustrated novels *The Good Times Are Killing Me* (1988), which she adapted into an off-Broadway play, and *Cruddy* (1999). Named Comics of the Year by the *Comics Journal,* her latest collections of work include *The Greatest of Marlys!* (2000) and *One Hundred Demons* (2002).

Cultural Context This graphic story deals with writer's block, the inability to put words down on paper. Experts say that writer's block can have many causes. For example, the writer simply isn't ready to write, the writer is anxious about writing, or the writer is simply trying to do too much at once. Some anxiety-reduction strategies that can be used to overcome writer's block include brainstorming, writing in a journal, talking through the writing project with a friend or colleague, visualizing the project in manageable steps, repeating affirmations that stimulate creativity, dispelling unrealistic goals of perfection, or simply taking a break. The fact is that no two writers are the same; what works for one writer might not work for another. The only effective way to deal with writers' block is to experiment and to discover what works.

Two Questions (2006)

This graphic story starts on the next page. →

Reading and Reacting

1. What are the "two questions" referred to in the story's title? Why do they matter so much to the narrator?
2. What is the central conflict of the story? How does the narrator resolve this conflict?
3. Look at the following characters in the "Two Questions":
   - The octopus
   - The ghosts
   - The monkey
   - The cat

How do each character's words and appearance help develop the central theme of the story? Which of these "minor characters" do you see as most important? Why?

4. **JOURNAL ENTRY** What do you think the narrator learns about inspiration and creativity?

5. **CRITICAL PERSPECTIVE** Scholar and writer Melinda L. de Jesús describes how Lynda Barry's "deliberately 'naïve' graphic style complements the brutally honest musings of . . . [her work's] young narrator and the often harsh subjects of the strips themselves."

In what ways is "Two Questions" both "deliberately 'naïve'" and "brutally honest"?

Related Works: "Araby" (p. 434), "Cathedral" (p. 527), "The White City" (p. 857), "Diving into the Wreck" (p. 1020), "Sea Grapes" (p. 1031), *The Cuban Swimmer*" (p. 1732)

WHEN I WAS LITTLE, I NOTICED THAT MAKING LINES ON PAPER GAVE ME A CERTAIN FLOATING FEELING. IT MADE ME FEEL LIKE I WAS BOTH THERE AND NOT THERE.
THE LINES MADE A PICTURE AND THE PICTURE MADE A STORY. I WASN'T THE ONLY KID IT HAPPENED TO. EVERY KID I KNEW COULD DO IT.
YES, I AGREE!
AND... BOMBS AWAY! OH NO! FIRE TORPEDO ONE! BBBOOOOSHZ! FIRE TORPEDO TWO!
UH-OH! IT'S STUCK
IT'S DRACULA!
HEY! LOOK OUT! WHAT'S THAT SMELL?
HE'S POOPING!
AND THE MUMMY IS POOPING BACK!
BUT IT'S LAVA!
AAHH!
OH NO! AHH!

BEFORE the TWO QUESTIONS, PICTURES AND STORIES HAPPENED IN A WAY THAT DIDN'T INVOLVE MUCH THINKING. ONE LINE LED TO ANOTHER UNTIL THEY SOMEHOW FINISHED. I NEVER FELT LIKE I WAS TRYING, AND THE DRAWING ITSELF DIDN'T MATTER TO ME MUCH AFTER-WARD.
WHY DON'T YOU COME WITH ME LITTLE GIRL ON A MAGIC CARPET RIDE
BUT THE TWO QUESTIONS FIND EVERYBODY
Where is She?
WHERE IS SHE?
LET'S SEE THAT PICTURE-STORY!!
SHOW ME!
SHOW ME!
SO TRUE
SSSUCK!
RAWK

Mine CAME IN THE GUISE OF THE TWO MOST POPULAR GIRLS IN MY 1ST GRADE CLASS.
HEY! THAT'S PRETTY!
YOU DRAW GOOD.
NOW HERE IT COMES
here comes the night
SUCK RAWK
They LIKED ME more AFTER I MADE THAT Picture. MY teacher LIKED me MORE TOO. IT LASTED a FEW Days
MISS ASTRINGENT, WHYDJA TAKE MY PICTURE DOWN?
IT'S TIME FOR SOMEONE ELSE TO HAVE A TURN.
BUT I MADEJA A NEW ONE.
IT'S VERY PRETTY.
WHAT IN THE---

IT TURNS OUT THERE ARE ALSO DRAWINGS WHICH CAN MAKE PEOPLE DISLIKE YOU. DRAWINGS THAT MAKE PEOPLE THINK YOU ARE DIRTY OR STUPID OR LAME.
ONE BY ONE MOST KIDS I KNEW QUIT DRAWING AND NEVER DREW AGAIN. IT LEFT BEHIND TOO MUCH EVIDENCE.
YES?
YES, THIS IS LYNDA'S MOTHER--
UH-HUH--
SHE DREW WHAT IN SCHOOL TODAY?!
Why DID I KEEP DRAWING??
BECAUSE I'D FIGURED OUT HOW TO MAKE THE GOOD KIND.
NICE. N'I HAVE IT?
YEAH.

As for the bad drawings, I tried my best not to ever make them, but some clawed their way up to the surface of my paper anyway. There were so many ways for a picture to be bad.
And what the *#C* is that s'posta be?
Be great!
I don't know yet.
You suck!
Please please me!
Then why the *#C* are you wasting time drawing it?!
Rule #1: If you don't know what it is, it sucks.
The Two Questions would help me make only good drawings if I'd give them something in exchange...
Know don't!
It's all we ask!
Give us this.
Give us this useless piece of *@#*.
You suck! Get in the box!

IT'S GOOD
GENIUSSS
REMEMBER
NAW.
IT'S SO BAD!
YOU LACK SPONTANEITY.
UH-OH.
NICE!
EEEDEEOT!
I WUV IT!
OH YOU WRECKED IT!
I POOPED IT!
WHERE'S THIS GOING?
FOR THE NEXT 30 YEARS I CHASED AFTER ONLY GOOD DRAWING. WHILE I DREW, MY MAIN FEELINGS WERE DOUBT AND WORRY, AND WHEN I FINISHED MY ONLY FEELINGS WERE RELIEF AND REGRET. I never drew for fun anymore - AND I'D FORGOTTEN ABOUT that STRANGE FLOATING FEELING MAKING LINES ON PAPER USED TO GIVE ME. I'D FORGOTTEN HOW STORIES USED TO BUBBLE UP OUT OF THE LINES AND SURPRISE ME. IT WAS WHY I STARTED DRAWING -- TO MEET THOSE LINES AND STORIES.
I JUST FEEL LIKE, SOMETHING'S MISSING.
HAW!
YAH? THEN GET A JOB.
HAW! LIKE TALENT!
HAW!
HAW!
YA GOT NOTHING TO GRIPE ABOUT.

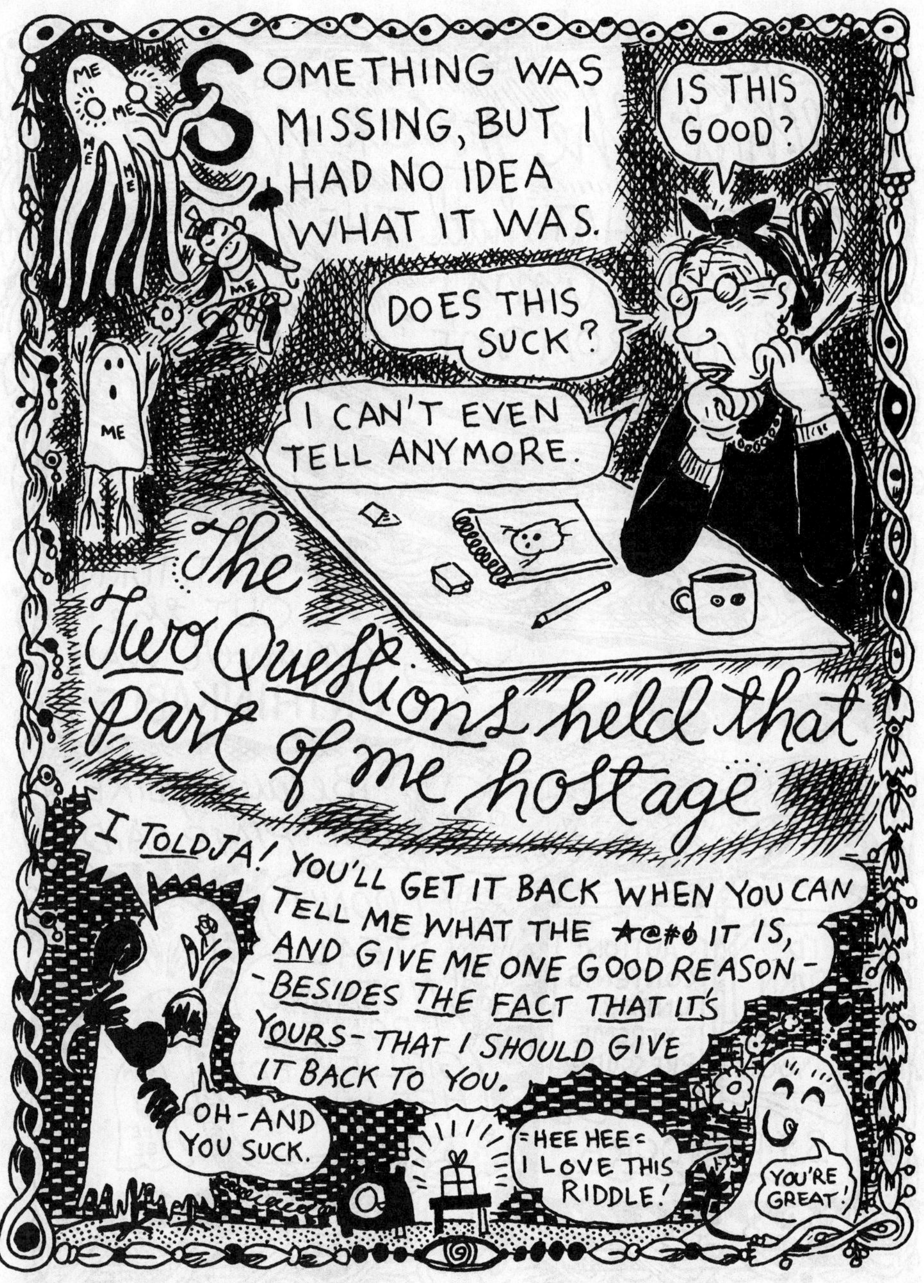
Something was missing, but I had no idea what it was.
Is this good?
Does this suck?
I can't even tell anymore.
The Two Questions held that part of me hostage
I toldja! You'll get it back when you can tell me what the ★@#¢ it is, and give me one good reason - besides the fact that it's yours - that I should give it back to you.
Oh - and you suck.
= Hee hee = I love this riddle!
You're great!
ME

What the #%@* Was it??
JUST WHAT had THE TWO Questions taken FROM me?
IT TURNS OUT the answer WAS UNTHINKABLE--
Because, LIKE THE PIMP SAID,
I DON'T STEAL NOTHING FROM THE GIRL EXCEPT HER MIND!
DANG PLAYAH!
I'D TURN BACK IF I WERE YOU!
CAUTION! CONTENTS UNDER EXTREME PRESSURE!
S.S. PANDORA
HEE HEE

It seems to be a very old riddle, this riddle of what's missing.
But in all the books I read, no one had ever solved the riddle by thinking their way out of it. If anything, just the opposite was true.
MAN THE TORPEDOES SHE'S GETTING CLOSER!
HEE HEE!
STUPID
BRILLIANT
MORON
GENIUS
RAWK
GRIMMS Fairy Tales
GREEK MYTHOLOGY
DANTE
Wm. Blake
LAO TSU
S. FREUD
ZEN BUDDHISM
D.W. WINNICOTT
MARION MILNER
ROALD DAHL
H.C. andersen
DR. SEUSS
WM. STEIG
JOHN LE CARRE'
AND MANY
MANY more

WHAT WAS THE ANSWER?
A FEELING OF DEADNESS SLOWLY CREPT OVER ME.
I ALMOST DIDN'T CARE ANYMORE.
OK. YEAH. WHAT'S MISSING FROM MY WORK.. UH..
DON'T KNOW
GIVE UP!
GIVE UP!
DON'T KNOW!
TECHNICAL ABILITY? UH.. UH... STORY STRUCTURE? ACTION POSES?
WRONG!
THAT WAS YOUR 9,999TH GUESS! YOU HAVE JUST ONE MORE, THEN IT'S OURS FOREVER!!
YOU SUCK!
HAS NO MEMORY OF HAVING SOLVED THIS PROBLEM BEFORE.
I GIVE UP! I DON'T KNOW! I DON'T KNOW, OK?!!
NO IDEA SHE'LL HAVE TO SOLVE IT AGAIN AND AGAIN AND HAVE TOTAL AMNESIA EACH TIME
WHO--
WHO TOLD YOU?

And THAT FEELING...
THAT STRANGE FLOATING FEELING OF BEING THERE AND NOT BEING THERE CAME BACK. ONE LINE LED TO ANOTHER AND A STORY SLOWLY FORMED UNDER MY HANDS.
DON'T KNOW
DON'T KNOW
ABRACAD
DON'T KNOW
TO BE ABLE TO STAND NOT KNOWING long ENOUGH to LET Something ALIVE TAKE SHAPE! without THE TWO QUESTIONS SO MUCH IS POSSIBLE. TO ALL THE KIDS WHO QUIT DRAWING... COME BACK!
HEY! LOOK!
DON'T KNOW!
DON'T KNOW!

Source: ©AP Photo

EUDORA WELTY (1909–2001) was born and raised in Jackson, Mississippi. After attending the Mississippi College for Women, the University of Wisconsin, and Columbia University (where she studied advertising), she returned to Jackson to pursue her long career as a writer, beginning as a journalist. In 1936, she wrote the first of her many short stories, which are gathered in *Collected Stories* (1980). Welty also wrote several novels, including *Delta Wedding* (1946), *Losing Battles* (1970), and the Pulitzer Prize–winning *The Optimist's Daughter* (1972). Her volume of memoirs, *One Writer's Beginnings* (1984), was a best-seller.

One of America's most accomplished writers, Welty focused much of her fiction on life in southern towns and villages peopled with dreamers, eccentrics, and close-knit families. Her sharply observed characters are sometimes presented with great humor, sometimes with poignant lyricism, but always with clarity and sympathy. "Of course any writer is in part all of his characters," she observed. "How otherwise would they be known to him, occur to him, become what they are?" In "A Worn Path," Welty creates a particularly memorable character in the tenacious Phoenix Jackson, and through her she explores a theme that transcends race and region.

Cultural Context During the 1930s, the years of the Great Depression, poverty and unemployment were widespread but were especially severe in isolated rural areas of the South. For the black population living in this poor and undeveloped region, difficult economic conditions were made worse by the system of segregation that prevented them from voting, receiving a good education, or enjoying the same rights and privileges as their white counterparts. Hoping to improve their situation, many African-American families left the South and moved into northern and midwestern cities where there were better opportunities for education and employment. Others, like the protagonist of this story, remained in the South in an atmosphere of residual racism and oppression.

A Worn Path (1940)

Film Series

DVD

See pp. 575–76 for film stills from the DVD version of this story.

It was December—a bright frozen day in the early morning. Far out in the country there was an old Negro woman with her head tied in a red rag, coming along a path through the pinewoods. Her name was Phoenix Jackson. She was very old and small and she walked slowly in the dark pine shadows, moving a little from side to side in her steps, with the balanced heaviness and lightness of a pendulum in a grandfather clock. She carried a thin, small cane made from an umbrella, and with this she kept tapping the frozen earth in front of her. This made a grave and persistent noise in the still air, that seemed meditative like the chirping of a solitary little bird.

She wore a dark striped dress reaching down to her shoe tops, and an equally long apron of bleached sugar sacks, with a full pocket: all neat and tidy, but every time she took a step she might have fallen over her shoelaces, which dragged from her unlaced shoes. She looked straight ahead. Her eyes were blue with age. Her skin had a pattern all its own of numberless branching wrinkles and as though a whole little tree stood in the middle of her forehead, but a golden color ran underneath, and the two knobs of her cheeks were illumined by a yellow burning under the dark. Under the red rag her hair came down on her neck in the frailest of ringlets, still black, and with an odor like copper.

Now and then there was a quivering in the thicket. Old Phoenix said, "Out of my way, all you foxes, owls, beetles, jack rabbits, coons and wild animals! . . . Keep out from under these feet, little bob-whites. . . . Keep the big wild hogs out of my path. Don't let none of those come running my direction. I got a long way." Under her small black-freckled hand her cane, limber as a buggy whip, would switch at the brush as if to rouse up any hiding things.

On she went. The woods were deep and still. The sun made the pine needles almost too bright to look at, up where the wind rocked. The cones dropped as light as feathers. Down in the hollow was the mourning dove—it was not too late for him.

5 The path ran up a hill. "Seem like there is chains about my feet, time I get this far," she said, in the voice of argument old people keep to use with themselves. "Something always take a hold of me on this hill—pleads I should stay."

After she got to the top she turned and gave a full, severe look behind her where she had come. "Up through pines," she said at length. "Now down through oaks."

Her eyes opened their widest, and she started down gently. But before she got to the bottom of the hill a bush caught her dress.

Her fingers were busy and intent, but her skirts were full and long, so that before she could pull them free in one place they were caught in another. It was not possible to allow the dress to tear. "I in the thorny bush," she said. "Thorns, you doing your appointed work. Never want to let folks pass, no sir. Old eyes thought you was a pretty little *green* bush."

Finally, trembling all over, she stood free, and after a moment dared to stoop for her cane.

10 "Sun so high!" she cried, leaning back and looking, while the thick tears went over her eyes. "The time getting all gone here."

At the foot of this hill was a place where a log was laid across the creek.

"Now comes the trial," said Phoenix.

Putting her right foot out, she mounted the log and shut her eyes. Lifting her skirt, leveling her cane fiercely before her, like a festival figure in some parade, she began to march across. Then she opened her eyes and she was safe on the other side.

"I wasn't as old as I thought," she said.

15 But she sat down to rest. She spread her skirts on the bank around her and folded her hands over her knees. Up above her was a tree in a pearly cloud of mistletoe. She did not dare to close her eyes, and when a little boy brought her a plate with a slice of marble-cake on it she spoke to him. "That would be acceptable," she said. But when she went to take it there was just her own hand in the air.

So she left that tree, and had to go through a barbed-wire fence. There she had to creep and crawl, spreading her knees and stretching her fingers like a baby trying to climb the steps. But she talked loudly to herself: she could not let her dress be torn now, so late in the day, and she could not pay for having her arm or her leg sawed off if she got caught fast where she was.

At last she was safe through the fence and risen up out in the clearing. Big dead trees, like black men with one arm, were standing in the purple stalks of the withered cotton field. There sat a buzzard.

"Who you watching?"

In the furrow she made her way along.

20 "Glad this not the season for bulls," she said, looking sideways, "and the good Lord made his snakes to curl up and sleep in the winter. A pleasure I don't see no two-headed snake coming around that tree, where it come once. It took a while to get by him, back in the summer."

She passed through the old cotton and went into a field of dead corn. It whispered and shook and was taller than her head. "Through the maze now," she said, for there was no path.

Then there was something tall, black, and skinny there, moving before her.

At first she took it for a man. It could have been a man dancing in the field. But she stood still and listened, and it did not make a sound. It was as silent as a ghost.

"Ghost," she said sharply, "who be you the ghost of? For I have heard of nary death close by."

25 But there was no answer — only the ragged dancing in the wind.

She shut her eyes, reached out her hand, and touched a sleeve. She found a coat and inside that an emptiness, cold as ice.

"You scarecrow," she said. Her face lighted. "I ought to be shut up for good," she said with laughter. "My senses is gone. I too old. I the oldest people I ever know. Dance, old scarecrow," she said, "while I dancing with you."

She kicked her foot over the furrow, and with mouth drawn down, shook her head once or twice in a little strutting way. Some husks blew down and whirled in streamers about her skirts.

Then she went on, parting her way from side to side with the cane, through the whispering field. At last she came to the end, to a wagon track where the silver grass blew between the red ruts. The quail were walking around like pullets, seeming all dainty and unseen.

30 "Walk pretty," she said. "This is the easy place. This the easy going."

She followed the track, swaying through the quiet bare fields, through the little strings of trees silver in their dead leaves, past cabins silver from weather, with the doors and windows boarded shut, all like old women under a spell sitting there. "I walking in their sleep," she said, nodding her head vigorously.

In a ravine she went where a spring was silently flowing through a hollow log. Old Phoenix bent and drank. "Sweet-gum makes the water sweet," she said, and drank more. "Nobody know who made this well, for it was here when I was born."

The track crossed a swampy part where the moss hung as white as lace from every limb. "Sleep on, alligators, and blow your bubbles." Then the track went into the road.

Deep, deep the road went down between the high green-colored banks. Overhead the live-oaks met, and it was as dark as a cave.

35 A black dog with a lolling tongue came up out of the weeds by the ditch. She was meditating, and not ready, and when he came at her she only hit him a little with her cane. Over she went in the ditch, like a little puff of milkweed.

Down there, her senses drifted away. A dream visited her, and she reached her hand up, but nothing reached down and gave her a pull. So she lay there and presently went to talking. "Old woman," she said to herself, "that black dog come up out of the weeds to stall you off, and now there he sitting on his fine tail, smiling at you."

A white man finally came along and found her—a hunter, a young man, with his dog on a chain.

"Well, Granny!" he laughed. "What are you doing there?"

"Lying on my back like a June-bug waiting to be turned over, mister," she said, reaching up her hand.

He lifted her up, gave her a swing in the air, and set her down. "Anything broken, Granny?"

"No sir, them old dead weeds is springy enough," said Phoenix, when she had got her breath. "I thank you for your trouble."

"Where do you live, Granny?" he asked, while the two dogs were growling at each other.

"Away back yonder, sir, behind the ridge. You can't even see it from here."

"On your way home?"

"No sir, I going to town."

"Why, that's too far! That's as far as I walk when I come out myself, and I get something for my trouble." He patted the stuffed bag he carried, and there hung down a little closed claw. It was one of the bob-whites, with its beak hooked bitterly to show it was dead. "Now you go on home, Granny!"

"I bound to go to town, mister," said Phoenix. "The time come around."

He gave another laugh, filling the whole landscape. "I know you old colored people! Wouldn't miss going to town to see Santa Claus!"

But something held old Phoenix very still. The deep lines in her face went into a fierce and different radiation. Without warning, she had seen with her own eyes a flashing nickel fall out of the man's pocket onto the ground.

"How old are you, Granny?" he was saying.

"There is no telling, mister," she said, "no telling."

Then she gave a little cry and clapped her hands and said, "Git on away from here, dog! Look! Look at that dog!" She laughed as if in admiration. "He ain't scared of nobody. He a big black dog." She whispered, "Sic him!"

"Watch me get rid of that cur," said the man. "Sic him, Pete! Sic him!"

Phoenix heard the dogs fighting, and heard the man running and throwing sticks. She even heard a gunshot. But she was slowly bending forward by that time, further and further forward, the lid stretched down over her eyes, as if she were doing this in her sleep. Her chin was lowered almost to her knees. The yellow palm of her hand came out from the fold of her apron. Her fingers slid down and along the ground under the piece of money with the grace and care they would have in lifting an egg from under a setting hen. Then she slowly straightened up, she stood erect, and the nickel was in her apron pocket. A bird flew by. Her lips moved. "God watching me the whole time. I come to stealing."

The man came back, and his own dog panted about them. "Well, I scared him off that time," he said, and then he laughed and lifted his gun and pointed it at Phoenix.

She stood straight and faced him.

"Doesn't the gun scare you?" he said, still pointing it.

"No, sir, I seen plenty go off closer by, in my day, and for less than what I done," she said, holding utterly still.

He smiled, and shouldered the gun. "Well, Granny," he said, "you must be a hundred years old, and scared of nothing. I'd give you a dime if I had any money with me. But you take my advice and stay home, and nothing will happen to you."

"I bound to go on my way, mister," said Phoenix. She inclined her head in the red rag. Then they went in different directions, but she could hear the gun shooting again and again over the hill.

She walked on. The shadows hung from the oak trees to the road like curtains. Then she smelled wood-smoke, and smelled the river, and she saw a steeple and the cabins on their steep steps. Dozens of little black children whirled around her. There ahead was Natchez shining. Bells were ringing. She walked on.

In the paved city it was Christmas time. There were red and green electric lights strung and crisscrossed everywhere, and all turned on in the daytime. Old Phoenix would have been lost if she had not distrusted her eyesight and depended on her feet to know where to take her.

She paused quietly on the sidewalk where people were passing by. A lady came along in the crowd, carrying an armful of red-, green- and silver-wrapped presents; she gave off perfume like the red roses in hot summer, and Phoenix stopped her.

"Please, missy, will you lace up my shoe?" She held up her foot.

"What do you want, Grandma?"

"See my shoe," said Phoenix. "Do all right for out in the country, but wouldn't look right to go in a big building."

"Stand still then, Grandma," said the lady. She put her packages down on the sidewalk beside her and laced and tied both shoes tightly.

"Can't lace 'em with a cane," said Phoenix. "Thank you, missy. I doesn't mind asking a nice lady to tie up my shoe, when I gets out on the street."

Moving slowly and from side to side, she went into the big building, and into a tower of steps, where she walked up and around and around until her feet knew to stop.

She entered a door, and there she saw nailed up on the wall the document that had been stamped with the gold seal and framed in the gold frame, which matched the dream that was hung up in her head.

"Here I be," she said. There was a fixed and ceremonial stiffness over her body.

"A charity case, I suppose," said an attendant who sat at the desk before her.

But Phoenix only looked above her head. There was sweat on her face, the wrinkles in her face shone like a bright net.

"Speak up, Grandma," the woman said. "What's your name? We must have your history, you know. Have you been here before? What seems to be the trouble with you?"

Old Phoenix only gave a twitch to her face as if a fly were bothering her.

"Are you deaf?" cried the attendant.

But then the nurse came in.

"Oh, that's just old Aunt Phoenix," she said. "She doesn't come for herself — she has a little grandson. She makes these trips just as regular as clockwork. She lives away back off the Old Natchez Trace." She bent down. "Well, Aunt Phoenix, why don't you just take a seat? We won't keep you standing after your long trip." She pointed.

The old woman sat down, bolt upright in the chair. 80

"Now, how is the boy?" asked the nurse.

Old Phoenix did not speak.

"I said, how is the boy?"

But Phoenix only waited and stared straight ahead, her face very solemn and withdrawn into rigidity.

"Is his throat any better?" asked the nurse. "Aunt Phoenix, don't you hear me? Is your grandson's throat any better since the last time you came for the medicine?"

With her hands on her knees, the old woman waited, silent, erect and 85
motionless, just as if she were in armor.

"You mustn't take up our time this way, Aunt Phoenix," the nurse said. "Tell us quickly about your grandson, and get it over. He isn't dead, is he?"

At last there came a flicker and then a flame of comprehension across her face, and she spoke.

"My grandson. It was my memory had left me. There I sat and forgot why I made my long trip."

"Forgot?" The nurse frowned. "After you came so far?"

Then Phoenix was like an old woman begging a dignified forgiveness for 90
waking up frightened in the night. "I never did go to school, I was too old at the Surrender,"° she said in a soft voice. "I'm an old woman without an education. It was my memory fail me. My little grandson, he is just the same, and I forgot it in the coming."

"Throat never heals, does it?" said the nurse, speaking in a loud, sure voice to old Phoenix. By now she had a card with something written on it, a little list. "Yes. Swallowed lye. When was it?—January — two-three years ago —"

Phoenix spoke unasked now. "No, missy, he not dead, he just the same. Every little while his throat begin to close up again, and he not able to swallow. He not get his breath. He not able to help himself. So the time come around, and I go on another trip for the soothing medicine."

"All right. The doctor said as long as you came to get it, you could have it," said the nurse. "But it's an obstinate case."

"My little grandson, he sit up there in the house all wrapped up, waiting by himself," Phoenix went on. "We is the only two left in the world. He suffer and it don't seem to put him back at all. He got a sweet look. He going to last. He wear a little patch quilt and peep out holding his mouth open like a little bird. I remembers so plain now. I not going to forget him again, no, the whole enduring time. I could tell him from all the others in creation."

---

the Surrender: The surrender of General Robert E. Lee to General Ulysses S. Grant at the end of the Civil War, April 9, 1865.

95 "All right." The nurse was trying to hush her now. She brought her a bottle of medicine. "Charity," she said, making a check mark in a book.

Old Phoenix held the bottle close to her eyes, and then carefully put it into her pocket.

"I thank you," she said.

"It's Christmas time, Grandma," said the attendant. "Could I give you a few pennies out of my purse?"

"Five pennies is a nickel," said Phoenix stiffly.

100 "Here's a nickel," said the attendant.

Phoenix rose carefully and held out her hand. She received the nickel and then fished the other nickel out of her pocket and laid it beside the new one. She stared at her palm closely, with her head on one side.

Then she gave a tap with her cane on the floor.

"This is what come to me to do," she said. "I going to the store and buy my child a little windmill they sells, made out of paper. He going to find it hard to believe there such a thing in the world. I'll march myself back where he waiting, holding it straight up in this hand."

She lifted her free hand, gave a little nod, turned around, and walked out of the doctor's office. Then her slow step began on the stairs, going down.

Reading and Reacting

1. How does the first paragraph set the scene for the rest of the story? How does it foreshadow the events that will take place later on?
2. Traditionally, a **quest** is a journey in which a knight overcomes a series of obstacles in order to perform a prescribed feat. In what way is Phoenix's journey a quest? What obstacles does she face? What feat must she perform?
3. Because Phoenix is old, she has trouble seeing. What things does she have difficulty seeing? How do her mistakes shed light on her character? How do they contribute to the impact of the story?
4. What is the major theme of this story? What other themes are expressed?
5. A **phoenix** is a mythical bird that would live for five hundred years, be consumed by fire, and then rise from its own ashes. In what way is the name of this creature appropriate for the main character of this story?
6. Phoenix is not intimidated by the man with the gun and has no difficulty asking a white woman to tie her shoe. In spite of her pride and her strength of character, however, Phoenix has no qualms about stealing a nickel or taking charity from the doctor. How do you account for this apparent contradiction?
7. How do the various people Phoenix encounters react to her? Do they treat her with respect? With disdain? Why do you think they react the way they do?
8. In paragraph 90, Phoenix says that she is an old woman without an education. Does she nevertheless seem to have any knowledge that the other characters lack?
9. **JOURNAL ENTRY** Could "A Worn Path" be seen as an **allegory**? If so, what might each of the characters represent?

10. Critical Perspective Writing about "A Worn Path," Eudora Welty said that the question she was asked most frequently by both students and teachers was whether Phoenix Jackson's grandson was actually dead. Here she attempts to answer this question:

> I had not meant to mystify readers by withholding any fact; it is not a writer's business to tease. The story is told through Phoenix's mind and she undertakes her errand. As the author at one with the character as I tell it, I must assume that the boy is alive. As the reader, you are free to think as you like, of course; the story invites you to believe that no matter what happens, Phoenix for as long as she is able to walk and can hold to her purpose will make her journey.

Do you think Phoenix's grandson is alive or dead? Why?

Related Works: "Miss Brill" (p. 266), "Araby" (p. 434), "Everyday Use" (p. 517), "Reapers" (p. 914), "The soul selects her own Society" (p. 1145), "We Wear the Mask" (p. 1150), "The Solitary Reaper" (p. 1211), *The Cuban Swimmer* (p. 1732)

 Fiction in Film: Eudora Welty's "A Worn Path"

"A Worn Path" is a story about Phoenix Jackson, an elderly African-American woman who repeatedly makes a long journey to town to get medicine for her ailing grandson. The theme of the story, however, is much more than the difficulty of Phoenix Jackson's journey. In one sense, Phoenix represents the strength of human spirit that perseveres regardless of the difficulties or the odds against success. In another sense, she represents African Americans in their long quest for integration and equal treatment. The DVD of "A Worn Path" presents the vivid incidents—both imaginary and real—that are described in the story. The stills included here depict scenes that appear on the DVD.

Reading and Reacting

1. If you were making a film of "A Worn Path," how would you show Phoenix's encounter with the thorn bush? The buzzard? The scarecrow?

Phoenix and the hunter.

Source: ©Bruce Schwartz / Worn Path Productions

Phoenix walking down the street in town.

Source: ©Victoria Mihich / Worn Path Productions

Phoenix in the doctor's office.
Source: ©James Patterson/Worn Path Productions

The film's last scene, with Phoenix, outlined against the sky, walking back to her cabin.
Source: ©Francisco Gonzales/Worn Path Productions

2. How would you indicate which events actually took place and which are imaginary? For example, how would you show Phoenix's imaginary encounter with the boy who offers her a piece of cake?
3. How much would you show of Phoenix's encounter with the hunter? How would she react to the dog? How would you show her stealing the nickel? What would her reaction be when the hunter asked her if she was afraid of guns?
4. Which of the story's themes could you easily suggest in a film? Which would be more difficult to suggest?
5. The story takes place around Christmas. How would you indicate this setting in a film?
6. "A Worn Path" is set during the Depression near Natchez, Mississippi, a segregated city in the South. If you were making a film version of the story, how would you suggest this racial situation?
7. The story ends with Phoenix walking down the stairs of the doctor's office. The DVD ends with Phoenix walking home, outlined against the sky (shown above). Is this ending an improvement? Explain.

Source: Courtesy of David Michael Kaplan

DAVID MICHAEL KAPLAN (1946–) is one of a group of American writers who, along with South American writers such as Gabriel García Márquez of Columbia, are called "magic realists." Magic realists work outside of the "hobbits and wizards" borders of traditional fantasy writing, seamlessly interweaving magical elements with detailed, realistically drawn "everyday" settings. These elements, says a reviewer of Kaplan's work, are invoked "to illuminate and underscore heightened moments of reality." The story "Doe Season," which appeared in Kaplan's debut collection, *Comfort* (1987), was included in *Best American Short Stories 1985*. Kaplan's first novel, *Skating in the Dark*, was published in 1991, and his writing text, *Revision: A Creative Approach to Writing and Re-writing Fiction*, was published in 1997. Kaplan teaches fiction writing at Loyola University Chicago, where he directs the Creative Writing Program. He is currently writing his second novel, *The Runny Men*.

Interestingly, the stories in *Comfort* break from classic "first-time author" tradition by sidestepping the autobiographical, young-man-comes-of-age theme. Instead, these stories are about young girls—or young women—coming to grips with parents (present or absent) and with loss and searching for ways to resolve their ambivalence about becoming women. In "Doe Season," Andy's surreal encounter with the doe may be a dream, but the beauty and horror of their meeting will affect the rest of her life.

Cultural Context When European settlers first came to America, deer roamed freely from coast to coast, and the settlers hunted them to put meat on the table. Today, deer are hunted in a regulated fashion in order to control their numbers and maintain a balance in their population. Deer hunting has long been viewed as a coming-of-age ritual for young men—and, more recently, for young women first entering adulthood, like the protagonist in this story. It used to be the tradition that a young hunter who missed his first deer had his shirttail cut off and, later, his face smeared with the blood of his first kill. Now few hunters observe these initiation rites.

Doe Season (1985)

They were always the same woods, she thought sleepily as they drove through the early morning darkness—deep and immense, covered with yesterday's snowfall, which had frozen overnight. They were the same woods that lay behind her house, *and they stretch all the way to here*, she thought, *for miles and miles, longer than I could walk in a day, or a week even, but they are still the same woods*. The thought made her feel good: it was like thinking of God; it was like thinking of the space between here and the moon; it was like thinking of all the foreign countries from her geography book where even now, Andy knew, people were going to bed, while they—she and her father and Charlie Spoon and Mac, Charlie's eleven-year-old son—were driving deeper into the Pennsylvania countryside, to go hunting.

They had risen long before dawn. Her mother, yawning and not trying to hide her sleepiness, cooked them eggs and French toast. Her father smoked a cigarette and flicked ashes into his saucer while Andy listened, wondering *Why doesn't he come?* and *Won't he ever come?* until at last a car pulled into the graveled drive and honked. "That will be Charlie Spoon," her father said; he always said "Charlie Spoon," even though his real name was Spreun, because Charlie was, in a sense, shaped like a spoon, with a large head and a narrow waist and chest.

Andy's mother kissed her and her father and said, "Well, have a good time" and "Be careful." Soon they were outside in the bitter dark, loading gear by the back-porch light, their breath steaming. The woods behind the house were then only a black streak against the wash of night.

Andy dozed in the car and woke to find that it was half light. Mac—also sleeping—had slid against her. She pushed him away and looked out the window. Her breath clouded the glass, and she was cold; the car's heater didn't work right. They were riding over gentle hills, the woods on both sides now—the same woods, she knew, because she had been watching the whole way, even while she slept. They had been in her dreams, and she had never lost sight of them.

5 Charlie Spoon was driving. "I don't understand why she's coming," he said to her father. "How old is she anyway—eight?"

"Nine," her father replied. "She's small for her age."

"So—nine. What's the difference? She'll just add to the noise and get tired besides."

"No, she won't," her father said. "She can walk me to death. And she'll bring good luck, you'll see. Animals—I don't know how she does it, but they come right up to her. We go walking in the woods, and we'll spot more raccoons and possums and such than I ever see when I'm alone."

Charlie grunted.

10 "Besides, she's not a bad little shot, even if she doesn't hunt yet. She shoots the .22 real good."

"Popgun," Charlie said, and snorted. "And target shooting ain't deer hunting."

"Well, she's not gonna be shooting anyway, Charlie," her father said. "Don't worry. She'll be no bother."

"I still don't know why she's coming," Charlie said.

"Because she wants to, and I want her to. Just like you and Mac. No difference."

15 Charlie turned onto a side road and after a mile or so slowed down. "That's it!" he cried. He stopped, backed up, and entered a narrow dirt road almost hidden by trees. Five hundred yards down, the road ran parallel to a fenced-in field. Charlie parked in a cleared area deeply rutted by frozen tractor tracks. The gate was locked. *In the spring,* Andy thought, *there will be cows here, and a dog that chases them,* but now the field was unmarked and bare.

"This is it," Charlie Spoon declared. "Me and Mac was up here just two weeks ago, scouting it out, and there's deer. Mac saw the tracks."

"That's right," Mac said.

"Well, we'll just see about that," her father said, putting on his gloves. He turned to Andy. "How you doing, honeybun?"

"Just fine," she said.

20 Andy shivered and stamped as they unloaded: first the rifles, which they unsheathed and checked, sliding the bolts, sighting through scopes, adjusting the slings; then the gear, their food and tents and sleeping bags and stove stored in four backpacks—three big ones for Charlie Spoon and her father and Mac, and a day pack for her.

"That's about your size," Mac said, to tease her.

She reddened and said, "Mac, I can carry a pack big as yours any day." He laughed and pressed his knee against the back of hers, so that her leg buckled. "Cut it out," she said. She wanted to make an iceball and throw it at him, but she knew that her father and Charlie were anxious to get going, and she didn't want to displease them.

Mac slid under the gate, and they handed the packs over to him. Then they slid under and began walking across the field toward the same woods that ran all the way back to her home, where even now her mother was probably rising again to wash their breakfast dishes and make herself a fresh pot of coffee. *She is there, and we are here:* the thought satisfied Andy. There was no place else she would rather be.

Mac came up beside her. "Over there's Canada," he said, nodding toward the woods.

"Huh!" she said. "Not likely." 25

"I don't mean *right* over there. I mean farther up north. You think I'm dumb?"

Dumb as your father, she thought.

"Look at that," Mac said, pointing to a piece of cow dung lying on a spot scraped bare of snow. "A frozen meadow muffin." He picked it up and sailed it at her. "Catch!"

"Mac!" she yelled. His laugh was as gawky as he was. She walked faster. He seemed different today somehow, bundled in his yellow-and-black-checkered coat, a rifle in hand, his silly floppy hat not quite covering his ears. They all seemed different as she watched them trudge through the snow—Mac and her father and Charlie Spoon—bigger, maybe, as if the cold landscape enlarged rather than diminished them, so that they, the only figures in that landscape, took on size and meaning just by being there. If they weren't there, everything would be quieter, and the woods would be the same as before. *But they are here,* Andy thought, looking behind her at the boot prints in the snow, *and I am too, and so it's all different.*

"We'll go down to the cut where we found those deer tracks," Charlie said as they 30
entered the woods. "Maybe we'll get lucky and get a late one coming through."

The woods descended into a gully. The snow was softer and deeper here, so that often Andy sank to her knees. Charlie and Mac worked the top of the gully while she and her father walked along the base some thirty yards behind them. "If they miss the first shot, we'll get the second," her father said, and she nodded as if she had known this all the time. She listened to the crunch of their boots, their breathing, and the drumming of a distant woodpecker. And the crackling. In winter the woods crackled as if everything were straining, ready to snap like dried chicken bones.

We are hunting, Andy thought. The cold air burned her nostrils.

They stopped to make lunch by a rock outcropping that protected them from the wind. Her father heated the bean soup her mother had made for them, and they ate it with bread already stiff from the cold. He and Charlie took a few pulls from a flask of Jim Beam while she scoured the plates with snow and repacked them. Then they all had coffee with sugar and powdered milk, and her father poured her a cup too. "We won't tell your momma," he said, and Mac laughed. Andy held the cup the way her father did, not by the handle but around the rim. The coffee tasted smoky. She felt a little queasy, but she drank it all.

Charlie Spoon picked his teeth with a fingernail. "Now, you might've noticed one thing," he said.

"What's that?" her father asked. 35

"You might've noticed you don't hear no rifles. That's because there ain't no other hunters here. We've got the whole damn woods to ourselves. Now, I ask you—do I know how to find 'em?"

"We haven't seen deer yet, neither."

"Oh, we will," Charlie said, "but not for a while now." He leaned back against the rock. "Deer're sleeping, resting up for the evening feed."

"I seen a deer behind our house once, and it was afternoon," Andy said.

"Yeah, honey, but that was *before* deer season," Charlie said, grinning. "They know something now. They're smart that way."

"That's right," Mac said.

Andy looked at her father—had she said something stupid?

"Well, Charlie," he said, "if they know so much, how come so many get themselves shot?"

"Them's the ones that don't *believe* what they know," Charlie replied. The men laughed. Andy hesitated, and then laughed with them.

They moved on, as much to keep warm as to find a deer. The wind became even stronger. Blowing through the treetops, it sounded like the ocean, and once Andy thought she could smell salt air. But that was impossible; the ocean was *hundreds* of miles away, farther than Canada even. She and her parents had gone last summer to stay for a week at a motel on the New Jersey shore. That was the first time she'd seen the ocean, and it frightened her. It was huge and empty, yet always moving. Everything lay hidden. If you walked in it, you couldn't see how deep it was or what might be below; if you swam, something could pull you under and you'd never be seen again. Its musky, rank smell made her think of things dying. Her mother had floated beyond the breakers, calling to her to come in, but Andy wouldn't go farther than a few feet into the surf. Her mother swam and splashed with animal-like delight while her father, smiling shyly, held his white arms above the waist-deep water as if afraid to get them wet. Once a comber rolled over and sent them both tossing, and when her mother tried to stand up, the surf receding behind, Andy saw that her mother's swimsuit top had come off, so that her breasts swayed free, her nipples like two dark eyes. Embarrassed, Andy looked around: except for two women under a yellow umbrella farther up, the beach was empty. Her mother stood up unsteadily, regained her footing. Taking what seemed the longest time, she calmly refixed her top. Andy lay on the beach towel and closed her eyes. The sound of the surf made her head ache.

And now it was winter; the sky was already dimming, not just with the absence of light but with a mist that clung to the hunters' faces like cobwebs. They made camp early. Andy was chilled. When she stood still, she kept wiggling her toes to make sure they were there. Her father rubbed her arms and held her to him briefly, and that felt better. She unpacked the food while the others put up the tents.

"How about rounding us up some firewood, Mac?" Charlie asked.

"I'll do it," Andy said. Charlie looked at her thoughtfully and then handed her the canvas carrier.

There wasn't much wood on the ground, so it took her a while to get a good load. She was about a hundred yards from camp, near a cluster of high, lichen-covered boulders, when she saw through a crack in the rock a buck and two does walking gingerly, almost daintily, through the alder trees. She tried to hush her breathing as they passed not more than twenty yards away. There was nothing she could do. If she yelled, they'd be gone; by the time she got back to camp, they'd be gone. The buck stopped, nostrils quivering, tail up and alert. He looked directly at her. Still she didn't move, not one muscle. He was a beautiful buck, the color of late-turned maple leaves. Unafraid, he lowered his tail, and he and his does silently merged into the trees. Andy walked back to camp and dropped the firewood.

"I saw three deer," she said. "A buck and two does." 50

"Where?" Charlie Spoon cried, looking behind her as if they might have followed her into camp.

"In the woods yonder. They're gone now."

"Well, hell!" Charlie banged his coffee cup against his knee.

"Didn't I say she could find animals?" her father said, grinning.

"Too late to go after them," Charlie muttered. "It'll be dark in a quarter hour. Damn!" 55

"Damn," Mac echoed.

"They just walk right up to her," her father said.

"Well, leastwise this proves there's deer here." Charlie began snapping long branches into shorter ones. "You know, I think I'll stick with you," he told Andy, "since you're so good at finding deer and all. How'd that be?"

"Okay, I guess," Andy murmured. She hoped he was kidding; no way did she want to hunt with Charlie Spoon. Still, she was pleased he had said it.

Her father and Charlie took one tent, she and Mac the other. When they were 60
in their sleeping bags, Mac said in the darkness, "I bet you really didn't see no deer, did you?"

She sighed. "I did, Mac. Why would I lie?"

"How big was the buck?"

"Four point. I counted."

Mac snorted.

"You just believe what you want, Mac," she said testily. 65

"Too bad it ain't buck season," he said. "Well, I got to go pee."

"So pee."

She heard him turn in his bag. "You ever see it?" he asked.

"It? What's 'it'?"

"It. A pecker." 70

"Sure," she lied.

"Whose? Your father's?"

She was uncomfortable. "No," she said.

"Well, whose then?"

"Oh I don't know! Leave me be, why don't you?" 75

"Didn't see a deer, didn't see a pecker," Mac said teasingly.

She didn't answer right away. Then she said, "My cousin Lewis. I saw his."

"Well, how old's he?"

"One and a half."

"Ha! A baby! A baby's is like a little worm. It ain't a real one at all." 80

If he says he'll show me his, she thought, *I'll kick him. I'll just get out of my bag and kick him*.

"I went hunting with my daddy and Versh and Danny Simmons last year in buck season," Mac said, "and we got ourselves one. And we hog-dressed the thing. You know what that is, don't you?"

"No," she said. She was confused. What was he talking about now?

"That's when you cut him open and take out all his guts, so the meat don't spoil. Makes him lighter to pack out, too."

85 She tried to imagine what the deer's guts might look like, pulled from the gaping hole. "What do you do with them?" she said. "The guts?"

"Oh, just leave 'em for the bears."

She ran her finger like a knife blade along her belly.

"When we left them on the ground," Mac said, "they smoked. Like they were cooking."

"Huh," she said.

90 "They cut off the deer's pecker, too, you know."

Andy imagined Lewis's pecker and shuddered. "Mac, you're disgusting."

He laughed. "Well, I gotta go pee." She heard him rustle out of his bag. "Broo!" he cried, flapping his arms. "It's cold!"

He makes so much noise, she thought, *just noise and more noise*.

Her father woke them before first light. He warned them to talk softly and said that they were going to the place where Andy had seen the deer, to try to cut them off on their way back from their night feeding. Andy couldn't shake off her sleep. Stuffing her sleeping bag into its sack seemed to take an hour, and tying her boots was the strangest thing she'd ever done. Charlie Spoon made hot chocolate and oatmeal with raisins. Andy closed her eyes and, between beats of her heart, listened to the breathing of the forest. *When I open my eyes, it will be lighter,* she decided. But when she did, it was still just as dark, except for the swaths of their flashlights and the hissing blue flame of the stove. *There has to be just one moment when it all changes from dark to light,* Andy thought. She had missed it yesterday, in the car; today she would watch more closely.

95 But when she remembered again, it was already first light and they had moved to the rocks by the deer trail and had set up shooting positions—Mac and Charlie Spoon on the up-trail side, she and her father behind them, some six feet up on a ledge. The day became brighter, the sun piercing the tall pines, raking the hunters, yet providing little warmth. Andy now smelled alder and pine and the slightly rotten odor of rock lichen. She rubbed her hand over the stone and considered that it must be very old, had probably been here before the giant pines, *before anyone was in these woods at all.* A chipmunk sniffed on a nearby branch. She aimed an imaginary rifle and pressed the trigger. The chipmunk froze, then scurried away. Her legs were cramping on the narrow ledge. Her father seemed to doze, one hand in his parka, the other cupped lightly around the rifle. She could smell his scent of old wool and leather. His cheeks were speckled with gray-black whiskers, and he worked his jaws slightly, as if chewing a small piece of gum.

Please let us get a deer, she prayed.

A branch snapped on the other side of the rock face. Her father's hand stiffened on the rifle, startling her—*He hasn't been sleeping at all,* she marveled—and then his jaw relaxed, as did the lines around his eyes, and she heard Charlie Spoon call, "Yo, don't shoot, it's us." He and Mac appeared from around the rock. They stopped beneath the ledge. Charlie solemnly crossed his arms.

"I don't believe we're gonna get any deer here," he said drily.

Andy's father lowered his rifle to Charlie and jumped down from the ledge. Then he reached up for Andy. She dropped into his arms and he set her gently on the ground.

Mac sidled up to her. “I knew you didn’t see no deer,” he said. 100

“Just because they don’t come when you want ’em to don’t mean she didn’t see them,” her father said.

Still, she felt bad. Her telling about the deer had caused them to spend the morning there, cold and expectant, with nothing to show for it.

They tramped through the woods for another two hours, not caring much about noise. Mac found some deer tracks, and they argued about how old they were. They split up for a while and then rejoined at an old logging road that deer might use, and followed it. The road crossed a stream, which had mostly frozen over but in a few spots still caught leaves and twigs in an icy swirl. They forded it by jumping from rock to rock. The road narrowed after that, and the woods thickened.

They stopped for lunch, heating up Charlie’s wife’s corn chowder. Andy’s father cut squares of applesauce cake with his hunting knife and handed them to her and Mac, who ate his almost daintily. Andy could faintly taste knife oil on the cake. She was tired. She stretched her leg; the muscle that had cramped on the rock still ached.

“Might as well relax,” her father said, as if reading her thoughts. “We won’t find 105
deer till suppertime.”

Charlie Spoon leaned back against his pack and folded his hands across his stomach. “Well, even if we don’t get a deer,” he said expansively, “it’s still great to be out here, breathe some fresh air, clomp around a bit. Get away from the house and the old lady.” He winked at Mac, who looked away.

“That’s what the woods are all about, anyway,” Charlie said. “It’s where the women don’t want to go.” He bowed his head toward Andy. “With your exception, of course, little lady.” He helped himself to another piece of applesauce cake.

“She ain’t a woman,” Mac said.

“Well, she damn well’s gonna be,” Charlie said. He grinned at her. “Or will you? You’re half a boy anyway. You go by a boy’s name. What’s your real name? Andrea, ain’t it?”

“That’s right,” she said. She hoped that if she didn’t look at him, Charlie would 110
stop.

“Well, which do you like? Andy or Andrea?”

“Don’t matter,” she mumbled. “Either.”

“She’s always been Andy to me,” her father said.

Charlie Spoon was still grinning. “So what are you gonna be, Andrea? A boy or a girl?”

“I’m a girl,” she said. 115

“But you want to go hunting and fishing and everything, huh?”

“She can do whatever she likes,” her father said.

“Hell, you might as well have just had a boy and be done with it!” Charlie exclaimed.

“That’s funny,” her father said, and chuckled. “That’s just what her momma tells me.”

They were looking at her, and she wanted to get away from them all, even from 120
her father, who chose to joke with them.

“I’m going to walk a bit,” she said.

She heard them laughing as she walked down the logging trail. She flapped her arms; she whistled. *I don't care how much noise I make*, she thought. Two grouse flew from the underbrush, startling her. A little farther down, the trail ended in a clearing that enlarged into a frozen meadow; beyond it the woods began again. A few moldering posts were all that was left of a fence that had once enclosed the field. The low afternoon sunlight reflected brightly off the snow, so that Andy's eyes hurt. She squinted hard. A gust of wind blew across the field, stinging her face. And then, as if it had been waiting for her, the doe emerged from the trees opposite and stepped cautiously into the field. Andy watched: it stopped and stood quietly for what seemed a long time and then ambled across. It stopped again about seventy yards away and began to browse in a patch of sugar grass uncovered by the wind. Carefully, slowly, never taking her eyes from the doe, Andy walked backward, trying to step into the boot prints she'd already made. When she was far enough back into the woods, she turned and walked faster, her heart racing. *Please let it stay*, she prayed.

"There's doe in the field yonder," she told them.

They got their rifles and hurried down the trail.

"No use," her father said. "We're making too much noise any way you look at it."

"At least we got us the wind in our favor," Charlie Spoon said, breathing heavily.

But the doe was still there, grazing.

"Good Lord," Charlie whispered. He looked at her father. "Well, whose shot?"

"Andy spotted it," her father said in a low voice. "Let her shoot it."

"What!" Charlie's eyes widened.

Andy couldn't believe what her father had just said. She'd only shot tin cans and targets; she'd never even fired her father's .30-.30, and she'd never killed anything.

"I can't," she whispered.

"That's right, she can't," Charlie Spoon insisted. "She's not old enough and she don't have a license even if she was!"

"Well, who's to tell?" her father said in a low voice. "Nobody's going to know but us." He looked at her. "Do you want to shoot it, punkin?"

Why doesn't it hear us? she wondered. *Why doesn't it run away?* "I don't know," she said.

"Well, I'm sure as hell gonna shoot it," Charlie said. Her father grasped Charlie's rifle barrel and held it. His voice was steady.

"Andy's a good shot. It's her deer. She found it, not you. You'd still be sitting on your ass back in camp." He turned to her again. "Now—do you want to shoot it, Andy? Yes or no."

He was looking at her; they were all looking at her. Suddenly she was angry at the deer, who refused to hear them, who wouldn't run away even when it could. "I'll shoot it," she said. Charlie turned away in disgust.

She lay on the ground and pressed the rifle stock against her shoulder bone. The snow was cold through her parka; she smelled oil and wax and damp earth. She pulled off one glove with her teeth. "It sights just like the .22," her father said gently. "Cartridge's already chambered." As she had done so many times before, she sighted down the scope; now the doe was in the reticle. She moved the barrel until the cross hairs lined up. Her father was breathing beside her.

"Aim where the chest and legs meet, or a little above, punkin," he was saying 140
calmly. "That's the killing shot."

But now, seeing it in the scope, Andy was hesitant. Her finger weakened on the trigger. Still, she nodded at what her father said and sighted again, the cross hairs lining up in exactly the same spot—the doe had hardly moved, its brownish-gray body outlined starkly against the blue-backed snow. *It doesn't know*, Andy thought. *It just doesn't know*. And as she looked, deer and snow and faraway trees flattened within the circular frame to become like a picture on a calendar, not real, and she felt calm, as if she had been dreaming everything—the day, the deer, the hunt itself. And she, finger on trigger, was only a part of that dream.

"Shoot!" Charlie hissed.

Through the scope she saw the deer look up, ears high and straining.

Charlie groaned, and just as he did, and just at the moment when Andy knew—*knew*—the doe would bound away, as if she could feel its haunches tensing and gathering power, she pulled the trigger. Later she would think, *I felt the recoil, I smelled the smoke, but I don't remember pulling the trigger*. Through the scope the deer seemed to shrink into itself, and then slowly knelt, hind legs first, head raised as if to cry out. It trembled, still straining to keep its head high, as if that alone would save it; failing, it collapsed, shuddered, and lay still.

"Whoee!" Mac cried. 145

"One shot! One shot!" her father yelled, clapping her on the back. Charlie Spoon was shaking his head and smiling dumbly.

"I told you she was a great little shot!" her father said. "I told you!" Mac danced and clapped his hands. She was dazed, not quite understanding what had happened. And then they were crossing the field toward the fallen doe, she walking dreamlike, the men laughing and joking, released now from the tension of silence and anticipation. Suddenly Mac pointed and cried out, "Look at that!"

The doe was rising, legs unsteady. They stared at it, unable to comprehend, and in that moment the doe regained its feet and looked at them, as if it too were trying to understand. Her father whistled softly. Charlie Spoon unslung his rifle and raised it to his shoulder, but the doe was already bounding away. His hurried shot missed, and the deer disappeared into the woods.

"Damn, damn, damn," he moaned.

"I don't believe it," her father said. "That deer was dead." 150

"Dead, hell!" Charlie yelled. "It was gutshot, that's all. Stunned and gutshot. Clean shot, my ass!"

What have I done? Andy thought.

Her father slung his rifle over his shoulder. "Well, let's go. It can't get too far."

"Hell, I've seen deer run ten miles gutshot," Charlie said. He waved his arms. "We may never find her!"

As they crossed the field, Mac came up to her and said in a low voice, "Gutshoot 155
a deer, you'll go to hell."

"Shut up, Mac," she said, her voice cracking. It was a terrible thing she had done, she knew. She couldn't bear to think of the doe in pain and frightened. *Please let it die*, she prayed.

But though they searched all the last hour of daylight, so that they had to recross the field and go up the logging trail in a twilight made even deeper by thick, smoky clouds, they didn't find the doe. They lost its trail almost immediately in the dense stands of alderberry and larch.

"I am cold, and I am tired," Charlie Spoon declared. "And if you ask me, that deer's in another county already."

"No one's asking you, Charlie," her father said.

160 They had a supper of hard salami and ham, bread, and the rest of the applesauce cake. It seemed a bother to heat the coffee, so they had cold chocolate instead. Everyone turned in early.

"We'll find it in the morning, honeybun," her father said, as she went to her tent.

"I don't like to think of it suffering." She was almost in tears.

"It's dead already, punkin. Don't even think about it." He kissed her, his breath sour and his beard rough against her cheek.

Andy was sure she wouldn't get to sleep; the image of the doe falling, falling, then rising again, repeated itself whenever she closed her eyes. Then she heard an owl hoot and realized that it had awakened her, so she must have been asleep after all. She hoped the owl would hush, but instead it hooted louder. She wished her father or Charlie Spoon would wake up and do something about it, but no one moved in the other tent, and suddenly she was afraid that they had all decamped, wanting nothing more to do with her. She whispered, "Mac, Mac," to the sleeping bag where he should be, but no one answered. She tried to find the flashlight she always kept by her side, but couldn't, and she cried in panic, "Mac, are you there?" He mumbled something, and immediately she felt foolish and hoped he wouldn't reply.

165 When she awoke again, everything had changed. The owl was gone, the woods were still, and she sensed light, blue and pale, light where before there had been none. *The moon must have come out,* she thought. And it was warm, too, warmer than it should have been. She got out of her sleeping bag and took off her parka—it was that warm. Mac was asleep, wheezing like an old man. She unzipped the tent and stepped outside.

The woods were more beautiful than she had ever seen them. The moon made everything ice-rimmed glimmer with a crystallized, immanent light, while underneath that ice the branches of trees were as stark as skeletons. She heard a crunching in the snow, the one sound in all that silence, and there, walking down the logging trail into their camp, was the doe. Its body, like everything around her, was silvered with frost and moonlight. It walked past the tent where her father and Charlie Spoon were sleeping and stopped no more than six feet from her. Andy saw that she had shot it, yes, had shot it cleanly, just where she thought she had, the wound a jagged, bloody hole in the doe's chest.

A heart shot, she thought.

The doe stepped closer, so that Andy, if she wished, could have reached out and touched it. It looked at her as if expecting her to do this, and so she did, running her hand, slowly at first, along the rough, matted fur, then down to the edge of the wound, where she stopped. The doe stood still. Hesitantly, Andy felt the edge of the wound. The torn flesh was sticky and warm. The wound parted under her touch. And then, almost without her knowing it, her fingers were within, probing, yet still the doe didn't move. Andy pressed deeper, through flesh and muscle and sinew, until her whole hand and more was inside the wound and she had found the doe's heart, warm and beating. She cupped it gently in her hand. *Alive*, she marveled. *Alive*.

The heart quickened under her touch, becoming warmer and warmer until it was hot enough to burn. In pain, Andy tried to remove her hand, but the wound closed about it and held her fast. Her hand was burning. She cried out in agony, sure they would all hear and come help, but they didn't. And then her hand pulled free, followed by a steaming rush of blood, more blood than she ever could have imagined—it covered her hand and arm, and she saw to her horror that her hand was steaming. She moaned and fell to her knees and plunged her hand into the snow. The doe looked at her gently and then turned and walked back up the trail.

In the morning, when she woke, Andy could still smell the blood, but she felt no 170
pain. She looked at her hand. Even though it appeared unscathed, it felt weak and withered. She couldn't move it freely and was afraid the others would notice. *I will hide it in my jacket pocket*, she decided, *so nobody can see*. She ate the oatmeal that her father cooked and stayed apart from them all. No one spoke to her, and that suited her. A light snow began to fall. It was the last day of their hunting trip. She wanted to be home.

Her father dumped the dregs of his coffee. "Well, let's go look for her," he said.

Again they crossed the field. Andy lagged behind. She averted her eyes from the spot where the doe had fallen, already filling up with snow. Mac and Charlie entered the woods first, followed by her father. Andy remained in the field and considered the smear of gray sky, the nearby flock of crows pecking at unyielding stubble. *I will stay here*, she thought, *and not move for a long while*. But now someone—Mac—was yelling. Her father appeared at the woods' edge and waved for her to come. She ran and pushed through a brake of alderberry and larch. The thick underbrush scratched her face. For a moment she felt lost and looked wildly about. Then, where the brush thinned, she saw them standing quietly in the falling snow. They were staring down at the dead doe. A film covered its upturned eye, and its body was lightly dusted with snow.

"I told you she wouldn't get too far," Andy's father said triumphantly. "We must've just missed her yesterday. Too blind to see."

"We're just damn lucky no animal got to her last night," Charlie muttered.

Her father lifted the doe's foreleg. The wound was blood-clotted, brown, and 175
caked like frozen mud. "Clean shot," he said to Charlie. He grinned. "My little girl."

Then he pulled out his knife, the blade gray as the morning. Mac whispered to Andy, "Now watch this," while Charlie Spoon lifted the doe from behind by its forelegs so that its head rested between his knees, its underside exposed. Her father's knife sliced thickly from chest to belly to crotch, and Andy was running from them, back to the field and across, scattering the crows who cawed and circled angrily. And now they were all calling to her—Charlie Spoon and Mac and her father—crying *Andy, Andy* (but that wasn't her name, she would no longer be called that); yet louder than any of them was the wind blowing through the treetops, like the ocean where her mother floated in green water, also calling *Come in, come in,* while all around her roared the mocking of the terrible, now inevitable, sea.

Reading and Reacting

1. The initiation of a child into adulthood is a common literary theme. In this story, hunting is presented as an initiation rite. In what way is hunting an appropriate coming-of-age ritual?
2. Which characters are in conflict in this story? Which ideas are in conflict? How do these conflicts help to communicate the story's initiation theme?
3. In the story's opening paragraph and elsewhere, Andy finds comfort and reassurance in the idea that the woods are "always the same"; later in the story, she remembers the ocean, "huge and empty, yet always moving. Everything lay hidden . . ." (par. 45). How does the contrast between the woods and the ocean suggest the transition she must make from childhood to adulthood?
4. How do the references to blood support the story's initiation theme? Do they suggest other themes as well?
5. Throughout the story, references are made to Andy's ability to inspire the trust of animals. As her father says, "Animals—I don't know how she does it, but they come right up to her" (par. 8). How does his comment foreshadow later events?
6. Why does Andy pray that she and the others will get a deer? What makes her change her mind? How does the change in Andy's character help to convey the story's theme?
7. Andy's mother is not an active participant in the story's events. Still, she is important to the story. *Why* is it important? How does paragraph 45 reveal the importance of the mother's role?
8. What has Andy learned as a result of her experience? What else do you think she still has to learn?
9. **JOURNAL ENTRY** How would the story be different if Andy were a boy? What would be the same?
10. **CRITICAL PERSPECTIVE** In a review of *Comfort*, the book in which "Doe Season" appears, Susan Wood makes the following observation:

    > The dozen or so stories in David Michael Kaplan's affecting first collection share a common focus on the extraordinary moments of recognition in ordinary lives. He is at his best suggesting how such moments may alter, for better or for worse, our relationships with those to whom we are most deeply bound—children, parents, lovers—in love and guilt.

    At what point does "the extraordinary moment of recognition" occur in "Doe Season"? How does this moment alter Andy's relationship with both her parents?

Related Works: "Jinx" (p. 178), "A&P" (p. 259), "Greasy Lake" (p. 687), "Half a Day" (p. 733), "Cinderella" (p. 866), "Traveling through the Dark" (p. 1052), "The Lamb" (p. 1128), *Proof* (p. 1476)

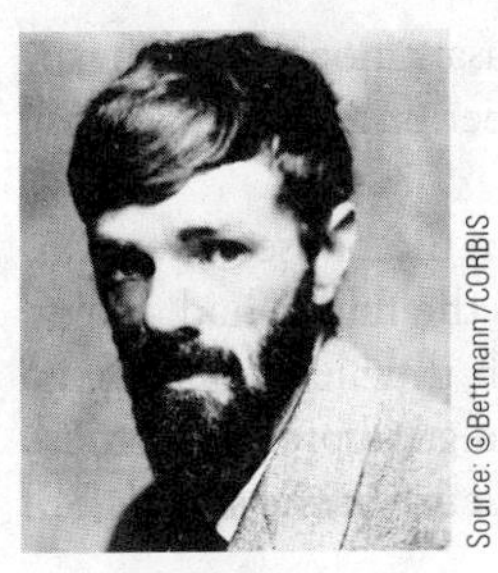
Source: ©Bettmann/CORBIS

D(AVID) H(ERBERT) LAWRENCE (1885–1930) was born in Nottinghamshire, England, the son of a coal miner and a schoolteacher. Determined to escape the harsh life of a miner, Lawrence taught for several years after graduating from high school. He soon began writing fiction and established himself in London literary circles.

During World War I, Lawrence and his wife were suspected of treason because of his pacifism and her connection to German aristocracy. Because Lawrence suffered from tuberculosis, he and his wife left England after the armistice in search of a healthier climate. They traveled in Australia, France, Italy, Mexico, and the United States throughout their lives.

Lawrence is recognized for his impassioned portrayal of our unconscious and instinctive natures. In his novel *Lady Chatterley's Lover* (1928), he attempted to incorporate explicit sexuality into English fiction, and the book was banned for years in Britain and the United States. His other novels include *Sons and Lovers* (1913), *The Rainbow* (1915), *Women in Love* (1921), and *The Plumed Serpent* (1926). Lawrence was also a gifted poet, essayist, travel writer, and short story writer, and his work had a strong influence on other writers.

Lawrence's fascination with the struggle between the unconscious and the intellect is revealed in his short story "The Rocking-Horse Winner" (1920). Lawrence sets his story in a house full of secrets and weaves symbolism with elements of the fairy tale and the gothic to produce a tale that has often been the subject of literary debate.

Cultural Context Horse racing in England has a long history, beginning with casual competitions organized by Roman soldiers in Yorkshire in A.D. 200. The first recorded horse race was run during the reign of Henry II in 1174. Today, horses can be raced over fences or hurdles (National Hunt Racing) or over unobstructed distances (flat racing). There are also cross-country races from point to point, which are called steeplechases. A derby, like the one mentioned in this story, usually denotes a race in which three-year-old horses compete. The name *derby* is derived from the Epsom Derby, which is still run at the Epsom racecourse and is named for Edward Smith Stanley, the twelfth Earl of Derby.

The Rocking-Horse Winner (1920)

There was a woman who was beautiful, who started with all the advantages, yet she had no luck. She married for love, and the love turned to dust. She had bonny children, yet she felt they had been thrust upon her, and she could not love them. They looked at her coldly, as if they were finding fault with her. And hurriedly she felt she must cover up some fault in herself. Yet what it was that she must cover up she never knew. Nevertheless, when her children were present, she always felt the centre of her heart go hard. This troubled her, and in her manner she was all the more gentle and anxious for her children, as if she loved them very much. Only she herself knew that at the centre of her heart was a hard little place that could not feel love, no, not for anybody. Everybody else said of her: "She is such a good mother. She adores her children." Only she herself, and her children themselves, knew it was not so. They read it in each other's eyes.

There were a boy and two little girls. They lived in a pleasant house, with a garden, and they had discreet servants, and felt themselves superior to anyone in the neighbourhood.

Although they lived in style, they felt always an anxiety in the house. There was never enough money. The mother had a small income, and the father had a small income, but not nearly enough for the social position which they had to keep up. The father went into town to some office. But though he had good prospects, these prospects never materialised. There was always the grinding sense of the shortage of money, though the style was always kept up.

At last the mother said: "I will see if *I* can't make something." But she did not know where to begin. She racked her brains, and tried this thing and the other, but could not find anything successful. The failure made deep lines come into her face. Her children were growing up, they would have to go to school. There must be more money, there must be more money. The father, who was always very handsome and expensive in his tastes, seemed as if he never *would* be able to do anything worth doing. And the mother, who had a great belief in herself, did not succeed any better, and her tastes were just as expensive.

And so the house came to be haunted by the unspoken phrase: *There must be more money! There must be more money!* The children could hear it all the time, though nobody said it aloud. They heard it at Christmas, when the expensive and splendid toys filled the nursery. Behind the shining modern rocking-horse, behind the smart doll's house, a voice would start whispering: "There *must* be more money! There *must* be more money!" And the children would stop playing, to listen for a moment. They would look into each other's eyes, to see if they had all heard. And each one saw in the eyes of the other two that they too had heard. "There *must* be more money! There *must* be more money!"

It came whispering from the springs of the still-swaying rocking-horse, and even the horse, bending his wooden, champing head, heard it. The big doll, sitting so pink and smirking in her new pram, could hear it quite plainly, and seemed to be smirking all the more self-consciously because of it. The foolish puppy, too, that took the place of the teddybear, he was looking so extraordinarily foolish for no other reason but that he heard the secret whisper all over the house: "There *must* be more money!"

Yet nobody ever said it aloud. The whisper was everywhere, and therefore no one spoke it. Just as no one ever says: "We are breathing!" in spite of the fact that breath is coming and going all the time.

"Mother," said the boy Paul one day, "why don't we keep a car of our own? Why do we always use uncle's, or else a taxi?"

"Because we're the poor members of the family," said the mother.

"But why *are* we, mother?"

"Well — I suppose," she said slowly and bitterly, "it's because your father has no luck."

The boy was silent for some time.

"Is luck money, mother?" he asked, rather timidly.

"No, Paul. Not quite. It's what causes you to have money."

"Oh!" said Paul vaguely. "I thought when Uncle Oscar said *filthy lucker*, it meant money."

"*Filthy lucre* does mean money," said the mother. "But it's lucre, not luck."

"Oh!" said the boy. "Then what *is* luck, mother?"

"It's what causes you to have money. If you're lucky you have money. That's why it's better to be born lucky than rich. If you're rich, you may lose your money. But if you're lucky, you will always get more money."

"Oh! Will you? And is father not lucky?"

"Very unlucky, I should say," she said bitterly.

The boy watched her with unsure eyes.

"Why?" he asked.

"I don't know. Nobody ever knows why one person is lucky and another unlucky."

"Don't they? Nobody at all? Does *nobody* know?"

"Perhaps God. But He never tells."

"He ought to, then. And aren't you lucky either, mother?"

"I can't be, if I married an unlucky husband."

"But by yourself, aren't you?"

"I used to think I was, before I married. Now I think I am very unlucky indeed."

"Why?"

"Well — never mind! Perhaps I'm not really," she said.

The child looked at her to see if she meant it. But he saw, by the lines of her mouth, that she was only trying to hide something from him.

"Well, anyhow," he said stoutly, "I'm a lucky person."

"Why?" said his mother, with a sudden laugh.

He stared at her. He didn't even know why he had said it.

"God told me," he asserted, brazening it out.

"I hope He did, dear!" she said, again with a laugh, but rather bitter.

"He did, mother!"

"Excellent!" said the mother, using one of her husband's exclamations.

The boy saw she did not believe him; or rather, that she paid no attention to his assertion. This angered him somewhat, and made him want to compel her attention.

He went off by himself, vaguely, in a childish way, seeking for the clue to "luck." Absorbed, taking no heed of other people, he went about with a sort of stealth, seeking inwardly for luck. He wanted luck, he wanted it, he wanted it. When the two girls were playing dolls in the nursery, he would sit on his big rocking-horse, charging madly into space, with a frenzy that made the little girls peer at him uneasily. Wildly the horse careered, the waving dark hair of the boy tossed, his eyes had a strange glare in them. The little girls dared not speak to him.

When he had ridden to the end of his mad little journey, he climbed down and stood in front of his rocking-horse, staring fixedly into its lowered face. Its red mouth was slightly open, its big eye was wide and glassy-bright.

"Now!" he would silently command the snorting steed. "Now, take me to where there is luck! Now take me!"

And he would slash the horse on the neck with the little whip he had asked Uncle Oscar for. He *knew* the horse could take him to where there was luck, if only he forced it. So he would mount again and start on his furious ride, hoping at last to get there. He knew he could get there.

"You'll break your horse, Paul!" said the nurse.

"He's always riding like that! I wish he'd leave off!" said his elder sister Joan.

But he only glared down on them in silence. Nurse gave him up. She could make nothing of him. Anyhow, he was growing beyond her.

One day his mother and his Uncle Oscar came in when he was on one of his furious rides. He did not speak to them.

"Hallo, you young jockey! Riding a winner?" said his uncle.

"Aren't you growing too big for a rocking-horse? You're not a very little boy any longer, you know," said his mother.

But Paul only gave a blue glare from his big, rather close-set eyes. He would speak to nobody when he was in full tilt. His mother watched him with an anxious expression on her face.

At last he suddenly stopped forcing his horse into the mechanical gallop and slid down.

"Well, I got there!" he announced fiercely, his blue eyes still flaring, and his sturdy long legs straddling apart.

"Where did you get to?" asked his mother.

"Where I wanted to go," he flared back at her.

"That's right, son!" said Uncle Oscar. "Don't you stop till you get there. What's the horse's name?"

"He doesn't have a name," said the boy.

"Gets on without all right?" asked the uncle.

"Well, he has different names. He was called Sansovino last week."

"Sansovino, eh? Won the Ascot.° How did you know this name?"

"He always talks about horse-races with Bassett," said Joan.

The uncle was delighted to find that his small nephew was posted with all the racing news. Bassett, the young gardener, who had been wounded in the left foot in the war and had got his present job through Oscar Cresswell, whose batman° he had been, was a perfect blade of the "turf." He lived in the racing events, and the small boy lived with him.

Oscar Cresswell got it all from Bassett.

"Master Paul comes and asks me, so I can't do more than tell him, sir," said Bassett, his face terribly serious, as if he were speaking of religious matters.

"And does he ever put anything on a horse he fancies?"

"Well — I don't want to give him away — he's a young sport, a fine sport, sir. Would you mind asking him himself? He sort of takes a pleasure in it, and perhaps he'd feel I was giving him away, sir, if you don't mind."

Bassett was serious as a church.

---

the Ascot: The annual horse race at Ascot Heath in England.

batman: A British military officer's personal assistant.

The uncle went back to his nephew and took him off for a ride in the car.

"Say, Paul, old man, do you ever put anything on a horse?" the uncle asked.

The boy watched the handsome man closely.

"Why, do you think I oughtn't to?" he parried.

"Not a bit of it! I thought perhaps you might give me a tip for the Lincoln."°

The car sped on into the country, going down to Uncle Oscar's place in Hampshire.

"Honour bright?" said the nephew.

"Honour bright, son!" said the uncle.

"Well, then, Daffodil."

"Daffodil! I doubt it, sonny. What about Mirza?"

"I only know the winner," said the boy. "That's Daffodil."

"Daffodil, eh?"

There was a pause. Daffodil was an obscure horse comparatively.

"Uncle!"

"Yes, son?"

"You won't let it go any further, will you? I promised Bassett."

"Bassett be damned, old man! What's he got to do with it?"

"We're partners. We've been partners from the first. Uncle, he lent me my first five shillings, which I lost. I promised him, honour bright, it was only between me and him; only you gave me that ten-shilling note I started winning with, so I thought you were lucky. You won't let it go any further, will you?"

The boy gazed at his uncle from those big, hot, blue eyes, set rather close together. The uncle stirred and laughed uneasily.

"Right you are, son! I'll keep your tip private. Daffodil, eh? How much are you putting on him?"

"All except twenty pounds," said the boy. "I keep that in reserve."

The uncle thought it a good joke.

"You keep twenty pounds in reserve, do you, you young romancer? What are you betting, then?"

"I'm betting three hundred," said the boy gravely. "But it's between you and me, Uncle Oscar! Honour bright?"

The uncle burst into a roar of laughter.

"It's between you and me all right, you young Nat Gould,"° he said, laughing. "But where's your three hundred?"

"Bassett keeps it for me. We're partners."

"You are, are you! And what is Bassett putting on Daffodil?"

"He won't go quite as high as I do, I expect. Perhaps he'll go a hundred and fifty."

"What, pennies?" laughed the uncle.

"Pounds," said the child, with a surprised look at his uncle. "Bassett keeps a bigger reserve than I do."

---

the Lincoln: The Lincolnshire Handicap, a horse race.

Nat Gould: Nathaniel Gould (1857–1919), British journalist and writer known for his stories about horse racing.

Between wonder and amusement Uncle Oscar was silent. He pursued the matter no further, but he determined to take his nephew with him to the Lincoln races.

"Now, son," he said, "I'm putting twenty on Mirza, and I'll put five on for you on any horse you fancy. What's your pick?"

"Daffodil, uncle."

"No, not the fiver on Daffodil!"

"I should if it was my own fiver," said the child.

"Good! Good! Right you are! A fiver for me and a fiver for you on Daffodil."

The child had never been to a race-meeting before, and his eyes were blue fire. He pursed his mouth tight and watched. A Frenchman just in front had put his money on Lancelot. Wild with excitement, he flayed his arms up and down, yelling *"Lancelot! Lancelot!"* in his French accent.

Daffodil came in first, Lancelot second, Mirza third. The child, flushed and with eyes blazing, was curiously serene. His uncle brought him four five-pound notes, four to one.

"What am I to do with these?" he cried, waving them before the boy's eyes.

"I suppose we'll talk to Bassett," said the boy. "I expect I have fifteen hundred now; and twenty in reserve; and this twenty."

His uncle studied him for some moments.

"Look here, son!" he said. "You're not serious about Bassett and that fifteen hundred, are you?"

"Yes, I am. But it's between you and me, uncle. Honour bright?"

"Honour bright all right, son! But I must talk to Bassett."

"If you'd like to be a partner, uncle, with Bassett and me, we could all be partners. Only, you'd have to promise, honour bright, uncle, not to let it go beyond us three. Bassett and I are lucky, and you must be lucky, because it was your ten shillings I started winning with. . . ."

Uncle Oscar took both Bassett and Paul into Richmond Park for an afternoon, and there they talked.

"It's like this, you see, sir," Bassett said. "Master Paul would get me talking about racing events, spinning yarns, you know, sir. And he was always keen on knowing if I'd made or if I'd lost. It's about a year since, now, that I put five shillings on Blush of Dawn for him: and we lost. Then the luck turned, with that ten shillings he had from you: that we put on Singhalese. And since that time, it's been pretty steady, all things considering. What do you say, Master Paul?"

"We're all right when we're sure," said Paul. "It's when we're not quite sure that we go down."

"Oh, but we're careful then," said Bassett.

"But when are you *sure?*" smiled Uncle Oscar.

"It's Master Paul, sir," said Bassett in a secret, religious voice. "It's as if he had it from heaven. Like Daffodil, now, for the Lincoln. That was as sure as eggs."

"Did you put anything on Daffodil?" asked Oscar Cresswell.

"Yes, sir. I made my bit."

"And my nephew?"

Bassett was obstinately silent, looking at Paul.

"I made twelve hundred, didn't I, Bassett? I told uncle I was putting three hundred on Daffodil."

"That's right," said Bassett, nodding.

"But where's the money?" asked the uncle.

"I keep it safe locked up, sir. Master Paul can have it any minute he likes to ask for it."

"What, fifteen hundred pounds?"

"And twenty! And *forty*, that is, with the twenty he made on the course."

"It's amazing!" said the uncle.

"If Master Paul offers you to be partners, sir, I would, if I were you: if you'll excuse me," said Bassett.

Oscar Cresswell thought about it.

"I'll see the money," he said.

They drove home again, and, sure enough, Bassett came round to the garden-house with fifteen hundred pounds in notes. The twenty pounds reserve was left with Joe Glee, in the Turf Commission deposit.

"You see, it's all right, uncle, when I'm *sure!* Then we go strong, for all we're worth. Don't we, Bassett?"

"We do that, Master Paul."

"And when are you sure?" said the uncle, laughing.

"Oh, well, sometimes I'm *absolutely* sure, like about Daffodil," said the boy; "and sometimes I have an idea; and sometimes I haven't even an idea, have I, Bassett? Then we're careful, because we mostly go down."

"You do, do you! And when you're sure, like about Daffodil, what makes you sure, sonny?"

"Oh, well, I don't know," said the boy uneasily. "I'm sure, you know, uncle; that's all."

"It's as if he had it from heaven, sir," Bassett reiterated.

"I should say so!" said the uncle.

But he became a partner. And when the Leger° was coming on Paul was "sure" about Lively Spark, which was a quite inconsiderable horse. The boy insisted on putting a thousand on the horse, Bassett went for five hundred, and Oscar Cresswell two hundred. Lively Spark came in first, and the betting had been ten to one against him. Paul had made ten thousand.

"You see," he said, "I was absolutely sure of him."

Even Oscar Cresswell had cleared two thousand.

"Look here, son," he said, "this sort of thing makes me nervous."

"It needn't, uncle! Perhaps I shan't be sure again for a long time."

"But what are you going to do with your money?" asked the uncle.

"Of course," said the boy, "I started it for mother. She said she had no luck, because father is unlucky, so I thought if *I* was lucky, it might stop whispering."

"What might stop whispering?"

---

the Leger: The St. Leger Stakes, a horse race.

"Our house. I *hate* our house for whispering."

"What does it whisper?"

"Why—why"—the boy fidgeted—"why, I don't know. But it's always short of money, you know, uncle."

"I know it, son, I know it."

155 "You know people send mother writs,° don't you, uncle?"

"I'm afraid I do," said the uncle.

"And then the house whispers, like people laughing at you behind your back. It's awful, that is! I thought if I was lucky . . ."

"You might stop it," added the uncle.

The boy watched him with big blue eyes, that had an uncanny cold fire in them, and he said never a word.

160 "Well, then!" said the uncle. "What are we doing?"

"I shouldn't like mother to know I was lucky," said the boy.

"Why not, son?"

"She'd stop me."

"I don't think she would."

165 "Oh!"—and the boy writhed in an odd way—"I *don't* want her to know, uncle."

"All right, son! We'll manage it without her knowing."

They managed it very easily. Paul, at the other's suggestion, handed over five thousand pounds to his uncle, who deposited it with the family lawyer, who was then to inform Paul's mother that a relative had put five thousand pounds into his hands, which sum was to be paid out a thousand pounds at a time, on the mother's birthday, for the next five years.

"So she'll have a birthday present of a thousand pounds for five successive years," said Uncle Oscar. "I hope it won't make it all the harder for her later."

Paul's mother had her birthday in November. The house had been "whispering" worse than ever lately, and, even in spite of his luck, Paul could not bear up against it. He was very anxious to see the effect of the birthday letter, telling his mother about the thousand pounds.

170 When there were no visitors, Paul now took his meals with his parents, as he was beyond the nursery control. His mother went into town nearly every day. She had discovered that she had an odd knack of sketching furs and dress materials, so she worked secretly in the studio of a friend who was the chief "artist" for the leading drapers. She drew the figures of ladies in furs and ladies in silk and sequins for the newspaper advertisements. This young woman artist earned several thousand pounds a year, but Paul's mother only made several hundreds, and she was again dissatisfied. She so wanted to be first in something, and she did not succeed, even in making sketches for drapery advertisements.

She was down to breakfast on the morning of her birthday. Paul watched her face as she read her letters. He knew the lawyer's letter. As his mother read it, her face hardened and became more expressionless. Then a cold, determined look came on her mouth. She hid the letter under the pile of others, and said not a word about it.

writs: Letters from creditors requesting payment.

"Didn't you have anything nice in the post for your birthday, mother?" said Paul.

"Quite moderately nice," she said, her voice cold and absent.

She went away to town without saying more.

But in the afternoon Uncle Oscar appeared. He said Paul's mother had had 175
a long interview with the lawyer, asking if the whole five thousand could not be advanced at once, as she was in debt.

"What do you think, uncle?" asked the boy.

"I leave it to you, son."

"Oh, let her have it, then! We can get some more with the other," said the boy.

"A bird in the hand is worth two in the bush, laddie!" said Uncle Oscar.

"But I'm sure to *know* for the Grand National; or the Lincolnshire; or else the 180
Derby.° I'm sure to know for *one* of them," said Paul.

So Uncle Oscar signed the agreement, and Paul's mother touched the whole five thousand. Then something very curious happened. The voices in the house suddenly went mad, like a chorus of frogs on a spring evening. There was certain new furnishings, and Paul had a tutor. He was *really* going to Eton, his father's school, in the following autumn. There were flowers in the winter, and a blossoming of the luxury Paul's mother had been used to. And yet the voices in the house, behind the sprays of mimosa and almond-blossom, and from under the piles of iridescent cushions, simply trilled and screamed in a sort of ecstasy: "There *must* be more money! Oh-h-h; there *must* be more money. Oh, now, now-w! Now-w-w—there *must* be more money!—more than ever! More than ever!"

It frightened Paul terribly. He studied away at his Latin and Greek with his tutor. But his intense hours were spent with Bassett. The Grand National had gone by: he had not "known," and had lost a hundred pounds. Summer was at hand. He was in agony for the Lincoln. But even for the Lincoln he didn't "know," and he lost fifty pounds. He became wild-eyed and strange, as if something were going to explode in him.

"Let it alone, son! Don't you bother about it!" urged Uncle Oscar. But it was as if the boy couldn't really hear what his uncle was saying.

"I've got to know for the Derby! I've got to know for the Derby!" the child reiterated, his big blue eyes blazing with a sort of madness.

His mother noticed how overwrought he was. 185

"You'd better go to the seaside. Wouldn't you like to go now to the seaside, instead of waiting? I think you'd better," she said, looking down at him anxiously, her heart curiously heavy because of him.

But the child lifted his uncanny blue eyes.

"I couldn't possibly go before the Derby, mother!" he said. "I couldn't possibly!"

"Why not?" she said, her voice becoming heavy when she was opposed. "Why not? You can still go from the seaside to see the Derby with your Uncle Oscar, if that's what you wish. No need for you to wait here. Besides, I think you care too much about these races. It's a bad sign. My family has been a gambling family, and you won't know till you grow up how much damage it has done. But it has done damage. I shall

Grand National . . . Derby: Famous British horse races. The Grand National is run at Aintree; the Derby, at Epsom Downs.

have to send Bassett away, and ask Uncle Oscar not to talk racing to you, unless you promise to be reasonable about it: go away to the seaside and forget it. You're all nerves!"

"I'll do what you like, mother, so long as you don't send me away till after the Derby," the boy said.

"Send you away from where? Just from this house?"

"Yes," he said, gazing at her.

"Why, you curious child, what makes you care about this house so much, suddenly? I never knew you loved it."

He gazed at her without speaking. He had a secret within a secret, something he had not divulged, even to Bassett or to his Uncle Oscar.

But his mother, after standing undecided and a little bit sullen for some moments, said:

"Very well, then! Don't go to the seaside till after the Derby, if you don't wish it. But promise me you won't let your nerves go to pieces. Promise you won't think so much about horse-racing and *events*, as you call them!"

"Oh no," said the boy casually. "I won't think much about them, mother. You needn't worry. I wouldn't worry, mother, if I were you."

"If you were me and I were you," said his mother, "I wonder what we *should* do!"

"But you know you needn't worry, mother, don't you?" the boy repeated.

"I should be awfully glad to know it," she said wearily.

"Oh, well, you *can*, you know. I mean, you *ought* to know you needn't worry," he insisted.

"Ought I? Then I'll see about it," she said.

Paul's secret of secrets was his wooden horse, that which had no name. Since he was emancipated from a nurse and a nursery-governess, he had had his rocking-horse removed to his own bedroom at the top of the house.

"Surely you're too big for a rocking-horse!" his mother had remonstrated.

"Well, you see, mother, till I can have a *real* horse, I like to have *some* sort of animal about," had been his quaint answer.

"Do you feel he keeps you company?" she laughed.

"Oh yes! He's very good, he always keeps me company, when I'm there," said Paul.

So the horse, rather shabby, stood in an arrested prance in the boy's bedroom.

The Derby was drawing near, and the boy grew more and more tense. He hardly heard what was spoken to him, he was very frail, and his eyes were really uncanny. His mother had sudden strange seizures of uneasiness about him. Sometimes, for half an hour, she would feel a sudden anxiety about him that was almost anguish. She wanted to rush to him at once, and know he was safe.

Two nights before the Derby, she was at a big party in town, when one of her rushes of anxiety about her boy, her firstborn, gripped her heart till she could hardly speak. She fought with the feeling, might and main, for she believed in common sense. But it was too strong. She had to leave the dance and go downstairs to telephone to the country. The children's nursery-governess was terribly surprised and startled at being rung up in the night.

"Are the children all right, Miss Wilmot?"

"Oh yes, they are quite all right."

"Master Paul? Is he all right?"

"He went to bed as right as a trivet. Shall I run up and look at him?"

"No," said Paul's mother reluctantly. "No! Don't trouble. It's all right. Don't sit up. We shall be home fairly soon." She did not want her son's privacy intruded upon.

"Very good," said the governess.

It was about one o'clock when Paul's mother and father drove up to their house. All was still. Paul's mother went to her room and slipped off her white fur cloak. She had told her maid not to wait up for her. She heard her husband downstairs, mixing a whisky and soda.

And then, because of the strange anxiety at her heart, she stole upstairs to her son's room. Noiselessly she went along the upper corridor. Was there a faint noise? What was it?

She stood, with arrested muscles, outside his door, listening. There was a strange, heavy, and yet not loud noise. Her heart stood still. It was a soundless noise, yet rushing and powerful. Something huge, in violent, hushed motion. What was it? What in God's name was it? She ought to know. She felt that she knew the noise. She knew what it was.

Yet she could not place it. She couldn't say what it was. And on and on it went, like a madness.

Softly, frozen with anxiety and fear, she turned the door-handle.

The room was dark. Yet in the space near the window, she heard and saw something plunging to and fro. She gazed in fear and amazement.

Then suddenly she switched on the light, and saw her son, in his green pyjamas, madly surging on the rocking-horse. The blaze of light suddenly lit him up, as he urged the wooden horse, and lit her up, as she stood, blonde, in her dress of pale green and crystal, in the doorway.

"Paul!" she cried. "Whatever are you doing?"

"It's Malabar!" he screamed in a powerful, strange voice. "It's Malabar!"

His eyes blazed at her for one strange and senseless second, as he ceased urging his wooden horse. Then he fell with a crash to the ground, and she, all her tormented motherhood flooding upon her, rushed to gather him up.

But he was unconscious, and unconscious he remained, with some brain-fever. He talked and tossed, and his mother sat stonily by his side.

"Malabar! It's Malabar! Bassett, Bassett, I *know!* It's Malabar!"

So the child cried, trying to get up and urge the rocking-horse that gave him his inspiration.

"What does he mean by Malabar?" asked the heart-frozen mother.

"I don't know," said the father stonily.

"What does he mean by Malabar?" she asked her brother Oscar.

"It's one of the horses running for the Derby," was the answer.

And, in spite of himself, Oscar Cresswell spoke to Bassett, and himself put a thousand on Malabar: at fourteen to one.

The third day of the illness was critical: they were waiting for a change. The boy, with his rather long, curly hair, was tossing ceaselessly on the pillow. He neither slept nor regained consciousness, and his eyes were like blue stones. His mother sat, feeling her heart had gone, turned actually into a stone.

In the evening, Oscar Cresswell did not come, but Bassett sent a message, saying could he come up for one moment, just one moment? Paul's mother was very angry at the intrusion, but on second thought she agreed. The boy was the same. Perhaps Bassett might bring him to consciousness.

The gardener, a shortish fellow with a little brown moustache and sharp little brown eyes, tiptoed into the room, touched his imaginary cap to Paul's mother, and stole to the bedside, staring with glittering, smallish eyes at the tossing, dying child.

"Master Paul!" he whispered. "Master Paul! Malabar came in first all right, a clean win. I did as you told me. You've made over seventy thousand pounds, you have; you've got over eighty thousand. Malabar came in all right, Master Paul."

"Malabar! Malabar! Did I say Malabar, mother? Did I say Malabar? Do you think I'm lucky, mother? I knew Malabar, didn't I? Over eighty thousand pounds! I call that lucky, don't you, mother? Over eighty thousand pounds! I knew, didn't I know I knew? Malabar came in all right. If I ride my horse till I'm sure, then I tell you, Bassett, you can go as high as you like. Did you go for all you were worth, Bassett?"

240 "I went a thousand on it, Master Paul."

"I never told you, mother, that if I can ride my horse, and *get there*, then I'm absolutely sure—oh, absolutely! Mother, did I ever tell you? I *am* lucky!"

"No, you never did," said his mother.

But the boy died in the night.

And even as he lay dead, his mother heard her brother's voice saying to her: "My God, Hester, you're eighty-odd thousand to the good, and a poor devil of a son to the bad. But, poor devil, poor devil, he's best gone out of a life where he rides his rocking-horse to find a winner."

Reading and Reacting

1. From what point of view is "The Rocking-Horse Winner" told? How does this point of view help to communicate the story's theme?
2. In what ways is "The Rocking-Horse Winner" like a fairy tale? How is it different?
3. Many fairy tales involve a hero who goes on a journey to search for something of great value. What journey does Paul go on? What thing of value does he search for? Is he successful?
4. In paragraph 5, the narrator says that the house is "haunted by the unspoken phrase: '*There must be more money!*'" In what way does this phrase "haunt" the house?
5. How would you characterize Paul's parents? His uncle? Bassett? Are they weak? Evil? What motivates them?
6. Beginning in paragraph 11, Paul's mother attempts to define the word *luck*. According to her definition, does she consider Paul lucky? Do you agree?
7. In what ways does Paul behave like other children? In what ways is he different? How do you account for these differences? How old do you think Paul is? Why is his age significant?

8. The rocking horse is an important literary **symbol** in the story. What possible meanings might the rocking horse suggest? In what ways does this symbol reinforce the story's theme?
9. What secrets do the various characters keep from one another? Why do they keep them? What do these secrets suggest about the story's theme?
10. How does Paul know who the winners will be? Does the rocking horse really tell him? Does he get his information "from heaven" as Bassett suggests (par. 119)? Or does he just guess?
11. **JOURNAL ENTRY** In your opinion, who or what is responsible for Paul's death?
12. **CRITICAL PERSPECTIVE** In a letter dated January 17, 1913, Lawrence wrote the following:

> My great religion is a belief in the blood, the flesh, as being wiser than the intellect. We can go wrong in our minds. But what our blood feels and believes and says, is always true. The intellect is only a bit and a bridle. What do I care about knowledge. All I want is to answer to my blood, direct, without fribbling intervention of mind, or moral, or what-not.

How does Lawrence's portrayal of Paul in "The Rocking-Horse Winner" support his belief in "the blood . . . being wiser than the intellect"? How does Lawrence remain true in this story to his metaphor of the intellect as "a bit and a bridle"?

Related Works: "Once upon a Time" (p. 232), "Teenage Wasteland" (p. 785), "Gretel in Darkness" (p. 839), "Suicide Note" (p. 846), "Birches" (p. 1050), "The Chimney Sweeper" (p. 1127), *Death of a Salesman* (p. 1531)

Source: ©AP Photo/Marcio Jose Sanchez

MICHAEL CHABON (1963–) is a novelist, short story writer, and member of the literary group McSweeney's. He has been widely praised for his ability to convey the complexity of love and loss in his fiction. His stories have appeared in publications such as the *New Yorker, Gentleman's Quarterly,* and *Mademoiselle.* Chabon has published several critically acclaimed novels, including the Pulitzer Prize–winning *The Amazing Adventures of Kavalier and Clay* (2000), the basis for a 2009 feature film for which he wrote the screenplay, and *The Yiddish Policemen's Union* (2007). His novel *Wonder Boys* (1995) was adapted into the Academy Award–winning feature film of the same name.

Cultural Context "The Little Knife" explores the psychological impact of divorce on children. The effects of divorce on children vary, ranging from feelings of loss and powerlessness to erratic and destructive behavior. Children of divorce often carry feelings of guilt and resentment into adolescence and adulthood, prompting psychologists to classify some children of divorce as "adult children." Recent studies have shown that it is not only young children who suffer from divorce. Older children, too, feel a sense of sadness and loss. Even adult children feel as if they have to reevaluate their own childhoods in light of their parents' actions.

The Little Knife (1991)

One Saturday in that last, interminable summer before his parents separated and the Washington Senators baseball team was expunged forever from the face of the earth, the Shapiros went to Nags Head, North Carolina, where Nathan, without planning to, perpetrated a great hoax. They drove down I-95, through the Commonwealth of Virginia, to a place called the Sandpiper—a ragged, charming oval of motel cottages painted white and green as the Atlantic, and managed by a kind, astonishingly fat old man named Colonel Larue, who smoked cherry cigars and would, if asked, play catch or keep-away. Outside his office, in the weedy gravel, stood an old red-and-radium-white Coke machine, which dispensed bottles from a vertical glass door that sighed when you opened it, and which reminded Nathan of the Automat his grandmother had taken him to once in New York City. The sight of the faded machine and of the whole Sandpiper—like that of the Automat—filled Nathan with a happy sadness, or, really, a sad happiness; he was not too young, at ten, to have developed a sense of nostalgia.

There were children in every cottage—with all manner of floats, pails, paddles, trucks, and flying objects—and his younger brother Ricky, to Nathan's envy, immediately fell in with a gang of piratical little boys with water pistols, who were always reproducing fart sounds and giggling chaotically when their mothers employed certain ordinary words such as "hot dog" and "rubber." The Shapiros went to the ocean every summer, and at the beginning of this trip, as on all those that had preceded it, Nathan and his brother got along better than they usually did, their mother broke out almost immediately in a feathery red heat rash, and their father lay pale and motionless in the sun, like a monument, and always forgot to take off his wristwatch when he went into the sea. Nathan had brought a stack of James Bond books and his colored pencils; there were board games—he and his father were in the middle of their Strat-O-Matic baseball playoffs—and miniature boxes of cereal; the family ate out every single night. But when they were halfway through the slow, dazzling week—which was as far as they were to get—Nathan began to experience an unfamiliar longing: He wanted to go home.

He awoke very early on Wednesday morning, went into the cottage's small kitchen, where the floor was sticky and the table rocked and trembled, and chose the last of the desirable cereals from the Variety pack, leaving for Ricky only those papery, sour brands with the scientific names—the sort that their grandparents liked. As he began to eat, Nathan heard, from the big bedroom down the hall, the unmistakable, increasingly familiar sound of his father burying his mother under a heap of scorn and ridicule. It was, oddly, a soft and pleading sound. Lately, the conversation and actions of Dr. Shapiro's family seemed to disappoint him terribly. His left hand was always flying up to smack his sad and outraged forehead, so hard that Nathan often thought he could hear his father's wedding ring crack against his skull. When they'd played their baseball game the day before—Nathan's Baltimore Bonfires against his father's Brooklyn Eagles—every decision Nathan made led to a disaster, and his father pointed out each unwise substitution and foolish attempt to steal in this new tone of miserable sarcasm, so that Nathan had spent the afternoon apologizing, and, finally, crying. Now he listened for his mother's voice, for the note of chastened shame.

The bedroom door slammed, and Mrs. Shapiro came out into the kitchen. She was in her bathrobe, a wild, sleepless smile on her face.

5 "Good morning, honey," she said, then hummed to herself as she boiled water and made a cup of instant coffee. Her spoon tinkled gaily against the cup.

"Where are you going, Mom?" said Nathan. She had taken up her coffee and was heading for the sliding glass door that led out of the kitchen and down to the beach.

"See you, honey," she sang.

"Mom!" said Nathan. He stood up—afraid, absurdly, that she might be leaving for good, because she seemed so happy. After a few seconds he heard her whistling, and he went to the door and pressed his face against the wire screen. His mother had a Disney whistle, melodious and full, like a Scotsman's as he walks across a meadow in a brilliant kilt. She paced briskly along the ramshackle slat-and-wire fence, back and forth through the beach grass, drinking from the huge white mug of coffee and whistling heartily into the breeze; her red hair rose from her head and trailed like a defiant banner. He watched her observe the sunrise—it was going to be a perfect, breezy day—then continued to watch as she set her coffee on the ground, removed her bathrobe, and, in her bathing suit, began to engage in a long series of yoga exercises—a new fad of hers—as though she were playing statues all alone. Nathan was soon lost, with the fervor of a young scientist, in contemplation of his pretty, whistling mother rolling around on the ground.

"Oh, how can she?" said Dr. Shapiro.

10 "Yes," said Nathan, gravely, before he blushed and whirled around to find his father, in pajamas, staring out at Mrs. Shapiro. His smile was angry and clenched, but in his eyes was the same look of bleak surprise, of betrayal, that had been there when Nathan took out Johnny Sain, a slugging pitcher, and the pinch-hitter, Enos Slaughter, immediately went down on strikes. There were a hundred new things that interested Nathan's mother—bonsai, the Zuni,° yoga, real estate—and although Dr. Shapiro had always been a liberal, generous, encouraging man (as Nathan had heard his mother say to a friend), and had at first happily helped her to purchase the necessary manuals, supplies, and coffee-table books, lately each new fad seemed to come as a blow to him—a going astray, a false step.

"How can she?" he said again, shaking his big bearded head.

"She says it's really good for you," said Nathan.

His father smiled down on his son ruefully, and tapped him once on the head. Then he turned and went to the refrigerator, hitching up his pajama bottoms. They were the ones patterned with a blue stripe and red chevrons—the ones that Nathan

Zuni: Native-American tribe living in west-central New Mexico.

always imagined were the sort worn by the awkward, doomed elephant in the Groucho Marx joke.°

Later that day, as they made egg-salad sandwiches to carry down to the beach, Dr. and Mrs. Shapiro fought bitterly, for the fifth time since their arrival. In the cottage's kitchen was a knife—a small, new, foreign knife, which Mrs. Shapiro admired. As she used it to slice neat little horseshoes of celery, she praised it again. "Such a good little knife," she said. "Why don't you just take it?" said Dr. Shapiro. The air in the kitchen was suddenly full of sharp, caramel smoke, and Dr. Shapiro ran to unplug the toaster.

15 "That would be stealing," said Nathan's mother, ignoring her husband's motions of alarm and the fact that their lunch was on fire. "We are not taking this knife, Martin."

"Give it to me." Dr. Shapiro held out his hand, palm up.

"I'm not going to let you—make me—dishonest anymore!" said his mother. She seemed to struggle, at first, not to finish the sentence she had begun, but in the end she turned, put her face right up to his, and cried out boldly. After her outburst, both adults turned to look, with a simultaneity that was almost funny, at their sons. Nathan hadn't the faintest notion of what his mother was talking about.

"Don't steal, Dad," Ricky said.

"I only wanted it to extract the piece of toast," said their father. He was looking at their mother again. "God damn it." He turned and went out of the kitchen.

20 Her knuckles white around the handle of the knife, their mother freed the toast and began scraping the burnt surfaces into the sink. Because their father had said "God damn," Ricky wiggled his eyebrows and smiled at Nathan. At the slamming of the bedroom door, Nathan clambered up suddenly from the rickety kitchen table as though he had found an insect crawling on his leg.

"Kill it!" said Ricky. "What is it?"

"What is it?" said his mother. She scanned Nathan's body quickly, one hand half raised to swat.

"Nothing," said Nathan. He took off his glasses. "I'm going for a walk."

When he got to the edge of the water, he turned to look toward the Sandpiper. At that time in Nags Head there were few hotels and no condominiums, and it seemed to Nathan that their little ring of cottages stood alone, like Stonehenge, in the middle of a giant wasteland. He set off down the beach, watching his feet print and following the script left in the sand by the birds for which the motel was named. He passed a sand castle, then a heart drawn with a stick enclosing the names Jimmy and Beth. Sometimes his heels sank deeply into the sand, and he noticed the odd marks this would leave—a pair of wide dimples. He discovered that he could walk entirely on his heels, and his trail became two lines of big periods. If he took short

---

Groucho Marx joke: Quotation from the 1930 Marx Brothers film *Animal Crackers,* in which Groucho Marx's character says, "One morning I shot an elephant in my pajamas. How he got in my pajamas, I don't know."

steps, it looked as though a creature—a bird with two peg legs—had come to fish along the shore.

He lurched a long way in this fashion, watching his feet, and nearly forgot his parents' quarrel. But when at last he grew bored with walking on his heels and turned to go back, he saw that his mother and father had also decided to take a walk, and that they were, in fact, coming toward him—clasping hands, letting go, clasping hands again. Nathan ran to meet them, and they parted to let him walk between them. They all continued down the beach, stopping to pick up shells, glass, dead crabs, twine, and all the colored or smelly things that Nathan had failed to take note of before. At first his parents exclaimed with him over these discoveries, and his father took each striped seashell into his hands, to keep it safe, until there were two dozen and they jingled there like money. But after a while they seemed to lose interest, and Nathan found himself walking a few feet ahead of them, stooping alone, glumly dusting his toes with sand as he tried to eavesdrop on their careless and incomprehensible conversation.

"Never again," his mother said at last.

Dr. Shapiro let the shells fall. He rubbed his hands together and then stared at them as though waking from a dream in which he had been holding a fortune in gold. Straightening up so quickly that his head spun, Nathan let out a cry and pointed down at the sand beneath their feet, among the scattered shells. "Look at those weird tracks!" he cried.

They all looked down.

Speculation on the nature of the beast that went toeless down the shore went on for several minutes, and although Nathan was delighted at first, he soon began to feel embarrassed and, obscurely, frightened by the ease with which he had deceived his parents. His treachery was almost exposed when Ricky, carrying a long stick and wearing a riot of Magic Marker tattoos on his face and all down his arms, ran over to find out what was happening. The little boy immediately tipped back onto his heels, and would have taken a few steps like that had Nathan not grabbed him by the elbow and dragged him aside.

"Why do you have a dog on your face?" said Nathan.

"It's a jaguar," said Ricky.

Nathan bent to whisper into his brother's ear. "I'm tricking Mom and Dad," he said.

"Good," said Ricky.

"They think there's some kind of weird creature on the beach."

Ricky pushed Nathan away and then surveyed their mother and father, who were talking again, quietly, as though they were trying not to alarm their sons. "It can't be real," said Nathan's father.

Ricky's skin under the crude tattoos was tanned, his hair looked stiff and ragged from going unwashed and sea-tangled, and as he regarded their parents he held his skinny stick like a javelin at his side. "They're dumb," he said flatly.

Dr. Shapiro approached, stepping gingerly across the mysterious tracks, and then knelt beside his sons. His face was red, though not from the sun, and he seemed to have trouble looking directly at the boys. Nathan began to cry before his father even spoke.

"Boys," he said. He looked away, then back, and bit his lip. "I'm afraid—I'm sorry. We're going to go home. Your mom and I—don't feel very well. We don't seem to be well."

"No! No! It was Nathan!" said Ricky, laying down his spear and throwing himself into his father's arms. "It wasn't me. Make *him* go home."

Nathan, summoning up his courage, decided to admit that the curious trail of the crippled animal was his, and he said, "I'm responsible."

"Oh, no!" cried both his parents together, startling him. His mother rushed over and fell to her knees, and they took Nathan into their arms and said that it was never, never him, and they ruffled his hair with their fingers, as though he had done something they could love him for.

After they came back from dinner, the Shapiros, save Nathan, went down to the sea for a final, sad promenade. At the restaurant, Ricky had pleaded with his parents to stay through the end of the week—they had not even been to see the monument at Kitty Hawk,° the Birthplace of Aviation. For Ricky's sake, Nathan had also tried to persuade them, but his heart wasn't in it—he himself wanted so badly to go home—and the four of them had all ended up crying and chewing their food in the brass-and-rope dining room of the Port O' Call; even Dr. Shapiro had shed a tear. They were going to leave that night. Nathan's family now stood, in sweatshirts, by the sliding glass door, his parents straining to adopt hard and impatient looks, and Nathan saw that they felt guilty about leaving him behind in the cottage.

"I'll pack my stuff," he said. "Just go." For a moment his stomach tightened with angry, secret glee as his mother and father, sighing, turned their backs on him and obeyed his small command. Then he was alone in the kitchen again, for the second time that day, and he wished that he had gone to look at the ocean, and he hated his parents, uncertainly, for leaving him behind. He got up and walked into the bedroom that he and Ricky had shared. There, in the twilight that fell in orange shafts through the open window, the tangle of their clothes and bedsheets, their scattered toys and books, the surfaces of the broken dresser and twin headboards seemed dusted with a film of radiant sand, as though the tide had washed across them and withdrawn, and the room was strewn with the seashells they had found. Nathan, after emptying his shoebox of baseball cards into his suitcase, went slowly around the room and harvested the shells with careful sweeps of his trembling hand. Bearing the shoebox back into the kitchen, he collected the few stray shards of salt-white and green beach glass that lay in a pile beside the electric can opener, and then added a hollow pink crab's leg in whose claw Ricky had fixed a colored pencil. When Nathan saw the little knife in the drainboard by the sink, he hesitated only a moment before dropping it into the box, where it swam, frozen, like a model shark

---

Kitty Hawk: Town in North Carolina and site of the Wright Brothers National Memorial commemorating the first powered airplane flight by Wilbur and Orville Wright in 1903.

in a museum diorama of life beneath the sea. Nathan chuckled. As clearly as if he were remembering them, he foresaw his mother's accusation, his father's enraged denial, and with an unhappy chuckle he foresaw, recalled, and fondly began to preserve all the discord for which, in his wildly preserving imagination, he was and would always be responsible.

Reading and Reacting

1. What information does the first sentence of the story include? How does this information prepare readers for the story to follow?
2. At the end of paragraph 2, the narrator says, "Nathan began to experience an unfamiliar longing—he wanted to go home." What causes him to feel this way?
3. Although the story is told by a third-person narrator, its point of view is, for the most part, limited to that of Nathan, a ten-year-old boy. How much of what Nathan sees does he understand? What things does he not understand?
4. How would you describe Nathan's father? His mother? His brother? How would you characterize the family?
5. What do you think Nathan's mother means when she says to her husband, "I'm not going to let you—make me—dishonest anymore!" (par. 17)? What could she be referring to?
6. Why do you think the parents decide to cut their vacation short? Does anything occur during the vacation to cause them to make this decision, or did they have problems before they arrived?
7. In paragraph 1, the narrator says that Nathan unintentionally "perpetrated a great hoax." What hoax is the narrator referring to? Do you believe, as the narrator states, that Nathan carried out this hoax "without planning to"?
8. Why does Nathan steal the knife? What does the knife symbolize to him? To his parents?
9. **JOURNAL ENTRY** What is the main theme of the story? What other stories have you read that have a similar theme?
10. **CRITICAL PERSPECTIVE** Writing for *Studies in Short Fiction*, Douglas Fowler describes the skill with which Michael Chabon captures painful human emotions in his fiction:

    > Chabon's protagonist always seems to be obsessively engaged in investigating a poisoned wound located just at the juncture where his individual life once drew sustenance from a family life-support system. In Chabon's fictional kingdom, the psychodrama Freud called the "Family Romance" is almost always crucial to the narrative. . . . And everywhere in Chabon's fiction there is a valedictory sense of seeing from the outside those emotions that seem to be experienced from the inside only once.

    Do you think "The Little Knife" realistically depicts Nathan's emotions as he witnesses the events leading up to his parents' divorce? How is the knife symbolic of "those emotions that seem to be experienced from the inside only once"?

Related Works: "Oliver's Evolution" (p. 191), "Gryphon" (p. 277), "Daddy" (p. 936), "I Go Back to May 1937 (p. 1039), "Men at Forty," (p. 1167), *Proof* (p. 1476)

Source: ©AP Photo/Marty Lederhandler

TOBIAS WOLFF (1945–) is a novelist, short story writer, and editor whose work has appeared in the *Atlantic Monthly*, the *New Yorker*, and the *Paris Review*. The author of four story collections, two novels, and two memoirs, Wolff received a PEN/Faulkner Award for his first novel, *The Barracks Thief* (1984). His award-winning memoir *This Boy's Life* (1989), which chronicles his unstable childhood growing up with various abusive stepfathers, was adapted into the feature film of the same name. In addition to writing his own successful short fiction, Wolff has edited a collection of Anton Chekhov's short stories and two collections of American short stories.

Cultural Context Bank robberies are particularly prevalent in the southern and north central United States. According to the Bank Crime Statistics database, only twenty percent of the approximately seventy million dollars stolen each year from banks is recovered. On average, thieves steal less than $8,000 in a single robbery. Data also show, surprisingly, that violence and injury are generally uncommon in bank robberies, with only two percent of all robberies involving shootings. In recent years, the number of bank robberies has declined. Modern security measures, such as hidden cameras, silent alarms, exploding dye packs, and SWAT teams, make robbing banks very difficult. In addition, bank robbery is a federal crime and is severely punished. Today, the arrest rate for bank robbery is second only to that for murder.

Bullet in the Brain (1996)

Anders couldn't get to the bank until just before it closed, so of course the line was endless and he got stuck behind two women whose loud, stupid conversation put him in a murderous temper. He was never in the best of tempers anyway, Anders—a book critic known for the weary, elegant savagery with which he dispatched almost everything he reviewed.

With the line still doubled around the rope, one of the tellers stuck a "POSITION CLOSED" sign in her window and walked to the back of the bank, where she leaned against a desk and began to pass the time with a man shuffling papers. The women in front of Anders broke off their conversation and watched the teller with hatred. "Oh, that's nice," one of them said. She turned to Anders and added, confident of his accord, "One of those little human touches that keep us coming back for more."

Anders had conceived his own towering hatred of the teller, but he immediately turned it on the presumptuous crybaby in front of him. "Damned unfair," he said. "Tragic, really. If they're not chopping off the wrong leg, or bombing your ancestral village, they're closing their positions."

She stood her ground. "I didn't say it was tragic," she said. "I just think it's a pretty lousy way to treat your customers."

5 "Unforgivable," Anders said. "Heaven will take note."

She sucked in her cheeks but stared past him and said nothing. Anders saw that the other woman, her friend, was looking in the same direction. And then the tellers stopped what they were doing, and the customers slowly turned, and silence came over the bank. Two men wearing black ski masks and blue business suits were standing to the side of the door. One of them had a pistol pressed against the guard's neck. The guard's eyes were closed, and his lips were moving. The other man had a sawed-off shotgun. "Keep your big mouth shut!" the man with the pistol said, though no one had spoken a word. "One of you tellers hits the alarm, you're all dead meat. Got it?"

The tellers nodded.

"Oh, bravo," Anders said. "*Dead meat*." He turned to the woman in front of him. "Great script, eh? The stern, brass-knuckled poetry of the dangerous classes."

She looked at him with drowning eyes.

The man with the shotgun pushed the guard to his knees. He handed up the shotgun to his partner and yanked the guard's wrists up behind his back and locked them together with a pair of handcuffs. He toppled him onto the floor with a kick between the shoulder blades. Then he took his shotgun back and went over to the security gate at the end of the counter. He was short and heavy and moved with peculiar slowness, even torpor. "Buzz him in," his partner said. The man with the shotgun opened the gate and sauntered along the line of tellers, handing each of them a Hefty bag. When he came to the empty position he looked over at the man with the pistol, who said, "Whose slot is that?"

Anders watched the teller. She put her hand to her throat and turned to the man she'd been talking to. He nodded. "Mine," she said.

"Then get your ugly ass in gear and fill that bag."

"There you go," Anders said to the woman in front of him. "Justice is done."

"Hey! Bright Boy! Did I tell you to talk?"

"No," Anders said.

"Then shut your trap."

"Did you hear that?" Anders said. "'Bright boy.' Right out of 'The Killers'."

"Please be quiet," the woman said.

"Hey, you deaf or what?" The man with the pistol walked over to Anders. He poked the weapon into Anders' gut. "You think I'm playing games?"

"No," Anders said, but the barrel tickled like a stiff finger and he had to fight back the titters. He did this by making himself stare into the man's eyes, which were clearly visible behind the holes in the mask: pale blue, and rawly red-rimmed. The man's left eyelid kept twitching. He breathed out a piercing, ammoniac smell that shocked Anders more than anything that had happened, and he was beginning to develop a sense of unease when the man prodded him again with the pistol.

"You like me, bright boy?" he said. "You want to suck my dick?"

"No," Anders said.

"Then stop looking at me."

Anders fixed his gaze on the man's shiny wing-tip shoes.

"Not down there. Up there." He stuck the pistol under Anders' chin and pushed it upward until Anders was looking at the ceiling.

Anders had never paid much attention to that part of the bank, a pompous old building with marble floors and counters and pillars, and gilt scrollwork over the tellers' cages. The domed ceiling had been decorated with mythological figures whose fleshy, toga-draped ugliness Anders had taken in at a glance many years earlier and afterward declined to notice. Now he had no choice but to scrutinize the painter's work. It was even worse than he remembered, and all of it executed with the utmost gravity. The artist had a few tricks up his sleeve and used them again and again—a certain rosy blush on the underside of the clouds, a coy backward glance on the faces of the cupids and fauns. The ceiling was crowded with various dramas, but the one that caught Anders' eye was Zeus and Europa°—portrayed, in this rendition, as a bull ogling a cow from behind a haystack. To make the cow sexy, the painter had canted her hips suggestively and given her long, droopy eyelashes through which she gazed back at the bull with sultry welcome. The bull wore a smirk and his eyebrows were arched. If there'd been a bubble coming out of his mouth, it would have said, "Hubba hubba."

"What's so funny, bright boy?"

"Nothing."

"You think I'm comical? You think I'm some kind of clown?"

"No."

"You think you can fuck with me?"

"No."

"Fuck with me again, you're history. *Capiche?*"°

Anders burst out laughing. He covered his mouth with both hands and said, "I'm sorry, I'm sorry," then snorted helplessly through his fingers and said, "*Capiche*— oh, God, *capiche*," and at that the man with the pistol raised the pistol and shot Anders right in the head.

The bullet smashed Anders' skull and ploughed through his brain and exited behind his right ear, scattering shards of bone into the cerebral cortex, the corpus callosum, back toward the basal ganglia, and down into the thalamus. But before all this occurred, the first appearance of the bullet in the cerebrum set off a cracking chain of ion transports and neuro-transmissions. Because of their peculiar origin these traced a peculiar pattern, flukishly calling to life a summer afternoon some forty years past, and long since lost to memory. After striking the cranium the bullet was moving at 900 feet per second, a pathetically sluggish, glacial pace compared to the synaptic lightning that flashed around it. Once in the brain, that is, the bullet came under the mediation of brain time, which gave Anders plenty of leisure to contemplate the scene that, in a phrase he would have abhorred, "passed before his eyes."

It is worth noting what Anders did not remember, given what he did remember. He did not remember his first lover, Sherry, or what he had most madly loved about her, before it came to irritate him—her unembarrassed carnality, and especially the cordial way she had with his unit, which she called Mr. Mole, as in, "Uh-oh, looks like Mr. Mole wants to play," and "Let's hide Mr. Mole!" Anders did not remember his wife, whom he had also loved before she exhausted him with her predictability, or his daughter, now a sullen professor of economics at Dartmouth. He did not remember standing just outside his daughter's door as she lectured her bear about his naughtiness and described the truly appalling punishments Paws would receive unless

---

Zeus and Europa: According to Greek mythology, the god Zeus, as a white bull, seduced Europa, who in turn gave birth to three sons.

Capiche?: Americanized spelling of *capisci*, Italian for "Do You Understand?"

he changed his ways. He did not remember a single line of the hundreds of poems he had committed to memory in his youth so that he could give himself the shivers at will—not "Silent, upon a peak in Darien," or "My God, I heard this day," or "All my pretty ones? Did you say all? O hell-kite! All?" None of these did he remember; not one. Anders did not remember his dying mother saying of his father, "I should have stabbed him in his sleep."

He did not remember Professor Josephs telling his class how Athenian prisoners in Sicily had been released if they could recite Aeschylus,° and then reciting Aeschylus himself, right there, in the Greek. Anders did not remember how his eyes had burned at those sounds. He did not remember the surprise of seeing a college classmate's name on the jacket of a novel not long after they graduated, or the respect he had felt after reading the book. He did not remember the pleasure of giving respect.

Nor did Anders remember seeing a woman leap to her death from the building opposite his own just days after his daughter was born. He did not remember shouting, "Lord have mercy!" He did not remember deliberately crashing his father's car into a tree, or having his ribs kicked in by three policemen at an anti-war rally, or waking himself up with laughter. He did not remember when he began to regard the heap of books on his desk with boredom and dread, or when he grew angry at writers for writing them. He did not remember when everything began to remind him of something else.

This is what he remembered. Heat. A baseball field. Yellow grass, the whirr of insects, himself leaning against a tree as the boys of the neighborhood gather for a pickup game. He looks on as the others argue the relative genius of Mantle and Mays.° They have been worrying this subject all summer, and it has become tedious to Anders: an oppression, like the heat.

Then the last two boys arrive, Coyle and a cousin of his from Mississippi. Anders 40
has never met Coyle's cousin before and will never see him again. He says hi with the rest but takes no further notice of him until they've chosen sides and someone asks the cousin what position he wants to play. "Shortstop," the boy says. "Short's the best position they is." Anders turns and looks at him. He wants to hear Coyle's cousin repeat what he's just said, but he knows better than to ask. The others will think he's being a jerk, ragging the kid for his grammar. But that isn't it, not at all—it's that Anders is strangely roused, elated, by those final two words, their pure unexpectedness and their music. He takes the field in a trance, repeating them to himself.

The bullet is already in the brain; it won't be outrun forever, or charmed to a halt. In the end it will do its work and leave the troubled skull behind, dragging its comet's tail of memory and hope and talent and love into the marble hall of commerce. That can't be helped. But for now Anders can still make time. Time for the shadows to lengthen on the grass, time for the tethered dog to bark at the flying ball, time for the boy in right field to smack his sweat-blackened mitt and softly chant, *They is, they is, they is.*

Aeschylus: Greek tragic dramatist (525/524 B.C.–456/455 B.C.).

Mantle and Mays: American professional baseball players Mickey Mantle (1931–1995) and Willie Mays (1931–).

Reading and Reacting

1. According to the narrator, Anders is a book critic "known for the weary, elegant savagery with which he dispatched almost everything he reviewed" (par. 1). Why does Wolff begin his story with this statement? In what way does it set the stage for what follows?
2. In paragraphs 3–5, Anders has an exchange with a woman waiting in line with him. Why does the woman react to Anders's comments the way she does?
3. Why does Anders sarcastically refer to the bank robber's words as a "great script" (par. 8)? What does this remark reveal about him?
4. At one point in the story the bank robber sticks a gun under Anders's chin and forces his head up. As he looks up, Anders begins to mentally critique the artwork on the ceiling. What does this action tell you about him?
5. After repeatedly threatening him, one of the bank robbers tells Anders that if he laughs again, he will shoot him. Why does Anders burst out laughing?
6. What does the bank robber not understand about Anders? What does Anders not understand about the bank robber?
7. In his dying moments, what events does Anders not remember? What does the narrator mean when he says, "He did not remember when everything began to remind him of something else" (par. 38)?
8. As he is dying, what event does Anders remember? Why do you think he remembers this? What insight does this memory provide into Anders's character?
9. **JOURNAL ENTRY** What is your opinion of Anders before he is shot? Does your opinion of him change by the end of the story?
10. **CRITICAL PERSPECTIVE** Editor of *A Doctor's Visit* (1988), a collection of Anton Chekhov's short stories, Tobias Wolff makes the following observation:

    > [Chekhov] gives an intuitive sense that the lives of his characters continue after the story, he does not forcibly bring things to a conclusion . . . . the moral arc of the story, though apparent, is not completed, the circle is not drawn; there is enough of it there, I think, for an imaginative and intelligent reader to continue to draw the circle.

    Do you think that, despite Anders's death, Wolff resists "forcibly bring[ing] things to a conclusion" in "Bullet in the Brain"? What techniques in the final paragraph allow the story to continue on for the reader?

Related Works: "The Story of an Hour" (p. 226), "Miss Brill" (p. 266), "Baca Grande" (p. 889), "Her Whole Life Is an Epigram" (p. 994), "The Love Song of J. Alfred Prufrock" (p. 1151), *Tape* (p. 1275)

WRITING SUGGESTIONS: Theme

1. In "The Little Knife," Nathan witnesses the first episodes of his parents' divorce. In "Doe Season," Andy who witnesses events in the adult world. As children, however, these characters cannot fully understand or interpret what they see. Write an essay in which you examine the limited nature of each character's view

of events. Then, discuss how this limited view helps each author develop the main theme of his story.

2. Two of the stories in this chapter deal with the importance of patience and persistence. Write an essay in which you examine the value of enduring despite difficulties, citing the experiences of the main characters in "Two Questions" and "A Worn Path."
3. Two of the stories in this chapter deal with characters who experience violence and death: Andy, in "Doe Season," kills her first deer, and Anders, in "Bullet in the Brain," is caught up in a bank robbery. Write an essay in which you discuss the ways these characters respond to the violence they see. Account, if you can, for the differences in the characters' reactions.
4. Both "The Rocking-Horse Winner" and "A Worn Path" deal with characters who make journeys. What is the significance of each journey? How do the protagonists of these two stories overcome the obstacles they encounter? In what sense are these journeys symbolic as well as actual?
5. Like "Doe Season," the following poem focuses on a child's experience with hunting. Write an essay in which you contrast its central theme with the central theme of "Doe Season."

ROBERT HUFF (1924–1993)

Rainbow*

After the shot the driven feathers rock
In the air and are by sunlight trapped.
Their moment of descent is eloquent.
It is the rainbow echo of a bird
Whose thunder, stopped, puts in my daughter's eyes
A question mark. She does not see the rainbow,
And the folding bird-fall was for her too quick.
It is about the stillness of the bird
Her eyes are asking. She is three years old;
Has cut her fingers; found blood tastes of salt;
But she has never witnessed quiet blood,
Nor ever seen before the peace of death.
I say: "The feathers—Look!" but she is torn
And wretched and draws back. And I am glad
That I have wounded her, have winged her heart,
And that she goes beyond my fathering.

*Publication date is not available.

CHAPTER 19

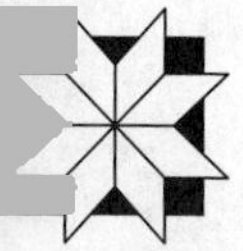

JOYCE CAROL OATES'S "WHERE ARE YOU GOING, WHERE HAVE YOU BEEN?": A CASEBOOK FOR READING, RESEARCH, AND WRITING

This chapter provides all the materials you will need to begin a research project about a work of fiction. It includes the 1966 short story "Where Are You Going, Where Have You Been?" by Joyce Carol Oates; questions to stimulate discussion and writing; a collection of source materials;* a model student paper that shows how one student, Michele Olivari, used the materials in this chapter in her research; and suggestions for further research on Oates.

Source Materials

- Oates, Joyce Carol. "When Characters from the Page Are Made Flesh on the Screen." *New York Times* 23 Mar. 1986, sec. 2:1+. An article by Oates in which she discusses her feelings about the film *Smooth Talk*, based on her story. .... (p. 630)
- Schulz, Gretchen, and R. J. R. Rockwood. From "In Fairyland, without a Map: Connie's Exploration Inward in Joyce Carol Oates's 'Where Are You Going, Where Have You Been?'" *Literature and Psychology* 30 (1980): 155–67. A psychological interpretation of the story. .... (p. 633)
- Tierce, Mike, and John Michael Crafton. From "Connie's Tambourine Man: A New Reading of Arnold Friend." *Studies in Short Fiction* 22 (1985): 219–24. A critical interpretation of the character of Arnold Friend. .... (p. 637)
- Dylan, Bob. "It's All Over Now, Baby Blue." Los Angeles: Warner Bros., 1965. Lyrics from a popular folk song, which, according to Oates, inspired the story. (This and other Dylan songs are discussed in Tierce and Crafton's article.) .... (p. 640)
- Kalpakian, Laura. From a review of *Where Are You Going, Where Have You Been?: Selected Early Stories*, by Joyce Carol Oates. *The Southern Review* 29.4

* Note that some of the critical articles in this casebook were written before the current MLA documentation style was adopted. See Chapter 7 for current MLA format.

Each of these sources provides insights (sometimes contradictory ones) into the short story "Where Are You Going, Where Have You Been?" Other sources can also enrich your understanding of the work—for instance, other works by Oates (such as the short monologue *When I Was a Little Girl and My Mother Didn't Want Me* (p. 1266), biographical data about the author, or stories by other writers dealing with similar themes. In addition, nonprint sources—such as the film *Smooth Talk*, which is based on the story—and Web sites devoted to Oates and her work can offer insight into the story. Links to several interesting Web sites about Oates are available at <http://academic.cengage.com/english/Kirszner/literaturereadingreactingwriting7e>.

Although no analytical or biographical source—not even the author's comments—can give you a magical key that will unlock a story's secrets, such sources can enhance your enjoyment and aid in your understanding of a work. They can also suggest topics that you can explore in writing.

In preparation for writing an essay on a topic of your choice about the story "Where Are You Going, Where Have You Been?" read the story and the accompanying source materials carefully. Then, consider the Reading and Reacting questions that follow the story (p. 629), and use your responses to help you find a topic you can develop in a short essay. Be sure to document any words or ideas borrowed from the story or from another source, and remember to enclose words that are not your own in quotation marks. (For guidelines on evaluating literary criticism, see page 15; for guidelines on using source materials, see Chapter 6, "Using Sources in Your Writing.")

A model student paper, "Mesmerizing Men and Vulnerable Teens: Power Relationships in 'Where Are You Going, Where Have You Been?' and 'Teenage Wasteland,'" based on the source materials in this Casebook, begins on page 654.

Source: ©Nancy Kaszerman/ZUMA/CORBIS

JOYCE CAROL OATES (1938–) is one of contemporary America's most prolific novelists and short story writers. Oates first gained prominence in the 1960s with the publication of *A Garden of Earthly Delights* (1967), *Expensive People* (1968), and *them* (1969), which won the National Book Award. In these and other works, Oates explores the multilayered nature of American society, writing about urban slums, decaying rural communities, and exclusive suburbs in a dense and compellingly realistic prose style. In some of her novels, including *Bellefleur* (1980) and *Myster-*

ies of Winterthurn (1984), Oates reveals her deep fascination with the traditions of nineteenth-century gothic writers Edgar Allan Poe, Fyodor Dostoevski, Mary Shelley, and others. Oates's recent works include *Missing Mom* (2005), *High Lonesome* (2006), *Black Girl / White Girl* (2006), *The Museum of Dr. Moses* (2007), and *The Gravedigger's Daughter* (2007), and *My Sister, My Love* (2008).

Born on June 16, 1938, Joyce Carol Oates grew up in the small hamlet of Millersport, near Lockport, New York, about ten miles east of Niagara Falls and twenty miles north of Buffalo. She is the eldest of three children (her sister Lynn, who is almost twenty years younger, has been institutionalized with autism since adolescence). Oates attended school in a one-room schoolhouse with other working-class children from the area. Her childhood was hard, yet she writes about it in a loving and respectful tone: "Though frequently denounced and often misunderstood by a somewhat genteel literary community, my writing is, at least in part, an attempt to memorialize my parents' vanished world; my parents' lives. Sometimes directly, sometimes in metaphor." Her childhood town, parents, siblings, relatives, and neighbors all appear in some form in three of Oates's books: *You Must Remember This* (1987) blends Buffalo and Lockport as its backdrop, along with the Erie Canal; *Marya: A Life* (1986) contains elements of Oates's mother's childhood as well as her own; and in *Wonderland* (1971), one of Oates's earliest novels, the main character stops off in Millersport and meets her family.

Oates is one of those writers who has always been a writer, and even before she could possibly know the alphabet, she drew and painted words. Once she did learn her letters, she was given a typewriter and learned how to use it, and she was soon writing book after book. She left her small town to attend Syracuse University on a scholarship and while there won the *Mademoiselle* fiction contest. She earned an MA in English at the University of Wisconsin. Oates moved to Detroit in 1962, during a time when social tensions were at the boiling point; Detroit was one of the first American cities to erupt in urban violence in the 1960s. Oates considers her time in Detroit to be significant, shaping her writing as well as her personal beliefs and political views.

In 1968, Oates crossed the Detroit River to teach at the University of Windsor in Ontario, Canada. While teaching a full load of courses, she embarked on an extremely productive period of writing. In less than a decade, she wrote over twenty novels, and her audience grew along with her success. In 1978, she moved to Princeton, New Jersey, to accept a teaching position at Princeton University. Today, Oates continues to teach at Princeton and publishes *The Ontario Review,* a literary magazine.

Washington Post critic Susan Wood has written that Oates "attempts more than most of our writers . . . to explore the profound issues of evil and innocence, betrayal and revenge and atonement, as they are manifest in contemporary American experience. . . ." Although Oates frequently centers her novels on larger issues and moral questions, she can also focus on the private worlds of her characters, as in *Black Water* (1992).

Critics responding to Oates's work have called it violent, lurid, even depraved. Yet, asks Laura Z. Hobson in a review of Oates's 1981 novel, *Angel of Light,* "Would there be such a hullabaloo about the violence in her books if they had been written by a man? From her earliest books onward, reviewers too often struck an insulting tone of surprise: *What's a nice girl like you doing in a place like this?* [Oates] replies that in these violent times only tales of violence have reality. Well, maybe. But the critics' preoccupation with a single facet of her work ignores everything else: her inventiveness, her insider's knowledge of college life, her evocations of nature . . . her ability to tell a story, to write a spellbinder. . . ."

Oates's work changes as the landscape changes around her. Her earliest novels focused on rural characters who seemingly could have sprung from her hometown, and the dozens of books she wrote while in Detroit and Ontario reveal the often harsh realities of those places and times. The novels she began to write in New Jersey went in an entirely new direction. Published in the 1980s, her series of ambitious gothic novels challenge established literary form and also envision a vastly different American identity and history from that of her earlier books. In short, her prolific career reveals an ability to experiment with new forms and subject matter, and it is exactly this ability that makes her universally appealing and that makes her books timeless as well as timebound.

Where Are You Going, Where Have You Been? (1966)

For Bob Dylan

Her name was Connie. She was fifteen and she had a quick nervous giggling habit of craning her neck to glance into mirrors, or checking other people's faces to make sure her own was all right. Her mother, who noticed everything and knew everything and who hadn't much reason any longer to look at her own face, always scolded Connie about it. "Stop gawking at yourself, who are you? You think you're so pretty?" she would say. Connie would raise her eye-brows at these familiar complaints and look right through her mother, into a shadowy vision of herself as she was right at that moment: she knew she was pretty and that was everything. Her mother had been pretty once too, if you could believe those old snapshots in the album, but now her looks were gone and that was why she was always after Connie.

"Why don't you keep your room clean like your sister? How've you got your hair fixed—what the hell stinks? Hair spray? You don't see your sister using that junk."

Her sister June was twenty-four and still lived at home. She was a secretary in the high school Connie attended, and if that wasn't bad enough—with her in the same building—she was so plain and chunky and steady that Connie had to hear her praised all the time by her mother and her mother's sisters. June did this, June did that, she saved money and helped clean the house and cooked and Connie couldn't do a thing, her mind was all filled with trashy daydreams. Their father was away at work most of the time and when he came home he wanted supper and he read the newspaper at supper and after supper he went to bed. He didn't bother talking much to them, but around his bent head Connie's mother kept picking at her until Connie wished her mother was dead and she herself was dead and it was all over. "She makes me want to throw up sometimes," she complained to her friends. She had a high, breathless, amused voice which made everything she said sound a little forced, whether it was sincere or not.

There was one good thing: June went places with girl friends of hers, girls who were just as plain and steady as she, and so when Connie wanted to do that her mother had no objections. The father of Connie's best girl friend drove the girls the three miles to town and left them off at a shopping plaza, so that they could walk through the stores or go to a movie, and when he came to pick them up again at eleven he never bothered to ask what they had done.

5 They must have been familiar sights, walking around that shopping plaza in their shorts and flat ballerina slippers that always scuffed the sidewalk, with charm bracelets jingling on their thin wrists; they would lean together to whisper and laugh secretly if someone passed by who amused or interested them. Connie had long dark blond hair that drew anyone's eye to it, and she wore part of it pulled up on her head and puffed out and the rest of it she let fall down her back. She wore a pull-over jersey blouse that looked one way when she was at home and another way when she was away from home. Everything about her had two sides to it, one for home and one for anywhere that was not home: her walk that could be childlike and bobbing, or languid enough to make anyone think she was hearing music in her head, her mouth which was pale and smirking most of the time, but bright and pink on these evenings out, her laugh which was cynical and drawling at home—"Ha, ha, very funny"—but high-pitched and nervous anywhere else, like the jingling of the charms on her bracelet.

Sometimes they did go shopping or to a movie, but sometimes they went across the highway, ducking fast across the busy road, to a drive-in restaurant where older kids hung out. The restaurant was shaped like a big bottle, though squatter than a real bottle, and on its cap was a revolving figure of a grinning boy who held a hamburger aloft. One night in mid-summer they ran across, breathless with daring, and right away someone leaned out a car window and invited them over, but it was just a boy from high school they didn't like. It made them feel good to be able to ignore him. They went up through the maze of parked and cruising cars to the bright-lit, fly-infested restaurant, their faces pleased and expectant as if they were entering a sacred building that loomed out of the night to give them what haven and what blessing they yearned for. They sat at the counter and crossed their legs at the ankles, their thin shoulders rigid with excitement, and listened to the music that made everything so good: the music was always in the background like music at a church service, it was something to depend upon.

A boy named Eddie came in to talk with them. He sat backwards on his stool, turning himself jerkily around in semi-circles and then stopping and turning again, and after a while he asked Connie if she would like something to eat. She said she did and so she tapped her friend's arm on her way out—her friend pulled her face up into a brave droll look—and Connie said she would meet her at eleven, across the way. "I just hate to leave her like that," Connie said earnestly, but the boy said that she wouldn't be alone for long. So they went out to his car and on the way Connie couldn't help but let her eyes wander over the windshields and faces all around her, her face gleaming with a joy that had nothing to do with Eddie or even this place; it might have been the music. She drew her shoulders up and sucked in her breath with the pure pleasure of being alive, and just at that moment she happened to glance at a face just a few feet from hers. It was a boy with shaggy black hair, in a convertible jalopy painted gold. He stared at her and then his lips widened into a grin. Connie slit her eyes at him and turned away, but she couldn't help glancing back and there he was still watching her. He wagged a finger and laughed and said, "Gonna get you, baby," and Connie turned away again without Eddie noticing anything.

She spent three hours with him, at the restaurant where they ate hamburgers and drank Cokes in wax cups that were always sweating, and then down an alley a mile or so away, and when he left her off at five to eleven only the movie house was still open at the plaza. Her girl friend was there, talking with a boy. When Connie came up the two girls smiled at each other and Connie said, "How was the movie?" and the girl said, "*You* should know." They rode off with the girl's father, sleepy and pleased, and Connie couldn't help but look at the darkened shopping plaza with its big empty parking lot and its signs that were faded and ghostly now, and over at the drive-in restaurant where cars were still circling tirelessly. She couldn't hear the music at this distance.

Next morning June asked her how the movie was and Connie said, "So-so."

She and that girl and occasionally another girl went out several times a week that way, 10
and the rest of the time Connie spent around the house—it was summer vacation—getting in her mother's way and thinking, dreaming, about the boys she met. But all the boys fell back and dissolved into a single face that was not even a face, but an idea, a feeling, mixed up with the urgent insistent pounding of the music and the humid night air of July. Connie's mother kept dragging her back to the daylight by finding things for her to do or saying, suddenly, "What's this about the Pettinger girl?"

And Connie would say nervously, "Oh, her. That dope." She always drew thick clear lines between herself and such girls, and her mother was simple and kindly enough to believe her. Her mother was so simple, Connie thought, that it was maybe cruel to fool her so much. Her mother went scuffling around the house in old bedroom slippers and complained over the telephone to one sister about the other, then the other called up and the two of them complained about the third one. If June's name was mentioned her mother's tone was approving, and if Connie's name was mentioned it was disapproving. This did not really mean she disliked Connie and actually Connie thought that her mother preferred her to June because she was prettier, but the two of them kept up a pretense of exasperation, a sense that they were tugging and struggling over something of little value to either of them. Sometimes, over coffee, they were almost friends, but something would come up—some vexation that was like a fly buzzing suddenly around their heads—and their faces went hard with contempt.

One Sunday Connie got up at eleven—none of them bothered with church—and washed her hair so that it could dry all day long, in the sun. Her parents and sister were going to a barbecue at an aunt's house and Connie said no, she wasn't interested, rolling her eyes to let her mother know just what she thought of it. "Stay home alone then," her mother said sharply. Connie sat out back in a lawn chair and watched them drive away, her father quiet and bald, hunched around so that he could back the car out, her mother with a look that was still angry and not at all softened through the windshield, and in the back seat poor old June all dressed up as if she didn't know what a barbecue was, with all the running yelling kids and the flies. Connie sat with her eyes closed in the sun, dreaming and dazed with the warmth about her as if this were a kind of love, the caresses of love, and her mind slipped over onto thoughts of the boy she had been with the night before and how nice he had been, how sweet it always was, not the way someone like June would suppose but sweet, gentle, the way it was in movies and promised in songs; and when she opened her eyes she hardly knew where she was, the back yard ran off into weeds and a fence-line of trees and behind it the sky was perfectly blue and still. The asbestos "ranch house" that was now three years old startled her — it looked small. She shook her head as if to get awake.

It was too hot. She went inside the house and turned on the radio to drown out the quiet. She sat on the edge of her bed, barefoot, and listened for an hour and a half to a program called *XYZ Sunday Jamboree*, record after record of hard, fast, shrieking songs she sang along with, interspersed by exclamations from "Bobby King": "An' look here you girls at Napoleon's — Son and Charley want you to pay real close attention to this song coming up!"

And Connie paid close attention herself, bathed in a glow of slow-pulsed joy that seemed to rise mysteriously out of the music itself and lay languidly about the airless little room, breathed in and breathed out with each gentle rise and fall of her chest.

After a while she heard a car coming up the drive. She sat up at once, startled, because it couldn't be her father so soon. The gravel kept crunching all the way in from the road — the driveway was long — and Connie ran to the window. It was a car she didn't know. It was an open jalopy, painted a bright gold that caught the sunlight opaquely. Her heart began to pound and her fingers snatched at her hair, checking it, and she whispered "Christ. Christ," wondering how bad she looked. The car came to a stop at the side door and the horn sounded four short taps as if this were a signal Connie knew.

She went into the kitchen and approached the door slowly, then hung out the screen door, her bare toes curling down off the step. There were two boys in the car and now she recognized the driver: he had shaggy, shabby black hair that looked crazy as a wig and he was grinning at her.

"I ain't late, am I?" he said.

"Who the hell do you think you are?" Connie said.

"Toldja I'd be out, didn't I?"

"I don't even know who you are."

She spoke sullenly, careful to show no interest or pleasure, and he spoke in a fast bright monotone. Connie looked past him to the other boy, taking her time. He had fair brown hair, with a lock that fell onto his forehead. His sideburns gave him a fierce, embarrassed look, but so far he hadn't even bothered to glance at her. Both boys wore sunglasses. The driver's glasses were metallic and mirrored everything in miniature.

"You wanta come for a ride?" he said.

Connie smirked and let her hair fall loose over one shoulder.

"Don'tcha like my car? New paint job," he said. "Hey."

"What?"

"You're cute."

She pretended to fidget, chasing flies away from the door.

"Don'tcha believe me, or what?" he said.

"Look, I don't even know who you are," Connie said in disgust.

"Hey, Ellie's got a radio, see. Mine's broke down." He lifted his friend's arm and showed her the little transistor the boy was holding, and now Connie began to hear the music. It was the same program that was playing inside the house.

"Bobby King?" she said.

"I listen to him all the time. I think he's great."

"He's kind of great," Connie said reluctantly.

"Listen, that guy's *great*. He knows where the action is."

Connie blushed a little, because the glasses made it impossible for her to see just 35 what this boy was looking at. She couldn't decide if she liked him or if he was just a jerk, and so she dawdled in the doorway and wouldn't come down or go back inside. She said, "What's all that stuff painted on your car?"

"Can'tcha read it?" He opened the door very carefully, as if he was afraid it might fall off. He slid out just as carefully, planting his feet firmly on the ground, the tiny metallic world in his glasses slowing down like gelatine hardening and in the midst of it Connie's bright green blouse. "This here is my name, to begin with," he said. ARNOLD FRIEND was written in tarlike black letters on the side, with a drawing of a round grinning face that reminded Connie of a pumpkin, except it wore sunglasses. "I wanta introduce myself, I'm Arnold Friend and that's my real name and I'm gonna be your friend, honey, and inside the car's Ellie Oscar, he's kinda shy." Ellie brought his transistor radio up to his shoulder and balanced it there. "Now these numbers are a secret code, honey," Arnold Friend explained. He read off the numbers 33, 19, 17 and raised his eyebrows at her to see what she thought of that, but she didn't think much of it. The left rear fender had been smashed and around it was written, on the gleaming gold background: DONE BY CRAZY WOMAN DRIVER. Connie had to laugh at that. Arnold Friend was pleased at her laughter and looked up at her. "Around the other side's a lot more— you wanta come and see them?"

"No."

"Why not?"

"Why should I?"

"Don'tcha wanta see what's on the car? Don'tcha wanta go for a ride?" 40

"I don't know."

"Why not?"

"I got things to do."

"Like what?"

"Things." 45

He laughed as if she had said something funny. He slapped his thighs. He was standing in a strange way, leaning back against the car as if he were balancing himself. He wasn't tall, only an inch or so taller than she would be if she came down to him. Connie liked the way he was dressed, which was the way all of them dressed: tight faded jeans stuffed into black, scuffed boots, a belt that pulled his waist in and showed how lean he was, and a white pull-over shirt that was a little soiled and showed the hard small muscles of his arms and shoulders. He looked as if he probably did hard work, lifting and carrying things. Even his neck looked muscular. And his face was a familiar face, somehow: the jaw and chin and cheeks slightly darkened, because he hadn't shaved for a day or two, and the nose long and hawk-like, sniffing as if she were a treat he was going to gobble up and it was all a joke.

"Connie, you ain't telling the truth. This is your day set aside for a ride with me and you know it," he said, still laughing. The way he straightened and recovered from his fit of laughing showed that it had been all fake.

"How do you know what my name is?" she said suspiciously.

"It's Connie."

"Maybe and maybe not."

"I know my Connie," he said, wagging his finger. Now she remembered him even better, back at the restaurant, and her cheeks warmed at the thought of how she sucked in her breath just at the moment she passed him—how she must have looked to him. And he had remembered her. "Ellie and I come out here especially for you," he said. "Ellie can sit in back. How about it?"

"Where?"

"Where what?"

"Where're we going?"

He looked at her. He took off the sunglasses and she saw how pale the skin around his eyes was, like holes that were not in shadow but instead in light. His eyes were chips of broken glass that catch the light in an amiable way. He smiled. It was as if the idea of going for a ride somewhere, to some place, was a new idea to him.

"Just for a ride, Connie sweetheart."

"I never said my name was Connie," she said.

"But I know what it is. I know your name and all about you, lots of things," Arnold Friend said. He had not moved yet but stood still leaning back against the side of his jalopy. "I took a special interest in you, such a pretty girl, and found out all about you like I know your parents and sister are gone somewheres and I know where and how long they're going to be gone, and I know who you were with last night, and your best girl friend's name is Betty. Right?"

He spoke in a simple lilting voice, exactly as if he were reciting the words to a song. His smile assured her that everything was fine. In the car Ellie turned up the volume on his radio and did not bother to look around at them.

"Ellie can sit in the back seat," Arnold Friend said. He indicated his friend with a casual jerk of his chin, as if Ellie did not count and she should not bother with him.

"How'd you find out all that stuff?" Connie said.

"Listen: Betty Schultz and Tony Fitch and Jimmy Pettinger and Nancy Pettinger," he said, in a chant. "Raymond Stanley and Bob Hutter—"

"Do you know all those kids?"

"I know everybody."

"Look, you're kidding. You're not from around here."

"Sure."

"But—how come we never saw you before?"

"Sure you saw me before," he said. He looked down at his boots, as if he were a little offended. "You just don't remember."

"I guess I'd remember you," Connie said.

"Yeah?" He looked up at this, beaming. He was pleased. He began to mark time with the music from Ellie's radio, tapping his fists lightly together. Connie looked away from his smile to the car, which was painted so bright it almost hurt her eyes to look at it. She looked at that name, ARNOLD FRIEND. And up at the front fender was an expression that was familiar—MAN THE FLYING SAUCERS. It was an expression kids had used the year before, but didn't use this year. She looked at it for a while as if the words meant something to her that she did not yet know.

"What're you thinking about? Huh?" Arnold Friend demanded. "Not worried about your hair blowing around in the car, are you?"

"No."

"Think I maybe can't drive good?"

"How do I know?"

"You're a hard girl to handle. How come?" he said. "Don't you know I'm your 75
friend? Didn't you see me put my sign in the air when you walked by?"

"What sign?"

"My sign." And he drew an X in the air, leaning out toward her. They were maybe ten feet apart. After his hand fell back to his side the X was still in the air, almost visible. Connie let the screen door close and stood perfectly still inside it, listening to the music from her radio and the boy's blend together. She stared at Arnold Friend. He stood there so stiffly relaxed, pretending to be relaxed, with one hand idly on the door handle as if he were keeping himself up that way and had no intention of ever moving again. She recognized most things about him, the tight jeans that showed his thighs and buttocks and the greasy leather boots and the tight shirt, and even that slippery friendly smile of his, that sleepy dreamy smile that all the boys used to get across ideas they didn't want to put into words. She recognized all this and also the singsong way he talked, slightly mocking, kidding, but serious and a little melancholy, and she recognized the way he tapped one fist against the other in homage to the perpetual music behind him. But all these things did not come together.

She said suddenly, "Hey, how old are you?"

His smile faded. She could see then that he wasn't a kid, he was much older—thirty, maybe more. At this knowledge her heart began to pound faster.

"That's a crazy thing to ask. Can'tcha see I'm your own age?" 80

"Like hell you are."

"Or maybe a coupla years older, I'm eighteen."

"Eighteen?" she said doubtfully.

He grinned to reassure her and lines appeared at the corners of his mouth. His teeth were big and white. He grinned so broadly his eyes became slits and she saw how thick the lashes were, thick and black as if painted with a black tarlike material. Then he seemed to become embarrassed, abruptly, and looked over his shoulder at Ellie. "*Him,* he's crazy," he said. "Ain't he a riot, he's a nut, a real character." Ellie was still listening to the music. His sunglasses told nothing about what he was thinking. He wore a bright orange shirt unbuttoned halfway to show his chest, which was a pale, bluish chest and not muscular like Arnold Friend's. His shirt collar was turned up all around and the very tips of the collar pointed out past his chin as if they were protecting him. He was pressing the transistor radio up against his ear and sat there in a kind of daze, right in the sun.

"He's kinda strange," Connie said. 85

"Hey, she says you're kinda strange! Kinda strange!" Arnold Friend cried. He pounded on the car to get Ellie's attention. Ellie turned for the first time and Connie saw with shock that he wasn't a kid either—he had a fair, hairless face, cheeks reddened slightly as if the veins grew too close to the surface of his skin, the face of a forty-year-old baby. Connie felt a wave of dizziness rise in her at this sight and she stared at him as if waiting for something to change the shock of the moment, make it all right again. Ellie's lips kept shaping words, mumbling along with the words blasting in his ear.

"Maybe you two better go away," Connie said faintly.

"What? How come?" Arnold Friend cried. "We come out here to take you for a ride. It's Sunday." He had the voice of the man on the radio now. It was the same voice, Connie thought. "Don'tcha know it's Sunday all day and honey, no matter who you were with last night today you're with Arnold Friend and don't you forget it!—Maybe you better step out here," he said, and this last was in a different voice. It was a little flatter, as if the heat was finally getting to him.

"No. I got things to do."

90 "Hey."

"You two better leave."

"We ain't leaving until you come with us."

"Like hell I am—"

"Connie, don't fool around with me. I mean, I mean, don't fool *around*," he said, shaking his head. He laughed incredulously. He placed his sunglasses on top of his head, carefully, as if he were indeed wearing a wig, and brought the stems down behind his ears. Connie stared at him, another wave of dizziness and fear rising in her so that for a moment he wasn't even in focus but was just a blur, standing there against his gold car, and she had the idea that he had driven up the driveway all right but had come from nowhere before that and belonged nowhere and that everything about him and even about the music that was so familiar to her was only half real.

95 "If my father comes and sees you—"

"He ain't coming. He's at a barbecue."

"How do you know that?"

"Aunt Tillie's. Right now they're—uh—they're drinking. Sitting around," he said vaguely, squinting as if he were staring all the way to town and over to Aunt Tillie's backyard. Then the vision seemed to get clear and he nodded energetically. "Yeah. Sitting around. There's your sister in a blue dress, huh? And high heels, the poor sad bitch—nothing like you sweetheart! And your mother's helping some fat woman with the corn, they're cleaning the corn—husking the corn—"

"What fat woman?" Connie cried.

100 "How do I know what fat woman. I don't know every goddam fat woman in the world!" Arnold Friend laughed.

"Oh, that's Mrs. Hornby. . . . Who invited her?" Connie said. She felt a little light-headed. Her breath was coming quickly.

"She's too fat. I don't like them fat. I like them the way you are, honey," he said, smiling sleepily at her. They stared at each other for a while, through the screen door. He said softly, "Now what you're going to do is this: you're going to come out that door. You're going to sit up front with me and Ellie's going to sit in the back, the hell with Ellie, right? This isn't Ellie's date. You're my date. I'm your lover, honey."

"What? You're crazy—"

"Yes, I'm your lover. You don't know what that is but you will," he said. "I know that too. I know all about you. But look: it's real nice and you couldn't ask for nobody better than me, or more polite. I always keep my word. I'll tell you how it is, I'm always nice at first, the first time. I'll hold you so tight you won't think you have to try to get away or pretend anything because you'll know you can't. And I'll come inside you where it's all secret and you'll give in to me and you'll love me—"

"Shut up! You're crazy!" Connie said. She backed away from the door. She put her 105
hands against her ears as if she'd heard something terrible, something not meant for her. "People don't talk like that, you're crazy," she muttered. Her heart was almost too big now for her chest and its pumping made sweat break out all over her. She looked out to see Arnold Friend pause and then take a step toward the porch lurching. He almost fell. But, like a clever drunken man, he managed to catch his balance. He wobbled in his high boots and grabbed hold of one of the porch posts.

"Honey?" he said. "You still listening?"

"Get the hell out of here!"

"Be nice, honey. Listen."

"I'm going to call the police—"

He wobbled again and out of the side of his mouth came a fast spat curse, an aside 110
not meant for her to hear. But even this "Christ!" sounded forced. Then he began to smile again. She watched this smile come, awkward as if he were smiling from inside a mask. His whole face was a mask, she thought wildly, tanned down onto his throat but then running out as if he had plastered makeup on his face but had forgotten about his throat.

"Honey—? Listen, here's how it is. I always tell the truth and I promise you this: I ain't coming in that house after you."

"You better not! I'm going to call the police if you—if you don't—"

"Honey," he said, talking right through her voice, "honey, I'm not coming in there but you are coming out here. You know why?"

She was panting. The kitchen looked like a place she had never seen before, some room she had run inside but which wasn't good enough, wasn't going to help her. The kitchen window had never had a curtain, after three years, and there were dishes in the sink for her to do—probably—and if you ran your hand across the table you'd probably feel something sticky there.

"You listening, honey? Hey?" 115

"—going to call the police—"

"Soon as you touch the phone I don't need to keep my promise and can come inside. You won't want that."

She rushed forward and tried to lock the door. Her fingers were shaking. "But why lock it," Arnold Friend said gently, talking right into her face. "It's just a screen door. It's just nothing." One of his boots was at a strange angle, as if his foot wasn't in it. It pointed out to the left, bent at the ankle. "I mean, anybody can break through a screen door and glass and wood and iron or anything else if he needs to, anybody at all and specially Arnold Friend. If the place got lit up with a fire honey you'd come running out into my arms, right into my arms and safe at home—like you knew I was your lover and'd stopped fooling around. I don't mind a nice shy girl but I don't like no fooling around." Part of those words were spoken with a slight rhythmic lilt, and Connie somehow recognized them—the echo of a song from last year, about a girl rushing into her boy friend's arms and coming home again—

Connie stood barefoot on the linoleum floor, staring at him. "What do you want?" she whispered.

120 "I want you," he said.

"What?"

"Seen you that night and thought, that's the one, yes sir. I never needed to look any more."

"But my father's coming back. He's coming to get me. I had to wash my hair first—" She spoke in a dry, rapid voice, hardly raising it for him to hear.

"No, your daddy is not coming and yes, you had to wash your hair and you washed it for me. It's nice and shining and all for me, I thank you, sweetheart," he said, with a mock bow, but again he almost lost his balance. He had to bend and adjust his boots. Evidently his feet did not go all the way down; the boots must have been stuffed with something so that he would seem taller. Connie stared out at him and behind him Ellie in the car, who seemed to be looking off toward Connie's right, into nothing. This Ellie said, pulling the words out of the air one after another as if he were just discovering them, "You want me to pull out the phone?"

125 "Shut your mouth and keep it shut," Arnold Friend said, his face red from bending over or maybe from embarrassment because Connie had seen his boots. "This ain't none of your business."

"What—what are you doing? What do you want?" Connie said. "If I call the police they'll get you, they'll arrest you—"

"Promise was not to come in unless you touch that phone, and I'll keep that promise," he said. He resumed his erect position and tried to force his shoulders back. He sounded like a hero in a movie, declaring something important. He spoke too loudly and it was as if he were speaking to someone behind Connie. "I ain't made plans for coming in that house where I don't belong but just for you to come out to me, the way you should. Don't you know who I am?"

"You're crazy," she whispered. She backed away from the door but did not want to go into another part of the house, as if this would give him permission to come through the door. "What do you. . . . You're crazy, you . . ."

"Huh? What're you saying, honey?"

130 Her eyes darted everywhere in the kitchen. She could not remember what it was, this room.

"This is how it is, honey: you come out and we'll drive away, have a nice ride. But if you don't come out we're gonna wait till your people come home and then they're all going to get it."

"You want that telephone pulled out?" Ellie said. He held the radio away from his ear and grimaced, as if without the radio the air was too much for him.

"I toldja shut up, Ellie," Arnold Friend said, "you're deaf, get a hearing aid, right? Fix yourself up. This little girl's no trouble and's gonna be nice to me, so Ellie keep to yourself, this ain't your date—right? Don't hem in on me. Don't hog. Don't crush. Don't bird dog. Don't trail me," he said in a rapid meaningless voice, as if he were running through all the expressions he'd learned but was no longer sure which one of them was in style, then rushing on to new ones, making them up with his eyes closed, "Don't crawl under my fence, don't squeeze in my chipmunk hole, don't sniff my glue, suck my popsicle, keep your own greasy fingers on yourself!" He shaded his eyes and peered in at Connie, who was backed against the kitchen table. "Don't mind him honey he's just a creep. He's a dope. Right? I'm the boy for you and like I said you come out here nice like a lady and give me your hand, and nobody else gets hurt, I mean, your nice old bald-headed daddy and your mummy and your sister in her high heels. Because listen: why bring them in this?"

"Leave me alone," Connie whispered.

"Hey, you know that old woman down the road, the one with the chickens and 135
stuff—you know her?"

"She's dead!"

"Dead? What? You know her?" Arnold Friend said.

"She's dead—"

"Don't you like her?"

"She's dead—she's—she isn't here any more—" 140

"But don't you like her, I mean, you got something against her? Some grudge or something?" Then his voice dipped as if he were conscious of a rudeness. He touched the sunglasses perched on top of his head as if to make sure they were still there. "Now you be a good girl."

"What are you going to do?"

"Just two things, or maybe three," Arnold Friend said. "But I promise it won't last long and you'll like me that way you get to like people you're close to. You will. It's all over for you here, so come on out. You don't want your people in any trouble, do you?"

She turned and bumped against a chair or something, hurting her leg, but she ran into the back room and picked up the telephone. Something roared in her ear, a tiny roaring, and she was so sick with fear that she could do nothing but listen to it—the telephone was clammy and very heavy and her fingers groped down to the dial but were too weak to touch it. She began to scream into the phone, into the roaring. She cried out, she cried for her mother, she felt her breath start jerking back and forth in her lungs as if it were something Arnold Friend were stabbing her with again and again with no tenderness. A noisy sorrowful wailing rose all about her and she was locked inside it the way she was locked inside the house.

After a while she could hear again. She was sitting on the floor with her wet back 145
against the wall.

Arnold Friend was saying from the door, "That's a good girl. Put the phone back."

She kicked the phone away from her.

"No, honey. Pick it up. Put it back right."

She picked it up and put it back. The dial tone stopped.

"That's a good girl. Now you come outside." 150

She was hollow with what had been fear, but what was now just an emptiness. All that screaming had blasted it out of her. She sat, one leg cramped under her, and deep inside her brain was something like a pinpoint of light that kept going and would not let her relax. She thought, I'm not going to see my mother again. She thought, I'm not going to sleep in my bed again. Her bright green blouse was all wet.

Arnold Friend said, in a gentle-loud voice that was like a stage voice, "The place where you came from ain't there any more, and where you had in mind to go is cancelled out. This place you are now—inside your daddy's house—is nothing but a cardboard box I can knock down any time. You know that and always did know it. You hear me?"

She thought, I have got to think. I have to know what to do.

"We'll go out to a nice field, out in the country here where it smells so nice and it's sunny," Arnold Friend said. "I'll have my arms around you so you won't need to try to get away and I'll show you what love is like, what it does. The hell with this house! It looks solid all right," he said. He ran a fingernail down the screen and the noise did not make Connie shiver, as it would have the day before. "Now put your hand on your heart, honey. Feel that? That feels solid too but we know better, be nice to me, be sweet like you can because what else is there for a girl like you but to be sweet and pretty and give in?—and get away before her people come back?"

155 She felt her pounding heart. Her hand seemed to enclose it. She thought for the first time in her life that it was nothing that was hers, that belonged to her, but just a pounding, living thing inside this body that wasn't really hers either.

"You don't want them to get hurt," Arnold Friend went on. "Now get up, honey. Get up all by yourself."

She stood.

"Now turn this way. That's right. Come over here to me—Ellie, put that away, didn't I tell you? You dope. You miserable creepy dope," Arnold Friend said. His words were not angry but only part of an incantation. The incantation was kindly. "Now come out through the kitchen to me honey and let's see a smile, try it, you're a brave sweet little girl and now they're eating corn and hotdogs cooked to bursting over an outdoor fire, and they don't know one thing about you and never did and honey you're better than them because not a one of them would have done this for you."

Connie felt the linoleum under her feet; it was cool. She brushed her hair back out of her eyes. Arnold Friend let go of the post tentatively and opened his arms for her, his elbows pointing in toward each other and his wrists limp, to show that this was an embarrassed embrace and a little mocking, he didn't want to make her self-conscious.

160 She put out her hand against the screen. She watched herself push the door slowly open as if she were safe back somewhere in the other doorway, watching this body and this head of long hair moving out into the sunlight where Arnold Friend waited.

"My sweet little blue-eyed girl," he said, in a half-sung sigh that had nothing to do with her brown eyes but was taken up just the same by the vast sunlit reaches of the land behind him and on all sides of him, so much land that Connie had never seen before and did not recognize except to know that she was going to it.

Reading and Reacting

1. Is Arnold Friend meant to be the devil? A rapist and murderer (see "The Pied Piper of Tucson" on page 644)? Is he actually Bob Dylan (as Tierce and Crafton suggest in their article on page 637)? Or is he just a misunderstood social misfit who terrifies Connie more because of her innocence than because of his evil?

2. In a note accompanying the article she coauthored (p. 633), Gretchen Schulz says that Oates told her the **allusions** to fairy tales in the story are intentional. What allusions to fairy tales can you identify? What do these allusions add to the story?

3. Many critical articles see "Where Are You Going, Where Have You Been?" as heavily symbolic, even allegorical, with elements of myth, dream, and fairy tale woven throughout. Do you think such analysis adds something vital to readers' understanding of the story, or do you think the story could be explained in much simpler terms?

4. Feminist critics might see this story as a familiar tale of a man who uses flattering seductive language followed by threats of physical violence to coerce a young woman into giving in to him. In what sense do you see this as a story of male power and female powerlessness?

5. Dark undertones aside, in what sense is this simply a story about the coming of age of a typical 1960s teenager?

6. What roles do music, sex, the weather, contemporary slang, and the characters' physical appearance play in the story?

7. Why do members of Connie's family make such brief appearances in the story? How might expanding their roles change the story?

8. Which aspects of teenage culture have changed in the more than forty years since Oates wrote the story? Which have stayed the same? Given the scope of these changes, is the story dated?

9. Most critics (like Oates herself) see the end of the story as alarmingly negative, suggesting rape and even murder. Do you see it this way?

10. Do you agree with Oates's view, expressed in her article on page 630, that the differences in the endings of the 1985 film *Smooth Talk* (based on the story) and the story itself are justified by the differences between the 1960s and the 1980s?

11. **Journal Entry** How is the generation gap—the failure of one generation to understand another's culture, customs, and heroes—central to the story?

12. **Critical Perspective** According to *New York Times* book critic Michiko Kakutani, Joyce Carol Oates has several "fictional trademarks":

> [She has] a penchant for mixing the mundane and Gothic, the ordinary and sensationalistic; a fascination with the dark undercurrents of violence, eroticism and emotional chaos in American life, and a tendency to divide her characters' lives into a Before and After with one "unspeakable turn of destiny."

In what sense do Kakutani's remarks apply to "Where Are You Going, Where Have You Been?" Do you see a fascination with "the dark undercurrents of . . . life" in this story? What is the "unspeakable turn of destiny" that divides Connie's life into a "Before and After"?

Related Works: "Jinx" (p. 178), "Kansas" (p. 237), "A&P" (p. 259), "Saint Helene" (p. 499), "The Lottery" (p. 509), "Young Goodman Brown" (p. 540), "To His Coy Mistress" (p. 941), *When I Was a Little Girl and My Mother Didn't Want Me* (p. 1266), *Beauty* (p. 1270)

JOYCE CAROL OATES

When Characters from the Page Are Made Flesh on the Screen

Some years ago in the American Southwest there surfaced a tabloid psychopath known as "The Pied Piper of Tucson." I have forgotten his name but his specialty was the seduction and occasional murder of teen-age girls. He may or may not have had actual accomplices, but his bizarre activities were known among a circle of teen-agers in the Tucson area; for some reason they kept his secrets, deliberately did not inform parents or police. It was this fact, not the fact of the mass murderer himself, that struck me at the time. And this was a pre-Manson time, this was early or mid-1960's.

The "Pied Piper" mimicked teen-agers in their talk, dress and behavior, but he was not a teen-ager—he was a man in his early 30's. Rather short, he stuffed rags in his leather boots to give himself height. (And sometimes walked unsteadily as a consequence: did none among his admiring constituency notice?) He charmed his victims, to the bewilderment of others who fancy themselves free of all lunatic attractions. "The Pied Piper of Tucson": a trashy dream, a tabloid archetype, sheer artifice, comedy, cartoon—surrounded, however improbably, and finally tragically, by real people. You think that, if you look twice, he won't be there. But there he is.

I don't remember any longer where I first read about "The Pied Piper"—very likely in *Life* magazine. I do recall deliberately not reading the full article because I didn't want to be distracted by too much detail. It was not after all the mass murderer himself who intrigued me, but the disturbing fact that a number of teen-agers—from "good" families—aided and abetted his crimes. This is the sort of thing authorities and responsible citizens invariably call "inexplicable" because they can't find explanations for it. *They* would not have fallen under this maniac's spell, after all.

An early draft of my short story "Where Are You Going, Where Have You Been?"—from which the current film "Smooth Talk" has been adapted by Joyce Chopra and Tom Cole—had the rather too explicit title "Death and the Maiden." It was cast in a mode of fiction to which I am still partial—indeed, every third or fourth story of mine is probably in this mode—"realistic allegory," it might be called. It is Hawthornian, romantic, shading into parable. Like the medieval German engraving from which my title was taken the story was minutely detailed yet clearly an allegory of the fatal attractions of death (or the devil). An innocent young girl is seduced by way of her own vanity; she mistakes death for erotic romance of a particularly American/trashy sort.

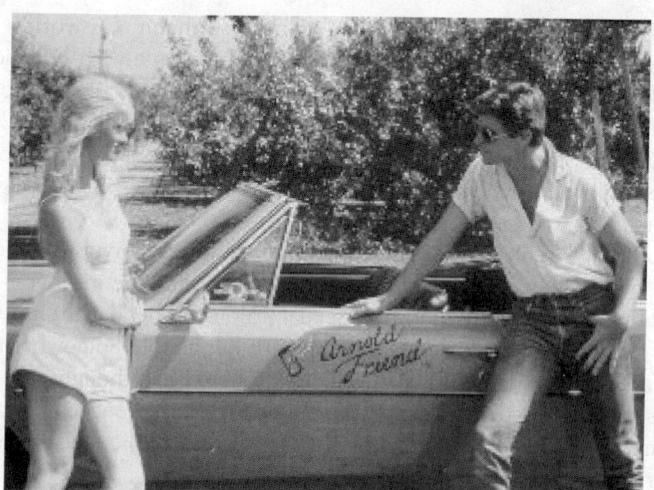

Laura Dern and Treat Williams in a still from the film *Smooth Talk (1985).*
Source: Goldcrest/The Kobal Collection/Ellison, Nancy

In subsequent drafts the story changed its tone, its focus, its language, its title. It 5
became "Where Are You Going, Where Have You Been?" Written at a time when the author was intrigued by the music of Bob Dylan, particularly the hauntingly elegiac song "It's All Over Now, Baby Blue," it was dedicated to Bob Dylan. The charismatic mass murderer drops into the background and his innocent victim, a 15-year-old, moves into the foreground. She becomes the true protagonist of the tale, courting and being courted by her fate, a self-styled 1950's pop figure, alternately absurd and winning.

There is no suggestion in the published story that "Arnold Friend" has seduced and murdered other young girls, or even that he necessarily intends to murder Connie. Is his interest "merely" sexual? (Nor is there anything about the complicity of other teen-agers. I saved that yet more provocative note for a current story, "Testimony.") Connie is shallow, vain, silly, hopeful, doomed—perhaps as I saw, and still see, myself?—but capable nonetheless of an unexpected gesture of heroism at the story's end.

Her smooth-talking seducer, who cannot lie, promises her that her family will be unharmed if she gives herself to him; and so she does. The story ends abruptly at the point of her "crossing over." We don't know the nature of her sacrifice, only that she is generous enough to make it.

In adapting a narrative so spare and thematically foreshortened as "Where Are You Going, Where Have You Been?" film director Joyce Chopra and screenwriter Tom Cole were required to do a good deal of filling in, expanding, inventing. Connie's story becomes lavishly, and lovingly, textured; she is not an allegorical figure so much as a "typical" teen-age girl (if Laura Dern, spectacularly good-looking, can be so defined).

Joyce Chopra, who has done documentary films on contemporary teen-age culture, and, yet more authoritatively, has an adolescent daughter of her own, creates in

"Smooth Talk" a believable world for Connie to inhabit. Or worlds: as in the original story there is Connie-at-home, and there is Connie-with-her-friends. Two 15-year-old girls, two finely honed styles, two voices, sometimes but not often overlapping. It is one of the marvelous visual features of the film that we *see* Connie and her friends transform themselves, once they are safely free of parental observation. What freedom, what joy! The girls claim their true identities in the neighborhood shopping mall!

10 "Smooth Talk" is, in a way, as much Connie's mother's story as it is Connie's; its center of gravity, its emotional nexus, is frequently with the mother—played by Mary Kay Place. (Though the mother's sexual jealousy of her daughter is slighted in the film.) Connie's ambiguous relationship with her affable, somewhat mysterious father (played by Levon Helm) is an excellent touch: I had thought, subsequent to the story's publication, that I should have built up the father, suggesting, as subtly as I could, an attraction there paralleling the attraction Connie feels for her seducer Arnold Friend.

Treat Williams impersonates Arnold Friend as Arnold Friend impersonates—is it James Dean? James Dean regarding himself in mirrors, doing James Dean impersonations? Laura Dern is so right as "my" Connie that I may come to think I modeled the fictitious girl on her, in the way that writers frequently delude themselves about notions of causality.

My difficulties with "Smooth Talk" have primarily to do with my chronic hesitation—a justifiable shyness, I'm sure—about seeing/hearing work of mine abstracted from its contexture of language. All writers know that language is their subject; quirky word choices, patterns of rhythm, enigmatic pauses, punctuation marks. Where the quick-scanner sees "quick" writing, the writer conceals nine-tenths of his iceberg.

Of course we all have "real" subjects, and we will fight to the death to defend these subjects, but beneath the tale-telling it is the tale-telling that grips us so very fiercely: "the soul at the *white heat*" in Emily Dickinson's words. Because of this it is always an eerie experience for me, as a writer, to hear "my" dialogue floating back to me from the external world; particularly when it is surrounded, as of course it must be, by "other" dialogue I seem not to recall having written. Perhaps a panic reaction sets in—perhaps I worry that I might be responsible for knowing what "I" meant, in writing things "I" didn't write? Like a student who has handed in work not entirely his own, and dreads interrogation from his teacher?

It is startling too to *see* fictitious characters inhabiting, with such seeming aplomb, roles that until now seemed private, flat on the page. (I don't, like many of my writing colleagues, feel affronted, thinking, "*That* isn't how he/she looks!" I think instead, guiltily, "Is *that* how he/she really looks?")

15 I have also had a number of plays produced and so characteristically doubtful am I about intruding into my directors' territories that I nearly always abrogate my authority to them. The writer works in a single dimension, the director works in three. I assume that they are professionals to their fingertips; authorities in their medium as I am an authority (if I am) in mine. I would fiercely defend the placement of a semicolon in one of my novels, but I would probably have deferred fairly quickly to Joyce

Chopra's decision to reverse the story's ending, turn it upside-down, in a sense, so that the film ends not with death, not with a sleepwalker's crossing-over to her fate, but upon a sense of reconciliation, rejuvenation. Laura Dern's Connie is no longer "my" Connie at the film's conclusion; she is very much alive, assertive, strong-willed—a girl, perhaps, of the mid-1980's, and not of the mid-1960's.

A girl's loss of virginity, bittersweet but not necessarily tragic. Not today. A girl's coming of age that involves her succumbing to, but then rejecting, the "trashy dreams" of her pop teen-age culture. "Where Are You Going, Where Have You Been?" deliberately betrays itself as allegorical in its conclusion: Death and Death's chariot (a funky souped-up convertible) have come for the Maiden. Awakening is, in the story's final lines, moving out into the sunlight where Arnold Friend waits:

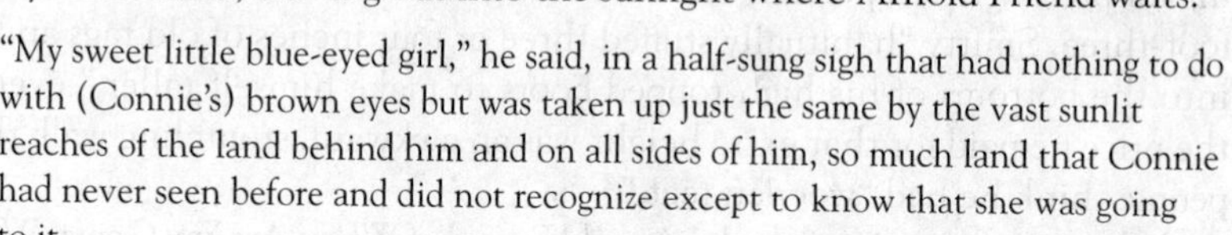

> "My sweet little blue-eyed girl," he said, in a half-sung sigh that had nothing to do with (Connie's) brown eyes but was taken up just the same by the vast sunlit reaches of the land behind him and on all sides of him, so much land that Connie had never seen before and did not recognize except to know that she was going to it.

I quite understand that this is an unfilmable conclusion, and "Where Are You Going, Where Have You Been?" is in fact an unfilmable short story. But Joyce Chopra's "Smooth Talk" is an accomplished and sophisticated movie that attempts to do just that.

* * *

GRETCHEN SCHULZ AND R. J. R. ROCKWOOD

from In Fairyland, without a Map: Connie's Exploration Inward in Joyce Carol Oates's "Where Are You Going, Where Have You Been?"

Joyce Carol Oates has stated that her prize-winning story *Where Are You Going, Where Have You Been?* (Fall, 1966) came to her "more or less in a piece" after hearing Bob Dylan's song *It's All Over Now, Baby Blue*, and then reading about a "killer in some Southwestern state," and thinking about "the old legends and folk songs of Death and the Maiden."[1] The "killer" that Miss Oates had in mind, the one on whom her character Arnold Friend is modeled, was twenty-three-year-old Charles Schmid of Tucson, Arizona. Schmid had been charged with the murders of three teen-age girls, and was the subject of a lengthy article in the March 4, 1966, issue of *Life* magazine. It is not surprising that this account should have generated mythic musings in Miss Oates—musings that culminated in a short story which has depths as mythic as any of the "old legends and folk songs." The *Life* reporter, Don Moser, himself had found in this raw material such an abundance of the reality which is the stuff of myth, that he entitled his article "The Pied Piper of Tucson."

The article states that Schmid—or "Smitty," as he was called—had sought deliberately "to create an exalted, heroic image of himself." To the teen-agers in Smitty's crowd, who "had little to do but look each other over," their leader was a "folk hero . . . more dramatic, more theatrical, more *interesting* than anyone else in their lives," and seemed to embody the very lyrics of a then popular song: "Hey, c'mon babe, follow me, / I'm the Pied Piper, follow me, / I'm the Pied Piper, / And I'll show you where it's at." With a face which was "his own creation: the hair dyed raven black, the skin darkened to a deep tan with pancake make-up, the lips whitened, the whole effect heightened by a mole he had painted on one cheek," Smitty would cruise "in a golden car," haunting "all the teen-age hangouts," looking for pretty girls, especially ones with long blond hair. Because he was only five-foot-three, Smitty "habitually stuffed three or four inches of old rags and tin cans into the bottoms of his high-topped boots to make himself taller," even though the price he paid for that extra height was an awkward, stumbling walk that made people think he had "wooden feet."[2]

In his transformation into the Arnold Friend of *Where Are You Going, Where Have You Been?*, Smitty underwent the kind of apotheosis° which he had tried, by means of bizarre theatrics, to achieve in actuality, for Arnold is the exact transpersonal° counterpart of the real-life "Pied Piper of Tucson." Thus, although Arnold is a "realistic" figure, drawn from the life of a specific psychopathic killer, that superficial realism is only incidental to the more essential realism of the mythic characteristics—the archetypal qualities—he shares with the man who was his model. Asked to comment on Arnold, Miss Oates reveals that, to her, the character is *truly* mythological. No longer quite human, he functions as a personified subjective factor: "Arnold Friend," she says, "is a fantastic figure: he is Death, he is the 'elf-[king]' of the ballads, he is the Imagination, he is a Dream, he is a Lover, a Demon, *and all that*."[3]

If *Where Are You Going, Where Have You Been?* is a "portrait of a psychopathic killer masquerading as a teenager,"[4] it is clear that this portrait is created in the mind of Connie, the teen-age protagonist of the story, and that it exists *there only*. It is thus Connie's inner world that determines how Arnold is, or has to be, at least in her eyes, for her personal problems are so compelling that they effectively rearrange and remodel the world of objective reality. Arnold Friend's own part in the creation of his image—whether he deliberately set about to become the "fantastic" figure he is, or seems to be, as his model, Smitty, did—Miss Oates ignores altogether. She is interested only in Connie, Arnold's young victim, and in how Connie's psychological state shapes her perceptions. We find—as we might expect with a writer who characterizes the mode in which she writes as "psychological realism"[5]—that the "fantastic" or mythological qualities of Arnold Friend (and of all those in the story) are presented as subjective rather than objective facts, aspects of the transpersonal psyche projected outward, products of the unconscious mental processes of a troubled adolescent girl.

---

apotheosis: The raising of a human to divine status.

transpersonal: Going beyond the individual or personal.

Toward Arnold Friend, and what he represents, Connie is ambivalent: she is both fascinated and frightened. She is, after all, at that confusing age when a girl feels, thinks, and acts both like a child, put off by a possible lover, and like a woman, attracted to him. Uncertain how to bridge the chasm between "home" and "anywhere that was not home," she stands—or wavers—at the boundary between childhood and adulthood, hesitant and yet anxious to enter the new world of experience which is opening before her: 5

> Everything about her had two sides to it, one for home and one for anywhere that was not home: her walk, which could be childlike and bobbing, or languid enough to make anyone think she was hearing music in her head; her mouth, which was pale and smirking most of the time, but bright and pink on these evenings out; her laugh, which was cynical and drawling at home—"Ha, ha, very funny,"—but high-pitched and nervous anywhere else, like the jingling of the charms on her bracelet.[6]

That her laugh is "high-pitched and nervous" when she is "anywhere that was not home" betrays the fact that Connie, like all young people, needs help as she begins to move from the past to the future, as she begins the perilous inward journey towards maturity. This journey is an essential part of the adolescent's search for personal identity, and though it is a quest that he must undertake by himself, traditionally it has been the responsibility of culture to help by providing symbolic maps of the territory through which he will travel, territory that lies on the other side of consciousness.

Such models of behavior and maps of the unknown are generally provided by the products of fantasy—myth, legend, and folklore. Folk fairy tales have been especially useful in this way. In his book, *The Uses of Enchantment: The Meaning and Importance of Fairy Tales* (1976), Bruno Bettelheim argues that children's fairy tales offer "symbolic images" that suggest "happy solutions"[7] to the problems of adolescence. Indeed, Joyce Carol Oates herself has Hugh Petrie, the caricaturist in her novel *The Assassins* (1975), observe that "fairy tales are analogous to life as it is lived in the family."[8] In her fiction both short and long Miss Oates makes frequent use of fairy tale material. Again and again she presents characters and situations which parallel corresponding motifs from the world of folk fantasy. And never is this more true than in the present story—never in all the eight novels and eleven collections of short stories which she has written at last count. Woven into the complex texture of *Where Are You Going, Where Have You Been?* are motifs from such tales as *The Spirit in the Bottle*, *Snow White*, *Cinderella*, *Sleeping Beauty*, *Rapunzel*, *Little Red Riding Hood*, and *The Three Little Pigs*.[9] *The Pied Piper of Hamelin*, which ends tragically and so according to Bettelheim does not qualify as a proper fairy tale,[10] serves as the "frame device" that contains all the other tales.

There is a terrible irony here, for although the story is full of fairy tales, Connie, its protagonist, is not. Connie represents an entire generation of young people who have grown up—or tried to—without the help of those bedtime stories which not only entertain the child, but also enable him vicariously to experience and work through problems which he will encounter in adolescence. The only "stories" Connie knows are those of the sexually provocative but superficial lyrics of the popular songs she loves or of the equally insubstantial movies she attends. Such songs and movies provide either no models of behavior for her to imitate, or dangerously inappropriate ones. Connie has thus been led to believe that life and, in particular, love will be "sweet, gentle, the way it was in the movies and promised in songs." She has no idea that life actually can be just as grim as in folk fairy tales. The society that is depicted in *Where Are You Going, Where Have You Been?* has failed to make available to children like Connie maps of the unconscious such as fairy tales provide, because it has failed to recognize that in the unconscious past and future coalesce, and that, psychologically, where the child is going is where he has already been. Since Connie has been left—in the words of yet another of the popular songs—to "wander through that wonderland alone"—it is small wonder, considering her lack of spiritual preparation, that Connie's journey there soon becomes a terrifying schizophrenic separation from reality, with prognosis for recovery extremely poor. . . .

Had she been nurtured on fairy tales instead of popular songs and movies she would not feel at such a loss; she would have "been" to this world before, through the vicarious experience offered by fairy tales, and she would have some sense of how to survive there now. Connie lacks the benefit of such experience, however, and even Arnold Friend appears to realize how that lack has hampered her development. He certainly speaks to the supposed woman as though she were still a child: "'Now, turn this way. That's right. Come over here to me. . . . and let's see a smile, try it, you're a brave, sweet little girl'." How fatherly he sounds. And how like the Woodcutter. But we know that he is still the Wolf, and that he still intends to "gobble up" this "little girl" as soon as he gets the chance. Connie is not going to live happily ever after. Indeed, it would seem that she is not going to live at all. She simply does not know how. She is stranded in Fairyland, without a map.[11]

Notes

[1] "Interview with Joyce Carol Oates about 'Where Are You Going, Where Have You Been?'" in *Mirrors: An Introduction to Literature*, ed. John R. Knott, Jr., and Christopher R. Keaske, 2nd ed. (San Francisco: Canfield Press, 1975), pp. 18–19.

[2] Don Moser, "The Pied Piper of Tucson," *Life*, 60, no. 9 (March 4, 1966), 18–19, 22–24, 80c–d.

[3] Interview in *Mirrors*, p. 19. For a perceptive analysis of Arnold Friend as a demonic figure, a subject which will not be developed here, see Joyce M. Wegs, "'Don't You Know Who I Am?' The Grotesque in Oates's 'Where Are You Going, Where Have You Been?'," *The Journal of Narrative Technique*, 5 (January 1975), pp. 66–72.

[4] Wegs, p. 69.

[5] Joyce Carol Oates, "Preface," *Where Are You Going, Where Have You Been?: Stories of Young America* (Greenwich, CT: Fawcett Publications, 1974), p. 10.

[6] Joyce Carol Oates, "Where Are You Going, Where Have You Been?," *Where Are You Going, Where Have You Been?: Stories of Young America* (Greenwich, CT: Fawcett Publications, 1974), p. 13. All further references are to this edition of the story and will appear in the text of the essay. The story was originally published in *Epoch*, Fall 1966. It has since been included in *Prize Stories: The O. Henry Awards 1968*; in *The Best American Short Stories of 1967*; and in a collection of Oates' stories, *The Wheel of Love* (New York: Vanguard Press, 1970; Greenwich, CT: Fawcett Publications, 1972). The story is also

being anthologized with increasing frequency in collections intended for use in the classroom, such as Donald McQuade and Robert Atwan, *Popular Writing in America: The Interaction of Style and Audience* (New York: Oxford University Press, 1974).

[7] Bruno Bettelheim, *The Uses of Enchantment: The Meaning and Importance of Fairy Tales* (New York: Alfred A. Knopf, 1976), p. 39.

[8] Joyce Carol Oates, *The Assassins* (New York: Vanguard Press, 1975), p. 378.

[9] At the MLA convention in New York, on December 26, 1976, I got a chance to ask Joyce Carol Oates if the many allusions to various fairy tales in "Where Are You Going, Where Have You Been?" were intentional. She replied that they were. (Gretchen Schulz)

[10] Bettelheim, n. 34, p. 316.

[11] Concerning the plight of the Connies of the world, Bettelheim states thus: "unfed by our common fantasy heritage, the folk fairy tale, the child cannot invent stories on his own which help him cope with life's problems. All the stories he can invent are just expressions of his own wishes and anxieties. Relying on his own resources, all the child can imagine are elaborations of where he presently is, since he cannot know where he needs to go, or how to go about getting there" (pp. 121–122).

* * *

MIKE TIERCE AND JOHN MICHAEL CRAFTON

from Connie's Tambourine Man: A New Reading of Arnold Friend

The critical reception of Joyce Carol Oates' "Where Are You Going, Where Have You Been?" reveals a consistent pattern for reducing the text to a manageable, univocal° reading. Generally, this pattern involves two assumptions: Arnold *must* symbolize Satan and Connie *must* be raped and murdered. No critic has yet questioned Joyce Wegs' assertion that "Arnold is clearly a symbolic Satan."[1] Marie Urbanski argues that Arnold's "feet resemble the devil's cloven hoofs," Joan Winslow calls the story "an encounter with the devil," Tom Quirk maintains the story describes a "demoniac character," and Christina Marsden Gillis refers to "the satanic visitor's incantation."[2] Wegs' assertion that Arnold is "a criminal with plans to rape and probably murder Connie"[3] is also accepted at face value. Gillis assumes that Arnold "leads his victim . . . to a quick and violent sexual assault,"[4] and Quirk refers to "the rape and subsequent murder of Connie."[5] Even though Gretchen Schulz and R. J. R. Rockwood correctly claim that the portrait of Arnold "is created in the mind of Connie . . . and that it exists *there only*," they still persist in having Arnold as a demon and Connie as doomed: "But we know that he is still the Wolf, and that he still intends to 'gobble up' this 'little girl' as soon as he gets the chance. Connie is not going to live happily ever after. Indeed, it would seem that she is not going to live at all."[6]

univocal: Having only one meaning.

While all of these critics insist on seeing satanic traces in Arnold, they refuse, on the other hand, to see that these traces are only part of a much more complex, more dynamic symbol. There are indeed diabolic shades to Arnold, but just as Blake and Shelley could see in Milton's Satan[7] a positive, attractive symbol of the poet, the rebellious embodiment of creative energy, so we should also be sensitive to Arnold's multifaceted and creative nature. Within the frame of the story, the fiction of Arnold burns in the day as the embodiment of poetic energy. The story is dedicated to Bob Dylan, the troubadour, the artist. Friend is the artist, the actor, the rhetorician, the teacher, all symbolized by Connie's overheated imagination. We should not assume that Arnold is completely evil because she is afraid of him. Her limited perceptions remind us of Blake's questioner in "The Tyger" who begins to perceive the frightening element of the experiential world but also is rather duped into his fear by his own limitations. Like the figure in Blake, Connie is the framer, the story creator—and the diabolic traces in her fiction frighten her not because they are the manifestations of an outside evil but because they are the symbolic extrapolations of her own psyche.

If the adamant insistence that Arnold Friend is Satan is rejected, then who is this intriguing mysterious visitor? In *Enter Mysterious Stranger: American Cloistral Fiction*, Roy Male asserts that many mysterious intruders throughout American literature "are almost always potential saviors, destroyers, or ambiguous combinations of both, and their initial entrance, however much it may be displaced toward realism, amounts to the entrance of God or the devil on a machine."[8] And if Arnold Friend is *not* satanic, then his arrival could be that of a savior. This possibility moreover is suggested by Connie's whispering "Christ. Christ"[9] when Arnold first arrives in his golden "machine." Not only is "33" part of Arnold's "secret code" of numbers, but his sign, an "X" that seems to hover in the air, is also one of the symbols for Christ. Because music is closely associated with religion—"the music was always in the background, like music at a church service"—it also adds a religious element to Arnold's arrival. The key question then is who is this musical messiah, and the key to the answer is the dedication "For Bob Dylan"—the element of the story so unsatisfactorily accounted for by our predecessors. Not only does the description of Arnold Friend also fit Bob Dylan—a type of rock-and-roll messiah—but three of Dylan's songs (popular when the story was written) are very similar to the story itself.

In the mid-sixties Bob Dylan's followers perceived him to be a messiah. According to his biographer, Dylan was "a rock-and-roll king."[10] It is no wonder then that Arnold speaks with "the voice of the man on the radio," the disc jockey whose name, Bobby King, is a reference to "Bobby" Dylan, the "king" of rock-and-roll. Dylan was more than just a "friend" to his listeners; he was "Christ revisited," "the prophet leading [his followers] into [a new] Consciousness."[11] In fact, "people were making him an idol; . . . thousands of men and women, young and old, felt their lives entwined with his because they saw him as a mystic, a messiah who would lead them to salvation."[12]

5 That Oates consciously associates Arnold Friend with Bob Dylan is clearly suggested by the similarities of their physical descriptions. Arnold's "shaggy, shabby

black hair that looked crazy as a wig," his "long and hawk-like" nose, his unshaven face, his "big and white" teeth, his lashes, "thick and black as if painted with a black tarlike material" and his size ("only an inch or so taller than Connie") are all characteristic of Bob Dylan. Even Arnold's "fast, bright monotone voice" is suggestive of Dylan, especially since he speaks "in a simple lilting voice, exactly as if he were reciting the words to a song."

The reference to "Mister Tambourine Man" implies another connection between the story and Dylan. A few of his song lyrics are very similar to the story itself. Oates herself suggests that part of the story's inspiration was "hearing for some weeks Dylan's song 'It's All Over Now, Baby Blue.'"[13] Such lines as "you must leave now," "something calls for you," "the vagabond who's rapping at your door," and "go start anew" are suggestive of the impending change awaiting Connie. Two other Dylan songs are equally as applicable though. The following lines from "Like a Rolling Stone"—the second most popular song of 1965 (the story was first published in 1966)—are also very similar to Connie's situation at the end of the story:

> You used to be so amused
> At Napoleon in rags and the language that he used
> Go to him now, he calls you, you can't refuse
> When you got nothing, you got nothing to lose
> You're invisible now, you got no secrets to conceal.

But Dylan's "Mr. Tambourine Man"—the number ten song in 1965—is even more similar. The following stanza establishes the notion of using music to rouse one's imagination into a blissful fantasy world:

> Take me on a trip upon your magic swirlin' ship,
> My senses have been stripped,
> My hands can't feel to grip,
> My toes too numb to step,
> Wait only for my boot heels to be wanderin'.
> I'm ready to go anywhere,
> I'm ready for to fade
> Into my own parade.
> Cast your dancin' spell my way,
> I promise to go under it.
> Hey, Mister Tambourine Man, play a song for me,
> I'm not sleepy and there ain't no place I'm going to.
> Hey, Mister Tambourine Man, play a song for me.
> In the jingle, jangle morning I'll come followin' you.

Arnold Friend's car—complete with the phrase "MAN THE FLYING SAUCERS"—is just such "a magic swirlin' ship." Arnold is the personification of popular music, particularly Bob Dylan's music; and as such, Connie's interaction with him is a musically induced fantasy, a kind of "magic carpet ride" in "a convertible jalopy painted gold." Rising out of Connie's radio, Arnold Friend/Bob Dylan is a magical, musical messiah; he persuades Connie to abandon her father's house. As a manifestation of her own desires, he frees her from the limitations of a fifteen-year-old girl, assisting her maturation by stripping her of her childlike vision.

Notes

[1] Joyce M. Wegs, "'Don't You Know Who I Am?' The Grotesque in Oates's 'Where Are You Going, Where Have You Been?'" in *Critical Essays on Joyce Carol Oates*, ed. Linda W. Wagner (Boston: G. K. Hall, 1979), p. 90. First printed in *Journal of Narrative Technique*, 5 (1975), pp. 66–72.

[2] Marie Urbanski, "Existential Allegory: Joyce Carol Oates' 'Where Are You Going, Where Have You Been?'" *Studies in Short Fiction*, 15 (1978), p. 202; Joan Winslow, "The Stranger Within: Two Stories by Oates and Hawthorne," *Studies in Short Fiction*, 17 (1980), p. 264; Tom Quirk, "A Source for 'Where Are You Going, Where Have You Been?'" *Studies in Short Fiction*, 18 (1981), p. 416; Christina Marsden Gillis, "'Where Are You Going, Where Have You Been?': Seduction, Space, and a Fictional Mode," *Studies in Short Fiction*, 18 (1981), p. 70.

[3] Wegs, p. 89.

[4] Gillis, p. 65.

[5] Quirk, p. 416.

[6] Gretchen Schulz and R. J. R. Rockwood, "In Fairyland, without a Map: Connie's Exploration Inward in Joyce Carol Oates' 'Where Are You Going, Where Have You Been?'" *Literature and Psychology*, 30 (1980), pp. 156, 165, & 166, respectively.

[7] In *Paradise Lost*, Milton clearly intends Satan to be a symbol of archetypal evil. Blake and Shelley, as true Romantics, saw in their predecessor's portrait of Lucifer a duality that embodied positive as well as negative traits.

[8] Roy Male, *Enter Mysterious Stranger: American Cloistral Fiction* (Norman: University of Oklahoma Press, 1979), p. 21.

[9] Joyce Carol Oates, "Where Are You Going, Where Have You Been?" in *The Wheel of Love* (New York: Vanguard Press, 1970), p. 40. Hereafter cited parenthetically within the text.

[10] Anthony Scaduto, *Bob Dylan* (New York: Grosset and Dunlop, 1971), p. 222.

[11] Scaduto, p. 274.

[12] Scaduto, p. 229.

[13] "Interview with Joyce Carol Oates about 'Where Are You Going, Where Have You Been?'" in *Mirrors: An Introduction to Literature*, ed. John R. Knott, Jr., and Christopher R. Keaske, 2nd ed. (San Francisco: Canfield Press, 1975), pp. 18–19.

* * *

BOB DYLAN

It's All Over Now, Baby Blue

You must leave now, take what you need you think will last
But whatever you wish to keep, you better grab it fast
Yonder stands your orphan with his gun
Crying like a fire in the sun.
Look out, the saints are comin' through
And it's all over now, baby blue.

The highway is for gamblers, better use your sins
Take what you have gathered from coincidence
The empty-handed painter from your streets
Is drawing crazy patterns on your sheets
This sky too is folding under you
And it's all over now, baby blue.

All your seasick sailors they are rowing home
Your empty-handed army men are going home
The lover who has just walked out your door
Has taken all his blankets from the floor
The carpet too is moving under you
And it's all over now, baby blue.

Leave your stepping stones behind, something calls for you
Forget the dead you've left, they will not follow you
The vagabond who's rapping at your door
Is standing in the clothes that you once wore
Strike another match, go start anew
And it's all over now, baby blue.

* * *

LAURA KALPAKIAN

from a review of Where Are You Going, Where Have You Been?: Selected Early Stories

In acknowledging her range, one must celebrate Ms. Oates's bravery. Range requires courage—and always did, though people perpetually insist things are worse now than they were thirty years ago. In any event and for a wide variety of reasons, current American literature seems self-consciously picketed off, writers hunkered over thimble-sized garden plots, No Trespassing signs stuck about tiny terrains of age or race, region, religion, gender, sexual persuasion, politics, each writer farming a tiny furrow: the pen as plow. Joyce Carol Oates, as these early stories [from the collection *Where Are You Going, Where Have You Been?: Selected Early Stories*] testify, has always declined to be pinned down to her plot, has kicked down the fences. She writes about the rich and poor, urban and rural, black and white, the literate, the tongue-tied, young and old, the primly conventional, the drugged, delinquent, and debilitated. They're all here. Moreover, they're cast out of the comfy old narrative conventions and into structures which demand more from the reader.

Given Ms. Oates's range of structure, character, and voice, we might ask ourselves what unites these pieces. Poured, all of them, into a vial, shaken, what might rise to the top? Drastic acts with drastic consequences, severed connections, doomed love, destructive sex, fear, evil, madness—but not much guilt. Oates's characters all twist about on short tethers, whatever the differences in their worldly circumstances. More often than not a single act or choice or instant plummets these characters not merely into the depths of despair, but into depravity and destruction. In "Upon the Sweeping Flood" (1966), we meet a complacent, well-to-do family man driving home from his father's funeral. Caught in a hurricane, he refuses to obey an order to evacuate and plunges into the maelstrom, thrust finally into the company of two unnamed, abandoned white-trash kids, a boy and a girl. The three survive the night, but in the morning the boy dies at the hands of this man who then lunges toward the girl—he can "already see himself grappling with her in the mud, forcing her down, tearing her ugly clothing from her body"—just as a rescue boat heaves into view. "Save me! Save me!" cries yesterday's prosperous bourgeois and today's murderer.

In the ironically titled "Love and Death" (1972), an equally short distance separates a man (again comfortable, conventional, unloved, and unflappable) from a previously unthinkable fate. Visiting his infirm father, he meets a prostitute he slept with years before, as a young man. Their versions of the past are different; hers is correct. Though he returns to his manicured life, the chance encounter evolves into an obsession, sucking him into abasement and humiliation.

At the conclusion of "In the Warehouse" (1973), the narrator tells us of her tidy married life in "a colonial house on a lane of colonial houses called Meadowbrook Lane." But as a twelve-year-old, she was bullied about by a stronger girl named Ronnie whose toughness sprung from a sort of delinquent passion and unfocused unhappiness. The narrator was completely cowed by Ronnie: "I have never thought about liking Ronnie. I have no choice. She has never given me the privilege of liking or disliking her and if she knew I was thinking such a thought, she would yank my hair out of my head." As the girls prowled the darkened loft of a deserted warehouse, Ronnie urged the narrator up the stairs, ordering, "Do it! Do it!" Atop the loft, the narrator pushed Ronnie, who was impaled on the machinery below and died in a pool of blood. The sleepy narrator then went home, went to bed. Eventually, she "[grew] out of the skinny little body that knocked the clumsy body down—and I have never felt sorry. Never any guilt."

5 The Joyce Carol Oates of these early stories believes that evil lurks everywhere, even in the sunniest lives, the ostensibly to-be-envied lives. The knowledge of this evil defines character for Oates—or, more to the point, the individual's reaction to this knowledge defines character. Oates cares nothing for justice, nor judgment, nor Christian virtue and Christian wickedness. There are only two possible responses to the darkness. One reaction is the murderer's cry, "Save me! Save me!", the wail of inescapable horror, the wish to be delivered. But there is no deliverance and there is no salvation. The narrator of "In the Warehouse" expresses for Oates the other possible reaction: "Never any guilt." She waits patiently to feel guilt for Ronnie's murder; but guilt, like a missed train, never arrives. In Oates's moral lexicon, the word "retribution" does not exist, nor "punishment," nor even anything so personal as "revenge." Evil is an impersonal, inescapable fact in every life. The central recognition of adulthood—no matter how old or young the character—is the recognition of this evil.

So omnipresent are the evil acts and consequences that Oates's characters seem often to be less created than enslaved by narrative: allegorical figures painted against realistic sunshine. In the title piece, "Where Are You Going, Where Have You Been?" (1970), for instance, there is a struggle between the menacing and cajoling Arnold Friend and the pubescent Connie. In the end Connie is, apparently, raped (in the Afterword Oates calls her "the presumably doomed Connie"). But Connie seems, despite the carefully drawn settings—shopping malls, drive-in restaurants, backyard barbecues—less a character than a cipher. She has no volition, no choices, and therefore it's hard to see her even as a victim. Instead, she suggests in her helplessness the awful inequalities of sex and power and violence. . . .

Emphatically in the stories in this volume, character and landscape serve the narrative rather than vice versa. Moreover, Joyce Carol Oates does not stoop to authorial pleading; she is neither pseudomaternal toward her characters nor pseudo-avuncular toward the reader, and she never importunes us with the unspoken: Please care for these characters. And, though the seasons are always noted and the geographical details of settings are always provided (including the oft-mentioned Detroit and its suburbs, as well as Erie County, New York), landscape in Oates's work seems dreamy, monochromatic, and unrealized—landscape as Tim Burton sometimes uses it in his movies. We may care about these characters or not, as we wish, but we are compelled by vigorous narrative through essentially indifferent landscapes. . . .

In Oates's stories there are no safe relationships, but the most perilous of all possibilities is sex. Sex is always destructive. In "Accomplished Desires" (1970), a two-edged narrative recounts the collision (and collusion) of two women: one a pretty college girl, vacuous but orderly, the other an accomplished woman poet married to a bullying professor. The wife is a prisoner in the upper reaches of her rented home; defeated by her home life, her three children, her inability to write, she drinks and looks out the high window. The smarmy husband not only beds the student but installs her as his secretary and housekeeper and moves her into his home to keep his life in order. According to the husband, this young woman "gets herself pregnant. On purpose." Because sages concerned with the state of modern literature await the professor's lecture at a meeting on the West Coast, the wife drives the student to an appointment with an abortionist. The women strike up a tentative, unspoken alliance (though not against the man, as we might have thought—or hoped). Indeed, the wife bows out of the struggle altogether, almost gracefully: a quiet overdose self-administered in a hotel room. The pretty former student, new wife—now, suddenly, a mother of four—finds herself prisoner in the upper reaches of the rented house, without the consolations of company or poetry or even gin.

Communication—especially sexual communication—is not only baffling and treacherous for Oates's characters; it often seems impossible. My personal favorite in this collection, "Translation" (1977), describes a middle-aged American academic who makes an official visit to an unnamed Central European country and is provided with a translator, Liebert. At a dreary communist cocktail party the American, Oliver, meets a woman whose beauty and fragility strike him to the very heart. He falls in love though he cannot even pronounce her name: "Alisa was as close as he could come to it." Oliver is euphoric, intoxicated, as he spends a memorable evening with her in a cafe (Liebert translating) where they speak of literature, politics, passion, history, and love. Oliver feels himself buoyed, enfolded, welcomed in a country where, in effect, he is a mute. The following day Liebert discreetly suggests that

Alisa's roommate could be persuaded to leave overnight if she had train fare, which Oliver provides. But on the morning of the intended assignation, Oliver discovers he has been given a new translator. No explanations offered. No questions answered. This new man—obscene in every way—talks of the weather, smirks lewdly, arranges another cafe date with Alisa that evening. Through the new translator, Alisa inquires after Oliver's life in America, his financial assets, his cars, his wife. She eyeballs his watch. As Oliver leaves the country the next day, desperate for Liebert, he cries, "What shall I do for the rest of my life . . . ?"

10 No doubt the young and gifted writer of these stories found herself facing that same question. The dust-jacket photo for these selected early stories shows Ms. Oates circa 1965, her hair in the "flip" fashionable in that era, shoulders framed by a boat-necked dress. She regards the reader with the serene gaze of a high-school valedictorian. Not at all the look of a woman who willingly, knowingly smashes up the conventions of narrative. She does not look like the author who will unmask the evil of everyday life, who will see allegory in the backyard and real darkness among the metaphoric daisies. But she is.

* * *

DON MOSER

from The Pied Piper of Tucson

Sullen and unshaved, 23 years old and arrested for murder, Charles Schmid did not now look like a hero. But to many of the teen-agers in Tucson, Ariz. he had been someone to admire and emulate. He was different. He was Smitty, with mean, "beautiful" eyes and an interesting way of talking, and if he sometimes did weird things, at least he wasn't dull. He had his own house where he threw good parties, he wore crazy make-up, he was known at all the joints up and down Tucson's Speedway, and girls dyed their hair blond for him. Three of the girls who knew him wound up dead in the desert outside of town. And so last week, in a sun-blessed town where big-city squalor and violence seem far away, Smitty, the cool pied piper, stood trial for murder.

Charles Schmid in police custody.
Source: ©Jon Kamman / Tucson Citizen

The death of the girls was shocking enough to Tucson, but the city had to face something more. There were indications that Smitty had boasted about the killings to his teen-age followers long before authorities even began to suspect that murder might have been done. Nobody spoke up. As the trial began for the murder of two of the victims—there will be another trial later for the murder of the third—Tucson's parents looked closely at their own children, and at the different young man so many of their children admired.

He Cruised in a Golden Car,
Looking for the Action

Hey, c'mon babe, follow me,
I'm the Pied Piper, follow me,
I'm the Pied Piper,
And I'll show you where it's at.
—Popular song,
Tucson, winter 1965

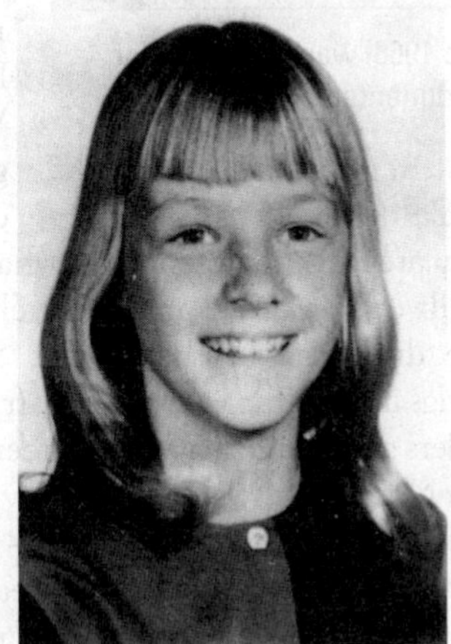

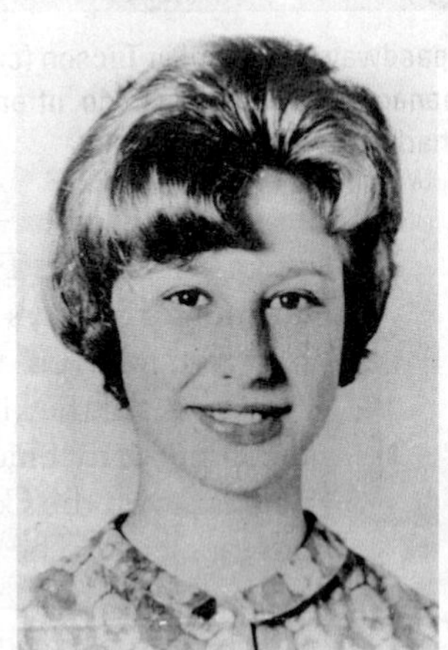

Schmid's teenage victims: Gretchen Fritz (*left*), Wendy Fritz (*center*), and Alleen Rowe (*right*).
Source: ©Tucson Citizen

At dusk in Tucson, as the stark, yellow-flared mountains begin to blur against the sky, the golden car slowly cruises Speedway. Smoothly it rolls down the long, divided avenue, past the supermarkets, the gas stations and the motels; past the twist joints, the sprawling drive-in restaurants. The car slows for an intersection, stops, then pulls away again. The exhaust mutters against the pavement as the young man driving takes the machine swiftly, expertly through the gears. A car pulls even with him; the teen-age girls in the front seat laugh, wave and call his name. The young man glances toward the rearview mirror, turned always so that he can look at his own reflection, and he appraises himself.

The face is his own creation: the hair dyed raven black, the skin darkened to a deep tan with pancake make-up, the lips whitened, the whole effect heightened by a mole he has painted on one cheek. But the deep-set blue eyes are all his own. Beautiful eyes, the girls say.

Approaching the Hi-Ho, the teen-agers' nightclub, he backs off on the accelerator, then slowly cruises on past Johnie's Drive-in. There the cars are beginning to orbit and accumulate in the parking lot—neat sharp cars with deep-throated

Speedway Boulevard in Tucson (circa 1966) was a hangout for teenagers with nothing to do, often frequented by murderer Charles Schmid.

Source: ©Bill Ray/Time Life Pictures/Getty Images

mufflers and Maltese-cross decals on the windows. But it's early yet. Not much going on. The driver shifts up again through the gears, and the golden car slides away along the glitter and gimcrack of Speedway. Smitty keeps looking for the action.

Whether the juries in the two trials decide that Charles Howard Schmid Jr. did or did not brutally murder Alleen Rowe, Gretchen Fritz and Wendy Fritz has from the beginning seemed of almost secondary importance to the people of Tucson. They are not indifferent. But what disturbs them far beyond the question of Smitty's guilt or innocence are the revelations about Tucson itself that have followed on the disclosure of the crimes. Starting with the bizarre circumstances of the killings and on through the ugly fragments of the plot—which in turn hint at other murders as yet undiscovered, at teen-age sex, blackmail, even connections with the Cosa Nostra—they have had to view their city in a new and unpleasant light. The fact is that Charles Schmid—who cannot be dismissed as a freak, an aberrant of no consequence—had for years functioned successfully as a member, even a leader, of the yeastiest stratum of Tucson's teen-age society.

5 As a high school student Smitty had been, as classmates remember, an outsider—but not that far outside. He was small but he was a fine athlete, and in his last year—1960—he was a state gymnastics champion. His grades were poor, but he was in no trouble to speak of until his senior year, when he was suspended for stealing tools from a welding class.

But Smitty never really left the school. After his suspension he hung around waiting to pick up kids in a succession of sharp cars which he drove fast and well. He haunted all the teen-age hangouts along Speedway, including the bowling alleys and the public swimming pool—and he put on spectacular diving exhibitions for girls far younger than he.

At the time of his arrest last November, Charles Schmid was 23 years old. He wore face make-up and dyed his hair. He habitually stuffed three or four inches of old rags and tin cans into the bottoms of his high-topped boots to make himself taller than his five-foot-three and stumbled about so awkwardly while walking that some people thought he had wooden feet. He pursed his lips and let his eyelids droop in order to emulate his idol, Elvis Presley. He bragged to girls that he knew 100 ways to make love, that he ran dope, that he was a Hell's Angel. He talked about being a rough customer in a fight (he was, though he was rarely in one), and he always carried in his pocket tiny bottles of salt and pepper, which he said he used to blind his opponents. He liked to use highfalutin language and had a favorite saying, "I can manifest my neurotical emotions, emancipate an epicureal instinct, and elaborate on my heterosexual tendencies."

He occasionally shocked even those who thought they knew him well. A friend says he once saw Smitty tie a string to the tail of his pet cat, swing it around his head and beat it bloody against a wall. Then he turned calmly and asked, "You feel compassion—why?"

Murderer Charles H. Schmid Jr., at the preliminary hearings before the trial.
Source: ©Bill Ray/Time Life Pictures/Getty Images

Yet even while Smitty tried to create an exalted, heroic image of himself, he had worked on a pitiable one. "He thrived on feeling sorry for himself," recalls a friend, "and making others feel sorry for him." At various times Smitty told intimates that he had leukemia and didn't have long to live. He claimed that he was adopted, that his real name was Angel Rodriguez, that his father was a "bean" (local slang for Mexican, an inferior race in Smitty's view), and that his mother was a famous lawyer who would have nothing to do with him.

What made Smitty a hero to Tucson's youth? 10

Isn't Tucson—out there in the Golden West, in the grand setting where the skies are not cloudy all day—supposed to be a flowering of the American Dream? One envisions teen-agers who drink milk, wear crewcuts, go to bed at half past 9, say "Sir" and "Ma'am," and like to go fishing with Dad. Part of Tucson is like this—but the city is not yet Utopia. It is glass and chrome and well-weathered stucco; it is also gimcrack, ersatz and urban sprawl at its worst. Its suburbs stretch for mile after mile—a level sea of bungalows, broken only by mammoth shopping centers, that ultimately peters out among the cholla and saguaro. The city has grown from 85,000 to 300,000 since World War II. Few who live there were born there, and a lot are just passing through. Its superb climate attracts the old and the infirm, many of whom, as one citizen put it, "have come here to retire from their responsibilities to life." Jobs are hard to find and there is little industry to stabilize employment. ("What do people do in Tucson?" the visitor asks. Answer: "They do each others' laundry.")

As for the youngsters, they must compete with the army of semi-retired who are willing to take on part-time work for the minimum wage. Schools are beautiful but overcrowded; and at those with split sessions, the kids are on the loose from noon on, or from 6 p.m. till noon the next day. When they get into trouble, Tucson teenagers are capable of getting into trouble in style: a couple of years ago they shocked the city fathers by throwing a series of beer-drinking parties in the desert, attended by scores of kids. The fests were called "boondockers" and if they were no more sinful than any other kids' drinking parties, they were at least on a magnificent scale. One statistic seems relevant: 50 runaways are reported to the Tucson police department each month.

Of an evening kids with nothing to do wind up on Speedway, looking for action. There is the teen-age nightclub ("Pickup Palace," the kids call it). There are the rock 'n' roll beer joints (the owners check ages meticulously, but young girls can enter if they don't drink; besides, anyone can buy a phony I.D. card for $2.50 around the high schools) where they can Jerk, Swim and Frug away the evening to the room-shaking electronic blare of *Hang On Sloopy*, *The Pied Piper* and a number called *The Bo Diddley Rock*. At the drive-in hamburger and pizza stands their cars circle endlessly, mufflers rumbling, as they check each other over.

Here on Speedway you find Richie and Ronny, out of work and bored and with nothing to do. Here you find Debby and Jabron, from the wrong side of the tracks, aimlessly cruising in their battered old car looking for something—anything—to relieve the tedium of their lives, looking for somebody neat. ("Well if the boys look bitchin,' you pull up next to them in your car and you roll down the window and say, 'Hey, how about a dollar for gas?' and if they give you the dollar then maybe you let them take you to Johnie's for a Coke.") Here you find Gretchen, pretty and rich and with problems, bad problems. Of a Saturday night, all of them cruising the long, bright street that seems endlessly in motion with the young. Smitty's people.

15 He had a nice car. He had plenty of money from his parents, who ran a nursing home, and he was always glad to spend it on anyone who'd listen to him. He had a pad of his own where he threw parties and he had impeccable manners. He was always willing to help a friend and he would send flowers to girls who were ill. He was older and more mature than most of his friends. He knew where the action was, and if he wore make-up—well, at least he was *different*.

Some of the older kids—those who worked, who had something else to do—thought Smitty was a creep. But to the youngsters—to the bored and the lonely, to the dropout and the delinquent, to the young girls with beehive hair-dos and tight pants they didn't quite fill out, and to the boys with acne and no jobs—to these people, Smitty was a kind of folk hero. Nutty maybe, but at least more dramatic, more theatrical, more *interesting* than anyone else in their lives: a semi-ludicrous sexy-eyed pied piper who, stumbling along in his rag-stuffed boots led them up and down Speedway. . . .

Out in the respectable Tucson suburbs parents have started to crack down on the youngsters and have declared Speedway hangouts off limits. "I thought my folks were bad before," laments one grounded 16-year-old, "but now they're just impossible."

As for the others—Smitty's people—most don't care very much. Things are duller without Smitty around, but things have always been dull.

"There's nothing to do in this town," says one of his girls, shaking her dyed blond hair. "The only other town I know is Las Vegas and there's nothing to do there either." For her, and for her friends, there's nothing to do in any town.

They are down on Speedway again tonight, cruising, orbiting the drive-ins, stopping 20
by the joints, where the words of *The Bo Diddley Rock* cut through the smoke and the electronic dissonance like some macabre reminder of their fallen hero.

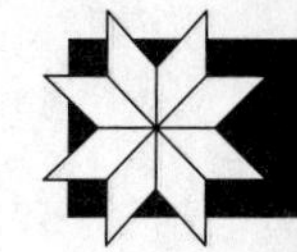

All you women stand in line,
And I'll love you all in an hour's time. . . .
I got a cobra snake for a necktie,
I got a brand-new house on the roadside
Covered with rattlesnake hide
I got a brand-new chimney made on top,
Made out of human skulls.
Come on baby, take a walk with me,
And tell me, who do you love?
Who do you love?
Who do you love?
Who do you love?

* * *

ANONYMOUS

The Pied Piper of Hamelin

Once upon a time . . . on the banks of a great river in the north of Germany lay a town called Hamelin. The citizens of Hamelin were honest folk who lived contentedly in their grey stone houses. The years went by, and the town grew very rich. Then one day, an extraordinary thing happened to disturb the peace. Hamelin had always had rats, and a lot too. But they had never been a danger, for the cats had always solved the rat problem in the usual way—by killing them. All at once, however, the rats began to multiply.

In the end, a black sea of rats swarmed over the whole town. First, they attacked the barns and storehouses, then, for lack of anything better, they gnawed the wood, cloth or anything at all. The one thing they didn't eat was metal. The terrified citizens flocked to plead with the town councillors to free them from the plague of rats. But the council had, for a long time, been sitting in the Mayor's room, trying to think of a plan.

"What we need is an army of cats!"

But all the cats were dead.

"We'll put down poisoned food then . . ." 5

But most of the food was already gone and even poison did not stop the rats.

"It just can't be done without help!" said the Mayor sadly.

Just then, while the citizens milled around outside, there was a loud knock at the door. "Who can that be?" the city fathers wondered uneasily, mindful of the angry crowds. They gingerly opened the door. And to their surprise, there stood a tall thin man dressed in brightly coloured clothes, with a long feather in his hat, and waving a gold pipe at them.

"I've freed other towns of beetles and bats," the stranger announced, "and for a thousand florins, I'll rid you of your rats!"

"A thousand florins!" exclaimed the Mayor. "We'll give you fifty thousand if you succeed!" At once the stranger hurried away, saying: "It's late now, but at dawn tomorrow, there won't be a rat left in Hamelin!"

Illustration of the Brothers Grimm version of the fairy tale "The Pied Piper of Hamelin."

Source: ©Bettmann/Corbis

The sun was still below the horizon, when the sound of a pipe wafted through the streets of Hamelin. The pied piper slowly made his way through the houses and behind him flocked the rats. Out they scampered from doors, windows and gutters, rats of every size, all after the piper. And as he played, the stranger marched down to the river and straight into the water, up to his middle. Behind him swarmed the rats and every one was drowned and swept away by the current.

By the time the sun was high in the sky, there was not a single rat in the town. There was even greater delight at the town hall, until the piper tried to claim his payment.

"Fifty thousand florins?" exclaimed the councillors, "Never . . ."

"A thousand florins at least!" cried the pied piper angrily. But the Mayor broke in. "The rats are all dead now and they can never come back. So be grateful for fifty florins, or you'll not get even that . . ."

His eyes flashing with rage, the pied piper pointed a threatening finger at the Mayor.

"You'll bitterly regret ever breaking your promise," he said, and vanished.

A shiver of fear ran through the councillors, but the Mayor shrugged and said excitedly: "We've saved fifty thousand florins!"

That night, freed from the nightmare of the rats, the citizens of Hamelin slept more soundly than ever. And when the strange sound of piping wafted through the streets at dawn, only the children heard it. Drawn as by magic, they hurried out of their homes. Again, the pied piper paced through the town. This time, it was children of all sizes that flocked at his heels to the sound of his strange piping. The long procession soon left the town and made its way through the wood and across the forest till it reached the foot of a huge mountain. When the piper came to the dark rock, he played his pipe even louder still and a great door creaked open. Beyond lay a cave. In trooped the children behind the pied piper, and when the last child had gone into the darkness, the door creaked shut. A great landslide came down the mountain blocking the entrance to the cave forever. Only one little lame boy escaped this fate. It was he who told the anxious citizens, searching for their children, what had happened. And no matter what people did, the mountain never gave up its victims. Many years were to pass before the merry voices of other children would ring through the streets of Hamelin but the memory of the harsh lesson lingered in everyone's heart and was passed down from father to son through the centuries.

* * *

CHARLES PERRAULT

Little Red Riding Hood

Once upon a time there was a little village girl, the prettiest that had ever been seen. Her mother doted on her. Her grandmother was even fonder, and made her a little red hood, which became her so well that everywhere she went by the name of Little Red Riding Hood.

One day her mother, who had just made and baked some cakes, said to her: "Go and see how your grandmother is, for I have been told that she is ill. Take her a cake and this little pot of butter."

Little Red Riding Hood set off at once for the house of her grandmother, who lived in another village. On her way through a wood she met old Father Wolf. He would have very much liked to eat her, but dared not do so on account of some wood-cutters who were in the forest. He asked her where she was going. The poor child, not knowing that it was dangerous to stop and listen to a wolf, said: "I am going to see my grandmother, and am taking her a cake and a pot of butter which my mother has sent to her." "Does she live far away?" asked the Wolf. "Oh, yes," replied Little Red Riding Hood; "it is yonder by the mill which you can see right below there, and it is the first house in the village."

Illustration from "Little Red Riding Hood."

Source: ©Archivo Iconografico, S.A./Corbis

"Well now," said the Wolf, "I think I shall go and see her too. I will go by this path, and you by that path, and we will see who gets there first." The Wolf set off running with all his might by the shorter road, and the little girl continued on her way by the longer road. As she went she amused herself by gathering nuts, running after the butterflies, and making nosegays of the wild flowers which she found.

The Wolf was not long in reaching the grandmother's house. He knocked. Toc Toc. "Who is there?" "It is your granddaughter, Red Riding Hood," said the Wolf, disguising his voice, "and I bring you a cake and a little pot of butter as a present from my mother." The worthy grandmother was in bed, not being very well, and cried out to him: "Pull out the peg and the latch will fall." The Wolf drew out the peg and the door flew open. Then he sprang upon the poor old lady and ate her up in less than no time, for he had been more than three days without food.

After that he shut the door, lay down in the grandmother's bed, and waited for Little Red Riding Hood. Presently she came and knocked. Toc Toc.

"Who is there?"

Now Little Red Riding Hood on hearing the Wolf's gruff voice was at first frightened, but thinking that her grandmother had a bad cold, she replied: "It is your granddaughter, Red Riding Hood, and I bring you a cake and a little pot of butter from my mother."

Softening his voice, the Wolf called out to her: "Pull out the peg and the latch will fall." Little Red Riding Hood drew out the peg and the door flew open. When he saw her enter, the Wolf hid himself in the bed beneath the counterpane. "Put the cake and the little pot of butter on the bin," he said, "and come up on the bed with me."

Little Red Riding Hood took off her cloak, but when she climbed up on the bed she was astonished to see how her grandmother looked in her nightgown.

"Grandmother dear!" she exclaimed, "what big arms you have!"

"The better to embrace you, my child!"

"Grandmother dear, what big legs you have!"

"The better to run with, my child!"

"Grandmother dear, what big ears you have!"

"The better to hear with, my child!"

"Grandmother dear, what big eyes you have!"

"The better to see with, my child!"

"Grandmother dear, what big teeth you have!"

"The better to eat you with!"

With these words the wicked Wolf leapt upon Little Red Riding Hood and gobbled her up.

Moral

From this story one learns that children, especially young lasses, pretty, courteous and well-bred, do very wrong to listen to strangers, and it is not an unheard thing if the Wolf is thereby provided with his dinner. I say Wolf, for all wolves are not of the same sort; there is one kind with an amenable disposition—neither noisy, nor hateful, nor angry, but tame, obliging and gentle, following the young maids in the streets, even into their homes. Alas! Who does not know that these gentle wolves are of all such creatures the most dangerous!

Topics for Further Research

1. In Schulz and Rockwood's essay "In Fairyland, without a Map: Connie's Exploration Inward in Joyce Carol Oates's 'Where Are You Going, Where Have You Been?'" (p. 617), the authors quote Oates on the subject of her story's allusions to fairy tales. After consulting Bruno Bettelheim's classic book *The Uses of Enchantment* (as well as the other sources in this Casebook) and after reading "Little Red Riding Hood" (p. 651 and "The Pied Piper of Hamelin" (p. 649), write an essay in which you consider the importance of fairy tales in the story.
2. In her article "When Characters from the Page Are Made Flesh on the Screen" (p. 630), Oates refers to her use of "realistic allegory" as a mode of fiction that is "Hawthornian . . . shading into parable" (par. 4). Research Hawthorne's views on allegory by reading some of his many essays on the subject, such as "The Custom House." Then, write an essay in which you consider how "Where Are You Going, Where Have You Been?" might be compared to Hawthorne's stories, such as "Young Goodman Brown" (p. 540), in terms of its portrayal of good, evil, and innocence. Try to identify elements in Oates's story that might be considered allegorical in the Hawthornian sense.
3. Oates has been described as a modern realist, and she herself has used the term "psychological realism" to describe her work. Research the history and emergence of literary realism in American literature. What elements of realism as it first appeared in literature at the end of the nineteenth century and the beginning of the twentieth century are found in Oates's work?
4. Critics often see Oates's short stories as gothic. Research the term *gothic* as it applies to works of literature. Then, write a paper in which you make the case for three of her stories, including "Where Are You Going, Where Have You Been?," as gothic works. (You may also wish to discuss gothic stories by other writers—for example, Poe's "The Cask of Amontillado," (p. 385), and Flannery O'Connor's "A Good Man Is Hard to Find," (p. 447).
5. In the excerpt from her book review included in this Casebook (p. 641) critic Laura Kalpakian takes a look at some of the themes of Oates's works as they are represented by her characters. Do some research to find out what other critics and reviewers have identified as recurring themes in Oates's work. Then, choose one of these themes, and write an essay discussing how three of Oates's characters illustrate the theme you have chosen.

Student Paper

Olivari 1

Michele Olivari

Professor Biemiller

English 102

8 March 2008

Mesmerizing Men and Vulnerable Teens: Power Relationships in "Where Are You Going, Where Have You Been?" and "Teenage Wasteland"

Introduction

In both Joyce Carol Oates's "Where Are You Going, Where Have You Been?" (1966) and Anne Tyler's "Teenage Wasteland" (1984), adolescents are in conflict with their parents. Both stories are set in "teenage wastelands" in which the protagonists ignore limits established by authority figures and avoid making decisions or finding a direction for their lives. An even more striking similarity between the two stories is the presence of a hypnotic older man—one who exerts enormous influence over the teenagers, pushing them out of their passive states and causing them to take action. Ironically, however, the actions these two adolescents take, though decisive, have serious negative consequences.

Thesis statement

Background: critics' interpretations of Arnold Friend

Arnold Friend, the mysterious loner who pursues Connie in "Where Are You Going, Where Have You Been?," is characterized by Gretchen Schulz and R. J. R. Rockwood as the fairy tale wolf who "intends to 'gobble up' this 'little girl' as soon as he gets the chance" (636). Many other critics, as Mike Tierce and John Michael Crafton point out, see Arnold as the devil; Tierce and Crafton, however, prefer to see

Olivari 2

him as a Bob Dylan figure "—a type of rock and roll messiah—" (638). Oates herself, in stating that Arnold is based on a "charismatic mass murderer" ("When Characters" 631), acknowledges both the threat he poses and his seductive powers. Regardless of whether Arnold is murderer, devil, wolf, or "musical messiah," it is clear that he is a strong, controlling personality who has an unnaturally powerful hold over Connie. In a less dramatic way, Cal, the tutor in "Teenage Wasteland," has a similar hold over Donny. Both men, supported by background music, use their power to mesmerize young people, separating them from home and family and seducing them into following different—and dangerous—paths. In both stories, it is the adolescents' tendency to drift without an anchor that makes them vulnerable to the men.

Comparison between Cal and Arnold established

Both Connie and Donny are passive dreamers, stuck in numbing adolescence, waiting for something to happen. Meanwhile, both break the rules set by their parents. Connie is fifteen, and her mind is "all filled with trashy daydreams" (617). At night she sneaks out to forbidden hangouts, lying to her parents about where she is going. As she drifts through her unstructured summer days, she is "dazed with the warmth about her" (619) and caught up in the music she listens to and in her romantic fantasies. Donny is also stalled, caught in a cycle of failure and defeat, "noisy, lazy, and disruptive" (785) and unresponsive in school, cutting classes, smoking, and drinking beer.

First parallel between Connie and Donny: passivity

Olivari 3

Second parallel between Connie and Donny: alienation from parents

Both Connie and Donny are emotionally separated from their parents. Connie's mother constantly nags her and compares her unfavorably to her sister June; her father does not even talk, choosing instead to read his newspaper and avoid conflict. In "Teenage Wasteland," Daisy's primary attitude toward her son Donny is disappointment. When she looks at him, she sees only "his pathetically poor posture, that slouch so forlorn that his shoulders [seem] about to meet his chin" (788). She feels sorry for him, but she is helpless to rescue him, let alone give him the emotional support he needs. Like Connie's mother, she disapproves of her child's behavior. Despite her efforts to defend and encourage him, she is ashamed of his failures and upset at how they reflect on her as a parent. Both Connie and Donny are disconnected from people and from social institutions, and both are allowed to remain this way by weak, ineffective parents whom they neither respect nor admire. For these reasons, both teenagers are vulnerable to the seductive power of a hypnotic older man.

Arnold's power over Connie

Arnold Friend, a strange-looking man who acts like a teenager, has great power over Connie. Initially, she is drawn to him by how he looks and dresses and by the music they share; later, his claims to know all about her, to know what she wants (which she herself does not know), draw her closer to him. Although she begins by flirting with him as she does with other boys, she soon realizes that he is

Olivari 4

different. At first "his face [is] a familiar face, somehow" (621), and "she recognize[s] most things about him" (623), but her confidence turns to fear when she realizes that he is older than he appears (623). By now, though, she is under his spell. Little by little, things that have been comforting and familiar—the music, Arnold's clothing and mannerisms, even Connie's own kitchen—become "only half real" (624). As Arnold becomes more and more threatening, Connie becomes more and more helpless; toward the end of the story, cut off from everything she has known, she is "hollow with what had been fear, but what [is] now just an emptiness" (628). Totally in Arnold's power, she crosses the line into uncertainty—and, perhaps, into death.

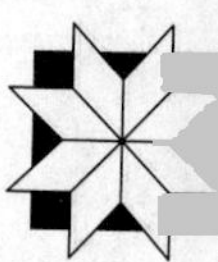

Cal's power over Donny

Cal Beadle, Donny's tutor, has none of the frightening mannerisms of Arnold Friend, and he apparently has no sinister intentions. Nevertheless, he too is a controlling figure. Like Arnold, Cal is an older man who dresses and acts as adolescents do and listens to the music they like. He immediately sides with Donny, setting himself in opposition to authority figures and social institutions, such as Donny's school and family. Never blaming or even criticizing Donny, Cal suggests that Donny's parents are too controlling and advises that they "give him more rope" (788). Cal does not help Donny to function in his world; he shelters him from it. Still, Donny identifies with Cal, adopting his attitudes and expressions: it becomes "Cal this, Cal that, Cal says this, Cal and I did that" (789).

Olivari 5

Cal's power over Donny, continued

Eventually, Cal becomes the role model Donny's own parents have failed to provide. Donny comes to depend on Cal, even going straight to Cal's house (rather than going home) when he is expelled from school, and Cal comes to enjoy this dependence. But Cal does not necessarily have Donny's best interests at heart. Daisy, who despite her own failures with Donny seems to know him (and Cal) well, views Cal as predatory and controlling, seeing his smile as "feverish and avid—a smile of hunger" (791). Although Cal does not cause Donny to leave home, he makes it impossible for him to stay. Once Cal has convinced Donny that it is acceptable to reject the values established by his parents and teachers, Donny's departure becomes inevitable. Having removed all Donny's anchors, Cal then removes himself from Donny's life, deciding the teenager is "emotionally disturbed" (791) and thus absolving himself of blame. At this point, Donny, "exhausted and defeated" (792), has no real choice but to disappear.

Conclusion

Both Arnold Friend and Cal Beadle seem to exist outside the adult world and its rules and values: Arnold is odd-looking and out-of-date, and Cal is estranged from his "controlling" wife and surrounded by teenagers. Perhaps as a result, each has a need for power and a desire to control. Each man selects someone weaker, less confident, and more confused than himself, a teenager with strained family relationships and no focused goals. Clearly, critics' characterizations of Arnold Friend, and the hypnotic power those characterizations suggest, apply not just to Arnold but also to Cal. Even though Cal may mean

Olivari 6

Donny no harm, his casual dismissal of him after he has separated the boy from all that is familiar to him pushes Donny from the known and safe to the unknown and dangerous. It is to this uncertain world that Connie too is driven: a place she "[does] not recognize except to know that she [is] going to it" (628).

Olivari 7

Works Cited

Kirszner, Laurie G., and Stephen R. Mandell, eds. *Literature: Reading, Reacting, Writing.* 7th ed. Boston: Wadsworth, 2010. Print.

Oates, Joyce Carol. "When Characters from the Page Are Made Flesh on the Screen." Kirszner and Mandell 630-33.

---. "Where Are You Going, Where Have You Been?" Kirszner and Mandell 617-28.

Schulz, Gretchen, and R. J. R. Rockwood. "In Fairyland, without a Map: Connie's Exploration Inward in Joyce Carol Oates's 'Where Are You Going, Where Have You Been?'" Kirszner and Mandell 633-37.

Tierce, Mike, and John Michael Crafton. "Connie's Tambourine Man: A New Reading of Arnold Friend." Kirszner and Mandell 637-40.

Tyler, Anne. "Teenage Wasteland." Kirszner and Mandell 785-92.

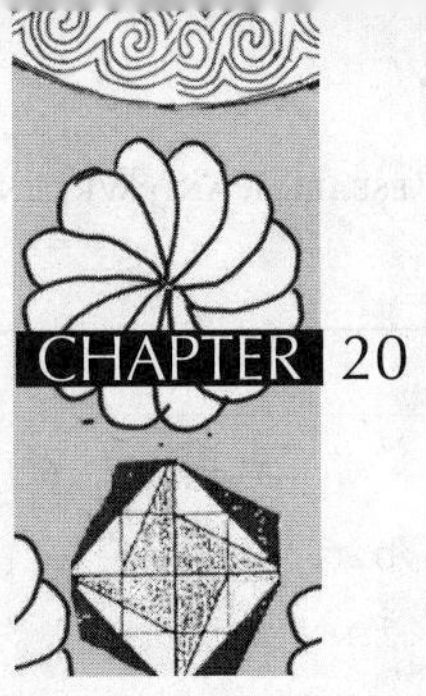

FICTION FOR FURTHER READING

CHINUA ACHEBE (1930–)

Dead Man's Path (1953) (1972)

Michael Obi's hopes were fulfilled much earlier than he had expected. He was appointed headmaster of Ndume Central School in January 1949. It had always been an unprogressive school, so the Mission authorities decided to send a young and energetic man to run it. Obi accepted this responsibility with enthusiasm. He had many wonderful ideas and this was an opportunity to put them into practice. He had had sound secondary school education which designated him a "pivotal teacher" in the official records and set him apart from the other headmasters in the mission field. He was outspoken in his condemnation of the narrow views of these older and often less-educated ones.

"We shall make a good job of it, shan't we?" he asked his young wife when they first heard the joyful news of his promotion.

"We shall do our best," she replied. "We shall have such beautiful gardens and everything will be just *modern* and delightful . . ." In their two years of married life she had become completely infected by his passion for "modern methods" and his denigration of "these old and superannuated people in the teaching field who would be better employed as traders in the Onitsha market." She began to see herself already as the admired wife of the young headmaster, the queen of the school.

The wives of the other teachers would envy her position. She would set the fashion in everything . . . Then, suddenly, it occurred to her that there might not be other wives. Wavering between hope and fear, she asked her husband, looking anxiously at him.

5 "All our colleagues are young and unmarried," he said with enthusiasm which for once she did not share. "Which is a good thing," he continued.

"Why?"

"Why? They will give all their time and energy to the school."

Nancy was downcast. For a few minutes she became skeptical about the new school; but it was only for a few minutes. Her little personal misfortune could not blind her to her husband's happy prospects. She looked at him as he sat folded up in a chair. He was stoop-shouldered and looked frail. But he sometimes surprised people with sudden bursts of physical energy. In his present posture, however, all his bodily strength seemed to have retired behind his deep-set eyes, giving them an extraordinary power of penetration. He was only twenty-six, but looked thirty or more. On the whole, he was not unhandsome.

"A penny for your thoughts, Mike," said Nancy after a while, imitating the woman's magazine she read.

"I was thinking what a grand opportunity we've got at last to show these people 10
how a school should be run."

Ndume School was backward in every sense of the word. Mr. Obi put his whole life into the work, and his wife hers too. He had two aims. A high standard of teaching was insisted upon, and the school compound was to be turned into a place of beauty. Nancy's dream-gardens came to life with the coming of the rains, and blossomed. Beautiful hibiscus and allamanda hedges in brilliant red and yellow marked out the carefully tended school compound from the rank neighbor-hood bushes.

One evening as Obi was admiring his work he was scandalized to see an old woman from the village hobble right across the compound, through a marigold flower-bed and the hedges. On going up there he found faint signs of an almost disused path from the village across the school compound to the bush on the other side.

"It amazes me," said Obi to one of his teachers who had been three years in the school, "that you people allowed the villagers to make use of this footpath. It is simply incredible." He shook his head.

"The path," said the teacher apologetically, "appears to be very important to them. Although it is hardly used, it connects the village shrine with their place of burial."

"And what has that got to do with the school?" asked the headmaster. 15

"Well, I don't know," replied the other with a shrug of the shoulders. "But I remember there was a big row some time ago when we attempted to close it."

"That was some time ago. But it will not be used now," said Obi as he walked away. "What will the Government Education Officer think of this when he comes to inspect the school next week? The villagers might, for all I know, decide to use the schoolroom for pagan ritual during the inspection."

Heavy sticks were planted closely across the path at the two places where it entered and left the school premises. These were further strengthened with barbed wire.

Three days later the village priest of *Ani* called on the headmaster. He was an old man and walked with a slight stoop. He carried a stout walking-stick which he usually tapped on the floor, by way of emphasis, each time he made a new point in his argument.

"I have heard," he said after the usual exchange of cordialities, "that our 20
ancestral footpath has recently been closed . . ."

"Yes," replied Mr. Obi. "We cannot allow people to make a highway of our school compound."

"Look here, my son," said the priest bringing down his walking-stick, "this path was here before you were born and before your father was born. The whole life of this village depends on it. Our dead relatives depart by it and our ancestors visit us by it. But most important, it is the path of children coming in to be born . . ."

Mr. Obi listened with a satisfied smile on his face.

"The whole purpose of our school," he said finally, "is to eradicate just such beliefs as that. Dead men do not require footpaths. The whole idea is just fantastic. Our duty is to teach your children to laugh at such ideas."

25 "What you say may be true," replied the priest, "but we follow the practices of our fathers. If you reopen the path we shall have nothing to quarrel about. What I always say is let the hawk perch and let the eagle perch." He rose to go.

"I am sorry," said the young headmaster. "But the school compound cannot be a thoroughfare. It is against our regulations. I would suggest your constructing another path, skirting our premises. We can even get our boys to help in building it. I don't suppose the ancestors will find the little detour too burdensome."

"I have no more words to say," said the old priest, already outside.

Two days later a young woman in the village died in childbed. A diviner was immediately consulted and he prescribed heavy sacrifices to propitiate ancestors insulted by the fence.

Obi woke up next morning among the ruins of his work. The beautiful hedges were torn up not just near the path but right round the school, the flowers trampled to death and one of the school buildings pulled down . . . That day, the white Supervisor came to inspect the school and wrote a nasty report on the state of the premises but more seriously about the "tribal-war situation developing between the school and the village, arising in part from the misguided zeal of the new headmaster."

* * *

MARGARET ATWOOD (1939–)

Happy Endings (1983)

John and Mary meet.
What happens next?
If you want a happy ending, try A.

A. John and Mary fall in love and get married. They both have worthwhile and remunerative jobs which they find stimulating and challenging. They buy a charming house. Real estate values go up. Eventually, when they can afford live-in help, they have two children, to whom they are devoted. The children turn out well. John and Mary have a stimulating and challenging sex life and worthwhile friends. They go on fun vacations together. They retire. They both have hobbies which they find stimulating and challenging. Eventually they die. This is the end of the story.

B. Mary falls in love with John but John doesn't fall in love with Mary. He merely 5
uses her body for selfish pleasure and ego gratification of a tepid kind. He comes to her apartment twice a week and she cooks him dinner, you'll notice that he doesn't even consider her worth the price of a dinner out, and after he's eaten the dinner he fucks her and after that he falls asleep, while she does the dishes so he won't think she's untidy, having all those dirty dishes lying around, and puts on fresh lipstick so she'll look good when he wakes up, but when he wakes up he doesn't even notice, he puts on his socks and his shorts and his pants and his shirt and his tie and his shoes, the reverse order from the one in which he took them off. He doesn't take off Mary's clothes, she takes them off herself, she acts as if she's dying for it every time, not because she likes sex exactly, she doesn't, but she wants John to think she does because if they do it often enough surely he'll get used to her, he'll come to depend on her and they will get married, but John goes out the door with hardly so much as a good-night and three days later he turns up at six o'clock and they do the whole thing over again.

Mary gets run-down. Crying is bad for your face, everyone knows that and so does Mary but she can't stop. People at work notice. Her friends tell her John is a rat, a pig, a dog, he isn't good enough for her, but she can't believe it. Inside John, she thinks, is another John, who is much nicer. This other John will emerge like a butterfly from a cocoon, a Jack from a box, a pit from a prune, if the first John is only squeezed enough.

One evening John complains about the food. He has never complained about the food before. Mary is hurt.

Her friends tell her they've seen him in a restaurant with another woman, whose name is Madge. It's not even Madge that finally gets to Mary: it's the restaurant. John has never taken Mary to a restaurant. Mary collects all the sleeping pills and aspirins she can find, and takes them and a half a bottle of sherry. You can see what kind of a woman she is by the fact that it's not even whiskey. She leaves a note for John. She hopes he'll discover her and get her to the hospital in time and repent and then they can get married, but this fails to happen and she dies.

John marries Madge and everything continues as in A.

C. John, who is an older man, falls in love with Mary, and Mary, who is only twenty- 10
two, feels sorry for him because he's worried about his hair falling out. She sleeps with him even though she's not in love with him. She met him at work. She's in love with someone called James, who is twenty-two also and not yet ready to settle down.

John on the contrary settled down long ago: this is what is bothering him. John has a steady, respectable job and is getting ahead in his field, but Mary isn't impressed by him, she's impressed by James, who has a motorcycle and a fabulous record collection. But James is often away on his motorcycle, being free. Freedom isn't the same for girls, so in the meantime Mary spends Thursday evenings with John. Thursdays are the only days John can get away.

John is married to a woman called Madge and they have two children, a charming house which they bought just before the real estate values went up, and hobbies which they find stimulating and challenging, when they have the time. John tells Mary how important she is to him, but of course he can't leave his wife because a commitment is a commitment. He goes on about this more than is necessary and Mary finds it boring, but older men can keep it up longer so on the whole she has a fairly good time.

One day James breezes in on his motorcycle with some top-grade California hybrid and James and Mary get higher than you'd believe possible and they climb into bed. Everything becomes very underwater, but along comes John, who has a key to Mary's apartment. He finds them stoned and entwined. He's hardly in any position to be jealous, considering Madge, but nevertheless he's overcome with despair. Finally he's middle-aged, in two years he'll be bald as an egg and he can't stand it. He purchases a handgun, saying he needs it for target practice — this is the thin part of the plot, but it can be dealt with later — and shoots the two of them and himself.

Madge, after a suitable period of mourning, marries an understanding man called Fred and everything continues as in A, but under different names.

15 D. Fred and Madge have no problems. They get along exceptionally well and are good at working out any little difficulties that may arise. But their charming house is by the seashore and one day a giant tidal wave approaches. Real estate values go down. The rest of the story is about what caused the tidal wave and how they escape from it. They do, though thousands drown, but Fred and Madge are virtuous and lucky. Finally on high ground they clasp each other, wet and dripping and grateful, and continue as in A.

E. Yes, but Fred has a bad heart. The rest of the story is about how kind and understanding they both are until Fred dies. Then Madge devotes herself to charity work until the end of A. If you like, it can be "Madge," "cancer," "guilty and confused," and "bird watching."

F. If you think this is all too bourgeois, make John a revolutionary and Mary a counterespionage agent and see how far that gets you. Remember, this is Canada. You'll still end up with A, though in between you may get a lustful brawling saga of passionate involvement, a chronicle of our times, sort of.

You'll have to face it, the endings are the same however you slice it. Don't be deluded by any other endings, they're all fake, either deliberately fake, with malicious intent to deceive, or just motivated by excessive optimism if not by downright sentimentality.

The only authentic ending is the one provided here:
John and Mary die. John and Mary die. John and Mary die.

20 So much for endings. Beginnings are always more fun. True connoisseurs, however, are known to favor the stretch in between, since it's the hardest to do anything with.

That's about all that can be said for plots, which anyway are just one thing after another, a what and a what and a what.

Now try How and Why.

JAMES BALDWIN (1924–1987)

Sonny's Blues (1957)

I read about it in the paper, in the subway, on my way to work. I read it, and I couldn't believe it, and I read it again. Then perhaps I just stared at it, at the newsprint spelling out his name, spelling out the story. I stared at it in the swinging lights of the subway car, and in the faces and bodies of the people, and in my own face, trapped in the darkness which roared outside.

It was not to be believed and I kept telling myself that, as I walked from the subway station to the high school. And at the same time I couldn't doubt it. I was scared, scared for Sonny. He became real to me again. A great block of ice got settled in my belly and kept melting there slowly all day long, while I taught my classes algebra it was a special kind of ice. It kept melting, sending trickles of ice water all up and down my veins, but it never got less. Sometimes it hardened and seemed to expand until I felt my guts were going to come spilling out or that I was going to choke or scream. This would always be at a moment when I was remembering some specific thing Sonny had once said or done.

When he was about as old as the boys in my classes his face had been bright and open, there was a lot of copper in it; and he'd had wonderfully direct brown eyes, and great gentleness and privacy. I wondered what he looked like now. He had been picked up, the evening before, in a raid on an apartment downtown, for peddling and using heroin.

I couldn't believe it: but what I mean by that is that I couldn't find any room for it anywhere inside me. I had kept it outside me for a long time. I hadn't wanted to know. I had had suspicions, but I didn't name them, I kept putting them away. I told myself that Sonny was wild, but he wasn't crazy. And he'd always been a good boy, he hadn't ever turned hard or evil or disrespectful, the way kids can, so quick, so quick, especially in Harlem. I didn't want to believe that I'd ever see my brother going down, coming to nothing, all that light in his face gone out, in the condition I'd already seen so many others. Yet it had happened and here I was, talking about algebra to a lot of boys who might, every one of them for all I knew, be popping off needles every time they went to the head.° Maybe it did more for them than algebra could.

I was sure that the first time Sonny had ever had horse,° he couldn't have been 5
much older than these boys were now. These boys, now, were living as we'd been living then, they were growing up with a rush and their heads bumped abruptly against the low ceiling of their actual possibilities. They were filled with rage. All they really knew were two darknesses, the darkness of their lives, which was now closing in on them, and the darkness of the movies, which had blinded them to that other darkness, and in which they now, vindictively, dreamed, at once more together than they were at any other time, and more alone.

---

the head: Restroom.

horse: Heroin.

When the last bell rang, the last class ended, I let out my breath. It seemed I'd been holding it for all that time. My clothes were wet—I may have looked as though I'd been sitting in a steam bath, all dressed up, all afternoon. I sat alone in the classroom a long time. I listened to the boys outside, downstairs, shouting and cursing and laughing. Their laughter struck me for perhaps the first time. It was not the joyous laughter which—God knows why—one associates with children. It was mocking and insular, its intent was to denigrate. It was disenchanted, and in this, also, lay the authority of their curses. Perhaps I was listening to them because I was thinking about my brother and in them I heard my brother. And myself.

One boy was whistling a tune, at once very complicated and very simple, it seemed to be pouring out of him as though he were a bird, and it sounded very cool and moving through all that harsh, bright air, only just holding its own through all those other sounds.

I stood up and walked over to the window and looked down into the courtyard. It was the beginning of the spring and the sap was rising in the boys. A teacher passed through them every now and again, quickly, as though he or she couldn't wait to get out of that courtyard, to get those boys out of their sight and off their minds. I started collecting my stuff. I thought I'd better get home and talk to Isabel.

The courtyard was almost deserted by the time I got downstairs. I saw this boy standing in the shadow of a doorway, looking just like Sonny. I almost called his name. Then I saw that it wasn't Sonny, but somebody we used to know, a boy from around our block. He'd been Sonny's friend. He'd never been mine, having been too young for me, and, anyway, I'd never liked him. And now, even though he was a grown-up man, he still hung around that block, still spent hours on the street corners, was always high and raggy. I used to run into him from time to time and he'd often work around to asking me for a quarter or fifty cents. He always had some real good excuse, too, and I always gave it to him. I don't know why.

10 But now, abruptly, I hated him. I couldn't stand the way he looked at me, partly like a dog, partly like a cunning child. I wanted to ask him what the hell he was doing in the school courtyard.

He sort of shuffled over to me, and he said, "I see you got the papers. So you already know about it."

"You mean about Sonny? Yes, I already know about it. How come they didn't get you?"

He grinned. It made him repulsive and it also brought to mind what he'd looked like as a kid. "I wasn't there. I stay away from them people."

"Good for you." I offered him a cigarette and I watched him through the smoke. "You come all the way down here just to tell me about Sonny?"

15 "That's right." He was sort of shaking his head and his eyes looked strange, as though they were about to cross. The bright sun deadened his damp dark brown skin and it made his eyes look yellow and showed up the dirt in his kinked hair. He smelled funky. I moved a little away from him and I said, "Well, thanks. But I already know about it and I got to get home."

"I'll walk you a little ways," he said. We started walking. There were a couple of kids still loitering in the courtyard and one of them said goodnight to me and looked strangely at the boy beside me.

"What're you going to do?" he asked me. "I mean, about Sonny?"

"Look. I haven't seen Sonny for over a year, I'm not sure I'm going to do anything. Anyway, what the hell *can* I do?"

"That's right," he said quickly, "ain't nothing you can do. Can't much help old Sonny no more, I guess."

It was what I was thinking and so it seemed to me he had no right to say it.

"I'm surprised at Sonny, though," he went on—he had a funny way of talking, he looked straight ahead as though he were talking to himself—"I thought Sonny was a smart boy, I thought he was too smart to get hung."

"I guess he thought so too," I said sharply, "and that's how he got hung. And how about you? You're pretty goddamn smart, I bet."

Then he looked directly at me, just for a minute. "I ain't smart," he said. "If I was smart, I'd have reached for a pistol a long time ago."

"Look. Don't tell *me* your sad story, if it was up to me, I'd give you one." Then I felt guilty—guilty, probably, for never having supposed that the poor bastard *had* a story of his own, much less a sad one, and I asked, quickly, "What's going to happen to him now?"

He didn't answer this. He was off by himself some place.

"Funny thing," he said, and from his tone we might have been discussing the quickest way to get to Brooklyn, "when I saw the papers this morning, the first thing I asked myself was if I had anything to do with it. I felt sort of responsible."

I began to listen more carefully. The subway station was on the corner, just before us, and I stopped. He stopped, too. We were in front of a bar and he ducked slightly, peering in, but whoever he was looking for didn't seem to be there. The juke box was blasting away with something black and bouncy and I half watched the barmaid as she danced her way from the juke box to her place behind the bar. And I watched her face as she laughingly responded to something someone said to her, still keeping time to the music. When she smiled one saw the little girl, one sensed the doomed, still struggling woman beneath the battered face of the semi-whore.

"I never *give* Sonny nothing," the boy said finally, "but a long time ago I come to school high and Sonny asked me how it felt." He paused, I couldn't bear to watch him, I watched the barmaid, and I listened to the music which seemed to be causing the pavement to shake. "I told him it felt great." The music stopped, the barmaid paused and watched the juke box until the music began again. "It did."

All this was carrying me some place I didn't want to go. I certainly didn't want to know how it felt. It filled everything, the people, the houses, the music, the dark, quicksilver barmaid, with menace; and this menace was their reality.

"What's going to happen to him now?" I asked again.

"They'll send him away some place and they'll try to cure him." He shook his head. "Maybe he'll even think he's kicked the habit. Then they'll let him loose"—he gestured, throwing his cigarette into the gutter. "That's all."

"What do you mean, that's *all?*"

But I knew what he meant.

"I *mean*, that's *all*." He turned his head and looked at me, pulling down the corners of his mouth. "Don't you know what I mean?" he asked softly.

"How the hell *would* I know what you mean?" I almost whispered it, I don't know why.

"That's right," he said to the air, "how would *he* know what I mean?" He turned toward me again, patient and calm, and yet I somehow felt him shaking, shaking as though he were going to fall apart. I felt that ice in my guts again, the dread I'd felt all afternoon; and again I watched the barmaid, moving about the bar, washing glasses, and singing. "Listen. They'll let him out and then it'll just start all over again. That's what I mean."

"You mean—they'll let him out. And then he'll just start working his way back in again. You mean he'll never kick the habit. Is that what you mean?"

"That's right," he said, cheerfully. "*You* see what I mean."

"Tell me," I said at last, "why does he want to die? He must want to die, he's killing himself, why does he want to die?"

He looked at me in surprise. He licked his lips. "He don't want to die. He wants to live. Don't nobody want to die, ever."

Then I wanted to ask him—too many things. He could not have answered, or if he had, I could not have borne the answers. I started walking. "Well, I guess it's none of my business."

"It's going to be rough on old Sonny," he said. We reached the subway station. "This is your station?" he asked. I nodded. I took one step down. "Damn!" he said, suddenly. I looked up at him. He grinned again. "Damn it if I didn't leave all my money home. You ain't got a dollar on you, have you? Just for a couple of days is all."

All at once something inside gave and threatened to come pouring out of me. I didn't hate him any more. I felt that in another moment I'd start crying like a child.

"Sure," I said. "Don't sweat." I looked in my wallet and didn't have a dollar, I only had a five. "Here," I said. "That hold you?"

He didn't look at it—he didn't want to look at it. A terrible, closed look came over his face, as though he were keeping the number on the bill a secret from him and me. "Thanks," he said, and now he was dying to see me go. "Don't worry about Sonny. Maybe I'll write him or something."

"Sure," I said. "You do that. So long."

"Be seeing you," he said. I went on down the steps.

And I didn't write Sonny or send him anything for a long time. When I finally did, it was just after my little girl died, and he wrote me back a letter which made me feel like a bastard.

Here's what he said:

> Dear brother,
>
> You don't know how much I needed to hear from you. I wanted to write you many a time but I dug how much I must have hurt you and so I didn't write. But now I feel like a man who's been trying to climb up out of some deep, real deep and funky hole and just saw the sun up there, outside I got to get outside.
>
> I can't tell you much about how I got here. I mean I don't know how to tell you. I guess I was afraid of something or I was trying to escape from something and you know I have never been very strong in the head (smile). I'm glad Mama and Daddy are dead and can't see what's happened to their son and I swear if I'd known what I was doing I would never have hurt you so, you and a lot of other fine people who were nice to me and who believed in me.

> I don't want you to think it had anything to do with me being a musician. It's more than that. Or maybe less than that. I can't get anything straight in my head down here and I try not to think about what's going to happen to me when I get outside again. Sometime I think I'm going to flip and *never* get outside and sometime I think I'll come straight back. I tell you one thing, though, I'd rather blow my brains out than go through this again. But that's what they all say, so they tell me. If I tell you when I'm coming to New York and if you could meet me, I sure would appreciate it. Give my love to Isabel and the kids and I was sure sorry to hear about little Gracie. I wish I could be like Mama and say the Lord's will be done, but I don't know it seems to me that trouble is the one thing that never does get stopped and I don't know what good it does to blame it on the Lord. But maybe it does some good if you believe it.
>
> Your brother,
>
> Sonny 55

Then I kept in constant touch with him and I sent him whatever I could and I went to meet him when he came back to New York. When I saw him many things I thought I had forgotten came flooding back to me. This was because I had begun, finally, to wonder about Sonny, about the life that Sonny lived inside. This life, whatever it was, had made him older and thinner and it had deepened the distant stillness in which he had always moved. He looked very unlike my baby brother. Yet, when he smiled, when we shook hands, the baby brother I'd never known looked out from the depths of his private life, like an animal waiting to be coaxed into the light.

"How you been keeping?" he asked me.

"All right. And you?"

"Just fine." He was smiling all over his face. "It's good to see you again." 60

"It's good to see you."

The seven years difference in our ages lay between us like a chasm: I wondered if these years would ever operate between us as a bridge. I was remembering, and it made it hard to catch my breath, that I had been there when he was born; and I had heard the first words he had ever spoken. When he started to walk, he walked from our mother straight to me. I caught him just before he fell when he took the first steps he ever took in this world.

"How's Isabel?"

"Just fine. She's dying to see you."

"And the boys?" 65

"They're fine, too. They're anxious to see their uncle."

"Oh, come on. You know they don't remember me."

"Are you kidding? Of course they remember you."

He grinned again. We got into a taxi. We had a lot to say to each other, far too much to know how to begin.

As the taxi began to move, I asked, "You still want to go to India?" 70

He laughed. "You still remember that. Hell, no. This place is Indian enough for me."

"It used to belong to them," I said.

And he laughed again. "They damn sure knew what they were doing when they got rid of it."

Years ago, when he was around fourteen, he'd been all hipped on the idea of going to India. He read books about people sitting on rocks, naked, in all kinds of weather, but mostly bad, naturally, and walking barefoot through hot coals and arriving at wisdom. I used to say that it sounded to me as though they were getting away from wisdom as fast as they could. I think he sort of looked down on me for that.

75 "Do you mind," he asked, "if we have the driver drive alongside the park? On the west side—I haven't seen the city in so long."

"Of course not," I said. I was afraid that I might sound as though I were humoring him, but I hoped he wouldn't take it that way.

So we drove along, between the green of the park and the stony, lifeless elegance of hotels and apartment buildings, toward the vivid, killing streets of our childhood. These streets hadn't changed, though housing projects jutted up out of them now like rocks in the middle of a boiling sea. Most of the houses in which we had grown up had vanished, as had the stores from which we had stolen, the basements in which we had first tried sex, the rooftops from which we had hurled tin cans and bricks. But houses exactly like the houses of our past yet dominated the landscape, boys exactly like the boys we once had been found themselves smothering in these houses, came down into the streets for light and air and found themselves encircled by disaster. Some escaped the trap, most didn't. Those who got out always left something of themselves behind, as some animals amputate a leg and leave it in the trap. It might be said, perhaps, that I had escaped, after all, I was a school teacher; or that Sonny had, he hadn't lived in Harlem for years. Yet, as the cab moved uptown through streets which seemed, with a rush, to darken with dark people, and as I covertly studied Sonny's face, it came to me that what we both were seeking through our separate cab windows was that part of ourselves which had been left behind. It's always at the hour of trouble and confrontation that the missing member aches.

We hit 110th Street and started rolling up Lenox Avenue. And I'd known this avenue all my life, but it seemed to me again, as it had seemed on the day I'd first heard about Sonny's trouble, filled with a hidden menace which was its very breath of life.

"We almost there," said Sonny.

80 "Almost." We were both too nervous to say anything more.

We live in a housing project. It hasn't been up long. A few days after it was up it seemed uninhabitably new, now, of course, it's already rundown. It looks like a parody of the good, clean, faceless life—God knows the people who live in it do their best to make it a parody. The beat-looking grass lying around isn't enough to make their lives green, the hedges will never hold out the streets, and they know it. The big windows fool no one, they aren't big enough to make space out of no space. They don't bother with the windows, they watch the TV screen instead. The playground is most popular with the children who don't play at jacks, or skip rope, or roller skate, or swing, and they can be found in it after dark. We moved in partly because it's not too far from where I teach, and partly for the kids; but it's really just like the houses in which Sonny and I grew up. The same things happen, they'll have the same things to remember. The moment Sonny and I started into the house I had the feeling that I was simply bringing him back into the danger he had almost died trying to escape.

Sonny has never been talkative. So I don't know why I was sure he'd be dying to talk to me when supper was over the first night. Everything went fine, the oldest boy remembered him, and the youngest boy liked him, and Sonny had remembered to bring something for each of them; and Isabel, who is really much nicer than I am, more open and giving, had gone to a lot of trouble about dinner and was genuinely glad to see him. And she's always been able to tease Sonny in a way that I haven't. It was nice to see her face so vivid again and to hear her laugh and watch her make Sonny laugh. She wasn't, or, anyway, she didn't seem to be, at all uneasy or embarrassed. She chatted as though there were no subject which had to be avoided and she got Sonny past his first, faint stiffness. And thank God she was there, for I was filled with that icy dread again. Everything I did seemed awkward to me, and everything I said sounded freighted with hidden meaning. I was trying to remember everything I'd heard about dope addiction and I couldn't help watching Sonny for signs. I wasn't doing it out of malice. I was trying to find out something about my brother. I was dying to hear him tell me he was safe.

"Safe!" my father grunted, whenever Mama suggested trying to move to a neighborhood which might be safer for children. "Safe, hell! Ain't no place safe for kids, nor nobody."

He always went on like this, but he wasn't, ever, really as bad as he sounded, not even on weekends, when he got drunk. As a matter of fact, he was always on the lookout for "something a little better," but he died before he found it. He died suddenly, during a drunken weekend in the middle of the war, when Sonny was fifteen. He and Sonny hadn't ever got on too well. And this was partly because Sonny was the apple of his father's eye. It was because he loved Sonny so much and was frightened for him, that he was always fighting with him. It doesn't do any good to fight with Sonny. Sonny just moves back, inside himself, where he can't be reached. But the principal reason that they never hit it off is that they were so much alike. Daddy was big and rough and loud-talking, just the opposite of Sonny, but they both had—that same privacy.

Mama tried to tell me something about this, just after Daddy died. I was home on 85
leave from the army.

This was the last time I ever saw my mother alive. Just the same, this picture gets all mixed up in my mind with pictures I had of her when she was younger. The way I always see her is the way she used to be on a Sunday afternoon, say, when the old folks were talking after the big Sunday dinner. I always see her wearing pale blue. She'd be sitting on the sofa. And my father would be sitting in the easy chair, not far from her. And the living room would be full of church folks and relatives. There they sit, in chairs all around the living room, and the night is creeping up outside, but nobody knows it yet. You can see the darkness growing against the windowpanes and you hear the street noises every now and again, or maybe the jangling beat of a tambourine from one of the churches close by, but it's real quiet in the room. For a moment nobody's talking, but every face looks darkening, like the sky outside. And my mother rocks a little from the waist, and my father's eyes are closed. Everyone is looking at something a child can't see. For a minute they've forgotten the children. Maybe a kid is lying on the rug half asleep. Maybe somebody's got a kid in his lap and is absent-mindedly stroking the kid's head. Maybe there's a kid, quiet and big-eyed, curled up in a big chair in the corner. The silence, the darkness coming, and the darkness in the faces frighten the child obscurely. He hopes that the hand which strokes his forehead will never stop—will never die. He hopes that there will never come a time when the old folks won't be sitting around the living room, talking about where they've come from, and what they've seen, and what's happened to them and their kinfolk.

But something deep and watchful in the child knows that this is bound to end, is already ending. In a moment someone will get up and turn on the light. Then the old folks will remember the children and they won't talk any more that day. And when light fills the room, the child is filled with darkness. He knows that every time this happens he's moved just a little closer to that darkness outside. The darkness outside is what the old folks have been talking about. It's what they've come from. It's what they endure. The child knows that they won't talk any more because if he knows too much about what's happened to *them*, he'll know too much too soon, about what's going to happen to *him*.

The last time I talked to my mother, I remember I was restless. I wanted to get out and see Isabel. We weren't married then and we had a lot to straighten out between us.

There Mama sat, in black, by the window. She was humming an old church song, *Lord, you brought me from a long ways off*. Sonny was out somewhere. Mama kept watching the streets.

90 "I don't know," she said, "if I'll ever see you again, after you go off from here. But I hope you'll remember the things I tried to teach you."

"Don't talk like that," I said, and smiled. "You'll be here a long time yet."

She smiled, too, but she said nothing. She was quiet for a long time. And I said, "Mama, don't you worry about nothing. I'll be writing all the time, and you be getting the checks. . . ."

"I want to talk to you about your brother," she said, suddenly. "If anything happens to me he ain't going to have nobody to look out for him."

"Mama," I said, "ain't nothing going to happen to you *or* Sonny. Sonny's all right. He's a good boy and he's got good sense."

95 "It ain't a question of his being a good boy," Mama said, "nor of his having good sense. It ain't only the bad ones, nor yet the dumb ones that gets sucked under." She stopped, looking at me. "Your Daddy once had a brother," she said, and she smiled in a way that made me feel she was in pain. "You didn't never know that, did you?"

"No," I said, "I never knew that," and I watched her face.

"Oh, yes," she said, "your Daddy had a brother." She looked out of the window again. "I know you never saw your Daddy cry. But *I* did—many a time, through all these years."

I asked her, "What happened to his brother? How come nobody's ever talked about him?"

This was the first time I ever saw my mother look old.

100 "His brother got killed," she said, "when he was just a little younger than you are now. I knew him. He was a fine boy. He was maybe a little full of the devil, but he didn't mean nobody no harm."

Then she stopped and the room was silent, exactly as it had sometimes been on those Sunday afternoons. Mama kept looking out into the streets.

"He used to have a job in the mill," she said, "and, like all young folks, he just liked to perform on Saturday nights. Saturday nights, him and your father would drift around to different places, go to dances and things like that, or just sit around with people they knew, and your father's brother would sing, he had a fine voice, and play along with himself on his guitar. Well, this particular Saturday night, him and your father was coming home from some place, and they were both a little drunk and there was a moon that night, it was bright like day. Your father's brother was feeling kind of good, and he was whistling to himself, and he had his guitar slung over his shoulder. They was coming down a hill and beneath them was a road that turned off from the highway. Well, your father's brother, being always kind of frisky, decided to run down this hill, and he did, with that guitar banging and clanging behind him, and he ran across the road, and he was making water behind a tree. And your father was sort of amused at him and he was still coming down the hill, kind of slow. Then he heard a car motor and that same minute his brother stepped from behind the tree, into the road, in the moonlight. And he started to cross the road. And your father started to run down the hill, he says he don't know why. This car was full of white men. They was all drunk, and when they seen your father's brother they let out a great whoop and holler and they aimed the car straight at him. They was having fun, they just wanted to scare him, the way they do sometimes, you know. But they was drunk. And I guess the boy, being drunk, too, and scared, kind of lost his head. By the time he jumped it was too late. Your father says he heard his brother scream when the car rolled over him, and he heard the wood of that guitar when it give, and he heard them strings go flying, and he heard them white men shouting, and the car kept on a-going and it ain't stopped till this day. And, time your father got down the hill, his brother weren't nothing but blood and pulp."

Tears were gleaming on my mother's face. There wasn't anything I could say.

"He never mentioned it," she said, "because I never let him mention it before you children. Your Daddy was like a crazy man that night and for many a night thereafter. He says he never in his life seen anything as dark as that road after the lights of that car had gone away. Weren't nothing, weren't nobody on that road, just your Daddy and his brother and that busted guitar. Oh, yes. Your Daddy never did really get right again. Till the day he died he weren't sure but that every white man he saw was the man that killed his brother."

She stopped and took out her handkerchief and dried her eyes and looked 105
at me.

"I ain't telling you all this," she said, "to make you scared or bitter or to make you hate nobody. I'm telling you this because you got a brother. And the world ain't changed."

I guess I didn't want to believe this. I guess she saw this in my face. She turned away from me, toward the window again, searching those streets.

"But I praise my Redeemer," she said at last, "that He called your Daddy home before me. I ain't saying it to throw no flowers at myself, but, I declare, it keeps me from feeling too cast down to know I helped your father get safely through this world. Your father always acted like he was the roughest, strongest man on earth. And everybody took him to be like that. But if he hadn't had me there — to see his tears!"

She was crying again. Still, I couldn't move. I said, "Lord, Lord, Mama, I didn't know it was like that."

"Oh, honey," she said, "there's a lot that you don't know. But you are going to find out." She stood up from the window and came over to me. "You got to hold on to your brother," she said, "and don't let him fall, no matter what it looks like is happening to him and no matter how evil you gets with him. You going to be evil with him many a time. But don't you forget what I told you, you hear?"

"I won't forget," I said. "Don't you worry, I won't forget. I won't let nothing happen to Sonny."

My mother smiled as though she was amused at something she saw in my face. Then, "You may not be able to stop nothing from happening. But you got to let him know you's *there*."

Two days later I was married, and then I was gone. And I had a lot of things on my mind and I pretty well forgot my promise to Mama until I got shipped home on a special furlough for her funeral.

And, after the funeral, with just Sonny and me alone in the empty kitchen, I tried to find out something about him.

"What do you want to do?" I asked him.

"I'm going to be a musician," he said.

For he had graduated, in the time I had been away, from dancing to the juke box to finding out who was playing what, and what they were doing with it, and he had bought himself a set of drums.

"You mean, you want to be a drummer?" I somehow had the feeling that being a drummer might be all right for other people but not for my brother Sonny.

"I don't think," he said, looking at me very gravely, "that I'll ever be a good drummer. But I think I can play a piano."

I frowned. I'd never played the role of the oldest brother quite so seriously before, had scarcely ever, in fact, *asked* Sonny a damn thing. I sensed myself in the presence of something I didn't really know how to handle, didn't understand. So I made my frown a little deeper as I asked: "What kind of musician do you want to be?"

He grinned. "How many kinds do you think there are?"

"Be *serious*," I said.

He laughed, throwing his head back, and then looked at me. "I *am* serious."

"Well, then, for Christ's sake, stop kidding around and answer a serious question. I mean, do you want to be a concert pianist, you want to play classical music and all that, or — or what?" Long before I finished he was laughing again. "For Christ's *sake*, Sonny!"

He sobered, but with difficulty. "I'm sorry. But you sound so — *scared*!" and he was off again.

"Well, you may think it's funny now, baby, but it's not going to be so funny when you have to make your living at it, let me tell you *that*." I was furious because I knew he was laughing at me and I didn't know why.

"No," he said, very sober now, and afraid, perhaps, that he'd hurt me, "I don't want to be a classical pianist. That isn't what interests me. I mean"—he paused, looking hard at me, as though his eyes would help me to understand, and then gestured helplessly, as though perhaps his hand would help—"I mean, I'll have a lot of studying to do, and I'll have to study *everything,* but, I mean, I want to play *with*—jazz musicians." He stopped. "I want to play jazz," he said.

Well, the word had never before sounded as heavy, as real, as it sounded that afternoon in Sonny's mouth. I just looked at him and I was probably frowning a real frown by this time. I simply couldn't see, why on earth he'd want to spend his time hanging around nightclubs, clowning around on bandstands, while people pushed each other around a dance floor. It seemed—beneath him, somehow. I had never thought about it before, had never been forced to, but I suppose I had always put jazz musicians in a class with what Daddy called "good-time people."

"Are you *serious?*"

"Hell, *yes*, I'm serious." 130

He looked more helpless than ever, and annoyed, and deeply hurt.

I suggested, helpfully: "You mean—like Louis Armstrong?"

His face closed as though I'd struck him. "No. I'm not talking about none of that old-time, down home crap."

"Well, look, Sonny, I'm sorry, don't get mad. I just don't altogether get it, that's all. Name somebody—you know, a jazz musician you admire."

"Bird." 135

"Who?"

"Bird! Charlie Parker!° Don't they teach you nothing in the goddamn army?"

I lit a cigarette. I was surprised and then a little amused to discover that I was trembling. "I've been out of touch," I said. "You'll have to be patient with me. Now. Who's this Parker character?"

"He's just one of the greatest jazz musicians alive," said Sonny, sullenly, his hands in his pockets, his back to me. "Maybe *the* greatest," he added, bitterly, "that's probably why *you* never heard of him."

"All right," I said, "I'm ignorant. I'm sorry. I'll go out and buy all the cat's records right away, all right?" 140

"It don't," said Sonny, with dignity, "make any difference to me. I don't care what you listen to. Don't do me no favors."

I was beginning to realize that I'd never seen him so upset before. With another part of my mind I was thinking that this would probably turn out to be one of those things kids go through and that I shouldn't make it seem important by pushing it too hard. Still, I didn't think it would do any harm to ask: "Doesn't all this take a lot of time? Can you make a living at it?"

Charlie "Bird" Parker (1920–1955): A renowned jazz saxophonist and composer who, with Dizzy Gillespie and others, developed the jazz style "bebop." He died of pneumonia and a bleeding ulcer, both of which were exacerbated by his addiction to narcotics and alcohol.

He turned back to me and half leaned, half sat, on the kitchen table. "Everything takes time," he said, "and—well, yes, sure, I can make a living at it. But what I don't seem to be able to make you understand is that it's the only thing I want to do."

"Well, Sonny," I said gently, "you know people can't always do exactly what they *want* to do—."

145 "*No,* I don't know that," said Sonny, surprising me. "I think people *ought* to do what they want to do, what else are they alive for?"

"You getting to be a big boy," I said desperately, "it's time you started thinking about your future."

"I'm thinking about my future," said Sonny, grimly. "I think about it all the time."

I gave up. I decided, if he didn't change his mind, that we could always talk about it later. "In the meantime," I said, "you got to finish school." We had already decided that he'd have to move in with Isabel and her folks. I knew this wasn't the ideal arrangement because Isabel's folks are inclined to be dicty° and they hadn't especially wanted Isabel to marry me. But I didn't know what else to do. "And we have to get you fixed up at Isabel's."

There was a long silence. He moved from the kitchen table to the window. "That's a terrible idea. You know it yourself."

150 "Do you have a *better* idea?"

He just walked up and down the kitchen for a minute. He was as tall as I was. He had started to shave. I suddenly had the feeling that I didn't know him at all.

He stopped at the kitchen table and picked up my cigarettes. Looking at me with a kind of mocking, amused defiance, he put one between his lips. "You mind?"

"You smoking already?"

He lit the cigarette and nodded, watching me through the smoke. "I just wanted to see if I'd have the courage to smoke in front of you." He grinned and blew a great cloud of smoke to the ceiling. "It was easy." He looked at my face. "Come on, now. I bet you was smoking at my age, tell the truth."

155 I didn't say anything but the truth was on my face, and he laughed. But now there was something very strained in his laugh. "Sure. And I bet that ain't all you was doing."

He was frightening me a little. "Cut the crap," I said. "We already decided that you was going to go and live at Isabel's. Now what's got into you all of a sudden?"

"*You* decided it," he pointed out. "*I* didn't decide nothing." He stopped in front of me, leaning against the stove, arms loosely folded. "Look, brother. I don't want to stay in Harlem no more, I really don't." He was very earnest. He looked at me, then over toward the kitchen window. There was something in his eyes I'd never seen before, some thoughtfulness, some worry all his own. He rubbed the muscle of one arm. "It's time I was getting out of here."

"Where do you want to *go*, Sonny?"

"I want to join the army. Or the navy, I don't care. If I say I'm old enough, they'll believe me."

dicty: Bossy.

160 Then I got mad. It was because I was so scared. "You must be crazy. You goddamn fool, what he hell do you want to go and join the *army* for?"

"I just told you. To get out of Harlem."

"Sonny, you haven't even finished *school.* And if you really want to be a musician, how do you expect to study if you're in the *army?*"

He looked at me, trapped, and in anguish. "There's ways. I might be able to work out some kind of deal. Anyway, I'll have the G.I. Bill when I come out."

"*If* you come out." We stared at each other. "Sonny, please. Be reasonable. I know the setup is far from perfect. But we got to do the best we can."

165 "I ain't learning nothing in school," he said. "Even when I go." He turned away from me and opened the window and threw his cigarette out into the narrow alley. I watched his back. "At least, I ain't learning nothing you'd want me to learn." He slammed the window so hard I thought the glass would fly out, and turned back to me. "And I'm sick of the stink of these garbage cans!"

"Sonny," I said, "I know how you feel. But if you don't finish school now, you're going to be sorry later that you didn't." I grabbed him by the shoulders. "And you only got another year. It ain't so bad. And I'll come back and I swear I'll help you do *whatever* you want to do. Just try to put up with it till I come back. Will you please do that? For me?"

He didn't answer and he wouldn't look at me.

"Sonny. You hear me?"

He pulled away. "I hear you. But you never hear anything I say."

170 I didn't know what to say to that. He looked out of the window and then back at me. "OK," he said, and sighed. "I'll try."

Then I said, trying to cheer him up a little, "They got a piano at Isabel's. You can practice on it."

And as a matter of fact, it did cheer him up for a minute. "That's right," he said to himself, "I forgot that." His face relaxed a little. But the worry, the thoughtfulness, played on it still, the way shadows play on a face which is staring into the fire.

But I thought I'd never hear the end of that piano. At first, Isabel would write me, saying how nice it was that Sonny was so serious about his music and how, as soon as he came in from school, or wherever he had been when he was supposed to be at school, he went straight to that piano and stayed there until suppertime. And, after supper, he went back to that piano and stayed there until everybody went to bed. He was at the piano all day Saturday and all day Sunday. Then he bought a record player and started playing records. He'd play one record over and over again, all day long sometimes, and he'd improvise along with it on the piano. Or he'd play one section of the record, one chord, one change, one progression, then he'd do it on the piano. Then back to the record. Then back to the piano.

Well, I really don't know how they stood it. Isabel finally confessed that it wasn't like living with a person at all, it was like living with sound. And the sound didn't make any sense to her, didn't make any sense to any of them—naturally. They began, in a way, to be afflicted by this presence that was living in their home. It was as though Sonny were some sort of god, or monster. He moved in an atmosphere which wasn't like theirs at all. They fed him and he ate, he washed himself, he walked in and out of their door; he certainly wasn't nasty or unpleasant or rude, Sonny isn't any of those things, but it was as though he were all wrapped up in some cloud, some fire, some vision all his own, and there wasn't any way to reach him.

175 At the same time, he wasn't really a man yet, he was still a child, and they had to watch out for him in all kinds of ways. They certainly couldn't throw him out. Neither did they dare to make a great scene about that piano because even they dimly sensed, as I sensed, from so many thousands of miles away, that Sonny was at that piano playing for his life.

But he hadn't been going to school. One day a letter came from the school board and Isabel's mother got it—there had, apparently, been other letters but Sonny had torn them up. This day, when Sonny came in, Isabel's mother showed him the letter and asked where he'd been spending his time. And she finally got it out of him that he'd been down in Greenwich Village, with musicians and other characters, in a white girl's apartment. And this scared her and she started to scream at him and what came up, once she began—though she denies it to this day—was what sacrifices they were making to give Sonny a decent home and how little he appreciated it.

Sonny didn't play the piano that day. By evening, Isabel's mother had calmed down but then there was the old man to deal with, and Isabel herself. Isabel says she did her best to be calm but she broke down and started crying. She says she just watched Sonny's face. She could tell, by watching him, what was happening with him. And what was happening was that they penetrated his cloud, they had reached him. Even if their fingers had been a thousand times more gentle than human fingers ever are, he could hardly help feeling that they had stripped him naked and were spitting on that nakedness. For he also had to see that his presence, that music, which was life or death to him, had been torture for them and that they had endured it, not at all for his sake, but only for mine. And Sonny couldn't take that. He can take it a little better today than he could then but he's still not very good at it and, frankly, I don't know anybody who is.

The silence of the next few days must have been louder than the sound of all the music ever played since time began. One morning, before she went to work, Isabel was in his room for something and she suddenly realized that all of his records were gone. And she knew for certain that he was gone. And he was. He went as far as the navy would carry him. He finally sent me a postcard from some place in Greece and that was the first I knew that Sonny was still alive. I didn't see him any more until we were both back in New York and the war had long been over.

He was a man by then, of course, but I wasn't willing to see it. He came by the house from time to time, but we fought almost every time we met. I didn't like the way he carried himself, loose and dreamlike all the time, and I didn't like his friends, and his music seemed to be merely an excuse for the life he led. It sounded just that weird and disordered.

180 Then we had a fight, a pretty awful fight, and I didn't see him for months. By and by I looked him up, where he was living, in a furnished room in the Village, and I tried to make it up. But there were lots of other people in the room and Sonny just lay on his bed, and he wouldn't come downstairs with me, and he treated these other people as though they were his family and I weren't. So I got mad and then he got

mad, and then I told him that he might just as well be dead as live the way he was living. Then he stood up and he told me not to worry about him any more in life, that he *was* dead as far as I was concerned. Then he pushed me to the door and the other people looked on as though nothing were happening, and he slammed the door behind me. I stood in the hallway, staring at the door. I heard somebody laugh in the room and then the tears came to my eyes. I started down the steps, whistling to keep from crying, I kept whistling to myself, *You going to need me, baby, one of these cold, rainy days*.

I read about Sonny's trouble in the spring. Little Grace died in the fall. She was a beautiful little girl. But she only lived a little over two years. She died of polio and she suffered. She had a slight fever for a couple of days, but it didn't seem like anything and we just kept her in bed. And we would certainly have called the doctor, but the fever dropped, she seemed to be all right. So we thought it had just been a cold. Then, one day, she was up, playing. Isabel was in the kitchen fixing lunch for the two boys when they'd come in from school, and she heard Grace fall down in the living room. When you have a lot of children you don't always start running when one of them falls, unless they start screaming or something. And, this time, Gracie was quiet. Yet, Isabel says that when she heard that *thump* and then that silence, something happened to her to make her afraid. And she ran to the living room and there was little Grace on the floor, all twisted up, and the reason she hadn't screamed was that she couldn't get her breath. And when she did scream, it was the worst sound, Isabel says, that she'd ever heard in all her life, and she still hears it sometimes in her dreams. Isabel will sometimes wake me up with a low, moaning, strangling sound and I have to be quick to awaken her and hold her to me and where Isabel is weeping against me seems a mortal wound.

I think I may have written Sonny the very day that little Grace was buried. I was sitting in the living room in the dark, by myself, and I suddenly thought of Sonny. My trouble made his real.

One Saturday afternoon, when Sonny had been living with us, or anyway, been in our house, for nearly two weeks. I found myself wandering aimlessly about the living room, drinking from a can of beer, and trying to work up courage to search Sonny's room. He was out, he was usually out whenever I was home, and Isabel had taken the children to see their grandparents. Suddenly I was standing still in front of the living room window, watching Seventh Avenue. The idea of searching Sonny's room made me still. I scarcely dared to admit to myself what I'd be searching for. I didn't know what I'd do if I found it. Or if I didn't.

On the sidewalk across from me, near the entrance to a barbecue joint, some people were holding an old fashioned revival meeting. The barbecue cook, wearing a dirty white apron, his conked° hair reddish and metallic in the pale sun, and a cigarette between his lips, stood in the doorway, watching them. Kids and older people paused in their errands and stood there, along with some older men and a couple of

---

conked: Chemically straightened and greased hair.

very tough looking women who watched everything that happened on the avenue, as though they owned it, or were maybe owned by it. Well, they were watching this, too. The revival was being carried on by three sisters in black, and a brother. All they had were their voices and their Bibles and a tambourine. The brother was testifying° and while he testified two of the sisters stood together, seeming to say, amen, and the third sister walked around with the tambourine outstretched and a couple of people dropped coins into it. Then the brother's testimony ended and the sister who had been taking up the collection dumped the coins into her palm and transferred them to the pocket of her long black robe. Then she raised both hands, striking the tambourine against the air, and then against one hand, and she started to sing. And the two other sisters and the brother joined in.

185 It was strange, suddenly, to watch, though I had been seeing these meetings all my life. So, of course, had everybody else down there. Yet, they paused and watched and listened and I stood still at the window. "*'Tis the old ship of Zion*," they sang, and the sister with the tambourine kept a steady, jangling beat, "*it has rescued many a thousand!*" Not a soul under the sound of their voices was hearing this song for the first time, not one of them had been rescued. Nor had they seen much in the way of rescue work being done around them. Neither did they especially believe in the holiness of the three sisters and the brother, they knew too much about them, knew where they lived, and how. The woman with the tambourine, whose voice dominated the air, whose face was bright with joy, was divided by very little from the woman who stood watching her, a cigarette between her heavy, chapped lips, her hair a cuckoo's nest, her face scarred and swollen from many beatings, and her black eyes glittering like coal. Perhaps they both knew this, which was why, when, as rarely, they addressed each other, they addressed each other as Sister. As the singing filled the air the watching, listening faces underwent a change, the eyes focusing on something within; the music seemed to soothe a poison out of them; and time seemed, nearly, to fall away from the sullen, belligerent, battered faces, as though they were fleeing back to their first condition, while dreaming of their last. The barbecue cook half shook his head and smiled, and dropped his cigarette and disappeared into his joint. A man fumbled in his pockets for change and stood holding it in his hand impatiently, as though he had just remembered a pressing appointment further up the avenue. He looked furious. Then I saw Sonny, standing on the edge of the crowd. He was carrying a wide, flat notebook with a green cover, and it made him look, from where I was standing, almost like a schoolboy. The coppery sun brought out the copper in his skin, he was very faintly smiling, standing very still. Then the singing stopped, the tambourine turned into a collection plate again. The furious man dropped in his coins and vanished, so did a couple of the women, and Sonny dropped some change in the plate, looking directly at the woman with a little smile. He started across the avenue, toward the house. He has a slow, loping walk, something like the way Harlem hipsters walk, only he's imposed on this his own half-beat. I had never really noticed it before.

---

testifying: Publicly proclaiming one's religious experience and belief.

I stayed at the window, both relieved and apprehensive. As Sonny disappeared from my sight, they began singing again. And they were still singing when his key turned in the lock.

"Hey," he said.

"Hey, yourself. You want some beer?"

"No. Well, maybe." But he came up to the window and stood beside me, looking out. "What a warm voice," he said.

They were singing *If I could only hear my mother pray again!*

"Yes," I said, "and she can sure beat that tambourine."

"But what a terrible song," he said, and laughed. He dropped his notebook on the sofa and disappeared into the kitchen. "Where's Isabel and the kids?"

"I think they went to see their grandparents. You hungry?"

"No." He came back into the living room with his can of beer. "You want to come some place with me tonight?"

I sensed, I don't know how, that I couldn't possibly say no. "Sure. Where?"

He sat down on the sofa and picked up his notebook and started leafing through it. "I'm going to sit in with some fellows in a joint in the Village."

"You mean, you're going to play, tonight?"

"That's right." He took a swallow of his beer and moved back to the window. He gave me a sidelong look. "If you can stand it."

"I'll try," I said.

He smiled to himself and we both watched as the meeting across the way broke up. The three sisters and the brother, heads bowed, were singing *God be with you till we meet again*. The faces around them were very quiet. Then the song ended. The small crowd dispersed. We watched the three women and the lone man walk slowly up the avenue.

"When she was singing before," said Sonny, abruptly, "her voice reminded me for a minute of what heroin feels like sometimes—when it's in your veins. It makes you feel sort of warm and cool at the same time. And distant. And—and sure." He sipped his beer, very deliberately not looking at me. I watched his face. "It makes you feel—in control. Sometimes you've got to have that feeling."

"Do you?" I sat down slowly in the easy chair.

"Sometimes." He went to the sofa and picked up his notebook again. "Some people do."

"In order," I asked, "to play?" And my voice was very ugly, full of contempt and anger.

"Well"—he looked at me with great, troubled eyes, as though, in fact, he hoped his eyes would tell me things he could never otherwise say—"they *think* so. And *if* they think so—!"

"And what do *you* think?" I asked.

He sat on the sofa and put his can of beer on the floor. "I don't know," he said, and I couldn't be sure if he were answering my question or pursuing his thoughts. His face didn't tell me. "It's not so much to *play*. It's to *stand* it, to be able to make it at all. On any level." He frowned and smiled! "In order to keep from shaking to pieces."

"But these friends of yours," I said, "they seem to shake themselves to pieces pretty goddamn fast."

"Maybe." He played with the notebook. And something told me that I should curb my tongue, that Sonny was doing his best to talk, that I should listen. "But of course you only know the ones that've gone to pieces. Some don't—or at least they haven't *yet* and that's just about all *any* of us can say. He paused. "And then there are some who just live, really, in hell, and they know it and they see what's happening and they go right on. I don't know." He sighed, dropped the notebook, folded his arms. "Some guys, you can tell from the way they play, they on something *all* the time. And you can see that, well, it makes something real for them. But of course," he picked up his beer from the floor and sipped it and put the can down again, "they *want* to, too, you've got to see that. Even some of them that say they don't—*some*, not all."

210 "And what about you?" I asked—I couldn't help it. "What about you? Do *you* want to?"

He stood up and walked to the window and I remained silent for a long time. Then he sighed. "Me," he said. Then: "While I was downstairs before, on my way here, listening to that woman sing, it struck me all of a sudden how much suffering she must have had to go through—to sing like that. It's *repulsive* to think you have to suffer that much."

I said: "But there's no way not to suffer—is there, Sonny?"

"I believe not," he said and smiled, "but that's never stopped anyone from trying." He looked at me. "Has it?" I realized, with this mocking look, that there stood between us, forever, beyond the power of time or forgiveness, the fact that I had held silence—so long!—when he had needed human speech to help him. He turned back to the window. "No, there's no way not to suffer. But you try all kinds of ways to keep from drowning in it, to keep on top of it, and to make it seem—well, like *you*. Like you did something, all right, and now you're suffering for it. You know?" I said nothing. "Well you know," he said, impatiently, "why *do* people suffer? Maybe it's better to do something to give it a reason, *any* reason."

"But we just agreed," I said, "that there's no way not to suffer. Isn't it better, then, just to—take it?"

215 "But nobody just takes it," Sonny cried, "that's what I'm telling you! *Everybody* tries not to. You're just hung up on the way some people try—it's not *your* way!"

The hair on my face began to itch, my face felt wet. "That's not true," I said, "that's not true. I don't give a damn what other people do, I don't even care how they suffer. I just care how *you* suffer." And he looked at me. "Please believe me," I said, "I don't want to see you—die—trying not to suffer."

"I won't," he said flatly, "die trying not to suffer. At least, not any faster than anybody else."

"But there's no need," I said, trying to laugh, "is there? in killing yourself."

I wanted to say more, but I couldn't. I wanted to talk about will power and how life could be—well, beautiful. I wanted to say that it was all within; but was it? or, rather, wasn't that exactly the trouble? And I wanted to promise that I would never fail him again. But it would all have sounded—empty words and lies.

220 So I made the promise to myself and prayed that I would keep it.

"It's terrible sometimes, inside," he said, "that's what's the trouble. You walk these streets, black and funky and cold, and there's not really a living ass to talk to, and there's nothing shaking, and there's no way of getting it out—that storm inside. You can't talk it and you can't make love with it, and when you finally try to get with it and play it, you realize *nobody's* listening. So *you've* got to listen. You got to find a way to listen."

And then he walked away from the window and sat on the sofa again, as though all the wind had suddenly been knocked out of him. "Sometimes you'll do *anything* to play, even cut your mother's throat." He laughed and looked at me. "Or your brother's." Then he sobered. "Or your own." Then: "Don't worry. I'm all right now and I think I'll be all right. But I can't forget—where I've been. I don't mean just the physical place I've been, I mean where I've *been*. And *what* I've been."

"What have you been, Sonny?" I asked.

He smiled—but sat sideways on the sofa, his elbow resting on the back, his fingers playing with his mouth and chin, not looking at me. "I've been something I didn't recognize, didn't know, I could be. Didn't know anybody could be." He stopped, looking inward, looking helplessly young, looking old. "I'm not talking about it now because I feel *guilty* or anything like that—maybe it would be better if I did, I don't know. Anyway, I can't really talk about it. Not to you, not to anybody," and now he turned and faced me. "Sometimes, you know, and it was actually when I was most *out* of the world, I felt that I was in it, that I was *with* it, really, and I could *play* or I didn't really have to *play*, it just came out of me, it was there. And I don't know how I played, thinking about it now, but I know I did awful things, those times, sometimes, to people. Or it wasn't that I *did* anything to them—it was that they weren't real." He picked up the beer can; it was empty; he rolled it between his palms: "And other times—well, I needed a fix, I needed to find a place to lean, I needed to clear a space to *listen*—and I couldn't find it, and I—went crazy, I did terrible things to *me*, I was terrible *for* me." He began pressing the beer can between his hands, I watched the metal begin to give. It glittered, as he played with it like a knife, and I was afraid he would cut himself, but I said nothing. "Oh well, I can never tell you. I was all by myself at the bottom of something, stinking and sweating and crying and shaking, and I smelled it, you know? *my* stink, and I thought I'd die if I couldn't get away from it and yet, all the same, I knew that everything I was doing was just locking me in with it. And I didn't know," he paused, still flattening the beer can, "I didn't know, I still *don't* know, something kept telling me that maybe it was good to smell your own stink, but I didn't think that *that* was what I'd been trying to do—and—who can stand it?" and he abruptly dropped the ruined beer can, locking at me with a small, still smile, and then rose, walking to the window as though it were the lodestone rock. I watched his face, he watched the avenue. "I couldn't tell you when Mama died—but the reason I wanted to leave Harlem so bad was to get away from drugs. And then, when I ran away, that's what I was running from—really. When I came back, nothing had changed, *I* hadn't changed, I was just—older." And he stopped, drumming with his fingers on the windowpane. The sun had vanished, soon darkness would fall. I watched his face. "It can come again," he said, almost as though speaking to himself. Then he turned to me. "It can come again," he repeated. "I just want you to know that."

225 "All right," I said, at last. "So it can come again. All right."

He smiled, but the smile was sorrowful. "I had to try to tell you," he said.

"Yes," I said, "I understand that."

"You're my brother," he said, looking straight at me, and not smiling at all.

"Yes," I repeated, "yes I understand that."

230 He turned back to the window, looking out. "All that hatred down there," he said, "all that hatred and misery and love. It's a wonder it doesn't blow the avenue apart."

We went to the only nightclub on a short, dark street, downtown. We squeezed through the narrow, chattering, jampacked bar to the entrance of the big room, where the bandstand was. And we stood there for a moment, for the lights were very dim in this room and we couldn't see. Then, "Hello, boy," said the voice and an enormous black man, much older than Sonny or myself, erupted out of all that atmospheric lighting and put an arm around Sonny's shoulder. "I been sitting right here," he said, "waiting for you."

He had a big voice, too, and heads in the darkness turned toward us.

Sonny grinned and pulled a little away, and said, "Creole, this is my brother. I told you about him."

Creole shook my hand. "I'm glad to meet you, son," he said, and it was clear that he was glad to meet me *there*, for Sonny's sake. And he smiled: "You got a real musician in *your* family," and he took his arm from Sonny's shoulders and slapped him, lightly, affectionately, with the back of his hand.

235 "Well. Now I've heard it all," said a voice behind us. This was another musician, and a friend of Sonny's, a coal-black, cheerful-looking man, built close to the ground. He immediately began confiding to me, at the top of his lungs, the most terrible things about Sonny, his teeth gleaming like a lighthouse and his laugh coming up out of him like the beginning of an earthquake. And it turned out that everyone at the bar knew Sonny, or almost everyone; some were musicians, working there, or nearby, or not working, some were simply hangers on, and some were there to hear Sonny play. I was introduced to all of them and they were all very polite to me. Yet, it was clear that, for them, I was only Sonny's brother. Here, I was in Sonny's world. Or, rather: his kingdom. Here, it was not even a question that his veins bore royal blood.

They were going to play soon and Creole installed me, by myself, at a table in a dark corner. Then I watched them, Creole, and the little black man, and Sonny, and the others, while they horsed around, standing just below the bandstand. The light from the bandstand spilled just a little short of them and watching them laughing and gesturing and moving about, I had the feeling that they, nevertheless, were being most careful not to step into that circle of light too suddenly; that if they moved into the light too suddenly, without thinking, they would perish in flame. Then, while I watched, one of them, the small black man, moved into the light and crossed the bandstand and started fooling around with his drums. Then — being funny and being, also, extremely ceremonious — Creole took Sonny by the arm and led him to the piano. A woman's voice called Sonny's name and a few hands started clapping. And Sonny, also being funny and being ceremonious, and so touched, I think, that he could have cried, but neither hiding it nor showing it, riding it like a man, grinned, and put both hands to his heart and bowed from the waist.

Creole then went to the bass fiddle and a lean, very bright-skinned brown man jumped up on the bandstand and picked up his horn. So there they were, and the atmosphere on the bandstand and in the room began to change and tighten. Someone stepped up to the microphone and announced them. Then there were all kinds of murmurs. Some people at the bar shushed others. The waitress ran around, frantically getting in the last orders, guys and chicks got closer to each other, and the lights on the bandstand, on the quartet, turned to a kind of indigo. Then they all looked different there. Creole looked about him for the last time, as though he were making certain that all his chickens were in the coop, and then he—jumped and struck the fiddle. And there they were.

All I know about music is that not many people ever really hear it. And even then, on the rare occasions when something opens within, and the music enters, what we mainly hear, or hear corroborated, are personal, private, vanishing evocations. But the man who creates the music is hearing something else, is dealing with the roar rising from the void and imposing order on it as it hits the air. What is evoked in him, then, is of another order, more terrible because it has no words, and triumphant, too, for that same reason. And his triumph, when he triumphs, is ours. I just watched Sonny's face. His face was troubled, he was working hard, but he wasn't with it. And I had the feeling that, in a way, everyone on the bandstand was waiting for him, both waiting for him and pushing him along. But as I began to watch Creole, I realized that it was Creole who held them all back. He had them on a short rein. Up there, keeping the heat with his whole body, wailing on the fiddle, with his eyes half closed, he was listening to everything, but he was listening to Sonny. He was having a dialogue with Sonny. He wanted Sonny to leave the shoreline and strike out for the deep water. He was Sonny's witness that deep water and drowning were not the same thing—he had been there, and he knew. And he wanted Sonny to know. He was waiting for Sonny to do the things on the keys which would let Creole know that Sonny was in the water.

And, while Creole listened, Sonny moved, deep within, exactly like someone in torment. I had never before thought of how awful the relationship must be between the musician and his instrument. He has to fill it, this instrument, with the breath of life, his own. He has to make it do what he wants it to do. And a piano is just a piano. It's made out of so much wood and wires and little hammers and big ones, and Ivory. While there's only so much you can do with it, the only way to find this out is to try, to try and make it do everything.

And Sonny hadn't been near a piano for over a year. And he wasn't on much 240
better terms with his life, not the life that stretched before him now. He and the piano stammered, started one way, got scared, stopped, started another way, panicked, marked time, started again, then seemed to have found a direction, panicked again, got stuck. And the face I saw on Sonny I'd never seen before. Everything had been burned out of it, and, at the same time, things usually hidden were being burned in, by the fire and fury of the battle which was occurring in him up there.

Yet, watching Creole's face as they neared the end of the first set, I had the feeling that something had happened, something I hadn't heard. Then they finished, there was scattered applause, and then, without an instant's warning. Creole started into something else, it was almost sardonic, it was *Am I Blue*.° And, as though he commanded, Sonny began to play. Something began to happen. And Creole let out the reins. The dry, low, black man said something awful on the drums, Creole answered, and the drums talked back. Then the horn insisted, sweet and high, slightly detached perhaps, and Creole listened, commenting now and then, dry, and driving, beautiful and calm and old. Then they all came together again, and Sonny was part of the family again. I could tell this from his face. He seemed to have found, right there beneath his fingers, a damn brand-new piano. It seemed that he couldn't get over it. Then, for a while, just being happy with Sonny, they seemed to be agreeing with him that brand-new pianos certainly were a gas.

Then Creole stepped forward to remind them that what they were playing was the blues. He hit something in all of them, he hit something in me, myself, and the music tightened and deepened, apprehension began to beat the air. Creole began to tell us what the blues were all about. They were not about anything very new. He and his boys up there were keeping it new, at the risk of ruin, destruction, madness, and death, in order to find new ways to make us listen. For, while the tale of how we suffer, and how we are delighted, and how we may triumph is never new, it always must be heard. There isn't any other tale to tell, it's the only light we've got in all this darkness.

And this tale, according to that face, that body, those strong hands on those strings, has another aspect in every country, and a new depth in every generation. Listen, Creole seemed to be saying, listen, Now these are Sonny's blues. He made the little black man on the drums know it, and the bright, brown man on the horn. Creole wasn't trying any longer to get Sonny in the water. He was wishing him Godspeed. Then he stepped back, very slowly, filling the air with the immense suggestion that Sonny speak for himself.

Then they all gathered around Sonny and Sonny played. Every now and again one of them seemed to say, amen. Sonny's fingers filled the air with life, his life. But that life contained so many others. And Sonny went all the way back, he really began with the spare, flat statement of the opening phrase of the song. Then he began to make it his. It was very beautiful because it wasn't hurried and it was no longer a lament. I seemed to hear with what burning he had made it his, and what burning we had yet to make it ours, how we could cease lamenting. Freedom lurked around us and I understood, at last, that he could help us to be free if we would listen, that he would never be free until we did. Yet, there was no battle in his face now, I heard what he had gone through, and would continue to go through until he came to rest in earth. He had made it his: that long line, of which we knew only Mama and Daddy. And he was giving it back, as everything must be given back, so that, passing through death, it can live forever. I saw my mother's face again, and felt, for the first time, how the stones of the road she had walked on must have bruised her feet. I saw

Am I Blue: A jazz standard.

the moonlit road where my father's brother died. And it brought something else back to me, and carried me past it, I saw my little girl again and felt Isabel's tears again, and I felt my own tears begin to rise. And I was yet aware that this was only a moment, that the world waited outside, as hungry as a tiger, and that trouble stretched above us, longer than the sky.

Then it was over. Creole and Sonny let out their breath, both soaking wet, and 245
grinning. There was a lot of applause and some of it was real. In the dark, the girl came by and I asked her to take drinks to the bandstand. There was a long pause, while they talked up there in the indigo light and after awhile I saw the girl put a Scotch and milk on top of the piano for Sonny. He didn't seem to notice it, but just before they started playing again, he sipped from it and looked toward me, and nodded. Then he put it back on top of the piano. For me, then, as they began to play again, it glowed and shook above my brother's head like the very cup of trembling.°

* * *

T. CORAGHESSAN BOYLE (1948–)

Greasy Lake (1985)

It's about a mile down on the dark side of Route 88.

—Bruce Springsteen

There was a time when courtesy and winning ways went out of style, when it was good to be bad, when you cultivated decadence like a taste. We were all dangerous characters then. We wore torn-up leather jackets, slouched around with toothpicks in our mouths, sniffed glue and ether and what somebody claimed was cocaine. When we wheeled our parents' whining station wagons out into the street we left a patch of rubber half a block long. We drank gin and grape juice, Tango, Thunderbird, and Bali Hai. We were nineteen. We were bad. We read André Gide° and struck elaborate poses to show that we didn't give a shit about anything. At night, we went up to Greasy Lake.

Through the center of town, up the strip, past the housing developments and shopping malls, street lights giving way to the thin streaming illumination of the headlights, trees crowding the asphalt in a black unbroken wall: that was the way out to Greasy Lake. The Indians had called it Wakan, a reference to the clarity of its waters. Now it was fetid and murky, the mud banks glittering with broken glass and

See Isaiah 51:17, 22–23: "Awake, awake, stand up, O Jerusalem, which hast drunk at the hand of the Lord the cup of his fury; thou hast drunken the dregs of the cup of trembling, and wrung them out . . . Behold, I have taken out of thine hand the cup of trembling, even the dregs of the cup of my fury; thou shalt no more drink it again: But I will put it into the hand of them that affect thee . . ."

André Gide: French novelist and critic (1869–1951) whose work—much of it semiautobiographical—examines the conflict between desire and discipline and shows individuals battling conventional morality.

strewn with beer cans and the charred remains of bonfires. There was a single ravaged island a hundred yards from shore, so stripped of vegetation it looked as if the air force had strafed it. We went up to the lake because everyone went there, because we wanted to snuff the rich scent of possibility on the breeze, watch a girl take off her clothes and plunge into the festering murk, drink beer, smoke pot, howl at the stars, savor the incongruous full-throated roar of rock and roll against the primeval susurrus° of frogs and crickets. This was nature.

I was there one night, late, in the company of two dangerous characters. Digby wore a gold star in his right ear and allowed his father to pay his tuition at Cornell; Jeff was thinking of quitting school to become a painter/musician/head-shop proprietor. They were both expert in the social graces, quick with a sneer, able to manage a Ford with lousy shocks over a rutted and gutted blacktop road at eighty-five while rolling a joint as compact as a Tootsie Roll Pop stick. They could lounge against a bank of booming speakers and trade "man"s with the best of them or roll out across the dance floor as if their joints worked on bearings. They were slick and quick and they wore their mirror shades at breakfast and dinner, in the shower, in closets and caves. In short, they were bad.

I drove. Digby pounded the dashboard and shouted along with Toots & the Maytals while Jeff hung his head out the window and streaked the side of my mother's Bel Air with vomit. It was early June, the air soft as a hand on your cheek, the third night of summer vacation. The first two nights we'd been out till dawn, looking for something we never found. On this, the third night, we'd cruised the strip sixty-seven times, been in and out of every bar and club we could think of in a twenty-mile radius, stopped twice for bucket chicken and forty-cent hamburgers, debated going to a party at the house of a girl Jeff's sister knew, and chucked two dozen raw eggs at mailboxes and hitchhikers. It was 2:00 A.M.; the bars were closing. There was nothing to do but take a bottle of lemon-flavored gin up to Greasy Lake.

5 The taillights of a single car winked at us as we swung into the dirt lot with its tufts of weed and washboard corrugations; '57 Chevy, mint, metallic blue. On the far side of the lot, like the exoskeleton of some gaunt chrome insect, a chopper leaned against its kickstand. And that was it for excitement: some junkie half-wit biker and a car freak pumping his girlfriend. Whatever it was we were looking for, we weren't about to find it at Greasy Lake. Not that night.

But then all of a sudden Digby was fighting for the wheel. "Hey, that's Tony Lovett's car! Hey!" he shouted, while I stabbed at the brake pedal and the Bel Air nosed up to the gleaming bumper of the parked Chevy. Digby leaned on the horn, laughing, and instructed me to put my brights on. I flicked on the brights. This was hilarious. A joke. Tony would experience premature withdrawal and expect to be confronted by grim-looking state troopers with flashlights. We hit the horn, strobed the lights, and then jumped out of the car to press our witty faces to Tony's windows; for all we knew we might even catch a glimpse of some little fox's tit, and then we could slap backs with red-faced Tony, roughhouse a little, and go on to new heights of adventure and daring.

susurrus: A whispering or rustling sound.

The first mistake, the one that opened the whole floodgate, was losing my grip on the keys. In the excitement, leaping from the car with the gin in one hand and a roach clip in the other, I spilled them in the grass—in the dark, rank, mysterious nighttime grass of Greasy Lake. This was a tactical error, as damaging and irreversible in its way as Westmoreland's decision to dig in at Khe Sanh.° I felt it like a jab of intuition, and I stopped there by the open door, peering vaguely into the night that puddled up round my feet.

The second mistake—and this was inextricably bound up with the first—was identifying the car as Tony Lovett's. Even before the very bad character in greasy jeans and engineer boots ripped out of the driver's door, I began to realize that this chrome blue was much lighter than the robin's-egg of Tony's car, and that Tony's car didn't have rear-mounted speakers. Judging from their expressions, Digby and Jeff were privately groping toward the same inevitable and unsettling conclusion as I was.

In any case, there was no reasoning with this bad greasy character—clearly he was a man of action. The first lusty Rockette° kick of his steel-toed boot caught me under the chin, chipped my favorite tooth, and left me sprawled in the dirt. Like a fool, I'd gone down on one knee to comb the stiff hacked grass for the keys, my mind making connections in the most dragged-out, testudineous° way, knowing that things had gone wrong, that I was in a lot of trouble, and that the lost ignition key was my grail and my salvation. The three or four succeeding blows were mainly absorbed by my right buttock and the tough piece of bone at the base of my spine.

Meanwhile, Digby vaulted the kissing bumpers and delivered a savage kung-fu 10
blow to the greasy character's collarbone. Digby had just finished a course in martial arts for phys-ed credit and had spent the better part of the past two nights telling us apocryphal tales of Bruce Lee types and of the raw power invested in lightning blows shot from coiled wrists, ankles, and elbows. The greasy character was unimpressed. He merely backed off a step, his face like a Toltec mask, and laid Digby out with a single whistling roundhouse blow. . . but by now Jeff had got into the act, and I was beginning to extricate myself from the dirt, a tinny compound of shock, rage, and impotence wadded in my throat.

Jeff was on the guy's back, biting at his ear. Digby was on the ground, cursing. I went for the tire iron I kept under the driver's seat. I kept it there because bad characters always keep tire irons under the driver's seat, for just such an occasion as this. Never mind that I hadn't been involved in a fight since sixth grade, when a kid with a sleepy eye and two streams of mucus depending from his nostrils hit me in the knee with a Louisville slugger,° never mind that I'd touched the tire iron exactly twice before, to change tires: it was there. And I went for it.

Khe Sanh: In late 1967, North Vietnamese and Viet Cong forces mounted a strong attack against American troops at Khe Sanh, thereby causing General William C. Westmoreland, commander of United States forces in Vietnam, to "dig in" to defend an area of relatively little tactical importance.

Rockette: The reference is to the Rockettes, a dance troupe at New York's Radio City Music Hall noted for precision and cancan-like high kicks.

testudineous: Slow, like the pace of a tortoise.

Louisville slugger: A popular brand of baseball bat.

I was terrified. Blood was beating in my ears, my hands were shaking, my heart turning over like a dirtbike in the wrong gear. My antagonist was shirtless, and a single cord of muscle flashed across his chest as he bent forward to peel Jeff from his back like a wet overcoat. "Motherfucker," he spat, over and over, and I was aware in that instant that all four of us—Digby, Jeff, and myself included—were chanting "motherfucker, motherfucker," as if it were a battle cry. (What happened next? the detective asks the murderer from beneath the turned-down brim of his porkpie hat. I don't know, the murderer says, something came over me. Exactly.)

Digby poked the flat of his hand in the bad character's face and I came at him like a kamikaze, mindless, raging, stung with humiliation—the whole thing, from the initial boot in the chin to this murderous primal instant involving no more than sixty hyperventilating, gland-flooding seconds—I came at him and brought the tire iron down across his ear. The effect was instantaneous, astonishing. He was a stunt man and this was Hollywood, he was a big grimacing toothy balloon and I was a man with a straight pin. He collapsed. Wet his pants. Went loose in his boots.

A single second, big as a zeppelin, floated by. We were standing over him in a circle, gritting our teeth, jerking our necks, our limbs and hands and feet twitching with glandular discharges. No one said anything. We just stared down at the guy, the car freak, the lover, the bad greasy character laid low. Digby looked at me; so did Jeff. I was still holding the tire iron, a tuft of hair clinging to the crook like dandelion fluff, like down. Rattled, I dropped it in the dirt, already envisioning the headlines, the pitted faces of the police inquisitors, the gleam of handcuffs, clank of bars, the big black shadows rising from the back of the cell . . . when suddenly a raw torn shriek cut through me like all the juice in all the electric chairs in the country.

15 It was the fox. She was short, barefoot, dressed in panties and a man's shirt. "Animals!" she screamed, running at us with her fists clenched and wisps of blow-dried hair in her face. There was a silver chain round her ankle, and her toenails flashed in the glare of the headlights. I think it was the toenails that did it. Sure, the gin and the cannabis and even the Kentucky Fried may have had a hand in it, but it was the sight of those flaming toes that set us off—the toad emerging from the loaf in *Virgin Spring*,° lipstick smeared on a child: she was already tainted. We were on her like Bergman's deranged brothers—see no evil, hear none, speak none—panting, wheezing, tearing at her clothes, grabbing for flesh. We were bad characters, and we were scared and hot and three steps over the line—anything could have happened.

It didn't.

Before we could pin her to the hood of the car, our eyes masked with lust and greed and the purest primal badness, a pair of headlights swung into the lot. There we were, dirty, bloody, guilty, dissociated from humanity and civilization, the first of the Ur-crimes° behind us, the second in progress, shreds of nylon panty and spandex

---

Virgin Spring: A film by Swedish director Ingmar Bergman.

Ur-crimes: Primitive crimes.

brassiere dangling from our fingers, our flies open, lips licked — there we were, caught in the spotlight. Nailed.

We bolted. First for the car, and then, realizing we had no way of starting it, for the woods. I thought nothing. I thought escape. The headlights came at me like accusing fingers. I was gone.

Ram-bam-bam, across the parking lot, past the chopper and into the feculent undergrowth at the lake's edge, insects flying up in my face, weeds whipping, frogs and snakes and red-eyed turtles splashing off into the night: I was already ankle-deep in muck and tepid water and still going strong. Behind me, the girl's screams rose in intensity, disconsolate, incriminating, the screams of the Sabine women,° the Christian martyrs, Anne Frank° dragged from the garret. I kept going, pursued by those cries, imagining cops and bloodhounds. The water was up to my knees when I realized what I was doing: I was going to swim for it. Swim the breadth of Greasy Lake and hide myself in the thick clot of woods on the far side. They'd never find me there.

I was breathing in sobs, in gasps. The water lapped at my waist as I looked out over 20
the moon-burnished ripples, the mats of algae that clung to the surface like scabs. Digby and Jeff had vanished. I paused. Listened. The girl was quieter now, screams tapering to sobs, but there were male voices, angry, excited, and the high-pitched ticking of the second car's engine. I waded deeper, stealthy, hunted, the ooze sucking at my sneakers. As I was about to take the plunge — at the very instant I dropped my shoulder for the first slashing stroke — I blundered into something. Something unspeakable, obscene, something soft, wet, moss-grown. A patch of weed? A log? When I reached out to touch it, it gave like a rubber duck, it gave like flesh.

In one of those nasty little epiphanies for which we are prepared by films and TV and childhood visits to the funeral home to ponder the shrunken painted forms of dead grandparents, I understood what it was that bobbed there so inadmissibly in the dark. Understood, and stumbled back in horror and revulsion, my mind yanked in six different directions (I was nineteen, a mere child, an infant, and here in the space of five minutes I'd struck down one greasy character and blundered into the waterlogged carcass of a second), thinking, The keys, the keys, why did I have to go and lose the keys? I stumbled back, but the muck took hold of my feet — a sneaker snagged, balance lost — and suddenly I was pitching face forward into the buoyant black mass, throwing out my hands in desperation while simultaneously conjuring the image of reeking frogs and muskrats revolving in slicks of their own deliquescing° juices. AAAAArrrgh! I shot from the water like a torpedo, the dead man rotating to expose a mossy beard and eyes cold as the

---

Sabine women: According to legend, members of an ancient Italian tribe abducted by Romans who took them for wives. The "Rape of the Sabine Women" has been depicted by various artists, most notably by seventeenth-century French painter Nicolas Poussin.

Anne Frank: German Jewish girl (1929–1945) whose family hid in an attic in Amsterdam during the Nazi occupation of the Netherlands. Frank, who along with her family was discovered by storm troopers and sent to die at the concentration camp at Belsen, is famous for her diary, which recounts her days in hiding. A new version of the diary containing five missing pages surfaced in 1998.

deliquescing: Melting.

moon. I must have shouted out, thrashing around in the weeds, because the voices behind me suddenly became animated.

"What was that?"

"It's them, it's them: they tried to, tried to . . . *rape* me!" Sobs.

A man's voice, flat Midwestern accent. "You sons a bitches, we'll kill you!"

25 Frogs, crickets.

Then another voice, harsh, *r*-less, Lower East Side: "Motherfucker!" I recognized the verbal virtuosity of the bad greasy character in the engineer boots. Tooth chipped, sneakers gone, coated in mud and slime and worse, crouching breathless in the weeds waiting to have my ass thoroughly and definitively kicked and fresh from the hideous stinking embrace of a three-days-dead-corpse, I suddenly felt a rush of joy and vindication: the son of a bitch was alive! Just as quickly, my bowels turned to ice. "Come on out of there, you pansy mothers!" the bad greasy character was screaming. He shouted curses till he was out of breath.

The crickets started up again, then the frogs. I held my breath. All at once there was a sound in the reeds, a swishing, a splash: thunk-a-thunk. They were throwing rocks. The frogs fell silent. I cradled my head. Swish, swish, thunk-a-thunk. A wedge of feldspar the size of a cue ball glanced off my knee. I bit my finger.

It was then that they turned to the car. I heard a door slam, a curse, and then the sound of the headlights shattering—almost a good-natured sound, celebratory, like corks popping from the necks of bottles. This was succeeded by the dull booming of the fenders, metal on metal, and then the icy crash of the windshield. I inched forward, elbows and knees, my belly pressed to the muck, thinking of guerrillas and commandos and *The Naked and the Dead.*° I parted the weeds and squinted the length of the parking lot.

The second car—it was a Trans-Am—was still running, its high beams washing the scene in a lurid stagy light. Tire iron flailing, the greasy bad character was laying into the side of my mother's Bel Air like an avenging demon, his shadow riding up the trunks of the trees. Whomp. Whomp. Whomp-whomp. The other two guys—blond types, in fraternity jackets—were helping out with tree branches and skull-sized boulders. One of them was gathering up bottles, rocks, muck, candy wrappers, used condoms, pop-tops, and other refuse and pitching it through the window on the driver's side. I could see the fox, a white bulb behind the windshield of the '57 Chevy. "Bobbie," she whined over the thumping, "come *on*." The greasy character paused a moment, took one good swipe at the left taillight, and then heaved the tire iron halfway across the lake. Then he fired up the '57 and was gone.

30 Blond head nodded at blond head. One said something to the other, too low for me to catch. They were no doubt thinking that in helping to annihilate my mother's car they'd committed a fairly rash act, and thinking too that there were three bad characters connected with that very car watching them from the woods. Perhaps

---

The Naked and the Dead: A popular and critically praised 1948 novel by Norman Mailer depicting Army life among U.S. soldiers during World War II.

other possibilities occurred to them as well—police, jail cells, justices of the peace, reparations, lawyers, irate parents, fraternal censure. Whatever they were thinking, they suddenly dropped branches, bottles, and rocks and sprang for their car in unison, as if they'd choreographed it. Five seconds. That's all it took. The engine shrieked, the tires squealed, a cloud of dust rose from the rutted lot and then settled back on darkness.

I don't know how long I lay there, the bad breath of decay all around me, my jacket heavy as a bear, the primordial ooze subtly reconstituting itself to accommodate my upper thighs and testicles. My jaws ached, my knee throbbed, my coccyx° was on fire. I contemplated suicide, wondered if I'd need bridgework, scraped the recesses of my brain for some sort of excuse to give my parents—a tree had fallen on the car, I was blindsided by a bread truck, hit and run, vandals had got to it while we were playing chess at Digby's. Then I thought of the dead man. He was probably the only person on the planet worse off than I was. I thought about him, fog on the lake, insects chirring eerily, and felt the tug of fear, felt the darkness opening up inside me like a set of jaws. Who was he, I wondered, this victim of time and circumstance bobbing sorrowfully in the lake at my back. The owner of the chopper, no doubt, a bad older character come to this. Shot during a murky drug deal, drowned while drunkenly frolicking in the lake. Another headline. My car was wrecked; he was dead.

When the eastern half of the sky went from black to cobalt and the trees began to separate themselves from the shadows, I pushed myself up from the mud and stepped out into the open. By now the birds had begun to take over for the crickets, and dew lay slick on the leaves. There was a smell in the air, raw and sweet at the same time, the smell of the sun firing buds and opening blossoms. I contemplated the car. It lay there like a wreck along the highway, like a steel sculpture left over from a vanished civilization. Everything was still. This was nature.

I was circling the car, as dazed and bedraggled as the sole survivor of an air blitz, when Digby and Jeff emerged from the trees behind me. Digby's face was crosshatched with smears of dirt; Jeff's jacket was gone and his shirt was torn across the shoulder. They slouched across the lot, looking sheepish, and silently came up beside me to gape at the ravaged automobile. No one said a word. After a while Jeff swung open the driver's door and began to scoop the broken glass and garbage off the seat. I looked at Digby. He shrugged. "At least they didn't slash the tires," he said.

It was true: the tires were intact. There was no windshield, the headlights were staved in, and the body looked as if it had been sledgehammered for a quarter a shot at the county fair, but the tires were inflated to regulation pressure. The car was drivable. In silence, all three of us bent to scrape the mud and shattered glass from the interior. I said nothing about the biker. When we were finished, I reached in my pocket for the keys, experienced a nasty stab of recollection, cursed myself, and turned to search the grass. I spotted them almost immediately, no more than five feet from the open door, glinting like jewels in the first tapering shaft of sunlight. There

coccyx: Tailbone.

was no reason to get philosophical about it: I eased into the seat and turned the engine over.

35 It was at that precise moment that the silver Mustang with the flame decals rumbled into the lot. All three of us froze; then Digby and Jeff slid into the car and slammed the door. We watched as the Mustang rocked and bobbed across the ruts and finally jerked to a halt beside the forlorn chopper at the far end of the lot. "Let's go," Digby said. I hesitated, the Bel Air wheezing beneath me.

Two girls emerged from the Mustang. Tight jeans, stiletto heels, hair like frozen fur. They bent over the motorcycle, paced back and forth aimlessly, glanced once or twice at us, and then ambled over to where the reeds sprang up in a green fence round the perimeter of the lake. One of them cupped her hands to her mouth. "Al," she called, "Hey, Al!"

"Come on," Digby hissed. "Let's get out of here."

But it was too late. The second girl was picking her way across the lot, unsteady on her heels, looking up at us and then away. She was older — twenty-five or -six — and as she came closer we could see there was something wrong with her: she was stoned or drunk, lurching now and waving her arms for balance. I gripped the steering wheel as if it were the ejection lever of a flaming jet, and Digby spat out my name, twice, terse and impatient.

"Hi," the girl said.

40 We looked at her like zombies, like war veterans, like deaf-and-dumb pencil peddlers.

She smiled, her lips cracked and dry. "Listen," she said, bending from the waist to look in the window, "you guys seen Al?" Her pupils were pinpoints, her eyes glass. She jerked her neck. "That's his bike over there — Al's. You seen him?"

Al. I didn't know what to say. I wanted to get out of the car and retch, I wanted to go home to my parents' house and crawl into bed. Digby poked me in the ribs. "We haven't seen anybody," I said.

The girl seemed to consider this, reaching out a slim veiny arm to brace herself against the car. "No matter," she said, slurring the *t*'s, "he'll turn up." And then, as if she'd just taken stock of the whole scene — the ravaged car and our battered faces, the desolation of the place — she said: "Hey, you guys look like some pretty bad characters — been fightin', huh?" We stared straight ahead, rigid as catatonics. She was fumbling in her pocket and muttering something. Finally she held out a handful of tablets in glassine wrappers: "Hey, you want to party, you want to do some of these with me and Sarah?"

I just looked at her. I thought I was going to cry. Digby broke the silence. "No, thanks," he said, leaning over me. "Some other time."

45 I put the car in gear and it inched forward with a groan, shaking off pellets of glass like an old dog shedding water after a bath, heaving over the ruts on its worn springs, creeping toward the highway. There was a sheen of sun on the lake. I looked back. The girl was still standing there, watching us, her shoulders slumped, hand outstretched.

* * *

CHITRA BANERJEE DIVAKARUNI (1956–)

The Disappearance (1995)

At first when they heard about the disappearance, people didn't believe it.

Why, we saw her just yesterday at the Ram Ratan Indian Grocery, friends said, picking out radishes for pickling. And wasn't she at the Mountain View park with her little boy last week, remember, we waved from our car and she waved back, she was in that blue *salwaar-kameez,*° yes, she never did wear American clothes. And the boy waved too, he must be, what, two and a half? Looks just like her with those big black eyes, that dimple. What a shame, they said, it's getting so that you aren't safe anywhere in this country nowadays.

Because that's what everyone suspected, including the husband. Crime. Otherwise, he said to the investigating policeman (he had called the police that very night), how could a young Indian woman wearing a yellow-flowered *kurta*° and Nike walking shoes just *disappear?* She'd been out for her evening walk, she took one every day after he got back from the office. Yes, yes, always alone, she said that was her time for herself. (He didn't quite understand that, but he was happy to watch his little boy, play ball with him, perhaps, until she returned to serve them dinner.)

Did you folks have a quarrel, asked the policeman, looking up from his notepad with a frown, and the husband looked directly back into his eyes and said, No, of course we didn't.

Later he would think about what the policeman had asked, while he sat in front of 5
his computer in his office, or while he lay in the bed which still seemed to smell of her. (But surely that was his imagination—the linen had been washed already.) He *had* told the truth about them not having a quarrel, hadn't he? (He prided himself on being an honest man, he often told his son how important it was not to lie, see what happened to Pinocchio's nose. And even now when the boy asked him where Mama was, he didn't say she had gone on a trip, as some of his friends' wives had advised him. I don't know, he said. And when the boy's thin face would crumple, want Mama, when she coming back, he held him in his lap awkwardly and tried to stroke his hair, like he had seen his wife do, but he couldn't bring himself to say what the boy needed to hear, *soon-soon*. I don't know, he said over and over.)

They hadn't really had a fight. She wasn't, thank God, the quarrelsome type, like some of his friends' wives. Quiet. That's how she was, at least around him, although sometimes when he came home unexpectedly he would hear her singing to her son, her voice slightly off-key but full and confident. Or laughing as she chased him around the family room, Mama's going to get you, get you, both of them shrieking with delight until they saw him. Hush now, she would tell the boy, settle down, and they would walk over sedately to give him his welcome-home kiss.

---

salwaar-kameez: Form of dress consisting of pajama-like pants, gathered at the waist and ankles; usually worn under a long, loose tunic.

kurta: A long shirt, usually knee length, worn over drawstring trousers.

He couldn't complain, though. Wasn't that what he had specified when his mother started asking, When are you getting married, I'm getting old, I want to see a grandson before I die.

If you can find me a quiet, pretty girl, he wrote, not brash, like Calcutta girls are nowadays, not with too many western ideas. Someone who would be relieved to have her husband make the major decisions. But she had to be smart, at least a year of college, someone he could introduce to his friends with pride.

He'd flown to Calcutta to view several suitable girls that his mother had picked out. But now, thinking back, he can only remember her. She had sat, head bowed, jasmine plaited into her hair, silk sari draped modestly over her shoulders, just like all the other prospective brides he'd seen. Nervous, he'd thought, yearning to be chosen. But when she'd glanced up there had been a cool, considering look in her eyes. Almost disinterested, almost as though *she* were wondering if he would make a suitable spouse. He had wanted her then, had married her within the week in spite of his mother's protests (had she caught that same look?) that something about the girl just didn't feel *right*.

10 He was a good husband. No one could deny it. He let her have her way, indulged her, even. When the kitchen was remodeled, for example, and she wanted pink and gray tiles even though he preferred white. Or when she wanted to go to Yosemite Park instead of Reno, although he knew he would be dreadfully bored among all those bearshit-filled trails and dried-up waterfalls. Once in a while, of course, he had to put his foot down, like when she wanted to get a job or go back to school or buy American clothes. But he always softened his no's with a remark like, What for, I'm here to take care of you, or, You look so much prettier in your Indian clothes, so much more feminine. He would pull her onto his lap and give her a kiss and a cuddle which usually ended with him taking her to the bedroom.

That was another area where he'd had to be firm. Sex. She was always saying, Please, not tonight, I don't feel up to it. He didn't mind that. She was, after all, a well-bred Indian girl. He didn't expect her to behave like those American women he sometimes watched on X-rated videos, screaming and biting and doing other things he grew hot just thinking about. But her reluctance went beyond womanly modesty. After dinner for instance she would start on the most elaborate household projects, soaping down the floors, changing the liners in cabinets. The night before she disappeared she'd started cleaning windows, taken out the Windex and the rags as soon as she'd put the boy to bed, even though he said, Let's go. Surely he couldn't be blamed for raising his voice at those times (though never so much as to wake his son), or for grabbing her by the elbow and pulling her to the bed, like he did that last night. He was always careful not to hurt her, he prided himself on that. Not even a little slap, not like some of the men he'd known growing up, or even some of his friends now. And he always told himself he'd stop if she really begged him, if she cried. After some time, though, she would quit struggling and let him do what he wanted. But that was nothing new. That could have nothing to do with the disappearance.

Two weeks passed and there was no news of the woman, even though the husband had put a notice in the *San Jose Mercury* as well as a half-page ad in *India West*, which he photocopied and taped to neighborhood lampposts. The ad had a photo of her, a close-up taken in too-bright sunlight where she gazed gravely at something beyond the camera. WOMAN MISSING, read the ad. REWARD $100,000. (How on earth would he come up with that kind of money, asked his friends. The husband confessed that it would be difficult, but he'd manage somehow. His wife was more important to him, after all, than all the money in the world. And to prove it he went to the bank the very same day and brought home a sheaf of forms to fill so that he could take out a second mortgage on the house.) He kept calling the police station, too, but the police weren't much help. They were working on it, they said. They'd checked the local hospitals and morgues, the shelters. They'd even sent her description to other states. But there were no leads. It didn't look very hopeful.

So finally he called India and over a faulty long-distance connection that made his voice echo eerily in his ear told his mother what had happened. My poor boy, she cried, left all alone (the word flickered unpleasantly across his brain, *left, left*), how can you possibly cope with the household and a child as well. And when he admitted that yes, it was very difficult, could she perhaps come and help out for a while if it wasn't too much trouble, she had replied that of course she would come right away and stay as long as he needed her, and what was all this American nonsense about too much trouble, he was her only son, wasn't he. She would contact the wife's family too, she ended, so he wouldn't have to deal with that awkwardness.

Within a week she had closed up the little flat she had lived in since her husband's death, got hold of a special family emergency visa, and was on her way. Almost as though she'd been waiting for something like this to happen, said some of the women spitefully. (These were his wife's friends, though maybe acquaintances would be a more accurate word. His wife had liked to keep to herself, which had been just fine with him. He was glad, he'd told her several times, that she didn't spend hours chattering on the phone like the other Indian wives.)

He was angry when this gossip reached him (perhaps because he'd had the same 15
insidious thought for a moment when, at the airport, he noticed how happy his mother looked, her flushed excited face appearing suddenly young). Really, he said to his friends, some people see only what they *want* to see. Didn't *they* think it was a good thing she'd come over? Oh yes, said his friends. Look how well the household was running now, the furniture dusted daily, laundry folded and put into drawers (his mother, a smart woman, had figured out the washing machine in no time at all). She cooked all his favorite dishes, which his wife had never managed to learn quite right, and she took *such* good care of the little boy, walking him to the park each afternoon, bringing him into her bed when he woke up crying at night. (He'd told her once or twice that his wife had never done that, she had this idea about the boy needing to be independent. What nonsense, said his mother.) Lucky man, a couple of his friends added and he silently agreed, although later he thought it was ironic that they would say that about a man whose wife had disappeared.

As the year went on, the husband stopped thinking as much about the wife. It wasn't that he loved her any less, or that the shock of her disappearance was less acute. It was just that it wasn't on his mind all the time. There would be stretches of time—when he was on the phone with an important client, or when he was watching after-dinner TV or driving his son to kiddie gym class—when he would forget that his wife was gone, that he had had a wife at all. And even when he remembered that he had forgotten, he would experience only a slight twinge, similar to what he felt in his teeth when he drank something too cold too fast. The boy, too, didn't ask as often about his mother. He was sleeping through the nights again, he had put on a few pounds (because he was finally being fed right, said the grandmother), and he had started calling her "Ma," just like his father did.

So it seemed quite natural for the husband to, one day, remove the photographs of his wife from the frames that sat on the mantelpiece and replace them with pictures of himself and his little boy that friends had taken on a recent trip to Great America, and also one of the boy on his grandma's lap, holding a red birthday balloon, smiling (she said) exactly like his father used to at that age. He put the old pictures into a manila envelope and slid them to the back of a drawer, intending to show them to his son when he grew up. The next time his mother asked (as she had been doing ever since she got there), shall I put away all those saris and *kameezes*, it'll give you more space in the closet, he said, if you like. When she said, it's now over a year since the tragedy, shouldn't we have a prayer service done at the temple, he said OK. And when she told him, you really should think about getting married again, you're still young, and besides, the boy needs a mother, shall I contact second aunt back home, he remained silent but didn't disagree.

Then one night while cooking cauliflower curry, her specialty, his mother ran out of *hing*,° which was, she insisted, essential to the recipe. The Indian grocery was closed, but the husband remembered that sometimes his wife used to keep extra spices on the top shelf. So he climbed on a chair to look. There were no extra spices, but he did find something he had forgotten about, an old tea tin in which he'd asked her to hide her jewelry in case the house ever got burgled. Nothing major was ever kept there. The expensive wedding items were all stored in a vault. Still, the husband thought it would be a good idea to take them into the bank in the morning.

But when he picked up the tin it felt surprisingly light, and when he opened it, there were only empty pink nests of tissue inside.

20 He stood there holding the tin for a moment, not breathing. Then he reminded himself that his wife had been a careless woman. He'd often had to speak to her about leaving things lying around. The pieces could be anywhere—pushed to the back of her makeup drawer or forgotten under a pile of books in the spare room where she used to spend inordinate amounts of time reading. Nevertheless he was not himself the rest of the evening, so much so that his mother said, What happened, you're awfully quiet, are you all right, your face looks funny. He told her he was fine, just a little pain in the chest area. Yes, he would make an appointment with the doctor tomorrow, no, he wouldn't forget, now could she please leave him alone for a while.

The next day he took the afternoon off from work, but he didn't go to the doctor. He went to the bank. In a small stuffy cubicle that smelled faintly of mold, he opened

hing: An Indian spice.

his safety deposit box to find that all her jewelry was gone. She hadn't taken any of the other valuables.

The edges of the cubicle seemed to fade and darken at the same time, as though the husband had stared at a lightbulb for too long. He ground his fists into his eyes and tried to imagine her on that last morning, putting the boy in his stroller and walking the twenty minutes to the bank (they only had one car, which he took to work; they could have afforded another, but why, he said to his friends, when she didn't even know how to drive). Maybe she had sat in this very cubicle and lifted out the emerald earrings, the pearl choker, the long gold chain. He imagined her wrapping the pieces carefully in plastic bags, the thin, clear kind one got at the grocery for vegetables, then slipping them into her purse. Or did she just throw them in anyhow, the strands of the necklace tangling, the brilliant green stones clicking against each other in the darkness inside the handbag, the boy laughing and clapping his hands at this new game.

At home that night he couldn't eat any dinner, and before he went to bed he did thirty minutes on the dusty exercise bike that sat in the corner of the family room. Have you gone crazy, asked his mother. He didn't answer. When he finally lay down, the tiredness did not put him to sleep as he had hoped. His calves ached from the unaccustomed strain, his head throbbed from the images that would not stop coming, and the bedclothes, when he pulled them up to his neck, smelled again of his wife's hair.

Where was she now? And with whom? Because surely she couldn't manage on her own. He'd always thought her to be like the delicate purple passion-flower vines that they'd put up on trellises along their back fence, and once, early in the marriage, had presented her with a poem he'd written about this. He remembered how, when he held out the sheet to her, she'd stared at him for a long moment and a look he couldn't quite read had flickered in her eyes. Then she'd taken the poem with a small smile. He went over and over all the men she might have known, but they (mostly his Indian friends) were safely married and still at home, every one.

25 The bed felt hot and lumpy. He tossed his feverish body around like a caught animal, punched the pillow, threw the blanket to the floor. Even thought, for a wild moment, of shaking the boy awake and asking him, *Who did your mama see?* And as though he had an inbuilt antenna that picked up his father's agitation, in the next room the boy started crying (which he hadn't done for months), shrill screams that left him breathless. And when his father and grandmother rushed to see what the problem was, he pushed them from him with all the strength in his small arms, saying, Go way, don't want you, want Mama, want Mama.

After the boy had been dosed with gripe water° and settled in bed again, the husband sat alone in the family room with a glass of brandy. He wasn't a drinker. He believed that alcohol was for weak men. But somehow he couldn't face the rumpled bed just yet, the pillows wrested onto the floor. The unknown areas of his wife's existence yawning blackly around him like chasms. Should he tell the police, he wondered, would it do any good? What if somehow his friends came to know? *Didn't I tell you, right from the first,* his mother would say. And anyway it was possible she was

---

gripe water: A traditional European remedy for colic.

already dead, killed by a stranger from whom she'd hitched a ride, or by a violent, jealous lover. He felt a small, bitter pleasure at the thought, and then a pang of shame.

Nevertheless he made his way to the dark bedroom (a trifle unsteadily; the drink had made him light-headed) and groped in the bottom drawer beneath his underwear until he felt the coarse manila envelope with her photos. He drew it out and, without looking at them, tore the pictures into tiny pieces. Then he took them over to the kitchen, where the trash compactor was.

The roar of the compactor seemed to shake the entire house. He stiffened, afraid his mother would wake and ask what was going on, but she didn't. When the machine ground to a halt, he took a long breath. Finished, he thought. Finished. Tomorrow he would contact a lawyer, find out the legal procedure for remarriage. Over dinner he would mention to his mother, casually, that it was OK with him if she wanted to contact second aunt. Only this time he didn't want a college-educated woman. Even good looks weren't that important. A simple girl, maybe from their ancestral village. Someone whose family wasn't well off, who would be suitably appreciative of the comforts he could provide. Someone who would be a real mother to his boy.

He didn't know then that it wasn't finished. That even as he made love to his new wife (a plump, cheerful girl, good-hearted, if slightly unimaginative), or helped his daughters with their homework, or disciplined his increasingly rebellious son, he would wonder about *her*. Was she alive? Was she happy? With a sudden anger that he knew to be irrational, he would try to imagine her body tangled in swaying kelp at the bottom of the ocean where it had been flung. Bloated. Eaten by fish. But all he could conjure up was the intent look on her face when she rocked her son back and forth, singing a children's rhyme in Bengali, *Khoka jabe biye korte, shonge chhasho dhol, my little boy is going to be married, six hundred drummers*. Years later, when he was an old man living in a home for seniors (his second wife dead, his daughters moved away to distant towns, his son not on speaking terms with him), he would continue to be dazzled by that brief unguarded joy in her face, would say to himself, again, how much she must have hated me to choose to give *that* up.

30 But he had no inkling of any of this yet. So he switched off the trash compactor with a satisfied click, the sense of a job well done and, after taking a shower (long and very hot, the way he liked it, the hard jets of water turning the skin of his chest a dull red), went to bed and fell immediately into a deep, dreamless sleep.

* * *

LOUISE ERDRICH (1954–)

Sister Godzilla (2001)

The door banged shut, and then the children were alone with their sixth-grade teacher. It was the first day of school, in the fall of 1963. The habits of Franciscan nuns still shrouded all but their faces, so each of the new nun's features was emphasized, read forty times over in astonishment. Outlined in a stiff white frame of starched linen, Sister's eyes, nose, and mouth leaped out, a mask from a dream, a great rawboned jackal's muzzle.

"Oh, Christ," Toddy Crieder said, just loud enough for Dot to hear.

Dot Adare, a troublemaker, knew Toddy was in love with her and usually ignored him, but the nun's extreme ugliness was irresistible.

"Godzilla," she whispered.

The teacher's name was Sister Mary Anita Groff. She was young, in her twenties 5
or thirties, and so swift of movement, for all her hulking size, that walking from the back of the room to the front, she surprised her students, made them picture an athlete's legs and muscles concealed in the flow of black wool. When she swept the air in a gesture meant to include them all in her opening remarks, her hands fixed their gazes. They were the opposite of her face. Her hands were beautiful, as white as milk glass, the fingers straight and tapered. They were the hands in the hallway print of Mary underneath the cross. They were the hands of the Apostles, cast in plastic and lit at night on the tops of television sets. Praying hands.

Ballplayer's hands. She surprised them further by walking onto the graveled yard at recess, her neckpiece cutting hard into the flesh beneath her heavy jaw. When, with a matter-of-fact grace, she pulled from the sleeve of her gown a mitt of dark mustard-colored leather and raised it, a thrown softball dropped in. Her skill was obvious. Good players rarely stretch or change their expressions. They simply tip their hands toward the ball like magnets, and there it is. As a pitcher, Mary Anita was a swift of wool, as graceful as the windblown cape of Zorro,° an emotional figure that stirred Dot so thoroughly that as she pounded home plate—a rubber dish mat—and beat the air twice in practice swings, choked up on the handle, tried to concentrate, Dot knew she would have no choice but to slam a home run.

She did not. In fact, she whiffed, in three strikes, never ticking the ball or fouling. Purely disgusted with herself, she sat on the edge of the bike rack and watched as Sister gave a few balls away and pitched easy hits to the rest of the team. It was as if the two had sensed from the beginning what was to come. Or, then again, perhaps Mary Anita's information came from Dot's former teachers, living in the red-brick convent across the road. Hard to handle. A smart-off. Watch out when you turn your back. They were right. After recess, her pride burned, Dot sat at her desk and drew a dinosaur draped in a nun's robe, its mouth open in a roar. The teeth, long and jagged, grayish-white, held her attention. She worked so hard on the picture that she barely noticed as the room hushed around her. She felt the presence, though, the shadow of attention that dropped over her as Mary Anita stood watching. As a mark of her arrogance, Dot kept drawing.

She shaded in the last tooth and leaned back to frown at her work. The page was plucked into the air before she could pretend to cover it. No one made a sound. Dot's heart beat with excitement.

"You will remain after school," the nun pronounced.

The last half hour passed. The others filed out the door. And then the desk in 10
front of Dot filled suddenly. There was the paper, the carefully rendered dinosaur caught in mid-roar. Dot stared at it furiously, her mind a blur of anticipation. She was not afraid.

"Look at me," Mary Anita said.

Zorro: Fictional hero known for his long black cape.

Dot found that she didn't want to, that she couldn't. Then her throat filled. Her face was on fire. Her lids hung across her eyeballs like lead shades. She traced the initials carved into her desktop.

"Look at me," Mary Anita said to her again, and Dot's gaze was drawn upward, upward on a string, until she met the eyes of her teacher, deep brown, electrically sad. Their very stillness shook Dot.

"I'm sorry," she said.

When those two unprecedented words dropped from her lips, Dot knew, beyond reason and past bearing, that something terrible had occurred. She felt dizzy. The blood rushed to her head so fast that her ears ached, yet the tips of her fingers fell asleep. Her eyelids prickled and her nose wept, but at the same time her mouth went dry. Her body was a thing of extremes, contradicting itself.

"When I was young," Sister Mary Anita said, "as young as you are, I felt a great deal of pain when I was teased about my looks. I've long since accepted my . . . deformity. A prognathic jaw runs in our family, and I share it with an uncle. But I must admit, the occasional insult, or a drawing such as yours, still hurts."

Dot began to mumble and then stopped, desperate. Sister Mary Anita waited, and then handed her her own handkerchief.

"I'm sorry," Dot said again. She wiped her nose. The square of white material was cool and fresh. "Can I go now?"

"Of course not," Mary Anita said.

Dot was confounded. The magical two words, an apology, had dropped from her lips. Yet more was expected. What?

"I want you to understand something," the nun said. "I've told you how I feel. And I expect that you will never hurt me again."

The nun waited, and waited, until their eyes met. Then Dot's mouth fell wide. Her eyes spilled over. She knew that the strange feelings that had come upon her were the same feelings that Mary Anita had felt. Dot had never felt another person's feelings, never in her life.

"I won't do anything to hurt you," she blubbered passionately. "I'll kill myself first."

"I'm sure that will not be necessary," Sister Mary Anita said.

Dot tried to rescue her pride then, by turning away very quickly. Without permission, she ran out the schoolroom door, down the steps, and on into the street, where at last the magnetic force of the encounter weakened, and suddenly she could breathe. Even that was different, though. As she walked, she began to realize that her body was still fighting itself. Her lungs filled with air like two bags, but every time they did so, a place underneath them squeezed so painfully that the truth suddenly came, clear.

"I love her now," she blurted out. She stopped on a crack, stepping on it, sickened. "Oh, God, I am in love."

Toddy Crieder was a hollow-chested, envious boy whose reputation had never recovered from the time he was sent home for eating tree bark. In the third grade he had put two crayons up his nose, pretend tusks. The pink one got stuck, and Toddy had to visit the clinic. This year, already, his stomach had been pumped in the emergency room. Dot despised him, but that only seemed to fuel his adoration of her.

Coming into the schoolyard the second day, a bright, cool morning, Toddy ran up to Dot, his thin legs knocking.

"Yeah," he cried. "Godzilla! Not bad, Adare."

He wheeled off, the laces of his tennis shoes dragging. Dot looked after him and 30
felt the buzz inside her head begin. How she wanted to stuff that name back into her mouth, or at least Toddy's mouth.

"I hope you trip and murder yourself!" Dot screamed.

But Toddy did not trip. For all of his clumsiness, he managed to stay upright, and as Dot stood rooted in the center of the walk, she saw him whiz from clump to clump of children, laughing and gesturing, filling the air with small and derisive sounds. Sister Mary Anita swept out the door, a wooden-handled brass bell in her hand, and when she shook it up and down, the children, who played together in twos and threes, swung toward her and narrowed or widened their eyes and turned eagerly to one another. Some began to laugh. It seemed to Dot that all of them did, in fact, and that the sound, jerked from their lips, was large, uncanny, totally and horribly delicious.

"Godzilla, Godzilla," they called under their breath. "Sister Godzilla."

Before them on the steps, the nun continued to smile into their faces. She did not hear them—yet. But Dot knew she would. Over the bell her eyes were brilliantly dark and alive. Her horrid jagged teeth showed in a smile when she saw Dot, and Dot ran to her, thrusting a hand into her lunch bag and grabbing the cookies that her mother had made from whatever she could find around the house—raisins, congealed Malt-O-Meal, the whites of eggs.

"Here!" Dot shoved a sweet, lumpy cookie into the nun's hand. It fell apart, 35
distracting Sister as the children pushed past.

The students seemed to forget the name off and on all week. Some days they would move on to new triumphs or disasters—other teachers occupied them, or some small event occurred in the classroom. But then Toddy Crieder would lope and careen among them at recess, would pump his arms and pretend to roar behind Sister Mary Anita's back as she stepped up to the plate. As she swung and connected with the ball and gathered herself to run, her veil lifting, the muscles in her shoulders like the curved hump of a raptor's wings. Toddy would move along behind her, rolling his legs the way Godzilla did in the movie. In her excitement, dashing base to base, her feet long and limber in black laced shoes, Mary Anita did not notice. But Dot looked on, the taste of a penny caught in her throat.

"Snakes live in holes. Snakes are reptiles. These are Science Facts." Dot read aloud to the class from her Discovery science book. "Snakes are not wet. Some snakes lay eggs. Some have live young."

"Very good," Sister said. "Can you name other reptiles?" Dot's tongue fused to the back of her throat.

"No," she croaked.

"Anyone else?" Sister asked. 40

Toddy Crieder raised his hand. Sister recognized him.

"How about Godzilla?"

Gasps. Small noises of excitement. Mouths agape. Admiration for Toddy's nerve rippled through the rows of children like a wind across a field. Sister Mary Anita's great jaw opened, opened, and then snapped shut. Her shoulders shook. No one knew what to do at first. Then she laughed. It was a high-pitched, almost birdlike sound, a thin laugh like the highest notes on the piano. The children all hesitated, and then they laughed with her, even Toddy Crieder. Eyes darting from one child to the next, to Dot, Toddy laughed.

Dot's eyes crossed with urgency. When Sister Mary Anita turned to new work, Dot crooked her arm beside her like a piston and leaned across Toddy's desk.

"I'm going to give you one right in the breadbasket," she said.

With a precise boxer's jab she knocked the wind out of Toddy, left him gasping, and turned to the front, face clear, as Sister began to speak.

Furious sunlight. Black cloth. Dot sat on the iron trapeze, the bar pushing a sore line into the backs of her legs. As she swung, she watched Sister Mary Anita. The wind was harsh, and the nun wore a pair of wonderful gloves, black, the fingers cut off of them so that her hands could better grip the bat. The ball arced toward her sinuously and dropped. Her bat caught it with a thick, clean sound, and off it soared. Mary Anita's habit° swirled open behind her. The cold bit her cheeks red. She swung to third, glanced, panting, over her shoulder, and then sped home. She touched down lightly and bounded off.

Dot's arms felt heavy, weak, and she dropped from the trapeze and went to lean against the brick wall of the school building. Her heart thumped in her ears. She saw what she would do when she grew up: declare her vocation, enter the convent. She and Sister Mary Anita would live in the nuns' house together, side by side. They would eat, work, eat, cook. To relax, Sister Mary Anita would hit pop flies and Dot would catch them.

Someday, one day, Dot and Mary Anita would be walking, their hands in their sleeves, long habits flowing behind.

"Dear Sister," Dot would say, "remember that old nickname you had the year you taught the sixth grade?"

"Why, no," Sister Mary Anita would say, smiling at her. "Why, no."

And Dot would know that she had protected her, kept her from harm.

It got worse. Dot wrote some letters, tore them up. Her hand shook when Sister passed her in the aisle, and her eyes closed, automatically, as she breathed in the air that closed behind the nun. Soap—a harsh soap. Faint carbolic mothballs. That's what she smelled like. Dizzying. Dot's fists clenched. She pressed her knuckles to her eyes and very loudly excused herself. She went to the girls' bathroom and stood in a stall. Her life was terrible. The thing was, she didn't want to be a nun.

"I don't want to!" she whispered, desperate, to the whitewashed tin walls that shuddered if a girl bumped them. "There must be another way."

She would have to persuade Mary Anita to forsake her vows, to come and live with Dot and her mother in the house just past the edge of town. How would she start, how would she persuade her teacher?

---

habits: Garb worn by traditional nuns.

Someone was standing outside the stall. Dot opened the door a bit and stared into the great craggy face.

"Are you feeling all right? Do you need to go home?" Sister Mary Anita was concerned.

Fire shot through Dot's limbs. The girls' bathroom, a place of secrets, of frosted glass, its light mute and yet brilliant, paralyzed her. But she gathered herself. Here was her chance, as if God had given it to her.

"Please," Dot said, "let's run away together!"

Sister paused. "Are you having troubles at home?"

"No," Dot said.

Sister's milk-white hand came through the doorway and covered Dot's forehead. Dot's anxious thoughts throbbed against the lean palm. Staring into the eyes of the nun, Dot gripped the small metal knob on the inside of the door and pushed. Then she felt herself falling forward, slowly turning like a leaf in the wind, upheld and buoyant in the peaceful roar. It was as though she would never reach Sister's arms, but when she did, she came back with a jolt.

"You are ill," Sister said. "Come to the office, and we'll call your mother."

As Dot had known it would, perhaps from that moment in the girls' bathroom, the day came. The day of her reckoning.

Outside, in the morning schoolyard, after mass and before first bell, everyone crowded around Toddy Crieder. In his arms he held a wind-up tin Godzilla, a big toy, almost knee-high, a green-and-gold replica painted with a fierce eye for detail. The scales were perfect overlapping crescents, and the eyes were large and manic, pitch-black, oddly human. Toddy had pinned a sort of cloak on the thing, a black scarf. Dot's arms thrust through the packed shoulders, but the bell rang, and Toddy stowed the toy under his coat. His eyes picked Dot from the rest.

"I had to send for this!" he cried. The punch hadn't turned him against Dot, only hardened his resolve to please her. He vanished through the heavy wine-red doors of the school. Dot stared at the ground. The world went stark, the colors harsh in her eyes. The small brown pebbles of the playground leaped off the tarred and sealed earth. She took a step. The stones seemed to crack and whistle under her feet.

"Last bell!" Sister Mary Anita called. "You'll be late!"

Morning prayer. The pledge. Toddy drew out the suspense of his audience, enjoying the glances and whispers. The toy was in his desk. Every so often he lifted the lid and then looked around to see how many children were watching him duck inside to make adjustments. By the time Sister started the daily reading lesson, the tension in the room was so acute that not even Toddy could bear it any longer.

The room was large, high-ceilinged, floored with slats of polished wood. Round lights hung on thick chains, and the great rectangular windows let through enormous sheaves of radiance. This large class had been in the room for more than two years. Dot had spent most of every day in the room. She knew its creaks, the muted dunk of desks rocking out of floor bolts, the mad thumping in the radiators like the sound of a thousand imprisoned elves, and so she heard and immediately registered the click and grind of Toddy's wind-up key. Sister Mary Anita did not. The teacher turned to the chalkboard, her book open on the desk and began to write instructions for the children to copy.

She was absorbed, calling out the instructions as she wrote. Her arm swept up and down, it seemed to Dot, in a frighteningly innocent joy. She was inventing a lesson, some way of doing things, not a word of which was being taken in. All eyes were on the third row, where Toddy Crieder sat. All eyes were on his hand as he wound the toy up to its limit and bent over and set it on the floor. Then the eyes were on the toy itself, as Toddy lifted his hand away and the thing moved forward on its own.

The scarf it wore did not hamper the beast's progress, the regular thrash of its legs. The tiny claw hands beat forward like pistons and the thick metal tail whipped from side to side as the toy moved down the center of the aisle toward the front of the room, toward Sister Mary Anita, who stood, back turned, immersed in her work at the board.

Dot had gotten herself placed in the first row, to be closer to her teacher, and so she saw the creature up close just before it headed into the polished open space of floor at the front of the room. Its powerful jaws thrust from the black scarf; its great teeth were frozen, exhibited in a terrible smile. Its painted eyes had an eager and purposeful look.

Its movement faltered as it neared Mary Anita. The children caught their breath, but the thing inched forward, made slow and fascinating progress, directly toward the hem of her garment. She did not seem to notice. She continued to talk, to write, circling numbers and emphasizing certain words with careful underlines. And as she did so, as the moment neared, Dot's brain finally rang. She jumped as though it were the last bell of the day. She vaulted from her desk. Two steps took her across that gleaming space of wood at the front of the room. But just as she bent down to scoop the toy to her chest, a neat black boot slashed, inches from her nose. Sister Mary Anita had whirled, the chalk fixed in her hand. Daintily, casually, she had lifted her habit and kicked the toy dinosaur into the air. The thing ascended, pedaling its clawed feet, the scarf blown back like a sprung umbrella. The trajectory was straight and true. The toy knocked headfirst into the ceiling and came back down in pieces. The children ducked beneath the rain of scattered tin. Only Dot and Mary Anita stood poised, unmoving, focused on the moment between them.

Dot could look nowhere but at her teacher. But when she lifted her eyes this time, Sister Mary Anita was not looking at her. She had turned her face away, the rough cheek blotched as if it had borne a slap, the gaze hooded and set low. Sister walked to the window, her back again to Dot, to the class, and as the laughter started, uncomfortable and groaning at first, then shriller, fuller, becoming its own animal, Dot felt an unrecoverable tenderness boil up in her. Inwardly she begged the nun to turn and stop the noise. But Sister did not. She let it wash across them both without mercy. Dot lost sight of her unspeakable profile as Mary Anita looked out into the yard. Bathed in brilliant light, the nun's face went as blank as a sheet of paper, as the sky, as featureless as all things that enter heaven.

* * *

GABRIEL GARCÍA MÁRQUEZ (1928–)

A Very Old Man with Enormous Wings (1968)

A Tale for Children

Translated from the Spanish by Gregory Rabassa

On the third day of rain they had killed so many crabs inside the house that Pelayo had to cross his drenched courtyard and throw them into the sea, because the newborn child had a temperature all night and they thought it was due to the stench. The world had been sad since Tuesday. Sea and sky were a single ash-gray thing and the sands of the beach, which on March nights glimmered like powdered light, had become a stew of mud and rotten shellfish. The light was so weak at noon that when Pelayo was coming back to the house after throwing away the crabs, it was hard for him to see what it was that was moving and groaning in the rear of the courtyard. He had to go very close to see that it was an old man, a very old man, lying face down in the mud, who, in spite of his tremendous efforts, couldn't get up, impeded by his enormous wings.

Frightened by that nightmare, Pelayo ran to get Elisenda, his wife, who was putting compresses on the sick child, and he took her to the rear of the courtyard. They both looked at the fallen body with mute stupor. He was dressed like a ragpicker.° There were only a few faded hairs left on his bald skull and very few teeth in his mouth, and his pitiful condition of a drenched great-grandfather had taken away any sense of grandeur he might have had. His huge buzzard wings, dirty and half-plucked, were forever entangled in the mud. They looked at him so long and so closely that Pelayo and Elisenda very soon overcame their surprise and in the end found him familiar. Then they dared speak to him, and he answered in an incomprehensible dialect with a strong sailor's voice. That was how they skipped over the inconvenience of the wings and quite intelligently concluded that he was a lonely castaway from some foreign ship wrecked by the storm. And yet, they called in a neighbor woman who knew everything about life and death to see him, and all she needed was one look to show them their mistake.

"He's an angel," she told them. "He must have been coming for the child, but the poor fellow is so old that the rain knocked him down."

On the following day everyone knew that a flesh-and-blood angel was held captive in Pelayo's house. Against the judgment of the wise neighbor woman, for whom angels in those times were the fugitive survivors of a celestial conspiracy, they did not have the heart to club him to death. Pelayo watched over him all afternoon from the kitchen, armed with his bailiff's club, and before going to bed he dragged him out of the mud and locked him up with the hens in the wire chicken coop. In the middle of the night, when the rain stopped, Pelayo and Elisenda were still killing crabs. A short time afterward the child woke up without a fever and with a desire to eat. Then they felt magnanimous and decided to

---

ragpicker: Someone who makes a living collecting rags and other refuse.

put the angel on a raft with fresh water and provisions for three days and leave him to his fate on the high seas. But when they went out into the courtyard with the first light of dawn, they found the whole neighborhood in front of the chicken coop having fun with the angel, without the slightest reverence, tossing him things to eat through the openings in the wire as if he weren't a supernatural creature but a circus animal.

5 Father Gonzaga arrived before seven o'clock, alarmed by the strange news. By that time onlookers less frivolous than those at dawn had already arrived and they were making all kinds of conjectures concerning the captive's future. The simplest among them thought that he should be named mayor of the world. Others of sterner mind felt that he should be promoted to the rank of five-star general in order to win all wars. Some visionaries hoped that he could be put to stud in order to implant on earth a race of winged wise men who could take charge of the universe. But Father Gonzaga, before becoming a priest, had been a robust woodcutter. Standing by the wire, he reviewed his catechism° in an instant and asked them to open the door so that he could take a close look at that pitiful man who looked more like a huge decrepit hen among the fascinated chickens. He was lying in a corner drying his open wings in the sunlight among the fruit peels and breakfast leftovers that the early risers had thrown him. Alien to the impertinences of the world, he only lifted his antiquarian° eyes and murmured something in his dialect when Father Gonzaga went into the chicken coop and said good morning to him in Latin. The parish priest had his first suspicion of an imposter when he saw that he did not understand the language of God or know how to greet His ministers. Then he noticed that seen close up he was much too human; he had an unbearable smell of the outdoors, the back side of his wings was strewn with parasites and his main feathers had been mistreated by terrestrial winds, and nothing about him measured up to the proud dignity of angels. Then he came out of the chicken coop and in a brief sermon warned the curious against the risks of being ingenuous. He reminded them that the devil had the bad habit of making use of carnival tricks in order to confuse the unwary. He argued that if wings were not the essential element in determining the difference between a hawk and an airplane, they were even less so in the recognition of angels. Nevertheless, he promised to write a letter to his bishop so that the latter would write to his primate so that the latter would write to the Supreme Pontiff° in order to get the final verdict from the highest courts.

His prudence fell on sterile hearts. The news of the captive angel spread with such rapidity that after a few hours the courtyard had the bustle of a marketplace and they had to call in troops with fixed bayonets to disperse the mob that was about to knock the house down. Elisenda, her spine all twisted from sweeping up so much

catechism: A book that summarizes the doctrines of Roman Catholicism in question-and-answer form.
antiquarian: Ancient.
the Supreme Pontiff: The pope.

marketplace trash, then got the idea of fencing in the yard and charging five cents admission to see the angel.

The curious came from far away. A traveling carnival arrived with a flying acrobat who buzzed over the crowd several times, but no one paid any attention to him because his wings were not those of an angel but, rather, those of a sidereal° bat. The most unfortunate invalids on earth came in search of health: a poor woman who since childhood had been counting her heartbeats and had run out of numbers; a Portuguese man who couldn't sleep because the noise of the stars disturbed him; a sleepwalker who got up at night to undo the things he had done while awake; and many others with less serious ailments. In the midst of that shipwreck disorder that made the earth tremble, Pelayo and Elisenda were happy with fatigue, for in less than a week they had crammed their rooms with money and the line of pilgrims waiting their turn to enter still reached beyond the horizon.

The angel was the only one who took no part in his own act. He spent his time trying to get comfortable in his borrowed nest, befuddled by the hellish heat of the oil lamps and sacramental candles that had been placed along the wire. At first they tried to make him eat some mothballs, which, according to the wisdom of the wise neighbor woman, were the food prescribed for angels. But he turned them down, just as he turned down the papal lunches that the penitents brought him, and they never found out whether it was because he was an angel or because he was an old man that in the end he ate nothing but eggplant mush. His only supernatural virtue seemed to be patience. Especially during the first days, when the hens pecked at him, searching for the stellar parasites that proliferated in his wings, and the cripples pulled out feathers to touch their defective parts with, and even the most merciful threw stones at him, trying to get him to rise so they could see him standing. The only time they succeeded in arousing him was when they burned his side with an iron for branding steers, for he had been motionless for so many hours that they thought he was dead. He awoke with a start, ranting in his hermetic° language and with tears in his eyes, and he flapped his wings a couple of times, which brought on a whirlwind of chicken dung and lunar dust and a gale of panic that did not seem to be of this world. Although many thought that his reaction had been one not of rage but of pain, from then on they were careful not to annoy him, because the majority understood that his passivity was not that of a hero taking his ease but that of a cataclysm in repose.

Father Gonzaga held back the crowd's frivolity with formulas of maid-servant inspiration while awaiting the arrival of a final judgment on the nature of the captive. But the mail from Rome showed no sense of urgency. They spent their time finding out if the prisoner had a navel, if his dialect had any connection with Aramaic,° how many times he could fit on the head of a pin, or whether he wasn't just a Norwegian

---

sidereal: Relating to the stars.

hermetic: Occult, magical.

Aramaic: An ancient Middle Eastern language believed to have been the language spoken by Jesus.

with wings. Those meager letters might have come and gone until the end of time if a providential event had not put an end to the priest's tribulations.

10 It so happened that during those days, among so many other carnival attractions, there arrived in town the traveling show of the woman who had been changed into a spider for having disobeyed her parents. The admission to see her was not only less than the admission to see the angel, but people were permitted to ask her all manner of questions about her absurd state and to examine her up and down so that no one would ever doubt the truth of her horror. She was a frightful tarantula the size of a ram and with the head of a sad maiden. What was most heart-rending, however, was not her outlandish shape but the sincere affliction with which she recounted the details of her misfortune. While still practically a child she had sneaked out of her parents' house to go to a dance, and while she was coming back through the woods after having danced all night without permission, a fearful thunderclap rent the sky in two and through the crack came the lightning bolt of brimstone that changed her into a spider. Her only nourishment came from the meatballs that charitable souls chose to toss into her mouth. A spectacle like that, full of so much human truth and with such a fearful lesson, was bound to defeat without even trying that of a haughty angel who scarcely deigned to look at mortals. Besides, the few miracles attributed to the angel showed a certain mental disorder, like the blind man who didn't recover his sight but grew three new teeth, or the paralytic who didn't get to walk but almost won the lottery, and the leper whose sores sprouted sunflowers. Those consolation miracles, which were more like mocking fun, had already ruined the angel's reputation when the woman who had been changed into a spider finally crushed him completely. That was how Father Gonzaga was cured forever of his insomnia and Pelayo's courtyard went back to being as empty as during the time it had rained for three days and crabs walked through the bedrooms.

The owners of the house had no reason to lament. With the money they saved they built a two-story mansion with balconies and gardens and high netting so that crabs wouldn't get in during the winter, and with iron bars on the windows so that angels wouldn't get in. Pelayo also set up a rabbit warren close to town and gave up his job as bailiff for good, and Elisenda bought some satin pumps with high heels and many dresses of iridescent silk, the kind worn on Sunday by the most desirable women in those times. The chicken coop was the only thing that didn't receive any attention. If they washed it down with creolin° and burned tears of myrrh° inside it every so often, it was not in homage to the angel but to drive away the dungheap stench that still hung everywhere like a ghost and was turning the new house into an old one. At first, when the child learned to walk, they were careful that he not get too close to the chicken coop. But then they began to lose their fears and got used to the smell, and before the child got his second teeth he'd gone inside the chicken coop to play, where the wires were falling apart. The angel was no less standoffish with him than with other mortals, but he tolerated the most ingenious infamies with

---

creolin: A disinfectant.

myrrh: A type of incense.

the patience of a dog who had no illusions. They both came down with chicken pox at the same time. The doctor who took care of the child couldn't resist the temptation to listen to the angel's heart, and he found so much whistling in the heart and so many sounds in his kidneys that it seemed impossible for him to be alive. What surprised him most, however, was the logic of his wings. They seemed so natural on that completely human organism that he couldn't understand why other men didn't have them too.

When the child began school it had been some time since the sun and rain had caused the collapse of the chicken coop. The angel went dragging himself about here and there like a stray dying man. They would drive him out of the bedroom with a broom and a moment later find him in the kitchen. He seemed to be in so many places at the same time that they grew to think that he'd been duplicated, that he was reproducing himself all through the house, and the exasperated and unhinged Elisenda shouted that it was awful living in that hell full of angels. He could scarcely eat and his antiquarian eyes had also become so foggy that he went about bumping into posts. All he had left were the bare cannulae° of his last feathers. Pelayo threw a blanket over him and extended him the charity of letting him sleep in the shed, and only then did they notice that he had a temperature at night, and was delirious with the tongue twisters of an old Norwegian. That was one of the few times they became alarmed, for they thought he was going to die and not even the wise neighbor woman had been able to tell them what to do with dead angels.

And yet he not only survived his worst winter, but seemed improved with the first sunny days. He remained motionless for several days in the farthest corner of the courtyard, where no one would see him, and at the beginning of December some large, stiff feathers began to grow on his wings, the feathers of a scarecrow, which looked more like another misfortune of decrepitude. But he must have known the reason for those changes, for he was quite careful that no one should notice them, that no one should hear the sea chanteys that he sometimes sang under the stars. One morning Elisenda was cutting some bunches of onions for lunch when a wind that seemed to come from the high seas blew into the kitchen. Then she went to the window and caught the angel in his first attempts at flight. They were so clumsy that his fingernails opened a furrow in the vegetable patch and he was on the point of knocking the shed down with the ungainly flapping that slipped on the light and couldn't get a grip on the air. But he did manage to gain altitude. Elisenda let out a sigh of relief, for herself and for him, when she saw him pass over the last houses, holding himself up in some way with the risky flapping of a senile vulture. She kept watching him even when she was through cutting the onions and she kept on watching until it was no longer possible for her to see him, because then he was no longer an annoyance in her life but an imaginary dot on the horizon of the sea.

* * *

---

cannulae: Quills.

HA JIN (1956–)

Saboteur (1997)

Mr. Chiu and his bride were having lunch in the square before Muji Train Station. On the table between them were two bottles of soda spewing out brown foam and two paper boxes of rice and sautéed cucumber and pork. "Let's eat," he said to her, and broke the connected ends of the chopsticks. He picked up a slice of streaky pork and put it into his mouth. As he was chewing, a few crinkles appeared on his thin jaw.

To his right, at another table, two railroad policemen were drinking tea and laughing; it seemed that the stout, middle-aged man was telling a joke to his young comrade, who was tall and of athletic build. Now and again they would steal a glance at Mr. Chiu's table.

The air smelled of rotten melon. A few flies kept buzzing above the couple's lunch. Hundreds of people were rushing around to get on the platform or to catch buses to downtown. Food and fruit vendors were crying for customers in lazy voices. About a dozen young women, representing the local hotels, held up placards which displayed the daily prices and words as large as a palm, like FREE MEALS, AIR-CONDITIONING, and ON THE RIVER. In the center of the square stood a concrete statue of Chairman Mao, at whose feet peasants were napping, their backs on the warm granite and their faces toward the sunny sky. A flock of pigeons perched on the Chairman's raised hand and forearm.

The rice and cucumber tasted good, and Mr. Chiu was eating unhurriedly. His sallow face showed exhaustion. He was glad that the honeymoon was finally over and that he and his bride were heading back for Harbin. During the two weeks' vacation, he had been worried about his liver, because three months ago he had suffered from acute hepatitis; he was afraid he might have a relapse. But he had had no severe symptoms, despite his liver being still big and tender. On the whole he was pleased with his health, which could endure even the strain of a honeymoon; indeed, he was on the course of recovery. He looked at his bride, who took off her wire glasses, kneading the root of her nose with her fingertips. Beads of sweat coated her pale cheeks.

5 "Are you all right, sweetheart?" he asked.

"I have a headache. I didn't sleep well last night."

"Take an aspirin, will you?"

"It's not that serious. Tomorrow is Sunday and I can sleep in. Don't worry."

As they were talking, the stout policeman at the next table stood up and threw a bowl of tea in their direction. Both Mr. Chiu's and his bride's sandals were wet instantly.

10 "Hooligan!" she said in a low voice.

Mr. Chiu got to his feet and said out loud, "Comrade Policeman, why did you do this?" He stretched out his right foot to show the wet sandal.

"Do what?" the stout man asked huskily, glaring at Mr. Chiu while the young fellow was whistling.

"See, you dumped tea on our feet."

"You're lying. You wet your shoes yourself."

"Comrade Policeman, your duty is to keep order, but you purposely tortured us common citizens. Why violate the law you are supposed to enforce?" As Mr. Chiu was speaking, dozens of people began gathering around.

With a wave of his hand, the man said to the young fellow, "Let's get hold of him!"

They grabbed Mr. Chiu and clamped handcuffs around his wrists. He cried, "You can't do this to me. This is utterly unreasonable."

"Shut up!" The man pulled out his pistol. "You can use your tongue at our headquarters."

The young fellow added, "You're a saboteur, you know that? You're disrupting public order."

The bride was too petrified to say anything coherent. She was a recent college graduate, had majored in fine arts, and had never seen the police make an arrest. All she could say was, "Oh, please, please!"

The policemen were pulling Mr. Chiu, but he refused to go with them, holding the corner of the table and shouting, "We have a train to catch. We already bought the tickets."

The stout man punched him in the chest. "Shut up. Let your ticket expire." With the pistol butt he chopped Mr. Chiu's hands, which at once released the table. Together the two men were dragging him away to the police station.

Realizing he had to go with them, Mr. Chiu turned his head and shouted to his bride, "Don't wait for me here. Take the train. If I'm not back by tomorrow morning, send someone over to get me out."

She nodded, covering her sobbing mouth with her palm.

After removing his belt, they locked Mr. Chiu into a cell in the back of the Railroad Police Station. The single window in the room was blocked by six steel bars; it faced a spacious yard, in which stood a few pines. Beyond the trees, two swings hung from an iron frame, swaying gently in the breeze. Somewhere in the building a cleaver was chopping rhythmically. There must be a kitchen upstairs, Mr. Chiu thought.

He was too exhausted to worry about what they would do to him, so he lay down on the narrow bed and shut his eyes. He wasn't afraid. The Cultural Revolution was over already, and recently the Party had been propagating the idea that all citizens were equal before the law. The police ought to be a law-abiding model for common people. As long as he remained coolheaded and reasoned with them, they probably wouldn't harm him.

Late in the afternoon he was taken to the Interrogation Bureau on the second floor. On his way there, in the stairwell, he ran into the middle-aged policeman who had manhandled him. The man grinned, rolling his bulgy eyes and pointing his fingers at him as if firing a pistol. Egg of a tortoise! Mr. Chiu cursed mentally.

The moment he sat down in the office, he burped, his palm shielding his mouth. In front of him, across a long desk, sat the chief of the bureau and a donkey-faced man. On the glass desktop was a folder containing information on his case. He felt it bizarre that in just a matter of hours they had accumulated a small pile of writing about him. On second thought he began to wonder whether they had kept a file on him all the time. How could this have happened? He lived and worked in Harbin, more than three hundred miles away, and this was his first time in Muji City.

The chief of the bureau was a thin, bald man who looked serene and intelligent. His slim hands handled the written pages in the folder in the manner of a lecturing scholar. To Mr. Chiu's left sat a young scribe, with a clipboard on his knee and a black fountain pen in his hand.

"Your name?" the chief asked, apparently reading out the question from a form.

"Chiu Maguang."

"Age?"

"Thirty-four."

"Profession?"

"Lecturer."

"Work unit?"

"Harbin University."

"Political status?"

"Communist Party member."

The chief put down the paper and began to speak. "Your crime is sabotage, although it hasn't induced serious consequences yet. Because you are a Party member, you should be punished more. You have failed to be a model for the masses and you—"

"Excuse me, sir," Mr. Chiu cut him off.

"What?"

"I didn't do anything. Your men are the saboteurs of our social order. They threw hot tea on my feet and on my wife's feet. Logically speaking, you should criticize them, if not punish them."

"That statement is groundless. You have no witness. Why should I believe you?" the chief said matter-of-factly.

"This is my evidence." He raised his right hand. "Your man hit my fingers with a pistol."

"That doesn't prove how your feet got wet. Besides, you could have hurt your fingers yourself."

"But I am telling the truth!" Anger flared up in Mr. Chiu. "Your police station owes me an apology. My train ticket has expired, my new leather sandals are ruined, and I am late for a conference in the provincial capital. You must compensate me for the damage and losses. Don't mistake me for a common citizen who would tremble when you sneeze. I'm a scholar, a philosopher, and an expert in dialectical materialism. If necessary, we will argue about this in *The Northeastern Daily*, or we will go to the highest People's Court in Beijing. Tell me, what's your name?" He got carried away with his harangue, which was by no means trivial and had worked to his advantage on numerous occasions.

"Stop bluffing us," the donkey-faced man broke in. "We have seen a lot of your kind. We can easily prove you are guilty. Here are some of the statements given by eyewitnesses." He pushed a few sheets of paper toward Mr. Chiu.

Mr. Chiu was dazed to see the different handwritings, which all stated that he had shouted in the square to attract attention and refused to obey the police. One of the witnesses had identified herself as a purchasing agent from a shipyard in Shanghai. Something stirred in Mr. Chiu's stomach, a pain rising to his rib. He gave out a faint moan.

"Now you have to admit you are guilty," the chief said. "Although it's a serious crime, we won't punish you severely, provided you write out a self-criticism and promise that you won't disrupt the public order again. In other words, your release will depend on your attitude toward this crime."

"You're daydreaming," Mr. Chiu cried. "I won't write a word, because I'm innocent. I demand that you provide me with a letter of apology so I can explain to my university why I'm late."

Both the interrogators smiled contemptuously. "Well, we've never done that," said the chief, taking a puff at his cigarette.

"Then make this a precedent."

"That's unnecessary. We are pretty certain that you will comply with our wishes." The chief blew a column of smoke toward Mr. Chiu's face.

At the tilt of the chief's head, two guards stepped forward and grabbed the criminal by the arms. Mr. Chiu meanwhile went on saying "I shall report you to the Provincial Administration. You'll have to pay for this! You are worse than the Japanese military police."

They dragged him out of the room.

After dinner, which consisted of a bowl of millet porridge, a corn bun, and a piece of pickled turnip, Mr. Chiu began to have a fever, shaking with a chill and sweating profusely. He knew that the fire of anger had gotten into his liver and that he was probably having a relapse. No medicine was available, because his briefcase had been left with his bride. At home it would have been time for him to sit in front of their color TV, drinking jasmine tea and watching the evening news. It was so lonesome in here. The orange bulb above the single bed was the only source of light, which enabled the guards to keep him under surveillance at night. A moment ago he had asked them for a newspaper or a magazine to read, but they turned him down.

Through the small opening on the door noises came in. It seemed that the police on duty were playing cards or chess in a nearby office; shouts and laughter could be heard now and then. Meanwhile, an accordion kept coughing from a remote corner in the building. Looking at the ballpoint and the letter paper left for him by the guards when they took him back from the Interrogation Bureau, Mr. Chiu remembered the old saying, "When a scholar runs into soldiers, the more he argues, the muddier his point becomes." How ridiculous this whole thing was. He ruffled his thick hair with his fingers.

He felt miserable, massaging his stomach continually. To tell the truth, he was more upset than frightened, because he would have to catch up with his work once he was back home—a paper that was due at the printers next week, and two dozen books he ought to read for the courses he was going to teach in the fall.

60 A human shadow flitted across the opening. Mr. Chiu rushed to the door and shouted through the hole, "Comrade Guard, Comrade Guard!"

"What do you want?" a voice rasped.

"I want you to inform your leaders that I'm very sick. I have heart disease and hepatitis. I may die here if you keep me like this without medication."

"No leader is on duty on the weekend. You have to wait till Monday."

"What? You mean I'll stay in here tomorrow?"

65 "Yes."

"Your station will be held responsible if anything happens to me."

"We know that. Take it easy, you won't die."

It seemed illogical that Mr. Chiu slept quite well that night, though the light above his head had been on all the time and the straw mattress was hard and infested with fleas. He was afraid of ticks, mosquitoes, cockroaches—any kind of insect but fleas and bedbugs. Once, in the countryside, where his school's faculty and staff had helped the peasants harvest crops for a week, his colleagues had joked about his flesh, which they said must have tasted nonhuman to fleas. Except for him, they were all afflicted with hundreds of bites.

More amazing now, he didn't miss his bride a lot. He even enjoyed sleeping alone, perhaps because the honeymoon had tired him out and he needed more rest.

70 The backyard was quiet on Sunday morning. Pale sunlight streamed through the pine branches. A few sparrows were jumping on the ground, catching caterpillars and ladybugs. Holding the steel bars, Mr. Chiu inhaled the morning air, which smelled meaty. There must have been an eatery or a cooked-meat stand nearby. He reminded himself that he should take this detention with ease. A sentence that Chairman Mao had written to a hospitalized friend rose in his mind: "Since you are already in here, you may as well stay and make the best of it."

His desire for peace of mind originated in his fear that his hepatitis might get worse. He tried to remain unperturbed. However, he was sure that his liver was swelling up, since the fever still persisted. For a whole day he lay in bed, thinking about his paper on the nature of contradictions. Time and again he was overwhelmed by anger, cursing aloud, "A bunch of thugs!" He swore that once he was out, he would write an article about this experience. He had better find out some of the policemen's names.

It turned out to be a restful day for the most part; he was certain that his university would send somebody to his rescue. All he should do now was remain calm and wait patiently. Sooner or later the police would have to release him, although they had no idea that he might refuse to leave unless they wrote him an apology. Damn those hoodlums, they had ordered more than they could eat!

When he woke up on Monday morning, it was already light. Somewhere a man was moaning; the sound came from the backyard. After a long yawn, and kicking off the tattered blanket, Mr. Chiu climbed out of bed and went to the window. In the middle of the yard, a young man was fastened to a pine, his wrists handcuffed around the trunk from behind. He was wriggling and swearing loudly, but there was no sight of anyone else in the yard. He looked familiar to Mr. Chiu.

Mr. Chiu squinted his eyes to see who it was. To his astonishment, he recognized the man, who was Fenjin, a recent graduate from the Law Department at Harbin University. Two years ago Mr. Chiu had taught a course in Marxist materialism, in which Fenjin had enrolled. Now, how on earth had this young devil landed here?

Then it dawned on him that Fenjin must have been sent over by his bride. What 75
a stupid woman! A bookworm, who only knew how to read foreign novels! He had expected that she would contact the school's Security Section, which would for sure send a cadre here. Fenjin held no official position; he merely worked in a private law firm that had just two lawyers; in fact, they had little business except for some detective work for men and women who suspected their spouses of having extramarital affairs. Mr. Chiu was overcome with a wave of nausea.

Should he call out to let his student know he was nearby? He decided not to, because he didn't know what had happened. Fenjin must have quarreled with the police to incur such a punishment. Yet this could never have occurred if Fenjin hadn't come to his rescue. So no matter what, Mr. Chiu had to do something. But what could he do?

It was going to be a scorcher. He could see purple steam shimmering and rising from the ground among the pines. Poor devil, he thought, as he raised a bowl of corn glue to his mouth, sipped, and took a bite of a piece of salted celery.

When a guard came to collect the bowl and the chopsticks, Mr. Chiu asked him what had happened to the man in the backyard. "He called our boss 'bandit,'" the guard said. "He claimed he was a lawyer or something. An arrogant son of a rabbit."

Now it was obvious to Mr. Chiu that he had to do something to help his rescuer. Before he could figure out a way, a scream broke out in the backyard. He rushed to the window and saw a tall policeman standing before Fenjin, an iron bucket on the ground. It was the same young fellow who had arrested Mr. Chiu in the square two days before. The man pinched Fenjin's nose, then raised his hand, which stayed in the air for a few seconds, then slapped the lawyer across the face. As Fenjin was groaning, the man lifted up the bucket and poured water on his head.

"This will keep you from getting sunstroke, boy. I'll give you some more every 80
hour," the man said loudly.

Fenjin kept his eyes shut, yet his wry face showed that he was struggling to hold back from cursing the policeman, or, more likely, that he was sobbing in silence. He sneezed, then raised his face and shouted, "Let me go take a piss."

"Oh yeah?" the man bawled. "Pee in your pants."

Still Mr. Chiu didn't make any noise, gripping the steel bars with both hands, his fingers white. The policeman turned and glanced at the cell's window; his pistol, partly holstered, glittered in the sun. With a snort he spat his cigarette butt to the ground and stamped it into the dust.

Then the door opened and the guards motioned Mr. Chiu to come out. Again they took him upstairs to the Interrogation Bureau.

The same men were in the office, though this time the scribe was sitting there 85
empty-handed. At the sight of Mr. Chiu the chief said, "Ah, here you are. Please be seated."

After Mr. Chiu sat down, the chief waved a white silk fan and said to him, "You may have seen your lawyer. He's a young man without manners, so our director had him taught a crash course in the backyard."

"It's illegal to do that. Aren't you afraid to appear in a newspaper?"

"No, we are not, not even on TV. What else can you do? We are not afraid of any story you make up. We call it fiction. What we do care about is that you cooperate with us. That is to say, you must admit your crime."

"What if I refuse to cooperate?"

"Then your lawyer will continue his education in the sunshine."

A swoon swayed Mr. Chiu, and he held the arms of the chair to steady himself. A numb pain stung him in the upper stomach and nauseated him, and his head was throbbing. He was sure that the hepatitis was finally attacking him. Anger was flaming up in his chest; his throat was tight and clogged.

The chief resumed, "As a matter of fact, you don't even have to write out your self-criticism. We have your crime described clearly here. All we need is your signature."

Holding back his rage, Mr. Chiu said, "Let me look at that."

With a smirk the donkey-faced man handed him a sheet, which carried these words:

> I hereby admit that on July 13 I disrupted public order at Muji Train Station, and that I refused to listen to reason when the railroad police issued their warning. Thus I myself am responsible for my arrest. After two days' detention, I have realized the reactionary nature of my crime. From now on, I shall continue to educate myself with all my effort and shall never commit this kind of crime again.

A voice started screaming in Mr. Chiu's ears, "Lie, lie!" But he shook his head and forced the voice away. He asked the chief, "If I sign this, will you release both my lawyer and me?"

"Of course, we'll do that." The chief was drumming his fingers on the blue folder—their file on him.

Mr. Chiu signed his name and put his thumbprint under his signature.

"Now you are free to go," the chief said with a smile, and handed him a piece of paper to wipe his thumb with.

Mr. Chiu was so sick that he couldn't stand up from the chair at first try. Then he doubled his effort and rose to his feet. He staggered out of the building to meet his lawyer in the backyard, having forgotten to ask for his belt back. In his chest he felt as though there were a bomb. If he were able to, he would have razed the entire police station and eliminated all their families. Though he knew he could do nothing like that, he made up his mind to do something.

"I'm sorry about this torture, Fenjin," Mr. Chiu said when they met.

"It doesn't matter. They are savages." The lawyer brushed a patch of dirt off his jacket with trembling fingers. Water was still dribbling from the bottoms of his trouser legs.

"Let's go now," the teacher said.

The moment they came out of the police station, Mr. Chiu caught sight of a tea stand. He grabbed Fenjin's arm and walked over to the old woman at the table. "Two bowls of black tea," he said and handed her a one-yuan note.

After the first bowl, they each had another one. Then they set out for the train station. But before they walked fifty yards, Mr. Chiu insisted on eating a bowl of tree-ear soup at a food stand. Fenjin agreed. He told his teacher, "You mustn't treat me like a guest."

"No, I want to eat something myself." 105

As if dying of hunger, Mr. Chiu dragged his lawyer from restaurant to restaurant near the police station, but at each place he ordered no more than two bowls of food. Fenjin wondered why his teacher wouldn't stay at one place and eat his fill.

Mr. Chiu bought noodles, wonton, eight-grain porridge, and chicken soup, respectively, at four restaurants. While eating, he kept saying through his teeth, "If only I could kill all the bastards!" At the last place he merely took a few sips of the soup without tasting the chicken cubes and mushrooms.

Fenjin was baffled by his teacher, who looked ferocious and muttered to himself mysteriously, and whose jaundiced face was covered with dark puckers. For the first time Fenjin thought of Mr. Chiu as an ugly man.

Within a month over eight hundred people contracted acute hepatitis in Muji. Six died of the disease, including two children. Nobody knew how the epidemic had started.

* * *

JAMES JOYCE (1884–1941)

Eveline (1914)

She sat at the window watching the evening invade the avenue. Her head was leaned against the window curtains and in her nostrils was the odor of dusty cretonne.° She was tired.

Few people passed. The man out of the last house passed on his way home; she heard his footsteps clacking along the concrete pavement and afterwards crunching on the cinder path before the new red houses. One time there used to be a field there in which they used to play every evening with other people's children. Then a man from Belfast° bought the field and built houses in it—not like their little brown houses but bright brick houses with shining roofs. The children of the avenue used to play together in that field—the Devines, the Waters, the Dunns, little Keogh the cripple, she and her brothers and sisters. Ernest, however, never played: he was too

cretonne: Heavy cloth used for curtains and upholstery.

Belfast: Capital of present-day Northern Ireland. This story refers to a time before the Partition of Ireland.

grown up. Her father used often to hunt them in out of the field with his blackthorn stick; but usually little Keogh used to keep *nix*° and call out when he saw her father coming. Still they seemed to have been rather happy then. Her father was not so bad then; and besides, her mother was alive. That was a long time ago; she and her brothers and sisters were all grown up; her mother was dead. Tizzie Dunn was dead, too, and the Waters had gone back to England. Everything changes. Now she was going to go away like the others, to leave her home.

Home! She looked around the room, reviewing all its familiar objects which she had dusted once a week for so many years, wondering where on earth all the dust came from. Perhaps she would never see again those familiar objects from which she had never dreamed of being divided. And yet during all those years she had never found out the name of the priest whose yellowing photograph hung on the wall above the broken harmonium beside the colored print of the promises made to Blessed Margaret Mary Alacoque. He had been a school friend of her father. Whenever he showed the photograph to a visitor her father used to pass it with a casual word:

"He is in Melbourne now."

5 She had consented to go away, to leave her home. Was that wise? She tried to weigh each side of the question. In her home anyway she had shelter and food; she had those whom she had known all her life about her. Of course she had to work hard both in the house and at business. What would they say of her in the Stores when they found out that she had run away with a fellow? Say she was a fool, perhaps; and her place would be filled up by advertisement. Miss Gavan would be glad. She had always had an edge on her, especially whenever there were people listening.

"Miss Hill, don't you see these ladies are waiting?"

"Look lively, Miss Hill, please."

She would not cry many tears at leaving the Stores.

But in her new home, in a distant unknown country, it would not be like that. Then she would be married — she, Eveline. People would treat her with respect then. She would not be treated as her mother had been. Even now, though she was over nineteen, she sometimes felt herself in danger of her father's violence. She knew it was that that had given her the palpitations. When they were growing up he had never gone for her, like he used to go for Harry and Ernest, because she was a girl; but latterly he had begun to threaten her and say what he would do to her only for her dead mother's sake. And now she had nobody to protect her. Ernest was dead and Harry, who was in the church decorating business, was nearly always down somewhere in the country. Besides, the invariable squabble for money on Saturday nights had begun to weary her unspeakably. She always gave her entire wages — seven shillings — and Harry always sent up what he could but the trouble was to get any money from her father. He said she used to squander the money, that she had no head, that he wasn't going to give her his hard-earned money to throw about the streets, and much more, for he was usually fairly bad of a Saturday night. In the end

keep nix: Keep watch (slang).

he would give her the money and ask her had she any intention of buying Sunday dinner. Then she had to rush out as quickly as she could and do her marketing, holding her black leather purse tightly in her hand as she elbowed her way through the crowds and returning home late under her load of provisions. She had hard work to keep the house together and to see that the two young children, who had been left to her charge went to school regularly and got their meals regularly. It was hard work—a hard life—but now that she was about to leave it she did not find it a wholly undesirable life.

She was about to explore another life with Frank. Frank was very kind, manly, open-hearted. She was to go away with him by the night-boat to be his wife and to live with him in Buenos Aires where he had a home waiting for her. How well she remembered the first time she had seen him; he was lodging in a house on the main road where she used to visit. It seemed a few weeks ago. He was standing at the gate, his peaked cap pushed back on his head and his hair tumbled forward over a face of bronze. Then they had come to know each other. He used to meet her outside the Stores every evening and see her home. He took her to see *The Bohemian Girl* and she felt elated as she sat in an unaccustomed part of the theater with him. He was awfully fond of music and sang a little. People knew that they were courting and, when he sang about the lass that loves a sailor, she always felt pleasantly confused. He used to call her Poppens out of fun. First of all it had been an excitement for her to have a fellow and then she had begun to like him. He had tales of distant countries. He had started as a deck boy at a pound a month on a ship of the Allan Line going out to Canada. He told her the names of the ships he had been on and the names of the different services. He had sailed through the Straits of Magellan° and he told her stories of the terrible Patagonians.° He had fallen on his feet in Buenos Aires, he said, and had come over to the old country just for a holiday. Of course, her father had found out the affair and had forbidden her to have anything to say to him.

"I know these sailor chaps," he said.

One day he had quarreled with Frank and after that she had to meet her lover secretly.

The evening deepened in the avenue. The white of two letters in her lap grew indistinct. One was to Harry; the other was to her father. Ernest had been her favorite but she liked Harry too. Her father was becoming old lately, she noticed; he would miss her. Sometimes he could be very nice. Not long before, when she had been laid up for a day, he had read her out a ghost story and made toast for her at the fire. Another day, when their mother was alive, they had all gone for a picnic to the Hill of Howth. She remembered her father putting on her mother's bonnet to make the children laugh.

Her time was running out but she continued to sit by the window, leaning her head against the window curtain, inhaling the odor of dusty cretonne. Down far in the avenue she could hear a street organ playing. She knew the air. Strange that it

Straits of Magellan: Sea channel at the southern tip of South America.
Patagonians: People from Patagonia, a tableland region in southern Argentina and Chile.

should come that very night to remind her of the promise to her mother, her promise to keep the home together as long as she could. She remembered the last night of her mother's illness; she was again in the close dark room at the other side of the hall and outside she heard a melancholy air of Italy. The organ player had been ordered to go away and given sixpence. She remembered her father strutting back into the sickroom saying:

"Damned Italians! coming over here!"

As she mused the pitiful vision of her mother's life laid its spell on the very quick of her being—that life of commonplace sacrifices closing in final craziness. She trembled as she heard again her mother's voice saying constantly with foolish insistence:

"Derevaun Seraun! Derevaun Seraun!"°

She stood up in a sudden impulse of terror. Escape! She must escape! Frank would save her. He would give her life, perhaps love, too. But she wanted to live. Why should she be unhappy? She had a right to happiness. Frank would take her in his arms, fold her in his arms. He would save her.

She stood among the swaying crowd in the station at the North Wall. He held her hand and she knew that he was speaking to her, saying something about the passage over and over again. The station was full of soldiers with brown baggages. Through the wide doors of the sheds she caught a glimpse of the black mass of the boat, lying in beside the quay° wall, with illumined portholes. She answered nothing. She felt her cheek pale and cold and, out of a maze of distress, she prayed to God to direct her, to show her what was her duty. The boat blew a long mournful whistle into the mist. If she went, tomorrow she would be on the sea with Frank, steaming toward Buenos Aires. Their passage had been booked. Could she still draw back after all he had done for her? Her distress awoke a nausea in her body and she kept moving her lips in silent, fervent prayer.

A bell clanged upon her heart. She felt him seize her hand:

"Come!"

All the seas of the world tumbled about her heart. He was drawing her into them: he would drown her. She gripped with both hands at the iron railing.

"Come!"

No! No! No! It was impossible. Her hands clutched the iron in frenzy. Amid the seas she sent a cry of anguish!

"Eveline! Evvy!"

He rushed beyond the barrier and called to her to follow. He was shouted at to go on but he still called to her. She set her white face to him, passive, like a helpless animal. Her eyes gave him no sign of love or farewell or recognition.

* * *

Derevaun Seraun: "The end of pleasure is pain!" (Irish).

quay: A paved stretch of shoreline facing navigable water, used for loading and unloading ships.

FRANZ KAFKA (1883–1924)

A Hunger Artist (1924)

Translated by Edwin and Willa Muir

During these last decades the interest in professional fasting has markedly diminished. It used to pay very well to stage such great performances under one's own management, but today that is quite impossible. We live in a different world now. At one time the whole town took a lively interest in the hunger artist; from day to day of his fast the excitement mounted; everybody wanted to see him at least once a day; there were people who bought season tickets for the last few days and sat from morning till night in front of his small barred cage; even in the nighttime there were visiting hours, when the whole effect was heightened by torch flares; on fine days the cage was set out in the open air, and then it was the children's special treat to see the hunger artist; for their elders he was often just a joke that happened to be in fashion, but the children stood open-mouthed, holding each other's hands for greater security, marveling at him as he sat there pallid in black tights, with his ribs sticking out so prominently, not even on a seat but down among straw on the ground, sometimes giving a courteous nod, answering questions with a constrained smile, or perhaps stretching an arm through the bars so that one might feel how thin it was, and then again withdrawing deep into himself, paying no attention to anyone or anything, not even to the all-important striking of the clock that was the only piece of furniture in his cage, but merely starting into vacancy with half shut eyes, now and then taking a sip from a tiny glass of water to moisten his lips.

Besides causal onlookers there were also relays of permanent watchers selected by the public, usually butchers, strangely enough, and it was their task to watch the hunger artist day and night, three of them at a time, in case he should have some secret recourse to nourishment. This was nothing but a formality, instituted to reassure the masses, for the initiates knew well enough that during his fast the artist would never in any circumstances, not even under forcible compulsion, swallow the smallest morsel of food: the honor of his profession forbade it. Not every watcher, of course, was capable of understanding this, there were often groups of night watchers who were very lax in carrying out their duties and deliberately huddled together in a retired corner to play cards with great absorption, obviously intending to give the hunger artist the chance of a little refreshment, which they supposed he could draw from some private hoard. Nothing annoyed the artist more than such watchers; they made him miserable; they made his fast seem unendurable; sometimes he mastered his feebleness sufficiently to sing during their watch for as long as he could keep going, to show them how unjust their suspicions were. But that was of little use; they only wondered at his cleverness in being able to fill his mouth even while singing. Much more to his taste were the watchers who sat close up to the bars, who were not content with the dim night lighting of the hall but focused him in the full glare of the electric pocket torch given them by the impresario. The harsh light did not trouble him at all, in any case he could never sleep properly, and he could always drowse a little, whatever the light, at any hour, even when the hall was thronged with noisy onlookers. He was quite happy at the prospect of spending a sleepless night with such watchers; he was ready to exchange jokes with them, to tell them stories out of his nomadic life, anything at all to keep them awake and demonstrate to them again that he had no eatables in his cage and that he was fasting as not one of them could fast. But his happiest moment was when the morning came and an enormous breakfast was brought them, at his expense, on which they flung themselves with the keen appetite of healthy men after a weary night of wakefulness. Of course there were people who argued that this breakfast was an unfair attempt to bribe the watchers, but that was going rather too far, and when they were invited to take on a night's vigil without a breakfast, merely for the sake of the cause, they made themselves scarce, although they stuck stubbornly to their suspicions.

Such suspicions, anyhow, were a necessary accompaniment to the profession of fasting. No one could possibly watch the hunger artist continuously, day and night, and so no one could produce first-hand evidence that the fast had really been rigorous and continuous; only the artist himself could know that, he was therefore bound to be the sole completely satisfied spectator of his own fast. Yet for other reasons he was never satisfied; it was not perhaps mere fasting that had brought him to such skeleton thinness that many people had regretfully to keep away from his exhibitions; because the sight of him was too much for them, perhaps it was dissatisfaction with himself that had worn him down. For he alone knew, what no other initiate knew, how easy it was to fast. It was the easiest thing in the world. He made no secret of this, yet people did not believe him, at the best they set him down as modest, most of them, however, thought he was out for publicity or else was some kind of cheat who found it easy to fast because he had discovered a way of making it easy, and then had the impudence to admit the fact, more or less. He had to put up with all that, and in the course of time had got used to it, but his inner dissatisfaction always rankled, and never yet, after any term of fasting—this must be granted to his credit—had he left the cage of his own free will. The longest period of fasting was fixed by his impresario at forty days, beyond that term he was not allowed to go, not even in great cities, and there was good reason for it, too. Experience had proved that for about forty days the interest of the public could be stimulated by a steadily increasing pressure of advertisement, but after that the town began to lose interest, sympathetic support began notably to fall off; there were of course local variations as between one town and another or one country and another, but as a general rule forty days marked the limit. So on the fortieth day the flower-bedecked cage was opened, enthusiastic spectators filled the hall, a military band played, two doctors entered the cage to measure the results of the fast, which were announced through a megaphone, and finally two young ladies appeared, blissful at having been selected for the honor, to help the hunger artist down the few steps leading to a small table on which was spread a carefully chosen invalid repast. And at this very moment the artist always turned stubborn. True, he would entrust his bony arms to the outstretched helping hands of the ladies bending over him, but stand up he would not. Why stop fasting at this particular moment, after forty days of it? He had held out for a long time, an illimitably long time; why stop now, when he was in his best fasting form, or rather, not yet quite in his best fasting form? Why should he be cheated of the fame he would get for fasting longer, for being not only the record hunger artist of all time, which presumably he was already, but for beating his own record by a performance beyond human imagination, since he felt that there were no limits to his capacity for fasting? His public pretended to admire him so much, why should it have so little patience with him; if he could endure fasting longer, why shouldn't the public endure it? Besides, he was tired, he was comfortable sitting in the straw, and now he was supposed to lift himself to his full height and go down to a meal the very thought of which gave him a nausea that only the presence of the ladies kept him from betraying, and even that with an effort. And he looked up into the eyes of the ladies who were apparently so friendly and in reality so cruel, and shook his head, which felt too heavy on its strengthless neck. But then there happened yet again what always happened. The impresario came forward, without a word—for the band made speech impossible—lifted his arms in the air above the artist, as if inviting Heaven to look down upon its creature here in the straw, this suffering martyr, which indeed he was, although in quite another sense; grasped him round the emaciated waist, with exaggerated caution, so that the frail condition he was in might be appreciated; and committed him to the care of the blenching ladies, not without secretly giving him a shaking so that his legs and body tottered and swayed. The artist now submitted completely; his head lolled on his breast as if it had landed there by chance; his body was hollowed out; his legs in a spasm of self-preservation clung close to each other at the knees, yet scraped on the ground as if it were not really solid ground, as if they were only trying to find solid ground; and the whole weight of his body, a feather-weight after all, relapsed onto one of the ladies, who, looking round for help and panting a little—this post of honor was not at all what she had expected it to be—first stretched her neck as far as she could to keep her face at least free from contact with the artist, when finding this impossible, and her more fortunate companion not coming to her aid but merely holding extended on her own trembling hand the little bunch of knuckle-bones that was the artist's, to the great delight of the spectators burst into tears and had to be replaced by an attendant who had long been stationed in readiness. Then came the food, a little of which the impresario managed to get between the artist's lips, while he sat in a kind of half-fainting trance, to the accompaniment of cheerful patter designed to distract the public's attention from the artist's condition; after that, a toast was drunk to the public, supposedly prompted by a whisper from the artist in the impresario's ear; the band confirmed it with a mighty flourish, the spectators melted away, and no one had any cause to be dissatisfied with the proceedings, no one except the hunger artist himself, he only, as always.

So he lived for many years, with small regular intervals of recuperation, in visible glory, honored by the world, yet in spite of that troubled in spirit, and all the more troubled because no one would take his trouble seriously. What comfort could he possibly need? What more could he possibly wish for? And if some good-natured person, feeling sorry for him, tried to console him by pointing out that his melancholy was probably caused by fasting, it could happen, especially when he had been fasting for some time, that he reacted with an outburst of fury and to the general alarm began to shake the bars of his cage like a wild animal. Yet the impresario had a way of punishing these outbreaks which he rather enjoyed putting into operation. He would apologize publicly for the artist's behavior, which was only to be excused, he admitted, because of the irritability caused by fasting: a condition hardly to be understood by well-fed people; then by natural transition he went on to mention the artist's equally incomprehensible boast that he could fast for much longer than he was doing; he praised the high ambition, the good will, the great self-denial undoubtedly implicit in such a statement; and then quite simply countered it by bringing out photographs, which were also on sale to the public, showing the artist on the fortieth day of a fast lying in bed almost dead from exhaustion. This perversion of the truth, familiar to the artist though it was, always unnerved him afresh and proved too much for him. What was a consequence of the premature ending of his fast was here presented as the cause of it! To fight against this lack of understanding, against a whole world of non-understanding, was impossible. Time and again in good faith he stood by the bars listening to the impresario, but as soon as the photographs appeared he always let go and sank with a groan back on to his straw, and the reassured public could once more come close and gaze at him.

5 A few years later when the witnesses of such scenes called them to mind, they often failed to understand themselves at all. For meanwhile the aforementioned change in public interest had set in; it seemed to happen almost overnight; there may have been profound causes for it, but who was going to bother about that; at any rate the pampered hunger artist suddenly found himself deserted one fine day by the amusement seekers, who went streaming past him to other more favored attractions. For the last time the impresario hurried him over half Europe to discover whether the old interest might still survive here and there; all in vain; everywhere, as if by secret agreement, a positive revulsion from professional fasting was in evidence. Of course it could not really have sprung up so suddenly as all that, and many premonitory symptoms which had not been sufficiently remarked or suppressed during the rush and glitter of success now came retrospectively to mind, but it was now too late to take any countermeasures. Fasting would surely come into fashion again at some future date, yet that was no comfort for those living in the present. What, then, was the hunger artist to do? He had been applauded by thousands in his time and could hardly come down to showing himself in a street booth at village fairs, and as for adopting another profession, he was not only too old for that but too fanatically devoted to fasting. So he took leave of the impresario, his partner in an unparalleled career, and hired himself to a large circus; in order to spare his own feelings he avoided reading the conditions of his contract.

A large circus with its enormous traffic in replacing and recruiting men, animals and apparatus can always find a use for people at any time, even for a hunger artist, provided of course that he does not ask too much, and in this particular case anyhow it was not only the artist who was taken on but his famous and long-known name as well, indeed considering the peculiar nature of his performance, which was not impaired by advancing age, it could not be objected that here was an artist past his prime, no longer at the height of his professional skill, seeking a refuge in some quiet corner of a circus; on the contrary, the hunger artist averred that he could fast as well as ever, which was entirely credible, he even alleged that if he were allowed to fast as he liked, and this was at once promised him without more ado, he could astound the world by establishing a record never yet achieved, a statement which certainly provoked a smile among the other professionals, since it left out of account the change in public opinion, which the hunger artist in his zeal conveniently forgot.

He had not, however, actually lost his sense of the real situation and took it as a matter of course that he and his cage should be stationed, not in the middle of the ring as a main attraction, but outside, near the animal cages, on a site that was after all easily accessible. Large and gaily painted placards made a frame for the cage and announced what was to be seen inside it. When the public came thronging out in the intervals to see the animals, they could hardly avoid passing the hunger artist's cage and stopping there for a moment, perhaps they might even have stayed longer had not those pressing behind them in the narrow gangway, who did not understand why they should be held up on their way toward the excitements of the menagerie, made it impossible for anyone to stand gazing quietly for any length of time. And that was the reason why the hunger artist, who had of course been looking forward to these visiting hours as the main achievement of his life, began instead to shrink from them. At first he could hardly wait for the intervals; it was exhilarating to watch the crowds come streaming his way, until only too soon—not even the most obstinate self-deception, clung to almost consciously, could hold out against the fact—the conviction was borne in upon him that these people, most of them, to judge from their actions, again and again, without exception, were all on their way to the menagerie. And the first sight of them from the distance remained the best. For when they reached his cage he was at once deafened by the storm of shouting and abuse that arose from the two contending factions, which renewed themselves continuously, of those who wanted to stop and stare at him—he soon began to dislike them more than the others—not out of real interest but only out of obstinate self-assertiveness, and those who wanted to go straight on to the animals: When the first great rush was past, the stragglers came along, and these, whom nothing could have prevented from stopping to look at him as long as they had breath, raced past with long strides, hardly even glancing at him, in their haste to get to the menagerie in time. And all too rarely did it happen that he had a stroke of luck, when some father of a family fetched up before him with his children, pointed a finger at the hunger artist and explained at length what the phenomenon meant, telling stories of earlier years when he himself had watched similar but much more thrilling performances, and the children, still rather uncomprehending, since neither inside nor outside school had they been sufficiently prepared for this lesson—what did they care about fasting?—yet showed by the brightness of their intent eyes that new and better times might be coming. Perhaps, said the hunger artist to himself many a time, things would be a little better if his cage were set not quite so near the menagerie. That made it too easy for people to make their choice, to say nothing of what he suffered from the stench of the menagerie, the animals' restlessness by night, the carrying past of raw lumps of flesh for the beasts of prey, the roaring at feeding times, which depressed him continually. But he did not dare to lodge a complaint with the management; after all, he had the animals to thank for the troops of people who passed his cage, among whom there might always be one here and there to take an interest in him, and who could tell where they might seclude him if he called attention to his existence and thereby to the fact that, strictly speaking, he was only an impediment on the way to the menagerie.

A small impediment, to be sure, one that grew steadily less. People grew familiar with the strange idea that they could be expected, in times like these, to take an interest in a hunger artist, and with this familiarity the verdict went out against him. He might fast as much as he could, and he did so; but nothing could save him now, people passed him by. Just try to explain to anyone the art of fasting! Anyone who has no feeling for it cannot be made to understand it. The fine placards grew dirty and illegible, they were torn down; the little notice board telling the number of fast days achieved, which at first was changed carefully every day, had long stayed at the same figure, for after the first few weeks even this small task seemed pointless to the staff; and so the artist simply fasted on and on, as he had once dreamed of doing, and it was no trouble to him, just as he had always foretold, but no one counted the days, no one, not even the artist himself, knew what records he was already breaking, and his heart grew heavy. And when once in a time some leisurely passer-by stopped, made merry over the old figure on the board and spoke of swindling, that was in its way the stupidest lie ever invented by indifference and inborn malice, since it was not the hunger artist who was cheating; he was working honestly, but the world was cheating him of his reward.

Many more days went by, however, and that too came to an end. An overseer's eye fell on the cage one day and he asked the attendants why this perfectly good cage should be left standing there unused with dirty straw inside it; nobody knew, until one man, helped out by the notice board, remembered about the hunger artist. They poked into the straw with sticks and found him in it. "Are you still fasting?" asked the overseer: "When on earth do you mean to stop?" "Forgive me, everybody," whispered the hunger artist; only the overseer, who had his ear to the bars, understood him. "Of course," said the overseer, and tapped his forehead with a finger to let the attendants know what state the man was in, "we forgive you." "I always wanted you to admire my fasting," said the hunger artist. "We do admire it," said the overseer, affably. "But you shouldn't admire it," said the hunger artist. "Well, then we don't admire it," said the overseer, "but why shouldn't we admire it?" "Because I have to fast, I can't help it," said the hunger artist. "What a fellow you are," said the overseer, "and why can't you help it?" "Because," said the hunger artist, lifting his head a little and speaking, with his lips pursed, as if for a kiss, right into the overseer's ear, so that no syllable might be lost, "because I couldn't find the food I liked. If I had found it, believe me, I should have made no fuss and stuffed myself like you or anyone else." These were his last words, but in his dimming eyes remained the firm though no longer proud persuasion that he was still continuing to fast.

10 "Well, clear this out now!" said the overseer, and they buried the hunger artist, straw and all. Into the cage they put a young panther. Even the most insensitive felt it refreshing to see this wild creature leaping around the cage that had so long been dreary. The panther was all right. The food he liked was brought him without hesitation by the attendants; he seemed not even to miss his freedom; his noble body,

furnished almost to the bursting point with all that it needed, seemed to carry freedom around with it too; somewhere in his jaws it seemed to lurk; and the joy of life streamed with such ardent passion from his throat that for the onlookers it was not easy to stand the shock of it. But they braced themselves, crowded round the cage, and did not want ever to move away.

* * *

JONATHAN LETHEM (1964–)

The Spray (2004)

The apartment was burgled and the police came. Four of them and a dog. The three youngest were like boys. They wore buzzing squawking radios on their belts. The oldest was in charge and the young ones did what he told them. The dog sat. They asked what was taken and we said we weren't sure—the television and the fax machine, at least. One of them was writing, taking down what we said. He had a tic, an eye that kept blinking. "What else?" the oldest policeman said. We didn't know what else. That's when they brought it out, a small unmarked canister, and began spraying around the house. First they put a mask over the mouth and nose of the dog. None of them wore a mask. They didn't offer us any protection. Just the dog, "Stand back," they said. They sprayed in a circle toward the edges of the room. We stood clustered with the policemen. "What's that?" we said. "Spray," said the oldest policeman. "Makes lost things visible."

The spray settled like a small rain through the house and afterward glowing in various spots were the things the burglar had taken. It was a salmon-colored glow. On the table was a salmon-colored image of a box, a jewelry box that Addie's mother had given us. There was a salmon-colored glowing television and fax machine in place of the missing ones. On the shelves the spray showed a Walkman and a camera and a pair of cuff links, salmon-colored and luminous. In the bedroom was Addie's vibrator, glowing like a fuel rod. We all walked around the apartment, looking for things. The eye-tic policeman wrote down the names of the items that appeared. Addie called the vibrator a massager. The dog in the mask, eyes watering. I couldn't smell the spray. "How long does it last?" we said.

"About a day," said the policeman who'd done the spraying, not the oldest. "You known you c-can't use this stuff anymore, even though you c-can see it," he said. "It's gone."

"Try and touch it," said the oldest policeman. He pointed at the glowing jewelry box.

We did and it wasn't there. Our hands passed through the visible missing objects. 5

They asked us about our neighbors. We told them we trusted everyone in the building. They looked at the fire escape. The dog sneezed. They took some pictures. The burglars had come through the window. Addie put a book on the bedside table on top of the glowing vibrator. It showed through, like it was projected onto the book. We asked if they wanted to dust for fingerprints. The older policeman shook his head. "They wore gloves," he said. "How do you know?" we said, "Rubber gloves leave residue, powder," he said. "That's what makes the dog sneeze." "Oh." They took more pictures. "Did you want something to drink?" The older one said no. One of the younger policemen said, "I'm allergic, just like the d-dog," and the other policemen laughed. Addie had a drink, a martini. The policemen shook our hands and then they went away. We'd been given a case number. The box and the cuff links and the rest still glowed. Then Addie saw that the policemen had left the spray.

She took the canister and said, "There was something wrong with those policemen."

"Do you mean how young they seemed?"

"No, I think they always look young. You just don't notice on the street. Outdoors you see the uniforms, but in the house you can see how they're just barely old enough to vote."

"What are you going to do with that?" I said.

She handled it. "Nothing. Didn't you think there was something strange about those policemen, though?"

"Do you mean the one with the lisp?"

"He didn't have a lisp, he had a twitchy eye."

"Well, there was one with an eye thing, but the one who stuttered—is that what you mean by strange?" Addie kept turning the canister over in her hands. "Why don't you let me take that," I said.

"It's okay," she said. "I guess I don't know what I mean. Just something about them. Maybe there were too many of them. Do you think they develop the pictures themselves, Aaron? Do they have a darkroom in the police station?"

I said, "Probably." She said, " Do you think the missing things show up in the photographs—the things the spray reveals?"

"Probably."

"Let's just keep it and see if they come back."

"I wish you would put it on the table, then."

"Let's find a place to hide it."

"They're probably doing some kind of inventory right now, at the police station. They'll probably be back for it any minute."

"So if we hide it—"

"If we hide it we look guiltier than if you just put it on the table."

"We didn't steal anything. Our house was broken into. They left it here."

"I wish you would put it on the table."

"I wonder if the police do their inventory by spraying around the police station to see what's missing?"

"So if we have their spray—"

"They'll never know what happened!" She shrieked with laughter. I laughed too. I moved next to her on the couch and we rolled and laughed like monkeys in a zoo. Still laughing. I put my hand on the spray canister. "Gimme," I said.

"Let go." Her laughter faded as she pulled at the can. The ends of several hairs were stuck to her tongue. I pulled on the can. And she pulled. We both pulled harder.

"Gimme," I said. I let go of the an and tickled her. "Gimme gimme gimme."

She grimaced and twisted away from me. "Not funny," she said.

"The police don't have their SPRAY!" I said, and kept tickling her.

"Not funny not funny." Slapping my hands away, she stood up.

"Okay. You're right, it's not funny. Put it on the table."

"Let's return it like you said."

"I'm too tired. Let's just hide it. We can return it tomorrow."

"Okay, I'll hide it. Cover your eyes."

"Not hide-and-seek. We have to agree on a place. A locked place."

"What's the big deal? Let's just leave it on the table." She put it on the table, beside the salmon-colored glowing box. "Maybe somebody will break in and take it. Maybe the police will break in."

"You're a little mixed up, I'd say." I moved closer to the table.

"I'm just tired." She pretended to yawn. "What a day."

"I don't miss the stuff that was taken," I said.

"You don't?"

"I hate television and faxes. I hate this little jewelry box."

"See if you're still saying that tomorrow, when you can't see them anymore."

"I only care about you, you, you," I grabbed the canister of spray. She grabbed it too. "Let go," she said.

"You're all I love, you're all that matters to me," I said.

We wrestled for the can again. We fell onto the couch together.

"Let's just put it down on the table," said Addie. "Okay," "Let go." "You first." "No, at the same time." We put it on the table.

"Are you thinking what I'm thinking," she said.

"I don't know, probably,"

"What are you thinking?"

"What you're thinking."

"I'm not thinking anything."

"Then I'm not either."

"Liar."

"It probably doesn't work that way," I said. "The police wouldn't have a thing like that. It isn't the same thing."

"So why not try."

"Don't."

"You said it wouldn't work."

"Just don't. It's toxic. You saw them cover the dog's mouth."

"They didn't cover themselves. Anyway, I asked them about that when you were in the other room. They said it was so you wouldn't see the stuff the dog ate that fell out of its mouth. Because the dog is a very sloppy eater. So the spray would show what it had been eating recently, around the mouth. It's disgusting, they said."

"Now you're the liar."

"Let's just see."

I jumped up. "If you spray me I'll spray you," I shouted. The spray hit me as I moved across the room. The wet mist fell behind me, like a parachute collapsing in the spot where I'd been, but enough got on me. An image of Lucinda formed, glowing and salmon-colored.

Lucinda was naked. Her hair was short, like when we were together. Her head lay on my shoulder, her arms were around my neck, and her body was across my front. My shirt and jacket. Her breasts were mashed against me, but I couldn't feel them. Her knee was across my legs. I jumped backward but she came with me, radiant and insubstantial. I turned my head to see her face. Her expression was peaceful, but her little salmon-colored eyelids were half open.

"Ha!" said Addie. "I told you it would work."

"GIVE ME THAT!" I lunged for the spray. Addie ducked. I grabbed her arm and pulled her with me onto the couch. Me and Addie and Lucinda were all there together, Lucinda placidly naked. As Addie and I wrestled for the spray we plunged through Lucinda's glowing body, her luminous arms and legs.

I got my hands on the spray canister. We both had our hands on it. Four hands covering the one can. Then it went off. One of us pressed the nozzle, I don't know who. It wasn't Lucinda, anyway.

70 As the spray settled over us Charles became visible, poised over Addie. He was naked, like Lucinda. His glowing shoulders and legs and ass were covered with glowing salmon hair, like the halo around a lightbulb. His mouth was open. His face was blurred, like he was a picture someone had taken while he was moving his face, saying something.

"There you go," I said. "You got what you wanted." "I didn't want anything," said Addie.

We put the spray on the table.

"How long did the police say it would last?" I said. I tried not to look at Lucinda. She was right beside my head.

"About twenty-four hours. What time is it?"

75 "It's late. I'm tired. The police didn't say twenty-four hours. About a day, they said."

"That's twenty-four hours."

"Probably they meant it's gone the next day."

"I don't think so."

I looked at the television. I looked at the cuff links. I looked at Charles's ass. "Probably the sunlight makes it wear off," I said.

80 "Maybe."

"Probably you can't see it in the dark, in complete darkness. Let's go to bed."

We went into the bedroom. All four of us. I took off my shoes and socks. "Probably it's just attached to our clothes. If I take off my clothes and leave them in the other room—

"Try it."

I took off my pants and jacket. Lucinda was attached to me, not the clothes. Her bare salmon knee was across my bare legs. I started to take off my shirt. Addie looked at me. Lucinda's face was on my bare shoulder.

85 "Put your clothes back on," said Addie.

I put them back on. Addie left her clothes on. We lay on top of the covers in our clothes. Lucinda and Charles were on top of us. I didn't know where to put my hands. I wondered how Addie felt about Charles's blurred face, his open mouth. I was glad Lucinda wasn't blurred. "Turn off the light," I said. "We won't be able to see them in the dark."

Addie turned off the light. The room was dark. Charles and Lucinda glowed salmon above us. Glowing in the blackness with the vibrator on the side table and the luminous dial of my watch.

"Just close your eyes," I said to Addie.

"You close yours first," she said.

* * *

NAGUIB MAHFOUZ (1911–2006)

Half a Day (Arabic version: 1989; English version: 1991)

Translated by Denys Johnson-Davies

I proceeded alongside my father, clutching his right hand, running to keep up with the long strides he was taking. All my clothes were new: the black shoes, the green school uniform, and the red tarboosh.° My delight in my new clothes, however, was not altogether unmarred, for this was no feast day but the day on which I was to be cast into school for the first time.

My mother stood at the window watching our progress, and I would turn toward her from time to time, as though appealing for help. We walked along a street lined with gardens; on both sides were extensive fields planted with crops, prickly pears, henna trees, and a few date palms.

"Why school?" I challenged my father openly. "I shall never do anything to annoy you."

"I'm not punishing you," he said, laughing. "School's not a punishment. It's the factory that makes useful men out of boys. Don't you want to be like your father and brothers?"

I was not convinced. I did not believe there was really any good to be had in tear- 5
ing me away from the intimacy of my home and throwing me into this building that stood at the end of the road like some huge, high-walled fortress, exceedingly stern and grim.

When we arrived at the gate we could see the courtyard, vast and crammed full of boys and girls. "Go in by yourself," said my father, "and join them. Put a smile on your face and be a good example to others."

---

tarboosh: A felt cap, which is usually red and shaped like a flat-topped cone with a tassel that hangs from the crown. Also known as a *fez*.

I hesitated and clung to his hand, but he gently pushed me from him. "Be a man," he said. "Today you truly begin life. You will find me waiting for you when it's time to leave."

I took a few steps, then stopped and looked but saw nothing. Then the faces of boys and girls came into view. I did not know a single one of them, and none of them knew me. I felt I was a stranger who had lost his way. But glances of curiosity were directed toward me, and one boy approached and asked, "Who brought you?"

"My father," I whispered.

10 "My father's dead," he said quite simply.

I did not know what to say. The gate was closed, letting out a pitiable screech. Some of the children burst into tears. The bell rang. A lady came along, followed by a group of men. The men began sorting us into ranks. We were formed into an intricate pattern in the great courtyard surrounded on three sides by high buildings of several floors; from each floor we were overlooked by a long balcony roofed in wood.

"This is your new home," said the woman. "Here too there are mothers and fathers. Here there is everything that is enjoyable and beneficial to knowledge and religion. Dry your tears and face life joyfully."

We submitted to the facts, and this submission brought a sort of contentment. Living beings were drawn to other living beings, and from the first moments my heart made friends with such boys as were to be my friends and fell in love with such girls as I was to be in love with, so that it seemed my misgivings had had no basis. I had never imagined school would have this rich variety. We played all sorts of different games: swings, the vaulting horse, ball games. In the music room we chanted our first songs. We also had our first introduction to language. We saw a globe of the Earth, which revolved and showed the various continents and countries. We started learning the numbers. The story of the Creator of the universe was read to us, we were told of His present world and of His Hereafter, and we heard examples of what He said. We ate delicious food, took a little nap, and woke up to go on with friendship and love, play and learning.

As our path revealed itself to us, however, we did not find it as totally sweet and unclouded as we had presumed. Dust-laden winds and unexpected accidents came about suddenly, so we had to be watchful, at the ready, and very patient. It was not all a matter of playing and fooling around. Rivalries could bring about pain and hatred or give rise to fighting. And while the lady would sometimes smile, she would often scowl and scold. Even more frequently she would resort to physical punishment.

15 In addition, the time for changing one's mind was over and gone and there was no question of ever returning to the paradise of home. Nothing lay ahead of us but exertion, struggle, and perseverance. Those who were able took advantage of the opportunities for success and happiness that presented themselves amid the worries.

The bell rang announcing the passing of the day and the end of work. The throngs of children rushed toward the gate, which was opened again. I bade farewell to friends and sweethearts and passed through the gate. I peered around but found no trace of my father, who had promised to be there. I stepped aside to wait. When I had waited for a long time without avail, I decided to return home on my own. After I had taken a few steps, a middle-aged man passed by, and I realized at once that I knew him. He came toward me, smiling, and shook me by the hand, saying, "It's a long time since we last met—how are you?"

With a nod of my head, I agreed with him and in turn asked, "And you, how are you?"

"As you can see, not all that good, the Almighty be praised!"

Again he shook me by the hand and went off. I proceeded a few steps, then came to a startled halt. Good Lord! Where was the street lined with gardens? Where had it disappeared to? When did all these vehicles invade it? And when did all these hordes of humanity come to rest upon its surface? How did these hills of refuse come to cover its sides? And where were the fields that bordered it? High buildings had taken over, the street surged with children, and disturbing noises shook the air. At various points stood conjurers showing off their tricks and making snakes appear from baskets. Then there was a band announcing the opening of a circus, with clowns and weight lifters walking in front. A line of trucks carrying central security troops crawled majestically by. The siren of a fire engine shrieked, and it was not clear how the vehicle would cleave its way to reach the blazing fire. A battle raged between a taxi driver and his passenger, while the passenger's wife called out for help and no one answered. Good God! I was in a daze. My head spun, I almost went crazy. How could all this have happened in half a day, between early morning and sunset? I would find the answer at home with my father. But where was my home? I could see only tall buildings and hordes of people. I hastened on to the crossroads between the gardens and Abu Khoda. I had to cross Abu Khoda to reach my house, but the stream of cars would not let up. The fire engine's siren was shrieking at full pitch as it moved at a snail's pace, and I said to myself, "Let the fire take its pleasure in what it consumes." Extremely irritated, I wondered when I would be able to cross. I stood there a long time, until the young lad employed at the ironing shop on the corner came up to me. He stretched out his arm and said gallantly, "Grandpa, let me take you across."

* * *

BOBBIE ANN MASON (1942–)

Shiloh (1982)

Leroy Moffitt's wife, Norma Jean, is working on her pectorals. She lifts three-pound dumbbells to warm up, then progresses to a twenty-pound barbell. Standing with her legs apart, she reminds Leroy of Wonder Woman.

"I'd give anything if I could just get these muscles to where they're real hard," says Norma Jean. "Feel this arm. It's not as hard as the other one."

"That's 'cause you're right-handed," says Leroy, dodging as she swings the barbell in an arc.

"Do you think so?"

"Sure." 5

Leroy is a truckdriver. He injured his leg in a highway accident four months ago, and his physical therapy, which involves weights and a pulley, prompted Norma Jean to try building herself up. Now she is attending a bodybuilding class. Leroy has been collecting temporary disability since his tractor-trailer jackknifed in Missouri, badly twisting his left leg in its socket. He has a steel pin in his hip. He will probably not be able to drive his rig again. It sits in the backyard, like a gigantic bird that has flown home to roost. Leroy has been home in Kentucky for three months, and his leg is almost healed, but the accident frightened him and he does not want to drive any more long hauls. He is not sure what to do next. In the meantime, he makes things from craft kits. He started by building a miniature log cabin from notched Popsicle sticks. He varnished it and placed it on the TV set, where it remains. It reminds him of a rustic Nativity scene. Then he tried string art (sailing ships on black velvet), a macramé owl kit, a snap-together B-17 Flying Fortress, and a lamp made out of a model truck, with a light fixture screwed in the top of the cab. At first the kits were diversions, something to kill time, but now he is thinking about building a full-scale log house from a kit. It would be considerably cheaper than building a regular house, and besides, Leroy has grown to appreciate how things are put together. He has begun to realize that in all the years he was on the road he never took time to examine anything. He was always flying past scenery.

"They won't let you build a log cabin in any of the new subdivisions," Norma Jean tells him.

"They will if I tell them it's for you," he says, teasing her. Ever since they were married, he has promised Norma Jean he would build her a new home one day. They have always rented, and the house they live in is small and nondescript. It does not even feel like a home, Leroy realizes now.

Norma Jean works at the Rexall drugstore, and she has acquired an amazing amount of information about cosmetics. When she explains to Leroy the three stages of complexion care, involving creams, toners, and moisturizers, he thinks happily of other petroleum products—axle grease, diesel fuel. This is a connection between him and Norma Jean. Since he has been home, he has felt unusually tender about his wife and guilty over his long absences. But he can't tell what she feels about him. Norma Jean has never complained about his traveling; she has never made hurt remarks, like calling his truck a "widow-maker." He is reasonably certain she has been faithful to him, but he wishes she would celebrate his permanent homecoming more happily. Norma Jean is often startled to find Leroy at home, and he thinks she seems a little disappointed about it. Perhaps he reminds her too much of the early days of their marriage, before he went on the road. They had a child who died as an infant, years ago. They never speak about their memories of Randy, which have almost faded, but now that Leroy is home all the time, they sometimes feel awkward around each other, and Leroy wonders if one of them should mention the child. He has the feeling that they are waking up out of a dream together—that they must create a new marriage, start afresh. They are lucky they are still married. Leroy has read that for most people losing a child destroys the marriage—or else he heard this on *Donahue*. He can't always remember where he learns things anymore.

10 At Christmas, Leroy bought an electric organ for Norma Jean. She used to play the piano when she was in high school. "It don't leave you," she told him once. "It's like riding a bicycle."

The new instrument had so many keys and buttons that she was bewildered by it at first. She touched the keys tentatively, pushed some buttons, then pecked out "Chopsticks." It came out in an amplified fox-trot rhythm, with marimba sounds.

"It's an orchestra!" she cried.

The organ had a pecan-look finish and eighteen preset chords, with optional flute, violin, trumpet, clarinet, and banjo accompaniments. Norma Jean mastered the organ almost immediately. At first she played Christmas songs. Then she bought *The Sixties Songbook* and learned every tune in it, adding variations to each with the rows of brightly colored buttons.

"I didn't like these old songs back then," she said. "But I have this crazy feeling I missed something."

"You didn't miss a thing," said Leroy. 15

Leroy likes to lie on the couch and smoke a joint and listen to Norma Jean play "Can't Take My Eyes Off You" and "I'll Be Back." He is back again. After fifteen years on the road, he is finally settling down with the woman he loves. She is still pretty. Her skin is flawless. Her frosted curls resemble pencil trimmings.

Now that Leroy has come home to stay, he notices how much the town has changed. Subdivisions are spreading across western Kentucky like an oil slick. The sign at the edge of town says "Pop: 11,500"— only seven hundred more than it said twenty years before. Leroy can't figure out who is living in all the new houses. The farmers who used to gather around the courthouse square on Saturday afternoons to play checkers and spit tobacco juice have gone. It has been years since Leroy has thought about the farmers, and they have disappeared without his noticing.

Leroy meets a kid named Stevie Hamilton in the parking lot at the new shopping center. While they pretend to be strangers meeting over a stalled car, Stevie tosses an ounce of marijuana under the front seat of Leroy's car. Stevie is wearing orange jogging shoes and a T-shirt that says CHATTAHOOCHEE SUPERRAT. His father is a prominent doctor who lives in one of the expensive subdivisions in a new white-columned brick house that looks like a funeral parlor. In the phone book under his name there is a separate number, with the listing "Teenagers."

"Where do you get this stuff?" asks Leroy. "From your pappy?"

"That's for me to know and you to find out," Stevie says. He is slit-eyed and skinny. 20

"What else you got?"

"What you interested in?"

"Nothing special. Just wondered."

Leroy used to take speed on the road. Now he has to go slowly. He needs to be mellow. He leans back against the car and says, "I'm aiming to build me a log house, soon as I get time. My wife, though, I don't think she likes the idea."

"Well, let me know when you want me again," Stevie says. He has a cigarette in his cupped palm, as though sheltering it from the wind. He takes a long drag, then stomps it on the asphalt and slouches away. 25

Stevie's father was two years ahead of Leroy in high school. Leroy is thirty-four. He married Norma Jean when they were both eighteen, and their child Randy was born a few months later, but he died at the age of four months and three days. He would be about Stevie's age now. Norma Jean and Leroy were at the drive-in, watching a double feature (*Dr. Strangelove* and *Lover Come Back*), and the baby was sleeping in the back seat. When the first movie ended, the baby was dead. It was the sudden infant death syndrome. Leroy remembers handing Randy to a nurse at the emergency room, as though he were offering her a large doll as a present. A dead baby feels like a sack of flour. "It just happens sometimes," said the doctor, in what Leroy always recalls as a nonchalant tone. Leroy can hardly remember the child anymore, but he still sees vividly a scene from *Dr. Strangelove* in which the President of the United States was talking in a folksy voice on the hot line to the Soviet premier about the bomber accidentally headed toward Russia. He was in the War Room, and the world map was lit up. Leroy remembers Norma Jean standing catatonically beside him in the hospital and himself thinking: Who is this strange girl? He had forgotten who she was. Now scientists are saying that crib death is caused by a virus. Nobody knows anything, Leroy thinks. The answers are always changing.

When Leroy gets home from the shopping center, Norma Jean's mother, Mabel Beasley, is there. Until this year, Leroy has not realized how much time she spends with Norma Jean. When she visits, she inspects the closets and then the plants, informing Norma Jean when a plant is droopy or yellow. Mabel calls the plants "flowers," although there are never any blooms. She always notices if Norma Jean's laundry is pilling up. Mabel is a short, overweight woman whose tight, brown-dyed curls look more like a wig than the actual wig she sometimes wears. Today she has brought Norma Jean an off-white dust ruffle she made for the bed; Mabel works in a custom-upholstery shop.

"This is the tenth one I made this year," Mabel says. "I got started and couldn't stop."

"It's real pretty," says Norma Jean.

30 "Now we can hide things under the bed," says Leroy, who gets along with his mother-in-law primarily by joking with her. Mabel has never really forgiven him for disgracing her by getting Norma Jean pregnant. When the baby died, she said that fate was mocking her.

"What's that thing?" Mabel says to Leroy in a loud voice, pointing to a tangle of yarn on a piece of canvas.

Leroy holds it up for Mabel to see. "It's my needlepoint," he explains. "This is a *Star Trek* pillow cover."

"That's what a woman would do," says Mabel. "Great day in the morning!"

"All the big football players on TV do it," he says.

35 "Why, Leroy, you're always trying to fool me. I don't believe you for one minute. You don't know what to do with yourself—that's the whole trouble. Sewing!"

"I'm aiming to build us a log house," says Leroy. "Soon as my plans come."

"Like *heck* you are," says Norma Jean. She takes Leroy's needlepoint and shoves it into a drawer. "You have to find a job first. Nobody can afford to build now anyway."

Mabel straightens her girdle and says, "I still think before you get tied down y'all ought to take a little run to Shiloh."

"One of these days, Mama," Norma Jean says impatiently.

Mabel is talking about Shiloh, Tennessee. For the past few years, she has been urging Leroy and Norma Jean to visit the Civil War battleground there. Mabel went there on her honeymoon — the only real trip she ever took. Her husband died of a perforated ulcer when Norma Jean was ten, but Mabel, who was accepted into the United Daughters of the Confederacy in 1975, is still preoccupied with going back to Shiloh.

"I've been to kingdom come and back in that truck out yonder," Leroy says to Mabel, "but we never yet set foot in that battleground. Ain't that something? How did I miss it?"

"It's not even that far," Mabel says.

After Mabel leaves, Norma Jean reads to Leroy from a list she has made.

"Things you could do," she announces. "You could get a job as a guard at Union Carbide, where they'd let you set on a stool. You could get on at the lumberyard. You could do a little carpenter work, if you want to build so bad. You could —"

"I can't do something where I'd have to stand up all day."

"You ought to try standing up all day behind a cosmetics counter. It's amazing that I have strong feet, coming from two parents that never had strong feet at all." At the moment Norma Jean is holding on to the kitchen counter, raising her knees one at a time as she talks. She is wearing two-pound ankle weights.

"Don't worry," says Leroy. "I'll do something."

"You could truck calves to slaughter for somebody. You wouldn't have to drive any big old truck for that."

"I'm going to build you this house," says Leroy. "I want to make you a real home."

"I don't want to live in any log cabin."

"It's not a cabin. It's a house."

"I don't care. It looks like a cabin."

"You and me together could lift those logs. It's just like lifting weights."

Norma Jean doesn't answer. Under her breath, she is counting. Now she is marching through the kitchen. She is doing goose steps.

Before his accident, when Leroy came home he used to stay in the house with Norma Jean, watching TV in bed and playing cards. She would cook fried chicken, picnic ham, chocolate pie—all his favorites. Now he is home alone much of the time. In the mornings, Norma Jean disappears, leaving a cooling place in the bed. She eats a cereal called Body Buddies, and she leaves the bowl on the table, with the soggy tan balls floating in a milk puddle. He sees things about Norma Jean that he never realized before. When she chops onions, she stares off into a corner, as if she can't bear to look. She puts on her house slippers almost precisely at nine o'clock every evening and nudges her jogging shoes under the couch. She saves bread heels for the birds. Leroy watches the birds at the feeder. He notices the peculiar way goldfinches fly past the window. They close their wings, then fall, then spread their wings to catch and lift themselves. He wonders if they close their eyes when they fall. Norma Jean closes her eyes when they are in bed. She wants the lights turned out. Even then, he is sure she closes her eyes.

He goes for long drives around town. He tends to drive a car rather carelessly. Power steering and an automatic shift make a car feel so small and inconsequential that his body is hardly involved in the driving process. His injured leg stretches out comfortably. Once or twice he has almost hit something, but even the prospect of an accident seems minor in a car. He cruises the new subdivisions, feeling like a criminal rehearsing for a robbery. Norma Jean is probably right about a log house being inappropriate here in the new subdivisions. All the houses look grand and complicated. They depress him.

One day when Leroy comes home from a drive he finds Norma Jean in tears. She is in the kitchen making a potato and mushroom-soup casserole, with grated-cheese topping. She is crying because her mother caught her smoking.

"I didn't hear her coming. I was standing here puffing away pretty as you please," Norma Jean says, wiping her eyes.

"I knew it would happen sooner or later," says Leroy, putting his arm around her.

60 "She don't know the meaning of the word 'knock,'" says Norma Jean. "It's a wonder she hadn't caught me years ago."

"Think of it this way," Leroy says. "What if she caught me with a joint?"

"You better not let her!" Norma Jean shrieks. "I'm warning you, Leroy Moffitt!"

"I'm just kidding. Here, play me a tune. That'll help you relax."

Norma Jean puts the casserole in the oven and sets the timer. Then she plays a ragtime tune, with horns and banjo, as Leroy lights up a joint and lies on the couch, laughing to himself about Mabel's catching him at it. He thinks of Stevie Hamilton—a doctor's son pushing grass. Everything is funny. The whole town seems crazy and small. He is reminded of Virgil Mathis, a boastful policeman Leroy used to shoot pool with. Virgil recently led a drug bust in a back room at a bowling alley, where he seized ten thousand dollars' worth of marijuana. The newspaper had a picture of him holding up the bags of grass and grinning widely. Right now, Leroy can imagine Virgil breaking down the door and arresting him with a lungful of smoke. Virgil would probably have been alerted to the scene because of all the racket Norma Jean is making. Now she sounds like a hard-rock band. Norma Jean is terrific. When she switches to a Latin-rhythm version of "Sunshine Superman," Leroy hums along. Norma Jean's foot goes up and down, up and down.

65 "Well, what do you think?" Leroy says, when Norma Jean pauses to search through her music.

"What do I think about what?"

His mind has gone blank. Then he says, "I'll sell my rig and build us a house." That wasn't what he wanted to say. He wanted to know what she thought—what she *really* thought—about them.

"Don't start in on that again," says Norma Jean. She begins playing, "Who'll Be the Next in Line?"

Leroy used to tell hitchhikers his whole life story—about his travels, his hometown, the baby. He would end with a question: "Well, what do you think?" It was just a rhetorical question. In time, he had the feeling that he'd been telling the same story over and over to the same hitchhikers. He quit talking to hitchhikers when he realized how his voice sounded—whining and self-pitying, like some teenage-tragedy song. Now Leroy has the sudden impulse to tell Norma Jean about himself, as if he had just met her. They have known each other so long they have forgotten a lot about each other. They could become reacquainted. But when the oven timer goes off and she runs to the kitchen, he forgets why he wants to do this.

The next day, Mabel drops by. It is Saturday and Norma Jean is cleaning. Leroy is 70
studying the plans of his log house, which have finally come in the mail. He has them spread out on the table—big sheets of stiff blue paper, with diagrams and numbers printed in white. While Norma Jean runs the vacuum, Mabel drinks coffee. She sets her coffee cup on a blueprint.

"I'm just waiting for time to pass," she says to Leroy, drumming her fingers on the table.

As soon as Norma Jean switches off the vacuum, Mabel says in a loud voice, "Did you hear about the datsun dog that killed the baby?"

Norma Jean says, "The word is 'dachshund.'"

"They put the dog on trial. It chewed the baby's legs off. The mother was in the next room all the time." She raises her voice. "They thought it was neglect."

Norma Jean is holding her ears. Leroy manages to open the refrigerator and get 75
some Diet Pepsi to offer Mabel. Mabel still has some coffee and she waves away the Pepsi.

"Datsuns are like that," Mabel says. "They're jealous dogs. They'll tear a place to pieces if you don't keep an eye on them."

"You better watch out what you're saying, Mabel," says Leroy.

"Well, facts is facts."

Leroy looks out the window at his rig. It is like a huge piece of furniture gathering dust in the backyard. Pretty soon it will be an antique. He hears the vacuum cleaner. Norma Jean seems to be cleaning the living room rug again.

Later, she says to Leroy, "She just said that about the baby because she caught me 80
smoking. She's trying to pay me back."

"What are you talking about?" Leroy says, nervously shuffling blueprints.

"You know good and well," Norma Jean says. She is sitting in a kitchen chair with her feet up and her arms wrapped around her knees. She looks small and helpless. She says, "The very idea, her bringing up a subject like that! Saying it was neglect."

"She didn't mean that," Leroy says.

"She might not have *thought* she meant it. She always says things like that. You don't know how she goes on."

"But she didn't really mean it. She was just talking." 85

Leroy opens a king-sized bottle of beer and pours it into two glasses, dividing it carefully. He hands a glass to Norma Jean and she takes it from him mechanically. For a long time, they sit by the kitchen window watching the birds at the feeder.

Something is happening. Norma Jean is going to night school. She has graduated from her six-week body-building course and now she is taking an adult-education course in composition at Paducah Community College. She spends her evenings outlining paragraphs.

"First you have a topic sentence," she explains to Leroy. "Then you divide it up. Your secondary topic has to be connected to your primary topic."

To Leroy, this sounds intimidating. "I never was any good in English," he says.

"It makes a lot of sense."

"What are you doing this for, anyhow?"

She shrugs. "It's something to do." She stands up and lifts her dumbbells a few times.

"Driving a rig, nobody cared about my English."

"I'm not criticizing your English."

Norma Jean used to say, "If I lose ten minutes' sleep, I just drag all day." Now she stays up late, writing compositions. She got a B on her first paper — a how-to theme on soup-based casseroles. Recently Norma Jean has been cooking unusual foods — tacos, lasagna, Bombay chicken. She doesn't play the organ anymore, though her second paper was called "Why Music Is Important to Me." She sits at the kitchen table, concentrating on her outlines, while Leroy plays with his log house plans, practicing with a set of Lincoln Logs. The thought of getting a truckload of notched, numbered logs scares him, and he wants to be prepared. As he and Norma Jean work together at the kitchen table, Leroy has the hopeful thought that they are sharing something, but he knows he is a fool to think this. Norma Jean is miles away. He knows he is going to lose her. Like Mabel, he is just waiting for time to pass.

One day, Mabel is there before Norma Jean gets home from work, and Leroy finds himself confiding in her. Mabel, he realizes, must know Norma Jean better than he does.

"I don't know what's got into that girl," Mabel says. "She used to go to bed with the chickens. Now you say she's up all hours. Plus her a-smoking. I like to died."

"I want to make her this beautiful home," Leroy says, indicating the Lincoln Logs. "I don't think she even wants it. Maybe she was happier with me gone."

"She don't know what to make of you, coming home like this."

"Is that it?"

Mabel takes the roof off his Lincoln Log cabin. "You couldn't get *me* in a log cabin," she says. "I was raised in one. It's no picnic, let me tell you."

"They're different now," says Leroy.

"I tell you what," Mabel says, smiling oddly at Leroy.

"What?"

"Take her on down to Shiloh. Y'all need to get out together, stir a little. Her brain's all balled up over them books."

Leroy can see traces of Norma Jean's features in her mother's face. Mabel's worn face has the texture of crinkled cotton, but suddenly she looks pretty. It occurs to Leroy that Mabel has been hinting all along that she wants them to take her with them to Shiloh.

"Let's all go to Shiloh," he says. "You and me and her. Come Sunday."

Mabel throws up her hands in protest. "Oh, no, not me. Young folks want to be by theirselves."

When Norma Jean comes in with groceries, Leroy says excitedly, "Your mama here's been dying to go to Shiloh for thirty-five years. It's about time we went, don't you think?"

"I'm not going to butt in on anybody's second honeymoon," Mabel says.

"Who's going on a honeymoon, for Christ's sake?" Norma Jean says loudly.

"I never raised no daughter of mine to talk that-a-way," Mabel says.

"You ain't seen nothing yet," says Norma Jean. She starts putting away boxes and cans, slamming cabinet doors.

"There's a log cabin at Shiloh," Mabel says. "It was there during the battle. There's bullet holes in it."

"When are you going to *shut up* about Shiloh, Mama?" asks Norma Jean. 115

"I always thought Shiloh was the prettiest place, so full of history," Mabel goes on. "I just hoped y'all could see it once before I die, so you could tell me about it." Later, she whispers to Leroy, "You do what I said. A little change is what she needs."

"Your name means 'the king,'" Norma Jean says to Leroy that evening, He is trying to get her to go to Shiloh, and she is reading a book about another century.

"Well, I reckon I ought to be right proud."

"I guess so."

"Am I still king around here?" 120

Norma Jean flexes her biceps and feels them for hardness. "I'm not fooling around with anybody, if that's what you mean," she says.

"Would you tell me if you were?"

"I don't know."

"What does *your* name mean?"

"It was Marilyn Monroe's real name." 125

"No kidding!"

"Norma comes from the Normans. They were invaders," she says. She closes her book and looks hard at Leroy. "I'll go to Shiloh with you if you'll stop staring at me."

On Sunday, Norma Jean packs a picnic and they go to Shiloh. To Leroy's relief, Mabel says she does not want to come with them. Norma Jean drives, and Leroy, sitting beside her, feels like some boring hitchhiker she has picked up. He tries some conversation, but she answers him in monosyllables. At Shiloh, she drives aimlessly through the park, past bluffs and trails and steep ravines. Shiloh is an immense place, and Leroy cannot see it as a battleground. It is not what he expected. He thought it would look like a golf course. Monuments are everywhere, showing through the thick clusters of trees. Norma Jean passes the log cabin Mabel mentioned. It is surrounded by tourists looking for bullet holes.

"That's not the kind of log house I've got in mind," says Leroy apologetically.

"I know *that*." 130

"This is a pretty place. Your mama was right."

"It's O.K.," says Norma Jean. "Well, we've seen it. I hope she's satisfied."

They burst out laughing together.

At the park museum, a movie on Shiloh is shown every half hour, but they decide that they don't want to see it. They buy a souvenir Confederate flag for Mabel, and then they find a picnic spot near the cemetery. Norma Jean has brought a picnic cooler, with pimiento sandwiches, soft drinks, and Yodels. Leroy eats a sandwich and then smokes a joint, hiding it behind the picnic cooler. Norma Jean has quit smoking altogether. She is picking cake crumbs from the cellophane wrapper, like a fussy bird.

135 Leroy says, "So the boys in gray ended up in Corinth.° The Union soldiers zapped' em finally. April 7, 1862."

They both know that he doesn't know any history. He is just talking about some of the historical plaques they have read. He feels awkward, like a boy on a date with an older girl. They are still just making conversation.

"Corinth is where Mama eloped to," says Norma Jean.

They sit in silence and stare at the cemetery for the Union dead and, beyond, at a tall cluster of trees. Campers are parked nearby, bumper to bumper, and small children in bright clothing are cavorting and squealing. Norma Jean wads up the cake wrapper and squeezes it tightly in her hand. Without looking at Leroy, she says, "I want to leave you."

Leroy takes a bottle of Coke out of the cooler and flips off the cap. He holds the bottle poised near his mouth but cannot remember to take a drink. Finally he says, "No, you don't."

140 "Yes, I do."

"I won't let you."

"You can't stop me."

"Don't do me that way."

Leroy knows Norma Jean will have her own way. "Didn't I promise to be home from now on?" he says.

145 "In some ways, a woman prefers a man who wanders," says Norma Jean. "That sounds crazy, I know."

"You're not crazy."

Leroy remembers to drink from his Coke. Then he says, "Yes, you *are* crazy. You and me could start all over again. Right back at the beginning."

"We *have* started all over again," says Norma Jean. "And this is how it turned out."

"What did I do wrong?"

150 "Nothing."

"Is this one of those women's lib things?" Leroy asks.

"Don't be funny."

The cemetery, a green slope dotted with white markers, looks like a subdivision site. Leroy is trying to comprehend that his marriage is breaking up, but for some reason he is wondering about white slabs in a graveyard.

"Everything was fine till Mama caught me smoking," says Norma Jean, standing up. "That set something off."

155 "What are you talking about?"

"She won't leave me alone—*you* won't leave me alone." Norma Jean seems to be crying, but she is looking away from him. "I feel eighteen again. I can't face that all over again." She starts walking away. "No, it *wasn't* fine. I don't know what I'm saying. Forget it."

Leroy takes a lungful of smoke and closes his eyes as Norma Jean's words sink in. He tries to focus on the fact that thirty-five hundred soldiers died on the grounds

Corinth: Corinth, Mississippi, where the Union troops seized control of the Confederate railroad.

around him. He can only think of that war as a board game with plastic soldiers. Leroy almost smiles, as he compares the Confederates' daring attack on the Union camps and Virgil Mathis's raid on the bowling alley. General Grant, drunk and furious, shoved the Southerners back to Corinth, where Mabel and Jet Beasley were married years later, when Mabel was still thin and good-looking. The next day, Mabel and Jet visited the battleground, and then Norma Jean was born, and then she married Leroy and they had a baby, which they lost, and now Leroy and Norma Jean are here at the same battleground. Leroy knows he is leaving out a lot. He is leaving out the insides of history. History was always just names and dates to him. It occurs to him that building a house out of logs is similarly empty — too simple. And the real inner workings of a marriage, like most of history, have escaped him. Now he sees that building a log house is the dumbest idea he could have had. It was clumsy of him to think Norma Jean would want a log house. It was a crazy idea. He'll have to think of something else, quickly. He will wad the blueprints into tight balls and fling them into the lake. Then he'll get moving again. He opens his eyes. Norma Jean has moved away and is walking through the cemetery, following a serpentine brick path.

Leroy gets up to follow his wife, but his good leg is asleep and his bad leg still hurts him. Norma Jean is far away, walking rapidly toward the bluff by the river, and he tries to hobble toward her. Some children run past him, screaming noisily. Norma Jean has reached the bluff, and she is looking out over the Tennessee River. Now she turns toward Leroy and waves her arms. Is she beckoning to him? She seems to be doing an exercise for her chest muscles. The sky is unusually pale — the color of the dust ruffle Mabel made for their bed.

* * *

HARUKI MURAKAMI (1949–)

The Year of Spaghetti (2006)

Translated by Philip Gabriel

1971 was the Year of Spaghetti.

In 1971 I cooked spaghetti to live, and lived to cook spaghetti. Steam rising from the aluminum pot was my pride and joy, tomato sauce bubbling up in the saucepan my one great hope in life.

I'd gone to a cooking specialty store and bought a kitchen timer and a huge aluminum cooking pot, big enough to bathe a German shepherd in, then went round all the supermarkets that cater to foreigners, gathering an assortment of odd-sounding spices. I picked up a pasta cookbook at the bookstore, and bought tomatoes by the dozen. I purchased every brand of spaghetti I could lay my hands on, simmered every kind of sauce known to man. Fine particles of garlic, onion, and olive oil swirled in the air, forming a harmonious cloud that penetrated every corner of my tiny apartment, permeating the floor and ceiling and walls, my clothes, my books, my records, my tennis racket, my bundles of old letters. It was a fragrance one might have smelled on ancient Roman aqueducts.

This is a story from the Year of Spaghetti, 1971 A.D.

5 As a rule I cooked spaghetti, and ate it, alone. I was convinced that spaghetti was a dish best enjoyed alone. I can't really explain why I felt that way, but there it is.

I always drank tea with my spaghetti and ate a simple lettuce-and-cucumber salad. I'd make sure I had plenty of both. I laid everything out neatly on the table, and enjoyed a leisurely meal, glancing at the paper as I ate. From Sunday to Saturday, one Spaghetti Day followed another. And each new Sunday started a brand-new Spaghetti Week.

Every time I sat down to a plate of spaghetti—especially on a rainy afternoon—I had the distinct feeling that somebody was about to knock on my door. The person who I imagined was about to visit me was different each time. Sometimes it was a stranger, sometimes someone I knew. Once, it was a girl with slim legs whom I'd dated in high school, and once it was myself, from a few years back, come to pay a visit. Another time, it was none other than William Holden, with Jennifer Jones on his arm.

William Holden?

Not one of these people, though, actually ventured into my apartment. They hovered just outside the door, without knocking, like fragments of memory, and then slipped away.

* * *

10 Spring, summer, and fall, I cooked away, as if cooking spaghetti were an act of revenge. Like a lonely jilted girl throwing old love letters into the fireplace, I tossed one handful of spaghetti after another into the pot.

I'd gather up the trampled-down shadows of time, knead them into the shape of a German shepherd, toss them into the roiling water, and sprinkle them with salt. Then I'd hover over the pot, oversize chopsticks in hand, until the timer dinged its plaintive tone.

Spaghetti strands are a crafty bunch, and I couldn't let them out of my sight. If I were to turn my back, they might well slip over the edge of the pot and vanish into the night. Like the tropical jungle waits to swallow up colorful butterflies into the eternity of time, the night lay in silence, hoping to waylay the prodigal strands.

Spaghetti alla parmigiana
Spaghetti alla napoletana
15 Spaghetti al cartoccio
Spaghetti aglio e olio
Spaghetti alla carbonara
Spaghetti della pina

And then there was the pitiful, nameless leftover spaghetti carelessly tossed into the fridge.

20 Born in heat, the strands of spaghetti washed down the river of 1971 and vanished.

And I mourn them all—all the spaghetti of the year 1971.

When the phone range at three twenty I was sprawled out on the tatami,° staring at the ceiling. A pool of winter sunlight had formed in the place where I lay. Like a dead fly I lay there, vacant, in a December 1971 spotlight.

At first, I didn't recognize it as the phone ringing. It was more like an unfamiliar memory that had hesitantly slipped in between the layers of air. Finally, though, it began to take shape, and, in the end, a ringing phone was unmistakably what it was. It was one hundred percent a phone ring in one-hundred-percent-real air. Still sprawled out, I reached over and picked up the receiver.

On the other end was a girl, a girl so indistinct that, by four thirty, she might very well have disappeared altogether. She was the ex-girlfriend of a friend of mine. Something had brought them together, this guy and this indistinct girl, and something had led them to break up. I had, I admit, reluctantly played a role in getting them together in the first place.

"Sorry to bother you," she said, "but do you know where he is now?

I looked at the phone, running my eyes along the length of the cord. The cord was, sure enough, attached to the phone. I managed a vague reply. There was something ominous in the girl's voice, and whatever trouble was brewing I knew I didn't want to get involved.

"Nobody will tell me where he is," she said in a chilly tone. "Everybody's pretending they don't know. But there's something important I have to tell him, so *please*—tell me where he is. I promise I won't drag you into this. Where is he?"

"I honestly don't know," I told her. " I haven't seen him in a long time." My voice didn't sound like my own. I was telling the truth about not having seen him for a long time, but not about the other part—I did know his address and phone number. Whenever I tell a lie, something weird happens to my voice.

No comment from her.

The phone was like a pillar of ice.

Then all the objects around me turned into pillars of ice, as if I were in a J. G. Ballard science fiction story.

"I really don't know," I repeated. "He went away a long time ago, without saying a word."

The girl laughed. "Give me a break. He's not that clever. We're talking about a guy who has to raise a noise no matter what he does."

She was right. The guy really was a bit of a dim bulb.

But I wasn't about to tell her where he was. Do that, and next I'd have *him* on the phone, giving me an earful. I was through with getting caught up in other people's messes. I'd already dug a hole in the backyard and buried everything that needed to be buried in it. Nobody could ever dig it up again.

"I'm sorry," I said.

"You don't like me, do you?" she suddenly said.

I had no idea what to say. I didn't particularly dislike her. I had no real impression of her at all. And it's hard to have a bad impression of somebody you have no impression of.

---

tatami: Straw floor covering.

"I'm sorry," I said again. "But I'm cooking spaghetti right now."

"What?

"I said I'm cooking spaghetti," I lied. I had no idea why I said that. But that lie was already a part of me — so much so that, at that moment at least, it didn't feel like a lie at all.

I went ahead and filled an imaginary pot with water, lit an imaginary stove with an imaginary match.

"So?" she asked.

I sprinkled imaginary salt into the boiling water, gently lowered a handful of imaginary spaghetti into the imaginary pot, set the imaginary kitchen timer for twelve minutes.

"So I can't talk. The spaghetti will be ruined."

She didn't say anything.

"I'm really sorry, but cooking spaghetti's a delicate operation."

The girl was silent. The phone in my hand began to freeze again.

"So could you call me back?" I added hurriedly.

"Because you're in the middle of making spaghetti?" she asked.

"Yeah."

"Are you making it for someone, or are you going to eat alone?"

"I'll eat it by myself," I said.

She held her breath for a long time, then slowly breathed out. "There's no way you could know this, but I'm really in trouble. I don't know what to do."

"I'm sorry I can't help you," I said.

"There's some money involved, too."

"I see."

"He owes me money," she said. "I lent him some money. I shouldn't have, but I had to."

I was quiet for a minute, my thoughts drifting toward spaghetti. "I'm sorry," I said. "But I've got the spaghetti going, so. . ."

She gave a listless laugh. "Goodbye," she said. "Say hi to your spaghetti for me. I hope it turns out OK."

"Bye," I said.

When I hung up the phone, the circle of light on the floor had shifted an inch or two. I lay down again in that pool of light and resumed staring at the ceiling.

* * *

Thinking about spaghetti that boils eternally but is never done is a sad, sad thing.

Now I regret, a little, that I didn't tell the girl anything, Perhaps I should have. I mean, her ex-boyfriend wasn't much to start with — an empty shell of a guy with artistic pretensions, a great talker whom nobody trusted. She sounded as if she really were strapped for money, and, no matter what the situation, you've got to pay back what you borrow.

Sometimes I wonder what happened to the girl — the thought usually pops into my mind when I'm facing a steaming-hot plate of spaghetti. After she hung up, did she disappear forever, sucked into the four thirty p.m. shadows? Was I partly to blame?

I want you to understand my position, though. At the time, I didn't want to get involved with anyone. That's why I kept on cooking spaghetti, all by myself. In that huge pot, big enough to hold a German shepherd.

* * *

Durum semolina, golden wheat wafting in Italian fields.

Can you imagine how astonished the Italians would be if they knew that what they were exporting in 1971 was really *loneliness*?

* * *

FLANNERY O'CONNOR (1925–1964)

Everything That Rises Must Converge (1965)

Her doctor had told Julian's mother that she must lose twenty pounds on account of her blood pressure, so on Wednesday nights Julian had to take her downtown on the bus for a reducing class at the Y. The reducing class was designed for working girls over fifty, who weighed from 165 to 200 pounds. His mother was one of the slimmer ones, but she said ladies did not tell their age or weight. She would not ride the buses by herself at night since they had been integrated, and because the reducing class was one of her few pleasures, necessary for her health, and *free*, she said Julian could at least put himself out to take her, considering all she did for him. Julian did not like to consider all she did for him, but every Wednesday night he braced himself and took her.

She was almost ready to go, standing before the hall mirror, putting on her hat, while he, his hands behind him, appeared pinned to the door frame, waiting like Saint Sebastian° for the arrows to begin piercing him. The hat was new and had cost her seven dollars and a half. She kept saying, "Maybe I shouldn't have paid that for it. No, I shouldn't have. I'll take it off and return it tomorrow. I shouldn't have bought it."

Julian raised his eyes to heaven. "Yes, you should have bought it," he said "Put it on and let's go." It was a hideous hat. A purple velvet flap came down on one side of it and stood up on the other; the rest of it was green and looked like a cushion with the stuffing out. He decided it was less comical than jaunty and pathetic. Everything that gave her pleasure was small and depressed him.

She lifted the hat one more time and set it down slowly on top of her head. Two wings of gray hair protruded on either side of her florid face, but her eyes, sky-blue, were as innocent and untouched by experience as they must have been when she was ten. Were it not that she was a widow who had struggled fiercely to feed and clothe

---

Saint Sebastian: A Roman Catholic Saint. Accused of being a Christian, Sebastian was tied to a tree, shot with arrows, and left for dead. He survived and recovered, returning to preach. The emperor then had him beaten to death.

and put him through school and who was supporting him still "until he got on his feet," she might have been a little girl that he had to take to town.

"It's all right, it's all right," he said. "Let's go." He opened the door himself and started down the walk to get her going. The sky was a dying violet and the houses stood out darkly against it, bulbous liver-colored monstrosities of a uniform ugliness though no two were alike. Since this had been a fashionable neighborhood forty years ago, his mother persisted in thinking they did well to have an apartment in it. Each house had a narrow collar of dirt around it in which sat, usually, a grubby child. Julian walked with his hands in his pockets, his head down and thrust forward and his eyes glazed with the determination to make himself completely numb during the time he would be sacrificed to her pleasure.

The door closed and he turned to find the dumpy figure, surmounted by the atrocious hat, coming toward him. "Well," she said, "you only live once and paying a little more for it, I at least won't meet myself coming and going."

"Some day I'll start making money," Julian said gloomily—he knew he never would—"and you can have one of those jokes whenever you take the fit." But first they would move. He visualized a place where the nearest neighbors would be three miles away on either side.

"I think you're doing fine," she said, drawing on her gloves. "You've only been out of school a year. Rome wasn't built in a day."

She was one of the few members of the Y reducing class who arrived in hat and gloves and who had a son who had been to college. "It takes time," she said, "and the world is in such a mess. This hat looked better on me than any of the others, though when she brought it out I said, 'Take that thing back. I wouldn't have it on my head,' and she said, 'Now wait till you see it on,' and when she put it on me, I said, 'We-ull,' and she said, 'If you ask me, that hat does something for you and you do something for the hat, and besides,' she said, 'with that hat, you won't meet yourself coming and going.'"

Julian thought he could have stood his lot better if she had been selfish, if she had been an old hag who drank and screamed at him. He walked along, saturated in depression, as if in the midst of his martyrdom he had lost his faith. Catching sight of his long, hopeless, irritated face, she stopped suddenly with a grief-stricken look, and pulled back on his arm. "Wait on me," she said. "I'm going back to the house and take this thing off and tomorrow I'm going to return it. I was out of my head. I can pay the gas bill with that seven-fifty."

He caught her arm in a vicious grip. "You are not going to take it back," he said. "I like it."

"Well," she said, "I don't think I ought . . ."

"Shut up and enjoy it," he muttered, more depressed than ever.

"With the world in the mess it's in," she said, "it's a wonder we can enjoy anything. I tell you, the bottom rail is on the top."

Julian sighed.

"Of course," she said, "if you know who are you, you can go anywhere." She said this every time he took her to the reducing class. "Most of them in it are not our kind of people," she said, "but I can be gracious to anybody. I know who I am."

"They don't give a damn for your graciousness," Julian said savagely. "Knowing who you are is good for one generation only. You haven't the foggiest idea where you stand now or who you are."

She stopped and allowed her eyes to flash at him. "I most certainly do know who I am," she said, "and if you don't know who you are, I'm ashamed of you."

"Oh hell," Julian said.

20 "Your great-grandfather was a former governor of this state," she said. "Your grandfather was a prosperous land-owner. Your grandmother was a Godhigh."

"Will you look around you," he said tensely, "and see where you are now?" and he swept his arm jerkily out to indicate the neighborhood, which the growing darkness at least made less dingy.

"You remain what you are," she said. "Your great-grandfather had a plantation and two hundred slaves."

"There are no more slaves," he said irritably.

"They were better off when they were," she said. He groaned to see that she was off on that topic. She rolled onto it every few days like a train on an open track. He knew every stop, every junction, every swamp along the way, and knew the exact point at which her conclusion would roll majestically into the station: "It's ridiculous. It's simply not realistic. They should rise, yes, but on their own side of the fence."

25 "Let's skip it," Julian said.

"The ones I feel sorry for," she said, "are the ones that are half white. They're tragic."

"Will you skip it?"

"Suppose we were half white. We would certainly have mixed feelings."

"I have mixed feelings now," he groaned.

30 "Well let's talk about something pleasant," she said. "I remember going to Grandpa's when I was a little girl. Then the house had double stairways that went up to what was really the second floor—all the cooking was done on the first. I used to like to stay down in the kitchen on account of the way the walls smelled. I would sit with my nose pressed against the plaster and take deep breaths. Actually the place belonged to the Godhighs but your grandfather Chestny paid the mortgage and saved it for them. They were in reduced circumstances," she said, "but reduced or not, they never forgot who they were."

"Doubtless that decayed mansion reminded them," Julian muttered. He never spoke of it without contempt or thought of it without longing. He had seen it once when he was a child before it had been sold. The double stairways had rotted and been torn down. Negroes were living in it. But it remained in his mind as his mother had known it. It appeared in his dreams regularly. He would stand on the wide porch, listening to the rustle of oak leaves, then wander through the high-ceilinged hall into the parlor that opened onto it and gaze at the worn rugs and faded draperies. It occurred to him that it was he, not she, who could have appreciated it. He preferred its threadbare elegance to anything he could name and it was because of it that all the neighborhoods they had lived in had been a torment to him—whereas she had hardly known the difference. She called her insensitivity "being adjustable."

"And I remember the old darky who was my nurse, Caroline. There was no better person in the world. I've always had a great respect for my colored friends," she said. "I'd do anything in the world for them and they'd . . ."

"Will you for God's sake get off that subject?" Julian said. When he got on a bus by himself, he made it a point to sit down beside a Negro, in reparation as it were for his mother's sins.

"You're mighty touchy tonight," she said. "Do you feel all right?"

"Yes I feel all right," he said. "Now lay off."

She pursed her lips. "Well, you certainly are in a vile humor," she observed. "I just won't speak to you at all."

They had reached the bus stop. There was no bus in sight and Julian, his hands still jammed in his pockets and his head thrust forward, scowled down the empty street. The frustration of having to wait on the bus as well as ride on it began to creep up his neck like a hot hand. The presence of his mother was borne in upon him as she gave a pained sigh. He looked at her bleakly. She was holding herself very erect under the preposterous hat, wearing it like a banner of her imaginary dignity. There was in him an evil urge to break her spirit. He suddenly unloosened his tie and pulled it off and put it in his pocket.

She stiffened. "Why must you look like *that* when you take me to town?" she said. "Why must you deliberately embarrass me?"

"If you'll never learn where you are," he said, "you can at least learn where I am."

"You look like a—thug," she said.

"Then I must be one," he murmured.

"I'll just go home," she said. "I will not bother you. If you can't do a little thing like that for me . . ."

Rolling his eyes upward, he put his tie back on. "Restored to my class," he muttered. He thrust his face toward her and hissed, "True culture is in the mind, the *mind*," he said, and tapped his head, "the mind."

"It's in the heart," she said, "and in how you do things and how you do things is because of who you *are*."

"Nobody in the damn bus cares who you are."

"I care who I am," she said icily.

The lighted bus appeared on top of the next hill and as it approached, they moved out into the street to meet it. He put his hand under her elbow and hoisted her up on the creaking step. She entered with a little smile, as if she were going into a drawing room where everyone had been waiting for her. While he put in the tokens, she sat down on one of the broad front seats for three which faced the aisle. A thin woman with protruding teeth and long yellow hair was sitting on the end of it. His mother moved up beside her and left room for Julian beside herself. He sat down and looked at the floor across the aisle where a pair of thin feet in red and white canvas sandals were planted.

His mother immediately began a general conversation meant to attract anyone who felt like talking. "Can it get any hotter?" she said and removed from her purse a folding fan, black with a Japanese scene on it, which she began to flutter before her.

"I reckon it might could," the woman with the protruding teeth said, "but I know for a fact my apartment couldn't get no hotter."

"It must get the afternoon sun," his mother said. She sat forward and looked up 50 and down the bus. It was half filled. Everybody was white. "I see we have the bus to ourselves," she said. Julian cringed.

"For a change," said the woman across the aisle, the owner of the red and white canvas sandals. "I come on one the other day and they were thick as fleas—up front and all through."

"The world is in a mess everywhere," his mother said. "I don't know how we've let it get in this fix."

"What gets my goat is all those boys from good families stealing automobile tires," the woman with the protruding teeth said. "I told my boy, I said you may not be rich but you been raised right and if I ever catch you in any such mess, they can send you on to the reformatory. Be exactly where you belong."

"Training tells," his mother said. "Is your boy in high school?"

"Ninth grade," the woman said. 55

"My son just finished college last year. He wants to write but he's selling typewriters until he gets started," his mother said.

The woman leaned forward and peered at Julian. He threw her such a malevolent look that she subsided against the seat. On the floor across the aisle there was an abandoned newspaper. He got up and got it and opened it out in front of him. His mother discreetly continued the conversation in a lower tone but the woman across the aisle said in a loud voice, "Well that's nice. Selling typewriters is close to writing. He can go right from one to the other."

"I tell him," his mother said, "that Rome wasn't built in a day."

Behind the newspaper Julian was withdrawing into the inner compartment of his mind where he spent most of his time. This was a kind of mental bubble in which he established himself when he could not bear to be a part of what was going on around him. From it he could see out and judge but in it he was safe from any kind of penetration from without. It was the only place where he felt free of the general idiocy of his fellows. His mother had never entered it but from it he could see her with absolute clarity.

The old lady was clever enough and he thought that if she had started from any 60 of the right premises, more might have been expected of her. She lived according to the laws of her own fantasy world, outside of which he had never seen her set foot. The law of it was to sacrifice herself for him after she had first created the necessity to do so by making a mess of things. If he had permitted her sacrifices, it was only because her lack of foresight had made them necessary. All of her life had been a struggle to act like a Chestny without the Chestny goods, and to give him everything she thought a Chestny ought to have; but since, said she, it was fun to struggle, why complain? And when you had won, as she had won, what fun to look back on the hard times! He could not forgive her that she had enjoyed the struggle and that she thought *she* had won.

What she meant when she said she had won was that she had brought him up successfully and had sent him to college and that he had turned out so well—good looking (her teeth had gone unfilled so that his could be straightened), intelligent (he realized he was too intelligent to be a success), and with a future ahead of him (there was of course no future ahead of him). She excused his gloominess on the grounds that he was still growing up and his radical ideas on his lack of practical experience. She said he didn't yet know a thing about "life," that he hadn't even entered the real world—when already he was as disenchanted with it as a man of fifty.

The further irony of all this was that in spite of her, he had turned out so well. In spite of going to only a third-rate college, he had, on his own initiative, come out with a first-rate education; in spite of growing up dominated by a small mind, he had ended up with a large one; in spite of all her foolish views, he was free of prejudice and unafraid to face facts. Most miraculous of all, instead of being blinded by love for her as she was for him, he had cut himself emotionally free of her and could see her with complete objectivity. He was not dominated by his mother.

The bus stopped with a sudden jerk and shook him from his meditation. A woman from the back lurched forward with little steps and barely escaped falling in his newspaper as she righted herself. She got off and a large Negro got on. Julian kept his paper lowered to watch. It gave him a certain satisfaction to see injustice in daily operation. It confirmed his view that with a few exceptions there was no one worth knowing within a radius of three hundred miles. The Negro was well dressed and carried a briefcase. He looked around and then sat down on the other end of the seat where the woman with the red and white canvas sandals was sitting. He immediately unfolded a newspaper and obscured himself behind it. Julian's mother's elbow at once prodded insistently into his ribs. "Now you see why I won't ride on these buses by myself," she whispered.

The woman with the red and white canvas sandals had risen at the same time the Negro sat down and had gone further back in the bus and taken the seat of the woman who had got off. His mother leaned forward and cast her an approving look.

65 Julian rose, crossed the aisle, and sat down in the place of the woman with the canvas sandals. From this position, he looked serenely across at his mother. Her face had turned an angry red. He stared at her, making his eyes the eyes of a stranger. He felt his tension suddenly lift as if he had openly declared war on her.

He would have liked to get in conversation with the Negro and to talk with him about art or politics or any subject that would be above the comprehension of those around them, but the man remained entrenched behind his paper. He was either ignoring the change of seating or had never noticed it. There was no way for Julian to convey his sympathy.

His mother kept her eyes fixed reproachfully on his face. The woman with the protruding teeth was looking at him avidly as if he were a type of monster new to her.

"Do you have a light?" he asked the Negro.

Without looking away from his paper, the man reached in his pocket and handed him a packet of matches.

70 "Thanks," Julian said. For a moment he held the matches foolishly. A NO SMOKING sign looked down upon him from over the door. This alone would not have deterred him; he had no cigarettes. He had quit smoking some months before

because he could not afford it. "Sorry," he muttered and handed back the matches. The Negro lowered the paper and gave him an annoyed look. He took the matches and raised the paper again.

His mother continued to gaze at him but she did not take advantage of his momentary discomfort. Her eyes retained their battered look. Her face seemed to be unnaturally red, as if her blood pressure had risen. Julian allowed no glimmer of sympathy to show on his face. Having got the advantage, he wanted desperately to keep it and carry it through. He would have liked to teach her a lesson that would last her a while, but there seemed no way to continue the point. The Negro refused to come out from behind his paper.

Julian folded his arms and looked stolidly before him, facing her but as if he did not see her, as if he had ceased to recognize her existence. He visualized a scene in which, the bus having reached their stop, he would remain in his seat and when she said, "Aren't you going to get off?" he would look at her as a stranger who had rashly addressed him. The corner they got off on was usually deserted, but it was well lighted and it would not hurt her to walk by herself the four blocks to the Y. He decided to wait until the time came and then decide whether or not he would let her get off by herself. He would have to be at the Y at ten to bring her back, but he could leave her wondering if he was going to show up. There was no reason for her to think she could always depend on him.

He retired again into the high-ceilinged room sparsely settled with large pieces of antique furniture. His soul expanded momentarily but then he became aware of his mother across from him and the vision shriveled. He studied her coldly. Her feet in little pumps dangled like a child's and did not quite reach the floor. She was training on him an exaggerated look of reproach. He felt completely detached from her. At that moment he could with pleasure have slapped her as he would have slapped a particularly obnoxious child in his charge.

He began to imagine various unlikely ways by which he could teach her a lesson. He might make friends with some distinguished Negro professor or lawyer and bring him home to spend the evening. He would be entirely justified but her blood pressure would rise to 300. He could not push her to the extent of making her have a stroke, and moreover, he had never been successful at making any Negro friends. He had tried to strike up an acquaintance on the bus with some of the better types, with ones that looked like professors or ministers or lawyers. One morning he had sat down next to a distinguished-looking dark brown man who had answered his questions with a sonorous solemnity but who had turned out to be an undertaker. Another day he had sat down beside a cigar-smoking Negro with a diamond ring on his finger, but after a few stilted pleasantries, the Negro had rung the buzzer and risen, slipping two lottery tickets into Julian's hand as he climbed over him to leave.

He imagined his mother lying desperately ill and his being able to secure only a 75
Negro doctor for her. He toyed with that idea for a few minutes and then dropped it for a momentary vision of himself participating as a sympathizer in a sit-in demonstration. This was possible but he did not linger with it. Instead, he approached the ultimate horror. He brought home a beautiful suspiciously Negroid woman. Prepare yourself, he said. There is nothing you can do about it. This is the woman I've chosen.

She's intelligent, dignified, even good, and she's suffered and she hasn't thought *fun*. Now persecute us, go ahead and persecute us. Drive her out of here, but remember, you're driving me too. His eyes were narrowed and through the indignation he had generated, he saw his mother across the aisle, purple-faced, shrunken to the dwarf-like proportions of her moral nature, sitting like a mummy beneath the ridiculous banner of her hat.

He was tilted out of his fantasy again as the bus stopped. The door opened with a sucking hiss and out of the dark a large, gaily dressed, sullen-looking colored woman got on with a little boy. The child, who might have been four, had on a short plaid suit and a Tyrolean hat with a blue feather in it. Julian hoped that he would sit down beside him and that the woman would push in beside his mother. He could think of no better arrangement.

As she waited for her tokens, the woman was surveying the seating possibilities — he hoped with the idea of sitting where she was least wanted. There was something familiar-looking about her but Julian could not place what it was. She was a giant of a woman. Her face was set not only to meet opposition but to seek it out. The downward tilt of her large lower lip was like a warning sign: DON'T TAMPER WITH ME. Her bulging figure was encased in a green crepe dress and her feet overflowed in red shoes. She had on a hideous hat. A purple velvet flap came down on one side of it and stood up on the other, the rest of it was green and looked like a cushion with the stuffing out. She carried a mammoth red pocket-book that bulged throughout as if it were stuffed with rocks.

To Julian's disappointment, the little boy climbed up on the empty seat beside his mother. His mother lumped all children, black and white, into the common category, "cute," and she thought little Negroes were on the whole cuter than little white children. She smiled at the little boy as he climbed on the seat.

Meanwhile the woman was bearing down upon the empty seat beside Julian. To his annoyance, she squeezed herself into it. He saw his mother's face change as the woman settled herself next to him and he realized with satisfaction that this was more objectionable to her than it was to him. Her face seemed almost gray and there was a look of dull recognition in her eyes, as if suddenly she had sickened at some awful confrontation. Julian saw that it was because she and the woman had, in a sense, swapped sons. Though his mother would not realize the symbolic significance of this, she would feel it. His amusement showed plainly on his face.

80 The woman next to him muttered something unintelligible to herself. He was conscious of a kind of bristling next to him, a muted growling like that of an angry cat. He could not see anything but the red pocketbook upright on the bulging green thighs. He visualized the woman as she had stood waiting for her tokens — the ponderous figure, rising from the red shoes upward over the solid hips, the mammoth bosom, the haughty face, to the green and purple hat.

His eyes widened.

The vision of the two hats, identical, broke upon him with the radiance of a brilliant sunrise. His face was suddenly lit with joy. He could not believe that Fate had thrust upon his mother such a lesson. He gave a loud chuckle so that she would look at him and see that he saw. She turned her eyes on him slowly. The blue in them seemed to have turned a bruised purple. For a moment he had an uncomfortable sense of her innocence, but it lasted only a second before principle rescued him. Justice entitled him to laugh. His grin hardened until it said to her as plainly as if he were saying aloud: Your punishment exactly fits your pettiness. This should teach you a permanent lesson.

Her eyes shifted to the woman. She seemed unable to bear looking at him and to find the woman preferable. He became conscious again of the bristling presence at his side. The woman was rumbling like a volcano about to become active. His mother's mouth began to twitch slightly at one corner. With a sinking heart, he saw incipient signs of recovery on her face and realized that this was going to strike her suddenly as funny and was going to be no lesson at all. She kept her eyes on the woman and an amused smile came over her face as if the woman were a monkey that had stolen her hat. The little Negro was looking up at her with large fascinated eyes. He had been trying to attract her attention for some time.

"Carver!" the woman said suddenly. "Come heah!"

When he saw that the spotlight was on him at last, Carver drew his feet up and 85
turned himself toward Julian's mother and giggled.

"Carver!" the woman said. "You heah me? Come heah!"

Carver slid down from the seat but remained squatting with his back against the base of it, his head turned slyly around toward Julian's mother, who was smiling at him. The woman reached a hand across the aisle and snatched him to her. He righted himself and hung backwards on her knees, grinning at Julian's mother. "Isn't he cute?" Julian's mother said to the woman with the protruding teeth.

"I reckon he is," the woman said without conviction.

The Negress yanked him upright but he eased out of her grip and shot across the aisle and scrambled, giggling wildly, onto the seat beside his love.

"I think he likes me," Julian's mother said, and smiled at the woman. It was the 90
smile she used when she was being particularly gracious to an inferior. Julian saw everything was lost. The lesson had rolled off her like rain on a roof.

The woman stood up and yanked the little boy off the seat as if she were snatching him from contagion. Julian could feel the rage in her at having no weapon like his mother's smile. She gave the child a sharp slap across his leg. He howled once and then thrust his head into her stomach and kicked his feet against her shins. "Behave," she said vehemently.

The bus stopped and the Negro who had been reading the newspaper got off. The woman moved over and set the little boy down with a thump between herself and Julian. She held him firmly by the knee. In a moment he put his hands in front of his face and peeped at Julian's mother through his fingers.

"I see yoooooooo!" she said and put her hand in front of her face and peeped at him.

The woman slapped his hand down. "Quit yo' foolishness," she said, "before I knock the living Jesus out of you!"

Julian was thankful that the next stop was theirs. He reached up and pulled the 95
cord. The woman reached up and pulled it at the same time. Oh my God, he thought. He had the terrible intuition that when they got off the bus together, his mother would

open her purse and give the little boy a nickel. The gesture would be as natural to her as breathing. The bus stopped and the woman got up and lunged to the front, dragging the child, who wished to stay on, after her. Julian and his mother got up and followed. As they neared the door, Julian tried to relieve her of her pocketbook.

"No," she murmured, "I want to give the little boy a nickel."

"No!" Julian hissed. "No!"

She smiled down at the child and opened her bag. The bus door opened and the woman picked him up by the arm and descended with him, hanging at her hip. Once in the street she set him down and shook him.

Julian's mother had to close her purse while she got down the bus step but as soon as her feet were on the ground, she opened it again and began to rummage inside. "I can't find but a penny," she whispered, "but it looks like a new one."

100 "Don't do it!" Julian said fiercely between his teeth. There was a streetlight on the corner and she hurried to get under it so that she could better see into her pocketbook. The woman was heading off rapidly down the street with the child still hanging backward on her hand.

"Oh little boy!" Julian's mother called and took a few quick steps and caught up with them just beyond the lamppost. "Here's a bright new penny for you," and she held out the coin, which shone bronze in the dim light.

The huge woman turned and for a moment stood, her shoulders lifted and her face frozen with frustrated rage, and stared at Julian's mother. Then all at once she seemed to explode like a piece of machinery that had been given one ounce of pressure too much. Julian saw the black fist swing out with the red pocketbook. He shut his eyes and cringed as he heard the woman shout, "He don't take nobody's pennies!" When he opened his eyes, the woman was disappearing down the street with the little boy staring wide-eyed over her shoulder. Julian's mother was sitting on the sidewalk.

"I told you not to do that," Julian said angrily. "I told you not to do that!"

He stood over her for a minute, gritting his teeth. Her legs were stretched out in front of her and her hat was on her lap. He squatted down and looked her in the face. It was totally expressionless. "You got exactly what you deserved," he said. "Now get up."

105 He picked up her pocketbook and put what had fallen out back in it. He picked the hat up off her lap. The penny caught his eye on the sidewalk and he picked that up and let it drop before her eyes into the purse. Then he stood up and leaned over and held his hands out to pull her up. She remained immobile. He sighed. Rising above them on either side were black apartment buildings, marked with irregular rectangles of light. At the end of the block a man came out of a door and walked off in the opposite direction. "All right," he said, "suppose somebody happens by and wants to know why you're sitting on the sidewalk?"

She took the hand and, breathing hard, pulled heavily up on it and then stood for a moment, swaying slightly as if the spots of light in the darkness were circling around her. Her eyes, shadowed and confused, finally settled on his face. He did not try to conceal his irritation. "I hope this teaches you a lesson," he said. She leaned forward and her eyes raked his face. She seemed trying to determine his identity. Then, as if she found nothing familiar about him, she started off with a headlong movement in the wrong direction.

"Aren't you going on to the Y?" he asked.

"Home," she muttered.

"Well, are we walking?"

110 For answer she kept going. Julian followed along, his hands behind him. He saw no reason to let the lesson she had had go without backing it up with an explanation of its meaning. She might as well be made to understand what had happened to her. "Don't think that was just an uppity Negro woman," he said. "That was the whole colored race which will no longer take your condescending pennies. That was your black double. She can wear the same hat as you, and to be sure," he added gratuitously (because he thought it was funny), "it looked better on her than it did on you. What all this means," he said, "is that the old world is gone. The old manners are obsolete and your graciousness is not worth a damn." He thought bitterly of the house that had been lost for him. "You aren't who you think you are," he said.

She continued to plow ahead, paying no attention to him. Her hair had come undone on one side. She dropped her pocketbook and took no notice. He stooped and picked it up and handed it to her but she did not take it.

"You needn't act as if the world had come to an end," he said, "because it hasn't. From now on you've got to live in a new world and face a few realities for a change. Buck up," he said, "it won't kill you."

She was breathing fast.

"Let's wait on the bus," he said.

115 "Home," she said thickly.

"I hate to see you behave like this," he said. "Just like a child. I should be able to expect more of you." He decided to stop where he was and make her stop and wait for a bus. "I'm not going any farther," he said stopping. "We're going on the bus."

She continued to go on as if she had not heard him. He took a few steps and caught her arm and stopped her. He looked into her face and caught his breath. He was looking into a face he had never seen before. "Tell Grandpa to come get me," she said.

He stared, stricken.

"Tell Caroline to come get me," she said.

120 Stunned, he let her go and she lurched forward again, walking as if one leg were shorter than the other. A tide of darkness seemed to be sweeping her from him. "Mother!" he cried. "Darling, sweetheart, wait!" Crumpling, she fell to the pavement. He dashed forward and fell at her side, crying, "Mamma, Mamma!" He turned her over. Her face was fiercely distorted. One eye, large and staring, moved slightly to the left as if it had become unmoored. The other remained fixed on him, raked his face again, found nothing and closed.

"Wait here, wait here!" he cried and jumped up and began to run for help toward a cluster of lights he saw in the distance ahead of him. "Help, help!" he shouted, but his voice was thin, scarcely a thread of sound. The lights drifted farther away the faster he ran and his feet moved numbly as if they carried him nowhere. The tide of darkness seemed to sweep him back to her, postponing from moment to moment his entry into the world of guilt and sorrow.

* * *

EDGAR ALLAN POE (1809–1849)

The Tell-Tale Heart (1843)

True!—nervous—very, very dreadfully nervous I had been and am; but why *will* you say that I am mad? The disease had sharpened my senses—not destroyed—not dulled them. Above all was the sense of hearing acute. I heard all things in the heaven and in the earth. I heard many things in hell. How, then, am I mad? Hearken! and observe how healthily—how calmly I can tell you the whole story.

It is impossible to say how first the idea entered my brain; but once conceived, it haunted me day and night. Object there was none. Passion there was none. I loved the old man. He had never wronged me. He had never given me insult. For his gold I had no desire. I think it was his eye! yes, it was this! One of his eyes resembled that of a vulture—a pale eye, with a film over it. Whenever it fell upon me, my blood ran cold; and so by degrees—very gradually—I made up my mind to take the life of the old man, and thus rid myself of the eye forever.

Now this is the point. You fancy me mad. Madmen know nothing. But you should have seen *me*. You should have seen how wisely I proceeded—with what caution—with what foresight—with what dissimulation I went to work! I was never kinder to the old man than during the whole week before I killed him. And every night, about midnight, I turned the latch of his door and opened it—oh, so gently! And then, when I had made an opening sufficient for my head, I put in a dark lantern, all closed, closed, so that no light shone out, and then I thrust in my head. Oh, you would have laughed to see how cunningly I thrust it in! I moved it slowly—very, very slowly, so that I might not disturb the old man's sleep. It took me an hour to place my whole head within the opening so far that I could see him as he lay upon his bed. Ha!—would a madman have been so wise as this? And then, when my head was well in the room, I undid the lantern cautiously—oh, so cautiously—cautiously (for the hinges creaked)—I undid it just so much that a single thin ray fell upon the vulture eye. And this I did for seven long nights—every night just at midnight—but I found the eye always closed; and so it was impossible to do the work; for it was not the old man who vexed me, but his Evil Eye. And every morning, when the day broke, I went boldly into the chamber, and spoke courageously to him, calling him by name in a hearty tone, and inquiring how he had passed the night. So you see he would have been a very profound old man, indeed, to suspect that every night, just at twelve, I looked in upon him while he slept.

Upon the eighth night I was more than usually cautious in opening the door. A watch's minute hand moves more quickly than did mine. Never before that night had I *felt* the extent of my own powers—of my sagacity. I could scarcely contain my feelings of triumph. To think that there I was, opening the door little by little, and he not even to dream of my secret deeds or thoughts. I fairly chuckled at the idea; and perhaps he heard me; for he moved on the bed suddenly, as if startled. Now you may think that I drew back—but no. His room was as black as pitch with the thick darkness (for the shutters were close fastened through fear of robbers), and so I knew that he could not see the opening of the door, and I kept pushing it on steadily, steadily.

I had my head in, and was about to open the lantern, when my thumb slipped 5
upon the tin fastening, and the old man sprang up in the bed, crying out—"Who's there?"

I kept quite still and said nothing. For a whole hour I did not move a muscle, and in the meantime I did not hear him lie down. He was still sitting up in the bed listening;—just as I have done, night after night, hearkening to the death watches° in the wall.

Presently I heard a slight groan, and I knew it was the groan of mortal terror. It was not a groan of pain or of grief—oh, no!—it was the low stifled sound that arises from the bottom of the soul when overcharged with awe. I knew the sound very well. Many a night, just at midnight, when all the world slept, it has welled up from my own bosom, deepening, with its dreadful echo, the terrors that distracted me. I say I knew it well. I knew what the old man felt, and pitied him, although I chuckled at heart. I knew that he had been lying awake ever since the first slight noise, when he had turned in the bed. His fears had been ever since growing upon him. He had been trying to fancy them causeless, but could not. He had been saying to himself—"It is nothing but the wind in the chimney—it is only a mouse crossing the floor," or "it is merely a cricket which has made a single chirp." Yes, he had been trying to comfort himself with these suppositions; but he had found all in vain. *All in vain*; because Death, in approaching him, had stalked with his black shadow before him, and enveloped the victim. And it was the mournful influence of the unperceived shadow that caused him to feel—although he neither saw nor heard—to *feel* the presence of my head within the room.

When I had waited a long time, very patiently, without hearing him lie down, I resolved to open a little—a very, very little crevice in the lantern. So I opened it—you cannot imagine how stealthily, stealthily—until, at length, a single dim ray, like the thread of the spider, shot from out of the crevice and fell upon the vulture eye.

It was open—wide, wide open—and I grew furious as I gazed upon it. I saw it with perfect distinctness—all a dull blue, with a hideous veil over it that chilled the very marrow in my bones; but I could see nothing else of the old man's face or person: for I had directed the ray as if by instinct, precisely upon the damned spot.

And now have I not told you that what you mistake for madness is but over- 10
acuteness of the senses?—now, I say, there came to my ears a low, dull, quick sound, such as a watch makes when enveloped in cotton. I knew *that* sound well, too. It was the beating of the old man's heart. It increased my fury, as the beating of a drum stimulates the soldier into courage.

But even yet I refrained and kept still. I scarcely breathed. I held the lantern motionless. I tried how steadily I could maintain the ray upon the eye. Meantime the hellish tattoo of the heart increased. It grew quicker and quicker, and louder and louder every instant. The old man's terror *must* have been extreme! It grew louder, I say, louder every moment!—do you mark me well? I have told you that I am nervous: so I am. And now at the dead hour of the night, amid the dreadful silence of that old house, so strange a noise as this excited me to uncontrollable terror. Yet, for some minutes longer

---

death watches: Wood-burrowing beetles. Their clicking sound was superstitiously thought of as an omen of death.

I refrained and stood still. But the beating grew louder, louder! I thought the heart must burst. And now a new anxiety seized me—the sound would be heard by a neighbor! The old man's hour had come! With a loud yell, I threw open the lantern and leaped into the room. He shrieked once—once only. In an instant I dragged him to the floor, and pulled the heavy bed over him. I then smiled gaily, to find the deed so far done. But, for many minutes, the heart beat on with a muffled sound. This, however, did not vex me; it would not be heard through the wall. At length it ceased. The old man was dead. I removed the bed and examined the corpse. Yes, he was stone, stone dead. I placed my hand upon the heart and held it there many minutes.

If still you think me mad, you will think so no longer when I describe the wise precautions I took for the concealment of the body. The night waned, and I worked hastily, but in silence. First of all I dismembered the corpse. I cut off the head and the arms and the legs.

I then took up three planks from the flooring of the chamber, and deposited all between the scantlings. I then replaced the boards so cleverly, so cunningly, that no human eye—not even *his*—could have detected anything wrong. There was nothing to wash out—no stain of any kind—no bloodspot whatever. I had been too wary for that. A tub had caught all—ha! ha!

When I had made an end of these labors, it was four o'clock—still dark as midnight. As the bell sounded the hour, there came a knocking at the street door. I went down to open it with a light heart,—for what had I *now* to fear? There entered three men, who introduced themselves, with perfect suavity, as officers of the police. A shriek had been heard by a neighbor during the night; suspicion of foul play had been aroused, information had been lodged at the police office, and they (the officers) had been deputed to search the premises.

15 I smiled,—for *what* had I to fear? I bade the gentlemen welcome. The shriek, I said, was my own in a dream. The old man, I mentioned, was absent in the country. I took my visitors all over the house. I bade them search—search *well*. I led them, at length, to *his* chamber. I showed them his treasures, secure, undisturbed. In the enthusiasm of my confidence, I brought chairs into the room, and desired them *here* to rest from their fatigues, while I myself, in the wild audacity of my perfect triumph, placed my own seat upon the very spot beneath which reposed the corpse of the victim.

The officers were satisfied. My *manner* had convinced them. I was singularly at ease. They sat, and while I answered cheerily, they chatted of familiar things. But, ere long, I felt myself getting pale and wished them gone. My head ached, and I fancied a ringing in my ears: but still they sat and still chatted. The ringing became more distinct:—it continued and became more distinct: I talked more freely to get rid of the feeling: but it continued and gained definitiveness—until, at length, I found that the noise was *not* within my ears.

No doubt I now grew *very* pale:—but I talked more fluently, and with a heightened voice. Yet the sound increased—and what could I do? It was a *low, dull, quick sound—much such a sound as a watch makes when enveloped in cotton*. I gasped for breath—and yet the officers heard it not. I talked more quickly—more vehemently; but the noise steadily increased. I arose and argued about trifles, in a high key and with violent gesticulations; but the noise steadily increased. Why *would* they not be gone? I paced the floor to and fro with heavy strides, as if excited to fury by the observations of the men — but the noise steadily increased. Oh God! what *could* I do? I foamed — I raved — I swore! I swung the chair upon which I had been sitting, and grated it upon the boards, but the noise arose over all and continually increased. It grew louder — louder — *louder!* And still the men chatted pleasantly, and smiled. Was it possible they heard not? Almighty God! — no, no! They heard! — they suspected! — they *knew!* — they were making a mockery of my horror! — this I thought, and this I think. But anything was better than this agony! Anything was more tolerable than this derision! I could bear those hypocritical smiles no longer! I felt that I must scream or die! — and now — again! — hark! louder! louder! louder! *louder!* —

"Villains!" I shrieked, "dissemble no more! I admit the deed! — tear up the planks! — here, here! — it is the beating of his hideous heart!"

* * *

KATHERINE ANNE PORTER (1890–1980)

The Jilting of Granny Weatherall (1930)

She flicked her wrist neatly out of Doctor Harry's pudgy careful fingers and pulled the sheet up to her chin. The brat ought to be in knee breeches. Doctoring around the country with spectacles on his nose! "Get along now, take your schoolbooks and go. There's nothing wrong with me."

Doctor Harry spread a warm paw like a cushion on her forehead where the forked green vein danced and made her eyelids twitch. "Now, now, be a good girl, and we'll have you up in no time."

"That's no way to speak to a woman nearly eighty years old just because she's down. I'd have you respect your elders, young man."

"Well, Missy, excuse me." Doctor Harry patted her cheek. "But I've got to warn you, haven't I? You're a marvel, but you must be careful or you're going to be good and sorry."

"Don't tell me what I'm going to be. I'm on my feet now, morally speaking. It's 5
Cornelia. I had to go to bed to get rid of her."

Her bones felt loose, and floated around in her skin, and Doctor Harry floated like a balloon around the foot of the bed. He floated and pulled down his waistcoat and swung his glasses on a cord. "Well, stay where you are, it certainly can't hurt you."

"Get along and doctor your sick," said Granny Weatherall. "Leave a well woman alone. I'll call for you when I want you. . . . Where were you forty years ago when I pulled through milk-leg and double pneumonia? You weren't even born. Don't let Cornelia lead you on," she shouted, because Doctor Harry appeared to float up to the ceiling and out. "I pay my own bills, and I don't throw my money away on nonsense!"

She meant to wave good-by, but it was too much trouble. Her eyes closed of themselves, it was like a dark curtain drawn around the bed. The pillow rose and floated under her, pleasant as a hammock in a light wind. She listened to the leaves rustling outside the window. No, somebody was swishing newspapers: no, Cornelia and Doctor Harry were whispering together. She leaped broad awake, thinking they whispered in her ear.

"She was never like this, *never* like this!" "Well, what can we expect?" "Yes, eighty years old. . . ."

Well, and what if she was? She still had ears. It was like Cornelia to whisper around doors. She always kept things secret in such a public way. She was always being tactful and kind. Cornelia was dutiful; that was the trouble with her. Dutiful and good: "So good and dutiful," said Granny, "that I'd like to spank her." She saw herself spanking Cornelia and making a fine job of it.

"What'd you say, Mother?"

Granny felt her face tying up in hard knots.

"Can't a body think, I'd like to know?"

"I thought you might want something."

"I do. I want a lot of things. First off, go away and don't whisper."

She lay and drowsed, hoping in her sleep that the children would keep out and let her rest a minute. It had been a long day. Not that she was tired. It was always pleasant to snatch a minute now and then. There was always so much to be done, let me see: tomorrow.

Tomorrow was far away and there was nothing to trouble about. Things were finished somehow when the time came; thank God there was always a little margin over for peace: then a person could spread out the plan of life and tuck in the edges orderly. It was good to have everything clean and folded away, with the hair brushes and tonic bottles sitting straight on the white embroidered linen: the day started without fuss and the pantry shelves laid out with rows of jelly glasses and brown jugs and white stone-china jars with blue whirligigs and words painted on them: coffee, tea, sugar, ginger, cinnamon, allspice: and the bronze clock with the lion on top nicely dusted off. The dust that lion could collect in twenty-four hours! The box in the attic with all those letters tied up, well, she'd have to go through that tomorrow. All those letters — George's letters and John's letters and her letters to them both — lying around for the children to find afterwards made her uneasy. Yes, that would be tomorrow's business. No use to let them know how silly she had been once.

While she was rummaging around she found death in her mind and it felt clammy and unfamiliar. She had spent so much time preparing for death there was no need for bringing it up again. Let it take care of itself now. When she was sixty she had felt very old, finished, and went around making farewell trips to see her children and grandchildren, with a secret in her mind: This is the very last of your mother, children! Then she made her will and came down with a long fever. That was all just a notion like a lot of other things, but it was lucky too, for she had once and for all got over the idea of dying for a long time. Now she couldn't be worried. She hoped she had better sense now. Her father had lived to be one hundred and two years old and had drunk a noggin of strong hot toddy on his last birthday. He told the reporters it was his daily habit, and he owed his long life to that. He had made quite a scandal and was very pleased about it. She believed she'd just plague Cornelia a little.

"Cornelia! Cornelia!" No footsteps, but a sudden hand on her cheek. "Bless you, where have you been?"

"Here, Mother." 20

"Well, Cornelia, I want a noggin of hot toddy."

"Are you cold, darling?"

"I'm chilly, Cornelia. Lying in bed stops the circulation. I must have told you that a thousand times."

Well, she could just hear Cornelia telling her husband that Mother was getting a little childish and they'd have to humor her. The thing that most annoyed her was that Cornelia thought she was deaf, dumb, and blind. Little hasty glances and tiny gestures tossed around her and over her head saying, "Don't cross her, let her have her way, she's eighty years old," and she sitting there as if she lived in a thin glass cage. Sometimes Granny almost made up her mind to pack up and move back to her own house where nobody could remind her every minute that she was old. Wait, wait, Cornelia, till your own children whisper behind your back!

In her day she had kept a better house and had got more work done. She 25
wasn't too old yet for Lydia to be driving eighty miles for advice when one of the children jumped the track, and Jimmy still dropped in and talked things over: "Now, Mammy, you've a good business head, I want to know what you think of this? . . ." Old. Cornelia couldn't change the furniture around without asking. Little things, little things! They had been so sweet when they were little. Granny wished the old days were back again with the children young and everything to be done over. It had been a hard pull, but not too much for her. When she thought of all the food she had cooked, and all the clothes she had cut and sewed, and all the gardens she had made—well, the children showed it. There they were, made out of her, and they couldn't get away from that. Sometimes she wanted to see John again and point to them and say, Well, I didn't do so badly, did I? But that would have to wait. That was for tomorrow. She used to think of him as a man, but now all the children were older than their father, and he would be a child beside her if she saw him now. It seemed strange and there was something wrong in the idea. Why, he couldn't possibly recognize her. She had fenced in a hundred acres once, digging the post holes herself and clamping the wires with just a negro boy to help. That changed a woman. John would be looking for a young woman with the peaked Spanish comb in her hair and the painted fan. Digging post holes changed a woman. Riding country roads in the winter when women had their babies was another thing: sitting up nights with sick horses and sick negroes and sick children and hardly ever losing one. John, I hardly ever lost one of them! John would see that in a minute, that would be something he could understand, she wouldn't have to explain anything!

It made her feel like rolling up her sleeves and putting the whole place to rights again. No matter if Cornelia was determined to be everywhere at once, there were a great many things left undone on this place. She would start tomorrow and do them. It was good to be strong enough for everything, even if all you made melted and changed and slipped under your hands, so that by the time you finished you almost forgot what you were working for. What was it I set out to do? she asked herself intently, but she could not remember. A fog rose over the valley, she saw it marching across the creek swallowing the trees and moving up the hill like an army of ghosts. Soon it would be at the near edge of the orchard, and then it was time to go in and light the lamps. Come in, children, don't stay out in the night air.

Lighting the lamps had been beautiful. The children huddled up to her and breathed like little calves waiting at the bars in the twilight. Their eyes followed the match and watched the flame rise and settle in a blue curve, then they moved away from her. The lamp was lit, they didn't have to be scared and hang on to mother any more. Never, never, never more. God, for all my life I thank Thee. Without Thee, my God, I could never have done it. Hail, Mary, full of grace.

I want you to pick all the fruit this year and see that nothing is wasted. There's always someone who can use it. Don't let good things rot for want of using. You waste life when you waste good food. Don't let things get lost. It's bitter to lose things. Now, don't let me get to thinking, not when I am tired and taking a little nap before supper. . . .

The pillow rose about her shoulders and pressed against her heart and the memory was being squeezed out of it: oh, push down the pillow, somebody: it would smother her if she tried to hold it. Such a fresh breeze blowing and such a green day with no threats in it. But he had not come, just the same. What does a woman do when she has put on the white veil and set out the white cake for a man and he doesn't come? She tried to remember. No, I swear he never harmed me but in that. He never harmed me but in that . . . and what if he did? There was the day, the day, but a whirl of dark smoke rose and covered it, crept up and over into the bright field where everything was planted so carefully in orderly rows. That was hell, she knew hell when she saw it. For sixty years she had prayed against remembering him and against losing her soul in the deep pit of hell, and now the two things were mingled in one and the thought of him was a smoky cloud from hell that moved and crept in her head when she had just got rid of Doctor Harry and was trying to rest a minute. Wounded vanity, Ellen, said a sharp voice in the top of her mind. Don't let your wounded vanity get the upper hand of you. Plenty of girls get jilted. You were jilted, weren't you? Then stand up to it. Her eyelids wavered and let in streamers of blue-gray light like tissue paper over her eyes. She must get up and pull the shades down or she'd never sleep. She was in bed again and the shades were not down. How could that happen? Better turn over, hide from the light, sleeping in the light gave you nightmares. "Mother, how do you feel now?" and a stinging wetness on her forehead. But I don't like having my face washed in cold water!

Hapsy? George? Lydia? Jimmy? No, Cornelia, and her features were swollen and full of little puddles. "They're coming, darling, they'll all be here soon." Go wash your face, child, you look funny.

Instead of obeying, Cornelia knelt down and put her head on the pillow. She seemed to be talking but there was no sound. "Well, are you tongue-tied? Whose birthday is it? Are you going to give a party?"

Cornelia's mouth moved urgently in strange shapes. "Don't do that, you bother me, daughter."

"O, no, Mother. Oh, no. . . ."

Nonsense. It was strange about children. They disputed your every word. "No what, Cornelia?"

"Here's Doctor Harry."

"I won't see that boy again. He just left five minutes ago."

"That was this morning, Mother. It's night now. Here's the nurse."

"This is Doctor Harry, Mrs. Weatherall. I never saw you look so young and happy!"

"Ah, I'll never be young again—but I'd be happy if they'd let me lie in peace and get rested."

She thought she spoke up loudly, but no one answered. A warm weight on her 40
forehead, a warm bracelet on her wrist, and a breeze went on whispering, trying to tell her something. A shuffle of leaves in the everlasting hand of God. He blew on them and they danced and rattled. "Mother, don't mind, we're going to give you a little hypodermic." "Look here, daughter, how do ants get in this bed? I saw sugar ants yesterday." Did you send for Hapsy too?

It was Hapsy she really wanted. She had to go a long way back through a great many rooms to find Hapsy standing with a baby on her arm. She seemed to herself to be Hapsy also, and the baby on Hapsy's arm was Hapsy and himself and herself, all at once, and there was no surprise in the meeting. Then Hapsy melted from within and turned flimsy as gray gauze and the baby was a gauzy shadow, and Hapsy came up close and said, "I thought you'd never come," and looked at her very searchingly and said, "You haven't changed a bit!" They leaned forward to kiss, when Cornelia began whispering from a long way off, "Oh, is there anything you want to tell me? Is there anything I can do for you?"

Yes, she had changed her mind after sixty years and she would like to see George. I want you to find George. Find him and be sure to tell him I forgot him. I want him to know I had my husband just the same and my children and my house like any other woman. A good house too and a good husband that I loved and fine children out of him. Better than I hoped for even. Tell him I was given back everything he took away and more. Oh, no, oh, God, no, there was something else besides the house and the man and the children. Oh, surely they were not all? What was it? Something not given back. . . . Her breath crowded down under her ribs and grew into a monstrous frightening shape with cutting edges; it bored up into her head, and the agony was unbelievable: Yes, John, get the Doctor now, no more talk, my time has come.

When this one was born it should be the last. The last. It should have been born first, for it was the one she had truly wanted. Everything came in good time. Nothing left out, left over. She was strong, in three days she would be as well as ever. Better. A woman needed milk in her to have her full health.

"Mother, do you hear me?"

"I've been telling you—" 45

"Mother, Father Connolly's here."

"I went to Holy Communion last week. Tell him I'm not so sinful as all that."

"Father just wants to speak to you."

He could speak as much as he pleased. It was like him to drop in and inquire about her soul as if it were a teething baby, and then stay on for a cup of tea and a round of cards and gossip. He always had a funny story of some sort, usually about an Irishman who made his little mistakes and confessed them, and the point lay in some absurd thing he would blurtout in the confessional showing his struggles between native piety and original sin. Granny felt easy about her soul. Cornelia, where are your manners? Give Father Connolly a chair. She had her secret comfortable understanding with a few favorite saints who cleared a straight road to God for her. All as surely signed and sealed as the papers for the new Forty Acres. Forever . . . heirs and assigns forever. Since the day the wedding cake was not cut, but thrown out and wasted. The whole bottom dropped out of the world, and there she was blind and sweating with nothing under her feet and the walls falling away. His hand had caught her under the breast, she had not fallen, there was the freshly polished floor with the green rug on it, just as before. He had cursed like a sailor's parrot and said, "I'll kill him for you." Don't lay a hand on him, for my sake leave something to God. "Now, Ellen, you must believe what I tell you. . . ."

50 So there was nothing, nothing to worry about any more, except sometimes in the night one of the children screamed in a nightmare, and they both hustled out shaking and hunting for the matches and calling, "There, wait a minute, here we are!" John, get the doctor now, Hapsy's time has come. But there was Hapsy standing by the bed in a white cap. "Cornelia, tell Hapsy to take off her cap. I can't see her plain."

Her eyes opened very wide and the room stood out like a picture she had seen somewhere. Dark colors with the shadows rising towards the ceiling in long angles. The tall black dresser gleamed with nothing on it but John's picture, enlarged from a little one, with John's eyes very black when they should have been blue. You never saw him, so how do you know how he looked? But the man insisted the copy was perfect, it was very rich and handsome. For a picture, yes, but it's not my husband. The table by the bed had a linen cover and a candle and a crucifix. The light was blue from Cornelia's silk lampshades. No sort of light at all, just frippery. You had to live forty years with kerosene lamps to appreciate honest electricity. She felt very strong and she saw Doctor Harry with a rosy nimbus around him.

"You look like a saint, Doctor Harry, and I vow that's as near as you'll ever come to it."

"She's saying something."

"I heard you, Cornelia. What's all this carrying-on?"

55 "Father Connolly's saying—"

Cornelia's voice staggered and bumped like a cart in a bad road. It rounded corners and turned back again and arrived nowhere. Granny stepped up in the cart very lightly and reached for the reins, but a man sat beside her and she knew him by his hands, driving the cart. She did not look in his face, for she knew without seeing, but looked instead down the road where the trees leaned over and bowed to each other and a thousand birds were singing a Mass. She felt like singing too, but she put her hand in the bosom of her dress and pulled out a rosary, and Father Connolly murmured Latin in a very solemn voice and tickled her feet. My God, will you stop that nonsense? I'm a married woman. What if he did run away and leave me to face the priest by myself? I found another a whole world better. I wouldn't have exchanged my husband for anybody except St. Michael himself, and you may tell him that for me with a thank you in the bargain.

Light flashed on her closed eyelids, and a deep roaring shook her. Cornelia, is that lightning? I hear thunder. There's going to be a storm. Close all the windows. Call the children in. . . . "Mother, here we are, all of us." "Is that you, Hapsy?" "Oh, no, I'm Lydia. We drove as fast as we could." Their faces drifted above her, drifted away. The rosary fell out of her hands and Lydia put it back. Jimmy tried to help, their hands fumbled together, and Granny closed two fingers around Jimmy's thumb.

Beads wouldn't do, it must be something alive. She was so amazed her thoughts ran round and round. So, my dear Lord, this is my death and I wasn't even thinking about it. My children have come to see me die. But I can't, it's not time. Oh, I always hated surprises. I wanted to give Cornelia the amethyst set—Cornelia, you're to have the amethyst set, but Hapsy's to wear it when she wants, and, Doctor Harry, do shut up. Nobody sent for you. Oh, my dear Lord, do wait a minute. I meant to do something about the Forty Acres, Jimmy doesn't need it and Lydia will later on, with that worthless husband of hers. I meant to finish the altar cloth and send six bottles of wine to Sister Borgia for her dyspepsia. I want to send six bottles of wine to Sister Borgia, Father Connolly, now don't let me forget.

Cornelia's voice made short turns and tilted over and crashed. "Oh, Mother, oh, Mother, oh, Mother. . . ."

"I'm not going, Cornelia. I'm taken by surprise. I can't go."

You'll see Hapsy again. What about her? "I thought you'd never come." Granny 60
made a long journey outward, looking for Hapsy. What if I don't find her? What then? Her heart sank down and down, there was no bottom to death, she couldn't come to the end of it. The blue light from Cornelia's lampshade drew into a tiny point in the center of her brain, it flickered and winked like an eye, quietly it fluttered and dwindled. Granny lay curled down within herself, amazed and watchful, staring at the point of light that was herself; her body was now only a deeper mass of shadow in an endless darkness and this darkness would curl around the light and swallow it up. God, give a sign!

For the second time there was no sign. Again no bridegroom and the priest in the house. She could not remember any other sorrow because this grief wiped them all away. Oh, no, there's nothing more cruel than this—I'll never forgive it. She stretched herself with a deep breath and blew out the light.

* * *

JOHN STEINBECK (1902–1968)

The Chrysanthemums (1937)

The high grey-flannel fog of winter closed off the Salinas Valley from the sky and from all the rest of the world. On every side it sat like a lid on the mountains and made of the great valley a closed pot. On the broad, level land floor the gang plows bit deep and left the black earth shining like metal where the shares had cut. On the foothill ranches across the Salinas River, the yellow stubble fields seemed to be bathed in pale cold sunshine, but there was no sunshine in the valley now in December. The thick willow scrub along the river flamed with sharp and positive yellow leaves.

It was a game of quiet and of waiting. The air was cold and tender. A light wind blew up from the southwest so that the farmers were mildly hopeful of a good rain before long; but fog and rain do not go together.

Across the river, on Henry Allen's foothill ranch there was little work to be done, for the hay was cut and stored and the orchards were plowed up to receive the rain deeply when it should come. The cattle on the higher slopes were becoming shaggy and rough-coated.

Elisa Allen, working in her flower garden, looked down across the yard and saw Henry, her husband, talking to two men in business suits. The three of them stood by the tractor shed, each man with one foot on the side of the little Fordson. They smoked cigarettes and studied the machine as they talked.

5 Elisa watched them for a moment and then went back to her work. She was thirty-five. Her face was lean and strong and her eyes were as clear as water. Her figure looked blocked and heavy in her gardening costume, a man's black hat pulled low down over her eyes, clod-hopper shoes,° a figured print dress almost completely covered by a big corduroy apron with four big pockets to hold the snips, the trowel and scratcher, the seeds and the knife she worked with. She wore heavy leather gloves to protect her hands while she worked.

She was cutting down the old year's chrysanthemum stalks with a pair of short and powerful scissors. She looked down toward the men by the tractor shed now and then. Her face was eager and mature and handsome; even her work with the scissors was over-eager, over-powerful. The chrysanthemum stems seemed too small and easy for her energy.

She brushed a cloud of hair out of her eyes with the back of her glove, and left a smudge of earth on her cheek in doing it. Behind her stood the neat white farm house with red geraniums close-banked around it as high as the windows. It was a hard-swept looking little house with hard-polished windows, and a clean mud-mat on the front steps.

Elisa cast another glance toward the tractor shed. The strangers were getting into their Ford coupe. She took off a glove and put her strong fingers down into the forest of new green chrysanthemum sprouts that were growing around the old roots. She spread the leaves and looked down among the close-growing stems. No aphids were there, no sowbugs or snails or cutworms. Her terrier fingers destroyed such pests before they could get started.

Elisa started at the sound of her husband's voice. He had come near quietly, and he leaned over the wire fence that protected her flower garden from cattle and dogs and chickens.

10 "At it again," he said. "You've got a strong new crop coming."

Elisa straightened her back and pulled on the gardening glove again. "Yes. They'll be strong this coming year." In her tone and on her face there was a little smugness.

"You've got a gift with things," Henry observed. "Some of those yellow chrysanthemums you had this year were ten inches across. I wish you'd work out in the orchard and raise some apples that big."

Her eyes sharpened. "Maybe I could do it, too. I've a gift with things, all right. My mother had it. She could stick anything in the ground and make it grow. She said it was having planters' hands that knew how to do it."

"Well, it sure works with flowers," he said.

15 "Henry, who were those men you were talking to?"

---

clod-hopper shoes: Heavy shoes, such as the ones that a plowman might wear.

"Why, sure, that's what I came to tell you. They were from the Western Meat Company. I sold those thirty head of three-year-old steers. Got nearly my own price, too."

"Good," she said. "Good for you."

"And I thought," he continued, "I thought how it's Saturday afternoon, and we might go into Salinas for dinner at a restaurant, and then to a picture show — to celebrate, you see."

"Good," she repeated. "Oh, yes. That will be good."

Henry put on his joking tone. "There's fights tonight. How'd you like to go to the fights?"

"Oh, no," she said breathlessly. "No, I wouldn't like fights."

"Just fooling, Elisa. We'll go to a movie. Let's see. It's two now. I'm going to take Scotty and bring down those steers from the hill. It'll take us maybe two hours. We'll go in town about five and have dinner at the Cominos Hotel. Like that?"

"Of course I'll like it. It's good to eat away from home."

"All right, then. I'll go get up a couple of horses."

She said, "I'll have plenty of time to transplant some of these sets, I guess."

She heard her husband calling Scotty down by the barn. And a little later she saw the two men ride up the pale yellow hillside in search of the steers.

There was a little square sandy bed kept for rooting the chrysanthemums. With her trowel she turned the soil over and over, and smoothed it and patted it firm. Then she dug ten parallel trenches to receive the sets. Back at the chrysanthemum bed she pulled out the little crisp shoots, trimmed off the leaves of each one with her scissors and laid it on a small orderly pile.

A squeak of wheels and plod of hoofs came from the road. Elisa looked up. The country road ran along the dense bank of willows and cottonwoods that bordered the river, and up this road came a curious vehicle, curiously drawn. It was an old spring-wagon, with a round canvas top on it like the cover of a prairie schooner.° It was drawn by an old bay horse and a little grey-and-white burro. A big stubble-bearded man sat between the cover flaps and drove the crawling team. Underneath the wagon, between the hind wheels, a lean and rangy mongrel dog walked sedately. Words were printed on the canvas, in clumsy, crooked letters. "Pots, pans, knives, sisors, lawn mores, Fixed." Two rows of articles, and the triumphantly definitive "Fixed" below. The black paint had run down in little sharp points beneath each letter.

Elisa, squatting on the ground, watched to see the crazy, loose-jointed wagon pass by. But it didn't pass. It turned into the farm road in front of her house, crooked old wheels skirling and squeaking. The rangy dog darted from between the wheels and ran ahead. Instantly the two ranch shepherds flew out at him. Then all three stopped, and with stiff and quivering tails, with taut straight legs, with ambassadorial dignity, they slowly circled, sniffing daintily. The caravan pulled up to Elisa's wire fence and stopped. Now the newcomer dog, feeling outnumbered, lowered his tail and retired under the wagon with raised hackles and bared teeth.

---

prairie schooner: Covered wagon used by American pioneers.

30 The man on the wagon seat called out, "That's a bad dog in a fight when he gets started."

Elisa laughed. "I see he is. How soon does he generally get started?"

The man caught up her laughter and echoed it heartily. "Sometimes not for weeks and weeks," he said. He climbed stiffly down, over the wheel. The horse and the donkey drooped like unwatered flowers.

Elisa saw that he was a very big man. Although his hair and beard were greying, he did not look old. His worn black suit was wrinkled and spotted with grease. The laughter had disappeared from his face and eyes the moment his laughing voice ceased. His eyes were dark, and they were full of the brooding that gets in the eyes of teamsters and of sailors. The calloused hands he rested on the wire fence were cracked, and every crack was a black line. He took off his battered hat.

"I'm off my general road, ma'am," he said. "Does this dirt road cut over across the river to the Los Angeles highway?"

35 Elisa stood up and shoved the thick scissors in her apron pocket. "Well, yes, it does, but it winds around and then fords the river. I don't think your team could pull through the sand."

He replied with some asperity. "It might surprise you what them beasts can pull through."

"When they get started?" she asked.

He smiled for a second. "Yes. When they get started."

"Well," said Elisa, "I think you'll save time if you go back to the Salinas road and pick up the highway there."

40 He drew a big finger down the chicken wire and made it sing. "I ain't in any hurry, ma'am. I go from Seattle to San Diego and back every year. Takes all my time. About six months each way. I aim to follow nice weather."

Elisa took off her gloves and stuffed them in the apron pocket with the scissors. She touched the under edge of her man's hat, searching for fugitive hairs. "That sounds like a nice kind of a way to live," she said.

He leaned confidentially over the fence. "Maybe you noticed the writing on my wagon. I mend pots and sharpen knives and scissors. You got any of them things to do?"

"Oh, no," she said quickly. "Nothing like that." Her eyes hardened with resistance.

"Scissors is the worst thing," he explained. "Most people just ruin scissors trying to sharpen 'em, but I know how. I got a special tool. It's a little bobbit kind of thing, and patented. But it sure does the trick."

45 "No. My scissors are all sharp."

"All right, then. Take a pot," he continued earnestly, "a bent pot, or a pot with a hole. I can make it like new so you don't have to buy no new ones. That's a saving for you."

"No," she said shortly. "I tell you I have nothing like that for you to do."

His face fell to an exaggerated sadness. His voice took on a whining undertone. "I ain't had a thing to do today. Maybe I won't have no supper tonight. You see I'm off my regular road. I know folks on the highway clear from Seattle to San Diego. They save their things for me to sharpen up because they know I do it so good and save them money."

"I'm sorry," Elisa said irritably. "I haven't anything for you to do."

50 His eyes left her face and fell to searching the ground. They roamed about until they came to the chrysanthemum bed where she had been working. "What's them plants, ma'am?"

The irritation and resistance melted from Elisa's face. "Oh, those are chrysanthemums, giant whites and yellows. I raise them every year, bigger than anybody around here."

"Kind of a long-stemmed flower? Looks like a quick puff of colored smoke?" he asked.

"That's it. What a nice way to describe them."

"They smell kind of nasty till you get used to them," he said.

55 "It's a good bitter smell," she retorted, "not nasty at all."

He changed his tone quickly. "I like the smell myself."

"I had ten-inch blooms this year," she said.

The man leaned farther over the fence. "Look. I know a lady down the road a piece, has got the nicest garden you ever seen. Got nearly every kind of flower but no chrysanthemums. Last time I was mending a copper-bottom washtub for her (that's a hard job but I do it good), she said to me, 'If you ever run acrost some nice chrysanthemums I wish you'd try to get me a few seeds.' That's what she told me."

Elisa's eyes grew alert and eager. "She couldn't have known much about chrysanthemums. You *can* raise them from seed, but it's much easier to root the little sprouts you see there."

60 "Oh," he said. "I s'pose I can't take none to her, then."

"Why yes you can," Elisa cried. "I can put some in damp sand, and you can carry them right along with you. They'll take root in the pot if you keep them damp. And then she can transplant them."

"She'd sure like to have some, ma'am. You say they're nice ones?"

"Beautiful," she said. "Oh, beautiful." Her eyes shone. She tore off the battered hat and shook out her dark pretty hair. "I'll put them in a flower pot, and you can take them right with you. Come into the yard."

While the man came through the picket gate Elisa ran excitedly along the geranium-bordered path to the back of the house. And she returned carrying a big red flower pot. The gloves were forgotten now. She kneeled on the ground by the starting bed and dug up the sandy soil with her fingers and scooped it into the bright new flower pot. Then she picked up the little pile of shoots she had prepared. With her strong fingers she pressed them into the sand and tamped around them with her knuckles. The man stood over her. "I'll tell you what to do," she said. "You remember so you can tell the lady."

65 "Yes, I'll try to remember."

"Well, look. These will take root in about a month. Then she must set them out, about a foot apart in good rich earth like this, see?" She lifted a handful of dark soil for him to look at. "They'll grow fast and tall. Now remember this: In July tell her to cut them down, about eight inches from the ground."

"Before they bloom?" he asked.

"Yes, before they bloom." Her face was tight with eagerness. "They'll grow right up again. About the last of September the buds will start."

She stopped and seemed perplexed. "It's the budding that takes the most care," she said hesitantly. "I don't know how to tell you." She looked deep into his eyes, searchingly. Her mouth opened a little, and she seemed to be listening. "I'll try to tell you," she said. "Did you ever hear of planting hands?"

70 "Can't say I have, ma'am."

"Well, I can only tell you what it feels like. It's when you're picking off the buds you don't want. Everything goes right down into your fingertips. You watch your fingers work. They do it themselves. You can feel how it is. They pick and pick the buds. They never make a mistake. They're with the plant. Do you see? Your fingers and the plant. You can feel that, right up your arm. They know. They never make a mistake. You can feel it. When you're like that you can't do anything wrong. Do you see that? Can you understand that?"

She was kneeling on the ground looking up at him. Her breast swelled passionately.

The man's eyes narrowed. He looked away self-consciously. "Maybe I know," he said. "Sometimes in the night in the wagon there—"

Elisa's voice grew husky. She broke in on him, "I've never lived as you do, but I know what you mean. When the night is dark—why, the stars are sharp-pointed, and there's quiet. Why, you rise up and up! Every pointed star gets driven into your body. It's like that. Hot and sharp and—lovely."

75 Kneeling there, her hand went out toward his legs in the greasy black trousers. Her hesitant fingers almost touched the cloth. Then her hand dropped to the ground. She crouched low like a fawning dog.

He said, "It's nice, just like you say. Only when you don't have no dinner, it ain't."

She stood up then, very straight, and her face was ashamed. She held the flower pot out to him and placed it gently in his arms. "Here. Put it in your wagon, on the seat, where you can watch it. Maybe I can find something for you to do."

At the back of the house she dug in the can pile and found two old and battered aluminum saucepans. She carried them back and gave them to him. "Here, maybe you can fix these."

His manner changed. He became professional. "Good as new I can fix them." At the back of his wagon he sat a little anvil, and out of an oily tool box dug a small machine hammer. Elisa came through the gate to watch him while he pounded out the dents in the kettles. His mouth grew sure and knowing. At a difficult part of the work he sucked his under-lip.

80 "You sleep right in the wagon?" Elisa asked.

"Right in the wagon, ma'am. Rain or shine I'm dry as a cow in there."

"It must be nice," she said. "It must be very nice. I wish women could do such things."

"It ain't the right kind of a life for a woman."

Her upper lip raised a little, showing her teeth. "How do you know? How can you tell?" she said.

85 "I don't know, ma'am," he protested. "Of course I don't know. Now here's your kettles, done. You don't have to buy no new ones."

"How much?"

"Oh, fifty cents'll do. I keep my prices down and my work good. That's why I have all them satisfied customers up and down the highway."

Elisa brought him a fifty-cent piece from the house and dropped it in his hand. "You might be surprised to have a rival some time. I can sharpen scissors, too. And I can beat the dents out of little pots. I could show you what a woman might do."

He put his hammer back in the oily box and shoved the little anvil out of sight. "It would be a lonely life for a woman, ma'am, and a scarey life, too, with animals creeping under the wagon all night." He climbed over the singletree,° steadying himself with a hand on the burro's white rump. He settled himself in the seat, picked up the lines. "Thank you kindly, ma'am," he said. "I'll do like you told me; I'll go back and catch the Salinas road."

"Mind," she called, "if you're long in getting there, keep the sand damp." 90

"Sand, ma'am? . . . Sand? Oh, sure. You mean around the chrysanthemums. Sure I will." He clucked his tongue. The beasts leaned luxuriously into their collars. The mongrel dog took his place between the back wheels. The wagon turned and crawled out the entrance road and back the way it had come, along the river.

Elisa stood in front of her wire fence watching the slow progress of the caravan. Her shoulders were straight, her head thrown back, her eyes half-closed, so that the scene came vaguely into them. Her lips moved silently, forming the words "Good-bye — good-bye." Then she whispered, "That's a bright direction. There's a glowing there." The sound of her whisper startled her. She shook herself free and looked about to see whether anyone had been listening. Only the dogs had heard. They lifted their heads toward her from their sleeping in the dust, and then stretched out their chins and settled asleep again. Elisa turned and ran hurriedly into the house.

In the kitchen she reached behind the stove and felt the water tank. It was full of hot water from the noonday cooking. In the bathroom she tore off her soiled clothes and flung them into the corner. And then she scrubbed herself with a little block of pumice, legs and thighs, loins and chest and arms, until her skin was scratched and red. When she had dried herself she stood in front of a mirror in her bedroom and looked at her body. She tightened her stomach and threw out her chest. She turned and looked over her shoulder at her back.

After a while she began to dress, slowly. She put on her newest underclothing and her nicest stockings and the dress which was the symbol of her prettiness. She worked carefully on her hair, penciled her eyebrows and rouged her lips.

Before she was finished she heard the little thunder of hoofs and the shouts of 95
Henry and his helper as they drove the red steers into the corral. She heard the gate bang shut and set herself for Henry's arrival.

His step sounded on the porch. He entered the house calling, "Elisa, where are you?"

"In my room, dressing. I'm not ready. There's hot water for your bath. Hurry up. It's getting late."

---

singletree: A wooden bar that connects a wagon to the horses' harnesses.

When she heard him splashing in the tub, Elisa laid his dark suit on the bed, and shirt and socks and tie beside it. She stood his polished shoes on the floor beside the bed. Then she went to the porch and sat primly and stiffly down. She looked toward the river road where the willow-line was still yellow with frosted leaves so that under the high grey fog they seemed a thin band of sunshine. This was the only color in the grey afternoon. She sat unmoving for a long time. Her eyes blinked rarely.

Henry came banging out of the door, shoving his tie inside his vest as he came. Elisa stiffened and her face grew tight. Henry stopped short and looked at her. "Why—why, Elisa. You look so nice!"

100 "Nice? You think I look nice? What do you mean by 'nice'?"

Henry blundered on. "I don't know. I mean you look different, strong and happy."

"I am strong? Yes, strong. What do you mean 'strong'?"

He looked bewildered. "You're playing some kind of a game," he said helplessly. "It's a kind of a play. You look strong enough to break a calf over your knee, happy enough to eat it like a watermelon."

For a second she lost her rigidity. "Henry! Don't talk like that. You didn't know what you said." She grew complete again. "I'm strong," she boasted. "I never knew before how strong."

105 Henry looked down toward the tractor shed, and when he brought his eyes back to her, they were his own again. "I'll get out the car. You can put on your coat while I'm starting."

Elisa went into the house. She heard him drive to the gate and idle down his motor, and then she took a long time to put on her hat. She pulled it here and pressed it there. When Henry turned the motor off she slipped into her coat and went out.

The little roadster° bounced along on the dirt road by the river, raising the birds and driving the rabbits into the brush. Two cranes flapped heavily over the willow-line and dropped into the river-bed.

Far ahead on the road Elisa saw a dark speck. She knew.

She tried not to look as they passed it, but her eyes would not obey. She whispered to herself sadly, "He might have thrown them off the road. That wouldn't have been much trouble, not very much. But he kept the pot," she explained. "He had to keep the pot. That's why he couldn't get them off the road."

110 The roadster turned a bend and she saw the caravan ahead. She swung full around toward her husband so she could not see the little covered wagon and the mismatched team as the car passed them.

In a moment it was over. The thing was done. She did not look back.

She said loudly, to be heard above the motor, "It will be good, tonight, a good dinner."

"Now you're changed again," Henry complained. He took one hand from the wheel and patted her knee. "I ought to take you in to dinner oftener. It would be good for both of us. We get so heavy out on the ranch."

---

roadster: An early roofless automobile, with a single seat for two or three passengers.

"Henry," she asked, "could we have wine at dinner?"

"Sure we could. Say! That will be fine."

She was silent for a while; then she said, "Henry, at those prize fights, do the men hurt each other very much?"

"Sometimes a little, not often. Why?"

"Well, I've read how they break noses, and blood runs down their chests. I've read how the fighting gloves get heavy and soggy with blood."

He looked around at her. "What's the matter, Elisa? I didn't know you read things like that." He brought the car to a stop, then turned to the right over the Salinas River bridge.

"Do any women ever go to the fights?" she asked.

"Oh, sure, some. What's the matter, Elisa? Do you want to go? I don't think you'd like it, but I'll take you if you really want to go."

She relaxed limply in the seat. "Oh, no. No. I don't want to go. I'm sure I don't." Her face was turned away from him. "It will be enough if we can have wine. It will be plenty." She turned up her coat collar so he could not see that she was crying weakly—like an old woman.

* * *

AMY TAN (1952–)

Two Kinds (1989)

My mother believed you could be anything you wanted to be in America. You could open a restaurant. You could work for the government and get good retirement. You could buy a house with almost no money down. You could become rich. You could become instantly famous.

"Of course you can be prodigy, too," my mother told me when I was nine. "You can be best anything. What does Auntie Lindo know? Her daughter, she is only best tricky."

America was where all my mother's hopes lay. She had come here in 1949 after losing everything in China: her mother and father, her family home, her first husband, and two daughters, twin baby girls. But she never looked back with regret. There were so many ways for things to get better.

We didn't immediately pick the right kind of prodigy. At first my mother thought I could be a Chinese Shirley Temple. We'd watch Shirley's old movies on TV as though they were training films. My mother would poke my arm and say, "*Ni kan*"—You watch. And I would see Shirley tapping her feet, or singing a sailor song, or pursing her lips into a very round O while saying, "Oh my goodness."

5 "*Ni kan*," said my mother as Shirley's eyes flooded with tears. "You already know how. Don't need talent for crying!"

Soon after my mother got this idea about Shirley Temple, she took me to a beauty training school in the Mission district and put me in the hands of a student who could barely hold the scissors without shaking. Instead of getting big fat curls, I emerged with an uneven mass of crinkly black fuzz. My mother dragged me off to the bathroom and tried to wet down my hair.

"You look like Negro Chinese," she lamented, as if I had done this on purpose.

The instructor of the beauty training school had to lop off these soggy clumps to make my hair even again. "Peter Pan is very popular these days," the instructor assured my mother. I now had hair the length of a boy's, with straight-across bangs that hung at a slant two inches above my eyebrows. I liked the haircut and it made me actually look forward to my future fame.

In fact, in the beginning, I was just as excited as my mother, maybe even more so. I pictured this prodigy part of me as many different images, trying each one on for size. I was a dainty ballerina girl standing by the curtains, waiting to hear the right music that would send me floating on my tiptoes. I was like the Christ child lifted out of the straw manger, crying with holy indignity. I was Cinderella stepping from her pumpkin carriage with sparkly cartoon music filling the air.

10 In all of my imaginings, I was filled with a sense that I would soon become *perfect*. My mother and father would adore me. I would be beyond reproach. I would never feel the need to sulk for anything.

But sometimes the prodigy in me became impatient. "If you don't hurry up and get me out of here, I'm disappearing for good," it warned. "And then you'll always be nothing."

Every night after dinner, my mother and I would sit at the Formica kitchen table. She would present new tests, taking her examples from stories of amazing children she had read in *Ripley's Believe It or Not*, or *Good Housekeeping*, *Reader's Digest*, and a dozen other magazines she kept in a pile in our bathroom. My mother got these magazines from people whose houses she cleaned. And since she cleaned many houses each week, we had a great assortment. She would look through them all, searching for stories about remarkable children.

The first night she brought out a story about a three-year-old boy who knew the capitals of all the states and even most of the European countries. A teacher was quoted as saying the little boy could also pronounce the names of the foreign cities correctly.

"What's the capital of Finland?" my mother asked me, looking at the magazine story.

15 All I knew was the capital of California, because Sacramento was the name of the street we lived on in Chinatown. "Nairobi!" I guessed, saying the most foreign word I could think of. She checked to see if that was possibly one way to pronounce "Helsinki" before showing me the answer.

The tests got harder—multiplying numbers in my head, finding the queen of hearts in a deck of cards, trying to stand on my head without using my hands, predicting the daily temperatures in Los Angeles, New York, and London.

One night I had to look at a page from the Bible for three minutes and then report everything I could remember. "Now Jehoshaphat had riches and honor in abundance and . . . that's all I remember, Ma," I said.

And after seeing my mother's disappointed face once again, something inside of me began to die. I hated the tests, the raised hopes and failed expectations. Before going to bed that night, I looked in the mirror above the bathroom sink and when I saw only my face staring back—and that it would always be this ordinary face—I began to cry. Such a sad, ugly girl! I made high-pitched noises like a crazed animal, trying to scratch out the face in the mirror.

And then I saw what seemed to be the prodigy side of me—because I had never seen that face before. I looked at my reflection, blinking so I could see more clearly. The girl staring back at me was angry, powerful. This girl and I were the same. I had new thoughts, willful thoughts, or rather thoughts filled with lots of won'ts. I won't let her change me, I promised myself. I won't be what I'm not.

So now on nights when my mother presented her tests, I performed listlessly, my 20
head propped on one arm. I pretended to be bored. And I was. I got so bored I started counting the bellows of the foghorns out on the bay while my mother drilled me in other areas. The sound was comforting and reminded me of the cow jumping over the moon. And the next day, I played a game with myself, seeing if my mother would give up on me before eight bellows. After a while I usually counted only one, maybe two bellows at most. At last she was beginning to give up hope.

Two or three months had gone by without any mention of my being a prodigy again. And then one day my mother was watching *The Ed Sullivan Show* on TV. The TV was old and the sound kept shorting out. Every time my mother got halfway up from the sofa to adjust the set, the sound would go back on and Ed would be talking. As soon as she sat down, Ed would go silent again. She got up, the TV broke into loud piano music. She sat down. Silence. Up and down, back and forth, quiet and loud. It was like a stiff embraceless dance between her and the TV set. Finally she stood by the set with her hand on the sound dial.

She seemed entranced by the music, a little frenzied piano piece with this mesmerizing quality, sort of quick passages and then teasing lilting ones before it returned to the quick playful parts.

"*Ni kan*," my mother said, calling me over with hurried hand gestures, "Look here."

I could see why my mother was fascinated by the music. It was being pounded out by a little Chinese girl, about nine years old, with a Peter Pan haircut. The girl had the sauciness of a Shirley Temple. She was proudly modest like a proper Chinese child. And she also did this fancy sweep of a curtsy, so that the fluffy skirt of her white dress cascaded slowly to the floor like the petals of a large carnation.

In spite of these warning signs, I wasn't worried. Our family had no piano and we 25
couldn't afford to buy one, let alone reams of sheet music and piano lessons. So I could be generous in my comments when my mother bad-mouthed the little girl on TV.

"Play note right, but doesn't sound good! No singing sound," complained my mother.

"What are you picking on her for?" I said carelessly. "She's pretty good. Maybe she's not the best, but she's trying hard." I knew almost immediately I would be sorry I said that.

"Just like you," she said. "Not the best. Because you not trying." She gave a little huff as she let go of the sound dial and sat down on the sofa.

The little Chinese girl sat down also to play an encore of "Anitra's Dance" by Grieg. I remember the song, because later on I had to learn how to play it.

30 Three days after watching *The Ed Sullivan Show*, my mother told me what my schedule would be for piano lessons and piano practice. She had talked to Mr. Chong, who lived on the first floor of our apartment building. Mr. Chong was a retired piano teacher and my mother had traded housecleaning services for weekly lessons and a piano for me to practice on every day, two hours a day, from four until six.

When my mother told me this, I felt as though I had been sent to hell. I whined and then kicked my foot a little when I couldn't stand it anymore.

"Why don't you like me the way I am? I'm *not* a genius! I can't play the piano. And even if I could, I wouldn't go on TV if you paid me a million dollars!" I cried.

My mother slapped me. "Who ask you be genius?" she shouted. "Only ask you be your best. For you sake. You think I want you be genius? Hnnh! What for! Who ask you!"

"So ungrateful," I heard her mutter in Chinese. "If she had as much talent as she has temper, she would be famous now."

35 Mr. Chong, whom I secretly nicknamed Old Chong, was very strange, always tapping his fingers to the silent music of an invisible orchestra. He looked ancient in my eyes. He had lost most of the hair on top of his head and he wore thick glasses and had eyes that always looked tired and sleepy. But he must have been younger than I thought, since he lived with his mother and was not yet married.

I met Old Lady Chong once and that was enough. She had this peculiar smell like a baby that had done something in its pants. And her fingers felt like a dead person's, like an old peach I once found in the back of the refrigerator; the skin just slid off the meat when I picked it up.

I soon found out why Old Chong had retired from teaching piano. He was deaf. "Like Beethoven!" he shouted to me. "We're both listening only in our head!" And he would start to conduct his frantic silent sonatas.

Our lessons went like this. He would open the book and point to different things, explaining their purpose: "Key! Treble! Bass! No sharps or flats! So this is C major! Listen now and play after me!"

And then he would play the C scale a few times, a simple chord, and then, as if inspired by an old, unreachable itch, he gradually added more notes and running trills and a pounding bass until the music was really something quite grand.

40 I would play after him, the simple scale, the simple chord, and then I just played some nonsense that sounded like a cat running up and down on top of garbage cans. Old Chong smiled and applauded and then said, "Very good! But now you must learn to keep time!"

So that's how I discovered that Old Chong's eyes were too slow to keep up with the wrong notes I was playing. He went through the motions in half-time. To help me keep rhythm, he stood behind me, pushing down on my right shoulder for every beat. He balanced pennies on top of my wrists so I would keep them still as I slowly played scales and arpeggios. He had me curve my hand around an apple and keep that shape when playing chords. He marched stiffly to show me how to make each finger dance up and down, staccato like an obedient little soldier.

He taught me all these things, and that was how I also learned I could be lazy and get away with mistakes, lots of mistakes. If I hit the wrong notes because I hadn't practiced enough, I never corrected myself. I just kept playing in rhythm. And Old Chong kept conducting his own private reverie.

So maybe I never really gave myself a fair chance. I did pick up the basics pretty quickly, and I might have become a good pianist at that young age. But I was so determined not to try, not to be anybody different that I learned to play only the most ear-splitting preludes, the most discordant hymns.

Over the next year, I practiced like this, dutifully in my own way. And then one day I heard my mother and her friend Lindo Jong both talking in a loud bragging tone of voice so others could hear. It was after church, and I was leaning against the brick wall wearing a dress with stiff white petticoats. Auntie Lindo's daughter, Waverly, who was about my age, was standing farther down the wall about five feet away. We had grown up together and shared all the closeness of two sisters squabbling over crayons and dolls. In other words, for the most part, we hated each other. I thought she was snotty. Waverly Jong had gained a certain amount of fame as "Chinatown's Littlest Chinese Chess Champion."

"She bring home too many trophy," lamented Auntie Lindo that Sunday. "All day 45
she play chess. All day I have no time do nothing but dust off her winnings." She threw a scolding look at Waverly, who pretended not to see her.

"You lucky you don't have this problem," said Auntie Lindo with a sigh to my mother.

And my mother squared her shoulders and bragged: "Our problem worser than yours. If we ask Jing-mei wash dish, she hear nothing but music. It's like you can't stop this natural talent."

And right then, I was determined to put a stop to her foolish pride.

A few weeks later, Old Chong and my mother conspired to have me play in a talent show which would be held in the church hall. By then, my parents had saved up enough to buy me a secondhand piano, a black Wurlitzer spinet with a scarred bench. It was the showpiece of our living room.

For the talent show, I was to play a piece called "Pleading Child" from 50
Schumann's *Scenes from Childhood*. It was a simple, moody piece that sounded more difficult than it was. I was supposed to memorize the whole thing, playing the repeat parts twice to make the piece sound longer. But I dawdled over it, playing a few bars and then cheating, looking up to see what notes followed. I never really listened to what I was playing. I daydreamed about being somewhere else, about being someone else.

The part I liked to practice best was the fancy curtsy: right foot out, touch the rose on the carpet with a pointed foot, sweep to the side, left leg bends, look up and smile.

My parents invited all the couples from the Joy Luck Club° to witness my debut. Auntie Lindo and Uncle Tin were there. Waverly and her two older brothers had also come. The first two rows were filled with children both younger and older than I was. The littlest ones got to go first. They recited simple nursery rhymes, squawked out tunes on miniature violins, twirled Hula Hoops, pranced in pink ballet tutus, and when they bowed or curtsied, the audience would sigh in unison, "Awww," and then clap enthusiastically.

When my turn came, I was very confident. I remember my childish excitement. It was as if I knew, without a doubt, that the prodigy side of me really did exist. I had no fear whatsoever, no nervousness. I remember thinking to myself, This is it! This is it! I looked out over the audience, at my mother's blank face, my father's yawn, Auntie Lindo's stiff-lipped smile, Waverly's sulky expression. I had on a white dress layered with sheets of lace, and a pink bow in my Peter Pan haircut. As I sat down I envisioned people jumping to their feet and Ed Sullivan rushing up to introduce me to everyone on TV.

And I started to play. It was so beautiful. I was so caught up in how lovely I looked that at first I didn't worry how I would sound. So it was a surprise to me when I hit the first wrong note and I realized something didn't sound quite right. And then I hit another and another followed that. A chill started at the top of my head and began to trickle down. Yet I couldn't stop playing, as though my hands were bewitched. I kept thinking my fingers would adjust themselves back, like a train switching to the right track. I played this strange jumble through two repeats, the sour notes staying with me all the way to the end.

55 When I stood up, I discovered my legs were shaking. Maybe I had just been nervous and the audience, like Old Chong, had seen me go through the right motions and had not heard anything wrong at all. I swept my right foot out, went down on my knee, looked up and smiled. The room was quiet, except for Old Chong, who was beaming and shouting, "Bravo! Bravo! Well done!" But then I saw my mother's face, her stricken face. The audience clapped weakly, and as I walked back to my chair, with my whole face quivering as I tried not to cry, I heard a little boy whisper loudly to his mother, "That was awful," and the mother whispered back, "Well, she certainly tried."

And now I realized how many people were in the audience, the whole world it seemed. I was aware of eyes burning into my back. I felt the shame of my mother and father as they sat stiffly throughout the rest of the show.

We could have escaped during intermission. Pride and some strange sense of honor must have anchored my parents to their chairs. And so we watched it all: the eighteen-year-old boy with a fake mustache who did a magic show and juggled flaming hoops while riding a unicycle. The breasted girl with white makeup who sang from *Madama Butterfly* and got honorable mention. And the eleven-year-old boy who won first prize playing a tricky violin song that sounded like a busy bee.

Joy Luck Club: A name denoting the mother's circle of friends, all of whom were Chinese immigrants to the United States.

After the show, the Hsus, the Jongs, and the St. Clairs from the Joy Luck Club came up to my mother and father.

"Lots of talented kids," Auntie Lindo said vaguely, smiling broadly.

"That was somethin' else," said my father, and I wondered if he was referring to 60
me in a humorous way, or whether he even remembered what I had done.

Waverly looked at me and shrugged her shoulders. "You aren't a genius like me," she said matter-of-factly. And if I hadn't felt so bad, I would have pulled her braids and punched her stomach.

But my mother's expression was what devastated me: a quiet, blank look that said she had lost everything. I felt the same way, and it seemed as if everybody were now coming up, like gawkers at the scene of an accident, to see what parts were actually missing. When we got on the bus to go home, my father was humming the busy-bee tune and my mother was silent. I kept thinking she wanted to wait until we got home before shouting at me. But when my father unlocked the door to our apartment, my mother walked in and then went to the back, into the bedroom. No accusations. No blame. And in a way, I felt disappointed. I had been waiting for her to start shouting, so I could shout back and cry and blame her for all my misery.

I assumed my talent-show fiasco meant I never had to play the piano again. But two days later, after school, my mother came out of the kitchen and saw me watching TV.

"Four clock," she reminded me as if it were any other day. I was stunned, as though she were asking me to go through the talent-show torture again. I wedged myself more tightly in front of the TV.

"Turn off TV," she called from the kitchen five minutes later. 65

I didn't budge. And then I decided. I didn't have to do what my mother said anymore. I wasn't her slave. This wasn't China. I had listened to her before and look what happened. She was the stupid one.

She came out from the kitchen and stood in the arched entryway of the living room. "Four clock," she said once again, louder.

"I'm not going to play anymore," I said nonchalantly. "Why should I? I'm not a genius."

She walked over and stood in front of the TV. I saw her chest was heaving up and down in an angry way.

"No!" I said, and I now felt stronger, as if my true self had finally emerged. So this 70
was what had been inside me all along.

"No! I won't!" I screamed.

She yanked me by the arm, pulled me off the floor, snapped off the TV. She was frighteningly strong, half pulling, half carrying me toward the piano as I kicked the throw rugs under my feet. She lifted me up and onto the hard bench. I was sobbing by now, looking at her bitterly. Her chest was heaving even more and her mouth was open, smiling crazily as if she were pleased I was crying.

"You want me to be someone that I'm not!" I sobbed. "I'll never be the kind of daughter you want me to be!"

"Only two kinds of daughters," she shouted in Chinese. "Those who are obedient and those who follow their own mind! Only one kind of daughter can live in this house. Obedient daughter!"

"Then I wish I wasn't your daughter. I wish you weren't my mother," I shouted. As I said these things I got scared. It felt like worms and toads and slimy things crawling out of my chest, but it also felt good, as if this awful side of me had surfaced, at last.

"Too late change this," said my mother shrilly.

And I could sense her anger rising to its breaking point. I wanted to see it spill over. And that's when I remembered the babies she had lost in China, the ones we never talked about. "Then I wish I'd never been born!" I shouted. "I wish I were dead! Like them."

It was as if I had said the magic words. Alakazam!—and her face went blank, her mouth closed, her arms went slack, and she backed out of the room, stunned, as if she were blowing away like a small brown leaf, thin, brittle, lifeless.

It was not the only disappointment my mother felt in me. In the years that followed, I failed her so many times, each time asserting my own will, my right to fall short of expectations. I didn't get straight As. I didn't become class president. I didn't get into Stanford. I dropped out of college.

For unlike my mother, I did not believe I could be anything I wanted to be. I could only be me.

And for all those years, we never talked about the disaster at the recital or my terrible accusations afterward at the piano bench. All that remained unchecked, like a betrayal that was now unspeakable. So I never found a way to ask her why she had hoped for something so large that failure was inevitable.

And even worse, I never asked her what frightened me the most: Why had she given up hope?

For after our struggle at the piano, she never mentioned my playing again. The lessons stopped. The lid to the piano was closed, shutting out the dust, my misery, and her dreams.

So she surprised me. A few years ago, she offered to give me the piano, for my thirtieth birthday. I had not played in all those years. I saw the offer as a sign of forgiveness, a tremendous burden removed.

"Are you sure?" I asked shyly. "I mean, won't you and Dad miss it?"

"No, this your piano," she said firmly. "Always your piano. You only one can play."

"Well, I probably can't play anymore," I said. "It's been years."

"You pick up fast," said my mother, as if she knew this was certain. "You have natural talent. You could been genius if you want to."

"No I couldn't."

"You just not trying," said my mother. And she was neither angry nor sad. She said it as if to announce a fact that could never be disproved. "Take it," she said.

But I didn't at first. It was enough that she had offered it to me. And after that, every time I saw it in my parents' living room, standing in front of the bay windows, it made me feel proud, as if it were a shiny trophy I had won back.

Last week I sent a tuner over to my parents' apartment and had the piano reconditioned, for purely sentimental reasons. My mother had died a few months before and I had been getting things in order for my father, a little bit at a time. I put the jewelry in special silk pouches. The sweaters she had knitted in yellow, pink, bright orange — all the colors I hated — I put those in moth-proof boxes. I found some old Chinese silk dresses, the kind with little slits up the sides. I rubbed the old silk against my skin, then wrapped them in tissue and decided to take them home with me.

After I had the piano tuned, I opened the lid and touched the keys. It sounded even richer than I remembered. Really, it was a very good piano. Inside the bench were the same exercise notes with handwritten scales, the same secondhand music books with their covers held together with yellow tape.

I opened up the Schumann book to the dark little piece I had played at the recital. It was on the left-hand side of the page, "Pleading Child." It looked more difficult than I remembered. I played a few bars, surprised at how easily the notes came back to me.

And for the first time, or so it seemed, I noticed the piece on the right-hand side. 95
It was called "Perfectly Contented." I tried to play this one as well. It had a lighter melody but the same flowing rhythm and turned out to be quite easy. "Pleading Child" was shorter but slower; "Perfectly Contented" was longer, but faster. And after I played them both a few times, I realized they were two halves of the same song.

* * *

ANNE TYLER (1941–)

Teenage Wasteland (1984)

He used to have very blond hair — almost white — cut shorter than other children's so that on his crown a little cowlick always stood up to catch the light. But this was when he was small. As he grew older, his hair grew darker, and he wore it longer — past his collar even. It hung in lank, taffy-colored ropes around his face, which was still an endearing face, fine-featured, the eyes an unusual aqua blue. But his cheeks, of course, were no longer round, and a sharp new Adam's apple jogged in his throat when he talked.

In October, they called from the private school he attended to request a conference with his parents. Daisy went alone; her husband was at work. Clutching her purse, she sat on the principal's couch and learned that Donny was noisy, lazy, and disruptive; always fooling around with his friends, and he wouldn't respond in class.

In the past, before her children were born, Daisy had been a fourth-grade teacher. It shamed her now to sit before this principal as a parent, a delinquent parent, a parent who struck Mr. Lanham, no doubt, as unseeing or uncaring. "It isn't that we're not concerned," she said. "Both of us are. And we've done what we could, whatever we could think of. We don't let him watch TV on school nights. We don't let him talk on the phone till he's finished his homework. But he tells us he doesn't *have* any homework or he did it all in study hall. How are we to know what to believe?"

From early October through November, at Mr. Lanham's suggestion, Daisy checked Donny's assignments every day. She sat next to him as he worked, trying to be encouraging, sagging inwardly as she saw the poor quality of everything he did—the sloppy mistakes in math, the illogical leaps in his English themes, the history questions left blank if they required any research.

5 Daisy was often late starting supper, and she couldn't give as much attention to Donny's younger sister. "You'll never guess what happened at . . ." Amanda would begin, and Daisy would have to tell her, "Not now, honey."

By the time her husband, Matt, came home, she'd be snappish. She would recite the day's hardships—the fuzzy instructions in English, the botched history map, the morass of unsolvable algebra equations. Matt would look surprised and confused, and Daisy would gradually wind down. There was no way, really, to convey how exhausting all this was.

In December, the school called again. This time, they wanted Matt to come as well. She and Matt had to sit on Mr. Lanham's couch like two bad children and listen to the news: Donny had improved only slightly, raising a D in history to a C, and a C in algebra to a B-minus. What was worse, he had developed new problems. He had cut classes on at least three occasions. Smoked in the furnace room. Helped Sonny Barnett break into a freshman's locker. And last week, during athletics, he and three friends had been seen off the school grounds; when they returned, the coach had smelled beer on their breath.

Daisy and Matt sat silent, shocked. Matt rubbed his forehead with his fingertips. Imagine, Daisy thought, how they must look to Mr. Lanham: an overweight housewife in a cotton dress and a too-tall, too-thin insurance agent in a baggy, frayed suit. Failures, both of them—the kind of people who are always hurrying to catch up, missing the point of things that everyone else grasps at once. She wished she'd worn nylons instead of knee socks.

It was arranged that Donny would visit a psychologist for testing. Mr. Lanham knew just the person. He would set this boy straight, he said.

10 When they stood to leave, Daisy held her stomach in and gave Mr. Lanham a firm, responsible handshake.

Donny said the psychologist was a jackass and the tests were really dumb; but he kept all three of his appointments, and when it was time for the follow-up conference with the psychologist and both parents, Donny combed his hair and seemed unusually sober and subdued. The psychologist said Donny had no serious emotional problems. He was merely going through a difficult period in his life. He required some academic help and a better sense of self-worth. For this reason, he was suggesting a man named Calvin Beadle, a tutor with considerable psychological training.

In the car going home, Donny said he'd be damned if he'd let them drag him to some stupid fairy tutor. His father told him to watch his language in front of his mother.

That night, Daisy lay awake pondering the term "self-worth." She had always been free with her praise. She had always told Donny he had talent, was smart, was good with his hands. She had made a big to-do over every little gift he gave her. In fact, maybe she had gone too far, although, Lord knows, she had meant every word. Was that his trouble?

She remembered when Amanda was born. Donny had acted lost and bewildered. Daisy had been alert to that, of course, but still, a new baby keeps you so busy. Had she really done all she could have? She longed—she ached—for a time machine. Given one more chance, she'd do it perfectly—hug him more, praise him more, or perhaps praise him less. Oh, who can say . . .

The tutor told Donny to call him Cal. All his kids did, he said. Daisy thought for a second that he meant his own children, then realized her mistake. He seemed too young, anyhow, to be a family man. He wore a heavy brown handlebar mustache. His hair was as long and stringy as Donny's, and his jeans as faded. Wire-rimmed spectacles slid down his nose. He lounged in a canvas director's chair with his fingers laced across his chest, and he casually, amiably questioned Donny, who sat upright and glaring in an armchair.

"So they're getting on your back at school," said Cal. "Making a big deal about anything you do wrong."

"Right," said Donny.

"Any idea why that would be?"

"Oh, well, you know, stuff like homework and all," Donny said.

"You don't do your homework?"

"Oh, well, I might do it sometimes but not just exactly like they want it." Donny sat forward and said, "It's like a prison there, you know? You've got to go to every class, you can never step off the school grounds."

"You cut classes sometimes?"

"Sometimes," Donny said, with a glance at his parents.

Cal didn't seem perturbed. "Well," he said, "I'll tell you what. Let's you and me try working together three nights a week. Think you can handle that? We'll see if we can show that school of yours a thing or two. Give it a month; then if you don't like it, we'll stop. If *I* don't like it, we'll stop. I mean, sometimes people just don't get along, right? What do you say to that?"

"Okay," Donny said. He seemed pleased.

"Make it seven o'clock till eight, Monday, Wednesday, and Friday," Cal told Matt and Daisy. They nodded. Cal shambled to his feet, gave them a little salute, and showed them to the door.

This was where he lived as well as worked, evidently. The interview had taken place in the dining room, which had been transformed into a kind of office. Passing the living room, Daisy winced at the rock music she had been hearing, without registering it, ever since she had entered the house. She looked in and saw a boy about Donny's age lying on a sofa with a book. Another boy and a girl were playing Ping-Pong in front of the fireplace. "You have several here together?" Daisy asked Cal.

"Oh, sometimes they stay on after their sessions, just to rap. They're a pretty sociable group, all in all. Plenty of goof-offs like young Donny here."

He cuffed Donny's shoulder playfully. Donny flushed and grinned.

Climbing into the car, Daisy asked Donny, "Well? What do you think?"

But Donny had returned to his old evasive self. He jerked his chin toward the garage. "Look," he said. "He's got a basketball net."

Now on Mondays, Wednesdays, and Fridays, they had supper early—the instant Matt came home. Sometimes, they had to leave before they were really finished. Amanda would still be eating her dessert. "Bye, honey. Sorry," Daisy would tell her.

Cal's first bill sent a flutter of panic through Daisy's chest, but it was worth it, of course. Just look at Donny's face when they picked him up: alight and full of interest. The principal telephoned Daisy to tell her how Donny had improved. "Of course, it hasn't shown up in his grades yet, but several of the teachers have noticed how his attitude's changed. Yes, sir, I think we're onto something here."

At home, Donny didn't act much different. He still seemed to have a low opinion of his parents. But Daisy supposed that was unavoidable—part of being fifteen. He said his parents were too "controlling"—a word that made Daisy give him a sudden look. He said they acted like wardens. On weekends, they enforced a curfew. And any time he went to a party, they always telephoned first to see if adults would be supervising. "For God's sake!" he said. "Don't you trust me?"

"It isn't a matter of trust, honey . . ." But there was no explaining to him.

His tutor called one afternoon. "I get the sense," he said, "that this kid's feeling . . . underestimated, you know? Like you folks expect the worst of him. I'm thinking we ought to give him more rope."

"But see, he's still so suggestible," Daisy said. "When his friends suggest some mischief—smoking or drinking or such—why, he just finds it hard not to go along with them."

"Mrs. Coble," the tutor said, "I think this kid is hurting. You know? Here's a serious, sensitive kid, telling you he'd like to take on some grown-up challenges, and you're giving him the message that he can't be trusted. Don't you understand how that hurts?"

"Oh," said Daisy.

"It undermines his self-esteem—don't you realize that?"

"Well, I guess you're right," said Daisy. She saw Donny suddenly from a whole new angle: his pathetically poor posture, that slouch so forlorn that his shoulders seemed about to meet his chin . . . oh, wasn't it awful being young? She'd had a miserable adolescence herself and had always sworn no child of hers would ever be that unhappy.

They let Donny stay out later, they didn't call ahead to see if the parties were supervised, and they were careful not to grill him about his evening. The tutor had set down so many rules! They were not allowed any questions at all about any aspect of school, nor were they to speak with his teachers. If a teacher had some complaint, she should phone Cal. Only one teacher disobeyed—the history teacher, Miss Evans. She called one morning in February. "I'm a little concerned about Donny, Mrs. Coble."

"Oh, I'm sorry, Miss Evans, but Donny's tutor handles these things now . . ."

"I always deal directly with the parents. You are the parent," Miss Evans said, speaking very slowly and distinctly. "Now, here is the problem. Back when you were helping Donny with his homework, his grades rose from a D to a C, but now they've slipped back, and they're closer to an F."

"They are?"

"I think you should start overseeing his homework again."

"But Donny's tutor says . . ."

"It's nice that Donny has a tutor, but you should still be in charge of his homework. With you, he learned it. Then he passed his tests. With the tutor, well, it seems the tutor is more of a crutch. 'Donny,' I say, 'a quiz is coming up on Friday. Hadn't you better be listening instead of talking?' 'That's okay, Miss Evans,' he says. 'I have a tutor now.' Like a talisman! I really think you ought to take over, Mrs. Coble."

"I see," said Daisy. "Well, I'll think about that. Thank you for calling."

Hanging up, she felt a rush of anger at Donny. A talisman! For a talisman, she'd given up all luxuries, all that time with her daughter, her evenings at home!

She dialed Cal's number. He sounded muzzy. "I'm sorry if I woke you," she told him, "but Donny's history teacher just called. She says he isn't doing well."

"She should have dealt with me."

"She wants me to start supervising his homework again. His grades are slipping."

"Yes," said the tutor, "but you and I both know there's more to it than mere grades, don't we? I care about the *whole* child—his happiness, his self-esteem. The grades will come. Just give them time."

When she hung up, it was Miss Evans she was angry at. What a narrow woman!

It was Cal this, Cal that, Cal says this, Cal and I did that. Cal lent Donny an album by The Who. He took Donny and two other pupils to a rock concert. In March, when Donny began to talk endlessly on the phone with a girl named Miriam, Cal even let Miriam come to one of the tutoring sessions. Daisy was touched that Cal would grow so involved in Donny's life, but she was also a little hurt, because she had offered to have Miriam to dinner and Donny had refused. Now he asked them to drive her to Cal's house without a qualm.

This Miriam was an unappealing girl with blurry lipstick and masses of rough red hair. She wore a short, bulky jacket that would not have been out of place on a motorcycle. During the trip to Cal's she was silent, but coming back, she was more talkative. "What a neat guy, and what a house! All those kids hanging out, like a club. And the stereo playing rock . . . gosh, he's not like a grown-up at all! Married and divorced and everything, but you'd think he was our own age."

"Mr. Beadle was married?" Daisy asked.

"Yeah, to this really controlling lady. She didn't understand him a bit."

"No, I guess not," Daisy said.

Spring came, and the students who hung around at Cal's drifted out to the basketball net above the garage. Sometimes, when Daisy and Matt arrived to pick up Donny, they'd find him there with the others—spiky and excited, jittering on his toes beneath the backboard. It was staying light much longer now, and the neighboring fence cast narrow bars across the bright grass. Loud music would be spilling from Cal's windows. Once it was The Who, which Daisy recognized from the time that Donny had borrowed the album. *"Teenage Wasteland,"*° she said aloud, identifying the song, and Matt gave a short, dry laugh. "It certainly is," he said. He'd misunderstood; he thought she was commenting on the scene spread before them. In fact, she might have

Teenage Wasteland: The song is actually "Baba O'Riley," from the band's *Who's Next* album.

been. The players looked like hoodlums, even her son. Why, one of Cal's students had recently been knifed in a tavern. One had been shipped off to boarding school in midterm; two had been withdrawn by their parents. On the other hand, Donny had mentioned someone who'd been studying with Cal for five years. "Five years!" said Daisy. "Doesn't anyone ever stop needing him?"

Donny looked at her. Lately, whatever she said about Cal was read as criticism. "You're just feeling competitive," he said. "And controlling."

She bit her lip and said no more.

In April, the principal called to tell her that Donny had been expelled. There had been a locker check, and in Donny's locker they found five cans of beer and half a pack of cigarettes. With Donny's previous record, his offense meant expulsion.

65 Daisy gripped the receiver tightly and said, "Well, where is he now?"

"We've sent him home," said Mr. Lanham. "He's packed up all his belongings, and he's coming home on foot."

Daisy wondered what she would say to him. She felt him looming closer and closer, bringing this brand-new situation that no one had prepared her to handle. What other place would take him? Could they enter him in public school? What were the rules? She stood at the living room window, waiting for him to show up. Gradually, she realized that he was taking too long. She checked the clock. She stared up the street again.

When an hour had passed, she phoned the school. Mr. Lanham's secretary answered and told her in a grave, sympathetic voice that yes, Donny Coble had most definitely gone home. Daisy called her husband. He was out of the office. She went back to the window and thought awhile, and then she called Donny's tutor.

"Donny's been expelled from school," she said, "and now I don't know where he's gone. I wonder if you've heard from him?"

70 There was a long silence. "Donny's with me, Mrs. Coble," he finally said.

"With you? How'd he get there?"

"He hailed a cab, and I paid the driver."

"Could I speak to him, please?"

There was another silence. "Maybe it'd be better if we had a conference," Cal said.

75 "I don't *want* a conference. I've been standing at the window picturing him dead or kidnapped or something, and now you tell me you want a—"

"Donny is very, very upset. Understandably so," said Cal. "Believe me, Mrs. Coble, this is not what it seems. Have you asked Donny's side of the story?"

"Well, of course not, how could I? He went running off to you instead."

"Because he didn't feel he'd be listened to."

"But I haven't even—"

80 "Why don't you come out and talk? The three of us," said Cal, "will try to get this thing in perspective."

"Well, all right," Daisy said. But she wasn't as reluctant as she sounded. Already, she felt soothed by the calm way Cal was taking this.

Cal answered the doorbell at once. He said, "Hi, there," and led her into the dining room. Donny sat slumped in a chair, chewing the knuckle of one thumb. "Hello, Donny," Daisy said. He flicked his eyes in her direction.

"Sit here, Mrs. Coble," said Cal, placing her opposite Donny. He himself remained standing, restlessly pacing. "So," he said.

Daisy stole a look at Donny. His lips were swollen, as if he'd been crying.

"You know," Cal told Daisy, "I kind of expected something like this. That's a very punitive school you've got him in—you realize that. And any half-decent lawyer will tell you they've violated his civil rights. Locker checks! Where's their search warrant?"

"But if the rule is—" Daisy said.

"Well, anyhow, let him tell you his side."

She looked at Donny. He said, "It wasn't my fault. I promise."

"They said your locker was full of beer."

"It was a put-up job! See, there's this guy that doesn't like me. He put all these beers in my locker and started a rumor going, so Mr. Lanham ordered a locker check."

"What was the boy's name?" Daisy asked.

"Huh?"

"Mrs. Coble, take my word, the situation is not so unusual," Cal said. "You can't imagine how vindictive kids can be sometimes."

"What was the boy's *name*," said Daisy, "so that I can ask Mr. Lanham if that's who suggested he run a locker check."

"You don't believe me," Donny said.

"And how'd this boy get your combination in the first place?"

"Frankly," said Cal, "I wouldn't be surprised to learn the school was in on it. Any kid that marches to a different drummer, why, they'd just love an excuse to get rid of him. The school is where I lay the blame."

"Doesn't *Donny* ever get blamed?"

"Now, Mrs. Coble, you heard what he—"

"Forget it," Donny told Cal. "You can see she doesn't trust me."

Daisy drew in a breath to say that of course she trusted him—a reflex. But she knew that bold-faced, wide-eyed look of Donny's. He had worn that look when he was small, denying some petty misdeed with the evidence plain as day all around him. Still, it was hard for her to accuse him outright. She temporized and said, "The only thing I'm sure of is that they've kicked you out of school, and now I don't know what we're going to do."

"We'll fight it," said Cal.

"We can't. Even you must see we can't."

"I could apply to Brantly," Donny said.

Cal stopped his pacing to beam down at him. "Brantly! Yes. They're really onto where a kid is coming from, at Brantly. Why, *I* could get you into Brantly. I work with a lot of their students."

Daisy had never heard of Brantly, but already she didn't like it. And she didn't like Cal's smile, which struck her now as feverish and avid—a smile of hunger.

On the fifteenth of April, they entered Donny in a public school, and they stopped his tutoring sessions. Donny fought both decisions bitterly. Cal, surprisingly enough, did not object. He admitted he'd made no headway with Donny and said it was because Donny was emotionally disturbed.

Donny went to his new school every morning, plodding off alone with his head down. He did his assignments, and he earned average grades, but he gathered no friends, joined no clubs. There was something exhausted and defeated about him.

The first week in June, during final exams, Donny vanished. He simply didn't come home one afternoon, and no one at school remembered seeing him. The police were reassuring, and for the first few days, they worked hard. They combed Donny's sad, messy room for clues; they visited Miriam and Cal. But then they started talking about the number of kids who ran away every year. Hundreds, just in this city. "He'll show up, if he wants to," they said. "If he doesn't, he won't."

Evidently, Donny didn't want to.

It's been three months now and still no word. Matt and Daisy still look for him in every crowd of awkward, heartbreaking teenage boys. Every time the phone rings, they imagine it might be Donny. Both parents have aged. Donny's sister seems to be staying away from home as much as possible.

At night, Daisy lies awake and goes over Donny's life. She is trying to figure out what went wrong, where they made their first mistake. Often, she finds herself blaming Cal, although she knows he didn't begin it. Then at other times she excuses him, for without him, Donny might have left earlier. Who really knows? In the end, she can only sigh and search for a cooler spot on the pillow. As she falls asleep, she occasionally glimpses something in the corner of her vision. It's something fleet and round, a ball—a basketball. It flies up, it sinks through the hoop, descends, lands in a yard littered with last year's leaves and striped with bars of sunlight as white as bones, bleached and parched and cleanly picked.

* * *

3| POETRY

CHAPTER 21

UNDERSTANDING POETRY

Source: ©The Granger Collection, New York

MARIANNE MOORE (1887–1972)

Poetry (1921)

I, too, dislike it: there are things that are important beyond all
this fiddle.
Reading it, however, with a perfect contempt for it, one
discovers
in it after all, a place for the genuine.
Hands that can grasp, eyes
that can dilate, hair that can rise
if it must, these things are important not because a

high-sounding interpretation can be put upon them but because they are
useful. When they become so derivative as to become unintelligible,
the same thing may be said for all of us, that we
do not admire what
we cannot understand: the bat
holding on upside down or in quest of something to

eat, elephants pushing, a wild horse taking a roll, a tireless wolf under
a tree, the immovable critic twitching his skin like a horse that
feels a flea, the base-
ball fan, the statistician—
nor is it valid
to discriminate against "business documents and

school-books";° all these phenomena are important. One must make
a distinction
however: when dragged into prominence by half poets, the result
is not poetry,
nor till the poets among us can be
"literalists of

"business documents and school-books": Moore quotes the *Diaries of Tolstoy* (New York, 1917): "Where the boundary between prose and poetry lies, I shall never be able to understand. . . . Poetry is verse; prose is not verse. Or else poetry is everything with the exception of business documents and school books."

the imagination"°— above
insolence and triviality and can present
for inspection, "imaginary gardens with real toads in them,"°
shall we have
it. In the meantime, if you demand on the one hand,
the raw material of poetry in
all its rawness and
that which is on the other hand
genuine, you are interested in poetry.

Source: ©Marion Ettlinger

See this poet's biography on p. 1221.

NIKKI GIOVANNI (1943–)

Poetry (1975)

poetry is motion graceful
as a fawn
gentle as a teardrop
strong like the eye
finding peace in a crowded room
we poets tend to think
our words are golden
though emotion speaks too
loudly to be defined
by silence

sometimes after midnight or just before
the dawn
we sit typewriter in hand
pulling loneliness around us
forgetting our lovers or children
who are sleeping
ignoring the weary wariness
of our own logic
to compose a poem
no one understands it
it never says "love me" for poets are
beyond love

"literalists of the imagination": A reference (given by Moore) to W. B. Yeats's "William Blake and His Illustrations" (in *Ideas of Good and Evil*, 1903): "The limitation of his view was from the very intensity of his vision; he was a too literal realist of the imagination as others are of nature; and because he believed that the figures seen by the mind's eye, when exalted by inspiration, were 'external existences,' symbols of divine essences, he hated every grace of style that might obscure their lineaments."

"imaginary gardens with real toads in them": Moore places these words in quotations, but the source is unknown.

it never says "accept me" for poems seek not
acceptance but controversy
it only says "i am" and therefore
i concede that you are too

a poem is pure energy
horizontally contained
between the mind
of the poet and the ear of the reader
if it does not sing discard the ear
for poetry is song
if it does not delight discard
the heart for poetry is joy
if it does not inform then close
off the brain for it is dead
if it cannot heed the insistent message
that life is precious

which is all we poets
wrapped in our loneliness
are trying to say

 Origins of Modern Poetry

The history of poetry begins where the history of all literature begins—with the **oral tradition.** In a time before literacy and the printing press, the oral tradition was relied on as a way of preserving stories, histories, values, and beliefs. These stories were usually put into the form of rhyming poems, with repeated words and sounds used to make the poems easier to memorize and remember.

These extended narratives were eventually transcribed as **epics**—long poems depicting the actions of heroic figures who determine the fate of a nation or of an entire race. Early epics include Homer's *Iliad* and *Odyssey*, the *Epic of Gilgamesh*, the *Bhagavad Gita*, and Virgil's *Aeneid*. Early poetry can also be found in various religious texts, including ancient Hindu holy books like the Upanishads; sections of the Bible, including the Song of Solomon; and the Koran.

During the **Anglo-Saxon era** (late sixth to mid-eleventh centuries), poetry flourished as a literary form. Unfortunately, only about 30,000 lines of poetry survive from this period. Those poems that did survive are marked by heroic deeds and the absence of romantic love. The major texts of this time include *Beowulf*, *The Battle of Maldon*, and *The Dream of the Rood*, which is one of the earliest Christian poems. The theme of Christian morality in poetry continued into the Middle Ages with poems such as William Langland's *Piers Plowman*, which consists of three religious dream visions, and Chaucer's *Canterbury Tales*, a collection of narrative poems told by pilgrims as they travel to Canterbury, England. Using a slightly different approach to similar subject matter, Dante Alighieri wrote the Italian epic poem *The Divine Comedy*, which depicts an imaginary journey

Image depicting the pilgrims from Geoffrey Chaucer's *The Canterbury Tales.*

Source: ©British Library, London, UK/Bridgeman Art Library

Illuminated manuscript (fifteenth century) from Dante's *Divine Comedy* depicting Dante and Virgil in Hell.

Source: ©Archivo Iconografico, S.A./CORBIS

through hell, purgatory, and heaven. In France, the **troubadours,** poets of the Provençal region, wrote complex lyric poems about courtly love.

The next major literary period, the **Renaissance** (late fourteenth to mid-sixteenth centuries), witnessed the rebirth of science, philosophy, and the classical arts. Perhaps the most important writer of this period was William Shakespeare. A prolific poet, Shakespeare also wrote plays in verse, continuing in the tradition of the ancient Greek tragedian Sophocles and the ancient Roman playwright Seneca. Other notable writers of the Renaissance included Sir Philip Sidney, Christopher Marlowe, and Edmund Spenser.

During the seventeenth century, several literary movements emerged that contributed to poetry's growing prevalence and influence. John Milton continued the tradition of Christian poetry with his epic *Paradise Lost*, which told the tale of Adam and Eve's exile from the Garden of Eden. The **metaphysical poets** (John Donne, Andrew Marvell, and George Herbert) used elaborate figures of speech and favored intellect over emotions in their writing. Their poems were characterized by reason, complex comparisons and allusions, and paradoxes, and they introduced the **meditative poem** (a poem that abstractly ponders a concept or idea) into the literary world.

In the early eighteenth century, British poets (such as Alexander Pope and Samuel Johnson) wrote poems, biographies, and literary criticism. Toward the end of the eighteenth century, the movement known as **Romanticism** began. Romantic poetry was marked by heightened emotion and sentiment; a strong sense of individualism; a respect for nature, history, and mysticism; and a return to first-person lyric poems. The early British Romantics included Samuel Taylor Coleridge, William

Illuminated manuscript from William Blake's "The Tyger."

Source: ©Fitzwilliam Museum, University of Cambridge, UK / Bridgeman Art Library

John Martin's painting *The Bard* (1817) illustrating the mystical view of nature characteristic of Romanticism.

Source: ©Yale Center for British Art, Paul Mellon Collection, USA / Bridgeman Art Library

Wordsworth, and William Blake. This generation was followed by the later Romantics, including Percy Bysshe Shelley, John Keats, and George Gordon, Lord Byron. American Romantics included Henry David Thoreau, Ralph Waldo Emerson, and Walt Whitman.

The nineteenth century was marked by yet another shift in poetic consciousness. This time, poets moved away from the contemplation of the self within nature that characterized Romanticism and returned to a more elevated sense of rhetoric and subject matter. Notable British poets included Matthew Arnold, Robert Browning, Elizabeth Barrett Browning, and Alfred, Lord Tennyson. American poets of the this period included Edgar Allan Poe, Henry Wadsworth Longfellow, Emily Dickinson, and Phillis Wheatley, a slave who became the first African-American poet.

Undated engraving of Edgar Allan Poe's "The Raven."

Source: ©Bettmann / CORBIS

The twentieth century had perhaps the largest number of literary movements to date, with each one reflecting its predecessors and influencing future generations of poets. In the early twentieth century, a literary movement that became known as **modernism** developed. As writers responded to the increasing complexity of a changing world, the overarching sentiment of modernism was that the "old ways" would no longer suffice in a world that had changed almost overnight as a result of the rise of industrialization and urbanization, as well as the devastation of World War I. Key modernist poets included W. H. Auden, William Butler Yeats, Ezra Pound, and T. S. Eliot, whose epic poem *The Waste Land* expressed the fragmentation of consciousness in the modern world.

After World War I, poets began to challenge the prevailing ideas of subject matter and form. Ezra Pound, along with Amy Lowell and other poets, founded **imagism,** a poetic movement that emphasized free verse and the writer's response to a visual scene or an object. William Carlos Williams wrote poems that were often deceptively simple, while the poetry of Wallace Stevens was often opaque and difficult to grasp. Dylan Thomas and E. E. Cummings also experimented with form, with Cummings intentionally manipulating the accepted constructs of grammar, syntax, and punctuation.

In the 1920s, the United States experienced the **Harlem Renaissance.** This rebirth of arts and culture was centered in Harlem, an area in New York City where, by the mid-1920s, the African-American population had reached 150,000. Harlem was teeming with creativity, especially in music (jazz and blues), literature, art, and drama. The poets who were part of the Harlem Renaissance—including Langston Hughes, Countee Cullen, James Weldon Johnson, and Jean Toomer—chose diverse subject matter and styles, but they were united in their celebration of African-American culture.

In the early 1930s, a group of poets gathered at a college in Black Mountain, North Carolina, with the aim of teaching and writing about poetry in a new way. The **Black Mountain Poets,** as they were called, stressed the process of writing poetry rather than the finished poem. Notable poets in this group included Robert Creeley, Denise Levertov, and Charles Olson. Meanwhile, in Latin America, poetry was growing in importance, with poets such as Pablo Neruda experimenting with subject matter, language, form, and imagery.

In the late 1940s, in the aftermath of World War II, a group of disillusioned American poets turned to eastern mysticism and newly available hallucinogenic drugs to achieve higher consciousness. They became known as the **Beat poets,** and their work was known for social and political criticism that challenged the established norms of the time. These poets included Allen Ginsberg, whose long poem *Howl* became an unofficial anthem of the revolutionary 1960s, and Lawrence Ferlinghetti.

Up until the late 1950s, subject matter in American poetry was largely impersonal, concentrating chiefly on symbols, ideas, and politics. This changed when a group of poets—including Robert Lowell, Anne Sexton, W. D. Snodgrass, and Sylvia Plath—began to write **confessional poems** about their own personal experiences, emotions, triumphs, and tragedies (including mental illness and attempted suicide). Although there was considerable backlash against these poets from writers who thought that such highly personal subjects were not suitable for poetry, contemporary poets such as Sharon Olds continue to write confessional poetry.

The early 1960s witnessed the rise of the **Black Arts Movement,** which had its roots in the ideas of the civil rights struggle, Malcolm X and the Nation of Islam, and the Black Power Movement. The Black Arts poets wrote political works that addressed the sociopolitical and cultural context of African-American life.

Notable authors in this group included Amiri Baraka, Gwendolyn Brooks, Jayne Cortez, and Etheridge Knight.

The next major literary movement in poetry had its beginnings in the mid to late 1980s with slam poetry. **Slam poetry,** with origins in the oral tradition, was influenced by the Beat poets, who stressed the live performance of poems. In a **slam,** poets compete either individually or in teams before an audience, which serves as the judge. (The structure of a traditional poetry slam was created by Marc Smith, a poet and construction worker, in 1986.) Slam poetry is concerned with current events and social and political themes, and often the winning poet is the one who best combines enthusiasm, presentation, and attitude with contemporary subject matter. A home base for slam poetry is the Nyuorican Poets Café in New York City, which has become a forum for poetry, music, video, and theater. Notable slam poets past and present include Miguel Piñero, Maggie Estep, Jeffrey McDaniel, and Bob Holman, whose poetry appears below.

BOB HOLMAN (1948–)

6 Short Poems

Modern Lovers

In order to save the relationship
We will never see each other again

Night Fears

Everyone is in love
Except you

Ten Things I Do Every Day

Suicide

My Shirt

I like to put it on
My arms get long that way

Love Poems

I love poems

Goo Ahead

Goo ahead

A spinoff of slam poetry is the **spoken word** movement, which, unlike slam poetry, is a rehearsed performance. Spoken word performances have captivated a broad audience due in part to television shows such as HBO's *Def Poetry Jam*. **Hip-hop** and **rap,** musical forms whose lyrics rely heavily on rhyme, alliteration,

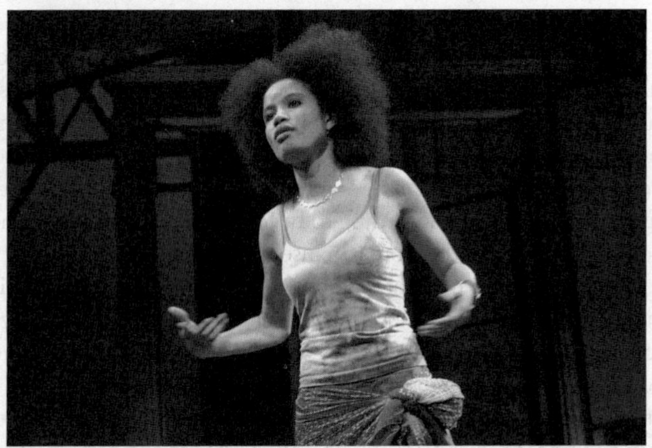

Staceyann Chin, acclaimed slam poet and the star of *Def Poetry Jam on Broadway.*

Source: ©AP Photo/In the Life TV, Pat Johnson

assonance, consonance, and other poetic devices, also owe a debt to slam poetry and the spoken word movement.

Contemporary poetry is an extremely diverse genre whose practitioners have been influenced by many of the literary movements discussed above. Some contemporary poets embrace narrative poetry; others favor the lyric. Some write free verse; others experiment with traditional forms like the **sonnet** or the **villanelle.** Still others write **concrete poetry,** which uses words as well as varying type sizes and type fonts to form pictures on a page, or other forms of **visual poetry.** The types of poetry being written today vary greatly, and this diversity is part of the appeal for those who read and write it.

Defining Poetry

Throughout history and across national and cultural boundaries, poetry has occupied an important place. In ancient China and Japan, for example, poetry was prized above all else. One story tells of a samurai warrior who, when defeated, asked for a pen and paper. Thinking that he wanted to write a will before being executed, his captor granted his wish. Instead of writing a will, however, the warrior wrote a farewell poem that so moved his captor that he immediately released him.

To the ancient Greeks and Romans, poetry was the medium of spiritual and philosophical expression. Today, throughout the world, poetry continues to delight and to inspire. For many people in countless places, poetry is the language of the emotions, the medium of expression they use when they speak from the heart.

But what exactly *is* poetry? Is a poem "pure energy / horizontally contained / between the mind / of the poet and the readers," as Nikki Giovanni (page 795) describes it? Or is a poem simply what Marianne Moore (page 794) calls "all this fiddle"?

One way of defining poetry is to examine how it is different from other forms of literature, such as fiction or drama. The first and most important element of poetry that distinguishes it from other genres is its **form.** Unlike prose, which is written from margin to margin, poetry is made up of individual **lines**. A poetic line begins and ends where the poet chooses: it can start at the left margin or halfway across the page, and it can end at the right margin or after only a word or two. A poet chooses when to stop, or break, the line according to his or her sense of rhythm and meter.

Poets also use the **sound** of the words themselves, alone and in conjunction with the other words of the poem, to create a sense of rhythm and melody. **Alliteration** (the repetition of initial consonant sounds in consecutive or neighboring words), **assonance** (the repetition of vowel sounds), and **consonance** (the repetition of consonant sounds within words) are three devices commonly used by poets to help create the music of a poem. Poets can also use **rhyme** (either at the ends of lines or within the lines themselves), which contributes to the pattern of sounds in a poem.

In addition, poets are more likely than writers of other kinds of literature to rely on **imagery,** words or phrases that describe the senses. These vivid descriptions or details help the reader to connect with the poet's ideas in a tangible way. Poets also make extensive use of **figurative language,** including metaphors and similes, to convey their ideas and to help their readers access these ideas.

Another way of defining poetry is to examine our assumptions about it. Different readers, different poets, different generations of readers and poets, and different cultures often have different expectations about poetry. As a result, they have varying assumptions about what poetry should be, and these assumptions raise questions. Must poetry be written to delight or inspire, or can a poem have a political or social message? Must a poem's theme be conveyed subtly, embellished with imaginatively chosen sounds and words, or can it be explicit and straightforward? Such questions, which have been debated by literary critics as well as by poets for many years, have no easy answers—and perhaps no answers at all. A **haiku**—a short poem, rich in imagery, adhering to a rigid formal structure—is certainly poetry, and so is a political poem like Wole Soyinka's "Telephone Conversation" (p. 7). To some Western readers, however, a haiku might seem too plain or understated to be "poetic," and Soyinka's poem might seem to be a political tract masquerading as poetry. Still, most of these readers would agree that the following lines qualify as poetry.

WILLIAM SHAKESPEARE (1564–1616)

That time of year thou mayst in me behold (1609)

That time of year thou mayst in me behold
When yellow leaves, or none, or few, do hang
Upon those boughs which shake against the cold,
Bare ruined choirs, where late the sweet birds sang.
In me thou see'st the twilight of such day

As after sunset fadeth in the west,
Which by and by black night doth take away,
Death's second self that seals up all in rest.
In me thou see'st the glowing of such fire,
That on the ashes of his youth doth lie,
As the deathbed whereon it must expire,
Consumed with that which it was nourished by.
This thou perceiv'st, which makes thy love more strong,
To love that well which thou must leave ere long.

This poem includes many of the characteristics that Western readers commonly associate with poetry. For instance, its lines have a regular pattern of rhyme and meter that identifies it as a **sonnet.** The poem also develops a complex network of related images and figures of speech that compare the lost youth of the aging speaker to the sunset and to autumn. Finally, the pair of rhyming lines at the end of the poem expresses a familiar poetic theme: the lovers' realization that they must eventually die makes their love stronger.

Although most readers would classify Shakespeare's sonnet as a poem, they might be less certain about the following lines.

E. E. CUMMINGS (1894–1962)

l(a (1923)

l(a
le
af
fa
ll
s)
one
l
iness

Unlike Shakespeare's poem, "l(a" does not seem to have any of the characteristics normally associated with poetry. It has no meter, rhyme, or imagery. It has no repeated sounds and no figures of speech. It cannot even be read aloud because its "lines" are fragments of words. In spite of its odd appearance, however, "l(a" does communicate a conventional poetic theme.

When reconstructed, the words Cummings broke apart have the following appearance: "l (a leaf falls) one l iness." In a sense, this poem is a complex visual and verbal pun. If the parenthetical insertion "(a leaf falls)" is removed, the remaining letters spell "loneliness." Moreover, the form of the letter *l* in loneliness suggests the number *1*—which, in turn, suggests the loneliness and isolation of the individual, as reflected in nature (the single leaf). Like Shakespeare, Cummings uses an image of a leaf to express his ideas about life and human experience. At the same time, by breaking words into bits and pieces, Cummings suggests the flexibility of language and conveys the need to break out of customary ways of using words to define experience.

As these two poems illustrate, defining what a poem is (and what it is not) can be difficult. Poems can rhyme or not rhyme. They can be divided into stanzas and have a distinct form, or they can flow freely and have no discernable form. These and other choices are what many poets find alluring about the proc- ess of writing poetry. As a form, poetry is compact and concise, and choosing the right words to convey ideas is a challenge. As a literary genre, it offers room for experimentation while at the same time remaining firmly grounded in a literary tradition that stretches back through time to antiquity.

 Recognizing Kinds of Poetry

Most poems are either **narrative** poems, which recount a story, or **lyric** poems, which communicate a speaker's mood, feelings, or state of mind.

Narrative Poetry

Although any brief poem that tells a story, such as Edwin Arlington Robinson's "Richard Cory" (p. 1192), may be considered a narrative poem, the two most familiar forms of narrative poetry are the *epic* and the *ballad*.

Epics are narrative poems that recount the accomplishments of heroic figures, typically including expansive settings, superhuman feats, and gods and supernatural beings. The language of epic poems tends to be formal, even elevated, and often quite elaborate. In ancient times, epics were handed down orally; more recently, poets have written literary epics, such as John Milton's *Paradise Lost* (1667) and Nobel Prize–winning poet Derek Walcott's *Omeros* (1990), that follow many of the same conventions.

The **ballad** is another type of narrative poetry with roots in an oral tradition. Originally intended to be sung, a ballad uses repeated words and phrases, including a refrain, to advance its story. Some—but not all—ballads use the **ballad stanza.** For examples of traditional ballads in this book, see "Bonny Barbara Allan" (p. 1121) and "Western Wind" (p. 1123). Dudley Randall's "Ballad of Birmingham" (p. 869) is an example of a contemporary ballad.

Lyric Poetry

Like narrative poems, lyric poems take various forms.

An **elegy** is a poem in which a poet mourns the death of a specific person, as in Etheridge Knight's "For Malcolm, a Year After" (p. 964), about the activist Malcolm X. Another example of this type of poem is A. E. Housman's "To an Athlete Dying Young" (p. 900).

An **ode** is a long lyric poem, formal and serious in style, tone, and subject matter. An ode typically has a fairly complex stanzaic pattern, such as the **terza rima** used by Percy Bysshe Shelley in "Ode to the West Wind" (p. 1194). Another ode in this text is John Keats's "Ode on a Grecian Urn" (p. 1171).

An **aubade** is a poem about morning, usually celebrating the coming of dawn. An example is Joy Harjo's "Morning Song" (p. 856).

An **occasional poem** is written to celebrate a particular event or occasion. An example is Billy Collins's poem "The Names" (p. 1139), read before a joint session of Congress to commemorate the first anniversary of the terrorist attacks on the World Trade Center.

A **meditation** is a lyric poem that focuses on a physical object, using this object as a vehicle for considering larger issues. Edmund Waller's seventeenth-century poem "Go, lovely rose" is a meditation.

A **pastoral**—for example, Christopher Marlowe's "The Passionate Shepherd to His Love" (p. 1179)—is a lyric poem that celebrates the simple, idyllic pleasures of country life.

A **dramatic monologue** is a poem whose speaker addresses one or more silent listeners, often revealing much more than he or she intends. Robert Browning's "My Last Duchess" (p. 843) and "Porphyria's Lover" (p. 860) and Alfred Lord Tennyson's "Ulysses" (p. 1203) are dramatic monologues.

As you read the poems in this text, you will encounter works with a wide variety of forms, styles, and themes. Some you will find appealing, amusing, uplifting, or moving; others may strike you as puzzling, intimidating, or depressing. But regardless of your critical reaction to the poems, one thing is certain: if you take the time to connect with the lines you are reading, you will come away from them thinking not just about the images and ideas they express but also about yourself and your world.

CHAPTER 22

POETRY SAMPLER: SONG LYRICS

You might be surprised to learn how much poetry you know by heart. In its broadest sense, poetry can include any written, spoken, or sung text. One type of poetry that most of us have memorized without even trying is song texts, or lyrics. In fact, any time you notice that the lyrics of a song are particularly good or bad, you make a literary judgment, and if you go on to tell a friend what you thought about those lyrics, then you are, if only for a moment, a literary critic.

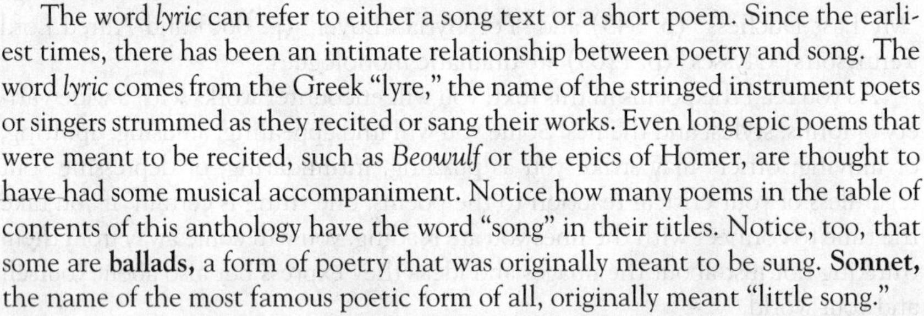

The word *lyric* can refer to either a song text or a short poem. Since the earliest times, there has been an intimate relationship between poetry and song. The word *lyric* comes from the Greek "lyre," the name of the stringed instrument poets or singers strummed as they recited or sang their works. Even long epic poems that were meant to be recited, such as *Beowulf* or the epics of Homer, are thought to have had some musical accompaniment. Notice how many poems in the table of contents of this anthology have the word "song" in their titles. Notice, too, that some are **ballads,** a form of poetry that was originally meant to be sung. **Sonnet,** the name of the most famous poetic form of all, originally meant "little song."

Some song lyrics start as poems that are eventually set to music. This was the case with the United States national anthem, "The Star Spangled Banner." Francis Scott Key wrote his poem after watching the British bombardment of Fort McHenry in 1812, and it was later set to the melody of a popular drinking song. In other cases, just the reverse happens: many of the anonymous poems that have come down to us from earlier times were originally sung although in most cases the melody has been lost. Of course, not all song texts make good poems, and the reverse is also true. The lyrics of some songs may seem trite or simplistic without the music that brings them to life, and a great poem, set badly to music, can seem awkward or pedestrian.

Within the general category of song texts, there are many different styles and genres. The traditional ballads of England, Scotland, and Ireland are the direct ancestors of much of today's country and folk music. Africans, brought to the Americas as slaves, combined their own traditions with those they found in the New World to produce a distinctive style that later became the blues, which in turn gave rise to jazz. Out of varying mixtures of all of these musical forms came styles as diverse as American musicals, rock and roll, rhythm and blues, and rap. Naturally, this summary does not include every possible genre, and it does not take into account all of the cross-pollination among genres, but it gives some idea of how varied song texts can be.

As you will see from the song lyrics in this chapter, certain themes crop up again and again in all types of music, as they do in poetry in general. Love, with its pain and heartache, is one of the most common themes, appearing here in Aimee Mann's "Invisible Ink," Hank Williams's "I'm So Lonesome I Could Cry," and David Gray's "Babylon." Political and social criticism are also popular subjects, as in "Imagine" by John Lennon, "Brother Can You Spare a Dime?" by Yip Harburg, and the two songs entitled "If I Ruled the World." Latin Playboys' "Forever Night Shade Mary" and Regina Spektor's "On the Radio" portray characters searching for meaning in their lives. Finally, the conflicts facing the artist are examined in many songs, as in Inspectah Deck's rap from "Triumph."

In addition to sharing common themes, poetry and songs also use similar technical devices. For example, both songs and poetry use **rhyme** and **meter.** They also both use allusions and figures of speech. When Regina Spektor refers to a Guns N' Roses song in "On the Radio," she is using a **literary allusion.** The "Invisible Ink" that Aimee Mann refers to is not actual ink, but a **metaphor.** Like poetry, songs use these and other literary devices to communicate ideas to their audience.

JOHN LENNON (1940–1980)

Imagine (1971)

Imagine there's no heaven
It's easy if you try
No hell below us
Above us only sky
Imagine all the people
Living for today . . .

Imagine there's no countries
It isn't hard to do
Nothing to kill or die for
And no religion too
Imagine all the people
Living life in peace . . .

You may say I'm a dreamer
But I'm not the only one
I hope someday you'll join us
And the world will be as one

Imagine no possessions
I wonder if you can
No need for greed or hunger
A brotherhood of man
Imagine all the people
Sharing all the world . . .

You may say I'm a dreamer
But I'm not the only one
I hope someday you'll join us
And the world will live as one

YIP HARBURG (1896–1981)

Brother, Can You Spare a Dime? (1931)

They used to tell me
I was building a dream.
And so I followed the mob
When there was earth to plow
Or guns to bear
I was always there
Right on the job.
They used to tell me
I was building a dream
With peace and glory ahead.
Why should I be standing in line
Just waiting for bread?
Once I built a railroad
I made it run
Made it race against time.
Once I built a railroad
Now it's done
Brother, can you spare a dime?
Once I built a tower up to the sun
Brick and rivet and lime°.
Once I built a tower,
Now it's done.
Brother, can you spare a dime?
Once in khaki suits
Gee we looked swell
Full of that yankee doodle dee dum.
Half a million boots went sloggin' through hell
And I was the kid with the drum!
Say don't you remember?
They called me Al.
It was Al all the time.
Why don't you remember?
I'm your pal.
Say buddy, can you spare a dime?

lime: A building material.

Once in khaki suits,
Ah, gee we looked swell
Full of that yankee doodle dee dum!
Half a million boots went sloggin' through hell
And I was the kid with the drum!
Oh, say don't you remember?
They called me Al.
It was Al all the time.
Say, don't you remember?
I'm your pal.
Buddy, can you spare a dime?

REGINA SPEKTOR (1980–)

On the Radio (2006)

This is how it works
It feels a little worse
Than when we drove our hearse
Right through that screaming crowd
While laughing up a storm
Until we were just bone
Until it got so warm
That none of us could sleep
And all the Styrofoam
Began to melt away
We tried to find some words
To aid in the decay
But none of them were home
Inside their catacomb°
A million ancient bees
Began to sting our knees
While we were on our knees
Praying that disease
Would leave the ones we love
And never come again

On the radio
We heard November Rain°
That solo's really long
But it's a pretty song
We listened to it twice
'Cause the DJ was asleep

---

catacomb: An underground cemetery with corridors and passageways.

November Rain: A song by the band Guns N' Roses.

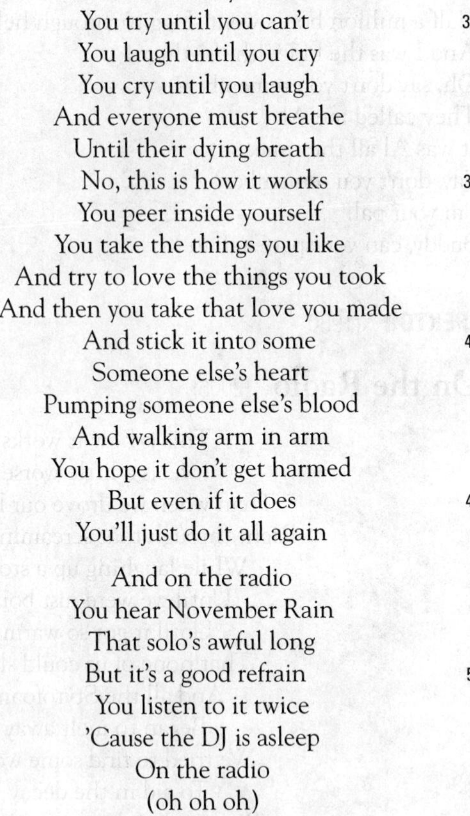

This is how it works
You're young until you're not
You love until you don't
You try until you can't
You laugh until you cry
You cry until you laugh
And everyone must breathe
Until their dying breath
No, this is how it works
You peer inside yourself
You take the things you like
And try to love the things you took
And then you take that love you made
And stick it into some
Someone else's heart
Pumping someone else's blood
And walking arm in arm
You hope it don't get harmed
But even if it does
You'll just do it all again

And on the radio
You hear November Rain
That solo's awful long
But it's a good refrain
You listen to it twice
'Cause the DJ is asleep
On the radio
(oh oh oh)
On the radio
On the radio—uh oh
On the radio—uh oh
On the radio—uh oh
On the radio

DAVID GRAY (1968–)

Babylon (2000)

Friday night I'm going nowhere
All the lights are changing green to red
Turning over TV stations
Situations running through my head
Well looking back through time
You know it's clear that I've been blind

I've been a fool
To ever open up my heart
To all that jealousy, that bitterness, that ridicule

Saturday I'm running wild
And all the lights are changing red to green
Moving through the crowd I'm pushing
Chemicals all rushing through my bloodstream
Only wish that you were here
You know I'm seeing it so clear
I've been afraid
To tell you how I really feel
Admit to some of those bad mistakes I've made

If you want it
Come and get it
Crying out loud
The love that I was
Giving you was
Never in doubt
Let go your heart
Let go your head
And feel it now

Babylon, Babylon

Sunday all the lights of London
Shining, Sky is fading red to blue
I'm kicking through the Autumn leaves
And wondering where it is you might be going to
Turning back for home
You know I'm feeling so alone
I can't believe
Climbing on the stair
I turn around to see you smiling there
In front of me

If you want it
Come and get it
Crying out loud
The love that I was
Giving you was
Never in doubt
And feel it now
Let go your heart
Let go your head
And feel it now
Let go your heart
Let go your head

And feel it now
Let go your heart
Let go your head
And feel it now
Let go your heart
Let go your head
And feel it now

Babylon, Babylon, Babylon

AIMEE MANN (1960–)

Invisible Ink (2002)

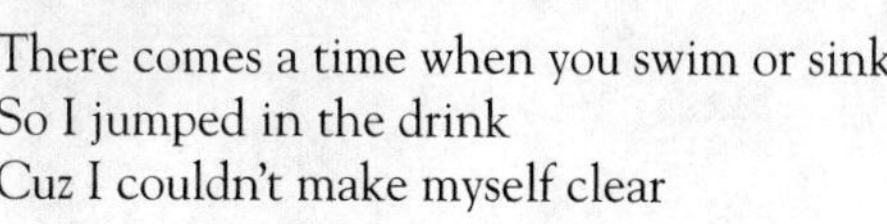

There comes a time when you swim or sink
So I jumped in the drink
Cuz I couldn't make myself clear

Maybe I wrote in invisible ink
Oh I've tried to think
How I could have made it appear

But another illustration is wasted
Cuz the results are the same
I feel like a ghost who's trying to move your hands
Over some Ouija° board in the hopes I can spell out my name

What some take for magic at first glance
Is just sleight of hand depending on what you believe
Something gets lost when you translate
It's hard to keep straight
Perspective is everything

And I know now which is which and what angle I oughta look at it from
I suppose I should be happy to be misread—
Better be that than some of the other things I have become

But nobody wants to hear this tale
The plot is clichéd, the jokes are stale
And baby we've all heard it all before
Oh I could get specific but
Nobody needs a catalog
With details of love I can't sell anymore

And aside from that, this chain of reaction,
Baby, is losing a link

Ouija board: A board with numbers and letters used to receive messages from the spirits of the dead.

Though I'd hope you'd know what I tried to tell you
And if you don't I could draw you a picture in invisible ink

But nobody wants to hear this tale
The plot is clichéd, the jokes are stale
And baby we've all heard it all before
Oh I could get specific but
Nobody needs a catalog
With details of love I can't sell anymore

HANK WILLIAMS (1923–1953)

I'm So Lonesome I Could Cry (1949)

Did you hear that lonesome whippoorwill?
He sounds too blue to fly
The midnight train is whining low
I'm so lonesome, I could cry

I've never seen a night so long
When time goes crawling by
The moon just went behind a cloud
To hide its face and cry

Did you ever see a robin weep
When leaves begin to die?
That means he's lost the will to live
I'm so lonesome, I could cry

The silence of a falling star
Light's up a purple sky
And as I wonder where you are
I'm so lonesome, I could cry

TONY BENNETT (1926–)

If I Ruled the World (1997)

If I ruled the world, ev'ry day would be the first day of spring
Every heart would have a new song to sing
And we'd sing of the joy every morning would bring

If I ruled the world, ev'ry man would be as free as a bird,
Ev'ry voice would be a voice to be heard
Take my word we would treasure each day that occurred

My world would be a beautiful place
Where we would weave such wonderful dreams

My world would wear a smile on its face
Like the man in the moon has when the moon beams
If I ruled the world every man would say the world was his friend
There'd be happiness that no man could end
No my friend, not if I ruled the world
Every head would be held up high
There'd be sunshine in everyone's sky
If the day ever dawned when I ruled the world

NAS (1973–)

from If I Ruled the World (Imagine That) (1996)

Life . . . . . I wonder . . . .
Will it take me under . . . . I don't know

The way to be, paradise like relaxin black, latino and anglo-saxon
Armani exchange the reins
Cash, Lost Tribe of Shabazz, free at last
Brand new whips to crash then we laugh in the iller path
The Villa house is for the crew, how we do
Trees for breakfast, dime sexes and Benz stretches
So many years of depression make me vision
The better livin, type of place to raise kids in
Open they eyes to the lies history's told foul
But I'm as wise as the old owl, plus the Gold Child
Seeing things like I was controlling, click rollin
Trickin six digits on kicks and still holdin
Trips to Paris, I civilized every savage
Gimme one shot I turn trife life to lavish
Political prisoner set free, stress free
No work release purple M3's and jet skis
Feel the wind breeze in West Indies
I make Coretta Scott-King mayor the cities and reverse
themes to Willies
It sounds foul but every girl I meet to go downtown
I'd open every cell in Attica send em to Africa

If I ruled the world
Imagine that
I'd free all my sons, I love em love em baby
Black diamonds and pearls
Could it be, if you could
be mine, we'd both shine
If I ruled the world
Still livin for today, in
these last days and times

INSPECTAH DECK (1970–)

from Triumph (1997) by Wu-Tang Clan

I bomb atomically, Socrates° philosophies
and hypotheses can't define how I be droppin these
mockeries, lyrically perform armed robbery
Flee with the lottery, possibly they spotted me
Battle-scarred shogun°, explosion when my pen hits
tremendous, ultra-violet° shine blind forensics
I inspect view through the future see millennium°
Killa Beez° sold fifty gold sixty platinum
Shackling the masses with drastic rap tactics
Graphic displays melt the steel like blacksmiths
Black Wu jackets Queen Beez ease the guns in
Rumblein° patrolmen tear gas laced the function
Heads by the score take flight incite a war
Chicks hit the floor, diehard fans demand more
Behold the bold soldier, control the globe slowly
Proceeds to blow swingin swords like Shinobi°
Stomp grounds I pound footprints in solid rock
Wu got it locked, Performin live on you hottest block

LATIN PLAYBOYS

Forever Night Shade Mary (1994)

Maybe a moonbeam
To light the way when evening comes
Hasn't a worry
Don't care 'bout the cold outside
Only a glad wish
For a magic ride on wings of gold

Only a daydream
Maybe a moonbeam
Just star bright
Forever nightshade Mary goodnight

Socrates: Greek philosopher (470 B.C.–399 B.C.).

shogun: In earlier times a military figure in Japan.

ultra-violet: A type of electromagnetic radiation that is ordinarily invisible.

millennium: A period of 1,000 years.

Killa Beez: A 2002 album by members of Wu-Tang Clan and other musicians.

Rumblein: Rumbling, fighting.

Shinobi: A combat video game.

She don't want money
Don't want rings or fancy things
Only a star bright
To shine behind big clouds of joy

Only a daydream
Maybe a moonbeam
Just a star bright
Forever nightshade Mary goodnight

Only a daydream
Maybe a moonbeam
Just a star bright
Forever nightshade Mary goodnight

Reading and Reacting

1. Which set of song lyrics in this chapter do you think is best able to stand on its own—without music—as a poem? Why?
2. Read the two sets of song lyrics, performed by Tony Bennett and Nas, entitled "If I Ruled the World." In what ways are these song lyrics similar? In what ways are they different?
3. The refrain of "On the Radio" by Regina Spektor mentions the song "November Rain" by Guns N' Roses. Find the lyrics of this song on the Web. How does the allusion to "November Rain" support your reading of "On the Radio"?
4. Watch a performance of one of the songs in this chapter on *YouTube*. How does the presence or absence of music change the way you experience the lyrics?
5. How are the views of love in Aimee Mann's "Invisible Ink" and Hank Williams's "I'm So Lonesome I Could Cry" similar? How are they different? What do we know about the people to whom the songs are addressed? What do we know about their relationships?
6. How do you picture the character in "Forever Night Shade Mary"? What details in the lyrics help you form this picture? What can you infer about the character? What else would you like to know about her?

WRITING SUGGESTIONS: Song Lyrics

1. Choose two sets of song lyrics in this chapter that share a common theme. Then, write an essay in which you compare how they develop this theme.
2. Choose a song whose lyrics you think can stand on their own as a poem. Then, write an **explication** of those lyrics.
3. Read some of the poems in Chapter 31, "Discovering Themes in Poetry," and read the chapter's introduction (p. 1037). Which of the four themes discussed in this chapter do you see as most suitable for song lyrics? Why?

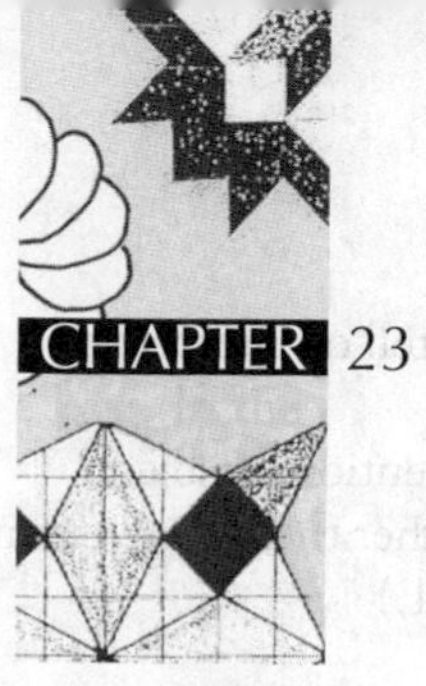

READING AND WRITING ABOUT POETRY

Reading Poetry

Sometimes readers approach poetry purely for pleasure. At other times, reading a poem is also the first step toward writing about it. The following guidelines, designed to help you explore poetic works, focus on issues explored in chapters to come:

- *Rephrase the poem in your own words.* What does your paraphrase reveal about the poem's subject and central concerns? What is lost or gained in your paraphrase of the poem?
- *Consider the poem's* ***voice.*** Who is the poem's speaker? How would you characterize the poem's tone? Is the poem ironic? (See Chapter 24.)
- *Study the poem's* ***diction.*** Look up any unfamiliar words in a dictionary. How does word choice affect your reaction to the poem? What do the connotations of words reveal about the poem? What level of diction is used? Is word order unusual or unexpected? How does the arrangement of words contribute to your understanding of the poem? (See Chapter 25.)
- *Examine the poem's* ***imagery.*** What kind of imagery predominates? What specific images are used? Is there a pattern of imagery? How does imagery enrich the poem? (See Chapter 26.)
- *Identify the poem's* ***figures of speech.*** Does the poet use metaphor? Simile? Personification? Hyperbole? Understatement? Metonymy or synecdoche? Apostrophe? How do figures of speech affect your reading of the poem? (See Chapter 27.)
- *Listen to the* ***sound*** *of the poem.* Are rhythm and meter regular or irregular? How do rhythm and meter reinforce the poem's central concerns? Does the poem use alliteration? Assonance? Rhyme? How do these elements enhance the poem? (See Chapter 28.)
- *Look at the poem's* ***form.*** Is the poem written in closed or open form? Is the poem constructed as a sonnet? A sestina? A villanelle? An epigram? A haiku? A prose poem? A concrete poem? How does the poem's form help to communicate (or reinforce) its ideas? (See Chapter 29.)
- *Consider the poem's use of* ***symbol, allegory, allusion,*** *or* ***myth.*** Does the poem make use of symbols? Allusions? How do symbols or allusions support

its theme? Is the poem an allegory? Does the poem retell or interpret a myth? (See Chapter 30.)

- *Identify the poem's* **theme.** Does the poem treat a conventional subject? What central theme does the poem explore? What other themes are examined? How are the themes expressed? (See Chapter 31.)

Active Reading

When you approach a poem that you plan to write about, you engage in the same **active reading** strategies you use when you read a short story or a play. When you finish recording your reactions to the poem, you focus on a topic, list possible ideas to explore, decide on a thesis, prepare an outline, and then go on to draft and revise your essay.

Catherine Whittaker, a student in an Introduction to Literature course, was asked to write a three- to five-page essay comparing any two of the poems that appear in "Poems about Parents" in Chapter 31 (pp. 1038–39). Her instructor told the class that the essay should reflect students' own ideas about the poems, not the opinions of literary critics. As Catherine planned and wrote her paper, she was guided by the process described in Chapter 2, "Reading and Writing about Literature."

Previewing

Catherine began her work by previewing the poems, eliminating those she considered obscure or difficult and those whose portrait of the speaker's parent did not seem sympathetic. This process helped Catherine to narrow down her choices. As she looked through "Those Winter Sundays," two phrases in the opening lines ("Sundays too"; "blueblack cold") caught her eye; she also noticed the words "The squat pen rests; snug as a gun" in line 2 of "Digging." In each case, the words made Catherine want to examine the poem further. She noticed too that both poems focused on fathers and that both were divided into stanzas of varying lengths. Keeping these general parallels in mind, Catherine began a close reading of each poem.

Highlighting and Annotating

As Catherine read and reread "Those Winter Sundays" and "Digging," she recorded her comments and questions. The poems, with her highlighting and annotations, appear below.

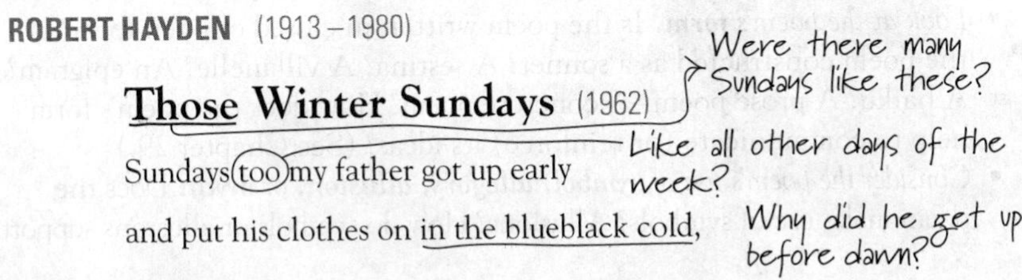
ROBERT HAYDEN (1913–1980)
Those Winter Sundays (1962)
Sundays too my father got up early
and put his clothes on in the blueblack cold,
Were there many Sundays like these?
Like all other days of the week?
Why did he get up before dawn?

then with cracked hands that ached
from labor in the weekday weather made
banked fires blaze. No one ever thanked him.
I'd wake and hear the cold splintering, breaking.
When the rooms were warm, he'd call,
and slowly I would rise and dress,
fearing the chronic angers of that house,
Speaking indifferently to him,
who had driven out the cold
and polished my good shoes as well.
What did I know, what did I know
of love's austere and lonely offices?

What kind of job did the father have?

Was there a large family?

Were there problems in the family?

Was there a mother around?

Offices=duties or functions assigned to someone

Austere=without adornment or ornamentation, simple; harsh

SEAMUS HEANEY (1939–)

Digging (1966)

Between my finger and my thumb
The squat pen rests; snug as a gun.

Under my window, a clean rasping sound
When the spade sinks into gravelly ground:
My father, digging. I look down

Till his straining rump among the flowerbeds
Bends low, comes up twenty years away
Stooping in rhythm through potato drills
Where he was digging.

The coarse boot nestled on the lug, the shaft
Against the inside knee was levered firmly.

gun=snug?

Why a "squat" pen?

Is he thinking about the past?

Like the poets' pen?

He rooted out tall tops, buried the bright edge deep
To scatter new potatoes that we picked → *Was this a family task?*
Loving their cool hardness in our hands.

By God, the old man could handle a spade.
Just like his old man. } *Two generations could "handle a spade." Can the poet dig?*

My grandfather cut more turf in a day
Than any other man on Toner's bog.
Once I carried him milk in a bottle
Corked sloppily with paper. He straightened up
To drink it, then fell to right away → *The grandfather was a hard worker.*
Nicking and slicing neatly, heaving sods → *Digging was an art*
Over his shoulder, going down and down
For the good turf. Digging.

The cold smell of potato mould, the squelch and slap
Of soggy peat, the curt cuts of an edge
Through living roots awaken in my head. → *What does it make him remember?*
But I've no spade to follow men like them. → *What are "men like them" like?*

Same as first 2 lines { Between my finger and my thumb
The squat pen rests. → *Why is this repeated?*
I'll dig with it. → *Dig for what?*

Catherine found the language of both poems appealing, and she believed her highlighting and annotating had given her some valuable insights. For example, she noticed some similarities between the two poems: both focus on the past, both portray fathers as hard workers, and neither mentions a mother.

Writing about Poetry

Planning an Essay

Catherine still had to find a specific topic for her paper, and her preliminary work suggested some interesting possibilities. She was especially intrigued by the way both poems depicted fathers as actively engaged in physical tasks.

Choosing a Topic

One idea Catherine thought she might want to write about was the significance of the sons' attitudes toward their fathers: although both see their fathers as hard workers, the son in "Those Winter Sundays" seems to have mixed feelings about his father's devotion to his family, whereas the son in "Digging" is more appreciative. Catherine explored this idea in two journal entries.

"Those Winter Sundays"

Why did the father get up early every morning? Maybe he had a large family and little money. There is no mention of a mother. The poems suggest the utter cold and "chronic angers" of the house. The father not only made fires to warm the house but also polished his child's (or children's) shoes—maybe for church. And yet, the child seemed not to care about or appreciate the father's efforts. Was he too young to say thank you, or were there other problems in the house for which the child blamed the father?

"Digging"

In the poem, the poet seems to be wondering what to write about when the sounds of digging capture his attention. He remembers the steady rhythm of his father's digging of the potatoes and how they (probably the poet and his brothers and sisters) picked out the cool potatoes. He seems to appreciate his father's and grandfather's hard work and skill. He does, however, feel regret that he is not like these dedicated men. Even though he cannot use a shovel, he hopes to use his pen to make his own contributions as a writer.

When Catherine reread her journal entries, she saw that she could focus on the two fathers' similar roles and the sons' contrasting attitudes toward their fathers. (In fact, she had so many ideas that she did not feel she had to brainstorm to generate more material.) Before she could write a draft of her paper, however, Catherine needed to identify specific similarities and differences between the two poems.

Seeing Connections

Catherine reread the highlighted and annotated poems and then compiled the following lists.

Differences

"Those Winter Sundays"	"Digging"
–memories of family problems	–only happy memories
–the child is ambivalent toward his father	–the child admires his father
–atmosphere of tension	–atmosphere of happiness and family unity

Similarities

```
–the fathers are hard workers
–the fathers appear to love their children
–the events seem to have happened years ago
–children, now grown, appreciate their fathers'
 dedication
–children, now grown, are inspired by their
 fathers' determination
```

At this point, as connections between the two poems came into focus, Catherine was able to decide on a thesis and on a possible order for her ideas.

Deciding on a Thesis

Catherine expressed her paper's main idea in the following thesis statement.

```
Although their family backgrounds are different, both
poets now realize the determination and dedication
of their fathers and are consequently impassioned in
their writing.
```

Preparing an Outline

Catherine reviewed her notes to help her identify the specific ideas she wanted to develop in her first draft. Then, she arranged those ideas in a logical order in a scratch outline.

```
"Those Winter Sundays"

    Poet reflects on childhood
        –father's hard work
        –his own misunderstanding and lack of
          appreciation for everything his father did
```

```
    Family's unhappiness
        –tension in the house
        –no mother mentioned in the poem
    Poet's realization of father's love and
    dedication

"Digging"

    Poet reminisces about childhood
        –father's skill and hard work
        –grandfather's cutting of turf
        –children's participation and acceptance
    Family's happiness
    Poet's desire to continue the family tradition
```

Drafting an Essay

With a thesis statement and a scratch outline to guide her, Catherine wrote the following first draft of her essay. Her instructor's comments appear in the margins and at the end of the paper.

first draft

A Comparison of Two Poems about Fathers

Careful! you're confusing poet and speaker.

Robert Hayden's "Those Winter Sundays" and "Digging" by Seamus Heaney are poems that were inspired by fathers and composed as tributes to fathers. Although their family backgrounds are different, both poets now realize the determination and dedication of their fathers and are consequently impassioned in their writing.

What do you mean?

In "Those Winter Sundays," Hayden reflects back on his childhood. He remembers the many Sundays when his father got up early to start the fires to make the house warm for his children's awakening. The poet pictures his father's hands made rough by his weekday work. These same hands not only made the fires on Sunday but also polished his son's good shoes, in preparation, no doubt, for church.

Hayden also quite clearly remembers that his father was never thanked for his work. The reader imagines that the father had many children and may have been poor. There were inner tensions in the house and, quite noticeably, there is no mention of a mother.

Looking back, the poet now realizes the love and dedication with which his father took care of the

Quotations from the poem would strengthen your discussion in ¶s 3 and 4.

family. As a child, he never thanked his father, but now, as an adult, the poet seems to appreciate the simple kindness of his father.

In a similar sense, Seamus Heaney's "Digging" is a tribute to his father and grandfather. He also reminisces about his father and clearly remembers the skill with which his father dug potatoes. The grandfather too is remembered, as is his technique for "heaving sods." There is an atmosphere of happiness in this poem. With the children helping the father harvest the potatoes, a sense of family togetherness is created. The reader feels that this family is a hardworking but nevertheless happy one.

Add line number in parentheses.

As the poet reminisces about his childhood, he realizes that, unlike his father and grandfather, he will never be a master of digging or a person who uses physical strength to earn a living. He wishes to be like his father before him, desiring to accomplish and contribute. However, for the poet, any "digging" to be done will be by his pen, in the form of literature.

To conclude, the fathers in these poets' pasts inspire them to write. However, an appreciation for their fathers' dedication is achieved only after the children mature into adults. It is then that the fathers' impact on their children's lives is realized for its true importance.

Good start! When you revise, focus on the following:

- Edit use of "poet" and "speaker" carefully. You can't assume that these poems reflect the poets' own lives or attitudes toward their fathers.
- Add more specific references to the poems, particularly quotations. (Don't forget to give line numbers.)
- Consider adding brief references to other poems about parents. (Check the textbook.)
- Consider rearranging your material into a point-by-point comparison, which will make the specific similarities and differences clearer.

Let's discuss this draft in a conference.

First Draft: Commentary

After submitting her first draft, Catherine met with her instructor. Together, they reviewed not only her first draft but also her annotations, journal entries, lists of similarities and differences, and scratch outline. During the conference, her instructor explained his written comments and, building on Catherine's own ideas, helped her develop a plan for revision.

Catherine's instructor agreed that the poems' similarities were worth exploring in detail. He thought, however, that her references to the poems' language and ideas needed to be much more specific and that her paper's subject-by-subject structure—discussing "Those Winter Sundays" first and then moving on to consider "Digging"—made the specific similarities between the two poems difficult to see. He also thought that her thesis statement should be more concrete and specific.

Because the class had studied other poems in which speakers try to resolve their ambivalent feelings toward their parents, Catherine's instructor also suggested that she mention these poems to provide a wider context for her ideas. Finally, he explained the difference between the perspective of the poet and that of the **speaker,** a persona the poet creates.

As she reexamined her ideas in light of her discussion with her instructor, Catherine looked again at both the annotated poems and her notes about them. She then recorded her thoughts about her progress in an additional journal entry.

After reviewing the poems again and talking to Professor Jackson, I discovered some additional points I want to include in my next draft. The connection between the poet's pen and the shovel is evident in "Digging," and so is the link between the cold and the tensions in the house in "Those Winter Sundays." The tone of each poem should also be discussed. For example, I think that the poet's choice of *austere* in "Those Winter Sundays" has significance and should be included. In my next draft, I'll expand my first draft—hopefully, without reading into the poems too much. I also need to reorganize my ideas so parallels between the two poems will be clearer.

Because this journal entry suggested a new arrangement for her ideas, Catherine prepared a new scratch outline to guide her revision.

Reflections on their fathers
- Both poems
  - –fathers' dedication and hard work

```
Family similarities and differences
    "Digging"
        —loving and caring
    "Those Winter Sundays"
        —family problems (tone of the poem)
Lessons learned from fathers
    "Digging"
        —inspiration (images of pen and shovel)
        —realization of father's inner strength
    "Those Winter Sundays"
        —"austere" caring (images of cold)
        —realization of father's inner strength
Brief discussion of other poems about fathers
```

Revising and Editing an Essay

After once again reviewing all the material she had accumulated, Catherine wrote a second draft.

second draft

A Comparison of Two Poems about Fathers

Robert Hayden's "Those Winter Sundays" and Seamus Heaney's "Digging" are two literary pieces that are tributes to the speakers' fathers. The inspiration and admiration the speakers feel are evident in each poem. Although the nature of the two family relationships may differ, the common thread of the love of fathers for their children weaves through each poem.

Reflections on one's childhood can bring assorted memories to light. Presumably, the speakers are now adults and reminisce about their childhood with a mature sense of enlightenment not found in children. Both speakers describe their fathers' hard work and dedication to their families. Hayden's speaker remembers that even after working hard all week, his father would get up early on Sunday to warm the house in preparation for his children's rising. The speaker vividly portrays his father's hands, describing "cracked hands that ached / from labor in the weekday weather" (lines 3–4). And yet, these same hands not only built the fires that drove out the cold but also polished the children's good shoes.

In a similar way, Heaney's speaker reminisces about his father's and grandfather's digging of turf, describing their skill and their dedication to their task.

The fathers in these poems appear to be the hardest of workers, laborers who sought to support their families. Not only did they have a dedication to their work, but they also cared about and undoubtedly loved their children. Looking back, Hayden's speaker realizes that, although his childhood may not have been perfect nor his family life entirely without problems, his father loved him. Heaney's description of the potato picking makes us imagine a loving family led by a father and grandfather who worked together and included the children in both work and celebration. Heaney's speaker grows to become a man who has nothing but respect for his father and grandfather, wishing to be like them and somehow follow their greatness.

Although some similarities exist between the sons and fathers in the two poems, the family life is quite different. Perhaps it is the tone of the poems that best typifies the family atmosphere. The tone of "Digging" is wholesome, earthy, natural, and happy, emphasizing the healthy and caring nature of the poet's childhood. In reminiscing, Heaney's speaker seems to have no bad memories concerning his father or family. In contrast, the tone of Hayden's poem is very much like the coldness of the Sunday mornings. Even though the father warmed the house, the "chronic angers of that house" (9) did not leave with the cold. The speaker, as a child, seems full of resentment toward the father, no doubt blaming him for the family problems. (Curiously, it is the father and not the mother who polishes the children's good shoes. Was there no mother?) The reader senses that the father-son communication evident in Heaney's family is missing in Hayden's.

There are many other poets who have written about their fathers. Simon J. Ortiz in "My Father's Song" writes a touching tribute to his father, who taught him to respect and care for the lives of animals and to appreciate earthly wonders. In other poems, such as Theodore Roethke's "My Papa's Waltz," the fathers are depicted as imperfect, vulnerable people who try to cope with life as well as possible.

"Digging" and "Those Winter Sundays" are poems written from the inspirations of sons, admiring and appreciating their fathers. Childhood memories act not only as images of the past but also as aids for the speakers' self-realization and enlightenment. Even after childhood, the fathers' influence over their sons is evident; only now do the speakers appreciate its true importance.

Second Draft: Commentary

When she reread her second draft, Catherine thought she had accomplished much of what she had set out to do. For example, she had tightened her thesis statement, rearranged her discussion, added specific details, and changed *poet* to *speaker* where necessary.

However, she still was not satisfied with her analysis of the poems' language and tone (she had not, for example, considered the importance of the word *austere* or examined the significance of Heaney's equation of *spade* and *pen*). She also thought that the material in paragraph 6 about other poems, though interesting, was distracting, so she decided to try to move it to follow her introduction, where it could provide a context for the discussion to follow.

After making further revisions, Catherine prepared a final draft of her paper, which appears on the following pages.

Whittaker 1

Catherine Whittaker

Professor Jackson

English 102

5 March 2008

Digging for Memories

Robert Hayden's "Those Winter Sundays" and Seamus Heaney's "Digging" are two poems that are tributes to the speakers' fathers. Although the depiction of the families and the tones of the two poems are different, the common thread of love between fathers and children extends through the two poems, and each speaker is inspired by his father's example.

Many other poets have written about children and their fathers. Some of these poems express regret and gratitude. For example, Simon J. Ortiz in "My Father's Song" writes a touching tribute to a father who taught the speaker to respect and care for the lives of animals and to appreciate earthly wonders. In other poems, such as Theodore Roethke's "My Papa's Waltz," fathers are depicted as imperfect, vulnerable people who try to cope with life as well as possible.

As these and other poems reveal, reflections on childhood can bring complex memories to light, as they do for Hayden's and Heaney's speakers. Now adults, they reminisce about their childhoods with a mature sense of enlightenment not found in children. Both speakers describe their fathers' hard work and dedication to their families. For example, Hayden's speaker remembers that even after working hard all week, his father would get up early on Sunday to warm

Introduction

Thesis statement

¶6 from second draft has been relocated. References to poems in Chapter 31 of this text include complete authors' names and titles.

First point of similarity: Both poems focus on memory

Whittaker 2

Parenthetical reference cites line numbers of poem. (First reference to lines of poetry includes word *line* or *lines*. Subsequent references include just line numbers.)

the house in preparation for his sleeping children. The speaker vividly portrays his father's hands, describing "cracked hands that ached / from labor in the weekday weather" (lines 3-4). And yet, these same hands not only built the fires that drove out the cold but also polished his children's good shoes. In a similar way, Heaney's speaker reminisces about his father's and grandfather's digging of soil and sod, pointing out their skill and their dedication to their tasks.

Second point of similarity: Both fathers are hard workers.

The fathers in these poems appear to be hard workers, laborers who struggled to support their families. Not only were they dedicated to their work, but they also loved their children. Looking back, Hayden's speaker realizes that, although his childhood may not have been perfect and his family life was not entirely without problems, his father loved him. Heaney's description of the potato picking allows us to imagine a loving family led by a father and grandfather who worked together and included the children in both work and celebration. Heaney's speaker grows into a man who has nothing but respect for his father and grandfather, wishing to be like them and to somehow fill their shoes.

Focus shifts to contrast between the two poems.

Although some similarities exist between the fathers (and the sons) in the poems, the family life the two poems depict is very different. Perhaps it is the tone of each poem that best reveals the family atmosphere. The tone of "Digging" is wholesome, earthy, natural, and happy, emphasizing the healthy

Whittaker 3

and caring nature of the speaker's childhood. Heaney's speaker seems to have no bad memories of his father or family. In contrast, the tone of Hayden's poem is very much like the coldness of the Sunday mornings. Even though the father warmed the house, the "chronic angers of that house" (9) did not leave with the cold. The speaker, as a child, seems to have resented his father, blaming him for the family's problems. The warm relationship readers see between the father and the son in Heaney's poem is absent in Hayden's.

In spite of these differences, readers cannot go away from either poem without the impression that both speakers learned important lessons from their fathers. Both fathers had a great amount of inner strength and were dedicated to their families. As the years pass, Hayden's speaker has come to realize the depth of his father's devotion to his family. He uses the image of the "blueblack cold" (2) that was splintered and broken by the fires lovingly prepared by his father to suggest the father's efforts to keep his family free from harm. The cold suggests the tensions of the family, but the father is determined to force these tensions out of the house through his "austere and lonely offices" (14).

Focus returns to parallels between the two poems.

Third point of similarity: Both speakers learn from fathers (discussed in two paragraphs).

In Heaney's poem, the father—and the grandfather—also had a profound impact on the young speaker. As the memories come pouring back, the speaker's admiration for the men who came before him forces him to reflect on his own life and work. He realizes that he will never have the ability (or the

Whittaker 4

desire) to do the physical labor of his relatives: "I've no spade to follow men like them" (28). However, just as the spade was the tool of his father and grandfather, the pen will be the tool with which the speaker will work. The shovel suggests the hard work, effort, and determination of the men who came before him, and the pen is the literary equivalent of the shovel. Heaney's speaker has been inspired by his father and grandfather, and he hopes to accomplish with a pen in the world of literature what they accomplished with a shovel on the land.

Conclusion reinforces thesis.

"Digging" and "Those Winter Sundays" are poems written from the perspective of adult sons who admire and appreciate their fathers. Childhood memories not only evoke vivid images of the past but also lead the speakers to insight and enlightenment. Long after childhood, the fathers' influence over their sons is evident; only now, however, do the speakers appreciate its true importance.

Whittaker 5

Works Cited

Hayden, Robert. "Those Winter Sundays." Kirszner and Mandell 1040.

Heaney, Seamus. "Digging." Kirszner and Mandell 1040-41.

Kirszner, Laurie G., and Stephen R. Mandell, eds. *Literature: Reading, Reacting, Writing*. 7th ed. Boston: Wadsworth, 2010. Print.

Final Draft: Commentary

As she wrote her final draft, Catherine expanded her analysis, looking more closely at the language and tone of the two poems. To support and clarify her points, she added more quotations, taking care to reproduce words and punctuation marks accurately and to cite line numbers in parentheses after each quotation. She also moved her discussion of other poems to paragraph 2, where it provides a smooth transition from her introduction to her discussion of Hayden and Heaney. When she was satisfied with the content of her paper, she proofread it carefully and prepared a works-cited page.

CHAPTER 24

VOICE

Source: ©Bettmann/Corbis

See this poet's biography on p. 1220.

EMILY DICKINSON (1830–1886)

I'm nobody! Who are you? (1891)

I'm nobody! Who are you?
Are you—Nobody—Too?
Then there's a pair of us?
Don't tell! they'd advertise—you know!

How dreary—to be—Somebody!
How public—like a Frog—
To tell one's name—the livelong June—
To an admiring Bog!

The Speaker in the Poem

When they read a work of fiction, readers decide whether the narrator is sophisticated or unsophisticated, trustworthy or untrustworthy, innocent or experienced. Just as fiction depends on a narrator, poetry depends on a **speaker** who describes events, feelings, and ideas to readers. Finding out as much as possible about this speaker can help readers to interpret a poem. For example, the speaker in Emily Dickinson's "I'm nobody! Who are you?" seems at first to be playful, even flirtatious. As the poem continues, however, the speaker becomes a more complex persona. In the first stanza, the speaker reveals her private self—internal, isolated, with little desire to be well known; in the second stanza, she expresses disdain for those who seek to become "somebody," whom she sees as self-centered, self-promoting, and inevitably superficial. Far from being defeated by her isolation, the speaker rejects fame and celebrates her status as a "nobody."

One question readers might ask about "I'm nobody! Who are you?" is how close the speaker's voice is to the poet's. Readers who conclude that the poem is about the conflict between a poet's public and private selves may be tempted to see the speaker and the poet as one. But this is not necessarily the case. Like the narrator of a short story, the speaker of a poem is a **persona,** or mask, that the poet puts on. Granted, in some poems little distance exists between the poet and the speaker. Without hard evidence to support a link between speaker and poet, however, readers should not simply assume they are one and the same.

In many cases, the speaker is quite different from the poet—even when the speaker's voice conveys the attitude of the poet, either directly or indirectly. In "The Chimney Sweeper" (p. 1127), for example, William Blake assumes the voice of a child to criticize the system of child labor that existed in eighteenth-century England. Even though the child speaker does not understand the economic and social forces that cause his misery, readers sense the poet's anger as the trusting speaker describes the appalling conditions under which he works. The poet's indignation is especially apparent in the biting irony of the last line, in which the victimized speaker innocently assures readers that if all people do their duty, "they need not fear harm."

Sometimes the poem's speaker is anonymous. In such cases—as in William Carlos Williams's "Red Wheelbarrow" (p. 906), for instance—the first-person voice is absent, and the speaker remains outside the poem. At other times, the speaker has a set identity—a king, a beggar, a highwayman, a sheriff, a husband, a wife, a rich man, a murderer, a child, a mythical figure, an explorer, a teacher, a faithless lover, a saint—or even a flower, an animal, or a clod of earth. Whatever the case, the speaker is not the poet but rather a creation that the poet uses to convey his or her ideas. (For this reason, poems by a single poet may have very different voices. Compare Sylvia Plath's bitter and sardonic poem "Daddy" [p. 936] with her nurturing and celebratory work "Morning Song" [p. 856], for example.)

Sometimes a poem's title tells readers that the poet is assuming a particular persona. In the following poem, for example, the title identifies the speaker as a fictional character, Gretel from the fairy tale "Hansel and Gretel."

Source: ©AP Photo

See this poet's biography on p. 1221.

LOUISE GLÜCK (1943–)

Gretel in Darkness (1971)

This is the world we wanted.
All who would have seen us dead
are dead. I hear the witch's cry
break in the moonlight through a sheet
of sugar: God rewards.
Her tongue shrivels into gas. . . .
Now, far from women's arms
And memory of women, in our father's hut
we sleep, are never hungry.
Why do I not forget?
My father bars the door, bars harm
from this house, and it is years.

No one remembers. Even you, my brother,
summer afternoons you look at me as though

you meant to leave,
as though it never happened.
But I killed for you. I see armed firs,
the spires of that gleaming kiln—

Nights I turn to you to hold me
but you are not there.
Am I alone? Spies
hiss in the stillness, Hansel
we are there still, and it is real, real,
that black forest, and the fire in earnest.

The speaker in this poem comments on her life after her encounter with the witch in the forest. Speaking to her brother, Gretel observes that they now live in the world they wanted: they live with their father in his hut, and the witch and the wicked stepmother are dead. Even so, the memory of the events in the forest haunts Gretel and makes it impossible for her to live "happily ever after."

By assuming the persona of Gretel, the poet is able to convey some interesting and complex ideas. On one level, Gretel represents any person who has lived through a traumatic experience. Memories of the event keep breaking through into the present, frustrating her attempts to reestablish her belief in the goodness of the world. The voice we hear is sad, alone, and frightened: "Nights I turn to you to hold me," she says, "but you are not there." Although the murder Gretel committed for her brother was justified, it seems to haunt her. "No one remembers," laments Gretel, not even her brother. At some level, she realizes that by killing the witch she has killed a part of herself, perhaps the part of women that men fear and consequently transform into witches and wicked stepmothers. The world that is left after the killing is her father's and her brother's, not her own, and she is now alone in a dark world haunted by the memories of the black forest. In this sense, Gretel—"Now, far from women's arms / And memory of women"—may be the voice of all victimized women who, because of men, act against their own best interests—and regret it.

As "Gretel in Darkness" illustrates, a title can identify a poem's speaker, but the speaker's own words can provide much more information. This is also the case in the following poem, where Spanish words help to characterize the speaker.

LEONARD ADAMÉ (1947–)

My Grandmother Would Rock Quietly and Hum (1973)

in her house
she would rock quietly and hum
until her swelled hands
calmed

in summer
she wore thick stockings

sweaters
and grey braids

(when "el cheque"° came
we went to Payless
and I laughed greedily
when given a quarter)

mornings,
sunlight barely lit
the kitchen
and where
there were shadows
it was not cold

she quietly rolled
flour tortillas—
the "papas"°
cracking in hot lard
would wake me

she had lost her teeth
and when we ate
she had bread
soaked in "café"°

always her eyes
were clear
and she could see
as I cannot yet see—
through her eyes
she gave me herself

she would sit
and talk
of her girlhood—
of things strange to me:
México
epidemics
relatives shot
her father's hopes
of this country—
how they sank
with cement dust
to his insides

---

el cheque: The check.
papas: Potatoes.
café: Coffee.

now
when I go
to the old house
the worn spots
by the stove
echo of her shuffling
and
México
still hangs in her
fading
calendar pictures

In this poem, the speaker is an adult recalling childhood memories of his grandmother. Spanish words—*el cheque*, *tortillas*, *papas*, and *café*—identify the speaker as Latino. His easy use of English, his comment that Mexico is strange to him, and his observation that he cannot yet see through his grandmother's eyes suggest, however, that he is not in touch with his Mexican identity. At one level, the grandmother evokes nostalgic memories of the speaker's youth. At another level, she is a living symbol of his ties with Mexico, connecting him to the ethnic culture he is trying to recover. The poem ends on an ambivalent note: even though the speaker is able to return to "the old house," the pictures of Mexico are fading, perhaps suggesting the speaker's inevitable assimilation into mainstream American culture.

Direct statements by speakers can also help to characterize them. In the next poem, the first line of each stanza establishes the identity of the speaker—and defines his perspective.

Source: ©AP Photo

See this poet's biography on p. 1075.

LANGSTON HUGHES (1902–1967)

Negro (1926)

I am a Negro:
  Black as the night is black,
  Black like the depths of my Africa.

I've been a slave:
  Caesar told me to keep his door-steps clean.
  I brushed the boots of Washington.

I've been a worker:
  Under my hand the pyramids arose.
  I made mortar for the Woolworth Building.

I've been a singer:
  All the way from Africa to Georgia
  I carried my sorrow songs.
  I made ragtime.

POETRY SAMPLER: POETRY AND ART

Many poets have found visual art to be a source of inspiration for their poems. In fact, the ancient Greeks used the word *ekphrasis* to denote poetry that focused on paintings, artistic objects, and highly visual scenes. In the *Illiad*, for example, Homer vividly describes the shield of Achilles. The Ancient Romans also saw the connection between art and poetry. The Roman poet Horace made this point in *Ars Poetica* when he observed, "as in painting, so in poetry." Other more contemporary examples of *ekphrasis* occur in John Keats's "Ode on a Grecian Urn" (p. 1171) and W. H. Auden's "Musée des Beaux Arts" (p. 1032).

A poem about a work of art often expresses a poet's deep emotional response to it. Sometimes the poet not only gives voice to his or her reactions but also gives voice to the work of art itself. This is true of Keats when he writes about a Grecian urn (which he probably saw in the British Museum in London). Keats attempts to come to terms not only with the static images he sees on the urn but also with the effect it has on him. For Keats, the quiet majesty of the urn reflects a basic principle of art: "Heard melodies are sweet, but those unheard / Are sweeter; therefore, ye soft pipes, play on" (lines 11–12). For Keats, the message of the urn is simple and very direct: "'Beauty is truth, truth beauty,'—that is all / Ye know on earth, and all ye need to know" (lines 49–50).

A poem about a work of art can also try convey its essence to readers. Auden attempts to achieve this in his "Musée des Beaux Arts." By pointing out the inherent contradictions in the Brueghel painting his poem describes, Auden seeks to penetrate the painting and to interpret it for readers. As Icarus plunges to his death into the sea, "dogs go on with their doggy life" (line 12) and the ploughman goes on plowing, never having heard "the splash, the forsaken cry" (line 16). For Auden, Brueghel's painting expresses a basic truth that the old masters knew: that no matter how momentous an occurrence, life goes on. While someone is suffering—whether it be Christ or Icarus—"someone else is eating or opening a window or just walking dully along" (line 4).

Each of the poems in this sampler is accompanied by the art that inspired it. In "Sonnet in Primary Colors," Rita Dove explores her reactions to paintings by the artist Frida Kahlo. In "Cézanne's Ports," Alan Ginsberg uses a painting by a well-known impressionist as inspiration just as Robert Hayden does in "Monet's 'Waterlilies'" In "Girl Powdering Her Neck," Cathy Song contemplates a portrait by Kitagawa Ultamaro of a geisha preparing herself for her next assignation. In "Tall Figures," May Swenson explores the meaning of a sculpture by Alberto Giacometti. Finally, in "Fun Gallery," Kevin Young reacts to the work of graffiti artist and painter Jean-Michel Basquiat.

RITA DOVE (1952–)

Sonnet in Primary Colors (1995)

This is for the woman with one black wing
perched over her eyes: lovely Frida,° erect
among parrots, in the stern petticoats of the peasant,
who painted herself a present—
wildflowers entwining the plaster corset
her spine resides in the romance of mirrors.

Each night she lay down in pain and rose
to her celluloid butterflies of her Beloved Dead,
Lenin° and Marx° and Stalin° arrayed at the footstead.
And rose to her easel, the hundred dogs panting
like children along the graveled walks of the garden, Diego's°
love a skull in the circular window
of the thumbprint searing her immutable brow.

Self Portrait with Monkey and Parrot (1938) by Frida Kahlo.

Frida: Frida Kahlo (1907–1954), Mexican painter, feminist and Communist.

Lenin: Vladimir Ilyich Lenin (1870–1924), Communist revolutionary and first leader of the Soviet Union.

Marx: Karl Marx (1818–1883), political theorist and author of *The Communist Manifesto.*

Stalin: Joseph Stalin (1878–1953), second leader of the Soviet Union.

Diego's: Diego Rivera (1886–1957), Communist Mexican artist, husband of Frida Kahlo.

ALLEN GINSBERG (1926–1997)

Cézanne's° Ports (1961)

In the foreground we see time and life
swept in a race
toward the left hand side of the picture
where shore meets shore.

But that meeting place
isn't represented;
it doesn't occur on the canvas.

For the other side of the bay
is Heaven and Eternity,
with a bleak white haze over its mountains.

And the immense water of L'Estaque° is a go-between
for minute rowboats.

L'Estaque **(1883–1885) by Paul Cézanne.**
Source: ©The Metropolitan Museum of Art/Art Resource, NY

Cézanne's: Paul Cézanne (1839–1906), French Postimpressionist painter.
L'Estaque: Fishing village in France where Cézanne painted many views of the sea.

ROBERT HAYDEN (1913–1980)

Monet's "Waterlilies"° (1966)

Today as the news from Selma° and Saigon°
poisons the air like fallout,
I come again to see
the serene, great picture that I love.

Here space and time exist in light
the eye like the eye of faith believes.
The seen, the known
dissolve in iridescence, become
illusive flesh of light
that was not, was, forever is.

O light beheld as through refracting tears.
Here is the aura of that world
each of us has lost.
Here is the shadow of its joy.

Water Lilies (1914–1917) by Claude Monet.
Source: ©Musee Marmottan, Paris, France/Bridgeman Art Library

"Waterlilies": A series of paintings by Claude Monet (1840–1926), a French impressionist painter.
Selma: Selma, Alabama. The site of civil rights marches in the mid 1960s, one of which was ended by police violence.
Saigon: Capital of South Vietnam from 1954 to 1975; now know as Ho Chi Mihn City.

CATHY SONG (1955–)

Girl Powdering Her Neck (1983)

from a ukiyo-e° print by Utamaro°

The light is the inside
sheen of an oyster shell,
sponged with talc and vapor,
moisture from a bath.

A pair of slippers
are placed outside
the rice-paper doors.
She kneels at a low table
in the room,
her legs folded beneath her
as she sits on a buckwheat pillow.

Her hair is black
with hints of red,
the color of seaweed
spread over rocks.

Morning begins the ritual
wheel of the body,
the application of translucent skins.
She practices pleasure:
the pressure of three fingertips
applying powder.
Fingerprints of pollen
some other hand will trace.

The peach-dyed kimono
patterned with maple leaves
drifting across the silk,
falls from right to left
in a diagonal, revealing
the nape of her neck
and the curve of a shoulder
like the slope of a hill
set deep in snow in a country
of huge white solemn birds.
Her face appears in the mirror,
a reflection in a winter pond,
rising to meet itself.

She dips a corner of her sleeve
like a brush into water
to wipe the mirror;
she is about to paint herself.
The eyes narrow
in a moment of self-scrutiny.
The mouth parts
as if desiring to disturb
the placid plum face;
break the symmetry of silence.
But the berry-stained lips,
stenciled into the mask of beauty,
do not speak.

Two chrysanthemums
touch in the middle of the lake
and drift apart.

Girl Powdering Her Neck (1790) by Kitagawa Utamaro.
Source: ©Erich Lessing/Art Resource, NY, ©Musee des Arts Asiatiques-Guimet, Paris, France

ukiyo-e: A type of Japanese woodblock print.
Utamaro: Kitagawa Utamaro (1754–1806), Japanese printmaker.

MAY SWENSON (1919–1989)

The Tall Figures of Giacometti° (1966)

We move by means of our mud bumps.
We bubble as do the dead but more slowly.

The products of excruciating purges
we are squeezed out thin hard and dry.

If we exude a stench it is petrified sainthood.
Our feet are large crude fused together

solid like anvils. Ugly as truth is ugly
we are meant to stand upright a long time

and shudder without motion
under the scintillating pins of light

that dart between our bodies
of pimpled mud and your eyes.

City Square (1948) by Alberto Giacometti.
Source: ©The Museum of Modern Art/Licensed by SCALA/Art Resource, NY

Giacometti: Alberto Giacometti (1901–1966), Swiss sculptor, painter, and printmaker.

KEVIN YOUNG (1970–)

The Fun Gallery° (2001)

A buzz in the air
already, Basquiat°
beaming. RAY GUN

set to stun—
—maximum—a hold
up in this hole

in the wall,
a billion
paintings pinned

to dry wall
like butterflies,
stomachs. He's made it

all from scratch
& paint.
The work's too low

his dealer warned—
everything should be higher
to keep up

your prices,
speed. All night
the crowds line

outside like Disneyland
& love it. Taken
over Manhattan

he's King
Kong or Mighty Joe
Young, social

climbing—gone
from trains
to scale the Empire

State. Keeping most
of the show
for hisself, hitches

a limo to Bklyn
by dawn—the armored
car hour—up

early—or late—
as if to his own
funeral—

"Papa I've made it"

hugs & hands
him a blooming
bouquet.

Untitled (1981) by Jean-Michel Basquiat.
Source: Banque d'Images, ADAGP/Art Resource, NY

Fun Gallery: Art gallery founded in New York City's East Village in 1981, which introduced graffiti as an art form to the mainstream art world.

Basquiat: Jean-Michel Basquiat (1960–1988) a graffiti and neo-Expressionist artist of Puerto Rican and Haitian heritage. He died of a drug overdose at age twenty-eight.

Reading and Reacting

1. What particular aspects of the work of art does the poet focus on? Which aspects does he or she ignore?
2. What purpose is the poet trying to achieve? For example, is he or she expressing emotion, offering an analysis, or attempting to shed light on a particular aspect of the art?
3. What insight into the art do you gain from reading the poem? Do you think the poet is missing anything?
4. Compare the poem to the artwork that inspired it. How are the two alike? How are they different?
5. What questions about the art does the poem raise?
6. Do you disagree with the speaker's interpretation of the work of art? With what do you disagree?

WRITING SUGGESTIONS: Poetry and Art

1. Look at one of the pieces of visual art that appears in this sampler. Then, write a poem about it. Before you write your poem, consider whether you want to try to describe the piece of visual art or whether you want to use it as inspiration for your own ideas. (You could, of course, do both.)
2. Write an essay in which you compare the poem you wrote to the one in the sampler that accompanies the work of visual art. What details about the piece of visual art did you choose to emphasize? What details does the poet emphasize? How do you account for the differences?
3. Select one of the poems in this sampler and write an **explication** (see Chapter 3).

I've been a victim:
 The Belgians cut off my hands in the Congo.
 They lynch me still in Mississippi.

I am a Negro:
 Black as the night is black,
 Black like the depths of my Africa.

Here the speaker, identifying himself as "a Negro," assumes each of the roles African-Americans have historically played in Western society—slave, worker, singer, and victim. By so doing, he gives voice to his ancestors who, by being forced to serve others, were deprived of their identities. By presenting not only their suffering but also their accomplishments, the speaker asserts his pride in being black. The speaker also implies that the suffering of black people has been caused by economic exploitation: Romans, Egyptians, Belgians, and Americans all used black labor to help build their societies. In this context, the speaker's implied warning is clear: except for the United States, all the societies that have exploited blacks have declined, and long after the fall of those empires, black people still endure.

In each of the preceding poems, the speaker is alone. The following poem, a **dramatic monologue,** presents a more complex situation in which the poet creates a complete dramatic scene. The speaker is developed as a character whose distinctive personality is revealed through his words as he addresses a silent listener.

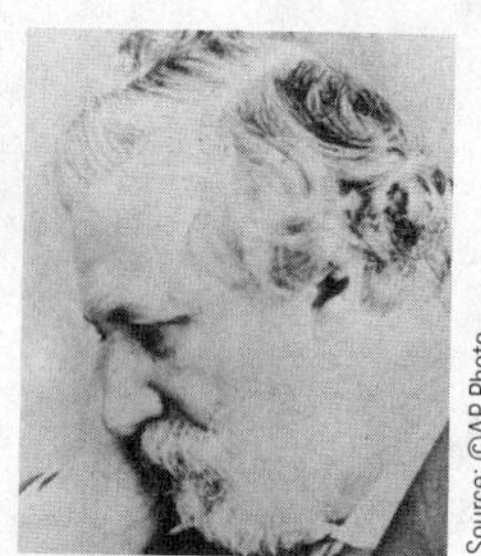
Source: ©AP Photo

See this poet's biography on p. 1219.

ROBERT BROWNING (1812–1889)

My Last Duchess (1842)

Ferrara

That's my last Duchess painted on the wall,
Looking as if she were alive. I call
That piece a wonder, now: Frà Pandolf's° hands
Worked busily a day, and there she stands.
Will't please you sit and look at her? I said
"Frà Pandolf" by design, for never read
Strangers like you that pictured countenance,
The depth and passion of its earnest glance,
But to myself they turned (since none puts by
The curtain I have drawn for you, but I)
And seemed as they would ask me, if they durst,
How such a glance came there; so, not the first
Are you to turn and ask thus. Sir, 'twas not
Her husband's presence only, called that spot
Of joy into the Duchess' cheek: perhaps

Frà Pandolf: "Brother" Pandolf, a fictive painter.

Frà Pandolf chanced to say "Her mantle laps
Over my lady's wrist too much," or "Paint
Must never hope to reproduce the faint
Half-flush that dies along her throat": such stuff
Was courtesy, she thought, and cause enough
For calling up that spot of joy. She had
A heart—how shall I say?—too soon made glad,
Too easily impressed; she liked whate'er
She looked on, and her looks went everywhere.
Sir, 'twas all one! My favor at her breast,
The dropping of the daylight in the West,
The bough of cherries some officious fool
Broke in the orchard for her, the white mule
She rode with round the terrace—all and each
Would draw from her alike the approving speech,
Or blush, at least. She thanked men—good! but thanked
Somehow—I know not how—as if she ranked
My gift of a nine-hundred-years-old name
With anybody's gift. Who'd stoop to blame
This sort of trifling? Even had you skill
In speech—(which I have not)—to make your will
Quite clear to such an one, and say, "Just this
Or that in you disgusts me; here you miss,
Or there exceed the mark"—and if she let
Herself be lessoned so, nor plainly set
Her wits to yours, forsooth, and made excuse
—E'en then would be some stooping; and I choose
Never to stoop. Oh sir, she smiled, no doubt,
Whene'er I passed her; but who passed without
Much the same smile? This grew; I gave commands;
Then all smiles stopped together. There she stands
As if alive. Will't please you rise? We'll meet
The company below, then. I repeat,
The Count your master's known munificence
Is ample warrant that no just pretense
Of mine for dowry will be disallowed;
Though his fair daughter's self, as I avowed
At starting, is my object. Nay, we'll go
Together down, sir. Notice Neptune,° though,
Taming a sea horse, thought a rarity,
Which Claus of Innsbruck° cast in bronze for me!

Neptune: In Roman mythology, the god of the sea.

Claus of Innsbruck: A fictive—or unidentified—sculptor. The count of Tyrol's capital was at Innsbrück, Austria.

The speaker is probably Alfonso II, duke of Ferrara, Italy, whose young wife, Lucrezia, died in 1561 after only three years of marriage. Shortly after her death, the duke began negotiations to marry again. When the poem opens, the duke is showing a portrait of his late wife to an emissary of an unnamed count who is there to arrange a marriage between the duke and the count's daughter. The duke remarks that the artist, Frà Pandolf, has caught a certain look on the duchess's face. This look aroused the jealousy of the duke, who thought that it should have been for him alone. Eventually, the duke could tolerate the situation no longer; he "gave commands," and "all smiles stopped together."

Though silent, the listener plays a subtle but important role in the poem: his presence establishes the dramatic situation that allows the character of the duke to be revealed. The purpose of the story is to communicate to the emissary exactly what the duke expects from his prospective bride and from her father. As he speaks, the duke provides only the information that he wants the emissary to take back to his master, the count. Although the duke appears vain and superficial, he is actually extraordinarily shrewd. Throughout the poem, he turns the conversation to his own ends and gains the advantage through flattery and false modesty. The success of the poem lies in the poet's ability to develop the voice of this complex character, who embodies both superficial elegance and shocking cruelty.

FURTHER READING: The Speaker in the Poem

LESLIE MARMON SILKO (1948–)

Where Mountain Lion Lay Down with Deer (1973)

I climb the black rock mountain
    stepping from day to day
                silently.
I smell the wind for my ancestors
    pale blue leaves
    crushed wild mountain smell.
Returning
  up the gray stone cliff
  where I descended
        a thousand years ago.
Returning to faded black stone.
  where mountain lion lay down with deer.
It is better to stay up here
                watching wind's reflection
                in tall yellow flowers.
The old ones who remember me are gone
      the old songs are all forgotten
and the story of my birth.

How I danced in snow-frost moonlight
distant stars to the end of the Earth,
How I swam away
in freezing mountain water
narrow mossy canyon tumbling down
out of the mountain
out of the deep canyon stone
down
the memory
spilling out
into the world.

Reading and Reacting

1. Who is speaking in line 4? In line 9? Can you explain this shift?
2. From where is the speaker returning? What is she trying to recover?
3. **Journal Entry** Is it important for you to know that the poet is Native American? How does this information affect your interpretation of the poem?
4. **Critical Perspective** In her 1983 essay "Answering the Deer," poet and critic Paula Gunn Allen observes that the possibility of cultural extinction is a reality Native Americans must face. Native American women writers, says Allen, face this fact directly but with a kind of hope:

> The sense of hope . . . comes about when one has faced ultimate disaster time and time again over the ages and has emerged . . . stronger and more certain of the endurance of the people, the spirits, and the land from which they both arise and which informs both with life. Transformation, or more directly, metamorphosis, is the oldest tribal ceremonial theme. . . . And it comes once again into use within American Indian poetry of extinction and regeneration that is ultimately the only poetry any contemporary Indian woman can write.

Does Silko's poem address the issue of cultural extinction and the possibility of regeneration or metamorphosis? How?

Related Works: "This Is What It Means to Say Phoenix, Arizona" (p. 322) "Two Kinds" (p. 777), "How to Write the Great American Indian Novel" (p. 871), "Immigrants" (p. 1006), "My Father's Song" (p. 1044), "Nikki-Rosa" (p. 1161), *Trying to Find Chinatown* (p. 1856)

Source: ©AP Photo/David Pau Morris

JANICE MIRIKITANI (1942–)

Suicide Note (1987)

. . . An Asian-American college student was reported to have jumped to her death from her dormitory window. Her body was found two days later under a deep cover of snow. Her suicide note contained an apology to her parents for having received less than a perfect four point grade average. . . .

How many notes written . . .
ink smeared like birdprints in snow.

not good enough   not pretty enough   not smart enough
dear mother and father.
I apologize
for disappointing you.
I've worked very hard,
not good enough
harder, perhaps to please you.
If only I were a son, shoulders broad
as the sunset threading through pine,
I would see the light in my mother's
eyes, or the golden pride reflected
in my father's dream
of my wide, male hands worthy of work
and comfort.
I would swagger through life
muscled and bold and assured,
drawing praises to me
like currents in the bed of wind, virile
with confidence.
not good enough   not strong enough   not good enough

I apologize.
Tasks do not come easily.
Each failure, a glacier.
Each disapproval, a bootprint.
Each disappointment,
ice above my river.
So I have worked hard.
not good enough
My sacrifice I will drop
bone by bone, perched
on the ledge of my womanhood,
fragile as wings.
not strong enough
It is snowing steadily
surely not good weather
for flying—this sparrow
sillied and dizzied by the wind
on the edge.
not smart enough
I make this ledge my altar
to offer penance.
This air will not hold me,
the snow burdens my crippled wings,
my tears drop like bitter cloth
softly into the gutter below.

not good enough not strong enough not smart enough
Choices thin as shaved
ice. Notes shredded
drift like snow
on my broken body,
cover me like whispers
of sorries
sorries.
Perhaps when they find me
they will bury
my bird bones beneath
a sturdy pine
and scatter my feathers like
unspoken song
over this white and cold and silent
breast of earth.

Reading and Reacting

1. This poem is a suicide note that contains an apology. Why does the speaker feel she must apologize? Do you agree that she needs to apologize?
2. What attitude does the speaker convey toward her parents?
3. **Journal Entry** Is the college student who speaks in this poem a stranger to you, or is her voice in any way like that of students you know?

Related Works: "Eye Ball" (p. 258), "The Rocking-Horse Winner" (p. 589), "Teenage Wasteland" (p. 785), "The Value of Education" (p. 892), "Dreams of Suicide" (p. 1025), "Death Be Not Proud" (p. 1148), *The Cuban Swimmer* (p. 1732)

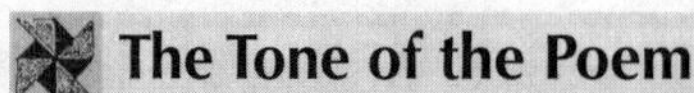

The Tone of the Poem

The **tone** of a poem conveys the speaker's attitude toward his or her subject or audience. In speech, this attitude can be conveyed easily: stressing a word in a sentence can modify or color a statement. For example, the statement "Of course, you would want to go to that restaurant" is quite straightforward, but changing the emphasis to "Of course *you* would want to go to *that* restaurant" transforms a neutral statement into a sarcastic one. For poets, however, conveying a particular tone to readers poses a challenge because readers rarely hear poets' spoken voices. Instead, poets indicate tone by using rhyme, meter, word choice, sentence structure, figures of speech, and imagery.

The range of possible tones is wide. For example, a poem's speaker may be joyful, sad, playful, serious, comic, intimate, formal, relaxed, condescending, or ironic. In the following poem, notice how the tone conveys the speaker's attitude toward his subject.

ROBERT FROST (1874–1963)

Fire and Ice (1923)

Some say the world will end in fire,
Some say in ice.
From what I've tasted of desire
I hold with those who favor fire.
But if it had to perish twice,
I think I know enough of hate
To say that for destruction ice
Is also great
And would suffice.

Here the speaker uses word choice, rhyme, and especially **understatement** to comment on the human condition. The conciseness as well as the simple, regular meter and rhyme suggest an **epigram**—a short poem that makes a pointed comment in an unusually clear, and often witty, manner. This pointedness is consistent with the speaker's glib, unemotional tone, as is the last line's wry understatement that ice "would suffice." The contrast between the poem's serious message—that hatred and indifference are equally destructive—and its informal style and offhand tone complement the speaker's detached, almost smug, posture.

Sometimes shifts in tone reveal changes in the speaker's attitude. In the next poem, subtle shifts in tone reveal a change in the speaker's attitude toward war.

Source: ©Underwood And Underwood/Time & Life Pictures/Getty Images

See this poet's biography on p. 1222.

THOMAS HARDY (1840–1928)

The Man He Killed (1902)

"Had he and I but met
By some old ancient inn,
We should have sat us down to wet
Right many a nipperkin!°

"But ranged as infantry,
And staring face to face,
I shot at him as he at me,
And killed him in his place.

"I shot him dead because—
Because he was my foe,
Just so: my foe of course he was;
That's clear enough; although

---

nipperkin: A small container of liquor.

"He thought he'd 'list,° perhaps,
Off-hand-like—just as I—
Was out of work—had sold his traps—
No other reason why.

"Yes; quaint and curious war is!
You shoot a fellow down
You'd treat if met where any bar is,
Or help to half-a crown."

The speaker in this poem is a soldier relating a wartime experience. Quotation marks indicate that he is engaged in conversation—perhaps in a pub—and his dialect indicates that he is a member of the English working class. For him, at least at first, the object of war is simple: kill or be killed. To Hardy, this speaker represents all men who are thrust into a war without understanding its underlying social, economic, or ideological causes. In this sense, the speaker and his enemy are both victims of forces beyond their comprehension or control.

The tone of "The Man He Killed" changes as the speaker tells his story. In the first two stanzas, sentences are smooth and unbroken, establishing the speaker's matter-of-fact tone and reflecting his confidence that he has done what he had to do. In the third and fourth stanzas, broken syntax reflects the narrator's increasingly disturbed state of mind as he tells about the man he killed. The poem's singsong meter and regular rhyme scheme *(met/wet, inn/nipperkin)* suggest that the speaker is struggling to maintain his composure; the smooth sentence structure of the last stanza and the use of a cliché ("Yes; quaint and curious war is!") indicate that the speaker is trying to trivialize an incident that has seriously traumatized him.

Sometimes a poem's tone can establish an ironic contrast between the speaker and his or her subject. The speaker's abrupt change of tone at the end of the next poem establishes such a contrast.

AMY LOWELL (1874–1925)

Patterns (1915)

I walk down the garden-paths,
And all the daffodils
Are blowing, and the bright blue squills.
I walk down the patterned garden-paths
In my stiff, brocaded gown.
With my powdered hair and jewelled fan,

'*list:* Enlist.

I too am a rare
Pattern. As I wander down
The garden-paths.

My dress is richly figured,
And the train
Makes a pink and silver stain
On the gravel, and the thrift
Of the borders.
Just a plate of current fashion
Tripping by in high-heeled, ribboned shoes.
Not a softness anywhere about me,
Only whalebone° and brocade.
And I sink on a seat in the shade
Of a lime tree. For my passion
Wars against the stiff brocade.
The daffodils and squills
Flutter in the breeze
As they please.
And I weep;
For the lime-tree is in blossom
And one small flower has dropped upon my bosom.

And the plashing of waterdrops
In the marble fountain
Comes down the garden-paths.
The dripping never stops.
Underneath my stiffened gown
Is the softness of a woman bathing in a marble basin,
A basin in the midst of hedges grown
So thick, she cannot see her lover hiding,
But she guesses he is near,
And the sliding of the water
Seems the stroking of a dear
Hand upon her.
What is Summer in a fine brocaded gown!
I should like to see it lying in a heap upon the ground.
All the pink and silver crumpled up on the ground.

I would be the pink and silver as I ran along the paths,
And he would stumble after,
Bewildered by my laughter.

whalebone: The type of bone used to stiffen corsets.

I should see the sun flashing from his sword-hilt and buckles
on his shoes.
I would choose
To lead him in a maze along the patterned paths,
A bright and laughing maze for my heavy-booted lover.
Till he caught me in the shade,
And the buttons of his waistcoat bruised my body as
he clasped me,
Aching, melting, unafraid.
With the shadows of the leaves and the sundrops,
And the plopping of the waterdrops,
All about us in the open afternoon—
I am very like to swoon
With the weight of this brocade,
For the sun sifts through the shade.

Underneath the fallen blossom
In my bosom,
Is a letter I have hid.
It was brought to me this morning by a rider from the Duke.
Madam, we regret to inform you that Lord Hartwell
Died in action Thursday se'nnight.°
As I read it in the white, morning sunlight,
The letters squirmed like snakes.
"Any answer, Madam," said my footman.
"No," I told him.
"See that the messenger takes some refreshment.
No, no answer."
And I walked into the garden,
Up and down the patterned paths,
In my stiff, correct brocade.
The blue and yellow flowers stood up proudly in the sun,
Each one.
I stood upright too,
Held rigid to the pattern
By the stiffness of my gown.
Up and down I walked.
Up and down.

In a month he would have been my husband.
In a month, here, underneath this lime,
We would have broken the pattern;
He for me, and I for him,

se'nnight: "Seven night," or a week ago Thursday.

He as Colonel, I as Lady,
On this shady seat.
He had a whim
That sunlight carried blessing.
And I answered, "It shall be as you have said."
Now he is dead.

In Summer and in Winter I shall walk
Up and down
The patterned garden-paths
In my stiff, brocaded gown.
The squills and daffodils
Will give place to pillared roses, and to asters, and to snow.
I shall go
Up and down,
In my gown.
Gorgeously arrayed,
Boned and stayed.
And the softness of my body will be guarded from embrace
By each button, hook, and lace.
For the man who should loose me is dead,
Fighting with the Duke in Flanders,°
In a pattern called a war.
Christ! What are patterns for?

The speaker begins by describing herself walking down garden paths. She wears a stiff brocaded gown, has powdered hair, and carries a jeweled fan. By her own admission, she is "a plate of current fashion." Although her tone is controlled, she is preoccupied by sensual thoughts. Beneath her "stiffened gown / Is the softness of a woman bathing in a marble basin," and the "sliding of the water" in a fountain reminds the speaker of the stroking of her lover's hand. She imagines herself shedding her brocaded gown and running with her lover along the maze of "patterned paths." The sensuality of the speaker's thoughts stands in ironic contrast to the images of stiffness and control that dominate the poem: her passion "Wars against the stiff brocade." She is also full of repressed rage. She knows that her lover has been killed, and she realizes the meaninglessness of the patterns of her life, patterns to which she has conformed, just as her lover conformed by going to war. Throughout the poem, the speaker's tone reflects her barely contained anger and frustration. In the last line, when she finally lets out her rage, the poem's point about the senselessness of conformity and war becomes apparent.

Flanders: A region in northwestern Europe, including part of northern France and western Belgium. Flanders was a site of fighting during World War I.

Source: ©Jerry Bauer

See this poet's biography on p. 1231.

FURTHER READING: The Tone of the Poem

ADAM ZAGAJEWSKI (1945–)

Try to Praise the Mutilated World (2001)

Translated from the Polish by Clare Cavanagh

Try to praise the mutilated world.
Remember June's long days,
and wild strawberries, drops of wine, the dew.
The nettles that methodically overgrow
the abandoned homesteads of exiles.
You must praise the mutilated world.
You watched the stylish yachts and ships;
one of them had a long trip ahead of it,
while salty oblivion awaited others.
You've seen the refugees heading nowhere,
you've heard the executioners sing joyfully.
You should praise the mutilated world.
Remember the moments when we were together
in a white room and the curtain fluttered.
Return in thought to the concert where music flared.
You gathered acorns in the park in autumn
and leaves eddied over the earth's scars.
Praise the mutilated world
and the gray feather a thrush lost,
and the gentle light that strays and vanishes
and returns.

Reading and Reacting

1. Who is the speaker? Whom is he addressing?
2. In line 1, the speaker says, "Try to praise . . ."; in line 6, he says, "You must praise . . ."; in line 12, he says, "You should praise . . ."; and in line 18, he says, "Praise . . . ." What is the significance, if any, of these changes in phrasing?
3. What is the mood of the speaker? Do you think he is optimistic or pessimistic?
4. **JOURNAL ENTRY** Though written earlier, this poem was printed in the issue of the *New Yorker* magazine that appeared immediately after the World Trade Center towers were destroyed by terrorists on September 11, 2001. Why do you think the editors chose to reprint the poem at that time?
5. **CRITICAL PERSPECTIVE** The critic and poet Adam Kirsch, writing in the *New Republic*, characterizes Adam Zagajewski as a mystical poet who looks for meaning in ordinary things and situations:

> Like Rilke, Zagajewski is overcome at times by a powerful sense that the singular being of objects conceals some higher truth. For him, too, things are the sites of illumination.

What "higher truth" do the objects in "Try to Praise the Mutilated World" conceal? What do you think is the underlying message of this poem?

Related Works: "Cathedral" (p. 526), "Hope" (p. 863), "Nothing Gold Can Stay" (p. 914), "For the Union Dead" (p. 1063), "The Second Coming" (p. 1215), *Nine Ten* (p. 1314)

WILLIAM WORDSWORTH (1770–1850)

The World Is Too Much with Us (1807)

The world is too much with us; late and soon,
Getting and spending, we lay waste our powers;
Little we see in Nature that is ours;
We have given our hearts away, a sordid boon!
This Sea that bares her bosom to the moon;
The winds that will be howling at all hours,
And are up-gathered now like sleeping flowers;
For this, for everything, we are out of tune;
It moves us not. Great God! I'd rather be
A Pagan suckled in a creed outworn;
So might I, standing on this pleasant lea,
Have glimpses that would make me less forlorn;
Have sight of Proteus° rising from the sea;
Or hear old Triton° blow his wreathèd horn.

Reading and Reacting

1. What is the speaker's attitude toward the contemporary world? How is this attitude revealed through the poem's tone?
2. This poem is a **sonnet,** a highly structured traditional form. How do the regular meter and rhyme scheme help to establish the poem's tone?
3. **JOURNAL ENTRY** Imagine you are a modern-day environmentalist, labor organizer, or corporate executive. Write a response to the sentiments expressed in this poem.
4. **CRITICAL PERSPECTIVE** In his 1972 essay "Two Roads to Wordsworth," M. H. Abrams notes that critics have tended to view Wordsworth in one of two ways:

> One Wordsworth is simple, elemental, forthright, the other is complex, paradoxical, problematic; one is an affirmative poet of life, love, and joy, the other is an equivocal or self-divided poet whose affirmations are implicitly qualified . . . by a pervasive sense of morality and an ever-incipient despair of life; . . . one is the Wordsworth of light, the other the Wordsworth of [shadow], or even darkness.

Proteus: Sometimes said to be Poseidon's son, this Greek sea-god had the ability to change shape at will and to tell the future.

Triton: The trumpeter of the sea, this sea-god is usually pictured blowing on a conch shell. Triton was the son of Poseidon, ruler of the sea.

Does your reading of "The World Is Too Much with Us" support one of these versions of Wordsworth over the other? Which one? Why?

Related Works: "New York Day Women" (p. 406), "The Rocking-Horse Winner" (p. 589), "Dover Beach" (p. 1123), "She dwelt among the untrodden ways" (p. 1211), "The Lake Isle of Innisfree" (p. 1213)

SYLVIA PLATH (1932–1963)

Morning Song (1962)

Love set you going like a fat gold watch.
The midwife slapped your footsoles, and your bald cry
Took its place among the elements.

Our voices echo, magnifying your arrival. New statue.
In a drafty museum, your nakedness
Shadows our safety. We stand round blankly as walls.

I'm no more your mother
Than the cloud that distills a mirror to reflect its own slow
Effacement at the wind's hand.

All night your moth-breath
Flickers among the flat pink roses. I wake to listen:
A far sea moves in my ear.

One cry, and I stumble from bed, cow-heavy and floral
In my Victorian nightgown.
Your mouth opens clean as a cat's. The window square
Whitens and swallows its dull stars. And now you try
Your handful of notes;
The clear vowels rise like balloons.

Reading and Reacting

1. Who is the speaker? To whom is she speaking? What does the poem reveal about her?
2. What is the poem's subject? What attitudes about this subject do you suppose the poet expects her readers to have?
3. How is the tone of the first stanza different from that of the third? How does the tone of each stanza reflect its content?
4. **JOURNAL ENTRY** In what sense does this poem reinforce traditional ideas about motherhood? How does it challenge them?
5. **CRITICAL PERSPECTIVE** Sylvia Plath's life, which ended in suicide, was marked by emotional turbulence and instability. As Anne Stevenson observes in *Bitter Fame*, her 1988 biography of Plath, in the weeks immediately preceding the composition of "Morning Song" a fit of rage over her husband's supposed infidelity caused Plath to destroy many of his books and

poetic works in progress. Then, only a few days later, she suffered a miscarriage. According to Stevenson, "Morning Song" is about sleepless nights and surely reflects Plath's depression. However, in a 1991 biography, *Rough Magic*, Paul Alexander says, "Beautiful, simple, touching, 'Morning Song' was Plath's—then—definitive statement of motherhood."

Which biographer's assessment of the poem do you think makes more sense? Why?

Related Works: "The Yellow Wallpaper" (p. 459), "Daddy" (p. 936), "My Son, My Executioner" (p. 945), "Those Winter Sundays" (p. 1040), "The courage that my mother had" (p. 1042), *Proof* (p. 1476)

Source: ©The Granger Collection, New York

See this poet's biography on p. 1224.

CLAUDE MCKAY (1890–1948)

The White City (1922)

I will not toy with it nor bend an inch.
Deep in the secret chambers of my heart
I muse my life-long hate, and without flinch
I bear it nobly as I live my part.
My being would be a skeleton, a shell,
If this dark Passion that fills my every mood,
And makes my heaven in the white world's hell,
Did not forever feed me vital blood.
I see the mighty city through a mist—
The strident trains that speed the goaded mass,
The poles and spires and towers vapor-kissed,
The fortressed port through which the great ships pass,
The tides, the wharves, the dens I contemplate,
Are sweet like wanton loves because I hate.

Reading and Reacting

1. How would you characterize the tone of this sonnet?
2. How is the speaker's description of the city in the third stanza consistent with the emotions he expresses in lines 1–8?
3. The closing couplet of a Shakespearean sonnet traditionally sums up the poem's concerns. Is this the case here? Explain.
4. **Journal Entry** What possible meanings does the phrase "the white world's hell" (line 7) have? How does it express the poem's central theme?
5. **Critical Perspective** According to Cary Nelson in *Modern American Poetry*, "'The White City' is not an attack on white people but rather a critique of race-based economic and political power." Which parts of the poem support this assessment? Which do not?

Related Works: "Deportation at Breakfast" (p. 229), "Battle Royal" (p. 332), "Saboteur" (p. 712), "The Man He Killed" (p. 849), "For Malcolm, a Year After" (p. 964), "Dinner Guest: Me" (p. 1088), "If We Must Die" (p. 1179)

ROBERT HERRICK (1591–1674)

To the Virgins, to Make Much of Time (1646)

Gather ye rosebuds while ye may,
Old Time is still a-flying;
And this same flower that smiles today,
Tomorrow will be dying.

The glorious lamp of heaven, the sun,
The higher he's a-getting,
The sooner will his race be run,
And nearer he's to setting.

That age is best which is the first,
When youth and blood are warmer;
But being spent, the worse, and worst
Times still succeed the former.

Then be not coy, but use your time,
And while ye may, go marry;
For having lost but once your prime,
You may forever tarry.

Reading and Reacting

1. How would you characterize the speaker? Do you think he expects his listeners to share his views? How might his expectations affect his tone?
2. This poem is developed like an argument. What is the speaker's main point? How does he support it?
3. What effect does the poem's use of rhyme have on its tone?
4. **JOURNAL ENTRY** Whose side are you on—the speaker's or those he addresses?

Related Works: "Jinx" (p. 178), "The Girl with Bangs" (p. 271), "Greasy Lake" (p. 687), "Cinderella" (p. 866), "Love Is Just Complicated" (p. 1060), "The Passionate Shepherd to His Love" (p. 1179), *The Brute* (p. 1250)

DEBORAH GARRISON (1965–)

Please Fire Me (1998)

Here comes another alpha male,
and all the other alphas
are snorting and pawing,
kicking up puffs of acrid dust
while the silly little hens
clatter back and forth

on quivering claws and raise
a titter about the fuss.

Here comes another alpha male—
a man's man, a dealmaker,
holds tanks of liquor,
charms them pantsless at lunch:
I've never been sicker.
Do I have to stare into his eyes
and sympathize? If I want my job
I do. Well I think I'm through

with the working world,
through with warming eggs
and being Zenlike in my detachment
from all things Ego.

I'd like to go
somewhere else entirely,
and I don't mean
Europe.

Reading and Reacting

1. Who are the "alpha males" in the poem? Who are the "silly little hens" (line 5)?
2. What does the speaker's choice of animal reveal about her attitude toward her situation? What does it reveal about her?
3. In the last stanza, the speaker says that she would like to "go / somewhere else" (lines 21–22). Where do you suppose she wants to go?
4. **Journal Entry** Why do you think the speaker wants to be fired? Why doesn't she simply quit?
5. **Critical Perspective** About her own poetry, Deborah Garrison has said, "I need to feel that the language in my poems is alive in the sense of talking on the phone to a friend, sharing gossip."
   In what sense do you think "Please Fire Me" is like "sharing gossip"?

Related Works: "A&P" (p. 259), "Shiloh" (p. 735), "Cinderella" (p. 866), "Sears Life" (p. 891), "The secretary chant" (p. 932), "Barbie doll" (p. 1187), *Beauty* (p. 1270), *Proof* (p. 1476)

Irony

Just as in fiction and drama, **irony** occurs in poetry when a discrepancy exists between two levels of meaning or experience. Consider the tone of the following lines by Stephen Crane:

Do not weep, maiden, for war is kind.
Because your lover threw wild hands toward the sky
And the afrightened steed ran on alone,
Do not weep.
War is kind.

Surely the speaker in this poem does not intend his words to be taken literally. How can war be "kind"? Isn't war exactly the opposite of "kind"? By making this ironic statement, the speaker actually conveys the opposite idea: war is a cruel, mindless exercise of violence.

Skillfully used, irony enables a poet to make a pointed comment about a situation or to manipulate a reader's emotions. Implicit in irony is the writer's assumption that readers will not be misled by the literal meaning of a statement. In order for irony to work, readers must recognize the disparity between what is said and what is meant, or between what a speaker thinks is occurring and what readers know to be occurring.

One kind of irony that appears in poetry is **dramatic irony,** which occurs when a speaker believes one thing and readers realize something else. In the following poem, the poet uses a deranged speaker to tell a story that is filled with irony.

ROBERT BROWNING (1812–1889)

Porphyria's Lover (1836)

The rain set early in to-night,
    The sullen wind was soon awake,
It tore the elm-tops down for spite,
    And did its worst to vex the lake:
    I listened with heart fit to break.
When glided in Porphyria; straight
    She shut the cold out and the storm,
And kneeled and made the cheerless grate
    Blaze up, and all the cottage warm;
    Which done, she rose, and from her form
Withdrew the dripping cloak and shawl,
    And laid her soiled gloves by, untied
Her hat and let the damp hair fall,
    And, last, she sat down by my side
    And called me. When no voice replied,
She put my arm about her waist,
    And made her smooth white shoulder bare,
And all her yellow hair displaced,
    And, stooping, made my cheek lie there,
    And spread, o'er all, her yellow hair,
Murmuring how she loved me—she
    Too weak, for all her heart's endeavour,
To set its struggling passion free
    From pride, and vainer ties dissever,
    And give herself to me for ever.
But passion sometimes would prevail,
    Nor could to-night's gay feast restrain
A sudden thought of one so pale

For love of her, and all in vain:
So, she was come through wind and rain.
Be sure I looked up at her eyes
Happy and proud; at last I knew
Porphyria worshipped me; surprise
Made my heart swell, and still it grew
While I debated what to do.
That moment she was mine, mine, fair,
Perfectly pure and good: I found
A thing to do, and all her hair
In one long yellow string I wound
Three times her little throat around,
And strangled her. No pain felt she;
I am quite sure she felt no pain.
As a shut bud that holds a bee,
I warily oped her lids: again
Laughed the blue eyes without a stain.
And I untightened next the tress
About her neck; her cheek once more
Blushed bright beneath my burning kiss:
I propped her head up as before,
Only, this time my shoulder bore
Her head, which droops upon it still:
The smiling rosy little head,
So glad it has its utmost will,
That all it scorned at once is fled,
And I, its love, am gained instead!
Porphyria's love: she guessed not how
Her darling one wish would be heard.
And thus we sit together now,
And all night long we have not stirred,
And yet God has not said a word!

Like Browning's "My Last Duchess" (p. 843), this poem is a **dramatic monologue,** a poem that assumes an implied listener as well as a speaker. The speaker recounts his story in a straightforward manner, seemingly unaware of the horror of his tale. In fact, much of the effect of this poem comes from the speaker's telling his tale of murder in a flat, unemotional tone — and from readers' gradual realization that the speaker is mad.

The irony of the poem, as well as its title, becomes apparent as the monologue progresses. At first, the speaker fears that Porphyria is too weak to free herself from pride and vanity to love him. As he looks into her eyes, however, he comes to believe that she worships him. The moment the speaker realizes that Porphyria loves him, he feels compelled to kill her and keep her his forever. According to him, she is at this point "mine, mine, fair, / Perfectly pure and good," and he believes that by murdering her, he actually fulfills "Her darling one wish" — to stay with him forever. As he attempts to justify his actions, the speaker reveals himself to be a deluded psychopathic killer.

Another kind of irony is **situational irony,** which occurs when the situation itself contradicts readers' expectations. For example, in "Porphyria's Lover" the meeting of two lovers ironically results not in joy and passion but in murder.

In the next poem, the situation also creates irony.

Source: ©The Granger Collection, New York

See this poet's biography on p. 1228.

PERCY BYSSHE SHELLEY (1792–1822)

Ozymandias° (1818)

I met a traveler from an antique land
Who said: Two vast and trunkless legs of stone
Stand in the desert. Near them, on the sand,
Half sunk, a shattered visage lies, whose frown,
And wrinkled lip, and sneer of cold command,
Tell that its sculptor well those passions read
Which yet survive, stamped on these lifeless things,
The hand that mocked them, and the heart that fed;
And on the pedestal these words appear:
"My name is Ozymandias, king of kings:
Look on my works, ye Mighty, and despair!"
Nothing beside remains. Round the decay
Of that colossal wreck, boundless and bare
The lone and level sands stretch far away.

Source: ©Bildagentur-online/McPhoto/Alamy

The speaker recounts a tale about a colossal statue that lies shattered in the desert. Its head lies separated from the trunk, and the face has a wrinkled lip and a "sneer of cold command." On the pedestal of the monument are words exhorting all those who pass: "Look on my works, ye Mighty, and despair!" The situational irony of the poem has its source in the contrast between the "colossal wreck" and the boastful inscription on its base: Ozymandias is a monument to the vanity of those who mistakenly think they can withstand the ravages of time.

Perhaps the most common kind of irony found in poetry is **verbal irony,** which is created when words say one thing but mean another, often exactly the opposite. When verbal irony is particularly biting, it is called **sarcasm**—for example, Stephen Crane's use of the word *kind* in his antiwar poem "War Is Kind." In speech, verbal irony is easy to detect through the speaker's change in tone or emphasis. In writing, when these signals are absent, verbal irony becomes more difficult to convey. Poets must depend on the context of a remark or on the contrast between a word and other images in the poem to create irony.

Consider how verbal irony is communicated in the following poem.

Ozymandias: The Greek name for Ramses II, ruler of Egypt in the thirteenth century B.C.

ARIEL DORFMAN (1942–)

Hope (1988)

Translated by Edith Grossman with the author

My son has been
missing
since May 8
of last year.

They took him
just for a few hours
they said
just for some routine
questioning.

After the car left,
the car with no license plate,
we couldn't

find out

anything else
about him.
But now things have changed.
We heard from a compañero
who just got out
that five months later
they were torturing him
in Villa Grimaldi,
at the end of September
they were questioning him
in the red house
that belonged to the Grimaldis.

They say they recognized
his voice his screams
they say.

Somebody tell me frankly
what times are these
what kind of world
what country?
What I'm asking is
how can it be
that a father's
joy
a mother's
joy

is knowing
that they
that they are still
torturing
their son?
Which means
that he was alive
five months later
and our greatest
hope
will be to find out
next year
that they're still torturing him
eight months later

and he may   might   could
still be alive.

Although it is not necessary to know the background of the poet to appreciate this poem, it does help to know that Ariel Dorfman is a native of Chile. After the assassination of Salvador Allende, Chile's elected socialist president, in September 1973, the civilian government was replaced by a military dictatorship. Civil rights were suspended, and activists, students, and members of opposition parties were arrested. Many were detained indefinitely; some simply disappeared. The irony of this poem originates in the discrepancy between what the word *hope* comes to mean in the poem and what it usually means. For most people, *hope* has positive connotations. For the speaker, however, *hope* means that his son is still being tortured eight months after his arrest. Thus, *hope* takes on a different meaning, and this irony is not lost on the speaker.

FURTHER READING: Irony

W. H. AUDEN (1907–1973)

The Unknown Citizen (1939)

(To JS/07/M/378 This Marble Monument Is Erected by the State)

He was found by the Bureau of Statistics to be
One against whom there was no official complaint,
And all the reports on his conduct agree
That, in the modern sense of an old-fashioned word, he was a saint,
For in everything he did he served the Greater Community.
Except for the War till the day he retired
He worked in a factory and never got fired,
But satisfied his employers, Fudge Motors Inc.

Yet he wasn't a scab or odd in his views,
For his Union reports that he paid his dues,
(Our report on his Union shows it was sound)
And our Social Psychology workers found
That he was popular with his mates and liked a drink.
The Press are convinced that he bought a paper every day
And that his reactions to advertisements were normal
in every way.
Policies taken out in his name prove that he was fully insured,
And his Health-card shows he was once in hospital but left it cured.
Both Producers Research and High-Grade Living declare
He was fully sensible to the advantages of the Installment Plan
And had everything necessary to the Modern Man,
A phonograph, a radio, a car and a frigidaire.
Our researchers into Public Opinion are content
That he held the proper opinions for the time of year;
When there was peace, he was for peace; when there was war,
he went.
He was married and added five children to the population,
Which our Eugenist° says was the right number for a parent of his
generation,
And our teachers report that he never interfered with their
education.
Was he free? Was he happy? The question is absurd:
Had anything been wrong, we should certainly have heard.

Reading and Reacting

1. The "unknown citizen" represents all modern citizens, who, according to the poem, are programmed like machines. How does the title help to establish the tone of the poem? How does the inscription on the monument also help to establish the tone?
2. Who is the speaker? What is his attitude toward the unknown citizen? How can you tell?
3. What kinds of irony are present in the poem? Identify several examples.
4. **JOURNAL ENTRY** This poem was written in 1939. Does its message apply to contemporary society, or does the poem seem dated?
5. **CRITICAL PERSPECTIVE** In 1939, the year this poem was published, Auden argued in his essay "The Public vs. The Late Mr. William Butler Yeats" that poetry can never really change anything. He reiterated this point as late as 1971 in his biographical *A Certain World:*

> By all means let a poet, if he wants to, write poems . . . that protest against this or that political evil or social injustice. But let him remember this. The only person who will benefit from them is himself; they will enhance his literary reputation among those who feel as he does. The evil or injustice, however, will remain exactly what it would have been if he had kept his mouth shut.

Eugenist: A person who studies eugenics, the science of human improvement through genetic manipulation.

Do you believe that poetry—or any kind of literature—has the power to combat "evil or injustice" in the world? Do you consider "The Unknown Citizen" a political poem? How might this poem effect positive social or political change?

Related Works: "A&P" (p. 259), "New York Day Women" (p. 406), "The Man He Killed" (p. 849), "Please Fire Me" (p. 858), "next to of course god america i" (p. 1141), "The Love Song of J. Alfred Prufrock" (p. 1151), *A Doll House* (p. 1402), *The Glass Menagerie* (p. 1961)

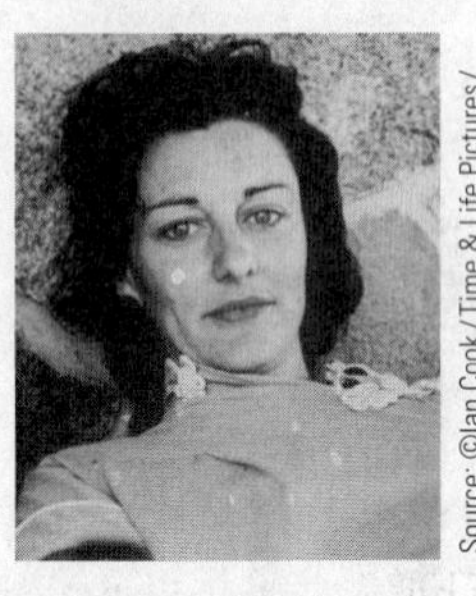
Source: ©Ian Cook/Time & Life Pictures/ Getty Images

ANNE SEXTON (1928–1974)

Cinderella (1970)

You always read about it:
the plumber with twelve children
who wins the Irish Sweepstakes.
From toilets to riches.
That story.

Or the nursemaid,
some luscious sweet from Denmark
who captures the oldest son's heart.
From diapers to Dior.°
That story.

Or a milkman who serves the wealthy,
eggs, cream, butter, yogurt, milk,
the white truck like an ambulance
who goes into real estate
and makes a pile.
From homogenized to martinis at lunch.

Or the charwoman
who is on the bus when it cracks up
and collects enough from the insurance.
From mops to Bonwit Teller.°
That story.

Once
the wife of a rich man was on her deathbed
and she said to her daughter Cinderella:
Be devout. Be good. Then I will smile

Dior: The fashion designer Christian Dior.

Bonwit Teller: An exclusive department store.

down from heaven in the seam of a cloud.
The man took another wife who had
two daughters, pretty enough
but with hearts like blackjacks.
Cinderella was their maid.
She slept on the sooty hearth each night
and walked around looking like Al Jolson.°
Her father brought presents home from town,
jewels and gowns for the other women
but the twig of a tree for Cinderella.
She planted that twig on her mother's grave
and it grew to a tree where a white dove sat.
Whenever she wished for anything the dove
would drop it like an egg upon the ground.
The bird is important, my dears, so heed him.

Next came the ball, as you all know.
It was a marriage market.
The prince was looking for a wife.
All but Cinderella were preparing
and gussying up for the big event.
Cinderella begged to go too.
Her stepmother threw a dish of lentils
into the cinders and said: Pick them
up in an hour and you shall go.
The white dove brought all his friends;
all the warm wings of the fatherland came,
and picked up the lentils in a jiffy.
No, Cinderella, said the stepmother,
you have no clothes and cannot dance.
That's the way with stepmothers.

Cinderella went to the tree at the grave
and cried forth like a gospel singer:
Mama! Mama! My turtledove,
send me to the prince's ball!
The bird dropped down a golden dress
and delicate little gold slippers.
Rather a large package for a simple bird.
So she went. Which is no surprise.
Her stepmother and sisters didn't
recognize her without her cinder face
and the prince took her hand on the spot
and danced with no other the whole day.

Al Jolson: American entertainer and songwriter (1886–1950) famous for his blackface minstrel performances.

As nightfall came she thought she'd better
get home. The prince walked her home
and she disappeared into the pigeon house
and although the prince took an axe and broke
it open she was gone. Back to her cinders.
These events repeated themselves for three days.
However on the third day the prince
covered the palace steps with cobbler's wax
and Cinderella's gold shoe stuck upon it.
Now he would find whom the shoe fit
and find his strange dancing girl for keeps.
He went to their house and the two sisters
were delighted because they had lovely feet.
The eldest went into a room to try the slipper on
but her big toe got in the way so she simply
sliced it off and put on the slipper.
The prince rode away with her until the white dove
told him to look at the blood pouring forth.
That is the way with amputations.
They don't just heal up like a wish.
The other sister cut off her heel
but the blood told as blood will.
The prince was getting tired.
He began to feel like a shoe salesman.
But he gave it one last try.
This time Cinderella fit into the shoe
like a love letter into its envelope.

At the wedding ceremony
the two sisters came to curry favor
and the white dove pecked their eyes out.
Two hollow spots were left
like soup spoons.

Cinderella and the prince
lived, they say, happily ever after,
like two dolls in a museum case
never bothered by diapers or dust,
never arguing over the timing of an egg,
never telling the same story twice,
never getting a middle-aged spread,
their darling smiles pasted on for eternity
Regular Bobbsey Twins.°
That story.

Bobbsey Twins: The two sets of twins — Nan and Bert, Flossie and Freddie — in a popular series of early twentieth-century children's books. They led an idealized, problem-free life.

Reading and Reacting

1. The first twenty-one lines of the poem act as a prelude. How does this prelude help to establish the speaker's ironic tone?

2. At times, the speaker talks directly to readers. What effect do these statements have on you? Would the poem be stronger without them?

3. Throughout the poem, the speaker mixes contemporary colloquial expressions with the conventional language of a fairy tale. Find examples of these two kinds of language. How does their juxtaposition create irony?

4. **Journal Entry** What details of the Cinderella fairy tale does Sexton change in her poem? Why do you think she makes these changes?

5. **Critical Perspective** In his 1973 book *Confessional Poets*, Robert Phillips comments on Anne Sexton's use of the Grimm Brothers' fairy tales in her book *Transformations*. According to Phillips, by transforming the Grimms' stories into symbols of our own time, Sexton "has managed to offer us understandable images of the world around us":

> ["Cinderella"] she takes to be a prototype of the old rags to riches theme ("From diapers to Dior. / That story."). Cinderella is said to have slept on the sooty hearth each night and "walked around looking like Al Jolson"—a comparison indicative of the level of invention and humor in the book. At the end, when Cinderella marries the handsome prince to live happily ever after, . . . Sexton pulls a double whammy and reveals that the ending, in itself, is another fairy tale within a fairy tale, totally unreal and unlikely.

Is the poem "Cinderella," written in 1970, still a "symbol of our own time"? Does it still offer us "understandable images of the world around us"?

Related Works: "The Story of an Hour" (p. 226), "Once upon a Time" (p. 232), "Birthmark" (p. 411), "The Jilting of Granny Weatherall" (p. 763), "Gretel in Darkness" (p. 839), "A Mown Lawn" (p. 974), *Beauty* (p. 1270), *Trifles* (p. 1319)

DUDLEY RANDALL (1914–2000)

Ballad of Birmingham (1969)

(On the bombing of a church in Birmingham, Alabama, 1963)

"Mother dear, may I go downtown
Instead of out to play,
And march the streets of Birmingham
In a Freedom March today?"

"No, baby, no, you may not go,
For the dogs are fierce and wild,
And clubs and hoses, guns and jails
Aren't good for a little child."

"But, mother, I won't be alone.
Other children will go with me,
And march the streets of Birmingham
To make our country free."

"No, baby, no, you may not go,
For I fear those guns will fire.
But you may go to church instead
And sing in the children's choir."

She has combed and brushed her night-dark hair,
And bathed rose petal sweet,
And drawn white gloves on her small brown hands,
And white shoes on her feet.

The mother smiled to know her child
Was in the sacred place,
But that smile was the last smile
To come upon her face.

For when she heard the explosion,
Her eyes grew wet and wild.
She raced through the streets of Birmingham
Calling for her child.

She clawed through bits of glass and brick,
Then lifted out a shoe.
"O, here's the shoe my baby wore,
But, baby, where are you?"

Reading and Reacting

1. Who are the speakers in the poem? How do their tones differ?
2. What kinds of irony are present in the poem? Give examples of each kind you identify.
3. What point do you think the poem makes about violence? About racial hatred? About the civil rights struggle?
4. This poem is a **ballad,** a form of poetry traditionally written to be sung or recited. Ballads typically repeat words and phrases and have regular meter and rhyme. How do the regular rhyme, repeated words, and singsong meter affect the poem's tone?
5. **JOURNAL ENTRY** This poem was written in response to the 1963 bombing of the 16th Street Baptist Church in Birmingham, Alabama, a bomb that killed four African-American children (pictured on p. 1085). How does this historical background help you to understand the irony of the poem?
6. **CRITICAL PERSPECTIVE** Speaking of "Ballad of Birmingham," critic James Sullivan says, "This poem uses the ballad convention of the innocent questioner and the wiser respondent (the pattern of, for example, 'Lord Randall' and 'La Belle Dame sans Merci'), but it changes the object of knowledge from fate to racial politics. The child is the conventional innocent, while the mother understands the violence of this political moment."

   How does Randall's use of these ballad conventions help him create irony?

Related Works: "Once upon a Time" (p. 232), "Birmingham Sunday (September 15, 1963)" (p. 1084), "Bonny Barbara Allan" (p. 1121), "Emmett Till" (p. 1155), "If We Must Die" (p. 1179), *Fences* (p. 1902)

Source: ©The Granger Collection, New York

SHERMAN J. ALEXIE (1966–)

How to Write the Great American Indian Novel (1996)

All of the Indians must have tragic features:
 tragic noses, eyes, and arms.
Their hands and fingers must be tragic
 when they reach for tragic food.

The hero must be a half-breed, half white and half Indian, preferably
from a horse culture. He should often weep alone. That is mandatory.

If the hero is an Indian woman, she is beautiful. She must be slender
and in love with a white man. But if she loves an Indian man

then he must be a half-breed, preferably from a horse culture.
If the Indian woman loves a white man, then he has to be so white

that we can see the blue veins running through his skin like rivers.
When the Indian woman steps out of her dress, the white man gasps

at the endless beauty of her brown skin. She should be compared to
 nature:
brown hills, mountains, fertile valleys, dewy grass, wind, and clear
 water.

If she is compared to murky water, however, then she must have a
 secret.
Indians always have secrets, which are carefully and slowly revealed.

Yet Indian secrets can be disclosed suddenly, like a storm.
Indian men, of course, are storms. They should destroy the lives

of any white women who choose to love them. All white women
 love
Indian men. That is always the case. White women feign disgust

at the savage in blue jeans and T-shirt, but secretly lust after him.
White women dream about half-breed Indian men from horse
 cultures.

Indian men are horses, smelling wild and gamey. When the Indian
 man
unbuttons his pants, the white woman should think of topsoil.

There must be one murder, one suicide, one attempted rape.
Alcohol should be consumed. Cars must be driven at high
 speeds.

Indians must see visions. White people can have the same
visions if they are in love with Indians. If a white person loves an Indian
then the white person is Indian by proximity. White people must carry
an Indian deep inside themselves. Those interior Indians are half-breed
and obviously from horse cultures. If the interior Indian is male
then he must be a warrior, especially if he is inside a white man.
If the interior Indian is female, then she must be a healer, especially if she is inside
a white woman. Sometimes there are complications.
An Indian man can be hidden inside a white woman. An Indian woman
can be hidden inside a white man. In these rare instances,
everybody is a half-breed struggling to learn more about his or her horse culture.
There must be redemption, of course, and sins must be forgiven.
For this, we need children. A white child and an Indian child, gender
not important, should express deep affection in a childlike way.
In the Great American Indian novel, when it is finally written,
all of the white people will be Indians and all of the Indians will be ghosts.

Reading and Reacting

1. Who is the speaker in this poem? What is the speaker's attitude toward Native Americans? Toward the white novelists who write about them?
2. What stereotypes of Native Americans does the speaker identify? How does the speaker's tone undercut these stereotypes?
3. What does the speaker mean in the last line of the poem when he says that when the great American Indian novel is finally written, "all of the white people will be Indians and all of the Indians will be ghosts"?
4. **Journal Entry** How are the characters discussed in the poem like and unlike those you have seen in films?

Related Works: "This Is What It Means to Say Phoenix, Arizona" (p. 322), "Sister Godzilla" (p. 700), "Where Mountain Lion Lay Down with Deer" (p. 845), "Indian Boarding School: The Runaways" (p. 1155), "The English Canon" (p. 1202), *The Cuban Swimmer* (p. 1732), *Trying to Find Chinatown* (p. 1856)

✔ **CHECKLIST Writing about Voice**

The Speaker in the Poem

- ☐ What do we know about the speaker?
- ☐ Is the speaker anonymous, or does he or she have a particular identity?
- ☐ How does assuming a particular persona help the poet to convey his or her ideas?
- ☐ Does the title give readers any information about the speaker's identity?
- ☐ How does word choice provide information about the speaker?
- ☐ Does the speaker make any direct statements to readers that help establish his or her identity or character?
- ☐ Does the speaker address anyone? How can you tell? How does the presence of a listener affect the speaker?

The Tone of the Poem

- ☐ What is the speaker's attitude toward his or her subject?
- ☐ How do word choice, rhyme, meter, sentence structure, figures of speech, and imagery help to convey the attitude of the speaker?
- ☐ Is the poem's tone consistent? How do shifts in tone reveal the changing mood or attitude of the speaker?

Irony

- ☐ Does the poem include dramatic irony? Situational irony? Verbal irony?

WRITING SUGGESTIONS: Voice

1. The poet Robert Frost once said that he wanted to write "poetry that talked." According to Frost, "whenever I write a line it is because that line has already been spoken clearly by a voice within my mind, an audible voice." Choose some poems in this chapter (or from elsewhere in the book) that you consider "poetry that talks." Then, write an essay about how successful they are in communicating "an audible voice."
2. Compare the speakers' voices in "Cinderella" (p. 866) and "Gretel in Darkness" (p. 839). How are their attitudes toward men similar? How are they different?
3. The theme of Herrick's poem "To the Virgins, to Make Much of Time" (p. 858) is known as **carpe diem**, or "seize the day." Read Andrew Marvell's "To His Coy Mistress" (p. 941), which has the same theme, and compare its tone with that of "To the Virgins, to Make Much of Time."
4. Read the following poem, and compare the speaker's use of the word *hope* with the way the speaker uses the word in Ariel Dorfman's "Hope" (p. 863).

EMILY DICKINSON (1830–1886)

"Hope" is the thing with feathers— (1861)

"Hope" is the thing with feathers—
That perches in the soul—
And sings the tune without the words—
And never stops—at all—

And sweetest—in the Gale—is heard—
And sore must be the storm—
That could abash the little Bird—
That kept so many warm—

I've heard it in the chillest land—
And on the strangest Sea—
Yet, never, in Extremity,
It asked a crumb—of Me.

5. Because the speaker and the poet are not the same, poems by the same author can have different voices. Compare the voices of several poems by one poet—for example, Sylvia Plath, W. H. Auden, or William Blake, whose works are included in this anthology.

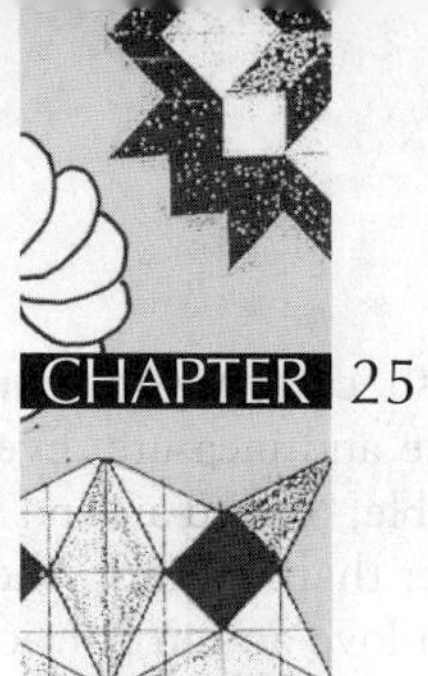

CHAPTER 25

WORD CHOICE, WORD ORDER

Source: Courtesy, ETONSA—The English Teacher's Online Network of South Africa

SIPHO SEPAMLA (1932–)

Words, Words, Words (1984)

We don't speak of tribal wars anymore
we say simple faction fights
there are no tribes around here
only nations
it makes sense you see
'cause from there
one moves to multinational
it makes sense you get me
'cause from there
one gets one's homeland
which is a reasonable idea
'cause from there
one can dabble with independence
which deserves warm applause
—the bloodless revolution

we are talking of words
words tossed around as if
denied location by the wind
we mean those words some spit
others grab
dress them up for the occasion
fling them on the lap of an audience
we are talking of those words
that stalk our lives like policemen
words no dictionary can embrace
words that change sooner than seasons
we mean words
that spell out our lives
words, words, words
for there's a kind of poetic licence
doing the rounds in these parts

Words identify and name, characterize and distinguish, compare and contrast. Words describe, limit, and embellish; words locate and measure. Even though words may be elusive and uncertain and changeable, "tossed around as if / denied location by the wind" and "can change sooner than seasons," they still can "stalk our lives like policemen." In poetry, as in love and in politics, words matter.

Beyond the quantitative—how many words, how many letters and syllables—is a much more important consideration: the *quality* of words. Which words are chosen, and why? Why are certain words placed next to others? What does a word suggest in a particular context? How are the words arranged? What exactly constitutes the "right word"?

Word Choice

In poetry, even more than in fiction or drama, words are the focus—sometimes even the true subject—of a work. For this reason, the choice of one word over another can be crucial. Because poems are brief, they must compress many ideas into just a few lines; poets know how much weight each individual word carries, so they choose with great care, trying to select words that imply more than they state.

In general, poets (like prose writers) select words because they communicate their ideas. However, poets may also choose words for their sound. For instance, a word may echo another word's sound, and such repetition may place emphasis on both words; a word may rhyme with another word and therefore be needed to preserve the poem's rhyme scheme; or a word may have a certain combination of stressed and unstressed syllables needed to maintain the poem's metrical pattern. Occasionally, a poet may even choose a word because of how it looks on the page.

At the same time, poets may choose words for their degree of concreteness or abstraction, specificity or generality. A **concrete** word refers to an item that is a perceivable, tangible entity—for example, a kiss or a flag. An **abstract** word refers to an intangible idea, condition, or quality, something that cannot be perceived by the senses—love or patriotism, for instance. **Specific** words refer to particular items; **general** words refer to entire classes or groups of items. As the following sequence illustrates, whether a word is specific or general is relative; its degree of specificity or generality depends on its relationship to other words.

> Poem → closed form poem → sonnet → seventeenth-century sonnet → Elizabethan sonnet → sonnet by Shakespeare → "My mistress' eyes are nothing like the sun"

Sometimes a poet wants a precise word, one that is both specific and concrete. At other times, a poet might prefer general or abstract language, which may allow for more subtlety—or even for intentional ambiguity.

Finally, a word may be chosen for its **connotation**—what it suggests. Every word has one or more **denotations**—what it signifies without emotional associations, judgments, or opinions. The word *family*, for example, denotes "a group of related things or people." Connotation is a more complex matter; after all, a single word may have many different associations. In general terms, a word may have a connotation that is positive, neutral, or negative. Thus, *family* may have a positive connotation when it describes a group of loving relatives, a neutral connotation when it describes a biological category, and an ironically negative connotation when it describes an organized crime family. Beyond this distinction, *family*, like any other word, may have a variety of emotional and social associations, suggesting loyalty, warmth, home, security, or duty. In fact, many words have somewhat different meanings in different contexts. When poets choose words, then, they must consider what a particular word may suggest to readers as well as what it denotes.

In the poem that follows, the poet chooses words for their sounds and for their relationships to other words as well as for their connotations.

WALT WHITMAN (1819–1892)

When I Heard the Learn'd Astronomer (1865)

When I heard the learn'd astronomer,
When the proofs, the figures, were ranged in columns before me,
When I was shown the charts and diagrams, to add, divide, and
measure them,
When I sitting heard the astronomer where he lectured with much
applause in the lecture-room,
How soon unaccountable I became tired and sick,
Till rising and gliding out I wander'd off by myself,
In the mystical moist night-air, and from time to time,
Look'd up in perfect silence at the stars.

This poem might be paraphrased as follows: "When I grew restless listening to an astronomy lecture, I went outside, where I found I learned more just by looking at the stars than I had learned inside." However, the paraphrase is obviously neither as rich nor as complex as the poem. Through careful use of diction, Whitman establishes a dichotomy that supports the poem's central theme about the relative merits of two ways of learning.

The poem can be divided into two groups of four lines each. The first four lines, unified by the repetition of "When," introduce the astronomer and his tools: "proofs," "figures," and "charts and diagrams" to be added, divided, or measured. In this section of the poem, the speaker is passive: he sits and listens ("I heard"; "I was shown"; "I sitting heard"). The repetition of "When" reinforces the dry monotony of the lecture. In the next four lines, the choice of words signals the change in the speaker's actions and reactions. The confined lecture hall is replaced by "the mystical moist night-air," and the dry lecture and the applause give way to "perfect silence"; instead of sitting passively, the speaker becomes active (he rises, glides, wanders); instead of listening, he looks. The mood of the first half of the poem is restrained: the language is concrete and physical, and the speaker is passively receiving information from a "learn'd" authority. The rest of the poem, celebrating intuitive knowledge and feelings, is more abstract, freer. Throughout the poem, the lecture hall is set in sharp contrast to the natural world outside its walls.

After considering the poem as a whole, readers should not find it hard to understand why the poet selected certain words. Whitman's use of "lectured" in line 4 rather than a more neutral word like "spoke" is appropriate both because it suggests formality and distance and because it echoes "lecture-room" in the same line. The word "sick" in line 5 is striking because it connotes physical as well as emotional distress, more effectively conveying the extent of the speaker's discomfort than "bored" or "restless" would. "Rising" and "gliding" (line 6) are used rather than "standing" and "walking out" both because of the way their stressed vowel sounds echo each other (and echo "time to time" in the next line) and because of their connotation of dreaminess, which is consistent with "wander'd" (line 6) and "mystical" (line 7). The word "moist" (line 7) is chosen not only because its consonant sounds echo the *m* and *st* sounds in "mystical," but also because it establishes a contrast with the dry, airless lecture hall. Finally, line 8's "perfect silence" is a better choice than a reasonable substitute like "complete silence" or "total silence," either of which would suggest the degree of the silence but not its quality.

In the next poem, the poet also pays careful attention to word choice.

WILLIAM STAFFORD (1914–1993)

For the Grave of Daniel Boone (1957)

The farther he went the farther home grew.
Kentucky became another room;
the mansion arched over the Mississippi;
flowers were spread all over the floor.
He traced ahead a deepening home,
and better, with goldenrod:

Leaving the snakeskin of place after place,
going on—after the trees
the grass, a bird flying after a song.
Rifle so level, sighting so well
his picture freezes down to now,
a story-picture for children.

They go over the velvet falls
into the tapestry of his time,
heirs to the landscape, feeling no jar:

it is like evening; they are the quail
surrounding his fire, coming in for the kill;
their little feet move sacred sand.

Children, we live in a barbwire time
but like to follow the old hands back—
the ring in the light, the knuckle, the palm,
all the way to Daniel Boone,
hunting our own kind of deepening home.
From the land that was his I heft this rock.

Here on his grave I put it down.

A number of words in "For the Grave of Daniel Boone" are noteworthy for their multiple denotations and connotations. In the first stanza, for example, "home" does not simply mean Boone's residence; it connotes an abstract state, a dynamic concept that grows and deepens, encompassing states and rivers while becoming paradoxically more and more elusive. In literal terms, Boone's "home" at the poem's end is a narrow, confined space: his grave. In a wider sense, his home is the United States, particularly the natural landscape he explored. Thus, the word "home" comes to have a variety of associations for readers beyond its denotative meaning, suggesting both the infinite possibilities beyond the frontier and the realities of civilization's walls and fences.

The word "snakeskin" denotes "the skin of a snake"; its most obvious connotations are smoothness and slipperiness. In this poem, however, the snakeskin signifies more, because it is Daniel Boone who is "Leaving the snakeskin of place after place." Like a snake, Boone belongs to the natural world—and, like a snake, he wanders from place to place, shedding his skin as he goes. Thus, the word "snakeskin," with its connotation of rebirth and its links to nature, passing time, and the inevitability of change, is consistent with the image of Boone as both a man of nature and a restless wanderer, "a bird flying after a song."

In the poem's third stanza, the phrases "velvet falls" and "tapestry of . . . time" seem at first to have been selected solely for their pleasing repetition of sounds ("velvet falls"; "tapestry of time"). However, both of these paradoxical phrases also support the poem's theme. Alive, Boone was in constant movement; he was also larger than life. Now, in death, he has been diminished; "his picture freezes down to . . . / a story-picture for children" (lines 11–12), and he is as static and inorganic as velvet or tapestry—no longer dynamic, like "falls" and "time."

The word "barbwire" (line 19) is another word whose multiple meanings enrich the poem's theme. In the simplest terms, "barbwire" denotes a metal fencing material. In light of the poem's concern with space and distance, however, "barbwire" (with its connotations of sharpness, danger, and confinement) is also the antithesis of Boone's free and peaceful wilderness, evoking images of enclosure and imprisonment and reinforcing the poem's central dichotomy between past freedom and present restriction.

The phrase "old hands" (line 20) might also have multiple meanings in the context of the poem. On one level, the hands could belong to an elderly person holding a storybook; on another level, "old hands" could refer to people with considerable life experience—like Boone, who was an "old hand" at scouting. On still another level, given the poem's concern with time, "old hands" could even suggest the hands of a clock.

Through what it says literally and through what its words suggest, "For the Grave of Daniel Boone" communicates a good deal about the speaker's identification with Daniel Boone and with the nation he called home. Boone's horizons, his concept of "home," expanded as he wandered. Now, when he is frozen in time and space, a character in a child's picture book, a body in a grave, we are still "hunting our own kind of deepening home," but our horizons, like Boone's, have narrowed in this "barbwire time."

FURTHER READING: Word Choice

RHINA ESPAILLAT (1932–)

Bilingual/Bilingue (1998)

My father liked them separate, one there,
one here (allá y aquí), as if aware

that words might cut in two his daughter's heart
(el corazón) and lock the alien part

to what he was—his memory, his name
(su nombre)—with a key he could not claim.

"English outside this door, Spanish inside,"
he said, "y basta."° But who can divide

the world, the word (mundo y palabra) from
any child? I knew how to be dumb

and stubborn (testaruda); late, in bed,
I hoarded secret syllables I read

until my tongue (mi lengua) learned to run
where his stumbled. And still the heart was one.

I like to think he knew that, even when,
proud (orgulloso) of his daughter's pen,
he stood outside mis versos,° half in fear
of words he loved but wanted not to hear.

"y basta.": and enough.

mis versos: my poems.

Reading and Reacting

1. Why do you think the poet includes parenthetical Spanish translations in this poem? Are they necessary? Why do you think the Spanish words "y basta" (line 8) and "mis versos" (line 17) are not translated as the others are?
2. Some of the words in this poem might be seen as having more than one connotation. Consider, for example, "alien" (line 4), "word" (line 9), "dumb" (line 10), and "syllables" (line 12). What meanings could each of these words have? Which meaning do you think the poet intended them to have?
3. What is the relationship between "the word" and "the world" in this poem?
4. **JOURNAL ENTRY** What is the father's fear? Do you think this fear is justified? Why do you think he doesn't want to hear his daughter's words?

Related Works: "The Secret Lion" (p. 197), "Water Names" (p. 318), "New York Day Women" (p. 406), "Two Questions" (p. 556), "Two Kinds" (p. 777), "Baca Grande" (p. 889), "My Father in the Navy: A Childhood Memory" (p. 1043)

JAMES WRIGHT (1927–1980)

Autumn Begins in Martins Ferry, Ohio (1963)

In the Shreve High football stadium,
I think of Polacks nursing long beers in Tiltonsville,
And gray faces of Negroes in the blast furnace at Benwood,
And the ruptured night watchman of Wheeling Steel,
Dreaming of heroes.

All the proud fathers are ashamed to go home.
Their women cluck like starved pullets,
Dying for love.

Therefore,
Their sons grow suicidally beautiful
At the beginning of October,
And gallop terribly against each other's bodies.

Reading and Reacting

1. Evaluate Wright's decision to use each of the following words: "Polacks" (line 2), "ruptured" (line 4), "pullets" (line 7), "suicidally" (line 10), "gallop" (line 12). Do any of these words seem unexpected, even unsettling, in the context in which the poet uses them? Can you explain why each is used instead of a more conventional word?
2. What thematic relationship, if any, do you see between line 5 ("Dreaming of heroes") and line 8 ("Dying for love")? What do these lines reveal about the people who live in Martins Ferry?
3. **JOURNAL ENTRY** What comment does this poem seem to be making about small towns? About high school football?
4. **CRITICAL PERSPECTIVE** In her 1980 essay "James Wright: Returning to the Heartland," Bonnie Costello discusses the poet's complex relationship to place and its effect on "Autumn

Begins in Martins Ferry, Ohio," characterizing Wright as a kind of "fugitive" or "exile" from the past his poems reveal:

> James Wright was an elegiac poet of place. Place names echo through his lines as through deserted villages and wintry valleys, for Martins Ferry, Ohio; Fargo, North Dakota; Wheeling, West Virginia, are all dying. While he admired D. H. Lawrence's essay "The Spirit of Place" and tried to follow its guidelines, his own subject raised a special problem since it was the departure of spirit that he best portrayed. Wright tried repeatedly to call his spirit back, but his finest poems are those which catch it crossing the last hill crest or disappearing into the mist. One might argue that there is, indeed, a spirit in this place, one hopeless, ignorant, and long suffering, nonetheless beautiful and mysterious.

How does "Autumn Begins in Martins Ferry, Ohio" convey the elegiac sense of place Costello describes?

Related Works: "The Secret Lion" (p. 197), "Teenage Wasteland" (p. 785), "To an Athlete Dying Young" (p. 900), "Ex-Basketball Player" (p. 930), *Fences* (p. 1902)

ADRIENNE RICH (1929–)

Living in Sin (1955)

She had thought the studio would keep itself,
no dust upon the furniture of love.
Half heresy, to wish the taps less vocal,
the panes relieved of grime. A plate of pears,
a piano with a Persian shawl, a cat
stalking the picturesque amusing mouse
had risen at his urging.
Not that at five each separate stair would writhe
under the milkman's tramp; that morning light
so coldly would delineate the scraps
of last night's cheese and three sepulchral bottles;
that on the kitchen shelf among the saucers
a pair of beetle-eyes would fix her own—
envoy from some black village in the mouldings . . .
Meanwhile, he, with a yawn,
sounded a dozen notes upon the keyboard,
declared it out of tune, shrugged at the mirror,
rubbed at his beard, went out for cigarettes;
while she, jeered by the minor demons,
pulled back the sheets and made the bed and found
a towel to dust the table-top,
and let the coffee-pot boil over on the stove.
By evening she was back in love again,
though not so wholly but throughout the night
she woke sometimes to feel the daylight coming
like a relentless milkman up the stairs.

Reading and Reacting

1. How might the poem's impact change if each of these words were deleted: "Persian" (line 5), "picturesque" (line 6), "sepulchral" (line 11), "minor" (line 19), "sometimes" (line 25)?
2. What words in the poem have strongly negative connotations? What do these words suggest about the relationship the poem describes? How does the image of the "relentless milkman" (line 26) sum up this relationship?
3. This poem, about a woman in love, uses very few words conventionally associated with love poems. Instead, many of its words denote the everyday routine of housekeeping. Give examples of such words. Why do you think they are used?
4. **JOURNAL ENTRY** What connotations does the title have? What other phrases have similar denotative meanings? How do their connotations differ? Why do you think Rich chose the title "Living in Sin"?
5. **CRITICAL PERSPECTIVE** In "Her Cargo: Adrienne Rich and the Common Language," a 1979 essay examining the poet's work over almost thirty years, Alicia Ostriker offers the following analysis of Rich's early poems, including "Living in Sin":

 > They seem about to state explicitly . . . a connection between feminine subordination in male-dominated middle-class relationships, and emotionally lethal inarticulateness for both sexes. But the poetry . . . is minor because it is polite. It illustrates symptoms but does not probe sources. There is no disputing the ideas of the predecessors, and Adrienne Rich at this point is a cautious good poet in the sense of being a good girl, a quality noted with approval by her reviewers.

 Does your reading of "Living in Sin" support Ostriker's characterization of the poem as "polite" and "cautious"? Do you think Rich is "being a good girl"?

Related Works: "Hills Like White Elephants" (p. 171), "Love and Other Catastrophies: A Mix Tape" (p. 182), "The Storm" (p. 313), "What Lips My Lips Have Kissed" (p. 1056), *The Stronger* (p. 1470)

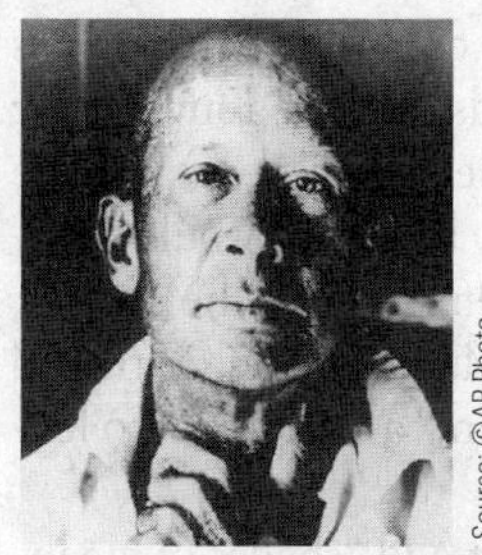

Source: ©AP Photo

See this poet's biography on p. 1220.

E. E. CUMMINGS (1894–1962)

in Just-° (1923)

in Just-
spring when the world is mud-
luscious the little
lame balloonman
whistles far and wee
and eddieandbill come
running from marbles and

---

in Just-: This poem is also known as "Chansons Innocentes I."

piracies and it's
spring
when the world is puddle-wonderful
the queer
old balloonman whistles
far   and   wee
and bettyandisbel come dancing

from hop-scotch and jump-rope and
it's
spring
and
    the
        goat-footed
balloonMan whistles
far
and
wee

Reading and Reacting

1. In this poem, Cummings coins a number of words that he uses to modify other words. Identify these coinages. What other, more conventional, words could be used in their place? What does Cummings accomplish by using the coined words instead?
2. What do you think Cummings means by "far and wee" in lines 5, 13, and 22–24? Why do you think he arranges these three words in a different way on the page each time he uses them?
3. **JOURNAL ENTRY** Evaluate this poem. Do you like it? Is it memorable? Moving? Or is it just clever?
4. **CRITICAL PERSPECTIVE** In "Latter-Day Notes on E. E. Cummings' Language" (1955), Robert E. Maurer suggests that Cummings often coined new words in the same way that children do: for example, "by adding the normal *-er* or *-est (beautifuler, chiefest)*, or stepping up the power of a word such as *last*, which is already superlative, and saying *lastest*," creating words such as *givingest* and *whirlingest*. In addition to "combining two or more words to form a single new one . . . to give an effect of wholeness, of one quality" (for example, *yellowgreen*), "in the simplest of his word coinages, he merely creates a new word by analogy as a child would without adding any shade of meaning other than that inherent in the prefix or suffix he utilizes, as in the words *unstrength* and *untimid*. . . . " Many early reviewers, Maurer notes, criticized such coinages because they "convey a thrill but not a precise impression," a criticism also leveled at Cummings's poetry more broadly.

   Consider the coinages in "in Just-." Do you agree that many do not add "shades of meaning" or provide a "precise impression"? Or do you find that the coinages contribute to the poem in a meaningful way?

Related Works: "The Secret Lion" (p. 197), *Words, Words, Words* (p. 875), "anyone lived in a pretty how town" (p. 899), "Constantly Risking Absurdity" (p. 925), "Jabberwocky" (p. 976), "the sky was can dy" (p. 1000)

Source: ©AP Photo/Julia Malakie

See this poet's biography on p. 1226.

ROBERT PINSKY (1940–)

ABC (1998)

Any body can die, evidently. Few
Go happily, irradiating joy,

Knowledge, love. Many
Need oblivion, painkillers,
Quickest respite.

Sweet time unafflicted,
Various world:

X = your zenith.

Reading and Reacting

1. What "rules" limit the choice of words used in this poem? What determines the order in which they are used? Where does the poet break (or bend) the rules he has established? Can you suggest a way for him to avoid doing so?
2. Given the constraints the poet places on himself here, how successful is he? Is the result of his efforts actually a poem or just a novelty? Explain.
3. **Journal Entry** This poem is tightly compressed, limited to very few words. Rewrite it as a paragraph, adding any words you think are necessary to communicate its theme. How is your version different from the original in what it says? In what it suggests?
4. **Critical Perspective** "ABC" has a very distinctive form. The poet and critic Louise Glück has stressed the importance of form in the poetry of Robert Pinsky:

   > [I]n Pinsky's art, form does what we have come to believe only tone can do. That is to say, form here is not intellectual construct but rather metaphor. For the poems to be understood at all they must be apprehended entire, as shapes.

   How does reflecting on the form, or "shape," of "ABC" help you to understand the poem?

Related Works: "A Primer for the Punctuation of Heart Disease" (p. 440), "Bullet in the Brain" (p. 608), "l(a" (p. 803), "Constantly Risking Absurdity" (p. 925), "Verities" (p. 1117), *Tape* (p. 1275)

THEODORE ROETHKE (1908–1963)

I Knew a Woman (1958)

I knew a woman, lovely in her bones,
When small birds sighed, she would sigh back at them;
Ah, when she moved, she moved more ways than one:
The shapes a bright container can contain!
Of her choice virtues only gods should speak,
Or English poets who grew up on Greek
(I'd have them sing in chorus, cheek to cheek).

How well her wishes went! She stroked my chin,
She taught me Turn, and Counter-turn, and Stand;
She taught me Touch, that undulant white skin;
I nibbled meekly from her proffered hand;
She was the sickle; I, poor I, the rake,
Coming behind her for her pretty sake
(But what prodigious mowing we did make).

Love likes a gander, and adores a goose:
Her full lips pursed, the errant note to seize;
She played it quick, she played it light and loose;
My eyes, they dazzled at her flowing knees;
Her several parts could keep a pure repose,
Or one hip quiver with a mobile nose
(She moved in circles, and those circles moved).

Let seed be grass, and grass turn into hay:
I'm martyr to a motion not my own;
What's freedom for? To know eternity.
I swear she cast a shadow white as stone.
But who would count eternity in days?
These old bones live to learn her wanton ways:
(I measure time by how a body sways).

Reading and Reacting

1. Many of the words in Roethke's poem have double meanings—for example, "gander" and "goose" in line 15. Identify other words that have more than one meaning, and consider the function these multiple meanings serve.

2. The poem's language contains many surprises; often, the word we expect is not the one we get. For example, "container" in line 4 is not a conventional way to describe a woman. What other words are used in unusual ways? What does Roethke achieve by choosing such words?

3. Is there a difference between the denotation or connotation of the word "bones" in the phrases "lovely in her bones" (line 1) and "These old bones" (line 27)? Explain.

4. **Journal Entry** How does this poem differ from your idea of what a love poem should be?

Related Works: "The Girl With Bangs" (p. 271), "My mistress' eyes are nothing like the sun" (p. 917), "Oh, my love is like a red, red rose" (p. 928), "Women" (p. 1007), "She Walks in Beauty" (p. 1133), *Beauty* (p. 1270)

KAY RYAN (1945–)

Crib (1997)

From the Greek for
woven or *plaited*,
which quickly translated

to *basket*. Whence the verb
crib, which meant to *filch*
under cover of wicker
anything—some liquor,
a cutlet.
For we want to make off
with things that are not
our own. There is a pleasure
theft brings, a vitality
to the home.
Cribbed objects or answers
keep their guilty shimmer
forever, have you noticed?
Yet religions downplay this.
Note, for instance, in our annual rehearsals of innocence,
the substitution of *manger* for *crib*—
as if we ever deserved that baby,
or thought we did.

Reading and Reacting

1. What different meanings of the word *crib* does Ryan consider? Which meaning do you think she had in mind when she titled her poem "Crib"?
2. How do you interpret the words, "For we want to make off / with things that are not / our own" (lines 9–11)? When the speaker refers to "a pleasure / theft brings" (lines 11–12), is she talking about poetry or about something else?
3. **Journal Entry** Is this a poem about word origins? About writing poetry? About religious values? Or about something else entirely?

Related Works: "A Primer for the Punctuation of Heart Disease" (p. 440), *Words, Words, Words* (p. 875), "Litany" (p. 918), "Naming of Parts" (p. 1190)

Levels of Diction

The diction of a poem may be formal or informal or fall anywhere in between, depending on the identity of the speaker and on the speaker's attitude toward the reader and toward his or her subject. At one extreme, very formal poems can seem lofty and dignified, far removed in style and vocabulary from everyday speech. At the other extreme, highly informal poems can be full of jargon, regionalisms, and slang. Many poems, of course, use language that falls somewhere between formal and informal diction.

Formal diction is characterized by a learned vocabulary and grammatically correct forms. In general, formal diction does not include colloquialisms, such as contractions and shortened word forms (*phone* for *telephone*). As the following poem illustrates, a speaker who uses formal diction can sound aloof and impersonal.

Source: ©AP Photo/Jennifer Graylock

See this poet's biography on p. 1217.

MARGARET ATWOOD (1939–)

The City Planners (1966)

Cruising these residential Sunday
streets in dry August sunlight:
what offends us is
the sanities:
the houses in pedantic rows, the planted
sanitary trees, assert
levelness of surface like a rebuke
to the dent in our car door.
No shouting here, or
shatter of glass; nothing more abrupt
than the rational whine of a power mower
cutting a straight swath in the discouraged grass.

But though the driveways neatly
sidestep hysteria
by being even, the roofs all display
the same slant of avoidance to the hot sky,
certain things:
the smell of spilled oil a faint

sickness lingering in the garages,
a splash of paint on brick surprising as a bruise,
a plastic hose poised in a vicious

coil; even the too-fixed stare of the wide windows
give momentary access to
the landscape behind or under
the future cracks in the plaster

when the houses, capsized, will slide
obliquely into the clay seas, gradual as glaciers
that right now nobody notices.

That is where the City Planners
with the insane faces of political conspirators
are scattered over unsurveyed
territories, concealed from each other,
each in his own private blizzard;

guessing directions, they sketch
transitory lines rigid as wooden borders
on a wall in the white vanishing air

tracing the panic of suburb
order in a bland madness of snows.

Atwood's speaker is clearly concerned about the poem's central issue, but rather than use *I*, the poem uses the first-person plural (*us*) to convey some degree of emotional detachment. Although phrases such as "sickness lingering in the garages" and "insane faces of political conspirators" subjectively communicate the speaker's disapproval, formal words—"pedantic," "rebuke," "display," "poised," "obliquely," "conspirators," "transitory"—help her to maintain her distance. Both the speaker herself and her attack on the misguided city planners gain credibility through her balanced, measured tone and through her use of language that is as formal and "professional" as theirs.

Informal diction is the language closest to everyday conversation. It includes **colloquialisms**—contractions, shortened word forms, and the like—and may also include slang, regional expressions, and even nonstandard words.

In the poem that follows, the speaker uses informal diction to highlight the contrast between James Baca, a law student speaking to the graduating class of his old high school, and the graduating seniors.

JIM SAGEL (1947–1998)

Baca Grande° (1982)

Una vaca se topó con un ratón y le dice:
"Tú—¿tan chiquito y con bigote?" Y le responde el ratón:
"Y tú tan grandota—¿y sin brassiere?"°

It was nearly a miracle
James Baca remembered anyone at all
from the old hometown gang
having been two years at Yale
    no less
and halfway through law school
at the University of California at Irvine
They hardly recognized him either
in his three-piece grey business suit
and surfer-swirl haircut
with just the menacing hint
of a tightly trimmed Zapata moustache
    for cultural balance
and relevance

He had come to deliver the keynote address
to the graduating class of 80

Baca Grande: Baca is both a phonetic spelling of the Spanish word *vaca* (cow) and the last name of one of the poem's characters. *Grande* means "large."

Una . . . brassiere?: A cow ran into a rat and said: "You — so small and with a moustache?" The rat responded: "And you — so big and without a bra?"

at his old alma mater
and show off his well-trained lips
which laboriously parted
    each Kennedyish "R"
and drilled the first person pronoun
through the microphone
like an oil bit
with the slick, elegantly honed phrases
that slid so smoothly
off his meticulously bleached
    tongue
He talked Big Bucks
with astronautish fervor and if he
    the former bootstrapless James A. Baca
could dazzle the ass
off the universe
then even you
    yes you
Joey Martinez toying with your yellow
    tassle
and staring dumbly into space
could emulate Mr. Baca someday
    possibly
well
there was of course
such a thing
as being an outrageously successful
gas station attendant too
    let us never forget
it doesn't really matter what you do
so long as you excel
    James said
never believing a word
of it
for he had already risen
        as high as they go

Wasn't nobody else
from this deprived environment
who'd ever jumped
        straight out of college
into the Governor's office
and maybe one day
he'd sit in that big chair
    himself
and when he did

he'd forget this damned town
and all the petty little people
in it
once and for all
That much he promised himself

"Baca Grande" uses numerous colloquialisms, including contractions; conversational placeholders, such as "no less" and "well"; shortened word forms, such as "gas"; slang terms, such as "Big Bucks"; whimsical coinages ("Kennedyish," "astronautish," "bootstrapless"); nonstandard grammatical constructions, such as "Wasn't nobody else"; and even profanity. The level of language is perfectly appropriate for the poem's speaker, one of the students Baca addresses — suspicious, streetwise, and unimpressed by Baca's "three-piece grey business suit" and "surfer-swirl haircut." In fact, the informal diction is a key element in the poem, expressing the gap between the slick James Baca, with "his well-trained lips / which laboriously parted / each Kennedyish 'R'" and members of his audience, with their unpretentious, forthright speech — and also the gap between Baca as he is today and the student he once was. In this sense, "Baca Grande" is as much a linguistic commentary as a social one.

FURTHER READING: Levels of Diction

WANDA COLEMAN (1946–)

Sears Life (2001)

it makes me nervous to go into a store
because i never know if i'm going to
come out. have you noticed how much
they look like prisons these days? no display
windows anymore. all that cold soulless
lighting—as atmospheric as county jail—
and all that ground-breaking status-quo
shattering rock 'n' roll reduced to neuron
pablum and piped in over the escalators.
breaks my rebel heart. and i especially
hate the aroma of fresh-nuked popcorn
rushing my nose, throwing my stomach
off balance. eyes follow me everywhere i go
like i'm a neon sign that shouts shoplifter.
and so many snide counter rats want to
service me, it almost makes me feel rich
and royal. that's why i rarely bother to
browse. i go straight to the department of
the object of conjecture, make my decision
quick, throw down the cash and split

one time i had barely left this store
when i heard somebody yelling stop! stop!
i turned around and this dough-fleshed
armed security guard was waving me down.
i waited while he caught his breath and
demanded to search my purse i stared him
into his socks. we're outside the store,
i reminded him. if you search me, you'd
better find some goddamned something.
he took a minute to examine my eyes, turned
around and went back to his job, snorting
dust and coondogging teenage loiterers

Reading and Reacting

1. List the words that identify this poem's diction as informal. Do you think this informality is a strength or a weakness? Explain.
2. Look closely at the poem's sentence structure, its use of all lowercase letters, and its punctuation. What does each of these elements contribute to the poem's overall effect?
3. What can you infer about the speaker from the poem's language—for example, from language like "neuron / pablum" (lines 8–9), "counter rats" (line 15), and "dough-fleshed" (line 23)?
4. **JOURNAL ENTRY** What comment does the poem's title make about Sears? About life? Do you think the speaker's observations are valid?

Related Works: "A&P" (p. 259), "Bullet in the Brain" (p. 608), "Saboteur" (p. 712)

MARK HALLIDAY (1949–)

The Value of Education (2000)

I go now to the library. When I sit in the library
I am not illegally dumping bags of kitchen garbage
in the dumpster behind Clippinger Laboratory,
and a very pissed-off worker at Facilities Management
is not picking through my garbage and finding
several yogurt-stained and tomato-sauce-stained envelopes
with my name and address on them.
When I sit in the library,
I might doze off a little,
and what I read might not penetrate my head
which is mostly porridge in a bowl of bone.
However, when I sit there trying to read
I am not, you see, somewhere else being a hapless ass.
I am not leaning on the refrigerator
in the apartment of a young female colleague

chatting with oily pep
because I imagine she may suddenly decide to
do sex with me while her boyfriend is on a trip.
Instead I am in the library! Sitting still!
No one in town is approaching my chair
with a summons, or a bill, or a huge fist.
This is good. You may say,
"But this is merely a negative definition of
the value of education." Maybe so,
but would you be able to say that
if you hadn't been to the library?

Reading and Reacting

1. Who is the speaker? What does he reveal about himself? Whom might he be addressing?
2. How is the speaker's life outside the library different from the life he leads inside the library?
3. In lines 23–24, the speaker imagines a challenge to his comments. Do you think this challenge is valid? What do you think of the speaker's reply?
4. What phrases are repeated in this poem? Why?
5. **Journal Entry** What argument is the speaker making for the benefits of the library (and for the value of education)? Is he joking, or is he serious?

Related Works: "Gryphon" (p. 277), "Teenage Wasteland" (p. 785), "When I Heard the Learn'd Astronomer" (p. 877), "Why I Went to College" (p. 994)

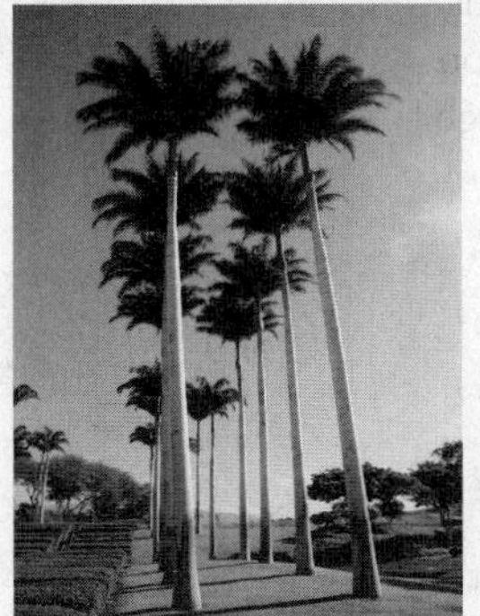
Source: ©Susan Van Etten

HART CRANE (1899–1932)

Royal Palm (1927)

Green rustlings, more-than-regal charities
Drift coolly from that tower of whispered light.
Amid the noontide's blazed asperities
I watched the sun's most gracious anchorite°

Climb up as by communings, year on year
Uneaten of the earth or aught° earth holds,
And the gray trunk, that's elephantine, rear
Its frondings sighing in ethereal folds.

Forever fruitless, and beyond that yield
Of sweat the jungle presses with hot love
And tendril till our deathward breath is sealed—
It grazes the horizons, launched above

anchorite: One who withdraws from society to pursue a life of religious devotion.
aught: Anything.

Mortality-ascending emerald-bright,
A fountain at salute, a crown in view—
Unshackled, casual of its azured height,
As though it soared suchwise through heaven too.

Reading and Reacting

1. What do you make of the poet's choice of formal words like "asperities" (line 3), "communings" (line 5), "elephantine" (line 7), and "ethereal" (line 8)? Given the poem's subject—the royal palm—are such words appropriate?
2. What other words in this poem do you see as formal? What words do you consider informal?
3. The general theme of this poem, which is dedicated to the poet's mother, is mortality. What is the connection between this theme and the royal palm?
4. **JOURNAL ENTRY** What exactly is it about the royal palm that captures the speaker's attention and inspires his awe?

Related Works: "My Son, My Executioner" (p. 945), "Do not go gentle into that good night" (p. 1046), "Trees" (p. 1052)

CHARLES BUKOWSKI (1920–1994)

Dog Fight (1984)

he draws up against my rear bumper in the fast lane,
I can see his head in the rear view mirror, his eyes
are blue and he sucks upon a dead cigar.
I pull over. he passes, then slows. I don't like this.
I pull back into the fast lane, engage myself upon
his rear bumper. we are as a team passing through
Compton.
I turn the radio on and light a cigarette.
he ups it 5 mph, I do likewise. we are as a team
entering Inglewood.
he pulls out of the fast lane and I drive past.
then I slow. when I check the rear view he is
upon my bumper again.
he has almost made me miss my turnoff at Century.
I hit the blinker and fire across 3 lanes of
traffic, just make the off-ramp . . .
blazing past the front of an inflammable tanker.
blue eyes comes down from behind the tanker and
we veer down the ramp in separate lanes to the signal
and we sit there side by side, not looking at each
other.
I am caught behind an empty school bus as he idles
behind a Mercedes.

the signal switches and he is gone. I cut to the
inner lane behind him, then I see that the parking
lane is open and I flash by inside of him and the
Mercedes, turn up the radio, make the green as the
Mercedes and blue eyes run the yellow into the red.
they make it as I power it and switch back ahead of
them in their lane in order to miss a parked vegetable
truck.
now we are running 1-2-3, not a cop in sight, we are
moving through a 1980 California July
we are driving with skillful nonchalance
we are moving in perfect anger
we are as a team
approaching LAX:°
1-2-3
2-3-1
3-2-1.

Reading and Reacting

1. "Dog Fight" describes a car race from the emotionally charged perspective of a driver. Given this perspective, comment on the appropriateness of the level of diction of the words "likewise" (line 9), "upon" (line 13), "nonchalance" (line 34), and "perfect" (line 35).
2. Many of the words in the poem are **jargon**—specialized language associated with a particular trade or profession. In this case, Bukowski uses automotive terms and the action words and phrases that typically describe driving maneuvers. Would you characterize these words as formal, informal, or neither? Explain.
3. What colloquialisms are present in the poem? Could noncolloquial expressions be substituted for any of them? How would such substitutions change the poem?
4. **Journal Entry** Look up the phrase *dog fight* in a dictionary. What meanings are listed? Which one do you think Bukowski had in mind? Why?
5. **Critical Perspective** In a review in the *Village Voice*, critic Michael Lally defended Bukowski's poetry:

   > Despite what some criticize as prose in Bukowski's poetry, there is in much of his work a poetic sensibility that, though arrogantly smart-ass and self-protective as well as self-promotional (he's the granddaddy of "punk" sensibility for sure), is also sometimes poignant, emotionally revealing, uniquely "American". . . .

   Does "Dog Fight" seem like prose to you, or do you see in it a "poetic sensibility"? In what sense, if any, do you find it "uniquely 'American'"? Give examples from the poem to support your conclusions.

Related Works: "Accident" (p. 181), "Greasy Lake" (p. 687), "American Haiku" (p. 997), "Chicago" (p. 999), "The Ride" (p. 1209), *The Cuban Swimmer* (p. 1732)

LAX: Los Angeles International Airport.

Source: ©Bill Tague

See this poet's biography on p. 1218.

GWENDOLYN BROOKS (1917–2000)

We Real Cool (1959)

The Pool Players.
Seven at the Golden Shovel.

We real cool. We
Left School. We

Lurk late. We
Strike straight. We

Sing sin. We
Thin gin. We

Jazz June. We
Die soon.

Reading and Reacting

1. What elements of nonstandard English grammar appear in this poem? How does the use of such language affect your attitude toward the speaker?
2. Every word in this poem is a single syllable. Why?
3. Why do you think the poet begins with "We" only in the first line instead of isolating each complete sentence on its own line? How does this strategy change the poem's impact?
4. **JOURNAL ENTRY** Write a prose version of this poem, adding words, phrases, and sentences to expand the poem into a paragraph.
5. **CRITICAL PERSPECTIVE** In *Gwendolyn Brooks: Poetry and the Heroic Voice*, critic D. H. Malhem writes of "We Real Cool," "Despite presentation in the voice of the gang, this is a maternal poem, gently scolding yet deeply sorrowing for the hopelessness of the boys."

   Do you agree with Malhem that the speaker's attitude is "maternal"?

Related Works: "Where Are You Going, Where Have You Been?" (p. 617), "Greasy Lake" (p. 687), "Teenage Wasteland" (p. 785), "Ex-Basketball Player" (p. 930), *Tape* (p. 1275), *Poker!* (p. 1282)

GWENDOLYN BROOKS (1917–2000)

What Shall I Give My Children? (1949)

What shall I give my children? who are poor,
Who are adjudged the leastwise of the land,
Who are my sweetest lepers, who demand
No velvet and no velvety velour;
But who have begged me for a brisk contour,
Crying that they are quasi, contraband

Because unfinished, graven by a hand
Less than angelic, admirable or sure.
My hand is stuffed with mode, design, device.
But I lack access to my proper stone.
And plenitude of plan shall not suffice
Nor grief nor love shall be enough alone
To ratify my little halves who bear
Across an autumn freezing everywhere.

Reading and Reacting

1. Unlike "We Real Cool" (p. 896), also by Gwendolyn Brooks, this sonnet's diction is quite formal. Given the subject of each poem, do the poet's decisions about level of diction make sense to you?
2. Which words in this poem do you see as elevated—that is, not likely to be used in conversation?
3. Apart from individual words, what else strikes you as formal about this poem?
4. **Journal Entry** Consulting a dictionary if necessary, write down a synonym for each of the formal words you identified in question 2. Then, write out three or four lines of this poem in more conversational language.

Related Works: "We Real Cool" (p. 896), "The *Chicago Defender* Sends a Man to Little Rock" (p. 1131), "Medgar Evers" (p. 1132)

 Word Order

The order in which words are arranged in a poem is as important as the choice of words. Because English sentences nearly always have a subject-verb-object sequence, with adjectives preceding the nouns they modify, a departure from this order calls attention to itself. Thus, poets can use readers' expectations about word order to their advantage.

For example, poets often manipulate word order to place emphasis on a word. Sometimes they achieve this emphasis by using a very unconventional sequence; sometimes they simply place the word first or last in a line or place it in a stressed position in the line. Poets may also choose a particular word order to make two related—or startlingly unrelated—words fall in adjacent or parallel positions, calling attention to the similarity (or the difference) between them. In other cases, poets may manipulate syntax to preserve a poem's rhyme or meter or to highlight sound correspondences that might otherwise not be noticeable. Finally, irregular syntax may be used throughout a poem to reveal a speaker's mood—for example, to give a playful quality to a poem or to suggest a speaker's disoriented state.

In the poem that follows, word order frequently departs from conventional English syntax.

EDMUND SPENSER (1552–1599)

One day I wrote her name upon the strand (1595)

One day I wrote her name upon the strand,°
But came the waves and washed it away:
Again I wrote it with a second hand,
But came the tide and made my pains his prey.
"Vain man," said she, "that doest in vain assay,
A mortal thing so to immortalize,
For I myself shall like to this decay,
And eek° my name be wiped out likewise."
"Not so," quod° I, "let baser things devise,
To die in dust, but you shall live by fame:
My verse your virtues rare shall eternize,
And in the heavens write your glorious name.
Where whenas death shall all the world subdue,
Our love shall live, and later life renew."

"One day I wrote her name upon the strand," a **sonnet,** has a fixed metrical pattern and rhyme scheme. To accommodate the sonnet's rhyme and meter, Spenser makes a number of adjustments in syntax. For example, to make sure certain rhyming words fall at the ends of lines, the poet sometimes moves words out of their conventional order, as the following three comparisons illustrate.

Conventional Word Order	Inverted Sequence
"'Vain man,' she said, 'that doest *assay in vain*.'"	"'Vain man,' said she, 'that doest *in vain assay*.'" ("Assay" appears at end of line 5, to rhyme with line 7's "decay.")
"My verse shall *eternize your rare virtues*."	"My verse *your virtues rare shall eternize*." ("Eternize" appears at end of line 11 to rhyme with line 9's "devise.")
"Where whenas death shall *subdue all the world*, / Our love shall live, and *later renew life*."	"Where whenas death shall *all the world subdue*, / Our love shall live, and *later life renew*." (Rhyming words "subdue" and "renew" are placed at ends of lines.)

strand: Beach.
eek: Also, indeed.
quod: Said.

To make sure the metrical pattern stresses certain words, the poet occasionally moves a word out of conventional order and places it in a stressed position. The following comparison illustrates this technique.

Conventional Word Order	**Inverted Sequence**
"But *the waves came* and washed it away."	"But *came the waves* and washed it away." (Stress in line 2 falls on "waves" rather than on "the.")

As the above comparisons show, Spenser's adjustments in syntax are motivated at least in part by a desire to preserve his sonnet's rhyme and meter.

The next poem does more than simply invert word order; it presents an intentionally disordered syntax.

E. E. CUMMINGS (1894–1962)

anyone lived in a pretty how town (1940)

anyone lived in a pretty how town
(with up so floating many bells down)
spring summer autumn winter
he sang his didn't he danced his did.

Women and men (both little and small)
cared for anyone not at all
they sowed their isn't they reaped their same
sun moon stars rain

children guessed (but only a few
and down they forgot as up they grew
autumn winter spring summer)
that noone loved him more by more

when by now and tree by leaf
she laughed his joy she cried his grief
bird by snow and stir by still
anyone's any was all to her

someones married their everyones
laughed their cryings and did their dance
(sleep wake hope and then) they
said their nevers they slept their dream

stars rain sun moon
(and only the snow can begin to explain
how children are apt to forget to remember
with up so floating many bells down)

one day anyone died i guess
(and noone stooped to kiss his face)
busy folk buried them side by side
little by little and was by was

all by all and deep by deep
and more by more they dream their sleep
noone and anyone earth by april
wish by spirit and if by yes.

Women and men (both dong and ding)
summer autumn winter spring
reaped their sowing and went their came
sun moon stars rain

Cummings, like Spenser, sometimes manipulates syntax in response to the demands of rhyme and meter—for example, in line 10. But Cummings goes much further, using unconventional syntax as part of a scheme that includes other unusual elements of the poem, such as its unexpected departures from the musical metrical pattern (for example, in lines 3 and 8) and from the rhyme scheme (for example, in lines 3 and 4) and its use of various parts of speech in unfamiliar contexts. Together, these techniques give the poem a playful quality. The refreshing disorder of the syntax (for instance, in lines 1–2, 10, and 24) adds to the poem's whimsical effect.

FURTHER READING: Word Order

A. E. HOUSMAN (1859–1936)

To an Athlete Dying Young (1896)

The time you won your town the race
We chaired you through the market-place;
Man and boy stood cheering by,
And home we brought you shoulder-high.

Today, the road all runners come,
Shoulder-high we bring you home,
And set you at your threshold down,
Townsman of a stiller town.

Smart lad, to slip betimes away
From fields where glory does not stay,
And early though the laurel grows
It withers quicker than the rose.

Eyes the shady night has shut
Cannot see the record cut,
And silence sounds no worse than cheers
After earth has stopped the ears.

Now you will not swell the rout
Of lads that wore their honors out,
Runners whom renown outran
And the name died before the man.

So set, before its echoes fade,
The fleet foot on the sill of shade,
And hold to the low lintel up
The still-defended challenge-cup.

And round that early-laureled head
Will flock to gaze the strengthless dead,
And find unwithered on its curls
The garland briefer than a girl's.

Reading and Reacting

1. Where does the poem's meter or rhyme scheme require the poet to depart from conventional syntax?
2. Edit the poem so its word order is more conventional. Do your changes improve the poem?
3. **JOURNAL ENTRY** Who do you think the speaker is? What is his relationship to the athlete?

Related Works: "Saint Helene" (p. 499), "Nothing Gold Can Stay" (p. 914), "Ex-Basketball Player" (p. 930), "For Malcolm, a Year After" (p. 964), "The Names" (p. 1139)

EMILY DICKINSON (1830–1886)

My Life had stood—a Loaded Gun (c. 1863)

My Life had stood—a Loaded Gun—
In Corners—till a Day
The Owner passed—identified—
And carried Me away—

And now We roam in Sovereign Woods—
And now We hunt the Doe—
And every time I speak for Him—
The Mountains straight reply—

And do I smile, such cordial light
Upon the Valley glow—
It is as a Vesuvian° face
Had let its pleasure through—

And when at Night—Our good Day done—
I guard My Master's Head—

Vesuvian: The volcano Mount Vesuvius erupted in A.D. 79, destroying the city of Pompeii.

'Tis better than the Eider-Duck's°
Deep Pillow—to have shared—

To foe of His—I'm deadly foe—
None stir the second time—
On whom I lay a Yellow Eye—
Or an emphatic Thumb—

Though I than He—may longer live
He longer must—than I—
For I have but the power to kill,
Without—the power to die—

Reading and Reacting

1. Identify lines in which word order departs from conventional English syntax. Can you explain in each case why the word order has been manipulated?
2. Do any words gain added emphasis by virtue of their unexpected position? Which ones? How are these words important to the poem's meaning?
3. **JOURNAL ENTRY** Why do you think the speaker might be comparing her life to a loaded gun?
4. **CRITICAL PERSPECTIVE** Writing in the *New York Times*, Elizabeth Schmidt offers this evaluation of Dickinson's poetry:

   > Her formal discipline—the economy of her language and her elaborate, idiosyncratic metrical schemes—turns out to be anything but off-putting. She chose forms that readers could learn by heart, creating one of literature's great, and most unlikely, combinations of style and content. Her poems are often conceptually difficult, and yet they are also surprisingly inviting, whether they coax you to guess a riddle or carry you along to the beat of a familiar tune.

   Do you find Dickinson's poetry as "inviting" as Schmidt does, or do you think a poem like "My Life had stood—a Loaded Gun" *is* "off-putting"?

Related Works: "Because I could not stop for Death—" (p. 1141), "I heard a Fly buzz—when I died—" (p. 1143), "I taste a liquor never brewed—" (p. 1144)

✔ CHECKLIST Writing about Word Choice and Word Order

Word Choice

- Which words are of key importance in the poem? What is the denotative meaning of each of these key words?
- Which key words have neutral connotations? Which have negative connotations? Which have positive connotations? Beyond its literal meaning, what does each word suggest?
- Why is each word chosen instead of a synonym? (For example, is the word chosen for its sound? Its connotation? Its relationship to other words in the poem? Its contribution to the poem's metrical pattern?)

continued on next page

Eider-Duck's: Eider ducks produce a soft down (eiderdown) used as pillow stuffing.

- What other words could be effectively used in place of words now in the poem? How would substitutions change the poem's meaning?
- Are any words repeated? Why?

Levels of Diction

- How would you characterize the poem's level of diction? Why is this level of diction used? Is it appropriate?
- Does the poem mix different levels of diction? If so, why?

Word Order

- Is the poem's word order conventional, or are words arranged in unexpected order?
- What is the purpose of the unusual word order? (For example, does it preserve the poem's meter or rhyme scheme? Does it highlight particular sound correspondences? Does it place emphasis on a particular word or phrase? Does it reflect the speaker's mood?)
- How would the poem's impact change if conventional syntax were used?

WRITING SUGGESTIONS: Word Choice, Word Order

1. Reread the two poems in this chapter by E. E. Cummings—"in Just-" (p. 883) and "anyone lived in a pretty how town" (p. 899). If you like, you may also read one or two additional poems in this book by Cummings. Do you believe Cummings chose words primarily for their sound? For their appearance on the page? What other factors might have influenced his choices?
2. The tone of "We Real Cool" (p. 896) is flat and unemotional; the problem on which it focuses, however, is serious. Expand this concise poem into a few paragraphs that retain the poem's informal, colloquial tone but use more detailed, more emotional language to communicate the hopeless situation of the speaker and his friends. Include dialogue as well as narrative.
3. Reread "Living in Sin" (p. 882) and "Sears Life" (p. 891), and choose one or two other poems in this book whose speaker is a woman. Compare the speakers' levels of diction and choice of words. What does their language reveal about their lives?
4. Reread "For the Grave of Daniel Boone" (p. 878) alongside another poem about a historical figure or event—for example, "For the Union Dead" (p. 1063) or "The Convergence of the Twain" (p. 1163). What does each poem's choice of words reveal about the speaker's attitude toward his subject?
5. Analyze the choice of words and the level of diction in several poems in this book that use language to express social or political criticism. Some poems that might work well include William Blake's "London" (p. 1128), Claude McKay's "If We Must Die" (p. 1179), Marge Piercy's "Barbie doll" (p. 1187), Robert Pinsky's "Shirt" (p. 1188), and Ariel Dorfman's "Hope" (p. 863).

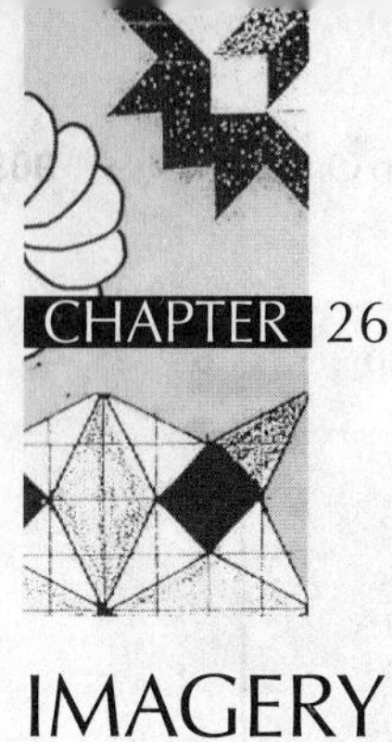

CHAPTER 26

IMAGERY

Source: ©Steven Flanders

JANE FLANDERS (1940–2001)

Cloud Painter (1984)

Suggested by the life and art of John Constable°

At first, as you know, the sky is incidental—
a drape, a backdrop for trees and steeples.
Here an oak clutches a rock (already he works outdoors),
a wall buckles but does not break,
water pearls through a lock, a haywain° trembles.

The pleasures of landscape are endless. What we see
around us should be enough.
Horizons are typically high and far away.

Still, clouds let us drift and remember. He is, after all,
a miller's son, used to trying
to read the future in the sky, seeing instead
ships, horses, instruments of flight.
Is that his mother's wash flapping on the line?
His schoolbook, smudged, illegible?

In this period the sky becomes significant.
Cloud forms are technically correct—mares' tails,
sheep-in-the-meadow, thunderheads.
You can almost tell which scenes have been interrupted
by summer showers.

Now his young wife dies.
His landscapes achieve belated success.
He is invited to join the Academy. I forget
whether he accepts or not.

In any case, the literal forms give way
to something spectral, nameless. His palette shrinks
to gray, blue, white—the colors of charity.

John Constable: British painter (1776–1837) noted for his landscapes.
haywain: An open horse-drawn wagon for carrying hay.

Horizons sink and fade,
trees draw back till they are little more than frames,
then they too disappear.
Finally the canvas itself begins to vibrate
with waning light,
as if the wind could paint.
And we too, at last, stare into a space
which tells us nothing,
except that the world can vanish along with our need for it.

Because the purpose of poetry—and, for that matter, of all literature—is to expand the perception of readers, poets appeal to the senses. In "Cloud Painter," Jane Flanders uses **images,** such as the mother's wash on the line and the smudged schoolbook, to enable readers to visualize particular scenes in John Constable's early paintings. (For additional poems written in response to works of art, see the Poetry Sampler: Poetry and Art, p. PS1). Clouds are described so readers can picture them—"mares' tails, / sheep-in-the-meadow, thunderheads." Thus, "Cloud Painter" is not only about the work of John Constable but also about the ability of an artist—poet or painter—to call up images in the minds of an audience. To achieve this end, a poet uses **imagery,** language that evokes a physical sensation produced by one or more of the five senses—sight, hearing, taste, touch, smell.

Although the effect can be complex, the way images work is simple: when you read the word *red,* your memory of the various red things that you have seen determines how you picture the image. In addition, the word *red* may have **connotations**—emotional associations that define your response. A red

John Constable (1776–1837). *Landscape, Noon, The Haywain.* 1821. Oil on canvas, 130½ × 185½ cm. London, National Gallery.

sunset, for example, can have a positive connotation or a negative one, depending on whether it is associated with the end of a perfect day or with air pollution. By choosing images carefully, poets not only create pictures in a reader's mind but also create a great number of imaginative associations. These associations help poets to establish the **atmosphere** or **mood** of the poem. The image of softly falling snow in "Stopping by Woods on a Snowy Evening" (p. 1159), for example, creates a quiet, almost mystical mood.

Readers come to a poem with their own unique experiences, so an image in a poem does not suggest exactly the same thing to all readers. In "Cloud Painter," for example, the poet presents the image of an oak tree clutching a rock. Although most readers will probably see a picture that is generally consistent with the one the poet sees, no two images will be identical. Every reader will have his or her own distinct mental image of a tree clinging to a rock; some images will be remembered experiences, whereas others will be imaginative creations. Some readers may even be familiar enough with the work of the painter John Constable to visualize a particular tree clinging to a particular rock in one of his paintings. By conveying what the poet imagines, images open readers' minds to perceptions and associations different from—and possibly more original and complex than—their own.

One advantage of imagery is its extreme economy. A few carefully chosen words enable poets to evoke a range of emotions and reactions. In the following poem, William Carlos Williams uses simple visual images to create a rich and compelling picture.

Source: ©Bettmann/Corbis

See this poet's biography on p. 1231.

WILLIAM CARLOS WILLIAMS (1883–1963)

Red Wheelbarrow (1923)

so much depends
upon

a red wheel
barrow

glazed with rain
water

beside the white
chickens

What is immediately apparent in this poem is its verbal economy. The poet does not tell readers what the barnyard smells like or what sounds the animals make. In fact, he does not even present a detailed picture of the scene. How large is the wheelbarrow? What is its condition? How many chickens are in the barnyard? In this poem, the answers to these questions are not important.

Even without answering these questions, the poet is able to use simple imagery to create a scene on which, he says, "so much depends." The wheelbarrow establishes a momentary connection between the poet and his world. Like a still-life painting, the red wheelbarrow beside the white chickens gives order to a world that is full of seemingly unrelated objects. In this poem, the poet suggests that our ability to perceive the objects of this world gives our lives meaning and that our ability to convey our perceptions to others is central to our lives as well as to poetry.

Images enable poets to present ideas that would be difficult to convey in any other way. One look at a dictionary will illustrate that concepts such as *beauty* and *mystery* are so abstract that they are difficult to define, let alone to discuss in specific terms. However, by choosing an image or a series of images to embody these ideas, poets can effectively make their feelings known, as Ezra Pound does in the two-line poem that follows.

Source: ©AP Photo

See this poet's biography on p. 1226.

EZRA POUND (1885–1972)

In a Station of the Metro (1916)

The apparition of these faces in the crowd;
Petals on a wet, black bough.

This poem is almost impossible to paraphrase because the information it communicates is less important than the feelings associated with this information. The poem's title indicates that the first line is meant to suggest a group of people standing in a station of the Paris subway. The scene, however, is presented not as a clear picture but as an "apparition," suggesting that it is unexpected or even dreamlike. In contrast with the image of the subway platform is the image of the people's faces as flower petals on the dark branch of a tree. Thus, the subway platform—dark, cold, wet, subterranean (associated with baseness, death, and hell)—is juxtaposed with flower petals—delicate, pale, radiant, lovely (associated with the ideal, life, and heaven). These contrasting images, presented without comment, bear the entire weight of the poem.

Although images can be strikingly visual, they can also appeal to the senses of hearing, smell, taste, and touch. The following poem uses images of sound and taste as well as sight.

GARY SNYDER (1930–)

Some Good Things to Be Said for the Iron Age (1970)

A ringing tire iron
    dropped on the pavement
Whang of a saw

brusht on limbs
the taste
of rust

Here Snyder presents two commonplace aural images: the ringing of a tire iron and the sound of a saw. These somewhat ordinary images gain power, however, through their visual isolation on separate lines in the poem. Together they produce a harsh and jarring chord that creates a sense of uneasiness in the reader. This poem does more than present sensory images, though; it also conveys the speaker's interpretations of these images. The last two lines imply not only that the time in which we live (the Iron Age) is base and mundane, but also that it is declining, decaying into an age of rust. The title of the poem makes an ironic comment, suggesting that compared to the time that is approaching, the age of iron may be "good." Thus, in the mind of the poet, ordinary events gain added significance, and images that spring from everyday experience become sources of insight.

In short poems, such as most of those discussed above, one or two images may serve as focal points. A longer poem may introduce a cluster of images, creating a more complex tapestry of sensory impressions—as in the following poem, where a number of related images are woven together.

SUZANNE E. BERGER (1944–)

The Meal (1984)

They have washed their faces until they are pale,
their homework is beautifully complete.
They wait for the adults to lean towards each other.
The hands of the children are oval
and smooth as pine-nuts.
The girls have braided and rebraided their hair,
and tied ribbons without a single mistake.
The boy has put away his coin collection.
They are waiting for the mother to straighten her lipstick,
and for the father to speak.

They gather around the table, carefully
as constellations waiting to be named.
Their minds shift and ready, like dunes.
It is so quiet, all waiting stars and dunes.

Their forks move across their plates without scraping,
they wait for the milk and the gravy
at the table with its forgotten spices.

They are waiting for a happiness to lift their eyes,
like sudden light flaring in the trees outside.

The white miles of the meal continue,
the figures still travel across a screen:
the father carving the Sunday roast,
her mouth uneven as a torn hibiscus,
their braids still gleaming in the silence.

"The Meal" begins with the image of faces washed "until they are pale" and goes on to describe the children's oval hands as "smooth as pine-nuts." Forks move across plates "without scraping," and the table hints at the memory of "forgotten spices." Despite the poem's title, these children are emotionally starved. The attentive, well-scrubbed children sit at a table where, neither eating nor speaking, they wait for "the milk and the gravy" and for happiness that never comes. The "white miles of the meal" seem to go on forever, reinforcing the sterility and emptiness of the Sunday ritual. Suggesting an absence of sensation or feeling, a kind of paralysis, the poem's images challenge conventional assumptions about the family and its rituals.

Much visual imagery is **static,** freezing the moment and thereby giving it the timeless quality of painting or sculpture. ("The Meal" presents such a tableau, and so do "Red Wheelbarrow" and "In a Station of the Metro.") Some imagery, in contrast, is **kinetic,** conveying a sense of motion or change.

WILLIAM CARLOS WILLIAMS (1883–1963)

The Great Figure (1938)

Among the rain
and lights
I saw the figure 5
in gold
on a red
firetruck
moving
tense
unheeded
to gong clangs
siren howls
and wheels rumbling
through the dark city.

Commenting on "The Great Figure" in his autobiography, Williams explained that while walking in New York, he heard the sound of a fire engine. As he turned the corner, he saw a golden figure 5 on a red background speed by. The impression was so forceful that he immediately jotted down a poem about it. In the poem, Williams attempts to re-create the sensation the figure 5 made as it moved into his consciousness. The poet presents images in the order in which he perceived them: first the 5, and then the red fire truck howling and clanging into the darkness. Thus, "The Great Figure" uses images of sight, sound, and movement to convey the poet's experience. The American painter Charles Demuth was fascinated by the poem. Working closely with Williams, he attempted to capture the poem's kinetic energy in a painting.

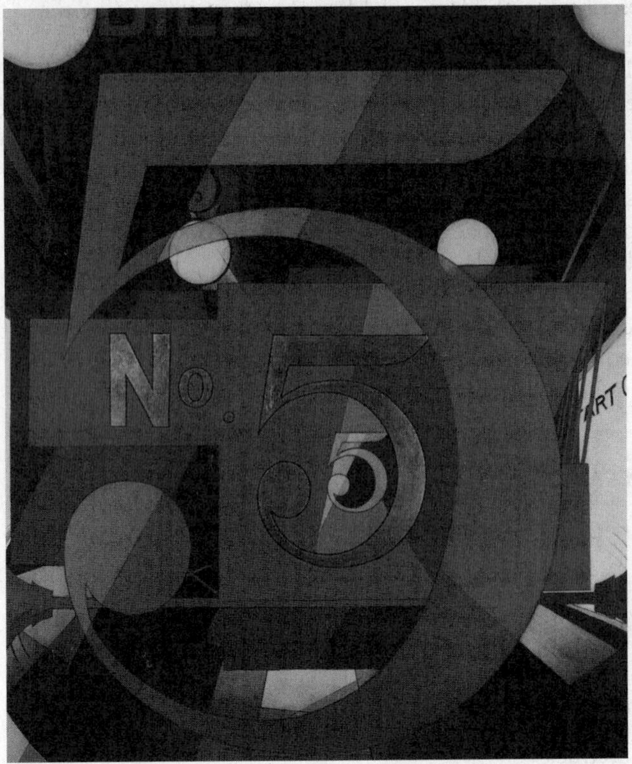

Charles Henry Demuth (1883–1935). *The Figure 5 in Gold*. Oil on composition board, 36 × 29¾ in.

Source: ©The Metropolitan Museum of Art, The Alfred Steiglitz Collection, 1949 (49.59.1)

NOTE: A special use of imagery, called **synesthesia,** occurs when one sense is described in a way that is more appropriate for another sense—for instance, when a sound is described with color. When people say they are feeling *blue* or describe music as *hot,* they are using synesthesia.

FURTHER READING: Imagery

RICHARD WILBUR (1921–)

Sleepless at Crown Point (1973)

All night, this headland
Lunges into the rumpling
Capework of the wind.

Reading and Reacting

1. What scene is the speaker describing?
2. What is the poem's central image? How do the words "lunges" and "capework" help to convey this image?
3. **JOURNAL ENTRY** What is the significance of the title?

Related Works: "I wandered lonely as a cloud" (p. 1048), "Fog" (p. 1053)

Source: ©University of Nebraska—Lincoln Publications and Photography

See this poet's biography on p. 1223.

TED KOOSER (1939–)

Wild Plums in Blossom (2006)

In a light, cold rain, at the edge of the woods,
a line of brides is waiting, hand in hand.
Their perfume carries far across the fields.
They have been brought here from the east
to marry farmers, and were left on the platform.
The dark old depot of the woods is locked
and no one has come for them but me.

Reading and Reacting

1. What scene is the poem describing?
2. What different kinds of images does the poem present?
3. In what way does the poem's title establish the central image of the poem?
4. **JOURNAL ENTRY** What do you think the poem's last line means?

Related Works: "Snow" (p. 177), "Pied Beauty" (p. 971), "After Bashō" (p. 996), "American Haiku" (p. 997), "Spring and All" (p. 1003)

MICHAEL CHITWOOD (1978–)

Division (2002)

Inside the shed, he'd rigged
an oil drip into the barrel stove
so that the used sludge from his trucks
burned with split hickory while he
passed the winter piecing together furniture.
Just a sideline, he'd say, aiming
down a board to judge it in or out of true.
"It fills in the down months and tacks
some cash on the end of the year."

In those same white weeks at school
I learned division. First, you made a lean-to
for the big number to go under. The little
number waited outside. You could add on
as many zeros as you wanted.
The answer appeared on the roof.
December and January passed into February
and a whole bedroom suite came together.
On the roof, the smoke swirled into 0s and 8s.

Reading and Reacting

1. This poem is divided into two stanzas. What is described in the first stanza? What is described in the second stanza?
2. In what sense is doing carpentry like learning long division?
3. List the images that appear in the poem. How do these images reinforce the similarities between the carpenter and the boy?
4. **JOURNAL ENTRY** Other than arithmetic, what else could the title of the poem suggest?

Related Works: "Gryphon" (p. 277), "When I Heard The Learn'd Astronomer" (p. 877), "My Father as a Guitar" (p. 935), "Digging" (p. 1040), *Proof* (p. 1476)

BILL COYLE (1968–)

Spring: The Star Magnolia (2006)

Wind stirs the branches and white petals fall,
filling the fountain, carpeting the lawn.
The snows of yesteryear have been and gone
and drift the ground in memory, if at all.

Reading and Reacting

1. The poem consists of two sentences. What images does each sentence contain?
2. What central idea does the poem attempt to convey?
3. What does the poem's title suggest?
4. **JOURNAL ENTRY** The fourth line of "Spring: The Star Magnolia" alludes to a poem by fifteenth-century poet François Villon, which contains the refrain, "Where are the snows of yesteryear?" In his poem, Villon asks why life fades so quickly. Why do you think Coyle alludes to Villon's line in his poem?

Related Works: "Snow" (p. 177), "A Rose for Emily" (p. 243), "To the Virgins, to Make Much of Time" (p. 858), "Spring and All" (p. 1003)

LAM THI MY DA (1949–)

Washing Rice (2001)

My mother is washing rice in late morning
A gentle wind ruffles the shade of the palms
The yellow rice glistens in rippled water
The ripe grains and the unripe look the same
They are both the color of silk, the same color
But why does she keep washing, washing so long?

How many unripe grains drift away from you, Mother?
How many ripe grains stay with you and talk?
When I go out tomorrow, full of life,
Will my lesson be your hand, washing rice?

Reading and Reacting

1. Why is the speaker's mother washing rice? What does the washing accomplish?
2. In line 6, the speaker asks, "But why does she keep washing, washing so long?" What do you think the answer to this question might be?
3. What is the significance of the speaker's observation that the ripe and unripe grains are the same color?
4. **JOURNAL ENTRY** According to the speaker, what lesson can he learn from watching his mother washing rice?

Related Works: "Gryphon" (p. 277), "Water Names" (p. 318), "Girl Powdering Her Neck" (p. PS5), "Those Winter Sundays" (p. 1040), "To see a World in a Grain of Sand" (p. 1129), *Trying to Find Chinatown* (p. 1856)

ROBERT FROST (1874–1963)

Nothing Gold Can Stay (1923)

Nature's first green is gold,
Her hardest hue to hold.
Her early leaf's a flower;
But only so an hour.
Then leaf subsides to leaf.
So Eden sank to grief.
So dawn goes down to day.
Nothing gold can stay.

Reading and Reacting

1. What central idea does this poem express?

2. What do you think the first line of the poem means? In what sense is this line ironic?

3. What is the significance of the colors green and gold in this poem? What do these colors have to do with "Eden" and "dawn"?

4. JOURNAL ENTRY How do the various images in the poem prepare readers for the last line? Do you think the title spoils the impact of the last line?

5. CRITICAL PERSPECTIVE In "The Figure a Poem Means," the introduction to the first edition of his *Collected Poems* (1930), Frost laid out a theory of poetry:

> It begins in delight, it inclines to the impulse, it assumes direction with the first line laid down, it runs a course of lucky events, and ends in a clarification of life—not necessarily a great clarification . . . but a momentary stay against confusion. . . . Like a piece of ice on a hot stove the poem must ride on its own melting. . . . Read it a hundred times: it will forever keep its freshness as a metal keeps its fragrance. It can never lose its sense of a meaning that once unfolded by surprise as it went.

Explain how Frost's remarks apply to "Nothing Gold Can Stay."

Related Works: "The Secret Lion" (p. 197), "Araby" (p. 434), "Greasy Lake" (p. 687), "Try to Praise the Mutilated World" (p. 854), "Shall I compare thee to a summer's day?" (p. 923), "This is my letter to the World" (p. 1147), "God's Grandeur" (p. 1166)

JEAN TOOMER (1894–1967)

Reapers (1923)

Black reapers with the sound of steel on stones
Are sharpening scythes. I see them place the hones°
In their hip-pockets as a thing that's done,

---

hones: Stones used to sharpen cutting instruments.

And start their silent swinging, one by one.
Black horses drive a mower through the weeds,
And there, a field rat, startled, squealing bleeds,
His belly close to ground. I see the blade,
Blood-stained, continue cutting weeds and shade.

Reading and Reacting

1. What determines the order in which the speaker arranges the images in this poem? At what point does he comment on these images?
2. The first four lines of the poem seem to suggest that the workers are content. What image contradicts this impression? How does it do so?
3. What ideas are traditionally associated with the image of the reaper? The scythe? The harvest? (To answer these questions, you may want to consult a reference source, such as <http://www.symbols.com>.) In what way does the speaker rely on these conventional associations to help him convey his ideas? Can you appreciate the poem without understanding these associations?
4. **JOURNAL ENTRY** Who do you think the speaker might be? Why?
5. **CRITICAL PERSPECTIVE** As Brian Joseph Benson and Mabel Mayle Dillard point out in their 1980 study *Jean Toomer*, the poet disagreed with some other artists of the Harlem Renaissance, choosing not to focus on "Negro" themes for a primarily black audience but rather to try to make his work universal in scope.

   Do you think he has achieved this goal in "Reapers"?

Related Works: "Buffalo Soldiers" (p. 187), "A Worn Path" (p. 568), "Traveling through the Dark" (p. 1052), "Because I could not stop for Death—" (p. 1141), "The Solitary Reaper" (p. 1211)

WILFRED OWEN (1893–1918)

Dulce et Decorum Est° (1920)

Bent double, like old beggars under sacks,
Knock-kneed, coughing like hags, we cursed through sludge,
Till on the haunting flares we turned our backs
And towards our distant rest began to trudge.
Men marched asleep. Many had lost their boots
But limped on, blood-shod. All went lame; all blind;
Drunk with fatigue; deaf even to the hoots
Of tired, outstripped Five-Nines° that dropped behind.

Dulce et Decorum Est: The title and last two lines are from Horace, *Odes* 3.2: "Sweet and fitting it is to die for one's country."

Five-Nines: Shells that explode on impact and release poison gas.

Gas! GAS Quick, boys!—An ecstasy of fumbling,
Fitting the clumsy helmets just in time;
But someone still was yelling out and stumbling
And flound'ring like a man in fire or lime . . .
Dim, through the misty panes and thick green light,
As under a green sea, I saw him drowning.
In all my dreams, before my helpless sight,
He plunges at me, guttering, choking, drowning.

If in some smothering dreams you too could pace
Behind the wagon that we flung him in,
And watch the white eyes writhing in his face,
His hanging face, like a devil's sick of sin;
If you could hear, at every jolt, the blood
Come gargling from the froth-corrupted lungs,
Obscene as cancer, bitter as the cud
Of vile, incurable sores on innocent tongues,—
My friend, you would not tell with such high zest
To children ardent for some desperate glory,
The old Lie: Dulce et decorum est
Pro patria mori.

Reading and Reacting

1. Who is the speaker in this poem? What is his attitude toward his subject?
2. What images are traditionally associated with war? How do the images in this poem depart from these associations? Why do you think Owen selected such images?
3. To what senses (other than sight) does the poem appeal? Is any of its imagery **kinetic?**
4. **Journal Entry** Does the knowledge that Owen died in World War I change your reaction to the poem, or are the poem's images compelling enough to eliminate the need for such biographical background?
5. **Critical Perspective** Like many other British poets who experienced fighting in the European trenches during World War I, Owen struggled to find a way to describe the horrors of this new kind of war. In his 1986 biography *Owen the Poet*, Dominic Hibberd praises the "controlled and powerful anger in 'Dulce et Decorum Est' which for some readers will be the poem's most valuable quality" and goes on to note that the "organization and clarity of the first half is replaced [beginning at line 15] by confused, choking syntax and a vocabulary of sickness and disgust, matching the nightmare which is in progress."

   Give some examples to support Hibberd's statements. How do the images in the poem help establish the movement from control to confusion?

Related Works: "Buffalo Soldiers" (p. 187), "The Things They Carried" (p. 473), "Try to Praise the Mutilated World" (p. 854), "The Soldier" (p. 1062), "How Did They Kill My Grandmother?" (p. 1065)

KOBAYASHI ISSA (1763–1827)

Haiku

Not yet having become a Buddha,
The ancient pine-tree
Idly dreaming

Reading and Reacting

1. Buddhists believe that every person goes through cycles of death and rebirth until he or she reaches the state of nirvana. A key element in achieving this state is the extinction of all desire. In line 1 of the poem, who (or what) has not yet achieved nirvana and become a Buddha?
2. What two images are being compared in the poem? What insight or spiritual message is suggested by this comparison?
3. What is the tone of this poem? Do you think the speaker intends to be taken literally?
4. **Journal Entry** Read the definition of *haiku* on page 802. In what respects is this poem a haiku? How is it unlike tradition haiku?
5. **Critical Perspective** In his essay series *Confessions of a Translator*, David G. Lanoue writes the following about Kobayashi Issa's haiku:

> Though Japanese children are made to memorize it, this haiku is no mere child's poem. It not only vocalizes Issa's Buddhist compassion for, and sense of karmic connection with, sentient life, it hints of a political meaning.

In what ways is this poem "political"? In what ways does it give voice to the Buddhist idea of "compassion for all life"?

Related Works: "Water Names" (p. 318), "Saint Helene" (p. 499), "A Worn Path" (p. 568), "Four Haiku" (p. 995), "American Haiku" (p. 997)

WILLIAM SHAKESPEARE (1564–1616)

My mistress' eyes are nothing like the sun (1609)

My mistress' eyes are nothing like the sun;
Coral is far more red than her lips' red;
If snow be white, why then her breasts are dun;
If hairs be wires, black wires grow on her head.
I have seen roses damasked red and white,
But no such roses see I in her cheeks;
And in some perfumes is there more delight
Than in the breath that from my mistress reeks.
I love to hear her speak, yet well I know
That music hath a far more pleasing sound;

I grant I never saw a goddess go:
My mistress, when she walks, treads on the ground.
  And yet, by heaven, I think my love as rare
  As any she, belied with false compare.

Reading and Reacting

1. What point does Shakespeare make in the first twelve lines of his sonnet?
2. What point does the rhymed couplet at the end of the poem make?
3. How is Shakespeare's imagery like and unlike that of traditional love poems? For example, how is the imagery in this poem different from that in Thomas Campion's "There is a garden in her face" (p. 1134).
4. **Journal Entry** How do you think the woman to whom the poem is addressed will react?
5. **Critical Perspective** During the Renaissance, poets commonly used the "Petrarchan conceit" to praise their lovers. In this type of metaphor, the author draws elaborate comparisons between his beloved and one or more dissimilar things. According to critic Felicia Jean Steele, "Traditional readings of Shakespeare's Sonnet 130 argue that Shakespeare cunningly employs Petrarchan imagery while deliberately undermining it."
   How does this poem use the Petrarchan conceit? How does it undercut this convention?

Related Works: "A&P" (p. 259), "The Storm" (p. 313), "Birthmark" (p. 411), "How Do I Love Thee?" (p. 1055), "In My Little Museum of Erotica" (p. 1057), *The Brute* (p. 1250)

BILLY COLLINS (1941–)

Litany (2002)

You are the bread and the knife,
The crystal goblet and the wine . . .
—Jacques Crickillon

You are the bread and the knife,
the crystal goblet and the wine.
You are the dew on the morning grass
and the burning wheel of the sun.
You are the white apron of the baker
and the marsh birds suddenly in flight.

However, you are not the wind in the orchard,
the plums on the counter,
or the house of cards.
And you are certainly not the pine-scented air.
There is just no way you are the pine-scented air.

It is possible that you are the fish under the bridge,
maybe even the pigeon on the general's head,

but you are not even close
to being the field of cornflowers at dusk.

And a quick look in the mirror will show
that you are neither the boots in the corner
nor the boat asleep in its boathouse.

It might interest you to know,
speaking of the plentiful imagery of the world,
that I am the sound of rain on the roof.

I also happen to be the shooting star,
the evening paper blowing down an alley,
and the basket of chestnuts on the kitchen table.

I am also the moon in the trees
and the blind woman's tea cup.
But don't worry, I am not the bread and the knife.
You are still the bread and the knife.
You will always be the bread and the knife,
not to mention the crystal goblet and—somehow—
the wine.

Reading and Reacting

1. A *litany* is a prayer, but it can also refer to a listing, catalog, or inventory. In what sense is this poem a litany?
2. What images does the speaker associate with himself? What images does he associate with the person he is addressing? What do these images reveal about the speaker? About his attitude toward the person he is addressing?
3. How would you describe the tone of this poem? How do the images help the poet create this tone?
4. **JOURNAL ENTRY** What images could you associate with yourself? What images could you definitely *not* associate with yourself? (Look at the fourth stanza of the poem, for example.)
5. **CRITICAL PERSPECTIVE** Novelist, poet, and critic John Updike wrote the following about poet Billy Collins:

> Billy Collins writes lovely poems—lovely in a way almost nobody's since Roethke's are. Limpid, gently and consistently startling, more serious than they seem, they describe all the worlds that are and were and some others besides.

What "worlds" are being described in this poem? In what sense is this poem "startling" or "more serious" than it seems to be?

Related Works: "Love and Other Catastrophes: A Mix Tape" (p. 182), "The Story of an Hour" (p. 226), "The Girl with Bangs" (p. 271), "Cinderella" (p. 866), "I Knew a Woman" (p. 885), "My mistress' eyes are nothing like the sun" (p. 917), "Metaphors" (p. 929), "How Do I Love Thee?" (p. 1055)

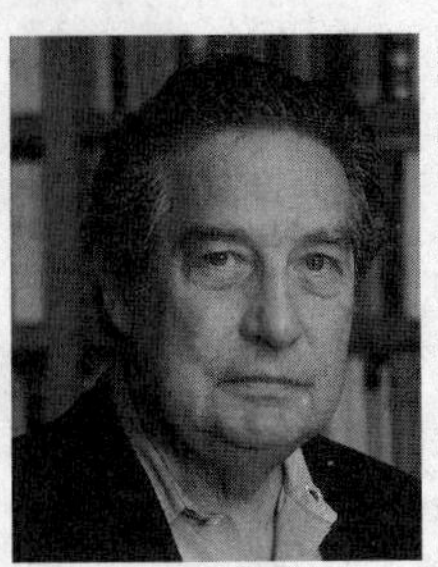
Source: ©Steve Northup/Timepix/Time Life Pictures/Getty Images

See this poet's biography on p. 1226.

OCTAVIO PAZ (1914–1998)

Daybreak

Hands and lips of wind
heart of water
eucalyptus
campground of the clouds
the life that is born every day
the death that is born every life

I rub my eyes:
the sky walks the land

Reading and Reacting

1. What are the connotations of the word *daybreak*?
2. What images does the speaker use to evoke daybreak? What other images could he have used?
3. The poem is visually divided into three parts. What idea does each part express?
4. **Journal Entry** How would you describe the tone of this poem? How do the images help establish this tone?

Related Works: "The Secret Lion" (p. 197), "Morning Song" (p. 856), "Haiku" (p. 917), "Spring and All" (p. 1003), "The Windhover" (p. 1050), "Parting at Morning" (p. 1055), "Anecdote of the Jar" (p. 1201), "October" (p. 1212)

OCTAVIO PAZ (1914–1998)

Nightfall

What sustains it,
half-open, the clarity of nightfall,
the light let loose in the gardens?

All the branches,
conquered by the weight of birds,
lean toward the darkness.

Pure, self-absorbed moments
still gleam
on the fences.

Receiving night,
the groves become
hushed fountains.

A bird falls,
the grass grows dark,
edges blur, lime is black,
the world is less credible

Reading and Reacting

1. Does the speaker present nightfall as something that has positive or negative connotations? Explain.
2. Each of the five stanzas in the poem presents an image. What feature of nightfall does each image express?
3. What does the speaker mean in the last line when he says that nightfall makes the world "less credible"?
4. **Journal Entry** What images do you associate with nightfall? How are these images like and unlike those in the poem?
5. **Critical Perspective** The poetry critic Helen Vendler noted the following about the relationships between reality and fantasy in the work of Octavio Paz:

   > For Paz, poetry is a brink, a precipice, an abyss, where silent before a void, the poet leaves historical time to reenter the time of desire, a time always with us, for which our myths of the Golden Age are only a representation.

   In what ways does the speaker of "Daybreak" and "Nightfall" "leave historical time" to "reenter a time of desire"? What is desired in these poems? How do these desires differ from waking desires? How do they differ from each other from nightfall to daybreak?

Related Works: "Araby" (p. 434), "Gretel in Darkness" (p. 839), "Harlem" (p. 924), Traveling through the Dark" (p. 1052), "Meeting at Night" (p. 1055), "Ode to The West Wind" (p. 1194)

✔ CHECKLIST Writing about Imagery

- Do the images in the poem appeal to the sense of sight? hearing? taste? touch? smell?
- Does the poem depend on a single image or on several different images?
- Does the poem depend on a cluster of related images?
- What details make the images memorable?
- What mood do the images create?
- Are the images static or kinetic?
- How do the poem's images help to convey its theme?
- How effective are the images? How do they enhance your enjoyment of the poem?

WRITING SUGGESTIONS: Imagery

1. Read the **haiku** in Chapter 29 (p. 995), focusing on their use of imagery. How are short poems such as "Some Good Things to Be Said for the Iron Age" (p. 907) and "In a Station of the Metro" (p. 907) like and unlike haiku?
2. After rereading "Cloud Painter" (p. 904) and "The Great Figure" (p. 909), read "Musée des Beaux Arts" (p. 1032), study the corresponding paintings *Landscape, Noon, the Haywain* (p. 905), *The Figure 5 in Gold* (p. 910), and *Landscape with the Fall of Icarus* (p. 1033). Then, write an essay in which you draw some conclusions about the differences between artistic and poetic images. If you like, you may also consider the pictures and poems in the Poetry Sampler: Poetry and Art, PS1–PS8.
3. Reread "The Meal" (p. 908) and the discussion that accompanies it. Then, analyze the role of imagery in the depiction of the parent/child relationships in "Washing Rice" (p. 913) and "My Papa's Waltz" (p. 1039). How does each poem's imagery convey the nature of the relationship it describes?
4. Write an essay in which you discuss the color imagery in "Nothing Gold Can Stay" (p. 914) and "Reapers" (p. 914). In what way does color reinforce the themes of these poems?
5. Sometimes imagery can be used to make a comment about the society in which a scene takes place. Choose two poems in which imagery functions in this way—"For the Union Dead" (p. 1063) or "The *Chicago Defender* Sends a Man to Little Rock" (p. 1131), for example—and discuss how the images chosen reinforce the social comment each poem makes.

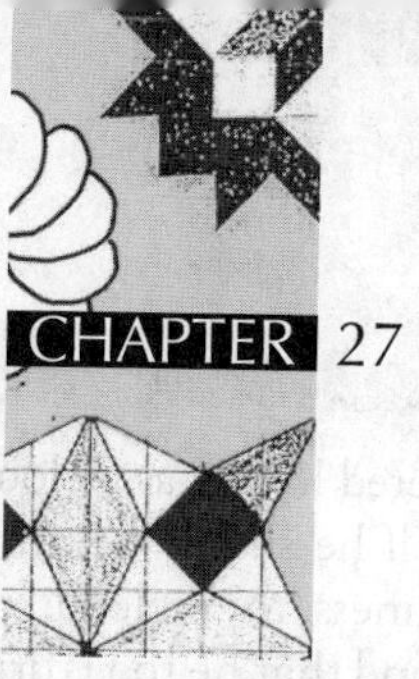

CHAPTER 27

FIGURES OF SPEECH

Source: ©Bettmann/Corbis

See this poet's biography on p. 1604.

WILLIAM SHAKESPEARE (1564–1616)

Shall I compare thee to a summer's day? (1609)

Shall I compare thee to a summer's day?
Thou art more lovely and more temperate.
Rough winds do shake the darling buds of May,
And summer's lease hath all too short a date.
Sometime too hot the eye of heaven shines,
And often is his gold complexion dimmed;
And every fair from fair sometimes declines,
By chance, or nature's changing course, untrimmed.
But thy eternal summer shall not fade,
Nor lose possession of that fair thou ow'st;°
Nor shall death brag thou wand'rest in his shade,
When in eternal lines to time thou grow'st.
So long as men can breathe or eyes can see,
So long lives this, and this gives life to thee.

Although writers experiment with language in all kinds of literary works, poets in particular recognize the power of a figure of speech to take readers beyond the literal meaning of a word. For this reason, **figures of speech**—expressions that use words to achieve effects beyond the power of ordinary language—are more prominent in poetry than in other kinds of writing. For example, the sonnet above compares a loved one to a summer's day in order to make the point that, unlike the fleeting summer, the loved one will—within the poem—remain forever young. But this sonnet goes beyond the obvious equation (loved one = summer's day): the speaker's assertion that his loved one will live forever in his poem actually says more about his confidence in his own talent and reputation (and about the power of language) than about the loved one's beauty.

---

that fair thou ow'st: That beauty you possess.

Simile, Metaphor, and Personification

When William Wordsworth opens a poem with "I wandered lonely as a cloud" (p. 1048), he conveys a good deal more than he would if he simply began, "I wandered, lonely." By comparing himself in his loneliness to a cloud, the speaker suggests that like the cloud he is a part of nature and that he too is drifting, passive, blown by winds, and lacking will or substance. Thus, by using a figure of speech, the poet can suggest a wide variety of feelings and associations in very few words.

The phrase "I wandered lonely as a cloud" is a **simile,** a comparison between two unlike items that uses *like* or *as*. When an imaginative comparison between two unlike items does not use *like* or *as*— that is, when it says "a *is* b" rather than "a is *like* b"—it is a **metaphor**.

Accordingly, when the speaker in Adrienne Rich's "Living in Sin" (p. 882) speaks of "daylight coming / like a relentless milkman up the stairs," she is using a strikingly original simile to suggest that daylight brings not the conventional associations of promise and awakening but rather a stale, never-ending routine that is greeted without enthusiasm. This idea is consistent with the rest of the poem, an account of an unfulfilling relationship. However, when the speaker in the Audre Lorde poem on page 926 says, "Rooming houses are old women," she uses a metaphor, equating two elements to stress their common associations with emptiness, transience, and hopelessness. At the same time, by identifying rooming houses as old women, Lorde is using **personification,** a special kind of comparison, closely related to metaphor, that gives life or human characteristics to inanimate objects or abstract ideas.

Sometimes, as in Wordsworth's "I wandered lonely as a cloud," a single brief simile or metaphor can be appreciated for what it communicates on its own. At other times, however, a simile or metaphor may be one of several related figures of speech that work together to convey a poem's meaning. The following poem, for example, presents a series of related similes. Together, they suggest the depth of the problem the poem explores in a manner that each individual simile could not do on its own.

LANGSTON HUGHES (1902–1967)

Harlem (1951)

What happens to a dream deferred?

Does it dry up
like a raisin in the sun?
Or fester like a sore—
And then run?
Does it stink like rotten meat?
Or crust and sugar over—

like a syrupy sweet?

Maybe it just sags
like a heavy load.

Or does it explode?

The dream to which Hughes alludes in this poem is the dream of racial equality. It is also the American Dream — or, by extension, any important unrealized dream. His speaker offers six tentative answers to the question asked in the poem's first line, and five of the six are presented as similes. As the poem unfolds, the speaker considers different alternatives: the dream can shrivel up and die, fester, decay, crust over — or sag under the weight of the burden those who hold the dream must carry. In each case, the speaker transforms an abstract entity — a dream — into a concrete item — a raisin in the sun, a sore, rotten meat, syrupy candy, a heavy load. The final line, italicized for emphasis, gains power less from what it says than from what it leaves unsaid. Unlike the other alternatives explored in the poem, "*Or does it explode?*" is not presented as a simile. Nevertheless, because of the pattern of figurative language the poem has established, readers can supply the other, unspoken half of the comparison: ". . . like a bomb."

Sometimes a single extended simile or extended metaphor is developed throughout a poem. The following poem develops an **extended simile,** comparing a poet to an acrobat.

LAWRENCE FERLINGHETTI (1919–)

Constantly Risking Absurdity (1958)

Constantly risking absurdity
and death
whenever he performs
above the heads
of his audience
the poet like an acrobat
climbs on rime
to a high wire of his own making
and balancing on eyebeams
above a sea of faces
paces his way
to the other side of day
performing entrechats
and sleight-of-foot tricks
and other high theatrics
and all without mistaking
any thing

for what it may not be

For he's the super realist
who must perforce perceive
taut truth
before the taking of each stance or step
in his supposed advance
toward that still higher perch
where Beauty stands and waits
with gravity
to start her death-defying leap

And he
a little charleychaplin man
who may or may not catch
her fair eternal form
spreadeagled in the empty air
of existence

In his extended comparison of a poet and an acrobat, Ferlinghetti characterizes the poet as a circus performer, at once swinging recklessly on a trapeze and balancing carefully on a tightrope.

What the poem suggests is that the poet, like an acrobat, works hard at his craft but manages to make it all look easy. Something of an exhibitionist, the poet is innovative and creative, taking impossible chances yet also building on traditional skills in his quest for truth and beauty. Moreover, like an acrobat, the poet is balanced "on eyebeams / above a sea of faces," for he too depends on audience reaction to help him keep his performance focused. The poet may be "the super realist," but he also has plenty of playful tricks up his sleeve: "entrechats / and sleight-of-foot tricks / and other high theatrics," including puns ("above the heads / of his audience"), unexpected rhyme ("climbs on rime"), alliteration ("taut truth"), coinages ("a little charleychaplin man"), and all the other linguistic acrobatics available to poets. (Even the arrangement of the poem's lines on the page suggests the acrobatics it describes.) Like these tricks, the poem's central simile is a whimsical one, perhaps suggesting that Ferlinghetti is poking fun at poets who take their craft too seriously. In any case, the simile helps him to illustrate the acrobatic possibilities of language in a fresh and original manner.

The following poem develops an **extended metaphor,** personifying rooming houses as old women.

AUDRE LORDE (1934–1992)

Rooming houses are old women (1968)

Rooming houses are old women
rocking dark windows into their whens

waiting incomplete circles
rocking
rent office to stoop to
community bathrooms to gas rings and
under-bed boxes of once useful garbage
city issued with a twice monthly check
and the young men next door
with their loud midnight parties
and fishy rings left in the bathtub
no longer arouse them
from midnight to mealtime no stops inbetween
light breaking to pass through jumbled up windows
and who was it who married the widow that Buzzie's
son messed with?

To Welfare and insult form the slow shuffle
from dayswork to shopping bags
heavy with leftovers
Rooming houses
are old women waiting
searching
through darkening windows
the end or beginning of agony
old women seen through half-ajar doors
hoping
they are not waiting
but being
the entrance to somewhere
unknown and desired
but not new.

So closely does Lorde equate rooming houses and old women in this poem that at times it is difficult to tell which of the two is actually the poem's subject. Despite the poem's assertion, rooming houses are *not* old women; however, they are *comparable to* the old women who live there because their walls enclose a lifetime of disappointments as well as the physical detritus of life. Like the old women, rooming houses are in decline, rocking away their remaining years. And, like the houses they inhabit, these women's boundaries are fixed—"rent office to stoop to / community bathrooms to gas rings"—and their hopes and expectations are few. They are surrounded by other people's loud parties, but their own lives have been reduced to a "slow shuffle" to nowhere, a hopeless, frightened—and perhaps pointless—"waiting / searching." Over time, the women and the places in which they live have become one. By using an unexpected comparison between two seemingly unrelated entities, the poem illuminates both the essence of the rooming houses and the essence of their elderly occupants.

FURTHER READING: Simile, Metaphor, and Personification

ROBERT BURNS (1759–1796)

Oh, my love is like a red, red rose (1796)

Oh, my love is like a red, red rose
That's newly sprung in June;
My love is like the melody
That's sweetly played in tune.

So fair art thou, my bonny lass,
So deep in love am I;
And I will love thee still, my dear,
Till a' the seas gang° dry.

Till a' the seas gang dry, my dear,
And the rocks melt wi' the sun;
And I will love thee still, my dear,
While the sands o' life shall run.

And fare thee weel, my only love!
And fare thee weel awhile!
And I will come again, my love
Though it were ten thousand mile.

Reading and Reacting

1. Why does the speaker compare his love to a rose? What other simile is used in the poem? For what purpose is it used?
2. Why do you suppose Burns begins his poem with similes? Would moving them to the end change the poem's impact?
3. Where does the speaker seem to exaggerate the extent of his love? Why does he exaggerate? Do you think this exaggeration weakens the poem? Explain.
4. **JOURNAL ENTRY** Create ten original similes that begin with, "My love is like________."

Related Works: "Araby" (p. 434), "Baca Grande" (p. 889), "My mistress' eyes are nothing like the sun" (p. 917), "To His Coy Mistress" (p. 941), "How Do I Love Thee?" (p. 1055), *The Brute* (p. 1250)

N. SCOTT MOMADAY (1934–)

Simile (1974)

What did we say to each other
that now we are as the deer
who walk in single file

---

gang: Go.

with heads high
with ears forward
with eyes watchful
with hooves always placed on firm ground
in whose limbs there is latent flight

Reading and Reacting

1. In what sense are the speaker and the person he is speaking to like the deer he describes in this extended simile? In what sense are their limbs in "latent flight" (line 8)?
2. Without using similes or metaphors, paraphrase this poem.
3. This entire poem consists of a single sentence, but it has no punctuation. Do you see this as a problem? What punctuation marks, if any, would you add? Why?

4. **JOURNAL ENTRY** What do you suppose the speaker and the person he addresses might have said to each other to inspire the feelings described in this poem?

Related Works: "The Disappearance" (p. 695), "Comparatives" (p. 967), "Let me not to the marriage of true minds" (p. 1193)

SYLVIA PLATH (1932–1963)

Metaphors (1960)

I'm a riddle in nine syllables,
An elephant, a ponderous house,
A melon strolling on two tendrils.
O red fruit, ivory, fine timbers!
This loaf's big with its yeasty rising.
Money's new-minted in this fat purse.
I'm a means, a stage, a cow in calf.
I've eaten a bag of green apples,
Boarded the train there's no getting off.

Reading and Reacting

1. The speaker in this poem is a pregnant woman. Do all the metaphors seem appropriate? For instance, in what sense is the speaker "a means, a stage" (line 7)?
2. If you were going to expand this poem, what other metaphors (or similes) would you add?
3. What are the "nine syllables" to which the speaker refers in the poem's first line? What significance does the number *nine* have in terms of the poem's subject? In terms of its form?

4. **JOURNAL ENTRY** Would you say the speaker has a positive, negative, or neutral attitude toward her pregnancy? Which metaphors give you this impression?

Related Works: "I Stand Here Ironing" (p. 344), "My Son, My Executioner" (p. 945), "Morning Song" (p. 1053), "A Blessing from My Sixteen Years' Son" (p. 1167)

RICHARD WILBUR (1921–)

Mind (1956)

Mind in its purest play is like some bat
That beats about in caverns all alone,
Contriving by a kind of senseless wit
Not to conclude against a wall of stone.

It has no need to falter or explore;
Darkly it knows what obstacles are there,
And so may weave and flitter, dip and soar
In perfect courses through the blackest air.

And has this simile a like perfection?
The mind is like a bat. Precisely. Save
That in the very happiest intellection
A graceful error may correct the cave.

Reading and Reacting

1. In what sense is a mind like a bat? List the parallels the speaker identifies.

2. According to the speaker, how is the mind *unlike* a bat? What do you think the speaker means by "A graceful error may correct the cave" (line 12)?

3. JOURNAL ENTRY If the mind is like a bat, what do you suppose the speaker sees as equivalent to the cave, or caverns?

Related Works: "Gryphon" (p. 277), "When I Heard the Learn'd Astronomer" (p. 877), "Explaining an Affinity for Bats" (p. 986), "For Once, Then, Something" (p. 1013), "Diving into the Wreck" (p. 1020), *Proof* (p. 1476)

Source: ©AP Photo/Seth Perlman

JOHN UPDIKE (1932–)

Ex-Basketball Player (1958)

Pearl Avenue runs past the high-school lot,
Bends with the trolley tracks, and stops, cut off
Before it has a chance to go two blocks,
At Colonel McComsky Plaza. Berth's Garage
Is on the corner facing west, and there,
Most days, you'll find Flick Webb, who helps Berth out.

Flick stands tall among the idiot pumps—
Five on a side, the old bubble-head style,
Their rubber elbows hanging loose and low.
One's nostrils are two S's, and his eyes
An E and O.° And one is squat, without
A head at all—more of a football type.

ESSO: Former name of Exxon.

Once Flick played for the high-school team, the Wizards.
He was good: in fact, the best. In '46
He bucketed three hundred ninety points,
A county record still. The ball loved Flick.
I saw him rack up thirty-eight or forty
In one home game. His hands were like wild birds.

He never learned a trade, he just sells gas,
Checks oil, and changes flats. Once in a while,
As a gag, he dribbles an inner tube,
But most of us remember anyway.
His hands are fine and nervous on the lug wrench.
It makes no difference to the lug wrench, though.
Off work, he hangs around Mae's luncheonette.
Grease-gray and kind of coiled, he plays pinball,
Smokes those thin cigars, nurses lemon phosphates.
Flick seldom says a word to Mae, just nods
Beyond her face toward bright applauding tiers
Of Necco Wafers, Nibs, and Juju Beads.

Reading and Reacting

1. Explain the use of personification in the second stanza and in the poem's last two lines. What two elements make up each figure of speech? In what sense are the two elements in each pair comparable?
2. What other figures of speech can you identify in the poem? How do these figures of speech work together to communicate the poem's central theme?
3. **JOURNAL ENTRY** Who do you think this poem's speaker might be? What is his attitude toward Flick Webb? Do you think Flick himself shares this assessment? Explain.

Related Works: "A&P" (p. 259), "Miss Brill" (p. 266), "Autumn Begins in Martins Ferry, Ohio" (p. 881), "To an Athlete Dying Young" (p. 900), "Sadie and Maud" (p. 957), *Fences* (p. 1902)

Source: ©Cape Canaveral Hangar, United States Air Force

RANDALL JARRELL (1914–1965)

The Death of the Ball Turret Gunner° (1945)

From my mother's sleep I fell into the State
And I hunched in its belly till my wet fur froze.
Six miles from earth, loosed from its dream of life,
I woke to black flak and the nightmare fighters.
When I died they washed me out of the turret
with a hose.

Ball turret gunner: World War II machine gunner positioned upside-down in a plexiglass sphere in the belly of a fighter plane.

Reading and Reacting

1. Who is the speaker? To what does he compare himself in the poem's first two lines? What words establish this comparison?
2. Contrast the speaker's actual identity with the one he creates for himself in lines 1–2. What elements of his actual situation do you think lead him to characterize himself as he does in these lines?
3. **Journal Entry** Both this poem and "Dulce et Decorum Est" (p. 915) use figures of speech to describe the horrors of war. Which poem has a greater impact on you? How does the poem's figurative language contribute to this impact?
4. **Critical Perspective** In a 1974 article, Frances Ferguson criticizes "The Death of the Ball Turret Gunner," arguing that the poem "thoroughly manifests the lack of a middle between the gunner's birth and his death. . . . Because the poem presents a man who seems to have lived in order to die, we forget the fiction that he must have lived." However, in a 1978 explication, Patrick J. Horner writes that the "manipulation of time reveals the stunning brevity of the gunner's waking life and the State's total disregard for that phenomenon. . . . Because of the telescoping of time, [the poem] resonates with powerful feeling."

   With which critic do you agree? Do you see the "lack of a middle" as a positive or negative quality of this poem?

Related Works: "Buffalo Soldiers" (p. 187), "The Things They Carried" (p. 473), "The Soldier" (p. 1062), "An Irish Airman Foresees His Death" (p. 1062)

MARGE PIERCY (1936–)

The secretary chant (1973)

My hips are a desk.
From my ears hang
chains of paper clips.
Rubber bands form my hair.
My breasts are wells of mimeograph ink.
My feet bear casters.
Buzz. Click.
My head is a badly organized file.
My head is a switchboard
where crossed lines crackle.
Press my fingers
and in my eyes appear
credit and debit.
Zing. Tinkle.
My navel is a reject button.
From my mouth issue canceled reams.
Swollen, heavy, rectangular
I am about to be delivered
of a baby

Xerox machine.
File me under W
because I wonce
was
a woman.

Reading and Reacting

1. Examine each of the poem's figures of speech. Do they all make reasonable comparisons, or are some far-fetched or hard to visualize? Explain the relationship between the secretary and each item with which she is compared.

2. **JOURNAL ENTRY** Using as many metaphors and similes as you can, write a "chant" about a job you have held.

3. **CRITICAL PERSPECTIVE** In a review of a recent collection of Piercy's poetry, critic Sandra Gilbert notes instances of "a kind of bombast" (pompous language) and remarks, "As most poets realize, political verse is almost the hardest kind to write."

   In what sense can "The secretary chant" be seen as "political verse"? Do you think Piercy successfully achieves her political purpose, or does she undercut it with "bombast"?

Related Works: "Girl" (p. 183), "Buffalo Soldiers" (p. 187), "A&P" (p. 259), "Battle Royal" (p. 332), "Please Fire Me" (p. 858), "Women" (p. 1007), *Workout* (p. 1265)

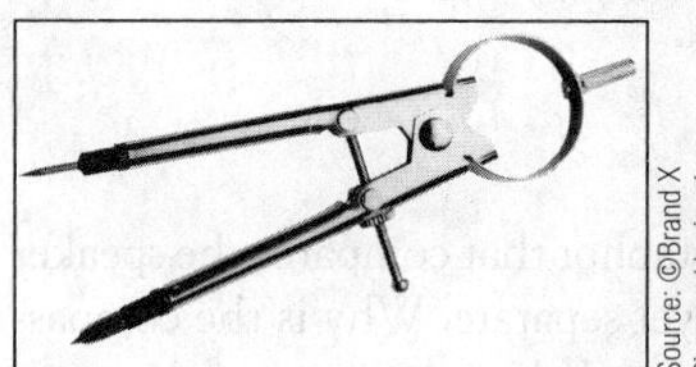

Source: ©Brand X Pictures/Jupiter Images

JOHN DONNE (1572–1631)

A Valediction: Forbidding Mourning (1611)

As virtuous men pass mildly away,
And whisper to their souls to go,
Whilst some of their sad friends do say
The breath goes now, and some say no:

So let us melt, and make no noise,
No tear-floods, nor sigh-tempests move;
'Twere profanation of our joys
To tell the laity° our love.

Moving of th' earth brings harms and fears;
Men reckon what it did and meant;
But trepidation of the spheres,
Though greater far, is innocent.

Dull sublunary lovers' love
(Whose soul is sense) cannot admit

---

laity: Here, "common people."

Absence, because it doth remove
Those things which elemented it.

But we, by a love so much refined
That ourselves know not what it is,
Inter-assurèd of the mind,
Care less, eyes, lips, and hands to miss.

Our two souls, therefore, which are one,
Though I must go, endure not yet
A breach, but an expansion,
Like gold to airy thinness beat.

If they be two, they are two so
As stiff twin compasses° are two:
Thy soul, the fixed foot, makes no show
To move, but doth, if th' other do.
And though it in the center sit,
Yet when the other far doth roam,
It leans and harkens after it,
And grows erect as that comes home.

Such wilt thou be to me, who must,
Like th' other foot, obliquely run;
Thy firmness makes my circle just,°
And makes me end where I begun.

Reading and Reacting

1. Beginning with line 25, the poem develops an extended metaphor that compares the speaker and his loved one to "twin compasses" (line 26), attached yet separate. Why is the compass (pictured on p. 933) an especially apt metaphor? What physical characteristics of the compass does the poet emphasize?
2. The poem uses other figures of speech to characterize both the lovers' union and their separation. To what other events does the speaker compare his separation from his loved one? To what other elements does he compare their attachment? Do you think these comparisons make sense?
3. **Journal Entry** To what other object could Donne have compared his loved one and himself? Explain the logic of the extended metaphor you suggest.
4. **Critical Perspective** In *John Donne and the Metaphysical Poets* (1970), Judah Stampfer writes of this poem's "thin, dry texture, its stanzas of pinched music," noting that its form "has too clipped a brevity to qualify as a song" and that its "music wobbles on a dry, measured beat." Yet, he argues, "the poem comes choked with emotional power" because "the speaker reads as a naturally reticent man, leaving his beloved in uncertainty and deep trouble." Stampfer

compasses: V-shaped instruments used for drawing circles.
just: Perfect.

concludes, "Easy self-expression here would be self-indulgent, if not reprehensible. . . . For all his careful dignity, we feel a heart is breaking here."

Do you find such emotional power in this highly intellectual poem?

Related Works: "The Third and Final Continent" (p. 290), "To My Dear and Loving Husband" (p. 940), "How Do I Love Thee?" (p. 1055), "A Parting Gift" (p. 1059), *A Doll House* (p. 1402)

Source: ©AP Photo/Nancy Palmieri

See this poet's biography on p. 1221.

MARTIN ESPADA (1957–)

My Father as a Guitar (2000)

The cardiologist prescribed
a new medication
and lectured my father
that he had to stop working.
And my father said: *I can't.*
The landlord won't let me.
The heart pills are dice
in my father's hand,
gambler who needs cash
by the first of the month.

On the night his mother died
in faraway Puerto Rico,
my father lurched upright in bed,
heart hammering
like the fist of a man at the door
with an eviction notice.
Minutes later,
the telephone sputtered
with news of the dead.

Sometimes I dream
my father is a guitar,
with a hole in his chest
where the music throbs
between my fingers.

Reading and Reacting

1. Where does this poem use simile? Metaphor? Personification?

2. What is the speaker's attitude toward his father? In what way does the poem's central comparison (between the father and a guitar) help the speaker express his feelings?

3. **Journal Entry** Why do you suppose the speaker dreams that his father is a guitar? How might his dreams be related to his father's dreams about his own mother?

4. **Critical Perspective** In a review of one of Espada's earlier collections of poetry, Leslie Ullman discusses how the poet brings his characters to life:

> The poems in this collection tell their stories and flesh out their characters deftly, without shrillness or rhetoric, and vividly enough to invite the reader into a shared sense of loss. Espada makes vanquished individuals and curtailed family histories present by offering us their remnants, their echoes, in such a way as to make us confront the ruined whole.

Does "My Father as a Guitar" present the speaker's father in the way Ullman describes?

Related Works: "A Primer for the Punctuation of Heart Disease" (p. 440), "Fun Home" (p. 494), "Nothing Gold Can Stay" (p. 914), "My Son, My Executioner" (p. 945), "My Papa's Waltz" (p. 1039), "Do not go gentle into that good night" (p. 1046), *Proof* (p. 1476)

Hyperbole and Understatement

Two additional kinds of figurative language, *hyperbole* and *understatement*, also give poets opportunities to suggest meaning beyond the literal level of language.

Hyperbole is intentional exaggeration—saying more than is actually meant. In the poem "Oh, my love is like a red, red rose" (p. 928), when the speaker says that he will love his lady until all the seas go dry, he is using hyperbole.

Understatement is the opposite—saying less than is meant. When the speaker in the poem "Fire and Ice" (p. 849), weighing two equally grim alternatives for the end of the world, says that "for destruction ice / Is also great / And would suffice," he is using understatement. In both cases, poets expect their readers to understand that their words are not to be taken literally.

By using hyperbole and understatement, poets enhance the impact of their poems. For example, poets can use hyperbole to convey exaggerated anger or graphic images of horror—and to ridicule and satirize as well as to inflame and shock. With understatement, poets can convey the same kind of powerful emotions subtly, without artifice or embellishment, thereby leading readers to read more closely than they might otherwise.

The emotionally charged poem that follows uses hyperbole to convey anger and bitterness that seem almost beyond the power of words.

Source: ©AP Photo

See this poet's biography on p. 1226.

SYLVIA PLATH (1932–1963)

Daddy (1965)

You do not do, you do not do
Any more, black shoe
In which I have lived like a foot
For thirty years, poor and white,
Barely daring to breathe or Achoo.

Daddy, I have had to kill you.
You died before I had time—
Marble-heavy, a bag full of God,

Ghastly statue with one grey toe
Big as a Frisco seal

And a head in the freakish Atlantic
Where it pours bean green over blue
In the waters off beautiful Nauset.
I used to pray to recover you.
Ach, du.°

In the German tongue, in the Polish town°
Scraped flat by the roller
Of wars, wars, wars.
But the name of the town is common.
My Polack friend

Says there are a dozen or two.
So I never could tell where you
Put your foot, your root,
I never could talk to you.
The tongue stuck in my jaw.

It stuck in a barb wire snare.
Ich, ich, ich, ich,°
I could hardly speak.
I thought every German was you.
And the language obscene

An engine, an engine
Chuffing me off like a Jew.
A Jew to Dachau, Auschwitz, Belsen.°
I began to talk like a Jew.
I think I may well be a Jew.

The snows of the Tyrol, the clear beer of Vienna
Are not very pure or true.
With my gypsy ancestress and my weird luck
And my Taroc pack and my Taroc pack
I may be a bit of a Jew.

I have always been scared of *you*,
With your Luftwaffe,° your gobbledygoo.
And your neat moustache
And your Aryan eye, bright blue.
Panzer°-man, panzer-man, O You—

Ach, du: "Ah, you" (German).

Polish town: Grabôw, where Plath's father was born.

ich: "I" (German).

Dachau, Auschwitz, Belsen: Nazi concentration camps.

Luftwaffe: The German air force.

Panzer: Protected by armor. The Panzer division was the German armored division.

Not God but a swastika
So black no sky could squeak through.
Every woman adores a Fascist,
The boot in the face, the brute
Brute heart of a brute like you.

You stand at the blackboard, daddy,
In the picture I have of you,
A cleft in your chin instead of your foot
But no less a devil for that, no not
Any less the black man who

Bit my pretty red heart in two.
I was ten when they buried you.
At twenty I tried to die
And get back, back, back to you.
I thought even the bones would do.

But they pulled me out of the sack,
And they stuck me together with glue.
And then I knew what to do.
I made a model of you,
A man in black with a Meinkampf° look

And a love of the rack and the screw.
And I said I do, I do.
So daddy, I'm finally through.
The black telephone's off at the root,
The voices just can't worm through.

If I've killed one man, I've killed two—
The vampire who said he was you
And drank my blood for a year,
Seven years, if you want to know.
Daddy, you can lie back now.

There's a stake in your fat black heart
And the villagers never liked you.
They are dancing and stamping on you.
They always *knew* it was you.
Daddy, daddy, you bastard, I'm through.

In her anger and frustration, the speaker sees herself as a helpless victim—a foot entrapped in a shoe, a Jew in a concentration camp—of her father's (and, later, her husband's) absolute tyranny. Thus, her hated father is characterized as a "black shoe," "a bag full of God," a "Ghastly statue," and, eventually, a Nazi, a torturer,

Meinkampf: Mein Kampf (My Struggle) is Adolf Hitler's autobiography.

the devil, a vampire. The poem "Daddy" is widely accepted by scholars as autobiographical, and the fact that Plath's own father was actually neither a Nazi nor a sadist (nor, obviously, the devil or a vampire) makes it clear that the figures of speech in the poem are wildly exaggerated. Even so, they may convey the poet's true feelings toward her father—and, perhaps, toward the patriarchal society in which she lived.

Plath uses hyperbole to communicate these emotions to readers who she knows cannot possibly feel the way she does. Her purpose, therefore, is not only to shock but also to enlighten, to persuade, and perhaps even to empower her readers. Throughout the poem, the inflammatory language is set in ironic opposition to the childish, affectionate term "Daddy"—most strikingly in the last line's choked out "Daddy, daddy, you bastard, I'm through." The result of the exaggerated rhetoric is a poem that is vivid and shocking. And, although some might believe that Plath's almost wild exaggeration undermines the poem's impact, others would argue that the powerful language is necessary to convey the extent of the speaker's rage.

Like "Daddy," the following poem presents a situation whose emotional impact is devastating. In this case, however, the poet does not use highly charged language; instead, he uses understatement, presenting events without embellishment.

DAVID HUDDLE (1942–)

Holes Commence Falling (1979)

The lead & zinc company
owned the mineral rights
to the whole town anyway,
and after drilling holes
for 3 or 4 years,
they finally found the right
place and sunk a mine shaft.
We were proud
of all that digging,
even though nobody from
town got hired. They
were going to dig right
under New River and hook up
with the mine at Austinville.
Then people's wells
started drying up just like
somebody'd shut off a faucet,
and holes commenced falling,
big chunks of people's yards
would drop 5 or 6 feet,

houses would shift and crack.
Now and then the company'd
pay out a little money
in damages; they got a truck
to haul water and sell it
to the people whose wells
had dried up, but most
everybody agreed the
situation wasn't
serious.

Although "Holes Commence Falling" relates a tragic sequence of events, the tone of the poem is matter-of-fact, and the language is understated. The speaker could have overdramatized the events, using inflated rhetoric to denounce big business and to predict disastrous events for the future. At the very least, he could have colored the facts with realistic emotions, assigning blame to the lead and zinc company with justifiable anger. Instead, the speaker is so restrained, so nonchalant, so passive that readers must supply the missing emotions themselves—realizing, for example, that when the speaker concludes "everybody agreed the / situation wasn't / serious," he means exactly the opposite.

Throughout the poem, unpleasant information is presented without comment or emotion. As it proceeds, the poem traces the high and low points in the town's fortunes, but for every hope ("We were proud / of all that digging"), there is a disappointment ("even though nobody from / town got hired"). The lead and zinc company offers some compensation for the damage it does, but it is never enough. The present tense verb of the poem's title indicates that the problems the town faces—wells drying up, yards dropping, houses shifting and cracking—are regular occurrences. Eventually, readers come to see that what is not expressed, what lurks just below the surface—anger, powerlessness, resentment, hopelessness—is the poem's real subject.

FURTHER READING: Hyperbole and Understatement

Source: ©The Granger Collection, New York

See this poet's biography on p. 1218.

ANNE BRADSTREET (1612–1672)

To My Dear and Loving Husband (1678)

If ever two were one, then surely we.
If ever man were lov'd by wife, then thee;
If ever wife was happy in a man,
Compare with me ye women if you can.
I prize thy love more than whole Mines of gold,
Or all the riches that the East doth hold.
My love is such that Rivers cannot quench,
Nor ought but love from thee, give recompense.

Thy love is such I can no way repay,
The heavens reward thee manifold I pray.
Then while we live, in love let's so persever,
That when we live no more, we may live ever.

Reading and Reacting

1. Review the claims the poem's speaker makes about her love in lines 5–8. Are such exaggerated declarations of love necessary, or would the rest of the poem be sufficient to convey the extent of her devotion to her husband?

2. **JOURNAL ENTRY** Compare this poem's declarations of love to those of John Donne's speaker in "A Valediction: Forbidding Mourning" (p. 933). Which speaker do you find more convincing? Why?

Related Works: "A Rose for Emily" (p. 243), "How Do I Love Thee?" (p. 1055), "Stop all the clocks, cut off the telephone" (p. 1057), "Bright Star! Would I Were Steadfast as Thou Art" (p. 1170)

ANDREW MARVELL (1621–1678)

To His Coy Mistress (1681)

Had we but world enough and time,
This coyness, lady, were no crime.
We would sit down and think which way
To walk, and pass our long love's day.
Thou by the Indian Ganges' side
Should'st rubies find; I by the tide
Of Humber° would complain. I would
Love you ten years before the Flood,
And you should, if you please, refuse
Till the conversion of the Jews.
My vegetable love should grow
Vaster than empires, and more slow.
An hundred years should go to praise
Thine eyes, and on thy forehead gaze,
Two hundred to adore each breast,

Humber: An estuary on the east coast of England.

But thirty thousand to the rest.
An age at least to every part,
And the last age should show your heart.
For, lady, you deserve this state,
Nor would I love at lower rate.
    But at my back I always hear
Time's wingèd chariot hurrying near,
And yonder all before us lie
Deserts of vast eternity.
Thy beauty shall no more be found,
Nor in thy marble vault shall sound
My echoing song; then worms shall try
That long preserved virginity,
And your quaint honor turn to dust,
And into ashes all my lust.
The grave's a fine and private place,
But none, I think, do there embrace.
    Now therefore, while the youthful hue
Sits on thy skin like morning glew°
And while thy willing soul transpires
At every pore with instant fires,
Now let us sport us while we may;
And now, like amorous birds of prey,
Rather at once our time devour
Than languish in his slow-chapped° power.
Let us roll all our strength and all
Our sweetness up into one ball
And tear our pleasures with rough strife
Thorough the iron gates of life.
Thus, though we cannot make our sun
Stand still, yet we will make him run.

Reading and Reacting

1. In this poem, Marvell's speaker sets out to convince a reluctant woman to become his lover. In order to make his case more persuasive, he uses hyperbole, exaggerating time periods, sizes, spaces, and the possible fate of the woman if she refuses him. Identify as many examples of hyperbole as you can.
2. The tone of "To His Coy Mistress" is more whimsical than serious. Given this tone, what do you see as the purpose of Marvell's use of hyperbole?

glew: Dew.
slow-chapped: Slowly crushing.

3. **Journal Entry**Using contemporary prose, paraphrase the first four lines of the poem. Then, beginning with the word *But*, compose a few new sentences of prose, continuing the argument Marvell's speaker makes.

4. **Critical Perspective** In her critical essay "*Andrew Marvell's 'To His Coy Mistress'*: A Feminist Reading," critic Margaret Wald presents the following analysis of the poem:

> Andrew Marvell's speaker in "To His Coy Mistress" invokes Petrarchan convention, a poetic mode originating in the fourteenth century in which a male lover uses exaggerated metaphors to appeal to his female beloved. Yet Marvell alludes to such excessive—and disempowering—pining only to defy this tradition of unrequited love. Instead of respectful adulation, he offers lustful invitation; rather than anticipating rejection, he assumes sexual dominion over the eponymous "mistress." The poem is as much a celebration of his rhetorical mastery as it is of his physical conquest.

In what sense is the speaker in this poem celebrating his beloved? In what sense is he celebrating himself? Is his portrayal of his loved one entirely positive? Which elements, if any, are negative?

Related Works: "Where Are You Going, Where Have You Been?" (p. 617), "To the Virgins, to Make Much of Time" (p. 858), "The Passionate Shepherd to His Love" (p. 1179), *The Brute* (p. 1250)

ROBERT FROST (1874–1963)

"Out, Out—" (1916)

The buzz saw snarled and rattled in the yard
And made dust and dropped stove-length sticks of wood,
Sweet-scented stuff when the breeze drew across it.
And from there those that lifted eyes could count
Five mountain ranges one behind the other
Under the sunset far into Vermont.
And the saw snarled and rattled, snarled and rattled,
As it ran light, or had to bear a load.
And nothing happened: day was all but done.
Call it a day, I wish they might have said
To please the boy by giving him the half hour
That a boy counts so much when saved from work.
His sister stood beside them in her apron
To tell them "Supper." At the word, the saw,
As if to prove saws knew what supper meant,
Leaped out at the boy's hand, or seemed to leap—
He must have given the hand. However it was,
Neither refused the meeting. But the hand!
The boy's first outcry was a rueful laugh,

As he swung toward them holding up the hand
Half in appeal, but half as if to keep
The life from spilling. Then the boy saw all—
Since he was old enough to know, big boy
Doing a man's work, though a child at heart—
He saw all spoiled. "Don't let him cut my hand off—
The doctor, when he comes. Don't let him, sister!"
So. But the hand was gone already.
The doctor put him in the dark of ether.
He lay and puffed his lips out with his breath.
And then—the watcher at his pulse took fright.
No one believed. They listened at his heart.
Little—less—nothing!—and that ended it.
No more to build on there. And they, since they
Were not the one dead, turned to their affairs.

Reading and Reacting

1. The poem's title is an **allusion** to a passage in Shakespeare's *Macbeth* (5.5.23–28) that attacks the brevity and meaninglessness of life in very emotional terms:

> Out, out brief candle!
> Life's but a walking shadow, a poor player,
> That struts and frets his hour upon the stage
> And then is heard no more. It is a tale
> Told by an idiot, full of sound and fury,
> Signifying nothing.

What idea do you think Frost wants to convey through the title "Out, Out—"?

2. Explain why each of the following qualifies as understatement:

- "Neither refused the meeting." (line 18)
- "He saw all spoiled." (line 25)
- "— and that ended it." (line 32)
- "No more to build on there." (line 33)

Can you identify any other examples of understatement in the poem?

3. JOURNAL ENTRY Do you think the poem's impact is strengthened or weakened by its understated tone?

4. CRITICAL PERSPECTIVE In an essay on Frost in his book *Affirming Limits*, poet and critic Robert Pack focuses on the single word "So" in line 27 of "Out, Out—":

> For a moment, his narration is reduced to the impotent word "So," and in that minimal word all his restrained grief is held. . . . That "So" is the narrator's cry of bearing witness to a story that must be what it is in a scene he cannot enter. He cannot rescue or protect the boy. . . . In the poem's

> sense of human helplessness in an indifferent universe, we are all "watchers," and what we see is death without redemption, "signifying nothing." So. So? So! How shall we read that enigmatic word?

How do you read this "enigmatic word"? Why?

Related Works: "Accident" (p. 181), "Incarnations of Burned Children" (p. 192), "Kansas" (p. 237), "The Lottery" (p. 509), "Happy Endings" (p. 662), "Hope" (p. 863), "The Death of the Ball Turret Gunner" (p. 931), "What Were They Like?" (p. 1066)

DONALD HALL (1928–)

My Son, My Executioner (1955)

My son, my executioner,
    I take you in my arms,
Quiet and small and just astir,
    And whom my body warms.

Sweet death, small son, our instrument
    Of immortality,
Your cries and hungers document
    Our bodily decay.

We twenty-five and twenty-two,
    Who seemed to live forever,
Observe enduring life in you
    And start to die together.

Reading and Reacting

1. Because the speaker is a young man holding his newborn son in his arms, the metaphor in line 1 comes as a shock. What is Hall's purpose in opening with such a startling statement?
2. In what sense is the comparison between baby and executioner a valid one? Could you argue that, given the underlying similarities between the two, Hall is *not* using hyperbole? Explain.
3. **Journal Entry** List some other metaphors that could describe a newborn baby. Then, divide them into positive and negative columns.

Related Works: "Doe Season" (p. 577), "That time of year thou mayst in me behold" (p. 802), "Morning Song" (p. 856), "Little Father" (p. 1175), "Sailing to Byzantium" (p. 1214), *Proof* (p. 1476)

MARGARET ATWOOD (1939–)

You fit into me (1971)

you fit into me
like a hook into an eye

a fish hook
an open eye

Reading and Reacting

1. What positive connotations does Atwood expect readers to associate with the phrase "you fit into me"? What does the speaker seem at first to mean by "like a hook into an eye" in line 2?
2. The speaker's shift to the brutal suggestions of lines 3 and 4 is calculated to shock readers. Does the use of hyperbole here have another purpose in the context of the poem? Explain.
3. **JOURNAL ENTRY** Do you find this poem unsettling? Do you think it is serious or just a joke?

Related Works: "Hills Like White Elephants" (p. 171), "Love and Other Catastrophes: A Mix Tape" (p. 182), "The Disappearance" (p. 695), "Daddy" (p. 936), *A Doll House* (p. 1402)

Metonymy and Synecdoche

Metonymy and synecdoche are two related figures of speech. **Metonymy** is the substitution of the name of one thing for the name of another thing that most readers associate with the first—for example, using *hired gun* to mean "paid assassin" or *suits* to mean "business executives." A specific kind of metonymy, called **synecdoche,** is the substitution of a part for the whole (for example, using *bread*—as in "Give us this day our daily bread"—to mean "food") or the whole for a part (for example, using *the law* to refer to a police officer.)

With metonymy and synecdoche, instead of describing something by saying it is like something else (as in simile) or by equating it with something else (as in metaphor), writers can characterize an object or concept by using a term that evokes it. The following poem illustrates the use of synecdoche.

RICHARD LOVELACE (1618–1658)

To Lucasta Going to the Wars (1649)

Tell me not, Sweet, I am unkind
    That from the nunnery
Of thy chaste breast and quiet mind,
    To war and arms I fly.

True, a new mistress now I chase,
  The first foe in the field;
And with a stronger faith embrace
  A sword, a horse, a shield.
Yet this inconstancy is such
  As you too shall adore;
I could not love thee, Dear, so much,
  Loved I not Honor more.

Here, Lovelace's use of synecdoche allows him to condense a number of complex ideas into a very few words. In line 3, when the speaker says that he is flying from his loved one's "chaste breast and quiet mind," he is using "breast" and "mind" to stand for all his loved one's physical and intellectual attributes. In line 8, when he says that he is embracing "A sword, a horse, a shield," he is using these three items to represent the trappings of war—and, thus, to represent war itself.

FURTHER READING: Metonymy and Synecdoche

CARMINE STARNINO

What My Mother's Hands Smell Like (2000)

Right now it's obviously garlic. She's chopping
a little of it for tonight's *pasta con alice*, my father's
favourite dish. The sauce calls for three cloves
and three fillets of anchovies, mashed with a fork,
all brought together to fry in some oil for about
two minutes. But after dinner—after she's scoured
the mucked pan and scrubbed the smeared plates,
after she's flushed the glasses free of wine-stains
and wiped the grease speckling the top of the oven—
take her hands, ruddy with the scalded burnish
of hot water, bring them to your face, breathe deeply,
and somewhere, worked into her red knuckles,
is the cool stowed in a pile of sheets just off the line,
is the scent of one's soul in a dry dwelling-place.

Reading and Reacting

1. This poem is an example of **synecdoche**. In what sense is a part being substituted for a whole here? Do you see this substitution as positive, negative, or neutral?

2. List the verbs used to describe the mother's actions. Then, list the adjectives used to describe her. What do you conclude about the mother? About the speaker's attitude toward her?

3. **JOURNAL ENTRY** What sights and smells characterize your family's kitchen? Do you see these sights and smells as appropriate material for poetry? Why or why not?

Related Works: "Snow" (p. 177), "Deportation at Breakfast" (p. 229), "Eye Ball" (p. 258), "Birthmark" (p. 411), "Digging" (p. 1040), "Those Winter Sundays" (p. 1040), "A Woman Mourned by Daughters" (p. 1045), "Marks" (p. 1187)

Apostrophe

With **apostrophe,** a poem's speaker addresses an absent person or thing—for example, a historical or literary figure or even an inanimate object or an abstract concept.

In the following poem, the speaker addresses Vincent Van Gogh.

SONIA SANCHEZ (1934–)

On Passing thru Morgantown, Pa. (1984)

i saw you
vincent van
gogh perched
on those pennsylvania
cornfields communing
amid secret black
bird societies. yes.
i'm sure that was
you exploding your
fantastic delirium
while in the
distance
red indian
hills beckoned.

Expecting her readers to be aware that Van Gogh, a nineteenth-century Dutch postimpressionist painter, is known for his mental instability as well as for his art, Sanchez is able to give added meaning to a phrase such as "fantastic delirium" as well as to the poem's visual images. Perhaps picturing his 1890 painting *Wheatfield with Crows*, the speaker sees Van Gogh perched like a black bird on a fence, and at the same time she also sees what he sees. Like Van Gogh, then, the speaker sees the Pennsylvania cornfields as both a natural landscape and an "exploding" work of art.

Wheatfield with Crows, 1890 (oil on canvas), Gogh, Vincent Van (1853–90).
Source: Rijksmuseum Vincent Van Gogh, Amsterdam, The Netherlands/Bridgeman Art Library

FURTHER READING: Apostrophe

JOHN KEATS (1795–1821)

Ode to a Nightingale (1819)

My heart aches, and a drowsy numbness pains
  My sense, as though of hemlock° I had drunk,
Or emptied some dull opiate° to the drains
  One minute past, and Lethe°–wards had sunk:
'Tis not through envy of thy happy lot.
But being too happy in thine happiness,—
  That thou, light-wingèd Dryad° of the trees,
    In some melodious plot
Of beechen° green, and shadows numberless,
  Singest of summer in full-throated ease.

---

hemlock: A medicinal plant used as a sedative or, in higher doses, a deadly poison.
opiate: A medicine containing opium, a substance derived from poppies, which aids sleep and relieves pain.
Lethe: In Greek mythology, a river in Hades, the land of the dead. Those who drank its water lost all memory of the past.
Dryad: A spirit believed to inhabit trees.
beechen: Of or relating to a beech tree.

O for a draught° of vintage! that hath been
Cool'd a long age in the deep-delvèd° earth,
Tasting of Flora° and the country-green,
Dance, and Provençal° song, and sunburnt mirth!
O for a beaker full of the warm South!
Full of the true, the blushful Hippocrene,°
With beaded bubbles winking at the brim,
And purple-stainèd mouth;
That I might drink, and leave the world unseen,
And with thee fade away into the forest dim:

Fade far away, dissolve, and quite forget
What thou among the leaves hast never known,
The weariness, the fever, and the fret
Here, where men sit and hear each other groan;
Where palsy shakes a few, sad, last grey hairs,
Where youth grows pale, and spectre-thin, and dies;
Where but to think is to be full of sorrow
And leaden-eyed despairs,
Where beauty cannot keep her lustrous eyes,
Or new Love pine at them beyond to-morrow.

Away! away! for I will fly to thee,
Not charioted by Bacchus° and his pards,°
But on the viewless wings of Poesy,
Though the dull brain perplexes and retards:
Already with thee! tender is the night,
And haply the Queen-Moon is on her throne,
Cluster'd around by all her starry Fays;°
But here there is no light,
Save what from heaven is with the breezes blown
Through verdurous° glooms and winding mossy ways.

I cannot see what flowers are at my feet,
Nor what soft incense hangs upon the boughs,
But, in embalmèd darkness, guess each sweet
Wherewith the seasonable month endows

---

draught: A large sip of liquid.

deep-delvèd: Excavated.

Flora: In Roman mythology, the goddess of flowers.

Provençal: From Provence, a region of southern France.

Hippocrene: A fountain on Mt. Helicon, in Greece, considered sacred to the Muses.

Bacchus: The god of wine.

pards: Leopards or panthers.

Fays: Fairies.

verdurous: Green with vegetation.

The grass, the thicket, and the fruit-tree wild;
White hawthorn, and the pastoral eglantine;°
Fast-fading violets cover'd up in leaves;
And mid-May's eldest child,
The coming musk-rose, full of dewy wine,
The murmurous haunt of flies on summer eves.

Darkling I listen; and, for many a time
I have been half in love with easeful Death,
Call'd him soft names in many a musèd rhyme,
To take into the air my quiet breath;
Now more than ever seems it rich to die,
To cease upon the midnight with no pain,
While thou art pouring forth the soul abroad
In such an ecstasy!
Still wouldst thou sing, and I have ears in vain—
To thy high requiem become a sod.

Thou wast not born for death, immortal Bird!
No hungry generations tread thee down;
The voice I hear this passing night was heard
In ancient days by emperor and clown:
Perhaps the self-same song that found a path
Through the sad heart of Ruth, when, sick for home,
She stood in tears amid the alien corn;°
The same that ofttimes hath
Charm'd magic casements,° opening on the foam
Of perilous seas, in faery lands forlorn.°

Forlorn! the very word is like a bell
To toll me back from thee to my sole self!
Adieu! the fancy cannot cheat so well
As she is famed to do, deceiving elf.
Adieu!° adieu! the plaintive anthem fades
Past the near meadows, over the still stream,
Up the hill-side; and now 'tis buried deep
In the next valley-glades:
Was it a vision, or a waking dream?
Fled is that music:—Do I wake or sleep?

eglantine: A plant also known as the sweet-briar.

corn: Grain.

casements: Windows.

forlorn: Lost.

Adieu: Farewell.

Reading and Reacting

1. Where does the speaker first address the nightingale? Where else does he speak directly to the nightingale?
2. In lines 19–20, the speaker expresses his desire to "leave the world unseen, / And with thee fade away into the forest dim. . . ." Why does he want to "fade away"? What is it about the "forest dim" that attracts him? Give some examples from the poem to contrast the speaker's world with the world of the nightingale.
3. What is it that the speaker admires about the nightingale? In what sense does he see the nightingale as superior to human beings?
4. **JOURNAL ENTRY** If you were to write an **ode**—a long, serious, and formal poem—to a creature or an object, what would you choose as your subject? Why? How do you see your own world as different from (and inferior to) the world of your subject?
5. **CRITICAL PERSPECTIVE** John Keats was a romantic poet, and it was the romantics who thought most intensely about the meaning and power of the human imagination. In his essay "Keats's Symbolism," James D. Boulger makes the following comments:

   > In Keats's poetry there is a tension between spirit and matter, between vision and existence. . . . Keats longed to shape existence into the permanent form of beauty, but he could never forget the sense of anguish and limitation in his individual self. The tension arising from this dualism caused him to search for symbols which might unite in permanent and meaningful form the play between the transient anguish of life and the world of his imagination.

   Do you sense this tension between vision and existence at work in "Ode to a Nightingale"? To what extent do you think the nightingale is the kind of symbol that Boulger says Keats was seeking?

Related Works: "Young Goodman Brown" (p. 540), "Sonny's Blues" (p. 665), "The World Is Too Much with Us" (p. 855), "Death Be Not Proud" (p. 1148), *Krapp's Last Tape* (p. 1894)

ALLEN GINSBERG (1926–1997)

A Supermarket in California (1956)

What thoughts I have of you tonight, Walt Whitman,° for I walked down the sidestreets under the trees with a headache self-conscious looking at the full moon.

In my hungry fatigue, and shopping for images, I went into the neon fruit supermarket, dreaming of your enumerations!

What peaches and what penumbras! Whole families shopping at night! Aisles full of husbands! Wives in the avocados, babies in the

Walt Whitman: American poet (1819–1892) whose poems frequently praise the commonplace and often contain lengthy "enumerations."

tomatoes!—and you, Garcia Lorca,° what were you doing down
by the watermelons?

I saw you, Walt Whitman, childless, lonely old grubber, poking
among the meats in the refrigerator and eyeing the grocery boys.°

I heard you asking questions of each: Who killed the pork chops?
What price bananas? Are you my Angel?

I wandered in and out of the brilliant stacks of cans following you,
and followed in my imagination by the store detective.

We strode down the open corridors together in our solitary fancy
tasting artichokes, possessing every frozen delicacy, and never passing
the cashier.

Where are we going, Walt Whitman? The doors close in an hour.
Which way does your beard point tonight?

(I touch your book° and dream of our odyssey in the supermarket
and feel absurd.)

Will we walk all night through solitary streets? The trees add
shade to shade, lights out in the houses, we'll both be lonely.

Will we stroll dreaming of the lost America of love past blue
automobiles in driveways, home to our silent cottage?

Ah, dear father, graybeard, lonely old courage-teacher, what
America did you have when Charon° quit poling his ferry and you
got out on a smoking bank and stood watching the boat disappear on
the black waters of Lethe?°

Reading and Reacting

1. In this poem, Ginsberg's speaker wanders through the aisles of a supermarket, speaking to the nineteenth-century American poet Walt Whitman and asking Whitman a series of questions. Why do you think the speaker addresses Whitman? What kind of answers do you think he is looking for?

2. In paragraph 2, the speaker says he is "shopping for images." What does he mean? Why does he look for these images in a supermarket? Does he find them?

3. Is this poem about supermarkets? About Walt Whitman? About poetry? About love? About America? What do you see as its primary theme? Why?

4. **JOURNAL ENTRY** Does the incongruous image of the respected poet "poking / among the meats" (paragraph 4) in the supermarket strengthen the poem's impact, or does it undercut any serious "message" the poem might have? Explain.

Federico Garcia Lorca: Spanish poet and dramatist (1899–1936).

eyeing the grocery boys: Whitman's sexual orientation is the subject of much debate. Ginsberg is suggesting here that Whitman was homosexual.

your book: Leaves of Grass.

Charon: In Greek mythology, the ferryman who transported the dead over the river Styx to Hades.

Lethe: In Greek mythology, the river of forgetfulness (one of five rivers in Hades).

5. CRITICAL PERSPECTIVE The critic Leslie Fiedler discusses some of the ways in which Ginsberg's style resembles that of Walt Whitman:

> Everything about Ginsberg is . . . blatantly Whitmanian: his meter is resolutely anti-iambic, his line groupings stubbornly anti-stanzaic, his diction aggressively colloquial and American, his voice public.

Can you suggest some ways in which "A Supermarket in California" is "American" and "public"?

Related Works: "A&P" (p. 259), "Chicago" (p. 999), *from* "Out of the Cradle Endlessly Rocking" (p. 1001), "Old Walt" (p. 1086), "Defending Walt Whitman" (p. 1117), *from* "Song of Myself" (p. 1207), *The Cuban Swimmer* (p. 1732)

✔ CHECKLIST Writing about Figures of Speech

- What figures of speech are present in the poem? Identify any examples of simile, metaphor, personification, hyperbole, understatement, metonymy, synecdoche, and apostrophe.
- What two elements are being compared in each use of simile, metaphor, and personification? What characteristics are shared by the two items being compared?
- Does the poet use hyperbole? Why? For example, is it used to move or to shock readers, or is its use intended to produce a humorous or satirical effect? Would more understated language be more effective?
- Does the poet use understatement? For what purpose? Would more emotionally charged language be more effective?
- In metonymy and synecdoche, what item is being substituted for another? What purpose does the substitution serve?
- If the poem includes apostrophe, whom or what does the speaker address? What does the use of apostrophe accomplish?
- How do figures of speech contribute to the impact of the poem as a whole?

WRITING SUGGESTIONS: Figures of Speech

1. Various figures of speech are often used to describe characters in literary works. Choose two or three works that focus on a single character—for example, "A Rose for Emily" (p. 243), "Miss Brill" (p. 266), "Gryphon" (p. 277), "Richard Cory" (p. 1192), or *When I Was a Little Girl and My Mother Didn't Want Me* (p. 1266), —and explain how figures of speech are used to characterize each work's central figure. If you like, you may write about works that focus on real (rather than fictional) people—for example, "Emmett Till" (p. 1155) or "Medgar Evers" (p. 1132).

2. Write an essay in which you discuss the different ways poets use figures of speech to examine the nature of poetry itself. What kinds of figures of speech do poets use to describe their craft? (You might begin by reading the two poems about poetry that open Chapter 21.)
3. Write a letter replying to the speaker in the poem by Marvell, Bradstreet, Donne, or Burns that appears in this chapter. Use figures of speech to express the depth of your love and the extent of your devotion.
4. Choose three or four poems that have a common subject—for example, love or nature—and write an essay in which you draw some general conclusions about the relative effectiveness of the poems' use of figures of speech to examine that subject. (If you like, you may focus on the poems clustered under the heads "Poems about Parents," "Poems about Nature," "Poems about Love," and "Poems about War" in Chapter 31.)
5. Select a poem and a short story that deal with the same subject, and write an essay in which you compare their use of figures of speech.

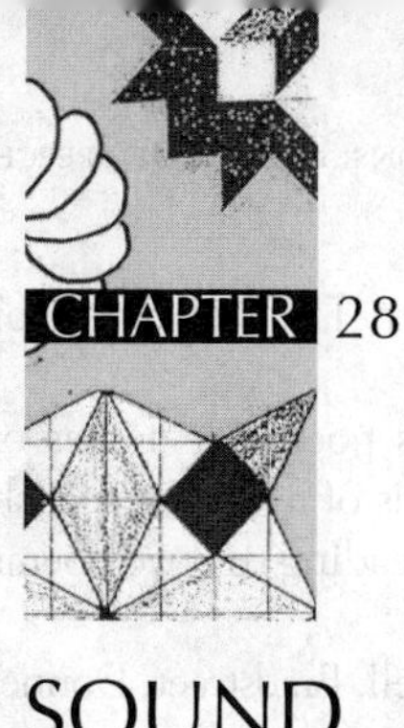

CHAPTER 28

SOUND

See this poet's biography on p. 1230.

WALT WHITMAN (1819–1892)

Had I the Choice*

Had I the choice to tally greatest bards,
To limn° their portraits, stately, beautiful, and emulate at will,
Homer with all his wars and warriors—Hector, Achilles, Ajax,
Or Shakespeare's woe-entangled Hamlet, Lear,
    Othello—Tennyson's fair ladies,
Meter or wit the best, or choice conceit to wield in perfect
    rhyme, delight of singers;
These, these, O sea, all these I'd gladly barter,
Would you the undulation of one wave, its trick to me transfer,
Or breathe one breath of yours upon my verse,
And leave its odor there.

Rhythm

Rhythm—the regular recurrence of sounds—is at the heart of all natural phenomena: the beating of a heart, the lapping of waves against the shore, the croaking of frogs on a summer's night, the whispering of wheat swaying in the wind. Even mechanical phenomena, such as the movement of rush-hour traffic through a city's streets, have a kind of rhythm. Poetry, which explores these phenomena, often tries to reflect the same rhythms. Walt Whitman expresses this idea in "Had I the Choice" when he says that he would gladly trade the "perfect rhyme" of Shakespeare for the ability to reproduce "the undulation of one wave" in his verse.

Public speakers frequently repeat key words and phrases to create rhythm. In his "I Have a Dream" speech, for example, Martin Luther King Jr. repeats the phrase "I have a dream" to create a rhythm that ties the central section of the speech together:

---

*Publication date is not available.

limn: To describe, depict.

> I say to you today, my friends, even though we face the difficulties of today and tomorrow, I still have a dream. It is a dream deeply rooted in the American dream. I have a dream that one day this nation will rise up and live out the true meaning of its creed: "We hold these truths to be self-evident, that all men are created equal." I have a dream that one day, on the red hills of Georgia, sons of former slaves and the sons of former slave owners will be able to sit down together at the table of brotherhood. I have a dream that one day even the state of Mississippi, a state sweltering with the heat of injustice, sweltering with the heat of oppression, will be transformed into an oasis of freedom and justice. I have a dream that my four little children will one day live in a nation where they will not be judged by the color of their skin, but by the content of their character.

Poets too create rhythm by using repeated words and phrases, as Gwendolyn Brooks does in the poem that follows.

GWENDOLYN BROOKS (1917–2000)

Sadie and Maud (1945)

Maud went to college.
Sadie stayed at home.
Sadie scraped life
With a fine-tooth comb.

She didn't leave a tangle in.
Her comb found every strand.
Sadie was one of the livingest chits
In all the land.

Sadie bore two babies
Under her maiden name.
Maud and Ma and Papa
Nearly died of shame.

When Sadie said her last so-long
Her girls struck out from home.
(Sadie had left as heritage
Her fine-tooth comb.)
Maud, who went to college,
Is a thin brown mouse.
She is living all alone
In this old house.

Much of the force of this poem comes from the repeated words "Sadie" and "Maud," which shift the focus from one subject to the other and back again ("Maud went to college / Sadie stayed home"). The poem's singsong rhythm recalls the rhymes children recite when jumping rope. This evocation of carefree childhood is ironically contrasted with the adult realities that both Sadie and Maud face as they grow up: Sadie stays at home and has two children out of wedlock; Maud goes to college and ends up "a thin brown mouse." The speaker implies that the alternatives Sadie and Maud represent are both undesirable. Although Sadie "scraped life / with a fine-tooth comb," she dies young and leaves nothing to her girls but her desire to experience life. Maud, who graduated from college, shuts out life and cuts herself off from her roots.

Just as the repetition of words and phrases can create rhythm, so can the appearance of words on the printed page. How a poem looks is especially important in **open form poetry** (see p. 998), which dispenses with traditional patterns of versification. In the following excerpt from a poem by E. E. Cummings, for example, an unusual arrangement of words forces readers to slow down and then to speed up, creating a rhythm that emphasizes a key phrase—"The / lily":

the moon is hiding
in her hair.
The
lily
of heaven
full of all dreams,
draws down.

Meter

Although rhythm can be affected by the regular repetition of words and phrases or by the arrangement of words into lines, poetic rhythm is largely created by **meter,** the recurrence of regular units of stressed and unstressed syllables. A **stress** (or accent) occurs when one syllable is emphasized more than another, unstressed, syllable: *fór • ceps, bá • sic, il • lú • sion, ma • lár • i • a*. In a poem, even one-syllable words can be stressed to create a particular effect. For example, in Elizabeth Barrett Browning's line "How do I love thee? Let me count the ways," the metrical pattern that places stress on "love" creates one meaning; stressing "I" would create another.

Scansion is the analysis of patterns of stressed and unstressed syllables within a line. The most common method of poetic notation indicates stressed syllables with a ′ and unstressed syllables with a ˘. Although scanning lines gives readers the "beat" of the poem, scansion only generally suggests the sound of spoken language, which contains an infinite variety of stresses. By providing a graphic representation of the stressed and unstressed syllables of a poem, scansion aids understanding, but it is no substitute for reading the poem aloud and experimenting with various patterns of emphasis.

The basic unit of meter is a **foot**—a group of syllables with a fixed pattern of stressed and unstressed syllables. The chart that follows illustrates the most common types of metrical feet in English and American verse.

Foot	Stress Pattern	Example
Iamb	˘ ´	They pace | in sleek | chi val | ric cer | tain ty (Adrienne Rich)
Trochee	´ ˘	Thou, when | thou re | turn'st, wilt | tell me. (John Donne)
Anapest	˘ ˘ ´	With a hey, | and a ho, | and a hey | no ni no (William Shakespeare)
Dactyl	´ ˘ ˘	Constantly | risking ab | surdity (Lawrence Ferlinghetti)

Iambic and *anapestic* meters are called **rising meters** because they progress from unstressed to stressed syllables. *Trochaic* and *dactylic* meters are called **falling meters** because they progress from stressed to unstressed syllables.

The following types of metrical feet, less common than those listed above, are used to add emphasis or to provide variety rather than to create the dominant meter of a poem.

Foot	Stress Pattern	Example
Spondee	´ ´	Pomp, pride | and circumstance of glorious war! (William Shakespeare)
Pyrrhic	˘ ˘	A horse! a horse! My king | dom for | a horse! (William Shakespeare)

A metric line of poetry is measured by the number of feet it contains.

Monometer	one foot	**Pentameter**	five feet
Dimeter	two feet	**Hexameter**	six feet
Trimeter	three feet	**Heptameter**	seven feet
Tetrameter	four feet	**Octameter**	eight feet

The name for a metrical pattern of a line of verse identifies the name of the foot used and the number of feet the line contains. For example, the most common foot in English poetry is the **iamb,** most often occurring in lines of three or five feet.

Metrical Pattern	**Example**
Iambic trimeter	Eight hun | dred of | the brave (William Cowper)
Iambic pentameter	O, how | much more | doth beau | ty beau | teous seem (William Shakespeare)

Because **iambic pentameter** is so well suited to the rhythms of English speech, writers frequently use it in plays and poems. Shakespeare's plays, for example, are written in unrhymed lines of iambic pentameter called **blank verse** (see pp. 981–82).

Many other metrical combinations are also possible; a few are illustrated below.

Metrical Pattern	**Example**
Trochaic trimeter	Like a | high-born | maiden (Percy Bysshe Shelley)
Anapestic tetrameter	The As sy | rian came down | like the wolf | on the fold (Lord Byron)
Dactylic hexameter	Maid en most | beau ti ful | moth er most | boun ti ful, | la dy of | lands, (A. C. Swinburne)
Iambic heptameter	The yel | low fog | that rubs | its back | up on | the win | dow-panes (T. S. Eliot)

Scansion can be an extremely technical process, and when readers become bogged down with anapests and dactyls, they can easily forget that poetic scansion is not an end in itself. Meter should be appropriate for the ideas expressed by the poem, and it should help to create a suitable tone. A light, skipping rhythm, for example, would be inappropriate for an **elegy,** and a slow, heavy rhythm would surely be out of place in an **epigram** or a limerick. The following lines of a poem by Samuel Taylor Coleridge illustrate the uses of different types of metrical feet:

Trochee trips from long to short;
From long to long in solemn sort
Slow Spondee stalks; strong foot! yet ill able
Ever to come up with Dactyl trisyllable.
Iambics march from short to long—
With a leap and a bound the swift Anapests throng;
One syllable long, with one short at each side,
Amphibrachys hastes with a stately stride—
First and last being long, middle short, Amphimacer
Strikes his thundering hoofs like a proud high-bred Racer.

A poet may use one kind of meter—iambic meter, for example—throughout a poem, but may vary line length to relieve monotony or to accommodate the poem's meaning or emphasis. In the following poem, the poet uses iambic lines of different lengths.

EMILY DICKINSON (1830–1886)

I like to see it lap the Miles— (1891)

I like to see it lap the Miles—
And lick the Valleys up—
And stop to feed itself at Tanks—
And then—prodigious step

Around a Pile of Mountains—
And supercilious peer
In Shanties—by the sides of Roads—
And then a Quarry pare

To fit its Ribs
And crawl between
Complaining all the while
In horrid—hooting stanza—
Then chase itself down Hill—

And neigh like Boanerges°—
Then—punctual as a Star
Stop—docile and omnipotent
At its own stable door—

This poem is a single sentence that, except for some pauses, stretches unbroken from beginning to end. Iambic lines of varying lengths actually suggest the movements of the train that the poet describes. Lines of iambic tetrameter, such as the first, give readers a sense of the train's steady, rhythmic movement across a flat landscape, and shorter lines ("To fit its Ribs / And crawl between") suggest the train's slowing motion. Beginning with two iambic dimeter lines and progressing to iambic trimeter lines, the third stanza increases in speed just like the train that is racing downhill "In horrid—hooting stanza—."

When a poet uses more than one type of metrical foot, any variation in a metrical pattern—the substitution of a trochee for an iamb, for instance—immediately calls attention to itself. For example, in line 16 of "I like to see it lap the Miles," the poet departs from iambic meter by placing unexpected stress on the first word, *stop*. By emphasizing this word, the poet brings the flow of the poem to an abrupt halt, suggesting the jolt riders experience when a train comes to a stop.

Another way of varying the meter of a poem is to introduce a pause known as a **caesura**—a Latin word meaning "a cutting"—within a line. When scanning a poem, you indicate a caesura with two parallel lines: ‖. Unless a line of poetry is extremely short, it probably will contain a caesura.

A caesura occurs after a punctuation mark or at a natural break in phrasing:

How do I love thee? ‖ Let me count the ways.

Elizabeth Barrett Browning

Two loves I have ‖ of comfort and despair.

William Shakespeare

High on a throne of royal state, ‖ which far
Outshone the wealth of Ormus ‖ and of Ind

John Milton

Sometimes more than one caesura occurs in a single line:

'Tis good. ‖ Go to the gate. ‖ Somebody knocks.

William Shakespeare

Although the end of a line may mark the end of a metrical unit, it does not always coincide with the end of a sentence. Lines that have distinct pauses at the end—usually signaled by punctuation—are called **end-stopped lines.** Lines that do not end with strong pauses are called **run-on lines.** (Sometimes the term

Boanerges: A vociferous preacher and orator. Also, the name, meaning "son of thunder," Jesus gave to apostles John and James because of their fiery zeal.

enjambment is used to describe run-on lines.) End-stopped lines can sometimes seem formal, or even forced, because their length is rigidly dictated by the poem's meter, rhythm, and rhyme scheme. In the following excerpt from John Keats's "La Belle Dame sans Merci" (p. 1169), for example, rhythm, meter, and rhyme dictate the pauses that occur at the ends of the lines:

O, what can ail thee, knight-at-arms,
    Alone and palely loitering?
The sedge has wither'd from the lake,
    And no birds sing.

In contrast to end-stopped lines, run-on lines often seem more natural. Because their ending points are determined by the rhythms of speech and by the meaning and emphasis the poet wishes to convey rather than by meter and rhyme, run-on lines are suited to the open form of much modern poetry. In the following lines from the poem "We Have Come Home," by Lenrie Peters, run-on lines give readers the sense of spoken language:

We have come home
From the bloodless war
With sunken hearts
Our boots full of pride—
From the true massacre of the soul
When we have asked
"What does it cost
To be loved and left alone?"

Rather than relying exclusively on end-stopped or run-on lines, poets often use a combination of the two to produce the effects they want. For example, the following lines from "Pot Roast," by Mark Strand, juxtapose end-stopped and run-on lines:

I gaze upon the roast,
that is sliced and laid out
on my plate
and over it
I spoon the juices
of carrot and onion.
And for once I do not regret
the passage of time.

FURTHER READING: Rhythm and Meter

ADRIENNE RICH (1929–)

Aunt Jennifer's Tigers (1951)

Aunt Jennifer's tigers prance across a screen,
Bright topaz denizens of a world of green.
They do not fear the men beneath the tree;
They pace in sleek chivalric certainty.

Aunt Jennifer's fingers fluttering through her wool
Find even the ivory needle hard to pull.
The massive weight of Uncle's wedding band
Sits heavily upon Aunt Jennifer's hand.

When Aunt is dead, her terrified hands will lie
Still ringed with ordeals she was mastered by.
The tigers in the panel that she made
Will go on prancing, proud and unafraid.

Reading and Reacting

1. What is the dominant metrical pattern of the poem? How does the meter enhance the contrast the poem develops?
2. The lines in the first stanza are end-stopped, and those in the second and third stanzas combine end-stopped and run-on lines. What does the poet achieve by varying the rhythm?
3. What ideas do the caesuras in the first and fourth lines of the last stanza emphasize?
4. **JOURNAL ENTRY** What is the speaker's opinion of Aunt Jennifer's marriage? Do you think she is commenting on this particular marriage or on marriage in general?
5. **CRITICAL PERSPECTIVE** In *The Aesthetics of Power,* Claire Keyes writes of this poem that although it is formally beautiful, almost perfect, its voice creates problems:

> [T]he tone seldom approaches intimacy, the speaker seeming fairly detached from the fate of Aunt Jennifer. . . . The dominant voice of the poem asserts the traditional theme that art outlives the person who produces it. . . . The speaker is almost callous in her disregard for Aunt's death. . . . Who cares that Aunt Jennifer dies? The speaker does not seem to; she gets caught up in those gorgeous tigers. . . . Here lies the dominant voice: Aunt is not compelling; her creation is.

Do you agree with Keyes's interpretation of the poem?

Related Works: "Prue" (p. 184), "Miss Brill" (p. 266), "Everyday Use" (p. 517), "Happy Endings" (p. 662), "Rooming houses are old women" (p. 926), "Ethics" (p. 1186)

ETHERIDGE KNIGHT (1931–1991)

For Malcolm,° a Year After (1986)

Compose for Red° a proper verse;
Adhere to foot and strict iamb;
Control the burst of angry words
Or they might boil and break the dam.
Or they might boil and overflow
And drench me, drown me, drive me mad.

Malcolm: Malcolm X (1925–1965).

Red: Malcolm X's nickname when he was a young man.

So swear no oath, so shed no tear,
And sing no song blue Baptist sad.
Evoke no image, stir no flame,
And spin no yarn across the air.
Make empty anglo tea lace words—
Make them dead white and dry bone bare.

Compose a verse for Malcolm man,
And make it rime and make it prim.
The verse will die—as all men do—
But not the memory of him!
Death might come singing sweet like C,
Or knocking like the old folk say,
The moon and stars may pass away,
But not the anger of that day.

Reading and Reacting

1. Why do you think Knight chooses to write a "proper verse" in "strict iamb"? Do you think this meter is an appropriate choice for his subject?
2. What sounds and words are repeated in this poem? How does this repetition enhance the poem's rhythm?
3. Where in the poem does Knight use caesuras? Why does he use a pause in each instance?
4. **Journal Entry** How would you describe the mood of the speaker? Is the poem's meter consistent with his mood or in conflict with it? Explain.

Related Works: "Battle Royal" (p. 332), "New York Day Women" (p. 406), "To an Athlete Dying Young" (p. 900), "Medgar Evers" (p. 1132), "If We Must Die" (p. 1179)

Alliteration and Assonance

Just as poetry depends on rhythm, it also depends on the sounds of individual words. An effect pleasing to the ear, such as "Did he who made the Lamb make thee?" from William Blake's "The Tyger" (p. 1129), is called **euphony.** A jarring or discordant effect, such as "The vorpal blade went snicker-snack!" from Lewis Carroll's "Jabberwocky" (p. 976), is called **cacophony.**

One of the earliest, and perhaps the most primitive, methods of enhancing sound is **onomatopoeia,** which occurs when the sound of a word echoes its meaning, as it does in common words such as *bang*, *crash*, and *hiss*. Poets make broad application of this technique by using combinations of words that suggest a correspondence between sound and meaning, as Edgar Allan Poe does in these lines from his poem "The Bells":

Yet the ear, it fully knows,
    By the twanging
    And the clanging,

How the danger ebbs and flows;
Yet the ear distinctly tells,
In the jangling
And the wrangling
How the danger sinks and swells
By the sinking or the swelling in the anger of the bells—
Of the bells,—
Of the bells, bells, bells, bells. . . .

Poe's primary objective in this poem is to re-create the sound of ringing bells. Although he succeeds, the poem (113 lines long in its entirety) is extremely tedious. A more subtle use of onomatopoetic words appears in the following passage from *An Essay on Criticism* by Alexander Pope:

Soft is the strain when Zephyr gently blows,
And the smooth stream in smoother numbers flows;
But when the loud surges lash the sounding shore,
The hoarse, rough verse should like the torrent roar:
When Ajax strives some rock's vast weight to throw,
The line too Labors, and the words move slow.

After earlier admonishing readers that sound must echo sense, Pope uses onomatopoetic words such as *lash* and *roar* to convey the fury of the sea, and he uses repeated consonants to echo the sounds these words suggest. Notice, for example, how the *s* and *m* sounds suggest the gently blowing Zephyr and the flowing of the smooth stream and how the series of *r* sounds echoes the torrent's roar.

Alliteration—the repetition of consonant sounds in consecutive or neighboring words, usually at the beginning of words—is another device used to enhance sound in a poem. Both Poe ("sinks and swells") and Pope ("smooth stream") make use of alliteration in the preceding excerpts, and so does Tennyson in the following poem.

Source: ©Cape Canaveral Hanger

See this poet's biography on p. 1229.

ALFRED, LORD TENNYSON (1809–1892)

The Eagle (1851)

He clasps the crag with crooked hands;
Close to the sun in lonely lands,
Ringed with the azure world, he stands.

The wrinkled sea beneath him crawls:
He watches from his mountain walls,
And like a thunderbolt he falls.

Throughout the poem, *c*, *l*, and *w* sounds occur repeatedly. The poem is drawn together by the recurrence of these sounds and, as a result, it flows smoothly from beginning to end.

The following poem also uses alliteration to create special aural effects.

Source: ©Brand X Pictures/Jupiter Images

See this poet's biography on p. 1224.

N. SCOTT MOMADAY (1934–)

Comparatives (1976)

Sunlit sea,
the drift of fronds,
and banners
of bobbing boats—
the seaside
upon the planks,
the coil and
crescent of flesh
extending
just into death.

Even so,
in the distant,
inland sea,
a shadow runs,
radiant,
rude in the rock:
fossil fish,
fissure of bone
forever.
It is perhaps
the same thing,
an agony
twice perceived.

It is most like
wind on waves—
mere commotion,
mute and mean,
perceptible—
that is all.

Throughout the poem, Momaday uses alliteration to create a pleasing effect and to link certain words and ideas. Each stanza has its own alliterative pattern: the first stanza contains repeated *s* and *b* sounds, the second stanza contains repeated initial *r* and *f* sounds, and the third stanza contains repeated initial *w* and *m* sounds. Not only does this use of alliteration create a pleasing effect, it also reinforces the development of the poem's theme from stanza to stanza.

Assonance—the repetition of the same or similar vowel sounds, especially in stressed syllables—can also enrich a poem. When used effectively, assonance can create both mood and tone in a subtle, musical way. Consider, for example, the use of assonance in the following lines from Dylan Thomas's "Do not go gentle into that good night": "Old age should burn and rave at close of day; / Rage, rage, against the dying of the light."

Sometimes assonance unifies an entire poem. In the following poem, assonance emphasizes the thematic connections among words and thus links the poem's ideas.

ROBERT HERRICK (1591–1674)

Delight in Disorder (1648)

A sweet disorder in the dress
Kindles in clothes a wantonness.
A lawn° about the shoulders thrown
Into a fine distractión;
An erring lace, which here and there
Enthralls the crimson stomacher;°
A cuff neglectful, and thereby
Ribbons to flow confusedly;
A winning wave, deserving note,
In the tempestuous petticoat;
A careless shoestring, in whose tie
I see a wild civility;
Do more bewitch me than when art
Is too precise in every part.

Repeated vowel sounds extend throughout this poem—for instance, "shoulders" and "thrown" in line 3; and "tie," "wild," and "precise" in lines 11, 12, and 14. Using alliteration as well as assonance, Herrick subtly links certain words—"tempestuous petticoat," for example. By connecting these words, he calls attention to the pattern of imagery that helps to convey the poem's theme.

Rhyme

In addition to alliteration and assonance, poets create sound patterns with **rhyme**—the use of matching sounds in two or more words: "tight" and "might"; "born" and "horn"; "sleep" and "deep." For a rhyme to be **perfect,** final vowel and consonant sounds must be the same, as they are in each of the preceding examples. **Imperfect rhyme** (also called *near rhyme*, *slant rhyme*, *approximate rhyme*, or **consonance**) occurs when the final consonant sounds in two words are the same but vowel sounds are different—"learn" / "barn" or "pads" / "lids," for example. William Stafford uses imperfect rhyme in "Traveling through the Dark" (p. 1052) when he rhymes "road" with "dead." Finally, **eye rhyme** occurs when two words look as if they should rhyme but do not—for example, "watch" and "catch."

lawn: A shawl made of fine fabric.
stomacher: A heavily embroidered garment worn by females over the chest and stomach.

Rhyme can also be classified according to the position of the rhyming syllables in a line of verse. The most common type of rhyme is **end rhyme,** which occurs at the end of a line:

Tyger! Tyger! burning bright
In the forests of the night

William Blake, "The Tyger"

Internal rhyme occurs within a line:

The Sun came up upon the left,
Out of the sea came he!
And he shone bright and on the right
Went down into the sea.

Samuel Taylor Coleridge, "The Rime of the Ancient Mariner"

Beginning rhyme occurs at the beginning of a line:

Red river, red river,
Slow flow heat is silence
No will is still as a river

T. S. Eliot, "Virginia"

Rhyme can also be classified according to the number of syllables that correspond. **Masculine rhyme** (also called **rising rhyme**) occurs when single syllables correspond ("can" / "ran"; "descend" / "contend"). **Feminine rhyme** (also called **double rhyme** or **falling rhyme**) occurs when two syllables, a stressed one followed by an unstressed one, correspond ("ocean" / "motion"; "leaping" / "sleeping"). **Triple rhyme** occurs when three syllables correspond. Less common than the other two, triple rhyme is often used for humorous or satiric purposes, as in the following lines from the long poem *Don Juan* by Lord Byron:

Sagest of women, even of widows, she
  Resolved that Juan should be quite a paragon,
And worthy of the noblest pedigree:
  (His sire of Castile, his dam from Aragon).

In some cases—for example, when it is overused or when it is used in unexpected places—rhyme can create unusual and even comic effects. In the following poem, humor is created by the incongruous connections established by rhymes such as "priest" / "beast" and "pajama" / "lllama."

OGDEN NASH (1902–1971)

The Lama (1931)

The one-l lama
He's a priest.
The two-l llama,
He's a beast.

And I will bet
A silk pajama
There isn't any
Three-l lllama.

The conventional way to describe a poem's rhyme scheme is to chart rhyming sounds that appear at the ends of lines. The sound that ends the first line is designated *a*, and all subsequent lines that end in that sound are also labeled *a*. The next sound to appear at the end of a line is designated *b*, and all other lines whose last sounds rhyme with it are also designated *b*—and so on through the alphabet. The lines of the poem that follows are labeled in this manner.

Source: ©AP Photo

See this poet's biography on p. 1230.

RICHARD WILBUR (1921–)

In Trackless Woods (2003)

In trackless woods, it puzzled me to find a
Four great rock maples seemingly aligned, a
As if they had been set out in a row b
Before some house a century ago, b
To edge the property and lend some shade. c
I looked to see if ancient wheels had made c
Old ruts to which these trees can parallel, d
But there were none, so far as I could tell— d
There'd been no roadway. Nor could I find the square e
Depression of a cellar anywhere, e
And so I tramped on further, to survey f
Amazing patterns in a hornbeam spray f
Or spirals in a pinecone, under trees g
Not subject to our stiff geometries. g

"In Trackless Woods" has a simple rhyme scheme (*aa*, *bb*, *cc*, and so on). In a sense, this fourteen-line poem is a sonnet—but one that that rejects the fixed rhyme scheme of the traditional sonnet. Despite its simplicity, the rhyme scheme of the poem is important. It reinforces the central point of the poem: to convey what the speaker sees in the trackless woods, he (as well as other poets) must reject the "stiff geometries" of formal poetry and employ a new, more natural, means of expression.

Other poems have a more complicated rhyme scheme. Notice in the following excerpt from "The Road Not Taken" (p. 1159) how Robert Frost uses rhyme:

Two roads diverged in a yellow wood, *a*
And sorry I could not travel both *b*
And be one traveler, long I stood, *a*
And looked down one as far as I could *a*
To where it bent in the undergrowth; *b*

This rhyme of this five-line stanza (and indeed of the whole poem) is *abaab*. In addition, there are four stressed syllables per line, mostly in iambic tetrameter. Despite its rather complex rhyme and metrical scheme, the poem sounds conversational, as if someone just spoke it without any effort or planning. The beauty of this poem comes from Frost's subtle use of rhyme and rhythm to create a musical effect that makes the lines flow together. In addition, the alternating *a* and *b* rhymes suggest the divergent roads that the speaker is forced to choose between.

FURTHER READING: Alliteration, Assonance, and Rhyme

GERARD MANLEY HOPKINS (1844–1889)

Pied Beauty (1918)

Glory be to God for dappled things—
　　For skies of couple-color as a brinded° cow;
　　　　For rose-moles all in stipple upon trout that swim;
Fresh-firecoal chestnut-falls; finches' wings;
　　Landscape plotted and pieced—fold, fallow, and plow;
　　　　And áll trádes, their gear and tackle and trim.°

All things counter, original, spare, strange;
　　Whatever is fickle, freckled (who knows how?)
　　　　With swift, slow; sweet, sour; adazzle, dim;
He fathers-forth whose beauty is past change:
　　　　　　　　Praise him.

Reading and Reacting

1. Identify examples of onomatopoeia, alliteration, assonance, imperfect rhyme, and perfect rhyme. Do you think all these techniques are essential to the poem? Are any of them annoying or distracting?

2. What is the central idea of this poem? How do the sounds of the poem help to communicate this idea?

3. Identify examples of masculine and feminine rhyme.

4. **Journal Entry** Hopkins uses both pleasing and discordant sounds in his poem. Identify uses of euphony and cacophony, and explain how these techniques affect your reactions to the poem.

Related Works: "Cathedral" (p. 526), "Women" (p. 1007), "I never saw a Moor—" (p. 1144), "Batter My Heart, Three-Personed God" (p. 1148)

---

brinded: Brindled (streaked).

trim: Equipment.

W. H. AUDEN (1907–1973)

As I Walked Out One Evening (1940)

As I walked out one evening,
Walking down Bristol Street,
The crowds upon the pavement
Were fields of harvest wheat.

And down by the brimming river
I heard a lover sing
Under an arch of the railway:
"Love has no ending.

"I'll love you, dear, I'll love you
Till China and Africa meet,
And the river jumps over the mountain
And the salmon sing in the street,

"I'll love you till the ocean
Is folded and hung up to dry,
And the seven stars go squawking
Like geese about the sky.

"The years shall run like rabbits,
For in my arms I hold
The Flower of the Ages,
And the first love of the world."

But all the clocks in the city
Began to whirr and chime:
"O let not Time deceive you,
You cannot conquer Time.

"In the burrows of the Nightmare
Where Justice naked is,
Time watches from the shadow
And coughs when you would kiss.

"In headaches and in worry
Vaguely life leaks away,
And Time will have his fancy
Tomorrow or today.

"Into many a green valley
Drifts the appalling snow;
Time breaks the threaded dances
And the diver's brilliant bow.

"O plunge your hands in water,
Plunge them in up to the wrist;

Stare, stare in the basin
And wonder what you've missed.

"The glacier knocks in the cupboard,
The desert sighs in the bed,
And the crack in the teacup opens
A lane to the land of the dead.

"Where the beggars raffle the banknotes
And the Giant is enchanting to Jack,
And the Lily-white Boy is a Roarer,
And Jill goes down on her back.

"O look, look in the mirror,
O look in your distress;
Life remains a blessing
Although you cannot bless.

"O stand, stand at the window
As the tears scald and start;
You shall love your crooked neighbor
With your crooked heart."

It was late, late in the evening,
The lovers they were gone;
The clocks had ceased their chiming,
And the deep river ran on.

Reading and Reacting

1. Chart the poem's rhyme scheme. Does Auden use perfect rhyme at the end of the second line and the fourth line of every stanza? If not, why do you think he chooses not to?

2. Does Auden use internal rhyme? Where does he use alliteration and assonance? In what other ways does he use sound?

3. Does Auden's use of sound reinforce the poem's content or undercut it? Explain.

4. **JOURNAL ENTRY** Could this poem be considered a love poem? How are its sentiments about love different from those conventionally expressed in poems about love?

5. **CRITICAL PERSPECTIVE** In a 1940 British review of Auden's work, T. C. Worsley made the following comments about this poem:

> There is no technical reason why such a poem as [this] should not be popular; the metre and the rhythm are easy and helpful, and the symbols have reference to a world of experience common to every inhabitant of these islands. Here . . . the poet has gone as far as he can along the road to creating a popular poetry.

Does Auden's poem strike you as a model for "popular" poetry—that is, poetry for people who do not usually read poetry?

Related Works: "The Story of an Hour" (p. 226), "Araby" (p. 434), "The World Is Too Much with Us" (p. 855), "Oh, my love is like a red, red rose" (p. 928), "To His Coy Mistress" (p. 941), "Not marble, nor the gilded monuments" (p. 1194)

GALWAY KINNELL (1927–)

Blackberry Eating (1980)

I love to go out in late September
among the fat, overripe, icy, black blackberries
to eat blackberries for breakfast,
the stalks very prickly, a penalty
they earn for knowing the black art
of blackberry-making; and as I stand among them
lifting the stalks to my mouth, the ripest berries
fall almost unbidden to my tongue,
as words sometimes do, certain peculiar words
like *strengths* or *squinched*,
many-lettered, one-syllabled lumps,
which I squeeze, squinch open, and splurge well
in the silent, startled, icy, black language
of blackberry-eating in late September.

Reading and Reacting

1. What sounds does Kinnell repeat in the poem? How do they help to create the poem's rhythm?
2. This poem consists entirely of run-on lines. Why do you think the poet uses this technique instead of end-stopped lines?
3. One part of the poem deals with blackberries, and the other part deals with the poet's love for words. What is the connection between these two subjects?
4. How do alliteration and assonance help Kinnell convey his ideas?
5. **Journal Entry** What do you think this poem is really about?
6. **Critical Perspective** Critic Daniela Gioseffi had the following to say about Galway Kinnell:

   > He has real things to say about an actual world of flesh and bone and excrement, full of nature's glories and horrors, always viewed from within the reality of our gutsy, animal being, our need to survive from the land and its vulnerable animal life, a world poignant with transient beauty and helpless mortality.

   Do you think this poem reflects both nature's "glories" and its "horrors"? How does it comment on the transient beauty of nature and on our own "helpless mortality"?

Related Works: "Snow" (p. 177), "Cathedral" (p. 526), "Two Questions" (p. 556), "Words, Words, Words" (p. 875), "Introduction to Poetry" (p. 1138)

LYDIA DAVIS (1947–)

A Mown Lawn (2001)

She hated a *mown lawn*. Maybe that was because *mow* was the reverse of *wom*, the beginning of the name of what she was—a *woman*. A *mown lawn* had a sad sound to it, like a *long moan*. From her, a *mown lawn* made a *long moan*. *Lawn* had some of the letters of *man*, though the reverse of *man* would be *Nam*, a bad war. A *raw war*. *Lawn* also contained the letters of *law*. In fact, *lawn* was a contraction of *lawman*. Certainly a *lawman* could and did *mow a lawn*. *Law and order* could be seen as starting from *lawn order*, valued by so many Americans. *More lawn* could be made using a *lawn mower*. A *lawn mower* did make *more lawn*. *More lawn* was a contraction of *more lawmen*. Did *more lawn* in America make *more lawmen* in America? Did *more lawn* make *more Nam? More mown lawn* made *more long moan*, from her. Or a *lawn mourn*. So often, she said, Americans wanted *more mown lawn*. All of America might be one *long mown lawn*. A *lawn* not *mown* grows *long*, she said: better a *long lawn*. Better a *long lawn* and a *mole*. Let the *lawman* have the *mown lawn*, she said. Or the *moron*, the *lawn moron*.

Reading and Reacting

1. Identify several different types of rhyme in this poem. Then, find examples of alliteration and assonance.
2. "A Mown Lawn" does not conform to most people's idea of what a poem should look like. Do you think "A Mown Lawn" is a poem, or is it something else?
3. Study the poem's italicized words and phrases. How are they related in terms of sound? What ideas do these words convey?
4. **Journal Entry** What comment does this poem make about life in the United States?

Related Works: "The Secret Lion" (p. 197), "The Spray" (p. 729), "The Year of Spaghetti" (p. 745), "The World Is Too Much with Us" (p. 855), "Sears Life" (p. 891), "Spring: The Star Magnolia" (p. 912), "A Supermarket in California" (p. 952)

Source: ©WOJDA/FREE/Corbis Sygma

See this poet's biography on p. 1228.

KAY RYAN (1945–)

Lighthouse Keeping (2005)

Seas pleat
winds keen
fogs deepen
ships lean no
doubt, and
the lighthouse
keeper keeps
a light for
those left out.
It is intimate
and remote both
for the keeper
and those afloat.

Reading and Reacting

1. Although this poem does not have a regular rhyme scheme, it still includes words that rhyme. Identify these words, and explain how they contribute to the overall effect of the poem.

2. In addition to using rhyme, Ryan also uses repetition. What words does she repeat? What ideas does this repetition emphasize?

3. Where does Ryan use alliteration and assonance? Do alliteration and assonance contribute something vital to the poem, or are they a distraction?

4. **JOURNAL ENTRY** What point do you think this poem is making about a lighthouse? About the lighthouse keeper?

5. **CRITICAL PERSPECTIVE** Speaking about "Lighthouse Keeping," poet Tom Padgett says:

> In her little lighthouse-shaped poem "Lighthouse Keeping," Kay Ryan. . . says lighthouse keepers obviously keep the light "for those left out." They guide "those afloat" to the safety of the harbor by protecting them from the submerged reefs and shoreline rocks that would sink their ship. The light is "intimate and remote" to both the keeper and the endangered sailor. As poets we, too, possess intimate light that is valuable to ourselves but also to others. We are part of a process that keeps language as light functioning to clarify our meanings, to communicate our feelings, and of course to preserve [to freeze] our time.

Do you agree with Padgett that "Lighthouse Keeping" is more about keeping the light than about a lighthouse keeper? Explain.

Related Works: "Water Names" (p. 318), "Two Questions" (p. 556), "Royal Palm" (p. 893), "Washing Rice" (p. 913), "Reapers" (p. 914), "American Haiku" (p. 997), "Women" (p. 1007), *The Cuban Swimmer* (p. 1732)

LEWIS CARROLL (1832–1898)

Jabberwocky (1871)

'Twas brillig, and the slithy toves
Did gyre and gimble in the wabe:
All mimsy were the borogoves,
And the mome raths outgrabe.

"Beware the Jabberwock, my son!
The jaws that bite, the claws that catch!
Beware the Jubjub bird, and shun
The frumious Bandersnatch!"

He took his vorpal sword in hand;
Long time the manxome foe he sought—
So rested he by the Tumtum tree
And stood awhile in thought.

And, as in uffish thought he stood,
The Jabberwock, with eyes of flame,
Came whiffling through the tulgey wood,
And burbled as it came!

One, two! One, two! And through and through
The vorpal blade went snicker-snack!
He left it dead, and with its head
He went galumphing back.

"And hast thou slain the Jabberwock?
Come to my arms, my beamish boy!
O frabjous day! Callooh, Callay!"
He chortled in his joy.

'Twas brillig, and the slithy toves
Did gyre and gimble in the wabe:
All mimsy were the borogoves,
And the mome raths outgrabe.

Reading and Reacting

1. Many words in this poem may be unfamiliar to you. Are they actual words? Use a dictionary to check before you dismiss any. Do some words that do not appear in the dictionary nevertheless seem to have meaning in the context of the poem? Explain.

2. This poem contains many examples of onomatopoeia. What meanings does the sound of each of these words suggest?

3. **JOURNAL ENTRY** Summarize the story the poem tells. In what sense is this poem a story of a young man's initiation into adulthood?

4. **CRITICAL PERSPECTIVE** According to Humpty Dumpty in Carroll's *Alice in Wonderland*, the nonsense words in the poem are **portmanteau words** (that is, words whose form and meaning are derived from two other distinct words—as *smog* is a portmanteau of *smoke* and *fog*). Critic Elizabeth Sewell, however, rejects this explanation: "*[F]rumious*, for instance, is not a word, and does not have two meanings packed up in it; it is a group of letters without any meaning at all. . . . [I]t looks like other words, and almost certainly more than two."

Which nonsense words in the poem seem to you to be portmanteau words, and which do not? Can you suggest possible sources for the words that are not portmanteau words?

Related Works: "A&P" (p. 259), "Gryphon" (p. 277), "Words, Words, Words" (p. 875)

✔ CHECKLIST Writing about Sound

Rhythm and Meter

- ☐ Does the poem contain repeated words and phrases? If so, how do they help to create rhythm?
- ☐ Does the poem use one kind of meter throughout, or does the meter vary from line to line?
- ☐ How does the meter contribute to the overall effect of the poem?

continued on next page

- Where do caesuras appear? What effect do they have?
- Are the lines of the poem end-stopped, run-on, or a combination of the two? What effects are created by the presence or absence of pauses at the ends of lines?

Alliteration, Assonance, and Rhyme

- Does the poem include alliteration or assonance?
- Does the poem have a regular rhyme scheme?
- Does the poem use internal rhyme? Beginning rhyme?
- Does the poem include examples of masculine, feminine, or triple rhyme?
- How does rhyme unify the poem?
- How does rhyme reinforce the poem's ideas?

WRITING SUGGESTIONS: Sound

1. William Blake's "The Tyger" appeared in a collection entitled *Songs of Experience*. Compare this poem (p. 1129) to "The Lamb" (p. 1128), which appeared in a collection called *Songs of Innocence*. In what sense are the speakers in these two poems either "innocent" or "experienced"? How does sound help to convey the voice of the speakers in these two poems?
2. "Sadie and Maud" (p. 957), like "My Papa's Waltz" (p. 1039), and "Daddy" (p. 936), communicates the speaker's attitude toward home and family. How does the presence or absence of rhyme in these poems help to convey the speakers' attitudes?
3. Robert Frost once said that writing **free verse** poems, which have no fixed metrical pattern, is like playing tennis without a net. What do you think he meant? Do you agree? After reading "Out, Out—" (p. 943), "Stopping by Woods on a Snowy Evening" (p. 1159), and "The Road Not Taken" (p. 1159), write an essay in which you discuss Frost's use of meter.
4. Select two or three contemporary poems that have no end rhyme. Write an essay in which you discuss what these poets gain and lose by not using end rhyme.
5. Prose writers as well as poets use assonance and alliteration. Choose two or three a passages of prose—from "Araby" (p. 434), "Barn Burning" (p. 391), or "The Things They Carried" (p. 473), for example—and discuss their use of assonance and alliteration. Where are these techniques used? How do they help the writer create a mood?

CHAPTER 29

FORM

Source: ©AP Photo/Steve Yeater

See this poet's biography on p. 1223.

JOHN KEATS (1795–1821)

On the Sonnet (1819)

If by dull rhymes our English must be chained,
And like Andromeda,° the sonnet sweet
Fettered, in spite of painéd loveliness,
Let us find, if we must be constrained,
Sandals more interwoven and complete
To fit the naked foot of Poesy:
Let us inspect the lyre, and weigh the stress
Of every chord, and see what may be gained
By ear industrious, and attention meet;
Misers of sound and syllable, no less
Than Midas° of his coinage, let us be
Jealous of dead leaves in the bay-wreath crown;
So, if we may not let the Muse be free,
She will be bound with garlands of her own.

Source: ©AP Photo/Beth A. Keiser

See this poet's biography on p. 1219.

BILLY COLLINS (1941–)

Sonnet (1999)

All we need is fourteen lines, well, thirteen now,
and after this one just a dozen
to launch a little ship on love's storm chased seas,
then only ten more left like rows of beans.
How easily it goes unless you get Elizabethan
and insist the iambic bongos must be played
and rhymes positioned at the ends of lines,
one for every station of the cross.

Andromeda: In Greek mythology, an Ethiopian princess chained to a rock to appease a sea monster.
Midas: A legendary king of Phrygia whose wish that everything he touched would turn to gold was granted by the god Dionysus.

But hang on here while we make the turn
into the final six where all will be resolved,
where longing and heartache will find an end,
where Laura will tell Petrarch to put down his pen,
take off those crazy medieval tights,
blow out the lights, and come at last to bed.

The **form** of a literary work is its structure or shape, the way its elements fit together to form a whole; **poetic form** is the design of a poem described in terms of rhyme, meter, and stanzaic pattern.

Until the twentieth century, most poetry was written in **closed form** (sometimes called **fixed form**), characterized by regular patterns of meter, rhyme, line length, and stanzaic divisions. Early poems that were passed down orally—epics and ballads, for example—relied on regular form to facilitate memorization. Even after poems began to be written down, poets tended to favor regular patterns. In fact, until relatively recently, regular form was what distinguished poetry from prose. Of course, strict adherence to regular patterns sometimes produced poems that were, in John Keats's words, "chained" by "dull rhymes" and "fettered" by the rules governing a particular form. But rather than feeling "constrained" by form, many poets—like Billy Collins in the playful sonnet above—have experimented with imagery, figures of speech, allusion, and other techniques, moving away from rigid patterns of rhyme and meter and thus stretching closed form to its limits.

As they sought new ways in which to express themselves, poets also borrowed forms from other cultures, adapting them to the demands of their own languages. English and American poets, for example, adopted (and still use) early French forms, such as the **villanelle** and the **sestina,** and early Italian forms, such as the **Petrarchan sonnet** and **terza rima.** The nineteenth-century American poet Henry Wadsworth Longfellow studied Icelandic epics; the twentieth-century poet Ezra Pound studied the works of French troubadours; and Pound and other twentieth-century American poets, such as Richard Wright and Carolyn Kizer, were inspired by Japanese haiku. Other American poets, such as Vachel Lindsay, Langston Hughes, and Maya Angelou, looked closer to home—to the rhythms of blues, jazz, and spirituals—for inspiration.

As time went on, more and more poets moved away from closed form to experiment with **open form** poetry (sometimes called **free verse** or *vers libre*), varying line length within a poem, dispensing with meter and stanzaic divisions, breaking lines in unexpected places, and even abandoning any semblance of formal structure. In English, nineteenth-century poets—such as William Blake and Matthew Arnold—experimented with lines of irregular meter and length, and Walt Whitman wrote **prose poems,** open form poems whose long lines made them look like prose. (Well before this time, Asian poetry and some biblical passages had used a type of free verse.) In nineteenth-century France, symbolist poets, such as Baudelaire, Rimbaud, Verlaine, and Mallarmé, also used free verse. In the early twentieth century, a group of American poets—including Ezra Pound, William Carlos

Williams, and Amy Lowell—who were associated with a movement known as **imagism** wrote poetry that dispensed with traditional principles of English versification, creating new rhythms and meters.

Although much contemporary English and American poetry is composed in open form, many poets also continue to write in closed form—even in very traditional, highly structured patterns. Still, new forms, and new variations of old forms, are being created all the time. And, because contemporary poets do not necessarily feel bound by rules or restrictions about what constitutes "acceptable" poetic form, they experiment freely, trying to discover the form that best suits the poem's purpose, subject, language, and theme.

Closed Form

A **closed form** (or *fixed form*) poem looks symmetrical; it has an identifiable, repeated pattern, with lines of similar length arranged in groups of two, three, four, or more. A closed form poem also tends to rely on regular metrical patterns and rhyme schemes.

Despite what its name suggests, closed form poetry does not have to be confining or conservative. In fact, contemporary poets often experiment with closed form—for example, by using characteristics of open form poetry (such as lines of varying length) within a closed form. Sometimes poets move back and forth within a single poem from open to closed to open form; sometimes (like their eighteenth-century counterparts) they combine different stanzaic forms (stanzas of two and three lines, for example) within a single poem.

Even when poets work within a traditional closed form, such as a sonnet, sestina, or villanelle, they can break new ground. For example, they can write a sonnet with an unexpected meter or rhyme scheme (or with no consistent pattern of rhyme or meter at all), add an extra line or even extra stanzas to a traditional sonnet form, combine two different traditional sonnet forms in a single poem, or write an abbreviated version of a sestina or villanelle. In other words, poets can use traditional forms as building blocks, combining them in innovative ways to create new patterns and new forms.

Sometimes a pattern (such as **blank verse**) simply determines the meter of a poem's individual lines. At other times, the pattern extends to the level of the **stanza,** with lines arranged into groups (**couplets, quatrains,** and so on). At still other times, as in the case of traditional closed forms like sonnets, a poetic pattern gives shape to an entire poem.

Blank Verse

Blank verse is unrhymed poetry with each line written in a pattern of five stressed and five unstressed syllables called **iambic pentameter** (see p. 960). Many passages from Shakespeare's plays, such as the following lines from *Hamlet*, are written in blank verse:

To sleep! perchance to dream:—ay, there's the rub;
For in that sleep of death what dreams may come,
When we have shuffled off this mortal coil,
Must give us pause: there's the respect
That makes calamity of so long life

For a contemporary use of blank verse, see John Updike's "Ex-Basketball Player" (p. 930).

Stanza

A **stanza** is a group of two or more lines with the same metrical pattern—and often with a regular rhyme scheme as well—separated by blank space from other such groups of lines. Stanzas in poetry are like paragraphs in prose: they group related ideas into units.

A two-line stanza with rhyming lines of similar length and meter is called a **couplet.** The **heroic couplet,** first used by Chaucer and later very popular throughout the eighteenth century, consists of two rhymed lines of iambic pentameter, with a weak pause after the first line and a strong pause after the second. The following example, from Alexander Pope's *An Essay on Criticism*, is a heroic couplet:

True ease in writing comes from art, not chance,
As those move easiest who have learned to dance.

A three-line stanza with lines of similar length and a set rhyme scheme is called a **tercet.** Percy Bysshe Shelley's "Ode to the West Wind" (p. 1194) is built largely of tercets:

O wild West Wind, thou breath of Autumn's being,
Thou, from whose unseen presence the leaves dead
Are driven, like ghosts from an enchanter fleeing,
Yellow, and black, and pale, and hectic red,
Pestilence-stricken multitudes: O Thou,
Who chariotest to their dark wintry bed

Although in many tercets all three lines rhyme, "Ode to the West Wind" uses a special rhyme scheme, also used by Dante, called **terza rima.** This rhyme scheme (*aba, bcb, cdc, ded,* and so on) creates an interlocking series of stanzas: line 2's *dead* looks ahead to the rhyming words *red* and *bed,* which close lines 4 and 6, and the pattern continues throughout the poem. Robert Frost's "Acquainted with the Night" (p. 1156) is a contemporary example of terza rima.

A four-line stanza with lines of similar length and a set rhyme scheme is called a **quatrain.** The quatrain, the most widely used and versatile unit in English and American poetry, is used by William Wordsworth in the following excerpt from "She dwelt among the untrodden ways" (p. 1211):

A violet by a mossy stone
Half hidden from the eye!
—Fair as a star, when only one
Is shining in the sky.

Quatrains are frequently used by contemporary poets as well—for instance, in Theodore Roethke's "My Papa's Waltz" (p. 1039), Adrienne Rich's "Aunt Jennifer's Tigers" (p. 963), and William Stafford's "Traveling through the Dark" (p. 1052).

One special kind of quatrain, called the **ballad stanza,** alternates lines of eight and six syllables; typically, only the second and fourth lines rhyme. The following lines from the traditional Scottish ballad "Sir Patrick Spence" illustrate the ballad stanza:

> The king sits in Dumferling toune,
> Drinking the blude-reid wine:
> "O whar will I get guid sailor
> To sail this schip of mine?"

Common measure, a four-line stanzaic pattern closely related to the ballad stanza, is used in hymns as well as in poetry. It differs from the ballad stanza in that its rhyme scheme is *abab* rather than *abcb*. This pattern appears in Donald Hall's poem "My Son, My Executioner" (p. 945).

Other stanzaic forms include **rhyme royal**, a seven-line stanza *(ababbcc)* set in iambic pentameter, used in Sir Thomas Wyatt's sixteenth-century poem "They Flee from Me That Sometimes Did Me Seke" as well as in Theodore Roethke's twentieth-century "I Knew a Woman" (p. 885); **ottava rima,** an eight-line stanza *(abababcc)* set in iambic pentameter; and the **Spenserian stanza,** a nine-line form *(ababbcbcc)* whose first eight lines are set in iambic pentameter and whose last line is in iambic hexameter. The Romantic poets John Keats and Percy Bysshe Shelley were among those who used the Spenserian stanza. (See Chapter 28 for definitions and examples of various metrical patterns.)

The Sonnet

Perhaps the most familiar kind of traditional closed form poem written in English is the **sonnet,** a fourteen-line poem with a distinctive rhyme scheme and metrical pattern. The English or **Shakespearean sonnet,** which consists of fourteen lines divided into three quatrains and a concluding couplet, is written in iambic pentameter and follows the rhyme scheme *abab cdcd efef gg*. The **Petrarchan sonnet,** popularized in the fourteenth century by the Italian poet Francesco Petrarch, also consists of fourteen lines of iambic pentameter, but these lines are divided into an eight-line unit called an **octave** and a six-line unit (composed of two tercets) called a **sestet.** The rhyme scheme of the octave is *abba abba*; the rhyme scheme of the sestet is *cde cde*.

The conventional structures of these sonnet forms reflect the arrangement of ideas within the poem. In the Shakespearean sonnet, the poet typically presents three "paragraphs" of related thoughts, introducing an idea in the first quatrain, developing it in the two remaining quatrains, and summing up in a succinct closing couplet. In the Petrarchan sonnet, the octave introduces a problem that is resolved in the sestet. (Many Shakespearean sonnets also have a problem-solution structure.) Some poets vary the traditional patterns somewhat to suit the poem's language or ideas. For example, they may depart from the pattern to sidestep a forced rhyme or unnatural stress on a syllable, or they may shift from problem to solution in a place other than between octave and sestet.

The following poem has the form of a traditional English sonnet.

WILLIAM SHAKESPEARE (1564–1616)

When, in disgrace with Fortune and men's eyes (1609)

When, in disgrace with Fortune and men's eyes,
I all alone beweep my outcast state,
And trouble deaf heaven with my bootless° cries,
And look upon myself and curse my fate,
Wishing me like to one more rich in hope,
Featured like him, like him with friends possessed,
Desiring this man's art, and that man's scope,
With what I most enjoy contented least,
Yet in these thoughts myself almost despising,
Haply° I think on thee, and then my state,
Like to the lark at break of day arising
From sullen earth, sings hymns at heaven's gate;
For thy sweet love rememb'red such wealth brings
That then I scorn to change my state with kings.

This sonnet is written in iambic pentameter and has a conventional rhyme scheme: *abab* (eyes-state-cries-fate), *cdcd* (hope-possessed-scope-least), *efef* (despising-state-arising-gate), *gg* (brings-kings). In this poem, in which the speaker explains how thoughts of his loved one can rescue him from despair, each quatrain is unified by subject matter as well as by rhyme.

In the first quatrain, the speaker presents his problem: he is down on his luck and out of favor with his peers, isolated in self-pity and cursing his fate. In the second quatrain, he develops this idea further: he is envious of others and dissatisfied with things that usually please him. In the third quatrain, the focus shifts. After the first two quatrains develop a dependent clause ("When . . .") that introduces a problem, line 9 begins to present the resolution. In the third quatrain, the speaker explains how, in the midst of his despair and self-hatred, he thinks of his loved one, and his spirits soar. The closing couplet sums up the mood transformation the poem describes and explains its significance: when the speaker realizes the emotional riches his loved one gives him, he is no longer envious of others.

FURTHER READING: The Sonnet

JOHN KEATS (1795–1821)

On First Looking into Chapman's Homer° (1816)

Much have I traveled in the realms of gold,
        And many goodly states and kingdoms seen;

---

bootless: Futile.
Haply: Luckily.
Chapman's Homer: The translation of Homer's works by Elizabethan poet George Chapman.

Round many western islands have I been
Which bards in fealty to Apollo° hold.
Oft of one wide expanse had I been told
That deep-browed Homer ruled as his demesne,°
Yet did I never breathe its pure serene°
Till I heard Chapman speak out loud and bold.
Then felt I like some watcher of the skies
When a new planet swims into his ken;
Or like stout Cortez° when with eagle eyes
He stared at the Pacific—and all his men
Looked at each other with a wild surmise—
Silent, upon a peak in Darien.°

Reading and Reacting

1. Is this a Petrarchan or a Shakespearean sonnet? Explain.

2. JOURNAL ENTRY The sestet's change of focus is introduced with the word "Then" in line 9. How does the mood of the sestet differ from the mood of the octave? How does the language differ?

3. CRITICAL PERSPECTIVE As Keats's biographer Aileen Ward observes, Homer's epic tales of gods and heroes were known to most readers of Keats's day only in a very formal eighteenth-century translation by Alexander Pope. This is Pope's description of Ulysses escaping from a shipwreck:

> his knees no more
> Perform'd their office, or his weight upheld:
> His swoln heart heav'd, his bloated body swell'd:
> From mouth to nose the briny torrent ran,
> And lost in lassitude lay all the man,
> Deprived of voice, of motion, and of breath,
> The soul scarce waking in the arms of death . . .

In a rare 1616 edition of Chapman's translation, Keats discovered a very different poem:

> both knees falt'ring, both
> His strong hands hanging down, and all with froth
> His cheeks and nostrils flowing, voice and breath
> Spent to all use, and down he sank to death.
> The sea had soak'd his heart through. . . .

This, as Ward notes, was "poetry of a kind that had not been written in England for two hundred years."

Can you understand why Keats was so moved by Chapman's translation? Do you think Keats's own poem seems closer in its form and language to Pope or to Chapman?

Apollo: Greek god of light, truth, reason, male beauty; associated with music and poetry.

demesne: Realm, domain.

serene: Air, atmosphere.

Cortez: It was Vasco de Balboa (not Hernando Cortez as Keats suggests) who first saw the Pacific Ocean, from "a peak in Darien."

Darien: Former name of the Isthmus of Panama.

Related Works: "Snow" (p. 177), "Gryphon" (p. 277), "Araby" (p. 434), "When I Heard the Learn'd Astronomer" (p. 877), *Trifles* (p. 1319)

A. E. STALLINGS (1968–)

Explaining an Affinity for Bats (2006)

That they are only glimpsed in silhouette,
And seem something else at first—a swallow—
And move like new runes, difficult to follow,
Staggering towards an obstacle they yet
Avoid in a last-minute pirouette,
Somehow telling solid things from hollow,
Sounding out how high a space, or shallow,
Revising into deepening violet.

That they sing—not the way the songbird sings
(Whose song is rote, to ornament, finesse)—
But travel by a sort of song that rings
True not in utterance, but harkenings,
Who find their way by calling into darkness
To hear their voice bounce off the shape of things.

Reading and Reacting

1. Describe the poem's rhyme scheme. How is it like and unlike the traditional Shakespearean and Petrarchan sonnet forms?
2. What determines the break between octave and sestet? For example, does the poem have a problem-solution structure, or is there some other thematic rationale for dividing the poem?
3. Sound is very important in this poem. Apart from rhyming words, what kinds of repeated sounds can you identify? How do these repetitions help to convey a sense of how the bats move and sing?
4. **JOURNAL ENTRY** What characteristics of bats does the speaker admire? Does this poem explain the speaker's "affinity for bats" to your satisfaction?

Related Works: "Doe Season" (p. 577), "Mind" (p. 930), "The Windhover" (p. 1050)

SOR JUANA INÉS DE LA CRUZ (c. 1651–1695)

Sonnet I*

Translated by Rhina Espaillat (2007)

To Celio, who, unregarded, does not wish to seem forgotten.

You say that I forget you, but you lie:
it would require thinking to forget you,
and nowhere in my thinking have I let you—

* Publication date is not available.

even as one forgotten—saunter by.
My thoughts are far—so far—from you, that I,
focused elsewhere, as if I'd never met you,
have no idea what thoughts of mine upset you,
or if your absence from them makes you sigh.
If anyone could love you, one could, yes,
forget you: what a triumph that would be,
affirming your existence; none the less,
you are so far from such a victory
that you're eclipsed, not through forgetfulness,
but sheer rejection by my memory.

Reading and Reacting

1. The first eight lines of this sonnet conform to the rhyme scheme of a Petrarchan sonnet, but the rest of the poem does not. How is it different?

2. How would you characterize the speaker's tone? For example, do you see her as serious or playful? Detached or involved?

3. This poem is dedicated "To Celio." Who do suppose Celio might be? What is the speaker's attitude toward him?

4. This poem was translated from the Spanish (the original Spanish version appears below). Is the rhyme scheme of the Spanish and English versions the same? Is the metrical pattern of the two versions the same? Explain.

Soneto

No quiere pasar por olvido lo descuidado.

Dices que yo te olvido, Celio, y mientes
en decir que me acuerdo de olvidarte,
pues no hay en mi memoria alguna parte
en que, aun como olvidado, te presentes.
Mis pensamientos son tan diferentes
y en todos tan ajeno de tratarte,
que ni saben si pueden agraviarte
ni, sit e olvidan, saben si lo sientes.
Si tú fueras capaz de ser querido
fueras capaz de olvido; y ya era gloria,
al menos, la potencia de haber sido;
mas tan lejos estás de esa victoria
que aqueste no acordame no es olvido
sino una negación de la memoria.

5. Journal Entry This poem was written in the seventeenth century. In what respects does it seem like a contemporary poem?

Related Works: "Love and Other Catastrophes: A Mix Tape" (p. 182), "The Girl with Bangs" (p. 271), "General Review of the Sex Situation" (p. 1056), "Love Is Just Complicated" (p. 1060), *The Brute* (p. 1250)

GWENDOLYN BROOKS (1917–2000)

First Fight. Then Fiddle (1949)

First fight. Then fiddle. Ply the slipping string
With feathery sorcery; muzzle the note
With hurting love; the music that they wrote
Bewitch, bewilder. Qualify to sing
Threadwise. Devise no salt, no hempen thing
For the dear instrument to bear. Devote
The bow to silks and honey. Be remote
A while from malice and from murdering.
But first to arms, to armor. Carry hate
In front of you and harmony behind.
Be deaf to music and to beauty blind.
Win war. Rise bloody, maybe not too late
For having first to civilize a space
Wherein to play your violin with grace.

Reading and Reacting

1. What is the subject of Brooks's poem?
2. Explain the poem's rhyme scheme. Is this rhyme scheme an essential element of the poem? Would the poem be equally effective if it did not include end rhyme? Why or why not?
3. Study the poem's use of capitalization and punctuation carefully. Why do you think Brooks chooses to end many of her sentences in midline? How do her decisions determine how you read the poem?
4. **Journal Entry** What do you think Brooks means by "fight" and "fiddle"?

Related Works: "Buffalo Soldiers" (p. 187), "The White City" (p. 857), "The Soldier" (p. 1062), "The *Chicago Defender* Sends a Man to Little Rock" (p. 1131)

The Sestina

The **sestina,** introduced in thirteenth-century France, is composed of six six-line stanzas and a three-line conclusion called an **envoi.** The sestina does not require end rhyme; however, it requires that each line end with one of six key words, which are repeated throughout the poem in a fixed order. The alternation of these six words in different positions—but always at the ends of lines—in each of the poem's six stanzas creates a rhythmic verbal pattern that unifies the poem, as the key words do in the poem that follows.

ALBERTO ALVARO RÍOS (1952–)

Nani (1982)

Sitting at her table, she serves
the sopa de arroz° to me
instinctively, and I watch her,
the absolute mamá, and eat words
I might have had to say more
out of embarrassment. To speak,
now-foreign words I used to speak,
too, dribble down her mouth as she serves
me albóndigas.° No more
than a third are easy to me.
By the stove she does something with words
and looks at me only with her
back. I am full. I tell her
I taste the mint, and watch her speak
smiles at the stove. All my words
make her smile. Nani never serves
herself, she only watches me
with her skin, her hair. I ask for more.

I watch the mamá warming more
tortillas for me. I watch her
fingers in the flame for me.
Near her mouth, I see a wrinkle speak
of a man whose body serves
the ants like she serves me, then more words
from more wrinkles about children, words
about this and that, flowing more
easily from these other mouths. Each serves
as a tremendous string around her,
holding her together. They speak
nani was this and that to me
and I wonder just how much of me
will die with her, what were the words
I could have been, was. Her insides speak
through a hundred wrinkles, now, more
than she can bear, steel around her,
shouting, then, What is this thing she serves?

She asks me if I want more.
I own no words to stop her.
Even before I speak, she serves.

---

sopa de arroz: Rice soup.

albóndigas: Meatballs.

In many respects, Ríos's poem closely follows the form of the traditional sestina. For instance, it interweaves six key words—"serves," "me," "her," "words," "more," and "speak"—through six groups of six lines each, rearranging the order in which the words appear so that the first line of each group of six lines ends with the same key word that also ended the preceding group of lines. The poem repeats the key words in exactly the order prescribed: *abcdef*, *faebdc*, *cfdabe*, and so on. In addition, the sestina closes with a three-line envoi that includes all six of the poem's key words, three at the ends of lines and three within the lines. Despite this generally strict adherence to the sestina form, Ríos departs from the form by grouping his six sets of six lines not into six separate stanzas but rather into two eighteen-line stanzas.

The sestina form suits Ríos's subject matter. The focus of the poem, on the verbal and nonverbal interaction between the poem's "me" and "her," is reinforced by each of the related words. "Nani" is a poem about communication, and the key words return to probe this theme again and again. Throughout the poem, these repeated words help to create a fluid, melodic, and tightly woven work.

FURTHER READING: The Sestina

Source: ©The Granger Collection, New York

See this poet's biography on p. 1217.

ELIZABETH BISHOP (1911–1979)

Sestina (1965)

September rain falls on the house.
In the failing light, the old grandmother
sits in the kitchen with the child
beside the Little Marvel Stove,
reading the jokes from the almanac,
laughing and talking to hide her tears.

She thinks that her equinoctial tears
and the rain that beats on the roof of the house
were both foretold by the almanac,
but only known to a grandmother.
The iron kettle sings on the stove.
She cuts some bread and says to the child,

It's time for tea now; but the child
is watching the teakettle's small hard tears
dance like mad on the hot black stove,
the way the rain must dance on the house.
Tidying up, the old grandmother
hangs up the clever almanac

on its string. Birdlike, the almanac
hovers half open above the child,
hovers above the old grandmother
and her teacup full of dark brown tears.
She shivers and says she thinks the house
feels chilly, and puts more wood in the stove.

It was to be, says the Marvel Stove.
I know what I know, says the almanac.
With crayons the child draws a rigid house
and a winding pathway. Then the child
puts in a man with buttons like tears
and shows it proudly to the grandmother.

But secretly, while the grandmother
busies herself about the stove,
the little moons fall down like tears
from between the pages of the almanac
into the flower bed the child
has carefully placed in the front of the house.

Time to plant tears, says the almanac.
The grandmother sings to the marvellous stove
and the child draws another inscrutable house.

Reading and Reacting

1. Does the poet's adherence to the traditional sestina form create any problems? For example, do you think word order seems forced at any point?
2. Consider the adjectives used in this poem. Are any of them unexpected? What is the effect of these surprising choices? Do you find them distracting, or do you think they strengthen the poem?
3. **Journal Entry** What are the poem's six key words? How are these words related to the poem's theme?

Related Works: "The Meal" (p. 908), "Nani" (p. 989), "My Papa's Waltz" (p. 1039)

The Villanelle

The **villanelle,** first introduced in France during the Middle Ages, is a nineteen-line poem composed of five tercets and a concluding quatrain; its rhyme scheme is *aba aba aba aba aba abaa*. Two different lines are systematically repeated in the poem: line 1 appears again in lines 6, 12, and 18, and line 3 reappears as lines 9, 15, and 19. Thus, each tercet concludes with an exact (or close) duplication of either line 1 or line 3, and the final quatrain concludes by repeating both line 1 and line 3.

THEODORE ROETHKE (1908–1963)

The Waking (1953)

I wake to sleep, and take my waking slow.
I feel my fate in what I cannot fear.
I learn by going where I have to go.

We think by feeling. What is there to know?
I hear my being dance from ear to ear.
I wake to sleep, and take my waking slow.

Of those so close beside me, which are you?
God bless the Ground! I shall walk softly there,
And learn by going where I have to go.

Light takes the Tree; but who can tell us how?
The lowly worm climbs up a winding stair;
I wake to sleep, and take my waking slow.

Great Nature has another thing to do
To you and me; so take the lively air,
And, lovely, learn by going where to go.

This shaking keeps me steady. I should know.
What falls away is always. And is near.
I wake to sleep, and take my waking slow.
I learn by going where I have to go.

"The Waking," like all villanelles, closely intertwines threads of sounds and words. The repeated lines and the very regular rhyme and meter give the poem a monotonous, almost hypnotic, rhythm. This poem uses end rhyme and repeats entire lines. It also makes extensive use of alliteration ("I feel my fate in what I cannot fear") and internal rhyme ("I hear my being dance from ear to ear"; "I wake to sleep and take my waking slow"). The result is a tightly constructed poem of overlapping sounds and images.

FURTHER READING: The Villanelle

MARY JO SALTER (1954–)

Refrain (1985)

But let his disposition have that scope
As dotage gives it.
—Generil to Albany

Never afflict yourself to know the cause,°
said Goneril,° her mind already set.
No one can tell us who her mother was

or, knowing, could account then by the laws
of nature for so false and hard a heart
Never afflict yourself to know the cause

Never afflict yourself to know the cause: From *King Lear,* Act I, Scene 4.
Goneril: One of Lear's disloyal daughters.

of Lear's undoing: if without a pause
he shunned Cordelia,° as soon he saw the fault.
No one can tell us who her mother was,

but here's a pretty reason seven stars
are seven stars, because they are not eight.
Never afflict yourself to know the cause—

like servants, even one's superfluous.°
The King makes a good fool the Fool is right.
No one can tell him who his mother was

when woman's water-drops° are all he has
against the storm, and daughters cast him out.
Never afflict yourself to know the cause,
no one can tell you who your mother was

Reading and Reacting

1. Review the definition of *villanelle*, and explain how "Refrain" conforms (or does not conform) to this definition.
2. A *refrain* is a group of words repeated at intervals throughout a poem or a song. What is this poem's refrain? Why is the poem called "Refrain"?
3. This poem refers to Shakespeare's play *King Lear*. If you have not read the play, find a brief plot summary on the Internet. What assumptions does this poem make about Goneril, Cordelia, and Lear himself?
4. **JOURNAL ENTRY** Given their form, what kinds of subjects do you see as most suitable for villanelles? Why? What subjects, if any, do you think would *not* be appropriate?

Related Works: "A Primer for the Punctuation of Heart Disease" (p. 440), "Fun Home" (p. 494) "Do not go gentle into that good night" (p. 1046), *When I Was a Little Girl and My Mother Didn't Want Me* (p. 1266), *Proof* (p. 1476)

The Epigram

Originally, an epigram was an inscription carved in stone on a monument or statue. As a literary form, an **epigram** is a very brief poem that makes a pointed, often sarcastic, comment in a surprising twist at the end. In a sense, it is a poem with a punch line. Although some epigrams rhyme, others do not. Many are only two lines long, but others are somewhat longer. What they have in common is their economy of language and their tone. One of the briefest of epigrams, written by Ogden Nash, appeared in the *New Yorker* magazine in 1931:

The Bronx?
No thonx.

Cordelia: Lear's loyal daughter, whom he exiles.
superfluous: Unnecessary.
water-drops: Tears.

Here, in four words, Nash manages to convey the unexpected, using rhyme and creative spelling to convey his assessment of one of New York City's five boroughs. The poem's two lines are perfectly balanced, making the contrast between the noncommittal tone of the first and the negative tone of the second quite striking.

FURTHER READING: The Epigram

SAMUEL TAYLOR COLERIDGE (1772–1834)

What Is an Epigram? (1802)

What is an epigram? a dwarfish whole,
Its body brevity, and wit its soul.

WILLIAM BLAKE (1757–1827)

Her Whole Life Is an Epigram (c. 1793–1811)

Her whole life is an epigram: smack, smooth & neatly penned,
Platted° quite neat to catch applause, with a sliding noose at the end.

Reading and Reacting

1. Explain the point made in each of the epigrams above.

2. Evaluate each poem. What qualities do you conclude make an epigram effective?

3. JOURNAL ENTRY In what sense are short-short stories (see Chapter 10) and ten-minute plays (see Chapter 36) like epigrams?

Related Works: "55 Miles to the Gas Pump" (p. 190), "Deportation at Breakfast" (p. 229), "Fire and Ice" (p. 849), "You fit into me" (p. 946), "General Review of the Sex Situation" (p. 1056), "Verities" (p. 1117), *Nine Ten* (p. 1314)

MARTIN ESPADA (1957–)

Why I Went to College (2000)

If you don't,
my father said,
you better learn
to eat soup
through a straw,
'cause I'm gonna
break your jaw

Platted: Braided.

Reading and Reacting

1. How is "Why I Went to College" different from Coleridge's and Blake's epigrams? How is it similar to them?
2. What function does the poem's title serve? Is it the epigram's "punch line," or does it serve another purpose?
3. What can you infer about the speaker's father from this poem? Why, for example, do you think he wants his son to go to college?
4. **JOURNAL ENTRY** Exactly why did the speaker go to college? Expand this short poem into a paragraph written from the speaker's point of view.

Related Works: "Baca Grande" (p. 889), "My Father as a Guitar" (p. 935), "My Papa's Waltz" (p. 1039), "'Faith' is a fine invention" (p. 1142), "Marks" (p. 1187)

Haiku

Like an epigram, a haiku compresses words into a very small package. Unlike an epigram, however, a haiku focuses on an image, not an idea. A traditional Japanese form, the **haiku** is a brief unrhymed poem that presents the essence of some aspect of nature, concentrating a vivid image in three lines. Although in the strictest sense a haiku consists of seventeen syllables divided into lines of five, seven, and five syllables, respectively, not all poets conform to this rigid structure.

The following poem is a translation of a classic Japanese haiku by Matsuo Bashō:

Silent and still: then
Even sinking into the rocks,
The cicada's screech.

Notice that this poem conforms to the haiku's three-line structure and traditional subject matter, vividly depicting a natural scene without comment or analysis.

FURTHER READING: Haiku

MATSUO BASHŌ (1644–1694)

Four Haiku*

Translated by Geoffrey Bownas and Anthony Thwaite

Spring:
A hill without a name
Veiled in morning mist.

The beginning of autumn:
Sea and emerald paddy
Both the same green.

*Publication date is not available.

The winds of autumn
Blow: yet still green
The chestnut husks.

A flash of lightning:
Into the gloom
Goes the heron's cry.

Reading and Reacting

1. Haiku are admired for their extreme economy and their striking images. What are the central images in each of Bashō's haiku? To what senses do these images appeal?
2. In another poem, Bashō says that art begins with "The depths of the country / and a rice-planting song." What do you think he means? How do these four haiku exemplify this idea?
3. Do you think the conciseness of these poems increases or decreases the impact of their images? Explain.
4. **JOURNAL ENTRY** "In a Station of the Metro" (p. 907) is Ezra Pound's version of a haiku. How successful do you think his poem is as a haiku? Do you think a longer poem could have conveyed the images more effectively?

Related Works: "Water Names" (p. 318), "Where Mountain Lion Lay Down with Deer" (p. 845), "Wild Plums in Blossom" (p. 911), "the sky was can dy" (p. 1000), "Easter Wings" (p. 1008), "Birches" (p. 1050).

CAROLYN KIZER (1925–)

After Bashō (1984)

Tentatively, you
slip onstage this evening,
pallid, famous moon.

Reading and Reacting

1. What possible meanings might the word "After" have in the title? What does the title tell readers about the writer's purpose?
2. What is the impact of "tentatively" in the first line and "famous" in the last line? How do the connotations of these words convey the image of the moon?
3. **JOURNAL ENTRY** What visual picture does the poem suggest? What mood does the poem's central image create?

Related Works: "Sleepless at Crown Point" (p. 911), "Nightfall" (p. 920), "Four Haiku" (p. 995), "The Moon" (p. 1049), "Meeting at Night" (p. 1055)

JACK KEROUAC (1922–1969)

American Haiku

Early morning yellow flowers,
thinking about
the drunkards of Mexico.

No telegram today
only more leaves
fell.

Nightfall,
boy smashing dandelions
with a stick.

Holding up my
purring cat to the moon
I sighed.

Drunk as a hoot owl,
writing letters
by thunderstorm.

Empty baseball field
a robin
hops along the bench.

All day long
wearing a hat
that wasn't on my head.

Crossing the football field
coming home from work—
the lonely businessman.

After the shower
among the drenched roses
the bird thrashing in the bath.

Snap your finger
stop the world—
rain falls harder.

Nightfall,
too dark to read the page
too cold.

Following each other
my cats stop
when it thunders.

Wash hung out
by moonlight
Friday night in May.

The bottoms of my shoes
are clean
from walking in the rain.

Glow worm
sleeping on this flower—
your light's on.

Reading and Reacting

1. How are these haiku different from those by Matsuo Bashō (p. 995)? Do they fit the definition of *haiku* on page 995?
2. What, if anything, makes these poems "American"? Is it their language? Their subject matter? Something else?
3. **JOURNAL ENTRY** Try writing a few "American haiku" of your own. Then, evaluate the success of your efforts. What problems did you encounter?
4. **CRITICAL PERSPECTIVE** Writing about his experiments with haiku, Jack Kerouac said, "Above all, a Haiku must be very simple and free of all poetic trickery and make a little picture and yet be as airy and graceful as a Vivaldi Pastorella."

   Do you think Kerouac's haiku satisfy these conditions?

Related Works: "Love and Other Catastrophes: A Mix Tape" (p. 182), "Comparatives" (p. 967), "Chicago" (p. 999), "Morning Song" (p. 1053), "American Poetry" (p. 1197), *from* "Song of Myself" (p. 1207)

Open Form

An **open form poem** may make occasional use of rhyme and meter, but it has no easily identifiable pattern or design: no conventional stanzaic divisions, no consistent metrical pattern or line length, no repeated rhyme scheme. Still, open form poetry is not necessarily shapeless, untidy, or randomly ordered. All poems have form, and the form of a poem may be determined by factors such as repeated sounds, the appearance of words on the printed page, or pauses in natural speech as well as by a conventional metrical pattern or rhyme scheme.

Open form poetry invites readers to participate in the creative process, to discover the relationship between form and meaning. In fact, some modern poets believe that only open form offers them freedom to express their ideas or that the subject matter or mood of their poetry demands a relaxed, experimental approach to form. For example, when Lawrence Ferlinghetti portrays the poet as an acrobat who "climbs on rime" (p. 925), he constructs his poem in a way that is consistent with the poet/acrobat's willingness to take risks. Thus, the poem's idiosyncratic form supports its ideas about the limitless possibilities of poetry and the poet as experimenter.

Without a predetermined pattern, however, poets must create forms that suit their needs, and they must continue to shape and reshape the look of the poem on the page as they revise its words. Thus, open form is a challenge, but it is also a way for poets to experiment with fresh arrangements of words and new juxtapositions of ideas.

For some poets, such as Carl Sandburg, open form provides an opportunity to create **prose poems,** poems that look like prose.

Source: ©Bettmann/Corbis

See this poet's biography on p. 1228.

CARL SANDBURG (1878–1967)

Chicago (1914)

Hog Butcher for the World,
Tool Maker, Stacker of Wheat,
Player with Railroads and the Nation's Freight Handler;
Stormy, husky, brawling,
City of the Big Shoulders:

They tell me you are wicked and I believe them, for I have seen
your painted women under the gas lamps luring the farm boys.
And they tell me you are crooked and I answer: Yes, it is true
I have seen the gunman kill and go free to kill again.
And they tell me you are brutal and my reply is: On the faces of
women and children I have seen the marks of wanton hunger.
And having answered so I turn once more to those who sneer at
this my city, and I give them back the sneer and say to them:
Come and show me another city with lifted head singing so
proud to be alive and coarse and strong and cunning.
Flinging magnetic curses amid the toil of piling job on job,
here is a tall bold slugger set vivid against the little soft cities;
Fierce as a dog with tongue lapping for action, cunning as a
savage pitted against the wilderness,
Bareheaded,
Shoveling,
Wrecking,
Planning,
Building, breaking, rebuilding,
Under the smoke, dust all over his mouth, laughing with white
teeth,
Under the terrible burden of destiny laughing as a young man
laughs,
Laughing even as an ignorant fighter laughs who has never lost
a battle,
Bragging and laughing that under his wrist is the pulse, and under
his ribs the heart of the people,
Laughing!

Laughing the stormy, husky, brawling laughter of Youth,
half-naked, sweating, proud to be Hog Butcher, Tool Maker,
Stacker of Wheat, Player with Railroads and Freight Handler
to the Nation.

"Chicago" uses capitalization and punctuation conventionally, and it generally (though not always) arranges words in lines in a way that is consistent with the natural divisions of phrases and sentences. However, the poem is not divided into stanzas, and its lines vary widely in length—from a single word isolated on a line to a line crowded with words—and follow no particular metrical pattern. Instead, its form is created through its pattern of alternating sections of long and short lines; through its repeated words and phrases ("They tell me" in lines 6–8, "under" in lines 18–19, and "laughing" in lines 18–23, for example); through alliteration (for instance, "slugger set vivid against the little soft cities" in line 11); and, most of all, through the piling up of words and images into catalogs in lines 1–5, 13–17, and 22.

In order to understand Sandburg's reasons for choosing such a form, readers need to consider the poem's subject matter and theme. "Chicago" celebrates the scope and power of a "Stormy, husky, brawling" city, one that is exuberant and outgoing, not sedate and civilized. Chicago is a city that does not follow anyone else's rules; it is, after all, "Bareheaded, / Shoveling, / Wrecking, / Planning, / Building, breaking, rebuilding," constantly active, in flux, on the move, "proud to be alive." "Fierce as a dog . . . cunning as a savage," the city is characterized as, among other things, a worker, a fighter, and a harborer of "painted women" and killers and hungry women and children. Just as Chicago itself does not conform to the rules, the poem departs from the orderly confines of stanzaic form and measured rhyme and meter, a kind of form that is, after all, better suited to "the little soft cities" than to the "tall bold slugger" that is Chicago.

Of course, open form poetry does not have to look like Sandburg's prose poem. The following poem, an extreme example of open form, looks almost as if it has spilled out of a box of words.

E. E. CUMMINGS (1894–1962)

the sky was can dy (1925)

the
sky
was
can dy lu
minous
edible
spry
pinks shy
lemons
greens coo l choc

olate
s.

    un   der,
    a   lo
co
mo
    tive   s pout
                ing
                vi
                o
                lets

Like many of Cummings's poems, this one seems ready to skip off the page. Its irregular line length and its unconventional capitalization, punctuation, and word divisions immediately draw readers' attention to its form. Despite these oddities, and despite the absence of orderly rhyme and meter, the poem does have its conventional elements.

A closer examination reveals that the poem's theme—the beauty of the sky—is quite conventional; that the poem is divided, though somewhat crudely, into two sections; and that the poet does use some rhyme—"spry" and "shy," for example. However, Cummings's sky is described not in traditional terms but rather as something "edible," not only in terms of color but of flavor as well. The breaks within words ("can dy lu / minous"; "coo l choc / olate / s") seem to expand the words' possibilities, visually stretching them to the limit, extending their taste and visual image over several lines and, in the case of the poem's last two words, visually reinforcing the picture the words describe. In addition, the isolation of syllables exposes hidden rhyme, as in "lo / co / mo" and "lu" / "coo." Thus, by using open form, Cummings illustrates the capacity of a poem to move beyond the traditional boundaries set by words and lines.

FURTHER READING: Open Form

WALT WHITMAN (1819–1892)

from "Out of the Cradle Endlessly Rocking" (1881)

Out of the cradle endlessly rocking,
Out of the mocking-bird's throat, the musical shuttle,
Out of the Ninth-month° midnight,

Ninth-month: The Quaker designation for September; in context, an allusion to the human birth cycle.

Over the sterile sands and the fields beyond, where the child
leaving his bed wander'd alone, bareheaded, barefoot,
Down from the shower'd halo,
Up from the mystic play of shadows twining and twisting as if
they were alive,
Out from the patches of briers and blackberries,
From the memories of the bird that chanted to me,
From your memories sad brother, from the fitful risings and
fallings I heard,
From under that yellow half-moon late-risen and swollen as if
with tears,
From those beginning notes of yearning and love there in the
mist,
From the thousand responses of my heart never to cease,
From the myriad thence-arous'd words,
From the word stronger and more delicious than any,
From such as now they start the scene revisiting,
As a flock, twittering, rising, or overhead passing,
Borne hither, ere all eludes me, hurriedly,
A man, yet by these tears a little boy again,
Throwing myself on the sand, confronting the waves,
I, chanter of pains and joys, uniter of here and hereafter,
Taking all hints to use them, but swiftly leaping beyond them,
A reminiscence sing.

Reading and Reacting

1. This excerpt, the first twenty-two lines of a poem nearly two hundred lines long, has no regular metrical pattern or rhyme scheme. What gives it its form?

2. How might you explain why the poem's lines vary in length?

3. **JOURNAL ENTRY** Compare this excerpt with the excerpt from Whitman's "Song of Myself" (p. 1207). In what respects are the forms of the two poems similar?

4. **CRITICAL PERSPECTIVE** Reviewing a recent biography of Whitman, Geoffrey O'Brien writes of a paradox in Whitman's poetry:

> [N]either fiction nor verse as they then existed could provide Whitman with what he needed, so he invented out of necessity his own form, a reversion to what he conceived of as the most archaic bardic impulses, representing itself as the poetry of the future.

Can you see the form of this section of "Out of the Cradle" as both "archaic" and "of the future"?

Related Works: "Chicago" (p. 999), "Old Walt" (p. 1086), "Defending Walt Whitman" (p. 1117), *from* "Song of Myself" (p. 1207)

WILLIAM CARLOS WILLIAMS (1883–1963)

Spring and All (1923)

By the road to the contagious hospital
under the surge of the blue
mottled clouds driven from the
northeast—a cold wind. Beyond, the
waste of broad, muddy fields
brown with dried weeds, standing and fallen

patches of standing water
the scattering of tall trees

All along the road the reddish
purplish, forked, upstanding, twiggy
stuff of bushes and small trees
with dead, brown leaves under them
leafless vines—

Lifeless in appearance, sluggish
dazed spring approaches—

They enter the new world naked,
cold, uncertain of all
save that they enter. All about them
the cold, familiar wind—

Now the grass, tomorrow
the stiff curl of wildcarrot leaf
One by one objects are defined—
It quickens: clarity, outline of leaf

But now the stark dignity of
entrance—Still, the profound change
has come upon them: rooted, they
grip down and begin to awaken

Reading and Reacting

1. Although this poem is written in free verse and lacks a definite pattern of meter or rhyme, it includes some characteristics of closed form poetry. Explain.

2. What does Williams accomplish by visually isolating lines 7–8 and lines 14–15?

3. "Spring and All" includes assonance, alliteration, and repetition. Give several examples of each technique, and explain what each adds to the poem.

4. **Journal Entry** What do you think the word *All* means in the poem's title?

5. **Critical Perspective** According to critic Bonnie Costello, "Williams thought about the creative process in painters' terms, and he asks us to experience the work as we might experience a modern painting. His great achievement was to bring some of its qualities into poetry."

Consider the images Williams uses in this poem. In what ways is this poem like a painting? Which images are conveyed in "painters' terms"? How does he use these images to create meaning in the poem?

Related Works: "Comparatives" (p. 967), "Pied Beauty" (p. 971), "Group Photo with Winter Trees" (p. 1009), "Trees" (p. 1052)

CAROLYN FORCHÉ (1950–)

The Colonel (1978)

What you have heard is true. I was in his house. His wife carried a tray of coffee and sugar. His daughter filed her nails, his son went out for the night. There were daily papers, pet dogs, a pistol on the cushion beside him. The moon swung bare on its black cord over the house. On the television was a cop show. It was in English. Broken bottles were embedded in the walls around the house to scoop the kneecaps from a man's legs or cut his hands to lace. On the windows there were gratings like those in liquor stores. We had dinner, rack of lamb, good wine, a gold bell was on the table for calling the maid. The maid brought green mangoes, salt, a type of bread. I was asked how I enjoyed the country. There was a brief commercial in Spanish. His wife took everything away. There was some talk then of how difficult it had become to govern. The parrot said hello on the terrace. The colonel told it to shut up, and pushed himself from the table. My friend said to me with his eyes: say nothing. The colonel returned with a sack used to bring groceries home. He spilled many human ears on the table. They were like dried peach halves. There is no other way to say this. He took one of them in his hands, shook it in our faces, dropped it into a water glass. It came alive there. I am tired of fooling around he said. As for the rights of anyone, tell your people they can go fuck themselves. He swept the ears to the floor with his arm and held the last of his wine in the air. Something for your poetry, no? he said. Some of the ears on the floor caught this scrap of his voice. Some of the ears on the floor were pressed to the ground.

Reading and Reacting

1. Treating Forché's prose poem as prose rather than poetry, try dividing it into paragraphs. What determines where you make your divisions?
2. If you were to reshape "The Colonel" into a conventional-looking poem, what options might you have? Rearrange a few sentences of the poem so that they "look like poetry," and compare your revision to the original. Which version do you find more effective? Why?
3. What is the main theme of "The Colonel"? How does the poem's form help Forché to communicate this theme?

4. **JOURNAL ENTRY** Do you think "The Colonel" is poetry or prose? Consider its subject matter and language as well as its form.

5. **CRITICAL PERSPECTIVE** Writing in the *New York Times Book Review*, critic Katha Pollitt focuses on "poetic clichés," which, she says, are "attempts to energize the poem by annexing a subject that is guaranteed to produce a knee-jerk response in the reader. This saves a lot of bother all around, and enables poet and reader to drowse together in a warm bath of mutual admiration for each other's capacity for deep feeling and right thinking." Among the poetic clichés Pollitt discusses is something she calls "the CNN poem, which retells in overheated free verse a prominent news story involving war, famine, torture, child abuse or murder."

   Do you think "The Colonel" is a "CNN poem," or do you see it as something more than just a "poetic cliché"?

Related Works: "All about Suicide" (p. 6), "Once upon a Time" (p. 232), "Saboteur" (p. 712), "Hope" (p. 863), "Poetry Searches for Radiance" (p. 1215)

TOMAS TRANSTRÖMER (1931–)

Answers to Letters (2003)

Translated by Robin Fulton

In the bottom drawer of my desk I come across a letter that first arrived twenty-six years ago. A letter in panic, and it's still breathing when it arrives the second time.

A house has five windows: through four of them the day shines clear and still. The fifth faces a black sky, thunder and storm. I stand at the fifth window. The letter.

Sometimes an abyss opens between Tuesday and Wednesday but twenty-six years may be passed in a moment. Time is not a straight line, it's more of a labyrinth, and if you press close to the wall at the right place you can hear the hurrying steps and the voices, you can hear yourself walking past there on the other side.

Was the letter ever answered? I don't remember, it *was* long ago. The countless thresholds of the sea went on migrating. The heart went on leaping from second to second like the road in the wet grass of an August night.

The unanswered letters pile up, like cirrostratus clouds presaging bad weather. They make the sunbeams lusterless. One day I will answer. One day when I am dead and can at last concentrate. Or at least so far away from here that I can find myself again. When I'm walking, newly arrived, in the big city, on 125th Street, in the wind on the street of dancing garbage. I who love to stray off and vanish in the crowd, a capital T in the mass of the endless text.

Reading and Reacting

1. This prose poem is divided into five stanzas, which are indented and set off like paragraphs. What is the subject of each stanza? How are the five stanzas related?
2. Does any part of this poem seem like a digression, or does all the information appear to be essential?
3. In lines 8–9, the speaker says, "Time is not a straight line, it's more of a labyrinth. . . ." In what sense does this characterization also apply to Tranströmer's poem? To poetry in general?
4. **JOURNAL ENTRY** Who is the speaker? How old do you think he is? Where is he? Write a paragraph in which you identify him and invent some background about the speaker's life.

Related Works: "Kansas" (p. 237), "Sonny's Blues" (p. 665), "The World Is Too Much with Us" (p. 855), "The Road Not Taken" (p. 1159)

Source: Courtesy of Pat Mora; Photo: ©Cheron Bayna

See this poet's biography on p. 1225.

PAT MORA (1942–)

Immigrants (1986)

wrap their babies in the American flag,
feed them mashed hot dogs and apple pie,
name them Bill and Daisy,
buy them blonde dolls that blink blue
eyes or a football and tiny cleats
before the baby can even walk,
speak to them in thick English,
    hallo, babee, hallo.
whisper in Spanish or Polish
when the babies sleep, whisper
in a dark parent bed, that dark
parent fear, "Will they like
our boy, our girl, our fine american
boy, our fine american girl?"

Reading and Reacting

1. What do the immigrant parents want for their children? What "dark/ parent fear" (lines 11–12) do they have? Do you think this fear is justified?
2. What, if anything, determines where the poet breaks the lines of this poem? Why, for example, is line 8 shorter than the others? Should the poet have broken any lines in different places?
3. Although this poem is not a sonnet, it does have fourteen lines. Does it resemble a sonnet in any other respects?
4. **JOURNAL ENTRY** Why do you think the word *american* is not capitalized in the last two lines?

Concrete Poetry

With roots in the ancient Greek *pattern poems* and the sixteenth- and seventeenth-century **emblem poems,** contemporary **concrete poetry** uses words—sometimes, different fonts and type sizes—to shape a picture on the page.

MAY SWENSON (1913–1989)

Women (1970)

Women Or they
should be should be
pedestals little horses
moving those wooden
pedestals sweet
moving oldfashioned
to the painted
motions rocking
of men horses

the gladdest things in the toyroom

The feelingly
pegs and then
of their unfeelingly
ears To be
so familiar joyfully
and dear ridden
to the trusting rockingly
fists ridden until
To be chafed the restored

egos dismount and the legs stride away

Immobile willing
sweetlipped to be set
sturdy into motion
and smiling Women
women should be
should always pedestals
be waiting to men

The form of a concrete poem is not something that emerges from the poem's words and images; it is something predetermined by the visual image the poet has decided to create. Although some concrete poems are little more than novelties, others—like the poem above—can be original and enlightening.

The curved shape of Swenson's poem immediately reinforces its title, and the arrangement of words on the page suggests a variety of visual directions readers might follow. The two columns seem at first to suggest two alternatives: "Women should be . . ." / "Or they should be. . . ." A closer look, however, reveals that the poem's central figures of speech, such as woman as rocking horse and woman as pedestal, move back and forth between the two columns of images. This exchange of positions might suggest that the two possibilities are really just two ways of looking at one limited role. Thus, the experimental form of the poem visually challenges the apparent complacency of its words, suggesting that women, like words, need not fall into traditional roles or satisfy conventional expectations.

FURTHER READING: Concrete Poetry

Source: ©Michael Nicholson/Corbis

See this poet's biography on p. 1222.

GEORGE HERBERT (1593–1633)

Easter Wings (1633)

Lord, who createdst man in wealth and store,
Though foolishly he lost the same,
Decaying more and more
Till he became
Most poor,
With thee
Oh, let me rise
As larks, harmoniously,
And sing this day thy victories;
Then shall the fall further the flight in me.
My tender age in sorrow did begin;
And still with sicknesses and shame
Thou didst so punish sin,
That I became
Most thin.
With thee
Let me combine,
And feel this day thy victory;
For if I imp my wing on thine,
Affliction shall advance the flight in me.

Reading and Reacting

1. In this example of a seventeenth-century emblem poem, lines are arranged so that shape and subject matter reinforce each other. Explain how this is accomplished. (For example, how does line length support the poem's images and ideas?)
2. This poem has a definite rhyme scheme. How would you describe it? What relationship do you see between the rhyme scheme and the poem's visual divisions?

Related Works: "l(a" p. 803), "A Valediction: Forbidding Mourning" (p. 933), "Batter My Heart, Three-Personed God" (p. 1148), "When I Have Fears" (p. 1172)

GREG WILLIAMSON (1964–)

XXV. Group Photo with Winter Trees (2002)

These were my neighbors. It's big group pose:
On mist-gray skies, the stark, black branches etch
Horizon, lawn, in loose haphazard rows.
As if in tin, or as in some old sketch,
That's The Great Bob. And that's our good Queen Paul
Whose lines, whose every nuance was precise,
With Champagne Anne and Rick the dog. They're all
But faded now. I've seen the trees in ice,
Decked out, (Liz, too, who helped me do the plumbing),
But I'll be gone when their spring blooms and scatters
Even the children. And, God, they're all becoming.
Shades, as the new leaves turn to other matters.

Reading and Reacting

1. Why are alternate lines of this poem set in boldface type? Why are some lines set flush left and others set flush right?
2. What is the poem's rhyme scheme?
3. Is this a single poem or two separate interlocking poems? Explain.
4. **JOURNAL ENTRY** How does the form of this poem suggest the "group photo with winter trees" of the title? What is in the foreground? What is in the background?
5. **CRITICAL PERSPECTIVE** The poem "Group Photo with Winter Trees" is part of the sequence "Double Exposures" from Greg Williamson's second book, *Errors in the Script*. A review of the book notes that it "is obsessed with double vision," and points to "Double Exposures" as "[t]he most dramatic example" of this obsession. "Each poem in the sequence," it notes, "consists of two six-line stanzas printed (one flush left and the other flush right) so that they overlap in the middle of the page; each stanza can be read separately, and the whole set of alternating lines can also be read straight through. Some of the poems succeed better at this high-wire act than others, but in many cases the technique has striking results, and the sequence is decidedly a tour de force."

   Do you feel that "Group Photo with Winter Trees" succeeds at its "high-wire act"? In other words, does the unusual approach Williamson takes help him communicate his point more effectively? What do you think his point is?

Related Works: "Nothing Gold Can Stay" (p. 914), "Photograph of My Father in His Twenty-Second Year" (p. 1042)

✔ CHECKLIST Writing about Form

- ☐ Is the poem written in open or closed form? On what characteristics do you base your conclusion?
- ☐ Why did the poet choose open or closed form? For example, is the poem's form consistent with its subject matter, tone, or theme? Is it determined by the conventions of the historical period in which it was written?
- ☐ If the poem is arranged in closed form, does the pattern apply to single lines, to groups of lines, or to the entire poem? What factors determine the breaks between groups of lines?
- ☐ Is the poem a sonnet? A sestina? A villanelle? An epigram? A haiku? How do the traditional form's conventions suit the poet's language and theme? Does the poem follow the rules of the form at all times, or does it break any new ground?
- ☐ If the poem is arranged in open form, what determines the breaks at the ends of lines?
- ☐ Are certain words or phrases isolated on lines? Why?
- ☐ How do elements such as assonance, alliteration, rhyme, and repetition of words give the poem form?
- ☐ What use does the poet make of punctuation and capitalization? Of white space on the page?
- ☐ Is the poem a prose poem? How does this form support the poem's subject matter?
- ☐ Is the poem a concrete poem? How does the poet use the visual shape of the poem to convey meaning?

WRITING SUGGESTIONS: Form

1. Reread the definitions of closed form and open form in this chapter. Do you think concrete poems are "open" or "closed"? Explain your position in a short essay, supporting your thesis with specific references to the concrete poems in this chapter.
2. Some poets—for example, Emily Dickinson and Robert Frost—write both open and closed form poems. Choose one open and one closed form poem by a single poet, and analyze the two poems, explaining the poet's possible reasons for choosing each type of form.
3. Do you see complex forms, such as the villanelle and the sestina, as exercises or even merely as opportunities for poets to show off their skills—or do you

believe the special demands of the forms add something valuable to a poem? To help you answer this question, read Dylan Thomas's "Do not go gentle into that good night" (p. 1046), and Elizabeth Bishop's "Sestina" (p. 990).

4. The following poem is an alternate version of May Swenson's "Women" (p. 1007). Read the two versions carefully, and write an essay in which you compare them. What differences do you notice? Which do you think was written first? Why? Do the two poems make the same point? Which makes the point with less ambiguity? Which is more effective? Why?

Women Should Be Pedestals

Women should be pedestals
moving pedestals
moving to the motions of men
Or they should be little horses
those wooden sweet oldfashioned painted rocking horses
the gladdest things in the toyroom
The pegs of their ears so familiar and dear
to the trusting fists
To be chafed feelingly
and then unfeelingly
To be joyfully ridden
until the restored egos dismount and the legs stride away
Immobile sweetlipped sturdy and smiling
women should always be waiting
willing to be set into motion
Women should be pedestals to men

5. Look through Chapter 33, "Poetry for Further Reading," and identify one or two **prose poems.** Write an essay in which you consider why the form seems suitable for the poem or poems you have chosen. Is there a particular kind of subject matter that seems especially appropriate for a prose poem?

CHAPTER 30

SYMBOL, ALLEGORY, ALLUSION, MYTH

Source: ©Michael Nicholson/Corbis

See this poet's biography on p. 1218.

WILLIAM BLAKE (1757–1827)

The Sick Rose (1794)

O Rose thou art sick.
The invisible worm
That flies in the night,
In the howling storm:

Has found out thy bed
Of crimson joy:
And his dark secret love
Does thy life destroy.

Symbol

A **symbol** is an idea or image that suggests something else—but not in the simple way that a dollar sign stands for money or a flag represents a country. A symbol is an image that transcends its literal, or denotative, meaning in a complex way. For instance, if someone gives a rose to a loved one, it could simply be a sign of love. But in the poem "The Sick Rose," the rose has a range of contradictory and complementary meanings. What does the rose represent? Beauty? Perfection? Passion? Something else? As this poem illustrates, the distinctive trait of a symbol is that its meaning cannot easily be pinned down or defined.

Such ambiguity can be frustrating, but it is precisely this characteristic of a symbol that enriches a poem by giving it additional layers of meaning. As Robert Frost has said, a symbol is a little thing that touches a larger thing. In the poem of his that follows, the central symbol does just this.

ROBERT FROST (1874–1963)

For Once, Then, Something (1923)

Others taunt me with having knelt at well-curbs
Always wrong to the light, so never seeing
Deeper down in the well than where the water
Gives me back in a shining surface picture
Me myself in the summer heaven, godlike,
Looking out of a wreath of fern and cloud puffs.
Once, when trying with chin against a well-curb,
I discerned, as I thought, beyond the picture,
Through the picture, a something white, uncertain,
Something more of the depths—and then I lost it.
Water came to rebuke the too clear water.
One drop fell from a fern, and lo, a ripple
Shook whatever it was lay there at bottom,
Blurred it, blotted it out. What was that whiteness?
Truth? A pebble of quartz? For once, then, something.

The central symbol in this poem is the "something" that the speaker thinks he sees at the bottom of a well. Traditionally, the act of looking down a well suggests a search for truth. In this poem, the speaker says that he always seems to look down the well at the wrong angle, so that all he can see is his own reflection—the surface, not the depths. Once, however, the speaker thought he saw something "beyond the picture," something "white, uncertain," but the image remained indistinct, disappearing when a drop of water from a fern caused the water to ripple. The poem ends with the speaker questioning the significance of what he saw. Like a reader encountering a symbol, the speaker is left trying to come to terms with images that cannot be clearly perceived and associations that cannot be readily understood. In light of the elusive nature of truth, all the speaker can do is ask questions that have no definite answers.

Symbols that appear in poetic works can be *conventional* or *universal*. **Conventional symbols** are those recognized by people who share certain cultural and social assumptions. For example, national flags evoke a general and agreed-upon response in most people of a particular country and—for better or for worse—American children have for years perceived the golden arches of McDonald's as a symbol of food and fun. **Universal symbols** are those likely to be recognized by people regardless of their culture. In 1890, the noted Scottish anthropologist Sir James George Frazer wrote the first version of his work *The Golden Bough*, in which he identified parallels between the rites and beliefs of early pagan cultures and those of Christianity. Fascinated by Frazer's work, the psychologist Carl Jung sought to explain these parallels by formulating a theory of **archetypes,** which held that certain images or ideas reside in the subconscious of all people. According to Jung, archetypal symbols include water, symbolizing rebirth; spring, symbolizing growth; and winter, symbolizing death.

Sometimes symbols that appear in poems can be obscure or highly idiosyncratic. William Blake is one of many poets (William Butler Yeats is another) whose works combine symbols from different cultural, theological, and philosophical sources to form complex networks of personal symbolic associations. To Blake, for example, the scientist Isaac Newton represents the tendency of scientists to quantify experience while ignoring the beauty and mystery of nature. Readers cannot begin to understand his use of Newton as a symbol until they have read a number of Blake's more difficult poems.

How do you know when an idea or image in a poem is a symbol? At what point do you decide that a particular object or idea goes beyond the literal level and takes on symbolic significance? When is a rose more than a rose or a well more than a well? Frequently you can recognize a symbol by its prominence or repetition. In "For Once, Then, Something," for example, the well is introduced in the first line of the poem, and it is the poem's focal point; in "The Sick Rose," the importance of the rose is emphasized by the title.

It is not enough, however, to identify an image or idea that seems to suggest something else. Your decision that a particular item has symbolic significance must be supported by the details of the poem and make sense in light of the ideas the poem develops. In the following poem, the symbolic significance of the volcano helps readers to understand the poem's central theme.

EMILY DICKINSON (1830–1886)

Volcanoes be in Sicily (1914)

Volcanoes be in Sicily
And South America
I judge from my Geography—
Volcanoes nearer here
A Lava step at any time
Am I inclined to climb—
A Crater I may contemplate
Vesuvius at Home.

This poem opens with a statement of fact: volcanoes are located in Sicily and South America. In line 3, however, the speaker introduces the improbable idea that volcanoes are located near where she is at the moment. Readers familiar with Dickinson know that her poems are highly autobiographical and that she lived in Massachusetts, where there are no volcanoes. This information leads readers to suspect that they should not take the speaker's observation literally and that in the context of the poem volcanoes may have symbolic significance. But what do volcanoes suggest here?

On the one hand, volcanoes represent the awesome creative power of nature; on the other hand, they suggest its destructiveness. The speaker's contemplation of the crater of Vesuvius—the volcano that buried the ancient Roman city of

Pompeii in A.D. 79—is therefore filled with contradictory associations. Because Dickinson was a recluse, volcanoes—active, destructive, unpredictable, and dangerous—may be seen as symbolic of everything she fears in the outside world—and, perhaps, within herself. Volcanoes may even suggest her own creative power, which, like a volcano, is something to be feared as well as contemplated. Dickinson seems to have a voyeur's attraction to danger and power, but she is also afraid of them. For this reason, she (and her speaker) may feel safer contemplating Vesuvius at home—not traveling to exotic lands but simply reading a geography book.

FURTHER READING: Symbol

LANGSTON HUGHES (1902–1967)

Island (1951)

Wave of sorrow,
Do not drown me now:

I see the island
Still ahead somehow.

I see the island
And its sands are fair:

Wave of sorrow,
Take me there.

Reading and Reacting

1. What makes you suspect that the island has symbolic significance in this poem?
2. Is the "wave of sorrow" also a symbol?
3. **Journal Entry** Beyond its literal meaning, what might the island in this poem suggest? Consider several possibilities.
4. **Critical Perspective** James Baldwin, a preeminent African-American writer, wrote the following about the poetry of Langston Hughes:

   > Hughes, in his sermons, blues and prayers, has working for him the power and the beat of Negro speech and Negro music. Negro speech is vivid largely because it is private. It is a kind of emotional shorthand—or sleight-of-hand—by means of which Negroes express, not only their relationship to each other, but their judgment of the white world.

   Can a symbol—such as the island in this poem—also function as "emotional shorthand"? What kind of judgment do you think it might reveal about the "white world"?

Related Works: "A Worn Path" (p. 568), "The White City" (p. 857), "Sea Grapes" (p. 1031), "Acquainted with the Night" (p. 1156), *The Cuban Swimmer* (p. 1732)

Source: ©AP Photo

See this poet's biography on p. 384.

EDGAR ALLAN POE (1809–1849)

The Raven (1844)

Once upon a midnight dreary, while I pondered, weak and weary,
Over many a quaint and curious volume of forgotten lore,
While I nodded, nearly napping, suddenly there came a tapping,
As of some one gently rapping, rapping at my chamber door.
" 'Tis some visitor," I muttered, "tapping at my chamber door—
Only this, and nothing more."

Ah, distinctly I remember it was in the bleak December,
And each separate dying ember wrought its ghost upon the floor.
Eagerly I wished the morrow;—vainly I had sought to borrow
From my books surcease of sorrow—sorrow for the lost Lenore—
For the rare and radiant maiden whom the angels name Lenore—
Nameless here for evermore.

And the silken sad uncertain rustling of each purple curtain
Thrilled me—filled me with fantastic terrors never felt before;
so that now, to still the beating of my heart, I stood repeating
" 'Tis some visitor entreating entrance at my chamber door;—
Some late visitor entreating entrance at my chamber door;
This it is, and nothing more."

Presently my soul grew stronger; hesitating then no longer,
"Sir," said I, "or Madam, truly your forgiveness I implore;
But the fact is I was napping, and so gently you came rapping,
And so faintly you came tapping, tapping at my chamber door,
That I scarce was sure I heard you"—here I opened wide the door;—
Darkness there, and nothing more.

Deep into that darkness peering, long I stood there wondering, fearing,
Doubting, dreaming dreams no mortal ever dared to dream before;
But the silence was unbroken, and the darkness gave no token,
And the only word there spoken was the whispered word, "Lenore!"
This I whispered, and an echo murmured back the word, "Lenore!"—
Merely this, and nothing more.

Back into the chamber turning, all my soul within me burning,
Soon I heard again a tapping somewhat louder than before.
"Surely," said I, "surely that is something at my window lattice;
Let me see, then, what thereat is, and this mystery explore—
Let my heart be still a moment and this mystery explore;—
'Tis the wind and nothing more!"

Open here I flung the shutter, when, with many a flirt and flutter,
In there stepped a stately raven of the saintly days of yore;
Not the least obeisance made he; not an instant stopped or stayed he;

But, with mien of lord or lady, perched above my chamber door—
Perched upon a bust of Pallas° just above my chamber door—
Perched, and sat, and nothing more.

Then this ebony bird beguiling my sad fancy into smiling,
By the grave and stern decorum of the countenance it wore,
"Though thy crest be shorn and shaven, thou," I said, "art sure no craven,
Ghastly grim and ancient raven wandering from the Nightly shore—
Tell me what thy lordly name is on the Night's Plutonian° shore!"
Quoth the raven, "Nevermore."

Much I marvelled this ungainly fowl to hear discourse so plainly,
Though its answer little meaning—little relevancy bore,
For we cannot help agreeing that no living human being
Ever yet was blessed with seeing bird above his chamber door—
Bird or beat upon the sculptured bust above his chamber door,
With such name as "Nevermore."

But the raven, sitting lonely on the placid bust, spoke only
That one word, as if his soul in that one word he did outpour.
Nothing farther then he uttered—not a feather then he fluttered—
Till I scarcely more than muttered "Other friends have flown before—
On the morrow *he* will leave me, as my hopes have flown before."
Then the bird said "Nevermore."

Startled at the stillness broken by reply so aptly spoken,
"Doubtless," said I, "what it utters is its only stock and store
Caught from some unhappy master whom unmerciful Disaster
Followed fast and followed faster till his songs one burden bore—
Till the dirges of his Hope that melancholy burden bore
Of 'Never—nevermore.'"

But the raven still beguiling all my sad soul into smiling,
Straight I wheeled a cushioned seat in front of bird and bust and door;
Then, upon the velvet sinking, I betook myself to linking
Fancy unto fancy, thinking what this ominous bird of yore—
What this grim, ungainly, ghastly, gaunt, and ominous bird of yore
Meant in croaking "Nevermore."

This I sat engaged in guessing, but no syllable expressing
To the fowl whose fiery eyes now burned into my bosom's core;
This and more I sat divining, with my head at ease reclining
On the cushion's velvet lining that the lamplight gloated o'er,
But whose velvet violet lining with the lamplight gloating o'er,
she shall press, ah, nevermore!

Pallas: Athena, Greek goddess of wisdom.

Plutonian: dark; Pluto was the Greek god of the dead and ruler of the underworld.

Then, methought, the air grew denser, perfumed from an unseen
censer
Swung by angels whose faint foot-falls tinkled on the tufted floor.
"Wretch," I cried, "thy God hath lent thee—by these angels he
hath sent thee
Respite—respite and nepenthe° from thy memories of Lenore!
Quaff, oh quaff this kind nepenthe and forget this lost Lenore!"
Quoth the raven, "Nevermore."

"Prophet!" said I, "thing of evil!—prophet still, if bird or devil!—
Whether Tempter sent, or whether tempest tossed thee here
ashore,
Desolate, yet all undaunted, on this desert land enchanted—
On this home by Horror haunted—tell me truly, I implore—
Is there—*is* there balm in Gilead?°—tell me—tell me, I implore!"
Quoth the raven, "Nevermore."

"Prophet!" said I, "thing of evil—prophet still, if bird or devil!
By that Heaven that bends above us—by that God we both adore—
Tell this soul with sorrow laden if, within the distant Aidenn,
It shall clasp a sainted maiden whom the angels name Lenore—
Clasp a rare and radiant maiden whom the angels name Lenore."
Quoth the raven, "Nevermore."

"Be that word our sign of parting, bird or fiend!" I shrieked upstarting—
"Get thee back into the tempest and the Night's Plutonian shore!
Leave no black plume as a token of that lie thy soul hath spoken!
Leave my loneliness unbroken!—quit the bust above my door!
Take thy beak from out my heart, and take thy form from off my
door!"
Quoth the raven, "Nevermore."

And the raven, never flitting, still is sitting, still is sitting
On the pallid bust of Pallas just above my chamber door;
And his eyes have all the seeming of a demon's that is dreaming,
And the lamp-light o'er him streaming throws his shadow on the floor;
And my soul from out that shadow that lies floating on the floor
Shall be lifted—nevermore!

Reading and Reacting

1. Who is the speaker in the poem? What is his state of mind? How does the raven mirror the speaker's mental state?
2. "The Raven" contains a good deal of alliteration. Identify some examples. How does this use of repeated initial consonant sounds help to convey the mood of the poem?

---

nepenthe: a drug mentioned in the *Odessy* as a remedy for grief.

Gilead: a region mentioned in the Bible; noted for its soothing ointments.

3. The speaker refers to the raven in a number of different ways. At one point, it is simply "an ebony bird" (line 42); at another, it is a "prophet" and "a thing of evil" (85). How else does the speaker characterize the raven?

4. **Journal Entry** What is the symbolic significance of the raven? Of the repeated word "nevermore"? Of the bust of Pallas, the ancient Greek god of wisdom?

5. **Critical Perspective** According to Christoffer Nilsson, who maintains a Web site dedicated to the works of Poe, "The Raven" was composed with almost mathematical precision. When writing the stanza in which the interrogation of the raven reaches its climax (third stanza from the end), Poe wanted to make certain that no preceding stanza would "surpass this in rythmical effect":

> Poe then worked backwards from this stanza and used the word "Nevermore" in many different ways, so that even with the repetition of this word, it would not prove to be monotonous. Poe builds the tension in this poem up, stanza by stanza, but after the climaxing stanza he tears the whole thing down, and lets the narrator know that there is no meaning in searching for a moral in the raven's "nevermore."

Do you agree with Nilsson that it makes no sense to look for a moral in the raven's "nevermore"? What kind of moral, if any, do you think "Nevermore" implies for the speaker?

Related Works: "A Hunger Artist" (p. 424), "Saint Helene" (p. 499), "Rooming houses are old women" (p. 926), "The Eagle" (p. 966), "The Fish" (p. 1125), "The Tyger" (p. 1129), *Hamlet* (p. 1605)

Allegory

Allegory is a form of narrative that conveys a message or doctrine by using people, places, or things to stand for abstract ideas. **Allegorical figures,** each with a strict equivalent, form an **allegorical framework,** a set of ideas that conveys the allegory's message or lesson. Thus, the allegory takes place on two levels: a **literal level** that tells a story and a **figurative level** on which the allegorical figures in the story stand for ideas, concepts, and other qualities.

Like symbols, allegorical figures suggest other things. But unlike symbols, which have a range of possible meanings, allegorical figures can always be assigned specific meanings. (Because writers use allegory to instruct, they gain nothing by hiding its significance.) Thus, symbols open up possibilities for interpretation, whereas allegories tend to restrict possibilities.

Quite often an allegory involves a journey or an adventure, as in the case of Dante's *Divine Comedy*, which traces a journey through Hell, Purgatory, and Heaven. Within an allegory, everything can have meaning: the road on which the characters walk, the people they encounter, or a phrase that one of them repeats throughout the journey. Once you understand the allegorical framework, your main task is to see how the various elements fit within this system. Some allegorical poems can be relatively straightforward, but others can be so complicated that it takes a great deal of effort to unlock their meaning. In the following poem, a journey is central to the allegory.

Source: ©The Granger Collection, New York

See this poet's biography on p. 1227.

CHRISTINA ROSSETTI (1830–1894)

Uphill (1861)

Does the road wind uphill all the way?
    Yes, to the very end.
Will the day's journey take the whole long day?
    From morn to night, my friend.

But is there for the night a resting-place?
    A roof for when the slow dark hours begin.
May not the darkness hide it from my face?
    You cannot miss that inn.

Shall I meet other wayfarers at night?
    Those who have gone before.
Then must I knock, or call when just in sight?
    They will not keep you standing at that door.

Shall I find comfort, travel-sore and weak?
    Of labor you shall find the sum.
Will there be beds for me and all who seek?
    Yea, beds for all who come.

"Uphill" uses a question-and-answer structure to describe a journey along an uphill road. Like the one described in John Bunyan's seventeenth-century allegory *The Pilgrim's Progress*, this is a spiritual journey, one that suggests the challenges a person faces throughout life. The day-and-night duration of the journey stands for life and death, and the inn at the end of the road stands for the grave, the final resting place.

FURTHER READING: Allegory

Source: ©AP Photo/Chuck Knoblock

See this poet's biography on p. 1227.

ADRIENNE RICH (1929–)

Diving into the Wreck (1973)

First having read the book of myths,
and loaded the camera,
and checked the edge of the knife-blade,
I put on
the body-armor of black rubber
the absurd flippers
the grave and awkward mask.
I am having to do this
not like Cousteau with his
assiduous team

aboard the sun-flooded schooner
but here alone.

There is a ladder.
The ladder is always there
hanging innocently
close to the side of the schooner.
We know what it is for,
we who have used it.
Otherwise
it's a piece of maritime floss
some sundry equipment.

I go down.
Rung after rung and still
the oxygen immerses me
the blue light
the clear atoms
of our human air.
I go down.
My flippers cripple me,
I crawl like an insect down the ladder
and there is no one
to tell me when the ocean
will begin.

First the air is blue and then
it is bluer and then green and then
black I am blacking out and yet
my mask is powerful
it pumps my blood with power
the sea is another story
the sea is not a question of power
I have to learn alone
to turn my body without force
in the deep element.

And now: it is easy to forget
what I came for
among so many who have always
lived here
swaying their crenellated fans
between the reefs
and besides
you breathe differently down here.

I came to explore the wreck.
The words are purposes.
The words are maps.

I came to see the damage that was done
and the treasures that prevail.
I stroke the beam of my lamp
slowly along the flank
of something more permanent
than fish or weed

the thing I came for:
the wreck and not the story of the wreck
the thing itself and not the myth
the drowned face always staring
toward the sun
the evidence of damage
worn by salt and sway into this threadbare beauty
the ribs of the disaster
curving their assertion
among the tentative haunters.

This is the place.
And I am here, the mermaid whose dark hair
streams black, the merman in his armored body
We circle silently
about the wreck
we dive into the hold.
I am she: I am he
whose drowned face sleeps with open eyes
whose breasts still bear the stress
whose silver, copper, vermeil cargo lies
obscurely inside barrels
half-wedged and left to rot
we are the half-destroyed instruments
that once held to a course
the water-eaten log
the fouled compass

We are, I am, you are
by cowardice or courage
the one who finds our way
back to this scene
carrying a knife, a camera
a book of myths
in which
our names do not appear.

Reading and Reacting

1. On one level, this poem is about a deep-sea diver's exploration of a wrecked ship. What details suggest that the poet wants you to see the poem as something more?

2. Explain the allegorical figures presented in the poem. What, for example, might the diver and the wreck represent?
3. Does the poem contain any symbols? How can you tell they are symbols and not allegorical figures?
4. **Journal Entry** In lines 62–63, the speaker says that she came for "the wreck and not the story of the wreck / the thing itself and not the myth." Explain this distinction. What do you think the speaker is really looking for?
5. **Critical Perspective** A number of critics have seen "Diving into the Wreck" as an attempt by Rich to reimagine or reinvent the myths of Western culture. Rachel Blau DuPlessis makes the following observation:

   > In this poem of journey and transformation Rich is tapping the energies and plots of myth, while re-envisioning the content. While there is a hero, a quest, and a buried treasure, the hero is a woman; the quest is a critique of old myths; the treasure is knowledge. . . .

   Why do you suppose Rich decided to "reinvent" myth?

Related Works: "Once upon a Time" (p. 232), "Young Goodman Brown" (p. 540), "Two Questions" (p. 556), "The Love Song of J. Alfred Prufrock" (p. 1151), "Lost Sister" (p. 1198), *The Cuban Swimmer* (p. 1732)

Allusion

An **allusion** is a brief reference to a person, place, or event (fictional or actual) that readers are expected to recognize. Like symbols and allegories, allusions enrich a work by introducing associations from another context.

When poets use allusions, they assume that they and their readers have a common body of knowledge. If, when reading a poem, you come across a reference with which you are not familiar, take the time to look it up online or in a dictionary or an encyclopedia. As you have probably realized by now, your understanding of a poem may depend on your ability to interpret an unfamiliar reference.

Although most poets expect readers to recognize their references, some use allusions to exclude certain readers from their work. In his 1922 poem "The Waste Land," for example, T. S. Eliot alludes to historical events, ancient languages, and obscure literary works. He even includes a set of notes to accompany his poem, but they do little more than complicate an already difficult text. (As you might expect, initial critical response to this poem was mixed: some critics said that it was a work of genius, while others thought that it was arcane and pretentious.)

Allusions can come from any source: history, the arts, other works of literature, the Bible, current events, or even the personal life of the poet. In the following poem, the Nigerian poet and playwright Wole Soyinka alludes to several political figures.

WOLE SOYINKA (1934–)

Future Plans (1972)

The meeting is called
To odium: Forgers, framers
Fabricators Inter-
national. Chairman,
A dark horse, a circus nag turned blinkered sprinter

Mach Three
We rate him — one for the Knife
Two for 'iavelli, Three —
Breaking speed
Of the truth barrier by a swooping detention decree

Projects in view:
Mao Tse Tung in league
With Chiang Kai. Nkrumah
Makes a secret
Pact with Verwood, sworn by Hastings Banda.
Proven: Arafat
In flagrante cum
Golda Meir. Castro drunk
With Richard Nixon
Contraceptives stacked beneath the papal bunk . . .
. . . *and more to come*

This poem is structured like an agenda for a meeting. From the moment it announces that a meeting has been called "To odium" (a pun on "to *order*"), it is clear that the poem will be a bitter political satire. Those in attendance are "Forgers, framers / Fabricators." The second stanza contains three allusions that shed light on the character of the chairman. The first is to Mack the Knife, a petty criminal in Bertolt Brecht and Kurt Weill's *Threepenny Opera* (1933). The second is to Niccolò Machiavelli, whose book *The Prince* (1532) advocates the use of unscrupulous means to strengthen the state. The last is to the term *mach*, which denotes the speed of an airplane in relation to the speed of sound—mach one, two, three, and so on. By means of these allusions, the poem implies that the meeting's chairman has been chosen for his ability to engage in violence, to be ruthless, and to break the "truth barrier"—that is, to lie.

The rest of the poem alludes to individuals involved in global politics around the time it was written, in 1972—specifically, the politics of developing nations. According to the speaker, instead of fighting for the rights of the oppressed, these people consolidate their own political power by collaborating with those who oppose their positions. Thus, Mao Tse-tung, the communist leader of China, is "in league / With" Chiang Kai-shek, his old Nationalist Chinese enemy; Yassir Arafat, the leader of the Palestine Liberation Organization, is linked with Golda Meir, the prime minister of Israel; Kwame Nkrumah, the first president of Ghana, conspires with Hendrick

Verwoerd, the prime minister of South Africa, assassinated in 1966; and United States president Richard Nixon gets drunk with Cuba's communist leader, Fidel Castro. These allusions suggest the self-serving nature of political alliances and the extreme disorder of world politics. Whether the poem is satirizing the United Nations and its agenda, criticizing the tendency of politics to make strange bedfellows, or showing how corrupt politicians are, its allusions enable the poet to broaden his frame of reference and thus make the poem more meaningful to readers.

The next poem uses allusions to prominent literary figures, as well as to myth, to develop its theme.

WILLIAM MEREDITH (1919–)

Dreams of Suicide (1980)

(in sorrowful memory of Ernest Hemingway, Sylvia Plath, and John Berryman)

I

I reach for the awkward shotgun not to disarm
you, but to feel the metal horn,
furred with the downy membrane of dream.
More surely than the unicorn,
you are the mythical beast.

II

Or I am sniffing an oven. On all fours
I am imitating a totemic animal
but she is not my totem or the totem
of my people, this is not my magic oven.

III

If I hold you tight by the ankles,
still you fly upward from the iron railing.
Your father made these wings,
after he made his own, and now from beyond
he tells you *fly down*, in the voice
my own father might say *walk, boy*.

This poem is dedicated to the memory of three writers who committed suicide. In each stanza, the speaker envisions in a dream the death of one of the writers. In the first stanza, he dreams of Ernest Hemingway, who killed himself with a shotgun. The speaker grasps the "metal horn" of Hemingway's shotgun and transforms Hemingway into a mythical beast who, like a unicorn, represents the rare, unique talent of the artist. In the second stanza, the speaker dreams of Sylvia Plath, who asphyxiated herself in a gas oven. He sees himself, like Plath, on his knees imitating an animal sniffing an oven. In the third stanza, the speaker dreams of John Berryman, who leaped to his death. Berryman is characterized as Icarus, a mythological figure who, along with his father Daedalus, fled Crete by building wings made of feathers and wax. Together they flew away; however, ignoring his father's warning, Icarus flew so close to the sun that the wax melted, and he fell to his death in the sea. In this poem, then, the speaker uses allusions to make a point about the difficult lives of writers—and, perhaps, to convey his own empathy for those who could not survive the struggle to reconcile art and life.

BILL COYLE (1968–)

Post-Colonial Studies° (2006)

Australia
The two surviving
speakers of Mati Ke,° ancient
sister and brother,
honor a tribal taboo°
and do not speak to each other.

Fiji
On an island bought
for him by a worthy follower,
Adi da Samraj,°
long awaited avatar,°
native New Yorker, holds sway.

Laos
In the country, homes
are often set on stilts. Some
of the stilts are bombs,
ordnance left from the war.°
Some of the bombs are still live.

Reading and Reacting

1. Use *Google* or some other search engine to get more information than the footnotes provide for Mati Ke and Adi Da Samraj. How do these allusions help Coyle make his point?

2. Explain the significance of the poem's title. Why does Coyle precede each stanza with the name of a country?

3. What do you think the poem's last stanza means? Why does Coyle choose to end the poem with a reference to Laos? (You may want to consult an encyclopedia to find information about United States involvement in Laos during the Vietnam War.)

4. **JOURNAL ENTRY** Does Coyle expects readers to be familiar with his allusions? Do you think he expects too much of readers, or is the effort worth the gain?

post-colonial studies: A school of literary criticism that examines literature written in and about the former colonies of Western powers.

Mati Ke: An indigenous language of Australia.

taboo: A prohibition against a certain action.

Adi Da Samraj: Literally, "the radiant avatar, primordial giver, universal ruler."

avatar: The embodiment of a divinity.

the war: The Laotian Civil War (1962–1975).

5. **Critical Perspective** Writing about Bill Coyle's book of poetry, *The God of This World to His Prophet*, poet and critic Richard Wilbur says:

> Bill Coyle's poems can strike every kind of note: they are grave or touching, acerbic or funny, and always civil. He writes with a clear flow of lively thought, and at the same time plays the whole instrument of poetry.

Do you agree with Wilbur's assessment of Coyle's poetry? Do you think that "Post-Colonial Studies" demonstrates "a clear flow of lively thought"?

Related Works: "Love and Other Catastrophes: A Mix Tape" (p. 182), "The Third and Final Continent" (p. 290), "The Things They Carried" (p. 473), "Try to Praise the Mutilated World" (p. 854), "Bilingual/Bilingue" (p. 880), "Buying Rations in Kabul" (p. 1067), *Trying to Find Chinatown* (p. 1856)

Myth

A **myth** is a narrative that embodies—and in some cases helps to explain—the religious, philosophical, moral, and political values of a culture. Using gods and supernatural beings, myths try to make sense of occurrences in the natural world. (The term *myth* can also refer to a private belief system devised by an individual poet as well as to any fully realized fictitious setting in which a literary work takes place, such as the myths of William Faulkner's Yoknapatawpha County or of novelist Lawrence Durrell's Alexandria.) Contrary to popular usage, *myth* does not mean "falsehood." In the broadest sense, myths are stories—usually whole groups of stories—that can be true or partly true as well as false; regardless of their degree of accuracy, however, myths frequently express the deepest beliefs of a culture. According to this definition, the *Iliad* and the *Odyssey*, the Koran, and the Old and New Testaments can all be referred to as myths.

The mythologist Joseph Campbell wrote that myths contain truths that link people together, whether they live today or lived 2,500 years ago. Myths attempt to explain phenomena that human beings care about, regardless of when and where they live. It is not surprising, then, that myths frequently contain **archetypal images**—images that cut across cultural and racial boundaries and touch us at a very deep level. Many Greek myths illustrate this power. For example, when Orpheus descends into Hades to rescue his wife, Eurydice, he acts out the universal human desire to transcend death; and when Telemachus sets out in search of his father, Odysseus, he reminds readers that we are all lost children searching for parents. When Icarus ignores his father and flies too near the sun and when Pandora cannot resist looking into a box that she has been told not to open, we are reminded of the human weaknesses we all share.

When poets use myths, they are actually making allusions. They expect readers to bring to the poem the cultural, emotional, and ethical context of the myths to which they are alluding. At one time, when all educated individuals studied the Greek and Latin classics as well as the Bible and other religious texts, poets could safely assume that readers would recognize the mythological allusions they made. Today, many readers are unable to understand the full significance of an allusion or its application within a poem. Many of the poems in this anthology are accompanied by notes, but these may not provide all the information you will need to understand the full significance of each mythological allusion. Occasionally, you may have to look elsewhere for answers, turning to dictionaries, encyclopedias, online information sites such as <http://www.answers.com>, or collections of myths such as the *New Larousse Encyclopedia of Mythology* or *Bulfinch's Mythology*.

Sometimes a poet alludes to a myth in a title; sometimes references to various myths appear throughout a poem; at other times, an entire poem focuses on a single myth. In each case, as in the following poem, the use of myth helps to develop the poem's theme.

COUNTEE CULLEN (1903–1946)

Yet Do I Marvel (1925)

I doubt not God is good, well-meaning, kind,
And did He stoop to quibble could tell why
The little buried mole continues blind,
Why flesh that mirrors Him must some day die,
Make plain the reason tortured Tantalus
Is baited by the fickle fruit, declare
If merely brute caprice dooms Sisyphus
To struggle up a never-ending stair.
Inscrutable His ways are, and immune
To catechism by a mind too strewn
With petty cares to slightly understand
What awful brain compels His awful hand.
Yet do I marvel at this curious thing:
To make a poet black, and bid him sing!

The speaker begins by affirming his belief in the benevolence of God but then questions why God engages in what appear to be capricious acts. As part of his catalog of questions, the speaker alludes to Tantalus and Sisyphus, two figures from Greek mythology. Tantalus was a king who for his crimes was condemned to Hades. There, he was forced to stand in a pool of water up to his chin. Overhead hung a tree branch laden with fruit. When Tantalus got thirsty and tried to drink, the level of the water dropped, and when he got hungry and reached for fruit, it moved just out of reach. Thus, Tantalus was doomed to be near what he most desired but forever unable to obtain it. Sisyphus also was condemned to Hades. For his disrespect to Zeus, he was sentenced to endless toil. Every day, Sisyphus pushed a boulder up a steep hill. Every time he neared the top, the boulder rolled back down the hill, and Sisyphus had to begin again. Like Tantalus, the speaker in "Yet Do I Marvel" cannot have what he wants; like Sisyphus, he is forced to toil in vain. He wonders why a well-meaning God would "make a poet black, and bid him sing" in a racist society that does not listen to his voice. Thus, the poet's two allusions to Greek mythology enrich the poem by connecting the suffering of the speaker to a universal drama that has been acted out again and again.

FURTHER READING: Myth

H. D. (HILDA DOOLITTLE) (1886–1961)

Helen° (1924)

All Greece hates
the still eyes in the white face,
the lustre as of olives
where she stands,
and the white hands.

All Greece reviles
the wan face when she smiles,
hating it deeper still
when it grows wan and white,
remembering past enchantments
and past ills.

Greece sees unmoved,
God's daughter, born of love,
the beauty of cool feet
and slenderest knees,
could love indeed the maid,
only if she were laid,
white ash amid funereal cypresses.

Reading and Reacting

1. Why do you think that H.D. chose to write about Helen, the mythic symbol of illicit love and beauty? What does she admire about her?

2. Why does all Greece hate Helen? Why is she reviled when she smiles?

3. What is the significance of the last stanza? Why could Greece love Helen only if she were dead?

4. **Journal Entry** How does H.D. portray Helen? What characteristics does she emphasize? What characteristics does she downplay?

5. **Critical Perspective** A number of critics have mentioned H.D.'s strong advocacy of feminist principles. According to performance artist and critic Joan Jonas, "her writings foreshadow a feminist project of reclamation and revision as she chose to express her feelings and

---

Helen: In Greek mythology, Helen was the most beautiful of all women. She was the daughter of the Greek god Zeus and the mortal Leda. After a decade or so of marriage to Menelaus, the King of Sparta, Helen was abducted by Paris, the son of King Priam of Troy. Menelaus enlisted an army to recapture her in what would become known as the Trojan War, a portion of which is recounted in Homer's epic poem *The Iliad.*

sense of self as a woman through rather than against a host of classical Greek female personages, key among them Helen of Troy."

In what sense do you think H.D. is attempting to "reclaim" Helen of Troy?

Related Works: "The Girl with Bangs" (p. 271), "The Yellow Wallpaper" (p. 459), "Saint Helene" (p. 499), "Girl Powdering Her Neck" (p. PS5), Porphyria's Lover" (p. 860), "Sonnet I" (p. 986), *Beauty* (p. 1270)

Source: ©Bettmann/Corbis

See this poet's biography on p. 1231.

WILLIAM BUTLER YEATS (1865–1939)

Leda and the Swan (1924)

A sudden blow: the great wings beating still
Above the staggering girl, her thighs caressed
By the dark webs, her nape caught in his bill,
He holds her helpless breast upon his breast.

How can those terrified vague fingers push
The feathered glory from her loosening thighs?
And how can body, laid in that white rush,
But feel the strange heart beating where it lies?

A shudder in the loins engenders there
The broken wall, the burning roof and tower
And Agamemnon dead.
Being so caught up,
So mastered by the brute blood of the air,
Did she put on his knowledge with his power
Before the indifferent beak could let her drop?

Reading and Reacting

1. What event is described in this poem? What is the mythological significance of this event?
2. How is Leda portrayed? Why is the swan described as a "feathered glory" (line 6)? Why in the poem's last line is Leda dropped by his "indifferent beak"?
3. The third stanza refers to the Trojan War, which was indirectly caused by the event described in the poem. How does the allusion to the Trojan War help develop the theme of the poem?
4. **JOURNAL ENTRY** Does the poem answer the question asked in its last two lines? Explain.
5. **CRITICAL PERSPECTIVE** According to Richard Ellmann, this poem deals with "transcendence of opposites." The bird's "rape of the human, the coupling of god and woman, the moment at which one epoch ended and another began . . . in the act which included all these Yeats had the violent symbol for the transcendence of opposites which he needed."

   What opposite or contrary forces exist in the myth of Leda and the swan? Do you think the poem implies that these forces can be reconciled?

Related Works: "Saint Helene" (p. 499), "Where Are You Going, Where Have You Been?" (p. 617), "Greasy Lake" (p. 687), "Easter Wings" (p. 1008), "The Second Coming" (p. 1215)

Source: ©AP Photo/Paula Alyle Scully

DEREK WALCOTT (1930–)

Sea Grapes° (1971)

That sail which leans on light,
tired of islands,
a schooner beating up the Caribbean
for home, could be Odysseus,
home-bound on the Aegean;
that father and husband's

longing, under gnarled sour grapes, is
like the adulterer hearing Nausicaa's name°
in every gull's outcry.

This brings nobody peace. The ancient war
between obsession and responsibility
will never finish and has been the same

for the sea-wanderer or the one on shore
now wriggling on his sandals to walk home,
since Troy sighed its last flame,

and the blind giant's boulder heaved the trough
from whose ground-swell the great hexameters come
to the conclusions of exhausted surf.

The classics can console. But not enough.

Reading and Reacting

1. Read a plot summary of the *Odyssey*. In the context of the myth of Odysseus, what is the "ancient war / between obsession and responsibility" (lines 10–11) to which the speaker refers? Does this conflict have a wider application in the context of the poem? Explain.
2. Consider the following lines from the poem: "and the blind giant's boulder heaved the trough / from whose ground-swell the great hexameters come / to the conclusions of exhausted surf" (lines 16–18). In what sense does the blind giant's boulder create the "great hexameters"? In what way does the trough end up as "exhausted surf"?
3. **JOURNAL ENTRY** This poem includes many references to Homer's *Odyssey*. Could you have appreciated it if you had not read a plot summary of the *Odyssey*?
4. **CRITICAL PERSPECTIVE** Asked in an interview about the final line of "Sea Grapes," Derek Walcott made the following comments:

> All of us have been to the point where, in extreme agony and distress, you turn to a book, and look for parallels, and you look for a greater grief than maybe your own. . . . But the truth of human agony is that a book does not assuage a toothache. It isn't that things don't pass

---

Sea Grapes: Small trees found on tropical sandy beaches.

Nausicaa's name: Nausicaa was a young princess who befriended the shipwrecked Odysseus.

and heal. Perhaps the only privilege that a poet has is that, in that agony, whatever chafes and hurts, if the person survives, [he] produces something that is hopefully lasting and moral from the experience.

How do Walcott's remarks help to explain his poem's last line?

Related Works: "Gryphon" (p. 277), "Bullet in the Brain" (p. 608), "Gretel in Darkness" (p. 839), "My Father in the Navy: A Childhood Memory" (p. 1043), "Dover Beach" (p. 1123), "Ulysses" (p. 1203)

Source: ©AP Photo

See this poet's biography on p. 1217.

W. H. AUDEN (1907–1973)

Musée des Beaux Arts (1940)

About suffering they were never wrong,
The Old Masters: how well they understood
Its human position; how it takes place
While someone else is eating or opening a window or just
    walking dully along
How, when the aged are reverently, passionately waiting
For the miraculous birth, there always must be
Children who did not specially want it to happen, skating
On a pond at the edge of the wood:
They never forgot
That even the dreadful martyrdom must run its course
Anyhow in a corner, some untidy spot
Where the dogs go on with their doggy life and the torturer's
    horse
Scratches its innocent behind on a tree.
In Brueghel's *Icarus*, for instance: how everything turns away
Quite leisurely from the disaster; the ploughman may
Have heard the splash, the forsaken cry,
But for him it was not an important failure; the sun shone
As it had to on the white legs disappearing into the green
Water; and the expensive delicate ship that must have seen
Something amazing, a boy falling out of the sky,
Had somewhere to get to and sailed calmly on.

Reading and Reacting

1. Reread the summary of the myth of Icarus on page 1025. What does Auden's allusion to this myth contribute to the poem?
2. What point does the poet make by referring to the "Old Masters" (line 2)?
3. **JOURNAL ENTRY** Brueghel's painting *Landscape with the Fall of Icarus* is shown on the next page. How does looking at this painting help you to understand the poem? To what specific details in the painting does the poet refer?

Brueghel, Pieter the Elder (1525?–1569). ***Landscape with the Fall of Icarus.***
Musée D'Art Ancien, Brussels, Belgium. © Scala/Art Resource, New York.

Related Works: "The Lottery" (p. 509), "One day I wrote her name upon the strand" (p. 898), "Shall I compare thee to a summer's day?" (p. 923), "Ethics" (p. 1186), "Not Waving but Drowning" (p. 1197), "The Second Coming" (p. 1215)

Source: ©AP Photo

See this poet's biography on p. 1220.

T. S. ELIOT (1888–1965)

Journey of the Magi° (1927)

"A cold coming we had of it,
Just the worst time of the year
For a journey, and such a long journey:
The ways deep and the weather sharp,
The very dead of winter." *
And the camels galled, sore-footed, refractory,
Lying down in the melting snow.
There were times we regretted
The summer palaces on slopes, the terraces,
And the silken girls bringing sherbet.
Then the camel men cursing and grumbling
And running away, and wanting their liquor and women,
And the night-fires going out, and the lack of shelters,

Magi: The three wise men who ventured east to pay tribute to the infant Jesus (see Matthew 12.1–12)

*The five quoted lines are adapted from a passage in a 1622 Christmas Day sermon by Bishop Lancelot Andrewes.

And the cities hostile and the towns unfriendly
And the villages dirty and charging high prices:
A hard time we had of it.
At the end we preferred to travel all night,
Sleeping in snatches,
With the voices singing in our ears, saying
That this was all folly.

Then at dawn we came down to a temperate valley,
Wet, below the snow line, smelling of vegetation;
With a running stream and a water-mill beating the darkness,
And three trees° on the low sky,
And an old white horse° galloped away in the meadow.
Then we came to a tavern with vine-leaves over the lintel,
Six hands at an open door dicing for pieces of silver,°
And feet kicking the empty wine-skins.
But there was no information, and so we continued
And arrived at evening, not a moment too soon
Finding the place; it was (you may say) satisfactory.
All this was a long time ago, I remember,
And I would do it again, but set down
This set down
This: were we led all that way for
Birth or Death? There was a Birth, certainly,
We had evidence and no doubt. I had seen birth and death,
But had thought they were different; this Birth was
Hard and bitter agony for us, like Death, our death.
We returned to our places, these Kingdoms,
But no longer at ease here, in the old dispensation,
With an alien people clutching their gods.
I should be glad of another death.

Reading and Reacting

1. The speaker in this poem is one of the three wise men who came to pay tribute to the infant Jesus. In what way are his recollections unexpected? How would you have expected him to react to the birth of Jesus?
2. In what way do the mythical references in the poem allude to future events? Do you need to understand these allusions in order to appreciate the poem?
3. What does the speaker mean in line 41 when he says that the three wise men were "no longer at ease here, in the old dispensation"? What has changed for them? Why does the speaker say that he would be glad for "another death" (line 43)?

---

three trees: The three crosses at Calvary (see Luke 23.32–33).

white horse: The horse ridden by the conquering Christ in Revelation 19.11–16.

dicing . . . silver: Echoes the soldiers dicing for Christ's garments, as well as his betrayal by Judas Iscariot for thirty pieces of silver (see Matthew 27.35 and 26.14–16).

4. **Journal Entry** How is this poem similar to and different from the story of the three wise men told in the New Testament (Matthew 2.1–18)?

5. **Critical Perspective** In an analysis of "Journey of the Magi," poet and critic Anthony Hecht discusses the most common interpretation of the poem, pointing to "a consensus of critical feeling about the tone of the conclusion of this poem, which, it is said, appears to border on despair and exhaustion of hope." Hecht, however, suspects that something more subtle is going on—namely, that Eliot is using the speaker of the poem to express his own imperfect acceptance of Christianity:

> Again, if I am right, about this, the poem might have a deeply personal meaning for Eliot himself, and might represent a kind of "confession," an acknowledgment that he had not yet perfectly embraced the fate to which he nominally adhered, that his imperfect spiritual status was, like the Magus's, that of a person whose faith was incomplete. . . .

Which of the two interpretations given above seems more plausible to you? Is the speaker of the poem wrestling with an incomplete faith, or is he experiencing "despair and exhaustion of hope"?

Related Works: "Araby" (p. 434), "The World Is Too Much with Us" (p. 855), "On First Looking into Chapman's Homer" (p. 984), "Do not go gentle into that good night" (p. 1046), "The Love Song of J. Alfred Prufrock" (p. 1151)

✔ CHECKLIST Writing about Symbol, Allegory, Allusion, Myth

Symbol

- ☐ Are there any symbols in the poem? What leads you to believe they are symbols?
- ☐ Are these symbols conventional?
- ☐ Are they universal or archetypal?
- ☐ Are any symbols obscure or highly idiosyncratic?
- ☐ What is the literal meaning of each symbol in the context of the poem?
- ☐ Beyond its literal meaning, what else could each symbol suggest?
- ☐ How does your interpretation of each symbol enhance your understanding of the poem?

Allegory

- ☐ Is the poem an allegory?
- ☐ Are there any allegorical figures within the poem? How can you tell?
- ☐ What do the allegorical figures signify on a literal level?
- ☐ What lesson does the allegory illustrate?

continued on next page

Allusion

- Are there any allusions in the poem?
- Do you recognize the names, places, historical events, or literary works to which the poet alludes?
- In what way does each allusion deepen the poem's meaning? Does any allusion interfere with your understanding or enjoyment of the poem? If so, how?
- Would the poem be more effective without a particular allusion?

Myth

- What myths or mythological figures are alluded to?
- How does the poem use myth to convey its meaning?
- How faithful is the poem to the myth? Does the poet add material to the myth? Are any details from the original myth omitted? Is any information distorted? Why?

WRITING SUGGESTIONS: Symbol, Allegory, Allusion, Myth

1. Read "Aunt Jennifer's Tigers" (p. 963) and "Diving into the Wreck" (p. 1020) by Adrienne Rich. Then, write an essay in which you discuss the similarities and differences in Rich's use of symbols in the two poems.
2. Many popular songs make use of allusion. Choose one or two popular songs that you know well, and analyze their use of allusion, paying particular attention to whether the allusions expand the impact and meaning of the song or create barriers to listeners' understanding.
3. Read the Emily Dickinson poem "Because I could not stop for Death—" (p. 1141), and then write an interpretation of the poem, identifying its allegorical figures.
4. What applications do the lessons of myth have for life today? Analyze a poem in which myth is central, and then discuss how you might use myth to make generalizations about your own life.
5. Both Judith Ortiz Cofer's "My Father in the Navy: A Childhood Memory" (p. 1043) and Derek Walcott's "Sea Grapes" (p. 1031) allude to Homer's *Odyssey*. Read a summary of the *Odyssey* in an encyclopedia or other reference work, and then write an essay in which you compare the poets' treatment of Homer's tale.

CHAPTER 31

DISCOVERING THEMES IN POETRY

Source: ©AP Photo/Paula Alyle Scully

See this poet's biography on p. 1223.

ROBERT HERRICK (1591–1674)

The Argument of His Book (1648)

I sing of brooks, of blossoms, birds, and bowers,
Of April, May, of June, and July-flowers;
I sing of May-poles, hock-carts, wassails, wakes,
Of bridegrooms, brides and of their bridal-cakes;
I write of youth, of love, and have access
By these to sing of cleanly wantonness;
I sing of dews, of rains, and piece by piece
Of balm, of oil, of spice and ambergris;
I sing of times trans-shifting, and I write
How roses first came red and lilies white;
I write of groves, of twilights, and I sing
The court of Mab,° and of the fairy king;
I write of Hell; I sing (and ever shall)
Of Heaven, and hope to have it after all.

As the poem above makes clear, a poem can be about anything, from the mysteries of the universe to poetry itself. Although no subject is really inappropriate for poetic treatment, certain conventional subjects—family, nature, love, war, death, the folly of human desires, and the inevitability of growing old—recur frequently.

A poem's theme, however, is more than its subject. In general terms, *theme* refers to the ideas that the poet explores, the concerns that the poem examines. More specifically, a poem's **theme** is its main point or idea. Poems "about death," for example, may examine the difficulty of facing one's own mortality, eulogize a friend, assert the need for the acceptance of life's cycles, or cry out against death's inevitability. Or, such poems may explore the **carpe diem** theme—the belief that life is brief, so we must "seize the day."

In order to understand the theme of a poem, readers should consider its form, voice, tone, language, images, allusions, sound—all of its individual elements. Together, these elements communicate the ideas that are important in the poem. Keep in mind, however, that a poem may not mean the same thing to every reader. Different readers will bring different backgrounds, attitudes, and experiences to a poem and will therefore see things in various ways. And, poets

Mab: Queen of the fairies.

may approach the same subject in drastically different ways, emphasizing different elements as they view the subject matter from their own unique perspectives. Ultimately, there are as many different themes, and ways to approach these themes, as there are writers (and readers) of poetry.

Poems about Parents

Although a poet's individual experience may be vastly different from the experiences of his or her readers, certain ideas seem universal in poems about parents. On the one hand, such poems can express positive sentiments: love, joy, wistfulness, nostalgia, and gratitude for childhood's happy memories and a parent's unconditional love. On the other hand, they may express negative emotions: anger, detachment, frustration, resentment, or regret. When they write about parents, poets may be emotionally engaged or distant, curious or apathetic, remorseful or grateful; they may idealize parents or despise them. Regardless of the particulars of the poem's specific theme, however, virtually all poems about parents address one general concept: the influence of a parent over his or her child.

For as long as poets have been writing poetry, their personal experiences (and childhoods) have influenced their subject matter and their poems. In American poetry, poems about parents became more common with the advent of **confessionalism,** a movement in the mid 1950s in which poets began to write subjective verse about their personal experiences. Poems in Robert Lowell's *Life Studies* and W. D. Snodgrass's *Heart's Needle* both addressed the positive and negative aspects of the poets' families (including their parents and children), thus opening the door for an influx of poems about similar themes. Poems by Sylvia Plath and Anne Sexton dealt with previously taboo subjects such as abortion, suicide, and mental illness. Though confessional poets often adapted or fictionalized their experiences when putting them into verse, the line between art and life could be thin, sometimes dangerously so: both Plath and Sexton committed suicide.

The poems in this section all deal with issues related to parents and family, but their styles, voices, and focuses are very different. Sometimes the speakers' voices express ambivalence, communicating conventional sentiments of love and admiration alongside perplexity, frustration, and even anger. This ambivalence is apparent in Theodore Roethke's "My Papa's Waltz" and Robert Hayden's "Those Winter Sundays," as adult speakers struggle to understand their fathers' long-ago behavior. In Edna St. Vincent Millay's "The courage that my mother had," Seamus Heaney's "Digging," and Louis Simpson's "Working Late," the speakers are more positive, finding traits in their parents that they would like to emulate. Raymond Carver's "Photograph of My Father in His Twenty-Second Year," Judith Ortiz Cofer's "My Father in the Navy: A Childhood Memory," and Sharon Olds's " I Go Back to May 1937" are meditations on visual images of the speakers' parents in their younger years, while Mitsuye Yamada's "The Night Before Goodbye" focuses on a mother's quiet sacrifice, and Simon J. Ortiz's "My Father's Song" is an elegiac poem that addresses the inevitable cycles of life. Finally, both Adrienne Rich's "A Woman Mourned by Daughters" and Dylan Thomas's "Do not go gentle into that good night" confront the death of a parent.

SHARON OLDS (1942–)

I Go Back to May 1937 (1987)

I see them standing at the formal gates of their colleges,
I see my father strolling out
under the ochre sandstone arch, the
red tiles glinting like bent
plates of blood behind his head, I
see my mother with a few light books at her hip
standing at the pillar made of tiny bricks,
the wrought-iron gate still open behind her, its
sword-tips aglow in the May air,
they are about to graduate, they are about to get married,
they are kids, they are dumb, all they know is they are
innocent, they would never hurt anybody.
I want to go up to them and say Stop,
don't do it—she's the wrong woman,
he's the wrong man, you are going to do things
you cannot imagine you would ever do,
you are going to do bad things to children,
you are going to suffer in ways you have not heard of,
you are going to want to die. I want to go
up to them there in the late May sunlight and say it,
her hungry pretty face turning to me,
her pitiful beautiful untouched body,
his arrogant handsome face turning to me,
his pitiful beautiful untouched body,
but I don't do it. I want to live. I
take them up like the male and female
paper dolls and bang them together
at the hips, like chips of flint, as if to
strike sparks from them, I say
Do what you are going to do, and I will tell about it.

Source: ©Bettmann/Corbis

See this poet's biography on p. 1227.

THEODORE ROETHKE (1908–1963)

My Papa's Waltz (1948)

The whiskey on your breath
Could make a small boy dizzy;
But I hung on like death:
Such waltzing was not easy.

We romped until the pans
Slid from the kitchen shelf;

My mother's countenance
Could not unfrown itself.

The hand that held my wrist
Was battered on one knuckle;
At every step you missed
My right ear scraped a buckle.

You beat time on my head
With a palm caked hard by dirt,
Then waltzed me off to bed
Still clinging to your shirt.

Source: ©Pach Brothers/Corbis

See this poet's biography on p. 1222.

ROBERT HAYDEN (1913–1980)

Those Winter Sundays (1962)

Sundays too my father got up early
and put his clothes on in the blueblack cold,
then with cracked hands that ached
from labor in the weekday weather made
banked fires blaze. No one ever thanked him.

I'd wake and hear the cold splintering,
    breaking.
When the rooms were warm, he'd call,
and slowly I would rise and dress,
fearing the chronic angers of that house,

Speaking indifferently to him,
who had driven out the cold
and polished my good shoes as well.
What did I know, what did I know
of love's austere and lonely offices?

Source: ©Simon Walker/Rex USA, Ltd.

See this poet's biography on p. 1222.

SEAMUS HEANEY (1939–   )

Digging (1966)

Between my finger and my thumb
The squat pen rests; snug as a gun.

Under my window, a clean rasping sound
When the spade sinks into gravelly ground:
My father, digging. I look down

Till his straining rump among the flowerbeds
Bends low, comes up twenty years away
Stooping in rhythm through potato drills
Where he was digging.

The coarse boot nestled on the lug, the shaft
Against the inside knee was levered firmly.
He rooted out tall tops, buried the bright edge deep
To scatter new potatoes that we picked
Loving their cool hardness in our hands.

By God, the old man could handle a spade.
Just like his old man.

My grandfather cut more turf in a day
Than any other man on Toner's bog.
Once I carried him milk in a bottle
Corked sloppily with paper. He straightened up
To drink it, then fell to right away

Nicking and slicing neatly, heaving sods
Over his shoulder, going down and down
For the good turf. Digging.

The cold smell of potato mould, the squelch and slap
Of soggy peat, the curt cuts of an edge
Through living roots awaken in my head.
But I've no spade to follow men like them.

Between my finger and my thumb
The squat pen rests.
I'll dig with it.

LOUIS SIMPSON (1923–)

Working Late (1980)

A light is on in my father's study.
"Still up?" he says, and we are silent,
looking at the harbor lights,
listening to the surf
and the creak of coconut boughs.

He is working late on cases.
No impassioned speech! He argues from evidence,
actually pacing out and measuring,
while the fans revolving on the ceiling
winnow the true from the false.

Once he passed a brass curtain rod
through a head made out of plaster
and showed the jury the angle of fire—
where the murderer must have stood.
For years, all through my childhood,
if I opened a closet . . . bang!

There would be the dead man's head
with a black hole in the forehead.

All the arguing in the world
will not stay the moon.
She has come all the way from Russia
to gaze for a while in a mango tree
and light the wall of a veranda,
before resuming her interrupted journey
beyond the harbor and the lighthouse
at Port Royal,° turning away
from land to the open sea.

Yet, nothing in nature changes, from that day to this,
she is still the mother of us all.
I can see the drifting offshore lights,
black posts where the pelicans brood.
And the light that used to shine
at night in my father's study
now shines as late in mine.

EDNA ST. VINCENT MILLAY (1892–1950)

The courage that my mother had (1954)

The courage that my mother had
Went with her, and is with her still:
Rock from New England quarried;
New granite in a granite hill.

The golden brooch my mother wore
She left behind for me to wear;
I have no thing I treasure more:
Yet, it is something I could spare.

Oh, if instead she'd left to me
The thing she took into the grave!—
That courage like a rock, which she
Has no more need of, and I have.

RAYMOND CARVER (1938–1988)

Photograph of My Father in His Twenty-Second Year (1983)

October. Here in this dank, unfamiliar kitchen
I study my father's embarrassed young man's face.

Port Royal: A city in Jamaica.

Sheepish grin, he holds in one hand a string
of spiny yellow perch, in the other
a bottle of Carlsbad beer.

In jeans and denim shirt, he leans
against the front fender of a 1934 Ford.
He would like to pose bluff and hearty for his posterity,
wear his old hat cocked over his ear.
All his life my father wanted to be bold.

But the eyes give him away, and the hands
that limply offer the string of dead perch
and the bottle of beer. Father, I love you,
yet how can I say thank you, I who can't hold my liquor either,
and don't even know the places to fish?

Source: ©Dorothy Alexander

See this poet's biography on p. 1219.

JUDITH ORTIZ COFER (1952–)

My Father in the Navy: A Childhood Memory (1982)

Stiff and immaculate
in the white cloth of his uniform
and a round cap on his head like a halo,
he was an apparition on leave from a shadow-world
and only flesh and blood when he rose from below
the waterline where he kept watch over the engines
and dials making sure the ship parted the waters
on a straight course.
Mother, brother and I kept vigil
on the nights and dawns of his arrivals,
watching the corner beyond the neon sign of a quasar
for the flash of white our father like an angel
heralding a new day.
His homecomings were the verses
we composed over the years making up
the siren's song that kept him coming back
from the bellies of iron whales
and into our nights
like the evening prayer.

MITSUYE YAMADA (1923–)

The Night Before Goodbye (1976)

Mama is mending
my underwear

while my brothers sleep.
Her husband taken away by the FBI
one son lured away by the Army
now another son and daughter
lusting for the free world outside.
She must let go.
The war goes on.
She will take one still small son
and join Papa in internment°
to make a family.
Still sewing
squinting in the dim light
in room C barrack 4 block 4
she whispers
Remember
keep your underwear
in good repair
in case of accident
don't bring shame
on us.

SIMON J. ORTIZ (1941–)

My Father's Song (1976)

Wanting to say things,
I miss my father tonight.
His voice, the slight catch,
the depth from his thin chest,
the tremble of emotion
in something he has just said
to his son, his song:

We planted corn one Spring at Acu—
we planted several times
but this one particular time
I remember the soft damp sand
in my hand.

My father had stopped at one point
to show me an overturned furrow;
the plowshare had unearthed

---

internment: Shortly after the attack on Pearl Harbor, President Roosevelt ordered that all people of Japanese ancestry — even American citizens — be removed from the West Coast. About 112,000 people were relocated to "internment camps," where they remained until after the war's end.

the burrow nest of a mouse
in the soft moist sand.

Very gently, he scooped tiny pink animals
into the palm of his hand
and told me to touch them.
We took them to the edge
of the field and put them in the shade
of a sand moist clod.

I remember the very softness
of cool and warm sand and tiny alive mice
and my father saying things.

ADRIENNE RICH (1929–)

A Woman Mourned by Daughters (1984)

Now, not a tear begun,
we sit here in your kitchen,
spent, you see, already.
You are swollen till you strain
this house and the whole sky.
You, whom we so often
succeeded in ignoring!
You are puffed up in death
like a corpse pulled from the sea;
we groan beneath your weight.
And yet you were a leaf,
a straw blown on the bed,
you had long since become
crisp as a dead insect.
What is it, if not you,
that settles on us now
like satins you pulled down
over our bridal heads?
What rises in our throats
like food you prodded in?
Nothing could be enough.
You breathe upon us now
through solid assertions
of yourself: teaspoons, goblets,
seas of carpet, a forest
of old plants to be watered,
an old man in an adjoining
room to be touched and fed.

And all this universe
dares us to lay a finger
anywhere, save exactly
as you would wish it done.

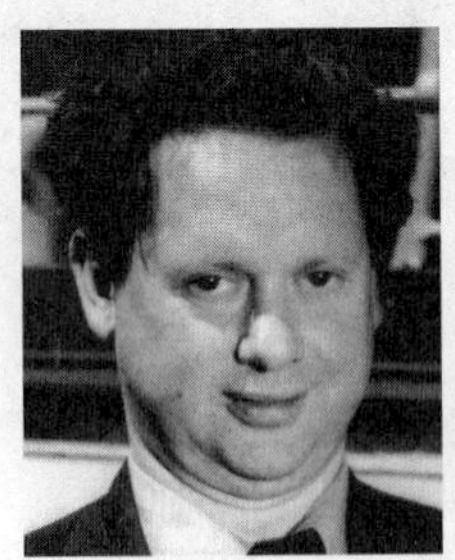

See this poet's biography on p. 1230.

DYLAN THOMAS (1914–1953)

Do not go gentle into that good night* (1952)

Do not go gentle into that good night,
Old age should burn and rave at close of day;
Rage, rage against the dying of the light.

Though wise men at their end know dark is right,
Because their words had forked no lightning they
Do not go gentle into that good night.

Good men, the last wave by, crying how bright
Their frail deeds might have danced in a green bay,
Rage, rage against the dying of the light.

Wild men who caught and sang the sun in flight,
And learn, too late, they grieved it on its way,
Do not go gentle into that good night.

Grave men, near death, who see with blinding sight
Blind eyes could blaze like meteors and be gay,
Rage, rage against the dying of the light.

And you, my father, there on the sad height,
Curse, bless, me now with your fierce tears, I pray,
Do not go gentle into that good night.
Rage, rage against the dying of the light.

Reading and Reacting: Poems about Parents

1. What is each speaker's attitude toward his or her parent?
2. Which words, images, and figures of speech in each poem have positive associations? Which help to create a negative impression?
3. How would you characterize each poem's tone? For example, is the tone sentimental? Playful? Angry? Resentful? Regretful? Admiring?
4. What problems associated with parent-child relationships are explored in each poem?
5. What does each poem say about the parent? What does it reveal about the child?
6. What is each poem's central theme?

*This poem was written during the last illness of the poet's father.

Related Works: "Oliver's Evolution" (p. 191), "I Stand Here Ironing" (p. 344), "New York Day Women" (p. 406), "A Primer for the Punctuation of Heart Disease" (p. 440), "Fun Home" (p. 494), "The Little Knife" (p. 602), "Two Kinds" (p. 777), "Daddy" (p. 936), *When I Was a Little Girl and My Mother Didn't Want Me* (p. 1266), *Proof* (p. 1476), *Fences* (p. 1902)

Poems about Nature

In his 1913 poem "Trees," the American poet Joyce Kilmer neatly summarized the symbiotic relationship that exists between poetry and nature: "I think that I shall never see / A poem lovely as a tree." Poets have always found inspiration in the beauty, majesty, and grandeur of the natural world; in fact, some forms of poetry are dedicated solely to the subject of nature. For example, a **pastoral** is a literary form that deals nostalgically with a simple rural life. Many of the early Greek and Roman pastorals were about shepherds who passed the time writing about love while watching their flocks. In these poems, the shepherd's life is idealized; thus, the pastoral tradition celebrates simple times and the beauty of the rural life. Similarly, an **idyll,** a short work in verse or prose (or a painting or a piece of music), depicts simple pastoral or rural scenes, often in idealized terms.

Certain literary movements also focused on the subject of nature. For the **romantic** poets, nature was a source of inspiration, authenticity, and spiritual refreshment, elements they by and large saw as lacking in the lives of Europeans—both the educated classes and those working in the mills and factories that came with industrialization. Later, the American **transcendentalists,** including Ralph Waldo Emerson and Henry David Thoreau, examined the relationships between philosophy, religion, and nature. In *Walden*, for example, Thoreau wrote about the pleasures and rewards of withdrawing from mainstream life in order to live simply in the woods.

While all poems about nature deal with the same general subject, their approaches, and their focuses, can differ greatly. Poems "about nature" may focus on the seasons, the weather, mountains or the sea, birds or animals, or trees and flowers. They may praise the beauty of nature, assert the superiority of its simplest creatures, consider its evanescence, or mourn its destruction. In this section, romantic poet William Wordsworth's "I wandered lonely as a cloud" extols the virtue of nature and the value of immersing oneself in its beauty, while in "The Windhover," Gerard Manley Hopkins celebrates the divinity of God's natural kingdom. In "Trees," Mark Haddon's speaker acknowledges the power of nature as he observes the quiet yet lasting presence of trees; in Carl Sandburg's "Fog," the speaker focuses on a single image of a natural phenomenon. In Robert Frost's "Birches," the speaker recalls the childhood enjoyment of climbing trees, and he longs for the simplicity of those times; in Jaime Sabines' "The Moon," the speaker recommends the moon as a "tonic" to be taken "in precise and regular doses." Mary Oliver's "Sleeping in the Forest" expresses a oneness with nature and its creatures, and Joy Harjo's "Morning Song" is a lyrical ode that celebrates the natural world. Conversely, in William Stafford's "Traveling through the Dark," the speaker presents human beings as adversaries of nature and its other creatures.

Source: ©The Granger Collection, New York

See this poet's biography on p. 1231.

WILLIAM WORDSWORTH (1770–1850)

I wandered lonely as a cloud (1807)

I wandered lonely as a cloud
That floats on high o'er vales and hills,
When all at once I saw a crowd,
A host, of golden daffodils,
Beside the lake, beneath the trees,
Fluttering and dancing in the breeze.

Continuous as the stars that shine
And twinkle on the milky way,
They stretched in never-ending line
Along the margin of a bay:
Ten thousand saw I at a glance,
Tossing their heads in sprightly dance.

The waves beside them danced; but they
Out-did the sparkling waves in glee;
A poet could not but be gay,
In such a jocund company;
I gazed—and gazed—but little thought
What wealth the show to me had brought:

For oft, when on my couch I lie
In vacant or in pensive mood,
They flash upon that inward eye
Which is the bliss of solitude;
And then my heart with pleasure fills,
And dances with the daffodils.

MARY OLIVER (1935–)

Sleeping in the Forest (1979)

I thought the earth remembered me,
she took me back so tenderly,
arranging her dark skirts, her pockets
full of lichens and seeds.

I slept as never before, a stone on the river bed,
nothing between me and the white fire of the stars
but my thoughts, and they floated light as moths
among the branches of the perfect trees.
All night I heard the small kingdoms
breathing around me, the insects,
and the birds who do their work in the darkness.
All night I rose and fell, as if in water,
grappling with a luminous doom. By morning
I had vanished at least a dozen times
into something better.

JAIME SABINES (1926–1999)

The Moon (1981)

Translated by W. S. Merwin

You can take the moon by the spoonful
or in capsules every two hours.
It's useful as a hypnotic and sedative
and besides it relieves
those who have had too much philosophy.
A piece of moon in your purse
works better than a rabbit's foot.
Helps you find a lover
or get rich without anyone knowing,
and it staves off doctors and clinics.
You can give it to children like candy
when they've not gone to sleep,
and a few drops of moon in the eyes of the old
helps them to die in peace.

Put a new leaf of moon
under your pillow
and you'll see what you want to.
Always carry a little bottle of air of the moon
to keep you from drowning.
Give the key to the moon
to prisoners and the disappointed.
For those who are sentenced to death
and for those who are sentenced to life
there is no better tonic than the moon
in precise and regular doses.

Source: ©The Granger Collection

See this poet's biography on p. 1223.

GERARD MANLEY HOPKINS (1844–1889)

The Windhover° (1877)

To Christ Our Lord

I caught this morning morning's minion,° kingdom
  of daylight's dauphin, dapple-dawn-drawn Falcon,
    in his riding
  Of the rolling level underneath him steady air, and striding
High there, how he rung upon the rein° of a wimpling° wing
In his ecstasy! then off, off forth on swing,
  As a skate's heel sweeps smooth on a bow-bend: the hurl and
    gliding
  Rebuffed the big wind. My heart in hiding
Stirred for a bird,—the achieve of, the mastery of the thing!
Brute beauty and valor and act, oh, air, pride, plume, here
  Buckle! and the fire that breaks from thee then, a billion
Times told lovelier, more dangerous, O my chevalier!
  No wonder of it: shéer plód, makes plow down sillion°
Shine, and blue-bleak embers, ah my dear,
  Fall, gall themselves, and gash gold-vermilion.

Source: ©Bettmann/Corbis

See this poet's biography on p. 1221.

ROBERT FROST (1874–1963)

Birches (1915)

When I see birches bend to left and right
Across the lines of straighter darker trees,
I like to think some boy's been swinging them.
But swinging doesn't bend them down to stay
As ice-storms do. Often you must have seen them
Loaded with ice a sunny winter morning
After a rain. They click upon themselves
As the breeze rises, and turn many-colored
As the stir cracks and crazes their enamel.
Soon the sun's warmth makes them shed crystal shells
Shattering and avalanching on the snow-crust—

Windhover: A kestrel, a European falcon able to hover in the air with its head to the wind.
minion: Favorite.
rung upon the rein: A horse is "rung upon the rein" when it circles at the end of a long rein held by the trainer.
wimpling: Rippling.
sillion: The ridge between two furrows.

Such heaps of broken glass to sweep away
You'd think the inner dome of heaven had fallen.
They are dragged to the withered bracken by the load,
And they seem not to break; though once they are bowed
So low for long, they never right themselves:
You may see their trunks arching in the woods
Years afterwards, trailing their leaves on the ground
Like girls on hands and knees that throw their hair
Before them over their heads to dry in the sun.
But I was going to say when Truth broke in
With all her matter-of-fact about the ice-storm
I should prefer to have some boy bend them
As he went out and in to fetch the cows—
Some boy too far from town to learn baseball,
Whose only play was what he found himself,
Summer or winter, and could play alone.
One by one he subdued his father's trees
By riding them down over and over again
Until he took the stiffness out of them,
And not one but hung limp, not one was left
For him to conquer. He learned all there was
To learn about not launching out too soon
And so not carrying the tree away
Clear to the ground. He always kept his poise
To the top branches, climbing carefully
With the same pains you use to fill a cup
Up to the brim, and even above the brim.
Then he flung outward, feet first, with a swish,
Kicking his way down through the air to the ground.
So was I once myself a swinger of birches.
And so I dream of going back to be.
It's when I'm weary of considerations,
And life is too much like a pathless wood
Where your face burns and tickles with the cobwebs
Broken across it, and one eye is weeping
From a twig's having lashed across it open.
I'd like to get away from earth awhile
And then come back to it and begin over.
May no fate willfully misunderstand me
And half grant what I wish and snatch me away
Not to return. Earth's the right place for love:
I don't know where it's likely to go better.
I'd like to go by climbing a birch tree,
And climb black branches up a snow-white trunk

Toward Heaven, till the tree could bear no more,
But dipped its top and set me down again.
That would be good both going and coming back.
One could do worse than be a swinger of birches.

Source: ©Dorothy Alexander

See this poet's biography on p. 1229.

WILLIAM STAFFORD (1914–1993)

Traveling through the Dark (1962)

Traveling through the dark I found a deer
dead on the edge of the Wilson River road.
It is usually best to roll them into the canyon:
that road is narrow; to swerve might make more dead.

By glow of the tail-light I stumbled back of the car
and stood by the heap, a doe, a recent killing;
she had stiffened already, almost cold.
I dragged her off; she was large in the belly.

My fingers touching her side brought me the reason—
her side was warm; her fawn lay there waiting,
alive, still, never to be born.
Beside that mountain road I hesitated.

The car aimed ahead its lowered parking lights;
under the hood purred the steady engine.
I stood in the glare of the warm exhaust turning red;
around our group I could hear the wilderness listen.

I thought hard for us all—my only swerving—
then pushed her over the edge into the river.

MARK HADDON (1962–)

Trees (2006)

They stand in parks and graveyards and gardens.
Some of them are taller than department stores,
yet they do not draw attention to themselves.

You will be fitting a heated towel rail one day
and see, through the louvre window,°
a shoal of olive-green fish changing direction
in the air that swims above the little gardens.

louvre window: A window with fixed or movable slats.

Or you will wake at your aunt's cottage,
your sleep broken by a coal train on the empty hill
as the oaks roar in the wind off the channel.

Your kindness to animals, your skill at the clarinet,
these are accidental things.
We lost this game a long way back.
Look at you. You're reading poetry.
Outside the spring air is thick
with the seeds of their children.

CARL SANDBURG (1878–1967)

Fog (1916)

The fog comes
on little cat feet.
It sits looking
over harbor and city
on silent haunches
and then moves on.

JOY HARJO (1951–)

Morning Song (2001)

The red dawn now is rearranging the earth
Thought by thought
Beauty by beauty
Each sunrise a link in the ladder
The ladder the backbone
Of shimmering deity
Child stirring in the web of your mother
Do not be afraid
Old man turning to walk through the door
Do not be afraid

Reading and Reacting: Poems about Nature

1. What aspect of nature does the poem focus on?
2. What is the speaker's attitude toward nature? For example, is nature seen as a benevolent, comforting, threatening, awe-inspiring, or overwhelming force?
3. Which words, images, and figures of speech in the poem have positive associations? Which help to create a negative impression of nature?
4. How would you characterize each poem's tone? For example, is the speaker hopeful? Thoughtful? Humbled? Frightened?

5. Is the natural world the poem's true subject, or is it just the setting? Explain.
6. What is each poem's central theme?

Related Works: "Snow" (p. 177), "Doe Season" (p. 577), "Greasy Lake" (p. 687), "Cézanne's Ports" (p. PS3), "Nothing Gold Can Stay" (p. 914), "Comparatives" (p. 967), "Blackberry Eating" (p. 974), "Explaining an Affinity for Bats" (p. 986), "Four Haiku" (p. 995), A *Midsummer Night's Dream* (p. 1787)

Poems about Love

Since the earliest times, romantic love has been one of the great themes of poetry. In the European tradition, Sappho, whose works exist largely in fragments, is one of the early classic Greek poets. Even more influential, in part because most of their works survived, were the Romans Catullus and Ovid. Although the Bible may strike some as an unlikely place to find love poetry, the *Song of Songs* is just that (although it is also commonly interpreted as an allegory of the love between God and his people). In *La Vita Nuova* (*The New Life*), Dante wrote about the life-changing effect of his meeting with Beatrice, a beautiful young woman who was to die young. It is this same Beatrice with whose help Dante embarks on his journey from hell to heaven in *The Divine Comedy*.

Love has played an equally important part in English poetry. During the Middle Ages, poems such as *Sir Gawain and the Green Knight* and *Le Morte d'Arthur* employed the conventions of "courtly love," in which a protagonist performs gallant deeds to win the hand of a fair maiden. Examples of Renaissance love poems include many of the sonnets of William Shakespeare and Edmund Spenser. Christopher Marlowe's "The Passionate Shepherd to His Love" (p. 1179) was answered by Sir Walter Raleigh's "The Nymph's Reply to the Shepherd" (p. 1189). Andrew Marvel produced a seduction poem on much the same theme with "To His Coy Mistress" (p. 941).

Although the Renaissance may arguably be considered the high point of love poetry in English, the tradition has continued to the present day. Increased opportunities for women to read, write, and publish poetry have brought new perspectives to what was once a male-dominated field. Confessional poetry has allowed a more direct, frank discussion of love. And, of course, love songs today are as much in fashion as they were in the time of Shakespeare, Dante, or Sappho—and heard by more people than ever.

In each of the poems in this section, the poets address the subject of love in their own styles and voices. Robert Browning and Elizabeth Barrett Browning (who were married to each other) are represented with traditional love poems, including "Meeting at Night," "Parting at Morning," and "How Do I Love Thee?" (which is one of the most often quoted poems in the English language).

In Edna St. Vincent Millay's "What Lips My Lips Have Kissed," the speaker reminisces about her past lovers with a mixture of nostalgia and wistfulness; Alan

Shapiro's "A Parting Gift" also looks back, expressing regret for a lost love, and W. H. Auden's "Stop all the clocks, cut off the telephone" is an eloquent elegy that expresses profound loss and despair. On a lighter note, Dorothy Parker's "General Review of the Sex Situation" is a tongue-in-cheek explanation of the differences between the sexes.

Contemporary love poems are equally varied in their approaches, ranging from the playfulness of Sandra Cisneros's "In My Little Museum of Erotica" and the irreverence of George Elliott Clarke's "Monologue for Selah Bringing Spring to Whylah Falls" to the visual experimentation of Tupac Shakur's "Love Is Just Complicated."

ROBERT BROWNING (1812–1889)

Meeting at Night (1845)

The gray sea and the long black land;
And the yellow half-moon large and low;
And the startled little waves that leap
In fiery ringlets from their sleep,
As I gain the cove with pushing prow,
And quench its speed i' the slushy sand.

Then a mile of warm sea-scented beach;
Three fields to cross till a farm appears;
A tap at the pane, the quick sharp scratch
And blue spurt of a lighted match,
And a voice less loud, through its joys and fears,
Than the two hearts beating each to each!

Parting at Morning (1845)

Round the cape of a sudden came the sea,
And the sun looked over the mountain's rim:
And straight was a path of gold for him,
And the need of a world of men for me.

ELIZABETH BARRETT BROWNING (1806–1861)

How Do I Love Thee? (1850)

How do I love thee? Let me count the ways.
I love thee to the depth and breadth and height
My soul can reach, when feeling out of sight
For the ends of being and ideal grace.
I love thee to the level of every day's

Most quiet need, by sun and candle-light.
I love thee freely, as men strive for right.
I love thee purely, as they turn from praise.
I love thee with the passion put to use
In my old griefs, and with my childhood's faith.
I love thee with a love I seemed to lose
With my lost saints. I love thee with the breath,
Smiles, tears, of all my life; and, if God choose,
I shall but love thee better after death.

Source: ©Car Van Vechten Archive at the Library of Congress

See this poet's biography on p. 1224.

EDNA ST. VINCENT MILLAY (1892–1950)

What Lips My Lips Have Kissed (1923)

What lips my lips have kissed, and where, and why,
I have forgotten, and what arms have lain
Under my head till morning; but the rain
Is full of ghosts tonight, that tap and sigh
Upon the glass and listen for reply,
And in my heart there stirs a quiet pain
For unremembered lads that not again
Will turn to me at midnight with a cry.
Thus in the winter stands the lonely tree,
Nor knows what birds have vanished one by one,
Yet knows its boughs more silent than before:
I cannot say what loves have come and gone,
I only know that summer sang in me
A little while, that in me sings no more.

DOROTHY PARKER (1893–1967)

General Review of the Sex Situation (1933)

Woman wants monogamy;
Man delights in novelty.
Love is woman's moon and sun;
Man has other forms of fun.

Woman lives but in her lord;
Count to ten, and man is bored.
With this the gist and sum of it,
What earthly good can come of it?

W. H. AUDEN (1907–1973)

Stop all the clocks, cut off the telephone (1936)

Stop all the clocks, cut off the telephone,
Prevent the dog from barking with a juicy bone,
Silence the pianos and with muffled drum
Bring out the coffin, let the mourners come.

Let aeroplanes circle moaning overhead
Scribbling on the sky the message He Is Dead,
Put the crepe bows round the white necks of the public doves,
Let the traffic policemen wear black cotton gloves.

He was my North, my South, my East and West,
My working week and my Sunday rest,
My noon, my midnight, my talk, my song;
I thought that love would last for ever. I was wrong.

The stars are not wanted now: put out every one;
Pack up the moon and dismantle the sun;
Pour away the ocean and sweep up the wood.
For nothing now can ever come to any good.

SANDRA CISNEROS (1954–)

In My Little Museum of Erotica*

In my little museum
of erotica
I would place your feet.

I would place your feet
sandwiching
my feet.

Their softness.
Their heat.

And I would
place your arms
as you do mornings,
beneath my neck.
around my waist,
tugging me towards you,
my back to your chest.

*Publication date is unavailable.

This
well-beingness
I would set
on a Corinthian
column.

And those
who are aesthetes
of mornings and feet
would say, Ah!
Yes!

GEORGE ELLIOTT CLARKE (1960–)

Monologue for Selah Bringing Spring to Whylah Falls° (1990)

I cry, in the vernacular, this plain manifesto,
No matter how many fishmen offer you their laps,
Or how contrary you are in the morning,
Or how your hair gleams like dark lightning,
Or how many lies the encyclopedia preserves,
Because, Selah, I won't play them parlour-seducer games—
Card tricks of chat, sleight-of-hand caresses—
Or stick my head in books. I love your raspy,
Backwoods accent, your laughter like ice breaking up!
I'd burn dictionaries to love you even once!
Selah, I tell myself I come to Whylah Falls
To spy the river crocheted with apple blossoms,
To touch you whose hair fans in mystery,
Whose smile is Cheshire and shadow and bliss,
Whose scent is brown bread, molasses, and milk,
Whose love is Coca-Cola and rose petals
In a ship's cabin soaked in saltwater.
But my lies lie. My colleged speech ripens before you,
Becomes Negro-natural, those green, soiled words
Whose roots mingle with turnip, carrot, and squash,
Keeping philology fresh and tasty.
You slouch and sigh that sassy, love speech,
And aroused, very aroused, I exalt
Your decisive eyes, your definitive lips,
Your thighs that'd be emboldened by childbirth,
For when you move, every line of poetry quakes,

Whylah Falls: A fictional black community in Nova Scotia.

And I inhale your perfume—ground roses,
Distilled petals, praise your blue skirt bright
Against your bare, black legs! *You won't wear stockings!*
I'm scripting this lyric because I'm too shy
To blurt my passion for you, Selah!
My history is white wine from a charred log,
A white horse galloping in a meadow,
A dozen chicks quitting an egg carton tomb,
But also selfish, suicidal love.
I don't want that!
Selah, I want to lie beside you
And hear you whisper this poem and giggle.
Selah, I thought this poem was finished!
Selah, I am bust upside the head with love!

ALAN SHAPIRO (1952–)

A Parting Gift (2005)

Songbirds are singing from a cave of leaves
inside a tree that I imagine there
beyond the upper-story window of
the bedroom where
the lovers we no longer are
are making love.

They're singing now because I say they do,
swallow and nightingale, wren, lark and thrush,
each song a different air of deepest pleasure
all through a lush,
long night we'll never have again
with one another,
a night of birdsong that won't let you sleep,
a night of hearing how each tremulous thread
of melody pulls back against the urge
to pull ahead,
how song weaves in and out of song
till all songs merge

into the sheerest billowing of air
that settles and never settles over all
the lovers do throughout that long-ago
spectacular
lost night that's now forever my
last gift to you.

See this poet's biography on p. 1228.

TUPAC SHAKUR (1971–1996)

Love Is Just Complicated

You ask me 2 communicate
What it is I feel within
I search 4 words 2 assist
But I find none 2 help me begin
I guess love is just complicated
Love
is
Just
complicated.

I thought I knew my heart's desire
I thought I quenched my burning fire
I thought I wanted "A"
But "A" was 2 mixed up with B
Then "C" made me more confused
So "A" turned off me and "B" feels
better. "C" is upset and lonely
and me, I think love is complicated
Love
is
Just
complicated.

2-Pac

Reading and Reacting: Poems about Love

1. What general ideas about love are expressed in each poem?
2. What conventional images and figures of speech are used to express feelings of love?
3. Does any poet use any unexpected (or even shocking) images or figures of speech?
4. How would you characterize the tone of each poem? For example, is the tone happy? Sad? Celebratory? Regretful?
5. What does each poem reveal about the speaker? About the person to whom the poem is addressed?
6. What is each poem's central theme?

Related Works: "Hills Like White Elephants" (p. 171), "Love and Other Catastrophes: A Mix Tape" (p. 182), "The Girl with Bangs" (p. 271), "The Storm" (p. 313), "Living in Sin" (p. 882), "I Knew a Woman" (p. 885), "My mistress' eyes are nothing like the sun" (p. 917), "Shall I compare thee to a summer's day?" (p. 923), "A Valediction: Forbidding Mourning" (p. 933), "To My Dear and Loving Husband" (p. 940), "You fit into me" (p. 946), "There is a garden in her face" (p. 1134), *The Brute* (p. 1250)

 Poems about War

In poetry, war is as ancient a theme as love and nature. In fact, the earliest poems, including Homer's *Iliad* and *Odyssey* and Virgil's *Aeneid,* have at their centers epic battles and struggles. These poems were created in metered verse so they could be remembered and passed down from one generation to the next. Portions of them would be recited at public gatherings and festivals, making them analogous to the war movies of today. Epic poems reflected the belief that war could be a noble and glorious endeavor, and they often glorified the heroes of the wars and battles they described. Even in the earliest of these poems, however, there is a sense of the futility and devastation that war brings with it; for example, in the *Iliad,* many of the Greeks laying siege to the city of Troy are sick of the war and want to go home. In the *Aeneid,* the scene where Aeneas witnesses the destruction of his native Troy by the Greeks, and by the gods aiding them, is one of the most moving in literature.

In modern times, poets have tended to concentrate on the horrors of war, no doubt in part because technology has allowed armies to do more damage more quickly than ever before. World War I, which saw the first widespread use of aircraft, poison gas, and machine guns in warfare, marked a turning point in war and in poetic responses to it. One of the best-known poems to come out of this war is "Dulce et Decorum Est" (p. 915), written toward the end of the war by Wilfred Owen, a soldier who was killed on the Western Front in 1918. The poem, which includes graphic images of war, ends with a bitterly ironic quotation that summarizes the mentality that fuels war: "It is sweet and fitting to die for one's country." Similarly, in William Butler Yeats's "An Irish Airman Foresees His Death," written at the same time as Owen's poem, the speaker expresses ambivalence about the war in which he is fighting and about the reasons why he is fighting it.

Of course, not all modern poems about war are poems of protest. For example, Walt Whitman's "Vigil Strange I Kept on the Field One Night" focuses not on the evils of war but on the loss of a beloved comrade. Robert Lowell's "For the Union Dead," written in 1959, is an elegy for Colonel Robert Gould Shaw, the leader of a regiment of African-American soldiers who fought and died for the Union Army during the Civil War. And "The Soldier," by Rupert Brooke (a contemporary of Wilfred Owen), celebrates the nobility of fighting for the sake of one's beloved country.

Although war poems tend to focus on death and destruction, in modern poems, the victims of war are not always soldiers. For example, Boris Slutsky's "How Did They Kill My Grandmother?" describes a World War II German assault on civilians—in this case, the Jews in a Russian village. In the post–World War II years, enemies (like victims) were not as clearly defined as they had been in the past. The war in Vietnam unfolded before the American people on their television screens, and as a result, many Americans questioned the war and its goals. This skepticism carried over into poems about the war, as seen in Denise Levertov's "What Were They Like?" (a call and response poem that asks questions about the people in Vietnam in an effort to heighten their humanity and diminish their identity as "the enemy") and in Yusef Komunyakaa's "Facing It," in which a Vietnam veteran visits the Vietnam War Memorial in Washington.

The post-Vietnam years have seen troops from various nations take part in war conflicts around the globe; Eliza Griswold writes of one such conflict in "Buying Rations in Kabul." Finally, Edwin Muir's "The Horses" is a bleak look at a post–nuclear war world, while Wislawa Szymborska's "The End and the Beginning" addresses the onerous job of cleaning up what is left behind in the aftermath of war.

RUPERT BROOKE (1887–1915)

The Soldier (1915)

If I should die, think only this of me;
  That there's some corner of a foreign field
That is forever England. There shall be
  In that rich earth a richer dust concealed;
A dust whom England bore, shaped, made aware,
  Gave, once, her flowers to love, her ways to roam,
A body of England's breathing English air,
  Washed by the rivers, blest by suns of home.

And think, this heart, all evil shed away,
  A pulse in the eternal mind, no less
    Gives somewhere back the thoughts by England given;
Her sights and sounds; dreams happy as her day;
  And laughter, learnt of friends; and gentleness,
    In hearts at peace, under an English heaven.

WILLIAM BUTLER YEATS (1865–1939)

An Irish Airman Foresees His Death (1919)

I know that I shall meet my fate
Somewhere among the clouds above;
Those that I fight I do not hate,
Those that I guard I do not love;
My country is Kiltartan Cross
My countrymen Kiltartan's poor,
No likely end could bring them loss
Or leave them happier than before.
Nor law, nor duty bade me fight,
Nor public men, nor cheering crowds,
A lonely impulse of delight
Drove to this tumult in the clouds;
I balanced all, brought all to mind,
The years to come seemed waste of breath,
A waste of breath the years behind
In balance with this life, this death.

ROBERT LOWELL (1917–1977)

For the Union Dead (1959)

"Relinquunt omnia servare rem publicam."°

The old South Boston Aquarium stands
in a Sahara of snow now. Its broken windows are boarded.
The bronze weathervane cod has lost half its scales.
The airy tanks are dry.

Once my nose crawled like a snail on the glass;
my hand tingled
to burst the bubbles
drifting from the noses of the cowed, compliant fish.

My hand draws back. I often sigh still
for the dark downward and vegetating kingdom
of the fish and reptile. One morning last March,
I pressed against the new barbed and galvanized

fence on the Boston Common. Behind their cage,
yellow dinosaur steamshovels were grunting
as they cropped up tons of mush and grass
to gouge their underworld garage.

Parking spaces luxuriate like civic
sandpiles in the heart of Boston.
A girdle of orange, Puritan-pumpkin colored girders
braces the tingling Statehouse,

shaking over the excavations, as it faces Colonel Shaw
and his bell-cheeked Negro infantry
on St. Gauden's shaking Civil War relief,
propped by a plant splint against the garage's earthquake.

Two months after marching through Boston,
half the regiment was dead;
at the dedication,
William James° could almost hear the bronze Negroes breathe.

Their monument sticks like a fishbone
in the city's throat.
Its Colonel is as lean
as a compass-needle.

Relinquunt omnia servare rem publicam: "They gave up everything to preserve the Republic" (Latin). A monument in Boston Common bears a similar form of this quotation. Designed by Augustus Saint-Gaudens, the monument is dedicated to Colonel Robert Gould Shaw and the African-American troops he commanded during a Civil War battle at Fort Wagner, South Carolina, on July 18, 1863.

William James: Harvard psychologist and philosopher (1842–1910), often called the father of modern psychology.

He has an angry wrenlike vigilance,
a greyhound's gentle tautness;
he seems to wince at pleasure,
and suffocate for privacy.

He is out of bounds now. He rejoices in man's lovely,
peculiar power to choose life and die—
when he leads his black soldiers to death,
he cannot bend his back.

On a thousand small town New England greens,
the old white churches hold their air
of sparse, sincere rebellion; frayed flags
quilt the graveyards of the Grand Army of the Republic.

The stone statues of the abstract Union Soldier
grow slimmer and younger each year—
wasp-waisted, they doze over muskets
and muse through their sideburns . . .

Shaw's father wanted no monument
except the ditch,
where his son's body was thrown
and lost with his "niggers."

The ditch is nearer.
There are no statues for the last war here;
on Boylston Street, a commercial photograph
shows Hiroshima boiling

over a Mosler Safe,° the "Rock of Ages"
that survived the blast. Space is nearer.
When I crouch to my television set,
the drained faces of Negro school-children rise like balloons.

Colonel Shaw
is riding on his bubble,
he waits
for the blessed break.

The Aquarium is gone. Everywhere,
giant finned cars nose forward like fish;
a savage servility
slides by on grease.

Mosler Safe: A brand of safe known for being especially strong.

BORIS SLUTSKY (1919–1986)

How Did They Kill My Grandmother?*

Translated by Elaine Feinstein

How did they kill my grandmother?
I'll tell you how they killed her.
One morning a tank rolled up to
a building where
the hundred and fifty Jews of our town who,
weightless
        from a year's starvation,
and white
        with the knowledge of death,
were gathered holding their bundles.
And the German polizei° were
herding the old people briskly;
and their tin mugs clanked as
the young men led them away
                        far away.

But my small grandmother
my seventy-year-old grandmother
began to curse and
scream at the Germans;
shouting that I was a soldier.
She yelled at them: My grandson
is off at the front fighting!
Don't you dare
touch me!
Listen, you
        can hear our guns!

Even as she went off, my grandmother
cried abuse,
        starting all over again
with her curses.
From every window then
Ivanovnas and Andreyevnas
Sidorovnas and Petrovnas
sobbed: You tell them, Polina
Matveyevna, keep it up!
They all yelled together:

---

*Publication date is not available.

polizei: Police.

"What can we do against
this enemy, the Hun?"
Which was why the Germans chose
to kill her inside the town.

A bullet struck her hair
and kicked her grey plait down.
My grandmother fell to the ground.
That is how she died there.

DENISE LEVERTOV (1923–1997)

What Were They Like? (1966)

1) Did the people of Viet Nam
use lanterns of stone?
2) Did they hold ceremonies
to reverence the opening of buds?
3) Were they inclined to rippling laughter?
4) Did they use bone and ivory,
jade and silver, for ornament?
5) Had they an epic poem?
6) Did they distinguish between speech and singing?

1) Sir, their light hearts turned to stone.
It is not remembered whether in gardens
stone lanterns illumined pleasant ways.
2) Perhaps they gathered once to delight in blossom,
but after the children were killed
there were no more buds.
3) Sir, laughter is bitter to the burned mouth.
4) A dream ago, perhaps. Ornament is for joy.
All the bones were charred.
5) It is not remembered. Remember,
most were peasants; their life
was in rice and bamboo.
When peaceful clouds were reflected in the paddies
and the water buffalo stepped surely along terraces,
maybe fathers told their sons old tales.
When bombs smashed the mirrors
there was time only to scream.
6) There is an echo yet, it is said,
of their speech which was like a song.
It is reported their singing resembled
the flight of moths in moonlight.
Who can say? It is silent now.

Source: ©Dan Getsug

See this poet's biography on p. 1223.

YUSEF KOMUNYAKAA (1947–)

Facing It (1988)

My black face fades,
hiding inside the black granite.
I said I wouldn't,
dammit: No tears.
I'm stone. I'm flesh.
My clouded reflection eyes me
like a bird of prey, the profile of night
slanted against morning. I turn
this way—the stone lets me go.
I turn that way—I'm inside
the Vietnam Veterans Memorial
again, depending on the light
to make a difference.
I go down the 58,022 names,
half-expecting to find
my own in letters like smoke.
I touch the name Andrew Johnson;
I see the booby trap's white flash.
Names shimmer on a woman's blouse
but when she walks away
the names stay on the wall.
Brushstrokes flash, a red bird's
wings cutting across my stare.
The sky. A plane in the sky.
A white vet's image floats
closer to me, then his pale eyes
look through mine. I'm a window.
He's lost his right arm
inside the stone. In the black mirror
a woman's trying to erase names:
No, she's brushing a boy's hair.

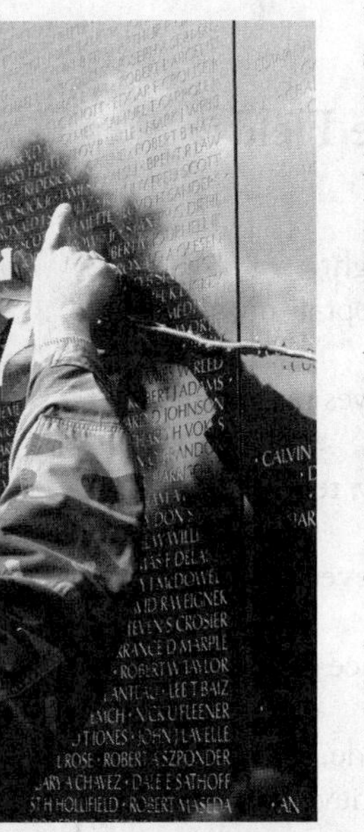

Hand tracing names of dead on the Vietnam War Memorial.
Source: ©AP Photo/Dennis Cook

ELIZA GRISWOLD

Buying Rations in Kabul

The Uzbek boys on Chicken Street
have never had enough to eat.
They stock from shelf to shining shelf
these G.I. meals, which boil themselves
in added water (bottled, please).

In twenty minutes, processed cheese
on jambalaya, followed by
a peanut-butter jamboree.

The boys, polite,
advise on which we might prefer—
beef teriyaki, turkey blight—
and thank us twice for bringing peace
as, meals in hand, we leave the store.
Of course they know that any peace
that must be kept by force
contains another name. It's war.

WALT WHITMAN (1819–1892)

Vigil Strange I Kept on the Field One Night (1865)

Vigil strange I kept on the field one night;
When you my son and my comrade dropt at my side that day,
One look I but gave which your dear eyes return'd with a look I shall never forget,
One touch of your hand to mine O boy, reach'd up as you lay on the ground,
Then onward I sped in the battle, the even-contested battle,
Till late in the night reliev'd to the place at last again I made my way,
Found you in death so cold dear comrade, found your body son of responding kisses (never again on earth responding),
Bared your face in the starlight, curious the scene, cool blew the moderate night-wind,
Long there and then in vigil I stood, dimly around me the battle-field spreading,
Vigil wondrous and vigil sweet there in the fragrant silent night,
But not a tear fell, not even a long-drawn sigh, long, long I gazed.
Then on the earth partially reclining sat by your side leaning my chin in my hands,
Passing sweet hours, immortal and mystic hours with you dearest comrade—not a tear, not a word.

Vigil of silence, love and death, vigil for you my
son and my soldier,
As onward silently stars aloft, eastward new ones
upward stole,
Vigil final for you brave boy, (I could not save
you, swift was your death,
I faithfully loved you and cared for you living,
I think we shall surely meet again,)
Till at latest lingering of the night, indeed just
as the dawn appear'd,
My comrade I wrapt in his blanket, envelop'd
well his form,
Folded the blanket well, tucking it carefully over
head and carefully under feet,
And there and then and bathed by the rising sun,
my son in his grave, in his rude-dug grave I deposited,
Ending my vigil strange with that, vigil of night
and battlefield dim,
Vigil for boy of responding kisses (never again
on earth responding),
Vigil for comrade swiftly slain, vigil I never
forget, how as day brighten'd,
I rose from the chill ground and folded my
soldier well in his blanket,
And buried him where he fell.

EDWIN MUIR (1887–1959)

The Horses (1925)

Barely a twelvemonth after
The seven days war that put the world to sleep,
Late in the evening the strange horses came.
By then we had made our covenant with silence,
But in the first few days it was so still
We listened to our breathing and were afraid.
On the second day
The radios failed; we turned the knobs, no answer.
On the third day a warship passed us, headed north,
Dead bodies piled on the deck. On the sixth day
A plane plunged over us into the sea. Thereafter
Nothing. The radios dumb;
And still they stand in corners of our kitchens,

And stand, perhaps, turned on, in a million rooms
All over the world. But now if they should speak,
If on a sudden they should speak again,
If on the stroke of noon a voice should speak,
We would not listen, we would not let it bring
That old bad world that swallowed its children quick
At one great gulp. We would not have it again.
Sometimes we think of the nations lying asleep,
Curled blindly in impenetrable sorrow,
And then the thought confounds us with its strangeness.
The tractors lie about our fields; at evening
They look like dank sea-monsters crouched and waiting.
We leave them where they are and let them rust:
"They'll molder away and be like other loam."
We make our oxen drag our rusty plows,
Long laid aside. We have gone back
Far past our fathers' land.
And then, that evening
Late in the summer the strange horses came.
We heard a distant tapping on the road,
A deepening drumming; it stopped, went on again
And at the corner changed to hollow thunder.
We saw the heads
Like a wild wave charging and were afraid.
We had sold our horses in our fathers' time
To buy new tractors. Now they were strange to us
As fabulous steeds set on an ancient shield
Or illustrations in a book of knights.
We did not dare go near them. Yet they waited,
Stubborn and shy, as if they had been sent
By an old command to find our whereabouts
And that long-lost archaic companionship.
In the first moment we had never a thought
That they were creatures to be owned and used.
Among them were some half a dozen colts
Dropped in some wilderness of the broken world,
Yet new as if they had come from their own Eden.
Since then they have pulled our plows and borne our loads,
But that free servitude still can pierce our hearts.
Our life is changed; their coming our beginning.

Source: ©WOJDA/FREE/Corbis Sygma

WISLAWA SZYMBORSKA (1923–)

The End and the Beginning (1993)

After every war
someone has to clean up.
Things won't
straighten themselves up, after all.

Someone has to push the rubble
to the side of the road,
so the corpse-filled wagons
can pass.

Someone has to get mired
in scum and ashes,
sofa springs,
splintered glass,
and bloody rags.

Someone has to drag in a girder
to prop up a wall,
Someone has to glaze a window,
rehang a door.

Photogenic it's not,
and takes years.
All the cameras have left
for another war.

We'll need the bridges back,
and new railway stations.
Sleeves will go ragged
from rolling them up.

Someone, broom in hand,
still recalls the way it was.

Someone else listens
and nods with unsevered head.
But already there are those nearby
starting to mill about
who will find it dull.

From out of the bushes
sometimes someone still unearths
rusted-out arguments
and carries them to the garbage pile.

Those who knew
what was going on here

must make way for
those who know little.
And less than little.
And finally as little as nothing.

In the grass that has overgrown
causes and effects,
someone must be stretched out
blade of grass in his mouth
gazing at the clouds.

Reading and Reacting: Poems about War

1. What is each speaker's attitude toward war? Does the speaker seem to be focusing on a particular war or on war in general?
2. What conventional images and figures of speech does each poem use to express its ideas about war?
3. Do any of the poems use unusual, unexpected, or shocking images or figures of speech?
4. How would you describe each poem's tone? For example, is the tone angry? Cynical? Sad? Disillusioned? Resigned?
5. What does each poem reveal about the speaker?
6. What is each poem's central theme?

Related Works: "Buffalo Soldiers" (p. 187), "The Things They Carried" (p. 473), "The Man He Killed" (p. 849), "Patterns" (p. 850), "The Death of the Ball Turret Gunner" (p. 931), "Naming of Parts" (p. 1190), *Nine Ten* (p. 1314)

WRITING SUGGESTIONS: Discovering Themes in Poetry

1. Compare any two poems in this chapter about parents, nature, love, or war.
2. Write an **explication** (see Chapter 3) of one of the poems in this chapter.
3. Write an essay in which you compare one of the poems in this chapter to a short story or play on the same general subject. (For possible topics, consult the Related Works list that follows each group of poems.)
4. Some poets write multiple poems on the same general subject. For example, Shakespeare wrote many love poems, and Robert Frost wrote a number of poems about nature. Choose two poems by a single poet that explore the same subject, and compare and contrast the themes of the two poems.
5. A number of poems in this book focus on the theme of poetry itself. Choose three poems on this theme, and write an essay that compares the poems' ideas about reading and writing poetry.

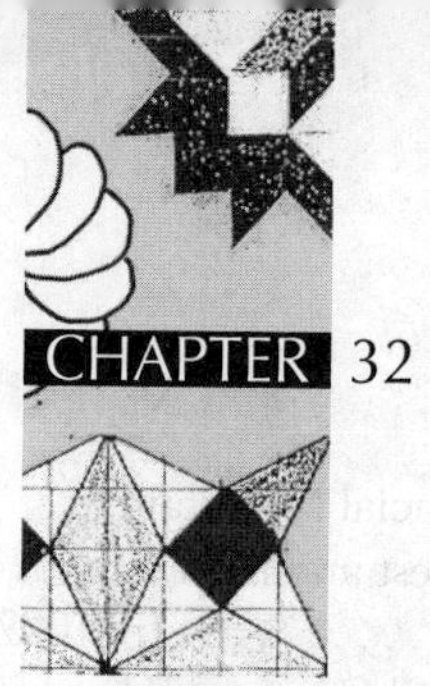

THE POETRY OF LANGSTON HUGHES: A CASEBOOK FOR READING, RESEARCH, AND WRITING

This chapter provides all the materials you will need to begin a research project about Langston Hughes. It includes sixteen poems by Hughes; questions to stimulate discussion and writing; a collection of source materials; a student paper that shows how one student, Ashley McIntyre, used the materials in this chapter as well as two outside sources in her research; and suggested topics for further research on Hughes.

Poems

Other poems by Hughes that appear elsewhere in this anthology are "Negro" (p. 842), "Harlem" (p. 924), and "Island" (p. 1015).

Source Materials

- Hughes, Langston. *From* "The Negro Artist and the Racial Mountain." *The Nation* 23 June 1926. Excerpts from Hughes's earliest and most famous poetic manifesto. . . . . (p. 1092)
- Hughes, Langston. "To Negro Writers." *American Writers' Congress*. Ed. Henry Hart. New York: International Publishers, 1935. A speech Hughes gave to the First American Writers' Congress in New York City in April 1935, quite different in tone from his 1926 manifesto. . . . . (p. 1094)
- Hughes, Langston. *From* "My Adventures as a Social Poet." *Phylon* Third Quarter, 1947. An excerpt from an essay in which Hughes considers the costs of his decision to deal frankly with social issues in his poetry. . . . . (p. 1096)
- Rampersad, Arnold. *From* "The Origins of Poetry in Langston Hughes." *The Southern Review* 21.3 (1985): 695–705. Excerpts from a critical essay that considers the development of Hughes as a major poet. . . . . (p. 1099)
- Beavers, Herman. *From* "Dead Rocks and Sleeping Men: Aurality in the Aesthetic of Langston Hughes." *Langston Hughes Review* 11.1 (1992): 1–5. Excerpts from a critical essay that discusses the importance of speaking and listening to Hughes's artistry. . . . . (p. 1104)
- Tracy, Steven C. *From* "'Midnight Ruffles of Cat-Gut Lace': The Boogie Poems of Langston Hughes." *College Language Association Journal* 32.1 (1988): 55–68. Excerpts from an article that examines Hughes's poetic use of boogie-woogie, an African-American musical form. . . . . (p. 1105)
- Ford, Karen Jackson. *From* "Do Right to Write Right: Langston Hughes's Aesthetics of Simplicity." *Twentieth Century Literature* 38.4 (1992): 436–56. Excerpts from an article that evaluates Hughes's commitment to "simple" poetics. . . . . (p. 1107)
- Hutchinson, George B. *From* "Langston Hughes and the 'Other' Whitman." In *The Continuing Presence of Walt Whitman: The Life after the Life*. Ed. Robert K. Martin. Iowa City: U of Iowa P, 1992. Excerpts from an essay that assesses the importance of Whitman's influence on Hughes. . . . . (p. 1109)

Each of these sources offers insights into the poems included in this Casebook. Three are Hughes's own words, one is largely biographical, one is a close reading of a particular poem, and others discuss Hughes's use of poetic devices and his influences. All were selected to help you to appreciate this poet as well as the themes and devices in his poetry. Other kinds of sources can also enrich your understanding of Hughes's accomplishments—for example, other poems by Hughes, biographical data about the writer, and works of literature by other writers dealing with similar themes. Several interesting Web sites on Hughes are listed below:

- *The Academy of American Poets*. <http://www.poets.org>. Search for Langston Hughes in the upper left search box to go to the Hughes page. A full site hosted by the Academy of American Poets, the Hughes page includes poems—some read aloud—and a link to the academy's online exhibit "Poets of the Harlem Renaissance and After," which includes Hughes.

- *Langston Hughes Honored*. <http://www.usps.com/news/2002/philatelic/sr02_004.htm>. This site, sponsored by the United States Postal Service, offers an interesting explanation of why the USPS chose to honor Hughes's centennial by putting his image on a postage stamp. The site includes a link to the government's other Black Heritage honorees from 1978 to 2002.
- *Langston Hughes*. <http://www.americaslibrary.gov/cgi-bin/page.cgi/aa/hughes>. In addition to containing a biography of Hughes, this site has a time line of events that took place during Hughes's lifetime.

In preparation for writing an essay on a topic of your choice, read the poems carefully. Then, consider the Reading and Reacting questions that follow them (pp. 1091–92) in light of what you have read. Use your responses to help you find a topic you can develop in a three- to six-page essay. When you write your paper, be sure to document any words or ideas that you borrow from your sources and to enclose words that are not your own in quotation marks. (For guidelines on evaluating literary criticism, see pp. 15–16; for guidelines on using source materials, see Chapters 6 and 7.)

A sample student paper, "The Rhythms of African-American Life: Langston Hughes and the Poetics of Blues and Jazz," which uses some of the sources included in this Casebook, begins on page 1112.

Source: ©AP Photo

LANGSTON HUGHES (1902–1967) was one of the best-known American writers of the twentieth century. As a member of the Harlem Renaissance in the 1920s, he helped establish a vital African-American literature. His earliest book of poetry, *The Weary Blues* (1926), established him as one of the most important poets of his generation. His first novel, *Not Without Laughter*, was published in 1930. Not only did Hughes deal honestly in this novel with the daily lives and struggles of African Americans, but he also wrote poems that owed much to African-American musical forms, such as jazz and blues. Art and politics were inseparable for Hughes, and he was active throughout his life in the struggle for racial and economic justice.

Hughes was born in Joplin, Missouri, in 1902, and during his early life, he experienced the racial and economic inequities that would become the focus of his writing and social activism. His father, James Hughes, had studied law, but he was not allowed to take the bar exam because he was African American, and eventually he left the United States to try his luck in Mexico. Hughes's mother, Carrie, refused to follow her husband, so the young Langston had little contact with his father until he was in his late teens. As a child, Hughes was a voracious reader. While attending Central High School in Cleveland, Ohio, he began to write poetry, with Carl Sandburg as one of his chief influences. Upon leaving high school, Hughes began the travels that would have such a great effect on his work. In 1920, he went to live with his father in Mexico City. On the way there, he wrote what was to become one of his best-known poems, "The Negro Speaks of Rivers." Father and son had little in common, so the trip was not successful on a personal level. (At one point, Hughes even considered suicide.) When he returned to the United States, he enrolled at Columbia University to study engineering, but his classes were of little interest to him, and he spent most of his time writing and absorbing the cultural life of New York's African-American community.

With the publication of his first book of poetry, *The Weary Blues,* in 1926, Hughes became a visible member of the Harlem Renaissance, a major literary movement of the twentieth century. Centered in the Harlem section of New York City, the movement represented the first great flowering of African-American literature and included writers such as James Weldon Johnson, Claude McKay, and Countee Culleen. This creative period ended with the onset of the Great Depression in the 1930s.

Although he would become arguably the best-known writer of the Harlem Renaissance, Hughes's work was not universally praised. In fact, many of the elements that have given his work its staying power—his use of African-American vernacular, his imitation of the forms of popular music, his concern for the economically disadvantaged—were controversial at the time. There were many who thought that African-American writing ought to deal primarily with uplifting stories and follow the conventions of white literature. These critics believed that Hughes's work was undercutting the advances African-Americans were achieving in both literary and social life.

Hughes's response to his critics was straightforward. "I sympathized deeply," he later said, "with those critics and those intellectuals, and I saw clearly the need for some of the kinds of books they wanted." He insisted, however, that not every book by an African-American could or should be about subjects that middle- or upper-class whites and blacks would find palatable: "I didn't know the upper-class Negroes well enough to write much about them. I knew only the people I had grown up with, and they weren't people whose shoes were always shined, who had been to Harvard, or who had heard of Bach. But they seemed to me good people, too."

In portraying these "good people," Hughes did not shy away from depicting the details of their difficult lives. His subjects are often poor and frequently face racism. Sometimes they are in trouble with the law, and they are typically less interested in intellectual discussion than in paying the rent. The poor had been portrayed before in poetry: T. S. Eliot's long poem *The Waste Land,* published in 1922, just four years before *The Weary Blues,* includes a particularly pointed exchange between two lower-class women. What distinguished Hughes's approach from Eliot's, apart from his direct style, was his sympathy for his subjects and his intimate familiarity with their living conditions.

In writing about lower-class African Americans, people who had never "heard of Bach," Hughes devised poetic forms that imitated the cadences of jazz and blues, the types of music with which they were familiar. Hughes found nothing wrong with Bach, but he was convinced that African-Americans had their own composers and performers. Nor was this simply a self-conscious attempt to find an appropriate poetic vehicle for his subject matter or to promote the art of African Americans; Hughes loved jazz and blues and nothing could have been more natural for him than to use their rhythms in his poetry. His later move into writing song lyrics was a natural transition.

In 1932, Hughes traveled to the Soviet Union and observed many aspects of the Soviet system that he felt were admirable. He was especially impressed by what he saw as the lack of racial injustice and economic inequality. He learned the Uzbek language while recuperating from an illness and began writing on a regular basis for Soviet newspapers, including *Izvestia*. He published a book devoted to impressions of the trip, *A Negro Looks at Soviet Central Asia* in 1934, and he also reflected on his experiences in newspaper columns for the *Chicago Defender*.

Hughes left the Soviet Union after a little more than a year, but he did not abandon his commitment to radical social change. Back in the United States, he settled for a time in California, where he devoted himself to a number of social causes. It would be a mistake, however, to suppose that Hughes was hostile to America. During World War II, when the United States was allied with the Soviet Union against Nazi Germany, Fascist Italy, and Imperial Japan, Hughes used his writing to support the American war effort even as he encouraged America to live up to its democratic ideals.

As part of his effort to depict the lives of average African Americans, Hughes invented a character, Jesse B. Semple, later known as Simple. Simple first appeared in newspaper columns that were so popular they were later anthologized in a series of books, beginning in 1950 with *Simple Speaks His Mind*. Here, Hughes uses a fictional narrator who talks with, and buys drinks for, his friend Semple. The popularity of the pieces derived in part from their humor and straightforward examination of racial issues and partly from Hughes's skillful use of African-American vernacular. Since his first publications, Hughes had included the actual speech of the black lower class in his work, and the "Simple" books brought this strategy to a wide audience.

During the cold war in the 1950s, his sympathetic comments on communism and the Soviet Union caused Hughes great political difficulties. His activities were monitored by the House Un-American Activities Committee (HUAC), and in 1953 he was called to testify before Senator Joseph McCarthy's Subcommittees on Subversive Activities. In his testimony to the committee, Hughes denied being a communist but explained why he felt communism appealed to some African Americans. There is some debate about Hughes's actual political views during this period. Commentators who maintain that Hughes had never been a communist also assume that his statements to the Committee were an accurate reflection of his political views. Others, however, are convinced that Hughes, afraid that the writing career he had worked so hard to establish would be destroyed, was downplaying the communist views he still held.

Despite the disruption to his career caused by the Committee's investigation, Hughes remained an important literary and political figure for the remainder of his life. In 1961, he published *Ask Your Mama,* a work that addressed many of the racial and cultural issues that would be so important in the 1960s. He also traveled widely, often as an official representative of the United States. When Hughes died in 1967, he was completing work on his last volume of poetry, *The Panther and the Lash*.

Today, Hughes is remembered chiefly as a poet, but he made important contributions to virtually every genre of writing. He was an accomplished dramatist who also founded several theaters. He wrote novels, short stories, newspaper articles, song lyrics, translations, and fiction for children. In addition to his work as a writer, Hughes edited numerous books and helped encourage and promote the work of younger African-American writers. In the years since his death, his reputation has become solidly established. Plain-spoken and highly rhythmic, his poetry continues to appeal to new readers and to provide an example of the ways in which social commitment and literary art can be combined.

The Negro Speaks of Rivers (1921)

I've known rivers:
I've known rivers ancient as the world and old as the flow of
human blood in human veins.

My soul has grown deep like the rivers.

I bathed in the Euphrates° when dawns were young.
I built my hut near the Congo° and it lulled me to sleep.
I looked upon the Nile and raised the pyramids above it.
I heard the singing of the Mississippi when Abe Lincoln went
down to New Orleans, and I've seen its muddy bosom turn
all golden in the sunset.

I've known rivers:
Ancient, dusky rivers.

My soul has grown deep like the rivers.

Mother to Son (1922)

Well, son, I'll tell you:
Life for me ain't been no crystal stair.
It's had tacks in it,
And splinters,
And boards torn up,
And places with no carpet on the floor—
Bare.
But all the time
I'se been a-climbin' on,
And reachin' landin's,
And turnin' corners,
And sometimes goin' in the dark
Where there ain't been no light.
So boy, don't you turn back.
Don't you set down on the steps

Euphrates: Major river of southwest Asia; with the Tigris, the Euphrates forms a valley sometimes referred to as the "cradle of civilization."
Congo: River in equatorial Africa, the continent's second longest.

Cause you finds it's kinder hard.
Don't you fall now—
For I'se still goin', honey,
I'se still climbin',
And life for me ain't been no crystal stair.

Dream Variations (1924)

To fling my arms wide
In some place of the sun,
To whirl and to dance
Till the white day is done.
Then rest at cool evening
Beneath a tall tree
While night comes on gently,
    Dark like me—
That is my dream!

To fling my arms wide
In the face of the sun,
Dance! Whirl! Whirl!
Till the quick day is done.
Rest at pale evening . . .
A tall, slim tree . . .
Night coming tenderly
    Black like me.

The Weary Blues (1926)

Droning a drowsy syncopated tune,
Rocking back and forth to a mellow croon,
    I heard a Negro play.
Down on Lenox Avenue° the other night
By the pale dull pallor of an old gas light
    He did a lazy sway . . .
    He did a lazy sway . . .
To the tune o' those Weary Blues.
With his ebony hands on each ivory key
He made that poor piano moan with melody.
    O Blues!
Swaying to and fro on his rickety stool
He played that sad raggy tune like a musical fool.
    Sweet Blues!
Coming from a black man's soul.

Lenox Avenue: Street in Harlem noted for nightlife and music during the 1920s.

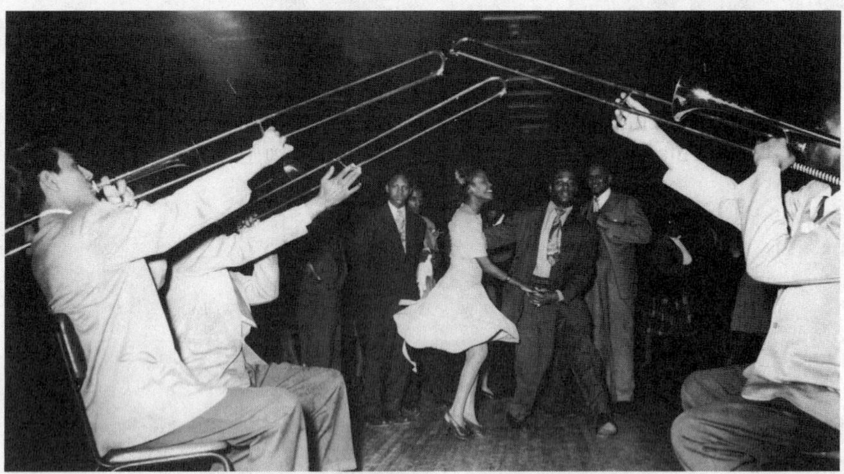

Dancers and musicians at the Savoy Ballroom in Harlem, 1947.
Source: ©Bettmann/Corbis

O Blues!
In a deep song voice with a melancholy tone
I heard that Negro sing, that old piano moan—
"Ain't got nobody in all this world,
Ain't got nobody but ma self.
I's gwine to quit ma frownin'
And put ma troubles on the shelf."
Thump, thump, thump, went his foot on the floor.
He played a few chords then he sang some more—
"I got the Weary Blues
And I can't be satisfied,
Got the Weary Blues
And can't be satisfied—
I ain't happy no mo'
And I wish that I had died."
And far into the night he crooned that tune.
The stars went out and so did the moon.
The singer stopped playing and went to bed
While the Weary Blues echoed through his head.
He slept like a rock or a man that's dead.

I, Too (1925)

I, too, sing America.

I am the darker brother.
They send me to eat in the kitchen
When company comes,

But I laugh,
And eat well,
And grow strong.

Tomorrow,
I'll be at the table
When company comes.
Nobody'll dare
Say to me,
"Eat in the kitchen,"
Then.

Besides,
They'll see how beautiful I am
And be ashamed—

I too, am America.

Song for a Dark Girl (1927)

Way Down South in Dixie
        (Break the heart of me)
They hung my black young lover
        To a cross roads tree.

Way Down South in Dixie
        (Bruised body high in air)
I asked the white Lord Jesus
        What was the use of prayer.

Way down South in Dixie
        (Break the heart of me)
Love is a naked shadow
        On a gnarled and naked tree.

Ballad of the Landlord (1940)

Landlord, landlord,
My roof has sprung a leak.
Don't you 'member I told you about it
Way last week?

Landlord, landlord,
These steps is broken down.
When you come up yourself
It's a wonder you don't fall down.

Ten Bucks you say I owe you?
Ten Bucks you say is due?

An exposed wall in a tenement like the one referred to in "Ballad of a Landlord."
Source: ©Masaaki Toyoura/Photonica/Getty Images

Well, that's Ten Bucks more'n I'll pay you
Till you fix this house up new.

What? You gonna get eviction orders?
You gonna cut off my heat?
You gonna take my furniture and
Throw it in the street?

Um-huh! You talking high and mighty.
Talk on—till you get through.
You ain't gonna be able to say a word
If I land my fist on you.

Police! Police!
Come and get this man!
He's trying to ruin the government
And overturn the land!

Copper's whistle!
Patrol bell!
Arrest.

Precinct Station.

Iron cell.
Headlines in press:

MAN THREATENS LANDLORD

TENANT HELD NO BAIL

JUDGE GIVES NEGRO 90 DAYS IN COUNTY JAIL

Theme for English B (1949)

The instructor said,

Go home and write
a page tonight.
And let that page come out of you—
Then, it will be true.

I wonder if it's that simple?
I am twenty-two, colored, born in Winston-Salem.
I went to school there, then Durham, then here
to this college on the hill above Harlem.
I am the only colored student in my class.
The steps from the hill lead down into Harlem,
through a park, then I cross St. Nicholas,

Eighth Avenue, Seventh, and I come to the Y,
the Harlem Branch Y, where I take the elevator
up to my room, sit down and write this page:

It's not easy to know what is true for you or me
at twenty-two, my age. But I guess I'm what
I feel and see and hear, Harlem, I hear you:
hear you, hear me—we two—you, me, talk on this page.
(I hear New York, too) Me—who?
Well, I like to eat, sleep, drink, and be in love.
I like to work, read, learn, and understand life.
I like a pipe for a Christmas present,
or records—Bessie,° bop,° or Bach.
I guess being colored doesn't make me *not* like
the same things other folks like who are other races.
So will my page be colored that I write?
Being me, it will not be white.
But it will be
a part of you, instructor.
You are white—
yet a part of me, as I am a part of you.
That's American.
Sometimes perhaps you don't want to be a part of me.
Nor do I often want to be a part of you.
But we are, that's true!
As I learn from you,
I guess you learn from me—
although you're older—and white—
and somewhat more free.

This is my page for English B.

Dream Boogie (1951)

Good morning, daddy!
Ain't you heard
The boogie-woogie° rumble
Of a dream deferred?

Bessie: Bessie Smith (1894–1937), blues singer.
bop: Short for "bebop," a jazz style developed in the early 1940s by Charlie Parker, Dizzy Gillespie, and others.
boogie-woogie: A popular black musical style with variants in both blues and jazz; more specifically, a vigorous piano style marked by heavy and repeated bass figures.

Listen closely:
You'll hear their feet
Beating out and beating out a—

You think
It's a happy beat?

Listen to it closely:
Ain't you heard
something underneath
like a—

What did I say?

Sure,
I'm happy!
Take it away!

Hey, pop!
Re-bop!
Mop!

Y-e-a-h!

Sixteenth Street Baptist Church, Birmingham, Alabama; site of the September 15, 1963 firebombing.

Source: ©Kevin Fleming/Corbis

Birmingham Sunday (September 15, 1963)° (1967)

Four little girls
Who went to Sunday School that day
And never came back home at all
But left instead
Their blood upon the wall
With spattered flesh
And bloodied Sunday dresses
Torn to shreds by dynamite
That China made aeons ago—
Did not know
That what China made
Before China was ever Red at all
Would redden with their blood
This Birmingham-on-Sunday wall.

September 15, 1963: On this date, only weeks after Martin Luther King Jr.'s historic March on Washington, four young African-American girls were killed at their Sunday school in Birmingham, Alabama, by a bomb, likely in response to recent civil rights activities in the area.

Four tiny girls
Who left their blood upon that wall,
In little graves today await
The dynamite that might ignite
The fuse of centuries of Dragon Kings°
Whose tomorrow sings a hymn
The missionaries never taught Chinese
In Christian Sunday School
To implement the Golden Rule.
Four little girls
Might be awakened someday soon
By songs upon the breeze
As yet unfelt among magnolia trees.

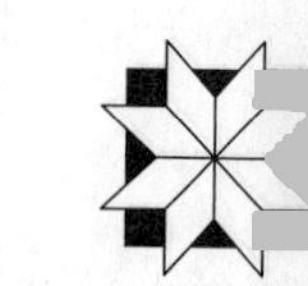

Photos taken in 1963 of the four girls killed in the bombing of the Sixteenth Street Baptist Church (clockwise from top left: Addie Mae Collins, 14; Cynthia Wesley, 14; Carole Robertson, 14; and Denise McNair, 11).
Source: ©AP Photo

Dragon Kings: In Chinese myth and lore, the dragon is a beneficent force that dispenses blessings in both the natural and supernatural worlds. Eventually, the dragon became a symbol of imperial China. The dragon has also been used in the mythology of white supremacist groups like the Ku Klux Klan.

Old Walt (1954)

Old Walt Whitman
Went finding and seeking,
Finding less than sought
Seeking more than found,
Every detail minding
Of the seeking or the finding.

Pleasured equally
In seeking as in finding,
Each detail minding,
Old Walt went seeking
And finding.

Genius Child (1947)

This is a song for the genius child.
Sing it softly, for the song is wild.
Sing it softly as ever you can—
Lest the song get out of hand.

Nobody loves a genius child.

Can you love an eagle,
Tame or wild?

Wild or tame,
Can you love a monster
Of a frightening name?

Nobody loves a genius child.

Kill him—and let his soul run wild!

Lenox Avenue: Midnight (1926)

The rhythm of life
Is a jazz rhythm,
Honey.
The gods are laughing at us.

The broken heart of love,
The weary, weary heart of pain,—
  Overtones,
  Undertones,
To the rumble of street cars,
To the swish of rain.

Lenox Avenue,
Honey.
Midnight,
And the gods are laughing at us.

Un-American Investigators (1953)

The committee's fat,
Smug, almost secure
Co-religionists
Shiver with delight
In warm manure
As those investigated—
Too brave to name a name—
Have pseudonyms revealed
In Gentile game
  Of who,
  Born Jew,
  Is who?
Is not your name Lipshitz?
  Yes.
Did you not change it
For subversive purposes?
  No.

Langston Hughes testifying before the House Un-American Activities Committee in Washington, D.C., in March of 1953.
Source: ©AP Photo

For nefarious gain?
    Not so.
Are you sure?
The committee shivers
With delight in
Its manure.

Dinner Guest: Me (1965)

I know I am
The Negro Problem
Being wined and dined,
Answering the usual questions

That come to white mind
Which seeks demurely
To probe in polite way
The why and wherewithal
Of darkness U.S.A.—
Wondering how things got this way
In current democratic night,
Murmuring gently
Over *fraises du bois*,
"I'm so ashamed of being white."

The lobster is delicious,
The wine divine,
And center of attention
At the damask table, mine.
To be a Problem on
Park Avenue at eight
Is not so bad.
Solutions to the Problem,
Of course, wait.

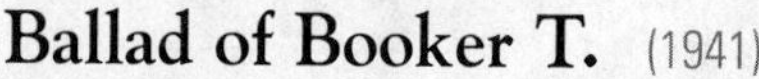

Ballad of Booker T. (1941)

Booker T.
Was a practical man.
He said, Till the soil
And learn from the land.
Let down your bucket
Where you are.
Your fate is here
And not afar.
To help yourself
And your fellow man,
Train your head,
Your heart, and your hand.
For smartness alone's
Surely not meet —
If you haven't at the same time
Got something to eat.
Thus at Tuskegee
He built a school
With book-learning there.
And the workman's tool.

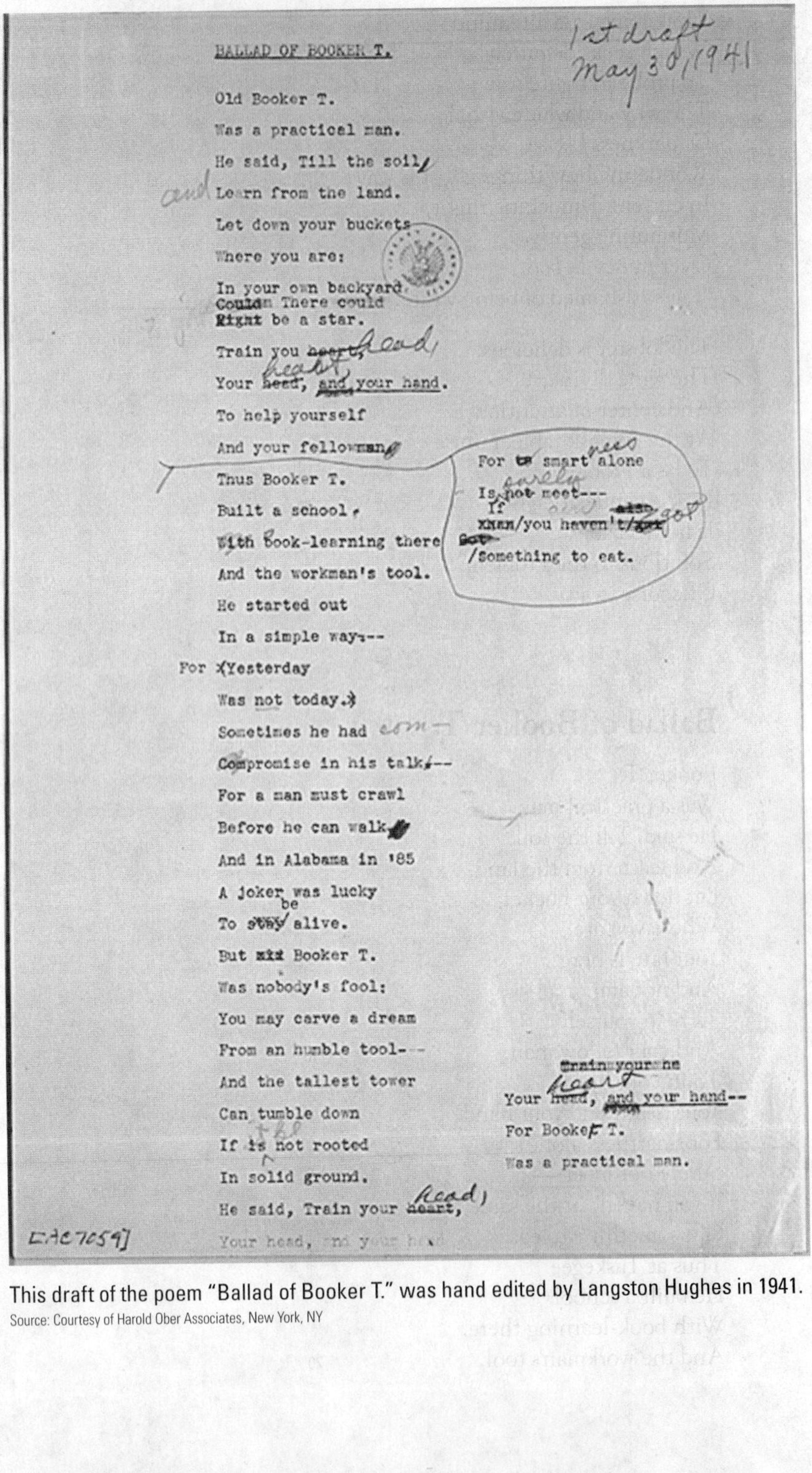

1st draft
May 30, 1941

BALLAD OF BOOKER T.

Old Booker T.
Was a practical man.
He said, Till the soil,
and Learn from the land.
Let down your buckets
Where you are:
In your own backyard
~~Could~~ There could
~~Might~~ be a star.
Train you ~~heart~~ head,
Your ~~head~~ heart, and your hand.
To help yourself
And your fellowman.

For ~~to~~ smart ness alone
Is ~~not~~ surely meet---
If ~~Xman~~/you haven't/~~got~~ got
~~Got~~/Something to eat.

Thus Booker T.
Built a school,
With book-learning there
And the workman's tool.
He started out
In a simple way--
For (Yesterday
Was not today.)
Sometimes he had com-
Compromise in his talk---
For a man must crawl
Before he can walk.
And in Alabama in '85
A joker was lucky
To ~~stay~~ be alive.
But ~~xix~~ Booker T.
Was nobody's fool:
You may carve a dream
From an humble tool---
And the tallest tower
Can tumble down
If ~~is~~ the not rooted
In solid ground.
He said, Train your ~~heart~~ head,
Your head, and your hand

~~Train your he~~
Your ~~head~~ heart, and your hand--
For Booker T.
Was a practical man.

[AC7059]

This draft of the poem "Ballad of Booker T." was hand edited by Langston Hughes in 1941.

Source: Courtesy of Harold Ober Associates, New York, NY

He started out
In a simple way —
For yesterday
Was not today.
Sometimes he had
Compromise in his talk—
For a man must crawl
Before he can walk —
And in Alabama in '85
A joker was lucky
To be alive.
But Booker T.
Was nobody's fool;
You may carve a dream
With an humble tool.
The tallest tower
Can tumble down
If it be not rooted
In solid ground,
So, being a far-seeing
Practical man,
He said, Train your head,
Your heart, and your hand.
Your fate is here
And not afar,
So let down your bucket
Where you are.

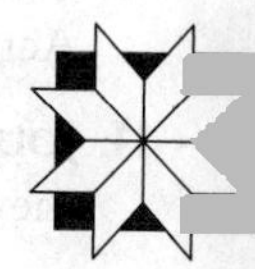

Reading and Reacting

1. How does Hughes use music and musical allusions? Are the poems themselves meant to be musical?
2. Which poems are poems of protest? Does Hughes seem to place his social or political goals above literary concerns?
3. How do historical and geographic allusions contribute to the power of "The Negro Speaks of Rivers"?
4. Is the question of identity (especially racial identity) handled differently in "The Negro Speaks of Rivers" and "Theme for English B"? Explain.
5. How would you characterize Hughes's attitude toward America in "Theme for English B" and "I, Too"? Do you think these poems are patriotic? Why or why not?
6. Hughes is often celebrated for his ability to express complex human dilemmas in accessible language and forms. Does he do this successfully in "Harlem" (p. 924)? Explain.
7. In the poem "Birmingham Sunday," why does Hughes include statements about Chinese mythology and history?

8. Is the "dream" in "Harlem" (p. 924) the same as the dream in "Dream Boogie"? Do you think the poems were meant to be read side by side? Do they shed light on each other? Do they represent different approaches to a similar problem?

9. In which poems do you think the first-person voice is autobiographical? In which poems do you think Hughes is creating a speaker?

10. What do you think Hughes expects of readers of his poetry? Reflection? A change of heart? Action? Something else?

11. **JOURNAL ENTRY** Are Langston Hughes's poems relevant only to African Americans, or do they also have relevance for other Americans—and even for readers in other countries?

12. **CRITICAL PERSPECTIVE** In his essay "The Negro Artist and the Racial Mountain" below, Hughes asserts his respect for the "common people," those he admires for their lack of self-importance:

> But then there are the low-down folks, the so-called common element, and they are the majority—may the Lord be praised! The people who have their nip of gin on Saturday nights are not too important to themselves or the community, or too well fed, or too learned to watch the lazy world go round. They live on Seventh Street in Washington or State Street in Chicago and they do not particularly care whether they are like white folks or anybody else. . . . They furnish a wealth of colorful, distinctive material for any artist because they still hold their own individuality in the face of American standardizations.

How does Hughes depict the "common people" in his poetry? What are their concerns? How have America's "standardizations" attempted to shape and change the common people, and what has been the result of those attempts?

Related Works: "Big Black Good Man" (p. 374), "A Worn Path" (p. 568), "The Unknown Citizen" (p. 864), "Ballad of Birmingham" (p. 869), "We Real Cool" (p. 896), "Sadie and Maud" (p. 957), "Photograph of My Father in His Twenty-Second Year" (p. 1042), "For the Union Dead" (p. 1063), *Fences* (p. 1902)

LANGSTON HUGHES

from The Negro Artist and the Racial Mountain

One of the most promising of the young Negro poets said to me once, "I want to be a poet—not a Negro poet," meaning, I believe, "I want to write like a white poet": meaning subconsciously, "I would like to be a white poet," meaning behind that, "I would like to be white." And I was sorry the young man said that, for no great poet has ever been afraid of being himself. And I doubted then that, with his desire to run away spiritually from his race, this boy would ever be a great poet. But this is the mountain standing in the way of any true Negro art in America—this urge within the race toward whiteness, the desire to pour racial individuality into the mold of American standardization, and to be as little Negro and as much American as possible.

But let us look at the immediate background of this young poet. His family is of what I suppose one would call the Negro middle class: people who are by no means rich yet never uncomfortable nor hungry—smug, contented, respectable folk, members of the Baptist church. The father goes to work every morning. He is a chief steward at a large white club. The mother sometimes does fancy sewing or supervises parties for the rich families of the town. The children go to a mixed school. In the home they read white papers and magazines. And the mother often says, "Don't be like niggers" when the children are bad. A frequent phrase from the father is, "Look how well a white man does things." And so the word white comes to be unconsciously a symbol of all the virtues. It holds for the children beauty, morality, and money. The whisper of "I want to be white" runs silently through their minds. This young poet's home is, I believe, a fairly typical home of the colored middle class. One sees immediately how difficult it would be for an artist born in such a home to interest himself in interpreting the beauty of his own people. He is never taught to see that beauty. He is taught rather not to see it, or if he does, to be ashamed of it when it is not according to Caucasian patterns.

For racial culture the home of a self-styled "high-class" Negro has nothing better to offer. Instead there will perhaps be more aping of things white than in a less cultured or less wealthy home. The father is perhaps a doctor, lawyer, landowner, or politician. The mother may be a social worker, or a teacher, or she may do nothing and have a maid. Father is often dark but he has usually married the lightest woman he could find. The family attend a fashionable church where few really colored faces are to be found. And they themselves draw a color line. In the North they go to white theaters and white movies. And in the South they have at least two cars and a house "like white folks." Nordic manners, Nordic faces, Nordic hair, Nordic art (if any), and an Episcopal heaven. A very high mountain indeed for the would-be racial artist to climb in order to discover himself and his people.

But then there are the low-down folks, the so-called common element, and they are the majority—may the Lord be praised! The people who have their nip of gin on Saturday nights are not too important to themselves or the community, or too well fed, or too learned to watch the lazy world go round. They live on Seventh Street in Washington or State Street in Chicago and they do not particularly care whether they are like white folks or anybody else. Their joy runs, bang! into ecstasy. Their religion soars to a shout. Work maybe a little today, rest a little tomorrow. Play awhile. Sing awhile. O, let's dance! These common people are not afraid of spirituals, as for a long time their more intellectual brethren were, and jazz is their child. They furnish a wealth of colorful, distinctive material for any artist because they still hold their own individuality in the face of American standardizations. And perhaps these common people will give to the world its truly great Negro artist, the one who is not afraid to be himself. Whereas the better-class Negro would tell the artist what to do, the people at least let him alone when he does appear. And they are not ashamed of him—if they know he exists at all. And they accept what beauty is their own without question.

Certainly there is, for the American Negro artist who can escape the restrictions the more advanced among his own group would put upon him, a great field

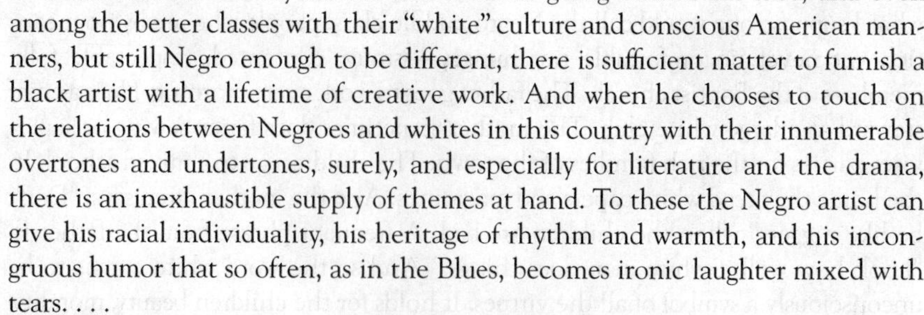

of unused material ready for his art. Without going outside his race, and even among the better classes with their "white" culture and conscious American manners, but still Negro enough to be different, there is sufficient matter to furnish a black artist with a lifetime of creative work. And when he chooses to touch on the relations between Negroes and whites in this country with their innumerable overtones and undertones, surely, and especially for literature and the drama, there is an inexhaustible supply of themes at hand. To these the Negro artist can give his racial individuality, his heritage of rhythm and warmth, and his incongruous humor that so often, as in the Blues, becomes ironic laughter mixed with tears. . . .

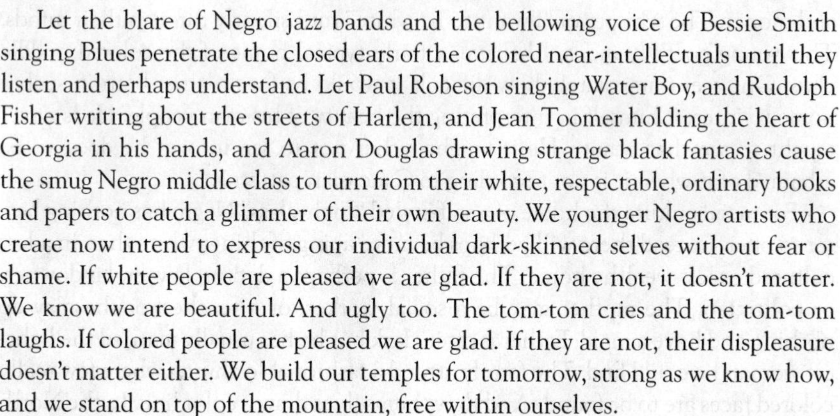
Let the blare of Negro jazz bands and the bellowing voice of Bessie Smith singing Blues penetrate the closed ears of the colored near-intellectuals until they listen and perhaps understand. Let Paul Robeson singing Water Boy, and Rudolph Fisher writing about the streets of Harlem, and Jean Toomer holding the heart of Georgia in his hands, and Aaron Douglas drawing strange black fantasies cause the smug Negro middle class to turn from their white, respectable, ordinary books and papers to catch a glimmer of their own beauty. We younger Negro artists who create now intend to express our individual dark-skinned selves without fear or shame. If white people are pleased we are glad. If they are not, it doesn't matter. We know we are beautiful. And ugly too. The tom-tom cries and the tom-tom laughs. If colored people are pleased we are glad. If they are not, their displeasure doesn't matter either. We build our temples for tomorrow, strong as we know how, and we stand on top of the mountain, free within ourselves.

LANGSTON HUGHES

To Negro Writers

There are certain practical things American Negro writers can do through their work.

We can reveal to the Negro masses, from which we come, our potential power to transform the now ugly face of the Southland into a region of peace and plenty.

We can reveal to the white masses those Negro qualities which go beyond the mere ability to laugh and sing and dance and make music, and which are a part of the useful heritage that we place at the disposal of a future free America.

Negro writers can seek to unite blacks and whites in our country, not on the nebulous basis of an inter-racial meeting, or the shifting sands of religious brotherhood, but on the *solid* ground of the daily working-class struggle to wipe out, now and forever, all the old inequalities of the past.

Furthermore, by way of exposure, Negro writers can reveal in their novels, stories, poems, and articles:

The lovely grinning face of Philanthropy—which gives a million dollars to a Jim Crow school, but not one job to a graduate of that school; which builds a Negro hospital with second-rate equipment, then commands black patients and student-doctors to go there whether they will or no; or which, out of the kindness of its heart, erects yet another separate, segregated, shut-off, Jim Crow Y.M.C.A.

Negro writers can expose those white labor leaders who keep their unions closed against Negro workers and prevent the betterment of all workers.

We can expose, too, the sick-sweet smile of organized religion—which lies about what it doesn't know, and about what it *does* know. And the half-voodoo, half-clown, face of revivalism, dulling the mind with the clap of its empty hands.

Expose, also, the false leadership that besets the Negro people—bought and paid for leadership, owned by capital, afraid to open its mouth except in the old conciliatory way so advantageous to the exploiters.

And all the economic roots of race hatred and race fear.

And the Contentment Tradition of the O-lovely-Negroes school of American fiction, which makes an ignorant black face and a Carolina head filled with superstition, appear more desirable than a crown of gold; the jazz-band; and the O-so-gay writers who make of the Negro's poverty and misery a dusky funny paper.

And expose war. And the old My-Country-'Tis-of-Thee lie. And the colored American Legion posts strutting around talking about the privilege of dying for the nobel Red, White and Blue, when they aren't even permitted the privilege of living for it. Or voting for it in Texas. Or working for it in the diplomatic service. Or even rising, like every other good little boy, from the log cabin to the White House.

White House is right!

Dear colored American Legion, you can swing from a lynching tree, uniform and all, with pleasure—and nobody'll fight for you. Don't you know that? Nobody even salutes you down South, dead or alive, medals or no medals, chevrons° or not, no matter how many wars you've fought in.

Let Negro writers write about the irony and pathos of the *colored* American Legion.

"*Salute*, Mr. *White Man!*"

"Salute, hell! . . . You're a nigger."

Or would you rather write about the moon?

Sure, the moon still shines over Harlem. Shines over Scottsboro. Shines over Birmingham, too, I reckon. Shines over Cordie Cheek's grave, down South.

Write about the moon if you want to. Go ahead. This is a free country.

But there are certain very practical things American Negro writers can do. And must do. There's a song that says, "the time ain't long." That song is right. Something has got to change in America—and change soon. We must help that change to come.

The moon's still shining as poetically as ever, but all the stars on the flag are dull. (And the stripes, too.)

We want a new and better America, where there won't be any poor, where there won't be any more Jim Crow, where there won't be any lynchings, where

chevrons: Stripes on a military uniform denoting rank.

there won't be any munition makers, where we won't need philanthropy, nor charity, nor the New Deal, nor Home Relief.

We want an America that will be ours, a world that will be ours—we Negro workers and white workers! Black writers and white! We'll make that world!

LANGSTON HUGHES

from My Adventures as a Social Poet

Some of my earliest poems were social poems in that they were about people's problems—whole groups of people's problems—rather than my own personal difficulties. Sometimes, though, certain aspects of my personal problems happened to be also common to many other people. And certainly, racially speaking, my own problems of adjustment to American life were the same as those of millions of other segregated Negroes. The moon belongs to everybody, but not this American earth of ours. That is perhaps why poems about the moon perturb no one, but poems about color and poverty do perturb many citizens. Social forces pull backwards or forwards, right or left, and social poems get caught in the pulling and hauling. Sometimes the poet himself gets pulled and hauled—even hauled off to jail. . . .

My adventures as a social poet are mild indeed compared to the body-breaking, soul-searing experiences of poets in the recent Fascist countries or of the resistance poets of the Nazi-invaded lands during the war. For that reason, I can use so light a word as "adventure" in regard to my own skirmishes with reaction and censorship.

My adventures as a social poet began in a colored church in Atlantic City shortly after my first book, *The Weary Blues*, was published in 1926. I had been invited to come down to the shore from Lincoln University where I was a student, to give a program of my poems in the church. During the course of my program I read several of my poems in the form of the Negro folk songs, including some blues poems about hard luck and hard work. As I read I noticed a deacon approach the pulpit with a note which he placed on the rostrum beside me, but I did not stop to open the note until I had finished and had acknowledged the applause of a cordial audience. The note read, "Do not read any more blues in my pulpit." It was signed by the minister. That was my first experience with censorship.

The kind and generous woman who sponsored my writing for a few years after my college days did not come to the point quite so directly as did the minister who disliked blues. Perhaps, had it not been in the midst of the great depression of the late '20's and '30's, the kind of poems that I am afraid helped to end her patronage might not have been written. But it was impossible for me to travel from hungry Harlem to the lovely homes on Park Avenue without feeling in my soul the great gulf between the very poor and the very rich in our society. In those days, on the way to visit this kind lady I would see the homeless sleeping in subways and the hungry begging in doorways on sleet-stung winter days. It was then that I wrote a poem called "Advertisement for the Waldorf-Astoria," satirizing the slick-paper magazine advertisements of the opening of that deluxe hotel. Also I wrote:

PARK BENCH

I live on a park bench,
You, Park Avenue.
Hell of a distance
Between us two.
I beg a dime for dinner—
You got a butler and maid.
But I'm wakin' up!
Say, ain't you afraid

That I might, just maybe,
In a year or two,
Move on over
To Park Avenue?

In a little while I did not have a patron any more.

But that year I won a prize, the Harmon Gold Award for Literature, which consisted of a medal and four hundred dollars. With the four hundred dollars I went to Haiti. On the way I stopped in Cuba and I was cordially received by the writers and artists. I had written poems about the exploitation of Cuba by the sugar barons and I had translated many poems of Nicolás Guillén such as:

CANE

Negro
In the cane fields.
White man
Above the cane fields
Earth
Beneath the cane fields.
Blood
That flows from us.

This was during the days of the dictatorial Machado regime. Perhaps someone called his attention to these poems and translations because, when I came back from Haiti weeks later, I was not allowed to land in Cuba, but was detained by the immigration authorities at Santiago and put on an island until the American consul came, after three days, to get me off with the provision that I cross the country to Havana and leave Cuban soil at once.

That was my first time being put out of any place. But since that time I have been put out of or barred from quite a number of places, all because of my poetry—not the roses and moonlight poems (which I write, too) but because of poems about poverty, oppression, and segregation. Nine Negro boys in Alabama were on trial for their lives when I got back from Cuba and Haiti. The famous Scottsboro "rape" case was in full session. I visited those boys in the death house at Kilby Prison, and I wrote many poems about them. One of these poems was:

CHRIST IN ALABAMA

Christ is a Nigger,
Beaten and black—
O, bare your back.

Mary is His Mother—
Mammy of the South,
Silence your mouth.
God's His Father—
White Master above,
Grant us your love.

Most holy bastard
Of the bleeding mouth:
Nigger Christ
On the cross of the South.

Contempo, a publication of some of the students at the University of North Carolina, published the poem on its front page on the very day that I was being presented in a program of my poems at the University in Chapel Hill. That evening there were police outside the building in which I spoke, and in the air the rising tension of race that is peculiar to the South. It had been rumored that some of the local citizenry were saying that I should be run out of town, and that one of the sheriffs agreed, saying, "Sure, he ought to be run out! It's bad enough to call Christ a *bastard*. But when he calls him a *nigger*, he's gone too far!"

The next morning a third of my fee was missing when I was handed my check. One of the departments of the university jointly sponsoring my program had refused to come through with its portion of the money. Nevertheless, I remember with pleasure the courtesy and kindness of many of the students and faculty at Chapel Hill and their lack of agreement with the anti-Negro elements of the town. There I began to learn at the University of North Carolina how hard it is to be a white liberal in the South.

It was not until I had been to Russia and around the world as a writer and journalist that censorship and opposition to my poems reached the point of completely preventing me from appearing in public programs on a few occasions. It happened first in Los Angeles shortly after my return from the Soviet Union. I was to have been one of several speakers on a memorial program to be held at the colored branch Y.M.C.A. for a young Negro journalist of the community. At the behest of white higher-ups, no doubt, some reactionary Negro politicians informed the Negro Y.M.C.A. that I was a Communist. The secretary of the Negro Branch Y then informed the committee of young people in charge of the memorial that they could have their program only if I did not appear.

I have never been a Communist, but I soon learned that anyone visiting the Soviet Union and speaking with favor of it upon returning is liable to be so labeled. Indeed when Mrs. Roosevelt, Walter White, and so Christian a lady as Mrs. Bethune who has never been in Moscow, are so labeled, I should hardly be surprised! I wasn't surprised. And the young people's committee informed the Y secretary that since the Y was a public community center which they helped to support, they saw no reason why it should censor their memorial program to the extent of eliminating any speaker.

Since I had been allotted but a few moments on the program, it was my intention simply to read this short poem of mine:

Dear lovely death
That taketh all things under wing,
Never to kill,
Only to change into some other thing
This suffering flesh—
To make it either more or less
But not again the same,
Dear lovely death,
Change is thy other name.

But the Negro branch Y, egged on by the reactionary politicians (whose incomes, incidentally, were allegedly derived largely from gambling houses and other underworld activities), informed the young people's committee that the police would be at the door to prevent my entering the Y on the afternoon of the scheduled program. So when the crowd gathered, the memorial was not held that Sunday. The young people simply informed the audience of the situation and said that the memorial would be postponed until a place could be found where all the participants could be heard. The program was held elsewhere a few Sundays later. . . .

So goes the life of social poet. I am sure none of these things would ever have happened to me had I limited the subject matter of my poems to roses and moonlight. But, unfortunately, I was born poor—and colored—and almost all the prettiest roses I have seen have been in rich white people's yards—not in mine. That is why I cannot write exclusively about roses and moonlight—for sometimes in the moonlight my brothers see a fiery cross and a circle of Klansmen's hoods. Sometimes in the moonlight a dark body sways from a lynching tree—but for his funeral there are no roses.

ARNOLD RAMPERSAD

from The Origins of Poetry in Langston Hughes

Revealing an increase in skill, Hughes's early poetry nevertheless gives no sign of a major poetic talent in the making. At some point in his development, however, something happened to Hughes that was as mysterious and as wonderful, in its own way, as the miracle that overtook John Keats after the watchful night spent with his friend Charles Cowden Clarke and a copy of Chapman's translation. With "The Negro Speaks of Rivers" the creativity in Langston Hughes, hitherto unexpressed, suddenly created itself.

In writing thus about Hughes, are we taking him too seriously? With a few exceptions, literary critics have resisted offering even a modestly complicated theory concerning his creativity. His relentless affability and charm, his deep, open love of the black masses, his devotion to their folk forms, and his insistence on writing poetry that they could understand, all have contributed to the notion that Langston Hughes was intellectually and emotionally shallow. One wonders, then, at the source of the creative energy that drove him from 1921 to 1967 to write so many poems, novels, short stories, plays, operas, popular histories, children's books, and assorted other work. As a poet, Hughes virtually reinvented Afro-American poetry with his pioneering use of the blues and other folk forms; as Howard Mumford Jones marveled in a 1927 review, Hughes added the verse form of the blues to poetry in English (a form that continues to attract the best black poets, including Michael Harper, Sherley Anne Williams, and Raymond Patterson). One wonders, too, in his aspect as a poet, why this apparently happy, apparently shallow man defined his creativity in terms of unhappiness. "I felt bad for the next three or four years," he would write in *The Big Sea* about the period beginning more or less with the publication of "The Negro Speaks of Rivers," and "those were the years when I wrote most of my poetry. (For my best poems were all written when I felt the worst. When I was happy, I didn't write anything)."...

The first of [Hughes's] two illnesses took place in the summer of 1919, when Hughes (at seventeen) saw his father for the first time in a dozen years. In 1903, James Hughes had gone to Mexico, where he would become a prosperous property owner. In a lonely, impoverished, passed-around childhood in the Midwest, his son had fantasized about the man "as a kind of strong, bronze cowboy, in a big Mexican hat, going back and forth from his business in the city to his ranch in the mountains, free—in a land where there were no white folks to draw the color line, and no tenements with rent always due—just mountains and cacti: Mexico!" Elated to be invited suddenly to Mexico in 1919 at the end of his junior year in high school, Langston left the United States with high hopes for his visit.

The summer was a disaster. James Hughes proved to be an unfeeling, domineering, and materialistic man, scornful of Indians and blacks (he was himself black) and the poor in general; and contemptuous of his son's gentler pace and artistic temperament. One day, Langston could take no more: "Suddenly my stomach began to turn over and over. And I could not swallow another mouthful. Waves of heat engulfed me. My eyes burned. My body shook. I wanted more than anything on earth to hit my father, but instead I got up from the table and went back to bed. The bed went round and round and the room turned dark. Anger clotted in every vein, and my tongue tasted like dry blood." But the boy, ill for a long time, never confessed the true cause of his affliction. Having been moved to Mexico City, he declined to help his doctors: "I never told them . . . that I was sick because I hated my father." He recovered only when it was time to return to the United States.

Hughes's second major illness came eleven years later. By this time he had finished high school, returned to Mexico to live with his father for a year, attended Columbia University for one year (supported grudgingly by James Hughes), dropped out of school, and served as a messman on voyages to Africa and to Europe, where he spent several months in 1924 as a dishwasher. All the while, however, Hughes was publishing poetry in a variety of places, especially in important black journals. This activity culminated in books of verse published in 1926 (*The Weary Blues*) and 1927 (*Fine Clothes to the Jew*) that established him, with Countee Cullen, as one of two major black poets of the decade. In 1929, he graduated after three and a half years at black Lincoln University, Pennsylvania. In 1930, Hughes published his first novel, *Not Without Laughter*.

This book had been virtually dragged out of him by his patron of the preceding three years, "Godmother" (as she wished to be called), an old, white, very generous but eccentric woman who ruled Hughes with a benevolent despotism inspired by her volatile beliefs in African spirituality, folk culture, mental telepathy, and the potential of his genius. But the result of her largesse was a paradox: the more comfortable he grew, the less Hughes was inclined to create. Estranged by his apparent languor, his patron finally seized on an episode of conflict to banish him once and for all. Hughes was devastated. Surviving drafts of his letters to "Godmother" reveal him deep in self-abasement before a woman with whom he was clearly in love. Ten years later, he confessed in *The Big Sea:* "I cannot write here about that last half-hour in the big bright drawing-room high above Park Avenue . . . because when I think about it, even now, something happens in the pit of my stomach that makes me ill. That beautiful room . . . suddenly became like a trap closing in, faster and faster, the room darker and darker, until the light went out with a sudden crash in the dark, and everything became like . . . that morning in Mexico when I suddenly hated my father.

"I was violently and physically ill, with my stomach turning over and over. . . . And there was no rationalizing anything. I couldn't." For several months, according to my research (Hughes erroneously presents a far briefer time frame in *The Big Sea*), he waited in excruciating hope for a reconciliation. As in Mexico, he wasted time and money on doctors without revealing to them the source of his chronic illness (which one very ingenious Harlem physician diagnosed as a Japanese tapeworm). Rather than break his silence, Hughes even agreed to have his tonsils removed. Gradually it became clear that reconciliation was impossible. Winning a prize of four hundred dollars for his novel, Hughes fled to seclusion in hot, remote Haiti. When his money ran out some months later, he returned home, healed at last but badly scarred.

Although they occurred more than a decade apart, the two illnesses were similar. Both showed a normally placid Hughes driven into deep rage by an opponent, a rage which he was unable to ventilate because the easy expression of personal anger and indignation was anathema to him. In both cases, he developed physical symptoms of hyperventilation and, eventually, anemia. More importantly, both were triggered in a period of relatively low poetic creativity (as when he was still a juvenile poet) or outright poetic inactivity (as with his patron). In each instance, Hughes had become satisfied with this low creativity or inactivity. At both times, a certain powerful figure, first his father, then "Godmother," had opposed his right to be content. His father had opposed any poetic activity at all; "Godmother" had opposed his right to enjoy the poetical state without true poetical action, or writing. In other words, a powerful will presented itself in forceful opposition to what was, in one sense, a vacuum of expressive will on Hughes's part. (Needless to say, the *apparent* absence of will in an individual can easily be a token of the presence of a very powerful will.) The result on both occasions, which was extraordinary, was first Hughes's endurance of, then his violent rebellion against, a force of will that challenged his deepest vision of the poetic life. . . .

In his bitter struggles with his father and "Godmother," Hughes turned to the black race for direction. But one needs to remember that this appeal in itself hardly gave Hughes distinction as a poet; what made Hughes distinct was the highly original manner in which he internalized the Afro-American racial dilemma and expressed it in poems such as "When Sue Wears Red," "The Negro Speaks of Rivers," "Mother to Son," "Dream Variations," and "The Weary Blues," poems of Hughes's young manhood on which his career would rest. Of these, the most important was "The Negro Speaks of Rivers."

> I've known rivers.
> I've known rivers ancient as the world and old
> as the flow of human blood in human veins.
>
> My soul has grown deep like the rivers.
>
> I bathed in the Euphrates when dawns were young.
> I built my hut near the Congo and it lulled me to sleep.
> I looked upon the Nile and raised the pyramids above it.
> I heard the singing of the Mississippi when Abe Lincoln went down
> to New Orleans, and I've seen its muddy bosom turn all golden
> in the sunset.
>
> I've known rivers:
> Ancient, dusky rivers.
>
> My soul has grown deep like the rivers.

Here, the persona moves steadily from dimly starred personal memory ("I've known rivers") toward a rendezvous with modern history (Lincoln going down the Mississippi and seeing the horror of slavery that, according to legend, would make him one day free the slaves). The death wish, benign but suffusing, of its images of rivers older than human blood, of souls grown as deep as these rivers, gives way steadily to an altering, ennobling vision whose final effect gleams in the evocation of the Mississippi's "muddy bosom" turning at last "all golden in the sunset." Personal anguish has been alchemized by the poet into a gracious meditation on his race, whose despised ("muddy") culture and history, irradiated by the poet's vision, changes within the poem from mud into gold. This is a classic example of the essential process of creativity in Hughes.

The poem came to him, according to Hughes (accurately, it seems clear) about ten months after his Mexican illness, when he was riding a train from Cleveland to Mexico to rejoin his father. The time was sundown, the place the Mississippi outside St. Louis. "All day on the train I had been thinking of my father," he would write in *The Big Sea*. "Now it was just sunset and we crossed the Mississippi, slowly, over a long bridge. I looked out of the window of the Pullman at the great muddy river flowing down toward the heart of the South, and I began to think what that river, the old Mississippi, had meant to Negroes in the past—how to be sold down the river was the worst fate that could overtake a slave in bondage. Then I remembered reading how Abraham Lincoln had made a trip down the Mississippi on a raft, and how he had seen slavery at its worst, and had decided within himself that it should be removed from American life. Then I began to think of other rivers in our past—the Congo, and the Niger, and the Nile in Africa—and the thought came to me: 'I've known rivers,' and I put it down on the back of an envelope I had in my pocket, and within the space of ten or fifteen minutes, as the train gathered speed in the dusk, I had written this poem."

Here, starting with anguish over his father, Hughes discovered the compressed ritual of passivity, challenge, turmoil, and transcendence he would probably have to re-create, doubtless in variant forms, during the great poetic trysts of his life. Even after he became a successful, published poet, the basic process remained the same, because his psychology remained largely the same even though he had become technically expert. In his second major illness, caused by his patron "Godmother," Hughes wrote poetry as he struggled for a transcendence that would be long in coming. The nature of that interim poetry is telling. When he sent some poems to a friend for a little book to be printed privately, she noticed at once that many spoke of death—"Dear lovely Death / That taketh all things under wing— / Never to kill. . . ." She called the booklet *Dear Lovely Death*. In "Afro-American Fragment," unlike in "The Negro Speaks of Rivers," Africa is seen plaintively:

> . . . Subdued and time-lost
> Are the drums—and yet
> Through some vast mist of race
> There comes this song
> I do not understand,
> This song of atavistic land,
> Of bitter yearnings lost
> Without a place—
> So long,
> So far away
> Is Africa's
> Dark face.

But when Hughes returned home, scarred but healed, after months in seclusion in Haiti, he no longer thought of loss and death. Instead, he plunged directly into the life of the black masses with a seven-month tour of the South in which he read his poetry in their churches and schools. Then he set out for the Soviet Union, where he would spend more than a year. Hughes then reached the zenith of his revolutionary ardor with poems (or verse) such as "Good Morning Revolution," "Goodbye Christ," and "Put One More 'S' in the USA."

HERMAN BEAVERS

from Dead Rocks and Sleeping Men: Aurality in the Aesthetic of Langston Hughes

In his 1940 autobiography, *The Big Sea*, Langston Hughes discusses the circumstances that led him, at the puerile age of 19, to the creation of his poem, "The Negro Speaks of Rivers" [see p. 1078]. The poem came into being during a trip to Mexico, Hughes writes, "when [he] was feeling very bad."[1] Thus, he connects poetic inspiration and emotional turbulence, both of which stemmed from his attempt to understand his father's self-hatred. He relates, "All day on the train I had been thinking about my father and his strange dislike of his own people. I didn't understand it because I was a Negro, and I liked Negroes very much" (54). What is striking about the end of this passage is that one finds Hughes adopting a posture both inside and outside the race: he does not make a statement of self-love (e.g. I like myself), rather he indicates through a kind of reflexivity, that he has self-worth. In short, he is unable to articulate self-valuation, he can only construct his positionality as the mirror opposite of his father's racial feeling. But then Hughes shifts the subject and recalls that "one of the happiest jobs [he] ever had," was the time he spent working behind the soda fountain of a refreshment parlor, in "the heart of the colored neighborhood" in Cleveland. He offers this description:

> People just up from the South used to come in for ice cream and sodas and watermelon. And I never tired of *hearing* their talk, *listening* to thunderclaps of their laughter, to their troubles, to their discussions of the war and the men who had gone to Europe from the Jim Crow South, their complaints over the high rent and the long overtime hours that brought what seemed big checks, until the weekly bills were paid. (54, my emphasis)

I quote this passage at length to point to the disjointed quality Hughes's narrative assumes. In one chapter, we find the self-hatred of his father, his own admiration for the recuperative powers of newly arrived Southern blacks, and the act of composing a famous poem. The elements that form Hughes's account can be read, at least on a cursory level, as an attempt to demonstrate that his "best poems were written when [he] felt the worst" (54). This notwithstanding, what I would like to propose is that we can place the poem into an aesthetic frame that brings these three disparate elements into a more geometrical alignment.

Hughes's autobiographical account can be found in the middle of a chapter entitled, "I've Known Rivers." Having established his father as someone he neither understands nor wishes to emulate, the autobiography paints the older man as an outsider, not only geographically, but spiritually as well. That Hughes would discuss his father in relation to such an important poem, alludes to body travel of a different sort than that which he undertakes in this chapter of his autobiography. Moving further away from Cleveland, the geographical space where he encountered the individuals he describes as "the gayest and bravest people possible . . ." (54), Hughes elides the distance his father has put between himself and other blacks. He resists the impulses that lead to the latter's self-imposed exile: he is immersed in a vernacular moment and simultaneously peripheral to that moment. What differentiates the younger Hughes is that he listens to the voices of the folk and is "empowered rather than debilitated" by what he hears.[2]

In composing the poem, Hughes looks at "the great muddy river flowing down toward the heart of the South" (*The Big Sea* 55). While he suggests that it is his gaze—looking out of the train window at the Mississippi—that initiates composition, I would assert that what catalyzes his act of writing is the act of recovering the spoken word. A point emphasized, moreover, by the fact that he recounts a moment where he is listener rather than speaker.

Later in the autobiography, Hughes relates, in much less detail, the events which lead to his poem, "The Weary Blues" (see p. 1079) There, he states, simply: "That winter, I wrote a poem called "The Weary Blues," about a piano-player I heard in Harlem . . ." (92). Again, Hughes's poetic composition moves forward from an aural moment where, as with "The Negro Speaks of Rivers," he is an outsider. Arnold Rampersad alludes to this when he observes:

> . . . [I]n his willingness to stand back and record, with minimal intervention as a craftsman, aspects of the drama of black religion or black music, Hughes had clearly shown already that he saw his *own art as inferior* [my emphasis] to that of either black musicians or religionists. . . . At the heart of his sense of inferiority . . . was the knowledge that he stood to a great extent *outside* the culture he worshipped.[3]

Rampersad concludes that Hughes's sense of alienation resulted from the fact that "his life had been spent away from consistent, normal involvement with the black masses whose affection and regard he craved" (64–5).

Notes

[1] Langston Hughes, *The Big Sea* (1940; New York: Hill and Wang, 1963) 54. All subsequent references to this text are from this volume.

[2] Arnold Rampersad, *The Life of Langston Hughes, Volume I: 1902–1941: I, Too, Sing America,* 2 vols. (New York: Oxford UP, 1986) 1: 64.

[3] Rampersad 64–65. My emphasis.

STEVEN C. TRACY

from "Midnight Ruffles of Cat-Gut Lace": The Boogie Poems of Langston Hughes

The influence of the blues tradition on Langston Hughes' poetry is by now an oft-discussed and readily accepted fact, although the depth and breadth of his employment of the tradition has not often been discussed with a similar depth and breadth. A close examination of a related sequence of Hughes' blues poems offers the opportunity to explore his fusion of oral and written traditions and to examine his tremendous skills as a literary-jazz improviser. That is not to suggest that Hughes' poems are spontaneous creations. Improvisation is normally thought of as a spontaneous act, but the jazz or blues musician's improvisations are in fact bounded by several things: the musician's "vocabulary"—style, patterns, techniques, and riffs; the accepted conventions of the specific genre (even if those conventions are deliberately violated, they are, in a large sense, at work); and the boundaries of the individual piece being performed. For example, boogie-woogie pianist Pete Johnson, in his 1947 version of "Swanee River Boogie," performs the melody of the song to a boogie-woogie beat, thereafter improvising solos built around the song's chord changes, the boogie-woogie beat, and variations on the melody of the piece, combined with his arsenal of boogie-woogie riffs and performed in his inimitable style.[1] Hughes, in his 1951 collection, *Montage of a Dream Deferred*, generated a set or sequence of six "boogie" poems—"Dream Boogie," "Easy Boogie," "Boogie 1 a.m.," "Lady's Boogie," "Nightmare Boogie," and "Dream Boogie: Variation"—that have in common much more than the "boogie" of the titles. The poems comprise an intricate series of interwoven "improvisations" over a set boogie-woogie rhythm, with Hughes modulating and modifying rhythm, words, imagery, moods, and themes, and constructing a complex interrelationship between music, the musical instrument, the performance, and a set of attitudes exemplified by them.

Structurally, Hughes' six boogie poems share the exciting, rushing rhythms of boogie-woogie: Hughes at work on his poems, pounding out rhythms on his typewriter keyboard. Briefly, boogie-woogie is a form of Afro-American music, normally performed on the piano, that emerged as a recognizable genre in the 1920s. As blues researcher Karl Gert zur Heide points out, "the theme of boogie is the blues, some features derive from ragtime, and the rhythmic inter-play of both hands can be traced back to African roots."[2] In boogie-woogie, the improvisations executed by the pianist's right hand on the treble keys of the piano are set off against the ostinato or repeated phrases of the left hand on the bass keys. Characteristically boogie-woogie follows the twelve-bar blues chord change pattern—in the key of C, CFC GFC—employing a repeated bass pattern recognizable most often for its eight beats to the bar and performed at a medium-to-fast tempo that builds an explosive drive and swing appropriate to the dance step after which it was named. Besides identifying a dance step and a type of music, however, the term "boogie" functions in other contexts: to boogie is to raise a ruckus or act wildly or uninhibitedly; it also has sexual connotations:

> I'm gonna pull off my pants and keep on my shirt,
> I'm gonna get so low you think I'm in the dirt.
> I'm gonna pitch a boogie-woogie,
> Gonna boogie-woogie all night long.[3]

In this tune, singer Big Bill Broonzy has taken a boogie-woogie beat suitable for dancing and provided both the "wild acting" and sexual connotations that go with it. In the tradition, the word carried these connotations, and typically Hughes tried to capture the ambience of the tradition.

Notes

[1]Pete Johnson, "Swanee River Boogie," *Boogie Woogie Trio,* Storyville SLP 4006, 1976.

[2]Karl Gert zur Heide, *Deep South Piano* (London: Studio Vista, 1970), p. 11.

[3]Big Bill Broonzy, "Let's Reel and Rock," Melotone, 7-06-64, 1936, 78 R.P.M. recording.

KAREN JACKSON FORD

from Do Right to Write Right: Langston Hughes's Aesthetics of Simplicity

The one thing most readers of twentieth-century American poetry can say about Langston Hughes is that he has known rivers. "The Negro Speaks of Rivers" has become memorable for its lofty, oratorical tone, mythic scope, and powerful rhythmic repetitions.

> I've known rivers:
> I've known rivers ancient as the world and old as the flow of human
> blood in human veins.

But however beautiful its cadences, the poem is remembered primarily because it is Hughes's most frequently anthologized work. The fact is, "The Negro Speaks of Rivers" is one of Hughes's most uncharacteristic poems, and yet it has defined his reputation, along with a small but constant selection of other poems included in anthologies. "A Negro Speaks of Rivers," "A House in Taos," "The Weary Blues," "Montage of a Dream Deferred," "Theme for English B," "Refugee in America," and "I, Too"—these poems invariably comprise his anthology repertoire despite the fact that none of them typifies his writing. What makes these poems atypical is exactly what makes them appealing and intelligible to the scholars who edit anthologies—their complexity. True, anthologies produced in the current market, which is hospitable to the African-American tradition and to canon reform, now include a brief selection of poems in black folk forms. But even though Hughes has fared better in anthologies than most African-American writers, only a small and predictable segment of his poetry has been preserved. A look back through the original volumes of poetry, and even through the severely redrawn *Selected Poems*, reveals a wealth of simpler poems we ought to be reading.[1]

Admittedly, an account of Hughes's poetic simplicity requires some qualification. Most obvious is the fact that he wrote poems that are not simple. "A Negro Speaks of Rivers" is oracular; "The Weary Blues" concludes enigmatically; "A House in Taos" is classically modernist in both its fragmented form and its decadent sensibility. Even more to the point, many of the poems that have been deemed simple are only ironically so. "The Black Christ," for example, is a little jingle that invokes monstrous cultural complexity. Likewise, two later books, *Ask Your Mama* (1961) and *The Panther and the Lash* (1967), contain an intricate vision of American history beneath their simple surfaces.[2] Nevertheless, the overwhelming proportion of poems in the Hughes canon consists of work in the simpler style, and even those poems that can yield complexities make use of simplicity in ways that ought not to be ignored.

The repression of the great bulk of Hughes's poems is the result of chronic critical scorn for their simplicity. Throughout his long career, but especially after his first two volumes of poetry (readers were at first willing to assume that a youthful poet might grow to be more complex), his books received their harshest reviews for a variety of "flaws" that all originate in an aesthetics of simplicity. From his first book, *The Weary Blues* (1926), to his last one, *The Panther and the Lash* (1967), the reviews invoke a litany of faults: the poems are superficial, infantile, silly, small, unpoetic, common, jejune, iterative, and, of course, simple.[3] Even his admirers reluctantly conclude that Hughes's poetics failed. Saunders Redding flatly opposes simplicity and artfulness. "While Hughes's rejection of his own growth shows an admirable loyalty to his self-commitment as the poet of the 'simple, Negro commonfolk' . . . it does a disservice to his art" (Mullen 74). James Baldwin, who recognizes the potential of simplicity as an artistic principle, faults the poems for "tak[ing] refuge . . . in a fake simplicity in order to avoid the very difficult simplicity of the experience" (Mullen 85).

Despite a lifetime of critical disappointments, then, Hughes remained loyal to the aesthetic program he had outlined in 1926 in his decisive poetic treatise, "The Negro Artist and the Racial Mountain." There he had predicted that the common people would "give to this world its truly great Negro artist, the one who is not afraid to be himself," a poet who would explore the "great field of unused [folk] material ready for his art" and recognize that this source would provide "sufficient matter to furnish a black artist with a lifetime of creative work" (692).* This is clearly a portrait of the poet Hughes would become, and he maintained his fidelity to this ideal at great cost to his literary reputation. . . .

In his column in the *Chicago Defender* on February 13, 1943, Hughes first introduced the prototype of the humorous and beloved fictional character Jesse B. Semple, nicknamed by his Harlem friends "Simple." For the next twenty-three years Hughes would continue to publish Simple stories both in the *Defender* and in several volumes of collected and edited pieces.[4] Hughes called Simple his "ace-boy," and it is surely not coincidental that the Simple stories span the years, the 1940s to the 1960s, when Langston Hughes needed a literary ace in the hole.[5] The success of the Simple stories was an important consolation of the writer's later years, when his poetry was reviewed with disappointment, his autobiography dismissed as "chit-chat," his plays refused on Broadway, and his fiction diminished in importance next to Richard Wright's *Native Son* (1940) and Ralph Ellison's *Invisible Man* (1952).[6]

It seems obvious, however, that in the long association with his ace-boy Hughes found more than popularity and financial success. In fact, his prefatory sketches of Simple attest to the character's importance, in the sheer number of times Hughes sets out to explain him and in the specific details these explanations

*See pages 1093–94 for the quoted passage in its entirety.

provide.[7] All of them depict Simple as an African American Everyman, the authentic—even unmediated—voice of the community that engendered him. For instance, in "Who Is Simple?" Hughes emphasizes the authenticity of his creation: "[Simple's] first words came directly out of the mouth of a young man who lived just down the block from me" (*Best* vii). Here and elsewhere Hughes asserts a vital connection between the fictional character and the people he represents: "If there were not a lot of genial souls in Harlem as talkative as Simple, I would never have these tales to write down that are 'just like him'" (*Best* viii). The author's dedication to Simple is surely rooted in his conviction that Simple embodies and speaks for the very people to whom Hughes had committed himself back in the 1920s.

Notes

[1] Easily ninety per cent of the poems in Hughes's canon are of the sort that I am describing as simple.

[2] Jemie, Hudson, and Miller, among others, have persuasively demonstrated the intricacies of Hughes's jazz structures in these two late books.

[3] Reviews in which these epithets appear are collected in Mullen.

[4] The stories are collected in five volumes, *The Best of Simple*, *Simple Speaks His Mind*, *Simple Stakes a Claim*, *Simple Takes a Wife*, and *Simple's Uncle Sam*. Additionally, Hughes takes Simple to the stage with *Simply Heavenly*, a comedy about Simple's marriage.

[5] In "Who Is Simple?"— the foreword to *The Best of Simple*— Hughes concludes, "He is my ace-boy, Simple. I hope you like him, too" (viii).

[6] For a chronicle of Hughes's disappointments during these years, see Rampersad, especially chapter 8 of the second volume "In Warm Manure: 1951 to 1953." Ellison characterized *The Big Sea* as a "chit-chat" book during an interview with Rampersad in 1983 (202).

[7] Hughes wrote at least four explanations of Simple: "The Happy Journey of 'Simply Heavenly,'" "Simple and Me," "Who Is Simple?" and the "Character Notes" to *Simply Heavenly*.

GEORGE B. HUTCHINSON

from Langston Hughes and the "Other" Whitman

At various points in his long career, Hughes put together no fewer than three separate anthologies of Whitman's poetry (one of them for children), included several Whitman poems in an anthology on *The Poetry of the Negro*, wrote a poem entitled "Old Walt" for the one hundredth anniversary of *Leaves of Grass*, and repeatedly—in lectures, newspaper columns, and introductions—encouraged black Americans to read his work. He called Whitman "America's greatest poet" and spoke of *Leaves of Grass* as the greatest expression of "the real meaning of democracy ever made on our shores." Feeling that Whitman had been ignored and, in current parlance, marginalized by the custodians of culture, Hughes indeed attempted in his own way to canonize the poet he considered "the Lincoln of our Letters" (*Chicago Defender*, July 4, 1953). . . .

One reason Whitman's poetry has resonated in the sensibilities of black American writers is that in certain of his poems he uses the condition of the slave as representative of the condition of his audience. The "you" of his songs, if it is to apply to *all* readers, must apply to slaves, those most graphically denied the right to self-determination. The poem "To You (Whoever You Are)" at times seems directly addressed to a slave:

> None has done justice to you, you have not done justice to yourself,
> None but has found you imperfect, I only find no imperfection
> in you,
> None but would subordinate you, I only am he who will never consent
> to subordinate you,
> I only am he who places over you no master, owner, better, God,
> beyond what waits intrinsically in yourself. (14–17)

Arguably, Whitman here distills the specific oppression of black people in the antebellum United States into a metaphor for the hidden condition of all people—"you, whoever you are." But his slave is not just any slave—his slave is the *most* enslaved, the one rejected by all others and even by himself or herself. . . . Hughes was the first African-American poet to sense the affinity between the inclusive "I" of Whitman (which Whitman claimed as his most important innovation—"the quite changed attitude of the ego, the one chanting or talking, towards himself and towards his fellow humanity") ("A Backward Glance," 564) and the "I" of the blues and even of the spirituals. The result of Hughes's appropriation of this triply descended "I" is amply demonstrated in one of his first published poems, "The Negro Speaks of Rivers":

> I've known rivers ancient as the world and old as the flow of human
> blood in human veins.
>
> My soul has grown deep like the rivers.
>
> I bathed in the Euphrates when dawns were young.
> I built my hut near the Congo and it lulled me to sleep.
> I looked upon the Nile and raised the pyramids above it.
> I heard the singing of the Mississippi when Abe Lincoln went down to
> New Orleans, and I've seen its muddy bosom turn all golden in the
> sunset. (*Weary Blues*, 51)

Though Hughes would later, for the most part, turn away from the Whitmanesque style of free verse, the example of Whitman's break with traditional definitions of the poetic, his attempts to achieve an orally based poetics with the cadence and diction of the voice on the street, at the pond-side, or at the pulpit, provided a partial model for the young black poet looking for a way to sing his own song, which would be at the same time a song of his people.

Topics for Further Research

1. As Hughes's own essays in this chapter suggest, much of his life was spent actively campaigning for various causes. Research his social and political activities and their effect on his poetry. How did his social and political work change between 1935 and 1955?

2. Investigate the ways in which Hughes's poetry was inspired by the accomplishments of African-American musicians. For example, how did the different musical forms of the female blues singers of the 1920s and the bebop musicians of the 1940s inspire him?
3. Hughes was a primary inspiration for the artistic movement known as *negritude*. Poets and writers like Nicolás Guillén, Jacques Roumain, Aimé Cesaire, and Leopold Senghor all acknowledged Hughes's influence. Find out what the negritude poets stood for, and write a paper in which you discuss why Hughes was so important to this movement.

4. Hughes's work was distinct from that of his two most important contemporaries, Gwendolyn Brooks and Robert Hayden, who were influenced by modernism. Using a dictionary or an encyclopedia of literary criticism, find out what modernist poetry is. Is *modernism* a useful term in discussing what distinguishes Brooks and Hayden from Hughes? Why might Hughes be skeptical about some aspects of modernism? Read the poems by Brooks and Hayden in this anthology. Then, read some additional poems by one of these poets, and compare some of these poems to those of Hughes.
5. Hughes was a central figure in a period of African-American artistic flowering called the Harlem Renaissance. Find out as much as you can about the Harlem Renaissance and Hughes's involvement with it. Then, write an essay in which you assess how the Harlem Renaissance was important to Hughes's development as a poet.
6. Read a collection of Hughes's "Simple" stories, newspaper columns that were later collected in book form. What is he able to do in fiction that he is unable to do in poetry? What is he able to do in poetry that he is unable to do in fiction?

Student Paper

McIntyre 1

Ashley McIntyre

Professor Hall

African-American Literature

15 February 2009

The Rhythms of African-American Life:

Langston Hughes and the Poetics of Blues and Jazz

Introduction

In "The Negro Artist and the Racial Mountain," Langston Hughes argues that African-American artists should draw on their own cultural heritage when looking for material. He writes that "Without going outside his race . . . there is sufficient matter to furnish a black artist with a lifetime of creative work" (Kirszner and Mandell 1094). Hughes wanted to write poetry that accurately portrayed African-American life, and to achieve this goal, he incorporated the rhythms of jazz and the blues into poems such as "The Weary Blues," "Lenox Avenue: Midnight," and Dream Boogie."

Thesis statement

Discussion of "The Weary Blues"

In "The Weary Blues," Hughes tells the story of a blues singer and pianist performing in a club on Lenox Avenue. Readers would have recognized Lenox Avenue in Harlem as a street well known for its nightlife and music during the 1920s. But Hughes does more than simply describe the blues singer to convey the African-American experience. He also uses the rhythms of the blues in the poem. For example, he repeats the words "He did a lazy sway . . . / He did a lazy sway . . ." (lines 6-7) to recreate the singer's "syncopated tune" (1). Hughes draws us into the experience of the performance when he includes lines that mirror the beat of the music. He follows his descriptions of the piano's melody with "O Blues!" (11) and "Sweet Blues!" (14). He goes further when he includes the singer's lyrics in lines 19-22 and lines 25-30.

McIntyre 2

In most blues songs, a "statement is made in the first four bars, repeated (sometimes with slight variation) in the next four, and answered or commented on in the last four" ("Jazz"). In the first four lines of "The Weary Blues," the blues singer says that although he is alone and lonely, he is going to put his "troubles on the shelf" (22). In the next four lines, he expands this statement by explaining that despite his best efforts, he continues to experience the "Weary Blues." Hughes also incorporates the irony so often found in blues music by juxtaposing the white piano keys with the black singer. According to the *Dictionary of Literary Biography,* the "black musician who plays his song ironically on the piano's white keys, [creates] a heightened moment that purges him, as well as the listener and reader, from human suffering" (Quartermain). Although the singer does not talk directly about race, Hughes might be alluding to race relations by repeatedly saying that the singer made the white-keyed piano "moan" (10 and 18). As the performance ends, the singer, exhausted by its emotional intensity, sleeps "like a rock or a man that's dead" (35).

Background on blues

Use of blues in the poem

Hughes also features Lenox Avenue in "Lenox Avenue: Midnight." In this poem, however, Hughes uses the rhythms of jazz rather than those of the blues. While the blues has a defined form, jazz has an improvisational style. Jazz is known for "its spontaneous, emotional, and improvisational character" ("Jazz"), and Hughes's poem is consistent with this form. The speaker begins by making the following announcement:

Discussion of "Lenox Avenue: Midnight"

McIntyre 3

The rhythm of life
Is a jazz rhythm,
Honey. (lines 1–3)

Use of jazz in the poem

According to the speaker, life (like jazz) is unpredictable and not straightforward. The speaker then juxtaposes concrete scenes such as "the rumble of street cars" (9) and "the swish of rain" (10) with his own abstract thoughts about urban life. These thoughts focus on the pain of life: "the broken heart of love / the weary, weary heart of pain,—" (5–6). As these lines show, although jazz and blues have different forms, they both use irony to convey meaning. Lenox Avenue, well known for its exciting nightlife, is not depicted rather as a street where people celebrate but rather as a wet, dark place where hearts are broken. This idea is further developed through the repetition of the line "the gods are laughing at us" (4 and 14).

Discussion of "Dream Boogie"

Definition of boogie-woogie

Use of boogie-woogie in the poem

In "Dream Boogie," Hughes draws on the musical style of boogie-woogie. According to the notes that accompany this poem, boogie-woogie combines elements of both blues and jazz (Kirszner and Mandell 1083–84). Vigorous piano playing, the note explains, is punctuated by heavy and "repeated bass figures" (Kirszner and Mandell 1083). Hughes uses italics to identify the heavy, repeated bass line. For example, the speaker says that if the audience listens closely, they can hear the "beating out and beating out a— / *You think / It's a happy beat?*" (lines 7–9). In these lines, the speaker challenges whites who might assume that boogie-woogie is simply an upbeat style of music. This question also supports

McIntyre 4

the theme established in the first lines of the poem when Hughes follows the upbeat announcement "Good morning, daddy!" (1) with these lines:

> Ain't you heard
> The boogie-woogie rumble
> Of a dream deferred? (lines 2-4)

Including colloquial words, such as "daddy" and "ain't," Hughes uses boogie-woogie to discuss the "dream deferred." Unlike whites, who have been able to achieve the promises of the American Dream, African Americans have been excluded because of racism. As Steven C. Tracy explains in "Midnight Ruffles," boogie is both a musical style and an attitude. To boogie, he writes, is to "raise a ruckus or act wildly or uninhibitedly" (Kirszner and Mandell 1106). In this poem, the speaker uses boogie-woogie to suggest that African Americans are not sitting idly by and accepting inequality but are protesting through music.

Conclusion

In "The Negro Artist and the Racial Mountain," Hughes called on the African-American artist to use his heritage of "rhythm and warmth, and his incongruous humor" (Kirszner and Mandell 1094) that was so often found in the music of blues and jazz. Although Hughes often drew on traditional poetic forms, much of his work is marked by the rhythms of African-American music. Through these forms, Hughes successfully and powerfully communicates the energy and beauty of African-American culture during the 1920s.

Evaluation of Hughes's use of jazz and boogie-woogie

McIntyre 5

Works Cited

Hughes, Langston. "Dream Boogie." Kirszner and Mandell 1083-84.

---. "Lenox Avenue: Midnight." Kirszner and Mandell 1087.

---. "The Negro Artist and the Racial Mountain." Kirszner and Mandell 1092-94.

---. "The Weary Blues." Kirszner and Mandell 1079-80.

"Jazz." *The Columbia Encyclopedia Online*. 6th ed. New York, 2005. *Bartleby.com*. Web. 3 Jan. 2009.

Kirszner, Laurie G., and Stephen R. Mandell, eds. *Literature: Reading, Reacting, Writing*. 7th ed. Boston: Wadsworth, 2010. Print.

Quartermain, Peter, ed. "Langston Hughes." *Dictionary of Literary Biography: American Poets, 1880-1945, Second Series*. 2007 ed. Vol. 48. *Contemporary Literary Criticism Select*. Web. 2 Jan. 2009.

Tracy, Steven C. "'Midnight Ruffles of Cat-Gut Lace': The Boogie Poems of Langston Hughes." Kirszner and Mandell 1105-07.

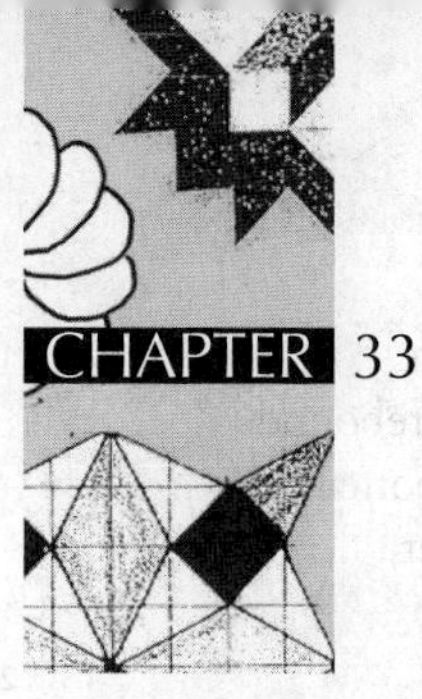

POETRY FOR FURTHER READING

KIM ADDONIZIO (1954–)

Veritiesº (2005)

Into every life a little ax must fall.
Every dog has its choke chain.
Every cloud has a shadow.
Better dead than fed.
He who laughs, will not last.
Sticks and stones will break you,
and then the names of things will be changed.
A stitch in time saves no one.
The darkest hour comes.

SHERMAN J. ALEXIE (1966–)

Defending Walt Whitman (1996)

Basketball is like this for young Indian boys, all arms and legs
and serious stomach muscles. Every body is brown!
These are the twentieth-century warriors who will never kill,
although a few sat quietly in the deserts of Kuwait,
waiting for orders to do something, do something.

God, there is nothing as beautiful as a jump shot
on a reservation summer basketball court
where the ball is moist with sweat
and makes a sound when it swishes through the net
that causes Walt Whitman to weep because it is so perfect.

There are veterans of foreign wars here,
whose bodies are still dominated
by collarbones and knees, whose bodies still respond
in the ways that bodies are supposed to respond when we
    are young.

Verities: Truths.

Every body is brown! Look there, that boy can run
up and down this court forever. He can leap for a rebound
with his back arched like a salmon, all meat and bone
synchronized, magnetic, as if the court were a river,
as if the rim were a dam, as if the air were a ladder
leading the Indian boy toward home.

Some of the Indian boys still wear their military haircuts
while a few have let their hair grow back.
It will never be the same as it was before!
One Indian boy has never cut his hair, not once, and he braids it
into wild patterns that do not measure anything.
He is just a boy with too much time on his hands.
Look at him. He wants to play this game in bare feet.

God, the sun is so bright! There is no place like this.
Walt Whitman stretches his calf muscles
on the sidelines. He has the next game.
His huge beard is ridiculous on the reservation.
Some body throws a crazy pass and Walt Whitman catches it
    with quick hands.
He brings the ball close to his nose
and breathes in all of its smells: leather, brown skin, sweat,
    black hair,
burning oil, twisted ankle, long drink of warm water,
gunpowder, pine tree. Walt Whitman squeezes the ball tightly.
He wants to run. He hardly has the patience to wait for his turn.
"What's the score?" he asks. He asks, "What's the score?"

Basketball is like this for Walt Whitman. He watches these
    Indian boys
as if they were the last bodies on earth. Every body is brown!
Walt Whitman shakes because he believes in God.
Walt Whitman dreams of the Indian boy who will defend him,
trapping him in the corner, all flailing arms and legs
and legendary stomach muscles. Walt Whitman shakes
because he believes in God. Walt Whitman dreams
of the first jump shot he will take, the ball arcing clumsily
from his fingers, striking the rim so hard that it sparks.
Walt Whitman shakes because he believes in God.
Walt Whitman closes his eyes. He is a small man and his beard
is ludicrous on the reservation, absolutely insane.
His beard makes the Indian boys laugh righteously. His beard
    frightens
the smallest Indian boys. His beard tickles the skin
of the Indian boys who dribble past him. His beard, his beard!

God, there is beauty in every body. Walt Whitman stands
at center court while the Indian boys run from basket to basket.

Walt Whitman cannot tell the difference between
offense and defense. He does not care if he touches the ball.
Half of the Indian boys wear T-shirts damp with sweat
and the other half are barebacked, skin slick and shiny.
There is no place like this. Walt Whitman smiles.
Walt Whitman shakes. This game belongs to him.

LEWIS ALLEN (1903–1986)

Strange Fruit* (1939)

Southern trees bear strange fruit,
Blood on the leaves and blood at the root,
Black bodies swinging in the southern breeze,
Strange fruit hanging from the poplar trees.

Pastoral scene of the gallant south,
The bulging eyes and the twisted mouth,
Scent of magnolias, sweet and fresh,
Then the sudden smell of burning flesh.

Here is fruit for the crows to pluck,
For the rain to gather, for the wind to suck,
For the sun to rot, for the trees to drop,
Here is a strange and bitter crop.

JULIA ALVAREZ (1950–)

Papi Working (1995)

The long day spent listening
to homesick hearts,
the tick tock of the clock—
the way Americans mark time.
long hours, long days.
Often they came only to hear him
say *nada* in their mother tongue.
I found nothing wrong.
To dole out *jarabe* for the children's coughs,
convince the *doña* to stay off that leg.

*In 1937, Abel Meeropol, a schoolteacher from New York, saw a photograph of the 1930 lynching of Thomas Shipp and Abram Smith in Marion, Indiana. Haunted by this image, he wrote the poem "Strange Fruit" under the pseudonym Lewis Allen. After hearing Billie Holiday (a renowned African-American blues singer) perform, he gave the poem to her, and she worked it into a haunting song.

In his white *saca* Mami ironed out,
smoothing the tired wrinkles
till he was young again,
he spent his days, long days
tending to the ills of immigrants,
his own heart heavy with what was gone,
this new country like a pill
that slowly kills but keeps you
from worse deaths.
What was to be done?

They came to hear him say
nada in their mother tongue.

Source: ©AP Photo

See this poet's biography on p. 1217.

MAYA ANGELOU (1928–)

Africa (1975)

Thus she had lain
sugar cane sweet
deserts her hair
golden her feet
mountains her breasts
two Niles° her tears
Thus she has lain
Black through the years.

Over the white seas
rime white and cold
brigands ungentled
icicle bold
took her young daughters
sold her strong sons
churched her with Jesus
bled her with guns.
Thus she has lain.

Now she is rising
remember her pain
remember the losses
her screams loud and vain
remember her riches
her history slain
now she is striding
although she had lain.

Niles: The Nile River, which originates in East Africa and flows through Egypt, is the world's longest river.

ANONYMOUS

Bonny Barbara Allan

(Traditional Scottish ballad)

It was in and about the Martinmas° time,
When the green leaves were afalling,
That Sir John Graeme, in the West Country,
Fell in love with Barbara Allan.

He sent his men down through the town,
To the place where she was dwelling;
"O haste and come to my master dear,
Gin° ye be Barbara Allan."

O hooly,° hooly rose she up,
To the place where he was lying,
And when she drew the curtain by:
"Young man, I think you're dying."

"O it's I'm sick, and very, very sick,
And 'tis a' for Barbara Allan."—
"O the better for me ye's never be,
Tho your heart's blood were aspilling.

"O dinna ye mind,° young man," said she,
"When ye was in the tavern adrinking,
That ye made the health gae round and round,
And slighted Barbara Allan?"

He turned his face unto the wall,
And death was with him dealing:
"Adieu, adieu, my dear friends all,
And be kind to Barbara Allan."

And slowly, slowly raise she up,
And slowly, slowly left him,
And sighing said she could not stay,
Since death of life had reft him.

She had not gane a mile but twa,°
When she heard the dead-bell ringing,

Martinmas: Saint Martin's Day, November 11.
Gin: If.
hooly: Slowly.
O dinna ye mind: Don't you remember?
twa: Two.

And every jow° that the dead-bell geid,
It cried, "Woe to Barbara Allan!"

"O mother, mother, make my bed!
O make it saft and narrow!
Since my love died for me today,
I'll die for him tomorrow."

ANONYMOUS

Go Down, Moses*

Go down, Moses,
Way down in Egyptland
Tell old Pharaoh
To let my people go.

When Israel was in Egyptland
Let my people go
Oppressed so hard they could not stand
Let my people go.

Go down, Moses,
Way down in Egyptland
Tell old Pharaoh
"Let my people go."

"Thus saith the Lord," bold Moses said,
"Let my people go;
If not I'll smite your first-born dead
Let my people go.

"No more shall they in bondage toil,
Let my people go;
Let them come out with Egypt's spoil,
Let my people go."

The Lord told Moses what to do
Let my people go;
To lead the children of Israel through,
Let my people go.

jow: Stroke.

*Music, especially religious songs, or "spirituals," was one of the few means of expression permitted for slaves. Many of these spirituals contained coded messages conveying antislavery sentiments or even directions on how to use the Underground Railroad. For example, the spiritual "Wade in the Water" seemed, on the surface, to be about crossing the River Jordan to reach the Promised Land. But its lyrics contained vital information, including the idea that crossing streams was a good way for runaway slaves to cover their scent and thus to lose the bloodhounds used to track them.

Go down, Moses,
Way down in Egyptland,
Tell old Pharaoh,
"Let my people go!"

ANONYMOUS

Western Wind

(English lyric)

Western wind, when wilt thou blow,
The° small rain down can rain?
Christ, if my love were in my arms,
And I in my bed again!

MATTHEW ARNOLD (1822–1888)

Dover Beach (1867)

The sea is calm tonight.
The tide is full, the moon lies fair
Upon the straits;— on the French coast the light
Gleams and is gone; the cliffs of England stand,
Glimmering and vast, out in the tranquil bay.
Come to the window, sweet is the night-air!
Only, from the long line of spray
Where the sea meets the moon-blanched° land,
Listen! you hear the grating roar
Of pebbles which the waves draw back, and fling,
At their return, up the high strand,°
Begin, and cease, and then again begin,
With tremulous cadence slow, and bring
The eternal note of sadness in.

Sophocles° long ago
Heard it on the Aegean,° and it brought
Into his mind the turbid ebb and flow
Of human misery; we
Find also in the sound a thought,
Hearing it by this distant northern sea.

The: [So that] the.
moon-blanched: Whitened by moonlight.
strand: Beach.
Sophocles: Greek playwright (496–406 B.C.), author of tragedies such as *Oedipus the King* and *Antigone*.
Aegean: Sea between Greece and Turkey.

The Sea of Faith
Was once, too, at the full, and round earth's shore
Lay like the folds of a bright girdle furled.
But now I only hear
Its melancholy, long, withdrawing roar,
Retreating, to the breath
Of the night-wind, down the vast edges drear
And naked shingles° of the world.

Ah, love, let us be true
To one another! for the world, which seems
To lie before us like a land of dreams,
So various, so beautiful, so new,
Hath really neither joy, nor love, nor light,
Nor certitude, nor peace, nor help for pain;
And we are here as on a darkling° plain
Swept with confused alarms of struggle and flight,
Where ignorant armies clash by night.

JOHN ASHBERY (1927–)

You Would Have Thought (1995)

Meanwhile, back in
soulless America, people are having fun
as usual.
A bird visits a birdbath.
A young girl takes a refresher course
in polyhistory. My mega-units are straining
at the leash of spring.
The annual race is on—
white flowers in someone's hair.
He comes in waltzing on empty airs,
mulling the blues notes of your case.
The leash is elastic and receptive
but I fear I am too wrapped up in cloudlets
of my own making this time.
In the other time it was rain dripping
from a tree to a house to the ground—
each thing helping itself and another thing
along a little. That would be inconceivable
these days of receptive answers and aggressive querying.
The routine is all too familiar,
the stone path wearying.

shingles: Gravel beaches.

darkling: Darkening.

ELIZABETH BISHOP (1911–1979)

The Fish (1946)

I caught a tremendous fish
and held him beside the boat
half out of water, with my hook
fast in a corner of his mouth.
He didn't fight.
He hadn't fought at all.
He hung a grunting weight,
battered and venerable
and homely. Here and there
his brown skin hung in strips
like ancient wallpaper,
and its pattern of darker brown
was like wallpaper:
shapes like full-blown roses
stained and lost through age.
He was speckled with barnacles,
fine rosettes of lime,
and infested
with tiny white sea-lice,
and underneath two or three
rags of green weed hung down.
While his gills were breathing in
the terrible oxygen
—the frightening gills,
fresh and crisp with blood,
that can cut so badly—
I thought of the coarse white flesh
packed in like feathers,
the big bones and the little bonies,
the dramatic reds and blacks
of his shiny entrails,
and the pink swim-bladder
like a big peony.
I looked into his eyes
which were far larger than mine
but shallower, and yellowed,
the irises backed and packed
with tarnished tinfoil
seen through the lenses
of old scratched isinglass.
They shifted a little, but not
to return my stare.
—It was more like the tipping

of an object toward the light.
I admired his sullen face,
the mechanism of his jaw,
and then I saw
that from his lower lip
—if you could call it a lip—
grim, wet, and weaponlike,
hung five old pieces of fish-line,
or four and a wire leader
with the swivel still attached,
with all their five big hooks
grown firmly in his mouth.
A green line, frayed at the end
and crimped from the strain and snap
when it broke and he got away.
Like medals with their ribbons
frayed and wavering,
a five-haired beard of wisdom
trailing from his aching jaw.
I stared and stared
and victory filled up
the little rented boat,
from the pool of bilge
where oil had spread a rainbow
around the rusted engine
to the bailer rusted orange,
the sun-cracked thwarts,
the oarlocks on their strings,
the gunnels—until everything
was rainbow, rainbow, rainbow!
And I let the fish go.

ELIZABETH BISHOP (1911–1979)

One Art (1976)

The art of losing isn't hard to master;
so many things seem filled with the intent
to be lost that their loss is no disaster.

Lose something every day. Accept the fluster
of lost door keys, the hour badly spent.
The art of losing isn't hard to master.

Then practice losing farther, losing faster:
places, and names, and where it was you meant
to travel. None of these will bring disaster.

I lost my mother's watch. And look! my last, or
next-to-last, of three loved houses went.
The art of losing isn't hard to master.

I lost two cities, lovely ones. And, vaster,
some realms I owned, two rivers, a continent.
I miss them, but it wasn't a disaster.

—Even losing you (the joking voice, a gesture
I love) I shan't have lied. It's evident
the art of losing's not too hard to master
though it may look like (*Write it!*) like disaster.

WILLIAM BLAKE (1757–1827)

The Chimney Sweeper* (1789)

When my mother died I was very young,
And my father sold me while yet my tongue
Could scarcely cry "'weep! 'weep! 'weep! 'weep!"
So your chimneys I sweep, and in soot I sleep.

There's little Tom Dacre, who cried when his head,
That curled like a lamb's back, was shaved: so I said
"Hush, Tom! never mind it, for when your head's bare
You know that the soot cannot spoil your white hair."

And so he was quiet, and that very night,
As Tom was a-sleeping, he had such a sight!
That thousands of sweepers, Dick, Joe, Ned, and Jack,
Were all of them locked up in coffins of black.

And by came an Angel who had a bright key,
And he opened the coffins and set them all free;
Then down a green plain leaping, laughing, they run,
And wash in a river, and shine in the sun.

Then naked and white, all their bags left behind,
They rise upon clouds and sport in the wind;
And the Angel told Tom, if he'd be a good boy,
He'd have God for his father, and never want joy.

And so Tom awoke; and we rose in the dark,
And got with our bags and our brushes to work.
Though the morning was cold, Tom was happy and warm;
So if all do their duty they need not fear harm.

*During the eighteenth and early nineteenth centuries, orphans as young as four years old were apprenticed to chimney sweepers.

WILLIAM BLAKE (1757–1827)

The Lamb (1789)

Little Lamb, who made thee?
Dost thou know who made thee?
Gave thee life & bid thee feed,
By the stream & o'er the mead;
Gave thee clothing of delight,
Softest clothing wooly bright;
Gave thee such a tender voice,
Making all the vales rejoice!
Little Lamb who made thee?
Dost thou know who made thee?

Little Lamb I'll tell thee,
Little Lamb I'll tell thee!
He is calléd by thy name,
For he calls himself a Lamb:
He is meek & he is mild,
He became a little child:
I a child & thou a lamb,
We are calléd by his name.
Little Lamb God bless thee.
Little Lamb God bless thee.

WILLIAM BLAKE (1757–1827)

London (1794)

I wander through each chartered street,
Near where the chartered Thames does flow,
And mark in every face I meet
Marks of weakness, marks of woe.

In every cry of every man,
In every infant's cry of fear,
In every voice, in every ban,
The mind-forged manacles I hear.

How the chimney-sweeper's cry
Every black'ning church appalls;
And the hapless soldier's sigh
Runs in blood down palace walls.

But most through midnight streets I hear
How the youthful harlot's curse
Blasts the new born infant's tear,
And blights with plagues the marriage hearse.

WILLIAM BLAKE (1757–1827)

To see a World in a Grain of Sand (1803)

To see a World in a Grain of Sand
And a Heaven in a Wild Flower,
Hold Infinity in the palm of your hand
And Eternity in an hour.

WILLIAM BLAKE (1757–1827)

The Tyger (1794)

Tyger! Tyger! burning bright
In the forests of the night,
What immortal hand or eye
Could frame thy fearful symmetry?

In what distant deeps or skies
Burnt the fire of thine eyes?
On what wings dare he aspire?
What the hand dare seize the fire?

And what shoulder, and what art,
Could twist the sinews of thy heart?
And when thy heart began to beat,
What dread hand? and what dread feet?

What the hammer? what the chain?
In what furnace was thy brain?
What the anvil? what dread grasp
Dare its deadly terrors clasp?

When the stars threw down their spears,
And watered heaven with their tears,
Did he smile his work to see?
Did he who made the Lamb make thee?

Tyger! Tyger! burning bright
In the forests of the night,
What immortal hand or eye
Dare frame thy fearful symmetry?

EAVAN BOLAND (1944–)

The Emigrant Irish (1987)

Like oil lamps, we put them out the back—

of our houses, of our minds. We had lights
better than, newer than and then

a time came, this time and now
we need them. Their dread, makeshift example:

they would have thrived on our necessities.
What they survived we could not even live.
By their lights now it is time to
imagine how they stood there, what they stood with,
that their possessions may become our power:
Cardboard. Iron. Their hardships parceled in them.
Patience. Fortitude. Long-suffering
in the bruise-colored dusk of the New World.

And all the old songs. And nothing to lose.

ANNE BRADSTREET (1612–1672)

The Author to Her Book° (1678)

Thou ill-formed offspring of my feeble brain,
Who after birth did'st by my side remain,
Till snatched from thence by friends, less wise than true,
Who thee abroad exposed to public view;
Made thee in rags, halting, to the press to trudge,
Where errors were not lessened, all may judge.
At thy return my blushing was not small,
My rambling brat (in print) should mother call;
I cast thee by as one unfit for light,
Thy visage was so irksome in my sight;
Yet being mine own, at length affection would
Thy blemishes amend, if so I could:
I washed thy face, but more defects I saw,
And rubbing off a spot, still made a flaw.
I stretched thy joints to make thee even feet,°
Yet still thou run'st more hobbling than is meet;°
In better dress to trim thee was my mind,
But nought save homespun cloth in the house I find.
In this array, 'mongst vulgars° may'st thou roam;
In critics' hands beware thou dost not come;
And take thy way where yet thou are not known.
If for thy Father asked, say thou had'st none;
And for thy Mother, she alas is poor,
Which caused her thus to send thee out of door.

Her Book: Bradstreet addresses *The Tenth Muse,* a collection of her poetry published without her consent in 1650.
even feet: Metrical feet.
meet: Appropriate or decorous.
vulgars: Common people.

GWENDOLYN BROOKS (1917–2000)

The *Chicago Defender*° Sends a Man to Little Rock (1960)

Fall, 1957°

In Little Rock the people bear
Babes, and comb and part their hair
And watch the want ads, put repair
To roof and latch. While wheat toast burns
A woman waters multiferns.

Time upholds or overturns
The many, tight, and small concerns.

In Little Rock the people sing
Sunday hymns like anything,
Through Sunday pomp and polishing.

And after testament and tunes,
Some soften Sunday afternoons
With lemon tea and Lorna Doones.

I forecast
And I believe
Come Christmas Little Rock will cleave
To Christmas tree and trifle, weave,
From laugh and tinsel, texture fast.

In Little Rock is baseball; Barcarolle.°
That hotness in July . . . the uniformed figures raw and implacable
And not intellectual,
Batting the hotness or clawing the suffering dust.
The Open Air Concert, on the special twilight green. . . .
When Beethoven is brutal or whispers to lady-like air.
Blanket-sitters are solemn, as Johann troubles to lean
To tell them what to mean. . . .

There is love, too, in Little Rock. Soft women softly
Opening themselves in kindness,
Or, pitying one's blindness,
Awaiting one's pleasure
In azure

Chicago Defender: A weekly newspaper for African-American readers.

Fall, 1957: When black students first entered the public high school in Little Rock, Arkansas, in 1957, the city erupted in race riots protesting desegregation.

Barcarolle: A Venetian gondolier's song, or a song suggesting the rhythm of rowing.

Glory with anguished rose at the root. . . .
To wash away old semi-discomfitures.
They re-teach purple and unsullen blue.
The wispy soils go. And uncertain
Half-havings have they clarified to sures.

In Little Rock they know
Not answering the telephone is a way of rejecting life,
That it is our business to be bothered, is our business
To cherish bores or boredom, be polite
To lies and love and many-faceted fuzziness.
I scratch my head, massage the hate-I-had.
I blink across my prim and pencilled pad.
The saga I was sent for is not down.
Because there is a puzzle in this town.
The biggest News I do not dare
Telegraph to the Editor's chair:
"They are like people everywhere."

The angry Editor would reply
In hundred harryings of Why.

And true, they are hurling spittle, rock,
Garbage and fruit in Little Rock.
And I saw coiling storm a-writhe
On bright madonnas. And a scythe
Of men harassing brownish girls.
(The bows and barrettes in the curls
And braids declined away from joy.)

I saw a bleeding brownish boy. . . .

The lariat lynch-wish I deplored.

The loveliest lynchee was our Lord.

GWENDOLYN BROOKS (1917–2000)

Medgar Evers° (1964)

For Charles Evers°

The man whose height his fear improved he
arranged to fear no further. The raw
intoxicated time was time for better birth or a final death.

Medgar Evers: African-American civil rights leader who was killed by a sniper in 1963.
Charles Evers: Medgar Evers's brother.

Old styles, old tempos, all the engagement of
the day— the sedate, the regulated fray—
the antique light, the Moral rose, old gusts,
tight whistlings from the past, the mothballs
in the Love at last our man forswore.

Medgar Evers annoyed confetti and assorted
brands of businessmen's eyes.

The shows came down: to maxims and surprise.
And palsy.

Roaring no rapt arise-ye to the dead, he
leaned across tomorrow. People said that
he was holding clean globes in his hands.

GEORGE GORDON, LORD BYRON (1788–1824)

She Walks in Beauty (1815)

1

She walks in beauty, like the night
Of cloudless climes and starry skies;
And all that's best of dark and bright
Meet in her aspect and her eyes:
Thus mellowed to that tender light
Which heaven to gaudy day denies.

2

One shade the more, one ray the less,
Had half impaired the nameless grace
Which waves in every raven tress,
Or softly lightens o'er her face;
Where thoughts serenely sweet express
How pure, how dear their dwelling place.

3

And on that cheek, and o'er that brow,
So soft, so calm, yet eloquent,
The smiles that win, the tints that glow,
But tell of days in goodness spent,
A mind at peace with all below,
A heart whose love is innocent!

THOMAS CAMPION (1567–1620)

There is a garden in her face (1617)

There is a garden in her face
Where roses and white lilies grow;
A heav'nly paradise is that place
Wherein all pleasant fruits do flow.
There cherries grow which none may buy
Till "Cherry-ripe" themselves do cry.

Those cherries fairly do enclose
Of orient pearl a double row,
Which when her lovely laughter shows,
They look like rose-buds filled with snow;
Yet them nor peer nor prince can buy,
Till "Cherry-ripe" themselves do cry.

Her eyes like angels watch them still;
Her brows like bended bows do stand,
Threat'ning with piercing frowns to kill
All that attempt, with eye or hand
Those sacred cherries to come nigh
Till "Cherry-ripe" themselves do cry.

GEOFFREY CHAUCER (c. 1343–1400)

Source: ©Bettmann/Corbis

See this poet's biography on p. 1219.

from The Canterbury Tales

Part I
from The General Prologue

Here bigynneth the Book of the Tales of Caunterbury.

Whan that Aprill with his shoures soote°
The droghte of March hath perced to the roote,
And bathed every veyne in swich licour°
Of which vertu° engendred is the flour;
Whan Zephirus eek° with his sweete breeth
Inspired hath in every holt and heeth°
The tendre croppes, and the yonge sonne
Hath in the Ram his halfe cours yronne,°

his shoures soote: its sweet showers.
veyne in swich licour: vein (as in the veins in a plant) in such liquid.
of which vertu: by the power of which.
Whan Zephirus eek: When the West Wind also.
every holt and heath: grove and field.
and the yonge sonne / Hath in the Ram his halfe cours yronne: Refers to the sun in its zodiac cycle. It is young because it has run only halfway through its course in Aries, the Ram, which is the first sign of the zodiac in the solar year.

And smale foweles maken melodye,
That slepen al the nyght with open eye—
So priketh hem nature in hir corages—°
Thanne longen folk to goon° on pilgrimages,
And palmeres° for to seken straunge strondes°
To ferne halwes, kowthe in sondry londes;°
And specially from every shires ende
Of Engelond to Caunterbury they wende
The hooly blisful martir° for to seke
That hem hath holpen° whan that they were seeke.°
  Bilfil that in that seson on a day
In Southwerk at the Tabard° as I lay
Redy to wenden on my pilgrymage
To Caunterbury with ful devout corage,
At nyght was come into that hostelrye
Wel nyne and twenty in a compaignye
Of sondry° folk, by aventure° yfalle
In felaweship, and pilgrimes were they alle,
That toward Caunterbury wolden° ryde.
The chambres and the stables weren wyde,°
And wel we weren esed atte beste.°
And shortly, whan the sonne was to reste,
So hadde I spoken with hem everichon°
That I was of hir felaweship anon,°
And made forward° erly for to ryse,
To take oure wey ther as I yow devyse.°
  But nathelees, whil I have tyme and space,

in hir corages: in their hearts.
goon: go.
palmeres: professional pilgrims, whose emblem was a palm frond.
strondes: lands.
ferne halwes, kowthe in sondry londes: far-off shrines known in various lands.
The hooly blissful martir: refers to St. Thomas à Becket, a martyr who was murdered in the Canterbury Cathedral in 1170.
holpen: helped.
seeke: sick.
Southwerk, Tabard: Southwark, site of the Tabard Inn, then a suburb of London, south of the Thames River.
sondry: various.
aventure: chance.
wolden: would.
wyde: spacious.
esed atte beste: accommodated in the best possible way.
everichon: everyone.
anon: at once.
made forward: (we) made an agreement.
as I yow devyse: as I will tell you.

Er° that I ferther in this tale pace,°
Me thynketh it acordaunt to resoun
To telle yow al the condicioun°
Of ech of hem, so as it semed me,
And whiche they weren, and of what degree,°
And eek in what array that they were inne,
And at a knyght than° wol I first bigynne.

LUCILLE CLIFTON (1936–)

praise song*

to my aunt blanche
who rolled from grass to driveway
into the street one sunday morning.
i was ten. i had never seen
a human woman hurl her basketball
of a body into the traffic of the world.
Praise to the drivers who stopped in time.
Praise to the faith with which she rose
after some moments then slowly walked
sighing back to her family.
Praise to the arms which understood
little or nothing of what it meant
but welcomed her in without judgment,
accepting it all like children might,
like God.

JUDITH ORTIZ COFER (1952–)

Claims (1990)

Last time I saw her, Grandmother
had grown seamed as a bedouin tent.
She had claimed the right
to sleep alone, to own
her nights, to never bear
the weight of sex again, nor to accept
its gift of comfort, for the luxury
of stretching her bones.
She's carried eight children,
three had sunk in her belly, *náufragos*,

Er / pace: Before, pass.
condicioun: circumstance.
whiche . . . degree: what status or rank.
than: then.
*Publication date is not available.

she called them, shipwrecked babies,
drowned in her black waters.
Children are made in the night and
steal your days
for the rest of your life, amen. She said this
to each of her daughters in turn. Once she had made a pact
with man and nature and kept it. Now like the sea,
she is claiming back her territory.

Source: ©The Granger Collection

See this poet's biography on p. 1219.

SAMUEL TAYLOR COLERIDGE (1772–1834)

Kubla Khan° (1797, 1798)

Or, a Vision in a Dream. A Fragment.

In Xanadu did Kubla Khan
A stately pleasure-dome decree:
Where Alph,° the sacred river, ran
Through caverns measureless to man
Down to a sunless sea.
So twice five miles of fertile ground
With walls and towers were girdled round;
And there were gardens bright with sinuous rills,
Where blossomed many an incense-bearing tree;
And here were forests ancient as the hills,
Enfolding sunny spots of greenery.

But oh! that deep romantic chasm which slanted
Down the green hill athwart a cedarn cover!
A savage place! as holy and enchanted
As e'er beneath a waning moon was haunted
By woman wailing for her demon-lover!
And from this chasm, with ceaseless turmoil seething,
As if this earth in fast thick pants were breathing,
A mighty fountain momently was forced:
Amid whose swift half-intermitted burst
Huge fragments vaulted like rebounding hail,
Or chaffy grain beneath the thresher's flail:
And 'mid these dancing rocks at once and ever
It flung up momently the sacred river.
Five miles meandering with a mazy motion
Through wood and dale the sacred river ran,

Kubla Khan: Coleridge mythologizes the actual Kublai Khan, a thirteenth-century Mongol emperor, as well as the Chinese city of Xanadu.
Alph: Probably derived from the Greek river Alpheus, whose waters, according to legend, rose from the Ionian Sea in Sicily as the fountain of Arethusa.

Then reached the caverns measureless to man,
And sank in tumult to a lifeless ocean:
And 'mid this tumult Kubla heard from far
Ancestral voices prophesying war!

The shadow of the dome of pleasure
Floated midway on the waves;
Where was heard the mingled measure
From the fountain and the caves.
It was a miracle of rare device,
A sunny pleasure-dome with caves of ice!

A damsel with a dulcimer
In a vision once I saw:
It was an Abyssinian maid,
And on her dulcimer she played,
Singing of Mount Abora.°
Could I revive within me
Her symphony and song,
To such a deep delight 'twould win me,
That with music loud and long,
I would build that dome in air,
That sunny dome! those caves of ice!
And all who heard should see them there,
And all should cry, Beware! Beware!
His flashing eyes, his floating hair!
Weave a circle round him thrice,°
And close your eyes with holy dread,
For he on honey-dew hath fed,
And drunk the milk of Paradise.

BILLY COLLINS (1941–)

Introduction to Poetry (1988)

I ask them to take a poem
and hold it up to the light
like a color slide

or press an ear against its hive.

I say drop a mouse into a poem
and watch him probe his way out,

Mount Abora: Some scholars see a reminiscence here of John Milton's *Paradise Lost* 4.280–82: "where Abassin kings their issue guard / Mount Amara, though this by some supposed / True Paradise under the Ethiop Line."
Weave . . . thrice: A magic ritual to keep away intruding spirits.

or walk inside the poem's room
and feel the walls for a light switch.

I want them to waterski
across the surface of a poem
waving at the author's name on the shore.

But all they want to do
is tie the poem to a chair with rope
and torture a confession out of it.

They begin beating it with a hose
to find out what it really means.

BILLY COLLINS (1941–)

The Names* (2002)

Yesterday, I lay awake in the palm of the night.
A fine rain stole in, unhelped by any breeze,
And when I saw the silver glaze on the windows,
I started with A, with Ackerman, as it happened,
Then Baxter and Calabro,
Davis and Eberling, names falling into place
As droplets fell through the dark.

Names printed on the ceiling of the night.
Names slipping around a watery bend.
Twenty-six willows on the banks of a stream.

In the morning, I walked out barefoot
Among thousands of flowers
Heavy with dew like the eyes of tears,
And each had a name—
Fiori inscribed on a yellow petal
Then Gonzalez and Han, Ishikawa and Jenkins.

Names written in the air
And stitched into the cloth of the day.
A name under a photograph taped to a mailbox.
Monogram on a torn shirt,
I see you spelled out on storefront windows
And on the bright unfurled awnings of this city.
I say the syllables as I turn a corner—
Kelly and Lee,
Medina, Nardella, and O'Connor.

*Billy Collins, former poet laureate of The United States, read this poem before a special joint session of Congress in New York City on September 6, 2002, in honor of the first anniversary of the terrorist attacks that took place on September 11, 2001.

When I peer into the woods,
I see a thick tangle where letters are hidden
As in a puzzle concocted for children.
Parker and Quigley in the twigs of an ash,
Rizzo, Schubert, Torres, and Upton,
Secrets in the boughs of an ancient maple.

Names written in the pale sky.
Names rising in the updraft amid buildings.
Names silent in stone
Or cried out behind a door.
Names blown over the earth and out to sea.

In the evening—weakening light, the last swallows.
A boy on a lake lifts his oars.
A woman by a window puts a match to a candle,
And the names are outlined on the rose clouds—
Vanacore and Wallace,
(let X stand, if it can, for the ones unfound)
Then Young and Ziminsky, the final jolt of Z.

Names etched on the head of a pin.
One name spanning a bridge, another undergoing a tunnel.
A blue name needled into the skin.
Names of citizens, workers, mothers and fathers,
The bright-eyed daughter, the quick son.
Alphabet of names in green rows in a field.
Names in the small tracks of birds.
Names lifted from a hat
Or balanced on the tip of the tongue.
Names wheeled into the dim warehouse of memory.
So many names, there is barely room on the walls of the heart.

E. E. CUMMINGS (1894–1962)

Buffalo Bill's (1923)

Buffalo Bill's
defunct
                    who used to
                    ride a watersmooth-silver
                                                            stallion
and break onetwothreefourfive pigeonsjustlikethat
                                                                                    Jesus

he was a handsome man
                                        and what i want to know is
how do you like your blueeyed boy
Mister Death

E. E. CUMMINGS (1894–1962)

next to of course god america i (1926)

"next to of course god america i
love you land of the pilgrims' and so forth oh
say can you see by the dawn's early my
country 'tis of centuries come and go
and are no more what of it we should worry
in every language even deafanddumb
thy sons acclaim your glorious name by gorry
by jingo by gee by gosh by gum
why talk of beauty what could be more beautiful than these heroic happy dead
who rushed like lions to the roaring slaughter
they did not stop to think they died instead
then shall the voice of liberty be mute?"

He spoke. And drank rapidly a glass of water

EMILY DICKINSON (1830–1886)

After great pain, a formal feeling comes— (1862)

After great pain, a formal feeling comes—
The Nerves sit ceremonious, like Tombs—
The stiff Heart questions was it He, that bore,
And Yesterday, or Centuries before?

The Feet, mechanical, go round—
Of Ground, or Air, or Ought—
A Wooden way
Regardless grown,
A Quartz contentment, like a stone—

This is the Hour of Lead—
Remembered, if outlived,
As Freezing persons, recollect the Snow—
First—Chill—then Stupor—then the letting go—

EMILY DICKINSON (1830–1886)

Because I could not stop for Death— (1863)

Because I could not stop for Death—
He kindly stopped for me—
The Carriage held but just Ourselves—
And Immortality.

We slowly drove—He knew no haste
And I had put away
My labor and my leisure too,
For His Civility—

We passed the School, where Children strove
At Recess—in the Ring—
We passed the Fields of Gazing Grain—
We passed the Setting Sun—

Or rather—He passed Us—
The Dews drew quivering and chill—
For only Gossamer, my Gown—
My Tippet°— only Tulle—

We passed before a House that seemed
A Swelling of the Ground—
The Roof was scarcely visible—
The Cornice—in the Ground—

Since then—'tis Centuries—and yet
Feels shorter than the Day
I first surmised the Horses' Heads
Were toward Eternity—

EMILY DICKINSON (1830–1886)

"Faith" is a fine invention (1860)

"Faith" is a fine invention
When Gentlemen can *see*—
But *Microscopes* are prudent
In an Emergency.

EMILY DICKINSON (1830–1886)

"Heaven"—is what I cannot reach! (1861)

"Heaven"—is what I cannot reach!
The Apple on the Tree—
Provided it do hopeless—hang—
That—"Heaven" is—to Me!

The Color, on the Cruising Cloud—
The interdicted Land—

Tippet: A short cape or scarf.

Behind the Hill—the House behind—
There—Paradise—is found!

Her teasing Purples—Afternoons—
The credulous—decoy—
Enamored—of the Conjuror—
That spurned us—Yesterday!

EMILY DICKINSON (1830–1886)

I dwell in Possibility— (1862)

I dwell in Possibility—
A fairer House than Prose—
More numerous of Windows—
Superior—for Doors—

Of Chambers as the Cedars—
Impregnable of Eye—
And for an Everlasting Roof
The Gambrels° of the Sky—

Of Visitors—the fairest—
For Occupation—This—
The spreading wide my narrow Hands
To gather Paradise—

EMILY DICKINSON (1830–1886)

I heard a Fly buzz—when I died— (1862)

I heard a Fly buzz—when I died—
The Stillness in the Room
Was like the Stillness in the Air—
Between the Heaves of Storm—

The Eyes around—had wrung them dry—
And Breaths were gathering firm
For that last Onset—when the King
Be witnessed—in the Room—

I willed my Keepsakes—Signed away
What portion of me be

Gambrels: A gambrel roof; a ridged roof with two slopes on each side.

Assignable—and then it was
There interposed a Fly—

With Blue—uncertain stumbling Buzz—
Between the light—and me—
And then the Windows failed—and then
I could not see to see—

EMILY DICKINSON (1830–1886)

I never saw a Moor— (1865)

I never saw a Moor—
I never saw the Sea—
Yet know I how the Heather looks
And what a Billow be.

I never spoke with God
Nor visited in Heaven—
Yet certain am I of the spot
As if the Checks were given—

EMILY DICKINSON (1830–1886)

I taste a liquor never brewed— (1861)

I taste a liquor never brewed—
From Tankards scooped in Pearl—
Not all the Frankfort Berries°
Yield such an Alcohol!

Inebriate of Air—am I—
and Debauchee of Dew—
Reeling—thro endless summer days—
From inns of Molten Blue—

When "Landlords" turn the drunken Bee
Out of the Foxglove's door—
When Butterflies—renounce their "drams"—
I shall but drink the more!

Till Seraphs swing their snowy Hats—
And Saints—to windows run—
To see the little Tippler
From Manzanilla come!

Frankfort Berries: The 1890 Higginson and Todd edition *Poems* changed "Frankfort Berries" to "vats upon the Rhine."

EMILY DICKINSON (1830–1886)

Much Madness is divinest Sense— (1862)

Much Madness is divinest Sense—
To a discerning Eye—
Much Sense—the starkest Madness—
'Tis the Majority
In this, as All, prevail—

Assent—and you are sane—
Demur—you're straightway dangerous—
And handled with a Chain—

EMILY DICKINSON (1830–1886)

Some keep the Sabbath going to Church— (1860)

Some keep the Sabbath going to Church—
I keep it, staying at Home—
With a Bobolink for a Chorister—
And an Orchard, for a Dome—

Some keep the Sabbath in Surplice°
I just wear my Wings—
And instead of tolling the Bell, for Church,
Our little Sexton—sings.

God preaches, a noted Clergyman—
And the sermon is never long,
So instead of getting to Heaven, at last—
I'm going, all along.

EMILY DICKINSON (1830–1886)

The Soul selects her own Society— (1862)

The Soul selects her own Society—
Then—shuts the Door—
To her divine Majority—
Present no more—

Unmoved—she notes the Chariots—pausing—
At her low Gate—
Unmoved—an Emperor be kneeling
Upon her Mat—

Surplice: A white, loose-fitting robe with broad sleeves worn by members of the clergy.

I've known her—from an ample nation—
Choose One—
Then—close the Valves of her attention—
Like Stone—

EMILY DICKINSON (1830–1886)

Success is counted sweetest (1859)

Success is counted sweetest
By those who ne'er succeed.
To comprehend a nectar°
Requires sorest need.

Not one of all the purple Host
Who took the Flag today
Can tell the definition
So clear of Victory

As he defeated—dying—
On whose forbidden ear
The distant strains of triumph
Burst agonized and clear!

EMILY DICKINSON (1830–1886)

Tell all the Truth but tell it slant— (1868)

Tell all the Truth but tell it slant—
Success in Circuit lies
Too bright for our infirm Delight
The Truth's superb surprise
As Lightning to the Children eased
With explanation kind
The Truth must dazzle gradually
Or every man be blind—

EMILY DICKINSON (1830–1886)

There is no Frigate like a Book (1873)

There is no Frigate like a Book
To take us Lands away

Nectar: In Greek mythology, the drink of the gods.

Nor any Coursers like a Page
Of prancing Poetry—
This Traverse may the poorest take
Without oppress of Toll—
How frugal is the Chariot
That bears the Human soul.

EMILY DICKINSON (1830–1886)

There's a certain Slant of light (c. 1861)

There's a certain Slant of light,
Winter Afternoons—
That oppresses, like the Heft
Of Cathedral Tunes—

Heavenly Hurt, it gives us—
We can find no scar,
But internal difference,
Where the Meanings, are—

None may teach it—Any—
'Tis the Seal Despair—
An imperial affliction
Sent us of the Air—

When it comes, the landscape listens—
Shadows—hold their breath—
When it goes, 'tis like the Distance
On the look of Death—

EMILY DICKINSON (1830–1886)

This is my letter to the World (1862)

This is my letter to the World
That never wrote to Me—
The simple News that Nature told—
With tender Majesty

Her Message is committed
To Hands I cannot see
For love of Her — Sweet — countrymen —
Judge tenderly — of Me

EMILY DICKINSON (1830–1886)

Wild Nights—Wild Nights! (1861)

Wild Nights—Wild Nights!
Were I with thee
Wild Nights should be
Our luxury!

Futile—the Winds—
To a Heart in port—
Done with the Compass—
Done with the Chart!

Rowing in Eden—
Ah, the Sea!
Might I but moor—Tonight—
In Thee!

Source: ©The Granger Collection

See this poet's biography on p. 1220.

JOHN DONNE (1572–1631)

Batter My Heart, Three-Personed God (c. 1610)

Batter my heart, three-personed God, for You
As yet but knock, breathe, shine, and seek to mend.
That I may rise and stand, o'erthrow me, and bend
Your force to break, blow, burn, and make me new.
I, like an usurped town to another due,
Labor to admit You, but Oh! to no end.
Reason, Your viceroy in me, me should defend,
But is captived, and proves weak or untrue.
Yet dearly I love You, and would be lovèd fain,
But am betrothed unto Your enemy;
Divorce me, untie or break that knot again;
Take me to You, imprison me, for I,
Except You enthrall me, never shall be free,
Nor ever chaste, except You ravish me.

JOHN DONNE (1572–1631)

Death Be Not Proud (c. 1610)

Death be not proud, though some have callèd thee
Mighty and dreadful, for thou art not so;
For those whom thou think'st thou dost overthrow
Die not, poor death, nor yet canst thou kill me.
From rest and sleep, which but thy pictures be,

Much pleasure, then from thee much more must flow,
And soonest our best men with thee do go,
Rest of their bones, and soul's delivery.
Thou art slave to fate, chance, kings, and desperate men,
And dost with poison, war, and sickness dwell,
And poppy, or charms can make us sleep as well,
And better than thy stroke; why swell'st thou then?
One short sleep past, we wake eternally,
And death shall be no more; death, thou shalt die.

JOHN DONNE (1572–1631)

The Flea (1633)

Mark but this flea, and mark in this°
How little that which thou deny'st me is;
It sucked me first, and now sucks thee,
And in this flea our two bloods mingled be;
Thou know'st that this cannot be said
A sin, nor shame, nor loss of maidenhead,
  Yet this enjoys before it woo,
  And pampered swells with one blood made of two,
  And this, alas, is more than we would do.°

Oh stay, three lives in one flea spare,
Where we almost, yea more than, married are.
This flea is you and I, and this
Our marriage bed, and marriage temple is;
Though parents grudge, and you, we're met
And cloistered in these living walls of jet.
  Though use make you apt to kill me,
  Let not to that, self-murder added be,
  And sacrilege, three sins in killing three.

Cruel and sudden, hast thou since
Purpled thy nail in blood of innocence?
Wherein could this flea guilty be,
Except in that drop which it sucked from thee?
Yet thou triumph'st, and say'st that thou
Find'st not thyself, nor me, the weaker now;
  'Tis true; then learn how false, fears be;
  Just so much honor, when thou yield'st to me,
  Will waste, as this flea's death took life from thee.

---

mark in this: Note the moral lesson in it.
more than we would do: If we do not join our blood.

JOHN DONNE (1572–1631)

Song (1633)

Go and catch a falling star,
Get with child a mandrake root,°
Tell me where all past years are,
Or who cleft the Devil's foot,
Teach me to hear mermaids singing,
Or to keep off envy's stinging,
And find
What wind
Serves to advance an honest mind.

If thou be'st borne to strange sights,
Things invisible to see,
Ride ten thousand days and nights,
Till age snow white hairs on thee,
Thou, when thou return'st, wilt tell me
All strange wonders that befell thee,
And swear
Nowhere
Lives a woman true, and fair.

If thou findst one, let me know,
Such a pilgrimage were sweet—
Yet do not, I would not go,
Though at next door we might meet;
Though she were true, when you met her,
And last, till you write your letter,
Yet she
Will be
False, ere I come, to two, or three.

PAUL LAURENCE DUNBAR (1872–1906)

We Wear the Mask (1896)

We wear the mask that grins and lies,
It hides our cheeks and shades our eyes—
This debt we pay to human guile;
With torn and bleeding hearts we smile,
And mouth with myriad subtleties.

mandrake root: Also called *mandragora,* the mandrake root is forked and resembles the lower part of the human body; it was thought to be an aphrodisiac.

Why should the world be over-wise,
In counting all our tears and sighs?
Nay, let them only see us, while
We wear the mask.

We smile, but, O great Christ, our cries
To thee from tortured souls arise.
We sing, but oh the clay is vile
Beneath our feet, and long the mile;
But let the world dream otherwise,
We wear the mask!

T. S. ELIOT (1888–1965)

The Love Song of J. Alfred Prufrock (1917)

S'io credessi che mia risposta fosse
A persona che mai tornasse al mondo,
Questa fiamma staria senza piu scosse.
Ma perciocche giammai di questo fondo
Non torno vivo alcun, s'i'odo il vero,
Senza tema d'infamia ti rispondo.°

Let us go then, you and I,
When the evening is spread out against the sky
Like a patient etherized upon a table;
Let us go, through certain half-deserted streets,
The muttering retreats
Of restless nights in one-night cheap hotels
And sawdust restaurants with oyster-shells:
Streets that follow like a tedious argument
Of insidious intent
To lead you to an overwhelming question . . .
Oh, do not ask, "What is it?"
Let us go and make our visit.

In the room the women come and go
Talking of Michelangelo.

The yellow fog that rubs its back upon the window-panes,
The yellow smoke that rubs its muzzle on the window-panes
Licked its tongue into the corners of the evening,
Lingered upon the pools that stand in drains,

S'io . . . rispondo: The epigraph is from Dante's *Inferno,* Canto 27. In response to the poet's question about his identity, Guido da Montefelto, who for his sin of fraud must spend eternity wrapped in flames, replies: "If I thought that I was speaking to someone who could go back to the world, this flame would shake me no more. But since from this place nobody ever returns alive, if what I hear is true, I answer you without fear of infamy."

Let fall upon its back the soot that falls from chimneys,
Slipped by the terrace, made a sudden leap,
And seeing that it was a soft October night,
Curled once about the house, and fell asleep.

And indeed there will be time
For the yellow smoke that slides along the street,
Rubbing its back upon the window-panes;
There will be time, there will be time
To prepare a face to meet the faces that you meet;
There will be time to murder and create,
And time for all the works and days° of hands
That lift and drop a question on your plate;
Time for you and time for me,
And time yet for a hundred indecisions,
And for a hundred visions and revisions,
Before the taking of a toast and tea.

In the room the women come and go
Talking of Michelangelo.

And indeed there will be time
To wonder, "Do I dare?" and, "Do I dare?"
Time to turn back and descend the stair,
With a bald spot in the middle of my hair—
(They will say: "How his hair is growing thin!")
My morning coat, my collar mounting firmly to the chin,
My necktie rich and modest, but asserted by a simple pin—
(They will say: "But how his arms and legs are thin!")
Do I dare
Disturb the universe?
In a minute there is time
For decisions and revisions which a minute will reverse.

For I have known them all already, known them all—
Have known the evenings, mornings, afternoons,
I have measured out my life with coffee spoons;
I know the voices dying with a dying fall°
Beneath the music from a farther room.
    So how should I presume?

And I have known the eyes already, known them all—
The eyes that fix you in a formulated phrase,
And when I am formulated, sprawling on a pin,

works and days: Works and Days, by the eighth-century B.C. Greek poet Hesiod, is a poem that celebrates farm life.
dying fall: An allusion to Orsino's speech in *Twelfth Night* (1.1): "That strain again! It had a dying fall."

When I am pinned and wriggling on the wall,
Then how should I begin
To spit out all the butt-ends of my days and ways?
  And how should I presume?

And I have known the arms already, known them all—
Arms that are braceleted and white and bare
(But in the lamplight, downed with light brown hair!)
Is it perfume from a dress
That makes me so digress?
Arms that lie along a table, or wrap about a shawl.
  And should I then presume?
  And how should I begin?

* * *

Shall I say, I have gone at dusk through narrow streets
And watched the smoke that rises from the pipes
Of lonely men in shirt-sleeves, leaning out of windows? . . .

I should have been a pair of ragged claws
Scuttling across the floors of silent seas.

* * *

And the afternoon, the evening, sleeps so peacefully!
Smoothed by long fingers,
Asleep . . . tired . . . or it malingers,
Stretched on the floor, here beside you and me.
Should I, after tea and cakes and ices,
Have the strength to force the moment to its crisis?
But though I have wept and fasted, wept and prayed,
Though I have seen my head (grown slightly bald) brought in
  upon a platter,°
I am no prophet—and here's no great matter;
I have seen the moment of my greatness flicker,
And I have seen the eternal Footman° hold my coat, and
  snicker,
And in short, I was afraid.

And would it have been worth it, after all,
After the cups, the marmalade, the tea,
Among the porcelain, among some talk of you and me,
Would it have been worth while,
To have bitten off the matter with a smile,
To have squeezed the universe into a ball

head . . . platter: Like John the Baptist, who was beheaded by King Herod (see Matthew 14.3–11).
eternal Footman: Perhaps death or fate.

To roll it toward some overwhelming question,
To say: "I am Lazarus,° come from the dead,
Come back to tell you all, I shall tell you all"—
If one, settling a pillow by her head,
Should say: "That is not what I meant at all.
That is not it, at all."

And would it have been worth it, after all,
Would it have been worth while,
After the sunsets and the dooryards and the sprinkled streets,
After the novels, after the teacups, after the skirts that trail along the floor—
And this, and so much more?—
It is impossible to say just what I mean!
But as if a magic lantern threw the nerves in patterns on a screen:
Would it have been worth while
If one, settling a pillow or throwing off a shawl,
And turning toward the window, should say:
"That is not it at all,
That is not what I meant, at all."

* * *

No! I am not Prince Hamlet, nor was meant to be;
Am an attendant lord, one that will do
To swell a progress,° start a scene or two,
Advise the prince; no doubt, an easy tool,
Deferential, glad to be of use,
Politic, cautious, and meticulous;
Full of high sentence,° but a bit obtuse;
At times, indeed, almost ridiculous—
Almost, at times, the Fool.

I grow old . . . I grow old . . .
I shall wear the bottoms of my trousers rolled.

Shall I part my hair behind? Do I dare to eat a peach?
I shall wear white flannel trousers, and walk upon the beach.
I have heard the mermaids singing, each to each.

I do not think that they will sing to me.

Lazarus: A man whom Christ raised from the dead (see John 11.1–44).
a progress: Here, in the Elizabethan sense of a royal journey.
sentence: Opinions.

I have seen them riding seaward on the waves
Combing the white hair of the waves blown back
When the wind blows the water white and black.

We have lingered in the chambers of the sea
By sea-girls wreathed with seaweed red and brown
Till human voices wake us, and we drown.

JAMES A. EMANUEL (1921–)

Emmett Till° (1968)

I hear a whistling
Through the water.
Little Emmett
Won't be still.
He keeps floating
Round the darkness,
Edging through
The silent chill.
Tell me, please,
That bedtime story
Of the fairy
River Boy
Who swims forever,
Deep in treasures,
Necklaced in
A coral toy.

LOUISE ERDRICH (1954–)

Indian Boarding School: The Runaways (1984)

Home's the place we head for in our sleep.
Boxcars stumbling north in dreams
don't wait for us. We catch them on the run.
The rails, old lacerations that we love,

Emmett Till: Emmett Till, a fourteen-year-old African-American boy from Chicago, was visiting relatives in Mississippi when he allegedly whistled at a white woman who ran a local store. Unfamiliar with the racial climate of the South, he did not realize that his actions would generate a savage response. Several days later, he was kidnapped, and his severely beaten and mutilated body was later found in the river with a heavy cotton gin fan tied around his neck with barbed wire. His death prompted a new chapter in the Civil Rights struggle; the investigation into his murder was reopened in 2004.

shoot parallel across the face and break
just under Turtle Mountains.° Riding scars
you can't get lost. Home is the place they cross.

The lame guard strikes a match and makes the dark
less tolerant. We watch through cracks in boards
as the land starts rolling, rolling till it hurts
to be here, cold in regulation clothes.
We know the sheriff's waiting at midrun
to take us back. His car is dumb and warm.
The highway doesn't rock, it only hums
like a wing of long insults. The worn-down welts
of ancient punishments lead back and forth.

All runaways wear dresses, long green ones,
the color you would think shame was. We scrub
the sidewalks down because it's shameful work.
Our brushes cut the stone in watered arcs
and in the soak frail outlines shiver clear
a moment, things us kids pressed on the dark
face before it hardened, pale, remembering
delicate old injuries, the spines of names and leaves.

ROBERT FROST (1874–1963)

Acquainted with the Night (1928)

I have been one acquainted with the night.
I have walked out in rain—and back in rain.
I have outwalked the furthest city light.

I have looked down the saddest city lane.
I have passed by the watchman on his beat
And dropped my eyes, unwilling to explain.

I have stood still and stopped the sound of feet
When far away an interrupted cry
Came over houses from another street,

But not to call me back or say good-by;
And further still at an unearthly height,
One luminary clock against the sky

Proclaimed the time was neither wrong nor right.
I have been one acquainted with the night.

Turtle Mountains: Erdrich is a descendant of the Turtle Mountain band of the Chippewa.

ROBERT FROST (1874–1963)

Desert Places (1936)

Snow falling and night falling fast, oh, fast
In a field I looked into going past,
And the ground almost covered smooth in snow,
But a few weeds and stubble showing last.

The woods around it have it—it is theirs.
All animals are smothered in their lairs,
I am too absent-spirited to count;
The loneliness includes me unawares.

And lonely as it is, that loneliness
Will be more lonely ere it will be less—
A blanker whiteness of benighted snow
With no expression, nothing to express.

They cannot scare me with their empty spaces
Between stars—on stars where no human race is.
I have it in me so much nearer home
To scare myself with my own desert places.

ROBERT FROST (1874–1963)

Design (1936)

I found a dimpled spider, fat and white,
On a white heal-all,° holding up a moth
Like a white piece of rigid satin cloth—
Assorted characters of death and blight
Mixed ready to begin to morning right,
Like the ingredients of a witches' broth—
A snow-drop spider, a flower like a froth,
And dead wings carried like a paper kite.

What had the flower to do with being white,
The wayside blue and innocent heal-all?
What brought the kindred spider to that height,
Then steered the white moth thither in the night?
What but design of darkness to appall?—
If design govern in a thing so small.

---

heal-all: A perennial weed with flowers ranging from light blue to purple in color.

ROBERT FROST (1874–1963)

Mending Wall (1914)

Something there is that doesn't love a wall,
That sends the frozen-ground-swell under it,
And spills the upper boulders in the sun;
And makes gaps even two can pass abreast.
The work of hunters is another thing:
I have come after them and made repair
Where they have left not one stone on a stone,
But they would have the rabbit out of hiding,
To please the yelping dogs. The gaps I mean,
No one has seen them made or heard them made,
But at spring mending-time we find them there.
I let my neighbor know beyond the hill;
And on a day we meet to walk the line
And set the wall between us once again.
We keep the wall between us as we go.
To each the boulders that have fallen to each.
And some are loaves and some so nearly balls
We have to use a spell to make them balance:
"Stay where you are until our backs are turned!"
We wear our fingers rough with handling them.
Oh, just another kind of outdoor game,
One on a side. It comes to little more:
There where it is we do not need the wall:
He is all pine and I am apple orchard.
My apple trees will never get across
And eat the cones under his pines, I tell him.
He only says, "Good fences make good neighbors."
Spring is the mischief in me, and I wonder
If I could put a notion in his head:
"*Why* do they make good neighbors? Isn't it
Where there are cows? But here there are no cows.
Before I built a wall I'd ask to know
What I was walling in or walling out,
And to whom I was like to give offense.
Something there is that doesn't love a wall,
That wants it down." I could say "Elves" to him,
But it's not elves exactly, and I'd rather
He said it for himself. I see him there
Bringing a stone grasped firmly by the top
In each hand, like an old-stone savage armed.
He moves in darkness as it seems to me,
Not of woods only and the shade of trees.

He will not go behind his father's saying,
And he likes having thought of it so well
He says again, "Good fences make good neighbors."

ROBERT FROST (1874–1963)

The Road Not Taken (1915)

Two roads diverged in a yellow wood,
And sorry I could not travel both
And be one traveler, long I stood
And looked down one as far as I could
To where it bent in the undergrowth;

Then took the other, as just as fair,
And having perhaps the better claim,
Because it was grassy and wanted wear;
Though as for that the passing there
Had worn them really about the same,

And both that morning equally lay
In leaves no step had trodden black.
Oh, I kept the first for another day!
Yet knowing how way leads on to way,
I doubted if I should ever come back.

I shall be telling this with a sigh
Somewhere ages and ages hence:
Two roads diverged in a wood, and I—
I took the one less traveled by,
And that has made all the difference.

ROBERT FROST (1874–1963)

Stopping by Woods on a Snowy Evening (1923)

Whose woods these are I think I know.
His house is in the village though;
He will not see me stopping here
To watch his woods fill up with snow.

My little horse must think it queer
To stop without a farmhouse near
Between the woods and frozen lake
The darkest evening of the year.

He gives his harness bells a shake
To ask if there is some mistake.
The only other sound's the sweep
Of easy wind and downy flake.

The woods are lovely, dark and deep,
But I have promises to keep,
And miles to go before I sleep,
And miles to go before I sleep.

FEDERICO GARCÍA LORCA (1898–1936)

Arbolé,° Arbolé . . . (1955)

Translated by William Logan

Tree, tree
dry and green.

The girl with the pretty face
is out picking olives.
The wind, playboy of towers,
grabs her around the waist.
Four riders passed by
on Andalusian ponies,
with blue and green jackets
and big, dark capes.
"Come to Cordoba, muchacha."
The girl won't listen to them.
Three young bullfighters passed,
slender in the waist,
with jackets the color of oranges
and swords of ancient silver.
"Come to Sevilla, muchacha."
The girl won't listen to them.
When the afternoon had turned
dark brown, with scattered light,
a young man passed by, wearing
roses and myrtle of the moon.
"Come to Granada, muchacha."
And the girl won't listen to him.
The girl with the pretty face
keeps on picking olives
with the grey arm of the wind

Arbolé: Spanish for tree.

wrapped around her waist.
Tree, tree
dry and green.

Arbolé, arbolé,
seco y verdí.

La niña del bello rostro
está cogiendo aceituna.
El viento, galán de torres,
la prende por la cintura.
Pasaron cuatro jinetes
sobre jacas andaluzas,
con trajes de azul y verde,
con largas capas oscuras.
"Vente a Córdoba, muchacha."
La niña no los escucha.
Pasaron tres torerillos
delgaditos de cintura,
con trajes color naranja
y espadas de plata antigua.
"Vente a Córdoba, muchacha."
La niña no los escucha.
Cuando la tarde se puso
morada, con lux difusa,
pasó un joven que llevaba
rosas y mirtos de luna.
"Vente a Granada, muchacha."
Y la niña no lo escucha.
La niña del bello rostro
sigue cogiendo aceituna,
con el brazo gris del viento
ceñido por la cintura.
Arbolé, arbolé.
Seco y verdé.

NIKKI GIOVANNI (1943–)

Nikki-Rosa (1968)

childhood remembrances are always a drag
if you're Black
you always remember things like living in Woodlawn°

Woodlawn: A predominantly black suburb of Cincinnati, Ohio.

with no inside toilet
and if you become famous or something
they never talk about how happy you were to have your mother
all to yourself and
how good the water felt when you got your bath from one of those
big tubs that folk in chicago barbecue in
and somehow when you talk about home
it never gets across how much you
understood their feelings
as the whole family attended meetings about Hollydale
and even though you remember
your biographers never understand
your father's pain as he sells his stock
and another dream goes
and though you're poor it isn't poverty that
concerns you
and though they fought a lot
it isn't your father's drinking that makes any difference
but only that everybody is together and you
and your sister have happy birthdays and very good christmasses
and I really hope no white person ever has cause to write
about me
because they never understand Black love is Black wealth and
they'll
probably talk about my hard childhood and never understand that
all the while I was quite happy

THOM GUNN (1929–2004)

The Man with Night Sweats (1992)

I wake up cold, I who
Prospered through dreams of heat
Wake to their residue,
Sweat, and a clinging sheet.

My flesh was its own shield:
Where it was gashed, it healed.

I grew as I explored
The body I could trust
Even while I adored
The risk that made robust,

A world of wonders in
Each challenge to the skin.

I cannot but be sorry
The given shield was cracked,
My mind reduced to hurry,
My flesh reduced and wrecked.

I have to change the bed,
But catch myself instead

Stopped upright where I am
Hugging my body to me
As if to shield it from
The pains that will go through me,

As if hands were enough
To hold an avalanche off.

THOMAS HARDY (1840–1928)

The Convergence of the Twain (1912)

(Lines on the loss of the "Titanic")

I

In a solitude of the sea
Deep from human vanity,
And the Pride of Life that planned her, stilly couches she.

II

Steel chambers, late the pyres°
Of her salamandrine fires,°
Cold currents thrid,° and turn to rhythmic tidal lyres.

III

Over the mirrors meant
To glass the opulent
The sea-worm crawls—grotesque, slimed, dumb, indifferent.

IV

Jewels in joy designed
To ravish the sensuous mind
Lie lightless, all their sparkles bleared and black and blind.

V

Dim moon-eyed fishes near
Gaze at the gilded gear
And query: "What does this vaingloriousness down here?" . . .

---

pyres: Funeral pyres; piles of wood on which corpses were burned in ancient rites.
salamandrine fires: An allusion to the old belief that salamanders could live in fire.
thrid: Thread (archaic verb form).

VI

Well: while was fashioning
This creature of cleaving wing,
The Immanent° Will that stirs and urges everything

VII

Prepared a sinister mate
For her—so gaily great—
A Shape of Ice, for the time far and dissociate.

VIII

And as the smart ship grew
In stature, grace, and hue,
In shadowy silent distance grew the Iceberg too.

IX

Alien they seemed to be:
No mortal eye could see
The intimate welding of their later history,

X

Or sign that they were bent
By paths coincident
On being anon° twin halves of one august° event,

XI

Till the Spinner of the Years
Said "Now!" And each one hears,
And consummation comes, and jars two hemispheres.

SEAMUS HEANEY (1939–)

Mid-Term Break (1966)

I sat all morning in the college sick bay
Counting bells knelling classes to a close.
At two o'clock our neighbors drove me home.

In the porch I met my father crying—
He had always taken funerals in his stride—
And Big Jim Evans saying it was a hard blow.

The baby cooed and laughed and rocked the pram
When I came in, and I was embarrassed
By old men standing up to shake my hand

Immanent: Inherent, dwelling within.
anon: Soon.
august: Awe-inspiring, majestic.

And tell me they were "sorry for my trouble,"
Whispers informed strangers I was the eldest,
Away at school, as my mother held my hand

In hers and coughed out angry tearless sighs.
At ten o'clock the ambulance arrived
With the corpse, stanched and bandaged by the nurses.

Next morning I went up into the room. Snowdrops
And candles soothed the bedside; I saw him
For the first time in six weeks. Paler now,

Wearing a poppy bruise on his left temple,
He lay in the four foot box as in his cot.
No gaudy scars, the bumper knocked him clear.

A four foot box, a foot for every year.

GARRETT KAORU HONGO (1951–)

And Your Soul Shall Dance* (1976)

for Wakako Yamauchi

Walking to school beside fields
of tomatoes and summer squash,
alone and humming a Japanese love song,
you've concealed copy of *Photoplay*
between your algebra and English texts.
Your knee socks, saddle shoes, plaid dress,
and blouse, long-sleeved and white
with ruffles down the front,
come from a Sears catalogue
and neatly complement your new Toni curls.
All of this sets you apart from the landscape:
flat valley grooved with irrigation ditches,
a tractor grinding through alkaline earth,
the short stands of windbreak eucalyptus
shuttering the desert wind
from a small cluster of wooden shacks
where your mother hangs the wash.
You want to go somewhere.
Somewhere far away from all the dust
and sorting machines and acres of lettuce.

*The title is based on *And the Soul Shall Dance*, a play by Wakako Yamauchi about two first-generation immigrant Japanese families struggling to make ends meet from crop to crop during the Great Depression.

Someplace where you might be kissed
by someone with smooth, artistic hands.
When you turn into the schoolyard,
the flagpole gleams like a knife blade in the sun,
and classmates scatter like chickens,
shooed by the storm brooding on your horizon.

GERARD MANLEY HOPKINS (1844–1889)

God's Grandeur (1877)

The world is charged with the grandeur of God.
　It will flame out, like shining from shook foil;
　It gathers to a greatness, like the ooze of oil
Crushed. Why do men then now not reck his rod?
Generations have trod, have trod, have trod;
　And all is seared with trade; bleared, smeared with toil;
　And wears man's smudge and shares man's smell: the soil
Is bare now, nor can foot feel, being shod.
And for all this, nature is never spent;
　There lives the dearest freshness deep down things;
And though the last lights off the black West went
　Oh, morning, at the brown brink eastward, springs—
Because the Holy Ghost over the bent
　World broods with warm breast and with ah! bright wings.

TED HUGHES (1930–1998)

Where I Sit Writing My Letter (1986)

Suddenly hooligan baby starlings
Rain all round me squealing,
Shouting how it's tremendous and everybody
Has to join in and they're off this minute!

Probably the weird aniseed corpse-odour
Of the hawthorn flower's disturbed them,
As it disturbs me. Now they all rise
Flutter-floating, oddly eddying,

Squalling their dry gargles. Then, mad, they
Hurl off, on a new wrench of excitement,
Leaving me out.
　　　　　　　I pluck apple-blossom,
Cool, blood-lipped, wet open.
And I'm just quieting thoughts towards my letter
When they all come storming back,

Giddy with hoarse hissings and snarls
And clot the top of an ash sapling—

Sizzling bodies, snaky black necks craning
For a fresh thrill—Where next? Where now? Where?—they're off
All rushing after it
Leaving me fevered, and addled.

They can't believe their wings.

Snow-bright clouds boil up.

DONALD JUSTICE (1925–2004)

Men at Forty (1967)

Men at forty
Learn to close softly
The doors to rooms they will not be
Coming back to.

At rest on a stair landing,
They feel it
Moving beneath them now like the deck of a ship,
Though the swell is gentle.

And deep in mirrors
They rediscover
The face of the boy as he practices tying
His father's tie there in secret

And the face of that father,
Still warm with the mystery of lather.
They are more fathers than sons themselves now.
Something is filling them, something

That is like the twilight sound
Of the crickets, immense,
Filling the woods at the foot of the slope
Behind their mortgaged houses.

MARY KARR (1965–)

A Blessing from My Sixteen Years' Son (2004)

I have this son who assembled inside me
during Hurricane Gloria. In a flash, he appeared,
in a heartbeat. Outside, pines toppled.

Phone lines snapped and hissed like cobras.
Inside, he was a raw pearl: microscopic, luminous.
Look at the muscled obelisk of him now

pawing through the icebox for more grapes.
Sixteen years and not a bone broken,
not a single stitch. By his age,

I was marked more ways, and small.
He's a slouching six foot three,
with implausible blue eyes, which settle

on the pages of Emerson's "Self-Reliance"
with profound belligerence.
A girl with a navel ring

could make his cell phone go *brr*,
or an Afro'd boy leaning on a mop at Taco Bell—
creatures strange as dragons or eels.

Balanced on a kitchen stool, each gives counsel
arcane as any oracle's. Bruce claims school
is harshing my mellow. Case longs to date

a tattooed girl, because he wants a woman
willing to do stuff she'll regret.
They've come to lead my son

into his broadening spiral.
Someday soon, the tether
will snap. I birthed my own mom

into oblivion. The night my son smashed
the car fender, then rode home
in the rain-streaked cop car, he asked, *Did you*

and Dad screw up so much?
He'd let me tuck him in,
my grandmother's wedding quilt

from 1912 drawn to his goateed chin. *Don't*
blame us, I said. *You're your own*
idiot now. At which he grinned.

The cop said the girl in the crimped Chevy
took it hard. He'd found my son
awkwardly holding her in the canted headlights,

where he'd draped his own coat
over her shaking shoulders. My *fault*,
he'd confessed right off.

Nice kid, said the cop.

JOHN KEATS (1795–1821)

La Belle Dame sans Merci: A Ballad° (1819, 1820)

1

O what can ail thee, knight at arms,
Alone and palely loitering?
The sedge has wither'd from the lake,
And no birds sing.

2

O what can ail thee, knight at arms,
So haggard and so woe-begone?
The squirrel's granary is full,
And the harvest's done.

3

I see a lily on thy brow
With anguish moist and fever dew,
And on thy cheeks a fading rose
Fast withereth too.

4

I met a lady in the meads,
Full beautiful, a fairy's child;
Her hair was long, her foot was light,
And her eyes were wild.

5

I made a garland for her head,
And bracelets too, and fragrant zone;°
She look'd at me as she did love,
And made sweet moan.

6

I set her on my pacing steed,
And nothing else saw all day long,
For sidelong would she bend, and sing
A fairy's song.

7

She found me roots of relish sweet,
And honey wild, and manna dew,
And sure in language strange she said—
I love thee true.

"La Belle Dame sans Merci": The title, which means "The Lovely Lady without Pity," was taken from a medieval poem by Alain Chartier.
fragrant zone: Belt.

8

She took me to her elfin grot,°
And there she wept, and sigh'd full sore,
And there I shut her wild wild eyes
With kisses four.

9

And there she lullèd me asleep,
And there I dream'd—Ah! woe betide!
The latest° dream I ever dream'd
On the cold hill's side.

10

I saw pale kings, and princes too,
Pale warriors, death pale were they all;
They cried—"La belle dame sans merci
Hath thee in thrall!"

11

I saw their starv'd lips in the gloam°
With horrid warning gapèd wide,
And I awoke and found me here
On the cold hill's side.

12

And this is why I sojourn here,
Alone and palely loitering,
Though the sedge is wither'd from the lake,
And no birds sing.

JOHN KEATS (1795–1821)

Bright Star! Would I Were Steadfast as Thou Art (1819)

Bright star! would I were steadfast as thou art—
Not in lone splendor hung aloft the night,
And watching, with eternal lids apart,
Like nature's patient, sleepless Eremite°
The moving waters at their priest-like task
Of pure ablution° round earth's human shores,

grot: Grotto.
latest: Last.
gloam: Twilight.
Eremite: Hermit, religious recluse.
ablution: Washing, cleansing.

Or gazing on the new soft-fallen mask
    Of snow upon the mountains and the moors—
No—yet still steadfast, still unchangeable,
    Pillowed upon my fair love's ripening breast,
To feel for ever its soft fall and swell,
    Awake for ever in a sweet unrest,
Still, still to hear her tender-taken breath,
And so live ever—or else swoon to death.

JOHN KEATS (1795–1821)

Ode on a Grecian Urn (1819)

Sketch by John Keats of the Sosibios Vase that may have inspired "Ode on a Grecian Urn."

Source: ©Keats-Shelley Memorial House, Rome

1

Thou still unravish'd bride of quietness,
    Thou foster-child of silence and slow time,
Sylvan° historian, who canst thus express
A flowery tale more sweetly than our rhyme:
What leaf-fring'd legend haunts about thy shape
    Of deities or mortals, or of both,
        In Tempe° or the dales of Arcady?°
    What men or gods are these? What maidens loth?
What mad pursuit? What struggle to escape?
What pipes and timbrels? What wild ecstasy?

2

Heard melodies are sweet, but those unheard
    Are sweeter; therefore, ye soft pipes, play on;
Not to the sensual ear, but, more endear'd,
    Pipe to the spirit ditties of no tone:
Fair youth, beneath the trees, thou canst not leave
    Thy song, nor ever can those trees be bare;
        Bold lover, never, never canst thou kiss,
Though winning near the goal—yet, do not grieve;
        She cannot fade, though thou hast not thy bliss,
    For ever wilt thou love, and she be fair!

3

Ah, happy, happy boughs! that cannot shed
    Your leaves, nor ever bid the spring adieu;

Sylvan: Pertaining to woods or forests.

Tempe: A beautiful valley in Greece.

Arcady: The valleys of Arcadia, a mountainous region on the Greek peninsula. Like Tempe, they represent a rustic pastoral ideal.

And, happy melodist, unwearied,
  For ever piping songs for ever new;
More happy love! more happy, happy love!
  For ever warm and still to be enjoy'd,
    For ever panting, and for ever young;
All breathing human passion far above,
  That leaves a heart high-sorrowful and cloy'd,
A burning forehead, and a parching tongue.

4

Who are these coming to the sacrifice?
  To what green altar, O mysterious priest,
Lead'st thou that heifer lowing at the skies,
  And all her silken flanks with garlands drest?
What little town by river or sea shore,
  Or mountain-built with peaceful citadel,
    Is emptied of this folk, this pious morn?
And, little town, thy streets for evermore
  Will silent be; and not a soul to tell
    Why thou art desolate, can e'er return.

5

O Attic° shape! Fair attitude! with brede°
  Of marble men and maidens overwrought,°
With forest branches and the trodden weed;
  Thou, silent form, dost tease us out of thought
As doth eternity: Cold Pastoral!
  When old age shall this generation waste,
    Thou shalt remain, in midst of other woe
Than ours, a friend to man, to whom thou say'st,
"Beauty is truth, truth beauty,"— that is all
  Ye know on earth, and all ye need to know.

JOHN KEATS (1795–1821)

When I Have Fears (1818)

When I have fears that I may cease to be
  Before my pen has gleaned my teeming brain,
Before high-pilèd books, in charact'ry,°

Attic: Characteristic of Athens or Athenians.
brede: Braid.
overwrought: Elaborately ornamented.
charact'ry: Print.

Hold like rich garners the full-ripened grain;
When I behold, upon the night's starred face,
Huge cloudy symbols of a high romance,
And think that I may never live to trace
Their shadows, with the magic hand of chance;
And when I feel, fair creature of an hour,
That I shall never look upon thee more,
Never have relish in the faery power
Of unreflecting love! — then on the shore
Of the wide world I stand alone, and think
Till Love and Fame to nothingness do sink.

TED KOOSER (1939–)

Selecting a Reader (1980)

First, I would have her be beautiful,
and walking carefully up on my poetry
at the loneliest moment of an afternoon,
her hair still damp at the neck
from washing it. She should be wearing
a raincoat, an old one, dirty
from not having money enough for the cleaners.
She will take out her glasses, and there
in the bookstore, she will thumb
over my poems, then put the book back
up on its shelf. She will say to herself,
"For that kind of money, I can get
my raincoat cleaned." And she will.

PHILIP LARKIN (1922–1985)

The Explosion (1974)

On the day of the explosion
Shadows pointed towards the pithead:
In the sun the slagheap slept.

Down the lane came men in pitboots
Coughing oath-edged talk and pipe-smoke,
Shouldering off the freshened silence.

One chased after rabbits; lost them;
Came back with a nest of lark's eggs;
Showed them; lodged them in the grasses.

So they passed in beards and moleskins,
Fathers, brothers, nicknames, laughter,
Through the tall gates standing open.

At noon, there came a tremor; cows
Stopped chewing for a second; sun,
Scarfed as in a heat-haze, dimmed.

The dead go on before us, they
Are sitting in God's house in comfort,
We shall see them face to face—

Plain as lettering in the chapels
It was said, and for a second
Wives saw men of the explosion

Larger than in life they managed—
Gold as on a coin, or walking
Somehow from the sun towards them,

One showing the eggs unbroken.

Source: ©Donna Lee

See this poet's biography on p. 1223.

LI-YOUNG LEE (1957–)

The Gift (1986)

To pull the metal splinter from my palm
my father recited a story in a low voice.
I watched his lovely face and not the blade.
Before the story ended, he'd removed
the iron sliver I thought I'd die from.

I can't remember the tale,
but hear his voice still, a well
of dark water, a prayer.
And I recall his hands,
two measures of tenderness
he laid against my face,
the flames of discipline
he raised above my head.

Had you entered that afternoon
you would have thought you saw a man
planting something in a boy's palm,
a silver tear, a tiny flame.
Had you followed that boy
you would have arrived here,
where I bend over my wife's right hand.

Look how I shave her thumbnail down
so carefully she feels no pain.
Watch as I lift the splinter out.
I was seven when my father
took my hand like this,

and I did not hold that shard
between my fingers and think,
Metal that will bury me,
christen it Little Assassin,
Ore Going Deep for My Heart.
And I did not lift up my wound and cry,
Death visited here!
I did what a child does
when he's given something to keep.
I kissed my father.

LI-YOUNG LEE (1957–)

Little Father (2001)

I buried my father
in the sky.
Since then, the birds
clean and comb him every morning
and pull the blanket up to his chin
every night.

I buried my father underground.
Since then, my ladders
only climb down,
and all the earth has become a house
whose rooms are the hours, whose doors
stand open at evening, receiving
guest after guest.
Sometimes I see past them
to the tables spread for a wedding feast.

I buried my father in my heart.
Now he grows in me, my strange son,
my little root who won't drink milk,
little pale foot sunk in unheard-of night,
little clock spring newly wet
in the fire, little grape, parent to the future
wine, a son the fruit of his own son,
little father I ransom with my life.

Source: ©AP Photo/Martin Cleaver

See this poet's biography on p. 1224.

DORIS LESSING (1919–)

Learning Geography, 1943 (2005)

Baria,° Sidi Rezegh,° El Alamein,°
One after another
These names reflected light from the eyes of the world.

Now they barter again in the market place
And at evening lovers pause
When an acre or so of crosses lean in the sand.

DORIS LESSING (1919–)

And in 2005 (2005)

Phuket, Andoman, Gallé,°
Sunkissed shores if ever there were,
Wars they knew as do we all,
Eating the world now here, now there.

But not the wave that rose up from the sea,
Not unfound, unnamed, unnumbered dead.

Some lost where the fishes are,
Some deep in sea-wet land.

PHILIP LEVINE (1928–)

The Old Testament (1994)

My twin brother swears that at age thirteen
I'd take on anyone who called me kike°
no matter how old or how big he was.
I only wish I'd been that tiny kid
who fought back through his tears, swearing
he would not go quietly. I go quietly
packing bark chips and loam into the rose beds,
while in his memory I remain the constant child
daring him to wrest Detroit from lean gentiles°

Baria: A part of India, formerly a distinct state.
Sidi Rezegh: Town in North Africa, site of a battle between British and German forces in World War II.
El Alamein: Town in Egypt, site of two important battles between allied and Axis forces in World War II.
Phuket, Andoman, Gallé: Islands in southern Thailand, the Indian Ocean, and Sri Lanka, respectively. All were devastated by a tsunami on December 26, 2004.
kike: Derogatory term for a Jewish person.
gentiles: Non-Jews.

in LaSalle convertibles and golf clothes
who step slowly into the world we have tainted,
and have their revenge. I remember none of this.
He insists, he names the drug store where I poured
a milkshake over the head of an Episcopalian
with quick fists as tight as croquet balls.
He remembers his license plate, his thin lips,
the exact angle at which this 17 year old dropped
his shoulder to throw the last punch. He's making
it up. Wasn't I always terrified?
"Of course," he tells me, "that's the miracle,
you were even more scared than me, so scared
you went insane, you became a whirlwind,
an avenging angel."
I remember planting
my first Victory Garden° behind the house, hauling
dark loam in a borrowed wagon, and putting in
carrots, corn that never grew, radishes that did.
I remember saving for weeks to buy a tea rose,
a little stick packed in dirt and burlap,
my mother's favorite. I remember the white bud
of my first peony that one morning burst
beside the mock orange that cost me 69¢
(Fifty years later the orange is still there,
the only thing left beside a cage for watch dogs,
empty now, in what had become a tiny yard.)
I remember putting myself to sleep dreaming
of the tomatoes coming into fullness, the pansies
laughing in the spring winds, the magical wisteria
climbing along the garage, and dreaming of Hitler,
of firing a single shot from a foot away, one
that would tear his face into a caricature of mine,
tear stained, bloodied, begging for a moment's peace.

THOMAS LUX (1946–)

Eyes Scooped Out and Replaced by Hot Coals (2006)

The above, the punishment, the mild
but just punishment, symbolic,
the great advancement our planet
most needs.

Victory Garden: Gardens planted during World War II to reduce dependency on rationed food.

The procedure is painless,
using methods currently available
only in cartoons. Polls were taken,
it was voted upon overwhelmingly in favor.
The justness of it,
known in the bone
by each of our nation—is undeniable. Thus, it is proclaimed,
on this day anno domino, etc., I, the final arbiter
and ultimate enforcer
of such things (appointed by the king!), make official
and binding, this: that the eyes shall be gouged out
and replaced by hot coals
in the head, *the blockhead,*
of each countryman or woman who,
upon reaching their majority,
has yet to read
Moby Dick, by Mr. Herman Melville (1819–1891),
American novelist and poet.

ARCHIBALD MACLEISH (1892–1982)

Ars Poetica° (1926)

A poem should be palpable and mute
As a globed fruit,

Dumb
As old medallions to the thumb,

Silent as the sleeve-worn stone
Of casement ledges where the moss has grown—

A poem should be wordless
As the flight of birds.

A poem should be motionless in time
As the moon climbs,

Leaving, as the moon releases
Twig by twig the night-entangled trees,

Leaving, as the moon behind the winter leaves,
Memory by memory the mind—

A poem should be motionless in time
As the moon climbs.

A poem should be equal to:
Not true.

Ars Poetica: "The Art of Poetry" (Latin).

For all the history of grief
An empty doorway and a maple leaf.

For love
The leaning grasses and two lights above the sea—

A poem should not mean
But be.

CHRISTOPHER MARLOWE (1564–1593)

The Passionate Shepherd to His Love (1600)

Come live with me and be my love,
And we will all the pleasures prove
That valleys, groves, hills, and fields,
Woods, or steepy mountain yields.

And we will sit upon the rocks,
Seeing the shepherds feed their flocks
By shallow rivers, to whose falls
Melodious birds sing madrigals.

And I will make thee beds of roses
And a thousand fragrant posies,
A cap of flowers and a kirtle°
Embroidered all with leaves of myrtle;

A gown made of the finest wool
Which from our pretty lambs we pull;
Fair-linèd slippers for the cold,
With buckles of the purest gold;

A belt of straw and ivy buds,
With coral clasps and amber studs.
And if these pleasures may thee move,
Come live with me and be my love.

The shepherds' swains shall dance and sing
For thy delight each May morning.
If these delights thy mind may move,
Then live with me and be my love.

CLAUDE McKAY (1890–1948)

If We Must Die (1922)

If we must die, let it not be like hogs
Hunted and penned in an inglorious spot,

kirtle: Skirt.

While round us bark the mad and hungry dogs,
Making their mock at our accursed lot.
If we must die, O let us nobly die,
So that our precious blood may not be shed
In vain; then even the monsters we defy
Shall be constrained to honor us though dead!
O kinsmen! we must meet the common foe!
Though far outnumbered let us show us brave,
And for their thousand blows deal one deathblow!
What though before us lies the open grave?
Like men we'll face the murderous, cowardly pack,
Pressed to the wall, dying, but fighting back!

JAMES MERRILL (1926–1995)

Page from the Koran (1985)

A small vellum environment
Overrun by black
Scorpions of Kufic script — their ranks
All trigger tail and gold vowel-sac —
At auction this mild winter morning went
For six hundred Swiss francs.

By noon, fire from the same blue heavens
Had half erased Beirut.
Allah be praised, it said on crude handbills,
For guns and Nazarenes to shoot.
"How gladly with proper words," said Wallace Stevens,
"The soldier dies." Or kills.

God's very word, then, stung the heart
To greed and rancor. Yet
Not where the last glow touches one spare man
Inked-in against his minaret
—Letters so handled they are life, and hurt,
Leaving the scribe immune?

W. S. MERWIN (1927–)

Blueberries after Dark (2007)

So this is the way the night tastes
one at a time
not early nor late

my mother told me
that I was not afraid of the dark
and when I looked it was true

how did she know
so long ago

with her father dead
almost before she could remember
and her mother following him
not long after
and then her grandmother
who had brought her up
and a little later
her only brother
and then her firstborn
gone as soon
as he was born

she knew

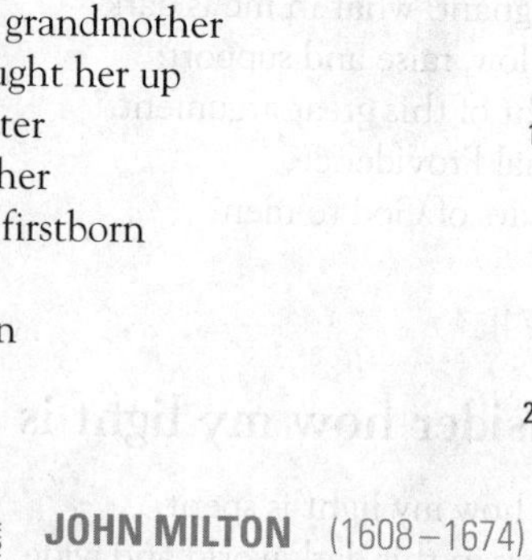

Source: ©The Granger Collection, New York

See this poet's biography on p. 1224.

JOHN MILTON (1608–1674)

from Paradise Lost (1667)

I

Of man's first disobedience, and the fruit°
Of that forbidden tree whose mortal taste
Brought death into the world, and all our woe,
With loss of Eden, till one greater Man°
Restore us, and regain the blissful seat,
Sing, Heav'nly Muse,° that, on the secret top
Of Oreb, or of Sinai,° didst inspire
That shepherd who first taught the chosen seed
In the beginning how the Heav'ns and Earth
Rose out of Chaos: or, if Sion hill°
Delight thee more, and Siloa's° brook that flowed
Fast° by the oracle of God, I thence
Invoke thy aid to my adventurous song,
That with no middle flight intends to soar
Above th' Aonian mount,° while it pursues

fruit: Refers to the apple eaten by Adam and Eve in the Garden of Eden as well as the consequences of their disobedience.
one greater Man: Refers to the coming of the Messiah.
Heav'nly Muse: Invoking one of the Muses and asking for help is a convention that usually appears in the first few lines of an epic poem.
Of Oreb, or of Sinai: Refers to the geographical location of Mt. Sinai, where Moses (*that shepherd*) received the Ten Commandments.
Sion hill: A mountain near Jerusalem.
Siloa: A brook near Jerusalem.
Fast by: Close, to.
Aonian mount: Refers to Mt. Helicon, the home of the Muses.

Things unattempted yet in prose or rhyme.
And chiefly thou, O Spirit° that dost prefer
Before all temples th' upright heart and pure,
Instruct me, for thou know'st; thou from the first
Wast present, and, with mighty wings outspread,
Dovelike sat'st brooding on the vast abyss,
And mad'st it pregnant: what in me is dark
Illumine; what is low, raise and support;
That, to the height of this great argument,°
I may assert Eternal Providence,
And justify the ways of God to men.

JOHN MILTON (1608–1674)

When I consider how my light is spent° (1655?)

When I consider how my light is spent,
   Ere half my days in this dark world and wide,
   And that one talent° which is death to hide
Lodged with me useless, though my soul more bent
To serve therewith my Maker, and present
   My true account, lest He returning chide;
   "Doth God exact day-labor, light denied?"
I fondly° ask. But Patience, to prevent
That murmur, soon replies, "God doth not need
   Either man's work or His own gifts. Who best
   Bear His mild yoke, they serve Him best. His state
Is kingly: thousands at His bidding speed,
And post o'er land and ocean without rest;
They also serve who only stand and wait."

THYLIAS MOSS (1954–)

Interpretation of a Poem by Frost° (1991)

A young black girl stopped by the woods,
so young she knew only one man: Jim Crow°
but she wasn't allowed to call him Mister.
The woods were his and she respected his boundaries

O Spirit: An allusion in classical form, this refers to the Spirit of God, or the Holy Spirit.
argument: Subject at hand.
how my light is spent: A meditation on his blindness.
one talent: See Jesus' parable of the talents in Matthew 25.14–30.
fondly: Foolishly.
Poem by Frost: "Stopping by Woods on a Snowy Evening."
Jim Crow: Name given to the system of segregation in the American South following the Civil War.

even in the absence of fence.
Of course she delighted in the filling up
of his woods, she so accustomed to emptiness,
to being taken at face value.
This face, her face eternally the brown
of declining autumn, watches snow inter the grass,
cling to bark making it seem indecisive
about race preference, a fast-to-melt idealism.
With the grass covered, black and white are the only options,
polarity is the only reality; corners aren't neutral
but are on edge.
She shakes off snow, defiance wasted
on the limited audience of horse.
The snow does not hypnotize her as it wants to,
as the blond sun does in making too many prefer daylight.
She has promises to keep,
the promise that she bear Jim no bastards,
the promise that she ride the horse only as long
as it is willing to accept riders
the promise that she bear Jim no bastards,
the promise to her face that it not be mistaken as shadow,
and miles to go, more than the distance from Africa to Andover,°
more than the distance from black to white
before she sleeps with Jim.

PABLO NERUDA (1904–1973)

The United Fruit Co.° (1950)

Translated by Robert Bly

When the trumpet sounded, it was
all prepared on the earth,
and Jehovah parceled out the earth
to Coca-Cola, Inc., Anaconda,
Ford Motors, and other entities:
The Fruit Company, Inc.
reserved for itself the most succulent,
the central coast of my own land,
the delicate waist of America.
It rechristened its territories
as the "Banana Republics"

Andover: A town in Massachusetts.

United Fruit Co.: Incorporated in New Jersey in 1899 by Andrew Preston and Minor C. Keith, United Fruit became a major force in growing, transporting, and merchandising Latin American produce, especially bananas. The company is notorious for its involvement in politics, and as a result its name came to represent "Yankee" imperialism and oppression.

and over the sleeping dead,
over the restless heroes
who brought about the greatness,
the liberty and the flags,
it established the comic opera:
abolished the independencies,
presented crowns of Caesar,
unsheathed envy, attracted
the dictatorship of the flies,
Trujillo flies, Tacho flies,
Carias flies, Martinez flies,
Ubico flies,° damp flies
of modest blood and marmalade,
drunken flies who zoom
over the ordinary graves,
circus flies, wise flies
well trained in tyranny.
Among the bloodthirsty flies
the Fruit Company lands its ships,
taking off the coffee and the fruit;
the treasure of our submerged
territories flows as though
on plates into the ships.
Meanwhile Indians are falling
into the sugared chasms
of the harbors, wrapped
for burial in the mist of the dawn:
a body rolls, a thing
that has no name, a fallen cipher,
a cluster of dead fruit
thrown down on the dump.

Source: ©AP Photo/Pat Wellenbach

See this poet's biography on p. 1225.

FRANK O'HARA (1926–1966)

Ave Maria° (1964)

Mothers of America
let your kids go to the movies!
get them out of the house so they won't know what
you're up to
it's true that fresh air is good for the body
but what about the soul
that grows in darkness, embossed by silvery images

Trujillo, Tacho, Carias, Martinez, Ubico: Political dictators.
Ave Maria: "Hail, Mary." The first words of the Roman Catholic prayer to the Virgin Mary.

and when you grow old as grow old you must
    they won't hate you
they won't criticize you they won't know
    they'll be in some glamorous country
they first saw on a Saturday afternoon
  or playing hookey
they may even be grateful to you
    for their first sexual experience
which only cost you a quarter
    and didn't upset the peaceful home
they will know where candy bars come from
    and gratuitous bags of popcorn
as gratuitous as leaving the movie before it's over
with a pleasant stranger whose apartment is in the
  Heaven on Earth Bldg
near the Williamsburg Bridge°
    oh mothers you will have made the little
      tykes
so happy because if nobody does pick them up in the movies
they won't know the difference
    and if somebody does it'll be sheer gravy
and they'll have been truly entertained either way
instead of hanging around the yard
    or up in their room hating you
prematurely since you won't have done anything horribly mean yet
except keeping them from the darker joys
    it's unforgivable the latter
so don't blame me if you won't take this advice
    and the family breaks up
and your children grow old and blind in front of a TV set
    seeing
movies you wouldn't let them see when they were young

Source: Courtesy of Alfred A. Knopf Publishing, Photo: ©David Bartolomi

See this poet's biography on p. 1225.

SHARON OLDS (1942–)

The One Girl at the Boys' Party (1983)

When I take my girl to the swimming party
I set her down among the boys. They tower and
bristle, she stands there smooth and sleek,
her math scores unfolding in the air around her.
They will strip to their suits, her body hard and
indivisible as a prime number,

Williamsburg Bridge: A suspension bridge in New York City.

they'll plunge in the deep end, she'll subtract
her height from ten feet, divide it into
hundreds of gallons of water, the numbers
bouncing in her mind like molecules of chlorine
in the bright blue pool. When they climb out,
her ponytail will hang its pencil lead
down her back, her narrow silk suit
with hamburgers and french fries printed on it
will glisten in the brilliant air, and they will
see her sweet face, solemn and
sealed, a factor of one, and she will
see their eyes, two each,
their legs, two each, and the curves of their sexes,
one each, and in her head she'll be doing her
wild multiplying, as the drops
sparkle and fall to the power of a thousand from her body.

Source: ©Goodman/Van Riper Photography

See this poet's biography on p. 1225.

LINDA PASTAN (1932–)

Ethics (1980)

In ethics class so many years ago
our teacher asked this question every fall:
if there were a fire in a museum
which would you save, a Rembrandt painting
or an old woman who hadn't many
years left anyhow? Restless on hard chairs
caring little for pictures or old age
we'd opt one year for life, the next for art
and always half-heartedly. Sometimes
the woman borrowed my grandmother's face
leaving her usual kitchen to wander
some drafty, half imagined museum.
One year, feeling clever, I replied
why not let the woman decide herself?
Linda, the teacher would report, eschews
the burdens of responsibility.
This fall in a real museum I stand
before a real Rembrandt, old woman,
or nearly so, myself. The colors
within this frame are darker than autumn,
darker even than winter—the browns of earth,
though earth's most radiant elements burn
through the canvas. I know now that woman
and painting and season are almost one
and all beyond saving by children.

LINDA PASTAN (1932–)

Marks (1978)

My husband gives me an A
for last night's supper,
an incomplete for my ironing,
a B plus in bed.
My son says I am average,
an average mother, but if
I put my mind to it
I could improve.
My daughter believes
in Pass/Fail and tells me
I pass. Wait 'til they learn
I'm dropping out.

Source: ©AP Photo/Ben Barnhart

See this poet's biography on p. 1226.

MARGE PIERCY (1936–)

Barbie doll (1973)

This girlchild was born as usual
and presented dolls that did pee-pee
and miniature GE stoves and irons
and wee lipsticks the color of cherry candy.
Then in the magic of puberty, a classmate said:
You have a great big nose and fat legs.

She was healthy, tested intelligent,
possessed strong arms and back,
abundant sexual drive and manual dexterity.
She went to and fro apologizing.
Everyone saw a fat nose on thick legs.

She was advised to play coy,
exhorted to come on hearty,
exercise, diet, smile and wheedle.
Her good nature wore out
like a fan belt.
So she cut off her nose and her legs
and offered them up.

In the casket displayed on satin she lay
with the undertaker's cosmetics painted on,
a turned-up putty nose,
dressed in a pink and white nightie.
Doesn't she look pretty? everyone said.
Consummation at last.
To every woman a happy ending.

ROBERT PINSKY (1940–)

Shirt (1990)

The back, the yoke, the yardage. Lapped seams,
The nearly invisible stitches along the collar
Turned in a sweatshop by Koreans or Malaysians

Gossiping over tea and noodles on their break
Or talking money or politics while one fitted
This armpiece with its overseam to the band

Of cuff I button at my wrist. The presser, the cutter,
The wringer, the mangle. The needle, the union,
The treadle, the bobbin. The code. The infamous blaze

At the Triangle Factory in nineteen-eleven.
One hundred and forty-six died in the flames
On the ninth floor, no hydrants, no fire escapes—

The witness in a building across the street
Who watched how a young man helped a girl to step
Up to the windowsill, then held her out

Away from the masonry wall and let her drop.
And then another. As if he were helping them up
To enter a streetcar, and not eternity.

A third before he dropped her put her arms
Around his neck and kissed him. Then he held
Her into space, and dropped her. Almost at once

He stepped to the sill himself, his jacket flared
And fluttered up from his shirt as he came down,
Air filling up the legs of his gray trousers—

Like Hart Crane's Bedlamite, "shrill shirt ballooning."
Wonderful how the pattern matches perfectly
Across the placket and over the twin bar-tacked

Corners of both pockets, like a strict rhyme
Or a major chord. Prints, plaids, checks,
Houndstooth, Tattersall, Madras. The clan tartans

Invented by mill-owners inspired by the hoax of Ossian,
To control their savage Scottish workers, tamed
By a fabricated heraldry: MacGregor,

Bailey, MacMartin. The kilt, devised for workers
To wear among the dusty clattering looms.
Weavers, carders, spinners. The loader,

The docker, the navvy. The planter, the picker, the sorter
Sweating at her machine in a litter of cotton
As slaves in calico headrags sweated in fields:

George Herbert, your descendant is a Black
Lady in South Carolina, her name is Irma
And she inspected my shirt. Its color and fit

And feel and its clean smell have satisfied
Both her and me. We have culled its cost and quality
Down to the buttons of simulated bone,

The buttonholes, the sizing, the facing, the characters
Printed in black on neckband and tail. The shape,
The label, the labor, the color, the shade. The shirt.

SYLVIA PLATH (1932–1963)

Mirror (1963)

I am silver and exact. I have no preconceptions.
Whatever I see I swallow immediately
Just as it is, unmisted by love or dislike.
I am not cruel, only truthful —
The eye of a little god, four-cornered.
Most of the time I meditate on the opposite wall.
It is pink, with speckles. I have looked at it so long
I think it is a part of my heart. But it flickers.
Faces and darkness separate us over and over.

Now I am a lake. A woman bends over me,
Searching my reaches for what she really is.
Then she turns to those liars, the candles or the moon.
I see her back, and reflect it faithfully.
She rewards me with tears and an agitation of hands.
I am important to her. She comes and goes.
Each morning it is her face that replaces the darkness.
In me she has drowned a young girl, and in me an
    old woman
Rises toward her day after day, like a terrible fish.

SIR WALTER RALEIGH (1552–1618)

The Nymph's Reply to the Shepherd (1600)

If all the world and love were young,
And truth in every shepherd's tongue,
These pretty pleasures might me move
To live with thee and be thy love.

Time drives the flocks from field to fold,
When rivers rage and rocks grow cold;
And Philomel° becometh dumb;
The rest complains of cares to come.

The flowers do fade, and wanton fields
To wayward winter reckoning yields:
A honey tongue, a heart of gall,
Is fancy's spring, but sorrow's fall.

Thy gowns, thy shoes, thy beds of roses,
Thy cap, thy kirtle, and thy posies
Soon break, soon wither, soon forgotten,
In folly ripe, in reason rotten.

Thy belt of straw and ivy buds,
Thy coral clasps and amber studs.
All these in me no means can move
To come to thee and be thy love.

But could youth last, and love still breed,
Had joys no date, nor age no need,
Then these delights my mind might move
To live with thee and be thy love.

HENRY REED (1914–1986)

Naming of Parts (1946)

Today we have naming of parts. Yesterday,
We had daily cleaning. And tomorrow morning,
We shall have what to do after firing. But today,
Today we have naming of parts. Japonica°
Glistens like coral in all of the neighboring gardens,
    And today we have naming of parts.

This is the lower sling swivel. And this
Is the upper sling swivel, whose use you will see,
When you are given your slings. And this is the piling swivel,
Which in your case you have not got. The branches
Hold in the gardens their silent, eloquent gestures,
    Which in our case we have not got.

This is the safety-catch, which is always released
With an easy flick of the thumb. And please do not let me

Philomel: The nightingale.
Japonica: A shrub having waxy flowers in a variety of colors.

See anyone using his finger. You can do it quite easy
If you have any strength in your thumb. The blossoms
Are fragile and motionless, never letting anyone see
  Any of them using their finger.

And this you can see is the bolt. The purpose of this
Is to open the breech, as you see. We can slide it
Rapidly backwards and forwards: we call this
Easing the spring. And rapidly backwards and forwards
The early bees are assaulting and fumbling the flowers:
  They call it easing the Spring.

They call it easing the Spring: it is perfectly easy
If you have any strength in your thumb: like the bolt,
And the breech, and the cocking-piece, and the point of balance,
Which in our case we have not got; and the almond-blossom
Silent in all of the gardens and the bees going backwards and
    forwards,
  For today we have the naming of parts.

Source: ©Bettmann/Corbis

See this poet's biography on p. 1227.

EDWIN ARLINGTON ROBINSON (1869–1935)

Miniver Cheevy (1910)

Miniver Cheevy, child of scorn,
  Grew lean while he assailed the seasons;
He wept that he was ever born,
  And he had reasons.

Miniver loved the days of old
  When swords were bright and
    steeds were prancing;
The vision of a warrior bold
  Would set him dancing.

Miniver sighed for what was not,
  And dreamed, and rested from his labors;
He dreamed of Thebes° and Camelot,°
And Priam's neighbors.°

Miniver mourned the ripe renown
  That made so many a name so fragrant;

Thebes: The setting of many Greek legends, including that of Oedipus.
Camelot: The legendary site of King Arthur's court.
Priam's neighbors: Priam was the last king of Troy; his "neighbors" included Helen, Aeneas, and Hector.

He mourned Romance, now on the town,
And Art, a vagrant.

Miniver loved the Medici,°
Albeit he had never seen one;
He would have sinned incessantly
Could he have been one.

Miniver cursed the commonplace
And eyed a khaki suit with loathing;
He missed the medieval grace
Of iron clothing.

Miniver scorned the gold he sought,
But sore annoyed was he without it;
Miniver thought, and thought, and thought,
And thought about it.

Miniver Cheevy, born too late,
Scratched his head and kept on thinking;
Miniver coughed, and called it fate,
And kept on drinking.

EDWARD ARLINGTON ROBINSON (1869–1935)

Richard Cory (1897)

Whenever Richard Cory went down town,
We people on the pavement looked at him:
He was a gentleman from sole to crown,
Clean favored, and imperially slim.

And he was always quietly arrayed,
And he was always human when he talked;
But still he fluttered pulses when he said,
"Good-morning," and he glittered when he walked.

And he was rich — yes, richer than a king —
And admirably schooled in every grace:
In fine, we thought that he was everything
To make us wish that we were in his place.

So on we worked, and waited for the light,
And went without the meat, and cursed the bread;
And Richard Cory, one calm summer night,
Went home and put a bullet through his head.

Medici: Rulers of Florence, Italy, from the fifteenth through the eighteenth centuries. During the Renaissance, Lorenzo de Medici was a renowned patron of the arts.

Source: Courtesy of Sonia Sanchez, Photo: ©Marion Ettlinger

See this poet's biography on p. 1228.

SONIA SANCHEZ (1934–)

right on: white america (1970)

this country might have
been a pio
    neer land
once.
    but.   there ain't
no mo
    indians   blowing
custer's° mind
            with a different
image of america.
                this country
might have
            needed shoot/
outs/ daily/
    once.
            but. there ain't
no mo real/ white/ allamerican
                bad/guys.
just.
    u & me.
        blk/ and un/armed.
this country might have
been a pion
        eer land.   once.
                and it still is.
check out
        the falling
gun/shells   on our blk/tomorrows.

WILLIAM SHAKESPEARE (1564–1616)

Let me not to the marriage of true minds (1609)

Let me not to the marriage of true minds
Admit impediments.° Love is not love

---

custer: General George Armstrong Custer (1839–1876) was killed by Sioux in his "last stand" at the Little Bighorn in Montana.

Admit impediments: A reference to "The Order of Solemnization of Matrimony" in the Anglican Book of Common Prayer: "I require that if either of you know any impediments why ye may not be lawfully joined together in Matrimony, ye do now confess it."

Which alters when it alteration finds,
Or bends with the remover to remove:
Oh, no! it is an ever-fixéd mark,
That looks on tempests and is never shaken;
It is the star to every wandering bark,
Whose worth's unknown, although his height be taken.°
Love's not Time's fool,° though rosy lips and cheeks
Within his bending sickle's compass come;
Love alters not with his brief hours and weeks,
But bears it out even to the edge of doom.°
If this be error and upon me proved,
I never writ, nor no man ever loved.

WILLIAM SHAKESPEARE (1564–1616)

Not marble, nor the gilded monuments (1609)

Not marble, nor the gilded monuments
Of princes, shall outlive this powerful rhyme;
But you shall shine more bright in these contents
Than unswept stone, besmeared with sluttish time.
When wasteful war shall statues overturn,
And broils root out the work of masonry,
Nor Mars° his sword nor war's quick fire shall burn
The living record of your memory.
'Gainst death and all-oblivious enmity
Shall you pace forth; your praise shall still find room
Even in the eyes of all posterity
That wear this world out to the ending doom.
So, till the judgment that yourself arise,
You live in this, and dwell in lovers' eyes.

PERCY BYSSHE SHELLEY (1792–1822)

Ode to the West Wind (1820)

I

O wild West Wind, thou breath of Autumn's being,
Thou, from whose unseen presence the leaves dead
Are driven, like ghosts from an enchanter fleeing,

Whose worth's . . . taken: Although the altitude of a star may be measured, its worth is unknowable.
Love's not Time's fool: Love is not mocked by Time.
doom: Doomsday.
Mars: The Roman god of war.

Yellow, and black, and pale, and hectic red,°
Pestilence-stricken multitudes: O Thou,
Who chariotest to their dark wintry bed

The winged seeds, where they lie cold and low,
Each like a corpse within its grave, until
Thine azure sister of the Spring° shall blow

Her clarion o'er the dreaming earth, and fill
(Driving sweet buds like flocks to feed in air)
With living hues and odours plain and hill:

Wild Spirit, which art moving everywhere;
Destroyer and Preserver; hear, O hear!

II

Thou on whose stream, mid the steep sky's commotion,
Loose clouds like Earth's decaying leaves are shed,
Shook from the tangled boughs of Heaven and Ocean,

Angels of rain and lightning: there are spread
On the blue surface of thine aery surge,
Like the bright hair uplifted from the head

Of some fierce Maenad,° even from the dim verge
Of the horizon to the zenith's height,
The locks of the approaching storm. Thou Dirge

Of the dying year, to which this closing night
Will be the dome of a vast sepulchre,
Vaulted with all thy congregated might

Of vapours, from whose solid atmosphere
Black rain and fire and hail will burst: O hear!

III

Thou who didst waken from his summer dreams
The blue Mediterranean, where he lay,
Lulled by the coil of his crystalline streams,

Beside a pumice isle in Baiae's bay,°
And saw in sleep old palaces and towers
Quivering within the wave's intenser day,

Yellow . . . hectic red: A reference to a tubercular fever that produces flushed cheeks.

azure . . . Spring: The west wind of the spring.

Maenad: A female votary who danced wildly in ceremonies for Dionysus (or Bacchus), Greek god of wine and vegetation, who according to legend died in the fall and was reborn in the spring.

Baiae's bay: A bay in the Mediterranean Sea, west of Naples. It was known for the opulent villas built by Roman emperors along its shores.

All overgrown with azure moss and flowers
So sweet, the sense faints picturing them! Thou
For whose path the Atlantic's level powers

Cleave themselves into chasms, while far below
The sea-blooms and the oozy woods which wear
The sapless foliage of the ocean, know

Thy voice, and suddenly grow grey with fear,
And tremble and despoil themselves: O hear!

IV

If I were a dead leaf thou mightest bear;
If I were a swift cloud to fly with thee;
A wave to pant beneath thy power, and share

The impulse of thy strength, only less free
Than thou, O Uncontrollable! If even
I were as in my boyhood, and could be

The comrade of thy wanderings over Heaven,
As then, when to outstrip thy skiey speed
Scarce seemed a vision; I would ne'er have striven

As thus with thee in prayer in my sore need,
Oh! lift me as a wave, a leaf, a cloud!
I fall upon the thorns of life! I bleed!

A heavy weight of hours has chained and bowed
One too like thee: tameless, and swift, and proud.

V

Make me thy lyre,° even as the forest is:
What if my leaves are falling like its own!
The tumult of thy mighty harmonies

Will take from both a deep, autumnal tone,
Sweet though in sadness. Be thou, Spirit fierce,
My spirit! Be thou me, impetuous one!

Drive my dead thoughts over the universe
Like withered leaves to quicken a new birth!
And, by the incantation of this verse,

Scatter, as from an unextinguished hearth
Ashes and sparks, my words among mankind!
Be through my lips to unawakened Earth

The trumpet of a prophecy! O Wind,
If Winter comes, can Spring be far behind?

lyre: An Aeolian harp, a stringed instrument that produces musical sounds when exposed to the wind.

CHARLES SIMIC (1938–)

Old Soldier (2004)

By the time I was ten,
I had fought in hundreds of battles,
Had innumerable wounds,
Had slain thousands.

My mother took me by the hand
And led me into the garden.
The cherry trees were in flower.
There was a cat lying in the grass
Whose tail I wanted to pull,
But I let her be for a moment.

After the air raid, the sky was full
Of birds and flying cinders
But the ants at our feet
Were their usual serene selves,
Running their quick errands
Along the crumbling walls.

I forgot to mention my sword.
True, it was of cardboard,
But its handle was painted gold.
What I needed was a horse—
The one I saw pull a hearse
With a merry wave of his tail.

LOUIS SIMPSON (1923–)

American Poetry (1963)

Whatever it is, it must have
A stomach that can digest
Rubber, coal, uranium, moons, poems.

Like the shark, it contains a shoe.
It must swim for miles through the desert
Uttering cries that are almost human.

STEVIE SMITH (1902–1971)

Not Waving but Drowning (1957)

Nobody heard him, the dead man,
But still he lay moaning:
I was much further out than you thought
And not waving but drowning.

Poor chap, he always loved larking
And now he's dead
It must have been too cold for him his heart gave way,
They said.

Oh, no no no, it was too cold always
(Still the dead one lay moaning)
I was much too far out all my life
And not waving but drowning.

CATHY SONG (1955–)

Lost Sister (1983)

1

In China,
even the peasants
named their first daughters
Jade—
the stone that in the far fields
could moisten the dry season,
could make men move mountains
for the healing green of the inner hills
glistening like slices of winter melon.

And the daughters were grateful:
they never left home.
To move freely was a luxury
stolen from them at birth.
Instead, they gathered patience,
learning to walk in shoes
the size of teacups,°
without breaking—
the arc of their movements
as dormant as the rooted willow,
as redundant as the farmyard hens.
But they traveled far
in surviving,
learning to stretch the family rice,
to quiet the demons,
the noisy stomachs.

shoes . . . teacups: A reference to the practice of binding young girls' feet so that they remain small. This practice, which crippled women, was common in China until the communist revolution.

2

There is a sister
across the ocean,
who relinquished her name,
diluting jade green
with the blue of the Pacific.
Rising with a tide of locusts,
she swarmed with others
to inundate another shore.
In America,
there are many roads
and women can stride along with men.

But in another wilderness,
the possibilities,
the loneliness,
can strangulate like jungle vines.
The meager provisions and sentiments
of once belonging—
fermented roots, Mah-Jongg° tiles and firecrackers—
set but a flimsy household
in a forest of nightless cities.
A giant snake rattles above,
spewing black clouds into your kitchen.
Dough-faced landlords
slip in and out of your keyholes,
making claims you don't understand,
tapping into your communication systems
of laundry lines and restaurant chains.

You find you need China:
your one fragile identification,
a jade link
handcuffed to your wrist.
You remember your mother
who walked for centuries,
footless—
and like her,
you have left no footprints,
but only because
there is an ocean in between,
the unremitting space of your rebellion.

Mah-Jongg: Or *mahjong,* an ancient Chinese game played with dice and tiles.

GARY SOTO (1952–)

Saturday at the Canal (1991)

I was hoping to be happy by seventeen.
School was a sharp check mark in the roll book,
An obnoxious tuba playing at noon because our team
Was going to win at night. The teachers were
Too close to dying to understand. The hallways
Stank of poor grades and unwashed hair. Thus,
A friend and I sat watching the water on Saturday,
Neither of us talking much, just warming ourselves
By hurling large rocks at the dusty ground
And feeling awful because San Francisco was a postcard
On a bedroom wall. We wanted to go there,
Hitchhike under the last migrating birds
And be with people who knew more than three chords
On a guitar. We didn't drink or smoke,
But our hair was shoulder length, wild when
The wind picked up and the shadows of
This loneliness gripped loose dirt. By bus or car,
By the sway of train over a long bridge,
We wanted to get out. The years froze
As we sat on the bank. Our eyes followed the water,
White-tipped but dark underneath, racing out of town.

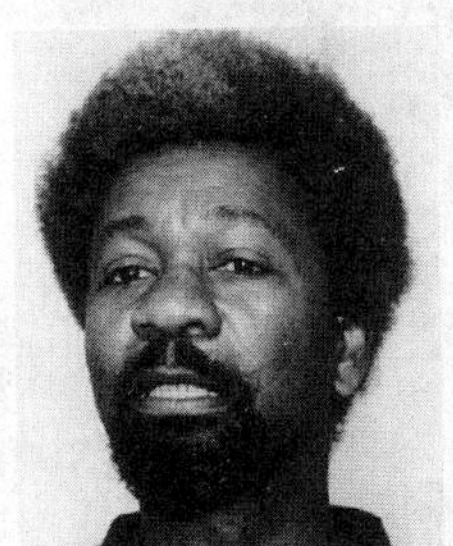
Source: ©AP Photo

See this poet's biography on p. 1229.

WOLE SOYINKA (1934–)

Hamlet (1972)

He stilled his doubts, they rose to halt and lame
A resolution on the rack. Passion's flame
Was doused in fear of error, his mind's unease
Bred indulgence to the state's disease
Ghosts embowelled his earth; he clung to rails
In a gallery of abstractions, dissecting tales
As "told by an idiot." Passionless he set a stage
Of passion for the guilt he would engage.

Justice despaired. The turn and turn abouts
Of reason danced default to duty's counterpoint
Till treachery scratched the slate of primal clay
Then Metaphysics waived a thought's delay—
It took the salt in the wound, the "point
Envenom'd too" to steel the prince of doubts.

Source: ©AP Photo

See this poet's biography on p. 1229.

WALLACE STEVENS (1879–1955)

Anecdote of the Jar (1923)

I placed a jar in Tennessee,
And round it was, upon a hill.
It made the slovenly wilderness
Surround that hill.

The wilderness rose up to it,
And sprawled around, no longer wild.
The jar was round upon the ground
And tall and of a port in air.

It took dominion everywhere.
The jar was gray and bare.
It did not give of bird or bush,
Like nothing else in Tennessee.

WALLACE STEVENS (1879–1955)

The Emperor of Ice-Cream (1923)

Call the roller of big cigars,
The muscular one, and bid him whip
In kitchen cups concupiscent curds.
Let the wenches dawdle in such dress
As they are used to wear, and let the boys
Bring flowers in last month's newspapers.
Let be be finale of seem.
The only emperor is the emperor of ice-cream.

Take from the dresser of deal,°
Lacking the three glass knobs, that sheet
On which she embroidered fantails° once
And spread it so as to cover her face.
If her horny feet protrude, they come
To show how cold she is, and dumb.
Let the lamp affix its beam.
The only emperor is the emperor of ice-cream.

deal: Fir or pine wood.
fantails: According to Stevens, "the word fantails does not mean fans, but fantail pigeons."

WALLACE STEVENS (1879–1955)

The House Was Quiet and the World Was Calm (1954)

The house was quiet and the world was calm.
The reader became the book; and summer night

Was like the conscious being of the book.
The house was quiet and the world was calm.

The words were spoken as if there was no book,
Except that the reader leaned above the page,

Wanted to lean, wanted much most to be
The scholar to whom his book is true, to whom

The summer night is like a perfection of thought.
The house was quiet because it had to be.

The quiet was part of the meaning, part of the mind:
The access of perfection to the page.

And the world was calm. The truth in a calm world,
In which there is no other meaning, itself

Is calm, itself is summer and night, itself
Is the reader leaning late and reading there.

ADRIENNE SU (1967–)

The English Canon° (2000)

It's not that the first speakers left out women
Unless they were goddesses, harlots, or impossible loves
Seen from afar, often while bathing,

And it's not that the only parts my grandfathers
    could have played
Were as extras in Xanadu,°
Nor that it gives no instructions for shopping or cooking.

The trouble is, I've spent my life
Getting over the lyrics
That taught me to brush my hair till it's gleaming,

Stay slim, dress tastefully, and not speak of sex,
Death, violence, or the desire for any of them,
And to let men do the talking and warring

English Canon: Those works in English traditionally thought worthy of study.
Xanadu: The summer capital of the emperor Kublai Kahn; also the setting for the poem "Kubla Khan" (p. 1137) by the English poet Samuel Taylor Coleridge.

And bringing of the news. I know a girl's got to protest
These days, but she also has to make money
And do her share of journalism and combat,

And she has to know from the gut whom to trust,
Because what do her teachers know, living in books,
And what does she know, starting from scratch?

ALFRED, LORD TENNYSON (1809–1892)

Ulysses° (1833)

It little profits that an idle king,
By this still hearth, among these barren crags,
Matched with an agèd wife, I mete and dole
Unequal laws unto a savage race
That hoard, and sleep, and feed, and know not me.
I cannot rest from travel; I will drink
Life to the lees. All times I have enjoyed
Greatly, have suffered greatly, both with those
That loved me, and alone; on shore, and when
Through scudding drifts the rainy Hyades°
Vexed the dim sea. I am become a name;
For always roaming with a hungry heart
Much have I seen and known — cities of men
And manners, climates, councils, governments,
Myself not least, but honored of them all—
And drunk delight of battle with my peers,
Far on the ringing plains of windy Troy.°
I am a part of all that I have met;
Yet all experience is an arch wherethrough
Gleams that untraveled world whose margin fades
Forever and forever when I move.
How dull it is to pause, to make an end,
To rust unburnished, not to shine in use!
As though to breathe were life! Life piled on life
Were all too little, and of one to me
Little remains; but every hour is saved
From that eternal silence, something more,

Ulysses: A legendary Greek king of Ithaca and hero of Homer's *Odyssey,* Ulysses (or Odysseus) is noted for his daring and cunning. After his many adventures — including encounters with the Cyclops, the cannibalistic Laestrygones, and the enchantress Circe — Ulysses returned home to his faithful wife, Penelope. Tennyson portrays an older Ulysses pondering his situation.

Hyades: A group of stars whose rising was supposedly followed by rain and thus stormy seas.

Troy: An ancient city in Asia Minor. According to legend, Paris, king of Troy, abducted Helen, the beautiful wife of Menelaus, king of Sparta, initiating the Trojan War, in which numerous Greek heroes, including Ulysses, fought.

A bringer of new things; and vile it were
For some three suns to store and hoard myself,
And this grey spirit yearning in desire
To follow knowledge like a sinking star,
Beyond the utmost bound of human thought.
   This is my son, mine own Telemachus,
To whom I leave the scepter and the isle—
Well-loved of me, discerning to fulfill
This labor, by slow prudence to make mild
A rugged people, and through soft degrees
Subdue them to the useful and the good.
Most blameless is he, centered in the sphere
Of common duties, decent not to fail
In offices of tenderness, and pay
Meet adoration to my household gods,
When I am gone. He works his work, I mine.
   There lies the port; the vessel puffs her sail;
There gloom the dark, broad seas. My mariners,
Souls that have toiled, and wrought, and thought with me—
That ever with a frolic welcome took
The thunder and the sunshine, and opposed
Free hearts, free foreheads—you and I are old;
Old age hath yet his honor and his toil.
Death closes all; but something ere the end,
Some work of noble note, may yet be done,
Not unbecoming men that strove with Gods.
The lights begin to twinkle from the rocks;
The long day wanes; the low moon climbs; the deep
Moans round with many voices. Come, my friends,
'Tis not too late to seek a newer world.
Push off, and sitting well in order smite
The sounding furrows; for my purpose holds
To sail beyond the sunset, and the baths
Of all the western stars, until I die.
It may be that the gulfs will wash us down;
It may be we shall touch the Happy Isles,°
And see the great Achilles,° whom we knew.
Though much is taken, much abides; and though
We are not now that strength which in old days
Moved earth and heaven, that which we are, we are—
One equal temper of heroic hearts,
Made weak by time and fate, but strong in will
To strive, to seek, to find, and not to yield.

Happy Isles: Elysium, or Paradise, believed to be in the far western ocean.
Achilles: Greek hero of the Trojan War.

DYLAN THOMAS (1914–1953)

Fern Hill (1946)

Now as I was young and easy under the apple boughs
About the lilting house and happy as the grass was green,
  The night above the dingle° starry,
    Time let me hail and climb
  Golden in the heydays of his eyes,
And honoured among wagons I was prince of the apple towns
And once below a time I lordly had the trees and leaves
    Trail with daisies and barley
  Down the rivers of the windfall light.

And as I was green and carefree, famous among the barns
About the happy yard and singing as the farm was home,
  In the sun that is young once only,
    Time let me play and be
  Golden in the mercy of his means,
And green and golden I was huntsman and herdsman, the calves
Sang to my horn, the foxes on the hills barked clear and cold,
    And the sabbath rang slowly
  In the pebbles of the holy streams.

All the sun long it was running, it was lovely, the hay
Fields high as the house, the tunes from the chimneys, it was air
  And playing, lovely and watery
    And fire green as grass.
  And nightly under the simple stars
As I rode to sleep the owls were bearing the farm away,
All the moon long I heard, blessed among stables, the nightjars°
  Flying with the ricks,° and the horses
    Flashing into the dark.

And then to awake, and the farm, like a wanderer white
With the dew, come back, the cock on his shoulder: it was all
  Shining, it was Adam and maiden,
    The sky gathered again
  And the sun grew round that very day.
So it must have been after the birth of the simple light
In the first, spinning place, the spellbound horses walking warm
  Out of the whinnying green stable
    On to the fields of praise.

---

dingle: A small valley or dell, typically wooded.
nightjars: A type of nocturnal bird.
ricks: A pile of hay or straw.

And honoured among foxes and pheasants by the gay house
Under the new made clouds and happy as the heart was long,
In the sun born over and over,
I ran my heedless ways,
My wishes raced through the house high hay
And nothing I cared, at my sky blue trades, that time allows
In all his tuneful turning so few and such morning songs
Before the children green and golden
Follow him out of grace,
Nothing I cared, in the lamb white days, that time would take me
Up to the swallow thronged loft by the shadow of my hand,
In the moon that is always rising,
Nor that riding to sleep
I should hear him fly with the high fields
And wake to the farm forever fled from the childless land.
Oh as I was young and easy in the mercy of his means,
Time held me green and dying
Though I sang in my chains like the sea.

Source: ©Dorothy Alexander

See this poet's biography on p. 1230.

MONA VAN DUYN (1921–2004)

Earth Tremors Felt in Missouri (1964)

The quake last night was nothing personal,
you told me this morning. I think one always wonders,
unless, of course, something is visible: tremors
that take us, private and willy-nilly, are usual.

But the earth said last night that what I feel,
you feel; what secretly moves you, moves me.
One small, sensuous catastrophe
makes inklings letters, spelled in a worldly tremble.

The earth, with others on it, turns in its course
as we turn toward each other, less than ourselves, gross,
mindless, more than we were. Pebbles, we swell
to planets, nearing the universal roll,
in our conceit even comprehending the sun,
whose bright ordeal leaves cool men woebegone.

PHILLIS WHEATLEY (1753–1784)

On Being Brought from Africa to America (1773)

'Twas mercy brought me from my *Pagan* land,
Taught my benighted soul to understand

That there's a God, that there's a *Saviour* too:
Once I redemption neither sought nor knew.
Some view our sable race with scornful eye,
"Their colour is a diabolic die."
Remember, *Christians*, *Negroes*, black as *Cain*,
May be refin'd, and join th' angelic train.

WALT WHITMAN (1819–1892)

A Noiseless Patient Spider (1881)

A noiseless patient spider,
I mark'd where on a little promontory it stood isolated,
Mark'd how to explore the vacant vast surrounding,
It launch'd forth filament, filament, filament, out of itself,
Ever unreeling them, ever tirelessly speeding them.

And you O my soul where you stand,
Surrounded, detached, in measureless oceans of space,
Ceaselessly musing, venturing, throwing, seeking the spheres to
connect them,
Till the bridge you will need be form'd, till the ductile anchor
hold,
Till the gossamer thread you fling catch somewhere, O my soul.

WALT WHITMAN (1819–1892)

from "Song of Myself" (1855)

1

I celebrate myself, and sing myself,
And what I assume you shall assume,
For every atom belonging to me as good belongs to you.

I loafe and invite my soul,
I lean and loafe at my ease observing a spear of summer grass.

My tongue, every atom of my blood, form'd from this soil, this air,
Born here of parents born here from parents the same, and their
parents the same,
I, now thirty-seven years old in perfect health begin,
Hoping to cease not till death.

Creeds and schools in abeyance,
Retiring back a while sufficed at what they are, but never
forgotten,
I harbor for good or bad, I permit to speak at every hazard,
Nature without check with original energy.

2

Houses and rooms are full of perfumes, the shelves are crowded
with perfumes,
I breathe the fragrance myself and know it and like it,
The distillation would intoxicate me also, but I shall not let it.

The atmosphere is not a perfume, it has no taste of the distillation,
it is odorless,
It is for my mouth forever, I am in love with it,
I will go to the bank by the wood and become undisguised
and naked,
I am mad for it to be in contact with me.

The smoke of my own breath,
Echoes, ripples, buzz'd whispers, love-root, silk-thread, crotch
and vine,
My respiration and inspiration, the beating of my heart, the
passing of blood and air through my lungs,
The sniff of green leaves and dry leaves, and of the shore and
dark-color'd sea-rocks, and of hay in the barn,
The sound of the belch'd words of my voice loos'd to the eddies
of the wind,
A few light kisses, a few embraces, a reaching around of arms,
The play of shine and shade on the trees as the supple
boughs wag,
The delight alone or in the rush of the streets, or along the fields
and hill-sides,
The feeling of health, the full-noon trill, the song of me rising
from bed and meeting the sun.

Have you reckon'd a thousand acres much? have you
reckon'd the
earth much?
Have you practis'd so long to learn to read?
Have you felt so proud to get at the meaning of poems?

Stop this day and night with me and you shall possess the origin
of all poems,
You shall possess the good of the earth and sun,
(there are millions
of suns left,)
You shall no longer take things at second or third hand, nor look
through the eyes of the dead, nor feed on the
spectres in books,
You shall not look through my eyes either, nor take things
from me,
You shall listen to all sides and filter them from your self.

RICHARD WILBUR (1921–)

The Ride (1987)

The horse beneath me seemed
To know what course to steer
Through the horror of snow I dreamed,
And so I had no fear.

Nor was I chilled to death
By the wind's white shudders, thanks
To the veils of his patient breath
And the mist of sweat from his flanks.

It seemed that all night through,
Within my hand no rein
And nothing in my view
But the pillar of his mane.

I rode with magic ease
At a quick, unstumbling trot
Through shattering vacancies
On into what was not,

Till the weave of the storm grew thin,
With a threading of cedar-smoke,
And the ice-blind pane of an inn
Shimmered, and I awoke.

How shall I now get back
To the inn-yard where he stands,
Burdened with every lack,
And waken the stable-hands

To give him, before I think
That there was no horse at all,
Some hay, some water to drink,
A blanket and a stall?

WILLIAM WORDSWORTH (1770–1850)

Composed upon Westminster Bridge, September 3, 1802 (1807)

Earth has not anything to show more fair:
Dull would he be of soul who could pass by
A sight so touching in its majesty:
This City now doth, like a garment, wear
The beauty of the morning; silent, bare,

Ships, towers, domes, theatres, and temples lie
Open unto the fields, and to the sky;
All bright and glittering in the smokeless air.
Never did sun more beautifully steep
In his first splendor, valley, rock, or hill;
Ne'er saw I, never felt, a calm so deep!
The river glideth at his own sweet will:
Dear God! the very houses seem asleep;
And all that mighty heart is lying still!

WILLIAM WORDSWORTH (1770–1850)

London, 1802 (1802)

Milton!° thou should'st be living at this hour:
England hath need of thee: she is a fen
Of stagnant waters: altar, sword and pen,
Fireside, the heroic wealth of hall and bower,
Have forfeited their ancient English dower
Of inward happiness. We are selfish men;
Oh! raise us up, return to us again;
And give us manners, virtue, freedom, power.
Thy soul was like a star, and dwelt apart:
Thou hadst a voice whose sound was like the sea:
Pure as the naked heavens, majestic, free,
So didst thou travel on life's common way,
In cheerful godliness; and yet thy heart
The lowliest duties on herself did lay.

WILLIAM WORDSWORTH (1770–1850)

My heart leaps up when I behold (1807)

My heart leaps up when I behold
    A rainbow in the sky:
So was it when my life began;
So is it now I am a man;
So be it when I shall grow old,
    Or let me die!
The Child is father of the Man;
And I could wish my days to be
Bound each to each by natural piety.

Milton: John Milton (1608–1674), poet, best known for *Paradise Lost.*

WILLIAM WORDSWORTH (1770–1850)

She dwelt among the untrodden ways (1800)

She dwelt among the untrodden ways
  Beside the springs of Dove,°
A Maid whom there were none to praise
  And very few to love:

A violet by a mossy stone
  Half hidden from the eye!
—Fair as a star, when only one
  Is shining in the sky.

She lived unknown, and few could know
  When Lucy ceased to be;
But she is in her grave, and, oh,
  The difference to me!

WILLIAM WORDSWORTH (1770–1850)

The Solitary Reaper° (1807)

Behold her, single in the field,
Yon solitary Highland lass!
Reaping and singing by herself;
Stop here, or gently pass!
Alone she cuts and binds the grain,
And sings a melancholy strain;
O listen! for the vale profound
Is overflowing with the sound.

No nightingale did ever chaunt
More welcome notes to weary bands
Of travelers in some shady haunt
Among Arabian sands.
A voice so thrilling ne'er was heard
In springtime from the cuckoo-bird,
Breaking the silence of the seas
Among the farthest Hebrides.°

Will no one tell me what she sings?—
Perhaps the plaintive numbers flow

Dove: A river in the Lake District of England.

Reaper: A worker who harvests grain.

Hebrides: A group of islands off the west coast of Scotland.

For old, unhappy, far-off things,
And battles long ago.
Or is it some more humble lay,
Familiar matter of today?
Some natural sorrow, loss, or pain,
That has been, and may be again?

Whate'er the theme, the maiden sang
As if her song could have no ending;
I saw her singing at her work,
And o'er the sickle° bending—
I listened, motionless and still;
And, as I mounted up the hill,
The music in my heart I bore
Long after it was heard no more.

CHARLES WRIGHT (1935–)

October (1981)

The leaves fall from my fingers
Cornflowers scatter across the field like stars,
like smoke stars,
By the train tracks, the leaves in a drift
Under the slow clouds
and the nine steps to heaven,
The light falling in great sheets through the trees,
Sheets almost tangible.

The transfiguration will start like this, I think
breathless,
Quick blade through the trees,
Something with red colors falling away from my hands,
The air beginning to go cold . . .
And when it does
I'll rise from this tired body, a blood-knot of light,
Ready to take the darkness in.

—Or for the wind to come
And carry me, bone by bone, through the sky,
Its wafer a burn on my tongue,
its wine deep forgetfulness.

sickle: A curved blade used for harvesting grain or cutting grass.

WILLIAM BUTLER YEATS (1865–1939)

Crazy Jane Talks with the Bishop (1933)

I met the Bishop on the road
And much said he and I.
"Those breasts are flat and fallen now,
Those veins must soon be dry;
Live in a heavenly mansion,
Not in some foul sty."

"Fair and foul are near of kin,
And fair needs foul," I cried.
"My friends are gone, but that's a truth
Nor grave nor bed denied,
Learned in bodily lowliness
And in the heart's pride.

"A woman can be proud and stiff
When on love intent;
But Love has pitched his mansion in
The place of excrement;
For nothing can be sole or whole
That has not been rent."

WILLIAM BUTLER YEATS (1865–1939)

The Lake Isle of Innisfree (1892)

I will arise and go now, and go to Innisfree,°
And a small cabin build there, of clay and wattles° made:
Nine bean-rows will I have there, a hive for the honey-bee,
And live alone in the bee-loud glade.

And I shall have some peace there, for peace comes
  dropping slow,
Dropping from the veils of the morning to where the
  cricket sings;
There midnight's all a glimmer, and noon a purple glow,
And evening full of the linnet's wings.

Innisfree: An island in Lough (Lake) Gill, County Sligo, in Ireland.

wattles: Stakes interwoven with twigs or branches, used for walls and roofing.

I will arise and go now, for always night and day
I hear lake water lapping with low sounds by the shore;
While I stand on the roadway, or on the pavements grey,
I hear it in the deep heart's core.

WILLIAM BUTLER YEATS (1865–1939)

Sailing to Byzantium° (1927)

That is no country for old men. The young
In one another's arms, birds in the trees
—Those dying generations — at their song,
The salmon-falls, the mackerel-crowded seas,
Fish, flesh, or fowl, commend all summer long
Whatever is begotten, born, and dies.
Caught in that sensual music all neglect
Monuments of unaging intellect.

An aged man is but a paltry thing,
A tattered coat upon a stick, unless
Soul clap its hands and sing, and louder sing
For every tatter in its mortal dress,
Nor is there singing school but studying
Monuments of its own magnificence;
And therefore I have sailed the seas and come
To the holy city of Byzantium.

O sages standing in God's holy fire
As in the gold mosaic of a wall,
Come from the holy fire, perne in a gyre,
And be the singing-masters of my soul.
Consume my heart away; sick with desire
And fastened to a dying animal
It knows not what it is; and gather me
Into the artifice of eternity.

Once out of nature I shall never take
My bodily form from any natural thing,
But such a form as Grecian goldsmiths make
Of hammered gold and gold enameling
To keep a drowsy Emperor awake;
Or set upon a golden bough to sing
To lords and ladies of Byzantium
Of what is past, or passing, or to come.

Byzantium: Ancient Greek city later rebuilt as Constantinople (now Istanbul).

WILLIAM BUTLER YEATS (1865–1939)

The Second Coming° (1921)

Turning and turning in the widening gyre°
The falcon cannot hear the falconer;
Things fall apart; the center cannot hold;
Mere anarchy is loosed upon the world,
The blood-dimmed tide is loosed, and everywhere
The ceremony of innocence is drowned;
The best lack all conviction, while the worst
Are full of passionate intensity.°

Surely some revelation is at hand;
Surely the Second Coming is at hand;
The Second Coming! Hardly are those words out
When a vast image out of *Spiritus Mundi*°
Troubles my sight: somewhere in sands of the desert
A shape with lion body and the head of a man,
A gaze blank and pitiless as the sun,
Is moving its slow thighs, while all about it
Reel shadows of the indignant desert birds.
The darkness drops again; but now I know
That twenty centuries° of stony sleep
Were vexed to nightmare by a rocking cradle,
And what rough beast, its hour come round at last,
Slouches towards Bethlehem to be born?

ADAM ZAGAJEWSKI (1945–)

Poetry Searches for Radiance*

Translated by Clare Cavanagh

Poetry searches for radiance,
poetry is the kingly road
that leads us farthest.
We seek radiance in a gray hour,
at noon or in the chimneys of the dawn,

The Second Coming: The phrase usually refers to the return of Christ. Yeats theorized cycles of history, much like the turning of a wheel. Here he offers a poetic comment on his view of the dissolution of civilization at the end of one such cycle.
gyre: Spiral.
Mere . . . intensity: Lines 4–8 refer to the Russian Revolution of 1917.
Spiritus Mundi: Literally, "Spirit of the World" (Latin). Yeats believed all souls to be connected by a "Great Memory."
twenty centuries: The centuries between the birth of Christ and the twentieth century, in which Yeats was writing.
*Publication date is not available.

even on a bus, in November,
while an old priest nods beside us.

The waiter in a Chinese restaurant bursts into tears
and no one can think why.
Who knows, this may also be a quest,
like that moment at the seashore
when a predatory ship appeared on the horizon
and stopped short, held still for a long while.
And also moments of deep joy

and countless moments of anxiety.
Let me see, I ask.
Let me persist, I say.
A cold rain falls at night.
In the streets and avenues of my city
quiet darkness is hard at work.
Poetry searches for radiance.

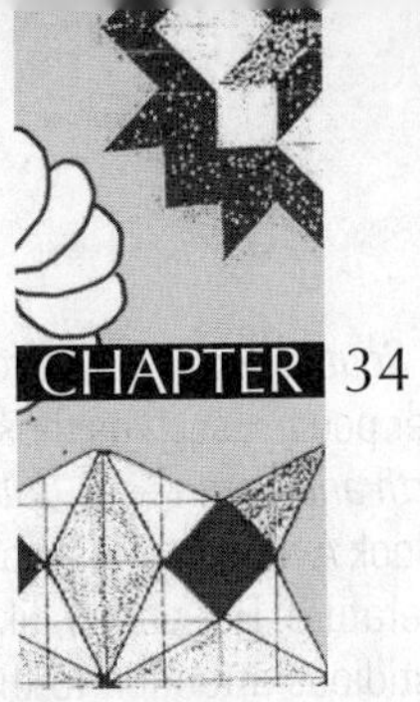

CHAPTER 34

BIOGRAPHICAL SKETCHES OF SELECTED POETS

MAYA ANGELOU (1928–), born Marguerite Johnson in St. Louis, lived with her grandmother in Stamps, Arkansas, where she graduated from Lafayette County Training School. She has worked as a cook, streetcar conductor, screenwriter, singer, dancer, and actress. Angelou was nominated for the National Book Award (for *I Know Why the Caged Bird Sings*) and the Pulitzer Prize (for *Just Give Me a Cool Drink of Water 'Fore I Die,* 1974). She won an Emmy for her role in *Roots* (1977) and a Grammy for an album of her poem "On the Pulse of Morning," which she read at the 1993 inauguration of President Bill Clinton. Angelou's collected poems, *The Complete Collected Poems of Maya Angelou,* was published in 1994. Angelou summarizes her work in this way: "I speak to the black experience, but I am always talking about the human condition — about what we can endure, dream, fail at, and still survive."

MARGARET ATWOOD (1939–) was born in Ottawa, Canada, and grew up in Toronto. After her first book of poetry, *Double Persephone* (1962), she published *The Circle Game* (1966), winner of Canada's highest literary honor, the Governor General's Award. She gained even greater prominence with novels — *The Handmaid's Tale* (1985), which was made into a movie, *Cat's Eye* (1988), and *The Robber Bride* (1993) — as well as other volumes of poetry, short stories, critical essays, radio and television scripts, and children's books. Her novel *The Blind Assassin* won the 2000 Booker Prize for fiction. Her most recent book is *The Tent,* published in 2006. In an interview with critic Linda Sandler, Atwood observed, "You can't write poetry unless you're willing to immerse yourself in language — not just in words, but in words of a certain potency. It's like learning a foreign language."

W(YSTAN) H(UGH) AUDEN (1907–1973) earned a scholarship to Oxford University, where he and his writer friends — Stephen Spender, Cecil Day-Lewis, Christopher Isherwood, and Louis MacNeice (known as the "Auden Generation") — exerted considerable influence on modern literature. Auden left England in 1939 and became a United States citizen in 1946. Among his many works probing the mysteries of religion, psychology, and politics are *The Double Man* (1941); *The Age of Anxiety* (1947), winner of the 1948 Pulitzer Prize; and *The Shield of Achilles* (1955), winner of the 1956 National Book Award. In a 1971 interview with Daniel Halpern, Auden commented, "Truth in poetry is very important to me. I think you must feel, when you read a poem, that it says something about life which you recognize to be true."

ELIZABETH BISHOP (1911–1979) was born in Worcester, Massachusetts, and raised by her grandparents in Nova Scotia. After graduating from Vassar College, she traveled widely, living in New York, Mexico, France, Spain, North Africa, Ireland, and Italy. For four years, she lived in Key West, Florida —

an experience that informed some of the poems in her first volume, *North and South* (1946)—and for sixteen years, she lived in Brazil. These varied settings continued to influence her poems, such as those in the 1965 volume *Questions of Travel,* and much of her later work. *Poems: North and South—A Cold Spring* (1955) won the Pulitzer Prize; *Complete Poems* (1969) won the National Book Award; her last volume, *Geography III* (1976), established her as a major figure in contemporary literature. Her poetry, like that of Marianne Moore, her longtime friend and mentor, is admired for its fastidious attention to the natural world, as well as for its muted irony and humor. Her *Collected Prose,* published in 1984, includes autobiographical sketches, travel accounts, a memoir of Marianne Moore, and short stories. Bishop was awarded the Fellowship of the Academy of American Poets in 1964. During the last years of her life, she lived in Cambridge, Massachusetts, and taught at Harvard University.

WILLIAM BLAKE (1757–1827) was born in London, England, and educated entirely at home. At fourteen, he was apprenticed to an engraver. His talent for art flourished, and he was eventually made a member of London's Royal Academy. His first book, *Poetical Sketches* (1783), was printed by friends. During this time, Blake began illustrating his poems with hand-colored engravings. Throughout the rest of his life, he experimented with this technique, which he called "illuminated printing," and produced books of stunning beauty and originality. In 1789, he published *Songs of Innocence,* followed in 1794 by *Songs of Experience.* Also issued during this period were his works *The Book of Thel* (1789) and *The Marriage of Heaven and Hell* (1791). In 1793, Blake moved to Lambeth, south of London, where he worked on *The Book of Job,* completed when he was nearly seventy. Largely dismissed in his time as the products of an eccentric, even a madman, Blake's books attracted no more than a small following of readers. He died a pauper and was buried in an unmarked grave. Still, his influence on poetry and art, and even on contemporary popular culture, has been enormous.

ANNE BRADSTREET (1612–1672) was born in Northampton, England. At sixteen, she married Simon Bradstreet and two years later sailed for America with her husband and father, both of whom eventually became governors of the Massachusetts Bay colony. In 1650, her first collection of poems, *The Tenth Muse,* was published in London without her knowledge by her brother-in-law, who thus bestowed on Bradstreet the unexpected honor of being the first American poet to be published in England. Along with poems on the familiar poetic preoccupations of the age—time and mutability—the volume contains elegies on Sidney and Queen Elizabeth. A second edition, with corrections and additions, appeared in Boston six years after the poet's death. In this collection, Bradstreet turns more frequently toward the personal, often addressing domestic topics from a religious point of view. The second edition contains elegies on her children and poems to her husband.

GWENDOLYN BROOKS (1917–2000) former Poet Laureate of Illinois, was, in 1950, the first African American to win a Pulitzer Prize (for her second book of poems, *Annie Allen*). Born in Topeka, Kansas, Brooks was raised in a section of Chicago called "Bronzeville," which provided the setting for her first published poetry collection, *A Street in Bronzeville* (1945). Other collections include *The Bean Eaters* (1960), *In the Mecca* (1968), and *The World of Gwendolyn Brooks* (1971). Brooks also published a novel, *Maud Martha* (1953), and *Report from Part One: An Autobiography* (1972). In a review of *Annie Allen,* Langston Hughes noted that "the people and the poems in Gwendolyn Brooks's book are alive, reaching and very much of today." Brooks's desire to reach all African-Americans is revealed in a 1974 interview in which she explained that she wanted "to develop a style that will appeal to black people in taverns, black people in gutters, schools, offices, factories, prisons, the consulate; I wish to reach black people in pulpits, black people in mines, on farms, on thrones."

ROBERT BROWNING (1812–1889) was born in Camberwell, a London suburb, into a family of religious dissenters. He received little formal education; much of his learning he gained from his father's library. His poetry attracted little attention until the publication of *Paracelsus* (1835) and *Bells and Pomegranates* (1841–1846). Eventually, Browning turned to the creation of dramatic characters and to the development of the dramatic monologue, a literary form now associated almost exclusively with him. In 1846, he married Elizabeth Barrett, and the couple moved to Florence, where he composed *Men and Women* (1855) and *Dramatis Personae* (1864). After the death of his wife, Browning returned to London, where he wrote his masterpiece, *The Ring and the Book* (1869). He died in 1889 while visiting his son in Venice. Browning was one of the most famous poets of the Victorian Age; his work — especially his dramatic monologues — had great influence on early twentieth-century writers, notably Ezra Pound.

GEOFFREY CHAUCER (c. 1343–1400), born in London sometime between 1340 and 1344, was the son of a prosperous wine merchant. Although little is known of his early education, his later works reflect his knowledge of French, Italian, and Latin. A skilled professional soldier, Chaucer fought in the Hundred Years War and did not begin working on *The Canterbury Tales* until he was in his early forties. The book, which was left unfinished when he died, depicts a journey by some pilgrims going to the shrine of the martyr St. Thomas Becket. On the way, they amuse themselves by telling stories that are interlinked with interludes in which the characters reveal much about themselves. Although Chaucer wrote numerous literary works, he is best remembered for his *Canterbury Tales*.

JUDITH ORTIZ COFER (1952–) was born in Hormigueros, Puerto Rico. In 1960, her family settled in Paterson, New Jersey; much of Cofer's memory of that time is vividly recorded in her collection of essays and poetry, *Silent Dancing: A Partial Remembrance of a Puerto Rican Childhood* (1991). She is the author of two additional collections of essays, *The Year of Revolution* (1998) and *Woman in Front of the Sun: On Becoming a Writer* (2000); a novel, *The Line of the Sun* (1989); two books of poetry, *Terms of Survival* and *Reaching for the Mainland* (both 1987); *The Latin Deli: Prose and Poetry* (1993); and *The Year of Our Revolution: Selected and New Prose and Poetry* (1998). Her most recent books are *The Meaning of Consuelo* (2003), *Call Me Maria* (2004), and *A Love Story Beginning in Spanish: Poems* (2005).

SAMUEL TAYLOR COLERIDGE (1772–1834) was born at Ottery St. Mary, Devon, England, where his father was vicar. He entered Jesus College, Cambridge, in 1791, intending a profession in the Church of England, but abandoned his studies in 1793. In collaboration with his friend William Wordsworth, Coleridge published *Lyrical Ballads* in 1798. Here and in their later poems, the two not only laid the foundations of English romanticism but also redefined the contours of English poetic form. Coleridge experimented with preexisting forms ranging from the ballad (*Lyrical Ballads* included his masterpiece, *The Rime of the Ancient Mariner*) to the ode. His visionary fragment "Kubla Khan" was written in 1797. Despite his falling out with Wordsworth after 1810 and the decline of his poetic powers (due in part to a long-term opium addiction), Coleridge continued to write philosophical and social tracts, as well as sermons and literary criticism.

BILLY COLLINS (1941–) was born in New York City and currently resides in Somers, New York. Since the publication of his first book, *The Apple That Astonished Paris* (1988), he has established himself as a prominent voice in contemporary American poetry. He has received many awards, among them the Bess Hokin Prize, the Frederick Bock Prize, the Oscar Blumenthal Prize, and the Levinson Prize awarded by *Poetry* magazine. His books of poetry include *The Trouble with Poetry and Other Poems* (2005), *Nine Horses* (2002), *Sailing Alone around the Room: New and Selected Poems* (2001), *Picnic, Lightning* (1998), *The Art of Drowning* (1995), a finalist for the Lenore Marshall Prize, and *Questions about Angels* (1991), selected for the National Poetry Series and reissued in 1999. Collins served as Poet Laureate of the United States between 2001 and 2003. His poems, often about ordinary people and situations, have made him one of the country's most popular poets.

E(DWARD) E(STLIN) CUMMINGS (1894–1962) was born in Cambridge, Massachusetts. He served as an ambulance driver during World War I and then spent several years studying art in Paris. *Tulips and Chimneys* (1923), his first book of poems, received both praise and criticism for its idiosyncratic capitalization (such as the use of only lowercase letters in his name), diction, punctuation, and typography. The publication of his *Complete Poems: 1904–1962* (1994), a collection of his twelve volumes of verse, affirms his lasting literary reputation. Best known as an experimental poet, the versatile Cummings was also a talented painter, prose writer, translator, and playwright. Noted poet Randall Jarrell observed, "No one else . . . has ever made avant-garde, experimental poems so attractive to the general and special reader."

EMILY DICKINSON (1830–1886), born into a prominent Amherst, Massachusetts, family, attended Amherst Academy and Mount Holyoke Female Seminary. She rarely left her hometown—and, except for extended stays in Cambridge in 1864 and 1865, she rarely left her home after that. In her lifetime, Dickinson published anonymously only seven of her poems, and most of these had been edited to make them more conventional. In 1955, Thomas H. Johnson edited the definitive Dickinson canon of 1,775 poems. Noted writer Joyce Carol Oates considers Dickinson a "poet of the soul"—indeed, "our most endlessly fascinating American poet." Fascinating, indeed, is the way Dickinson saw poetry as a moment of great intensity. As she told her literary adviser Thomas Wentworth Higginson, "If I read a book and it makes my whole body so cold no fire can warm me, I know *that* is poetry. If I feel physically as if the top of my head were taken off, I know *that* is poetry."

JOHN DONNE (1572–1631) was born in London, England. During the 1590s, he traveled widely, read voraciously, and was a courtier in Queen Elizabeth's court. In 1601, he married Ann Moore, still a minor, an offense for which he was briefly imprisoned and left unemployed. The next twenty years were difficult for Donne: he supported his steadily growing family with a series of makeshift jobs; when Ann died in 1617, he was left with seven children. In 1621, however, Donne's prospects changed: King James, convinced of Donne's promise as a preacher, made him the dean of St. Paul's Cathedral in London, a position he held until his death in 1631. Donne's poetry, known as "metaphysical," is characterized by passionate thought and intellectual playfulness; it delights in puns, paradox, poses, and conceits. His career is generally seen as divided between the love poetry of his early years and his later poems of religious devotion.

T(HOMAS) S(TEARNS) ELIOT (1888–1965), born in St. Louis, emigrated to England, where he worked in London as a bank clerk and book editor. In 1927, he became a British citizen and declared himself an "Anglo-Catholic in religion, royalist in politics, and classicist in literature." He won prestigious professorships at Cambridge and Harvard, the Nobel Prize in Literature (1948), the

British Order of Merit, the Emerson-Thoreau Medal from the American Academy of Arts and Sciences (1959), and the U.S. Medal of Freedom (1964). His best-known works of poetry include "The Love Song of J. Alfred Prufrock" (1917), *The Waste Land* (1922), *The Four Quartets* (1943), and *Old Possum's Book of Practical Cats* (1939), the basis for the long-running musical *Cats.* His friend Ezra Pound, upon reading the manuscript of *The Waste Land,* suggested revisions but immediately recognized it as a work of genius, saying that Eliot's poem was enough "to make the rest of us shut up shop."

MARTIN ESPADA (1957–) was born in Brooklyn, New York, and was early immersed in political activism by his father, a leader in the Puerto Rican community. In his poetry, Espada strikes out against oppression, giving voice to the struggles of the poor and the working class. *Imagine the Angels of Bread,* his 1996 collection, won the American Book Award. Other books of poetry include *Rebellion Is the Circle of a Lover's Hand* (1990), *City of Coughing and Dead Radiators* (1993), and *A Mayan Astronomer in Hell's Kitchen: Poems* (2000). He has edited several anthologies, including *El Coro: A Chorus of Latino and Latina Poets* (1997) and *Poetry like Bread: Poets of the Imagination from Curbstone Press* (1994). His collection of essays, *Zapata's Disciple,* appeared in 1998. In 2003, Espada published *Albanza: New and Selected Poems 1982–2002,* for which he received the Patterson Award for Sustained Literary Achievement.

ROBERT FROST (1874–1963) was born in San Francisco. He attended Dartmouth College and Harvard without receiving a degree. In 1900, he settled on a New Hampshire dairy farm, writing many of his works there. Frost enjoyed enormous popularity as a revered poet, receiving honorary degrees from prestigious universities and winning major prizes, including the Pulitzer for *New Hampshire, Collected Poems, A Further Range,* and *Witness Tree.* He served as Poet Laureate of the United States between 1958 and 1959. In 1961, at the inauguration of President John F. Kennedy, he recited from memory his poem "The Gift Outright" because poor eyesight at age eighty-seven prevented him from reading. "Stopping by Woods on a Snowy Evening," observed critic Donald J. Greiner, "has immortality written all over it." Frost himself, in a letter to poet-critic Louis Untermeyer in 1923, called this poem his "best bid for remembrance."

NIKKI GIOVANNI (1943–) was born in Knoxville, Tennessee, and raised in the Lincoln Heights neighborhood of Cincinnati, Ohio. During the late 1960s, Giovanni became involved in the Black Arts movement; in her first three collections of poems—*Black Feeling, Black Talk* (1968), *Black Judgement* (1968), and *Re: Creation* (1970)— she explores the interpretation of identity and experience through a black consciousness. Her work of the 1970s treats her experience as a single mother; the volumes *Spin a Soft Black Song* (1971), *Ego-Tripping* (1973), and *Vacation Time* (1980) are collections of poems for children. Giovanni returned to more explicitly political subjects in *Those Who Ride the Night Winds* (1983); more recently, she published *Selected Poems of Nikki Giovanni* (1996), *Love Poems* (1997), *Blues for All the Changes: New Poems* (1999), *Quilting the Black-Eyed Pea: Poems and Not-Quite Poems* (2002), *The Collected Poetry of Nikki Giovanni: 1968–1998* (2003), and *Acolytes* (2007). Her honors include the NAACP Image Award for Literature (1998) and the Langston Hughes Award for Distinguished Contributions to Arts and Letters (1996).

LOUISE GLÜCK (1943–) was born in New York City. Among her many awards and honors are Columbia University's Academy of American Poets Prize (1967), a Rockefeller Foundation grant (1968), a National Endowment for the Arts grant (1969–1970), and a Guggenheim Fellowship (1975–1976). Glück's first collection of poetry, *First Born,* appeared in 1968. It was followed in 1975 by *The House on Marshland,* which brought her national recognition. She won the American Academy Award in 1981 and the National Book Critics Circle Award in 1985 for *The Triumph of Achilles*. Glück also served as Poet Laureate of the United States between 2003 and 2004. Her most recent collections include *Meadowlands* (1996), *Vita Nova* (1999), the *Seven Ages* (2001), and *Averno* (2006).

THOMAS HARDY (1840–1928), born in Dorsetshire, England, became a full-time writer after working as an architect in London. He published fourteen novels, eight volumes of poetry, four short story collections, two plays, and a variety of essays, prefaces, and other nonfiction prose. His best-known novels are *Far from the Madding Crowd* (1874), *The Return of the Native* (1878), *The Mayor of Casterbridge* (1886), *Tess of the D'Urbervilles* (1891), and *Jude the Obscure* (1896). Recipient of many honors, Hardy was the last great Victorian poet. The American poet-critic John Crowe Ransom connected Hardy to the next generation of poets "by reason of his naturalism and rebellion against the dogma." Often called a pessimist, Hardy regarded himself as a "meliorist"— someone who believes the world can be improved by human effort.

ROBERT HAYDEN (1913–1980), born Asa Bundy Sheffey in Detroit, was renamed by his adoptive parents. He published four significant volumes of poetry and in 1966 gained international recognition by winning the Grand Prize for Poetry in English at the First World Festival of Negro Arts in Dakar, Senegal, for *A Ballad of Remembrance*. Elected in 1975 to the Academy of American Poets, Hayden became the first African-American appointed Consultant in Poetry to the Library of Congress (1976–1978), the position now known as Poet Laureate of the United States. His *Collected Poems,* reissued in 1995 with an introduction by noted scholar Arnold Rampersad, reaffirms his literary reputation. Critic Wilbur Williams noted that "Hayden's characteristically soft-spoken and fluid voice derives much of its power from the evident contrast between the maelstrom of anguish [from] which it originates and the quiet reflecting pool of talk into which it is inevitably channeled."

SEAMUS HEANEY (1939–) comes from a Roman Catholic family in the predominantly Protestant town of Mossbawn, County Derry, Northern Ireland. This influential contemporary Irish poet has received most of the literary prizes awarded in Ireland and England as well as the 1995 Nobel Prize in Literature — the third Irish writer to receive this award, joining W. B. Yeats (1923) and Samuel Beckett (1969). Heaney's works include *Crediting Poetry: The Nobel Lecture* (1996) and *Open Ground: Selected Poems 1966–1996* (1998), which was named a *New York Times* Notable Book. Heaney's poetry, William Grimes observed, "is rooted in the Irish soil . . . as though Ireland's wet peat were a storehouse of images and memories." Heaney's most recent works include a poetry collection, *Electric Light* (2001); essays, *Finders Keepers: Selected Prose 1971–2001* (2002); and a translation, *The Burial at Thebes: A Version of Sophocles' Antigone* (2004).

GEORGE HERBERT (1593–1633) was born in Wales and raised in Oxford and London. His father died when he was three years old, and he was raised by his mother, an accomplished, cultured woman who was a friend of John Donne. Herbert had political ambitions and served for a time as a member of Parliament, but eventually he became a priest in the Church of England. Among his works was *The Temple,* a collection of verse that would eventually establish his reputation as one of the greatest religious poets in English. His poetry is characterized by its perfect marriage of form and content and by the poet's struggle to reconcile his art and faith.

ROBERT HERRICK (1591–1674) was the seventh child and fourth son born to a London goldsmith, Nicholas, and his wife, Julia Stone Herrick. As a young man, Herrick took holy orders and became a vicar in the Church of England. His most famous work was *Hesperides; or, the Works Both Human and Divine of Robert Herrick, Esq.* (1648). Influenced by classical Roman poetry, he wrote on pastoral themes, dealing primarily with English country life and village customs.

GERARD MANLEY HOPKINS (1844–1889) attended Oxford, where he was influenced by Cardinal John Henry Newman. As a result, Hopkins converted to Roman Catholicism and became a Jesuit priest. His long poem *The Wreck of the Deutschland* appeared in 1875; his shorter, more accessible nature poems were published in 1918. "The Windhover," his most famous sonnet, has a typically religious theme, exploring ways to praise, revere, and serve God. Hopkins is best known for his unusual metrical system, which he named "sprung rhythm." Critic Jerome Bump has observed that this "idiosyncratic creativity" made Hopkins's style "so radically different from that of his contemporaries" that much of his work was not fully recognized until after his death.

JOHN KEATS (1795–1821) was born in London, England, the eldest of four children. Keats studied medicine at Guy's Hospital, intending to become a surgeon, but gave up that goal in 1816 for a life of writing. In 1816, *The Examiner* printed his sonnet "On First Looking into Chapman's Homer" and hailed Keats, alongside Percy Bysshe Shelley, as one of the most promising writers of his generation. His *Poems* (1817), however, appeared to little applause. In 1818, after his brother's death from tuberculosis, Keats moved to Hampstead, where he met and fell in love with Fanny Brawne. He finished *Hyperion,* wrote lyrics such as "La Belle Dame sans Merci," and completed the great odes of 1819, for which he is chiefly remembered. In the winter of 1820, he fell seriously ill with tuberculosis and sailed for Italy. He died in Rome that summer, at age twenty-five.

YUSEF KOMUNYAKAA (1947–) was born the oldest of five children in Bogalusa, Louisiana. After high school, he enlisted in the Army. He served as a war correspondent for the *Southern Cross* during the Vietnam War, and he was awarded a Bronze Star. His experiences during the war became the basis for one of his most important collections of poetry, *Dien Cai Dau* (1988). In addition to this collection, Komunyakaa's numerous books of poems include *Copacetic* (1984), *I Apologize for the Eyes in My Head* (1986), *Magic City* (1992), *Thieves of Paradise* (1998), *Talking Dirty to the Gods* (2000), *Taboo* (2004), and two collections of new and collected poems — one of which, *Neon Vernacular* (1993), won the Pulitzer Prize in 1994. His most recent poetry collection, *Pleasure Dome: New and Collected Poems, 1975–1999,* was published in 2001.

TED KOOSER (1939–) was born in Ames, Iowa. He is the author of ten collections of poetry, including *Delights and Shadows* (2004), *Winter Morning Walks: One Hundred Postcards to Jim Harrison* (2000), *Weather Central* (1994), *One World at a Time* (1985), and *Sure Signs* (1980). His fiction and nonfiction books include *Braided Creek: A Conversation in Poetry* (2003) and *Local Wonders: Seasons in the Bohemian Alps* (2002). In 2004, Kooser was named Poet Laureate of the United States. His latest works are *Flying at Night: Poems 1965–1985* (Pitt Poetry Series) (2005) and *The Poetry Repair Manual: Practical Advice for Beginning Poets* (2005).

LI-YOUNG LEE (1957–) was born in Jakarta, Indonesia, of Chinese parents. In 1959, the Lee family fled Indonesia to escape anti-Chinese sentiment. After a five-year journey through Hong Kong, Macau, and Japan, they settled in the United States in 1964. His collections of poetry include *Behind My Eyes* (2008),

Book of My Nights (2001), *The City in Which I Love You* (1991), and *Rose* (1986). He is also the author of a memoir entitled *The Winged Seed: A Remembrance* (1995), which received an American Book Award from the Before Columbus Foundation. Other honors include a Lannan Literary Award, a Whiting Writer's Award, and a Guggenheim Foundation fellowship.

DORIS LESSING (1919–) was born Doris May Tayler, the child of British parents in what is now Iran. Her family moved to Rhodesia (present-day Zimbabwe) where they started a farm, which failed. In 1947, she moved to England, where she has lived since, and where she established herself as a writer. Lessing's work falls into three distinct phases: one when she was a member of the Communist Party; one in which she was influenced by psychoanalytic theory; and the most recent phase, lasting up to the present, in which she has drawn inspiration from Sufism, the mystical branch of Islam. She has written in a wide variety of genres, from realistic novels to science fiction, memoirs, and poetry. In 2007, she was awarded the Nobel Prize in Literature.

CLAUDE MCKAY (1890–1948), born in Jamaica, received part of his education from a well-read older brother. In 1914, he traveled to New York City, and his works *Harlem Shadows* (1922) and *Home to Harlem* (1927) established him as an important writer of the Harlem Renaissance. His best work is collected in *The Passion of Claude McKay: Selected Poetry and Prose, 1912–1948.* Written in traditional meter and rhyme, his poetry expresses powerful, compressed passion about topics both personal and social. According to critic Arthur D. Prayton, "McKay does not seek to hide his bitterness, but having preserved his vision as a poet and his status as a human being, he can transcend bitterness."

EDNA ST. VINCENT MILLAY (1892–1950) was born in Rockland, Maine. Her mother raised three daughters on her own, and she encouraged her girls to be ambitious and self-sufficient, teaching them an appreciation of music and literature. After college, Millay published several collections of poems and a play in verse. She moved to New York City's Greenwich Village, where she led a notoriously bohemian lifestyle, living for a time in a nine-foot-wide attic and maintaining an "open marriage" with her husband for twenty-six years. Her most famous collection of poetry is *Renascence and Other Poems* (1917).

JOHN MILTON (1608–1674) was born in London's Cheapside district, the son of a businessman. He was educated at St. Paul's, where he showed a great aptitude for languages, mastering both Latin and Greek before turning to Hebrew and modern European tongues. In 1634, he wrote the masque popularly known as *Comus,* and in 1637, he wrote the great elegy *Lycidas* for a college classmate who had drowned. From 1640 to 1660, Milton was embroiled in the political-religious controversies of the time, publishing tract after tract in what are known as the pamphlet wars. For a time, he was imprisoned at peril of his life, but at the intervention of friends (the poet Andrew Marvell among them), he was released. In 1663, blind and impoverished, Milton began work on his masterpiece, a long poem aimed at "justifying the ways of God to men." *Paradise Lost* was published in 1667 and was at once recognized as a supreme epic achievement. It was followed by *Paradise Regained* in 1671 and *Samson Agonistes,* a tragedy, in 1674.

N(AVARRE) SCOTT MOMADAY (1934–) was born in Lawton, Oklahoma. In 1969, he became the first Native American writer to win a Pulitzer Prize, awarded for his first novel, *House*

Made of Dawn (1969). His autobiographical work *The Names: A Memoir* (1976) recounts his growing up in New Mexico. His other publications include volumes of poetry—*Angle of Geese and Other Poems* (1974) and *Gourd Dancer* (1976)—and *The Way to Rainy Mountain* (1969), a collection of personal and historical narratives interwoven with tales from Kiowa mythology. He also wrote another novel, *The Ancient Child* (1989), and a collection of poems and narratives that he illustrated, *In the Presence of Sun* (1991). In 1993, he published *Circle of Wonder: A Native American Christmas Story* and *The Native Americans: Indian Country.* A collection of essays, *The Man Made of Words,* was published in 1997. Momaday, who considers himself primarily a poet, has stated that he returns again and again to his Kiowa culture for inspiration because it has "a certain strength and beauty I find missing in the modern world."

PAT MORA (1942–), a leading figure in contemporary Hispanic poetry, was born in El Paso, Texas. Her works include *My Own True Name: New and Selected Poems for Young Adults, 1984–1999* (2000)*; Aunt Carmen's Book of Practical Saints* (1997)*;* and *Agua Santa: Holy Water* (1995). In addition to her books of poetry, Mora is the author of numerous children's books, including *A Birthday Basket for Tia* (1992), and a memoir. Her most recent works include *Doña Flor: A Tall Tale About a Giant Woman with a Great Big Heart* (2005) and *The Song of Francis and the Animals* (2005).

FRANK O'HARA (1926–1966) was born in Baltimore, Maryland, and grew up in Grafton, Massachusetts. He served in the Navy, in the South Pacific, during World War II. After returning to civilian life, he received his BA and MA in English. Moving to New York, he became an art critic and a member of the group of poets—including John Ashbery and Kenneth Koch—known as the New York School. O'Hara's poems are wide-ranging and chatty and reflect his love of the visual arts and music and the delight he took in friendship. He was struck and killed by a dune buggy while walking at night on the beach at Fire Island, New York.

SHARON OLDS (1942–) was born in San Francisco. Her poetry collections include *The Dead and the Living* (1983), winner of both the Lamont Poetry Award and the National Book Critics Circle Award; *The Gold Cell* (1987); *The Father* (1992); *The Wellspring* (1995); *Blood, Tin, Straw* (1999); and *Unswept Room* (2002). She served as the New York State Poet Laureate from 1998 to 2000. More recently, she published the poetry collection *Strike Sparks: Selected Poems* in 2004. Because she so graphically details personal traumas, some critics place her in the confessional tradition of Sylvia Plath. However, Olds's poems have a less tormented tone and are more easily understood. Her style combines grotesque humor and straightforward reporting in a manner that *Poetry* magazine critic Lisel Mueller has called "a proud, urgent human voice."

LINDA PASTAN (1932–) was born in the Bronx, New York. Her publications include *A Perfect Circle of Sun* (1971); *On the Way to the Zoo* (1975); *Aspects of Eve* (1977); *The Five Stages of Grief* (1978), winner of the Poetry Society of America award; *PM/AM: New and Selected Poems* (1983), American Book Award nominee; *The Imperfect Paradise* (1988); *Heroes in Disguise* (1991); and *An Early Afterlife* (1995). Her most recent collection is *Queen of a Rainy Country* (2006). She was Poet Laureate for Maryland from 1991 through 1994. According to critic Sandra M. Gilbert, Pastan "broods on the rewards as well as the risks of domesticity" because she is "quite self-consciously a *woman* poet" who "austerely ordains the necessity of acquiescence in the ordinary."

OCTAVIO PAZ (1914–1998) was born in Mexico City. Under the encouragement of poet Pablo Neruda, he began his poetic career in his teens by founding an avant-garde literary magazine, *Barandal,* and publishing his first book of poems, *Luna silvestre* (1933). In his youth, Paz spent time in the United States and in Spain, where he was influenced by the modernist and surrealist movements. His sequence of prose poems, *Aguila o sol?* (*Eagle or Sun?*) (1951) is a visionary mapping of Mexico in terms of its past, present, and future, and *Piedra de Sol* (*Sun Stone*) (1957) borrows its structure from the Aztec calendar. This long poem, and Paz's sociocultural analysis of Mexico, *El laberinto de la soledad* (*The Labyrinth of Solitude*) (1950), established him as a major literary figure in the 1950s. In 1962, he became Mexico's ambassador to India but resigned six years later in protest when government forces massacred student demonstrators in Mexico City. He was awarded the Nobel Prize in Literature in 1990.

MARGE PIERCY (1936–) grew up poor and white in a predominantly black neighborhood in Detroit. Her publications include *Woman on the Edge of Time* (1976), *Circles on the Water* (1982), *Braided Lives* (1982), and *The Longings of Women* (1994). In addition to her novels and a collection of essays, Piercy has written numerous collections of poetry, including *What are Big Girls Made Of?* (1997). Her volume of poetry, *The Art of Blessing the Day: Poems with a Jewish Theme* (1999), celebrates the traditions of her religion. Her most recent work, *Sex Wars: A Novel of the Turbulent Post–Civil War Period,* was published in 2005.

ROBERT PINSKY (1940–) was born in Long Branch, New Jersey. Pinsky is the author of seven books of poetry: *Sadness and Happiness* (1975); *An Explanation of America* (1980); *History of My Heart* (1984); *The Want Bone* (1990); *The Figured Wheel: New and Collected Poems 1966–1996* (1996), which won the 1997 Lenore Poetry Prize and was a Pulitzer Prize nominee; *Jersey Rain* (2000); and *Gulf Music* (2007). Two of his four books of criticism are *The Sounds of Poetry* (1998), which was a finalist for the National Book Critics Circle Award, and *The Situation of Poetry* (1977). Pinsky's honors include an American Academy of Arts and Letters award, the Oscar Blumenthal Prize, the William Carlos Williams Award, and a Guggenheim Foundation Fellowship. In 1997, he was named the thirty-ninth Poet Laureate of the United States, a position he held for an unprecedented three years.

SYLVIA PLATH (1932–1963) was born in Boston to Polish-German parents who taught at Boston University. Having won a *Mademoiselle* magazine prize (1953), an award from *Poetry* magazine (1957), and a Yaddo writers' colony fellowship (1959), she began a promising career. After *A Winter Ship* (1960) came *The Colossus and Other Poems* (1962) and a novel, *The Bell Jar* (1963). Plath committed suicide at age thirty-one, soon after her seven-year marriage to poet Ted Hughes ended. Her posthumous works are *Ariel* (1965); *Crossing the Water* (1971); *Winter Trees* (1971); *Letters Home by Sylvia Plath: Correspondence 1950–1963* (1975); *Johnny Panic and the Bible of Dreams and Other Prose Writings* (1977); and her *Collected Poems,* a 1982 Pulitzer Prize winner. In the introduction to *Ariel,* Robert Lowell praised her as "one of those super-real, hypnotic, great classical heroines."

EZRA POUND (1885–1972), born in Hailey, Idaho, spent his childhood near Philadelphia. Leader of the Imagist poets, Pound experimented with poetic images to express "an intellectual and emotional complex in an instant of time." After his first volume, *A Lume Spento* (1908), he published *Personae and Exultations of Ezra Pound* (1913), *Homage to Sextus Propertius* (1919), and *Hugh Selwyn Mauberley* (1920). In 1917, he began his best-known work — a series of cantos that eventually included *The*

Pisan Cantos (1948) and *Thrones: Cantos 96–109* (1959). During World War II, Pound fervently supported Mussolini and broadcast Fascist propaganda over Italian radio. After the war, he was arrested for treason against the United States and was incarcerated in a mental hospital in Washington, D.C., from 1946 to 1958. A motivating force behind modern poetry, Pound won the Bollingen–Library of Congress Award in 1948.

ADRIENNE RICH (1929–), born and raised in Baltimore, began her prolific publishing career during her senior year at Radcliffe when her first book, *A Change of World,* was published by W. H. Auden in the Yale Series of Younger Poets. She has received Guggenheim fellowships, a Poetry Society of America award, a National Institute of Arts and Letters award, a Bollingen Foundation grant, and a National Endowment for the Arts grant. Rich writes about feminist issues in her many poetry collections, including *Dark Fields of the Republic: Poems, 1991–1995* (1995); *Time's Power: Poems, 1985–88* (1989); and *Midnight Salvage: Poems 1995–1998.* Her most recent collections are *Fox: Poems 1998–2000,* published in 2001, and *The School Among the Ruins: Poems 2000–2004,* published in 2004. *The Diamond Cutters and Other Poems* (1955) won the Poetry Society of America Award, and *Diving into the Wreck: Poems 1971–1972* (1973) won the 1974 National Book Award. William Heyen noted that Rich's work describes years of conflict as woman, wife, mother, and poet.

EDWIN ARLINGTON ROBINSON (1869–1935), a descendant of the Puritan poet Anne Bradstreet, was born in Head Tide, Maine. He grew up in Gardiner, Maine (the inspiration for his fictitious Tilbury Town) and then studied for two years at Harvard before his family's financial difficulties halted his education. He went on to publish *The Torrent and the Night Before* (1896), *The Children of the Night* (1897), and *Captain Craig* (1902). In 1916, *The Man against the Sky* confirmed his reputation as a major poet. He won Pulitzer Prizes for his *Collected Poems* (1921), *The Man Who Died Twice* (1924), and *Tristram* (1927). Robert Frost, in his introduction to Robinson's posthumous *King Jasper* (1935), characterized Robinson as a poet who "stayed content with the old-fashioned way to be new," unlike contemporary experimentalists who used poetry to express their grievances against society.

THEODORE ROETHKE (1908–1963) was born and grew up in Saginaw, Michigan. He won the Pulitzer Prize (1954) and two National Book Awards (1959 and 1965) for *Words for the Wind* (1958) and *The Far Field* (1964), respectively. Poet and critic Stanley Kunitz praised his rare gifts as a writer: "The ferocity of Roethke's imagination makes most contemporary poetry seem pale and tepid in contrast. Even his wit is murderous. . . ." Roethke once explained that he wrote about "trivial and vulgar" details "as barely and honestly as possible, symbolically, what few nuggets of observation and, let us hope, spiritual wisdom I have managed to seize upon in the course of a conventional albeit sometimes disordered existence."

CHRISTINA ROSSETTI (1830–1894) was born in London, England, the daughter of a Neapolitan political exile and sister of the poet-painter Dante Gabriel Rossetti. She was educated at home by her mother. *Goblin Market and Other Poems* was published in 1862; before that, lyrics such as "An End" and "Dream Lane" had been published in magazines under her pseudonym, Ellen Alleyne. *Goblin Market* was followed by *The Prince's Progress and Other Poems* (1866) and *Sing Song: A Nursery Rhyme Book* (1872). By the 1880s, ill health had made her an invalid, but she continued to write poetry. *A Pageant and Other Poems,* published in 1881, contains her sonnet sequence *Monna Innominata.* It was followed by *Time Flies: A Reading Diary* (1885) and *The Face of the Deep: A Devotional Commentary on the Apocalypse* (1892), her last published work. Her brother William edited her complete works (1904) after her death.

KAY RYAN (1945–) grew up in the Mojave Desert and San Joaquin Valley in California. Her reputation built slowly, and her first books were brought out by small presses, but she is currently one of the most highly regarded and popular poets in the United States. Her poems are typically short, highly compressed, and witty, with rhymes appearing where they are least expected. Ryan's poetry is seldom without humor, though that humor is often a means of grappling with serious, even dark, subject matter. Ryan's poems and essays have appeared in *The New Yorker, The Atlantic, Poetry, The Yale Review, Paris Review,* and *The American Scholar.* She has published several collections of poetry, including *The Niagara River* (Grove Press, 2005) and *Flamingo Watching* (1994), which was a finalist for both the Lamont Poetry Selection and the Lenore Marshall Prize.

SONIA SANCHEZ (1934–) moved from her birthplace of Birmingham, Alabama, to New York City. Her publications include *Homecoming* (1969); *It's a New Day: Poems for Young Brothas and Sistuhs* (1971); *A Blues Book for Blue Black Magical Women* (1973); *I'm Black When I'm Singing, I'm Blue When I Ain't* (1982); *homegirls & handgrenades* (1984); *Like the Singing Coming off the Drums: Love Poems* (1998); and *Shake Loose My Skin: New and Selected Poems* (1999). She has received grants from the National Institute of Arts and Letters and the National Endowment for the Arts and won the American Book Award. A strong black feminist advocate, Sanchez supports change, not through rage, violence, or substance abuse but through political astuteness, moral power, and strong family relationships. She has won the American Book Award and was the 2001 recipient of the Robert Frost medal in poetry.

CARL SANDBURG (1878–1967) was born in Galesburg, Illinois, to Swedish immigrant parents. His volumes of verse, often about industrialized America, include *Chicago Poems* (1915), *Corn Huskers* (1918), *Smoke and Steel* (1920), and *Good Morning, America* (1928); in 1951 he won the Pulitzer Prize for his *Complete Poems.* He also wrote prose works, such as *Abraham Lincoln: The Prairie Years* (1926) and *Abraham Lincoln: The War Years* (1940). According to historian Henry Steele Commager, Sandburg "celebrates what is best in us, and recalls us to our heritage and our humanity." On his eighty-fifth birthday, in 1963, when he published his final book, *Honey and Salt,* Sandburg confessed, "Being a poet is a damn dangerous business."

TUPAC SHAKUR (1971–1996) was born Lesane Parish Crooks in Brooklyn, New York, but his mother soon changed his name to Tupac Amaru after an Inca Indian revolutionary. His father, a Black Panther, was sentenced to sixty years in prison for his part in a fatal armored car robbery when Shakur was two years old, and the singer was raised by his mother, also a Black Panther. After winning a scholarship to the prestigious Baltimore School of the Arts, he began writing raps and acting. The single "Brenda's Got a Baby" launched his career and landed him a role in the motion picture *Juice* (1992). From there, he appeared in *Poetic Justice* (1993) and went on to release a platinum album, *Me Against the World* (1995). In addition to writing rap lyrics, Shakur wrote poetry that combined elements of the street and hip-hop culture with lyrical forms. Shakur, who was arrested eight times by the time he was twenty, was notorious for promoting the "Thug Life," which glorified living and dying by the gun. On September 7, 1996, he was shot and killed by unknown gunmen in Las Vegas.

PERCY BYSSHE SHELLEY (1792–1822) attended Oxford but was expelled after he published his pamphlet *The Necessity of Atheism* (1811). He eloped to Scotland with Harriet Westbrook, a move that, combined with his refusal to retract his pamphlet, caused a permanent break with his family.

While in Scotland, Shelley corresponded with the radical thinker William Godwin, published a series of political works, and composed his poem *Queen Mab* (1813). After moving to London, Shelley fell in love with Godwin's sixteen-year-old daughter, Mary (later Mary Shelley, author of *Frankenstein*). Despite the birth of Shelley's daughter by Harriet, Shelley and Mary Godwin ran off to the Continent in 1814, spending the summer of 1816 at Lake Geneva with the poet and celebrity George Gordon, Lord Byron. Harriet drowned herself that autumn, and Shelley immediately married Mary. In 1818, they left England permanently and settled in Italy. Shelley completed his long poem *Prometheus Unbound* in 1819; that year and the next constituted his most productive period. "Ode to the West Wind" and many of his important lyrics were completed during this time. He drowned at age twenty-nine when his boat sank in the Gulf of Spezia. His poetry was a major influence on later nineteenth-century poets such as Tennyson and Robert Browning.

(AKINWANDE OLUWOLE) WOLE SOYINKA (1934–) was born in western Nigeria. In *Aké: The Years of Childhood* (1981), he wrote about growing up under colonial rule. His *Collected Plays* (Vol. 1, 1973; Vol. 2, 1974), along with major works such as *Death and the King's Horseman* (1975) and *The Interpreters* (1965), led to his winning the Nobel Prize in Literature in 1986. In addition to his analytical work *Myth, Literature, and the African World* (1976), he has published two volumes based on lectures at the W. E. B. Du Bois Institute at Harvard. A deeply committed political writer and activist, Soyinka endured repeated imprisonment for his outspoken beliefs. Despite this persecution, in 1999 he returned to his homeland after a long absence. His most recent play, *King Baabu*, was published in 2001.

WILLIAM STAFFORD (1914–1993) was born in Hutchinson, Kansas. During World War II, Stafford, a conscientious objector, worked in civilian public service camps — an experience he recorded in the prose memoir *Down My Heart* (1947). In 1948, Stafford moved to Oregon to teach at Lewis and Clark College. Though he traveled and read his work widely, he continued to teach at Lewis and Clark until 1980. His first major collection of poems, *Traveling Through the Dark* (1962), was published when Stafford was forty-eight and won the National Book Award in 1963. He went on to publish more than sixty-five volumes of poetry and prose. He served as Poet Laureate of the United States from 1970 to 1971.

WALLACE STEVENS (1879–1955) was born in Reading, Pennsylvania. He attended Harvard, where he began writing poetry, and New York Law School. In 1916, he took a job with the Hartford Accident and Indemnity Company, which afforded him and his family a prosperous life, and he continued writing poetry. For his life work, he was awarded the Bollingen Prize in 1949, and in 1955 he won both the Pulitzer Prize and the National Book Award for his *Collected Poems*. In a letter to his wife, Stevens wrote, "The priest in me worshipped one God at one shrine; the poet another God at another shrine. The priest worshipped Mercy and Love; the poet Beauty and Might."

ALFRED, LORD TENNYSON (1809–1892) was born in Somersby, Lincolnshire, England. Tennyson's early collection *Poems, Chiefly Lyrical* (1830) was not well received. Neither was *Poems* (1832), which included major works such as "The Lady of Shallott" and "The Lotos-Eaters." In the ten years following the publication of *Poems,* Tennyson revised earlier works and continued to write poetry. Finally, in 1842, two volumes of *Poems* were published and well received. Among the new works in these volumes were "Ulysses," "Locksley Hall," and "Morte d'Arthur." Tennyson had begun writing a poem in memory of his best friend, Arthur Hallam in 1834; in 1850, *In Memoriam* was published. Also in 1850,

Tennyson succeeded William Wordsworth as Poet Laureate of England. In 1855, he published *Maud and Other Poems,* which included the title work and "The Charge of the Light Brigade." From 1859 to 1885, he issued his series of Arthurian poems, *Idylls of the King.* He continued to write poems and plays until his death in 1892.

DYLAN THOMAS (1914–1953) was born in Swansea, in Wales. Thomas obtained much of his poetic education through access to his father's library, and his formal education ended when he was seventeen. His poetry was popular but controversial, with many critics objecting to what they saw as the obscurity and self-consciousness of the poems. No one could deny the startling imagery and rich sound of the best of them, however. Early in his career Thomas began to drink heavily and behave outrageously, and by the time he achieved his greatest fame, he was more or less finished as a poet. He died of alcohol poisoning in New York City just two days after his thirty-ninth birthday.

MONA VAN DUYN (1921–2004) was born in Waterloo, Iowa. She is the author of nine books of poems: *Firefall* (1994); *If It Be Not I: Collected Poems, 1959–1982* (1994); *Near Changes* (1990), for which she won a Pulitzer Prize; *Letters from a Father and Other Poems* (1982); *Merciful Disguises* (1973, reissued 1982); *Bedtime Stories* (1972); *To See, to Take* (1970), recipient of the National Book Award; *A Time of Bees* (1964); and *Valentines to the Wide World* (1959). With her husband, Jarvis Thurston, she founded *Perspective: A Quarterly of Literature* in 1947 and coedited it until 1970. She received numerous prizes and awards, including the Bollingen Prize, the Hart Crane Memorial Award, and the Shelley Memorial Prize, as well as fellowships from the Academy of American Poets, the American Academy of Arts and Sciences, the Guggenheim Foundation, and the National Endowment for the Arts. She served as Poet Laureate of the United States (1992–1993) and was a chancellor of the Academy of American Poets.

WALT WHITMAN (1819–1892) was born in Long Island, New York. After only six years of formal education, he left school and eventually became a newspaper reporter and editor. He worked as a part-time carpenter while writing his major work *Leaves of Grass,* which he continued to revise and expand until his death. In 1862, when his brother was wounded in the Civil War, Whitman went to Washington to work as a hospital nurse volunteer, an experience that led to *Drum-Taps* (1865); a later edition of this volume included the poem "When Lilacs Last in the Door-Yard Bloom'd." Whitman has been a major influence not only for most significant American poets after him, but also for writers of fiction. Justifying the nontraditional forms of poetry he created, Whitman asserted, "The rhyme and conformity of perfect poems show the free growth of metrical laws and bud from them as unerringly and loosely as lilacs or roses on a bush. . . ."

RICHARD WILBUR (1921–) was born in New York City and grew up on a farm in North Caldwell, New Jersey. He served in the infantry during World War II, and began writing poetry in the army. He won the Pulitzer Prize, the Edna St. Vincent Millay Memorial Award, and the National Book Award in 1957 for *Things of This World* (1956). Other works include *The Beautiful Changes and Other Poems* (1947); *Ceremony and Other Poems* (1950); *Poems, 1943–1956* (1957); *The Poems of Richard Wilbur* (1963); and *New and Collected Poems* (1989). Named Poet Laureate of the United States in 1987, Wilbur also has written translations, nonfiction, and operetta lyrics. Beyond his scholarly life, Wilbur seeks "non-verbal" activities because, as he has explained, it is "good for a writer to move into words out of silence as much as he can." His most recent collection, *Collected Poems: 1943–2004,* was published in 2004.

WILLIAM CARLOS WILLIAMS (1883–1963) was born in Rutherford, New Jersey. He read the classics at home and attended private schools in Geneva and Paris. Williams was a pediatrician for over forty years. He published widely in several genres—poetry, fiction, autobiography, essays, and drama. His many honors include the National Book Award (1950), the Bollingen Prize in Poetry (1952), and a posthumous Pulitzer Prize (1963) for *Pictures from Brueghel and Other Poems.* In his poetry, Williams tried to escape from what he saw as the worn-out constraints of fixed European forms. He tried to invent a fresh form, one that was suited to the reality of everyday objects and that depended on the natural breaks of speech. Reflecting on the origins of modern poetry and of his own work, Williams speculated that "it was the French painters rather than the writers who influenced us, and their influence was very great; they created an atmosphere of release, color-release, from stereotypical forms, trite subjects."

WILLIAM WORDSWORTH (1770–1850) was born in Cockermouth, Cumberland, England. In 1790, he embarked on a walking tour through France and Switzerland, commemorated in his early collection of poems, *Descriptive Sketches* (published in 1793). On returning to England, he took up residence with his sister, Dorothy, who was to have a profound effect on his early poetry. Settling at Somerset, he developed a friendship with Samuel Taylor Coleridge, and the two began to compose the poems that would appear in *Lyrical Ballads* (1798); the volume's preface, written by Wordsworth, is essentially the manifesto of early English Romantic poetry. In 1802, after a year in Germany with Coleridge and Dorothy, Wordsworth married Mary Hutchinson and began work on his long autobiographical poem *The Prelude,* in which he traces the growth of a poet's mind. He was appointed Poet Laureate of England in 1843, receiving visits from admirers and political sympathizers at his home, Rydal Mount, in the English Lake District.

WILLIAM BUTLER YEATS (1865–1939) came from an upper-middle-class Anglo-Irish family in Dublin. In 1923, he won the Nobel Prize in Literature in recognition not only of his achievements as a poet but also of his tireless efforts to promote Irish literature. As leader of the Celtic Renaissance in Ireland, Yeats celebrated nationalism in his early poetry, such as *The Wanderings of Oislin* (1889), based on Irish legend. His later poems, often mystical and deeply symbolic, reflect more expansive universal themes. Besides his highly regarded volumes of poetry, such as *The Wild Swans at Coole* (1917), *The Tower* (1928), and *The Winding Stair and Other Poems* (1929), his legacy includes plays and essays.

ADAM ZAGAJEWSKI (1945–) was born in Lwów, Poland, and spent his childhood in Silesia and then in Krakow. Zagajewski first became well known as one of the leading poets of the "Generation of 1968," or the Polish New Wave, and is one of Poland's best-known contemporary poets. His books of poetry in English include *Mysticism for Beginners* (1997); *Tremor* (1985); and *Canvas* (1991). He is also the author of a memoir, *Another Beauty* (2000); and of the prose collections, *Two Cities* (1991) and *Solitude and Solidarity* (1986). His poems and essays have been translated into many languages. He is currently coeditor of *Zeszyty literackie* (Literary Review), which is published in Paris. More recently, he published another poetry collection, *Without End,* as well as a collection of essays, *A Defense of Ardor* in 2004.

4 | DRAMA

UNDERSTANDING DRAMA

Dramatic Literature

The distinctive appearance of a script, with its stage directions, character parts, and divisions into acts and scenes, identifies **drama** as a unique form of literature. A play is written to be performed in front of an audience by actors who take on the roles of the characters and who present the story through dialogue and action. (An exception is a **closet drama,** which is meant to be read, not performed.) In fact, the term *theater* comes from the Greek word *theasthai*, which means "to view" or "to see." Thus, drama is different from novels and short stories, which are meant to be read.

Origins of Modern Drama

The Ancient Greek Theater

The dramatic presentations of ancient Greece developed out of religious rites performed to honor gods or to mark the coming of spring. Playwrights such as Aeschylus (525–456 B.C.), Sophocles (496–406 B.C.), and Euripides (480?–406 B.C.) wrote plays to be performed and judged at competitions held during the yearly Dionysian festivals. Works were chosen by a selection board and evaluated by a panel of judges. To compete in the contest, writers had to submit three tragedies, which could be either based on a common theme or unrelated, and one comedy. Unfortunately, relatively few of these ancient Greek plays survive today.

The open-air semicircular ancient Greek theater, built into the side of a hill, looked much like a primitive version of a modern sports stadium. Some Greek theaters, such as the Athenian theater, could seat almost seventeen thousand spectators. Sitting in tiered seats, the audience would look down on the **orchestra,** or "dancing place," occupied by the **chorus** — originally a group of men (led by an individual called the **choragos**) who danced and chanted and later a group of onlookers who commented on the drama.

Raised a few steps above the orchestra was a platform on which the actors performed. Behind this platform was a **skene,** or building, that originally served as a resting place or dressing room. (The modern word *scene* is derived from the Greek *skene*.) Behind the skene was a line of pillars called a **colonnade,** which was

Grand Theater at Ephesus (3rd century B.C.), a Greek settlement in what is now Turkey.
Source: ©David G. Houser/Corbis

covered by a roof. Actors used the skene for entrances and exits; beginning with the plays of Sophocles, painted backdrops were hung there. These backdrops, however, were most likely more decorative than realistic. Historians believe that realistic props and scenery were probably absent from the ancient Greek theater. Instead, the setting was suggested by the play's dialogue, and the audience had to imagine the physical details of a scene.

Two mechanical devices were used. One, a rolling cart or platform, was sometimes employed to introduce action that had occurred offstage. For example, actors frozen in position could be rolled onto the roof of the skene to illustrate an event such as the killing of Oedipus's father, which occurred before the play began. Another mechanical device, a small crane, was used to show gods ascending to or descending from heaven. Such devices enabled playwrights to dramatize the myths that were celebrated at the Dionysian festivals.

The ancient Greek theater was designed to enhance acoustics. The flat stone wall of the skene reflected the sound from the orchestra and the stage, and the curved shape of the amphitheater captured the sound, enabling the audience to hear the lines spoken by the actors. Each actor wore a stylized mask, or **persona,** to convey to the audience the personality traits of the particular character being portrayed— a king, a soldier, a wise old man, a young girl (female roles were played by men). The mouths of these masks were probably constructed so they amplified the voice and projected it into the audience. In addition, the actors wore *kothorni,* high shoes that elevated them above the stage, perhaps also helping to project their voices. Due to the excellent acoustics, audiences who see plays performed in these ancient theaters today can hear clearly without microphones or speaker systems.

Because actors wore masks and because males played the parts of women and gods as well as men, acting methods in the ancient Greek theater were probably not realistic. In their masks, high shoes, and full-length tunics (called *chiton*), actors could not hope to appear natural or to mimic the attitudes of everyday life. Instead, they probably recited their lines while standing in stylized poses, with emotions conveyed more by gesture and tone than by action. Typically, three actors had all the speaking roles. One actor — the **protagonist** — would play the central role and have the largest speaking part. Two other actors would divide the remaining lines between them. Although other characters would come on and off the stage, they would usually not have speaking roles.

Ancient Greek tragedies were typically divided into five parts. The first part was the **prologos,** or prologue, in which an actor gave the background or explanations that the audience needed to follow the rest of the drama. Then came the **párodos,** in which the chorus entered and commented on the events presented in the prologue. Following this were several **episodia,** or episodes, in which characters spoke to one another on the stage and developed the central conflict of the play. Alternating with episodes were **stasimon** (choral odes), in which the chorus commented on the exchanges that had taken place during the preceding episode. Frequently, the choral odes were divided into *strophes*, or stanzas, which were recited or sung as the chorus moved across the orchestra in one direction, and *antistrophes*, which were recited as it moved in the opposite direction. (Interestingly, the chorus stood between the audience and the actors, often functioning as an additional audience, expressing the political, social, and moral views of the community.) The fifth part was the **exodos,** the last scene of the play, during which the conflict was resolved and the actors left the stage.

Using music, dance, and verse — as well as a variety of architectural and technical innovations — the ancient Greek theater was able to convey the traditional themes of tragedy. Thus, the Greek theater powerfully expressed ideas that were central to the religious festivals in which they first appeared: the reverence for the cycles of life and death, the unavoidable dictates of the gods, and the inscrutable workings of fate.

The Elizabethan Theater

The Elizabethan theater, influenced by the classical traditions of Roman and Greek dramatists, traces its roots back to local religious pageants performed at medieval festivals during the twelfth and thirteenth centuries. Town guilds — organizations of craftsmen who worked in the same profession — reenacted Old and New Testament stories: the fall of man, Noah and the flood, David and Goliath, and the crucifixion of Christ, for example. Church fathers encouraged these plays because they brought the Bible to a largely illiterate audience. Sometimes these spectacles, called **mystery plays,** were presented in the market square or on the church steps, and at other times actors appeared on movable stages or wagons called **pageants,** which could be wheeled to a given location. (Some of these wagons were quite elaborate, with trapdoors and pulleys and an upper tier that simulated heaven.) As mystery plays became more popular, they were performed in series over several days, presenting an entire cycle of a holiday — the crucifixion and resurrection of Christ during Easter, for example.

Related to mystery plays are **morality plays,** which developed in the fourteenth and fifteenth centuries. Unlike mystery plays, which depict scenes from the Bible, morality plays allegorize the Christian way of life. Typically, characters representing various virtues and vices struggle or debate over the soul of man. *Everyman* (1500), the best known of these plays, dramatizes the good and bad qualities of Everyman and shows his struggle to determine what is of value to him as he journeys toward death.

By the middle of the sixteenth century, mystery and morality plays had lost ground to a new secular drama. One reason for this decline was that mystery and morality plays were associated with Catholicism and consequently discouraged by the Protestant clergy. In addition, newly discovered plays of ancient Greece and Rome introduced a dramatic tradition that supplanted the traditions of religious drama. English plays that followed the classic model were sensational and bombastic, often dealing with murder, revenge, and blood retribution. Appealing to privileged classes and commoners alike, these plays were extremely popular. (One source estimates that in London, between 20,000 and 25,000 people attended performances each week.)

In spite of the popularity of the theater, actors and playwrights encountered a number of difficulties. First, they faced opposition from city officials who were averse to theatrical presentations because they thought that the crowds attending these performances spread disease. Puritans opposed the theater because they thought plays were immoral and sinful. Finally, some people attached to the royal court opposed the theater because they thought that the playwrights undermined the authority of Queen Elizabeth by spreading seditious ideas. As a result, during Elizabeth's reign, performances were placed under the strict control of the **Master of Revels,** a public official who had the power to censor plays (and did so with great regularity) and to grant licenses for performances.

Acting companies that wanted to put on a performance had to obtain a license — possible only with the patronage of a powerful nobleman — and to perform the play in an area designated by the queen. Despite these difficulties, a number of actors and playwrights gained a measure of financial independence by joining together and forming acting companies. These companies of professional actors performed works such as Christopher Marlowe's *Tamburlaine* and Thomas Kyd's *The Spanish Tragedy* in tavern courtyards and then eventually in permanent theaters. According to scholars, the structures of the Elizabethan theater evolved from these tavern courtyards.

William Shakespeare's plays were performed at the Globe Theatre (a corner of which was unearthed in December 1988). Although scholars do not know the exact design of the original Globe, drawings from the period provide a good idea of its physical features. The major difference between the Globe and today's theaters is the multiple stages on which action could be performed. The Globe consisted of a large main **stage** that extended out into the open-air **yard** where the **groundlings,** or common people, stood. Spectators who paid more sat on small stools in two or three levels of galleries that extended in front of and around the stage. (The theater could probably seat almost two thousand people at a performance.) Most of the play's action occurred on the stage, which had no curtain and could be seen from three sides. Beneath the stage was a space called the **hell,** which could be reached when the floorboards were removed. This space enabled actors to "disappear" or descend into a hole or grave when the play called for such action. Above the stage was a roof called the **heavens,** which protected the actors from the weather and contained ropes and pulleys used to lower props or to create special effects.

At the rear of the stage was a narrow **alcove** covered by a curtain that could be open or closed. This curtain, often painted, functioned as a decorative rather than a realistic backdrop. The main function of this alcove was to enable actors to hide or disappear when the script called for them to do so. Some Elizabethan theaters contained a **rear stage** instead of an alcove. Because the rear stage was concealed by a curtain, props could be arranged on it ahead of time. When the action on the rear stage was finished, the curtain would be closed and the action would continue on the front stage.

On either side of the rear stage was a door through which the actors could enter and exit the front stage. Above the rear stage was a curtained stage called the **chamber,** which functioned as a balcony or as any other setting located above the action taking place on the stage below. On either side of the chamber were casement windows, which actors could use when a play called for a conversation with someone leaning out a window or standing on a balcony. Above the chamber was the **music gallery,** a balcony that housed the musicians who provided musical interludes throughout the play (and that doubled as a stage if the play required it). The **huts,** windows located above the music gallery, could be used by characters playing lookouts or sentries. Because of the many acting sites, more than one action could take place simultaneously. For example, lookouts could stand in the towers of Hamlet's castle while Hamlet and Horatio walked the walls below.

During Shakespeare's time, the theater had many limitations that challenged the audience's imagination. First, young boys — usually between the ages of ten and twelve — played all the women's parts. In addition, there was no artificial lighting, so plays had to be performed in daylight. Rain, wind, or clouds could disrupt a performance or ruin an image — such as "the morn in russet mantle clad" — that the audience was asked to imagine. Finally, because few sets and props were used, the audience often had to visualize the high walls of a castle or the trees of a forest. The plays were performed without intermission, except for musical interludes that occurred at various points. Thus, the experience of seeing one of Shakespeare's plays staged in the Elizabethan theater was different from seeing it staged today in a modern theater.

Today, a reconstruction of the Globe Theatre stands on the south bank of the Thames River in London. In the 1940s, the American actor Sam Wanamaker visited London and was shocked to find nothing that commemorated the site of the original Globe. He eventually decided to try to raise enough money to reconstruct

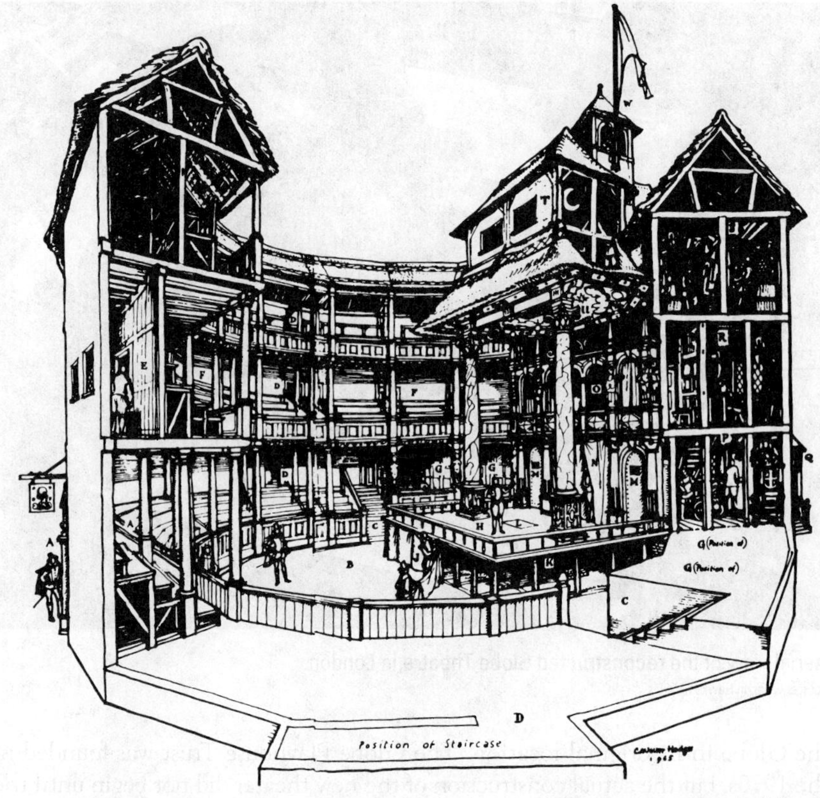

The Globe Playhouse,

1599-1613

A CONJECTURAL

RECONSTRUCTION

KEY

AA Main entrance
B The Yard
CC Entrances to lowest gallery
D Entrances to staircase and upper galleries
E Corridor serving the different sections of the middle gallery
F Middle gallery ('Twopenny Rooms')
G 'Gentlemen's Rooms' or 'Lords' Rooms'
H The stage
J The hanging being put up round the stage
K The 'Hell' under the stage
L The stage trap, leading down to the Hell
MM Stage doors
N Curtained 'place behind the stage'
O Gallery above the stage, used as required sometimes by musicians, sometimes by spectators, and often as part of the play
P Back-stage area (the tiring-house)
Q Tiring-house door
R Dressing-rooms
S Wardrobe and storage
T The hut housing the machine for lowering enthroned gods, etc., to the stage
U The 'Heavens'
W Hoisting the playhouse flag

The Globe Playhouse, 1599–1613; a conjectural reconstruction. From C. Walter Hodges *The Globe Restored: A Study of the Elizabethan Theatre.* New York: Norton, 1973.

Source: C. Walter Hodges, *The Globe Restored: A Study of the Elizabethan Theatre.* New York: Norton, 1973.

Aerial view of the reconstructed Globe Theatre in London.
Source: ©Jason Hawkes/Corbis

the Globe in its original location. The Globe Playhouse Trust was founded in the 1970s, but the actual construction of the new theater did not begin until the 1980s. After a number of setbacks — for example, the Trust ran out of funds after the construction of a large underground "diaphragm" wall needed to keep out the river water — the project was finally completed. The first performance at the reconstructed Globe was given on June 14, 1996, which would have been the late Sam Wanamaker's 77th birthday.

The Modern Theater

Unlike the theaters of ancient Greece and Elizabethan England, seventeenth- and eighteenth-century theaters — such as the Palais Royal, where the great French playwright Molière presented many of his plays — were covered by a roof, beautifully decorated, and illuminated by candles so that plays could be performed at night. The theater remained brightly lit even during performances, partly because there was no easy way to extinguish hundreds of candles and partly because people went to the theater as much to see each other as to see the play. A curtain opened and closed between acts. The audience of about five hundred spectators sat in a long room and viewed the play on a **picture-frame stage.** This type of stage, which resembles the stages on which plays are performed today, contained the action within a **proscenium arch** that surrounded the opening through which the audience viewed the performance. Thus, the action seemed to take place in an adjoining room with one of its walls cut away. Painted scenery (some of it quite elaborate), intricately detailed costumes, and stage makeup were commonplace, and for the first time women performed female roles. In addition, a complicated series of ropes, pulleys, and cranks enabled stagehands to change scenery quickly, and sound-effects machines could give audiences the impression that they were hearing a galloping horse or a raging thunderstorm. Because the theaters were small, audiences were relatively close to the stage, so actors could use subtle movements and facial expressions to enhance their performances.

Many of the first innovations in the theater were quite basic. For example, the first stage lighting was produced by candles lining the front of the stage. This method of lighting was not only ineffective — actors were lit from below and had to step forward to be fully illuminated — but also dangerous. Costumes and even entire theaters could (and did) catch fire. Later, covered lanterns with reflectors provided better and safer lighting. In the nineteenth century, a device that used an oxyhydrogen flame directed on a cylinder of lime created extremely bright illumination that could, with the aid of a lens, be concentrated into a spotlight. (It is from this method of stage lighting that we get the expression *to be in the limelight*.)

Eventually, in the twentieth century, electric lights provided a dependable and safe way of lighting the stage. Electric spotlights, footlights, and ceiling light bars made the actors clearly visible and enabled playwrights to create special effects. In Arthur Miller's *Death of a Salesman* (p. 1531), for example, lighting focuses attention on action in certain areas of the stage while other areas are left in complete darkness.

Along with electric lighting came other innovations, such as electronic amplification. Microphones made it possible for actors to speak conversationally and to avoid using unnaturally loud "stage diction" to project their voices to the rear of the theater. Microphones placed at various points around the stage enabled actors and actresses to interact naturally and to deliver their lines audibly even without facing the audience. More recently, small wireless microphones have eliminated the unwieldy wires and the "dead spaces" left between upright or hanging microphones, allowing characters to move freely around the stage.

The true revolutions in staging came with the advent of **realism** in the middle of the nineteenth century. Until this time, scenery had been painted on canvas backdrops that trembled visibly, especially when they were intersected by doors through which actors and actresses entered. With realism came settings that were accurate down to the smallest detail. (Improved lighting, which revealed the inadequacies of painted backdrops, made such realistic stage settings necessary.) Backdrops were replaced by the **box set,** three flat panels arranged to form connected walls, with the fourth wall removed to give the audience the illusion of looking into a room. The room itself was decorated with real furniture, plants, and pictures on the walls; the door of one room might connect to another completely furnished room, or a window might open to a garden filled with realistic foliage. In addition, new methods of changing scenery were employed. Elevator stages, hydraulic lifts, and moving platforms enabled directors to make complicated changes in scenery out of the audience's view.

During the late nineteenth and early twentieth centuries, however, some playwrights reacted against what they saw as the excesses of realism. They introduced **surrealistic** stage settings, in which color and scenery mirrored the uncontrolled images of dreams, and **expressionistic** stage settings, in which costumes and scenery were exaggerated and distorted to reflect the workings of a troubled, even unbalanced mind. In addition, playwrights used lighting to create areas of light, shadow, and color that reinforced the themes of the play or reflected the emotions of the protagonist. Eugene O'Neill's 1933 play *The Emperor Jones*, for example, used a series of expressionistic scenes to show the mental state of the terrified protagonist.

Sets in contemporary plays run the gamut from realistic to fantastic, from a detailed re-creation of a room in a production of Tennessee Williams's *The Glass Menagerie* (p. 1961) to a dreamlike set for *The Emperor Jones* and Edward Albee's *The Sandbox* (1959). Motorized devices, such as revolving turntables, and *wagons*— scenery mounted on wheels — make possible rapid changes of scenery. The Broadway musical *Les Misérables*, for example, required scores of elaborate sets — Parisian slums, barricades, walled gardens — to be shifted as the audience watched. A gigantic barricade constructed on stage at one point in the play was

Thrust-Stage Theater. Rendering of the thrust stage at the Guthrie Theatre in Minneapolis. With seats on three sides of the stage area, the thrust stage and its background can assume many forms. Entrances can be made from the aisles, from the sides, through the stage floor, and from the back.

Source: ©Penton Media, Inc.

Arena Theater. The arena theater at the Riverside Community Players in Riverside, California. The audience surrounds the stage area, which may or may not be raised. Use of scenery is limited—perhaps to a single piece of scenery standing alone in the middle of the stage.
Source: Courtesy The Arena Theatre, Riverside Community Players, Riverside, CA

later rotated to show the carnage that had taken place on both sides of a battle. Light, sound, and smoke were used to heighten the impact of the scene.

Today, as dramatists attempt to break down the barriers that separate audiences from the action they are viewing, plays are not limited to the picture-frame stage; in fact, they are performed on many different kinds of stages. Some plays take place on a **thrust stage,** (pictured on the previous page), which has an area that projects out into the audience. Other plays are performed on an **arena stage,** with the audience surrounding the actors. (This kind of performance is often called **theater in the round.**) In addition, experiments have been done with **environmental staging,** in which the stage surrounds the audience or several stages are situated at various locations throughout the audience. Plays may also be performed outdoors, in settings ranging from parks to city streets.

Some playwrights even try to blur the line that divides the audience from the stage by having actors move through or sit in the audience—or even by eliminating the stage entirely. For example, *Tony 'n Tina's Wedding*, a **participatory drama** created in 1988 by the theater group Artificial Intelligence, takes place not in a theater but at a church where a wedding is performed and then at a catering hall where the wedding reception is held. Throughout the play, the members of the audience function as guests, joining in the wedding celebration and mingling with the actors, who improvise freely. Recent examples of such interactive drama include *Grandma Sylvia's Funeral* and *Off the Wall,* in which audiences "attend" an art auction. Today, no single architectural form defines the theater. The modern stage is a flexible space suited to the many varieties of contemporary theatrical production.

 Tragedy and Comedy

Tragedy

In his *Poetics*, Aristotle (384–322 B.C.) sums up ancient Greek thinking about drama when he defines a **tragedy**— a drama treating a serious subject and involving persons of significance. According to Aristotle, when the members of an audience see a tragedy, they should feel both pity (and thus closeness to the protagonist) and fear (and thus revulsion) because they recognize in themselves the potential for similar reactions. The purging of these emotions that audience members experience as they see the dramatic action unfold is called **catharsis.** For catharsis to occur, the protagonist of a tragedy must be worthy of the audience's attention and sympathy.

Because of his or her exalted position, the fall of a tragic protagonist is greater than that of an average person; therefore, it arouses more pity and fear in the audience. Often the entire society suffers as a result of the actions of the protagonist. Before the action of Sophocles' *Oedipus the King* (p. 1745), for example, Oedipus has freed Thebes from the deadly grasp of the Sphinx by answering her riddle and, as a result, has been welcomed as king. But because of his sins, Oedipus is an affront to the gods and brings famine and pestilence to the city. When his fall finally comes, it is sudden and absolute.

According to Aristotle, the protagonist of a tragedy is neither all good nor all evil, but a mixture of the two. The protagonist is like the rest of us — only more exalted and possessing some weakness or flaw **(hamartia)**. This tragic flaw— perhaps narrowness of vision or overwhelming pride **(hubris)**— is typically the element that creates the conditions for tragedy. Shakespeare's Romeo and Juliet, for example, are so much in love they think they can ignore the blood feud that rages between their two families. However, their naive efforts to sustain their love despite the feud lead them to their tragic deaths. Similarly, Richard III's blind ambition to gain the throne causes him to murder all those who stand in his way. His unscrupulousness sets into motion the forces that eventually cause his death.

Irony— a discrepancy between what characters say and what the audience believes to be true — is central to tragedy. **Dramatic irony** (also called **tragic irony**) emerges from a situation in which the audience knows more about the dramatic situation than a character does. As a result, the character's words and actions may be consistent with what he or she expects but at odds with what the audience knows will happen. Thus, a character may say or do something that causes the audience to infer a meaning beyond what the character intends or realizes. The dramatic irony is clear, for example, when Oedipus announces that whoever has disobeyed the dictates of the gods will be exiled. The audience knows, although Oedipus does not, that he has just condemned himself. **Cosmic irony,** also called **irony of fate,** occurs when God, fate, or some larger, uncontrollable force seems to be intentionally deceiving characters into believing they can escape their fate. Too late, they realize that trying to avoid their destiny is futile. Years before Oedipus was born, for example, the oracle of Apollo foretold that Oedipus would kill his parents. Naturally, his parents attempted to thwart the prophecy, but ironically, their actions ensured that the prophecy would be fulfilled.

At some point in a tragedy—after the climax—the protagonist begins to recognize and understand the reasons for his or her downfall. This moment of recognition (called the **catastrophe**) elevates tragic protagonists to grandeur and gives their suffering meaning. Without this recognition, there would be no tragedy, just **pathos**—suffering that exists simply to satisfy the sentimental or morbid sensibilities of the audience. In spite of the death of the protagonist, then, tragedy enables the audience to see the nobility of the character and thus to experience a sense of elation. In Shakespeare's *King Lear,* for example, a king at the height of his powers decides to divide his kingdom among his three daughters. Later, he realizes that without his power, he is just a bothersome old man to his ambitious children. Only after going mad does he understand the vanity of his former existence; he dies a humbled but enlightened man.

According to Aristotle, a tragedy achieves the illusion of reality when it has **unity of action**—that is, when the play contains only those actions that lead to its tragic outcome. Later critics interpreted this constraint to mean that including subplots or mixing tragic and comic elements would destroy this unity. To the concept of unity of action, these later critics added two other requirements: **unity of place**—the requirement that the play have a single setting—and **unity of time**—the requirement that the events depicted by the play take no longer than the actual duration of the play (or, at most, a single day).

The **three unities** have had a long and rather uneven history. For example, although Shakespeare observed the unities in some of his plays—such as *The Tempest* and *The Comedy of Errors*—he had no compunctions about writing plays with subplots and frequent changes of location. He also wrote **tragicomedies,** such as *The Merchant of Venice*, which have a serious theme appropriate for tragedy but end happily, usually because of a sudden turn of events. During the eighteenth century, with its emphasis on classic form, the unities were adhered to quite strictly. In the late eighteenth and early nineteenth centuries, with the onset of romanticism and its emphasis on the natural, interest in the unities of place and time waned. Even though some modern plays (particularly one-act plays) do observe the unities—*Trifles* (p. 1319), for instance, has a single setting and takes place during a period of time that corresponds to the length of the play—few modern dramatists strictly adhere to them.

Ideas about appropriate subjects for tragedy have also changed. For Aristotle, the protagonist of a tragedy had to be exceptional—a king, for example. The protagonists of Greek tragedies were usually historical or mythical figures. Shakespeare often used kings and princes as protagonists—Richard II and Hamlet, for example—but he also used people of lesser rank, as in *Romeo and Juliet* and *A Midsummer Night's Dream* (p. 1787). In our times, interest in the lives of monarchs has been overshadowed by involvement in the lives of ordinary people. Modern tragedies—*Death of a Salesman*, for example—are more likely to focus on a traveling salesman than on a king.

With the rise of the middle class in the nineteenth century, ideas about the nature of tragedy changed. Responding to the age's desire for sentimentality, playwrights produced **melodramas,** sensational plays that appealed mainly to the emotions. Melodramas include many of the elements of tragedy but end happily and often rely on conventional plots and stock characters. Because the protagonists in melodramas — often totally virtuous heroines suffering at the hands of impossibly wicked villains — helplessly endure their tribulations without ever gaining insight or enlightenment, they never achieve tragic status. As a result, they remain cardboard cutouts who exist only to exploit the emotions of the audience. Melodrama survives today in many films and in television soap operas.

Realism, which arose in the late nineteenth century as a response to the artificiality of melodrama, presented serious (and sometimes tragic) themes and believable characters in the context of everyday contemporary life. Writers of realistic drama used their plays to educate their audiences about the problems of the society in which they lived. For this reason, realistic drama focuses on the commonplace and eliminates the unlikely coincidences and excessive sentimentality of melodrama. Dramatists such as Henrik Ibsen scrutinize the lives of ordinary people, not larger-than-life characters. After great suffering, these characters rise above the limitations of their mediocre lives and exhibit courage or emotional strength. The insight they gain often focuses attention on a social problem — the restrictive social conventions that define the behavior of women in nineteenth-century marriages, for example. Realistic drama also features settings and props similar to those used in people's daily lives and includes dialogue that reflects the way people actually speak.

Developing alongside realism was a literary movement called **naturalism.** Like realism, naturalism rejected the unrealistic plots and sentimentality of melodrama, but unlike realism, naturalism sought to explore the depths of the human condition. Influenced by Charles Darwin's ideas about evolution and natural selection and Karl Marx's ideas about economic forces that shape people's lives, naturalism is a pessimistic philosophy that presents a world that is at worst hostile and at best indifferent to human concerns. It portrays human beings as higher-order animals who are driven by basic instincts — especially hunger, fear, greed, and sexuality — and who are subject to economic, social, and biological forces beyond their understanding or control. For these reasons, it is well suited to tragic themes.

The nineteenth-century French writer Émile Zola did much to develop the theory of naturalism, as did the American writers Stephen Crane, Frank Norris, and Theodore Dreiser. Naturalism also finds its way into the work of contemporary dramatists, such as Arthur Miller. Unlike other tragic characters, the protagonists of naturalist works are crushed not by the gods or by fate but by poverty, animal drives, or social class. Willy Loman in *Death of a Salesman*, (p. 1531), for example, is subject to the economic forces of a society that does not value its workers and discards those it no longer finds useful.

Comedy

A **comedy** treats themes and characters with humor and typically has a happy ending. Whereas tragedy focuses on the hidden dimensions of the tragic hero's character, comedy focuses on the public persona, the protagonist as a social being. Tragic figures are typically seen in isolation, questioning the meaning of their lives and trying to comprehend their suffering. Hamlet — draped in sable, longing for death, and self-consciously contemplating his duty—epitomizes the isolation of the tragic hero.

Unlike tragic heroes, comic figures are seen in the public arena, where people intentionally assume the masks of pretension and self-importance. The purpose of comedy is to strip away these masks and expose human beings for what they are. Whereas tragedy reveals the nobility of the human condition, comedy reveals its inherent folly, portraying human beings as selfish, hypocritical, vain, weak, irrational, and capable of self-delusion. Thus, the basic function of comedy is critical — to tell people that things are not what they seem and that appearances are not necessarily reality. In the comic world, nothing is solid or predictable, and accidents and coincidences are more important to the plot than reason. Many of Shakespeare's comedies, for example, depend on exchanged or confused identities. The wordplay and verbal nonsense of comedy add to this general confusion.

Comedies typically rely on certain familiar plot devices. Many comedies begin with a startling or unusual situation that attracts the audience's attention. In Shakespeare's *A Midsummer Night's Dream* (p. 1787), for example, Theseus, the duke of Athens, rules that Hermia will either marry the man her father has chosen for her or be put to death. Such an event could lead to tragedy if comedy did not intervene to save the day.

Comedy often depends on obstacles and hindrances to further its plot: the more difficult the problems the lovers face, the more satisfying their eventual triumph will be. For this reason, the plot of a comedy is usually more complex than the plot of a tragedy. Compare the rather straightforward plot of *Hamlet* (p. 1605)— a prince ordered to avenge his murdered father's death is driven mad with indecision and, after finally acting decisively, is killed himself — with the mix-ups, mistaken identities, and general confusion of *A Midsummer Night's Dream*.

Finally, comedies have happy endings. Whereas tragedy ends with death, comedy ends with an affirmation of life. Eventually, the confusion and misunderstandings reach a point where some resolution must be achieved: the difficulties of the lovers are overcome, the villains are banished, and the lovers marry — or at least express their intention to do so. In this way, the lovers establish their connection with the rest of society, and its values are affirmed.

The first comedies, written in Greece in the fifth century B.C., heavily satirized the religious and social issues of the day and were characterized by bawdy humor. In the fourth and third centuries B.C., this **Old Comedy** gave way to **New Comedy,** a comedy of romance with stock characters — lovers and untrustworthy servants, for example — and conventional settings. Lacking the bitter satire and bawdiness of Old Comedy, New Comedy depends on outrageous plots, mistaken identities, young lovers, interfering parents, and conniving servants. Ultimately, the young lovers outwit all those who stand between them and, in so doing, affirm the primacy of youth and love over old age and death.

Old and New Comedy represent two distinct lines of humor that extend to modern times. Old Comedy depends on **satire** — biting humor that diminishes a person, idea, or institution by ridiculing it or holding it up to scorn. Unlike most comedy, which exists simply to make people laugh, satire is social criticism, deriding hypocrisy, pretension, and vanity or condemning vice. At its best, satire appeals to the intellect, has a serious purpose, and arouses thoughtful laughter. New Comedy may also be satiric, but the satire is often tempered by elements of **farce,** comedy in which stereotypical characters engage in boisterous horseplay and slapstick humor, all the while making jokes and sexual innuendoes — as they do in Anton Chekhov's *The Brute* (p. 1250).

English comedy got its start in the sixth century A.D. in the form of farcical episodes that appeared in morality plays. During the Renaissance, comedy developed rapidly, beginning in 1533 with Nicholas Udall's *Ralph Roister Doister* and eventually evolving into Shakespeare's **romantic comedy** — such as *A Midsummer Night's Dream*—in which love is the main subject and idealized heroines and lovers endure great difficulties until the inevitable happy ending is reached.

Also during the Renaissance, particularly in the latter part of the sixteenth century, writers such as Ben Jonson experimented with a different type of comedy — the **comedy of humours,** which focused on characters whose behavior was controlled by a characteristic trait, or *humour*. During the Renaissance, a person's temperament was thought to be determined by the mix of fluids, or humours, in the body. When one humour dominated, a certain type of disposition resulted. Playwrights capitalized on this belief, writing comedies in which characters are motivated by stereotypical behaviors that result from the imbalance of the humours. In comedies such as Jonson's *Volpone* and *The Alchemist*, characters such as the suspicious husband and the miser can be manipulated by others because of their predictable dispositions.

Closely related to the comedy of humours is the satiric **comedy of manners,** which developed during the sixteenth century and achieved great popularity in the nineteenth century. This form focused on the manners and customs of society and directed its satire against characters who violated social conventions and rules of behavior. These plays tend to be memorable more for their witty dialogue than for their development of characters or setting. Oliver Goldsmith's *She Stoops to Conquer*, George Bernard Shaw's *Pygmalion*, and even some of the television sitcoms of today are examples of this type of comedy.

In the eighteenth century, a reaction against the perceived immorality of the comedy of manners led to **sentimental comedy,** which eventually achieved great popularity. This kind of comedy relied on sentimental emotion rather than on wit or humor to move an audience. It also dwelled on the virtues rather than on the vices of life. The heroes of sentimental comedy are unimpeachably noble, moral, and honorable; the pure, virtuous, middle-class heroines suffer trials and tribulations calculated to move the audience to tears rather than to laughter. Eventually, the distress of the hero and heroine is resolved in a sometimes contrived (but always happy) ending. Sir Richard Steele's *The Conscious Lovers* (1722) is an example of sentimental comedy.

In his 1877 essay *The Idea of Comedy*, novelist and critic George Meredith suggests that comedy that appeals to the intellect should be called **high comedy.** Thus, Shakespeare's *As You Like It* and George Bernard Shaw's *Pygmalion* can be characterized as high comedy. When comedy has little or no intellectual appeal, according to Meredith, it is **low comedy.** Low comedy appears in parts of Shakespeare's *The Taming of the Shrew* and as comic relief in *Macbeth*.

The twentieth century developed its own characteristic comic forms, reflecting the uncertainty and pessimism of a period marked by two world wars, the Holocaust, and nuclear destruction, as well as threats posed by environmental pollution and ethnic and racial conflict — and, in this century, the terrorist attacks of September 11, 2001. Combining laughter and hints of tragedy, these modern tragicomedies feature **antiheroes,** characters who, instead of manifesting dignity and power, are ineffectual or petty. Their plight frequently elicits laughter, not pity and fear, from the audience. **Black** or **dark comedies,** for example, rely on the morbid and the absurd. These works are usually so satiric and bitter that they threaten to slip over into tragedy. The screenplay of Joseph Heller's novel *Catch-22*, which ends with a character dropping bombs on his own men, is a classic example of such comedy. **Theater of the absurd,** which includes comedies such as Samuel Beckett's *Waiting for Godot* and Tom Stoppard's *Rosencrantz and Guildenstern Are Dead*, begins with the assumption that the human condition is irrational. Typically, this type of drama does not have a conventional plot; instead, it presents a series of apparently unrelated images and illogical exchanges of dialogue meant to reinforce the idea that human beings live in a remote, confusing, and often incomprehensible universe. Absurdist dramas seem to go in circles, never progressing to a climax or achieving a resolution, thus reinforcing the theme of the endless and meaningless repetition that characterizes modern life.

Defining Drama

Dramatic works differ from other prose works in a number of fairly obvious ways. For one thing, plays look different on the page: generally, they are divided into **acts** and **scenes;** they include **stage directions** that specify characters' entrances and exits and describe what settings look like and how characters look and act; and they consist primarily of **dialogue,** lines spoken by the characters. And, of course, plays are different from other prose works in that they are written not to be read but to be performed in front of an audience.

Unlike novels and short stories, plays do not usually have narrators to tell the audience what a character is thinking or what happened in the past; for the most part, the audience knows only what characters reveal. To compensate for the absence of a narrator, playwrights can use **monologues** (extended speeches by one character), **soliloquies** (monologues in which a character expresses private thoughts while alone on stage), or **asides** (brief comments by a character who reveals thoughts by speaking directly to the audience without being heard by the other characters). In addition to these dramatic techniques, a play can also use costumes, scenery, props, music, lighting, and other techniques to enhance its impact on the audience.

The play that follows, Anton Chekhov's *The Brute* (1888), is typical of modern drama in many respects. A one-act play translated from Russian, it is essentially a struggle of wills between two headstrong characters, a man and a woman, with action escalating through the characters' increasingly heated exchanges of dialogue. Stage directions briefly describe the setting—"*the drawing room of a country house*"— and announce the appearance of various props. They also describe the major characters' appearances as well as their actions, gestures, and emotions. Because the play is a **farce,** it features broad physical comedy, asides, wild dramatic gestures, and elaborate figures of speech, all designed to enhance its comic effect.

Source: ©Bettmann/Corbis

ANTON CHEKHOV (1860–1904) is an important nineteenth-century Russian playwright and short story writer. He became a doctor and, as a young adult, supported the rest of his family after his father's bankruptcy. After his early adult years in Moscow, Chekhov spent the rest of his life in the country, moving to Yalta, a resort town in Crimea, for his health (he suffered from tuberculosis). He continued to write plays, mostly for the Moscow Art Theatre, although he could not supervise their production as he would have wished. His plays include *The Seagull* (1896), *Uncle Vanya* (1898), *The Three Sisters* (1901), and *The Cherry Orchard* (1904).

The Brute, or *The Bear* (1888), is one of a number of one-act farces Chekhov wrote just before his major plays. It is based on a French farce (*Les Jurons de Cadillac* by Pierre Breton) about a man who cannot refrain from swearing. The woman he loves offers to marry him if he can avoid swearing for one hour; he is unable to do it, but he fails so charmingly that she agrees to marry him anyway.

Cultural Context The custom of dueling has been popular throughout history in many countries. Generally speaking, as in *The Brute*, duels are fought as a matter of honor — in response to an insult, an offense to one's character, or an affront to one's dignity. Once a challenge to a duel has been issued, negotiators (called *seconds*) agree on the time, place, and weaponry involved, as well as the point of surrender (first blood drawn or death). In a pistol duel, the participants stand back to back, count off a predetermined number of paces, turn, and fire. Today, dueling is illegal in most countries, and killing someone in the course of a duel is considered murder.

The Brute

A Joke in One Act (1888)

Translated by Eric Bentley

CHARACTERS

Mrs. Popov, *widow and landowner, small, with dimpled cheeks*
Mr. Grigory S. Smirnov, *gentleman farmer, middle-aged*
Luka, *Mrs. Popov's footman, an old man*
Gardener
Coachman
Hired Men

SCENE

The drawing room of a country house. Mrs. Popov, in deep mourning, is staring hard at a photograph. Luka is with her.

LUKA: It's not right, ma'am, you're killing yourself. The cook has gone off with the maid to pick berries. The cat's having a high old time in the yard catching birds. Every living thing is happy. But you stay moping here in the house like it was a convent, taking no pleasure in nothing. I mean it, ma'am! It must be a full year since you set foot out of doors.

MRS. POPOV: I must never set foot out of doors again, Luka. Never! I have nothing to set foot out of doors *for*. My life is done. *He* is in his grave. I have buried myself alive in this house. We are *both* in our graves.

LUKA: You're off again, ma'am. I just won't listen to you no more. Mr. Popov is dead, but what can we do about that? It's God's doing. God's will be done. You've cried over him, you've done your share of mourning, haven't you? There's a limit to everything. You can't go on weeping and wailing forever. My old lady died, for that matter, and I wept and wailed over her a whole month long. Well, that was it. I couldn't weep and wail all my life. She just wasn't worth it. *(He sighs.)* As for the neighbors, you've forgotten all about them, ma'am. You don't visit them and you don't let them visit you. You and I are like a pair of spiders — excuse the expression, ma'am — here we are in this house like a pair of spiders, we never see the light of day. And it isn't like there was no nice people around either. The whole county's swarming with 'em. There's a regiment quartered at Riblov, and the officers are so good-looking! The girls can't take their eyes off them — There's a ball at the camp every Friday — The military band plays most every day of the week — What do you say, ma'am? You're young, you're pretty, you could enjoy yourself! Ten years from now you may want to strut and show your feathers to the officers, and it'll be too late.

MRS. POPOV: *(firmly)* You must never bring this subject up again, Luka. Since Popov died, life has been an empty dream to me, you know that. *You* may think I am alive. Poor ignorant Luka! You are wrong. I am dead. I'm in my grave. Never more shall I see the light of day, never strip from my body this . . . raiment of death! Are you listening, Luka? Let his ghost learn how I love him! Yes, *I* know, and *you* know, he was often unfair to me, he was cruel to me, and he was unfaithful to me. What of it? *I* shall be faithful to *him*, that's all. I will show him how *I* can love. Hereafter, in a better world than this, he will welcome me back, the same loyal girl I always was —

LUKA: Instead of carrying on this way, ma'am, you should go out in the garden 5
and take a bit of a walk, ma'am. Or why not harness Toby and take a drive? Call on a couple of the neighbours, ma'am?

MRS. POPOV: *(breaking down)* Oh, Luka!

LUKA: Yes, ma'am? What have I said, ma'am? Oh, dear!

MRS. POPOV: Toby! You said Toby! He adored that horse. When he drove me out to the Korchagins and the Vlasovs, it was always with Toby! He was a wonderful driver, do you remember, Luka? So graceful! So strong! I can see him now, pulling at those reins with all his might and main! Toby! Luka, tell them to give Toby an extra portion of oats today.

Luka: Yes, ma'am.

A bell rings.

Mrs. Popov: Who is that? Tell them I'm not at home.

Luka: Very good, ma'am. *(Exit.)*

Mrs. Popov: *(gazing again at the photograph)* You shall see, my Popov, how a wife can love and forgive. Till death do us part. Longer than that. Till death re-unite us forever! *(Suddenly a titter breaks through her tears.)* Aren't you ashamed of yourself, Popov? Here's your little wife, being good, being faithful, so faithful she's locked up here waiting for her own funeral, while you — doesn't it make you ashamed, you naughty boy? You were terrible, you know. You were unfaithful, and you made those awful scenes about it, you stormed out and left me alone for weeks —

Enter Luka.

Luka: *(upset)* There's someone asking for you, ma'am. Says he must —

Mrs. Popov: I suppose you told him that since my husband's death I see no one?

Luka: Yes, ma'am. I did, ma'am. But he wouldn't listen, ma'am. He says it's urgent.

Mrs. Popov: *(shrilly)* I see no one!!

Luka: He won't take no for an answer, ma'am. He just curses and swears and comes in anyway. He's a perfect monster, ma'am. He's in the dining room right now.

Mrs. Popov: In the dining room, is he? I'll give him his come-uppance. Bring him in here this minute.

Exit Luka.

(Suddenly sad again.) Why do they do this to me? Why? Insulting my grief, intruding on my solitude? *(She sighs.)* I'm afraid I'll have to enter a convent. I will, I *must* enter a convent!

Enter Mr. Smirnov and Luka.

Smirnov: *(to Luka)* Dolt! Idiot! You talk too much! *(Seeing Mrs. Popov. With dignity.)* May I have the honor of introducing myself, madam? Grigory S. Smirnov, landowner and lieutenant of artillery, retired. Forgive me, madam, if I disturb your peace and quiet, but my business is both urgent and weighty.

Mrs. Popov: *(declining to offer him her hand)* What is it you wish, sir?

Smirnov: At the time of his death, your late husband — with whom I had the honor to be acquainted, ma'am — was in my debt to the tune of twelve hundred rubles. I have two notes to prove it. Tomorrow, ma'am, I must pay the interest on a bank loan. I have therefore no alternative, ma'am, but to ask you to pay me the money today.

MRS. POPOV: Twelve hundred rubles? But what did my husband owe it to you for?

SMIRNOV: He used to buy his oats from me, madam.

MRS. POPOV: *(to Luka, with a sigh)* Remember what I said, Luka: tell them to give Toby an extra portion of oats today!

Exit Luka.

My dear Mr. — what was the name again?

SMIRNOV: Smirnov, ma'am.

MRS. POPOV: My dear Mr. Smirnov, if Mr. Popov owed you money, you shall be paid — to the last ruble, to the last kopeck. But today — you must excuse me, Mr. — what was it?

SMIRNOV: Smirnov, ma'am.

MRS. POPOV: Today, Mr. Smirnov, I have no ready cash in the house. *(Smirnov starts to speak.)* Tomorrow, Mr. Smirnov, no, the day after tomorrow, all will be well. My steward will be back from town. I shall see that he pays what is owing. Today, no. In any case, today is exactly seven months from Mr. Popov's death. On such a day you will understand that I am in no mood to think of money.

SMIRNOV: Madam, if you don't pay up now, you can carry me out feet foremost. They'll seize my estate.

MRS. POPOV: You can have your money. *(He starts to thank her.)* Tomorrow. *(He again starts to speak.)* That is: the day after tomorrow.

SMIRNOV: I don't need the money the day after tomorrow. I need it today.

MRS. POPOV: I'm sorry, Mr. —

SMIRNOV: *(shouting)* Smirnov!

MRS. POPOV: *(sweetly)* Yes, of course. But you can't have it today.

SMIRNOV: But I can't wait for it any longer!

MRS. POPOV: Be sensible, Mr. Smirnov. How can I pay you if I don't have it?

SMIRNOV: You don't have it?

MRS. POPOV: I don't have it.

SMIRNOV: Sure?

MRS. POPOV: Positive.

SMIRNOV: Very well. I'll make a note to that effect. *(Shrugging.)* And then they want me to keep cool. I meet the tax commissioner on the street, and he says, "Why are you always in such a bad humor, Smirnov?" Bad humor! How can I help it, in God's name? I need money, I need it desperately. Take yesterday: I leave home at the crack of dawn, I call on all my debtors. Not a one of them pays up. Footsore and weary. I creep at midnight into some little dive, and try to snatch a few winks of sleep on the floor by the vodka barrel. Then today, I come here, fifty miles from home, saying to myself, "At last, at last, I can be sure of something," and you're not in the mood! You give me a mood! Christ, how can I help getting all worked up?

MRS. POPOV: I thought I'd made it clear, Mr. Smirnov, that you'll get your money the minute my steward is back from town.

SMIRNOV: What the hell do I care about your steward? Pardon the expression, ma'am. But it was you I came to see.

MRS. POPOV: What language! What a tone to take to a lady! I refuse to hear another word. *(Quickly, exit.)*

45 **SMIRNOV:** Not in the mood, huh? "Exactly seven months since Popov's death," huh? How about me? *(Shouting after her.)* Is there this interest to pay, or isn't there? I'm asking you a question: is there this interest to pay, or isn't there? So your husband died, and you're not in the mood, and your steward's gone off some place, and so forth and so on, but what can *I* do about all that, huh? What do *you* think I should do? Take a running jump and shove my head through the wall? Take off in a balloon? You don't know my *other* debtors. I call on Gruzdeff. Not at home. I look for Yaroshevitch. He's hiding out. I find Kooritsin. He kicks up a row, and I have to throw him through the window. I work my way right down the list. Not a kopeck. Then I come to you, and God damn it to hell, if you'll pardon the expression, you're not in the mood! *(Quietly, as he realizes he's talking to air.)* I've spoiled them all, that's what, I've let them play me for a sucker. Well, I'll show them. I'll show this one. I'll stay right here till she pays up. Ugh! *(He shudders with rage.)* I'm in a rage! I'm in a positively towering rage! Every nerve in my body is trembling at forty to the dozen! I can't breathe, I feel ill, I think I'm going to faint, hey, you there!

Enter Luka.

LUKA: Yes, sir? Is there anything you wish, sir?

SMIRNOV: Water! Water! No, make it vodka.

Exit Luka.

Consider the logic of it. A fellow creature is desperately in need of cash, so desperately in need that he has to seriously contemplate hanging himself, and this woman, this mere chit of a girl, won't pay up, and why not? Because, forsooth, she isn't in the mood! Oh, the logic of women! Come to that, I never have liked them, I could do without the whole sex. Talk to a woman? I'd rather sit on a barrel of dynamite, the very thought gives me gooseflesh. Women! Creatures of poetry and romance! Just to see one in the distance gets me mad. My legs start twitching with rage. I feel like yelling for help.

Enter Luka, handing Smirnov a glass of water.

LUKA: Mrs. Popov is indisposed, sir. She is seeing no one.

SMIRNOV: Get out.

Exit Luka.

Indisposed, is she? Seeing no one, huh? Well, she can see me or not, but I'll be here, I'll be right here till she pays up. If you're sick for a week, I'll be here for a week. If you're sick for a year, I'll be here for a year. You won't get around *me* with your widow's weeds and your schoolgirl dimples. I know all about dimples. *(Shouting through the window.)* Semyon, let the horses out of those shafts, we're not leaving, we're staying, and tell them to give the horses some oats, yes, oats, you fool, what do you think? *(Walking away from the window.)* What a mess, what an unholy mess! I didn't sleep last night, the heat is terrific today, not a damn one of 'em has paid up, and here's this — this skirt in mourning that's not in the mood! My head aches, where's that — *(He drinks from the glass.)* Water, ugh! You there!

Enter Luka.

LUKA: Yes, sir. You wish for something, sir?
SMIRNOV: Where's that confounded vodka I asked for?

Exit Luka.

(Smirnov sits and looks himself over.) Oof! A fine figure of a man *I* am! Unwashed, uncombed, unshaven, straw on my vest, dust all over me. The little woman must've taken me for a highwayman. *(Yawns.)* I suppose it wouldn't be considered polite to barge into a drawing room in this state, but who cares? I'm not a visitor, I'm a creditor — most unwelcome of guests, second only to Death.

Enter Luka.

LUKA: *(handing him the vodka)* If I may say so, sir, you take too many liberties, sir.
SMIRNOV: What?!
LUKA: Oh, nothing, sir, nothing.
SMIRNOV: Who in hell do you think you're talking to? Shut your mouth!
LUKA: *(aside)* There's an evil spirit abroad. The Devil must have sent him. Oh! *(Exit Luka.)*
SMIRNOV: What a rage I'm in! I'll grind the whole world to powder. Oh, I feel ill again. You there!

Enter Mrs. Popov.

MRS. POPOV: *(looking at the floor)* In the solitude of my rural retreat, Mr. Smirnov, I've long since grown unaccustomed to the sound of the human voice. Above all, I cannot bear shouting. I must beg you not to break the silence.
SMIRNOV: Very well. Pay me my money and I'll go.
MRS. POPOV: I told you before, and I tell you again, Mr. Smirnov. I have no cash, you'll have to wait till the day after tomorrow. Can I express myself more plainly?
SMIRNOV: And *I* told *you* before, and *I* tell *you* again, that I need the money today, that the day after tomorrow is too late, and that if you don't pay, and pay now, I'll have to hang myself in the morning!
MRS. POPOV: But I have no cash. This is quite a puzzle.
SMIRNOV: You won't pay, huh?
MRS. POPOV: I *can't* pay, Mr. Smirnov.

SMIRNOV: In that case, I'm going to sit here and wait. *(Sits down.)* You'll pay up the day after tomorrow? Very good. Till the day after tomorrow, here I sit. *(Pause. He jumps up.)* Now look, do I have to pay that interest tomorrow, or don't I? Or do you think I'm joking?

MRS. POPOV: I must ask you not to raise your voice, Mr. Smirnov. This is not a stable.

SMIRNOV: Who said it was? Do I have to pay the interest tomorrow or not?

MRS. POPOV: Mr. Smirnov, do you know how to behave in the presence of a lady?

SMIRNOV: No, madam, I do not know how to behave in the presence of a lady.

MRS. POPOV: Just what I thought. I look at you, and I say: ugh! I hear you talk, and I say to myself: "That man doesn't know how to talk to a lady."

SMIRNOV: You'd like me to come simpering to you in French, I suppose. "*Enchanté, madame! Merci beaucoup* for not paying zee money, *madame! Pardonnez-moi* if I 'ave disturbed you, *madame!* How *charmante* you look in mourning, *madame!*"

MRS. POPOV: Now you're being silly, Mr. Smirnov.

SMIRNOV: *(mimicking)* "Now you're being silly, Mr. Smirnov." "You don't know how to talk to a lady, Mr. Smirnov." Look here, Mrs. Popov, I've known more women than you've known pussy cats. I've fought three duels on their account. I've jilted twelve, and been jilted by nine others. Oh, yes, Mrs. Popov, I've played the fool in my time, whispered sweet nothings, bowed and scraped and endeavored to please. Don't tell me I don't know what it is to love, to pine away with longing, to have the blues, to melt like butter, to be weak as water. I was full of tender emotion. I was carried away with passion. I squandered half my fortune on the sex. I chattered about women's emancipation. But there's an end to everything, dear madam. Burning eyes, dark eyelashes, ripe, red lips, dimpled cheeks, heaving bosoms, soft whisperings, the moon above; the lake below — I don't give a rap for that sort of nonsense any more, Mrs. Popov. I've found out about women. Present company excepted, they're liars. Their behavior is mere play acting; their conversation is sheer gossip. Yes, dear lady, women, young or old, are false, petty, vain, cruel, malicious, unreasonable. As for intelligence, any sparrow could give them points. Appearances, I admit, can be deceptive. In appearance, a woman may be all poetry and romance, goddess and angel, muslin and fluff. To look at her exterior is to be transported to heaven. But I have looked at her interior, Mrs. Popov, and what did I find there — in her very soul? A crocodile. *(He has gripped the back of the chair so firmly that it snaps.)* And, what is more revolting, a crocodile with an illusion, a crocodile that imagines tender sentiments are its own special province, a crocodile that thinks itself queen of the realm of love! Whereas, in sober fact, dear madam, if a woman can love anything except a lapdog you can hang me by the feet on that nail. For a man, love is suffering, love is sacrifice. A woman just swishes her train around and tightens her grip on your nose. Now, you're a woman, aren't you, Mrs. Popov? You must be an expert on some of this. Tell me, quite frankly, did you ever know a woman to be — faithful, for instance? Or even sincere? Only old hags, huh? Though some women are old hags from birth. But as for the others? You're right: a faithful woman is a freak of nature — like a cat with horns.

MRS. POPOV: Who *is* faithful, then? Who *have* you cast for the faithful lover? Not man?

SMIRNOV: Right first time, Mrs. Popov: man.

MRS. POPOV: *(going off into a peal of bitter laughter)* Man! Man is faithful! that's a new one! *(Fiercely.)* What right do you have to say this, Mr. Smirnov? Men faithful? Let me tell you something. Of all the men I have ever known my late husband Popov was the best. I loved him, and there are women who know how to love, Mr. Smirnov. I gave him my youth, my happiness, my life, my fortune. I worshipped the ground he trod on — and what happened? The best of men was unfaithful to me, Mr. Smirnov. Not once in a while. All the time. After he died, I found his desk drawer full of love letters. While he was alive, he was always going away for the week-end. He squandered my money. He made love to other women before my very eyes. But, in spite of all, Mr. Smirnov, *I* was faithful. Unto death. And beyond. I am *still* faithful, Mr. Smirnov! Buried alive in this house, I shall wear mourning till the day I, too, am called to my eternal rest.

SMIRNOV: *(laughing scornfully)* Expect me to believe that? As if I couldn't see through all this hocus-pocus. Buried alive! Till you're called to your eternal rest! Till when? Till some little poet — or some little subaltern with his first moustache — comes riding by and asks: "Can that be the house of the mysterious Tamara who for love of her late husband has buried herself alive, vowing to see no man?" Ha!

MRS. POPOV: *(flaring up)* How dare you? How dare you insinuate —?

SMIRNOV: You may have buried yourself alive, Mrs. Popov, but you haven't forgotten to powder your nose.

MRS. POPOV: *(incoherent)* How dare you? How — ?

SMIRNOV: Who's raising his voice now? Just because I call a spade a spade. Because I shoot straight from the shoulder. Well, don't shout at me, I'm not your steward.

MRS. POPOV: I'm not shouting, you're shouting! Oh, leave me alone!

SMIRNOV: Pay me the money, and I will.

MRS. POPOV: You'll get no money out of me!

SMIRNOV: Oh, so that's it!

MRS. POPOV: Not a ruble, not a kopeck. Get out! Leave me alone!

SMIRNOV: Not being your husband, I must ask you not to make scenes with me. *(He sits.)* I don't like scenes.

MRS. POPOV: *(choking with rage)* You're sitting down?

SMIRNOV: Correct, I'm sitting down.

MRS. POPOV: I asked you to leave!

SMIRNOV: Then give me the money. *(Aside.)* Oh, what a rage I'm in, what a rage!

MRS. POPOV: The impudence of the man! I won't talk to you a moment longer. Get out. *(Pause.)* Are you going?

SMIRNOV: No.

MRS. POPOV: No?!

SMIRNOV: No.

MRS. POPOV: On your head be it. Luka!

Enter Luka.

Show the gentleman out, Luka.

LUKA: *(approaching)* I'm afraid, sir, I'll have to ask you, um, to leave, sir, now, um—

SMIRNOV: *(jumping up)* Shut your mouth, you old idiot! Who do you think you're talking to? I'll make mincemeat of you.

LUKA: *(clutching his heart)* Mercy on us! Holy saints above! *(He falls into an armchair.)* I'm taken sick! I can't breathe!!

MRS. POPOV: Then where's Dasha? Dasha! Dasha! Come here at once! *(She rings.)*

LUKA: They gone picking berries, ma'am, I'm alone here—Water, water, I'm taken sick!

MRS. POPOV: *(to Smirnov)* Get out, you!

SMIRNOV: Can't you even be polite with me, Mrs. Popov?

MRS. POPOV: *(clenching her fists and stamping her feet)* With you? You're a wild animal, you were never house-broken!

SMIRNOV: What? What did you say?

MRS. POPOV: I said you were a wild animal, you were never house-broken.

SMIRNOV: *(advancing upon her)* And what right do you have to talk to me like that?

MRS. POPOV: Like what?

SMIRNOV: You have insulted me, madam.

MRS. POPOV: What of it? Do you think I'm scared of you?

SMIRNOV: So you think you can get away with it because you're a woman. A creature of poetry and romance, huh? Well, it doesn't go down with me. I hereby challenge you to a duel.

LUKA: Mercy on us! Holy saints alive! Water!

SMIRNOV: I propose we shoot it out.

MRS. POPOV: Trying to scare me again? Just because you have big fists and a voice like a bull? You're a brute.

SMIRNOV: No one insults Grigory S. Smirnov with impunity! And I don't care if you *are* a female.

MRS. POPOV: *(trying to outshout him)* Brute, brute, brute!

SMIRNOV: The sexes are equal, are they? Fine: then it's just prejudice to expect men alone to pay for insults. I hereby challenge—

MRS. POPOV: *(screaming)* All right! You want to shoot it out? All right! Let's shoot it out!

SMIRNOV: And let it be here and now!

MRS. POPOV: Here and now! All right! I'll have Popov's pistols here in one minute! *(Walks away, then turns.)* Putting one of Popov's bullets through your silly head will be a pleasure! Au revoir. *(Exit.)*

SMIRNOV: I'll bring her down like a duck, a sitting duck. I'm not one of your little poets, I'm no little subaltern with his first moustache. No, sir, there's no weaker sex where I'm concerned!

LUKA: Sir! Master! *(He goes down on his knees.)* Take pity on a poor old man, and do me a favor: go away. It was bad enough before, you nearly scared me to death. But a duel—!

SMIRNOV: *(ignoring him)* A duel! That's equality of the sexes for you! That's women's emancipation! Just as a matter of principle I'll bring her down like a duck. But what a woman! "Putting one of Popov's bullets through your silly head . . ." Her cheeks were flushed, her eyes were gleaming! And, by God, she's accepted the challenge! I never knew a woman like this before!

LUKA: Sir! Master! Please go away! I'll always pray for you!

SMIRNOV: *(again ignoring him)* What a woman! Phew!! *She's* no sour puss, *she's* no cry baby. She's fire and brimstone. She's a human cannon ball. What a shame I have to kill her!

LUKA: *(weeping)* Please, kind sir, please, go away!

SMIRNOV: *(as before)* I like her, isn't that funny? With those dimples and all? I like her. I'm even prepared to consider letting her off that debt. And where's my rage? It's gone. I never knew a woman like this before.

Enter Mrs. Popov with pistols.

MRS. POPOV: *(boldly)* Pistols, Mr. Smirnov! *(Matter of fact.)* But before we start, you'd better show me how it's done. I'm not too familiar with these things. In fact I never gave a pistol a second look.

LUKA: Lord, have mercy on us, I must go hunt up the gardener and the coachman. Why has this catastrophe fallen upon us, O Lord? *(Exit.)*

SMIRNOV: *(examining the pistols)* Well, it's like this. There are several makes: one is the Mortimer, with capsules, especially constructed for dueling. What you have here are Smith and Wesson triple-action revolvers, with extractor, first-rate job, worth ninety rubles at the very least. You hold it this way. *(Aside.)* My God, what eyes she has! They're setting me on fire.

MRS. POPOV: This way?

SMIRNOV: Yes, that's right. You cock the trigger, take aim like this, head up, arm out like this. Then you just press with this finger here, and it's all over. The main thing is, keep cool, take slow aim, and don't let your arm jump.

MRS. POPOV: I see. And if it's inconvenient to do the job here, we can go out in the garden.

SMIRNOV: Very good. Of course, I should warn you: I'll be firing in the air.

MRS. POPOV: What? This is the end. Why?

SMIRNOV: Oh, well—because—for private reasons.

MRS. POPOV: Scared, huh? *(She laughs heartily.)* Now don't you try to get out of it, Mr. Smirnov. My blood is up. I won't be happy till I've drilled a hole through that skull of yours. Follow me. What's the matter? Scared?

SMIRNOV: That's right. I'm scared.

MRS. POPOV: Oh, come on, what's the matter with you?

SMIRNOV: Well, um, Mrs. Popov, I, um, I like you.

MRS. POPOV: *(laughing bitterly)* Good God! He likes me, does he? The gall of the man. *(Showing him the door.)* You may leave, Mr. Smirnov.

SMIRNOV: *(Quietly puts the gun down, takes his hat, and walks to the door. Then he stops and the pair look at each other without a word. Then, approaching gingerly.)* Listen, Mrs. Popov. Are you still mad at me? I'm in the devil of a temper myself, of course. But then, you see — what I mean is — it's this way — the fact is — *(Roaring.)* Well, is it my fault, damn it, if I like you? *(Clutches the back of a chair. It breaks.)* Christ, what fragile furniture you have here. I like you. Know what I mean? I could fall in love with you.

MRS. POPOV: I hate you. Get out!

SMIRNOV: What a woman! I never saw anything like it. Oh, I'm lost, I'm done for, I'm a mouse in a trap.

MRS. POPOV: Leave this house, or I shoot!

SMIRNOV: Shoot away! What bliss to die of a shot that was fired by that little velvet hand! To die gazing into those enchanting eyes. I'm out of my mind. I know: you must decide at once. Think for one second, then decide. Because if I leave now, I'll never be back. Decide! I'm a pretty decent chap. Landed gentleman, I should say. Ten thousand a year. Good stable. Throw a kopeck up in the air, and I'll put a bullet through it. Will you marry me?

MRS. POPOV: *(indignant, brandishing the gun)* We'll shoot it out! Get going! Take your pistol!

SMIRNOV: I'm out of my mind. I don't understand anything any more. *(Shouting.)* You there! That vodka!

MRS. POPOV: No excuses! No delays! We'll shoot it out!

SMIRNOV: I'm out of my mind. I'm falling in love. I *have* fallen in love. *(He takes her hand vigorously; she squeals.)* I love you. *(He goes down on his knees.)* I love you as I've never loved before. I jilted twelve, and was jilted by nine others. But I didn't love a one of them as I love you. I'm full of tender emotion. I'm melting like butter. I'm weak as water. I'm on my knees like a fool, and I offer you my hand. It's a shame, it's a disgrace. I haven't been in love in five years. I took a vow against it. And now, all of a sudden, to be swept off my feet, it's a scandal. I offer you my hand, dear lady. Will you or won't you? You won't? Then don't! *(He rises and walks toward the door.)*

MRS. POPOV: I didn't say anything.

SMIRNOV: *(stopping)* What?

MRS. POPOV: Oh, nothing, you can go. Well, no, just a minute. No, you can go. Go! I detest you! But, just a moment. Oh, if you knew how furious I feel! *(Throws the gun on the table.)* My fingers have gone to sleep holding that horrid thing. *(She is tearing her handkerchief to shreds.)* And what are you standing around for? Get out of here!

SMIRNOV: Goodbye.

MRS. POPOV: Go, go, go! *(Shouting.)* Where are you going? Wait a minute! No, no, it's all right, just go. I'm fighting mad. Don't come near me, don't come near me!

Smirnov: *(who is coming near her)* I'm pretty disgusted with myself—falling in love like a kid, going down on my knees like some moongazing whippersnapper, the very thought gives me gooseflesh. *(Rudely.)* I love you. But it doesn't make sense. Tomorrow, I have to pay that interest, and we've already started mowing. *(He puts his arm about her waist.)* I shall never forgive myself for this.

Mrs. Popov: Take your hands off me, I hate you! Let's shoot it out!

A long kiss. Enter Luka with an axe, the Gardener with a rake, the coachman with a pitchfork, hired men with sticks.

Luka: *(seeing the kiss)* Mercy on us! Holy saints above!

Mrs. Popov: *(dropping her eyes)* Luka, tell them in the stable that Toby is *not* to have any oats today.

* * *

A Note on Translations

Many dramatic works that we read or see are translations from other languages. For example, Ibsen wrote in Norwegian, Sophocles in Greek, Molière in French, and Chekhov in Russian. Before English-speaking viewers or readers can evaluate the language of a translated play, they must understand that the language they hear or read is the translator's interpretation of what the playwright intended to communicate. Translation is interpretation, not just a search for literal equivalents; as a result, a translation is always different from the original. Moreover, because translators make different choices, two translations of the same work into English can vary considerably.

Compare these two versions of an exchange of dialogue from two translations of the same Chekhov play, called *The Brute* in the translation that begins on page 1250 and *The Bear* in the alternate version.

From *The Brute*

Smirnov: You'd like me to come simpering to you in French, I suppose. *"Enchanté, madame! Merci beaucoup* for not paying zee money, *madame! Pardonnez-moi* if I 'ave disturbed you, *madame!* How *charmante* you look in mourning, *madame!"*

Mrs. Popov: Now you're being silly, Mr. Smirnov.

Smirnov: *(mimicking)* "Now you're being silly, Mr. Smirnov." "You don't know how to talk to a lady, Mr. Smirnov." Look here, Mrs. Popov. I've known more women than you've known pussy cats. I've fought three duels on their account. I've jilted twelve, and been jilted by nine others. Oh, yes, Mrs. Popov, I've played the fool in my time, whispered sweet nothings, bowed and scraped and endeavored to please. Don't tell me I don't know what it is to love, to pine away with longing, to have the blues, to melt like butter, to be weak as water. I was full of tender emotion. I was carried away with passion. I squandered half my fortune on the sex. I chattered about women's emancipation. But there's an end to everything, dear madam. . . . (1.71–73)

From *The Bear*

SMIRNOV: Ach, it's astonishing! How would you like me to talk to you? In French, perhaps? *(Lisps in anger.) Madame, je vous prie. . . . how happy I am that you're not paying me the money. . . . Ah, pardon, I've made you uneasy! Such lovely weather we're having today! And you look so becoming in your mourning dress. (Bows and scrapes.)*

MRS. POPOV: That's rude and not very clever!

SMIRNOV: *(teasing)* Rude and not very clever! I don't know how to behave in the company of ladies. Madam, in my time I've seen far more women than you've seen sparrows. Three times I've fought duels over women; I've jilted twelve women, nine have jilted me! Yes! There was a time when I played the fool; I became sentimental over women, used honeyed words, fawned on them, bowed and scraped. . . . I loved, suffered, sighed at the moon; I became limp, melted, shivered . . . I loved passionately, madly, every which way, devil take me, I chattered away like a magpie about the emancipation of women, ran through half my fortune as a result of my tender feelings; but now, if you will excuse me, I'm on to your ways! I've had enough!

Although both translations convey Smirnov's anger and frustration, they use different words (with different connotations), different phrasing—and even different stage directions. In *The Bear*, for instance, only one French phrase is used, whereas *The Brute* uses several and specifies a French accent as well; other differences between the two translations include *The Bear*'s use of "teasing," "sparrows," and "I've had enough!" where *The Brute* uses "mimicking," "pussy cats," and "But there's an end to everything, dear madam." (Elsewhere in the play, *The Bear* uses profanity while *The Brute* uses more polite language.) Many words and idiomatic expressions used in daily speech cannot be translated exactly from one language to another; as a result, the two translators make different choices to try to convey a sense of the original.

Recognizing Kinds of Drama

The dramatic tradition stretches back to antiquity, with some of the earliest known plays dating back to the sixth century B.C. This long lifespan has produced numerous developments in the form and conventions of drama.

Traditionally, plays are divided into **acts,** which are further divided into **scenes.** In between acts, there is sometimes an **intermission,** a pause in the action that can be used to heighten the dramatic tension created at the end of the previous scene (as well as to represent the passage of time between one act and the next). The number of acts in a play can range from one to five, depending on the length and scope of the play itself. Shakespeare's *Hamlet* and *A Midsummer's Night's Dream* both have five acts, but most full-length contemporary plays have just two or three.

Some shorter plays have only one act. In a **one-act play** such as Chekov's *The Brute*, the playwright is faced with the challenge of creating a dramatic work that includes all the elements that are part of longer plays — exposition, conflict, climax, and resolution. Because these plays are shorter, their imagery and dialogue are often more concise. In fact, because there is less time to devote to character development, subtext, or the consequences of events, one-act plays differ from full-length plays in the same way that short stories differ from novels.

An even more recent development in drama is the **ten-minute play** — a play in which all the actors are onstage and all events take place within a ten-minute time period (see Chapter 36). On an even smaller scale, a **monologue** — an extended speech delivered by one character — can stand alone as a complete dramatic work, as in Wendy Wasserstein's *Workout* (p. 1265) and Joyce Carol Oates's *When I was a Little Girl and My Mother Didn't Want Me* (p. 1266). Some contemporary plays — including Eve Ensler's *The Vagina Monologues* and Claudia Shear's *Blown Sideways through Life* — are composed entirely of a series of interrelated dramatic monologues.

Some contemporary drama is **improvisational,** which means that it is either partially or completely unscripted. This dramatic tradition is a descendant of **commedia dell'arte,** an Italian form of improvisational theater that began in the sixteenth century and was popular until the eighteenth century. Today, many theater actors are trained in "improv" work, which challenges them to sharpen their concentration and trust in their own instincts rather than relying solely on a script. Some improvisational plays rely on audience participation, requiring actors to improvise in response to audience members' spontaneous contributions to the play.

DRAMA SAMPLER: TEN-MINUTE PLAYS

Throughout the long history of playwriting, many types and forms of drama have emerged. In recent years, theater has become more experimental, as evidenced by the proliferation of one-act and ten-minute plays, which strive to convey complex ideas in a short amount of time. While traditional one-act plays such as Anton Chekhov's *The Brute* (p. 1250) and Susan Glaspell's *Trifles* (p. 1319) may have the luxury of unfolding in a more extended period, the **ten-minute play,** which must be performed in ten minutes or less, offers a very small window of opportunity in which the playwright can create meaning. In fact, as director Jon Jory has noted, the ten-minute play is in a sense the dramatic equivalent of the **haiku** in that it is intended to be taken in all at once, and thus to have a particularly intense effect on the audience. According to Jory, considered to be the father of the ten-minute play genre, these plays "must, by nature, imply rather than explain. They often depend on metaphor to extend their reach. They stick like glue in the mind because the viewer remembers the *whole* play."

Since a page of script roughly translates into a minute of time onstage, a ten-minute play is generally limited to about ten pages. Despite its brevity, however, a ten-minute play is more than just a scene or an excerpt from a longer play: it is written to stand alone as a complete dramatic work. Although its brief length means it has little or no room for **exposition,** it must introduce a **conflict** (usually relatively early in the play), and it must provide a **resolution,** just as any other play does.

Ten-minute plays are generally staged in groups, allowing the audience to watch several plays in sequence. Casts are usually small; often, the same actors appear in a number of different plays. For this reason, elaborate costumes and staging are impractical (and therefore rare). The most popular venue for a ten-minute play is a drama festival, and numerous competitions offer prizes that include the staging of the winning play. The most prominent contest is sponsored by the Actors Theatre of Louisville, which stages the annual Humana Festival of New American Plays.

The ten-minute plays in this sampler treat a variety of topics. Wendy Wasserstein's *Workout* and Joyce Carol Oates's *When I Was a Little Girl and My Mother Didn't Want Me* are monologues, single-character plays that reveal emotional truths about the protagonists as the plays unfold. In Jane Martin's *Beauty*, the two protagonists trade lives, with unexpected consequences; in *Tape*, by Jose Rivera, the protagonist is forced to confront his entire life and face up to his own truths; and in Billy Goda's *No Crime*, a job interview takes an unexpected turn. Finally, in Zora Neale Hurston's *Poker!* a group of men gather for a card game that threatens to escalate into a different kind of contest. (Warren Leight's *Nine Ten* on page 1314, and David Henry Hwang's *Trying to Find Chinatown* on page 1856 are also ten-minute plays.)

Source: ©AP Photo/Gino Domenico

WENDY WASSERSTEIN (1950–2006) is a Tony Award– and Pulitzer Prize–winning dramatist known for plays about educated women and the challenges they face. The characters in her plays often struggle to define themselves in relation to (and sometimes in opposition to) the stereotypical roles of wife, mother, and career woman. Her plays include *Uncommon Women and Others* (1977), her Yale School of Drama thesis; *Isn't It Romantic* (1983); *The Heidi Chronicles* (1988), for which she won both a Tony Award and a Pulitzer Prize; *Tender Offer* (1991); *The Sisters Rosensweig* (1993); *An American Daughter* (1998); and *Old Money* (1999). In addition to her dramatic works, Wasserstein published two books of essays and two novels, *An American Daughter* (1998) and *Elements of Style* (2006). She died of lymphoma at the age of 56.

Workout (1995)

A woman enters a small room wearing leotards and a midi sweat top. She turns on disco music and lies on the floor. She begins to exercise, and begins to talk.

Ready for your workout? We'll start with buttock tucks. These are my favorite. Now lie back, breathe deep. Big breath. Mmmmmm. Relax, feet forward. Remember, make the muscles burn. *(She begins to bounce her buttocks.)*

And lift and lower. And lift and lower. Squeeze it. Squeeze it. Push up, release. Push up and release. Really squeeze it, Denise. Lift up, lift up and bounce bounce bounce. *(She begins doing leg lifts.)*

This is what I like to think about when I'm doing my workout. I think about how I got up at four-thirty in the morning and ran for five miles. And how great that run felt. Keep bouncing, up down up down. I like to think about the brewer's yeast I gave my children for breakfast. Squeeze it! Squeeze it! And how proud I am that the words "french toast" are never used in our house. I think about my husband's stamina. It's better now than when we first got married because we're organized. Work deep. Work deep! *(She does lifts in fire hydrant position.)*

And I think about the novel I'm writing between nine and eleven this morning. And the chain of appliance stores I'm opening at twelve. I just think it's so important that we take charge of our own appliances. Last week I restored the electricity for the city of Fresno. And a year ago I couldn't use a can opener. Just keep bouncing, Denise. And one, and two. And this afternoon after my yoghurt shake. . . *(She goes into a split.)*

5 Ooooooooooooh I felt the burn that time. I'm going to learn ancient Egyptian so I can star in the Nefertiti° story, which I am also producing, directing, writing, editing, and distributing. I'll need all my strength. Let's do twenty more. Denise, put the gun down. Your life isn't my fault. Be angry with your buttocks. Let them know your feelings. *(She squats, elbow to knee.)*

At five o'clock I'm going to my daughter's dance recital, where my husband will announce his candidacy for governor — I hope you all will vote for him — and I will announce the publication of my new workout book for children under six and their pets. On our way home, the entire family will stop at the home of a woman friend of mine for women's friendship and Tofutti ice cream. Release, release, we're almost there. Don't give in. Push it. Push it. *(She begins doing jumping jacks.)*

And then my very favorite part of the day. Tuck in. Feel it all over. The children are outside playing nonviolent baseball with radishes and zucchinis, my husband is preparing his part of the family meal and debating with Connie Chung and the six o'clock news team by satellite. Just two more. Get ready to release. And it is time for my moment. Just me. *(She stops exercising for the first time.)*

And I sit for the first time in the day. On my favorite chair, with my favorite quilt. And I take a deep breath, and I cry. *(She pauses.)* But just a little. *(She stands up.)*

And then I tuck in my stomach and pull up from the chair. Vertebra by vertebra. And I take a deep inhalation and exhale. And now we're ready for fifty more jumping jacks. And one, and two, and three, let's go, Denise. *(She continues jumping happily.)*

END

* * *

JOYCE CAROL OATES (1938–)

When I Was a Little Girl and My Mother Didn't Want Me (1997)

See this writer's biography and photo on p. 615.

Lights up. An elderly woman speaks. Her voice alternates between urgency and bemusement; emotion and reflection.

My father was killed and I never knew why.
Then, I was given away. By my mother.
I was so little . . . six months.
There were too many of us, nine of us,
    my mother gave me away.
When I was old enough to know . . . I cried a lot.

Nefertiti: Queen of Egypt from 1353–1336 B.C.

My father was killed and I never knew why.
No one would tell me.
Now there's no one I can ask.
"Why? Why?"
It happened in a fight, in a tavern, he was only
forty-four years old.
My father I never knew. Forty-four! Now, he could be
my son.

I wasn't always an . . . old woman. Eighty-one.
I was a girl for so long.
I was a little girl for so long.
I was six months old when my father died.
And there were too many of us to feed, and my mother . . .
gave me away.

There were nine children. I was the baby.
I was born late, I was the baby.
My mother gave me to her sister Lena who didn't have
children. This was in 1918.
This was in the Black Rock section of Buffalo,
the waterfront on the Niagara River.
Germans, Poles, Hungarians . . . immigrants.
We were Hungarians. We were called "Hunkies."
I don't know why people hated us . . .

(Woman pauses; decides not to explore this.)

Uncle John and Aunt Lena were my "parents."
We moved to a farm far away in the country.
And my real mother and my brothers and sisters
moved to a farm a few miles away.

Uncle John and Aunt Lena were good to me.
I don't know if I loved them . . . I think I loved them.
I think . . . I think they loved me.
They wanted children but couldn't have them so it was
right, I think, that my mother gave me to them . . .
It was a, a good thing, it was a . . . (*Pause.*)
necessary thing.
I would learn one day that it happened often.
In immigrant families in those days.
In poor immigrant families.

My father was killed and I never knew why.
They said he was a bad drinker, he got drunk
and was always in fights.
The Hungarians were the worst, they
said—the drinking, and the fighting.

They said he was so handsome, my father.
My mother Elizabeth was so pretty.
Curly hair like mine.
They said he had a temper "like the devil."
In the tavern there was a fight, and he died.
A man took up a poker and beat my father to death.
I never knew why, I never knew who it had been.
Yet this was how my life was decided.

There is the moment of conception — you don't know.
There is the moment of birth — you don't know.
There is the moment your life is decided — you don't know.
Yet you say, "This is my life."
You say, "This is me."

(Woman regards herself in wonder like a stroke victim regaining some of her awareness.)

When I was a little girl and my mother didn't want me
I hid away to cry.
I felt so bad and I felt so ashamed.
When I was old enough I would walk to the other farm.
There was a bridge over the Tonawanda Creek a few miles away.
They didn't really want to see me I guess.
My name was Carolina, but they didn't call me that.
I don't remember if there was a name they called me.
They weren't very nice to me I guess.
They didn't want me, I guess I was a reminder of . . . something.

Elizabeth, my mother, never learned English.
She spoke Hungarian all her life.
She never learned to read. She never learned to drive a car.
My Aunt Lena never learned to drive, so the sisters didn't see much of each other.
They lived only a few miles apart, and were the only sisters of their family in America, but they didn't see much of each other.
That was how women were in the old days.

I loved my mother.
She was a short, plump woman.
Curly brown hair like mine.
People would say, "You look just like your momma!"
Then they would be surprised, I'd start to cry.
My mother scolded me in Hungarian —
"Go away, go home where you belong. You have a home.
Your home is not here."

I loved my big brothers and sisters.
There was Leslie, he was the oldest.
He took over when my father died.
There was Mary, I didn't get to know real well.
They were born in Budapest.
There was Steve, who'd been kicked and trampled by a horse.
His brain was injured, he would never leave home.
There was Elsie who was my "big sister."
There was Frank who was my "big brother."
There was Johnny . . . and Edith . . .
There was George, I wasn't too close with George.
There was Joseph, I wasn't too close with.

(*Pause.*)

They are all dead now.
I loved them, but . . .
I am the only one remaining.
Sometimes I think: The soul is just a burning match!
It burns awhile and then . . .
And then that's all.

It's a long time ago now, but I remember hiding away to cry.
When I was a little girl and my mother didn't want me.

* * *

JANE MARTIN, a prize-winning playwright, has never made a public appearance or spoken about any of her works. In fact, she has never given an interview, and no picture of her has ever been published. As one critic wryly observed, Martin is "America's best known, unknown playwright." Martin first came to the attention of American theater audiences with her collection of monologues, *Talking With . . .*, a work that premiered at the 1981 Humana Festival of New American Plays at the Actors Theatre of Louisville, Kentucky. Her other works include *Vital Signs; What Mama Don't Know; Cementville;* the Pulitzer Prize–nominated *Keely and Du* (winner of the 1994 American Theatre Critics Association New Play Award); *Criminal Hearts; Middle Aged White Guys; Jack and Jill; Mr. Bundy; Flaming Guns of the Purple Sage; Good Boys; Flags;* and *Sez She.* Martin's name is widely believed to be a pseudonym. Jon Jory, former artistic director of the Actors Theatre of Louisville — and director of the premieres of all of Martin's plays — is spokesperson for the playwright and, according to some people, may actually be the playwright behind the pen name. Jory has repeatedly denied this; in a 1994 interview, he said that Martin "feels she could not write plays if people knew who she was, regardless of her identity or gender." In Jory's opinion, "The point in the end is the plays themselves. . . . But if Jane's anonymity is a P. T. Barnum publicity stunt, it's one of the longest circus acts going."

Beauty (2000)

CHARACTERS

Carla

Bethany

An apartment. Minimalist set. A young woman, Carla, on the phone.

CARLA: In love with me? You're in love with me? Could you describe yourself again? Uh-huh. Uh-huh. And you spoke to me? *(A knock at the door.)* Listen, I always hate to interrupt a marriage proposal, but . . . could you possibly hold that thought? *(Puts phone down and goes to door. Bethany, the same age as Carla and a friend, is there. She carries the sort of Mideastern lamp we know of from Aladdin.)*

BETHANY: Thank God you were home. I mean, you're not going to believe this!

CARLA: Somebody on the phone. *(Goes back to it.)*

BETHANY: I mean, I just had a beach urge, so I told them at work my uncle was dying . . .

CARLA: *(motions to Bethany for quiet)* And you were the one in the leather jacket with the tattoo? What was the tattoo? *(Carla again asks Bethany, who is gesturing wildly that she should hang up, to cool it.)* Look, a screaming eagle from shoulder to shoulder, maybe. There were a lot of people in the bar.

BETHANY: *(gesturing and mouthing)* I have to get back to work.

CARLA: *(on phone)* See, the thing is, I'm probably not going to marry someone I can't remember . . . particularly when I don't drink. Sorry. Sorry. Sorry. *(She hangs up.)* Madness.

BETHANY: So I ran out to the beach . . .

CARLA: This was some guy I never met who apparently offered me a beer . . .

BETHANY: . . . low tide and this . . . *(The lamp.)* . . . was just sitting there, lying there . . .

CARLA: . . . and he tracks me down . . .

BETHANY: . . . on the beach, and I lift this lid thing . . .

CARLA: . . . and seriously proposes marriage.

BETHANY: . . . and a genie comes out.

CARLA: I mean, that's twice in a . . . what?

BETHANY: A genie comes out of this thing.

CARLA: A genie?

BETHANY: I'm not kidding, the whole Disney kind of thing, swirling smoke, and then this twenty-foot-high, see-through guy in like an Arabian outfit.

CARLA: Very funny.

BETHANY: Yes, funny, but twenty feet high! I look up and down the beach, I'm alone. I don't have my pepper spray or my hand alarm. You know me, when I'm petrified I joke. I say his voice is too high for Robin Williams, and he says he's a castrati. Naturally. Who else would I meet?

CARLA: What's a castrati?
BETHANY: You know . . .

The appropriate gesture.

CARLA: Bethany, dear one, I have three modeling calls. I am meeting Ralph Lauren!
BETHANY: Okay, good. Ralph Lauren. Look, I am not kidding!
CARLA: You're not kidding what?!
BETHANY: There is a genie in this thingamajig.
CARLA: Uh-huh. I'll be back around eight.
BETHANY: And he offered me *wishes!*
CARLA: Is this some elaborate practical joke because it's my birthday?
BETHANY: No, happy birthday, but I'm like crazed because I'm on this deserted beach with a twenty-foot-high, see-through genie, so like sarcastically . . . you know how I need a new car . . . I said fine, gimme 25,000 dollars . . .
CARLA: On the beach with the genie?
BETHANY: Yeah, right, exactly, and it rains down out of the sky.
CARLA: Oh sure.
BETHANY: *(pulling a wad out of her purse)* Count it, those are thousands. I lost one in the surf.

Carla sees the top bill. Looks at Bethany, who nods encouragement. Carla thumbs through them.

CARLA: These look real.
BETHANY: Yeah.
CARLA: And they rained down out of the sky?
BETHANY: Yeah.
CARLA: You've been really strange lately, are you dealing?
BETHANY: Dealing what, I've even given up chocolate.
CARLA: Let me see the genie.
BETHANY: Wait, wait.
CARLA: Bethany, I don't have time to screw around. Let me see the genie or let me go on my appointments.
BETHANY: Wait! So I pick up the money . . . see, there's sand on the money . . . and I'm like nuts so I say, you know, "Okay, look, ummm, big guy, my uncle is in the hospital" . . . because as you know when I said to the people at work my uncle was dying, I was on one level telling the truth although it had nothing to do with the beach, but he was in Intensive Care after the accident, and that's on my mind, so I say, okay, Genie, heal my uncle . . . which is like impossible given he was hit by two trucks, and the genie says, "Yes, Master" . . . like they're supposed to say, and he goes into this like kind of whirlwind, kicking up sand and stuff, and I'm like, "Oh my God!" and the air clears, and he bows, you know, and says, "It is done, Master," and I say, "Okay, whatever-you-are, I'm calling on my cell phone," and I get it out and I get this doctor who is like dumbstruck who says my uncle came to, walked out of Intensive Care and left the hospital! I'm not kidding, Carla.

CARLA: On your mother's grave?

BETHANY: On my mother's grave.

They look at each other.

CARLA: Let me see the genie.

BETHANY: No, no, look, that's the whole thing . . . I was just, like, reacting, you know, responding, and that's already two wishes . . . although I'm really pleased about my uncle, the $25,000 thing, I could have asked for $10 million, and there is only one wish left.

CARLA: So ask for $10 million.

BETHANY: I don't think so. I don't think so. I mean, I gotta focus in here. Do you have a sparkling water?

CARLA: No. Bethany, I'm missing Ralph Lauren now. Very possibly my one chance to go from catalogue model to the very, very big time, so, if you are joking, stop joking.

BETHANY: Not joking. See, see, the thing is, I know what I want. In my guts. Yes. Underneath my entire bitch of a life is this unspoken, ferocious, all-consuming urge . . .

CARLA: *(trying to get her to move this along)* Ferocious, all-consuming urge . . .

BETHANY: I want to be like you.

CARLA: Me?

BETHANY: Yes.

CARLA: Half the time you don't even like me.

BETHANY: Jealous. The ogre of jealousy.

CARLA: You're the one with the $40,000 job straight out of school. You're the one who has published short stories. I'm the one hanging on by her fingernails in modeling. The one who has creeps calling her on the phone. The one who had to have a nose job.

BETHANY: I want to be beautiful.

CARLA: You are beautiful.

BETHANY: Carla, I'm not beautiful.

CARLA: You have charm. You have personality. You know perfectly well you're pretty.

BETHANY: "Pretty," see, that's it. Pretty is the minor leagues of beautiful. Pretty is what people discover about you after they know you. Beautiful is what knocks them out across the room. Pretty, you get called a couple of times a year; *beautiful* is twenty-four hours a day.

CARLA: Yeah? So?

BETHANY: So?! We're talking *beauty* here. Don't say "So?" Beauty is the real deal. You are the center of any moment of your life. People stare. Men flock. I've seen you get offered discounts on makeup for no reason. Parents treat beautiful children better. Studies show your income goes up. You can have sex anytime you want it. Men have to know me. That takes up to a year. I'm continually horny.

Carla: Bethany, I don't even like sex. I can't have a conversation without men coming on to me. I have no privacy. I get hassled on the street. They start pressuring me from the beginning. Half the time, it never occurs to them to start with a conversation. Smart guys like you. You've had three long-term relationships, and you're only twenty-three. I haven't had one. The good guys, the smart guys are scared to death of me. I'm surrounded by male bimbos who think a preposition is when you go to school away from home. I have no woman friends except you. I don't even want to talk about this!

Bethany: I knew you'd say something like this. See, you're "in the club" so you can say this. It's the way beauty functions as an elite. You're trying to keep it all for yourself.

Carla: I'm trying to tell you it's no picnic.

Bethany: But it's what everybody wants. It's the nasty secret at large in the world. It's the unspoken tidal desire in every room and on every street. It's the unspoken, the soundless whisper . . . millions upon millions of people longing hopelessly and forever to stop being whatever they are and be beautiful, but the difference between those ardent multitudes and me is that I have a goddamn genie and one more wish!

Carla: Well, it's not what I want. This is me, Carla. I have never read a whole book. Page six, I can't remember page four. The last thing I read was *The Complete Idiot's Guide to WordPerfect*. I leave dinner parties right after the dessert because I'm out of conversation. You know the dumb blond joke about the application where it says, "Sign here," she put Sagittarius? I've done that. Only beautiful guys approach me, and that's because they want to borrow my eye shadow. I barely exist outside a mirror! You don't want to *be me*.

Bethany: None of you tell the truth. That's why you have no friends. We can all see you're just trying to make us feel better because we aren't in your league. This only proves to me it should be my third wish. Money can only buy things. Beauty makes you the center of the universe.

Bethany picks up the lamp.

Carla: Don't do it. Bethany, don't wish it! I am telling you you'll regret it.

Bethany lifts the lid. There is a tremendous crash, and the lights go out. Then they flicker and come back up, revealing Bethany and Carla on the floor where they have been thrown by the explosion. We don't realize it at first, but they have exchanged places.

Carla/Bethany: Oh God.

Bethany/Carla: Oh God.

Carla/Bethany: Am I bleeding? Am I dying?

Bethany/Carla: I'm so dizzy. You're not bleeding.

Carla/Bethany: Neither are you.

Bethany/Carla: I feel so weird.

CARLA/BETHANY: Me too. I feel . . . *(Looking at her hands.)* Oh, my God, I'm wearing your jewelry. I'm wearing your nail polish.

BETHANY/CARLA: I know I'm over here, but I can see myself over there.

CARLA/BETHANY: I'm wearing your dress. I have your legs!!

BETHANY/CARLA: These aren't my shoes. I can't meet Ralph Lauren wearing these shoes!

CARLA/BETHANY: I wanted to be beautiful, but I didn't want to be you.

BETHANY/CARLA: Thanks a lot!!

CARLA/BETHANY: I've got to go. I want to pick someone out and get laid.

BETHANY/CARLA: You can't just walk out of here in my body!

CARLA/BETHANY: Wait a minute. Wait a minute. What's eleven eighteenths of 1,726?

BETHANY/CARLA: Why?

CARLA/BETHANY: I'm a public accountant. I want to know if you have my brain.

BETHANY/CARLA: One hundred thirty-two and a half.

CARLA/BETHANY: You have my brain.

BETHANY/CARLA: What shade of Rubenstein lipstick does Cindy Crawford wear with teal blue?

CARLA/BETHANY: Raging Storm.

BETHANY/CARLA: You have my brain. You poor bastard.

CARLA/BETHANY: I don't care. Don't you see?

BETHANY/CARLA: See what?

CARLA/BETHANY: We both have the one thing, the one and only thing everybody wants.

BETHANY/CARLA: What is that?

CARLA/BETHANY: It's better than beauty for me; it's better than brains for you.

BETHANY/CARLA: What? What?!

CARLA/BETHANY: Different problems.

Blackout.

* * *

JOSÉ RIVERA (1955–) was born in San Juan, Puerto Rico and grew up in a household where the only book was a Bible. When he was four years old, his family moved to New York. Early in his life, he saw a staged version of the play *Rumpelstiltskin* and decided to become a playwright. He has written numerous plays and won several awards, including two Obie Awards, a Fulbright Fellowship, and the Whiting Foundation Writing Award. In 2002, Rivera wrote the screenplay for *The Motorcycle Diaries,* a movie based on a motorcycle trip that Cuban revolutionary Che Guevara took as a young man. In 2005, Rivera became the first Puerto Rican to be nominated for an Academy Award for best adapted screenplay.

Tape (1993)

CHARACTERS
Person
Attendant

A small dark room. No windows. One door. A Person is being led in by an Attendant. In the room is a simple wooden table and chair. On the table is a large reel-to-reel tape recorder, a glass of water, and a pitcher of water.

PERSON: Dark in here.
ATTENDANT: I'm sorry.
PERSON: No, I know it's not your fault.
ATTENDANT: I'm afraid of those lights . . .
PERSON: I guess, what does it matter now?
ATTENDANT: . . . not very bright.
PERSON: Who cares, really?
ATTENDANT: We don't want to cause you any undue suffering. If it's too dark in here, I'll make sure one of the other attendants replaces the light bulb.

(The Person looks at the Attendant.)

PERSON: Any "undue suffering"?
ATTENDANT: That's right. *(The Person looks at the room.)*
PERSON: Is this where I'll be?
ATTENDANT: That's right.
PERSON: Will you be outside?
ATTENDANT: Yes.
PERSON: The entire time?
ATTENDANT: The entire time.
PERSON: Is it boring?
ATTENDANT: I'm sorry?
PERSON: Is it boring? You know. Waiting outside all the time.
ATTENDANT: *(Soft smile.)* It's my job. It's what I do.
PERSON: Of course. *(Beat.)* Will I get anything to eat or drink?
ATTENDANT: Well, we're not really set up for that. We don't have what you'd call a kitchen. But we can send out for things. Little things. Cold food.
PERSON: I understand.
ATTENDANT: Soft drinks.
PERSON: *(Hopefully.)* Beer?
ATTENDANT: I'm afraid not.
PERSON: Not even on special occasions like my birthdays?
ATTENDANT: *(Thinking.)* I guess maybe on your birthday.
PERSON: *(Truly appreciative.)* Great, thanks. *(Beat.)*
ATTENDANT: Do you have any more questions before we start? Because if you do, that's okay. It's okay to ask as many questions as you want. I'm sure you're very curious. I'm sure you'd like to know as much as possible, so you

can figure out how it all fits together and what it all means. So please ask. That's why I'm here. Don't worry about the time. We have a lot of time. *(Beat.)*

Person: I don't have any questions.

Attendant: *(Disappointed.)* Are you sure?

Person: There's not much I really have to know is there? Really?

Attendant: No, I guess not. I just thought . . .

Person: It's okay. I appreciate it. I guess I really want to sit.

Attendant: Sit. *(The person sits on the chair and faces the tape recorder.)*

Person: Okay, I'm sitting.

Attendant: Is it . . . comfortable?

Person: Does it matter? Does it really fucking matter?

Attendant: No. I suppose not. *(The Attendant looks sad. The Person looks at the Attendant and feels bad.)*

Person: Hey I'm sorry. I know it's not your fault. I know you didn't mean it. I'm sorry.

Attendant: It's all right.

Person: What's your name anyway? Do you have a name?

Attendant: Not really. It's not allowed.

Person: Really? Not allowed? Who says?

Attendant: The rules say.

Person: Have you actually seen these rules? Are they in writing?

Attendant: Oh yes. There's a long and extensive training course.

Person: *(Surprised.)* There is?

Attendant: Oh yes. It's quite rigorous.

Person: Imagine that.

Attendant: You have to be a little bit of everything. Confidant, confessor, friend, stern taskmaster. Guide.

Person: I guess that would take time.

Attendant: My teachers were all quite strong and capable. They really pushed me. I was grateful. I knew I had been chosen for something unique and exciting. Something significant. Didn't mind the hard work and sleepless nights.

Person: *(Surprised.)* Oh? You sleep?

Attendant: *(Smiles.)* When I can. *(Beat.)*

Person: Do you dream? *(Beat.)*

Attendant: No. *(Beat.)* That's not allowed. *(Beat.)*

Person: I'm sorry.

Attendant: No. It's something you get used to.

Person: *(Trying to be chummy.)* I know. I went years and years without being able to remember one single dream I had. It really scared the shit out of me when I was ten and . . .

Attendant: I know.

Person: I'm sorry.

Attendant: I said I know. I know that story. When you were ten.

Person: Oh. Yeah. I guess you would know everything. Every story.

Attendant: *(Apologetic.)* It's part of the training.

PERSON: I figured. *(A long uncomfortable silence.)*

ATTENDANT: *(Softly.)* Have you ever operated a reel-to-reel tape recorder before?

PERSON: No I haven't. I mean—no.

ATTENDANT: It's not hard.

PERSON: I, uhm, these things were pretty obsolete by the time I was old enough to afford stereo equipment, you know, I got into cassettes, and, later, CDs, but never one of these jobbies.

ATTENDANT: It's not hard. *(Demonstrates.)* On here. Off here. Play. Pause. Rewind.

PERSON: *(Surprised.)* Rewind?

ATTENDANT: In some cases the quality of the recording is so poor . . . you'll want to rewind it until you understand.

PERSON: No fast forward?

ATTENDANT: No.

PERSON: It looks like a pretty good one. Sturdy. Very strong.

ATTENDANT: They get a lot of use.

PERSON: I bet. *(Beat.)* Is this the only tape? *(The Attendant laughs out loud—then quickly stops.)*

ATTENDANT: No.

PERSON: I didn't think so.

ATTENDANT: There are many more.

PERSON: How many? A lot?

ATTENDANT: There are ten thousand boxes.

PERSON: *Ten* thousand?

ATTENDANT: I'm afraid so.

PERSON: Did I really . . .

ATTENDANT: I'm afraid you did.

PERSON: So . . . everyone goes into a room like this?

ATTENDANT: Exactly like this. There's no differentiation. Everyone's equal.

PERSON: For once.

ATTENDANT: What isn't equal, of course, is the . . . amount of time you spend here listening.

PERSON: Oh God.

ATTENDANT: *(Part of the training.)* Listening, just to yourself. To your voice.

PERSON: I know.

ATTENDANT: Listening, word by word, to every lie you ever told while you were alive.

PERSON: Oh God!

ATTENDANT: Every ugly lie to every person, every single time, every betrayal, every lying thought, every time you lied to yourself, deep in your mind, we were listening, we were recording, and it's all in these tapes, ten thousand boxes of them, in your own words, one lie after the next, over and over, until we're finished. So the amount of time varies. The amount of time you spend here all depends on how many lies you told. How many boxes of tape we have to get through together.

PERSON: *(Almost in tears.)* I'm sorry . . .

ATTENDANT: Too late.

PERSON: I said I'm sorry! I said I'm sorry! I said it a million times! What happened to forgiveness? I don't want to be here! I don't want this! I don't want to listen! I don't want to hear myself! I didn't mean to say the things that I said! I don't want to listen!

ATTENDANT: Yes, well. Neither did we. Neither did we. *(The Attendant looks sadly at the Person. The Attendant turns on the tape recorder. The Attendant hits the Play button, the reels spin slowly, and the tape starts snaking its way through the machine. Silence. The Attendant leaves the room, leaving the Person all alone. The Person nervously pours a glass of water, accidentally spilling water on the floor. From the depths of the machine comes a long-forgotten voice.)*

WOMAN'S VOICE: "Where have you been? Do you know I've been looking all over? Jesus Christ! I went to Manny's! I went to the pharmacy! The school! I even called the police! Look at me, Jesus Christ, I'm shaking! Now look at me—look at me and tell me where the hell you were! Tell me right now!" *(Silence. As the Person waits for the lying response, the lights fade to black.)*

* * *

BILLY GODA is a screenwriter and playwright who earned an MFA in playwriting at Columbia University, where he also studied screenwriting. While he was at Columbia, his play *Georgia Cowboy* was selected as his graduating class's production. Recent screenplays include *The Cretan Bull* and *Two-Arm Bandit. No Crime* was originally published in the *Best American Short Play Series 1998–1999.* Goda's recent works include *Final Appeal,* optioned by Avenue A Productions, and *Dust,* which he is currently writing.

No Crime

CHARACTERS

Cal Roberts, a good looking thirty-year-old man

Jim Abner, a big, egotistical fifty-year-old man

Cal is in Jim Abner's office. It is a large office with a great deal of room, light, and a nice view. Jim has his cowboy boots up on his desk.

JIM: A time comes in a man's life when fifteen minutes can change his future, change his life; these could be your fifteen minutes, Cal.

Pause as Jim takes a tin of Skoal chewing tobacco out of his desk, packs it down, and takes a dip. He will spit throughout the scene.

You're one of three finalists for this position. Now it all depends upon your interview. Whichever one of you has the best interview, that's the one I'll hire. (Jim *spits*). Nasty habit. I've already met with the other two, so it's up to you now, Cal. It's up to you. (Jim *spits.*) What do you have to say about that?

CAL: I look forward to the challenge . . .

JIM: Yeah, yeah, yeah, one of the others said that also. Every time we interview I get that answer: "looking forward to something." You must get it out of a book. Were you reading one of those "what to say in an interview" books?

CAL: I wasn't . . .

JIM: I hope not. We need original thinking here. This law firm's been around for fifty-two years, and we've become so damn successful by original thinking; not by memorizing some damn answers in a how to be interviewed book. Are you aware of the success this firm has accomplished?

CAL: I am very aware of that . . .

JIM: We've been involved in some of the most important criminal cases in this country, and you know what nearly every one of them have in common? (*Pause.*) I'm asking what do these cases have in common? You said you know about our firm . . .

CAL: That you've improved the situation of the defendant. You've either plea bargained for a much lesser charge or you've had your client acquitted.

JIM: That's good, very good. Dave told you to say that, didn't he? (*Laughing.*) That s.o.b.'s ruining all my fun. That question usually scares the pants off the applicant . . .

CAL: However, in 1988, the state versus Max Mainer, he received a life sentence. In 1994, Tony Giovano received three consecutive life sentences for multiple murders, and I wonder if you shouldn't have gone with the insanity plea . . .

JIM: All right, Cal, you've done your homework; I don't need a history lesson. (*Pause.*) There is only one thing that matters when a client walks through that door. Do you know what that is?

CAL: That he can pay the bill for our legal services.

JIM: (*Laughing.*) Well, yes that too. Make that two things that matter. If he can pay our bill and if there is at least a slight chance of our improving his situation. If there is not that possibility we will reject the case no matter how much money they offer. If you lose cases you lose your reputation. We do not take kindly to losing cases here.

CAL: I understand.

JIM: When we went down with the Giovano fiasco, two very prestigious clients walked out the door with his guilty verdict. (*Jim spits.*) How is Dave?

CAL: He's fine.

JIM: Dave speaks very highly of you.

CAL: Thank you.

JIM: I said Dave does, not me. I don't know you yet. That's one of the main reasons you're sitting in that chair right now—that crazy bastard's a very good friend of mine. At Harvard Law, he saved my butt more than once forcing me to study something other than women and beer. I never understood why he decided to become a professor, without a doubt he could have been one of the top litigates in the country. We could have been partners. (*Pause.*) I have numerous applications with excellent resumes, but you have an ace in your pocket by the name of Dave Horowitz. That recommendation gives you the rail position. What do you have to say about that?

CAL: I think Dave's an excellent judge of character.

JIM: (*Laughing.*) I'm sure you do. He says you'll do whatever it takes to improve your situation—that's the feeling he gets from you. That's an important feeling, very important. What did Dave teach you, Cal? You better not give me a course title.

CAL: How to shoot a gun. How to aim and hit a target.

JIM: Well that's good, but I'm not interviewing you for our rifle team.

CAL: Everyone has a price, that becomes, that is, a weakness, and it's up to me, as a lawyer, as a thinking man, to find out what that is, and then, if need be, to use it. Ready, aim, fire, so to speak.

Long pause.
Jim spits.

JIM: A client walks into your office, sits down in your leather arm chair, Cal, lights a cigar, and then tells you the truth of his case, let's say he cracked some lady on the head with a baseball bat splattering her brains all over the sidewalk . . . (*Jim spits.*) . . . and he played Mickey Mantle on her head because he was ordered to by his, let's call it a supervisor, and he did not question his supervisor's authority. What would you do? How would you feel, Cal? This client has confessed his guilt to you. He has confessed to this horrible, this heinous crime of an innocent lady's head being smashed open. What would you do in defending a client that was guilty, and your only hope of winning the case was by twisting the truth?

Long pause.

CAL: I cannot accurately answer that question.

JIM: Why not?

CAL: He is my client?

JIM: That's what I said . . .

CAL: He has already agreed to use our firm as his representation?

JIM: Correct . . .

CAL: He is not guilty.

JIM: Cal, he has confessed to you . . .

CAL: He is innocent . . .

JIM: He has told you about the murder . . .

CAL: He did not commit . . .

JIM: He bashed a lady's head in with a bat! Splattering her blood . . .

CAL: Blood on the sidewalk from someone else's bat . . .

JIM: Are you stupid, son?! What is wrong with you? I have told you, he has told you . . .

CAL: You say that my client is guilty, well I say that is impossible, Jim. It is impossible to say he is guilty. He is innocent until someone from the DA's office can persuade a jury of twelve to say he is not innocent. He is innocent until a verdict of guilty is returned. This is why I can not accurately answer your question; this is why your question becomes irrelevant. If he is my client then he is innocent, and it was someone else's bat. Who are the witnesses, Jim? Do you have eyewitnesses? Did he confess to the police? I don't think he confessed or he wouldn't be in my office. Only if he confessed to the police would I start with the idea of his guilt as a possibility. A possibility that I would evaluate and attempt to repudiate. Has our hypothetical client confessed to the police?

JIM: We'll say he has not.

CAL: Then he is not guilty. Then the only thing which can be proved is that some lady's head has been struck with a blunt object causing her death. What other evidence exists, Jim? Is there any other evidence?

Jim spits.

JIM: Your conscience.

CAL: My conscience is not on trial.

Pause.

JIM: Would you like a dip of tobacco? Green, Skoal, longcut. Dave's the idiot that started me dipping; he thinks he's a Jewish cowboy from New York. I always chew tobacco when I think—that's as long as no women are around.

CAL: Yes, thank you.

Jim passes the tin to Cal. Cal packs it down and places a dip in his mouth.

JIM: I spit in this bronze cup. It was a present from my daughter. See that: "World's Greatest Dad."

CAL: That's a nice spit cup, sir.

JIM: I never hired a lawyer that dips tobacco.

CAL: It helps me think.

JIM: So your hypothetical client is not guilty?

CAL: No, he isn't.

JIM: I like that answer. I like the logic. The logic of truth not existing until it's been proven again.

CAL: And it can be a very difficult thing to prove.

Pause.

Jim spits and then gives Cal an empty-cup to spit in.

JIM: My instincts seem to be the same as Dave's, and I go with my instincts, Cal. I'm betting you'll be a fine addition to this team.

CAL: Thank you. I'll do my best . . .

JIM: Is that another answer out of that damn book?

CAL: No, it's not.

JIM: When you start at this firm, you start on probation, so I can see if you have what it takes to succeed.

CAL: That's fine.

JIM: You'll do some leg work for me, gathering some background information. Let's see what questions you come up with, what possibilities you create. (Jim *spits.*) I ask everyone if they'd like a dip of tobacco. No one ever says yes. Most people think it's disgusting.

CAL: Maybe that's why we like it.

JIM: Yes, yes, maybe that is why. I want you to meet someone, Cal. (Jim *buzzes the secretary*.) Send him in.

A man enters the office.

Cal, this will be your first client. His name is John Stutts. He bashed an elderly lady's head in with a baseball bat.

Lights down.

* * *

Source: ©Corbis

ZORA NEALE HURSTON (1891–1960) was born in Notasulga, Alabama, and grew up in Eatonville, Florida, the first incorporated African-American town in the United States and the subject of much of her literary work. After overcoming various personal setbacks that uprooted her from one home to another, she attended Howard University, where she published her work in the school's journals and where she joined the theater group the Howard Players. After winning second prize in the *Opportunity* literary contest for her short story "Drenched in Light," Hurston moved to New York City in 1925. There, she attended Barnard College and met Langston Hughes, Countee Cullen, and other preeminent African-American writers who came to be known as the Harlem Renaissance writers. Despite continued personal setbacks, she went on to publish various plays, poems, short stories, folk tales, and the novels *Jonah's Gourd Vine* (1934); *Their Eyes Were Watching God* (1937); *Moses, Man of the Mountain* (1939); and *Seraph on the Suwannee* (1948). The following play was one of several unpublished dramatic works written by Hurston that surfaced in 1997 at the Library of Congress.

Poker! (1931)

Time—Present

Place—New York

CHARACTERS

Nunkie
Too-Sweet
Peckerwood*
Black Baby
Sack Daddy
Tush Hawg
Aunt Dilsey

SCENE

A shabby front room in a shotgun house.°

A door covered by dingy portieres° *upstage C. Small panel window in side Wall L. Plain centre table with chairs drawn up about it. Gaudy calendars on wall. Battered piano against wall R. Kerosene lamp with reflector against wall on either side of room.*

*"Peckerwood" and "Beckerwood" are used interchangeably in the original manuscript.

shotgun house: Narrow rectangular house most common in the South.

portieres: Curtains.

At rise of curtain Nunkie is at piano playing. . . . Others at table with small stacks of chips before each man. Tush Hawg is seated at table so that he faces audience. He is expertly riffing° *the cards. . . looks over his shoulder and speaks to Nunkie.*

TUSH HAWG: Come on here, Nunkie — and take a hand! You're holding up the game. You been woofin' round here about the poker you can play — now do it!

NUNKIE: Yeah, I plays poker. I plays the piano and Gawd knows I plays the devil.

BLACK BABY: Aw, you can be had! Come on and get in the game! My britches is cryin' for your money!

NUNKIE: Soon as I play the deck I'm comin' and take you alls money! Don' rush me.

Ace means the first time that I met you
Duece means there was nobody there but us two
Trey means the third party — Charlie was his name
Four spot means the fourth time you tried that same old game —
Five spot means five years you played me for a clown
Six spot means six feet of earth when the deal goes down
Now I'm holding the seven spot for each day of the week
Eight means eight hours that she Sheba-ed with your Sheik—
Nine spot means nine hours that I work hard every day—
Ten spot means tenth of every month I brought you home my pay—
The Jack is three-card Charlie who played me for a goat
The Queen, that's my pretty Mama, also trying to cut my throat—
The King stands for Sweet Papa Nunkie and he's goin' to wear the crown,
So be careful you all ain't broke when the deal goes down!

He laughs—X'es to table, bringing piano stool for seat.

TUSH HAWG: Aw now, brother, two dollars for your seat before you try to sit in this game.

NUNKIE: *Laughs sheepishly—puts money down—Tush Hawg pushes stack of chips toward him. Bus.*

I didn't put it down because I knew you all goin' to be puttin' it right back in my pocket.

PECKERWOOD: Aw, Y'all go ahead and play. (*to Tush Hawg*) Deal!

Tush Hawg beings to deal for draw poker. The game gets tense. Sack Daddy is first man at Tush's left—he throws back three cards and is dealt three more.

SACK DADDY: My luck sure is rotten! My gal must be cheatin' on me. I ain't had a pair since John Henry° had a hammer!

riffing: Skimming.

John Henry: Hero of a popular African-American folk ballad who competes against a steam drill and breaks more rock with his hammer but who consequently dies.

BLACK BABY: (*drawing three new cards*) You might be fooling the rest with the cryin' you're doin' but I'm squattin' for you! You're cryin' worse than cryin' Emma!

TOO-SWEET: (*studying his three new cards — Sings*)

When yo' cards gets lucky, oh Partner, you oughter be in a rollin' game. Get you foot offa my chair.

AUNT DILSEY: (*enters through portieres — stands and looks disapprovingly*) You all oughter be ashamed of yourself, gamblin' and carryin' on like this!

BLACK BABY: Aw, this ain't no harm, Aunt Dilsey! You go on back to bed and git your night's rest.

AUNT DILSEY: No harm! I know all about these no-harm sins! If you don't stop this card playin', all of you all goin' to die and go to Hell.

Shakes warning finger — exits through portieres. While she is talking the men have been hiding cards out of their hands and pulling aces out of sleeves and vest pockets and shoes. It is done quickly. One does not see the other do it.

NUNKIE: (*shoving a chip forward*) A dollar!

SACK DADDY: Raise you two!

BLACK BABY: I don't like to strain with nobody but it's goin' to cost you five. Come on, you shag-nags!

TOO-SWEET: You all act like you're spuddin'![o] Bet some money! Put your money where your mouth is els my fist where yo mouf is.

TUSH HAWG: Twenty-five dollars to keep my company! Dog-gone, I'm spreadin' my knots!

SACK DADDY: And I bet you a fat man I'll take your money — I call you.

Turns up his cards — he has four aces and king.

TUSH HAWG: (*showing his cards*)

Youse a liar! I ain't dealt you no aces. Don't try to carry the Pam-Pam to me 'cause I'll gently chain-gang[o] for you!

SACK DADDY: Oh yeah! I ain't goin' to fit no jail for you and nobody else. I'm to get me a green club and season it over your head. Then I'll give my case to Miss Bush and let Mother Green stand my bond! I got deal them aces!

NUNKIE: That's a lie! Both of you is lyin'! Lyin' like the cross-ties[o] from New York to Key West! How can you all hold aces when I got *four*? Somebody is goin' to West hell before midnight!

---

spuddin': Betting with small change.

chain-gang: Group of convicts chained together to perform outside work.

cross-ties: beams connecting the rails of a railroad.

PECKERWOOD: Don't you woof at Tush Hawg. If you do I'm goin' to bust hell wide open with a man!

BLACK BABY: (*pulls out razor—bus.*) My chop-axe tells me I got the only clean aces they is on this table! Before I'll leave you all rob me outa my money, I'm goin' to die it off!

TOO-SWEET: I promised the devil one man and I'm goin' to give him five!

Draws gun.

TUSH HAWG: Don't draw your bosom on me! God sent me a pistol and I'm goin' to send him a man!

Fires. Bus. for all.

AUNT DILSEY: (*enters after shooting bus. Stands. Bus. Drops to chair.*)
They wouldn't lissen — (*looks men over — bus.*) It sure is goin' to be a whole lot tougher in hell now!

CURTAIN

Reading and Reacting

1. Do you think any of the characters in the six plays in this chapter are fully developed, or do you see most (or all) of them as stereotypes? Given the limits of its form, can a ten-minute play ever really develop a character?
2. Most of the plays in this chapter have only one or two characters. Should any additional parts have been written for these plays?
3. The play *Tape* was written for two actors of either gender. Could the roles in the other plays in this chapter also be portrayed by actors of either gender? By actors of any age? Of any race?
4. Identify the central conflict in each play. What do you see as the **climax,** or highest point of tension, in each? Where does the climax generally occur in these plays?
5. Each play in this chapter has a single setting, and each of these settings is described only minimally. Do any settings seem to require more detailed descriptions? If you were going to expand each play, what additional settings might you show?
6. Considering the subject matter of each of the plays in this chapter, what kinds of topics seem to be most appropriate for ten-minute plays? Why do you think this is so? What kinds of topics would *not* be suitable for ten-minute plays?
7. The Web site *10-Minute-Plays.com,* whose slogan is "High-octane drama for a fast-food nation," summarizes the structure of a ten-minute play as follows:

   Pages 1 to 2: Set up the world of your main character.
   Pages 2 to 3: Something happens to throw your character's world out of balance.
   Pages 4 to 7: Your character struggles to restore order to his world.
   Page 8: Just when your character is about to restore order, something happens to complicate matters.
   Pages 9 to 10: Your character either succeeds or fails in his attempt to restore order.

   Although the plays in this chapter are not all ten pages long, do they nevertheless conform to the general structure outlined above?

WRITING SUGGESTIONS: Ten-Minute Plays

1. Assume you are a director writing notes for an actor who is to play a role in one of this chapter's plays. Write a character sketch in which you outline the character's background and explain his or her emotions, actions, conflicts, and motivation.
2. Choose a scene from one of the longer plays in this text that has a definite beginning, middle, and end. Rewrite this scene as a self-contained ten-minute play. (If you like, you can update the scene to the present time, change the characters' names or genders, and make other changes you see as necessary.)
3. Write an original ten-minute play for two characters.

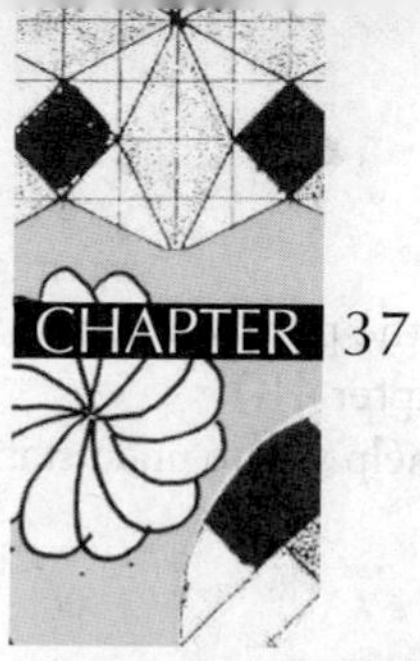

READING AND WRITING ABOUT DRAMA

Reading Drama

When you read a play, you will notice features it shares with works of fiction—for instance, the use of language and symbols, the interaction among characters, and the development of a theme or themes. In addition, you will notice features that distinguish it from fiction—for example, the presence of stage directions and the division of the play into acts and scenes.

The following guidelines, designed to help you explore works of dramatic literature, focus on issues that are examined in depth in chapters to come:

- *Trace the play's* ***plot.*** What conflicts are present? Where does the rising action reach a climax? Where does the falling action begin? What techniques move the action along? (See Chapter 38.)
- *Analyze the play's* ***characters.*** Who are the central characters? What are their most distinctive traits? How do you learn about their personalities, backgrounds, appearances, and strengths and weaknesses? (See Chapter 39.)
- *Consider how the characters interact with one another.* Do the characters change and grow in response to the play's events, or do they remain essentially unchanged? (See Chapter 39.)
- *Examine the play's* ***language.*** How does **dialogue** reveal characters' emotions, conflicts, opinions, and motivations? (See Chapter 39.)
- *Look for* ***soliloquies*** *or* ***asides.*** What do they contribute to your knowledge of the play's characters and events? (See Chapter 39.)
- *Read the play's* ***stage directions.*** What do you learn from the descriptions of the characters, including their dress, gestures, and facial expressions? (See Chapter 39.) What information do you gain from studying the playwright's descriptions of the play's setting? Do the stage directions include information about lighting, props, music, or sound effects? (See Chapter 40.)
- *Consider the play's* ***staging.*** Where and when does the action take place? What techniques are used to convey a sense of time and place to the audience? (See Chapter 40.)

- *Try to identify the play's* **themes**. What main idea does the play communicate? What additional themes are explored? (See Chapter 41.)
- *Identify any* **symbols** *in the play*. How do these symbols help you to understand the play's themes? (See Chapter 41.)

Active Reading

As you read a play about which you plan to write, you follow the same process that guides you when you read any work of literature. You read actively, marking the text as you proceed. Then, you go on to select a topic and develop ideas about it, decide on a thesis, prepare an outline, and write and revise several drafts.

Kimberly Allison, a student in an Introduction to Literature course, was given the following assignment.

> Without consulting any outside sources, write a three- to five-page essay about any play in our literature anthology. You may focus on action, character, staging, or theme, or you may consider more than one of these elements.

Previewing

Kim decided to write her paper on Susan Glaspell's play *Trifles*, which begins on page 1319. She began by previewing *Trifles*, noting its brief length, its one-act structure, its list of characters, and its setting in John Wright's farmhouse. Kim noticed immediately that John Wright does not appear in the play, and his absence aroused her curiosity.

Highlighting and Annotating

As Kim read *Trifles*, she highlighted the dialogue and stage directions she thought she might later want to examine more closely, noted possible links among ideas, identified patterns of action and language, and jotted down her own observations and questions. She found herself especially interested in the female and male characters' different reactions to the objects discovered in the house and in the interaction between the women and the men.

The following highlighted and annotated passage illustrates some of her responses to the play.

The men laugh; the women looked abashed. — Why do the men and women react so differently?

COUNTY ATTORNEY: (*rubbing his hands over the stove*) Frank's fire didn't do much up there, did it? Well, let's go out to the barn and get that cleared up.

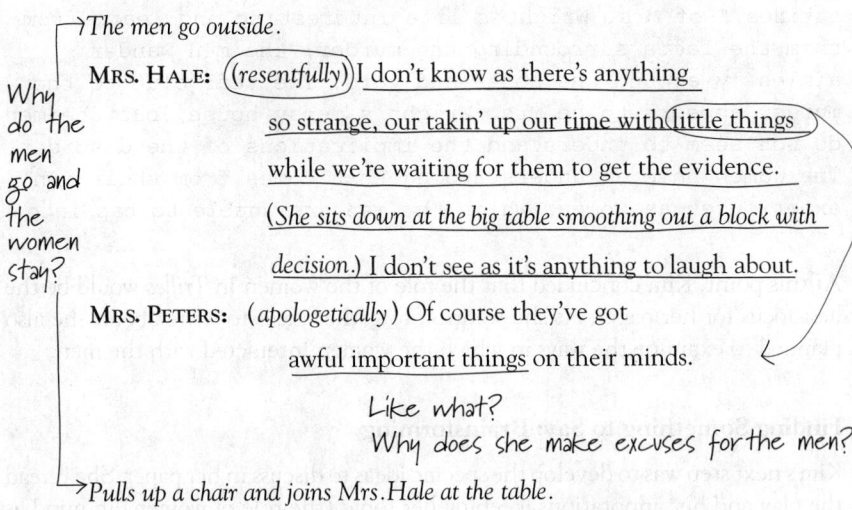

The men go outside.

Mrs. Hale: *(resentfully)* I don't know as there's anything so strange, our takin' up our time with little things while we're waiting for them to get the evidence. (*She sits down at the big table smoothing out a block with decision.*) I don't see as it's anything to laugh about.

Mrs. Peters: *(apologetically)* Of course they've got awful important things on their minds.

Pulls up a chair and joins Mrs. Hale at the table.

Why do the men go and the women stay?

Like what?
Why does she make excuses for the men?

Kim's highlighting and annotations of the entire play — most of which, like those above, focused on the play's characters — suggested some interesting possibilities for her essay.

Writing about Drama

Planning an Essay

Even after Kim decided to write about the play's characters, she knew she had to narrow her focus. Her notes suggested that gender roles in general, and the role of the women in particular, would make an interesting topic, so she decided to explore this idea further.

Choosing a Topic

To help her decide on a direction for her paper, Kim wrote the following entry in her journal.

What is the role of the women in this play? Although the two women have gone with their husbands to pick up some items for Mrs. Wright, they seem to be primarily interested in why Mrs. Wright would leave her house in such disarray. They find several objects that suggest that Mrs. Wright was lonely and that she was dominated by her husband. But these women are left on their own and seem to band together. Their guilt about not visiting Mrs. Wright also seems to connect them with the murder suspect. The women find the details, or "trifles," of Mrs. Wright's life interesting and learn from them the facts surrounding the murder; the men wander aimlessly around the house and yard. The real clue to the murder appears to be Mrs. Wright's messy house, but the men do not seem to understand the implications of the disorder. The women have an understanding that comes from their own experiences as women, which the men are unable to tap into.

At this point, Kim concluded that the role of the women in *Trifles* would be the best focus for her paper. As she went on to gather ideas to write about, she also planned to examine the ways in which the women interacted with the men.

Finding Something to Say: Brainstorming

Kim's next step was to develop the specific ideas to discuss in her paper. She reread the play and her annotations, keeping her topic (the role of women) in mind as she brainstormed.

Sheriff Peters says there is nothing in the kitchen but "kitchen stuff"; he thinks Mrs. Wright is a typical woman, worried about her preserves while imprisoned for murder.

Mrs. Hale feels animosity toward the men for laughing about the women's interest in the quilt; she regrets not visiting Mrs. Wright; she feels sorry for Mrs. Wright because she had no children.

Mr. Henderson eventually sides with the other two men, claiming that women's worries are "trifles."

Mr. Hale mentions Mr. Wright's stinginess; he seems to know Mr. Wright best.

Men think women are shallow and worry only about trifles.

Women empathize with Mrs. Wright because they understand how she was treated.

Mrs. Peters (wife of Sheriff) empathizes with Mrs. Wright's loss of bird; notes that keeping house was Mrs. Wright's duty.

Mrs. Wright seems trapped in the house; loses control after her bird is killed.

John Wright strips wife of her identity; controls her every move; stops her from singing, which she enjoys; kills canary.

Mr. Wright

Mrs. Wrig

When she reread her notes, the first thing Kim noticed was that the women and men have two entirely different attitudes about women's lives and concerns: the men think their own work is much more important than that of the women, which they see as trivial; the women realize they are not much different from Mrs. Wright. Now, Kim saw that in order to discuss the role of women in the play, she first had to define that role in relation to the role of the men.

Seeing Connections: Listing

At this point, Kim decided that listing ideas under the heads *Men* and *Women* could help her clarify the differences between men's and women's roles.

Men	Women
Work outside the home	Make preserves
Make decisions about financial expenditures	Clean house
Think women should do just housework	Make quilts
Create and enforce law	Raise children
Dictate wives' actions	Go to ladies' clubs for socializing
Have separate identities and power	Follow laws that men create
Act in ways that are accepted by society	Subordinate their desires to their husbands'
	Act defiantly to break boundaries set by social role

Making these two lists enabled Kim to confirm her idea that the men's and the women's roles are defined very differently in *Trifles*. In fact, the men and women seem to agree that they have different responsibilities, and both seem to understand and accept the fact that power is unevenly distributed.

Deciding on a Thesis

Kim's work clarified her understanding of the limited role women have in the society portrayed in *Trifles*. This, in turn, enabled her to develop the following **thesis statement.**

The central focus of *Trifles* is not on finding out who killed Mr. Wright, but on defining the limited, even subservient, role of women like Mrs. Wright.

Preparing an Outline

Guided by her thesis statement and the information she had collected in her notes, Kim made a scratch outline, arranging her supporting details in a logical order under appropriate headings.

```
Mrs. Hale and Mrs. Peters had limited roles
   —Subservient to husbands
   —Restricted to performing domestic chores
   —Confined to kitchen
   —Identified with Minnie Wright's loneliness
Minnie Wright had limited role
   —Did what husband told her to do
   —Had no link with outside world
   —Couldn't sing
   —Had no friends
   —Had no identity
```

Drafting an Essay

Following her tentative thesis and her scratch outline, Kim wrote the following first draft of her essay. Before she began, she reviewed her notes and her highlighting of the play to look for details that would illustrate and support her generalizations about it.

first draft

The Women's Role in *Trifles*

Susan Glaspell's *Trifles* seems to focus on the murder of John Wright. Mr. Wright had little concern for his wife's opinions. Mr. Hale suggested that Minnie Wright was powerless against her husband, and Sheriff Henry Peters questioned whether Minnie was allowed to quilt her log cabin pattern. Perhaps, because Mr. Wright did not spend his money freely, he would have made Minnie knot the quilt because it cost less. Minnie was controlled by her husband. He forced her to perform repetitive domestic chores. The central focus of *Trifles* is not on finding out who killed Mr. Wright but on defining the limited, even subservient role of women like Mrs. Wright.

Mrs. Peters and Mrs. Hale were similar to Minnie. Mrs. Peters and Mrs. Hale also performed domestic chores and had to do what their husbands wanted them to do, and they too were confined to Mrs. Wright's kitchen. The kitchen was the focal point of the play. Mrs. Peters and Mrs. Hale remained confined to the kitchen while their husbands exercised their freedom to enter and exit the house at will. This mirrored Minnie's life because she stayed home while her husband went to work and into town. The two women discussed Minnie's isolation. Beginning to identify with Minnie's loneliness, Mrs. Peters and Mrs. Hale recognized that while they were busy in their own homes, they had, in fact, participated in isolating and confining Minnie.

Eventually, the women found that the kitchen held the clues to Mrs. Wright's loneliness and to the details of the murder. The two women discovered that Minnie's only connection to the outside world was her bird. Minnie too was a caged bird because she was kept from singing and communicating with others by her husband. And piecing together the evidence, the women came to believe that John Wright had broken the bird's neck.

At the same time, Mrs. Peters and Mrs. Hale discovered the connection between the dead canary and Minnie's situation, and they began to recognize that they had to band together in order to exert their strength against the men. They realized that Minnie's independence and identity were crushed by her husband and that their own husbands believed women's lives were trivial and unimportant. The revelation that Mrs. Peters and Mrs. Hale experienced encouraged them to commit an act as rebellious as the one that got Minnie in trouble: they concealed their discovery from their husbands and from the law.

Because Mrs. Hale and Mrs. Peters empathized with Minnie's situation, they suppressed the evidence they found and endured the men's insults. And in this way, the women attempted to break through the boundaries of their social roles, just as Minnie had done before them.

First Draft: Commentary

When Kim reread her first draft, she realized that she had gone beyond the scope of her tentative thesis statement and scratch outline, considering not just the women's subservient role but also the actions they take to break free of this role. She decided to revise her thesis statement to reflect this new emphasis — and then to expand her paper to develop this aspect of her revised thesis more fully.

Kim's peer review group made the general suggestion that she develop her paper further. In addition, they thought that her paper's sentences seemed choppy—many needed to be linked with transitional words and phrases — and that her introduction was unfocused.

When Kim met with her instructor to discuss her revision plans, he encouraged her to expand her paper's focus and to use quotations and specific examples to support her ideas. He also reminded her to use the present tense in her paper — not "Mrs. Peters and Mrs. Hale *were* similar to Minnie" but "Mrs. Peters and Mrs. Hale *are* similar to Minnie." (Only events that occurred *before* the time in which the play takes place — for example, the murder itself or Minnie's girlhood experiences — should be described in past tense.)

After meeting with her instructor, Kim made a new scratch outline to guide her as she continued to revise.

```
Subservient role of women
   —Minnie's husband didn't respect her opinion
   —Her husband didn't let her sing
   —Minnie could perform only domestic chores
Confinement of women in home
   —Mrs. Hale and Mrs. Peters are confined to kitchen
   —Minnie was lonely at home because she had no children
   —Minnie didn't belong to Ladies Aid
   —Minnie was a caged bird
Women's defiance
   —Mrs. Hale and Mrs. Peters solve "mystery"
   —They realize they must band together
   —They take action
   —They defy men's law
```

Revising and Editing an Essay

Before she wrote her next draft, Kim reviewed the suggestions she had recorded in meetings with classmates and with her instructor. Then, she incorporated this material, along with her own new ideas, into her second draft, which follows.

second draft

Confinement and Rebellion in *Trifles*

Susan Glaspell's play *Trifles* involves the solving of a murder. Two women, Mrs. Peters and Mrs. Hale, discover that Mrs. Wright, who remains in jail throughout the play, has indeed murdered her husband. Interestingly, the women make this discovery through the examination of evidence in Mrs. Wright's kitchen, which their husbands, Sheriff Henry Peters and farmer Lewis Hale, along with the county attorney, Mr. Henderson, dismiss as women's "trifles." The focus of *Trifles*, however, is not on the murder of John Wright but on the subservient role of women, the confinement of the wife in the home, and the desperate measures women must take to achieve autonomy.

The role of Minnie Wright becomes evident in the first few minutes of the play, when Mr. Hale declares, "I didn't know as what his wife wanted made much difference to John—" (1320). Minnie's powerlessness is further revealed when the women discuss how Mr. Wright forced her to give up the thing she loved—singing. Both of these observations suggest that Minnie's every action was controlled and stifled by her husband. She was not allowed to make decisions or be an individual; instead, she was expected only to perform domestic chores.

Doing domestic chores was the only part of life that Minnie was allowed to exert some power over, a condition that is shared by Mrs. Peters and Mrs. Hale, whom we assume work only in the home and whose behavior as wives is determined by their husbands.

The men are free to walk throughout the house and outside of it while the women are, not surprisingly, confined to the kitchen, just as Mrs. Wright had been confined to the house. Early in the play, Mrs. Hale refers to Minnie's isolation, saying she "kept so much to herself. She didn't even belong to the Ladies Aid" (1324). Mrs. Hale goes on to mention Mrs. Wright's lack of nice clothing, which further suggests her confinement in the home: if she never left her home, she wouldn't need to look nice, and why would she want to leave home if she had no nice clothes? Minnie's isolation is further revealed when Mrs. Hale mentions her lack of children: "Not having children makes less work—but it makes a quiet house, and Wright out to work all day, and no company when he did come in" (1326). Minnie's only connection to the outside world was her bird, which becomes the symbol of her confinement because she herself was a caged bird. In a sense, Mr. Wright strangled her, as he did the bird, by preventing her from talking to other people in the community. Unlike the men, Mrs. Peters and Mrs. Hale realize the connection between the dead canary and Minnie's situation as "*Their eyes meet*" and they share "*A look of growing comprehension, of horror*" (1327).

The comprehension that Mrs. Peters and Mrs. Hale experience urges them to rebel by concealing their discovery from their husbands and from the law. Mrs. Peters does concede that "the law is the law"

(1324), but she also seems to believe that because Mr. Wright treated his wife badly, treating her as a domestic slave and isolating her from the world, Minnie was justified in killing him. And Mrs. Peters knows that even if Minnie had been able to communicate the abuse she suffered, the law would not take the abuse into account because the men on the jury would not be sympathetic to a woman's complaints about how her husband treated her.

The dialogue in *Trifles* reveals a huge difference in how women and men view their experiences. From the opening of the play, the gulf between the men and women emerges, and as the play progresses, the polarization of the male and female characters becomes clearer. Once the men leave the kitchen to find what they consider to be significant criminal evidence, the men and women are divided physically as well as emotionally. The men create their own community, as do the women. With the women alone in the kitchen, the focus of the dialogue is on the female experience. The women discuss the preserves, the quilt, and the disarray in the kitchen, emphasizing that Mrs. Wright would not have left her home in disorder unless she had been distracted by some more pressing situation.

Minnie Wright seems to have accepted her servitude voluntarily, making work in the home her main interest. But the men trivialize Mrs. Wright's and other women's significance when they criticize her role as a homemaker. The county attorney condemns her, sarcastically observing, "I shouldn't say she had the homemaking instinct" (1322). Minnie attempted to keep her home clean and do her chores, but the cold exploded her preserves, and her husband dirtied the towels. What caused Minnie to neglect her chores is something of great importance: her longing for independence and freedom from the servitude she once accepted voluntarily.

What makes this play most interesting is that Mrs. Hale and Mrs. Peters come to realize that they too have volunteered to be subservient to their husbands. They understand that their husbands will trivialize their discovery about the murder, as the men earlier trivialized their discussions of Minnie's daily tasks. Therefore, the women band together and conceal the information, breaking through their subservient roles as wives. And, in the end, they find their own independence and significance in society.

Second Draft: Commentary

When she read her second draft, Kim had mixed feelings about it. She thought it was an improvement over her first draft, primarily because she had expanded the focus of her discussion and added specific details and quotations to support her points. She also believed her essay was now clearer, with a more specific thesis statement and smoother transitions.

Still, Kim thought that the logic of her discussion was somewhat difficult to follow, and she thought clearer topic sentences might correct this problem by guiding readers more smoothly through her essay. She also thought her organization, which did not follow her revised scratch outline, was somewhat confusing. (For example, she discussed the women's subservient role in two different parts of her essay—paragraphs 2 and 7.) In addition, Kim thought her third paragraph could be developed further, and she believed her essay needed additional supporting details and quotations throughout. After rereading her notes, she wrote her final draft, which appears on the following pages.

Allison 1

Kimberly Allison

Professor Johnson

English 1013

3 March 2008

Desperate Measures: Acts of Defiance in *Trifles*

Susan Glaspell wrote her best-known play, *Trifles*, in 1916, at a time when married women were beginning to challenge their socially defined roles, realizing that their identities as wives kept them in a subordinate position in society. Because women were demanding more autonomy, traditional institutions such as marriage, which confined women to the home and made them mere extensions of their husbands, were beginning to be reexamined.

Opening sentence identifies author and work.

Introduction places play in historical context.

Evidently touched by these concerns, Glaspell chose as her play's protagonist a married woman, Minnie Wright, who challenged society's expectations in a very extreme way: by murdering her husband. Minnie's defiant act has occurred before the action begins; during the play, two women, Mrs. Peters and Mrs. Hale, who accompany their husbands on an investigation of the murder scene, piece together the details of the situation surrounding the murder. As the events unfold, however, it becomes clear that the focus of *Trifles* is not on who killed John Wright but on the themes of the subordinate role of women, the confinement of the wife in the home, and the experiences all women share. With these themes, Glaspell shows her audience the desperate measures women had to take to achieve autonomy.

Thesis statement

Allison 2

Topic sentence identifies first point paper will discuss: women's subordinate role.

The subordinate role of women, particularly Minnie's role in her marriage, becomes evident in the first few minutes of the play, when Mr. Hale observes that the victim, John Wright, had little concern for his wife's opinions: "I didn't know as what his wife wanted made much difference to John—" (1320). Here Mr. Hale suggests that Mrs. Wright was powerless against the wishes of her husband. Indeed, as these characters imply, Mrs. Wright's every act and thought was controlled by her husband, who tried to break her spirit by forcing her to stay alone in the house, performing repetitive domestic chores. Mrs. Wright's only source of power in the household was her kitchen work, a situation that Mrs. Peters and Mrs. Hale understand because their own behavior is also determined by their husbands. Therefore, when Sheriff Peters makes fun of Minnie's concern about her preserves, saying, "Well, can you beat the women! Held for murder and worryin' about her preserves" (1322), he is, in a sense, criticizing all three of the women for worrying about domestic matters rather than about the murder that has been committed. Indeed, the sheriff's comment suggests that he assumes women's lives are trivial, an attitude that influences the thoughts and speech of all three men.

Topic sentence introduces second point paper will discuss: women's confinement in the home.

Mrs. Peters and Mrs. Hale are similar to Minnie Wright in another way as well: throughout the play, they are confined to the kitchen of the Wrights' house. As a result, the kitchen becomes the focal point of the play—and, ironically, the women find

Allison 3

that the kitchen holds the clues to Mrs. Wright's loneliness and to the details of the murder. Mrs. Peters and Mrs. Hale remain confined to the kitchen while their husbands enter and exit the house at will. This situation mirrors Minnie Wright's daily life, as she remained in the home while her husband went to work and into town. As they move about the kitchen, the two women discuss Minnie Wright's isolation: "Not having children makes less work—but it makes a quiet house, and Wright out to work all day, and no company when he did come in" (1326). Beginning to identify with Mrs. Wright's loneliness, Mrs. Peters and Mrs. Hale recognize that, busy in their own homes, they have participated in isolating and confining Minnie Wright. Mrs. Hale declares, "Oh, I wish I'd come over here once in a while! That was a crime! That was a crime! Who's going to punish that? . . . I might have known she needed help" (1329)!

Soon the two women discover that Mrs. Wright's only connection to the outside world was her bird, the symbol of her confinement; she herself was a caged bird who was kept from singing and communicating with others because of her husband. And piecing together the evidence—the disorderly kitchen, the misstitched quilt pieces, and the dead canary—the women come to believe that John Wright broke the bird's neck, just as he had broken his wife's spirit. At this point, Mrs. Peters and Mrs. Hale understand the connection between the dead canary and Minnie Wright's motivation. The stage directions describe the moment when the women become aware of the truth behind the

Transitional paragraph discusses women's observations and conclusions.

Allison 4

murder: *"Their eyes meet,"* and the women share *"A look of growing comprehension, of horror"* (1327).

Topic sentence introduces third point paper will discuss: experiences women share.

Through their observations and discussions in Mrs. Wright's kitchen, Mrs. Hale and Mrs. Peters come to understand the commonality of women's experiences. Mrs. Hale speaks for both of them when she says, "I know how things can be—for women. . . . We all go through the same things—it's all just a different kind of the same thing" (1329). And once the two women realize the experiences they share, they begin to recognize that they must join together in order to challenge their male-oriented society; although their experiences may seem trivial to the men, the "trifles" of their lives are significant to them. They realize that Minnie's independence and identity were crushed by her husband and that their own husbands also believe that women's lives are trivial and unimportant. This realization leads them to commit an act as defiant as the one that got Minnie into trouble: they conceal their discovery from their husbands and from the law.

Significantly, Mrs. Peters does acknowledge that "the law is the law" (1324), yet she still seems to believe that because Mr. Wright treated his wife badly, she is justified in killing him. They also realize, however, that for men the law is black and white and that an all-male jury will not take into account the extenuating circumstances that prompted Minnie Wright to kill her husband. And even if Mrs. Wright were allowed to communicate to the all-male court the psychological abuse she has suffered, the

Allison 5

law would undoubtedly view her experience as trivial because a woman who complained about how her husband treated her would be seen as ungrateful.

Nevertheless, because Mrs. Hale and Mrs. Peters empathize with Mrs. Wright's situation, they suppress the evidence they find, enduring their husbands' condescension rather than standing up to them. And through this desperate action, the women break through the boundaries of their social role, just as Minnie Wright has done. Although Mrs. Wright is imprisoned for her crime, she has freed herself; and although Mrs. Peters and Mrs. Hale conceal their knowledge, fearing the men will laugh at them, these women are really challenging society and, in this way, freeing themselves as well.

In *Trifles*, Susan Glaspell addresses many of the problems shared by early-twentieth-century women, including their subordinate status and their confinement in the home. In order to emphasize the pervasiveness of these problems and the desperate measures women had to take to break out of restrictive social roles, Glaspell does more than focus on the plight of a woman who has ended her isolation and loneliness by committing a heinous crime against society. By presenting characters who demonstrate the vast differences between male and female experience, she illustrates how men define the roles of women and how women must challenge these roles in search of their own significance in society and their eventual independence.

Conclusion places play in historical context.

Allison 6

Work Cited

Glaspell, Susan. *Trifles*. *Literature: Reading, Reacting, Writing*. Ed. Laurie G. Kirszner and Stephen R. Mandell. 7th ed. Boston: Wadsworth, 2010. 1319-30. Print.

Final Draft: Commentary

Kim made many changes in her final draft. Although her focus is much the same as it was in her previous draft, she expanded her paper considerably. Most important, she added a discussion of the commonality of women's experience in paragraph 6 and elsewhere, and this material helps to explain what motivates Mrs. Hale and Mrs. Peters to conceal evidence from their husbands.

As she expanded her essay, Kim added explanations, details, and quotations, taking care to provide accurate page numbers in parentheses after each quotation and to include a work-cited page. She also worked hard to make her topic sentences clearer, and she used information from her class notes to help her write a new introduction and conclusion that discussed the status of women at the time in which *Trifles* was written. Finally, she added a new title and revised her thesis statement again to emphasize the focus of her essay on the "desperate measures" all three women are driven to in response to their social situation.

CHAPTER 38

PLOT

Plot denotes the way events are arranged in a work of literature. Although the conventions of drama require that the plot of a play be presented somewhat differently from the plot of a short story, the same components of plot are present in both. Plot in a dramatic work, like plot in a short story, is shaped by conflicts that are revealed, intensified, and resolved through the characters' actions. (See Chapter 12 for a discussion of conflict.)

In this scene from the Provincetown Players' 1917 production of Susan Glaspell's *Trifles* (p. 1319), the three men discuss the crime while Mrs. Peters and Mrs. Hale look on.

Source: ©Billy Rose Theatre Collection, New York Public Library for the Performing Arts, Astor, Lenox & Tilden Foundations

Cast members from the 2008 television adaptation of Lorraine Hansberry's *A Raisin in the Sun* (p. 1331).
Source: ABC-TV/ The Kobal Collection /Alston, Kuaku

In this scene from Henrik Ibsen's *A Doll House* (p. 1402), Doctor Rank, Helmer, and Nora have just returned from the party; Nora is wearing her tarantella costume.

Source: ©T. Charles Erickson

Plot Structure

In 1863, the German critic Gustav Freytag devised a pyramid to represent a prototype for the plot of a dramatic work. According to Freytag, a play typically begins with **exposition,** which presents characters and setting and introduces the basic situation in which the characters are involved. Then, during the **rising action,** complications develop, conflicts emerge, suspense builds, and crises occur. The rising action culminates in a **climax,** a point at which the plot's tension peaks. Finally, during the **falling action,** the intensity subsides, eventually winding down to a **resolution,** or **denouement,** in which all loose ends are tied up.

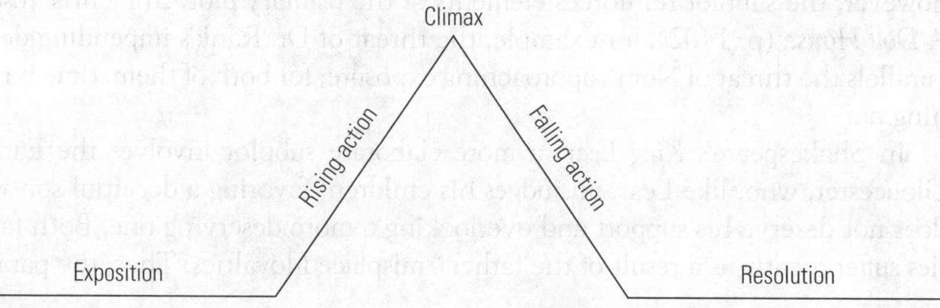

The familiar plot of a detective story follows Freytag's concept of plot: the exposition section includes the introduction of the detective and the explanation of the crime; the rising action develops as the investigation of the crime proceeds, with suspense increasing as the solution approaches; the high point of the action, the climax, comes with the revelation of the crime's solution; and the falling action presents the detective's explanation of the solution. The story concludes with a resolution that typically includes the capture of the criminal and the restoration of order.

The action of Susan Glaspell's one-act play *Trifles* (p. 1319), which in many ways resembles a detective story, can be diagrammed like this.

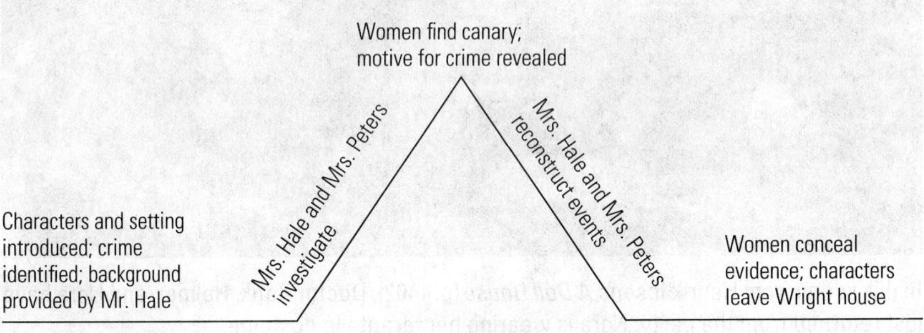
Women find canary;
motive for crime revealed
Characters and setting
introduced; crime
identified; background
provided by Mr. Hale
Mrs. Hale and Mrs. Peters
investigate
Mrs. Hale and Mrs. Peters
reconstruct events
Women conceal
evidence; characters
leave Wright house

Of course, the plot of a complex dramatic work rarely conforms to the neat pattern represented by Freytag's pyramid. For example, a play can lack exposition entirely. Because long stretches of exposition can be dull, a playwright may decide to arouse audience interest by moving directly into conflict, as Sophocles does in *Oedipus the King* (p. 1745) and as Milcha Sanchez-Scott does in *The Cuban Swimmer* (p. 1732). Similarly, because audiences tend to lose interest after the play's climax is reached, a playwright may choose to dispense with extended falling action. Thus, after Hamlet's death, the play ends quite abruptly, with no real resolution.

Plot and Subplot

While the main plot is developing, a parallel plot, called a **subplot,** may be developing alongside it. This structural device is common in the works of Shakespeare and in many other plays as well. The subplot's function may not immediately be clear, so at first it may seem to draw attention away from the main plot. Ultimately, however, the subplot reinforces elements of the primary plot. In Henrik Ibsen's *A Doll House* (p. 1402), for example, the threat of Dr. Rank's impending death parallels the threat of Nora's approaching exposure; for both of them, time is running out.

In Shakespeare's *King Lear*, a more elaborate subplot involves the Earl of Gloucester, who, like Lear, misjudges his children, favoring a deceitful son who does not deserve his support and overlooking a more deserving one. Both families suffer greatly as a result of the fathers' misplaced loyalties. Thus, the parallel plot places additional emphasis on Lear's poor judgment and magnifies the consequences of his misguided acts: both fathers, and all but one of the five children, are dead by the play's end. A subplot can also set up a contrast with the main plot — as it does in *Hamlet* (p. 1605), where Fortinbras acts decisively to avenge his father, an action that underscores Hamlet's hesitation and procrastination when faced with a similar challenge.

Plot Development

In a dramatic work, plot unfolds through **action:** what characters say and do. Generally, a play does not include a narrator. Instead, dialogue, stage directions, and various staging techniques work together to move the play's action along.

Exchanges of **dialogue** reveal what is happening — and, sometimes, indicate what happened in the past or suggest what will happen in the future. Characters can recount past events to other characters, announce an intention to take some action in the future, or summarize events that are occurring offstage. Thus, dialogue takes the place of formal narrative.

On the printed page, **stage directions** efficiently move readers from one location and time period to another by specifying entrances and exits and identifying the play's structural divisions — acts and scenes — and their accompanying changes of setting.

Staging techniques can also advance a play's action. For example, a change in **lighting** can shift the focus to another part of the stage — and thus to another place and time. An adjustment of **scenery** or **props** — for instance, a breakfast table, complete with morning paper, replacing a bedtime setting — can indicate that the action has moved forward in time, as can a change of costumes. **Music** can also move a play's action along, predicting excitement or doom or a romantic interlude — or a particular character's entrance.

In Tennessee Williams's *The Glass Menagerie* (p. 1961), unusual staging devices — such as words projected on a screen that preview words to be spoken by a character and visual images on screen that predict scenes to follow — were designed to help keep the action moving. For example, a screen image of blue roses leads into a scene in which Laura tells her mother how Jim gave her the nickname "Blue Roses." Other unconventional staging techniques are also used to advance the plot. For example, toward the end of scene 5, stage directions announce, "*The Dance-Hall Music Changes To A Tango That Has A Minor and Somewhat Ominous Tone,*" and a "music legend" repeated throughout the play serves as a signature in scenes focusing on Laura.

Occasionally, a play does have a formal narrator. In Thornton Wilder's play *Our Town* (1938), a character known as the Stage Manager functions as a narrator, not only describing the play's setting and introducing the characters to the audience but also soliciting questions from characters scattered around the audience, prompting characters, and interrupting dialogue. In *The Glass Menagerie*, the protagonist, Tom Wingfield, also serves as a narrator, summarizing what has happened and moving the audience on to the next scene, as in these lines that introduce scene 3: "After the fiasco at Rubicam's Business College, the idea of getting a gentleman caller for Laura began to play a more important part in Mother's calculations."

Flashbacks

Many plays — such as *The Glass Menagerie* and Arthur Miller's *Death of a Salesman* (p. 1531)— include **flashbacks,** which depict events that occurred before the play's main action. Dialogue can also summarize events that occurred earlier, thereby overcoming the limitations set by the time frame in which the play's action unfolds. Thus, Mr. Hale in *Trifles* tells the other characters how he discovered John Wright's murder, and Nora in *A Doll House* confides her secret past to her friend Kristine. As characters on stage are brought up to date, the audience is also given necessary information — facts that are essential to an understanding of the characters' motivation. (In less realistic dramas, characters can interrupt the action to deliver long monologues or soliloquies that fill in background details — or even address the audience directly, as Tom does in *The Glass Menagerie*.)

Foreshadowing

In addition to revealing past events, dialogue can **foreshadow,** or look ahead to, future action. In many cases, seemingly unimportant comments have significance that becomes clear as the play develops. For example, in act 3 of *A Doll House*, Torvald Helmer says to Kristine, "An exit should always be effective, Mrs. Linde, but that's what I can't get Nora to grasp." At the end of the play, Nora's exit is not only effective but also memorable.

Elements of staging can also suggest events to come. In *The Glass Menagerie*, the ever-present photograph of the absent father — who, Tom tells the audience in scene 1, may be seen as a symbol of "the long delayed but always expected something that we live for"—foreshadows Tom's own eventual escape. Finally, various bits of **stage business**— gestures or movements designed to attract the audience's attention — may also foreshadow future events. In *A Doll House*, Nora's sneaking forbidden macaroons seems at first to suggest her fear of her husband, but her actions actually foreshadow her eventual defiance of his authority.

✔ CHECKLIST Writing about Plot

- What happens in the play?
- What is the play's central conflict? How is it resolved? What other conflicts are present?
- What section of the play constitutes its rising action?

- Where does the play's climax occur?
- What crises can you identify?
- How is suspense created?
- What section of the play constitutes its falling action?
- Does the play contain a subplot? What is its purpose? How is it related to the main plot?
- How do characters' actions advance the play's plot?
- How does dialogue advance the play's plot?
- How do stage directions advance the play's plot?
- How do staging techniques advance the play's plot?
- Does the play include a narrator?
- Does the play include flashbacks? Foreshadowing? Does the play's dialogue contain summaries of past events or references to events in the future? How does the use of flashbacks or foreshadowing advance the play's plot?

Source: ©Getty Images

WARREN LEIGHT (1957–), a widely acclaimed writer and director, is a writer/producer for the television series *Law and Order: Criminal Intent*. His play *Side Man* (1998) was nominated for a Pulitzer Prize and won Broadway's 1999 Tony Award for Best Play. His other plays include *Glimmer, Glimmer and Shine* (2001) *and No Foreigners Beyond This Point* (2006). His screen credits include *Dear God* (1996) and *The Night We Never Met* (1993).

Cultural Context The right of the accused to a trial by jury is stated in the Sixth Amendment to the United States Constitution as well as in the constitutions of individual states. However, even though it is a civic duty and an important cultural mainstay, many Americans see jury duty as a burden because it requires them to take time off from their work and family responsibilities to serve. Although failing to appear for jury service is a crime, a study conducted by the American Judicature Society reported that, on any given day, an average of twenty percent of Americans summoned for jury duty do not appear. (That number drops to fewer than ten percent in some urban areas.) Some common excuses people use to try to get out of serving include obligations at school, work, or home; child or elder care; illness or disability; and bias (which may result from prior knowledge of the case or having a previous or ongoing relationship with someone involved in the case). In one 2007 criminal case in Miami, Florida, a prospective juror was dismissed after she told the judge that, if she served, her pet ferret would be left home alone.

Nine Ten (2001)

CHARACTERS

Leslie
John
Kearrie
Nick
Lyris

Jury Duty Grand Hall. Morning.

John, a slightly awkward bond trader, sits on a bench. Very neat, buttoned down. He reads a perfectly folded Wall Street Journal. *Lyris Touzet, a dancer, enters, almost spills her coffee on him.*

LYRIS: Is this Part B?

JOHN: What?

LYRIS: Part B, or not part B?

JOHN: Ah . . . that is the question.

LYRIS: Are you making fun of me?

JOHN: No no. Um, let me look at your . . . (*She hands him a slip of paper, he reads it.*) Where you are is where you're supposed to be.

She sits next to him. He needs a little more personal space than she does.

LYRIS: Why do they call us at eight-thirty? It's like, nine already, and they haven't said anything.

JOHN: They build in a grace period.

LYRIS: They what?

JOHN: They say eight-thirty so that most people get here by nine. And around nine ten they start calling names.

LYRIS: You knew this, and you came at eight-thirty?

JOHN: Eight actually.

LYRIS: Eight A.M.? You must hate your wife.

JOHN: I don't see her much. We both have to be at work at six.

LYRIS: You punch in at six?

JOHN: Well, I don't . . . punch in exactly. But, the desk opens at six so . . . .

LYRIS: Your desk opens?

JOHN: Sorry. Trading desk. Bonds. Euros, mostly. From my desk, I'm up so high, on a clear day, you can see Europe.

At a bench opposite, Nick Theron works the Times *crossword puzzle as Leslie Rudin arrives, pissed off and hyper.*

LESLIE: Part B?

NICK: Must be.

LYRIS: Have they called any —

NICK: Does it look like it? (*She looks to the court officer's desk, downstage left.*) Every once in a while this guy comes out and says we should wait. Which is . . . helpful.

LESLIE: I tried to get out of it on the phone and they said it was my third postponement and I had to come down here in person on the day of and that I wasn't going to get out anyway. And I finally get here — do they just change the names of the subway lines for spite lately?— and there's a line a mile long to get through security and they go through my purse like I'm a serial killer and it turns out if I want to smoke I'm going to have to go down and outside, and then wait on line again for them to check my bag. This just sucks.

NICK: I'm going to tell the judge that I'm a felon. He won't even question it. And he'll tell me felons can't serve. I'll act offended at this. And then he'll just let me go back to my life.

LESLIE: (*impressed*) That's good.

NICK: Racial profiling. A two-way street.

Over to John and Lyris.

LYRIS: My brother's in the same building. Security guard. You probably don't know him.

Kearrie, a tough businesswoman, enters, rushed.

KEARRIE: Part B?

LYRIS AND JOHN: Or not part B?

KEARRIE: It's too early for cute. (*They look at her, she means it.*) Have they started to give out postponements yet?

LYRIS: No one gets postponement.

KEARRIE: I'm on a flight tomorrow. (*Pulls something out of her bag.*) I've got a ticket.

John takes another look at her.

JOHN: Kearrie?

KEARRIE: What?

JOHN: It's me, John. . . .

KEARRIE: Right. John. That narrows it down.

JOHN: John McCormack. From Wharton.

Kearrie still doesn't place him.

LYRIS: (*to John*) You sure leave an impression.

JOHN: Story of my life. (*To Kearrie.*) Case study. Euro-economic unity.

KEARRIE: You got an A, I got a B plus. Even though we worked together.

JOHN: (*to Lyris*) You know about Irish Alzheimer's . . . you forget everything except your grudges.

KEARRIE: You went to Gold and Strauss when we graduated, right?

JOHN: Still there.

KEARRIE: (*grades him a loser*) You're kidding. You are not still at —

JOHN: Just the last ten years. Kearrie this is —

LYRIS: Lyris Touzet. Spiritual dancer. And healer.

JOHN: Lyris this is Kearrie Whitman. We went to Wharton together. Class of 91.

Lyris: I must have missed you two by like . . . one year.

Leslie and Nick. He has no hope of attending to his crossword puzzle. Leslie must talk or die.

Leslie: I'm out in the Hamptons. One week after Labor Day. Paradise found. The assholes are gone. The beaches are empty. The water is warm.

Nick: Sharks are hungry.

Leslie: No sharks in the Hamptons. Professional courtesy.

Nick: Touché.

Leslie: I think I'll stay another day. Then I remember . . . fuck me—eight-thirty summons. Drive in at midnight. Get stuck in traffic. The L.I.E. has got to be the only road in the world that has traffic jams at two A.M. By the time I get to my garage it's locked for the night. You ever try to find a space on the right side of the street at two A.M.?

Back to John and Lyris chatting. Kearrie plays with her Palm Pilot.

John: It's funny, I always wanted to be a spiritual dancer.

Lyris: You're making fun of me.

John: I'm not. . . . swear to god. But what is a—

Lyris: I heal people, through movement. Rhythm. Every person has their own . . . pulse. Below the surface, that—

Kearrie: Fuck me!

Lyris: I help them to get in touch with their inner—

Kearrie: (*Turns to them.*) Fuck me fuck me fuck . . .

John: What's hers?

Kearrie now rants in their direction, about her Palm Pilot.

Kearrie: Money on the table. I've got a watch list. It's programmed to signal me when there's a discrepancy between euro prices and ADRs. The spread is sitting there. Sitting there. It's blinking—buy me. Buy me. I try to buy and my damn signal fades. What's the point of fucking having a watch list if you can't follow up on it. This whole building should be wired. This city is . . . in the stone ages.

Lyris: (*to John*) Some people are harder cases than others.

Over to Nick and Leslie.

Nick: My neighborhood, downtown, they're *always* filming. Some sequel to a sequel to a disaster flick. *Mortal Danger Times Four*. Whatever. Which means like—

Leslie: They take every parking place. Big lights up—

Nick: —all night long.

Leslie: Idiots in walkie-talkies saying don't walk there. On your own street. Call the cops to complain, they don't care. No one in this city cares. The film crew can be, like, setting off concussion bombs, and nobody does anything.

Back to John and Lyris.

John: (*to Lyris*) I can't.

LYRIS: Everybody can move. Even you . . . Stand up.

He doesn't.

LYRIS: (*loud*) STAND UP!

Nick and Leslie hear this. Look over to John and Lyris. John doesn't want to attract attention, so he stands. John and Lyris now overlap with Nick and Leslie. Kearrie is in her own world.

LYRIS: (*to John*) Just start to, sway a little . . . from your hips.
LESLIE: (*to Nick*) That is sick the way he's flirting with her.

John sits back down.

JOHN: I can't.
LYRIS: Yes you can.
NICK: (*to Leslie*) How do you know it's his fault?
LESLIE: (*to Nick*) It's always the guy's fault. I date cops. Believe me. I know.
JOHN: (*to Lyris*) I don't like to. Move. I like things as they are. I've had the same job for ten years.
KEARRIE: (*on her cell phone, to her office*) Here? It's a fucking hellhole. What do you think? Ah-huh. Ah-huh. Ah-huh. Look—keep that on hold.
JOHN: (*to Lyris, oblivious to Kearrie*) Same office, same view. Married my junior high school sweetheart. We take the same train to work. We have the same lunch. Tuna. On rye. No mayo.
LYRIS: No mayo?
JOHN: It's not so bad, once you get used to it.
KEARRIE: (*into phone*) Yeah as soon as they call roll, I show my plane ticket . . . and I'm out of here.

Now, from downstage left, a court officer enters.

COURT OFFICER: Hello folks. Welcome to New York County Jury Duty. Before you all come up to me . . .
KEARRIE: Excuse me, I have a flight to—
NICK: I have a record—
COURT OFFICER: (*He drowns her out.*)—with your reasons for why you shouldn't be here, let me tell you: I've heard them all. On the bright side, most of you will get to go back to your life in two or three days.

Leslie, Nick, Kearrie, John, and Lyris all groan. Two days is eternity.

COURT OFFICER: And we are as happy to have you, as you are happy to be here. First things first. Check your summons, and be sure you're in the right place. This is Civil Court. Part B. 60 Centre Street. Today is Monday, September 10th . . . Two thousand and one.

Blackout.

* * *

Reading and Reacting

1. The exposition provided in the play's stage directions is quite minimal, giving few clues about setting. How do you picture the setting?
2. What basic information does the audience learn about each character? Given the revelation at the end of the play, why is this information important?
3. In the absence of a narrator, how do we learn about each character?
4. This play has a single setting and very little physical action. What moves the plot along?
5. What preconceived ideas do you think most people have about jury duty? How do the characters reinforce these ideas? How does the play use the audience's stereotypical assumptions about jury duty to advance the plot?
6. John complains that he is bored with his life, stuck in a routine. Given the play's ending, these complaints are deeply ironic. What other examples of irony can you identify in this play?
7. Foreshadowing is extremely important in *Nine Ten*. Consider how each of the following details foreshadows the play's ending: John works on a very high floor of his building; Lyris's brother is a security guard in John's building; Kearrie has a ticket for a flight the following day; Nick lives downtown; Leslie dates cops. What is the probable significance of each of these details?
8. At the beginning of the play, John explains the rules for jury duty, saying, "around nine ten they start calling names." What is the significance of this statement?
9. **JOURNAL ENTRY** Do you think the play's title gives away too much about the ending? Why or why not? What alternate titles might be appropriate, and why?
10. **CRITICAL PERSPECTIVE** In her article on literature about the 9/11 terrorist attacks, award-winning novelist Julia Glass tries to find common ground among writers who address her era's "most resounding moments":

    > Storytellers who dramatize their own era embrace its most resounding moments, moments when the spiritual compass by which we live (and write) has spun out of alignment. Realigning that compass, searching for a new magnetic north, is some of the best work fiction writers do. We seize something that everyone around us has taken for granted and, whether tenderly or violently, ironically or tragically, we upend it, dissect or shatter it. We write not about *you or them* or *then*. We write about *us*; we write about *now*. *Reader*, we say, *the view has changed; let me show you how*.

    In what sense does *Nine Ten* "upend," "dissect," or "shatter" common perceptions of the world as it was before 9/11?

Related Works: "55 Miles to the Gas Pump" (p. 190), "Deportation at Breakfast" (p. 229), "Bullet in the Brain" (p. 608), "Try to Praise the Mutilated World" (p. 854), "The End and the Beginning" (p. 1071), "The Names" (p. 1139), *Trifles* (p. 1319)

SUSAN GLASPELL (1882–1948) was born in Davenport, Iowa, and graduated from Drake University in 1899. First a reporter and then a freelance writer, she lived in Chicago (where she was part of the Chicago Renaissance that included poet Carl Sandburg and novelist Theodore Dreiser) and later in Greenwich Village. Her works include two plays in addition to *Trifles, The Verge* (1921) and *Alison's House* (1930), and several novels, including *Fidelity* (1915) and *The Morning Is Near Us* (1939). With her husband, George Cram Cook, she founded the Provincetown Players, which became the staging ground for innovative plays by Eugene O'Neill, among others.

Glaspell herself wrote plays for the Provincetown Players, beginning with *Trifles,* which she created for the 1916 season although she had never previously written a drama. The play opened on August 8, 1916, with Glaspell and her husband in the cast. Glaspell said she wrote *Trifles* in one afternoon, sitting in the empty theater and looking at the bare stage: "After a time, the stage became a kitchen — a kitchen there all by itself." She remembered a murder trial she had covered in Iowa in her days as a reporter, and the story began to play itself out on the stage as she gazed. Throughout her revisions, she said, she returned to look at the stage to see whether the events she was recording came to life on it. Although Glaspell later rewrote *Trifles* as a short story called "A Jury of Her Peers," the play remains her most successful and memorable work.

Cultural Context One of the main themes of this play is the contrast between the sexes in terms of their roles, rights, and responsibilities. In 1916, when *Trifles* was first produced, women were not allowed to serve on juries in most states. This circumstance was in accordance with other rights denied to women, including the right to vote, which was not ratified in all states until 1920. Unable to participate in the most basic civic functions, women largely discussed politics only among themselves and were relegated to positions of lesser status in their personal and professional lives.

Trifles (1916)

CHARACTERS

George Henderson, *county attorney*
Henry Peters, *sheriff*
Lewis Hale, *a neighboring farmer*
Mrs. Peters
Mrs. Hale

SCENE

The kitchen in the now abandoned farmhouse of John Wright, a gloomy kitchen, and left without having been put in order — unwashed pans under the sink, a loaf of bread outside the breadbox, a dish towel on the table — other signs of incompleted work. At the rear the outer door opens and the Sheriff comes in followed by the County Attorney and Hale. The Sheriff and Hale are men in middle life, the County Attorney is a young man; all are much bundled up and go at once to the stove. They are followed by two women — the Sheriff's wife first; she is a slight wiry woman, a thin nervous face. Mrs. Hale is larger and would ordinarily be called more comfortable looking, but she is disturbed now and looks fearfully about as she enters. The women have come in slowly, and stand close together near the door.

COUNTY ATTORNEY: *(rubbing his hands)* This feels good. Come up to the fire, ladies.

MRS. PETERS: *(after taking a step forward)* I'm not — cold.

SHERIFF: *(unbuttoning his overcoat and stepping away from the stove as if to mark the beginning of official business)* Now, Mr. Hale, before we move things about, you explain to Mr. Henderson just what you saw when you came here yesterday morning.

COUNTY ATTORNEY: By the way, has anything been moved? Are things just as you left them yesterday?

SHERIFF: *(looking about)* It's just the same. When it dropped below zero last night I thought I'd better send Frank out this morning to make a fire for us — no use getting pneumonia with a big case on, but I told him not to touch anything except the stove — and you know Frank.

COUNTY ATTORNEY: Somebody should have been left here yesterday.

SHERIFF: Oh — yesterday. When I had to send Frank to Morris Center for that man who went crazy — I want you to know I had my hands full yesterday. I knew you could get back from Omaha by today and as long as I went over everything here myself —

COUNTY ATTORNEY: Well, Mr. Hale, tell just what happened when you came here yesterday morning.

HALE: Harry and I had started to town with a load of potatoes. We came along the road from my place and as I got here I said, "I'm going to see if I can't get John Wright to go in with me on a party telephone." I spoke to Wright about it once before and he put me off, saying folks talked too much anyway, and all he asked was peace and quiet — I guess you know about how much he talked himself; but I thought maybe if I went to the house and talked about it before his wife, though I said to Harry that I didn't know as what his wife wanted made much difference to John —

COUNTY ATTORNEY: Let's talk about that later, Mr. Hale. I do want to talk about that, but tell now just what happened when you got to the house.

HALE: I didn't hear or see anything; I knocked at the door, and still it was all quiet inside. I knew they must be up, it was past eight o'clock. So I knocked again, and I thought I heard somebody say, "Come in." I wasn't sure, I'm not sure yet, but I opened the door — this door *(indicating the door by which the two women are still standing)* and there in that rocker — *(pointing to it)* sat Mrs. Wright.

They all look at the rocker.

COUNTY ATTORNEY: What — was she doing?

HALE: She was rockin' back and forth. She had her apron in her hand and was kind of — pleating it.

COUNTY ATTORNEY: And how did she — look?

HALE: Well, she looked queer.

COUNTY ATTORNEY: How do you mean — queer?

HALE: Well, as if she didn't know what she was going to do next. And kind of done up.

County Attorney: How did she seem to feel about your coming?

Hale: Why, I don't think she minded — one way or other. She didn't pay much attention. I said, "How do, Mrs. Wright, it's cold, ain't it?" And she said, "Is it?"— and went on kind of pleating at her apron. Well, I was surprised; she didn't ask me to come up to the stove, or to set down, but just sat there, not even looking at me, so I said, "I want to see John." And then she — laughed. I guess you would call it a laugh. I thought of Harry and the team outside, so I said a little sharp: "Can't I see John?" "No," she says, kind o' dull like. "Ain't he home?" says I. "Yes," says she, "he's home." "Then why can't I see him?" I asked her, out of patience. "'Cause he's dead," says she. *"Dead?"* says I. She just nodded her head, not getting a bit excited, but rockin' back and forth. "Why — where is he?" says I, not knowing what to say. She just pointed upstairs — like that. *(Himself pointing to the room above.)* I got up, with the idea of going up there. I walked from there to here — then I says, "Why, what did he die of?" "He died of a rope round his neck," says she, and just went on pleatin' at her apron. Well, I went out and called Harry. I thought I might — need help. We went upstairs and there he was lyin'—

County Attorney: I think I'd rather have you go into that upstairs, where you can point it all out. Just go on now with the rest of the story.

Hale: Well, my first thought was to get that rope off. It looked . . . *(stops, his face twitches)* . . . but Harry, he went up to him, and he said, "No, he's dead all right, and we'd better not touch anything." So we went back down stairs. She was still sitting that same way. "Has anybody been notified?" I asked. "No," says she, unconcerned. "Who did this, Mrs. Wright?" said Harry. He said it businesslike — and she stopped pleatin' of her apron. "I don't know," she says. "You don't *know?*" says Harry. "No," says she. "Weren't you sleepin' in the bed with him?" says Harry. "Yes," says she, "but I was on the inside." "Somebody slipped a rope round his neck and strangled him and you didn't wake up?" says Harry. "I didn't wake up," she said after him. We must 'a looked as if we didn't see how that could be, for after a minute she said, "I sleep sound." Harry was going to ask her more questions but I said maybe we ought to let her tell her story first to the coroner, or the sheriff, so Harry went fast as he could to Rivers' place, where there's a telephone.

County Attorney: And what did Mrs. Wright do when she knew that you had gone for the coroner?

Hale: She moved from that chair to this one over here *(pointing to a small chair in the corner)* and just sat there with her hands held together and looking down. I got a feeling that I ought to make some conversation, so I said I had come in to see if John wanted to put in a telephone, and at that she started to laugh, and then she stopped and looked at me — scared. *(The County Attorney, who has had his notebook out, makes a note.)* I dunno, maybe it wasn't scared. I wouldn't like to say it was. Soon Harry got back, and then Dr. Lloyd came, and you, Mr. Peters, and so I guess that's all I know that you don't.

COUNTY ATTORNEY: *(looking around)* I guess we'll go upstairs first — and then out to the barn and around there. *(To the Sheriff.)* You're convinced that there was nothing important here — nothing that would point to any motive.

SHERIFF: Nothing here but kitchen things.

The County Attorney, *after again looking around the kitchen, opens the door of a cupboard closet. He gets up on a chair and looks on a shelf. Pulls his hand away, sticky.*

COUNTY ATTORNEY: Here's a nice mess.

The women draw nearer.

MRS. PETERS: *(to the other woman)* Oh, her fruit; it did freeze. *(To the County Attorney.)* She worried about that when it turned so cold. She said the fire'd go out and her jars would break.

SHERIFF: Well, can you beat the women! Held for murder and worryin' about her preserves.

COUNTY ATTORNEY: I guess before we're through she may have something more serious than preserves to worry about.

HALE: Well, women are used to worrying over trifles.

The two women move a little closer together.

COUNTY ATTORNEY: *(with the gallantry of a young politician)* And yet, for all their worries, what would we do without the ladies? *(The women do not unbend. He goes to the sink, takes a dipperful of water from the pail and pouring it into a basin, washes his hands. Starts to wipe them on the roller towel, turns it for a cleaner place.)* Dirty towels! *(Kicks his foot against the pans under the sink.)* Not much of a housekeeper, would you say, ladies?

MRS. HALE: *(stiffly)* There's a great deal of work to be done on a farm.

COUNTY ATTORNEY: To be sure. And yet *(with a little bow to her)* I know there are some Dickson county farmhouses which do not have such roller towels.

He gives it a pull to expose its full length again.

MRS. HALE: Those towels get dirty awful quick. Men's hands aren't always as clean as they might be.

COUNTY ATTORNEY: Ah, loyal to your sex, I see. But you and Mrs. Wright were neighbors. I suppose you were friends, too.

MRS. HALE: *(shaking her head)* I've not seen much of her of late years. I've not been in this house — it's more than a year.

COUNTY ATTORNEY: And why was that? You didn't like her?

MRS. HALE: I liked her all well enough. Farmers' wives have their hands full, Mr. Henderson. And then —

COUNTY ATTORNEY: Yes — ?

MRS. HALE: *(looking about)* It never seemed a very cheerful place.

COUNTY ATTORNEY: No — it's not cheerful. I shouldn't say she had the homemaking instinct.

MRS. HALE: Well, I don't know as Wright had, either.

COUNTY ATTORNEY: You mean that they didn't get on very well?

MRS. HALE: No, I don't mean anything. But I don't think a place'd be any cheerfuller for John Wright's being in it.

COUNTY ATTORNEY: I'd like to talk more of that a little later. I want to get the lay of things upstairs now.

He goes to the left, where three steps lead to a stair door.

SHERIFF: I suppose anything Mrs. Peters does'll be all right. She was to take in some clothes for her, you know, and a few little things. We left in such a hurry yesterday.

COUNTY ATTORNEY: Yes, but I would like to see what you take, Mrs. Peters, and keep an eye out for anything that might be of use to us.

MRS. PETERS: Yes, Mr. Henderson.

The women listen to the men's steps on the stairs, then look about the kitchen.

MRS. HALE: I'd hate to have men coming into my kitchen, snooping around and criticizing.

She arranges the pans under sink which the County Attorney had shoved out of place.

MRS. PETERS: Of course it's no more than their duty.

MRS. HALE: Duty's all right, but I guess that deputy sheriff that came out to make the fire might have got a little of this on. *(Gives the roller towel a pull.)* Wish I'd thought of that sooner. Seems mean to talk about her for not having things slicked up when she had to come away in such a hurry.

MRS. PETERS: *(who has gone to a small table in the left rear corner of the room, and lifted one end of a towel that covers a pan)* She had bread set.

Stands still.

MRS. HALE: *(eyes fixed on a loaf of bread beside the breadbox, which is on a low shelf at the other side of the room. Moves slowly toward it.)* She was going to put this in there. *(Picks up loaf, then abruptly drops it. In a manner of returning to familiar things.)* It's a shame about her fruit. I wonder if it's all gone. *(Gets up on the chair and looks.)* I think there's some here that's all right, Mrs. Peters. Yes — here; *(holding it toward the window)* this is cherries, too. *(Looking again.)* I declare I believe that's the only one. *(Gets down, bottle in her hand. Goes to the sink and wipes it off on the outside.)* She'll feel awful bad after all her hard work in the hot weather. I remember the afternoon I put up my cherries last summer.

She puts the bottle on the big kitchen table, center of the room. With a sigh, is about to sit down in the rocking-chair. Before she is seated realizes what chair it is; with a slow look at it, steps back. The chair which she has touched rocks back and forth.

MRS. PETERS: Well, I must get those things from the front room closet. *(She goes to the door at the right, but after looking into the other room, steps back.)* You coming with me, Mrs. Hale? You could help me carry them.

They go in the other room; reappear, Mrs. Peters carrying a dress and skirt, Mrs. Hale following with a pair of shoes.

MRS. PETERS: My, it's cold in there.

She puts the clothes on the big table, and hurries to the stove.

MRS. HALE: *(examining her skirt)* Wright was close. I think maybe that's why she kept so much to herself. She didn't even belong to the Ladies Aid. I suppose she felt she couldn't do her part, and then you don't enjoy things when you feel shabby. She used to wear pretty clothes and be lively, when she was Minnie Foster, one of the town girls singing in the choir. But that—oh, that was thirty years ago. This all you was to take in?

MRS. PETERS: She said she wanted an apron. Funny thing to want, for there isn't much to get you dirty in jail, goodness knows. But I suppose just to make her feel more natural. She said they was in the top drawer in this cupboard. Yes, here. And then her little shawl that always hung behind the door. *(Opens stair door and looks.)* Yes, here it is.

Quickly shuts door leading upstairs.

MRS. HALE: *(abruptly moving toward her)* Mrs. Peters?

MRS. PETERS: Yes, Mrs. Hale?

MRS. HALE: Do you think she did it?

MRS. PETERS: *(in a frightened voice)* Oh, I don't know.

MRS. HALE: Well, I don't think she did. Asking for an apron and her little shawl. Worrying about her fruit.

MRS. PETERS: *(starts to speak, glances up, where footsteps are heard in the room above. In a low voice.)* Mr. Peters says it looks bad for her. Mr. Henderson is awful sarcastic in a speech and he'll make fun of her sayin' she didn't wake up.

MRS. HALE: Well, I guess John Wright didn't wake when they was slipping that rope under his neck.

MRS. PETERS: No, it's strange. It must have been done awful crafty and still. They say it was such a—funny way to kill a man, rigging it all up like that.

MRS. HALE: That's just what Mr. Hale said. There was a gun in the house. He says that's what he can't understand.

MRS. PETERS: Mr. Henderson said coming out that what was needed for the case was a motive; something to show anger, or—sudden feeling.

MRS. HALE: *(who is standing by the table)* Well, I don't see any signs of anger around here. *(She puts her hand on the dish towel which lies on the table, stands looking down at table, one half of which is clean, the other half messy.)* It's wiped to here. *(Makes a move as if to finish work, then turns and looks at loaf of bread outside the breadbox. Drops towel. In that voice of coming back to familiar things.)* Wonder how they are finding things upstairs. I hope she had it a little more red-up° up there. You know, it seems kind of *sneaking*. Locking her up in town and then coming out here and trying to get her own house to turn against her!

MRS. PETERS: But Mrs. Hale, the law is the law.

---

red-up: Spruced-up (slang).

MRS. HALE: I s'pose 'tis. *(Unbuttoning her coat.)* Better loosen up your things, Mrs. Peters. You won't feel them when you go out.

Mrs. Peters takes off her fur tippet, goes to hang it on hook at back of room, stands looking at the under part of the small corner table.

MRS. PETERS: She was piecing a quilt.

She brings the large sewing basket and they look at the bright pieces.

MRS. HALE: It's log cabin pattern. Pretty, isn't it? I wonder if she was goin' to quilt it or just knot it?

Footsteps have been heard coming down the stairs. The Sheriff enters followed by Hale and the County Attorney.

SHERIFF: They wonder if she was going to quilt it or just knot it!

The men laugh; the women look abashed.

COUNTY ATTORNEY: *(rubbing his hands over the stove)* Frank's fire didn't do much up there, did it? Well, let's go out to the barn and get that cleared up.

The men go outside.

MRS. HALE: *(resentfully)* I don't know as there's anything so strange, our takin' up our time with little things while we're waiting for them to get the evidence. *(She sits down at the big table smoothing out a block with decision.)* I don't see as it's anything to laugh about.

MRS. PETERS: *(apologetically)* Of course they've got awful important things on their minds.

Pulls up a chair and joins Mrs. Hale at the table.

MRS. HALE: *(examining another block)* Mrs. Peters, look at this one. Here, this is the one she was working on, and look at the sewing! All the rest of it has been so nice and even. And look at this! It's all over the place! Why, it looks as if she didn't know what she was about!

After she has said this they look at each other, then start to glance back at the door. After an instant Mrs. Hale has pulled at a knot and ripped the sewing.

MRS. PETERS: Oh, what are you doing, Mrs. Hale?

MRS. HALE: *(mildly)* Just pulling out a stitch or two that's not sewed very good. *(Threading a needle.)* Bad sewing always made me fidgety.

MRS. PETERS: *(nervously)* I don't think we ought to touch things.

MRS. HALE: I'll just finish up this end. *(Suddenly stopping and leaning forward.)* Mrs. Peters?

MRS. PETERS: Yes, Mrs. Hale?

MRS. HALE: What do you suppose she was so nervous about?

MRS. PETERS: Oh—I don't know. I don't know as she was nervous. I sometimes sew awful queer when I'm just tired. *(Mrs. Hale starts to say something, looks at Mrs. Peters, then goes on sewing.)* Well, I must get these things wrapped up. They may be through sooner than we think. *(Putting apron and other things together.)* I wonder where I can find a piece of paper, and string.

MRS. HALE: In that cupboard, maybe.

MRS. PETERS: *(looking in cupboard)* Why, here's a birdcage. *(Holds it up.)* Did she have a bird, Mrs. Hale?

MRS. HALE: Why, I don't know whether she did or not — I've not been here for so long. There was a man around last year selling canaries cheap, but I don't know as she took one; maybe she did. She used to sing real pretty herself.

MRS. PETERS: *(glancing around)* Seems funny to think of a bird here. But she must have had one, or why would she have a cage? I wonder what happened to it.

MRS. HALE: I s'pose maybe the cat got it.

MRS. PETERS: No, she didn't have a cat. She's got that feeling some people have about cats — being afraid of them. My cat got in her room and she was real upset and asked me to take it out.

MRS. HALE: My sister Bessie was like that. Queer, ain't it?

MRS. PETERS: *(examining the cage)* Why, look at this door. It's broke. One hinge is pulled apart.

MRS. HALE: *(looking too)* Looks as if someone must have been rough with it.

MRS. PETERS: Why, yes.

She brings the cage forward and puts it on the table.

MRS. HALE: I wish if they're going to find any evidence they'd be about it. I don't like this place.

MRS. PETERS: But I'm awful glad you came with me, Mrs. Hale. It would be lonesome for me sitting here alone.

MRS. HALE: It would, wouldn't it? *(Dropping her sewing.)* But I tell you what I do wish, Mrs. Peters. I wish I had come over sometimes when *she* was here. I — *(looking around the room)* — wish I had.

MRS. PETERS: But of course you were awful busy, Mrs. Hale — your house and your children.

MRS. HALE: I could've come. I stayed away because it weren't cheerful — and that's why I ought to have come. I — I've never liked this place. Maybe because it's down in a hollow and you don't see the road. I dunno what it is but it's a lonesome place and always was. I wish I had come over to see Minnie Foster sometimes. I can see now —

Shakes her head.

MRS. PETERS: Well, you mustn't reproach yourself, Mrs. Hale. Somehow we just don't see how it is with other folks until — something comes up.

MRS. HALE: Not having children makes less work — but it makes a quiet house, and Wright out to work all day, and no company when he did come in. Did you know John Wright, Mrs. Peters?

Mrs. Peters: Not to know him; I've seen him in town. They say he was a good man.

Mrs. Hale: Yes — good; he didn't drink, and kept his word as well as most, I guess, and paid his debts. But he was a hard man, Mrs. Peters. Just to pass the time of day with him — *(Shivers.)* Like a raw wind that gets to the bone. *(Pauses, her eye falling on the cage.)* I should think she would 'a wanted a bird. But what do you suppose went with it?

Mrs. Peters: I don't know, unless it got sick and died.

She reaches over and swings the broken door, swings it again. Both women watch it.

Mrs. Hale: You weren't raised round here, were you? *(Mrs. Peters shakes her head.)* You didn't know — her?

Mrs. Peters: Not till they brought her yesterday.

Mrs. Hale: She — come to think of it, she was kind of like a bird herself — real sweet and pretty, but kind of timid and — fluttery. How — she — did — change. *(Silence; then as if struck by a happy thought and relieved to get back to everyday things.)* Tell you what, Mrs. Peters, why don't you take the quilt in with you? It might take up her mind.

Mrs. Peters: Why, I think that's a real nice idea, Mrs. Hale. There couldn't possibly be any objection to it, could there? Now, just what would I take? I wonder if her patches are in here — and her things.

They look in the sewing basket.

Mrs. Hale: Here's some red. I expect this has got sewing things in it. *(Brings out a fancy box.)* What a pretty box. Looks like something somebody would give you. Maybe her scissors are in here. *(Opens box. Suddenly puts her hand to her nose.)* Why — *(Mrs. Peters bends nearer, then turns her face away.)* There's something wrapped up in this piece of silk.

Mrs. Peters: Why, this isn't her scissors.

Mrs. Hale: *(lifting the silk)* Oh, Mrs. Peters — it's —

Mrs. Peters bends closer.

Mrs. Peters: It's the bird.

Mrs. Hale: *(jumping up)* But, Mrs. Peters — look at it! Its neck! Look at its neck! It's all — other side *to*.

Mrs. Peters: Somebody — wrung — its — neck.

Their eyes meet. A look of growing comprehension, of horror. Steps are heard outside. Mrs. Hale slips box under quilt pieces, and sinks into her chair. Enter Sheriff and County Attorney. Mrs. Peters rises.

County Attorney: *(as one turning from serious things to little pleasantries)* Well, ladies, have you decided whether she was going to quilt it or knot it?

Mrs. Peters: We think she was going to — knot it.

County Attorney: Well, that's interesting, I'm sure. *(Seeing the birdcage.)* Has the bird flown?

MRS. HALE: *(putting more quilt pieces over the box)* We think the — cat got it.
COUNTY ATTORNEY: *(preoccupied)* Is there a cat?

Mrs. Hale glances in a quick covert way at Mrs. Peters.

120 **MRS. PETERS:** Well, not *now*. They're superstitious, you know. They leave.
COUNTY ATTORNEY: *(to Sheriff Peters, continuing an interrupted conversation)* No sign at all of anyone having come from the outside. Their own rope. Now let's go up again and go over it piece by piece. *(They start upstairs.)* It would have to have been someone who knew just the —

Mrs. Peters sits down. The two women sit there not looking at one another, but as if peering into something and at the same time holding back. When they talk now it is in the manner of feeling their way over strange ground, as if afraid of what they are saying, but as if they can not help saying it.

MRS. HALE: She liked the bird. She was going to bury it in that pretty box.
MRS. PETERS: *(in a whisper)* When I was a girl — my kitten — there was a boy took a hatchet, and before my eyes — and before I could get there — *(Covers her face an instant.)* If they hadn't held me back I would have — *(catches herself, looks upstairs where steps are heard, falters weakly)* — hurt him.
MRS. HALE: *(with a slow look around her)* I wonder how it would seem never to have had any children around. *(Pause.)* No, Wright wouldn't like the bird — a thing that sang. She used to sing. He killed that, too.
125 **MRS. PETERS:** *(moving uneasily)* We don't know who killed the bird.
MRS. HALE: I knew John Wright.
MRS. PETERS: It was an awful thing was done in this house that night, Mrs. Hale. Killing a man while he slept, slipping a rope around his neck that choked the life out of him.
MRS. HALE: His neck. Choked the life out of him.

Her hand goes out and rests on the birdcage.

MRS. PETERS: *(with rising voice)* We don't know who killed him. We don't know.
130 **MRS. HALE:** *(her own feeling not interrupted)* If there'd been years and years of nothing, then a bird to sing to you, it would be awful — still, after the bird was still.
MRS. PETERS: *(something within her speaking)* I know what stillness is. When we homesteaded in Dakota, and my first baby died — after he was two years old, and me with no other then —
MRS. HALE: *(moving)* How soon do you suppose they'll be through, looking for the evidence?
MRS. PETERS: I know what stillness is. *(Pulling herself back.)* The law has got to punish crime, Mrs. Hale.
MRS. HALE: *(not as if answering that)* I wish you'd seen Minnie Foster when she wore a white dress with blue ribbons and stood up there in the choir and sang. *(A look around the room.)* Oh, I *wish* I'd come over here once in a while! That was a crime! That was a crime! Who's going to punish that?
135 **MRS. PETERS:** *(looking upstairs)* We mustn't — take on.

MRS. HALE: I might have known she needed help! I know how things can be — for women. I tell you, it's queer, Mrs. Peters. We live close together and we live far apart. We all go through the same things — it's all just a different kind of the same thing. *(Brushes her eyes; noticing the bottle of fruit, reaches out for it.)* If I was you I wouldn't tell her her fruit was gone. Tell her it *ain't*. Tell her it's all right. Take this in to prove it to her. She — she may never know whether it was broke or not.

MRS. PETERS: *(takes the bottle, looks about for something to wrap it in; takes petticoat from the clothes brought from the other room, very nervously begins winding this around the bottle. In a false voice)* My, it's a good thing the men couldn't hear us. Wouldn't they just laugh! Getting all stirred up over a little thing like a — dead canary. As if that could have anything to do with — with — wouldn't they *laugh!*

The men are heard coming down stairs.

MRS. HALE: *(under her breath)* Maybe they would — maybe they wouldn't.

COUNTY ATTORNEY: No, Peters, it's all perfectly clear except a reason for doing it. But you know juries when it comes to women. If there was some definite thing. Something to show — something to make a story about — a thing that would connect up with this strange way of doing it —

The women's eyes meet for an instant. Enter Hale from outer door.

HALE: Well, I've got the team around. Pretty cold out there.

COUNTY ATTORNEY: I'm going to stay here a while by myself. *(To the Sheriff.)* You can send Frank out for me, can't you? I want to go over everything. I'm not satisfied that we can't do better.

SHERIFF: Do you want to see what Mrs. Peters is going to take in?

The County Attorney goes to the table, picks up the apron, laughs.

COUNTY ATTORNEY: Oh, I guess they're not very dangerous things the ladies have picked out. *(Moves a few things about, disturbing the quilt pieces which cover the box. Steps back.)* No, Mrs. Peters doesn't need supervising. For that matter, a sheriff's wife is married to the law. Ever think of it that way, Mrs. Peters?

MRS. PETERS: Not — just that way.

SHERIFF: *(chuckling)* Married to the law. *(Moves toward the other room.)* I just want you to come in here a minute, George. We ought to take a look at these windows.

COUNTY ATTORNEY: *(scoffingly)* Oh, windows!

SHERIFF: We'll be right out, Mr. Hale.

Hale goes outside. The Sheriff follows the County Attorney into the other room. Then Mrs. Hale rises, hands tight together, looking intensely at Mrs. Peters, whose eyes make a slow turn, finally meeting Mrs. Hale's. A moment Mrs. Hale holds her, then her own eyes point the way to where the box is concealed. Suddenly Mrs. Peters throws back quilt pieces and tries to put the box in the bag she is wearing. It is too big. She opens box, starts to take bird out, cannot touch it, goes to pieces, stands there helpless. Sound of a knob turning in the other room. Mrs. Hale snatches the box and puts it in the pocket of her big coat. Enter County Attorney and Sheriff.

COUNTY ATTORNEY: *(facetiously)* Well, Henry, at least we found out that she was not going to quilt it. She was going to—what is it you call it, ladies?

MRS. HALE: *(her hand against her pocket)* We call it—knot it, Mr. Henderson.

Reading and Reacting

1. What key events have occurred before the start of the play? Why do you suppose these events are not presented in the play itself?
2. What are the "trifles" to which the title refers? How do these "trifles" advance the play's plot?
3. Glaspell's short story version of *Trifles* is called "A Jury of Her Peers." Who are Mrs. Wright's peers? What do you suppose the verdict would be if she were tried for her crime in 1916, when only men were permitted to serve on juries? If the trial were held today, do you think a jury might reach a different verdict? What would your own verdict be? Do you think Mrs. Hale and Mrs. Peters do the right thing by concealing the evidence?
4. *Trifles* is a one-act play, and all its action occurs in the Wrights' kitchen. What do you see as the advantages and disadvantages of this confined setting?
5. All background information about Mrs. Wright is provided by Mrs. Hale. Do you consider her to be a reliable source of information? Why or why not?
6. Mr. Hale's summary of his conversation with Mrs. Wright is the reader's only chance to hear her version of events. How might the play be different if Mrs. Wright appeared as a character?
7. How does each of the following events advance the play's action: the men's departure from the kitchen, the discovery of the quilt pieces, the discovery of the dead bird?
8. What assumptions about women do the male characters make? In what ways do the female characters support or challenge these assumptions?
9. **JOURNAL ENTRY** In what sense is the process of making a quilt an appropriate metaphor for the plot of *Trifles*?
10. **CRITICAL PERSPECTIVE** In *American Drama from the Colonial Period through World War I*, Gary A. Richardson says that in *Trifles*, Glaspell developed a new structure for her action:

> While action in the traditional sense is minimal, Glaspell is nevertheless able to rivet attention on the two women, wed the audience to their perspective, and make a compelling case for the fairness of their actions. Existing on the margins of their society, Mrs. Peters and Mrs. Hale become emotional surrogates for the jailed Minnie Wright, effectively exonerating her action as "justifiable homicide."
>
> *Trifles* is carefully crafted to match Glaspell's subject matter — the action meanders, without a clearly delineated beginning, middle, or end. . . .

Exactly how does Glaspell "rivet attention on" Mrs. Hale and Mrs. Peters? In what sense is the play's "meandering" structure "carefully crafted to match Glaspell's subject matter"?

Related Works: "Persepolis" (p. 310), "I Stand Here Ironing" (p. 344), "The Yellow Wallpaper" (p. 459), "Everyday Use"(p. 517), "The Disappearance" (p. 695), "Eveline" (p. 719), "Harlem" (p. 924), "Daddy" (p. 936), "After great pain, a formal feeling comes—" (p. 1141), *A Doll House* (p. 1402), *The Stronger* (p. 1470)

Source: ©Bettmann/Corbis

LORRAINE HANSBERRY (1930–1965) was born in Chicago and was raised by politically active parents who surrounded themselves with some of the most influential and important African-American intellectuals of the time. Her inspiration for *A Raisin in the Sun* came from her own experiences: her father moved their family into the white, middle-class suburb of Woodlawn at a time when Chicago was still legally segregated. Her family frequently faced the threats of racist mobs, but as a result of her father's lawsuit against the city's housing practices, the Illinois Supreme Court declared the housing segregation laws unconstitutional. *A Raisin in the Sun,* the first play written by an African-American woman to be produced on Broadway, received the best play award from the New York Drama Critics' Circle. In 1961, a film version of the play, starring Sidney Poitier, Claudia McNeil, and Ruby Dee, received a special award at the Cannes Film Festival. A 2008 television film of this play starred Sean "P. Diddy" Combs as Walter and Audra McDonald as Ruth. Lorraine Hansberry died of cancer at the age of 34.

Cultural Context The action of this play is probably set around 1957, during a time of segregation and overt racism in the United States. Some particularly harmful manifestations of this racism were seen in the housing market, where unlawful practices kept African Americans from buying homes. In one such practice, *blockbusting,* realtors persuaded white homeowners to sell their homes by warning them that the presence of African Americans in their neighborhoods would increase the crime rate and decrease their property value. Another practice, known as *steering,* directed minorities to or away from particular neighborhoods. Finally, *redlining* was the practice of denying mortgage loans or home insurance to minorities buying in certain neighborhoods (regardless of their financial qualifications). These practices were in effect at the time this play was written and were not outlawed until the Fair Housing Amendments Act of 1988.

A Raisin in the Sun (1959)

CHARACTERS (in order of appearance)

Ruth Younger	**George Murchison**
Travis Younger	**Mrs. Johnson**
Walter Lee Younger, *brother*	**Karl Lindner**
Beneatha Younger	**Bobo**
Lena Younger, *Mama*	**Moving men**
Joseph Asagas	

The action of the play is set in Chicago's Southside, sometime between World War II and the present.

ACT 1

SCENE 1 (FRIDAY MORNING)

The Younger living room would be a comfortable and well-ordered room if it were not for a number of indestructible contradictions to this state of being. Its furnishings are typical and undistinguished and their primary feature now is that they have clearly had to accommodate the living of too many people for too many years — and they are tired. Still, we can see that at some time, a time probably no longer remembered by the family (except perhaps for Mama), the furnishings of this room were actually selected with care and love and even hope—and brought to this apartment and arranged with taste and pride.

That was a long time ago. Now the once loved pattern of the couch upholstery has to fight to show itself from under acres of crocheted doilies and couch covers which have themselves finally come to be more important than the upholstery. And here a table or a chair has been moved to disguise the worn places in the carpet, but the carpet has fought back by showing its weariness, with depressing uniformity, elsewhere on its surface.

Weariness has, in fact, won in this room. Everything has been polished, washed, sat on, used, scrubbed too often. All pretenses but living itself have long since vanished from the very atmosphere of this room.

Moreover, a section of this room, for it is not really a room unto itself, though the landlord's lease would make it seem so, slopes backward to provide a small kitchen area, where the family prepares the meals that are eaten in the living room proper, which must also serve as dining room. The single window that has been provided for these "two" rooms is located in this kitchen area. The sole natural light the family may enjoy in the course of a day is only that which fights its way through this little window.

At left, a door leads to a bedroom which is shared by Mama and her daughter, Beneatha. At right, opposite, is a second room (which in the beginning of the life of this apartment was probably a breakfast room) which serves as a bedroom for Walter and his wife, Ruth.

Time: Sometime between World War II and the present.

Place: Chicago's Southside.

At Rise: It is morning dark in the living room. Travis is asleep on the make-down bed at center. An alarm clock sounds from within the bedroom at right, and presently Ruth enters from that room and closes the door behind her. She crosses sleepily toward the window. As she passes her sleeping son she reaches down and shakes him a little. At the window she raises the shade and a dusky Southside morning light comes in feebly. She fills a pot with water and puts it on to boil. She calls to the boy, between yawns, in a slightly muffled voice.

Ruth is about thirty. We can see that she was a pretty girl, even exceptionally so, but now it is apparent that life has been little that she expected, and disappointment has already begun to hang in her face. In a few years, before thirty-five even, she will be known among her people as a "settled woman."

She crosses to her son and gives him a good, final, rousing shake.

RUTH: Come on now, boy, it's seven thirty! *(Her son sits up at last, in a stupor of sleepiness.)* I say hurry up, Travis! You ain't the only person in the world got to use a bathroom! *(The child, a sturdy, handsome little boy of ten or eleven, drags himself out of the bed and almost blindly takes his towels and "today's clothes" from drawers and a closet and goes out to the bathroom, which is in an outside hall and which is shared by another family or families on the same floor. Ruth crosses to the bedroom door at right and opens it and calls in to her husband.)* Walter Lee! . . . It's after seven thirty! Lemme see you do some waking up in there now! *(She waits.)* You better get up from there, man!

It's after seven thirty I tell you. *(She waits again.)* All right, you just go ahead and lay there and next thing you know Travis be finished and Mr. Johnson'll be in there and you'll be fussing and cussing round here like a madman! And be late too! *(She waits, at the end of patience.)* Walter Lee — it's time for you to GET UP!

She waits another second and then starts to go into the bedroom, but is apparently satisfied that her husband has begun to get up. She stops, pulls the door to, and returns to the kitchen area. She wipes her face with a moist cloth and runs her fingers through her sleep-disheveled hair in a vain effort and ties an apron around her housecoat. The bedroom door at right opens and her husband stands in the doorway in his pajamas, which are rumpled and mismated. He is a lean, intense young man in his middle thirties, inclined to quick nervous movements and erratic speech habits—and always in his voice there is a quality of indictment.

WALTER: Is he out yet?

RUTH: What you mean *out*? He ain't hardly got in there good yet.

WALTER: *(wandering in, still more oriented to sleep than to a new day)* Well, what was you doing all that yelling for if I can't even get in there yet? *(Stopping and thinking.)* Check coming today?

RUTH: They *said* Saturday and this is just Friday and I hopes to God you ain't going to get up here first thing this morning and start talking to me 'bout no money — 'cause I 'bout don't want to hear it.

WALTER: Something the matter with you this morning?

RUTH: No — I'm just sleepy as the devil. What kind of eggs you want?

WALTER: Not scrambled. *(Ruth starts to scramble eggs.)* Paper come? *(Ruth points impatiently to the rolled up* Tribune *on the table, and he gets it and spreads it out and vaguely reads the front page.)* Set off another bomb yesterday.

RUTH: *(maximum indifference)* Did they?

WALTER: *(looking up)* What's the matter with you?

RUTH: Ain't nothing the matter with me. And don't keep asking me that this morning.

WALTER: Ain't nobody bothering you. *(Reading the news of the day absently again.)* Say Colonel McCormick is sick.

RUTH: *(affecting tea-party interest)* Is he now? Poor thing.

WALTER: *(sighing and looking at his watch)* Oh, me *(He waits.)* Now what is that boy doing in that bathroom all this time? He just going to have to start getting up earlier. I can't be being late to work on account of him fooling around in there.

RUTH: *(turning on him)* Oh, no he ain't going to be getting up no earlier no such thing! It ain't his fault that he can't get to bed no earlier nights 'cause he got a bunch of crazy good-for-nothing clowns sitting up running their mouths in what is supposed to be his bedroom after ten o'clock at night.

WALTER: That's what you mad about, ain't it? The things I want to talk about with my friends just couldn't be important in your mind, could they?

He rises and finds a cigarette in her handbag on the table and crosses to the little window and looks out, smoking and deeply enjoying this first one.

RUTH: *(almost matter of factly, a complaint too automatic to deserve emphasis)* Why you always got to smoke before you eat in the morning?

WALTER: *(at the window)* Just look at 'em down there . . . Running and racing to work . . . *(He turns and faces his wife and watches her a moment at the stove, and then, suddenly)* You look young this morning, baby.

RUTH: *(indifferently)* Yeah?

WALTER: Just for a second — stirring them eggs. Just for a second it was — you looked real young again. *(He reaches for her, she crosses away. Then, drily.)* It's gone now — you look like yourself again!

RUTH: Man, if you don't shut up and leave me alone.

WALTER: *(looking out to the street again)* First thing a man ought to learn in life is not to make love to no colored woman first thing in the morning. You all some eeeevil people at eight o'clock in the morning.

Travis appears in the hall doorway, almost fully dressed and quite wide awake now, his towels and pajamas across his shoulders. He opens the door and signals for his father to make the bathroom in a hurry.

TRAVIS: *(watching the bathroom)* Daddy, come on!

Walter gets his bathroom utensils and flies out to the bathroom.

RUTH: Sit down and have your breakfast, Travis.

TRAVIS: Mama, this is Friday. *(Gleefully.)* Check coming tomorrow, huh?

RUTH: You get your mind off money and eat your breakfast.

TRAVIS: *(eating)* This is the morning we supposed to bring the fifty cents to school.

RUTH: Well, I ain't got no fifty cents this morning.

TRAVIS: Teacher say we have to.

RUTH: I don't care what teacher say. I ain't got it. Eat your breakfast, Travis.

TRAVIS: I *am* eating.

RUTH: Hush up now and just eat!

The boy gives her an exasperated look for her lack of understanding, and eats grudgingly.

TRAVIS: You think Grandmama would have it?

RUTH: No! And I want you to stop asking your grandmother for money, you hear me?

TRAVIS: *(outraged)* Gaaaleee! I don't ask her, she just gimme it sometimes!

RUTH: Travis Willard Younger — I got too much on me this morning to be —

TRAVIS: Maybe Daddy —

RUTH: *Travis!*

The boy hushes abruptly. They are both quiet and tense for several seconds.

TRAVIS: *(presently)* Could I maybe go carry some groceries in front of the supermarket for a little while after school then?

RUTH: Just hush, I said *(Travis jabs his spoon into his cereal bowl viciously, and rests his head in anger upon his fists.)* If you through eating, you can get over there and make up your bed.

The boy obeys stiffly and crosses the room, almost mechanically, to the bed and more or less folds the bedding into a heap, then angrily gets his books and cap.

TRAVIS: *(sulking and standing apart from her unnaturally)* I'm gone.

RUTH: *(looking up from the stove to inspect him automatically)* Come here. *(He crosses to her and she studies his head.)* If you don't take this comb and fix this here head, you better! *(Travis puts down his books with a great sign of oppression, and crosses to the mirror. His mother mutters under her breath about his "slubbornness.")* 'Bout to march out of here with that head looking just like chickens slept in it! I just don't know where you get your slubborn way . . . And get your jacket, too. Looks chilly out this morning.

TRAVIS: *(with conspicuously brushed hair and jacket)* I'm gone.

RUTH: Get carfare and milk money—*(Waving one finger.)*—and not a single penny for no caps, you hear me?

TRAVIS: *(with sullen politeness)* Yes'm.

He turns in outrage to leave. His mother watches after him as in his frustration he approaches the door almost comically. When she speaks to him, her voice has become a very gentle tease.

RUTH: *(mocking; as she thinks he would say it)* Oh, Mama makes me so mad sometimes, I don't know what to do! *(She waits and continues to his back as he stands stock-still in front of the door.)* I wouldn't kiss that woman goodbye for nothing in this world this morning! *(The boy finally turns around and rolls his eyes at her, knowing the mood has changed and he is vindicated, he does not, however, move toward her yet.)* Not for nothing in this world! *(She finally laughs aloud at him and holds out her arms to him and we see that it is a way between them, very old and practiced. He crosses to her and allows her to embrace him warmly but keeps his face fixed with masculine rigidity. She holds him back from her presently and looks at him and runs her fingers over the features of his face. With utter gentleness—.)* Now — whose little old angry man are you?

TRAVIS: *(the masculinity and gruffness start to fade at last)* Aw gaalee—Mama. . .

RUTH: *(mimicking)* Aw — gaaaaalleeeee, Mama! *(She pushes him, with rough playfulness and finality, toward the door.)* Get on out of here or you going to be late.

TRAVIS: *(in the face of love, new aggressiveness)* Mama, could I *please* go carry groceries?

RUTH: Honey, it's starting to get so cold evenings.

WALTER: *(coming in from the bathroom and drawing a make-believe gun from a make-believe holster and shooting at his son)* What is it he wants to do?

RUTH: Go carry groceries after school at the supermarket.

WALTER: Well, let him go . . .

TRAVIS: *(quickly, to the ally)* I *have* to — she won't gimme the fifty cents . . .

WALTER: *(to his wife only)* Why not?

RUTH: *(simply, and with flavor)* 'Cause we don't have it.

WALTER: *(to Ruth only)* What you tell the boy things like that for? *(Reaching down into his pants with a rather important gesture.)* Here, son—

He hands the boy the coin, but his eyes are directed to his wife's. Travis takes the money happily.

TRAVIS: Thanks, Daddy.

He starts out. Ruth watches both of them with murder in her eyes. Walter stands and stares back at her with defiance, and suddenly reaches into his pocket again on an afterthought.

WALTER: *(without even looking at his son, still staring hard at his wife)* In fact, here's another fifty cents . . . Buy yourself some fruit today — or take a taxicab to school or something!

TRAVIS: Whoopee—

He leaps up and clasps his father around the middle with his legs, and they face each other in mutual appreciation; slowly Walter Lee peeks around the boy to catch the violent rays from his wife's eyes and draws his head back as if shot.

WALTER: You better get down now—and get to school, man.

TRAVIS: *(at the door)* O.K. Good-bye.

He exits.

WALTER: *(after him, pointing with pride)* That's *my* boy. *(She looks at him in disgust and turns back to her work.)* You know what I was thinking 'bout in the bathroom this morning?

RUTH: No.

WALTER: How come you always try to be so pleasant!

RUTH: What is there to be pleasant 'bout!

WALTER: You want to know what I was thinking 'bout in the bathroom or not!

RUTH: I know what you thinking 'bout.

WALTER: *(ignoring her)* 'Bout what me and Willy Harris was talking about last night.

RUTH: *(immediately—a refrain)* Willy Harris is a good-for-nothing loudmouth.

WALTER: Anybody who talks to me has got to be a good-for-nothing loudmouth, ain't he? And what you know about who is just a good-for-nothing loudmouth? Charlie Atkins was just a "good-for-nothing loudmouth" too, wasn't he! When he wanted me to go in the dry-cleaning business with him. And now — he's grossing a hundred thousand a year. A hundred thousand dollars a year! You still call *him* a loudmouth!

RUTH: *(bitterly)* Oh, Walter Lee . . .

She folds her head on her arms over the table.

WALTER: *(rising and coming to her and standing over her)* You tired, ain't you? Tired of everything. Me, the boy, the way we live — this beat-up hole — everything. Ain't you? *(She doesn't look up, doesn't answer)* So tired — moaning and groaning all the time, but you wouldn't do nothing to help, would you? You couldn't be on my side that long for nothing, could you?

RUTH: Walter, please leave me alone.

WALTER: A man needs for a woman to back him up . . .

RUTH: Walter —

WALTER: Mama would listen to you. You know she listen to you more than she do me and Bennie. She think more of you. All you have to do is just sit down with her when you drinking your coffee one morning and talking 'bout things like you do and — *(He sits down beside her and demonstrates graphically what he thinks her methods and tone should be.)* — you just sip your coffee, see, and say easy like that you been thinking 'bout that deal Walter Lee is so interested in, 'bout the store and all, and sip some more coffee, like what you saying ain't really that important to you — And the next thing you know, she be listening good and asking you questions and when I come home — I can tell her the details. This ain't no fly-by-night proposition, baby. I mean we figured it out, me and Willy and Bobo.

RUTH: *(with a frown)* Bobo?

WALTER: Yeah. You see, this little liquor store we got in mind cost seventy-five thousand and we figured the initial investment on the place be 'bout thirty thousand, see. That be ten thousand each. Course, there's a couple of hundred you got to pay so's you don't spend your life just waiting for them clowns to let your license get approved —

RUTH: You mean graft?

WALTER: *(frowning impatiently)* Don't call it that. See there, that just goes to show you what women understand about the world. Baby, don't *nothing* happen for you in the world 'less you pay *somebody* off!

RUTH: Walter, leave me alone! *(She raises her head and stares at him vigorously — then says, more quietly.)* Eat your eggs, they gonna be cold.

WALTER: *(straightening up from her and looking off)* That's it. There you are. Man say to his woman: I got me a dream. His woman say: Eat your eggs. *(Sadly, but gaining in power.)* Man say: I got to take hold of this here world, baby I And a woman will say: Eat your eggs and go to work. *(Passionately now.)* Man say: I got to change my life, I'm choking to death, baby! And his woman say — *(In utter anguish as he brings his fists down on his thighs.)* — Your eggs is getting cold!

RUTH: *(softly)* Walter, that ain't none of our money.

WALTER: *(not listening at all or even looking at her)* This morning, I was lookin' in the mirror and thinking about it . . . I'm thirty-five years old; I been married eleven years and I got a boy who sleeps in the living room — *(Very, very quietly.)* — and all I got to give him is stories about how rich white people live . . .

RUTH: Eat your eggs, Walter.

WALTER: *(slams the table and jumps up)* — DAMN MY EGGS — DAMN ALL THE EGGS THAT EVER WAS!

RUTH: Then go to work.

WALTER: *(looking up at her)* See — I'm trying to talk to you 'bout myself — *(Shaking his head with the repetition.)*— and all you can say is eat them eggs and go to work.

RUTH: *(wearily)* Honey, you never say nothing new. I listen to you every day, every night and every morning, and you never say nothing new. *(Shrugging)* So you would rather *be* Mr. Arnold than be his chauffeur. So — I would *rather* be living in Buckingham Palace.

WALTER: That is just what is wrong with the colored woman in this world . . . Don't understand about building their men up and making 'em feel like they somebody. Like they can do something.

RUTH: *(drily, but to hurt)* There *are* colored men who do things.

WALTER: No thanks to the colored woman.

RUTH: Well, being a colored woman, I guess I can't help myself none.

She rises and gets the ironing board and sets it up and attacks a huge pile of rough-dried clothes, sprinkling them in preparation for the ironing and then rolling them into tight fat balls.

WALTER: *(mumbling)* We one group of men tied to a race of women with small minds!

His sister Beneatha enters. She is about twenty, as slim and intense as her brother. She is not as pretty as her sister-in-law, but her lean, almost intellectual face has a handsomeness of its own. She wears a bright-red flannel nightie, and her thick hair stands wildly about her head. Her speech is a mixture of many things; it is different from the rest of the family's insofar as education has permeated her sense of English — and perhaps the Midwest rather than the South has finally — at last — won out in her inflection; but not altogether, because over all of it is a soft slurring and transformed use of vowels which is the decided influence of the Southside. She passes through the room without looking at either Ruth or Walter and goes to the outside door and looks, a little blindly, out to the bathroom. She sees that it has been lost to the Johnsons. She closes the door with a sleepy vengeance and crosses to the table and sits down a little defeated.

BENEATHA: I am going to start timing those people.

WALTER: You should get up earlier.

BENEATHA: *(her face in her hands. She is still fighting the urge to go back to bed)* Really — would you suggest dawn? Where's the paper?

WALTER: *(pushing the paper across the table to her as he studies her almost clinically, as though he has never seen her before)* You a horrible-looking chick at this hour.

BENEATHA: *(drily)* Good morning, everybody.

WALTER: *(senselessly)* How is school coming?

BENEATHA: *(in the same spirit)* Lovely. Lovely. And you know, biology is the greatest. *(Looking up at him.)* I dissected something that looked just like you yesterday.

WALTER: I just wondered if you've made up your mind and everything.

Beneatha: *(gaining in sharpness and impatience)* And what did I answer yesterday morning — and the day before that?

Ruth: *(from the ironing board, like someone disinterested and old)* Don't be so nasty, Bennie.

Beneatha: *(still to her brother)* And the day before that and the day before that!

Walter: *(defensively)* I'm interested in you. Something wrong with that? Ain't many girls who decide—

Walter and Beneatha *(in unison):* "to be a doctor."

Silence.

Walter: Have we figured out yet just exactly how much medical school is going to cost?

Ruth: Walter Lee, why don't you leave that girl alone and get out of here to work?

Beneatha: *(exits to the bathroom and bangs on the door)* Come on out of there, please!

She comes back into the room.

Walter: *(looking at his sister intently)* You know the check is coming tomorrow.

Beneatha: *(turning on him with a sharpness all her own)* That money belongs to Mama, Walter, and it's for her to decide how she wants to use it. I don't care if she wants to buy a house or a rocket ship or just nail it up somewhere and look at it. It's hers. Not ours —*hers.*

Walter: *(bitterly)* Now ain't that fine! You just got your mother's interest at heart, ain't you, girl? You such a nice girl — but if Mama got that money she can always take a few thousand and help you through school too — can't she?

Beneatha: I have never asked anyone around here to do anything for me!

Walter: No! And the line between asking and just accepting when the time comes is big and wide—ain't it!

Beneatha: *(with fury)* What do you want from me, Brother—that I quit school or just drop dead, which!

Walter: I don't want nothing but for you to stop acting holy 'round here. Me and Ruth done made some sacrifices for you— why can't you do something for the family?

Ruth: Walter, don't be dragging me in it.

Walter: You are in it — Don't you get up and go work in somebody's kitchen for the last three years to help put clothes on her back?

Ruth: Oh, Walter — that's not fair . . .

Walter: It ain't that nobody expects you to get on your knees and say thank you, Brother; thank you, Ruth; thank you, Mama — and thank you, Travis, for wearing the same pair of shoes for two semesters —

Beneatha: *(dropping to her knees)* Well—I *do*— all right?— thank everybody! And forgive me for ever wanting to be anything at all *(Pursuing him on her knees across the floor.)* FORGIVE ME, FORGIVE ME, FORGIVE ME!

RUTH: Please stop it! Your mama'll hear you.

WALTER: Who the hell told you you had to be a doctor? If you so crazy 'bout messing 'round with sick people — then go be a nurse like other women — or just get married and be quiet . . .

BENEATHA: Well — you finally got it said . . . It took you three years but you finally got it said. Walter, give up; leave me alone — it's Mama's money.

WALTER: *He was my father, too!*

BENEATHA: So what? He was mine, too — and Travis' grandfather — but the insurance money belongs to Mama. Picking on me is not going to make her give it to you to invest in any liquor stores — (*Under breath, dropping into a chair.*) — and I for one say, God bless Mama for that!

WALTER: (*to Ruth*) See — did you hear? Did you hear!

RUTH: Honey, please go to work.

WALTER: Nobody in this house is ever going to understand me.

BENEATHA: Because you're a nut.

WALTER: Who's a nut?

BENEATHA: You — you are a nut. Thee is mad, boy.

WALTER: (*looking at his wife and his sister from the door, very sadly*) The world's most backward race of people, and that's a fact.

BENEATHA: (*turning slowly in her chair*) And then there are all those prophets who would lead us out of the wilderness — (*Walter slams out of the house*) — into the swamps!

RUTH: Bennie, why you always gotta be pickin' on your brother? Can't you be a little sweeter sometimes? (*Door opens. Walter walks in. He fumbles with his cap, starts to speak, clear throat, looks everywhere but at Ruth. Finally:*)

WALTER: (*to Ruth*) I need some money for carfare.

RUTH: (*looks at him, then warms; teasing, but tenderly*) Fifty cents? (*She goes to her bag and gets money.*) Here — take a taxi!

Walter exits. Mama enters. She is a woman in her early sixties, full-bodied and strong. She is one of those women of a certain grace and beauty who wear it so unobtrusively that it takes a while to notice. Her dark-brown face is surrounded by the total whiteness of her hair, and, being a woman who has adjusted to many things in life and overcome many more, her face is full of strength. She has, we can see, wit and faith of a kind that keep her eyes lit and full of interest and expectancy. She is, in a word, a beautiful woman. Her bearing is perhaps most like the noble bearing of the women of the Hereros of Southwest Africa — rather as if she imagines that as she walks she still bears a basket or a vessel upon her head. Her speech, on the other hand, is as careless as her carriage is precise — she is inclined to slur everything — but her voice is perhaps not so much quiet as simply soft.

MAMA: Who that 'round here slamming doors at this hour?

She crosses through the room, goes to the window, opens it, and brings in a feeble little plant growing doggedly in a small pot on the window sill. She feels the dirt and puts it back out.

RUTH: That was Walter Lee. He and Bennie was at it again.

MAMA: My children and they tempers. Lord, if this little old plant don't get more sun than it's been getting it ain't never going to see spring again. *(She turns from the window.)* What's the matter with you this morning, Ruth? You looks right peaked. You aiming to iron all them things? Leave some for me. I'll get to 'em this afternoon. Bennie honey, it's too drafty for you to be sitting 'round half dressed. Where's you robe?

BENEATHA: In the cleaners.

MAMA: Well, go get mine and put it on.

BENEATHA: I'm not cold, Mama, honest.

MAMA: I know—but you so thin

BENEATHA: *(irritably)* Mama, I'm not cold.

MAMA: *(seeing the make down bed as Travis has left it)* Lord have mercy, look at that poor bed. Bless his heart—he tries, don't he?

She moves to the bed Travis has sloppily made up.

RUTH:. No—he don't half try at all 'cause he knows you going to come along behind him and fix everything. That's just how come he don't know how to do nothing right now—you done spoiled that boy so.

MAMA: *(folding bedding)* Well—he's a little boy. Ain't supposed to know 'bout housekeeping. My baby, that's what he is. What you fix for his breakfast this morning?

RUTH: *(angrily)* I feed my son, Lena!

MAMA: I ain't meddling—*(Under breath; busy-bodyish.)* I just noticed all last week he had cold cereal, and when it starts getting this chilly in the fall a child ought to have some hot grits of something when he goes out in the cold—

RUTH: *(furious)* I gave him hot oats—is that all right!

MAMA: I ain't meddling. *(Pause.)* Put a lot of nice butter on it? *(Ruth shoots her an angry look and does not reply.)* He likes lots of butter.

RUTH: *(exasperated)* Lena—

MAMA: *(to Beneatha. Mama is inclined to wander conversationally sometimes)* What was you and your brother fussing 'bout this morning?

BENEATHA: It's not important, Mama.

She gets up and goes to look out at the bathroom, which is apparently free, and she picks up her towels and rushes out.

MAMA: What was they fighting about?

RUTH: Now you know as well as I do.

MAMA: *(shaking her head)* Brother still worrying hisself sick about that money?

RUTH: You know he is.

MAMA: You had breakfast?

RUTH: Some coffee.

MAMA: Girl, you better start eating and looking after yourself better. You almost thin as Travis.

RUTH: Lena—

Mama: Un-hunh?

Ruth: What are you going to do with it?

Mama: Now don't you start, child. It's too early in the morning to be talking about money. It ain't Christian.

Ruth: It's just that he got his heart set on that store—

Mama: You mean that liquor store that Willy Harris want him to invest in?

Ruth: Yes—

Mama: We ain't no business people, Ruth. We just plain working folks.

Ruth: Ain't nobody business people till they go into business. Walter Lee say colored people ain't never going to start getting ahead till they start gambling on some different kinds of things in the world—investments and things.

Mama: What done got into you, girl? Walter Lee done finally sold you on investing.

Ruth: No. Mama, something is happening between Walter and me. I don't know what it is—but he needs something—something I can't give him any more. He needs this chance, Lena.

Mama: *(frowning deeply)* But liquor, honey—

Ruth: Well—like Walter say—I spec people going to always be drinking themselves some liquor.

Mama: Well—whether they drinks it or not ain't none of my business. But whether I go into business selling it to 'em *is*, and I don't want that on my ledger this late in life. *(Stopping suddenly and studying her daughter (in law.)* Ruth Younger, what's the matter with you today? You look like you could fall over right there.

Ruth: I'm tired.

Mama: Then you better stay home from work today.

Ruth: I can't stay home. She'd be calling up the agency and screaming at them, "My girl didn't come in today—send me somebody! My girl didn't come in!" Oh, she just have a fit. . .

Mama: Well, let her have it. I'll just call her up and say you got the flu—

Ruth: *(laughing)* Why the flu?

Mama: 'Cause it sounds respectable to 'em. Something white people get, too. They know 'bout the flu. Otherwise they think you been cut up or something when you tell 'em you sick.

Ruth: I got to go in. We need the money.

Mama: Somebody would of thought my children done all but starved to death the way they talk about money here late. Child, we got a great big old check coming tomorrow.

Ruth: *(sincerely, but also self-righteously)* Now that's your money. It ain't got nothing to do with me. We all feel like that—Walter and Bennie and me—even Travis.

Mama: *(thoughtfully, and suddenly very far away)* Ten thousand dollars—

Ruth: Sure is wonderful.

Mama: Ten thousand dollars.

Ruth: You know what you should do, Miss Lena? You should take yourself a trip somewhere. To Europe or South America or someplace—

Mama: *(throwing up her hands at the thought)* Oh, child!

Ruth: I'm serious. Just pack up and leave! Go on away and enjoy yourself some. Forget about the family and have yourself a ball for once in your life—

Mama: *(drily)* You sound like I'm just about ready to die. Who'd go with me? What I look like wandering 'round Europe by myself?

Ruth: Shoot—these here rich white women do it all the time. They don't think nothing of packing up they suitcases and piling on one of them big steamships and—swoosh!—they gone, child.

Mama: Something always told me I wasn't no rich white woman.

Ruth: Well—what are you going to do with it then?

Mama: I ain't rightly decided. *(Thinking. She speaks now with emphasis.)* Some of it got to be put away for Beneatha and her schoolin'—and ain't nothing going to touch that part of it. Nothing *(She waits several seconds, trying to make up her mind about something, and looks at Ruth a little tentatively before going on.)* Been thinking that we maybe could meet the notes on a little old two-story somewhere, with a yard where Travis could play in the summertime, if we use part of the insurance for a down payment and everybody kind of pitch in. I could maybe take on a little day work again, few days a week—

Ruth: *(studying her mother-in-law furtively and concentrating on her ironing, anxious to encourage without seeming to)* Well, Lord knows, we've put enough rent into this here rat trap to pay for four houses by now.

Mama: *(looking up at the words "rat trap" and then looking around and leaning back and sighing—in a suddenly reflective mood—)* "Rat trap"—yes, that's all it is. *(Smiling.)* I remember just as well the day me and Big Walter moved in here. Hadn't been married but two weeks and wasn't planning on living here no more than a year. *(She shakes her head at the dissolved dream.)* We was going to set away, little by little, don't you know, and buy a little place out in Morgan Park. We had even picked out the house. *(Chuckling a little.)* Looks right dumpy today. But Lord, child, you should know all the dreams I had 'bout buying that house and fixing it up and making me a little garden in the back—*(She waits and stops smiling.)* And didn't none of it happen.

Dropping her hands in a futile gesture.

Ruth: *(keep her head down, ironing)* Yes, life can be a barrel of disappointments, sometimes.

Mama: Honey, Big Walter would come in here some nights back then and slump down on that couch there and just look at the rug, and look at me and look at the rug and then back at me—and I'd know he was down then . . . really down. *(After a second very long and thoughtful pause; she is seeing back to times that only she can see.)* And then, Lord, when I lost that baby—little Claude—I almost thought I was going to lose Big Walter too. Oh, that man grieved hisself! He was one man to love his children.

Ruth: Ain't nothin' can tear at you like losin' your baby.

MAMA: I guess that's how come that man finally worked hisself to death like he done. Like he was fighting his own war with this here world that took his baby from him.

RUTH: He sure was a fine man, all right. I always liked Mr. Younger.

MAMA: Crazy 'bout his children! God knows there was plenty wrong with Walter Younger—hard-headed, mean, kind of wild with women—plenty wrong with him. But he sure loved his children. Always wanted them to have something—be something. That's where Brother gets all these notions, I reckon. Big Walter used to say, he'd get right wet in the eyes sometimes, lean his head back with the water standing in his eyes and say, "Seem like God didn't see fit to give the black man nothing but dreams—but He did give us children to make them dreams seem worthwhile." *(She smiles.)* He could talk like that, don't you know.

RUTH: Yes, he sure could. He was a good man, Mr. Younger.

MAMA: Yes, a fine man—just couldn't never catch up with his dreams, that's all.

Beneatha comes in, brushing her hair and looking up to the ceiling, where the sound of a vacuum cleaner has started up.

BENEATHA: What could be so dirty on that woman's rugs that she has to vacuum them every single day?

RUTH: I wish certain young women 'round here who I could name would take inspiration about certain rugs in a certain apartment I could also mention.

BENEATHA: *(shrugging)* How much cleaning can a house need, for Christ's sakes.

MAMA: *(not liking the Lord's name used thus)* Bennie!

RUTH: Just listen to her—just listen!

BENEATHA: Oh, God!

MAMA: If you use the Lord's name just one more time—

BENEATHA: *(a bit of a whine)* Oh, Mama—

RUTH: Fresh—just fresh as salt, this girl!

BENEATHA: *(drily)* Well—if the salt loses its savor—

MAMA: Now that will do. I just ain't going to have you 'round here reciting the scriptures in vain—you hear me?

BENEATHA: How did I manage to get on everybody's wrong side by just walking into a room?

RUTH: If you weren't so fresh—

BENEATHA: Ruth, I'm twenty years old.

MAMA: What time you be home from school today?

BENEATHA: Kind of late. *(With enthusiasm.)* Madeline is going to start my guitar lessons today.

Mama and Ruth look up with the same expression.

MAMA: Your *what* kind of lessons?

BENEATHA: Guitar.

RUTH: Oh, Father!

MAMA: How come you done taken it in your mind to learn to play the guitar?

BENEATHA: I just want to, that's all.

Mama: *(smiling)* Lord, child, don't you know what to do with yourself? How long it going to be before you get tired of this now—like you got tired of that little play-acting group you joined last year? *(Looking at Ruth.)* And what was it the year before that?

Ruth: The horseback-riding club for which she bought that fifty-five-dollar riding habit that's been hanging in the closer ever since!

Mama: *(to Beneatha)* Why you got to flit so from one thing to another, baby?

Beneatha: *(sharply)* I just want to learn to play the guitar. Is there anything wrong with that?

Mama: Ain't nobody trying to stop you. I just wonders sometimes why you has to flit so from one thing to another all the time. You ain't never done nothing with all that camera equipment you brought home—

Beneatha: I don't flit! I—I experiment with different forms of expression—

Ruth: Like riding a horse?

Beneatha: —People have to express themselves one way or another.

Mama: What is it you want to express?

Beneatha: *(angrily)* Me! *(Mama and Ruth look at each other and burst into raucous laughter.)* Don't worry—I don't expect you to understand.

Mama: *(to change the subject)* Who you going out with tomorrow night?

Beneatha: *(with displeasure)* George Murchison again.

Mama: *(pleased)* Oh you getting a little sweet on him?

Ruth: You ask me, this child ain't sweet on nobody but herself—*(under breath.)* Express herself!

They laugh.

Beneatha: Oh I like George all right, Mama. I mean I like him enough to go out with him and stuff, but—

Ruth: *(for devilment)* What does *and stuff* mean?

Beneatha: Mind your own business.

Mama: Stop picking at her now, Ruth. *(She chuckles—then a suspicious sudden look at her daughter as she turns in her chair for emphasis.)* What DOES it mean?

Beneatha: *(wearily)* Oh, I just mean I couldn't ever really be serious about George. He's—he's so shallow.

Ruth: Shallow—what do you mean he's shallow? He's *rich!*

Mama: Hush, Ruth.

Beneatha: I know he's rich. He knows he's rich, too.

Ruth: Well—what other qualities a man got to have to satisfy you, little girl?

Beneatha: You wouldn't even begin to understand. Anybody who married Walter could not possibly understand.

Mama: *(outraged)* What kind of way is that to talk about your brother?

Beneatha: Brother is a flip—let's face it.

Mama: *(to Ruth, helplessly)* What's a flip?

Ruth: *(glad to add kindling)* She's saying he's crazy.

Beneatha: Not crazy. Brother isn't really crazy yet—he—he's an elaborate neurotic.

MAMA: Hush your mouth!

BENEATHA: As for George. Well. George looks good—he's got a beautiful car and he takes me to nice places and, as my sister-in-law says, he is probably the richest boy I will ever get to know and I even like him sometimes—but if the Youngers are sitting around waiting to see if their little Bennie is going to tie up the family with the Murchisons, they are wasting their time.

RUTH: You mean you wouldn't marry George Murchison if he asked you someday? That pretty, rich thing? Honey, I knew you was odd—

BENEATHA: No I would not marry him if all I felt for him was what I feel now. Besides, George's family wouldn't really like it.

MAMA: Why not?

BENEATHA: Oh, Mama—The Murchisons are honest-to-God-real-*live*-rich colored people, and the only people in the world who are more snobbish than rich white people are rich colored people. I thought everybody knew that. I've met Mrs. Murchison. She's a scene!

MAMA: You must not dislike people 'cause they well off, honey.

BENEATHA: Why not? It makes just as much sense as disliking people 'cause they are poor, and lots of people do that.

RUTH: *(a wisdom-of-the-ages manner. To Mama)* Well, she'll get over some of this—

BENEATHA: Get over it? What are you talking about, Ruth? Listen, I'm going to be a doctor. I'm not worried about who I'm going to marry yet—if I ever get married.

MAMA AND RUTH: *If!*

MAMA: Now, Bennie—

BENEATHA: Oh, I probably will . . . but first I'm going to be a doctor, and George, for one, still thinks that's pretty funny. I couldn't be bothered with that. I am going to be a doctor and everybody around here better understand that!

MAMA: *(kindly)* 'Course you going to be a doctor, honey, God willing.

BENEATHA: *(drily)* God hasn't got a thing to do with it.

MAMA: Beneatha—that just wasn't necessary.

BENEATHA: Well—neither is God. I get sick of hearing about God.

MAMA: Beneatha!

BENEATHA: I mean it! I'm just tired of hearing about God all the time. What has He got to do with anything? Does He pay tuition?

MAMA: You 'bout to get your fresh little jaw slapped!

RUTH: That's just what she needs, all right!

BENEATHA: Why? Why can't I say what I want to around here, like everybody else?

MAMA: It don't sound nice for a young girl to say things like that—you wasn't brought up that way. Me and your father went to trouble of get you and Brother to church every Sunday.

BENEATHA: Mama, you don't understand. It's all a matter of ideas, and God is just one idea I don't accept. It's not important. I am not going out and being immoral or commit crimes because I don't believe in God. I don't even think about it. It's just that I get tired of Him getting credit for all the things the human race achieves through its own stubborn effort. There simply is no blasted God—there is only man and it is *He* who makes miracles!

Mama absorbs this speech, studies her daughter, and rises slowly and crosses to Beneatha and slaps her powerfully across the face. After, there is only silence and the daughter drops her eyes from her mother's face, and Mama is very tall before her.

MAMA: Now—you say after me, in my mother's house there is still God. *(There is a long pause and Beneatha stares at the floor wordlessly. Mama repeats the phrase with precision and cool emotion.)* In my mother's house there is still God.

BENEATHA: In my mother's house there is still God.

A long pause.

MAMA: *(walking away from Beneatha, too disturbed for triumphant posture. Stopping and turning back to her daughter)* There are some ideas we ain't going to have in this house. Not long as I am at the head of this family.

BENEATHA: Yes, ma'am.

Mama walks out of the room.

RUTH: *(almost gently, with profound understanding)* You think you a woman. Bennie—but you still a little girl. What you did was childish—so you got treated like a child.

BENEATHA: I see. *(Quietly.)* I also see that everybody thinks it's all right for Mama to be a tyrant. But all the tyranny in the world will never put a God in the heavens!

She picks up her books and goes out. Pause.

RUTH: *(goes to Mama's door)* She said she was sorry.

MAMA: *(coming out, going to her plant)* They frightens me, Ruth. My children.

RUTH: You got good children, Lena. They just a little off sometimes—but they're good.

MAMA: No—there's something come down between me and them that don't let us understand each other and I don't know what it is. One done almost lost his mind thinking 'bout money all the time and the other done commence to talk about things I can't seem to understand in no form or fashion. What is it that's changing, Ruth?

RUTH: *(soothingly, older than her years)* Now . . . you taking it all too seriously. You just got strong-willed children and it takes a strong woman like you to keep 'em in hand.

MAMA: *(looking at her plant and sprinkling a little water on it)* They spirited all right, my children. Got to admit they got spirit—Bennie and Walter Like this little old plant that ain't never had enough sunshine or nothing—and look at it. . .

She has her back to Ruth, who has had to stop ironing and lean against something and put the back of her hand to her forehead.

RUTH: *(trying to keep Mama from noticing)* You . . . sure . . . loves that little old thing, don't you?

MAMA: Well, I always wanted me a garden like I used to see sometimes at the back of the houses down home. This plant is close as I ever got to having one. *(She looks out of the window as she replaces the plant.)* Lord, ain't nothing as dreary as the view from this window on a dreary day, is there? Why ain't you singing this morning, Ruth? Sing that "No Ways Tired." That song always lifts me up so—*(She turns at last to see that Ruth has slipped quietly to the floor, in a state of semiconsciousness.)* Ruth! Ruth honey—what's the matter with you . . . Ruth!

Curtain.

SCENE 2 **(*The following morning.*)**

It is the following morning; a Saturday morning, and house cleaning is in progress at the Youngers'. Furniture has been shoved hither and yon and Mama is giving the kitchen area walls a washing down. Beneatha, in dungarees, with a handkerchief tied around her face, is spraying insecticide into the cracks in the walls. As they work, the radio is on and a Southside disk jockey program is inappropriately filling the house with a rather exotic saxophone blues. Travis, the sole idle one, is leaning on his arms, looking out of the window.

TRAVIS: Grandmama, that stuff Bennie is using smells awful. Can I go downstairs, please?

MAMA: Did you get all them chores done already? I ain't seen you doing much.

TRAVIS: Yes'm—finished early. Where did Mama go this morning?

MAMA: *(looking at Beneatha)* She had to go on a little errand.

The phone rings. Beneatha runs to answer it and reaches it before Walter, who has entered from bedroom.

TRAVIS: Where?

MAMA: To tend to her business.

BENEATHA: Haylo . . . *(Disappointed.)* Yes, he is. *(She tosses the phone to Walter, who barely catches it.)* It's Willie Harris again.

WALTER: *(as privately as possible under Mama's gaze)* Hello, Willie. Did you get the papers from the lawyer? . . . No, not yet. I told you the mailman doesn't get here till ten-thirty . . . No, I'll come there . . . Yeah! Right away. *(He hangs up and goes for his coat.)*

BENEATHA: Brother, where did Ruth go?

WALTER: *(as he exits)* How should I know!

TRAVIS: Aw come on, Grandma. Can I go outside?

MAMA: Oh, I guess so. You stay right in front of the house, though, and keep a good lookout for the postman.

TRAVIS: Yes'm. *(He darts into bedroom for stickball and bat, reenters, and sees Beneatha on her knees spraying under sofa with behind upraised. He edges closer to the target, takes aim, and lets her have it. She screams.)* Leave them poor little cockroaches alone, they ain't bothering you none! *(He runs as she swings the spraygun at him viciously and playfully.)* Grandma! Grandma!

MAMA: Look out there, girl, before you be spilling some of that stuff on that child!

TRAVIS: *(safely behind the bastion of Mama)* That's right—look out, now! *(He exits.)*

BENEATHA: *(drily)* I can't imagine that it would hurt him—it has never hurt the roaches.

MAMA: Well, little boys' hides ain't as tough as Southside roaches. You better get over there behind the bureau. I seen one marching out of there like Napoleon yesterday.

BENEATHA: There's really only one way to get rid of them, Mama—

MAMA: How?

BENEATHA: Set fire to this building! Mama, where did Ruth go?

MAMA: *(looking at her with meaning)* To the doctor, I think.

BENEATHA: The doctor? What's the matter? *(They exchange glances.)* You don't think—

MAMA: *(with her sense drama)* Now I ain't saying what I think. But I ain't never been wrong 'bout a woman neither.

The phone rings.

BENEATHA: *(at the phone)* Hay-lo . . . *(Pause, and a moment of recognition.)* Well—when did you get back! . . . And how was it? . . . Of course I've missed you—in my way . . . This morning? No . . . house cleaning and all that and Mama hates it if I let people come over when the house is like this . . . You *have*? Well, that's different . . . What is it — Oh, what the hell, come on over . . . Right, see you then. *Arrividerci.*

She hangs up.

MAMA: *(who has listened vigorously, as is her habit)* Who is that you inviting over here with this house looking like this? You ain't got the pride you was born with!

BENEATHA: Asagai doesn't care how houses look, Mama—he's an intellectual.

MAMA: *Who*?

BENEATHA: Asagai — Joseph Asagai. He's an African boy I met on campus. He's been studying in Canada all summer.

MAMA: What's his name?

BENEATHA: Asagai, Joseph. Ah-sah-guy . . . He's from Nigeria.

MAMA: Oh, that's the little country that was founded by slaves way back . . .

BENEATHA: No, Mama—that's Liberia.

MAMA: I don't think I never met no African before.

BENEATHA: Well, do me a favor and don't ask him a whole lot of ignorant questions about Africans. I mean, do they wear clothes and all that—

MAMA: Well, now, I guess if you think we so ignorant 'round here maybe you shouldn't bring your friends here—

BENEATHA: It's just that people ask such crazy things. All anyone seems to know about when it comes to Africa is Tarzan—

MAMA: *(indignantly)* Why should I know anything about Africa?

BENEATHA: Why do you give money at church for the missionary work?

MAMA: Well, that's to help save people.

BENEATHA: You mean save them from *heathenism*—

MAMA: *(innocently)* Yes.

BENEATHA: I'm afraid they need more salvation from the British and the French.

Ruth comes in forlornly and pulls off her coat with dejection. They both turn to look at her.

RUTH: *(dispiritedly)* Well, I guess from all the happy faces—everybody knows.

BENEATHA: You pregnant?

MAMA: Lord have mercy, I sure hope it's a little old girl. Travis ought to have a sister.

Beneatha and Ruth give her a hopeless look for this grandmotherly enthusiasm.

BENEATHA: How far along are you?

RUTH: Two months.

BENEATHA: Did you mean to? I mean did you plan it or was it an accident?

MAMA: What do you know about planning or not planning?

BENEATHA: Oh, Mama.

RUTH: *(wearily)* She's twenty years old, Lena.

BENEATHA: Did you plan it, Ruth?

RUTH: Mind your own business.

BENEATHA: It is my business—where is he going to live, on the *roof*? *(There is silence following the remark as the three women react to the sense of it.)* Gee—I didn't mean that, Ruth, honest. Gee, I don't feel like that at all. I—I think it is wonderful.

RUTH: *(dully)* Wonderful.

BENEATHA: Yes—really.

MAMA: *(looking at Ruth, worried)* Doctor say everything going to be all right?

RUTH: *(far away)* Yes—she says everything is going to be fine . . .

MAMA: *(immediately suspicious)* "She"—What doctor you went to?

Ruth folds over, near hysteria.

MAMA: *(worriedly hovering over Ruth)* Ruth honey—what's the matter with you—you sick?

Ruth has her fists clenched on her thighs and is fighting hard to suppress a scream that seems to be rising in her.

BENEATHA: What's the matter with her, Mama?

MAMA: *(working her fingers in Ruth's shoulders to relax her)* She be all right. Women gets right depressed sometimes when they get her way. *(Speaking softly, expertly, rapidly.)* Now you just relax. That's right . . . just lean back, don't think 'bout nothing at all . . . nothing at all—

RUTH: I'm all right . . .

The glassy eyed look melts and then she collapses into a fit of heavy sobbing. The bell rings.

BENEATHA: Oh, my God— that must be Asagai.

MAMA: *(to Ruth)* Come on now, honey. You need to lie down and rest awhile . . . then have some nice hot food.

They exit, Ruth's weight on her mother-in-law. Beneatha, herself profoundly disturbed, opens the door to admit a rather dramatic-looking young man with a large package.

ASAGAI: Hello, Alaiyo–

BENEATHA: *(holding the door open and regarding him with pleasure)* Hello . . . *(Long pause.)* Well—come in. And please excuse everything. My mother was very upset about my letting anyone come here with the place like this.

ASAGAI: *(coming into the room)* You look disturbed too . . . Is something wrong?

BENEATHA: *(still at the door, absently)* Yes . . . we've all got acute ghetto-itsu. *(She smiles and comes toward him, finding a cigarette and sitting.)* So—sit down! No! Wait! *(She whips the spraygun off sofa where she had left it and puts the cushions back. At last perches on arm of sofa. He sits.)* So, how was Canada?

ASAGAI: *(a sophisticate)* Canadian.

BENEATHA: *(looking at him)* Asagai, I'm very glad you are back.

ASAGAI: *(looking back at her in turn)* Are you really?

BENEATHA: Yes—very.

ASAGAI: Why?—you were quite glad when I went away. What happened?

BENEATHA: You went away.

ASAGAI: Ahhhhhhhh.

BENEATHA: Before—you wanted to be so serious before there was time.

ASAGAI: How much time must there be before one knows what one feels?

BENEATHA: *(stalling this particular conversation. Her hands pressed together, in a deliberately childish gesture)* What did you bring me?

ASAGAI: *(handing her the package)* Open it and see.

BENEATHA: *(eagerly opening the package and drawing out some records and the colorful robes of a Nigerian woman)* Oh Asagai! . . . You got them for me! . . . How beautiful . . . and the records too! *(She lifts out the robes and runs to the mirror with them and holds the drapery up in front of herself.)*

ASAGAI: *(coming to her at the mirror)* I shall have to teach you how to drape it properly. *(He flings the material about her for the moment and stands back to look at her.)* Ah-Oh-pay-gay-day, oh-gbab-mu-shay. *(A Yoruba exclamation for admiration.)* You wear it well . . . very well . . . mutilated hair and all.

BENEATHA: *(turning suddenly)* My hair — what's wrong with my hair?

ASAGAI: *(shrugging)* Were you born with it like that?

BENEATHA: *(reaching up to touch it)* No . . . of course not.

She looks back to the mirror, disturbed.

ASAGAI: *(smiling)* How then?

BENEATHA: You know perfectly well how . . . as crinkly as yours . . . that's how.

ASAGAI: And it is ugly to you that way?

BENEATHA: *(quickly)* Oh, no—not ugly . . . *(More slowly, apologetically.)* But it's so hard to manage when it's, well—raw.

ASAGAI: And so to accommodate that—you mutilate it every week?

BENEATHA: It's not mutilation!

ASAGAI: *(laughing aloud at her seriousness)* Oh . . . please! I am only teasing you because you are so very serious about these things. *(He stands back from her and folds his arms across his chest as he watches her pulling at her hair and frowning in the mirror.)* Do you remember the first time you met me at school? *(He laughs.)* You came up to me and you said—and I thought you were the most serious little thing I had ever seen—you said: *(He imitates her.)* "Mr. Asagai—I want very much to talk with you. About Africa. You see, Mr. Asagai, I am looking for my *identity!*"

He laughs.

BENEATHA: *(turning to him, not laughing)* Yes—

Her face is quizzical, profoundly disturbed.

ASAGAI: *(still teasing and reaching out and taking her face in his hands and turning her profile to him)* Well . . . it is true that this is not so much a profile of a Hollywood queen as perhaps a queen of the Nile—*(A mock dismissal of the importance of the question.)* But what does it matter. Assimilationism is so popular in your country.

BENEATHA: *(wheeling, passionately, sharply)* I am not an assimilationist!

ASAGAI: *(the protest hangs in the room for a moment and Asagai studies her, his laughter fading)* Such a serious one. *(There is a pause.)* So—you like the robes? You must take excellent care of them—they are from my sister's personal wardrobe.

BENEATHA: *(with incredulity)* You—you sent all the way home—for me?

ASAGAI: *(with charm)* For you—I would do much more . . . Well, that is what I came for. I must go.

BENEATHA: Will you call me Monday?

ASAGAI: Yes . . . We have a great deal to talk about. I mean about identity and time and all that.

BENEATHA: Time?

ASAGAI: Yes. About how much time one needs to know what one feels.

BENEATHA: You see! You never understood that there is more than one kind of feeling which can exist between a man and a woman—or, at least, there should be.

ASAGAI: *(shaking his head negatively but gently)* No. Between a man and a woman there need be only one kind of feeling. I have that for you . . . Now even . . . right this moment . . .

BENEATHA: I know—and by itself—it won't do. I can find that anywhere.

ASAGAI: For a woman it should be enough.

BENEATHA: I know—because that's what it says in all the novels that men write. But it isn't. Go ahead and laugh—but I'm not interested in being someone's little episode in America or—*(With feminine vengeance.)*—one of them! *(Asagai has burst into laughter again.)* That's funny as hell, huh!

ASAGAI: It's just that every American girl I have known has said that to me. White—black—in this you are all the same. And the same speech, too!

BENEATHA: *(angrily)* Yuk, yuk, yuk!

ASAGAI: It's how you can be sure that the world's most liberated women are not liberated at all. You all talk about it too much!

Mama enters and is immediately all social charm because of the presence of a guest.

BENEATHA: Oh—Mama—this is Mr. Asagai.

MAMA: How do you do?

ASAGAI: *(total politeness to an elder)* How do you do, Mrs. Younger. Please forgive me for coming at such an outrageous hour on a Saturday.

MAMA: Well, you are quite welcome. I just hope you understand that our house don't always look like this. *(Chatterish.)* You must come again. I would love to hear all about—*(Not sure of the name.)*—your country. I think it's so sad the way our American Negroes don't know nothing about Africa 'cept Tarzan and all that. And all that money they pour into these churches when they ought to be helping you people over there drive out them French and Englishmen done taken away your land.

The mother flashes a slightly superior look at her daughter upon completion of the recitation.

ASAGAI: *(taken aback by this sudden and acutely unrelated expression of sympathy)* Yes . . . yes . . .

MAMA: *(smiling at him suddenly and relaxing and looking him over)* How many miles is it from here to where you come from?

ASAGAI: Many thousands.

MAMA: *(looking at him as she would Walter)* I bet you don't half look after yourself, being away from your mama either. I spec you better come 'round here from time to time to get yourself some decent homecooked meals . . .

ASAGAI: *(moved)* Thank you. Thank you very much. *(They are all quiet, then.)* Well . . . I must go. I will call you Monday, Alaiyo.

MAMA: What's that he call you?

ASAGAI: Oh—"Alaiyo." I hope you don't mind. It is what you would call a nickname, I think. It is a Yoruba word. I am a Yoruba.

MAMA: *(looking at Beneatha)* I—I thought he was from—*(Uncertain.)*

ASAGAI: *(understanding)* Nigeria is my country. Yoruba is my tribal origin—

BENEATHA: You didn't tell us what Alaiyo means . . . for all I know, you might be calling me Little Idiot or something . . .

ASAGAI: Well . . . let me see . . . I do not know how just to explain it . . . The sense of a thing can be so different when it changes languages.

Beneatha: You're evading.

Asagai: No—really it is difficult . . . *(Thinking.)* It means . . . it means One for Whom Bread—Food—Is Not Enough. *(He looks at her.)* Is that all right?

Beneatha: *(understanding, softly)* Thank you.

Mama: *(looking from one to the other and not understanding any of it)* Well . . . that's nice . . . You must come see us again—Mr.—

Asagai: Ah-sah-guy . . .

Mama: Yes . . . Do come again.

Asagai: Good-bye.

He exits.

Mama: *(after him)* Lord, that's a pretty thing just went out here! *(Insinuatingly, to her daughter.)* Yes, I guess I see why we done commence to get so interested in Africa 'round here. Missionaries my aunt Jenny!

She exits.

Beneatha: Oh, Mama! . . .

She picks up the Nigerian dress and holds it up to her in front of the mirror again. She sets the headdress on haphazardly and then notices her hair again and clutches at it and then replaces the headdress and frowns at herself. Then she starts to wriggle in front of the mirror as she thinks a Nigerian woman might. Travis enters and stands regarding her.

Travis: What's the matter, girl, you cracking up?

Beneatha: Shut up.

She pulls the headdress off and looks at herself in the mirror and clutches at her hair again and squinches her eyes as if trying to imagine something. Then, suddenly, she gets her raincoat and kerchief and hurriedly prepares for going out.

Mama: *(coming back into the room)* She's resting now. Travis, baby, run next door and ask Miss Johnson to please let me have a little kitchen cleanser. This here can is empty as Jacob's kettle.

Travis: I just came in.

Mama: Do as you told. *(He exits and she looks at her daughter.)* Where you going?

Beneatha: *(halting at the door)* To become a queen of the Nile!

She exits in a breathless blaze of glory. Ruth appears in the bedroom doorway.

Mama: Who told you to get up?

Ruth: Ain't nothing wrong with me to be lying in no bed for. Where did Bennie go?

Mama: *(drumming her fingers)* Far as I could make out—to Egypt. *(Ruth just looks at her.)* What time is it getting to?

Ruth: Ten twenty. And the mailman going to ring that bell this morning just like he done ever morning for the last umpteen years.

Travis comes in with the cleanser can.

TRAVIS: She say to tell you that she don't have much.

MAMA: *(angrily)* Lord, some people I could name sure is tight-fisted! *(Directing her grandson.)* Mark two cans of cleanser on the list there. If she that hard up for kitchen cleanser, I sure don't want to forget to get her none!

RUTH: Lena—maybe the woman is just short on cleanser—

MAMA: *(not listening)*—Much baking powder as she done borrowed from me all these years, she could of done gone into the baking business!

The bell sounds suddenly and sharply and all three are stunned—serious and silent—midspeech. In spite of all the other conversations and distractions of the morning, this is what they have been waiting for, even Travis, who looks helplessly from his mother to his grandmother. Ruth is the first to come to life again.

RUTH: *(to Travis) Get down them steps, boy!*

Travis snaps to life and flies out to get the mail.

MAMA: *(her eyes wide, her hand to her breast)* You mean it done really come?

RUTH: *(excited)* Oh, Miss Lena!

MAMA: *(collecting herself)* Well . . . I don't know what we all so excited about round here for. We known it was coming for months.

RUTH: That's a whole lot different from having it come and being able to hold it in your hands . . . a piece of paper worth ten thousand dollars . . . *(Travis bursts back into the room. He holds the envelope high above his head, like a little dancer, his face is radiant and he is breathless. He moves to his grandmother with sudden slow ceremony and puts the envelope into her hands. She accepts it, and then merely holds it and looks at it.)* Come on! Open it . . . Lord have mercy, I wish Walter Lee was here!

TRAVIS: Open it, Grandmama!

MAMA: *(staring at it)* Now you all be quiet. It's just a check.

RUTH: Open it. . .

MAMA: *(still staring at it)* Now don't act silly . . . We ain't never been no people to act silly 'bout no money—

RUTH: *(swiftly)* We ain't never had none before—OPEN IT!

Mama finally makes a good strong tear and pulls out the thin blue slice of paper and inspects it closely. The boy and his mother study it raptly over Mama's shoulders.

MAMA: Travis! *(She is counting off with doubt.)* Is that the right number of zeros?

TRAVIS: Yes'm . . . ten thousand dollars. Gaalee, grandmama, you rich.

MAMA: *(She holds the check away from her, still looking at it. Slowly her face sobers into a mask of unhappiness)* Ten thousand dollars. *(She hands it to Ruth.)* Put it away somewhere, Ruth. *(She does not look at Ruth; her eyes seem to be seeing something somewhere very far off.)* Ten thousand dollars they give you, Ten thousand dollars.

TRAVIS: *(to his mother, sincerely)* What's the matter with Grandmama—don't she want to be rich?

RUTH: *(distractedly)* You go on out and play now, baby. *(Travis exits. Mama starts wiping dishes absently, humming intently to herself. Ruth turns to her; with kind exasperation.)* You've gone and got yourself upset.

MAMA: *(not looking at her)* I spec if it wasn't for you all . . . I would just put that money away or give it to the church or something.

RUTH: Now what kind of talk is that. Mr. Younger would just be plain mad if he could hear you talking foolish like that.

MAMA: *(stopping and staring off)* Yes . . . he sure would. *(Sighing.)* We got enough to do with that money, all right. *(She halts then, and turns and looks at her daughter-in-law hard; Ruth avoids her eyes and Mama wipes her hands with finality and starts to speak firmly to Ruth.)* Where did you go today, girl?

RUTH: To the doctor.

MAMA: *(impatiently)* Now, Ruth . . . you know better than that. Old Doctor Jones is strange enough in his way but there ain't nothing 'bout him make somebody slip and call him "she"—like you done this morning.

RUTH: Well, that's what happened—my tongue slipped.

MAMA: You went to see that woman, didn't you?

RUTH: *(defensively, giving herself away)* What woman you talking about?

MAMA: *(angrily)*: That woman who—

Walter enters in great excitement.

WALTER: Did it come?

MAMA: *(quietly)* Can't you give people a Christian greeting before you start asking about money?

WALTER: *(to Ruth)* Did it come? *(Ruth unfolds the check and lays it quietly before him, watching him intently with thoughts of her own. Walter sits down and grasps it close and counts off the zeros.)* Ten thousand dollars —*(He turns suddenly, frantically to his mother and draws some papers out of his breast pocket.)* Mama—look. Old Willy Harris put everything on paper —

MAMA: Son—I think you ought to talk to your wife . . . I'll go on out and leave you alone if you want —

WALTER: I can talk to her later —Mama, look —

MAMA: Son —

WALTER: WILL SOMEBODY PLEASE LISTEN TO ME TODAY!

MAMA: *(quietly)* I don't 'low no yellin' in this house, Walter Lee, and you know it —*(Walter stares at them in frustration and starts to speak several times.)* And there ain't going to be no investing in no liquor stores.

WALTER: But, Mama, you ain't even looked at it.

MAMA: I don't aim to have to speak on that again.

A long pause.

WALTER: You ain't looked at it and you don't aim to have to speak on that again? You ain't even looked at it and *you* have decided —*(Crumpling his papers.)* Well, *you* tell that to my boy tonight when you put him to sleep on the living-room couch . . . *(Turning to Mama and speaking directly on her.)*

Yeah—and tell it to my wife, Mama, tomorrow when she has to go out of here to look after somebody else's kids. And tell it to *me*, Mama, every time we need a new pair of curtains and I have to watch *you* go out and work in somebody's kitchen. Yeah, you tell me then!

Walter starts out.

RUTH: Where you going?

WALTER: I'm going out!

RUTH: Where?

WALTER: Just out of this house somewhere—

RUTH: *(getting her coat)* I'll come too.

WALTER: I don't want you to come!

RUTH: I got something to talk to you about, Walter.

WALTER: That's too bad.

MAMA: *(still quietly)* Walter Lee—*(She waits and he finally turns and looks at her.)* Sit down.

WALTER: I'm a grown man, Mama.

MAMA: Ain't nobody said you wasn't grown. But you still in my house and my presence. And as long as you are—you'll talk to your wife civil. Now sit down.

RUTH: *(suddenly)* Oh, let him go on out and drink himself to death! He makes me sick to my stomach! *(She flings her coat against him and exits to bedroom.)*

WALTER: *(violently flinging the coat after her)* And you turn mine too, baby! *(The door slams behind her.)* That was my biggest mistake—

MAMA: *(still quietly)* Walter, what is the matter with you?

WALTER: Matter with me? Ain't nothing the matter with *me*!

MAMA: Yes there is. Something eating you up like a crazy man. Something more than me not giving you this money. The past few years I been watching it happen to you. You get all nervous acting and kind of wild in the eyes—*(Walter jumps up impatiently at her words.)* I said sit there now, I'm talking to you!

WALTER: Mama—I don't need no nagging at me today.

MAMA: Seem like you getting to a place where you always tied up in some kind of knot about something. But if anybody ask you 'bout it you just yell at 'em and bust out the house and go out and drink somewheres. Walter Lee, people can't live with that. Ruth's a good, patient girl in her way—but you getting to be too much. Boy, don't make the mistake of driving that girl away from you.

WALTER: Why—what she do for me?

MAMA: She loves you.

WALTER: Mama—I'm going out I want to go off somewhere and be by myself for a while.

MAMA: I'm sorry 'bout your liquor store, son. It just wasn't the thing for us to do. That's what I want to tell you about—

WALTER: I got to go out, Mama—

He rises.

MAMA: It's dangerous, son.

WALTER: What's dangerous?

MAMA: When a man goes outside his home to look for peace.

WALTER: *(beseechingly)* Then why can't there never be no peace in this house then?

MAMA: You done found it in some other house?

WALTER: No — there ain't no woman! Why do women always think there's a woman somewhere when a man gets restless *(Picks up the check.)* Do you know what this money means to me? Do you know what this money can do for us? *(Puts it back.)* Mama—Mama—I want so many things . . .

MAMA: Yes, son—

WALTER: I want so many things that they are driving me kind of crazy . . . Mama—look at me.

MAMA: I'm looking at you. You a good-looking boy. You got a job, a nice wife, a fine boy, and—

WALTER: A job. *(Looks at her.)* Mama, a job? I open and close car doors all day long. I drive a man around in his limousine and I say, "Yes, sir, no, sir, very good, sir; shall I take the Drive, sir?" Mama, that ain't no kind of job . . . that ain't nothing at all. *(Very quietly.)* Mama, I don't know if I can make you understand.

MAMA: Understand what, baby?

WALTER: *(quietly)* Sometimes it's like I can see the future stretched out in front of me—just plain as day. The future Mama. Hanging over there at the edge of my days. Just waiting for me—a big, looming blank space—full of *nothing*. Just waiting for *me*. But it don't have to be. *(Pause. Kneeling beside her chair.)* Mama—sometimes when I'm downtown and I pass them cool, quiet looking restaurants where them white boys are sitting back and talking 'bout things . . . sitting there turning deals worth millions of dollars . . . sometimes I see guys don't look much older than me—

MAMA: Son—how come you talk so much 'bout money?

WALTER: *(with immense passion)* Because it is life, Mama!

MAMA: *(quietly)* Oh —*(Very quietly.)* So now it's life. Money is life. Once upon a time freedom used to be life—now it's money. I guess the world really do change . . .

WALTER: No—it was always money, Mama. We just didn't know about it.

MAMA: No . . . something has changed. *(She looks at him.)* You something new, boy. In my time we was worried about not being lynched and getting to the North if we could and how to stay alive and still have a pinch of dignity too . . . Now here come you and Beneatha—talking 'bout things we ain't never even thought about hardly, me and your daddy. You ain't satisfied or proud of nothing we done. I mean that you had a home; that we kept you out of trouble till you was grown; that you don't have to ride to work on the back of nobody's streetcar—You my children—but how different we done become.

WALTER: *(a long beat. He pats her hand and gets up)* You just don't understand, Mama, you just don't understand.

MAMA: Son — do you know your wife is expecting another baby? *(Walter stands, stunned, and absorbs what his mother has said.)* That's what she wanted to talk to you about. *(Walter sinks down into a chair.)* This ain't for me to be telling—but you ought to know. *(She waits.)* I think Ruth is thinking 'bout getting rid of that child.

WALTER: *(slowly understanding)* — No — no — Ruth wouldn't do that.

MAMA: When the world gets ugly enough — a woman will do anything for her family. *The part that's already living.*

WALTER: You don't know Ruth, Mama, if you think she would do that.

Ruth opens the bedroom door and stands there a little limp.

RUTH: *(beaten)* Yes I would too, Walter. *(Pause.)* I gave her a five-dollar down payment.

There is total silence as the man stares at his wife and the mother stares at her son.

MAMA: *(presently)* Well—*(Tightly.)* Well—son, I'm waiting to hear you say something . . . *(She waits.)* I'm waiting to hear how you be your father's son. Be the man he was . . . *(Pause. The silence shouts.)* Your wife say she going to destroy your child. And I'm waiting to hear you talk like him and say we a people who give children life, not who destroys them —*(She rises.)* I'm waiting to see you stand up and look like your daddy and say we done give up one baby to poverty and that we ain't going to give up nary another one . . . I'm waiting.

WALTER: Ruth—*(He can say nothing.)*

MAMA: If you a son of mine, tell her! *(Walter picks up his keys and his coat and walks out. She continues, bitterly.)* You . . . you are a disgrace to your father's memory. Somebody get me my hat!

Curtain.

ACT 2

SCENE 1

TIME: Later the same day.

At rise. Ruth is ironing again. She has the radio going. Presently Beneatha's bedroom door opens and Ruth's mouth falls and she puts down the iron in fascination.

RUTH: What have we got on tonight!

BENEATHA: *(emerging grandly from the doorway so that we can see her thoroughly robed in the costume Asagai brought)* You are looking at what a well-dressed Nigerian woman wears —*(She parades for Ruth, her hair completely hidden by the headdress; she is coquettishly fanning herself with an ornate oriental fan, mistakenly more like Butterfly than any Nigerian that ever was.)* Isn't it beautiful? *(She promenades to the radio and, with an arrogant flourish, turns off the good loud blues that is playing.)* Enough of this assimilationist junk! *(Ruth follows her with her eyes as she goes to the phonograph and puts on a record and turns and waits ceremoniously for the music to come up. Then, with a shout —)* OCOMOGOSIAY!

Ruth jumps. The music comes up, a lovely Nigerian melody. Beneatha listens, enraptured, her eyes far way—"back to the past." She begins to dance. Ruth is dumfounded.

Ruth: What kind of dance is that?

Beneatha: A folk dance.

Ruth: What kind of folks do that, honey?

Beneatha: It's from Nigeria. It's a dance of welcome.

Ruth: Who you welcoming?

Beneatha: The men back to the village.

Ruth: Where they been?

Beneatha: How should I know—out hunting or something. Anyway, they are coming back now . . .

Ruth: Well, that's good.

Beneatha: *(with the record)*

Alundi, alundi
Alundi alunya
Jop pu a jeepua
Ang gu soooooooooo
Ai yai yae . . .
Ayehaye—alundi . . .

Walter comes in during this performance, he has obviously been drinking. He leans against the door heavily and watches his sister, at first with distaste. Then his eyes look off—"back to the past"—as he lifts both his fists to the roof, screaming.

Walter: YEAH . . . AND ETHIOPIA, STRETCH FORTH HER HANDS AGAIN! . . .

Ruth: *(drily, looking at him)* Yes—and Africa sure is claiming her own tonight. *(She gives them both up and starts ironing again.)*

Walter: *(all in a drunken, dramatic shout)* Shut up! . . . I'm diggin them drums . . . them drums move me! . . . *(He makes his weaving way to his wife's face and leans in close to her.)* In my *heart of hearts*—*(He thumps his chest.)*—I am much warrior!

Ruth: *(without even looking up)* In your heart of hearts you are much drunkard.

Walter: *(coming away from her and starting to wander around the room, shouting)* Me and Jomo . . . *(Intently, in his sister's face. She has stopped dancing to watch him in this unknown mood.)* That's my man, Kenyatta. *(Shouting and thumping his chest.)* FLAMING SPEAR! HOT DAMN! *(He is suddenly in possession of an imaginary spear and actively spearing enemies all over the room.)* OCOMOGOSIAY . . .

Beneatha: *(to encourage Walter, thoroughly caught up with this side of him)* OCOMOGOSIAY, FLAMING SPEAR!

Walter: THE LION IS WAKING . . . OWIMOWEH!

He pulls his shirt open and leaps up on the table and gestures with his spear.

Beneatha: OWIMOWEH!

WALTER: *(on the table, very far gone, his eyes pure glass sheets. He sees what we cannot, that he is a leader of his people, a great chief, a descendant of Chaka, and that the hour to march has come)* Listen, my black brothers —

BENEATHA: OCOMOGOSIAY!

WALTER: Do you hear the waters rushing against the shores of the coastlands—

BENEATHA: OCOMOGOSIAY!

WALTER: Do you hear the screeching of the cocks in yonder hills beyond where the chiefs meet in council for the coming of the mighty war —

BENEATHA: OCOMOGOSIAY!

And now the lighting shifts subtly to suggest the world of Walter's imagination, and the mood shifts from pure comedy. It is the inner Walter speaking: the Southside chauffeur has assumed an unexpected majesty.

WALTER: —Do you hear the beating of the wings of the birds flying low over the mountains and the low places of our land—

BENEATHA: OCOMOGOSIAY!

WALTER: —Do you hear the singing of the women, singing the war songs of our fathers to the babies in the great houses? Singing the sweet war songs! *(The doorbell rings.)* OH, DO YOU HEAR, MY *BLACK* BROTHERS!

BENEATHA: *(completely gone)* We hear you, Flaming spear —

Ruth shuts off the phonograph and opens the door. George Murchison enters.

WALTER: Telling us to prepare for the GREATNESS OF THE TIME! *(Lights back to normal. He turns and sees George.)* Black Brother!

He extends his hand for the fraternal clasp.

GEORGE: Black Brother, hell!

RUTH: *(having had enough, and embarrassed for the family)* Beneatha, you got company — what's the matter with you? Walter Lee Younger, get down off that table and stop acting like a fool . . .

Walter comes down off the table suddenly and makes a quick exit to the bathroom.

RUTH: He's had a little to drink . . . I don't know what her excuse is.

GEORGE: *(to Beneatha)* Look honey, we're going to the theater—we're not going to be *in* it . . . so go change, huh?

Beneatha looks at him and slowly, ceremoniously, lifts her hands and pulls off the head-dress. Her hair is close-cropped and unstraightened. George freezes mid-sentence and Ruth's eyes all but fall out of her head.

GEORGE: What in the name of—

RUTH: *(touching Beneatha's hair)* Girl, you done lost your natural mind? Look at your head!

GEORGE: What have you done to your head—I mean your hair!

BENEATHA: Nothing—except cut it off.

RUTH: Now that's the truth—it's what ain't been done to it! You expect this boy to go out with you with your head all nappy like that?

BENEATHA: *(looking at George)* That's up to George. If he's ashamed of his heritage —

GEORGE: Oh, don't be so proud of yourself, Bennie—just because you look eccentric.

BENEATHA: How can something that's natural be eccentric?

GEORGE: That's what being eccentric means—being natural. Get dressed.

BENEATHA: I don't like that, George.

RUTH: Why must you and your brother make an argument out of everything people say?

BENEATHA: Because I hate assimilationist Negroes!

RUTH: Will somebody please tell me what assimila-whoever means!

GEORGE: Oh, it's just a college girl's way of calling people Uncle Toms—but that isn't what it means at all.

RUTH: Well, what does it means?

BENEATHA: *(cutting George off and staring at him as she replies to Ruth)* It means someone who is willing to give up his own culture and submerge himself completely in the dominant, and in this case *oppressive* culture!

GEORGE: Oh, dear, dear, dear! Here we go! A lecture on the African past! On our Great West African Heritage! In one second we will hear all about the great Ashanti empires, the great Songhay civilizations; and the great sculpture of Benin — and then some poetry in the Bantu—and the whole monologue will end with the word *heritage*! *(Nastily.)* Let's face it, baby, your heritage is nothing but a bunch of raggedy-assed spirituals and some grass huts!

BENEATHA: GRASS HUTS! *(Ruth crosses to her and forcibly pushes her toward the bedroom.)* See there . . . you are standing there in your splendid ignorance talking about people who were the first to smelt iron on the face of the earth! *(Ruth is pushing her through the door.)* The Ashanti were performing surgical operations when the English—*(Ruth pulls the door to, with Beneatha on the other side, and smiles graciously at George. Beneatha opens the door and shouts the end of the sentence defiantly at George.)*—were still tatooing themselves with blue dragons! *(She goes back inside.)*

RUTH: Have a seat, George. *(They both sit. Ruth folds her hands rather primly on her lap, determined to demonstrate the civilization of the family.)* Warm, ain't it? I mean for September. *(Pause.)* Just like they always say about Chicago weather. If it's too hot or cold for you, just wait a minute and it'll change. *(She smiles happily at this cliché of cliché.)* Everybody say it's got to do with them bombs and things they keep setting off. *(Pause.)* Would you like a nice cold beer?

GEORGE: No, thank you. I don't care for beer. *(He looks at his watch.)* I hope she hurries up.

RUTH: What time is the show?

GEORGE: It's an eight-thirty curtain. That's just Chicago, though. In New York standard curtain time is eight forty.

He is rather proud of this knowledge.

RUTH: (*properly appreciating it*) You get to New York a lot?
GEORGE: (*offhand*) Few times a year.
RUTH: Oh—that's nice. I've never been to New York.

Walter enters. We feel he has relieved himself, but the edge of unreality is still with him.

WALTER: New York ain't got nothing Chicago ain't. Just a bunch of hustling people all squeezed up together—being "Eastern."

He turns his face into a screw of displeasure.

GEORGE: Oh—you've been?
WALTER: Plenty of times.
RUTH: (*Shocked at the lie*) Walter Lee Younger!
WALTER: (*staring her down*) Plenty! (*Pause.*) What we got to drink in this house? Why don't you offer this man some refreshment. (*To George.*) They don't know how to entertain people in this house, man.
GEORGE: Thank you—I don't really care for anything.
WALTER: (*feeling his head, sobriety coming*) Where's Mama?
RUTH: She ain't come back yet.
WALTER: (*looking Murchison over from head to toe, scrutinizing his carefully casual tweed sports jacket over cashmere V-neck sweater over soft eyelet shirt and tie, and soft slacks, finished off with white buckskin shoes*) Why all you college boys wear them faggoty-looking white shoes?
RUTH: Walter Lee!

George Murchison ignores the remark.

WALTER: (*to Ruth*) Well, they look crazy as hell—white shoes, cold as it is.
RUTH: (*crushed*) You have to excuse him—
WALTER: No he don't! Excuse me for what? What you always excusing me for! I'll excuse myself when I needs to be excused! (*A pause.*) They look as funny as them black knee socks Beneatha wears out of here all the time.
RUTH: It's the college *style*, Walter.
WALTER: Style, hell. She looks like she got burnt legs or something!
RUTH: Oh, Walter—
WALTER: (*an irritable mimic*) Oh, Walter! Oh, Walter! (*To Murchison.*) How's your old man making out? I understand you all going to buy that big hotel on the Drive? (*He finds a beer in the refrigerator, wanders over to Murchison, sipping and wiping his lips with the back of his hand, and straddling a chair backwards to talk to the other man.*) Shrewed move. Your old man is all right, man. (*Tapping his head and half winking for emphasis.*) I mean he knows how to operate. I mean he thinks *big*, you know what I mean, I mean for a *home*, you know? But I think he's kind of running out of ideas now. I'd like to talk to him, Listen, man, I got some plans that could turn this city upside down. I mean think like he does. *Big*. Invest big, gamble big, hell, lose *big* if you have to, you know what I mean. It's hard to find a man on this whole

Southside who understands my kinds of thinking—you dig? *(He scrutinizes Murchison again, drinks his beer, squints his eyes and leans in close, confidential, man to man.)* Me and you ought to sit down and talk sometimes, man. Man, I got me some ideas . . .

MURCHISON: *(with boredom)* Yeah—sometimes we'll have to do that, Walter.

WALTER: *(understanding the indifference, and offended)* Yeah—well, when you get the time, man. I know you a busy little boy.

RUTH: Walter, please—

WALTER: *(bitterly, hurt)* I know ain't nothing in this world as busy as you colored college boys with your fraternity pins and white shoes . . .

RUTH: *(covering her face with humiliation)* Oh, Walter Lee—

WALTER: I see you all all the time—with the books tucked under your arms—going to your *(British A—a mimic.)* "clahsses." And for what! What the hell you learning over there? Filling up your heads—*(Counting off on his fingers.)*—with the sociology and the psychology—but they teaching you how to be a man? How to take over and run the world? They teaching you how to run a rubber plantation or a steel mill? Naw—just to talk proper and read books and wear them faggoty-looking white shoes . . .

GEORGE: *(looking at him with distaste, a little above it all)* You're all wacked up with bitterness, man.

WALTER: *(intently, almost quietly, between the teeth, glaring at the boy)* And you—ain't you bitter, man! Ain't you just about had it yet? Don't you see no stars gleaming that you can't reach out and grab? You happy?—You contented son-of-a-bitch—you happy? You got it made? Bitter? Man, I'm a volcano. Bitter? Here I am a giant—surrounded by ants! Ants who can't even understand what it is the giant is talking about.

RUTH: *(passionately and suddenly)* Oh, Walter—ain't you with nobody!

WALTER: *(violently)* No! 'Cause ain't nobody with me! Not even my own mother!

RUTH: Walter, that's a terrible thing to say!

Beneatha enters, dressed for the evening in a cocktail dress and earrings, hair natural.

GEORGE: Well—hey—*(Crosses to Beneatha; thoughtful, with emphasis, since this is a reversal.)* You look great!

WALTER: *(seeing his sister's hair for the first time)* What's the matter with your head?

BENEATHA: *(tired of the jokes now)* I cut it off, Brother.

WALTER: *(coming close to inspect it and walking around her)* Well, I'll be damned. So that's what they mean by the African bush.

BENEATHA: Ha ha. Let's go, George.

GEORGE: *(looking at her)* You know something? I like it. It's sharp. I mean it really is. *(Helps her into her wrap.)*

RUTH: Yes—I think so, too. *(She goes to the mirror and starts to clutch at her hair.)*

WALTER: Oh no! You leave yours alone, baby. You might turn out to have a pin-shaped head or something!

BENEATHA: See you all later.

Ruth: Have a nice time.

George: Thanks. Good night. (*Half out the door, he reopens it. To Walter.*) Good night, Prometheus!

Beneatha and George exit.

Walter: (*to Ruth*) Who is Prometheus?

Ruth: I don't know. Don't worry about it.

Walter: (*in fury, pointing after George*) See there — they get to a point where they can't insult you man to man — they got to go talk about something ain't nobody never heard of!

Ruth: How do you know it was an insult? (*To humor him.*) Maybe Prometheus is a nice fellow.

Walter: Prometheus! I bet there ain't even no such thing! I bet that simple-minded clown —

Ruth: Walter —

She stops what she is doing and looks at him.

Walter: (*yelling*) Don't start!

Ruth: Start what?

Walter: Your nagging! Where was I? Who was I with? How much money did I spend?

Ruth: (*plaintively*) Walter Lee — why don't we just try to talk about it. . .

Walter: (*not listening*) I been out talking with people who understand me. People who care about the things I got on my mind.

Ruth: (*wearily*) I guess that means people like Willy Harris.

Walter: Yes, people like Willy Harris.

Ruth: (*with a sudden flash of impatience*) Why don't you all just hurry up and go into the banking business and stop talking about it!

Walter: Why? You want to know why? Cause we all tied up in a race of people that don't know how to do nothing but moan, pray and have babies!

The line is too bitter even for him and he looks at her and sits down.

Ruth: Oh, Walter. . . (*Softly.*) Honey, why can't you stop fighting me?

Walter: (*without thinking*) Who's fighting you? Who even cares about you?

This line begins the retardation of his mood.

Ruth: Well — (*She waits a long time, and then with resignation starts to put away her things.*) I guess I might as well go on to bed . . . (*More or less to herself.*) I don't know where we lost it . . . but we have . . . (*Then, to him.*) I — I'm sorry about this new baby, Walter. I guess maybe I better go on and do what I started . . . I guess I just didn't realize how bad things was with us . . . I guess I just didn't really realize — (*She starts out to the bedroom and stops.*) You want some hot milk?

Walter: Hot milk?

Ruth: Yes — hot milk.

Walter: Why hot milk?

RUTH: 'Cause after all that liquor you come home with you ought to have something hot in your stomach.

WALTER: I don't want hot milk.

RUTH: You want some coffee then?

WALTER: No, I don't want no coffee. I don't want nothing hot to drink. *(Almost plaintively.)* Why you always trying to give me something to eat?

RUTH: *(standing and looking at him helplessly)* What *else* can I give you, Walter Lee Younger?

She stands and looks at him and presently turns to go out again. He lifts his head and watches her going away from him in a new mood which began to emerge when he asked her "Who cares about you?"

WALTER: It's been rough, ain't it, baby? *(She hears and stops but does not turn around and he continues to her back.)* I guess between two people there ain't never as much understood as folks generally thinks there is. I mean like between me and you —*(She turns to face him.)* How we gets to the place where we scared to talk softness to each other. *(He waits, thinking hard himself.)* Why you think it got to be like that? *(He is thoughtful, almost as a child would be.)* Ruth, what is it gets into people ought to be close?

RUTH: I don't know, honey, I think about it a lot.

WALTER: On account of you and me, you mean? The way things are with us. The way something done come down between us.

RUTH: There ain't so much between us, Walter . . . Not when you come to me and try to talk to me. Try to be with me . . . a little even.

WALTER: *(total honesty)* Sometimes . . . sometimes . . . I don't even know how to try.

RUTH: Walter—

WALTER: Yes?

RUTH: *(coming to him, gently and with misgiving, but coming to him)* Honey . . . life don't have to be like this. I mean sometimes people can do things so that things are better . . . You remember how we used to talk when Travis was born . . . about the way we were going to live . . . the kind of house. . . *(She is stroking his head.)* Well, it's all starting to slip away from us. . .

He turns her to him and they look at each other and kiss, tenderly and hungrily. The door opens and Mama enters—Walter breaks away and jumps up. A beat.

WALTER: Mama, where have you been?

MAMA: My—them steps is longer than they used to be. Whew! *(She sits down and ignores him.)* How you feeling this evening, Ruth?

Ruth shrugs, disturbed at having been interrupted and watching her husband knowingly.

WALTER: Mama, where have you been all day?

MAMA: *(still ignoring him and leaning on the table and changing to more comfortable shoes)* Where's Travis?

RUTH: I let him go out earlier and he ain't come back yet. Boy, is he going to get it!

Walter: Mama!

Mama: *(as if she has heard him for the first time)* Yes, son?

Walter: Where did you go this afternoon?

Mama: I went downtown to tend to some business that I had to tend to.

Walter: What kind of business?

Mama: You know better than to question me like a child, Brother.

Walter: *(rising and bending over the table)* Where were you, Mama? *(Bringing his fists down and shouting.)* Mama, you didn't go do something with that insurance money, something crazy?

The front door opens slowly, interrupting him, and Travis peeks his head in, less than hopefully.

Travis: *(to his mother)* Mama, I—

Ruth: "Mama I" nothing! You're going to get it, boy! Get on in that bedroom and get yourself ready!

Travis: But I—

Mama: Why don't you all never let the child explain hisself.

Ruth: Keep out of it now, Lena.

Mama clamps her lips together, and Ruth advances toward her son menacingly.

Ruth: A thousand times I have told you not to go off like that—

Mama: *(holding out her arms to her grandson)* Well—at least let me tell him something. I want him to be the first one to hear . . . Come here, Travis. *(The boy obeys, gladly.)* Travis—*(She takes him by the shoulder and looks into his face.)*—you know that money we got in the mail this morning?

Travis: Yes'm—

Mama: Well—what you think your grandmama gone and done with that money?

Travis: I don't know, Grandmama.

Mama: *(putting her finger on his nose for emphasis)* She went out and she bought you a house! *(The explosion comes from Walter at the end of the revelation and he jumps up and turns away from all of them in a fury. Mama continues, to Travis.)* You glad about the house? It's going to be yours when you get to be a man.

Travis: Yeah—I always wanted to live in a house.

Mama: All right, gimme some sugar then—*(Travis puts his arms around her neck as she watches her son over the boy's shoulder. Then, to Travis, after the embrace.)* Now when you say your prayers tonight, you thank God and your grandfather—'cause it was him who give you the house—in his way.

Ruth: *(taking the boy from Mama and pushing him toward the bedroom)* Now you get out of here and get ready for your beating.

Travis: Aw, Mama—

Ruth: Get on in there—*(Closing the door behind him and turning radiantly to her mother-in-law.)* So you went and did it!

Mama: *(quietly, looking at her son with pain)* Yes, I did.

RUTH: *(raising both arms classically)* PRAISE GOD! *(Looks at Walter a moment, who says nothing. She crosses rapidly to her husband.)* Please, honey—let me be glad . . . you be glad too. *(She has laid her hands on his shoulders, but he shakes himself free of her roughly, without turning to face her.)* Oh, Walter . . . a home . . . *a home*. *(She comes back to Mama.)* Well—where is it? How big is it? How much it going to cost?

MAMA: Well—

RUTH: When we moving?

MAMA: *(smiling at her)* First of the month.

RUTH: *(throwing back her head with jubilance) Praise God!*

MAMA: *(tentatively, still looking at her son's back turned against her and Ruth)* It's—it's a nice house too . . . *(She cannot help speaking directly to him. An imploring quality in her voice, her manner, makes her almost like a girl now.)* Three bedrooms—nice big one for you and Ruth . . . Me and Beneatha still have to share our room, but Travis have one of his own—and *(With difficulty.)* I figure if the—new baby—is a boy, we could get one of them double-decker outfits . . . And there's a yard with a little patch of dirt where I could maybe get to grow me a few flowers . . . And a nice big basement . . .

RUTH: Walter honey, be glad—

MAMA: *(still to his back, fingering things on the table)* 'Course I don't want to make it sound fancier than it is . . . It's just a plain little old house—but it's made good and solid—and it will be *ours*. Walter Lee—it makes a difference in a man when he can walk on floors that belong to *him* . . .

RUTH: Where is it?

MAMA: *(frightened at this telling)* Well—well—it's out there in Clybourne Park—

Ruth's radiance fades abruptly, and Walter finally turns slowly to face his mother with incredulity and hostility.

RUTH: Where?

MAMA: *(matter of factly)* Four o six Clybourne Street, Clybourne Park.

RUTH: Clybourne Park? Mama, there ain't no colored people living in Clybourne Park.

MAMA: *(almost idiotically)* Well, I guess there's going to be some now.

WALTER: *(bitterly)* So that's the peace and comfort you went out and bought for us today!

MAMA: *(raising her eyes to meet his finally)* Son—I just tried to find the nicest place for the least amount of money for my family.

RUTH: *(trying to recover from the shock)* Well—well—'course I ain't one never been 'fraid of no crackers, mind you—but—well, wasn't there no other houses nowhere?

MAMA: Them houses they put up for colored in them areas way out all seem to cost twice as much as other houses. I did the best I could.

RUTH: *(struck senseless with the news, in its various degrees of goodness and trouble, she sits a moment, her fists propping her chin in thought, and then she* *starts to rise, bringing her fists down with vigor, the radiance spreading from cheek to cheek again)* Well —well — All I can say is —if this is my time in life —MY TIME— to say good-bye —*(And she builds with momentum as she starts to circle the room with an exuberant, almost tearfully happy release.)*— to these God-damned cracking walls! —*(She pounds the walls.)*— and these marching roaches! —*(She wipes at an imaginary army of marching reaches.)*— and this cramped little closet which ain't now or never was no kitchen!. . . then I say it loud and good, HALLELUJAH! AND GOOD-BYE MISERY . . . I DON'T NEVER WANT TO SEE YOUR UGLY FACE AGAIN! *(She laughs joyously, having practically destroyed the apartment, and flings her arms up and lets them come down happily, slowly, reflectively, over her abdomen, aware for the first time perhaps that the life therein pulses with happiness and not despair.)* Lena?

MAMA: *(moved, watching her happiness)* Yes, honey?

RUTH: *(looking off)* Is there—is there a whole lot of sunlight?

MAMA: *(understanding)* Yes, child, there's a whole lot of sunlight.

Long pause.

RUTH: *(collecting herself and going to the door of the room Travis is in)* Well — I guess I better see 'bout Travis. *(To Mama.)* Lord, I sure don't feel like whipping nobody today!

She exits.

MAMA: *(the mother and son are left alone now and the mother waits a long time, considering deeply, before she speaks)* Son — you — you understand what I done, don't you? *(Walter is silent and sullen.)* I — I just seen my family falling apart today . . . just falling to pieces in front of my eyes . . . We couldn't of gone on like we was today. We was going backwards 'stead of forwards — talking 'bout killing babies and wishing each other was dead . . . When it gets like that in life — you just got to do something different, push on out and do something bigger . . . *(She waits.)* I wish you say something, son . . . I wish you'd say how deep inside you you think I done the right thing —

WALTER: *(crossing slowly to his bedroom door and finally turning there and speaking measuredly)* What you need me to say you done right for? *You* the head of this family. You run our lives like you want to. It was your money and you did what you wanted with it. So what you need for me to say it was all right for? *(Bitterly, to hurt her as deeply as he knows is possible.)* So you butchered up a dream of mine — you — who always talking 'bout your children's dreams . . .

MAMA: Walter Lee —

He just closes the door behind him. Mama sits alone, thinking heavily.

Curtain.

SCENE 2

TIME: Friday night, a few weeks later.

At rise: Packing crates mark the intention of the family to move. Beneatha and George come in, presumably from an evening out again.

GEORGE: O.K. . . . O.K., whatever you say . . . *(They both sit on the couch. He tries to kiss her. She moves away.)* Look, we've had a nice evening, let's not spoil it, huh? . . .

He again turns her head and tries to nuzzle in and she turns away from him, not with distaste but with momentary lack of interest; in a mood to pursue what they were talking about.

BENEATHA: I'm *trying* to talk to you.

GEORGE: We always talk.

BENEATHA: Yes — and I love to talk.

GEORGE: *(exasperated rising)* I know it and I don't mind it sometimes . . . I want you to cut it out, see — The moody stuff, I mean. I don't like it. You're a nice-looking girl . . . all over. That's all you need, honey, forget the atmosphere. Guys aren't going to go for the atmosphere — they're going to go for what they see. Be glad for that. Drop the Garbo routine. It doesn't go with you. As for myself, I want a nice —*(Groping.)* — simple *(Thoughtfully.)* — sophisticated girl . . . not a poet — O.K.?

He starts to kiss her, she rebuffs him again and he jumps up.

BENEATHA: Why are you angry, George?

GEORGE: Because this is stupid! I don't go out with you to discuss the nature of "quiet desperation" or to hear all about your thoughts — because the world will go on thinking what it thinks regardless —

BENEATHA: Then why read books? Why go to school?

GEORGE: *(with artificial patience, counting on his fingers)* It's simple. You read books — to learn facts — to get grades — to pass the course — to get a degree. That's all — it has nothing to do with thoughts.

A long pause.

BENEATHA: I see. *(He starts to sit.)* Good night, George.

George looks at her a little oddly, and starts to exit. He meets Mama coming in.

GEORGE: Oh — hello, Mrs. Younger.

MAMA: Hello George how you feeling?

GEORGE: Fine — fine, how are you?

MAMA: Oh, a little tired. You know them steps can get you after a day's work. You all have a nice time tonight?

GEORGE: Yes — a fine time. A fine time.

MAMA: Well, good night.

GEORGE: Good night. *(He exits. Mama closes the door behind her.)* Hello, honey. What you sitting like that for?

BENEATHA: I'm just sitting.

MAMA: Didn't you have a nice time?

BENEATHA: No.

MAMA: No? What's the matter?

BENEATHA: Mama, George is a fool—honest. (*She rises.*)

MAMA: (*hustling around unloading the packages she has entered with. She stops.*) Is he, baby?

BENEATHA: Yes.

Beneatha makes up Travis's bed as she talks.

MAMA: You sure?

BENEATHA: Yes.

MAMA: Well—I guess you better not waste your time with no fools.

Beneatha looks up at her mother, watching her put groceries in the refrigerator. Finally she gathers up her things and starts into the bedroom. At the door she stops and looks back at her mother.

BENEATHA: Mama—

MAMA: Yes, baby—

BENEATHA: Thank you.

MAMA: For what?

BENEATHA: For understanding me this time.

She exits quickly and the mother stands, smiling a little, looking at the place where Beneatha just stood. Ruth enters.

RUTH: Now don't you fool with any of this stuff, Lena—

MAMA: Oh, I just thought I'd sort a few things out. Is Brother here?

RUTH: Yes.

MAMA: (*with concern*) Is he—

RUTH: (*reading her eyes*) Yes.

Mama is silent and someone knocks on the door. Mama and Ruth exchange weary and knowing glances and Ruth opens it to admit the neighbor, Mrs. Johnson, who is a rather squeaky wide-eyed lady of no particular age, with a newspaper under her arm.

MAMA: (*changing her expression to acute delight and a ringing cheerful greeting*) Oh—hello there, Johnson.

JOHNSON: (*this is a woman who decided long ago to be enthusiastic about EVERYTHING in life and she is inclined to wave her wrist vigorously at the height of her exclamatory comments*) Hello there, yourself! H'you this evening, Ruth?

RUTH: (*not much of a deceptive type*) Fine, Mis' Johnson, h'you?

JOHNSON: Fine. (*Reaching out quickly, playfully, and patting Ruth's stomach.*) Ain't you starting to poke out none yet! (*She mugs with delight at the over familiar remark and her eyes dart around looking at the crates and packing preparation; Mama's face is a cold sheet of endurance.*) Oh, ain't we getting ready round here, though! Yessir! Lookathere! I'm telling you the Youngers is really getting ready to "move on up a little higher!"—Bless God!

MAMA: (*a little drily, doubting the total sincerity of the Blesser*) Bless God.

Johnson: He's good, ain't He?

Mama: Oh yes, He's good.

Johnson: I mean sometimes He works in mysterious ways . . . but He works, don't He!

Mama: *(the same)* Yes, he does.

Johnson: I'm just soooooo happy for y'all. And this here child—*(About Ruth.)* looks like she could just pop open with happiness, don't she. Where's all the rest of the family?

Mama: Bennie's gone to bed —

Johnson: Ain't no . . . *(The implication is pregnancy.)* sickness done hit you — I hope . . . ?

Mama: No — she just tired. She was out this evening.

Johnson: *(all is a coo, an emphatic coo)* Aw — ain't that lovely. She still going out with the little Murchison boy?

Mama: *(drily)* Ummmm huh.

Johnson: That's lovely. You sure got lovely children, Younger. Me and Isaiah talks all the time 'bout what fine children you was blessed with. We sure do.

Mama: Ruth, give Mis' Johnson a piece of sweet potato pie and some milk.

Johnson: Oh honey, I can't stay hardly a minute — I just dropped in to see if there was anything I could do. *(Accepting the food easily.)* I guess y'all seen the news what's all over the colored paper this week . . .

Mama: No — didn't get mine yet this week.

Johnson: *(lifting her head and blinking with the spirit of catastrophe)* You mean you ain't read 'bout them colored people that was bombed out their place out there?

Ruth straightens with concern and takes the paper and reads it. Johnson notices her and feeds commentary.

Johnson: Ain't it something how bad these here white folks is getting here in Chicago! Lord, getting so you think you right down in Mississippi! *(With a tremendous and rather insincere sense of melodrama.)* 'Course I thinks it's wonderful how our folk keeps on pushing out. You hear some of these Negroes round here talking 'bout how they don't go where they ain't wanted and all that —but not me, honey! *(This is a lie.)* Wilhemenia Othella Johnson goes anywhere, any time she feels like it! *(With head movement for emphasis.)* Yes I do! Why if we left it up to these here crackers, the poor niggers wouldn't have nothing —*(She clasps her hand over her mouth.)* Oh, I always forgets you don't 'low that word in your house.

Mama: *(quietly, looking at her)* No — I don't 'low it.

Johnson: *(vigorously again)* Me neither! I was just telling Isaiah yesterday when he come using it in front of me — I said, "Isaiah, it's just like Mis' Younger says all the time —"

Mama: Don't you want some more pie?

Johnson: No — no thank you; this was lovely. I got to get on over home and have my midnight coffee, I hear some people say it don't let them sleep but

I finds I can't close my eyes right lessen I done had that laaaast cup of coffee . . . *(She waits. A beat. Undaunted.)* My Goodnight coffee, I calls it!

MAMA: *(with much eye-rolling and communication between herself and Ruth)* Ruth, why don't you give Mis' Johnson some coffee.

Ruth gives Mama an unpleasant look for her kindness.

JOHNSON: *(accepting the coffee)* Where's Brother tonight?

MAMA: He's lying down.

JOHNSON: MMmmmmm, he sure gets his beauty rest, don't he? Good-looking man. Sure is a good-looking man! *(Reaching out to pat Ruth's stomach again.)* I guess that's how come we keep on having babies around here. *(She winks at Mama.)* One thing 'bout Brother, he always know how to have a *good* time. And soooooo ambitious! I bet it was his idea y'all moving out to Clybourne Park. Lord — I bet this time next month y'all's names will have been in the papers plenty — *(Holding up her hands to mark off each word of the headline she can see in front of her.)* "NEGROES INVADE CLYBOURNE PARK — BOMBED!"

MAMA: *(she and Ruth look at the woman in amazement)* We ain't exactly moving out there to get bombed.

JOHNSON: Oh honey — you know I'm praying to God every day that don't nothing like that happen! But you have to think of life like it is — and these here Chicago peckerwoods is some baaaad peckerwoods.

MAMA: *(wearily)* We done thought about all that Mis' Johnson.

Beneatha comes out of the bedroom in her robe and passes through to the bathroom. Mrs. Johnson turns.

JOHNSON: Hello there, Bennie!

BENEATHA: *(crisply)* Hello, Mrs. Johnson.

JOHNSON: How is school?

BENEATHA: *(crisply)* Fine, thank you. *(She goes out.)*

JOHNSON: *(insulted)* Getting so she don't have much to say to nobody.

MAMA: The child was on her way to the bathroom.

JOHNSON: I know — but sometimes she act like ain't got time to pass the time of day with nobody ain't been to college. Oh — I ain't criticizing her none. It's just — you know how some of our young people gets when they get a little education. *(Mama and Ruth say nothing, just look at her.)* Yes — well. Well, I guess I better get on home. *(Unmoving.)* 'Course I can understand how she must be proud and everything — being the only one in the family to make something of herself. I know just being a chauffeur ain't never satisfied Brother none. He shouldn't feel like that, though. Ain't nothing wrong with being a chauffeur.

MAMA: There's plenty wrong with it.

JOHNSON: What?

MAMA: Plenty. My husband always said being any kind of a servant wasn't a fit thing for a man to have to be. He always said a man's hands was made to make things, or to turn the earth with —not to drive nobody's car for 'em — or —*(She looks at her own hands.)* carry they slop jars. And my boy is just like him —he wasn't meant to wait on nobody.

JOHNSON: *(rising, somewhat offended)* Mmmmmmmmm. The Youngers is too much for me! *(She looks around.)* You sure one proud acting bunch of colored folks. Well —I always thinks like Booker T. Washington said that time —"Education has spoiled many a good plow hand"—

MAMA: Is that what old Booker T. said?

JOHNSON: He sure did.

MAMA: Well, it sounds just like him. The fool.

JOHNSON: *(indignantly)* Well —he was one of our great men.

MAMA: Who said so?

JOHNSON: *(nonplussed)* You know, me and you ain't never agreed about some things, Lena *Younger*. I guess I better be going —

RUTH: (quickly) Good night.

JOHNSON: Good night. Oh —*(Thrusting it at her.)* You can keep the paper! *(With a trill.)* 'Night.

MAMA: Good night, Mis' Johnson.

Mrs. Johnson exits.

RUTH: If ignorance was gold.

MAMA: Shush. Don't talk about folks behind their backs.

RUTH: You do.

MAMA: I'm old and corrupted. *(Beneatha enters.)* You was rude to Mis' Johnson, Beneatha, and I don't like it at all.

BENEATHA: *(at her door)* Mama, if there are two things we, as a people, have got to overcome, one is the Klu Klux Klan —and the other is Mrs. Johnson. *(She exits.)*

MAMA: Smart aleck.

The phone rings.

RUTH: I'll get it.

MAMA: Lord, ain't this a popular place tonight.

RUTH: *(at the phone)* Hello —Just a minute. *(Goes to door.)* Walter, it's Mrs. Arnold. *(Waits. Goes back to the phone. Tense.)* Hello. Yes, this is his wife speaking. He's lying down now. Yes . . . well, he'll be in tomorrow. He's been very sick. Yes — I know we should have called, but we were so sure he'd be able to come in today. Yes —yes, I'm very sorry. Yes . . . Thank you very much. *(She hangs up. Walter is standing in the doorway of the bedroom behind her.)* That was Mrs. Arnold.

WALTER: *(indifferently)* Was it?

RUTH: She said if you don't come in tomorrow that they are getting a new man . . .

WALTER: Ain't that sad — ain't that crying sad.

RUTH: She said Mr. Arnold has had to take a cab for three days . . . Walter, you ain't been to work for three days! *(This is a revelation to her.)* Where you been, Walter Lee Younger? *(Walter looks at her and starts to laugh.)* You're going to lose your job.

WALTER: That's right . . . *(He turns on the radio.)*

RUTH: Oh, Walter, and with your mother working like a dog every day —

A steamy, deep blues pours into the room.

WALTER: That's sad too — Everything is sad.

MAMA: What you been doing for these three days, son?

WALTER: Mama — you don't know all the things a man what got leisure can find to do in this city . . . What's this — Friday night? Well — Wednesday I borrowed Willey Harris' car and I went for a drive . . . just me and myself and I drove and drove . . . Way out . . . way past South Chicago, and I parked the car and I sat and looked at the steel mills all day long. I just sat in the car and looked at them big black chimneys for hours. Then I drove back and I went to the Green Hat. *(Pause.)* And Thursday — Thursday I borrowed the car again and I got in it and I pointed it the other way and I drove the other way — for hours — way, way up to Wisconsin, and I looked at the farms. I just drove and looked at the farms. Then I drove back and I went to the Green Hat. *(Pause.)* And today — today I didn't get the car. Today I just walked. All over the Southside. And I looked at the Negroes and they looked at me and finally I just sat down on the curb at Thirty-ninth and South Parkway and I just sat there and watched the Negroes go by. And then I went to the Green Hat. You all sad? You all depressed? And you know where I am going right now —

Ruth goes out quietly.

MAMA: Oh, Big Walter, is this the harvest of our days?

WALTER: You know what I like about the Green Hat? I like this little cat they got there who blows a sax . . . He blows. He talks to me. He ain't but 'bout five feet tall and he's got a conked head and his eyes is always closed and he's all music —

MAMA: *(rising and getting some papers out of her handbag)* Walter —

WALTER: And there's this other guy who plays the piano . . . and they got a sound. I mean they can work on some music . . . They got the best little combo in the world in the Green Hat . . . You can just sit there and drink and listen to them three men play and you realize that don't nothing matter worth a damn, but just being there —

MAMA: I've helped do it to you, haven't I, son? Walter I been wrong.

WALTER: Naw — you ain't never been wrong about nothing, Mama.

MAMA: Listen to me, now. I say I been wrong son. That I been doing to you what the rest of the world been doing to you. *(She turns off the radio.)* Walter — *(She stops and he looks up slowly at her and she meets his eyes pleadingly.)*

What you ain't never understood is that I ain't got nothing, don't own nothing, ain't never really wanted nothing that wasn't for you. There ain't nothing as precious to me . . . There ain't nothing worth holding on to, money, dreams, nothing else —if it means —if it means it's going to destroy my boy. *(She takes an envelope out of her handbag and puts it in front of him and he watches her without speaking or moving.)* I paid the man thirty-five hundred dollars down on the house. That leaves sixty-five hundred dollars. Monday morning I want you to take this money and take three thousand dollars and put it in a savings account for Beneatha's medical schooling. The rest you put in a checking account — with your name on it. And from now on any penny that come out of it or that go in it is for you to look after. For you to decide. *(She drops her hands a little helplessly.)* It ain't much, but it's all I got in the world and I'm putting it in your hands. I'm telling you to be the head of this family from now on like you supposed to be.

WALTER: *(stares at the money)* You trust me like that Mama?

MAMA: I ain't never stop trusting you. Like I ain't never stop loving you.

She goes out, and Walter sits looking at the money on the table. Finally, in a decisive gesture, he gets up, and, in mingled joy and desperation, picks up the money. At the same moment, Travis enters for bed.

TRAVIS: What's the matter, Daddy? You drunk?

WALTER: *(sweetly, more sweetly than we have ever known him)* No, Daddy ain't drunk. Daddy ain't going to never be drunk again . . .

TRAVIS: Well, good night, Daddy.

The father has come from behind the couch and leans over, embracing his son.

WALTER: Son, I feel like talking to you tonight.

TRAVIS: About what?

WALTER: Oh, about a lot of things. About you and what kind of man you going to be when you grow up . . . Son —son, what do you want to be when you grow up?

TRAVIS: A bus driver.

WALTER: *(laughing a little)*: A what? Man, that ain't nothing to want to be!

TRAVIS: Why not?

WALTER: 'Cause, man —it ain't big enough —you know what I mean.

TRAVIS: I don't know then. I can't make up my mind. Sometimes Mama asks me that too. And sometimes when I tell her I just want to be like you — she says she don't want me to be like that and sometimes she says she does. . . .

WALTER: *(gathering him up in his arms)* You know what, Travis? In seven years you going to be seventeen years old. And things is going to be very different with us in seven years, Travis. . . . One day when you are seventeen I'll come home — home from my office downtown somewhere —

TRAVIS: You don't work in no office, Daddy.

WALTER: No —but after tonight. After what your daddy gonna do tonight, there's going to be offices — a whole lot of offices. . . .

TRAVIS: What you gonna do tonight, Daddy?

WALTER: You wouldn't understand yet, son, but your daddy's gonna make a transaction . . . a business transaction that's going to change our lives. . . . That's how come one day when you 'bout seventeen years old I'll come home and I'll be pretty tired, you know what I mean, after a day of conference and secretaries getting things wrong the way they do . . . just a plain black Chrysler, I think, with white walls—no—black tires. More elegant. Rich people don't have to be flashy . . . though I'll have to get something a little sportier for Ruth—maybe a Cadillac convertible to do her shopping in. . . . And I'll come up the steps to the house and the gardener will be clipping away at the hedges and he'll say, "Good evening, Mr. Younger." And I'll say, "Hello, Jefferson, how are you this evening?" And I'll go inside and Ruth will come downstairs and meet me at the door and we'll kiss each other and she'll take my arm and we'll go up to your room to see you sitting on the floor with the catalogues of all the great schools in America around you. . . . All the great schools in the world! And—and I'll say, all right son—it's your seventeenth birthday, what is it you've decided? . . . Just tell me where you want to go to school and you'll *go*. Just tell me, what it is you want to be—and you'll *be* it. . . . Whatever you want to be—Yessir! *(He holds his arms open for Travis.)* You just name it, son . . . *(Travis leaps into them.)* and I hand you the world!

Walter's voice has risen in pitch and hysterical promise and on the last line he lifts Travis high.

Blackout.

SCENE 3

TIME: *Saturday, moving day, one week later.*

Before the curtain rises, Ruth's voice, a strident, dramatic church alto, cuts through the silence.

It is, in the darkness, a triumphant surge, a penetrating statement of expectation: "Oh, Lord, I don't feel no ways tired! Children, oh, glory hallelujah!"

As the curtain rises we see that Ruth is alone in the living room, finishing up the family's packing. It is moving day. She is nailing crates and trying cartons. Beneatha enters, carrying a guitar case, and watches her exuberant sister-in-law.

RUTH: Hey!
BENEATHA: *(putting away the case)* Hi.
RUTH: *(pointing at a package)* Honey—look in that package there and see what I found on sale this morning at the South Center. *(Ruth gets up and moves to the package and draws out some curtains.)* Lookahere—hand-turned hems!
BENEATHA: How do you know the window size out there?
RUTH: *(who hadn't thought of that)* Oh—Well, they bound to fit something in the whole house. Anyhow, they was too good a bargain to pass up. *(Ruth slaps her head, suddenly remembering something.)* Oh, Bennie—I meant to put a special note on that carton over there. That's your mama's good china and she wants 'em to be very careful with it.

BENEATHA: I'll do it.

Beneatha finds a piece of paper and starts to draw large letters on it.

RUTH: You know what I'm going to do soon as I get in that new house?

BENEATHA: What?

RUTH: Honey—I'm going to run me a tub of water up to here . . . *(With her fingers practically up to her nostrils.)* And I'm going to get in it—and I am going to sit . . . and sit . . . and sit in that hot water and the first person who knocks to tell *me* to hurry up and come out—

BENEATHA: Gets shot at sunrise.

RUTH: *(laughing happily)* You said it, sister! *(Noticing how large Beneatha is absent-mindedly making the note):* Honey, they ain't going to read that from no air-plane.

BENEATHA: *(laughing herself)* I guess I always think things have more emphasis if they are big, somehow.

RUTH: *(looking up at her and smiling).* You and your brother seem to have that as a philosophy of life. Lord, that man—done changed so 'round here. You know—you know what we did last might? Me and Walter Lee?

BENEATHA: What?

RUTH: *(smiling to herself)* We went to the movies. *(Looking at Beneatha to see if she understands.)* We went to the movies. You know the last time me and Walter went to the movies together?

BENEATHA: No.

RUTH: Me neither. That's how long it been. *(Smiling again.)* But we went last night. The picture wasn't much good, but that didn't seem to matter. We went—and we held hands.

BENEATHA: Oh, Lord!

RUTH: We held hands—and you know what?

BENEATHA: What?

RUTH: When we come out of the show it was late and dark and all the stores and things was closed up . . . and it was kind of chilly and there wasn't many people on the streets . . . and we was still holding hands, me and Walter.

BENEATHA: You're killing me.

Walter enters with a large package. His happiness is deep in him; he cannot keep still with his newfound exuberance. He is singing and wiggling and snapping his fingers. He puts his package in a corner and puts a phonograph record, which he has brought in with him, on the record player. As the music, soulful and sensuous, comes up he dances over to Ruth and tries to get her to dance with him. She gives in at last to his raunchiness and in a fit of giggling allows herself to be drawn into his mood. They dip and she melts into his arms in a classic, body melting "slow drag."

BENEATHA: *(regarding them a long time as they dance, then drawing in her breath for a deeply exaggerated comment which she does not particularly mean)* Talk about—oldddddddddd-fashion edddddddd—Negroes!

WALTER: *(stopping momentarily)* What kind of Negroes?

He says this in fun, He is not angry with her today, nor with anyone. He starts to dance with his wife again.

BENEATHA: Old-fashioned.

WALTER: *(as he dances with Ruth)* You know, when these *New Negroes* have their convention —*(Pointing at his sister.)*— that is going to be the chairman of the Committee on Unending Agitation. *(He goes on dancing, then stops.)* Race, race, race! . . . Girl, I do believe you are the first person in the history of the entire human race to successfully brainwash yourself. *(Beneatha breaks up and he goes on dancing. He stops again, enjoying his tease.)* Damn, even the N double A C P takes a holiday sometimes! *(Beneatha and Ruth laugh. He dances with Ruth some more and starts to laugh and stops and pantomimes someone over an operating table.)* I can just see that chick someday looking down at some poor cat on an operating table and before she starts to slice him, she says . . . *(Pulling his sleeves back maliciously.)* "By the way, what are your views on civil rights down there? . . ."

He laughs at her again and starts to dance happily. The bell sounds.

BENEATHA: Sticks and stones may break my bones but . . . words will never hurt me!

Beneatha goes to the door and opens it as Walter and Ruth go on with the clowning. Beneatha is somewhat surprised to see a quiet looking middle-aged white man in a business suit holding his hat and a briefcase in his hand and consulting a small piece of paper.

MAN: Uh — how do you do, miss. I am looking for a Mrs. —*(He looks at the slip of paper.)* Mrs. Lena Younger? *(He stops short, struck dumb at the sight of the oblivious Walter and Ruth.)*

BENEATHA: *(smoothing her hair with slight embarrassment)* Oh — yes, that's my mother. Excuse me. *(She closes the door and turns to quiet the other two.)* Ruth! Brother! *(Enunciating precisely but soundlessly: "There's a white man at the door!" They stop dancing, Ruth cuts off the phonograph, Beneatha opens the door. The man casts a curious quick glance at all of them.)* Uh — come in please.

MAN: *(coming in)* Thank you.

BENEATHA: My mother isn't here just now. Is it business?

MAN: Yes . . . well, of a sort.

WALTER: *(freely, the Man of the House)* Have a seat. I'm Mrs. Younger's son. I look after most of her business matters.

Ruth and Beneatha exchange amused glances.

MAN: *(regarding Walter, and sitting)* Well my name is Karl Lindner . . .

WALTER: *(stretching out his hand)* Walter Younger. This is my wife —*(Ruth nods politely.)*— and my sister.

LINDNER: How do you do.

WALTER: *(amiably, as he sits himself easily on a chair, leaning forward on his knees with interest and looking expectantly into the newcomer's face)* What can we do for you, Mr. Lindner!

LINDNER: *(some minor shuffling of the hat and briefcase on his knees)* Well — I am a representative of the Clybourne Park Improvement Association —

WALTER: *(pointing)* Why don't you sit your things on the floor?

LINDNER: Oh — yes. Thank you. *(He slides the briefcase and hat under the chair.)* And as I was saying — I am from the Clybourne Park Improvement Association and we have had it brought to our attention at the last meeting that you people — or at least your mother — has bought a piece of residential property at — *(He digs for the slip of paper again.)* — four o six Clybourne Street . . .

WALTER: That's right. Care for something to drink? Ruth, get Mr. Lindner a beer.

LINDNER: *(upset for some reason)* Oh — no, really. I mean thank you very much, but no thank you.

RUTH: *(innocently)* Some coffee?

LINDNER: Thank you, nothing at all.

Beneatha is watching the man carefully.

LINDNER: Well, I don't know how much you folks know about our organization. *(He is a gentle man; thoughtful and somewhat labored in his manner.)* It is one of these community organizations set up to look after — oh, you know, things like block upkeep and special projects and we also have what we call our New Neighbors Orientation Committee . . .

BENEATHA: *(drily)* Yes — and what do they do?

LINDNER: *(turning a little to her and then returning the main force to Walter)* Well — it's what you might call a sort of welcoming committee, I guess. I mean they, we — I'm the chairman of the committee — go around and see the new people who move into the neighborhood and sort of give them the lowdown on the way we do things out in Clybourne Park.

BENEATHA: *(with appreciation of the two meanings, which escape Ruth and Walter)* Un-huh.

LINDNER: And we also have the category of what the association calls — *(He looks elsewhere.)* — uh — special community problems . . .

BENEATHA: Yes — and what are some of those?

WALTER: Girl, let the man talk.

LINDNER: *(with understated relief)* Thank you. I would sort of like to explain this thing in my own way. I mean I want to explain to you in a certain way.

WALTER: Go ahead.

LINDNER: Yes. Well. I'm going to try to get right to the point. I'm sure we'll all appreciate that in the long run.

BENEATHA: Yes.

WALTER: Be still now!

LINDNER: Well —

RUTH: *(still innocently)* Would you like another chair — you don't look comfortable.

LINDNER: *(more frustrated than annoyed)* No, thank you very much. Please. Well — to get right to the point, I — *(A great breath, and he is off at last.)* I am sure you people must be aware of some of the incidents which have happened in various parts of the city when colored people have moved into certain areas—*(Beneatha exhales heavily and starts tossing a piece of fruit up and down in the air.)* Well—because we have what I think is going to be a unique type of organization in American community life—not only do we deplore that kind of thing—but we are trying to do something about it. *(Beneatha stops tossing and turns with a new and quizzical interest to the man.)* We feel—*(gaining confidence in his mission because of the interest in the faces of the people he is talking to.)*—we feel that most of the trouble in this world, when you come right down to it—*(He hits his knee for emphasis.)*—most of the trouble exists because people just don't sit down and talk to each other.

RUTH: *(nodding as she might in church, pleased with the remark)* You can say that again, mister.

LINDNER: *(more encouraged by such affirmation)* That we don't try hard enough in this world to understand the other fellow's problem. The other guy's point of view.

RUTH: Now that's right.

Beneatha and Walter merely watch and listen with genuine interest.

LINDNER: Yes — that's the way we feel out in Clybourne Park. And that's why I was elected to come here this afternoon and talk to you people. Friendly like, you know, the way people should talk to each other and see if we couldn't find some way to work this thing out. As I say, the whole business is a matter of *caring* about the other fellow. Anybody can see that you are a nice family of folks, hard working and honest I'm sure. *(Beneatha frowns slightly, quizzically, her head tilted regarding him.)* Today everybody knows what it means to be on the outside of *something*. And of course, there is always somebody who is out to take advantage of people who don't always understand.

WALTER: What do you mean?

LINDNER: Well—you see our community is made up of people who've worked hard as the dickens for years to build up that little community. They're not rich and fancy people; just hard-working, honest people who don't really have much but those little homes and a dream of the kind of community they want to raise their children in. Now, I don't say we are perfect and there is a lot wrong in some of the things they want. But you've got to admit that a man, right or wrong, has the right to want to have the neighborhood he lives in a certain kind of way. And at the moment the overwhelming majority of our people out there feel that people get along better, take more of a common interest in the life of the community, when they share a common background. I want you to believe me when I tell you that race prejudice simply doesn't enter into it. It is a matter of the people of Clybourne Park believing, rightly or wrongly, as I say, that for the happiness of all concerned that our Negro families are happier when they live in their *own* communities.

Beneatha: *(with a grand and bitter gesture)* This, friends, is the Welcoming Committee!

Walter: *(dumfounded, looking at Lindner)* Is this what you came marching all the way over here to tell us?

Lindner: Well, now we've been having a fine conversation. I hope you'll hear me all the way through.

Walter: *(tightly)* Go ahead, man.

Lindner: You see—in the face of all the things I have said, we are prepared to make your family a very generous offer . . .

Beneatha: Thirty pieces and not a coin less!

Walter: Yeah?

Lindner: *(putting on his glasses drawing a form out of the briefcase)* Our association is prepared, through the collective effort of our people, to buy the house from you at a financial gain to your family.

Ruth: Lord have mercy, ain't this the living gall!

Walter: All right, you through?

Lindner: Well, I want to give you the exact terms of the financial arrangement—

Walter: We don't want to hear no exact terms of no arrangements. I want to know if you got any more to tell us 'bout getting together?

Lindner: *(taking off his glasses)* Well—I don't suppose that you feel . . .

Walter: Never mind how I feel—you got any more or say 'bout how people ought to sit down and talk to each other? . . . Get out of my house, man.

He turns his back and walks to the door.

Lindner: *(looking around at the hostile faces and reaching and assembling his hat and briefcase)* Well—I don't understand why you people are reacting this way. What do you think you are going to gain by moving into a neighborhood where you just aren't wanted and where some elements—well—people can get awful worked up when they feel that their whole way of life and everything they've ever worked for is threatened.

Walter: Get out.

Lindner: *(at the door, holding a small card)* Well—I'm sorry it went like this.

Walter: Get out.

Lindner: *(almost sadly regarding Walter)* You just can't force people to change their hearts, son.

He turns and puts his card on a table and exits. Walter pushes the door to with stinging hatred, and stands looking at it. Ruth just sits and Beneatha just stands. They say nothing. Mama and Travis enter.

Mama: Well—this all the packing got done since I left out of here this morning. I testify before God that my children got all the energy of the *dead!* What time the moving men due?

Beneatha: Four o'clock. You had a caller, Mama.

She is smiling teasingly.

MAMA: Sure enough—who?

BENEATHA: *(her arms folded saucily)* The Welcoming Committee.

Walter and Ruth giggle.

MAMA: *(innocently)* Who?

BENEATHA: The Welcoming Committee. They said they're sure going to be glad to see you when you get there.

WALTER: *(devilishly)* Yeah, they said they can't hardly wait to see your face.

Laughter

MAMA: *(sensing their facetiousness)* What's the matter with you all?

WALTER: Ain't nothing the matter with us. We just telling you 'bout the gentleman who came to see you this afternoon. From the Clybourne Park Improvement Association.

MAMA: What he want?

RUTH: *(in the same mood as Beneatha and Walter)* To welcome you, honey.

WALTER: He said they can't hardly wait. He said the one thing they don't have, that they just *dying* to have out there is a fine family of fine colored people! *(To Ruth and Beneatha.)* Ain't that right!

RUTH: *(mockingly)* Yeah! He left his card—

BENEATHA: *(handing card to Mama)* In case.

Mama reads and throws it on the floor—understanding and looking off as she draws her chair up to the table on which she has put her plant and some sticks and some card.

MAMA: Father, give us strength. *(Knowingly—and without fun.)* Did he threaten us?

BENEATHA: Oh—Mama—they don't do it like that any more. He talked Brotherhood. He said everybody ought to learn how to sit down and hate each other with good Christian fellowship.

She and Walter shake hands to ridicule the remark.

MAMA: *(sadly)* Lord, protect us . . .

RUTH: You should hear the money those folks raised to buy the house from us. All we paid and then some.

BENEATHA: What they think we going to do—eat 'em?

RUTH: No, honey, marry 'em.

MAMA: *(shaking her head)* Lord, Lord, Lord . . .

RUTH: Well — that's the way the crackers crumble. *(A beat.)* Joke.

BENEATHA: *(laughingly noticing what her mother is doing)* Mama, what are you doing?

MAMA: Fixing my plant so it won't get hurt none on the way . . .

BENEATHA: Mama, you going to take *that* to the new house?

MAMA: Un-huh—

BENEATHA: That raggedy-looking old thing?

MAMA: *(stopping and looking at her)* It expresses ME!

RUTH: *(with delight, to Beneatha)* So there, Miss Thing!

Walter comes to Mama suddenly and bends down behind her and squeezes her in his arms with all his strength. She is overwhelmed by the suddenness of it and, though delighted, her manner is like that of Ruth and Travis.

MAMA: Look out now, boy! You make me mess up my thing here!

WALTER: *(his face lit, he slips down on his knees beside her, his arms still about her)* Mama . . . you know what it means to climb up in the chariot?

MAMA: *(gruffly, very happy)* Get on away from me now . . .

RUTH: *(near the gift-wrapped package, trying to catch Walter's eye)* Psst—

WALTER: What the old song say, Mama . . .

RUTH: Walter—Now?

She is pointing at the package.

WALTER: *(speaking the lines, sweetly, playfully, in his mother's face)*

I got wings . . . you got wings . . .
All God's children got wings . . .

MAMA: Boy—get out of my face and do some work . . .

WALTER:

When I get to heaven gonna put on my wings,
Gonna fly all over God's heaven . . .

BENEATHA: *(teasingly, from across the room)* Everybody talking 'bout heaven ain't going there!

WALTER: *(to Ruth, who is carrying the box across to them)* I don't know, you think we ought to give her that . . . Seems to me she ain't been very appreciative around here.

MAMA: *(eying the box, which is obviously a gift)* What is that?

WALTER: *(taking it from Ruth and putting it on the table in front of Mama)* Well—what you all think? Should we give it to her?

RUTH: Oh—she was pretty good today.

MAMA: I'll good you—

She turns her eyes to the box again.

BENEATHA: Open it, Mama.

She stands up, looks at it, turns and looks at all of them, and then presses her hands together does not open the package.

WALTER: *(sweetly)* Open it, Mama. It's for you. *(Mama looks in his eyes. It is the first present in her life without its being Christmas. Slowly she opens her package and lifts out, one by one, a brand-new sparkling set of gardening tools. Walter continues, prodding.)* Ruth made up the note—read it . . .

MAMA: *(picking up the card and adjusting her glasses)* "To our own Mrs. Miniver—Love from Brother, Ruth, and Beneatha." Ain't that lovely . . .

TRAVIS: *(tugging at his father's sleeve)* Daddy, can I give her mine now?

WALTER: All right, son. *(Travis flies to get his gift.)*

MAMA: Now I don't have to use my knives and forks no more . . .

WALTER: Travis didn't want to go in with the rest of us, Mama. He got his own. *(Somewhat amused.)* We don't know what it is . . .

TRAVIS: *(racing back in the room with a large hatbox and putting it in front of his grandmother)* Here!

MAMA: Lord have mercy, baby. You done gone and bought your grandmother a hat?

TRAVIS: *(very proud)* Open it!

She does and lifts out an elaborate, but very elaborate, wide gardening hat, and all the adults break up at the sight of it.

RUTH: Travis, honey, what is that?

TRAVIS: *(who thinks it is beautiful and appropriate)* It's a gardening hat! Like the ladies always have on in the magazines when they work in their gardens.

BENEATHA: *(giggling fiercely)* Travis—we were trying to make Mama Mrs. Miniver—not Scarlett O'Hara!

MAMA: *(indignantly)* What's the matter with you all! This here is a beautiful hat! *(Absurdly.)* I always wanted me one just like it!

She pops it on her head to prove it to her grandson, and the hat is ludicrous and considerably oversized.

RUTH: Hot dog! Go, Mama!

WALTER: *(doubled over with laughter)* I'm sorry, Mama—but you look like you ready to go out and chop you some cotton sure enough!

They all laugh except Mama, out of deference to Travis's feelings.

MAMA: *(gathering the boy up to her)* Bless your heart—this is the prettiest hat I ever owned —*(Walter, Ruth, and Beneatha chime in—noisily, festively, and insincerely congratulating Travis on his gift.)* What are we all standing around here for? We ain't finished packin' yet. Bennie, you ain't packed one book.

The bell rings.

BENEATHA: That couldn't be the movers . . . it's not hardly two good yet —

Beneatha goes into her room. Mama starts for door.

WALTER: *(turning, stiffening)* Wait—wait—I'll get it.

He stands and looks at the door.

MAMA: You expecting company, son?

WALTER: *(just looking at the door)* Yeah—yeah . . .

Mama looks at Ruth, and they exchange innocent and unfrightened glances.

MAMA: *(not understanding)* Well, let them in, son.
BENEATHA: *(from her room)* We need some more string.
MAMA: Travis—you run to the hardware and get me some string cord.

Mama goes out and Walter turns and looks at Ruth. Travis goes to a dish for money.

RUTH: Why don't you answer the door, man?
WALTER: *(suddenly bounding across the floor to embrace her)* 'Cause sometimes it hard to let the future begin! *(Stooping down in her face.)*

I got wings! You got wings!
All God's children got wings!

He crosses to the door and throws it open. Standing there is a very slight little man in a not-too-prosperous business suit and with haunted frightened eyes and a hat pulled down tightly, brim up, around his forehead. Travis passes between the men and exits. Walter leans deep in the man's face, still in his jubilance.

When I get to heaven gonna put on my wings,
Gonna fly all over God's heaven . . .

The little man just stares at him.

Heaven—

Suddenly he stops and looks past the little man into the empty hallways.

Where's Willy, man?

BOBO: He ain't with me.
WALTER: *(not disturbed)* Oh—come on in. You know my wife.
BOBO: *(dumbly, taking off his hat)* Yes—h'you, Miss Ruth.
RUTH: *(quietly, a mood apart form her husband, already seening Bobo)* Hello, Bobo.
WALTER: You right on time today . . . Right on time. That's the way! *(He slaps Bobo on his back.)* Sit down . . . lemme hear.

Ruth stands stiffly and quietly in back of them, as though somehow she senses death, her eyes fixed on her husband.

BOBO: *(his frightened eyes on the floor, his hat in his hands)* Could I please get a drink of water, before I tell you about it, Walter Lee?

Walter does not take his eyes off the man. Ruth goes blindly to the tap and gets a glass of water and brings it to Bobo.

WALTER: There ain't nothing wrong, is there?
BOBO: Lemme tell you—
WALTER: Man—didn't nothing go wrong?
BOBO: Lemme tell you—Walter Lee. *(Looking at Ruth and talking to her more than to Walter.)* You know how it was. I got to tell you how it was. I mean

first I got to tell you how it was all the way . . . . I mean about the money I put in, Walter Lee . . .

WALTER: *(with taut agitation now)* What about the money you put in?

BOBO: Well—it wasn't much as we told you—me and Willy—*(He stops.)* I'm sorry, Walter. I got a bad feeling about it. I got a real bad feeling about it . . .

WALTER: Man, what you telling me about all this for? . . . Tell me what happened in Springfield . . .

BOBO: Springfield.

RUTH: *(like a dead woman)* What was supposed to happen in Springfield?

BOBO: *(to her)* This deal that me and Walter went into with Willy — Me and Willy was going to go down to Springfield and spread some money 'round so's we wouldn't have to wait so long for the liquor license . . . That's what we were going to do. Everybody said that was the way you had to do, you understand, Miss Ruth?

WALTER: Man — what happened down there?

BOBO: *(a pitiful man, near tears)* I'm trying to tell you, Walter.

WALTER: *(screaming at him suddenly)* THEN TELL ME, GODDAMMIT . . . WHAT'S THE MATTER WITH YOU?

BOBO: Man . . . I didn't go to no Springfield, yesterday.

WALTER: *(halted, life hanging in the moment)* Why not?

BOBO: *(the long way, the hard way to tell)* 'Cause I didn't have no reasons to . . .

WALTER: Man, what are you talking about!

BOBO: I'm talking about the fact that when I got to the train station yesterday morning—eight o'clock like we planned . . . Man—*Willy didn't never show up.*

WALTER: Why . . . where was he . . . where is he?

BOBO: That's what I'm trying to tell you . . . I don't know . . . I waited six hours . . . I called his house . . . and I waited . . . six hours . . . I waited in that train station six hours . . . *(Breaking into tears.)* That was all the extra money I had in the world . . . *(Looking up at Walter with the tears running down his face.)* Man, *Willy is gone*.

WALTER: Gone, what you mean Willy is gone? Gone where? You mean he went by himself. You mean he went off to Springfield by himself — to take care of getting the license—*(Turns and looks anxiously at Ruth.)* You mean maybe he didn't want too many people in on the business down there? *(Looks to Ruth again, as before.)* You know Willy got his own ways. *(Looks back to Bobo.)* Maybe you was late yesterday and he just went on down there without you. Maybe—maybe —he's been callin' you at home tryin' to tell you what happened or something. Maybe —maybe—he just got sick. He's somewhere — he's got to be somewhere. We just got to find him — me and you got to find him. *(Grabs Bobo senselessly by the cellar and starts to shake him.)* We got to!

BOBO: *(in sudden angry, frightened agony)* Wha's the matter with you, Walter! *When a cat take off with your money he don't leave you no road maps!*

WALTER: *(turning madly, as though he is looking for Willy in the very room)* Willy! . . . Willy . . . don't do it . . . Please don't do it . . . Man, not with that money . . . Man, please, not with that money . . . Oh, God . . . Don't let it be true . . . *(He is wandering around, crying out for Willy and looking for him or perhaps for help from God.)* Man . . . I trusted you . . . Man, I put my life in your hands . . . *(He starts to crumple down on the floor as Ruth just covers her face in horror. Mama opens the door and comes into the room, with Beneatha behind her.)* Man . . . *(He starts to pound the floor with his fists, sobbing wildly.)* THAT MONEY IS MADE OUT OF MY FATHER'S FLESH —

BOBO: *(standing over him helplessly)* I'm sorry, Walter . . . *(only Walter's sobs reply. Bobo puts on his hat.)* I had my life staked on this deal, too . . .

He exits.

MAMA: *(to Walter)* Son — *(She goes to him, bends down to him, talks to his bent head.)* Son . . . Is it gone? Son, I gave you sixty-five hundred dollars. Is it gone? All of it? Beneatha's money too?

WALTER: *(lifting his head slowly)* Mama . . . I never . . . went to the bank at all . . .

MAMA: *(not wanting to believe him)* You mean . . . your sister's school money . . . you used that too . . . Walter? . . .

WALTER: Yessss! All of it . . . It's all gone . . .

There is total silence. Ruth stands with her face covered with her hands; Beneatha leans forlornly against a wall, fingering a piece of red ribbon from the mother's gift. Mama stops and looks at her son without recognition and then, quite without thinking about it, starts to beat him senselessly in the face. Beneatha goes to them and stops it.

BENEATHA: Mama!

Mama stops and looks at both of her children and rises slowly and wanders vaguely, aimlessly away from them.

MAMA: I seen . . . him . . . night after night . . . come in . . . and look at that rug . . . and then look at me . . . the red showing in his eyes . . . the veins moving in his head . . . I seen him grow thin and old before he was forty . . . working and working and working like somebody's old horse . . . killing himself . . . and you — you give it all away in a day — *(She raises her arms to strike him again.)*

BENEATHA: Mama —

MAMA: Oh, God . . . *(She looks up to Him.)* Look down here — and show me the strength.

BENEATHA: Mama —

MAMA: *(folding over)* Strength . . .

BENEATHA: *(plaintively)* Mama . . .

MAMA: Strength!

Curtain.

ACT 3

TIME: *An hour later.*

At curtain, there is a sullen light of gloom in the living room, gray light not unlike that which began the first scene of Act 1. At left we can see Walter within his room, alone with himself. He is stretched out on the bed, his shirt out and open, his arms under his head. He does not smoke, he does not cry out, he merely lies there, looking up at the ceiling, much as if he were alone in the world.

In the living room Beneatha sits at the table, still surrounded by the now almost ominous packing crates. She sits looking off. We feel that this is a mood struck perhaps an hour before, and it lingers now, full of the empty sound of profound disappointment. We see on a line from her brother's bedroom the sameness of their attitudes. Presently the bell rings and Beneatha rises without ambition or interest in answering. It is Asagai, smiling broadly, striding into the room with energy and happy expectation and conversations.

ASAGAI: I came over . . . I had some free time. I thought I might help with the packing. Ah, I like the look of packing crates! A household in preparation for a journey! It depresses some people . . . but for me . . . it is another feeling. Something full of the flow of life, do you understand? Movement, progress . . . It makes me think of Africa.

BENEATHA: Africa!

ASAGAI: What kind of a mood is this? Have I told you how deeply you move me?

BENEATHA: He gave away the money, Asagai . . .

ASAGAI: Who gave away what money?

BENEATHA: The insurance money. My brother gave it away.

ASAGAI: Gave it away?

BENEATHA: He made an investment! With a man even Travis wouldn't have trusted with his most worn out marbles.

ASAGAI: And it's gone?

BENEATHA: Gone!

ASAGAI: I'm very sorry . . . And you, now?

BENEATHA: Me? . . . Me? . . . Me, I'm nothing . . . Me. When I was very small . . . we used to take our sleds out in the wintertime and the only hills we had were the ice-covered stone steps of some houses down the street. And we used to fill them in with snow and make them smooth and slide down them all day . . . and it was very dangerous, you know . . . far too steep . . . and sure enough one day a kid named Rufus came down too fast and hit the sidewalk and we saw his face just split open right there in front of us . . . And I remember standing there looking at his bloody open face thinking that was the end of Rufus. But the ambulance came and they took him to the hospital and they fixed the broken bones and they sewed it all up . . . and the next time I saw Rufus he just had a little line down the middle of his face . . . I never got over that . . .

ASAGAI: What?

Beneatha: That that was what one person could do for another, fix him up — sew up the problem, make him all right again. That was the most marvelous thing in the world . . . I wanted to do that, I always thought it was the one concrete thing in the world that a human being could do. Fix up the sick, you know — and make them whole again. This was truly being God . . .

Asagai: You wanted to be God?

Beneatha: No — I wanted to cure. It used to be so important to me. I wanted to cure. It used to matter. I used to care. I mean about people and how their bodies hurt . . .

Asagai: And you've stopped caring?

Beneatha: Yes — I think so.

Asagai: Why?

Beneatha: *(bitterly)* Because it doesn't seem deep enough, close enough to what ails mankind! It was a child's way of seeing things — or an idealist's.

Asagai: Children see things very well sometimes — and idealists even better.

Beneatha: I know that's what you think. Because you are still where I left off. You with all your talk and dreams about Africa! You still think you can patch up the world. Cure the Great Sore of Colonialism — *(Loftily, mocking it.)* with the Penicillin of Independence — !

Asagai: Yes!

Beneatha: Independence *and then what?* What about all the crooks and thieves and just plain idiots who will come into power and steal and plunder the same as before — only now they will be black and do it in the name of the new Independence — WHAT ABOUT THEM?!

Asagai: That will be the problem for another time. First we must get there.

Beneatha: And where does it end?

Asagai: End? Who even spoke of an end? To life? To living?

Beneatha: An end to misery! To stupidity! Don't you see there isn't any real progress, Asagai, there is only one large circle that we march in, around and around, each of us with our own little picture in front of us — our own little mirage that we think is the future.

Asagai: That is the mistake.

Beneatha: What?

Asagai: What you just said — about the circle. It isn't a circle — it is simply a long line — as in geometry, you know, one that reaches into infinity. And because we cannot see the end — we also cannot see how it changes. And it is very odd but those who see the changes — who dream, who will not give up — are called idealists . . . and those who see only the circle — we call *them* the "realists"!

Beneatha: Asagai, while I was sleeping in that bed in there, people went out and took the future right out of my hands! And nobody asked me, nobody consulted me — they just went out and changed my life!

Asagai: Was it your money?

Beneatha: What?

ASAGAI: Was it your money he gave away?

BENEATHA: It belonged to all of us.

ASAGAI: But did you earn it? Would you have had it at all if your father had not died?

BENEATHA: No.

ASAGAI: Then isn't there something wrong in a house—in a world—where all dreams, good or bad, must depend on the death of a man? I never thought to see *you* like this, Alaiyo. You! Your brother made a mistake and you are grateful to him so that now you can give up the ailing human race on account of it! You talk about what good is struggle, what good is anything! Where are we all going and why are we bothering!

BENEATHA: AND YOU CANNOT ANSWER IT!

ASAGAI: *(shouting over her) I LIVE THE ANSWER! (Pause.)* In my village at home it is the exceptional man who can even read a newspaper . . . or who ever sees a book at all. I will go home and much of what I will have to say will seem strange to the people of my village. But I will teach and work and things will happen, slowly and swiftly. At times it will seem that nothing changes at all . . . and then again the sudden dramatic events which make history leap into the future. And then quiet again. Retrogression even. Guns, murder, revolution. And I even will have moments when I wonder if the quiet was not better than all that death and hatred. But I will look about my village at the illiteracy and disease and ignorance and I will not wonder long. And perhaps . . . perhaps I will be a great man . . . I mean perhaps I will hold on to the substance of truth and find my way always with the right course . . . and perhaps for it I will be butchered in my bed some night by the servants of empire . . .

BENEATHA: *The martyr!*

ASAGAI: *(he smiles)* . . . or perhaps I shall live to be a very old man, respected and esteemed in my new nation . . . And perhaps I shall hold office and this is what I'm trying to tell you, Alaiyo: perhaps the things I believe now for my country will be wrong and outmoded, and I will not understand and do terrible things to have things my way or merely to keep my power. Don't you see that there will be young men and women—not British soldiers then, but my own black countrymen—to step out of the shadows some evening and slit my then useless throat? Don't you see they have always been there . . . that they always will be. And that such a thing as my own death will be an advance? They who might kill me even . . . actually replenish all that I was.

BENEATHA: Oh, Asagai, I know all that.

ASAGAI: Good! Then stop moaning and groaning and tell me what you plan to do.

BENEATHA: Do?

ASAGAI: I have a bit of a suggestion.

BENEATHA: What?

ASAGAI: *(rather quietly for him)* That when it is all over—that you come home with me—

BENEATHA: *(staring at him and crossing away with exasperation)* Oh—Asagai—at this moment you decide to be romantic!

ASAGAI: *(quickly understanding the misunderstanding)* My dear, young creature of the New World—I do not mean across the city—I mean across the ocean: home—to Africa.

BENEATHA: *(slowly understanding and turning to him with murmured amazement)* To Africa?

ASAGAI: Yes! . . . *(smiling and lifting his arms playfully.)* Three hundred years later the African Prince rose up out of the seas and swept the maiden back across the middle passage over which her ancestors had come—

BENEATHA: *(unable to play)* To—to Nigeria?

ASAGAI: Nigeria, Home. *(Coming to her with genuine romantic flippancy.)* I will show you our mountains and our stars, and give you cool drinks from gourds and teach you the old songs and the ways of our people—and, in time, we will pretend that—*(Very softly)*—you have only been away for a day. Say that you'll come—*(He swings her around and takes her full in his arms in a kiss which proceeds to passion.)*

BENEATHA: *(pulling away suddenly)* You're getting me all mixed up—

ASAGAI: Why?

BENEATHA: Too many things—too many things have happened today. I must sit down and think. I don't know what I feel about anything right this minute.

She promptly sits down and props her chin on her fist.

ASAGAI: *(charmed)* All right, I shall leave you. No—don't get up. *(Touching her, gently, sweetly)* Just sit awhile and think . . . Never be afraid to sit awhile and think. *(He goes to door and looks at her.)* How often I have looked at you and said, "Ah—so this is what the New World hath finally wrought . . ."

He exits. Beneatha sits on alone. Presently Walter enters from his room and starts to rummage through things, feverishly looking for something. She looks up and turns in her seat.

BENEATHA: *(hissingly)* Yes—just look at what the New World hath wrought! . . . Just look! *(She gestures with bitter disgust.)* There he is! *Monsieur le petit bourgeois noir*°—himself! There he is—Symbol of a Rising Class! Entrepreneur! Titan of the system! *(Walter ignores her completely and continues frantically and destructively looking for something and hurling things to floor and tearing things out of their place in his search. Beneatha ignores the eccentricity of his actions and goes on with the monologue of insult.)* Did you dream of yachts on Lake Michigan, Brother? Did you see yourself on that Great Day sitting down at the Conference Table, surrounded by all the mighty bald-headed-men in America? All halted, waiting, breathless, waiting for your pronouncements on industry? Waiting for you—Chairman of the Board! *(Walter finds what he is looking for—a small piece of white paper—and pushes it in his pocket and puts on his coat and rushes out without ever having looked at her. She shouts after him.)* I look at you and I see the final triumph of stupidity in the world!

°*Monsieur le petit bourgeois noir.* French for Mr. *Black Bourgoisie.*

The door slams and she returns to just sitting again. Ruth comes quickly out of Mama's room.

RUTH: Who was that?

BENEATHA: Your husband.

RUTH: Where did he go?

BENEATHA: Who knows—maybe he has an appointment at U.S. Steel.

RUTH: *(anxiously, with frightened eyes)* You didn't say nothing bad to him, did you?

BENEATHA: Bad? Say anything bad to him? No—I told him he was a sweet boy and full of dreams and everything is strictly peachy keen, as the ofay kids say!

Mama enters from her bedroom. She is lost, vague, trying to catch hold, to make some sense of her former command of the world, but it still eludes her. A sense of waste overwhelms her gait; a measure of apology rides on her shoulders. She goes to her plant, which has remained on the table, looks at it, picks it up and takes it to the window sill and sits it outside, and she stands and looks at it a long moment. Then she closes the window, straightens her body with effort and turns around to her children.

MAMA: Well—ain't it a mess in here, though? *(A false cheerfulness, a beginning of something.)* I guess we all better stop moping around and get some work done. All this unpacking and everything we got to do. *(Ruth raises her head slowly in response to the sense of the line; and Beneatha in similar manner turns very slowly to look at her mother.)* One of you all better call the moving people and tell 'em not to come.

RUTH: Tell 'em not to come?

MAMA: Of course, baby. Ain't no need in 'em coming all the way here and having to go back. They charges for that too. *(She sits down, fingers to her brow, thinking.)* Lord, ever since I was a little girl, I always remembers people saying, "Lena—Lena Eggleston, you aims too high all the time. You needs to slow down and see life a little more like it is. Just slow down some." That's what they always used to say down home—"Lord, that Lena Eggleston is a high-minded thing. She'll get her due one day!"

RUTH: No, Lena . . .

MAMA: Me and Big Walter just didn't never learn right.

RUTH: Lena, no! We gotta go. Bennie — tell her . . .

She rises and crosses to Beneatha with her arms outstretched. Beneatha doesn't respond.

Tell her we can still move . . . the notes ain't but a hundred and twenty-five a month. We got four grown people in this house — we can work . . .

MAMA: *(to herself)* Just aimed too high all the time—

RUTH: *(turning and going to Mama fast — the words pouring out with urgency and desperation)* Lena—I'll work . . . I'll work twenty hours a day in all the kitchens in Chicago . . . I'll strap my baby on my back if I have to and scrub all the floors in America and wash all the sheets in America if I have to—but we got to MOVE! We got to get OUT OF HERE!!

Mama reaches out absently and pats Ruth's hand.

Mama: No—I sees things differently now. Been thinking 'bout some of the things we could do to fix this place up some. I seen a second-hand bureau over on Maxwell Street just the other day that could fit right there. *(She points to where the new furniture might go. Ruth wanders away from her.)* Would need some new handles on it and then a little varnish and it look like something brand-new. And—we can put up them new curtains in the kitchen . . . Why this place be looking fine. Cheer us all up so that we forget trouble ever come . . . *(To Ruth.)* And you could get some nice screens to put up in your room round the baby's bassinet . . . *(She looks at both of them pleadingly.)* Sometimes you just got to know when to give up some things . . . and hold on to what you got. . .

Walter enters from the outside, looking spent and leaning against the door, his coat hanging from him.

Mama: Where you been, son?

Walter: *(breathing hard)* Made a call.

Walter: To The Man. *(He heads for his room.)*

Mama: What man, baby?

Walter: *(stops in the door)* The Man, Mama. Don't you know who The Man is?

Ruth: Walter Lee?

Walter: *The Man*. Like the guys in the streets say—The Man. Captain Boss—Mistuh Charley . . . Old Cap'n Please Mr. Bossman . . .

Beneatha: *(suddenly)* Lindner!

Walter: That's right! That's good. I told him to come right over.

Beneatha: *(fiercely, understanding)* For what? What do you want to see him for!

Walter: *(looking at his sister)* We going to do business with him.

Mama: What you talking 'bout, son?

Walter: Talking 'bout life, Mama. You all always telling me to see life like it is. Well—I laid in there on my back today . . . and I figured it out. Life just like it is. Who gets and who don't get. *(He sits down with his coat on and laughs.)* Mama, you know it's all divided up. Life is. Sure enough, Between the takers and the "tooken." *(He laughs.)* I've figured it our finally. *(He looks around at them.)* Yeah. Some of us always getting "tooken." *(He laughs.)* People like Willy Harris, they don't never get "tooken." And you know why the rest of us do? 'Cause we all mixed up. Mixed up bad. We get to looking 'round for the right and the wrong, and we worry about it and cry about it and stay up nights trying to figure out 'bout the wrong and the right of things all the time . . . And all the time, man, them takers is out there operating, just taking and taking. Willy Harris? Shoot—Willy Harris don't even count. He don't even count in the big scheme of things. But I'll say one thing for old Willy Harris . . . he's taught me something. He's taught me to keep my eye on what counts in this world. Yeah—*(Shouting out a little.)* Thanks, Willy!

Ruth: What did you call that man for, Walter Lee?

WALTER: Called him to tell him to come on over to the show: Gonna put on a show for the man. Just what he wants to see. You see, Mama, the man came here today and he told us that them people out there where you want us to move—well they so upset they willing to pay us *not* to move! *(He laughs again.)* And—and oh, Mama—you would have been proud of the way me and Ruth and Bennie acted. We told him to get out . . . Lord have mercy! We told the man to get out! Oh, we was some proud folks this afternoon, yeah. *(He lights a cigarette.)* We were still full of that old-time stuff . . .

RUTH: *(coming toward him slowly)* You talking 'bout taking them people's money to keep us from moving in that house?

WALTER: I ain't just talking 'bout it, baby—I'm telling you that's what's going to happen!

BENEATHA: Oh, God! Where is the bottom! Where is the real honest-to-God bottom so he can't go any farther!

WALTER: See—that's the old stuff. You and that boy that was here today. You all want everybody to carry a flag and a spear and sing some marching songs, huh? You wanna spend your life looking into things and trying to find the right and the wrong part, huh? Yeah. You know what's going to happen to that boy someday—he'll find himself sitting in a dungeon, locked in forever—and the takers will have the key! Forget it, baby! There ain't no causes—there ain't nothing but taking in this world, and he who takes most is smartest—and it don't make a damn bit of difference *how*.

MAMA: You making something inside me cry, son. Some awful pain inside me.

WALTER: Don't cry, Mama. Understand. That white man is going to walk in that door able to write checks for more money than we ever had. It's important to him and I'm going to help him . . . I'm going to put on the show, Mama.

MAMA: Son—I come from five generations of people who was slaves and sharecroppers—but ain't nobody in my family never let nobody pay 'em no money that was a way of telling us we wasn't fit to walk the earth. We ain't never been that poor. *(Raising her eyes and looking at him.)* We ain't never been that—dead inside.

BENEATHA: Well—we are dead now. All the talk about dreams and sunlight that goes on in this house. It's all dead now.

WALTER: What's the matter with you all! I didn't make this world! It was give to me this way! Hell, yes, I want me some yachts someday! Yes, I want to hang some real pearls round my wife's neck. Ain't she supposed to wear no pearls? Somebody tell me—tell me, who decides which women is suppose to wear pearls in this world. I tell you I am a *man*—and I think my wife should wear some pearls in this world!

This last line hangs a good while and Walter begins to move about the room. The word "Man" has penetrated his consciousness; he mumbles it to himself repeatedly between strange agitated pauses as he moves about.

MAMA: Baby, how you going to feel on the inside?

WALTER: Fine! . . . Going to feel fine . . . a man . . .

MAMA: You won't have nothing left then, Walter Lee.

WALTER: *(coming to her)* I'm going to feel fine, Mama. I'm going to look that son-of-a-bitch in the eyes and say —*(He falters.)*— and say, "All right, Mr. Lindner —*(He falters even more.)*— that's *your* neighborhood out there! You got the right to keep it like you want! You got the right to have it like you want! Just write the check and — the house is yours." And — and I am going to say —*(His voice almost breaks.)* And you — you people just put the money in my hand and you won't have to live next to this bunch of stinking niggers! . . ." *(He straightens up and moves away from his mother, walking, around the room.)* And maybe — maybe I'll just get down on my black knees . . . *(He does so, Ruth and Bennie and Mama watch him in frozen horror.)* "Captain, Mistuh, Bossman —*(Groveling and grinning and wringing his hands in profoundly anguished imitation of the slow-witted movie stereotype.)* A hee-hee-hee! Oh, Yassuhboss! Yasssssuh! Great white —*(Voice breaking, he forces himself to go on.)*— Father, just gi' ussen de money, fo' God's sake, and we's — we's ain't gwine come out deh and dirty up yo' white folks neighborhood . . ." *(He breaks down completely.)* And I'll feel fine! Fine! FINE! *(He gets up and goes into the bedroom.)*

BENEATHA: That is not a man. That is nothing but a roothless rat.

MAMA: Yes — death done come in this here house. *(She is nodding, slowly, reflectively.)* Done come walking in my house on the lips of my children. You what supposed to be my beginning again. You — what supposed to be my harvest. *(To Beneatha.)* You — you mourning your brother?

BENEATHA: He's no brother of mine.

MAMA: What you say?

BENEATHA: I said that that individual in that room is no brother of mine.

MAMA: That's what I thought you said. You feeling like you better than he is today? *(Beneatha does not answer.)* Yes? What you tell him a minute ago? That he wasn't a man? Yes? You give him up for me? You done wrote his epitaph too—like the rest of the world? Well, who give you the privilege?

BENEATHA: Be on my side for once! You saw what he just did, Mama! You saw him — down on his knees. Wasn't it you who taught me to despise any man who would do that? Do what he's going to do?

MAMA: Yes —I taught you that Me and your daddy. But I thought I taught you something else too . . . I thought I taught you to love him.

BENEATHA: Love him? There is nothing left to love.

MAMA: There is *always* something left to love. And if you ain't learned that, you ain't learned nothing. *(Looking at her.)* Have you cried for that boy today? I don't mean for yourself and for the family 'cause we lost the money. I mean for him: what he been through and what it done to him. Child, when do you think is the time to love somebody the most? When they done good and made things easy for everybody? Well then you ain't through learning —because that ain't the time at all. It's when he's at his lowest and can't believe in hisself 'cause the world done whipped him so! When you starts measuring somebody, measure him right, child, measure him right. Make sure you done taken into account what hills and valleys he come through before he got to wherever he is.

Travis bursts into the room at the end of the speech, leaving the door open.

TRAVIS: Grandmama — the moving men are downstairs! The truck just pulled up.

MAMA: *(turning and looking at him)* Are they, baby? They downstairs?

She sighs and sits. Lindner appears in the doorway. He peers in and knocks lightly, to gain attention, and comes in. All turn to look at him.

LINDNER: *(hat and briefcase in hand)* Uh — hello . . .

Ruth crosses mechanically to the bedroom door and opens it and lets it swing open freely and slowly as the lights come up on Walter within, still in his coat, sitting at the far corner of the room. He looks up and out through the room to Lindner.

RUTH: He's here.

A long minute passes and Walter slowly gets up.

LINDNER: *(coming to the table with efficiency, putting his briefcase on the table and starting to unfold papers and unscrew fountain pens).* Well, I certainly was glad to hear from you people. *(Walter has begun the trek out of the room, slowly and awkwardly, rather like a small boy, passing the back of his sleeve across his mouth from time to time.)* Life can really be so much simpler than people let it be most of the time. Well — with whom do I negotiate? You, Mrs. Younger, or your son here? *(Mama sits with her hands folded on her lap and her eyes closed as Walter advances. Travis goes closer to Lindner and looks at the papers curiously.)* Just some official papers, sonny.

RUTH: Travis, you go downstairs —

MAMA: *(opening her eyes and looking into Walter's)* No. Travis, you stay right here. And you make him understand what you doing, Walter Lee. You teach him good. Like Willy Harris taught you. You show where our five generations done come to. *(Walter looks from her to the boy, who grins at him innocently.)* Go ahead, son — *(She folds her hands and closes her eyes.)* Go ahead.

WALTER: *(at last crosses to Lindner, who is reviewing the contract)* Well, Mr. Lindner. *(Beneatha turns away.)* We called you — *(There is a profound, simple groping quality in his speech.)* — because, well me and my family *(He looks around and shifts from one foot to the other.)* Well — we are very plain people . . .

LINDNER: Yes —

WALTER: I mean — I have worked as a chauffeur most of my life — and my wife here, she does domestic work in people's kitchens. So does my mother. I mean — we are plain people . . .

LINDNER: Yes, Mr. Younger —

WALTER: *(really like a small boy, looking down at his shoes and then up at the man)* And — uh — well, my father, well, he was a laborer most of his life . . .

Lindner: *(absolutely confused)* Uh, yes—yes, I understand. *(He turns back to the contract.)*

Walter: *(a beat; staring at him)* And my father—*(With sudden intensity.)* My father almost *beat a man to death* once because this man called him a bad name or something, you know what I mean?

Lindner: *(looking up, frozen)* No, no, I'm afraid I don't—

Walter: *(a beat. The tension hangs; then Walter steps back from it)* Yeah. Well—what I mean is that we come from people who had a lot of *pride*, I mean—we are very proud people. And that's my sister over there and she's going to be a doctor—and we are very proud—

130 **Lindner:** Well—I am sure that is very nice, but—

Walter: What I am telling you is that we called you over here to tell you that we are very proud and that this—*(Signaling to Travis.)* Travis, come here. *(Travis crosses and Walter draws him before him facing the man.)* This is my son, and he makes the sixth generation our family in this country. And we have all thought about your offer—

Lindner: Well, good . . . good—

Walter: And we have decided to move into our house because my father—my father—he earned it for us brick by brick. *(Mama has her eyes closed and is rocking back and forth as though she were in church, with her head nodding the Amen yes.)* We don't want to make no trouble for nobody or fight no causes, and we will try to be good neighbors. And that's *all* we got to say about that. *(He looks the man absolutely in the eyes.)* We don't want your money. *(He turns and walks away.)*

Lindner: *(looking around at all of them)* I take it then—that you have decided to occupy.

135 **Beneatha:** That's what the man said.

Lindner: *(to Mama in her reverie)* Then I would like to appeal to you, Mrs. Younger. You are older and wiser and understand things better I am sure . . .

Mama: I am afraid you don't understand. My son said we was going to move and there ain't nothing left for me to say. *(Briskly.)* You know how these young folks is nowadays, mister. Can't do a thing with 'em! *(As he opens his mouth, she rises.)* Good-bye.

Lindner: *(folding up his materials)* Well—if you are that final about it . . . there is nothing left for me to say. *(He finishes, almost ignored by the family, who are concentrating on Walter Lee. At the door Lindner halts and looks around.)* I sure hope you people know what you're getting into.

He shakes his head and exits.

Ruth: *(looking around and coming to life)* Well, for God's sake—if the moving men are here—LET'S GET THE HELL OUT OF HERE!

140 **Mama:** *(into action)* Ain't it the truth! Look at all this here mess. Ruth, put Travis' good jacket on him . . . Walter Lee, fix your tie and tuck your shirt in, you look like somebody's hoodlum! Lord have mercy, where is my plant? *(She flies to get it amid the general bustling of the family, who are deliberately trying*

to ignore the nobility of the past moment.) You all start on down . . . Travis child, don't go empty-handed . . . Ruth, where did I put that box with my skillets in it? I want to be in charge of it myself . . . I'm going to make us the biggest dinner we ever ate tonight . . . Beneatha, what's the matter with them stockings? Pull them things up girl . . .

The family starts to file out as two moving men appear and begin to carry out the heavier pieces of furniture, bumping into the family as they move about.

Beneatha: Mama, Asagai asked me to marry him today and go to Africa —

Mama: *(in the middle of her getting-ready activity)* He did? You ain't old enough to marry nobody — *(Seeing the moving men lifting one of her chairs precariously.)* Darling, that ain't no bale of cotton, please handle it so we can sit in it again! I had that chair twenty-five years . . .

The movers sigh with exasperation and go on with their work.

Beneatha: *(girlishly and unreasonably trying to pursue the conversation)* To go to Africa, Mama — be a doctor in Africa . . .

Mama: *(distracted)* Yes, baby —

Walter: *Africa!* What he want you to go to Africa for?

Beneatha: To practice there . . .

Walter: Girl, if you don't get all them silly ideas our your head! You better marry yourself a man with some loot . . .

Beneatha: *(angrily, precisely as in the first scene of the play)* What have you got to do with who I marry!

Walter: Plenty. Now I think George Murchison —

Beneatha: *George Murchison!* I wouldn't marry him if he was Adam and I was Eve!

Walter and Beneatha go out yelling at each other vigorously and the anger is loud and real till their voices diminish. Ruth stands at the door and turns to Mama and smiles knowingly.

Mama: *(fixing her hat at last)* Yeah — they something all right, my children . . .

Ruth: Yeah — they're something. Let's go, Lena.

Mama: *(stalling, starting to look around at the house)* Yes — I'm coming. Ruth —

Ruth: Yes?

Mama: *(quietly, woman to woman)* He finally come into his manhood today, didn't he? Kind of like a rainbow after the rain . . .

Ruth: *(biting her lip lest her own pride explode in front of Mama)* Yes, Lena.

Walter's voice calls for them raucously.

Walter: *(off stage)* Y'all come on! These people charges by the hour, you know!

Mama: *(waving Ruth out vaguely)* All right, honey — go on down. I be down directly.

Ruth hesitates, then exits. Mama stands, at last alone in the living room, her plant on the table before her as the lights starts to come down. She looks around at all the walls and ceilings and suddenly, despite herself, while the children call below, a great heaving thing rises in her and she puts her fist to her mouth to stifle it, takes a final desperate look, pulls her coat about her, pats her hat, and goes out. The lights dim down. The door opens and she comes back in, grabs her plant, and goes out for the last time.

Curtain.

Reading and Reacting

1. The title of this play is an allusion to Langston Hughes's poem "Harlem" (p. 924). How does this title help to explain what motivates the main characters at various points in the play?
2. What conflicts are developed in *A Raisin in the Sun?* How is each of these conflicts central to the plot?
3. What ideas does Walter have about education, success, and raising children? How are his ideas different from Ruth's?
4. Does Walter love Ruth? Why do you think he treats her the way he does? Do you see him as a sympathetic character?
5. Why does Walter refuse to sign the paper Mr. Lindner brings? What do you think Mama means when she says to Ruth at the end of the play, "He [Walter] finally come into his manhood today, didn't he? Kind of like a rainbow after the rain."
6. What does the subplot about Beneatha's choice between George and Asagai contribute to the plot?
7. When the play was first staged in 1959, several cuts were made to shorten it. For instance, the scene in which Beneatha unveils her natural hair was eliminated. The scene in which Travis recounts the killing of the rat and the scene describing Mrs. Johnson's visit were also cut. Finally, Walter's bedtime scene with Travis (act 2, scene 2) was cut (although Hansberry thought it should be restored). What does each of these scenes contribute to the play? Are they essential to the plot?
8. Do you see this play as relevant only to the struggles of an urban black family in the period after World War II, or do you see its themes as universal? Do you think it is dated in any way? Explain.
9. **JOURNAL ENTRY** Some critics contend than Hansberry attempts to force a happy ending by transforming her characters into an acceptable middle-class family. Hansberry herself, however, denied the play's ending was optimistic. Do you think the play has a happy ending? Do you think it should?
10. **CRITICAL PERSPECTIVE** In his 1967 study *The Crisis of the Negro Intellectual*, African-American social and cultural critic Harold Cruse criticized Hansberry's play, calling it "psychologically uncomplicated" and "bourgeois" because it sees integration as a positive good. Cruse also discussed the critical reaction to the play:

    > When *Raisin* burst on the scene with a Negro star, a Negro director plus a young Negro woman playwright, everybody on Broadway was startled and very apprehensive about what this play might say. What obviously elated the drama critics was the very relieving discovery that what the publicity buildup actually heralded was not the arrival of belligerent forces from across the color line to settle some long-standing racial accounts on stage, but a good

> old-fashioned, home-spun saga of some good working-class folk in pursuit of the American Dream. And what could possibly be thematically objectionable about that? Only because it was about Negroes was this play acceptable. . . . If this play—which is so "American" that many whites did not consider it a "Negro play"—had ever been staged by white actors it would be judged second-rate.

Do you see this play as simply "a good old-fashioned" saga of working-class people in search of the American Dream, or do you see it as a uniquely African-American work? Do you agree that the race of the characters is all that distinguishes the play and keeps it from being "second-rate"?

Related Works: "I Stand Here Ironing" (p. 344), "A Primer for the Punctuation of Heart Disease" (p. 440), "Everyday Use" (p. 517), "Sonny's Blues" (p. 665), "Harlem" (p. 924), "The courage that my mother had" (p. 1042), *Death of a Salesman* (p. 1531), *Fences* (p. 1902)

Source: ©AP Photo

HENRIK IBSEN (1828–1906), Norway's foremost dramatist, was born into a prosperous family; however, his father lost his fortune when Ibsen was six. When Ibsen was fifteen, he was apprenticed to an apothecary away from home and was permanently estranged from his family. During his apprenticeship, he studied to enter the university and wrote plays. Although he did not pass the university entrance exam, his second play, *The Warrior's Barrow* (1850), was produced by the Christiania Theatre in 1850. He began a life in the theater, writing plays and serving as artistic director of a theatrical company. Disillusioned by the public's lack of interest in theater, he left Norway, living with his wife and son in Italy and Germany between 1864 and 1891. By the time he returned to Norway, he was famous and revered. Ibsen's most notable plays include *Brand* (1865), *Peer Gynt* (1867), *A Doll House* (1879), *Ghosts* (1881), *An Enemy of the People* (1882), *The Wild Duck* (1884), *Hedda Gabler* (1890), and *When We Dead Awaken* (1899).

A Doll House marks the beginning of Ibsen's successful realist period, during which he explored the ordinary lives of small-town people — in this case, writing what he called "a modern tragedy." Ibsen based the play on a true story, which closely paralleled the main events of the play: a wife borrows money to finance a trip for an ailing husband, repayment is demanded, she forges a check and is discovered. (In the real-life story, however, the husband demanded a divorce, and the wife had a nervous breakdown and was committed to a mental institution.) The issue in *A Doll House,* he said, is that there are "two kinds of moral law, . . . one in man and a completely different one in woman. They do not understand each other. . . ." Nora and Helmer's marriage is destroyed because they cannot comprehend or accept their differences. The play begins conventionally but does not fulfill the audience's expectations for a tidy resolution; as a result, it was not a success when it was first performed. Nevertheless, the publication of *A Doll House* made Ibsen internationally famous.

Cultural Context During the nineteenth century, the law treated women only a little better than it did children. Women could not vote, and they were not considered able to handle their own financial affairs. A woman could not borrow money in her own name, and when she married, her finances were placed under the control of her husband. Moreover, working outside the home was out of the question for a middle-class woman. So, if a woman were to leave her husband, she was not likely to have any way of supporting herself, and she would lose the custody of her children. At the time when *A Doll House* was first performed, most viewers were offended by the way Nora spoke to her husband, and Ibsen was considered an anarchist for suggesting that a woman could leave her family in search of herself. However, Ibsen argued that he was merely asking people to look at, and think about, the social structure they supported.

A Doll House (1879)

Translated by Rolf Fjelde

CHARACTERS

Torvald Helmer, *a lawyer*
Nora, *his wife*
Dr. Rank
Mrs. Linde
Nils Krogstad, *a bank clerk*
The Helmers' three small children
Anne-Marie, *their nurse*
Helene, *a maid*
A Delivery Boy

The action takes place in Helmer's residence.

ACT 1

A comfortable room, tastefully but not expensively furnished. A door to the right in the back wall leads to the entryway; another to the left leads to Helmer's study. Between these doors, a piano. Midway in the left-hand wall a door, and further back a window. Near the window a round table with an armchair and a small sofa. In the right-hand wall, toward the rear, a door, and nearer the foreground a porcelain stove with two armchairs and a rocking chair beside it. Between the stove and the side door, a small table. Engravings on the walls. An étagère with china figures and other small art objects; a small bookcase with richly bound books; the floor carpeted; a fire burning in the stove. It is a winter day.

A bell rings in the entryway; shortly after we hear the door being unlocked. Nora comes into the room, humming happily to herself; she is wearing street clothes and carries an armload of packages, which she puts down on the table to the right. She has left the hall door open; and through it a Delivery Boy is seen, holding a Christmas tree and a basket, which he gives to the Maid who let them in.

NORA: Hide the tree well, Helene. The children mustn't get a glimpse of it till this evening, after it's trimmed. *(To the Delivery Boy, taking out her purse.)* How much?

DELIVERY BOY: Fifty, ma'am.

NORA: There's a crown. No, keep the change. *(The Boy thanks her and leaves. Nora shuts the door. She laughs softly to herself while taking off her street things. Drawing a bag of macaroons from her pocket, she eats a couple, then steals over and listens at her husband's study door.)* Yes, he's home. *(Hums again as she moves to the table right.)*

HELMER: *(from the study)* Is that my little lark twittering out there?

NORA: *(busy opening some packages)* Yes, it is.

HELMER: Is that my squirrel rummaging around?

NORA: Yes!

HELMER: When did my squirrel get in?

NORA: Just now. *(Putting the macaroon bag in her pocket and wiping her mouth.)* Do come in, Torvald, and see what I've bought.

HELMER: Can't be disturbed. *(After a moment he opens the door and peers in, pen in hand.)* Bought, you say? All that there? Has the little spendthrift been out throwing money around again?

NORA: Oh, but Torvald, this year we really should let ourselves go a bit. It's the first Christmas we haven't had to economize.

HELMER: But you know we can't go squandering.

NORA: Oh yes, Torvald, we can squander a little now. Can't we? Just a tiny, wee bit. Now that you've got a big salary and are going to make piles and piles of money.

HELMER: Yes — starting New Year's. But then it's a full three months till the raise comes through.

NORA: Pooh! We can borrow that long.

HELMER: Nora! *(Goes over and playfully takes her by the ear.)* Are your scatterbrains off again? What if today I borrowed a thousand crowns, and you squandered them over Christmas week, and then on New Year's Eve a roof tile fell on my head, and I lay there —

NORA: *(putting her hand on his mouth)* Oh! Don't say such things!

HELMER: Yes, but what if it happened — then what?

NORA: If anything so awful happened, then it just wouldn't matter if I had debts or not.

HELMER: Well, but the people I'd borrowed from?

NORA: Them? Who cares about them! They're strangers.

HELMER: Nora, Nora, how like a woman! No, but seriously, Nora, you know what I think about that. No debts! Never borrow! Something of freedom's lost — and something of beauty, too — from a home that's founded on borrowing and debt. We've made a brave stand up to now, the two of us; and we'll go right on like that the little while we have to.

NORA: *(going toward the stove)* Yes, whatever you say, Torvald.

HELMER: *(following her)* Now, now, the little lark's wings mustn't droop. Come on, don't be a sulky squirrel. *(Taking out his wallet.)* Nora, guess what I have here.

NORA: *(turning quickly)* Money!

HELMER: There, see. *(Hands her some notes.)* Good grief, I know how costs go up in a house at Christmastime.

NORA: Ten — twenty — thirty — forty. Oh, thank you, Torvald; I can manage no end on this.

HELMER: You really will have to.

NORA: Oh yes, I promise I will! But come here so I can show you everything I bought. And so cheap! Look, new clothes for Ivar here — and a sword. Here a horse and a trumpet for Bob. And a doll and a doll's bed here for Emmy; they're nothing much, but she'll tear them to bits in no time anyway. And here I have dress material and handkerchiefs for the maids. Old Anne-Marie really deserves something more.

HELMER: And what's in that package there?

NORA: *(with a cry)* Torvald, no! You can't see that till tonight!

HELMER: I see. But tell me now, you little prodigal, what have you thought of for yourself?

NORA: For myself? Oh, I don't want anything at all.

HELMER: Of course you do. Tell me just what — within reason — you'd most like to have.

NORA: I honestly don't know. Oh, listen, Torvald —

HELMER: Well?

NORA: *(fumbling at his coat buttons, without looking at him)* If you want to give me something, then maybe you could — you could —

HELMER: Come on, out with it.

NORA: *(hurriedly)* You could give me money, Torvald. No more than you think you can spare; then one of these days I'll buy something with it.

HELMER: But Nora —

NORA: Oh, please, Torvald darling, do that! I beg you, please. Then I could hang the bills in pretty gilt paper on the Christmas tree. Wouldn't that be fun?

HELMER: What are those little birds called that always fly through their fortunes?

NORA: Oh yes, spendthrifts; I know all that. But let's do as I say, Torvald; then I'll have time to decide what I really need most. That's very sensible, isn't it?

HELMER: *(smiling)* Yes, very — that is, if you actually hung onto the money I give you, and you actually used it to buy yourself something. But it goes for the house and for all sorts of foolish things, and then I only have to lay out some more.

NORA: Oh, but Torvald —

HELMER: Don't deny it, my dear little Nora. *(Putting his arm around her waist.)* Spendthrifts are sweet, but they use up a frightful amount of money. It's incredible what it costs a man to feed such birds.

NORA: Oh, how can you say that! Really, I save everything I can.

HELMER: *(laughing)* Yes, that's the truth. Everything you can. But that's nothing at all.

NORA: *(humming, with a smile of quiet satisfaction)* Hm, if you only knew what expenses we larks and squirrels have, Torvald.

HELMER: You're an odd little one. Exactly the way your father was. You're never at a loss for scaring up money; but the moment you have it, it runs right out through your fingers; you never know what you've done with it. Well, one takes you as you are. It's deep in your blood. Yes, these things are hereditary, Nora.

NORA: Ah, I could wish I'd inherited many of Papa's qualities.

HELMER: And I couldn't wish you anything but just what you are, my sweet little lark. But wait; it seems to me you have a very — what should I call it? — a very suspicious look today —

NORA: I do?

HELMER: You certainly do. Look me straight in the eye.

NORA: *(looking at him)* Well?

HELMER: *(shaking an admonitory finger)* Surely my sweet tooth hasn't been running riot in town today, has she?

NORA: No. Why do you imagine that?

HELMER: My sweet tooth really didn't make a little detour through the confectioner's?

NORA: No, I assure you, Torvald —

HELMER: Hasn't nibbled some pastry?

NORA: No, not at all.

HELMER: Nor even munched a macaroon or two?

NORA: No, Torvald, I assure you, really —

HELMER: There, there now. Of course I'm only joking.

NORA: *(going to the table, right)* You know I could never think of going against you.

HELMER: No, I understand that; and you *have* given me your word. *(Going over to her.)* Well, you keep your little Christmas secrets to yourself, Nora darling. I expect they'll come to light this evening, when the tree is lit.

NORA: Did you remember to ask Dr. Rank?

HELMER: No. But there's no need for that; it's assumed he'll be dining with us. All the same, I'll ask him when he stops by here this morning. I've ordered some fine wine. Nora, you can't imagine how I'm looking forward to this evening.

NORA: So am I. And what fun for the children, Torvald!

HELMER: Ah, it's so gratifying to know that one's gotten a safe, secure job, and with a comfortable salary. It's a great satisfaction, isn't it?

NORA: Oh, it's wonderful!

HELMER: Remember last Christmas? Three whole weeks before, you shut yourself in every evening till long after midnight, making flowers for the Christmas tree, and all the other decorations to surprise us. Ugh, that was the dullest time I've ever lived through.

NORA: It wasn't at all dull for me.

HELMER: *(smiling)* But the outcome *was* pretty sorry, Nora.

NORA: Oh, don't tease me with that again. How could I help it that the cat came in and tore everything to shreds.

HELMER: No, poor thing, you certainly couldn't. You wanted so much to please us all, and that's what counts. But it's just as well that the hard times are past.

NORA: Yes, it's really wonderful.

HELMER: Now I don't have to sit here alone, boring myself, and you don't have to tire your precious eyes and your fair little delicate hands —

NORA: *(clapping her hands)* No, is it really true, Torvald, I don't have to? Oh, how wonderfully lovely to hear! *(Taking his arm.)* Now I'll tell you just how I've thought we should plan things. Right after Christmas —*(The doorbell rings.)* Oh, the bell. *(Straightening the room up a bit.)* Somebody would have to come. What a bore!

Helmer: I'm not at home to visitors, don't forget.

Maid: *(from the hall doorway)* Ma'am, a lady to see you —

Nora: All right, let her come in.

Maid: *(to Helmer)* And the doctor's just come too.

Helmer: Did he go right to my study?

Maid: Yes, he did.

Helmer goes into his room. The Maid shows in Mrs. Linde, dressed in traveling clothes, and shuts the door after her.

Mrs. Linde: *(in a dispirited and somewhat hesitant voice)* Hello, Nora.

Nora: *(uncertain)* Hello —

Mrs. Linde: You don't recognize me.

Nora: No, I don't know — but wait, I think — *(Exclaiming.)* What! Kristine! Is it really you?

Mrs. Linde: Yes, it's me.

Nora: Kristine! To think I didn't recognize you. But then, how could I? *(More quietly.)* How you've changed, Kristine!

Mrs. Linde: Yes, no doubt I have. In nine — ten long years.

Nora: Is it so long since we met! Yes, it's all of that. Oh, these last eight years have been a happy time, believe me. And so now you've come in to town, too. Made the long trip in the winter. That took courage.

Mrs. Linde: I just got here by ship this morning.

Nora: To enjoy yourself over Christmas, of course. Oh, how lovely! Yes, enjoy ourselves, we'll do that. But take your coat off. You're not still cold? *(Helping her.)* There now, let's get cozy here by the stove. No, the easy chair there! I'll take the rocker here. *(Seizing her hands.)* Yes, now you have your old look again; it was only in that first moment. You're a bit more pale, Kristine — and maybe a bit thinner.

Mrs. Linde: And much, much older, Nora.

Nora: Yes, perhaps a bit older; a tiny, tiny bit; not much at all. *(Stopping short; suddenly serious.)* Oh, but thoughtless me, to sit here, chattering away. Sweet, good Kristine, can you forgive me?

Mrs. Linde: What do you mean, Nora?

Nora: *(softly)* Poor Kristine, you've become a widow.

Mrs. Linde: Yes, three years ago.

Nora: Oh, I knew it, of course: I read it in the papers. Oh, Kristine, you must believe me; I often thought of writing you then, but I kept postponing it, and something always interfered.

Mrs. Linde: Nora dear, I understand completely.

Nora: No, it was awful of me, Kristine. You poor thing, how much you must have gone through. And he left you nothing?

Mrs. Linde: No.

Nora: And no children?

Mrs. Linde: No.

Nora: Nothing at all, then?

Mrs. Linde: Not even a sense of loss to feed on.

Nora: *(looking incredulously at her)* But Kristine, how could that be?

Mrs. Linde: *(smiling wearily and smoothing her hair)* Oh, sometimes it happens, Nora.

Nora: So completely alone. How terribly hard that must be for you. I have three lovely children. You can't see them now; they're out with the maid. But now you must tell me everything —

Mrs. Linde: No, no, no, tell me about yourself.

Nora: No, you begin. Today I don't want to be selfish. I want to think only of you today. But there *is* something I must tell you. Did you hear of the wonderful luck we had recently?

Mrs. Linde: No, what's that?

Nora: My husband's been made manager in the bank, just think!

Mrs. Linde: Your husband? How marvelous!

Nora: Isn't it? Being a lawyer is such an uncertain living, you know, especially if one won't touch any cases that aren't clean and decent. And of course Torvald would never do that, and I'm with him completely there. Oh, we're simply delighted, believe me! He'll join the bank right after New Year's and start getting a huge salary and lots of commissions. From now on we can live quite differently—just as we want. Oh, Kristine, I feel so light and happy! Won't it be lovely to have stacks of money and not a care in the world?

Mrs. Linde: Well, anyway, it would be lovely to have enough for necessities.

Nora: No, not just for necessities, but stacks and stacks of money!

Mrs. Linde: *(smiling)* Nora, Nora, aren't you sensible yet? Back in school you were such a free spender.

Nora: *(with a quiet laugh)* Yes, that's what Torvald still says. *(Shaking her finger.)* But "Nora, Nora" isn't as silly as you all think. Really, we've been in no position for me to go squandering. We've had to work, both of us.

Mrs. Linde: You too?

Nora: Yes, at odd jobs — needlework, crocheting, embroidery, and such — *(casually)* and other things too. You remember that Torvald left the department when we were married? There was no chance of promotion in his office, and of course he needed to earn more money. But that first year he drove himself terribly. He took on all kinds of extra work that kept him going morning and night. It wore him down, and then he fell deathly ill. The doctors said it was essential for him to travel south.

Mrs. Linde: Yes, didn't you spend a whole year in Italy?

Nora: That's right. It wasn't easy to get away, you know. Ivar had just been born. But of course we had to go. Oh, that was a beautiful trip, and it saved Torvald's life. But it cost a frightful sum, Kristine.

Mrs. Linde: I can well imagine.

Nora: Four thousand, eight hundred crowns it cost. That's really a lot of money.

MRS. LINDE: But it's lucky you had it when you needed it.

NORA: Well, as it was, we got it from Papa.

MRS. LINDE: I see. It was just about the time your father died.

NORA: Yes, just about then. And, you know, I couldn't make that trip out to nurse him. I had to stay here, expecting Ivar any moment, and with my poor sick Torvald to care for. Dearest Papa, I never saw him again, Kristine. Oh, that was the worst time I've known in all my marriage.

MRS. LINDE: I know how you loved him. And then you went off to Italy?

NORA: Yes. We had the means now, and the doctors urged us. So we left a month after.

MRS. LINDE: And your husband came back completely cured?

NORA: Sound as a drum!

MRS. LINDE: But — the doctor?

NORA: Who?

MRS. LINDE: I thought the maid said he was a doctor, the man who came in with me.

NORA: Yes, that was Dr. Rank — but he's not making a sick call. He's our closest friend, and he stops by at least once a day. No, Torvald hasn't had a sick moment since, and the children are fit and strong, and I am, too. *(Jumping up and clapping her hands.)* Oh, dear God, Kristine, what a lovely thing to live and be happy! But how disgusting of me — I'm talking of nothing but my own affairs. *(Sits on a stool close by Kristine, arms resting across her knees.)* Oh, don't be angry with me! Tell me, is it really true that you weren't in love with your husband? Why did you marry him, then?

MRS. LINDE: My mother was still alive, but bedridden and helpless — and I had my two younger brothers to look after. In all conscience, didn't think I could turn him down.

NORA: No, you were right there. But was he rich at the time?

MRS. LINDE: He was very well off, I'd say. But the business was shaky, Nora. When he died, it all fell apart, and nothing was left.

NORA: And then — ?

MRS. LINDE: Yes, so I had to scrape up a living with a little shop and a little teaching and whatever else I could find. The last three years have been like one endless workday without a rest for me. Now it's over, Nora. My poor mother doesn't need me, for she's passed on. Nor the boys, either; they're working now and can take care of themselves.

NORA: How free you must feel —

MRS. LINDE: No — only unspeakably empty. Nothing to live for now. *(Standing up anxiously.)* That's why I couldn't take it any longer out in that desolate hole. Maybe here it'll be easier to find something to do and keep my mind occupied. If I could only be lucky enough to get a steady job, some office work —

Nora: Oh, but Kristine, that's so dreadfully tiring, and you already look so tired. It would be much better for you if you could go off to a bathing resort.

Mrs. Linde: *(going toward the window)* I have no father to give me travel money, Nora.

Nora: *(rising)* Oh, don't be angry with me.

Mrs. Linde: *(going to her)* Nora dear, don't you be angry with me. The worst of my kind of situation is all the bitterness that's stored away. No one to work for, and yet you're always having to snap up your opportunities. You have to live; and so you grow selfish. When you told me the happy change in your lot, do you know I was delighted less for your sakes than for mine?

Nora: How so? Oh, I see. You think Torvald could do something for you.

Mrs. Linde: Yes, that's what I thought.

Nora: And he will, Kristine! Just leave it to me; I'll bring it up so delicately—find something attractive to humor him with. Oh, I'm so eager to help you.

Mrs. Linde: How very kind of you, Nora, to be so concerned over me—doubly kind, considering you really know so little of life's burdens yourself.

Nora: I—? I know so little—?

Mrs. Linde: *(smiling)* Well my heavens—a little needlework and such—Nora, you're just a child.

Nora: *(tossing her head and pacing the floor)* You don't have to act so superior.

Mrs. Linde: Oh?

Nora: You're just like the others. You all think I'm incapable of anything serious—

Mrs. Linde: Come now—

Nora: That I've never had to face the raw world.

Mrs. Linde: Nora dear, you've just been telling me all your troubles.

Nora: Hm! Trivial! *(Quietly.)* I haven't told you the big thing.

Mrs. Linde: Big thing? What do you mean?

Nora: You look down on me so, Kristine, but you shouldn't. You're proud that you worked so long and hard for your mother.

Mrs. Linde: I don't look down on a soul. But it *is* true: I'm proud—and happy, too—to think it was given to me to make my mother's last days almost free of care.

Nora: And you're also proud thinking of what you've done for your brothers.

Mrs. Linde: I feel I've a right to be.

Nora: I agree. But listen to this, Kristine—I've also got something to be proud and happy for.

Mrs. Linde: I don't doubt it. But whatever do you mean?

Nora: Not so loud. What if Torvald heard! He mustn't, not for anything in the world. Nobody must know, Kristine. No one but you.

Mrs. Linde: But what is it, then?

Nora: Come here. *(Drawing her down beside her on the sofa.)* It's true—I've also got something to be proud and happy for. I'm the one who saved Torvald's life.

MRS. LINDE: Saved —? Saved how?

NORA: I told you about the trip to Italy. Torvald never would have lived if he hadn't gone south —

MRS. LINDE: Of course; your father gave you the means —

NORA: *(smiling)* That's what Torvald and all the rest think, but —

MRS. LINDE: But —?

NORA: Papa didn't give us a pin. I was the one who raised the money.

MRS. LINDE: You? That whole amount?

NORA: Four thousand, eight hundred crowns. What do you say to that?

MRS. LINDE: But Nora, how was it possible? Did you win the lottery?

NORA: *(disdainfully)* The lottery? Pooh! No art to that.

MRS. LINDE: But where did you get it from then?

NORA: *(humming, with a mysterious smile)* Hmm, tra-la-la-la.

MRS. LINDE: Because you couldn't have borrowed it.

NORA: No? Why not?

MRS. LINDE: A wife can't borrow without her husband's consent.

NORA: *(tossing her head)* Oh, but a wife with a little business sense, a wife who knows how to manage —

MRS. LINDE: Nora, I simply don't understand —

NORA: You don't have to. Whoever said I *borrowed* the money? I could have gotten it other ways. *(Throwing herself back on the sofa.)* I could have gotten it from some admirer or other. After all, a girl with my ravishing appeal —

MRS. LINDE: You lunatic.

NORA: I'll bet you're eaten up with curiosity, Kristine.

MRS. LINDE: Now listen here, Nora — you haven't done something indiscreet?

NORA: *(sitting up again)* Is it indiscreet to save your husband's life?

MRS. LINDE: I think it's indiscreet that without his knowledge you —

NORA: But that's the point: he mustn't know! My Lord, can't you understand? He mustn't ever know the close call he had. It was to *me* the doctors came to say his life was in danger — that nothing could save him but a stay in the south. Didn't I try strategy then! I began talking about how lovely it would be for me to travel abroad like other young wives; I begged and I cried; I told him please to remember my condition, to be kind and indulge me; and then I dropped a hint that he could easily take out a loan. But at that, Kristine, he nearly exploded. He said I was frivolous, and it was his duty as man of the house not to indulge me in whims and fancies — as I think he called them. Aha, I thought, now you'll just have to be saved — and that's when I saw my chance.

MRS. LINDE: And your father never told Torvald the money wasn't from him?

NORA: No, never. Papa died right about then. I'd considered bringing him into my secret and begging him never to tell. But he was too sick at the time — and then, sadly, it didn't matter.

MRS. LINDE: And you've never confided in your husband since?

NORA: For heaven's sake, no! Are you serious? He's so strict on that subject. Besides—Torvald, with all his masculine pride—how painfully humiliating for him if he ever found out he was in debt to me. That would just ruin our relationship. Our beautiful, happy home would never be the same.

MRS. LINDE: Won't you ever tell him?

NORA: *(thoughtfully, half smiling)* Yes—maybe sometime, years from now, when I'm no longer so attractive. Don't laugh! I only mean when Torvald loves me less than now, when he stops enjoying my dancing and dressing up and reciting for him. Then it might be wise to have something in reserve—*(Breaking off.)* How ridiculous! That'll never happen—Well, Kristine, what do you think of my big secret? I'm capable of something too, hm? You can imagine, of course, how this thing hangs over me. It really hasn't been easy meeting the payments on time. In the business world there's what they call quarterly interest and what they call amortization, and these are always so terribly hard to manage. I've had to skimp a little here and there, wherever I could, you know. I could hardly spare anything from my house allowance, because Torvald has to live well. I couldn't let the children go poorly dressed; whatever I got for them, I felt I had to use up completely—the darlings!

MRS. LINDE: Poor Nora, so it had to come out of your own budget, then?

NORA: Yes, of course. But I was the one most responsible, too. Every time Torvald gave me money for new clothes and such, I never used more than half; always bought the simplest, cheapest outfits. It was a godsend that everything looks so well on me that Torvald never noticed. But it did weigh me down at times, Kristine. It *is* such a joy to wear fine things. You understand.

MRS. LINDE: Oh, of course.

NORA: And then I found other ways of making money. Last winter I was lucky enough to get a lot of copying to do. I locked myself in and sat writing every evening till late in the night. Ah, I was tired so often, dead tired. But still it was wonderful fun, sitting and working like that, earning money. It was almost like being a man.

MRS. LINDE: But how much have you paid off this way so far?

NORA: That's hard to say, exactly. These accounts, you know, aren't easy to figure. I only know that I've paid out all I could scrape together. Time and again I haven't known where to turn. *(Smiling.)* Then I'd sit here dreaming of a rich old gentleman who had fallen in love with me—

MRS. LINDE: What! Who is he?

NORA: Oh, really! And that he'd died, and when his will was opened, there in big letters it said, "All my fortune shall be paid over in cash, immediately, to that enchanting Mrs. Nora Helmer."

MRS. LINDE: But Nora dear—who *was* this gentleman?

NORA: Good grief, can't you understand? The old man never existed; that was only something I'd dream up time and again whenever I was at my wits' end for money. But it makes no difference now; the old fossil can go where he pleases for all I care; I don't need him or his will—because now I'm free. *(Jumping up.)* Oh, how lovely to think of that, Kristine! Carefree! To know you're carefree, utterly carefree; to be able to romp and play with the children, and to keep up a beautiful, charming home—everything just the way Torvald likes it! And think, spring is coming, with big blue skies. Maybe we can travel a little then. Maybe I'll see the ocean again. Oh yes, it *is* so marvelous to live and be happy!

The front doorbell rings.

Mrs. Linde: *(rising)* There's the bell. It's probably best that I go.

Nora: No, stay. No one's expected. It must be for Torvald.

Maid: *(from the hall doorway)* Excuse me, ma'am—there's a gentleman here to see Mr. Helmer, but I didn't know—since the doctor's with him—

Nora: Who is the gentleman?

Krogstad: *(from the doorway)* It's me, Mrs. Helmer.

Mrs. Linde starts and turns away toward the window.

Nora: *(stepping toward him, tense, her voice a whisper)* You? What is it? Why do you want to speak to my husband?

Krogstad: Bank business—after a fashion. I have a small job in the investment bank, and I hear now your husband is going to be our chief—

Nora: In other words, it's—

Krogstad: Just dry business, Mrs. Helmer. Nothing but that.

Nora: Yes, then please be good enough to step into the study. *(She nods indifferently as she sees him out by the hall door, then returns and begins stirring up the stove.)*

Mrs. Linde: Nora—who was that man?

Nora: That was a Mr. Krogstad—a lawyer.

Mrs. Linde: Then it really was him.

Nora: Do you know that person?

Mrs. Linde: I did once—many years ago. For a time he was a law clerk in our town.

Nora: Yes, he's been that.

Mrs. Linde: How he's changed.

Nora: I understand he had a very unhappy marriage.

Mrs. Linde: He's a widower now.

Nora: With a number of children. There now, it's burning. *(She closes the stove door and moves the rocker a bit to one side.)*

Mrs. Linde: They say he has a hand in all kinds of business.

Nora: Oh? That may be true: I wouldn't know. But let's not think about business. It's so dull.

Dr. Rank enters from Helmer's study.

Rank: *(still in the doorway)* No, no, really—I don't want to intrude, I'd just as soon talk a little while with your wife. *(Shuts the door, then notices Mrs. Linde.)* Oh, beg pardon. I'm intruding here too.

NORA: No, not at all. *(Introducing him.)* Dr. Rank, Mrs. Linde.

RANK: Well now, that's a name much heard in this house. I believe I passed the lady on the stairs as I came.

MRS. LINDE: Yes, I take the stairs very slowly. They're rather hard on me.

RANK: Uh-hm, some touch of internal weakness?

MRS. LINDE: More overexertion, I'd say.

RANK: Nothing else? Then you're probably here in town to rest up in a round of parties?

MRS. LINDE: I'm here to look for work.

RANK: Is that the best cure for overexertion?

MRS. LINDE: One has to live, Doctor.

RANK: Yes, there's a common prejudice to that effect.

NORA: Oh, come on, Dr. Rank—you really do want to live yourself.

RANK: Yes, I really do. Wretched as I am, I'll gladly prolong my torment indefinitely. All my patients feel like that. And it's quite the same, too, with the morally sick. Right at this moment there's one of those moral invalids in there with Helmer—

MRS. LINDE: *(softly)* Ah!

NORA: Who do you mean?

RANK: Oh, it's a lawyer, Krogstad, a type you wouldn't know. His character is rotten to the root—but even he began chattering all-importantly about how he had to *live*.

NORA: Oh? What did he want to talk to Torvald about?

RANK: I really don't know. I only heard something about the bank.

NORA: I didn't know that Krog—that this man Krogstad had anything to do with the bank.

RANK: Yes, he's gotten some kind of berth down there. *(To Mrs. Linde.)* I don't know if you also have, in your neck of the woods, a type of person who scuttles about breathlessly, sniffing out hints of moral corruption, and then maneuvers his victim into some sort of key position where he can keep an eye on him. It's the healthy these days that are out in the cold.

MRS. LINDE: All the same, it's the sick who most need to be taken in.

RANK: *(with a shrug)* Yes, there we have it. That's the concept that's turning society into a sanatorium.

Nora, lost in her thoughts, breaks out into quiet laughter and claps her hands.

RANK: Why do you laugh at that? Do you have any real idea of what society is?

NORA: What do I care about dreary old society? I was laughing at something quite different—something terribly funny. Tell me, Doctor—is everyone who works in the bank dependent now on Torvald?

RANK: Is that what you find so terribly funny?

NORA: *(smiling and humming)* Never mind, never mind! *(Pacing the floor.)* Yes, that's really immensely amusing: that we—that Torvald has so much power now over all those people. *(Taking the bag out of her pocket.)* Dr. Rank, a little macaroon on that?

RANK: See here, macaroons! I thought they were contraband here.

NORA: Yes, but these are some that Kristine gave me.

MRS. LINDE: What? I — ?

NORA: Now, now, don't be afraid. You couldn't possibly know that Torvald had forbidden them. You see, he's worried they'll ruin my teeth. But hmp! Just this once! Isn't that so, Dr. Rank? Help yourself! *(Puts a macaroon in his mouth.)* And you too, Kristine. And I'll also have one, only a little one — or two, at the most. *(Walking about again.)* Now I'm really tremendously happy. Now there's just one last thing in the world that I have an enormous desire to do.

RANK: Well! And what's that?

NORA: It's something I have such a consuming desire to say so Torvald could hear.

RANK: And why can't you say it?

NORA: I don't dare. It's quite shocking.

MRS. LINDE: Shocking?

RANK: Well, then it isn't advisable. But in front of us you certainly can. What do you have such a desire to say so Torvald could hear?

NORA: I have such a huge desire to say — to hell and be damned!

RANK: Are you crazy?

MRS. LINDE: My goodness, Nora!

RANK: Go on, say it. Here he is.

NORA: *(hiding the macaroon bag)* Shh, shh, shh!

Helmer comes in from his study, hat in hand, overcoat over his arm.

NORA: *(going toward him)* Well, Torvald dear, are you through with him?

HELMER: Yes, he just left.

NORA: Let me introduce you — this is Kristine, who's arrived here in town.

HELMER: Kristine — ? I'm sorry, but I don't know —

NORA: Mrs. Linde, Torvald dear. Mrs. Kristine Linde.

HELMER: Of course. A childhood friend of my wife's, no doubt?

MRS. LINDE: Yes, we knew each other in those days.

NORA: And just think, she made the long trip down here in order to talk with you.

HELMER: What's this?

MRS. LINDE: Well, not exactly —

NORA: You see, Kristine is remarkably clever in office work, and so she's terribly eager to come under a capable man's supervision and add more to what she already knows —

HELMER: Very wise, Mrs. Linde.

NORA: And then when she heard that you'd become a bank manager — the story was wired out to the papers — then she came in as fast as she could and — Really, Torvald, for my sake you can do a little something for Kristine, can't you?

HELMER: Yes, it's not at all impossible. Mrs. Linde, I suppose you're a widow?

MRS. LINDE: Yes.

HELMER: Any experience in office work?

MRS. LINDE: Yes, a good deal.

HELMER: Well, it's quite likely that I can make an opening for you —

NORA: *(clapping her hands)* You see, you see!

HELMER: You've come at a lucky moment, Mrs. Linde.

MRS. LINDE: Oh, how can I thank you?

HELMER: Not necessary. *(Putting his overcoat on.)* But today you'll have to excuse me —

RANK: Wait, I'll go with you. *(He fetches his coat from the hall and warms it at the stove.)*

NORA: Don't stay out long, dear.

HELMER: An hour; no more.

NORA: Are you going too, Kristine?

MRS. LINDE: *(putting on her winter garments)* Yes, I have to see about a room now.

HELMER: Then perhaps we can all walk together.

NORA: *(helping her)* What a shame we're so cramped here, but it's quite impossible for us to —

MRS. LINDE: Oh, don't even think of it! Good-bye, Nora dear, and thanks for everything.

NORA: Good-bye for now. Of course you'll be back this evening. And you too, Dr. Rank. What? If you're well enough? Oh, you've got to be! Wrap up tight now.

In a ripple of small talk the company moves out into the hall; children's voices are heard outside on the steps.

NORA: There they are! There they are! *(She runs to open the door. The children come in with their nurse, Anne-Marie.)* Come in, come in! *(Bends down and kisses them.)* Oh, you darlings—! Look at them, Kristine. Aren't they lovely!

RANK: No loitering in the draft here.

HELMER: Come, Mrs. Linde—this place is unbearable now for anyone but mothers.

Dr. Rank, Helmer, and Mrs. Linde go down the stairs. Anne-Marie goes into the living room with the children. Nora follows, after closing the hall door.

NORA: How fresh and strong you look. Oh, such red cheeks you have! Like apples and roses. *(The children interrupt her throughout the following.)* And it was so much fun? That's wonderful. Really? You pulled both Emmy and Bob on the sled? Imagine, all together! Yes, you're a clever boy, Ivar. Oh, let me hold her a bit, Anne-Marie. My sweet little doll baby! *(Takes the smallest from the nurse and dances with her.)* Yes, yes, Mama will dance with Bob as well. What? Did you throw snowballs? Oh, if I'd only been there! No, don't bother, Anne-Marie —I'll undress them myself. Oh yes, let me. It's such fun. Go in and rest; you look half frozen. There's hot coffee waiting for you on the stove. *(The nurse goes into the room to the left. Nora takes the children's* *winter things off, throwing them about, while the children talk to her all at once.)* Is that so? A big dog chased you? But it didn't bite? No, dogs never bite little, lovely doll babies. Don't peek in the packages, Ivar! What is it? Yes, wouldn't you like to know. No, no, it's an ugly something. Well? Shall we play? What shall we play? Hide-and-seek? Yes, let's play hide-and-seek. Bob must hide first. I must? Yes, let me hide first. *(Laughing and shouting, she and the children play in and out of the living room and the adjoining room to the right. At last Nora hides under the table. The children come storming in, search, but cannot find her, then hear her muffled laughter, dash over to the table, lift the cloth up and find her. Wild shouting. She creeps forward as if to scare them. More shouts. Meanwhile, a knock at the hall door; no one has noticed it. Now the door half opens, and Krogstad appears. He waits a moment; the game goes on.)*

KROGSTAD: Beg pardon, Mrs. Helmer —

NORA: *(with a strangled cry, turning and scrambling to her knees)* Oh! What do you want?

KROGSTAD: Excuse me. The outer door was ajar; it must be someone forgot to shut it —

NORA: *(rising)* My husband isn't home, Mr. Krogstad.

KROGSTAD: I know that.

NORA: Yes — then what do you want here?

KROGSTAD: A word with you.

NORA: With —? *(To the children, quietly.)* Go in to Anne-Marie. What? No, the strange man won't hurt Mama. When he's gone, we'll play some more. *(She leads the children into the room to the left and shuts the door after them. Then, tense and nervous.)* You want to speak to me?

KROGSTAD: Yes, I want to.

NORA: Today? But it's not yet the first of the month —

KROGSTAD: No, it's Christmas Eve. It's going to be up to you how merry a Christmas you have.

NORA: What is it you want? Today I absolutely can't —

KROGSTAD: We won't talk about that till later. This is something else. You do have a moment to spare, I suppose?

NORA: Oh yes, of course — I do, except —

KROGSTAD: Good. I was sitting over at Olsen's Restaurant when I saw your husband go down the street —

NORA: Yes?

KROGSTAD: With a lady.

NORA: Yes. So?

KROGSTAD: If you'll pardon my asking: wasn't that lady a Mrs. Linde?

NORA: Yes.

KROGSTAD: Just now come into town?

NORA: Yes, today.

KROGSTAD: She's a good friend of yours?

NORA: Yes, she is. But I don't see —

KROGSTAD: I also knew her once.

NORA: I'm aware of that.

KROGSTAD: Oh? You know all about it. I thought so. Well, then let me ask you short and sweet: is Mrs. Linde getting a job in the bank?

NORA: What makes you think you can cross-examine me, Mr. Krogstad — you, one of my husband's employees? But since you ask, you might as well know — yes, Mrs. Linde's going to be taken on at the bank. And I'm the one who spoke for her, Mr. Krogstad. Now you know.

KROGSTAD: So I guessed right.

NORA: *(pacing up and down)* Oh, one does have a tiny bit of influence, I should hope. Just because I am a woman, don't think it means that — When one has a subordinate position, Mr. Krogstad, one really ought to be careful about pushing somebody who — hm —

KROGSTAD: Who has influence?

NORA: That's right.

KROGSTAD: *(in a different tone)* Mrs. Helmer, would you be good enough to use your influence on my behalf?

NORA: What? What do you mean?

KROGSTAD: Would you please make sure that I keep my subordinate position in the bank?

NORA: What does that mean? Who's thinking of taking away your position?

KROGSTAD: Oh, don't play the innocent with me. I'm quite aware that your friend would hardly relish the chance of running into me again; and I'm also aware now whom I can thank for being turned out.

NORA: But I promise you —

KROGSTAD: Yes, yes, yes, to the point: there's still time, and I'm advising you to use your influence to prevent it.

NORA: But Mr. Krogstad, I have absolutely no influence.

KROGSTAD: You haven't? I thought you were just saying —

NORA: You shouldn't take me so literally. I! How can you believe that I have any such influence over my husband?

KROGSTAD: Oh, I've known your husband from our student days. I don't think the great bank manager's more steadfast than any other married man.

NORA: You speak insolently about my husband, and I'll show you the door.

KROGSTAD: The lady has spirit.

NORA: I'm not afraid of you any longer. After New Year's, I'll soon be done with the whole business.

KROGSTAD: *(restraining himself)* Now listen to me, Mrs. Helmer. If necessary, I'll fight for my little job in the bank as if it were life itself.

NORA: Yes, so it seems.

KROGSTAD: It's not just a matter of income; that's the least of it. It's something else — All right, out with it! Look, this is the thing. You know, just like all the others, of course, that once, a good many years ago, I did something rather rash.

NORA: I've heard rumors to that effect.

KROGSTAD: The case never got into court; but all the same, every door was closed in my face from then on. So I took up those various activities you know about. I had to grab hold somewhere; and I dare say I haven't been among the worst. But now I want to drop all that. My boys are growing up. For their sakes, I'll have to win back as much respect as possible here in town. That job in the bank was like the first rung in my ladder. And now your husband wants to kick me right back down in the mud again.

NORA: But for heaven's sake, Mr. Krogstad, it's simply not in my power to help you.

KROGSTAD: That's because you haven't the will to — but I have the means to make you.

NORA: You certainly won't tell my husband that I owe you money?

KROGSTAD: Hm — what if I told him that?

NORA: That would be shameful of you. *(Nearly in tears.)* This secret — my joy and my pride — that he should learn it in such a crude and disgusting way — learn it from you. You'd expose me to the most horrible unpleasantness —

KROGSTAD: Only unpleasantness?

NORA: *(vehemently)* But go on and try. It'll turn out the worse for you, because then my husband will really see what a crook you are, and then you'll *never* be able to hold your job.

KROGSTAD: I asked if it was just domestic unpleasantness you were afraid of.

NORA: If my husband finds out, then of course he'll pay what I owe at once, and then we'd be through with you for good.

KROGSTAD: *(a step closer)* Listen, Mrs. Helmer — you've either got a very bad memory, or else no head at all for business. I'd better put you a little more in touch with the facts.

NORA: What do you mean?

KROGSTAD: When your husband was sick, you came to me for a loan of four thousand, eight hundred crowns.

NORA: Where else could I go?

KROGSTAD: I promised to get you that sum —

NORA: And you got it.

KROGSTAD: I promised to get you that sum, on certain conditions. You were so involved in your husband's illness, and so eager to finance your trip, that I guess you didn't think out all the details. It might just be a good idea to remind you. I promised you the money on the strength of a note I drew up.

NORA: Yes, and that I signed.

KROGSTAD: Right. But at the bottom I added some lines for your father to guarantee the loan. He was supposed to sign down there.

NORA: Supposed to? He did sign.

KROGSTAD: I left the date blank. In other words, your father would have dated his signature himself. Do you remember that?

NORA: Yes, I think —

KROGSTAD: Then I gave you the note for you to mail to your father. Isn't that so?

NORA: Yes.

KROGSTAD: And naturally you sent it at once — because only some five, six days later you brought me the note, properly signed. And with that, the money was yours.

NORA: Well, then; I've made my payments regularly, haven't I?

KROGSTAD: More or less. But — getting back to the point — those were hard times for you then, Mrs. Helmer.

NORA: Yes, they were.

KROGSTAD: Your father was very ill, I believe.

NORA: He was near the end.

KROGSTAD: He died soon after?

NORA: Yes.

KROGSTAD: Tell me, Mrs. Helmer, do you happen to recall the date of your father's death? The day of the month, I mean.

NORA: Papa died the twenty-ninth of September.

KROGSTAD: That's quite correct; I've already looked into that. And now we come to a curious thing — *(taking out a paper)* which I simply cannot comprehend.

NORA: Curious thing? I don't know —

KROGSTAD: This is the curious thing: that your father co-signed the note for your loan three days after his death.

NORA: How — ? I don't understand.

KROGSTAD: Your father died the twenty-ninth of September. But look. Here your father dated his signature October second. Isn't that curious, Mrs. Helmer? *(Nora is silent.)* Can you explain it to me? *(Nora remains silent.)* It's also remarkable that the words "October second" and the year aren't written in your father's hand, but rather in one that I think I know. Well, it's easy to understand. Your father forgot perhaps to date his signature, and then someone or other added it, a bit sloppily, before anyone knew of his death. There's nothing wrong in that. It all comes down to the signature. And there's no question about *that,* Mrs. Helmer. It really *was* your father who signed his own name here, wasn't it?

NORA: *(after a short silence, throwing her head back and looking squarely at him)* No, it wasn't. *I* signed Papa's name.

KROGSTAD: Wait, now — are you fully aware that this is a dangerous confession?

NORA: Why? You'll soon get your money.

KROGSTAD: Let me ask you a question — why didn't you send the paper to your father?

NORA: That was impossible. Papa was so sick. If I'd asked him for his signature, I also would have had to tell him what the money was for. But I couldn't tell him, sick as he was, that my husband's life was in danger. That was just impossible.

KROGSTAD: Then it would have been better if you'd given up the trip abroad.

NORA: I couldn't possibly. The trip was to save my husband's life. I couldn't give that up.

KROGSTAD: But didn't you ever consider that this was a fraud against me?

NORA: I couldn't let myself be bothered by that. You weren't any concern of mine. I couldn't stand you, with all those cold complications you made, even though you knew how badly off my husband was.

KROGSTAD: Mrs. Helmer, obviously you haven't the vaguest idea of what you've involved yourself in. But I can tell you this: it was nothing more and nothing worse than I once did—and it wrecked my whole reputation.

NORA: You? Do you expect me to believe that you ever acted bravely to save your wife's life?

KROGSTAD: Laws don't inquire into motives.

NORA: Then they must be very poor laws.

KROGSTAD: Poor or not—if I introduce this paper in court, you'll be judged according to law.

NORA: This I refuse to believe. A daughter hasn't a right to protect her dying father from anxiety and care? A wife hasn't a right to save her husband's life? I don't know much about laws, but I'm sure that somewhere in the books these things are allowed. And you don't know anything about it—you who practice the law? You must be an awful lawyer, Mr. Krogstad.

KROGSTAD: Could be. But business—the kind of business we two mixed up in—don't you think I know about that? All right. Do what you want now. But I'm telling you *this:* if I get shoved down a second time, you're going to keep me company. *(He bows and goes out through the hall.)*

NORA: *(pensive for a moment, then tossing her head)* Oh, really! Trying to frighten me! I'm not so silly as all that. *(Begins gathering up the children's clothes, but soon stops.)* But—? No, but that's impossible! I did it out of love.

THE CHILDREN: *(in the doorway, left)* Mama, that strange man's gone out the door.

NORA: Yes, yes, I know it. But don't tell anyone about the strange man. Do you hear? Not even Papa!

THE CHILDREN: No, Mama. But now will you play again?

NORA: No, not now.

THE CHILDREN: Oh, but Mama, you promised.

NORA: Yes, but I can't now. Go inside; I have too much to do. Go in, go in, my sweet darlings. *(She herds them gently back in the room and shuts the door after them. Settling on the sofa, she takes up a piece of embroidery and makes some stitches, but soon stops abruptly.)* No! *(Throws the work aside, rises, goes to the hall door and calls out.)* Helene! Let me have the tree in here. *(Goes to the table, left, opens the table drawer, and stops again.)* No, but that's utterly impossible!

MAID: *(with the Christmas tree)* Where should I put it, ma'am?

NORA: There. The middle of the floor.

MAID: Should I bring anything else?

NORA: No, thanks. I have what I need.

The Maid, who has set the tree down, goes out.

NORA: *(absorbed in trimming the tree)* Candles here — and flowers here. That terrible creature! Talk, talk, talk! There's nothing to it at all. The tree's going to be lovely. I'll do anything to please you, Torvald. I'll sing for you, dance for you —

Helmer comes in from the hall, with a sheaf of papers under his arm.

NORA: Oh! You're back so soon?

HELMER: Yes. Has anyone been here?

NORA: Here? No.

ER: That's odd. I saw Krogstad leaving the front door.

NORA: So? Oh yes, that's true. Krogstad was here a moment.

HELMER: Nora, I can see by your face that he's been here, begging you to put in a good word for him.

NORA: Yes.

HELMER: And it was supposed to seem like your own idea? You were to hide it from me that he'd been here. He asked you that, too, didn't he?

NORA: Yes, Torvald, but —

HELMER: Nora, Nora, and you could fall for that? Talk with that sort of person and promise him anything? And then in the bargain, tell me an untruth.

NORA: An untruth —?

HELMER: Didn't you say that no one had been here? *(Wagging his finger.)* My little songbird must never do that again. A songbird needs a clean beak to warble with. No false notes. *(Putting his arm about her waist.)* That's the way it should be, isn't it? Yes, I'm sure of it. *(Releasing her.)* And so, enough of that. *(Sitting by the stove.)* Ah, how snug and cozy it is here. *(Leafing among his papers.)*

NORA: *(busy with the tree, after a short pause)* Torvald!

HELMER: Yes.

NORA: I'm so much looking forward to the Stenborgs' costume party, day after tomorrow.

HELMER: And I can't wait to see what you'll surprise me with.

NORA: Oh, that stupid business!

HELMER: What?

NORA: I can't find anything that's right. Everything seems so ridiculous, so inane.

HELMER: So my little Nora's come to *that* recognition?

NORA: *(going behind his chair, her arms resting on its back)* Are you very busy, Torvald?

HELMER: Oh—

NORA: What papers are those?

HELMER: Bank matters.

NORA: Already?

HELMER: I've gotten full authority from the retiring management to make all necessary changes in personnel and procedure. I'll need Christmas week for that. I want to have everything in order by New Year's.

NORA: So that was the reason this poor Krogstad —

HELMER: Hm.

NORA: *(still leaning on the chair and slowly stroking the nape of his neck)* If you weren't so very busy, I would have asked you an enormous favor, Torvald.

HELMER: Let's hear. What is it?

NORA: You know, there isn't anyone who has your good taste — and I want so much to look well at the costume party. Torvald, couldn't you take over and decide what I should be and plan my costume?

HELMER: Ah, is my stubborn little creature calling for a lifeguard?

NORA: Yes, Torvald, I can't get anywhere without your help.

HELMER: All right — I'll think it over. We'll hit on something.

NORA: Oh, how sweet of you. *(Goes to the tree again. Pause.)* Aren't the red flowers pretty —? But tell me, was it really such a crime that this Krogstad committed?

HELMER: Forgery. Do you have any idea what that means?

NORA: Couldn't he have done it out of need?

HELMER: Yes, or thoughtlessness, like so many others. I'm not so heartless that I'd condemn a man categorically for just one mistake.

NORA: No, of course not, Torvald!

HELMER: Plenty of men have redeemed themselves by openly confessing their crimes and taking their punishment.

NORA: Punishment —?

HELMER: But now Krogstad didn't go that way. He got himself out by sharp practices, and that's the real cause of his moral breakdown.

NORA: Do you really think that would —?

HELMER: Just imagine how a man with that sort of guilt in him has to lie and cheat and deceive on all sides, has to wear a mask even with the nearest and dearest he has, even with his own wife and children. And with the children, Nora — that's where it's most horrible.

NORA: Why?

HELMER: Because that kind of atmosphere of lies infects the whole life of a home. Every breath the children take in is filled with the germs of something degenerate.

NORA: *(coming closer behind him)* Are you sure of that?

HELMER: Oh, I've seen it often enough as a lawyer. Almost everyone who goes bad early in life has a mother who's a chronic liar.

NORA: Why just — the mother?

HELMER: It's usually the mother's influence that's dominant, but the father's works in the same way, of course. Every lawyer is quite familiar with it. And still this Krogstad's been going home year in, year out, poisoning his own children with lies and pretense; that's why I call him morally lost. *(Reaching* *his hands out toward her.)* So my sweet little Nora must promise me never to plead his cause. Your hand on it. Come, come, what's this? Give me your hand. There, now. All settled. I can tell you it'd be impossible for me to work alongside of him. I literally feel physically revolted when I'm anywhere near such a person.

NORA: *(withdraws her hand and goes to the other side of the Christmas tree)* How hot it is here! And I've got so much to do.

HELMER: *(getting up and gathering his papers)* Yes, and I have to think about getting some of these read through before dinner. I'll think about your costume, too. And something to hang on the tree in gilt paper, I may even see about that. *(Putting his hand on her head.)* Oh you, my darling little songbird. *(He goes into his study and closes the door after him.)*

NORA: *(softly, after a silence)* Oh, really! It isn't so. It's impossible. It must be impossible.

ANNE-MARIE: *(in the doorway, left)* The children are begging so hard to come in to Mama.

NORA: No, no, no, don't let them in to me! You stay with them, Anne-Marie.

ANNE-MARIE: Of course, ma'am. *(Closes the door.)*

NORA: *(pale with terror)* Hurt my children —! Poison my home? *(A moment's pause; then she tosses her head.)* That's not true. Never. Never in all the world.

ACT 2

Same room. Beside the piano the Christmas tree now stands stripped of ornaments, burned-down candle stubs on its ragged branches. Nora's street clothes lie on the sofa. Nora, alone in the room, moves restlessly about; at last she stops at the sofa and picks up her coat.

NORA: *(dropping the coat again)* Someone's coming! *(Goes toward the door, listens.)* No — there's no one. Of course — nobody's coming today, Christmas Day — or tomorrow, either. But maybe —*(Opens the door and looks out.)* No, nothing in the mailbox. Quite empty. *(Coming forward.)* What nonsense! He won't do anything serious. Nothing terrible could happen. It's impossible. Why, I have three small children.

Anne-Marie, with a large carton, comes in from the room to the left.

ANNE-MARIE: Well, at last I found the box with the masquerade clothes.

NORA: Thanks. Put it on the table.

ANNE-MARIE: *(does so)* But they're all pretty much of a mess.

NORA: Ahh! I'd love to rip them in a million pieces!

ANNE-MARIE: Oh, mercy, they can be fixed right up. Just a little patience.

NORA: Yes, I'll go get Mrs. Linde to help me.

ANNE-MARIE: Out again now? In this nasty weather? Miss Nora will catch cold — get sick.

NORA: Oh, worse things could happen — How are the children?

ANNE-MARIE: The poor mites are playing with their Christmas presents, but —

NORA: Do they ask for me much?

ANNE-MARIE: They're so used to having Mama around, you know.

NORA: Yes. But Anne-Marie, I *can't* be together with them as much as I was.

ANNE-MARIE: Well, small children get used to anything.

NORA: You think so? Do you think they'd forget their mother if she was gone for good?

ANNE-MARIE: Oh, mercy—gone for good!

NORA: Wait, tell me, Anne-Marie — I've wondered so often — how could you ever have the heart to give your child over to strangers?

ANNE-MARIE: But I had to, you know, to become little Nora's nurse.

NORA: Yes, but how could you *do* it?

ANNE-MARIE: When I could get such a good place? A girl who's poor and who's gotten in trouble is glad enough for that. Because that slippery fish, he didn't do a thing for me, you know.

NORA: But your daughter's surely forgotten you.

ANNE-MARIE: Oh, she certainly has not. She's written to me, both when she was confirmed and when she was married.

NORA: *(clasping her about the neck)* You old Anne-Marie, you were a good mother for me when I was little.

ANNE-MARIE: Poor little Nora, with no other mother but me.

NORA: And if the babies didn't have one, then I know that you'd — What silly talk! *(Opening the carton.)* Go in to them. Now I'll have to—Tomorrow you can see how lovely I'll look.

ANNE-MARIE: Oh, there won't be anyone at the party as lovely as Miss Nora. *(She goes off into the room, left.)*

NORA: *(begins unpacking the box, but soon throws it aside)* Oh, if I dared to go out. If only nobody would come. If only nothing would happen here while I'm out. What craziness — nobody's coming. Just don't think. This muff — needs a brushing. Beautiful gloves, beautiful gloves. Let it go. Let it go! One, two, three, four, five, six —*(With a cry.)* Oh, there they are! *(Poises to move toward the door, but remains irresolutely standing. Mrs. Linde enters from the hall, where she has removed her street clothes.)*

NORA: Oh, it's you, Kristine. There's no one else out there? How good that you've come.

MRS. LINDE: I hear you were up asking for me.

NORA: Yes, I just stopped by. There's something you really can help me with. Let's get settled on the sofa. Look, there's going to be a costume party tomorrow evening at the Stenborgs' right above us, and now Torvald wants me to go as a Neapolitan peasant girl and dance the tarantella that I learned in Capri.

MRS. LINDE: Really, are you giving a whole performance?

NORA: Torvald says yes, I should. See, here's the dress. Torvald had it made for me down there; but now it's all so tattered that I just don't know —

MRS. LINDE: Oh, we'll fix that up in no time. It's nothing more than the trimmings — they're a bit loose here and there. Needle and thread? Good, now we have what we need.

NORA: Oh, how sweet of you!

MRS. LINDE: *(sewing)* So you'll be in disguise tomorrow, Nora. You know what? I'll stop by then for a moment and have a look at you all dressed up. But listen, I've absolutely forgotten to thank you for that pleasant evening yesterday.

NORA: *(getting up and walking about)* I don't think it was as pleasant as usual yesterday. You should have come to town a bit sooner, Kristine—Yes, Torvald really knows how to give a home elegance and charm.

MRS. LINDE: And you do, too, if you ask me. You're not your father's daughter for nothing. But tell me, is Dr. Rank always so down in the mouth as yesterday?

NORA: No, that was quite an exception. But he goes around critically ill all the time — tuberculosis of the spine, poor man. You know, his father was a disgusting thing who kept mistresses and so on—and that's why the son's been sickly from birth.

MRS. LINDE: *(lets her sewing fall to her lap)* But my dearest Nora, how do you know about such things?

NORA: *(walking more jauntily)* Hmp! When you've had three children, then you've had a few visits from —from women who know something of medicine, and they tell you this and that.

MRS. LINDE: *(resumes sewing; a short pause)* Does Dr. Rank come here every day?

NORA: Every blessed day. He's Torvald's best friend from childhood, and *my* good friend, too. Dr. Rank almost belongs to this house.

MRS. LINDE: But tell me—is he quite sincere? I mean, doesn't he rather enjoy flattering people?

NORA: Just the opposite. Why do you think that?

MRS. LINDE: When you introduced us yesterday, he was proclaiming that he'd often heard my name in this house; but later I noticed that your husband hadn't the slightest idea who I really was. So how could Dr. Rank—?

NORA: But it's all true, Kristine. You see, Torvald loves me beyond words, and, as he puts it, he'd like to keep me all to himself. For a long time he'd almost be jealous if I even mentioned any of my old friends back home. So of course I dropped that. But with Dr. Rank I talk a lot about such things, because he likes hearing about them.

MRS. LINDE: Now listen, Nora; in many ways you're still like a child. I'm a good deal older than you, with a little more experience. I'll tell you something: you ought to put an end to all this with Dr. Rank.

NORA: What should I put an end to?

MRS. LINDE: Both parts of it, I think. Yesterday you said something about a rich admirer who'd provide you with money—

NORA: Yes, one who doesn't exist—worse luck. So?

MRS. LINDE: Is Dr. Rank well off?

NORA: Yes, he is.

MRS. LINDE: With no dependents?

NORA: No, no one. But—

MRS. LINDE: And he's over here every day?

NORA: Yes, I told you that.

MRS. LINDE: How can a man of such refinement be so grasping?

NORA: I don't follow you at all.

MRS. LINDE: Now don't try to hide it, Nora. You think I can't guess who loaned you the forty-eight hundred crowns?

NORA: Are you out of your mind? How could you think such a thing! A friend of ours, who comes here every single day. What an intolerable situation that would have been!

MRS. LINDE: Then it really wasn't him.

NORA: No, absolutely not. It never even crossed my mind for a moment— And he had nothing to lend in those days; his inheritance came later.

MRS. LINDE: Well, I think that was a stroke of luck for you, Nora dear.

NORA: No, it never would have occurred to me to ask Dr. Rank—Still, I'm quite sure that if I had asked him—

MRS. LINDE: Which you won't, of course.

NORA: No, of course not. I can't see that I'd ever need to. But I'm quite positive that if I talked to Dr. Rank—

MRS. LINDE: Behind your husband's back?

NORA: I've got to clear up this other thing; *that's* also behind his back. I've *got* to clear it all up.

MRS. LINDE: Yes, I was saying that yesterday, but—

NORA: *(pacing up and down)* A man handles these problems so much better than a woman—

MRS. LINDE: One's husband does, yes.

NORA: Nonsense. *(Stopping.)* When you pay everything you owe, then you get your note back, right?

MRS. LINDE: Yes, naturally.

NORA: And can rip it into a million pieces and burn it up—that filthy scrap of paper!

MRS. LINDE: *(looking hard at her, laying her sewing aside, and rising slowly)* Nora, you're hiding something from me.

NORA: You can see it in my face?

MRS. LINDE: Something's happened to you since yesterday morning. Nora, what is it?

NORA: *(hurrying toward her)* Kristine! *(Listening.)* Shh! Torvald's home. Look, go in with the children a while. Torvald can't bear all this snipping and stitching. Let Anne-Marie help you.

MRS. LINDE: *(gathering up some of the things)* All right, but I'm not leaving here until we've talked this out. *(She disappears into the room, left, as Torvald enters from the hall.)*

NORA: Oh, how I've been waiting for you, Torvald dear.

HELMER: Was that the dressmaker?

NORA: No, that was Kristine. She's helping me fix up my costume. You know, it's going to be quite attractive.

HELMER: Yes, wasn't that a bright idea I had?

NORA: Brilliant! But then wasn't I good as well to give in to you?

HELMER: Good—because you give in to your husband's judgment? All right, you little goose, I know you didn't mean it like that. But I won't disturb you. You'll want to have a fitting, I suppose.

NORA: And you'll be working?

HELMER: Yes. *(Indicating a bundle of papers.)* See. I've been down to the bank. *(Starts toward his study.)*

NORA: Torvald.

HELMER: *(stops)* Yes.

NORA: If your little squirrel begged you, with all her heart and soul, for something—?

HELMER: What's that?

NORA: Then would you do it?

HELMER: First, naturally, I'd have to know what it was.

NORA: Your squirrel would scamper about and do tricks, if you'd only be sweet and give in.

HELMER: Out with it.

NORA: Your lark would be singing high and low in every room—

HELMER: Come on, she does that anyway.

NORA: I'd be a wood nymph and dance for you in the moonlight.

HELMER: Nora—don't tell me it's that same business from this morning?

NORA: *(coming closer)* Yes, Torvald, I beg you, please!

HELMER: And you actually have the nerve to drag that up again?

NORA: Yes, yes, you've got to give in to me; you *have* to let Krogstad keep his job in the bank.

HELMER: My dear Nora, I've slated his job for Mrs. Linde.

NORA: That's awfully kind of you. But you could just fire another clerk instead of Krogstad.

HELMER: This is the most incredible stubbornness! Because you go and give an impulsive promise to speak up for him, I'm expected to—

NORA: That's not the reason, Torvald. It's for your own sake. That man does writing for the worst papers; you said it yourself. He could do you any amount of harm. I'm scared to death of him—

HELMER: Ah, I understand. It's the old memories haunting you.

NORA: What do you mean by that?

HELMER: Of course, you're thinking about your father.

NORA: Yes, all right. Just remember how those nasty gossips wrote in the papers about Papa and slandered him so cruelly. I think they'd have had him dismissed if the department hadn't sent you up to investigate, and if you hadn't been so kind and open-minded toward him.

HELMER: My dear Nora, there's a notable difference between your father and me. Your father's official career was hardly above reproach. But mine is; and I hope it'll stay that way as long as I hold my position.

Nora: Oh, who can ever tell what vicious minds can invent? We could be so snug and happy now in our quiet, carefree home — you and I and the children, Torvald! That's why I'm pleading with you so —

Helmer: And just by pleading for him you make it impossible for me to keep him on. It's already known at the bank that I'm firing Krogstad. What if it's rumored around now that the new bank manager was vetoed by his wife —

Nora: Yes, what then — ?

Helmer: Oh yes — as long as our little bundle of stubbornness gets her way — ! I should go and make myself ridiculous in front of the whole office — give people the idea I can be swayed by all kinds of outside pressure. Oh, you can bet I'd feel the effects of that soon enough! Besides — there's something that rules Krogstad right out at the bank as long as I'm the manager.

Nora: What's that?

Helmer: His moral failings I could maybe overlook if I had to —

Nora: Yes, Torvald, why not?

Helmer: And I hear he's quite efficient on the job. But he was a crony of mine back in my teens — one of those rash friendships that crop up again and again to embarrass you later in life. Well, I might as well say it straight out: we're on a first-name basis. And that tactless fool makes no effort at all to hide it in front of others. Quite the contrary — he thinks that entitles him to take a familiar air around me, and so every other second he comes booming out with his "Yes, Torvald!" and "Sure thing, Torvald!" I tell you, it's been excruciating for me. He's out to make my place in the bank unbearable.

Nora: Torvald, you can't be serious about all this.

Helmer: Oh no? Why not?

Nora: Because these are such petty considerations.

Helmer: What are you saying? Petty? You think I'm petty!

Nora: No, just the opposite, Torvald dear. That's exactly why —

Helmer: Never mind. You call my motives petty; then I might as well be just that. Petty! All right! We'll put a stop to this for good. *(Goes to the hall door and calls.)* Helene!

Nora: What do you want?

Helmer: *(searching among his papers)* A decision. *(The Maid comes in.)* Look here; take this letter; go out with it at once. Get hold of a messenger and have him deliver it. Quick now. It's already addressed. Wait, here's some money.

Maid: Yes, sir. *(She leaves with the letter.)*

Helmer: *(straightening his papers)* There, now, little Miss Willful.

Nora: *(breathlessly)* Torvald, what was that letter?

Helmer: Krogstad's notice.

Nora: Call it back, Torvald! There's still time. Oh, Torvald, call it back! Do it for my sake — for your sake, for the children's sake! Do you hear, Torvald; do it! You don't know how this can harm us.

Helmer: Too late.

NORA: Yes, too late.

HELMER: Nora dear, I can forgive you this panic, even though basically you're insulting me. Yes, you are! Or isn't it an insult to think that *I* should be afraid of a courtroom hack's revenge? But I forgive you anyway, because this shows so beautifully how much you love me. (*Takes her in his arms.*) This is the way it should be, my darling Nora. Whatever comes, you'll see: when it really counts, I have strength and courage enough as a man to take on the whole weight myself.

NORA: (*terrified*) What do you mean by that?

HELMER: The whole weight, I said.

NORA: (*resolutely*) No, never in all the world.

HELMER: Good. So we'll share it, Nora, as man and wife. That's as it should be. (*Fondling her.*) Are you happy now? There, there, there—not these frightened dove's eyes. It's nothing at all but empty fantasies—Now you should run through your tarantella and practice your tambourine. I'll go to the inner office and shut both doors, so I won't hear a thing; you can make all the noise you like. (*Turning in the doorway.*) And when Rank comes, just tell him where he can find me. (*He nods to her and goes with his papers into the study, closing the door.*)

NORA: (*standing as though rooted, dazed with fright, in a whisper*) He really could do it. He will do it. He'll do it in spite of everything. No, not that, never, never! Anything but that! Escape! A way out—(*The doorbell rings.*) Dr. Rank! Anything but that! *Anything*, whatever it is! (*Her hands pass over her face, smoothing it; she pulls herself together, goes over and opens the hall door. Dr. Rank stands outside, hanging his fur coat up. During the following scene, it begins getting dark.*)

NORA: Hello, Dr. Rank. I recognized your ring. But you mustn't go in to Torvald yet; I believe he's working.

RANK: And you?

NORA: For you, I always have an hour to spare—you know that. (*He has entered, and she shuts the door after him.*)

RANK: Many thanks. I'll make use of these hours while I can.

NORA: What do you mean by that? While you can?

RANK: Does that disturb you?

NORA: Well, it's such an odd phrase. Is anything going to happen?

RANK: What's going to happen is what I've been expecting so long—but I honestly didn't think it would come so soon.

NORA: (*gripping his arm*) What is it you've found out? Dr. Rank, you have to tell me!

RANK: (*sitting by the stove*) It's all over with me. There's nothing to be done about it.

NORA: (*breathing easier*) Is it you—then—?

RANK: Who else? There's no point in lying to one's self. I'm the most miserable of all my patients, Mrs. Helmer. These past few days I've been auditing my internal accounts. Bankrupt! Within a month I'll probably be laid out and rotting in the churchyard.

NORA: Oh, what a horrible thing to say.

RANK: The thing itself is horrible. But the worst of it is all the other horror before it's over. There's only one final examination left; when I'm finished with that, I'll know about when my disintegration will begin. There's something I want to say. Helmer with his sensitivity has such a sharp distaste for anything ugly. I don't want him near my sickroom.

NORA: Oh, but Dr. Rank—

RANK: I won't have him in there. Under no condition. I'll lock my door to him—As soon as I'm completely sure of the worst, I'll send you my calling card marked with a black cross, and you'll know then the wreck has started to come apart.

NORA: No, today you're completely unreasonable. And I wanted you so much to be in a really good humor.

RANK: With death up my sleeve? And then to suffer this way for somebody else's sins. Is there any justice in that? And in every single family, in some way or another, this inevitable retribution of nature goes on—

NORA: *(her hands pressed over her ears)* Oh, stuff! Cheer up! Please—be gay!

RANK: Yes, I'd just as soon laugh at it all. My poor, innocent spine, serving time for my father's gay army days.

NORA: *(by the table, left)* He was so infatuated with asparagus tips and *pâté de foie gras*, wasn't that it?

RANK: Yes—and with truffles.

NORA: Truffles, yes. And then with oysters, I suppose?

RANK: Yes, tons of oysters, naturally.

NORA: And then the port and champagne to go with it. It's so sad that all these delectable things have to strike at our bones.

RANK: Especially when they strike at the unhappy bones that never shared in the fun.

NORA: Ah, that's the saddest of all.

RANK: *(looks searchingly at her)* Hm.

NORA: *(after a moment)* Why did you smile?

RANK: No, it was you who laughed.

NORA: No, it was you who smiled, Dr. Rank!

RANK: *(getting up)* You're even a bigger tease than I'd thought.

NORA: I'm full of wild ideas today.

RANK: That's obvious.

NORA: *(putting both hands on his shoulders)* Dear, dear Dr. Rank, you'll never die for Torvald and me.

RANK: Oh, that loss you'll easily get over. Those who go away are soon forgotten.

NORA: *(looks fearfully at him)* You believe that?

RANK: One makes new connections, and then—

NORA: Who makes new connections?

RANK: Both you and Torvald will when I'm gone. I'd say you're well under way already. What was that Mrs. Linde doing here last evening?

NORA: Oh, come—you can't be jealous of poor Kristine?

RANK: Oh yes, I am. She'll be my successor here in the house. When I'm down under, that woman will probably—

NORA: Shh! Not so loud. She's right in there.

RANK: Today as well. So you see.

NORA: Only to sew on my dress. Good gracious, how unreasonable you are. *(Sitting on the sofa.)* Be nice now, Dr. Rank. Tomorrow you'll see how beautifully I'll dance; and you can imagine then that I'm dancing only for you—yes, and of course for Torvald, too—that's understood. *(Takes various items out of the carton.)* Dr. Rank, sit over here and I'll show you something.

RANK: *(sitting)* What's that?

NORA: Look here. Look.

RANK: Silk stockings.

NORA: Flesh-colored. Aren't they lovely? Now it's so dark here, but tomorrow— No, no, no, just look at the feet. Oh well, you might as well look at the rest.

RANK: Hm—

NORA: Why do you look so critical? Don't you believe they'll fit?

RANK: I've never had any chance to form an opinion on that.

NORA: *(glancing at him a moment)* Shame on you. *(Hits him lightly on the ear with the stockings.)* That's for you. *(Puts them away again.)*

RANK: And what other splendors am I going to see now?

NORA: Not the least bit more, because you've been naughty. *(She hums a little and rummages among her things.)*

RANK: *(after a short silence)* When I sit here together with you like this, completely easy and open, then I don't know—I simply can't imagine—whatever would have become of me if I'd never come into this house.

NORA: *(smiling)* Yes, I really think you feel completely at ease with us.

RANK: *(more quietly, staring straight ahead)* And then to have to go away from it all—

NORA: Nonsense, you're not going away.

RANK: *(his voice unchanged)*—and not even be able to leave some poor show of gratitude behind, scarcely a fleeting regret—no more than a vacant place that anyone can fill.

NORA: And if I asked you now for—? No—

RANK: For what?

NORA: For a great proof of your friendship—

RANK: Yes, yes?

NORA: No, I mean—for an exceptionally big favor—

RANK: Would you really, for once, make me so happy?

NORA: Oh, you haven't the vaguest idea what it is.

RANK: All right, then tell me.

NORA: No, but I can't, Dr. Rank—it's all out of reason. It's advice and help, too—and a favor—

RANK: So much the better. I can't fathom what you're hinting at. Just speak out. Don't you trust me?

NORA: Of course. More than anyone else. You're my best and truest friend, I'm sure. That's why I want to talk to you. All right, then, Dr. Rank: there's something you can help me prevent. You know how deeply, how inexpressibly dearly Torvald loves me; he'd never hesitate a second to give up his life for me.

RANK: *(leaning close to her)* Nora—do you think he's the only one—

NORA: *(with a slight start)* Who—?

RANK: Who'd gladly give up his life for you.

NORA: *(heavily)* I see.

RANK: I swore to myself you should know this before I'm gone. I'll never find a better chance. Yes, Nora, now you know. And also you know now that you can trust me beyond anyone else.

NORA: *(rising, natural and calm)* Let me by.

RANK: *(making room for her, but still sitting)* Nora—

NORA: *(in the hall doorway)* Helene, bring the lamp in. *(Goes over to the stove.)* Ah, dear Dr. Rank, that was really mean of you.

RANK: *(getting up)* That I've loved you just as deeply as somebody else? Was *that* mean?

NORA: No, but that you came out and told me. That was quite unnecessary—

RANK: What do you mean? Have you known—?

The Maid comes in with the lamp, sets it on the table, and goes out again.

RANK: Nora—Mrs. Helmer—I'm asking you: have you known about it?

NORA: Oh, how can I tell what I know or don't know? Really, I don't know what to say—Why did you have to be so clumsy, Dr. Rank! Everything was so good.

RANK: Well, in any case, you now have the knowledge that my body and soul are at your command. So won't you speak out?

NORA: *(looking at him)* After that?

RANK: Please, just let me know what it is.

NORA: You can't know anything now.

RANK: I have to. You mustn't punish me like this. Give me the chance to do whatever is humanly possible for you.

NORA: Now there's nothing you can do for me. Besides, actually, I don't need any help. You'll see—it's only my fantasies. That's what it is. Of course! *(Sits in the rocker, looks at him, and smiles.)* What a nice one you are, Dr. Rank. Aren't you a little bit ashamed, now that the lamp is here?

RANK: No, not exactly. But perhaps I'd better go—for good?

NORA: No, you certainly can't do that. You must come here just as you always have. You know Torvald can't do without you.

RANK: Yes, but *you?*

NORA: You know how much I enjoy it when you're here.

RANK: That's precisely what threw me off. You're a mystery to me. So many times I've felt you'd almost rather be with me than with Helmer.

NORA: Yes—you see, there are some people that one loves most and other people that one would almost prefer being with.

RANK: Yes, there's something to that.

NORA: When I was back home, of course I loved Papa most. But I always thought it was so much fun when I could sneak down to the maids' quarters, because they never tried to improve me, and it was always so amusing, the way they talked to each other.

RANK: Aha, so it's *their* place that I've filled.

NORA: *(jumping up and going to him)* Oh, dear, sweet Dr. Rank, that's not what I mean at all. But you can understand that with Torvald it's just the same as with Papa—

The Maid enters from the hall.

MAID: Ma'am — please! *(She whispers to Nora and hands her a calling card.)*

NORA: *(glancing at the card)* Ah! *(Slips it into her pocket.)*

RANK: Anything wrong?

NORA: No, no, not at all. It's only some—it's my new dress—

RANK: Really? But—there's your dress.

NORA: Oh, that. But this is another one—I ordered it—Torvald mustn't know—

RANK: Ah, now we have the big secret.

NORA: That's right. Just go in with him—he's back in the inner study. Keep him there as long as—

RANK: Don't worry. He won't get away. *(Goes into the study.)*

NORA: *(to the Maid)* And he's standing waiting in the kitchen?

MAID: Yes, he came up by the back stairs.

NORA: But didn't you tell him somebody was here?

MAID: Yes, but that didn't do any good.

NORA: He won't leave?

MAID: No, he won't go till he's talked with you, ma'am.

NORA: Let him come in, then—but quietly. Helene, don't breathe a word about this. It's a surprise for my husband.

MAID: Yes, yes, I understand—*(Goes out.)*

NORA: This horror — it's going to happen. No, no, no, it can't happen, it mustn't. *(She goes and bolts Helmer's door. The Maid opens the hall door for Krogstad and shuts it behind him. He is dressed for travel in a fur coat, boots, and a fur cap.)*

NORA: *(going toward him)* Talk softly. My husband's home.

KROGSTAD: Well, good for him.

NORA: What do you want?

KROGSTAD: Some information.

NORA: Hurry up, then. What is it?

KROGSTAD: You know, of course, that I got my notice.

NORA: I couldn't prevent it, Mr. Krogstad. I fought for you to the bitter end, but nothing worked.

Krogstad: Does your husband's love for you run so thin? He knows everything I can expose you to, and all the same he dares to—

Nora: How can you imagine he knows anything about this?

Krogstad: Ah, no—I can't imagine it either, now. It's not at all like my fine Torvald Helmer to have so much guts—

Nora: Mr. Krogstad, I demand respect for my husband!

Krogstad: Why, of course—all due respect. But since the lady's keeping it so carefully hidden, may I presume to ask if you're also a bit better informed than yesterday about what you've actually done?

Nora: More than you ever could teach me.

Krogstad: Yes, I *am* such an awful lawyer.

Nora: What is it you want from me?

Krogstad: Just a glimpse of how you are, Mrs. Helmer. I've been thinking about you all day long. A cashier, a night-court scribbler, a—well, a type like me also has a little of what they call a heart, you know.

Nora: Then show it. Think of my children.

Krogstad: Did you or your husband ever think of mine? But never mind. I simply wanted to tell you that you don't need to take this thing too seriously. For the present, I'm not proceeding with any action.

Nora: Oh no, really! Well—I knew that.

Krogstad: Everything can be settled in a friendly spirit. It doesn't have to get around town at all; it can stay just among us three.

Nora: My husband must never know anything of this.

Krogstad: How can you manage that? Perhaps you can pay me the balance?

Nora: No, not right now.

Krogstad: Or you know some way of raising the money in a day or two?

Nora: No way that I'm willing to use.

Krogstad: Well, it wouldn't have done you any good, anyway. If you stood in front of me with a fistful of bills, you still couldn't buy your signature back.

Nora: Then tell me what you're going to do with it.

Krogstad: I'll just hold onto it—keep it on file. There's no outsider who'll even get wind of it. So if you've been thinking of taking some desperate step—

Nora: I have.

Krogstad: Been thinking of running away from home—

Nora: I have!

Krogstad: Or even of something worse—

Nora: How could you guess that?

Krogstad: You can drop those thoughts.

Nora: How could you guess I was thinking of *that*?

Krogstad: Most of us think about *that* at first. I thought about it too, but I discovered I hadn't the courage—

Nora: *(lifelessly)* I don't either.

Krogstad: *(relieved)* That's true, you haven't the courage? You too?

Nora: I don't have it—I don't have it.

KROGSTAD: It would be terribly stupid, anyway. After that first storm at home blows out, why, then—I have here in my pocket a letter for your husband—

NORA: Telling everything?

KROGSTAD: As charitably as possible.

NORA: *(quickly)* He mustn't ever get that letter. Tear it up. I'll find some way to get money.

KROGSTAD: Beg pardon, Mrs. Helmer, but I think I just told you—

NORA: Oh, I don't mean the money I owe you. Let me know how much you want from my husband, and I'll manage it.

KROGSTAD: I don't want any money from your husband.

NORA: What do you want, then?

KROGSTAD: I'll tell you what. I want to recoup, Mrs. Helmer; I want to get on in the world—and there's where your husband can help me. For a year and a half I've kept myself clean of anything disreputable—all that time struggling with the worst conditions; but I was satisfied, working my way up step by step. Now I've been written right off, and I'm just not in the mood to come crawling back. I tell you, I want to move on. I want to get back in the bank—in a better position. Your husband can set up a job for me—

NORA: He'll never do that!

KROGSTAD: He'll do it. I know him. He won't dare breathe a word of protest. And once I'm in there together with him, you just wait and see! Inside of a year, I'll be the manager's right-hand man. It'll be Nils Krogstad, not Torvald Helmer, who runs the bank.

NORA: You'll never see the day!

KROGSTAD: Maybe you think you can—

NORA: I have the courage now—for *that*.

KROGSTAD: Oh, you don't scare me. A smart, spoiled lady like you—

NORA: You'll see; you'll see!

KROGSTAD: Under the ice, maybe? Down in the freezing, coal-black water? There, till you float up in the spring, ugly, unrecognizable, with your hair falling out—

NORA: You don't frighten me.

KROGSTAD: Nor do you frighten me. One doesn't do these things, Mrs. Helmer. Besides, what good would it be? I'd still have him safe in my pocket.

NORA: Afterwards? When I'm no longer—?

KROGSTAD: Are you forgetting that *I'll* be in control then over your final reputation? *(Nora stands speechless, staring at him.)* Good; now I've warned you. Don't do anything stupid. When Helmer's read my letter, I'll be waiting for his reply. And bear in mind that it's your husband himself who's forced me back to my old ways. I'll never forgive him for that. Good-bye, Mrs. Helmer. *(He goes out through the hall.)*

NORA: *(goes to the hall door, opens it a crack, and listens)* He's gone. Didn't leave the letter. Oh no, no, that's impossible too! *(Opening the door more and more.)* What's that? He's standing outside—not going downstairs. He's thinking it over? Maybe he'll—? *(A letter falls in the mailbox; then Krogstad's* *footsteps are heard, dying away down a flight of stairs. Nora gives a muffled cry and runs over toward the sofa table. A short pause.)* In the mailbox. *(Slips warily over to the hall door.)* It's lying there. Torvald, Torvald—now we're lost!

MRS. LINDE: *(entering with the costume from the room, left)* There now, I can't see anything else to mend. Perhaps you'd like to try—

NORA: *(in a hoarse whisper)* Kristine, come here.

MRS. LINDE: *(tossing the dress on the sofa)* What's wrong? You look upset.

NORA: Come here. See that letter? *There!* Look—through the glass in the mailbox.

MRS. LINDE: Yes, yes, I see it.

NORA: That letter's from Krogstad—

MRS. LINDE: Nora—it's Krogstad who loaned you the money!

NORA: Yes, and now Torvald will find out everything.

MRS. LINDE: Believe me, Nora, it's best for both of you.

NORA: There's more you don't know. I forged a name.

MRS. LINDE: But for heaven's sake—?

NORA: I only want to tell you that, Kristine, so that you can be my witness.

MRS. LINDE: Witness? Why should I—?

NORA: If I should go out of my mind—it could easily happen—

MRS. LINDE: Nora!

NORA: Or anything else occurred—so I couldn't be present here—

MRS. LINDE: Nora, Nora, you aren't yourself at all!

NORA: And someone should try to take on the whole weight, all of the guilt, you follow me—

MRS. LINDE: Yes, of course, but why do you think—?

NORA: Then you're the witness that it isn't true, Kristine. I'm very much myself; my mind right now is perfectly clear; and I'm telling you: nobody else has known about this; I alone did everything. Remember that.

MRS. LINDE: I will. But I don't understand all this.

NORA: Oh, how could you ever understand it? It's the miracle now that's going to take place.

MRS. LINDE: The miracle?

NORA: Yes, the miracle. But it's so awful, Kristine. It mustn't take place, not for anything in the world.

MRS. LINDE: I'm going right over and talk with Krogstad.

NORA: Don't go near him; he'll do you some terrible harm!

MRS. LINDE: There was a time once when he'd gladly have done anything for me.

NORA: He?

MRS. LINDE: Where does he live?

NORA: Oh, how do I know? Yes. *(Searches in her pocket.)* Here's his card. But the letter, the letter—!

HELMER: *(from the study, knocking on the door)* Nora!

NORA: *(with a cry of fear)* Oh! What is it? What do you want?

HELMER: Now, now, don't be so frightened. We're not coming in. You locked the door—are you trying on the dress?

NORA: Yes, I'm trying it. I'll look just beautiful, Torvald.

MRS. LINDE: *(who has read the card)* He's living right around the corner.

NORA: Yes, but what's the use? We're lost. The letter's in the box.

MRS. LINDE: And your husband has the key?

NORA: Yes, always.

MRS. LINDE: Krogstad can ask for his letter back unread; he can find some excuse—

NORA: But it's just this time that Torvald usually—

MRS. LINDE: Stall him. Keep him in there. I'll be back as quick as I can. *(She hurries out through the hall entrance.)*

NORA: *(goes to Helmer's door, opens it, and peers in)* Torvald!

HELMER: *(from the inner study)* Well—does one dare set foot in one's own living room at last? Come on, Rank, now we'll get a look—*(In the doorway.)* But what's this?

NORA: What, Torvald dear?

HELMER: Rank had me expecting some grand masquerade.

RANK: *(in the doorway)* That was my impression, but I must have been wrong.

NORA: No one can admire me in my splendor—not till tomorrow.

HELMER: But Nora dear, you look so exhausted. Have you practiced too hard?

NORA: No, I haven't practiced at all yet.

HELMER: You know, it's necessary—

NORA: Oh, it's absolutely necessary, Torvald. But I can't get anywhere without your help. I've forgotten the whole thing completely.

HELMER: Ah, we'll soon take care of that.

NORA: Yes, take care of me, Torvald, please! Promise me that? Oh, I'm so nervous. That big party—You must give up everything this evening for me. No business—don't even touch your pen. Yes? Dear Torvald, promise?

HELMER: It's a promise. Tonight I'm totally at your service—you little helpless thing. Hm—but first there's one thing I want to—*(Goes toward the hall door.)*

NORA: What are you looking for?

HELMER: Just to see if there's any mail.

NORA: No, no, don't do that, Torvald!

HELMER: Now what?

NORA: Torvald, please. There isn't any.

HELMER: Let me look, though. *(Starts out. Nora, at the piano, strikes the first notes of the tarantella. Helmer, at the door, stops.)* Aha!

NORA: I can't dance tomorrow if I don't practice with you.

HELMER: *(going over to her)* Nora dear, are you really so frightened?

NORA: Yes, so terribly frightened. Let me practice right now; there's still time before dinner. Oh, sit down and play for me, Torvald. Direct me. Teach me, the way you always have.

HELMER: Gladly, if it's what you want. *(Sits at the piano.)*

NORA: *(snatches the tambourine up from the box, then a long, varicolored shawl, which she throws around herself, whereupon she springs forward and cries out)* Play for me now! Now I'll dance!

Helmer plays and Nora dances. Rank stands behind Helmer at the piano and looks on.

HELMER: *(as he plays)* Slower. Slow down.

NORA: Can't change it.

HELMER: Not so violent, Nora!

NORA: Has to be just like this.

HELMER: *(stopping)* No, no, that won't do at all.

NORA: *(laughing and swinging her tambourine)* Isn't that what I told you?

RANK: Let me play for her.

HELMER: *(getting up)* Yes, go on. I can teach her more easily then.

Rank sits at the piano and plays; Nora dances more and more wildly. Helmer has stationed himself by the stove and repeatedly gives her directions; she seems not to hear them; her hair loosens and falls over her shoulders; she does not notice, but goes on dancing. Mrs. Linde enters.

MRS. LINDE: *(standing dumbfounded at the door)* Ah—!

NORA: *(still dancing)* See what fun, Kristine!

HELMER: But Nora darling, you dance as if your life were at stake.

NORA: And it is.

HELMER: Rank, stop! This is pure madness. Stop it, I say!

Rank breaks off playing, and Nora halts abruptly.

HELMER: *(going over to her)* I never would have believed it. You've forgotten everything I taught you.

NORA: *(throwing away the tambourine)* You see for yourself.

HELMER: Well, there's certainly room for instruction here.

NORA: Yes, you see how important it is. You've got to teach me to the very last minute. Promise me that, Torvald?

HELMER: You can bet on it.

NORA: You mustn't, either today or tomorrow, think about anything else but me; you mustn't open any letters—or the mailbox—

HELMER: Ah, it's still the fear of that man—

NORA: Oh yes, yes, that too.

HELMER: Nora, it's written all over you—there's already a letter from him out there.

NORA: I don't know. I guess so. But you mustn't read such things now; there mustn't be anything ugly between us before it's all over.

RANK: *(quietly to Helmer)* You shouldn't deny her.

HELMER: *(putting his arm around her)* The child can have her way. But tomorrow night, after you've danced—

NORA: Then you'll be free.

MAID: *(in the doorway, right)* Ma'am, dinner is served.

NORA: We'll be wanting champagne, Helene.

MAID: Very good, ma'am. *(Goes out.)*

HELMER: So—a regular banquet, hm?

NORA: Yes, a banquet—champagne till daybreak! *(Calling out.)* And some macaroons, Helene. Heaps of them—just this once.

HELMER: *(taking her hands)* Now, now, now—no hysterics. Be my own little lark again.

NORA: Oh, I will soon enough. But go on in—and you, Dr. Rank. Kristine, help me put up my hair.

RANK: *(whispering, as they go)* There's nothing wrong—really wrong, is there?

HELMER: Oh, of course not. It's nothing more than this childish anxiety I was telling you about. *(They go out, right.)*

NORA: Well?

MRS. LINDE: Left town.

NORA: I could see by your face.

MRS. LINDE: He'll be home tomorrow evening. I wrote him a note.

NORA: You shouldn't have. Don't try to stop anything now. After all, it's a wonderful joy, this waiting here for the miracle.

MRS. LINDE: What is it you're waiting for?

NORA: Oh, you can't understand that. Go in to them: I'll be along in a moment.

Mrs. Linde goes into the dining room. Nora stands a short while as if composing herself; then she looks at her watch.

NORA: Five. Seven hours to midnight. Twenty-four hours to the midnight after, and then the tarantella's done. Seven and twenty-four? Thirty-one hours to live.

HELMER: *(in the doorway, right)* What's become of the little lark?

NORA: *(going toward him with open arms)* Here's your lark!

ACT 3

Same scene. The table, with chairs around it, has been moved to the center of the room. A lamp on the table is lit. The hall door stands open. Dance music drifts down from the floor above. Mrs. Linde sits at the table, absently paging through a book, trying to read, but apparently unable to focus her thoughts. Once or twice she pauses, tensely listening for a sound at the outer entrance.

MRS. LINDE: *(glancing at her watch)* Not yet—and there's hardly any time left. If only he's not—*(Listening again.)* Ah, there he is. *(She goes out in the hall and cautiously opens the outer door. Quiet footsteps are heard on the stairs. She whispers:)* Come in. Nobody's here.

KROGSTAD: *(in the doorway)* I found a note from you at home. What's back of all this?

MRS. LINDE: I just *had* to talk to you.

KROGSTAD: Oh? And it just *had* to be here in this house?

MRS. LINDE: At my place it was impossible; my room hasn't a private entrance. Come in; we're all alone. The maid's asleep, and the Helmers are at the dance upstairs.

Krogstad: *(entering the room)* Well, well, the Helmers are dancing tonight? Really?

Mrs. Linde: Yes, why not?

Krogstad: How true—why not?

Mrs. Linde: All right, Krogstad, let's talk.

Krogstad: Do we two have anything more to talk about?

Mrs. Linde: We have a great deal to talk about.

Krogstad: I wouldn't have thought so.

Mrs. Linde: No, because you've never understood me, really.

Krogstad: Was there anything more to understand—except what's all too common in life? A calculating woman throws over a man the moment a better catch comes by.

Mrs. Linde: You think I'm so thoroughly calculating? You think I broke it off lightly?

Krogstad: Didn't you?

Mrs. Linde: Nils—is that what you really thought?

Krogstad: If you cared, then why did you write me the way you did?

Mrs. Linde: What else could I do? If I had to break off with you, then it was my job as well to root out everything you felt for me.

Krogstad: *(wringing his hands)* So that was it. And this—all this, simply for money!

Mrs. Linde: Don't forget I had a helpless mother and two small brothers. We couldn't wait for you, Nils; you had such a long road ahead of you then.

Krogstad: That may be; but you still hadn't the right to abandon me for somebody else's sake.

Mrs. Linde: Yes—I don't know. So many, many times I've asked myself if I did have that right.

Krogstad: *(more softly)* When I lost you, it was as if all the solid ground dissolved from under my feet. Look at me; I'm a half-drowned man now, hanging onto a wreck.

Mrs. Linde: Help may be near.

Krogstad: It was near—but then you came and blocked it off.

Mrs. Linde: Without my knowing it, Nils. Today for the first time I learned that it's you I'm replacing at the bank.

Krogstad: All right—I believe you. But now that you know, will you step aside?

Mrs. Linde: No, because that wouldn't benefit you in the slightest.

Krogstad: Not "benefit" me, hm! I'd step aside anyway.

Mrs. Linde: I've learned to be realistic. Life and hard, bitter necessity have taught me that.

Krogstad: And life's taught me never to trust fine phrases.

Mrs. Linde: Then life's taught you a very sound thing. But you do have to trust in actions, don't you?

Krogstad: What does that mean?

Mrs. Linde: You said you were hanging on like a half-drowned man to a wreck.

KROGSTAD: I've good reason to say that.

MRS. LINDE: I'm also like a half-drowned woman on a wreck. No one to suffer with; no one to care for.

KROGSTAD: You made your choice.

MRS. LINDE: There wasn't any choice then.

KROGSTAD: So—what of it?

MRS. LINDE: Nils, if only we two shipwrecked people could reach across to each other.

KROGSTAD: What are you saying?

MRS. LINDE: Two on one wreck are at least better off than each on his own.

KROGSTAD: Kristine!

MRS. LINDE: Why do you think I came into town?

KROGSTAD: Did you really have some thought of me?

MRS. LINDE: I have to work to go on living. All my born days, as long as I can remember, I've worked, and it's been my best and my only joy. But now I'm completely alone in the world; it frightens me to be so empty and lost. To work for yourself—there's no joy in that. Nils, give me something—someone to work for.

KROGSTAD: I don't believe all this. It's just some hysterical feminine urge to go out and make a noble sacrifice.

MRS. LINDE: Have you ever found me to be hysterical?

KROGSTAD: Can you honestly mean this? Tell me—do you know everything about my past?

MRS. LINDE: Yes.

KROGSTAD: And you know what they think I'm worth around here.

MRS. LINDE: From what you were saying before, it would seem that with me you could have been another person.

KROGSTAD: I'm positive of that.

MRS. LINDE: Couldn't it happen still?

KROGSTAD: Kristine—you're saying this in all seriousness? Yes, you are! I can see it in you. And do you really have the courage, then—?

MRS. LINDE: I need to have someone to care for; and your children need a mother. We both need each other. Nils, I have faith that you're good at heart—I'll risk everything together with you.

KROGSTAD: *(gripping her hands)* Kristine, thank you, thank you—Now I know I can win back a place in their eyes. Yes—but I forgot—

MRS. LINDE: *(listening)* Shh! The tarantella. Go now! Go on!

KROGSTAD: Why? What is it?

MRS. LINDE: Hear the dance up there? When that's over, they'll be coming down.

KROGSTAD: Oh, then I'll go. But—it's all pointless. Of course, you don't know the move I made against the Helmers.

MRS. LINDE: Yes, Nils, I know.

KROGSTAD: And all the same, you have the courage to—?

MRS. LINDE: I know how far despair can drive a man like you.

KROGSTAD: Oh, if I only could take it all back.

MRS. LINDE: You easily could—your letter's still lying in the mailbox.

KROGSTAD: Are you sure of that?

MRS. LINDE: Positive. But—

KROGSTAD: *(looks at her searchingly)* Is that the meaning of it, then? You'll save your friend at any price. Tell me straight out. Is that it?

MRS. LINDE: Nils—anyone who's sold herself for somebody else once isn't going to do it again.

KROGSTAD: I'll demand my letter back.

MRS. LINDE: No, no.

KROGSTAD: Yes, of course. I'll stay here till Helmer comes down; I'll tell him to give me my letter again—that it only involves my dismissal—that he shouldn't read it—

MRS. LINDE: No, Nils, don't call the letter back.

KROGSTAD: But wasn't that exactly why you wrote me to come here?

MRS. LINDE: Yes, in that first panic. But it's been a whole day and night since then, and in that time I've seen such incredible things in this house. Helmer's got to learn everything; this dreadful secret has to be aired; those two have to come to a full understanding; all these lies and evasions can't go on.

KROGSTAD: Well, then, if you want to chance it. But at least there's one thing I can do, and do right away—

MRS. LINDE: *(listening)* Go now, go, quick! The dance is over. We're not safe another second.

KROGSTAD: I'll wait for you downstairs.

MRS. LINDE: Yes, please do; take me home.

KROGSTAD: I can't believe it; I've never been so happy. *(He leaves by way of the outer door; the door between the room and the hall stays open.)*

MRS. LINDE: *(straightening up a bit and getting together her street clothes)* How different now! How different! Someone to work for, to live for—a home to build. Well, it is worth the try! Oh, if they'd only come! *(Listening.)* Ah, there they are. Bundle up. *(She picks up her hat and coat. Nora's and Helmer's voices can be heard outside; a key turns in the lock, and Helmer brings Nora into the hall almost by force. She is wearing the Italian costume with a large black shawl about her; he has on evening dress, with a black domino open over it.)*

NORA: *(struggling in the doorway)* No, no, no, not inside! I'm going up again. I don't want to leave so soon.

HELMER: But Nora dear—

NORA: Oh, I beg you, please, Torvald. From the bottom of my heart, *please*—only an hour more!

HELMER: Not a single minute, Nora darling. You know our agreement. Come on, in we go; you'll catch cold out here. *(In spite of her resistance, he gently draws her into the room.)*

MRS. LINDE: Good evening.

NORA: Kristine!

HELMER: Why, Mrs. Linde—are you here so late?

MRS. LINDE: Yes, I'm sorry, but I did want to see Nora in costume.

NORA: Have you been sitting here, waiting for me?

MRS. LINDE: Yes. I didn't come early enough; you were all upstairs; and then I thought I really couldn't leave without seeing you.

HELMER: *(removing Nora's shawl)* Yes, take a good look. She's worth looking at, I can tell you that, Mrs. Linde. Isn't she lovely?

MRS. LINDE: Yes, I should say—

HELMER: A dream of loveliness, isn't she? That's what everyone thought at the party, too. But she's horribly stubborn—this sweet little thing. What's to be done with her? Can you imagine, I almost had to use force to pry her away.

NORA: Oh, Torvald, you're going to regret you didn't indulge me, even for just a half hour more.

HELMER: There, you see. She danced her tarantella and got a tumultuous hand—which was well earned, although the performance may have been a bit too naturalistic—I mean it rather overstepped the proprieties of art. But never mind—what's important is, she made a success, an overwhelming success. You think I could let her stay on after that and spoil the effect? Oh no; I took my lovely little Capri girl—my capricious little Capri girl, I should say—took her under my arm; one quick tour of the ballroom, a curtsy to every side, and then—as they say in novels—the beautiful vision disappeared. An exit should always be effective, Mrs. Linde, but that's what I can't get Nora to grasp. Phew, it's hot in here. *(Flings the domino on a chair and opens the door to his room.)* Why's it dark in here? Oh yes, of course. Excuse me. *(He goes in and lights a couple of candles.)*

NORA: *(in a sharp, breathless whisper)* So?

MRS. LINDE: *(quietly)* I talked with him.

NORA: And—?

MRS. LINDE: Nora—you must tell your husband everything.

NORA: *(dully)* I knew it.

MRS. LINDE: You've got nothing to fear from Krogstad, but you have to speak out.

NORA: I won't tell.

MRS. LINDE: Then the letter will.

NORA: Thanks, Kristine. I know now what's to be done. Shh!

HELMER: *(reentering)* Well, then, Mrs. Linde—have you admired her?

MRS. LINDE: Yes, and now I'll say good night.

HELMER: Oh, come, so soon? Is this yours, this knitting?

MRS. LINDE: Yes, thanks. I nearly forgot it.

HELMER: Do you knit, then?

MRS. LINDE: Oh yes.

HELMER: You know what? You should embroider instead.

MRS. LINDE: Really? Why?

HELMER: Yes, because it's a lot prettier. See here, one holds the embroidery so, in the left hand, and then one guides the needle with the right—so—in an easy, sweeping curve—right?

MRS. LINDE: Yes, I guess that's—

HELMER: But, on the other hand, knitting—it can never be anything but ugly. Look, see here, the arms tucked in, the knitting needles going up and down—there's something Chinese about it. Ah, that was really a glorious champagne they served.

MRS. LINDE: Yes, good night, Nora, and don't be stubborn any more.

HELMER: Well put, Mrs. Linde!

MRS. LINDE: Good night, Mr. Helmer.

HELMER: *(accompanying her to the door)* Good night, good night. I hope you get home all right. I'd be very happy to—but you don't have far to go. Good night, good night. *(She leaves. He shuts the door after her and returns.)* There, now, at last we got her out the door. She's a deadly bore, that creature.

NORA: Aren't you pretty tired, Torvald?

HELMER: No, not a bit.

NORA: You're not sleepy?

HELMER: Not at all. On the contrary, I'm feeling quite exhilarated. But you? Yes, you really look tired and sleepy.

NORA: Yes, I'm very tired. Soon now I'll sleep.

HELMER: See! You see! I was right all along that we shouldn't stay longer.

NORA: Whatever you do is always right.

HELMER: *(kissing her brow)* Now my little lark talks sense. Say, did you notice what a time Rank was having tonight?

NORA: Oh, was he? I didn't get to speak with him.

HELMER: I scarcely did either, but it's a long time since I've seen him in such high spirits. *(Gazes at her a moment, then comes nearer her.)* Hm—it's marvelous, though, to be back home again—to be completely alone with you. Oh, you bewitchingly lovely young woman!

NORA: Torvald, don't look at me like that!

HELMER: Can't I look at my richest treasure? At all that beauty that's mine, mine alone—completely and utterly.

NORA: *(moving around to the other side of the table)* You mustn't talk to me that way tonight.

HELMER: *(following her)* The tarantella is still in your blood, I can see—and it makes you even more enticing. Listen. The guests are beginning to go. *(Dropping his voice.)* Nora—it'll soon be quiet through this whole house.

NORA: Yes, I hope so.

HELMER: You do, don't you, my love? Do you realize—when I'm out at a party like this with you—do you know why I talk to you so little, and keep such a distance away; just send you a stolen look now and then—you know why I do it? It's because I'm imagining then that you're my secret darling, my secret young bride-to-be, and that no one suspects there's anything between us.

NORA: Yes, yes; oh, yes, I know you're always thinking of me.

HELMER: And then when we leave and I place the shawl over those fine young rounded shoulders—over that wonderful curving neck—then I pretend that you're my young bride, that we're just coming from the wedding, that for the first time I'm bringing you into my house—that for the first time I'm alone with you—completely alone with you, your trembling young beauty! All this evening I've longed for nothing but you. When I saw you turn and sway in the tarantella—my blood was pounding till I couldn't stand it—that's why I brought you down here so early—

NORA: Go away, Torvald! Leave me alone. I don't want all this.

HELMER: What do you mean? Nora, you're teasing me. You will, won't you? Aren't I your husband—?

A knock at the outside door.

NORA: *(startled)* What's that?

HELMER: *(going toward the hall)* Who is it?

RANK: *(outside)* It's me. May I come in a moment?

HELMER: *(with quiet irritation)* Oh, what does he want now? *(Aloud.)* Hold on. *(Goes and opens the door.)* Oh, how nice that you didn't just pass us by!

RANK: I thought I heard your voice, and then I wanted so badly to have a look in. *(Lightly glancing about.)* Ah, me, these old familiar haunts. You have it snug and cozy in here, you two.

HELMER: You seemed to be having it pretty cozy upstairs, too.

RANK: Absolutely. Why shouldn't I? Why not take in everything in life? As much as you can, anyway, and as long as you can. The wine was superb—

HELMER: The champagne especially.

RANK: You noticed that too? It's amazing how much I could guzzle down.

NORA: Torvald also drank a lot of champagne this evening.

RANK: Oh?

NORA: Yes, and that always makes him so entertaining.

RANK: Well, why shouldn't one have a pleasant evening after a well spent day?

HELMER: Well spent? I'm afraid I can't claim that.

RANK: *(slapping him on the back)* But I can, you see!

NORA: Dr. Rank, you must have done some scientific research today.

RANK: Quite so.

HELMER: Come now—little Nora talking about scientific research!

NORA: And can I congratulate you on the results?

RANK: Indeed you may.

NORA: Then they were good?

RANK: The best possible for both doctor and patient—certainty.

NORA: *(quickly and searchingly)* Certainty?

RANK: Complete certainty. So don't I owe myself a gay evening afterwards?

NORA: Yes, you're right, Dr. Rank.

HELMER: I'm with you—just so long as you don't have to suffer for it in the morning.

RANK: Well, one never gets something for nothing in life.

NORA: Dr. Rank—are you very fond of masquerade parties?

RANK: Yes, if there's a good array of odd disguises—

NORA: Tell me, what should we two go as at the next masquerade?

HELMER: You little featherhead—already thinking of the next!

RANK: We two? I'll tell you what: you must go as Charmed Life—

HELMER: Yes, but find a costume for *that!*

RANK: Your wife can appear just as she looks every day.

HELMER: That was nicely put. But don't you know what you're going to be?

RANK: Yes, Helmer, I've made up my mind.

HELMER: Well?

RANK: At the next masquerade I'm going to be invisible.

HELMER: That's a funny idea.

RANK: They say there's a hat—black, huge—have you never heard of the hat that makes you invisible? You put it on, and then no one on earth can see you.

HELMER: *(suppressing a smile)* Ah, of course.

RANK: But I'm quite forgetting what I came for. Helmer, give me a cigar, one of the dark Havanas.

HELMER: With the greatest of pleasure. *(Holds out his case.)*

RANK: Thanks. *(Takes one and cuts off the tip.)*

NORA: *(striking a match)* Let me give you a light.

RANK: Thank you. *(She holds the match for him; he lights the cigar.)* And now good-bye.

HELMER: Good-bye, good-bye, old friend.

NORA: Sleep well, Doctor.

RANK: Thanks for that wish.

NORA: Wish me the same.

RANK: You? All right, if you like—Sleep well. And thanks for the light. *(He nods to them both and leaves.)*

HELMER: *(his voice subdued)* He's been drinking heavily.

NORA: *(absently)* Could be. *(Helmer takes his keys from his pocket and goes out in the hall.)* Torvald—what are you after?

HELMER: Got to empty the mailbox; it's nearly full. There won't be room for the morning papers.

NORA: Are you working tonight?

HELMER: You know I'm not. Why—what's this? Someone's been at the lock.

NORA: At the lock—?

HELMER: Yes, I'm positive. What do you suppose—? I can't imagine one of the maids—? Here's a broken hairpin. Nora, it's yours—

NORA: *(quickly)* Then it must be the children—

HELMER: You'd better break them of that. Hm, hm—well, opened it after all. *(Takes the contents out and calls into the kitchen.)* Helene! Helene, would you put out the lamp in the hall. *(He returns to the room, shutting the hall door, then displays the handful of mail.)* Look how it's piled up. *(Sorting through them.)* Now what's this?

NORA: *(at the window)* The letter! Oh, Torvald, no!

HELMER: Two calling cards—from Rank.

NORA: From Dr. Rank?

HELMER: *(examining them)* "Dr. Rank, Consulting Physician." They were on top. He must have dropped them in as he left.

NORA: Is there anything on them?

HELMER: There's a black cross over the name. See? That's a gruesome notion. He could almost be announcing his own death.

NORA: That's just what he's doing.

HELMER: What! You've heard something? Something he's told you?

NORA: Yes. That when those cards came, he'd be taking his leave of us. He'll shut himself in now and die.

HELMER: Ah, my poor friend! Of course I knew he wouldn't be here much longer. But so soon—And then to hide himself away like a wounded animal.

NORA: If it has to happen, then it's best it happens in silence—don't you think so, Torvald?

HELMER: *(pacing up and down)* He'd grown right into our lives. I simply can't imagine him gone. He with his suffering and loneliness—like a dark cloud setting off our sunlit happiness. Well, maybe it's best this way. For him, at least. *(Standing still.)* And maybe for us too, Nora. Now we're thrown back on each other, completely. *(Embracing her.)* Oh you, my darling wife, how can I hold you close enough? You know what, Nora—time and again I've wished you were in some terrible danger, just so I could stake my life and soul and everything, for your sake.

NORA: *(tearing herself away, her voice firm and decisive)* Now you must read your mail, Torvald.

HELMER: No, no, not tonight. I want to stay with you, dearest.

NORA: With a dying friend on your mind?

HELMER: You're right. We've both had a shock. There's ugliness between us—these thoughts of death and corruption. We'll have to get free of them first. Until then—we'll stay apart.

NORA: *(clinging about his neck)* Torvald—good night! Good night!

HELMER: *(kissing her on the cheek)* Good night, little songbird. Sleep well, Nora. I'll be reading my mail now. *(He takes the letters into his room and shuts the door after him.)*

NORA: *(with bewildered glances, groping about, seizing Helmer's domino, throwing it around her, and speaking in short, hoarse, broken whispers)* Never see him again. Never, never. *(Putting her shawl over her head.)* Never see the children either—them, too. Never, never. Oh, the freezing black water! The depths—down—Oh, I wish it were over—He has it now; he's reading it—now. Oh no, no, not yet. Torvald, good-bye, you and the children—*(She starts for the hall; as she does, Helmer throws open his door and stands with an open letter in his hand.)*

HELMER: Nora!

NORA: *(screams)* Oh—!

HELMER: What is this? You know what's in this letter?

NORA: Yes, I know. Let me go! Let me out!

HELMER: *(holding her back)* Where are you going?

NORA: *(struggling to break loose)* You can't save me, Torvald!

HELMER: *(slumping back)* True! Then it's true what he writes? How horrible! No, no, it's impossible — it can't be true.

NORA: It *is* true. I've loved you more than all this world.

HELMER: Ah, none of your slippery tricks.

NORA: *(taking one step toward him)* Torvald —!

HELMER: What *is* this you've blundered into!

NORA: Just let me loose. You're not going to suffer for my sake. You're not going to take on my guilt.

HELMER: No more playacting. *(Locks the hall door.)* You stay right here and give me a reckoning. You understand what you've done? Answer! You understand?

NORA: *(looking squarely at him, her face hardening)* Yes. I'm beginning to understand everything now.

HELMER: *(striding about)* Oh, what an awful awakening! In all these eight years — she who was my pride and joy — a hypocrite, a liar — worse, worse — a criminal! How infinitely disgusting it all is! The shame! *(Nora says nothing and goes on looking straight at him. He stops in front of her.)* I should have suspected something of the kind. I should have known. All your father's flimsy values — Be still! All your father's flimsy values have come out in you. No religion, no morals, no sense of duty — Oh, how I'm punished for letting him off! I did it for your sake, and you repay me like this.

NORA: Yes, like this.

HELMER: Now you've wrecked all my happiness — ruined my whole future. Oh, it's awful to think of. I'm in a cheap little grafter's hands; he can do anything he wants with me, ask for anything, play with me like a puppet — and I can't breathe a word. I'll be swept down miserably into the depths on account of a featherbrained woman.

NORA: When I'm gone from this world, you'll be free.

HELMER: Oh, quit posing. Your father had a mess of those speeches too. What good would that ever do me if you were gone from this world, as you say? Not the slightest. He can still make the whole thing known; and if he does, I could be falsely suspected as your accomplice. They might even think that I was behind it — that I put you up to it. And all that I can thank you for — you that I've coddled the whole of our marriage. Can you see now what you've done to me?

NORA: *(icily calm)* Yes.

HELMER: It's so incredible, I just can't grasp it. But we'll have to patch up whatever we can. Take off the shawl. I said, take if off! I've got to appease him somehow or other. The thing has to be hushed up at any cost. And as for you and me, it's got to seem like everything between us is just as it was — to the outside world, that is. You'll go right on living in this house, of course. But you can't be allowed to bring up the children; I don't dare trust you with them — Oh, to have to say this to someone I've loved so much! Well, that's done with. From now on happiness doesn't matter; all that matters is saving the bits and pieces, the appearance — *(The doorbell rings. Helmer starts.)* What's that? And so late. Maybe the worst—? You think he'd—? Hide, Nora! Say you're sick. *(Nora remains standing motionless. Helmer goes and opens the door.)*

MAID: *(half dressed, in the hall)* A letter for Mrs. Helmer.

HELMER: I'll take it. *(Snatches the letter and shuts the door.)* Yes, it's from him. You don't get it; I'm reading it myself.

NORA: Then read it.

HELMER: *(by the lamp)* I hardly dare. We may be ruined, you and I. But—I've got to know. *(Rips open the letter, skims through a few lines, glances at an enclosure, then cries out joyfully.)* Nora! *(Nora looks inquiringly at him.)* Nora! Wait—better check it again—Yes, yes, it's true. I'm saved. Nora, I'm saved!

NORA: And I?

HELMER: You too, of course. We're both saved, both of us. Look. He's sent back your note. He says he's sorry and ashamed—that a happy development in his life—oh, who cares what he says! Nora, we're saved! No one can hurt you. Oh, Nora, Nora—but first, this ugliness all has to go. Let me see—*(Takes a look at the note.)* No, I don't want to see it; I want the whole thing to fade like a dream. *(Tears the note and both letters to pieces, throws them into the stove and watches them burn.)* There—now there's nothing left—He wrote that since Christmas Eve you—Oh, they must have been three terrible days for you, Nora.

NORA: I fought a hard fight.

HELMER: And suffered pain and saw no escape but—No, we're not going to dwell on anything unpleasant. We'll just be grateful and keep on repeating: it's over now, it's over! You hear me, Nora? You don't seem to realize—it's over. What's it mean—that frozen look? Oh, poor little Nora, I understand. You can't believe I've forgiven you. But I have, Nora; I swear I have. I know that what you did, you did out of love for me.

NORA: That's true.

HELMER: You loved me the way a wife ought to love her husband. It's simply the means that you couldn't judge. But you think I love you any the less for not knowing how to handle your affairs? No, no—just lean on me; I'll guide you and teach you. I wouldn't be a man if this feminine helplessness didn't make you twice as attractive to me. You mustn't mind those sharp words I said—that was all in the first confusion of thinking my world had collapsed. I've forgiven you, Nora; I swear I've forgiven you.

NORA: My thanks for your forgiveness. *(She goes out through the door, right.)*

HELMER: No, wait—*(Peers in.)* What are you doing in there?

NORA: *(inside)* Getting out of my costume.

HELMER: *(by the open door)* Yes, do that. Try to calm yourself and collect your thoughts again, my frightened little songbird. You can rest easy now; I've got wide wings to shelter you with. *(Walking about close by the door.)* How snug and nice our home is, Nora. You're safe here; I'll keep you like a hunted dove I've rescued out of a hawk's claws. I'll bring peace to your poor, shuddering heart. Gradually it'll happen, Nora; you'll see. Tomorrow all this will look different to you; then everything will be as it was. I won't have to go on repeating I forgive you; you'll feel it for yourself. How can you imagine I'd ever conceivably want to disown you — or even blame you in any way? Ah, you don't know a man's heart, Nora. For a man there's something indescribably sweet and satisfying in knowing he's forgiven his wife — and forgiven her out of a full and open heart. It's as if she belongs to him in two ways now: in a sense he's given her fresh into the world again, and she's become his wife and his child as well. From now on that's what you'll be to me — you little, bewildered, helpless thing. Don't be afraid of anything, Nora; just open your heart to me, and I'll be conscience and will to you both —*(Nora enters in her regular clothes.)* What's this? Not in bed? You've changed your dress?

NORA: Yes, Torvald, I've changed my dress.

HELMER: But why now, so late?

NORA: Tonight I'm not sleeping.

HELMER: But Nora dear —

NORA: *(looking at her watch)* It's still not so very late. Sit down, Torvald; we have a lot to talk over. *(She sits at one side of the table.)*

HELMER: Nora — what is this? That hard expression —

NORA: Sit down. This'll take some time. I have a lot to say.

HELMER: *(sitting at the table directly opposite her)* You worry me, Nora. And I don't understand you.

NORA: No, that's exactly it. You don't understand me. And I've never understood you either — until tonight. No, don't interrupt. You can just listen to what I say. We're closing out accounts, Torvald.

HELMER: How do you mean that?

NORA: *(after a short pause)* Doesn't anything strike you about our sitting here like this?

HELMER: What's that?

NORA: We've been married now eight years. Doesn't it occur to you that this is the first time we two, you and I, man and wife, have ever talked seriously together?

HELMER: What do you mean — seriously?

NORA: In eight whole years — longer even — right from our first acquaintance, we've never exchanged a serious word on any serious thing.

HELMER: You mean I should constantly go and involve you in problems you couldn't possibly help me with?

NORA: I'm not talking of problems. I'm saying that we've never sat down seriously together and tried to get to the bottom of anything.

HELMER: But dearest, what good would that ever do you?

NORA: That's the point right there: you've never understood me. I've been wronged greatly, Torvald — first by Papa, and then by you.

HELMER: What! By us — the two people who've loved you more than anyone else?

NORA: *(shaking her head)* You never loved me. You've thought it fun to be in love with me, that's all.

HELMER: Nora, what a thing to say!

NORA: Yes, it's true now, Torvald. When I lived at home with Papa, he told me all his opinions, so I had the same ones too; or if they were different

I hid them, since he wouldn't have cared for that. He used to call me his doll-child, and he played with me the way I played with my dolls. Then I came into your house—

HELMER: How can you speak of our marriage like that?

NORA: *(unperturbed)* I mean, then I went from Papa's hands into yours. You arranged everything to your own taste, and so I got the same taste as you—or I pretended to; I can't remember. I guess a little of both, first one, then the other. Now when I look back, it seems as if I'd lived here like a beggar—just from hand to mouth. I've lived by doing tricks for you, Torvald. But that's the way you wanted it. It's a great sin what you and Papa did to me. You're to blame that nothing's become of me.

HELMER: Nora, how unfair and ungrateful you are! Haven't you been happy here?

NORA: No, never. I thought so—but I never have.

HELMER: Not—not happy!

NORA: No, only lighthearted. And you've always been so kind to me. But our home's been nothing but a playpen. I've been your doll-wife here, just as at home I was Papa's doll-child. And in turn the children have been my dolls. I thought it was fun when you played with me, just as they thought it fun when I played with them. That's been our marriage, Torvald.

HELMER: There's some truth in what you're saying—under all the raving exaggeration. But it'll all be different after this. Playtime's over; now for the schooling.

NORA: Whose schooling—mine or the children's?

HELMER: Both yours and the children's, dearest.

NORA: Oh, Torvald, you're not the man to teach me to be a good wife to you.

HELMER: And you can say that?

NORA: And I—how am I equipped to bring up children?

HELMER: Nora!

NORA: Didn't you say a moment ago that that was no job to trust me with?

HELMER: In a flare of temper! Why fasten on that?

NORA: Yes, but you were so very right. I'm not up to the job. There's another job I have to do first. I have to try to educate myself. You can't help me with that. I've got to do it alone. And that's why I'm leaving you now.

HELMER: *(jumping up)* What's that?

NORA: I have to stand completely alone, if I'm ever going to discover myself and the world out there. So I can't go on living with you.

HELMER: Nora, Nora!

NORA: I want to leave right away. Kristine should put me up for the night—

HELMER: You're insane! You've no right! I forbid you!

NORA: From here on, there's no use forbidding me anything. I'll take with me whatever is mine. I don't want a thing from you, either now or later.

HELMER: What kind of madness is this!

NORA: Tomorrow I'm going home—I mean, home where I came from. It'll be easier up there to find something to do.

HELMER: Oh, you blind, incompetent child!

NORA: I must learn to be competent, Torvald.

HELMER: Abandon your home, your husband, your children! And you're not even thinking what people will say.

NORA: I can't be concerned about that. I only know how essential this is.

HELMER: Oh, it's outrageous. So you'll run out like this on your most sacred vows.

NORA: What do you think are my most sacred vows?

HELMER: And I have to tell you that! Aren't they your duties to your husband and children?

NORA: I have other duties equally sacred.

HELMER: That isn't true. What duties are they?

NORA: Duties to myself.

HELMER: Before all else, you're a wife and a mother.

NORA: I don't believe in that any more. I believe that, before all else, I'm a human being, no less than you — or anyway, I ought to try to become one. I know the majority thinks you're right, Torvald, and plenty of books agree with you, too. But I can't go on believing what the majority says, or what's written in books. I have to think over these things myself and try to understand them.

HELMER: Why can't you understand your place in your own home? On a point like that, isn't there one everlasting guide you can turn to? Where's your religion?

NORA: Oh, Torvald, I'm really not sure what religion is.

HELMER: What —?

NORA: I only know what the minister said when I was confirmed. He told me religion was this thing and that. When I get clear and away by myself, I'll go into that problem too. I'll see if what the minister said was right, or, in any case, if it's right for me.

HELMER: A young woman your age shouldn't talk like that. If religion can't move you, I can try to rouse your conscience. You do have some moral feeling? Or, tell me — has that gone too?

NORA: It's not easy to answer that, Torvald. I simply don't know. I'm all confused about these things. I just know I see them so differently from you. I find out, for one thing, that the law's not at all what I'd thought — but I can't get it through my head that the law is fair. A woman hasn't a right to protect her dying father or save her husband's life! I can't believe that.

HELMER: You talk like a child. You don't know anything of the world you live in.

NORA: No, I don't. But now I'll begin to learn for myself. I'll try to discover who's right, the world or I.

HELMER: Nora, you're sick; you've got a fever. I almost think you're out of your head.

NORA: I've never felt more clearheaded and sure in my life.

HELMER: And — clearheaded and sure — you're leaving your husband and children?

NORA: Yes.

HELMER: Then there's only one possible reason.

NORA: What?

HELMER: You no longer love me.

NORA: No. That's exactly it.

HELMER: Nora! You can't be serious!

NORA: Oh, this is so hard, Torvald—you've been so kind to me always. But I can't help it. I don't love you any more.

HELMER: *(struggling for composure)* Are you also clearheaded and sure about that?

NORA: Yes, completely. That's why I can't go on staying here.

HELMER: Can you tell me what I did to lose your love?

NORA: Yes, I can tell you. It was this evening when the miraculous thing didn't come—then I knew you weren't the man I'd imagined.

HELMER: Be more explicit; I don't follow you.

NORA: I've waited now so patiently eight long years—for, my Lord, I know miracles don't come every day. Then this crisis broke over me, and such a certainty filled me: *now* the miraculous event would occur. While Krogstad's letter was lying out there, I never for an instant dreamed that you could give in to his terms. I was so utterly sure you'd say to him: go on, tell your tale to the whole wide world. And when he'd done that—

HELMER: Yes, what then? When I'd delivered my own wife into shame and disgrace—!

NORA: When he'd done that, I was so utterly sure that you'd step forward, take the blame on yourself and say: I am the guilty one.

HELMER: Nora—!

NORA: You're thinking I'd never accept such a sacrifice from you? No, of course not. But what good would my protests be against you? That was the miracle I was waiting for, in terror and hope. And to stave that off, I would have taken my life.

HELMER: I'd gladly work for you day and night, Nora—and take on pain and deprivation. But there's no one who gives up honor for love.

NORA: Millions of women have done just that.

HELMER: Oh, you think and talk like a silly child.

NORA: Perhaps. But you neither think nor talk like the man I could join myself to. When your big fright was over—and it wasn't from any threat against me, only for what might damage you—when all the danger was past, for you it was just as if nothing had happened. I was exactly the same, your little lark, your doll, that you'd have to handle with double care now that I'd turned out so brittle and frail. *(Gets up.)* Torvald—in that instant it dawned on me that for eight years I've been living here with a stranger, and that I'd even conceived three children—oh, I can't stand the thought of it! I could tear myself to bits.

HELMER: *(heavily)* I see. There's a gulf that's opened between us—that's clear. Oh, but Nora, can't we bridge it somehow?

NORA: The way I am now, I'm no wife for you.

HELMER: I have the strength to make myself over.

NORA: Maybe—if your doll gets taken away.

HELMER: But to part! To part from you! No, Nora, no—I can't imagine it.

NORA: *(going out, right)* All the more reason why it has to be. *(She reenters with her coat and a small overnight bag, which she puts on a chair by the table.)*

HELMER: Nora, Nora, not now! Wait till tomorrow.

NORA: I can't spend the night in a strange man's room.

HELMER: But couldn't we live here like brother and sister—

NORA: You know very well how long that would last. *(Throws her shawl about her.)* Good-bye, Torvald. I won't look in on the children. I know they're in better hands than mine. The way I am now, I'm no use to them.

HELMER: But someday, Nora—someday—?

NORA: How can I tell? I haven't the least idea what'll become of me.

HELMER: But you're my wife, now and wherever you go.

NORA: Listen, Torvald—I've heard that when a wife deserts her husband's house just as I'm doing, then the law frees him from all responsibility. In any case, I'm freeing you from being responsible. Don't feel yourself bound, any more than I will. There has to be absolute freedom for us both. Here, take your ring back. Give me mine.

HELMER: That too?

NORA: That too.

HELMER: There it is.

NORA: Good. Well, now it's all over. I'm putting the keys here. The maids know all about keeping up the house—better than I do. Tomorrow, after I've left town, Kristine will stop by to pack up everything that's mine from home. I'd like those things shipped up to me.

HELMER: Over! All over! Nora, won't you ever think about me?

NORA: I'm sure I'll think of you often, and about the children and the house here.

HELMER: May I write you?

NORA: No—never. You're not to do that.

HELMER: Oh, but let me send you—

NORA: Nothing. Nothing.

HELMER: Or help you if you need it.

NORA: No. I accept nothing from strangers.

HELMER: Nora—can I never be more than a stranger to you?

NORA: *(picking up the overnight bag)* Ah, Torvald—it would take the greatest miracle of all—

HELMER: Tell me the greatest miracle!

NORA: You and I both would have to transform ourselves to the point that—Oh, Torvald, I've stopped believing in miracles.

HELMER: But I'll believe. Tell me! Transform ourselves to the point that—?

NORA: That our living together could be a true marriage. *(She goes out down the hall.)*

HELMER: *(sinks down on a chair by the door, face buried in his hands)* Nora! Nora! *(Looking about and rising.)* Empty. She's gone. *(A sudden hope leaps in him.)* The greatest miracle—?

From below, the sound of a door slamming shut.

Reading and Reacting

1. What is your attitude toward Nora at the beginning of the play? How does your attitude toward her change as the play progresses? What actions and lines of dialogue change your assessment of her?

2. List the key events that have occurred before the start of the play. How do we learn of each event?

3. Explain the role of each of the following in advancing the play's action: the Christmas tree, the locked mailbox, the telegram Dr. Rank receives, Dr. Rank's calling cards.

4. In act 2, Torvald says, "Whatever comes, you'll see: when it really counts, I have strength and courage enough as a man to take on the whole weight myself." How does this statement influence Nora's subsequent actions?

5. Explain how each of the following foreshadows events that will occur later in the play: Torvald's comments about Krogstad's children (act 1); Torvald's attitude toward Nora's father (act 2); Krogstad's suggestions about suicide (act 2).

6. In addition to the play's main plot—which concerns the blackmail of Nora by Krogstad and her attempts to keep her crime secret from Torvald—the play contains several subplots. Some of them began to develop before the start of the play, and some unfold alongside the main plot. Identify these subplots. How do they advance the themes of survival, debt, sacrifice, and duty that run through the play?

7. Is Kristine Linde as much of a "modern woman" as Nora? Is she actually *more* of a modern woman? Is she essential to the play? How might the play be different without her?

8. JOURNAL ENTRY Do you see *A Doll House* as primarily about the struggle between the needs of the individual and the needs of society, or about the conflict between women's roles in the family and in the larger society? Explain.

9. CRITICAL PERSPECTIVE Since its earliest performances, there has been much comment on the conclusion of *A Doll House*. Many viewers have found the play's ending unrealistically harsh. In fact, a famous German actress refused to play the scene as written because she insisted she would never leave her children. (Ibsen reluctantly rewrote the ending for her; in this version, Helmer forces Nora to the doorway of the children's bedroom, and she sinks to the floor as the curtain falls.) Moreover, many critics have found it hard to accept Nora's sudden transformation from, in the words of Elizabeth Hardwick in her essay "Ibsen's Women," "the girlish, charming wife to the radical, courageous heroine setting out alone."

What is your response to the play's ending? Do you think it makes sense in light of what we have learned about Nora and her marriage? Or, do you agree with Hardwick that Nora's abandonment of her children is not only implausible but also a "rather casual" gesture that "drops a stain on our admiration of Nora"?

Related Works: "The Story of an Hour" (p. 226), "The Yellow Wallpaper" (p. 459), "The Rocking-Horse Winner" (p. 589), "The Chrysanthemums" (p. 769), "Marks" (p. 1187), "Barbie doll" (p. 1187), *The Stronger* (p. 1470)

WRITING SUGGESTIONS: Plot

1. Central to the plots of both *Trifles* and *A Doll House* is a woman who commits a crime. Compare and contrast the desperate situations that motivate the two women. Then, consider the reactions of other characters in the two plays to each woman's crime. If you like, you may also discuss the crime committed by Emily Grierson in "A Rose for Emily" (p. 243).

2. Write an essay in which you compare the influence of Nora's father on the plot of *A Doll House* with the influence of Catherine's father on the plot of *Proof* (p. 1476).

3. Write a monologue for Mama in *A Raisin in the Sun* (or Nora in *A Doll House*), including everything you think she would like to tell her children. Or, write a monologue for Mrs. Wright in *Trifles* in which she describes her marriage and explains the motivation for her crime.

4. Although Beneatha in *A Raisin in the Sun* wants to be a doctor, she is constantly encouraged by Mama and Walter, as well as by George and Asagai, to marry and settle down. Write an essay in which you examine how Beneatha's struggle to achieve her full potential is similar to and different from that of a more contemporary female character, such as Dee in "Everyday Use" (p. 517). Or, compare Beneatha's dilemma to the one faced by the protagonists of such works as *A Doll House*, "A&P" (p. 259), and "Eveline" (p. 719), who struggle between conforming to the expectations of their families (or society) and doing what is best for themselves.

5. Write a play called *Nine Twelve*. Keep all the major characters of *Nine Ten*, but put them together on September 12 in another setting, where they discuss what happened to them since they last met and how their attitudes toward jury duty, work, and life in general have changed as a result.

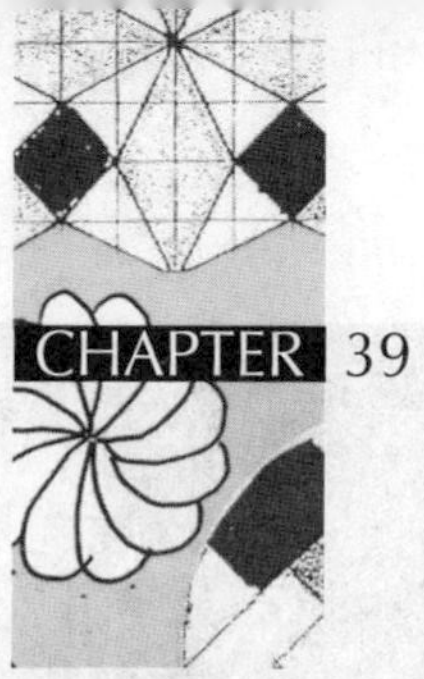

CHAPTER 39

CHARACTER

In Tennessee Williams's 1945 play *The Glass Menagerie* (p. 1961), the protagonist, Tom Wingfield, functions as the play's narrator. Stepping out of his role as a character and speaking directly to the audience, he directs the play's action, music, lighting, and other elements. In addition, he summarizes characters' actions, explains what motivates them, and discusses the significance of their behavior in the context of the play — commenting on his own character's actions as well.

Scene from John Madden's 2005 film adaption of David Auburn's *Proof* (p. 1476) with Gwyneth Paltrow as Catherine and Jake Gyllenhaal as Hal.
Source: MIRAMAX/The Kobal

Jo Mielziner's celebrated set for the premiere production of Arthur Miller's *Death of a Salesman*, (p. 1531) starring Lee J. Cobb, showing the cutaway house and the downstage playing area.

Source: ©Eileen Darby Lester

Richard Burton (left), Laurence Olivier (middle), and Mel Gibson (right) have all played the role of Hamlet.

Source: Left, ©Bettmann/Corbis; center, ©Bettmann/Corbis; right, ©Paramount/The Kobal Collection

As narrator, Tom also presents useful background information about the characters. For instance, when he introduces his coworker, Jim, he prepares the audience for Jim's entrance and helps them to understand his subsequent actions:

> In high school Jim was a hero. He had tremendous Irish good nature and vitality with the scrubbed and polished look of white chinaware. He seemed to move in a continual spotlight. . . . But Jim apparently ran into more interference after his graduation. . . . His speed had definitely slowed. Six years after he left high school he was holding a job that wasn't much better than mine. (scene 6)

Most plays, however, do not include narrators who present background. Instead, the audience learns about characters from their own words and from comments by others about them, as well as from the characters' actions. When reading a play, we learn about the characters from the playwright's stage directions; when watching a performance, we gain insight into characters from the way actors interpret them.

Characters in plays, like characters in novels and short stories, may be **round** or **flat, static,** or **dynamic.** Generally speaking, major characters are likely to be round, whereas minor characters are likely to be flat. Through the language and the actions of the characters, audiences learn whether the characters are multidimensional, skimpily developed, or perhaps merely **foils,** players whose main purpose is to shed light on more important characters. Audiences also learn about the emotions, attitudes, and values that help to shape the characters — their hopes and fears, their strengths and weaknesses. In addition, by comparing characters' early words and actions with later ones, audiences learn from the play whether or not characters grow and change emotionally.

Characters' Words

Characters' words reveal the most about their attitudes, feelings, beliefs, and values. Sometimes information is communicated (to other characters as well as to the audience) in a **monologue**— an extended speech by one character. This device is used throughout August Strindberg's *The Stronger* (p. 1470). A **soliloquy**— a monologue revealing a character's thoughts and feelings, directed at the audience and presumed not to be heard by other characters — can also convey information about a character. For example, Hamlet's well-known soliloquy that begins "To be or not to be" eloquently communicates his distraught mental state — his resentment of his mother and uncle, his confusion about what course of action to take, and his suicidal thoughts. Finally, **dialogue**— an exchange of words between two characters — can reveal misunderstanding or conflict between them, or it can show their agreement, mutual support, or similar beliefs.

In Henrik Ibsen's *A Doll House* (p. 1402), dialogue reveals a good deal about the characters. Nora Helmer, the spoiled young wife, has broken the law and kept her crime secret from her husband. Through her words, we learn about her motivation, her values, her emotions, and her reactions to other characters and to her potentially dangerous situation. We learn, for instance, that she is flirtatious — "If your little squirrel begged you, with all her heart and soul . . ." — and that she is childishly unrealistic about the consequences of her actions. When her husband, Torvald, asks what she would do if he was seriously injured, leaving her in debt, she says, "If anything so awful happened, then it just wouldn't matter if I had debts or not." When Torvald presses, "Well, but the people I'd borrowed from?" she dismisses them: "Them? Who cares about them! They're strangers." As the play progresses, Nora's lack of understanding of the power of the law becomes more and more significant as she struggles with her moral and ethical dilemma.

The inability of both Nora and Torvald to confront ugly truths is also revealed through their words. When, in act 1, Nora tells Krogstad, her blackmailer, that his revealing her secret could expose her to "the most horrible unpleasantness," he responds, "Only unpleasantness?" Yet later on, in act 3, Torvald echoes her language, fastidiously dismissing the horror with, "No, we're not going to dwell on anything unpleasant."

The ease with which Torvald is able to dismiss his dying friend Dr. Rank in act 3 ("He with his suffering and loneliness — like a dark cloud setting off our sunlit happiness. Well, maybe it's best this way.") foreshadows the lack of support he will give Nora immediately thereafter. Especially revealing is his use of *I* and *my* and *me*, which convey his self-centeredness:

> Now you've wrecked all my happiness — ruined my whole future. Oh, it's awful to think of. I'm in a cheap little grafter's hands; he can do anything he wants with me, ask for anything, play with me like a puppet — and I can't breathe a word. I'll be swept down miserably into the depths on account of a featherbrained woman.

Just as Torvald's words reveal that he has not been changed by the play's events, Nora's words show that she has changed significantly. Her dialogue near the end of act 3 shows that she has become a responsible, determined woman — one who understands her situation and her options and is no longer blithely oblivious to her duties. When she says, "I've never felt more clearheaded and sure in my life," she is calm and decisive. When she says, "Our home's been nothing but a playpen. I've been your doll-wife here, just as at home I was Papa's doll-child," she reveals a new self-awareness. And, when she confronts her husband, she displays — perhaps for the first time in their relationship — complete honesty.

Sometimes what other characters say to (or about) a character can reveal more to an audience than the character's own words. For instance, in *A Doll House*, when the dying Dr. Rank says, apparently without malice, "[Torvald] Helmer with his sensitivity has such a sharp distaste for anything ugly," the audience not only thinks ill of the man who is too "sensitive" to visit his sick friend but also questions his ability to withstand situations that may be emotionally or morally "ugly" as well.

When a character is offstage for much (or even all) of the action, the audience must rely on other characters' assessments of the absent character. In Susan Glaspell's *Trifles* (p. 1319), the play's focus is on an absent character, Minnie Wright, who is described solely through other characters' remarks. The evidence suggests that Mrs. Wright killed her husband, and only Mrs. Hale's and Mrs. Peters's comments about Mrs. Wright's dreary life can delineate her character and suggest a likely motive for the murder. Although Mrs. Wright never appears on stage, we learn essential information from the other women about her: that as a young girl she liked to sing and that more recently she was so distraught about the lack of beauty in her life that even her sewing revealed her distress. Similarly, the father in *The Glass Menagerie* never appears (and therefore never speaks), but the play's other characters describe him as "A telephone man who — fell in love with long-distance!" — the absent husband and father who symbolizes abandonment and instability to Laura and Amanda and the possibility of freedom and escape to Tom.

Whether a character's words are in the form of a monologue, a soliloquy, or dialogue, and whether they reveal information about the character who is speaking or about someone else, such words are always revealing. Explicitly or implicitly, they convey a character's nature, attitudes, and relationships with other characters.

The language characters use can vary widely. A character may, for instance, use learned words, foreign words, elaborate figures of speech, irony or sarcasm, regionalisms, slang, jargon, clichés, or profanity. Words can also be used to indicate tone — for example, to express irony. Any of these uses of language may communicate vital information to the audience about a character's background, attitudes, and motivation. And, of course, a character's language may change as a play progresses, and this change too may be revealing.

Formal and Informal Language

One character in a dramatic work may speak very formally, using absolutely correct grammar, a learned vocabulary, and long, complex sentences; another may speak in an informal style, using conversational speech, colloquialisms, and slang. At times, two characters with different levels of language may be set in opposition for dramatic effect, as they are in Irish playwright George Bernard Shaw's classic play *Pygmalion* (1912), which updates the ancient Greek myth of a sculptor who creates (and falls in love with) a statue of a woman. In Shaw's version, a linguistics professor sets out to teach "proper" speech and manners to a woman who sells flowers on the street. Throughout the play, the contrasting language of Henry

Higgins, the professor, and Eliza Doolittle, the flower seller, reveals their differing social standing. The following exchange illustrates this contrast:

LIZA: I ain't got no mother. Her that turned me out was my sixth stepmother. But I done without them. And I'm a good girl, I am.
HIGGINS: Very well, then, what on earth is all this fuss about?

A character's accent or dialect may also be significant. In **comedies of manners,** for instance, rustic or provincial characters, identified by their speech, are often objects of humor. In *Pygmalion*, Eliza Doolittle uses cockney dialect, the dialect spoken in the East End of London. At first, her colorful, distinctive language (complete with expressions like *Nah-ow*, *garn*, and *ah-ah-ah-ow-ow-ow-oo*) and her nonstandard grammatical constructions make her an object of ridicule; later, the transformation of her speech reveals the dramatic changes in her character.

Plain and Elaborate Language

A character's speech may be simple and straightforward or complex and convoluted; it may be plain and unadorned or embellished with elaborate **figures of speech.** The relative complexity or lack of complexity of a character's speech may have different effects on the audience. For example, a character whose language is simple and unsophisticated may seem to be unintelligent, unenlightened, gullible, or naive — especially if he or she also uses slang, dialect, or colloquial expressions. Conversely, a character's plain, down-to-earth language may convey common sense or intelligence. Plain language may also be quite emotionally powerful. Thus, Willy Loman's speech in act 2 of *Death of a Salesman* (p. 1531), about an eighty-four-year-old salesman named Dave Singleman, moves the audience with its sincerity and directness:

> Do you know? When he died — and by the way he died the death of a salesman, in his green velvet slippers in the smoker of the New York, New Haven and Hartford, going into Boston — when he died, hundreds of salesmen and buyers were at his funeral. Things were sad on a lotta trains for months after that.

Like plain speech, elaborate language may have different effects in different contexts. Sometimes, use of figures of speech can make a character seem to have depth and insight and analytical skills absent in other characters. In the following excerpt from a soliloquy in act 1 scene 2 of *Hamlet*, for example, complex language reveals the depth of Hamlet's anguished self-analysis:

HAMLET: O, that this too too solid flesh would melt,
Thaw, and resolve itself into a dew!
Or that the Everlasting had not fix'd
His canon 'gainst self-slaughter! O God! O God!

How weary, stale, flat, and unprofitable
Seem to me all the uses of this world!
Fie on't, O fie, 'tis an unweeded garden,
That grows to seed. . .

In these lines, Hamlet compares the world to a garden gone to seed. His use of imagery and figures of speech vividly communicates his feelings about the world and his internal struggle against the temptation to commit suicide.

Sometimes, however, elaborate language may make a character seem aloof, pompous, or even untrustworthy. In the following passages from Shakespeare's *King Lear,* Goneril and Regan, the deceitful daughters, use complicated verbal constructions to conceal their true feelings from their father, King Lear. In contrast, Cordelia — the loyal, loving daughter — uses simple, straightforward language that suggests her sincerity and lack of artifice. Compare the three speeches:

Goneril: Sir, I love you more than words can wield the matter;
Dearer than eyesight, space, and liberty;
Beyond what can be valued, rich or rare;
No less than life, with grace, health, beauty, honour;
As much as child e'er lov'd, or father found;
A love that makes breath poor, and speech unable.
Beyond all manner of so much I love you. . . .

Regan: Sir, I am made
Of the selfsame metal that my sister is,
And prize me at her worth. In my true heart
I find she names my very deed of love;
Only she comes too short, that I profess
Myself an enemy to all other joys
Which the most precious square of sense possesses,
And find I am alone felicitate
In your dear Highness' love. . . .

Cordelia: Unhappy that I am, I cannot heave
My heart into my mouth. I love your Majesty
According to my bond; no more no less. . .

Cordelia's unwillingness, even when she is prodded by Lear, to exaggerate her feelings or misrepresent her love through inflated language shows the audience her honesty and nobility. The contrast between her language and that of her sisters makes their very different motives clear.

Tone

Tone reveals a character's mood or attitude. Tone can be flat or emotional, bitter or accepting, affectionate or aloof, anxious or calm. Contrasts in tone can indicate differences in outlook or emotional state between two characters; changes in tone from one point in a play to another can suggest corresponding changes within a character. At the end of *A Doll House,* for instance, Nora is resigned to what she must do, and her language is appropriately controlled. Her husband, however, is desperate to change her mind, and his language reflects this desperation. The following exchanges of dialogue from the end of act 3 illustrate the two characters contrasting emotional states:

HELMER: But to part! To part from you! No, Nora, no — I can't imagine it.
NORA: *(going out, right)* All the more reason why it has to be.

HELMER: Over! All over! Nora, won't you ever think about me?
NORA: I'm sure I'll think of you often, and about the children and the house here.

In earlier scenes between the two characters, Nora is emotional — at times, hysterical — and her husband is considerably more controlled. As the above exchanges indicate, both Nora and Torvald Helmer change drastically during the course of the play.

Irony

Irony, a contradiction or discrepancy between two levels of meaning, can reveal a great deal about character. **Verbal irony** — a contradiction between what a character says and what he or she means — is very important in drama, where the verbal interplay between characters may carry the weight of the play. For example, when Nora and Dr. Rank discuss the latest news about his health in *A Doll House,* there is deep irony in his use of the phrase "complete certainty." Although the phrase usually suggests reassuring news, here it is meant to suggest death, and both Nora and Dr. Rank understand this.

Dramatic irony depends on the audience's knowing something that a character has not yet realized, or on one character's knowing something that other characters do not know. In some cases, dramatic irony is created by an audience's awareness of historical background or events of which characters are unaware. Familiar with the story of Oedipus, for instance, the audience knows that the man who has caused all the problems in Thebes — the man Oedipus vows to find and take revenge on — is Oedipus himself. In other cases, dramatic irony emerges when the audience learns something — something the characters do not yet know or comprehend — from a play's unfolding action. The central irony in *A Doll House,* for example, is that the family's "happy home" rests on a foundation of secrets, lies, and deception. Torvald does not know about the secrets, and Nora does not understand how they have poisoned her marriage. The audience, however, quickly becomes aware of the atmosphere of deceit — and aware of how it threatens the family's happiness.

Dramatic irony may also be conveyed through dialogue. Typically, dramatic irony is revealed when a character says something that gives the audience information that other characters, offstage at the time, do not know. In *A Doll House*, the audience knows — because Nora has explained her situation to Kristine — that Nora spent the previous Christmas season hard at work, earning money to pay her secret debt. Torvald, however, remains unaware of her activities and believes her story that she was using the time to make holiday decorations, which the cat destroyed. This belief is consistent with his impression of Nora as an irresponsible child, yet the audience has quite a different impression of her. This discrepancy, one of many contradictions between the audience's view of Nora and Torvald's view of her, helps to create dramatic tension in the play.

Finally, **asides** (comments to the audience that other characters do not hear) can create dramatic irony by undercutting dialogue, providing ironic contrast between what the characters on stage know and what the audience knows. In Anton Chekhov's *The Brute* (p. 1250), for example, the audience knows that Mr. Smirnov is succumbing to Mrs. Popov's charms because he says, in an aside, "My God, what eyes she has! They're setting me on fire." Mrs. Popov, however, is not yet aware of his infatuation. The discrepancy between the audience's awareness and the character's adds to the play's humor.

Characters' Actions

Through their actions, characters convey their values and attitudes to the audience. Actions also reveal aspects of a character's personality. When Laura Wingfield, a character in *The Glass Menagerie*, hides rather than face the "gentleman caller," the audience sees how shy she is; when Nora in *A Doll House* plays hide-and-seek with her children, eats forbidden macaroons, and takes childish joy in Christmas, her immaturity is apparent.

Audiences also learn about characters from what they do *not* do. Thus, Nora's failure to remain in touch with her friend Kristine, who has had a hard life, reveals her selfishness, and the failure of Mrs. Peters and Mrs. Hale in *Trifles* to give their evidence to the sheriff indicates their defiant support for Mrs. Wright and their understanding of what motivated her to take such drastic action.

Audiences also learn a good deal about characters by observing how they interact with other characters. In William Shakespeare's *Othello*, Iago is the embodiment of evil, and as the play's action unfolds, we discover his true nature. He reveals the secret marriage of Othello and Desdemona to her father; he schemes to arouse Othello's jealousy, making him believe Desdemona has been unfaithful with his lieutenant, Cassio; he persuades Cassio to ask Desdemona to plead his case with Othello, knowing this act will further arouse Othello's suspicions; he encourages Othello to be suspicious of Desdemona's defense of Cassio; he plants Desdemona's handkerchief in Cassio's room; and, finally, he persuades Othello to kill Desdemona and then kills his own wife, Emilia, to prevent her from exposing his role in the intrigue. As the play progresses, then, Iago's dealings with others consistently reveal him to be evil and corrupt.

Stage Directions

When we read a play, we also read the playwright's italicized **stage directions,** the notes that concern **staging**— the scenery, props, lighting, music, sound effects, costumes, and other elements that contribute to the way the play looks and sounds to an audience (see Chapter 40). In addition to commenting on staging, stage directions may supply physical details about the characters, suggesting their age, appearance, movements, gestures, and facial expressions. These details may in turn convey additional information about characters: appearance may reveal social position or economic status, expressions may reveal attitudes, and so on. Stage directions may also indicate the manner in which a line of dialogue is to be delivered —*confidently* or *hesitantly*, for instance. The way a line is spoken may reveal a character to be excited, upset, angry, shy, or disappointed. Finally, stage directions may indicate *changes* in characters — for instance, a character whose speech is described as timid in early scenes may deliver lines emphatically and forcefully later on in the play.

Some stage directions provide a good deal of detail about character; others do little more than list characters' names. Arthur Miller is one playwright who often provides detailed information about character through stage directions. In *Death of a Salesman*, for instance, Miller's stage directions at the beginning of act 1 characterize Willy Loman immediately and specifically:

> *He is past sixty years of age, dressed quietly. Even as he crosses the stage to the doorway of the house, his exhaustion is apparent. He unlocks the door, comes into the kitchen, and thankfully lets his burden down, feeling the soreness of his palms. A word-sigh escapes his lips. . . .*

Subsequent stage directions indicate how lines are to be spoken. For example, in the play's opening lines, Willy's wife Linda calls out to him "*with some trepidation*"; Linda speaks "*very carefully, delicately*," and Willy speaks "*with casual irritation*." These instructions to readers (and actors) are meant to suggest the strained relationship between the two characters.

George Bernard Shaw is notorious for the full character description in his stage directions. In these directions — seen by readers of the play but of course not heard by audiences — he communicates complex information about characters' attitudes and values, motivation and reactions, and relationships with other characters. In doing so, Shaw functions as a narrator, explicitly communicating his own attitudes toward various characters. (Unlike the voice of Tom Wingfield in *The Glass Menagerie*, however, the voice in Shaw's stage directions is not also the voice of a character in the play; it is the voice of the playwright.) Shaw's stage directions for *Pygmalion* initially describe Eliza Doolittle as follows:

> *She is not at all an attractive person. She is perhaps eighteen, perhaps twenty, hardly older. She wears a little sailor hat of black straw that has long been exposed to the dust and soot of London and has seldom if ever been brushed. Her hair needs washing rather badly; its mousy color can hardly be natural. She wears a shoddy black coat that reaches nearly to her knees and is shaped to her waist. She has a brown skirt with*

a coarse apron. Her boots are much the worse for wear. She is no doubt as clean as she can afford to be; but compared to the ladies she is very dirty. Her features are no worse than theirs; but their condition leaves something to be desired; and she needs the services of a dentist.

Rather than providing an objective summary of the character's most notable physical attributes, Shaw injects subjective comments (*"seldom if ever brushed"*; *"color can hardly be natural"*; *"no doubt as clean as she can afford to be"*) that reveal his attitude toward Eliza. This initially supercilious attitude, which he has in common with Professor Higgins, is tempered considerably by the end of the play, helping to make Eliza's transformation more obvious to readers than it would be if measured by her words and actions alone. By act 5, the tone of the stage directions characterizing Eliza has changed to admiration: *"Eliza enters, sunny, self-possessed, and giving a staggeringly convincing exhibition of ease of manner."*

Stage directions in other plays are not nearly as comprehensive. In *Hamlet*, for example, characters are introduced with only the barest identifying tags: "Claudius, *King of Denmark*"; "Hamlet, *Son to the former, and nephew to the present King*"; "Gertrude, *Queen of Denmark, mother to Hamlet*." Most stage directions do little more than chronicle the various characters' entrances and exits or specify particular physical actions: *"Enter Ghost"*; *"Spreads his arms"*; *"Ghost beckons Hamlet"*; *"He kneels"*; *"Sheathes his sword"*; *"Leaps in the grave."* Occasionally, stage directions specify a prop (*"Puts down the skull"*); a sound effect (*"A noise within"*); or a costume (*"Enter the ghost in his night-gown"*). Such brevity is typical of Shakespeare's plays, in which characters are delineated almost solely by their words — and, not incidentally, by the way actors have interpreted the characters over the years. In fact, because Shakespeare's stage directions only suggest characters' gestures, physical reactions, movements, and facial expressions, actors have been left quite free to experiment, reading various interpretations into Shakespeare's characters.

Actors' Interpretations

When we watch a play, we gain insight into a character not merely through what the character says and does or how other characters react, but also through the way an actor interprets the role. If a playwright does not specify a character's mannerisms, gestures, or movements, or does not indicate how a line is to be delivered (and sometimes even if he or she does), an actor is free to interpret the role as he or she believes it should be played. Even when a playwright *does* specify such actions, the actor has a good deal of freedom to decide which gestures or expressions will convey a particular emotion.

In "Some Thoughts on Playwriting," American dramatist Thornton Wilder argues that "the theatre is an art which reposes upon the work of many collaborators" rather than on "one governing selecting will." Citing examples from Shakespeare and Ibsen, Wilder illustrates the great degree of "intervention" that may occur in dramatic productions. For instance, Wilder observes, Shakespeare's

Shylock has been portrayed by two different actors as "noble, wronged and indignant" and as "a vengeful and hysterical buffoon"— and both performances were considered plausible interpretations. As noted earlier, the absence of detailed stage directions in Shakespeare's plays makes possible (and perhaps even encourages) such widely divergent interpretations. However, as Wilder points out, even when playing roles created by a dramatist such as Ibsen, whose stage directions are typically quite specific, actors and directors have a good deal of leeway. Thus, actress Janet McTeer, who played the part of Ibsen's Nora in the 1997 London production of *A Doll House*, saw Nora and Torvald, despite their many problems, as "the perfect couple," deeply in love and involved in a passionate marriage. "You have to make that marriage sexually credible," McTeer told the *New York Times*, "to imagine they have a wonderful time in bed, so there becomes something to lose. If you play them as already past it or no longer attracted to each other, then there is no play." This interpretation is not inconsistent with the play, but it does go beyond what Ibsen actually wrote.

Similarly, the role of Catherine in David Auburn's *Proof* (p. 1476) has been played by several actresses — among them Mary-Louise Parker, Jennifer Jason Leigh, Anne Heche, Gwyneth Paltrow, and Lea Salonga — and each actress has interpreted this complex character in a different way. As *New York Times* theater critic John Rockwell observes, "Catherine can be loopy-ethereal-sexy (Ms. Parker), earthy and even a little bitter (Ms. Leigh), or adorable-needy-fragile (Ms. Heche), and Mr. Auburn's structure and characters and ideas still work."

Irish playwright Samuel Beckett devotes a good deal of attention to indicating actors' movements and gestures and their physical reactions to one another. In his 1952 play *Waiting for Godot*, for example, Beckett's stage directions seem to choreograph every gesture, every emotion, every intention:

- *(he looks at them ostentatiously in turn to make it clear they are both meant)*
- *Vladimir seizes Lucky's hat. Silence of Lucky. He falls. Silence. Panting of the victors.*
- *Estragon hands him the boot. Vladimir inspects it, throws it down angrily.*
- *Estragon pulls, stumbles, falls. Long silence.*
- *He goes feverishly to and fro, halts finally at extreme left, broods.*

Beckett provides full and obviously carefully thought-out stage directions and, in so doing, attempts to retain a good deal of control over his characters. Still, in a 1988 production of *Godot*, director Mike Nichols and comic actors Robin Williams and Steve Martin felt free to improvise, adding gestures and movements not specified or even hinted at — and most critics believed that this production remained true to the tragicomic spirit of Beckett's existentialist play. In a sense, then, the playwright's words on the page are just the beginning of the characters' lives on the stage.

✔ CHECKLIST Writing about Character

- Does any character serve as a narrator? If so, what information does this narrator supply about the other characters? How reliable is the narrator?
- Who are the major characters? What do we know about them?
- Do the major characters change and grow during the course of the play, or do they remain essentially unchanged?
- What do the minor characters contribute to the play?
- Does the play include monologue or soliloquies? What do these extended speeches reveal about the characters?
- What is revealed about the characters through dialogue?
- Do characters use foreign words, regionalisms, slang, jargon, clichés, or profanity? What does such use of language reveal about the characters? About the play's theme?
- Is the characters' language formal or informal?
- Do characters speak in dialect? Do they have accents?
- Is the characters' language plain or elaborate?
- Do different characters have different styles or levels of language? What is the significance of these differences?
- How does language reveal characters' emotional states?
- Does the tone of any character's language change significantly as the play progresses? What does this change reveal?
- Does the play include verbal irony? Dramatic irony? How is irony conveyed? What purpose does irony achieve?
- What is revealed about the characters through what others say about them?
- What is revealed about characters through their actions?
- What is revealed about characters through the play's stage directions?
- How might different actors' interpretations change an audience's understanding of the characters?

Source: ©Hulton-Deutsch Collection/Corbis

AUGUST STRINDBERG (1849–1912) was born in Stockholm, Sweden, the child of a shipping merchant and his former maid. He studied at Uppsala University but left the university without a degree. By 1872, he had moved into the artistic circles in Stockholm and had begun work as a journalist.

In 1874, Strindberg was appointed assistant librarian at the Royal Library in Stockholm. Beginning the first of several stormy marriages, he struggled over the next few years; in 1879, he declared bankruptcy. During the same period, he wrote *The Red Room* (1879), the novel that marked his breakthrough as a writer. In 1881, he left the Royal Library to devote himself to writing, and in 1883, he left Sweden to join an artists' colony near Paris. His restlessness continued, however, and he soon moved to Switzerland, later living in Denmark, Germany, and Austria before returning at last to Stockholm.

Strindberg was a prolific artist, and his work includes novels, plays, poetry, and paintings. He is considered one of the most influential dramatists in literature.

The Stronger has been called a monodrama, a dramatic monologue, and a battle of brains in one scene. This play was the kind of experimental work being encouraged in the late nineteenth century at the Théâtre Libre in Paris, for which Strindberg wrote several plays while hoping to form his own experimental theater in Stockholm. Though written in 1889, *The Stronger* did not premiere on stage until 1907.

Cultural Context Strindberg's subject matter (*The Stronger*, for example, is about a meeting between an actress and her husband's mistress) shocked and sometimes scandalized his nineteenth-century contemporaries. As a result, Strindberg often had difficulty getting his plays performed in commercial theaters, and for this reason, he and other playwrights became involved with the Independent Theater movement. By producing plays outside the control of official censors, they were able to attract an audience for their work, and their subject matter reflected their rebellion against the mores and standards of their societies.

The Stronger (1889)

Translated by Elizabeth Sprigge

CHARACTERS

Mrs. X., *actress, married*
Miss Y., *actress, unmarried*
A Waitress

SCENE

A corner of a ladies' café [in Stockholm in the eighteen eighties].° *Two small wrought-iron tables, a red plush settee and a few chairs.*

Miss Y. is sitting with a half-empty bottle of beer on the table before her, reading an illustrated weekly which from time to time she exchanges for another.

Mrs. X. enters, wearing a winter hat and coat and carrying a decorative Japanese basket.

°[*In Stockholm in the eighteen eighties*] Brackets indicate translator's addition to scene.

MRS. X: Why, Millie, my dear, how are you? Sitting here all alone on Christmas Eve like some poor bachelor.

Miss Y. looks up from her magazine, nods, and continues to read.

MRS. X: You know it makes me feel really sad to see you. Alone. Alone in a café and on Christmas Eve of all times. It makes me feel as sad as when once in Paris I saw a wedding party at a restaurant. The bride was reading a comic paper and the bridegroom playing billiards with the witnesses. Ah me, I said to myself, with such a beginning how will it go, and how will it end? He was playing billiards on his wedding day! And she, you were going to say, was reading a comic paper on hers. But that's not quite the same.

A waitress brings a cup of chocolate to Mrs. X. and goes out.

MRS. X: Do you know, Amelia, I really believe now you would have done better to stick to him. Don't forget I was the first who told you to forgive him. Do you remember? Then you would be married now and have a home. Think how happy you were that Christmas when you stayed with your financé's people in the country. How warmly you spoke of domestic happiness! You really quite longed to be out of the theatre. Yes, Amelia dear, home is best—next best to the stage, and as for children—but you couldn't know anything about that.

Miss Y.'s expression is disdainful. Mrs. X. sips a few spoonfuls of chocolate, then opens her basket and displays some Christmas presents.

MRS. X: Now you must see what I have bought for my little chicks. *(Takes out a doll.)* Look at this. That's for Lisa. Do you see how she can roll her eyes and turn her head. Isn't she lovely? And here's a toy pistol for Maja.° *(She loads the pistol and shoots it at Miss Y. who appears frightened.)*

MRS. X: Were you scared? Did you think I was going to shoot you? Really, I didn't think you'd believe that of me. Now if *you* were to shoot *me* it wouldn't be so surprising, for after all I did get in your way, and I know you never forget it—although I was entirely innocent. You still think I intrigued to get you out of the Grand Theatre, but I didn't. I didn't, however much you think I did. Well, it's no good talking, you will believe it was me . . . *(Takes out a pair of embroidered slippers.)* And these are for my old man, with tulips on them that I embroidered myself. As a matter of fact I hate tulips, but he has to have tulips on everything.

Miss Y. looks up, irony and curiosity in her face.

MRS. X: *(putting one hand in each slipper)* Look what small feet Bob has, hasn't he? And you ought to see the charming way he walks—you've never seen him in slippers, have you?

Miss Y. laughs.

°*Maja:* Pronounced "Maya."

Mrs. X: Look, I'll show you. *(She makes the slippers walk across the table, and Miss Y. laughs again.)*

Mrs. X: But when he gets angry, look, he stamps his foot like this. "Those damn girls who can never learn how to make coffee! Blast! That silly idiot hasn't trimmed the lamp properly!" Then there's a draught under the door and his feet get cold. "Hell, it's freezing, and the damn fools can't even keep the stove going!" *(She rubs the sole of one slipper against the instep of the other. Miss Y roars with laughter.)*

Mrs. X: And then he comes home and has to hunt for his slippers, which Mary has pushed under the bureau . . . Well, perhaps it's not right to make fun of one's husband like this. He's sweet anyhow, and a good, dear husband. You ought to have had a husband like him, Amelia. What are you laughing at? What is it? Eh? And, you see, I know he is faithful to me. Yes, I know it. He told me himself—what *are* you giggling at?—that while I was on tour in Norway that horrible Frederica came and tried to seduce him. Can you imagine anything more abominable? *(Pause.)* I'd have scratched her eyes out if she had come around while I was at home. *(Pause.)* I'm glad Bob told me about it himself, so I didn't just hear it from gossip. *(Pause.)* And, as a matter of fact, Frederica wasn't the only one. I can't think why, but all the women in the Company° seem to be crazy about my husband. They must think his position gives him some say in who is engaged at the Theatre. Perhaps you have run after him yourself? I don't trust you very far, but I know he has never been attracted by you, and you always seemed to have some sort of grudge against him, or so I felt. *(Pause. They look at one another guardedly.)*

10 **Mrs. X:** Do come and spend Christmas Eve with us tonight, Amelia—just to show that you're not offended with us, or anyhow not with me. I don't know why, but it seems specially unpleasant not to be friends with you. Perhaps it's because I did get in your way that time . . . *(slowly)* or—I don't know—really, I don't know at all why it is.

Pause. Miss Y. gazes curiously at Mrs. X.

Mrs. X: *(thoughtfully)* It was so strange when we were getting to know one another. Do you know, when we first met, I was frightened of you, so frightened I didn't dare let you out of my sight. I arranged all my goings and comings to be near you. I dared not be your enemy, so I became your friend. But when you came to our home, I always had an uneasy feeling, because I saw my husband didn't like you, and that irritated me—like when a dress doesn't fit. I did all I could to make him be nice to you, but it was no good—until you went and got engaged. Then you became such tremendous friends that at first it looked as if you only dared show your real feelings then—when you were safe. And then, let me see, how was it after that? I wasn't jealous—that's queer. And I remember at the christening,

° *in the Company:* Translator's addition.

when you were the godmother, I told him to kiss you. He did, and you were so upset . . . As a matter of fact I didn't notice that then . . . I didn't think about it afterwards either . . . I've never thought about it — until *now!* *(Rises abruptly.)* Why don't you say something? You haven't said a word all this time. You've just let me go on talking. You have sat there with your eyes drawing all these thoughts out of me — they were there in me like silk in a cocoon — thoughts. . . Mistaken thoughts? Let me think. Why did you break off your engagement? Why did you never come to our house after that? Why don't you want to come to us tonight?

Miss Y. makes a motion, as if about to speak.

Mrs. X: No. You don't need to say anything, for now I see it all. That was why — and why — and why. Yes. Yes, that's why it was. Yes, yes, all the pieces fit together now. That's it. I won't sit at the same table as you. *(Moves her things to the other table.)* That's why I have to embroider tulips, which I loathe, on his slippers — because you liked tulips. *(Throws the slippers on the floor.)* That's why we have to spend the summer on the lake — because you couldn't bear the seaside. That's why my son had to be called Eskil — because it was your father's name. That's why I had to wear your colours, read your books, eat the dishes you liked, drink your drinks — your chocolate, for instance. That's why — oh my God, it's terrible to think of, terrible! Everything, everything came to me from you — even your passions. Your soul bored into mine like a worm into an apple, and ate and ate and burrowed and burrowed, till nothing was left but the skin and a little black mould. I wanted to fly from you, but I couldn't. You were there like a snake, your black eyes fascinating me. When I spread my wings, they only dragged me down. I lay in the water with my feet tied together, and the harder I worked my arms, the deeper I sank — down, down, till I reached the bottom, where you lay in waiting like a giant crab to catch me in your claws — and now here I am. Oh how I hate you! I hate you, I hate you! And you just go on sitting there, silent, calm, indifferent, not caring whether the moon is new or full, if it's Christmas or New Year, if other people are happy or unhappy. You don't know how to hate or to love. You just sit there without moving — like a cat° at a mouse-hole. You can't drag your prey out, you can't chase it, but you can out-stay it. Here you sit in your corner — you know they call it the rat-trap after you — reading the papers to see if anyone's ruined or wretched or been thrown out of the Company. Here you sit sizing up your victims and weighing your chances — like a pilot his shipwrecks for the salvage. *(Pause.)* Poor Amelia! Do you know, I couldn't be more sorry for you. I know you are miserable, miserable like some wounded creature, and vicious because you are wounded. I can't be angry with you. I should like to be, but after all you are the small one — and as for your affair with Bob, that doesn't worry me in the least. Why should it matter to me?

°*cat:* In Swedish, "stork."

And if you, or somebody else taught me to drink chocolate, what's the difference? *(Drinks a spoonful. Smugly.)* Chocolate is very wholesome anyhow. And if I learnt from you how to dress, *tant mieux!*—that only gave me a stronger hold over my husband, and you have lost what I gained. Yes, to judge from various signs, I think you have now lost him. Of course, you meant me to walk out, as you once did, and which you're now regretting. But I won't do that, you may be sure. One shouldn't be narrow-minded, you know. And why should nobody else want what I have? *(Pause.)* Perhaps, my dear, taking everything into consideration, at this moment it is I who am the stronger. You never got anything from me, you just gave away—from yourself. And now, like the thief in the night, when you woke up I had what you had lost. Why was it then that everything you touched became worthless and sterile? You couldn't keep a man's love—for all your tulips and your passions—but I could. You couldn't learn the art of living from your books—but I learnt it. You bore no little Eskil, although that was your father's name. *(Pause.)* And why is it you are silent—everywhere, always silent? Yes, I used to think this was strength, but perhaps it was because you hadn't anything to say, because you couldn't think of anything. *(Rises and picks up the slippers.)* Now I am going home, taking the tulips with me—*your* tulips. You couldn't learn from others, you couldn't bend, and so you broke like a dry stick. I did not. Thank you, Amelia, for all your good lessons. Thank you for teaching my husband how to love. Now I am going home—to love him.

Exit.

Reading and Reacting

1. Summarize the plot of *The Stronger*. What actually happens during the play? What events have occurred before the play begins?
2. Explain the nature of the conflict between Mrs. X and Miss Y. Is this conflict entirely personal, or is it professional as well?
3. Why do you suppose Strindberg structures this play as a monologue? Would exchanges of dialogue strengthen the play? What do you suppose Miss Y would like to tell Mrs. X?
4. Both Miss Y and Mrs. X are actresses. What significance, if any, do you see in this fact?
5. What does the audience learn about Bob, Mrs. X's husband, during the course of the play? What more can we infer about him?
6. As she continues to speak, Mrs. X's similes—for example, "Your soul bored into mine like a worm into an apple"—grow increasingly vivid. Identify as many similes as you can. What does this language reveal about Mrs. X's character? How does it move the play's action along?
7. As the play progresses, Mrs. X gains knowledge and self-awareness. What does she learn?
8. List all the play's props—for example, the toy gun and the slippers. What function does each of these props serve? Are they all necessary?

9. **JOURNAL ENTRY** Which of the two women do you see as "the stronger" in this play? Explain your position.

10. **CRITICAL PERSPECTIVE** In her notes on the play, director Tracy Campbell makes the following observations about the play's two characters:

> To be stronger, two things have to be compared with one overcoming the other. The two are both women, both have hopes and dreams, both have very real fears. But that's where the comparisons end. Mrs. X and Miss Y are not the same kind of woman; they have similar hopes and dreams but they are motivated differently; their fears of loneliness may be the same, but how the two women face this fear is very different.

How are these two women similar? How are they different? What do you think each woman fears, and how does each one face her fears?

Related Works: "Hills Like White Elephants" (p. 171), "The Storm" (p. 313), "Big Black Good Man" (p. 374), "Happy Endings" (p. 662), "Sonnet I" (p. 986), "Women" (p. 1007), "General Review of the Sex Situation" (p. 1056)

Source: ©AP Photo/Alan Solomon

DAVID AUBURN (1969–) was born in Chicago and grew up in Columbus, Ohio, and in Arkansas before returning to Chicago for college. Having spent time in Los Angeles on a screenwriting fellowship, Auburn moved to New York to become a playwright. He enrolled in the playwriting program at Juilliard and had his first full-length play, *Skyscraper* (1998), produced off-Broadway in 1997. The production attracted the attention of the Manhattan Theatre Club, which told Auburn, "Keep us in mind for your next play and send it to us." He did, and that play was *Proof* (2000), his first Broadway production. *Proof* was awarded the 2001 Pulitzer Prize for drama and the 2001 Tony Award; Auburn also received a Dramatists Guild's Hull-Warriner Award. He adapted *Proof* into the 2005 feature film of the same name. His other plays include *Fifth Planet* (1998), *Miss You* (1998), and *The Next Life*. His short play *What Do You Believe about the Future?* (1996) appeared in *Harper's* magazine and was adapted for the screen. Auburn also wrote the screenplay for the 2006 feature film *The Lake House*. Winner of the Joseph Kesselring Prize for drama, Auburn has also received the Helen Merrill Playwriting Award and a Guggenheim Foundation Fellowship.

Cultural Context *Proof* is a play about mathematics and mathematicians. The number of women in mathematics — traditionally a male-dominated field — has grown slowly but steadily in the last thirty years. According to a study published in 2006, since 2000, women have been earning more bachelor's degrees than men in science and engineering fields from colleges and universities in the United States. The percentage of American women earning PhDs in science and engineering fields has also risen, climbing above forty percent. Despite these gains, the notion that women can excel in math and science is still not universally accepted. In January 2005, Dr. Lawrence Summers, then President of Harvard University, hypothesized that innate genetic differences between men and women might be one reason why "fewer women succeed in math and science careers." These comments — from the leader of a prestigious university — sparked international controversy.

Proof (2001)

SETTING

THE BACK PORCH OF A HOUSE IN CHICAGO

CHARACTERS

Robert, *fifties* **Hal,** *twenty-eight*
Catherine, *twenty-five* **Claire,** *twenty-nine*

ACT 1

SCENE 1

Night. Catherine sits in a chair. She is exhausted, haphazardly dressed. Eyes closed. Robert is standing behind her. He is Catherine's father. Rumpled academic look. Catherine does not know he is there. After a moment:

ROBERT: Can't sleep?
CATHERINE: Jesus, you scared me.
ROBERT: Sorry.
CATHERINE: What are you doing here?
ROBERT: I thought I'd check up on you. Why aren't you in bed?
CATHERINE: Your student is still here. He's up in your study.
ROBERT: He can let himself out.
CATHERINE: I might as well wait up till he's done.
ROBERT: He's not my student anymore. He's teaching now. Bright kid.

Beat.

CATHERINE: What time is it?
ROBERT: It's almost one.
CATHERINE: Huh.
ROBERT: After midnight . . .
CATHERINE: So?
ROBERT: So: (*He indicates something on the table behind him: a bottle of champagne.*) Happy birthday.
CATHERINE: Dad.
ROBERT: Do I ever forget?
CATHERINE: Thank you.
ROBERT: Twenty-five. I can't believe it.
CATHERINE: Neither can I. Should we have it now?
ROBERT: It's up to you.
CATHERINE: Yes.
ROBERT: You want me to open it?
CATHERINE: Let me. Last time you opened a bottle of champagne out here you broke a window.
ROBERT: That was a long time ago. I resent your bringing it up.
CATHERINE: You're lucky you didn't lose an eye.

Pop. The bottle foams.

ROBERT: Twenty-five!

CATHERINE: I feel old.

ROBERT: You're a kid.

CATHERINE: Glasses?

ROBERT: Goddamn it, I forgot the glasses. Do you want me to—

CATHERINE: Nah.

Catherine drinks from the bottle. A long pull. Robert watches her.

ROBERT: I hope you like it. I wasn't sure what to get you.

CATHERINE: This is the worst champagne I have ever tasted.

ROBERT: I am proud to say I don't know anything about wines. I hate those kind of people who are always talking about "vintages."

CATHERINE: It's not even champagne.

ROBERT: The bottle was the right shape.

CATHERINE: "Great Lakes Vineyards." I didn't know they made wine in Wisconsin.

ROBERT: A girl who's drinking from the bottle shouldn't complain. Don't guzzle it. It's an elegant beverage. Sip.

CATHERINE: *(offering the bottle)* Do you—

ROBERT: No, go ahead.

CATHERINE: You sure?

ROBERT: Yeah. It's your birthday.

CATHERINE: Happy birthday to me.

ROBERT: What are you going to do on your birthday?

CATHERINE: Drink this. Have some.

ROBERT: No. I hope you're not spending your birthday alone.

CATHERINE: I'm not alone.

ROBERT: I don't count.

CATHERINE: Why not?

ROBERT: I'm your old man. Go out with some friends.

CATHERINE: Right.

ROBERT: Your friends aren't taking you out?

CATHERINE: No.

ROBERT: Why not?

CATHERINE: Because in order for your friends to take you out you generally have to have friends.

ROBERT: *(dismissive)* Oh—

CATHERINE: It's funny how that works.

ROBERT: You have friends. What about that cute blonde, what was her name?

CATHERINE: What?

ROBERT: She lives over on Ellis Avenue—you used to spend every minute together.

CATHERINE: Cindy Jacobsen?

ROBERT: Cindy Jacobsen!

CATHERINE: That was in *third grade*, Dad. Her family moved to Florida in 1983.

ROBERT: What about Claire?

CATHERINE: She's not my friend, she's my sister. And she's in New York. And I don't like her.

ROBERT: I thought she was coming in.

CATHERINE: Not till tomorrow.

Beat.

ROBERT: My advice, if you find yourself awake late at night, is to sit down and do some mathematics.

CATHERINE: Oh please.

ROBERT: We could do some together.

CATHERINE: No.

ROBERT: Why not?

CATHERINE: I can't think of anything worse. You sure you don't want any?

ROBERT: Yeah, thanks. You used to love it.

CATHERINE: Not anymore.

ROBERT: You knew what a prime number was before you could read.

CATHERINE: Well now I've forgotten.

ROBERT: *(Hard)* Don't waste your talent, Catherine.

Beat.

CATHERINE: I knew you'd say something like that.

ROBERT: I realize you've had a difficult time.

CATHERINE: Thanks.

ROBERT: That's not an excuse. Don't be lazy.

CATHERINE: I haven't been lazy, I've been taking care of you.

ROBERT: Kid, I've seen you. You sleep till noon, you eat junk, you don't work, the dishes pile up in the sink. If you go out it's to buy magazines. You come back with a stack of magazines this high—I don't know how you read that crap. And those are the good days. Some days you don't get up, you don't get out of bed.

CATHERINE: Those are the good days.

ROBERT: Bullshit. Those days are lost. You threw them away. And you'll never know what else you threw away with them—the work you lost, the ideas you didn't have, discoveries you never made because you were moping in your bed at four in the afternoon. *(Beat.)* You know I'm right. *(Beat.)*

CATHERINE: I've lost a few days.

ROBERT: How many?

CATHERINE: Oh, I don't know.

ROBERT: I bet you do.

CATHERINE: What?

ROBERT: I bet you count.

CATHERINE: Knock it off.

ROBERT: Well do you know or don't you?

CATHERINE: I don't.

ROBERT: Of course you do. How many days have you lost?

CATHERINE: A month. Around a month.

ROBERT: Exactly.

CATHERINE: Goddamn it, I don't—

ROBERT: *How many?*

CATHERINE: Thirty-three days.

ROBERT: Exactly?

CATHERINE: I don't know.

ROBERT: Be precise, for Chrissake.

CATHERINE: I slept till noon today.

ROBERT: Call it thirty-three and a quarter days.

CATHERINE: Yes, all right.

ROBERT: You're kidding!

CATHERINE: No.

ROBERT: Amazing number!

CATHERINE: It's a depressing fucking number.

ROBERT: Catherine, if every day you say you've lost were a year, it would be a very interesting fucking number.

CATHERINE: Thirty-three and a quarter years is not interesting.

ROBERT: Stop it. You know exactly what I mean.

CATHERINE: *(conceding)* 1729 weeks.

ROBERT: 1729. Great number. The smallest number expressible—

CATHERINE: —expressible as the sum of two cubes in two different ways.

ROBERT: 12 cubed plus 1 cubed equals 1729.

CATHERINE: And 10 cubed plus 9 cubed. Yes, we've got it, thank you.

ROBERT: You see? Even your depression is mathematical. Stop moping and get to work. The kind of potential you have—

CATHERINE: I haven't done anything good.

ROBERT: You're young. You've got time.

CATHERINE: I do?

ROBERT: *Yes*.

CATHERINE: By the time you were my age you were famous.

ROBERT: By the time I was your age I'd already done my best work.

Beat.

CATHERINE: What about after?

ROBERT: After what?

CATHERINE: After you got sick.

ROBERT: What about it?

CATHERINE: You couldn't work then.

ROBERT: No, if anything I was sharper.

CATHERINE: (*She can't help it: she laughs.*) Dad.

ROBERT: I was. Hey, it's true. The clarity—that was the amazing thing. No doubts.

CATHERINE: You were happy?

ROBERT: Yeah, I was busy.

CATHERINE: Not the same thing.

ROBERT: I don't see the difference. I knew what I wanted to do and I did it.

If I wanted to work a problem all day long, I did it.

If I wanted to look for information—secrets, complex and tantalizing messages—I could find them all around me. In the air. In a pile of fallen leaves some neighbor raked together. In box scores in the paper, written in the steam coming up off a cup of coffee. The whole world was talking to me.

If I just wanted to close my eyes, sit quietly on the porch and listen for the messages, I did that.

It was wonderful.

Beat.

CATHERINE: How old were you? When it started.

ROBERT: Mid-twenties. Twenty-three, four. *(Beat.)* Is that what you're worried about?

CATHERINE: I've thought about it.

ROBERT: Just getting a year older means nothing, Catherine.

CATHERINE: It's not just getting older.

ROBERT: It's me.

Beat.

CATHERINE: I've thought about it.

ROBERT: Really?

CATHERINE: How could I not?

ROBERT: Well if that's why you're worried you're not keeping up with the medical literature. There are all kinds of factors. It's not simply something you inherit. Just because I went bughouse doesn't mean you will.

CATHERINE: Dad . . .

ROBERT: Listen to me. Life changes fast in your early twenties and it shakes you up. You're feeling down. It's been a bad week. You've had a lousy couple years, no one knows that better than me. But you're gonna be okay.

CATHERINE: Yeah?

ROBERT: Yes. I promise you. Push yourself. Don't read so many magazines. Sit down and get the machinery going and I swear to God you'll feel fine. The simple fact that we can talk about this together is a good sign.

CATHERINE: A good sign?

ROBERT: Yes!

CATHERINE: How could it be a good sign?

ROBERT: Because! Crazy people don't sit around wondering if they're nuts.

CATHERINE: They don't?

ROBERT: Of course not. They've got better things to do. Take it from me. A very good sign that you're crazy is an inability to ask the question "Am I crazy?"

CATHERINE: Even if the answer is yes?

ROBERT: Crazy people don't ask. You see?

CATHERINE: Yes.

ROBERT: So if you're asking . . .
CATHERINE: I'm not.
ROBERT: But if you were, it would be a very good sign.
CATHERINE: A good sign . . .
ROBERT: A good sign that you're fine.
CATHERINE: Right.
ROBERT: You see? You've just gotta think these things through. Now come on, what do you say? Let's call it a night; you go up, get some sleep, and then in the morning you can—
CATHERINE: Wait. No.
ROBERT: What's the matter?
CATHERINE: It doesn't work.
ROBERT: Why not?
CATHERINE: It doesn't make sense.
ROBERT: Sure it does.
CATHERINE: No.
ROBERT: Where's the problem?
CATHERINE: The problem is you are crazy!
ROBERT: What difference does that make?
CATHERINE: You admitted—You just told me that you are.
ROBERT: So?
CATHERINE: You said a crazy person would never admit that.
ROBERT: Yeah, but it's . . . Oh. I see.
CATHERINE: So?
ROBERT: It's a point.
CATHERINE: So how can you admit it?
ROBERT: Well. Because I'm also dead. *(Beat.)* Aren't I?
CATHERINE: You died a week ago.
ROBERT: Heart failure. Quick. The funeral's tomorrow.
CATHERINE: That's why Claire's flying in from New York.
ROBERT: Yes.
CATHERINE: You're sitting here. You're giving me advice. You brought me champagne.
ROBERT: Yes.

Beat.

CATHERINE: Which means . . .
ROBERT: For you?
CATHERINE: Yes.
ROBERT: For you, Catherine, my daughter, who I love very much . . . It could be a bad sign.

They sit together for a moment. Noise off. Hal enters, semi-hip clothes. He carries a backpack and a jacket, folded. He lets the door go and it bangs shut. Catherine sits up with a jolt.

CATHERINE: What?

HAL: Oh God, sorry—did I wake you?

CATHERINE: What?

HAL: Were you asleep?

Beat. Robert is gone.

CATHERINE: You scared me, for Chrissake. What are you doing?

HAL: I'm sorry. I didn't realize it had gotten so late. I'm done for the night.

CATHERINE: Good.

HAL: Drinking alone?

Catherine realizes she is holding the champagne bottle. She puts it down quickly.

CATHERINE: Yes.

HAL: Champagne, huh?

CATHERINE: Yes.

HAL: Celebrating?

CATHERINE: No. I just like champagne.

HAL: It's festive.

CATHERINE: What?

HAL: *Festive. (He makes an awkward "party" gesture.)*

CATHERINE: Do you want some?

HAL: Sure.

CATHERINE: *(gives him the bottle)* I'm done. You can take the rest with you.

HAL: Oh. No thanks.

CATHERINE: Take it, I'm done.

HAL: No, I shouldn't. I'm driving. *(Beat.)* Well I can let myself out.

CATHERINE: Good.

HAL: When should I come back?

CATHERINE: Come back?

HAL: Yeah. I'm nowhere near finished. Maybe tomorrow?

CATHERINE: We have a funeral tomorrow.

HAL: God, you're right, I'm sorry. I was going to attend, if that's all right.

CATHERINE: Yes.

HAL: What about Sunday? Will you be around?

CATHERINE: You've had three days.

HAL: I'd love to get in some more time up there.

CATHERINE: How much longer do you need?

HAL: Another week. At least.

CATHERINE: Are you joking?

HAL: No. Do you know how much stuff there is?

CATHERINE: A week?

HAL: I know you don't need anybody in your hair right now. Look, I spent the last couple days getting everything sorted out. It's mostly notebooks. He dated them all; now that I've got them in order I don't have to work here. I could take some stuff home, read it, bring it back.

CATHERINE: No.

HAL: I'll be careful.

CATHERINE: My father wouldn't want anything moved and I don't want anything to leave this house.

HAL: Then I should work here. I'll stay out of the way.

CATHERINE: You're wasting your time.

HAL: Someone needs to go through your dad's papers.

CATHERINE: There's nothing up there. It's garbage.

HAL: There are a hundred and three notebooks.

CATHERINE: I've looked at those. It's gibberish.

HAL: Someone should read them.

CATHERINE: He was crazy.

HAL: Yes, but he wrote them.

CATHERINE: He was a graphomaniac, Harold. Do you know what that is?

HAL: I know. He wrote compulsively. Call me Hal.

CATHERINE: There's no connection between the ideas. There's no ideas. It's like a monkey at a typewriter. A hundred and three notebooks full of bullshit.

HAL: Let's make sure they're bullshit.

CATHERINE: I'm sure.

HAL: I'm prepared to look at every page. Are you?

CATHERINE: No. *I'm* not crazy.

Beat.

HAL: Well, I'm gonna be late . . . Some friends of mine are in this band. They're playing at a bar up on Diversey. Way down the bill, they're probably going on around two, two-thirty. I said I'd be there.

CATHERINE: Great.

HAL: They're all in the math department. They're really good. They have this great song—you'd like it—called "i"—lower-case I. They just stand there and don't play anything for three minutes.

CATHERINE: "Imaginary Number."

HAL: It's a math joke. You see why they're way down the bill.

CATHERINE: Long drive to see some nerds in a band.

HAL: God I hate when people say that. It is not that long a drive.

CATHERINE: So they are nerds.

HAL: Oh they're raging geeks. But they're geeks who, you know, can dress themselves . . . hold down a job at a major university . . . Some of them have switched from glasses to contacts. They play sports, they play in a band, they get laid surprisingly often, so in that sense they sort of make you question the whole set of terms: geek, nerd, wonk, dweeb, dilbert, paste-eater.

CATHERINE: You're in this band, aren't you?

HAL: Okay, yes. I play drums. You want to come? I never sing, I swear to God.

CATHERINE: No thanks.

HAL: All right. Look, Catherine, Monday: what do you say?

CATHERINE: Don't you have a job?

HAL: Yeah, I have a full teaching load this quarter plus my own work.

CATHERINE: Plus band practice.

HAL: I don't have time to do this but I'm going to. If you'll let me. (*Beat.*) I loved your dad. I don't believe a mind like his can just shut down. He had lucid moments. He had a lucid year, a whole year four years ago.

CATHERINE: It wasn't a year. It was more like nine months.

HAL: A school year. He was advising students . . . I was stalled on my Ph.D. I was this close to quitting. I met with your dad and he put me on the right track with my research. I owe him.

CATHERINE: Sorry.

HAL: Look. Let me—You're twenty-five, right?

CATHERINE: How old are you?

HAL: It doesn't matter. Listen.

CATHERINE: Fuck you, how old are you?

HAL: I'm twenty-eight, all right? When your dad was younger than both of us, he made major contributions to three fields: game theory, algebraic geometry, and nonlinear operator theory. Most of us never get our heads around one. He basically invented the mathematical techniques for studying rational behavior, and he gave the astrophysicists plenty to work over too. Okay?

CATHERINE: Don't lecture me.

HAL: I'm not. I'm telling you, if I came up with one-tenth of the shit your dad produced, I could write my own ticket to any math department in the country.

Beat.

CATHERINE: Give me your backpack.

HAL: What?

CATHERINE: Give me your backpack.

HAL: Why?

CATHERINE: I want to look inside it.

HAL: What?

CATHERINE: Open it and give it to me.

HAL: Oh come on.

CATHERINE: You're not taking anything out of this house.

HAL: I wouldn't do that.

CATHERINE: You're hoping to find something upstairs that you can publish.

HAL: Sure.

CATHERINE: Then you can write your own ticket.

HAL: What? No! It would be under your dad's name. It would be for your dad.

CATHERINE: I don't believe you. You have a notebook in that backpack.

HAL: What are you talking about?

CATHERINE: Give it to me.

HAL: You're being a little bit paranoid.

CATHERINE: *Paranoid?*

HAL: Maybe a little.

CATHERINE: Fuck you, *Hal. I know* you have one of my notebooks.

HAL: I think you should calm down and think about what you're saying.

CATHERINE: I'm saying you're lying to me and stealing my family's property.

HAL: And I think that sounds paranoid.

CATHERINE: Just because I'm paranoid doesn't mean there isn't something in that backpack.

HAL: *You just said yourself there's nothing up there.* Didn't you?

CATHERINE: I—

HAL: Didn't you say that?

CATHERINE: Yes.

HAL: So what would I take? Right?

Beat.

CATHERINE: You're right.

HAL: Thank you.

CATHERINE: So you don't need to come back.

HAL: *(Sighs.)* Please. Someone should know for sure whether—

CATHERINE: *I lived with him.* I spent my life with him. I fed him. Talked to him. Tried to listen when he talked. Talked to people who weren't there . . . Watched him shuffling around like a ghost. A very smelly ghost. He was filthy. I had to make sure he bathed. My own father.

HAL: I'm sorry. I shouldn't have . . .

CATHERINE: After my mother died it was just me here. I tried to keep him happy no matter what idiotic project he was doing. He used to read all day. He kept demanding more and more books. I took them out of the library by the carload. We had hundreds upstairs. Then I realized he wasn't reading: he believed aliens were sending him messages through the Dewey decimal numbers on the library books. He was trying to work out the code.

HAL: What kind of messages?

CATHERINE: Beautiful mathematics. The most elegant proofs, perfect proofs, proofs like music.

HAL: Sounds good.

CATHERINE: Plus fashion tips, knock-knock jokes—I mean it was *nuts*, okay?

HAL: He was ill. It was a tragedy.

CATHERINE: Later the writing phase: scribbling nineteen, twenty hours a day . . . I ordered him a case of notebooks and he used every one.

I dropped out of school . . .

I'm glad he's dead.

HAL: I understand why you'd feel that way.

CATHERINE: Fuck you.

HAL: You're right. I can't imagine dealing with that. It must have been awful. I know you—

CATHERINE: You don't know me. I want to be alone. I don't want him around.

HAL: *(confused)* Him? I don't—

CATHERINE: You. I don't want you here.

HAL: Why?

CATHERINE: He's dead.

HAL: But I'm not—

CATHERINE: *He's* dead; I don't need any *protégés* around.

HAL: There will be others.

CATHERINE: What?

HAL: You think I'm the only one? People are already working over his stuff. Someone's gonna read those notebooks.

CATHERINE: I'll do it.

HAL: No, you—

CATHERINE: He's my father, I'll do it.

HAL: You can't.

CATHERINE: Why not?

HAL: You don't have the math. It's all just squiggles on a page. You wouldn't know the good stuff from the junk.

CATHERINE: It's all junk.

HAL: If it's not we can't afford to miss any through carelessness.

CATHERINE: I know mathematics.

HAL: If there was anything up there it would be pretty high-order. It would take a professional to recognize it.

CATHERINE: I think I could recognize it.

HAL: *(Patient)* Cathy . . .

CATHERINE: *What?*

HAL: I know your dad taught you some basic stuff, but come on.

CATHERINE: You don't think I could do it.

HAL: I'm sorry: I know that you couldn't. *(Beat. Catherine snatches his backpack.)* Hey! Oh come on. Give me a break. *(Catherine opens the backpack and rifles through it.)* This isn't an airport.

Catherine removes items one by one. A water bottle. Some workout clothes. An orange. Drumsticks. Nothing else. She puts everything back in and gives it back. Beat.

CATHERINE: You can come tomorrow.

Beat. They are both embarrassed.

HAL: The university health service is uh very good.

My mom died a couple years ago and I was pretty broken up. Also my work wasn't going that well . . . I went over and talked to this doctor. I saw her for a couple months and it really helped.

CATHERINE: I'm fine.

Beat.

HAL: Also exercise is great. I run along the lake a couple of mornings a week. It's not too cold yet. If you wanted to come sometime I could pick you up. We wouldn't have to talk . . .

CATHERINE: No thanks.

HAL: All right. I'm gonna be late for the show. I better go.

CATHERINE: Okay.

Beat.

HAL: It's seriously like twenty minutes up to the club. We go on, we play, we're terrible but we buy everyone drinks afterward to make up for it. You're home by four, four-thirty, tops . . .

CATHERINE: Good night.

HAL: Good night. *(He starts to exit. He has forgotten his jacket.)*

CATHERINE: Wait, your coat.

HAL: No, you don't have to—

Catherine picks up his jacket. As she does, a composition book that was folded up in the coat falls to the floor. Beat. She picks it up, trembling with rage.

CATHERINE: I'm *paranoid?*

HAL: Wait.

CATHERINE: You think I should go *jogging?*

HAL: Just hold on.

CATHERINE: Get out!

HAL: Can I please just—

CATHERINE: Get the fuck out of my house.

HAL: Listen to me for a *minute.*

CATHERINE: *(Waving the book)* You stole this!

HAL: Let me *explain!*

CATHERINE: You stole it from *me*, you stole it from my *father—*

Hal snatches the book.

HAL: I want to show you something. Will you calm down?

CATHERINE: Give it back.

HAL: Just wait a minute.

CATHERINE: I'm calling the police. *(She picks up the phone and dials.)*

HAL: Don't. Look, I borrowed the book, all right? I'm sorry, I just picked it up before I came downstairs and thought I'd—

CATHERINE: *(On phone)* Hello?

HAL: I did it for a reason.

CATHERINE: Hello, police? I—Yes, I'd like to report a robbery in progress.

HAL: I noticed something—something your father wrote. All right? Not math, something he *wrote*. Here, let me show you.

CATHERINE: A *robbery*.

HAL: Will you put the fucking phone down and listen to me?

CATHERINE: *(On phone)* Yes, I'm at 5724 South—

HAL: It's about you. See? *You*. It was written about you. Here's your name: *Cathy*. See?

CATHERINE: South . . .

Catherine pauses. She seems to be listening. Hal reads.

HAL: "A good day. Some very good news from Catherine." I didn't know what that referred to, but I thought you might . . .

CATHERINE: When did he write this?

HAL: I think four years ago. The handwriting is steady. It must have been during his remission. There's more. *(A moment. Catherine hangs up the phone.)* "Machinery not working yet but I am patient." "The machinery" is what he called his mind, his ability to do mathematics.

CATHERINE: I know.

HAL: *(reads)* "I know I'll get there. I am an auto mechanic who after years of greasy work on a hopeless wreck turns the ignition and hears a faint cough. I am not driving yet, but there's cause for optimism. Talking with students helps. So does being outside, eating meals in restaurants, riding buses, all the activities of 'normal' life.

"Most of all Cathy. The years she has lost caring for me. I almost wrote 'wasted.' Yet her refusal to let me be institutionalized—her keeping me at home, caring for me herself, has certainly saved my life. Made writing this possible. Made it possible to imagine doing math again. Where does her strength come from? I can never repay her.

"Today is her birthday: she is twenty-one. I'm taking her to dinner." Dated September 4. That's tomorrow.

CATHERINE: It's today.

HAL: You're right. *(He gives her the book.)* I thought you might want to see it. I shouldn't have tried to sneak it out. Tomorrow I was going to—it sounds stupid now. I was going to wrap it. Happy birthday.

Hal exits. Catherine is alone. She puts her head in her hands. She weeps. Eventually she stops, wipes her eyes. From off: a police siren, drawing closer.

CATHERINE: Shit.

Fade

SCENE 2

The next morning. Claire, stylish, attractive, drinks coffee from a mug. She has brought bagels and fruit on a tray out to the porch. She arranges them on two plates. She notices the champagne bottle lying on the floor. She picks it up and sets it on a table. Catherine enters. Her hair is wet from a shower.

CLAIRE: Better. Much.

CATHERINE: Thanks.

CLAIRE: Feel better?

CATHERINE: Yeah.

CLAIRE: You look a million times better. Have some coffee.

CATHERINE: Okay.

CLAIRE: How do you take it?

CATHERINE: Black.

CLAIRE: Have a little milk. *(She pours.)* Want a banana? It's a good thing I brought food: there was nothing in the house.

CATHERINE: I've been meaning to go shopping.

CLAIRE: Have a bagel.

CATHERINE: No. I hate breakfast. *(Beat.)*
CLAIRE: You didn't put on the dress.
CATHERINE: Didn't really feel like it.
CLAIRE: Don't you want to try it on? See if it fits?
CATHERINE: I'll put it on later.

Beat.

CLAIRE: If you want to dry your hair I have a hair dryer.
CATHERINE: Nah.
CLAIRE: Did you use that conditioner I brought you?
CATHERINE: No, shit, I forgot.
CLAIRE: It's my favorite. You'll love it, Katie. I want you to try it.
CATHERINE: I'll use it next time.
CLAIRE: You'll like it. It has jojoba.
CATHERINE: What is "jojoba"?
CLAIRE: It's something they put in for healthy hair.
CATHERINE: Hair is dead.
CLAIRE: What?
CATHERINE: It's dead tissue. You can't make it "healthy."
CLAIRE: Whatever, it's something that's good for your hair.
CATHERINE: What, a chemical?
CLAIRE: No, it's organic.
CATHERINE: Well it can be organic and still be a chemical.
CLAIRE: I don't know what it is.
CATHERINE: Haven't you ever heard of organic chemistry?
CLAIRE: It makes my hair feel, look, and smell good. That's the extent of my information about it. You might like it if you decide to use it.
CATHERINE: Thanks, I'll try it.
CLAIRE: Good. *(Beat.)* If the dress doesn't fit we can go downtown and exchange it.
CATHERINE: Okay.
CLAIRE: I'll take you to lunch.
CATHERINE: Great.
CLAIRE: Maybe Sunday before I go back. Do you need anything?
CATHERINE: Like clothes?
CLAIRE: Or anything. While I'm here.
CATHERINE: Nah, I'm cool.

Beat.

CLAIRE: I thought we'd have some people over tonight. If you're feeling okay.
CATHERINE: I'm feeling okay, Claire, stop saying that.
CLAIRE: You don't have any plans?
CATHERINE: No.
CLAIRE: I ordered some food. Wine, beer.

CATHERINE: We are burying Dad this afternoon.

CLAIRE: I think it will be all right. Anyone who's been to the funeral and wants to come over for something to eat can. And it's the only time I can see any old Chicago friends. It'll be nice. It's a funeral but we don't have to be completely grim about it. *If* it's okay with you.

CATHERINE: Yes, sure.

CLAIRE: It's been a stressful time. It would be good to relax in a low-key way. Mitch says Hi.

CATHERINE: Hi Mitch.

CLAIRE: He's really sorry he couldn't come.

CATHERINE: Yeah, he's gonna miss all the fun.

CLAIRE: He wanted to see you. He sends his love. I told him you'd see him soon enough. *(Beat.)* We're getting married.

CATHERINE: No shit.

CLAIRE: Yes! We just decided.

CATHERINE: Yikes.

CLAIRE: Yes!

CATHERINE: When?

CLAIRE: January.

CATHERINE: Huh.

CLAIRE: We're not going to do a huge thing. His folks are gone too. Just City Hall, then a big dinner at our favorite restaurant for all our friends. And you, of course. I hope you'll be in the wedding.

CATHERINE: Yeah. Of course. Congratulations, Claire, I'm really happy for you.

CLAIRE: Thanks. Me too. We just decided it was time. His job is great. I just got promoted . . .

CATHERINE: Huh.

CLAIRE: You will come?

CATHERINE: Yes, sure. January? I mean, I don't have to check my calendar or anything. Sure.

CLAIRE: That makes me very happy. *(Beat. From here on Claire treads gingerly.)*

CLAIRE: How are you?

CATHERINE: Okay.

CLAIRE: How are you feeling about everything?

CATHERINE: About "everything"?

CLAIRE: About Dad.

CATHERINE: What about him?

CLAIRE: How are you feeling about his death? Are you all right?

CATHERINE: Yes, I am.

CLAIRE: Honestly?

CATHERINE: Yes.

CLAIRE: I think in some ways it was the "right time." If there is ever a right time. Do you know what you want to do now?

CATHERINE: No.

CLAIRE: Do you want to stay here?

CATHERINE: I don't know.
CLAIRE: Do you want to go back to school?
CATHERINE: I haven't thought about it.
CLAIRE: Well there's a lot to think about.
How do you feel?
CATHERINE: Physically? Great. Except my hair seems kind of unhealthy, I wish there were something I could do about that.
CLAIRE: Come on, Catherine.
CATHERINE: What is the point of all these questions?

Beat.

CLAIRE: Katie, some policemen came by while you were in the shower.
CATHERINE: Yeah?
CLAIRE: They said they were "checking up" on things here. Seeing how everything was this morning.
CATHERINE: *(neutral)* That was nice.
CLAIRE: They told me they responded to a call last night and came to the house.
CATHERINE: Yeah?
CLAIRE: Did you call the police last night?
CATHERINE: Yeah.
CLAIRE: Why?
CATHERINE: I thought the house was being robbed.
CLAIRE: But it wasn't.
CATHERINE: No. I changed my mind.

Beat.

CLAIRE: First you call 911 with an emergency and then you hang up on them—
CATHERINE: I didn't really want them to come.
CLAIRE: So why did you call?
CATHERINE: I was trying to get this guy out of the house.
CLAIRE: Who?
CATHERINE: One of Dad's students.
CLAIRE: Dad hasn't had any students for years.
CATHERINE: No, he *was* Dad's student. Now he's—he's a mathematician.
CLAIRE: Why was he in the house in the first place?
CATHERINE: Well he's been coming here to look at Dad's notebooks.
CLAIRE: In the middle of the night?
CATHERINE: It was late. I was waiting for him to finish, and last night I thought he might have been stealing them.
CLAIRE: Stealing the notebooks.
CATHERINE: *Yes*. So I told him to go.
CLAIRE: Was he stealing them?
CATHERINE: Yes. That's why I called the police—
CLAIRE: What is this man's name?
CATHERINE: Hal. Harold. Harold Dobbs.

CLAIRE: The police said you were the only one here.

CATHERINE: He left before they got here.

CLAIRE: With the notebooks?

CATHERINE: No, Claire, don't be stupid, there are over a hundred notebooks. He was only stealing *one*, but he was stealing it so he could give it *back* to me, so I let him go so he could play with his band on the north side.

CLAIRE: His band?

CATHERINE: He was late. He wanted me to come with him but I was like, Yeah, right.

Beat.

CLAIRE: *(gently)* Is "Harold Dobbs" your boyfriend?

CATHERINE: No!

CLAIRE: Are you sleeping with him?

CATHERINE: What? Euughh! No! He's a math geek!

CLAIRE: And he's in a band? A rock band?

CATHERINE: No, a marching band. He plays trombone. Yes, a rock band!

CLAIRE: What is the name of his band?

CATHERINE: How should I know?

CLAIRE: "Harold Dobbs" didn't tell you the name of his rock band?

CATHERINE: No. I don't know. Look in the paper. They were playing last night. They do a song called "Imaginary Number" that doesn't exist.

Beat.

CLAIRE: I'm sorry, I'm just trying to understand: is "Harold Dobbs"—

CATHERINE: Stop saying "Harold Dobbs."

CLAIRE: Is this . . . person . . .

CATHERINE: *Harold Dobbs exists.*

CLAIRE: I'm sure he does.

CATHERINE: He's a mathematician at the University of Chicago. Call the fucking math department.

CLAIRE: Don't get upset. I'm just trying to understand! I mean if you found out some creepy grad student was trying to take some of Dad's papers and you called the police, I'd understand, and if you were out here partying, drinking with your boyfriend, I'd understand. But the two stories don't go together.

CATHERINE: Because you made up the "boyfriend" story. I was here *alone*.

CLAIRE: Harold Dobbs wasn't here?

CATHERINE: No, he—*Yes,* he was here, but we weren't partying!

CLAIRE: You weren't drinking with him?

CATHERINE: No!

CLAIRE: *(She holds up the champagne bottle.)* This was sitting right here. Who were you drinking champagne with?

Catherine hesitates.

CATHERINE: With no one.

CLAIRE: Are you sure?

CATHERINE: Yes.

Beat.

CLAIRE: The police said you were abusive. *(Catherine doesn't say anything.)* They said you're lucky they didn't haul you in.

CATHERINE: These guys were assholes, Claire. They wouldn't go away. They wanted me to fill out a report . . .

CLAIRE: Were you abusive?

CATHERINE: This one cop kept spitting on me when he talked. It was disgusting.

CLAIRE: Did you use the word "dickhead"?

CATHERINE: Oh I don't remember.

CLAIRE: Did you tell one cop . . . to go fuck the other cop's mother?

CATHERINE: *No.*

CLAIRE: That's what they said.

CATHERINE: Not with that phrasing.

CLAIRE: Did you strike one of them?

CATHERINE: They were trying to come in the house!

CLAIRE: Oh my God.

CATHERINE: I might have *pushed* him a little.

CLAIRE: They said you were either drunk or disturbed.

CATHERINE: They wanted to come in here and *search my house*—

CLAIRE: *You* called *them*.

CATHERINE: Yes but I didn't actually *want* them to come. But they did come and then they started acting like they owned the place, pushing me around, calling me "girly," smirking at me, laughing: they were assholes.

CLAIRE: These guys seemed perfectly nice. They were off-duty and they took the trouble to come back here at the end of their shift to check up on you. They were very polite.

CATHERINE: Well people are nicer to you.

Beat.

CLAIRE: Katie. Would you like to come to New York?

CATHERINE: Yes, I told you, I'll come in January.

CLAIRE: You could come sooner. We'd love to have you. You could stay with us. It'd be fun.

CATHERINE: I don't want to.

CLAIRE: Mitch has become an *excellent* cook. It's like his hobby now. He buys all these gadgets. Garlic press, olive oil sprayer . . . Every night there's something new. Delicious, wonderful meals. The other day he made vegetarian chili!

CATHERINE: What the fuck are you talking about?

CLAIRE: Stay with us for a while. We would have so much fun.

Catherine: Thanks, I'm okay here.

Claire: Chicago is dead. New York is so much more fun, you can't believe it.

Catherine: The "fun" thing is really not where my focus is at the moment.

Claire: I think New York would be a really fun and . . . safe . . . place for you to—

Catherine: I don't need a safe place and I don't want to have any fun! I'm perfectly fine here.

Claire: You look tired. I think you could use some downtime.

Catherine: Downtime?

Claire: Katie, please. You've had a very hard time.

Catherine: I'm *perfectly okay*.

Claire: I think you're upset and exhausted.

Catherine: I was *fine* till you got here.

Claire: Yes, but you—

Hal: *(from off)* Catherine?

Claire: Who is that?

Beat. Hal enters.

Hal: Hey, I—

Catherine stands and points triumphantly at him.

Catherine: *Harold Dobbs!*

Hal: *(confused)* Hi.

Catherine: *Okay?* I really don't need this, Claire. I'm fine, you know, I'm totally fine, and then you swoop in here with these questions, and "Are you okay?" and your soothing tone of voice and "Oh, the poor policemen"—I think the police can handle themselves!—and bagels and bananas and jojoba and "Come to New York" and vegetarian *chili*. I mean it really pisses me off so just *save* it.

Beat.

Claire: *(Smoothly, to Hal)* I'm Claire. Catherine's sister.

Hal: Oh, hi. Hal. Nice to meet you. *(Uncomfortable beat.)* I . . . hope it's not too early. I was just going to try to get some work done before the uh—if uh if . . .

Claire: Yes!

Catherine: Sure, okay.

Hal exits. A moment.

Claire: That's Harold Dobbs?

Catherine: Yes.

Claire: He's cute.

Catherine: *(disgusted)* Eugh.

Claire: He's a mathematician?

Catherine: I think you owe me an apology, Claire.

CLAIRE: We need to make some decisions. But I shouldn't have tried to start first thing in the morning. I don't want an argument. *(Beat.)* Maybe Hal would like a bagel?

Beat. Catherine doesn't take the hint. She exits.

Fade

SCENE 3

Night. Inside the house a party is in progress. Loud music from a not-very-good but enthusiastic band. Catherine is alone on the porch. She wears a flattering black dress. Inside, the band finishes a number. Cheers, applause. After a moment Hal comes out. He wears a dark suit. He has taken off his tie. He is sweaty and revved up from playing. He holds two bottles of beer. Catherine regards him. A beat.

CATHERINE: I feel that for a funeral reception this might have gotten a bit out of control.
HAL: Aw come on. It's great. Come on in.
CATHERINE: I'm okay.
HAL: We're done playing, I promise.
CATHERINE: No thanks.
HAL: Do you want a beer?
CATHERINE: I'm okay.
HAL: I brought you one.

Beat. Catherine hesitates.

CATHERINE: Okay. *(She takes it, sips.)* How many people are in there?
HAL: It's down to about forty.
CATHERINE: Forty?
HAL: Just the hardcore partyers.
CATHERINE: My sister's friends.
HAL: No, mathematicians. Your sister's friends left hours ago. The guys were really pleased to be asked to participate. They worshipped your dad.
CATHERINE: It was Claire's idea.
HAL: It was good.
CATHERINE: *(concedes)* The performance of "Imaginary Number" was . . . sort of . . . moving.
HAL: Good funeral. I mean not "good," but—
CATHERINE: No. Yeah.
HAL: Can you believe how many people came?
CATHERINE: I was surprised.
HAL: I think he would have liked it. *(Catherine looks at him.)* Sorry, it's not my place to—
CATHERINE: No, you're right. Everything was better than I thought.

Beat.

HAL: You look great.

Catherine: *(indicates the dress)* Claire gave it to me.

Hal: I like it.

Catherine: It doesn't really fit.

Hal: No, Catherine, it's good.

A moment. Noise from inside.

Catherine: When do you think they'll leave?

Hal: No way to know. Mathematicians are insane. I went to this conference in Toronto last fall. I'm young, right? I'm in shape, I thought I could hang with the big boys. Wrong. I've never been so exhausted in my life. Forty-eight straight hours of partying, drinking, drugs, papers, lectures . . .

Catherine: Drugs?

Hal: Yeah. Amphetamines mostly. I mean, I don't. Some of the older guys are really hooked.

Catherine: Really?

Hal: Yeah, they think they need it.

Catherine: Why?

Hal: They think math's a young man's game. Speed keeps them racing, makes them feel sharp. There's this fear that your creativity peaks around twenty-three and it's all downhill from there. Once you hit fifty it's over, you might as well teach high school.

Catherine: That's what my father thought.

Hal: I dunno. Some people stay prolific.

Catherine: Not many.

Hal: No, you're right. Really original work—it's all young guys.

Catherine: Young guys.

Hal: Young people.

Catherine: But it is men, mostly.

Hal: There are some women.

Catherine: Who?

Hal: There's a woman at Stanford, I can't remember her name.

Catherine: Sophie Germain.

Hal: Yeah? I've probably seen her at meetings, I just don't think I've met her.

Catherine: She was born in Paris in 1776.

Beat.

Hal: So I've definitely never met her.

Catherine: She was trapped in her house.

The French Revolution was going on, the Terror. She had to stay inside for safety and she passed the time reading in her father's study. The Greeks . . . Later she tried to get a real education but the schools didn't allow women. So she wrote letters. She wrote to Gauss. She used a man's name. Uh—Antoine-August Le Blanc. She sent him some proofs involving a certain kind of prime number, important work. He was delighted to correspond with such a brilliant young man. Dad gave me a book about her.

HAL: I'm stupid. Sophie Germain, of course.

CATHERINE: You know her?

HAL: Germain Primes.

CATHERINE: Right.

HAL: They're famous. Double them and add one, and you get another prime. Like two. Two is prime, doubled plus one is five: also prime.

CATHERINE: Right. Or $92{,}305 \times 2^{16{,}998} + 1$.

HAL: *(startled)* Right.

CATHERINE: That's the biggest one. The biggest one known . . .

Beat.

HAL: Did he ever find out who she was? Gauss.

CATHERINE: Yeah. Later a mutual friend told him the brilliant young man was a woman.

He wrote to her: "A taste for the mysteries of numbers is excessively rare, but when a person of the sex which, according to our customs and prejudices, must encounter infinitely more difficulties than men to familiarize herself with these thorny researches, succeeds nevertheless in penetrating the most obscure parts of them, then without a doubt she must have the noblest courage, quite extraordinary talents, and superior genius."

(Now self-conscious.) I memorized it . . .

Hal stares at her. He suddenly kisses her, then stops, embarrassed. He moves away.

HAL: Sorry. I'm a little drunk.

CATHERINE: It's okay. *(Uncomfortable beat.)* I'm sorry about yesterday.

I wasn't helpful. About the work you're doing. Take as long as you need upstairs.

HAL: You were fine. I was pushy.

CATHERINE: I was awful.

HAL: No. My timing was terrible. Anyway, you're probably right.

CATHERINE: What?

HAL: About it being junk.

CATHERINE: *(nods)* Yes.

HAL: I read through a lot of stuff today, just skimming. Except for the book I stole—

CATHERINE: Oh God, I'm sorry about that.

HAL: No, you were right.

CATHERINE: I shouldn't have called the police.

HAL: It was my fault.

CATHERINE: No.

HAL: The point is, that book—I'm starting to think it's the only lucid one, really. And there's no math in it.

CATHERINE: No.

HAL: I mean, I'll keep reading, but if I don't find anything in a couple of days . . .

CATHERINE: Back to the drums.

HAL: Yeah.

CATHERINE: And your own research.

HAL: Such as it is.

CATHERINE: What's wrong with it?

HAL: It's not exactly setting the world on fire.

CATHERINE: Oh come on.

HAL: It sucks, basically.

CATHERINE: Harold.

HAL: My papers get turned down. For the right reasons—my stuff is trivial. The big ideas aren't there.

CATHERINE: It's not about big ideas. It's work. You've got to chip away at a problem.

HAL: That's not what your dad did.

CATHERINE: I think it was, in a way. He'd attack a question from the side, from some weird angle, sneak up on it, grind away at it. He was slogging. He was just so much faster than anyone else that from the outside it looked magical.

HAL: I don't know.

CATHERINE: I'm just guessing.

HAL: Plus the work was beautiful. You can read it for pleasure. It's streamlined: no wasted moves, like a ninety-five-mile-an-hour fastball. It's just . . . elegant.

CATHERINE: Yeah.

HAL: And that's what you can never duplicate. At least I can't. It's okay. At a certain point you realize it's not going to happen, you readjust your expectations. I enjoy teaching.

CATHERINE: You might come up with something.

HAL: I'm twenty-eight, remember? On the downhill slope.

CATHERINE: Have you tried speed? I've heard it helps.

HAL: *(laughs)* Yeah.

Beat.

CATHERINE: So, Hal.

HAL: Yeah?

CATHERINE: What do you do for sex?

HAL: What?

CATHERINE: At your conferences.

HAL: Uh, I uh—

CATHERINE: Isn't that why people hold conferences? Travel. Room service. Tax-deductible sex in big hotel beds.

HAL: *(laughs, nervous)* Maybe. I don't know.

CATHERINE: So what do you do? All you guys.

Beat. Is she flirting with him? Hal is not sure.

HAL: Well we are scientists.
CATHERINE: So?
HAL: So there's a lot of experimentation.
CATHERINE: *(laughs)* I see.

Beat. Catherine goes to him. She kisses him. A longer kiss. It ends. Hal is surprised and pleased.

HAL: Huh.
CATHERINE: That was nice.
HAL: Really?
CATHERINE: Yes.
HAL: Again?
CATHERINE: Yes.

Kiss.

HAL: I always liked you.
CATHERINE: You did?
HAL: Even before I knew you. I'd catch glimpses of you when you visited your dad's office at school. I wanted to talk to you, but I thought, No, you do not flirt with your doctoral adviser's daughter.
CATHERINE: Especially when your adviser's crazy.
HAL: Especially then.

Kiss.

CATHERINE: You came here once. Four years ago. Remember?
HAL: Sure. I can't believe you do. I was dropping off a draft of my thesis for your dad. Jesus I was nervous.
CATHERINE: You looked nervous.
HAL: I can't believe you remember that.
CATHERINE: I remember you. *(Kiss.)* I thought you seemed . . . not boring.

They continue to kiss.

Fade

SCENE 4

The next morning. Catherine alone on the porch, in a robe. Hal enters, half-dressed. He walks up behind her quietly. She hears him and turns.

HAL: How long have you been up?
CATHERINE: A while.
HAL: Did I oversleep?
CATHERINE: No.

Beat. Morning-after awkwardness.

HAL: Is your sister up?

CATHERINE: No. She's flying home in a couple hours. I should probably wake her.

HAL: Let her sleep. She was doing some pretty serious drinking with the theoretical physicists last night.

CATHERINE: I'll make her some coffee when she gets up.

Beat.

HAL: Sunday mornings I usually go out. Get the paper, have some breakfast.

CATHERINE: Okay.

Beat.

HAL: Do you want to come?

CATHERINE: Oh. No. I ought to stick around until Claire leaves.

HAL: All right. Do you mind if I stay?

CATHERINE: No. You can work if you want.

HAL: *(Taken aback)* Okay.

CATHERINE: Okay.

HAL: Should I?

CATHERINE: If you want to.

HAL: Do you want me to go?

CATHERINE: Do you want to go?

HAL: I want to stay here with you.

CATHERINE: Oh . . .

HAL: I want to spend the day with you if possible. I'd like to spend as much time with you as I can unless of course I'm coming on *way* too strong right now and scaring you in which case I'll begin backpedaling immediately . . . *(Catherine laughs. Her relief is evident; so is his. They kiss.)* How embarrassing is it if I say last night was wonderful?

CATHERINE: It's only embarrassing if I don't agree.

HAL: Uh, so . . .

CATHERINE: Don't be embarrassed. *(They kiss. After a moment she breaks off. She hesitates, making a decision. Then she takes a chain from around her neck. There is a key on the chain. She tosses it to Hal.)* Here.

HAL: What's this?

CATHERINE: It's a key.

HAL: Ah.

CATHERINE: Try it.

HAL: Where?

CATHERINE: Bottom drawer of the desk in my dad's office.

HAL: What's in there?

CATHERINE: There's one way to find out, Professor.

HAL: Now? *(Catherine shrugs. He laughs, unsure if this is a joke or not.)* Okay.

Hal kisses her quickly, then goes inside. Catherine smiles to herself. She is happy, on the edge of being giddy. Claire enters, hungover. She sits down, squinting.

CATHERINE: Good morning.

CLAIRE: Please don't yell please!

CATHERINE: Are you all right?

CLAIRE: No. *(Beat. She clutches her head.)* Those fucking physicists.

CATHERINE: What happened?

CLAIRE: Thanks a *lot* for leaving me all alone with them.

CATHERINE: Where were your friends?

CLAIRE: My stupid friends left—it was only eleven o'clock!—they all had to get home and pay their babysitters or bake bread or something. I'm left alone with these lunatics . . .

CATHERINE: Why did you drink so much?

CLAIRE: I thought I could keep up with them. I thought they'd stop. They didn't. Oh God. "Have another tequila . . ."

CATHERINE: Do you want some coffee?

CLAIRE: In a minute. *(Beat.)* That *band*.

CATHERINE: Yeah.

CLAIRE: They were terrible.

CATHERINE: They were okay. They had fun. I think.

CLAIRE: Well as long as everyone had fun. *(Beat.)* Your dress turned out all right.

CATHERINE: I love it.

CLAIRE: You do.

CATHERINE: Yeah, it's wonderful.

CLAIRE: I was surprised you even wore it.

CATHERINE: I love it, Claire. Thanks.

CLAIRE: *(surprised)* You're welcome. You're in a good mood.

CATHERINE: Should I not be?

CLAIRE: Are you kidding? No. I'm thrilled. *(Beat.)* I'm leaving in a few hours.

CATHERINE: I know.

CLAIRE: The house is a wreck. Don't clean it up yourself. I'll hire someone to come in.

CATHERINE: Thanks. You want your coffee?

CLAIRE: No, thanks.

CATHERINE: *(starting in)* It's no trouble.

CLAIRE: Hold on a sec, Katie. I just . . . *(She takes a breath.)* I'm leaving soon. I—

CATHERINE: You said. I know.

CLAIRE: I'd still like you to come to New York.

CATHERINE: Yes: January.

CLAIRE: I'd like you to move to New York.

CATHERINE: Move?

CLAIRE: Would you think about it? For me? You could stay with me and Mitch at first. There's plenty of room. Then you could get your own place. I've already scouted some apartments for you, really cute places.

CATHERINE: What would I do in New York?

CLAIRE: What are you doing here?

CATHERINE: I live here.

CLAIRE: You could do whatever you want. You could work, you could go to school.

CATHERINE: I don't know, Claire. This is pretty major.

CLAIRE: I realize that.

CATHERINE: I know you mean well. I'm just not sure what I want to do. I mean to be honest you were right yesterday. I do feel a little confused. I'm tired. It's been a pretty weird couple of years. I think I'd like to take some time to figure things out.

CLAIRE: You could do that in New York.

CATHERINE: And I could do it here.

CLAIRE: But it would be much easier for me to get you set up in an apartment in New York, and—

CATHERINE: I don't need an apartment, I'll stay in the house.

CLAIRE: We're selling the house.

Beat.

CATHERINE: What?

CLAIRE: We—I'm selling it.

CATHERINE: *When?*

CLAIRE: I'm hoping to do the paperwork this week. I know it seems sudden.

CATHERINE: No one was here looking at the place, who are you selling it to?

CLAIRE: The university. They've wanted the block for years.

CATHERINE: *I live here.*

CLAIRE: Honey, now that Dad's gone it doesn't make sense. It's in bad shape. It costs a fortune to heat. It's time to let it go. Mitch agrees, it's a very smart move. We're lucky, we have a great offer—

CATHERINE: Where am I supposed to live?

CLAIRE: Come to New York.

CATHERINE: I can't believe this.

CLAIRE: It'll be so good. You deserve a change. This would be a whole new adventure for you.

CATHERINE: Why are you doing this?

CLAIRE: I want to help.

CATHERINE: By kicking me out of my *house?*

CLAIRE: It was my house too.

CATHERINE: You haven't lived here for years.

CLAIRE: I know that. You were on your own. I really regret that, Katie.

CATHERINE: Don't.

CLAIRE: I know I let you down. I feel awful about it. Now I'm trying to help.

CATHERINE: You want to help *now?*

CLAIRE: Yes.

CATHERINE: Dad is dead.

CLAIRE: I know.

CATHERINE: He's dead. Now that he's dead you fly in for the weekend and decide you want to help? *You're late*. Where have you been?

CLAIRE: I —

CATHERINE: Where were you five years ago? You weren't helping then.

CLAIRE: I was working.

CATHERINE: I was *here*. I lived with him *alone*.

CLAIRE: I was working fourteen-hour days. I paid every bill here. I paid off the mortgage on this three-bedroom house while I was living in a studio in Brooklyn.

CATHERINE: You had your life. You got to finish school.

CLAIRE: You could have stayed in school!

CATHERINE: How?

CLAIRE: I would have done anything—I told you that. I told you a million times to do anything you wanted.

CATHERINE: What about Dad? Someone had to take care of him.

CLAIRE: He was ill. He should have been in a full-time professional-care situation.

CATHERINE: He didn't belong in the nuthouse.

CLAIRE: He might have been better off.

CATHERINE: How can you say that?

CLAIRE: This is where I'm meant to feel guilty, right?

CATHERINE: Sure, go for it.

CLAIRE: I'm heartless. My own father.

CATHERINE: He needed to be here. In his own house, near the university, near his students, near everything that made him happy.

CLAIRE: Maybe. Or maybe some real professional care would have done him more good than rattling around in a filthy house with *you* looking after him.

I'm sorry, Catherine, it's not your fault. It's my fault for letting you do it.

CATHERINE: I was right to keep him here.

CLAIRE: No.

CATHERINE: What about his remission? Four years ago. He was healthy for almost a year.

CLAIRE: And then he went right downhill again.

CATHERINE: He might have been worse in a hospital.

CLAIRE: And he *might* have been *better*. Did he ever do any work again?

CATHERINE: No.

CLAIRE: *No. (Beat.)* And you might have been better.

CATHERINE: *(keeping her voice under control)* Better than what?

CLAIRE: Living here with him didn't do you any good. You said that yourself. You had so much talent . . .

CATHERINE: You think I'm like Dad.

CLAIRE: I think you have some of his talent and some of his tendency toward . . . instability.

Beat.

Catherine: Claire, in addition to the "cute apartments" that you've "scouted" for me in New York, would you by any chance also have devoted some of your considerable energies toward scouting out another type of—

Claire: *No.*

Catherine: —living facility for your bughouse little sister?

Claire: *No!* Absolutely not. That is not what this is about.

Catherine: Don't lie to me, Claire. I'm smarter than you.

Beat.

Claire: The resources . . . I've investigated—

Catherine: Oh my *God.*

Claire: —if you *wanted* to, all I'm saying is, the doctors in New York and the people are the *best,* and they—

Catherine: *Fuck you.*

Claire: It would be entirely up to you. You wouldn't *live* anywhere, you can—

Catherine: I hate you.

Claire: Don't yell, please. Calm down.

Catherine: *I hate you.* I—

Hal enters, holding a notebook. Claire and Catherine stop suddenly. Beat.

Claire: What are you doing here? . . .

Claire stares at Catherine

Hal: How long have you known about this?

Catherine: A while.

Hal: Why didn't you tell me about it?

Catherine: I wasn't sure I wanted to.

Beat.

Hal: Thank you.

Catherine: You're welcome.

Claire: What's going on?

Hal: God, Catherine, thank you.

Catherine: I thought you'd like to see it.

Claire: What is it?

Hal: It's incredible.

Claire: What *is* it?

Hal: Oh, uh, it's a result. A proof. I mean it looks like a proof. I mean it is a proof, a very long proof, I haven't read it all of course, or checked it, I don't even know if I *could* check it, but if it *is* a proof of what I think it's a proof of, it's . . . a very . . . *important* . . . proof.

Claire: What does it prove?

Hal: It looks like it proves a theorem . . . a mathematical theorem about prime numbers, something mathematicians have been trying to prove since . . .

since there were mathematicians, basically. Most people thought it couldn't be done.

CLAIRE: Where did you find it?

HAL: In your father's desk. Cathy told me about it.

CLAIRE: You know what this is?

CATHERINE: Sure.

CLAIRE: Is it good?

CATHERINE: Yes.

HAL: It's historic. If it checks out.

CLAIRE: What does it say?

HAL: I don't know yet. I've just read the first few pages.

CLAIRE: But what does it mean?

HAL: It means that during a time when everyone thought your dad was crazy . . . or barely functioning . . . he was doing some of the most important mathematics in the world. If it checks out, it means you publish instantly. It means newspapers all over the world are going to want to talk to the person who found this notebook.

CLAIRE: Cathy.

HAL: Cathy.

CATHERINE: I didn't find it.

HAL: Yes you did.

CATHERINE: No.

CLAIRE: Well did you find it or did Hal find it?

HAL: I didn't find it.

CATHERINE: I didn't find it.

I wrote it.

Curtain

ACT 2

SCENE 1

Robert is alone on the porch. He sits quietly, enjoying a drink, the quiet, the September afternoon. A notebook nearby, unopened. He closes his eyes, apparently dozing. It is four years earlier than the events in Act One. Catherine enters quietly. She stands behind her father for a moment.

ROBERT: Hello.

CATHERINE: How did you know I was here?

ROBERT: I heard you.

CATHERINE: I thought you were asleep.

ROBERT: On an afternoon like this? No.

CATHERINE: Do you need anything?

ROBERT: No.

CATHERINE: I'm going to the store.

ROBERT: What's for dinner?

CATHERINE: What do you want?
ROBERT: Not spaghetti.
CATHERINE: All right.
ROBERT: Disgusting stuff.
CATHERINE: That's what I was going to make.
ROBERT: I had a feeling. Good thing I spoke up. You make it too much.
CATHERINE: What do you want?
ROBERT: What do you have a taste for?
CATHERINE: Nothing.
ROBERT: Nothing at all?
CATHERINE: I don't care. I thought pasta would be easy.
ROBERT: Pasta, oh God, don't even say the word "pasta." It sounds so hopeless, like surrender: "Pasta would be easy." Yes, yes, it would. Pasta. It doesn't *mean* anything. It's just a euphemism people invented when they got sick of eating spaghetti.
CATHERINE: Dad, what do you want to eat?
ROBERT: I don't know.
CATHERINE: Well I don't know what to get.
ROBERT: I'll shop.
CATHERINE: No.
ROBERT: I'll do it.
CATHERINE: No, Dad, rest.
ROBERT: I wanted to take a walk anyway.
CATHERINE: Are you sure?
ROBERT: Yes. What about a walk to the lake? You and me.
CATHERINE: All right.
ROBERT: I would love to go to the lake. Then on the way home we'll stop at the store, see what jumps out at us.
CATHERINE: It's warm. It would be nice, if you're up for it.
ROBERT: You're damn right I'm up for it. We'll work up an appetite. Give me ten seconds, let me put this stuff away and we're out the door.
CATHERINE: I'm going to school.

Beat.

ROBERT: When?
CATHERINE: I'm gonna start at Northwestern at the end of the month.
ROBERT: Northwestern?
CATHERINE: They were great about my credits. They're taking me in as a sophomore. I wasn't sure when to talk to you about it.
ROBERT: Northwestern?
CATHERINE: Yes.
ROBERT: What's wrong with Chicago?
CATHERINE: You still teach there. I'm sorry, it's too weird, taking classes in your department.
ROBERT: It's a long drive.

CATHERINE: Not that long, half an hour.
ROBERT: Still, twice a day . . .
CATHERINE: Dad, I'd live there.

Beat.

ROBERT: You'd actually want to live in Evanston?
CATHERINE: Yes. I'll still be close. I can come home whenever you want. You've been well—really well—for almost seven months. I don't think you need me here every minute of the day.

Beat.

ROBERT: This is all a done deal? You're in.
CATHERINE: Yes.
ROBERT: You're sure.
CATHERINE: *Yes.*
ROBERT: Who pays for it?
CATHERINE: They're giving me a free ride, Dad. They've been great.
ROBERT: On tuition, sure. What about food, books, clothes, gas, meals out—do you plan to have a social life?
CATHERINE: I don't know.
ROBERT: You gotta pay your own way on dates, at least the early dates, say the first three, otherwise they expect something.
CATHERINE: The money will be fine. Claire's gonna help out.
ROBERT: When did you talk to Claire?
CATHERINE: I don't know, a couple weeks ago.
ROBERT: You talk to her before you talk to me?
CATHERINE: There were a lot of details to work out. She was great, she offered to take care of all the expenses.
ROBERT: This is a big step. A different *city*—
CATHERINE: It's not even a long-distance phone call.
ROBERT: It's a huge place. They're serious up there. I mean serious. Yeah the football's a disaster but the math guys don't kid around. You haven't been in school. You sure you're ready? You can get buried up there.
CATHERINE: I'll be all right.
ROBERT: You're way behind.
CATHERINE: I know.
ROBERT: A year, at least.
CATHERINE: Thank you, *I know*. Look, I don't know if this is a good idea. I don't know if I can handle the work. I don't know if I can handle *any* of it.
ROBERT: For Chrissake, Catherine, you should have talked to me.
CATHERINE: Dad. Listen. If you ever . . . if for any reason it ever turned out that you needed me here full-time again—
ROBERT: *I won't.* That's not—
CATHERINE: I can always take a semester off, or—

Robert: No. Stop it. I just—the end of the *month?* Why didn't you say something before?

Catherine: Dad, come on. It took a while to set this up, and until recently, until very recently, you weren't—

Robert: You just said yourself I've been fine.

Catherine: Yes, but I didn't know—*I hoped,* but I didn't *know,* no one knew if this would last. I told myself to wait until I was sure about you. That you were feeling okay again. Consistently okay.

Robert: So I'm to take this conversation as a vote of confidence? I'm honored.

Catherine: Take it however you want. I believed you'd get better.

Robert: Well thank you very much.

Catherine: Don't thank me. I had to. I was living with you.

Robert: All right, that's enough, Catherine. Let's stay on the subject.

Catherine: This is the subject! There were *library books* upstairs stacked up to the ceiling, do you remember that? You were trying to decode *messages*—

Robert: The fucking books are gone, I took them back myself. Why do you bring that garbage up?

Knocking offstage. Beat. Catherine goes inside to answer the door. She returns with Hal. He carries a manila envelope. He is nervous.

Robert: Mr. Dobbs.

Hal: Hi. I hope it's not a bad time.

Robert: Yes it is, actually, you couldn't have picked worse.

Hal: Oh, I uh—

Robert: You interrupted an argument.

Hal: I'm sorry. I can come back.

Robert: It's all right. We needed a break.

Hal: Are you sure?

Robert: Yes. The argument was about dinner. We don't know what to eat. What's your suggestion?

A beat while Hal is on the spot.

Hal: Uh, there's a great pasta place not too far from here.

Robert: *No!*

Catherine: *(with Robert):* That is a *brilliant* idea.

Robert: Oh dear Jesus God, no.

Catherine: *(with Robert):* What's it called? Give me the address.

Robert: No! Sorry. Wrong answer, but thank you for trying.

Hal stands there, looking at both of them.

Hal: I can come back.

Robert: Stay. *(To Catherine.)* Where are you going?

Catherine: Inside.

Robert: What about dinner?

CATHERINE: What about him?

ROBERT: What are you doing here, Dobbs?

HAL: My timing sucks. I am really sorry.

ROBERT: Don't be silly.

HAL: I'll come to your office.

ROBERT: Stop. Sit down. Glad you're here. Don't let the dinner thing throw you, you'll bounce back. *(To Catherine.)* This should be easier. Let's back off the problem, let it breathe, come at it again when it's not looking.

CATHERINE: Fine. *(Exiting.)* Excuse me.

ROBERT: Sorry, I'm rude. Hal, this is my daughter Catherine. *(To Catherine.)* Don't go, have a drink with us. Catherine, Harold Dobbs.

CATHERINE: Hi.

HAL: Hi.

ROBERT: Hal is a grad student. He's doing his Ph.D., very promising stuff. Unfortunately for him, his work coincided with my return to the department and he got stuck with me.

HAL: No, no, it's been—I've been very lucky.

CATHERINE: How long have you been at U. of C.?

HAL: Well I've been working on my thesis for—

ROBERT: Hal's in our "Infinite" program. As he approaches completion of his dissertation, time approaches infinity. Would you like a drink, Hal?

HAL: Yes I would. And uh, with all due respect . . .

Hal hands Robert the envelope.

ROBERT: Really? *(He opens it and looks inside.)* You must have had an interesting few months.

HAL: *(cheerfully)* Worst summer of my life.

ROBERT: Congratulations.

HAL: It's just a draft. Based on everything we talked about last spring. *(Robert pours a drink. Hal babbles.)* I wasn't sure if I should wait till the quarter started, or if I should give it to you *now*, or hold off, do another draft, but I figured fuck it, I, I mean I just . . . let's just get it *over* with, so I thought I'd just come over and see if you were home, and—

ROBERT: Drink this.

HAL: Thanks. *(He drinks.)* I decided, I don't know, if it feels done, maybe it is.

ROBERT: Wrong. If it feels done, there are major errors.

HAL: Uh, I—

ROBERT: That's okay, that's good, we'll find them and fix them. Don't worry. You're on your way to a solid career, you'll be teaching younger, more irritating versions of yourself in no time.

HAL: Thank you.

ROBERT: Catherine's in the math department at Northwestern, Hal.

Catherine looks up, startled.

HAL: Oh, who are you working with?

CATHERINE: I'm just starting this fall. Undergrad.

ROBERT: She's starting in . . . three weeks?

CATHERINE: A little more.

Beat.

ROBERT: They have some good people at Northwestern. O'Donohue. Kaminsky.

CATHERINE: Yes.

ROBERT: They will work your ass off.

CATHERINE: I know.

ROBERT: You'll have to run pretty hard to catch up.

CATHERINE: I think I can do it.

ROBERT: Of course you can. *(Beat.)*

HAL: You must be excited.

CATHERINE: I am.

HAL: First year of school can be great.

CATHERINE: Yeah?

HAL: Sure, all the new people, new places, getting out of the house.

CATHERINE: *(Embarrassed)* Yes.

HAL: *(Embarrassed)* Or, no I—

ROBERT: Absolutely, getting the hell out of here, thank God, it's about time. I'll be glad to see the back of her.

CATHERINE: You will?

ROBERT: Of course. Maybe I want to have the place to myself for a while, did that ever occur to you? *(To Hal.)* It's awful the way children sentimentalize their parents. *(To Catherine.)* We could use some quiet around here.

CATHERINE: Oh don't worry, I'll come back. I'll be here every Sunday cooking up big vats of pasta to last you through the week.

ROBERT: And I'll drive up, strut around Evanston, embarrass you in front of your classmates.

CATHERINE: Good. So we'll be in touch.

ROBERT: Sure. And if you get stuck with a problem, give me a call.

CATHERINE: Okay. Same to you.

ROBERT: Fine. Make sure to get me your number. *(To Hal.)* I'm actually looking forward to getting some work done.

HAL: Oh, what are you working on?

ROBERT: Nothing. *(Beat.)* Nothing at the moment.

Which I'm glad of, really. This is the time of year when you don't want to be tied down to anything. You want to be outside. I love Chicago in September. Perfect skies. Sailboats on the water. Cubs losing. Warm, the sun still hot . . . with the occasional blast of Arctic wind to keep you on your toes, remind you of winter. Students coming back, bookstores full, everybody busy.

I was in a bookstore yesterday. Completely full, students buying books . . . browsing . . . Students do a hell of a lot of browsing, don't they? Just browsing. You see them shuffling around with their backpacks, goofing off, taking up space. You'd call it loitering except every once in a while they pick up a book and flip the pages: "browsing." I admire it. It's an honest way to kill an afternoon. In the back of a used bookstore, or going through a crate of somebody's old record albums — not looking for anything, just looking, what the hell, touching the old book jackets, seeing what somebody threw out, seeing what they underlined . . . Maybe you find something great, like an old thriller with a painted cover from the forties, or a textbook one of your professors used when *he* was a student — his name is written in it very carefully . . . Yeah, I like it. I like watching the students. Wondering what they're gonna buy, what they're gonna read. What kind of ideas they'll come up with when they settle down and get to work . . .

I'm not doing much right now. It does get harder. It's a stereotype that happens to be true, unfortunately for me — unfortunately for you, for all of us.

CATHERINE: Maybe you'll get lucky.

ROBERT: Maybe I will. Maybe you'll pick up where I left off.

CATHERINE: Don't hold your breath.

ROBERT: Don't underestimate yourself.

CATHERINE: Anyway.

Beat.

ROBERT: Another drink? Cathy? Hal?

CATHERINE: No thanks.

HAL: Thanks, I really should get going.

ROBERT: Are you sure?

HAL: Yes.

ROBERT: I'll call you when I've looked at this. Don't think about it till then. Enjoy yourself, see some movies.

HAL: Okay.

ROBERT: You can come by my office in a week. Call it—

HAL: The eleventh?

ROBERT: Yes, we'll . . . *(Beat. He turns to Catherine. Grave)* I am sorry. I used to have a pretty good memory for numbers. Happy birthday.

CATHERINE: Thank you.

ROBERT: I am so sorry. I'm embarrassed.

CATHERINE: Dad, don't be stupid.

ROBERT: I didn't get you anything.

CATHERINE: Don't worry about it.

ROBERT: I'm taking you out.

CATHERINE: You don't have to.

ROBERT: We are going out. I didn't want to shop and cook. Let's go to dinner. Let's get the hell out of this neighborhood. What do you want to eat? Let's go to the North Side. Or Chinatown. Or Greektown. I don't know what's good anymore.

CATHERINE: Whatever you want.

ROBERT: Whatever *you* want goddamnit, Catherine, it's your birthday.

Beat.

CATHERINE: Steak.

ROBERT: Steak. Yes.

CATHERINE: No, first beer, really cold beer. Really cheap beer.

ROBERT: Done.

CATHERINE: That Chicago beer that's watery with no flavor and you can just drink *gallons* of it.

ROBERT: They just pump the water out of Lake Michigan and bottle it.

CATHERINE: It's so awful.

ROBERT: I have a taste for it myself.

CATHERINE: Then the steak, grilled really black, and potatoes and creamed spinach.

ROBERT: I remember a place. If it's still there I think it will do the trick.

CATHERINE: And dessert.

ROBERT: That goes without saying. It's your birthday, hooray. And there's the solution to our dinner problem. Thank you for reminding me, Harold Dobbs.

CATHERINE: *(To Hal.)* We're being rude. Do you want to come?

HAL: Oh, no, I shouldn't.

ROBERT: Why not? Please, come.

CATHERINE: Come on.

A tiny moment between Hal and Catherine. Hal wavers, then

HAL: No, I can't, I have plans. Thank you, though. Happy birthday.

CATHERINE: Thanks. Well. I'll let you out.

ROBERT: I'll see you on the eleventh, Hal.

HAL: Great.

CATHERINE: I'm gonna change my clothes, Dad. I'll be ready in a sec.

Hal and Catherine exit. A moment. It's darker. Robert looks out at the evening. Eventually he picks up the notebook and a pen. He sits down. He opens to a blank page. He writes.

ROBERT: "September fourth. A good day . . ." *(He continues to write.)*

Fade

SCENE 2

Morning. An instant after the end of Act One: Catherine, Claire, and Hal.

HAL: You wrote this?

CATHERINE: Yes.

CLAIRE: You mean Dad dictated it to you?

CATHERINE: No, its my proof. It's mine, I wrote it.

CLAIRE: When?

CATHERINE: I started after I quit school. I finished a few months before Dad died.

CLAIRE: Did he see it?

CATHERINE: No. He didn't know I was working on it. It wouldn't have mattered to him anyway, he was too sick.

HAL: I don't understand—you did this by yourself?

CATHERINE: *Yes*.

CLAIRE: It's in Dad's notebook.

CATHERINE: I used one of his blank books. There were a bunch of them upstairs.

Beat.

CLAIRE: *(To Hal.)* Tell me exactly where you found this.

HAL: In his study.

CATHERINE: In his desk. I gave him the—

CLAIRE: *(To Catherine.)* Hold on. *(To Hal.)* Where did you find it?

HAL: In the bottom drawer of the desk in the study, a locked drawer: Catherine gave me the key.

CLAIRE: Why was the drawer locked?

CATHERINE: It's mine, it's the drawer I keep my private things in. I've used it for years.

CLAIRE: *(To Hal.)* Was there anything else in the drawer?

HAL: No.

CATHERINE: No, that's the only—

CLAIRE: Can I see it? *(Hal gives Claire the book. She pages through it. Beat.)* I'm sorry, I just . . . *(To Catherine.)* The book was in the . . . You told him where to find it . . . You gave him the key . . . You wrote this incredible thing and you didn't *tell* anyone?

CATHERINE: I'm telling you both now. After I dropped out of school I had nothing to do. I was depressed, really depressed, but at a certain point I decided, Fuck it, I don't need them. It's just math, I can do it on my own. So I kept working here. I worked at night, after Dad had gone to sleep. It was hard but I did it.

Beat.

CLAIRE: Catherine, I'm sorry but I just find this very hard to believe.

CATHERINE: Claire. I wrote. The proof.

CLAIRE: I'm sorry, I—

CATHERINE: Claire . . .

CLAIRE: This is Dad's handwriting.

CATHERINE: It's not.

CLAIRE: It looks exactly like it.

CATHERINE: It's my writing.

CLAIRE: I'm sorry—

CATHERINE: Ask Hal, he's been looking at Dad's writing for weeks.

Claire gives Hal the book. He looks at it. Beat.

HAL: I don't know.

CATHERINE: Hal, come on.

CLAIRE: What does it look like?

HAL: It looks . . . I don't know what Catherine's handwriting looks like.

CATHERINE: It *looks* like *that.*

HAL: Okay. It . . . Okay. *(Beat. He hands the book back.)*

CLAIRE: I think—you know what? I think it's early, and people are tired and not in the best state to make decisions about emotional things, so maybe we should all just take a breath . . .

CATHERINE: You don't believe me?

CLAIRE: I don't know. I really don't know anything about this.

CATHERINE: Never mind. I don't know why I expected you to believe me about *anything.*

CLAIRE: Could you *tell* us the proof? That would show it was yours.

CATHERINE: You wouldn't understand it.

CLAIRE: Tell it to Hal.

CATHERINE: *(taking the book)* We could talk through it together. It might take a while.

CLAIRE: *(taking the book)* You can't use the book.

CATHERINE: For God's sake, it's forty pages long. I didn't *memorize* it. It's not a muffin recipe.

This is stupid. It's my book, my writing, my key, my drawer, my proof. Hal, tell her!

HAL: Tell her what?

CATHERINE: Whose book is that?

HAL: I don't know.

CATHERINE: What is the matter with you? You've been looking at his other stuff, you know there's nothing even remotely like this!

HAL: Look, Catherine—

CATHERINE: We'll go through the proof together. We'll sit down—if Claire will *please* let me have my book back—

CLAIRE: *(giving her the book)* All right, talk him through it.

HAL: That might take days and it still wouldn't show that she wrote it.

CATHERINE: Why not?

HAL: Your dad might have written it and explained it to you later. I'm not saying he did, I'm just saying there's no proof that you wrote this.

CATHERINE: Of course there isn't, but come on! He didn't do this, he couldn't have. He didn't do any mathematics at all for years. Even in the good year he couldn't work: you *know* that. You're supposed to be a scientist.

Beat.

HAL: You're right. Okay. Here's my suggestion. I know three or four guys at the department, very sharp, disinterested people who knew your father, knew his work. Let me take this to them.

CATHERINE: What?

HAL: I'll tell them we've found something, something potentially major, we're not sure about the authorship; I'll sit down with them. We'll go through the thing carefully—

CLAIRE: Good.

HAL: —and figure out exactly what we've got. It would only take a couple of days, probably, and then we'd have a lot more information.

CLAIRE: I think that's an excellent suggestion.

CATHERINE: You can't.

CLAIRE: Catherine.

CATHERINE: No! You can't take it.

HAL: I'm not "taking" it.

CATHERINE: This is what you wanted.

HAL: Oh come on, Jesus.

CATHERINE: You don't waste any time, do you? No hesitation. You can't wait to show them your brilliant discovery.

HAL: I'm trying to determine what this is.

CATHERINE: I'm telling you what it is.

HAL: You don't know!

CATHERINE: *I wrote it.*

HAL: *It's your father's handwriting. (Beat. Pained.)* At least it looks an awful lot like the writing in the other books. Maybe your writing looks exactly like his, I don't know.

CATHERINE: *(softly)* It does look like his. I didn't show this to anyone else. I could have. I wanted you to be the first to see it. I didn't know I wanted that until last night. It's *me*. I trusted you.

HAL: I know.

CATHERINE: Was I wrong?

HAL: No. I—

CATHERINE: I should have known she wouldn't believe me but why don't you?

HAL: This is one of his notebooks. The exact same kind he used.

CATHERINE: I told you. I just used one of his blank books. There were extras.

HAL: There aren't any extra books in the study.

CATHERINE: There were when I started writing the proof. I bought them for him. He must have used the rest up later.

HAL: And the writing.

CATHERINE: You want to test the handwriting?

HAL: No. It doesn't matter. He could have dictated it to you for Chrissake. It still doesn't make sense.

CATHERINE: Why not?

HAL: I'm a mathematician.

CATHERINE: Yes.

HAL: I know how hard it would be to come up with something like this. I mean it's impossible. You'd have to be . . . you'd have to be your dad, basically. Your dad at the peak of his powers.

CATHERINE: I'm a mathematician too.

HAL: Not like your dad.

CATHERINE: Oh, he's the only one who could have done this?

HAL: The only one I know.

CATHERINE: Are you sure?

HAL: Your father was the most—

CATHERINE: Just because you and the rest of the geeks worshipped him doesn't mean he wrote this proof, Hal!

HAL: He was the *best.* My generation hasn't produced anything like him. He revolutionized the field twice before he was twenty-two. I'm sorry, Catherine, but you took some classes at Northwestern for a few months.

CATHERINE: My education wasn't at Northwestern. It was living in this house for twenty-five years.

HAL: Even so, it doesn't matter. This is too advanced. I don't even understand most of it.

CATHERINE: You think it's too advanced.

HAL: Yes.

CATHERINE: It's too advanced for *you.*

HAL: You could not have done this work.

CATHERINE: But what if I did?

HAL: Well what if?

CATHERINE: It would be a real disaster for you, wouldn't it? And for the other geeks who *barely* finished their Ph.D.'s, who are marking time doing *lame* research, bragging about the conferences they go to—*wow*—playing in an *awful* band, and whining that they're intellectually past it at twenty-eight, *because they are.*

Beat. Hal hesitates, then abruptly exits. Beat. Catherine is furious and so upset she looks dazed.

CLAIRE: Katie. Let's go inside. Katie?

Catherine opens the book, tries to rip out the pages, destroy it. Claire goes to take it from her. They struggle. Catherine gets the book away. They stand apart, breathing hard. After a moment, Catherine throws the book to the floor. She exits.

Fade

SCENE 3

The next day. The porch is empty. Knocking off. No one appears. After a moment Hal comes around the side of the porch and knocks on the back door.

HAL: Catherine?

Claire enters.

HAL: I thought you were leaving.
CLAIRE: I had to delay my flight.

Beat.

HAL: Is Catherine here?
CLAIRE: I don't think this is a good time, Hal.
HAL: Could I see her?
CLAIRE: Not now.
HAL: What's the matter?
CLAIRE: She's sleeping.
HAL: Can I wait here until she gets up?
CLAIRE: She's been sleeping since yesterday. She won't get up. She won't eat, won't talk to me. I couldn't go home. I'm going to wait until she seems okay to travel.
HAL: Jesus, I'm sorry.
CLAIRE: Yes.
HAL: I'd like to talk to her.
CLAIRE: I don't think that's a good idea.
HAL: Has she said anything?
CLAIRE: About you? No.
HAL: Yesterday . . . I know I didn't do what she wanted.
CLAIRE: Neither of us did.
HAL: I didn't know what to say. I feel awful.
CLAIRE: Why did you sleep with her?

Beat.

HAL: I'm sorry, that's none of your business.
CLAIRE: Bullshit. I have to take care of her. It's a little bit harder with you jerking her around.
HAL: I wasn't jerking her around. It just happened.
CLAIRE: Your timing was not great.
HAL: It wasn't *my* timing, it was *both* of our—
CLAIRE: Why'd you do it? You know what she's like. She's fragile and you took advantage of her.
HAL: No. It's what we both wanted. I didn't mean to hurt her.
CLAIRE: You did.
HAL: I'd like to talk to Catherine, please.
CLAIRE: You can't.
HAL: Are you taking her away?
CLAIRE: Yes.
HAL: To New York.

CLAIRE: Yes.

HAL: Just going to drag her to New York.

CLAIRE: If I have to.

HAL: Don't you think she should have some say in whether or not she goes?

CLAIRE: If she's not going to speak, what else can I do?

HAL: Let me try. Let me talk to her.

CLAIRE: Hal, give up. This has nothing to do with you.

HAL: I know her. She's tougher than you think, Claire.

CLAIRE: What?

HAL: She can handle herself. She can handle talking to me—maybe it would help. Maybe she'd like it.

CLAIRE: Maybe she'd *like* it? Are you out of your *mind?* You're the reason she's up there right now! You have *no idea* what she needs. You don't know her! She's my sister. Jesus, you fucking mathematicians: you *don't think*. You don't know what you're doing. You stagger around creating these catastrophes and it's people like me who end up flying in to clean them up. *(Beat.)* She needs to get out of Chicago, out of this house. I'll give you my number in New York. You can call her once she's settled there. That's it, that's the deal.

HAL: Okay. *(Beat. He doesn't move.)*

CLAIRE: I don't mean to be rude but I have a lot to do.

HAL: There's one more thing. You're not going to like it.

CLAIRE: Sure, take the notebook.

HAL: *(startled)* I—

CLAIRE: Hold on a sec, I'll get it for you. *(She goes inside and returns with the notebook. She gives it to Hal.)*

HAL: I thought this would be harder.

CLAIRE: Don't worry, I understand. It's very sweet you want to see Catherine but of course you'd like to see the notebook too.

HAL: *(Huffy)* It's—No, it's my responsibility—as a professional I can't turn my back on the necessity of the—

CLAIRE: Relax. I don't care. Take it. What would I do with it?

HAL: You sure?

CLAIRE: Yes, of course.

HAL: You trust me with this?

CLAIRE: Yes.

HAL: You just said I don't know what I'm doing.

CLAIRE: I think you're a little bit of an idiot but you're not dishonest. Someone needs to figure out what's in there. I can't do it. It should be done here, at Chicago: my father would like that. When you decide what we've got let me know what the family should do.

HAL: Thanks.

CLAIRE: Don't thank me, it's by far the most convenient option available. I put my card in there, call me whenever you want.

HAL: Okay.

Hal starts to exit. Claire hesitates, then

CLAIRE: Hal.

HAL: Yeah?

CLAIRE: Can you tell me about it? The proof. I'm just curious.

HAL: It would take some time. How much math have you got?

Beat.

CLAIRE: I'm a currency analyst. It helps to be very quick with numbers. I am. I probably inherited about one one-thousandth of my father's ability. It's enough.

Catherine got more. I'm not sure how much.

Fade

SCENE 4

Winter. About three and a half years earlier. Robert is on the porch. He wears a T-shirt. He writes in a notebook. After a moment we hear Catherine's voice from offstage.

CATHERINE: Dad? (*She enters wearing a parka. She sees her father and stops.*) What are you doing out here?

ROBERT: Working.

CATHERINE: It's December. It's thirty degrees.

ROBERT: I know.

Catherine stares at him, baffled.

CATHERINE: Don't you need a coat?

ROBERT: Don't you think I can make that assessment for myself?

Beat.

CATHERINE: Aren't you cold?

ROBERT: Of course I am! I'm freezing my ass off!

CATHERINE: So what are you *doing* out here?

ROBERT: Thinking! Writing!

CATHERINE: You're gonna freeze.

ROBERT: It's too hot in the house. The radiators dry out the air. Also the clanking—I can't concentrate. If the house weren't so old, we'd have central air heating, but we don't, so I have to come out here to get any work done.

CATHERINE: I'll turn off the radiators. They won't make any noise. Come inside, it isn't safe.

ROBERT: I'm okay.

CATHERINE: I've been calling. Didn't you hear the phone?

ROBERT: It's a distraction.

CATHERINE: I didn't know what was going on. I had to drive all the way down here.

ROBERT: I can see that.

CATHERINE: I had to skip class. (*She brings Robert a coat and he puts it on.*) Why don't you answer the phone?

ROBERT: Well I'm sorry, Catherine, but it's a question of priorities, and work takes priority, you know that.

CATHERINE: You're working?

ROBERT: Goddamnit, I am working! I say "I"—The machinery. The machinery is working. Catherine, it's on full-blast. All the cylinders are firing, I'm on fire. That's why I came out here, to cool off. I haven't felt like this for years.

CATHERINE: You're kidding.

ROBERT: No!

CATHERINE: I don't believe it.

ROBERT: I don't believe it either! But it's true. It started about a week ago. I woke up, came downstairs, made a cup of coffee, and before I could pour in the milk it was like someone turned the *light* on in my head.

CATHERINE: Really?

ROBERT: Not the light, the whole *power grid. I lit up*, and it's like no time has passed since I was twenty-one.

CATHERINE: You're kidding!

ROBERT: No! I'm back! I'm back in touch with the source—the font, the—whatever the source of my creativity was all those years ago. I'm in contact with it again. I'm *sitting* on it. It's a geyser and I'm shooting right up into the air on top of it.

CATHERINE: My God.

ROBERT: I'm not talking about divine inspiration. It's not funneling down into my head and onto the page. It'll take *work* to shape these things; I'm not saying it won't be a tremendous amount of work. It *will* be a tremendous amount of work. It's not going to be easy. But the raw material is there. It's like I've been driving in traffic and now the lanes are opening up before me and I can *accelerate*. I see whole landscapes—places for the work to go, new techniques, revolutionary possibilities. I'm going to get whole branches of the profession talking to each other. I—I'm sorry, I'm being rude. How's school?

CATHERINE: *(taken aback)* Fine.

ROBERT: You're working hard?

CATHERINE: Sure.

ROBERT: Faculty treating you all right?

CATHERINE: Yes. Dad—

ROBERT: Made any friends?

CATHERINE: Of course. I—

ROBERT: Dating?

CATHERINE: Dad, hold on.

ROBERT: No details necessary if you don't want to provide them. I'm just interested.

CATHERINE: School's great. I want to talk about what you're doing.

ROBERT: Great, let's talk.

CATHERINE: This work.

ROBERT: Yes.

CATHERINE: *(indicating the notebooks)* Is it here?

ROBERT: Part of it, yes.

CATHERINE: Can I see it?

ROBERT: It's all at a very early stage.

CATHERINE: I don't mind.

ROBERT: Nothing's actually complete, to be honest. It's all in progress. I think we're talking years.

CATHERINE: That's okay. I don't care. Just let me see anything.

ROBERT: You really want to?

CATHERINE: Yes.

ROBERT: You're genuinely interested.

CATHERINE: Dad, of course!

ROBERT: Of course. It's your field.

CATHERINE: Yes.

ROBERT: You know how happy that makes me.

Beat.

CATHERINE: Yes.

ROBERT: I think there's enough here to keep me working the rest of my life.

Not just me.

I was starting to imagine I was finished, Catherine. Really finished. Don't get me wrong, I was grateful I could go to my office, have a life, but secretly I was terrified I'd never work again. Did you know that?

CATHERINE: I wondered.

ROBERT: I was absolutely fucking terrified.

Then I remembered something and a part of the terror went away. I remembered you.

Your creative years were just beginning. You'd get your degree, do your own work. You were just getting started. If you hadn't gone into math, that would have been all right. Claire's done well for herself. I'm satisfied with her.

I'm proud of you.

I don't mean to embarrass you. It's part of the reason we have children. We hope they'll survive us, accomplish what we can't.

Now that I'm back in the game I admit I've got another idea, a better one.

CATHERINE: What?

ROBERT: I know you've got your own work. I don't want you to neglect that. You can't neglect it. But I could probably use some help. Work with me. If you want to, if you can work it out with your class schedule and everything else, I could help you with that, make some calls, talk to your teachers . . .

I'm getting ahead of myself.

Well, Jesus, look, enough bullshit. You asked to see something. Let's start with this. I've roughed something out. General outline for a proof. Major result. Important. It's not finished but you can see where it's going. Let's see. *(He selects a notebook.)* Here. *(He gives it to Catherine. She opens it and reads.)* It's very rough.

After a long moment Catherine closes the notebook. A beat. She sits down next to Robert.

CATHERINE: Dad. Let's go inside.

ROBERT: The gaps might make it hard to follow. We can talk it through.

CATHERINE: You're cold. Let's go in.

ROBERT: Maybe we could work on this together. This might be a great place to start. What about it? What do you think? Let's talk it through.

CATHERINE: Not now. I'm cold too. It's really freezing out here. Let's go inside.

ROBERT: I'm telling you it's stifling in there, goddamn it. The radiators. Look, read out the first couple of lines. That's how we start: you read, and we go line by line, out loud, through the argument. See if there's a better way, a shorter way. Let's collaborate.

CATHERINE: No. Come on.

ROBERT: I've been waiting years for this. This is something I want to do. Come on, let's do some work together.

CATHERINE: We can't do it out here. It's freezing cold. I'm taking you in.

ROBERT: Not until we *talk about the proof.*

CATHERINE: No.

ROBERT: *Goddamnit, Catherine, open the goddamn book and read me the lines.*

Beat. Catherine, opens the book. She reads slowly, without inflection.

CATHERINE: "Let X equal the quantity of all quantities of X. Let X equal the cold. It is cold in December. The months of cold equal November through February. There are four months of cold and four of heat, leaving four months of indeterminate temperature. In February it snows. In March the lake is a lake of ice. In September the students come back and the bookstores are full. Let X equal the month of full bookstores. The number of books approaches infinity as the number of months of cold approaches four. I will never be as cold now as I will in the future. The future of cold is infinite. The future of heat is the future of cold. The bookstores are infinite and so are never full except in September . . ." *(She stops reading and slowly closes the book. Robert is shivering uncontrollably. She puts her arms around him and helps him to his feet.)* It's all right. We'll go inside.

ROBERT: I'm cold.

CATHERINE: We'll warm you up.

ROBERT: Don't leave. Please.

CATHERINE: I won't. Let's go inside.

Fade

SCENE 5

The present. A week after the events in Scene 3. Claire on the porch. Coffee in takeout cups. Claire takes a plane ticket out of her purse, checks the itinerary. A moment. Catherine enters with bags for travel. Claire gives her a cup of coffee. Catherine drinks in silence. Beat.

CATHERINE: Good coffee.

CLAIRE: It's all right, isn't it? *(Beat.)* We have a place where we buy all our coffee. They roast it themselves, they have an old roaster down in the basement. You can smell it on the street. Some mornings you can smell it from our place, four stories up. It's wonderful. "Manhattan's Best": some magazine wrote it up. Who knows. But it is very good.

CATHERINE: Sounds good.

CLAIRE: You'll like it.

CATHERINE: Good.

Beat.

CLAIRE: You look nice.

CATHERINE: Thanks, so do you.

Beat.

CLAIRE: It's bright.

CATHERINE: Yes.

CLAIRE: It's one of the things I do miss. All the space, the light. You could sit out here all morning.

CATHERINE: It's not that warm.

CLAIRE: Are you cold?

CATHERINE: Not really. I just—

CLAIRE: It has gotten chilly. I'm sorry. Do you want to go in?

CATHERINE: I'm okay.

CLAIRE: I just thought it might be nice to have a quick cup of coffee out here.

CATHERINE: No, it is.

CLAIRE: Plus the kitchen's all put away. If you're cold—

CATHERINE: I'm not. Not really.

CLAIRE: Want your jacket?

CATHERINE: Yeah, okay. *(Claire gives it to her. She puts it on.)* Thanks.

CLAIRE: It's that time of year.

CATHERINE: Yes. You can feel it coming. *(Beat. She stares out at the yard.)*

CLAIRE: Honey, there's no hurry.

CATHERINE: I know.

CLAIRE: If you want to hang out, be alone for a while—

CATHERINE: No. It's no big deal.

CLAIRE: We don't have to leave for twenty minutes or so.

CATHERINE: I know. Thanks, Claire.

CLAIRE: You're all packed.

CATHERINE: Yes.

CLAIRE: If you missed anything it doesn't really matter. The movers will send us everything next month. *(Catherine doesn't move. Beat.)* I know this is hard.

CATHERINE: It's fine.

CLAIRE: This is the right decision.

CATHERINE: I know . . .

Claire: I want to do everything I can to make this a smooth transition for you. So does Mitch.

Catherine: Good.

Claire: The actual departure is the hardest part. Once we get there we can relax. Enjoy ourselves.

Catherine: I know.

Beat.

Claire: You'll love New York.

Catherine: I can't wait.

Claire: You'll love it. It's the most exciting city.

Catherine: I know.

Claire: It's not like Chicago, it's really alive.

Catherine: I've read about that.

Claire: I think you'll truly feel at home there.

Catherine: You know what I'm looking forward to?

Claire: What?

Catherine: Seeing Broadway musicals.

Beat.

Claire: Mitch can get us tickets to whatever you'd like.

Catherine: And Rockefeller Center in winter—all the skaters!

Claire: Well, you—

Catherine: Also, the many fine museums!

Beat.

Claire: I know how hard this is for you.

Catherine: Listening to you say how hard it is for me is what's hard for me.

Claire: Once you're there you'll see all the possibilities that are available.

Catherine: Restraints, lithium, electroshock.

Claire: *Schools*. In the New York area alone there's NYU, Columbia—

Catherine: Bright college days! Football games, road trips, necking on the "quad."

Claire: Or if that's not what you want we can help you find a job. Mitch has terrific contacts all over town.

Catherine: Does he know anyone in the phone-sex industry?

Claire: I want to make this as easy a transition as I can.

Catherine: It's going to be *easy*, Claire, it's gonna be so fucking easy you won't believe it.

Claire: Thank you.

Catherine: I'm going to sit quietly on the plane to New York. And live quietly in a cute apartment. And answer Dr. Von Heimlich's questions very politely.

Claire: You can see any doctor you like, or you can see no doctor.

Catherine: I would like to see a doctor called Dr. Von Heimlich: please find one. And I would like him to wear a monocle. And I'd like him to have a very soft, very well-upholstered couch, so that I'll be perfectly comfortable while I'm blaming everything on you.

Beat.

CLAIRE: Don't come.

CATHERINE: No, I'm coming.

CLAIRE: Stay here, see how you do.

CATHERINE: I could.

CLAIRE: You can't take care of yourself for *five days*.

CATHERINE: Bullshit!

CLAIRE: You *slept all week*. I had to cancel my flight. I missed a week of work—I was this close to taking you to the hospital! I couldn't believe it when you finally dragged yourself up.

CATHERINE: I was tired!

CLAIRE: You were completely out of it, Catherine, you weren't speaking!

CATHERINE: I didn't want to talk to you.

Beat.

CLAIRE: Stay here if you hate me so much.

CATHERINE: And do what?

CLAIRE: You're the genius, figure it out.

Claire is upset, near tears. She digs in her bag, pulls out a plane ticket, throws it on the table. She exits. Catherine is alone. She can't quite bring herself to leave the porch. A moment. Hal enters—not through the house, from the side. He is badly dressed and looks very tired. He is breathless from running.

HAL: You're still here. *(Catherine is surprised. She doesn't speak.)* I saw Claire leaving out front. I wasn't sure if you—*(He holds up the notebook.)* This fucking thing . . . checks out.

I have been over it, *twice*, with two different sets of guys, old geeks *and* young geeks. It is *weird*. I don't know where the techniques came from. Some of the moves are very hard to follow. But we can't find anything wrong with it! There might be something wrong with it but we can't find it. I have not slept. *(He catches his breath.)* It works. I thought you might want to know.

CATHERINE: I already knew.

Beat.

HAL: I had to swear these guys to secrecy. They were jumping out of their skins. See, one e-mail and it's all over. I threatened them. I think we're safe, they're physical cowards. *(Beat.)* I had to see you.

CATHERINE: I'm leaving.

HAL: I know. Just wait for a minute, please?

CATHERINE: What do you want? You have the book. She told me you came by for it and she gave it to you. You can do whatever you want with it. Publish it.

HAL: Catherine.

CATHERINE: Get Claire's permission and publish it. She doesn't care. She doesn't know anything about it anyway.

Hal: I don't want Claire's permission.

Catherine: You want mine? Publish. Go for it. Have a press conference. Tell the world what my father discovered.

Hal: I don't want to.

Catherine: Or fuck my father, pass it off as your own work. Who cares? Write your own ticket to any math department in the country.

Hal: I don't think your father wrote it.

Beat.

Catherine: You thought so last week.

Hal: That was last week. I spent this week reading the proof. I think I understand it, more or less. It uses a lot of newer mathematical techniques, things that were developed in the last decade. Elliptic curves. Modular forms. I think I learned more mathematics this week than I did in four years of grad school.

Catherine: So?

Hal: So the proof is very . . . hip.

Catherine: Get some sleep, Hal.

Hal: What was your father doing the last ten years? He wasn't well, was he?

Catherine: Are you done?

Hal: I don't think he would have been able to master those new techniques.

Catherine: But he was a genius.

Hal: But he was nuts.

Catherine: So he read about them later.

Hal: Maybe. The books he would have needed are upstairs.

Beat.

Your dad dated everything. Even his most incoherent entries he dated. There are no dates in this.

Catherine: The handwriting—

Hal: —looks like your dad's. Parents and children sometimes have similar handwriting, especially if they've spent a lot of time together.

Beat.

Catherine: Interesting theory.

Hal: I like it.

Catherine: I like it too. It's what I told you last week.

Hal: I know.

Catherine: You blew it.

Hal: I—

Catherine: It's too bad, the rest of it was really good. All of it: "I loved your dad." "I always liked you." "I'd like to spend every minute with you . . ." It's killer stuff. You got laid *and* you got the notebook! You're a genius!

Hal: You're giving me way too much credit. *(Beat.)* I don't expect you to be happy with me. I just wanted . . . I don't know. I was hoping to discuss some of this with you before you left. Purely professional. I don't expect anything else.

CATHERINE: Forget it.

HAL: I mean we have questions. Working on this must have been amazing. I'd love just to hear you talk about some of it.

CATHERINE: No.

HAL: You'll have to deal with it eventually, you know. You can't ignore it, you'll have to get it published. You'll have to talk to someone.

Take it, at least. Then I'll go. Here.

CATHERINE: I don't want it.

HAL: Come on, Catherine. I'm trying to correct things.

CATHERINE: You *can't*. Do you hear me?

You think you've figured something out? You run over here so pleased with yourself because you changed your mind. Now you're certain. You're so . . . *sloppy*. You don't know anything. The book, the math, the dates, the writing, all that stuff you decided with your buddies, it's just evidence. It doesn't finish the job. It doesn't prove anything.

HAL: Okay, what would?

CATHERINE: *Nothing*.

You should have trusted me.

Beat.

HAL: I know *(Beat. Catherine gathers her things.)* So Claire sold the house?

CATHERINE: Yes.

HAL: Stay in Chicago. You're an adult.

CATHERINE: She wants me in New York. She wants to look after me.

HAL: Do you need looking after?

CATHERINE: She thinks I do.

HAL: You looked after your dad for five years.

CATHERINE: So maybe it's my turn.

I kick and scream, but I don't know. Being taken care of, it doesn't sound so bad. I'm tired.

And the house is a wreck, let's face it. It was my dad's house . . .

Beat.

HAL: Nice house.

CATHERINE: It's old.

HAL: I guess.

CATHERINE: It's drafty as hell. The winters are rough.

HAL: That's just Chicago.

CATHERINE: Either it's freezing inside, or the steam's on full-blast and you're stifling.

HAL: I don't mind cold weather. Keeps you alert.

CATHERINE: Wait a few years.

HAL: I've lived here all my life.

CATHERINE: Yeah?

HAL: Sure. Just like you.

Catherine: Still. I don't think I should spend another winter here.

Beat.

Hal: There is nothing wrong with you.
Catherine: I think I'm like my dad.
Hal: I think you are too.
Catherine: I'm . . . *afraid* I'm like my dad.
Hal: You're not him.
Catherine: Maybe I will be.
Hal: Maybe. Maybe you'll be better.

Pause. Hal hands her the book. This time Catherine takes it. She sits. She looks down at the book, runs her fingers over the cover.

Catherine: It didn't feel "amazing" or—what word did you use?
Hal: Yeah, amazing.
Catherine: Yeah. It was just connecting the dots.
Some nights I could connect three or four. Some nights they'd be really far apart, I'd have no idea how to get to the next one, if there was a next one.
Hal: He really never knew?
Catherine: No. I worked after midnight. He was usually in bed.
Hal: Every night?
Catherine: No. When I got stuck I watched TV. Sometimes if he couldn't sleep he'd come downstairs, sit with me. We'd talk. Not about math, he couldn't. About the movie we were watching. I'd explain the stories.
Or about fixing the heat. Decide we didn't want to. We liked the radiators even though they clanked in the middle of the night, made the air dry.
Or we'd plan breakfast, talk about what we were gonna eat together in the morning.
Those nights were usually pretty good.
I know . . . it works . . . But all I can see are the compromises, the approximations, places where it's stitched together. It's lumpy. Dad's stuff was way more elegant. When he was young.

Beat.

Hal: Talk me through it? Whatever's bothering you. Maybe you'll improve it.
Catherine: I don't know . . .
Hal: Pick anything. Give it a shot? Maybe you'll discover something elegant.

A moment, Hal sits next to Catherine. Eventually she opens the book, turns the pages slowly, finding a section. She looks at him.

Catherine: Here.

She begins to speak.

Curtain

Reading and Reacting

1. How are Catherine and her father alike? Why are their similarities important?
2. What role does the academic discipline of mathematics play in *Proof*? How would the play be different if Catherine and Robert shared another academic or professional interest instead of mathematics?
3. Robert had a mental breakdown when he was in his mid-twenties; now, Catherine is afraid the same thing is happening to her. Do you think her fears are justified? Why or why not?
4. How do you interpret the play's title? Consider all its possible meanings.
5. Why do you think Hal doubts that Catherine could have written the proof? Could it be because he worships Robert? Because Catherine is so young? Because she has no reputation as a mathematician? Because she does not have a PhD? Because she is female? Because she has a family history of mental illness? Which of these explanations seems most likely? Which seems least likely? Why?
6. Is Claire essential to the play? Do you see her as a fully developed character or merely as a foil for Catherine?
7. Act 1 ends with Catherine announcing, "I wrote it." What stage directions would you write for this dramatic moment if you wanted to indicate Catherine's gestures, expression, and tone — and Hal's and Claire's reactions?
8. Which stereotypes about mathematicians does this play promote? Which does it challenge? For example, are Hal and his friends "typical" mathematicians? Is Robert? Is Catherine?
9. In act 1, scene 3, Hal explains why some mathematicians take amphetamines:

   > They think math's a young man's game. Speed keeps them racing, makes them feel sharp. There's this fear that your creativity peaks around twenty-three and it's all downhill from there. Once you hit fifty it's over, you might as well teach high school.

   How does this speech provide insight into the motivation of the three mathematicians in this play (Robert, Hal, and Catherine)?
10. What purpose does Catherine's story about Sophie Germain (act 1, scene 3) serve in the play?
11. Robert is dead when the play begins, yet he functions as a character who interacts with his daughter. Would the play have worked without him? Would it have been stronger? What, if anything, does his presence add?
12. What do you see as the central theme of this play? For example, is its focus on mathematics? Genius? Heredity? Family relationships? Professional rivalry? Feminism? Mental illness? Explain your reasoning.
13. **JOURNAL ENTRY** Do you believe Catherine really wrote the proof? Why or why not? Do you think *Proof* has a happy ending?
14. **CRITICAL PERSPECTIVE** In his review of *Proof* for the *New York Times*, critic Bruce Weber discusses the play's characterizations of mathematicians:

    > Without any baffling erudition—if you know what a prime number is, there won't be a single line of dialogue you find perplexing—the play presents mathematicians as both blessed and bedeviled by the gift for abstraction that ties them achingly to one another and separates them, also achingly, from concrete-minded folks like you and me. And perhaps most satisfying of all, it does so without a moment of meanness.

How are the play's characters "blessed" by mathematics? How are they "bedeviled" by it? How does mathematics unite them? How does it separate them from ordinary people?

Related Works: "Gryphon" (p. 277), "Doe Season" (p. 577), "ABC" (p. 885), "Division" (p. 912), "My Father as a Guitar" (p. 935), "My Son, My Executioner" (p. 945), "Do not go gentle into that good night" (p. 1046), *Trifles* (p. 1319)

Source: ©AP Photo

ARTHUR MILLER (1915–2005) was born in New York City and graduated in 1938 from the University of Michigan, where he began to write plays. His first big success, which won the New York Drama Critics Circle Award, was *All My Sons* (1947), about a man who has knowingly manufactured faulty airplane parts during World War II. Other significant plays are *The Crucible* (1953), based on the Salem witch trials of 1692, which Miller saw as parallel to contemporary investigations of suspected Communists by the House Un-American Activities Committee; *A View from the Bridge* (1955); and *After the Fall* (1955). He was married for a time to actress Marilyn Monroe and wrote the screenplay for her movie *The Misfits* (1961). His play *The Last Yankee* opened off-Broadway in 1993, *Broken Glass* was both published and performed in 1994, and *Mr. Peter's Connection* was published in 1998. In 2001, Miller was awarded an NEH fellowship and the John H. Finney Award for Exemplary Service to New York City.

Death of a Salesman is Miller's most significant work, a play that quickly became an American classic. Miller said he was very much influenced by the structure of Greek tragedy, and in his play he shows that a tragedy can also be the story of an ordinary person told in realistic terms. The play is frequently produced, and each production interprets it a bit differently. When Miller directed *Death of a Salesman* in China in 1983, audiences perceived it as primarily the story of the mother. In the 1983 Broadway production, Miller himself realized "at a certain point that it was far more the story of Biff, the son, than it was of Willy Loman, the salesman of the title."

Cultural Context At the time *Death of a Salesman* was written in 1949, the United States was experiencing the largest economic expansion in its history. After World War II, soldiers returned home, women left the factory jobs they had held while men were at war, and more and more consumer goods were developed and manufactured. As companies expanded and were consolidated, large, impersonal corporations began to replace the mom-and-pop businesses that had dominated the American scene. The foot soldiers of these corporations were the traveling salesmen (today called manufacturers' representatives) who moved from town to town and covered large territories in a relentless effort to sign up clients and generate sales. During the same period, the American suburbs began to appear, with a mass movement of population from older urban neighborhoods to massive housing developments such as those constructed in Levittown, Long Island, in 1946. It is against this background that the events of *Death of a Salesman* unfold.

Death of a Salesman (1949)

Certain Private Conversations in Two Acts and a Requiem

CHARACTERS

Willy Loman
Linda, *his wife*
Biff } *his sons*
Happy
Uncle Ben
Charley
Bernard
The Woman
Howard Wagner
Jenny
Stanley
Miss Forsythe
Letta

The action takes place in Willy Loman's house and yard and in various places he visits in the New York and Boston of today.

Throughout the play, in the stage directions, left and right mean stage left and stage right.

ACT 1

A melody is heard, played upon a flute. It is small and fine, telling of grass and trees and the horizon. The curtain rises.

Before us is the Salesman's house. We are aware of towering, angular shapes behind it, surrounding it on all sides. Only the blue light of the sky falls upon the house and forestage; the surrounding area shows an angry glow of orange. As more light appears, we see a solid vault of apartment houses around the small, fragile-seeming home. An air of the dream clings to the place, a dream rising out of reality. The kitchen at center seems actual enough, for there is a kitchen table with three chairs, and a refrigerator. But no other fixtures are seen. At the back of the kitchen there is a draped entrance, which leads to the living room. To the right of the kitchen, on a level raised two feet, is a bedroom furnished only with a brass bedstead and a straight chair. On a shelf over the bed a silver athletic trophy stands. A window opens onto the apartment house at the side.

Behind the kitchen, on a level raised six and a half feet, is the boys' bedroom, at present barely visible. Two beds are dimly seen, and at the back of the room a dormer window. (This bedroom is above the unseen living room.) At the left a stairway curves up to it from the kitchen.

The entire setting is wholly or, in some places, partially transparent. The roofline of the house is one-dimensional; under and over it we see the apartment buildings. Before the house lies an apron, curving beyond the forestage into the orchestra. This forward area serves as the back yard as well as the locale of all Willy's imaginings and of his city scenes. Whenever the action is in the present the actors observe the imaginary wall-lines, entering the house only through the door at the left. But in the scenes of the past these boundaries are broken, and characters enter or leave a room by stepping "through" a wall onto the forestage.

From the right, Willy Loman, the Salesman, enters, carrying two large sample cases. The flute plays on. He hears but is not aware of it. He is past sixty years of age, dressed quietly. Even as he crosses the stage to the doorway of the house, his exhaustion is apparent. He unlocks the door, comes into the kitchen, and thankfully lets his burden down, feeling the soreness of his palms. A word-sigh escapes his lips—it might be "Oh, boy, oh, boy." He closes the door, then carries his cases out into the living room, through the draped kitchen doorway.

Linda, his wife, has stirred in her bed at the right. She gets out and puts on a robe, listening. Most often jovial, she has developed an iron repression of her exceptions to Willy's behavior—she more than loves him, she admires him, as though his mercurial nature, his temper, his massive dreams and little cruelties, served her only as sharp reminders of the turbulent longings within him, longings which she shares but lacks the temperament to utter and follow to their end.

Linda: *(hearing Willy outside the bedroom, calls with some trepidation)* Willy!

Willy: It's all right. I came back.

Linda: Why? What happened? *(Slight pause.)* Did something happen, Willy?

Willy: No, nothing happened.

Linda: You didn't smash the car, did you?

Willy: *(with casual irritation)* I said nothing happened. Didn't you hear me?

Linda: Don't you feel well?

Willy: I am tired to the death. *(The flute has faded away. He sits on the bed beside her, a little numb.)* I couldn't make it. I just couldn't make it, Linda.

Linda: *(very carefully, delicately)* Where were you all day? You look terrible.

Willy: I got as far as a little above Yonkers. I stopped for a cup of coffee. Maybe it was the coffee.

Linda: What?

Willy: *(after a pause)* I suddenly couldn't drive any more. The car kept going onto the shoulder, y'know?

Linda: *(helpfully)* Oh. Maybe it was the steering again. I don't think Angelo knows the Studebaker.

Willy: No, it's me, it's me. Suddenly I realize I'm goin' sixty miles an hour and I don't remember the last five minutes. I'm—I can't seem to—keep my mind to it.

Linda: Maybe it's your glasses. You never went for your new glasses.

Willy: No, I see everything. I came back ten miles an hour. It took me nearly four hours from Yonkers.

Linda: *(resigned)* Well, you'll just have to take a rest, Willy, you can't continue this way.

Willy: I just got back from Florida.

Linda: But you didn't rest your mind. Your mind is overactive, and the mind is what counts, dear.

Willy: I'll start out in the morning. Maybe I'll feel better in the morning. *(She is taking off his shoes.)* These goddam arch supports are killing me.

Linda: Take an aspirin. Should I get you an aspirin? It'll soothe you.

Willy: *(with wonder)* I was driving along, you understand? And I was fine. I was even observing the scenery. You can imagine, me looking at scenery, on the road every week of my life. But it's so beautiful up there, Linda, the trees are so thick, and the sun is warm. I opened the windshield and just let the warm air bathe over me. And then all of a sudden I'm goin' off the road! I'm tellin' ya, I absolutely forgot I was driving. If I'd've gone the other way over the white line I might've killed somebody. So I went on again—and five minutes later I'm dreamin' again, and I nearly—*(He presses two fingers against his eyes.)* I have such thoughts, I have such strange thoughts.

LINDA: Willy, dear. Talk to them again. There's no reason why you can't work in New York.

WILLY: They don't need me in New York. I'm the New England man. I'm vital in New England.

LINDA: But you're sixty years old. They can't expect you to keep traveling every week.

WILLY: I'll have to send a wire to Portland. I'm supposed to see Brown and Morrison tomorrow morning at ten o'clock to show the line. Goddammit, I could sell them! *(He starts putting on his jacket.)*

LINDA: *(taking the jacket from him)* Why don't you go down to the place tomorrow and tell Howard you've simply got to work in New York? You're too accommodating, dear.

WILLY: If old man Wagner was alive I'd a been in charge of New York now! That man was a prince, he was a masterful man. But that boy of his, that Howard, he don't appreciate. When I went north the first time, the Wagner Company didn't know where New England was!

LINDA: Why don't you tell those things to Howard, dear?

WILLY: *(encouraged)* I will, I definitely will. Is there any cheese?

LINDA: I'll make you a sandwich.

WILLY: No, go to sleep. I'll take some milk. I'll be up right away. The boys in?

LINDA: They're sleeping. Happy took Biff on a date tonight.

WILLY: *(interested)* That so?

LINDA: It was so nice to see them shaving together, one behind the other, in the bathroom. And going out together. You notice? The whole house smells of shaving lotion.

WILLY: Figure it out. Work a lifetime to pay off a house. You finally own it, and there's nobody to live in it.

LINDA: Well, dear, life is a casting off. It's always that way.

WILLY: No, no, some people — some people accomplish something. Did Biff say anything after I went this morning?

LINDA: You shouldn't have criticized him, Willy, especially after he just got off the train. You mustn't lose your temper with him.

WILLY: When the hell did I lose my temper? I simply asked him if he was making any money. Is that a criticism?

LINDA: But, dear, how could he make any money?

WILLY: *(worried and angered)* There's such an undercurrent in him. He became a moody man. Did he apologize when I left this morning?

LINDA: He was crestfallen, Willy. You know how he admires you. I think if he finds himself, then you'll both be happier and not fight any more.

WILLY: How can he find himself on a farm? Is that a life? A farmhand? In the beginning, when he was young, I thought, well, a young man, it's good for him to tramp around, take a lot of different jobs. But it's more than ten years now and he has yet to make thirty-five dollars a week!

LINDA: He's finding himself, Willy.

WILLY: Not finding yourself at the age of thirty-four is a disgrace!

LINDA: Shh!

WILLY: The trouble is he's lazy, goddammit!

LINDA: Willy, please!

WILLY: Biff is a lazy bum!

LINDA: They're sleeping. Get something to eat. Go on down.

WILLY: Why did he come home? I would like to know what brought him home.

LINDA: I don't know. I think he's still lost, Willy. I think he's very lost.

WILLY: Biff Loman is lost. In the greatest country in the world a young man with such—personal attractiveness, gets lost. And such a hard worker. There's one thing about Biff—he's not lazy.

LINDA: Never.

WILLY: *(with pity and resolve)* I'll see him in the morning; I'll have a nice talk with him. I'll get him a job selling. He could be big in no time. My God! Remember how they used to follow him around in high school? When he smiled at one of them their faces lit up. When he walked down the street . . . *(He loses himself in reminiscences.)*

LINDA: *(trying to bring him out of it)* Willy, dear, I got a new kind of American-type cheese today. It's whipped.

WILLY: Why do you get American when I like Swiss?

LINDA: I just thought you'd like a change—

WILLY: I don't want a change! I want Swiss cheese. Why am I always being contradicted?

LINDA: *(with a covering laugh)* I thought it would be a surprise.

WILLY: Why don't you open a window in here, for God's sake?

LINDA: *(with infinite patience)* They're all open, dear.

WILLY: The way they boxed us in here. Bricks and windows, windows and bricks.

LINDA: We should've bought the land next door.

WILLY: The street is lined with cars. There's not a breath of fresh air in the neighborhood. The grass don't grow any more, you can't raise a carrot in the back yard. They should've had a law against apartment houses. Remember those two beautiful elm trees out there? When I and Biff hung the swing between them?

LINDA: Yeah, like being a million miles from the city.

WILLY: They should've arrested the builder for cutting those down. They massacred the neighborhood. *(Lost.)* More and more I think of those days, Linda. This time of year it was lilac and wisteria. And then the peonies would come out, and the daffodils. What fragrance in this room!

LINDA: Well, after all, people had to move somewhere.

WILLY: No, there's more people now.

LINDA: I don't think there's more people. I think—

WILLY: There's more people! That's what's ruining this country! Population is getting out of control. The competition is maddening! Smell the stink from that apartment house! And another on the other side . . . How can they whip cheese?

On Willy's last line, Biff and Happy raise themselves up in their beds, listening.

LINDA: Go down, try it. And be quiet.

WILLY: *(turning to Linda, guiltily)* You're not worried about me, are you, sweetheart?

BIFF: What's the matter?

HAPPY: Listen!

LINDA: You've got too much on the ball to worry about.

WILLY: You're my foundation and my support, Linda.

LINDA: Just try to relax, dear. You make mountains out of molehills.

WILLY: I won't fight with him any more. If he wants to go back to Texas, let him go.

LINDA: He'll find his way.

WILLY: Sure. Certain men just don't get started till later in life. Like Thomas Edison, I think. Or B. F. Goodrich. One of them was deaf. *(He starts for the bedroom doorway.)* I'll put my money on Biff.

LINDA: And Willy—if it's warm Sunday we'll drive in the country. And we'll open the windshield, and take lunch.

WILLY: No, the windshields don't open on the new cars.

LINDA: But you opened it today.

WILLY: Me? I didn't. *(He stops.)* Now isn't that peculiar! Isn't that remarkable— *(He breaks off in amazement and fright as the flute is heard distantly.)*

LINDA: What, darling?

WILLY: That is the most remarkable thing.

LINDA: What, dear?

WILLY: I was thinking of the Chevvy. *(Slight pause.)* Nineteen twenty-eight . . . when I had that red Chevvy—*(Breaks off.)* That funny? I coulda sworn I was driving that Chevvy today.

LINDA: Well, that's nothing. Something must've reminded you.

WILLY: Remarkable. Ts. Remember those days? The way Biff used to simonize that car? The dealer refused to believe there was eighty thousand miles on it. *(He shakes his head.)* Heh! *(To Linda.)* Close your eyes, I'll be right up. *(He walks out of the bedroom.)*

HAPPY: *(to Biff)* Jesus, maybe he smashed up the car again!

LINDA: *(calling after Willy)* Be careful on the stairs, dear! The cheese is on the middle shelf! *(She turns, goes over to the bed, takes his jacket, and goes out of the bedroom.)*

Light has risen on the boys' room. Unseen, Willy is heard talking to himself, "Eighty thousand miles," and a little laugh. Biff gets out of bed, comes downstage a bit, and stands attentively. Biff is two years older than his brother Happy, well built, but in these days bears a worn air and seems less self-assured. He has succeeded less, and his dreams are stronger and less acceptable than Happy's. Happy is tall, powerfully made. Sexuality is like a visible color on him, or a scent that many women have discovered. He, like his brother, is lost, but in a different way, for he has never allowed himself to turn his face toward defeat and is thus more confused and hard-skinned, although seemingly more content.

HAPPY: *(getting out of bed)* He's going to get his license taken away if he keeps that up. I'm getting nervous about him, y'know, Biff?

BIFF: His eyes are going.

HAPPY: No, I've driven with him. He sees all right. He just doesn't keep his mind on it. I drove into the city with him last week. He stops at a green light and then it turns red and he goes. *(He laughs.)*

BIFF: Maybe he's color-blind.

HAPPY: Pop? Why he's got the finest eye for color in the business. You know that.

BIFF: *(sitting down on his bed)* I'm going to sleep.

HAPPY: You're not still sour on Dad, are you, Biff?

BIFF: He's all right, I guess.

WILLY: *(underneath them, in the living room)* Yes, sir, eighty thousand miles—eighty-two thousand!

BIFF: You smoking?

HAPPY: *(holding out a pack of cigarettes)* Want one?

BIFF: *(taking a cigarette)* I can never sleep when I smell it.

WILLY: What a simonizing job, heh!

HAPPY: *(with deep sentiment)* Funny, Biff, y'know? Us sleeping in here again? The old beds. *(He pats his bed affectionately.)* All the talk that went across those two beds, huh? Our whole lives.

BIFF: Yeah. Lotta dreams and plans.

HAPPY: *(with a deep and masculine laugh)* About five hundred women would like to know what was said in this room.

They share a soft laugh.

BIFF: Remember that big Betsy something—what the hell was her name—over on Bushwick Avenue?

HAPPY: *(combing his hair)* With the collie dog!

BIFF: That's the one. I got you in there, remember?

HAPPY: Yeah, that was my first time—I think. Boy, there was a pig! *(They laugh, almost crudely.)* You taught me everything I know about women. Don't forget that.

BIFF: I bet you forgot how bashful you used to be. Especially with girls.

HAPPY: Oh, I still am, Biff.

BIFF: Oh, go on.

HAPPY: I just control it, that's all. I think I got less bashful and you got more so. What happened, Biff? Where's the old humor, the old confidence? *(He shakes Biff's knee. Biff gets up and moves restlessly about the room.)* What's the matter?

BIFF: Why does Dad mock me all the time?

HAPPY: He's not mocking you, he—

BIFF: Everything I say there's a twist of mockery on his face. I can't get near him.

HAPPY: He just wants you to make good, that's all. I wanted to talk to you about Dad for a long time, Biff. Something's—happening to him. He—talks to himself.

BIFF: I noticed that this morning. But he always mumbled.

HAPPY: But not so noticeable. It got so embarrassing I sent him to Florida. And you know something? Most of the time he's talking to you.

BIFF: What's he say about me?

HAPPY: I can't make it out.

BIFF: What's he say about me?

HAPPY: I think the fact that you're not settled, that you're still kind of up in the air . . .

BIFF: There's one or two other things depressing him, Happy.

HAPPY: What do you mean?

BIFF: Never mind. Just don't lay it all to me.

HAPPY: But I think if you just got started—I mean—is there any future for you out there?

BIFF: I tell ya, Hap, I don't know what the future is. I don't know—what I'm supposed to want.

HAPPY: What do you mean?

BIFF: Well, I spent six or seven years after high school trying to work myself up. Shipping clerk, salesman, business of one kind or another. And it's a measly manner of existence. To get on that subway on the hot mornings in summer. To devote your whole life to keeping stock, or making phone calls, or selling or buying. To suffer fifty weeks of the year for the sake of a two-week vacation, when all you really desire is to be outdoors, with your shirt off. And always to have to get ahead of the next fella. And still—that's how you build a future.

HAPPY: Well, you really enjoy it on a farm? Are you content out there?

BIFF: *(with rising agitation)* Hap, I've had twenty or thirty different kinds of jobs since I left home before the war, and it always turns out the same. I just realized it lately. In Nebraska when I herded cattle, and the Dakotas, and Arizona, and now in Texas. It's why I came home now, I guess, because I realized it. This farm I work on, it's spring there now, see? And they've got about fifteen new colts. There's nothing more inspiring or—beautiful than the sight of a mare and a new colt. And it's cool there now, see? Texas is cool now, and it's spring. And whenever spring comes to where I am, I suddenly get the feeling, my God, I'm not gettin' anywhere! What the hell am I doing, playing around with horses, twenty-eight dollars a week! I'm thirty-four years old, I oughta be makin' my future. That's when I come running home. And now, I get here, and I don't know what to do with myself. *(After a pause.)* I've always made a point of not wasting my life, and every time I come back here I know that all I've done is to waste my life.

HAPPY: You're a poet, you know that, Biff? You're a—you're an idealist!

BIFF: No, I'm mixed up very bad. Maybe I oughta get married. Maybe I oughta get stuck into something. Maybe that's my trouble. I'm like a boy. I'm not married, I'm not in business, I just—I'm like a boy. Are you content, Hap? You're a success, aren't you? Are you content?

HAPPY: Hell, no!

BIFF: Why? You're making money, aren't you?

HAPPY: *(moving about with energy, expressiveness)* All I can do now is wait for the merchandise manager to die. And suppose I get to be merchandise manager? He's a good friend of mine, and he just built a terrific estate on Long Island. And he lived there about two months and sold it, and now he's building another one. He can't enjoy it once it's finished. And I know that's just what I would do. I don't know what the hell I'm workin' for. Sometimes I sit in my apartment—all alone. And I think of the rent I'm paying. And it's crazy. But then, it's what I always wanted. My own apartment, a car, and plenty of women. And still, goddammit, I'm lonely.

BIFF: *(with enthusiasm)* Listen, why don't you come out West with me?

HAPPY: You and I, heh?

BIFF: Sure, maybe we could buy a ranch. Raise cattle, use our muscles. Men built like we are should be working out in the open.

HAPPY: *(avidly)* The Loman Brothers, heh?

BIFF: *(with vast affection)* Sure, we'd be known all over the counties!

HAPPY: *(enthralled)* That's what I dream about, Biff. Sometimes I want to just rip my clothes off in the middle of the store and outbox that goddam merchandise manager. I mean I can outbox, outrun, and outlift anybody in that store, and I have to take orders from those common, petty sons-of-bitches till I can't stand it any more.

BIFF: I'm telln' you, kid, if you were with me I'd be happy out there.

HAPPY: *(enthused)* See, Biff, everybody around me is so false that I'm constantly lowering my ideals . . .

BIFF: Baby, together we'd stand up for one another, we'd have someone to trust.

HAPPY: If I were around you—

BIFF: Hap, the trouble is we weren't brought up to grub for money. I don't know how to do it.

HAPPY: Neither can I!

BIFF: Then let's go!

HAPPY: The only thing is—what can you make out there?

BIFF: But look at your friend. Builds an estate and then hasn't the peace of mind to live in it.

HAPPY: Yeah, but when he walks into the store the waves part in front of him. That's fifty-two thousand dollars a year coming through the revolving door, and I got more in my pinky finger than he's got in his head.

BIFF: Yeah, but you just said—

HAPPY: I gotta show some of those pompous, self-important executives over there that Hap Loman can make the grade. I want to walk into the store the way he walks in. Then I'll go with you, Biff. We'll be together yet, I swear. But take those two we had tonight. Now weren't they gorgeous creatures?

BIFF: Yeah, yeah, most gorgeous I've had in years.

HAPPY: I get that any time I want, Biff. Whenever I feel disgusted. The only trouble is, it gets like bowling or something. I just keep knockin' them over and it doesn't mean anything. You still run around a lot?

BIFF: Naa. I'd like to find a girl—steady, somebody with substance.

HAPPY: That's what I long for.

BIFF: Go on! You'd never come home.

HAPPY: I would! Somebody with character, with resistance! Like Mom, y'know? You're gonna call me a bastard when I tell you this. That girl Charlotte I was with tonight is engaged to be married in five weeks. *(He tries on his new hat.)*

BIFF: No kiddin'!

HAPPY: Sure, the guy's in line for the vice-presidency of the store. I don't know what gets into me, maybe I just have an overdeveloped sense of competition or something, but I went and ruined her, and furthermore I can't get rid of her. And he's the third executive I've done that to. Isn't that a crummy characteristic? And to top it all, I go to their weddings! *(Indignantly, but laughing.)* Like I'm not supposed to take bribes. Manufacturers offer me a hundred-dollar bill now and then to throw an order their way. You know how honest I am, but it's like this girl, see. I hate myself for it. Because I don't want the girl, and, still, I take it and—I love it!

BIFF: Let's go to sleep.

HAPPY: I guess we didn't settle anything, heh?

BIFF: I just got one idea that I think I'm going to try.

HAPPY: What's that?

BIFF: Remember Bill Oliver?

HAPPY: Sure, Oliver is very big now. You want to work for him again?

BIFF: No, but when I quit he said something to me. He put his arm on my shoulder, and he said, "Biff, if you ever need anything, come to me."

HAPPY: I remember that. That sounds good.

BIFF: I think I'll go to see him. If I could get ten thousand or even seven or eight thousand dollars I could buy a beautiful ranch.

HAPPY: I bet he'd back you. 'Cause he thought highly of you, Biff, I mean, they all do. You're well liked, Biff. That's why I say to come back here, and we both have the apartment. And I'm telln' you, Biff, any babe you want . . .

BIFF: No, with a ranch I could do the work I like and still be something. I just wonder though. I wonder if Oliver still thinks I stole that carton of basketballs.

HAPPY: Oh, he probably forgot that long ago. It's almost ten years. You're too sensitive. Anyway, he didn't really fire you.

BIFF: Well, I think he was going to. I think that's why I quit. I was never sure whether he knew or not. I know he thought the world of me, though. I was the only one he'd let lock up the place.

WILLY: *(below)* You gonna wash the engine, Biff?
HAPPY: Shh!

Biff looks at Happy, who is gazing down, listening. Willy is mumbling in the parlor.

HAPPY: You hear that?

They listen. Willy laughs warmly.

BIFF: *(growing angry)* Doesn't he know Mom can hear that?
WILLY: Don't get your sweater dirty, Biff!

A look of pain crosses Biff's face.

HAPPY: Isn't that terrible? Don't leave again, will you? You'll find a job here. You gotta stick around. I don't know what to do about him, it's getting embarrassing.
WILLY: What a simonizing job!
BIFF: Mom's hearing that!
WILLY: No kiddin', Biff, you got a date? Wonderful!
HAPPY: Go on to sleep. But talk to him in the morning, will you?
BIFF: *(reluctantly getting into bed)* With her in the house. Brother!
HAPPY: *(getting into bed)* I wish you'd have a good talk with him.

The light on their room begins to fade.

BIFF: *(to himself in bed)* That selfish, stupid . . .
HAPPY: Sh . . . Sleep, Biff.

Their light is out. Well before they have finished speaking, Willy's form is dimly seen below in the darkened kitchen. He opens the refrigerator, searches in there, and takes out a bottle of milk. The apartment houses are fading out, and the entire house and surroundings become covered with leaves. Music insinuates itself as the leaves appear.

WILLY: Just wanna be careful with those girls, Biff, that's all. Don't make any promises. No promises of any kind. Because a girl, y'know, they always believe what you tell'em, and you're very young, Biff, you're too young to be talking seriously to girls.

Light rises on the kitchen. Willy, talking, shuts the refrigerator door and comes downstage to the kitchen table. He pours milk into a glass. He is totally immersed in himself, smiling faintly.

WILLY: Too young entirely, Biff. You want to watch your schooling first. Then when you're all set, there'll be plenty of girls for a boy like you. *(He smiles broadly at a kitchen chair.)* That so? The girls pay for you? *(He laughs.)* Boy, you must really be makin' a hit.

Willy is gradually addressing—physically—a point offstage, speaking through the wall of the kitchen, and his voice has been rising in volume to that of a normal conversation.

WILLY: I been wondering why you polish the car so careful. Ha! Don't leave the hubcaps, boys. Get the chamois to the hubcaps. Happy, use newspaper on the windows, it's the easiest thing. Show him how to do it, Biff! You see, Happy? Pad it up, use it like a pad. That's it, that's it, good work. You're doin' all right, Hap. *(He pauses, then nods in approbation for a few seconds, then looks upward.)* Biff, first thing we gotta do when we get time is clip that big branch over the house. Afraid it's gonna fall in a storm and hit the roof. Tell you what. We get a rope and sling her around, and then we climb up there with a couple of saws and take her down. Soon as you finish the car, boys, I wanna see ya. I got a surprise for you, boys.

BIFF: *(offstage)* Whatta ya got, Dad?

WILLY: No, you finish first. Never leave a job till you're finished—remember that. *(Looking toward the "big trees.")* Biff, up in Albany I saw a beautiful hammock. I think I'll buy it next trip, and we'll hang it right between those two elms. Wouldn't that be something? Just swingin' there under those branches. Boy, that would be . . .

Young Biff and Young Happy appear from the direction Willy was addressing. Happy carries rags and a pail of water. Biff, wearing a sweater with a block "S," carries a football.

BIFF: *(pointing in the direction of the car offstage)* How's that, Pop, professional?

WILLY: Terrific. Terrific job, boys. Good work, Biff.

HAPPY: Where's the surprise, Pop?

WILLY: In the back seat of the car.

HAPPY: Boy! *(He runs off.)*

BIFF: What is it, Dad? Tell me, what'd you buy?

WILLY: *(laughing, cuffs him)* Never mind, something I want you to have.

BIFF: *(turns and starts off)* What is it, Hap?

HAPPY: *(offstage)* It's a punching bag!

BIFF: Oh, Pop!

WILLY: It's got Gene Tunney's° signature on it!

Happy runs onstage with a punching bag.

BIFF: Gee, how'd you know we wanted a punching bag?

WILLY: Well, it's the finest thing for the timing.

HAPPY: *(lies down on his back and pedals with his feet)* I'm losing weight, you notice, Pop?

WILLY: *(to Happy)* Jumping rope is good too.

BIFF: Did you see the new football I got?

WILLY: *(examining the ball)* Where'd you get a new ball?

BIFF: The coach told me to practice my passing.

WILLY: That so? And he gave you the ball, heh?

BIFF: Well, I borrowed it from the locker room. *(He laughs confidentially.)*

WILLY: *(laughing with him at the theft)* I want you to return that.

HAPPY: I told you he wouldn't like it!

BIFF: *(angrily)* Well, I'm bringing it back!

°*Gene Tunney's:* James Joseph ("Gene") Tunney (1897–1978)—American boxer, world heavyweight champion from his defeat of Jack Dempsey in 1926 until his retirement in 1928.

Willy: *(stopping the incipient argument, to Happy)* Sure, he's gotta practice with a regulation ball, doesn't he? *(To Biff.)* Coach'll probably congratulate you on your initiative!

Biff: Oh, he keeps congratulating my initiative all the time, Pop.

Willy: That's because he likes you. If somebody else took that ball there'd be an uproar. So what's the report, boys, what's the report?

Biff: Where'd you go this time, Dad? Gee we were lonesome for you.

Willy: *(pleased, puts an arm around each boy and they come down to the apron)* Lonesome, heh?

Biff: Missed you every minute.

Willy: Don't say? Tell you a secret, boys. Don't breathe it to a soul. Someday I'll have my own business, and I'll never have to leave home any more.

Happy: Like Uncle Charley, heh?

Willy: Bigger than Uncle Charley! Because Charley is not—liked. He's liked, but he's not—well liked.

Biff: Where'd you go this time, Dad?

Willy: Well, I got on the road, and I went north to Providence. Met the Mayor.

Biff: The Mayor of Providence!

Willy: He was sitting in the hotel lobby.

Biff: What'd he say?

Willy: He said, "Morning!" And I said, "You've got a fine city here, Mayor." And then he had coffee with me. And then I went to Waterbury. Waterbury is a fine city. Big clock city, the famous Waterbury clock. Sold a nice bill there. And then Boston—Boston is the cradle of the Revolution. A fine city. And a couple of other towns in Mass., and on to Portland and Bangor and straight home!

Biff: Gee, I'd love to go with you sometime, Dad.

Willy: Soon as summer comes.

Happy: Promise?

Willy: You and Hap and I, and I'll show you all the towns. America is full of beautiful towns and fine, upstanding people. And they know me, boys, they know me up and down New England. The finest people. And when I bring you fellas up, there'll be open sesame for all of us, 'cause one thing, boys: I have friends. I can park my car in any street in New England, and the cops protect it like their own. This summer, heh?

Biff and Happy: *(together)* Yeah! You bet!

Willy: We'll take our bathing suits.

Happy: We'll carry your bags, Pop!

Willy: Oh, won't that be something! Me comin' into the Boston store with you boys carryin' my bags. What a sensation!

Biff is prancing around, practicing passing the ball.

Willy: You nervous, Biff, about the game?

Biff: Not if you're gonna be there.

Willy: What do they say about you in school, now that they made you captain?

HAPPY: There's a crowd of girls behind him everytime the classes change.

BIFF: *(taking Willy's hand)* This Saturday, Pop, this Saturday—just for you, I'm going to break through for a touchdown.

HAPPY: You're supposed to pass.

BIFF: I'm takin' one play for Pop. You watch me, Pop, and when I take off my helmet, that means I'm breakin' out. Then you watch me crash through that line!

WILLY: *(kisses Biff)* Oh, wait'll I tell this in Boston!

Bernard enters in knickers. He is younger than Biff, earnest and loyal, a worried boy.

BERNARD: Biff, where are you? You're supposed to study with me today.

WILLY: Hey, looka Bernard. What're you lookin' so anemic about, Bernard?

BERNARD: He's gotta study, Uncle Willy. He's got Regents next week.

HAPPY: *(tauntingly, spinning Bernard around)* Let's box, Bernard!

BERNARD: Biff! *(He gets away from Happy.)* Listen, Biff, I heard Mr. Birnbaum say that if you don't start studyin' math he's gonna flunk you, and you won't graduate. I heard him!

WILLY: You better study with him, Biff. Go ahead now.

BERNARD: I heard him!

BIFF: Oh, Pop, you didn't see my sneakers! *(He holds up a foot for Willy to look at.)*

WILLY: Hey, that's a beautiful job of printing!

BERNARD: *(wiping his glasses)* Just because he printed University of Virginia on his sneakers doesn't mean they've got to graduate him, Uncle Willy!

WILLY: *(angrily)* What're you talking about? With scholarships to three universities they're gonna flunk him?

BERNARD: But I heard Mr. Birnbaum say—

WILLY: Don't be a pest, Bernard! *(To his boys.)* What an anemic!

BERNARD: Okay, I'm waiting for you in my house, Biff.

Bernard goes off. The Lomans laugh.

WILLY: Bernard is not well liked, is he?

BIFF: He's liked, but he's not well liked.

HAPPY: That's right, Pop.

WILLY: That's just what I mean. Bernard can get the best marks in school, y'understand, but when he gets out in the business world, y'understand, you are going to be five times ahead of him. That's why I thank Almighty God you're both built like Adonises. Because the man who makes an appearance in the business world, the man who creates personal interest, is the man who gets ahead. Be liked and you will never want. You take me, for instance. I never have to wait in line to see a buyer. "Willy Loman is here!" That's all they have to know, and I go right through.

BIFF: Did you knock them dead, Pop?

WILLY: Knocked 'em cold in Providence, slaughtered 'em in Boston.

HAPPY: *(on his back, pedaling again)* I'm losing weight, you notice, Pop?

Linda enters, as of old, a ribbon in her hair, carrying a basket of washing.

LINDA: *(with youthful energy)* Hello, dear!

WILLY: Sweetheart!

LINDA: How'd the Chevvy run?

WILLY: Chevrolet, Linda, is the greatest car ever built. *(To the boys.)* Since when do you let your mother carry wash up the stairs?

BIFF: Grab hold there, boy!

HAPPY: Where to, Mom?

LINDA: Hang them up on the line. And you better go down to your friends, Biff. The cellar is full of boys. They don't know what to do with themselves.

BIFF: Ah, when Pop comes home they can wait!

WILLY: *(laughs appreciatively)* You better go down and tell them what to do, Biff.

BIFF: I think I'll have them sweep out the furnace room.

WILLY: Good work, Biff.

BIFF: *(goes through wall-line of kitchen to doorway at back and calls down)* Fellas! Everybody sweep out the furnace room! I'll be right down!

VOICES: All right! Okay, Biff.

BIFF: George and Sam and Frank, come out back! We're hangin' up the wash! Come on, Hap, on the double! *(He and Happy carry out the basket.)*

LINDA: The way they obey him!

WILLY: Well, that's training, the training. I'm tellin' you, I was sellin' thousands and thousands, but I had to come home.

LINDA: Oh, the whole block'll be at that game. Did you sell anything?

WILLY: I did five hundred gross in Providence and seven hundred gross in Boston.

LINDA: No! Wait a minute, I've got a pencil. *(She pulls pencil and paper out of her apron pocket.)* That makes your commission . . . Two hundred — my God! Two hundred and twelve dollars!

WILLY: Well, I didn't figure it yet, but . . .

LINDA: How much did you do?

WILLY: Well, I—I did—about a hundred and eighty gross in Providence. Well, no—it came to—roughly two hundred gross on the whole trip.

LINDA: *(without hesitation)* Two hundred gross. That's . . . *(She figures.)*

WILLY: The trouble was that three of the stores were half closed for inventory in Boston. Otherwise I woulda broke records.

LINDA: Well, it makes seventy dollars and some pennies. That's very good.

WILLY: What do we owe?

LINDA: Well, on the first there's sixteen dollars on the refrigerator —

WILLY: Why sixteen?

LINDA: Well, the fan belt broke, so it was a dollar eighty.

WILLY: But it's brand new.

LINDA: Well, the man said that's the way it is. Till they work themselves in, y'know.

They move through the wall-line into the kitchen.

WILLY: I hope we didn't get stuck on that machine.

LINDA: They got the biggest ads of any of them!

WILLY: I know, it's a fine machine. What else?

LINDA: Well, there's nine-sixty for the washing machine. And for the vacuum cleaner there's three and a half due on the fifteenth. Then the roof, you got twenty-one dollars remaining.

WILLY: It don't leak, does it?

LINDA: No, they did a wonderful job. Then you owe Frank for the carburetor.

WILLY: I'm not going to pay that man! That goddam Chevrolet, they ought to prohibit the manufacture of that car!

LINDA: Well, you owe him three and a half. And odds and ends, comes to around a hundred and twenty dollars by the fifteenth.

WILLY: A hundred and twenty dollars! My God, if business don't pick up I don't know what I'm gonna do!

LINDA: Well, next week you'll do better.

WILLY: Oh, I'll knock them dead next week. I'll go to Hartford. I'm very well liked in Hartford. You know, the trouble is, Linda, people don't seem to take to me.

They move onto the forestage.

LINDA: Oh, don't be foolish.

WILLY: I know it when I walk in. They seem to laugh at me.

LINDA: Why? Why would they laugh at you? Don't talk that way, Willy.

Willy moves to the edge of the stage. Linda goes into the kitchen and starts to darn stockings.

WILLY: I don't know the reason for it, but they just pass me by. I'm not noticed.

LINDA: But you're doing wonderful, dear. You're making seventy to a hundred dollars a week.

WILLY: But I gotta be at it ten, twelve hours a day. Other men—I don't know—they do it easier. I don't know why—I can't stop myself—I talk too much. A man oughta come in with a few words. One thing about Charley. He's a man of few words, and they respect him.

LINDA: You don't talk too much, you're just lively.

WILLY: *(smiling)* Well, I figure, what the hell, life is short, a couple of jokes. *(To himself.)* I joke too much! *(The smile goes.)*

LINDA: Why? You're—

WILLY: I'm fat. I'm very—foolish to look at, Linda. I didn't tell you, but Christmas time I happened to be calling on F. H. Stewarts, and a salesman I know, as I was going in to see the buyer, I heard him say something about—walrus. And I—I cracked him right across the face. I won't take that. I simply will not take that. But they do laugh at me. I know that.

LINDA: Darling . . .

WILLY: I gotta overcome it. I know I gotta overcome it. I'm not dressing to advantage, maybe.

LINDA: Willy, darling, you're the handsomest man in the world—

WILLY: Oh, no, Linda.

LINDA: To me you are. *(Slight pause.)* The handsomest.

From the darkness is heard the laughter of a woman. Willy doesn't turn to it, but it continues through Linda's lines.

LINDA: And the boys, Willy. Few men are idolized by their children the way you are.

Music is heard as behind a scrim, to the left of the house, The Woman, dimly seen, is dressing.

WILLY: *(with great feeling)* You're the best there is, Linda, you're a pal, you know that? On the road—on the road I want to grab you sometimes and just kiss the life outa you.

The laughter is loud now, and he moves into a brightening area at the left, where The Woman has come from behind the scrim and is standing, putting on her hat, looking into a "mirror" and laughing.

WILLY: 'Cause I get so lonely—especially when business is bad and there's nobody to talk to. I get the feeling that I'll never sell anything again, that I won't make a living for you, or a business, a business for the boys. *(He talks through The Woman's subsiding laughter; The Woman primps at the "mirror.")* There's so much I want to make for—

THE WOMAN: Me? You didn't make me, Willy. I picked you.

WILLY: *(pleased)* You picked me?

THE WOMAN: *(who is quite proper-looking, Willy's age)* I did. I've been sitting at that desk watching all the salesmen go by, day in, day out. But you've got such a sense of humor, and we do have such a good time together, don't we?

WILLY: Sure, sure. *(He takes her in his arms.)* Why do you have to go now?

THE WOMAN: It's two o'clock . . .

WILLY: No, come on in! *(He pulls her.)*

THE WOMAN: . . . my sisters'll be scandalized. When'll you be back?

WILLY: Oh, two weeks about. Will you come up again?

THE WOMAN: Sure thing. You do make me laugh. It's good for me. *(She squeezes his arm, kisses him.)* And I think you're a wonderful man.

WILLY: You picked me, heh?

THE WOMAN: Sure. Because you're so sweet. And such a kidder.

WILLY: Well, I'll see you next time I'm in Boston.

THE WOMAN: I'll put you right through to the buyers.

WILLY: *(slapping her bottom)* Right. Well, bottoms up!

THE WOMAN: *(slaps him gently and laughs)* You just kill me, Willy. *(He suddenly grabs her and kisses her roughly.)* You kill me. And thanks for the stockings. I love a lot of stockings. Well, good night.

WILLY: Good night. And keep your pores open!

THE WOMAN: Oh, Willy!

The Woman bursts out laughing, and Linda's laughter blends in. The Woman disappears into the dark. Now the area at the kitchen table brightens. Linda is sitting where she was at the kitchen table, but now is mending a pair of silk stockings.

LINDA: You are, Willy. The handsomest man. You've got no reason to feel that—

WILLY: *(coming out of The Woman's dimming area and going over to Linda)* I'll make it all up to you, Linda, I'll—

LINDA: There's nothing to make up, dear. You're doing fine, better than—

WILLY: *(noticing her mending)* What's that?

LINDA: Just mending my stockings. They're so expensive—

WILLY: *(angrily, taking them from her)* I won't have you mending stockings in this house! Now throw them out!

Linda puts the stockings in her pocket.

BERNARD: *(entering on the run)* Where is he? If he doesn't study!

WILLY: *(moving to the forestage, with great agitation)* You'll give him the answers!

BERNARD: I do, but I can't on a Regents! That's a state exam! They're liable to arrest me!

WILLY: Where is he? I'll whip him, I'll whip him!

LINDA: And he'd better give back that football, Willy, it's not nice.

WILLY: Biff! Where is he? Why is he taking everything?

LINDA: He's too tough with the girls, Willy. All the mothers are afraid of him!

WILLY: I'll whip him!

BERNARD: He's driving the car without a license!

The Woman's laugh is heard.

WILLY: Shut up!

LINDA: All the mothers—

WILLY: Shut up!

BERNARD: *(backing quietly away and out)* Mr. Birnbaum says he's stuck up.

WILLY: Get outa here!

BERNARD: If he doesn't buckle down he'll flunk math! *(He goes off.)*

LINDA: He's right, Willy, you've gotta—

WILLY: *(exploding at her)* There's nothing the matter with him! You want him to be a worm like Bernard? He's got spirit, personality . . .

As he speaks, Linda, almost in tears, exits into the living room. Willy is alone in the kitchen, wilting and staring. The leaves are gone. It is night again, and the apartment houses look down from behind.

WILLY: Loaded with it. Loaded! What is he stealing? He's giving it back, isn't he? Why is he stealing? What did I tell him? I never in my life told him anything but decent things.

Happy in pajamas has come down the stairs; Willy suddenly becomes aware of Happy's presence.

Happy: Let's go now, come on.

Willy: *(sitting down at the kitchen table)* Huh! Why did she have to wax the floors herself? Everytime she waxes the floors she keels over. She knows that!

Happy: Shh! Take it easy. What brought you back tonight?

Willy: I got an awful scare. Nearly hit a kid in Yonkers. God! Why didn't I go to Alaska with my brother Ben that time! Ben! That man was a genius, that man was success incarnate! What a mistake! He begged me to go.

Happy: Well, there's no use in—

Willy: You guys! There was a man started with the clothes on his back and ended up with diamond mines!

Happy: Boy, someday I'd like to know how he did it.

Willy: What's the mystery? The man knew what he wanted and went out and got it! Walked into a jungle, and comes out, the age of twenty-one, and he's rich! The world is an oyster, but you don't crack it open on a mattress!

Happy: Pop, I told you I'm gonna retire you for life.

Willy: You'll retire me for life on seventy goddam dollars a week? And your women and your car and your apartment, and you'll retire me for life! Christ's sake, I couldn't get past Yonkers today! Where are you guys, where are you? The woods are burning! I can't drive a car!

Charley has appeared in the doorway. He is a large man, slow of speech, laconic, immovable. In all he says, despite what he says, there is pity, and now, trepidation. He has a robe over his pajamas, slippers on his feet. He enters the kitchen.

Charley: Everything all right?

Happy: Yeah, Charley, everything's . . .

Willy: What's the matter?

Charley: I heard some noise. I thought something happened. Can't we do something about the walls? You sneeze in here, and in my house hats blow off.

Happy: Let's go to bed, Dad. Come on.

Charley signals to Happy to go.

Willy: You go ahead, I'm not tired at the moment.

Happy: *(to Willy)* Take it easy, huh? *(He exits.)*

Willy: What're you doin' up?

395 **Charley:** *(sitting down at the kitchen table opposite Willy)* Couldn't sleep good. I had a heartburn.

Willy: Well, you don't know how to eat.

Charley: I eat with my mouth.

Willy: No, you're ignorant. You gotta know about vitamins and things like that.

Charley: Come on, let's shoot. Tire you out a little.

Willy: *(hesitantly)* All right. You got cards?

Charley: *(taking a deck from his pocket)* Yeah, I got them. Someplace. What is it with those vitamins?

Willy: *(dealing)* They build up your bones. Chemistry.

Charley: Yeah, but there's no bones in a heartburn.

Willy: What are you talkin' about? Do you know the first thing about it?

Charley: Don't get insulted.

Willy: Don't talk about something you don't know anything about.

They are playing. Pause.

Charley: What're you doin' home?

Willy: A little trouble with the car.

Charley: Oh. *(Pause.)* I'd like to take a trip to California.

Willy: Don't say.

Charley: You want a job?

Willy: I got a job, I told you that. *(After a slight pause.)* What the hell are you offering me a job for?

Charley: Don't get insulted.

Willy: Don't insult me.

Charley: I don't see no sense in it. You don't have to go on this way.

Willy: I got a good job. *(Slight pause.)* What do you keep comin' in here for?

Charley: You want me to go?

Willy: *(after a pause, withering)* I can't understand it. He's going back to Texas again. What the hell is that?

Charley: Let him go.

Willy: I got nothin' to give him, Charley, I'm clean, I'm clean.

Charley: He won't starve. None a them starve. Forget about him.

Willy: Then what have I got to remember?

Charley: You take it too hard. To hell with it. When a deposit bottle is broken you don't get your nickel back.

Willy: That's easy enough for you to say.

Charley: That ain't easy for me to say.

Willy: Did you see the ceiling I put up in the living room?

Charley: Yeah, that's a piece of work. To put up a ceiling is a mystery to me. How do you do it?

Willy: What's the difference?

Charley: Well, talk about it.

Willy: You gonna put up a ceiling?

Charley: How could I put up a ceiling?

Willy: Then what the hell are you bothering me for?

Charley: You're insulted again.

Willy: A man who can't handle tools is not a man. You're disgusting.

Charley: Don't call me disgusting, Willy.

Uncle Ben, carrying a valise and an umbrella, enters the forestage from around the right corner of the house. He is a stolid man, in his sixties, with a mustache and an authoritative air. He is utterly certain of his destiny, and there is an aura of far places about him. He enters exactly as Willy speaks.

Willy: I'm getting awfully tired, Ben.

Ben's music is heard. Ben looks around at everything.

CHARLEY: Good, keep playing; you'll sleep better. Did you call me Ben?

Ben looks at his watch.

WILLY: That's funny. For a second there you reminded me of my brother Ben.

BEN: I have only a few minutes. *(He strolls, inspecting the place. Willy and Charley continue playing.)*

CHARLEY: You never heard from him again, heh? Since that time?

WILLY: Didn't Linda tell you? Couple of weeks ago we got a letter from his wife in Africa. He died.

CHARLEY: That so.

BEN: *(chuckling)* So this is Brooklyn, eh?

CHARLEY: Maybe you're in for some of his money.

WILLY: Naa, he had seven sons. There's just one opportunity I had with that man . . .

BEN: I must make a train, William. There are several properties I'm looking at in Alaska.

WILLY: Sure, sure! If I'd gone with him to Alaska that time, everything would've been totally different.

CHARLEY: Go on, you'd froze to death up there.

WILLY: What're you talking about?

BEN: Opportunity is tremendous in Alaska, William. Surprised you're not up there.

WILLY: Sure, tremendous.

CHARLEY: Heh?

WILLY: There was the only man I ever met who knew the answers.

CHARLEY: Who?

BEN: How are you all?

WILLY: *(taking a pot, smiling)* Fine, fine.

CHARLEY: Pretty sharp tonight.

BEN: Is Mother living with you?

WILLY: No, she died a long time ago.

CHARLEY: Who?

BEN: That's too bad. Fine specimen of a lady, Mother.

WILLY: *(to Charley)* Heh?

BEN: I'd hoped to see the old girl.

CHARLEY: Who died?

BEN: Heard anything from Father, have you?

WILLY: *(unnerved)* What do you mean, who died?

CHARLEY: *(taking a pot)* What're you talkin' about?

BEN: *(looking at his watch)* William, it's half-past eight!

WILLY: *(as though to dispel his confusion he angrily stops Charley's hand)* That's my build!

CHARLEY: I put the ace—

WILLY: If you don't know how to play the game I'm not gonna throw my money away on you!

CHARLEY: *(rising)* It was my ace, for God's sake!

WILLY: I'm through, I'm through!

BEN: When did Mother die?

WILLY: Long ago. Since the beginning you never knew how to play cards.

CHARLEY: *(picks up the cards and goes to the door)* All right! Next time I'll bring a deck with five aces.

WILLY: I don't play that kind of game!

CHARLEY: *(turning to him)* You should be ashamed of yourself!

WILLY: Yeah?

CHARLEY: Yeah! *(He goes out.)*

WILLY: *(slamming the door after him)* Ignoramus!

BEN: *(as Willy comes toward him through the wall-line of the kitchen)* So you're William.

WILLY: *(shaking Ben's hand)* Ben! I've been waiting for you so long! What's the answer? How did you do it?

BEN: Oh, there's a story in that.

Linda enters the forestage, as of old, carrying the wash basket.

LINDA: Is this Ben?

BEN: *(gallantly)* How do you do, my dear.

LINDA: Where've you been all these years? Willy's always wondered why you—

WILLY: *(pulling Ben away from her impatiently)* Where is Dad? Didn't you follow him? How did you get started?

BEN: Well, I don't know how much you remember.

WILLY: Well, I was just a baby, of course, only three or four years old—

BEN: Three years and eleven months.

WILLY: What a memory, Ben!

BEN: I have many enterprises, William, and I have never kept books.

WILLY: I remember I was sitting under the wagon in—was it Nebraska?

BEN: It was South Dakota, and I gave you a bunch of wild flowers.

WILLY: I remember you walking away down some open road.

BEN: *(laughing)* I was going to find Father in Alaska.

WILLY: Where is he?

BEN: At that age I had a very faulty view of geography, William. I discovered after a few days that I was heading due south, so instead of Alaska, I ended up in Africa.

LINDA: Africa!

WILLY: The Gold Coast!

BEN: Principally, diamond mines.

LINDA: Diamond mines!

BEN: Yes, my dear. But I've only a few minutes—

WILLY: No! Boys! Boys! *(Young Biff and Happy appear.)* Listen to this. This is your Uncle Ben, a great man! Tell my boys, Ben!

BEN: Why, boys, when I was seventeen I walked into the jungle, and when I was twenty-one I walked out. *(He laughs.)* And by God I was rich.

WILLY: *(to the boys)* You see what I been talking about? The greatest things can happen!

BEN: *(glancing at his watch)* I have an appointment in Ketchikan Tuesday week.

WILLY: No, Ben! Please tell about Dad. I want my boys to hear. I want them to know the kind of stock they spring from. All I remember is a man with a big beard, and I was in Mamma's lap, sitting around a fire, and some kind of high music.

BEN: His flute. He played the flute.

WILLY: Sure, the flute, that's right!

New music is heard, a high, rollicking tune.

BEN: Father was a very great and a very wild-hearted man. We would start in Boston, and he'd toss the whole family into the wagon, and then he'd drive the team right across the country; through Ohio, and Indiana, Michigan, Illinois, and all the Western states. And we'd stop in the towns and sell the flutes that he'd made on the way. Great inventor, Father. With one gadget he made more in a week than a man like you could make in a lifetime.

WILLY: That's just the way I'm bringing them up, Ben—rugged, well liked, all-around.

BEN: Yeah? *(To Biff.)* Hit that, boy—hard as you can. *(He pounds his stomach.)*

BIFF: Oh, no, sir!

BEN: *(taking boxing stance)* Come on, get to me! *(He laughs.)*

WILLY: Go to it, Biff! Go ahead, show him!

BIFF: Okay! *(He cocks his fist and starts in.)*

LINDA: *(to Willy)* Why must he fight, dear?

BEN: *(sparring with Biff)* Good boy! Good boy!

WILLY: How's that, Ben, heh?

HAPPY: Give him the left, Biff!

LINDA: Why are you fighting?

BEN: Good boy! *(Suddenly comes in, trips Biff, and stands over him, the point of his umbrella poised over Biff's eye.)*

LINDA: Look out, Biff!

BIFF: Gee!

BEN: *(patting Biff's knee)* Never fight fair with a stranger, boy. You'll never get out of the jungle that way. *(Taking Linda's hand and bowing.)* It was an honor and a pleasure to meet you, Linda.

LINDA: *(withdrawing her hand coldly, frightened)* Have a nice—trip.

BEN: *(to Willy)* And good luck with your—what do you do?

WILLY: Selling.

BEN: Yes. Well . . . *(He raises his hand in farewell to all.)*

WILLY: No, Ben, I don't want you to think . . . *(He takes Ben's arm to show him.)* It's Brooklyn, I know, but we hunt too.

BEN: Really, now.

WILLY: Oh, sure, there's snakes and rabbits and—that's why I moved out here. Why, Biff can fell any one of these trees in no time! Boys!

Go right over to where they're building the apartment house and get some sand. We're gonna rebuild the entire front stoop right now! Watch this, Ben!

BIFF: Yes, sir! On the double, Hap!

HAPPY: *(as he and Biff run off)* I lost weight, Pop, you notice?

Charley enters in knickers, even before the boys are gone.

CHARLEY: Listen, if they steal any more from that building the watchman'll put the cops on them!

LINDA: *(to Willy)* Don't let Biff . . .

Ben laughs lustily.

WILLY: You shoulda seen the lumber they brought home last week. At least a dozen six-by-tens worth all kinds of money.

CHARLEY: Listen, if that watchman—

WILLY: I gave them hell, understand. But I got a couple of fearless characters there.

CHARLEY: Willy, the jails are full of fearless characters.

BEN: *(clapping Willy on the back, with a laugh at Charley)* And the stock exchange, friend!

WILLY: *(joining in Ben's laughter)* Where are the rest of your pants?

CHARLEY: My wife bought them.

WILLY: Now all you need is a golf club and you can go upstairs and go to sleep. *(To Ben.)* Great athlete! Between him and his son Bernard they can't hammer a nail!

BERNARD: *(rushing in)* The watchman's chasing Biff!

WILLY: *(angrily)* Shut up! He's not stealing anything!

LINDA: *(alarmed, hurrying off left)* Where is he? Biff, dear! *(She exits.)*

WILLY: *(moving toward the left, away from Ben)* There's nothing wrong. What's the matter with you?

BEN: Nervy boy. Good!

WILLY: *(laughing)* Oh, nerves of iron, that Biff!

CHARLEY: Don't know what it is. My New England man comes back and he's bleedin', they murdered him up there.

WILLY: It's contacts, Charley, I got important contacts!

CHARLEY: *(sarcastically)* Glad to hear it, Willy. Come in later, we'll shoot a little casino. I'll take some of your Portland money. *(He laughs at Willy and exits.)*

WILLY: *(turning to Ben)* Business is bad, it's murderous. But not for me, of course.

BEN: I'll stop by on my way back to Africa.

WILLY: *(longingly)* Can't you stay a few days? You're just what I need, Ben, because I—I have a fine position here, but I—well, Dad left when I was such a baby and I never had a chance to talk to him and I still feel—kind of temporary about myself.

BEN: I'll be late for my train.

They are at opposite ends of the stage.

WILLY: Ben, my boys—can't we talk? They'd go into the jaws of hell for me, see, but I—

BEN: William, you're being first-rate with your boys. Outstanding, manly chaps!

WILLY: *(hanging on to his words)* Oh, Ben, that's good to hear! Because sometimes I'm afraid that I'm not teaching them the right kind of—Ben, how should I teach them?

BEN: *(giving great weight to each word, and with a certain vicious audacity)* William, when I walked into the jungle, I was seventeen. When I walked out I was twenty-one. And, by God, I was rich! *(He goes off into darkness around the right corner of the house.)*

WILLY: . . . was rich! That's just the spirit I want to imbue them with! To walk into a jungle! I was right! I was right! I was right!

Ben is gone, but Willy is still speaking to him as Linda, in nightgown and robe, enters the kitchen, glances around for Willy, then goes to the door of the house, looks out and sees him. Comes down to his left. He looks at her.

LINDA: Willy, dear? Willy?

WILLY: I was right!

LINDA: Did you have some cheese? *(He can't answer.)* It's very late, darling. Come to bed, heh?

WILLY: *(looking straight up)* Gotta break your neck to see a star in this yard.

LINDA: You coming in?

WILLY: What ever happened to that diamond watch fob? Remember? When Ben came from Africa that time? Didn't he give me a watch fob with a diamond in it?

LINDA: You pawned it, dear. Twelve, thirteen years ago. For Biff's radio correspondence course.

WILLY: Gee, that was a beautiful thing. I'll take a walk.

LINDA: But you're in your slippers.

WILLY: *(starting to go around the house at the left)* I was right! I was! *(Half to Linda, as he goes, shaking his head.)* What a man! There was a man worth talking to. I was right!

LINDA: *(calling after Willy)* But in your slippers, Willy!

Willy is almost gone when Biff, in his pajamas, comes down the stairs and enters the kitchen.

BIFF: What is he doing out there?

LINDA: Sh!

BIFF: God Almighty, Mom, how long has he been doing this?

LINDA: Don't, he'll hear you.

BIFF: What the hell is the matter with him?

LINDA: It'll pass by morning.

BIFF: Shouldn't we do anything?

LINDA: Oh, my dear, you should do a lot of things, but there's nothing to do, so go to sleep.

Happy comes down the stairs and sits on the steps.

HAPPY: I never heard him so loud, Mom.

LINDA: Well, come around more often; you'll hear him. *(She sits down at the table and mends the lining of Willy's jacket.)*

BIFF: Why didn't you ever write me about this, Mom?

LINDA: How would I write to you? For over three months you had no address.

BIFF: I was on the move. But you know I thought of you all the time. You know that, don't you, pal?

LINDA: I know, dear, I know. But he likes to have a letter. Just to know that there's still a possibility for better things.

BIFF: He's not like this all the time, is he?

LINDA: It's when you come home he's always the worst.

BIFF: When I come home?

LINDA: When you write you're coming, he's all smiles, and talks about the future, and—he's just wonderful. And then the closer you seem to come, the more shaky he gets, and then, by the time you get here, he's arguing, and he seems angry at you. I think it's just that maybe he can't bring himself to—to open up to you. Why are you so hateful to each other? Why is that?

BIFF: *(evasively)* I'm not hateful, Mom.

LINDA: But you no sooner come in the door than you're fighting!

BIFF: I don't know why. I mean to change. I'm tryin', Mom, you understand?

LINDA: Are you home to stay now?

BIFF: I don't know. I want to look around, see what's doin'.

LINDA: Biff, you can't look around all your life, can you?

BIFF: I just can't take hold, Mom. I can't take hold of some kind of a life.

LINDA: Biff, a man is not a bird, to come and go with the springtime.

BIFF: Your hair . . . *(He touches her hair.)* Your hair got so gray.

LINDA: Oh, it's been gray since you were in high school. I just stopped dyeing it, that's all.

BIFF: Dye it again, will ya? I don't want my pal looking old. *(He smiles.)*

LINDA: You're such a boy! You think you can go away for a year and . . . You've got to get it into your head now that one day you'll knock on this door and there'll be strange people here—

BIFF: What are you talking about? You're not even sixty, Mom.

LINDA: But what about your father?

BIFF: *(lamely)* Well, I meant him too.

HAPPY: He admires Pop.

LINDA: Biff, dear, if you don't have any feeling for him, then you can't have any feeling for me.

BIFF: Sure I can, Mom.

LINDA: No. You can't just come to see me, because I love him. *(With a threat, but only a threat, of tears.)* He's the dearest man in the world to me, and I won't have anyone making him feel unwanted and low and blue. You've got to make up your mind now, darling, there's no leeway any more. Either he's your father and you pay him that respect, or else you're not to come here.

I know he's not easy to get along with—nobody knows that better than me—but . . .

WILLY: *(from the left, with a laugh)* Hey, hey, Biffo!

BIFF: *(starting to go out after Willy)* What the hell is the matter with him? *(Happy stops him.)*

LINDA: Don't—don't go near him!

BIFF: Stop making excuses for him! He always, always wiped the floor with you. Never had an ounce of respect for you.

HAPPY: He's always had respect for—

BIFF: What the hell do you know about it?

HAPPY: *(surlily)* Just don't call him crazy!

BIFF: He's got no character — Charley wouldn't do this. Not in his own house—spewing out that vomit from his mind.

HAPPY: Charley never had to cope with what he's got to.

BIFF: People are worse off than Willy Loman. Believe me, I've seen them!

LINDA: Then make Charley your father, Biff. You can't do that, can you? I don't say he's a great man. Willy Loman never made a lot of money. His name was never in the paper. He's not the finest character that ever lived. But he's a human being, and a terrible thing is happening to him. So attention must be paid. He's not to be allowed to fall into his grave like an old dog. Attention, attention must be finally paid to such a person. You called him crazy—

BIFF: I didn't mean—

LINDA: No, a lot of people think he's lost his—balance. But you don't have to be very smart to know what his trouble is. The man is exhausted.

HAPPY: Sure!

LINDA: A small man can be just as exhausted as a great man. He works for a company thirty-six years this March, opens up unheard-of territories to their trademark, and now in his old age they take his salary away.

HAPPY: *(indignantly)* I didn't know that, Mom.

LINDA: You never asked, my dear! Now that you get your spending money someplace else you don't trouble your mind with him.

HAPPY: But I gave you money last—

LINDA: Christmas time, fifty dollars! To fix the hot water it cost ninety-seven fifty! For five weeks he's been on straight commission, like a beginner, an unknown!

BIFF: Those ungrateful bastards!

LINDA: Are they any worse than his sons? When he brought them business, when he was young, they were glad to see him. But now his old friends, the old buyers that loved him so and always found some order to hand him in a pinch — they're all dead, retired. He used to be able to make six, seven calls a day in Boston. Now he takes his valises out of the car and puts them back and takes them out again and he's exhausted. Instead of walking he talks now. He drives seven hundred miles, and when he gets there no one knows him any more, no one welcomes him. And what goes through a man's mind, driving seven hundred miles home without having earned a cent? Why shouldn't he talk to himself? Why? When he has to go to

Charley and borrow fifty dollars a week and pretend to me that it's his pay? How long can that go on? How long? You see what I'm sitting here and waiting for? And you tell me he has no character? The man who never worked a day but for your benefit? When does he get the medal for that? Is this his reward—to turn around at the age of sixty-three and find his sons, who he loved better than his life, one a philandering bum—

HAPPY: Mom!

LINDA: That's all you are, my baby! *(To Biff.)* And you! What happened to the love you had for him? You were such pals! How you used to talk to him on the phone every night! How lonely he was till he could come home to you!

BIFF: All right, Mom. I'll live here in my room, and I'll get a job. I'll keep away from him, that's all.

LINDA: No, Biff. You can't stay here and fight all the time.

BIFF: He threw me out of this house, remember that.

LINDA: Why did he do that? I never knew why.

BIFF: Because I know he's a fake and he doesn't like anybody around who knows!

LINDA: Why a fake? In what way? What do you mean?

BIFF: Just don't lay it all at my feet. It's between me and him—that's all I have to say. I'll chip in from now on. He'll settle for half my pay check. He'll be all right. I'm going to bed. *(He starts for the stairs.)*

LINDA: He won't be all right.

BIFF: *(turning on the stairs, furiously)* I hate this city and I'll stay here. Now what do you want?

LINDA: He's dying, Biff.

Happy turns quickly to her, shocked.

BIFF: *(after a pause)* Why is he dying?

LINDA: He's been trying to kill himself.

BIFF: *(with great horror)* How?

LINDA: I live from day to day.

BIFF: What're you talking about?

LINDA: Remember I wrote you that he smashed up the car again? In February?

BIFF: Well?

LINDA: The insurance inspector came. He said that they have evidence. That all these accidents in the last year—weren't—weren't—accidents.

HAPPY: How can they tell that? That's a lie.

LINDA: It seems there's a woman . . . *(She takes a breath as—)*

BIFF: *(sharply but contained)* What woman?

LINDA: *(simultaneously)* . . . and this woman . . .

LINDA: What?

BIFF: Nothing. Go ahead.

LINDA: What did you say?

BIFF: Nothing. I just said what woman?

HAPPY: What about her?

LINDA: Well, it seems she was walking down the road and saw his car. She says that he wasn't driving fast at all, and that he didn't skid. She says he came to that little bridge, and then deliberately smashed into the railing, and it was only the shallowness of the water that saved him.

BIFF: Oh, no, he probably just fell asleep again.

LINDA: I don't think he fell asleep.

BIFF: Why not?

LINDA: Last month . . . *(With great difficulty.)* Oh, boys, it's so hard to say a thing like this! He's just a big stupid man to you, but I tell you there's more good in him than in many other people. *(She chokes, wipes her eyes.)* I was looking for a fuse. The lights blew out, and I went down the cellar. And behind the fuse box—it happened to fall out—was a length of rubber pipe—just short.

HAPPY: No kidding?

LINDA: There's a little attachment on the end of it. I knew right away. And sure enough, on the bottom of the water heater there's a new little nipple on the gas pipe.

HAPPY: *(angrily)* That—jerk.

BIFF: Did you have it taken off?

LINDA: I'm—I'm ashamed to. How can I mention it to him? Every day I go down and take away that little rubber pipe. But, when he comes home, I put it back where it was. How can I insult him that way? I don't know what to do. I live from day to day, boys. I tell you, I know every thought in his mind. It sounds so old-fashioned and silly, but I tell you he put his whole life into you and you've turned your backs on him. *(She is bent over in the chair, weeping, her face in her hands.)* Biff, I swear to God! Biff, his life is in your hands!

HAPPY: *(to Biff)* How do you like that damned fool!

BIFF: *(kissing her)* All right, pal, all right. It's all settled now. I've been remiss. I know that, Mom, but now I'll stay, and I swear to you, I'll apply myself. *(Kneeling in front of her, in a fever of self-reproach.)* It's just—you see, Mom, I don't fit in business. Not that I won't try. I'll try, and I'll make good.

HAPPY: Sure you will. The trouble with you in business was you never tried to please people.

BIFF: I know, I—

HAPPY: Like when you worked for Harrison's. Bob Harrison said you were tops, and then you go and do some damn fool thing like whistling whole songs in the elevator like a comedian.

BIFF: *(against Happy)* So what? I like to whistle sometimes.

HAPPY: You don't raise a guy to a responsible job who whistles in the elevator!

LINDA: Well, don't argue about it now.

HAPPY: Like when you'd go off and swim in the middle of the day instead of taking the line around.

BIFF: *(his resentment rising)* Well, don't you run off? You take off sometimes, don't you? On a nice summer day?

HAPPY: Yeah, but I cover myself!

LINDA: Boys!

HAPPY: If I'm going to take a fade the boss can call any number where I'm supposed to be and they'll swear to him that I just left. I'll tell you something that I hate to say, Biff, but in the business world some of them think you're crazy.

BIFF: *(angered)* Screw the business world!

HAPPY: All right, screw it! Great, but cover yourself!

LINDA: Hap, Hap!

BIFF: I don't care what they think! They've laughed at Dad for years, and you know why? Because we don't belong in this nut-house of a city! We should be mixing cement on some open plain, or — or carpenters. A carpenter is allowed to whistle!

Willy walks in from the entrance of the house, at left.

WILLY: Even your grandfather was better than a carpenter. *(Pause. They watch him.)* You never grew up. Bernard does not whistle in the elevator, I assure you.

BIFF: *(as though to laugh Willy out of it)* Yeah, but you do, Pop.

WILLY: I never in my life whistled in an elevator! And who in the business world thinks I'm crazy?

BIFF: I didn't mean it like that, Pop. Now don't make a whole thing out of it, will ya?

WILLY: Go back to the West! Be a carpenter, a cowboy, enjoy yourself!

LINDA: Willy, he was just saying —

WILLY: I heard what he said!

HAPPY: *(trying to quiet Willy)* Hey, Pop, come on now . . .

WILLY: *(continuing over Happy's line)* They laugh at me, heh? Go to Filene's, go to the Hub, go to Slattery's, Boston. Call out the name Willy Loman and see what happens! Big shot!

BIFF: All right, Pop.

WILLY: Big!

BIFF: All right!

WILLY: Why do you always insult me?

BIFF: I didn't say a word. *(To Linda.)* Did I say a word?

LINDA: He didn't say anything, Willy.

WILLY: *(going to the doorway of the living room)* All right, good night, good night.

LINDA: Willy, dear, he just decided . . .

WILLY: *(to Biff)* If you get tired hanging around tomorrow, paint the ceiling I put up in the living room.

BIFF: I'm leaving early tomorrow.

HAPPY: He's going to see Bill Oliver, Pop.

WILLY: *(interestedly)* Oliver? For what?

BIFF: *(with reserve, but trying, trying)* He always said he'd stake me. I'd like to go into business, so maybe I can take him up on it.

LINDA: Isn't that wonderful?

WILLY: Don't interrupt. What's wonderful about it? There's fifty men in the City of New York who'd stake him. *(To Biff.)* Sporting goods?

BIFF: I guess so. I know something about it and—

WILLY: He knows something about it! You know sporting goods better than Spalding, for God's sake! How much is he giving you?

BIFF: I don't know, I didn't even see him yet, but—

WILLY: Then what're you talkin' about?

BIFF: *(getting angry)* Well, all I said was I'm gonna see him, that's all!

WILLY: *(turning away)* Ah, you're counting your chickens again.

BIFF: *(starting left for the stairs)* Oh, Jesus, I'm going to sleep!

WILLY: *(calling after him)* Don't curse in this house!

BIFF: *(turning)* Since when did you get so clean!

HAPPY: *(trying to stop them)* Wait a . . .

WILLY: Don't use that language to me! I won't have it!

HAPPY: *(grabbing Biff, shouts)* Wait a minute! I got an idea. I got a feasible idea. Come here, Biff, let's talk this over now, let's talk some sense here. When I was down in Florida last time, I thought of a great idea to sell sporting goods. It just came back to me. You and I, Biff—we have a line, the Loman Line. We train a couple of weeks, and put on a couple of exhibitions, see?

WILLY: That's an idea!

HAPPY: Wait! We form two basketball teams, see? Two water-polo teams. We play each other. It's a million dollars' worth of publicity. Two brothers, see? The Loman Brothers. Displays in the Royal Palms—all the hotels. And banners over the ring and the basketball court: "Loman Brothers." Baby, we could sell sporting goods!

WILLY: That is a one-million-dollar idea.

LINDA: Marvelous!

BIFF: I'm in great shape as far as that's concerned.

HAPPY: And the beauty of it is, Biff, it wouldn't be like a business. We'd be out playin' ball again . . .

BIFF: *(enthused)* Yeah, that's . . .

WILLY: Million-dollar . . .

HAPPY: And you wouldn't get fed up with it, Biff. It'd be the family again. There'd be the old honor, and comradeship, and if you wanted to go off for a swim or somethin'—well, you'd do it! Without some smart cooky gettin' up ahead of you!

WILLY: Lick the world! You guys together could absolutely lick the civilized world.

BIFF: I'll see Oliver tomorrow. Hap, if we could work that out . . .

LINDA: Maybe things are beginning to—

WILLY: *(wildly enthused, to Linda)* Stop interrupting! *(To Biff.)* But don't wear sport jacket and slacks when you see Oliver.

BIFF: No, I'll—

WILLY: A business suit, and talk as little as possible, and don't crack any jokes.

BIFF: He did like me. Always liked me.

LINDA: He loved you!

WILLY: *(to Linda)* Will you stop! *(To Biff.)* Walk in very serious. You are not applying for a boy's job. Money is to pass. Be quiet, fine, and serious. Everybody likes a kidder, but nobody lends him money.

HAPPY: I'll try to get some myself, Biff. I'm sure I can.

WILLY: I can see great things for you, kids, I think your troubles are over. But remember, start big and you'll end big. Ask for fifteen. How much you gonna ask for?

BIFF: Gee, I don't know—

WILLY: And don't say "Gee." "Gee" is a boy's word. A man walking in for fifteen thousand dollars does not say "Gee!"

BIFF: Ten, I think, would be top though.

WILLY: Don't be so modest. You always started too low. Walk in with a big laugh. Don't look worried. Start off with a couple of your good stories to lighten things up. It's not what you say, it's how you say it—because personality always wins the day.

LINDA: Oliver always thought the highest of him—

WILLY: Will you let me talk?

BIFF: Don't yell at her, Pop, will ya?

WILLY: *(angrily)* I was talking, wasn't I!

BIFF: I don't like you yelling at her all the time, and I'm tellin' you, that's all.

WILLY: What're you, takin' over this house?

LINDA: Willy—

WILLY: *(turning on her)* Don't take his side all the time, goddammit!

BIFF: *(furiously)* Stop yelling at her!

WILLY: *(suddenly pulling on his cheek, beaten down, guilt ridden)* Give my best to Bill Oliver—he may remember me. *(He exits through the living room doorway.)*

LINDA: *(her voice subdued)* What'd you have to start that for? *(Biff turns away.)* You see how sweet he was as soon as you talked hopefully? *(She goes over to Biff.)* Come up and say good night to him. Don't let him go to bed that way.

HAPPY: Come on, Biff, let's buck him up.

LINDA: Please, dear. Just say good night. It takes so little to make him happy. Come. *(She goes through the living room doorway, calling upstairs from within the living room.)* Your pajamas are hanging in the bathroom. Willy!

HAPPY: *(looking toward where Linda went out)* What a woman! They broke the mold when they made her. You know that, Biff?

BIFF: He's off salary. My God, working on commission!

HAPPY: Well, let's face it: he's no hot-shot selling man. Except that sometimes, you have to admit, he's a sweet personality.

BIFF: *(deciding)* Lend me ten bucks, will ya? I want to buy some new ties.

HAPPY: I'll take you to a place I know. Beautiful stuff. Wear one of my striped shirts tomorrow.

BIFF: She got gray. Mom got awful old. Gee, I'm gonna go in to Oliver tomorrow and knock him for a—

HAPPY: Come on up. Tell that to Dad. Let's give him a whirl. Come on.

BIFF: *(steamed up)* You know, with ten thousand bucks, boy!

HAPPY: *(as they go into the living room)* That's the talk, Biff, that's the first time I've heard the old confidence out of you! *(From within the living room, fading off.)* You're gonna live with me, kid, and any babe you want you just say the word . . . *(The last lines are hardly heard. They are mounting the stairs to their parents' bedroom.)*

LINDA: *(entering her bedroom and addressing Willy, who is in the bathroom. She is straightening the bed for him)* Can you do anything about the shower? It drips.

WILLY: *(from the bathroom)* All of a sudden everything falls to pieces! Goddam plumbing, oughta be sued, those people. I hardly finished putting it in and the thing . . . *(His words rumble off.)*

LINDA: I'm just wondering if Oliver will remember him. You think he might?

WILLY: *(coming out of the bathroom in his pajamas)* Remember him? What's the matter with you, you crazy? If he'd've stayed with Oliver he'd be on top by now! Wait'll Oliver gets a look at him. You don't know the average caliber any more. The average young man today—*(he is getting into bed)*—is got a caliber of zero. Greatest thing in the world for him was to bum around.

Biff and Happy enter the bedroom. Slight pause.

WILLY: *(stops short, looking at Biff)* Glad to hear it, boy.

HAPPY: He wanted to say good night to you, sport.

WILLY: *(to Biff)* Yeah. Knock him dead, boy. What'd you want to tell me?

BIFF: Just take it easy, Pop. Good night. *(He turns to go.)*

WILLY: *(unable to resist)* And if anything falls off the desk while you're talking to him—like a package or something—don't you pick it up. They have office boys for that.

LINDA: I'll make a big breakfast—

WILLY: Will you let me finish? *(To Biff.)* Tell him you were in the business in the West. Not farm work.

BIFF: All right, Dad.

LINDA: I think everything—

WILLY: *(going right through her speech)* And don't undersell yourself. No less than fifteen thousand dollars.

BIFF: *(unable to bear him)* Okay. Good night, Mom. *(He starts moving.)*

WILLY: Because you got a greatness in you, Biff, remember that. You got all kinds a greatness . . . *(He lies back, exhausted. Biff walks out.)*

LINDA: *(calling after Biff)* Sleep well, darling!

HAPPY: I'm gonna get married, Mom. I wanted to tell you.

LINDA: Go to sleep, dear.

HAPPY: *(going)* I just wanted to tell you.

WILLY: Keep up the good work. *(Happy exits.)* God . . . remember that Ebbets Field game? The championship of the city?

LINDA: Just rest. Should I sing to you?

WILLY: Yeah. Sing to me. *(Linda hums a soft lullaby.)* When that team came out—he was the tallest, remember?

Linda: Oh, yes. And in gold.

Biff enters the darkened kitchen, takes a cigarette, and leaves the house. He comes downstage into a golden pool of light. He smokes, staring at the night.

Willy: Like a young god. Hercules—something like that. And the sun, the sun all around him. Remember how he waved to me? Right up from the field, with the representatives of three colleges standing by? And the buyers I brought, and the cheers when he came out—Loman, Loman, Loman! God Almighty, he'll be great yet. A star like that, magnificent, can never really fade away!

The light on Willy is fading. The gas heater begins to glow through the kitchen wall, near the stairs, a blue flame beneath red coils.

Linda: *(timidly)* Willy, dear, what has he got against you?
Willy: I'm so tired. Don't talk any more.

Biff slowly returns to the kitchen. He stops, stares toward the heater.

Linda: Will you ask Howard to let you work in New York?
Willy: First thing in the morning. Everything'll be all right.

Biff reaches behind the heater and draws out a length of rubber tubing. He is horrified and turns his head toward Willy's room, still dimly lit, from which the strains of Linda's desperate but monotonous humming rise.

Willy: *(staring through the window into the moonlight)* Gee, look at the moon moving between the buildings!

Biff wraps the tubing around his hand and quickly goes up the stairs. Curtain.

ACT 2

Music is heard, gay and bright. The curtain rises as the music fades away. Willy, in shirt sleeves, is sitting at the kitchen table, sipping coffee, his hat in his lap. Linda is filling his cup when she can.

Willy: Wonderful coffee. Meal in itself.
Linda: Can I make you some eggs?
Willy: No. Take a breath.
Linda: You look so rested, dear.
Willy: I slept like a dead one. First time in months. Imagine, sleeping till ten on a Tuesday morning. Boys left nice and early, heh?
Linda: They were out of here by eight o'clock.
Willy: Good work!
Linda: It was so thrilling to see them leaving together. I can't get over the shaving lotion in this house.
Willy: *(smiling)* Mmm—

Linda: Biff was very changed this morning. His whole attitude seemed to be hopeful. He couldn't wait to get downtown to see Oliver.

Willy: He's heading for a change. There's no question, there simply are certain men that take longer to get—solidified. How did he dress?

Linda: His blue suit. He's so handsome in that suit. He could be a—anything in that suit!

Willy gets up from the table. Linda holds his jacket for him.

Willy: There's no question, no question at all. Gee, on the way home tonight I'd like to buy some seeds.

Linda: *(laughing)* That'd be wonderful. But not enough sun gets back there. Nothing'll grow any more.

Willy: You wait, kid, before it's all over we're gonna get a little place out in the country, and I'll raise some vegetables, a couple of chickens . . .

Linda: You'll do it yet, dear.

Willy walks out of his jacket. Linda follows him.

Willy: And they'll get married, and come for a weekend. I'd build a little guest house. 'Cause I got so many fine tools, all I'd need would be a little lumber and some peace of mind.

Linda: *(joyfully)* I sewed the lining . . .

Willy: I could build two guest houses, so they'd both come. Did he decide how much he's going to ask Oliver for?

Linda: *(getting him into the jacket)* He didn't mention it, but I imagine ten or fifteen thousand. You going to talk to Howard today?

Willy: Yeah. I'll put it to him straight and simple. He'll just have to take me off the road.

Linda: And Willy, don't forget to ask for a little advance, because we've got the insurance premium. It's the grace period now.

Willy: That's a hundred . . .?

Linda: A hundred and eight, sixty-eight. Because we're a little short again.

Willy: Why are we short?

Linda: Well, you had the motor job on the car . . .

Willy: That goddam Studebaker!

Linda: And you got one more payment on the refrigerator . . .

Willy: But it just broke again!

Linda: Well, it's old, dear.

Willy: I told you we should've bought a well-advertised machine. Charley bought a General Electric and it's twenty years old and it's still good, that son-of-a-bitch.

Linda: But, Willy—

Willy: Whoever heard of a Hastings refrigerator? Once in my life I would like to own something outright before it's broken! I'm always in a race with the junkyard! I just finished paying for the car and it's on its last legs. The refrigerator consumes belts like a goddam maniac. They time those things. They time them so when you finally paid for them, they're used up.

LINDA: *(buttoning up his jacket as he unbuttons it)* All told, about two hundred dollars would carry us, dear. But that includes the last payment on the mortgage. After this payment, Willy, the house belongs to us.

WILLY: It's twenty-five years!

LINDA: Biff was nine years old when we bought it.

WILLY: Well, that's a great thing. To weather a twenty-five year mortgage is—

LINDA: It's an accomplishment.

WILLY: All the cement, the lumber, the reconstruction I put in this house! There ain't a crack to be found in it any more.

LINDA: Well, it served its purpose.

WILLY: What purpose? Some stranger'll come along, move in, and that's that. If only Biff would take this house, and raise a family . . . *(He starts to go.)* Good-by, I'm late.

LINDA: *(suddenly remembering)* Oh, I forgot! You're supposed to meet them for dinner.

WILLY: Me?

LINDA: At Frank's Chop House on Forty-eighth near Sixth Avenue.

WILLY: Is that so! How about you?

LINDA: No, just the three of you. They're gonna blow you to a big meal!

WILLY: Don't say! Who thought of that?

LINDA: Biff came to me this morning, Willy, and he said, "Tell Dad, we want to blow him to a big meal." Be there six o'clock. You and your two boys are going to have dinner.

WILLY: Gee whiz! That's really somethin'. I'm gonna knock Howard for a loop, kid. I'll get an advance, and I'll come home with a New York job. Goddammit, now I'm gonna do it!

LINDA: Oh, that's the spirit, Willy!

WILLY: I will never get behind a wheel the rest of my life!

LINDA: It's changing, Willy, I can feel it changing!

WILLY: Beyond a question. G'by, I'm late. *(He starts to go again.)*

LINDA: *(calling after him as she runs to the kitchen table for a handkerchief)* You got your glasses?

WILLY: *(feels for them, then comes back in)* Yeah, yeah, got my glasses.

LINDA: *(giving him the handkerchief)* And a handkerchief.

WILLY: Yeah, handkerchief.

LINDA: And your saccharine?

WILLY: Yeah, my saccharine.

LINDA: Be careful on the subway stairs.

She kisses him, and a silk stocking is seen hanging from her hand. Willy notices it.

WILLY: Will you stop mending stockings? At least while I'm in the house. It gets me nervous. I can't tell you. Please.

Linda hides the stocking in her hand as she follows Willy across the forestage in front of the house.

LINDA: Remember, Frank's Chop House.

WILLY: *(passing the apron)* Maybe beets would grow out there.

LINDA: *(laughing)* But you tried so many times.

WILLY: Yeah. Well, don't work hard today. *(He disappears around the right corner of the house.)*

LINDA: Be careful!

As Willy vanishes, Linda waves to him. Suddenly the phone rings. She runs across the stage and into the kitchen and lifts it.

LINDA: Hello? Oh, Biff! I'm so glad you called, I just . . . Yes, sure, I just told him. Yes, he'll be there for dinner at six o'clock, I didn't forget. Listen, I was just dying to tell you. You know that little rubber pipe I told you about? That he connected to the gas heater? I finally decided to go down the cellar this morning and take it away and destroy it. But it's gone! Imagine? He took it away himself, it isn't there! *(She listens.)* When? Oh, then you took it. Oh—nothing, it's just that I'd hoped he'd taken it away himself. Oh, I'm not worried, darling, because this morning he left in such high spirits, it was like the old days! I'm not afraid any more. Did Mr. Oliver see you? . . . Well, you wait there then. And make a nice impression on him, darling. Just don't perspire too much before you see him. And have a nice time with Dad. He may have big news too! . . . That's right, a New York job. And be sweet to him tonight, dear. Be loving to him. Because he's only a little boat looking for a harbor. *(She is trembling with sorrow and joy.)* Oh, that's wonderful, Biff, you'll save his life. Thanks, darling. Just put your arm around him when he comes into the restaurant. Give him a smile. That's the boy . . . Good-by, dear. . . . You got your comb? . . . That's fine. Good-by, Biff dear.

In the middle of her speech, Howard Wagner, thirty-six, wheels in a small typewriter table on which is a wire-recording machine and proceeds to plug it in. This is on the left forestage. Light slowly fades on Linda as it rises on Howard. Howard is intent on threading the machine and only glances over his shoulder as Willy appears.

WILLY: Pst! Pst!

HOWARD: Hello, Willy, come in.

WILLY: Like to have a little talk with you, Howard.

HOWARD: Sorry to keep you waiting. I'll be with you in a minute.

WILLY: What's that, Howard?

HOWARD: Didn't you ever see one of these? Wire recorder.

WILLY: Oh. Can we talk a minute?

HOWARD: Records things. Just got delivery yesterday. Been driving me crazy, the most terrific machine I ever saw in my life. I was up all night with it.

WILLY: What do you do with it?

HOWARD: I bought it for dictation, but you can do anything with it. Listen to this. I had it home last night. Listen to what I picked up. The first one is my daughter. Get this. *(He flicks the switch and "Roll out the Barrel" is heard being whistled.)* Listen to that kid whistle.

WILLY: That is lifelike, isn't it?

HOWARD: Seven years old. Get that tone.

WILLY: Ts, ts. Like to ask a little favor if you . . .

The whistling breaks off, and the voice of Howard's Daughter is heard.

HIS DAUGHTER: "Now you, Daddy."

HOWARD: She's crazy for me! *(Again the same song is whistled.)* That's me! Ha! *(He winks.)*

WILLY: You're very good!

The whistling breaks off again. The machine runs silent for a moment.

HOWARD: Sh! Get this now, this is my son.

HIS SON: "The capital of Alabama is Montgomery; the capital of Arizona is Phoenix; the capital of Arkansas is Little Rock; the capital of California is Sacramento . . ." *(And on, and on.)*

HOWARD: *(holding up five fingers)* Five years old, Willy!

WILLY: He'll make an announcer some day!

HIS SON: *(continuing)* "The capital . . ."

HOWARD: Get that—alphabetical order! *(The machine breaks off suddenly.)* Wait a minute. The maid kicked the plug out.

WILLY: It certainly is a—

HOWARD: Sh, for God's sake!

HIS SON: "It's nine o'clock, Bulova watch time. So I have to go to sleep."

WILLY: That really is—

HOWARD: Wait a minute! The next is my wife.

They wait.

HOWARD'S VOICE: "Go on, say something." *(Pause.)* "Well, you gonna talk?"

HIS WIFE: "I can't think of anything."

HOWARD'S VOICE: "Well, talk—it's turning."

HIS WIFE: *(shyly, beaten)* "Hello." *(Silence.)* "Oh, Howard, I can't talk into this . . ."

HOWARD: *(snapping the machine off)* That was my wife.

WILLY: That is a wonderful machine. Can we—

HOWARD: I tell you, Willy, I'm gonna take my camera, and my bandsaw, and all my hobbies, and out they go. This is the most fascinating relaxation I ever found.

WILLY: I think I'll get one myself.

HOWARD: Sure, they're only a hundred and a half. You can't do without it. Supposing you wanna hear Jack Benny, see? But you can't be at home at that hour. So you tell the maid to turn the radio on when Jack Benny comes on, and this automatically goes on with the radio . . .

WILLY: And when you come home you . . .

HOWARD: You can come home twelve o'clock, one o'clock, any time you like, and you get yourself a Coke and sit yourself down, throw the switch, and there's Jack Benny's program in the middle of the night!

Willy: I'm definitely going to get one. Because lots of time I'm on the road, and I think to myself, what I must be missing on the radio!

Howard: Don't you have a radio in the car?

Willy: Well, yeah, but who ever thinks of turning it on?

Howard: Say, aren't you supposed to be in Boston?

Willy: That's what I want to talk to you about, Howard. You got a minute?

He draws a chair in from the wing.

Howard: What happened? What're you doing here?

Willy: Well . . .

Howard: You didn't crack up again, did you?

Willy: Oh, no. No . . .

Howard: Geez, you had me worried there for a minute. What's the trouble?

Willy: Well, to tell you the truth, Howard, I've come to the decision that I'd rather not travel any more.

Howard: Not travel! Well, what'll you do?

Willy: Remember, Christmas time, when you had the party here? You said you'd try to think of some spot for me here in town.

Howard: With us?

Willy: Well, sure.

Howard: Oh, yeah, yeah. I remember. Well, I couldn't think of anything for you, Willy.

Willy: I tell ya, Howard. The kids are all grown up, y'know. I don't need much any more. If I could take home—well, sixty-five dollars a week, I could swing it.

Howard: Yeah, but Willy, see I—

Willy: I tell ya why, Howard. Speaking frankly and between the two of us, y'know—I'm just a little tired.

Howard: Oh, I could understand that, Willy. But you're a road man, Willy, and we do a road business. We've only got a half-dozen salesmen on the floor here.

Willy: God knows, Howard, I never asked a favor of any man. But I was with the firm when your father used to carry you in here in his arms.

Howard: I know that, Willy, but—

Willy: Your father came to me the day you were born and asked me what I thought of the name of Howard, may he rest in peace.

Howard: I appreciate that, Willy, but there just is no spot here for you. If I had a spot I'd slam you right in, but I just don't have a single, solitary spot.

He looks for his lighter. Willy has picked it up and gives it to him. Pause.

Willy: *(with increasing anger)* Howard, all I need to set my table is fifty dollars a week.

Howard: But where am I going to put you, kid?

Willy: Look, it isn't a question of whether I can sell merchandise, is it?

HOWARD: No, but it's a business, kid, and everybody's gotta pull his own weight.

WILLY: *(desperately)* Just let me tell you a story, Howard—

HOWARD: 'Cause you gotta admit, business is business.

WILLY: *(angrily)* Business is definitely business, but just listen for a minute. You don't understand this. When I was a boy—eighteen, nineteen—I was already on the road. And there was a question in my mind as to whether selling had a future for me. Because in those days I had a yearning to go to Alaska. See, there were three gold strikes in one month in Alaska, and I felt like going out. Just for the ride, you might say.

HOWARD: *(barely interested)* Don't say.

WILLY: Oh, yeah, my father lived many years in Alaska. He was an adventurous man. We've got quite a little streak of self-reliance in our family. I thought I'd go out with my older brother and try to locate him, and maybe settle in the North with the old man. And I was almost decided to go, when I met a salesman in the Parker House. His name was Dave Singleman. And he was eighty-four years old, and he'd drummed merchandise in thirty-one states. And old Dave, he'd go up to his room, y'understand, put on his green velvet slippers—I'll never forget—and pick up his phone and call the buyers, and without ever leaving his room, at the age of eighty-four, he made his living. And when I saw that, I realized that selling was the greatest career a man could want. 'Cause what could be more satisfying than to be able to go, at the age of eighty-four, into twenty or thirty different cities, and pick up a phone, and be remembered and loved and helped by so many different people? Do you know? when he died—and by the way he died the death of a salesman, in his green velvet slippers in the smoker of the New York, New Haven and Hartford, going into Boston—when he died, hundreds of salesmen and buyers were at his funeral. Things were sad on a lotta trains for months after that. *(He stands up. Howard has not looked at him.)* In those days there was personality in it, Howard. There was respect, and comradeship, and gratitude in it. Today, it's all cut and dried, and there's no chance for bringing friendship to bear—or personality. You see what I mean? They don't know me any more.

HOWARD: *(moving away, to the right)* That's just the thing, Willy.

WILLY: If I had forty dollars a week—that's all I'd need. Forty dollars, Howard.

HOWARD: Kid, I can't take blood from a stone, I—

WILLY: *(desperation is on him now)* Howard, the year Al Smith was nominated, your father came to me and—

HOWARD: *(starting to go off)* I've got to see some people, kid.

WILLY: *(stopping him)* I'm talking about your father! There were promises made across this desk! You mustn't tell me you've got people to see—I put thirty-four years into this firm, Howard, and now I can't pay my insurance! You can't eat the orange and throw the peel away—a man is not a piece of fruit! *(After a pause.)* Now pay attention. Your father—in 1928 I had a big year. I averaged a hundred and seventy dollars a week in commissions.

HOWARD: *(impatiently)* Now, Willy, you never averaged—

WILLY: *(banging his hand on the desk)* I averaged a hundred and seventy dollars a week in the year of 1928! And your father came to me—or rather, I was in the office here—it was right over this desk—and he put his hand on my shoulder—

HOWARD: *(getting up)* You'll have to excuse me, Willy, I gotta see some people. Pull yourself together. *(Going out.)* I'll be back in a little while.

On Howard's exit, the light on his chair grows very bright and strange.

WILLY: Pull myself together! What the hell did I say to him? My God, I was yelling at him! How could I! *(Willy breaks off, staring at the light, which occupies the chair, animating it. He approaches this chair, standing across the desk from it.)* Frank, Frank, don't you remember what you told me that time? How you put your hand on my shoulder, and Frank . . . *(He leans on the desk and as he speaks the dead man's name he accidentally switches on the recorder, and instantly—)*

HOWARD'S SON: ". . . of New York is Albany. The capital of Ohio is Cincinnati, the capital of Rhode Island is . . ." *(The recitation continues.)*

WILLY: *(leaping away with fright, shouting)* Ha! Howard! Howard! Howard!

HOWARD: *(rushing in)* What happened?

WILLY: *(pointing at the machine, which continues nasally, childishly, with the capital cities)* Shut it off! Shut it off!

HOWARD: *(pulling the plug out)* Look, Willy . . .

WILLY: *(pressing his hands to his eyes)* I gotta get myself some coffee. I'll get some coffee . . .

Willy starts to walk out. Howard stops him.

HOWARD: *(rolling up the cord)* Willy, look . . .

WILLY: I'll go to Boston.

HOWARD: Willy, you can't go to Boston for us.

WILLY: Why can't I go?

HOWARD: I don't want you to represent us. I've been meaning to tell you for a long time now.

WILLY: Howard, are you firing me?

HOWARD: I think you need a good long rest, Willy.

WILLY: Howard—

HOWARD: And when you feel better, come back, and we'll see if we can work something out.

WILLY: But I gotta earn money, Howard. I'm in no position—

HOWARD: Where are your sons? Why don't your sons give you a hand?

WILLY: They're working on a very big deal.

HOWARD: This is no time for false pride, Willy. You go to your sons and tell them that you're tired. You've got two great boys, haven't you?

WILLY: Oh, no question, no question, but in the meantime . . .

HOWARD: Then that's that, heh?

WILLY: All right, I'll go to Boston tomorrow.

HOWARD: No, no.

WILLY: I can't throw myself on my sons. I'm not a cripple!

HOWARD: Look, kid, I'm busy this morning.

WILLY: *(grasping Howard's arm)* Howard, you've got to let me go to Boston!

HOWARD: *(hard, keeping himself under control)* I've got a line of people to see this morning. Sit down, take five minutes, and pull yourself together, and then go home, will ya? I need the office, Willy. *(He starts to go, turns, remembering the recorder, starts to push off the table holding the recorder.)* Oh, yeah. Whenever you can this week, stop by and drop off the samples. You'll feel better, Willy, and then come back and we'll talk. Pull yourself together, kid, there's people outside.

Howard exits, pushing the table off left. Willy stares into space, exhausted. Now the music is heard—Ben's music—first distantly, then closer, closer. As Willy speaks, Ben enters from the right. He carries valise and umbrella.

WILLY: Oh, Ben, how did you do it? What is the answer? Did you wind up the Alaska deal already?

BEN: Doesn't take much time if you know what you're doing. Just a short business trip. Boarding ship in an hour. Wanted to say good-by.

WILLY: Ben, I've got to talk to you.

BEN: *(glancing at his watch)* Haven't the time, William.

WILLY: *(crossing the apron to Ben)* Ben, nothing's working out. I don't know what to do.

BEN: Now, look here, William. I've bought timberland in Alaska and I need a man to look after things for me.

WILLY: God, timberland! Me and my boys in those grand outdoors!

BEN: You've a new continent at your doorstep, William. Get out of these cities, they're full of talk and time payments and courts of law. Screw on your fists and you can fight for a fortune up there.

WILLY: Yes, yes! Linda! Linda!

Linda enters as of old, with the wash.

LINDA: Oh, you're back?

BEN: I haven't much time.

WILLY: No, wait! Linda, he's got a proposition for me in Alaska.

LINDA: But you've got—*(To Ben.)* He's got a beautiful job here.

WILLY: But in Alaska, kid, I could—

LINDA: You're doing well enough, Willy!

BEN: *(to Linda)* Enough for what, my dear?

LINDA: *(frightened of Ben and angry at him)* Don't say those things to him! Enough to be happy right here, right now. *(To Willy, while Ben laughs.)* Why must everybody conquer the world? You're well liked, and the boys love you, and someday—*(to Ben)*—why, old man Wagner told him just the other day that if he keeps it up he'll be a member of the firm, didn't he, Willy?

WILLY: Sure, sure. I am building something with this firm, Ben, and if a man is building something he must be on the right track, mustn't he?

BEN: What are you building? Lay your hand on it. Where is it?

WILLY: *(hesitantly)* That's true, Linda, there's nothing.

LINDA: Why? *(To Ben.)* There's a man eighty-four years old—

WILLY: That's right, Ben, that's right. When I look at that man I say, what is there to worry about?

BEN: Bah!

WILLY: It's true, Ben. All he has to do is go into any city, pick up the phone, and he's making his living and you know why?

BEN: *(picking up his valise)* I've got to go.

WILLY: *(holding Ben back)* Look at this boy!

Biff, in his high school sweater, enters carrying suitcase. Happy carries Biff's shoulder guards, gold helmet, and football pants.

WILLY: Without a penny to his name, three great universities are begging for him, and from there the sky's the limit, because it's not what you do, Ben. It's who you know and the smile on your face! It's contacts, Ben, contacts! The whole wealth of Alaska passes over the lunch table at the Commodore Hotel, and that's the wonder, the wonder of this country, that a man can end with diamonds here on the basis of being liked! *(He turns to Biff.)* And that's why when you get out on that field today it's important. Because thousands of people will be rooting for you and loving you. *(To Ben, who has again begun to leave.)* And Ben! when he walks into a business office his name will sound out like a bell and all the doors will open to him! I've seen it, Ben, I've seen it a thousand times! You can't feel it with your hand like timber, but it's there!

BEN: Good-by, William.

WILLY: Ben, am I right? Don't you think I'm right? I value your advice.

BEN: There's a new continent at your doorstep, William. You could walk out rich. Rich. *(He is gone.)*

WILLY: We'll do it here, Ben! You hear me? We're gonna do it here!

Young Bernard rushes in. The gay music of the boys is heard.

BERNARD: Oh, gee, I was afraid you left already!

WILLY: Why? What time is it?

BERNARD: It's half-past one!

WILLY: Well, come on, everybody! Ebbets Field° next stop! Where's the pennants? *(He rushes through the wall-line of the kitchen and out into the living room.)*

LINDA: *(to Biff)* Did you pack fresh underwear?

BIFF: *(who has been limbering up)* I want to go!

BERNARD: Biff, I'm carrying your helmet, ain't I?

HAPPY: No, I'm carrying the helmet.

BERNARD: Oh, Biff, you promised me.

°*Ebbets Field:* The home park of the Brooklyn Dodgers.

HAPPY: I'm carrying the helmet.

BERNARD: How am I going to get in the locker room?

LINDA: Let him carry the shoulder guards. *(She puts her coat and hat on in the kitchen.)*

BERNARD: Can I, Biff? 'Cause I told everybody I'm going to be in the locker room.

HAPPY: In Ebbets Field it's the clubhouse.

BERNARD: I meant the clubhouse. Biff!

HAPPY: Biff!

BIFF: *(grandly, after a slight pause)* Let him carry the shoulder guards.

HAPPY: *(as he gives Bernard the shoulder guards)* Stay close to us now.

Willy rushes in with the pennants.

WILLY: *(handing them out)* Everybody wave when Biff comes out on the field. *(Happy and Bernard run off.)* You set now, boy?

The music has died away.

BIFF: Ready to go, Pop. Every muscle is ready.

WILLY: *(at the edge of the apron)* You realize what this means?

BIFF: That's right, Pop.

WILLY: *(feeling Biff's muscles)* You're comin' home this afternoon captain of the All-Scholastic Championship Team of the City of New York.

BIFF: I got it, Pop. And remember, pal, when I take off my helmet, that touchdown is for you.

WILLY: Let's go! *(He is starting out, with his arm around Biff, when Charley enters, as of old, in knickers.)* I got no room for you, Charley.

CHARLEY: Room? For what?

WILLY: In the car.

CHARLEY: You goin' for a ride? I wanted to shoot some casino.

WILLY: *(furiously)* Casino! *(Incredulously.)* Don't you realize what today is?

LINDA: Oh, he knows, Willy. He's just kidding you.

WILLY: That's nothing to kid about!

CHARLEY: No, Linda, what's goin' on?

LINDA: He's playing in Ebbets Field.

CHARLEY: Baseball in this weather?

WILLY: Don't talk to him. Come on, come on! *(He is pushing them out.)*

CHARLEY: Wait a minute, didn't you hear the news?

WILLY: What?

CHARLEY: Don't you listen to the radio? Ebbets Field just blew up.

WILLY: You go to hell! *(Charley laughs. Pushing them out.)* Come on, come on! We're late.

CHARLEY: *(as they go)* Knock a homer, Biff, knock a homer!

WILLY: *(the last to leave, turning to Charley)* I don't think that was funny, Charley. This is the greatest day of his life.

CHARLEY: Willy, when are you going to grow up?

WILLY: Yeah, heh? When this game is over, Charley, you'll be laughing out of the other side of your face. They'll be calling him another Red Grange.° Twenty-five thousand a year.

CHARLEY: *(kidding)* Is that so?

WILLY: Yeah, that's so.

CHARLEY: Well, then, I'm sorry, Willy. But tell me something.

WILLY: What?

CHARLEY: Who is Red Grange?

WILLY: Put up your hands. Goddam you, put up your hands!

Charley, chuckling, shakes his head and walks away, around the left corner of the stage. Willy follows him. The music rises to a mocking frenzy.

WILLY: Who the hell do you think you are, better than everybody else? You don't know everything, you big, ignorant, stupid . . . Put up your hands!

Light rises, on the right side of the forestage, on a small table in the reception room of Charley's office. Traffic sounds are heard. Bernard, now mature, sits whistling to himself. A pair of tennis rackets and an overnight bag are on the floor beside him.

WILLY: *(offstage)* What are you walking away for? Don't walk away! If you're going to say something say it to my face! I know you laugh at me behind my back. You'll laugh out of the other side of your goddam face after this game. Touchdown! Touchdown! Eighty thousand people! Touchdown! Right between the goal posts.

Bernard is a quiet, earnest, but self-assured young man. Willy's voice is coming from right upstage now. Bernard lowers his feet off the table and listens. Jenny, his father's secretary, enters.

JENNY: *(distressed)* Say, Bernard, will you go out in the hall?

BERNARD: What is that noise? Who is it?

JENNY: Mr. Loman. He just got off the elevator.

BERNARD: *(getting up)* Who's he arguing with?

JENNY: Nobody. There's nobody with him. I can't deal with him any more, and your father gets all upset everytime he comes. I've got a lot of typing to do, and your father's waiting to sign it. Will you see him?

WILLY: *(entering)* Touchdown! Touch — *(He sees Jenny.)* Jenny, Jenny, good to see you. How're ya? Workin'? Or still honest?

JENNY: Fine. How've you been feeling?

WILLY: Not much any more, Jenny. Ha, ha! *(He is surprised to see the rackets.)*

BERNARD: Hello, Uncle Willy.

WILLY: *(almost shocked)* Bernard! Well, look who's here! *(He comes quickly, guiltily, to Bernard and warmly shakes his hand.)*

BERNARD: How are you? Good to see you.

WILLY: What are you doing here?

°*Red Grange:* Harold Edward ("Red") Grange (1903–1991)—American football player. A running back for the New York Giants football team and the Chicago Bears, Grange was elected to the Football Hall of Fame in 1963.

BERNARD: Oh, just stopped by to see Pop. Get off my feet till my train leaves. I'm going to Washington in a few minutes.

WILLY: Is he in?

BERNARD: Yes, he's in his office with the accountant. Sit down.

WILLY: *(sitting down)* What're you going to do in Washington?

BERNARD: Oh, just a case I've got there, Willy.

WILLY: That so? *(indicating the rackets)* You going to play tennis there?

BERNARD: I'm staying with a friend who's got a court.

WILLY: Don't say. His own tennis court. Must be fine people, I bet.

BERNARD: They are, very nice. Dad tells me Biff's in town.

WILLY: *(with a big smile)* Yeah, Biff's in. Working on a very big deal, Bernard.

BERNARD: What's Biff doing?

WILLY: Well, he's been doing very big things in the West. But he decided to establish himself here. Very big. We're having dinner. Did I hear your wife had a boy?

BERNARD: That's right. Our second.

WILLY: Two boys! What do you know!

BERNARD: What kind of a deal has Biff got?

WILLY: Well, Bill Oliver—very big sporting-goods man—he wants Biff very badly. Called him in from the West. Long distance, carte blanche, special deliveries. Your friends have their own private tennis court?

BERNARD: You still with the old firm, Willy?

WILLY: *(after a pause)* I'm—I'm overjoyed to see how you made the grade, Bernard, overjoyed. It's an encouraging thing to see a young man really—really—Looks very good for Biff—very—*(He breaks off, then.)* Bernard—*(He is so full of emotion, he breaks off again.)*

BERNARD: What is it, Willy?

WILLY: *(small and alone)* What—what's the secret?

BERNARD: What secret?

WILLY: How—how did you? Why didn't he ever catch on?

BERNARD: I wouldn't know that, Willy.

WILLY: *(confidentially, desperately)* You were his friend, his boyhood friend. There's something I don't understand about it. His life ended after that Ebbets Field game. From the age of seventeen nothing good ever happened to him.

BERNARD: He never trained himself for anything.

WILLY: But he did, he did. After high school he took so many correspondence courses. Radio mechanics; television; God knows what, and never made the slightest mark.

BERNARD: *(taking off his glasses)* Willy, do you want to talk candidly?

WILLY: *(rising, faces Bernard)* I regard you as a very brilliant man, Bernard. I value your advice.

BERNARD: Oh, the hell with the advice, Willy. I couldn't advise you. There's just one thing I've always wanted to ask you. When he was supposed to graduate, and the math teacher flunked him—

WILLY: Oh, that son-of-a-bitch ruined his life.

Bernard: Yeah, but, Willy, all he had to do was go to summer school and make up that subject.

Willy: That's right, that's right.

Bernard: Did you tell him not to go to summer school?

Willy: Me? I begged him to go. I ordered him to go!

Bernard: Then why wouldn't he go?

Willy: Why? Why! Bernard, that question has been trailing me like a ghost for the last fifteen years. He flunked the subject, and laid down and died like a hammer hit him!

Bernard: Take it easy, kid.

Willy: Let me talk to you—I got nobody to talk to. Bernard, Bernard, was it my fault? Y'see? It keeps going around in my mind, maybe I did something to him. I got nothing to give him.

Bernard: Don't take it so hard.

Willy: Why did he lay down? What is the story there? You were his friend!

Bernard: Willy, I remember, it was June, and our grades came out. And he'd flunked math.

Willy: That son-of-a-bitch!

Bernard: No, it wasn't right then. Biff just got very angry, I remember, and he was ready to enroll in summer school.

Willy: *(surprised)* He was?

Bernard: He wasn't beaten by it at all. But then, Willy, he disappeared from the block for almost a month. And I got the idea that he'd gone up to New England to see you. Did he have a talk with you then?

Willy stares in silence.

Bernard: Willy?

Willy: *(with a strong edge of resentment in his voice)* Yeah, he came to Boston. What about it?

Bernard: Well, just that when he came back—I'll never forget this, it always mystifies me. Because I'd thought so well of Biff, even though he'd always taken advantage of me. I loved him, Willy, y'know? And he came back after that month and took his sneakers—remember those sneakers with "University of Virginia" printed on them? He was so proud of those, wore them every day. And he took them down in the cellar, and burned them up in the furnace. We had a fist fight. It lasted at least half an hour. Just the two of us, punching each other down the cellar, and crying right through it. I've often thought of how strange it was that I knew he'd given up his life. What happened in Boston, Willy?

Willy looks at him as at an intruder.

Bernard: I just bring it up because you asked me.

Willy: *(angrily)* Nothing. What do you mean, "What happened?" What's that got to do with anything?

Bernard: Well, don't get sore.

WILLY: What are you trying to do, blame it on me? If a boy lays down is that my fault?

BERNARD: Now, Willy, don't get—

WILLY: Well, don't—don't talk to me that way! What does that mean, "What happened?"

Charley enters. He is in his vest, and he carries a bottle of bourbon.

CHARLEY: Hey, you're going to miss that train. *(He waves the bottle.)*

BERNARD: Yeah, I'm going. *(He takes the bottle.)* Thanks, Pop. *(He picks up his rackets and bag.)* Good-by, Willy, and don't worry about it. You know, "If at first you don't succeed . . ."

WILLY: Yes, I believe in that.

BERNARD: But sometimes, Willy, it's better for a man just to walk away.

WILLY: Walk away?

BERNARD: That's right.

WILLY: But if you can't walk away?

BERNARD: *(after a slight pause)* I guess that's when it's tough. *(Extending his hand.)* Good-by, Willy.

WILLY: *(shaking Bernard's hand)* Good-by, boy.

CHARLEY: *(an arm on Bernard's shoulder)* How do you like this kid? Gonna argue a case in front of the Supreme Court.

BERNARD: *(protesting)* Pop!

WILLY: *(genuinely shocked, pained, and happy)* No! The Supreme Court!

BERNARD: I gotta run, 'By, Dad!

CHARLEY: Knock 'em dead, Bernard!

Bernard goes off.

WILLY: *(as Charley takes out his wallet)* The Supreme Court! And he didn't even mention it!

CHARLEY: *(counting out money on the desk)* He don't have to—he's gonna do it.

WILLY: And you never told him what to do, did you? You never took any interest in him.

CHARLEY: My salvation is that I never took any interest in anything. There's some money—fifty dollars. I got an accountant inside.

WILLY: Charley, look . . . *(With difficulty.)* I got my insurance to pay. If you can manage it—I need a hundred and ten dollars.

Charley doesn't reply for a moment; merely stops moving.

WILLY: I'd draw it from my bank but Linda would know, and I . . .

CHARLEY: Sit down, Willy.

WILLY: *(moving toward the chair)* I'm keeping an account of everything, remember. I'll pay every penny back. *(He sits.)*

CHARLEY: Now listen to me, Willy.

WILLY: I want you to know I appreciate . . .

CHARLEY: *(sitting down on the table)* Willy, what're you doin'? What the hell is goin' on in your head?

WILLY: Why? I'm simply . . .

CHARLEY: I offered you a job. You can make fifty dollars a week. And I won't send you on the road.

WILLY: I've got a job.

CHARLEY: Without pay? What kind of a job is a job without pay? *(He rises.)* Now, look, kid, enough is enough. I'm no genius but I know when I'm being insulted.

WILLY: Insulted!

CHARLEY: Why don't you want to work for me?

WILLY: What's the matter with you? I've got a job.

CHARLEY: Then what're you walkin' in here every week for?

WILLY: *(getting up)* Well, if you don't want me to walk in here—

CHARLEY: I am offering you a job.

WILLY: I don't want your goddam job!

CHARLEY: When the hell are you going to grow up?

WILLY: *(furiously)* You big ignoramus, if you say that to me again I'll rap you one! I don't care how big you are! *(He's ready to fight.)*

Pause.

CHARLEY: *(kindly, going to him)* How much do you need, Willy?

WILLY: Charley, I'm strapped. I'm strapped. I don't know what to do. I was just fired.

CHARLEY: Howard fired you?

WILLY: That snotnose. Imagine that? I named him. I named him Howard.

CHARLEY: Willy, when're you gonna realize that them things don't mean anything? You named him Howard, but you can't sell that. The only thing you got in this world is what you can sell. And the funny thing is that you're a salesman, and you don't know that.

WILLY: I've always tried to think otherwise, I guess. I always felt that if a man was impressive, and well liked, that nothing—

CHARLEY: Why must everybody like you? Who liked J. P. Morgan?° Was he impressive? In a Turkish bath he'd look like a butcher. But with his pockets on he was very well liked. Now listen, Willy, I know you don't like me, and nobody can say I'm in love with you, but I'll give you a job because—just for the hell of it, put it that way. Now what do you say?

WILLY: I—I just can't work for you, Charley.

CHARLEY: What're you, jealous of me?

WILLY: I can't work for you, that's all, don't ask me why.

CHARLEY: *(angered, takes out more bills)* You been jealous of me all your life, you damned fool! Here, pay your insurance. *(He puts the money in Willy's hand.)*

WILLY: I'm keeping strict accounts.

CHARLEY: I've got some work to do. Take care of yourself. And pay your insurance.

°*J. P. Morgan:* John Pierpont Morgan (1837–1913)—American financier.

WILLY: *(moving to the right)* Funny, y'know? After all the highways, and the trains, and the appointments, and the years, you end up worth more dead than alive.

CHARLEY: Willy, nobody's worth nothin' dead. *(After a slight pause.)* Did you hear what I said?

Willy stands still, dreaming.

CHARLEY: Willy!

WILLY: Apologize to Bernard for me when you see him. I didn't mean to argue with him. He's a fine boy. They're all fine boys, and they'll end up big—all of them. Someday they'll all play tennis together. Wish me luck, Charley. He saw Bill Oliver today.

CHARLEY: Good luck.

WILLY: *(on the verge of tears)* Charley, you're the only friend I got. Isn't that a remarkable thing? *(He goes out.)*

CHARLEY: Jesus!

Charley stares after him a moment and follows. All light blacks out. Suddenly raucous music is heard, and a red glow rises behind the screen at right. Stanley, a young waiter, appears, carrying a table, followed by Happy, who is carrying two chairs.

STANLEY: *(putting the table down)* That's all right, Mr. Loman, I can handle it myself. *(He turns and takes the chairs from Happy and places them at the table.)*

HAPPY: *(glancing around)* Oh, this is better.

STANLEY: Sure, in the front there you're in the middle of all kinds a noise. Whenever you got a party, Mr. Loman, you just tell me and I'll put you back here. Y'know, there's a lotta people they don't like it private, because when they go out they like to see a lotta action around them because they're sick and tired to stay in the house by theirself. But I know you, you ain't from Hackensack. You know what I mean?

HAPPY: *(sitting down)* So, how's it coming, Stanley?

STANLEY: Ah, it's a dog's life. I only wish during the war they'd a took me in the Army. I coulda been dead by now.

HAPPY: My brother's back, Stanley.

STANLEY: Oh, he come back, heh? From the Far West.

HAPPY: Yeah, big cattle man, my brother, so treat him right. And my father's coming too.

STANLEY: Oh, your father too!

HAPPY: You got a couple of nice lobsters?

STANLEY: Hundred per cent, big.

HAPPY: I want them with the claws.

STANLEY: Don't worry, I don't give you no mice. *(Happy laughs.)* How about some wine? It'll put a head on the meal.

HAPPY: No. You remember, Stanley, that recipe I brought you from overseas? With the champagne in it?

STANLEY: Oh, yeah, sure. I still got it tacked up yet in the kitchen. But that'll have to cost a buck apiece anyways.

Happy: That's all right.

Stanley: What'd you, hit a number or somethin'?

Happy: No, it's a little celebration. My brother is—I think he pulled off a big deal today. I think we're going into business together.

Stanley: Great! That's the best for you. Because a family business, you know what I mean?—that's the best.

Happy: That's what I think.

Stanley: 'Cause what's the difference? Somebody steals? It's in the family. Know what I mean? *(Sotto voce.)* Like this bartender here. The boss is goin' crazy what kinda leak he's got in the cash register. You put it in but it don't come out.

Happy: *(raising his head)* Sh!

Stanley: What?

Happy: You notice I wasn't lookin' right or left, was I?

Stanley: No.

Happy: And my eyes are closed.

Stanley: So what's the—

Happy: Strudel's comin'.

Stanley: *(catching on, looks around)* Ah, no, there's no—

He breaks off as a furred, lavishly dressed Girl enters and sits at the next table. Both follow her with their eyes.

Stanley: Geez, how'd ya know?

Happy: I got radar or something. *(Staring directly at her profile.)* Oooooooo . . . Stanley.

Stanley: I think that's for you, Mr. Loman.

Happy: Look at that mouth. Oh, God. And the binoculars.

Stanley: Geez, you got a life, Mr. Loman.

Happy: Wait on her.

Stanley: *(going to The Girl's table)* Would you like a menu, ma'am?

Girl: I'm expecting someone, but I'd like a—

Happy: Why don't you bring her—excuse me, miss, do you mind? I sell champagne, and I'd like you to try my brand. Bring her a champagne, Stanley.

Girl: That's awfully nice of you.

Happy: Don't mention it. It's all company money. *(He laughs.)*

Girl: That's a charming product to be selling, isn't it?

Happy: Oh, gets to be like everything else. Selling is selling, y'know.

Girl: I suppose.

Happy: You don't happen to sell, do you?

Girl: No, I don't sell.

Happy: Would you object to a compliment from a stranger? You ought to be on a magazine cover.

Girl: *(looking at him a little archly)* I have been.

Stanley comes in with a glass of champagne.

HAPPY: What'd I say before, Stanley? You see? She's a cover girl.
STANLEY: Oh, I could see, I could see.
HAPPY: *(to The Girl)* What magazine?
GIRL: Oh, a lot of them. *(She takes the drink.)* Thank you.
HAPPY: You know what they say in France, don't you? "Champagne is the drink of the complexion"—Hya, Biff!

Biff has entered and sits with Happy.

BIFF: Hello, kid. Sorry I'm late.
HAPPY: I just got here. Uh, Miss—?
GIRL: Forsythe.
HAPPY: Miss Forsythe, this is my brother.
BIFF: Is Dad here?
HAPPY: His name is Biff. You might've heard of him. Great football player.
GIRL: Really? What team?
HAPPY: Are you familiar with football?
GIRL: No, I'm afraid I'm not.
HAPPY: Biff is quarterback with the New York Giants.
GIRL: Well, that is nice, isn't it? *(She drinks.)*
HAPPY: Good health.
GIRL: I'm happy to meet you.
HAPPY: That's my name. Hap. It's really Harold, but at West Point they called me Happy.
GIRL: *(now really impressed)* Oh, I see. How do you do? *(She turns her profile.)*
BIFF: Isn't Dad coming?
HAPPY: You want her?
BIFF: Oh, I could never make that.
HAPPY: I remember the time that idea would never come into your head. Where's the old confidence, Biff?
BIFF: I just saw Oliver—
HAPPY: Wait a minute. I've got to see that old confidence again. Do you want her? She's on call.
BIFF: Oh, no. *(He turns to look at The Girl.)*
HAPPY: I'm telling you. Watch this. *(Turning to The Girl.)* Honey? *(She turns to him.)* Are you busy?
GIRL: Well, I am . . . but I could make a phone call.
HAPPY: Do that, will you, honey? And see if you can get a friend. We'll be here for a while. Biff is one of the greatest football players in the country.
GIRL: *(standing up)* Well, I'm certainly happy to meet you.
HAPPY: Come back soon.
GIRL: I'll try.
HAPPY: Don't try, honey, try hard.

The Girl exits. Stanley follows, shaking his head in bewildered admiration.

HAPPY: Isn't that a shame now? A beautiful girl like that? That's why I can't get married. There's not a good woman in a thousand. New York is loaded with them, kid!

BIFF: Hap, look —

HAPPY: I told you she was on call!

BIFF: *(strangely unnerved)* Cut it out, will ya? I want to say something to you.

HAPPY: Did you see Oliver?

BIFF: I saw him all right. Now look, I want to tell Dad a couple of things and I want you to help me.

HAPPY: What? Is he going to back you?

BIFF: Are you crazy? You're out of your goddam head, you know that?

HAPPY: Why? What happened?

BIFF: *(breathlessly)* I did a terrible thing today, Hap. It's been the strangest day I ever went through. I'm all numb, I swear.

HAPPY: You mean he wouldn't see you?

BIFF: Well, I waited six hours for him, see? All day. Kept sending my name in. Even tried to date his secretary so she'd get me to him, but no soap.

HAPPY: Because you're not showin' the old confidence, Biff. He remembered you, didn't he?

BIFF: *(stopping Happy with a gesture)* Finally, about five o'clock, he comes out. Didn't remember who I was or anything. I felt like such an idiot, Hap.

HAPPY: Did you tell him my Florida idea?

BIFF: He walked away. I saw him for one minute. I got so mad I could've torn the walls down! How the hell did I ever get the idea I was a salesman there? I even believed myself that I'd been a salesman for him! And then he gave me one look and — I realized what a ridiculous lie my whole life has been! We've been talking in a dream for fifteen years. I was a shipping clerk.

HAPPY: What'd you do?

BIFF: *(with great tension and wonder)* Well, he left, see. And the secretary went out. I was all alone in the waiting-room. I don't know what came over me, Hap. The next thing I know I'm in his office — paneled walls, everything. I can't explain it. I — Hap, I took his fountain pen.

HAPPY: Geez, did he catch you?

BIFF: I ran out. I ran down all eleven flights. I ran and ran and ran.

HAPPY: That was an awful dumb — what'd you do that for?

BIFF: *(agonized)* I don't know, I just — wanted to take something, I don't know. You gotta help me, Hap. I'm gonna tell Pop.

HAPPY: You crazy? What for?

BIFF: Hap, he's got to understand that I'm not the man somebody lends that kind of money to. He thinks I've been spiting him all these years and it's eating him up.

HAPPY: That's just it. You tell him something nice.

BIFF: I can't.

HAPPY: Say you got a lunch date with Oliver tomorrow.

BIFF: So what do I do tomorrow?

HAPPY: You leave the house tomorrow and come back at night and say Oliver is thinking it over. And he thinks it over for a couple of weeks, and gradually it fades away and nobody's the worse.

BIFF: But it'll go on forever!

HAPPY: Dad is never so happy as when he's looking forward to something!

Willy enters.

HAPPY: Hello, scout!

WILLY: Gee, I haven't been here in years!

Stanley has followed Willy in and sets a chair for him. Stanley starts off but Happy stops him.

HAPPY: Stanley!

Stanley stands by, waiting for an order.

BIFF: *(going to Willy with guilt, as to an invalid)* Sit down, Pop. You want a drink?

WILLY: Sure, I don't mind.

BIFF: Let's get a load on.

WILLY: You look worried.

BIFF: N-no. *(To Stanley.)* Scotch all around. Make it doubles.

STANLEY: Doubles, right. *(He goes.)*

WILLY: You had a couple already, didn't you?

BIFF: Just a couple, yeah.

WILLY: Well, what happened, boy? *(Nodding affirmatively, with a smile.)* Everything go all right?

BIFF: *(takes a breath, then reaches out and grasps Willy's hand)* Pal . . . *(He is smiling bravely, and Willy is smiling too.)* I had an experience today.

HAPPY: Terrific, Pop.

WILLY: That so? What happened?

BIFF: *(high, slightly alcoholic, above the earth)* I'm going to tell you everything from first to last. It's been a strange day. *(Silence. He looks around, composes himself as best he can, but his breath keeps breaking the rhythm of his voice.)* I had to wait quite a while for him, and—

WILLY: Oliver?

BIFF: Yeah, Oliver. All day, as a matter of cold fact. And a lot of—instances—facts, Pop, facts about my life came back to me. Who was it, Pop? Who ever said I was a salesman with Oliver?

WILLY: Well, you were.

BIFF: No, Dad, I was a shipping clerk.

WILLY: But you were practically—

BIFF: *(with determination)* Dad, I don't know who said it first, but I was never a salesman for Bill Oliver.

WILLY: What're you talking about?

BIFF: Let's hold on to the facts tonight, Pop. We're not going to get anywhere bullin' around. I was a shipping clerk.

Willy: *(angrily)* All right, now listen to me—

Biff: Why don't you let me finish?

Willy: I'm not interested in stories about the past or any crap of that kind because the woods are burning, boys, you understand? There's a big blaze going on all around. I was fired today.

Biff: *(shocked)* How could you be?

Willy: I was fired, and I'm looking for a little good news to tell your mother, because the woman has waited and the woman has suffered. The gist of it is that I haven't got a story left in my head, Biff. So don't give me a lecture about facts and aspects. I am not interested. Now what've you got to say to me?

Stanley enters with three drinks. They wait until he leaves.

Willy: Did you see Oliver?

Biff: Jesus, Dad!

Willy: You mean you didn't go up there?

Happy: Sure he went up there.

Biff: I did. I—saw him. How could they fire you?

Willy: *(on the edge of his chair)* What kind of a welcome did he give you?

Biff: He won't even let you work on commission?

Willy: I'm out! *(Driving.)* So tell me, he gave you a warm welcome?

Happy: Sure, Pop, sure!

Biff: *(driven)* Well, it was kind of—

Willy: I was wondering if he'd remember you. *(To Happy.)* Imagine, man doesn't see him for ten, twelve years and gives him that kind of a welcome!

Happy: Damn right!

Biff: *(trying to return to the offensive)* Pop, look—

Willy: You know why he remembered you, don't you? Because you impressed him in those days.

Biff: Let's talk quietly and get this down to the facts, huh?

Willy: *(as though Biff had been interrupting)* Well, what happened? It's great news, Biff. Did he take you into his office or'd you talk in the waiting-room?

Biff: Well, he came in, see, and—

Willy: *(with a big smile)* What'd he say? Betcha he threw his arm around you.

Biff: Well, he kinda—

Willy: He's a fine man. *(To Happy.)* Very hard man to see, y'know.

Happy: *(agreeing)* Oh, I know.

Willy: *(to Biff)* Is that where you had the drinks?

Biff: Yeah, he gave me a couple of—no, no!

Happy: *(cutting in)* He told him my Florida idea.

Willy: Don't interrupt. *(To Biff.)* How'd he react to the Florida idea?

Biff: Dad, will you give me a minute to explain?

Willy: I've been waiting for you to explain since I sat down here! What happened? He took you into his office and what?

BIFF: Well—I talked. And—and he listened, see.
WILLY: Famous for the way he listens, y'know. What was his answer?
BIFF: His answer was—*(He breaks off, suddenly angry.)* Dad, you're not letting me tell you what I want to tell you!
WILLY: *(accusing, angered)* You didn't see him, did you?
BIFF: I did see him!
WILLY: What'd you insult him or something? You insulted him, didn't you?
BIFF: Listen, will you let me out of it, will you just let me out of it!
HAPPY: What the hell!
WILLY: Tell me what happened!
BIFF: *(to Happy)* I can't talk to him!

A single trumpet note jars the ear. The light of green leaves stains the house, which holds the air of night and a dream. Young Bernard enters and knocks on the door of the house.

YOUNG BERNARD: *(frantically)* Mrs. Loman, Mrs. Loman!
HAPPY: Tell him what happened!
BIFF: *(to Happy)* Shut up and leave me alone!
WILLY: No, no! You had to go and flunk math!
BIFF: What math? What're you talking about?
YOUNG BERNARD: Mrs. Loman, Mrs. Loman!

Linda appears in the house, as of old.

WILLY: *(wildly)* Math, math, math!
BIFF: Take it easy, Pop!
YOUNG BERNARD: Mrs. Loman!
WILLY: *(furiously)* If you hadn't flunked you'd've been set by now!
BIFF: Now, look, I'm gonna tell you what happened, and you're going to listen to me.
YOUNG BERNARD: Mrs. Loman!
BIFF: I waited six hours—
HAPPY: What the hell are you saying?
BIFF: I kept sending in my name but he wouldn't see me. So finally he . . . *(He continues unheard as light fades low on the restaurant.)*
YOUNG BERNARD: Biff flunked math!
LINDA: No!
YOUNG BERNARD: Birnbaum flunked him! They won't graduate him!
LINDA: But they have to. He's gotta go to the university. Where is he? Biff! Biff!
YOUNG BERNARD: No, he left. He went to Grand Central.
LINDA: Grand—You mean he went to Boston!
YOUNG BERNARD: Is Uncle Willy in Boston?
LINDA: Oh, maybe Willy can talk to the teacher. Oh, the poor, poor boy!

Light on house area snaps out.

BIFF: *(at the table, now audible, holding up a gold fountain pen)* . . . so I'm washed up with Oliver, you understand? Are you listening to me?

WILLY: *(at a loss)* Yeah, sure. If you hadn't flunked—

BIFF: Flunked what? What're you talking about?

WILLY: Don't blame everything on me! I didn't flunk math—you did! What pen?

HAPPY: That was awful dumb, Biff, a pen like that is worth—

WILLY: *(seeing the pen for the first time)* You took Oliver's pen?

BIFF: *(weakening)* Dad, I just explained it to you.

WILLY: You stole Bill Oliver's fountain pen!

BIFF: I didn't exactly steal it! That's just what I've been explaining to you!

HAPPY: He had it in his hand and just then Oliver walked in, so he got nervous and stuck it in his pocket!

WILLY: My God, Biff!

BIFF: I never intended to do it, Dad!

OPERATOR'S VOICE: Standish Arms, good evening!

WILLY: *(shouting)* I'm not in my room!

BIFF: *(frightened)* Dad, what's the matter? *(He and Happy stand up.)*

OPERATOR: Ringing Mr. Loman for you!

WILLY: I'm not there, stop it!

BIFF: *(horrified, gets down on one knee before Willy)* Dad, I'll make good, I'll make good. *(Willy tries to get to his feet. Biff holds him down.)* Sit down now.

WILLY: No, you're no good, you're no good for anything.

BIFF: I am, Dad, I'll find something else, you understand? Now don't worry about anything. *(He holds up Willy's face.)* Talk to me, Dad.

OPERATOR: Mr. Loman does not answer. Shall I page him?

WILLY: *(attempting to stand, as though to rush and silence the Operator)* No, no, no!

HAPPY: He'll strike something, Pop.

WILLY: No, no . . .

BIFF: *(desperately, standing over Willy)* Pop, listen! Listen to me! I'm telling you something good. Oliver talked to his partner about the Florida idea. You listening? He—he talked to his partner, and he came to me . . . I'm going to be all right, you hear? Dad, listen to me, he said it was just a question of the amount!

WILLY: Then you . . . got it?

HAPPY: He's gonna be terrific, Pop!

WILLY: *(trying to stand)* Then you got it, haven't you? You got it! You got it!

BIFF: *(agonized, holds Willy down)* No, no. Look, Pop. I'm supposed to have lunch with them tomorrow. I'm just telling you this so you'll know that I can still make an impression, Pop. And I'll make good somewhere, but I can't go tomorrow, see?

WILLY: Why not? You simply—

BIFF: But the pen, Pop!

WILLY: You give it to him and tell him it was an oversight!

HAPPY: Sure, have lunch tomorrow!

BIFF: I can't say that—

WILLY: You were doing a crossword puzzle and accidentally used his pen!

BIFF: Listen, kid, I took those balls years ago, now I walk in with his fountain pen? That clinches it, don't you see? I can't face him like that! I'll try elsewhere.

PAGE'S VOICE: Paging Mr. Loman!

WILLY: Don't you want to be anything?

BIFF: Pop, how can I go back?

WILLY: You don't want to be anything, is that what's behind it?

BIFF: *(now angry at Willy for not crediting his sympathy)* Don't take it that way! You think it was easy walking into that office after what I'd done to him? A team of horses couldn't have dragged me back to Bill Oliver!

WILLY: Then why'd you go?

BIFF: Why did I go? Why did I go? Look at you! Look at what's become of you!

Off left, The Woman laughs.

WILLY: Biff, you're going to go to that lunch tomorrow, or—

BIFF: I can't go. I've got no appointment!

HAPPY: Biff, for . . .!

WILLY: Are you spiting me?

BIFF: Don't take it that way! Goddammit!

WILLY: *(strikes Biff and falters away from the table)* You rotten little louse! Are you spiting me?

THE WOMAN: Someone's at the door, Willy!

BIFF: I'm no good, can't you see what I am?

HAPPY: *(separating them)* Hey, you're in a restaurant! Now cut it out, both of you! *(The Girls enter.)* Hello, girls, sit down.

The Woman laughs, off left.

MISS FORSYTHE: I guess we might as well. This is Letta.

THE WOMAN: Willy, are you going to wake up?

BIFF: *(ignoring Willy)* How're ya, miss, sit down. What do you drink?

MISS FORSYTHE: Letta might not be able to stay long.

LETTA: I gotta get up very early tomorrow. I got jury duty. I'm so excited! Were you fellows ever on a jury?

BIFF: No, but I been in front of them! *(The Girls laugh.)* This is my father.

LETTA: Isn't he cute? Sit down with us, Pop.

HAPPY: Sit him down, Biff!

BIFF: *(going to him)* Come on, slugger, drink us under the table. To hell with it! Come on, sit down, pal.

On Biff's last insistence, Willy is about to sit.

THE WOMAN: *(now urgently)* Willy, are you going to answer the door!

The Woman's call pulls Willy back. He starts right, befuddled.

BIFF: Hey, where are you going?

WILLY: Open the door.

BIFF: The door?

WILLY: The washroom . . . the door . . . where's the door?

BIFF: *(leading Willy to the left)* Just go straight down.

Willy moves left.

THE WOMAN: Willy, Willy, are you going to get up, get up, get up, get up?

Willy exits left.

LETTA: I think it's sweet you bring your daddy along.

MISS FORSYTHE: Oh, he isn't really your father!

BIFF: *(at left, turning to her resentfully)* Miss Forsythe, you've just seen a prince walk by. A fine, troubled prince. A hard-working, unappreciated prince. A pal, you understand? A good companion. Always for his boys.

LETTA: That's so sweet.

HAPPY: Well, girls, what's the program? We're wasting time. Come on, Biff. Gather round. Where would you like to go?

BIFF: Why don't you do something for him?

HAPPY: Me!

BIFF: Don't you give a damn for him, Hap?

HAPPY: What're you talking about? I'm the one who—

BIFF: I sense it, you don't give a good goddam about him. *(He takes the rolled-up hose from his pocket and puts it on the table in front of Happy.)* Look what I found in the cellar, for Christ's sake. How can you bear to let it go on?

HAPPY: Me? Who goes away? Who runs off and—

BIFF: Yeah, but he doesn't mean anything to you. You could help him—I can't! Don't you understand what I'm talking about? He's going to kill himself, don't you know that?

HAPPY: Don't I know it! Me!

BIFF: Hap, help him! Jesus . . . help him . . . Help me, help me, I can't bear to look at his face! *(Ready to weep, he hurries out, up right.)*

HAPPY: *(starting after him)* Where are you going?

MISS FORSYTHE: What's he so mad about?

HAPPY: Come on, girls, we'll catch up with him.

MISS FORSYTHE: *(as Happy pushes her out)* Say, I don't like that temper of his!

HAPPY: He's just a little overstrung, he'll be all right!

WILLY: *(off left, as The Woman laughs)* Don't answer! Don't answer!

LETTA: Don't you want to tell your father—

HAPPY: No, that's not my father. He's just a guy. Come on, we'll catch Biff, and, honey, we're going to paint this town! Stanley, where's the check! Hey, Stanley!

They exit. Stanley looks toward left.

STANLEY: *(calling to Happy indignantly)* Mr. Loman! Mr. Loman!

Stanley picks up a chair and follows them off. Knocking is heard off left. The Woman enters, laughing. Willy follows her. She is in a black slip; he is buttoning his shirt. Raw, sensuous music accompanies their speech.

WILLY: Will you stop laughing? Will you stop?

THE WOMAN: Aren't you going to answer the door? He'll wake the whole hotel.

WILLY: I'm not expecting anybody.

THE WOMAN: Whyn't you have another drink, honey, and stop being so damn self-centered?

WILLY: I'm so lonely.

THE WOMAN: You know you ruined me, Willy? From now on, whenever you come to the office, I'll see that you go right through to the buyers. No waiting at my desk any more, Willy. You ruined me.

WILLY: That's nice of you to say that.

THE WOMAN: Gee, you are self-centered! Why so sad? You are the saddest self-centeredest soul I ever did see-saw. *(She laughs. He kisses her.)* Come on inside, drummer boy. It's silly to be dressing in the middle of the night. *(As knocking is heard.)* Aren't you going to answer the door?

WILLY: They're knocking on the wrong door.

THE WOMAN: But I felt the knocking. And he heard us talking in here. Maybe the hotel's on fire!

WILLY: *(his terror rising)* It's a mistake.

THE WOMAN: Then tell him to go away!

WILLY: There's nobody there.

THE WOMAN: It's getting on my nerves, Willy. There's somebody standing out there and it's getting on my nerves!

WILLY: *(pushing her away from him)* All right, stay in the bathroom here, and don't come out. I think there's a law in Massachusetts about it, so don't come out. It may be that new room clerk. He looked very mean. So don't come out. It's a mistake, there's no fire.

The knocking is heard again. He takes a few steps away from her, and she vanishes into the wing. The light follows him, and now he is facing Young Biff, who carries a suitcase. Biff steps toward him. The music is gone.

BIFF: Why didn't you answer?

WILLY: Biff! What are you doing in Boston?

BIFF: Why didn't you answer? I've been knocking for five minutes, I called you on the phone—

WILLY: I just heard you. I was in the bathroom and had the door shut. Did anything happen home?

BIFF: Dad—I let you down.

WILLY: What do you mean?

BIFF: Dad . . .

WILLY: Biffo, what's this about? *(Putting his arm around Biff.)* Come on, let's go downstairs and get you a malted.

BIFF: Dad, I flunked math.

WILLY: Not for the term?

BIFF: The term. I haven't got enough credits to graduate.

Willy: You mean to say Bernard wouldn't give you the answers?

Biff: He did, he tried, but I only got a sixty-one.

Willy: And they wouldn't give you four points?

Biff: Birnbaum refused absolutely. I begged him, Pop, but he won't give me those points. You gotta talk to him before they close the school. Because if he saw the kind of man you are, and you just talked to him in your way, I'm sure he'd come through for me. The class came right before practice, see, and I didn't go enough. Would you talk to him? He'd like you, Pop. You know the way you could talk.

Willy: You're on. We'll drive right back.

Biff: Oh, Dad, good work! I'm sure he'll change it for you!

Willy: Go downstairs and tell the clerk I'm checkin' out. Go right down.

Biff: Yes, Sir! See, the reason he hates me, Pop—one day he was late for class so I got up at the blackboard and imitated him. I crossed my eyes and talked with a lithp.

Willy: *(laughing)* You did? The kids like it?

Biff: They nearly died laughing!

Willy: Yeah? What'd you do?

Biff: The thquare root of thixthy twee is . . . *(Willy bursts out laughing; Biff joins him.)* And in the middle of it he walked in!

Willy laughs and The Woman joins in offstage.

Willy: *(without hesitating)* Hurry downstairs and—

Biff: Somebody in there?

Willy: No, that was next door.

The Woman laughs offstage.

Biff: Somebody got in your bathroom!

Willy: No, it's the next room, there's a party—

The Woman: *(enters, laughing. She lisps this)* Can I come in? There's something in the bathtub, Willy, and it's moving!

Willy looks at Biff, who is staring open-mouthed and horrified at The Woman.

Willy: Ah—you better go back to your room. They must be finished painting by now. They're painting her room so I let her take a shower here. Go back, go back . . . *(He pushes her.)*

The Woman: *(resisting)* But I've got to get dressed, Willy, I can't—

Willy: Get out of here! Go back, go back . . . *(Suddenly striving for the ordinary.)* This is Miss Francis, Biff, she's a buyer. They're painting her room. Go back, Miss Francis, go back . . .

The Woman: But my clothes, I can't go out naked in the hall!

Willy: *(pushing her offstage)* Get outa here! Go back, go back!

Biff slowly sits down on his suitcase as the argument continues offstage.

The Woman: Where's my stockings? You promised me stockings, Willy!

WILLY: I have no stockings here!

THE WOMAN: You had two boxes of size nine sheers for me, and I want them!

WILLY: Here, for God's sake, will you get outa here!

THE WOMAN: *(enters holding a box of stockings)* I just hope there's nobody in the hall. That's all I hope. *(To Biff.)* Are you football or baseball?

BIFF: Football.

THE WOMAN: *(angry, humiliated)* That's me too. G'night. *(She snatches her clothes from Willy, and walks out.)*

WILLY: *(after a pause)* Well, better get going. I want to get to the school first thing in the morning. Get my suits out of the closet. I'll get my valise. *(Biff doesn't move.)* What's the matter? *(Biff remains motionless, tears falling.)* She's a buyer. Buys for J. H. Simmons. She lives down the hall—they're painting. You don't imagine—*(He breaks off. After a pause.)* Now listen, pal, she's just a buyer. She sees merchandise in her room and they have to keep it looking just so . . . *(Pause. Assuming command.)* All right, get my suits. *(Biff doesn't move.)* Now stop crying and do as I say. I gave you an order. Biff, I gave you an order! Is that what you do when I give you an order? How dare you cry! *(Putting his arm around Biff.)* Now look, Biff, when you grow up you'll understand about these things. You mustn't—you mustn't overemphasize a thing like this. I'll see Birnbaum first thing in the morning.

BIFF: Never mind.

WILLY: *(getting down beside Biff)* Never mind! He's going to give you those points. I'll see to it.

BIFF: He wouldn't listen to you.

WILLY: He certainly will listen to me. You need those points for the U. of Virginia.

BIFF: I'm not going there.

WILLY: Heh? If I can't get him to change that mark you'll make it up in summer school. You've got all summer to—

BIFF: *(his weeping breaking from him)* Dad . . .

WILLY: *(infected by it)* Oh, my boy . . .

BIFF: Dad . . .

WILLY: She's nothing to me, Biff. I was lonely, I was terribly lonely.

BIFF: You—you gave her Mama's stockings! *(His tears break through and he rises to go.)*

WILLY: *(grabbing for Biff)* I gave you an order!

BIFF: Don't touch me, you—liar!

WILLY: Apologize for that!

BIFF: You fake! You phony little fake! You fake! *(Overcome, he turns quickly and weeping fully goes out with his suitcase. Willy is left on the floor on his knees.)*

WILLY: I gave you an order! Biff, come back here or I'll beat you! Come back here! I'll whip you!

Stanley comes quickly in from the right and stands in front of Willy.

WILLY: *(shouts at Stanley)* I gave you an order . . .

STANLEY: Hey, let's pick it up, pick it up, Mr. Loman. *(He helps Willy to his feet.)* Your boys left with the chippies. They said they'll see you home.

A second waiter watches some distance away.

WILLY: But we were supposed to have dinner together.

Music is heard, Willy's theme.

STANLEY: Can you make it?

WILLY: I'll—sure, I can make it. *(Suddenly concerned about his clothes.)* Do I—I look all right?

STANLEY: Sure, you look all right. *(He flicks a speck off Willy's lapel.)*

WILLY: Here—here's a dollar.

STANLEY: Oh, your son paid me. It's all right.

WILLY: *(putting it in Stanley's hand)* No, take it. You're a good boy.

STANLEY: Oh, no, you don't have to . . .

WILLY: Here—here's some more, I don't need it any more. *(After a slight pause.)* Tell me—is there a seed store in the neighborhood?

STANLEY: Seeds? You mean like to plant?

As Willy turns, Stanley slips the money back into his jacket pocket.

WILLY: Yes. Carrots, peas . . .

STANLEY: Well, there's hardware stores on Sixth Avenue, but it may be too late now.

WILLY: *(anxiously)* Oh, I'd better hurry. I've got to get some seeds. *(He starts off to the right.)* I've got to get some seeds, right away. Nothing's planted. I don't have a thing in the ground.

Willy hurries out as the light goes down. Stanley moves over to the right after him, watches him off. The other waiter has been staring at Willy.

STANLEY: *(to the waiter)* Well, whatta you looking at?

The waiter picks up the chairs and moves off right. Stanley takes the table and follows him. The light fades on this area. There is a long pause, the sound of the flute coming over. The light gradually rises on the kitchen, which is empty. Happy appears at the door of the house, followed by Biff. Happy is carrying a large bunch of long-stemmed roses. He enters the kitchen, looks around for Linda. Not seeing her, he turns to Biff, who is just outside the house door, and makes a gesture with his hands, indicating "Not here, I guess." He looks into the living room and freezes. Inside, Linda, unseen, is seated, Willy's coat on her lap. She rises ominously and quietly and moves toward Happy, who backs up into the kitchen, afraid.

HAPPY: Hey, what're you doing up? *(Linda says nothing but moves toward him implacably.)* Where's Pop? *(He keeps backing to the right, and now Linda is in full view in the doorway to the living room.)* Is he sleeping?

LINDA: Where were you?

HAPPY: *(trying to laugh it off)* We met two girls, Mom, very fine types. Here, we brought you some flowers. *(Offering them to her.)* Put them in your room, Ma.

She knocks them to the floor at Biff's feet. He has now come inside and closed the door behind him. She stares at Biff, silent.

HAPPY: Now what'd you do that for? Mom, I want you to have some flowers—

LINDA: *(cutting Happy off, violently to Biff)* Don't you care whether he lives or dies?

HAPPY: *(going to the stairs)* Come upstairs, Biff.

BIFF: *(with a flare of disgust, to Happy)* Go away from me! *(To Linda.)* What do you mean, lives or dies? Nobody's dying around here, pal.

LINDA: Get out of my sight! Get out of here!

BIFF: I wanna see the boss.

LINDA: You're not going near him!

BIFF: Where is he? *(He moves into the living room and Linda follows.)*

LINDA: *(shouting after Biff)* You invite him for dinner. He looks forward to it all day—*(Biff appears in his parents' bedroom, looks around, and exits)*—and then you desert him there. There's no stranger you'd do that to!

HAPPY: Why? He had a swell time with us. Listen, when I—*(Linda comes back into the kitchen)*—desert him I hope I don't outlive the day!

LINDA: Get out of here!

HAPPY: Now look, Mom . . .

LINDA: Did you have to go to women tonight? You and your lousy rotten whores!

Biff re-enters the kitchen.

HAPPY: Mom, all we did was follow Biff around trying to cheer him up! *(To Biff.)* Boy, what a night you gave me!

LINDA: Get out of here, both of you, and don't come back! I don't want you tormenting him any more. Go on now, get your things together! *(To Biff.)* You can sleep in his apartment. *(She starts to pick up the flowers and stops herself.)* Pick up this stuff, I'm not your maid any more. Pick it up, you bum, you!

Happy turns his back to her in refusal. Biff slowly moves over and gets down on his knees, picking up the flowers.

LINDA: You're a pair of animals! Not one, not another living soul would have had the cruelty to walk out on that man in a restaurant!

BIFF: *(not looking at her)* Is that what he said?

LINDA: He didn't have to say anything. He was so humiliated he nearly limped when he came in.

HAPPY: But, Mom he had a great time with us—

BIFF: *(cutting him off violently)* Shut up!

Without another word, Happy goes upstairs.

LINDA: You! You didn't even go in to see if he was all right!

BIFF: *(still on the floor in front of Linda, the flowers in his hand; with self-loathing)* No. Didn't. Didn't do a damned thing. How do you like that, heh? Left him babbling in a toilet.

LINDA: You louse. You . . .

BIFF: Now you hit it on the nose! *(He gets up, throws the flowers in the wastebasket.)* The scum of the earth, and you're looking at him!

LINDA: Get out of here!

BIFF: I gotta talk to the boss, Mom. Where is he?

LINDA: You're not going near him. Get out of this house!

BIFF: *(with absolute assurance, determination)* No. We're gonna have an abrupt conversation, him and me.

LINDA: You're not talking to him!

Hammering is heard from outside the house, off right. Biff turns toward the noise.

LINDA: *(suddenly pleading)* Will you please leave him alone?

BIFF: What's he doing out there?

LINDA: He's planting the garden!

BIFF: *(quietly)* Now? Oh, my God!

Biff moves outside, Linda following. The light dies down on them and comes up on the center of the apron as Willy walks into it. He is carrying a flashlight, a hoe and a handful of seed packets. He raps the top of the hoe sharply to fix it firmly, and then moves to the left, measuring off the distance with his foot. He holds the flashlight to look at the seed packets, reading off the instructions. He is in the blue of night.

WILLY: Carrots . . . quarter-inch apart. Rows . . . one-foot rows. *(He measures it off.)* One foot. *(He puts down a package and measures off.)* Beets. *(He puts down another package and measures again.)* Lettuce. *(He reads the package, puts it down.)* One foot— *(He breaks off as Ben appears at the right and moves slowly down to him.)* What a proposition, ts, ts. Terrific, terrific. 'Cause she's suffered, Ben, the woman has suffered. You understand me? A man can't go out the way he came in, Ben, a man has got to add up to something. You can't, you can't— *(Ben moves toward him as though to interrupt.)* You gotta consider, now. Don't answer so quick. Remember, it's a guaranteed twenty-thousand-dollar proposition. Now look, Ben, I want you to go through the ins and outs of this thing with me. I've got nobody to talk to, Ben, and the woman has suffered, you hear me?

BEN: *(standing still, considering)* What's the proposition?

WILLY: It's twenty thousand dollars on the barrelhead. Guaranteed, gilt-edged, you understand?

BEN: You don't want to make a fool of yourself. They might not honor the policy.

WILLY: How can they dare refuse? Didn't I work like a coolie to meet every premium on the nose? And now they don't pay off? Impossible!

BEN: It's called a cowardly thing, William.

WILLY: Why? Does it take more guts to stand here the rest of my life ringing up a zero?

BEN: *(yielding)* That's a point, William. *(He moves, thinking, turns.)* And twenty thousand—that *is* something one can feel with the hand, it is there.

WILLY: *(now assured, with rising power)* Oh, Ben, that's the whole beauty of it! I see it like a diamond, shining in the dark, hard and rough, that I can pick up and touch in my hand. Not like—like an appointment! This would not be another damned-fool appointment, Ben, and it changes all the aspects. Because he thinks I'm nothing, see, and so he spites me. But the funeral—*(Straightening up.)* Ben, that funeral will be massive! They'll come from Maine, Massachusetts, Vermont, New Hampshire! All the old-timers with the strange license plates—that boy will be thunder-struck, Ben, because he never realized—I am known! Rhode Island, New York, New Jersey—I am known, Ben, and he'll see it with his eyes once and for all. He'll see what I am, Ben! He's in for a shock, that boy!

BEN: *(coming down to the edge of the garden)* He'll call you a coward.

WILLY: *(suddenly fearful)* No, that would be terrible.

BEN: Yes. And a damned fool.

WILLY: No, no, he mustn't, I won't have that! *(He is broken and desperate.)*

BEN: He'll hate you, William.

The gay music of the boys is heard.

WILLY: Oh, Ben, how do we get back to all the great times? Used to be so full of light, and comradeship, the sleigh-riding in winter, and the ruddiness on his cheeks. And always some kind of good news coming up, always something nice coming up ahead. And never even let me carry the valises in the house, and simonizing, simonizing that little red car! Why, why can't I give him something and not have him hate me?

BEN: Let me think about it. *(He glances at his watch.)* I still have a little time. Remarkable proposition, but you've got to be sure you're not making a fool of yourself.

Ben drifts off upstage and goes out of sight. Biff comes down from the left.

WILLY: *(suddenly conscious of Biff, turns and looks up at him, then begins picking up the packages of seeds in confusion)* Where the hell is that seed? *(Indignantly.)* You can't see nothing out here! They boxed in the whole goddam neighborhood!

BIFF: There are people all around here. Don't you realize that?

WILLY: I'm busy. Don't bother me.

BIFF: *(taking the hoe from Willy)* I'm saying good-by to you, Pop. *(Willy looks at him, silent, unable to move.)* I'm not coming back any more.

WILLY: You're not going to see Oliver tomorrow?

BIFF: I've got no appointment, Dad.

WILLY: He put his arm around you, and you've got no appointment?

BIFF: Pop, get this now, will you? Everytime I've left it's been a fight that sent me out of here. Today I realized something about myself and I tried to explain it to you and I—I think I'm just not smart enough to make any sense out of it for you. To hell with whose fault it is or anything like that.

(He takes Willy's arm.) Let's just wrap it up, heh? Come on in, we'll tell Mom. *(He gently tries to pull Willy to the left.)*

WILLY: *(frozen, immobile, with guilt in his voice)* No, I don't want to see her.

BIFF: Come on! *(He pulls again, and Willy tries to pull away.)*

WILLY: *(highly nervous)* No, no, I don't want to see her.

BIFF: *(tries to look into Willy's face, as if to find the answer there)* Why don't you want to see her?

WILLY: *(more harshly now)* Don't bother me, will you?

BIFF: What do you mean, you don't want to see her? You don't want them calling you yellow, do you? This isn't your fault; it's me, I'm a bum. Now come inside! *(Willy strains to get away.)* Did you hear what I said to you?

Willy pulls away and quickly goes by himself into the house. Biff follows.

LINDA: *(to Willy)* Did you plant, dear?

BIFF: *(at the door, to Linda)* All right, we had it out. I'm going and I'm not writing any more.

LINDA: *(going to Willy in the kitchen)* I think that's the best way, dear. 'Cause there's no use drawing it out, you'll just never get along.

Willy doesn't respond.

BIFF: People ask where I am and what I'm doing, you don't know, and you don't care. That way it'll be off your mind and you can start brightening up again. All right? That clears it, doesn't it? *(Willy is silent, and Biff goes to him.)* You gonna wish me luck, scout? *(He extends his hand.)* What do you say?

LINDA: Shake his hand, Willy.

WILLY: *(turning to her, seething with hurt)* There's no necessity to mention the pen at all, y'know.

BIFF: *(gently)* I've got no appointment, Dad.

WILLY: *(erupting fiercely)* He put his arm around . . .?

BIFF: Dad, you're never going to see what I am, so what's the use of arguing? If I strike oil I'll send you a check. Meantime forget I'm alive.

WILLY: *(to Linda)* Spite, see?

BIFF: Shake hands, Dad.

WILLY: Not my hand.

BIFF: I was hoping not to go this way.

WILLY: Well, this is the way you're going. Good-by.

Biff looks at him a moment, then turns sharply and goes to the stairs.

WILLY: *(stops him with)* May you rot in hell if you leave this house!

BIFF: *(turning)* Exactly what is it that you want from me?

WILLY: I want you to know, on the train, in the mountains, in the valleys, wherever you go, that you cut down your life for spite!

BIFF: No, no.

WILLY: Spite, spite, is the word of your undoing! And when you're down and out, remember what did it. When you're rotting somewhere beside the railroad tracks, remember, and don't you dare blame it on me!

BIFF: I'm not blaming it on you!

WILLY: I won't take the rap for this, you hear?

Happy comes down the stairs and stands on the bottom step, watching.

BIFF: That's just what I'm telling you!

WILLY: *(sinking into a chair at the table, with full accusation)* You're trying to put a knife in me—don't think I don't know what you're doing!

BIFF: All right, phony! Then let's lay it on the line. *(He whips the rubber tube out of his pocket and puts it on the table.)*

HAPPY: You crazy—

LINDA: Biff! *(She moves to grab the hose, but Biff holds it down with his hand.)*

BIFF: Leave it there! Don't move it!

WILLY: *(not looking at it)* What is that?

BIFF: You know goddam well what that is.

WILLY: *(caged, wanting to escape)* I never saw that.

BIFF: You saw it. The mice didn't bring it into the cellar! What is this supposed to do, make a hero out of you? This supposed to make me sorry for you?

WILLY: Never heard of it.

BIFF: There'll be no pity for you, you hear it? No pity!

WILLY: *(to Linda)* You hear the spite!

BIFF: No, you're going to hear the truth—what you are and what I am!

LINDA: Stop it!

WILLY: Spite!

HAPPY: *(coming down toward Biff)* You cut it now!

BIFF: *(to Happy)* The man don't know who we are! The man is gonna know! *(To Willy.)* We never told the truth for ten minutes in this house!

HAPPY: We always told the truth!

BIFF: *(turning on him)* You big blow, are you the assistant buyer? You're one of the two assistants to the assistant, aren't you?

HAPPY: Well, I'm practically—

BIFF: You're practically full of it! We all are! And I'm through with it. *(To Willy.)* Now hear this, Willy, this is me.

WILLY: I know you!

BIFF: You know why I had no address for three months? I stole a suit in Kansas City and I was in jail. *(To Linda, who is sobbing.)* Stop crying. I'm through with it.

Linda turns away from them, her hands covering her face.

WILLY: I suppose that's my fault!

BIFF: I stole myself out of every good job since high school!

WILLY: And whose fault is that?

BIFF: And I never got anywhere because you blew me so full of hot air I could never stand taking orders from anybody! That's whose fault it is!

WILLY: I hear that!

LINDA: Don't, Biff!

BIFF: It's goddam time you heard that! I had to be boss big shot in two weeks, and I'm through with it!

WILLY: Then hang yourself! For spite, hang yourself!

BIFF: No! Nobody's hanging himself, Willy! I ran down eleven flights with a pen in my hand today. And suddenly I stopped, you hear me? And in the middle of that office building, do you hear this? I stopped in the middle of that building and I saw—the sky. I saw the things that I love in this world. The work and the food and time to sit and smoke. And I looked at the pen and said to myself, what the hell am I grabbing this for? Why am I trying to become what I don't want to be? What am I doing in an office, making a contemptuous, begging fool of myself, when all I want is out there, waiting for me the minute I say I know who I am! Why can't I say that, Willy? *(He tries to make Willy face him, but Willy pulls away and moves to the left.)*

WILLY: *(with hatred, threateningly)* The door of your life is wide open!

BIFF: Pop! I'm a dime a dozen, and so are you!

WILLY: *(turning on him now in an uncontrolled outburst)* I am not a dime a dozen! I am Willy Loman, and you are Biff Loman!

Biff starts for Willy, but is blocked by Happy. In his fury, Biff seems on the verge of attacking his father.

BIFF: I am not a leader of men, Willy, and neither are you. You were never anything but a hard-working drummer who landed in the ash can like all the rest of them! I'm one dollar an hour, Willy! I tried seven states and couldn't raise it. A buck an hour! Do you gather my meaning? I'm not bringing home any prizes any more, and you're going to stop waiting for me to bring them home!

WILLY: *(directly to Biff)* You vengeful, spiteful mutt!

Biff breaks from Happy. Willy, in fright, starts up the stairs. Biff grabs him.

BIFF: *(at the peak of his fury)* Pop, I'm nothing! I'm nothing, Pop. Can't you understand that? There's no spite in it any more. I'm just what I am, that's all.

Biff's fury has spent itself, and he breaks down, sobbing, holding on to Willy, who dumbly fumbles for Biff's face.

WILLY: *(astonished)* What're you doing? What're you doing? *(To Linda.)* Why is he crying?

BIFF: *(crying, broken)* Will you let me go, for Christ's sake? Will you take that phony dream and burn it before something happens? *(Struggling to contain himself, he pulls away and moves to the stairs.)* I'll go in the morning. Put him—put him to bed. *(Exhausted, Biff moves up the stairs to his room.)*

WILLY: *(after a long pause, astonished, elevated)* Isn't that remarkable? Biff—he likes me!

LINDA: He loves you, Willy!

HAPPY: *(deeply moved)* Always did, Pop.

WILLY: Oh, Biff! *(Staring wildly.)* He cried! Cried to me! *(He is choking with his love, and now cries out his promise.)* That boy—that boy is going to be magnificent!

Ben appears in the light just outside the kitchen.

BEN: Yes, outstanding, with twenty thousand behind him.

LINDA: *(sensing the racing of his mind, fearfully, carefully)* Now come to bed, Willy. It's all settled now.

WILLY: *(finding it difficult not to rush out of the house)* Yes, we'll sleep. Come on. Go to sleep, Hap.

BEN: And it does take a great kind of man to crack the jungle.

In accents of dread, Ben's idyllic music starts up.

HAPPY: *(his arm around Linda)* I'm getting married, Pop, don't forget it. I'm changing everything. I'm gonna run that department before the year is up. You'll see, Mom. *(He kisses her.)*

BEN: The jungle is dark but full of diamonds, Willy.

Willy turns, moves, listening to Ben.

LINDA: Be good. You're both good boys, just act that way, that's all.

HAPPY: 'Night, Pop. *(He goes upstairs.)*

LINDA: *(to Willy)* Come, dear.

BEN: *(with greater force)* One must go in to fetch a diamond out.

WILLY: *(to Linda, as he moves slowly along the edge of the kitchen, toward the door)* I just want to get settled down, Linda. Let me sit alone for a little.

LINDA: *(almost uttering her fear)* I want you upstairs.

WILLY: *(taking her in his arms)* In a few minutes, Linda. I couldn't sleep right now. Go on, you look awful tired. *(He kisses her.)*

BEN: Not like an appointment at all. A diamond is rough and hard to the touch.

WILLY: Go on now. I'll be right up.

LINDA: I think this is the only way, Willy.

WILLY: Sure, it's the best thing.

BEN: Best thing!

WILLY: The only way. Everything is gonna be—go on, kid, get to bed. You look so tired.

LINDA: Come right up.

WILLY: Two minutes.

Linda goes into the living room, then reappears in her bedroom. Willy moves just outside the kitchen door.

WILLY: Loves me. *(Wonderingly.)* Always loved me. Isn't that a remarkable thing? Ben, he'll worship me for it!

BEN: *(with promise)* It's dark there, but full of diamonds.

Willy: Can you imagine that magnificence with twenty thousand dollars in his pocket?

Linda: *(calling from her room)* Willy! Come up!

Willy: *(calling from the kitchen)* Yes! Yes! Coming! It's very smart, you realize that, don't you, sweetheart? Even Ben sees it. I gotta go, baby. 'By! By! *(Going over to Ben, almost dancing.)* Imagine? When the mail comes he'll be ahead of Bernard again!

Ben: A perfect proposition all around.

Willy: Did you see how he cried to me? Oh, if I could kiss him, Ben!

Ben: Time, William, time!

Willy: Oh, Ben, I always knew one way or another we were gonna make it, Biff and I!

Ben: *(looking at his watch)* The boat. We'll be late. *(He moves slowly off into the darkness.)*

Willy: *(elegiacally, turning to the house)* Now when you kick off, boy, I want a seventy-yard boot, and get right down the field under the ball, and when you hit, hit low and hit hard, because it's important, boy. *(He swings around and faces the audience.)* There's all kinds of important people in the stands, and the first thing you know . . . *(Suddenly realizing he is alone.)* Ben! Ben, where do I . . . ? *(He makes a sudden movement of search.)* Ben, how do I . . . ?

Linda: *(calling)* Willy, you coming up?

Willy: *(uttering a gasp of fear, whirling about as if to quiet her)* Sh! *(He turns around as if to find his way; sounds, faces, voices, seem to be swarming in upon him and he flicks at them, crying.)* Sh! Sh! *(Suddenly music, faint and high, stops him. It rises in intensity, almost to an unbearable scream. He goes up and down on his toes, and rushes off around the house.)* Shhh!

Linda: Willy?

There is no answer. Linda waits. Biff gets up off his bed. He is still in his clothes. Happy sits up. Biff stands listening.

Linda: *(with real fear)* Willy, answer me! Willy!

There is the sound of a car starting and moving away at full speed.

Linda: No!

Biff: *(rushing down the stairs)* Pop!

As the car speeds off, the music crashes down in a frenzy of sound, which becomes the soft pulsation of a single cello string. Biff slowly returns to his bedroom. He and Happy gravely don their jackets. Linda slowly walks out of her room. The music has developed into a dead march. The leaves of day are appearing over everything. Charley and Bernard, somberly dressed, appear and knock on the kitchen door. Biff and Happy slowly descend the stairs to the kitchen as Charley and Bernard enter. All stop a moment when Linda, in clothes of mourning, bearing a little bunch of roses, comes through the draped doorway into the kitchen. She goes to Charley and takes his arm. Now all move toward the audience, through the wall-line of the kitchen. At the limit of the apron, Linda lays down the flowers, kneels, and sits back on her heels. All stare down at the grave.

REQUIEM

Charley: It's getting dark, Linda.

Linda doesn't react. She stares at the grave.

Biff: How about it, Mom? Better get some rest, heh? They'll be closing the gate soon.

Linda makes no move. Pause.

Happy: *(deeply angered)* He had no right to do that! There was no necessity for it. We would've helped him.

Charley: *(grunting)* Hmmm.

Biff: Come along, Mom.

Linda: Why didn't anybody come?

Charley: It was a very nice funeral.

Linda: But where are all the people he knew? Maybe they blame him.

Charley: Naa. It's a rough world, Linda. They wouldn't blame him.

Linda: I can't understand it. At this time especially. First time in thirty-five years we were just about free and clear. He only needed a little salary. He was even finished with the dentist.

Charley: No man only needs a little salary.

Linda: I can't understand it.

Biff: There were a lot of nice days. When he'd come home from a trip; or on Sundays, making the stoop; finishing the cellar; putting on the new porch; when he built the extra bathroom; and put up the garage. You know something, Charley, there's more of him in that front stoop than in all the sales he ever made.

Charley: Yeah. He was a happy man with a batch of cement.

Linda: He was so wonderful with his hands.

Biff: He had the wrong dreams. All, all, wrong.

Happy: *(almost ready to fight Biff)* Don't say that!

Biff: He never knew who he was.

Charley: *(stopping Happy's movement and reply. To Biff.)* Nobody dast blame this man. You don't understand: Willy was a salesman. And for a salesman, there is no rock bottom to the life. He don't put a bolt to a nut, he don't tell you the law or give you medicine. He's a man out there in the blue, riding on a smile and a shoeshine. And when they start not smiling back—that's an earthquake. And then you get yourself a couple of spots on your hat, and you're finished. Nobody dast blame this man. A salesman is got to dream, boy. It comes with the territory.

Biff: Charley, the man didn't know who he was.

HAPPY: *(infuriated)* Don't say that!

BIFF: Why don't you come with me, Happy?

HAPPY: I'm not licked that easily. I'm staying right in this city, and I'm gonna beat this racket! *(He looks at Biff, his chin set.)* The Loman Brothers!

BIFF: I know who I am, kid.

HAPPY: All right, boy. I'm gonna show you and everybody else that Willy Loman did not die in vain. He had a good dream. It's the only dream you can have — to come out number-one man. He fought it out here, and this is where I'm gonna win it for him.

BIFF: *(with a hopeless glance at Happy, bends toward his mother)* Let's go, Mom.

LINDA: I'll be with you in a minute. Go on, Charley. *(He hesitates.)* I want to, just for a minute. I never had a chance to say good-by.

Charley moves away, followed by Happy. Biff remains a slight distance up and left of Linda. She sits there, summoning herself. The flute begins, not far away, playing behind her speech.

LINDA: Forgive me, dear. I can't cry. I don't know what it is, but I can't cry. I don't understand it. Why did you ever do that? Help me, Willy, I can't cry. It seems to me that you're just on another trip. I keep expecting you. Willy, dear, I can't cry. Why did you do it? I search and search and I search, and I can't understand it, Willy. I made the last payment on the house today. Today, dear. And there'll be nobody home. *(A sob rises in her throat.)* We're free and clear. *(Sobbing more fully, released.)* We're free. *(Biff comes slowly toward her.)* We're free . . . We're free . . .

Biff lifts her to her feet and moves out up right with her in his arms. Linda sobs quietly. Bernard and Charley come together and follow them, followed by Happy. Only the music of the flute is left on the darkening stage as over the house the hard towers of the apartment buildings rise into sharp focus, and—

The Curtain Falls

Reading and Reacting

1. Is Willy a likeable character? What words and actions — both Willy's and those of other characters — help you to reach your conclusion?
2. How does the existence of The Woman affect your overall impression of Willy? What does she reveal about his character?
3. What does Willy's attitude toward his sons indicate about his character? How is this attitude revealed?
4. In the absence of a narrator, what devices does Miller use to provide exposition — basic information about character and setting?

5. The conversation between Biff and Happy in act 1 reveals many of their differences. List some of the differences between these two characters.

6. In numerous remarks, Willy expresses his philosophy of business. Summarize some of his key ideas about the business world. How realistic do you think these ideas are? How do these ideas help to delineate his character?

7. In act 1, Linda tells Willy, "Few men are idolized by their children the way you are." Is she sincere, is she being ironic, or is she just trying to make Willy feel better?

8. How do the frequent flashbacks help to explain what motivates Willy? How else could this background information have been presented in the play? Are there advantages to using flashbacks instead of the alternative you suggest?

9. Is Linda simply a stereotype of the long-suffering wife, or is she a multidimensional character? Explain.

10. Willy Loman lives in Brooklyn, New York; his "territory" is New England. What is the significance to him of the "faraway places"— Africa, Alaska, California, Texas, and the like — mentioned in the play?

11. What purpose does Bernard serve in the play?

12. The play concludes with a requiem. What is a requiem? What information about each of the major characters is supplied in this brief section? Is this information essential to your understanding or appreciation of the play, or would the play have been equally effective without the requiem? Explain.

13. JOURNAL ENTRY Do you believe Willy Loman is an innocent victim of the society in which he lives, or do you believe there are flaws in his character that make him at least partially responsible for his own misfortune? Explain.

14. CRITICAL PERSPECTIVE Writing just after Miller's death in 2005, playwright David Mamet notes that at the end of *Death of a Salesman*, Miller has offered no solution to Willy's problems but instead "has reconciled us to the notion that there is no solution — that it is the human lot to try and fail, and that no one is immune from self-deception." Mamet goes on to explain the value of Miller's plays by comparing "bad drama" and "good drama":

> Bad drama reinforces our prejudices. It informs us of what we knew when we came into the theater. . . .
>
> The good drama survives because it appeals not to the fashion of the moment, but to the problems both universal and eternal, as they are insoluble.
>
> To find beauty in the sad, hope in the midst of loss, and dignity in failure is great poetic art.

According to Mamet's criteria, do you agree that *Death of a Salesman* qualifies as "good drama"? Do you think it is great drama?

Related Works: "A Primer for the Punctuation of Heart Disease" (p. 440), "Those Winter Sundays" (p. 818), "Do not go gentle into that good night" (p. 1046), "The Love Song of J. Alfred Prufrock" (p. 1151), *Oedipus the King* (p. 1745), *Fences* (p. 1902)

Source: ©Bettmann/Corbis

WILLIAM SHAKESPEARE (1564–1616) is recognized as the greatest of English writers, but many details about his life are based on conjecture or tradition. The earliest dependable information concerning Shakespeare is found in the parish registers of Stratford-upon-Avon's Holy Trinity Church, where his baptism was recorded on April 26, 1564. Although his date of birth cannot be determined with certainty, tradition has assigned it to April 23, 1564. Little is known about his early life, but reliable information about significant events is available in church documents. For example, he married Ann Hathaway in 1582 and had three children — Susanna in 1583 and the twins Judith and Hamnet in 1585.

Soon after the birth of his children, Shakespeare left Stratford for London. Upon his arrival in the capital, he set out to establish himself in London's literary world. His first step toward achieving this goal occurred in 1592, when he published his narrative poem *Venus and Adonis;* the following year, he published a second poem, *The Rape of Lucrece.*

By 1594, Shakespeare had become quite involved with the London stage. For approximately twenty years, he enjoyed a successful professional career in London — as actor, playwright, shareholder in the Lord Chamberlain's Men (an acting company), part owner of the Globe Theatre (from 1599), and author of at least thirty-six plays. The income derived from these activities brought him significant wealth and enabled him, sometime between 1610 and 1613, to retire from the theater and to return to Stratford-upon-Avon, where he owned considerable property. On April 23, 1616, Shakespeare died at age fifty-two in Stratford and was buried two days later in Holy Trinity Church.

It is difficult to date many of Shakespeare's plays exactly because they must be dated by records of their first performance (often hard to come by) and by topical references in the text. Shakespeare's company probably first staged *Hamlet* at the Globe Theatre in 1600 or 1601, but some scholars believe the play was composed as early as 1598.

An audience at the reconstructed Globe Theatre in London.
Source: ©Andreas Hub/laif/Aurora

Hamlet has been called Shakespeare's most complex and most confusing play, yet it is also the play most frequently performed, read, and written about. Shakespeare's audience would have recognized *Hamlet* as a **revenge tragedy** — a play in which the hero discovers that a close relative has been murdered, experiences considerable trouble in identifying the murderer, and, after overcoming numerous obstacles, avenges the death by killing the murderer. Frequently, revenge tragedies featured murders, physical mutilations, and ghosts, all enacted with grand style and bold rhetoric. These plays were extremely popular productions that were the action movies of their day.

Hamlet, however, is different from the typical revenge tragedy. Because the Ghost gives him the necessary information, Hamlet has no need to search for the cause of his father's death or find the murderer. In fact, the only impediments to Hamlet's revenge are those he himself creates. And, by the time the delay ends and Hamlet avenges his father's death, the loss is immense: his mother, the woman he loves, her father and brother, and Hamlet himself are all dead. Although the argument that there would be no play if Hamlet had immediately avenged his father may be valid, it fails to satisfy those who ponder the tragic cost of Hamlet's inaction.

Cultural Context The appearance of a ghost was a longstanding tradition in Renaissance drama. The ghost appeared in Elizabethan revenge tragedies as a plot device to help further the action and prompt a reaction from the hero. For a Renaissance audience, the dramatic representation of a ghost from purgatory would evoke a rich context of legends and lore derived from paintings, illuminated manuscript, prints, and narratives. Moreover, stories involving ghosts were a frequent element of medieval sermons. However, the ghost in *Hamlet* transcends the traditions of the revenge tragedy. Here, Shakespeare's use of the ghost not only as a plot device but also as a character who may or may not be telling the truth adds depth and complexity to the play.

Hamlet

Prince of Denmark* (c. 1600)

CHARACTERS

Claudius, *King of Denmark*
Hamlet, *son to the late King Hamlet, and nephew to the present King*
Polonius, *Lord Chamberlain*
Horatio, *friend to Hamlet*
Laertes, *son to Polonius*
Voltemand, **Cornelius**, **Rosencrantz**, **Guildenstern**, **Osric**, **Gentleman** — *courtiers*
Marcellus, **Barnardo** — *officers*
Francisco, *a soldier*
Reynaldo, *servant to Polonius*
Fortinbras, *Prince of Norway*
Norwegian Captain
Doctor of Divinity
Players
Two Clowns, *grave-diggers*
English Ambassadors
Gertrude, *Queen of Denmark, and mother to Hamlet*
Ophelia, *daughter to Polonius*
Ghost *of Hamlet's Father*
Lords, Ladies, Officers, Soldiers, Sailors, Messengers, and Attendants

Scene: *Denmark*

*Words and passages enclosed in square brackets in the text are either emendations of the copy-text or additions to it.

ACT 1

SCENE 1°

Enter Barnardo and Francisco, two sentinels [meeting].°

BARNARDO: Who's there?
FRANCISCO: Nay, answer me.° Stand and unfold yourself.°
BARNARDO: Long live the King!°
FRANCISCO: Barnardo.
BARNARDO: He.
FRANCISCO: You come most carefully upon your hour.
BARNARDO: 'Tis now strook twelf.° Get thee to bed, Francisco.
FRANCISCO: For this relief much thanks. 'Tis bitter cold,
And I am sick at heart.°
BARNARDO: Have you had quiet guard?
FRANCISCO: Not a mouse stirring.
BARNARDO: Well, goodnight.
If you do meet Horatio and Marcellus,
The rivals° of my watch, bid them make haste.

Enter Horatio and Marcellus.

FRANCISCO: I think I hear them. Stand ho! Who is there?
HORATIO: Friends to this ground.
MARCELLUS: And liegemen° to the Dane.
FRANCISCO: Give° you good night.
MARCELLUS: O, farewell, honest [soldier].
Who hath reliev'd you?
FRANCISCO: Barnardo hath my place.
Give you goodnight. *(Exit Francisco.)*
MARCELLUS: Holla, Barnardo!
BARNARDO: Say—
What, is Horatio there?
HORATIO: A piece of him.
BARNARDO: Welcome, Horatio, welcome, good Marcellus.
HORATIO: What, has this thing appear'd again to-night?
BARNARDO: I have seen nothing.
MARCELLUS: Horatio says 'tis but our fantasy,°
And will not let belief take hold of him
Touching this dreaded sight twice seen of us;

°*Location:* Elsinore; a guard-platform of the castle. °*answer me: You* answer *me.* Francisco is on watch; Barnardo has come to relieve him. °*unfold yourself:* Make known who you are. °*Long . . . King:* Perhaps a password, perhaps simply an utterance to allow the voice to be recognized. °*strook twelf:* Struck twelve. °*sick at heart:* In low spirits. °*rivals:* Partners. °*liegemen . . . Dane:* Loyal subjects to the king of Denmark. °*Give:* God give. °*fantasy:* Imagination.

Therefore I have entreated him along,
With us to watch the minutes of this night,
That if again this apparition come,
He may approve° our eyes and speak to it.

HORATIO: Tush, tush, 'twill not appear.

BARNARDO: Sit down a while,
And let us once again assail your ears,
That are so fortified against our story,
What we have two nights seen.

HORATIO: Well, sit we down,
And let us hear Barnardo speak of this.

BARNARDO: Last night of all,
When yond same star that's westward from the pole.°
Had made his° course t' illume that part of heaven
Where now it burns, Marcellus and myself,
The bell then beating one —

Enter Ghost.

MARCELLUS: Peace, break thee off! Look where it comes again!

BARNARDO: In the same figure like° the King that's dead.

MARCELLUS: Thou art a scholar,° speak to it, Horatio.

BARNARDO: Looks 'a° not like the King? Mark it, Horatio.

HORATIO: Most like; it [harrows] me with fear and wonder.

BARNARDO: It would be spoke to.°

MARCELLUS: Speak to it, Horatio.

HORATIO: What art thou that usurp'st° this time of night,
Together with that fair and warlike form
In which the majesty of buried Denmark°
Did sometimes° march? By heaven I charge thee speak!

MARCELLUS: It is offended.

BARNARDO: See, it stalks away!

HORATIO: Stay! Speak, speak, I charge thee speak!

Exit Ghost.

MARCELLUS: 'Tis gone, and will not answer.

BARNARDO: How now, Horatio, you tremble and look pale.
Is not this something more than fantasy?
What think you on't?

HORATIO: Before my God, I might not this believe
Without the sensible° and true avouch°
Of mine own eyes.

°*approve:* Corroborate. °*pole:* Pole star. °*his:* Its (the commonest form of the neuter possessive singular in Shakespeare's day) °*like:* In the likeness of. °*a scholar:* One who knows how best to address it. °*a:* He. °*It . . . to:* A ghost had to be spoken to before it could speak. °*usurp'st:* The ghost, a supernatural being, has invaded the realm of nature. °*majesty . . . Denmark:* Late king of Denmark. °*sometimes:* formerly. °*sensible:* Relating to the senses. °*avouch:* Guarantee.

MARCELLUS: Is it not like the King?
HORATIO: As thou art to thyself.
Such was the very armor he had on
When he the ambitious Norway° combated.
So frown'd he once when in an angry parle°
He smote the sledded° [Polacks]° on the ice.
'Tis strange.
MARCELLUS: Thus twice before, and jump° at this dead hour,
With martial stalk hath he gone by our watch.
HORATIO: In what particular thought to work I know not,
But in the gross and scope of mine opinion,°
This bodes some strange eruption° to our state.
MARCELLUS: Good row, sit down, and tell me, he that knows,
Why this same strict and most observant watch
So nightly toils° the subject° of the land,
And [why] such daily [cast] of brazen cannon,
And foreign mart° for implements of war,
Why such impress° of shipwrights, whose sore task
Does not divide the Sunday from the week,
What might be toward,° that this sweaty haste
Doth make the night joint-laborer with the day:
Who is't that can inform me?
HORATIO: That can I,
At least the whisper goes so: our last king,
Whose image even but now appear'd to us,
Was, as you know, by Fortinbras of Norway,
Thereto prick'd on by a most emulate° pride,
Dar'd to the combat; in which our valiant Hamlet
(For so this side of our known world esteem'd him)
Did slay this Fortinbras, who, by a seal'd compact
Well ratified by law and heraldry,°
Did forfeit (with his life) all [those] his lands
Which he stood seiz'd of,° to the conqueror;
Against the which a moi'ty° competent°
Was gaged° by our king, which had° [return'd]
To the inheritance° of Fortinbras,
Had he been vanquisher; as by the same comart°

°*Norway:* King of Norway. °*parle:* Parley. °*sledded:* Using sleds or sledges. °*Polacks:* Poles. °*jump:* Precisely. °*In . . . opinion:* While I have no precise theory about it, my general feeling is that; *gross* = wholeness, totality; *scope* = range. °*eruption:* Upheaval. °*toils:* Causes to work. °*subject:* Subjects. °*foreign mart:* Dealing with foreign markets. °*impress:* Forced service. °*toward:* In preparation. °*emulate:* Emulous, proceeding from rivalry. °*law and heraldy:* Heraldic law (governing combat). *Heraldy* is a variant of *heraldry*. °*seiz'd of:* Possessed of. °*moi'ty:* Portion. °*competent:* Adequate, equivalent. °*gaged:* Pledged. °*had:* Would have. °*inheritance:* Possession. °*comart:* Bargain.

And carriage° of the article [design'd],°
His fell to Hamlet. Now, sir, young Fortinbras,
Of unimproved° mettle hot and full,
Hath in the skirts° of Norway here and there
Shark'd up° a list of lawless resolutes
For food and diet to some enterprise
That hath a stomach° in't, which is no other,
As it doth well appear unto our state,
But to recover of us, by strong hand
And terms compulsatory, those foresaid lands
So by his father lost; and this, I take it,
Is the main motive of our preparations,
The source of this our watch, and the chief head°
Of this post-haste and romage° in the land.

BARNARDO: I think it be no other but e'en so.
Well may it sort° that this portentous° figure
Comes armed through our watch so like the King
That was and is the question of these wars.

HORATIO: A mote it is to trouble the mind's eye.
In the most high and palmy state of Rome,
A little ere the mightiest Julius fell,°
The graves stood [tenantless] and the sheeted dead
Did squeak and gibber in the Roman streets.
As stars with trains of fire, and dews of blood,
Disasters° in the sun; and the moist star°
Upon whose influence Neptune's empire stands°
Was sick almost to doomsday° with eclipse.°
And even the like precurse° of [fear'd] events,
As harbingers° preceding still° the fates
And prologue to the omen° coming on,
Have heaven and earth together demonstrated
Unto our climatures° and countrymen.

Enter Ghost.

But, soft, behold! lo where it comes again!

It spreads his° arms.

°*carriage:* Tenor. °*design'd:* Drawn up. °*unimproved:* Untried (?) or not directed to any useful end (?). °*skirts:* Outlying territories. °*Shark'd up:* Gathered up hastily and indiscriminately. °*stomach:* Relish of danger (?) or demand for courage (?) °*head:* Source. °*romage:* Rummage, bustling activity. °*sort:* Fit. °*portentous:* Ominous. °*fell:* One or more lines may have been lost between this line and the next. °*Disasters:* Ominous signs. °*moist star:* Moon. °*Neptune's empire stands:* The seas are dependent. °*sick . . . doomsday:* Almost totally darkened. When the Day of Judgment is imminent, says Matthew 24:29, "the moon shall not give her light." °*eclipse:* There were a solar and two total lunar eclipses visible in England in 1598; they caused gloomy speculation. °*precurse:* Foreshadowing. °*harbingers:* Advance messengers. °*still:* Always. °*omen:* The events portended. °*climatures:* Regions. °*s.d.* (stage direction) *his:* Its.

I'll cross it° though it blast° me. Stay, illusion!
If thou hast any sound or use of voice,
Speak to me.
If there be any good thing to be done
That may to thee do ease, and grace to me,
Speak to me.
If thou art privy to thy country's fate,
Which happily° foreknowing may avoid,
O speak!
Or if thou has uphoarded in thy life
Extorted treasure in the womb of earth,
For which, they say, your° spirits oft walk in death,
Speak of it, stay and speak! *(The cock crows.)* Stop it, Marcellus.

MARCELLUS: Shall I strike it with my partisan?°
HORATIO: Do, if it will not stand.
BARNARDO: 'Tis here!
HORATIO: 'Tis here!

Exit Ghost.

MARCELLUS: 'Tis gone!
We do it wrong, being so majestical,
To offer it the show of violence,
For it is as the air, invulnerable,
And our vain blows malicious mockery.°
BARNARDO: It was about to speak when the cock crew.
HORATIO: And then it started like a guilty thing
Upon a fearful summons. I have heard
The cock, that is the trumpet° to the morn,
Doth with his lofty and shrill-sounding throat
Awake the god of day, and at his warning,
Whether in sea or fire, in earth or air,
Th' extravagant° and erring° spirit hies°
To his confine; and of the truth herein
This present object° made probation.°
MARCELLUS: It faded on the crowing of the cock.
Some say that ever 'gainst° that season comes
Wherein our Saviour's birth is celebrated,
This bird of dawning singeth all night long,

°*cross it:* Cross its path, confront it directly. °*blast:* Wither (by supernatural means). °*happily:* Haply, perhaps. °*your:* Colloquial and impersonal; cf. 1. 5. 186, 4. 3. 23–25. Most editors adopt *you* from F1. °*partisan:* Long-handled spear. °*malicious mockery:* Mockery of malice, empty pretenses of harming it. °*trumpet:* Trumpeter. °*extravagant:* Wandering outside its proper bounds. °*erring:* Wandering abroad. °*hies:* Hastens. °*object:* Sight. °*probation:* Proof. °*gainst:* Just before.

And then they say no spirit dare stir abroad,
The nights are wholesome, then no planets strike,°
No fairy takes,° nor witch hath power to charm,
So hallowed, and so gracious,° is that time.

Horatio: So have I heard and do in part believe it.
But look, the morn in russet° mantle clad
Walks o'er the dew of yon high eastward hill.
Break we our watch up, and by my advice
Let us impart what we have seen to-night
Unto young Hamlet, for, upon my life,
This spirit, dumb to us, will speak to him.
Do you consent we shall acquaint him with it,
As needful in our loves, fitting our duty?

Marcellus: Let's do't, I pray, and I this morning know
Where we shall find him most convenient.

Exeunt.

[SCENE 2]°

Flourish.° Enter Claudius, King of Denmark, Gertrude the Queen, Council: as Polonius; and his son Laertes, Hamlet, cum aliis° [including Voltemand and Cornelius].

King: Though yet of Hamlet our dear brother's death
The memory be green, and that it us befitted°
To bear our hearts in grief, and our whole kingdom
To be contracted in° one brow of woe,°
Yet so far hath discretion fought with nature
That we with wisest sorrow think on him
Together with remembrance of ourselves.
Therefore our sometime sister, now our queen,
Th' imperial jointress° of this warlike state,
Have we, as 'twere with defeated° joy,
With an auspicious, and a dropping° eye,
With mirth in funeral, and with dirge in marriage,
In equal scale weighing delight and dole,
Taken to wife; nor have we herein barr'd
Your better wisdoms, which have freely° gone
With this affair along. For all, our thanks.
Now follows that you know° young Fortinbras,

°*strike:* Exert malevolent influence. °*takes:* Bewitches, charms. °*gracious:* Blessed. °*russet:* Coarse greyish-brown cloth. °1.2. *Location:* The castle. o.s.d. (opening-stage direction). °*Flourish:* Trumpet fanfare. °*cum aliis:* With others. °*befitted:* Would befit. °*contracted in:* (1) Reduced to; (2) knit or wrinkled in. °*brow of woe:* Mournful brow. °*jointress:* Joint holder. °*defeated:* Impaired. °*auspicious . . . dropping:* Cheerful . . . weeping. °*freely:* Fully, without reservation. °*know:* Be informed, learn.

Holding a weak supposal° of our worth,
Or thinking by our late dear brother's death
Our state to be disjoint and out of frame,
Co-leagued° with this dream of his advantage,
He hath not fail'd to pester us with message°
Importing° the surrender of those lands
Lost by his father, with all bands° of law,
To our most valiant brother. So much for him.
Now for ourself, and for this time of meeting,
Thus much the business is: we have here writ
To Norway, uncle of young Fortinbras—
Who, impotent and bedred,° scarcely hears
Of this his nephew's purpose—to suppress
His further gait° herein, in that the levies,
The lists, and full proportions are all made
Out of his subject;° and we here dispatch
You, good Cornelius, and you, Voltemand,
For bearers of this greeting to old Norway,
Giving to you no further personal power
To business with the King, more than the scope
Of these delated° articles allow. [*Giving a paper.*]
Farewell, and let your haste commend your duty.

CORNELIUS, VOLTEMAND: In that and all things, will we show our duty.

KING: We doubt it nothing;° heartily farewell.

Exeunt Voltemand and Cornelius.

And now, Laertes, what's the news with you?
You told us of some suit, what is't, Laertes?
You cannot speak of reason to the Dane
And lose° your voice. What wouldst thou beg, Laertes,
That shall not be my offer, not thy asking?
The head is not more native° to the heart,
The hand more instrumental° to the mouth,
Than is the throne of Denmark to thy father.
What wouldst thou have, Laertes?

LAERTES: My dread lord,
Your leave and favor° to return to France,
From whence though willingly I came to Denmark

°*supposal:* Conjecture, estimate. °*Co-leagued:* Joined. °*pester . . . message:* Trouble me with persistent messages (the original sense of *pester* is overcrowd". °*Importing:* Having as import. °*bands:* Bonds, binding terms. °*impotent and bedred:* Feeble and bedridden. °*gait:* Proceeding. °*in . . . subject:* Since the troops are all drawn from his subjects. °*delated:* Extended, detailed (a variant of *dilated*). °*nothing:* Not at all. °*lose:* Waste. °*native:* Closely related. °*instrumental:* Serviceable. °*leave and favor:* Gracious permission.

To show my duty in your coronation,
Yet now I must confess, that duty done,
My thoughts and wishes bend again toward France,
And bow them to your gracious leave and pardon.°

King: Have you your father's leave? What says Polonius?

Polonius: H'ath,° my lord, wrung from me my slow leave
By laborsome petition, and at last
Upon his will I seal'd my hard° consent
I do beseech you give him leave to go.

King: Take thy fair hour, Laertes, time be thine,
And thy best graces spend it at thy will!
But now, my cousin° Hamlet, and my son—

Hamlet [*Aside.*]: A little more than kin, and less than kind.°

King: How is it that the clouds still hang on you?

Hamlet: Not so, my lord, I am too much in the sun.°

Queen: Good Hamlet, cast thy nighted color off,
And let thine eye look like a friend on Denmark.
Do not for ever with thy vailed° lids
Seek for thy noble father in the dust.
Thou know'st 'tis common,° all that lives must die,
Passing through nature to eternity.

Hamlet: Ay, madam, it is common.

Queen: If it be,
Why seems it so particular° with thee?

Hamlet: Seems, madam? nay, it is, I know not "seems."
'Tis not alone my inky cloak, [good] mother,
Nor customary suits of solemn black,
Nor windy suspiration of forc'd breath,
No, nor the fruitful° river in the eye,
Nor the dejected havior of the visage,
Together with all forms, moods, [shapes] of grief,
That can [denote] me truly. These indeed seem,
For they are actions that a man might play,
But I have that within which passes show,
These but the trappings and the suits of woe.

King: 'Tis sweet and commendable in your nature, Hamlet,
To give these mourning duties to your father.
But you must know your father lost a father,
That father lost, lost his, and the survivor bound

°*pardon:* Permission to depart. °*H'ath:* He hath. °*hard:* Reluctant. °*cousin:* Kinsman (used in familiar address to any collateral relative more distant than a brother or sister; here to a nephew.) °*A little . . . kind:* Closer than a nephew, since you are my mother's husband; yet more distant than a son, too (and not well disposed to you). °*sun:* With obvious quibble on *son.* °*vailed:* Downcast. °*common:* General, universal. °*particular:* Individual, personal. °*fruitful:* Copious.

In filial obligation for some term
To do obsequious° sorrow. But to persever
In obstinate condolement° is a course
Of impious stubbornness, 'tis unmanly grief,
It shows a will most incorrect° to heaven,
A heart unfortified, a mind impatient,
An understanding simple and unschool'd:
For what we know must be, and is as common
As any the most vulgar thing to sense,°
Why should we in our peevish opposition
Take it to° heart? Fie, 'tis a fault to heaven,
A fault against the dead, a fault to nature,
To reason most absurd,° whose common theme
Is death of fathers, and who still hath cried,
From the first corse till he that died to-day,
"This must be so." We pray you throw to earth
This unprevailing° woe, and think of us
As of a father, for let the world take note
You are the most immediate to our throne,
And with no less nobility of love
Than that which dearest° father bears his son
Do I impart° toward you. For your intent
In going back to school in Wittenberg,
It is most retrograde to our desire,
And we beseech you bend you to remain
Here in the cheer and comfort of our eye,
Our chiefest courtier, cousin, and our son.

QUEEN: Let not thy mother lose her prayers, Hamlet,
I pray thee stay with us, go not to Wittenberg.

HAMLET: I shall in all my best obey you, madam.

KING: Why, 'tis a loving and a fair reply:
Be as ourself in Denmark. Madam, come.
This gentle and unforc'd accord of Hamlet
Sits smiling to my heart, in grace whereof,
No jocund health that Denmark drinks to-day,
But the great cannon to the clouds shall tell,
And the King's rouse° the heaven shall bruit° again,
Respeaking earthly thunder. Come away.

Flourish. Exeunt all but Hamlet.

°*obsequious:* Proper to obsequies. °*condolement:* Grief. °*incorrect:* Unsubmissive. °*any . . . sense:* What is perceived to be commonest. °*to:* Against. °*absurd:* Contrary. °*unprevailing:* Unavailing. °*dearest:* Most loving. °*impart:* Impart love. °*rouse:* Bumper, drink. °*Bruit:* Loudly declare.

Hamlet: O that this too too sallied° flesh would melt,
Thaw, and resolve itself into a dew!
Or that the Everlasting had not fix'd
His canon° 'gainst [self-]slaughter! O God, God,
How [weary], stale, flat, and unprofitable
Seem to me all the uses° of this world!
Fie on't, ah fie! 'tis an unweeded garden
That grows to seed, things rank and gross in nature
Possess it merely.° That it should come [to° this]!
But two months dead, nay, not so much, not two.
So excellent a king, that was to this
Hyperion° to a satyr, so loving to my mother
That he might not beteem° the winds of heaven
Visit her face too roughly. Heaven and earth,
Must I remember? Why, she should hang on him
As if increase of appetite had grown
By what it fed on, and yet, within a month—
Let me not think on't! Frailty, thy name is woman!—
A little month, or ere° those shoes were old
With which she followed my poor father's body,
Like Niobe,° all tears, why, she, [even she]—
O God, a beast that wants discourse of reason°
Would have mourn'd longer—married with my uncle,
My father's brother, but no more like my father
Than I to Hercules. Within a month,
Ere yet the salt of most unrighteous° tears
Had left the flushing° in her galled° eyes,
She married— O most wicked speed: to post
With such dexterity to incestious° sheets,
It is not, nor it cannot come to good,
But break my heart, for I must hold my tongue.

Enter Horatio, Marcellus and Barnardo.

Horatio: Hail to your lordship!
Hamlet: I am glad to see you well.
Horatio— or I do forget myself.
Horatio: The same, my lord, and your poor servant ever.

°*sallied:* Sullied. Many editors prefer the F1 reading, *solid.* °*canon:* Law. °*uses:* Customs. °*merely:* Utterly. °*to:* In comparison with. °*Hyperion:* The sun-god. °*beteem:* Allow. °*or ere:* Before. °*Niobe:* She wept endlessly for her children, whom Apollo and Artemis had killed. °*wants . . .reason:* Lacks the power of reason (which distinguishes men from beasts). °*unrighteous:* Hypocritical. °*flushing:* Redness. °*galled:* Inflamed. °*incestious:* Incestuous. The marriage of a man to his brother's widow was so regarded until long after Shakespeare's day.

HAMLET: Sir, my good friend—I'll change° that name with you.
And what make you from° Wittenberg, Horatio?
Marcellus.

MARCELLUS: My good lord.

HAMLET: I am very glad to see you. [*to Barnardo*] Good even, sir.—But what, in faith, make you from Wittenberg?

HORATIO: A truant disposition,° good my lord.

HAMLET: I would not hear your enemy say so,
Nor shall you do my ear that violence
To make it truster of your own report
Against yourself. I know you are no truant.
But what is your affair in Elsinore?
We'll teach you to drink [deep] ere you depart.

HORATIO: My lord, I came to see your father's funeral.

HAMLET: I prithee do not mock me, fellow-studient,°
I think it was to [see] my mother's wedding.

HORATIO: Indeed, my lord, it followed hard upon.

HAMLET: Thrift, thrift, Horatio, the funeral bak'd-meats
Did coldly° furnish forth the marriage tables.
Would I had met my dearest° foe in heaven
Or°ever I had seen that day, Horatio!
My father—methinks I see my father.

HORATIO: Where, my lord?

HAMLET: In my mind's eye, Horatio.

HORATIO: I saw him once, 'a was a goodly king.

HAMLET: 'A was a man, take him for all in all,
I shall not look upon his like again.

HORATIO: My lord, I think I saw him yesternight.

HAMLET: Saw, who?

HORATIO: My lord, the King your father.

HAMLET: The King my father?

HORATIO: Season° your admiration° for a while
With an attent ear, till I may deliver,°
Upon the witness of these gentlemen,
This marvel to you.

HAMLET: For God's love let me hear!

HORATIO: Two nights together had these gentlemen,
Marcellus and Barnardo, on their watch,
In the dead waste° and middle of the night,
Been thus encount'red: a figure like your father,

°*change:* Exchange. °*what . . . from:* What are you doing away from. °*truant disposition:* Inclination to play truant. °*studient:* Student. °*coldly:* When cold. °*dearest:* Most intensely hated. °*Or:* Ere, before. °*Season:* Temper. °*admiration:* Wonder. °*deliver:* Report. °*waste:* Empty expanse.

Armed at point exactly,° cap-a-pe,°
Appears before them, and with solemn march
Goes slow and stately by them; thrice he walk'd
By their oppress'd and fear-surprised° eyes
Within his truncheon's° length, whilst they, distill'd
Almost to jelly with the act° of fear,
Stand dumb, and speak not to him. This to me
In dreadful° secrecy impart they did,
And I with them the third night kept the watch,
Where, as they had delivered, both in time,
Form of the thing, each word made true and good,
The apparition comes. I knew your father,
These hands are not more like.°

HAMLET: But where was this?

MARCELLUS: My lord, upon the platform where we watch.

HAMLET: Did you not speak to it?

HORATIO: My lord, I did,
But answer made it none. Yet once methought
It lifted up it° head and did address
Itself to motion° like as it would speak;
But even then the morning cock crew loud,
And at the sound it shrunk in haste away
And vanish'd from our sight.

HAMLET: 'Tis very strange.

HORATIO: As I do live, my honor'd lord, 'tis true,
And we did think it writ down in our duty
To let you know of it.

HAMLET: Indeed, [indeed,] sirs. But this troubles me.
Hold you the watch to-night?

[MARCELLUS, BARNARDO]: We do, my lord.

HAMLET: Arm'd, say you?

[MARCELLUS, BARNARDO]: Arm'd, my lord.

HAMLET: From top to toe?

[MARCELLUS, BARNARDO]: My lord, from head to foot.

HAMLET: Then saw you not his face.

HORATIO: O yes, my lord, he wore his beaver° up.

HAMLET: What, look'd he frowningly?

HORATIO: A countenance more
In sorrow than in anger.

HAMLET: Pale, or red?

°*at point exactly:* In every particular. °*cap-a-pe:* From head to foot. °*fear-surprised:* Overwhelmed by fear. °*truncheon's:* Short staff carried as a symbol of military command. °*act:* Action, operation. °*dreadful:* Held in awe, solemnly sworn. °*are . . . like:* Do not resemble each other more closely than the apparition resembled him. °*it:* Its. °*address: . . . motion:* Begin to make a gesture. °*beaver:* visor.

HORATIO: Nay, very pale.
HAMLET: And fix'd his eyes upon you?
HORATIO: Most constantly.
HAMLET: I would I had been there.
HORATIO: It would have much amaz'd you.
HAMLET: Very like, [very like]. Stay'd it long?
HORATIO: While one with moderate haste might tell a hundredth.°
BOTH [MARCELLUS, BARNARDO]: Longer, longer.
HORATIO: Not when I saw't.
HAMLET: His beard was grisl'd,° no?
HORATIO: It was, as I have seen it in his life,
A sable silver'd.
HAMLET: I will watch to-night,
Perchance 'twill walk again.
HORATIO: I warr'nt it will.
HAMLET: If it assume my noble father's person,
I'll speak to it though hell itself should gape
And bid me hold my peace. I pray you all,
If you have hitherto conceal'd this sight,
Let it be tenable° in your silence still,
And whatsomever else shall hap to-night,
Give it an understanding but no tongue.
I will requite your loves. So fare you well.
Upon the platform 'twixt aleven° and twelf
I'll visit you.
ALL: Our duty to your honor.
HAMLET: Your loves, as mine to you; farewell.

Exeunt [all but Hamlet].

My father's spirit—in arms! All is not well,
I doubt° some foul play. Would the night were come!
Till then sit still, my soul. [Foul] deeds will rise,
Though all the earth o'erwhelm them, to men's eyes.

Exit.

[SCENE 3]°

Enter Laertes and Ophelia, his sister.

LAERTES: My necessaries are inbark'd.° Farewell.
And, sister, as the winds give benefit

°*tell a hundredth:* Count a hundred. °*grisl'd:* Grizzled, mixed with grey. °*tenable:* Held close. °*aleven:* Eleven. °*doubt:* Suspect. °*1.3. Location:* Polonius's quarters in the castle. °*inbark'd:* Embarked, abroad.

And convey [is] assistant,° do not sleep,
But let me hear from you.
OPHELIA: Do you doubt that?
LAERTES: For Hamlet, and the trifling of his favor,
Hold it a fashion° and a toy in blood,°
A violet in the youth of primy° nature,
Forward,° not permanent, sweet, not lasting,
The perfume and suppliance° of a minute—
No more.
OPHELIA: No more but so?
LAERTES: Think it no more:
For nature crescent° does not grow alone
In thews° and [bulk], but as this temple waxes,
The inward service of the mind and soul
Grows wide withal.° Perhaps he loves you now,
And now no soil° nor cautel° doth besmirch
The virtue of his will,° but you must fear,
His greatness weigh'd,° his will is not his own,
[For he himself is subject to his birth:]
He may not, as unvalued° persons do,
Carve for himself,° for on his choice depends
The safety and health of this whole state,
And therefore must his choice be circumscrib'd
Unto the voice° and yielding° of that body°
Whereof he is the head. Then if he says he loves you,
It fits your wisdom so far to believe it
As he in his particular act and place°
May give his saying deed, which is no further
Than the main° voice of Denmark goes withal.°
Then weigh what loss your honor may sustain
If with too credent° ear you list his songs,
Or lose your heart, or your chaste treasure open
To his unmast'red importunity.
Fear it, Ophelia, fear it, my dear sister,
And keep you in the rear of your affection,
Out of the shot° and danger of desire.
The chariest maid is prodigal enough

°*convey is assistant:* Means of transport is available. °*a fashion:* Standard behavior for a young man. °*toy in blood:* Idle fancy of youthful passion. °*primy:* Springlike. °*Forward:* Early of growth. °*suppliance:* Pastime. °*crescent:* Growing, increasing. °*thews:* Muscles, sinews. °*as . . . withal:* As the body develops, the powers of mind and spirit grow along with it. °*soil:* Stain. °*cautel:* Deceit. °*will:* Desire. °*His greatness weigh'd:* Considering his princely status. °*unvalued:* Of low rank. °*Carve for himself:* Indulge his own wishes. °*voice:* Vote, approval. °*yielding:* Consent. °*that body:* The state. °*in . . . place:* Acting as he must act in the position he occupies. °*main:* General. °*goes withal:* Accord with. °*credent:* Credulous. °*shot:* Range.

If she unmask her beauty to the moon.
Virtue itself scapes not calumnious strokes.
The canker° galls the infants of the spring
Too oft before their buttons° be disclos'd,°
And in the morn and liquid dew of youth
Contagious blastments° are most imminent.
Be wary then, best safety lies in fear:
Youth to itself rebels, though none else near.

OPHELIA: I shall the effect of this good lesson keep
As watchman to° my heart. But, good my brother,
Do not, as some ungracious° pastors do,
Show me the steep and thorny way to heaven,
Whiles, [like] a puff'd° and reckless libertine,
Himself the primrose path of dalliance treads,
And reaks° not his own rede.°

LAERTES: O, fear me not.°

Enter Polonius.

I stay too long—but here my father comes.
A double blessing is a double grace,
Occasion° smiles upon° a second leave.

POLONIUS: Yet here, Laertes? Aboard, aboard, for shame!
The wind sits in the shoulder of your sail,
And you are stay'd for. There—[*Laying his hand on Laertes' head*] my blessing with thee!
And these few precepts in thy memory
Look thou character.° Give thy thoughts no tongue,
Nor any unproportion'd° thought his act.
Be thou familiar,° but by no means vulgar.°
Those friends thou hast, and their adoption tried,°
Grapple them unto thy soul with hoops of steel,
But do not dull thy palm with entertainment
Of each new-hatch'd, unfledg'd courage.° Beware
Of entrance to a quarrel, but being in,
Bear't that° th' opposed may beware of thee.
Give every man thy ear, but few thy voice,
Take° each man's censure,° but reserve thy judgment.

°*canker:* Canker-worm. °*buttons:* Buds. °*disclos'd:* Opened. °*blastments:* Withering blights. °*to:* Of. °*ungracious:* Graceless. °*puff'd:* Bloated. °*reaks:* Recks, heeds. °*rede:* Advice. °*fear me not:* Don't worry about me. °*Occasion:* Opportunity (here personified, as often). °*smiles upon:* Graciously bestows. °*character:* Inscribe. °*unproportion'd:* Unfitting. °*familiar:* Affable, sociable. °*vulgar:* Friendly with everybody. °*their adoption tried:* Their association with you tested and proved. °*courage:* Spirited, young blood. °*Bear't that:* Manage it in such a way that. °*Take:* Listen to. °*censure:* Opinion.

Costly thy habit as thy purse can buy,
But not express'd in fancy, rich, not gaudy,
For the apparel oft proclaims the man,
And they in France of the best rank and station
[Are] of a most select and generous° chief° in that.
Neither a borrower nor a lender [be],
For a [loan] oft loses both itself and friend,
And borrowing dulleth [th'] edge of husbandry.°
This above all: to thine own self be true,
And it must follow, as the night the day,
Thou canst not then be false to any man.
Farewell, my blessing season° this in thee!

LAERTES: Most humbly do I take my leave, my lord.

POLONIUS: The time invests° you, go, your servants tend.°

LAERTES: Farewell, Ophelia, and remember well
What I have said to you.

OPHELIA: 'Tis in my memory lock'd,
And you yourself shall keep the key of it.

LAERTES: Farewell. (*Exit Laertes.*)

POLONIUS: What is't, Ophelia, he hath said to you?

OPHELIA: So please you, something touching the Lord Hamlet.

POLONIUS: Marry,° well bethought.
'Tis told me, he hath very oft of late
Given private time to you, and you yourself
Have of your audience been most free and bounteous.
If it be so — as so 'tis put on° me,
And that in way of caution — I must tell you,
You do not understand yourself so clearly
As it behooves my daughter and your honor.
What is between you? Give me up the truth.

OPHELIA: He hath, my lord, of late made many tenders°
Of his affection to me.

POLONIUS: Affection, puh! You speak like a green girl,
Unsifted° in such perilous circumstance.
Do you believe his tenders, as you call them?

OPHELIA: I do not know, my lord, what I should think.

POLONIUS: Marry, I will teach you: think yourself a baby
That you have ta'en these tenders° for true pay,
Which are not sterling. Tender° yourself more dearly,

°*generous:* Noble °*chief:* Eminence (?). But the line is probably corrupt. Perhaps *of a* is intrusive, in which case *chief* = chiefly. °*husbandry:* thrift. °*season:* preserve (?) or ripen, make fruitful (?). °*invests:* Besieges. °*tend:* Wait. °*Marry:* Indeed (originally the name of the Virgin Mary used as an oath). °*put on:* Told to. °*tenders:* Offers. °*Unsifted:* Untried. °*tenders:* With play on the sense "money offered in payment" (as in *legal tender*). °*Tender:* Hold, value.

Or (not to crack the wind of the poor phrase,
[Wringing]° it thus) you'll tender me a fool.°

OPHELIA: My lord, he hath importun'd me with love
In honorable fashion.°

POLONIUS: Ay, fashion you may call it. Go to, go to.

OPHELIA: And hath given countenance° to his speech, my lord,
With almost all the holy vows of heaven.

POLONIUS: Ay, springes° to catch woodcocks.° I do know,
When the blood burns, how prodigal the soul
Lends the tongue vows. These blazes, daughter,
Giving more light than heat, extinct in both
Even in their promise, as it is a-making,
You must not take for fire. From this time
Be something scanter of your maiden presence,
Set your entreatments at a higher rate
Than a command to parle.° For Lord Hamlet,
Believe so much in him,° that he is young,
And with a larger teder° may he walk
Than may be given you. In few, Ophelia,
Do not believe his vows, for they are brokers,°
Not of that dye which their investments show,°
But mere° [implorators] of unholy suits,
Breathing like sanctified and pious bonds,°
The better to [beguile]. This is for all:
I would not, in plain terms, from this time forth,
Have you so slander° any moment° leisure
As to give words or talk with the Lord Hamlet.
Look to't, I charge you. Come your ways.°

OPHELIA: I shall obey, my lord.

Exeunt.

[SCENE 4]°

Enter Hamlet, Horatio, and Marcellus.

HAMLET: The air bites shrowdly,° it is very cold.

HORATIO: It is [a] nipping and an eager° air.

°*Wringing:* Straining, forcing to the limit. °*tender . . . fool:* (1) Show me that you are a fool; (2) make me look like a fool; (3) present me with a (bastard) grandchild. °*fashion:* See note on line 7. °*countenance:* Authority. °*springes:* Snares. °*woodcocks:* Proverbially gullible birds. °*Set . . . parle:* Place a higher value on your favors; do not grant interviews simply because he asks for them. Polonius uses a military figure: *entreatments* = negotiations for surrender; *parle* = parley, discuss terms. °*so . . . him:* No more than this with respect to him. °*larger teder:* Longer tether. °*brokers:* Procurers. °*Not . . . show:* Not of the color that their garments (*investments*) exhibit; not what they seem. °*mere:* Out-and-out. °*bonds:* (Lover's) vows or assurances. Many editors follow Theobald in reading *bawds.* °*slander:* Disgrace. °*moment:* Momentary. °*Come your ways:* Come along. °*1.4 Location:* The guard-platform of the castle. °*shrowdly:* Shrewdly, wickedly. °*eager:* Sharp.

HAMLET: What hour now?
HORATIO: I think it lacks of twelf.
MARCELLUS: No, it is strook.
HORATIO: Indeed? I heard it not: It then draws near the season
Wherein the spirit held his wont to walk.

A flourish of trumpets, and two pieces° goes *off* [*within*].

What does this mean, my lord?
HAMLET: The King doth wake to-night and takes his rouse,°
Keeps wassail,° and the swagg'ring up-spring° reels;
And as he drains his draughts of Rhenish° down,
The kettle-drum and trumpet thus bray out
The triumph of his pledge.°
HORATIO: Is it a custom?
HAMLET: Ay, marry, is't,
But to my mind, though I am native here
And to the manner° born, it is a custom
More honor'd in the breach than the observance.°
This heavy-headed revel east and west
Makes us traduc'd and tax'd of° other nations.
They clip° us drunkards, and with swinish phrase
Soil our addition,° and indeed it takes
From our achievements, though perform'd at height,°
The pith and marrow of our attribute.°
So, oft it chances in particular° men,
That for some vicious mole of nature° in them,
As in their birth, wherein they are not guilty
(Since nature cannot choose his° origin),
By their o'ergrowth of some complexion°
Oft breaking down the pales° and forts of reason,
Or by some habit, that too much o'er-leavens°
The form of plausive° manners — that these men,
Carrying, I say, the stamp of one defect,
Being nature's livery, or fortune's star,°
His virtues else, be they as pure as grace,
As infinite as man may undergo,°

°*pieces:* cannon. °*doth . . . rouse:* Holds revels far into the night. °*wassail:* Carousal. °*up-spring:* Wild dance. °*Rhenish:* Rhine wine. °*triumph . . . pledge:* Accomplishment of his toast (by draining his cup at a single draught.) °*manner:* Custom (of carousing). °*More . . . observance:* Which it is more honorable to break than to observe. °*tax'd of:* Censured by. °*clip:* Clepe, call. °*addition:* Titles of honor. *at height:* Most excellently. °*attribute:* Reputation. °*particular:* Individual. °*vicious. . . nature:* Small natural blemish. °*his:* Its. °*By . . . complexion:* By the excess of some one of the humors (which were thought to govern the disposition). °*pales:* Fences. °*o'er-leavens:* Makes itself felt throughout (as leaven works in the whole mass of dough). °*plausive:* Pleasing. °*Being:. . . star:* Whether they were born with it, or got it by misfortune. *Star* means "blemish." °*undergo:* Carry the weight of, sustain.

Shall in the general censure° take corruption
From that particular fault: the dram° of [ev'l]°
Doth all the noble substance of a doubt°
To his own scandal.°

Enter Ghost.

HORATIO: Look, my lord, it comes!

HAMLET: Angels and ministers of grace defend us!
Be thou a spirit of health,° or goblin damn'd,
Bring with thee airs from heaven, or blasts from hell,
Be thy intents wicked, or charitable,
Thou com'st in such a questionable° shape
That I will speak to thee. I'll call thee Hamlet,
King, father, royal Dane. O, answer me!
Let me not burst in ignorance, but tell
Why thy canoniz'd° bones, hearsed in death,
Have burst their cerements;° why the sepulchre,
Wherein we saw thee quietly [inurn'd,]
Hath op'd his ponderous and marble jaws
To cast thee up again. What may this mean,
That thou, dead corpse, again in complete steel°
Revisits° thus the glimpses of the moon,
Making night hideous, and we fools of nature°
So horridly to shake our disposition°
With thoughts beyond the reaches of our souls?
Say why is this? wherefore? what should we do?

[*Ghost*] *beckons* [*Hamlet*].

HORATIO: It beckons you to go away with it,
As if it some impartment° did desire
To you alone.

MARCELLUS: Look with what courteous action
It waves you to a more removed ground,
But do not go with it.

HORATIO: No, by no means.

HAMLET: It will not speak, then I will follow it.

HORATIO: Do not, my lord.

°*general censure:* Popular opinion. °*dram:* Minute amount. °*ev'l:* Evil, with a pun on *eale,* "yeast" (cf. *o'-er-leavens* in line 31). °*of a doubt:* A famous crux, for which many emendations have been suggested, the most widely accepted being Steevens' *often dout* (extinguish). °*To . . . scandal:* So that it all shares in the disgrace. °*of health:* Wholesome, good. °*questionable:* Inviting talk. °*canoniz'd:* Buried with the prescribed rites. °*cerements:* Grave-clothes. °*complete steel:* Full armor. °*Revisits:* The *-s* ending in the second-person singular is common. °*fools of nature:* The children (or the dupes) of a purely natural order, baffled by the supernatural. °*disposition:* Nature. °*impartment:* Communication.

HAMLET: Why, what should be the fear?
I do not set my life at a pin's fee,°
And for my soul, what can it do to that,
Being a thing immortal as itself?
It waves me forth again, I'll follow it.
HORATIO: What if it tempt you toward the flood, my lord,
Or to the dreadful summit of the cliff
That beetles o'er his base into the sea,
And there assume some other horrible form
Which might deprive your sovereignty of reason,°
And draw you into madness? Think of it.
The very place puts toys of desperation,°
Without more motive, into every brain
That looks so many fadoms° to the sea
And hears it roar beneath.
HAMLET: It waves me still.—
Go on, I'll follow thee.
MARCELLUS: You shall not go, my lord.
HAMLET: Hold off your hands.
HORATIO: Be rul'd, you shall not go.
HAMLET: My fate cries out,
And makes each petty artere° in this body
As hardy as the Nemean lion's° nerve.°
Still am I call'd. Unhand me, gentlemen.
By heaven, I'll make a ghost of him that lets° me!
I say away!— Go on, I'll follow thee.

Exeunt Ghost and Hamlet.

HORATIO: He waxes desperate with [imagination].
MARCELLUS: Let's follow. 'Tis not fit thus to obey him.
HORATIO: Have after. To what issue will this come?
MARCELLUS: Something is rotten in the state of Denmark.
HORATIO: Heaven will direct it.°
MARCELLUS: Nay, let's follow him.

Exeunt.

[SCENE 5]°

Enter Ghost and Hamlet.

HAMLET: Whither wilt thou lead me? Speak, I'll go no further.
GHOST: Mark me.

°*fee:* Worth. °*deprive . . . reason:* Unseat reason from the rule of your mind. °*toys of desperation:* Fancies of desperate action, inclinations to jump off. °*fadoms:* Fathoms. °*artere:* Variant spelling of *artery;* here, ligament, sinew. °*Nemean lion:* Slain by Hercules as one of his twelve labors. °*nerve:* Sinew. °*lets:* Hinders. °*it:* The issue. °*1.5. Location:* On the battlements of the castle.

HAMLET: I will.
GHOST: My hour is almost come
When I to sulph'rous and tormenting flames
Must render up myself.
HAMLET: Alas, poor ghost!
GHOST: Pity me not, but lend thy serious hearing
To what I shall unfold.
HAMLET: Speak, I am bound to hear.
GHOST: So art thou to revenge, when thou shalt hear.
HAMLET: What?
GHOST: I am thy father's spirit,
Doom'd for a certain term to walk the night,
And for the day confin'd to fast° in fires,
Till the foul crimes° done in my days of nature
Are burnt and purg'd away. But that I am forbid
To tell the secrets of my prison-house,
I could a tale unfold whose lightest word
Would harrow up thy soul, freeze thy young blood,
Make thy two eyes like stars start from their spheres,°
Thy knotted and combined locks to part,
And each particular hair to stand an end,°
Like quills upon the fearful porpentine.°
But this eternal blazon° must not be
To ears of flesh and blood. List, list, O, list!
If thou didst ever thy dear father love—
HAMLET: O God!
GHOST: Revenge his foul and most unnatural murther.
HAMLET: Murther!
GHOST: Murther most foul, as in the best it is,
But this most foul, strange, and unnatural.
HAMLET: Haste me to know't, that I with wings as swift
As meditation,° or the thoughts of love,
May sweep to my revenge.
GHOST: I find thee apt,
And duller shouldst thou be than the fat weed
That roots itself in ease on Lethe° wharf,°
Wouldst thou not stir in this. Now, Hamlet, hear:
'Tis given out that, sleeping in my orchard,°
A serpent stung me, so the whole ear of Denmark

°*fast:* Do penance. °*crimes:* Sins. °*spheres:* Eye-sockets; with allusion to the revolving spheres in which, according to the Ptolemaic astronomy, the stars were fixed. °*an end:* On end °*fearful porpentine:* Frightened porcupine. °*eternal blazon:* Revelation of eternal things. °*meditation:* Thought. °*Lethe:* River of Hades, the water of which made the drinker forget the past. °*wharf:* Bank. °*orchard:* Garden.

Is by a forged process° of my death
Rankly abus'd;° but know, thou noble youth,
The serpent that did sting thy father's life
Now wears his crown.

Hamlet: O my prophetic soul!
My uncle?

Ghost: Ay, that incestuous, that adulterate° beast,
With witchcraft of his wit, with traitorous gifts—
O wicked wit and gifts that have the power
So to seduce!—won to his shameful lust
The will of my most seeming virtuous queen.
O Hamlet, what [a] falling-off was there
From me, whose love was of that dignity
That it went hand in hand even with the vow
I made to her in marriage, and to decline
Upon a wretch whose natural gifts were poor
To those of mine!
But virtue, as it never will be moved,
Though lewdness court it in a shape of heaven,°
So [lust], though to a radiant angel link'd,
Will [sate] itself in a celestial bed
And prey on garbage.
But soft, methinks I scent the morning air,
Brief let me be. Sleeping within my orchard,
My custom always of the afternoon,
Upon my secure° hour thy uncle stole,
With juice of cursed hebona° in a vial,
And in the porches of my ears did pour
The leprous distillment, whose effect
Holds such an enmity with blood of man
That, swift as quicksilver it courses through
The natural gates and alleys of the body,
And with a sudden vigor it doth [posset°]
And curd, like eager° droppings into milk,
The thin and wholesome blood. So did it mine,
And a most instant tetter° bark'd° about,
Most lazar-like,° with vile and loathsome crust
All my smooth body.
Thus was I, sleeping, by a brother's hand,
Of life, of crown, of queen, at once° dispatch'd,°

°*forged process:* False account. °*abus'd:* Deceived. °*adulterate:* Adulterous. °*shape of heaven:* Angelic form. °*secure:* Carefree. °*hebona:* Ebony (which Shakespeare, following a literary tradition, and perhaps also associating the word with *henbane*, thought the name of a poison). °*posset:* Curdle. °*eager:* Sour. °*tetter:* Scabby eruption. °*bark'd:* Formed a hard covering, like bark on a tree. °*lazar-like:* Leperlike. °*at once:* All at the same time. °*dispatch'd:* Deprived.

Cut off even in the blossoms of my sin,
Unhous'led,° disappointed,° unanel'd,°
No reck'ning made, but sent to my account
With all my imperfections on my head.
O, horrible, O, horrible, most horrible!
If thou hast nature° in thee, bear it not,
Let not the royal bed of Denmark be
A couch for luxury° and damned incest.
But howsomever thou pursues this act,
Taint not thy mind, nor let thy soul contrive
Against thy mother aught. Leave her to heaven,
And to those thorns that in her bosom lodge
To prick and sting her. Fare thee well at once!
The glow-worm shows the matin° to be near,
And gins° to pale his uneffectual fire.
Adieu, adieu, adieu! remember me.
Exit.

HAMLET: O all you host of heaven! O earth! What else?
And shall I couple hell? O fie, hold, hold, my heart,
And you, my sinows,° grow not instant old,
But bear me [stiffly] up. Remember thee!
Ay, thou poor ghost, whiles memory holds a seat
In this distracted globe.° Remember thee!
Yea, from the table° of my memory
I'll wipe away all trivial fond° records,
All saws° of books, all forms,° all pressures° past
That youth and observation copied there,
And thy commandement all alone shall live
Within the book and volume of my brain,
Unmix'd with baser matter. Yes, by heaven!
O most pernicious woman!
O villain, villain, smiling, damned villain!
My tables—meet it is I set it down
That one may smile, and smile, and be a villain!
At least I am sure it may be so in Denmark. [*He writes.*]
So, uncle, there you are. Now to my word:°
It is, "Adieu, adieu! remember me."
I have sworn't.

°*Unhous'led:* Without the Eucharist. °*disappointed:* Without (spiritual) preparation. °*unanel'd:* Unanointed, without extreme unction. °*nature:* Natural feeling. °*luxury:* Lust. °*matin:* Morning. °*gins:* Begins. °*sinows:* Sinews. °*globe:* Head. °*table:* Writing tablet. °*fond:* Foolish. °*saws:* Wise sayings. °*forms:* Shapes, images. °*pressures:* Impressions. °*word:* Word of command from the Ghost.

HORATIO [*Within.*]: My lord, my lord!
MARCELLUS [*Within.*]: Lord Hamlet!

Enter Horatio and Marcellus.

HORATIO: Heavens secure him!
HAMLET: So be it!
MARCELLUS: Illo, ho, ho, my lord!
HAMLET: Hillo, ho, ho, boy! Come,° [bird], come.
MARCELLUS: How is't, my noble lord?
HORATIO: What news, my lord?
HAMLET: O, wonderful!
HORATIO: Good my lord, tell it.
HAMLET: No, you will reveal it.
HORATIO: Not I, my lord, by heaven.
MARCELLUS: Nor I, my lord.
HAMLET: How say you then, would heart of man once think it?—
But you'll be secret?
BOTH [HORATIO, MARCELLUS]: Ay, by heaven, [my lord].
HAMLET: There's never a villain dwelling in all Denmark
But he's an arrant knave.
HORATIO: There needs no ghost, my lord, come from the grave
To tell us this.
HAMLET: Why, right, you are in the right,
And so, without more circumstance° at all,
I hold it fit that we shake hands and part,
You, as your business and desire shall point you,
For every man hath business and desire,
Such as it is, and for my own poor part,
I will go pray.
HORATIO: These are but wild and whirling words, my lord.
HAMLET: I am sorry they offend you, heartily,
Yes, faith, heartily.
HORATIO: There's no offense, my lord.
HAMLET: Yes, by Saint Patrick, but there is, Horatio,
And much offense too. Touching this vision here,
It is an honest° ghost, that let me tell you.
For your desire to know what is between us,
O'ermaster't as you may. And now, good friends,
As you are friends, scholars, and soldiers,
Give me one poor request.
HORATIO: What is't,° my lord, we will.
HAMLET: Never make known what you have seen tonight.

°*Hillo . . . come:* Hamlet answers Marcellus' halloo with a falconer's cry. °*circumstance:* Ceremony. °*honest:* True, genuine. °*What is't:* Whatever it is.

BOTH [HORATIO, MARCELLUS]: My lord, we will not.
HAMLET: Nay, but swear't.
HORATIO: In faith,
My lord, not I.
MARCELLUS: Nor I, my lord, in faith.
HAMLET: Upon my sword.
MARCELLUS: We have sworn, my lord, already.
HAMLET: Indeed, upon my sword,° indeed.

Ghost cries under the stage.

GHOST: Swear.
HAMLET: Ha, ha, boy, say'st thou so? Art thou there, truepenny?°
Come on, you hear this fellow in the cellarage,
Consent to swear.
HORATIO: Propose the oath, my lord.
HAMLET: Never to speak of this that you have seen,
Swear by my sword.
GHOST [*beneath*]: Swear.
HAMLET *Hic et ubique?*° Then we'll shift our ground.
Come hither, gentlemen,
And lay your hands again upon my sword.
Swear by my sword
Never to speak of this that you have heard.
GHOST [*beneath*]: Swear by his sword.
HAMLET: Well said, old mole, canst work i' th' earth so fast?
A worthy pioner!° Once more remove, good friends.
HORATIO: O day and night, but this is wondrous strange!
HAMLET: And therefore as a stranger give it welcome.°
There are more things in heaven and earth, Horatio,
Than are dreamt of in your° philosophy.°
But come—
Here, as before, never, so help you mercy,
How strange or odd some'er I bear myself—
As I perchance hereafter shall think meet
To put an antic disposition on°—
That you, at such times seeing me, never shall,
With arms encumb'red° thus, or this headshake,
Or by pronouncing of some doubtful phrase,
As "Well, well, we know," or "We could, and if° we would,"
Or "If we list° to speak," or "There be, and if they might,"

°*upon my sword:* On the cross formed by the hilt. °*truepenny:* Trusty fellow. °*Hic et ubique:* Here and everywhere. °*pioner:* Digger, miner (variant of *pioneer*). °*as . . . welcome:* Give it the welcome due in courtesy to strangers. °*your:* See note on. 1. 1. 151. °*philosophy:* Natural philosophy, science. °*put . . . on:* Behave in some fantastic manner, act like a madman. °*encumb'red:* Folded. °*and if:* If. °*list:* Cared, had a mind.

Or such ambiguous giving out, to note°
That you know aught of me — this do swear,
So grace and mercy at your most need help you,

GHOST [*beneath*]: Swear. [*They swear.*]

HAMLET: Rest, rest, perturbed spirit! So, gentlemen,
With all my love I do commend to you,
And what so poor a man as Hamlet is
May do t' express his love and friending to you,
God willing, shall not lack. Let us go in together,
And still° your fingers on your lips, I pray.
The time is out of joint — O cursed spite,
That ever I was born to set it right!
Nay, come, let's go together.°

Exeunt.

ACT 2

SCENE 1°

Enter old Polonius with his man [*Reynaldo*].

POLONIUS: Give him this money and these notes, Reynaldo.

REYNALDO: I will, my lord.

POLONIUS: You shall do marvell's° wisely, good Reynaldo,
Before you visit him, to make inquire
On his behavior.

REYNALDO: My lord, I did intend it.

POLONIUS: Marry, well said, very well said. Look you, sir,
Inquire me first what Danskers° are in Paris,
And how, and who, what means, and where they keep,°
What company, at what expense; and finding
By this encompassment° and drift of question°
That they do know my son, come you more nearer
Than your particular demands° will touch it.
Take you as 'twere some distant knowledge of him,
As thus, "I know his father and his friends,
And in part him." Do you mark this, Reynaldo?

REYNALDO: Ay, very well, my lord.

POLONIUS: "And in part him — but," you may say, "not well.
But if't be he I mean, he's very wild,
Addicted so and so," and there put on him

°*note:* Indicate. °*still:* Always. °*Nay . . . together:* They are holding back to let him go first. °*2. 1. Location:* Polonius's quarters in the castle. °*marvell's:* Marvellous(ly). °*Danskers:* Danes. °*keep:* Lodge. °*encompassment:* Circuitousness. °*drift of question:* Directing of the conversation. °*particular demands:* Direct questions.

What forgeries° you please: marry, none so rank
As may dishonor him, take heed of that,
But, sir, such wanton,° wild, and usual slips
As are companions and most known
To youth and liberty.

Reynaldo: As gaming, my lord.

Polonius: Ay, or drinking, fencing, swearing, quarreling,
Drabbing°—you may go so far.

Reynaldo: My lord, that would dishonor him.

Polonius: Faith,° as you may season° it in the charge:
You must not put another scandal on him,
That he is open to incontinency°—
That's not my meaning. But breathe his faults so quaintly°
That they may seem the taints of liberty,
The flash and outbreak of a fiery mind,
A savageness in unreclaimed° blood,
Of general assault.°

Reynaldo: But, my good lord—

Polonius: Wherefore should you do this?

Reynaldo: Ay, my lord,
I would know that.

Polonius: Marry, sir, here's my drift,
And I believe it is a fetch of wit:°
You laying these slight sallies° on my son,
As 'twere a thing a little soil'd [wi' th'] working,°
Mark you,
Your party in converse, him you would sound,
Having° ever seen in the prenominate crimes°
The youth you breathe of guilty, be assur'd
He closes° with you in this consequence:°
"Good sir," or so, or "friend," or "gentleman,"
According to the phrase or the addition°
Of man and country.

Reynaldo: Very good, my lord.

Polonius: And then, sir, does 'a this—'a does—what was I about to say?
By the mass, I was about to say something.
Where did I leave?

Reynaldo: At "closes in the consequence."

°*forgeries:* Invented charges. °*wanton:* Sportive. °*Drabbing:* Whoring. °*Faith:* Most editors read *Faith, no,* following F1; this makes easier sense. °*season:* Qualify, temper. °*open to incontinency:* Habitually profligate. °*quaintly:* Artfully. °*unreclaimed:* Untamed. °*Of general assault:* To which young men are generally subject. °*fetch of wit:* Ingenious device. °*sallies:* Sullies, blemishes. °*soil'd . . . working:* Shopworn. °*Having:* If he has. °*prenominate crimes:* Aforementioned faults. °*closes:* Falls in. °*in this consequence:* As follows. °*addition:* Style of address.

POLONIUS: At "closes in the consequence," ay, marry.
He closes thus: "I know the gentleman.
"I saw him yesterday, or th' other day,
Or then, or then, with such or such, and as you say,
There was 'a gaming, there o'ertook in 's rouse,°
There falling out at tennis" or, perchance,
I saw him enter such a house of sale,"
Videlicet, a brothel, or so forth. See you now,
Your bait of falsehood take this carp of truth,
And thus do we of wisdom and of reach,°
With windlasses° and with assays of bias,°
By indirections find directions° out;
So by my former lecture and advice
Shall you my son. You have me,° have you not?
REYNALDO: My lord, I have.
POLONIUS: God buy ye,° fare ye well.
REYNALDO: Good my lord.
POLONIUS: Observe his inclination in° yourself.
REYNALDO: I shall, my lord.
POLONIUS: And let him ply° his music.
REYNALDO: Well, my lord.
POLONIUS: Farewell.

Exit Reynaldo.

Enter Ophelia.

How now, Ophelia, what's the matter?
OPHELIA: O my lord, I have been so affrighted!
POLONIUS: With what, i' th' name of God?
OPHELIA: My lord, as I was sewing in my closet,°
Lord Hamlet, with his doublet all unbrac'd,°
No hat upon his head, his stockins fouled,°
Ungart'red, and down-gyved° to his ankle,
Pale as his shirt, his knees knocking each other,
And with a look so piteous in purport
As if he had been loosed out of hell
To speak of horrors—he comes before me.
POLONIUS: Mad for thy love?

°*o'ertook in 's rouse:* Overcome by drink. °*reach:* Capacity, understanding. °*windlasses:* Roundabout methods. °*assays of bias:* Indirect attempts (a figure from the game of bowls in which the player must make allowance for the curving course his bowl will take toward its mark. °*directions:* The way things are going. *have me:* Understand me. °*God buy ye:* Good-bye (a contraction of *God be with you*). °*in:* By; Polonius asks him to observe Laertes directly as well as making inquiries. °*let him ply:* See that he goes on with. °*closet:* Private room. °*unbrac'd:* Unlaced. °*stockins fouled:* Stockings dirty. °*down-gyved:* Hanging down like fetters on a prisoner's legs.

OPHELIA: My lord, I do not know,
But truly I do fear it.
POLONIUS: What said he?
OPHELIA: He took me by the wrist, and held me hard,
Then goes he to the length of all his arm,
And with his other hand thus o'er his brow,
He falls to such perusal of my face
As 'a would draw it. Long stay'd he so.
At last, a little shaking of mine arm,
And thrice his head thus waving up and down,
He rais'd a sigh so piteous and profound
As it did seem to shatter all his bulk°
And end his being. That done, he lets me go,
And with his head over his shoulder turn'd,
He seem'd to find his way without his eyes,
For out a' doors he went without their helps,
And to the last bended their light on me.
POLONIUS: Come, go with me. I will go seek the King.
This is the very ecstasy° of love,
Whose violent property° fordoes° itself,
And leads the will to desperate undertakings,
As oft as any passions under heaven
That does afflict our natures. I am sorry—
What, have you given him any hard words of late?
OPHELIA: No, my good lord, but as you did command
I did repel his letters, and denied
His access to me.
POLONIUS: That hath made him mad.
I am sorry that with better heed and judgment
I had not coted° him. I fear'd he did but trifle
And meant to wreck thee, but, beshrow° my jealousy!°
By heaven, it is as proper to our age°
To cast beyond ourselves° in our opinions,
As it is common for the younger sort
To lack discretion. Come, go we to the King.
This must be known, which, being kept close,° might move
More grief to hide, than hate to utter love.°
Come

Exeunt.

°*bulk:* Body. °*ecstasy:* Madness. °*property:* Quality. °*fordoes:* Destroys. °*coted:* Observed. °*beshrow:* Beshrew, plague take. °*jealousy:* Suspicious mind. °*proper . . . age:* Characteristic of men of my age. °*cast beyond ourselves:* Overshoot, go too far (by way of caution). °*close:* Secret. °*move . . . love:* Cause more grievous consequences by its concealment than we shall incur displeasure by making it known.

SCENE 2°

Flourish. Enter King and Queen, Rosencrantz and Guildenstern [cum aliis].

KING: Welcome, dear Rosencrantz and Guildenstern!
Moreover that we much did long to see you,°
The need we have to use you did provoke
Our hasty sending. Something have you heard
Of Hamlet's transformation; so call it,
Sith° nor th' exterior nor the inward man
Resembles that it was. What it should be,
More than his father's death, that thus hath put him
So much from th' understanding of himself,
I cannot dream of. I entreat you both
That, being of° so young days brought up with him,
And sith so neighbored to his youth and havior,
That you voutsafe your rest° here in our court
Some little time, so by your companies
To draw him on to pleasures, and to gather
So much as from occasion you may glean,
Whether aught to us unknown afflicts him thus,
That, open'd, lies within our remedy.

QUEEN: Good gentlemen, he hath much talk'd of you,
And sure I am two men there is not living
To whom he more adheres.° If it will please you
To show us so much gentry° and good will
As to expend your time with us a while,
For the supply and profit° of our hope,
Your visitation shall receive such thanks
As fits a king's remembrance.

ROSENCRANTZ: Both your Majesties
Might, by the sovereign power you have of us,
Put your dread pleasures more into command
Than to entreaty.

GUILDENSTERN: But we both obey,
And here give up ourselves, in the full bent,°
To lay our service freely at your feet,
To be commanded.

KING: Thanks, Rosencrantz and gentle Guildenstern.

QUEEN: Thanks, Guildenstern and gentle Rosencrantz.
And I beseech you instantly to visit

°*2.2. Location:* The castle. °*Moreover . . . you:* Besides the fact that we wanted to see you for your own sakes. °*Sith:* Since. °*of:* From. °*voutsafe your rest:* Vouchsafe to remain. °*more adheres:* Is more attached. °*gentry:* Courtesy. °*supply and profit:* Support and advancement. °*in . . . bent:* To our utmost.

My too much changed son. Go some of you
And bring these gentlemen where Hamlet is.

GUILDENSTERN: Heavens make our presence and our practices
Pleasant and helpful to him!

QUEEN: Ay, amen!

Exeunt Rosencrantz and Guildenstern [with some Attendants].

Enter Polonius.

POLONIUS: Th' embassadors° from Norway, my good lord,
Are joyfully return'd.

KING: Thou still° has been the father of good news.

POLONIUS: Have I, my lord? Issure my good liege°
I hold my duty as I hold my soul,
Both to my God and to my gracious king;
And I do think, or else this brain of mine
Hunts not the trail of policy° so sure
As it hath us'd to do, that I have found
The very cause of Hamlet's lunacy.

KING: O, speak of that, that do I long to hear.

POLONIUS: Give first admittance to th' ambassadors;
My news shall be the fruit° to that great feast.

KING: Thyself do grace to them, and bring them in. *Exit Polonius.*
He tells me, my dear Gertrude, he hath found
The head° and source of all your son's distemper.°

QUEEN: I doubt° it is no other but the main,°
His father's death and our [o'erhasty] marriage.

Enter [Polonius, with Voltemand and Cornelius, the] Embassadors.

KING: Well, we shall sift him.— Welcome, my good friends!
Say, Voltemand, what from our brother Norway?

VOLTEMAND: Most fair return of greetings and desires.
Upon our first,° he sent out to suppress
His nephew's levies, which to him appear'd
To be a preparation 'gainst the Polack;
But better look'd into, he truly found
It was against your Highness. Whereat griev'd,°
That so his sickness, age, and impotence
Was falsely borne in hand,° sends out arrests
On Fortinbras, which he, in brief, obeys,

°*embassadors:* Ambassadors. °*still:* Always. °*liege:* Sovereign. °*policy:* Statecraft. °*fruit:* Dessert. °*head:* Synonymous with *source.* °*distemper:* (Mental) illness. °*doubt:* Suspect. °*main:* Main cause. °*Upon our first:* At our first representation. °*griev'd:* Aggrieved, offended. °*borne in hand:* Taken advantage of.

Receives rebuke from Norway, and in fine,°
Makes vows before his uncle never more
To give th' assay° of arms against your majesty.
Whereon old Norway, overcome with joy,
Gives him three score thousand crowns in annual fee,
And his commission to employ those soldiers,
So levied, as before, against the Polack,
With an entreaty, herein further shown, [*giving a paper*]
That it might please you to give quiet pass
Through your dominions for this enterprise,
On such regards of safety and allowance°
As therein are set down.

KING: It likes° us well,
And at our more consider'd° time we'll read,
Answer, and think upon this business.
Mean time, we thank you for your well-took labor.
Go to your rest, at night we'll feast together.
Most welcome home!

Exeunt Embassadors [and Attendants].

POLONIUS: This business is well ended.
My liege, and madam, to expostulate°
What majesty should be, what duty is,
Why day is day, night night, and time is time,
Were nothing but to waste night, day, and time;
Therefore, [since] brevity is the soul of wit,°
And tediousness the limbs and outward flourishes,
I will be brief. Your noble son is mad:
Mad call I it, for to define true madness,
What is't but to be nothing else but mad?
But let that go.
QUEEN: More matter with less art.°
POLONIUS: Madam, I swear I use no art at all.
That he's mad, 'tis true, 'tis true 'tis pity,
And pity 'tis 'tis true—a foolish figure,°
But farewell it, for I will use no art.
Mad let us grant him then, and now remains
That we find out the cause of this effect,
Or rather say, the cause of this defect,

°*in fine:* In the end. °*assay:* Trial. °*On . . . allowance:* With such safeguards and provisos. °*likes:* Pleases. °*consider'd:* Suitable for consideration. °*expostulate:* Expound. °*wit:* Understanding, wisdom. °*art:* Rhetorical art. °*figure:* Figure of speech.

For this effect defective comes by cause:°
Thus it remains, and the remainder thus.
Perpend.°
I have a daughter — have while she is mine —
Who in her duty and obedience, mark,
Hath given me this. Now gather, and surmise.

[*reads the salutation of the letter*]

"To the celestial, and my soul's idol, the most beautified Ophelia"—
That's an ill phrase, a vile phrase, "beautified"° is a vile phrase. But you shall hear. Thus:
In her excellent white bosom, these, etc.

QUEEN: Came this from Hamlet to her?
POLONIUS: Good madam, stay awhile. I will be faithful.

([*reads the*] *letter)*

"Doubt° thou the stars are fire,
Doubt that the sun doth move,
Doubt truth to be a liar,
But never doubt I love.

O dear Ophelia, I am ill at these numbers.° I have not art to reckon° my groans, but that I love thee best, O most best, believe it. Adieu.
Thine evermore, most dear lady,
whilst this machine° is to him, Hamlet"

This in obedience hath my daughter shown me,
And more [above],° hath his solicitings,
As they fell out by time, by means, and place,
All given to mine ear.
KING: But how hath she
Receiv'd his love?
POLONIUS: What do you think of me?
KING: As of a man faithful and honorable.
POLONIUS: I would fain° prove so. But what might you think,
When I had seen this hot love on the wing —
As I perceiv'd it (I must tell you that)
Before my daughter told me — what might you,
Or my dear Majesty your queen here, think,
If I had play'd the desk or table-book,°
Or given my heart a [winking,°] mute and dumb,
Or look'd upon this love with idle sight,°

°*For . . . cause:* for this effect (which shows as a defect in Hamlet's reason) is not merely accidental, and has a cause we may trace. °*Perpend:* Consider. °*beautified:* Beautiful (not an uncommon usage). °*Doubt:* Suspect. °*ill . . . numbers:* Bad at versifying. °*reckon:* count (with a quibble on *numbers*). °*machine:* Body. °*more above:* Furthermore. °*fain:* Willingly, gladly. °*play'd . . . table-book:* Noted the matter secretly. °*winking:* Closing of the eyes. °*idle sight:* Noncomprehending eyes.

What might you think? No, I went round° to work,
And my young mistress thus I did bespeak:°
"Lord Hamlet is a prince out of thy star;°
This must not be"; and then I prescripts gave her,
That she should lock herself from [his] resort,
Admit no messengers, receive no tokens.
Which done, she took the fruits of° my advice;
And he repell'd,° a short tale to make,
Fell into a sadness, then into a fast,
Thence to a watch,° thence into a weakness,
Thence to [a] lightness,° and by this declension,
Into the madness wherein now he raves,
And all we mourn for.

KING: Do you think ['tis] this?

QUEEN: It may be, very like.

POLONIUS: Hath there been such a time — I would fain know that —
That I have positively said, " 'Tis so,"
When it prov'd otherwise?

KING: Not that I know.

POLONIUS [*points to his head and shoulder*]: Take this from this, if this be otherwise.
If circumstances lead me, I will find
Where truth is hid, though it were hid indeed
Within the centre.°

KING: How may we try it further?

POLONIUS: You know sometimes he walks four hours together
Here in the lobby.

QUEEN: So he does indeed.

POLONIUS: At such a time I'll loose my daughter to him.
Be you and I behind an arras° then,
Mark the encounter: if he love her not,
And be not from his reason fall'n thereon,°
Let me be no assistant for a state,
But keep a farm and carters.

KING: We will try it.

Enter Hamlet, [*reading on a book*].

QUEEN: But look where sadly the poor wretch comes reading.

POLONIUS: Away, I do beseech you, both away.
I'll board° him presently,°

°*round:* Straightforwardly. °*bespeak:* Address. °*star:* Sphere, lot in life. °*took . . . of:* Profited by, carried out. °*repell'd:* Repulsed. °*watch:* Sleeplessness. °*lightness:* Lightheadedness. °*centre:* Of the earth (which in the Ptolemaic system is also the centre of the universe). °*arras:* Hanging tapestry. °*thereon:* Because of that. °*board:* Accost. °*presently:* At once.

Exeunt King, and Queen.

O, give me leave,
How does my good Lord Hamlet?

HAMLET: Well, God-a-mercy.°

POLONIUS: Do you know me, my lord?

HAMLET: Excellent well, you are a fishmonger.°

POLONIUS: Not I, my lord.

HAMLET: Then I would you were so honest a man.

POLONIUS: Honest, my lord!

HAMLET: Ay, sir, to be honest, as this world goes, is to be one man pick'd out of ten thousand.

POLONIUS: That's very true, my lord.

HAMLET: For if the sun breed maggots in a dead dog, being a good kissing carrion°— Have you a daughter?

POLONIUS: I have, my lord.

HAMLET: Let her not walk i' th' sun. Conception° is a blessing, but as your daughter may conceive friend, look to't.

POLONIUS [*aside*]**:** How say you by that? still harping on my daughter. Yet he knew me not at first, 'a said I was a fishmonger. 'A is far gone. And truly in my youth I suff'red much extremity for love—very near this. I'll speak to him again.—What do you read, my lord?

HAMLET: Words, words, words.

POLONIUS: What is the matter,° my lord?

HAMLET: Between who?

POLONIUS: I mean, the matter that you read, my lord.

HAMLET: Slanders, sir; for the satirical rogue says here that old men have grey beards, that their faces are wrinkled, their eyes purging thick amber and plumtree gum, and that they have a plentiful lack of wit, together with most weak hams; all which, sir, though I most powerfully and potently believe, yet I hold it not honesty° to have it thus set down, for yourself, sir, shall grow old as I am, if like a crab you could go backward.

POLONIUS [*aside*]: Though this be madness, yet there is method° in't.—Will you walk out of the air, my lord?

HAMLET: Into my grave?

POLONIUS: Indeed, that's out of the air.° [*aside*] How pregnant° sometimes his replies are! a happiness that often madness hits on, which reason and [sanity] could not so prosperously be deliver'd of. I will leave him, [and suddenly° contrive the means of meeting between him] and my daughter.—My lord, I will take my leave of you.

°*God-a-mercy:* Thank you. °*fishmonger:* Usually explained as slang for "bawd," but no evidence has been produced for such a usage in Shakespeare's day. °*good kissing carrion:* Flesh good enough for the sun to kiss. °*Conception:* Understanding (with following play on the sense "conceiving a child"). °*matter:* Subject; but Hamlet replies as if he had understood Polonius to mean "cause for a quarrel." °*honesty:* A fitting thing. °*method:* Orderly arrangement, sequence of ideas. °*out . . . air:* Outdoor air was thought to be bad for invalids. °*pregnant:* Apt. °*suddenly:* At once.

HAMLET: You cannot, take from me any thing that I will not more willingly part withal—except my life, except my life, except my life.

POLONIUS: Fare you well, my lord.

HAMLET: These tedious old fools!

Enter Guildenstern and Rosencrantz.

POLONIUS: You go to seek the Lord Hamlet, there he is.

ROSENCRANTZ [*to Polonius*]: God save you, sir!

Exit Polonius.

GUILDENSTERN: My honor'd lord!

ROSENCRANTZ: My most dear lord!

HAMLET: My [excellent] good friends! How dost thou, Guildenstern? Ah, Rosencrantz? Good lads, how do you both?

ROSENCRANTZ: As the indifferent° children of the earth.

GUILDENSTERN: Happy, in that we are not [over-]happy; on Fortune's [cap] we are not the very button.

HAMLET: Nor the soles of her shoe?

ROSENCRANTZ: Neither, my lord.

HAMLET: Then you live about her waist, or in the middle of her favors?

GUILDENSTERN: Faith, her privates° we.

HAMLET: In the secret parts of Fortune? O, most true, she is a strumpet.° What's the news?

ROSENCRANTZ: None, my lord, but that the world's grown honest.

HAMLET: Then is doomsday near. But your news is not true. Let me question more in particular. What have you, my good friends, deserv'd at the hands of Fortune, that she sends you to prison hither?

GUILDENSTERN: Prison, my lord?

HAMLET: Denmark's a prison.

ROSENCRANTZ: Then is the world one.

HAMLET: A goodly one, in which there are many confines, wards,° and dungeons, Denmark being one o' th' worst.

ROSENCRANTZ: We think not so, my lord.

HAMLET: Why, then 'tis none to you; for there is nothing either good or bad, but thinking makes it so. To me it is a prison.

ROSENCRANTZ: Why then your ambition makes it one. 'Tis too narrow for your mind.

HAMLET: O God, I could be bounded in a nutshell, and count myself a king of infinite space—were it not that I have bad dreams.

GUILDENSTERN: Which dreams indeed are ambition, for the very substance of the ambitious is merely the shadow of a dream.

°*indifferent:* Average. °*privates:* (1) Intimate friends; (2) genitalia. °*strumpet:* A common epithet for Fortune, because she grants favors to all men. °*wards:* Cells.

HAMLET: A dream itself is but a shadow.

ROSENCRANTZ: Truly, and I hold ambition of so airy and light a quality that it is but a shadow's shadow.

HAMLET: Then are our beggars bodies,° and our monarchs and outstretch'd° heroes the beggars' shadows. Shall we to th' court? for, by my fay,° I cannot reason.

BOTH [ROSENCRANTZ GUILDENSTERN]: We'll wait upon you.°

HAMLET: No such matter. I will not sort° you with the rest of my servants; for to speak to you like an honest man, I am most dreadfully° attended. But in the beaten way of friendship, what make you at Elsinore?

ROSENCRANTZ: To visit you, my lord, no other occasion.

HAMLET: Beggar that I am, I am [even] poor in thanks— but I thank you, and sure, dear friends, my thanks are too dear a halfpenny.° Were you not sent for? is it your own inclining? is it a free visitation? Come, come, deal justly° with me. Come, come, nay, speak.

GUILDENSTERN: What should we say, my lord?

HAMLET: Anything but° to th' purpose. You were sent for, and there is a kind of confession in your looks, which your modesties° have not craft enough to color: I know the good King and Queen have sent for you.

ROSENCRANTZ: To what end, my lord?

HAMLET: That you must teach me. But let me conjure you, by the rights of our fellowship, by the consonancy of our youth,° by the obligation of our ever-preserv'd love, and by what more dear a better proposer could charge° you withal, be even° and direct with me, whether you were sent for or no?

ROSENCRANTZ [*aside to Guildenstern*]**:** What say you?

HAMLET [*aside*]**:** Nay then I have an eye of° you!—If you love me, hold not off.

GUILDENSTERN: My lord, we were sent for.

HAMLET: I will tell you why, so shall my anticipation prevent your discovery,° and your secrecy to the King and Queen moult no feather.° I have of late— but wherefore I know not— lost all my mirth, forgone all custom of exercises;° and indeed it goes so heavily with my disposition, that this goodly frame, the earth, seems to me a sterile promontory; this most excellent canopy, the air, look you, this brave° o'erhanging firmament, this majestical roof fretted° with golden fire, why, it appeareth nothing to me but a foul and pestilent congregation of vapors. What [a] piece of work° is a

---

°*bodies:* Not shadows (since they lack ambition). °*outstretch'd:* With their ambition extended to the utmost (and hence producing stretched-out or elongated shadows). °*fay:* Faith. °*wait upon you:* Attend you thither. °*sort:* Associate. °*dreadfully:* Execrably. °*too . . . halfpenny:* Too expensive priced at a halfpenny; not worth much. °*justly:* Honestly. °*but:* Ordinarily punctuated with a comma preceding, to give the sense "provided that it is"; but Q2 has no comma, and Hamlet may intend, or include, the sense "except." °*modesties:* Sense of shame. °*consonancy . . . youth:* Similarity of our ages. °*charge:* Urge, adjure. °*even:* Frank, honest (cf. modern "level with me"). °*of:* On. °*prevent your discovery:* Forestall your disclosure (of what the king and queen have said to you in confidence). °*moult no feather:* Not be impaired in the least. °*custom of exercises:* My usual athletic activities. °*brave:* Splendid. °*fretted:* Ornamented as with fretwork. °*piece of work:* Masterpiece.

man, how noble in reason, how infinite in faculties, in form and moving, how express° and admirable in action, how like an angel in apprehension, how like a god! the beauty of the world; the paragon of animals; and yet to me what is this quintessence° of dust? Man delights not me — nor woman neither, though by your smiling you seem to say so.

ROSENCRANTZ: My lord, there was no such stuff in my thoughts.

HAMLET: Why did you laugh then, when I said, "Man delights not me"?

ROSENCRANTZ: To think, my lord, if you delight not in man, what lenten entertainment° the players shall receive from you. We coted° them on the way, and hither are they coming to offer you service.

HAMLET: He that plays the king shall be welcome — his Majesty shall have tribute on° me, the adventerous° knight shall use his foil and target,° the lover shall not sigh gratis,° the humorous° man shall end his part in peace, [the clown shall make those laugh whose lungs are [tickle a' th' sere,]° and the lady shall say her mind freely, or the [blank] verse shall halt° for't. What players are they?

ROSENCRANTZ: Even those you were wont to take such delight in, the tragedians of the city.

HAMLET: How chances it they travel? Their residence, both in reputation and profit, was better both ways.

ROSENCRANTZ: I think their inhibition° comes by the means of the late innovation.°

HAMLET: Do they hold the same estimation they did when I was in the city? Are they so follow'd?

ROSENCRANTZ: No indeed are they not.

HAMLET: How° comes it? do they grow rusty?

ROSENCRANTZ: Nay, their endeavor keeps in the wonted pace; but there is, sir, an aery° of children, little eyases,° that cry out on the top of question,°

°*express:* Exact. °*quintessence:* Finest and purest extract. °*lenten entertainment:* Meagre reception. °*coted:* Outstripped. °*on:* Of, from. °*adventerous:* Adventurous, wandering in search of adventure. °*foil and target:* Light fencing sword and small shield. °*gratis:* Without reward. °*humorous:* Dominated by some eccentric trait (like the melancholy Jaques in *As You Like It*). °*tickle . . . sere:* Easily made to laugh (literally, describing a gun that goes off easily; *sere* = a catch in the gunlock; *tickle* = easily affected, highly sensitive to stimulus. °*halt:* Limp, come off lamely (the verse will not scan if she omits indecent words). °*inhibition:* Hindrance (to playing in the city). The word could be used of an official prohibition. See next note. °*innovation:* Shakespeare elsewhere uses this word of a political uprising or revolt, and lines 332–33 are often explained as meaning that the company had been forbidden to play in the city as the result of some disturbance. It is commonly conjectured that the allusion is to the Essex rebellion of 1601, but it is known that Shakespeare's company, though to some extent involved on account of the special performance of *Richard II* they were commissioned to give on the eve of the rising, were not in fact punished by inhibition. A second interpretation explains *innovation* as referring to the new theatrical vogue described in lines 320 ff., and conjectures that *inhibition* may allude to a Privy Council order of 1600 restricting the number of London playhouses to two and the number of performances to two a week. °*How . . . too:* This passage refers topically to the "War of the Theatres" between the child actors and their poet Jonson on the one side, and on the other the adults, with Dekker, Marston, and possibly Shakespeare as spokesmen, in 1600–1601. °*aery:* Nest. °*eyases:* Unfledged hawks. °*cry . . . question:* Cry shrilly above others in controversy.

and are most tyrannically° clapp'd for't. These are now the fashion, and so —[berattle°] the common stages° so they call them— that many wearing rapiers are afraid of goose-quills° and dare scarce come thither.

HAMLET: What, are they children? Who maintains 'em? How are they escoted?° Will they pursue the quality° no longer than they can sing?° Will they not say afterwards, if they should grow themselves to common players (as it is [most like], if their means are [no] better), their writers do them wrong, to make them exclaim against their own succession?°

ROSENCRANTZ: Faith, there has been much to do° on both sides, and the nation holds it no sin to tarre° them to controversy. There was for awhile no money bid for argument,° unless the poet and the player went to cuffs in the question.°

HAMLET: Is't possible?

GUILDENSTERN: O, there has been much throwing about of brains.

HAMLET: Do the boys carry it away?°

ROSENCRANTZ: Ay, that they do, my lord, Hercules and his load too.°

HAMLET: It is not strange, for my uncle is King of Denmark, and those that would make mouths° at him while my father liv'd, give twenty, forty, fifty, hundred ducats a-piece for his picture in little. 'Sblood,° there is something in this more than natural, if philosophy could find it out.

(*a flourish* [*for the Players*])

GUILDENSTERN: There are the players.

HAMLET: Gentlemen, you are welcome to Elsinore. Your hands, come then: th' appurtenance of welcome is fashion and ceremony. Let me comply° with you in this garb,° [lest my] extent° to the players, which, I tell you, must show fairly outwards, should more appear like entertainment than yours.° You are welcome; but my uncle-father and aunt-mother are deceiv'd.

GUILDENSTERN: In what, my dear lord?

HAMLET: I am but mad north-north-west. When the wind is southerly I know a hawk from a hand-saw.°

Enter Polonius.

POLONIUS: Well be with you, gentlemen!

°*tyrannically:* Outrageously. °*berattle:* Cry down, satirize. °*common stages:* Public theatres (the children played at the Blackfriars, a private theatre). °*goose-quills:* Pens (of satirical playwrights). °*escoted:* Supported. °*quality:* Profession (of acting). °*no . . . sing:* Only until their voices change. °*succession:* Future. °*to do:* Ado. °*tarre:* Incite. °*argument:* Plot of a play. °*in the question:* As part of the script °*carry it away:* Win. °*Hercules . . . too:* Hercules in the course of one of his twelve labors supported the world for Atlas; the children do better, for they carry away the world and Hercules as well. There is an allusion to the Globe playhouse, which reportedly had for its sign the figure of Hercules upholding the world. °*mouths:* Derisive faces. °*'Sblood:* By God's (Christ's) blood. °*comply:* Observe the formalities. °*garb:* Fashion, manner. °*my extent:* The degree of courtesy I show. °*more . . . yours:* Seem to be a warmer reception than I have given you. °*hawk, hand-saw:* both cutting tools; but also both birds, if *hand-saw* quibbles on *hernshaw,* "heron," a bird preyed upon by the hawk.

HAMLET [*aside to them*]: Hark you, Guildenstern, and you too— at each ear a hearer—that great baby you see there is not yet out of his swaddling-clouts.°

ROSENCRANTZ: Happily° he is the second time come to them, for they say an old man is twice° a child.

HAMLET: I will prophesy, he comes to tell me of the players, mark it. [*aloud*] You say right, sir, a' Monday morning, 'twas then indeed.

POLONIUS: My lord, I have news to tell you.

HAMLET: My lord, I have news to tell you. When Roscius° was an actor in Rome—

POLONIUS: The actors are come hither, my lord.

HAMLET: Buzz,° buzz!

POLONIUS: Upon my honor—

HAMLET: "Then came each actor on his ass"—

POLONIUS: The best actors in the world, either for tragedy, comedy, history, pastoral, pastoral-comical, historical-pastoral, [tragical-historical, tragical-comical-historical-pastoral,] scene individable,° or poem unlimited;° Seneca° cannot be too heavy, nor Plautus° too light, for the law of writ and the liberty:° these are the only° men.

HAMLET: O Jephthah, judge of Israel,° what a treasure hadst thou!

POLONIUS: What a treasure had he, my lord?

HAMLET: Why—

"One fair daughter, and no more,
The which he loved passing well."

POLONIUS [*aside*]: Still on my daughter.

HAMLET: Am I not i' th' right, old Jephthah?

POLONIUS: If you call me Jephthah, my lord, I have a daughter that I love passing well.

HAMLET: Nay, that follows not.

POLONIUS: What follows, then, my lord?

HAMLET: Why—

"As by lot, God wot,"

and then, you know,

"It came to pass, as most like it was,"—

°*swaddling-clouts:* Swaddling clothes. °*Happily:* Haply, perhaps. °*twice:* For the second time. °*Roscius:* The most famous of Roman actors (died 62 B.C.). News about him would be stale news indeed. °*Buzz:* Exclamation of impatience at someone who tells news already known. °*scene individable:* Play observing the unity of place. °*poem unlimited:* Play ignoring rules such as the three unities. °*Seneca:* Roman writer of tragedies. °*Plautus:* Roman writer of comedies. °*for . . . liberty:* For strict observance of the rules, or for freedom from them (with possible allusion to the location of playhouses, which were not built in properties under city jurisdiction, but in the "liberties"—land once monastic and now outside the jurisdiction of the city authorities). °*only:* very best (a frequent use). °*Jephthah . . . Israel:* Title of a ballad, from which Hamlet goes on to quote. For the story of Jephthah and his daughter, see Judges 11.

the first row° of the pious chanson° will show you more, for look where my abridgment° comes.

Enter the Players, [four or five].

You are welcome, masters, welcome, all. I am glad to see thee well. Welcome, good friends. O, why old friend! thy face is valanc'd° since I saw thee last; com'st thou to beard° me in Denmark? What, my young lady and mistress! by' lady,° your ladyship is nearer to heaven than when I saw you last, by the altitude of a chopine.° Pray God your voice, like a piece of uncurrent gold, be not crack'd within the ring.° Masters, you are all welcome. We'll e'en to't like [French] falc'ners—fly at any thing we see: we'll have a speech straight.° Come give us a taste of your quality,° come, a passionate speech.

[1.] **Player:** What speech, my good lord?

Hamlet: I heard thee speak me a speech once, but it was never acted, or if it was, not above once; for the play, I remember, pleas'd not the million, 'twas caviarey to the general,° but it was—as I receiv'd it, and others, whose judgments in such matters cried in the top of° mine—an excellent play, well digested in the scenes, set down with as much modesty as cunning. I remember one said there were no sallets° in the lines to make the matter savory,° nor no matter in the phrase that might indict the author of affection,° but call'd it an honest method, as wholesome as sweet, and by very much more handsome than fine.° One speech in't I chiefly lov'd, 'twas Aeneas' [tale] to Dido, and thereabout of it especially where he speaks of Priam's slaughter.° If it live in your memory, begin at this line—let me see, let me see:

"The rugged Pyrrhus,° like th' Hyrcanian beast,°—"
'Tis not so it begins with Pyrrhus:
"The rugged Pyrrhus, he whose sable arms,°
Black as his purpose, did the night resemble
When he lay couched in th' ominous horse,
Hath now this dread and black complexion smear'd
With heraldy° more dismal:° head to foot

°*row:* Stanza. °*chanson:* Song, ballad. °*abridgment:* (1) Interruption; (2) pastime. °*valanc'd:* Fringed, bearded. °*beard:* Confront boldly (with obvious pun). °*by' lady:* By Our Lady. °*chopine:* Thick-soled shoe. °*crack'd . . . ring:* Broken to the point where you can no longer play female roles. A coin with a crack extending far enough in from the edge to cross the circle surrounding the stamp of the sovereign's head was unacceptable in exchange (*uncurrent*). °*straight:* Straightway. °*quality:* Professional skill. °*caviary . . . general:* Caviare to the common people, too choice for the multitude. °*cried . . . of:* Were louder than, carried more authority than. °*sallets:* Salads, spicy jokes. °*savory:* Zesty. °*affection:* Affectation. °*fine:* Showily dressed (in language). °*Priam's slaughter:* The slaying of Priam (at the fall of Troy). °*Pyrrhus:* Another name for Neoptolemus, Achilles' son. °*Hyrcanian beast:* Hyrcania in the Caucasus was notorious for its tigers. °*sable arms:* The Greeks within the Trojan horse had blackened their skin so as to be inconspicuous when they emerged at night. °*heraldy:* Heraldry. °*dismal:* Ill-boding.

Now is he total gules,° horridly trick'd°
With blood of fathers, mothers, daughters, sons,
Bak'd° and impasted° with the parching streets,°
That lend a tyrannous and a damned light
To their lord's murther. Roasted in wrath and fire,
And thus o'er-sized° with coagulate gore,
With eyes like carbuncles,° the hellish Pyrrhus
Old grandsire Priam seeks."
So proceed you.

POLONIUS: 'Fore God, my lord, well spoken, with good accent and good discretion.

[1.] PLAYER: "Anon he finds him
Striking too short at Greeks. His antique sword,
Rebellious to his arm, lies where it falls,
Repugnant° to command. Unequal match'd,
Pyrrhus at Priam drives, in rage strikes wide,
But with the whiff and wind of his fell° sword
Th' unnerved° father falls. [Then senseless° Ilium,°]
Seeming to feel this blow, with flaming top
Stoops to his base, and with a hideous crash
Takes prisoner Pyrrhus' ear; for lo his sword,
Which was declining on the milky head
Of reverent° Priam, seem'd i' th' air to stick.
So as a painted tyrant. Pyrrhus stood,
[And,] like a neutral to his will and matter,°
Did nothing.
But as we often see, against° some storm,
A silence in the heavens, the rack° stand still,
The bold winds speechless, and the orb below
As hush as death, anon the dreadful thunder
Doth rend the region;° so after Pyrrhus' pause,
A roused vengeance sets him new a-work,
And never did the Cyclops° hammers fall
On Mar's his armor forg'd for proof eterne°
With less remorse° than Pyrrhus' bleeding sword
Now falls on Priam.
Out, out, thou strumpet. Fortune! All you gods,

°*gules:* Red (heraldic term). °*trick'd:* Adorned. °*Bak'd:* Caked. °*impasted:* Crusted. °*with . . . streets:* By the heat from the burning streets. °*o'er-sized:* Covered over as with a coat of sizing. °*carbuncles:* Jewels believed to shine in the dark. °*Repugnant:* Resistant, hostile. °*fell:* Cruel. °*unnerved:* Drained of strength. °*senseless:* Insensible. °*Ilium:* The citadel of Troy. °*reverent:* Reverend, aged. *like . . . matter:* Poised midway between intention and performance. °*against:* Just before. °*rack:* Cloud-mass. °*region:* Air. °*Cyclops:* Giants who worked in Vulcan's smithy, where armor was made for the gods. °*proof eterne:* Eternal endurance. °*remorse:* Pity.

In general synod take away her power!
Break all the spokes and [fellies°] from her wheel,
And bowl the round nave° down the hill of heaven
As low as to the fiends!

POLONIUS: This is too long.

HAMLET: It shall to the barber's with your beard. Preythee, say on, he's for a jig° or a tale of bawdry, or he sleeps. Say on, come to Hecuba.

[1.] PLAYER: "But who, ah woe," had seen the mobled° queen"—

HAMLET: "The mobled queen?"

POLONIUS: That's good [mobled] queen [is good.]

[1.] PLAYER: "Run barefoot up and down, threatening the flames"
With bissom rheum,° a clout° upon that head
Where late the diadem stood, and for a robe,
About her lank and all o'er-teemed° loins,
A blanket, in the alarm of fear caught up—
Who this had seen, with tongue in venom steep'd,
'Gainst Fortune's state° would treason have pronounc'd.
But if the gods themselves did see her then,
When she saw Pyrrhus make malicious sport
In mincing with his sword her [husband's] limbs,
The instant burst of clamor that she made,
Unless things mortal move them not at all,
Would have made milch° the burning eyes of heaven,
And passion° in the gods."

POLONIUS: Look whe'er he has not° turn'd his color and has tears in 's eyes. Prithee no more.

HAMLET: 'Tis well, I'll have thee speak out the rest of this soon. Good my lord, will you see the players well bestow'd?° Do you hear, let them be well us'd,° for they are the abstracts and brief chronicles of the time. After your death you were better have a bad epitaph than their ill report while you live.

POLONIUS: My lord, I will use them according to their desert.

HAMLET: God's bodkin,° man, much better: use every man after his desert, and who shall scape whipping? Use them after your own honor and dignity—the less they deserve, the more merit is in your bounty. Take them in.

POLONIUS: Come, sirs.

Exit.

HAMLET: Follow him, friends, we'll hear a play tomorrow.

°*fellies:* Rims. °*nave:* Hub. °*jig:* Song-and-dance entertainment performed after the main play. °*mobled:* Muffled. °*bissom rheum:* Blinding tears. °*clout:* Cloth. °*o'er-teemed:* Worn out by child-bearing. °*state:* rule, government. °*milch:* Moist (literally, milky). °*passion:* Grief. °*Look . . . not:* Note how he has. °*bestow'd:* Lodged. °*us'd:* Treated. °*God's bodkin:* By God's (Christ's) little body.

Exeunt all the Players but the First.

Dost thou hear me, old friend? Can you play "The Murther of Gonzago"?

[1.] **PLAYER:** Ay, my lord.

HAMLET: We'll ha't to-morrow night. You could for a need° study a speech of some dozen lines, or sixteen lines, which I would set down and insert in't, could you not?

[1.] **PLAYER:** Ay, my lord.

HAMLET: Very well. Follow that lord, and look you mock him not.

Exit First Player.

My good friends, I'll leave you [till] night. You are welcome to Elsinore.

ROSENCRANTZ: Good my lord!

HAMLET: Ay, so, God buy to you.

Exeunt [Rosencrantz and Guildenstern.]

Now I am alone
O, what a rogue and peasant slave am I!
Is it not monstrous that this player here,
But in a fiction, in a dream of passion,
Could force his soul so to his own conceit°
That from her working all his visage wann'd,
Tears in his eyes, distraction in his aspect,
A broken voice, an' his whole function° suiting
With forms° to his conceit? And all for nothing,
For Hecuba?
What's Hecuba to him, or he to [Hecuba],
That he should weep for her? What would he do
Had he the motive and [the cue] for passion
That I have? He would drown the stage with tears,
And cleave the general ear with horrid speech,
Make mad the guilty, and appall the free,°
Confound the ignorant, and amaze,° indeed
The very faculties of eyes and ears. Yet I,
A dull and muddy-mettled° rascal, peak°
Like John-a-dreams,° unpregnant of° my cause,
And can say nothing; no, not for a king,
Upon whose property and most dear life
A damn'd defeat° was made. Am I a coward?

°*for need:* If necessary. °*conceit:* Imaginative conception. °*his whole function:* The operation of his whole body. °*forms:* Actions, expressions. °*free:* Innocent. °*amaze:* Confound. °*muddy-mettled:* Dull-spirited. °*peak:* Mope. °*John-a-dreams:* A sleepy fellow. °*unpregnant of:* Unquickened by. °*defeat:* Destruction.

Who calls me villain, breaks my pate across,
Plucks off my beard and blows it in my face,
Tweaks me by the nose, gives me the lie i' th' throat,
As deep as to the lungs.° Who does me this?
Hah, 'swounds,° I should° take it: for it cannot be
But I am pigeon-liver'd, and lack gall°
To make oppression bitter, or ere this
I should 'a' fatted all the region kites
With this slave's offal.° Bloody, bawdy villain!
Remorseless, treacherous, lecherous, kindless° villain!
Why, what an ass am I! This is most brave,
That I, the son of a dear [father] murthered,
Prompted to my revenge by heaven and hell,
Must like a whore unpack my heart with words,
And fall a-cursing like a very drab,
A stallion.° Fie upon't, foh!
About,° my brains! Hum—I have heard
That guilty creatures sitting at a play
Have by the very cunning of the scene
Been strook so to the soul, that presently°
They have proclaim'd their malefactions:
For murther, though it have no tongue, will speak
With most miraculous organ. I'll have these players
Play something like the murther of my father
Before mine uncle: I'll observe his looks,
I'll tent° him to the quick. If 'a do blench,°
I know my course. The spirit° that I have seen
May be a [dev'l], and the [dev'l] hath power
T' assume a pleasing shape, yea, and perhaps,
Out of my weakness and my melancholy,
As he is very potent with such spirits,
Abuses° me to damn me. I'll have grounds
More relative° than this — the play's the thing
Wherein I'll catch the conscience of the King.

[*Exit*.]

°*gives . . . lungs:* Calls me a liar in the extremest degree. °*'swounds:* By God's (Christ's) wounds. °*should:* Would certainly °*am . . . gall:* Am constitutionally incapable of resentment: That doves were mild because they had no gall was a popular belief. °*offal:* Entrails. °*kindless:* Unnatural. °*stallion:* Male whore. Most editors adopt the F1 reading *scullion*, "kitchen menial." °*About:* To work. °*presently:* At once, then and there. °*tent:* Probe. °*blench:* Flinch. °*spirit:* States of temperament. °*Abuses:* Deludes. °*relative:* Closely related (to fact), conclusive.

ACT 3

SCENE 1°

Enter King, Queen, Polonius, Ophelia, Rosencrantz, Guildenstern, Lords.

KING: An'° can you by no drift of conference°
Get from him why he puts on this confusion,
Grating so harshly all his days of quiet
With turbulent and dangerous lunacy?
ROSENCRANTZ: He does confess he feels himself distracted,
But from what cause 'a will by no means speak.
GUILDENSTERN: Nor do we find him forward° to be sounded°
But with a crafty madness° keeps aloof
When we would bring him on to some confession
Of his true state.
QUEEN: Did he receive you well?
ROSENCRANTZ: Most like a gentleman.
GUILDENSTERN: But with much forcing of his disposition.°
ROSENCRANTZ: Niggard of question,° but of our demands°
Most free in his reply.

QUEEN: Did you assay° him
To any pastime?
ROSENCRANTZ: Madam, it so fell out that certain players
We o'erraught° on the way; of these we told him,
And there did seem in him a kind of joy
To hear of it: They are here about the court,
And as I think, they have already order
This night to play before him.

POLONIUS: 'Tis most true,
And he beseech'd me to entreat your Majesties
To hear and see the matter.

KING: With all my heart, and it doth much content me
To hear him so inclin'd.
Good gentlemen, give him a further edge,°
And drive his purpose into° these delights.
ROSENCRANTZ: We shall, my lord.

Exeunt Rosencrantz and Guildenstern.

°*3.1. Location:* The castle. °*An':* And. °*drift of conference:* Leading on of conversation. °*forward:* Readily willing. °*sounded:* Plumbed, probed. °*crafty madness:* Mad craftiness, the shrewdness that mad people sometimes exhibit. °*disposition:* Inclination. °*question:* Conversation. °*demands:* Questions. °*assay:* Attempt to win. °*o'erraught:* Passed (literally, overreached). °*edge:* Stimulus. °*into:* On to.

KING: Sweet Gertrude, leave us too,
For we have closely° sent for Hamlet hither,
That he, as 'twere by accident, may here
Affront° Ophelia. Her father and myself,
We'll so bestow ourselves that, seeing unseen,
We may of their encounter frankly° judge,
And gather by him, as he is behav'd,
If't be th' affliction of his love or no
That thus he suffers for.

QUEEN: I shall obey you.
And for your part, Ophelia, I do wish
That your good beauties be the happy cause
Of Hamlet's wildness: So shall I hope your virtues
Will bring him to his wonted way again,
To both your honors.

OPHELIA: Madam, I wish it may. *Exit Queen.*

POLONIUS: Ophelia, walk you here.— Gracious, so please you,
We will bestow ourselves. [*to Ophelia*] Read on this book,
That show of such an exercise° may color
Your [loneliness].° We are oft to blame in this—
'Tis too much prov'd°—that with devotion's visage
And pious action° we do sugar o'er
The devil himself.

KING: [*aside*] O, 'tis too true!
How smart a lash that speech doth give my conscience!
The harlot's cheek, beautied with plast'ring art,
Is not more ugly to the thing that helps it°
Than is my deed to my most painted word.
O heavy burthen!

POLONIUS: I hear him coming. Withdraw, my lord.

Exeunt King and Polonius.

Enter Hamlet.

HAMLET: To be, or not to be, that is the question:
Whether 'tis nobler in the mind to suffer°
The slings and arrows of outrageous fortune,
Or to take arms against a sea of troubles,
And by opposing, end them. To die, to sleep—
No more, and by a sleep to say we end

°*closely:* Privately. °*Affront:* Meet. °*frankly:* Freely. °*exercise:* Religious exercise (as the next sentence makes clear). °*color Your loneliness:* Make your solitude seem natural. °*too much prov'd:* Too often proved true. °*action:* Demeanor. °*to . . . it:* In comparison with the paint that makes it look beautiful. °*suffer:* Submit to, endure patiently.

The heart-ache and the thousand natural shocks
That flesh is heir to; 'tis a consummation°
Devoutly to be wish'd. To die, to sleep—
To sleep, perchance to dream—ay, there's the rub,°
For in that sleep of death what dreams may come,
When we have shuffled off° this mortal coil,°
Must give us pause; there's the respect°
That makes calamity of so long life:°
For who would bear the whips and scorns of time,°
Th' oppressor's wrong, the proud man's contumely,
The pangs of despis'd love, the law's delay,
The insolence of office, and the spurns
That patient merit of th' unworthy takes,
When he himself might his quietus make°
With a bare bodkin;° who would fardels° bear,
To grunt and sweat under a weary life,
But that the dread of something after death,
The undiscover'd° country, from whose bourn°
No traveller returns, puzzles° the will,
And makes us rather bear those ills we have,
Than fly to others that we know not of?
Thus conscience° does make cowards [of us all],
And thus the native hue° of resolution
Is sicklied o'er with the pale cast° of thought,°
And enterprises of great pitch° and moments
With this regard their currents turn awry,
And lose the name of action.—Soft you now,
The fair Ophelia. Nymph, in thy orisons°
Be all my sins rememb'red.

OPHELIA: Good my lord,
How does your honor for this many a day?

HAMLET: I humbly thank you, well, [well, well].

OPHELIA: My lord, I have remembrances of yours
That I have longed long to redeliver.
I pray you now receive them.

°*consummation:* Completion, end. °*rub:* Obstacle (a term from the game of bowls). °*shuffled off:* Freed ourselves from. °*this mortal coil:* The turmoil of this mortal life. °*respect:* Consideration. °*of . . . life:* So long-lived. °*time:* The world. °*his quietus make:* Write paid to his account. °*bare bodkin:* Mere dagger. °*fardels:* Burdens. °*undiscover'd:* Not disclosed to knowledge; about which men have no information. °*bourn:* Boundary, region. °*puzzles:* Paralyzes. °*conscience:* Reflection (but with some of the modern sense, too). °*native hue:* natural (ruddy) complexion. °*pale cast:* Pallor. °*thought:* Melancholy thought, brooding. °*pitch:* Loftiness (a term from falconry, signifying the highest point of a hawk's flight). °*orisons:* Prayers.

HAMLET: No, not I,
I never gave you aught.

OPHELIA: My honor'd lord, you know right well you did,
And with them words of so sweet breath compos'd
As made these things more rich. Their perfume lost,
Take these again, for to the noble mind
Rich gifts wax poor when givers prove unkind.
There, my lord.

HAMLET: Ha, ha! are you honest?°

OPHELIA: My lord?

HAMLET: Are you fair?

OPHELIA: What means your lordship?

HAMLET: That if you be honest and fair, [your honesty] should admit no discourse to your beauty.

OPHELIA: Could beauty, my lord, have better commerce than with honesty?

HAMLET: Ay, truly, for the power of beauty will sooner transform honesty from what it is to a bawd than the force of honesty can translate beauty into his likeness. This was sometime° a paradox,° but now the time gives it proof. I did love you once.

OPHELIA: Indeed, my lord, you made me believe so.

HAMLET: You should not have believ'd me, for virtue cannot so [inoculate] our old stock but we shall relish of it.° I lov'd you not.

OPHELIA: I was the more deceiv'd.

HAMLET: Get thee [to] a nunn'ry, why wouldst thou be a breeder of sinners? I am myself indifferent honest,° but yet I could accuse me of such things that it were better my mother had not borne me: I am very proud, revengeful, ambitious, with more offenses at my beck than I have thoughts to put them in, imagination to give them shape, or time to act them in. What should such fellows as I do crawling between earth and heaven? We are arrant knaves, believe none of us. Go thy ways to a nunn'ry. Where's your father?

OPHELIA: At home, my lord.

HAMLET: Let the doors be shut upon him, that he may play the fool no where but in 's own house. Farewell.

OPHELIA: O, help him, you sweet heavens!

HAMLET: If thou dost marry, I'll give thee this plague for thy dowry: be thou as chaste as ice, as pure as snow, thou shalt not escape calumny. Get thee to a nunn'ry, farewell. Or if thou wilt needs marry, marry a fool, for wise men know well enough what monsters° you° make of them. To a nunn'ry, go, and quickly too. Farewell.

°*honest:* Chaste. °*sometime:* Formerly °*paradox:* Tenet contrary to accepted belief. °*virtue . . . it:* Virtue, engrafted on our old stock (of viciousness), cannot so change the nature of the plant that no trace of the original will remain. °*indifferent honest:* Tolerably virtuous. °*monsters:* Alluding to the notion that the husbands of unfaithful wives grew horns. °*you:* You women.

Ophelia: Heavenly powers, restore him!

Hamlet: I have heard of your paintings, well enough. God hath given you one face, and you make yourselves another. You jig you amble, and you [lisp,] you nickname God's creatures° and make your wantonness [your] ignorance.° Go to, I'll no more on't, it hath made me mad. I say we will have no moe° marriage. Those that are married already (all but one) shall live, the rest shall keep as they are. To a nunn'ry, go.

[*Exit.*]

Ophelia: O, what a noble mind is here o'erthrown!
The courtier's, soldier's, scholar's, eye, tongue, sword,
Th' expectation° and rose° of the fair° state,
The glass° of fashion and the mould of form,°
Th' observ'd of all observers,° quite, quite down!
And I, of ladies most deject and wretched,
That suck'd the honey of his [music] vows,
Now see [that] noble and most sovereign reason
Like sweet bells jangled out of tune, and harsh;
That unmatch'd form and stature of blown° youth
Blasted° with ecstasy.° O, woe is me
T' have seen what I have seen, see what I see!

Ophelia withdraws.

Enter King and Polonius.

King: Love? his affections° do not that way tend,
Nor what he spake, though it lack'd form a little,
Was not like madness. There's something in his soul
O'er which his melancholy sits on brood,
And I do doubt° the hatch and the disclose°
Will be some danger; which for to prevent,
I have in quick determination
Thus set it down: he shall with speed to England
For the demand of our neglected tribute.
Haply the seas, and countries different,
With variable objects, shall expel
This something-settled matter in his heart,
Whereon his brains still beating puts him thus
From fashion of himself. What think you on't?

°*you . . . creatures:* You walk and talk affectedly. °*make . . . ignorance:* Excuse your affectation as ignorance. °*moe:* More. °*expectation:* Hope. °*rose:* Ornament. °*fair:* Probably proleptic: "(the kingdom) made fair by his presence." °*glass:* Mirror. °*mould of form:* Pattern of (courtly) behavior. °*observ'd . . . observers:* Shakespeare uses *observe* to mean not only "behold, mark attentively" but also "pay honor to." °*blown:* In full bloom. °*Blasted:* Withered. °*ecstasy:* Madness. °*affections:* Inclinations, feelings. °*doubt:* fear. °*disclose:* Synonymous with *batch*; see also 5.1.247.

POLONIUS: It shall do well; but yet do I believe
The origin and commencement of his grief
Sprung from neglected° love. [*Ophelia comes forward.*]
How now, Ophelia?
You need not tell us what Lord Hamlet said,
We heard it all. My lord, do as you please,
But if you hold it fit, after the play
Let his queen-mother all alone entreat him
To show his grief.° Let her be round° with him,
And I'll be plac'd (so please you) in the ear
Of all their conference. If she find him° not,
To England send him, or confine him where
Your wisdom best shall think.
KING: It shall be so.
Madness in great ones must not [unwatch'd] go.

Exeunt.

SCENE 2°

Enter Hamlet and three of the Players.

HAMLET: Speak the speech, I pray you, as I pronounc'd it to you, trippingly on the tongue, but if you mouth° it, as many of your players do, I had as live° the town-crier spoke my lines. Nor do not saw the air too much with your hand, thus, but use all gently, for in the very torrent, tempest, and, as I may say, whirlwind of your passion, you must acquire and beget a temperance that may give it smoothness. O, it offends me to the soul to hear a robustious periwig-pated fellow tear a passion to totters,° to very rags, to spleet° the ears of the groundlings,° who for the most part are capable° of nothing but inexplicable dumb shows and noise. I would have such a fellow whipt for o'erdoing Termagant,° it out-Herods Herod, pray you avoid it.

[1.] PLAYER: I warrant your honor.

HAMLET: Be not too tame neither, but let your own discretion be your tutor. Suit the action to the word, the word to the action, with this special observance, that you o'erstep not the modesty° of nature: for any thing so o'erdone is from° the purpose of playing, whose end, both at the first and now, was and is, to hold, as 'twere the mirror up to nature: to show virtue her feature, scorn° her own image, and the very age and body of the time his form

°*neglected:* Unrequited. °*his grief:* What is troubling him. °*round:* Blunt, outspoken. °*find him:* Learn the truth about him. °*3.2. Location:* The castle. °*mouth:* Pronounce with exaggerated distinctness or declamatory effect. °*live:* Lief, willingly. °*totters:* Tatters. °*spleet:* Split. °*groundlings:* Those who paid the lowest admission price and stood on the ground in the "yard" or pit of the theatre. °*capable of:* Able to take in. °*Termagant:* A supposed god of the Saracens, whose role in medieval drama, like that of Herod (line 10), was noisy and violent. °*modesty:* Moderation. °*from:* Contrary to. °*scorn:* That which is worthy of scorn.

and pressure.° Now this overdone, or come tardy° off, though it makes the unskillful laugh, cannot but make the judicious grieve; the censure° of which one° must in your allowance° o'erweigh a whole theatre of others. O, there be players that I have seen play — and heard others [praise], and that highly — not to speak it profanely,° that, neither having th' accent of Christians nor the gait of Christian, pagan, nor man, have so strutted and bellow'd that I have thought some of Nature's journeymen had made men, and not made them well, they imitated humanity so abominably.°

[1.] **PLAYER:** I hope we have reform'd that indifferently° with us, [sir].

HAMLET: O, reform it altogether. And let those that play your clowns speak no more than is set down for them, for there be of them° that will themselves laugh to set on some quantity of barren spectators to laugh too, though in the mean time some necessary question of the play be then to be consider'd. That's villainous, and shows a most pitiful ambition in the fool° that uses it. Go make you ready.

Exeunt Players.

Enter Polonius, Guildenstern, and Rosencrantz.

How now, my lord! Will the King hear this piece of work?°

POLONIUS: And the Queen too, and that presently.°

HAMLET: Bid the players make haste. [*Exit Polonius.*]
Will you two help to hasten them?

ROSENCRANTZ: Ay, my lord. [*Exeunt they two.*]

HAMLET: What, ho, Horatio!

Enter Horatio.

HORATIO: Here, sweet lord, at your service.

HAMLET: Horatio, thou art e'en as just a man°
As e'er my conversation cop'd withal.°

HORATIO: O my dear lord—

HAMLET: Nay, do not think I flatter,
For what advancement may I hope from thee
That no revenue hast but thy good spirits
To feed and clothe thee? Why should the poor be flatter'd?
No, let the candied° tongue lick absurd° pomp,
And crook the pregnant° hinges of the knee

°*pressure:* Impression (as of a seal), exact image. °*tardy:* Inadequately. °*censure:* Judgment. °*which one:* (Even) one of whom. °*allowance:* Estimation. °*profanely:* Irreverently. °*some . . . abominably:* They were so unlike men that it seemed Nature had not made them herself, but had delegated the task to mediocre assistants. °*indifferently:* Pretty well. °*of them:* Some of them. °*fool:* (1) Stupid person; (2) actor playing a fool's role. °*piece of work:* Masterpiece (said jocularly). °*presently:* At once. °*thou. . . man:* You come as close to being what a man should be (*just* = exact, precise). °*my . . . withal:* My association with people has brought me into contact with. °*candied:* Sugared, flattering. °*absurd:* Tasteless (Latin sense). °*pregnant:* Moving readily.

Where thrift° may follow fawning. Dost thou hear?
Since my dear soul was mistress of her choice
And could of men distinguish her election,
Sh' hath seal'd thee for herself, for thou hast been
As one in suff'ring all that suffers nothing,
A man that Fortune's buffets and rewards
Hast ta'en with equal thanks; and blest are those
Whose blood° and judgment are so well co-meddled,°
That they are not a pipe for Fortune's finger
To sound what stop she please. Give me that man
That is not passion's slave, and I will wear him
In my heart's core, ay, in my heart of heart,°
As I do thee. Something too much of this.
There is a play to-night before the King,
One scene of it comes near the circumstance
Which I have told thee of my father's death.
I prithee, when thou seest that act afoot,
Even with the very comment of thy soul°
Observe my uncle. If his occulted° guilt
Do not itself unkennel° in one speech,
It is a damned ghost° that we have seen,
And my imaginations are as foul
As Vulcan's stithy.° Give him heedful note,
For I mine eyes will rivet to his face,
And after we will both our judgments join
In censure of his seeming.°

Horatio: Well, my lord.
If 'a steal aught the whilst this play is playing,
And scape [detecting], I will pay the theft.

[*Sound a flourish. Danish march.*] *Enter Trumpets and Kettle-drums, King, Queen, Polonius, Ophelia,* [*Rosencrantz, Guidenstern, and other Lords, attendant, with his Guard carrying torches*].

Hamlet: They are coming to the play. I must be idle;° Get you a place.

King: How fares° our cousin Hamlet?

Hamlet: Excellent, i' faith, of the chameleon's dish:° I eat the air,° promise-cramm'd— you cannot feed capons so.

King: I have nothing with° this answer, Hamlet, these words are not mine.°

°*thrift:* Thriving, profit. °*blood:* Passions. °*co-meddled:* Mixed, blended. °*my heart of heart:* The heart of my heart. °*very... soul:* Your most intense critical observation. °*occulted:* Hidden. °*unkennel:* Bring into the open. °*damned ghost:* Evil spirit, devil. °*stithy:* Forge. °*censure . . . seeming:* Reaching a verdict on his behavior. °*be idle:* Act foolish, pretend to be crazy. °*fares:* Hamlet takes up this word in another sense. °*chameleon's dish:* Chameleons were thought to feed on air. Hamlet says that he subsists on an equally nourishing diet, the promise of succession. There is probably a pun on *air/heir.* °*have nothing with:* Do not understand. °*mine:* An answer to my question.

HAMLET: No, nor mine now. [*to Polonius*] My lord, you play'd once i' th' university, you say?

POLONIUS: That did I, my lord, and was accounted a good actor.

HAMLET: What did you enact?

POLONIUS: I did enact Julius Caesar: I was kill'd i' th' Capitol; Brutus kill'd me.

HAMLET: It was a brute part° of him to kill so capital a calf there. Be the players ready?

ROSENCRANTZ: Ay, my lord, they stay upon your patience.

QUEEN: Come hither, my dear Hamlet, sit by me.

HAMLET: No, good mother, here's metal more attractive. [*lying down at Ophelia's feet*]

POLONIUS: [*to the King*] O ho, do you mark that?

HAMLET: Lady, shall I lie in your lap?

OPHELIA: No, my lord.

[**HAMLET:** I mean, my head upon your lap?

OPHELIA: Ay, my lord.

HAMLET: Do you think I meant country matters?°

OPHELIA: I think nothing, my lord.

HAMLET: That's a fair thought to lie between maids' legs.

OPHELIA: What is, my lord?

HAMLET: Nothing.

OPHELIA: You are merry, my lord.

HAMLET: Who, I?

OPHELIA: Ay, my lord.

HAMLET: O God, your only° jig-maker.° What should a man do but be merry,? for look you how cheerfully my mother looks, and my father died within 's° two hours.

OPHELIA: Nay, 'tis twice two months, my lord.

HAMLET: So long? Nay then let the dev'l wear black, for I'll have a suit of sables.° O heavens, die two months ago, and not forgotten yet? Then there's hope a great man's memory may outlive his life half a year, but, by'r lady, 'a must build churches then, or else shall 'a suffer not thinking on,° with the hobby-horse, whose epitaph is, "For O, for O, the hobby-horse is forgot."°

The trumpets sound. Dumb show follows.

Enter a King and a Queen [*very lovingly*], *the Queen embracing him and he her.* [*She kneels and makes show of protestation unto him.*] *He takes her up and declines his head*

°*part:* Action. °*country matters:* Indecency. °*only:* Very best. °*jig-maker:* One who composed or played in the farcical song-and-dance entertainments that followed plays. ° *'s:* This. °*let . . . sables:* To the devil with my garments; after so long a time I am ready for the old man's garb of sables (fine fur). °*not thinking on:* Not being thought of, being forgotten. °*For . . . forgot:* Line from a popular ballad lamenting puritanical suppression of such country sports as the May-games, in which the hobby-horse, a character costumed to resemble a horse, traditionally appeared.

upon her neck. He lies him down upon a bank of flowers. She, seeing him asleep, leaves him. Anon comes in another man, takes off his crown, kisses it, pours poison in the sleeper's ears, and leaves him. The Queen returns, finds the King dead, makes passionate action. The pois'ner with some three or four [mutes] come in again, seem to condole with her. The dead body is carried away. The pois'ner woos the Queen with gifts; she seems harsh [and unwilling] awhile, but in the end accepts love. [*Exeunt.*]

Ophelia: What means this, my lord?
Hamlet: Marry, this' [miching] mallecho,° it means mischief.
Ophelia: Belike this show imports the argument° of the play.

Enter Prologue.

Hamlet: We shall know by this fellow. The players cannot keep [counsel°], they'll tell all.
Ophelia: Will 'a tell us what this show meant?
Hamlet: Ay, or any show that you will show him. Be not you° asham'd to show, he'll not shame to tell you what it means.
Ophelia: You are naught, you are naught.° I'll mark the play.
Prologue: For us, and for our tragedy,
Here stooping to your clemency,
We beg your hearing patiently. [*Exit.*]
Hamlet: Is this a prologue, or the posy of a ring?°
Ophelia: 'Tis brief, my lord.
Hamlet: As woman's love.

Enter [*two Players,*] *King and Queen.*

[P.] King: Full thirty times hath Phoebus' cart° gone round
Neptune's salt wash and Tellus° orbed ground,
And thirty dozen moons with borrowed sheen
About the world have times twelve thirties been,
Since love our hearts and Hymen° did our hands
Unite comutual in most sacred bands.°
[P.] Queen: So many journeys may the sun and moon
Make us again count o'er ere love be done!
But woe is me, you are so sick of late,
So far from cheer and from [your] former state,
That I distrust° you. Yet though I distrust,
Discomfort you, my lord, it nothing must,
[For] women's fear and love hold quantity,°
In neither aught, or in extremity.

°*this' [miching] mallecho:* This is sneaking mischief. °*argument:* Subject, plot. °*counsel:* Secrets. °*Be not you:* If you are not. °*naught:* Wicked. °*posy . . . ring:* Verse motto inscribed in a ring (necessarily short). °*Phoebus' cart:* The sun-god's chariot. °*Tellus:* Goddess of the earth. °*Hymen:* God of marriage. °*bands:* Bonds. °*distrust:* Fear for. °*hold quantity:* Are related in direct proportion.

Now what my [love] is, proof° hath made you know,
And as my love is siz'd, my fear is so.
Where love is great, the littlest doubts are fear;
Where little fears grow great, great love grows there.
[P.] King: Faith, I must leave thee, love, and shortly too;
My operant° powers their functions leave to do,
And thou shalt live in this fair world behind,
Honor'd, belov'd, and haply one as kind
For husband shalt thou—
[P.] Queen: O, confound the rest!°
Such love must needs be treason in my breast.
In second husband let me be accurs'd!
None wed the second but who kill'd the first.
Hamlet [*aside*]: That's wormwood!
[P.] Queen: The instances° that second marriage move°
Are base respects of thrift,° but none of love.
A second time I kill my husband dead,
When second husband kisses me in bed.
[P.] King: I do believe you think what now you speak,
But what we do determine, oft we break.
Purpose is but the slave to memory,
Of violent birth, but poor validity,°
Which now, the fruit unripe, sticks on the tree,
But fall unshaken when they mellow be.
Most necessary 'tis that we forget
To pay ourselves what to ourselves is debt.°
What to ourselves in passion° we propose,
The passion ending, doth the purpose lose.
The violence of either grief or joy
Their own enactures with themselves destroy.°
Where joy most revels, grief doth most lament;
Grief [joys], joy grieves, on slender accident.°
This world is not for aye, nor 'tis not strange
That even our loves should with our fortunes change:
For 'tis a question left us yet to prove,
Whether love lead fortune, or else fortune love.
The great man down, you mark his favorite flies,
The poor advanc'd makes friends of enemies.

°*proof:* Experience. °*operant:* Active, vital. *leave to do:* Cease to perform. °*confound the rest:* May destruction befall what you are about to speak of—a second marriage on my part. °*instances:* Motives. *move:* Give rise to. °*respects of thrift:* Considerations of advantage. °*validity:* Strength, power to last. °*Most . . . debt:* Such resolutions are debts we owe to ourselves, and it would be foolish to pay such debts. °*passion:* Violent emotion. °*The violence . . . destroy:* Both violent grief and violent joy fail of their intended acts because they destroy themselves by their very violence. °*slender accident:* Slight occasion.

And hitherto doth love on fortune tend,
For who not needs shall never lack a friend,
And who in want a hollow friend doth try,
Directly seasons° him his enemy.
But orderly to end where I begun,
Our wills and fates do so contrary run
That our devices° still° are overthrown,
Our thoughts are ours, their ends none of our own:
So think thou wilt no second husband wed,
But die thy thoughts when thy first lord is dead.

[P.] QUEEN: Nor earth to me give food, nor heaven light,
Sport and repose lock from me day and night,
To desperation turn my trust and hope,
[An] anchor's cheer° in prison be my scope!°
Each opposite that blanks° the face of joy
Meet what I would have well and it destroy!
Both here and hence pursue me lasting strife,
If once I be a widow, ever I be a wife!

HAMLET: If she should break it now!

[P.] KING: 'Tis deeply sworn. Sweet, leave me here a while,
My spirits grow dull, and fain I would beguile
The tedious day with sleep. [*sleeps*]

[P.] QUEEN: Sleep rock thy brain,
And never come mischance between us twain! [*Exit.*]

HAMLET: Madam, how like you this play?

QUEEN: The lady doth protest too much, methinks.

HAMLET: O but she'll keep her word.

KING: Have you heard the argument? is there no offense° in't?

HAMLET: No, no, they do but jest, poison in jest°—no offense i' th' world.

KING: What do you call the play?

HAMLET: "The Mouse-trap." Marry, how? tropically:° this play is the image° of a murther done in Vienna; Gonzago is the duke's name, his wife, Baptista. You shall see anon. 'Tis a knavish piece of work, but what of that? Your Majesty, and we that have free souls,° it touches us not. Let the gall'd jade° winch,° our withers° are unwrung.°

Enter Lucianus.

This is one Lucianus, nephew to the king.

°*seasons:* Ripens, converts into. °*devices:* Devisings, intentions. °*still:* Always. °*anchor's cheer:* Hermit's fare. *my scope:* The extent of my comforts. °*blanks:* Blanches, makes pale (a symptom of grief). °*offense:* Offensive matter (but Hamlet quibbles on the sense "crime"). °*jest:* pretend. °*tropically:* Figuratively (with play on *trapically*—which is the reading of Q1—and probably with allusion to the children's saying *marry trap,* meaning "now you're caught"). °*image:* Representation. °*free souls:* Clear consciences. °*gall'd jade:* Chafed horse. °*winch:* Wince. °*withers:* Ridge between a horse's shoulders. ° *unwrung:* Not rubbed sore.

OPHELIA: You are as good as a chorus,° my lord.

HAMLET: I could interpret between you and your love, if I could see the puppets dallying.°

OPHELIA: You are keen,° my lord, you are keen.

HAMLET: It would cost you a groaning to take off mine edge.

OPHELIA: Still better, and worse.°

HAMLET: So° you mistake° your husbands. Begin, murtherer, leave thy damnable faces° and begin. Come, the croaking raven doth bellow for revenge.°

LUCIANUS: Thoughts black, hands apt, drugs fit, and time agreeing,
[Confederate] season,° else no creature seeing,
Thou mixture rank, of midnight weeds collected,
With Hecat's ban° thrice blasted, thrice [infected],
Thy natural magic and dire property
On wholesome life usurps immediately.

[*pours the poison into his ears*.]

HAMLET: 'A poisons him i' th' garden for his estate. His name's Gonzago, the story is extant, and written in very choice Italian. You shall see anon how the murtherer gets the love of Gonzago's wife.

OPHELIA: The King rises.

[**HAMLET:** What, frighted with false fire?]°

QUEEN: How fares my lord?

POLONIUS: Give o'er the play.

KING: Give me some light. Away!

POLONIUS: Lights, lights, lights!

Exeunt all but Hamlet and Horatio.

HAMLET: "Why, let the strooken° deer go weep,
The hart ungalled° play,
For some must watch° while some
must sleep,
Thus runs the world away."
Would not this, sir, and a forest of feathers°— if the rest of my fortunes turn Turk° with me—with [two] Provincial roses° on my raz'd° shoes, get me a fellowship° in a cry° of players?

°*chorus:* One who explains the forthcoming action. °*I . . . dallying:* I could speak the dialogue between you and your lover like a puppet-master (with an indecent jest). °*keen:* Bitter, sharp. °*better, and worse:* More pointed and less decent. °*So:* "For better, for worse," in the words of the marriage service *mistake:* Mistake, take, take wrongfully. Their vows, Hamlet suggests, prove false. °*faces:* Facial expressions. °*the croaking . . . revenge:* Misquoted from an old play, *The True Tragedy of Richard III.* °*Confederate season:* The time being my ally. °*Hecat's ban:* The curse of Hecate, goddess of witchcraft. °*false fire:* A blank cartridge. °*strooken:* Struck, wounded. °*ungalled:* Unwounded. °*watch:* Stay awake. °*feathers:* The plumes worn by tragic actors. °*turn Turk:* Go to the bad. °*Provincial roses:* Rosettes designed to look like a variety of French rose. °*raz'd:* With decorating slashing. °*fellowship:* Partnership. °*cry:* Company.

HORATIO: Half a share.
HAMLET: A whole one, I.
"For thou dost know, O Damon dear,
This realm dismantled° was
Of Jove himself, and now reigns here
A very, very"— pajock.°
HORATIO: You might have rhym'd.
HAMLET: O good Horatio, I'll take the ghost's word for a thousand pound. Didst perceive?
HORATIO: Very well, my lord.
HAMLET: Upon the talk of the pois'ning?
HORATIO: I did very well note him.
HAMLET: Ah, ha! Come, some music! Come, the recorders!
For if the King like not the comedy,
Why then belike he likes it not, perdy.°
Come, some music!

Enter Rosencrantz and Guildenstern.

GUILDENSTERN: Good my lord, voutsafe me a word with you.
HAMLET: Sir, a whole history.
GUILDENSTERN: The King, sir—
HAMLET: Ay, sir, what of him?
GUILDENSTERN: Is in his retirement marvellous distemp'red.
HAMLET: With drink, sir?
GUILDENSTERN: No, my lord, with choler.°
HAMLET: Your wisdom should show itself more richer to signify this to the doctor, for for me to put him to his purgation° would perhaps plunge him into more choler.
GUILDENSTERN: Good my lord, put your discourse into some frame,° and [start] not so wildly from my affair.
HAMLET: I am tame, sir. Pronounce.
GUILDENSTERN: The Queen, your mother, in most great affliction of spirit, hath sent me to you.
HAMLET: You are welcome.
GUILDENSTERN: Nay, good my lord, this courtesy is not of the right breed. If it shall please you to make me a wholesome° answer, I will do your mother's commandement; if not, your pardon° and my return shall be the end of [my] business.
HAMLET: Sir, I cannot.

°*dismantled:* Divested, deprived. °*pajock:* Peacock (substituting for the rhyme-word *ass*). The natural history of the time attributed many vicious qualities to the peacock. °*perdy:* Assuredly (French *pardieu*, "by God."). °*choler:* Anger (but Hamlet willfully takes up the word in the sense "biliousness"). °*put . . . purgation:* Prescribe for what's wrong with him. °*frame:* Logical structure. °*wholesome:* Sensible, rational. °*pardon:* Permission for departure.

ROSENCRANTZ: What, my lord?

HAMLET: Make you a wholesome answer—my wit's diseas'd. But, sir, such answer as I can make, you shall command, or rather, as you say, my mother. Therefore no more, but to the matter: my mother, you say—

ROSENCRANTZ: Then thus she says: your behavior hath strook her into amazement and admiration.°

HAMLET: O wonderful son, that can so stonish° a mother! But is there no sequel at the heels of this mother's admiration? Impart.

ROSENCRANTZ: She desires to speak with you in her closet° ere you go to bed.

HAMLET: We shall obey, were she ten times our mother. Have you any further trade with us?

ROSENCRANTZ: My lord, you once did love me.

HAMLET: And do still, by these pickers and stealers.°

ROSENCRANTZ: Good my lord, what is your cause of distemper? You do surely bar the door upon your own liberty if you deny your griefs to your friend.

HAMLET: Sir, I lack advancement.

ROSENCRANTZ: How can that be, when you have the voice of the King himself for your succession in Denmark?

HAMLET: Ay, sir, but "While the grass grows"— the proverb° is something musty.°

Enter the Players with recorders.

O, the recorders! Let me see one.— To withdraw with you— why do you go about to recover the wind° of me, as if you would drive me into a toil?°

GUILDENSTERN: O my lord, if my duty be too bold, my love is too unmannerly.

HAMLET: I do not well understand that. Will you play upon this pipe?

GUILDENSTERN: My lord, I cannot.

HAMLET: I pray you.

GUILDENSTERN: Believe me, I cannot.

HAMLET: I do beseech you.

GUILDENSTERN: I know no touch of it, my lord.

HAMLET: It is as easy as lying. Govern these ventages° with your fingers and [thumbs], give it breath with your mouth, and it will discourse most eloquent music. Look you, these are the stops.

GUILDENSTERN: But these cannot I command to any utt'rance of harmony. I have not the skill.

HAMLET: Why, look you now, how unworthy a thing you make of me! You would play upon me, you would seem to know my stops, you would pluck out the heart of my mystery; you would sound me from my lowest note to [the top of]

°*amazement and admiration:* Bewilderment and wonder. °*stonish:* Astound. °*closet:* Private room. °*pickers and stealers:* Hands, which, as the Catechism says, we must keep "from picking and stealing." °*proverb:* While the grass grows, the steed starves." °*something musty:* Somewhat stale. °*recover the wind:* Get to windward. °*toil:* Snare. °*ventages:* Stops.

my compass; and there is much music, excellent voice, in this little organ,° yet cannot you make it speak. 'Sblood, do you think I am easier to be play'd on than a pipe? Call me what instrument you will, though you fret° me, [yet] you cannot play upon me.

Enter Polonius.

God bless you, sir.

POLONIUS: My lord, the Queen would speak with you, and presently.°

HAMLET: Do you see yonder cloud that's almost in shape of a camel?

POLONIUS: By th' mass and 'tis, like a camel indeed.

HAMLET: Methinks it is like a weasel.

POLONIUS: It is back'd like a weasel.

HAMLET: Or like a whale.

POLONIUS: Very like a whale.

HAMLET: Then I will come to my mother by and by. [*aside*] They fool me to the top of my bent.°— I will come by and by.°

POLONIUS: I will say so. [*Exit.*°]

HAMLET: "By and by" is easily said. Leave me, friends.

[*Exeunt all but Hamlet.*]

'Tis now the very witching° time of night,
When churchyards yawn and hell itself [breathes] out
Contagion to this world. Now could I drink hot blood,
And do such [bitter business as the] day
Would quake to look on. Soft, now to my mother.
O heart, lose not thy nature!° let not ever
The soul of Nero° enter this firm bosom,
Let me be cruel, not unnatural;
I will speak [daggers] to her, but use none.
My tongue and soul in this be hypocrites—
How in my words someever she be shent,°
To give them seals° never my soul consent!

Exit.

SCENE 3°

Enter King, Rosencrantz, and Guildenstern.

KING: I like him° not, nor stands it safe with us
To let his madness range. Therefore prepare you.

°*organ:* Instrument. °*fret:* (1) Finger (an instrument); (2) vex. °*presently:* At once. °*They . . . bent:* They make me play the fool to the limit of my ability. °*by and by:* At once. °*witching:* When the powers of evil are at large. °*nature:* Natural affection, filial feeling. °*Nero:* Murderer of his mother. °*shent:* Rebuked. °*give them seals*: Confirm them by deeds. °*3.3. Location:* The castle. °*him:* His state of mind, his behavior.

I your commission with forthwith dispatch,°
And he to England shall along with you.
The terms° of our estate° may not endure
Hazard so near's as doth hourly grow
Out of his brows.°

GUILDENSTERN: We will ourselves provide.
Most holy and religious fear° it is
To keep those many many bodies safe
That live and feed upon your Majesty.

ROSENCRANTZ: The single and peculiar° life is bound
With all the strength and armor of the mind
To keep itself from noyance,° but much more,
That spirit upon whose weal depends and rests
The lives of many. The cess° of majesty
Dies not alone, but like a gulf° doth draw
What's near it with it. Or it is a massy wheel
Fix'd on the summit of the highest mount,
To whose [huge] spokes ten thousand lesser things
Are mortis'd° and adjoin'd, which when it falls,
Each small annexment, petty consequence,
Attends° the boist'rous [ruin].° Never alone
Did the King sigh, but [with] a general groan.

KING: Arm° you, I pray you, to this speedy voyage,°
For we will fetters put about this fear,°
Which now goes too free-footed.

ROSENCRANTZ: We will haste us.

Exeunt Gentleman [Rosencrantz and Guildenstern].

Enter Polonius.

POLONIUS: My lord, he's going to his mother's closet.
Behind the arras I'll convey myself
To hear the process.° I'll warrant she'll tax him home.°
And as you said, and wisely was it said,
'Tis meet that some more audience than a mother,
Since nature makes them partial, should o'erhear
The speech, of vantage.° Fare you well, my liege,
I'll call upon you ere you go to bed,
And tell you what I know.

°*dispatch:* Have drawn up. °*terms:* Conditions, nature. °*our estate*: My position (as king). °*his brows*: The madness visible in his face (?). °*fear:* Concern. °*single and peculiar:* Individual and private. °*noyance:* Injury. °*cess:* Cessation, death. °*gulf:* Whirlpool. °*mortis'd:* Fixed. °*Attends:* Accompanies. °*ruin:* Fall. °*Arm:* Prepare. °*viage:* Voyage. °*fear:* Object of fear. °*process:* Course of the talk. °*tax him home:* Take him severely to task. °*of vantage:* From an advantageous position (?) or in addition (?).

KING: Thanks, dear my lord.

Exit [Polonius].

O, my offense is rank, it smells to heavens,
It hath the primal eldest curse° upon't,
A brother's murther. Pray can I not,
Though inclination be as sharp as will.°
My stronger guilt defeats my strong intent,
And, like a man to double business bound,°
I stand in pause where I shall first begin,
And both neglect.° What if this cursed hand
Were thicker than itself with brother's blood,
Is there not rain enough in the sweet heavens
To wash it white as snow? Whereto serves mercy
But to confront the visage of offense?°
And what's in prayer but this twofold force,
To be forestalled ere we come to fall,
Or [pardon'd] being down? then I'll look up.
My fault is past, but, O, what form of prayer
Can serve my turn? "Forgive me my foul murther"?
That cannot be, since I am still possess'd
Of those effects for which I did the murther:
My crown, mine own ambition, and my queen.
May one be pardon'd and retain th' offense?°
In the corrupted currents° of this world
Offense's gilded° hand may [shove] by justice,
And oft 'tis seen the wicked prize° itself
Buys out the law, but 'tis not so above:
There is no shuffling,° there the action lies°
In his true nature, and we ourselves compell'd,
Even to the teeth and forehead° of our faults,
To give in evidence. What then? What rests?°
Try what repentance can. What can it not?
Yet what can it, when one can not repent?
O wretched state! O bosom black as death!
O limed° soul, that struggling to be free
Art more engag'd!° Help, angels! Make assay,
Bow, stubborn knees, and heart, with strings of steel,

°*primal eldest curse:* God's curse on Cain, who also slew his brother. °*Though . . . will:* Though my desire is as strong as my resolve to do so. °*bound:* Committed. °*neglect:* Omit. °*Whereto . . . offense:* What function has mercy except when there has been sin. °*th' offense:* The "effects" or fruits of the offense. °*currents:* Courses. °*gilded:* Bribing. °*wicked prize:* Rewards of vice. °*shuffling:* Evasion. °*the action lies:* The charge comes for legal consideration. °*Even . . . forehead:* Fully recognizing their features, extenuating nothing. °*rests:* Remains. °*limed:* Caught (as in birdlime, a sticky substance used for catching birds). °*engag'd:* Entangled.

Be soft as sinews of the new-born babe!
All may be well. [*He kneels*.]

Enter Hamlet.

HAMLET: Now might I do it [pat], now 'a is a-praying;
And now I'll do't — and so 'a goes to heaven,
And so am I [reveng'd]. That would be scann'd:°
A villain kills my father, and for that
I, his sole son, do this same villain send
To heaven.
Why, this is [hire and salary], not revenge.
'A took my father grossly,° full of bread,
With all his crimes° broad blown,° as flush° as May,
And how his audit° stands who knows save heaven?
But in our circumstance and course of thought°
'Tis heavy with him. And am I then revenged,
To take him in the purging of his soul,
When he is fit and season'd for his passage?
No!
Up,° sword, and know thou a more horrid hent:°
When he is drunk asleep, or in his rage,
Or in th' incestious pleasure of his bed,
At game a-swearing, or about some act
That has no relish° of salvation in't —
Then trip him, that his heels may kick at heaven,
And that his soul may be as damn'd and black
As hell, whereto it goes. My mother stays,
This physic° but prolongs thy sickly days. *Exit*.

KING [*rising*]**:** My words fly up, my thoughts remain below:
Words without thoughts never to heaven go.
Exit.

[SCENE 4]°

Enter [Queen] Gertrude and Polonius.

POLONIUS: 'A will come straight. Look you lay home to him.°
Tell him his pranks have been too broad° to bear with,
And that your Grace hath screen'd and stood between

°*would be scann'd:* Must be carefully considered. °*grossly:* In a gross state; not spiritually prepared. °*crimes:* Sins. °*broad blown:* In full bloom. °*flush:* Lusty, vigorous. °*audit:* Account. °*in . . . thought:* To the best of our knowledge and belief. °*Up:* into the sheath. °*know . . . hent:* Be grasped at a more dreadful time. °*relish:* Trace. °*physic:* (Attempted) remedy, prayer. °*3. 4. Location:* The queen's closet in the castle. °*lay . . . him:* Reprove him severely. °*broad:* Unrestrained.

Much heat and him. I'll silence me even here;
Pray you be round° [with him].

QUEEN: I'll [warr'nt] you, fear me not.° Withdraw,
I hear him coming. [*Polonius hides behind the arras.*]

Enter Hamlet.

HAMLET: Now, mother, what's the matter?

QUEEN: Hamlet, thou hast thy father much offended.

HAMLET: Mother, you have my father much offended.

QUEEN: Come, come, you answer with an idle° tongue.

HAMLET: Go, go, you question with a wicked tongue.

QUEEN: Why, how now, Hamlet?

HAMLET: What's the matter now?

QUEEN: Have you forgot me?

HAMLET: No, by the rood,° not so:
You are the Queen, your husband's brother's wife,
And would it were not so, you are my mother.

QUEEN: Nay, then I'll set those to you that can speak.

HAMLET: Come, come, and sit you down, you shall not boudge;°
You go not till I set you up a glass
Where you may see the [inmost] part of you.

QUEEN: What wilt thou do? Thou wilt not murther me?
Help ho!

POLONIUS [*behind*]: What ho, help!

HAMLET [*drawing*]: How now! A rat? Dead, for a ducat,° dead! [*Kills Polonius through the arras.*]

POLONIUS [*behind*]: O, I am slain.

QUEEN: O me, what hast thou done?

HAMLET: Nay, I know not, is it the King?

QUEEN: O, what a rash and bloody deed is this!

HAMLET: A bloody deed! almost as bad, good mother,
As kill a king, and marry with his brother.

QUEEN: As kill a king!

HAMLET: Ay, lady, it was my word.

[*parts the arras and discovers Polonius*]

Thou wretched, rash, intruding fool, farewell!
I took thee for thy better. Take thy fortune;
Thou find'st to be too busy° is some danger.—
Leave wringing of your hands. Peace, sit you down,
And let me wring your heart, for so I shall
If it be made of penetrable stuff,

°*round:* Plainspoken. °*fear me not:* Have no fears about my handling of the situation. °*idle:* foolish. °*rood:* Cross. °*boudge:* Budge. °*for a ducat:* I'll wager a ducat. °*busy:* Officious, meddlesome.

If damned custom° have not brass'd° it so
That it be proof° and bulwark against sense.°

Queen: What have I done, that thou dar'st wag thy tongue
In noise so rude against me?

Hamlet: Such an act
That blurs the grace and blush of modesty,
Calls virtue hypocrite, takes off the rose
From the fair forehead of an innocent love
And sets a blister° there, makes marriage vows
As false as dicers' oaths, O, such a deed
As from the body of contraction° plucks
The very soul, and sweet religion° makes
A rhapsody° of words. Heaven's face does glow°
O'er this solidity and compound mass°
With heated visage, as against the doom;°
Is thought-sick at the act.

Queen: Ay me, what act,
That roars so loud and thunders in the index?°

Hamlet: Look here upon this picture, and on this,
The counterfeit presentment° of two brothers.
See what a grace was seated on this brow:
Hyperion's° curls, the front° of Jove himself,
An eye like Mars, to threaten and command,
A station° like the herald Mercury
New lighted on a [heaven-]kissing hill,
A combination and a form indeed,
Where every god did seem to set his seal
To give the world assurance of a man.
This was your husband. Look you now what follows:
Here is your husband, like a mildewed ear,°
Blasting his wholesome brother. Have you eyes?
Could you not on this fair mountain leave to feed,
And batten° on this moor? ha, have you eyes?
You cannot call it love, for at your age
The heyday° in the blood is tame, it's humble,
And waits upon the judgment, and what judgment
Would step from this to this? Sense° sure you have,

°*damned custom:* The habit of ill-doing. °*brass'd:* Hardened, literally, plated with brass. °*proof:* Armor. °*sense:* Feeling. °*blister:* Brand of shame. °*contraction:* The making of contracts, the assuming of solemn obligation. °*religion:* Sacred vows. °*rhapsody:* Miscellaneous collection, jumble. °*glow:* With anger. °*this . . . mass:* The earth; *compound* = compounded of the four elements. °*as . . . doom:* As if for Judgment Day. °*index:* Table of contents. The index was formerly placed at the beginning of a book. °*counterfeit presentment:* Painted likenesses. °*Hyperion's:* The sun-god's. °*front:* Forehead. °*station:* Bearing. °*ear:* Of grain. °*batten:* Gorge. °*heyday:* Excitement. °*Sense:* Sense perception, the five senses.

Else could you not have motion, but sure that sense
Is apoplex'd° for madness would not err,
Nor sense to ecstasy was ne'er so thrall'd
But it reserv'd some quantity of choice
To serve in such a difference.° What devil was't
That thus hath cozen'd° you at hoodman-blind?°
Eyes without feeling, feeling without sight,
Ears without hands or eyes, smelling sans° all,
Or but a sickly part of one true sense
Could not so mope.° O shame, where is thy blush?
Rebellious hell,
If thou canst mutine° in a matron's bones,
To flaming youth let virtue be as wax
And melt in her own fire. Proclaim no shame
When the compulsive ardure gives the charge,
Since frost itself as actively doth burn,
And reason [panders] will.°

QUEEN: O Hamlet, speak no more!
Thou turn'st my [eyes into my very] soul,
And there I see such black and [grained°] spots
As will [not] leave their tinct.°

HAMLET: Nay, but to live
In the rank sweat of an enseamed° bed,
Stew'd in corruption, honeying and making love
Over the nasty sty!

QUEEN: O, speak to me no more!
These words like daggers enter in my ears.
No more, sweet Hamlet!

HAMLET: A murtherer and a villain!
A slave that is not twentith° part the [tithe]
Of your precedent° lord, a Vice° of kings,
A cutpurse of the empire and the rule,
That from a shelf the precious diadem stole,
And put it in his pocket—

QUEEN: No more!

Enter Ghost. [*in his night-gown*°].

°*apoplex'd:* Paralyzed. °*madness . . . difference:* Madness itself could not go so far astray, nor were the senses ever so enslaved by lunacy that they did not retain the power to make so obvious a distinction. °*cozen'd:* Cheated °*hoodman-blind:* Blindman's bluff. °*sans:* Without. °*mope:* Be dazed. °*mutine:* Rebel. °*Proclaim . . . will:* Do not call it sin when the hot blood of youth is responsible for lechery, since here we see people of calmer age on fire for it; and reason acts as procurer for desire, instead of restraining it. °*Ardure* = ardor. °*grained:* Fast-dyed, indelible. °*leave their tinct:* Lose their color. °*enseamed:* Greasy. °*twentith:* Twentieth. °*precedent:* Former. °*Vice:* Buffoon (like the Vice of the morality plays). °*night-gown:* Dressing gown.

HAMLET: A king of shreds and patches°—
Save me, and hover o'er me with your wings,
You heavenly guards! What would your gracious figure?
QUEEN: Alas, he's mad!
HAMLET: Do you not come your tardy son to chide,
That, laps'd in time and passion,° lets go by
Th' important° acting of your dread command?
O, say!
GHOST: Do not forget! This visitation
Is but to whet thy almost blunted purpose.
But look, amazement° on thy mother sits,
O, step between her and her fighting soul.
Conceit° in weakest bodies strongest works,
Speak to her, Hamlet.
HAMLET: How is it with you, lady?
QUEEN: Alas, how is't with you,
That you do bend your eye on vacancy,
And with th' incorporal air do hold discourse?
Forth at your eyes your spirits wildly peep,
And as the sleeping soldiers in th' alarm,°
Your bedded hair, like life in excrements,°
Start up and stand an end.° O gentle son,
Upon the heat and flame of thy distemper
Sprinkle cool patience.° Whereon do you look?
HAMLET: On him, on him! look you how pale he glares!
His form and cause° conjoin'd, preaching to stones,
Would make them capable.°—Do not look upon me,
Lest with this piteous action you convert°
My stern effects,° then what I have to do
Will want true color°—tears perchance for blood.
QUEEN: To whom do you speak this?
HAMLET: Do you see nothing there?
QUEEN: Nothing at all, yet all that is I see.
HAMLET: Nor did you nothing hear?
QUEEN: No, nothing but ourselves.
HAMLET: Why, look you there, look how it steals away!
My father, in his habit° as he lived!
Look where he goes, even now, out at the portal!

°*of . . . patches:* Clownish (alluding to the motley worn by jesters) (?) or patched-up, beggarly (?). °*laps'd . . . passion:* "Having suffered time to slip and passion to cool" (Johnson). °*important:* Urgent. °*amazement:* Utter bewilderment. °*Conceit:* Imagination. °*in th' alarm:* When the call to arms is sounded. °*excrements:* Outgrowths; here, hair (also used of nails). °*an end:* On end. °*patience:* Self-control. °*His . . . cause:* His appearance and what he has to say. °*capable:* Sensitive, receptive. °*convert:* Alter. °*effects:* (Purposed) actions. °*want true color:* Lack its proper appearance. °*habit:* Dress.

Exit Ghost.

QUEEN: This is the very coinage of your brain,
This bodiless creation ecstasy°
Is very cunning in.
HAMLET: [Ecstasy!]
My pulse as yours doth temperately keep time,
And makes as healthful music. It is not madness
That I have utt'red. Bring me to the test,
And [I] the matter will reword, which madness
Would gambol° from. Mother, for love of grace,
Lay not that flattering unction° to your soul,
That not your trespass but my madness speaks;
It will but skin and film the ulcerous place,
Whiles rank corruption, mining all within,
Infects unseen. Confess yourself to heaven,
Repent what's past, avoid what is to come,
And do not spread the compost° on the weeds
To make them ranker. Forgive me this my virtue,
For in the fatness of these pursy° times
Virtue itself of vice must pardon beg,
Yea, curb and woo° for leave to do him good.
QUEEN: O Hamlet, thou hast cleft my heart in twain.
HAMLET: O, throw away the worser part of it,
And [live] the purer with the other half.
Good night, but go not to my uncle's bed—
Assume a virtue, if you have it not.
That monster custom, who all sense doth eat,°
Of habits devil,° is angel yet in this,
That to the use of actions fair and good
He likewise gives a frock or livery
That aptly is put on.° Refrain [to-]night,
And that shall lend a kind of easiness
To the next abstinence, the next more easy;
For use° almost can change the stamp of nature,
And either [. . .]° the devil or throw him out
With wondrous potency. Once more good night,
And when you are desirous to be blest,°
I'll blessing beg of you. For this same lord,

°*ecstasy:* Madness. °*gambol:* Start, jerk away. °*flattering unction:* Soothing ointment. °*compost:* Manure. °*pursy:* Puffy, out of condition. °*curb and woo:* Bow and entreat. °*all . . . eat:* Wears away all natural feeling. °*Of habits devil:* Though it acts like a devil in establishing bad habits. Most editors read (in lines 162–63) *eat / Of habits evil*, following Theobald. °*frock . . . on:* A "habit" or customary garment, readily put on without need of any decision. °*use:* Habit. °[. . .]: A word seems to be wanting after *either.* °*desirous . . . blest:* Repentant.

[*pointing to Polonius*]

I do repent; but heaven hath pleas'd it so,
To punish me with this, and this with me,
That I must be their scourge and minister.°
I will bestow° him, and will answer° well
The death I gave him. So again good night.
I must be cruel only to be kind.
This bad begins and worse remains behind.°
One word more, good lady.

QUEEN: What shall I do?

HAMLET: Not this, by no means, that I bid you do:
Let the bloat king tempt you again to bed,
Pinch wanton on your cheek, call you his mouse,
And let him, for a pair of reechy° kisses,
Or paddling in your neck with his damn'd fingers,
Make you to ravel all this matter out,
That I essentially am not in madness,
But mad in craft. 'Twere good you let him know,
For who that's but a queen, fair, sober, wise,
Would from a paddock,° from a bat, a gib,°
Such dear concernings° hide? Who would do so?
No, in despite of sense and secrecy,
Unpeg the basket° on the house's top,
Let the birds fly, and like the famous ape,°
To try conclusions° in the basket creep,
And break your own neck down.°

QUEEN: Be thou assur'd, if words be made of breath,
And breath of life, I have not life to breathe
What thou hast said to me.

HAMLET: I must to England, you know that?

QUEEN: Alack,
I had forgot: 'Tis so concluded on.

HAMLET: There's letters seal'd, and my two schoolfellows,
Whom I will trust as I will adders fang'd,
They bear the mandate, they must sweep my way
And marshal me to knavery.° Let it work,
For 'tis the sport to have the enginer°

°*scourge and minister:* The agent of heavenly justice against human crime. *Scourge* suggests a permissive cruelty (Tamburlaine was the "scourge of God"), but "woe to him by whom the offense cometh"; the scourge must suffer for the evil it performs. °*bestow:* Dispose of. °*answer:* Answer for. °*behind:* To come. °*reechy:* Filthy. °*paddock:* Toad. °*gib:* Tomcat. °*dear concernings:* Matters of intense concern. °*Unpeg the basket:* Open the door of the cage. °*famous ape:* The actual story has been lost. °*conclusions:* Experiments (to see whether he too can fly if he enters the cage and then leaps out). °*down:* By the fall. °*knavery:* Some knavish scheme against me. °*enginer:* Deviser of military "engines" or contrivances.

Hoist with° his own petar,° an't shall go hard
But I will delve one yard below their mines,
And blow them at the moon: O, 'tis most sweet
When in one line two crafts° directly meet.
This man shall set me packing;°
I'll lug the guts into the neighbor room.
Mother, good night indeed. This counsellor
Is now most still, most secret, and most grave,
Who was in life a foolish prating knave.
Come, sir, to draw toward an end° with you.
Good night, mother.

Exeunt [severally, Hamlet tugging in Polonius].

ACT 4

SCENE 1°

Enter King and Queen with Rosencrantz and Guildenstern.

KING: There's matter in these sighs, these profound heaves—
You must translate, 'tis fit we understand them.
Where is your son?
QUEEN: Bestow this place on us a little while.

Exeunt Rosencrantz and Guildenstern.

Ah, mine own lord, what have I seen to-night!
KING: What, Gertrude? How does Hamlet?
QUEEN: Mad as the sea and wind, when both contend
Which is the mightier. In his lawless fit,
Behind the arras hearing something stir,
Whips out his rapier cries, "A rat, a rat!"
And in this brainish apprehension° kills
The unseen good old man.
KING: O heavy deed!
It had been so with us had we been there.
His liberty is full of threats to all,
To you yourself, to us, to every one.
Alas, how shall this bloody deed be answer'd?°
It will be laid to us, whose providence°
Should have kept short,° restrain'd, and out of haunt°
This mad young man; but so much was our love,

°*Hoist with:* Blown up by. °*petar:* Petard, bomb. °*crafts:* Plots. °*packing:* (1) Taking on a load; (2) leaving in a hurry. °*draw . . . end:* Finish my conversation. °*4.1. Location:* The castle. °*brainish apprehension:* Crazy notion. °*answer'd:* Satisfactorily accounted for to the public. °*providence:* Foresight. °*short:* On a short leash. °*out of haunt:* Away from other people.

We would not understand what was most fit,
But, like the owner of a foul disease,
To keep it from divulging,° let it feed
Even on the pith of life. Where is he gone?

QUEEN: To draw apart the body he hath kill'd,
O'er whom his very madness, like some ore°
Among a mineral° of metals base,
Shows itself pure: 'a weeps for what is done.

KING: O Gertrude, come away!
The sun no sooner shall the mountains touch,
But we will ship him hence, and this vile deed,
We must, with all our majesty and skill
Both countenance and excuse. Ho, Guildenstern!

Enter Rosencrantz and Guildenstern.

Friends both, go join you with some further aid:
Hamlet in madness hath Polonius slain,
And from his mother's closet hath he dragg'd him.
Go seek him out, speak fair, and bring the body
Into the chapel. I pray you, haste in this.

Exeunt Rosencrantz and Guildenstern.

Come, Gertrude, we'll call up our wisest friends
And let them know both what we mean to do
And what's untimely done, [. . .]°
Whose whisper o'er the world's diameter,
As level° as the cannon to his blank,°
Transports his pois'ned shot, may amiss our name,
And hit the woundless° air. O, come away!
My soul is full of discord and dismay.

Exeunt.

SCENE 2°

Enter Hamlet.

HAMLET: Safely stow'd.

[**GENTLEMEN** (*Within.*): Hamlet! Lord Hamlet!]

HAMLET: But soft, what noise? Who calls on Hamlet? O, here they come.

Enter Rosencrantz and [*Guildenstern*].

°*divulging:* Being revealed. °*ore:* Vein of gold. °*mineral:* Mine. °Some words are wanting at the end of the line Capell's conjecture, *so, haply, slander,* probably indicates the intended sense of the passage. °*As level:* With aim as good. °*blank:* Target. °*woundless:* Incapable of being hurt. °*4.2. Location:* The castle.

ROSENCRANTZ: What have you done, my lord, with the dead body?
HAMLET: [Compounded] it with dust, whereto 'tis kin.
ROSENCRANTZ: Tell us where 'tis, that we may take it thence,
And bear it to the chapel.
HAMLET: Do not believe it.
ROSENCRANTZ: Believe what?
HAMLET: That I can keep your counsel and not mine own. Besides, to be demanded of° a spunge,° what replication° should be made by the son of a king?
ROSENCRANTZ: Take you me for a spunge, my lord?
HAMLET: Ay, sir, that soaks up the King's countenance,° his rewards, his authorities. But such officers do the King best service in the end: he keeps them, like [an ape] an apple in the corner of his jaw, first mouth'd, to be last swallow'd. When he needs what you have glean'd, it is but squeezing you, and, spunge, you shall be dry again.
ROSENCRANTZ: I understand you not, my lord.
HAMLET: I am glad of it a knavish speech sleeps° in a foolish ear.
ROSENCRANTZ: My lord, you must tell us where the body is, and go with us to the King.
HAMLET: The body is with the King, but the King is not with the body.° The King is a thing—
GUILDENSTERN: A thing, my lord!
HAMLET: Of nothing,° bring me to him. [Hide fox, and all after.°]

Exeunt.

SCENE 3°

Enter King and two or three.

KING: I have sent to seek him, and to find the body.
How dangerous is it that this man goes loose!
Yet must not we put the strong law on him.
He's lov'd of the distracted° multitude,
Who like not in their judgment, but their eyes,
And where 'tis so, th' offender's scourge° is weigh'd,
But never the offense. To bear° all smooth and even,
This sudden sending him away must seem
Deliberate pause.° Diseases desperate grown

°*demanded of:* Questioned by. °*spunge:* Sponge. °*replication:* Reply. °*countenance:* Favor. °*sleeps:* Is meaningless. °*The body . . . the body:* Possibly alluding to the legal fiction that the king's dignity is separate from his mortal body. °*Of nothing:* Of no account Cf. "Man is like a thing of nought, his time passeth away like a shadow" (Psalm 14:4 in the Prayer Book version) "Hamlet at once insults the King and hints that his days are numbered" (Dover Wilson). °*Hide . . . after:* Probably a cry in some game resembling hide-and-seek. °*4.3. Location:* The castle. °*distracted:* Unstable. °*scourge:* Punishment. °*bear:* Manage. °*must . . . pause:* Must be represented as a maturely considered decision.

By desperate appliance are reliev'd,
Or not at all.

Enter Rosencrantz.

How now! what hath befall'n!

ROSENCRANTZ: Where the dead body is bestow'd, my lord,
We cannot get from him.

KING: But where is he?

ROSENCRANTZ: Without, my lord, guarded, to know your pleasure.

KING: Bring him before us.

ROSENCRANTZ: Ho, bring in my lord.

They [Hamlet and Guildenstern] enter.

KING: Now, Hamlet, where's Polonius?

HAMLET: At supper.

KING: At supper? where?

HAMLET: Not where he eats, but where 'a is eaten; a certain convocation of politic° worms are e'en° at him. Your worm is your only emperor for diet:° we fat all creatures else to fat us, and we fat ourselves for maggots; your fat king and your lean beggar is but variable service,° two dishes, but to one table—that's the end.

KING: Alas, alas!

HAMLET: A man may fish with the worm that hath eat of a king, and eat of the fish that hath fed of that worm.

KING: What does thou mean by this?

HAMLET: Nothing but to show you how a king may go a progress° through the guts of a beggar.

KING: Where is Polonius?

HAMLET: In heaven, send thither to see; if your messenger find him not there, seek him i' th' other place yourself. But if, indeed, if you find him not within this month, you shall nose him as you go up the stairs into the lobby.

KING [*to Attendants*]**:** Go seek him there.

HAMLET: 'A will stay till you come.

Exeunt Attendants.

KING: Hamlet, this deed, for thine especial safety—
Which we do tender,° as we dearly° grieve
For that which thou hast done—must send thee hence
[With fiery quickness]; therefore prepare thyself,
The bark is ready, and the wind at help,°

°*politic:* Crafty, prying; "such worms as might breed in a politician's corpse" (Dowden). °*e'en:* even now. °*for diet:* with respect to what it eats. °*variable service:* Different courses of a meal. °*progress:* Royal journey of state. °*tender:* Regard with tenderness, hold dear. °*dearly:* With intense feeling. °*at help:* Favorable.

Th'° associates tend,° and every thing is bent°
For England.

HAMLET: For England.

KING: Ay, Hamlet.

HAMLET: Good.

KING: So is it, if thou knew'st our purposes.

HAMLET: I see a cherub that sees them.° But come, for England! Farewell, dear mother.

KING: Thy loving father, Hamlet.

HAMLET: My mother: father and mother is man and wife, man and wife is one flesh—so, my mother. Come, for England! (*Exit.*)

KING: Follow him at foot,° tempt him with speed aboard.
Delay it not I'll have him hence to-night.
Away, for every thing is seal'd and done
That else leans on° th' affair. Pray you, make haste.

Exeunt Rosencrantz and Guildenstern.

And, England,° if my love thou hold'st at aught—
As my great power thereof may give thee sense,
Since yet thy cicatrice° looks raw and red
After the Danish sword, and thy free awe
Pays° homage to us—thou mayst not coldly set°
Our sovereign process,° which imports at full,
By letters to congruing to° that effect,
The present° death of Hamlet. Do it, England,
For like the hectic° in my blood he rages,
And thou must cure me. Till I know 'tis done,
How e'er my haps,° my joys [were] ne'er [begun].

Exit.

SCENE 4°

Enter Fortinbras with his army over the stage.

FORTINBRAS: Go, captain, from me greet the Danish king.
Tell him that by his license Fortinbras
Craves the conveyance° of a promis'd march
Over his kingdom. You know the rendezvous
If that his Majesty would aught with us,

°*Th':* Thy. °*tend:* Await. °*bent:* Made ready. °*I . . . them:* Heaven sees them. °*at foot:* At his heels, close behind. °*leans on:* Relates to. °*England:* King of England. °*cicatrice:* Scar. °*thy . . . Pays:* Your fear makes you pay voluntarily. °*coldly set:* Undervalue, disregard. °*process:* Command. °*congruing to:* In accord with. °*present:* Immediate. °*hectic:* Continuous: fever. °*haps:* Fortunes. °*4.4. Location:* The Danish coast, near the castle. °*conveyance of:* Escort for.

We shall express our duty in his eye,°
And let him know so.

CAPTAIN: I will do't, my lord.

FORTINBRAS: Go softly° on. [*Exeunt all but the Captain.*]

Enter Hamlet, Rosencrantz, [*Guildenstern,*] *etc.*

HAMLET: Good sir, whose powers° are these?

CAPTAIN: They are of Norway, sir.

HAMLET: How purpos'd, sir, I pray you?

CAPTAIN: Against some part of Poland.

HAMLET: Who commands them, sir?

CAPTAIN: The nephew to old Norway, Fortinbras.

HAMLET: Goes it against the main° of Poland, sir,
Or for some frontier?

CAPTAIN: Truly to speak, and with no addition,
We go to gain a little patch of ground
That hath in it no profit but the name.
To pay° five ducats, five, I would not farm° it;
Nor will it yield to Norway or the Pole
A ranker° rate, should it be sold in fee.°

HAMLET: Why, then the Polack never will defend it.

CAPTAIN: Yes, it is already garrison'd.

HAMLET: Two thousand souls and twenty thousand ducats
Will not debate° the question of this straw.
This is th' imposthume° of much wealth and peace,
That inward breaks, and shows no cause without
Why the man dies. I humbly thank you, sir.

CAPTAIN: God buy you, sir. [*Exit.*]

ROSENCRANTZ: Will't please you go, my lord?

HAMLET: I'll be with you straight—go a little before.

[*Exeunt all but Hamlet.*]

How all occasions do inform against° me,
And spur my dull revenge! What is a man,
If his chief good and market° of his time
Be but to sleep and feed? a beast, no more.
Sure He that made us with such large discourse,°
Looking before and after, gave us not
That capability and godlike reason
To fust° in us unus'd. Now, whether it be

°*eye:* Presence. °*softly:* Slowly. °*powers:* Forces. °*main:* Main territory. °*To pay:* For an annual rent of. °*farm:* Lease. °*ranker:* Higher. °*in fee:* Outright. °*Will not debate:* Will scarcely be enough to fight out. °*imposthume:* Abscess. °*inform against:* Denounce, accuse. °*market:* Purchase, profit. °*discourse:* Reasoning power. °*fust:* Grow mouldy.

Bestial oblivion,° or some craven scruple
Of thinking too precisely on th' event°—
A thought which quarter'd hath but one part wisdom
And ever three parts coward—I do not know
Why yet I live to say, "This thing's to do,"
Sith I have cause, and will, and strength, and means
To do't. Examples, gross° as earth exhort me:
Witness this army of such mass and charge,°
Led by a delicate and tender prince,
Whose spirit with divine ambition puff'd
Makes mouths at° the invisible° event,
Exposing what is mortal and unsure
To all that fortune, death, and danger dare,
Even for an egg-shell. Rightly to be great
Is not to° stir without great argument,°
But greatly° to find quarrel in a straw
When honor's at the stake. How stand I then,
That have a father kill'd, a mother stain'd,
Excitements° of my reason and my blood,
And let all sleep, while to my shame I see
The imminent death of twenty thousand men,
That, for a fantasy° and trick° of fame
Go to their graves like beds, fight for a plot
Whereon the numbers cannot try the cause,°
Which is not tomb enough and continent°
To hide the slain? O, from this time forth,
My thoughts be bloody, or be nothing worth!

Exit.

[SCENE 5]°

Enter Horatio, [Queen] Gertrude, and a Gentlemen.

QUEEN: I will not speak with her.
GENTLEMEN: She is importunate, indeed distract.
Her mood will needs be pitied.
QUEEN: What would she have?
GENTLEMAN: She speaks much of her father, says she hears
There's tricks i' th' world, and hems, and beats her heart,

°*oblivion:* Forgetfulness. °*event:* Outcome. °*gross:* Large, obvious. °*mass and charge:* Size and expense. °*Makes mouths at:* Treats scornfully. °*invisible:* Unforeseeable. °*Is not to:* Is *not* not to. °*argument:* Cause. °*greatly:* Nobly. °*Excitements of:* Urgings by. °*fantasy:* Caprice. °*trick:* Trifle. °*Whereon . . . cause:* Which isn't large enough to let the opposing armies engage upon it. °*continent:* Container. °*5.5. Location:* The castle.

Spurns enviously at straws,° speaks things in doubt°
That carry but half sense. Her speech° is nothing,
Yet the unshaped use° of it doth move
The hearers to collection;° they yawn at° it,
And botch° the words up fit to their own thoughts,
Which° as her winks and nods and gestures yield them,
Indeed would make one think there might be thought,°
Though nothing sure, yet much unhappily.

HORATIO: 'Twere good she were spoken with, for she may strew
Dangerous conjectures in ill-breeding° minds.

[QUEEN]: Let her come in. [*Exit Gentleman.*]
[*aside*] To my sick soul, as sin's true nature is,
Each toy° seems prologue to some great amiss,°
So full of artless jealousy° is guilt,
It spills° itself in fearing to be spilt.

Enter Ophelia [distracted, with her hair down, playing on a lute].

OPHELIA: Where is the beauteous majesty of Denmark?

QUEEN: How now, Ophelia?

OPHELIA: "How should I your true-love°
know *She sings.*
From another one?
By his cockle hat° and staff,°
And his sandal shoon.°"

QUEEN: Alas, sweet lady, what imports this song?

OPHELIA: Say you? Nay, pray you mark.
"He is dead and gone, lady, *Song.*
He is dead and gone,
At his head a grass-green turf,
At his heels a stone."
O ho!

QUEEN: Nay, but, Ophelia—

OPHELIA: Pray you, mark. [*Sings.*]
"White his shroud as the mountain snow"—

°*Spurns . . . straws:* Spitefully takes offense at trifles. °*in doubt:* Obscurely. °*Her speech:* What she says. °*unshaped use:* Distracted manner. °*collection:* Attempts to gather the meaning. °*yawn at:* Gape eagerly (as if to swallow). Most editors adopt the F1 reading *aim at.* °*botch:* Patch. °*Which:* The words. °*thought:* Inferred, conjectured. °*ill-breeding:* Conceiving ill thoughts, prone to think the worst. °*toy:* Trifle. °*amiss:* Calamity. °*artless jealousy:* Uncontrolled suspicion. °*spills:* Destroys. °*23–27:* These lines resemble a passage in an earlier ballad beginning "As you came from the holy land / Of Walsingham." Probably all the song fragments sung by Ophelia were familiar to the Globe audience, but only one other line (187) is from a ballad still extant. °*cockle hat:* Hat bearing a cockle shell, the badge of a pilgrim to the shrine of St. James of Compostela in Spain. °*staff:* Another mark of a pilgrim. °*shoon:* Shoes (already an archaic form in Shakespeare's day).

Enter King.

QUEEN: Alas, look here, my lord.

OPHELIA: "Larded° with sweet flowers, *Song.*
Which bewept to the ground did not° go
With true-love showers."

KING: How do you, pretty lady?

OPHELIA: Well, God dild° you! They say the owl° was a baker's daughter. Lord, we know what we are, but know not what we may be. God be at your table!

KING: Conceit° upon her father.

OPHELIA: Pray let's have no words of this, but when they ask you what it means, say you this: *Song.*

"To-morrow is Saint Valentine's
day,
All in the morning betime,
And I a maid at your window,
To be your Valentine.
"Then up he rose and donn'd his clo'es,
And dupp'd° the chamber-door,
Let in the maid, that out a maid
Never departed more."

KING: Pretty Ophelia!

OPHELIA: Indeed without an oath, I'll make an end on't. [*Sings.*]

"By Gis,° and by Saint Charity,
Alack, and fie for shame!
Young men will do't if they come to't,
By Cock,° they are to blame.
"Quoth she, 'Before you tumbled me,
You promis'd me to wed.'"

He answers.

So would I 'a'done, by yonder sun,
And° thou hadst not come to my bed.' "

KING: How long hath she been thus?

OPHELIA: I hope all will be well. We must be patient, but I cannot choose but weep to think they would lay him i' th' cold ground. My brother shall know of it, and so I thank you for your good counsel. Come, my coach! Good night, ladies, good night. Sweet ladies, good night, good night. [*Exit.*]

KING: Follow her close, give her good watch, I pray you. [*Exit Horatio.*]

°*Larded:* Adorned. °*not:* Contrary to the expected sense, and unmetrical; explained as Ophelia's alteration of the line to accord with the facts of Polonius' burial (see line 83). °*dild:* Yield, reward. °*owl:* Alluding to the legend of a baker's daughter whom Jesus turned into an owl because she did not respond generously to his request for bread. °*Conceit:* Fanciful brooding. °*dupp'd:* Opened. °*Gis:* Contraction of *Jesus.* °*Cock:* Corruption of *God.* °*And:* If.

O, this is the poison of deep grief, it springs
All from her father's death—and now behold!
O Gertrude, Gertrude,
When sorrows come, they come not single spies,°
But in battalions: first, her father slain;
Next, your son gone, and he most violent author
Of his own just remove; the people muddied,°
Thick and unwholesome in [their] thoughts and whispers
For good Polonius' death; and we have done but greenly°
In hugger-mugger° to inter him; poor Ophelia
Divided from herself and her fair judgment,
Without the which we are pictures, or mere beasts;
Last, and as much containing as all these,
Her brother is in secret come from France,
Feeds on his wonder, keeps himself in clouds,°
And wants° not buzzers° to infect his ear
With pestilent speeches of his father's death,
Wherein necessity, of matter beggar'd,°
Will nothing stick our person to arraign°
In ear and ear. O my dear Gertrude, this,
Like to a murd'ring-piece,° in many places
Gives me superfluous death. *(a noise within)*

[**QUEEN:** Alack, what noise is this?]

KING: Attend!
Where is my Swissers?° Let them guard the door.

Enter a Messenger.

What is the matter?

MESSENGER: Save yourself, my lord!
The ocean, overpeering of his list,°
Eats not the flats with more impiteous haste
Than young Laertes, in a riotous head,°
O'erbears your officers. The rabble call him lord,
And as° the world were now but to begin,
Antiquity forgot, custom not known,
The ratifiers and props of every word,°
[They] cry, "Choose we, Laertes shall be king!"
Caps, hands, and tongues applaud it to the clouds,
"Laertes shall be king, Laertes king!" *(a noise within)*

°*spies:* Soldiers sent ahead of the main force to reconnoiter; scouts. °*muddied:* Confused. °*greenly:* Unwisely. °*In hugger-mugger:* Secretly and hastily. °*in clouds:* In cloudy surmise and suspicion (rather than the light of fact). °*wants:* Lacks. °*buzzers:* Whispering informers. °*of matter beggar'd:* Destitute of facts. °*nothing . . . arraign:* Scruple not at all to charge me with the crime. °*murd'ring-piece:* Cannon firing a scattering charge. °*Swissers:* Swiss guards. °*overpeering . . . list:* Rising higher than its shores. °*in . . . head:* With a rebellious force. °*as:* As if. °*word:* Pledge, promise.

QUEEN: How cheerfully on the false trail they cry!
O, this is counter,° you false Danish dogs!

Enter Laertes with others.

KING: The doors are broke.
LAERTES: Where is this king? Sirs, stand you all without.
ALL: No, let's come in.
LAERTES: I pray you give me leave.
ALL: We will, we will.
LAERTES: I thank you keep the door. [*Exeunt Laertes' followers.*] O thou vile king,
Give me my father!
QUEEN: Calmly, good Laertes.
LAERTES: That drop of blood that's calm proclaims me bastard,
Cries cuckold, to my father, brands the harlot
Even here between the chaste unsmirched brow
Of my true mother.
KING: What is the cause, Laertes,
That thy rebellion looks so giant-like?
Let him go, Gertrude, do not fear° our person:
There's such divinity doth hedge a king
That treason can but peep to what it would,°
Acts little of his will. Tell me, Laertes,
Why thou art thus incens'd. Let him go, Gertrude.
Speak, man.
LAERTES: Where is my father?
KING: Dead.
QUEEN: But not by him.
KING: Let him demand his fill.
LAERTES: How came he dead? I'll not be juggled with.
To hell, allegiance! vows, to the blackest devil!
Conscience and grace, to the profoundest pit!
I dare damnation. To this point I stand,
That both the worlds I give to negligence,°
Let come what comes, only I'll be reveng'd
Most throughly° for my father.
KING: Who shall stay you?
LAERTES: My will, not all the world's:°
And for my means, I'll husband them so well,
They shall go far with little.
KING: Good Laertes,
If you desire to know the certainty

°*counter:* On the wrong scent (literally, following the scent backward). °*fear:* Fear for. °*would:* Would like to do. °*both . . . negligence:* I don't care what the consequences are in this world or in the next. °*thoroughly:* Thoroughly. °*world's:* World's will.

Of your dear father, is't writ in your revenge
That, swoopstake,° you will draw both friend and foe,
Winner or loser?

LAERTES: None but his enemies.

KING: Will you know them then?

LAERTES: To his good friends thus wide I'll ope my arms,
And like the kind life-rendoring pelican,°
Repast them with my blood.

KING: Why, now you speak
Like a good child° and a true gentleman.
That I am guiltless of your father's death,
And am most sensibly° in grief for it,
It shall as level° to your judgment 'pear
As day does to your eye.
(*a noise within:*) "Let her come in!"

LAERTES: How now, what noise is that?

Eenter Ophelia.

O heat, dry up my brains! tears seven times salt
Burn out the sense and virtue° of mine eye!
By heaven, thy madness shall be paid by weight
[Till] our scale turn the beam. O rose of May!
Dear maid, kind sister, sweet Ophelia!
O heavens, is't possible a young maid's wits
Should be as mortal as [an old] man's life?
[Nature is fine in° love, and where 'tis fine,
It sends some precious instance° of itself
After the thing it loves.]

OPHELIA: "They bore him barefac'd on the *Song.*
bier,
[Hey nor nonny, nonny, hey nonny,]
And in his grave rain'd many a tear"—
Fare you well, my dove!

LAERTES: Hadst thou thy wits and didst persuade° revenge,
It could not move thus.

OPHELIA: You must sing, "A down-a-down," and you call him a-down-a.° O, how the wheel° becomes it! It is the false steward, that stole his master's daughter.

LAERTES: This nothing's more than matter.°

°*swoopstake:* Sweeping up everything without discrimination (modern *sweepstake*). °*pelican:* The female pelican was believed to draw blood from her own breast to nourish her young. °*good child:* Faithful son. °*sensibly:* Feelingly. °*level:* Plain. °*virtue:* Faculty. °*fine in:* Refined or spiritualized by. °*instance:* Proof, token. So delicate is Ophelia's love for her father that her sanity has pursued him into the grave. °*persuade:* Argue logically for. °*and . . . a-down-a:* "If he indeed agrees that Polonius is 'a-down,' fallen low" (Dover Wilson). °*wheel:* Refrain (?) or spinning-wheel, at which women sang ballads (?). °*matter:* Lucid speech.

Ophelia: There's rosemary, that's for remembrance; pray you, love, remember.
And there is pansies, that's for thoughts.
Laertes: A document in madness,° thoughts and remembrance fitted.
Ophelia [*to Claudius*]**:** There's fennel for you, and columbines.° [*to Gertrude*] There's rue° for you, and here's some of me of we may call it herb-grace a' Sundays. You may wear your rue with a difference.° There's a daisy.° I would give you some violets, but they wither'd all when my father died. They say, 'a made a good end— [*Sings*]
"For bonny sweet Robin is all my joy."
Laertes: Thought° and afflictions, passion, hell itself,
She turns to favor° and to prettiness.
Ophelia: And will 'a not come again? *Song.*
And will 'a not come again?
No, no, he is dead,
Go to thy death-bed,
He never will come again.
"His beard was as white as snow,
[All] flaxen° was his pole,°
He is gone, he is gone,
And we cast away moan,
God 'a' mercy on his soul!"

And of all Christian's souls, [I pray God]. God buy you. [*Exit.*]

Laertes: Do you [see] this, O God?
King: Laertes, I must commune with your grief,
Or you deny me right. Go but apart,
Make choice of whom your wisest friends you will,
And they shall hear and judge 'twixt you and me.
If by direct or by collateral° hand
They find us touch'd,° we will our kingdom give,
Our crown, our life, and all that we call ours,
To you in satisfaction; but if not,
Be you content to lend your patience to us,
And we shall jointly labor with your soul
To give it due content.
Laertes: Let this be so.
His means of death, his obscure funeral—

°*A document in madness:* A lesson contained in mad talk. °*fennel, columbines:* Symbols respectively of flattery and ingratitude. °*rue:* Symbolic of sorrow and repentance. °*with a difference:* To represent a different cause of sorrow. *Difference* is a term from heraldry, meaning a variation in a coat of arms made to distinguish different members of a family. °*daisy, violets:* Symbolic respectively of dissembling and faithfulness. It is not clear who are the recipients of these. °*Thought:* Melancholy. °*favor:* Grace; charm. °*flaxen:* White. °*pole:* Poll, head. °*collateral:* Indirect. °*touch'd:* Guilty.

No trophy,° sword, nor hatchment° o'er his bones,
No noble rite nor formal ostentation°—
Cry to be heard, as 'twere from heaven to earth,
That° I must call't in question.

KING: So you shall,
And where th' offense is, let the great axe fall.
I pray you, go with me.

Exeunt.

[SCENE 6]°

Enter Horatio and others.

HORATIO: What are they that would speak with me?

GENTLEMAN: Sea-faring men, sir. They say they have letters for you.

HORATIO: Let them come in. [*Exit Gentleman.*]
I do not know from what part of the world
I should be greeted, if not from Lord Hamlet.

Enter Sailors.

[1.] SAILOR: God bless you, sir.

HORATIO: Let him bless thee too.

[1.] SAILOR: 'A shall, sir, and['t] please him. There's a letter for you, sir—it came from th' embassador that was bound for England—if your name be Horatio, as I am let to know it is.

HORATIO [*reads*]: "Horatio, when thou shalt have overlook'd this, give these fellows some means to the King, they have letters for him. Ere we were two days old at sea, a pirate of very warlike appointment gave us chase. Finding ourselves too slow of sail, we put on a compell'd valor, and in the grapple I boarded them. On the instant they got clear of our ship, so I alone became their prisoner. They have dealt with me like thieves of mercy,° but they knew what they did: I am to do a [good] turn for them. Let the King have the letters I have sent, and repair thou to me with as much speed as thou wouldst fly death. I have words to speak in thine ear will make thee dumb, yet are they much too light for the [bore°] of the matter. These good fellows will bring thee where I am. Rosencrantz and Guildenstern hold their course for England, of them I have much to tell thee. Farewell.

[He] that thou knowest thine,

Hamlet."

Come, I will [give] you way for these your letters,
And do't the speedier that you may direct me
To him from whom you brought them.

Exeunt.

°*trophy:* Memorial. °*hatchment:* Heraldic memorial tablet. °*formal ostentation:* Fitting and customary ceremony. °*That:* So that. °*4. 6. Location:* The castle. °*thieves of mercy:* Merciful thieves. °*bore:* Calibre, size (gunnery term).

[SCENE 7]°

Enter King and Laertes.

KING: Now must your conscience my acquittance° seal,
And you must put me in your heart for friend,
Sith you have heard, and with a knowing ear,
That he which hath your noble father slain
Pursued my life.

LAERTES: It well appears. But tell me
Why you [proceeded] not against these feats°
So criminal and so capital in nature,
As by your safety,° greatness, wisdom, all things else
You mainly° were stirr'd up.

KING: O, for two special reasons,
Which may to you perhaps seem much unsinow'd,°
But yet to me th' are strong. The Queen his mother
Lives almost by his looks, and for myself—
My virtue or my plague, be it either which°—
She is so [conjunctive°]—to my life and soul,
That, as the star moves not but in his sphere,°
I could not but by her. The other motive,
Why to a public count° I might not go,
Is the great love the general gender° bear him,
Who, dipping all his faults in their affection,
Work like the spring that turneth wood to stone,
Convert his gyves° to graces, so that my arrows,
Too slightly timber'd for so [loud a wind],
Would have reverted to my bow again,
But not where I have aim'd them.

LAERTES: And so have I a noble father lost,
A sister driven into desp'rate terms,°
Whose worth, if praises may go back again,°
Stood challenger on mount° of all the age
For her perfections—but my revenge will come.

KING: Break not your sleeps for that.° You must not think
That we are made of stuff so flat° and dull
That we can let our beard be shook° with° danger,

°*4.7. Location:* The castle. °*my acquittance seal:* ratify my acquittal; i.e., acknowledge my innocence in Polonius's death. °*feats:* Acts. °*safety:* Regard for your own safety. °*mainly:* Powerfully. °*unsinow'd:* Unsinewed, weak. °*either which:* One or the other. °*conjunctive:* Closely joined. °*in his sphere:* By the movement of the sphere in which it is fixed (as the Ptolemaic astronomy taught). °*count:* Reckoning. °*the general gender:* Everybody. °*gyves:* Fetters. °*terms:* Condition. °*go back again:* Refer to what she was before she went mad. °*on mount:* Preeminent. °*for that:* For fear of losing your revenge. °*flat:* Spiritless. °*let . . . shook:* To ruffle or tweak a man's beard was an act of insolent defiance that he could not disregard without loss of honor. Cf. 2.2.521. °*with:* By.

And think it pastime. You shortly shall hear more.
I lov'd your father, and we love ourself,
And that, I hope, will teach you to imagine —

Enter a Messenger with letters.

[How now! what news?

MESSENGER: Letters, my lord, from Hamlet:]
These to your Majesty, this to the Queen.

KING: From Hamlet! Who brought them?

MESSENGER: Sailors, my lord, they say, I saw them not,
They were given me by Claudio. He receiv'd them
Of him that brought them.

KING: Laertes, you shall hear them.
— Leave us. [*Exit Messenger.*]

[*reads*] "High and mighty, You shall know I am set naked° on your kingdom. To-morrow shall I beg leave to see your kingly eyes, when I shall, first asking you pardon thereunto,° recount the occasion of my sudden [and more strange] return.

[Hamlet]"

What should this mean? Are all the rest come back?
Or is it some abuse,° and no such thing?

LAERTES: Know you the hand?

KING: 'Tis Hamlet's character. °Naked"!
And in a postscript here he says, "alone."
Can you devise me?°

LAERTES: I am lost in it, my lord. But let him come,
It warms the very sickness in my heart
That I [shall] live and tell him to his teeth,
"Thus diddest thou."

KING: If it be so, Laertes —
As how should it be so? how otherwise?° —
Will you be rul'd by me?

LAERTES: Ay, my lord,
So° you will not o'errule me to a peace.

KING: To thine own peace. If he be now returned,
As [checking] at° his voyage, and that he means
No more to undertake it. I will work him
To an exploit, now ripe in my device,
Under the which he shall not choose but fall;

°*naked:* Destitute. °*pardon thereunto:* Permission to do so. °*abuse:* Deceit. °*character:* Handwriting. °*devise me:* Explain it to me. °*As . . . otherwise:* How can he have come back? Yet he obviously has. °*So:* Provided that. °*checking at:* Turning from (like a falcon diverted from its quarry by other prey).

And for his death no wind of blame shall breathe,
But even his mother shall uncharge the practice,°
And call it accident.

LAERTES: My lord, I will be rul'd,
The rather if you could devise it so
That I might be the organ.°

KING: It falls right.
You have been talk'd of since your travel much,
And that in Hamlet's hearing, for a quality°
Wherein they say you shine. Your sum of parts°
Did not together pluck such envy from him
As did that one, and that, in my regard,
Of the unworthiest° siege.°

LAERTES: What part is that, my lord?

KING: A very riband in the cap of youth,
Yet needful too, for youth no less becomes
The light and careless livery that it wears
Than settled age his sables and his weeds,°
Importing health and graveness.° Two months since
Here was a gentleman of Normandy:
I have seen myself, and serv'd against, the French,
And they can well on horseback,° but this gallant
Had witchcraft in't, he grew unto his seat,
And to such wondrous doing brought his horse,
As had he been incorps'd° and demi-natur'd°
With the brave beast. So far he topp'd [my] thought,
That I in forgery° of shapes and tricks
Come short of what he did.

LAERTES: A Norman was't?

KING: A Norman.

LAERTES: Upon my life, Lamord.

KING: The very same.

LAERTES: I know him well. He is the brooch° indeed
And gem of all the nation.

KING: He made confession of you,°
And gave you such a masterly report
For art and exercise in your defense,
And for your rapier most especial,

°*uncharge the practice:* Adjudge the plot no plot, fail to see the plot. °*organ:* Instrument, agent. °*quality:* Skill. °*Your . . . parts:* All your (other) accomplishments put together. °*unworthiest:* Least important (with no implication of unsuitableness). °*siege:* Status, position. °*weeds:* Characteristic) garb. °*Importing . . . graveness:* Signifying prosperity and dignity. °*can . . . horseback:* Are excellent riders. °*incorps'd:* Made one body. °*demi-natur'd:* Become half of a composite animal. °*forgery:* Mere imagining. °*brooch:* Ornament (worn in the hat). °*made . . . you:* Acknowledged your excellence.

That he cried out 'twould be a sight indeed
If one could match you. The scrimers° of their nation
He swore had neither motion, guard, nor eye,
If you oppos'd them. Sir, this report of his
Did Hamlet so envenom with his envy
That he could nothing do but wish and beg
Your sudden° coming o'er to play with you.
Now, out of this—

LAERTES: What out of this, my lord?

KING: Laertes, was your father dear to you?
Or are you like the painting of a sorrow,
A face without a heart?

LAERTES: Why ask you this?

KING: Not that I think you did not love your father,
But that I know love is begun by time,°
And that I see, in passages of proof,°
Time qualifies° the spark and fire of it.
There lives within the very flame of love
A kind of week° or snuff that will abate it,
And nothing is at a like goodness still,°
For goodness, growing to a plurisy,°
Dies in his own too much.° That we would do,
We should do when we would; for this "would" changes,
And hath abatements and delays as many
As there are tongues, are hands, are accidents,
And then this "should" is like a spendthrift's sigh,°
That hurts by easing.° But to the quick of th' ulcer:
Hamlet comes back. What would you undertake
To show yourself in deed your father's son
More than in words?

LAERTES: To cut his throat i' th' church.

KING: No place indeed should murder sanctuarize,°
Revenge should have no bounds. But, good Laertes,
Will you do this,° keep close within your chamber.
Hamlet return'd shall know you are come home,
We'll put on those° shall praise your excellence,
And set a double varnish° on the fame
The Frenchman gave you, bring you in fine° together,

°*scrimers:* Fencers. °*sudden:* Speedy. °*time:* A particular set of circumstances. °*in . . . proof:* By the test of experience, by actual examples. °*qualifies:* Moderates. °*week:* Wick. °*nothing . . . still:* Nothing remains forever at the same pitch of perfection. °*plurisy:* Plethora (a variant spelling of *pleurisy,* which was erroneously related to *plus,* stem *plur,* "more, overmuch"). °*too much:* Excess. °*spendthrift's sigh:* A sigh was supposed to draw blood from the heart. °*hurts by easing:* Injures us at the same time that it gives us relief. °*sanctuarize:* Offer asylum to. °*Will . . . this:* If you want to undertake this. °*put on those:* Incite those who. °*double varnish:* Second coat of varnish. °*in fine:* Finally.

And wager o'er yours heads. He, being remiss,°
Most generous,° and free from all contriving,°
Will not peruse° the foils so that with ease,
Or with a little shuffling,° you may choose
A sword unbated,°and, in a [pass] of practice°
Requite him for your father.

LAERTES: I will do't
And for [that] purpose I'll anoint my sword.
I bought an unction° of a mountebank,°
So mortal° that, but dip a knife in it,
Where it draws blood, no cataplasm° so rare,
Collected from all simples° that have virtue°
Under the moon, can save the thing from death
That is but scratch'd withal. I'll touch my point
With this contagion, that if I gall° him slightly,
It may be death.

KING: Let's further think of this,
Weigh what convenience both of time and means
May fit us to our shape.° If this should fail,
And that our drift° look through° our bad performance,
'Twere better not assay'd; therefore this project
Should have a back or second,° that might hold
If this did blast in proof.° Soft, let me see.
We'll make a solemn wager on your cunnings—
I ha't!
When in your motion you are hot and dry—
As° make your bouts more violent to that end—
And that he calls for drink, I'll have preferr'd° him
A chalice for the nonce,° whereon but sipping,
If he by chance escape your venom'd stuck,°
Our purpose may hold there. But stay, what noise?

Enter Queen.

QUEEN: One woe doth tread upon another's heel,
So fast they follow. Your sister's drown'd, Laertes.

LAERTES: Drown'd! O, where?

°*remiss:* Careless, overtrustful. °*generous:* Noble-minded. °*free . . . contriving:* Innocent of sharp practices. °*peruse:* Examine. °*shuffling:* Cunning exchange. °*unbated:* Not blunted. °*pass of practice:* Tricky thrust. °*unction:* Ointment. °*mountebank:* Traveling quack-doctor. °*mortal:* Deadly. °*cataplasm:* Poultice. °*simples:* Medicinal herbs. °*virtue:* Curative power. °*gall:* Graze. °*fit . . . shape:* Suit our purposes best. °*drift:* purpose. °*look through:* Become visible, be detected. °*back or second:* A second plot in reserve for emergency. °*blast in proof:* Blow up while being tried (an image from gunnery). °*As:* And you should. °*preferr'd:* Offered to. Most editors adopt the F1 reading *prepar'd.* °*nonce:* Occasion. °*stuck:* Thrust (from *stoccado,* a fencing term).

Queen: There is a willow grows askaunt° the brook,
That shows his hoary° leaves in the glassy stream,
Therewith° fantastic garlands did she make
Of crow-flowers, nettles, daisies, and long purples°
That liberal° shepherds give a grosser name,
But our cull-cold° maids do dead men's fingers call them.
There on the pendant boughs her cownet° weeds
Clamb'ring to hang, an envious sliver° broke,
When down her weedy trophies and herself
Fell in the weeping brook. Her clothes spread wide,
And mermaid-like awhile they bore her up,
Which time she chaunted snatches of old lauds,°
As one incapable° of her own distress,
Or like a creature native and indued°
Unto that element. But long it could not be
Till that her garments, heavy with their drink,
Pull'd the poor wretch from her melodious lay
To muddy death.
Laertes: Alas, then, she is drown'd?
Queen: Drown'd, drown'd.
Laertes: Too much of water hast thou, poor Ophelia,
And therefore I forbid my tears; but yet
It° is our trick,° Nature her custom holds,
Let shame say what it will; when these° are gone,
The woman will be out.° Adieu, my lord,
I have a speech a' fire that fain would blaze,
But that this folly drowns it. (*Exit.*)
King: Let's follow, Gertrude.
How much I had to do to calm his rage!
Now fear I this will give it start again,
Therefore let's follow.

Exeunt.

ACT 5

SCENE 1°

Enter two Clowns° [with spades and mattocks].

1. Clown: Is she to be buried in Christian burial when she willfully seeks her own salvation?

°*askaunt:* Sideways over. °*hoary:* Grey-white. °*Therewith:* With willow branches. °*long purples:* Wild orchids. °*liberal:* Free-spoken. °*cull-cold:* Chaste. °*crownet:* Made into coronets. °*envious silver:* Malicious branch. °*lauds:* Hymns. °*incapable:* Insensible. °*indued:* Habituated. °*It:* Weeping. °*trick:* Natural way. °*these:* These tears. °*The woman . . . out:* My womanish traits will be gone for good. °*5.1. Location:* A churchyard. °*Clowns:* Rustics.

2. CLOWN: I tell thee she is, therefore make her grave straight.° The crowner° hath sate on her, and finds it Christian burial.

1. CLOWN: How can that be, unless she drown'd herself in her own defense?

2. CLOWN: Why, 'tis found so.

1. CLOWN: It must be [*se offendendo*],° it cannot be else. For here lies the point: if I drown myself wittingly, it argues an act, and an act hath three branches—it is to act, to do, to perform; [argal],° she drown'd herself wittingly.

2. CLOWN: Nay, but hear you, goodman delver—

1. CLOWN: Give me leave. Here lies the water; good. Here stands the man; good. If the man go to this water and drown himself, it is, will he, nill he,° he goes, mark you that. But if the water come to him and drown him, he drowns not himself; argal, he that is not guilty of his own death shortens not his own life.°

2. CLOWN: But is this law?

1. CLOWN: Ay, marry, is't—crowner's quest° law.

2. CLOWN: Will you ha' the truth an't? If this had not been a gentlewoman, she should have been buried out a' Christian burial.

1. CLOWN: Why, there thou say'st, and the more pity that great folk, should have count'nance in this world to drown or hang themselves, more than their even-Christen.° Come, my spade. There is no ancient gentlemen but gard'ners, ditchers, and grave-makers; they hold up Adam's profession.

2. CLOWN: Was he a gentleman?

1. CLOWN: 'A was the first that ever bore arms.

2. CLOWN: Why, he had none.°

1. CLOWN: What, art a heathen? How dost thou understand the Scripture? The Scripture says Adam digg'd could he dig without arms?] I'll put another question to thee. If thou answerest me not to the purpose, confess thyself—

2. CLOWN: Go to.

1. CLOWN: What is he that builds stronger than either the mason, the shipwright, or the carpenter?

2. CLOWN: The gallows-maker, for that outlives a thousand tenants.

1. CLOWN: I like thy wit well, in good faith. The gallows does well; but how does it well? it does well to those that do ill. Now thou dost ill to say the gallows is built stronger than the church; argal, the gallows may do well to thee. To't again, come.

2. CLOWN: Who builds stronger than a mason, a shipwright, or a carpenter?

1. CLOWN: Ay, tell me that, and unyoke.°

2. CLOWN: Marry, now I can tell.

°*straight:* Immediately. °*crowner:* Coroner. °*se offendendo:* Blunder for *se defendendo,* "in self-defense." °*argal:* Blunder for *ergo,* "therefore." °*Here . . . life*: Alluding to a very famous suicide case, that of Sir James Hales, a judge who drowned himself in 1554; it was long cited in the courts. The clown gives a garbled account of the defense summing-up and the verdict. °*nill he:* Will he not. °*quest:* Inquest. °*even-Christen:* Fellow-Christians. °*none:* No coat of arms. °*unyoke:* Cease to labor, call it a day.

1. CLOWN: To't.
2. CLOWN: Mass,° I cannot tell.

Enter Hamlet and Horatio [after off].

1. CLOWN: Cudgel thy brains no more about it, for your dull ass will not mend his pace with beating, and when you are ask'd this question next, say "a grave-maker" the houses he makes lasts till doomsday. Go get thee in, and fetch me a sup of liquor.

[*Exit Second Clown.First clown digs.*]

"In youth when I did love, did love, *Song*
Methought it was very sweet,
To contract—O—the time for—a—my behove,°
O, methought there—a—was nothing—a—meet."

HAMLET: Has this fellow no feeling of his business? 'a sings in grave-making.
HORATIO: Custom° hath made it in him a property of easiness.°
HAMLET: 'Tis e'en so, the hand of little employment hath the daintier sense.°
1. CLOWN: "But age with his stealing steps *Song*
Hath clawed me in his clutch,
And hath shipped me into the land,
As if I had never been such."

[*throws up a shovelful of earth with a skull in it*]

HAMLET: That skull had a tongue in it, and could sing once. How the knave jowls° it to the ground, as if 'twere Cain's jaw-bone, that did the first murder! This might be the pate of a politician,° which this ass now o'er-reaches,° one that would circumvent God,° might it not?
HORATIO: It might, my lord.
HAMLET: Or of a courtier, which could say, "Good morrow, sweet lord! How dost thou, sweet lord?" This might be my Lord Such-a-one, that prais'd my Lord Such-a-one's horse when 'a [meant] to beg it, might it not?
HORATIO: Ay, my lord.
HAMLET: Why, e'en so, and now my Lady Worm's, chopless,° and knock'd about the [mazzard]° with a sexton's spade. Here's fine revolution,° and° we had the trick° to see't. Did these bones cost° no more the breeding, but to play at loggats° with them? Mine ache to think on't.

°*Mass:* By the mass. °*contract . . . behove:* Shorten, spend agreeably . . . advantage. The song, punctuated by the grunts of the clown as he digs, is a garbled version of a poem by Thomas Lord Vaux, entitled "The Aged Lover Renounceth Love." °*Custom:* Habit. °*a property of easiness:* A thing he can do with complete ease of mind. °*daintier sense:* More delicate sensitivity. °*jowls:* Dashes. °*politician:* Schemer, intriguer. °*o'er-reaches:* Gets the better of (with play on the literal sense). °*circumvent God:* Bypass God's law. °*chopless:* Lacking the lower jaw. °*mazzard:* Head °*revolution:* Change. °*and:* If. °*trick:* Knack, ability. °*Did . . . cost:* Were . . . worth. °*loggats:* A game in which blocks of wood were thrown at a stake.

1. Clown: "A pickaxe and a spade, a spade, *(song)*
For and a shrouding sheet:
O, a pit of clay for to be made
For such a guest is meet."
[*throws up another skull*].

Hamlet: There's another. Why may not that be the skull of a lawyer? Where be his quiddities° now, his quillities,° his cases, his tenures,° and his tricks? Why does he suffer this knave now to knock him about the sconce° mode with a dirty shovel, and will not tell him of his action of battery? Hum! This fellow might be in 's time a great buyer of land, with his statutes, his recognizances,° his fines, his double vouchers, his recoveries. [Is this the fine° of his fines, and the recovery of his recoveries,] to have his fine pate full of fine dirt? Will [his] vouchers vouch him no more of his purchases, and [double ones too], than the length and breadth of a pair of indentures?° The very conveyances° of his lands will scarcely lie in this box,° and must th' inheritor° himself have no more, ha?

Horatio: Not a jot more, my lord.

Hamlet: Is not parchment made of sheep-skins?

Horatio: Ay, my lord, and of calves'-skins too.

Hamlet: They are sheep and calves which seek out assurance in that. I will speak to this fellow. Whose grave's this, sirrah?°

1. Clown: Mine, sir. [*sings*]
"[O]", a pit of clay for to be made
[For such a guest is meet]."

Hamlet: I think it be thine indeed, for thou liest in't.

1. Clown: You lie out on't, sir, and therefore 'tis not yours; for my part, I do not lie in't, yet it is mine.

Hamlet: Thou dost lie in't, to be in't, and say it is thine. 'Tis for the dead, not for the quick; therefore thou liest.

1. Clown: 'Tis a quick lie, sir, 'twill away again from me to you.

Hamlet: What man dost thou dig it for?

1. Clown: For no man, sir.

Hamlet: What woman then?

1. Clown: For none neither.

Hamlet: Who is to be buried in't?

1. Clown: One that was a woman, sir, but, rest her soul, she's dead.

°*quiddities:* Subtleties, quibbles. °*quillities:* Fine distinctions. °*tenures:* Titles to real estate. °*sconce:* Head. °*statutes, recognizances:* Bonds securing debts by attaching land and property. °*fines, recoveries:* Procedures for converting an entailed estate to freehold °*double vouchers:* documents guaranteeing title to real estate, signed by two persons. °*fine:* End. °*pair of indentures:* Legal document cut into two parts which fitted together on a serrated edge. Perhaps Hamlet thus refers to the two rows of teeth in the skull, or to the bone sutures. °*conveyances:* Documents relating to transfer of property. °*this box:* The skull itself. °*inheritor:* Owner. °*sirrah:* Term of address to inferiors.

HAMLET: How absolute° the knave is! we must speak by the card,° or equivocation° will undo us. By the Lord, Horatio, this three years I have took note of it: the age is grown so pick'd° that the toe of the peasant comes so near the heel of the courtier, he galls his kibe.° How long hast thou been grave maker?

1. CLOWN: Of [all] the days i' th' year, I came to't that day that our last king Hamlet overcame Fortinbras.

HAMLET: How long is that since?

1. CLOWN: Cannot you tell that? Every fool can tell that. It was the very day that young Hamlet was born—he that is mad, and sent into England.

HAMLET: Ay, marry, why was he sent into England?

1. CLOWN: Why, because 'a was mad. 'A shall recover his wits there, or if'a do not, 'tis no great matter there.

HAMLET: Why?

1. CLOWN: 'Twill not be seen in him there, there the men are as mad as he.

HAMLET: How came he mad?

1. CLOWN: Very strangely, they say.

HAMLET: How strangely?

1. CLOWN: Faith, e'en with losing his wits.

HAMLET: Upon what ground?

1. CLOWN: Why, here in Denmark. I have been sexton here, man and boy, thirty years.

HAMLET: How long will a man lie i' th' earth ere he rot?

1. CLOWN: Faith, if 'a be not rotten before 'a die'—as we have many pocky° corses, that will scarce hold the laying in°—'a will last you some eight year or nine year. A tanner will last you nine year.

HAMLET: Why he more than another?

1. CLOWN: Why, sir, his hide is so tann'd with his trade that 'a will keep out water a great while, and your water is a sore decayer of your whoreson dead body. Here's a skull now hath lien you i' th' earth three and twenty years.

HAMLET: Whose was it?

1. CLOWN: A whoreson mad fellow's it was. Whose do you think it was?

HAMLET: Nay, I know not.

1. CLOWN: A pestilence on him for a mad rogue! 'a pour'd a flagon of Rhenish on my head once. This same skull, sir, was, sir, Yorick's skull, the King's jester.

HAMLET: This? [*takes the skull*]

1. CLOWN: E'en that.

HAMLET: Alas, poor Yorick! I knew him, Horatio, a fellow of infinite jest, of most excellent fancy. He hath bore me on his back a thousand times, and now how abhorr'd in my imagination it is! my gorge rises at it. Here hung

°*absolute:* Positive. °*by the card:* By the compass, punctiliously. °*equivocation:* Ambiguity. °*pick'd:* Refined. °*galls his kibe:* Rubs the courtier's chilblain. °*pocky:* Rotten with venereal disease. °*hold: . . . in:* Last out the burial.

those lips that I have kiss'd I know not how oft. Where be your gibes now, your gambols, your songs, your flashes of merriment, that were wont to set the table on a roar? Not one now to mock your own grinning—quite chop-fall'n.° Now get you to my lady's [chamber], and tell her, let her paint an inch thick, to this favor° she must come; make her laugh at that. Prithee, Horatio, tell me one thing.

Horatio: What's that, my lord?

Hamlet: Dost thou think Alexander look'd a' this fashion i' th' earth?

Horatio: E'en so.

Hamlet: And smelt so? pah! [*puts down the skull*]

Horatio: E'en so, my lord.

Hamlet: To what base uses we may return, Horatio! Why may not imagination trace the noble dust of Alexander, till 'a find it stopping a bunghole?

Horatio: 'Twere to consider too curiously,° to consider so.

Hamlet: No, faith, not a jot, but to follow him thither with modesty° enough and likelihood to lead it: Alexander died, Alexander was buried, Alexander returneth to dust, the dust is earth, of earth we make loam,° and why of that loam whereto he was converted might they not stop a beer-barrel?
Imperious° Caesar, dead and turn'd to clay,
Might stop a hole to keep the wind away.
O that that earth which kept the world in awe
Should patch a wall t' expel the [winter's] flaw!°
But soft, but soft, awhile here, comes the King,

Enter King, Queen, Laertes, and [a Doctor of Divinity, following] the corse, [with Lords attendant].

The Queen, the courtiers. Who is this they follow?
And with such maimed rites?° This doth betoken
The corse they follow did with desp'rate hand
Foredo° it° own life. 'Twas of some estate.°
Couch we° a while and mark. [*retiring with Horatio*]

Laertes: What ceremony else?

Hamlet: That is Laertes, a very noble youth. Mark.

Laertes: What ceremony else?

Doctor: Her obsequies have been as far enlarg'd
As we have warranty. Her death was doubtful,°
And but that great command o'ersways the order,°
She should° in ground unsanctified have lodg'd

°*chop-fall'n:* (1) Lacking the lower jaw; (2) downcast. °*favor:* Appearance. °*curiously:* Closely, minutely. °*modesty:* Moderation. °*loam:* A mixture of moistened clay with sand, straw, etc. °*Imperious:* Imperial. °*flaw:* Gust. °*maimed rites:* lack of customary ceremony. °*Foredo:* Fordo, destroy. °*it:* Its. °*estate:* Rank. °*Couch we:* Let us conceal ourselves. °*doubtful:* The subject of an "open verdict." °*order:* Customary procedure. °*should:* Would certainly.

Till the last trumpet; for° charitable prayers,
[Shards,] flints, and pebbles, should be thrown on her.
Yet here she is allow'd her virgin crants,°
Her maiden strewments,° and the bringing home
Of bell and burial.°

LAERTES: Must there no more be done?

DOCTOR: No more be done:
We should profane the service of the dead
To sing a requiem° and such rest to her
As to peace-parted souls.

LAERTES: Lay her i' th' earth,
And from her fair and unpolluted flesh
May violets spring! I tell thee, churlish priest,
A minist'ring angel shall my sister be
When thou liest howling.

HAMLET: What, the fair Ophelia!

QUEEN [*scattering flowers*]**:** Sweets° to the sweet, farewell!
I hop'd thou shouldst have been my Hamlet's wife.
I thought thy bride-bed to have deck'd, sweet maid,
And not have strew'd thy grave.

LAERTES: O, treble woe
Fall ten times [treble] on that cursed head
Whose wicked deed thy most ingenious° sense
Depriv'd thee of! Hold off the earth a while,
Till I have caught her once more in mine arms.

[*leaps in the grave*]

Now pile your dust upon the quick and dead,
Till of this flat a mountain you have made
T' o'ertop old Pelion, or the skyish head
Of blue Olympus.°

HAMLET [*coming forward*]**:** What is he whose grief
Bears such an emphasis, whose phrase° of sorrow
Conjures° the wand'ring stars° and makes them stand
Like wonder-wounded hearers? This is I,
Hamlet the Dane.°

[*Hamlet leaps in after Laertes*.]

LAERTES: The devil take thy soul! [*grappling with him*]

°*for:* Instead of. °*crants:* Garland. °*maiden strewments:* Flowers scattered on the grave of an unmarried girl. °*bringing . . . burial:* Burial in consecrated ground, with the bell tolling. °*requiem:* Dirge. °*Sweets:* Flowers. °*ingenious:* Intelligent. °*Pelion, Olympus:* Mountains in northeastern Greece. °*emphasis, phrase:* Rhetorical terms, here used in disparaging reference to Laertes' inflated language. °*Conjures:* Puts a spell upon. °*wand'ring stars:* Planets. °*the Dane:* This title normally signifies the king.

HAMLET: Thou pray'st not well.
I prithee take thy fingers from my throat.
For though I am not splenitive° [and] rash,
Yet have I in me something dangerous,
Which let thy wisdom fear. Hold off thy hand!
KING: Pluck them asunder.
QUEEN: Hamlet! Hamlet!
ALL: Gentlemen!
HORATIO: Good my lord, be quiet.

[*The Attendants part them, and they come out of the grave.*]

HAMLET: Why, I will fight with him upon this theme
Until my eyelids will no longer wag.
QUEEN: O my son, what theme?
HAMLET: I lov'd Ophelia. Forty thousand brothers
Could not with all their quantity of love
Make up my sum. What wilt thou do for her?
KING: O, he is mad, Laertes.
QUEEN: For love of God, forbear him.
HAMLET: 'Swounds, show me what thou't° do.
Woo't° weep, woo't fight, woo't fast, woo't tear thyself?
Woo't drink up eisel,° eat a crocadile?°
I'll do't. Dost [thou] come here to whine?
To outface me with leaping in her grave?
Be buried quick with her, and so will I.
And if thou prate of mountains,° let them throw
Millions of acres on us, till our ground,
Singeing his pate against the burning zone,°
Make Ossa° like a wart! Nay, an thou'lt mouth,°
I'll rant as well as thou.
QUEEN: This is mere° madness,
And [thus] a while the fit will work on him;
Anon, as patient° as the female dove,
When that her golden couplets° are disclosed,°
His silence will sit drooping.
HAMLET: Hear you, sir,
What is the reason that you use me thus?
I lov'd you ever. But it is no matter.

°*splenitive:* Impetuous. °*thou't:* Thou wilt. °*Woo't:* Wilt thou. °*eisel:* Vinegar. °*crocadile:* Crocodile. °*if . . . mountains:* Referring to lines 203–205. °*burning zone:* Sphere of the sun. °*Ossa:* Another mountain in Greece, near Pelion and Olympus. °*mouth:* Talk bombast (synonymous with rant in the next line). °*mere:* Utter. °*patient:* Calm. °golden couplets: Pair of baby birds, covered with yellow down. °*disclosed:* Hatched.

Let Hercules himself do what he may,
The cat will mew, and dog will have his day.°

Exit Hamlet.

KING: I pray thee, good Horatio, wait upon him.

[Exit] Horatio.

[to Laertes] Strengthen your patience in° our last night's speech,
We'll put the matter to the present push.°—
Good Gertrude, set some watch over your son.
This grave shall have a living° monument.
An hour of quiet [shortly] shall we see,
Till then in patience our proceeding be.

Exeunt.

SCENE 2°

Enter Hamlet and Horatio.

HAMLET: So much for this, sir, now shall you see the other°—
You do remember all the circumstance?
HORATIO: Remember it, my lord!
HAMLET: Sir, in my heart there was a kind of fighting
That would not let me sleep. [Methought] I lay
Worse than the mutines° in the [bilboes°]. Rashly°
And prais'd be rashness for it—let us know°
Our indiscretion sometime serves us well
When our deep plots do pall,° and that should learn° us
There's a divinity that shapes our ends,°
Rough-hew them° how we will.—
HORATIO: That is most certain.
HAMLET: Up from my cabin,
My sea-gown scarf'd about me, in the dark
Grop'd I to find out them, had my desire,
Finger'd° their packet, and in fine withdrew
To mine own room again, making so bold,
My fears forgetting manners, to [unseal]

°*Let . . . day:* Nobody can prevent another from making the scenes he feels he has a right to. °*in:* By recalling. *present push:* Immediate test. °*living:* Enduring (?) or in the form of a lifelike effigy (?). °*5.2. Location:* The castle. °*see the other:* Hear the other news I have to tell you (hinted at in the letter to Horatio. 4.6. 19–20). °*mutines:* Mutineers (but the term *mutiny* was in Shakespeare's day used of almost any act of rebellion against authority). °*bilboes:* Fetters attached to a heavy iron bar. °*Rashly:* On impulse. °*know:* Recognize, acknowledge. °*pall:* Lose force, come to nothing. °*learn:* Teach. °*shapes our ends:* Gives final shape to our designs. °*Rough-hew them:* Block them out in initial form. °*Finger'd:* Filched, "pinched."

Their grand commission; where I found, Horatio—
Ah, royal knavery!—an exact command,
Larded° with many several sorts of reasons,
Importing° Denmark's health and England's too,
With, ho, such bugs and goblins in my life,°
That, on the supervise,° no leisure bated,°
No, not to stay° the grinding of the axe,
My head should be strook off.

HORATIO: Is't possible?

HAMLET: Here's the commission, read it at more leisure.
But wilt thou hear me how I did proceed?

HORATIO: I beseech you.

HAMLET: Being thus benetted round with [villainies],
Or° I could make a prologue to my brains,
They had begun the play. I sat me down,
Devis'd a new commission, wrote it fair.°
I once did hold it, as our statists° do,
A baseness° to write fair, and labor'd much
How to forget that learning, but, sir, now
I did me yeman's° service. Wilt thou know
Th' effect° of what I wrote?

HORATIO: Ay, good my lord.

HAMLET: An earnest conjuration from the King,
As England was his faithful tributary,
As love between them like the palm might flourish,
As peace should still her wheaten garland wear
And stand a comma° 'tween their amities,
And many such-like [as's] of great charge,°
That on the view and knowing of these contents,
Without debatement further, more or less,
He should those bearers put to sudden death,
Not shriving time° allow'd.

HORATIO: How was this seal'd?

HAMLET: Why, even in that was heaven ordinant.°
I had my father's signet in my purse,
Which was the model° of that Danish seal;
Folded the writ up in the form of th' other;
[Subscrib'd°] it, gave't th' impression, plac'd it safely,

°*Larded:* Garnished. °*Importing:* Relating to. °*bugs . . . life:* Terrifying things in prospect if I were permitted to remain alive; *bugs* = bugaboos. °*supervise:* Perusal. °*bated:* Deducted (from the stipulated speediness). °*stay:* Wait for. °*Or:* Before. °*fair:* In a beautiful hand (such as a professional scribe would use). °*statists:* Statesmen, public officials. °*A baseness:* A skill befitting of men of low rank. °*yeman's:* Yeoman's; solid, substantial. °*effect:* Purport, gist. °*comma:* Connective, link. °*as's . . . charge:* (1) Weighty clauses beginning with *as;* (2) asses with heavy loads. °*shriving time:* Time for confession and absolution. °*ordinant:* In charge, guiding. °*model:* Small copy. °*Subscrib'd:* Signed.

The changeling° never known.° Now the next day
Was our sea-fight, and what to this was sequent
Thou knowest already.

HORATIO: So Guildenstern and Rosencrantz go to't.°

HAMLET: [Why, man, they did make love to this employment,]
They are not near my conscience. Their defeat°
Does by their own insinuation° grow.
'Tis dangerous when the baser° nature comes
Between the pass° and fell° incensed points
Of mighty opposites.

HORATIO: Why, what a king is this!

HAMLET: Does it not, think thee, stand me now upon°—
He that hath kill'd my king and whor'd my mother,
Popp'd in between th' election° and my hopes,
Thrown out his angle° for my proper° life,
And with such coz'nage°—is't not perfect conscience
[To quit him° with this arm? And is't not to be damn'd,
To let this canker° of our nature come
In° further evil?

HORATIO: It must be shortly known to him from England
What is the issue of the business there.

HAMLET: It will be short; the interim's mine,
And a man's life's no more° than to say "one."°
But I am very sorry, good Horatio,
That to Laertes I forgot myself,
For by the image° of my cause I see
The portraiture of his. I'll [court] his favors.
But sure the bravery° of his grief did put me
Into a tow'ring passion.

HORATIO: Peace, who comes here?]

Enter [young Osric,] a courtier.

OSRIC: Your lordship is right welcome back to Denmark.

HAMLET: I [humbly] thank you, sir.—Dost know this water-fly?°

HORATIO: No, my good lord.

°*changeling:* Hamlet's letter, substituted secretly for the genuine letter, as fairies substituted their children for human children. °*never known:* Never recognized as a substitution (unlike the fairies' changelings). °*go to't:* Are going to their death. °*defeat:* Ruin, overthrow. °*insinuation:* Winding their way into the affair. °*baser:* Inferior. °*pass:* Thrust. °*fell:* Fierce. °*stand . . . upon:* Rest upon me as a duty. °*election:* As king of Denmark. °*angle:* Hook and line. °*proper:* Very. °*coz'nage:* Trickery. °*quit him:* Pay him back. °*canker:* Cancerous sore. °*come In:* Grow into. °*a man's . . . more*: To kill a man takes no more time. °*say "one."* Perhaps this is equivalent to "deliver one sword thrust"; see line 246 below, where Hamlet says. "One" as he makes the first hit. °*image:* Likeness. °*bravery:* Ostentatious expression. °*water-fly:* Tiny, vainly agitated creature.

HAMLET: Thy state is the more gracious,° for 'tis a vice to know him. He hath much land, and fertile; let a beast be lord of beasts, and his crib shall stand at the king's mess.° Tis a chough,° but, as I say, spacious in the possession of dirt.

OSRIC: Sweet lord, if your lordship were at leisure, I should impart a thing to you from his Majesty.

HAMLET: I will receive it, Sir, with all diligence of spirit. [Put] your bonnet° to his right use, 'tis for the head.

OSRIC: I thank your lordship, it is very hot.

HAMLET: No, believe me, 'tis very cold, the wind is northerly.

OSRIC: It is indifferent° cold, my lord, indeed.

HAMLET: But yet methinks it is very [sultry] and hot [for] my complexion.°

OSRIC: Exceedingly, my lord, it is very sultry,— as 'twere— I cannot tell how. My lord, his Majesty bade me signify to you that 'a has laid a great wager on your head. Sir, this is the matter—

HAMLET: I beseech you remember.

[*Hamlet moves him to put on his hat.*]

OSRIC: Nay, good my lord, for my ease,° in good faith. Sir, here is newly come to court Laertes, believe me, an absolute° [gentleman], full of most excellent differences,° of very soft° society, and great showing;° indeed, to speak sellingly° of him, he is the card or calendar° of gentry;° for you shall find in him the continent of what part° a gentleman would see.

HAMLET: Sir, his definement suffers no perdition° in you, though I know to divide him inventorially would dozy° th' the arithmetic of memory, and yet but yaw° neither° in respect of° his quick sail; but in the verity of extolment,° I take him to be a soul of great article,° and his infusion° of such dearth° and rareness as, to make true diction° of him, his semblable° is his mirror, and who else would trace him,° his umbrage,° nothing more.

OSRIC: Your lordship speaks most infallibly of him.

HAMLET: The concernancy,° sir? Why do we wrap the gentleman in our more rawer breath?°

°*gracious:* Virtuous. °*let . . . mess:* If a beast owned as many cattle as Osric, he could feast with the King. °*chough:* Jackdaw, a bird that could be taught to speak. °*bonnet:* Hat. °*indifferent:* Somewhat. °*complexion:* Temperament. °*for my ease:* I am really more comfortable with my hat off (a polite insistence on maintaining ceremony). °*absolute:* Complete, possessing every quality a gentleman should have. °*differences:* Distinguishing characteristics, personal qualities. °*soft:* Agreeable. °*great showing:* Splendid appearance. °*sellingly:* Like a seller to a prospective buyer; in a fashion to do full justice. Most editors follow Q3 in reading *feelingly* = with exactitude, as he deserves. °*card or calendar:* Chart or register, compendious guide. °*gentry:* Gentlemanly behavior. °*the continent . . . part:* One who contains every quality. °*perdition:* Loss. °*dozy:* Make dizzy. °*yaw:* Keep deviating erratically from its course (said of a ship). °*neither:* For all that. °*in respect of:* Compared with. °*in . . . extolment:* To praise him truly. °*article:* Scope (?) or importance (?). °*infusion:* Essence, quality. °*dearth:* Scarceness. °*make true diction:* Speak truly. °*his semblable:* His only likeness or equal. °*who . . . him:* Anyone else who tries to follow him. °*umbrage:* Shadow. °*concernancy:* Relevance. °*more rawer breath:* Words too crude to describe him properly.

Osric: Sir?

Horatio: Is't not possible to understand in another tongue?° You will to't, sir, really.°

Hamlet: What imports the nomination° of this gentleman?

Osric: Of Laertes?

Horatio: His purse is empty already: all 's golden words are spent.

Hamlet: Of him, sir.

Osric: I know you are not ignorant—

Hamlet: I would you did, sir, yet, in faith, if you did, it would not much approve° me. Well, sir?

Osric: You are not ignorant of what excellence Laertes is—

Hamlet: I dare not confess that, lest I should compare with him in excellence,° but° to know a man well were to know himself.°

Osric: I mean, sir, for [his] weapon, but in the imputation laid on him by them,° in his meed° he's unfellow'd.

Hamlet: What's his weapon?

Osric: Rapier and dagger.

Hamlet: That's two of his weapons—but well.

Osric: The King, sir, hath wager'd with him six Barbary horses, against the which he has impawn'd,° as I take it, six French rapiers and poniards, with their assigns,° as girdle, [hangers°], and so. Three of the carriages,° in faith, are very dear to fancy,° very responsive to° the hilts, most delicate carriages, and of very liberal conceit.°

Hamlet: What call you the carriages?

Horatio: I knew you must be edified by the margent° ere you had done.

Osric: The [carriages], sir, are the hangers.

Hamlet: The phrase would be more germane to the matter if we could carry a cannon by our sides; I would it [might be] hangers till then. But on: six Barb'ry horses against six French swords, their assigns, and three liberal-conceited carriages; that's the French bet against the Danish. Why is this all [impawn'd, as] you call it?

Osric: The King, sir, hath laid,° sir, that in a dozen passes between yourself and him, he shall not exceed you three hits;° he hath laid on twelve for nine;° and it would come to immediate trial, if your lordship would vouchsafe the answer.°

°*in another tongue:* When someone else is the speaker. °*You . . . really:* You can do it if you try. °*nomination:* Naming, mention. °*approve:* Commend. °*compare . . . excellence:* Seem to claim the same degree of excellence for myself. °*but:* The sense seems to require *for.* °*himself:* Onself. °*in. them:* In popular estimation. °*meed:* Merit. °*impawn'd:* Staked. °*assigns:* Appurtenances. °*hangers:* Straps on which the swords hang from the girdle. °*carriages:* Properly, gun-carriages; here used affectedly in place of *hangers.* °*fancy:* Taste. °*very responsive to:* Matching well. °*liberal conceit:* Elegant design. °*must . . . margent:* Would require enlightenment from a marginal note. °*laid:* Wagered. *he . . . hits:* Laertes must win by at least eight to four (if none of the "passes" or bouts are draws), since at seven to five he would be only two up. °*he . . . nine*: Not satisfactorily explained despite much discussion. One suggestion is that Laertes has raised the odds against himself by wagering that out of twelve bouts he will win nine. °*answer:* Encounter (as Hamlet's following quibble forces Osric to explain in his next speech).

HAMLET: How if I answer no?

OSRIC: I mean, my lord, the opposition of your person in trial.

HAMLET: Sir, I will walk here in the hall. If it please his Majesty, it is the breathing time of day with me.° Let the foils be brought, the gentleman willing, and the King hold his purpose, I will win for him and I can; if not, I will gain nothing but my shame and the odd hits.

OSRIC: Shall I deliver you so?

HAMLET: To this effect, sir—after what flourish° your nature will.

OSRIC: I commend my duty° to your lordship.

HAMLET: Yours. [*Exoit Osric.*]. ['A] does well to commend it himself, there are no tongues else for 's turn.

HORATIO: This lapwing° runs away with the shell on his head.

HAMLET: 'A did [comply], sir, with his dug° before 'a suck'd it. Thus has he, and many more of the same breed that I know the drossy° age dotes on, only got the tune of the time,° and out of an habit of encounter,° a kind of [yesty°] collection,° which carries them through and through the most [profound] and [winnow'd°] opinions,° and do but blow them to their trial,° the bubbles are out.°

Enter a Lord.

LORD: My lord, his Majesty commended him to you by young Osric, who brings back to him that you attend him in the hall. He sends to know if your pleasure hold to play with Laertes, or that you will take longer time.

HAMLET: I am constant to my purposes, they follow the King's pleasure. If his fitness speaks, mine is ready;° now or whensoever, provided I be so able as now.

LORD: The King and Queen and all are coming down.

HAMLET: In happy time.

LORD: The Queen desires you to use some gentle entertainment° to Laertes before you fall to play.

HAMLET: She well instructs me. [*Exit Lord.*]

HORATIO: You will lose, my lord.

HAMLET: I do not think so; since he went into France I have been in continual practice. I shall win at the odds. Thou wouldst not think how ill all's here about my heart—but it is no matter.

HORATIO: Nay, good my lord—

°*breathing . . . me:* My usual hour for exercise. °*after what flourish:* With whatever embellishment of language. °*commend my duty:* Offer my dutiful respects (but Hamlet picks up the phrase in the sense "praise my manner of bowing"). °*lapwing:* A foolish bird which upon hatching was supposed to run with part of the eggshell still over its head. (Osric has put his hat on at last.) °*comply . . . dug:* Bow politely to his mother's nipple. °*drossy:* Worthless. °*tune . . . time:* Fashionable ways of talk. °*habit of encounter:* Mode of social intercourse. *yesty:* Yeasty, frothy. °*collection:* Anthology of fine phrases. °*winnow'd:* Sifted choice. °*opinions:* Judgments. °*blow . . . trial:* Test them by blowing on them; make even the least demanding trial of them. °*out:* Blown away (?) or at an end, done for (?). °*If . . . ready:* If this is a good moment for him, it is for me also. °*gentle entertainment:* Courteous greeting.

HAMLET: It is but foolery, but it is such a kind of [gain-]giving,° as would perhaps trouble a woman.

HORATIO: If your mind dislike any thing, obey it. I will forestall their repair hither, and say you are not fit.

HAMLET: Not a whit, we defy augury. There's a special providence in the fall of a sparrow.° If it be [now], 'tis not to come; if it be not to come, it will be now; if it be not now, yet it [will] come — the readiness is all. Since no man, of aught° he leaves, knows what is't to leave betimes,° let be.

A table prepar'd, [and flangons of wine on it. Enter] Trumpets, Drums, and Officers with cushions, foils, daggers; King, Queen, Laertes, [Osric,] and all the State°

KING: Come, Hamlet, come, and take this hand from me.

[The King puts Laertes' hand into Hamlet's.]

HAMLET: Give me your pardon, sir. I have done you wrong,
But pardon't as you are a gentleman.
This presence° knows,
And you must needs have heard, how I am punish'd°
With sore distraction. What I have done
That might your nature, honor, and exception°
Roughly awake, I here proclaim was madness.
Was't Hamlet wrong'd Laertes? Never Hamlet!
If Hamlet from himself be ta'en away,
And when he's not himself does wrong Laertes,
Then Hamlet does it not, Hamlet denies it.
Who does it then? His madness. If't be so,
Hamlet is of the faction that is wronged,
His madness is poor Hamlet's enemy.
[Sir, in this audience,]
Let my disclaiming from a purpos'd evil°
Free° me so far in your most generous thoughts,
That I have shot my arrow o'er the house
And hurt my brother.

LAERTES: I am satisfied in nature,°
Whose motive in this case should stir me most
To my revenge, but in my terms of honor°
I stand aloof, and will no reconcilement
Till by some elder masters of known honor
I have a voice and precedent of peace

°*gain-giving:* Misgiving. °*special . . . sparrow:* See Matthew 10:29. °*of aught:* Whatever. °*knows . . . betimes:* Knows what is the best time to leave it. °*State:* Nobles. °*presence:* Assembled court. °*punish'd:* Afflicted. °*exception:* Objection. °*my . . . evil:* My declaration that I intended no harm. °*Free:* Absolve. °*in nature:* So far as my personal feelings are concerned. °*in . . . honor:* As a man governed by an established code of honor.

To [keep] my name ungor'd.° But [till] that time
I do receive your offer'd love like love,
And will not wrong it.

HAMLET: I embrace it freely,
And will this brothers'° wager frankly° play.
Give us the foils. [Come on.]

LAERTES: Come, one for me.

HAMLET: I'll be your foil,° Laertes; in mine ignorance
Your skill shall like a star i' th' darkest night
Stick fiery off° indeed.

LAERTES: You mock me, sir.

HAMLET: No, by this hand.

KING: Give them the foils, young Osric. Cousin Hamlet,
You know the wager?

HAMLET: Very well, my lord.
Your Grace hath laid the odds° a' th' weaker side.

KING: I do not fear it, I have seen you both;
But since he is [better'd],° we have therefore odds.°

LAERTES: This is too heavy; let me see another.

HAMLET: This likes° me well. These foils have all a length? [*Prepare to play.*]

OSRIC: Ay, my good lord.

KING: Set me the stoups° of wine upon that table.
If Hamlet give the first or second hit,
Or quit in answer of the third exchange,°
Let all the battlements their ord'nance fire.
The King shall drink to Hamlet's better breath,
And in the cup an [union°] shall he throw,
Richer than that which four successive kings
In Denmark's crown have worn. Give me the cups,
And let the kettle° to the trumpet speak,
The trumpet to the cannoneer without,
The cannons to the heavens, the heaven to earth,
"Now the King drinks to Hamlet." Come begin;

(*trumpets the while*)

And you, the judges, bear a wary eye.

HAMLET: Come on, sir.

LAERTES: Come, my lord.

°*have . . . ungor'd:* Can secure an opinion backed by precedent that I can make peace with you without injury to my reputation. °*brothers':* Amicable, as if between brothers. °*frankly:* Freely, without constraint. °*foil:* Thin sheet of metal placed behind a jewel to set it off. °*Stick. . . off:* Blaze out in contrast. °*laid the odds:* Wagered a higher stake (horses to rapiers). °*is better'd:* Has perfected his skill. °*odds:* The arrangement that Laertes must take more bouts than Hamlet to win. °*likes:* Pleases. °*a length:* The same length. °*stoups:* Tankards. °*quit . . . exchange:* Pays back wins by Laertes in the first and second bouts by taking the third. °*union:* An especially fine pearl. °*kettle:* Kettle-drum.

[*They play and Hamlet scores a bit*.]

Hamlet: One.
Laertes: No.
Hamlet: Judgment.
Osric: A hit, a very palpable hit.
Laertes: Well — again.
King: Stay, give me a drink. Hamlet, this pearl is thine,
Here's to thy health. Give him the cup.

(*Drum, trumpets* [*sound*] *flourish. A piece goes off* [*within*].)

Hamlet: I'll play this bout first, set it by a while.
Come. [*They play again*.] Another hit; what say you?
Laertes: [A touch, a touch,] I do confess 't.
King: Our son shall win.
Queen: He's fat,° and scant of breath.—
Here, Hamlet, take my napkin, rub thy brows.
The Queen carouses° to thy fortune, Hamlet.
Hamlet: Good madam!
King: Gertrude, do not drink.
Queen: I will, my lord, I pray you pardon me.
King [*aside*]: It is the pois'ned cup, it is too late.
Hamlet: I dare not drink yet, madam; by and by.
Queen: Come, let me wipe thy face.
Laertes: My lord, I'll hit him now.
King: I do not think't.
Laertes [*aside*]: And yet it is almost against my conscience.
Hamlet: Come, for the third, Laertes, you do but dally.
I pray you pass with your best violence;
I am sure you make a wanton of me.°
Laertes: Say you so? Come on. [*They play*.]
Osric: Nothing, neither way.
Laertes: Have at you now!

[*Laertes wounds Hamlet; then, in scuffling, they change rapiers*.]

King: Part them, they are incens'd.
Hamlet: Nay, come again.

[*Hamlet wounds Laertes. The Queen falls*.]

Osric: Look to the Queen there ho!
Horatio: They bleed on both sides. How is it, my lord?
Osric: How is't, Laertes?

°*fat:* Sweaty. °*carouses:* Drinks a toast. °*make . . . me:* Are holding back in order to let me win, as one does with a spoiled child (*wanton*).

LAERTES: Why, as a woodcock to mine own springe,° Osric:
I am justly kill'd with mine own treachery.
HAMLET: How does the Queen?
KING: She sounds° to see them bleed.
QUEEN: No, no, the drink, the drink— O my dear Hamlet—
The drink, the drink! I am pois'ned. [*Dies.*]
HAMLET: O villainy! Ho, let the door be lock'd!
Treachery! Seek it out.
LAERTES: It is here, Hamlet. [Hamlet,] thou art slain.
No med'cine in the world can do thee good;
In thee there is not half an hour of life.
The treacherous instrument is in [thy] hand,
Unbated° and envenom'd. The foul practice°
Hath turn'd itself on me. Lo here I lie,
Never to rise again. Thy mother's pois'ned.
I can no more— the King, the King's to blame.
HAMLET: The point envenom'd too!
Then, venom, to thy work. [*hurts° the King*]
ALL: Treason! treason!
KING: O, yet defend me, friends, I am but hurt.
HAMLET: Here, thou incestuous, [murd'rous], damned Dane,
Drink [off] this potion! Is [thy union] here?
Follow my mother! [*King dies.*]
LAERTES: He is justly served,
It is a poison temper'd° by himself.
Exchange forgiveness with me, noble Hamlet.
Mine and my father's death come not upon thee,
Nor thine on me! [*dies*]
HAMLET: Heaven make thee free° of it! I follow thee.
I am dead, Horatio. Wretched queen, adieu!
You that look pale, and tremble at this chance,
That are but mutes or audience° to this act,
Had I but time—as this fell° sergeant,° Death,
Is strict in his arrest—O, I could tell you—
But let it be. Horatio, I am dead,
Thou livest. Report me and my cause aright
To the unsatisfied.
HORATIO: Never believe it;
I am more an antique Roman° than a Dane.
Here's yet some liquor left.
HAMLET: As th' art a man,
Give me the cup. Let go! By heaven, I'll ha 't!

°*springe:* Snare. °*sounds:* Swoons. °*Unbated:* Not blunted. °*foul practice:* Vile plot. °*hurts:* Wounds. °*temper'd:* Mixed. °*make thee free:* Absolve you. °*mutes or audience:* Silent spectators. °*fell:* Cruel. °*sergeant:* Sheriff's officer. °*antique Roman:* One who will commit suicide on such an occasion.

O God, Horatio, what a wounded name,
Things standing thus unknown, shall I leave behind me!
If thou didst ever hold me in thy heart,
Absent thee from felicity a while,
And in this harsh world draw thy breath in pain
To tell my story. (*a march afar off*, [*and shot within*.]
What warlike noise is this?

[*Osric goes to the door and returns*.]

OSRIC: Young Fortinbras, with conquest come from Poland,
To th' ambassadors of England gives
This warlike volley.

HAMLET: O, I die, Horatio,
The potent poison quite o'er-crows° my spirit.°
I cannot live to hear the news from England,
But I do prophesy th' election lights
On Fortinbras, he has my dying voice.°
So tell him, with th' occurrents° more and less
Which have solicited°—the rest is silence. [*dies*]

HORATIO: Now cracks a noble heart. Good night, sweet prince,
And flights of angels sing thee to thy rest!

[*march within*.]

Why does the drum come hither?

[*Enter Fortinbras with the* [*English*] *Embassadors*, [*with Drum, Colors, and Attendants*.]

FORTINBRAS: Where is this sight?

HORATIO: What is it you would see?
If aught of woe or wonder, cease your search.

FORTINBRAS: This quarry cries on havoc.° O proud death,
What feast is toward° in thine eternal cell,
That thou so many princes at a shot
So bloodily hast strook?

[1.] **AMBASSADOR:** The sight is dismal,
And our affairs from England come too late.
The ears are senseless that should give us hearing,
To tell him his° commandment is fulfill'd,
That Rosencrantz and Guildenstern are dead.
Where should we have our thanks?

HORATIO: Not from his mouth,
Had it th' ability of life to thank you.
He never gave commandment for their death.

°*o'er-crows:* Triumphs over (a term derived from cockfighting). °*spirit:* Vital energy. °*voice:* Vote. °*occurrents:* Occurrences. °*solicited:* Instigated. °*This . . . havoc:* This heap of corpses proclaims a massacre. °*toward:* In preparation. °*his:* The king's.

But since so jump° upon this bloody question,°
You from the Polack wars, and you from England,
Are here arrived, give order that these bodies
High on a stage° be placed to the view,
And let me speak to [th'] yet unknowing world
How these things came about. So shall you hear
Of carnal, bloody, and unnatural acts,
Of accidental judgments,° casual° slaughters,
Of deaths put on° by cunning and [forc'd] cause,
And in this upshot, purposes mistook
Fall'n on the inventors' heads: all this can I
Truly deliver.

FORTINBRAS: Let us haste to hear it,
And call the noblest to the audience.
For me, with sorrow I embrace my fortune.
I have some rights of memory° in this kingdom,
Which now to claim my vantage° doth invite me.

HORATIO: Of that I shall have also cause to speak,
And from his mouth whose voice will draw [on] more.°
But let this same be presently° perform'd
Even while men's minds are wild,° lest more mischance
On plots and errors happen.

FORTINBRAS: Let four captains
Bear Hamlet like a soldier to the stage,
For he was likely, had he been put on,°
To have prov'd most royal; and for his passage,°
The soldiers' music and the rite of war
Speak loudly for him.
Take up the bodies. Such a sight as this
Becomes the field, but here shows much amiss.°
Go bid the soldiers shoot.

Exeunt [marching; after the which a peal of ordnance are shot off].

Reading and Reacting

1. What are Hamlet's most notable character traits? Do you see these traits as generally positive or negative?
2. Review each of Hamlet's soliloquies. Do you believe his assessments of his own problems are accurate? Are his assessments of other characters' behavior accurate? Point to examples from the soliloquies that reveal Hamlet's insight or lack of insight.

°*jump:* Precisely, pat. °*question:* Matter. °*stage:* Platform. °*judgments:* Retributions. °*causal:* Happening by chance. °*put on:* Instigated. °*of memory:* Unforgotten. °*my vantage:* My opportune presence at a moment when the throne is empty. °*his . . . more:* The mouth of one (Hamlet) whose vote will induce others to support your claim. °*presently:* At once. °*wild:* Distraught. °*put on:* Put to the test (by becoming king). *passage:* Death. °*Becomes . . . amiss:* Befits the battlefield, but appears very much out of place here.

3. Is Hamlet a sympathetic character? Where (if anywhere) do you find yourself growing impatient with him or disagreeing with him?
4. Why does Hamlet behave so cruelly toward Ophelia after his "To be or not to be" soliloquy (act 3, scene 1)? How does this behavior affect your view of his character?
5. What do other characters' comments reveal about Hamlet's character *before* the key events in the play begin to unfold? For example, in what way has Hamlet changed since he returned to the castle and found out about his father's death?
6. Claudius is presented as the play's villain. Is he all bad, or does he have any redeeming qualities?
7. List those in the play whom you believe to be flat characters. Why do you characterize each individual in this way? What does each of these flat characters contribute to the play?
8. Is Fortinbras simply Hamlet's foil, or does he have another essential role? Explain.
9. Each of the play's major characters has one or more character flaws that influence plot development. What specific weaknesses do you see in Claudius, Gertrude, Polonius, Laertes, Ophelia, and Hamlet himself? Through what words or actions is each weakness revealed? How does each weakness contribute to the play's plot?
10. Why doesn't Hamlet kill Claudius as soon as the ghost tells him what Claudius did? Why doesn't he kill him when he has the chance in act 3? What words and actions reveal Hamlet's motivation for hesitating? What are the implications of his failure to act?
11. Why does Hamlet pretend to be insane? Why does he arrange for the "play within a play" to be performed? Why does he agree to the duel with Laertes? In each case, what words or actions reveal his motivation to the audience?
12. Is the ghost an essential character, or could the information he reveals and the reactions he arouses come from another source? Explain. (Keep in mind that the ghost is a stock character in Elizabethan revenge tragedies.)
13. Describe Hamlet's relationship with his mother. Do you consider this a typical mother/son relationship? Why or why not?
14. In the graveyard scene (act 5, scene 1), the gravediggers make many ironic comments. How do these comments shed light on the events taking place in the play?
15. **Journal Entry** Both Gertrude and Ophelia are usually seen as weak women, firmly under the influence of the men in their lives. Do you think this characterization of them as passive and dependent is accurate? Why or why not?
16. **Critical Perspective** In *The Meaning of Shakespeare*, (1951), Harold Goddard reads *Hamlet* as, in part, a play about war, with a grimly ironic conclusion in that "all the Elder Hamlet's conquests have been for nothing—for less than nothing. Fortinbras, his former enemy, is to inherit the kingdom! Such is the end to which the ghost's thirst for vengeance has led." Goddard goes on to describe the play's ending:

> The dead Hamlet is borne out "like a soldier" and the last rites over his body are to be the rites of war. The final word of the text is "shoot." The last sounds we hear are a dead march and the reverberations of ordnance being shot off. The end crowns the whole. The sarcasm of fate could go no further. Hamlet, who aspired to nobler things, is treated at death as if he were the mere image of his father: a warrior. Shakespeare knew what he was about in making the conclusion of his play martial. Its theme has been war as well as revenge. It is the story of the Minotaur over again, of that monster who from the beginning of human strife has exacted his annual tribute of youth. No sacrifice ever offered to it was more precious than Hamlet. But he was not the last.
>
> If ever a play seems expressly written for the twentieth century, it is *Hamlet*. It should be unnecessary to underscore its pertinence to an age in which, twice within three decades, the

> older generation has called on the younger generation to settle a quarrel with the making of which it had nothing to do. So taken, *Hamlet* is an allegory of our time. Imagination or violence, Shakespeare seems to say, there is no other alternative.

Can you find other evidence in the play to support the idea that war (and, more specifically, the futility of war) is one of its major themes? Do you agree that the play is, in this respect, "an allegory of our time"?

Related Works: "The Cask of Amontillado" (p. 385), "Young Goodman Brown" (p. 540), *Words, Words, Words* (p. 1725), *Oedipus the King* (p. 1745)

WRITING SUGGESTIONS: Character

1. In *Death of a Salesman*, each character pursues his or her version of the American Dream. Choose two characters, define their concept of the American Dream, and explain how each tries to make the dream a reality. In each case, consider the obstacles the character encounters, and try to account for the character's success or lack of success. If you like, you may also consider other works in which the American Dream is central—for example, "The Third and Final Continent" (p. 290), "Two Kinds" (p. 777), *The Cuban Swimmer* (p. 1732), or *Fences* (p. 1902).
2. Many of the female characters in this chapter's plays—for example, Mrs. X (*The Stronger*), Catherine (*Proof*), Linda (*Death of a Salesman*), and Ophelia (*Hamlet*)—are, in one way or another, in conflict with men. Focusing on female characters in two different plays, define each conflict, and consider whether it is resolved in the play. (If you like, you may also discuss a female character who appears in a play in another chapter.)
3. Minor characters are often flat characters; in many cases, their sole function is to advance the plot or to highlight a particular trait in a major character. Sometimes, however, minor characters may be of more than minor importance. Choose one minor character from *Death of a Salesman* or *Hamlet* (or from a play in another chapter), and write an essay in which you discuss what this character contributes and how the play would be different without him or her.
4. Watch a film version of one of the four plays in this chapter, and write an essay in which you evaluate the actor's interpretation of the central character.
5. Three of this chapter's four plays explore complex relationships between parents and children. Write an essay in which you compare and contrast two of these three relationships: Catherine's relationship with her father, Willy Loman's relationships with his sons, or Hamlet's relationship with his mother.
6. In several other plays in this anthology, as in *Proof*, the past is an important influence on characters' lives in the present. Write an essay in which you discuss the impact of the past on the present in *Proof* and one or two other plays—for example, *When I Was a Little Girl and My Mother Didn't Want Me* (p. 1266), *The Glass Menagerie* (p. 1961), or *A Doll House* (p. 1402).

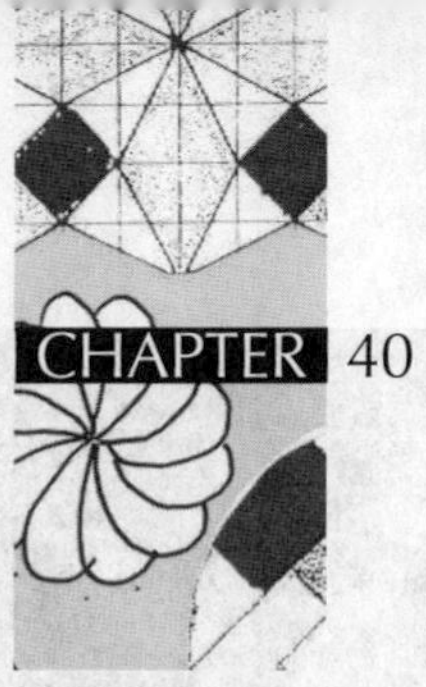

CHAPTER 40

STAGING

Staging refers to the physical elements of a play's production that determine how the play looks and sounds to an audience. It encompasses the **stage settings,** or **sets**—furnishings, scenery, props, and lighting—as well as the costumes, sound effects, and music that bring the play to life on the stage. In short, staging is everything that goes into making a written script a play.

Contemporary staging in the West has traditionally concentrated on recreating the outside world. This concept of staging, which has dominated Western theatrical productions for centuries, would seem alien in many non-Western theaters. Japanese **Kabuki dramas** and **No plays,** for example, depend on staging conventions that make no attempt to mirror reality. Scenery and costumes are largely symbolic, and often actors wear highly stylized makeup or masks. Although some European and American playwrights have been strongly influenced by non-Western staging, the majority of plays being produced in the West still try to create the illusion of reality.

Scene from the 2000 production of David Ives's *Words, Words, Words* by the English Theatre of Rome.

Source: The English Theatre of Rome. www.rometheatre.com, photo by Jason Cardone.

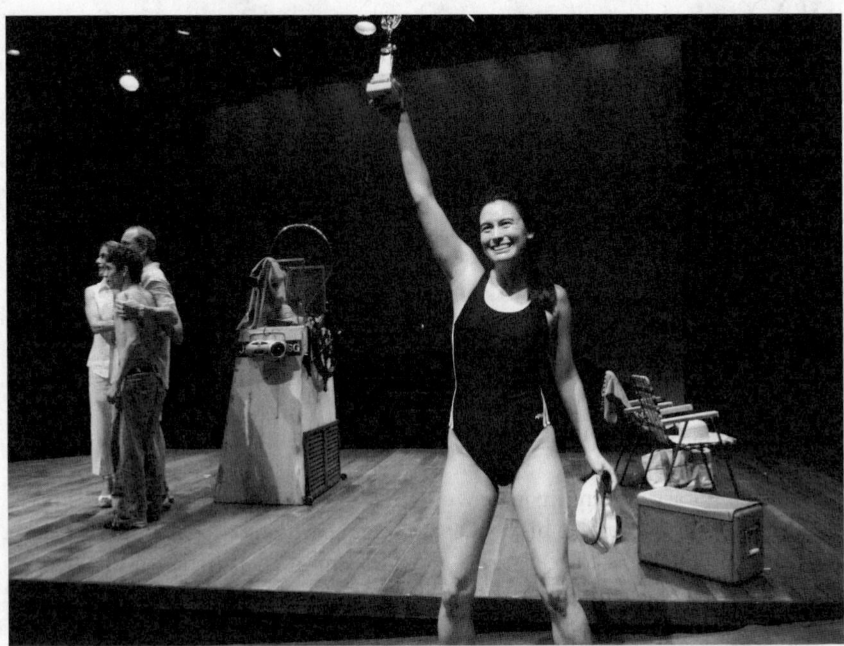

Performance photo of Milcha Sanchez-Scott's *The Cuban Swimmer* (p. 1732), featuring (from left to right) Socorro Santiago as Aìda Suarez, Stephen Novelli as Eduardo Suarez, Mark Del Guzzo as Sìmon Suarez, and Joanna Liao as Margarita Suarez.

Source: Milcha Sanchez-Scott's THE CUBAN SWIMMER at People's Light & Theatre Company. Photo by Mark Garvin.

Laurence Olivier as Oedipus, framed by a masked member of the Chorus and Jocasta. In this scene from the 1945 production of *Oedipus the King* (p. 1745), the doomed King seems to finally recognize the "truth" that he has been seeking.

Source: ©John Vickers Theatre Collection

A still from Michael Hoffman's 1999 film adaptation of Shakespeare's *A Midsummer Night's Dream* (p. 1787), with Kevin Kline as Bottom and Michelle Pfeiffer as Titania.
Source: ©Sygma/Corbis

Bottom being pampered by fairy attendants in the Hartford Stage production of *A Midsummer Night's Dream.*
Source: ©T. Charles Erickson

Stage Directions

Usually a playwright presents instructions for the staging of a play in **stage directions**—notes that comment on the scenery, the movements of the performers, the lighting, and the placement of props. (In the absence of detailed stage directions, dialogue can provide information about staging.) Sometimes these stage directions are quite simple, leaving much to the imagination of the director. Consider how little specific information about the setting of the play is provided in these stage directions from act 1 of Samuel Beckett's 1952 absurdist play *Waiting for Godot*:

A country road. A tree. Evening.

Often, however, playwrights furnish more detailed information about staging. Consider these stage directions from act 1 of Anton Chekhov's *The Cherry Orchard:*

A room, which has always been called the nursery. One of the doors leads into Anya's room. Dawn, sun rises during the scene. May, the cherry trees in flower, but it is cold in the garden with the frost of the early morning. Windows closed.

Enter Dunyasha with a candle and Lopahin with a book in his hand.

These comments indicate that the first act takes place in a room with more than one door and that several windows reveal cherry trees in bloom. They also specify that the lighting should simulate the sun rising at dawn and that certain characters should enter carrying particular props. Still, Chekhov leaves it up to those staging the play to decide on the costumes for the characters and on the furniture to be placed around the room.

Some stage directions are even more specific. Irish playwright George Bernard Shaw's long, complex stage directions are legendary in the theater. Note the degree of detail he provides in these stage directions from his 1906 comedy *The Doctor's Dilemma:*

The consulting-room has two windows looking on Queen Anne Street. Between the two is a marble-topped console, with haunched gilt legs ending in sphinx claws. The huge pier-glass [a long narrow mirror that fits between two windows] which surmounts it is mostly disabled from reflection by elaborate painting on its surface of palms, ferns, lilies, tulips, and sunflowers. The adjoining wall contains the fireplace, with two arm-chairs before it. As we happen to face the corner we see nothing of the other two walls. On the right of the fireplace, or rather on the right of any person facing the fireplace, is the door. On the left is the writing-table at which Redpenny [a medical student] sits. It is an untidy table with a microscope, several test tubes, and a spirit lamp [an alcohol burner] standing up through its litter of papers. There is a couch in the middle of the room, at right angles to the console, and parallel to the fireplace. A chair stands between the couch and the window. Another in the corner. Another at the other end of the windowed wall. . . . The wallpaper and carpets are mostly green. . . . The house, in fact, was so well furnished in the middle of the XIXth century that it stands unaltered to this day and is still quite presentable.

Not only does Shaw indicate exactly what furniture is to be placed on stage, but he also includes a good deal of physical description—specifying, for example, "gilt legs ending in sphinx claws" and "test tubes and a spirit lamp" that clutter the writing table. In addition, he defines furniture placement and specifies color.

Regardless of how detailed the stage directions are, they do not eliminate the need for creative interpretations on the part of the producer, director, set designers, and actors (see "Actors' Interpretations," p. 1467). Many directors see stage directions as suggestions, not requirements, and some consider them more confusing than helpful. Therefore, some directors may choose to interpret a play's stage directions quite loosely—or even to ignore them entirely. For example, in 2007, the Classical Theater of Harlem staged Samuel Beckett's 1952 existentialist drama *Waiting for Godot* in New Orleans. The performances were held outdoors in areas of the city that had been seriously damaged by Hurricane Katrina, and the still-devastated setting gave new power to Beckett's drama of characters' search for meaning against a backdrop of emptiness and despair.

 The Uses of Staging

Various elements of staging provide important information about characters and their motivations as well as about the play's theme.

Costumes

Costumes establish the historical period in which a play is set and provide insight into the characters who wear them. For example, when Hamlet first appears on stage, he is profoundly disillusioned and quite melancholy. This fact was immediately apparent to Shakespeare's audience because Hamlet is dressed in sable, which to the Elizabethans signified a melancholy nature. In Tennessee Williams's *The Glass Menagerie* (p. 1961), Laura's dress of soft violet material and her hair ribbon reflect her delicate, childlike innocence. In contrast, her mother's "*imitation velvety-looking cloth* [*coat*] *with imitation fur collar*" and her "*enormous black patent-leather pocketbook*" reveal her somewhat pathetic attempt to achieve respectability. Later in the play, awaiting the "gentleman caller," Laura's mother wears a dress that is both outdated and inappropriately youthful, suggesting both her need to relive her own past and her increasingly desperate desire to marry off her daughter.

Props and Furnishings

Props (short for *properties*) can also help audiences interpret a play's characters and themes. For example, the handkerchief in Shakespeare's *Othello* gains significance as the play progresses: it begins as an innocent object and ends as the piece of evidence that convinces Othello his wife is committing adultery. Sometimes props can have symbolic significance. During the Renaissance, for example, flowers had symbolic meaning. In act 4 of *Hamlet*, Ophelia, who is mad, gives flowers to various characters. In a note to the play, the critic Thomas Parrott points out the symbolic significance of her gifts: to Claudius, the murderer of Hamlet's father, she gives fennel and columbines, which signify flattery and ingratitude; to the Queen, she gives rue and daisies, which symbolize sadness and unfaithfulness. Although modern audiences would not understand the significance of these flowers, many people in Shakespeare's Elizabethan audience were aware of their meaning.

The **furnishings** in a room can also reveal a lot about a play's characters and themes. Willy Loman's house in Arthur Miller's *Death of a Salesman* (p. 1531) is sparsely furnished, revealing the declining financial status of the family. The kitchen contains a table and three chairs and the bedroom only a brass bed and a straight chair. Over the bed on a shelf is Biff's silver athletic trophy, a constant reminder of his loss of status. Like Willy Loman's house, the Wingfield apartment in *The Glass Menagerie* reflects its inhabitants' modest economic circumstances. For example, the living room, which contains a sofa that opens into a bed, also serves as a bedroom for Laura. In addition, one piece of furniture highlights a central theme of the play: an old-fashioned cabinet in the living room displays a collection of transparent glass animals that, like Laura, are too fragile to be removed from their surroundings.

Scenery and Lighting

Playwrights often use **scenery** and **lighting** to create imaginative stage settings. In *Death of a Salesman*, the house is surrounded by *"towering angular shapes"* of apartment houses that emphasize the *"small, fragile-seeming home."* Arthur Miller calls for a set that is *"wholly, or in some places, transparent."* Whenever the action is in the present, the actors observe the imaginary boundaries that separate rooms or mark the exterior walls of the house. When the characters reenact past events, however, they walk over the boundaries and come to the front of the stage. By lighting up and darkening different parts of the stage, Miller shifts from the present to the past and back again.

The set of *The Glass Menagerie* is also innovative, combining imaginative backdrops with subtle lighting. As the curtain rises, the audience sees the dark rear wall of the Wingfield tenement, which is flanked on both sides by alleys lined with clotheslines, garbage cans, and fire escapes. After Tom delivers his opening narrative, the rear wall becomes transparent, revealing the interior of the Wingfield apartment. To create this effect, Williams used a **scrim,** a curtain that when illuminated from the front appears solid but when illuminated from the back becomes transparent. For Williams, such "atmospheric touches" represented a new direction in theater that contrasted with the theater of "realistic conventions."

Contemporary playwrights often use sets that combine realistic and nonrealistic elements. In his Tony Award–winning play M. *Butterfly*, for example, David Henry Hwang employs not only scrims but also a large red lacquered ramp that runs from the bottom to the top of the stage. The action takes place beneath, on, and above the ramp, creating an effect not unlike that created by Shakespeare's multiple stages. At several points in the play, a character who acts as the narrator sits beneath the ramp, addressing the audience, while at the same time a character on top of the ramp acts out the narrator's words.

Music and Sound Effects

Staging involves more than visual elements such as costumes and scenery; it also involves **music** and **sound effects.** The stage directions for *Death of a Salesman*, for example, begin, "*A melody is heard, played upon a flute*." Although not specifically identified, the music is described as "*small and fine, telling of grass and trees and the horizon*." Significantly, this music stands in stark contrast to the claustrophobic urban setting of the play. Music also plays a major role in *The Glass Menagerie*, where a single recurring tune, like circus music, weaves in and out of the play. This musical motif gives emotional impact to certain lines and suggests the fantasy world into which Laura has retreated.

Sound effects play an important part in Henrik Ibsen's *A Doll House* (p. 1402). At the very end of the play, after his wife has left him, Torvald Helmer sits alone on the stage. In the following stage directions, the final sound effect cuts short Helmer's attempt at self-deluding optimism:

> **Helmer:** *(sinks down on a chair by the door, face buried in his hands)* Nora! Nora! *(Looking about and rising.)* Empty. She's gone. *(A sudden hope leaps in him.)* The greatest miracle—?
>
> *From below, the sound of a door slamming shut.*

When you read a play, it may be difficult to appreciate the effect that staging can have on a performance. As you read, pay particular attention to the stage directions, and use your imagination to visualize the scenes the playwright describes. In addition, try to imagine the play's sights and sounds, and consider the options for staging that are suggested as characters speak to one another. Although careful reading cannot substitute for seeing a play performed, it can help you imagine the play as it might appear on the stage.

A Final Note

Because of a play's limited performance time, and because of space and financial limitations, not every action or event can be represented on stage. Frequently, incidents that would involve many actors or require elaborate scenery are only suggested. For example, a violent riot may be suggested by a single scuffle, a full-scale wedding by the kiss between bride and groom, a gala evening at the opera by a well-dressed group in box seats, and a trip to an exotic locale by a departure scene. Other events may be suggested by sounds offstage—for example, the roar of a crowd may suggest an athletic event.

✔ CHECKLIST Writing about Staging

- ☐ What information about staging is specified in the stage directions of the play?
- ☐ What information about staging is suggested by the play's dialogue?
- ☐ What information about staging is left to the imagination?
- ☐ How might different decisions about staging change the play?
- ☐ Do the stage directions provide information about how characters are supposed to look or behave?
- ☐ What costumes are specified? In what ways do costumes provide insight into the characters who wear them?
- ☐ What props play an important part in the play? Do these props have symbolic meaning?
- ☐ Is the scenery special or unusual in any way?
- ☐ What kind of lighting is specified by the stage directions? In what way does this lighting affect your reaction to the play?
- ☐ How are music and sound effects used in the play? Are musical themes associated with any characters? Do music or sound effects heighten the emotional impact of certain lines?
- ☐ What events occur offstage? Why? How are they suggested?
- ☐ How does staging help to communicate the play's themes?

Source: ©AP Photo/Ed Wray

DAVID IVES (1950–), recipient of a Guggenheim Fellowship in playwriting, has published and produced numerous plays, many of which are one-act comedies. His plays are collected in *All in the Timing* (1994), *Mere Mortals* (1998), *Time Flies and Other Short Plays* (2001), and *Polish Joke and Other Plays* (2004). His play *Don Juan in Chicago* (1995) won the Outer Critics Circle Playwriting Award.

Cultural Context The basis for this play is the "infinite monkey theorem," the idea that, given enough time and enough monkeys, at least one monkey placed in front of a typewriter will eventually produce William Shakespeare's *Hamlet*. Credit for this idea is generally given to French mathematician Émile Borel, whose 1913 essay explains the theorem. Since then, numerous writers (including Richard Russo and Douglas Adams) have alluded to this idea in literature, using it as a metaphor to explore the probability of random, spontaneous acts of artistic genius.

Words, Words, Words (1994)

Lights come up on three monkeys pecking away at three typewriters. Behind them, a tire swing is hanging. The monkeys are named Milton, Swift, and Kafka. Kafka is a girl-monkey. (They shouldn't be in monkey suits, by the way. Instead, they wear the sort of little-kid clothes that chimps wear in circuses: white shirts and bow ties for the boys, a flouncy little dress for Kafka.) They type for a few moments, each at his own speed. Then Milton runs excitedly around the floor on his knuckles, swings onto the tire swing, leaps back onto his stool, and goes on typing. Kafka eats a banana thoughtfully. Swift pounds his chest and shows his teeth, then goes back to typing.

SWIFT: I don't know. I just don't know. . . .

KAFKA: Quiet, please. I'm trying to concentrate here. (*She types a moment with her toes.*)

MILTON: Okay, so what've you got?

SWIFT: Me?

MILTON: Yeah, have you hit anything? Let's hear it.

SWIFT (*reads what he's typed*): "Ping drobba fft fft fft inglewarp carcinoma." That's as far as I got.

KAFKA: I like the "fft fft fft."

MILTON: Yeah. Kind of onomatopoeic.

SWIFT: I don't know. Feels to me like it needs some punching up.

MILTON: You can always throw in a few jokes later on. You gotta get the throughline first.

SWIFT: But do you think it's *Hamlet?*

MILTON: Don't ask me. I'm just a chimp.

KAFKA: They could've given us a clue or something.

SWIFT: Yeah. Or a story conference.

MILTON: But that'd defeat the whole purpose of the experiment.

SWIFT: I know, I know, I know. Three monkeys typing into infinity will sooner or later produce *Hamlet*.

MILTON: Right.

SWIFT: Completely by chance.

MILTON: And Dr. David Rosenbaum up in that booth is going to prove it.

SWIFT: But what *is Hamlet?*

MILTON: I don't know.

SWIFT (*to* KAFKA): What is *Hamlet?*

KAFKA: I don't know. (*Silence.*)

SWIFT (*dawning realization*): You know—this is really *stupid*!

MILTON: Have you got something better to do in this cage? The sooner we produce the goddamn thing, the sooner we get out.

KAFKA: Sort of publish or perish, with a twist.

SWIFT: But what do we owe this Rosenbaum? A guy who stands outside those bars and tells people, "That one's Milton, that one's Swift, and that one's Kafka"—? Just to get a laugh?

KAFKA: What's a Kafka anyway? Why am I a Kafka?

Swift: Search me.

Kafka: What's a Kafka?

Swift: All his four-eyed friends sure think it's a stitch.

Kafka: And how are we supposed to write *Hamlet* if we don't even know what it is?

Milton: Okay, okay, so the chances are a little slim.

Swift: Yeah—and this from a guy who's supposed to be *smart*? This from a guy at *Columbia University*?

Milton: The way I figure it, there is a Providence that oversees our pages, rough-draft them how we may.

Kafka: But how about you, Milton? What've you got?

Milton: Let's see . . . (*Reads.*)

"Of Man's first disobedience, and the fruit
Of that forbidden tree whose mortal taste
Brought death into the—"

Kafka: Hey, that's good! It's got rhythm! It really sings!

Milton: Yeah?

Swift: But is it Shakespeare?

Kafka: Who cares? He's got a real voice there!

Swift: Does Dr. Rosenbaum care about voice? Does he care about anybody's individual creativity?

Milton: Let's look at this from Rosenbaum's point of view for a minute—

Swift: No! He brings us in here to produce copy, then all he wants is a clean draft of somebody else's stuff. (*Dumps out a bowl of peanuts.*) We're getting peanuts here, to be somebody's hack!

Milton: Writing is a mug's game° anyway, Swifty.

Swift: Well it hath made me mad.

Milton: Why not just buckle down and get the project over with? Set up a schedule for yourself. Type in the morning for a couple of hours when you're fresh, then take a break. Let the old juices flow. Do a couple more hours in the afternoon, and retire for a shot of papaya and some masturbation. What's the big deal?

Swift: If this Rosenbaum was worth anything, we'd be working on word processors, not these antiques. He's lucky he could find three who type this good, and then he treats us like those misfits at the Bronx Zoo. I mean, a *tire swing*? What does he take us for?

Milton: I like the tire swing. I think it was a very nice touch.

Swift: I can't work under these conditions! No wonder I'm producing garbage!

Kafka: How does the rest of yours go, Milton?

Milton: What, this?

Kafka: Yeah, read us some more.

Milton: Blah, blah, blah . . .

"whose mortal taste

---

mug's game: Pointless endeavor.

Brought death into the blammagam.
Bedsocks knockwurst tinkerbelle."

Small pause.

What do you think?

KAFKA: "Blammagam" is good.

SWIFT: Well. I don't know. . . .

MILTON: What's the matter? Is it the tone? I knew this was kind of a stretch for me.

SWIFT: I'm just not sure it has the same expressive intensity and pungent lyricism as the first part.

MILTON: Well sure, it needs rewriting. What doesn't? This is a rough draft! (*A red light goes on and a buzzer sounds.*)
Light's on.

Swift claps his hands over his eyes, Milton puts his hands over his ears, and Kafka puts her hands over her mouth so that they form "See no evil, hear no evil, speak no evil."

SWIFT: *This* bit.

KAFKA (*through her hands*): Are they watching?

MILTON (*hands over ears*): What?

KAFKA: Are they watching?

SWIFT: I don't know, I can't see. I have got my paws over my eyes.

MILTON: What?

KAFKA: What is the point of this?

SWIFT: Why do they videotape our bowel movements?

MILTON: *What?!*

SWIFT: Light's off. (*They take their hands away.*)

MILTON: But how are *you* doing, Franz? What've you got?

KAFKA: Well . . . (*Reads what she's typed.*) "K.K.K.K.K.K.K.K.K.K.K.K.K.K.K.K."

SWIFT: What is that—postmodernism?

KAFKA: Twenty lines of that.

SWIFT: At least it'll fuck up his data.

KAFKA: Twenty lines of that and I went dry. I got blocked. I felt like I was repeating myself.

MILTON: Do you think that that's in *Hamlet*?

KAFKA: I don't understand what I'm doing here in the first place! I'm not a writer, I'm a monkey! I'm supposed to be swinging on branches and digging up ants, not sitting under fluorescent lights ten hours a day!

MILTON: It sure is a long way home to the gardens of sweet Africa. Where lawns and level downs and flocks grazing the tender herb were sweetly interposèd . . .

KAFKA: Paradise, wasn't it?

MILTON: Lost!

SWIFT: Lost!

KAFKA: Lost!

MILTON: I'm trying to deal with some of that in this new piece here, but it's all still pretty close to the bone.

SWIFT: Just because they can keep us locked up, they think they're more powerful than we are.

MILTON: They *are* more powerful than we are.

SWIFT: Just because they control the means of production, they think they can suppress the workers.

MILTON: Things are how they are. What are you going to do?

SWIFT: Hey—how come you're always so goddamn ready to justify the ways of Rosenbaum to the apes?

MILTON: Do you have a key to that door?

SWIFT: No.

MILTON: Do you have an independent food source?

SWIFT: No.

MILTON: So call me a collaborator. I happen to be a professional. If Rosenbaum wants *Hamlet*, I'll give it a shot. Just don't forget—we're not astrophysicists. We're not brain surgeons. We're chimps. And for apes in captivity, this is not a bad gig.

SWIFT: What's really frightening is that if we stick around this cage long enough, we're gonna evolve into Rosenbaum.

KAFKA: Evolve into Rosenbaum?

SWIFT: Brush up your Darwin, baby. We're more than kin and less than kind.

MILTON: Anybody got a smoke?

KAFKA: I'm all out.

SWIFT: Don't look at me. I'm not going to satisfy those voyeurs with the old smoking-chimp act. No thank you.

MILTON: Don't be a sap, Swifty. You gotta use 'em! Use the system!

SWIFT: What do you mean?

MILTON: Watch me, while I put my antic disposition on. (*He jumps up onto his chair and scratches his sides, screeches, makes smoking motions, pounds his chest, jumps up and down—and a cigarette descends.*) See what I mean? Gauloise, too! My fave. (*He settles back to enjoy it.*)

SWIFT: They should've thrown in a Kewpie doll° for that performance.

MILTON: It got results, didn't it?

SWIFT: Sure. You do your Bonzo routine and get a Gauloise out of it. Last week I totalled a typewriter and got a whole carton of Marlboros.

MILTON: The trouble was, you didn't smoke 'em, you took a crap on 'em.

SWIFT: It was a political statement.

MILTON: Okay, you made your statement and I got my smoke. All's well that ends well, right?

KAFKA: It's the only way we know they're watching.

MILTON: Huh?

Kewpie doll: Style of doll based on magazine illustrations from the early twentieth century.

KAFKA: We perform, we break typewriters, we type another page—and a cigarette appears. At least it's a sign that somebody out there is paying attention.

MILTON: Our resident philosopher.

SWIFT: But what if one of us really *does* write *Hamlet*? Here we are, set down to prove the inadvertent virtues of randomness, and to produce something we wouldn't even recognize if it passed right through our hands—but what if one of us actually does it?

MILTON: Will we really be released?

KAFKA: Will they give us the key to the city and a ticker-tape parade?

SWIFT: Or will they move us on to *Ulysses*? (*They shriek in terror at the thought.*) Why did they pick *Hamlet* in the first place? What's *Hamlet* to them or they to *Hamlet* that we should care? Boy, there's the respect that makes calamity of so long life! For who would bear the whips and scorns of time, the oppressor's wrong, the proud man's contumely—

MILTON: Hey, Swifty!

SWIFT: —the pangs of despisèd love, the law's delay—

MILTON: Hey, Swifty! Relax, will you?

KAFKA: Have a banana.

SWIFT: I wish I could get Rosenbaum in here and see how *he* does at producing *Hamlet . . . That's it!*

KAFKA: What?

SWIFT: That's it! Forget about this random *Hamlet* crap. What about *revenge*?

KAFKA: Revenge? On Rosenbaum?

SWIFT: Who else? Hasn't he bereft us of our homes and families? Stepped in between us and our expectations?

KAFKA: How would we do it?

SWIFT: Easy. We lure him in here to look at our typewriters, test them out like something's wrong—but! *we poison the typewriter keys*!

MILTON: Oh Jesus.

SWIFT: Sure. Some juice of cursèd hebona° spread liberally over the keyboard? Ought to work like a charm.

MILTON: Great.

SWIFT: If that doesn't work, we envenom the tire swing and invite him for a ride. Plus—I challenge him to a duel.

MILTON: Brilliant.

SWIFT: Can't you see it? In the course of combat, I casually graze my rapier over the poisoned typewriter keys, and (*jabs*) a hit! A palpable hit! For a reserve, we lay by a cup with some venomous distillment. We'll put the pellet with the poison in the vessel with the pestle!

MILTON: Listen, I gotta get back to work. The man is gonna want his pages. (*He rolls a fresh page into his typewriter.*)

---

hebona: Type of poisonous plant.

KAFKA: It's not a bad idea, but . . .

SWIFT: What's the matter with you guys? I'm onto something here!

KAFKA: I think it's hopeless, Swifty.

SWIFT: But this is the goods!

MILTON: Where was I . . . "Bedsocks knockwurst tinkerbelle."

KAFKA: The readiness is all, I guess.

MILTON: Damn straight. Just let me know when that K-button gives out, honey.

SWIFT: Okay. You two serfs go back to work. I'll do all the thinking around here. Swifty—revenge! (*He paces, deep in thought.*)

MILTON: "Tinkerbelle . . . shtuckelschwanz . . . hemorrhoid." Yeah, that's good. *That is good.* (*Types.*) "Shtuckelshwanz . . ."

KAFKA (*types*): "Act one, scene one. Elsinore Castle, Denmark . . ."

MILTON (*types*): "Hemorrhoid."

KAFKA (*types*): "Enter Bernardo and Francisco."

MILTON: (*types*): "Pomegranate."

KAFKA (*types*): "Bernardo says, 'Who's there?' . . ."

MILTON (*types*): "Bazooka."

Kafka continues to type Hamlet, *as*

The Lights Fade

Reading and Reacting

1. Look up the names of the three monkeys in an encyclopedia. Why do you think Ives chose these names for his characters?
2. What personality traits define each of the monkeys? How are they alike? How are they different?
3. Why do you think Ives specifies that he does not want the monkeys dressed in monkey suits? Is this a good decision?
4. The monkeys sometimes use jargon typically used by writers for the movies or for television. Find several examples of this type of jargon. How does this use of language add to the humor of the play?
5. At various points in the play, the monkeys echo lines from Shakespeare's plays. Find several examples. What is the significance of this use of language?
6. The title of the play is an allusion to a line in *Hamlet*. In the play, Polonius asks Hamlet what he is reading. Hamlet answers, "words, words, words." Why do you think Ives chose this line as the title for his play?
7. What do the monkeys know about their situation? How do they attempt to manipulate Dr. Rosenbaum?
8. Like many of Shakespeare's characters, Swift decides to take revenge. Why does he decide to do so? What do the other monkeys think of Swift's plan?

9. **JOURNAL ENTRY** Read the stage directions at the beginning of the play. Then, decide what you would do differently if you were staging the play. Finally, write a set of stage directions reflecting the changes you would make.

10. CRITICAL PERSPECTIVE In a review of Ives's plays, *New York Times* theater critic Ben Brantley makes the following point:

> Mr. Ives's theories may owe much to the philosophical arcana of such dense thinkers as Einstein and Derrida, but he is no coolly detached academic. His obsessions with randomness and relativity are translated into revuelike sketches that percolate with comic brio and zesty bits of stagecraft.

Do you see evidence in *Words, Words, Words* that Ives is obsessed with "randomness and relativity"?

Related Works: "Accident" (p. 181), "Deportation at Breakfast" (p. 229), "Two Questions" (p. 556), "The Fun Gallery" (p. PS7), "Cinderella" (p. 866), "The Value of Education" (p. 892), *Hamlet* (p. 1605)

MILCHA SANCHEZ-SCOTT (1955–) is a Los Angeles–based writer of plays that include *Dog Lady* and *The Cuban Swimmer,* both one-act plays (1984); *Roosters,* published in *On New Ground: Contemporary Hispanic American Plays* (1987) and adapted into the 1993 feature film of the same name; and *Stone Wedding,* produced at the Los Angeles Theater Center (1988). Also produced by the Los Angeles Theater Center was her play *Carmen,* adapted from Georges Bizet's opera of the same title.

Born in Bali, Sanchez-Scott is the daughter of an Indonesian mother and a Colombian-Mexican father. Her early childhood was spent in Mexico, South America, and Britain; her family moved to San Diego when she was fourteen.

Writing in *Time* magazine, William A. Henry observes that the visionary or hallucinatory elements in Sanchez-Scott's plays derive from the Latin American "magic realism" tradition of Jorge Luis Borges and Gabriel García Márquez. For example, Henry notes that in *Roosters,* what seems "a straightforward depiction of the life of farmlands gives way to mysterious visitations, symbolic cockfights enacted by dancers, virginal girls wearing wings, archetypal confrontations between father and son."

In 1984, the New York production of *The Cuban Swimmer* was noteworthy for an ingeniously designed set that realistically re-created on stage Pacific Ocean waves, a helicopter, and a boat. According to the *New York Times,* "The audience [could] almost feel the resisting tides and the California oil slick . . . represented by a watery-blue floor and curtain." Jeannette Mirabel, as the Cuban swimmer, made an "auspicious" debut in the play, according to the *Times:* "In a tour de force of balletic movements, she [kept] her arms fluttering in the imaginary waters throughout the play."

Cultural Context In 1980, in the wake of numerous incidences of dissent and rebellion, Fidel Castro deported a large number of Cubans and encouraged many others to leave. In the resulting exodus, which became known as the Mariel boatlift, more than 120,000 undocumented Cubans arrived in Florida, placing tremendous strain on U.S. resources. In 1984, an agreement was made between the two countries that limited the number of Cuban immigrants to 20,000 per year. Over time, the United States relaxed this quota, but the resulting abundance of refugees prompted the U.S. government to reinstate the quota in the mid-1990s. In 1996, the Cuban Adjustment Act was passed, stating that Cubans who reached dry land would be allowed to become permanent residents of the United States, but those who were intercepted while still at sea would be returned to Cuba. In 1999, the plight of Cuban refugees was reflected in the story of Elian Gonzalez, a six-year-old boy who was found clinging to an inner tube but was later returned to Cuba in accordance with the 1996 act.

The Cuban Swimmer (1984)

CHARACTERS

Margarita Suárez, *the swimmer*
Eduardo Suárez, *her father, the coach*
Simón Suárez, *her brother*
Aída Suárez, *her mother*
Abuela, *her grandmother*
Voice of Mel Munson
Voice of Mary Beth White
Voice of Radio Operator

SETTING

The Pacific Ocean between San Pedro and Catalina Island.

TIME

Summer.

Live conga drums can be used to punctuate the action of the play.

SCENE 1

Pacific Ocean. Midday. On the horizon, in perspective, a small boat enters upstage left, crosses to upstage right, and exits. Pause. Lower on the horizon, the same boat, in larger perspective, enters upstage right, crosses and exits upstage left. Blackout.

SCENE 2

Pacific Ocean. Midday. The swimmer, Margarita Suárez, is swimming. On the boat following behind her are her father, Eduardo Suárez, holding a megaphone, and Simón, her brother, sitting on top of the cabin with his shirt off, punk sunglasses on, binoculars hanging on his chest.

Eduardo: *(leaning forward, shouting in time to Margarita's swimming) Uno, dos, uno, dos. Y uno, dos . . .* keep your shoulders parallel to the water.

Simón: I'm gonna take these glasses off and look straight into the sun.

Eduardo: *(through megaphone) Muy bien, muy bien . . .* but punch those arms in, baby.

Simón: *(looking directly at the sun through binoculars)* Come on, come on, zap me. Show me something. *(He looks behind at the shoreline and ahead at the sea.)* Stop! Stop, *Papi!* Stop!

Aída Suárez and Abuela, the swimmer's mother and grandmother, enter running from the back of the boat.

Aída and Abuela: *Qué? Qué es?*

Aída: *Es un* shark?

Eduardo: Eh?

Abuela: *Que es un* shark *dicen?*

Eduardo blows whistle. Margarita looks up at the boat.

Simón: No, *Papi,* no shark, no shark. We've reached the halfway mark.

Abuela: *(looking into the water) A dónde está?*

AÍDA: It's not in the water.

ABUELA: Oh, no? Oh, no?

AÍDA: No! A *poco* do you think they're gonna have signs in the water to say you are halfway to Santa Catalina? No. It's done very scientific. *A ver, hijo,* explain it to your grandma.

SIMÓN: Well, you see, Abuela — *(He points behind.)* There's San Pedro. *(He points ahead.)* And there's Santa Catalina. Looks halfway to me.

Abuela shakes her head and is looking back and forth, trying to make the decision, when suddenly the sound of a helicopter is heard.

ABUELA: *(looking up)* Virgencita de la Caridad del Cobre. *Qué es eso?*

Sound of helicopter gets closer. Margarita looks up.

MARGARITA: *Papi, Papi!*

A small commotion on the boat, with everybody pointing at the helicopter above. Shadows of the helicopter fall on the boat. Simón looks up at it through binoculars.

Papi—qué es? What is it?

EDUARDO: *(through megaphone)* Uh . . . uh . . . uh, *un momentico . . . mi hija. . . .* Your *papi's* got everything under control, understand? Uh . . . you just keep stroking. And stay . . . uh . . . close to the boat.

SIMÓN: Wow, *Papi!* We're on TV, man! Holy Christ, we're all over the fucking U.S.A.! It's Mel Munson and Mary Beth White!

AÍDA: *Por Dios!* Simón, don't swear. And put on your shirt.

Aída fluffs her hair, puts on her sunglasses and waves to the helicopter. Simón leans over the side of the boat and yells to Margarita.

SIMÓN: Yo, Margo! You're on TV, man.

EDUARDO: Leave your sister alone. Turn on the radio.

MARGARITA: *Papi! Qué está pasando?*

ABUELA: *Que es la televisión dicen? (She shakes her head.) Porque como yo no puedo ver nada sin mis espejuelos.*

Abuela rummages through the boat, looking for her glasses. Voices of Mel Munson and Mary Beth White are heard over the boat's radio.

MEL'S VOICE: As we take a closer look at the gallant crew of *La Havana* . . . and there . . . yes, there she is . . . the little Cuban swimmer from Long Beach, California, nineteen-year-old Margarita Suárez. The unknown swimmer is our Cinderella entry . . . a bundle of tenacity, battling her way through the choppy, murky waters of the cold Pacific to reach the Island of Romance . . . Santa Catalina . . . where should she be the first to arrive, two thousand dollars and a gold cup will be waiting for her.

AÍDA: Doesn't even cover our expenses.

ABUELA: *Qué dice?*

EDUARDO: Shhhh!

Mary Beth's Voice: This is really a family effort, Mel, and—

Mel's Voice: Indeed it is. Her trainer, her coach, her mentor, is her father, Eduardo Suárez. Not a swimmer himself, it says here, Mr. Suárez is head usher of the Holy Name Society and the owner-operator of Suárez Treasures of the Sea and Salvage Yard. I guess it's one of those places—

Mary Beth's Voice: If I might interject a fact here, Mel, assisting in this swim is Mrs. Suárez, who is a former Miss Cuba.

Mel's Voice: And a beautiful woman in her own right. Let's try and get a closer look.

Helicopter sound gets louder. Margarita, frightened, looks up again.

Margarita: *Papi!*

Eduardo: *(through megaphone) Mi hija,* don't get nervous . . . it's the press. I'm handling it.

Aída: I see how you're handling it.

Eduardo: *(through megaphone)* Do you hear? Everything is under control. Get back into your rhythm. Keep your elbows high and kick and kick and kick and kick . . .

Abuela: *(finds her glasses and puts them on) Ay sí, es la televisión . . . (She points to helicopter.) Qué lindo mira . . . (She fluffs her hair, gives a big wave.) Aló América! Viva mi Margarita, viva todo los Cubanos en los Estados Unidos!*

Aída: *Ay por Dios,* Cecilia, the man didn't come all this way in his helicopter to look at you jumping up and down, making a fool of yourself.

Abuela: I don't care. I'm proud.

Aída: He can't understand you anyway.

Abuela: *Viva . . . (She stops.) Simón, comó se dice viva?*

Simón: Hurray.

Abuela: Hurray for *mi Margarita y* for all the Cubans living *en* the United States, *y un abrazo . . . Simón, abrazo . . .*

Simón: A big hug.

Abuela: *Sí,* a big hug to all my friends in Miami, Long Beach, Union City, except for my son Carlos, who lives in New York in sin! He lives . . . *(she crosses herself)* in Brooklyn with a Puerto Rican woman in sin! *No decente . . .*

Simón: Decent.

Abuela: Carlos, *no decente.* This family, *decente.*

Aída: Cecilia, *por Dios.*

Mel's Voice: Look at that enthusiasm. The whole family has turned out to cheer little Margarita on to victory! I hope they won't be too disappointed.

Mary Beth's Voice: She seems to be making good time, Mel.

Mel's Voice: Yes, it takes all kinds to make a race. And it's a testimonial to the all-encompassing fairness . . . the greatness of this, the Wrigley Invitational Women's Swim to Catalina, where among all the professionals there is still room for the amateurs . . . like these, the simple people we see below us on the ragtag *La Havana*, taking their long-shot chance to victory. *Vaya con Dios!*

Helicopter sound fading as family, including Margarita, watch silently. Static as Simón turns radio off. Eduardo walks to bow of boat, looks out on the horizon.

EDUARDO: *(to himself)* Amateurs.

AÍDA: Eduardo, that person insulted us. Did you hear, Eduardo? That he called us a simple people in a ragtag boat? Did you hear . . . ?

ABUELA: *(clenching her fist at departing helicopter) Mal-Rayo los parta!*

SIMÓN: *(same gesture)* Asshole!

Aída follows Eduardo as he goes to side of boat and stares at Margarita.

AÍDA: This person comes in his helicopter to insult your wife, your family, your daughter . . .

MARGARITA: *(pops her head out of the water) Papi?*

AÍDA: Do you hear me, Eduardo? I am not simple.

ABUELA: *Sí.*

AÍDA: I am complicated.

ABUELA: *Sí, demasiada complicada.*

AÍDA: Me and my family are not so simple.

SIMÓN: Mom, the guy's an asshole.

ABUELA: *(shaking her fist at helicopter)* Asshole!

AÍDA: If my daughter was simple, she would not be in that water swimming.

MARGARITA: Simple? *Papi . . . ?*

AÍDA: *Ahora,* Eduardo, this is what I want you to do. When we get to Santa Catalina, I want you to call the TV station and demand an apology.

EDUARDO: *Cállete mujer! Aquí mando yo.* I will decide what is to be done.

MARGARITA: *Papi*, tell me what's going on.

EDUARDO: Do you understand what I am saying to you, Aída?

SIMÓN: *(leaning over side of boat, to Margarita)* Yo Margo! You know that Mel Munson guy on TV? He called you a simple amateur and said you didn't have a chance.

ABUELA: *(leaning directly behind Simón.) Mi hija, insultó a la familia. Desgraciado!*

AÍDA: *(leaning in behind Abuela)* He called us peasants! And your father is not doing anything about it. He just knows how to yell at me.

EDUARDO: *(through megaphone)* Shut up! All of you! Do you want to break her concentration? Is that what you are after? Eh?

Abuela, Aída, and Simón shrink back. Eduardo paces before them.

Swimming is rhythm and concentration. You win a race *aquí*. *(Pointing to his head.)* Now . . . *(to Simón)* you, take care of the boat, Aída y *Mama* . . . do something. Anything. Something practical.

Abuela and Aída get on knees and pray in Spanish.

Hija, give it everything, eh? . . . *por la familia. Uno . . . dos.* . . . You must win.

Simón goes into cabin. The prayers continue as lights change to indicate bright sunlight, later in the afternoon.

SCENE 3

Tableau for a couple of beats. Eduardo on bow with timer in one hand as he counts strokes per minute. Simón is in the cabin steering, wearing his sunglasses, baseball cap on backward. Abuela and Aída are at the side of the boat, heads down, hands folded, still muttering prayers in Spanish.

AÍDA and **ABUELA:** *(crossing themselves) En el nombre del Padre, del Hijo y del Espíritu Santo amén.*

EDUARDO: *(through megaphone)* You're stroking seventy-two!

SIMÓN: *(singing)* Mama's stroking, Mama's stroking seventy-two. . . .

EDUARDO: *(through megaphone)* You comfortable with it?

SIMÓN: *(singing)* Seventy-two, seventy-two, seventy-two for you.

AÍDA: *(looking at the heavens)* Ay, Eduardo, *ven acá,* we should be grateful that *Nuestro Señor* gave us such a beautiful day.

ABUELA: *(crosses herself) Si, gracias a Dios.*

EDUARDO: She's stroking seventy-two, with no problem. *(He throws a kiss to the sky.)* It's a beautiful day to win.

AÍDA: *Qué hermoso!* So clear and bright. Not a cloud in the sky. *Mira! Mira!* Even rainbows on the water . . . a sign from God.

SIMÓN: *(singing)* Rainbows on the water . . . you in my arms . . .

ABUELA and **EDUARDO:** *(Looking the wrong way.) Dónde?*

AÍDA: *(pointing toward Margarita)* There, dancing in front of Margarita, leading her on . . .

EDUARDO: Rainbows on . . . Ay *coño!* It's an oil slick! You . . . you . . . *(To Simón.)* Stop the boat. *(Runs to bow, yelling.)* Margarita! Margarita!

On the next stroke, Margarita comes up all covered in black oil.

MARGARITA: *Papi! Papi . . . !*

Everybody goes to the side and stares at Margarita, who stares back. Eduardo freezes.

AÍDA: *Apúrate,* Eduardo, move . . . what's wrong with you . . . *no me oíste,* get my daughter out of the water.

EDUARDO: *(softly)* We can't touch her. If we touch her, she's disqualified.

AÍDA: But I'm her mother.

EDUARDO: Not even by her own mother. Especially by her own mother. . . . You always want the rules to be different for you, you always want to be the exception. *(To Simón.)* And you . . . you didn't see it, eh? You were playing again?

SIMÓN: *Papi,* I was watching . . .

AÍDA: *(interrupting) Pues,* do something Eduardo. You are the big coach, the monitor.

SIMÓN: Mentor! Mentor!

EDUARDO: How can a person think around you? *(He walks off to bow, puts head in hands.)*

ABUELA: *(looking over side) Mira como todos los* little birds are dead. *(She crosses herself.)*
AÍDA: Their little wings are glued to their sides.
SIMÓN: Christ, this is like the La Brea tar pits.
AÍDA: They can't move their little wings.
ABUELA: *Esa niña tiene que moverse.*
SIMÓN: Yeah, Margo, you gotta move, man.

Abuela and Simón gesture for Margarita to move. Aída gestures for her to swim.

ABUELA: *Anda niña, muévete.*
AÍDA: Swim, *hija*, swim or the *aceite* will stick to your wings.
MARGARITA: *Papi?*
ABUELA: *(taking megaphone)* Your *papi* say "move it!"

Margarita with difficulty starts moving.

ABUELA, AÍDA AND SIMÓN: *(laboriously counting) Uno, dos . . . uno, dos . . . anda . . . uno, dos.*
EDUARDO: *(running to take megaphone from Abuela) Uno, dos . . .*

Simón races into cabin and starts the engine. Abuela, Aída and Eduardo count together.

SIMÓN: *(looking ahead) Papi*, it's over there!
EDUARDO: Eh?
SIMÓN: *(pointing ahead and to the right)* It's getting clearer over there.
EDUARDO: *(through megaphone)* Now pay attention to me. Go to the right.

Simón, Abuela, Aída and Eduardo all lean over side. They point ahead and to the right, except Abuela, who points to the left.

FAMILY: *(shouting together) Para yá! Para yá!*

Lights go down on boat. A special light on Margarita, swimming through the oil, and on Abuela, watching her.

ABUELA: *Sangre de mi sangre*, you will be another to save us. En Bolondron, where your great-grandmother Luz Suárez was born, they say one day it rained blood. All the people, they run into their houses. They cry, they pray, *pero* your great-grandmother Luz she had *cojones* like a man. She run outside. She look straight at the sky. She shake her fist. And she say to the evil one, "*Mira . . . (beating her chest) coño, Diablo, aquí estoy si me quieres.*" And she open her mouth, and she drunk the blood.

Blackout

SCENE 4

Lights up on boat. Aída and Eduardo are on deck watching Margarita swim. We hear the gentle, rhythmic lap, lap, lap of the water, then the sound of inhaling and exhaling as Margarita's breathing becomes louder. Then Margarita's heartbeat is heard, with the lapping of the water and the breathing under it. These sounds continue beneath the dialogue to the end of the scene.

Aída: *Dios mío*. Look how she moves through the water. . . .

Eduardo: You see, it's very simple. It is a matter of concentration.

Aída: The first time I put her in water she came to life, she grew before my eyes. She moved, she smiled, she loved it more than me. She didn't want my breast any longer. She wanted the water.

Eduardo: And of course, the rhythm. The rhythm takes away the pain and helps the concentration.

Pause. Aída and Eduardo watch Margarita.

Aída: Is that my child or a seal. . . .

Eduardo: Ah, a seal, the reason for that is that she's keeping her arms very close to her body. She cups her hands, and then she reaches and digs, reaches and digs.

Aída: To think that a daughter of mine . . .

Eduardo: It's the training, the hours in the water. I used to tie weights around her little wrists and ankles.

Aída: A spirit, an ocean spirit, must have entered my body when I was carrying her.

Eduardo: *(to Margarita)* Your stroke is slowing down.

Pause. We hear Margarita's heartbeat with the breathing under, faster now.

Aída: Eduardo, that night, the night on the boat . . .

Eduardo: Ah, the night on the boat again . . . the moon was . . .

Aída: The moon was full. We were coming to America. . . . *Qué romantico*.

Heartbeat and breathing continue.

Eduardo: We were cold, afraid, with no money, and on top of everything, you were hysterical, yelling at me, tearing at me with your nails. *(Opens his shirt, points to the base of his neck.)* Look, I still bear the scars . . . telling me that I didn't know what I was doing . . . saying that we were going to die. . . .

Aída: You took me, you stole me from my home . . . you didn't give me a chance to prepare. You just said we have to go now, now! Now, you said. You didn't let me take anything. I left everything behind. . . . I left everything behind.

Eduardo: Saying that I wasn't good enough, that your father didn't raise you so that I could drown you in the sea.

Aída: You didn't let me say even a good-bye. You took me, you stole me, you tore me from my home.

Eduardo: I took you so we could be married.

Aída: That was in Miami. But that night on the boat, Eduardo. . . . We were not married, that night on the boat.

Eduardo: *No pasó nada!* Once and for all get it out of your head, it was cold, you hated me, and we were afraid. . . .

Aída: *Mentiroso!*

EDUARDO: A man can't do it when he is afraid.

AÍDA: Liar! You did it very well.

EDUARDO: I did?

AÍDA: *Sí*. Gentle. You were so gentle and then strong . . . my passion for you so deep. Standing next to you . . . I would ache . . . looking at your hands I would forget to breathe, you were irresistible.

EDUARDO: I was?

AÍDA: You took me into your arms, you touched my face with your fingertips . . . you kissed my eyes . . . *la esquina de la boca y* . . .

EDUARDO: *Sí, sí*, and then . . .

AÍDA: I look at your face on top of mine, and I see the lights of Havana in your eyes. That's when you seduced me.

EDUARDO: Shhh, they're gonna hear you.

Lights go down. Special on Aída.

AÍDA: That was the night. A woman doesn't forget those things . . . and later that night was the dream . . . the dream of a big country with fields of fertile land and big, giant things growing. And there by a green, slimy pond I found a giant pea pod and when I opened it, it was full of little, tiny baby frogs.

Aída crosses herself as she watches Margarita. We hear louder breathing and heartbeat.

MARGARITA: Santa Teresa. Little Flower of God, pray for me. San Martín de Porres, pray for me. Santa Rosa de Lima, *Virgencita de la Caridad del Cobre*, pray for me. . . . Mother pray for me.

SCENE 5

Loud howling of wind is heard, as lights change to indicate unstable weather, fog and mist. Family on deck, braced and huddled against the wind. Simón is at the helm.

AÍDA: *Ay Dios mío, qué viento.*

EDUARDO: *(through megaphone)* Don't drift out . . . that wind is pushing you out. *(To Simón.)* You! Slow down. Can't you see your sister is drifting out?

SIMÓN: It's the wind, *Papi*.

AÍDA: Baby, don't go so far. . . .

ABUELA: *(to heaven) Ay Gran Poder de Dios, quita este maldito viento.*

SIMÓN: Margo! Margo! Stay close to the boat.

EDUARDO: Dig in. Dig in hard. . . . Reach down from your guts and dig in.

ABUELA: *(to heaven) Ay Virgen de la Caridad del Cobre, por lo más tú quieres a pararla.*

AÍDA: *(putting her hand out, reaching for Margarita)* Baby, don't go far.

Abuela crosses herself. Action freezes. Lights get dimmer, special on Margarita. She keeps swimming, stops, starts again, stops, then, finally exhausted, stops altogether. The boat stops moving.

EDUARDO: What's going on here? Why are we stopping?

SIMÓN: *Papi,* she's not moving! Yo Margo!

The family all run to the side.

EDUARDO: *Hija! . . . Hijita!* You're tired, eh?

AÍDA: *Por supuesto* she's tired. I like to see you get in the water, waving your arms and legs from San Pedro to Santa Catalina. A person isn't a machine, a person has to rest.

SIMÓN: Yo, Mama! Cool out, it ain't fucking brain surgery.

EDUARDO: *(to Simón)* Shut up, you. *(Louder to Margarita.)* I guess your mother's right for once, huh? . . . I guess you had to stop, eh? . . . Give your brother, the idiot . . . a chance to catch up with you.

SIMÓN: *(clowning like Mortimer Snerd)* Dum dee dum dee dum ooops, ah shucks . . .

EDUARDO: I don't think he's Cuban.

SIMÓN: *(like Ricky Ricardo) Oye,* Lucy! I'm home! Ba ba lu!

EDUARDO: *(joins in clowning, grabbing Simón in a headlock)* What am I gonna do with this idiot, eh? I don't understand this idiot. He's not like us, Margarita. *(Laughing.)* You think if we put him into your bathing suit with a cap on his head . . . *(He laughs hysterically.)* You think anyone would know . . . huh? Do you think anyone would know? *(Laughs.)*

SIMÓN: *(vamping) Ay, mi amor.* Anybody looking for tits would know.

Eduardo slaps Simón across the face, knocking him down. Aída runs to Simón's aid. Abuela holds Eduardo back.

MARGARITA: *Mía culpa! Mía culpa!*

ABUELA: *Qué dices hija?*

MARGARITA: *Papi,* it's my fault, it's all my fault. . . . I'm so cold, I can't move. . . . I put my face in the water . . . and I hear them whispering . . . laughing at me. . . .

AÍDA: Who is laughing at you?

MARGARITA: The fish are all biting me . . . they hate me . . . they whisper about me. She can't swim, they say. She can't glide. She has no grace. . . . Yellowtails, bonita, tuna, man-o'-war, snub-nose sharks, *los baracudas* . . . they all hate me . . . only the dolphins care . . . and sometimes I hear the whales crying . . . she is lost, she is dead. I'm so numb, I can't feel. *Papi! Papi!* Am I dead?

EDUARDO: *Vamos,* baby, punch those arms in. Come on . . . do you hear me?

MARGARITA: *Papi . . . Papi . . .* forgive me. . . .

All is silent on the boat. Eduardo drops his megaphone, his head bent down in dejection. Abuela, Aída, Simón, all leaning over the side of the boat. Simón slowly walks away.

AÍDA: *Mi hija, qué tienes?*

SIMÓN: Oh, Christ, don't make her say it. Please don't make her say it.

ABUELA: Say what? *Qué cosa?*

SIMÓN: She wants to quit, can't you see she's had enough?

ABUELA: *Mira, para eso. Esta niña* is turning blue.

AÍDA: *Oyeme, mi hija.* Do you want to come out of the water?

MARGARITA: *Papi?*

SIMÓN: *(to Eduardo)* She won't come out until *you* tell her.

AÍDA: Eduardo . . . answer your daughter.

EDUARDO: *Le dije* to concentrate . . . concentrate on your rhythm. Then the rhythm would carry her . . . ay, it's a beautiful thing, Aída. It's like yoga, like meditation, the mind over matter . . . the mind controlling the body . . . that's how the great things in the world have been done. I wish you . . . I wish my wife could understand.

MARGARITA: *Papi?*

SIMÓN: *(to Margarita)* Forget him.

AÍDA: *(imploring)* Eduardo, *por favor*.

EDUARDO: *(walking in circles)* Why didn't you let her concentrate? Don't you understand, the concentration, the rhythm is everything. But no, you wouldn't listen. *(Screaming to the ocean.)* Goddamn Cubans, why, God, why do you make us go everywhere with our families? *(He goes to back of boat.)*

AÍDA: *(opening her arms) Mi hija, ven,* come to *Mami. (Rocking.)* Your *mami* knows.

Abuela has taken the training bottle, puts it in a net. She and Simón lower it to Margarita.

SIMÓN: Take this. Drink it. *(As Margarita drinks, Abuela crosses herself.)*

ABUELA: *Sangre de mi sangre.*

Music comes up softly. Margarita drinks, gives the bottle back, stretches out her arms, as if on a cross. Floats on her back. She begins a graceful backstroke. Lights fade on boat as special lights come up on Margarita. She stops. Slowly turns over and starts to swim, gradually picking up speed. Suddenly as if in pain she stops, tries again, then stops in pain again. She becomes disoriented and falls to the bottom of the sea. Special on Margarita at the bottom of the sea.

MARGARITA: *Ya no puedo* . . . I can't. . . . A person isn't a machine . . . *es mi culpa* . . . Father forgive me . . . *Papi! Papi!* One, two. *Uno, dos. (Pause.) Papi! A dónde estás? (Pause.)* One, two, one, two. *Papi! Ay, Papi!* Where are you . . . ? Don't leave me. . . . Why don't you answer me? *(Pause. She starts to swim, slowly.) Uno, dos, uno, dos.* Dig in, dig in. *(Stops swimming.) Por favor, Papi! (Starts to swim again.)* One, two, one, two. Kick from your hip, kick from your hip. *(Stops swimming. Starts to cry.)* Oh God, please. . . . *(Pause.)* Hail Mary, full of grace . . . dig in, dig in . . . the Lord is with thee. . . . *(She swims to the rhythm of her Hail Mary.)* Hail Mary, full of grace . . . dig in, dig in . . . the Lord is with thee . . . dig in, dig in. . . . Blessed art thou among women. . . . *Mami,* it hurts. You let go of my hand. I'm lost. . . . And blessed is the fruit of thy womb, now and at the hour of our death. Amen. I don't want to die, I don't want to die.

Margarita is still swimming. Blackout. She is gone.

SCENE 6

Lights up on boat, we hear radio static. There is a heavy mist. On deck we see only black outline of Abuela with shawl over her head. We hear the voices of Eduardo, Aída, and Radio Operator.

EDUARDO'S VOICE: *La Havana!* Coming from San Pedro. Over.

RADIO OPERATOR'S VOICE: Right, DT6-6, you say you've lost a swimmer.

AÍDA'S VOICE: Our child, our only daughter . . . listen to me. Her name is Margarita Inez Suárez, she is wearing a black one-piece bathing suit cut high in the legs with a white racing stripe down the sides, a white bathing cap with goggles and her whole body covered with a . . . with a . . .

EDUARDO'S VOICE: With lanolin and paraffin.

AÍDA'S VOICE: *Sí . . . con lanolin and paraffin.*

More radio static. Special on Simón, on the edge of the boat.

SIMÓN: Margo! Yo Margo! *(Pause.)* Man don't do this. *(Pause.)* Come on. . . . Come on. . . . *(Pause.)* God, why does everything have to be so hard? *(Pause.)* Stupid. You know you're not supposed to die for this. Stupid. It's his dream and he can't even swim. *(Pause.)* Punch those arms in. Come home. Come home. I'm your little brother. Don't forget what Mama said. You're not supposed to leave me behind. *Vamos*, Margarita, take your little brother, hold his hand tight when you cross the street. He's so little. *(Pause.)* Oh, Christ, give us a sign. . . . I know! I know! Margo, I'll send you a message . . . like mental telepathy. I'll hold my breath, close my eyes, and I'll bring you home. *(He takes a deep breath; a few beats.)* This time I'll beep . . . I'll send out sonar signals like a dolphin. *(He imitates dolphin sounds.)*

The sound of real dolphins takes over from Simón, then fades into sound of Abuela saying the Hail Mary in Spanish, as full lights come up slowly.

SCENE 7

Eduardo coming out of cabin, sobbing, Aída holding him. Simón anxiously scanning the horizon. Abuela looking calmly ahead.

EDUARDO: *Es mi culpa, sí, es mi culpa. (He hits his chest.)*

AÍDA: *Ya, ya viejo* . . . it was my sin . . . I left my home.

EDUARDO: Forgive me, forgive me. I've lost our daughter, our sister, our granddaughter, *mi carne, mi sangre, mis ilusiones. (To heaven.) Dios mío*, take me . . . take me, I say . . . Goddammit, take me!

SIMÓN: I'm going in.

AÍDA AND EDUARDO: No!

EDUARDO: *(grabbing and holding Simón, speaking to heaven)* God, take me, not my children. They are my dreams, my illusions . . . and not this one, this one is my mystery . . . he has my secret dreams. In him are the parts of me I cannot see.

Eduardo embraces Simón. Radio static becomes louder.

AÍDA: I . . . I think I see her.

SIMÓN: No, it's just a seal.

ABUELA: *(looking out with binoculars) Mi nietacita, dónde estás? (She feels her heart.)* I don't feel the knife in my heart . . . my little fish is not lost.

Radio crackles with static. As lights dim on boat, Voices of Mel and Mary Beth are heard over the radio.

MEL'S VOICE: Tragedy has marred the face of the Wrigley Invitational Women's Race to Catalina. The Cuban swimmer, little Margarita Suárez, has reportedly been lost at sea. Coast Guard and divers are looking for her as we speak. Yet in spite of this tragedy the race must go on because . . .

MARY BETH'S VOICE: *(interrupting loudly)* Mel!

MEL'S VOICE: *(startled)* What!

MARY BETH'S VOICE: Ah . . . excuse me, Mel . . . we have a winner. We've just received word from Catalina that one of the swimmers is just fifty yards from the breakers . . . it's, oh, it's . . . Margarita Suárez!

Special on family in cabin listening to radio.

MEL'S VOICE: What? I thought she died!

Special on Margarita, taking off bathing cap, trophy in hand, walking on the water.

MARY BETH'S VOICE: Ahh . . . unless . . . unless this is a tragic . . . No . . . there she is, Mel. Margarita Suárez! The only one in the race wearing a black bathing suit cut high in the legs with a racing stripe down the side.

Family cheering, embracing.

SIMÓN: *(screaming)* Way to go, Margo!

MEL'S VOICE: This is indeed a miracle! It's a resurrection! Margarita Suárez, with a flotilla of boats to meet her, is now walking on the waters, through the breakers . . . onto the beach, with crowds of people cheering her on. What a jubilation! This is a miracle!

Sound of crowds cheering. Lights and cheering sounds fade.

Blackout

Reading and Reacting

1. What lighting and sound effects do the stage directions specify? In what way do these effects advance the action of the play? How do they help to communicate the play's theme?
2. Although most of the play is in English, the characters frequently speak Spanish. What are the advantages and disadvantages of this use of Spanish? How does the mixing of English and Spanish reflect one of the play's themes?

3. What function do the voices of Mel and Mary Beth serve in the play?
4. What conflicts develop among the family members as the play proceeds? Do you think these conflicts are meant to represent the problems of other immigrant groups?
5. In what sense is Mel's final comment "This is a miracle!" true? In what sense is it ironic?
6. Could this play be seen as an allegory? What is the value of seeing it in this way?
7. During much of the play, Margarita is swimming in full view of the audience. Suggest three ways in which a director could convey this effect on stage. Which way would you choose if you were directing the play? Why?
8. As the headnote to the play explains, the 1984 New York production of *The Cuban Swimmer* had an extremely realistic set. Could the play be staged unrealistically, with the characters on a raised platform instead of a boat? How do you think this kind of set would change the audience's reaction?
9. **JOURNAL ENTRY** Are you able to empathize with Margarita's struggle? What elements of the play make it easy (or difficult) for you to do so?
10. **CRITICAL PERSPECTIVE** In a 1998 article in the *New York Times*, theater critic Brooks Atkinson said, "Nothing is better for good actors than a stage with no scenery."

    How do you interpret Atkinson's comment? Do you think this remark could be applied to the staging of *The Cuban Swimmer*?

Related Works: "Snow" (p. 177), "The Secret Lion" (p. 197), "Deportation at Breakfast" (p. 229), "Two Kinds" (p. 777), "How to Write the Great American Indian Novel" (p. 871), "Baca Grande" (p. 889), "Harlem" (p. 924), "Post-Colonial Studies" (p. 1026)

Source: ©Araldo de Luca/Corbis

SOPHOCLES (496–406 B.C.), along with Aeschylus and Euripides, is one of the three great ancient Greek tragic dramatists. He lived during the flowering and subsequent decline of fifth-century B.C. Athens—the high point of Greek civilization. Born as Greece struggled against the Persian Empire and moved to adopt democracy, he lived as an adult under Pericles during the golden age of Athens and died as it became clear that Athens would lose the Peloponnesian War. Sophocles was an active participant in the public life of Athens, serving as a collector of tribute from Athenian subjects and later as a general. He wrote at least 120 plays, but only seven have survived, including three plays about Oedipus: *Oedipus the King* (c. 430 B.C.), *Oedipus at Colonus* (411? B.C.), and *Antigone* (441 B.C.).

Oedipus the King, or *Oedipus Rex* (sometimes called *Oedipus the Tyrant*), was performed shortly after a great plague in Athens (probably in 429 or 425 B.C.) and as Athens was falling into decline. The play opens with an account of a plague in Thebes, Oedipus's kingdom. Over the years, *Oedipus the King* has attracted impressive critical attention, from Aristotle's use of it as a model for his definition of tragedy to Freud's use of its power as evidence of the validity of the "Oedipus complex."

Cultural Context During the period in which *Oedipus* was written, the Greeks were especially interested in the relationship between greatness and *hubris,* the excessive pride and ambition that leads to the downfall of a hero in classical tragedy. They were fascinated by the idea that hubris can bring destruction: that the same traits that can elevate a person to greatness can also cause his or her ruin.

This theme recurs throughout classical literature and was especially relevant between 431 and 404 B.C., when the second Peloponnesian War (which Athens lost) was being fought between Athens and Sparta. After a Spartan army invaded Attica in 431 B.C., the Athenians retreated behind the walls of their city while the Athenian fleet began raids. Between 430 and 428 B.C., a plague (which the Athenians believed was inflicted upon them by the gods) wiped out at least a quarter of the Athenian population. It was during this tumultuous time that Sophocles wrote of Oedipus and his troubles.

Oedipus the King* (c. 430 B.C.)

Translated by Thomas Gould

CHARACTERS

Oedipus,° *the King of Thebes*
Priest of Zeus, *leader of the suppliants*
Creon, *Oedipus's brother-in-law*
Chorus, *a group of Theban elders*
Choragos, *spokesman of the Chorus*
Tiresias, *a blind seer or prophet*
Jocasta, *the queen of Thebes*
Messenger, *from Corinth, once a shepherd*
Herdsman, *once a servant of Laius*
Second Messenger, *a servant of Oedipus*

MUTES

Suppliants, *Thebans seeking Oedipus's help*
Attendants, *for the Royal Family*
Servants, *to lead Tiresias and Oedipus*
Antigone, *daughter of Oedipus and Jocasta*
Ismene, *daughter of Oedipus and Jocasta*

The action takes place during the day in front of the royal palace in Thebes. There are two altars (left and right) on the proscenium and several steps leading down to the orchestra. As the play opens, Thebans of various ages who have come to beg Oedipus for help are sitting on these steps and in part of the orchestra. These suppliants are holding branches of laurel or olive which have strips of wool° wrapped around them. Oedipus enters from the palace (the central door of the skene).

PROLOGUE°

OEDIPUS: My children, ancient Cadmus'° newest care,
why have you hurried to those seats, your boughs
wound with the emblems of the suppliant?
The city is weighed down with fragrant smoke,
with hymns to the Healer° and the cries of mourners.

---

*Note that individual lines are numbered in the following play. When a line is shared by two or more characters, it is counted as one line.

Oedipus: The name, meaning "swollen foot," refers to the mutilation of Oedipus's feet by his father, Laius, before the infant was sent to Mount Cithaeron to be put to death by exposure.

wool: Branches wrapped with wool are traditional symbols of prayer or supplication.

Prologue: The portion of the play containing the exposition, or explanation, of what has gone before and what is now happening.

Cadmus: Oedipus's great-great-grandfather (although Oedipus does not know this) and the founder of Thebes.

Healer: Apollo, god of prophecy, light, healing, justice, purification, and destruction.

I thought it wrong, my sons, to hear your words
through emissaries, and have come out myself,
I, Oedipus, a name that all men know.

Oedipus addresses the Priest.

Old man—for it is fitting that you speak
for all—what is your mood as you entreat me,
fear or trust? You may be confident
that I'll do anything. How hard of heart
if an appeal like this did not rouse my pity!

PRIEST: You, Oedipus, who hold the power here,
you see our several ages, we who sit
before your altars—some not strong enough
to take long flight, some heavy in old age,
the priests, as I of Zeus,° and from our youths
a chosen band. The rest sit with their windings
in the markets, at the twin shrines of Pallas,°
and the prophetic embers of Ismēnos.°
Our city, as you see yourself, is tossed
too much, and can no longer lift its head
above the troughs of billows red with death.
It dies in the fruitful flowers of the soil,
it dies in its pastured herds, and in its women's
barren pangs. And the fire-bearing god°
has swooped upon the city, hateful plague,
and he has left the house of Cadmus empty.
Black Hades° is made rich with moans and weeping.
Not judging you an equal of the gods,
do I and the children sit here at your hearth,
but as the first of men, in troubled times
and in encounters with divinities.
You came to Cadmus' city and unbound
the tax we had to pay to the harsh singer,°

Zeus: Father and king of the gods.

Pallas: Athena, goddess of wisdom, arts, crafts, and war.

Ismēnos: A reference to the temple of Apollo near the river Ismēnos in Thebes. Prophecies were made here by "reading" the ashes of the altar fires.

fire-bearing god: Contagious fever viewed as a god.

Black Hades: Refers both to the underworld where the spirits of the dead go and to the god of the underworld.

harsh singer: The Sphinx, a monster with a woman's head, a lion's body, and wings. The "tax" from which Oedipus freed Thebes was the destruction of all the young men who failed to solve the Sphinx's riddle and were subsequently devoured. The Sphinx always asked the same riddle: "What goes on four legs in the morning, two legs at noon, and three legs in the evening, and yet is weakest when supported by the largest number of feet?" Oedipus discovered the correct answer—man, who crawls in infancy, walks in his prime, and uses a stick in old age—and thus ended the Sphinx's reign of terror. The Sphinx destroyed herself when Oedipus answered the riddle. Oedipus's reward for freeing Thebes of the Sphinx was the throne and the hand of the recently widowed Jocasta.

did it without a helpful word from us,
with no instruction; with a god's assistance
you raised up our life, so we believe.
Again now Oedipus, our greatest power,
we plead with you, as suppliants, all of us,
to find us strength, whether from a god's response,
or learned in some way from another man.
I know that the experienced among men
give counsels that will prosper best of all.
Noblest of men, lift up our land again!
Think also of yourself; since now the land
calls you its Savior for your zeal of old,
oh let us never look back at your rule
as men helped up only to fall again!
Do not stumble! Put our land on firm feet!
The bird of omen was auspicious then,
when you brought that luck; be that same man again!
The power is yours; if you will rule our country,
rule over men, not in an empty land.
A towered city or a ship is nothing
if desolate and no man lives within.

OEDIPUS: Pitiable children, oh I know, I know
the yearnings that have brought you. Yes, I know
that you are sick. And yet, though you are sick,
there is not one of you so sick as I.
For your affliction comes to each alone,
for him and no one else, but my soul mourns
for me and for you, too, and for the city.
You do not waken me as from a sleep,
for I have wept, bitterly and long,
tried many paths in the wanderings of thought,
and the single cure I found by careful search
I've acted on: I sent Menoeceus' son,
Creon, brother of my wife, to the Pythian
halls of Phoebus,° so that I might learn
what I must do or say to save this city.
Already, when I think what day this is,
I wonder anxiously what he is doing.
Too long, more than is right, he's been away.
But when he comes, then I shall be a traitor
if I do not do all that the god reveals.

PRIEST: Welcome words! But look, those men have signaled
that it is Creon who is now approaching!

Pythian halls . . . Phoebus: The temple of Phoebus, Apollo's oracle or prophet at Delphi.

Oedipus: Lord Apollo! May he bring Savior Luck,
a Luck as brilliant as his eyes are now!
Priest: His news is happy, it appears. He comes,
forehead crowned with thickly berried laurel.°
Oedipus: We'll know, for he is near enough to hear us.

Enter Creon along one of the parados.

Lord, brother in marriage, son of Menoeceus!
What is the god's pronouncement that you bring?
Creon: It's good. For even troubles, if they chance
to turn out well, I always count as lucky.
Oedipus: But what was the response? You seem to say
I'm not to fear—but not to take heart either.
Creon: If you will hear me with these men present,
I'm ready to report—or go inside.

Creon moves up the steps toward the palace.

Oedipus: Speak out to all! The grief that burdens me
concerns these men more than it does my life.
Creon: Then I shall tell you what I heard from the god.
The task Lord Phoebus sets for us is clear:
drive out pollution sheltered in our land,
and do not shelter what is incurable.
Oedipus: What is our trouble? How shall we cleanse ourselves?
Creon: We must banish or murder to free ourselves
from a murder that blows storms through the city.
Oedipus: What man's bad luck does he accuse in this?
Creon: My Lord, a king named Laius ruled our land
before you came to steer the city straight.
Oedipus: I know. So I was told—I never saw him.
Creon: Since he was murdered, you must raise your hand
against the men who killed him with their hands.
Oedipus: Where are they now? And how can we ever find
the track of ancient guilt now hard to read?
Creon: In our own land, he said. What we pursue,
that can be caught; but not what we neglect.
Oedipus: Was Laius home, or in the countryside—
or was he murdered in some foreign land?

laurel: Creon is wearing a garland of laurel leaves, sacred to Apollo.

CREON: He left to see a sacred rite, he said;
He left, but never came home from his journey.
OEDIPUS: Did none of his party see it and report—
someone we might profitably question?
CREON: They were all killed but one, who fled in fear,
and he could tell us only one clear fact.
OEDIPUS: What fact? One thing could lead us on to more
if we could get a small start on our hope.
CREON: He said that bandits chanced on them and killed him—
with the force of many hands, not one alone.
OEDIPUS: How could a bandit dare so great an act—
unless this was a plot paid off from here!
CREON: We thought of that, but when Laius was killed,
we had no one to help us in our troubles.
OEDIPUS: It was your very kingship that was killed!
What kind of trouble blocked you from a search?
CREON: The subtle-singing Sphinx asked us to turn
from the obscure to what lay at our feet.
OEDIPUS: Then I shall begin again and make it plain.
It was quite worthy of Phoebus, and worthy of you,
to turn our thoughts back to the murdered man,
and right that you should see me join the battle
for justice to our land and to the god.
Not on behalf of any distant kinships,
it's for myself I will dispel this stain.
Whoever murdered him may also wish
to punish me—and with the selfsame hand.
In helping him I also serve myself.
Now quickly, children: up from the altar steps,
and raise the branches of the suppliant!
Let someone go and summon Cadmus' people:
say I'll do anything.

Exit an Attendant along one of the parados.

Our luck will prosper
if the god is with us, or we have already fallen.
PRIEST: Rise, my children; that for which we came,
he has himself proclaimed he will accomplish.
May Phoebus, who announced this, also come
as Savior and reliever from the plague.

Exit Oedipus and Creon into the palace. The Priest and the Suppliants exit left and right along the parados. After a brief pause, the Chorus (including the Choragos) enters the orchestra from the parados.

PARADOS°

STROPHE 1°

Chorus: Voice from Zeus,° sweetly spoken, what are you
that have arrived from golden
Pytho° to our shining
Thebes? I am on the rack, terror
shakes my soul.
Delian Healer,° summoned by "iē!"
I await in holy dread what obligation, something new
or something back once more with the revolving years,
you'll bring about for me.
Oh tell me, child of golden Hope,
deathless Response!

ANTISTROPHE 1

I appeal to you first, daughter of Zeus,
deathless Athena,
and to your sister who protects this land,
Artemis,° whose famous throne is the whole circle
of the marketplace,
and Phoebus, who shoots from afar: iō!
Three-fold defenders against death, appear!
If ever in the past, to stop blind ruin
sent against the city,
you banished utterly the fires of suffering,
come now again!

STROPHE 2

Ah! Ah! Unnumbered are the miseries
I bear. The plague claims all
our comrades. Nor has thought found yet a spear
by which a man shall be protected. What our glorious
earth gives birth to does not grow. Without a birth
from cries of labor
do the women rise.
One person after another
you may see, like flying birds,

Parados: A song sung by the Chorus on first entering.
Strophe: Probably refers to the direction in which the Chorus danced while reciting specific stanzas. *Strophe* may have indicated dance steps to stage left, *antistrophe* to stage right.
Voice from Zeus: A reference to Apollo's prophecy. Zeus taught Apollo how to prophesy.
Pytho: Delphi.
Delian Healer: Apollo.
Artemis: Goddess of virginity, childbirth, and hunting.

faster than indomitable fire, sped
to the shore of the god that is the sunset.°

ANTISTROPHE 2

And with their deaths unnumbered dies the city.
Her children lie unpitied on the ground,
spreading death, unmourned.
Meanwhile young wives, and gray-haired mothers with them,
on the shores of the altars, from this side and that,
suppliants from mournful trouble,
    cry out their grief.
A hymn to the Healer shines,
    the flute a mourner's voice.
Against which, golden goddess, daughter of Zeus,
    send lovely Strength.

STROPHE 3

Causing raging Ares°—who,
    armed now with no shield of bronze,
burns me, coming on amid loud cries—
to turn his back and run from my land,
with a fair wind behind, to the great
    hall of Amphitritē,°
or to the anchorage that welcomes no one,
Thrace's troubled sea!
If night lets something get away at last,
    it comes by day.
Fire-bearing god . . .
    you who dispense the might of lightning,
Zeus! Father! Destroy him with your thunderbolt!

Enter Oedipus from the palace.

ANTISTROPHE 3

Lycēan Lord!° From your looped
    bowstring, twisted gold,
I wish indomitable missiles might be scattered
and stand forward, our protectors; also fire-bearing
radiance of Artemis, with which
    she darts across the Lycian mountains.
I call the god whose head is bound in gold,

---

god . . . sunset: Hades, god of the underworld.

Ares: God of war and destruction.

Amphitritē: The Atlantic Ocean.

Lycēan Lord: Apollo.

with whom this country shares its name,
Bacchus,° wine-flushed, summoned by "euoi!,"
    Maenads' comrade,
to approach ablaze
    with gleaming . . .
pine, opposed to that god-hated god.

EPISODE 1°

OEDIPUS: I hear your prayer. Submit to what I say
and to the labors that the plague demands
and you'll get help and a relief from evils.
I'll make the proclamation, though a stranger
to the report and to the deed. Alone,
had I no key, I would soon lose the track.
Since it was only later that I joined you,
to all the sons of Cadmus I say this:
whoever has clear knowledge of the man
who murdered Laius, son of Labdacus,
I command him to reveal it all to me—
nor fear if, to remove the charge, he must
accuse himself: his fate will not be cruel—
he will depart unstumbling into exile.
But if you know another, or a stranger,
to be the one whose hand is guilty, speak:
I shall reward you and remember you.
But if you keep your peace because of fear,
and shield yourself or kin from my command,
hear you what I shall do in that event:
I charge all in this land where I have throne
and power, shut out that man—no matter who—
both from your shelter and all spoken words,
nor in your prayers or sacrifices make
him partner, nor allot him lustral° water.
All men shall drive him from their homes: for he
is the pollution that the god-sent Pythian
response has only now revealed to me.
In this way I ally myself in war
with the divinity and the deceased.°
And this curse, too, against the one who did it,
whether alone in secrecy, or with others:

Bacchus: Dionysus, god of fertility and wine.
Episode: The portion of ancient Greek plays that appears between choric songs.
lustral: Purifying.
the deceased: Laius.

may he wear out his life unblest and evil!
I pray this, too: if he is at my hearth
and in my home, and I have knowledge of him,
may the curse pronounced on others come to me.
All this I lay to you to execute,
for my sake, for the god's, and for this land
now ruined, barren, abandoned by the gods.
Even if no god had driven you to it,
you ought not to have left this stain uncleansed,
the murdered man a nobleman, a king!
You should have looked! But now, since, as it happens,
It's I who have the power that he had once,
and have his bed, and a wife who shares our seed,
and common bond had we had common children
(had not his hope of offspring had bad luck—
but as it happened, luck lunged at his head);
because of this, as if for my own father,
I'll fight for him, I'll leave no means untried,
to catch the one who did it with his hand,
for the son of Labdacus, of Polydōrus,
of Cadmus before him, and of Agēnor.°
This prayer against all those who disobey:
the gods send out no harvest from their soil,
nor children from their wives. Oh, let them die
victims of this plague, or of something worse.
Yet for the rest of us, people of Cadmus,
we the obedient, may Justice, our ally,
and all the gods, be always on our side!

CHORAGOS:° I speak because I feel the grip of your curse:
the killer is not I. Nor can I point
to him. The one who set us to this search,
Phoebus, should also name the guilty man.

OEDIPUS: Quite right, but to compel unwilling gods—
no man has ever had that kind of power.

CHORAGOS: May I suggest to you a second way?

OEDIPUS: A second or a third—pass over nothing!

CHORAGOS: I know of no one who sees more of what
Lord Phoebus sees than Lord Tiresias.
My Lord, one might learn brilliantly from him.

OEDIPUS: Nor is this something I have been slow to do.
At Creon's word I sent an escort—twice now!
I am astonished that he has not come.

---

son . . . Agēnor: Refers to Laius by citing his genealogy.

Choragos: Leader of the Chorus and principal commentator on the play's action.

CHORAGOS: The old account is useless. It told us nothing.
OEDIPUS: But tell it to me. I'll scrutinize all stories.
CHORAGOS: He is said to have been killed by travelers.
OEDIPUS: I have heard, but the one who did it no one sees.
CHORAGOS: If there is any fear in him at all,
he won't stay here once he has heard that curse.
OEDIPUS: He won't fear words: he had no fear when he did it.

Enter Tiresias from the right, led by a Servant and two of Oedipus's Attendants.

CHORAGOS: Look there! There is the man who will convict him!
It's the god's prophet they are leading here,
one gifted with the truth as no one else.
OEDIPUS: Tiresias, master of all omens—
public and secret, in the sky and on the earth—
your mind, if not your eyes, sees how the city
lives with a plague, against which Thebes can find
no Saviour or protector, Lord, but you.
For Phoebus, as the attendants surely told you,
returned this answer to us: liberation
from the disease would never come unless
we learned without a doubt who murdered Laius—
put them to death, or sent them into exile.
Do not begrudge us what you may learn from birds
or any other prophet's path you know!
Care for yourself, the city, care for me,
care for the whole pollution of the dead!
We're in your hands. To do all that he can
to help another is man's noblest labor.
TIRESIAS: How terrible to understand and get
no profit from the knowledge! I knew this,
but I forgot, or I had never come.
OEDIPUS: What's this? You've come with very little zeal.
TIRESIAS: Let me go home! If you will listen to me,
You will endure your troubles better—and I mine.
OEDIPUS: A strange request, not very kind to the land
that cared for you—to hold back this oracle!
TIRESIAS: I see your understanding comes to you
inopportunely. So that won't happen to me . . .
OEDIPUS: Oh, by the gods, if you understand about this,
don't turn away! We're on our knees to you.
TIRESIAS: None of you understands! I'll never bring
my grief to light—I will not speak of yours.
OEDIPUS: You know and won't declare it! Is your purpose
to betray us and to destroy this land!
TIRESIAS: I will grieve neither of us. Stop this futile
cross-examination. I'll tell you nothing!

Oedipus: Nothing? You vile traitor! You could provoke
a stone to anger! You still refuse to tell?
Can nothing soften you, nothing convince you?
Tiresias: You blamed anger in me — you haven't seen.
The kind that lives with you, so you blame me.
Oedipus: Who wouldn't fill with anger, listening
to words like yours which now disgrace this city?
Tiresias: It will come, even if my silence hides it.
Oedipus: If it will come, then why won't you declare it?
Tiresias: I'd rather say no more. Now if you wish,
respond to that with all your fiercest anger!
Oedipus: Now I am angry enough to come right out
with this conjecture: you, I think, helped plot
the deed; you did it — even if your hand,
cannot have struck the blow. If you could see,
I should have said the deed was yours alone.
Tiresias: Is that right! Then I charge you to abide
by the decree you have announced: from this day
say no word to either these or me,
for you are the vile polluter of this land!
Oedipus: Aren't you appalled to let a charge like that
come bounding forth? How will you get away?
Tiresias: You cannot catch me. I have the strength of truth.
Oedipus: Who taught you this? Not your prophetic craft!
Tiresias: You did. You made me say it. I didn't want to.
Oedipus: Say what? Repeat it so I'll understand.
Tiresias: I made no sense? Or are you trying me?
Oedipus: No sense I understood. Say it again!
Tiresias: I say you are the murderer you seek.
Oedipus: Again that horror! You'll wish you hadn't said that.
Tiresias: Shall I say more, and raise your anger higher?
Oedipus: Anything you like! Your words are powerless.
Tiresias: You live, unknowing, with those nearest to you
in the greatest shame. You do not see the evil.
Oedipus: You won't go on like that and never pay!
Tiresias: I can if there is any strength in truth.
Oedipus: In truth, but not in you! You have no strength,
blind in your ears, your reason, and your eyes.
Tiresias: Unhappy man! Those jeers you hurl at me
before long all these men will hurl at you.
Oedipus: You are the child of endless night; it's not
for me or anyone who sees to hurt you.
Tiresias: It's not my fate to be struck down by you.
Apollo is enough. That's his concern.
Oedipus: Are these inventions Creon's or your own?
Tiresias: No, your affliction is yourself, not Creon.

Oedipus: Oh success!—in wealth, kingship, artistry,
in any life that wins much admiration—
the envious ill will stored up for you!
to get at my command, a gift I did not
seek, which the city put into my hands,
my loyal Creon, colleague from the start,
longs to sneak up in secret and dethrone me.
So he's suborned this fortuneteller—schemer!
deceitful beggar-priest!—who has good eyes
for gains alone, though in his craft he's blind.
Where were your prophet's powers ever proved?
Why, when the dog who chanted verse° was here,
did you not speak and liberate this city?
Her riddle wasn't for a man chancing by
to interpret; prophetic art was needed,
but you had none, it seems—learned from birds
or from a god. I came along, yes I,
Oedipus the ignorant, and stopped her—
by using thought, not augury from birds.
And it is I whom you now wish to banish,
so you'll be close to the Creontian throne.
You—and the plot's concocter—will drive out
pollution to your grief: you look quite old
or you would be the victim of that plot!

Choragos: It seems to us that this man's words were said
in anger, Oedipus, and yours as well.
Insight, not angry words, is what we need,
the best solution to the god's response.

Tiresias: You are the king, and yet I am your equal
in my right to speak. In that I too am Lord.
for I belong to Loxias,° not you.
I am not Creon's man. He's nothing to me.
Hear this, since you have thrown my blindness at me:
Your eyes can't see the evil to which you've come,
nor where you live, nor who is in your house.
Do you know your parents? Not knowing, you are
their enemy, in the underworld and here.
A mother's and a father's double-lashing
terrible-footed curse will soon drive you out.
Now you can see, then you will stare into darkness.
What place will not be harbor to your cry,
or what Cithaeron° not reverberate

dog . . . verse: The Sphinx.

Loxias: Apollo.

Cithaeron: The mountain on which Oedipus was to be exposed as an infant.

when you have heard the bride-song in your palace
to which you sailed? Fair wind to evil harbor!
Nor do you see how many other woes
will level you to yourself and to your children.
So, at my message, and at Creon, too,
splatter muck! There will never be a man
ground into wretchedness as you will be.

OEDIPUS: Am I to listen to such things from him!
May you be damned! Get out of here at once!
Go! Leave my palace! Turn around and go!

Tiresias begins to move away from Oedipus.

TIRESIAS: I wouldn't have come had you not sent for me.

OEDIPUS: I did not know you'd talk stupidity,
or I wouldn't have rushed to bring you to my house.

TIRESIAS: Stupid I seem to you, yet to your parents
who gave you natural birth I seemed quite shrewd.

OEDIPUS: Who? Wait! Who is the one who gave me birth?

TIRESIAS: This day will give you birth,° and ruin too.

OEDIPUS: What murky, riddling things you always say!

TIRESIAS: Don't you surpass us all at finding out?

OEDIPUS: You sneer at what you'll find has brought me greatness.

TIRESIAS: And that's the very luck that ruined you.

OEDIPUS: I wouldn't care, just so I saved the city.

TIRESIAS: In that case I shall go. Boy, lead the way!

OEDIPUS: Yes, let him lead you off. Here, underfoot,
you irk me. Gone, you'll cause no further pain.

TIRESIAS: I'll go when I have said what I was sent for.
Your face won't scare me. You can't ruin me.
I say to you, the man whom you have looked for
as you pronounced your curses, your decrees
on the bloody death of Laius—he is here!
A seeming stranger, he shall be shown to be
a Theban born, though he'll take no delight
in that solution. Blind, who once could see,
a beggar who was rich, through foreign lands
he'll go and point before him with a stick.
To his beloved children, he'll be shown
a father who is also brother; to the one
who bore him, son and husband; to his father,
his seed-fellow and killer. Go in
and think this out; and if you find I've lied,
say then I have no prophet's understanding!

Exit Tiresias, led by a Servant. Oedipus exits into the palace with his Attendants.

This day . . . birth: On this day, you will learn who your parents are.

STASIMON 1°

STROPHE 1

Chorus: Who is the man of whom the inspired
rock of Delphi° said
he has committed the unspeakable
with blood-stained hands?
Time for him to ply a foot
mightier than those of the horses
of the storm in his escape;
upon him mounts and plunges the weaponed
son of Zeus,° with fire and thunderbolts,
and in his train the dreaded goddesses
of Death, who never miss.

ANTISTROPHE 1

The message has just blazed,
gleaming from the snows
of Mount Parnassus: we must track
everywhere the unseen man.
He wanders, hidden by wild
forests, up through caves
and rocks, like a bull,
anxious, with an anxious foot, forlorn.
He puts away from him the mantic° words come from earth's
navel,° at its center, yet these live
forever and still hover round him.

STROPHE 2

Terribly he troubles me,
the skilled interpreter of birds!°
I can't assent, nor speak against him.
Both paths are closed to me.
I hover on the wings of doubt,
not seeing what is here nor what's to come.
What quarrel started in the house of Labdacus°
or in the house of Polybus,°

Stasimon: Greek choral ode between episodes.
rock of Delphi: Apollo's oracle at Delphi.
son of Zeus: Apollo.
mantic: Prophetic.
earth's navel: Delphi.
interpreter of birds: Tiresias. The Chorus is troubled by his accusations.
house of Labdacus: The line of Laius.
Polybus: Oedipus's foster father.

either ever in the past
or now, I never
heard, so that . . . with this fact for my touchstone
I could attack the public
fame of Oedipus, by the side of the Labdaceans
an ally, against the dark assassination.

ANTISTROPHE 2

No, Zeus and Apollo
understand and know things
mortal; but that another man
can do more as a prophet than I can—
for that there is no certain test,
though, skill to skill,
one man might overtake another.
No, never, not until
I see the charges proved,
when someone blames him shall I nod assent.
For once, as we all saw, the winged maiden° came
against him: he was seen then to be skilled,
proved, by that touchstone, dear to the people. So,
never will my mind convict him of the evil.

EPISODE 2

Enter Creon from the right door of the skene and speaks to the Chorus.

CREON: Citizens, I hear that a fearful charge
is made against me by King Oedipus!
I had to come. If, in this crisis,
he thinks that he has suffered injury
from anything that I have said or done,
I have no appetite for a long life—
bearing a blame like that! It's no slight blow
the punishment I'd take from what he said:
it's the ultimate hurt to be called traitor
by the city, by you, by my own people!
CHORAGOS: The thing that forced that accusation out
could have been anger, not the power of thought.
CREON: But who persuaded him that thoughts of mine
had led the prophet into telling lies?
CHORAGOS: I do not know the thought behind his words.
CREON: But did he look straight at you? Was his mind right
when he said that I was guilty of this charge?

winged maiden: The Sphinx.

CHORAGOS: I have no eyes to see what rulers do.
But here he comes himself out of the house.

Enter Oedipus from the palace.

OEDIPUS: What? You here? And can you really have
the face and daring to approach my house
when you're exposed as its master's murderer
and caught, too, as the robber of my kingship?
Did you see cowardice in me, by the gods,
or foolishness, when you began this plot?
Did you suppose that I would not detect
your stealthy moves, or that I'd not fight back?
It's your attempt that's folly, isn't it—
tracking without followers or connections,
kingship which is caught with wealth and numbers?
CREON: Now wait! Give me as long to answer back!
Judge me for yourself when you have heard me!
OEDIPUS: You're eloquent, but I'd be slow to learn
from you, now that I've seen your malice toward me.
CREON: That I deny. Hear what I have to say.
OEDIPUS: Don't you deny it! You are the traitor here!
CREON: If you consider mindless willfulness
a prized possession, you are not thinking sense.
OEDIPUS: If you think you can wrong a relative
and get off free, you are not thinking sense.
CREON: Perfectly just, I won't say no. And yet
what is this injury you say I did you?
OEDIPUS: Did you persuade me, yes or no, to send
someone to bring that solemn prophet here?
CREON: And I still hold to the advice I gave.
OEDIPUS: How many years ago did your King Laius . . .
CREON: Laius! Do what? Now I don't understand.
OEDIPUS: Vanish—victim of a murderous violence?
CREON: That is a long count back into the past.
OEDIPUS: Well, was this seer then practicing his art?
CREON: Yes, skilled and honored just as he is today.
OEDIPUS: Did he, back then, ever refer to me?
CREON: He did not do so in my presence ever.
OEDIPUS: You did inquire into the murder then.
CREON: We had to, surely, though we discovered nothing.
OEDIPUS: But the "skilled" one did not say this then? Why not?
CREON: I never talk when I am ignorant.
OEDIPUS: But you're not ignorant of your own part.
CREON: What do you mean? I'll tell you if I know.
OEDIPUS: Just this: if he had not conferred with you
he'd not have told about my murdering Laius.

Creon: If he said that, you are the one who knows.
But now it's fair that you should answer me.
Oedipus: Ask on! You won't convict me as the killer.
Creon: Well then, answer. My sister is your wife?
Oedipus: Now there's a statement that I can't deny.
Creon: You two have equal power in this country?
Oedipus: She gets from me whatever she desires.
Creon: And I'm a third? The three of us are equals?
Oedipus: That's where you're treacherous to your kinsman!
Creon: But think about this rationally, as I do.
First look at this: do you think anyone
prefers the anxieties of being king
to untroubled sleep—if he has equal power?
I'm not the kind of man who falls in love
with kingship. I am content with a king's power.
And so would any man who's wise and prudent.
I get all things from you, with no distress;
as king I would have onerous duties, too.
How could the kingship bring me more delight
than this untroubled power and influence?
I'm not misguided yet to such a point
that profitable honors aren't enough.
As it is, all wish me well and all salute;
those begging you for something have me summoned,
for their success depends on that alone.
Why should I lose all this to become king?
A prudent mind is never traitorous.
Treason's a thought I'm not enamored of;
nor could I join a man who acted so.
In proof of this, first go yourself to Pytho
and ask if I brought back the true response.
Then, if you find I plotted with that portent
reader,° don't have me put to death by your vote
only—I'll vote myself for my conviction.
Don't let an unsupported thought convict me!
It's not right mindlessly to take the bad
for good or to suppose the good are traitors.
Rejecting a relation who is loyal
is like rejecting life, our greatest love.
In time you'll know securely without stumbling,
for time alone can prove a just man just,
though you can know a bad man in a day.

---

portent reader: Apollo's oracle or prophet.

CHORAGOS: Well said, to one who's anxious not to fall.
Swift thinkers, Lord, are never safe from stumbling.
OEDIPUS: But when a swift and secret plotter moves
against me, I must make swift counterplot.
If I lie quiet and await his move,
he'll have achieved his aims and I'll have missed.
CREON: You surely cannot mean you want me exiled!
OEDIPUS: Not exiled, no. Your death is what I want!
CREON: If you would first define what envy is . . .
OEDIPUS: Are you still stubborn? Still disobedient?
CREON: I see you cannot think!
OEDIPUS: For me I can.
CREON: You should for me as well!
OEDIPUS: But you're a traitor!
CREON: What if you're wrong?
OEDIPUS: Authority must be maintained.
CREON: Not if the ruler's evil.
OEDIPUS: Hear that, Thebes!
CREON: It is my city too, not yours alone!
CHORAGOS: Please don't, my Lords! Ah, just in time, I see
Jocasta there, coming from the palace.
With her help you must settle your quarrel.

Enter Jocasta from the palace.

JOCASTA: Wretched men! What has provoked this ill-
advised dispute? Have you no sense of shame,
with Thebes so sick, to stir up private troubles?
Now go inside! And Creon, you go home!
Don't make a general anguish out of nothing!
CREON: My sister, Oedipus your husband here
sees fit to do one of two hideous things:
to have me banished from the land — or killed!
OEDIPUS: That's right: I caught him, Lady, plotting harm
against my person — with a malignant science.
CREON: May my life fail, may I die cursed, if I
did any of the things you said I did!
JOCASTA: Believe his words, for the god's sake, Oedipus,
in deference above all to his oath
to the gods. Also for me, and for these men!

KOMMOS°

STROPHE 1

CHORUS: Consent, with will and mind,
my king, I beg of you!

Kommos: A dirge or lament sung by the Chorus and one or more of the chief characters.

OEDIPUS: What do you wish me to surrender?
CHORUS: Show deference to him who was not feeble in time past
and is now great in the power of his oath!
OEDIPUS: Do you know what you're asking?
CHORUS: Yes.
OEDIPUS: Tell me then.
CHORUS: Never to cast into dishonored guilt, with an unproved
assumption, a kinsman who has bound himself by curse.
OEDIPUS: Now you must understand, when you ask this,
you ask my death or banishment from the land.

STROPHE 2

CHORUS: No, by the god who is the foremost of all gods,
the Sun! No! Godless,
friendless, whatever death is worst of all,
let that be my destruction, if this
thought ever moved me!
But my ill-fated soul
this dying land
wears out — the more if to these older troubles
she adds new troubles from the two of you!
OEDIPUS: Then let him go, though it must mean my death,
or else disgrace and exile from the land.
My pity is moved by your words, not by his —
he'll only have my hate, wherever he goes.
CREON: You're sullen as you yield; you'll be depressed
when you've passed through this anger. Natures like yours
are hardest on themselves. That's as it should be.
OEDIPUS: Then won't you go and let me be?
CREON: I'll go.
Though you're unreasonable, they know I'm righteous.

Exit Creon.

ANTISTROPHE 1

CHORUS: Why are you waiting, Lady?
Conduct him back into the palace!
JOCASTA: I will, when I have heard what chanced.
CHORUS: Conjectures — words alone, and nothing based on thought.
But even an injustice can devour a man.
JOCASTA: Did the words come from both sides?
CHORUS: Yes.
JOCASTA: What was said?
CHORUS: To me it seems enough! enough! the land already troubled,
that this should rest where it has stopped.
OEDIPUS: See what you've come to in your honest thought,
in seeking to relax and blunt my heart?

ANTISTROPHE 2

CHORUS: I have not said this only once, my Lord.
That I had lost my sanity,
without a path in thinking—
be sure this would be clear
if I put you away
who, when my cherished land
wandered crazed
with suffering, brought her back on course.
Now, too, be a lucky helmsman!

JOCASTA: Please, for the god's sake, Lord, explain to me
the reason why you have conceived this wrath?

OEDIPUS: I honor you, not them,° and I'll explain
to you how Creon has conspired against me.

JOCASTA: All right, if that will explain how the quarrel started.

OEDIPUS: He says I am the murderer of Laius!

JOCASTA: Did he claim knowledge or that someone told him?

OEDIPUS: Here's what he did: he sent that vicious seer
so he could keep his own mouth innocent.

JOCASTA: Ah then, absolve yourself of what he charges!
Listen to this and you'll agree, no mortal
is ever given skill in prophecy.
I'll prove this quickly with one incident.
It was foretold to Laius—I shall not say
by Phoebus himself, but by his ministers—
that when his fate arrived he would be killed
by a son who would be born to him and me.
And yet, so it is told, foreign robbers
murdered him, at a place where three roads meet.
As for the child I bore him, not three days passed
before he yoked the ball-joints of its feet,°
then cast it, by others' hands, on a trackless mountain.
That time Apollo did not make our child
a patricide, or bring about what Laius
feared, that he be killed by his own son.
That's how prophetic words determined things!
Forget them. The things a god must track
he will himself painlessly reveal.

OEDIPUS: Just now, as I was listening to you, Lady,
what a profound distraction seized my mind!

JOCASTA: What made you turn around so anxiously?

OEDIPUS: I thought you said that Laius was attacked
and butchered at a place where three roads meet.

---

them: The Chorus.

ball-joints of its feet: The ankles.

Jocasta: That is the story, and it is told so still.
Oedipus: Where is the place where this was done to him?
Jocasta: The land's called Phocis, where a two-forked road
comes in from Delphi and from Daulia.
Oedipus: And how much time has passed since these events?
Jocasta: Just prior to your presentation here
as king this news was published to the city.
Oedipus: Oh, Zeus, what have you willed to do to me?
Jocasta: Oedipus, what makes your heart so heavy?
Oedipus: No, tell me first of Laius' appearance,
what peak of youthful vigor he had reached.
Jocasta: A tall man, showing his first growth of white.
He had a figure not unlike your own.
Oedipus: Alas! It seems that in my ignorance
I laid those fearful curses on myself.
Jocasta: What is it, Lord? I flinch to see your face.
Oedipus: I'm dreadfully afraid the prophet sees.
But I'll know better with one more detail.
Jocasta: I'm frightened too. But ask: I'll answer you.
Oedipus: Was his retinue small, or did he travel
with a great troop, as would befit a prince?
Jocasta: There were just five in all, one a herald.
There was a carriage, too, bearing Laius.
Oedipus: Alas! Now I see it! But who was it,
Lady, who told you what you know about this?
Jocasta: A servant who alone was saved unharmed.
Oedipus: By chance, could he be now in the palace?
Jocasta: No, he is not. When he returned and saw
you had the power of the murdered Laius,
he touched my hand and begged me formally
to send him to the fields and to the pastures,
so he'd be out of sight, far from the city.
I did. Although a slave, he well deserved
to win this favor, and indeed far more.
Oedipus: Let's have him called back in immediately.
Jocasta: That can be done, but why do you desire it?
Oedipus: I fear, Lady, I have already said
too much. That's why I wish to see him now.
Jocasta: Then he shall come; but it is right somehow
that I, too, Lord, should know what troubles you.
Oedipus: I've gone so deep into the things I feared
I'll tell you everything. Who has a right
greater than yours, while I cross through this chance?
Polybus of Corinth was my father,
my mother was the Dorian Meropē.
I was first citizen, until this chance
attacked me—striking enough, to be sure,

but not worth all the gravity I gave it.
This: at a feast a man who'd drunk too much
denied, at the wine, I was my father's son.
I was depressed and all that day I barely
held it in. Next day I put the question
to my mother and father. They were enraged
at the man who'd let this fiction fly at me.
I was much cheered by them. And yet it kept
grinding into me. His words kept coming back.
Without my mother's or my father's knowledge
I went to Pytho. But Phoebus sent me away
dishonoring my demand. Instead, other
wretched horrors he flashed forth in speech.
He said that I would be my mother's lover,
show offspring to mankind they could not look at,
and be his murderer whose seed I am.°
When I heard this, and ever since, I gauged
the way to Corinth by the stars alone,
running to a place where I would never see
the disgrace in the oracle's words come true.
But I soon came to the exact location
where, as you tell of it, the king was killed.
Lady, here is the truth. As I went on,
when I was just approaching those three roads,
a herald and a man like him you spoke of
came on, riding a carriage drawn by colts.
Both the man out front and the old man himself°
tried violently to force me off the road.
The driver, when he tried to push me off,
I struck in anger. The old man saw this, watched
me approach, then leaned out and lunged down
with twin prongs° at the middle of my head!
He got more than he gave. Abruptly — struck
once by the staff in this my hand—he tumbled
out, head first, from the middle of the carriage.
And then I killed them all. But if there is
a kinship between Laius and this stranger,
who is more wretched than the man you see?
Who was there born more hated by the gods?
For neither citizen nor foreigner
may take me in his home or speak to me.

---

be . . . am: I would murder my father.

old man himself: Laius.

lunged . . . prongs: Laius strikes Oedipus with a two-pronged horse goad, or whip.

No, they must drive me off. And it is I
who have pronounced these curses on myself!
I stain the dead man's bed with these my hands,
by which he died. Is not my nature vile?
Unclean?—if I am banished and even
in exile I may not see my own parents,
or set foot in my homeland, or else be yoked
in marriage to my mother, and kill my father,
Polybus, who raised me and gave me birth?
If someone judged a cruel divinity
did this to me, would he not speak the truth?
You pure and awful gods, may I not ever
see that day, may I be swept away
from men before I see so great and so
calamitous a stain fixed on my person!

CHORAGOS: These things seem fearful to us, Lord, and yet,
until you hear it from the witness, keep hope!

OEDIPUS: That is the single hope that's left to me,
to wait for him, that herdsman—until he comes.

JOCASTA: When he appears, what are you eager for?

OEDIPUS: Just this: if his account agrees with yours
then I shall have escaped this misery.

JOCASTA: But what was it that struck you in my story?

OEDIPUS: You said he spoke of robbers as the ones
who killed him. Now: if he continues still
to speak of many, then I could not have killed him.
One man and many men just do not jibe.
But if he says one belted man, the doubt
is gone. The balance tips toward me. I did it.

JOCASTA: No! He told it as I told you. Be certain.
He can't reject that and reverse himself.
The city heard these things, not I alone.
But even if he swerves from what he said,
he'll never show that Laius' murder, Lord,
occurred just as predicted. For Loxias
expressly said my son was doomed to kill him.
The boy—poor boy—he never had a chance
to cut him down, for he was cut down first.
Never again, just for some oracle
will I shoot frightened glances right and left.

OEDIPUS: That's full of sense. Nonetheless, send a man
to bring that farm hand here. Will you do it?

JOCASTA: I'll send one right away. But let's go in.
Would I do anything against your wishes?

Exit Oedipus and Jocasta through the central door into the palace.

STASIMON 2

STROPHE 1

CHORUS: May there accompany me
the fate to keep a reverential purity in what I say,
in all I do, for which the laws have been set forth
and walk on high, born to traverse the brightest,
highest upper air; Olympus° only
is their father, nor was it
mortal nature
that fathered them, and never will
oblivion lull them into sleep;
the god in them is great and never ages.

ANTISTROPHE 1

The will to violate, seed of the tyrant,
if it has drunk mindlessly of wealth and power,
without a sense of time or true advantage,
mounts to a peak, then
plunges to an abrupt . . . destiny,
where the useful foot
is of no use. But the kind
of struggling that is good for the city
I ask the god never to abolish.
The god is my protector: never will I give that up.

STROPHE 2

But if a man proceeds disdainfully
in deeds of hand or word
and has no fear of Justice
or reverence for shrines of the divinities
(may a bad fate catch him
for his luckless wantonness!),
if he'll not gain what he gains with justice
and deny himself what is unholy,
or if he clings, in foolishness, to the untouchable
(what man, finally, in such an action, will have strength
enough to fend off passion's arrows from his soul?),
if, I say, this kind of
deed is held in honor—
why should I join the sacred dance?

Olympus: Mount Olympus, home of the gods, and treated as a god itself.

ANTISTROPHE 2

No longer shall I visit and revere
Earth's navel,° the untouchable,
nor visit Abae's° temple,
or Olympia,°
if the prophecies are not matched by events
for all the world to point to.
No, you who hold the power, if you are rightly called
Zeus the king of all, let this matter not escape you
and your ever-deathless rule,
for the prophecies to Laius fade . . .
and men already disregard them;
nor is Apollo anywhere
glorified with honors.
Religion slips away.

EPISODE 3

Enter Jocasta from the palace carrying a branch wound with wool and a jar of incense. She is attended by two women.

JOCASTA: Lords of the realm, the thought has come to me
to visit shrines of the divinities
with suppliant's branch in hand and fragrant smoke.
For Oedipus excites his soul too much
with alarms of all kinds. He will not judge
the present by the past, like a man of sense.
He's at the mercy of all terror-mongers.

Jocasta approaches the altar on the right and kneels.

Since I can do no good by counseling,
Apollo the Lycēan!—you are the closest—
I come a suppliant, with these my vows,
for a cleansing that will not pollute him.
For when we see him shaken we are all
afraid, like people looking at their helmsman.

Enter a Messenger along one of the parados. He sees Jocasta at the altar and then addresses the Chorus.

MESSENGER: I would be pleased if you would help me, stranger.
Where is the palace of King Oedipus?
Or tell me where he is himself, if you know.

Earth's navel: Delphi.

Abae's: Abae was a town in Phocis where there was another oracle of Apollo.

Olympia: Site of the oracle of Zeus.

CHORUS: This is his house, stranger. He is within.
This is his wife and mother of his children.
MESSENGER: May she and her family find prosperity,
if, as you say, her marriage is fulfilled.
JOCASTA: You also, stranger, for you deserve as much
for your gracious words. But tell me why you've come.
What do you wish? Or what have you to tell us?
MESSENGER: Good news, my Lady, both for your house and husband.
JOCASTA: What is your news? And who has sent you to us?
MESSENGER: I come from Corinth. When you have heard my news
you will rejoice, I'm sure—and grieve perhaps.
JOCASTA: What is it? How can it have this double power?
MESSENGER: They will establish him their king, so say
the people of the land of Isthmia.°
JOCASTA: But is old Polybus not still in power?
MESSENGER: He's not, for death has clasped him in the tomb.
JOCASTA: What's this? Has Oedipus' father died?
MESSENGER: If I have lied then I deserve to die.
JOCASTA: Attendant! Go quickly to your master,
and tell him this.

Exit an Attendant into the palace.

Oracles of the gods!
Where are you now? The man whom Oedipus
fled long ago, for fear that he should kill him—
he's been destroyed by chance and not by him!

Enter Oedipus from the palace.

OEDIPUS: Darling Jocasta, my beloved wife,
Why have you called me from the palace?
JOCASTA: First hear what this man has to say. Then see
what the god's grave oracle has come to now!
OEDIPUS: Where is he from? What is this news he brings me?
JOCASTA: From Corinth. He brings news about your father:
that Polybus is no more! that he is dead!
OEDIPUS: What's this, old man? I want to hear you say it.
MESSENGER: If this is what must first be clarified,
please be assured that he is dead and gone.
OEDIPUS: By treachery or by the touch of sickness?
MESSENGER: Light pressures tip agéd frames into their sleep.
OEDIPUS: You mean the poor man died of some disease.
MESSENGER: And of the length of years that he had tallied.

---

land of Isthmia: Corinth, Greek city-state situated on an isthmus.

OEDIPUS: Aha! Then why should we look to Pytho's vapors,°
or to the birds that scream above our heads?°
If we could really take those things for guides,
I would have killed my father. But he's dead!
He is beneath the earth, and here am I,
who never touched a spear. Unless he died
of longing for me and I "killed" him that way!
No, in this case, Polybus, by dying, took
the worthless oracle to Hades with him.
JOCASTA: And wasn't I telling you that just now?
OEDIPUS: You were indeed. I was misled by fear.
JOCASTA: You should not care about this anymore.
OEDIPUS: I must care. I must stay clear of my mother's bed.
JOCASTA: What's there for man to fear? The realm of chance
prevails. True foresight isn't possible.
His life is best who lives without a plan.
This marriage with your mother—don't fear it.
How many times have men in dreams, too, slept
with their own mothers! Those who believe such things
mean nothing endure their lives most easily.
OEDIPUS: A fine, bold speech, and you are right, perhaps,
except that my mother is still living,
so I must fear her, however well you argue.
JOCASTA: And yet your father's tomb is a great eye.
OEDIPUS: Illuminating, yes. But I still fear the living.
MESSENGER: Who is the woman who inspires this fear?
OEDIPUS: Meropē, Polybus' wife, old man.
MESSENGER: And what is there about her that alarms you?
OEDIPUS: An oracle, god-sent and fearful, stranger.
MESSENGER: Is it permitted that another know?
OEDIPUS: It is. Loxias once said to me
I must have intercourse with my own mother
and take my father's blood with these my hands.
So I have long lived far away from Corinth.
This has indeed brought much good luck, and yet,
to see one's parents' eyes is happiest.
MESSENGER: Was it for this that you have lived in exile?
OEDIPUS: So I'd not be my father's killer, sir.
MESSENGER: Had I not better free you from this fear,
my Lord? That's why I came—to do you service.
OEDIPUS: Indeed, what a reward you'd get for that!

Pytho's vapors: Prophecies of the oracle at Delphi.

birds . . . heads: Prophecies derived from interpreting the flights of birds.

MESSENGER: Indeed, this is the main point of my trip,
to be rewarded when you get back home.
OEDIPUS: I'll never rejoin the givers of my seed!°
MESSENGER: My son, clearly you don't know what you're doing.
OEDIPUS: But how is that, old man? For the gods' sake, tell me!
MESSENGER: If it's because of them you won't go home.
OEDIPUS: I fear that Phoebus will have told the truth.
MESSENGER: Pollution from the ones who gave you seed?
OEDIPUS: That is the thing, old man, I always fear.
MESSENGER: Your fear is groundless. Understand that.
OEDIPUS: Groundless? Not if I was born their son.
MESSENGER: But Polybus is not related to you.
OEDIPUS: Do you mean Polybus was not my father?
MESSENGER: No more than I. We're both the same to you.
OEDIPUS: Same? One who begot me and one who didn't?
MESSENGER: He didn't beget you any more than I did.
OEDIPUS: But then, why did he say I was his son?
MESSENGER: He got you as a gift from my own hands.
OEDIPUS: He loved me so, though from another's hands?
MESSENGER: His former childlessness persuaded him.
OEDIPUS: But had you bought me, or begotten me?
MESSENGER: Found you. In the forest hallows of Cithaeron.
OEDIPUS: What were you doing traveling in that region?
MESSENGER: I was in charge of flocks which grazed those mountains.
OEDIPUS: A wanderer who worked the flocks for hire?
MESSENGER: Ah, but that day I was your savior, son.
OEDIPUS: From what? What was my trouble when you took me?
MESSENGER: The ball-joints of your feet might testify.
OEDIPUS: What's that? What makes you name that ancient trouble?
MESSENGER: Your feet were pierced and I am your rescuer.
OEDIPUS: A fearful rebuke those tokens left for me!
MESSENGER: That was the chance that names you who you are.
OEDIPUS: By the gods, did my mother or my father do this?
MESSENGER: That I don't know. He might who gave you to me.
OEDIPUS: From someone else? You didn't chance on me?
MESSENGER: Another shepherd handed you to me.
OEDIPUS: Who was he? Do you know? Will you explain!
MESSENGER: They called him one of the men of—was it Laius?
OEDIPUS: The one who once was king here long ago?
MESSENGER: That is the one! The man was shepherd to him.
OEDIPUS: And is he still alive so I can see him?
MESSENGER: But you who live here ought to know that best.

---

givers of my seed: i.e., "my parents." Oedipus still thinks Meropē and Polybus are his parents.

OEDIPUS: Does any one of you now present know
about the shepherd whom this man has named?
Have you seen him in town or in the fields? Speak out!
The time has come for the discovery!
CHORAGOS: The man he speaks of, I believe, is the same
as the field hand you have already asked to see.
But it's Jocasta who would know this best.
OEDIPUS: Lady, do you remember the man we just
now sent for—is that the man he speaks of?
JOCASTA: What? The man he spoke of? Pay no attention!
His words are not worth thinking about. It's nothing.
OEDIPUS: With clues like this within my grasp, give up?
Fail to solve the mystery of my birth?
JOCASTA: For the love of the gods, and if you love your life,
give up this search! My sickness is enough.
OEDIPUS: Come! Though my mothers for three generations
were in slavery, you'd not be lowborn!
JOCASTA: No, listen to me! Please! Don't do this thing!
OEDIPUS: I will not listen; I will search out the truth.
JOCASTA: My thinking is for you—it would be best.
OEDIPUS: This "best" of yours is starting to annoy me.
JOCASTA: Doomed man! Never find out who you are!
OEDIPUS: Will someone go and bring that shepherd here?
Leave her to glory in her wealthy birth!
JOCASTA: Man of misery! No other name
shall I address you by, ever again.

Exit Jocasta into the palace after a long pause.

CHORAGOS: Why has your lady left, Oedipus,
hurled by a savage grief? I am afraid
disaster will come bursting from this silence.
OEDIPUS: Let it burst forth! However low this seed
of mine may be, yet I desire to see it.
She, perhaps—she has a woman's pride—
is mortified by my base origins.
But I who count myself the child of Chance,
the giver of good, shall never know dishonor.
She is my mother,° and the months my brothers
who first marked out my lowness, then my greatness.
I shall not prove untrue to such a nature
by giving up the search for my own birth.

She . . . mother: Chance is my mother.

STASIMON 3

STROPHE

CHORUS: If I have mantic power°
and excellence in thought,
by Olympus,
you shall not, Cithaeron, at tomorrow's
full moon,
fail to hear us celebrate you as the countryman
of Oedipus, his nurse and mother,
or fail to be the subject of our dance,
since you have given pleasure
to our king.
Phoebus, whom we summon by "iē!,"
may this be pleasing to you!

ANTISTROPHE

Who was your mother, son?
which of the long-lived nymphs
after lying with Pan,°
the mountain roaming . . . Or was it a bride
of Loxias?°
For dear to him are all the upland pastures.
Or was it Mount Cyllēnē's lord,°
or the Bacchic god,°
dweller of the mountain peaks,
who received you as a joyous find
from one of the nymphs of Helicon,
the favorite sharers of his sport?

EPISODE 4

OEDIPUS: If someone like myself, who never met him,
may calculate—elders, I think I see
the very herdsman we've been waiting for.
His many years would fit that man's age,
and those who bring him on, if I am right,
are my own men. And yet, in real knowledge,
you can outstrip me, surely: you've seen him.

Enter the old Herdsman escorted by two of Oedipus's Attendants. At first, the Herdsman will not look at Oedipus.

If . . . mantic power: If I am a prophet.

Pan: God of shepherds and woodlands, half man and half goat.

Loxias: Apollo.

Mount Cyllēnē's lord: Hermes, messenger of the gods.

Bacchic god: Dionysus.

Choragos: I know him, yes, a man of the house of Laius,
a trusty herdsman if he ever had one.
Oedipus: I ask you first, the stranger come from Corinth:
is this the man you spoke of?
Messenger: That's he you see.
Oedipus: Then you, old man. First look at me! Now answer:
did you belong to Laius' household once?
Herdsman: I did. Not a purchased slave but raised in the palace.
Oedipus: How have you spent your life? What is your work?
Herdsman: Most of my life now I have tended sheep.
Oedipus: Where is the usual place you stay with them?
Herdsman: On Mount Cithaeron. Or in that district.
Oedipus: Do you recall observing this man there?
Herdsman: Doing what? Which is the man you mean?
Oedipus: This man right here. Have you had dealings with him?
Herdsman: I can't say right away. I don't remember.
Messenger: No wonder, master. I'll bring clear memory
to his ignorance. I'm absolutely sure
he can recall it, the district was Cithaeron,
he with a double flock, and I, with one,
lived close to him, for three entire seasons,
six months along, from spring right to Arcturus.°
Then for the winter I'd drive mine to my fold,
and he'd drive his to Laius' pen again.
Did any of the things I say take place?
Herdsman: You speak the truth, though it's from long ago.
Messenger: Do you remember giving me, back then,
a boy I was to care for as my own?
Herdsman: What are you saying? Why do you ask me that?
Messenger: There, sir, is the man who was that boy!
Herdsman: Damn you! Shut your mouth! Keep your silence!
Oedipus: Stop! Don't you rebuke his words.
Your words ask for rebuke far more than his.
Herdsman: But what have I done wrong, most royal master?
Oedipus: Not telling of the boy of whom he asked.
Herdsman: He's ignorant and blundering toward ruin.
Oedipus: Tell it willingly—or under torture.
Herdsman: Oh god! Don't—I am old—don't torture me!
Oedipus: Here! Someone put his hands behind his back!
Herdsman: But why? What else would you find out, poor man?
Oedipus: Did you give him the child he asks about?
Herdsman: I did. I wish that I had died that day!
Oedipus: You'll come to that if you don't speak the truth.

Arcturus: A star that is first seen in September in the sky over Greece.

HERDSMAN: It's if I speak that I shall be destroyed.
OEDIPUS: I think this fellow struggles for delay.
HERDSMAN: No, no! I said already that I gave him.
OEDIPUS: From your own home, or got from someone else?
HERDSMAN: Not from my own. I got him from another.
OEDIPUS: Which of these citizens? What sort of house?
HERDSMAN: Don't—by the gods!—don't, master, ask me more!
OEDIPUS: It means your death if I must ask again.
HERDSMAN: One of the children of the house of Laius.
OEDIPUS: A slave—or born into the family?
HERDSMAN: I have come to the dreaded thing, and I shall say it.
OEDIPUS: And I to hearing it, but hear I must.
HERDSMAN: He was reported to have been—his son.
Your lady in the house could tell you best.
OEDIPUS: Because she gave him to you?
HERDSMAN: Yes, my lord.
OEDIPUS: What was her purpose?
HERDSMAN: I was to kill the boy.
OEDIPUS: The child she bore?
HERDSMAN: She dreaded prophecies.
OEDIPUS: What were they?
HERDSMAN: The word was that he'd kill his parents.
OEDIPUS: Then why did you give him up to this old man?
HERDSMAN: In pity, master—so he would take him home,
to another land. But what he did was save him
for this supreme disaster. If you are the one
he speaks of—know your evil birth and fate!
OEDIPUS: Ah! All of it was destined to be true!
Oh light, now may I look my last upon you,
shown monstrous in my birth, in marriage monstrous,
a murderer monstrous in those I killed.

Exit Oedipus, running into the palace.

STASIMON 4

STROPHE 1

CHORUS: Oh generations of mortal men,
while you are living, I will
appraise your lives at zero!
What man
comes closer to seizing lasting blessedness
than merely to seize its semblance,
and after living in this semblance, to plunge?
With your example before us,
with your destiny, yours,
suffering Oedipus, no mortal
can I judge fortunate.

ANTISTROPHE 1

For he,° outranging everybody,
shot his arrow° and became the lord
    of wide prosperity and blessedness,
oh Zeus, after destroying
the virgin with the crooked talons,°
singer of oracles; and against death,
in my land, he arose a tower of defense.
From which time you were called my king
and granted privileges supreme—in mighty
Thebes the ruling lord.

STROPHE 2

But now—whose story is more sorrowful than yours?
Who is more intimate with fierce calamities,
with labors, now that your life is altered?
Alas, my Oedipus, whom all men know:
one great harbor°—
one alone sufficed for you,
as son and father,
when you tumbled,° plowman° of the woman's chamber.
How, how could your paternal
    furrows, wretched man,
endure you silently so long.

ANTISTROPHE 2

Time, all-seeing, surprised you living an unwilled life
and sits from of old in judgment on the marriage, not a marriage,
where the begetter is the begot as well.
Ah, son of Laius . . . ,
would that—oh, would that
I had never seen you!
I wail, my scream climbing beyond itself
from my whole power of voice. To say it straight:
    from you I got new breath—
but I also lulled my eye to sleep.°

---

he: Oedipus.

shot his arrow: Took his chances; made a guess at the Sphinx's riddle.

virgin . . . talons: The Sphinx.

one great harbor: Metaphorical allusion to Jocasta's body.

tumbled: Were born and had sex.

plowman: Plowing is used here as a sexual metaphor.

I . . . sleep: I failed to see the corruption you brought.

EXODOS°

Enter the Second Messenger from the palace.

SECOND MESSENGER: You who are first among the citizens,
what deeds you are about to hear and see!
What grief you'll carry, if, true to your birth,
you still respect the house of Labdacus!
Neither the Ister nor the Phasis river
could purify this house, such suffering
does it conceal, or soon must bring to light —
willed this time, not unwilled. Griefs hurt worst
which we perceive to be self-chosen ones.

CHORAGOS: They were sufficient, the things we knew before,
to make us grieve. What can you add to those?

SECOND MESSENGER: The thing that's quickest said and quickest heard:
our own, our royal one, Jocasta's dead.

CHORAGOS: Unhappy queen! What was responsible?

SECOND MESSENGER: Herself. The bitterest of these events
is not for you, you were not there to see,
but yet, exactly as I can recall it,
you'll hear what happened to that wretched lady.
She came in anger through the outer hall,
and then she ran straight to her marriage bed,
tearing her hair with the fingers of both hands.
Then, slamming shut the doors when she was in,
she called to Laius, dead so many years,
remembering the ancient seed which caused
his death, leaving the mother to the son
to breed again an ill-born progeny.
She mourned the bed where she, alas, bred double —
husband by husband, children by her child.
From this point on I don't know how she died,
for Oedipus then burst in with a cry,
and did not let us watch her final evil.
Our eyes were fixed on him. Wildly he ran
to each of us, asking for his spear
and for his wife — no wife: where he might find
the double mother-field, his and his children's.
He raved, and some divinity then showed him —
for none of us did so who stood close by.
With a dreadful shout — as if some guide were leading —
he lunged through the double doors; he bent the hollow

Exodos: The final scene, containing the play's resolution.

bolts from the sockets, burst into the room,
and there we saw her, hanging from above,
entangled in some twisted hanging strands.
He saw, was stricken, and with a wild roar
ripped down the dangling noose. When she, poor woman,
lay on the ground, there came a fearful sight:
he snatched the pins of worked gold from her dress,
with which her clothes were fastened: these he raised
and struck into the ball-joints of his eyes.°
He shouted that they would no longer see
the evils he had suffered or had done,
see in the dark those he should not have seen,
and know no more those he once sought to know.
While chanting this, not once but many times
he raised his hand and struck into his eyes.
Blood from his wounded eyes poured down his chin,
not freed in moistening drops, but all at once
a stormy rain of black blood burst like hail.
These evils, coupling them, making them one,
have broken loose upon both man and wife.
The old prosperity that they had once
was true prosperity, and yet today,
mourning, ruin, death, disgrace, and every
evil you could name — not one is absent.

CHORAGOS: Has he allowed himself some peace from all this grief?

SECOND MESSENGER: He shouts that someone slide the bolts and show
to all the Cadmeians the patricide,
his mother's — I can't say it, it's unholy —
so he can cast himself out of the land,
not stay and curse his house by his own curse.
He lacks the strength, though, and he needs a guide,
for his is a sickness that's too great to bear.
Now you yourself will see: the bolts of the doors
are opening. You are about to see
a vision even one who hates must pity.

Enter the blinded Oedipus from the palace, led in by a household Servant.

CHORAGOS: Terrifying suffering for men to see,
more terrifying than any I've ever
come upon. Oh man of pain
what madness reached you? Which god from far off,
surpassing in range his longest spring,
struck hard against your god-abandoned fate?

---

ball-joints of his eyes: His eyeballs. Oedipus blinds himself in both eyes at the same time.

Oh man of pain,
I cannot look upon you—though there's so much
I would ask you, so much to hear,
so much that holds my eyes—
such is the shudder you produce in me.

OEDIPUS: Ah! Ah! I am a man of misery.
Where am I carried? Pity me! Where
is my voice scattered abroad on wings?
Divinity, where has your lunge transported me?

CHORAGOS: To something horrible, not to be heard or seen.

KOMMOS

STROPHE 1

OEDIPUS: Oh, my cloud
of darkness, abominable, unspeakable as it attacks me,
not to be turned away, brought by an evil wind!
Alas!
Again alas! Both enter me at once:
the sting of the prongs,° the memory of evils!

CHORUS: I do not marvel that in these afflictions
you carry double griefs and double evils.

ANTISTROPHE 1

OEDIPUS: Ah, friend,
so you at least are there, resolute servant!
Still with a heart to care for me, the blind man.
Oh! Oh!
I know that you are there. I recognize
even inside my darkness, that voice of yours.

CHORUS: Doer of horror, how did you bear to quench
your vision? What divinity raised your hand?

STROPHE 2

OEDIPUS: It was Apollo there, Apollo, friends,
who brought my sorrows, vile sorrows to their perfection,
these evils that were done to me.
But the one who struck them with his hand,
that one was none but I, in wretchedness.
For why was I to see
when nothing I could see would bring me joy?

CHORUS: Yes, that is how it was.

OEDIPUS: What could I see, indeed,
or what enjoy—what greeting
is there I could hear with pleasure, friends?

---

prongs: Refers both to the whip that Laius used and to the two gold pins that Oedipus used to blind himself.

Conduct me out of the land
as quickly as you can!
Conduct me out, my friends,
the man utterly ruined,
supremely cursed,
the man who is by gods
the most detested of all men!

CHORUS: Wretched in disaster and in knowledge:
oh, I could wish you'd never come to know!

ANTISTROPHE 2

OEDIPUS: May he be destroyed, whoever freed the savage shackles
from my feet when I'd been sent to the wild pasture,
whoever rescued me from murder
and became my savior—
a bitter gift:
if I had died then,
I'd not have been such grief to self and kin.

CHORUS: I also would have had it so.

OEDIPUS: I'd not have returned to be my father's
murderer; I'd not be called by men
my mother's bridegroom.
Now I'm without a god,
child of a polluted parent,
fellow progenitor with him
who gave me birth in misery.
If there's an evil that
surpasses evils, that
has fallen to the lot of Oedipus.

CHORAGOS: How can I say that you have counseled well?
Better not to be than live a blind man.

OEDIPUS: That this was not the best thing I could do—
don't tell me that, or advise me any more!
Should I descend to Hades and endure
to see my father with these eyes? Or see
my poor unhappy mother? For I have done,
to both of these, things too great for hanging.
Or is the sight of children to be yearned for,
to see new shoots that sprouted as these did?
Never, never with these eyes of mine!
Nor city, nor tower, nor holy images
of the divinities! For I, all-wretched,
most nobly raised—as no one else in Thebes—
deprived myself of these when I ordained
that all expel the impious one—god-shown

to be polluted, and the dead king's son!°
Once I exposed this great stain upon me,
could I have looked on these with steady eyes?
No! No! And if there were a way to block
the source of hearing in my ears, I'd gladly
have locked up my pitiable body,
so I'd be blind and deaf. Evils shut out—
that way my mind could live in sweetness.
Alas, Cithaeron, why did you receive me?
Or when you had me, not killed me instantly?
I'd not have had to show my birth to mankind.
Polybus, Corinth, halls—ancestral,
they told me—how beautiful was your ward,
a scar that held back festering disease!
Evil my nature, evil my origin.
You, three roads, and you, secret ravine,
you oak grove, narrow place of those three paths
that drank my blood° from these hands, from him
who fathered me, do you remember still
the things I did to you? When I'd come here,
what I then did once more? Oh marriages! Marriages!
You gave us life and when you'd planted us
you sent the same seed up, and then revealed
fathers, brothers, sons, and kinsman's blood,
and brides, and wives, and mothers, all the most
atrocious things that happen to mankind!
One should not name what never should have been.
Somewhere out there, then, quickly, by the gods,
cover me up, or murder me, or throw me
to the ocean where you will never see me more!

Oedipus moves toward the Chorus and they back away from him.

Come! Don't shrink to touch this wretched man!
Believe me, do not be frightened! I alone
of all mankind can carry these afflictions.

Enter Creon from the palace with Attendants.

CHORAGOS: Tell Creon what you wish for. Just when we need him
he's here. He can act, he can advise you.
He's now the land's sole guardian in your place.

I . . . son: Oedipus refers to his own curse against the murderer as well as his sins of patricide and incest.
my blood: I.e., "the blood of my father, Laius."

Oedipus: Ah! Are there words that I can speak to him?
What ground for trust can I present? It's proved
that I was false to him in everything.

Creon: I have not come to mock you, Oedipus,
nor to reproach you for your former falseness.
You men, if you have no respect for sons
of mortals, let your awe for the all-feeding
flames of lordy Hēlius° prevent
your showing unconcealed so great a stain,
abhorred by earth and sacred rain and light.
Escort him quickly back into the house!
If blood kin only see and hear their own
afflictions, we'll have no impious defilement.

Oedipus: By the gods, you've freed me from one terrible fear,
so nobly meeting my unworthiness:
grant me something—not for me; for you!

Creon: What do you want that you should beg me so?

Oedipus: To drive me from the land at once, to a place
where there will be no man to speak to me!

Creon: I would have done just that—had I not wished
to ask first of the god what I should do.

Oedipus: His answer was revealed in full—that I,
the patricide, unholy, be destroyed.

Creon: He said that, but our need is so extreme,
it's best to have sure knowledge what must be done.

Oedipus: You'll ask about a wretched man like me?

Creon: Is it not time you put your trust in the god?

Oedipus: But I bid you as well, and shall entreat you.
Give her who is within what burial
you will—you'll give your own her proper rites;
but me—do not condemn my fathers' land
to have me dwelling here while I'm alive,
but let me live on mountains—on Cithaeron
famed as mine, for my mother and my father,
while they yet lived, made it my destined tomb,
and I'll be killed by those who wished my ruin!
And yet I know: no sickness will destroy me,
nothing will: I'd never have been saved
when left to die unless for some dread evil.
Then let my fate continue where it will!
As for my children, Creon, take no pains
for my sons—they're men and they will never lack
the means to live, wherever they may be—

Hēlius: The sun.

but my two wretched, pitiable girls,
who never ate but at my table, never
were without me—everything that I
would touch, they'd always have a share of it—
please care for them! Above all, let me touch
them with my hands and weep aloud my woes!
Please, my Lord!
Please, noble heart! Touching with my hands,
I'd think I held them as when I could see.

Enter Antigone and Ismene from the palace with Attendants.

What's this?
Oh gods! Do I hear, somewhere, my two dear ones
sobbing? Has Creon really pitied me
and sent to me my dearest ones, my children?
Is that it?

CREON: Yes, I prepared this for you, for I knew
you'd feel this joy, as you have always done.

OEDIPUS: Good fortune, then, and, for your care, be guarded
far better by divinity than I was!
Where are you, children? Come to me! Come here
to these my hands, hands of your brother, hands
of him who gave you seed, hands that made
these once bright eyes to see now in this fashion.

Oedipus embraces his daughters.

He, children, seeing nothing, knowing nothing,
he fathered you where his own seed was plowed.
I weep for you as well, though I can't see you,
imagining your bitter life to come,
the life you will be forced by men to live.
What gatherings of townsmen will you join,
what festivals, without returning home
in tears instead of watching holy rites?
And when you've reached the time for marrying,
where, children, is the man who'll run the risk
of taking on himself the infamy
that will wound you as it did my parents?
What evil is not here? Your father killed
his father, plowed the one who gave him birth,
and from the place where he was sown, from there
he got you, from the place he too was born.
These are the wounds: then who will marry you?
No man, my children. No, it's clear that you
must wither in dry barrenness, unmarried.

Oedipus addresses Creon.

Son of Menoeceus! You are the only father
left to them—we two who gave them seed
are both destroyed: watch that they don't become
poor, wanderers, unmarried—they are your kin.
Let not my ruin be their ruin, too!
No, pity them! You see how young they are,
bereft of everyone, except for you.
Consent, kind heart, and touch me with your hand!

Creon grasps Oedipus's right hand.

You, children, if you had reached an age of sense,
I would have counseled much. Now, pray you may live
always where it's allowed, finding a life
better than his was, who gave you seed.

CREON: Stop this now. Quiet your weeping. Move away, into the house.
OEDIPUS: Bitter words, but I obey them.
CREON: There's an end to all things.
OEDIPUS: I have first this request.
CREON: Tell me. I shall judge when I will hear it.
OEDIPUS: Banish me from my homeland.
CREON: You must ask that of the god.
OEDIPUS: But I am the gods' most hated man!
CREON: Then you will soon get what you want.
OEDIPUS: Do you consent?
CREON: I never promise when, as now, I'm ignorant.
OEDIPUS: Then lead me in.
CREON: Come. But let your hold fall from your children.
OEDIPUS: Do not take them from me, ever!
CREON: Do not wish to keep all of the power.
You had power, but that power did not follow you through life.

Oedipus's daughters are taken from him and led into the palace by Attendants. Oedipus is led into the palace by a Servant. Creon and the other Attendants follow. Only the Chorus remains.

CHORUS: People of Thebes, my country, see: here is that Oedipus—
he who "knew" the famous riddle, and attained the highest power,
whom all citizens admired, even envying his luck!
See the billows of wild troubles which he has entered now!
Here is the truth of each man's life: we must wait, and see his end,
scrutinize his dying day, and refuse to call him happy
till he has crossed the border of his life without pain.

Exit the Chorus along each of the parados.

Reading and Reacting

1. The ancient Greeks used no scenery in their theatrical productions. In the absence of scenery, how is the setting established at the beginning of *Oedipus the King*?
2. In some recent productions of *Oedipus the King*, actors wear copies of ancient Greek masks. What are the advantages and disadvantages of using such masks in a contemporary production of the play?
3. In the ancient Greek theater, the *strophe* and *antistrophe* were sung or chanted by the chorus as it danced back and forth across the stage. If you were staging the play today, would you retain the chorus or do away with it entirely? What would be gained or lost with each alternative?
4. Why does Sophocles have Oedipus blind himself offstage? What would be the effect of having Oedipus perform this act in full view of the audience?
5. How does Sophocles observe the unities of time, place, and action described on page 1245? How does Sophocles manage to present information about what happened years before the action of the play while still maintaining the three unities?
6. The ancient Greek audience that viewed *Oedipus the King* was familiar with the plot of the play. Given this situation, how does Sophocles create suspense? What are the advantages and disadvantages of using a story that the audience already knows?
7. By the end of the play, what has Oedipus learned about himself? About the gods? About the quest for truth? Is he a tragic or a pathetic figure? (See pages 1244–49 for a discussion of **tragedy** and **pathos**.)
8. Today, many directors employ **color-blind casting**—that is, they cast an actor in a role without regard to his or her race. Do you think this practice could be used in casting *Oedipus the King?* How, for example, would you react to an African-American Oedipus or to an Asian Creon?
9. **JOURNAL ENTRY** Do you think Oedipus deserves his fate? Why or why not?
10. **CRITICAL PERSPECTIVE** In "On Misunderstanding the *Oedipus Rex*," F. R. Dodds argues that Sophocles did not intend that Oedipus's tragedy be seen as rising from a "grave moral flaw." Neither, says Dodds, was Oedipus a "mere puppet" of the gods. Rather, "what fascinates us is the spectacle of a man freely choosing, from the highest motives, a series of actions which lead to his own ruin":

    > Oedipus is great, not in virtue of a great worldly position—for his worldly position is an illusion which will vanish like a dream—but in virtue of his inner strength: strength to pursue the truth at whatever personal cost, and strength to accept and endure it when found. . . . Oedipus is great because he accepts the responsibility for all his acts, including those which are objectively most horrible, though subjectively innocent.

    Do you agree with Dodds's arguments? Do you see Oedipus as someone who has inner strength or as a morally flawed victim of the gods?

Related Works: "Barn Burning" (p. 391), "Young Goodman Brown" (p. 540), "'Out, Out—'" (p. 943), "Leda and the Swan" (p. 1030), "Ulysses" (p. 1203), *Hamlet* (p. 1605), *Antigone* (p. 1863)

WILLIAM SHAKESPEARE (1564–1616) was the best-known dramatist of his era (see biography and photo on p. 1604). *A Midsummer Night's Dream* was first performed in celebration of an aristocratic marriage, in either January 1595 or February 1596; its three levels of love stories, all worked out by the end, make it a suitable wedding entertainment. Uncharacteristically for Shakespeare, there is no central earlier source for the story although parts of it probably come from Chaucer, Ovid, and English folk legends. The play has always been popular with audiences and has frequently been adapted into other forms, such as ballet and opera. In Seattle in 1979, for example, a musical adaptation used popular songs from the 1950s: Puck sang, "Why Do Fools Fall in Love?" and Oberon entered on a motorcycle and sang "Love Potion Number Nine."

Cultural Context The conditions and restrictions of Elizabethan theater undoubtedly shaped the kinds of plays and characters Shakespeare created. For example, during this period, women were not permitted to perform on the English stage, so all of the female roles in his plays were written for, and performed by, boy actors whose voices had not yet changed. Ironically, some of literature's most beloved female characters, including Ophelia, Desdemona, and Juliet, were originally performed by males. Moreover, many of Shakespeare's plays feature female characters who cross-dress, or pose as males to accomplish certain tasks, further compounding the gender confusion. Actresses were not allowed to play female roles onstage until 1660 when the theaters reopened after being closed during the Puritan Revolution of 1642.

A Midsummer Night's Dream*

DRAMATIS PERSONAE

Theseus, *Duke of Athens*
Egeus, *father to Hermia*
Lysander, **Demetrius** } *in love with Hermia*
Philostrate, *Master of the Revels to Theseus*
Quince, *a carpenter (Prologue)*
Bottom, *a weaver (Pyramus)*
Flute, *a bellows-mender (Thisby)*
Snout, *a tinker (Wall)*
Snug, *a joiner (Lion)*
Starveling, *a tailor (Moonshine)*
Hippolyta, *Queen of the Amazons, betrothed to Theseus*
Hermia, *daughter to Egeus, in love with Lysander*
Helena, *in love with Demetrius*
Oberon, *King of the Fairies*
Titania, *Queen of the Fairies*
Puck, *or* **Robin Goodfellow**
Peaseblossom, **Cobweb**, **Moth**, **Mustardseed** } *Fairies*
Other Fairies *attending their King and Queen; Attendants on Theseus and Hippolyta*

(Athens, and a wood near it.)

ACT 1

SCENE 1°

Enter Theseus, Hippolyta, [Philostrate,] with others.

THESEUS: Now, fair Hippolyta, our nuptial hour
Draws on apace. Four happy days bring in

*Note: Words and passages enclosed in square brackets in the text above are either emendations of the copy-text or additions to it. °*i. Location:* Athens. The palace of Theseus.

Another moon; but O, methinks, how slow
This old moon [wanes]! She lingers° my desires
Like to a step-dame,° or a dowager,°
Long withering out° a young man's revenue.

HIPPOLYTA: Four days will quickly steep themselves in night;
Four nights will quickly dream away the time;
And then the moon, like to a silver bow
[New] bent in heaven, shall behold the night
Of our solemnities.°

THESEUS: Go, Philostrate,
Stir up the Athenian youth to merriments,
Awake the pert° and nimble spirit of mirth.
Turn melancholy forth to funerals:
The pale companion° is not for our pomp.°

[*Exit Philostrate.*]

Hippolyta, I woo'd thee with my sword,
And won thy love doing thee injuries;°
But I will wed thee in another key,
With pomp, with triumph,° and with revelling.

Enter Egeus and his daughter Hermia and Lysander and Demetrius.

EGEUS: Happy be Theseus, our renowned Duke!

THESEUS: Thanks, good Egeus. What's the news with thee?

EGEUS: Full of vexation come I, with complaint
Against my child, my daughter Hermia.
Stand forth, Demetrius. My noble lord,
This man hath my consent to marry her.
Stand forth, Lysander. And, my gracious Duke,
This man hath bewitch'd the bosom of my child.
Thou, thou, Lysander, thou hast given her rhymes,
And interchang'd love-tokens with my child;
Thou hast by moonlight at her window sung
With faining voice verses of faining° love,
And stol'n the impression of her fantasy°
With bracelets of thy hair,° rings, gawds,° conceits,°
Knacks,° trifles, nosegays, sweetmeats—messengers

°*lingers:* Delays the fulfillment of. °*step-dame:* Stepmother. °*dowager:* Widow with property rights charged upon an estate during her lifetime. °*withering out:* Diminishing. °*solemnities:* i.e. marriage rites. °*pert:* Lively, brisk. °*companion:* Fellow (contemptuous). °*pomp:* Ceremonial splendor. °*I . . . injuries.* Theseus had made war against the Amazons and taken their queen captive. °*triumph*: Public spectacle. °*faining . . . faining:* (1) loving . . . longing; (2) feigning . . . feigned. °*stol'n . . . fantasy:* Stealthily stamped your image on her imagination, i.e. made her fall in love with you. °*bracelets . . . hair:* Hair bracelets were a common love token. °*gawds:* Toys, trinkets. °*conceits:* Ingenious trifles. °*Knacks:* Knickknacks.

Of strong prevailment in unhardened youth.
With cunning hast thou filch'd my daughter's heart,
Turn'd her obedience (which is due to me)
To stubborn harshness.° And, my gracious Duke,
Be it so° she will not here before your Grace
Consent to marry with Demetrius,
I beg the ancient privilege of Athens:
As she is mine, I may dispose of her;
Which shall be either to this gentleman,
Or to her death, according to our law
Immediately° provided in that case.

THESEUS: What say you, Hermia? Be advis'd,° fair maid.
To you your father should be as a god;
One that compos'd your beauties; yea, and one
To whom you are but as a form° in wax,
By him imprinted, and within his power,
To leave° the figure, or disfigure° it.
Demetrius is a worthy gentleman.

HERMIA: So is Lysander.

THESEUS: In himself he is;
But in this kind,° wanting° your father's voice,°
The other must be held the worthier.

HERMIA: I would my father look'd but with my eyes.

THESEUS: Rather your eyes must with his judgment look.

HERMIA: I do entreat your Grace to pardon me.
I know not by what power I am made bold,
Nor how it may concern° my modesty,
In such a presence here to plead my thoughts;
But I beseech your Grace that I may know
The worst that may befall me in this case,
If I refuse to wed Demetrius.

THESEUS: Either to die the death,° or to abjure
For ever the society of men.
Therefore, fair Hermia, question your desires,
Know of your youth,° examine well your blood,°
Whether (if you yield not to your father's choice)
You can endure the livery° of a nun,
For aye to be in shady cloister mew'd,°

°*harshness:* Discordance, i.e. disobedience. °*Be it so:* If. °*Immediately:* Expressly. °*Be advis'd:* Consider well. °*a form:* i.e. the impression of a seal. °*leave:* i.e. leave unchanged. °*disfigure:* Obliterate. °*in this kind:* In this respect, i.e. as your wooer. °*wanting:* Lacking. °*voice:* Authorization, consent. °*how . . . concern:* Whether it befit. °*die the death:* Be put to death by judicial sentence. °*Know . . . youth:* Inquire of your youthful feelings. °*blood:* Passions. °*livery:* Dress, distinctive garb. °*mew'd:* Shut up, confined.

To live a barren sister all your life,
Chaunting faint hymns to the cold fruitless moon.°
Thrice blessed they that master so their blood
To undergo such maiden pilgrimage;°
But earthlier happy is the rose distill'd,°
Than that which withering on the virgin thorn°
Grows, lives, and dies in single blessedness.°

HERMIA: So will I grow, so live, so die, my lord,
Ere I will yield my virgin patent° up
Unto his lordship, whose unwished yoke
My soul consents not to give sovereignty.

THESEUS: Take time to pause, and by the next new moon—
The sealing-day betwixt my love and me
For everlasting bond of fellowship—
Upon that day either prepare to die
For disobedience to your father's will,
Or else to wed Demetrius, as he would,
Or on Diana's altar to protest°
For aye austerity and single life.

DEMETRIUS: Relent, sweet Hermia, and, Lysander, yield
Thy crazed° title° to my certain right.

LYSANDER: You have her father's love, Demetrius,
Let me have Hermia's; do you marry him.

EGEUS: Scornful Lysander, true, he hath my love;
And what is mine, my love shall render him.
And she is mine, and all my right of her
I do estate unto° Demetrius.

LYSANDER: I am, my lord, as well deriv'd° as he,
As well possess'd;° my love is more than his;
My fortunes every way as fairly° rank'd
(If not with vantage°) as Demetrius';
And (which is more than all these boasts can be)
I am belov'd of beauteous Hermia.
Why should not I then prosecute my right?
Demetrius, I'll avouch it to his head,°
Made love to Nedar's daughter, Helena,
And won her soul; and she, sweet lady, dotes,

°*moon:* i.e. Diana, the virgin goddess, whose votary Hermia would become. °*maiden pilgrimage:* i.e. journey through life as a virgin. Lines 74–75 are a saving compliment to the Virgin Queen. Elizabeth, though lines 76–78 rather diminish its effect. °*distill'd:* Made into perfume. With the image in this passage cf. Sonnet 5. °*thorn:* Brier rose bush. °*single blessedness:* "Divine blessing accorded to a life of celibacy" (O.E.D.). °*virgin patent:* Privilege of virginity. °*protest:* Vow. °*crazed:* Cracked, flawed. °*title:* Claim to possession. °*estate unto:* Settle or bestow upon. °*well deriv'd:* Well born. °*possess'd:* Endowed with wealth. °*fairly:* Handsomely. °*with vantage:* Better. °*head:* Face.

Devoutly dotes, dotes in idolatry,
Upon this spotted and inconstant° man.

THESEUS: I must confess that I have heard so much,
And with Demetrius thought to have spoke thereof;
But, being over-full of self-affairs,°
My mind did lose it. But, Demetrius, come,
And come, Egeus, you shall go with me;
I have some private schooling° for you both.
For° you, fair Hermia, look you arm° yourself
To fit your fancies° to your father's will;
Or else the law of Athens yields you up
(Which by no means we may extenuate°)
To death, or to a vow of single life.
Come, my Hippolyta; what cheer, my love?
Demetrius and Egeus, go along;°
I must employ you in some business
Against° our nuptial, and confer with you
Of something nearly that° concerns yourselves.

EGEUS: With duty and desire° we follow you.

Exeunt. [*Manent° Lysander and Hermia.*]

LYSANDER: How now, my love? why is your cheek so pale?
How chance the roses there do fade so fast?

HERMIA: Belike° for want of rain; which I could well
Beteem° them from the tempest of my eyes.

LYSANDER: Ay me! for aught that I could ever read,
Could ever hear by tale or history,
The course of true love never did run smooth;
But either it was different in blood°—

HERMIA: O cross!° too high to be enthrall'd to [low].

LYSANDER: Or else misgraffed° in respect of years—

HERMIA: O spite! too old to be engag'd to young.

LYSANDER: Or else it stood upon the choice of friends°—

HERMIA: O hell, to choose love by another's eyes!

LYSANDER: Or if there were a sympathy in choice,
War, death, or sickness did lay siege to it,
Making it momentany° as a sound,

°*spotted and inconstant:* Stained with inconstancy. °*self-affairs:* My own affairs. °*schooling:* Admonition. °*For:* As for. °*look you arm:* See that you prepare. °*fancies:* Affections. °*extenuate:* Mitigate. °*go along:* Come with us. °*Against:* In preparation for. °*nearly that:* That closely. °*duty and desire:* Eagerness to serve. °*Manent:* Remain. °*Belike:* Very likely. °*Beteem:* Afford. °*blood:* Birth, hereditary station. °*cross:* Vexation, thwarting. °*misgraffed:* Ill grafted, i.e. badly matched. °*friends:* i.e. relatives. °*momentany:* momentary.

Swift as a shadow, short as any dream,
Brief as the lightning in the collied° night,
That, in a spleen,° unfolds° both heaven and earth;
And ere a man hath power to say "Behold!"
The jaws of darkness do devour it up:
So quick° bright things come to confusion.°

Hermia: If then true lovers have been ever° cross'd,
It stands as an edict in destiny.
Then let us teach our trial patience,°
Because it is a customary cross,
As due to love° as thoughts° and dreams and sighs,
Wishes and tears, poor fancy's° followers.

Lysander: A good persuasion;° therefore hear me, Hermia:
I have a widow aunt, a dowager,
Of great revenue, and she hath no child.
From Athens is her house remote seven leagues;
And she respects° me as her only son.
There, gentle Hermia, may I marry thee;
And to that place the sharp Athenian law
Cannot pursue us. If thou lovest me, then
Steal forth thy father's house to-morrow night,
And in the wood, a league without the town
(Where I did meet thee once with Helena
To do observance to a morn of May°),
There will I stay° for thee.

Hermia: My good Lysander,
I swear to thee, by Cupid's strongest bow,
By his best arrow with the golden head,°
By the simplicity° of Venus' doves,
By that which knitteth souls and prospers loves,
And by that fire which burn'd the Carthage queen°
When the false Troyan under sail was seen,
By all the vows that ever men have broke
(In number more than ever women spoke),
In that same place thou hast appointed me
To-morrow truly will I meet with thee.

°*collied:* Dark (literally, blackened with coal). °*in a spleen:* i.e. as if in a sudden fit of passion (?) or in a flash (?). The spleen was thought to be the seat of sudden impulsive feelings and actions. °*unfolds:* Reveals. °*quick:* Quickly, suddenly (perhaps with additional sense of "living" or "lively," modifying things). °*confusion:* Ruin. °*ever:* Always. °*teach . . . patience:* i.e. discipline ourselves to meet this trial patiently. °*As . . . love:* As much love's due. °*thoughts:* Melancholy moods. °*fancy's:* Love's. °*persuasion:* Opinion, doctrine. °*respects:* Regards. °*do . . . May:* Perform the ceremonies of May-day. °*stay:* Wait. °*arrow . . . head:* According to Ovid's Metamorphoses, Cupid's sharp, gold-tipped arrow produced love, his blunt, lead-tipped arrow aversion. °*simplicity:* Harmlessness, innocence. °*Carthage queen:* Dido, who immolated herself on a funeral pyre after the Trojan hero Aeneas, her lover, secretly sailed away from Carthage.

LYSANDER: Keep promise, love. Look, here comes Helena.

Enter Helena.

HERMIA: God speed fair Helena! whither away?
HELENA: Call you me fair? That fair again unsay.
Demetrius loves your fair,° O happy° fair!
Your eyes are lodestars,° and your tongue's sweet air°
More tuneable° than lark to shepherd's ear
When wheat is green, when hawthorn buds appear.
Sickness is catching; O, were favor° so,
[Yours would] I catch, fair Hermia, ere I go;
My ear should catch your voice, my eye your eye,
My tongue should catch your tongue's sweet melody.
Were the world mine, Demetrius being bated,°
The rest I'll give to be to you translated.°
O, teach me how you look, and with what art°
You sway the motion° of Demetrius' heart.
HERMIA: I frown upon him; yet he loves me still.
HELENA: O that your frowns would teach my smiles such skill!
HERMIA: I give him curses; yet he gives me love.
HELENA: O that my prayers could such affection° move°!
HERMIA: The more I hate, the more he follows me.
HELENA: The more I love, the more he hateth me.
HERMIA: His folly, Helena, is no fault of mine.
HELENA: None but your beauty; would that fault were mine!
HERMIA: Take comfort; he no more shall see my face;
Lysander and myself will fly this place.
Before the time I did Lysander see,
Seem'd Athens as a paradise to me;
O then, what graces in my love do dwell,
That he hath turn'd a heaven unto a hell!
LYSANDER: Helen, to you our minds we will unfold:
To-morrow night, when Phoebe° doth behold
Her silver visage in the wat'ry glass,°
Decking with liquid pearl the bladed grass
(A time that lovers' flights doth still° conceal),
Through Athens° gates have we devis'd° to steal.

°*fair . . . fair:* Beauty . . . fair one (with special reference to her blonde coloring). °*happy:* Lucky. °*lodestars:* Guiding stars. °*air:* Melody, music. °*tuneable:* Tuneful. °*favor:* Attributes, features (with play on "being favored"). °*bated:* Excepted. °*translated:* Transformed. °*art:* Skill (i.e., in magic). °*motion:* Impulse, desire. °*affection:* Passion. °*move:* Arouse. °*Phoebe:* Diana, the moon. °*glass:* Mirror. °*still:* Always. °*Athens:* Adjectival; cf. "Verona streets," Romeo and Juliet, III.i.89. °*devis'd:* Decided.

Hermia: And in the wood, where often you and I
Upon faint° primrose beds were wont to lie,
Emptying our bosoms of their counsel° [sweet],
There my Lysander and myself shall meet;
And thence from Athens turn away our eyes,
To seek new friends and [stranger companies°].
Farewell, sweet playfellow, pray thou for us;
And good luck grant thee thy Demetrius!
Keep word, Lysander; we must starve our sight
From lovers' food° till morrow deep midnight.

Lysander: I will, my Hermia. *Exit Hermia.*
Helena, adieu:
As you on him, Demetrius dote on you!

Exit Lysander.

Helena: How happy some o'er other some can be!
Through Athens I am thought as fair as she.
But what of that? Demetrius thinks not so;
He will not know what all but he do know;
And as he errs, doting on Hermia's eyes,
So I, admiring of° his qualities.
Things base and vile, holding no quantity,°
Love can transpose° to form and dignity.°
Love looks not with the eyes but with the mind;
And therefore is wing'd Cupid painted blind.
Nor hath Love's mind of any judgment taste;°
Wings, and no eyes, figure° unheedy haste;
And therefore is Love said to be a child,
Because in choice he is so oft beguil'd.
As waggish boys in game° themselves forswear,
So the boy Love is perjur'd every where;
For ere Demetrius look'd on Hermia's eyne,°
He hail'd down oaths that he was only mine;
And when this hail some heat from Hermia felt,
So he dissolv'd, and show'rs of oaths did melt.
I will go tell him of fair Hermia's flight;
Then to the wood will he to-morrow night
Pursue her; and for this intelligence°

°*faint:* Pale (?) or faintly scented (?). °*counsel:* Inmost thought. °*stranger companies:* The company of strangers. °*starve . . . food:* i.e. refrain from seeing each other. °*admiring of:* Wondering at. °*holding no quantity:* Lacking proportion, unshapely. °*transpose:* Change, transform. °*dignity:* Worth. *taste:* Any trace. °*figure:* Symbolize. °*game:* Fun, sport. °*eyne:* Eyes (archaic even in Elizabethan English; used for the sake of rhyme). °*intelligence:* Information.

If I have thanks, it is a dear expense.°
But herein mean I to enrich my pain,
To have his sight° thither and back again. *Exit.*

SCENE 2°

Enter Quince the carpenter and Snug the joiner and Bottom the weaver and Flute the bellows-mender and Snout the tinker and Starveling the tailor.°

QUINCE: Is all our company here?

BOTTOM: You were best° to call them generally,° man by man, according to the scrip.°

QUINCE: Here is the scroll of every man's name, which is thought fit, through all Athens, to play in our enterlude° before the Duke and the Duchess, on his wedding-day at night.

BOTTOM: First, good Peter Quince, say what the play treats on; then read the names of the actors; and so grow to a point.°

QUINCE: Marry,° our play is The *most lamentable*° *comedy and most cruel death of Pyramus and Thisby.*

BOTTOM: A very good piece of work, I assure you, and a merry. Now, good Peter Quince, call forth your actors by the scroll. Masters, spread yourselves.

QUINCE: Answer as I call you. Nick Bottom the weaver.

BOTTOM: Ready. Name what part I am for, and proceed.

QUINCE: You, Nick Bottom, are set down for Pyramus.

BOTTOM: What is Pyramus? a lover, or a tyrant?

QUINCE: A lover, that kills himself most gallant for love.

BOTTOM: That will ask some tears in the true performing of it. If I do it, let the audience look to their eyes.° I will move storms; I will condole° in some measure. To the rest—yet my chief humor° is for a tyrant. I could play Ercles° rarely, or a part to tear a cat° in, to make all split.°

"The raging rocks
And shivering shocks
Shall break the locks
Of prison gates;

°*dear expense:* Painful purchase, costly gain. °*his sight:* The sight of him. °*Location:* Athens. Quince's house. °The names of the craftsmen are derived in one way or another from their work. Quince's name is probably a form of *quoins* or *quines*, wedge-shaped pieces of wood used in carpentry. Snug's name suggests the expert joining of pieces of wood by a maker of fine furniture. Bottom is named for the *bottom* or core on which thread is wound. Flute would repair fluted church organs as well as domestic bellows. Snout's name suggests the spout of a kettle, an article very familiar to tinkers. Starveling takes his name from the proverbial leanness of tailors ("Nine tailors make a man"). °*You were best:* It would be best for you. °*generally.* The first of Bottom's characteristic verbal blunders. Here he obviously means "individually"—just the opposite of what he says. °*scrip:* Script, written list. °*enterlude:* Interlude, brief play. °*grow . . . point:* Come systematically to a conclusion. °*Marry:* Why, indeed (originally the name of the Virgin Mary used as an oath). °*lamentable:* Mournful. °*look . . . eyes:* Take care not to injure their eyes with weeping. °*condole:* Speak pathetically, arouse pity. °*humor:* Temperamental bent. °*Ercles:* Hercules. The tradition for ranting in this part grew from Seneca's Hercules Furens. °*tear a cat:* i.e. rant. °*make all split:* Cause great commotion.

And Phibbus' car°
Shall shine from far,
And make and mar
The foolish Fates."

This was lofty! Now name the rest of the players. This is Ercles' vein, a tyrant's vein; a lover is more condoling.°

QUINCE: Francis Flute the bellows-mender.

FLUTE: Here, Peter Quince.

QUINCE: Flute, you must take Thisby on you.

FLUTE: What° is Thisby? a wand'ring knight?°

QUINCE: It is the lady that Pyramus must love.

FLUTE: Nay, faith; let not me play a woman; I have a beard coming.°

QUINCE: That's all one;° you shall play it in a mask, and you may speak as small° as you will.

BOTTOM: And° I may hide my face, let me play Thisby too. I'll speak in a monstrous little voice, "Thisne! Thisne! Ah, Pyramus, my lover dear! thy Thisby dear, and lady dear!"

QUINCE: No, no, you must play Pyramus; and, Flute, you Thisby.

BOTTOM: Well, proceed.

QUINCE: Robin Starveling the tailor.

STAR: Here, Peter Quince.

QUINCE: Robin Starveling, you must play Thisby's mother. Tom Snout the tinker.

SNOUT: Here, Peter Quince.

QUINCE: You, Pyramus' father; myself, Thisby's father; Snug the joiner, you the lion's part. And I hope here is a play fitted.°

SNUG: Have you the lion's part written? Pray you, if it be, give it me, for I am slow of study.

QUINCE: You may do it extempore, for it is nothing but roaring.

BOTTOM: Let me play the lion too. I will roar, that° I will do any man's heart good to hear me. I will roar, that I will make the Duke say, "Let him roar again; let him roar again."

QUINCE: And you should do it too terribly,° you would fright the Duchess and the ladies, that they would shrike;° and that were enough to hang us all.

ALL: That would hang us, every mother's son.

BOTTOM: I grant you, friends, if you should fright the ladies out of their wits, they would have no more discretion but to hang us; but I will aggravate° my voice so that I will roar you as gently as any sucking dove; I will roar you and° twere any nightingale.

°*Phibbus' car:* The chariot of Phoebus, the sun-god. °*condoling:* Pathetic. °*What:* What sort of man. °*wand'ring knight:* Knight-errant. °*I. . .coming:* On the Elizabethan stage, female parts were played by boys. °*That's all one:* That makes no difference. °*small:* High-pitched. °*And:* If. °*fitted:* Cast. °*that:* So that. °*terribly:* Terrifyingly. °*shrike:* Shriek. °*aggravate:* He means just the opposite. °*and:* As if.

QUINCE: You can play no part but Pyramus; for Pyramus is a sweet-fac'd man; a proper° man as one shall see in a summer's day; a most lovely gentleman-like man: therefore you must needs play Pyramus.

BOTTOM: Well;° I will undertake it. What beard were I best to play it in?

QUINCE: Why, what you will.

BOTTOM: I will discharge° it in either your straw color beard, your° orange-tawny beard, your purple-in-grain° beard, or your French-crown-color° beard, your perfit° yellow.

QUINCE: Some of your French crowns have no hair at all;° and then you will play barefac'd. But, masters, here are your parts, and I am to° entreat you, request you, and desire you, to con° them by tomorrow night; and meet me in the palace wood, a mile without the town, by moonlight, there will we rehearse; for if we meet in the city, we shall be dogg'd with company, and our devices known. In the mean time I will draw a bill° of properties, such as our play wants. I pray you fail me not.

BOTTOM: We will meet, and there we may rehearse most obscenely° and courageously. Take pains, be perfit;° adieu.

QUINCE: At the Duke's oak we meet.

BOTTOM: Enough; hold, or cut bow-strings.° *Exeunt.*

ACT 2

SCENE 1°

Enter a Fairy at one door and Robin Goodfellow [Puck] at another.

PUCK: How now, spirit, whither wander you?

FAIRY: Over hill, over dale,
Thorough° bush, thorough brier,
Over park, over pale,°
Thorough flood, thorough fire,
I do wander every where,
Swifter than the moon's sphere;°
And I serve the Fairy Queen,
To dew her orbs° upon the green.
The cowslips tall her pensioners° be,
In their gold coats spots you see:

°*proper:* Handsome. °*Well:* Very well. °*discharge:* Perform. °*your:* The indefinite use, meaning vaguely "that you know of"; a colloquialism. °*purple-in-grain:* Dyed a fast purple or deep red. °*French-crown-color:* Yellowish color of a gold coin. °*perfit:* Perfect. °*Some. . .all:* Alluding to loss of hair from the "French disease," syphilis. °*am to:* Must. °*con:* Learn by heart. °*bill:* List. °*obscenely:* Bottom may connect this word with *seen* and mean "without being observed," or with scene and mean "dramatically." °*perfit:* i.e. letter-perfect in your parts. °*hold. . . bow-strings:* An expression of uncertain meaning, from archery; perhaps equivalent to "hold to our agreement or the project is done for." °*Location:* A wood near Athens. °*Thorough:* Through. °*pale:* Enclosure °*sphere.* In the Ptolemaic system of astronomy, the moon and the other heavenly bodies were thought to revolve about the earth fixed in transparent spheres. °*orbs:* Circles, i.e. fairy rings. °*pensioners.* Members of the royal bodyguard were called gentlemen pensioners.

Those be rubies, fairy favors,°
In those freckles live their savors.°

I must go seek some dewdrops here,
And hang a pearl in every cowslip's ear.
Farewell, thou lob° of spirits; I'll be gone.
Our Queen and all her elves come here anon.°

PUCK: The King doth keep his revels here to-night;
Take heed the Queen come not within his sight;
For Oberon is passing fell and wrath,°
Because that she as her attendant hath
A lovely boy stolen from an Indian king;
She never had so sweet a changeling.°
And jealous Oberon would have the child
Knight of his train, to trace° the forests wild;
But she, perforce,° withholds the loved boy,
Crowns him with flowers, and makes him all her joy.
And now they never meet in grove or green,
By fountain° clear, or spangled starlight sheen,
But they do square,° that° all their elves for fear
Creep into acron-cups, and hide them there.

FAIRY: Either I mistake your shape and making° quite,
Or else you are that shrewd° and knavish sprite
Call'd Robin Goodfellow. Are not you he
That frights the maidens of the villagery,°
Skim milk, and sometimes labor in the quern,°
And bootless° make the breathless huswife° churn,
And sometime° make the drink to bear no barm,°
Mislead night-wanderers, laughing at their harm?
Those that Hobgoblin call you, and sweet Puck,
You do their work, and they shall have good luck.
Are not you he?

PUCK: Thou speakest aright;
I am that merry wanderer of the night.
I jest to Oberon and make him smile
When I a fat and bean-fed horse beguile,
Neighing in likeness of a filly foal;
And sometime lurk I in a gossip's° bowl,

°*favors:* Love tokens. °*savors:* Perfumes. °*lob:* Country bumpkin. °*anon:* At once. °*passing ... wrath:* Exceedingly fierce and angry. °*changeling:* Child exchanged for another by fairies. °*trace:* Traverse. °*perforce:* Forcibly. °*fountain:* Spring. °*square:* Quarrel. °*that:* So that. °*making:* Form. °*shrewd:* Mischievous. °*villagery:* Village folk, peasantry. °*quern:* Handmill for grinding grain. °*bootless:* Unavailingly. °*huswife:* Housewife, woman who manages a household. °*sometime:* At times. °*bear no barm:* Fail to ferment (?) or go flat (?). *Barm* yeast. °*gossip's:* Garrulous old woman's.

In very likeness of a roasted crab,°
And when she drinks, against her lips I bob,
And on her withered dewlop° pour the ale.
The wisest aunt, telling the saddest° tale,
Sometime for three-foot stool mistaketh me;
Then slip I from her bum, down topples she,
And "tailor"° cries, and falls into a cough;°
And then the whole quire° hold their hips and loff,°
And waxen° in their mirth, and neeze,° and swear
A merrier hour was never wasted° there.
But room, fairy! here comes Oberon.

FAIRY: And here my mistress. Would that he were gone!

Enter the King of Fairies [Oberon] at one door with his Train, and the Queen [Titania] at another with hers.

OBERON: Ill met by moonlight, proud Titania.

TITANIA: What, jealous Oberon? [Fairies,] skip hence—
I have forsworn his bed and company.

OBERON: Tarry, rash wanton!° Am not I thy lord?

TITANIA: Then I must be thy lady; but I know
When thou hast stolen away from fairy land,
And in the shape of Corin° sat all day,
Playing on pipes of corn,° and versing love,°
To amorous Phillida. Why art thou here
Come from the farthest steep° of India?
But that, forsooth, the bouncing Amazon,
Your buskin'd° mistress, and your warrior love,
To Theseus must be wedded, and you come
To give their bed joy and prosperity.

OBERON: How canst thou thus for shame, Titania,
Glance at my credit with Hippolyta,°
Knowing I know thy love to Theseus?
Didst not thou lead him through the glimmering night
From Perigenia,° whom he ravished?

°*crab:* Crab apple. °*dewlop:* Dewlap, loose skin on the neck. °*aunt:* Old woman, gossip. °*saddest:* Soberest. °*tailor:* Probably referring to the fact that she finds herself sitting cross-legged on the floor as tailors did to sew. °*cough.* Probably with a suggestion of breaking wind. °*quire:* Choir, i.e. company. °*loff:* Laugh. °*waxen:* Increase (with archaic plural ending in -en). °*neeze:* Sneeze. °*wasted:* Spent. °*rash wanton:* Impetuous and willful creature. °*Corin, Phillida:* Conventional names in pastoral poetry. °*corn:* Oat stalks. °*versing love:* Making love verses. °*steep:* Mountain range. °*buskin'd:* Wearing buskins or half-boots. °*Glance . . . Hippolyta:* Cast aspersion on my good name by accusing me with Hippolyta. °*Perigenia:* Perigouna, daughter of the brigand Sinis, whom the youthful Theseus slew on his first journey to Athens. Shakespeare took this and the following names of Theseus' mistresses from the "Life of Theseus" in North's translation of Plutarch (which, however, reads *Perigouna*).

And make him with fair [Aegles°] break his faith,
With Ariadne,° and Antiopa?

TITANIA: These are the forgeries of jealousy;
And never, since the middle summer's spring,°
Met we on hill, in dale, forest, or mead,
By paved fountain° or by rushy° brook,
Or in° the beached margent° of the sea,
To dance our ringlets° to the whistling wind,
But with thy brawls° thou hast disturb'd our sport.
Therefore the winds, piping to us in vain,
As in revenge, have suck'd up from the sea
Contagious° fogs; which, falling in the land,
Hath every pelting° river made so proud
That they have overborne their continents.°
The ox hath therefore stretch'd his yoke in vain,
The ploughman lost his sweat, and the green corn°
Hath rotted ere his° youth attain'd a beard.
The fold stands empty in the drowned field,
And crows are fatted with the murrion° flock;
The nine men's morris° is fill'd up with mud,
And the quaint mazes° in the wanton° green,
For lack of tread, are undistinguishable.
The human mortals want their winter here;°
No night is now with hymn or carol blest.
Therefore° the moon (the governess of floods),
Pale in her anger, washes all the air,
That° rheumatic diseases° do abound.
And thorough this distemperature,° we see

°*Aegles:* Aegle, a nymph for whose love Theseus, in some accounts, deserted Ariadne. °*Ariadne:* Daughter of Minos, king of Crete. Having slain the Minotaur with her aid, Theseus fled Crete with her, but abandoned her on the voyage back to Athens. Antiopa: another name for the Amazon queen captured by Theseus; here obviously taken to be distinct from Hippolyta. °*middle summer's spring:* Beginning of midsummer. °*paved fountain:* Spring with pebbled bottom. °*rushy:* Edged with rushes. °*in:* On. °*margent:* Margin, edge. °*ringlets:* Circular dances. °*brawls:* Noisy quarrels (with probably play on *brawl* as the name of a dance [French *branle*] described as "base" by contemporary writers). °*Contagious:* Noxious. °*pelting:* Paltry. °*overborne their continents:* Overflowed their banks. °*corn:* Grain. °*his:* Its. °*murrion:* Dead of the murrain, a disease of cattle and sheep. °*nine men's morris:* i.e. the turf marked with squares on which the rustic game of this name was played. °*quaint mazes:* Complicated pattern of paths to be traced rapidly by a line of boys as a sport. °*wanton:* Luxuriant. °*want their winter here.* A controversial passage. Perhaps it means "lack under these circumstances their proper winter season" (with an allusion in *hymn* or *carol* in line 102 to Christmas observances). Most editors, following Theobald, emend *here to cheer.* °*Therefore.* As in lines 88 and 93, this means "in consequence of the breach between us." °*That:* So that. °*rheumatic diseases:* Colds, catarrh, and other such disorders characterized by a flow of watery "rheum." °*distemperature:* Disturbance in the natural order, i.e. bad weather (perhaps with play on the sense "ill humor," harking back to the moon's "anger" in line 104).

The seasons alter: hoary-headed frosts
Fall in the fresh lap of the crimson rose,
And on old Hiems'° [thin] and icy crown
An odorous chaplet of sweet summer buds
Is, as in mockery, set, the spring, the summer,
The childing° autumn, angry winter, change
Their wonted liveries,° and the mazed° world,
By their increase,° now knows not which is which.
And this same progeny of evils comes
From our debate,° from our dissension;
We are their parents and original.°

OBERON: Do you amend it then, it lies in you.
Why should Titania cross° her Oberon?
I do but beg a little changeling boy,
To be my henchman.°

TITANIA: Set your heart at rest;°
The fairy land buys not the child of me.
His mother was a vot'ress of my order,
And in the spiced Indian air, by night,
Full often hath she gossip'd by my side,
And sat with me on Neptune's yellow sands;
Marking th' embarked traders° on the flood;°
When we have laugh'd to see the salls conceive
And grow big-bellied with the wanton° wind,
Which she, with pretty and with swimming gait,
Following (her womb then rich with my young squire)
Would imitate, and sail upon the land
To fetch me trifles, and return again,
As from a voyage, rich with merchandise.
But she, being mortal, of that boy did die,
And for her sake do I rear up her boy,
And for her sake I will not part with him.

OBERON: How long within this wood intend you stay?

TITANIA: Perchance till after Theseus' wedding-day.
If you will patiently dance in our round,°
And see our moonlight revels, go with us;
If not, shun me, and I will spare° your haunts.

OBERON: Give me that boy, and I will go with thee.

°*Hiems:* The god of winter. °*childing:* Fruitful (literally, pregnant). °*wonted liveries:* Customary apparel. °*mazed:* Bewildered, confused. °*their increase:* What they produce. °*debate:* Disagreement, quarrelling. °*original:* Origin. °*cross:* Thwart. °*henchman:* Page of honor. °*Set . . . rest:* i.e. give up that notion. °*traders:* Trading vessels. °*flood:* Flood tide. °*wanton:* Amorous. °*round:* Circular dance. °*spare:* Stay away from.

TITANIA: Not for thy fairy kingdom. Fairies, away!
We shall chide° downright, if I longer stay.

Exeunt [Titania and her Train].

OBERON: Well; go thy way. Thou shalt not from° this grove
Till I torment thee for this injury.°
My gentle Puck, come hither. Thou rememb'rest
Since° once I sat upon a promontory,
And heard a mermaid on a dolphin's back
Uttering such dulcet and harmonious breath°
That the rude° sea grew civil° at her song,
And certain stars shot madly from their spheres,
To hear the sea-maid's music?

PUCK: I remember.

OBERON: That very time I saw (but thou couldst not),
Flying between the cold moon and the earth,
Cupid all° arm'd. A certain aim he took
At a fair vestal° throned by [the] west,
And loos'd his love-shaft smartly from his bow,
As° it should pierce a hundred thousand hearts;
But I might see young Cupid's fiery shaft
Quench'd in the chaste beams of the wat'ry moon,°
And the imperial vot'ress passed on,
In maiden meditation, fancy-free.°
Yet mark'd I where the bolt of Cupid fell.
It fell upon a little western flower,
Before milk-white, now purple with love's wound,
And maidens call it love-in-idleness.°
Fetch me that flow'r; the herb I showed thee once.
The juice of it on sleeping eyelids laid
Will make or man or° woman madly dote
Upon the next live creature that it sees.
Fetch me this herb, and be thou here again
Ere the leviathan° can swim a league.

PUCK: I'll put a girdle round about the earth
In forty° minutes. [*Exit.*]

°*chide:* Quarrel. °*from:* Go from. °*injury:* Affront. °*Since:* When. °*breath:* Voice, music. °*rude:* Rough, boisterous. °*civil:* Well- behaved, gentle. °*all:* Fully, completely. °*vestal:* i.e. vestal virgin. The passage is a compliment to Queen Elizabeth, and may allude to some actual entertainment in her honor, such as the water pageant with which the Earl of Hertford amused her when she visited him at Elvetham in 1591. °*As:* As if. °*moon:* i.e. Diana, the virgin goddess, whose votaress the "fair vestal" is. °*fancy-free:* Free of love-thoughts. °*love-in-idleness:* A name for the pansy. °*or . . . or:* Either . . . or. °*leviathan:* Gigantic sea-beast (see Job 41), usually identified with the whale. °*forty:* Used frequently as an indefinite number.

OBERON: Having once this juice,°
I'll watch Titania when she is asleep,°
And drop the liquor of it in her eyes;
The next thing then she waking looks upon
(Be it on lion, bear, or wolf, or bull,
On meddling monkey, or on busy ape),
She shall pursue it with the soul of love.
And ere I take this charm from off her sight
(As I can take it with another herb),
I'll make her render up her page to me.
But who comes here? I am invisible,°
And I will overhear their conference.

Enter Demetrius, Helena following him.

DEMETRIUS: I love thee not; therefore pursue me not.
Where is Lysander and fair Hermia?
The one I'll [slay]; the other [slayeth] me.
Thou toldst me they were stol'n unto this wood
And here am I, and wode° within this wood,
Because I cannot meet my Hermia.
Hence, get thee gone, and follow me no more.
HELENA: You draw me, you hard-hearted adamant;°
But yet you draw not iron,° for my heart
Is true as steel. Leave° you your power to draw,
And I shall have no power to follow you.
DEMETRIUS: Do I entice you? Do I speak you fair?°
Or rather do I not in plainest truth
Tell you I do not [nor] I cannot love you?
HELENA: And even for that do I love you the more:
I am your spaniel; and, Demetrius,
The more you beat me, I will fawn on you.
Use me but as your spaniel; spurn me, strike me,
Neglect° me, lose me; only give me leave,
Unworthy as I am, to follow you.
What worser place can I beg in your love
(And yet a place of high respect with me)
Than to be used as you use your dog?
DEMETRIUS: Tempt° not too much the hatred of my spirit,
For I am sick when I do look on thee.

°*watch . . . asleep:* i.e. watch for a time when I can catch her sleeping. °*I am invisible.* Spoken for the benefit of the audience to explain how he can eavesdrop unseen. °*wode:* Mad (pronounced wood). °*adamant:* (1) lodestone, magnet; (2) the hardest substance. °*you . . . iron:* i.e. what you draw (my heart) is not iron, but steel of the finest temper. °*Leave:* Give up. °*fair:* Courteously. °*Neglect:* Ignore. °*Tempt:* Try, put to the test.

HELENA: And I am sick when I look not on you.
DEMETRIUS: You do impeach° your modesty too much,
To leave the city and commit yourself
Into the hands of one that loves you not;
To trust the opportunity of night,
And the ill counsel of a desert° place,
With the rich worth of your virginity.
HELENA: Your virtue is my privilege° For that°
It is not night when I do see your face,
Therefore I think I am not in the night,
Nor doth this wood lack worlds of company,
For you in my respect° are all the world.
Then how can it be said I am alone,
When all the world is here to look on me?
DEMETRIUS: I'll run from thee, and hide me in the brakes,°
And leave thee to the mercy of wild beasts.
HELENA: The wildest hath not such a heart as you.
Run when you will; the story shall be chang'd:
Apollo flies, and Daphne holds the chase;°
The dove pursues the griffin;° the mild hind°
Makes speed to catch the tiger—bootless speed,
When cowardice pursues and valor flies.
DEMETRIUS: I will not stay thy questions.° Let me go;
Or if thou follow me, do not believe
But I shall do thee mischief in the wood.
HELENA: Ay, in the temple, in the town, the field,
You do me mischief. Fie, Demetrius!
Your wrongs do set a scandal on my sex.°
We cannot fight for love, as men may do.
We should be woo'd, and were not made to woo.

[*Exit Demetrius.*]

I'll follow thee and make a heaven of hell,
To die upon° the hand I love so well. [*Exit.*]
OBERON: Fare thee well, nymph. Ere he do leave this grove,
Thou shalt fly him, and he shall seek thy love.

Enter Puck.

°*impeach:* Discredit, call into question. °*desert:* Deserted, unpeopled. °*Your . . . privilege:* Your excellence in my eyes is my warrant for doing so. °*For that:* Because. °*in my respect:* As far as I am concerned. °*brakes:* Thickets. °*Apollo . . . chase:* According to the myth, Daphne, pursued by Apollo, was saved from rape by being transformed into a laurel tree. °*griffin:* Fabulous monster with the body of a lion and the head of an eagle. °*hind:* Female of the red deer. °*stay thy questions:* Delay to listen to your talk. °*Your . . . sex:* Because he forces her to be the wooer instead of the wooed. °*upon:* By.

Hast thou the flower there? Welcome, wanderer.
PUCK: Ay, there it is.
OBERON: I pray thee give it me.
I know a bank where the wild thyme blows,°
Where oxlips° and the nodding violet grows,
Quite over-canopied with luscious woodbine,°
With sweet musk-roses° and with eglantine;°
There sleeps Titania sometime of° the night,
Lull'd in these flowers with dances and delight;
And there the snake throws° her enamell'd skin,
Weed° wide enough to wrap a fairy in;
And with the juice of this I'll streak° her eyes,
And make her full of hateful fantasies.
Take thou some of it, and seek through this grove:
A sweet Athenian lady is in love
With a disdainful youth; anoint his eyes,
But do it when the next thing he espies
May be the lady. Thou shalt know the man
By the Athenian garments he hath on.
Effect it with some care, that he may prove
More fond on° her than she upon her love;
And look thou meet me ere the first cock crow.
PUCK: Fear not, my lord! your servant shall do so.

Exeunt.

SCENE 2°

Enter Titania, Queen of Fairies, with her Train.

TITANIA: Come, now a roundel° and a fairy song;
Then, for the third part of a minute, hence,
Some to kill cankers° in the musk-rose buds,
Some war with rere-mice° for their leathren° wings
To make my small elves coats, and some keep back
The clamorous owl, that nightly hoots and wonders
At our quaint° spirits. Sing me now asleep;
Then to your offices,° and let me rest.

Fairies sing.

[I. FAIRY:] You spotted snakes with double° tongue,

°*blows:* Blooms. °*oxlips:* Flowering plant resembling the cowslip. °*woodbine:* Honeysuckle. °*musk-roses:* Variety of large, fragrant rose. °*eglantine:* Sweet-brier, another variety of rose. °*sometime of:* At some time during. °*throws:* Sheds. °*Weed:* Garment. °*streak:* Anoint. °*fond on:* Infatuated with. °*Location:* The wood. °*roundel:* Dance in a circle. °*cankers:* Cankerworms. °*rere-mice:* Bats. °*leathren:* leathern. °*quaint:* Pretty, dainty. °*offices:* Duties. °*double:* Forked.

Thorny hedgehogs, be not seen,
Newts° and blind-worms, do no wrong,
Come not near our fairy queen.
[CHORUS] Philomele,° with melody,
Sing in our sweet lullaby,
Lulla, lulla, lullaby, lulla, lulla, lullaby.
Never harm,
Nor spell, nor charm,
Come our lovely lady nigh.
So good night, with lullaby.
1. FAIRY: Weaving spiders, come not here;
Hence, you long-legg'd spinners,° hence!
Beetles black, approach not near;
Worm nor snail, do no offense.
[CHORUS] Philomele, with melody, etc.
2. FAIRY: Hence, away! now all is well.
One aloof stand sentinel.

[*Exeunt Fairies. Titania sleeps.*]

Enter Oberon [*and squeezes the flower on Titania's eyelids*].

OBERON: What thou seest when thou dost wake,
Do it for thy true-love take;
Love and languish for his sake.
Be it ounce,° or cat,° or bear,
Pard,° or boar with bristled hair,
In thy eye that shall appear
When thou wak'st, it is thy dear
Wake when some vile thing is near. [*Exit.*]

Enter Lysander and Hermia.

LYSANDER: Fair love, you faint with wand'ring in the wood;
And to speak troth° I have forgot our way.
We'll rest us, Hermia, if you think it good,
And tarry for the comfort of the day.
HERMIA: Be't so, Lysander. Find you out a bed;
For I upon this bank will rest my head.
LYSANDER: One turf shall serve as pillow for us both,
One heart, one bed, two bosoms, and one troth.°
HERMIA: Nay, [good] Lysander; for my sake, my dear,
Lie further off yet; do not lie so near.

°*Newts:* Water lizards. Newts, blind-worms, and spiders (line 20) were all thought to be poisonous. °*Philomele:* The nightingale. Philomela, daughter of King Pandion of Athens, was transformed into a nightingale, according to Ovid, after her rape by her brother-in-law Tereus. °*spinners:* Spiders or (Cairncross) daddy-longlegs. °*ounce:* Lynx. °*cat:* Wildcat. °*Pard:* Leopard. °*troth:* Truth. °*troth:* Pledged faith.

LYSANDER: O, take the sense, sweet, of my innocence!°
Love takes the meaning in love's conference:°
I mean, that my heart unto yours [is] knit,
So that but one heart we can make of it;
Two bosoms interchained with an oath,
So then two bosoms and a single troth.
Then by your side no bed-room me deny;
For lying so, Hermia, I do not lie.°

HERMIA: Lysander riddles very prettily.°
Now much beshrew° my manners and my pride,
If Hermia meant to say Lysander lied.
But, gentle friend, for love and courtesy,
Lie further off, in humane° modesty;
Such separation as may well be said
Becomes a virtuous bachelor and a maid,
So far be distant; and good night, sweet friend.
Thy love ne'er alter till thy sweet life end!

LYSANDER: Amen, amen, to that fair prayer, say I,
And then end life when I end loyalty!
Here is my bed; sleep give thee all his rest!

HERMIA: With half that wish the wisher's eyes be press'd!° [*They sleep.*]

Enter Puck.

PUCK: Through the forest have I gone,
But Athenian found I none,
On whose eyes I might approve°
This flower's force in stirring love.
Night and silence—Who is here?
Weeds of Athens he doth wear:
This is he, my master said,
Despised° the Athenian maid;
And here the maiden, sleeping sound,
On the dank and dirty ground.
Pretty soul, she durst not lie,
Near this lack-love, this kill-courtesy.
Churl, upon thy eyes I throw
All the power this charm doth owe.°

°*take . . . innocence:* Interpret my meaning as entirely innocent. °*Love . . . conference:* i.e. a lover should be able to understand what is meant when he and his beloved talk together. °*I . . . lie:* i.e. I am not false. °*prettily:* Ingeniously, skillfully. °*beshrew:* Mischief take. °*humane:* Courteous, decorous. °*With . . . press'd:* i.e. may half of all sleep's rest (which "all" you have wished for me) be yours. °*approve:* Test. °*Despised:* Who despised. °*owe:* Possess.

When thou wak'st, let love forbid
Sleep his seat on thy eyelid.
So awake when I am gone,
For I must now to Oberon. *Exit.*

Enter Demetrius and Helena, running.

HELENA: Stay—though thou kill me, sweet Demetrius.
DEMETRIUS: I charge thee hence, and do not haunt° me thus.
HELENA: O, wilt thou darkling° leave me? do not so.
DEMETRIUS: Stay, on thy peril;° I alone will go. [*Exit.*]
HELENA: O, I am out of breath in this fond° chase!
The more my prayer, the lesser is my grace.°
Happy is Hermia, wheresoe'er she lies,°
For she hath blessed and attractive° eyes.
How came her eyes so bright? Not with salt tears;
If so, my eyes are oft'ner wash'd than hers.
No, no; I am as ugly as a bear;
For beasts that meet me run away for fear.
Therefore no marvel though Demetrius
Do, as a monster,° fly my presence thus.
What wicked and dissembling glass of mine
Made me compare° with Hermia's sphery eyne!°
But who is here? Lysander! on the ground?
Dead, or asleep? I see no blood, no wound.
Lysander, if you live, good sir, awake.
LYSANDER: [*Awaking.*] And run through fire I will for thy sweet sake.
Transparent° Helena, nature shows art,
That through thy bosom makes me see thy heart.
Where is Demetrius? O, how fit a word
Is that vile name to perish on my sword!
HELENA: Do not say so, Lysander, say not so.
What though he love your Hermia? Lord, what though?°
Yet Hermia still loves you; then be content.
LYSANDER: Content with Hermia? No, I do repent
The tedious minutes I with her have spent.
Not Hermia, but Helena I love.
Who will not change a raven for a dove?
The will° of man is by his reason sway'd;
And reason says you are the worthier maid.

°*haunt:* Follow persistently. °*darkling:* In the dark. °*Stay . . . peril:* i.e. it will be dangerous for you if you don't remain here. °*fond:* Doting, foolishly loving. °*my grace:* The favor I am granted. °*lies:* Dwells. °*attractive:* Magnetic. °*as a monster:* i.e. as he would fly from a monster. °*Made me compare:* Induced me to compare my eyes. °*sphery eyne:* Eyes as bright as stars in their spheres. °*Transparent:* (1) bright, radiant; (2) capable of being seen through. °*What though:* What does it matter if. °*will:* Desire.

Things growing are not ripe until their season,
So I, being young, till now ripe not to reason;
And touching now the point° of human skill,°
Reason becomes the marshal to my will,
And leads me to your eyes, where I o'erlook°
Love's stories written in Love's richest book.

HELENA: Wherefore was I to this keen° mockery born?
When at your hands did I deserve° this scorn?
Is't not enough, is't not enough, young man,
That I did never, no, not never can,
Deserve a sweet look from Demetrius' eye,
But you must flout my insufficiency?
Good troth, you do me wrong (good sooth,° you do)
In such disdainful manner me to woo.
But fare you well; perforce I must confess
I thought you lord of more true gentleness.°
O that a lady, of° one man refus'd,
Should of another therefore be abus'd!° *Exit.*

LYSANDER: She sees not Hermia. Hermia, sleep thou there,
And never mayst thou come Lysander near!
For as a surfeit of the sweetest things
The deepest loathing to the stomach brings,
Or as the heresies that men do leave
Are hated most of those they did deceive,
So thou, my surfeit and my heresy,
Of all be hated, but the most of me!
And, all my powers, address your love and might
To honor Helen and to be her knight. *Exit.*

HERMIA: [*Starting up.*] Help me, Lysander, help me! do thy best
To pluck this crawling serpent from my breast!
Ay me, for pity! what a dream was here!
Lysander, look how I do quake with fear.
Methought a serpent eat° my heart away,
And you sate° smiling at his cruel prey.°
Lysander! what, remov'd? Lysander! lord!
What, out of hearing gone? No sound, no word?
Alack, where are you? Speak, and if° you hear;
Speak, of all loves!° I swoon almost with fear.
No? then I well perceive you are not nigh:
Either death, or you, I'll find immediately. *Exit.*

°*point:* Summit. °*skill:* Discernment, judgment. °*o'erlook:* Survey, read. °*keen:* Bitter. °*deserve:* Earn. °*Good troth, good sooth.* Both phrases mean "in very truth." °*gentleness:* Courtesy. °*of:* By (so also in lines 134, 140, 142). °*abus'd:* Ill used. °*eat:* Ate (common preterite form, pronounced et). °*sate:* Sat. °*prey:* Preying. °*and if:* If. °*of all loves:* For the sake of all true love.

ACT 3

SCENE 1°

Enter the Clowns [Quince, Snug, Bottom, Flute, Snout, and Starveling].

BOTTOM: Are we all met?

QUINCE: Pat, pat; and here's a marvail's° convenient place for our rehearsal. This green plot shall be our stage, this hawthorn brake our tiring-house,° and we will do it in action as we will do it before the Duke.

BOTTOM: Peter Quince!

QUINCE: What sayest thou, bully° Bottom?

BOTTOM: There are things in this comedy of Pyramus and Thisby that will never please. First, Pyramus must draw a sword to kill himself; which the ladies cannot abide. How answer you that?

SNOUT: By'r lakin,° a parlous° fear.

STAR: I believe we must leave the killing out, when all is done.°

BOTTOM: Not a whit! I have a device to make all well. Write me a prologue, and let the prologue seem to say we will do no harm with our swords, and that Pyramus is not kill'd indeed; and for the more better assurance, tell them that I Pyramus am not Pyramus, but Bottom the weaver. This will put them out of fear.

QUINCE: Well; we will have such a prologue, and it shall be written in eight and six.°

BOTTOM: No; make it two more; let it be written in eight and eight.

SNOUT: Will not the ladies be afeard of the lion?

STARVELING: I fear it, I promise you.

BOTTOM: Masters, you ought to consider with your-[selves], to bring in (God shield us!) a lion among ladies,° is a most dreadful thing; for there is not a more fearful° wild-fowl than your lion living; and we ought to look to't.

SNOUT: Therefore another prologue must tell he is not a lion.

BOTTOM: Nay; you must name his name, and half his face must be seen through the lion's neck, and he himself must speak through, saying thus, or to the same defect:° "Ladies," or "Fair ladies, I would wish you," or "I would request you," or "I would entreat you, not to fear, not to tremble: my life for yours.° If you think I come hither as a lion, it were pity of my life.° No! I

°*Location:* Scene continues. (Although Fl marks an act break here, III.i is obviously a continuation of II.ii, since Titania remains asleep on stage, to wake at line 129.) °*marvail's:* Marvellous. °*tiring-house:* Dressing room. °*bully:* A friendly term meaning "fine fellow." °*By'r lakin:* By our ladykin, i.e. the Virgin Mary. °*parlous:* Perilous. °*when . . . done:* After all. °*eight and six:* The common ballad measure of alternating eight- and six-syllable lines. °*lion among ladies:* It has been suggested that Shakespeare here alludes to an episode at a court entertainment in Scotland in 1594, when a tame lion which was to have drawn a chariot was replaced by a black African so as not to frighten the spectators. °*fearful:* (1) dreadful (as referring to a lion); (2) full of fear (as referring to a bird). your. See note on I.ii.93. °*defect:* Blunder for effect. °*my . . . yours:* I pledge my life in defense of yours. °*were . . . life:* Would endanger my life.

am no such thing; I am a man as other men are"; and there indeed let him name his name, and tell them plainly he is Snug the joiner.

QUINCE: Well; it shall be so. But there is two hard things: that is, to bring the moonlight into a chamber; for you know, Pyramus and Thisby meet by moonlight.

SNOUT: Doth the moon shine that night we play our play?

BOTTOM: A calendar, a calendar! Look in the almanac. Find out moonshine, find out moonshine.

QUINCE: Yes; it doth shine that night.

[**BOTTOM:**] Why then may you leave a casement of the great chamber window (where we play) open; and the moon may shine in at the casement.

QUINCE: Ay; or else one must come in with a bush of thorns° and a lantern, and say he comes to disfigure,° or to present,° the person of Moonshine. Then, there is another thing: we must have a wall in the great chamber; for Pyramus and Thisby (says the story) did talk through the chink of a wall.

SNOUT: You can never bring in a wall. What say you, Bottom?

BOTTOM: Some man or other must present Wall, and let him have some plaster, or some loam, or some rough-cast° about him, to signify wall; or let him hold his fingers thus, and through that cranny shall Pyramus and Thisby whisper.

QUINCE: If that may be, then all is well. Come, sitdown, every mother's son, and rehearse your parts. Pyramus, you begin. When you have spoken your speech, enter into that brake; and so every one according to his cue.

Enter Robin [Puck, behind].

PUCK: What hempen home-spuns° have we swagg'ring° here,
So near the cradle of the Fairy Queen?
What, a play toward?° I'll be an auditor,
An actor too perhaps, if I see cause.

QUINCE: Speak, Pyramus. Thisby, stand forth.

BOTTOM: "Thisby, the flowers of odious° savors sweet"—

QUINCE: [Odorous], odorous.

BOTTOM: —"odors savors sweet;
So hath thy breath, my dearest Thisby dear.
But hark; a voice! Stay thou but here a while,
And by and by I will to thee appear." *Exit.*

[**PUCK:**] A stranger Pyramus than e'er played here.

[*Exit.*]

°*bush of thorns*: English peasants saw "the man in the moon" as bearing a bundle of sticks on his back. °*disfigure:* Blunder for prefigure. °*present:* Represent. °*rough-cast:* Plaster mixed with pebbles for coating the outside of buildings. °*hempen home-spuns:* Uncouth rustics (literally, persons wearing home-spun cloth made of hemp) °*swagg'ring:* Blustering about. °*toward:* About to take place. °*odious:* Blunder for odorous Dogberry makes the reverse error in *Much Ado,* III.v.16: "Comparisons are odorous."

FLUTE: Must I speak now?

QUINCE: Ay, marry, must you; for you must understand he goes but to see a noise that he heard, and is to come again.

FLUTE: "Most radiant Pyramus, most lily-white of hue,
Of color like the red rose on triumphant brier,
Most brisky juvenal,° and eke° most lovely Jew,°
As true as truest horse, that yet would never tire,
I'll meet thee, Pyramus, at Ninny's tomb."

QUINCE: "Ninus'° tomb," man. Why, you must not speak that yet. That you answer to Pyramus. You speak all your part at once, cues and all. Pyramus, enter. Your cue is past; it is "never tire."

FLUTE: O—"As true as truest horse, that yet would never tire."

[*Enter Puck, and Bottom with an ass's head.*]

BOTTOM: "If I were fair,° Thisby, I were° only thine."

QUINCE: O monstrous! O strange! We are haunted. Pray, masters, fly, masters! Help!

[*Exeunt Quince, Snug, Flute, Snout, and Starveling*]

PUCK: I'll follow you, I'll lead you about a round,° Through bog, through bush, through brake, through brier:
Sometime a horse I'll be, sometime a hound,
A hog, a headless bear, sometime a fire,°
And neigh, and bark, and grunt, and roar, and burn,
Like horse, hound, hog, bear, fire, at every turn.

Exit.

BOTTOM: Why do they run away? This is a knavery of them to make me afeard.

Enter Snout.

SNOUT: O Bottom, thou art chang'd! What do I see on thee?

BOTTOM: What do you see? You see an ass head of your own,° do you?

[*Exit Snout.*]

Enter Quince.

QUINCE: Bless thee, Bottom, bless thee! Thou art translated.° *Exit.*

BOTTOM: I see their knavery. This is to make an ass of me, to fright me, if they could, but I will not stir from this place, do what they can. I will walk up and down here, and I will sing, that they shall hear I am not afraid.

[*Sings.*]

°*brisky juvenal:* Lively youth. °*eke:* Also. °*Jew.* Probably suggested by the first syllable of *juvenal* and used to provide a rhyme. °*Ninus:* Mythical founder of Nineveh; his wife. Semiramis, reputedly erected Babylon, the scene of the story of Pyramus and Thisbe. °*fair:* Handsome. °*were:* Would be. °*about a round:* Roundabout. °*fire:* Will-o'-the-wisp. °*an ass-head . . . own:* i.e. something dreamed up inside your own asiuine head. °*translated:* Transformed.

The woosel cock° so black of hue,
With orange-tawny bill,
The throstle° with his note so true,
The wren with little quill°—

TITANIA: [*Awaking*.] What angel wakes me from my flow'ry bed?
BOTTOM: [*Sings*.]

The finch, the sparrow, and the lark,
The plain-song° cuckoo grey,
Whose note full many a man doth mark,
And dares not answer nay°—

for indeed, who would set his wit to so foolish a bird? Who would give a bird the lie,° though he cry "cuckoo" never so?°

TITANIA: I pray thee, gentle mortal, sing again.
Mine ear is much enamored of thy note;
So is mine eye enthralled to thy shape;
And thy fair virtue's force° (perforce) doth move me
On the first view to say, to swear, I love thee.

BOTTOM: Methinks, mistress, you should have little reason for that. And yet, to say the truth, reason and love keep little company together now-a-days. The more the pity that some honest neighbors will not make them friends. Nay, I can gleek° upon occasion.

TITANIA: Thou art as wise as thou art beautiful.

BOTTOM: Not so, neither; but if I had wit enough to get out of this wood, I have enough to serve mine owe° turn.

TITANIA: Out of this wood do not desire to go;
Thou shalt remain here, whether thou wilt or no.
I am a spirit of no common rate;°
The summer still° doth tend upon my state;°
And I do love thee; therefore go with me.
I'll give thee fairies to attend on thee;
And they shall fetch thee jewels from the deep,
And sing while thou on pressed flowers dost sleep.
And I will purge thy mortal grossness° so,
That thou shalt like an aery spirit go.
Peaseblossom! Cobweb! Moth!° and Mustardseed!

Enter four Fairies [*Peaseblossom, Cobweb, Moth, and Mustardseed*].

°*woosel cock:* Male ousel or blackbird. °*throstle:* Song thrush. °*quill:* Piping voice (literally, pipe made of a hollow stalk). °*plain-song:* Melody without variations. °*Whose . . . nay.* The similarity between *cuckoo* and *cuckold* gave rise to a common jest. °*give . . . lie:* Call a bird a liar. °*never so:* i.e. ever so much, continually. °*thy . . . force:* The power of your beauty. °*gleek:* Gibe, jest. °*owe:* Own. °*rate:* Value, worth. °*still:* Ever, always. °*doth . . . state:* Attends upon me as one of my retinue. °*grossness:* Corporeal nature. °*Moth:* Pronounced *mote* or *mot* by the Elizabethans, and probably intended by Shakespeare to represent here the word now written *mote,* which he seems regularly to have spelled *moth.*

[PEASEBLOSSOM:] Ready,
[COBWEB:] And I.
[MOTH:] And I.
[MUSTARDSEED:] And I.
[ALL:] Where shall we go?
TITANIA: Be kind and courteous to this gentleman,
Hop in his walks and gambol in his eyes;
Feed him with apricocks° and dewberries,
With purple grapes, green figs, and mulberries;
The honey-bags steal from the humble-bees,
And for night-tapers crop their waxen thighs,
And light them at the fiery glow-worm's eyes,
To have° my love to bed and to arise;
And pluck the wings from painted butterflies,
To fan the moonbeams from his sleeping eyes.
Nod to him, elves, and do him courtesies.
[PEASEBLOSSOM:] Hail, mortal!
[COBWEB:] Hail!
[MOTH:] Hail!
[MUSTARDSEED:] Hail!

BOTTOM: I cry your worships mercy,° heartily. I beseech your worship's name.

COBWEB: Cobweb.

BOTTOM: I shall desire you of more acquaintance,° good Master Cobweb. If I cut my finger, I shall make bold with you.° Your name, honest gentleman?

PEASEBLOSSOM: Peaseblossom.

BOTTOM: I pray you commend me° to Mistress Squash,° your mother, and to Master Peascod,° your father. Good Master Peaseblossom, I shall desire you of more acquaintance too. Your name, I beseech you, sir?

MUSTARDSEED: Mustardseed.

BOTTOM: Good Master Mustardseed, I know your patience° well. That same cowardly, giant-like oxbeef hath devour'd many a gentleman of your house. I promise you your kindred hath made my eyes water ere now. I desire you [of] more acquaintance, good Master Mustardseed.

TITANIA: Come wait upon him; lead him to my bower.
The moon methinks looks with a wat'ry eye;
And when she weeps,° weeps every little flower,
Lamenting some enforced° chastity.
Tie up my lover's tongue, bring him silently. *Exeunt.*

°*apricocks:* Apricots. °*have:* i.e. attend (with lights). °*cry . . . mercy:* Beg pardon of your honors. °*of more acquaintance:* To be better acquainted with me. °*If . . . you:* Cobwebs were applied to cuts to inhibit bleeding. °*commend me:* Give my regards. °*Squash:* Unripe pea pod. °*Peascod:* Mature pea pod. °*patience:* Calmness in suffering. °*she weeps:* i.e. causes dew. °*enforced:* Violated.

SCENE 2°

Enter King of Fairies [Oberon].

Oberon: I wonder if Titania be awak'd;
Then what it was that next° came in her eye,
Which she must dote on in extremity.°

[Enter Puck.]

Here comes my messenger. How now, mad spirit?
What night-rule° now about this haunted° grove?

Puck: My mistress with a monster is in love.
Near to her close° and consecrated bower,
While she was in her dull° and sleeping hour,
A crew of patches,° rude mechanicals,°
That work for bread upon Athenian stalls,°
Were met together to rehearse a play
Intended for great Theseus' nuptial day.
The shallowest thick-skin° of that barren sort,°
Who Pyramus presented, in their sport,
Forsook his scene,° and ent'red in a brake;
When I did him at this advantage take,
An ass's nole° I fixed on his head.
Anon his Thisby must be answered,
And forth my mimic° comes. When they him spy,
As wild geese that the creeping fowler eye,
Or russet-pated choughs,° many in sort°
(Rising and cawing at the gun's report),
Sever themselves and madly sweep the sky,
So, at his sight, away his fellows fly;
And at our stamp,° here o'er and o'er one falls;
He murther cries, and help from Athens calls.°
Their sense thus weak, lost with their fears thus strong,
Made senseless things begin to do them wrong,
For briers and thorns at their apparel snatch;
Some sleeves, some hats, from yielders all things catch.
I led them on in this distracted fear,

°*Location:* The wood. °*next:* Nearest, i.e. first. °*in extremity:* To the utmost degree. °*night-rule:* Night activity, night sport. °*haunted:* Much frequented. °*close:* Secret. °*dull:* Drowsy. °*patches:* Clowns, fools. °*rude mechanicals:* Ignorant workingmen. °*stalls:* Street or market booths where wares were sold. °*thick-skin:* Blockhead. °*barren sort:* Stupid crew. °*scene:* Playing place. °*nole:* Noddle, head. °*mimic:* Actor. °*russet-pated choughs:* Grey-headed jackdaws. °*in sort:* In company, together. °*at our stamp.* Puck's use of *our* instead of *my* has puzzled editors, as has the notion that a fairy's stamp would be frightening. (This is the first occurrence of the word in that sense recorded in the *O.E.D.*). Many editors adopt Theobald's conjecture at a *stump.* °*calls:* Calls for.

And left sweet Pyramus translated there;
When in that moment (so it came to pass)
Titania wak'd, and straightway lov'd an ass.

OBERON: This falls out better than I could devise.
But hast thou yet latch'd° the Athenian's eyes
With the love-juice, as I did bid thee do?

PUCK: I took him sleeping (that is finish'd too)
And the Athenian woman by his side;
That when he wak'd, of force° she must be ey'd.

Enter Demetrius and Hermia.

OBERON: Stand close; this is the same Athenian.

PUCK: This is the woman; but not this the man.

DEMETRIUS: O, why rebuke you him that loves you so?
Lay breath so bitter on your bitter foe.

HERMIA: Now I but chide; but I should use thee worse,
For thou (I fear) hast given me cause to curse.
If thou hast slain Lysander in his sleep,
Being o'er shoes in blood, plunge in the deep,
And kill me too.
The sun was not so true unto the day
As he to me. Would he have stolen away
From sleeping Hermia? I'll believe as soon
This whole° earth may be bor'd,° and that the moon
May through the centre creep, and so displease
Her brother's° noontide with th' Antipodes.°
It cannot be but thou hast murd'red him;
So should a murtherer look—so dead,° so grim.

DEMETRIUS: So should the murthered look, and so should I,
Pierc'd through the heart with your stern cruelty.
Yet you, the murtherer, look as bright, as clear,°
As yonder Venus in her glimmering sphere.

HERMIA: What's this to° my Lysander? Where is he?
Ah, good Demetrius, wilt thou give him me?

DEMETRIUS: I had rather give his carcass to my hounds.

HERMIA: Out, dog, out, cur! thou driv'st me past the bounds
Of maiden's patience. Hast thou slain him then?
Henceforth be never numb'red among men!
O, once tell true; tell true, even for my sake!
Durst thou have look'd upon him being awake?

°*latch'd:* Anointed. °*of force:* Perforce, necessarily. °*whole:* Solid. °*be bor'd:* Have a hole bored through it. °*her brother's:* i.e. the sun's. °*with th' Antipodes:* Among the people on the other side of the earth. °*dead:* Deadly (?) or deathly pale (?). °*clear:* Shining. °*What's this to:* What has all this to do with.

And hast thou kill'd him sleeping? O brave touch!°
Could not a worm,° an adder, do so much?
An adder did it! for with doubler tongue
Than thine, thou serpent, never adder stung.

DEMETRIUS: You spend your passion° on a mispris'd mood.°
I am not guilty of Lysander's blood;
Nor is he dead, for aught that I can tell.

HERMIA: I pray thee, tell me then that he is well.

DEMETRIUS: And if I could, what should I get therefore?

HERMIA: A privilege never to see me more.
And from thy hated presence part I [so]:
See me no more, whether he be dead or no. *Exit.*

DEMETRIUS: There is no following her in this fierce vein.
Here therefore for a while I will remain.
So sorrow's heaviness doth heavier° grow
For debt that bankrout° [sleep] doth sorrow owe;
Which now in some slight measure it will pay,
If for his tender° here I make some stay.

Lie down [*and sleep*].

OBERON: What hast thou done? Thou hast mistaken quite,
And laid the love-juice on some true-love's sight.
Of thy misprision° must perforce ensue
Some true love turn'd, and not a false turn'd true.

PUCK: Then fate o'errules, that one man holding troth,°
A million fail, confounding oath on oath.°

OBERON: About the wood go swifter than the wind,
And Helena of Athens look thou find.
All fancy-sick° she is and pale of cheer°
With sighs of love, that costs the fresh blood dear.°
By some illusion see thou bring her here.
I'll charm his eyes against she do appear.°

PUCK: I go, I go, look how I go,
Swifter than arrow from the Tartar's bow.° [*Exit.*]

OBERON: Flower of this purple dye,
Hit with Cupid's archery,
Sink in apple of his eye.
When his love he doth espy,

°*brave touch:* Noble exploit. °*worm:* Snake, serpent. °*passion:* Passionate outburst. °*on . . . mood:* In mistaken anger. °*heavier:* With play on the sense "drowsier." °*bankrout:* Bankrupt. °*for his tender:* Until sleep offers itself (in payment of the deficit). °*misprision:* Mistake. °*troth:* Faith. °*confounding . . . oath:* Invalidating one oath with another. °*fancy-sick:* Lovesick. °*cheer:* Face. °*costs . . . dear:* Each sigh was thought to draw a drop of blood from the heart. °*against . . . appear:* In preparation for her coming. °*arrow . . . bow:* Proverbial for swiftness.

Let her shine as gloriously
As the Venus of the sky.
When thou wak'st, if she be by,
Beg of her for remedy.

Enter Puck.

PUCK: Captain of our fairy band,
Helena is here at hand,
And the youth, mistook by me,
Pleading for a lover's fee.°
Shall we their fond pageant° see?
Lord, what fools these mortals be!
OBERON: Stand aside. The noise they make
Will cause Demetrius to awake.
PUCK: Then will two at once woo one;
That must needs be sport alone.°
And those things do best please me
That befall prepost'rously.°

Enter Lysander and Helena.

LYSANDER: Why should you think that I should woo in scorn?
Scorn and derision never come in tears.
Look when I vow, I weep, and vows so born,
In their nativity all truth appears.°
How can these things in me seem scorn to you,
Bearing the badge° of faith to prove them true?
HELENA: You do advance° your cunning more and more;
When truth kills truth, O devilish-holy fray!
These vows are Hermia's. Will you give her o'er?
Weigh oath with oath, and you will nothing weigh.
Your vows to her and me, put in two scales,
Will even weigh; and both as light as tales.°
LYSANDER: I had no judgment when to her I swore.
HELENA: Nor none, in my mind, now you give her o'er.
LYSANDER: Demetrius loves her; and he loves not you.
DEMETRIUS: [*Awaking.*] O Helen, goddess, nymph, perfect, divine!
To what, my love, shall I compare thine eyne?
Crystal is muddy. O, how ripe in show
Thy lips, those kissing cherries, tempting grow!

°*fee:* Right, privilege. °*fond pageant:* Foolish show. °*alone:* Unparalleled. °*prepost'rously:* Out of the natural order. °*vows . . . appears:* i.e. when vows are so born, the nature of their birth makes their sincerity manifest. °*badge:* Identifying mark (like the family crest or other device worn on livery to identify a gentleman's retainers). °*advance:* Hold high, i.e. display. °*tales:* Lies.

That pure congealed white, high Taurus'° snow,
Fann'd with the eastern wind, turns to a crow°
When thou hold'st up thy hand. O, let me kiss
This princess of pure white, this seal° of bliss!

HELENA: O spite! O hell! I see you all are bent
To set against me for your merriment.
If you were civil and knew courtesy,
You would not do me thus much injury.
Can you not hate me, as I know you do,
But you must join in souls to mock me too?
If you were men, as men you are in show,°
You would not use a gentle lady so;
To vow, and swear, and superpraise° my parts,°
When I am sure you hate me with your hearts.
You both are rivals, and love Hermia;
And now both rivals, to mock Helena.
A trim° exploit, a manly enterprise,
To conjure tears up in a poor maid's eyes
With your derision! None of noble sort
Would so offend a virgin, and extort°
A poor soul's patience, all to make you sport.

LYSANDER: You are unkind, Demetrius; be not so;
For you love Hermia; this you know I know.
And here, with all good will, with all my heart,
In Hermia's love I yield you up my part;
And yours of Helena to me bequeath,
Whom I do love, and will do till my death.

HELENA: Never did mockers waste more idle breath.

DEMETRIUS: Lysander, keep thy Hermia; I will none.°
If e'er I lov'd her, all that love is gone.
My heart to her but as guest-wise sojourn'd,
And now to Helen is it home return'd,
There to remain.

LYSANDER: Helen, it is not so.

DEMETRIUS: Disparage not the faith thou dost not know,
Lest, to thy peril, thou aby° it dear.
Look where thy love comes; yonder is thy dear.

Enter Hermia.

HERMIA: Dark night, that from the eye his° function takes,
The ear more quick of apprehension makes;

°*Taurus:* A mountain range in Asiatic Turkey. °*turns . . . crow:* i.e. seems black in comparison. °*seal:* Pledge. °*show:* Appearance. °*superpraise:* Overpraise. °*parts:* Qualities. °*trim:* Fine. °*extort:* Wring, torture. °*none:* i.e. of her. °*aby:* Pay for, atone for. °*his:* Its.

Wherein it doth impair the seeing sense,
It pays the hearing double recompense.
Thou art not by mine eye, Lysander, found;
Mine ear, I thank it, brought me to thy sound.
But why unkindly didst thou leave me so?

LYSANDER: Why should he stay, whom love doth press to go?

HERMIA: What love could press Lysander from my side?

LYSANDER: Lysander's love, that would not let him bide—
Fair Helena! who more engilds the night
Than all yon fiery oes° and eyes of light.
Why seek'st thou me? Could not this make thee know,
The hate I bare thee made me leave thee so?

HERMIA: You speak not as you think. It cannot be.

HELENA: Lo! she is one of this confederacy.
Now I perceive, they have conjoin'd all three
To fashion this false sport, in spite of me.°
Injurious° Hermia, most ungrateful maid!
Have you conspir'd, have you with these contriv'd°
To bait° me with this foul derision?
Is all the counsel° that we two have shar'd,
The sisters' vows, the hours that we have spent,
When we have chid the hasty-footed time
For parting us—O, is all forgot?
All school-days friendship, childhood innocence?
We, Hermia, like two artificial° gods,
Have with our needles created both one flower,
Both on one sampler, sitting on one cushion,
Both warbling of one song, both in one key,
As if our hands, our sides, voices, and minds
Had been incorporate.° So we grew together,
Like to a double cherry, seeming° parted,
But yet an union in partition,
Two lovely° berries moulded on one stem;
So with two seeming bodies, but one heart,
Two of the first, [like] coats in heraldry,
Due but to one, and crowned with one crest.°
And will you rent° our ancient love asunder,
To join with men in scorning your poor friend?
It is not friendly, 'tis not maidenly.

°*oes:* Circles, i.e. stars. °*in . . . me:* To vex me. °*Injurious:* Insulting. °*contriv'd:* Plotted. °*bait:* Torment. °*counsel:* Private thoughts, confidences. °*artificial:* Skilled in art, able to create. °*incorporate:* United in one body. °*seeming:* Apparently. °*lovely:* Loving. °*Two . . . crest:* "We had two of the first, i.e. bodies, like double coats in heraldry that belong to a man and wife as *one person,* But which, like our *single heart,* have but *one crest*" (Douce). °*rent:* Rend.

Our sex, as well as I, may chide you for it,
Though I alone do feel the injury.
Hermia: I am amazed° at your [passionate] words.
I scorn you not; it seems that you scorn me.
Helena: Have you not set Lysander, as in scorn,
To follow me and praise my eyes and face?
And made your other love, Demetrius
(Who even but now° did spurn me with his foot),
To call me goddess, nymph, divine and rare,
Precious, celestial? Wherefore speaks he this
To her he hates? And wherefore doth Lysander
Deny your love° (so rich within his soul)
And tender me (forsooth) affection,
But by your setting on, by your consent?
What though I be not so in grace° as you,
So hung upon with love, so fortunate
(But miserable most, to love unlov'd)?
This you should pity rather than despise.
Hermia: I understand not what you mean by this.
Helena: Ay, do! persever, counterfeit sad° looks,
Make mouths° upon° me when I turn my back,
Wink each at other, hold the sweet jest up;°
This sport, well carried,° shall be chronicled.
If you have any pity, grace, or manners,
You would not make me such an argument.°
But fare ye well; 'tis partly my own fault,
Which death, or absence, soon shall remedy.
Lysander: Stay, gentle Helena; hear my excuse,
My love, my life, my soul, fair Helena!
Helena: O excellent!
Hermia: Sweet, do not scorn her so.
Demetrius: If she cannot entreat, I can compel.°
Lysander: Thou canst compel no more than she entreat.
Thy threats have no more strength than her weak [prays°].
Helen, I love thee, by my life I do!
I swear by that which I will lose for thee,
To prove him false that says I love thee not.
Demetrius: I say I love thee more than he can do.
Lysander: If thou say so, withdraw, and prove it too.

°*amazed:* Utterly bewildered. °*even but now:* Just now. °*your love:* His love of you. °*grace:* Favor. °*sad:* Serious, grave. °*mouths:* A common corruption of *mows.* "Grimaces." °*upon:* At. °*hold . . . up:* Carry . . . on. °*carried:* Managed. °*argument:* Subject matter (for jesting). °*If . . . compel:* i.e. if Hermia cannot influence you by pleas, I can do so by force. °*prays:* Prayings, prayers.

DEMETRIUS: Quick, come!
HERMIA: Lysander, whereto tends all this?
LYSANDER: Away, you Ethiop!°
DEMETRIUS: No, no; he'll
Seem to break loose — take on as you would follow,
But yet come not. You are a tame man, go!
LYSANDER: Hang off,° thou cat, thou bur! Vile thing, let loose;
Or I will shake thee from me like a serpent!
HERMIA: Why are you grown so rude? What change is this,
Sweet love?
LYSANDER: Thy love? Out, tawny Tartar, out!
Out, loathed med'cine! O hated potion, hence!
HERMIA: Do you not jest?
HELENA: Yes, sooth; and so do you.
LYSANDER: Demetrius, I will keep my word with thee.
DEMETRIUS: I would I had your bond, for I perceive
A weak bond° holds you. I'll not trust your word.
LYSANDER: What? should I hurt her, strike her, kill her dead?
Although I hate her, I'll not harm her so.
HERMIA: What? can you do me greater harm than hate?
Hate me, wherefore? O me, what news,° my love!
Am not I Hermia? Are not you Lysander?
I am as fair now as I was erewhile.
Since night° you lov'd me; yet since night you left me:
Why then, you left me (O, the gods forbid!)
In earnest, shall I say?
LYSANDER: Ay, by my life;
And never did desire to see thee more.
Therefore be out of hope, of question, of doubt;
Be certain! nothing truer; 'tis no jest
That I do hate thee, and love Helena.
HERMIA: O me, you juggler, you canker-blossom,°
You thief of love! What, have you come by night
And stol'n my love's heart from him?
HELENA: Fine, i' faith!
Have you no modesty, no maiden shame,
No touch of bashfulness? What, will you tear
Impatient answers from my gentle tongue?
Fie, fie, you counterfeit, you puppet,° you!

°*Ethiop:* Blackamoor. Hermia is a brunette. °*Hang off:* Let go. °*weak bond:* i.e. Hermia's arms. Demetrius implies that Lysander is not trying very hard to break away from her. *what news:* What is the matter. °*Since night:* i.e. last night. °*canker-blossom:* Worm that destroys the bud. °*puppet:* i.e. a mere doll rather than a woman (cf. the preceding *counterfeit*), but Hermia takes it as a reference to her small stature.

HERMIA: "Puppet"? Why so? Ay, that way goes the game.
Now I perceive that she hath made compare
Between our statures: she hath urg'd her height,
And with her personage,° her tall personage,
Her height, forsooth, she hath prevail'd with him.
And are you grown so high in his esteem,
Because I am so dwarfish and so low?°
How low am I, thou painted maypole? Speak!
How low am I? I am not yet so low
But that my nails can reach unto thine eyes.
HELENA: I pray you, though you mock me, [gentlemen],
Let her not hurt me. I was never curst;°
I have no gift at all in shrewishness;
I am a right° maid for° my cowardice.
Let her not strike me. You perhaps may think,
Because she is something° lower than myself,
That I can match° her.
HERMIA: "Lower"? hark again.
HELENA: Good Hermia, do not be so bitter with me.
I evermore did love you, Hermia,
Did ever keep your counsels, never wrong'd you;
Save that, in love unto Demetrius,
I told him of your stealth° unto this wood.
He followed you; for love I followed him.
But he hath chid me hence, and threat'ned me
To strike me, spurn me, nay, to kill me too.
And now, so you will let me quiet go,
To Athens will I bear my folly back,
And follow you no furt her. Let me go.
You see how simple and how fond I am.
HERMIA: Why, get you gone. Who is't that hinders you?
HELENA: A foolish heart, that I leave here behind.
HERMIA: What, with Lysander?
HELENA: With Demetrius.
LYSANDER: Be not afraid; she shall not harm thee, Helena.
DEMETRIUS: No, sir, she shall not, though you take her part.
HELENA: O, when she is angry, she is keen and shrewd!°
She was a vixen° when she went to school;
And though she be but little, she is fierce.
HERMIA: "Little" again? Nothing but "low" and "little"?

°*personage:* Figure. °*low:* Short. °*curst:* Shrewish, sharp-tongued. °*right:* Real, true. °*for:* With respect to. °*something:* Somewhat. °*match:* Be a match for. °*stealth:* Stealing away. °*shrewd:* Sharp-tongued (synonymous with *curst* In line 300). °*vixen:* Shrew (literally, she-fox).

Why will you suffer her to flout me thus?
Let me come to her.

LYSANDER: Get you gone, you dwarf;
You minimus,° of hind'ring knot-grass° made;
You bead, you acorn.

DEMETRIUS: You are too officious
In her behalf that scorns your services.
Let her alone; speak not of Helena,
Take not her part. For if thou dost intend°
Never so little show of love to her,
Thou shalt aby° it.

LYSANDER: Now she holds me not;
Now follow, if thou dar'st, to try whose right,
Of thine or mine, is most in Helena.

DEMETRIUS: Follow? Nay; I'll go with thee, cheek by jowl.°

[*Exeunt Lysander and Demetrius*.]

HERMIA: You, mistress, all this coil° is long of° you.
Nay, go not back.

HELENA: I will not trust you, I,
Nor longer stay in your curst company.
Your hands than mine are quicker for a fray;
My legs are longer though, to run away. [*Exit*.]

HERMIA: I am amaz'd, and know not what to say. *Exit*.

OBERON: This is thy negligence. Still° thou mistak'st,
Or else commit'st thy knaveries willfully.

PUCK: Believe me, king of shadows, I mistook.
Did not you tell me I should know the man
By the Athenian garments he had on?
And so far° blameless proves my enterprise,
That I have 'nointed an Athenian's eyes;
And so far am I glad it so did sort,°
As° this their jangling° I esteem a sport.

OBERON: Thou seest these lovers seek a place to fight;
Hie° therefore, Robin, overcast the night;
The starry welkin° cover thou anon
With drooping fog as black as Acheron,°
And lead these testy rivals so astray
As one come not within another's way.

°*minimus:* Diminutive creature. °*knot-grass:* A weed that was thought to stunt the growth of animals or children. °*intend:* Offer or possibly pretend. °*aby:* Pay for. °*cheek by jowl:* Side by side. °*coil:* Uproar. °*long of:* Because of. °*Still:* Continually. °*so far:* To this extent. °*sort:* Turn out. °*As:* That. °*jangling:* Disputing, wrangling. °*Hie:* Hasten. °*welkin:* Sky. °*Acheron:* A river of Hades: here, Hades itself.

Like to Lysander sometime frame thy tongue;
Then stir Demetrius up with bitter wrong;°
And sometime rail thou like Demetrius;
And from each other look thou lead them thus,
Till o'er their brows death-counterfeiting sleep
With leaden legs and batty° wings doth creep.
Then crush this herb° into Lysander's eye;
Whose liquor hath this virtuous° property,
To take from thence all error with his might,°
And make his eyeballs roll with wonted sight.
When they next wake, all this derision°
Shall seem a dream and fruitless° vision,
And back to Athens shall the lovers wend
With league whose date° till death shall never end.
Whiles I in this affair do thee employ,
I'll to my queen and beg her Indian boy;
And then I will her charmed eye release
From monster's view, and all things shall be peace.

PUCK: My fairy lord, this must be done with haste,
For Night's swift dragons° cut the clouds full° fast,
And yonder shines Aurora's harbinger,°
At whose approach, ghosts, wand'ring here and there,
Troop home to churchyards. Damned spirits all,
That in crossways and floods have burial,°
Already to their wormy beds are gone,
For fear lest day should look their shames upon,
They willfully themselves exile from light,
And must for aye consort with black-brow'd Night.

OBERON: But we are spirits of another sort.
I with the Morning's love° have oft made sport,
And like° a forester,° the groves may tread
Even till the eastern gate, all fiery red,
Opening on Neptune with fair blessed beams,
Turns into yellow gold his salt green streams.
But notwithstanding, haste, make no delay;
We may effect this business yet ere day. [*Exit.*]

°*wrong:* Insults. °*batty:* Batlike. °*this herb:* i.e. the herb that Oberon has mentioned (II.i.184) as the antidote to love-in-idleness. °*virtuous:* Powerful. °*with his might:* By its efficacy. °*derision:* Laughable mockery. °*fruitless:* Having no effect, inconsequential. °*date:* Duration. °*dragons:* i.e. those that were supposed to draw the chariot of the goddess of night. °*full:* Very. °*Aurora's harbinger:* The precursor of dawn, i.e. the morning star. °*Damned . . . burial:* Suicides were commonly buried at cross-roads; to these Puck adds those who have drowned themselves and whose bodies have not been recovered. °*the Morning's love:* Cephalus, a mighty hunter, and lover of Aurora; or perhaps Aurora herself. If the first, Oberon means that he has often hunted in early morning with Cephalus; if the second, he means that he has often enjoyed the pleasures of the dawn, instead of being driven off by it. °*like:* In the guise of. °*forester:* Keeper of a royal forest or hunting preserve.

PUCK: Up and down, up and down,
I will lead them up and down;
I am fear'd in field and town.
Goblin, lead them up and down.
Here comes one.

Enter Lysander.

LYSANDER: Where art thou, proud Demetrius? Speak thou now.
PUCK: Here, villain, drawn° and ready. Where art thou?
LYSANDER: I will be with thee straight.°
PUCK: Follow me then
To plainer° ground.

[*Exit Lysander, as following the voice.*]

Enter Demetrius.

DEMETRIUS: Lysander, speak again!
Thou runaway, thou coward, art thou fled?
Speak! In some bush? Where dost thou hide thy head?
PUCK: Thou coward, art thou bragging to the stars,
Telling the bushes that thou look'st for wars,
And wilt not come? Come, recreant,° come, thou child,
I'll whip thee with a rod. He is defil'd
That draws a sword on thee.
DEMETRIUS: Yea, art thou there?
PUCK: Follow my voice; we'll try° no manhood here. *Exeunt.*

[*Enter Lysander.*]

LYSANDER: He goes before me, and still dares me on:
When I come where he calls, then he is gone.
The villain is much lighter-heel'd than I;
I followed fast, but faster he did fly,
That fallen am I in dark uneven° way,
And here will rest me. [*Lie down.*] Come, thou gentle day!
For if but once thou show me thy grey light,
I'll find Demetrius and revenge this spite. [*Sleeps.*]

[*Enter*] *Robin* [*Puck*] *and Demetrius.*

PUCK: Ho, ho, ho! Coward, why com'st thou not?
DEMETRIUS: Abide me,° if thou dar'st; for well I wot°
Thou run'st before me, shifting every place,
And dar'st not stand, nor look me in the face.
Where art thou now?

°*drawn:* With drawn sword. °*straight:* Straightway. °*plainer:* More level. °*recreant:* Coward. °*try:* Test. °*uneven:* Rough. °*Abide me:* Face me in fight. °*wot:* Know.

PUCK: Come hither; I am here.
DEMETRIUS: Nay then thou mock'st me. Thou shalt buy this dear,
If ever I thy face by daylight see.
Now, go thy way. Faintness constraineth me
To measure out my length° on this cold bed.
By day's approach look to be visited.

[*Lies down and sleeps*.]

Enter Helena.

HELENA: O weary night, O long and tedious night,
Abate° thy hours! Shine, comforts, from the east,
That I may back to Athens by daylight,
From these that my poor company detest.
And sleep, that sometimes shuts up sorrow's eye,
Steal me a while from mine own company. *Sleep*.
PUCK: Yet but three? Come one more;
Two of both kinds makes up four.

[*Enter Hermia*.]

Here she comes, curst° and sad.
Cupid is a knavish lad,
Thus to make poor females mad.
HERMIA: Never so weary, never so in woe,
Bedabbled with the dew and torn with briers,
I can no further crawl, no further go;°
My legs can keep no pace with my desires.
Here will I rest me till the break of day.
Heavens shield Lysander, if they mean a fray!

[*Lies down and sleeps*.]

PUCK: On the ground,
Sleep sound;
I'll apply,
[To] your eye,
Gentle lover, remedy.

[*Squeezing the juice on Lysander's eyes*.]

When thou wak'st,
Thou tak'st
True delight
In the sight
Of thy former lady's eye;
And the country proverb known,

°*measure . . . length:* i.e. stretch out. °*Abate:* Shorten. °*curst:* Ill-tempered. °*go:* Walk.

That every man should take his own,
In your waking shall be shown.
Jack shall have Jill;
Nought shall go ill:
The man shall have his mare again, and all shall be well. [*Exit*.]

ACT 4
SCENE 1°

Enter Queen of Fairies [*Titania*] *and Clown* [*Bottom*], *and Fairies* [*Peaseblossom, Cobweb, Moth, Mustardseed, and others, attending*]; *and the King* [*Oberon*] *behind them* [*unseen*].

TITANIA: Come sit thee down upon this flow'ry bed,
While I thy amiable° cheeks do coy,°
And stick musk-roses in thy sleek smooth head,
And kiss thy fair large ears, my gentle joy.

BOTTOM: Where's Peaseblossom?

PEASEBLOSSOM: Ready.

BOTTOM: Scratch my head, Peaseblossom. Where's Mounsieur Cobweb?

COBWEB: Ready.

BOTTOM: Mounsieur Cobweb, good mounsieur, get you your weapons in your hand, and kill me a red-hipp'd humble-bee on the top of a thistle; and, good mounsieur, bring me the honey-bag. Do not fret yourself too much in the action, mounsieur; and, good mounsieur, have a care the honey-bag break not, I would be loath to have you overflowen with° a honey-bag, signior. Where's Mounsieur Mustardseed?

MUSTARDSEED: Ready.

BOTTOM: Give me your neaf,° Mounsieur Mustardseed.
Pray you, leave your curtsy,° good mounsieur.

MUSTARDSEED: What's your will?

BOTTOM: Nothing, good mounsieur, but to help Cavalery° Cobweb° to scratch. I must to the barber's, mounsieur; for methinks I am marvail's hairy about the face; and I am such a tender ass, if my hair do but tickle me, I must scratch.

TITANIA: What, wilt thou hear some music, my sweet love?

BOTTOM: I have a reasonable good ear in music. Let's Eiave the tongs and the bones.°

[*Music. Tongs. Rural music.*]

°*Location:* Scene continues. (Again FI marks an act break where the action is clearly continuous, the lovers remaining asleep on the stage. The FI act division is preceded by the notation "They sleepe all the Act.": this may mean that they sleep during some kind of inter-act music, as well as into the next scene, but it need be nothing more than an inexact reference to the fact that they sleep during the first 138 lines of the next scene.) °*amiable:* Lovely. °*coy:* Caress. °*overflowen with:* Submerged by. °*neaf:* Fist. °*leave your curtsy:* i.e. put on your hat. °*Cavalery:* Cavalier (form of address for a fashionable gentleman). °*Cobweb:* Peaseblossom has been asked to do the scratching. This may be Shakespeare's slip or Bottom's. °*tongs, bones:* Rustic musical instruments: the tongs were struck with a key (as a triangle), and the bones were rattled between the fingers (as clappers).

Titania: Or say, sweet love, what thou desirest to eat.
Bottom: Truly, a peck of provender; I could munch your good dry oats. Methinks I have a great desire to a bottle° of hay. Good hay, sweet hay, hath no fellow.°
Titania: I have a venturous fairy that shall seek
The squirrel's hoard, and fetch thee new nuts.
Bottom: I had rather have a handful or two of dried Peaseblossom: But, I pray you, let none of your people stir me; I have an exposition° of sleep come upon me.
Titania: Sleep thou, and I will wind thee in my arms. Fairies, be gone, and be [all ways] away.°

[*Exeunt Fairies.*]

So doth the woodbine° the sweet honeysuckle
Gently entwist; the female ivy so
Enrings the barky fingers of the elm.
O, how I love thee! how I dote on thee! [*They sleep.*]

Enter Robin Goodfellow [Puck].

Oberon: [*Advancing.*] Welcome, good Robin. Seest thou this sweet sight?
Her dotage now I do begin to pity.
For meeting her of late behind the wood,
Seeking sweet favors° for this hateful fool,
I did upbraid her, and fall out with her.
For she his hairy temples then had rounded°
With coronet of fresh and fragrant flowers;
And that same dew which sometime° on the buds
Was wont to swell like round and orient pearls,°
Stood now within the pretty flouriets'° eyes,
Like tears that did their own disgrace bewail.
When I had at my pleasure taunted her,
And she in mild terms begg'd my patience,
I then did ask of her her changeling child;
Which straight she gave me, and her fairy sent
To bear him to my bower in fairy land.
And now I have the boy, I will undo
This hateful imperfection of her eyes.
And, gentle Puck, take this transformed scalp°
From off the head of this Athenian swain,
That he, awaking when the other° do,

°*bottle:* Bundle. °*fellow:* Equal. °*exposition:* Blunder for disposition, i.e. desire, inclination. °*all ways away:* Off in all directions. °*woodbine.* Obviously not the honeysuckle here (as at II.i.251). Various vines were known by this name. °*favors:* i.e. flowers as love gifts. °*rounded:* Encircled. °*sometime:* Formerly. °*orient pearls:* i.e. the most beautiful of pearls. °*flouriets':* Flowerets'. °*scalp:* Skull. °*other:* Others.

May all to Athens back again repair,
And think no more of this night's accidents°
But as the fierce° vexation of a dream.
But first I will release the Fairy Queen.

[*Touching her eyes.*]

Be as thou wast wont to be;
See as thou wast wont to see.
Dian's bud° [o'er] Cupid's flower
Hath such force and blessed power.
Now, my Titania, wake you, my sweet queen.

TITANIA: My Oberon, what visions have I seen!
Methought I was enamor'd of an ass.

OBERON: There lies your love.

TITANIA: How came these things to pass?
O, how mine eyes do loathe his visage now!

OBERON: Silence a while. Robin, take off this head.
Titania, music call, and strike more dead
Than common sleep of all these [five]° the sense.

TITANIA: Music, ho, music, such as charmeth sleep!

[*Music, still.*°]

PUCK: Now, when thou wak'st, with thine own fool's eyes peep.

OBERON: Sound, music! [*Louder music.*] Come, my queen, take hands with me,
And rock the ground whereon these sleepers be.
Now thou and I are new in amity,
And will to-morrow midnight solemnly°
Dance in Duke Theseus' house triumphantly,°
And bless it to all fair prosperity.
There shall the pairs of faithful lovers be
Wedded, with Theseus, all in jollity.

PUCK: Fairy King, attend and mark;
I do hear the morning lark.

OBERON: Then, my queen, in silence sad,°
Trip we after night's shade.
We the globe can compass soon,
Swifter than the wand'ring moon.

°*accidents:* Events, incidents. °*fierce:* Excessive, wild. °*Dian's bud:* i.e. the herb of II.i.184, III.ii.366, perhaps the flower of the *agnus castus* or chaste tree, thought to preserve chastity. °*these five:* i.e. the four lovers and Bottom. °*Music, still:* i.e. soft music. °*solemnly:* Ceremoniously. °*triumphantly:* Festively. °*sad:* Sober.

TITANIA: Come, my lord, and in our flight,
Tell me how it came this night
That I sleeping here was found,
With these mortals on the ground.

Exeunt. Wind° horn [within].

Enter Theseus, [Hippolyta, Egeus,] and all his Train.

THESEUS: Go, one of you, find out the forester,
For now our observation° is perform'd,
And since we have the vaward° of the day,
My love shall hear the music of my hounds.
Uncouple° in the western valley, let them go.
Dispatch,° I say, and find the forester.

[Exit an Attendant.]

We will, fair queen, up to the mountain's top,
And mark the musical confusion
Of hounds and echo in conjunction.

HIPPOLYTA: I was with Hercules and Cadmus once,
When in a wood of Crete they bay'd° the bear
With hounds of Sparta.° Never did I hear
Such gallant chiding;° for besides the groves,
The skies, the fountains, every region near
Seem° all one mutual cry. I never heard
So musical a discord, such sweet thunder.

THESEUS: My hounds are bred out of the Spartan kind;
So flew'd,° so sanded;° and their heads are hung
With ears that sweep away the morning dew;
Crook-knee'd, and dewlapp'd° like Thessalian bulls;
Slow in pursuit; but match'd in mouth like bells,
Each° under each. A cry° more tuneable°
Was never hollow'd to, nor cheer'd with horn,
In Crete, in Sparta, nor in Thessaly.
Judge when you hear. But soft!° What nymphs are these?

EGEUS: My lord, this'° my daughter here asleep,
And this Lysander, this Demetrius is,
This Helena, old Nedar's Helena.
I wonder of their being here together.

°*Wind:* Blow. °*observation:* Observance, May-day rites (cf. I.i.167). °*vaward:* Early part. °*Uncouple:* Unleash them. °*Dispatch:* Make haste. °*bay'd:* Brought to bay. °*hounds of Sparta:* Famous for hunting ability. °*chiding:* Baying. °*Seem:* Usually emended to *Seem'd.* °*flew'd:* Having large chaps. °*sanded:* Of a sandy color. °*dewlapp'd:* Having a pendulous flap of skin at the throat. °*match'd. . .Each:* With voices of varying but harmonious pitch, like a peal of bells. °*cry:* Pack of hounds. °*tuneable:* Melodious. °*soft:* Stop. °*this':* This is.

THESEUS: No doubt they rose up early to observe
The rite of May; and hearing our intent,
Came here in grace of our solemnity.°
But speak, Egeus, is not this the day
That Hermia should give answer of her choice?
EGEUS: It is, my lord.
THESEUS: Go, bid the huntsmen wake them with their horns.
[*Exit an Attendant.*] *Shout within. Wind horns. They all start up.*
Good morrow, friends. Saint Valentine° is past;
Begin these wood-birds but to couple now?
LYSANDER: Pardon, my lord. [*They kneel.*]
THESEUS: I pray you all, stand up.
I know you two are rival enemies.
How comes this gentle concord in the world,
That hatred is so far from jealousy°
To sleep by hate° and fear no enmity?
LYSANDER: My lord, I shall reply amazedly,°
Half sleep, half waking; but, as yet, I swear,
I cannot truly say how I came here.
But, as I think—for truly would I speak,
And now I do bethink me, so it is—
I came with Hermia hither. Our intent
Was to be gone from Athens, where we might,°
Without the peril° of the Athenian law—
EGEUS: Enough, enough, my lord; you have enough.
I beg the law, the law, upon his head.
They would have stol'n away, they would, Demetrius,
Thereby to have defeated° you and me:
You of your wife, and me of my consent,
Of my consent that she should be your wife.
DEMETRIUS: My lord, fair Helen told me of their stealth,
Of this their purpose hither to this wood,
And I in fury hither followed them,
Fair Helena in fancy° following me.
But, my good lord, I wot not by what power
(But by some power it is), my love to Hermia
(Melted as the snow) seems to me now
As the remembrance of an idle gaud,°
Which in my childhood I did dote upon;

°*in. . .solemnity:* To honor our observance of the same rites. °*Saint Valentine.* It was supposed that birds chose their mates on St. Valentine's Day. °*jealousy:* Suspicion, apprehension of evil. °*To. . .hate:* As to sleep side by side with a foe. °*amazedly:* Perplexedly. °*where we might:* Wherever we could. °*Without the peril:* Beyond the dangerous reach. °*defeated:* Defrauded. °*fancy:* Love. °*idle gaud:* Worthless trinket.

And all the faith, the virtue of my heart,
The object and the pleasure of mine eye,
Is only Helena. To her, my lord,
Was I betrothed ere I [saw] Hermia;
But like a sickness did I loathe this food;
But, as in health, come to my natural taste,
Now I do wish it, love it, long for it,
And will for evermore be true to it.

THESEUS: Fair lovers, you are fortunately met;
Of this discourse we more will hear anon.
Egeus, I will overbear your will;
For in the temple, by and by, with us
These couples shall eternally be knit.
And, for° the morning now is something worn,
Our purpos'd hunting shall be set aside.
Away with us to Athens. Three and three,
We'll hold a feast in great solemnity.
Come, Hippolyta.

[*Exeunt Theseus, Hippolyta, Egeus, and Train:*]

DEMETRIUS: These things seem small and undistinguishable,
Like far-off mountains turned into clouds.

HERMIA: Methinks I see these things with parted° eye,
When every thing seems double.

HELENA: So methinks;
And I have found Demetrius like a jewel,
Mine own, and not mine own.°

DEMETRIUS: Are you sure
That we are awake? It seems to me
That yet we sleep, we dream. Do not you think
The Duke was here, and bid us follow him?

HERMIA: Yea, and my father.

HELENA: And Hippolyta.

LYSANDER: And he did bid us follow to the temple.

DEMETRIUS: Why then, we are awake. Let's follow him,
And by the way let's recount our dreams.

[*Exeunt Lovers.*]

BOTTOM: [*Awaking.*] When my cue comes, call me, and I will answer. My next is, "Most fair Pyramus." Heigh-ho!° Peter Quince! Flute the bellows-mender! Snout the tinker! Starveling! God's° my life, stol'n hence, and left me asleep! I have had a most rare vision. I have had a dream, past the wit of man to say

°*for:* Since. °*parted:* Out of focus. °*like. . . mine own:* Like some precious thing found by accident, and hence not certainly belonging to me, though in my possession. °*Heigh-ho:* A yawn. °*God's:* God save.

what dream it was. Man is but an ass, if he go about° [t'] expound this dream. Methought I was—there is no man can tell what. Methought I was, and methought I had—but man is but [a patch'd°] fool, if he will offer° to say what methought I had. The eye of man hath not heard, the ear of man hath not seen, man's hand is not able to taste, his tongue to conceive, nor his heart to report, what my dream was.° I will get Peter Quince to write a ballet° of this dream. It shall be call'd "Bottom's Dream," because it hath no bottom;° and I will sing it in the latter end of a play, before the Duke. Peradventure, to make it the more gracious,° I shall sing it at her° death. [*Exit.*]

SCENE 2°

Enter Quince, Thisby [*Flute*], *and the rabble* [*Snout, Starveling*].

QUINCE: Have you sent to Bottom's house? Is he come home yet?

[STAR.] He cannot be heard of. Out of doubt he is transported.°

FLUTE: If he come not, then the play is marr'd. It goes not forward, doth it?

QUINCE: It is not possible. You have not a man in all Athens able to discharge° Pyramus but he.

FLUTE: No, he hath simply the best wit of any handicraft man in Athens.

QUINCE: Yea, and the best person too; and he is a very paramour for a sweet voice.

FLUTE: You must say "paragon." A paramour is (God bless us!) a thing of naught.°

Enter Snug the joiner.

SNUG: Masters, the Duke is coming from the temple, and there is two or three lords and ladies more married. If our sport had gone forward, we had all been made men.

FLUTE: O sweet bully Bottom! Thus hath he lost sixpence a day° during his life; he could not have scap'd° sixpence a day. And° the Duke had not given him sixpence a day for playing Pyramus, I'll be hang'd. He would have deserv'd it. Sixpence a day in Pyramus, or nothing.

Enter Bottom.

BOTTOM: Where are these lads? Where are these hearts?°

QUINCE: Bottom! O most courageous day! O most happy hour!

BOTTOM: Masters, I am to discourse wonders;° but ask me not what; for if I tell you, I am [no] true Athenian. I will tell you every thing, right° as it fell out.

QUINCE: Let us hear, sweet Bottom.

°*go about:* Attempt. °*patch'd:* Wearing motley. °*offer:* Venture. °*The eye. . .was.* A parody of 1 Corinthians 2:9: "The eye hath not seen, and the ear hath not heard, neither have entered into the heart of man. . ." (Bishops'). °*ballet:* Ballad. °*hath no bottom:* i.e. is all tangled up because it lacks a core (*bottom*). °*gracious:* Attractive, elegant. °*her:* i.e. Thisbe's. °*Location:* Athens. Quince's house. °*transported:* Carried away by the fairies. °*discharge:* Successfully perform the role of. °*a thing of naught:* Something wicked. °*sixpence a day:* i.e. as a royal pension. °*he. . .scap'd:* His reward would certainly not have been less than. °*And:* If. °*hearts:* Good fellows. °*am. . .wonders:* Have wonders to recount. °*right:* Exactly, just.

BOTTOM: Not a word of° me. All that I will tell you is, that the Duke hath din'd. Get your apparel together, good strings° to your beards, new ribands° to your pumps; meet presently° at the palace; every man look o'er his part; for the short and the long is, our play is preferr'd.° In any case, let Thisby have clean linen; and let not him that plays the lion pare his nails, for they shall hang out for the lion's claws. And, most dear actors, eat no onions nor garlic, for we are to utter sweet breath; and I do not doubt but to hear them say, it is a sweet comedy. No more words. Away, go, away! [*Exeunt.*]

ACT 5

SCENE 1°

Enter Theseus, Hippolyta, and Philostrate, [*Lords, and Attendants*].

HIPPOLYTA: 'Tis strange, my Theseus, that° these lovers speak of.
THESEUS: More strange than true. I never may° believe
These antic° fables, nor these fairy toys.°
Lovers and madmen have such seething brains,
Such shaping fantasies,° that apprehend°
More than cool reason ever comprehends.°
The lunatic, the lover, and the poet
Are of imagination all compact.°
One sees more devils than vast hell can hold;
That is the madman. The lover, all as frantic,
Sees Helen's° beauty in a brow of Egypt.°
The poet's eye, in a fine frenzy rolling,
Doth glance from heaven to earth, from earth to heaven;
And as imagination bodies forth
The forms of things unknown, the poet's pen
Turns them to shapes, and gives to aery nothing
A local habitation and a name.
Such tricks hath strong imagination,
That if it would but° apprehend some joy,
It comprehends some bringer of that joy;°
Or in the night, imagining some fear,°
How easy is a bush suppos'd a bear!
HIPPOLYTA: But all the story of the night told over,

°*of:* From. °*strings:* To attach their false beards (?). °*ribands:* Ribbons. °*presently:* Immediately. °*preferr'd:* Recommended, put forward. °*Location:* Athens. The palace of Theseus. °*that:* What. °*may:* Can. °*antic:* Grotesque. °*fairy toys:* Trifling tales about fairy doings. °*shaping fantasies:* Fertile imaginations. °*apprehend:* Perceive, imagine. °*comprehends:* Takes in, includes. °*compact:* Formed, composed. °*Helen:* Helen of Troy, a paragon of beauty. °*brow of Egypt:* Gipsy's face. °*would but:* Merely wishes to. °*comprehends. . . joy:* Has no trouble including or creating in his fantasy some source of the joy. °*some fear:* Something to be feared.

And all their minds transfigur'd so together,
More witnesseth° than fancy's images;°
And grows to° something of great constancy;°
But howsoever,° strange and admirable.°

Enter lovers, Lysander, Demetrius, Hermia, and Helena.

THESEUS: Here come the lovers, full of joy and mirth.
Joy, gentle friends, joy and fresh days of love
Accompany your hearts!
LYSANDER: More than to us
Wait in your royal walks, your board, your bed!
THESEUS: Come now; what masques, what dances shall we have,
To wear away this long age of three hours
Between [our] after-supper° and bed-time?
Where is our usual manager of mirth?
What revels are in hand? Is there no play
To ease the anguish of a torturing hour?
Call Philostrate.
PHILOSTRATE: Here, mighty Theseus.
THESEUS: Say, what abridgment° have you for this evening?
What masque? what music? How shall we beguile
The lazy time, if not with some delight?
PHILOSTRATE: There is a brief° how many sports are ripe.°
Make choice of which your Highness will see first.

[*Giving a paper.*]

THESEUS: [*Reads.*] "The battle with the Centaurs,° to be sung
By an Athenian eunuch to the harp."
We'll none of that: that have I told my love,
In glory of my kinsman° Hercules.
"The riot of the tipsy Bacchanals,
Tearing the Thracian singer in their rage."°
That is an old device;° and it was play'd
When I from Thebes came last a conqueror.

°*More witnesseth:* Gives evidence of more. °*fancy's images:* Ideas created by imagination. °*grows to:* Arrives at. °*constancy:* Consistency, hence certainty. °*howsoever:* In any event. °*admirable:* To be wondered at. °*after-supper:* Light repast following supper (?). °*abridgment:* Pastime (to abridge or shorten the time). °*brief:* List, abstract. °*ripe:* Ready for presentation. °*battle. . .Centaurs:* Battle between the Centaurs and the Lapithae at the wedding feast of Theseus' friend Pirithous, where the Centaurs attempted to carry off the bride, Hippodamia. °*glory. . .kinsman:* One version of the tradition placed Hercules at the battle against the Centaurs. He and Theseus, according to Plutarch's life of the latter, were kinsmen. °*The riot. . .rage:* Orpheus, the Thracian musician, was torn to pieces by Bacchantes at the height of their orgiastic frenzy. °*device:* i.e. something devised for dramatic representation.

"The thrice three Muses mourning for the death
Of Learning, late deceas'd in beggary."°
That is some satire, keen and critical,°
Not sorting with° a nuptial ceremony.
"A tedious brief scene of young Pyramus
And his love Thisby; very tragical mirth."
Merry and tragical? Tedious and brief?
That is hot ice and wondrous strange° snow.
How shall we find the concord of this discord?

PHILOSTRATE: A play there is, my lord, some ten words long,
Which is as brief as I have known a play;
But by ten words, my lord, it is too long,
Which makes it tedious; for in all the play
There is not one word apt, one player fitted.°
And tragical, my noble lord, it is;
For Pyramus therein doth kill himself;
Which when I saw rehears'd, I must confess,
Made mine eyes water; but more merry tears
The passion of loud laughter never shed.

THESEUS: What are they that do play it?

PHILOSTRATE: Hard-handed men that work in Athens here,
Which never labor'd in their minds till now;
And now have toiled° their unbreathed° memories
With this same play, against° your nuptial.

THESEUS: And we will hear it.

PHILOSTRATE: No, my noble lord,
It is not for you. I have heard it over,
And it is nothing, nothing in the world;
Unless you can find sport in their intents,
Extremely stretch'd,° and conn'd° with cruel pain,
To do you service.

THESEUS: I will hear that play;
For never any thing can be amiss,
When simpleness° and duty tender it.
Go bring them in; and take your places, ladies.

[*Exit Philostrate.*]

°*The thrice. . .beggary:* Perhaps a topical allusion, though laments on the low estate of learning were commonplace. °*critical:* Censorious. °*sorting with:* Befitting. °*strange.* Perhaps an error, replacing some word which with *snow* would produce a "discord" similar to *hot ice.* °*fitted:* Well cast. °*toiled:* Taxed. °*unbreathed:* Unexercised. °*against:* In preparation for. °*Extremely stretch'd:* Strained to the uttermost. °*conn'd:* Learned by heart. °*simpleness:* Sincerity.

HIPPOLYTA: I love not to see wretchedness o'ercharged,°
And duty in his service° perishing.
THESEUS: Why, gentle sweet, you shall see no such thing.
HIPPOLYTA: He says they can do nothing in this kind.°
THESEUS: The kinder we, to give them thanks for nothing.
Our sport shall be to take what they mistake;
And what poor duty cannot do, noble respect°
Takes it in might, not merit.°
Where I have come, great clerks° have purposed
To greet me with premeditated welcomes;
Where I have seen them shiver and look pale,
Make periods in the midst of sentences,
Throttle their practic'd accent in their fears,
And in conclusion dumbly have broke off,
Not paying me a welcome. Trust me, sweet,
Out of this silence yet I pick'd a welcome;
And in the modesty of fearful° duty
I read as much as from the rattling tongue
Of saucy and audacious eloquence.
Love, therefore, and tongue-tied simplicity
In least° speak most, to my capacity.°

[*Enter Philostrate.*]

PHILOSTRATE: So please your Grace, the Prologue° is address'd.°
THESEUS: Let him approach. [*Flourish° trumpet.*]

Enter [*Quince for*] *the Prologue.*

PROLOGUE: If we offend, it is with our good will.
That you should think, we come not to offend,
But with good will. To show our simple skill,
That is the true beginning of our end.
Consider then, we come but in despite.°
We do not come, as minding° to content you,
Our true intent is. All for your delight
We are not here. That you should here repent you,

°*wretchedness o'ercharged:* Feebleness overburdened. °*his service:* Its attempt to perform due service. °*in this kind:* Of this sort. °*noble respect:* Generous consideration. °*Takes. . .merit:* Judges it in relation to the abilities of the performers, not the merit of the performance. °*clerks:* Scholars. °*fearful:* Timorous, frightened. °*least:* i.e. saying least. °*to my capacity:* In my opinion. In the kindly speech of Theseus, a tribute was very likely intended to the graciousness of Queen Elizabeth. Attempts have been made to identify the passage with some particular occasion. °*Prologue:* Speaker of the prologue. °*address'd:* Ready. °*Flourish:* Sound a fanfare. °*despite:* Ill will, defiance of your wishes. °*minding:* Intending.

The actors are at hand; and, by their show,
You shall know all, that you are like to know.°

THESEUS: This fellow doth not stand upon points.°

LYSANDER: He hath rid his prologue like a rough° colt; he knows not the stop.° A good moral, my lord: it is not enough to speak, but to speak true.°

HIPPOLYTA: Indeed he hath play'd on this prologue like a child on a recorder°—a sound, but not in government.°

THESEUS: His speech was like a tangled chain; nothing impair'd,° but all disorder'd. Who is next?

Enter [*with a Trumpet before them*] *Pyramus and Thisby and Wall and Moonshine and Lion.*

PROLOGUE: Gentles, perchance you wonder at this show;
But wonder on till truth make all things plain.
This man is Pyramus, if you would know;
This beauteous lady Thisby is certain.
This man, with lime and rough-cast, doth present
Wall, that vile Wall, which did these lovers sunder;
And through Wall's chink, poor souls, they are content
To whisper. At the which let no man wonder.
This man, with lantern, dog, and bush of thorn,
Presenteth Moonshine; for if you will know,
By moonshine did these lovers think no scorn°
To meet at Ninus' tomb, there, there to woo.
This grisly beast, which Lion hight° by name,
The trusty Thisby, coming first by night,
Did scare away, or rather did affright;
And as she fled, her mantle she did fall,°
Which Lion vile with bloody mouth did stain.
Anon comes Pyramus, sweet youth and tall,°
And finds his trusty Thisby's mantle slain;
Whereat, with blade, with bloody blameful blade,
He bravely broach'd° his boiling bloody breast;
And Thisby, tarrying in mulberry shade,
His dagger drew, and died. For all the rest,
Let Lion, Moonshine, Wall, and lovers twain
At large° discourse, while here they do remain.

Exit [*with Pyramus,*] *Thisby, Lion, and Moonshine.*

°*If. . .know.* The humor of the passage is in the blunders of its punctuation. °*stand upon points:* (1) bother about trifles; (2) heed his punctuation. °*rough:* Unbroken. °*stop:* (1) reining in a horse to a quick halt; (2) period. °*true:* (1) the truth; (2) correctly. °*recorder:* Wind instrument resembling a flute or flageolet. °*government:* Control, management. °*nothing impair'd:* i.e. still unbroken (*nothing* is here, as often, adverbial, meaning "in no respect, not at all"). °*think no scorn:* Regard it as no disgrace. °*hight:* Is called. °*fall:* Let fall. °*tall:* Brave. °*broach'd:* Stabbed. °*At large:* At length.

THESEUS: I wonder if the lion be to speak.
DEMETRIUS: No wonder,° my lord; one lion may, when many asses do.
WALL: In this same enterlude it doth befall
That I, one [Snout] by name, present a wall;
And such a wall, as I would have you think,
That had in it a crannied hole or chink,
Through which the lovers, Pyramus and Thisby,
Did whisper often, very secretly.
This loam, this rough-cast, and this stone doth show
That I am that same wall; the truth is so;
And this the cranny is, right and sinister,°
Through which the fearful lovers are to whisper.
THESEUS: Would you desire lime and hair to speak better?
DEMETRIUS: It is the wittiest° partition that ever I heard discourse, my lord.

[*Enter Pyramus.*]

THESEUS: Pyramus draws near the wall. Silence!
PYRAMUS: O grim-look'd° night! O night with hue so black!
O night, which ever art when day is not!
O night, O night! alack, alack, alack,
I fear my Thisby's promise is forgot!
And thou, O wall, O sweet, O lovely wall,
That stand'st between her father's ground and mine!
Thou wall, O wall, O sweet and lovely wall,
Show me thy chink, to blink through with mine eyne!

[*Wall holds up his fingers.*]

Thanks, courteous wall; Jove shield thee well for this!
But what see I? No Thisby do I see.
O wicked wall, through whom I see no bliss!
Curs'd be thy stones for thus deceiving me!
THESEUS: The wall methinks, being sensible,° should curse again.°
PYRAMUS: No, in truth, sir, he should not. "Deceiving me" is Thisby's cue. She is to enter now, and I am to spy her through the wall. You shall see it will fall pat° as I told you. Yonder she comes.

Enter Thisby.

THISBY: O wall, full often hast thou heard my moans,
For parting my fair Pyramus and me!
My cherry lips have often kiss'd thy stones,
Thy stones with lime and° hair knit [up in thee].

°*No wonder:* It will be no wonder if he does. °*right and sinister:* Running right and left, i.e. horizontal. °*wittiest:* Cleverest. °*grim-look'd:* Grim-looking. °*sensible:* Capable of feeling. °*again:* In return. °*fall pat:* Happen exactly. °*and:* If.

PYRAMUS: I see a voice! Now will I to the chink,
To spy and I can hear my Thisby's face.
Thisby!
THISBY: My love thou art, my love I think.°
PYRAMUS: Think what thou wilt, I am thy lover's grace;°
And, like Limander, am I trusty still.
THISBY: And I, like Helen,° till the Fates me kill.
PYRAMUS: Not Shafalus to Procrus° was so true.
THISBY: As Shafalus to Procrus, I to you.
PYRAMUS: O, kiss me through the hole of this vild° wall!
THISBY: I kiss the wall's hole, not your lips at all.
PYRAMUS: Wilt thou at Ninny's tomb meet me straightway?
THISBY: 'Tide° life, 'tide death, I come without delay.

[*Exeunt Pyramus and Thisby*.]

WALL: Thus have I, Wall, my part discharged so;
And being done, thus Wall away doth go. [*Exit*.]
THESEUS: Now is the moon used° between the two neighbors.
DEMETRIUS: No remedy, my lord, when walls are so willful to hear° without warning.°
HIPPOLYTA: This is the silliest stuff that ever I heard.
THESEUS: The best in this kind° are but shadows;° and the worst are no worse, if imagination amend them.
HIPPOLYTA: It must be your imagination then, and not theirs.
THESEUS: If we imagine no worse of them than they of themselves, they may pass for excellent men. Here come two noble beasts in, a man and a lion.

Enter Lion and Moonshine.

LION: You, ladies, you, whose gentle hearts do fear
The smallest monstrous mouse that creeps on floor,
May now, perchance, both quake and tremble here,
When lion rough in wildest rage doth roar.
Then know that I as Snug the joiner am
A lion fell,° nor else no lion's dam,°

°*My . . . think:* The Q1 punctuation is here retained, although it "doth not stand upon points." °*grace:* i.e. lover. °*Limander, Helen:* Blunders for *Leander* and *Hero*. °*Shafalus, Procrus:* Blunders for *Cephalus* and *Procris*. °*vild:* Vile. °*Tide:* Betide, come. °*Now . . . used:* i.e. Moonshine, Wall being down, will now come into play. Most editors follow Pope in emending *moon used* to *mural* [i.e. wall] *down* (which is close to the F1 reading, *morall downe*). °*so . . . hear:* So willing to hear (?) or so perverse as to hear (?)—in either case, with humorous allusion to the proverb "Walls have ears" (certainly true of Snout!). °*without warning*: Surreptitiously (?) or without warning the parents (?). °*in this kind:* Of this profession, i.e. actors. °*shadows:* Likenesses, representations. °*lion fell:* Cruel lion (but with additional sense "lionskin"—an unintentionally humorous reference to Snug's costume). °*I . . . dam:* i.e. only as Snug the joiner am I a lion, or even a lioness.

For, if I should, as lion, come in strife
Into this place, 'twere pity on my life.

THESEUS: A very gentle° beast, and of a good conscience.

DEMETRIUS: The very best at a beast, my lord, that e'er I saw.

LYSANDER: This lion is a very fox for his valor.°

THESEUS: True; and a goose for his discretion.°

DEMETRIUS: Not so, my lord; for his valor cannot carry his discretion, and the fox carries the goose.

THESEUS: His discretion, I am sure, cannot carry his valor; for the goose carries not the fox. It is well, leave it to his discretion, and let us listen to the Moon.

MOON: This lanthorn° doth the horned moon present—

DEMETRIUS: He should have worn the horns on his head.

THESEUS: He is no crescent, and his horns are invisible within the circumference.

MOON: This lanthorn doth the horned moon present;
Myself the man i' th' moon do seem to be.

THESEUS: This is the greatest error of all the rest. The man should be put into the lanthorn. How is it else the man i' th' moon?

DEMETRIUS: He dares not come there for the candle;° for, you see, it is already in snuff.°

HIPPOLYTA: I am a-weary of this moon. Would he would change!

THESEUS: It appears, by his small light of discretion, that he is in the wane; but yet in courtesy, in all reason, we must stay° the time.

LYSANDER: Proceed, Moon.

MOON: All that I have to say is to tell you that the lanthorn is the moon, I the man i' th' moon, this thorn-bush my thorn-bush, and this dog my dog.

DEMETRIUS: Why, all these should be in the lanthorn; for all these are in the moon. But silence! here comes Thisby.

Enter Thisby.

THISBY: This is old Ninny's tomb. Where is my love?

LION: O! [*The Lion roars. Thisby runs off.*]

DEMETRIUS: Well roar'd, Lion.

THESEUS: Well run, Thisby.

HIPPOLYTA: Well shone, Moon. Truly; the moon shines with a good grace.

[*The Lion shakes Thisby's mantle.*]

THESEUS: Well mous'd,° Lion.

°*gentle:* Polite. °*very . . . valor:* i.e. more crafty (diplomatic) than courageous. °*goose . . . discretion:* i.e. more foolish than crafty. °*lanthorn:* A variant of *lantern*, influenced by the fact that lanterns usually had sides of transparent horn rather than *glass:* hence there is wordplay in the reference to the "horned" (i.e. crescent) moon, as well as in the jest about the cuckold's horns in the next speech. °*for the candle:* On account of the candle. °*in snuff:* (1) offended; (2) in need of snuffing. °*stay:* Wait for. °*mous'd:* Shaken, torn (like a mouse in the jaws of a cat).

Enter Pyramus.

DEMETRIUS: And then came Pyramus. [*Exit Lion.*]
LYSANDER: And so the lion vanish'd.
PYRAMUS: Sweet Moon, I thank thee for thy sunny beams;
I thank thee, Moon, for shining now so bright;
For by thy gracious, golden, glittering [gleams],
I trust to take of truest Thisby sight.
But stay! O spite!°
But mark, poor knight,
What dreadful dole° is here!
Eyes, do you see?
How can it be?
O dainty duck! O dear!
Thy mantle good,
What, stain'd with blood?
Approach, ye Furies fell!
O Fates, come, come,
Cut thread and thrum,°
Quail,° crush, conclude,° and quell!°

THESEUS: This passion,° and the death of a dear friend, would go near to make° a man look sad.

HIPPOLYTA: Beshrew my heart, but I pity the man.
PYRAMUS: O, wherefore, Nature, didst thou lions frame?
Since lion vild hath here deflow' r'd my dear;
Which is—no, no—which was the fairest dame
That liv'd, that lov'd, that lik'd, that look'd with cheer.°
Come, tears, confound,°
Out, sword, and wound
The pap of Pyramus;
Ay, that left pap,
Where heart doth hop. [*Stabs himself.*]
Thus die I, thus, thus, thus.
Now am I dead,
Now am I fled;
My soul is in the sky.
Tongue, lose thy light,
Moon, take thy flight,° [*Exit Moonshine.*]
Now die, die, die, die, die. [*Dies.*]

°*spite:* Malicious stroke of fortune. °*dole:* Grievous sight. °*thread and thrum:* Warp and the loose ends of the warp; here, the complete thread (of life). °*Quail:* Overpower. °*conclude:* Bring to an end. °*quell:* Kill. °*passion:* Violent expression of sorrow. °*go . . . make:* Almost succeed in making. °*cheer:* Almost certainly the meaning here is "countenance." °*confound:* Destroy (me). °*Tongue . . . flight:* Pyramus reverses the order of *Tongue* and *Moon,* with the result that Moonshine receives his walking orders. "Tongue, take your flight" would mean "be made dumb (by death)."

DEMETRIUS: No die, but an ace,° for him; for he is but one.°

LYSANDER: Less than an ace, man; for he is dead, he is nothing.

THESEUS: With the help of a surgeon he might yet recover, and yet prove an ass.°

HIPPOLYTA: How chance Moonshine is gone before Thisby comes back and finds her lover?

[*Enter Thisby*.]

THESEUS: She will find him by starlight. Here she comes, and her passion° ends the play.

HIPPOLYTA: Methinks she should not use a long one for such a Pyramus. I hope she will be brief.

DEMETRIUS: A mote will turn the balance, which Pyramus, which° Thisby, is the better: he for a man, God warr'nt° us; she for a woman, God bless us.

LYSANDER: She hath spied him already with those sweet eyes.

DEMETRIUS: And thus she means,° videlicet°—

THISBY:

Asleep, my love?
What, dead, my dove?
O Pyramus, arise!
Speak, speak! Quite dumb?
Dead, dead? A tomb
Must cover thy sweet eyes.
These lily lips,
This cherry nose,
These yellow cowslip cheeks,
Are gone, are gone!
Lovers, make moan;
His eyes were green as leeks.
O Sisters Three,°
Come, come to me,
With hands as pale as milk;
Lay them in gore,
Since you have shore°
With shears his thread of silk.
Tongue, not a word!
Come, trusty sword,
Come, blade, my breast imbrue!°

°*No . . . ace:* Not a whole die but a single face—the one-spot. °*one*: (1) a single person: (2) in a class by himself. °*ass:* With pun on *ace*. °*passion:* Passionate speech. °*which . . . which:* Whether . . . or. °*warr'nt:* Defend. "God warrant us" and "God bless us" were both used conventionally to ward off an evil omen, and hence here imply Demetrius' opinion of the performances. °*means:* Laments. °*videlicet:* As follows. °*Sisters Three:* The Fates. °*shore:* Shorn. °*imbrue:* Stain with blood.

[*Stabs herself.*]

And farewell, friends;
Thus Thisby ends;
Adieu, adieu, adieu. [*Dies.*]

Theseus: Moonshine and Lion are left to bury the dead.

Demetrius: Ay, and Wall too.

[Bottom:] [*Starting up.*] No, I assure you, the wall is down that parted their fathers. Will it please you to see the epilogue, or to hear° a Bergomask dance° between two of our company?

Theseus: No epilogue, I pray you; for your play needs no excuse.° Never excuse; for when the players are all dead, there need none to be blam'd. Marry, if he that writ it had play'd Pyramus, and hang'd himself in Thisby's garter, it would have been a fine tragedy; and so it is, truly, and very notably discharg'd. But come, your Bergomask; let your epilogue alone.
[*A dance.*]
The iron tongue of midnight hath told° twelve.
Lovers, to bed, 'tis almost fairy time.
I fear we shall outsleep the coming morn
As much as we this night have overwatch'd.°
This palpable-gross° play hath well beguil'd
The heavy° gait of night. Sweet friends, to bed.
A fortnight hold we this solemnity,
In nightly revels and new jollity. *Exeunt.*

Enter Puck.

Puck: Now the hungry [lion] roars,
And the wolf [behowls] the moon;
Whilst the heavy ploughman snores,
All with weary task foredone.°
Now the wasted brands do glow,°
Whilst the screech-owl, screeching loud,
Puts the wretch that lies in woe
In remembrance of a shroud.
Now it is the time of night
That the graves, all gaping wide,
Every one lets forth his sprite,°
In the church-way paths to glide.
And we fairies, that do run

°*see. . . hear:* Order reversed by *Bottom.* °*Bergomask dance:* A rustic dance taking its name from Bergamo in Italy. °*no excuse:* No extenuation of faults. °*told:* Struck. °*overwatch'd:* Stayed up too late. °*palpable-gross:* Obviously dull. °*heavy:* Torpid, dull. °*foredone:* Exhausted. °*wasted . . . glow:* Logs have burned down into glowing embers. °*his sprite:* Its ghost.

By the triple Hecat's team°
From the presence of the sun,
Following darkness like a dream,
Now are frolic.° Not a mouse
Shall disturb this hallowed house.
I am sent with broom before,
To sweep the dust behind° the door.

Enter King and Queen of Fairies [Oberon and Titania] with all their Train.

Oberon: Through the house give glimmering light
By the dead and drowsy fire,
Every elf and fairy sprite
Hop as light as bird from brier,
And this ditty, after me,
Sing, and dance it trippingly.

Titania: First, rehearse your song by rote,
To each word a warbling note.
Hand in hand, with fairy grace,
Will we sing, and bless this place.

[*Song and dance*.]

Oberon: Now, until the break of day,
Through this house each fairy stray.
To the best bride-bed will we,
Which by us shall blessed be;
And the issue, there create,°
Ever shall be fortunate.
So shall all the couples three
Ever true in loving be;
And the blots of Nature's hand
Shall not in their issue stand;
Never mole, hare-lip, nor scar,
Nor mark prodigious,° such as are
Despised in nativity,
Shall upon their children be.
With this field-dew consecrate,
Every fairy take his gait,°
And each several° chamber bless,

°*triple Hecat's team:* Hecate ruled in three capacities: as Luna (or Cynthia) in heaven, as Diana on earth, and as Proserpina in hell. Here she is the queen of night, drawn by her team of dragons (cf. III.ii.379). °*frolic:* Merry. °*behind:* i.e. from behind. Robin Goodfellow was a household spirit, and was thus sent to clean the house in preparation for the coming of his king and queen. °*create:* Created. °*prodigious:* Abnormal. °*take his gait:* Go his way. °*several:* Separate.

Through this palace, with sweet peace,
And the owner of it blest
Ever shall in safety rest.
Trip away; make no stay;
Meet me all by break of day.

Exeunt [*Oberon, Titania, and Train*]

PUCK: If we shadows have offended,
Think but this, and all is mended,
That you have but slumb'red here°
While these visions did appear.
And this weak and idle theme,
No more yielding but° a dream,
Gentles, do not reprehend.
If you pardon, we will mend.°
And, as I am an honest Puck,
If we have unearned luck
Now to scape the serpent's tongue,°
We will make amends ere long;
Else the Puck a liar call.
So, good night unto you all.
Give me your hands,° if we be friends.
And Robin shall restore amends.° [*Exit.*]

Reading and Reacting

1. In what two locations is *A Midsummer Night's Dream* set? How do these two settings help to define the action of the play?
2. This play contains very few stage directions. In the absence of stage directions, how does Shakespeare establish the settings? How does he indicate the actions of the various characters?
3. What costumes might highlight the most distinctive character traits of the following characters: Theseus, Hermia, Bottom, Hippolyta, Oberon, and Puck?
4. Musical interludes occur throughout *A Midsummer Night's Dream* (see act 2, scene 3, for example). How does music help to establish the mood of the play? In what way does it underscore the play's themes?
5. What is the significance of Oberon's flower? What kind of prop would you design to represent it?
6. Would you use a realistic ass's head on Bottom, or would some other alternative be more effective? (Look at the two pictures on page 1719 before you answer this question.)

°*That . . . here:* i.e. that it is but a "midsummer night's dream." °*No . . . but:* Yielding nothing more than. °*mend:* Do better the next time. °*serpent's tongue:* Hissing. °*Give . . . hands:* Applaud. °*restore amends:* Make amends in the future.

7. Today, the role of Puck is frequently played by a female. How might you explain this casting decision? How would you cast Puck?

8. How would you use lighting to establish the mood of act 3?

9. **JOURNAL ENTRY** A critic has observed that *A Midsummer Night's Dream* "does not read as well as it plays." What do you think he means? What, if anything, do you think one loses by reading this play instead of seeing it?

10. **CRITICAL PERSPECTIVE** In his commentary on *A Midsummer Night's Dream*, Charles Boyce says, "Scholars generally agree that *A Midsummer Night's Dream* was written to be performed at an aristocratic wedding. Everything in the play is related to the theme of marriage."

What elements of the play do you think are "related to the theme of marriage"? What "message" does Shakespeare's play have for those who are about to be married?

Related Works: "Araby" (p. 434), "Cathedral" (p. 526), "Young Goodman Brown" (p. 540), "La Belle Dame sans Merci: A Ballad" (p. 1169), "The Passionate Shepherd to His Love" (p. 1179), "Not marble, nor the gilded monuments" (p. 1194), "The English Canon" (p. 1202), *The Brute* (p. 1250).

WRITING SUGGESTIONS: Staging

1. Discuss the problems that the original staging of *Oedipus the King* or *A Midsummer Night's Dream* poses for contemporary audiences, and offer some possible solutions.
2. More than one critic has observed that the simplicity of Shakespeare's theater was one of its main strengths. If a character wanted to make himself invisible, all he had to do was declare himself so. If a scene called for a particular setting — a palace or forest, for example — the setting could be established with dialogue. Find some examples of this technique, and write an essay in which you discuss whether or not suggestions are more effective in the staging of *A Midsummer Night's Dream* than special effects or realistic settings would be.
3. Discuss and analyze the staging options for a play that is not in this chapter — for example, *Trifles* (p. 1319) or *Tape* (p. 1275).
4. Choose a short story that appears in this anthology, and explain how you would stage it if it were a play. What furnishings, props, costumes, lighting, and sound effects would you choose? What events would occur offstage? Possible subjects for this paper might include "The Story of an Hour" (p. 226), "A&P" (p. 259), or "The Storm" (p. 313).
5. Assume you have a very limited budget for staging *The Cuban Swimmer*. What challenges would you face? Write an essay in which you outline plans for staging *The Cuban Swimmer* with a very limited budget.

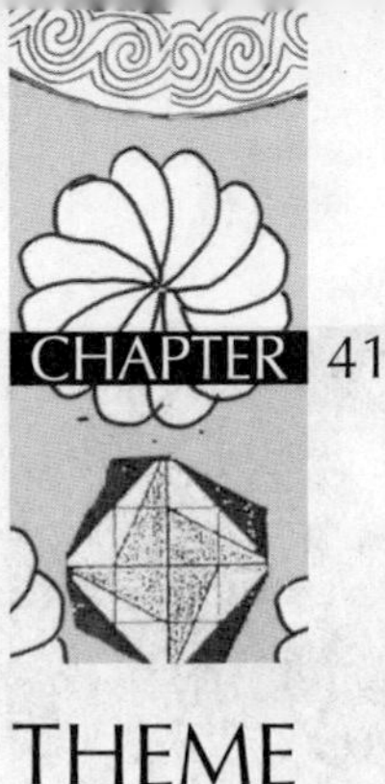

CHAPTER 41

THEME

Like a short story or a novel, a play is open to interpretation. Readers' reactions are influenced by the language of the text, and audiences' reactions are influenced by the performance on stage. Just as in fiction, every element of a play—its title, its conflicts, its dialogue, its characters, and its staging—can shed light on its themes.

James Earl Jones as Troy in a 1986 production of *Fences* (p. 1902) at the Goodman Theatre.

Source: Courtesy of the Goodman Theatre

Scene from the 1999 production of Sophocles' *Antigone* (p. 1863) at the Old Vic Theatre in London.
Source: ©John Vickers Theatre Collection

Scene from the 1999 production of *Krapp's Last Tape* (p. 1894) at the Barbican Theatre in London.
Source: Last Tape

Titles

The **title** of a play can provide insight into its themes. The ironic title of Susan Glaspell's *Trifles* (p. 1319), for example, suggests that women's concerns with "trifles" may get to the truth more effectively than the preoccupations of self-important men do. Lorraine Hansberry's *A Raisin in the Sun* is another title that offers clues to the theme of a play. An allusion to Langston Hughes's poem "Harlem" (p. 924)—which asks, "what happens to a dream deferred? / Does it dry up / like a raisin in the sun?"—the title suggests what happens to an African-American family whose dreams are repeatedly crushed. Likewise, the title *Fences* (p. 1902) offers clues to a major theme of August Wilson's play, suggesting that the main character is kept from his goals by barriers that are constructed by himself as well as by society. Finally, the title of Anton Chekhov's *The Brute* (p. 1250) calls attention to the play's ideas about male-female relationships. The title may refer to Smirnov, who says that he has never liked women — whom he characterizes as "creatures of poetry and romance." Or, it may refer to Mrs. Popov's late husband, to whose memory she has dedicated her life despite the fact that he was unfaithful. Either alternative reinforces the play's tongue-in-cheek characterization of men as "brutes."

Conflicts

The unfolding plot of a play — especially the **conflicts** that develop — can reveal the play's themes. In Henrik Ibsen's *A Doll House* (p. 1402), for example, at least three major conflicts are present: one between Nora and her husband Torvald, one between Nora and Krogstad (an old acquaintance), and one between Nora and society. Each of these conflicts sheds light on the themes of the play.

Through Nora's conflict with Torvald, Ibsen examines the constraints placed on women and men by marriage in the nineteenth century. Both Nora and Torvald are imprisoned within their respective roles: Nora must be passive and childlike, and Torvald must be proper and always in control. Nora, therefore, expects her husband to be noble and generous and, in a crisis, to sacrifice himself for her. When he fails to live up to her expectations, she is profoundly disillusioned.

Nora's conflict with Krogstad underscores Ibsen's criticisms of the class system in nineteenth-century Norway. At the beginning of the play, Nora finds it "immensely amusing: that we — that Torvald has so much power over . . . people." Krogstad, a bank clerk who is in the employ of Torvald, visits Nora in act 1 to enlist her aid in saving his job. It is clear that she sees him as her social inferior. For example, when Krogstad questions her about a woman with whom he has seen her, she replies, "What makes you think you can cross-examine me, Mr. Krogstad — you, one of my husband's employees?" Nora does not realize that she and Krogstad are, ironically, very much alike: both occupy subordinate positions and therefore have no power to determine their own destinies.

Finally, through Nora's conflict with society, Ibsen examines the destructive nature of the forces that subjugate women. Nineteenth-century society was male dominated. A married woman could not borrow money without her husband's signature, own real estate in her own name, or enter into contracts. In addition, all her assets — including inheritances and trust funds — automatically became the property of her husband at the time of marriage. As a result of her sheltered life, Nora at the beginning of the play is completely unaware of the consequences of her actions. Most readers share Dr. Rank's confusion when he asks Nora, "Why do you laugh at that? Do you have any idea of what society is?" It is Nora's disillusionment at finding out that Torvald and the rest of society are not what she has been led to believe they are that ultimately causes her to rebel. By walking out the door at the end of the play, Nora rejects not only her husband and her children (to whom she has no legal right once she leaves), but also society and its laws.

These three conflicts underscore many of the themes that dominate *A Doll House*. First, the conflicts show that marriage in the nineteenth century imprisons both men and women in narrow, constricting roles. They also show that middle-class Norwegian society is narrow, smug, and judgmental. (Krogstad is looked down upon for a crime years after he committed it, and Nora is looked down upon because she borrows money to save her husband's life.) Finally, the conflicts show that society does not offer individuals — especially women — the freedom to lead happy and fulfilling lives. Only when the social and economic conditions that govern society change, Ibsen suggests, can both women and men live together in mutual esteem.

Dialogue

Dialogue can also give insight into a play's themes. Sometimes a character suggests — or even explicitly states — a theme. In act 3 of *A Doll House*, for example, Nora's friend, Mrs. Linde, comes as close as any character to expressing the central concern of the play when she says, "Helmer's got to learn everything; this dreadful secret has to be aired; those two have to come to a full understanding; all these lies can't go on." As the play goes on to demonstrate, the lies that exist both in marriage and in society are obstacles to love and happiness.

One of the main themes of Arthur Miller's *Death of a Salesman* (p. 1531)— the questionable validity of the American Dream, given the nation's social, political, and economic realities — is suggested by the play's dialogue. As his son Biff points out, Willy Loman's stubborn belief in upward mobility and material success is based more on fantasy than on fact:

WILLY: *(with hatred, threatening)* The door of your life is wide open!

BIFF: Pop! I am a dime a dozen, and so are you!

Willy: *(turning on him now in an uncontrolled outburst)* I am not a dime a dozen! I am Willy Loman, and you are Biff Loman!

Biff starts for Willy, but is blocked by Happy. In his fury, Biff seems on the verge of attacking his father.

Biff: I am not a leader of men, Willy, and neither are you. You were never anything but a hard-working drummer who landed in the ash can like all the rest of them! I'm one dollar an hour, Willy! I tried seven states and couldn't raise it. A buck an hour! Do you gather my meaning? I'm not bringing home any prizes any more, and you're going to stop waiting for me to bring them home!

Although it does not explicitly state the theme of the play, this exchange strongly suggests that Biff rejects the desperate optimism to which Willy clings.

Characters

Because a dramatic work focuses on a central character, or **protagonist,** the development of this character can shed light on a play's themes. Willy Loman in *Death of a Salesman* is developed in great detail. At the beginning of the play, he feels trapped, exhausted, and estranged from his surroundings. As Willy gradually sinks from depression into despair, the action of the play shifts from the present to the past, showing the events that shaped his life. His attitudes, beliefs, dreams, and dashed hopes reveal him to be an embodiment of the major theme of the play — that an unquestioning belief in the American Dream of success is unrealistic and possibly destructive.

Nora in *A Doll House* changes a great deal during the course of the play. At the beginning, she is more her husband's possession than an adult capable of shaping her own destiny. Nora's status becomes apparent in the first act when Torvald gently scolds his "little spendthrift" and refers to her as his "little lark" and his "squirrel." She is reduced to childish deceptions, such as hiding her macaroons when her husband enters the room. After Krogstad accuses her of committing forgery and threatens to expose her, she expects her husband to rise to the occasion and take the blame for her. When Torvald instead accuses her of being a hypocrite, a liar, and a criminal, Nora's neat little world comes crashing down. As a result of this experience, Nora changes; no longer is she the submissive and obedient wife. Instead, she becomes assertive — even rebellious — ultimately telling Torvald that their marriage is a sham and that she can no longer stay with him. This abrupt shift in Nora's personality gives the audience a clear understanding of the major themes of the play.

Unlike Willy and Nora, Laura in Tennessee Williams's *The Glass Menagerie* (p. 1961) is a character who changes very little during the course of the play. Laura suffers from such pathological shyness that she is unable to attend typing class, let alone talk to a potential suitor. Although the "gentleman caller" draws her out of her shell for a short time, she soon withdraws again. Laura's inability to change reinforces the play's theme that contemporary society, with its emphasis on progress, has no place for people like her who live in private worlds "of glass animals and old, worn-out phonograph records."

 Staging

Various staging elements, such as props and furnishings, may also convey the themes of a play. In *Death of a Salesman*, Biff's trophy, which is constantly in the audience's view, is a prop that ironically underscores the futility of Willy's efforts to achieve success. Similarly, the miniature animals in *The Glass Menagerie* suggest the fragility of Laura's character and the futility of her efforts to fit into the modern world. And, in *Trifles*, the depressing farm house, the broken birdcage, and the dead canary hint at Mrs. Wright's misery and the reason she murdered her husband.

Special lighting effects and music can also suggest a play's themes. Throughout *The Glass Menagerie*, for example, words and pictures are projected onto a section of the set between the front room and dining room walls. In scene 1, as Tom's mother, Amanda, tells him about her experiences with her "gentlemen callers," an image of her as a girl greeting callers appears on the screen. As Amanda continues, the words *"Où sont Les Neiges"*—"Where are the snows [of yesteryear]?"— appear on the screen. Later in the play, when Laura and her mother discuss a boy Laura knew, his picture is projected on the screen, showing him as a high school hero carrying a silver cup. In addition to the slides, Williams uses music — a recurring tune, dance music, and "Ave Maria"— to increase the emotional impact of certain scenes. He also uses shafts of light focused on selected areas or characters to create a dreamlike atmosphere for the play. Collectively, the slides, music, and lighting reinforce the theme that those who retreat into the past inevitably become estranged from the present.

A Final Note

As you read, your own values and beliefs influence your interpretation of a play's themes. For instance, your interest in the changing status of women could lead you to focus on the submissive, almost passive, role of Willy's wife, Linda, in *Death of a Salesman*. As a result, you could conclude that the play shows how, in the post–World War II United States, women like Linda often sacrificed their own happiness for that of their husbands. Remember, however, that the play itself, not just your own feelings or assumptions about it, must support your interpretation.

✔ **CHECKLIST Writing about Theme**

- What is the central theme of the play?
- What other themes can you identify?
- Does the title of the play suggest a theme?
- What conflicts exist in the play? How do they shed light on the themes of the play?
- Do any characters' statements express or imply a theme of the play?
- Do any characters change during the play? How do these changes suggest the play's themes?
- Do certain characters resist change? How does their failure to change suggest a theme of the play?
- Do scenery and props help to communicate the play's themes?
- Does music reinforce certain ideas in the play?
- Does lighting underscore the themes of the play?

Source: ©Michele-Salmieri

DAVID HENRY HWANG (1957–) was born in Los Angeles. The son of Chinese-American immigrants, Hwang wrote his first play before he graduated from Stanford. *FOB* (Fresh Off the Boat), which was first performed in 1979, won the 1981 Obie as Best New Play of the Season. Hwang attended the Yale School of Drama from 1980 to 1981, and his next two plays, *The Dance and the Railroad* (1981) and *Family Devotions* (1981), were both based on the problems of immigrants trying at the same time to assimilate and to avoid assimilation into a new culture. In 1988, his Broadway hit, *M. Butterfly*, won the Tony Award for best play and established him as a major modern American playwright. The play was adapted into the 1993 feature film *M. Butterfly*. In his latest play, *Yellow Face* (2007), the protagonist's experiences are based closely on Hwang's own life.

Cultural Context With the advent of the Gold Rush and the burgeoning development of the railroad in the early nineteenth century, a large number of Chinese immigrants arrived to work in the United States. Many of these immigrants viewed their residency as temporary and did not wish to assimilate into American culture. Others wanted to stay but longed for a neighborhood of their own, and as a result, Chinatowns were born, with the largest in San Francisco and New York. Chinatowns, such as the one referred to in this play, are distinguished by bilingual signs, as well as by numerous restaurants, stores, and businesses that serve the Asian population.

Trying to Find Chinatown (1996)

CHARACTERS
Benjamin
Ronnie

SETTING
A street corner on the Lower East Side, New York City. The present.

NOTE ON MUSIC
Obviously, it would be foolish to require that the actor portraying Ronnie perform the specified violin music live. The score of this play can be played on tape over the house speakers, and the actor can feign playing the violin using a bow treated with soap. However, to effect a convincing illusion, it is desirable that the actor possess some familiarity with the violin, or at least another stringed instrument.

Darkness. Over the house speakers, fade in Hendrix-like virtuoso rock 'n' roll riffs—heavy feedback, distortion, phase shifting, wah-wah—amplified over a tiny Fender pug-nose.

Lights fade up to reveal that the music's being played over a solid-body electric violin by Ronnie, a Chinese American male in his mid-twenties, dressed in retro sixties clothing, with a few requisite nineties body mutilations. He's playing on a sidewalk for money, his violin case open before him, change and a few stray bills having been left by previous passers-by.

Enter Benjamin, early twenties, blond, blue-eyed, looking like a midwestern tourist in the big city. He holds a scrap of paper in his hands, scanning street signs for an address. He pauses before Ronnie, listens for a while. With a truly bravura run, Ronnie concludes the number, falls on his knees, gasping. Benjamin applauds.

BENJAMIN: Good. That was really great. (*Pause.*) I didn't . . . I mean, a fiddle . . . I mean, I'd heard them at square dances, on country stations and all, but I never . . . wow, this must really be New York City!

He applauds, starts to walk on. Still on his knees Ronnie clears his throat loudly.

BENJAMIN: Oh, I . . . you're not just doing this for your health, right?

He reaches in his pocket, pulls out a couple of coins. Ronnie clears his throat again.

BENJAMIN: Look, I'm not a millionaire, I'm just . . .

Benjamin pulls out his wallet, removes a dollar bill. Ronnie nods his head, gestures toward the violin case, as he sits on the sidewalk, takes out a pack of cigarettes, lights one.

RONNIE: And don't call it a "fiddle," OK?

BENJAMIN: Oh, well. I didn't mean to—

RONNIE: You sound like a wuss. A hick. A dipshit.

BENJAMIN: It just slipped out. I didn't really—

RONNIE: If this was a fiddle, I'd be sitting here with a cob pipe, stomping my cowboy boots and kicking up hay. Then I'd go home and fuck my cousin.

BENJAMIN: Oh! Well, I don't really think—

RONNIE: Do you see a cob pipe? Am I fucking my cousin?

BENJAMIN: Well, no, not at the moment, but—

RONNIE: All right. Then this is a violin, you hand over the money, and I ignore the insult, herein endeth the lesson. (*Pause.*)

BENJAMIN: Listen, a dollar's more than I've ever given to a . . . to someone asking for money.

RONNIE: Yeah, well, this is New York. Welcome to the cost of living.

BENJAMIN: What I mean is, maybe in exchange, you could help me—?

RONNIE: Jesus Christ! Do you see a sign around my neck reading "Big Apple Fucking Tourist Bureau?"

BENJAMIN: I'm just looking for an address, I don't think it's far from here, maybe you could . . . ?

Ronnie snatches the scrap of paper from Benjamin.

RONNIE: You're lucky I'm such a goddamn softie. (*He looks at the paper.*) Oh, fuck you. Just suck my dick, you and the cousin you rode in on.

BENJAMIN: I don't get it! What are you—?

RONNIE: Eat me. You know exactly what I—

BENJAMIN: I'm just asking for a little—

RONNIE: 13 Doyers St.? Like you don't know where that is?

BENJAMIN: Of course I don't know! That's why I'm asking—

RONNIE: C'mon, you trailer-park refugee. You don't know that's Chinatown?

BENJAMIN: Sure I know that's Chinatown.

RONNIE: I know you know that's Chinatown.

BENJAMIN: So? That doesn't mean I know where Chinatown—

RONNIE: So why is it that you picked me, of all the street musicians in the city—to point you in the direction of Chinatown? Lemme guess—is it the earring? No, I don't think so. The Hendrix riffs? Guess again, you fucking moron.

BENJAMIN: Now, wait a minute. I see what you're—

RONNIE: What are you gonna ask me next? Where you can find the best dim sum in the city? Whether I can direct you to a genuine opium den? Or do I know how you can meet Miss Saigon for a night of nookie-nookie followed by a good old-fashioned ritual suicide? (*He picks up his violin.*) Now, get your white ass off my sidewalk. One dollar doesn't even begin to make up for all this aggravation. Why don't you go back home and race bullfrogs, or whatever it is you do for—?

BENJAMIN: Brother, I can absolutely relate to your anger. Righteous rage, I suppose would be a more appropriate term. To be marginalized, as we are, by a white racist patriarchy, to the point where the accomplishments of our people are obliterated from the history books, this is cultural genocide of the first order, leading to the fact that you must do battle with all Euro-America's emasculating and brutal stereotypes of Asians—the opium den, the sexual objectification of the Asian female, the exoticized image of a tourist's Chinatown which ignores the exploitation of workers, the failure to unionize, the high rate of mental illness and tuberculosis — against these, each day, you rage, no, not as a victim, but as a survivor, yes, brother, a glorious warrior survivor!

Silence.

RONNIE: Say what?
BENJAMIN: So, I hope you can see that my request is not —
RONNIE: Wait, wait.
BENJAMIN: — motivated by sorts of racist assumptions —
RONNIE: But, but where . . . how did you learn all that?
BENJAMIN: All what?
RONNIE: All that — you know — oppression stuff — tuberculosis . . .
BENJAMIN: It's statistically irrefutable. TB occurs in the community at a rate —
RONNIE: Where did *you* learn it?
BENJAMIN: Well . . . I took Asian-American studies. In college.
RONNIE: Where did you go to college?
BENJAMIN: University of Wisconsin. Madison.
RONNIE: Madison, Wisconsin?
BENJAMIN: That's not where the bridges are, by the way.
RONNIE: Huh? Oh, right. . . .
BENJAMIN: You wouldn't believe the number of people who —
RONNIE: They have Asian-American studies in Madison, Wisconsin? Since when?
BENJAMIN: Since the last Third World Unity sit-in and hunger strike. (*Pause.*) Why do you look so surprised? We're down.
RONNIE: I dunno. It just never occurred to me, the idea of Asian students in the Midwest going on a hunger strike.
BENJAMIN: Well, a lot of them had midterms that week, so they fasted in shifts. (*Pause.*) The administration never figured it out. The Asian students put that "they all look alike" stereotype to good use.
RONNIE: OK, so they got Asian-American studies. That still doesn't explain —
BENJAMIN: What?
RONNIE: What *you* were doing taking it?
BENJAMIN: Just like everyone else. I wanted to explore my roots. After a lifetime of assimilation, I wanted to find out who I really am. (*Pause.*)
RONNIE: And did you?
BENJAMIN: Sure. I learned to take pride in my ancestors who built the railroads, my Popo who would make me a hot bowl of jok with thousand-day-old eggs when the white kids chased me home yelling. "Gook! Chink! Slant-eyes!"
RONNIE: OK, OK, that's enough!
BENJAMIN: Painful to listen to, isn't it?
RONNIE: I don't know what kind of bullshit ethnic studies program they're running over in Wisconsin, but did they teach you that in order to find your Asian "roots," it's a good idea first to be Asian? (*Pause.*)

BENJAMIN: Are you speaking metaphorically?

RONNIE: No! Literally! Look at your skin!

Ronnie grabs Benjamin's hands, holds them up before his face.

BENJAMIN: You know, it's very stereotypical to think that all Asian skin tones conform to a single hue.

RONNIE: You're white! Is this some kind of redneck joke or something? Am I the first person in the world to tell you this?

BENJAMIN: Oh! Oh! Oh!

RONNIE: I know real Asians are scarce in the Midwest, but . . . Jesus!

BENJAMIN: No, of course, I . . . I see where your misunderstanding arises.

RONNIE: Yeah. It's called "You white."

BENJAMIN: It's just that—in my hometown of Tribune, Kansas, and then at school—see, everyone knows me—so this sort of thing never comes up. (*He offers his hand.*) Benjamin Wong. I forget that a society wedded to racial constructs constantly forces me to explain my very existence.

RONNIE: Ronnie Chang. Otherwise known as "The Bowman."

BENJAMIN: You see, I was adopted by Chinese-American parents at birth. So clearly, I'm an Asian American—

RONNIE: Even though they could put a picture of you in the dictionary next to the definition of "WASP."

BENJAMIN: Well, you can't judge my race by my genetic heritage.

RONNIE: If genes don't determine race, what does?

BENJAMIN: Maybe you'd prefer that I continue in denial, masquerading as a white man?

RONNIE: Listen, you can't just wake up and say, "Gee, I *feel* Black today."

BENJAMIN: Brother, I'm just trying to find what you've already got.

RONNIE: What do I got?

BENJAMIN: A home. With your people. Picketing with the laundry workers. Taking refuge from the daily slights against your masculinity in the noble image of Gwan Gung.

RONNIE: Gwan *who*?

BENJAMIN: C'mon—the Chinese God of warriors and—what do you take me for? There're altars to him up all over the community.

RONNIE: I dunno what community you're talking about, but it's sure as hell not mine. (*Pause.*)

BENJAMIN: What do you mean?

RONNIE: I mean, if you wanna call Chinatown *your* community, OK, knock yourself out, learn to use chopsticks. Go ahead, try and find your roots in some dim sum parlor with headless ducks hanging in the window. Those places don't tell you a thing about who *I* am.

BENJAMIN: Oh, I get it.

RONNIE: You get what?

BENJAMIN: You're one of those self-hating, *assimilated* Chinese Americans, aren't you?

RONNIE: Oh, Jesus.

BENJAMIN: You probably call yourself, "Oriental," right? Look, maybe I can help you. I have some books I can—

RONNIE: Hey, I read all those Asian identity books when you were still slathering on industrial-strength sunblock. (*Pause.*) Sure, I'm Chinese. But folks like you act like that means something. Like all of a sudden, you know who I am. You think identity's that simple? That you can wrap it all up in a neat package and say, "I have ethnicity, therefore I am?" All you fucking ethnic fundamentalists. Always looking for easy answers. You say you're looking for identity, but you can't begin to face the real mysteries of the search. So instead you go skin-deep, and call it a day.

Pause. Ronnie turns away from Benjamin, starts to play his violin—slow and bluesy.

BENJAMIN: So what are you? "Just a human being?" That's like saying you *have* no identity. If you asked me to describe my dog, I'd say more than "He's just a dog."

RONNIE: What—you think if I deny the importance of my race, I'm nobody? There're worlds out there, worlds you haven't even begun to understand. Open your eyes. Hear with your ears.

He holds his violin at chest level, does not attempt to play during the following monologue. As he speaks, a montage of rock and jazz tracks fades in and out over the house speakers, bringing to life the styles of music he describes.

I concede—it was called a fiddle long ago—but that was even before the birth of jazz. When the hollering in the fields, the rank injustice of human bondage, the struggle of God's children against the plagues of the devil's white man, when all these boiled up into that bittersweet brew, called by later generations, the blues. That's when fiddlers like Son Sims held their chin rests at their chests and sawed away like the hillbillies still do today. And with the coming of ragtime appeared the pioneer Stuff Smith, who sang as he stroked the catgut, with his raspy Louis Armstrong voice—gruff and sweet like the timbre of horsehair riding south below the fingerboard, and who finally sailed for Europe to find ears that would hear. Europe—where Stephane Grapelli initialed a magical French violin, to be passed from generation to generation—first he, to Jean-Luc Ponty, then Ponty to Didier Lockwood. Listening to Grapelli play "A Nightingale Sang in Berkeley Square" is to understand not only the song of birds, but also how they learn to fly, fall in love on the wing, and finally falter one day, to wait for darkness beneath a London street lamp. And Ponty, he showed us how the modern violin man can accompany the shadow of his own lead lines, which cascade, one over another, into some netherworld beyond the range of human hearing. Joe Venuti, Noel Pointer, Svend Asmussen. Even the Kronos Quartet with their arrangement of "Purple Haze." Now, tell me, could any legacy be more rich, more crowded with mythology and heroes to inspire pride? What can I say if the banging of a gong or the clinking of a pickax on the Transcontinental Railroad fails to move me even as much as one note, played through the violin MIDI controller of Michal Urbaniak?

Ronnie puts his violin to his chin, begins to play a jazz composition of his own invention.

Does it have to sound like Chinese opera before people like you decide that I know who I am? (*Benjamin stands for a long moment, listening to Ronnie play. Then, he drops his dollar into the case, turns, and exits. Ronnie continues to play a long moment. Then Benjamin enters, illuminated in his own special. He sits on the floor of the stage, his feet dangling off the lip. As he speaks, Ronnie continues playing his tune, which becomes underscoring for Benjamin's monologue. As the music continues, does it slowly begin to reflect the influence of Chinese music?*)

BENJAMIN: When I finally found Doyers St., I scanned the buildings for Number 13. Walking down an alley where the scent of freshly steamed char siu bao lingered in the air, I felt immediately that I had entered a world where all things were finally familiar. (*Pause.*) An old woman bumped me with her shopping bag—screaming to her friend in Cantonese, though they walked no more than a few inches apart. Another man—shouting to a vendor in Sze-Yup. A youth, in a white undershirt, perhaps a recent newcomer, bargaining with a grocer in Hokkien. I walked through this ocean of dialects, breathing in the richness with deep gulps, exhilarated by the energy this symphony brought to my step. And when I finally saw the number 13, I nearly wept at my good fortune. An old tenement, paint peeling, inside walls no doubt thick with a century of grease and broken dreams—and yet, to me, a temple—the house where my father was born. I suddenly saw it all: Gung Gung, coming home from his 16-hour days pressing shirts he could never afford to own, bringing with him candies for my father, each sweet wrapped in the hope of a better life. When my father left the ghetto, he swore he would never return. But he had, this day, in the thoughts and memories of his son, just six months after his death. And as I sat on the stoop, I pulled a hua-moi from my pocket, sucked on it, and felt his spirit returning. To the place where his ghost, and the dutiful hearts of all his descendants, would always call home. (*He listens for a long moment.*) And I felt an ache in my heart for all those lost souls, denied this most important of revelations: to know who they truly are. (*Benjamin sits on the stage, sucking his salted plum and listening to the sounds around him. Ronnie continues to play. The two remain oblivious of one another. Lights fade slowly to black.*)

Reading and Reacting

1. What does Benjamin hope to find in Chinatown? Do you think he is successful?
2. During the first half of the play, Benjamin dominates the action. At what point does this situation change? What do you think causes this change?
3. What is the main theme of this play? What other themes are developed?
4. What is the significance of the play's title? How does it express the play's main theme? For example, is Benjamin really trying to find Chinatown, or is he looking for something else?

5. What is the central conflict of the play? Is it ever resolved? Explain.

6. Both Ronnie and Benjamin deliver long monologues. What do these characters reveal about themselves in their monologues?

7. How does Hwang use music in the play? How does music help him to convey his ideas?

8. What can you tell about the social class of the two characters? For example, which character do you think has a better education? Which one seems to come from a more privileged background? Is this difference in social class essential to the play?

9. **JOURNAL ENTRY** Is Ronnie correct when he says that Benjamin is white? Is it possible for Benjamin to be both white and Chinese? Explain.

10. **CRITICAL PERSPECTIVE** In an introduction to a collection of Hwang's plays, novelist Maxine Hong Kingston discusses his contributions to Chinese-American theater:

> Chinese American actors are given too few dignified parts to play. If no playwrights like David Hwang came along, a generation of actors who speak our accents would be lost. A novelist can only invent an approximate orthography. For voices, the play's the thing. Chinese American theater, which started out with a bang—firecrackers, drums—keeps dying out. David Henry Hwang gives it life once again.

Do you think that these comments apply to *Trying to Find Chinatown?* For example, does the play convey the authentic voices and accents of its characters? Do you agree that this kind of authenticity is not possible in a novel or short story?

Related Works: "Water Names" (p. 318), "The Disappearance" (p. 695), "Girl Powdering Her Neck" (p. PS5), "Suicide Note" (p. 846), "How to Write the Great American Indian Novel" (p. 871), "Harlem" (p. 924), "Little Father" (p. 1175), *The Cuban Swimmer* (p. 1732)

SOPHOCLES (496–406 B.C.) (picture and biography on p. 1744) was one of nine generals elected for a military campaign against Samos, a Greek island that was in revolt against Athens. Sophocles' election was due at least in part to the popularity of his play *Antigone.* (Greek plays often centered on problems of the city-state, and the theater was in many ways the center of the state's religious and political life.)

Even though it was written long before *Oedipus the King, Antigone* traces the events that befall Oedipus's younger daughter after his banishment from Thebes. Caught between the laws of the gods and the edict of her uncle the king, Antigone follows her conscience despite the fatal consequences to herself. In the 1960s, the story of Antigone was especially meaningful to those Americans who engaged in civil disobedience in struggles for civil rights and in protest against the war in Vietnam.

Cultural Context The central struggle in this play revolves around Antigone's desire to bury her brother in an honorable way. The ancient Greeks believed that at the moment of death, the spirit of the dead person left the body as a little puff of wind. The body was then prepared for burial according to time-honored rituals, which were primarily performed by female relatives. The burial rituals consisted of three parts: the *prothesis*, or laying out of the body; the *ekphora*, or funeral procession; and the interment of the body or cremated remains of the deceased. Coins were placed over the eyelids of the deceased as payment for the ferryman who would usher the body across the River Styx and into the underworld. Very few other objects were placed in the grave, but elaborate monuments were often erected to ensure that the dead would be remembered.

Antigone* (441 B.C.)

Translated by Dudley Fitts and Robert Fitzgerald

CHARACTERS

Antigone	**Teiresias**
Ismene	**A Sentry**
Eurydice	**A Messenger**
Creon	**Chorus**
Haimon	

SCENE

Before the palace of Creon, King of Thebes. A central double door, and two lateral doors. A platform extends the length of the facade, and from this platform three steps lead down into the "orchestra," or chorus-ground.

TIME

Dawn of the day after the repulse of the Argive army from the assault on Thebes.

PROLOGUE°

Antigone and Ismene enter from the central door of the palace.

ANTIGONE: Ismene, dear sister,
You would think that we had already suffered enough
For the curse on Oedipus.°
I cannot imagine any grief
That you and I have not gone through. And now—
Have they told you of the new decree of our King Creon?

ISMENE: I have heard nothing: I know
That two sisters lost two brothers, a double death
In a single hour; and I know that the Argive army
Fled in the night; but beyond this, nothing.

ANTIGONE: I thought so. And that is why I wanted you
To come out here with me. There is something we must do.

ISMENE: Why do you speak so strangely?

---

*Note that individual lines are numbered in the following play. When a line is shared by two or more characters, it is counted as one line.

Prologue: The portion of the play containing the exposition, or explanation, of what has gone before and what is now happening.

the curse on Oedipus: As Sophocles tells in *Oedipus the King,* the king of Thebes discovered that he had lived his life under a curse. Unknowingly, he had slain his father and married his mother. On realizing this terrible truth, Oedipus put out his own eyes and departed into exile. Now, years later, as *Antigone* opens, Antigone and Ismene, daughters of Oedipus, are recalling how their two brothers died. After the abdication of their father, the brothers ruled Thebes together, but they fell to quarreling. When Eteocles expelled Polyneices, the latter returned with an army and attacked the city. The two brothers killed each other in combat, leaving the throne to Creon. The new king of Thebes buried Eteocles with full honors but, calling Polyneices a traitor, decreed that Polyneices' body be left to the crows. This was an especially terrible decree, for a rotting corpse might offend Zeus, bring down plague, blight, and barrenness upon Thebes, and prevent the soul of a dead hero from entering the Elysian Fields, abode of those favored by the gods.

ANTIGONE: Listen, Ismene:
Creon buried our brother Eteocles
With military honors, gave him a soldier's funeral,
And it was right that he should; but Polyneices,
Who fought as bravely and died as miserably,—
They say that Creon has sworn
No one shall bury him, no one mourn for him,
But his body must lie in the fields, a sweet treasure
For carrion birds to find as they search for food.
That is what they say, and our good Creon is coming here
To announce it publicly; and the penalty—
Stoning to death in the public square!
There it is,
And now you can prove what you are:
A true sister, or a traitor to your family.

ISMENE: Antigone, you are mad! What could I possibly do?

ANTIGONE: You must decide whether you will help me or not.

ISMENE: I do not understand you. Help you in what?

ANTIGONE: Ismene, I am going to bury him. Will you come?

ISMENE: Bury him! You have just said the new law forbids it.

ANTIGONE: He is my brother. And he is your brother, too.

ISMENE: But think of the danger! Think what Creon will do!

ANTIGONE: Creon is not strong enough to stand in my way.

ISMENE: Ah sister!
Oedipus died, everyone hating him
For what his own search brought to light, his eyes
Ripped out by his own hand; and Jocasta died,
His mother and wife at once: she twisted the cords
That strangled her life; and our two brothers died,
Each killed by the other's sword. And we are left:
But oh, Antigone,
Think how much more terrible than these
Our own death would be if we should go against Creon
And do what he has forbidden! We are only women,
We cannot fight with men, Antigone!
The law is strong, we must give in to the law
In this thing, and in worse. I beg the Dead
To forgive me, but I am helpless: I must yield
To those in authority. And I think it is dangerous business
To be always meddling.

ANTIGONE: If that is what you think,
I should not want you, even if you asked to come.
You have made your choice, you can be what you want to be.
But I will bury him; and if I must die,
I say that this crime is holy: I shall lie down
With him in death, and I shall be as dear

To him as he to me.
It is the dead,
Not the living, who make the longest demands:
We die for ever . . .
You may do as you like,
Since apparently the laws of the gods mean nothing to you.

ISMENE: They mean a great deal to me; but I have no strength
To break laws that were made for the public good.

ANTIGONE: That must be your excuse, I suppose. But as for me,
I will bury the brother I love.

ISMENE: Antigone,
I am so afraid for you!

ANTIGONE: You need not be:
You have yourself to consider, after all.

ISMENE: But no one must hear of this, you must tell no one!
I will keep it a secret, I promise!

ANTIGONE: O tell it! Tell everyone!
Think how they'll hate you when it all comes out
If they learn that you knew about it all the time!

ISMENE: So fiery! You should be cold with fear.

ANTIGONE: Perhaps. But I am doing only what I must.

ISMENE: But can you do it? I say that you cannot.

ANTIGONE: Very well: when my strength gives out,
I shall do no more.

ISMENE: Impossible things should not be tried at all.

ANTIGONE: Go away, Ismene:
I shall be hating you soon, and the dead will too,
For your words are hateful. Leave me my foolish plan:
I am not afraid of the danger; if it means death,
It will not be the worst of deaths — death without honor.

ISMENE: Go then, if you feel that you must.
You are unwise,
But a loyal friend indeed to those who love you.

Exit into the palace. Antigone goes off, left. Enter the Chorus.

PARADOS°

STROPHE 1

CHORUS: Now the long blade of the sun, lying
Level east to west, touches with glory
Thebes of the Seven Gates. Open, unlidded

Parados: A song sung by the Chorus on the entering. Its *strophe* (according to scholarly theory) was sung while the Chorus danced from stage right to stage left; its *antistrophe,* while the Chorus danced back again. Another parados follows the prologue of *Oedipus the King.*

Eye of golden day! O marching light
Across the eddy and rush of Dirce's stream,°
Striking the white shields of the enemy
Thrown headlong backward from the blaze of morning!

CHORAGOS:° Polyneices their commander
Roused them with windy phrases,
He the wild eagle screaming
Insults above our land,
His wings their shields of snow,
His crest their marshalled helms.

ANTISTROPHE 1

CHORUS: Against our seven gates in a yawning ring
The famished spears came onward in the night;
But before his jaws were sated with our blood,
Or pinefire took the garland of our towers,
He was thrown back; and as he turned, great Thebes—
No tender victim for his noisy power—
Rose like a dragon behind him, shouting war.

CHORAGOS: For God hates utterly
The bray of bragging tongues;
And when he beheld their smiling,
Their swagger of golden helms,
The frown of his thunder blasted
Their first man from our walls.

STROPHE 2

CHORUS: We heard his shout of triumph high in the air
Turn to a scream; far out in a flaming arc
He fell with his windy torch, and the earth struck him.
And others storming in fury no less than his
Found shock of death in the dusty joy of battle.

CHORAGOS: Seven captains at seven gates
Yielded their clanging arms to the god
That bends the battle-line and breaks it.
These two only, brothers in blood,
Face to face in matchless rage,
Mirroring each the other's death,
Clashed in long combat.

Dirce's stream: A river near Thebes.

Choragos: Leader of the Chorus and principal commentator on the play's action.

ANTISTROPHE 2

Chorus: But now in the beautiful morning of victory
Let Thebes of the many chariots sing for joy!
With hearts for dancing we'll take leave of war:
Our temples shall be sweet with hymns of praise,
And the long nights shall echo with our chorus.

SCENE 1

Choragos: But now at last our new King is coming:
Creon of Thebes, Menoeceus' son.

In this auspicious dawn of his reign
What are the new complexities
That shifting Fate has woven for him?
What is his counsel? Why has he summoned
The old men to hear him?

Enter Creon from the palace, center. He addresses the Chorus from the top step.

Creon: Gentlemen: I have the honor to inform you that our Ship of State, which recent storms have threatened to destroy, has come safely to harbor at last, guided by the merciful wisdom of Heaven. I have summoned you here this morning because I know that I can depend upon you: your devotion to King Laius was absolute; you never hesitated in your duty to our late ruler Oedipus; and when Oedipus died, your loyalty was transferred to his children. Unfortunately, as you know, his two sons, the princes Eteocles and Polyneices, have killed each other in battle; and I, as the next in blood, have succeeded to the full power of the throne.

I am aware, of course, that no Ruler can expect complete loyalty from his subjects until he has been tested in office. Nevertheless, I say to you at the very outset that I have nothing but contempt for the kind of Governor who is afraid, for whatever reason, to follow the course that he knows is best for the State; and as for the man who sets private friendship above the public welfare,—I have no use for him, either. I call God to witness that I saw my country headed for ruin, I should not be afraid to speak out plainly; and I need hardly remind you that I would never have any dealings with an enemy of the people. No one values friendship more highly than I; but we must remember that friends made at the risk of wrecking our Ship are not real friends at all.

These are my principles, at any rate, and that is why I have made the following decision concerning the sons of Oedipus: Eteocles, who died as a man should die, fighting for his country, is to be buried with full military honors, with all the ceremony that is usual when the greatest heroes die; but his brother Polyneices, who broke his exile to come back with fire and sword against his native city and the shrines of his fathers' gods, whose one idea was to spill the blood of his blood and sell his own people into slavery — Polyneices, I say, is to have no burial: no man is to touch him or say the least prayer for him; he shall lie on the plain, unburied; and the birds and the scavenging dogs can do with him whatever they like.

This is my command, and you can see the wisdom behind it. As long as I am King, no traitor is going to be honored with the loyal man. But whoever shows by word and deed that he is on the side of the State,— he shall have my respect while he is living and my reverence when he is dead.

CHORAGOS: If that is your will, Creon son of Menoeceus,
You have the right to enforce it: we are yours.

CREON: That is my will. Take care that you do your part.

CHORAGOS: We are old men: let the younger ones carry it out.

CREON: I do not mean that: the sentries have been appointed.

CHORAGOS: Then what is it that you would have us do?

CREON: You will give no support to whoever breaks this law.

CHORAGOS: Only a crazy man is in love with death!

CREON: And death it is; yet money talks, and the wisest
Have sometimes been known to count a few coins too many.

Enter Sentry from left.

SENTRY: I'll not say that I'm out of breath from running, King, because every time I stopped to think about what I have to tell you, I felt like going back. And all the time a voice kept saying, "You fool, don't you know you're walking straight into trouble?"; and then another voice: "Yes, but if you let somebody else get the news to Creon first, it will be even worse than that for you!" But good sense won out, at least I hope it was good sense, and here I am with a story that makes no sense at all; but I'll tell it anyhow, because, as they say, what's going to happen's going to happen and—

CREON: Come to the point. What have you to say?

SENTRY: I did not do it. I did not see who did it. You must not punish me for what someone else has done.

CREON: A comprehensive defense! More effective, perhaps,
If I knew its purpose. Come: what is it?

SENTRY: A dreadful thing . . . I don't know how to put it—

CREON: Out with it!

SENTRY: Well, then;
The dead man—
Polyneices—

Pause. The Sentry is overcome, fumbles for words. Creon waits impassively.

out there—

someone,—
New dust on the slimy flesh!

Pause. No sign from Creon.

Someone has given it burial that way, and
Gone . . .

Long pause. Creon finally speaks with deadly control.

CREON: And the man who dared do this?
SENTRY: I swear I
Do not know! You must believe me!
Listen:
The ground was dry, not a sign of digging, no,
Not a wheeltrack in the dust, no trace of anyone.
It was when they relieved us this morning: and one of them,
The corporal, pointed to it.
There it was,
The strangest—
Look:
The body, just mounded over with light dust: you see?
Not buried really, but as if they'd covered it
Just enough for the ghost's peace. And no sign
Of dogs or any wild animal that had been there.
And then what a scene there was! Every man of us
Accusing the other: we all proved the other man did it,
We all had proof that we could not have done it.
We were ready to take hot iron in our hands,
Walk through fire, swear by all the gods,
It was not I!
I do not know who it was, but it was not I!

Creon's rage has been mounting steadily, but the Sentry is too intent upon his story to notice it.

And then, when this came to nothing, someone said
A thing that silenced us and made us stare
Down at the ground: you had to be told the news,
And one of us had to do it! We threw the dice,
And the bad luck fell to me. So here I am,
No happier to be here than you are to have me:
Nobody likes the man who brings bad news.
CHORAGOS: I have been wondering, King: can it be that the gods have done this?
CREON: *(Furiously)* Stop!
Must you doddering wrecks
Go out of your heads entirely? "The gods"!

Intolerable!
The gods favor this corpse? Why? How had he served them?
Tried to loot their temples, burn their images,
Yes, and the whole State, and its laws with it!
Is it your senile opinion that the gods love to honor bad men?
A pious thought!—
No, from the very beginning
There have been those who have whispered together,
Stiff-necked anarchists, putting their heads together,
Scheming against me in alleys. These are the men,
And they have bribed my own guard to do this thing.
(Sententiously) Money!
There's nothing in the world so demoralizing as money.
Down go your cities,
Homes gone, men gone, honest hearts corrupted,
Crookedness of all kinds, and all for money!
(To Sentry) But you—
I swear by God and by the throne of God,
The man who has done this thing shall pay for it!
Find that man, bring him here to me, or your death
Will be the least of your problems: I'll string you up
Alive, and there will be certain ways to make you
Discover your employer before you die;
And the process may teach you a lesson you seem to have missed:
The dearest profit is sometimes all too dear:
That depends on the source. Do you understand me?
A fortune won is often misfortune.

SENTRY: King, may I speak?
CREON: Your very voice distresses me.
SENTRY: Are you sure that it is my voice, and not your conscience?
CREON: By God, he wants to analyze me now!
SENTRY: It is not what I say, but what has been done, that hurts you.
CREON: You talk too much.
SENTRY: Maybe; but I've done nothing.
CREON: Sold your soul for some silver: that's all you've done.
SENTRY: How dreadful it is when the right judge judges wrong!
CREON: Your figures of speech
May entertain you now; but unless you bring me the man,
You will get little profit from them in the end.

Exit Creon into the palace.

SENTRY: "Bring me the man"—!
I'd like nothing better than bringing him the man!
But bring him or not, you have seen the last of me here.
At any rate, I am safe!

Exit Sentry.

ODE 1°

STROPHE 1

Chorus: Numberless are the world's wonders, but none
More wonderful than man; the stormgray sea
Yields to his prows, the huge crests bear him high;
Earth, holy and inexhaustible, is graven
With shining furrows where his plows have gone
Year after year, the timeless labor of stallions.

ANTISTROPHE 1

The lightboned birds and beasts that cling to cover,
The lithe fish lighting their reaches of dim water,
All are taken, tamed in the net of his mind;
The lion on the hill, the wild horse windy-maned,
Resign to him; and his blunt yoke has broken
The sultry shoulders of the mountain bull.

STROPHE 2

Words also, and thought as rapid as air,
He fashions to his good use; statecraft is his,
And his the skill that deflects the arrows of snow,
The spears of winter rain: from every wind
He has made himself secure — from all but one:
In the late wind of death he cannot stand.

ANTISTROPHE 2

O clear intelligence, force beyond all measure!
O fate of man, working both good and evil!
When the laws are kept, how proudly his city stands!
When the laws are broken, what of his city then?
Never may the anárchic man find rest at my hearth,
Never be it said that my thoughts are his thoughts.

SCENE 2

Reenter Sentry leading Antigone.

Choragos: What does this mean? Surely this captive woman
Is the Princess, Antigone. Why should she be taken?
Sentry: Here is the one who did it! We caught her
In the very act of burying him.— Where is Creon?
Choragos: Just coming from the house.

Enter Creon, center.

Ode 1: The first song sung by the Chorus, who at the same time danced. Here again, as in the parados, *strophe* and *antistrophe* probably divide the song into two movements of the dance: right to left, then left to right.

Creon: What has happened?
Why have you come back so soon?
Sentry: *(Expansively)* O King,
A man should never be too sure of anything:
I would have sworn
That you'd not see me here again: your anger
Frightened me so, and the things you threatened me with;
But how could I tell then
That I'd be able to solve the case so soon?
No dice-throwing this time: I was only too glad to come!
Here is this woman. She is the guilty one:
We found her trying to bury him.
Take her, then; question her; judge her as you will.
I am through with the whole thing now, and glad of it.
Creon: But this is Antigone! Why have you brought her here?
Sentry: She was burying him, I tell you!
Creon: *(Severely)* Is this the truth?
Sentry: I saw her with my own eyes. Can I say more?
Creon: The details: come, tell me quickly!
Sentry: It was like this:
After those terrible threats of yours, King,
We went back and brushed the dust away from the body.
The flesh was soft by now, and stinking,
So we sat on a hill to windward and kept guard.
No napping this time! We kept each other awake.
But nothing happened until the white round sun
Whirled in the center of the round sky over us:
Then, suddenly,
A storm of dust roared up from the earth, and the sky
Went out, the plain vanished with all its tress
In the stinging dark. We closed our eyes and endured it.
The whirlwind lasted a long time, but it passed;
And then we looked, and there was Antigone!
I have seen
A mother bird come back to a stripped nest, heard
Her crying bitterly a broken note or two
For the young ones stolen. Just so, when this girl
Found the bare corpse, and all her love's work wasted,
She wept, and cried on heaven to damn the hands
That had done this thing.
And then she brought more dust
And sprinkled wine three times for her brother's ghost.
We ran and took her at once. She was not afraid,
Not even when we charged her with what she had done.
She denied nothing.
And this was a comfort to me,

And some uneasiness: for it is a good thing
To escape from death, but it is no great pleasure
To bring death to a friend.
Yet I always say
There is nothing so comfortable as your own safe skin!

CREON: *(Slowly, dangerously)* And you, Antigone,
You with your head hanging,—do you confess this thing?

ANTIGONE: I do. I deny nothing.

CREON: *(To Sentry)* You may go.

Exit Sentry.

(To Antigone.) Tell me, tell me briefly:
Had you heard my proclamation touching this matter?

ANTIGONE: It was public. Could I help hearing it?

CREON: And yet you dared defy the law.

ANTIGONE: I dared.
It was not God's proclamation. That final Justice
That rules the world below makes no such laws.
Your edict, King, was strong,
But all your strength is weakness itself against
The immortal unrecorded laws of God.
They are not merely now: they were, and shall be,
Operative for ever, beyond man utterly.
I knew I must die, even without your decree:
I am only mortal. And if I must die
Now, before it is my time to die,
Surely this is no hardship: can anyone
Living, as I live, with evil all about me,
Think Death less than a friend? This death of mine
Is of no importance; but if I had left my brother
Lying in death unburied, I should have suffered.
Now I do not.
You smile at me. Ah Creon,
Think me a fool, if you like; but it may well be
That a fool convicts me of folly.

CHORAGOS: Like father, like daughter: both headstrong, deaf to reason!
She has never learned to yield:

CREON: She has much to learn.
The inflexible heart breaks first, the toughest iron
Cracks first, and the wildest horses bend their necks
At the pull of the smallest curb.
Pride? In a slave?
This girl is guilty of a double insolence,
Breaking the given laws and boasting of it.
Who is the man here,
She or I, if this crime goes unpunished?

Sister's child, or more than sister's child,
Or closer yet in blood — she and her sister
Win bitter death for this!
(To Servants) Go, some of you,
Arrest Ismene. I accuse her equally.
Bring her: you will find her sniffling in the house there.
Her mind's a traitor: crimes kept in the dark
Cry for light, and the guardian brain shudders;
But how much worse than this
Is brazen boasting of barefaced anarchy!

ANTIGONE: Creon, what more do you want than my death?

CREON: Nothing.
That gives me everything.

ANTIGONE: Then I beg you: kill me.
This talking is a great weariness: your words
Are distasteful to me, and I am sure that mine
Seem so to you. And yet they should not seem so:
I should have praise and honor for what I have done.
All these men here would praise me
Were their lips not frozen shut with fear of you.
(Bitterly) Ah the good fortune of kings,
Licensed to say and do whatever they please!

CREON: You are alone here in that opinion.

ANTIGONE: No, they are with me. But they keep their tongues in leash.

CREON: Maybe. But you are guilty, and they are not.

ANTIGONE: There is no guilt in reverence for the dead.

CREON: But Eteocles — was he not your brother too?

ANTIGONE: My brother too.

CREON: And you insult his memory?

ANTIGONE: *(Softly)* The dead man would not say that I insult it.

CREON: He would: for you honor a traitor as much as him.

ANTIGONE: His own brother, traitor or not, and equal in blood.

CREON: He made war on his country. Eteocles defended it.

ANTIGONE: Nevertheless, there are honors due all the dead.

CREON: But not the same for the wicked as for the just.

ANTIGONE: Ah Creon, Creon
Which of us can say what the gods hold wicked?

CREON: An enemy is an enemy, even dead.

ANTIGONE: It is my nature to join in love, not hate.

CREON: *(Finally losing patience)* Go join them then; if you must have your love,
Find it in hell!

CHORAGOS: But see, Ismene comes:

Enter Ismene, guarded.

Those tears are sisterly, the cloud
That shadows her eyes rains down gentle sorrow.

CREON: You too, Ismene,
Snake in my ordered house, sucking my blood
Stealthily — and all the time I never knew
That these two sisters were aiming at my throne!
Ismene,
Do you confess your share in this crime, or deny it?
Answer me.

ISMENE: Yes, if she will let me say so. I am guilty.

ANTIGONE: *(Coldly)* No, Ismene. You have no right to say so.
You would not help me, and I will not have you help me.

ISMENE: But now I know what you meant; and I am here
To join you, to take my share of punishment.

ANTIGONE: The dead man and the gods who rule the dead
Know whose act this was. Words are not friends.

ISMENE: Do you refuse me, Antigone? I want to die with you:
I too have a duty that I must discharge to the dead.

ANTIGONE: You shall not lessen my death by sharing it.

ISMENE: What do I care for life when you are dead?

ANTIGONE: Ask Creon. You're always hanging on his opinions.

ISMENE: You are laughing at me. Why, Antigone?

ANTIGONE: It's a joyless laughter, Ismene.

ISMENE: But can I do nothing?

ANTIGONE: Yes. Save yourself. I shall not envy you.
There are those who will praise you; I shall have honor, too.

ISMENE: But we are equally guilty!

ANTIGONE: No more, Ismene.
You are alive, but I belong to Death.

CREON: *(to the Chorus)* Gentlemen, I beg you to observe these girls:
One has just now lost her mind; the other
It seems, has never had a mind at all.

ISMENE: Grief teaches the steadiest minds to waver, King.

CREON: Yours certainly did, when you assumed guilt with the guilty!

ISMENE: But how could I go on living without her?

CREON: You are.
She is already dead.

ISMENE: But your own son's bride!

CREON: There are places enough for him to push his plow.
I want no wicked women for my sons!

ISMENE: O dearest Haimon, how your father wrongs you!

CREON: I've had enough of your childish talk of marriage!

CHORAGOS: Do you really intend to steal this girl from your son?

CREON: No; Death will do that for me.

CHORAGOS: Then she must die?

Creon: *(Ironically)* You dazzle me.
—But enough of this talk!
(To Guards) You, there, take them away and guard them well:
For they are but women, and even brave men run
When they see Death coming.

Exeunt Ismene, Antigone, and Guards.

ODE 2

STROPHE 1

Chorus: Fortunate is the man who has never tasted God's vengeance!
Where once the anger of heaven has struck, that house is shaken
For ever: damnation rises behind each child
Like a wave cresting out of the black northeast,
When the long darkness under sea roars up
And bursts drumming death upon the windwhipped sand.

ANTISTROPHE 1

I have seen this gathering sorrow from time long past
Loom upon Oedipus' children: generation from generation
Takes the compulsive rage of the enemy god.
So lately this last flower of Oedipus' line
Drank the sunlight! but now a passionate word
And a handful of dust have closed up all its beauty.

STROPHE 2

What mortal arrogance
Transcends the wrath of Zeus?
Sleep cannot lull him nor the effortless long months
Of the timeless gods: but he is young for ever,
And his house is the shining day of high Olympos.
All that is and shall be,
And all the past, is his.
No pride on earth is free of the curse of heaven.

ANTISTROPHE 2

The straying dreams of men
May bring them ghosts of joy:
But as they drowse, the waking embers burn them;
Or they walk with fixed eyes, as blind men walk.
But the ancient wisdom speaks for our own time:
Fate works most for woe
With Folly's fairest show.
Man's little pleasure is the spring of sorrow.

SCENE 3

CHORAGOS: But here is Haimon, King, the last of all your sons.
Is it grief for Antigone that brings him here,
And bitterness at being robbed of his bride?

Enter Haimon.

CREON: We shall soon see, and no need of diviners.
—Son,
You have heard my final judgment on that girl:
Have you come here hating me, or have you come
With deference and with love, whatever I do?

HAIMON: I am your son, father. You are my guide.
You make things clear for me, and I obey you.
No marriage means more to me than your continuing wisdom.

CREON: Good. That is the way to behave: subordinate
Everything else, my son, to your father's will.
This is what a man prays for, that he may get
Sons attentive and dutiful in his house,
Each one hating his father's enemies,
Honoring his father's friends. But if his sons
Fail him, if they turn out unprofitably,
What has he fathered but trouble for himself
And amusement for the malicious?
So you are right
Not to lose your head over this woman.
Your pleasure with her would soon grow cold, Haimon,
And then you'd have a hellcat in bed and elsewhere.
Let her find her husband in Hell!
Of all the people in this city, only she
Has had contempt for my law and broken it.
Do you want me to show myself weak before the people?
Or to break my sworn word? No, and I will not.
The woman dies.
I suppose she'll plead "family ties." Well, let her.
If I permit my own family to rebel,
How shall I earn the world's obedience?
Show me the man who keeps his house in hand,
He's fit for public authority.
I'll have no dealings
With lawbreakers, critics of the government:
Whoever is chosen to govern should be obeyed—
Must be obeyed, in all things, great and small,
Just and unjust! O Haimon,
The man who knows how to obey, and that man only,

Knows how to give commands when the time comes.
You can depend on him, no matter how fast
The spears come: he's a good soldier, he'll stick it out.
Anarchy, anarchy! Show me a greater evil!
This is why cities tumble and the great houses rain down,
This is what scatters armies!
No, no: good lives are made so by discipline.
We keep the laws then, and the lawmakers,
And no woman shall seduce us. If we must lose,
Let's lose to a man, at least! Is a woman stronger than we?

CHORAGOS: Unless time has rusted my wits,
What you say, King, is said with point and dignity.

HAIMON: *(Boyishly earnest)* Father:
Reason is God's crowning gift to man, and you are right
To warn me against losing mine. I cannot say—
I hope that I shall never want to say!—that you
Have reasoned badly. Yet there are other men
Who can reason, too; and their opinions might be helpful.
You are not in a position to know everything
That people say or do, or what they feel:
Your temper terrifies—everyone
Will tell you only what you like to hear.
But I, at any rate, can listen; and I have heard them
Muttering and whispering in the dark about this girl.
They say no woman has ever, so unreasonably,
Died so shameful a death for a generous act:
"She covered her brother's body. Is this indecent?
She kept him from dogs and vultures. Is this a crime?
Death?—She should have all the honor that we can give her!"

This is the way they talk out there in the city.

You must believe me:
Nothing is closer to me than your happiness.
What could be closer? Must not any son
Value his father's fortune as his father does his?
I beg you, do not be unchangeable:
Do not believe that you alone can be right.
The man who thinks that,
The man who maintains that only he has the power
To reason correctly, the gift to speak, the soul—
A man like that, when you know him, turns out empty.
It is not reason never to yield to reason!

In flood time you can see how some trees bend,
And because they bend, even their twigs are safe,
While stubborn trees are torn up, roots and all.

And the same thing happens in sailing:
Make your sheet fast, never slacken, — and over you go,
Head over heels and under: and there's your voyage.
Forget you are angry! Let yourself be moved!
I know I am young; but please let me say this:
The ideal condition
Would be, I admit, that men should be right by instinct;
But since we are all too likely to go astray,
The reasonable thing is to learn from those who can teach.

CHORAGOS: You will do well to listen to him, King,
If what he says is sensible. And you, Haimon,
Must listen to your father. — Both speak well.

CREON: You consider it right for a man of my years and experience
To go to school to a boy?

HAIMON: It is not right
If I am wrong. But if I am young, and right,
What does my age matter?

CREON: You think it right to stand up for an anarchist?

HAIMON: Not at all. I pay no respect to criminals.

CREON: Then she is not a criminal?

HAIMON: The City would deny it, to a man.

CREON: And the City proposes to teach me how to rule?

HAIMON: Ah. Who is it that's talking like a boy now?

CREON: My voice is the one voice giving orders in this City!

HAIMON: It is no City if it takes orders from one voice.

CREON: The State is the King!

HAIMON: Yes, if the State is a desert.

Pause.

CREON: This boy, it seems, has sold out to a woman.

HAIMON: If you are a woman: my concern is only for you.

CREON: So? Your "concern"! In a public brawl with your father!

HAIMON: How about you, in a public brawl with justice?

CREON: With justice, when all that I do is within my rights?

HAIMON: You have no right to trample on God's right.

CREON: *(Completely out of control)* Fool, adolescent fool! Taken in by a woman!

HAIMON: You'll never see me taken in by anything vile.

CREON: Every word you say is for her!

HAIMON: *(Quietly, darkly)* And for you.
And for me. And for the gods under the earth.

CREON: You'll never marry her while she lives.

HAIMON: Then she must die. — But her death will cause another.

CREON: Another?
Have you lost your senses? Is this an open threat?

HAIMON: There is no threat in speaking to emptiness.

CREON: I swear you'll regret this superior tone of yours!
You are the empty one!
HAIMON: If you were not my father,
I'd say you were perverse.
CREON: You girl-struck fool, don't play at words with me!
HAIMON: I am sorry. You prefer silence.
CREON: Now, by God—
I swear, by all the gods in heaven above us,
You'll watch it, I swear you shall!
(To the Servants) Bring her out!
Bring the woman out! Let her die before his eyes!
Here, this instant, with her bridegroom beside her!
HAIMON: Not here, no; she will not die here, King.
And you will never see my face again.
Go on raving as long as you've a friend to endure you.

Exit Haimon.

CHORAGOS: Gone, gone.
Creon, a young man in a rage is dangerous!
CREON: Let him do, or dream to do, more than a man can.
He shall not save these girls from death.
CHORAGOS: These girls?
You have sentenced them both?
CREON: No, you are right.
I will not kill the one whose hands are clean.
CHORAGOS: But Antigone?
CREON: *(Somberly)* I will carry her far away
Out there in the wilderness, and lock her
Living in a vault of stone. She shall have food,
As the custom is, to absolve the State of her death.
And there let her pray to the gods of hell:
They are her only gods:
Perhaps they will show her an escape from death,
Or she may learn,
though late,
That piety shown the dead is pity in vain.

Exit Creon.

ODE 3

STROPHE

CHORUS: Love, unconquerable
Waster of rich men, keeper
Of warm lights and all-night vigil
In the soft face of a girl:
Sea-wanderer, forest-visitor!

Even the pure Immortals cannot escape you,
And mortal man, in his one day's dusk,
Trembles before your glory.

ANTISTROPHE

Surely you swerve upon ruin
The just man's consenting heart,
As here you have made bright anger
Strike between father and son—
And none has conquered but Love!
A girl's glánce wórking the will of heaven:
Pleasure to her alone who mocks us,
Merciless Aphrodite.°

SCENE 4

Choragos: *(As Antigone enters guarded)* But I can no longer stand in awe of this,
Nor, seeing what I see, keep back my tears.
Here is Antigone, passing to that chamber
Where all find sleep at last.

STROPHE 1

Antigone: Look upon me, friends, and pity me
Turning back at the night's edge to say
Good-by to the sun that shines for me no longer;
Now sleepy Death
Summons me down to Acheron,° that cold shore:
There is no bridesong there, nor any music.

Chorus: Yet not unpraised, not without a kind of honor,
You walk at last into the underworld;
Untouched by sickness, broken by no sword.
What woman has ever found your way to death?

ANTISTROPHE 1

Antigone: How often I have heard the story of Niobe,°
Tantalos' wretched daughter, how the stone
Clung fast about her, ivy-close: and they say
The rain falls endlessly
And sifting soft snow; her tears are never done.
I feel the loneliness of her death in mine.

Aphrodite: Goddess of love and beauty.

Acheron: A river in Hades, domain of the dead.

story of Niobe: When her fourteen children were slain, Niobe wept so copiously that she was transformed into a stone on Mount Sipylus. Her tears became the mountain's streams.

CHORUS: But she was born of heaven, and you
Are woman, woman-born. If her death is yours,
A mortal woman's, is this not for you
Glory in our world and in the world beyond?

STROPHE 2

ANTIGONE: You laugh at me. Ah, friends, friends,
Can you not wait until I am dead? O Thebes,
O men many-charioted, in love with Fortune,
Dear springs of Dirce, sacred Theban grove,
Be witnesses for me, denied all pity,
Unjustly judged! and think a word of love
For her whose path turns
Under dark earth, where there are no more tears.

CHORUS: You have passed beyond human daring and come at last
Into a place of stone where Justice sits.
I cannot tell
What shape of your father's guilt appears in this.

ANTISTROPHE 2

ANTIGONE: You have touched it at last: that bridal bed
Unspeakable, horror of son and mother mingling:
Their crime, infection of all our family!
O Oedipus, father and brother!
Your marriage strikes from the grave to murder mine.
I have been a stranger here in my own land:
All my life
The blasphemy of my birth has followed me.

CHORUS: Reverence is a virtue, but strength
Lives in established law: that must prevail.
You have made your choice,
Your death is the doing of your conscious hand.

EPODE

ANTIGONE: Then let me go, since all your words are bitter,
And the very light of the sun is cold to me.
Lead me to my vigil, where I must have
Neither love nor lamentation; no song, but silence.

Creon interrupts impatiently.

CREON: If dirges and planned lamentations could put off death,
Men would be singing for ever.
(To the Servants) Take her, go!
You know your orders: take her to the vault
And leave her alone there. And if she lives or dies,
That's her affair, not ours: our hands are clean.

ANTIGONE: O tomb, vaulted bride-bed in eternal rock,
Soon I shall be with my own again
Where Persephone° welcomes the thin ghosts underground:
And I shall see my father again, and you, mother,
And dearest Polyneices —
dearest indeed
To me, since it was my hand
That washed him clean and poured the ritual wine:
And my reward is death before my time!
And yet, as men's hearts know, I have done no wrong,
I have not sinned before God. Or if I have,
I shall know the truth in death. But if the guilt
Lies upon Creon who judged me, then, I pray,
May his punishment equal my own.

CHORAGOS: O passionate heart,
Unyielding, tormented still by the same winds!

CREON: Her guards shall have good cause to regret their delaying.

ANTIGONE: Ah! That voice is like the voice of death!

CREON: I can give you no reason to think you are mistaken.

ANTIGONE: Thebes, and you my fathers' gods,
And rulers of Thebes, you see me now, the last
Unhappy daughter of a line of kings,
Your kings, led away to death. You will remember
What things I suffer, and at what men's hands,
Because I would not transgress the laws of heaven.
(To the Guards, simply) Come: let us wait no longer.

Exit Antigone, left, guarded.

ODE 4

STROPHE 1

CHORUS: All Danae's beauty was locked away
In a brazen cell where the sunlight could not come:
A small room still as any grave, enclosed her.
Yet she was a princess too,
And Zeus in a rain of gold poured love upon her.°
O child, child,
No power in wealth or war
Or tough sea-blackened ships
Can prevail against untiring Destiny!

Persephone: Pluto, god of the underworld, abducted her to be his queen.

All Danae's beauty . . . poured love upon her: In legend, when an oracle told Acrisius, king of Argos, that his daughter Danae would bear a son who would grow up to slay him, he locked the princess into a chamber made of bronze, lest any man impregnate her. But Zeus, father of the gods, entered Danae's prison in a shower of gold. The resultant child, the hero Perseus, was accidentally to fulfill the prophecy by killing Acrisius with an ill-aimed discus throw.

ANTISTROPHE 1

And Dryas' son ° also, that furious king,
Bore the god's prisoning anger for his pride:
Sealed up by Dionysos in deaf stone,
His madness died among echoes.
So at the last he learned what dreadful power
His tongue had mocked:
For he had profaned the revels,
And fired the wrath of the nine
Implacable Sisters ° that love the sound of the flute.

STROPHE 2

And old men tell a half-remembered tale
Of horror ° where a dark ledge splits the sea
And a double surf beats on the gráy shóres:
How a king's new woman, sick
With hatred for the queen he had imprisoned,
Ripped out his two sons' eyes with her bloody hands
While grinning Ares watched the shuttle plunge
Four times: four blind wounds crying for revenge,

ANTISTROPHE 2

Crying, tears and blood mingled.—Piteously born,
Those sons whose mother was of heavenly birth!
Her father was the god of the North Wind
And she was cradled by gales,
She raced with young colts on the glittering hills
And walked untrammeled in the open light:
But in her marriage deathless Fate found means
To build a tomb like yours for all her joy.

SCENE 5

Enter blind Teiresias, led by a boy. The opening speeches of Teiresias should be in sing-song contrast to the realistic lines of Creon.

Teiresias: This is the way the blind man comes, Princes, Princes,
Lockstep, two heads lit by the eyes of one.

Dryas' son: King Lycurgus of Thrace, whom Dionysos, god of wine, caused to be stricken with madness.

Sisters: The Muses, nine sister-goddesses who presided over poetry and music, arts and sciences.

a half-remembered tale Of horror: As the Chorus recalls in the rest of this song, the point of this tale is that being nobly born will not save one from disaster. King Phineas cast off his first wife Cleopatra (not the later Egyptian queen but the daughter of Boreas, god of the north wind) and imprisoned her in a cave. Out of hatred for Cleopatra, the cruel Eidothea, second wife of the king, blinded her stepsons. Ares, god of war, was said to gloat over bloodshed.

CREON: What new thing have you to tell us, old Teiresias?
TEIRESIAS: I have much to tell you: listen to the prophet, Creon.
CREON: I am not aware that I have ever failed to listen.
TEIRESIAS: Then you have done wisely, King, and ruled well.
CREON: I admit my debt to you. But what have you to say?
TEIRESIAS: This, Creon: you stand once more on the edge of fate.
CREON: What do you mean? Your words are a kind of dread.
TEIRESIAS: Listen, Creon:

I was sitting in my chair of augury, at the place
Where the birds gather about me. They were all a-chatter,
As is their habit, when suddenly I heard
A strange note in their jangling, a scream, a
Whirring fury; I knew that they were fighting,
Tearing each other, dying
In a whirlwind of wings clashing. And I was afraid.
I began the rites of burnt-offering at the altar,
But Hephaistos° failed me: instead of bright flame,
There was only the sputtering slime of the fat thigh-flesh
Melting: the entrails dissolved in gray smoke,
The bare bone burst from the welter. And no blaze!

This was a sign from heaven. My boy described it,
Seeing for me as I see for others.

I tell you, Creon, you yourself have brought
This new calamity upon us. Our hearths and altars
Are stained with the corruption of dogs and carrion birds
That glut themselves on the corpse of Oedipus' son.
The gods are deaf when we pray to them, their fire
Recoils from our offering, their birds of omen
Have no cry of comfort, for they are gorged
With the thick blood of the dead.
O my son,
These are no trifles! Think: all men make mistakes,
But a good man yields when he knows his course is wrong,
And repairs the evil. The only crime is pride.
Give in to the dead man, then: do not fight with a corpse—
What glory is it to kill a man who is dead?
Think, I beg you:
It is for your own good that I speak as I do.
You should be able to yield for your own good.

CREON: It seems that prophets have made me their especial province.
All my life long

Hephaistos: God of fire.

I have been a kind of butt for the dull arrows
Of doddering fortune-tellers!
No, Teiresias:
If your birds — if the great eagles of God himself
Should carry him stinking bit by bit to heaven,
I would not yield. I am not afraid of pollution:
No man can defile the gods.
Do what you will,
Go into business, make money, speculate
An India gold or that synthetic gold from Sardis,
Get rich otherwise than by my consent to bury him.
Teiresias, it is a sorry thing when a wise man
Sells his wisdom, lets out his words for hire!
TEIRESIAS: Ah Creon! Is there no man left in the world—
CREON: To do what?— Come, let's have the aphorism!
TEIRESIAS: No man who knows that wisdom outweighs any wealth?
CREON: As surely as bribes are baser than any baseness.
TEIRESIAS: You are sick, Creon! You are deathly sick!
CREON: As you say: it is not my place to challenge a prophet.
TEIRESIAS: Yet you have said my prophecy is for sale.
CREON: The generation of prophets has always loved gold.
TEIRESIAS: The generation of kings has always loved brass.
CREON: You forget yourself! You are speaking to your King.
TEIRESIAS: I know it. You are a king because of me.
CREON: You have a certain skill; but you have sold out.
TEIRESIAS: King, you will drive me to words that—
CREON: Say them, say them!
Only remember: I will not pay you for them.
TEIRESIAS: No, you will find them too costly.
CREON: No doubt. Speak:
Whatever you say, you will not change my will.
TEIRESIAS: Then take this, and take it to heart!
The time is not far off when you shall pay back
Corpse for corpse, flesh of your own flesh.
You have thrust the child of this world into living night,
You have kept from the gods below the child that is theirs:
The one in a grave before her death, the other,
Dead, denied the grave. This is your crime:
And the Furies and the dark gods of Hell
Are swift with terrible punishment for you.
Do you want to buy me now, Creon?
Not many days,
And your house will be full of men and women weeping,
And curses will be hurled at you from far
Cities grieving for sons unburied, left to rot
Before the walls of Thebes.

There are my arrows, Creon: they are all for you.
(To Boy) But come, child: lead me home.
Let him waste his fine anger upon younger men.
Maybe he will learn at last
To control a wiser tongue in a better head.

Exit Teiresias.

CHORAGOS: The old man has gone, King, but his words
Remain to plague us. I am old, too,
But I cannot remember that he was ever false.
CREON: That is true. . . . It troubles me.
Oh it is hard to give in! but it is worse
To risk everything for stubborn pride.
CHORAGOS: Creon: take my advice.
CREON: What shall I do?
CHORAGOS: Go quickly: free Antigone from her vault
And build a tomb for the body of Polyneices.
CREON: You would have me do this!
CHORAGOS: Creon, yes!
And it must be done at once: God moves
Swiftly to cancel the folly of stubborn men.
CREON: It is hard to deny the heart! But I
Will do it: I will not fight with destiny.
CHORAGOS: You must go yourself, you cannot leave it to others.
CREON: I will go.
—Bring axes, servants:
Come with me to the tomb. I buried her, I
Will set her free.
Oh quickly!
My mind misgives—
The laws of the gods are mighty, and a man must serve them
To the last day of his life!

Exit Creon.

PAEAN°

STROPHE 1

CHORAGOS: God of many names
CHORUS: O Iacchos
son
of Kadmeian Sémele
O born of the Thunder!
Guardian of the West
Regent

Paean: A song of praise or prayer, here to Dionysos, god of wine.

Of Eleusis' plain
O Prince of maenad Thebes
and the Dragon Field by rippling Ismenós: °

ANTISTROPHE 1

CHORAGOS: God of many names
CHORUS: the flame of torches
flares on our hills
the nymphs of Iacchos
dance at the spring of Castalia: °
from the vine-close mountain
come ah come in ivy:
Evohé evohé! ° sings through the streets of Thebes

STROPHE 2

CHORAGOS: God of many names
CHORUS: Iacchos of Thebes
heavenly Child
of Sémele bride of the Thunderer!
The shadow of plague is upon us:
come
with clement feet
oh come from Parnasos
down the long slopes
across the lamenting water

ANTISTROPHE 2

CHORAGOS: Io ° Fire! Chorister of the throbbing stars!
O purest among the voices of the night!
Thou son of God, blaze for us!
CHORUS: Come with choric rapture of circling Maenads
Who cry *Iô Iacche!*
God of many names!

God of many names . . . Dragon Field by rippling Ismenós: Dionysos was also called Iacchos (or, by the Romans, Bacchus). He was the son of Zeus ("the Thunderer") and of Sémele, daughter of Kadmos (or Cadmus), legendary founder of Thebes. "Regent of Eleusis' plain" is another name for Dionysos, honored in secret rites at Eleusis, a town northwest of Athens. "Prince of maenad Thebes" is yet another: the Maenads were women of Thebes said to worship Dionysos with wild orgiastic rites. Kadmos, so the story goes, sowed dragon's teeth in a field beside the river Ismenós. Up sprang a crop of fierce warriors who fought among themselves until only five remained. These victors became the first Thebans.

Castalia: A spring on Mount Parnassus, named for a maiden who drowned herself in it to avoid rape by the god Apollo. She became a nymph, or nature spirit, dwelling in its waters. In the temple of Delphi, at the mountain's foot, priestesses of Dionysos (the "nymphs of Iacchos") used the spring's waters in rites of purification.

Evohé evohé!: The cry of the Maenads in supplicating Dionysos: "Come forth, come forth!"

Io: "Hail" or "Praise be to. . . ."

EXODOS°

Enter Messenger from left.

Messenger: Men of the line of Kadmos, you who live
Near Amphion's citadel,°
I cannot say
Of any condition of human life "This is fixed,
This is clearly good, or bad." Fate raises up,
And Fate casts down the happy and unhappy alike:
No man can foretell his Fate.
Take the case of Creon:
Creon was happy once, as I count happiness:
Victorious in battle, sole governor of the land,
Fortunate father of children nobly born.
And now it has all gone from him! Who can say
That a man is still alive when his life's joy fails?
He is a walking dead man. Grant him rich,
Let him live like a king in his great house:
If his pleasure is gone, I would not give
So much as the shadow of smoke for all he owns.

Choragos: Your words hint at sorrow: what is your news for us?

Messenger: They are dead. The living are guilty of their death.

Choragos: Who is guilty? Who is dead? Speak!

Messenger: Haimon.
Haimon is dead; and the hand that killed him
Is his own hand.

Choragos: His father's? or his own?

Messenger: His own, driven mad by the murder his father had done.

Choragos: Teiresias, Teiresias, how clearly you saw it all!

Messenger: This is my news: you must draw what conclusions you can from it.

Choragos: But look: Eurydice, our Queen:
Has she overheard us?

Enter Eurydice from the palace, center.

Eurydice: I have heard something, friends:
As I was unlocking the gate of Pallas'° shrine,
For I needed her help today, I heard a voice
Telling of some new sorrow. And I fainted
There at the temple with all my maidens about me.
But speak again: whatever it is, I can bear it:
Grief and I are no strangers.

Exodos: The final scene, containing the play's resolution.

Amphion's citadel: A name for Thebes. Amphion, son of Zeus, had built a wall around the city by playing so beautifully on his lyre that the charmed stones leaped into their slots.

Pallas': Pallas Athene, goddess of wisdom, and hence an excellent source of advice.

MESSENGER: Dearest Lady,
I will tell you plainly all that I have seen.
I shall not try to comfort you: what is the use,
Since comfort could lie only in what is not true?
The truth is always best.
I went with Creon
To the outer plain where Polyneices was lying,
No friend to pity him, his body shredded by dogs.
We made our prayers in that place to Hecate
And Pluto,° that they would be merciful. And we bathed
The corpse with holy water, and we brought
Fresh-broken branches to burn what was left of it,
And upon the urn we heaped up a towering barrow
Of the earth of his own land.
When we were done, we ran
To the vault where Antigone lay on her couch of stone.
One of the servants had gone ahead,
And while he was yet far off he heard a voice
Grieving within the chamber, and he came back
And told Creon. And as the King went closer,
The air was full of wailing, the words lost,
And he begged us to make all haste. "Am I a prophet?"
He said, weeping, "And must I walk this road,
The saddest of all that I have gone before?
My son's voice calls me on. Oh quickly, quickly!
Look through the crevice there, and tell me
If it is Haimon, or some deception of the gods!"
We obeyed; and in the cavern's farthest corner
We saw her lying:
She had made a noose of her fine linen veil
And hanged herself. Haimon lay beside her,
His arms about her waist, lamenting her,
His love lost under ground, crying out
That his father had stolen her away from him.
When Creon saw him the tears rushed to his eyes
And he called to him: "What have you done, child? Speak to me.
What are you thinking that makes your eyes so strange?
O my son, my son, I come to you on my knees!"
But Haimon spat in his face. He said not a word,
Staring—
And suddenly drew his sword
And lunged. Creon shrank back, the blade missed; and the boy,

Hecate And Pluto: Two fearful divinities — the goddess of witchcraft and sorcery and the king of Hades, underworld of the dead.

Desperate against himself, drove it half its length
Into his own side, and fell. And as he died
He gathered Antigone close in his arms again,
Choking, his blood bright red on her white cheek.
And now he lies dead with the dead, and she is his
At last, his bride in the house of the dead.

Exit Eurydice into the palace.

CHORAGOS: She has left us without a word. What can this mean?
MESSENGER: It troubles me, too; yet she knows what is best,
Her grief is too great for public lamentation,
And doubtless she has gone to her chamber to weep
For her dead son, leading her maidens in his dirge.

Pause.

CHORAGOS: It may be so: but I fear this deep silence.
MESSENGER: I will see what she is doing. I will go in.

Exit Messenger into the palace.

Enter Creon with attendants, bearing Haimon's body.

CHORAGOS: But here is the king himself: oh look at him,
Bearing his own damnation in his arms.
CREON: Nothing you say can touch me any more.
My own blind heart has brought me
From darkness to final darkness. Here you see
The father murdering, the murdered son—
And all my civic wisdom!

Haimon my son, so young, so young to die,
I was the fool, not you; and you died for me.
CHORAGOS: That is the truth; but you were late in learning it.
CREON: This truth is hard to bear. Surely a god
Has crushed me beneath the hugest weight of heaven,
And driven me headlong a barbaric way
To trample out the thing I held most dear.
The pains that men will take to come to pain!

Enter Messenger from the palace.

MESSENGER: The burden you carry in your hands is heavy,
But it is not all: you will find more in your house.
CREON: What burden worse than this shall I find there?
MESSENGER: The Queen is dead.
CREON: O port of death, deaf world,
Is there no pity for me? And you, Angel of evil,
I was dead, and your words are death again.

Is it true, boy? Can it be true?
Is my wife dead? Has death bred death?
MESSENGER: You can see for yourself.

The doors are opened and the body of Eurydice is disclosed within.

CREON: Oh pity!
All true, all true, and more than I can bear!
O my wife, my son!
MESSENGER: She stood before the altar, and her heart
Welcomed the knife her own hand guided,
And a great cry burst from her lips for Megareus° dead,
And for Haimon dead, her sons; and her last breath
Was a curse for their father, the murderer of her sons.
And she fell, and the dark flowed in through her closing eyes.
CREON: O God, I am sick with fear.
Are there no swords here? Has no one a blow for me?
MESSENGER: Her curse is upon you for the deaths of both.
CREON: It is right that it should be. I alone am guilty.
I know it, and I say it. Lead me in,
Quickly, friends.
I have neither life nor substance. Lead me in.
CHORAGOS: You are right, if there can be right in so much wrong.
The briefest way is best in a world of sorrow.
CREON: Let it come,
Let death come quickly, and be kind to me.
I would not ever see the sun again.
CHORAGOS: All that will come when it will; but we, meanwhile,
Have much to do. Leave the future to itself.
CREON: All my heart was in that prayer!
CHORAGOS: Then do not pray any more: the sky is deaf.
CREON: Lead me away. I have been rash and foolish.
I have killed my son and my wife.
I look for comfort; my comfort lies here dead.
Whatever my hands have touched has come to nothing.
Fate has brought all my pride to a thought of dust.

As Creon is being led into the house, the Choragos advances and speaks directly to the audience.

CHORAGOS: There is no happiness where there is no wisdom;
No wisdom but in submission to the gods.
Big words are always punished,
And proud men in old age learn to be wise.

Megareus: Son of Creon and brother of Haimon, Megareus was slain in the unsuccessful attack on Thebes.

Reading and Reacting

1. What ideas does *Antigone* express about duty? About obedience? How do these ideas conform (or fail to conform) to your own concepts of duty and obedience?
2. The Chorus expresses the values of the community. According to the Chorus, is Antigone a danger to the community? How far do you believe a community should go to protect its values?
3. Both Creon and Antigone defend rights that they believe are sacred. What rights are in conflict? Is there any room for compromise? Do you sympathize with Antigone or with Creon?
4. Aristotle believed that to be effective, tragic heroes must have elements of both good and evil. Does Antigone conform to Aristotle's requirement? Explain.
5. What is Antigone's fatal flaw? How does this flaw lead to the tragic resolution of the play?
6. As the play progresses, do Creon and Antigone change, or do they remain essentially unchanged by events?
7. At the very end of *Antigone*, the Chorus says, "Big words are always punished, / And proud men in old age learn to be wise." Do you think Creon has gained wisdom from his experiences? Why or why not?
8. How does Antigone's gender affect her actions? How does it determine how she is treated? Are the play's attitudes toward women consistent with those of contemporary American society? Explain.
9. **JOURNAL ENTRY** If you were Antigone, would you have stuck to your principles, or would you have given in? Explain your reasoning.
10. **CRITICAL PERSPECTIVE** In *Sophocles the Playwright*, S. M. Adams argues that, to the ancient Greek audience, Antigone and Creon were both tragic heroes. Do you agree? If so, do you see the fact that the play has two tragic heroes as a problem?

Related Works: "Persepolis" (p. 310), "A Hunger Artist" (p. 424), "A Worn Path" (p. 568), "Do not go gentle into that good night" (p. 1046), "Medgar Evers" (p. 1132), "Hamlet" (p. 1605), *Oedipus the King* (p. 1745)

Source: ©AP Photo/Barbara Jackson

SAMUEL BECKETT (1906–1989) is regarded as one of the most influential playwrights of the modern era. Born in Dublin, he studied English and French, paving the way for a long literary career in both languages. The recipient of the Nobel Prize in Literature in 1969, Beckett has written numerous short stories and novels but is most famous for his plays, including *Waiting for Godot* (1952) and the one-act play *Endgame* (1957).

Cultural Context Samuel Beckett is among a group of European and American dramatists who, during the 1950s and early 1960s, belonged to a literary movement known as Theatre of the Absurd, in which characters search for meaning in a meaningless world and fragmented language and plots capture the absurdity of existence. Although the term is applied to a wide range of plays, all absurdist drama shares some characteristics: comedy mixed with tragic images; nonsense plots and dialogue; meaningless, repetitive action; and characters who are caught in situations beyond their understanding. The movement's central ideas come from the Algerian-French existentialist philosopher

Albert Camus, whose essay "The Myth of Sisyphus" (1942) makes the claim that human existence is purposeless and absurd. Other Theatre of the Absurd dramatists include Arthur Adamov, Edward Albee, Jean Genet, Eugène Ionesco, and Harold Pinter.

Krapp's Last Tape (1958)

A PLAY IN ONE ACT

SCENE

A late evening in the future.

Krapp's den. Front center a small table, the two drawers of which open towards audience. Sitting at the table, facing front, i.e. across from the drawers, a wearish° old man: Krapp.

Rusty black narrow trousers too short for him. Rusty black sleeveless waistcoat, four capacious° pockets. Heavy silver watch and chain. Grimy white shirt open at neck, no collar. Surprising pair of dirty white boots, size ten at least, very narrow and pointed.

White face. Purple nose. Disordered gray hair. Unshaven.

Very near-sighted (but unspectacled). Hard of hearing.

Cracked voice. Distinctive intonation.

Laborious walk.

On the table a tape-recorder with microphone and a number of cardboard boxes containing reels of recorded tapes.

Table and immediately adjacent area in strong white light. Rest of stage in darkness.

Krapp remains a moment motionless, heaves a great sigh, looks at his watch, fumbles in his pockets, takes out an envelope, puts it back, fumbles, takes out a small bunch of keys, raises it to his eyes, chooses a key, gets up and moves to front of table. He stoops, unlocks first drawer, peers into it, feels about inside it, takes out a reel of tape, peers at it, puts it back, locks drawer, unlocks second drawer, peers into it, feels about inside it, takes out a large banana, peers at it, locks drawer, puts keys back in his pocket. He turns, advances to edge of stage, halts, strokes banana, peels it, drops skin at his feet, puts end of banana in his mouth and remains motionless, staring vacuously before him. Finally he bites off the end, turns aside, and begins pacing to and fro at edge of stage, in the light, i.e. not more than four or five paces either way, meditatively eating banana. He treads on skin, slips, nearly falls, recovers himself, stoops and peers at skin and finally pushes it, still stooping, with his foot over the edge of stage into pit. He resumes his pacing, finishes banana, returns to table, sits down, remains a moment motionless, heaves a great sigh, takes keys from his pockets, raises them to his eyes, chooses key, gets up and moves to front of table, unlocks second drawer, takes out a second large banana, peers at it, locks drawer, puts back keys in his pocket, turns, advances to edge of stage, halts, strokes banana, peels it, tosses skin into pit, puts end of banana in his mouth, and

wearish: Weak and withered.
capacious: Large and deep.

remains motionless, staring vacuously before him. Finally he has an idea, puts banana in his waistcoat pocket, the end emerging, and goes with all the speed he can muster backstage into darkness. Ten seconds. Loud pop of cork. Fifteen seconds. He comes back into light carrying an old ledger and sits down at table. He lays ledger on table, wipes his mouth, wipes his hands on the front of his waistcoat, brings them smartly together and rubs them.

Krapp *(briskly)*: Ah! *(He bends over ledger, turns the pages, finds the entry he wants, reads.)* Box . . . thrree . . . spool . . . five. *(He raises his head and stares front. With relish.)* Spool! *(Pause.)* Spooool! *(Happy smile. Pause. He bends over table, starts peering and poking at the boxes.)* Box . . . thrree . . . thrree . . . four . . . two . . . *(with surprise)* nine! good God! . . . seven . . . ah! the little rascal! *(He takes up box, peers at it.)* Box thrree. *(He lays it on table, opens it, and peers at spools inside.)* Spool . . . *(he peers at ledger)* . . . five *(he peers at spools)* . . . five . . . five! . . . ah! the little scoundrel! *(He takes out a spool, peers at it.)* Spool five. *(He lays it on table, closes box three, puts it back with the others, takes up the spool.)* Box thrree, spool five. *(He bends over the machine, looks up. With relish.)* Spooool! *(Happy smile. He bends, loads spool on machine, rubs his hands.)* Ah! *(He peers at ledger, reads entry at foot of page.)* Mother at rest at last . . . Hm . . . The black ball . . . *(He raises his head, stares blankly front. Puzzled.)* Black ball? . . . *(He peers again at ledger, reads.)* The dark nurse . . . *(He raises his head, broods, peers again at ledger, reads.)* Slight improvement in bowel condition . . . Hm . . . Memorable . . . what? *(He peers closer.)* Equinox, memorable equinox. *(He raises his head, stares blankly front. Puzzled.)* Memorable equinox? . . . *(Pause. He shrugs his shoulders, peers again at ledger, reads.)*Farewell to—*(he turns the page)*—love.

He raises his head, broods, bends over machine, switches on, and assumes listening posture; i.e. leaning forward, elbows on table, hand cupping ear towards machine, face front.

Tape *(strong voice, rather pompous, clearly Krapp's at a much earlier time)*: Thirty-nine today, sound as a—*(Settling himself more comfortably he knocks one of the boxes off the table, curses, switches off, sweeps boxes and ledger violently to the ground, winds tape back to beginning, switches on, resumes posture.)* Thirty-nine today, sound as a bell, apart from my old weakness, and intellectually I have now every reason to suspect at the . . . *(hesitates)* . . . crest of the wave—or thereabouts. Celebrated the awful occasion, as in recent years, quietly at the Winehouse. Not a soul. Sat before the fire with closed eyes, separating the grain from the husks. Jotted down a few notes, on the back of an envelope. Good to be back in my den, in my old rags. Have just eaten I regret to say three bananas and only with difficulty refrained from a fourth. Fatal things for a man with my condition. *(Vehemently.)* Cut 'em out! *(Pause.)* The new light above my table is a great improvement. With all this darkness round me I feel less alone. *(Pause.)* In a way. *(Pause.)* I love to get up and move about in it, then back here to . . . *(hesitates)* . . . me. *(Pause.)* Krapp.

Pause.

The grain, now what I wonder do I mean by that, I mean . . . *(hesitates)* . . . I suppose I mean those things worth having when all the dust has—when all *my* dust has settled. I close my eyes and try and imagine them.

Pause. Krapp closes his eyes briefly.

Extraordinary silence this evening, I strain my ears and do not hear a sound. Old Miss McGlome always sings at this hour. But not tonight. Songs of her girlhood, she says. Hard to think of her as a girl. Wonderful woman though. Connaught,° I fancy. *(Pause.)* Shall I sing when I am her age, if I ever am? No. *(Pause.)* Did I sing as a boy? No. *(Pause.)* Did I ever sing? No.

Pause.

Just been listening to an old year, passages at random. I did not check in the book, but it must be at least ten or twelve years ago. At that time I think I was still living on and off with Bianca in Kedar Street. Well out of that, Jesus yes! Hopeless business. *(Pause.)* Not much about her, apart from a tribute to her eyes. Very warm. I suddenly saw them again. *(Pause.)* Incomparable! *(Pause.)* Ah well . . . *(Pause.)* These old P.M.s are gruesome, but I often find them—*(Krapp switches off, broods, switches on)*—a help before embarking on a new . . . *(hesitates)* . . . retrospect. Hard to believe I was ever that young whelp. The voice! Jesus! And the aspirations! *(Brief laugh in which Krapp joins.)* And the resolutions! *(Brief laugh in which Krapp joins.)* To drink less, in particular. *(Brief laugh of Krapp alone.)* Statistics. Seventeen hundred hours, out of the preceding eight thousand odd, consumed on licensed premises alone. More than 20%, say 40% of his waking life. *(Pause.)* Plans for a less . . . *(hesitates)* . . . engrossing sexual life. Last illness of his father. Flagging pursuit of happiness. Unattainable laxation. Sneers at what he calls his youth and thanks to God that it's over. *(Pause.)* False ring there. *(Pause.)* Shadows of the opus . . . magnum.° Closing with a—*(brief laugh)*—yelp to Providence. *(Prolonged laugh in which Krapp joins.)* What remains of all that misery? A girl in a shabby green coat, on a railway-station platform? No?

Pause.

When I look –

Krapp switches off, broods, looks at his watch, gets up, goes backstage into darkness. Ten seconds. Pop of cork. Ten seconds. Second cork. Ten seconds. Third cork. Ten seconds. Brief burst of quavering song.

Connaught: Province in West Ireland.

opus . . . magnum: Great work.

KRAPP *(sings):* Now the day is over,
Night is drawing nigh-igh,
Shadows°—

Fit of coughing. He comes back into light, sits down, wipes his mouth, switches on, resumes his listening posture.

TAPE:—back on the year that is gone, with what I hope is perhaps a glint of the old eye to come, there is of course the house on the canal where mother lay a-dying, in the late autumn, after her long viduity° *(Krapp gives a start)*, and the—*(Krapp switches off, winds back tape a little, bends his ear closer to machine, switches on)*—a-dying, after her long viduity, and the—

Krapp switches off, raises his head, stares blankly before him. His lips move in the syllables of "viduity." No sound. He gets up, goes backstage into darkness, comes back with an enormous dictionary, lays it on table, sits down and looks up the word.

KRAPP *(reading from dictionary)*: "State—or condition of being—or remaining a widow—or widower." *(Looks up. Puzzled.)* Being—or remaining? . . . *(Pause. He peers again at dictionary. Reading.)* "Deep weeds of viduity . . . Also of an animal, especially a bird . . . the vidua or weaver-bird . . . Black plumage of male . . ." *(He looks up. With relish.)* The vidua-bird!

Pause. He closes dictionary, switches on, resumes listening posture.

TAPE:—bench by the weir from where I could see her window. There I sat, in the biting wind, wishing she were gone. *(Pause.)* Hardly a soul, just a few regulars, nursemaids, infants, old men, dogs. I got to know them quite well—oh by appearance of course I mean! One dark young beauty I recollect particularly, all white and starch, incomparable bosom, with a big black hooded perambulator, most funereal thing. Whenever I looked in her direction she had her eyes on me. And yet when I was bold enough to speak to her—not having been introduced—she threatened to call a policeman. As if I had designs on her virtue! *(Laugh. Pause.)* The face she had! The eyes! Like . . . *(hesitates)* . . . chrysolite! *(Pause.)* Ah well . . . *(Pause.)* I was there when—*(Krapp switches off, broods, switches on again)*—the blind went down, one of those dirty brown roller affairs, throwing a ball for a little white dog, as chance would have it. I happened to look up and there it was. All over and done with, at last. I sat on for a few moments with the ball in my hand and the dog yelping and pawing at me. *(Pause.)* Moments. Her moments, my moments. *(Pause.)* The dog's moments. *(Pause.)* In the end I held it out to him and he took it in his mouth, gently, gently. A small, old, black, hard, solid rubber ball. *(Pause.)* I shall feel it, in my hand, until my dying day. *(Pause.)* I might have kept it. *(Pause.)* But I gave it to the dog.

Now . . . Shadows: Lyrics from the hymn "Now the Day Is Over" (1865) by Sabine Baring-Gould.
viduity: Widowhood.

Pause.

Ah well . . .

Pause.

Spiritually a year of profound gloom and indigence until that memorable night in March, at the end of the jetty, in the howling wind, never to be forgotten, when suddenly I saw the whole thing. The vision, at last. This I fancy is what I have chiefly to record this evening, against the day when my work will be done and perhaps no place left in my memory, warm or cold, for the miracle that . . . *(hesitates)* . . . for the fire that set it alight. What I suddenly saw then was this, that the belief I had been going on all my life, namely—*(Krapp switches off impatiently, winds tape forward, switches on again)*—great granite rocks the foam flying up in the light of the lighthouse and the wind-gauge spinning like a propeller, clear to me at last that the dark I have always struggled to keep under is in reality my most—*(Krapp curses, switches off, winds tape forward, switches on again)*—unshatterable association until my dissolution of storm and night with the light of the understanding and the fire—*(Krapp curses louder, switches off, winds tape forward, switches on again)*—my face in her breasts and my hand on her. We lay there without moving. But under us all moved, and moved us, gently, up and down, and from side to side.

Pause.

Past midnight. Never knew such silence. The earth might be uninhabited.

Pause.

Here I end—

Krapp switches off, winds tape back, switches on again.

—upper lake, with the punt, bathed off the bank, then pushed out into the stream and drifted. She lay stretched out on the floorboards with her hands under her head and her eyes closed. Sun blazing down, bit of a breeze, water nice and lively. I noticed a scratch on her thigh and asked her how she came by it. Picking gooseberries, she said. I said again I thought it was hopeless and no good going on, and she agreed, without opening her eyes. *(Pause.)* I asked her to look at me and after a few moments—*(pause)*—after a few moments she did, but the eyes just slits, because of the glare. I bent over her to get them in the shadow and they opened. *(Pause. Low.)* Let me in. *(Pause.)* We drifted in among the flags and stuck. The way they went down, sighing, before the stem! *(Pause.)* I lay down across her with my face in her breasts and my hand on her. We lay there without moving. But under us all moved, and moved us, gently, up and down, and from side to side.

Pause.

Past midnight. Never knew—

Krapp switches off, broods. Finally he fumbles in his pockets, encounters the banana, takes it out, peers at it, puts it back, fumbles, brings out the envelope, fumbles, puts back envelope, looks at his watch, gets up and goes backstage into darkness. Ten seconds. Sound of bottle against glass, then brief siphon. Ten seconds. Bottle against glass alone. Ten seconds. He comes back a little unsteadily into light, goes to front of table, takes out keys, raises them to his eyes, chooses key, unlocks first drawer, peers into it, feels about inside, takes out reel, peers at it, locks drawer, puts keys back in his pocket, goes and sits down, takes reel off machine, lays it on dictionary, loads virgin reel on machine, takes envelope from his pocket, consults back of it, lays it on table, switches on, clears his throat, and begins to record.

KRAPP: Just been listening to that stupid bastard I took myself for thirty years ago, hard to believe I was ever as bad as that. Thank God that's all done with anyway. *(Pause.)* The eyes she had! *(Broods, realizes he is recording silence, switches off, broods. Finally.)* Everything there, everything, all the—*(Realizes this is not being recorded, switches on.)* Everything there, everything on this old muckball, all the light and dark and famine and feasting of . . . *(hesitates)* . . . the ages! *(In a shout.)* Yes! *(Pause.)* Let that go! Jesus! Take his mind off his homework! Jesus! *(Pause. Weary.)* Ah well, maybe he was right. *(Pause.)* Maybe he was right. *(Broods. Realizes. Switches off. Consults envelope.)* Pah! *(Crumples it and throws it away. Broods. Switches on.)* Nothing to say, not a squeak. What's a year now? The sour cud and the iron stool. *(Pause.)* Revelled in the word spool. *(With relish.)* Spooool! Happiest moment of the past half million. *(Pause.)* Seventeen copies sold, of which eleven at trade price to free circulating libraries beyond the seas. Getting known. *(Pause.)* One pound six and something, eight I have little doubt. *(Pause.)* Crawled out once or twice, before the summer was cold. Sat shivering in the park, drowned in dreams and burning to be gone. Not a soul. *(Pause.)* Last fancies. *(Vehemently.)* Keep 'em under! *(Pause.)* Scalded the eyes out of me reading *Effie* again, a page a day, with tears again. Effie . . . *(Pause.)* Could have been happy with her, up there on the Baltic, and the pines, and the dunes. *(Pause.)* Could I? *(Pause.)* And she? *(Pause.)* Pah! *(Pause.)* Fanny came in a couple of times. Bony old ghost of a whore. Couldn't do much, but I suppose better than a kick in the crutch. The last time wasn't so bad. How do you manage it, she said, at your age? I told her I'd been saving up for her all my life. *(Pause.)* Went to Vespers° once, like when I was in short trousers. *(Pause. Sings.)*

Now the day is over,
Night is drawing nigh-igh,
Shadows—*(coughing, then almost inaudible)*—of the evening
Steal across the sky.

Vespers: Evening religious service.

(*Gasping.*) Went to sleep and fell off the pew. (*Pause.*) Sometimes wondered in the night if a last effort mightn't—(*Pause.*) Ah finish your booze now and get to your bed. Go on with this drivel in the morning. Or leave it at that. (*Pause.*) Leave it at that. (*Pause.*) Lie propped up in the dark—and wander. Be again in the dingle° on a Christmas Eve, gathering holly, the red-berried. (*Pause.*) Be again on Croghan on a Sunday morning, in the haze, with the bitch, stop and listen to the bells. (*Pause.*) And so on. (*Pause.*) Be again, be again. (*Pause.*) All that old misery. (*Pause.*) Once wasn't enough for you. (*Pause.*) Lie down across her.

Long pause. He suddenly bends over machine, switches off, wrenches off tape, throws it away, puts on the other, winds it forward to the passage he wants, switches on, listens staring front.

TAPE:—gooseberries, she said. I said again I thought it was hopeless and no good going on, and she agreed, without opening her eyes. (*Pause.*) I asked her to look at me and after a few moments—(*pause*)—after a few moments she did, but the eyes just slits, because of the glare. I bent over her to get them in the shadow and they opened. (*Pause. Low.*) Let me in. (*Pause.*) We drifted in among the flags and stuck. The way they went down, sighing, before the stem! (*Pause.*) I lay down across her with my face in her breasts and my hand on her. We lay there without moving. But under us all moved, and moved us, gently, up and down, and from side to side.

Pause. Krapp's lips move. No sound.

Past midnight. Never knew such silence. The earth might be uninhabited.
Pause.

Here I end this reel. Box—(*pause*)—three, spool—(*pause*)—five. (*Pause.*) Perhaps my best years are gone. When there was a chance of happiness. But I wouldn't want them back. Not with the fire in me now. No, I wouldn't want them back.

Krapp motionless staring before him. The tape runs on in silence.

Curtain

Reading and Reacting

1. *Krapp's Last Tape* is an example of a literary movement called Theatre of the Absurd. In what sense are this play and its main character absurd? What point do you think Beckett is trying to make with this play?
2. Is this a one-character play, or is there actually more than one character? Explain.

---

dingle: Small valley.

3. How would you describe Krapp? How is he similar to and different from his younger self, whose voice you hear on the tape?
4. What is the significance of the protagonist's name? Other than the obvious play on words, does the name have any other significance?
5. At one point in the play, Krapp mentions that he recently went to church. While there, he reveals, he "went to sleep and fell off the pew." Why does Krapp mention this incident?
6. At several points in the play, the younger Krapp says that he gave up love to pursue his career as a writer. (Ironically, he has sold just seventeen copies of his "great work.") Does the older Krapp regret his decision? Explain.
7. Krapp talks in short, sometimes unconnected phrases. In addition, he repeatedly turns the tape recorder on and off or rewinds it or skips forward. What is the effect of this fragmented speech? How does it help to express the play's theme?
8. For a short play, *Krapp's Last Tape* has a very long and detailed set of stage directions. What does Beckett emphasize in these stage directions? Are all the stage directions necessary? Which, if any, do you think could be eliminated?
9. **JOURNAL ENTRY** Choose any line in the play and write a new sequence of fragmented sentences that could follow it. Be sure your sentences are consistent with the play's theme.
10. **CRITICAL PERSPECTIVE** In his book *The Theater of the Absurd*, critic Martin Esslin says that at one time, Beckett planned to write "a long play with three Krapps: Krapp and his wife, Krapp with his wife and child, Krapp alone—further variations on the theme of the identity of the self."

    Do you think that this longer play would have been an improvement over the shorter play? Explain.

Related Works: "Kansas" (p. 237), "Miss Brill" (p. 266), "Bullet in the Brain" (p. 608), "The Love Song of J. Alfred Prufrock" (p. 1151), "The Road Not Taken" (p. 1159), "Men at Forty" (p. 1167), "Miniver Cheevy" (p. 1191), *Tape* (p. 1275), *The Glass Menagerie* (p. 1961)

Source: ©AP Photo

AUGUST WILSON (1945–2005) was born in Pittsburgh, Pennsylvania, to a German immigrant father and a black mother and lived in the African-American neighborhood known as the Hill District. After leaving school at fifteen when he was accused of plagiarizing a paper, he participated in the Black Arts movement in Pittsburgh, submitting poems to local African-American publications. In 1969, Wilson and his friend Rob Penny founded the Black Horizons Theatre Company, for which Wilson produced and directed plays. Although Wilson wrote plays while living in Pittsburgh, his work began to gain recognition only after 1978, when he moved to St. Paul, Minnesota. There, in 1982, Lloyd Richards, dean of the Yale School of Drama and artistic director of the Yale Repertory Company, staged a performance of Wilson's *Ma Rainey's Black Bottom.*

Wilson's achievement was epic. Beginning with *Ma Rainey's Black Bottom* in 1984, he wrote a ten-play cycle that chronicled the African-American experience in the United States decade by decade. In addition to *Ma Rainey's Black Bottom,* a Tony Award winner, the plays in this cycle include *Fences* (1985), which won a Pulitzer Prize in 1987; *Joe Turner's Come and Gone* (1986); *Two Trains Running* (1989), which won Wilson his fifth New York Drama Critics Circle Award; *The Piano Lesson* (1987), which won a second Pulitzer Prize for Wilson in 1990; *Seven Guitars* (1996); and *Radio Golf,* the last play in the cycle, which opened in 2005, the year of Wilson's death. To honor his achievements, Broadway's Virginia Theater was renamed the August Wilson Theater.

Fences explores how the long-upheld color barrier in professional baseball affected the main character, Troy, who struggles with the pain of never realizing his dream of becoming a big-league player. Throughout the play, Troy retreats behind literal and figurative barriers that impair his relationships with his family.

Cultural Context The history of African Americans in baseball began in the period between emancipation and the civil rights movement. Banned from professional baseball by segregationist laws, African-American players formed the Negro Leagues, with stars such as Satchel Paige and Josh Gibson emerging in the 1930s. Then, in 1946, Branch Rickey, the club president and general manager of the Brooklyn Dodgers, changed everything when he set out to sign the Negro Leagues' top players to his team. The first player he chose was Jackie Robinson, who broke the racial barrier and debuted at first base for the Dodgers on April 15, 1947, at the age of 28. Robinson's phenomenal performance earned him the Rookie of the Year award. In 1957, the year in which *Fences* is set, Robinson announced his retirement from baseball after he was traded to the New York Giants. In 1962, he was inducted into the Baseball Hall of Fame.

Fences (1985)

CHARACTERS

Troy Maxson
Jim Bono, *Troy's friend*
Rose, *Troy's wife*
Lyons, *Troy's oldest son by previous marriage*
Gabriel, *Troy's brother*
Cory, *Troy and Rose's son*
Raynell, *Troy's daughter*

SETTING

The setting is the yard which fronts the only entrance to the Maxson household, an ancient two-story brick house set back off a small alley in a big-city neighborhood. The entrance to the house is gained by two or three steps leading to a wooden porch badly in need of paint.

A relatively recent addition to the house and running its full width, the porch lacks congruence. It is a sturdy porch with a flat roof. One or two chairs of dubious value sit at one end where the kitchen window opens onto the porch. An old-fashioned icebox stands silent guard at the opposite end.

The yard is a small dirt yard, partially fenced, except for the last scene, with a wooden sawhorse, a pile of lumber, and other fence-building equipment set off to the side. Opposite is a tree from which hangs a ball made of rags. A baseball bat leans against the tree. Two oil drums serve as garbage receptacles and sit near the house at right to complete the setting.

THE PLAY

Near the turn of the century, the destitute of Europe sprang on the city with tenacious claws and an honest and solid dream. The city devoured them. They swelled its belly until it burst into a thousand furnaces and sewing machines, a thousand butcher shops and bakers' ovens, a thousand churches and hospitals and funeral parlors and money-lenders. The city grew. It nourished itself and offered each man a partnership limited only by his talent, his guile, and his willingness and capacity for hard work. For the immigrants of Europe, a dream dared and won true.

The descendants of African slaves were offered no such welcome or participation. They came from places called the Carolinas and the Virginias, Georgia, Alabama, Mississippi, and Tennessee. They came strong, eager, searching. The city rejected them and they fled and settled along the riverbanks and under bridges in shallow, ramshackle houses made of sticks and tarpaper. They collected rags and wood. They sold the use of their muscles and their bodies. They cleaned houses and washed clothes, they shined shoes, and in quiet desperation and vengeful pride, they stole, and lived in pursuit of their own dream. That they could breathe free, finally, and stand to meet life with the force of dignity and whatever eloquence the heart could call upon.

By 1957, the hard-won victories of the European immigrants had solidified the industrial might of America. War had been confronted and won with new energies that used loyalty and patriotism as its fuel. Life was rich, full, and flourishing. The Milwaukee Braves won the World Series, and the hot winds of change that would make the sixties a turbulent, racing, dangerous, and provocative decade had not yet begun to blow full.

ACT 1

SCENE 1

It is 1957. Troy and Bono enter the yard, engaged in conversation. Troy is fifty-three years old, a large man with thick, heavy hands; it is this largeness that he strives to fill out and make an accommodation with. Together with his blackness, his largeness informs his sensibilities and the choices he has made in his life.

Of the two men, Bono is obviously the follower. His commitment to their friendship of thirty-odd years is rooted in his admiration of Troy's honesty, capacity for hard work, and his strength, which Bono seeks to emulate.

It is Friday night, payday, and the one night of the week the two men engage in a ritual of talk and drink. Troy is usually the most talkative and at times he can be crude and almost vulgar, though he is capable of rising to profound heights of expression. The men carry lunch buckets and wear or carry burlap aprons and are dressed in clothes suitable to their jobs as garbage collectors.

BONO: Troy, you ought to stop that lying!

TROY: I ain't lying! The nigger had a watermelon this big. *(He indicates with his hands.)* Talking about . . . "What watermelon, Mr. Rand?" I liked to fell out! "What watermelon, Mr. Rand?" . . . And it sitting there big as life.

BONO: What did Mr. Rand say?

TROY: Ain't said nothing. Figure if the nigger too dumb to know he carrying a watermelon, he wasn't gonna get much sense out of him. Trying to hide that great big old watermelon under his coat. Afraid to let the white man see him carry it home.

BONO: I'm like you . . . I ain't got no time for them kind of people.

TROY: Now what he look like getting mad 'cause he see the man from the union talking to Mr. Rand?

BONO: He come to me talking about . . . "Maxson gonna get us fired." I told him to get away from me with that. He walked away from me calling you a troublemaker. What Mr. Rand say?

TROY: Ain't said nothing. He told me to go down the Commissioner's office next Friday. They called me down there to see them.

BONO: Well, as long as you got your complaint filed, they can't fire you. That's what one of them white fellows tell me.

TROY: I ain't worried about them firing me. They gonna fire me 'cause I asked a question? That's all I did. I went to Mr. Rand and asked him, "Why? Why you got the white mens driving and the colored lifting?" Told him, "what's the matter, don't I count? You think only white fellows got sense enough to drive a truck. That ain't no paper job! Hell, anybody can drive a truck. How come you got all whites driving and the colored lifting?" He told me "take it to the union." Well, hell, that's what I done! Now they wanna come up with this pack of lies.

BONO: I told Brownie if the man come and ask him any questions . . . just tell the truth! It ain't nothing but something they done trumped up on you 'cause you filed a complaint on them.

TROY: Brownie don't understand nothing. All I want them to do is change the job description. Give everybody a chance to drive the truck. Brownie can't see that. He ain't got that much sense.

BONO: How you figure he be making out with that gal be up at Taylors' all the time . . . that Alberta gal?

TROY: Same as you and me. Getting just as much as we is. Which is to say nothing.

BONO: It is, huh? I figure you doing a little better than me . . . and I ain't saying what I'm doing.

TROY: Aw, nigger, look here . . . I know you. If you had got anywhere near that gal, twenty minutes later you be looking to tell somebody. And the first one you gonna tell . . . that you gonna want to brag to . . . is me.

BONO: I ain't saying that. I see where you be eyeing her.

TROY: I eye all the women. I don't miss nothing. Don't never let nobody tell you Troy Maxson don't eye the women.

BONO: You been doing more than eyeing her. You done bought her a drink or two.

TROY: Hell yeah, I bought her a drink! What that mean? I bought you one, too. What that mean 'cause I buy her a drink? I'm just being polite.

BONO: It's all right to buy her one drink. That's what you call being polite. But when you wanna be buying two or three . . . that's what you call eyeing her.

TROY: Look here, as long as you known me . . . you ever known me to chase after women?

BONO: Hell yeah! Long as I done known you. You forgetting I knew you when.

TROY: Naw, I'm talking about since I been married to Rose?

BONO: Oh, not since you been married to Rose. Now, that's the truth, there. I can say that.

TROY: All right then! Case closed.

BONO: I see you be walking up around Alberta's house. You supposed to be at Taylors' and you be walking up around there.

TROY: What you watching where I'm walking for? I ain't watching after you.

BONO: I seen you walking around there more than once.

TROY: Hell, you liable to see me walking anywhere! That don't mean nothing cause you see me walking around there.

BONO: Where she come from anyway? She just kinda showed up one day.

TROY: Tallahassee. You can look at her and tell she one of them Florida gals. They got some big healthy women down there. Grow them right up out the ground. Got a little bit of Indian in her. Most of them niggers down in Florida got some Indian in them.

BONO: I don't know about that Indian part. But she damn sure big and healthy. Woman wear some big stockings. Got them great big old legs and hips as wide as the Mississippi River.

TROY: Legs don't mean nothing. You don't do nothing but push them out of the way. But them hips cushion the ride!

BONO: Troy, you ain't got no sense.

TROY: It's the truth! Like you riding on Goodyears!

Rose enters from the house. She is ten years younger than Troy, her devotion to him stems from her recognition of the possibilities of her life without him: a succession of abusive men and their babies, a life of partying and running the streets, the Church, or aloneness with its attendant pain and frustration. She recognizes Troy's spirit as a fine and illuminating one and she either ignores or forgives his faults, only some of which she recognizes. Though she doesn't drink, her presence is an integral part of the Friday night rituals. She alternates between the porch and the kitchen, where supper preparations are under way.

ROSE: What you all out here getting into?

TROY: What you worried about what we getting into for? This is men talk, woman.

ROSE: What I care what you all talking about? Bono, you gonna stay for supper?

BONO: No, I thank you, Rose. But Lucille say she cooking up a pot of pigfeet.

TROY: Pigfeet! Hell, I'm going home with you! Might even stay the night if you got some pigfeet. You got something in there to top them pigfeet, Rose?

ROSE: I'm cooking up some chicken. I got some chicken and collard greens.°

TROY: Well, go on back in the house and let me and Bono finish what we was talking about. This is men talk. I got some talk for you later. You know what kind of talk I mean. You go on and powder it up.

ROSE: Troy Maxson, don't you start that now!

TROY: *(puts his arm around her)* Aw, woman . . . come here. Look here, Bono . . . when I met this woman . . . I got out that place, say, "Hitch up my pony, saddle up my mare . . . there's a woman out there for me somewhere. I looked here. Looked there. Saw Rose and latched on to her."

---

collard greens: A leafy green vegetable.

I latched on to her and told her — I'm gonna tell you the truth — I told her, "Baby, I don't wanna marry, I just wanna be your man." Rose told me . . . tell him what you told me, Rose.

ROSE: I told him if he wasn't the marrying kind, then move out the way so the marrying kind could find me.

TROY: That's what she told me. "Nigger, you in my way. You blocking the view! Move out the way so I can find me a husband." I thought it over two or three days. Come back—

ROSE: Ain't no two or three days nothing. You was back the same night.

TROY: Come back, told her . . . "Okay, baby . . . but I'm gonna buy me a banty rooster and put him out there in the backyard . . . and when he see a stranger come, he'll flap his wings and crow . . ." Look here, Bono, I could watch the front door by myself . . . it was that back door I was worried about.

ROSE: Troy, you ought not talk like that. Troy ain't doing nothing but telling a lie.

TROY: Only thing is . . . when we first got married . . . forget the rooster . . . we ain't had no yard!

BONO: I hear you tell it. Me and Lucille was staying down there on Logan Street. Had two rooms with the outhouse in the back. I ain't mind the outhouse none. But when that goddamn wind blow through there in the winter . . . that's what I'm talking about! To this day I wonder why in the hell I ever stayed down there for six long years. But see, I didn't know I could do no better. I thought only white folks had inside toilets and things.

ROSE: There's a lot of people don't know they can do no better than they doing now. That's just something you got to learn. A lot of folks still shop at Bella's.

TROY: Ain't nothing wrong with shopping at Bella's. She got fresh food.

ROSE: I ain't said nothing about if she got fresh food. I'm talking about what she charge. She charge ten cents more than the A&P.

TROY: The A&P ain't never done nothing for me. I spends my money where I'm treated right. I go down to Bella, say, "I need a loaf of bread, I'll pay you Friday." She give it to me. What sense that make when I got money to go and spend it somewhere else and ignore the person who done right by me? That ain't in the Bible.

ROSE: We ain't talking about what's in the Bible. What sense it make to shop there when she overcharge?

TROY: You shop where you want to. I'll do my shopping where the people been good to me.

ROSE: Well, I don't think it's right for her to overcharge. That's all I was saying.

BONO: Look here . . . I got to get on. Lucille going be raising all kind of hell.

TROY: Where you going, nigger? We ain't finished this pint. Come here, finish this pint.

BONO: Well, hell, I am . . . if you ever turn the bottle loose.

TROY: *(hands him the bottle)* The only thing I say about the A&P is I'm glad Cory got that job down there. Help him take care of his school clothes and things. Gabe done moved out and things getting tight around here. He got that job . . . He can start to look out for himself.

ROSE: Cory done went and got recruited by a college football team.

TROY: I told that boy about that football stuff. The white man ain't gonna let him get nowhere with that football. I told him when he first come to me with it. Now you come telling me he done went and got more tied up in it. He ought to go and get recruited in how to fix cars or something where he can make a living.

ROSE: He ain't talking about making no living playing football. It's just something the boys in school do. They gonna send a recruiter by to talk to you. He'll tell you he ain't talking about making no living playing football. It's a honor to be recruited.

TROY: It ain't gonna get him nowhere. Bono'll tell you that.

BONO: If he be like you in the sports . . . he's gonna be all right. Ain't but two men ever played baseball as good as you. That's Babe Ruth° and Josh Gibson.° Them's the only two men ever hit more home runs than you.

TROY: What it ever get me? Ain't got a pot to piss in or a window to throw it out of.

ROSE: Times have changed since you was playing baseball, Troy. That was before the war. Times have changed a lot since then.

TROY: How in hell they done changed?

ROSE: They got lots of colored boys playing ball now. Baseball and football.

BONO: You right about that, Rose. Times have changed, Troy. You just come along too early.

TROY: There ought not never have been no time called too early! Now you take that fellow . . . what's that fellow they had playing right field for the Yankees back then? You know who I'm talking about, Bono. Used to play right field for the Yankees.

ROSE: Selkirk?

TROY: Selkirk! That's it! Man batting .269, understand? .269. What kind of sense that make? I was hitting .432 with thirty-seven home runs! Man batting .269 and playing right field for the Yankees! I saw Josh Gibson's daughter yesterday. She walking around with raggedy shoes on her feet. Now I bet you Selkirk's daughter ain't walking around with raggedy shoes on her feet! I bet you that!

ROSE: They got a lot of colored baseball players now. Jackie Robinson° was the first. Folks had to wait for Jackie Robinson.

TROY: I done seen a hundred niggers play baseball better than Jackie Robinson. Hell, I know some teams Jackie Robinson couldn't even make! What you talking about Jackie Robinson. Jackie Robinson wasn't nobody. I'm talking about if you could play ball then they ought to have let you play. Don't care what color you were. Come telling me I come along too early. If you could play . . . then they ought to have let you play.

Babe Ruth: George Herman Ruth (1895–1948), American baseball player. He played for the New York Yankees during the 1910s and 1920s and is remembered for his home-run hitting and flamboyant lifestyle.

Josh Gibson: (1911–1947), American baseball player. He played between the Negro Leagues between the 1920s and 1940s and was known as "the Negro Babe Ruth." An unwritten rule against hiring black players kept him out of the major leagues.

Jackie Robinson: John Roosevelt Robinson (1919–1972). He became the first African American to play major-league baseball when he was hired by the Brooklyn Dodgers in 1947.

Troy takes a long drink from the bottle.

ROSE: You gonna drink yourself to death. You don't need to be drinking like that.

80 **TROY:** Death ain't nothing. I done seen him. Done wrassled with him. You can't tell me nothing about death. Death ain't nothing but a fastball on the outside corner. And you know what I'll do to that! Lookee here, Bono . . . am I lying? You get one of them fastballs, about waist high, over the outside corner of the plate where you can get the meat of the bat on it . . . and good god! You can kiss it goodbye. Now, am I lying?

BONO: Naw, you telling the truth there. I seen you do it.

TROY: If I'm lying . . . that 450 feet worth of lying! *(Pause.)* That's all death is to me. A fastball on the outside corner.

ROSE: I don't know why you want to get on talking about death.

TROY: Ain't nothing wrong with talking about death. That's part of life. Everybody gonna die. You gonna die, I'm gonna die. Bono's gonna die. Hell, we all gonna die.

85 **ROSE:** But you ain't got to talk about it. I don't like to talk about it.

TROY: You the one brought it up. Me and Bono was talking about baseball . . . you tell me I'm gonna drink myself to death. Ain't that right, Bono? You know I don't drink this but one night out of the week. That's Friday night. I'm gonna drink just enough to where I can handle it. Then I cuts it loose. I leave it alone. So don't you worry about me drinking myself to death. 'Cause I ain't worried about Death. I done seen him. I done wrestled with him.

Look here, Bono . . . I looked up one day and Death was marching straight at me. Like Soldiers on Parade! The Army of Death was marching straight at me. The middle of July, 1941. It got real cold just like it be winter. It seem like Death himself reached out and touched me on the shoulder. He touch me just like I touch you. I got cold as ice and Death standing there grinning at me.

ROSE: Troy, why don't you hush that talk.

TROY: I say . . . what you want, Mr. Death? You be wanting me? You done brought your army to be getting me? I looked him dead in the eye. I wasn't fearing nothing. I was ready to tangle. Just like I'm ready to tangle now. The Bible say be ever vigilant. That's why I don't get but so drunk. I got to keep watch.

ROSE: Troy was right down there in Mercy Hospital. You remember he had pneumonia? Laying there with a fever talking plumb out of his head.

90 **TROY:** Death standing there staring at me . . . carrying that sickle in his hand. Finally he say, "You want bound over for another year?" See, just like that . . . "You want bound over for another year?" I told him, "Bound over hell! Let's settle this now!"

It seem like he kinda fell back when I said that, and all the cold went out of me. I reached down and grabbed that sickle and threw it just as far as I could throw it . . . and me and him commenced to wrestling.

We wrestled for three days and three nights. I can't say where I found the strength from. Every time it seemed like he was gonna get the best of me,

I'd reach way down deep inside myself and find the strength to do him one better.

ROSE: Every time Troy tell that story he find different ways to tell it. Different things to make up about it.

TROY: I ain't making up nothing. I'm telling you the facts of what happened. I wrestled with Death for three days and three nights and I'm standing here to tell you about it. *(Pause.)* All right. At the end of the third night we done weakened each other to where we can't hardly move. Death stood up, throwed on his robe . . . had him a white robe with a hood on it. He throwed on that robe and went off to look for his sickle. Say, "I'll be back." Just like that. "I'll be back." I told him, say, "Yeah, but . . . you gonna have to find me!" I wasn't no fool. I wan't going looking for him. Death ain't nothing to play with. And I know he's gonna get me. I know I got to join his army . . . his camp followers. But as long as I keep my strength and see him coming . . . as long as I keep up my vigilance . . . he's gonna have to fight to get me. I ain't going easy.

BONO: Well, look here, since you got to keep up your vigilance . . . let me have the bottle.

TROY: Aw hell, I shouldn't have told you that part. I should have left out that part.

ROSE: Troy be talking that stuff and half the time don't even know what he be talking about.

TROY: Bono know me better than that.

BONO: That's right. I know you. I know you got some Uncle Remus° in your blood. You got more stories than the devil got sinners.

TROY: Aw hell, I done seen him too! Done talked with the devil.

ROSE: Troy, don't nobody wanna be hearing all that stuff.

Lyons enters the yard from the street. Thirty-four years old, Troy's son by a previous marriage, he sports a neatly trimmed goatee, sport coat, white shirt, tieless and buttoned at the collar. Though he fancies himself a musician, he is more caught up in the rituals and "idea" of being a musician than in the actual practice of the music. He has come to borrow money from Troy, and while he knows he will be successful, he is uncertain as to what extent his lifestyle will be held up to scrutiny and ridicule.

LYONS: Hey, Pop.

TROY: What you come "Hey, Popping" me for?

LYONS: How you doing, Rose? *(He kisses her.)* Mr. Bono. How you doing?

BONO: Hey, Lyons . . . how you been?

TROY: He must have been doing all right. I ain't seen him around here last week.

ROSE: Troy, leave your boy alone. He come by to see you and you wanna start all that nonsense.

Uncle Remus: The fictional narrator of *Uncle Remus: His Songs and His Sayings* (1880) and a number of sequels by Joel Chandler Harris. Uncle Remus tells tales about characters such as Brer Rabbit and the Tarbaby in exaggerated dialect, now widely considered to be a derogatory representation of African Americans.

TROY: I ain't bothering Lyons. *(Offers him the bottle.)* Here . . . get you a drink. We got an understanding. I know why he come by to see me and he know I know.

LYONS: Come on, Pop . . . I just stopped by to say hi . . . see how you was doing.

TROY: You ain't stopped by yesterday.

ROSE: You gonna stay for supper, Lyons? I got some chicken cooking in the oven.

LYONS: No, Rose . . . thanks. I was just in the neighborhood and thought I'd stop by for a minute.

TROY: You was in the neighborhood all right, nigger. You telling the truth there. You was in the neighborhood cause it's my payday.

LYONS: Well, hell, since you mentioned it . . . let me have ten dollars.

TROY: I'll be damned! I'll die and go to hell and play blackjack with the devil before I give you ten dollars.

BONO: That's what I wanna know about . . . that devil you done seen.

LYONS: What . . . Pop done seen the devil? You too much, Pops.

TROY: Yeah, I done seen him. Talked to him too!

ROSE: You ain't seen no devil. I done told you that man ain't had nothing to do with the devil. Anything you can't understand, you want to call it the devil.

TROY: Look here, Bono . . . I went down to see Hertzberger about some furniture. Got three rooms for two-ninety-eight. That what it say on the radio. "Three rooms . . . two-ninety-eight." Even made up a little song about it. Go down there . . . man tell me I can't get no credit. I'm working every day and can't get no credit. What to do? I got an empty house with some raggedy furniture in it. Cory ain't got no bed. He's sleeping on a pile of rags on the floor. Working every day and can't get no credit. Come back here — Rose'll tell you — madder than hell. Sit down . . . try to figure what I'm gonna do. Come a knock on the door. Ain't been living here but three days. Who know I'm here? Open the door . . . devil standing there bigger than life. White fellow . . . white fellow . . . got on good clothes and everything. Standing there with a clipboard in his hand. I ain't had to say nothing. First words come out of his mouth was . . . "I understand you need some furniture and can't get no credit." I liked to fell over. He say, "I'll give you all the credit you want, but you got to pay the interest on it." I told him, "Give me three rooms worth and charge whatever you want." Next day a truck pulled up here and two men unloaded them three rooms. Man what drove the truck give me a book. Say send ten dollars, first of every month to the address in the book and everything will be all right. Say if I miss a payment the devil was coming back and it'll be hell to pay. That was fifteen years ago. To this day . . . the first of the month I send my ten dollars, Rose'll tell you.

ROSE: Troy lying.

TROY: I ain't never seen that man since. Now you tell me who else that could have been but the devil? I ain't sold my soul or nothing like that, you understand. Naw, I wouldn't have truck with the devil about nothing like that. I got my furniture and pays my ten dollars the first of the month just like clockwork.

BONO: How long you say you been paying this ten dollars a month?

TROY: Fifteen years!

BONO: Hell, ain't you finished paying for it yet? How much the man done charged you?

TROY: Ah hell, I done paid for it. I done paid for it ten times over! The fact is I'm scared to stop paying it.

ROSE: Troy lying. We got that furniture from Mr. Glickman. He ain't paying no ten dollars a month to nobody.

TROY: Aw hell, woman. Bono know I ain't that big a fool.

LYONS: I was just getting ready to say . . . I know where there's a bridge for sale.

TROY: Look here, I'll tell you this . . . it don't matter to me if he was the devil. It don't matter if the devil give credit. Somebody has got to give it.

ROSE: It ought to matter. You going around talking about having truck with the devil . . . God's the one you gonna have to answer to. He's the one gonna be at the Judgment.

LYONS: Yeah, well, look here, Pop . . . let me have that ten dollars. I'll give it back to you. Bonnie got a job working at the hospital.

TROY: What I tell you, Bono? The only time I see this nigger is when he wants something. That's the only time I see him.

LYONS: Come on, Pop, Mr. Bono don't want to hear all that. Let me have the ten dollars. I told you Bonnie working.

TROY: What that mean to me? "Bonnie working." I don't care if she working. Go ask her for the ten dollars if she working. Talking about "Bonnie working." Why ain't you working?

LYONS: Aw, Pop, you know I can't find no decent job. Where am I gonna get a job at? You know I can't get no job.

TROY: I told you I know some people down there. I can get you on the rubbish if you want to work. I told you that the last time you came by here asking me for something.

LYONS: Naw, Pop . . . thanks. That ain't for me. I don't wanna be carrying nobody's rubbish. I don't wanna be punching nobody's time clock.

TROY: What's the matter, you too good to carry people's rubbish? Where you think that ten dollars you talking about come from? I'm just supposed to haul people's rubbish and give my money to you 'cause you too lazy to work. You too lazy to work and wanna know why you ain't got what I got.

ROSE: What hospital Bonnie working at? Mercy?

LYONS: She's down at Passavant working in the laundry.

TROY: I ain't got nothing as it is. I give you that ten dollars and I got to eat beans the rest of the week. Naw . . . you ain't getting no ten dollars here.

LYONS: You ain't got to be eating no beans. I don't know why you wanna say that.

TROY: I ain't got no extra money. Gabe done moved over to Miss Pearl's paying her the rent and things done got tight around here. I can't afford to be giving you every payday.

LYONS: I ain't asked you to give me nothing. I asked you to loan me ten dollars. I know you got ten dollars.

TROY: Yeah, I got it. You know why I got it? 'Cause I don't throw my money away out there in the streets. You living the fast life . . . wanna be a musician . . . running around in them clubs and things . . . then, you learn to take care of yourself. You ain't gonna find me going and asking nobody for nothing. I done spent too many years without.

LYONS: You and me is two different people, Pop.

TROY: I done learned my mistake and learned to do what's right by it. You still trying to get something for nothing. Life don't owe you nothing. You owe it to yourself. Ask Bono. He'll tell you I'm right.

LYONS: You got your way of dealing with the world . . . I got mine. The only thing that matters to me is the music.

TROY: Yeah, I can see that! It don't matter how you gonna eat . . . where your next dollar is coming from. You telling the truth there.

LYONS: I know I got to eat. But I got to live too. I need something that gonna help me to get out of the bed in the morning. Make me feel like I belong in the world. I don't bother nobody. I just stay with the music 'cause that's the only way I can find to live in the world. Otherwise there ain't no telling what I might do. Now I don't come criticizing you and how you live. I just come by to ask you for ten dollars. I don't wanna hear all that about how I live.

TROY: Boy, your mama did a hell of a job raising you.

LYONS: You can't change me, Pop. I'm thirty-four years old. If you wanted to change me, you should have been there when I was growing up. I come by to see you . . . ask for ten dollars and you want to talk about how I was raised. You don't know nothing about how I was raised.

ROSE: Let the boy have ten dollars, Troy.

TROY: *(to Lyons)* What the hell you looking at me for? I ain't got no ten dollars. You know what I do with my money. *(To Rose.)* Give him ten dollars if you want him to have it.

ROSE: I will. Just as soon as you turn it loose.

TROY: *(handing Rose the money)* There it is. Seventy-six dollars and forty-two cents. You see this, Bono? Now, I ain't gonna get but six of that back.

ROSE: You ought to stop telling that lie. Here, Lyons. *(She hands him the money.)*

LYONS: Thanks, Rose. Look . . . I got to run . . . I'll see you later.

TROY: Wait a minute. You gonna say "thanks, Rose" and ain't gonna look to see where she got that ten dollars from? See how they do me, Bono?

LYONS: I know she got it from you, Pop. Thanks. I'll give it back to you.

TROY: There he go telling another lie. Time I see that ten dollars . . . he'll be owing me thirty more.

LYONS: See you, Mr. Bono.

BONO: Take care, Lyons!

LYONS: Thanks, Pop. I'll see you again.

Lyons exits the yard.

TROY: I don't know why he don't go and get him a decent job and take care of that woman he got.

BONO: He'll be all right, Troy. The boy is still young.

TROY: The *boy* is thirty-four years old.

ROSE: Let's not get off into all that.

BONO: Look here . . . I got to be going. I got to be getting on. Lucille gonna be waiting.

TROY: *(puts his arm around Rose)* See this woman, Bono? I love this woman. I love this woman so much it hurts. I love her so much . . . I done run out of ways of loving her. So I got to go back to basics. Don't you come by my house Monday morning talking about time to go to work . . . 'cause I'm still gonna be stroking!

ROSE: Troy! Stop it now!

BONO: I ain't paying him no mind, Rose. That ain't nothing but gin-talk. Go on, Troy. I'll see you Monday.

TROY: Don't you come by my house, nigger! I done told you what I'm gonna be doing.

The lights go down to black.

SCENE 2

The lights come up on Rose hanging up clothes. She hums and sings softly to herself. It is the following morning.

ROSE: *(sings)*

Jesus, be a fence all around me every day
Jesus, I want you to protect me as I travel on my way.
Jesus, be a fence all around me every day.

Troy enters from the house.

Jesus, I want you to protect me
As I travel on my way.

(To Troy.) 'Morning, You ready for breakfast? I can fix it soon as I finish hanging up these clothes?

TROY: I got the coffee on. That'll be all right. I'll just drink some of that this morning.

ROSE: That 651 hit yesterday. That's the second time this month. Miss Pearl hit for a dollar . . . seem like those that need the least always get lucky. Poor folks can't get nothing.

TROY: Them numbers don't know nobody. I don't know why you fool with them. You and Lyons both.

ROSE: It's something to do.

TROY: You ain't doing nothing but throwing your money away.

ROSE: Troy, you know I don't play foolishly. I just play a nickel here and a nickel there.

TROY: That's two nickels you done thrown away.

ROSE: Now I hit sometimes . . . that makes up for it. It always comes in handy when I do hit. I don't hear you complaining then.

TROY: I ain't complaining now. I just say it's foolish. Trying to guess out of six hundred ways which way the number gonna come. If I had all the money niggers, these Negroes, throw away on numbers for one week — just one week — I'd be a rich man.

ROSE: Well, you wishing and calling it foolish ain't gonna stop folks from playing numbers. That's one thing for sure. Besides . . . some good things come from playing numbers. Look where Pope done bought him that restaurant off of numbers.

TROY: I can't stand niggers like that. Man ain't had two dimes to rub together. He walking around with his shoes all run over bumming money for cigarettes. All right. Got lucky there and hit the numbers . . .

ROSE: Troy, I know all about it.

TROY: Had good sense, I'll say that for him. He ain't throwing his money away. I seen niggers hit the numbers and go through two thousand dollars in four days. Man bought him that restaurant down there . . . fixed it up real nice . . . and then didn't want nobody to come in it! A Negro go in there and can't get no kind of service. I seen a white fellow come in there and order a bowl of stew. Pope picked all the meat out the pot for him. Man ain't had nothing but a bowl of meat! Negro come behind him and ain't got nothing but the potatoes and carrots. Talking about what numbers do for people, you picked a wrong example. Ain't done nothing but make a worser fool out of him than he was before.

ROSE: Troy, you ought to stop worrying about what happened at work yesterday.

TROY: I ain't worried. Just told me to be down there at the Commissioner's office on Friday. Everybody think they gonna fire me. I ain't worried about them firing me. You ain't got to worry about that. *(Pause.)* Where's Cory? Cory in the house? *(Calls.)* Cory?

ROSE: He gone out.

TROY: Out, huh? He gone out 'cause he know I want him to help me with this fence. I know how he is. That boy scared of work.

Gabriel enters. He comes halfway down the alley and, hearing Troy's voice, stops.

TROY: *(continues)* He ain't done a lick of work in his life.

ROSE: He had to go to football practice. Coach wanted them to get in a little extra practice before the season start.

TROY: I got his practice . . . running out of here before he get his chores done.

ROSE: Troy, what is wrong with you this morning? Don't nothing set right with you. Go on back in there and go to bed . . . get up on the other side.

TROY: Why something got to be wrong with me? I ain't said nothing wrong with me.

ROSE: You got something to say about everything. First it's the numbers . . . then it's the way the man runs his restaurant . . . then you done got on Cory. What's it gonna be next? Take a look up there and see if the weather suits you . . . or is it gonna be how you gonna put up the fence with the clothes hanging in the yard.

TROY: You hit the nail on the head then.

ROSE: I know you like I know the back of my hand. Go on in there and get you some coffee . . . see if that straighten you up. 'Cause you ain't right this morning.

Troy starts into the house and sees Gabriel. Gabriel starts singing. Troy's brother, he is seven years younger than Troy. Injured in World War II, he has a metal plate in his head. He carries an old trumpet tied around his waist and believes with every fiber of his being that he is the Archangel Gabriel.° He carries a chipped basket with an assortment of discarded fruits and vegetables he has picked up in the strip district and which he attempts to sell.

Gabriel: *(singing)*

Yes, ma'am, I got plums
You ask me how I sell them
Oh ten cents apiece
Three for a quarter
Come and buy now
'Cause I'm here today
And tomorrow I'll be gone

Gabriel enters.

Hey, Rose!

Rose: How you doing, Gabe?

Gabriel: There's Troy . . . Hey, Troy!

Troy: Hey, Gabe.

Exit into kitchen.

Rose: *(To Gabriel.)* What you got there?

Gabriel: You know what I got, Rose. I got fruits and vegetables.

Rose: *(looking in basket)* Where's all these plums you talking about?

Gabriel: I ain't got no plums today, Rose. I was just singing that. Have some tomorrow. Put me in a big order for plums. Have enough plums tomorrow for St. Peter and everybody.

Troy reenters from kitchen, crosses to steps.

(To Rose.) Troy's mad at me.

Troy: I ain't mad at you. What I got to be mad at you about? You ain't done nothing to me.

Gabriel: I just moved over to Miss Pearl's to keep out from in your way. I ain't mean no harm by it.

Troy: Who said anything about that? I ain't said anything about that.

Gabriel: You ain't mad at me, is you?

Troy: Naw . . . I ain't mad at you, Gabe. If I was mad at you I'd tell you about it.

Gabriel: Got me two rooms. In the basement. Got my own door too. Wanna see my key? *(He holds up a key.)* That's my own key! Ain't nobody else got a key like that. That's my key! My two rooms!

Troy: Well, that's good, Gabe. You got your own key . . . that's good.

Archangel Gabriel: A messenger of God.

ROSE: You hungry, Gabe? I was just fixing to cook Troy his breakfast.

GABRIEL: I'll take some biscuits. You got some biscuits? Did you know when I was in heaven . . . every morning me and St. Peter° would sit down by the gate and eat some big fat biscuits? Oh, yeah! We had us a good time. We'd sit there and eat us them biscuits and then St. Peter would go off to sleep and tell me to wake him up when it's time to open the gates for the judgment.

ROSE: Well, come on . . . I'll make up a batch of biscuits.

Rose exits into the house.

GABRIEL: Troy . . . St. Peter got your name in the book. I seen it. It say . . . Troy Maxson. I say . . . I know him! He got the same name like what I got. That's my brother!

TROY: How many times you gonna tell me that, Gabe?

GABRIEL: Ain't got my name in the book. Don't have to have my name. I done died and went to heaven. He got your name though. One morning St. Peter was looking at his book . . . marking it up for the judgment . . . and he let me see your name. Got it in there under M. Got Rose's name . . . I ain't seen it like I seen yours . . . but I know it's in there. He got a great big book. Got everybody's name what was ever been born. That's what he told me. But I seen your name. Seen it with my own eyes.

TROY: Go on in the house there. Rose going to fix you something to eat.

GABRIEL: Oh, I ain't hungry. I done had breakfast with Aunt Jemima. She come by and cooked me up a whole mess of flapjacks. Remember how we used to eat them flapjacks?

TROY: Go on in the house and get you something to eat now.

GABRIEL: I got to sell my plums. I done sold some tomatoes. Got me two quarters. Wanna see? *(He shows Troy his quarters.)* I'm gonna save them and buy me a new horn so St. Peter can hear me when it's time to open the gates. *(Gabriel stops suddenly. Listens.)* Hear that? That's the hellhounds. I got to chase them out of here. Go on get out of here! Get out!

Gabriel exits singing.

Better get ready for the Judgment
Better get ready for the Judgment
My Lord is coming down

Rose enters from the house.

TROY: He's gone off somewhere.

GABRIEL: *(offstage)*

Better get ready for the Judgment
Better get ready for the Judgment morning
Better get ready for the Judgment
My God is coming down

St. Peter: Disciple of Christ, believed to be the guard at the gates of heaven.

ROSE: He ain't eating right. Miss Pearl say she can't get him to eat nothing.

TROY: What you want me to do about it, Rose? I done did everything I can for the man. I can't make him get well. Man got half his head blown away . . . what you expect?

ROSE: Seem like something ought to be done to help him.

TROY: Man don't bother nobody. He just mixed up from that metal plate he got in his head. Ain't no sense for him to go back into the hospital.

ROSE: Least he be eating right. They can help him take care of himself.

TROY: Don't nobody wanna be locked up, Rose. What you wanna lock him up for? Man go over there and fight the war . . . messin' around with them Japs, get half his head blown off . . . and they give him a lousy three thousand dollars. And I had to swoop down on that.

ROSE: Is you fixing to go into that again?

TROY: That's the only way I got a roof over my head . . . 'cause of that metal plate.

ROSE: Ain't no sense you blaming yourself for nothing. Gabe wasn't in no condition to manage that money. You done what was right by him. Can't nobody say you ain't done what was right by him. Look how long you took care of him . . . till he wanted to have his own place and moved over there with Miss Pearl.

TROY: That ain't what I'm saying, woman! I'm just stating the facts. If my brother didn't have that metal plate in his head . . . I wouldn't have a pot to piss in or a window to throw it out of. And I'm fifty-three years old. Now see if you can understand that!

Troy gets up from the porch and starts to exit the yard.

ROSE: Where you going off to? You been running out of here every Saturday for weeks. I thought you was gonna work on this fence?

TROY: I'm gonna walk down to Taylors'. Listen to the ball game. I'll be back in a bit. I'll work on it when I get back.

He exits the yard. The lights go to black.

SCENE 3

The lights come up on the yard. It is four hours later. Rose is taking down the clothes from the line. Cory enters carrying his football equipment.

ROSE: Your daddy like to had a fit with you running out of here this morning without doing your chores.

CORY: I told you I had to go to practice.

ROSE: He say you were supposed to help him with this fence.

CORY: He been saying that the last four or five Saturdays, and then he don't never do nothing, but go down to Taylors'. Did you tell him about the recruiter?

ROSE: Yeah, I told him.

Cory: What he say?

Rose: He ain't said nothing too much. You get in there and get started on your chores before he gets back. Go on and scrub down them steps before he gets back here hollering and carrying on.

Cory: I'm hungry. What you got to eat, Mama?

Rose: Go on and get started on your chores. I got some meat loaf in there. Go on and make you a sandwich . . . and don't leave no mess in there.

Cory exits into the house. Rose continues to take down the clothes. Troy enters the yard and sneaks up and grabs her from behind.

Troy! Go on, now. You liked to scared me to death. What was the score of the game? Lucille had me on the phone and I couldn't keep up with it.

Troy: What I care about the game? Come here, woman. *(He tries to kiss her.)*

Rose: I thought you went down Taylors' to listen to the game. Go on, Troy! You supposed to be putting up this fence.

Troy: *(attempting to kiss her again)* I'll put it up when I finish with what is at hand.

Rose: Go on, Troy. I ain't studying you.

Troy: *(chasing after her)* I'm studying you . . . fixing to do my homework!

Rose: Troy, you better leave me alone.

Troy: Where's Cory? That boy brought his butt home yet?

Rose: He's in the house doing his chores.

Troy: *(calling)* Cory! Get your butt out here, boy!

Rose exits into the house with the laundry. Troy goes over to the pile of wood, picks up a board, and starts sawing. Cory enters from the house.

Troy: You just now coming in here from leaving this morning?

Cory: Yeah, I had to go to football practice.

Troy: Yeah, what?

Cory: Yessir.

Troy: I ain't but two seconds off you noway. The garbage sitting in there overflowing . . . you ain't done none of your chores . . . and you come in here talking about "Yeah."

Cory: I was just getting ready to do my chores now, Pop . . .

Troy: Your first chore is to help me with this fence on Saturday. Everything else come after that. Now get that saw and cut them boards.

Cory takes the saw and begins cutting the boards. Troy continues working. There is a long pause.

Cory: Hey, Pop . . . why don't you buy a TV?

Troy: What I want with a TV? What I want one of them for?

Cory: Everybody got one. Earl, Ba Bra . . . Jesse!

Troy: I ain't asked you who had one. I say what I want with one?

Cory: So you can watch it. They got lots of things on TV. Baseball games and everything. We could watch the World Series.

TROY: Yeah . . . and how much this TV cost?

CORY: I don't know. They got them on sale for around two hundred dollars.

TROY: Two hundred dollars, huh?

CORY: That ain't that much, Pop.

TROY: Naw, it's just two hundred dollars. See that roof you got over your head at night? Let me tell you something about that roof. It's been over ten years since that roof was last tarred. See now . . . the snow comes this winter and sit up there on that roof like it is . . . and it's gonna seep inside. It's just gonna be a little bit . . . ain't gonna hardly notice it. Then the next thing you know, it's gonna be leaking all over the house. Then the wood rot from all that water and you gonna need a whole new roof. Now, how much you think it cost to get that roof tarred?

CORY: I don't know.

TROY: Two hundred and sixty-four dollars . . . cash money. While you thinking about a TV, I got to be thinking about the roof . . . and whatever else go wrong here. Now if you had two hundred dollars, what would you do . . . fix the roof or buy a TV?

CORY: I'd buy a TV. Then when the roof started to leak . . . when it needed fixing . . . I'd fix it.

TROY: Where you gonna get the money from? You done spent it for a TV. You gonna sit up and watch the water run all over your brand new TV.

CORY: Aw, Pop. You got money. I know you do.

TROY: Where I got it at, huh?

CORY: You got it in the bank.

TROY: You wanna see my bankbook? You wanna see that seventy-three dollars and twenty-two cents I got sitting up in there.

CORY: You ain't got to pay for it all at one time. You can put a down payment on it and carry it on home with you.

TROY: Not me. I ain't gonna owe nobody nothing if I can help it. Miss a payment and they come and snatch it right out your house. Then what you got? Now, soon as I get two hundred dollars clear, then I'll buy a TV. Right now, as soon as I get two hundred and sixty-four dollars, I'm gonna have this roof tarred.

CORY: Aw . . . Pop!

TROY: You go on and get you two hundred and buy one if ya want it. I got better things to do with my money.

CORY: I can't get no two hundred dollars. I ain't never seen two hundred dollars.

TROY: I'll tell you what . . . you get you a hundred dollars and I'll put the other hundred with it.

CORY: All right, I'm gonna show you.

TROY: You gonna show me how you can cut them boards right now.

Cory begins to cut the boards. There is a long pause.

CORY: The Pirates won today. That makes five in a row.

TROY: I ain't thinking about the Pirates. Got an all-white team. Got that boy . . . that Puerto Rican boy . . . Clemente.° Don't even half-play him. That boy could be something if they give him a chance. Play him one day and sit him on the bench the next.

CORY: He gets a lot of chances to play.

TROY: I'm talking about playing regular. Playing every day so you can get your timing. That's what I'm talking about.

CORY: They got some white guys on the team that don't play every day. You can't play everybody at the same time.

TROY: If they got a white fellow sitting on the bench . . . you can bet your last dollar he can't play! The colored guy got to be twice as good before he get on the team. That's why I don't want you to get all tied up in them sports. Man on the team and what it get him? They got colored on the team and don't use them. Same as not having them. All them teams the same.

CORY: The Braves got Hank Aaron° and Wes Covington.° Hank Aaron hit two home runs today. That makes forty-three.

TROY: Hank Aaron ain't nobody. That what you supposed to do. That's how you supposed to play the game. Ain't nothing to it. It's just a matter of timing . . . getting the right follow-through. Hell, I can hit forty-three home runs right now!

CORY: Not off no major-league pitching, you couldn't.

TROY: We had better pitching in the Negro leagues. I hit seven home runs off of Satchel Paige.° You can't get no better than that!

CORY: Sandy Koufax.° He's leading the league in strikeouts.

TROY: I ain't thinking of no Sandy Koufax.

CORY: You got Warren Spahn° and Lew Burdette.° I bet you couldn't hit no home runs off of Warren Spahn.

Roberto Clemente: (1934–1972), Major League baseball player for the Pittsburg Pirates, known as much for his humanitarianism as his unique batting style and ability. Clemente received the Most Valuable Player Award in 1966 and died in a plane crash in 1972 while shuttling supplies to Nicaraguan earthquake victims.

Hank Aaron: Henry Aaron (1934–), American baseball player who broke Babe Ruth's career home run record with a lifetime total of 755 home runs. The holder of 12 other Major League records, Aaron spent his Major League career with the Braves, first in Milwaukee and later in their hometown of Atlanta.

Wes Covington: John Wesley Covington (1932–), American baseball player known for his ability to frustrate pitchers by wasting time at the plate. In an eleven-year career, Covington played for six Major League teams, beginning with the Milwaukee Braves and retiring with the Los Angeles Dodgers in 1966.

Satchel Page: Leroy Robert Paige (1906–1982), American baseball player. He played in the Negro Leagues from the 1920s until 1948, when he joined the Cleveland Indians; he reportedly pitched 55 no-hit games during his career. Joe DiMaggio called him "the best pitcher I have ever faced."

Sandy Koufax: Sanford Koufax (1935–), left-handed pitcher who won 129 games and lost only 47 for the Los Angeles Dodgers in the six seasons between 1961 and 1966; he won three Cy Young Awards and pitched four no-hit games, the last of which (1965) was a perfect game. *Warren Spahn:* (1921–2003), left-handed pitcher who at the time of his retirement in 1966 held the National League record of 363 wins; he won 20 or more games in four consecutive seasons (1947–1950) and in several other seasons during the 1950s.

Lew Burdette: Selva Lewis Burdette (1926–), American baseball player who pitched and won three games for the Milwaukee Braves against the New York Yankees in the 1957 World Series; for that Series, his ERA was an amazingly low .067.

TROY: I'm through with it now. You go on and cut them boards. (Pause.) Your mama tell me you done got recruited by a college football team? Is that right?

CORY: Yeah. Coach Zellman say the recruiter gonna be coming by to talk to you. Get you to sign the permission papers.

TROY: I thought you supposed to be working down there at the A&P. Ain't you suppose to be working down there after school?

CORY: Mr. Stawicki say he gonna hold my job for me until after the football season. Say starting next week I can work weekends.

TROY: I thought we had an understanding about this football stuff? You suppose to keep up with your chores and hold that job down at the A&P. Ain't been around here all day on a Saturday. Ain't none of your chores done . . . and now you telling me you done quit your job.

CORY: I'm going to be working weekends.

TROY: You damn right you are! And ain't no need for nobody coming around here to talk to me about signing nothing.

CORY: Hey, Pop . . . you can't do that. He's coming all the way from North Carolina.

TROY: I don't care where he coming from. The white man ain't gonna let you get nowhere with that football noway. You go on and get your book-learning so you can work yourself up in that A&P or learn how to fix cars or build houses or something, get you a trade. That way you have something can't nobody take away from you. You go on and learn how to put your hands to some good use. Besides hauling people's garbage.

CORY: I get good grades, Pop. That's why the recruiter wants to talk with you. You got to keep up your grades to get recruited. This way I'll be going to college. I'll get a chance . . .

TROY: First you gonna get your butt down there to the A&P and get your job back.

CORY: Mr. Stawicki done already hired somebody else 'cause I told him I was playing football.

TROY: You a bigger fool than I thought . . . to let somebody take away your job so you can play some football. Where you gonna get your money to take out your girlfriend and whatnot? What kind of foolishness is that to let somebody take away your job?

CORY: I'm still gonna be working weekends.

TROY: Naw . . . naw. You getting your butt out of here and finding you another job.

CORY: Come on, Pop! I got to practice. I can't work after school and play football too. The team needs me. That's what Coach Zellman say . . .

TROY: I don't care what nobody else say. I'm the boss . . . you understand? I'm the boss around here. I do the only saying what counts.

CORY: Come on, Pop!

TROY: I asked you . . . did you understand?

CORY: Yeah . . .

TROY: What?!

CORY: Yessir.

TROY: You go on down there to that A&P and see if you can get your job back. If you can't do both . . . then you quit the football team. You've got to take the crookeds with the straights.

CORY: Yessir. (*Pause.*) Can I ask you a question?

TROY: What the hell you wanna ask me? Mr. Stawicki the one you got the questions for.

CORY: How come you ain't never liked me?

TROY: Liked you? Who the hell say I got to like you? What law is there say I got to like you? Wanna stand up in my face and ask a damn fool-ass question like that. Talking about liking somebody. Come here, boy, when I talk to you.

Cory comes over to where Troy is working. He stands slouched over and Troy shoves him on his shoulder.

Straighten up, goddammit! I asked you a question . . . what law is there say I got to like you?

CORY: None.

TROY: Well, all right then! Don't you eat every day? (*Pause.*) Answer me when I talk to you! Don't you eat every day?

CORY: Yeah.

TROY: Nigger, as long as you in my house, you put that sir on the end of it when you talk to me!

CORY: Yes . . . sir.

TROY: You eat every day.

CORY: Yessir!

TROY: Got a roof over your head.

CORY: Yessir!

TROY: Got clothes on your back.

CORY: Yessir.

TROY: Why you think that is?

CORY: 'Cause of you.

TROY: Ah, hell I know it's 'cause of me . . . but why do you think that is?

CORY: (*hesitant*) 'Cause you like me.

TROY: Like you? I go out of here every morning . . . bust my butt . . . putting up with them crackers° every day . . . 'cause I like you? You are the biggest fool I ever saw. (*Pause.*) It's my job. It's my responsibility! You understand that? A man got to take care of his family. You live in my house . . . sleep you behind on my bedclothes . . . fill you belly up with my food . . . 'cause you my son. You my flesh and blood. Not 'cause I like you! 'Cause it's my duty to take care of you. I owe a responsibility to you! Let's get this straight right here . . . before it go along any further . . . I ain't got to like you. Mr. Rand don't give me my money come payday cause he likes me. He give me 'cause

---

crackers: Derogatory term for white people, generally poor southern whites.

he owe me. I done give you everything I had to give you. I gave you your life! Me and your mama worked that out between us. And liking your black ass wasn't part of the bargain. Don't you try and go through life worrying about if somebody like you or not. You best be making sure they doing right by you. You understand what I'm saying, boy?

CORY: Yessir.

TROY: Then get the hell out of my face, and get on down to that A&P.

Rose has been standing behind the screen door for much of the scene. She enters as Cory exits.

ROSE: Why don't you let the boy go ahead and play football, Troy? Ain't no harm in that. He's just trying to be like you with the sports.

TROY: I don't want him to be like me! I want him to move as far away from my life as he can get. You the only decent thing that ever happened to me. I wish him that. But I don't wish him a thing else from my life. I decided seventeen years ago that boy wasn't getting involved in no sports. Not after what they did to me in the sports.

ROSE: Troy, why don't you admit you was too old to play in the major leagues? For once . . . why don't you admit that?

TROY: What do you mean too old? Don't come telling me I was too old. I just wasn't the right color. Hell, I'm fifty-three years old and can do better than Selkirk's .269 right now!

ROSE: How's was you gonna play ball when you were over forty? Sometimes I can't go no sense out of you.

TROY: I got good sense, woman. I got sense enough not to let my boy get hurt over playing no sports. You been mothering that boy too much. Worried about if people like him.

ROSE: Everything that boy do . . . he do for you. He wants you to say "Good job, son." That's all.

TROY: Rose, I ain't got time for that. He's alive. He's healthy. He's got to make his own way. I made mine. Ain't nobody gonna hold his hand when he get out there in that world.

ROSE: Times have changed from when you was young, Troy. People change. The world's changing around you and you can't even see it.

TROY: *(slow, methodical)* Woman . . . I do the best I can do. I come in here every Friday. I carry a sack of potatoes and a bucket of lard. You all line up at the door with your hands out. I give you the lint from my pockets. I give you my sweat and my blood. I ain't got no tears. I done spent them. We go upstairs in that room at night . . . and I fall down on you and try to blast a hole into forever. I get up Monday morning . . . find my lunch on the table. I go out. Make my way. Find my strength to carry me through to the next Friday. *(Pause.)* That's all I got, Rose. That's all I got to give. I can't give nothing else.

Troy exits into the house. The lights go down to black.

SCENE 4

It is Friday. Two weeks later. Cory starts out of the house with his football equipment. The phone rings.

CORY: *(calling)* I got it! *(He answers the phone and stands in the screen door talking.)* Hello? Hey, Jesse. Naw . . . I was just getting ready to leave now.

ROSE: *(calling)* Cory!

CORY: I told you, man, them spikes° is all tore up. You can use them if you want, but they ain't no good. Earl got some spikes.

ROSE: *(calling)* Cory!

CORY: *(calling to Rose)* Mam? I'm talking to Jesse. *(Into phone.)* When she say that? *(Pause.)* Aw, you lying, man. I'm gonna tell her you said that.

ROSE: *(calling)* Cory, don't you go nowhere!

CORY: I got to go to the game, Ma! *(Into the phone.)* Yeah, hey, look, I'll talk to you later. Yeah, I'll meet you over Earl's house. Later. Bye, Ma.

Cory exits the house and starts out the yard.

ROSE: Cory, where you going off to? You got that stuff all pulled out and thrown all over your room.

CORY: *(in the yard)* I was looking for my spikes. Jesse wanted to borrow my spikes.

ROSE: Get up there and get that cleaned up before your daddy get back in here.

CORY: I got to go to the game! I'll clean it up *when I get back.*

Cory exits.

ROSE: That's all he need to do is see that room all messed up.

Rose exits into the house. Troy and Bono enter the yard. Troy is dressed in clothes other than his work clothes.

BONO: He told him the same thing he told you. Take it to the union.

TROY: Brownie ain't got that much sense. Man wasn't thinking about nothing. He wait until I confront them on it . . . then he wanna come crying seniority. *(Calls.)* Hey, Rose!

BONO: I wish I could have seen Mr. Rand's face when he told you.

TROY: He couldn't get it out of his mouth! Liked to bit his tongue! When they called me down there to the Commissioner's office . . . he thought they was gonna fire me. Like everybody else.

BONO: I didn't think they was gonna fire you. I thought they was gonna put you on the warning paper.

TROY: Hey, Rose! *(To Bono.)* Yeah, Mr. Rand like to bit his tongue.

Troy breaks the seal on the bottle, takes a drink, and hands it to Bono.

---

spikes: Athletic shoes with sharp metal grips set into the soles.

BONO: I see you run right down to Taylors' and told that Alberta gal.

TROY: *(calling)* Hey, Rose! *(To Bono.)* I told everybody. Hey, Rose! I went down there to cash my check.

ROSE: *(entering from the house)* Hush all that hollering, man! I know you out here. What they say down there at the Commissioner's office?

TROY: You supposed to come when I call you, woman. Bono'll tell you that. *(To Bono.)* Don't Lucille come when you call her?

ROSE: Man, hush your mouth, I ain't no dog . . . talk about "come when you call me."

TROY: *(puts his arm around Rose)* You hear this, Bono? I had me an old dog used to get uppity like that. You say, "C'mere, Blue!" . . . and he just lay there and look at you. End up getting a stick and chasing him away trying to make him come.

ROSE: I ain't studying you and your dog. I remember you used to sing that old song.

TROY: *(he sings)*

Hear it ring! Hear it ring!
I had a dog his name was Blue.

ROSE: Don't nobody wanna hear you sing that old song.

TROY: *(sings)*

You know Blue was mighty true.

ROSE: Used to have Cory running around here singing that song.

BONO: Hell, I remember that song myself.

TROY: *(sings)*

You know Blue was a good old dog.
Blue treed a possum in a hollow log.

That was my daddy's song. My daddy made up that song.

ROSE: I don't care who made it up. Don't nobody wanna hear you sing it.

TROY: *(makes a song like calling a dog)* Come here, woman.

ROSE: You come in here carrying on, I reckon they ain't fired you. What they say down there at the Commissioner's office?

TROY: Look here, Rose . . . Mr. Rand called me into his office today when I got back from talking to them people down there . . . it come from up top . . . he called me in and told me they was making me a driver.

ROSE: Troy, you kidding!

TROY: No I ain't. Ask Bono.

ROSE: Well, that's great, Troy. Now you don't have to hassle them people no more.

Lyons enters from the street.

TROY: Aw hell, I wasn't looking to see you today. I thought you was in jail. Got it all over the front page of the *Courier* about them raiding Sefus's place . . . where you be hanging out with all them thugs.

LYONS: Hey, Pop . . . that ain't got nothing to do with me. I don't go down there gambling. I go down there to sit in with the band. I ain't got nothing to do with the gambling part. They got some good music down there.

TROY: They got some rogues . . . is what they got.

LYONS: How you been, Mr. Bono? Hi, Rose.

BONO: I see where you playing down at the Crawford Grill tonight.

ROSE: How come you ain't brought Bonnie like I told you? You should have brought Bonnie with you, she ain't been over in a month of Sundays.

LYONS: I was just in the neighborhood . . . thought I'd stop by.

TROY: Here he come . . .

BONO: Your daddy got a promotion on the rubbish. He's gonna be the first colored driver. Ain't got to do nothing but sit up there and read the paper like them white fellows.

LYONS: Hey, Pop . . . if you knew how to read you'd be all right.

BONO: Naw . . . naw . . . you mean if the nigger knew how to *drive* he'd be all right. Been fighting with them people about driving and ain't even got a license. Mr. Rand know you ain't got no driver's license?

TROY: Driving ain't nothing. All you do is point the truck where you want it to go. Driving ain't nothing.

BONO: Do Mr. Rand know you ain't got no driver's license? That's what I'm talking about. I ain't asked if driving was easy. I asked if Mr. Rand know you ain't got no driver's license.

TROY: He ain't got to know. The man ain't got to know my business. Time he find out, I have two or three driver's licenses.

LYONS: *(going into his pocket)* Say, look here, Pop . . .

TROY: I knew it was coming. Didn't I tell you, Bono? I know what kind of "Look here, Pop" that was. The nigger fixing to ask me for some money. It's Friday night. It's my payday. All them rogues down there on the avenue . . . the ones that ain't in jail . . . and Lyons is hopping in his shoes to get down there with them.

LYONS: See, Pop . . . if you give somebody else a chance to talk sometimes, you'd see that I was fixing to pay you back your ten dollars like I told you. Here . . . I told you I'd pay you when Bonnie got paid.

TROY: Naw . . . you go ahead and keep that ten dollars. Put it in the bank. The next time you feel like you wanna come by here and ask me for something . . . you go on down there and get that.

LYONS: Here's your ten dollars, Pop. I told you I don't want you to give me nothing. I just wanted to borrow ten dollars.

TROY: Naw . . . you go on and keep that for the next time you want to ask me.

LYONS: Come on, Pop . . . here go your ten dollars.

ROSE: Why don't you go on and let the boy pay you back, Troy?

LYONS: Here you go, Rose. If you don't take it I'm gonna have to hear about it for the next six months. *(He hands her the money.)*

ROSE: You can hand yours over here too, Troy.

TROY: You see this, Bono. You see how they do me.

BONO: Yeah, Lucille do me the same way.

Gabriel is heard singing offstage. He enters.

GABRIEL: Better get ready for the Judgment! Better get ready for . . . Hey! . . . Hey! . . . There's Troy's boy!

LYONS: How are you doing, Uncle Gabe?

GABRIEL: Lyons . . . The King of the Jungle! Rose . . . hey, Rose. Got a flower for you. *(He takes a rose from his pocket.)* Picked it myself. That's the same rose like you is!

ROSE: That's right nice of you, Gabe.

LYONS: What you been doing, Uncle Gabe?

GABRIEL: Oh, I been chasing hellhounds and waiting on the time to tell St. Peter to open the gates.

LYONS: You been chasing hellhounds, huh? Well . . . you doing the right thing, Uncle Gabe. Somebody got to chase them.

GABRIEL: Oh, yeah . . . I know it. The devil's strong. The devil ain't no pushover. Hellhounds snipping at everybody's heels. But I got my trumpet waiting on the judgment time.

LYONS: Waiting on the Battle of Armageddon, huh?

GABRIEL: Ain't gonna be too much of a battle when God get to waving that Judgment sword. But the people's gonna have a hell of a time trying to get into heaven if them gates ain't open.

LYONS: *(putting his arm around Gabriel)* You hear this, Pop. Uncle Gabe, you all right!

GABRIEL: *(laughing with Lyons)* Lyons! King of the Jungle.

ROSE: You gonna stay for supper, Gabe? Want me to fix you a plate?

GABRIEL: I'll take a sandwich, Rose. Don't want no plate. Just wanna eat with my hands. I'll take a sandwich.

ROSE: How about you, Lyons? You staying? Got some short ribs cooking.

LYONS: Naw, I won't eat nothing till after we finished playing. *(Pause.)* You ought to come down and listen to me play, Pop.

TROY: I don't like that Chinese music. All that noise.

ROSE: Go on in the house and wash up, Gabe . . . I'll fix you a sandwich.

GABRIEL: *(to Lyons, as he exits)* Troy's mad at me.

LYONS: What you mad at Uncle Gabe for, Pop?

ROSE: He thinks Troy's mad at him cause he moved over to Miss Pearl's.

TROY: I ain't mad at the man. He can live where he want to live at.

LYONS: What he move over there for? Miss Pearl don't like nobody.

ROSE: She don't mind him none. She treats him real nice. She just don't allow all that singing.

TROY: She don't mind that rent he be paying . . . that's what she don't mind.

ROSE: Troy, I ain't going through that with you no more. He's over there cause he want to have his own place. He can come and go as he please.

TROY: Hell, he could come and go as he please here. I wasn't stopping him. I ain't put no rules on him.

Rose: It ain't the same thing, Troy. And you know it.

Gabriel comes to the door.

Now, that's the last I wanna hear about that. I don't wanna hear nothing else about Gabe and Miss Pearl. And next week . . .

Gabriel: I'm ready for my sandwich, Rose.

Rose: And next week . . . when that recruiter come from that school . . . I want you to sign that paper and go on and let Cory play football. Then that'll be the last I have to hear about that.

Troy: *(to Rose as she exits into the house)* I ain't thinking about Cory nothing.

Lyons: What . . . Cory got recruited? What school he going to?

Troy: That boy walking around here smelling his piss . . . thinking he's grown. Thinking he's gonna do what he want, irrespective of what I say. Look here, Bono . . . I left the Commissioner's office and went down to the A&P . . . that boy ain't working down there. He lying to me. Telling me he got his job back . . . telling me he working weekends . . . telling me he working after school . . . Mr. Stawicki tell me he ain't working down there at all!

Lyons: Cory just growing up. He's just busting at the seams trying to fill out your shoes.

Troy: I don't care what he's doing. When he get to the point where he wanna disobey me . . . then it's time for him to move on. Bono'll tell you that. I bet he ain't never disobeyed his daddy without paying the consequences.

Bono: I ain't never had a chance. My daddy came on through . . . but I ain't never knew him to see him . . . or what he had on his mind or where he went. Just moving on through. Searching out the New Land. That's what the old folks used to call it. See a fellow moving around from place to place . . . woman to woman . . . called it searching out the New Land. Can't say if he ever found it. I come along, didn't want no kids. Didn't know if I was gonna be in one place long enough to fix on them right as their daddy. I figured I was going searching too. As it turned out I been hooked up with Lucille near about as long as your daddy been with Rose. Going on sixteen years.

Troy: Sometimes I wish I hadn't known my daddy. He ain't cared nothing about no kids. A kid to him wasn't nothing. All he wanted was for you to learn how to walk so he could start you to working. When it come time for eating . . . he ate first. If there was anything left over, that's what you got. Man would sit down and eat two chickens and give you the wing.

Lyons: You ought to stop that, Pop. Everybody feed their kids. No matter how hard times is . . . everybody care about their kids. Make sure they have something to eat.

Troy: The only thing my daddy cared about was getting them bales of cotton in to Mr. Lubin. That's the only thing that mattered to him. Sometimes I used to wonder why he was living. Wonder why the devil hadn't come and got him. "Get them bales of cotton in to Mr. Lubin" and find out he owe him money . . .

LYONS: He should have just went on and left when he saw he couldn't get nowhere. That's what I would have done.

TROY: How he gonna leave with eleven kids? And where he gonna go? He ain't knew how to do nothing but farm. No, he was trapped and I think he knew it. But I'll say this for him . . . he felt a responsibility toward us. Maybe he ain't treated us the way I felt he should have . . . but without that responsibility he could have walked off and left us . . . made his own way.

BONO: A lot of them did. Back in those days what you talking about . . . they walk out their front door and just take on down one road or another and keep on walking.

LYONS: There you go? That's what I'm talking about.

BONO: Just keep on walking till you come to something else. Ain't you never heard of nobody having the walking blues? Well, that's what you call it when you just take off like that.

TROY: My daddy ain't had them walking blues! What you talking about? He stayed right there with his family. But he was just as evil as he could be. My mama couldn't stand him. Couldn't stand that evilness. She run off when I was about eight. She sneaked off one night after he had gone to sleep. Told me she was coming back for me. I ain't never seen her no more. All his women run off and left him. He wasn't good for nobody.

When my turn come to head out, I was fourteen and got to sniffing around Joe Canewell's daughter. Had us an old mule we called Greyboy. My daddy sent me out to do some plowing and tied up Greyboy and went to fooling around with Joe Canewell's daughter. We done found us a nice little spot, got real cozy with each other. She about thirteen and we done figured we was grown anyway . . . so we down there enjoying ourselves . . . ain't thinking about nothing. We didn't know Greyboy had got loose and wandered back to the house and my daddy was looking for me. We down there by the creek enjoying ourselves when my daddy come up on us. Surprised us. He had them leather straps off the mule and commenced to whupping me like there was no tomorrow. I jumped up, mad and embarrassed. I was scared of my daddy. When he commenced to whupping on me . . . quite naturally I run to get out of the way. *(Pause.)* Now I thought he was mad 'cause I ain't done my work. But I see where he was chasing me off so he could have that gal for himself. When I see what the matter of it was, I lost all fear of my daddy. Right there is where I become a man . . . at fourteen years of age. *(Pause.)* Now it was my turn to run him off. I picked up them same reins that he had used on me. I picked up them reins and commenced to whupping on him. The gal jumped up and run off . . . and when my daddy turned to face me, I could see why the devil had never come to get him . . . cause he was the devil himself. I don't know what happened. When I woke up, I was laying right there by the creek, and Blue . . . this old dog we had . . . was licking my face. I thought I was blind. I couldn't see nothing. Both my eyes were swollen shut. I laid there and cried. I didn't know what I was gonna do. The only thing I knew was the time had come for me to leave my daddy's house. And right there the world suddenly got big. And it was a long time before I could cut it down to where I could handle it.

Part of that cutting down was when I got to the place where I could feel him kicking in my blood and knew that the only thing that separated us was the matter of a few years.

Gabriel enters from the house with a sandwich.

LYONS: What you got there, Uncle Gabe?

GABRIEL: Got me a ham sandwich. Rose gave me a ham sandwich.

TROY: I don't know what happened to him. I done lost touch with everybody except Gabriel. But I hope he's dead. I hope he found some peace.

LYONS: That's a heavy story, Pop. I didn't know you left home when you was fourteen.

TROY: And didn't know nothing. The only part of the world I knew was the forty-two acres of Mr. Lubin's land. That's all I knew about life.

LYONS: Fourteen's kinda young to be out on your own. *(Phone rings.)* I don't even think I was ready to be out on my own at fourteen. I don't know what I would have done.

TROY: I got up from the creek and walked on down to Mobile.° I was through with farming. Figured I could do better in the city. So I walked the two hundred miles to Mobile.

LYONS: Wait a minute . . . you ain't walked no two hundred miles, Pop. Ain't nobody gonna walk no two hundred miles. You talking about some walking there.

BONO: That's the only way you got anywhere back in them days.

LYONS: Shhh. Damn if I wouldn't have hitched a ride with somebody!

TROY: Who you gonna hitch it with? They ain't got no cars and things like they got now. We talking about 1918.

ROSE: *(entering)* What you all out here getting into?

TROY: *(to Rose)* I'm telling Lyons how good he got it. He don't know nothing about this I'm talking.

ROSE: Lyons, that was Bonnie on the phone. She say you supposed to pick her up.

LYONS: Yeah, okay, Rose.

TROY: I walked on down to Mobile and hitched up with some of them fellows that was heading this way. Got up here and found out . . . not only couldn't you get a job . . . you couldn't find no place to live. I thought I was in freedom. Shhh. Colored folks living down there on the riverbanks in whatever kind of shelter they could find for themselves. Right down there under the Brady Street Bridge. Living in shacks made of sticks and tarpaper. Messed around there and went from bad to worse. Started stealing. First it was food. Then I figured, hell, if I steal money I can buy me some food. Buy

Mobile: City and seaport in southwestern Alabama.

me some shoes too! One thing led to another. Met your mama. I was young and anxious to be a man. Met your mama and had you. What I do that for? Now I got to worry about feeding you and her. Got to steal three times as much. Went out one day looking for somebody to rob . . . that's what I was, a robber. I'll tell you the truth. I'm ashamed of it today. But it's the truth. Went to rob this fellow . . . pulled out my knife . . . and he pulled out a gun. Shot me in the chest. I felt just like somebody had taken a hot branding iron and laid it on me. When he shot me I jumped at him with my knife. They told me I killed him and they put me in the penitentiary and locked me up for fifteen years. That's where I met Bono. That's where I learned how to play baseball. Got out that place and your mama had taken you and went on to make life without me. Fifteen years was a long time for her to wait. But that fifteen years cured me of that robbing stuff. Rose'll tell you. She asked me when I met her if I had gotten all that foolishness out of my system. And I told her, "Baby, it's you and baseball all what count with me." You hear me, Bono? I meant it too. She say, "Which one comes first?" I told her, "Baby, ain't no doubt it's baseball . . . but you stick and get old with me and we'll both outlive this baseball." Am I right, Rose? And it's true.

ROSE: Man, hush your mouth. You ain't said no such thing. Talking about "Baby, you know you'll always be number one with me." That's what you was talking.

TROY: You hear that, Bono. That's why I love her.

BONO: Rose'll keep you straight. You get off the track, she'll straighten you up.

ROSE: Lyons, you better get on up and get Bonnie. She waiting on you.

LYONS: *(gets up to go)* Hey, Pop, why don't you come on down to the Grill and hear me play.

TROY: I ain't going down there. I'm too old to be sitting around in them clubs.

BONO: You got to be good to play down at the Grill.

LYONS: Come on, Pop . . .

TROY: I got to get up in the morning.

LYONS: You ain't got to stay long.

TROY: Naw, I'm gonna get my supper and go on to bed.

LYONS: Well, I got to go. I'll see you again.

TROY: Don't you come around my house on my payday.

ROSE: Pick up the phone and let somebody know you coming. And bring Bonnie with you. You know I'm always glad to see her.

LYONS: Yeah, I'll do that, Rose. You take care now. See you, Pop. See you, Mr. Bono. See you, Uncle Gabe.

GABRIEL: Lyons! King of the Jungle!

Lyons exits.

TROY: Is supper ready, woman? Me and you got some business to take care of. I'm gonna tear it up too.

ROSE: Troy, I done told you now!

TROY: *(puts his arm around Bono)* Aw hell, woman . . . this is Bono. Bono like family. I done known this nigger since . . . how long I done know you?

BONO: It's been a long time.

TROY: I done know this nigger since Skippy was a pup. Me and him done been through some times.

BONO: You sure right about that.

TROY: Hell, I done know him longer than I known you. And we still standing shoulder to shoulder. Hey, look here, Bono . . . a man can't ask for no more than that. *(Drinks to him.)* I love you, nigger.

BONO: Hell, I love you too . . . I got to get home see my woman. You got yours in hand. I got to go get mine.

Bono starts to exit as Cory enters the yard, dressed in his football uniform. He gives Troy a hard, uncompromising look.

CORY: What you do that for, Pop?

He throws his helmet down in the direction of Troy.

ROSE: What's the matter? Cory . . . what's the matter?

CORY: Papa done went up to the school and told Coach Zellman I can't play football no more. Wouldn't even let me play the game. Told him to tell the recruiter not to come.

ROSE: Troy . . .

TROY: What you Troying me for. Yeah, I did it. And the boy know why I did it.

CORY: Why you wanna do that to me? That was the one chance I had.

ROSE: Ain't nothing wrong with Cory playing football, Troy.

TROY: The boy lied to me. I told the nigger if he wanna play football . . . to keep up his chores and hold down that job at the A&P. That was the conditions. Stopped down there to see Mr. Stawicki . . .

CORY: I can't work after school during the football season, Pop! I tried to tell you that Mr. Stawicki's holding my job for me. You don't never want to listen to nobody. And then you wanna go and do this to me!

TROY: I ain't done nothing to you. You done it to yourself.

CORY: Just cause you didn't have a chance! You just scared I'm gonna be better than you, that's all.

TROY: Come here.

ROSE: Troy . . .

Cory reluctantly crosses over to Troy.

TROY: All right! See. You done made a mistake.

CORY: I didn't even do nothing!

TROY: I'm gonna tell you what your mistake was. See . . . you swung at the ball and didn't hit it. That's strike one. See, you in the batter's box now. You swung and you missed. That's strike one. Don't you strike out!

Lights fade to black.

ACT 2

SCENE 1

The following morning. Cory is at the tree hitting the ball with the bat. He tries to mimic Troy, but his swing is awkward, less sure. Rose enters from the house.

ROSE: Cory, I want you to help me with this cupboard.

CORY: I ain't quitting the team. I don't care what Poppa say.

ROSE: I'll talk to him when he gets back. He had to go see about your Uncle Gabe. The police done arrested him. Say he was disturbing the peace. He'll be back directly. Come on in here and help me clean out the top of this cupboard.

Cory exits into the house. Rose sees Troy and Bono coming down the alley.

Troy . . . what they say down there?

TROY: Ain't said nothing. I give them fifty dollars and they let him go. I'll talk to you about it. Where's Cory?

ROSE: He's in there helping me clean out these cupboards.

TROY: Tell him to get his butt out here.

Troy and Bono go over to the pile of wood. Bono picks up the saw and begins sawing.

TROY: *(to Bono)* All they want is the money. That makes six or seven times I done went down there and got him. See me coming they stick out their *hands*.

BONO: Yeah. I know what you mean. That's all they care about . . . that money. They don't care about what's right. *(Pause.)* Nigger, why you got to go and get some hard wood? You ain't doing nothing but building a little old fence. Get you some soft pine wood. That's all you need.

TROY: I know what I'm doing. This is outside wood. You put pine wood inside the house. Pine wood is inside wood. This here is outside wood. Now you tell me where the fence is gonna be?

BONO: You don't need this wood. You can put it up with pine wood and it'll stand as long as you gonna be here looking at it.

TROY: How you know how long I'm gonna be here, nigger? Hell, I might just live forever. Live longer than old man Horsely.

BONO: That's what Magee used to say.

TROY: Magee's a damn fool. Now you tell me who you ever heard of gonna pull their own teeth with a pair of rusty pliers.

BONO: The old folks . . . my granddaddy used to pull his teeth with pliers. They ain't had no dentists for the colored folks back then.

TROY: Get clean pliers! You understand? Clean pliers! Sterilize them! Besides we ain't living back then. All Magee had to do was walk over to Doc Goldblum's.

BONO: I see where you and that Tallahassee gal . . . that Alberta . . . I see where you all done got tight.

TROY: What you mean "got tight"?

BONO: I see where you be laughing and joking with her all the time.

TROY: I laughs and jokes with all of them, Bono. You know me.

BONO: That ain't the kind of laughing and joking I'm talking about.

Cory enters from the house.

CORY: How you doing, Mr. Bono?

TROY: Cory? Get that saw from Bono and cut some wood. He talking about the wood's too hard to cut. Stand back there, Jim, and let that young boy show you how it's done.

BONO: He's sure welcome to it.

Cory takes the saw and begins to cut the wood.

Whew-e-e! Look at that. Big old strong boy. Look like Joe Louis.° Hell, must be getting old the way I'm watching that boy whip through that wood.

CORY: I don't see why Mama want a fence around the yard noways.

TROY: Damn if I know either. What the hell she keeping out with it? She ain't got nothing nobody want.

BONO: Some people build fences to keep people out . . . and other people build fences to keep people in. Rose wants to hold on to you all. She loves you.

TROY: Hell, nigger, I don't need nobody to tell me my wife loves me. Cory . . . go on in the house and see if you can find that other saw.

CORY: Where's it at?

TROY: I said find it! Look for it till you find it!

Cory exits into the house.

What's that supposed to mean? Wanna keep us in?

BONO: Troy . . . I done known you seem like damn near my whole life. You and Rose both. I done know both of you all for a long time. I remember when you met Rose. When you was hitting them baseballs out the park. A lot of them gals was after you then. You had the pick of the litter. When you picked Rose, I was happy for you. That was the first time I knew you had any sense. I said . . . My man Troy knows what he's doing . . . I'm gonna follow this nigger . . . he might take me somewhere. I been following you too. I done learned a whole heap of things about life watching you. I done learned how to tell where the shit lies. How to tell it from the alfalfa. You done learned me a lot of things. You showed me how to not make the same mistakes . . . to take life as it comes along and keep putting one foot in front of the other. *(Pause.)* Rose a good woman, Troy.

TROY: Hell, nigger, I know she a good woman. I been married to her for eighteen years. What you got on your mind, Bono?

BONO: I just say she a good woman. Just like I say anything. I ain't got to have nothing on my mind.

Joe Louis: Joseph Louis Barrow (1914–1981), American boxer known as the "Brown Bomber." In 1937, he became the youngest boxer ever to win the Heavyweight Championship, which he defended twenty-five times; he retired undefeated in 1949.

TROY: You just gonna say she a good woman and leave it hanging out there like that? Why you telling me she a good woman?

BONO: She loves you, Troy. Rose loves you.

TROY: You saying I don't measure up. That's what you trying to say. I don't measure up 'cause I'm seeing this other gal. I know what you trying to say.

BONO: I know what Rose means to you, Troy. I'm just trying to say I don't want to see you mess up.

TROY: Yeah, I appreciate that, Bono. If you was messing around on Lucille I'd be telling you the same thing.

BONO: Well, that's all I got to say. I just say that because I love you both.

TROY: Hell, you know me . . . I wasn't out there looking for nothing. You can't find a better woman than Rose. I know that. But seems like this woman just stuck onto me where I can't shake her loose. I done wrestled with it, tried to throw her off me . . . but she just stuck on tighter. Now she's stuck on for good.

BONO: You's in control . . . that's what you tell me all the time. You responsible for what you do.

TROY: I ain't ducking the responsibility of it. As long as it sets right in my heart . . . then I'm okay. 'Cause that's all I listen to. It'll tell me right from wrong every time. And I ain't talking about doing Rose no bad turn. I love Rose. She done carried me a long ways and I love and respect her for that.

BONO: I know you do. That's why I don't want to see you hurt her. But what you gonna do when she find out? What you got then? If you try and juggle both of them . . . sooner or later you gonna drop one of them. That's common sense.

TROY: Yeah, I hear what you saying, Bono. I been trying to figure a way to work it out.

BONO: Work it out right, Troy. I don't want to be getting all up between you and Rose's business . . . but work it so it come out right.

TROY: Ah hell, I get all up between you and Lucille's business. When you gonna get that woman that refrigerator she been wanting? Don't tell me you ain't got no money now. I know who your banker is. Mellon don't need that money bad as Lucille want that refrigerator. I'll tell you that.

BONO: Tell you what I'll do . . . when you finish building this fence for Rose . . . I'll buy Lucille that refrigerator.

TROY: You done stuck your foot in your mouth now!

Troy grabs up a board and begins to saw. Bono starts to walk out the yard.

Hey, nigger . . . where you going?

BONO: I'm going home. I know you don't expect me to help you now. I'm protecting my money. I wanna see you put that fence up by yourself. That's what I want to see. You'll be here another six months without me.

TROY: Nigger, you ain't right.

Bono: When it comes to my money . . . I'm right as fireworks on the Fourth of July.

Troy: All right, we gonna see now. You better get out your bankbook.

Bono exits, and Troy continues to work. Rose enters from the house.

Rose: What they say down there? What's happening with Gabe?

Troy: I went down there and got him out. Cost me fifty dollars. Say he was disturbing the peace. Judge set up a hearing for him in three weeks. Say to show cause why he shouldn't be recommitted.

Rose: What was he doing that cause them to arrest him?

Troy: Some kids were teasing him and he run them off home. Say he was howling and carrying on. Some folks seen him and called the police. That's all it was.

Rose: Well, what's you say? What'd you tell the judge?

Troy: Told him I'd look after him. It didn't make no sense to recommit the man. He stuck out his big greasy palm and told me to give him fifty dollars and take him on home.

Rose: Where's he at now? Where'd he go off to?

Troy: He's gone about his business. He don't need nobody to hold his hand.

Rose: Well, I don't know. Seem like that would be the best place for him if they did put him into the hospital. I know what you're gonna say. But that's what I think would be best.

Troy: The man done had his life ruined fighting for what? And they wanna take and lock him up. Let him be free. He don't bother nobody.

Rose: Well, everybody got their own way of looking at it I guess. Come on and get your lunch. I got a bowl of lima beans and some cornbread in the oven. Come and get something to eat. Ain't no sense you fretting over Gabe.

Rose turns to go into the house.

Troy: Rose . . . got something to tell you.

Rose: Well, come on . . . wait till I get this food on the table.

Troy: Rose!

She stops and turns around.

I don't know how to say this. *(Pause.)* I can't explain it none. It just sort of grows on you till it gets out of hand. It starts out like a little bush . . . and the next thing you know it's a whole forest.

Rose: Troy . . . what is you talking about?

Troy: I'm talking, woman, let me talk. I'm trying to find a way to tell you . . . I'm gonna be a daddy. I'm gonna be somebody's daddy.

Rose: Troy . . . you're not telling me this? You're gonna be . . . what?

Troy: Rose . . . now . . . see . . .

Rose: You telling me you gonna be somebody's daddy? You telling your *wife* this?

Gabriel enters from the street. He carries a rose in his hand.

GABRIEL: Hey, Troy! Hey, Rose!

ROSE: I have to wait eighteen years to hear something like this.

GABRIEL: Hey, Rose . . . I got a flower for you. *(He hands it to her.)* That's a rose. Same rose like you is.

ROSE: Thanks, Gabe.

GABRIEL: Troy, you ain't mad at me is you? Them bad mens come and put me away. You ain't mad at me is you?

TROY: Naw, Gabe, I ain't mad at you.

ROSE: Eighteen years and you wanna come with this.

GABRIEL: *(takes a quarter out of his pocket)* See what I got? Got a brand new quarter.

TROY: Rose . . . it's just . . .

ROSE: Ain't nothing you can say, Troy. Ain't no way of explaining that.

GABRIEL: Fellow that give me this quarter had a whole mess of them. I'm gonna keep this quarter till it stop shining.

ROSE: Gabe, go on in the house there. I got some watermelon in the Frigidaire. Go on and get you a piece.

GABRIEL: Say, Rose . . . you know I was chasing hellhounds and them bad mens come and get me and take me away. Troy helped me. He come down there and told them they better let me go before he beat them up. Yeah, he did!

ROSE: You go on and get you a piece of watermelon, Gabe. Them bad mens is gone now.

GABRIEL: Okay, Rose . . . gonna get me some watermelon. The kind with the stripes on it.

Gabriel exits into the house.

ROSE: Why, Troy? Why? After all these years to come dragging this in to me now. It don't make no sense at your age. I could have expected this ten or fifteen years ago, but not now.

TROY: Age ain't got nothing to do with it, Rose.

ROSE: I done tried to be everything a wife should be. Everything a wife could be. Been married eighteen years and I got to live to see the day you tell me you been seeing another woman and done fathered a child by her. And you know I ain't never wanted no half nothing in my family. My whole family is half. Everybody got different fathers and mothers . . . my two sisters and my brother. Can't hardly tell who's who. Can't never sit down and talk about Papa and Mama. It's your papa and your mama and my papa and my mama . . .

TROY: Rose . . . stop it now.

ROSE: I ain't never wanted that for none of my children. And now you wanna drag your behind in here and tell me something like this.

TROY: You ought to know. It's time for you to know.

ROSE: Well, I don't want to know, goddamn it!

TROY: I can't just make it go away. It's done now. I can't wish the circumstance of the thing away.

ROSE: And you don't want to either. Maybe you want to wish me and my boy away. Maybe that's what you want? Well, you can't wish us away. I've got eighteen years of my life invested in you. You ought to have stayed upstairs in my bed where you belong.

TROY: Rose . . . now listen to me . . . we can get a handle on this thing. We can talk this out . . . come to an understanding.

ROSE: All of a sudden it's "we." Where was "we" at when you was down there rolling around with some godforsaken woman? "We" should have come to an understanding before you started making a damn fool of yourself. You're a day late and a dollar short when it comes to an understanding with me.

TROY: It's just . . . She gives me a different idea . . . a different understanding about myself. I can step out of this house and get away from the pressures and problems . . . be a different man. I ain't got to wonder how I'm gonna pay the bills or get the roof fixed. I can just be a part of myself that I ain't never been.

ROSE: What I want to know . . . is do you plan to continue seeing her. That's all you can say to me.

TROY: I can sit up in her house and laugh. Do you understand what I'm saying. I can laugh out loud . . . and it feels good. It reaches all the way down to the bottom of my shoes. *(Pause.)* Rose, I can't give that up.

ROSE: Maybe you ought to go on and stay down there with her . . . if she's a better woman than me.

TROY: It ain't about nobody being a better woman or nothing. Rose, you ain't the blame. A man couldn't ask for no woman to be a better wife than you've been. I'm responsible for it. I done locked myself into a pattern trying to take care of you all that I forgot about myself.

ROSE: What the hell was I there for? That was my job, not somebody else's.

TROY: Rose, I done tried all my life to live decent . . . to live a clean . . . hard . . . useful life. I tried to be a good husband to you. In every way I knew how. Maybe I come into the world backwards, I don't know. But . . . you born with two strikes on you before you come to the plate. You got to guard it closely . . . always looking for the curve ball on the inside corner. You can't afford to let none get past you. You can't afford a call strike. If you going down . . . you going down swinging. Everything lined up against you. What you gonna do. I fooled them, Rose. I bunted. When I found you and Cory and a halfway decent job . . . I was safe. Couldn't nothing touch me. I wasn't gonna strike out no more. I wasn't going back to the penitentiary. I wasn't gonna lay in the streets with a bottle of wine. I was safe. I had me a family. A job. I wasn't gonna get that last strike. I was on first looking for one of them boys to knock me in. To get me home.

ROSE: You should have stayed in my bed, Troy.

TROY: Then when I saw that gal . . . she firmed up my backbone. And I got to thinking that if I tried . . . I just might be able to steal second. Do you understand after eighteen years I wanted to steal second.

ROSE: You should have held me tight. You should have grabbed me and held on.

TROY: I stood on first base for eighteen years and I thought . . . well, goddamn it . . . go on for it!

ROSE: We're not talking about baseball! We're talking about you going off to lay in bed with another woman . . . and then bring it home to me. That's what we're talking about. We ain't talking about no baseball.

TROY: Rose, you're not listening to me. I'm trying the best I can to explain it to you. It's not easy for me to admit that I been standing in the same place for eighteen years.

ROSE: I been standing with you! I been right here with you, Troy. I got a life too. I gave eighteen years of my life to stand in the same spot with you. Don't you think I ever wanted other things? Don't you think I had dreams and hopes? What about my life? What about me. Don't you think it ever crossed my mind to want to know other men? That I wanted to lay up somewhere and forget about my responsibilities? That I wanted someone to make me laugh so I could feel good? You not the only one who's got wants and needs. But I held on to you, Troy. I took all my feelings, my wants and needs, my dreams . . . and I buried them inside you. I planted a seed and watched and prayed over it. I planted myself inside you and waited to bloom. And it didn't take me no eighteen years to find out the soil was hard and rocky and it wasn't never gonna bloom.

But I held on to you, Troy. I held you tighter. You was my husband. I owed you everything I had. Every part of me I could find to give you. And upstairs in that room . . . with the darkness falling in on me . . . I gave everything I had to try and erase the doubt that you wasn't the finest man in the world. And wherever you was going . . . I wanted to be there with you. 'Cause you was my husband. 'Cause that's the only way I was gonna survive as your wife. You always talking about what you give . . . and what you don't have to give. But you take too. You take . . . and don't even know nobody's giving!

Rose turns to exit into the house; Troy grabs her arm.

TROY: You say I take and don't give!

ROSE: Troy! You're hurting me!

TROY: You say I take and don't give!

ROSE: Troy . . . you're hurting my arm! Let go!

TROY: I done give you everything I got. Don't you tell that lie on me.

ROSE: Troy!

TROY: Don't you tell that lie on me!

Cory enters from the house.

CORY: Mama!

ROSE: Troy. You're hurting me.

TROY: Don't you tell me about no taking and giving.

Cory comes up behind Troy and grabs him. Troy, surprised, is thrown off balance just as Cory throws a glancing blow that catches him on the chest and knocks him down. Troy is stunned, as is Cory.

ROSE: Troy. Troy. No!

Troy gets to his feet and starts at Cory.

Troy . . . no. Please! Troy!

Rose pulls on Troy to hold him back. Troy stops himself.

TROY: *(to Cory)* All right. That's strike two. You stay away from around me, boy. Don't you strike out. You living with a full count. Don't you strike out.

Troy exits out the yard as the lights go down.

SCENE 2

It is six months later, early afternoon. Troy enters from the house and starts to exit the yard. Rose enters from the house.

ROSE: Troy, I want to talk to you.

TROY: All of a sudden, after all this time, you want to talk to me, huh? You ain't wanted to talk to me for months. You ain't wanted to talk to me last night. You ain't wanted no part of me then. What you wanna talk to me about now?

ROSE: Tomorrow's Friday.

TROY: I know what day tomorrow is. You think I don't know tomorrow's Friday? My whole life I ain't done nothing but look to see Friday coming and you got to tell me it's Friday.

ROSE: I want to know if you're coming home.

TROY: I always come home, Rose. You know that. There ain't never been a night I ain't come home.

ROSE: That ain't what I mean . . . and you know it. I want to know if you're coming straight home after work.

TROY: I figure I'd cash my check . . . hang out at Taylors' with the boys . . . maybe play a game of checkers . . .

ROSE: Troy, I can't live like this. I won't live like this. You livin' on borrowed time with me. It's been going on six months now you ain't been coming home.

TROY: I be here every Friday. Every night of the year. That's 365 days.

ROSE: I want you to come home tomorrow after work.

TROY: Rose . . . I don't mess up my pay. You know that now. I take my pay and I give it to you. I don't have no money but what you give me back. I just want to have a little time to myself . . . a little time to enjoy life.

ROSE: What about me? When's my time to enjoy life?

TROY: I don't know what to tell you, Rose. I'm doing the best I can.

ROSE: You ain't been home from work but time enough to change your clothes and run out . . . and you wanna call that the best you can do?

TROY: I'm going over to the hospital to see Alberta. She went into the hospital this afternoon. Look like she might have the baby early. I won't be gone long.

ROSE: Well, you ought to know. They went over to Miss Pearl's and got Gabe today. She said you told them to go ahead and lock him up.

TROY: I ain't said no such thing. Whoever told you that is telling a lie. Pearl ain't doing nothing but telling a big fat lie.

ROSE: She ain't had to tell me. I read it on the papers.

TROY: I ain't told them nothing of the kind.

ROSE: I saw it right there on the papers.

TROY: What it say, huh?

ROSE: It said you told them to take him.

TROY: Then they screwed that up, just the way they screw up everything. I ain't worried about what they got on the paper.

ROSE: Say the government send part of his check to the hospital and the other part to you.

TROY: I ain't got nothing to do with that if that's the way it works. I ain't made up the rules about how it work.

ROSE: You did Gabe just like you did Cory. You wouldn't sign the paper for Cory . . . but you signed for Gabe. You signed that paper.

The telephone is heard ringing inside the house.

TROY: I told you I ain't signed nothing, woman! The only thing I signed was the release form. Hell, I can't read. I don't know what they had on that paper! I ain't signed nothing about sending Gabe away.

ROSE: I said send him to the hospital . . . you said let him be free . . . now you done went down there and signed him to the hospital for half his money. You went back on yourself, Troy. You gonna have to answer for that.

TROY: See now . . . you been over there talking to Miss Pearl. She done got mad cause she ain't getting Gabe's rent money. That's all it is. She's liable to say anything.

ROSE: Troy, I seen where you signed the paper.

TROY: You ain't seen nothing I signed. What she doing got papers on my brother anyway? Miss Pearl telling a big fat lie. And I'm gonna tell her about it too! You ain't seen nothing I signed. Say . . . you ain't seen nothing I signed.

Rose exits into the house to answer the telephone. Presently she returns.

ROSE: Troy . . . that was the hospital. Alberta had the baby.

TROY: What she have? What is it?

ROSE: It's a girl.

TROY: I better get on down to the hospital to see her.

ROSE: Troy . . .

TROY: Rose . . . I got to go see her now. That's only right . . . what's the matter . . . the baby's all right, ain't it?

Rose: Alberta died having the baby.

Troy: Died . . . you say she's dead? Alberta's dead?

Rose: They said they done all they could. They couldn't do nothing for her.

Troy: The baby? How's the baby?

Rose: They say it's healthy. I wonder who's gonna bury her.

Troy: She had family, Rose. She wasn't living in the world by herself.

Rose: I know she wasn't living in the world by herself.

Troy: Next thing you gonna want to know if she had any insurance.

Rose: Troy, you ain't got to talk like that.

Troy: That's the first thing that jumped out your mouth. "Who's gonna bury her?" Like I'm fixing to take on that task for myself.

Rose: I am your wife. Don't push me away.

Troy: I ain't pushing nobody away. Just give me some space. That's all. Just give me some room to breathe.

Rose exits into the house. Troy walks about the yard.

Troy: *(with a quiet rage that threatens to consume him)* All right . . . Mr. Death. See now . . . I'm gonna tell you what I'm gonna do. I'm gonna take and build me a fence around this yard. See? I'm gonna build me a fence around what belongs to me. And then I want you to stay on the other side. See? You stay over there until you're ready for me. Then you come on. Bring your army. Bring your sickle. Bring your wrestling clothes. I ain't gonna fall down on my vigilance this time. You ain't gonna sneak up on me no more. When you ready for me . . . when the top of your list say Troy Maxson . . . that's when you come around here. You come up and knock on the front door. Ain't nobody else got nothing to do with this. This is between you and me. Man to man. You stay on the other side of the fence until you ready for me. Then you come up and knock on the front door. Anytime you want. I'll be ready for you.

The lights go down to black.

SCENE 3

The lights come up on the porch. It is late evening three days later. Rose sits listening to the ball game waiting for Troy. The final out of the game is made and Rose switches off the radio. Troy enters the yard carrying an infant wrapped in blankets. He stands back from the house and calls.

Rose enters and stands on the porch. There is a long, awkward silence, the weight of which grows heavier with each passing second.

Troy: Rose . . . I'm standing here with my daughter in my arms. She ain't but a wee bittie little old thing. She don't know nothing about grownups' business. She innocent . . . and she ain't got no mama.

Rose: What you telling me for, Troy?

She turns and exits into the house.

TROY: Well . . . I guess we'll just sit out here on the porch.

He sits down on the porch. There is an awkward indelicateness about the way he handles the baby. His largeness engulfs and seems to swallow it. He speaks loud enough for Rose to hear.

A man's got to do what's right for him. I ain't sorry for nothing I done. It felt right in my heart. *(To the baby.)* What you smiling at? Your daddy's a big man. Got these great big old hands. But sometimes he's scared. And right now your daddy's scared 'cause we sitting out here and ain't got no home. Oh, I been homeless before. I ain't had no little baby with me. But I been homeless. You just be out on the road by your lonesome and you see one of them trains coming and you just kinda go like this . . .

He sings a lullaby.

Please, Mr. Engineer let a man ride the line
Please, Mr. Engineer let a man ride the line
I ain't got no ticket please let me ride the blinds

Rose enters from the house. Troy, hearing her steps behind him, stands and faces her.

She's my daughter, Rose. My own flesh and blood. I can't deny her no more than I can deny them boys. *(Pause.)* You and them boys is my family. You and them and this child is all I got in the world. So I guess what I'm saying is . . . I'd appreciate it if you'd help me take care of her.

ROSE: Okay, Troy . . . you're right. I'll take care of your baby for you . . . 'cause . . . like you say . . . she's innocent . . . and you can't visit the sins of the father upon the child. A motherless child has got a hard time. *(She takes the baby from him.)* From right now . . . this child got a mother. But you a womanless man.

Rose turns and exits into the house with the baby. Lights go down to black.

SCENE 4

It is two months later. Lyons enters from the street. He knocks on the door and calls.

LYONS: Hey, Rose! *(Pause.)* Rose!

ROSE: *(from inside the house)* Stop that yelling. You gonna wake up Raynell. I just got her to sleep.

LYONS: I just stopped by to pay Papa this twenty dollars I owe him. Where's Papa at?

ROSE: He should be here in a minute. I'm getting ready to go down to the church. Sit down and wait on him.

LYONS: I got to go pick up Bonnie over her mother's house.

ROSE: Well, sit it down there on the table. He'll get it.

LYONS: *(enters the house and sets the money on the table)* Tell Papa I said thanks. I'll see you again.

ROSE: All right, Lyons. We'll see you.

Lyons starts to exit as Cory enters.

CORY: Hey, Lyons.

LYONS: What's happening, Cory? Say man, I'm sorry I missed your graduation. You know I had a gig and couldn't get away. Otherwise, I would have been there, man. So what you doing?

CORY: I'm trying to find a job.

LYONS: Yeah I know how that go, man. It's rough out there. Jobs are scarce.

CORY: Yeah, I know.

LYONS: Look here, I got to run. Talk to Papa . . . he know some people. He'll be able to help get you a job. Talk to him . . . see what he say.

CORY: Yeah . . . all right, Lyons.

LYONS: You take care. I'll talk to you soon. We'll find some time to talk.

Lyons exits the yard. Cory wanders over to the tree, picks up the bat, and assumes a batting stance. He studies an imaginary pitcher and swings. Dissatisfied with the result, he tries again. Troy enters. They eye each other for a beat. Cory puts the bat down and exits the yard. Troy starts into the house as Rose exits with Raynell. She is carrying a cake.

TROY: I'm coming in and everybody's going out.

ROSE: I'm taking this cake down to the church for the bake sale. Lyons was by to see you. He stopped by to pay you your twenty dollars. It's laying in there on the table.

TROY: *(going into his pocket)* Well . . . here go this money.

ROSE: Put it in there on the table, Troy. I'll get it.

TROY: What time you coming back?

ROSE: Ain't no use in you studying me. It don't matter what time I come back.

TROY: I just asked you a question, woman. What's the matter . . . can't I ask you a question?

ROSE: Troy, I don't want to go into it. Your dinner's in there on the stove. All you got to do is heat it up. And don't you be eating the rest of them cakes in there. I'm coming back for them. We having a bake sale at the church tomorrow.

Rose exits the yard. Troy sits down on the steps, takes a pint bottle from his pocket, opens it, and drinks. He begins to sing.

TROY:

Hear it ring! Hear it ring!
Had an old dog his name was Blue
You know Blue was mighty true
You know Blue was a good old dog
Blue treed a possum in a hollow log
You know from that he was a good old dog

Bono enters the yard.

BONO: Hey, Troy.

TROY: Hey, what's happening, Bono?

BONO: I just thought I'd stop by to see you.

TROY: What you stop by and see me for? You ain't stopped by in a month of Sundays. Hell, I must owe you money or something.

BONO: Since you got your promotion I can't keep up with you. Used to see you every day. Now I don't even know what route you working.

TROY: They keep switching me around. Got me out in Greentree now . . . hauling white folks' garbage.

BONO: Greentree, huh? You lucky, at least you ain't got to be lifting them barrels. Damn if they ain't getting heavier. I'm gonna put in my two years and call it quits.

TROY: I'm thinking about retiring myself.

BONO: You got it easy. You can *drive* for another five years.

TROY: It ain't the same, Bono. It ain't like working the back of the truck. Ain't got nobody to talk to . . . feel like you working by yourself. Naw, I'm thinking about retiring. How's Lucille?

BONO: She all right. Her arthritis get to acting up on her sometime. Saw Rose on my way in. She going down to the church, huh?

TROY: Yeah, she took up going down there. All them preachers looking for somebody to fatten their pockets. *(Pause.)* Got some gin here.

BONO: Naw, thanks. I just stopped by to say hello.

TROY: Hell, nigger . . . you can take a drink. I ain't never known you to say no to a drink. You ain't got to work tomorrow.

BONO: I just stopped by. I'm fixing to go over to Skinner's. We got us a domino game going over his house every Friday.

TROY: Nigger, you can't play no dominoes. I used to whup you four games out of five.

BONO: Well, that learned me. I'm getting better.

TROY: Yeah? Well, that's all right.

BONO: Look here . . . I got to be getting on. Stop by sometime, huh?

TROY: Yeah, I'll do that, Bono. Lucille told Rose you bought her a new refrigerator.

BONO: Yeah, Rose told Lucille you had finally built your fence . . . so I figured we'd call it even.

TROY: I knew you would.

BONO: Yeah . . . okay. I'll be talking to you.

TROY: Yeah, take care, Bono. Good to see you. I'm gonna stop over.

BONO: Yeah. Okay, Troy.

Bono exits. Troy drinks from the bottle.

TROY:

Old Blue died and I dig his grave
Let him down with a golden chain
Every night when I hear old Blue bark
I know Blue treed a possum in Noah's Ark.
Hear it ring! Hear it ring!

Cory enters the yard. They eye each other for a beat. Troy is sitting in the middle of the steps. Cory walks over.

CORY: I got to get by.

TROY: Say what? What's you say?

CORY: You in my way. I got to get by.

TROY: You got to get by where? This is my house. Bought and paid for. In full. Took me fifteen years. And if you wanna go in my house and I'm sitting on the steps . . . you say excuse me. Like your mama taught you.

CORY: Come on, Pop . . . I got to get by.

Cory starts to maneuver his way past Troy. Troy grabs his leg and shoves him back.

TROY: You just gonna walk over top of me?

CORY: I live here too!

TROY: *(advancing toward him)* You just gonna walk over top of me in my own house?

CORY: I ain't scared of you.

TROY: I ain't asked if you was scared of me. I asked you if you was fixing to walk over top of me in my own house? That's the question. You ain't gonna say excuse me? You just gonna walk over top of me?

CORY: If you wanna put it like that.

TROY: How else am I gonna put it?

CORY: I was walking by you to go into the house 'cause you sitting on the steps drunk, singing to yourself. You can put it like that.

TROY: Without saying excuse me???

Cory doesn't respond.

I asked you a question. Without saying excuse me???

CORY: I ain't got to say excuse me to you. You don't count around here no more.

TROY: Oh, I see . . . I don't count around here no more. You ain't got to say excuse me to your daddy. All of a sudden you done got so grown that your daddy don't count around here no more . . . Around here in his own house and yard that he done paid for with the sweat of his brow. You done got so grown to where you gonna take over. You gonna take over my house. Is that right? You gonna wear my pants. You gonna go in there and stretch out on my bed. You ain't got to say excuse me 'cause I don't count around here no more. Is that right?

CORY: That's right. You always talking this dumb stuff. Now, why don't you just get out my way?

TROY: I guess you got someplace to sleep and something to put in your belly. You got that, huh? You got that? That's what you need. You got that, huh?

CORY: You don't know what I got. You ain't got to worry about what I got.

TROY: You right! You one hundred percent right! I done spent the last seventeen years worrying about what you got. Now it's your turn, see? I'll tell you what to do. You grown . . . we done established that. You a man. Now, let's see you act like one. Turn your behind around and walk out this yard. And when you get out there in the alley . . . you can forget about this house. See? 'Cause this is my house. You go on and be a man and get your own house. You can forget about this. 'Cause this is mine. You go on and get yours 'cause I'm through with doing for you.

CORY: You talking about what you did for me . . . what'd you ever give me?

TROY: Them feet and bones! That pumping heart, nigger! I give you more than anybody else is ever gonna give you.

CORY: You ain't never gave me nothing! You ain't never done nothing but hold me back. Afraid I was gonna be better than you. All you ever did was try and make me scared of you. I used to tremble every time you called my name. Every time I heard your footsteps in the house. Wondering all the time . . . what's Papa gonna say if I do this? . . . What's he gonna say if I do that? . . . What's Papa gonna say if I turn on the radio? And Mama, too . . . she tries . . . but she's scared of you.

TROY: You leave your mama out of this. She ain't got nothing to do with this.

CORY: I don't know how she stand you . . . after what you did to her.

TROY: I told you to leave your mama out of this!

He advances toward Cory.

CORY: What you gonna do . . . give me a whupping? You can't whup me no more. You're too old. You just an old man.

TROY: *(shoves him on his shoulder)* Nigger! That's what you are. You just another nigger on the street to me!

CORY: You crazy! You know that?

TROY: Go on now! You got the devil in you. Get on away from me!

CORY: You just a crazy old man . . . talking about I got the devil in me.

TROY: Yeah, I'm crazy! If you don't get on the other side of that yard . . . I'm gonna show you how crazy I am! Go on . . . get the hell out of my yard.

CORY: It ain't your yard. You took Uncle Gabe's money he got from the army to buy this house and then you put him out.

TROY: *(advances on Cory)* Get your black ass out of my yard!

Troy's advance backs Cory up against the tree. Cory grabs up the bat.

CORY: I ain't going nowhere! Come on . . . put me out! I ain't scared of you.

TROY: That's my bat!

CORY: Come on!

TROY: Put my bat down!

CORY: Come on, put me out.

Cory swings at Troy, who backs across the yard.

What's the matter? You so bad . . . put me out!

Troy advances toward Cory.

CORY: *(backing up)* Come on! Come on!

TROY: You're gonna have to use it! You wanna draw that bat back on me . . . you're gonna have to use it.
CORY: Come on! . . . Come on!

Cory swings the bat at Troy a second time. He misses. Troy continues to advance toward him.

TROY: You're gonna have to kill me! You wanna draw that bat back on me. You're gonna have to kill me.

Cory, backed up against the tree, can go no farther. Troy taunts him. He sticks out his head and offers him a target.

Come on! Come on!

Cory is unable to swing the bat. Troy grabs it.

TROY: Then I'll show you.

Cory and Troy struggle over the bat. The struggle is fierce and fully engaged. Troy ultimately is the stronger and takes the bat away from Cory and stands over him ready to swing. He stops himself.

Go on and get away from around my house.

Cory, stung by his defeat, picks himself up, walks slowly out of the yard and up the alley.

CORY: Tell Mama I'll be back for my things.
TROY: They'll be on the other side of that fence.

Cory exits.

TROY: I can't taste nothing. Helluljah! I can't taste nothing no more. (*Troy assumes a batting posture and begins to taunt Death, the fastball on the outside corner.*) Come on! It's between you and me now! Come on! Anytime you want! Come on! I be ready for you . . . but I ain't gonna be easy.

The lights go down on the scene.

SCENE 5

The time is 1965. The lights come up in the yard. It is the morning of Troy's funeral. A funeral plaque with a light hangs beside the door. There is a small garden plot off to the side. There is noise and activity in the house as Rose, Gabriel, and Bono have gathered. The door opens and Raynell, seven years old, enters dressed in a flannel nightgown. She crosses to the garden and pokes around with a stick. Rose calls from the house.

ROSE: Raynell!
RAYNELL: Mam?
ROSE: What you doing out there?
RAYNELL: Nothing.

Rose comes to the door.

ROSE: Girl, get in here and get dressed. What you doing?
RAYNELL: Seeing if my garden growed.
ROSE: I told you it ain't gonna grow overnight. You got to wait.
RAYNELL: It don't look like it never gonna grow. Dag!
ROSE: I told you a watched pot never boils. Get in here and get dressed.
RAYNELL: This ain't even no pot, Mama.
ROSE: You just have to give it a chance. It'll grow. Now you come on and do what I told you. We got to be getting ready. This ain't no morning to be playing around. You hear me?
RAYNELL: Yes, mam.

Rose exits into the house. Raynell continues to poke at her garden with a stick. Cory enters. He is dressed in a Marine corporal's uniform, and carries a duffel bag. His posture is that of a military man, and his speech has a clipped sternness.

CORY: *(to Raynell)* Hi. *(Pause.)* I bet your name is Raynell.
RAYNELL: Uh huh.
CORY: Is your mama home?

Raynell runs up on the porch and calls through the screen door.

RAYNELL: Mama . . . there's some man out here. Mama?

Rose comes to the door.

ROSE: Cory? Lord have mercy! Look here, you all!

Rose and Cory embrace in a tearful reunion as Bono and Lyons enter from the house dressed in funeral clothes.

BONO: Aw, looka here . . .
ROSE: Done got all grown up!
CORY: Don't cry, Mama. What you crying about?
ROSE: I'm just so glad you made it.
CORY: Hey Lyons. How you doing, Mr. Bono.

Lyons goes to embrace Cory.

LYONS: Look at you, man. Look at you. Don't he look good, Rose. Got them Corporal stripes.
ROSE: What took you so long?
CORY: You know how the Marines are, Mama. They got to get all their paperwork straight before they let you do anything.
ROSE: Well, I'm sure glad you made it. They let Lyons come. Your Uncle Gabe's still in the hospital. They don't know if they gonna let him out or not. I just talked to them a little while ago.
LYONS: A Corporal in the United States Marines.
BONO: Your daddy knew you had it in you. He used to tell me all the time.

LYONS: Don't he look good, Mr. Bono?

BONO: Yeah, he remind me of Troy when I first met him. *(Pause.)* Say, Rose, Lucille's down at the church with the choir. I'm gonna go down and get the pallbearers lined up. I'll be back to get you all.

ROSE: Thanks, Jim.

CORY: See you, Mr. Bono.

LYONS: *(with his arm around Raynell)* Cory . . . look at Raynell. Ain't she precious? She gonna break a whole lot of hearts.

ROSE: Raynell, come and say hello to your brother. This is your brother, Cory. You remember Cory.

RAYNELL: No, Mam.

CORY: She don't remember me, Mama.

ROSE: Well, we talk about you. She heard us talk about you. *(To Raynell.)* This is your brother, Cory. Come on and say hello.

RAYNELL: Hi.

CORY: Hi. So you're Raynell. Mama told me a lot about you.

ROSE: You all come on into the house and let me fix you some breakfast. Keep up your strength.

CORY: I ain't hungry, Mama.

LYONS: You can fix me something, Rose. I'll be in there in a minute.

ROSE: Cory, you sure you don't want nothing? I know they ain't feeding you right.

CORY: No, Mama . . . thanks. I don't feel like eating. I'll get something later.

ROSE: Raynell . . . get on upstairs and get that dress on like I told you.

Rose and Raynell exit into the house.

LYONS: So . . . I hear you thinking about getting married.

CORY: Yeah, I done found the right one, Lyons. It's about time.

LYONS: Me and Bonnie been split up about four years now. About the time Papa retired. I guess she just got tired of all them changes I was putting her through. *(Pause.)* I always knew you was gonna make something out yourself. Your head was always in the right direction. So . . . you gonna stay in . . . make it a career . . . put in your twenty years?

CORY: I don't know. I got six already, I think that's enough.

LYONS: Stick with Uncle Sam and retire early. Ain't nothing out here. I guess Rose told you what happened with me. They got me down the workhouse. I thought I was being slick cashing other people's checks.

CORY: How much time you doing?

LYONS: They give me three years. I got that beat now. I ain't got but nine more months. It ain't so bad. You learn to deal with it like anything else. You got to take the crookeds with the straights. That's what Papa used to say. He used to say that when he struck out. I seen him strike out three times in a row . . . and the next time up he hit the ball over the grandstand. Right out there in Homestead Field. He wasn't satisfied hitting in the seats . . . he want to hit it over everything! After the game he had two hundred people standing around waiting to shake his hand. You got to take the crookeds with the straights. Yeah, Papa was something else.

CORY: You still playing?

LYONS: Cory . . . you know I'm gonna do that. There's some fellows down there we got us a band . . . we gonna try and stay together when we get out . . . but yeah, I'm still playing. It still helps me to get out of bed in the morning. As long as it do that I'm gonna be right there playing and trying to make some sense out of it.

ROSE: *(calling)* Lyons, I got these eggs in the pan.

LYONS: Let me go on and get these eggs, man. Get ready to go bury Papa. *(Pause.)* How you doing? You doing all right?

Cory nods. Lyons touches him on the shoulder and they share a moment of silent grief. Lyons exits into the house. Cory wanders about the yard. Raynell enters.

RAYNELL: Hi.

CORY: Hi.

RAYNELL: Did you used to sleep in my room?

CORY: Yeah . . . that used to be my room.

RAYNELL: That's what Papa call it. "Cory's room." It got your football in the closet.

Rose comes to the door.

ROSE: Raynell, get in there and get them good shoes on.

RAYNELL: Mama, can't I wear these? Them other ones hurt my feet.

ROSE: Well, they just gonna have to hurt your feet for a while. You ain't said they hurt your feet when you went down to the store and got them.

RAYNELL: They didn't hurt then. My feet done got bigger.

ROSE: Don't you give me no backtalk now. You get in there and get them shoes on.

Raynell exits into the house.

Ain't too much changed. He still got that piece of rag tied to that tree. He was out here swinging that bat. I was just ready to go back in the house. He swung that bat and then he just fell over. Seem like he swung it and stood there with this grin on his face . . . and then he just fell over. They carried him on down to the hospital, but I knew there wasn't no need . . . why don't you come on in the house?

CORY: Mama . . . I got something to tell you. I don't know how to tell you this . . . but I've got to tell you . . . I'm not going to Papa's funeral.

ROSE: Boy, hush your mouth. That's your daddy you talking about. I don't want hear that kind of talk this morning. I done raised you to come to this? You standing there all healthy and grown talking about you ain't going to your daddy's funeral?

CORY: Mama . . . listen . . .

ROSE: I don't want to hear it, Cory. You just get that thought out of your head.

CORY: I can't drag Papa with me everywhere I go. I've got to say no to him. One time in my life I've got to say no.

ROSE: Don't nobody have to listen to nothing like that. I know you and your daddy ain't seen eye to eye, but I ain't got to listen to that kind of talk this morning. Whatever was between you and your daddy . . . the time has come to put it aside. Just take it and set it over there on the shelf and forget about it. Disrespecting your daddy ain't gonna make you a man, Cory. You got to find a way to come to that on your own. Not going to your daddy's funeral ain't gonna make you a man.

CORY: The whole time I was growing up . . . living in his house . . . Papa was like a shadow that followed you everywhere. It weighed on you and sunk into your flesh. It would wrap around you and lay there until you couldn't tell which one was you anymore. That shadow digging in your flesh. Trying to crawl in. Trying to live through you. Everywhere I looked, Troy Maxson was staring back at me . . . hiding under the bed . . . in the closet. I'm just saying I've got to find a way to get rid of that shadow, Mama.

ROSE: You just like him. You got him in you good.

CORY: Don't tell me that, Mama.

ROSE: You Troy Maxson all over again.

CORY: I don't want to be Troy Maxson. I want to be me.

ROSE: You can't be nobody but who you are, Cory. That shadow wasn't nothing but you growing into yourself. You either got to grow into it or cut it down to fit you. But that's all you got to make life with. That's all you got to measure yourself against that world out there. Your daddy wanted you to be everything he wasn't . . . and at the same time he tried to make you into everything he was. I don't know if he was right or wrong . . . but I do know he meant to do more good than he meant to do harm. He wasn't always right. Sometimes when he touched he bruised. And sometimes when he took me in his arms he cut.

When I first met your daddy I thought . . . Here is a man I can lay down with and make a baby. That's the first thing I thought when I seen him. I was thirty years old and had done seen my share of men. But when he walked up to me and said, "I can dance a waltz that'll make you dizzy." I thought, Rose Lee, here is a man that you can open yourself up to and be filled to bursting. Here is a man that can fill all them empty spaces you been tipping around the edges of. One of them empty spaces was being somebody's mother.

I married your daddy and settled down to cooking his supper and keeping clean sheets on the bed. When your daddy walked through the house he was so big he filled it up. That was my first mistake. Not to make him leave some room for me. For my part in the matter. But at that time I wanted that. I wanted a house that I could sing in. And that's what your daddy gave me. I didn't know to keep up his strength I had to give up little pieces of mine. I did that. I took on his life as mine and mixed up the pieces so that you couldn't hardly tell which was which anymore. It was my choice. It was my life and I didn't have to live it like that. But that's what life offered me in the way of being a woman and I took it. I grabbed hold of it with both hands.

By the time Raynell came into the house, me and your daddy had done lost touch with one another. I didn't want to make my blessing off of nobody's misfortune . . . but I took on to Raynell like she was all them babies I had wanted and never had.

The phone rings.

Like I'd been blessed to relive a part of my life. And if the Lord see fit to keep up my strength . . . I'm gonna do her just like your daddy did you . . . I'm gonna give her the best of what's in me.

RAYNELL: *(entering, still with her old shoes)* Mama . . . Reverend Tollivier on the phone.

Rose exits into the house.

RAYNELL: Hi.
CORY: Hi.
RAYNELL: You in the Army or the Marines?
CORY: Marines.
RAYNELL: Papa said it was the Army. Did you know Blue?
CORY: Blue? Who's Blue?
RAYNELL: Papa's dog what he sing about all the time.
CORY: *(singing)*

Hear it ring! Hear it ring!
I had a dog his name was Blue
You know Blue was mighty true
You know Blue was a good old dog
Blue treed a possum in a hollow log
You know from that he was a good old dog.
Hear it ring! Hear it ring!

Raynell joins in singing.

CORY AND RAYNELL:

Blue treed a possum out on a limb
Blue looked at me and I looked at him
Grabbed that possum and put him in a sack
Blue stayed there till I came back
Old Blue's feets was big and round
Never allowed a possum to touch the ground.
Old Blue died and I dug his grave
I dug his grave with a silver spade
Let him down with a golden chain
And every night I call his name
Go on Blue, you good dog you
Go on Blue, you good dog you

RAYNELL:

Blue laid down and died like a man
Blue laid down and died . . .

BOTH:

Blue laid down and died like a man
Now he's treeing possums in the Promised Land
I'm gonna tell you this to let you know
Blue's gone where the good dogs go
When I hear old Blue bark
When I hear old Blue bark
Blue treed a possum in Noah's Ark°
Blue treed a possum in Noah's Ark.

Rose comes to the screen door.

ROSE: Cory, we gonna be ready to go in a minute.
CORY: *(to Raynell)* You go on in the house and change them shoes like Mama told you so we can go to Papa's funeral.
RAYNELL: Okay, I'll be back.

Raynell exits into the house. Cory gets up and crosses over to the tree. Rose stands in the screen door watching him. Gabriel enters from the alley.

GABRIEL: *(calling)* Hey, Rose!
ROSE: Gabe?
GABRIEL: I'm here, Rose. Hey Rose, I'm here!

Rose enters from the house.

ROSE: Lord . . . Look here, Lyons!
LYONS: See, I told you, Rose . . . I told you they'd let him come.
CORY: How you doing, Uncle Gabe?
LYONS: How you doing, Uncle Gabe?
GABRIEL: Hey, Rose. It's time. It's time to tell St. Peter to open the gates. Troy, you ready? You ready, Troy. I'm gonna tell St. Peter to open the gates. You get ready now.

Gabriel, with great fanfare, braces himself to blow. The trumpet is without a mouthpiece. He puts the end of it into his mouth and blows with great force, like a man who has been waiting some twenty-odd years for this single moment. No sound comes out of the trumpet. He braces himself and blows again with the same result. A third time he blows. There is a weight of impossible description that falls away and leaves him bare and exposed to a frightful realization. It is a trauma that a sane and normal mind would be unable to withstand. He begins to dance. A slow, strange dance, eerie and life-giving. A dance of atavistic signature and ritual. Lyons attempts to embrace him. Gabriel pushes Lyons away. He begins to howl in what is an attempt at song, or perhaps a song-turning back into itself in an attempt at speech. He finishes his dance and the gates of heaven stand open as wide as God's closet.

That's the way that go!

Noah's Ark: See Genesis 6.14–20.

Reading and Reacting

1. Obviously, fences are a central metaphor of the play. To what different kinds of fences does the play's title refer?
2. How are the fathers and sons in this play alike? How are they different? Does the play imply that sons must inevitably follow in their fathers' footsteps?
3. This play is set in 1957. Given the racial climate of the country at that time, how realistic are Cory's ambitions? How reasonable are his father's criticisms?
4. In what ways has Troy's character been shaped by his contact with the white world?
5. Is Troy a tragic hero? If so, what is his flaw?
6. Which of the play's characters, if any, do you consider to be stereotypes? What comment do you think the play makes about stereotypes?
7. How does the conflict between Troy and Cory reflect conflicts within the African-American community? Does the play suggest any possibilities for compromise?
8. Do you consider the message of this play to be optimistic or pessimistic? Explain.
9. **JOURNAL ENTRY** Which characters do you like? Which do you dislike? Why?
10. **CRITICAL PERSPECTIVE** Robert Brustein, theater critic and artistic director of Harvard's American Repertory Theater, has criticized Wilson on the ground that "his recurrent theme is the familiar American charge of victimization"; in *Fences*, he argues, "Wilson's larger purpose depends on his conviction that Troy's potential was stunted not [by] 'his own behavior' but by centuries of racist oppression."

    Do you agree with Brustein's characterization of Wilson's theme? Or, do you think there is another theme that Brustein ignores?

Related Works: "Big Black Good Man" (p. 374), "Ex-Basketball Player" (p. 930), "Yet Do I Marvel" (p. 1028), "The *Chicago Defender* Sends a Man to Little Rock" (p. 1131), *Death of a Salesman* (p. 1531)

WRITING SUGGESTIONS: Theme

1. In an interview, writer Lorrie Moore calls *Fences* "an African-American *Death of a Salesman.*" What do you think she means? Do you agree? Write an essay in which you examine the two plays in light of Moore's comment.
2. Write an essay in which you analyze the baseball images in *Fences*. How do the references to baseball help to develop the play's themes?
3. One of the themes of *Fences* is the dream a family has for its children. Compare the development of this theme in *Fences* and in another play in this book — for example, *The Cuban Swimmer* (p. 1732) or *The Glass Menagerie* (p. 1961).
4. *Antigone* explores the theme of obedience to authority: Antigone is executed for denying Creon's orders and thus defying the authority of the state. Do you

think she was right to act as she did, or do you think she should have compromised her principles?

5. Like *Trying to Find Chinatown*, *The Cuban Swimmer* (p. 1732) also explores elements of the characters' ethnic heritage. Compare and contrast the characters' attitudes toward their ethnicity in these two plays.

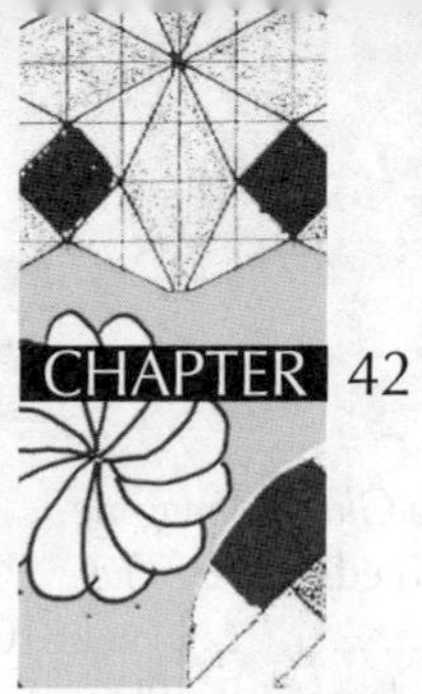

CHAPTER 42

TENNESSEE WILLIAMS'S *THE GLASS MENAGERIE:* A CASEBOOK FOR READING, RESEARCH, AND WRITING

Laura in the arms of the gentleman caller while Tom and Amanda look on in Tennessee Williams's *The Glass Menagerie* presented in 1956 at the Williamstown Theatre festival.

Source: ©Richard Feldman

This chapter provides all the materials you will need to begin a research project about Tennessee Williams's *The Glass Menagerie*. It includes the 1945 play; questions to stimulate discussion and writing; a collection of source materials;* a paper that shows how one student, Heather Jenkins, used the materials in this chapter in her research; and suggestions for further research on Williams.

* Note that some of the less current sources included in this Casebook do not use the parenthetical documentation style recommended by the most recent guidelines set by the Modern Language Association and explained in Chapter 7.

Source Materials

- Williams, Tennessee. "Author's Production Notes." *The Glass Menagerie*. New York: Random, 1945. The preface to the published edition of *The Glass Menagerie*. . . . . (p. 2010)
- O'Connor, Jacqueline. From *Dramatizing Dementia: Madness in the Plays of Tennessee Williams*. Bowling Green, OH: Bowling Green State U Popular P, 1997. Excerpt in which the author discusses Laura's loneliness in *The Glass Menagerie*. . . . . (p. 2012)
- Williams, Tennessee. From *Tennessee Williams: Memoirs*. New York: Doubleday, 1975. A memoir written by the playwright. . . . . (p. 2013)
- Evans, Jean. "Interview 1945." *New York PM* (1945). A magazine interview with Tennessee Williams conducted during the initial New York run of *The Glass Menagerie*. . . . . (p. 2016)
- King, Thomas L. From "Irony and Distance in *The Glass Menagerie*." *Educational Theatre Journal* 25.2 (May 1973): 85–94. Excerpts from an article that discusses the importance of Tom's soliloquies. . . . . (p.2017)
- Tischler, Nancy Marie Patterson. From *Student Companion to Tennessee Williams*. Westport, CT: Greenwood, 2000. Excerpt in which the author discusses the use of symbolism and other stylistic approaches in the work of the playwright. . . . . (p. 2020)
- Stein, Roger B. From "*The Glass Menagerie* Revisited: Catastrophe without Violence." *Western Humanities Review* 18 (Spring 1964): 141–53. Excerpt in which the author discusses religious themes in *The Glass Menagerie*. . . . . (p. 2022)
- Scanlan, Tom. From *Family, Drama, and American Dreams*. New York: Greenwood, 1978. A discussion of the portrayal of family life in *The Glass Menagerie*. . . . . (p. 2024)
- Fisher, James. From "'The Angels of Fructification': Tennessee Williams, Tony Kushner, and Images of Homosexuality on the American Stage." *Mississippi Quarterly* 49.1 (Winter 1995): 13–20. Excerpts from an article that discusses homosexuality in the work of Williams and other American playwrights. . . . . (p. 2027)
- Williams, Tennessee. "Portrait of a Girl in Glass." *Collected Stories*. New York: New Directions, 1985. A 1943 short story that Williams later developed into *The Glass Menagerie*. . . . . (p. 2031)

Each of these sources offers insights that can help you to understand, enjoy, and write about *The Glass Menagerie*. Some offer historical perspectives; some are biographical; others discuss literary devices or offer interpretations. All were selected to help you to understand this classic American play and appreciate its characters and themes. Other kinds of sources can also enrich your understanding of Williams's accomplishments — for example, other plays by Williams, biographical data about the author, or works of imaginative literature by other writers dealing with similar themes. In addition, a number of Web sites devoted to Williams can offer insights into his work.

In preparation for writing an essay on a topic of your choice about *The Glass Menagerie*, read the play and the accompanying source materials carefully. After doing so, explore — in your journal, in group discussions, or in brainstorming notes — the possibilities suggested by the Reading and Reacting questions on pages 2009–10. Think about the ideas expressed in the critical articles, memoirs, and interviews as well as those in the play itself. Your goal is to decide on a topic you can develop in a four- to six-page essay. Remember to document any words or ideas that you borrow from the play or from other sources, enclosing your borrowed words in quotation marks. (For guidelines on evaluating literary criticism, see pages 14–16; for guidelines on using source materials, see Chapter 6, "Using Sources in Your Writing," and Chapter 7, "Documenting Sources and Avoiding Plagiarism.")

A sample student paper, "Laura's Gentleman Caller," based on some of the source materials in this Casebook, begins on page 2039.

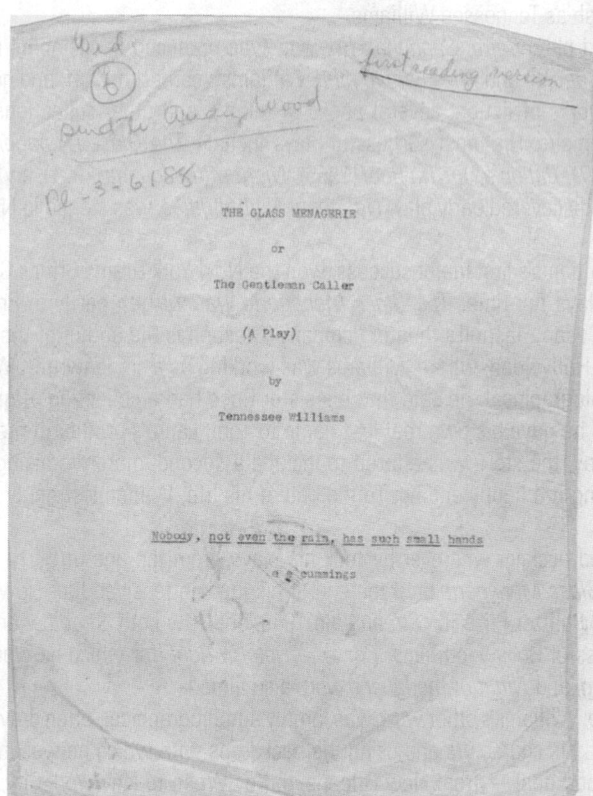

THE GLASS MENAGERIE

or

The Gentleman Caller

(A Play)

by

Tennessee Williams

Nobody, not even the rain, has such small hands

e e cummings

This title page, from a 1944 manuscript, includes as its epigraph the last line from the E. E. Cummings poem "somewhere i have never travelled, gladly beyond."

Source: Courtesy of the Albert and Shirley Small Special Collections Library, University of Virginia Library

Source: ©UPI/Bettmann/Corbis

TENNESSEE WILLIAMS (1911–1983) was born Thomas Lanier Williams in Columbus, Mississippi, on March 26, 1911. His father, who came from a well-to-do and well-connected Tennessee family, was a shoe salesman who was often on the road. His mother was the daughter of a minister, and her genteel ways left her ill-equipped to handle her three rowdy children, who spent more and more time with their maternal grandfather. Williams's grandfather had a stern manner and strong views about right and wrong. His grandson, however, did not always abide by these rules and mocked him playfully whenever he could.

When Williams was eight, his family moved to St. Louis, Missouri, where, only eight years later — at the age of sixteen — Williams made his first mark on the literary world by winning five dollars and placing third in a national essay contest sponsored by *Smart Set* magazine. His essay was entitled "Can a Good Wife Be a Good Sport?" After winning this award, he began to submit his writing widely. He enrolled at the University of Missouri, but he found that college did not give him enough opportunity to write, so he left school and worked at his father's shoe company — and as a waiter, an elevator operator, and a theater usher — while he wrote. Hoping to learn playwriting, he eventually went back to college and graduated from the University of Iowa in 1938. A year later, he adopted his college nickname and began to publish as Tennessee Williams.

Williams's earliest staged play, *Cairo, Shanghai, Bombay,* was produced in Memphis in 1937, followed closely by *Candles to the Sun* and *The Fugitive Kind.* Williams's career took off, and he went on to write over fifty plays, ten works of fiction, several books of poetry, and other collections of writing, including his letters and memoirs. His most successful plays include *The Glass Menagerie* (1945), *A Streetcar Named Desire* (1947), *Cat on a Hot Tin Roof* (1955), *Night of the Iguana* (1961), and *Sweet Bird of Youth* (1959). A recently rediscovered early play, *Not about Nightingales,* was staged in New York City in 1999.

The Glass Menagerie, Williams's first major success, won the New York Drama Critics Circle Award, freeing Williams to write plays full-time. *The Glass Menagerie* was written partly in Provincetown, Massachusetts, the site of Susan Glaspell's theater company (Glaspell is the author of the play *Trifles,* in Chapter 38), and partly in Hollywood, where Williams was working as a screenwriter. Williams saw his play as somewhat autobiographical: he said that his sister Rose had a collection of glass animals in her room in St. Louis, and he gave his own real first name to Tom, Laura's brother in the play. In the first movie version of the play, the story was altered to include a second, more promising Gentleman Caller at its conclusion, giving it a happy ending. To the end of his life, Williams strongly disliked this change.

Tennessee Williams found acclaim wherever he took his plays, from the age of thirty-four and the remarkable success of *The Glass Menagerie* until the end of his life. He received four New York Drama Critics Circle Awards, won a Pulitzer Prize for *Streetcar* in 1948, and saw both *Streetcar* and *The Glass Menagerie* made into successful Hollywood films. *Cat on a Hot Tin Roof* (for which he won his second Pulitzer), *Orpheus Descending,* and *Night of the Iguana* were also filmed.

Like *The Glass Menagerie,* Williams's other work was largely autobiographical, often drawing comparisons between his family and his characters and using the backdrops with which he was most familiar. Williams moved around a good deal — from New Orleans, to Key West, to New York City, to Provincetown. Each locale had a significant homosexual population, where Williams, who was gay, felt comfortable. He was a committed partner and suffered greatly when his love of many years, Frank Merlo, died of cancer in 1961.

Tennessee Williams battled alcoholism, drug abuse, and mental illness through much of his life. He fought constantly against the fear that he might go insane. His older sister Rose, who was diagnosed as schizophrenic, underwent a prefrontal lobotomy in her late twenties and was institutionalized for the remainder of her life; Williams himself suffered a mental breakdown at a young age. In the end, he choked to death on a bottle cap in his room at the Hotel Elysée in New York City.

His life and his work helped make Tennessee Williams one of America's best playwrights and one of the signature writers of the American South. His plays were bold and sometimes considered tawdry while those of his predecessors had been considered genteel and polite. Still, just as he was able to burst onto Broadway, he was able to spring on his readers a new type of drama that would forever change the way they saw the South.

The Glass Menagerie (1945)

Nobody, not even the rain, has such small hands.
E. E. Cummings

CHARACTERS

Amanda Wingfield, *the mother. A little woman of great but confused vitality clinging frantically to another time and place. Her characterization must be carefully created, not copied from type. She is not paranoiac, but her life is paranoia. There is much to admire in Amanda, and as much to love and pity as there is to laugh at. Certainly she has endurance and a kind of heroism, and though her foolishness makes her unwittingly cruel at times, there is tenderness in her slight person.*

Laura Wingfield, *her daughter. Amanda, having failed to establish contact with reality, continues to live vitally in her illusions, but Laura's situation is even graver. A childhood illness has left her crippled, one leg slightly shorter than the other, and held in a brace. This defect need not be more than suggested on the stage. Stemming from this, Laura's separation increases till she is like a piece of her own glass collection, too exquisitely fragile to move from the shelf.*

Tom Wingfield, *her son. And the narrator of the play. A poet with a job in a warehouse. His nature is not remorseless, but to escape from a trap he has to act without pity.*

Jim O'Connor, *the gentleman caller. A nice, ordinary, young man.*

SCENE

An alley in St. Louis.

PART I

Preparation for a Gentleman Caller.

PART II

The Gentleman Calls.

TIME

Now and the Past.

SCENE 1

The Wingfield apartment is in the rear of the building, one of those vast hive-like conglomerations of cellular living-units that flower as warty growths in overcrowded urban centers of lower middle-class population and are symptomatic of the impulse of this largest and fundamentally enslaved section of American society to avoid fluidity and differentiation and to exist and function as one interfused mass of automatism.

The apartment faces an alley and is entered by a fire-escape, a structure whose name is a touch of accidental poetic truth, for all of these huge buildings are always burning with the slow and implacable fires of human desperation. The fire-escape is included in the set—that is, the landing of it and steps descending from it.

The scene is memory and is therefore nonrealistic. Memory takes a lot of poetic license. It omits some details; others are exaggerated, according to the emotional value of the articles it touches, for memory is seated predominantly in the heart. The interior is therefore rather dim and poetic.

At the rise of the curtain, the audience is faced with the dark, grim rear wall of the Wingfield tenement. This building, which runs parallel to the footlights, is flanked on both sides by dark, narrow alleys which run into murky canyons of tangled clotheslines, garbage cans and the sinister latticework of neighboring fire-escapes. It is up and down these side alleys that exterior entrances and exits are made, during the play. At the end of Tom's opening commentary, the dark tenement wall slowly reveals (by means of a transparency) the interior of the ground floor Wingfield apartment.

Downstage is the living room, which also serves as a sleeping room for Laura, the sofa unfolding to make her bed. Upstage, center, and divided by a wide arch or second proscenium with transparent faded portieres (or second curtain), is the dining room. In an old-fashioned what-not in the living room are seen scores of transparent glass animals. A blown-up photograph of the father hangs on the wall of the living room, facing the audience, to the left of the archway. It is the face of a very handsome young man in a doughboy's First World War cap. He is gallantly smiling, ineluctably smiling, as if to say, "I will be smiling forever."

The audience hears and sees the opening scene in the dining room through both the transparent fourth wall of the building and the transparent gauze portieres of the dining-room arch. It is during this revealing scene that the fourth wall slowly ascends, out of sight. This transparent exterior wall is not brought down again until the very end of the play, during Tom's final speech.

The narrator is an undisguised convention of the play. He takes whatever license with dramatic convention as is convenient to his purposes.

Tom enters dressed as a merchant sailor from the alley, stage left, and strolls across the front of the stage to the fire-escape. There he stops and lights a cigarette. He addresses the audience.

TOM: Yes, I have tricks in my pocket, I have things up my sleeve. But I am the opposite of a stage magician. He gives you illusion that has the appearance of truth. I give you truth in the pleasant disguise of illusion. To begin with, I turn back time. I reverse it to that quaint period, the thirties, when the huge middle class of America was matriculating in a school for the blind.

Their eyes had failed them, or they had failed their eyes, and so they were having their fingers pressed forcibly down on the fiery Braille alphabet of a dissolving economy. In Spain there was revolution.° Here there was only shouting and confusion. In Spain there was Guernica.° Here there were disturbances of labor, sometimes pretty violent, in otherwise peaceful cities such as Chicago, Cleveland, Saint Louis. . . . This is the social background of the play.

Music.

The play is memory. Being a memory play, it is dimly lighted, it is sentimental, it is not realistic. In memory everything seems to happen to music. That explains the fiddle in the wings. I am the narrator of the play, and also a character in it. The other characters are my mother, Amanda, my sister, Laura, and a gentleman caller who appears in the final scenes. He is the most realistic character in the play, being an emissary from a world of reality that we were somehow set apart from. But since I have a poet's weakness for symbols, I am using this character also as a symbol; he is the long delayed but always expected something that we live for. There is a fifth character in the play who doesn't appear except in this larger-than-life photograph over the mantel. This is our father who left us a long time ago. He was a telephone man who fell in love with long distances; he gave up his job with the telephone company and skipped the light fantastic out of town. . . . The last we heard of him was a picture post-card from Mazatlan, on the Pacific coast of Mexico, containing a message of two words — "Hello — Good-bye!" and an address. I think the rest of the play will explain itself. . . .

Amanda's voice becomes audible through the portieres.

Legend On Screen: "Où Sont Les Neiges."°

He divides the portieres and enters the upstage area.

Amanda and Laura are seated at a drop-leaf table. Eating is indicated by gestures without food or utensils. Amanda faces the audience. Tom and Laura are seated in profile.

The interior has lit up softly and through the scrim we see Amanda and Laura seated at the table in the upstage area.

AMANDA: *(calling)* Tom?
TOM: Yes, Mother.
AMANDA: We can't say grace until you come to the table!

---

revolution: The Spanish Civil War (1936–1939).

Guernica: A Basque town in northern Spain, bombed and practically destroyed on April 27, 1937, by German planes aiding fascist General Francisco Franco's Nationalists. The destruction is depicted in one of Pablo Picasso's most famous paintings, *Guernica* (1937).

"Où Sont Les Neiges": "Where the snows [of yesteryear]." A famous line by French poet François Villon (1431–1463?).

TOM: Coming, Mother. *(He bows slightly and withdraws, reappearing a few moments later in his place at the table.)*

AMANDA: *(to her son)* Honey, don't *push* with your *fingers*. If you have to push with something, the thing to push with is a crust of bread. And chew — chew! Animals have sections in their stomachs which enable them to digest food without mastication, but human beings are supposed to chew their food before they swallow it down. Eat food leisurely, son, and really enjoy it. A well-cooked meal has lots of delicate flavors that have to be held in the mouth for appreciation. So chew your food and give your salivary glands a chance to function!

Tom deliberately lays his imaginary fork down and pushes his chair back from the table.

TOM: I haven't enjoyed one bite of this dinner because of your constant directions on how to eat it. It's you that makes me rush through meals with your hawk-like attention to every bite I take. Sickening — spoils my appetite — all this discussion of animals' secretion — salivary glands — mastication!

AMANDA: *(lightly)* Temperament like a Metropolitan star! *(He rises and crosses downstage.)* You're not excused from the table.

TOM: I am getting a cigarette.

AMANDA: You smoke too much.

Laura rises.

LAURA: I'll bring in the blanc mange.

He remains standing with his cigarette by the portieres during the following.

AMANDA: *(rising)* No, sister, no, sister — you be the lady this time and I'll be the darky.

LAURA: I'm already up.

AMANDA: Resume your seat, little sister — I want you to stay fresh and pretty — for gentlemen callers!

LAURA: I'm not expecting any gentlemen callers.

AMANDA: *(crossing out to kitchenette. Airily)* Sometimes they come when they are least expected! Why, I remember one Sunday afternoon in Blue Mountain — *(Enters kitchenette.)*

TOM: I know what's coming!

LAURA: Yes. But let her tell it.

TOM: Again?

LAURA: She loves to tell it.

Amanda returns with bowl of dessert.

AMANDA: One Sunday afternoon in Blue Mountain — your mother received — *seventeen!* — gentlemen callers! Why, sometimes there weren't chairs enough to accommodate them all. We had to send the nigger over to bring in folding chairs from the parish house.

TOM: *(remaining at portieres)* How did you entertain those gentlemen callers?

AMANDA: I understood the art of conversation!

TOM: I bet you could talk.

AMANDA: Girls in those days *knew* how to talk, I can tell you.

TOM: Yes?

Image: Amanda As A Girl On A Porch Greeting Callers.

AMANDA: They knew how to entertain their gentlemen callers. It wasn't enough for a girl to be possessed of a pretty face and a graceful figure — although I wasn't slighted in either respect. She also needed to have a nimble wit and a tongue to meet all occasions.

TOM: What did you talk about?

AMANDA: Things of importance going on in the world! Never anything coarse or common or vulgar. *(She addresses Tom as though he were seated in the vacant chair at the table though he remains by portieres. He plays this scene as though he held the book.)* My callers were gentlemen — all! Among my callers were some of the most prominent young planters of the Mississippi Delta — planters and sons of planters!

Tom motions for music and a spot of light on Amanda. Her eyes lift, her face glows, her voice becomes rich and elegiac.

Screen Legend: "Où Sont Les Neiges."

There was young Champ Laughlin who later became vice-president of the Delta Planters Bank. Hadley Stevenson who was drowned in Moon Lake and left his widow one hundred and fifty thousand in Government bonds. There were the Cutrere brothers, Wesley and Bates. Bates was one of my bright particular beaux! He got in a quarrel with that wild Wainright boy. They shot it out on the floor of Moon Lake Casino. Bates was shot through the stomach. Died in the ambulance on his way to Memphis. His widow was also well-provided for, came into eight or ten thousand acres, that's all. She married him on the rebound — never loved her — carried my picture on him the night he died! And there was that boy that every girl in the Delta had set her cap for! That beautiful, brilliant young Fitzhugh boy from Green County!

TOM: What did he leave his widow?

AMANDA: He never married! Gracious, you talk as though all of my old admirers had turned up their toes to the daisies!

TOM: Isn't this the first you mentioned that still survives?

AMANDA: That Fitzhugh boy went North and made a fortune — came to be known as the Wolf of Wall Street! He had the Midas touch, whatever he touched turned to gold! And I could have been Mrs. Duncan J. Fitzhugh, mind you! But — I picked your *father!*

LAURA: *(rising)* Mother, let me clear the table.

AMANDA: No dear, you go in front and study your typewriter chart. Or practice your shorthand a little. Stay fresh and pretty! — It's almost time for our gentlemen callers to start arriving. *(She flounces girlishly toward the kitchenette.)* How many do you suppose we're going to entertain this afternoon?

Tom throws down the paper and jumps up with a groan.

LAURA: *(alone in the dining room)* I don't believe we're going to receive any, Mother.

AMANDA: *(reappearing, airily)* What? No one — not one? You must be joking! *(Laura nervously echoes her laugh. She slips in a fugitive manner through the half-open portieres and draws them gently behind her. A shaft of very clear light is thrown on her face against the faded tapestry of the curtains.) (Music: "The Glass Menagerie" under faintly.) (Lightly.)* Not one gentleman caller? It can't be true! There must be a flood, there must have been a tornado!

LAURA: It isn't a flood, it's not a tornado, Mother. I'm just not popular like you were in Blue Mountain. . . . *(Tom utters another groan. Laura glances at him with a faint, apologetic smile. Her voice catching a little.)* Mother's afraid I'm going to be an old maid.

The Scene Dims Out With "Glass Menagerie" Music.

SCENE 2

"Laura, Haven't You Ever Liked Some Boy?"

On the dark stage the screen is lighted with the image of blue roses.

Gradually Laura's figure becomes apparent and the screen goes out.

The music subsides.

Laura is seated in the delicate ivory chair at the small clawfoot table.

She wears a dress of soft violet material for a kimono — her hair tied back from her forehead with a ribbon.

She is washing and polishing her collection of glass.

Amanda appears on the fire-escape steps. At the sound of her ascent, Laura catches her breath, thrusts the bowl of ornaments away and seats herself stiffly before the diagram of the typewriter keyboard as though it held her spellbound. Something has happened to Amanda. It is written in her face as she climbs to the landing: a look that is grim and hopeless and a little absurd.

She has on one of those cheap or imitation velvety-looking cloth coats with imitation fur collar. Her hat is five or six years old, one of those dreadful cloche hats that were worn in the late twenties, and she is clasping an enormous black patent-leather pocketbook with nickel clasp and initials. This is her fulldress outfit, the one she usually wears to the D.A.R.°

Before entering she looks through the door.

She purses her lips, opens her eyes wide, rolls them upward and shakes her head.

D.A.R.: Daughters of the American Revolution, an organization for female descendants of participants in the American Revolution, founded in 1890. That Amanda is a member says much about her concern with the past, as well as about her pride and affectations.

Then she slowly lets herself in the door. Seeing her mother's expression Laura touches her lips with a nervous gesture.

LAURA: Hello, Mother, I was — (*She makes a nervous gesture toward the chart on the wall. Amanda leans against the shut door and stares at Laura with a martyred look.*)

AMANDA: Deception? Deception? (*She slowly removes her hat and gloves, continuing the swift suffering stare. She lets the hat and gloves fall on the floor — a bit of acting.*)

LAURA: (*shakily*) How was the D.A.R. meeting? (*Amanda slowly opens her purse and removes a dainty white handkerchief which she shakes out delicately and delicately touches to her lips and nostrils.*) Didn't you go to the D.A.R. meeting, Mother?

AMANDA: (*faintly, almost inaudibly*) — No. — No. (*Then more forcibly.*) I did not have the strength — to go the D.A.R. In fact, I did not have the courage! I wanted to find a hole in the ground and hide myself in it forever! (*She crosses slowly to the wall and removes the diagram of the typewriter keyboard. She holds it in front of her for a second, staring at it sweetly and sorrowfully — then bites her lips and tears it in two pieces.*)

LAURA: (*faintly*) Why did you do that, Mother? (*Amanda repeats the same procedure with the chart of the Gregg Alphabet.*) Why are you —

AMANDA: Why? Why? How old are you, Laura?

LAURA: Mother, you know my age.

AMANDA: I thought that you were an adult; it seems that I was mistaken. (*She crosses slowly to the sofa and sinks down and stares at Laura.*)

LAURA: Please don't stare at me, Mother.

Amanda closes her eyes and lowers her head. Count ten.

AMANDA: What are we going to do, what is going to become of us, what is the future?

Count ten.

LAURA: Has something happened, Mother? (*Amanda draws a long breath and takes out the handkerchief again. Dabbing process.*) Mother, has — something happened?

AMANDA: I'll be all right in a minute. I'm just bewildered — (*count five*) — by life. . . .

LAURA: Mother, I wish that you would tell me what's happened.

AMANDA: As you know, I was supposed to be inducted into my office at the D.A.R. this afternoon. (*Image: A Swarm Of Typewriters.*) But I stopped off at Rubicam's Business College to speak to your teachers about your having a cold and ask them what progress they thought you were making down there.

LAURA: Oh. . . .

AMANDA: I went to the typing instructor and introduced myself as your mother. She didn't know who you were. Wingfield, she said. We don't have any such student enrolled at the school! I assured her she did, that you had been going to classes since early in January. "I wonder," she said, "if you could be talking about that terribly shy little girl who dropped out of school after only a few days' attendance?" "No," I said, "Laura, my daughter, has been going to school every day for the past six weeks!" "Excuse me," she said. She took the attendance book out and there was your name, unmistakably printed, and all the dates you were absent until they decided that you had dropped out of school. I still said, "No, there must have been some mistake! There must have been some mix-up in the records!" And she said, "No — I remember her perfectly now. Her hand shook so that she couldn't hit the right keys! The first time we gave a speed-test, she broke down completely — was sick at the stomach and almost had to be carried into the wash-room! After that morning she never showed up any more. We phoned the house but never got any answer" — while I was working at Famous and Barr, I suppose, demonstrating those — Oh! I felt so weak I could barely keep on my feet. I had to sit down while they got me a glass of water! Fifty dollars' tuition, all of our plans — my hopes and ambitions for you — just gone up the spout, just gone up the spout like that. *(Laura draws a long breath and gets awkwardly to her feet. She crosses to the Victrola and winds it up.)* What are you doing?

LAURA: Oh! *(She releases the handle and returns to her seat.)*

AMANDA: Laura, where have you been going when you've gone out pretending that you were going to business college?

LAURA: I've just been going out walking.

AMANDA: That's not true.

LAURA: It is. I just went walking.

AMANDA: Walking? Walking? In winter? Deliberately courting pneumonia in that light coat? Where did you walk to, Laura?

LAURA: It was the lesser of two evils, Mother. *(Image: Winter Scene In Park.)* I couldn't go back up. I — threw up — on the floor!

AMANDA: From half past seven till after five every day you mean to tell me you walked around in the park, because you wanted to make me think that you were still going to Rubicam's Business College?

LAURA: It wasn't as bad as it sounds. I went inside places to get warmed up.

AMANDA: Inside where?

LAURA: I went in the art museum and the bird-houses at the Zoo. I visited the penguins every day! Sometimes I did without lunch and went to the movies. Lately I've been spending most of my afternoons in the Jewel-box, that big glass house where they raise the tropical flowers.

AMANDA: You did all this to deceive me, just for the deception? *(Laura looks down.)* Why?

LAURA: Mother, when you're disappointed, you get that awful suffering look on your face, like the picture of Jesus' mother in the museum!

AMANDA: Hush!

LAURA: I couldn't face it.

Pause. A whisper of strings.

Legend: "The Crust Of Humility."

AMANDA: *(hopelessly fingering the huge pocketbook)* So what are we going to do the rest of our lives? Stay home and watch the parades go by? Amuse ourselves with the glass menagerie, darling? Eternally play those worn-out phonograph records your father left as a painful reminder of him? We won't have a business career — we've given that up because it gave us nervous indigestion! *(Laughs wearily.)* What is there left but dependency all our lives? I know so well what becomes of unmarried women who aren't prepared to occupy a position. I've seen such pitiful cases in the South — barely tolerated spinsters living upon the grudging patronage of sister's husband or brother's wife! — stuck away in some little mouse-trap of a room — encouraged by one in-law to visit another — little birdlike women without any nest — eating the crust of humility all their life! Is that the future that we've mapped out for ourselves? I swear it's the only alternative I can think of! It isn't a very pleasant alternative, is it? Of course — some girls *do marry*. *(Laura twists her hands nervously.)* Haven't you ever liked some boy?

LAURA: Yes I liked one once. *(Rises.)* I came across his picture a while ago.

AMANDA: *(with some interest)* He gave you his picture?

LAURA: No, it's in the year-book.

AMANDA: *(disappointed)* Oh — a high-school boy.

Screen Image: Jim As A High-School Hero Bearing A Silver Cup.

LAURA: Yes. His name was Jim. *(Laura lifts the heavy annual from the clawfoot table.)* Here he is in *The Pirates of Penzance*.°

AMANDA: *(absently)* The what?

LAURA: The operetta the senior class put on. He had a wonderful voice and we sat across the aisle from each other Mondays, Wednesdays and Fridays in the Aud. Here he is with the silver cup for debating! See his grin?

AMANDA: *(absently)* He must have had a jolly disposition.

LAURA: He used to call me — Blue Roses.

Image: Blue Roses.

AMANDA: Why did he call you such a name as that?

LAURA: When I had that attack of pleurosis — he asked me what was the matter when I came back. I said pleurosis — he thought that I said Blue Roses! So that's what he always called me after that. Whenever he saw me, he'd holler, "Hello, Blue Roses!" I didn't care for the girl that he went out with. Emily Meisenbach. Emily was the best-dressed girl at Soldan. She never struck me, though, as being sincere . . . It says in the Personal Section — they're engaged. That's — six years ago! They must be married by now.

The Pirates of Penzance: A musical by Gilbert and Sullivan.

Amanda: Girls that aren't cut out for business careers usually wind up married to some nice man. *(Gets up with a spark of revival.)* Sister, that's what you'll do!

Laura utters a startled, doubtful laugh. She reaches quickly for a piece of glass.

Laura: But, Mother —

Amanda: Yes? *(Crossing to photograph.)*

Laura: *(in a tone of frightened apology)* I'm — crippled!

Image: Screen.

Amanda: Nonsense! Laura, I've told you never, never to use that word. Why, you're not crippled, you just have a little defect — hardly noticeable, even! When people have some slight disadvantage like that, they cultivate other things to make up for it — develop charm — and vivacity — and — charm! That's all you have to do! *(She turns again to the photograph.)* One thing your father had *plenty* of — was *charm!*

Tom motions to the fiddle in the wings.

The Scene Fades Out With Music.

SCENE 3

Legend On The Screen: "After The Fiasco —"

Tom speaks from the fire-escape landing.

Tom: After the fiasco at Rubicam's Business College, the idea of getting a gentleman caller for Laura began to play a more important part in Mother's calculations. It became an obsession. Like some archetype of the universal unconscious, the image of the gentleman caller haunted our small apartment. . . . *(Image: Young Man At Door With Flowers.)* An evening at home rarely passed without some allusion to this image, this spectre, this hope. . . . Even when he wasn't mentioned, his presence hung in Mother's preoccupied look and in my sister's frightened, apologetic manner — hung like a sentence passed upon the Wingfields! Mother was a woman of action as well as words. She began to take logical steps in the planned direction. Late that winter and in the early spring — realizing that extra money would be needed to properly feather the nest and plume the bird — she conducted a vigorous campaign on the telephone, roping in subscribers to one of those magazines for matrons called *The Home-maker's Companion*, the type of journal that features the serialized sublimations of ladies of letters who think in terms of delicate cup-like breasts, slim, tapering waists, rich, creamy thighs, eyes like wood-smoke in autumn, fingers that soothe and caress like strains of music, bodies as powerful as Etruscan sculpture.

Screen Image: A Glamour Magazine Cover.

Amanda enters with phone on long extension cord. She is spotted in the dim stage.

AMANDA: Ida Scott? This is Amanda Wingfield! We *missed* you at the D.A.R. last Monday! I said to myself: She's probably suffering with that sinus condition! How is that sinus condition? Horrors! Heaven have mercy!—You're a Christian martyr, yes, that's what you are, a Christian martyr! Well, I just now happened to notice that your subscription to the *Companion's* about to expire! Yes, it expires with the next issue, honey!—just when that wonderful new serial by Bessie Mae Hopper is getting off to such an exciting start. Oh, honey, it's something that you can't miss! You remember how *Gone With the Wind* took everybody by storm? You simply couldn't go out if you hadn't read it. All everybody *talked* was Scarlett O'Hara. Well, this is a book that critics already compare to *Gone With the Wind*. It's the *Gone With the Wind* of the post–World War generation!—What?—Burning?—Oh, honey, don't let them burn, go take a look in the oven and I'll hold the wire! Heavens—I think she's hung up!

Dim Out.

Legend On Screen: "You Think I'm In Love With Continental Shoemakers?"

Before the stage is lighted, the violent voices of Tom and Amanda are heard. They are quarreling behind the portieres. In front of them stands Laura with clenched hands and panicky expression.

A clear pool of light on her figure throughout this scene.

TOM: What in Christ's name am I—
AMANDA: *(shrilly)* Don't you use that—
TOM: Supposed to do!
AMANDA: Expression! Not in my—
TOM: Ohhh!
AMANDA: Presence! Have you gone out of your senses?
TOM: I have, that's true, *driven* out!
AMANDA: What is the matter with you, you—big—big—IDIOT!
TOM: Look—I've got *no thing*, no single thing—
AMANDA: Lower your voice!
TOM: In my life here that I can call my OWN! Everything is—
AMANDA: Stop that shouting!
TOM: Yesterday you confiscated my books! You had the nerve to—
AMANDA: I took that horrible novel back to the library—yes! That hideous book by that insane Mr. Lawrence.° *(Tom laughs wildly.)* I cannot control the output of diseased minds or people who cater to them—*(Tom laughs still more wildly.)* BUT I WON'T ALLOW SUCH FILTH BROUGHT INTO MY HOUSE! No, no, no, no, no!
TOM: House, house! Who pays rent on it, who makes a slave of himself to—

Mr. Lawrence: English novelist D. H. Lawrence (1885–1930). The reference is to his 1928 novel *Lady Chatterley's Lover,* which was banned in the United States and England because of its frank treatment of sexuality.

AMANDA: *(fairly screeching)* Don't you DARE to —

TOM: No, no, *I* mustn't say things! *I've* got to just —

AMANDA: Let me tell you —

TOM: I don't want to hear any more! *(He tears the portieres open. The upstage area is lit with a turgid smoky red glow.)*

Amanda's hair is in metal curlers and she wears a very old bathrobe, much too large for her slight figure, a relic of the faithless Mr. Wingfield.

An upright typewriter and a wild disarray of manuscripts are on the drop-leaf table. The quarrel was probably precipitated by Amanda's interruption of his creative labor. A chair lying overthrown on the floor.

Their gesticulating shadows are cast on the ceiling by the fiery glow.

AMANDA: You *will* hear more, you —

TOM: No, I won't hear more, I'm going out!

AMANDA: You come right back in —

TOM: Out, out out! Because I'm —

AMANDA: Come back here, Tom Wingfield! I'm not through talking to you!

TOM: Oh, go —

LAURA: *(desperately)* Tom!

AMANDA: You're going to listen, and no more insolence from you! I'm at the end of my patience! *(He comes back toward her.)*

TOM: What do you think I'm at? Aren't I supposed to have any patience to reach the end of, Mother? I know, I know. It seems unimportant to you, what I'm *doing*— what I *want* to do — having a little *difference* between them! You don't think that —

AMANDA: I think you've been doing things that you're ashamed of. That's why you act like this. I don't believe that you go every night to the movies. Nobody goes to the movies night after night. Nobody in their right mind goes to the movies as often as you pretend to. People don't go to the movies at nearly midnight, and movies don't let out at two A.M. Come in stumbling. Muttering to yourself like a maniac! You get three hours' sleep and then go to work. Oh, I can picture the way you're doing down there. Moping, doping, because you're in no condition.

TOM: *(wildly)* No, I'm in no condition!

AMANDA: What right have you got to jeopardize your job? Jeopardize the security of us all? How do you think we'd manage if you were —

TOM: Listen! You think I'm crazy *about* the *warehouse? (He bends fiercely toward her slight figure.)* You think I'm in love with the Continental Shoemakers? You think I want to spend fifty-five *years* down there in that — *celotex interior!* with — *fluorescent* — *tubes!* Look! I'd rather somebody picked up a crowbar and battered out my brains — than go back mornings! I *go!* Every time you come in yelling that God damn *"Rise and Shine!" "Rise and Shine!"* I say to myself "How *lucky dead* people are!" But I get up. I *go!* For sixty-five dollars a month I give up all that I dream of doing and being *ever!* And you say self — *self's* all I ever think of. Why, listen, if self is what I thought of,

Mother, I'd be where he is — GONE! *(Pointing to father's picture.)* As far as the system of transportation reaches! *(He starts past her. She grabs his arm.)* Don't grab at me, Mother!

AMANDA: Where are you going?

TOM: I'm going to the *movies!*

AMANDA: I don't believe that lie!

TOM: *(crouching toward her, overtowering her tiny figure. She backs away, gasping)* I'm going to opium dens! Yes, opium dens, dens of vice and criminals' hang-outs, Mother. I've joined the Hogan gang, I'm a hired assassin, I carry a tommy-gun in a violin case! I run a string of cat-houses in the Valley! They call me Killer, Killer Wingfield, I'm leading a double-life, a simple, honest warehouse worker by day, by night a dynamic *czar of the underworld, Mother.* I go to gambling casinos, I spin away fortunes on the roulette table! I wear a patch over one eye and a false mustache, sometimes I put on green whiskers. On those occasions they call me — *El Diablo!* Oh, I could tell you things to make you sleepless! My enemies plan to dynamite this place. They're going to blow us all sky-high some night! I'll be glad, very happy, and so will you! You'll go up, up on a broomstick, over Blue Mountain with seventeen gentlemen callers! You ugly — babbling old — *witch. . . . (He goes through a series of violent, clumsy movements, seizing his overcoat, lunging to the door, pulling it fiercely open. The women watch him, aghast. His arm catches in the sleeve of the coat as he struggles to pull it on. For a moment he is pinioned by the bulky garment. With an outraged groan he tears the coat off again, splitting the shoulders of it, and hurls it across the room. It strikes against the shelf of Laura's glass collection, there is a tinkle of shattering glass. Laura cries out as if wounded.)*

Music Legend: "The Glass Menagerie."

LAURA: My *glass!* — menagerie. . . . *(She covers her face and turns away.)*

But Amanda is still stunned and stupefied by the "ugly witch" so that she barely notices this occurrence. Now she recovers her speech.

AMANDA: *(in an awful voice) I won't speak to you — until you apologize! (She crosses through portieres and draws them together behind her. Tom is left with Laura. Laura clings weakly to the mantel with her face averted. Tom stares at her stupidly for a moment. Then he crosses to shelf. Drops awkwardly to his knees to collect the fallen glass, glancing at Laura as if he would speak but couldn't.)*

"The Glass Menagerie" steals in as The Scene Dims Out.

SCENE 4

The interior is dark. Faint in the alley.

A deep-voiced bell in a church is tolling the hour of five as the scene commences.

Tom appears at the top of the alley. After each solemn boom of the bell in the tower, he shakes a little noise-maker or rattle as if to express the tiny spasm of man in contrast to the sustained power and dignity of the Almighty. This and the unsteadiness of his advance make it evident that he has been drinking.

As he climbs the few steps to the fire-escape landing light steals up inside. Laura appears in night-dress, observing Tom's empty bed in the front room.

Tom fishes in his pockets for the door-key, removing a motley assortment of articles in the search, including a perfect shower of movie-ticket stubs and an empty bottle. At last he finds the key, but just as he is about to insert it, it slips from his fingers. He strikes a match and crouches below the door.

TOM: *(bitterly)* One crack — and it falls through!

Laura opens the door.

LAURA: Tom! Tom, what are you doing?

TOM: Looking for a door-key.

LAURA: Where have you been all this time?

TOM: I have been to the movies.

LAURA: All this time at the movies?

TOM: There was a very long program. There was a Garbo picture and a Mickey Mouse and a travelogue and a newsreel and a preview of coming attractions. And there was an organ solo and a collection for the milk-fund — simultaneously — which ended up in a terrible fight between a fat lady and an usher!

LAURA: *(innocently)* Did you have to stay through everything?

TOM: Of course! And, oh, I forgot! There was a big stage show! The headliner on this stage show was Malvolio the Magician. He performed wonderful tricks, many of them, such as pouring water back and forth between pitchers. First it turned to wine and then it turned to beer and then it turned to whiskey. I know it was whiskey it finally turned into because he needed somebody to come up out of the audience to help him, and I came up — both shows! It was Kentucky Straight Bourbon. A very generous fellow, he gave souvenirs. *(He pulls from his back pocket a shimmering rainbow-colored scarf.)* He gave me this. This is his magic scarf. You can have it, Laura. You wave it over a canary cage and you get a bowl of gold-fish. You wave it over the gold-fish bowl and they fly away canaries. . . . But the wonderfullest trick of all was the coffin trick. We nailed him into a coffin and he got out of the coffin without removing one nail. *(He has come inside.)* There is a trick that would come in handy for me — get me out of this 2 by 4 situation! *(Flops onto bed and starts removing shoes.)*

LAURA: Tom — Shhh!

TOM: What you shushing me for?

LAURA: You'll wake up Mother.

TOM: Goody, goody! Pay 'er back for all those "Rise an' Shines." *(Lies down, groaning.)* You know it don't take much intelligence to get yourself into a nailed-up coffin, Laura. But who in hell ever got himself out of one without removing one nail?

As if in answer, the father's grinning photograph lights up.

Scene Dims Out.

Immediately following: The church bell is heard striking six. At the sixth stroke the alarm clock goes off in Amanda's room, and after a few moments we hear her calling: "Rise and Shine! Rise and Shine! Laura, go tell your brother to rise and shine!"

TOM: *(sitting up slowly)* I'll rise — but I won't shine.

The light increases.

AMANDA: Laura, tell your brother his coffee is ready.

Laura slips into front room.

LAURA: Tom! It's nearly seven. Don't make Mother nervous. *(He stares at her stupidly. Beseechingly.)* Tom, speak to Mother this morning. Make up with her, apologize, speak to her!

TOM: She won't to me. It's her that started not speaking.

LAURA: If you just say you're sorry she'll start speaking.

TOM: Her not speaking — is that such a tragedy?

LAURA: Please — please!

AMANDA: *(calling from kitchenette)* Laura, are you going to do what I asked you to do, or do I have to get dressed and go out myself?

LAURA: Going, going — soon as I get on my coat! *(She pulls on a shapeless felt hat with nervous, jerky movement, pleadingly glancing at Tom. Rushes awkwardly for coat. The coat is one of Amanda's inaccurately made-over, the sleeves too short for Laura.)* Butter and what else?

AMANDA: *(entering upstage)* Just butter. Tell them to charge it.

LAURA: Mother, they make such faces when I do that.

AMANDA: Sticks and stones may break my bones, but the expression on Mr. Garfinkel's face won't harm us! Tell your brother his coffee is getting cold.

LAURA: *(at door)* Do what I asked you, will you, will you, Tom?

He looks sullenly away.

AMANDA: Laura, go now or just don't go at all!

LAURA: *(rushing out)* Going — going! *(A second later she cries out. Tom springs up and crosses to the door. Amanda rushes anxiously in. Tom opens the door.)*

TOM: Laura?

LAURA: I'm all right. I slipped, but I'm all right.

AMANDA: *(peering anxiously after her)* If anyone breaks a leg on those fire-escape steps, the landlord ought to be sued for every cent he possesses! *(She shuts door. Remembers she isn't speaking and returns to other room.)*

As Tom enters listlessly for his coffee, she turns her back to him and stands rigidly facing the window on the gloomy gray vault of the areaway. Its light on her face with its aged but childish features is cruelly sharp, satirical as a Daumier print.

Music Under: "Ave Maria."

Tom glances sheepishly but sullenly at her averted figure and slumps at the table. The coffee is scalding hot; he sips it and gasps and spits it back in the cup. At his gasp, Amanda catches her breath and half turns. Then catches herself and turns back to window.

Tom blows on his coffee, glancing sidewise at his mother. She clears her throat. Tom clears his. He starts to rise. Sinks back down again, scratches his head, clears his throat again. Amanda coughs. Tom raises his cup in both hands to blow on it, his eyes staring over the rim of it at his mother for several moments. Then he slowly sets the cup down and awkwardly and hesitantly rises from the chair.

TOM: *(hoarsely)* Mother. I — I apologize. Mother. *(Amanda draws a quick, shuddering breath. Her face works grotesquely. She breaks into childlike tears.)* I'm sorry for what I said, for everything that I said, I didn't mean it.

AMANDA: *(sobbingly)* My devotion has made me a witch and so I make myself hateful to my children!

TOM: No, you *don't.*

AMANDA: I worry so much, don't sleep, it makes me nervous!

TOM: *(gently)* I understand that.

AMANDA: I've had to put up a solitary battle all these years. But you're my right-hand bower! Don't fall down, don't fail!

TOM: *(gently)* I try, Mother.

AMANDA: *(with great enthusiasm)* Try and you will SUCCEED! *(The notion makes her breathless.)* Why, you — you're just *full* of natural endowments! Both of my children — they're *unusual* children! Don't you think I know it? I'm so — *proud!* Happy and — feel I've — so much to be thankful for but — Promise me one thing, son!

TOM: What, Mother?

AMANDA: Promise, son, you'll — never be a drunkard!

TOM: *(turns to her grinning)* I will never be a drunkard, Mother.

AMANDA: That's what frightened me so, that you'd be drinking! Eat a bowl of Purina!

TOM: Just coffee, Mother.

AMANDA: Shredded wheat biscuit?

TOM: No. No, Mother, just coffee.

AMANDA: You can't put in a day's work on an empty stomach. You've got ten minutes — don't gulp! Drinking too-hot liquids makes cancer of the stomach. . . . Put cream in.

TOM: No, thank you.

AMANDA: To cool it.

TOM: No! No, thank you, I want it black.

AMANDA: I know, but it's not good for you. We have to do all that we can to build ourselves up. In these trying times we live in, all that we have to cling to is — each other. . . . That's why it's so important to — Tom, I — I sent out your sister so I could discuss something with you. If you hadn't spoken I would have spoken to you. *(Sits down.)*

TOM: *(gently)* What is it, Mother, that you want to discuss?

AMANDA: Laura!

Tom puts his cup down slowly.

Legend On Screen: "Laura."

Music: "The Glass Menagerie."

TOM: — Oh. — Laura . . .

AMANDA: *(touching his sleeve)* You know how Laura is. So quiet but — still water runs deep! She notices things and I think she — broods about them. *(Tom looks up.)* A few days ago I came in and she was crying.

TOM: What about?

AMANDA: You.

TOM: Me?

AMANDA: She has an idea that you're not happy here.

TOM: What gave her that idea?

AMANDA: What gives her any idea? However, you do act strangely. I — I'm not criticizing, understand *that!* I know your ambitions do not lie in the warehouse, that like everybody in the whole wide world — you've had to — make sacrifices, but — Tom — Tom — life's not easy, it calls for — Spartan endurance! There's so many things in my heart that I cannot describe to you! I've never told you but I — *loved* your father. . . .

TOM: (gently) I know that, Mother.

AMANDA: And you — when I see you taking after his ways! Staying out late — and — well, you *had* been drinking the night you were in that — terrifying condition! Laura says that you hate the apartment and that you go out nights to get away from it! Is that true, Tom?

TOM: No. You say there's so much in your heart that you can't describe to me. That's true of me, too. There's so much in my heart that I can't describe to *you!* So let's respect each other's —

AMANDA: But, why — *why*, Tom — are you always so *restless?* Where do you go to, nights?

TOM: I — go to the movies.

AMANDA: Why do you go to the movies so much, Tom?

TOM: I go to the movies because — I like adventure. Adventure is something I don't have much of at work, so I go to the movies.

AMANDA: But, Tom, you go to the movies *entirely* too *much!*

TOM: I like a lot of adventure.

Amanda looks baffled, then hurt. As the familiar inquisition resumes he becomes hard and impatient again. Amanda slips back into her querulous attitude toward him.

Image On Screen: Sailing Vessel With Jolly Roger.

AMANDA: Most young men find adventure in their careers.

TOM: Then most young men are not employed in a warehouse.

AMANDA: The world is full of young men employed in warehouses and offices and factories.

TOM: Do all of them find adventure in their careers?

AMANDA: They do or they do without it! Not everybody has a craze for adventure.

TOM: Man is by instinct a lover, a hunter, a fighter, and none of those instincts are given much play at the warehouse!

AMANDA: Man is by instinct! Don't quote instinct to me! Instinct is something that people have got away from! It belongs to animals! Christian adults don't want it!

TOM: What do Christian adults want, then, Mother?

AMANDA: Superior things! Things of the mind and the spirit! Only animals have to satisfy instincts! Surely your aims are somewhat higher than theirs! Than monkeys — pigs —

TOM: I reckon they're not.

AMANDA: You're joking. However, that isn't what I wanted to discuss.

TOM: *(rising)* I haven't much time.

AMANDA: *(pushing his shoulders)* Sit down.

TOM: You want me to punch in red at the warehouse, Mother?

AMANDA: You have five minutes. I want to talk about Laura.

Legend: "Plans And Provisions."

TOM: All right! What about Laura?

AMANDA: We have to be making plans and provisions for her. She's older than you, two years, and nothing has happened. She just drifts along doing nothing. It frightens me terribly how she just drifts along.

TOM: I guess she's the type that people call home-girls.

AMANDA: There's no such type, and if there is, it's a pity! That is unless the home is hers, with a husband!

TOM: What?

AMANDA: Oh, I can see the handwriting on the wall as plain as I see the nose in front of my face! It's terrifying! More and more you remind me of your father! He was out all hours without explanation — Then *left! Good-bye!* And me with the bag to hold. I saw that letter you got from the Merchant Marine. I know what you're dreaming of. I'm not standing here blindfolded. Very well, then. Then *do* it! But not till there's somebody to take your place.

TOM: What do you mean?

AMANDA: I mean that as soon as Laura has got somebody to take care of her, married, a home of her own, independent — why, then you'll be free to go wherever you please, on land, on sea, whichever way the wind blows! But until that time you've got to look out for your sister. I don't say me because I'm old and don't matter! I say for your sister because she's young and dependent. I put her in business college — a dismal failure! Frightened her so it made her sick to her stomach. I took her over to the Young People's League at the church. Another fiasco. She spoke to nobody, nobody spoke to her. Now all she does is fool with those pieces of glass and play those worn-out records. What kind of a life is that for a girl to lead!

TOM: What can I do about it?

AMANDA: Overcome selfishness! Self, self, self is all that you ever think of! *(Tom springs up and crosses to get his coat. It is ugly and bulky. He pulls on a cap with earmuffs.)* Where is your muffler? Put your wool muffler on! *(He snatches it angrily from the closet and tosses it around his neck and pulls both ends tight.)* Tom! I haven't said what I had in mind to ask you.

TOM: I'm too late to —

AMANDA: *(catching his arms — very importunately. Then shyly)* Down at the warehouse, aren't there some — nice young men?

TOM: No!

AMANDA: There *must* be — *some* . . .

TOM: Mother—

Gesture.

AMANDA: Find out one that's clean-living — doesn't drink and — ask him out for sister!

TOM: What?

AMANDA: For *sister!* To *meet!* Get *acquainted!*

TOM: *(stamping to door)* Oh, my *go-osh!*

AMANDA: Will you? *(He opens door. Imploringly.)* Will you? *(He starts down.)* Will you? *Will* you, dear?

TOM: *(calling back)* YES!

Amanda closes the door hesitantly and with a troubled but faintly hopeful expression.

(Screen Image: A Glamour Magazine Cover.)

Spot Amanda at phone.

AMANDA: Ella Cartwright? This is Amanda Wingfield! How are you, honey? How is that kidney condition? *(Count five.) Horrors! (Count five.)* You're a Christian martyr, yes, honey, that's what you are, a Christian martyr! Well, I just happened to notice in my little red book that your subscription to the *Companion* has just run out! I knew that you wouldn't want to miss out on the wonderful serial starting in this new issue. It's by Bessie Mae Hopper, the first thing she's written since *Honeymoon for Three*. Wasn't that a strange and interesting story? Well, this one is even lovelier, I believe. It has a sophisticated society background. It's all about the horsey set on Long Island!

Fade Out.

SCENE 5

(Legend On Screen: "Annunciation.") Fade with music.

It is early dusk of a spring evening. Supper has just been finished in the Wingfield apartment. Amanda and Laura in light colored dresses are removing dishes from the table, in the upstage area, which is shadowy, their movements formalized almost as a dance or ritual, their moving forms as pale and silent as moths.

Tom, in white shirt and trousers, rises from the table and crosses toward the fire-escape.

AMANDA: *(as he passes her)* Son, will you do me a favor?

TOM: What?

AMANDA: Comb your hair! You look so pretty when your hair is combed! *(Tom slouches on sofa with evening paper. Enormous caption "Franco Triumphs.")* There is only one respect in which I would like you to emulate your father.

TOM: What respect is that?

AMANDA: The care he always took of his appearance. He never allowed himself to look untidy. *(He throws down the paper and crosses to fire-escape.)* Where are you going?

TOM: I'm going out to smoke.

AMANDA: You smoke too much. A pack a day at fifteen cents a pack. How much would that amount to in a month? Thirty times fifteen is how much, Tom? Figure it out and you will be astounded at what you could save. Enough to give you a night-school course in accounting at Washington U! Just think what a wonderful thing that would be for you, son!

Tom is unmoved by the thought.

TOM: I'd rather smoke. *(He steps out on landing, letting the screen door slam.)*

AMANDA: *(sharply)* I know! That's the tragedy of it. . . . *(Alone, she turns to look at her husband's picture.)*

Dance Music: "All The World Is Waiting For The Sunrise!"

TOM: *(to the audience)* Across the alley from us was the Paradise Dance Hall. On evenings in spring the windows and doors were open and the music came outdoors. Sometimes the lights were turned out except for a large glass sphere that hung from the ceiling. It would turn slowly about and filter the dusk with delicate rainbow colors. Then the orchestra played a waltz or a tango, something that had a slow and sensuous rhythm. Couples would come outside, to the relative privacy of the alley. You could see them kissing behind ash-pits and telephone poles. This was the compensation for lives that passed like mine, without any change or adventure. Adventure and change were imminent in this year. They were waiting around the corner for all these kids. Suspended in the mist over Berchtesgaden,° caught in the folds of Chamberlain's umbrella°— In Spain there was Guernica! But here there was only hot swing music and liquor, dance halls, bars,

---

Berchtesgaden: A resort in Germany, in the Bavarian Alps; the site of Adolf Hitler's fortified retreat, the Berghof.
Chamberlain's umbrella: (Arthur) Neville Chamberlain (1869–1940)— Conservative Party prime minister of England (1937–1940) who advocated a policy of appeasement toward Hitler. Political cartoons often showed him carrying an umbrella.

and movies, and sex that hung in the gloom like a chandelier and flooded the world with brief, deceptive rainbows. . . . All the world was waiting for bombardments!

Amanda turns from the picture and comes outside.

AMANDA: *(sighing)* A fire-escape landing's a poor excuse for a porch. *(She spreads a newspaper on a step and sits down, gracefully and demurely as if she were settling into a swing on a Mississippi veranda.)* What are you looking at?

TOM: The moon.

AMANDA: Is there a moon this evening?

TOM: It's rising over Garfinkel's Delicatessen.

AMANDA: So it is! A little silver slipper of a moon. Have you made a wish on it yet?

TOM: Um-hum.

AMANDA: What did you wish for?

TOM: That's a secret.

AMANDA: A secret, huh? Well, I won't tell mine either. I will be just as mysterious as you.

TOM: I bet I can guess what yours is.

AMANDA: Is my head so transparent?

TOM: You're not a sphinx.

AMANDA: No, I don't have secrets. I'll tell you what I wished for on the moon. Success and happiness for my precious children! I wish for that whenever there's a moon, and when there isn't a moon, I wish for it, too.

TOM: I thought perhaps you wished for a gentleman caller.

AMANDA: Why do you say that?

TOM: Don't you remember asking me to fetch one?

AMANDA: I remember suggesting that it would be nice for your sister if you brought home some nice young man from the warehouse. I think I've made that suggestion more than once.

TOM: Yes, you have made it repeatedly.

AMANDA: Well?

TOM: We are going to have one.

AMANDA: What?

TOM: A gentleman caller!

The Annunciation Is Celebrated With Music.

Amanda rises.

Image On Screen: Caller With Bouquet.

AMANDA: You mean you have asked some nice young man to come over?

TOM: Yep. I've asked him to dinner.

AMANDA: You really did?

TOM: I did!

AMANDA: You did, and did he —*accept?*

TOM: He did!

AMANDA: Well, well — well, well! That's — lovely!

TOM: I thought that you would be pleased.

AMANDA: It's definite, then?

TOM: Very definite.

AMANDA: Soon?

TOM: Very soon.

AMANDA: For heaven's sake, stop putting on and tell me some things, will you?

TOM: What things do you want me to tell you?

AMANDA: Naturally I would like to know when he's *coming!*

TOM: He's coming tomorrow.

AMANDA: *Tomorrow?*

TOM: Yep. Tomorrow.

AMANDA: But, Tom!

TOM: Yes, Mother?

AMANDA: Tomorrow gives me no time!

TOM: Time for what?

AMANDA: Preparations! Why didn't you phone me at once, as soon as you asked him, the minute that he accepted? Then, don't you see, I could have been getting ready!

TOM: You don't have to make any fuss.

AMANDA: Oh, Tom, Tom, Tom, of course I have to make a fuss! I want things nice, not sloppy! Not thrown together. I'll certainly have to do some fast thinking, won't I?

TOM: I don't see why you have to think at all.

AMANDA: You just don't know. We can't have a gentleman caller in a pig-sty! All my wedding silver has to be polished, the monogrammed table linen ought to be laundered! The windows have to be washed and fresh curtains put up. And how about clothes? We have to *wear* something, don't we?

TOM: Mother, this boy is no one to make a fuss over!

AMANDA: Do you realize he's the first young man we've introduced to your sister? It's terrible, dreadful, disgraceful that poor little sister has never received a single gentleman caller! Tom, come inside! *(She opens the screen door.)*

TOM: What for?

AMANDA: I want to ask you some things.

TOM: If you're going to make such a fuss, I'll call it off, I'll tell him not to come.

AMANDA: You certainly won't do anything of the kind. Nothing offends people worse than broken engagements. It simply means I'll have to work like a Turk! We won't be brilliant, but we'll pass inspection. Come on inside. *(Tom follows, groaning.)* Sit down.

TOM: Any particular place you would like me to sit?

AMANDA: Thank heavens I've got that new sofa! I'm also making payments on a floor lamp I'll have sent out! And put the chintz covers on, they'll brighten things up! Of course I'd hoped to have these walls re-papered. . . . What is the young man's name?

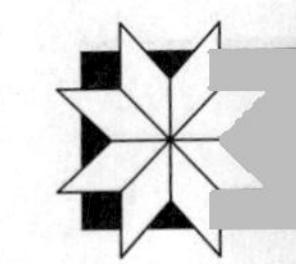

TOM: His name is O'Connor.

AMANDA: That, of course, means fish — tomorrow is Friday! I'll have that salmon loaf — with Durkee's dressing! What does he do? He works at the warehouse?

TOM: Of course! How else would I—

AMANDA: Tom, he — doesn't drink?

TOM: Why do you ask me that?

AMANDA: Your father *did!*

TOM: Don't get started on that!

AMANDA: He *does* drink, then?

TOM: Not that I know of!

AMANDA: Make sure, be certain! The last thing I want for my daughter's a boy who drinks!

TOM: Aren't you being a little premature? Mr. O'Connor has not yet appeared on the scene!

AMANDA: But will tomorrow. To meet your sister, and what do I know about his character? Nothing! Old maids are better off than wives of drunkards!

TOM: Oh, my God!

AMANDA: Be still!

TOM: *(leaning forward to whisper)* Lots of fellows meet girls whom they don't marry!

AMANDA: Oh, talk sensibly, Tom — and don't be sarcastic! *(She has gotten a hairbrush.)*

TOM: What are you doing?

AMANDA: I'm brushing that cow-lick down! What is this young man's position at the warehouse?

TOM: *(submitting grimly to the brush and the interrogation)* This young man's position is that of a shipping clerk, Mother.

AMANDA: Sounds to me like a fairly responsible job, the sort of a job *you* would be in if you just had more *get-up*. What is his salary? Have you got any idea?

TOM: I would judge it to be approximately eighty-five dollars a month.

AMANDA: Well — not princely, but—

TOM: Twenty more than I make.

AMANDA: Yes, how well I know! But for a family man, eighty-five dollars a month is not much more than you can just get by on. . . .

TOM: Yes, but Mr. O'Connor is not a family man.

AMANDA: He might be, mightn't he? Some time in the future?

TOM: I see. Plans and provisions.

AMANDA: You are the only young man that I know of who ignores the fact that the future becomes the present, the present the past, and the past turns into everlasting regret if you don't plan for it!

TOM: I will think that over and see what I can make of it.

AMANDA: Don't be supercilious with your mother! Tell me some more about this — what do you call him?

TOM: James D. O'Connor. The D. is for Delaney.

AMANDA: Irish on *both* sides! *Gracious!* And doesn't drink?

TOM: Shall I call him up and ask him right this minute?

AMANDA: The only way to find out about those things is to make discreet inquiries at the proper moment. When I was a girl in Blue Mountain and it was suspected that a young man drank, the girl whose attentions he had been receiving, if any girl *was*, would sometimes speak to the minister of his church, or rather her father would if her father was living, and sort of feel him out on the young man's character. That is the way such things are discreetly handled to keep a young woman from making a tragic mistake!

TOM: Then how did you happen to make a tragic mistake?

AMANDA: That innocent look of your father's had everyone fooled! He *smiled*— the world was *enchanted!* No girl can do worse than put herself at the mercy of a handsome appearance! I hope that Mr. O'Connor is not too good-looking.

TOM: No, he's not too good-looking. He's covered with freckles and hasn't too much of a nose.

AMANDA: He's not right-down homely, though?

TOM: Not right-down homely. Just medium homely, I'd say.

AMANDA: Character's what to look for in a man.

TOM: That's what I've always said, Mother.

AMANDA: You've never said anything of the kind and I suspect you would never give it a thought.

TOM: Don't be suspicious of me.

AMANDA: At least I hope he's the type that's up and coming.

TOM: I think he really goes in for self-improvement.

AMANDA: What reason have you to think so?

TOM: He goes to night school.

AMANDA: *(beaming)* Splendid! What does he do, I mean study?

TOM: Radio engineering and public speaking!

AMANDA: Then he has visions of being advanced in the world! Any young man who studies public speaking is aiming to have an executive job some day! And radio engineering? A thing for the future! Both of these facts are very illuminating. Those are the sort of things that a mother should know concerning any young man who comes to call on her daughter. Seriously or — not.

TOM: One little warning. He doesn't know about Laura. I didn't let on that we had dark ulterior motives. I just said, why don't you come have dinner with us? He said okay and that was the whole conversation.

AMANDA: I bet it was! You're eloquent as an oyster. However, he'll know about Laura when he gets here. When he sees how lovely and sweet and pretty she is, he'll thank his lucky stars he was asked to dinner.

TOM: Mother, you mustn't expect too much of Laura.

AMANDA: What do you mean?

TOM: Laura seems all those things to you and me because she's ours and we love her. We don't even notice she's crippled any more.

AMANDA: Don't say crippled! You know that I never allow that word to be used!

TOM: But face facts, Mother. She is and — that's not all —

AMANDA: What do you mean "not all"?

TOM: Laura is very different from other girls.

AMANDA: I think the difference is all to her advantage.

TOM: Not quite all — in the eyes of others — strangers — she's terribly shy and lives in a world of her own and those things make her seem a little peculiar to people outside the house.

AMANDA: Don't say peculiar.

TOM: Face the facts. She is.

The Dance-Hall Music Changes To A Tango That Has A Minor And Somewhat Ominous Tone.

AMANDA: In what way is she peculiar — may I ask?

TOM: *(gently)* She lives in a world of her own — a world of — little glass ornaments, Mother. . . . *(Gets up. Amanda remains holding brush, looking at him, troubled.)* She plays old phonograph records and — that's about all — *(He glances at himself in the mirror and crosses to door.)*

AMANDA: *(sharply)* Where are you going?

TOM: I'm going to the movies. *(Out screen door.)*

AMANDA: Not to the movies, every night to the movies! *(Follows quickly to screen door.)* I don't believe you always go to the movies! *(He is gone. Amanda looks worriedly after him for a moment. Then vitality and optimism return and she turns from the door. Crossing to portieres.)* Laura! Laura! *(Laura answers from kitchenette.)*

LAURA: Yes, Mother.

AMANDA: Let those dishes go and come in front! *(Laura appears with dish towel. Gaily.)* Laura, come here and make a wish on the moon!

LAURA: *(entering)* Moon — moon?

AMANDA: A little silver slipper of a moon. Look over your left shoulder, Laura, and make a wish! *(Laura looks faintly puzzled as if called out of sleep. Amanda seizes her shoulders and turns her at an angle by the door.)* Now! Now, darling, *wish!*

LAURA: What shall I wish for, Mother?

AMANDA: *(her voice trembling and her eyes suddenly filling with tears)* Happiness! Good Fortune!

The violin rises and the stage dims out.

SCENE 6

Image: High-School Hero.

TOM: And so the following evening I brought Jim home to dinner. I had known Jim slightly in high school. In high school Jim was a hero. He had tremendous Irish good nature and vitality with the scrubbed and polished look of white chinaware. He seemed to move in a continual spotlight.

He was a star in basketball, captain of the debating club, president of the senior class and the glee club and he sang the male lead in the annual light operas. He was always running or bounding, never just walking. He seemed always at the point of defeating the law of gravity. He was shooting with such velocity through his adolescence that you would logically expect him to arrive at nothing short of the White House by the time he was thirty. But Jim apparently ran into more interference after his graduation from Soldan. His speed had definitely slowed. Six years after he left high school he was holding a job that wasn't much better than mine.

Image: Clerk.

He was the only one at the warehouse with whom I was on friendly terms. I was valuable to him as someone who could remember his former glory, who had seen him win basketball games and the silver cup in debating. He knew of my secret practice of retiring to a cabinet of the washroom to work on poems when business was slack in the warehouse. He called me Shakespeare. And while the other boys in the warehouse regarded me with suspicious hostility, Jim took a humorous attitude toward me. Gradually his attitude affected the others, their hostility wore off and they also began to smile at me as people smile at an oddly fashioned dog who trots across their path at some distance.

I knew that Jim and Laura had known each other at Soldan, and I had heard Laura speak admiringly of his voice. I didn't know if Jim remembered her or not. In high school Laura had been as unobtrusive as Jim had been astonishing. If he did remember Laura, it was not as my sister, for when I asked him to dinner, he grinned and said, "You know, Shakespeare, I never thought of you as having folks!" He was about to discover that I did. . . .

Light Up Stage.

Legend On Screen: "The Accent Of A Coming Foot."

Friday evening. It is about five o'clock of a late spring evening which comes "scattering poems in the sky."

A delicate lemony light is in the Wingfield apartment.

Amanda has worked like a Turk in preparation for the gentleman caller. The results are astonishing. The new floor lamp with its rose-silk shade is in place, a colored paper lantern conceals the broken light fixture in the ceiling, new billowing white curtains are at the windows, chintz covers are on chairs and sofa, a pair of new sofa pillows make their initial appearance.

Open boxes and tissue paper are scattered on the floor.

Laura stands in the middle with lifted arms while Amanda crouches before her, adjusting the hem of the new dress, devout and ritualistic. The dress is colored and designed by memory. The arrangement of Laura's hair is changed; it is softer and more becoming. A fragile, unearthly prettiness has come out in Laura: she is like a piece of translucent glass touched by light, given a momentary radiance, not actual, not lasting.

AMANDA: *(impatiently)* Why are you trembling?

LAURA: Mother, you've made me so nervous!

AMANDA: How have I made you nervous?

LAURA: By all this fuss! You make it seem so important!

AMANDA: I don't understand you, Laura. You couldn't be satisfied with just sitting home, and yet whenever I try to arrange something for you, you seem to resist it. *(She gets up.)* Now take a look at yourself. No, wait! Wait just a moment — I have an idea!

LAURA: What is it now?

Amanda produces two powder puffs which she wraps in handkerchiefs and stuffs in Laura's bosom.

LAURA: Mother, what are you doing?

AMANDA: They call them "Gay Deceivers"!

LAURA: I won't wear them!

AMANDA: You will!

LAURA: Why should I?

AMANDA: Because, to be painfully honest, your chest is flat.

LAURA: You make it seem like we were setting a trap.

AMANDA: All pretty girls are a trap, a pretty trap, and men expect them to be. *(Legend: "A Pretty Trap.")* Now look at yourself, young lady. This is the prettiest you will ever be! I've got to fix myself now! You're going to be surprised by your mother's appearance! *(She crosses through portieres, humming gaily.)*

Laura moves slowly to the long mirror and stares solemnly at herself.

A wind blows the white curtains inward in a slow, graceful motion and with a faint, sorrowful sighing.

AMANDA: *(offstage)* It isn't dark enough yet. *(She turns slowly before the mirror with a troubled look.)*

Legend On Screen: "This Is My Sister: Celebrate Her With Strings!" Music.

AMANDA: *(laughing, off)* I'm going to show you something. I'm going to make a spectacular appearance!

LAURA: What is it, Mother?

AMANDA: Possess your soul in patience — you will see! Something I've resurrected from that old trunk! Styles haven't changed so terribly much after all. . . . *(She parts the portieres.)* Now just look at your mother! *(She wears a girlish frock of yellowed voile with a blue silk sash. She carries a bunch of jonquils — the legend of her youth is nearly revived. Feverishly.)* This is the dress in which I led the cotillion. Won the cakewalk twice at Sunset Hill, wore one spring to the Governor's ball in Jackson! See how I sashayed around the ballroom, Laura? *(She raises her skirt and does a mincing step around the room.)* I wore it on Sundays for my gentlemen callers! I had it on the day I met your father — I had malaria fever all that spring. The change of climate from East Tennessee to the Delta — weakened resistance — I had a little temperature all the time — not enough to be serious — just enough to make me restless and giddy! Invitations poured in — parties all over the Delta! — "Stay in bed," said Mother, "you have fever!" — but I just wouldn't. — I took quinine but kept on going, going! — Evenings, dances! — Afternoons, long, long rides! Picnics — lovely! — So lovely, that country in May. All lacy with dogwood, literally flooded with jonquils! — That was the spring I had the craze for jonquils. Jonquils became an absolute obsession. Mother said, "Honey, there's no more room for jonquils." And still I kept bringing in more jonquils. Whenever, wherever I saw them, I'd say, "Stop! Stop! I see jonquils!" I made the young men help me gather the jonquils! It was a joke, Amanda and her jonquils! Finally there were no more vases to hold them, every available space was filled with jonquils. No vases to hold them? All right, I'll hold them myself! And then I — *(She stops in front of the picture.) (Music)* met your father! Malaria fever and jonquils and then — this — boy. . . . *(She switches on the rose-colored lamp.)* I hope they get here before it starts to rain. *(She crosses upstage and places the jonquils in bowl on table.)* I gave your brother a little extra change so he and Mr. O'Connor could take the service car home.

LAURA: *(with altered look)* What did you say his name was?
AMANDA: O'Connor.
LAURA: What is his first name?
AMANDA: I don't remember. Oh, yes, I do. It was — Jim!

Laura sways slightly and catches hold of a chair.

Legend On Screen: "Not Jim!"

LAURA: *(faintly)* Not — Jim!
AMANDA: Yes, that was it, it was Jim! I've never known a Jim that wasn't nice!

Music: Ominous.

LAURA: Are you sure his name is Jim O'Connor?
AMANDA: Yes. Why?
LAURA: Is he the one that Tom used to know in high school?
AMANDA: He didn't say so. I think he just got to know him at the warehouse.
LAURA: There was a Jim O'Connor we both knew in high school — *(Then, with effort.)* If that is the one that Tom is bringing to dinner — you'll have to excuse me, I won't come to the table.
AMANDA: What sort of nonsense is this?
LAURA: You asked me once if I'd ever liked a boy. Don't you remember I showed you this boy's picture?
AMANDA: You mean the boy you showed me in the year book?
LAURA: Yes, that boy.
AMANDA: Laura, Laura, were you in love with that boy?
LAURA: I don't know, Mother. All I know is I couldn't sit at the table if it was him!

AMANDA: It won't be him! It isn't the least bit likely. But whether it is or not, you will come to the table. You will not be excused.

LAURA: I'll have to be, Mother.

AMANDA: I don't intend to humor your silliness, Laura. I've had too much from you and your brother, both! So just sit down and compose yourself till they come. Tom has forgotten his key so you'll have to let them in, when they arrive.

LAURA: *(panicky)* Oh, Mother — *you* answer the door!

AMANDA: *(lightly)* I'll be in the kitchen — busy!

LAURA: Oh, Mother, please answer the door, don't make me do it!

AMANDA: *(crossing into kitchenette)* I've got to fix the dressing for the salmon. Fuss, fuss — silliness! — over a gentleman caller!

Door swings shut. Laura is left alone.

Legend: "Terror!"

She utters a low moan and turns off the lamp — sits stiffly on the edge of the sofa, knotting her fingers together.

Legend On Screen: "The Opening Of A Door!"

Tom and Jim appear on the fire-escape steps and climb to landing. Hearing their approach, Laura rises with a panicky gesture. She retreats to the portieres.

The doorbell. Laura catches her breath and touches her throat. Low drums.

AMANDA: *(calling)* Laura, sweetheart! The door!

Laura stares at it without moving.

JIM: I think we just beat the rain.

TOM: Uh-huh. *(He rings again, nervously. Jim whistles and fishes for a cigarette.)*

AMANDA: *(very, very gaily)* Laura, that is your brother and Mr. O'Connor! Will you let them in, darling?

Laura crosses toward kitchenette door.

LAURA: *(breathlessly)* Mother — you go to the door!

Amanda steps out of kitchenette and stares furiously at Laura. She points imperiously at the door.

LAURA: Please, please!

AMANDA: *(in a fierce whisper)* What is the matter with you, you silly thing?

LAURA: *(desperately)* Please, you answer it, *please!*

AMANDA: I told you I wasn't going to humor you, Laura. Why have you chosen this moment to lose your mind?

LAURA: Please, please, please, you go!

AMANDA: You'll have to go to the door because I can't!

LAURA: *(despairingly)* I can't either!

AMANDA: Why?

LAURA: I'm *sick!*

AMANDA: I'm sick, too — of your nonsense! Why can't you and your brother be normal people? Fantastic whims and behavior! *(Tom gives a long ring.)* Preposterous goings on! Can you give me one reason — *(Calls out lyrically.)* COMING! JUST ONE SECOND! — why should you be afraid to open a door? Now you answer it, Laura!

LAURA: Oh, oh, oh . . . *(She returns through the portieres. Darts to the Victrola and winds it frantically and turns it on.)*

AMANDA: Laura Wingfield, you march right to that door!

LAURA: Yes — yes, Mother!

A faraway, scratchy rendition of "Dardanella" softens the air and gives her strength to move through it. She slips to the door and draws it cautiously open. Tom enters with the caller, Jim O'Connor.

TOM: Laura, this is Jim. Jim, this is my sister, Laura.

JIM: *(stepping inside)* I didn't know that Shakespeare had a sister!

LAURA: *(retreating stiff and trembling from the door)* How — how do you do?

JIM: *(heartily extending his hand)* Okay!

Laura touches it hesitantly with hers.

JIM: Your hand's *cold*, Laura!

LAURA: Yes, well — I've been playing the Victrola. . . .

JIM: Must have been playing classical music on it! You ought to play a little hot swing music to warm you up!

LAURA: Excuse me — I haven't finished playing the Victrola. . . .

She turns awkwardly and hurries into the front room. She pauses a second by the Victrola. Then catches her breath and darts through the portieres like a frightened deer.

JIM: *(grinning)* What was the matter?

TOM: Oh — with Laura? Laura is — terribly shy.

JIM: Shy, huh? It's unusual to meet a shy girl nowadays. I don't believe you ever mentioned you had a sister.

TOM: Well, now you know. I have one. Here is the *Post Dispatch*. You want a piece of it?

JIM: Uh-huh.

TOM: What piece? The comics?

JIM: Sports! *(Glances at it.)* Ole Dizzy Dean° is on his bad behavior.

TOM: *(disinterested)* Yeah? *(Lights cigarette and crosses back to fire-escape door.)*

JIM: Where are you going?

TOM: I'm going out on the terrace.

JIM: *(goes after him)* You know, Shakespeare — I'm going to sell you a bill of goods!

Dizzy Dean: Jay Hanna Dean (1910–1974), American baseball player who pitched for the St. Louis Cardinals (1930, 1932–1937), winning 30 games in 1934 and averaging 24 wins in his first five full seasons. From 1938 to 1941, he played for the Chicago Cubs.

TOM: What goods?

JIM: A course I'm taking.

TOM: Huh?

JIM: In public speaking! You and me, we're not the warehouse type.

TOM: Thanks — that's good news. But what has public speaking got to do with it?

JIM: It fits you for — executive positions!

TOM: Awww.

JIM: I tell you it's done a helluva lot for me.

Image: Executive At Desk.

TOM: In what respect?

JIM: In every! Ask yourself what is the difference between you an' me and men in the office down front? Brains?— No! — Ability?— No! Then what? Just one little thing —

TOM: What is that one little thing?

JIM: Primarily it amounts to — social poise! Being able to square up to people and hold your own on any social level!

AMANDA: *(offstage)* Tom?

TOM: Yes, Mother?

AMANDA: Is that you and Mr. O'Connor?

TOM: Yes, Mother.

AMANDA: Well, you just make yourselves comfortable in there.

TOM: Yes, Mother.

AMANDA: Ask Mr. O'Connor if he would like to wash his hands.

JIM: Aw — no — thank you — I took care of that at the warehouse. Tom —

TOM: Yes?

JIM: Mr. Mendoza was speaking to me about you.

TOM: Favorably?

JIM: What do you think?

TOM: Well—

JIM: You're going to be out of a job if you don't wake up.

TOM: I am waking up—

JIM: You show no signs.

TOM: The signs are interior.

Image On Screen: The Sailing Vessel With Jolly Roger Again.

TOM: I'm planning to change. *(He leans over the rail speaking with quiet exhilaration. The incandescent marquees and signs of the first-run movie houses light his face from across the alley. He looks like a voyager.)* I'm right at the point of committing myself to a future that doesn't include the warehouse and Mr. Mendoza or even a night-school course in public speaking.

JIM: What are you gassing about?

TOM: I'm tired of the movies.

JIM: Movies!

TOM: Yes, movies! Look at them — (*A wave toward the marvels of Grand Avenue.*) All of those glamorous people — having adventures — hogging it all, gobbling the whole thing up! You know what happens? People go to the *movies instead of moving!* Hollywood characters are supposed to have all the adventures for everybody in America, while everybody in America sits in a dark room and watches them have them! Yes, until there's a war. That's when adventure becomes available to the masses! *Everyone's* dish, not only Gable's! Then the people in the dark room come out of the dark room to have some adventures themselves — Goody, goody — It's our turn now, to go to the South Sea Island — to make a safari — to be exotic, far-off — But I'm not patient. I don't want to wait till then. I'm tired of the *movies* and I am *about* to *move!*

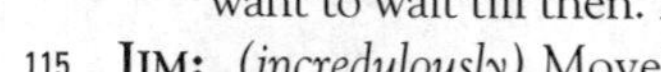

JIM: (*incredulously*) Move?

TOM: Yes.

JIM: When?

TOM: Soon!

JIM: Where? Where?

Theme three music seems to answer the question, while Tom thinks it over. He searches among his pockets.

TOM: I'm starting to boil inside. I know I seem dreary, but inside — well, I'm boiling! Whenever I pick up a shoe, I shudder a little thinking how short life is and what I am doing! — Whatever that means. I know it doesn't mean shoes — except as something to wear on a traveler's feet! (*Finds paper.*) Look —

JIM: What?

TOM: I'm a member.

JIM: (*reading*) The Union of Merchant Seamen.

TOM: I paid my dues this month, instead of the light bill.

JIM: You will regret it when they turn the lights off.

TOM: I won't be here.

JIM: How about your mother?

TOM: I'm like my father. The bastard son of a bastard! See how he grins? And he's been absent going on sixteen years!

JIM: You're just talking, you drip. How does your mother feel about it?

TOM: Shhh — Here comes Mother! Mother is not acquainted with my plans!

AMANDA: (*enters portieres*) Where are you all?

TOM: On the terrace, Mother.

They start inside. She advances to them. Tom is distinctly shocked at her appearance. Even Jim blinks a little. He is making his first contact with girlish Southern vivacity and in spite of the night-school course in public speaking is somewhat thrown off the beam by the unexpected outlay of social charm.

Certain responses are attempted by Jim but are swept aside by Amanda's gay laughter and chatter. Tom is embarrassed but after the first shock Jim reacts very warmly. Grins and chuckles, is altogether won over.

Image: Amanda As A Girl.

AMANDA: *(coyly smiling, shaking her girlish ringlets)* Well, well, well, so this is Mr. O'Connor. Introductions entirely unnecessary. I've heard so much about you from my boy. I finally said to him, Tom — good gracious! — why don't you bring this paragon to supper? I'd like to meet this nice young man at the warehouse! — Instead of just hearing him sing your praises so much! I don't know why my son is so stand-offish — that's not Southern behavior! Let's sit down and — I think we could stand a little more air in here! Tom, leave the door open. I felt a nice fresh breeze a moment ago. Where has it gone? Mmm, so warm already! And not quite summer, even. We're going to burn up when summer really gets started. However, we're having — we're having a very light supper. I think light things are better fo' this time of year. The same as light clothes are. Light clothes an' light food are what warm weather calls fo'. You know our blood gets so thick during th' winter — it takes a while fo' us to *adjust* ou'selves! — when the season changes . . . It's come so quick this year. I wasn't prepared. All of a sudden — heavens! Already summer! — I ran to the trunk an' pulled out this light dress — Terribly old! Historical almost! But feels so good — so good an' co-ol, y'know. . . .

TOM: Mother —

AMANDA: Yes, honey?

TOM: How about — supper?

AMANDA: Honey, you go ask Sister if supper is ready! You know that Sister is in full charge of supper! Tell her you hungry boys are waiting for it. *(To Jim.)* Have you met Laura?

JIM: She —

AMANDA: Let you in? Oh, good, you've met already! It's rare for a girl as sweet an' pretty as Laura to be domestic! But Laura is, thank heavens, not only pretty but also very domestic. I'm not at all. I never was a bit. I never could make a thing but angel-food cake. Well, in the South we had so many servants. Gone, gone, gone. All vestiges of gracious living! Gone completely! I wasn't prepared for what the future brought me. All of my gentlemen callers were sons of planters and so of course I assumed that I would be married to one and raise my family on a large piece of land with plenty of servants. But man proposes — and woman accepts the proposal! — To vary that old, old saying a little bit — I married no planter! I married a man who worked for the telephone company! — that gallantly smiling gentleman over there! *(Points to the picture.)* A telephone man who — fell in love with long-distance! — Now he travels and I don't even know where! — But what am I going on for about my — tribulations? Tell me yours — I hope you don't have any! Tom?

TOM: *(returning)* Yes, Mother?

AMANDA: Is supper nearly ready?

TOM: It looks to me like supper is on the table.

AMANDA: Let me look — *(She rises prettily and looks through portieres.)* Oh, lovely — But where is Sister?

TOM: Laura is not feeling well and says that she thinks she'd better not come to the table.

145 **AMANDA:** What?— Nonsense! — Laura? Oh, Laura!

LAURA: *(offstage, faintly)* Yes, Mother.

AMANDA: You really must come to the table. We won't be seated until you come to the table! Come in, Mr. O'Connor. You sit over there and I'll — Laura? Laura Wingfield! You're keeping us waiting, honey! We can't say grace until you come to the table!

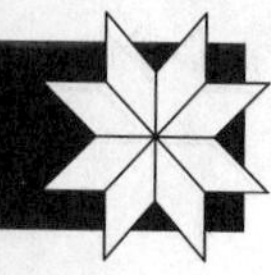

The back door is pushed weakly open and Laura comes in. She is obviously quite faint, her lips trembling, her eyes wide and staring. She moves unsteadily toward the table. Legend: "Terror!"

Outside a summer storm is coming abruptly. The white curtains billow inward at the windows and there is a sorrowful murmur and deep blue dusk.

Laura suddenly stumbles — She catches at a chair with a faint moan.

TOM: Laura!

AMANDA: Laura! *(There is a clap of thunder.) (Legend: "Ah!") (Despairingly.)* Why, Laura, you are sick, darling! Tom, help your sister into the living room, dear! Sit in the living room, Laura — rest on the sofa. Well! *(To the gentleman caller.)* Standing over the hot stove made her ill! — I told her that it was just too warm this evening, but — *(Tom comes back in. Laura is on the sofa.)* Is Laura all right now?

150 **TOM:** Yes.

AMANDA: What *is* that? Rain? A nice cool rain has come up! *(She gives the gentleman caller a frightened look.)* I think we may — have grace — now . . . *(Tom looks at her stupidly.)* Tom, honey — you say grace!

TOM: Oh . . . "For these and all thy mercies —" *(They bow their heads, Amanda stealing a nervous glance at Jim. In the living room Laura, stretched on the sofa, clenches her hand to her lips, to hold back a shuddering sob.)* God's Holy Name be praised —

The Scene Dims Out.

SCENE 7

A Souvenir.

Half an hour later. Dinner is just being finished in the upstage area which is concealed by the drawn portieres.

As the curtain rises Laura is still huddled upon the sofa, her feet drawn under her, her head resting on a pale blue pillow, her eyes wide and mysteriously watchful. The new floor lamp with its shade of rose-colored silk gives a soft, becoming light to her face, bringing out the fragile, unearthly prettiness which usually escapes attention. There is a steady murmur of rain, but it is slackening and stops soon after the scene begins; the air outside becomes pale and luminous as the moon breaks out.

A moment after the curtain rises, the lights in both rooms flicker and go out.

JIM: Hey, there, Mr. Light Bulb!

Amanda laughs nervously.

Legend: "Suspension Of A Public Service."

AMANDA: Where was Moses when the lights went out? Ha-ha. Do you know the answer to that one, Mr. O'Connor?

JIM: No, Ma'am, what's the answer?

AMANDA: In the dark! *(Jim laughs appreciatively.)* Everybody sit still. I'll light the candles. Isn't it lucky we have them on the table? Where's a match? Which of you gentlemen can provide a match?

JIM: Here.

AMANDA: Thank you, sir.

JIM: Not at all, Ma'am!

AMANDA: I guess the fuse has burnt out. Mr. O'Connor, can you tell a burnt-out fuse? I know I can't and Tom is a total loss when it comes to mechanics. *(Sound: Getting Up: Voices Recede A Little To Kitchenette.)* Oh, be careful you don't bump into something. We don't want our gentleman caller to break his neck. Now wouldn't that be a fine howdy-do?

JIM: Ha-ha! Where is the fuse-box?

AMANDA: Right here next to the stove. Can you see anything?

JIM: Just a minute.

AMANDA: Isn't electricity a mysterious thing? Wasn't it Benjamin Franklin who tied a key to a kite? We live in such a mysterious universe, don't we? Some people say that science clears up all the mysteries for us. In my opinion it only creates more! Have you found it yet?

JIM: No, Ma'am. All these fuses look okay to me.

AMANDA: Tom!

TOM: Yes, Mother?

AMANDA: That light bill I gave you several days ago. The one I told you we got the notices about?

TOM: Oh.—Yeah.

Legend: "Ha!"

AMANDA: You didn't neglect to pay it by any chance?

TOM: Why, I—

AMANDA: Didn't! I might have known it!

JIM: Shakespeare probably wrote a poem on that light bill, Mrs. Wingfield.

AMANDA: I might have known better than to trust him with it! There's such a high price for negligence in this world!

JIM: Maybe the poem will win a ten-dollar prize.

AMANDA: We'll just have to spend the remainder of the evening in the nineteenth century, before Mr. Edison made the Mazda lamp!

JIM: Candlelight is my favorite kind of light.

AMANDA: That shows you're romantic! But that's no excuse for Tom. Well, we got through dinner. Very considerate of them to let us get through dinner before they plunged us into everlasting darkness, wasn't it, Mr. O'Connor?

JIM: Ha-ha!

AMANDA: Tom, as a penalty for your carelessness you can help me with the dishes.

JIM: Let me give you a hand.

AMANDA: Indeed you will not!

JIM: I ought to be good for something.

AMANDA: Good for something? *(Her tone is rhapsodic.)* *You?* Why, Mr. O'Connor, nobody, *nobody's* given me this much entertainment in years — as you have!

JIM: Aw, now, Mrs. Wingfield!

AMANDA: I'm not exaggerating, not one bit! But Sister is all by her lonesome. You go keep her company in the parlor! I'll give you this lovely old candelabrum that used to be on the altar at the church of the Heavenly Rest. It was melted a little out of shape when the church burnt down. Lightning struck it one spring. Gypsy Jones was holding a revival at the time and he intimated that the church was destroyed because the Episcopalians gave card parties.

JIM: Ha-ha.

AMANDA: And how about coaxing Sister to drink a little wine? I think it would be good for her! Can you carry both at once?

JIM: Sure. I'm Superman!

AMANDA: Now, Thomas, get into this apron!

The door of kitchenette swings closed on Amanda's gay laughter; the flickering light approaches the portieres.

Laura sits up nervously as he enters. Her speech at first is low and breathless from the almost intolerable strain of being alone with a stranger.

The Legend: "I Don't Suppose You Remember Me At All!"

In her first speeches in this scene, before Jim's warmth overcomes her paralyzing shyness, Laura's voice is thin and breathless as though she has run up a steep flight of stairs.

Jim's attitude is gently humorous. In playing this scene it should be stressed that while the incident is apparently unimportant, it is to Laura the climax of her secret life.

JIM: Hello, there, Laura.

LAURA: *(faintly)* Hello. *(She clears her throat.)*

JIM: How are you feeling now? Better?

LAURA: Yes. Yes, thank you.

JIM: This is for you. A little dandelion wine. *(He extends it toward her with extravagant gallantry.)*

LAURA: Thank you.

JIM: Drink it — but don't get drunk! *(He laughs heartily. Laura takes the glass uncertainly; laughs shyly.)* Where shall I set the candles?

LAURA: Oh — oh, anywhere . . .

JIM: How about here on the floor? Any objections?

LAURA: No.

JIM: I'll spread a newspaper under to catch the drippings. I like to sit on the floor. Mind if I do?

LAURA: Oh, no.

JIM: Give me a pillow?

LAURA: What?

JIM: A pillow!

LAURA: Oh . . . *(Hands him one quickly.)*

JIM: How about you? Don't you like to sit on the floor?

LAURA: Oh — yes.

JIM: Why don't you, then?

LAURA: I — will.

JIM: Take a pillow! *(Laura does. Sits on the other side of the candelabrum. Jim crosses his legs and smiles engagingly at her.)* I can't hardly see you sitting way over there.

LAURA: I can — see you.

JIM: I know, but that's not fair, I'm in the limelight. *(Laura moves her pillow closer.)* Good! Now I can see you! Comfortable?

LAURA: Yes.

JIM: So am I. Comfortable as a cow. Will you have some gum?

LAURA: No, thank you.

JIM: I think that I will indulge, with your permission. *(Musingly unwraps it and holds it up.)* Think of the fortune made by the guy that invented the first piece of chewing gum. Amazing, huh? The Wrigley Building is one of the sights of Chicago. — I saw it summer before last when I went up to the Century of Progress. Did you take in the Century of Progress?

LAURA: No, I didn't.

JIM: Well, it was quite a wonderful exposition. What impressed me most was the Hall of Science. Gives you an idea of what the future will be in America, even more wonderful than the present time is! *(Pause. Smiling at her.)* Your brother tells me you're shy. Is that right, Laura?

LAURA: I — don't know.

JIM: I judge you to be an old-fashioned type of girl. Well, I think that's a pretty good type to be. Hope you don't think I'm being too personal — do you?

LAURA: *(hastily, out of embarrassment)* I believe I *will* take a piece of gum, if you — don't mind. *(Clearing her throat.)* Mr. O'Connor, have you — kept up with your singing?

JIM: Singing? Me?

LAURA: Yes. I remember what a beautiful voice you had.

JIM: When did you hear me sing?

Voice Offstage In The Pause.

VOICE *(offstage):*

O blow, ye winds, heigh-ho,
A-roving I will go!
I'm off to my love
With a boxing glove —
Ten thousand miles away!

JIM: You say you've heard me sing?

LAURA: Oh, yes! Yes, very often . . . I — don't suppose you remember me — at all?

JIM: *(smiling doubtfully)* You know I have an idea I've seen you before. I had that idea soon as you opened the door. It seemed almost like I was about to remember your name. But the name that I started to call you — wasn't a name! And so I stopped myself before I said it.

LAURA: Wasn't it — Blue Roses?

JIM: *(springs up, grinning)* Blue Roses! My gosh, yes — Blue Roses! That's what I had on my tongue when you opened the door! Isn't it funny what tricks your memory plays? I didn't connect you with the high school somehow or other. But that's where it was; it was high school. I didn't even know you were Shakespeare's sister! Gosh, I'm sorry.

LAURA: I didn't expect you to. You — barely knew me!

JIM: But we did have a speaking acquaintance, huh?

LAURA: Yes, we — spoke to each other.

JIM: When did you recognize me?

LAURA: Oh, right away!

JIM: Soon as I came in the door?

LAURA: When I heard your name I thought it was probably you. I knew that Tom used to know you a little in high school. So when you came in the door — Well, then I was — sure.

JIM: Why didn't you *say* something, then?

LAURA: *(breathlessly)* I didn't know what to say, I was — too surprised!

JIM: For goodness' sakes! You know, this sure is funny!

LAURA: Yes! Yes, isn't it, though . . .

JIM: Didn't we have a class in something together?

LAURA: Yes, we did.

JIM: What class was that?

LAURA: It was — singing — Chorus!

JIM: Aw!

LAURA: I sat across the aisle from you in the Aud.

JIM: Aw.

LAURA: Mondays, Wednesdays and Fridays.

JIM: Now I remember — you always came in late.

LAURA: Yes, it was so hard for me, getting upstairs. I had that brace on my leg — it clumped so loud!

JIM: I never heard any clumping.

LAURA: *(wincing at the recollection)* To me it sounded like — thunder!

JIM: Well, well, well. I never even noticed.

LAURA: And everybody was seated before I came in. I had to walk in front of all those people. My seat was in the back row. I had to go clumping all the way up the aisle with everyone watching!

JIM: You shouldn't have been self-conscious.

LAURA: I know, but I was. It was always such a relief when the singing started.

JIM: Aw, yes, I've placed you now! I used to call you Blue Roses. How was it that I got started calling you that?

LAURA: I was out of school a little while with pleurosis. When I came back you asked me what was the matter. I said I had pleurosis — you thought I said Blue Roses. That's what you always called me after that!

JIM: I hope you didn't mind.

LAURA: Oh, no — I liked it. You see, I wasn't acquainted with many — people. . . .

JIM: As I remember you sort of stuck by yourself.

LAURA: I — I — never had much luck at — making friends.

JIM: I don't see why you wouldn't.

LAURA: Well, I — started out badly.

JIM: You mean being —

LAURA: Yes, it sort of — stood between me —

JIM: You shouldn't have let it!

LAURA: I know, but it did, and —

JIM: You were shy with people!

LAURA: I tried not to be but never could —

JIM: Overcome it?

LAURA: No, I — I never could!

JIM: I guess being shy is something you have to work out of kind of gradually.

LAURA: *(sorrowfully)* Yes — I guess it —

JIM: Takes time!

LAURA: Yes —

JIM: People are not so dreadful when you know them. That's what you have to remember! And everybody has problems, not just you, but practically everybody has got some problems. You think of yourself as having the only problems, as being the only one who is disappointed. But just look around you and you will see lots of people as disappointed as you are. For instance, I hoped when I was going to high school that I would be further along at this time, six years later, than I am now — You remember that wonderful write-up I had in *The Torch?*

LAURA: Yes! *(She rises and crosses to table.)*

JIM: It said I was bound to succeed in anything I went into! *(Laura returns with the annual.)* Holy Jeez! *The Torch! (He accepts it reverently. They smile across it with mutual wonder. Laura crouches beside him and they begin to turn through it. Laura's shyness is dissolving in his warmth.)*

LAURA: Here you are in *Pirates of Penzance!*

JIM: *(wistfully)* I sang the baritone lead in that operetta.

LAURA: *(rapidly)* So — *beautifully!*

JIM: *(protesting)* Aw —

LAURA: Yes, yes — beautifully — beautifully!

JIM: You heard me?

LAURA: All three times!

JIM: No!

LAURA: Yes!

JIM: All three performances?

LAURA: *(looking down)* Yes.

JIM: Why?

LAURA: I — wanted to ask you to — autograph my program.

JIM: Why didn't you ask me to?

LAURA: You were always surrounded by your own friends so much that I never had a chance to.

JIM: You should have just —

LAURA: Well, I — thought you might think I was —

JIM: Thought I might think you was — what?

LAURA: Oh —

JIM: *(with reflective relish)* I was beleaguered by females in those days.

LAURA: You were terribly popular!

JIM: Yeah —

LAURA: You had such a — friendly way —

JIM: I was spoiled in high school.

LAURA: Everybody — liked you!

JIM: Including you?

LAURA: I — yes, I — I did, too — *(She gently closes the book in her lap.)*

JIM: Well, well, well! — Give me that program, Laura. *(She hands it to him. He signs it with a flourish.)* There you are — better late than never!

LAURA: Oh, I — what a — surprise!

JIM: My signature isn't worth very much right now. But some day — maybe — it will increase in value! Being disappointed is one thing and being discouraged is something else. I am disappointed but I'm not discouraged. I'm twenty-three years old. How old are you?

LAURA: I'll be twenty-four in June.

JIM: That's not old age!

LAURA: No, but —

JIM: You finished high school?

LAURA: *(with difficulty)* I didn't go back.

JIM: You mean you dropped out?

LAURA: I made bad grades in my final examinations. *(She rises and replaces the book and the program. Her voice strained.)* How is — Emily Meisenbach getting along?

JIM: Oh, that kraut-head!

LAURA: Why do you call her that?

JIM: That's what she was.

LAURA: You're not still — going with her?

JIM: I never see her.

LAURA: It said in the Personal Section that you were — engaged!

JIM: I know, but I wasn't impressed by that — propaganda!

LAURA: It wasn't — the truth?

JIM: Only in Emily's optimistic opinion!

LAURA: Oh —

Legend: "What Have You Done Since High School?"

Jim lights a cigarette and leans indolently back on his elbows smiling at Laura with a warmth and charm which light her inwardly with altar candles. She remains by the table and turns in her hands a piece of glass to cover her tumult.

JIM: *(after several reflective puffs on a cigarette)* What have you done since high school? *(She seems not to hear him.)* Huh? *(Laura looks up.)* I said what have you done since high school, Laura?

LAURA: Nothing much.

JIM: You must have been doing something these six long years.

LAURA: Yes.

JIM: Well, then, such as what?

LAURA: I took a business course at business college—

JIM: How did that work out?

LAURA: Well, not very—well—I had to drop out, it gave me—indigestion—

Jim laughs gently.

JIM: What are you doing now?

LAURA: I don't do anything—much. Oh, please don't think I sit around doing nothing! My glass collection takes up a good deal of my time. Glass is something you have to take good care of.

JIM: What did you say—about glass?

LAURA: Collection I said—I have one— *(She clears her throat and turns away again, acutely shy.)*

JIM: *(abruptly)* You know what I judge to be the trouble with you? Inferiority complex! Know what that is? That's what they call it when someone low-rates himself! I understand it because I had it, too. Although my case was not so aggravated as yours seems to be. I had it until I took up public speaking, developed my voice, and learned that I had an aptitude for science. Before that time I never thought of myself as being outstanding in any way whatsoever! Now I've never made a regular study of it, but I have a friend who says I can analyze people better than doctors that make a profession of it. I don't claim that to be necessarily true, but I can sure guess a person's psychology, Laura! *(Takes out his gum.)* Excuse me, Laura. I always take it out when the flavor is gone. I'll use this scrap of paper to wrap it in. I know how it is to get it stuck on a shoe. Yep—that's what I judge to be your principal trouble. A lack of confidence in yourself as a person. You don't have the proper amount of faith in yourself. I'm basing that fact on a number of your remarks and also on certain observations I've made. For instance that clumping you thought was so awful in high school. You say that you even dreaded to walk into class. You see what you did? You dropped out of school, you gave up an education because of a clump, which as far as I know was practically nonexistent! A little physical defect is what you have. Hardly noticeable even! Magnified thousands of times by imagination! You know what my strong advice to you is? Think of yourself as *superior* in some way!

LAURA: In what way would I think?

JIM: Why, man alive, Laura! Just look about you a little. What do you see? A world full of common people! All of 'em born and all of 'em going to die! Which of them has one-tenth of your good points! Or mine! Or anyone else's, as far as that goes — Gosh! Everybody excels in some one thing. Some in many! *(Unconsciously glances at himself in the mirror.)* All you've got to do is discover in *what!* Take me, for instance. *(He adjusts his tie at the mirror.)* My interest happens to lie in electro-dynamics. I'm taking a course in radio engineering at night school, Laura, on top of a fairly responsible job at the warehouse. I'm taking that course and studying public speaking.

LAURA: Ohhhh.

JIM: Because I believe in the future of television! *(Turning back to her.)* I wish to be ready to go up right along with it. Therefore I'm planning to get in on the ground floor. In fact, I've already made the right connections and all that remains is for the industry itself to get underway! Full steam — *(His eyes are starry.) Knowledge* — Zzzzzp! *Money* — Zzzzzzp! — *Power!* That's the cycle democracy is built on! *(His attitude is convincingly dynamic. Laura stares at him, even her shyness eclipsed in her absolute wonder. He suddenly grins.)* I guess you think I think a lot of myself!

LAURA: No — o-o-o, I —

JIM: Now how about you? Isn't there something you take more interest in than anything else?

LAURA: Well, I do — as I said — have my — glass collection —

A peal of girlish laughter from the kitchen.

JIM: I'm not right sure I know what you're talking about. What kind of glass is it?

LAURA: Little articles of it, they're ornaments mostly! Most of them are little animals made out of glass, the tiniest little animals in the world. Mother calls them a glass menagerie! Here's an example of one, if you'd like to see it! This one is one of the oldest. It's nearly thirteen. *(He stretches out his hand.) (Music: "The Glass Menagerie.")* Oh, be careful — if you breathe, it breaks!

JIM: I'd better not take it. I'm pretty clumsy with things.

LAURA: Go on, I trust you with him! *(Places it in his palm.)* There now — you're holding him gently! Hold him over the light, he loves the light! You see how the light shines through him?

JIM: It sure does shine!

LAURA: I shouldn't be partial, but he is my favorite one.

JIM: What kind of a thing is this one supposed to be?

LAURA: Haven't you noticed the single horn on his forehead?

JIM: A unicorn, huh?

LAURA: Mmm-hmmm!

JIM: Unicorns, aren't they extinct in the modern world?

LAURA: I know!

JIM: Poor little fellow, he must feel sort of lonesome.

LAURA: *(smiling)* Well, if he does he doesn't complain about it. He stays on a shelf with some horses that don't have horns and all of them seem to get along nicely together.

JIM: How do you know?

LAURA: *(lightly)* I haven't heard any arguments among them!

JIM: *(grinning)* No arguments, huh? Well, that's a pretty good sign! Where shall I set him?

LAURA: Put him on the table. They all like a change of scenery once in a while!

JIM: *(stretching)* Well, well, well, well — Look how big my shadow is when I stretch!

LAURA: Oh, oh, yes — it stretches across the ceiling!

JIM: *(crossing to door)* I think it's stopped raining. *(Opens fire-escape door.)* Where does the music come from?

LAURA: From the Paradise Dance Hall across the alley.

JIM: How about cutting the rug a little, Miss Wingfield?

LAURA: Oh, I—

JIM: Or is your program filled up? Let me have a look at it. *(Grasps imaginary card.)* Why, every dance is taken! I'll just have to scratch some out. *(Waltz Music: "La Golondrina.")* Ahhh, a waltz! *(He executes some sweeping turns by himself, then holds his arms toward Laura.)*

LAURA: *(breathlessly)* I — can't dance!

JIM: There you go, that inferiority stuff!

LAURA: I've never danced in my life!

JIM: Come on, try!

LAURA: Oh, but I'd step on you!

JIM: I'm not made out of glass.

LAURA: How — how — how do we start?

JIM: Just leave it to me. You hold your arms out a little.

LAURA: Like this?

JIM: A little bit higher. Right. Now don't tighten up, that's the main thing about it — relax.

LAURA: *(laughing breathlessly)* It's hard not to.

JIM: Okay.

LAURA: I'm afraid you can't budge me.

JIM: What do you bet I can't? *(He swings her into motion.)*

LAURA: Goodness, yes, you can!

JIM: Let yourself go, now, Laura, just let yourself go.

LAURA: I'm—

JIM: Come on!

LAURA: Trying!

JIM: Not so stiff — Easy does it!

LAURA: I know but I'm—

JIM: Loosen th' backbone! There now, that's a lot better.

LAURA: Am I?

JIM: Lots, lots better! *(He moves her about the room in a clumsy waltz.)*

LAURA: Oh, my!

JIM: Ha-ha!

LAURA: Goodness, yes you can!

JIM: Ha-ha-ha! *(They suddenly bump into the table, Jim stops.)* What did we hit on?

LAURA: Table.

JIM: Did something fall off it? I think—

LAURA: Yes.

JIM: I hope that it wasn't the little glass horse with the horn!

LAURA: Yes.

JIM: Aw, aw, aw. Is it broken?

LAURA: Now it is just like all the other horses.

JIM: It's lost its—

LAURA: Horn! It doesn't matter. Maybe it's a blessing in disguise.

JIM: You'll never forgive me. I bet that that was your favorite piece of glass.

LAURA: I don't have favorites much. It's no tragedy, Freckles. Glass breaks so easily. No matter how careful you are. The traffic jars the shelves and things fall off them.

JIM: Still I'm awfully sorry that I was the cause.

LAURA: *(smiling)* I'll just imagine he had an operation. The horn was removed to make him feel less — freakish! *(They both laugh.)* Now he will feel more at home with the other horses, the ones that don't have horns . . .

JIM: Ha-ha, that's very funny! *(Suddenly serious.)* I'm glad to see that you have a sense of humor. You know — you're — well — very different! Surprisingly different from anyone else I know! *(His voice becomes soft and hesitant with a genuine feeling.)* Do you mind me telling you that? *(Laura is abashed beyond speech.)* You make me feel sort of — I don't know how to put it! I'm usually pretty good at expressing things, but — This is something that I don't know how to say! *(Laura touches her throat and clears it — turns the broken unicorn in her hands.) (Even softer.)* Has anyone ever told you that you were pretty? *(Pause: Music.) (Laura looks up slowly, with wonder, and shakes her head.)* Well, you are! In a very different way from anyone else. And all the nicer because of the difference, too. *(His voice becomes low and husky. Laura turns away, nearly faint with the novelty of her emotions.)* I wish you were my sister. I'd teach you to have some confidence in yourself. The different people are not like other people, but being different is nothing to be ashamed of. Because other people are not such wonderful people. They're one hundred times one thousand. You're one times one! They walk all over the earth. You just stay here. They're common as — weeds, but — you — well, you're — *Blue Roses!*

Image On Screen: Blue Roses.

Music Changes.

LAURA: But blue is wrong for — roses . . .

JIM: It's right for you — You're — pretty!

LAURA: In what respect am I pretty?

JIM: In all respects — believe me! Your eyes — your hair — are pretty! Your hands are pretty! *(He catches hold of her hand.)* You think I'm making this up because I'm invited to dinner and have to be nice. Oh, I could do that! I could put on an act for you, Laura, and say lots of things without being very sincere. But this time I am. I'm talking to you sincerely. I happened to notice you had this inferiority complex that keeps you from feeling comfortable with people. Somebody needs to build your confidence up and make you proud instead of shy and turning away and — blushing — Somebody ought to — ought to — *kiss* you, Laura! *(His hand slips slowly up her arm to her shoulder.) (Music Swells Tumultuously.) (He suddenly turns her about and kisses her on the lips. When he releases her Laura sinks on the sofa with a bright, dazed look. Jim backs away and fishes in his pocket for a cigarette.) (Legend On Screen: "Souvenir.")* Stumble-john! *(He lights the cigarette, avoiding her look. There is a peal of girlish laughter from Amanda in the kitchen. Laura slowly raises and opens her hand. It still contains the little broken glass animal. She looks at it with a tender, bewildered expression.)* Stumble-john! I shouldn't have done that — That was way off the beam. You don't smoke, do you? *(She looks up, smiling, not hearing the question. He sits beside her a little gingerly. She looks at him speechlessly — waiting. He coughs decorously and moves a little farther aside as he considers the situation and senses her feelings, dimly, with perturbation. Gently.)* Would you — care for a — mint? *(She doesn't seem to hear him but her look grows brighter even.)* Peppermint — Life Saver? My pocket's a regular drug store — wherever I go . . . *(He pops a mint in his mouth. Then gulps and decides to make a clean breast of it. He speaks slowly and gingerly.)* Laura, you know, if I had a sister like you, I'd do the same thing as Tom, I'd bring out fellows — introduce her to them. The right type of boys of a type to — appreciate her. Only — well — he made a mistake about me. Maybe I've got no call to be saying this. That may not have been the idea in having me over. But what if it was? There's nothing wrong about that. The only trouble is that in my case — I'm not in a situation to do the right thing. I can't take down your number and say I'll phone. I can't call up next week and — ask for a date. I thought I had better explain the situation in case you misunderstood it and — hurt your feelings. . . . *(Pause. Slowly, very slowly, Laura's look changes, her eyes returning slowly from his to the ornament in her palm.)*

Amanda utters another gay laugh in the kitchen.

LAURA: *(faintly)* You — won't — call again?

JIM: No, Laura. I can't. *(He rises from the sofa.)* As I was just explaining, I've — got strings on me, Laura, I've — been going steady! I go out all the time with a girl named Betty. She's a home-girl like you, and Catholic, and Irish, and in a great many ways we — get along fine. I met her last summer on a moonlight boat trip up the river to Alton, on the *Majestic*. Well — right away from the start it was — love! *(Legend: Love!) (Laura sways slightly forward and grips the arm of the sofa. He fails to notice, now enrapt in his own comfortable being.)* Being in love has made a new man of me! *(Leaning stiffly*

forward, clutching the arm of the sofa, Laura struggles visibly with her storm. But Jim is oblivious, she is a long way off.) The power of love is really pretty tremendous! Love is something that — changes the whole world, Laura! *(The storm abates a little and Laura leans back. He notices her again.)* It happened that Betty's aunt took sick, she got a wire and had to go to Centralia. So Tom — when he asked me to dinner — I naturally just accepted the invitation, not knowing that you — that he — that I —*(He stops awkwardly.)* Huh — I'm a stumble-john! *(He flops back on the sofa. The holy candles in the altar of Laura's face have been snuffed out! There is a look of almost infinite desolation. Jim glances at her uneasily.)* I wish that you would — say something. *(She bites her lip which was trembling and then bravely smiles. She opens her hand again on the broken glass ornament. Then she gently takes his hand and raises it level with her own. She carefully places the unicorn in the palm of his hand, then pushes his fingers closed upon it.)* What are you — doing that for? You want me to have him?— Laura? *(She nods.)* What for?

LAURA: A — souvenir . . .

She rises unsteadily and crouches beside the Victrola to wind it up.

Legend On Screen: "Things Have A Way Of Turning Out So Badly."

Or Image: "Gentleman Caller Waving Good-bye! — Gaily."

At this moment Amanda rushes brightly back in the front room. She bears a pitcher of fruit punch in an old-fashioned cut-glass pitcher and a plate of macaroons. The plate has a gold border and poppies painted on it.

AMANDA: Well, well, well! Isn't the air delightful after the shower? I've made you children a little liquid refreshment. *(Turns gaily to the gentleman caller.)* Jim, do you know that song about lemonade?

"Lemonade, lemonade
Made in the shade and stirred with a spade—
Good enough for any old maid!"

JIM: *(uneasily)* Ha-ha! No — I never heard it.

AMANDA: Why, Laura! You look so serious!

JIM: We were having a serious conversation.

AMANDA: Good! Now you're better acquainted!

JIM: *(uncertainly)* Ha-ha! Yes.

AMANDA: You modern young people are much more serious-minded than my generation. I was so gay as a girl!

JIM: You haven't changed, Mrs. Wingfield.

AMANDA: Tonight I'm rejuvenated! The gaiety of the occasion, Mr. O'Connor! *(She tosses her head with a peal of laughter. Spills lemonade.)* Oooo! I'm baptizing myself!

JIM: Here — let me—

AMANDA: *(setting the pitcher down)* There now. I discovered we had some maraschino cherries. I dumped them in, juice and all!

JIM: You shouldn't have gone to that trouble. Mrs. Wingfield.

AMANDA: Trouble, trouble? Why it was loads of fun! Didn't you hear me cutting up in the kitchen? I bet your ears were burning! I told Tom how outdone with him I was for keeping you to himself so long a time! He should have brought you over much, much sooner! Well, now that you've found your way, I want you to be a very frequent caller! Not just occasional but all the time. Oh, we're going to have a lot of gay times together! I see them coming! Mmm, just breathe that air! So fresh, and the moon's so pretty! I'll skip back out — I know where my place is when young folks are having a — serious conversation!

JIM: Oh, don't go out, Mrs. Wingfield. The fact of the matter is I've got to be going.

AMANDA: Going, now? You're joking! Why, it's only the shank of the evening, Mr. O'Connor!

JIM: Well, you know how it is.

AMANDA: You mean you're a young workingman and have to keep workingmen's hours. We'll let you off early tonight. But only on the condition that next time you stay later. What's the best night for you? Isn't Saturday night the best night for you workingmen?

JIM: I have a couple of time-clocks to punch, Mrs. Wingfield. One at morning, another one at night!

AMANDA: My, but you are ambitious! You work at night, too?

JIM: No, Ma'am, not work but — Betty! *(He crosses deliberately to pick up his hat. The band at the Paradise Dance Hall goes into a tender waltz.)*

AMANDA: Betty? Betty? Who's Betty! *(There is an ominous cracking sound in the sky.)*

JIM: Oh, just a girl. The girl I go steady with! *(He smiles charmingly. The sky falls.)*

Legend: "The Sky Falls."

AMANDA: *(a long-drawn exhalation)* Ohhhh . . . Is it a serious romance Mr. O'Connor?

JIM: We're going to be married the second Sunday in June.

AMANDA: Ohhhh — how nice! Tom didn't mention that you were engaged to be married.

JIM: The cat's not out of the bag at the warehouse yet. You know how they are. They call you Romeo and stuff like that. *(He stops at the oval mirror to put on his hat. He carefully shapes the brim and the crown to give a discreetly dashing effect.)* It's been a wonderful evening, Mrs. Wingfield. I guess this is what they mean by Southern hospitality.

AMANDA: It really wasn't anything at all.

JIM: I hope it don't seem like I'm rushing off. But I promised Betty I'd pick her up at the Wabash depot, an' by the time I get my jalopy down there her train'll be in. Some women are pretty upset if you keep 'em waiting.

AMANDA: Yes, I know — The tyranny of women! *(Extends her hand.)* Good-bye, Mr. O'Connor. I wish you luck — and happiness — and success! All three of them, and so does Laura! — Don't you, Laura?

LAURA: Yes!

JIM: *(taking her hand)* Good-bye, Laura. I'm certainly going to treasure that souvenir. And don't you forget the good advice I gave you. *(Raises his voice to a cheery shout.)* So long, Shakespeare! Thanks again, ladies — Good night!

He grins and ducks jauntily out.

Still bravely grimacing, Amanda closes the door on the gentleman caller. Then she turns back to the room with a puzzled expression. She and Laura don't dare to face each other. Laura crouches beside the Victrola to wind it.

AMANDA: *(faintly)* Things have a way of turning out so badly. I don't believe that I would play the Victrola. Well, well — well — Our gentleman caller was engaged to be married! Tom!

TOM: *(from back)* Yes, Mother?

AMANDA: Come in here a minute. I want to tell you something awfully funny.

TOM: *(enters with macaroon and a glass of the lemonade)* Has the gentleman caller gotten away already?

AMANDA: The gentleman caller has made an early departure. What a wonderful joke you played on us!

TOM: How do you mean?

AMANDA: You didn't mention that he was engaged to be married.

TOM: Jim? Engaged?

AMANDA: That's what he just informed us.

TOM: I'll be jiggered! I didn't know about that.

AMANDA: That seems very peculiar.

TOM: What's peculiar about it?

AMANDA: Didn't you call him your best friend down at the warehouse?

TOM: He is, but how did I know?

AMANDA: It seems extremely peculiar that you wouldn't know your best friend was going to be married!

TOM: The warehouse is where I work, not where I know things about people!

AMANDA: You don't know things anywhere! You live in a dream; you manufacture illusions! *(He crosses to door.)* Where are you going?

TOM: I'm going to the movies.

AMANDA: That's right, now that you've had us make such fools of ourselves. The effort, the preparations, all the expense! The new floor lamp, the rug, the clothes for Laura! All for what? To entertain some other girl's fiancé! Go to the movies, go! Don't think about us, a mother deserted, an unmarried sister who's crippled and has no job! Don't let anything interfere with your selfish pleasure! Just go, go, go — to the movies!

TOM: All right, I will! The more you shout about my selfishness to me the quicker I'll go, and I won't go to the movies!

AMANDA: Go, then! Then go to the moon — you selfish dreamer!

Tom smashes his glass on the floor. He plunges out on the fire-escape, slamming the door. Laura screams — cut by door.

Dance-hall music up. Tom goes to the rail and grips it desperately, lifting his face in the chill white moonlight penetrating the narrow abyss of the alley.

Legend On Screen: "And So Good-bye . . ."

Tom's closing speech is timed with the interior pantomime. The interior scene is played as though viewed through sound-proof glass. Amanda appears to be making a comforting speech to Laura who is huddled upon the sofa. Now that we cannot hear the mother's speech, her silliness is gone and she has dignity and tragic beauty. Laura's dark hair hides her face until at the end of the speech she lifts it to smile at her mother. Amanda's gestures are slow and graceful, almost dancelike, as she comforts the daughter. At the end of her speech she glances a moment at the father's picture — then withdraws through the portieres. At close of Tom's speech, Laura blows out the candles, ending the play.

TOM: I didn't go to the moon, I went much further — for time is the longest distance between two places — Not long after that I was fired for writing a poem on the lid of a shoe-box. I left Saint Louis. I descended the steps of this fire-escape for a last time and followed, from then on, in my father's footsteps, attempting to find in motion what was lost in space — I traveled around a great deal. The cities swept about me like dead leaves, leaves that were brightly colored but torn away from the branches. I would have stopped, but was pursued by something. It always came upon me unawares, taking me altogether by surprise. Perhaps it was a familiar bit of music. Perhaps it was only a piece of transparent glass. Perhaps I am walking along a street at night, in some strange city, before I have found companions. I pass the lighted window of a shop where perfume is sold. The window is filled with pieces of colored glass, tiny transparent bottles in delicate colors, like bits of a shattered rainbow. Then all at once my sister touches my shoulder. I turn around and look into her eyes . . . Oh, Laura, Laura, I tried to leave you behind me, but I am more faithful than I intended to be! I reach for a cigarette, I cross the street, I run into the movies or a bar, I buy a drink, I speak to the nearest stranger — anything that can blow your candles out! *(Laura bends over the candles.)* — for nowadays the world is lit by lightning! Blow out your candles, Laura — and so good-bye . . .

She blows the candles out.

The Scene Dissolves.

Reading and Reacting

1. Whom do you think this play is really about — Tom, Laura, or Amanda?

2. What is the function of the absent father in the play?

3. Besides serving as a possible suitor for Laura, what other roles does Jim play?

4. Identify references to historical events occurring at the time of the play's action. How are these events related to the play's central theme?

5. Does Tom function primarily as an actor, a character, a playwright, or a narrator? Explain.

6. What do the music, the lighting, and the words and pictures projected on slides — which Tennessee Williams called "extra-literary accents" — contribute to the play's action? Are they essential? (Note that at the urging of the director, Williams eliminated these "accents" when the play opened on Broadway.)

7. In his production notes below, Tennessee Williams calls *The Glass Menagerie* a "memory play." What do you think he means?

8. Discuss how props help to develop the play's themes. For example, consider the picture of the father, the Victrola, the fire escape, the telephone, the alarm clock, the high school yearbook, the unicorn, and the candles.

9. What events and dialogue foreshadow Tom's escape? Do you see this escape as inevitable? Do you see it as successful? Explain.

10. Do Amanda and Laura change as the play develops? What do you think will happen to them after the play is over? What is the significance of Laura's blowing out the candles at the end of the play?

11. **JOURNAL ENTRY** Do you think Tom's decision to leave his family is a sign of strength or of weakness?

12. **CRITICAL PERSPECTIVE** Literary critic Roger Boxill contrasts the short story "Portrait of a Girl in Glass" (p. 2031) and *The Glass Menagerie*. According to Boxill, "'Portrait' is a wistful memory, *Menagerie* is a moving elegy."

Do you agree with Boxill's assessment of these two works? What do you see as the major differences between the short story and the play that was developed from it?

Related Works: "A&P" (p. 259), "Barn Burning" (p. 391), "A Primer for the Punctuation of Heart Disease" (p. 440), "Eveline" (p. 719), "The Soul selects her own Society —" (p. 1145), "The Road Not Taken" (p. 1159), *A Raisin in the Sun* (p. 1331)

TENNESSEE WILLIAMS

Author's Production Notes

(Preface to the Published Edition)

Being a "memory play," *The Glass Menagerie* can be presented with unusual freedom of convention. Because of its considerably delicate or tenuous material, atmospheric touches and subtleties of direction play a particularly important part. Expressionism and all other unconventional techniques in drama have only one valid aim, and that is a closer approach to truth. When a play employs unconventional techniques, it is not, or certainly shouldn't be, trying to escape its responsibility of dealing with reality, or interpreting experience, but is actually or should be attempting to find a closer approach, a more penetrating and vivid expression of things as they are. The straight realistic play with its genuine Frigidaire and authentic ice-cubes, its characters that speak exactly as its audience speaks, corresponds to the academic landscape and has the same virtue of a photographic likeness. Everyone should know nowadays the unimportance of the photographic in art: that truth, life, or reality is an organic thing which the poetic imagination can represent or suggest, in essence, only through transformation, through changing into other forms than those which were merely present in appearance.

These remarks are not meant as a preface only to this particular play. They have to do with a conception of a new, plastic theatre which must take the place of the exhausted theater of realistic conventions if the theatre is to resume vitality as a part of our culture.

The Screen Device: There is *only one important difference between the original and acting version of the play* and that is the *omission* in the latter of the device which I tentatively included in my *original* script. This device was the use of a screen on which were projected magic-lantern slides bearing images or titles. I do not regret the omission of this device from the present Broadway production. The extraordinary power of Miss Taylor's performance° made it suitable to have the utmost simplicity in the physical production. But I think it may be interesting to some readers to see how this device was conceived. So I am putting it into the published manuscript. These images and legends, projected from behind, were cast on a section of wall between the front-room and dining-room areas, which should be indistinguishable from the rest when not in use.

The purpose of this will probably be apparent. It is to give accent to certain values in each scene. Each scene contains a particular point (or several) which is structurally the most important. In an episodic play, such as this, the basic structure or narrative line may be obscured from the audience; the effect may seem fragmentary rather than architectural. This may not be the fault of the play so much as a lack of attention in the audience. The legend or image upon the screen will strengthen the effect of what is merely allusion in the writing and allow the primary point to be made more simply and lightly than if the entire responsibility were on the spoken lines. Aside from this structural value, I think the screen will have a definite emotional appeal, less definable but just as important. An imaginative producer or director may invent many other uses for this device than those indicated in the present script. In fact the possibilities of the device seem much larger to me than the instance of this play can possibly utilize.

The Music: Another extra-literary accent in this play is provided by the use of music. A single recurring tune, "The Glass Menagerie," is used to give emotional emphasis to suitable passages. This tune is like circus music, not when you are on the grounds or in the immediate vicinity of the parade, but when you are at some distance and very likely thinking of something else. It seems under those circumstances to continue almost interminably and it weaves in and out of the preoccupied consciousness; then it is the lightest, most delicate music in the world and perhaps the saddest. It expresses the surface vivacity of life with the underlying strain of immutable and inexpressible sorrow. When you look at a piece

---

Miss Taylor's performance: In the original production, the role of Amanda Wingfield was played by the American stage actress Laurette Taylor (1884–1946).

of delicately spun glass you think of two things: how beautiful it is and how easily it can be broken. Both of those ideas should be woven into the recurring tune, which dips in and out of the play as if it were carried on a wind that changes. It serves as a thread of connection and allusion between the narrator with his separate point in time and space and the subject of his story. Between each episode it returns as reference to the emotion, nostalgia, which is the first condition of the play. It is primarily Laura's music and therefore comes out most clearly when the play focuses upon her and the lovely fragility of glass which is her image.

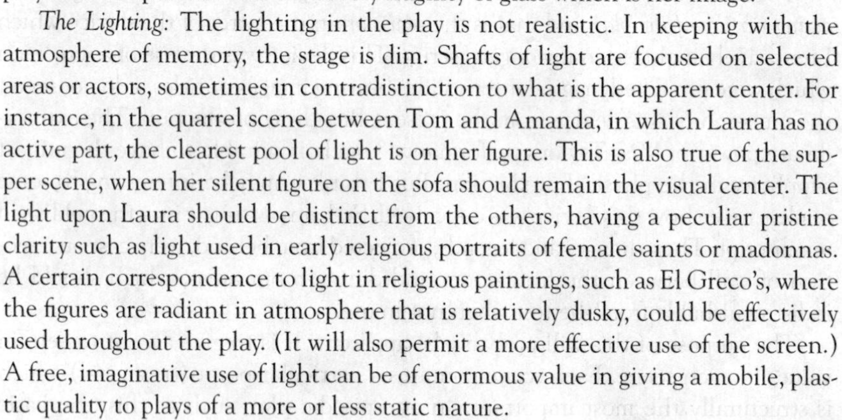

The Lighting: The lighting in the play is not realistic. In keeping with the atmosphere of memory, the stage is dim. Shafts of light are focused on selected areas or actors, sometimes in contradistinction to what is the apparent center. For instance, in the quarrel scene between Tom and Amanda, in which Laura has no active part, the clearest pool of light is on her figure. This is also true of the supper scene, when her silent figure on the sofa should remain the visual center. The light upon Laura should be distinct from the others, having a peculiar pristine clarity such as light used in early religious portraits of female saints or madonnas. A certain correspondence to light in religious paintings, such as El Greco's, where the figures are radiant in atmosphere that is relatively dusky, could be effectively used throughout the play. (It will also permit a more effective use of the screen.) A free, imaginative use of light can be of enormous value in giving a mobile, plastic quality to plays of a more or less static nature.

T.W.

JACQUELINE O'CONNOR

from Dramatizing Dementia: Madness in the Plays of Tennessee Williams

Many of Williams's plays take place in confined space, and the setting often suggests that the characters will face permanent confinement at the play's end. *The Glass Menagerie* is set in "one of those hive-like conglomerations of cellular living-units . . . symptomatic of the impulse of this largest and fundamentally enslaved section of American society to avoid fluidity and differentiation." Confinement figures as a major theme in this drama; Tom speaks frequently about the confinement that keeps him from fulfilling his dreams. In scene three, he berates his mother for the lack of privacy he feels in the apartment, telling her: "I've got no thing, no single thing — in my life that I can call my own!" He feels confined in his job, sarcastically wondering if Amanda thinks he wants to spend "fifty-five *years* down there in that — *celotex interior!* with — *fluorescent* — *tubes!*" When he returns from a night out, he brags to Laura about the magician who performed the coffin trick: "We nailed him into a coffin and he got out of the coffin without removing one nail." This, he claims, constitutes a "trick that would come in handy for me — get me out of this 2 × 4 situation!" Tom escapes from the oppressive apartment and the dead-end job, but does not find the freedom he expects, for he cannot forget his sister or the ties he feels to her, which bind him even in her absence.

Laura is voluntarily confined in the apartment, which, according to her mother, will lead to permanent confinement if she does not pursue a career or marriage. She will end up one of those "barely tolerated spinsters . . . stuck away in some little mouse-trap of a room." To the audience Laura's plight seems as constricted as the future her mother predicts, but if Laura's life proceeds as Lucretia's and Blanche's do, the "mouse-trap of a room" might well be in the state asylum. As Tom realizes, Laura is not just crippled: "In the eyes of others — strangers — she's terribly shy and lives in a world of her own and those things make her seem a little peculiar to people outside the house." Amanda's comment highlights Laura's social shortcomings, while Tom's remark focuses on her psychological ones: both assessments emphasize Laura's isolation.

TENNESSEE WILLIAMS

from Tennessee Williams: Memoirs

Rose was a popular girl in high school but only for a brief while. Her beauty was mainly in her expressive green-gray eyes and in her curly auburn hair. She was too narrow-shouldered and her state of anxiety when in male company inclined her to hunch them so they looked even narrower; this made her strong-featured, very Williams head seem too large for her thin, small-breasted body. She also, when she was on a date, would talk with an almost hysterical animation which few young men knew how to take.

The first real breakdown occurred shortly after I had suffered the heart attack that ended my career as a clerk-errand boy at the shoe company.

My first night back from St. Vincent's, as I mentioned, Rose came walking like a somnambulist into my tiny bedroom and said, "We must all die together."

I can assure you that the idea did not offer to me an irresistible appeal. Being now released at last from my three years as a clerk-typist at Continental, God damn it I was in no mood to consider group suicide with the family, not even at Rose's suggestion — however appropriate the suggestion may have been.

For several days Rose was demented. One afternoon she put a kitchen knife in her purse and started to leave for her psychiatrist's office with apparent intent of murder.

The knife was noticed by Mother and snatched away.

Then a day or so later this first onset of dementia praecox passed off and Rose was, at least on the surface, her usual (now very quiet) self again.

A few days later I departed for Memphis to recuperate at my grandparents' little house on Snowden Avenue near Southwestern University in Memphis.

I think it was about this time that our wise old family doctor told Mother that Rose's physical and mental health depended upon what struck Miss Edwina as a monstrous thing — an arranged, a sort of "therapeutic" marriage. Obviously old Doc Alexander had hit upon the true seat of Rose's afflictions. She was a very normal — but highly sexed — girl who was tearing herself apart mentally and physically by those repressions imposed upon her by Miss Edwina's monolithic Puritanism.

I may have inadvertently omitted a good deal of material about the unusually close relations between Rose and me. Some perceptive critic of the theatre made the observation that the true theme of my work is "incest." My sister and I had a close relationship, quite unsullied by any carnal knowledge. As a matter of fact, we were rather shy of each other, physically, there was no casual physical intimacy of the sort that one observes among the Mediterranean people in their family relations. And yet our love was, and is, the deepest in our lives and was, perhaps, very pertinent to our withdrawal from extra-familial attachments.

There were years when I was in the shoe company and summers when I was a student at the State University of Missouri when my sister and I spent nearly all our evenings together aside from those which I spent with Hazel.

What did we do those evenings, Rose and I? Well, we strolled about the business streets of University City. It was a sort of ritual with a pathos that I assure you was never caught in *Menagerie* nor in my story "Portrait of Girl in Glass," on which *Menagerie* was based.

I think it was Delmar — that long, long street which probably began near the Mississippi River in downtown St. Louis and continued through University City and on out into the country — that Rose and I strolled along in the evenings. There was a root-beer stand at which we always stopped. Rose was inordinately fond of root-beer, especially on warm summer evenings. And before and after our root-beer stop, we would window-shop. Rose's passion, as well as Blanche's, was clothes. And all along that part of Delmar that cut through University City were little shops with lighted windows at night in which were displayed dresses and accessories for women. Rose did not have much of a wardrobe and so her window-shopping on Delmar was like a hungry child's gazing through the window-fronts of restaurants. Her taste in clothes was excellent.

"How about *that* dress, Rose?"

"Oh no, that's tacky. But this one here's very nice."

The evening excursions lasted about an hour and a half, and although, as I've noted, we had a physical shyness of each other, never even touching hands except when dancing together in the Enright apartment, I'd usually follow her into her bedroom when we came home, to continue our warmly desultory chats. I felt most at home in that room, which was furnished with the white ivory bedroom set that had been acquired with the family's "furnished apartment" on Westminster Place when we first moved to St. Louis in 1918.

It was the only attractive room in the apartment — or did it seem so because it was my sister's?

I have mentioned our dancing together.

Rose taught me to dance to the almost aboriginal standing (nonhorned) Victrola that had been acquired in Mississippi and shipped to St. Louis at the time of the disastrous family move there.

As I drifted away from my sister, during this period, she drew close to our little Boston terrier Jiggs. She was constantly holding and hugging him and now and then Miss Edwina would say:

"Miss Florence, I'm afraid that you forget we have neighbors and Mrs. Ebbs upstairs sometimes complains when Cornelius° raises his voice."

Miss Florence would be likely to reply something to the effect that Mrs. Ebbs upstairs could go to hell, for all it mattered to her. . .

The last time I was in St. Louis, for a visit at Christmas, I had my brother Dakin drive me about all the old places where we had lived in my childhood. It was a melancholy tour. Westminster Place and Forest Park Boulevard had lost all semblance of their charm in the twenties. The big old residences had been converted into sleazy rooming-houses or torn down for nondescript duplexes and small apartment buildings.

The Kramer residence was gone: in fact, all of the family, including dear Hazel, were by then dead.

This can only serve as a preamble, in this "thing," to the story of my great love for Hazel, and not at all an adequate one at that. . . .

In my adolescence in St. Louis, at the age of sixteen, several important events in my life occurred. It was in the sixteenth year that I wrote "The Vengeance of Nitocris" and received my first publication in a magazine and the magazine was *Weird Tales*. The story wasn't published till June of 1928. That same year my grandfather Dakin took me with him on a tour of Europe with a large party of Episcopalian ladies from the Mississippi Delta. . . . And, it was in my sixteenth year that my deep nervous problems approached what might well have been a crisis as shattering as that which broke my sister's mind, lastingly, when she was in her twenties.

I was at sixteen a student at University City High School in St. Louis and the family was living in a cramped apartment at 6254 Enright Avenue.

University City was not a fashionable suburb of St. Louis and our neighborhood, while a cut better than that of the Wingfields in *Menagerie*, was only a little cut better: it was an ugly region of hive-like apartment buildings, for the most part, and fire escapes and pathetic little patches of green among concrete driveways.

My younger brother, Dakin, always an indomitable enthusiast at whatever he got into, had turned our little patch of green behind the apartment on Enright into quite an astonishing little vegetable garden. If there were flowers in it, they were, alas, obscured by the profuse growth of squash, pumpkins, and other edible flora.

I would, of course, have preempted all the space with rosebushes but I doubt they would have borne roses. The impracticalities, let's say the fantastic impracticalities, of my adolescence were not at all inclined to successful ends: and I can recall no roses in all the years that I spent in St. Louis and its environs except the two living Roses in my life, my grandmother, Rose O. Dakin, and, of course, my sister, Rose Isabel.

Cornelius: Cornelius Coffin — father of Tennessee Williams.

My adolescent problems took their most violent form in a shyness of a pathological degree. Few people realize, now, that I have always been and even remain in my years as a crocodile an extremely shy creature — in my crocodile years I compensate for this shyness by the typical Williams heartiness and bluster and sometimes explosive fury of behavior. In my high school days I had no disguise, no facade. And it was at University City High School that I developed the habit of blushing whenever anyone looked me in the eyes, as if I harbored behind them some quite dreadful or abominable secret.

JEAN EVANS

Interview 1945

I'd read four of Mr. Williams's one-act plays. All but one had been about poverty-stricken people whose situations seemed hopeless. I asked Mr. Williams if he always wrote about unhappy, trapped, hopeless people. He'd been half-reclining against a pillow on his bed, but he sat up now.

"I hadn't thought of them as being hopeless," he said. "That's not really what I was writing about. It's human valor that moves me. The one dominant theme in most of my writings, the most magnificent thing in all human nature, is valor — and endurance.

"The mother's valor is the core of *The Glass Menagerie*," he went on. "She's confused, pathetic, even stupid, but everything has *got* to be all right. She fights to make it that way in the only way she knows how."

We talked a little about his other plays and then, a trifle anxiously, he asked if I had found them without humor. I said no. There was a great deal of humor in them if he meant the wry kind that sprang out of incredibly miserable situations, the kind that made an audience want to cry while it was laughing. He nodded.

"George Jean Nathan,° in his review of *Menagerie*, said I was *deficient* in humor," Williams remarked. His manner was casual, but there was an edge of annoyance in his voice. "He said that all the humor had been embroidered into the play by Mr. Dowling." (Dowling is co-producer of the play, plays the narrator, and the son, Tom.) "I'd love for somebody who knows my other work to refute him."

He paused, and then went on defensively, "Not one line of *Glass Menagerie* was changed after the final draft came back from the typist. A scene was inserted, the drunk scene. That was Mr. Dowling's idea, but entirely of my authorship. And one line by Mr. Dowling, was added. The last line, where he says to the audience, 'Here's where memory stops and your imagination begins.'" He paused. "Mr. Dowling did a great job. A magnificent job. But there was humor *contained* in the play. I had that in mind, along with the rest, when I was writing it."

George Jean Nathan: American editor and drama critic (1882–1958). His review of the play appeared in the *New York Journal American* on April 9, 1945.

Mr. Nathan had also written that the play, as originally written, was *freakish*. I wanted to know if Mr. Williams liked writing plays unconventional in form.

"If you mean unconventional in that my plays are light on plot and heavy on characterization, yes. But not in structure. *Glass Menagerie* is not at all freakish in structure.

"Have you read Saroyan's° *Get Away, Old Man?*" Williams gave a peal of gay, sudden laughter that rang through the room. "There's a play that would give Mr. Nathan pause. The curtain goes up and down, up and down, all through the play."

He said he liked Saroyan very much, "his short stories perhaps, more than his plays."

I said I'd like Saroyan better if he were able to admit there was evil under the sun. Mr. Williams smiled. "His point of view — his attitude — I suppose you could say, is childish," he said. "Saroyan's characters are all little Saroyans. He multiplies himself like rabbits. But he is himself so interesting, that he usually gets away with writing only about himself."

How did he think the human situation could be improved? I asked. He looked as though the question had startled him.

"It's a social and economic problem, of course," he said, "not something mystical. I don't think there will be any equity in American life until at least 90 percent of our population are living under different circumstances. The white collar worker, for instance. Most people consider him pretty well off. I think his situation is horrible.

"I'd like to see people getting a lot more for what they invest in the way of effort and time. It's insane for human beings to work their whole lives away at dull, stupid, routine, anesthetizing jobs for just a little more than the necessities of life. There should be time — and money — for development. For living."

THOMAS L. KING

from Irony and Distance in *The Glass Menagerie*

Tennessee Williams's *The Glass Menagerie*, though it has achieved a firmly established position in the canon of American plays, is often distorted, if not misunderstood, by readers, directors, and audiences. The distortion results from an overemphasis on the scenes involving Laura and Amanda and their plight, so that the play becomes a sentimental tract on the trapped misery of two women in St. Louis. This leads to the neglect of Tom's soliloquies — speeches that can be ignored or discounted only at great peril, since they occupy such a prominent position in the play. When not largely ignored, they are in danger of being treated as nostalgic yearnings for a former time. But they are not sentimental excursions into the past, paralleling Amanda's, for while they contain sentiment and nostalgia, they also evince a pervasive humor and irony and, indeed, form and contain the entire play. . . .

Saroyan's: William Saroyan (1908–1981), American writer of short stories, plays, novels, and memoirs.

The play . . . is not Amanda's. Amanda is a striking and a powerful character, but the play is Tom's. Tom opens the play and he closes it; he also opens the second act and two further scenes in the first act — his is the first word and the last. Indeed, Amanda, Laura, and the Gentleman Caller do not appear in the play at all as separate characters. In a sense, as [reviewer], Stark Young noted, Tom is the only character in the play, for we see not the characters but Tom's memory of them — Amanda and the rest are merely aspects of Tom's consciousness. Tom's St. Louis is not an objective one, but a solipsist's created by Tom, the artist-magician, and containing Amanda, Laura, and the Gentleman Caller. Tom is the Prospero of *The Glass Menagerie*, and its world is the world of Tom's mind even more than *Death of a Salesman*'s is the world of Willy Loman's mind. The play is warped and distorted when any influence gives Amanda, Laura, or the glass menagerie any undue prominence. If Amanda looms large, she looms large in Tom's mind, not in her own right: though of course the image that finally dominates Tom's mind is that of Laura and the glass menagerie.

The full meaning of the scenes between the soliloquies lies not in themselves alone but also in the commentary provided by Tom standing outside the scenes and speaking with reasonable candor to the audience and reader. Moreover, the comment that the soliloquies makes is not a sentimental one; that is, they are not only expressions of a wistful nostalgia for the lost, doomed world of Amanda, Laura, and the glass menagerie but also contain a good deal of irony and humor which work in the opposite direction. They reveal Tom as an artist figure whose utterances show how the artist creates, using the raw material of his own life. . . .

Generally, each soliloquy oscillates between a sentimental memory of the past, which draws the narrator into it, and a wry irony which keeps him from being fully engulfed and controlled by it. This tension is found in all the soliloquies, though it is not always handled in the same way: sometimes the fond memory is predominant and sometimes the irony, but both are always present. At times, Tom seems almost deliberately to court disaster by creating for himself and the audience a memory so lovely and poignant that the pain of giving it up to return to reality is too much to bear, but return he does with mockery and a kind of wit that interrupts the witchery of memory just short of a withdrawn madness surrounded by soft music and a mind filled with "delicate rainbow colors." In short, Tom toys with the same madness in which his sister Laura is trapped but saves himself with irony. . . .

The opening soliloquy . . . reveals a number of elements that are to be important in the play: it establishes a tension between sentimental nostalgia and detached irony as well as a narrator who is to function as stage magician. The narrator disavows this, but we cannot take him at his word. He says that he is the opposite of a stage magician, but only because his truth looks like illusion rather than the other way round; he is still the magician who creates the play. He says that the play is sentimental rather than realistic, but that is a half truth, for while it contains large doses of sentiment, for the narrator at least, irony sometimes quenches the sentiment. Indeed, Irving Babbit's° phrase describing romantic

---

Babbit's: Irving Babbit (1865–1933), American scholar-critic and professor of French literature at Harvard.

irony is appropriate here: "Hot baths of sentiment . . . followed by cold douches of irony." . . .

The culmination of all the soliloquies, and of the tension between irony and nostalgia that is carefully developed in them, is in the final one. Tom's last speech contains just two touches of ironic detachment, but these are critical and are the foci on which this speech and, indeed, for Tom, the whole play turns. The speech begins with a touch of ironic humor. In the preceding scene, Amanda has told Tom to go to the moon. He begins his final speech with "I didn't go to the moon." This is a decidedly humorous line, indicating that Tom still has access to his detachment, but the audience is not laughing anymore, its detachment has been broken down. The speech then quickly moves into a tone of lyric regret:

> I didn't go to the moon, I went much further — for time is the longest distance between two places. Not long after that I was fired for writing a poem on the lid of a shoe-box. I left Saint Louis. I descended the steps of this fire-escape for a last time and followed, from then on, in my father's footsteps, attempting to find in motion what was lost in space. I traveled around a great deal. The cities swept about me like dead leaves, leaves that were brightly colored but torn away from the branches. I would have stopped, but I was pursued by something. It always came upon me unawares, taking me altogether by surprise. Perhaps it was a familiar bit of music. Perhaps it was only a piece of transparent glass. Perhaps I am walking along a street at night, in some strange city, before I have found companions. I pass the lighted window of a shop where perfume is sold. The window is filled with pieces of colored glass, tiny transparent bottles in delicate colors, like bits of a shattered rainbow. Then all at once my sister touches my shoulder. I turn around and look into her eyes. Oh, Laura, Laura, I tried to leave you behind me, but I am more faithful than I intended to be! I reach for a cigarette, I cross the street, I run into the movies or a bar, I buy a drink, I speak to the nearest stranger — anything that can blow your candles out!
>
> For nowadays the world is lit by lightning! Blow out your candles, Laura — and so good-bye.

The irony in this passage is no longer humorous. When Tom says "I didn't go to the moon," no one is laughing, and the final, ironic "and so good-bye" is not even potentially humorous. Tom seems to have been captured by the memory and the audience has almost certainly been captured, but Tom, in the end, still has his detachment. Laura's candles go out and Tom is relieved of his burden, uttering a final, flip farewell, but the audience has been more faithful than it intended to be; they are left behind, tricked by Tom who is free for the moment while they must face their grief, their cruelty, for they are the world that the Wingfields were somehow set apart from, they are the ones who shattered the rainbow.

The soliloquies, then, are of a piece: they all alternate between sentiment and irony, between mockery and nostalgic regret, and they all end with an ironic tag, which, in most cases, is potentially humorous. They show us the artist manipulating his audience, seeming to be manipulated himself to draw them in, but in the end resuming once more his detached stance. When Tom departs, the audience is left with Laura and Amanda alone before the dead, smoking candles, and Tom escapes into his artist's detachment having exorcized the pain with the creation of the play. This is the trick that Tom has in his pocket.

NANCY MARIE PATTERSON TISCHLER

from Student Companion to Tennessee Williams

Williams loved symbols. Having started his writing as a lyric poet, he explained that he had a "poet's weakness for symbols." This trait was undoubtedly also a result of his early saturation with the symbolism and thought of the Episcopal Church. He came to see almost every aspect of life as symbolic of some greater truth.

He had originally designed *The Glass Menagerie* as a Christmas story (Letter to Audrey Wood, 12/43), with the opening scene one of gift giving. The change in his point of attack to a family meal, though more secular, is nonetheless introduced by a demand that Tom come to the table so that they can say "grace," which incidentally, they then omit; but it is also to make his failed, secular "communion" a commentary on the painful relationship in this community of believers. Nothing should be more ordinary and comfortable than breaking bread together, yet the Wingfield children can perform no function without scrutiny and advice from the hovering mother. An echo of this scene is a second announcement of the impending blessing, this time a summons for Laura to come to the table when Jim O'Connor is their guest for dinner. Pretending that Laura has prepared the meal for their visitor, Amanda again dominates the event, making it her solo performance rather than a shared experience of hospitality. She turns the ritual of eating into a contest of wills. She has transformed a communion into a celebration of her personal sacrifices and a reinforcement of her children's obligations to her as their appropriately grateful response.

Amanda soon reveals herself as a symbol of the "devouring mother." Though apparently nurturing, she thwarts and hobbles her children, dominating not only their eating habits, but their entire lives, keeping them safely in the nest with her. Portraying herself as a martyr to their needs, she actually requires their submission to feed her own pride, crippling Laura by her outrageous expectations. If she could, she would emasculate Tom as well. As her own beauty fades, her appetite for adulation increases, making her a harpy rather than a saint. In a fit of anger, Tom calls his mother an ugly old "witch." Williams was to continue embellishing his archetypal monster-woman as he met more complex and powerful ogres throughout his career.

The central image in this play, from which the work takes its name, is Laura's glass menagerie. Williams' biographers have traced the origins of this image to a tragic young woman in Clarksdale, Mississippi (Leverich 1995, 55). Within the play, it allows us to see the childlike fixation on a private world of make-believe animals, and delicacy of this isolated girl.

This culture, frozen in time, would limit Tom's reading to proper works by polite writers and Laura's choices. In scene after scene, Williams shows Amanda as a victim of her own assumptions about how women should behave, how they should spend their lives, whom they should marry, what domestic chores they should perform, how they should dress, entertain, and talk. She is not just a peculiar old woman: she is a symbol of a dying civilization.

On an even more universal level, this story is about the effects of the industrial revolution on the American family. Although Williams emphasizes the Depression context of the narrative, we know that the pressures on Tom Wingfield extend beyond the span of the 1930s. The growth of big industries in the nineteenth and twentieth centuries had both forced families from the farms and small towns and lured them to great cities, where the personal needs of fragile folk are easily neglected. The polluted air, boring work, and separation from a caring community proved harmful to the mental and physical health of many displaced people.

The emphasis on the "hivelike" buildings of ugly colors with their fire escapes underscores the separation from nature, beauty, and human values. This is not the proper habitat for the dreamer, the poet, or the fragile cripple. Yet, all too often, it is the setting for the young man or woman in urban America. Williams, in *The Glass Menagerie*, is providing us a microcosm in which we can visualize the larger questions of the entire era.

Taking it as a symbol of Laura herself, fragile and beautiful, the author plays with the more specific figure of the unicorn. Here we see the complete development of a complex idea, hinted at in the dialogue. We know from medieval iconography that this mythical figure is identified with virgins and therefore with sexuality. Although it looks like a horse the unicorn is not a horse, but is a unique (if mythical) creature. Thus, when Jim accidentally breaks off its horn, he has not transformed it into a horse: it remains a unicorn, but is now a damaged unicorn that manages to look like an ordinary horse. In some ways, this is what Amanda has done to Laura, distorted her true childish nature to make her seem like all the normal young ladies being courted by nice young gentlemen. (The "gay deceivers" are delightful symbols of Laura's underdeveloped sexuality and Amanda's pressures to appear sexy.) Laura's pained responses to her mother's cruel questions about her plans for the evening expose the anguish that this teasing causes the sensitive girl.

The mock-courtship scene between Laura and Jim contains another cluster of images. Tom, having misused the money for the electric bill, has plunged them into darkness. Amanda, always eager to adopt romantic attitudes, furnishes them with a candelabra, a relic from a church fire, and thereby returns them to the nineteenth century — the family's native habitat. Jim briefly enters into their game of playing at pre-electric life, settles on the floor, and enjoys a childlike moment of shared memories with Laura. But we soon learn that he lives fully in the "Century of Progress," which Laura is blocked from entering. Jim tries, in an act of egocentric kindness, to move her into the adult world of dancing and kissing, but Laura remains a lonely little girl who had a playmate over to visit for the evening. That scene foreshadows the final words, "For nowadays the world is lit by lightning! Blow out your candles, Laura — and so goodbye". . . .

Other images also populate the play. Williams loved the ocean and frequently used the sea as an escape symbol. His sailors, pirates, and buccaneers are the gallant figures who sail away from the dreary land to have adventures denied to most of mankind. Certainly Americans have known this imagery from their earliest days, America itself being the grand adventure for most of our ancestors. For at least three of Williams' literary heroes° — Melville, O'Neill, and Crane — the sea voyage was also the escape into the life of literature.

Tennessee Williams' delight in earlier poets, novelists, and dramatists gives additional richness to the texture of the phrasing in *The Glass Menagerie*. For example, Tom's final portrayal of cities as leaves blown by the wind, "brightly colored, but torn away from the branches" echoes Shelley's "Ode to the West Wind."° Fortunately, such similes work effectively even if the listener fails to pick up the source of the allusion. We need not picture the famous medieval unicorn tapestry in order to delight in the unicorn reference. Nor do we need to know about D. H. Lawrence's rainbow° of sexuality in order to understand the rainbow colors at the Paradise Dance Hall. Blue Mountain is the right name for a romantic past, and Moon Lake is the ideal name for adventures in love. The words carry the message, regardless of our specific knowledge of Clarksdale's geography. Williams lets his words tell their own stories. The viewer can delight in the surface brilliance or dig deep into allusions, allowing several levels of possible resonance. . . .

ROGER B. STEIN

from The Glass Menagerie Revisited: Catastrophe without Violence

The religious overtones of *The Glass Menagerie* are even more pervasive. Though they never obscure the literal line of the story or seem self-conscious, as they do in some of the later plays, these overtones add a dimension to the play which reaches beyond individual pathos and social tragedy. Williams's stage directions clearly indicate his intention. As with Hannah in *The Night of the Iguana*, he tells us that the lighting for Laura should resemble that "used in early religious portraits of female saints or madonnas." The scene where Tom tells his mother that a gentleman caller will appear Williams entitles "Annunciation." The dressing of Laura for the caller's appearance should be "devout and ritualistic." During her scene with Jim she is lit "inwardly with altar candles," and when Jim withdraws after kissing her Williams informs us that the "holy candles in the altar of Laura's face have been snuffed out. There is a look of almost infinite desolation."

Those overtones extend beyond Williams's hints to the director and become a crucial part of the fabric of dramatic action. The first scene in both the Acting

literary heroes: Herman Melville (1819–1891), Eugene O'Neill (1888–1953), and Stephen Crane (1871–1900).

Shelley's "Ode to the West Wind": See Chapter 33, page 1194.

D. H. Lawrence's rainbow: Lawrence's novel *The Rainbow* was published in 1915.

Version and the Library Edition of the play opens on this note. In the former, Amanda narrates her "funny experience" of being denied a seat in the Episcopal church because she has not rented a pew. The idea of the Wingfields' exclusion from Christian ceremony is established thus at the outset, and it is underlined by the ensuing talk of digesting food, mastication, and salivary glands. In the Wingfield apartment, eating is an animal process only; it lacks ritual significance. The Library Edition opens with Amanda's call to Tom, "We can't say grace until you come to the table," and then moves on to the question of digestion. The lines are different, but their import is the same. When the gentleman caller comes, the scene is repeated, only this time it is Laura whose absence holds up "grace."

Amanda, who condemns instinct and urges Tom to think in terms of the mind and spirit, as "Christian adults" do, is often characterized in Christian terms. Her music, in the Library Edition, is "Ave Maria." As a girl she could only cook angel food cake. She urges Laura, "Possess your soul in patience," and then speaks of her dress for the dinner scene as "resurrected" from a trunk. Her constant refrain to Tom is "Rise an' Shine," and she sells subscriptions to her friends by waking them early in the morning and then sympathizing with them as "Christian martyrs." Laura is afraid to tell her mother she has left the business school because "when you're disappointed, you get that awful suffering look on your face, like the picture of Jesus' mother in the museum!"

The next picture Laura mentions is the one of Jim in the yearbook; though the context seems secular enough at this point — Jim is a high school hero — his religious function emerges later on. In the "Annunciation" scene, when Amanda learns that the gentleman caller's name is O'Connor, she says, "That, of course, means fish — tomorrow is Friday!" The remark functions not only literally, since Jim is Irish Catholic, but also figuratively, for the fish is the traditional symbol of Christ. In a very real sense both Amanda and Laura are searching for a Savior who will come to help them, to save them, to give their drab lives meaning.

Tom is unable to play this role himself. Though he appears as the angel of the Annunciation, he denies the world of belief and in a bitter speech to his mother calls himself "El Diablo." With him Christian terms appear only as imprecations: "what in Christ's name" or "that God damn Rise and Shine." When Tom returns home drunk one night, he tells Laura of a stage show he has seen which is shot through with Christian symbolism, none of which he perceives. Here the magician, Malvolio, whose name suggests bad will, dislike, or even hate, plays the role of the modern Christ. He performs the miracle of turning water into wine and then goes on to blasphemy by turning the wine into beer and then whiskey. He also produces his proper symbol, the fish, but it is goldfish, as if stained by modern materialism. Most important, perhaps, he escapes from a nailed coffin. But Tom reads the symbolism of this trick in personal terms only. When Laura tries to keep him from awakening Amanda, Tom retorts:

> Goody goody! Pay 'er back for all those "Rise an' Shine's." You know it don't take much intelligence to get yourself into a nailed-up coffin, Laura. But who in hell ever got himself out of one without removing one nail?

The illumination of the father's photograph at this point suggests one answer to this question, but the pattern of Christian imagery in the drama, especially when reinforced here by the "Rise an' Shine" refrain, should suggest to us another answer — the resurrection itself — which Tom's rejection of Christian belief prevents him from seeing.

It remains therefore for Jim to come as the Savior to this Friday night supper. The air of expectancy is great, with the ritualistic dressing of Laura, the tension, and the oppressive heat. Jim's arrival is marked by the coming of rain, but the hopes of fertility and renewal which this might suggest are soon dashed. Laura's attempt to come to the dinner table is a failure, signaled by a clap of thunder, and Tom's muttered grace, "For these and all thy mercies, God's Holy Name be praised," is bitterly ironic, mocked by what follows. The only paradise within reach is Paradise Dance Hall, with its "Waste Land" mood of slow and sensuous rhythms and couples kissing behind ashpits and telephone poles, "the compensation for lives that passed . . . without any change or adventure," as Tom remarks. The failure of electric power after dinner — previsioning the blackout of the world — leads to Amanda's joking question, "Where was Moses when the lights went off?" This suggests another savior who would lead his people from the desert into the promised land, but the answer to her question is "In the dark."

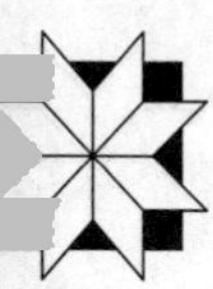

Jim's attempt to play the modern savior is an abysmal failure. In the after-dinner scene, he offers Laura the sacrament — wine and "life-savers," in this case — and a Dale Carnegie version of the Sermon on the Mount — self-help rather than divine help — but to no avail. At the end of the play Laura and Amanda are, as the joke bitterly reminds us, "in the dark," and Tom's last lines announce the final failure, the infinite desolation: "For nowadays the world is lit by lightning. Blow out your candles, Laura — and so goodbye."

TOM SCANLAN

from Family, Drama, and American Dreams

The major dilemmas of family life are imbedded in the dramatic action of Williams's plays, and the ideal that haunts his characters is family-related. Moreover, those plays which have been most successful artistically have been those mostly about the family. . . .

In the earlier plays Williams dramatized the family world in a state of collapse; in later ones family collapse is antecedent to the action. These two situations are combined in *The Glass Menagerie*, Williams's first successful play (and probably his most popular one[1]). The play is a perfect fusion of the two subjects and so is a figure for Williams's entire career. In it the family is long lost and, also, we witness its struggle before it is lost. Williams captures the poignancy of family memories in a way all his own, without sacrificing the core of dramatic conflict which makes such memories less static.

The play is a prime example of Williams's artistry in establishing the relation between his own dramatic world and the conventions of realistic domestic drama to which his audience owes great allegiance, as he well knew. The play occurs in the mind of Tom Wingfield, who drifts in and out of the action both as narrator and participant in a peculiarly appropriate way. From the moment at the beginning when the scrim of the tenement wall dissolves and we enter the Wingfields' apartment, we are reminded of the household of so many family plays. The realistic convention of the fourth wall is evoked as Tom remembers his family.

Tom's evocation is self-conscious, for as "stage manager" he has control over the setting. But Tom is also at the mercy of his memories and irresistibly must relive them. The play keeps us poised between these two styles, these two times, throughout. This is, in fact, its strongest and most subtle conflict. Like Tom, we are continually tempted into the world of a realistic family struggle, but never allowed to enter it completely. The projections and lighting keep the effect slightly stylized during the scenes, the fragmented structure blocks us from too long an absorption in the action, and the re-appearance of Tom as narrator forces us back to the present. It is Tom's final reappearance in this role, when the action of the memory play is completed, which releases the tension created between the two styles and dramatizes, in a final rush of emotion, the irretrievable loss of the family which Tom can never escape.

Tom cannot shake the memory of his family from his mind; the dissolution of time and space in the play — that is, in his consciousness — heightens the importance of what he is remembering to make it the most significant thing about his existence. What he remembers — the bulk of the play — centers around two lines of action. The first is his desire to escape from his family just as his father had done before him: "He was a telephone man who fell in love with long distances."[2] Tom, a would-be writer, is caught between a domineering mother and a stultifying warehouse job. He escapes to the porch, to the movies, to the saloon. And finally, in the end, we learn that he has followed his father out into long distances. The second line of action, the principal one, concerns his mother, Amanda, and her attempts to establish some kind of life for Tom's crippled sister, Laura. Amanda pins her hopes on getting "sister" married, after Laura fails because of painful shyness to continue in business school. A "gentleman caller" is found, Jim O'Connor, "an emissary from the world of reality," but all of Amanda's hopes are crushed as he turns out to be already engaged.

The plot is slight stuff, as Williams himself knew.[3] The effect of the play derives in part from the contrast between its two lines of action. Amanda is given over to memories of her past life of happiness as a young southern debutante in Blue Mountain, Mississippi, where on one incredible Sunday she had seventeen gentlemen callers. She imitates the manners and graciousness of those days, a faintly ludicrous parody of southern gentility, the played-out tradition of the antebellum South and its family of security. But she has spirit, too, and responds to the problems of raising two children in a St. Louis tenement during the Depression. Her practicality is what gives her dignity; as she cares for Laura we realize how much Amanda herself needs to be cared for. Her refusal to give in to her nostalgia, even while she indulges in it, enhances her character and makes us susceptible to her longing.

Tom is smothered by such a woman. He fights with her, in part, because she continually tells him what to do: how to eat; how to sleep; how to get ahead. But he fights, also, because her standards represent the conventionality of family responsibility. . . . The absent father, who still represents the memory of romantic family love to Amanda, is the possibility of romantic escape from family to Tom.[4] He loves his sister Laura, yet he will not accept the responsibility for her which Amanda demands of him. The Wingfields are only a ghost of the family of security, but even this demand to be close-knit repels the restless Tom.

Tom's love for Laura needs to be emphasized, I think, not only because it is one part of the final image of the play — the moment of revelation toward which the action tends — but because it shows Williams's interest in the special qualities of those whom the world has hurt. They are the delicate and fragile people, too sensitive to be able to withstand the crude and harsh necessities by which life drives us along. They have an extraordinary awareness of hidden, almost mystical, qualities of spiritual beauty; and this openness dooms them to be crushed or perverted by the animal vigor of the world.

Laura's specialness is seen largely in contrast with Jim, her gentleman caller. He is, by all odds, the kindest of Williams's emissaries from reality, perhaps because his faith in the American dream of self-improvement and success is so complete as to be itself a touching illusion. . . .

There will be no normal love of marriage and family for Laura nor for any of the Wingfields. Laura is too tender, too special, too fragile like her glass menagerie. It is Tom's painful sensitivity to Laura's predicament which makes him love her and which drives him from her. But he cannot escape Laura. The necessity of leaving her, and the guilt over doing so, haunt him:

> Oh, Laura, Laura, I tried to leave you behind me, but I am more faithful than I intended to be! I reach for a cigarette, I cross the street, I run into the movies or a bar, I buy a drink, I speak to the nearest stranger — anything that can blow your candles out!
>
> (*Laura bends over the candles.*)
>
> For nowadays the world is lit by lightning! Blow out your candles, Laura — and so good-bye. . . .
>
> (*She blows the candles out.*)[5]

Laura's painful encounter with the world's lightning represents all of the Wingfields. Amanda's last glance at her husband's picture reveals as much of her as does Tom's final speech of him. The family is the supreme case of love trying to struggle against the world, and the family fails. Fundamentally romantic, Williams evokes the beauty of failure, the beauty which must fail. . . .

Notes

[1] Jackson, *Broken World*, p. viii, note 1.

[2] Williams, *Menagerie*, p. 145.

[3] "A free, imaginative use of light can be of enormous value in giving a mobile, plastic quality to plays of a more or less static nature." Williams, "Production Notes," *Menagerie*, p. 134.

[4] Tischler, *Williams*, p. 97.

[5] Williams, *Menagerie*, p. 237.

JAMES FISHER

from "The Angels of Fructification°": Tennessee Williams, Tony Kushner, and Images of Homosexuality on the American Stage

Who, if I were to cry out, would hear me among the angelic orders?[1]
—*Rainer Maria Rilke*

Still obscured by glistening exhaltations, the angels of fructification had now begun to meet the tumescent phallus of the sun. Vastly the wheels of the earth sang Allelulia! And the seven foaming oceans bellowed Oh![2]
—*Tennessee Williams*

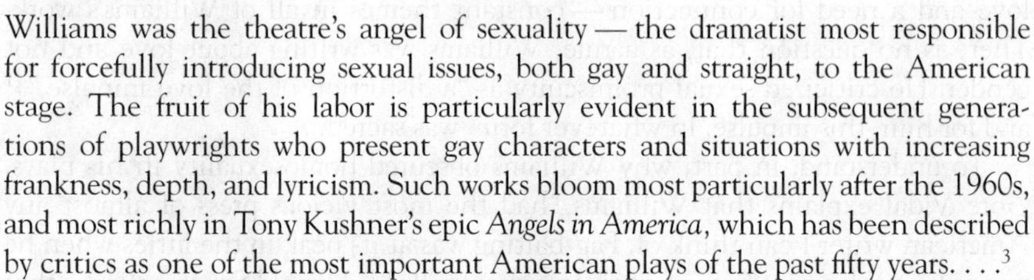

Williams was the theatre's angel of sexuality — the dramatist most responsible for forcefully introducing sexual issues, both gay and straight, to the American stage. The fruit of his labor is particularly evident in the subsequent generations of playwrights who present gay characters and situations with increasing frankness, depth, and lyricism. Such works bloom most particularly after the 1960s, and most richly in Tony Kushner's epic *Angels in America*, which has been described by critics as one of the most important American plays of the past fifty years. . . .[3]

In reflecting on the history of homosexuals in American theatre, Kushner believes that "there's a natural proclivity for gay people — who historically have often spent their lives hiding — to feel an affinity for the extended make-believe and donning of roles that is part of theater. It's reverberant with some of the central facts of our lives."[4] It is not surprising that, in a society in which homosexuals were firmly closeted before the 1960s, the illusions of the stage provided a safe haven. Williams could not be as open about his sexuality in his era as Kushner can be now, and thus had to work with overtly heterosexual situations and characters. Williams's creative achievements grow out of a guarded self-awareness and desire for self-preservation, as well as the constraints of the prevailing values of his day.

Donald Windham believes that Williams "loved being homosexual. I think he loved it more than he loved anybody, more than he loved anything except writing,"[5] and Edward A. Sklepowich seems to agree when he writes that "Williams treats homosexuality with a reverence that at times approaches chauvinism."[6] In fact, Williams was often ambivalent about homosexuality — either his own or anyone else's — in his writings. Although his sexuality was well known in the theatrical community, it is unclear when Williams first "came out" publicly. His 1970 appearance on David Frost's television program seems the earliest public declaration. When Frost asked him to comment on his sexuality, Williams replied, "I don't want to be involved in some sort of a scandal, but I've covered the waterfront."[7] He also told Frost that "everybody has some elements of homosexuality in him, even the most heterosexual of us" (p. 40), but a few years later he wrote, "I have never found the subject of homosexuality a satisfactory theme for a

Fructification: The producing of fruit.

full-length play, despite the fact that it appears as frequently as it does in my short fiction. Yet never even in my short fiction does the sexual activity of a person provide the story with its true inner substance."[8] A couple of years later, in an interview in the *Village Voice,* Williams made the point with bluntness: "I've nothing to conceal. Homosexuality isn't the theme of my plays. They're about all human relationships. I've never faked it,"[9] and in 1975 he stated, "Sexuality is part of my work, of course, because sexuality is a part of my life and everyone's life. I see no essential difference between the love of two men for each other and the love of a man for a woman; no essential difference, and that's why I've examined both. . . ."[10] In his novel, *Moise and the World of Reason* (1975), Williams is franker in his depiction of homosexuality than in any of his plays. However, more important than issues of homosexuality, the characters in the novel feel the absence of love and a need for connection — constant themes in all of Williams's work. There is no question that, as a rule, Williams was writing about love and not gender. He criticized sexual promiscuity as "a distortion of the love impulse,"[11] and for him, this impulse, in whatever form, was sacred. . . .

To understand, in part, why Williams obscured homosexuality in his plays, Gore Vidal explains that Williams "had the most vicious press of almost any American writer I can think of. Fag-baiting was at its peak in the fifties when he was at his peak and it has never given up, actually."[12] Donald Spoto believes that Williams's ambivalence had to do, in part, with the fact that he wanted "to be controversial — the hard-drinking, openly homosexual writer with nothing to hide — and at the same time, a man of his own time, a Southern gentleman from a politer era who would never abandon propriety and privacy."[13] This view might indicate why Williams seemed uncomfortable with public displays of drag or campiness, which, he writes, are

> imposed upon homosexuals by our society. The obnoxious forms of it will rapidly disappear as Gay Lib begins to succeed in its serious crusade to assert, for its genuinely misunderstood and persecuted minority, a free position in society which will permit them to respect themselves, at least to the extent that, individually, they deserve respect — and I think that degree is likely to be much higher than commonly supposed.[14]

And it was in the arena of the arts, Williams believed, that the gay sensibility was most likely to first engender such respect. In his *Memoirs* he states, "There is no doubt in my mind that there is more sensibility — which is equivalent to more talent — among the 'gays' of both sexes than among the 'norms' . . ." (p. 63). At the same time, Williams wished to attract a broader audience than gays for his work and seems to have believed that a so-called gay play would limit his access to universal acceptance.

Williams's concern about acceptance was not without some justice. He did not have to look too far back into the preceding decades of American drama to see that the audience was, at best, uncertain about its willingness to accept homosexual characters and issues. The first American play to deal openly with homosexuality is believed to be Mae West's *The Drag,* which generated so much controversy that it closed before completing a tumultuous pre-Broadway tour in 1927. A few other curiosities appeared in the subsequent decades, most notably Lillian Hellman's *The Children's Hour* (1934), in which the question of a lesbian relationship is at the center. Of course, secondary homosexual characters appear in a few plays of the 1930s and 1940s, but they are rarely identified as such. Simon Stimson, the alcoholic choir master of Thornton Wilder's *Our Town* (1938), is a vivid example of such types, typical in that he is comparatively unimportant to the plot and that he is seen mostly as a tragi-comic victim. With the appearance of Robert Anderson's *Tea and Sympathy* (1953), in which a sensitive young man is viewed by his peers as a homosexual (even though it later becomes clear that he is not), gay issues and characters slowly come out of the shadows.

During the 1950s, other playwrights introduced gay characters and issues, but often not in their most visible work. William Inge, inspired to become a playwright by Williams's example, did not feature openly homosexual characters in any of his major plays, but in a few lesser-known one-acts he does so vividly. Inge's *The Tiny Closet* (1959), for example, features a man boarding in a rooming house where the nosy landlady has been attempting to break into a padlocked closet in his room. As soon as the man goes out, the landlady and her friend manage to break in and discover an array of elegant women's hats. The landlady's violation — and the presumption that she will cause him public disgrace — leaves the man's ultimate fate in question. Inge's blunt attack on intolerance[15] was written in the aftermath of the McCarthy era and was a forerunner of later gay plays, particularly those written after the late 1960s, which argue for greater acceptance for homosexuals.

Mid-twentieth century dramatists employed various techniques to present gay characters and situations. One device often used is "transference," the act of hiding gay viewpoints and situations behind a mask of heterosexuality. Edward Albee, often accused of using transference in the writing of such plays as *Who's Afraid of Virginia Woolf?* (1962), is a gay dramatist who also emerged in the 1950s. With the homosexual triumvirate of Williams, Inge, and Albee dominating the non-musical Broadway stage — and despite the fact that none of them had publicly acknowledged their own sexuality —*New York Times* drama critic Stanley Kauffmann "outed" them in 1966. Although he does not give their names, it is clear to whom he is referring in his article "Homosexual Drama and Its Disguises." Kauffmann implies that homosexual writers have no right to write about anything but gay characters — an attitude which would logically imply that men are unable to write about women and vice versa. Kauffmann's notion, undoubtedly all too prevalent in the mid 1960s, becomes clearer when he writes:

> Conventions and puritanisms in the Western world have forced [homosexuals] to wear masks for generations, to hate themselves, and thus to hate those who make them hate themselves. Now that they have a certain relative freedom, they vent their feelings in camouflaged form. . . . They emphasize manner and style because these elements of art, at which they are often adept, are legal tender in their transactions with the world. These elements are, or can be, esthetically divorced from such other considerations as character and idea.[16]

Albee firmly refutes the idea that he, or Williams, employs transference in his plays: "Tennessee never did that, and I can't think of any self-respecting worthwhile writer who would do that sort of thing. It's beneath contempt to suggest it, and it's beneath contempt to do it.[17] Gore Vidal's explanation of the centrality of women characters in Williams's plays seems a valid alternative to understanding his work and the reasons critics see transference in his plays. Vidal believes that for Williams, a woman was "always more interesting as she was apt to be the victim of a society."[18] Williams understood, as Strindberg did, that there are many aspects of the female in the male and vice-versa. And, also like Strindberg, Williams's pained, driven, poetic, and passionate characters are unquestionably extensions of his own persona regardless of their gender.

Notes

[1] Ranier Maria Rilke, "Duino Elegies. The Ninth Elegy," in *Selected Works. Vol. 11. Poetry*, trans. J. B. Leishman (Norfolk, Connecticut, and New York: A New Directions Book, 1960), pp. 244–245.

[2] Tennessee Williams, "The Angels of Fructification," in *In the Winter of Cities. Selected Poems of Tennessee Williams* (New York: New Directions, 1956, 1964), p. 34.

[3] Kushner's theatrical output thus far includes the plays *Yes, Yes, No, No* (1985; children's play), *Stella* (1987; adapted from a play by Goethe), *A Bright Room Called Day* (1987), *Hydriotaphia* (1987), *The Illusion* (1988; freely adapted from a play by Pierre Corneille), *Angels in America. Part One. Millenium Approaches* (1990), *Angels in America. Part Two. Perestroika* (1991), *Widows* (1991; written with Ariel Dorfman, adapted from Dorfman's novel), *Slavs* (1994), and *The Dybbuk* (1995; adapted from S. Ansky's play).

[4] Bob Blanchard, "Playwright of Pain and Hope," *Progressive Magazine*. October 1994, p. 42.

[5] Donald Windham interviewed in "Tennessee Williams. Orpheus of the American Stage," a film by Merrill Brockway broadcast on "American Masters" (PBS-TV), 1994.

[6] Edward A. Sklepowich, "In Pursuit of the Lyric Quarry: The Image of the Homosexual in Tennessee Williams' Prose Fiction," in *Tennessee Williams: A Tribute*, ed. Jac Tharpe (Jackson: University Press of Mississippi, 1977), p. 541.

[7] David Frost, *The Americans* (New York: Stein and Day, 1970), p. 40.

[8] Tennessee Williams, "Let Me Hang It All Out." *New York Times*, March 4, 1975, Section 11, p. 1.

[9] Tennessee Williams interviewed by Arthur Bell, *Village Voice*, February 24, 1972.

[10] Tennessee Williams interviewed by Robert Berkvist, *New York Times*, December 21, 1975.

[11] Tennessee Williams interviewed on "The Lively Arts" program (BBC-TV), 1976.

[12] Gore Vidal interviewed in "Tennessee Williams. Orpheus of the American Stage," a film by Merrill Brockway for "American Masters" (PBS-TV), 1994.

[13] Donald Spoto, *The Kindness of Strangers, The Life of Tennessee Williams* (Boston/Toronto: Little, Brown and Co., 1985), p. 292.

[14] Tennessee Williams, *Memoirs* (New York: Doubleday, 1975), p. 63.

[15] Inge's one-act *The Boy in the Basement* (1962) makes a similar plea for tolerance.

[16] Stanley Kauffmann, "Homosexual Drama and Its Disguises," *New York Times*, January 23, 1966, Section 2, p. 1.

[17] Edward Albee, cited in *The Playwright's Art. Conversations with Contemporary American Dramatists*, ed. Jackson R. Bryer (New Brunswick, New Jersey: Rutgers University Press, 1995), p. 21.

[18] Gore Vidal interviewed in "Tennessee Williams. Orpheus of the American Stage," a film by Merrill Brockway for "American Masters" (PBS-TV), 1994.

TENNESSEE WILLIAMS

Portrait of a Girl in Glass

We lived in a third floor apartment on Maple Street in Saint Louis, on a block which also contained the Ever-ready Garage, a Chinese laundry, and a bookie shop disguised as a cigar store.

Mine was an anomalous character, one that appeared to be slated for radical change or disaster, for I was a poet who had a job in a warehouse. As for my sister Laura, she could be classified even less readily than I. She made no positive motion toward the world but stood at the edge of the water, so to speak, with feet that anticipated too much cold to move. She'd never have budged an inch, I'm pretty sure, if my mother who was a relatively aggressive sort of woman had not shoved her roughly forward, when Laura was twenty years old, by enrolling her as a student in a nearby business college. Out of her "magazine money" (she sold subscriptions to women's magazines), Mother had paid my sister's tuition for a term of six months. It did not work out. Laura tried to memorize the typewriter keyboard, she had a chart at home, she used to sit silently in front of it for hours, staring at it while she cleaned and polished her infinite number of little glass ornaments. She did this every evening after dinner. Mother would caution me to be very quiet. "Sister is looking at her typewriter chart!" I felt somehow that it would do her no good, and I was right. She would seem to know the positions of the keys until the weekly speed drill got underway, and then they would fly from her mind like a bunch of startled birds.

At last she couldn't bring herself to enter the school any more. She kept this failure a secret for a while. She left the house each morning as before and spent six hours walking around the park. This was in February, and all the walking outdoors regardless of weather brought on influenza. She was in bed for a couple of weeks with a curiously happy little smile on her face. Of course Mother phoned the business college to let them know she was ill. Whoever was talking on the other end of the line had some trouble, it seems, in remembering who Laura was, which annoyed my mother and she spoke up pretty sharply. "Laura has been attending that school of yours for two months, you certainly ought to recognize her name!" Then came the stunning disclosure. The person sharply retorted, after a moment or two, that now she *did* remember the Wingfield girl, and that she had not been at the business college *once* in about a month. Mother's voice became strident. Another person was brought to the phone to verify the statement of the first. Mother hung up and went to Laura's bedroom where she lay with a tense and frightened look in place of the faint little smile. Yes, admitted my sister, what they said was true. "I couldn't go any longer, it scared me too much, it made me sick at the stomach!"

After this fiasco, my sister stayed at home and kept in her bedroom mostly. This was a narrow room that had two windows on a dusky areaway between two wings of the building. We called this areaway Death Valley for a reason that seems worth telling. There were a great many alley cats in the neighborhood and one particularly vicious dirty white Chow who stalked them continually. In the open or on the fire escapes they could usually elude him but now and again he cleverly contrived to run some youngster among them into the cul-de-sac of this narrow areaway at the far end of which, directly beneath my sister's bedroom windows, they made the blinding discovery that what had appeared to be an avenue of escape was really a locked arena, a gloomy vault of concrete and brick with walls too high for any cat to spring, in which they must suddenly turn to spit at their death until it was hurled upon them. Hardly a week went by without a repetition of this violent drama. The areaway had grown to be hateful to Laura because she could not look out on it without recalling the screams and the snarls of killing. She kept the shades drawn down, and as Mother would not permit the use of electric current except when needed, her days were spent almost in perpetual twilight. There were three pieces of dingy ivory furniture in the room, a bed, a bureau, a chair. Over the bed was a remarkably bad religious painting, a very effeminate head of Christ with teardrops visible just below the eyes. The charm of the room was produced by my sister's collection of glass. She loved colored glass and had covered the walls with shelves of little glass articles, all of them light and delicate in color. These she washed and polished with endless care. When you entered the room there was always this soft, transparent radiance in it which came from the glass absorbing whatever faint light came through the shades on Death Valley. I have no idea how many articles there were of this delicate glass. There must have been hundreds of them. But Laura could tell you exactly. She loved each one.

She lived in a world of glass and also a world of music. The music came from a 1920 Victrola and a bunch of records that dated from about the same period, pieces such as "Whispering" or "The Love Nest" or "Dardanella." These records were souvenirs of our father, a man whom we barely remembered, whose name was spoken rarely. Before his sudden and unexplained disappearance from our lives, he had made this gift to the household, the phonograph and the records, whose music remained as a sort of apology for him. Once in a while, on payday at the warehouse, I would bring home a new record. But Laura seldom cared for these new records, maybe because they reminded her too much of the noisy tragedies in Death Valley or the speed drills at the business college. The tunes she loved were the ones she had always heard. Often she sang to herself at night in her bedroom. Her voice was thin, it usually wandered off-key. Yet it had a curious childlike sweetness. At eight o'clock in the evening I sat down to write in my own mousetrap of a room. Through the closed doors, through the walls, I would hear my sister singing to herself, a piece like "Whispering" or "I Love You" or "Sleepy Time Gal," losing the tune now and then but always preserving the minor atmosphere of the music. I think that was why I always wrote such strange and sorrowful poems in those days. Because I had in my ears the wispy sound of my sister serenading her pieces of colored glass, washing them while she sang or merely looking down at them with her vague blue eyes until the points of gem-like radiance in them gently drew the arching particles of reality from her mind and finally produced a state of hypnotic calm in which she even stopped singing or washing the glass and merely sat without motion until my mother knocked at the door and warned her against the waste of electric current.

I don't believe that my sister was actually foolish. I think the petals of her mind had simply closed through fear, and it's no telling how much they had closed upon in the way of secret wisdom. She never talked very much, not even to me, but once in a while she did pop out with something that took you by surprise.

After work at the warehouse or after I'd finished my writing in the evening, I'd drop in her room for a little visit because she had a restful and soothing effect on nerves that were worn rather thin from trying to ride two horses simultaneously in two opposite directions.

I usually found her seated in the straight-back ivory chair with a piece of glass cupped tenderly in her palm.

"What are you doing? Talking to it?" I asked.

"No," she answered gravely, "I was just looking at it."

On the bureau were two pieces of fiction which she had received as Christmas or birthday presents. One was a novel called the *Rose-Garden Husband* by someone whose name escapes me. The other was *Freckles* by Gene Stratton Porter. I never saw her reading the *Rose-Garden Husband,* but the other book was one that she actually lived with. It had probably never occurred to Laura that a book was something you read straight through and then laid aside as finished. The character Freckles, a one-armed orphan youth who worked in a lumber camp, was someone that she invited into her bedroom now and then for a friendly visit just as she did me. When I came in and found this novel open upon her lap, she would gravely remark that Freckles was having some trouble with the foreman of the lumber camp or that he had just received an injury to his spine when a tree fell on him. She frowned with genuine sorrow when she reported these misadventures of her storybook hero, possibly not recalling how successfully he came through them all, that the injury to the spine fortuitously resulted in the discovery of rich parents and that the bad-tempered foreman has a heart of gold at the end of the book. Freckles became involved in romance with a girl he called The Angel, but my sister usually stopped reading when this girl became too prominent in the story. She closed the book or turned back to the lonelier periods in the orphan's story. I only remember her making one reference to this heroine of the novel. "The Angel is nice," she said, "but seems to be kind of conceited about her looks."

Then one time at Christmas, while she was trimming the artificial tree, she picked up the Star of Bethlehem that went on the topmost branch and held it gravely toward the chandelier.

"Do stars have five points really?" she enquired.

This was the sort of thing that you didn't believe and that made you stare at Laura with sorrow and confusion.

"No," I told her, seeing she really meant it, "they're round like the earth and most of them much bigger."

She was gently surprised by this new information. She went to the window to look up at the sky which was, as usual during Saint Louis winters, completely shrouded by smoke.

"It's hard to tell," she said, and returned to the tree.

So time passed on till my sister was twenty-three. Old enough to be married, but the fact of the matter was she had never even had a date with a boy. I don't believe this seemed as awful to her as it did to Mother.

At breakfast one morning Mother said to me, "Why don't you cultivate some nice young friends? How about down at the warehouse? Aren't there some young men down there you could ask to dinner?"

This suggestion surprised me because there was seldom quite enough food on her table to satisfy three people. My mother was a terribly stringent housekeeper, God knows we were poor enough in actuality, but my mother had an almost obsessive dread of becoming even poorer. A not unreasonable fear since the man of the house was a poet who worked in a warehouse, but one which I thought played too important a part in all her calculations.

Almost immediately Mother explained herself.

"I think it might be nice," she said, "for your sister."

I brought Jim home to dinner a few nights later. Jim was a big red-haired Irishman who had the scrubbed and polished look of well-kept chinaware. His big square hands seemed to have a direct and very innocent hunger for touching his friends. He was always clapping them on your arms or shoulders and they burned through the cloth of your shirt like plates taken out of an oven. He was the best-liked man in the warehouse and oddly enough he was the only one that I was on good terms with. He found me agreeably ridiculous I think. He knew of my secret practice of retiring to a cabinet in the lavatory and working on rhyme schemes when work was slack in the warehouse, and of sneaking up on the roof now and then to smoke my cigarette with a view across the river at the undulant open country of Illinois. No doubt I was classified as screwy in Jim's mind as much as in the others', but while their attitude was suspicious and hostile when they first knew me, Jim's was warmly tolerant from the beginning. He called me Slim, and gradually his cordial acceptance drew the others around, and while he remained the only one who actually had anything to do with me, the others had now begun to smile when they saw me as people smile at an oddly fashioned dog who crosses their path at some distance.

Nevertheless it took some courage for me to invite Jim to dinner. I thought about it all week and delayed the action till Friday noon, the last possible moment, as the dinner was set for that evening.

"What are you doing tonight?" I finally asked him.

"Not a God damn thing," said Jim. "I had a date but her Aunt took sick and she's hauled her freight to Centralia!"

"Well," I said, "why don't you come over for dinner?"

"Sure!" said Jim. He grinned with astonishing brightness.

I went outside to phone the news to Mother.

Her voice that was never tired responded with an energy that made the wires crackle.

"I suppose he's Catholic?" she said.

"Yes," I told her, remembering the tiny silver cross on his freckled chest.

"Good!" she said. "I'll bake a salmon loaf!"

And so we rode home together in his jalopy.

I had a curious feeling of guilt and apprehension as I led the lamb-like Irishman up three flights of cracked marble steps to the door of Apartment F, which was not thick enough to hold inside it the odor of baking salmon.

Never having a key, I pressed the bell.

"Laura!" came Mother's voice. "That's Tom and Mr. Delaney! Let them in!"

There was a long, long pause.

"Laura?" she called again. "I'm busy in the kitchen, you answer the door!"

Then at last I heard my sister's footsteps. They went right past the door at which we were standing and into the parlor. I heard the creaking noise of the phonograph crank. Music commenced. One of the oldest records, a march of Sousa's, put on to give her the courage to let in a stranger.

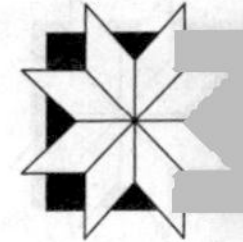

The door came timidly open and there she stood in a dress from Mother's wardrobe, a black chiffon ankle-length and high-heeled slippers on which she balanced uncertainly like a tipsy crane of melancholy plumage. Her eyes stared back at us with a glass brightness and her delicate wing-like shoulders were hunched with nervousness.

"Hello!" said Jim, before I could introduce him.

He stretched out his hand. My sister touched it only for a second.

"Excuse me!" she whispered, and turned with a breathless rustle back to her bedroom door, the sanctuary beyond it briefly revealing itself with the tinkling, muted radiance of glass before the door closed rapidly but gently on her wraithlike figure.

Jim seemed to be incapable of surprise.

"Your sister?" he asked.

"Yes, that was her," I admitted. "She's terribly shy with strangers."

"She looks like you," said Jim, "except she's pretty."

Laura did not reappear till called to dinner. Her place was next to Jim at the drop-leaf table and all through the meal her figure was slightly tilted away from his. Her face was feverishly bright and one eyelid, the one on the side toward Jim, had developed a nervous wink. Three times in the course of the dinner she dropped her fork on her plate with a terrible clatter and she was continually raising the water glass to her lips for hasty little gulps. She went on doing this even after the water was gone from the glass. And her handling of the silver became more awkward and hurried all the time.

I thought of nothing to say.

To Mother belonged the conversational honors, such as they were. She asked the caller about his home and family. She was delighted to learn that his father had a business of his own, a retail shoe store somewhere in Wyoming. The news that he went to night school to study accounting was still more edifying. What was his heart set on beside the warehouse? Radio-engineering? My, my, my! It was easy to see that here was a very up-and-coming young man who was certainly going to make his place in the world!

Then she started to talk about her children. Laura, she said, was not cut out for business. She was domestic, however, and making a home was really a girl's best bet.

Jim agreed with all this and seemed not to sense the ghost of an implication. I suffered through it dumbly, trying not to see Laura trembling more and more beneath the incredible unawareness of Mother.

And bad as it was, excruciating in fact, I thought with dread of the moment when dinner was going to be over, for then the diversion of food would be taken away, we would have to go into the little steam-heated parlor. I fancied the four of us having run out of talk, even Mother's seemingly endless store of questions about Jim's home and his job all used up finally — the four of us, then, just sitting there in the parlor, listening to the hiss of the radiator and nervously clearing our throats in the kind of self-consciousness that gets to be suffocating.

But when the blancmange was finished, a miracle happened.

Mother got up to clear the dishes away. Jim gave me a clap on the shoulders and said, "Hey, Slim, let's go have a look at those old records in there!"

He sauntered carelessly into the front room and flopped down on the floor beside the Victrola. He began sorting through the collection of worn-out records and reading their titles aloud in a voice so hearty that it shot like beams of sunlight through the vapors of self-consciousness engulfing my sister and me.

He was sitting directly under the floor-lamp and all at once my sister jumped up and said to him, "Oh — you have freckles!"

Jim grinned. "Sure that's what my folks call me — Freckles!"

"Freckles?" Laura repeated. She looked toward me as if for the confirmation of some too wonderful hope. I looked away quickly, not knowing whether to feel relieved or alarmed at the turn that things were taking.

Jim had wound the Victrola and put on *Dardanella*.

He grinned at Laura.

"How about you an' me cutting the rug a little?"

"What?" said Laura breathlessly, smiling and smiling.

"Dance!" he said, drawing her into his arms.

As far as I knew she had never danced in her life. But to my everlasting wonder she slipped quite naturally into those huge arms of Jim's, and they danced round and around the small steam-heated parlor, bumping against the sofa and chairs and laughing loudly and happily together. Something opened up in my sister's face. To say it was love is not too hasty a judgment, for after all he had freckles and that was what his folks called him. Yes, he had undoubtedly assumed the identity — for all practical purposes — of the one-armed orphan youth who lived in the Limberlost, that tall and misty region to which she retreated whenever the walls of Apartment F became too close to endure.

Mother came back in with some lemonade. She stopped short as she entered the portieres.

"Good heavens! Laura? Dancing?"

Her look was absurdly grateful as well as startled.

"But isn't she stepping all over you, Mr. Delaney?"

"What if she does?" said Jim, with bearish gallantry. "I'm not made of eggs!"

"Well, well, well!" said Mother, senselessly beaming.

"She's light as a feather!" said Jim. "With a little more practice she'd dance as good as Betty!"

There was a little pause of silence.

"Betty?" said Mother.

"The girl I go out with!" said Jim.

"Oh!" said Mother.

She set the pitcher of lemonade carefully down and with her back to the caller and her eyes on me, she asked him just how often he and the lucky young lady went out together.

"Steady!" said Jim.

Mother's look, remaining on my face, turned into a glare of fury.

"Tom didn't mention that you went out with a girl!"

"Nope," said Jim. "I didn't mean to let the cat out of the bag. The boys at the warehouse'll kid me to death when Slim gives the news away."

He laughed heartily but his laughter dropped heavily and awkwardly away as even his dull senses were gradually penetrated by the unpleasant sensation the news of Betty had made.

"Are you thinking of getting married?" said Mother.

"First of next month!" he told her.

It took her several moments to pull herself together. Then she said in a dismal tone, "How nice! If Tom had only told us we could have asked you *both!*"

Jim had picked up his coat.

"Must you be going?" said Mother.

"I hope it don't seem like I'm rushing off," said Jim, "but Betty's gonna get back on the eight o'clock train an' by the time I get my jalopy down to the Wabash depot —"

"Oh, then, we mustn't keep you."

Soon as he'd left, we all sat down, looking dazed.

Laura was the first to speak.

"Wasn't he nice?" she asked. "And all those freckles!"

"Yes," said Mother. Then she turned to me.

"You didn't mention that he was engaged to be married!"

"Well, how did I know that he was engaged to be married?"

"I thought you called him your best friend down at the warehouse?"

"Yes, but I didn't know he was going to be married!"

"How peculiar!" said Mother. "How very peculiar!"

"No," said Laura gently, getting up from the sofa. "There's nothing peculiar about it."

She picked up one of the records and blew on its surface a little as if it were dusty, then set it softly back down.

"People in love," she said, "take everything for granted."

What did she mean by that? I never knew.

She slipped quietly back to her room and closed the door.

Not very long after that I lost my job at the warehouse. I was fired for writing a poem on the lid of a shoe-box. I left Saint Louis and took to moving around. The cities swept about me like dead leaves, leaves that were brightly colored but torn away from the branches. My nature changed. I grew to be firm and sufficient.

In five years' time I had nearly forgotten home. I had to forget it, I couldn't carry it with me. But once in a while, usually in a strange town before I have found companions, the shell of deliberate hardness is broken through. A door comes softly and irresistibly open. I hear the tired old music my unknown father left in the place he abandoned as faithlessly as I. I see the faint and sorrowful radiance of the glass, hundreds of little transparent pieces of it in very delicate colors. I hold my breath, for if my sister's face appears among them — the night is hers!

June 1943 (Published 1948)

Topics for Further Research

1. In the Jean Evans article "Interview 1945" (p. 2016), Williams responds to the question of his use of "plays unconventional in form." In his response, he states that his plays are "light on plot and heavy on characterization." Does such an emphasis benefit *The Glass Menagerie*, or do you think its plot should be developed further? What other Williams plays share this emphasis on character over plot? Do you see this emphasis as a strength or a weakness?
2. Williams has called himself a "moral symbolist" in the tradition of Nathaniel Hawthorne. Williams, however, has made sexuality's mystery one of his central themes. How has he portrayed sexuality in his plays? What is his moral message?
3. Williams writes about his characters' attempt to escape their reality, and most often their reality is a life of loneliness. What methods do his characters use to try to escape their loneliness? Do any of them succeed? If so, how? When they do not succeed, what causes their failure?
4. Often, writers use biographical information to give their work authenticity or to explore elements of their own lives in fiction. Like the character Tom Wingfield, the young Tennessee Williams fled his family for the refuge of artistic creation, fame, and material success. Research the life of Tennessee Williams. What job did he hold that appears in *The Glass Menagerie?* What characters' names in the play come from his past? How are other elements of Williams's life used in *The Glass Menagerie*, and what do they contribute to the play?
5. One of the criticisms of *The Glass Menagerie* when it was first produced was that its staging was too complicated. Other critics, however, maintain that the complex staging is an integral part of this "memory play," which was intentionally designed to resemble a "magic act" much like the one Tom refers to in scene 4. Do you see all the staging elements as necessary to the play? How do these devices contribute to the theme Williams establishes of memory versus reality and reality versus illusion?
6. In addition to "Portrait of a Girl in Glass," Williams wrote another short story based on the story of *The Glass Menagerie*: "The Resemblance between a Violin Case and a Coffin." Read this story, and compare it to both the play and "Portrait of a Girl in Glass." What are the similarities and differences? Which version do you prefer? Why?

Jenkins 1

Heather Jenkins

Professor Spand

English 202

17 April 2008

Laura's Gentleman Caller

One of the major points of debate about Tennessee Williams's play *The Glass Menagerie* centers on the character Jim O'Connor, the "gentleman caller." Jim is an outgoing young man who approaches life lightheartedly, and his friendliness and charm make him a good suitor for Laura. But besides being Laura's suitor, what role does Jim play in the drama? Is Jim merely another character lost in the play's world of illusion, or is he something more? The answers to these questions become clear when we examine Jim's behavior and his influence on the other characters.

Thesis statement

One possible interpretation of Jim's role is that as someone who has created his own illusions, he encourages other characters to dream and fantasize. Jim's vision of the future is a grand (and unrealistic) one. He dreams of becoming part of the newly formed television industry, and throughout his appearance on stage, he rambles on about himself and his plans for the future:

First possible interpretation of gentleman caller: dreamer

> Because I believe in the future of television! *(Turning back to her.)* I wish to be ready to go up right along with it. Therefore I'm planning to get in on the ground floor. In fact, I've already made

> the right connections and all that remains is for the industry itself to get underway! Full steam— *(His eyes are starry.)* *Knowledge*—Zzzzzp! *Money*—Zzzzzp!—*Power*! That's the cycle democracy is built on! *(His attitude is convincingly dynamic. Laura stares at him, even her shyness eclipsed in her absolute wonder. He suddenly grins.)* I guess you think I think a lot of myself! (2002)

Jim's fantasies about the future play into and reinforce Amanda's romantic fantasies. Amanda's plans to find Laura a husband surface long before Jim enters the Wingfield apartment, but when Amanda learns that Jim will attend their dinner, her dream of entertaining gentlemen callers in the Southern tradition becomes a reality. As a result, she begins to have unrealistically high expectations for Jim's visit. When Jim charms Amanda and attempts to impress her with his dreams of success, he unknowingly fulfills her fantasy.

Second possible interpretation of gentleman caller: savior

Another possible interpretation of Jim's role is that he acts as a savior. In his article "*The Glass Menagerie* Revisited: Catastrophe without Violence," Roger B. Stein, discussing the "religious overtones" (2022) in the play, sees Jim in exactly this way. According to Stein, the play's action and language (as well as Williams's stage directions) make it clear that Laura's meeting with Jim can be seen in religious—specifically Christian—terms. It is

Jenkins 3

obvious that Laura needs a savior, but, as Stein observes, Tom is not able to play this role, and it "remains therefore for Jim to come as the Savior to this Friday night supper" (2024). In the simplest terms, Jim's role as possible savior for Laura—and, perhaps, for her family—is suggested by his ability to reach out to Laura and encourage her to enjoy the pleasures of the real world, such as dancing and romance.

Jim's role as Laura's savior can also be seen in the short story "Portrait of a Girl in Glass," from which the play developed. In the story, Jim and Laura begin to dance almost immediately after they are left alone. Although their encounter in the story is less intimate than the one in the play, Laura responds to Jim with joy and hope. In the play, Laura's visit with Jim evokes a similar response: she enjoys the feeling of being valued and accepted. Therefore, when Jim announces his departure (and his engagement), Laura realizes what she has lost and is overwhelmed with emotion.

Jim's failure in role as savior

Ironically, however, just as Jim offers Laura a way to escape her world of illusions, he abandons her, leaving her trapped in her own world. For this reason, Jim fails as a savior. In fact, it could even be argued that he consciously rejects his role as a savior. Still, we must remember that Jim enters the play unaware of the family's expectations; he views the visit purely as an opportunity to pass the time and to meet his friend's family, not as a prelude to romance. Jim's perception of his visit is made clear in "Portrait of a Girl in Glass," where he agrees to visit the Wingfields only because he has nothing else to do:

> "What are you doing tonight?" I finally asked him.
>
> "Not a God damn thing," said Jim. "I had a date but her Aunt took sick and she's hauled her freight to Centralia!"
>
> "Well," I said, "why don't you come over for dinner?"
>
> "Sure!" said Jim. He grinned with astonishing brightness. (2034)

Third possible interpretation of gentleman caller: realist

Although both these interpretations of Jim's role offer insights into the play, neither adequately explains Jim's function. Perhaps the best explanation of Jim's role comes from the play itself, where Jim is called "an emissary from a world of reality" (1963). In this sense, his solid presence in the play emphasizes the fragility of the other characters, who live in a world of illusion and fading memories. Jim may be a dreamer, but his dreams are grounded in reality: he lives in the real world and realizes the importance of striving for a better life. He attends public speaking and radio engineering classes so that he can advance beyond his low-level job at the warehouse. He scolds Tom for wanting to be a poet, an impractical goal for anyone living during the economic depression of the 1930s. Likewise, Jim

Jenkins 5

challenges Laura to cast off her feelings of inferiority and difference; he does not understand why Laura has given up hope and isolated herself. The contrast between Jim and Laura emphasizes not only Laura's vulnerability but also her family's consuming and ultimately debilitating delusions.

Contrast between Jim and Tom

Because Jim lives in a world of reality, he is the only character who escapes the kind of illusions that engulf the Wingfields. Jim's connection with reality allows him to continue to search for a better life, something that none of the Wingfields will ever attain. Even though Tom escapes the confines of the apartment, he is unable to leave behind the imaginary world his mother and his sister have created. Moreover, like his father, Tom leaves not to seek reality but to escape from one dream world into another, a world that is little different from the movies in which he has lost himself. As the play ends, Tom delivers a monologue about how he has been unable to leave the memory of his sister behind—and we are reminded of Jim, the happy and healthy gentleman caller, who has moved on.

Conclusion

Although Jim is referred to as the gentleman caller, his role in the play is much more complex. In one sense, Jim is a dreamer, detached from reality, enchanted by his own egotistical vision of how people should behave. In another sense, he is a kind of savior who reaches out to Laura, conveying the warmth and compassion of a saint. But these two images are

Jenkins 6

overshadowed by Jim's role as a visitor from the real world who journeys to the seductive world of fantasy and whose presence there emphasizes the destructive power of dreams that have become delusions. In this role, as Tom Scanlan observes, Jim is "the kindest of Williams's emissaries from reality, perhaps because his faith in the American dream of self-improvement and success is so complete as to be itself a touching illusion" (2026).

Jenkins 7

Works Cited

Kirszner, Laurie G., and Stephen R. Mandell, eds. *Literature: Reading, Reacting, Writing*. 7th ed. Boston: Wadsworth, 2010. Print.

Scanlan, Tom. Excerpt from *Family, Drama, and American Dreams*. Kirszner and Mandell 2024-26.

Stein, Roger B. "*The Glass Menagerie* Revisited: Catastrophe without Violence." Kirszner and Mandell 2022-24.

Williams, Tennessee. *The Glass Menagerie*. Kirszner and Mandell 1961-2009.

---. "Portrait of a Girl in Glass." Kirszner and Mandell 2031-38.

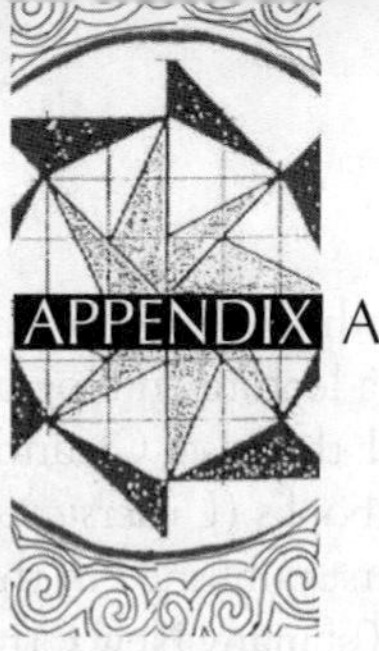

APPENDIX A

USING LITERARY CRITICISM IN YOUR WRITING

As you become aware of various schools of literary criticism, you see new ways to think — and to write — about fiction, poetry, and drama. Just as you value the opinions of your peers and your instructors, you also will find that the ideas of literary critics can enrich your own reactions to and evaluations of literature. Keep in mind that no single school of literary criticism offers the "right" way of approaching what you read; moreover, no single critic provides the definitive analysis of any short story, poem, or play. As you become aware of the richly varied possibilities of literary criticism, you will begin to ask new questions and discover new insights about the works you read.

Formalism and New Criticism

Formalism stresses the importance of literary form to the meaning of a work. Formalist scholars consider each work of literature in isolation. They consider biographical, historical, and social matters to be irrelevant to the real meaning of a play, short story, novel, or poem. For example, a formalist would see the relationship between Adam and Eve in *Paradise Lost* as entirely unrelated to John Milton's own marital concerns, and they would view theological themes in the same work as entirely separate from Milton's deep involvement with the Puritan religious and political cause in seventeenth-century England. Formalists would also regard Milton's intentions and readers' responses to the epic poem as irrelevant. Instead, formalists would read the text closely, paying attention to organization and structure, to verbal nuances (suggested by word choice and use of figurative language), and to multiple meanings (often created through the writer's use of paradox and irony). Formalist critics try to reconcile the tensions and oppositions inherent in the text in order to develop a unified reading.

The formalist movement in English-language criticism began in England with I. A. Richards's *Practical Criticism* (1929). To explain and introduce his theory, Richards asked students to interpret famous poems without telling them the poets' names. This strategy encouraged close reading of the text rather than reliance on information about a poet's reputation, the details of a poet's life, or the poem's historical context. The American formalist movement, called **New Criticism,** was made popular by college instructors who realized that formalist criticism provided a useful way for students to work along with an instructor in interpreting a literary work rather than passively listening to a lecture on biographical, literary, and historical influences. The New Critical theorists Cleanth Brooks and Robert Penn Warren put together a series of textbooks (*Understanding Poetry*, *Understanding Fiction*, and *Understanding Drama*, first published in the late 1930s) that were used in colleges for years. After the 1950s, many New Critics began to reevaluate their theories and to broaden their approaches. Although few scholars currently maintain a strictly formalist approach, nearly every critical movement, including feminist, Marxist, psychoanalytic, structuralist, and deconstructionist criticism, owes a debt to the close reading techniques introduced by the formalists.

A New Critical Reading: Kate Chopin's "The Storm" (p. 313)

If you were to apply formalist criticism to Chopin's "The Storm," you might begin by noting the story's three distinctive sections. What relationship do the sections bear to one another? What do we learn from the word choice, the figures of speech, and the symbols in these sections? And, most important, how do these considerations lead readers to a unified view of the story?

> In the first section of "The Storm," readers meet Bobinôt and his son Bibi. The description of the approaching clouds as "sombre," "sinister," and "sullen" (313) suggests an atmosphere of foreboding, yet the alliteration of these words also introduces a poetic tone. The conversation between father and son in the final part of this section contrasts, yet does not conflict, with the rather formal language of the introduction. Both Bobinôt and Bibi speak in Cajun dialect, suggesting their humble origins, yet their words have a rhythm that echoes the poetic notes struck in the description of the storm. As the section closes, Bobinôt, thinking of his wife, Calixta, at home, buys a can of the shrimp he knows she likes and holds the treasure "stolidly" (314), ironically suggesting the protection he cannot offer his wife in his separation from her during the coming storm.
>
> The long second section brings readers to the story's central events. Calixta, as she watches the rain, sees her former lover, Alcée, riding up to seek shelter. As in the first section, the language of the narrator is somewhat formal and always poetic, filled with sensuous diction and images. For instance, we see Calixta "unfasten[ing] her white sacque at the throat" (314) and, later, Alcée envisions her lips "as red and moist as pomegranate seed" (315). Again, as in the first section, the conversation of the characters is carried on in dialect, suggesting their lack of sophistication and their connection to the powerful natural forces that surround them. The lovemaking that follows, then, seems both natural and poetic. There is nothing sordid about this interlude and, as the final sections of the story suggest through their rather ordinary, matter-of-fact language, nothing has been harmed by Calixta and Alcée's yielding to passion.
>
> In the third section, Bobinôt brings home the shrimp, a symbol of his love for Calixta, and, although we recognize the tension between Bobinôt's shy, gentle approach and Alcée's passion, readers can accept the final sentence as literal rather than ironic. The "storms" (both the rain and the storm of passion) have passed, and no one has been hurt. The threat suggested in the opening

sentences has been diffused; both the power and the danger evoked by the poetic diction of the first two sections have disappeared, to be replaced entirely by the rhythms of daily life and speech.

For Further Reading: Formalism and New Criticism

Brooks, Cleanth. *The Well Wrought Urn*. 1947.
Empson, William. *Seven Types of Ambiguity*. 1930.
Hartman, Geoffrey H. *Beyond Formalism*. 1970.
Stallman, Robert W. *Critiques and Essays in Criticism. 1920–1948*. 1949.
Wellek, René. *A History of Modern Criticism*. Vol. 6. 1986.
Wimsatt, W. K. *The Verbal Icon*. 1954.

Reader-Response Criticism

Reader-response criticism opposes formalism, seeing the reader's interaction with the text as central to interpretation. Unlike formalists, reader-response critics do not believe that a work of literature exists as a separate, closed entity. Instead, they consider the reader's contribution to the text as essential. A poem, short story, novel, or play is not a solid piece of fabric but rather a series of threads separated by gaps that readers must fill in, drawing on their own experiences and knowledge.

As readers approach a literary text, they contribute their own interpretations. As they read one sentence and then the next, they develop expectations; and, in realistic stories, these expectations are generally met. Nevertheless, nearly every reader supplies personal meanings and observations, making each reader's experience with a work unique and distinctive from every other reader's experience with the same work. For example, imagine Shakespeare's *Romeo and Juliet* as it might be read by a fourteen-year-old high school student and by her father. The young woman, whose age is the same as Juliet's, is almost certain to identify closely with the female protagonist and to "read" Lord Capulet, Juliet's father, as overbearing and rigid. The young reader's father, however, may be drawn to the poignant passage where Capulet talks with a prospective suitor, urging that he wait while Juliet has time to enjoy her youth. Capulet describes the loss of his other children and calls Juliet "the hopeful lady of my earth." Although the young woman reading this line may interpret it as yet another indication of Capulet's possessiveness, her father may see it as a sign of love and even generosity. The twenty-first-century father may "read" Capulet as a man willing to risk offending a friend in order to keep his daughter safe from the rigors of early marriage (and early childbearing). Whose interpretation is correct? Reader-response theorists would say that both readings are entirely plausible and therefore equally "right."

The differing interpretations produced by different readers can be seen as simply the effect of the different personalities (and personal histories) involved in constructing meaning from the same series of clues. Not only does the reader "create" the work of literature, in large part, but the literature itself may work on the reader as he or she reads, altering the reader's experience and thus the reader's interpretation. For example, the father reading *Romeo and Juliet* may alter his sympathetic view of Capulet as he continues through the play and observes Capulet's later, angry exchanges with Juliet.

Reader-response theorists believe in the importance of **recursive reading**— that is, reading and rereading with the idea that no interpretation is carved in stone. A second or third interaction with the text may well produce a new interpretation. This changing view is particularly likely when the rereading takes place significantly later than the initial reading. For example, if the young woman just described reread *Romeo and Juliet* when she was middle-aged and herself the mother of teenage children, her reaction to Capulet would quite likely be different from her reaction when she read the work at age fourteen.

In one particular application of reader-response theory, called **reception theory,** the idea of developing readings is applied to the general reading public rather than to individual readers. Reception theory, as proposed by Hans Robert Jauss ("Literary History as a Challenge to Literary Theory," *New Literary History*, Vol. 2 [1970–71]), suggests that each new generation reads the same works of literature differently. Because each generation of readers has experienced different historical events, read different books, and been aware of different critical theories, each generation will view the same works very differently from its predecessors. Certainly a quick look at the summary of literary history in Appendix B will support this idea. (Consider, for example, the changing views toward Shakespeare from the seventeenth century to the present.)

Reader-response criticism has received serious attention since the 1960s, when Norman Holland formulated the theory in *The Dynamics of Literary Response* (1968). The German critic Wolfgang Iser (*The Implied Reader*, 1974) argued that in order to be an effective reader, one must be familiar with the conventions and "codes" of writing. This, then, is one reason for studying literature in a classroom: not to produce approved interpretations but to develop strategies and information that will make sense of a text. Stanley Fish, an American critic, goes even further, arguing that there may not be any "objective" text at all (*Is There a Text in This Class?*, 1980). Fish says that no two readers read the same book, though readers can be trained to have relatively similar responses to a text if they have had relatively similar experiences. For instance, readers who went to college and took an introduction to literature course in which they learned to respond to the various elements of literature, such as character, theme, irony, and figurative language, are likely to have similar responses to a text.

Reader-Response Readings: Kate Chopin's "The Storm" (p. 313)

To demonstrate possible reader-response readings, we can look at the same story previously considered from a formalist perspective. (Of course, if several formalist critics read the story, they too would each write a somewhat different interpretation.)

Written by a twenty-five-year-old man who has studied American literature

In Kate Chopin's "The Storm," attention must be paid to the two adult male characters, Bobinôt and Alcée. Usually, in a love triangle situation, one man is portrayed more sympathetically than the other. But Chopin provides us with a dilemma. Alcée is not a cavalier seducer; he genuinely cares for Calixta. Neither is he a brooding hero. There is nothing gruff or angry about Alcée, and he returns to his family home with no apparent harm done following the passionate interlude. On the other hand, Bobinôt is not a cruel or abusive husband. We can see no clear reason for Calixta's affair except for her desire to fulfill a sexual longing for Alcée.

Written by an eighteen-year-old male student in a first-year literature course

Bibi doesn't seem to be a very important character in the story, but we should pay attention to him as a reflection of his father. At the beginning of the story, Bibi worries about his mother and he expresses his concern to his father. Bobinôt tries to reassure his son, but he gets up and buys a treat for Calixta as much to comfort himself as to get something for her. Then Bibi sits with his father, and it seems as if he has transferred all his worries to Bobinôt. In the third section of the story, after Calixta and Alcée have had their love affair, Bibi and Bobinôt come home. They both seem like children, worried about how Calixta will react. She, of course, is nice to them because she feels so guilty. At the end of the third section, both father and son are happy and enjoying themselves. You can't help but feel great sympathy for them both because they are so loving and simple and because they have been betrayed by Calixta, who has not behaved the way a loving mother and wife should.

Written by a forty-five-year-old woman who has studied Kate Chopin's life and work

A decade after the controversial novel *The Awakening* was published in 1899, one critic protested, "To think of Kate Chopin, who once contented herself with mild yarns about genteel Creole life . . . blowing us a hot blast like that!" (qtd. in Gilbert and Gubar 981). This literary observer was shocked, as one might expect from an early-twentieth-century reader, by Chopin's frank picture of sexual relations, and particularly of the sexual feelings of the novel's heroine. One cannot help but wonder, however, whether the scandalized reader was really widely acquainted with Chopin.

Certainly he could not have read "The Storm." This short story is surprising for many reasons, but primarily because it defies the sexual mores of the late nineteenth century by showing a woman who is neither evil nor doomed enjoying, even glorying in, her sexuality. Calixta is presented as a good wife and loving mother, concerned about her husband and son who are away from home during the storm. Yet her connection to Bobinôt and Bibi does not keep her from passionately enjoying her interlude with Alcée. She goes to his arms unhesitatingly, with no false modesty or guilt (feigned or real) to hold her back. Somehow, this scenario does not seem to fit the definition of "a mild yarn about genteel Creole life."

For Further Reading: Reader-Response Criticism

Bleich, David. *Subjective Criticism*. 1978.
Fish, Stanley. *Is There a Text in This Class?* 1980.

Holland, Norman. *The Dynamics of Literary Response*. 1968.
Iser, Wolfgang. *The Implied Reader*. 1974.
———. *The Act of Reading: A Theory of Aesthetic Response*. 1978.
Rosenblatt, Louise. *The Reader, the Text, the Poem*. 1978.
Sulleiman, Susan, and Inge Crosman, eds. *The Reader in the Text*. 1980.
Tomkins, Jane P., ed. *Reader-Response Criticism*. 1980.

Feminist Criticism

Throughout the nineteenth century, women such as the Brontë sisters, George Eliot (Mary Ann Evans), Elizabeth Barrett Browning, and Christina Rossetti struggled for the right to be taken as seriously as their male counterparts. Then, in 1929, Virginia Woolf, an experimental novelist and literary critic, published *A Room of One's Own*, which described the difficulties that women writers faced and defined a tradition of literature written by women.

Feminist criticism emerged as a distinct approach to literature only in the late 1960s. Modern feminist criticism began with works such as Mary Ellman's *Thinking about Women* (1968), which focuses on the negative female stereotypes in books authored by men and points out alternative female characteristics suggested by women authors. Another pioneering feminist work was Kate Millet's *Sexual Politics* (1969), which analyzes the societal mechanisms that perpetuate male domination of women. Since that time, feminist writings, though not unified in one theory or methodology, have appeared in ever-growing numbers. Some feminist critics have adapted psychoanalytic, Marxist, or other poststructuralist theories, and others have broken new ground. In general, feminist critics take the view that our culture — and by extension our literature — is primarily patriarchal (controlled by males).

According to feminist critics, what is at issue is not anatomical sex but gender. As Simone de Beauvoir explained, a person is not born feminine, as our society defines it, but rather becomes so because of cultural conditioning. According to feminist critics, paternalist Western culture has defined the feminine as "other" to the male, as passive and emotional in opposition to the dominating and rational masculine.

Feminist critics claim that paternalist cultural stereotypes pervade works of literature in the **canon**— those works generally acknowledged to be the best and most significant. Feminists point out that the traditional canon typically consisted of works written by males and about male experiences. Female characters, when they did appear, were often subordinated to male characters. A female reader of these works must either identify with the male protagonist or accept a marginalized role.

One response of feminist critics is to reinterpret works in the traditional canon. As Judith Fetterley explains in *The Resisting Reader* (1978), the reader "revisions" the text, focusing on the covert sexual bias in a literary work. For example, a feminist scholar studying Shakespeare's *Macbeth* might look closely at the role played by Lady Macbeth and argue that she was not simply a cold-hearted villain but a victim of the circumstances of her time: women in her day were not permitted to follow their own ambitions but were relegated to supporting roles, living their lives vicariously through the achievements of their husbands and sons.

A second focus of feminist scholars has been the redefinition of the canon. By seeking out, analyzing, and evaluating little-known works by women, feminist scholars have rediscovered women writers who were ignored or shunned by the reading public and by critics of their own times. Thus, writers such as Kate Chopin and Charlotte Perkins Gilman (see "The Yellow Wallpaper," p. 459), who wrote during the late nineteenth and early twentieth centuries, are now recognized as worthy of serious consideration and study.

A Feminist Reading: Tillie Olsen's "I Stand Here Ironing" (p. 344)

To approach Tillie Olsen's "I Stand Here Ironing" from a feminist perspective, you might focus on the passages in which the narrator describes her relationships and encounters with men.

> Some readings of Tillie Olsen's "I Stand Here Ironing" suggest that the narrator made choices that doomed her oldest daughter to a life of confusion. If we look at the narrator's relationships with the men in her life, however, we can see that she herself is the story's primary victim.
>
> At nineteen, the narrator was a mother abandoned by her husband, who left her a note saying that he "could no longer endure . . . sharing want" (345) with his wife and infant daughter. This is the first desertion we hear about in the narrator's life, and although she agonizingly describes her painful decisions and the mistakes she made with her daughter Emily, we cannot help but recognize that she was the one who stayed and tried to make things right. Her actions contrast sharply with those of her husband, who ran away, saying that his wife and daughter were burdens too great for him to bear.
>
> The second abandonment is more subtle than the first but no less devastating. After the narrator remarried, she was again left alone to cope with a growing family when her second husband went off to war. True, this desertion was for a "noble" purpose and probably was not voluntary, but the narrator, nevertheless, had to seek one of the low-paying jobs available to women to supplement her allotment checks. She was again forced to leave her children because her husband had to serve the needs of the male-dominated military establishment.
>
> The narrator was alone at crucial points in Emily's life and had to turn away from her daughter in order to survive. She has been brought up in a world that teaches women to depend on men, but she learns that she is ultimately alone. Although the desertions she endured were not always intentional, she had to bear the brunt of circumstances that were not her choice but were foisted on her by the patriarchal society in which she lives.

For Further Reading: Feminist Criticism

Benstock, Shari, ed. *Feminist Issues in Literary Scholarship*. 1987.

Engleton, Mary, ed. *Feminist Issues in Literary Theory: A Reader*. 1986.

Gilbert, Sandra, and Susan Gubar. *The Madwoman in the Attic*. 1979.
———. *No Man's Land*. 3 vols. 1988, 1989, 1994.
———, eds. *The Norton Anthology of Literature by Women*. 1985.
Heilbrun, Carolyn G. *Hamlet's Mother and Other Women*. 1990.
Jacobus, Mary. *Reading Woman: Essays in Feminist Criticism*. 1986.
Miller, Nancy, K., ed. *The Poetics of Gender*. 1986.
———. *Subject to Change*. 1988.
Showalter, Elaine. *A Literature of Their Own*. 1977.
———. *Sister's Choice: Tradition and Change in American Women's Writing*. 1991.

Marxist Criticism

Marxist criticism bases interpretations of literature on the social and economic theories of Karl Marx (*Das Kapital*, 1867–94) and his colleague and coauthor Friedrich Engels (*The Communist Manifesto*, 1884). Marx and Engels believed that the dominant capitalist middle class would eventually be challenged and overthrown by the working class. In the meantime, however, middle-class capitalists would continue to exploit the working class, who produce excess products and profits yet do not share in the benefits of their labor. Marx and Engels further regarded all parts of the society in which they lived — religious, legal, educational, governmental — as tainted by what they saw as the corrupt values of middle-class capitalists.

Marxist critics apply these views about class struggle to their readings of poetry, fiction, and drama. They tend to analyze the literary works of any historical era as products of the ideology, or network of concepts, that supports the interests of the cultural elite and suppresses those of the working class. Some Marxist critics see all Western literature as distorted by the privileged views of the elite class, but most believe that a few creative writers reject the distorted views of their society and see clearly the wrongs to which working-class people have been subjected. For example, George Lukacs, a Hungarian Marxist critic, proposed that great works of literature create their own worlds and reflect life with clarity. These great works, though not written by Marxists, can be studied for their revealing examples of class conflict and other Marxist concerns. A Marxist critic would look with favor on Charles Dickens, who in nearly every novel pointed out inequities in the political, legal, and educational establishments of his time. Readers who remember Oliver Twist's pitiful plea for "more" workhouse porridge (refused by evil Mr. Bumble, who skims money from funds intended to feed the impoverished inmates) cannot help but see fertile ground for the Marxist critic, who would certainly applaud Dickens's scathing criticism of Victorian social and economic inequality.

Marxist criticism developed in the 1920s and 1930s in Germany and the Soviet Union. Since 1960, British and American Marxism has received greatest attention, with works such as Raymond Williams's *Culture and Society, 1780–1950* (1960) and Terry Eagleton's *Criticism and Ideology* (1976).

A Marxist Reading: Tillie Olsen's "I Stand Here Ironing" (p. 344)

In a Marxist reading of Tillie Olsen's "I Stand Here Ironing," you might concentrate on events that demonstrate how the narrator's and Emily's fates have been directly affected by the capitalist society of the United States.

> Tillie Olsen's "I Stand Here Ironing" stands as a powerful indictment of the capitalist system. The narrator and her daughter Emily are repeatedly exploited and defeated by the pressures of the economic system in which they live.
>
> The narrator's first child, Emily, is born into the world of the 1930s depression — an economic disaster brought on by the excesses and greed of Wall Street. When the young mother is deserted by her first husband, there are no government programs in place to help her. She says it was the "pre-relief, pre-WPA world of the depression" that forced her away from her child and into "a job hashing at night" (345). Although she is willing to work, she is paid so poorly that she must finally send Emily to live with her husband's family. Raising the money to bring Emily back takes a long time; and after this separation, Emily's health, both physical and emotional, is precarious.
>
> When Emily gets the measles, we get a hard look at what the few social programs that existed during the Depression were like. The child is sent — at the urging of a government social worker — to a convalescent home. The narrator notes bitterly, "They still send children to that place. I see pictures on the society page of sleek young women planning affairs to raise money for it, or dancing at the affairs, or decorating Easter eggs or filling Christmas stockings for the children" (346–47). The privileged class basks in the artificial glow of their charity work for the poor, yet the newspapers never show pictures of the hospitalized children who are kept isolated from everyone they loved and forced to eat "runny eggs . . . or mush with lumps" (347). Once again the mother is separated from her daughter by a system that discriminates against the poor. Because the family cannot afford private treatment, Emily is forced to undergo treatment in a public institution that not only denies her any contact with her family but also cruelly forbids her to save the letters she receives from home. Normal family relationships are severely disrupted by an uncaring economic structure that only grudgingly offers aid to the poor.
>
> It is clear that the division between mother and daughter is created by, and worsened by, the social conditions in which they live. Because they are poor, they are separated at crucial times and, therefore, never get to know each other fully. Thus, neither can truly understand the ordeals the other has been forced to endure.

For Further Reading: Marxist Criticism

Agger, Ben. *The Discourse of Domination*. 1992.

Bullock, Chris, and David Peck, eds. *Guide to Marxist Literary Criticism*. 1980.

Eagleton, Terry. *Marxism and Literary Criticism*. 1976.

Frow, John. *Marxism and Literary History*. 1986.

Holub, Renate, and Antonio Gramsci. *Beyond Marxism and Postmodernism*. 1992.

Jameson, Fredric. *Marxism and Form*. 1971.
Lentricchia, Frank. *Criticism and Social Change*. 1983.
Ohmann, Richard M. *Politics of Letters*. 1987.
Strelka, Joseph P., ed. *Literary Criticism and Sociology*. 1973.
Williams, Raymond. *Culture and Society, 1780–1950*. 1960.
———. *Marxism and Literature*. 1977.

Psychoanalytic Criticism

Psychoanalytic criticism focuses on a work of literature as an expression in fictional form of the inner workings of the human mind. The premises and procedures used in psychoanalytic criticism were developed by Sigmund Freud (1846–1939), though some critics disagree strongly with his conclusions and their therapeutic and literary applications. Feminists, for example, take issue with Freud's notion that women are inherently masochistic.

Some of the major points of Freud's theories depend on the idea that much of what is most significant to us does not take place in our conscious life. Freud believed that we are forced (mostly by the rigors of having to live in harmony with other people) to repress much of our experience and many of our desires in order to coexist peacefully with others. Some of this repressed experience Freud saw as available to us through dreams and other unconscious structures. He believed that literature could often be interpreted as the reflection of our unconscious life.

Freud was among the first psychoanalytic critics, often using techniques developed for interpreting dreams to interpret literature. Among other analyses, he wrote an insightful study of Dostoevsky's *The Brothers Karamazov* as well as brief commentaries on several of Shakespeare's plays, including *A Midsummer Night's Dream*, *Macbeth*, *King Lear*, and *Hamlet*. The study of *Hamlet* may have inspired a classic of psychoanalytic criticism: Ernest Jones's *Hamlet and Oedipus* (1949), in which Jones explains Hamlet's strange reluctance to act against his uncle Claudius as resulting from Hamlet's unresolved longings for his mother and subsequent drive to eliminate his father. Because Hamlet's own father is dead, Jones argues, Claudius becomes, in the young man's subconscious mind, a father substitute. Hamlet, then, cannot make up his mind to kill his uncle because he sees not a simple case of revenge (for Claudius's murder of his father) but rather a complex web that includes incestuous desire for his own mother (now wed to Claudius). Jones extends his analysis to include the suggestion that Shakespeare himself experienced such a conflict and reflected his own Oedipal feelings in *Hamlet*.

A French psychoanalyst, Jacques Lacan (1901–1981), combined Freudian theories with structuralist literary theories to argue that the essential alienating experience of the human psyche is the acquisition of language. Lacan believed that once you can name yourself and distinguish yourself from others, you enter the difficult social world that requires you to repress your instincts. Like Lacan, who modified and adapted psychoanalytic criticism to connect it to structuralism, many twentieth-century literary scholars, including Marxists and feminists, have found useful approaches in psychoanalytic literary theory (for example, see Mary Jacobus's *Reading Woman: Essays in Feminist Criticism*, 1986).

Psychoanalytic Terms

To fully appreciate psychoanalytic criticism, readers need to understand the following terms:

- *id*— The part of the mind that determines sexual drives and other unconscious compulsions that urge individuals to unthinking gratification.
- *ego*— The conscious mind that strives to deal with the demands of the id and to balance its needs with messages from the superego.
- *superego*— The part of the unconscious that seeks to repress the demands of the id and to prevent gratification of basic physical appetites. The superego is a sort of censor that represents the prohibitions of society, religion, family beliefs, and so on.
- *condensation*— A process that takes place in dreams (and in literature) when several elements from the repressed unconscious are linked together to form a new yet disguised whole.
- *symbolism*— The use of representative objects to stand for forbidden (often sexual) objects. This process takes place in dreams and in literature. For instance, a pole, knife, or gun may stand for the penis.
- *displacement*— The substitution of a socially acceptable desire for a desire that is not acceptable. This process takes place in dreams or in literature. For example, a woman who experiences sexual desires for her son may instead dream of being intimate with a neighbor who has the same first name as (or who looks like) her son.
- *Oedipus complex*— The repressed desire of a son to unite sexually with his mother and kill his father. According to Freud, all young boys go through this stage, but most resolve these conflicts before puberty.
- *projection*— A defense mechanism in which people mistakenly see in others antisocial impulses they fail to recognize in themselves.
- *subject*— The term used in Lacanian theory to designate a speaking person, or a person who has assumed a position within language. The Lacanian subject of language is split, or characterized by unresolvable tension between the conscious perception of the self (Freud's ego) and the unconscious desires that motivate behavior.

A Psychoanalytic Reading: Edgar Allan Poe's "The Cask of Amontillado" (p. 385)

Edgar Allan Poe died in 1849, six years before Freud was born, so Poe could not possibly have known Freud's work. Nevertheless, psychoanalytic critics argue that the principles discovered by Freud and those who followed him are inherent in human nature. Therefore, they believe it is perfectly plausible to use modern psychiatric terms when analyzing a work written before their invention. If you approached Poe's "The Cask of Amontillado" from a psychoanalytic perspective, you might write the following interpretation.

Montresor, the protagonist of Poe's "The Cask of Amontillado," has long fascinated readers who have puzzled over his motives for the story's climactic action when he imprisons his rival, Fortunato, and leaves him to die. Montresor claims that Fortunato insulted him and dealt him a "thousand injuries" (385). Yet when we meet Fortunato, although he appears something of a pompous fool, none of his actions — or even his comments — seems powerful enough to motivate Montresor's thirst for revenge.

If, however, we consider a defense mechanism, first named "projection" and described by Sigmund Freud, we gain a clearer picture of Montresor. Those who employ projection are often people who experience antisocial impulses yet are not conscious of these impulses. It seems highly likely that Fortunato did not persecute Montresor; rather, Montresor himself experienced the impulse to act in a hostile manner toward Fortunato. We know, for instance, that Fortunato belongs to the exclusive Order of Masons because he gives Montresor the secret Masonic sign. Montresor's failure to recognize the sign shows that he is a mason only in the grimmest literal sense. Montresor clearly resents Fortunato's high standing and projects onto Fortunato all of his own hostility toward those who (he thinks) have more or know more than he does. Thus, he imagines that Fortunato's main business in life is to persecute and insult him.

Montresor's obsessive behavior further indicates his pathology. He plans Fortunato's punishment with the cunning one might ordinarily reserve for a major battle, cleverly figuring out a way to keep his servants from the house and to lure the ironically named Fortunato to his death. Each step of the revenge is carefully plotted. This is no sudden crime of passion but rather the diabolically planned act of a deeply disturbed mind.

If we understand Montresor's need to take all of the hatred and anger that is inside himself and to rid himself of those socially unacceptable emotions by projecting them onto someone else, then we can see how he rationalizes a crime that seems otherwise nearly unmotivated. By killing Fortunato, Montresor symbolically kills the evil in himself. It is interesting to note that the final lines of the story support this reading. Montresor observes that "For the half of a century no mortal has disturbed" the bones. In other words, the unacceptable emotions have not again been aroused. His last words, a Latin phrase from the Mass for the Dead meaning "rest in peace," suggest that only through his heinous crime has he found release from the torment of his own hatred.

For Further Reading: Psychoanalytic Criticism

Freud, Sigmund. *The Interpretation of Dreams*. 1900.
Gardner, Shirley N., ed. *The (M)other Tongue: Essays in Feminist Psychoanalytic Interpretation*. 1985.
Hartman, Geoffrey H., ed. *Psychoanalysis and the Question of the Text*. 1979.
Kris, Ernst. *Psychoanalytic Explorations in Art*. 1952.
Kristeva, Julia. *Desire in Language*. 1980.
Nelson, Benjamin, ed. *Sigmund Freud on Creativity and the Unconscious*. 1958.
Wright, Elizabeth. *Psychoanalytic Criticism: Theory in Practice*. 1984.

Structuralism

Structuralism, a literary movement with roots in linguistics and anthropology, concentrates on literature as a system of signs that have no inherent meaning except in their agreed-upon or conventional relation to one another. Structuralism is usually described by its proponents not as a new way to interpret literary works but rather as a way to understand how works of literature come to have meaning. Because structuralism developed from linguistic theory, some structuralists use linguistic approaches to literature. When they talk about literary texts, they use the terms (such as *morpheme* and *phoneme*) that linguists use as they study the nature of language. Many structuralists, however, use the linguistic model as an analogy. To understand the analogy, you need to know a bit of linguistic theory.

The French linguist Ferdinand de Saussure (*Course in General Linguistics*, 1915) suggested that the relationship between an object and the name we use to designate it is purely arbitrary. What, for example, makes "C-A-T" signify a small, furry animal with pointed ears and whiskers? Only our learned expectation makes us associate *cat* with the family feline pet. Had we grown up in France, we would make the same association with *chat*, or in Mexico with *gato*. The words we use to designate objects (linguists call these words *signs*) make sense only within the large context of our entire language system and will not be understood as meaningful by someone who does not know that language system. Further, Saussure pointed out, signs become truly useful only when we use them to designate difference. For instance, the word *cat* becomes useful when we want to differentiate a small furry animal that meows from a small furry animal that barks. Saussure was interested in how language, as a structure of conventions, worked. He asked intriguing questions about the underlying rules that allow this made-up structure of signs to work, and, as a result, his pioneering study caught the interest of scholars in many fields.

Many literary scholars saw linguistic structuralism as analogous to the study of literary works. Literary structuralism leads readers to think of poems, short stories, novels, and plays not as self-contained and individual entities that have some kind of inherent meaning but rather as part of a larger literary system. To fully appreciate and analyze the work, the reader must understand the system within which it operates. Like linguistic structuralism, literary structuralism focuses on the importance of difference. We must, for example, understand the difference between the structure of poetry and the structure of prose before we can make sense of William Carlos Williams's "Red Wheelbarrow" (p. 906):

> so much depends
> upon
> a red wheel
> barrow

Readers unacquainted with the conventions of poetry would find those lines meaningless and confusing, although if they knew the conventions of prose, they would readily understand this sentence:

> So much depends upon a red wheelbarrow.

The way we interpret any group of "signs," then, depends on how they are structured and on the way we understand the system that governs their structure.

Structuralists believe that literature is basically artificial because although it uses the same "signs" as everyday language, whose purpose is to give information, the purpose of literature is *not* primarily to relay data. For example, a poem like Dylan Thomas's "Do not go gentle into that good night" (p. 1046) is written in the linguistic form of a series of commands, yet the poem goes much further than that. Its meaning is created not only by our understanding the lines as a series of commands but also by our recognition of the poetic form, the rhyming conventions, and the figures of speech that Thomas uses. We can only fully discuss the poem within the larger context of our literary knowledge.

Structuralism also provides the foundation for poststructuralism, a theoretical movement that informs the fields of deconstructionist and New Historicist criticism and has influenced the work of many psychoanalytic and sociological critics. Although structuralists claim that language functions by arbitrarily connecting words (signifiers) to ideas (signifieds), poststructuralists develop the implications of this claim, arguing that because the connection of a word to an idea is purely arbitrary, any operation of language is inherently unstable. Poststructuralists believe that to study a literary text is to study a continuously shifting set of meanings.

A Structuralist Reading: William Faulkner's "Barn Burning" (p. 391)

A structuralist reading tries to bring to light some of the assumptions about language and form that we are likely to take for granted. Looking at the opening paragraph of Faulkner's "Barn Burning," from the point of view of structuralist criticism, you might first look at an interpretation that reads the passage as a stream of Sarty's thoughts. The structuralist critic might then consider the assumptions a reader would have to make to see what Faulkner has written as the thoughts of an illiterate child. Next, the structuralist might look at evidence to suggest the language in this section operates outside the system of language that would be available to Sarty and that, therefore, "Barn Burning" opens not with a simple recounting of the main character's thoughts but rather with something far more complex.

> The opening paragraph of William Faulkner's "Barn Burning" is often read as an excursion into the mind of Sarty, the story's young protagonist. When we read the passage closely, however, we note that a supposedly simple consciousness is represented in a highly complex way. For Sarty — uneducated and illiterate — the "scarlet devils" and "silver curve of fish" on the labels of food tins serve as direct signs appealing to his hunger. It is unlikely, however, that Sarty could consciously understand what he sees and express it as metaphor. We cannot, then, read this opening passage as a recounting of the thoughts that pass through Sarty's mind. Instead, these complex sentences and images offer possibilities that reach beyond the limits of Sarty's linguistic system.
>
> Because our own knowledge is wider than Sarty's, the visual images the narrator describes take on meanings for us that are unavailable to the young boy. For example, like Sarty, we know that the "scarlet devils" stand for deviled ham. Yet the devils also carry another possible connotation. They may indicate evil and thus serve to emphasize the despair and grief Sarty feels are ever present. So we are given images that flash through the mind of an illiterate young boy, apparently intended to suggest his poverty and ignorance (he cannot read the words on the labels), yet we are led to see a highly complicated set of meanings. When we encounter later in the passage Sarty's articulated thought, "*our enemy . . . ourn! mine and hisn both! . . .*" his down-to-earth dialect shows clearly the sharp distinction between the system of language the narrator uses to describe Sarty's view of the store shelves and the system of language Sarty uses to describe what he sees and feels.

For Further Reading: Structuralism

Barthes, Roland. *Critical Essays*. 1964.
Culler, Jonathan. *Structuralist Poetics*. 1975.
Greimas, A. J. *Structured Semantics: An Attempt at a Method*. Trans. McDowell, Schleifer, and Velie. 1983.
Hawkes, Terence. *Structuralism and Semiotics*. 1977.
Lentricchia, Frank. *After the New Criticism*. 1980.
Pettit, Philip. *The Concept of Structuralism: A Critical Analysis*. 1975.
Scholes, Robert. *Structuralism in Literature: An Introduction*. 1974.

Deconstruction

Deconstruction is a literary movement that developed from structuralism. Deconstructionists argue that every text contains within it some ingredient undermining its purported system of meaning. In other words, the structure that seems to hold the text together is unstable because it depends on the conclusions of a particular ideology (for instance, the idea that women are inferior to men or that peasants are content with their lowly position in life), conclusions that are not as natural as the text may pretend. The practice of finding the point at which the text falls apart because of these internal inconsistencies is called deconstruction.

Deconstructive theorists share with formalists and structuralists a concern for the work itself rather than for biographical, historical, or ideological influences. Like formalists, deconstructionists focus on possibilities for multiple meanings within texts. However, while formalists seek to explain paradox by discovering tensions and ironies that can lead to a unified reading, deconstructionists insist on the primacy of multiple possibilities. They maintain that any given text is capable of yielding many divergent readings, all of which are equally valid yet may in some way undermine and oppose one another.

Like structuralists, deconstructionists see literary texts as part of larger systems of discourse. A key structuralist technique is identifying opposites in an attempt to show the structure of language used in a work. Having identified the opposites, the structuralist rests the case. Deconstructionists, however, go further. Jacques Derrida, a French philosopher, noticed that these oppositions do not simply reflect linguistic structures but are the linguistic response to the way people deal with their beliefs (their ideologies). For instance, if you believe strongly that democracy is the best possible form of government, you tend to lump other forms of government into the category "nondemocracies." If a government is nondemocratic, that — not its other distinguishing characteristics — would be significant to you. This typical ideological response operates in all kinds of areas of belief, even ones we are not aware of. Deconstructionists contend that texts tend to give away their ideological biases by means of this opposition.

Derrida called this distinction between "A" and "Not-A" (rather than between "A" and "B") *différance*, a word he coined to suggest a concept represented by the French verb *différer*, which has two meanings: "to be different" and "to defer." (Note that in Derrida's new term an *a* is substituted for an *e*— a distinction that can be seen in writing but not heard in speaking.) When a deconstructionist uncovers *différance* through careful examination of a text, he or she also finds an (often unwitting) ideological bias. Deconstructionists argue that the reader must transcend such ideological biases and must instead acknowledge contradictory possibilities as equally worthy of consideration. No one meaning can or should be designated as correct.

Deconstruction, then, is not really a system of criticism (and, in fact, deconstructionists resist being labeled as a school of criticism). Rather, deconstruction offers a way to take apart a literary text and thereby reveal its separate layers. Deconstructionists often focus on the metaphorical nature of language, claiming that all language is basically metaphoric because the sign we use to designate any given object or action stands apart from the object itself. In fact, deconstructionists believe that all writing is essentially literary and metaphorical because language, by its very nature, can only *stand for* what we call reality or truth; it cannot *be* reality or truth.

A major contribution of deconstructive critics lies in their playful approach to language and to literary criticism. They refuse to accept as absolute any one way of reading poetry, fiction, or drama, and they guard against what they see as the fixed conclusions and arbitrary operating assumptions of many schools of criticism.

A Deconstructionist Reading: Flannery O'Connor's "A Good Man Is Hard to Find" (p. 447)

A deconstructionist reading of Flannery O'Connor's "A Good Man Is Hard to Find" might challenge the essentially religious interpretations the author offered of her own stories in essays and letters. If you were applying deconstructionist criticism to the story, you might argue that the author's reading of the story is no more valid than anyone else's, and that the story can just as legitimately be read as an investigation of the functions of irony in language.

> Flannery O'Connor explained that the grotesque and violent aspects of her stories are intended to shock the reader into recognizing the inhospitable nature of the world and thereby recognizing the universal human need for divine grace. The last sentence of "A Good Man Is Hard to Find" is spoken by The Misfit, who has just murdered a family of travelers: "It's no real pleasure in life." However, the language of O'Connor's stories is extremely ironic — that is, her narrators and characters often say one thing but mean another. So, it is possible that their statements are not empirically true but are representations of a persona or elements of a story they have created using language.
>
> The Grandmother, for example, lives almost entirely in fictions — newspaper clippings, stories for the grandchildren, her belief that The Misfit is a good man. In contrast, The Misfit is more literal than the Grandmother in his perception of reality. He knows, for example, whether the car turned over once or twice. But he too is posing, at first as the tough guy who rejects religious and societal norms by saying, ". . . it's nothing for you to do but enjoy the few minutes you got left the best way you can — by killing somebody or burning down his house or doing some other meanness to him. No pleasure but meanness . . ." (p. 457). Finally, he poses as the pessimist — or, according to O'Connor's reading, the Christian — who claims, "It's no real pleasure in life." The contradictions in The Misfit's language make it impossible to tell which of these facades is "real."

For Further Reading: Deconstruction

Abrams, M. H. "Rationality and the Imagination in Cultural History." *Critical Inquiry* 2 (1976): 447–64. (Abrams claims deconstructionists are parasites who depend on other critics to come up with interpretations that can be deconstructed.)

Arac, Jonathan, Wlad Godzich, and Wallace Martin, eds. *The Yale Critics: Deconstruction in America*. 1983.

Berman, Art. *From the New Criticism to Deconstruction*. 1988.

Culler, Jonathan. *On Deconstruction: Theory and Criticism after Structuralism*. 1982.
Jefferson, Ann. "Structuralism and Post-Structuralism." *Modern Literary Theory: A Comparative Introduction*. 1982.
Johnson, Barbara. *The Critical Difference: Essays in the Contemporary Rhetoric of Reading*. 1980.
Leitsch, Vincent B. *Deconstructive Theory and Practice*. 1982.
Lynn, Steven. "A Passage into Critical Theory." *College English* 52 (1990): 258–71.
Miller, J. Hillis. "The Critic as Host." *Deconstruction and Criticism*. Ed. Harold Bloom et al. 1979. (a response to Abrams's article, listed above)
Norris, Christopher. *Deconstruction: Theory and Practice*. 1982.

Cultural Studies

Cultural studies is a particularly difficult field of criticism to define for a number of reasons. Chief among these is the scope of the field. Literary theory has typically focused on literature—however defined—while bringing in knowledge about a work's historical context or the life and views of the author as a means of better understanding the work. Cultural studies, on the other hand, treats any and all objects produced by a society as worthy of the same kind of analysis that literary texts receive. Thus, the advertisements for Arthur Miller's *Death of a Salesman*, or the diary of an actual traveling salesman might, to a cultural critic, be as interesting and complex as Miller's play itself.

Given that the work of art no longer occupies a privileged position relative to other artifacts, it is not surprising that cultural critics have tended to call into question the relative merit of what we have traditionally thought of as masterpieces. To say that one work is "better" than another, such critics would argue, is an almost meaningless statement, and one that reveals more about the values of the person making it than about the work itself. Many cultural critics would therefore reject altogether the idea of a literary canon, or a list of great works that an educated person should know. At the very least, cultural critics would argue, is any canon must be subject to constant examination and revision.

Cultural studies has roots in both the French structuralism of critics such as Roland Barthes and the Cultural Materialism of British critics such as Raymond Williams. In his classic text *Mythologies* (1957), Barthes began to apply structural analysis not simply to texts but to phenomena in popular culture—professional wrestling, for example. Williams came at similar subject matter from a different angle. Mass culture has traditionally been viewed by Marxists as something imposed on the working classes and the disadvantaged by upper and bourgeoisie classes seeking to maintain their own position. Williams, while acknowledging the truth in such an assertion, distinguished between mass culture and popular culture, noting that the latter can be used by those outside of power as a means of self-expression and even rebellion. It is not surprising that there is a distinctly political edge to cultural studies, and that many of its practitioners see themselves as activists and their research as a means to effect social change.

There are a number of distinct schools—New Historicism, postcolonialism, American multiculturalism, and queer theory—that are often, though not always, placed under the heading of cultural studies. Of these four, the broadest is New Historicism. Its assumptions—that a work cannot be discussed in isolation from the culture that gave rise to it—are shared by most critics in the other schools, and it might be described as much as a method as a school. Postcolonialism, American multiculturalism, and queer theory can all be seen as applications of the principles of cultural studies—particularly its awareness of power relationships and its questioning of traditional canons—to specific geographical areas and cultures.

New Historicism

New Historicism relates a text to the historical and cultural contexts of the period in which it was created and the periods in which it was critically evaluated. These contexts are not considered simply as "background" but as integral parts of a text. According to the New Historicists, history is not objective facts; rather, like literature, history is subject to interpretation and reinterpretation depending on the power structure of a society. Louis Althusser, for example, suggests that ideology intrudes in the discourse of an era, subjecting readers to the interests of the ruling establishment. Michel Foucault reflects that the discourse of an era defines the nature of "truth" and what behaviors are acceptable, sane, or criminal. "Truth," according to Foucault, is produced by the interaction of power and the systems in which the power flows, and it changes as society changes. Mikhail Bakhtin suggests that all discourse is dialogic, containing within it many independent and sometimes conflicting voices.

Literature, in the opinion of the New Historicist critics, cannot be interpreted without reference to the time and place in which it was written. Criticism likewise cannot be evaluated without reference to the time and place in which it was written. A flaw of much criticism, according to the New Historicists, is the consideration of a literary text as if it were an organic whole. Such an approach ignores the diversity of conflicting voices in a text and in the cultural context in which a text is embedded. Indeed, Stephen Greenblatt prefers the term "cultural poetics" to New Historicism because it acknowledges the integral role that literature and art play in the culture of any era. Works of art and literature, according to Greenblatt, actively foster subversive elements or voices but somehow constrain those forces in ways that defuse challenges to the dominant culture.

New Historicists also point out that readers, like texts, are influenced and shaped by the cultural context of their eras and that a thoroughly objective "reading" of a text is therefore impossible. Acknowledging that all readers to some degree "appropriate" a text, some New Historicists present their criticism of texts as "negotiations" between past and present contexts. Thus, criticism of a particular work of literature would draw from both the cultural context of the era in which the text was written and the critic's present cultural context, and the critic would acknowledge how the latter context influences interpretation of the former.

Since the early 1970s, feminist critics have adopted some New Historicist positions, focusing on male-female power conflicts. And critics interested in multicultural texts have stressed the role of the dominant white culture in suppressing or marginalizing the texts of nonwhites. Marxist critics, including Raymond Williams, have adopted the term "cultural materialism" in discussing their mode of New Historicism, which focuses on the political significance of a literary text.

A New Historicist Reading: Charlotte Perkins Gilman's "The Yellow Wallpaper" (p. 459)

A New Historicist scholar might write an essay about "The Yellow Wallpaper" as an illustration of the destructive effects of the patriarchal culture of the late nineteenth century on women. This reading would be vastly different from that of most nineteenth-century critics, who interpreted the story as a harrowing case study of female mental illness. Even some early-twentieth-century readings posited that the narrator's mental illness is the result of her individual psychological problems. In a New Historicist reading, however, you might focus on the social conventions of the time, which produced conflicting discourses that drove the narrator to madness.

> The female narrator of "The Yellow Wallpaper," who is writing in her private journal (which is the text of the short story), explains that her husband, a physician, has diagnosed her as having a "temporary nervous depression — a slight hysterical tendency" (460). She says she should believe such a physician "of high standing" (460) and cooperate with his treatment, which is to confine her to a room in an isolated country estate and compel her to rest and have no visitors and not to write. The "cure" is intended to reduce her nervousness, she further explains. But as the story unfolds, the narrator reveals that she suspects the treatment will not cure her because it leaves her alone with her thoughts without even her writing to occupy her mind. Her husband's "cure" forces her into a passive role and eliminates any possibility of asserting her own personality. However, she guiltily suggests that her own lack of confidence in her husband's diagnosis may be what is preventing her cure.
>
> The text of "The Yellow Wallpaper" can be divided into at least two conflicting discourses: (1) the masculine discourse of the husband, who has the authority both of a highly respected physician and of a husband, two positions reinforced by the patriarchal culture of the time; and (2) the feminine discourse of the narrator, whose hesitant personal voice contradicts the masculine voice but undermines itself because it keeps reminding her that women should obey their husbands and their physicians. A third discourse underlies the two dominant ones — that of the gothic horror tale, a popular genre of the late nineteenth century. The narrator in "The Yellow Wallpaper" is isolated against her will in a room with barred windows in an almost deserted palatial country mansion she describes as "The most beautiful place!" (460). She is at the mercy of her captor, in this case her husband. She is not sure whether she is hallucinating, and she thinks the mansion may be haunted. She does not know

whom to trust, not being sure whether her husband really wants to "cure" her or to punish her for expressing her rebellion.

The narrator learns to hide her awareness of the conflicting discourses. She avoids mentioning her thoughts and fears about her illness or her fancies about the house being haunted, and she hides her writing. She speaks reasonably and in "a very quiet voice" (467). But this inability to speak freely to anyone is a kind of torture, and alone in her room with the barred windows, she takes up discourse with the wallpaper. At first she describes it as "One of those sprawling flamboyant patterns committing every artistic sin" (461). But she is fascinated by the pattern, which has been distorted by mildew and by the tearing away of some sections. The narrator begins to strip off the wallpaper to free a woman she thinks is trapped inside; and, eventually, she visualizes herself as that woman, trapped yet freed by the destruction of the wallpaper. The narrator retreats, or escapes into madness, driven there by the multiple discourses she cannot resolve.

For Further Reading: New Historicist Criticism

Brook, Thomas. *The New Historicism and Other Old Fashioned Topics*. 1991.

Coates, Christopher. "What Was the New Historicism?" *Centennial Review* 32.2 (Spring 1993): 267–80.

Geertz, Clifford. "Thick Description: Toward an Interpretive Theory of Culture." *The Interpretation of Cultures*. By Clifford Geertz. 1973.

Greenblatt, Stephen, ed. *Representing the English Renaissance*. 1988.

Levin, David. "American Historicism: Old and New." *American Literary History* 6.3 (Fall 1994): 527–38.

Rabinov, Paul, ed. *The Foucault Reader*. 1986.

Veeser, H. Aram, ed. *The New Historicism*. 1989.

Queer Theory

The roots of queer theory go back to the 1960s and 1970s, when movements for gay liberation and changing attitudes toward sexuality in general made it easier for artists and critics to identify themselves as gay and lesbian and to deal directly with gay and lesbian themes in their work. Critical examination of these subjects intensified during the 1980s, partly in response to the AIDS crisis. By the early 1990s, the term "queer theory," coined by Teresa de Lauretis, came to be used as an umbrella term for the work being done by critics such as Eve Kosofsky Sedgwick and Judith Butler.

The actual scope of queer theory is significantly broader than the name might imply: queer theorists tend to doubt prevailing notions of sexual identity as something fixed by biology or even by personal inclination since a person might find different means of sexual expression appealing at different points. Queer theory therefore calls into question terms such as *homosexual*, *heterosexual*, *bisexual*, *transsexual*, and *transgender*. It also examines sympathetically those aspects of sexuality that, while not necessarily "queer" in the sense of "gay," have nonetheless been marginalized—cross-dressing, for example, or sadomasochism.

When applying queer theory to texts, critics tend to be particularly interested in those ways in which the text blurs or subverts traditional notions of sexual identity, notions that tend to rely on "heteronormativity"—the idea that heterosexuality is the statistical, and even moral, standard and that all departures from it are perverse or problematic. These blurrings in the text occur not only in contemporary literature but also in works from the past, where they were perhaps missed because of the ideological prejudices of earlier critics.

Given queer theory's emphasis on gender, there are inevitably points of contact with feminist criticism. Critics such as Judith Butler, however, have argued that feminists have been too quick to regard gender, however defined, as something fixed. Queer theory has connections to gay and lesbian activism, but those connections are sometimes strained because activists are often trying to gain recognition or respect for those with a given sexual identity, while queer theorists are more likely to call into question *all* identities. Like other schools within the field of cultural studies, critics employing queer theory often examine cultural artifacts such as film, music, and television programs, in this case for messages that may subtly subvert heteronormativity. For example, there has been considerable interest within queer studies in the ways that Madonna has portrayed sexuality.

In theoretical terms, queer theory's biggest debt has been to the deconstructionists, particularly to Michel Foucault, and to his groundbreaking work, *The History of Sexuality*. Among the foundational works in the field are Butler's *Gender Trouble* and Sedgwick's *Epistemology of the Closet*.

A Queer Theory Reading: Zadie Smith's "The Girl with Bangs"(p. 271)

A queer theory reading of Zadie Smith's "The Girl with Bangs" might focus on the ways in which sexual desire in the story seems related less to gender as it is commonly conceived than to the attraction between individuals. A critic might argue, in fact, that the story as a whole calls into question the validity of gender roles.

> In Zadie Smith's "The Girl with Bangs," the narrator enters into her first relationship with another woman, one that leaves her with a new perspective on sexual relationships and on herself. However, the narrator does not think in terms of gay and straight. Rather, she describes herself as being "a boy" in her relationship with Charlotte Greaves.
>
> Male and female, in the eyes of the narrator, are designations that have less to do with physical gender than with gender roles. Because she is the one who pursues Charlotte, and because she is the one who figuratively waits beneath Charlotte's window, she sees herself in the male role, that of the pursuer. Because she finds herself helpless to resist Charlotte—a situation she has never encountered with a man—she thinks, "So this is what it's like being a boy" (p. 273). When Maurice comes to ask her to give up Charlotte, she describes their talk—with only partial irony—as "man-to-man."
>
> The narrator agrees to end her relationship with Charlotte, but when she and Maurice go to speak with Charlotte, they find her in bed with

another man. Charlotte's sexual openness—she apparently has sex with anyone, of either gender, whenever she wants—represents another challenge to the heteronormativity of society and to its conventions of monogamy. Her eventual marriage to Maurice might seem at first a surrender to that norm, but the story certainly hints that Maurice will regret the marriage because nothing indicates that Charlotte will suddenly stop sleeping with other people.

Interestingly, the story concludes with the narrator identifying not—as she has during the affair with Charlotte—with men, but with a woman, the woman Maurice has been sleeping with in Thailand. For the duration of the affair, she viewed men as helpless, a view at odds with much of the stereotypical rhetoric of manliness—though not with the conventions of traditional courting. She pictured men, and herself with them, as standing beneath the beloved's window, waiting to catch whatever she might throw down. Now she says that "in the real world, or so it seems to me, it is almost always women and not men who are waiting under windows, and they are almost always disappointed. In this matter Charlotte was unusual" (p. 275).

To say that Charlotte was "unusual" is to say that she was odd, or, in the broadest sense of the word, "queer." What is "queerest" about Charlotte, then, may not be her bisexuality or promiscuity, but her ability to remain free of the negative emotional consequences her existence as a woman in a male-dominated society would typically bring with it.

For Further Reading: Queer Theory

Butler, Judith. *Bodies That Matter: On the Discursive Limits of "Sex."* 1993.

Halperin, David. *Homosexuality: A Cultural Construct*. 1990.

———. *One Hundred Years of Homosexuality*. 1990.

Jagose, Annamarie. *Queer Theory: An Introduction*. 1997.

Parker, Andrew. *After Sex?: On Writing Since Queer Theory*. 2007.

Sedgwick, Eve Kosofsky. *Between Men: English Literature and Male Homosocial Desire*. 1985.

Spargo, Tamsin. *Foucault and Queer Theory*. 1999.

Thomas, Calvin (ed.). *Straight with a Twist: Queer Theory and the Subject of Heterosexuality*. 1999.

Postcolonial Studies

In the years following World War II, the period of European colonization came to a close as first one country and then another gained its independence from the countries—England, France, Belgium—that had controlled them. In most cases, these newly independent countries were substantially different from how they had been prior to colonization; some, in fact, had actually been created by colonization, their borders having been determined by foreign powers. The colonial powers typically introduced their own languages as the languages of government in these countries, and the educational systems they introduced for both the European and native populations of the colonies were likewise modeled on those in Europe.

Writers in former colonies who began to write after the end of colonial rule, then, inherited an often uncomfortable mix of cultural tools and assumptions. On the one hand, many of them had been educated to appreciate European works of literature, and many of them wrote most naturally in European languages. On the other hand, they saw everywhere around them a culture that was very different from that of its former European masters, and which those masters tended to regard as inferior and less civilized. The tension that results from this cultural mix is one of the chief subjects of postcolonial theory and research. In addition, although colonialism has more or less formally ended, many critics would argue that European and other western countries continue to dominate their former colonial possessions in a cultural and economic sense, a domination called **neo-colonialism.**

Postcolonial critics do not necessarily restrict themselves to the literatures of those countries that the European powers have left. Australia, New Zealand, and Canada, for example, were all colonies, and some critics would regard any literature produced in such countries, including that by authors of European descent, to be an appropriate subject of study for postcolonialism. Others would argue that such writers belong to a European tradition and would use the adjective *postcolonial* to describe only the works written by authors from the indigenous populations of those countries.

Nor do postcolonial critics restrict themselves to looking at works produced since the end of the colonial period. Canonical European texts are of special interest to these critics, especially for the light they shed on the ways in which the colonizers viewed the colonized. The character of Caliban in Shakespeare's *The Tempest*, for instance, has been the focus of much debate about what his brutish nature reveals about the views of Shakespeare and the England in which he lived toward the native peoples being encountered by European explorers.

One of the foundational texts of postcolonialism is Edward Said's *Orientalism* (1978), which examined the ways in which Europeans and Americans view, and have viewed, peoples in developing nations (often known as the Third World). Other important works include *The Location of Culture* (1994) by Homi Bhaba and the essay "Under Western Eyes" (1986) by Chandra Talpade Mohanty.

A Postcolonial Reading: Jhumpa Lahiri's "The Third and Final Continent" (p. 290)

A postcolonial reading of "The Third and Final Continent" by Jhumpa Lahiri might look at the differences the narrator notices between his native culture and those of England and the United States. It might also examine the process of his gradual assimilation to American culture, and his own sense of the cultural distance he has traveled.

> Jhumpa Lahiri's short story "The Third and Final Continent" relates the thoughts of an Indian emigrant as he adjusts to western society. As a citizen of a country that gained its independence from Great Britain less than twenty

years earlier—and after his own birth—the narrator is very much in the position of a provincial visiting the imperial homeland. He lives with other Indians—specifically with other Bengalis—and they eat Indian food and listen to Indian music, but many of their habits are English. "On weekends," he remembers, "we lounged barefoot in drawstring pajamas, drinking tea and smoking Rothmans, or set out to watch cricket at Lord's" (p. 290).

The narrator arrives in the United States on the day of the first moon landing. The symbolism of this is particularly appropriate since the American astronauts have literally gone to another world, something the narrator does metaphorically. The moment also marks, again literally, the height of American power. At that moment, America is the most powerful country in the world, much as Great Britain was when it first subjugated India. To plant a flag on a piece of land has traditionally been a way of claiming that land for the country represented by the flag.

In the time the narrator spends with Mrs. Croft each evening while staying in her house, the acknowledgement of American supremacy becomes a kind of religious ritual. Each time Mrs. Croft notes, "There's an American flag on the moon, boy!" the narrator is expected to reply, loudly enough that the old woman can hear him, "Splendid!" (p. 294). The narrator himself had not thought very much about the moon landing despite the reports of it in the paper—and despite the fact that he is a librarian at the Massachusetts Institute of Technology. His values and the values of the American culture in which he finds himself are very different.

His stay with Mrs. Croft also reveals to him the enormous difference between Indian and American attitudes toward family. It shocks the narrator to learn that a woman one hundred and three years old would be living alone, and the story of her fortitude after the death of her husband is in marked contrast to his own mother's descent into madness after the death of her husband. At the same time, the narrator and Mrs. Croft seem to have a special understanding. The culture he comes from, with its strict rules of propriety, is in some ways reminiscent of the America in which Mrs. Croft lived as a young woman, a point made clear when the old woman, on seeing the narrator's new wife dressed in her traditional Indian clothes, declares, "She is a perfect Lady!" (p. 301).

For Further Reading: Postcolonial Studies

Ashcroft, Bill, Gareth Griffiths, and Helen Tiffin. *The Empire Writes Back: Theory and Practice in Post-Colonial Literatures*. 1989.

Chaterjee, Para. *Nationalist Thought in the Colonial World: A Derivative Discourse*. 1993.

Gandhi, Leela. *Postcolonial Theory: A Critical Introduction*. 1998.

Loomba, Ania. *Colonialism/Postcolonialism*. 1998.

Nandy, Ashis. *The Intimate Enemy: Loss and Recovery of Self under Colonialism*. 1983.

Poddar, Prem, and David Johnson. *A Historical Companion of Postcolonial Thought*. 2005.

Said, Edward. *Culture and Imperialism*. 1994.

Williams, Patrick, and Laura Chrisman, eds. *Colonial Discourse and Post-colonial Theory: A Reader*. 1994.

Young, Robert. *Colonial Desire: Hybridity in Theory, Culture, and Race*. 1995.

——— *Postcolonialism: An Historical Introduction*. 2001.

American Multiculturalism

Since its beginnings, America has been home to people from an increasing number of different cultures, many of which have retained distinct identities and traditions over time. Many of these groups came willingly, as immigrants from Europe and other places, while others—African slaves in particular—did not. And, of course, the Native Americans were here before any of the waves of European immigration. That America is multiethnic has long been recognized—it is an unarguable fact. That America is, and ought to be, multicultural—that is, that it is not one culture but many, and that all its cultures are equally valuable—is a position that has gained increasing support in recent decades, particularly since the civil rights movements of the 1950s and 1960s.

One of the chief goals of multicultural critics has been to increase the visibility of literature produced by members of minority groups in the United States. Another has been to create a critical environment in which these works can be properly appreciated. (Since many works by minority authors were written out of a set of assumptions different from those of the dominant culture, such a critical environment could not be assumed.) Multicultural critics have drawn attention to those features of writing by different groups that are distinctive.

Much multicultural criticism so far has focused on the writing of African Americans. The emphasis on this group has been due in part to the sheer number of its members, and in part to the sense that they had been excluded from American public life in a more profound and violent way than any other group. No doubt a further reason is that the African-American struggle for equality and freedom has been so central to America's attempts at self-definition. At the same time, Native American, Asian-American, and Latino writers, as well as writers of other backgrounds, have attracted an increasing amount of both critical attention and popular success. More recently, the field of ethnic studies has brought attention to the unique accomplishments of groups such as Irish-, Italian-, and Arab-Americans. At the same time, religious studies scholars have looked at the cultures and cultural products of different religious groups, groups that often cut across ethnic and racial boundaries.

Multiculturalism shares many points of contact with cultural studies in general—for example, a willingness to investigate literature traditionally excluded from the canon and a suspicion of the categories of "high" and "low" art. Along with Marxist and New Historicist criticism, it shares an awareness of the ways in which writers and the texts they produce are shaped by societal conditions, and the ways in which those conditions are enforced and defended by those in power.

Important texts in the study of multicultural literature include Henry Louis Gates's *The Signifying Monkey: A Theory of African-American Literary Criticism* (1988), *Beyond Ethnicity: Consent and Descent in American Culture* (1987) by Werner Sollar, and Robert Allen Warrior's *Tribal Secrets: Recovering American Indian Intellectual Traditions* (1995).

An American Multicultural Reading: Alice Walker's "Everyday Use" (p. 517)

A multicultural reading of "Everyday Use" might focus on the quilt that the narrator decides to give to Maggie, rather than to Dee, and on its connection to African-American history. Such a reading might also look at the ways in which the narrator's relationship to that history differs from Dee's.

> African-American art has often been functional—that is, it is meant to be used. The quilts that become the subject of contention in Alice Walker's "Everyday Use" are an example of this type of art. In fact, the little of the story is a specific reference to the functionality of the handmade things that Dee wants to take with her from her family home. Given Dee's newfound interest in African and African-American culture, it is striking that she is unable to appreciate this fact, which seems so obvious to her mother and sister.
>
> Dee seems interested in the history of her people, and of her family, chiefly when she is able to view them as exotic. At times, it seems that she has come to visit her family largely because she sees their home as a kind of museum of black culture. She wants nearly everything in and around the house that she lays eyes on, but she wants them as curios or decorations, not as the functioning butter churns, dashers, and quilts that they are. She was named after her mother's sister, and after her grandmother, but she has taken a new, supposedly more African name: Wangero. She wants the artifacts these women have left behind but not their name.
>
> It would be going too far to say that Walker is simply condemning Dee as shallow. Dee does genuinely admire the artifacts she wants to take with her, and she does want them in part because of the connection they have to members of her own family. Her failing—and this is where the story is at its most subtle—is that, in contrast with Maggie, she *needs* these artifacts to maintain a connection with her family's past. What convinces the narrator of the story to save the quilts for Maggie is the way in which Maggie relinquishes her claim to them: "She can have them, Mama . . . I can 'member Grandma Dee without the quilts" (p. 523).
>
> Dee's last words to her mother and sister neatly sum up her contradictory relationship to them and to the tradition they represent. After saying that her mother doesn't understand her own heritage, she turns to Dee and says, "You ought to try to make something of yourself, too, Maggie. It's really a new day for us. But from the way you and mama still live you'd never know it" (p. 523). Dee wants to be free of all the negative aspects that have defined the African-American experience, yet at the same time she wants to position herself as the heir to that culture. It isn't—it can't be—that simple.

For Further Reading: American Multiculturalism

Allen, Paula Gunn. *The Sacred Hoop: Recovering the Feminine in American Indian Traditions*. 1986.

Anzaldúa, Gloria. *Borderlands/La Frontera: The New Mestiza*. 1987.

Awkward, Michael. *Inspiriting Influences: Tradition, Revision, and Afro-American Literature*. 1989.

Berkovitch, Sacvan. *The Rites of Ascent: Transformations in the Symbolic Construction of America*. 1981.

Ferraro, Thomas J. *Ethnic Passages: Literary Immigrants in Twentieth-Century America*. 1993.

Gates, Henry Louis, Jr. (ed.). *Race, Writing and Difference*. 1985.

Goldberg, David Theo, ed. *Multiculturalism: A Critical Reader*. 1994.

Morrison, Toni. *Playing in the Dark: Whiteness and the Literary Imagination*. 1993.

Pulitano, Elvira. *Toward a Native American Critical Theory*. 2003.

West, Thomas R. *Signs of Struggle: The Rhetorical Politics of Cultural Difference*. 2002.

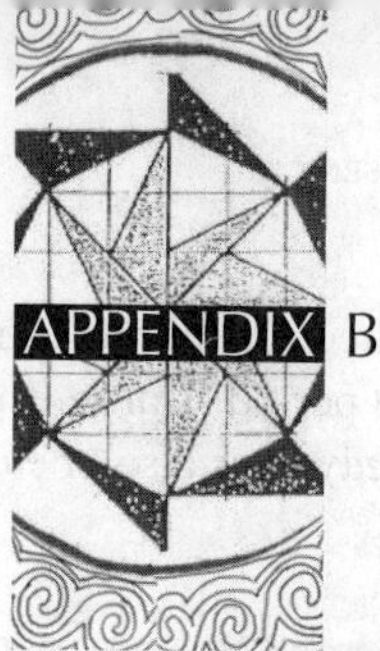

LITERARY HISTORY: FROM ARISTOTLE TO THE PRESENT

Beginnings: The Greeks and Romans (c. 450 B.C.–A.D. 400)

The Western critical tradition began in ancient Greece. In the *Republic,* Plato (427–347 B.C.) described the ideal state as well as the role of philosophers and poets. His pupil Aristotle (384–322 B.C.) was by far the most significant classical influence on Europeans of the Middle Ages and the Renaissance. Even today, drama critics and students pay careful attention to the theories presented in Aristotle's *Poetics* about how literature imitates life, how an audience responds with pity and fear to a tragedy, and how a well-written play is constructed.

The Romans contributed works on what would now be called "loftiness of style" (*On the Sublime,* Longinus, first century A.D.) and a treatise on the art of poetry (*Ars Poetica,* Horace, 65–8 B.C.). Roman writers were typically more interested in the craft of poetry — in how to construct a poem that would have a pleasing effect on a reader — than in the power of the poet. In contrast to the Greek philosophical approach, Roman literary criticism brings to mind a practical handbook.

The Middle Ages (c. A.D. 400–1500)

After the fall of the western Roman Empire in the fifth century A.D., Christianity became the unifying force of Western culture. Much European literature of the Middle Ages took the form of morality and mystery plays, both of which had religious themes. Worldly art was discouraged because the church believed that the role of literature was to instruct people in the way to lead a virtuous life. Significant departures from moralistic literature appeared in the French romances, which depicted adventures undertaken in the cause of love, and in Chaucer's (c. 1342–1400) *Canterbury Tales,* which drew on English, French, and Italian sources. These served as antidotes to the traditional religious cautionary plays and tales.

Because of the central importance of religion during the Middle Ages, much of the period's literary criticism is concerned with the interpretation of the Bible. The habits of reading that were developed in the process, many of which were derived from the ways in which New Testament texts were used to interpret the Old Testament, were also applied to secular literature of the period. Dante, the author of the period's greatest literary work, *The Divine Comedy*, was also one of its most important literary theorists.

The Renaissance (c. 1500–1660)

During the fourteenth and fifteenth centuries, Europe emerged from the church-centered Middle Ages with a rebirth (*renaissance* is French for "rebirth") of learning. Renewed access to Greek and Roman texts led Renaissance humanists to a broad interest in intellectual considerations. Sir Philip Sidney's (1554–1586) *The Defense of Poesy* (c. 1580) is considered the most important work of literary criticism from this period. In the *Defense*, Sidney argues that poetry must not simply give pleasure but also contribute positively to the life of society. Unlike the writers of medieval allegories, Sidney believed that literature could — and should — have a moral impact without being didactic or prescriptive.

Despite Sidney's contributions, Aristotle remained the arbiter of critical questions, although his role was complicated by the emergence of William Shakespeare (1564–1616) as a dramatist of exceptional talent. Shakespeare's work posed a problem because many critics realized that he was a fine playwright despite his frequent disregard for Aristotle's rules governing well-constructed plays. As a result, a major concern of criticism up to the eighteenth century became the reconciling of Aristotle's standards with the practices of contemporary playwrights.

The Enlightenment (1660–1798)

Samuel Johnson (1709–1784), who devoted much of the preface of his edition of Shakespeare's plays to the question of Shakespeare's departures from Aristotle's rules, was a major figure of the Enlightenment, a period of neoclassicism characterized by a revitalized interest in the values and ideas of the classical world, particularly of the Romans. Along with Johnson, poets John Dryden (1631–1700) and Alexander Pope (1688–1744), as well as philosopher Edmund Burke (1729–1797), compared contemporary practice with the ideas of their Roman forebears. Burke, for instance, addressed the subject of Longinus's *On the Sublime* in his own treatise, *The Origin of Our Ideas of the Sublime and the Beautiful* (1757). Eighteenth-century critics stressed the value of reason and what they called "common sense." Their neoclassic architectural style, familiar to us in the Capitol building in Washington, D.C., and other structures, provides a visual example of what they sought in literature: clarity, symmetry, discipline. They demanded that a play or poem be tightly constructed, and they saw the heroic couplet (two lines of rhymed iambic pentameter) as the perfect building block with which to construct didactic poems such as Pope's *Essay on Criticism* (1711), a scathing statement of neoclassical literary principles.

The literature of the American revolutionary age, when Thomas Paine, Thomas Jefferson, Alexander Hamilton, Philip Freneau, and Joel Barlow were writing, reflected the patriotic concerns of the infant democracy. For example, Paine's *Common Sense: Addressed to the Inhabitants of America* (1776) inspired Americans to revolution, and his *Rights of Man* (1791, 1792) made a stirring case for freedom as the right of every individual.

The Romantic Period (1798–1837)

The romantics were a counterreaction to the Enlightenment. They believed that poetry was *not* an objective construction like a building with a precise and unchanging meaning but, instead, was a subjective creation whose meaning depends on the poet's emotional state and a reader's personal response. Romantic poet William Blake (1757–1827) illustrated the conflict between romanticism and neoclassicism through his criticism of the opinions of Enlightenment artist Joshua Reynolds. In his notes on Reynolds's views, Blake observed that the Enlightenment emphasis on materialism and on physical evidence (empiricism) impoverishes art. Blake believed that the neoclassicists denied both imagination and subjective experience their preeminent roles in the creative process. Unlike most eighteenth-century writers, Blake and his fellow romantics believed in the importance of the individual example rather than the general principle.

Like Blake, Samuel Taylor Coleridge (1772–1834) and William Wordsworth (1770–1850) placed value on the mysterious and on the common person's experience. Wordsworth in particular stressed the importance of concrete, simple language and offered, in his preface to the second edition of *Lyrical Ballads* (1800), a definition of poetry that has since become famous. A poem, Wordsworth says, should originate in "the spontaneous overflow of powerful feelings" whose energy comes from "emotion recollected in tranquility." George Gordon, Lord Byron (1788–1824), who himself lived a flamboyant life of publicly expressed powerful emotions, created in his poetry the melancholy romantic hero, defiant and haunted by secret guilt. Percy Bysshe Shelley (1792–1822) makes perhaps the greatest claims for the poet's power and obligation to society in "A Defense of Poetry" (1821), in which he argues that the "great instrument of moral good is the imagination."

The difference in attitude between neoclassicists and romantics can also be seen through a comparison of the Shakespearean criticism of Samuel Johnson and Samuel Taylor Coleridge. In his *Preface to Shakespeare* (1765), Johnson argues that Shakespeare's faults include being much more concerned with pleasing an audience than with teaching it morals; he observes that often in Shakespeare's works virtue is not rewarded nor is wickedness suitably punished. In addition, Johnson notes, Shakespeare's diction is too elevated, and he lets the characters in the tragedies talk too much without advancing the action. Coleridge, in contrast, sees in the tragic character of Hamlet the prototype of the romantic hero and argues in his lecture "Shakespeare's Judgment Equal to his Genius" (1836) that Shakespeare describes how people actually behave rather than how they ought to behave.

John Keats (1795–1821), another romantic poet, continued Coleridge's defense of Shakespeare. Keats believed that Shakespeare's intensity, particularly evident in the tragedies, moved his work onto another level altogether, where the work itself takes on life through its relationship with "beauty and truth" rather than with teaching proper behavior.

The romantics in general, both in Britain and in the United States (where they were called *transcentalists*) saw the poet as particularly close to God and nature. The American philosopher Ralph Waldo Emerson (1803–1882) thought nature offered the poet a mystical symbolism, while Henry David Thoreau (1817–1862) extolled the view that man should live close to nature and follow his personal conscience rather than the dictates of society. Mary Shelley (1797–1851) and Edgar Allan Poe (1809–1849) were influential in another strand of romanticism: the macabre, melancholy, and mysterious.

The Victorian Period (1837–1901)

The literary problem facing the post-romantic generation of critics was how to deal with a world where sublime isolation and communing with nature were less and less possible. During the Victorian era, industrialization, poverty, population growth, and mass transportation contributed to a general sense that the world was changing rapidly. In England, critics such as the poet Matthew Arnold (1822–1888) argued that literature could help anchor people to their world and that literary criticism, as an occupation, should be a "disinterested endeavor" whose responsibility was to minister to a modern society that had lost its faith in other things, particularly religion. Arnold believed that poetry had a palliative function—in other words, that it should help people live productive, satisfying lives.

Just before the turn of the nineteenth century, the pendulum swung away from Arnold's view that poetry has moral utility to the view that art should exist for its own sake. The dichotomy seen by the romantics between intellect and feeling became in the 1890s the split between art and science. Oscar Wilde (1854–1900), Stéphane Mallarmé (1842–1898), and Charles Baudelaire (1821–1867) all dealt with this dichotomy by retreating into the world of art and denying art's connection with anything else. These members of the symbolist movement valued suggestion, private symbols, and evocative references in their poetry. They attempted to connect their writing with a spiritual world that was not accessible by the rational methods of science.

Charles Darwin (1809–1882) presented his theory of natural selection in *Origin of Species* (1859), and his ideas influenced novels and poetry of the latter part of the nineteenth century. Those who believed natural selection contradicted the Bible were outraged, and others interpreted his theories as evidence of humans' latent bestiality. Darwin's ideas undermined the certainty that humankind was the center of the universe and that the universe had been intelligently planned for a good purpose.

American writers of the late nineteenth century, including William Dean Howells and Henry James, were noted for realism. Others, including naturalists

Frank Norris and Theodore Dreiser, built on Darwin's views, exploring the idea of individuals being at the mercy of their instinctual drives and of sociological forces.

The Modern Period (Since 1901)

In the next major attempt to establish some objective significance to poetry, T. S. Eliot (1888–1965) argued against the lingering romantic idea that a poem is the original product of a poet's inspiration. Instead, he proposed in "Tradition and the Individual Talent" (1917) that the poem supersedes the poet, who is merely the agent of its creation. Eliot argues that Wordsworth is wrong to put the poet in the central role of life-experiencer and re-creator. According to Eliot, the poem itself will join the tradition, and it will be up to the *critic* to make sense of that tradition. For example, Eliot's analysis of *Hamlet* focuses neither on the character of Hamlet and his personal agony (as did the romantics) nor on the moral tone of the play (as did the neoclassicists), but rather on the story of Hamlet as treated by dramatists before Shakespeare. Eliot concludes that the problems with Shakespeare's play come about because Shakespeare cannot successfully balance the early source materials with his own desire to write a play about the effect of Gertrude's guilt on her son. Thus, Eliot judges Shakespeare within a literary and historical tradition rather than within a moral or personal context.

The twentieth century produced many important critics and theoreticians of literature who built on the legacy of the past, although some only to the extent that they attempted to contradict earlier approaches. The dominant critical views (discussed in Appendix A), can be divided into three categories: **formal,** those concerned with the structure or form of texts (formalism, structuralism, deconstruction); **social,** those concerned with texts in relation to social contexts (New Historicism, feminism, queer theory, Marxism); and **personal,** those concerned with the interaction of the individual (author or reader) and texts (reader-response criticism, psychoanalytic criticism). Each of these theoretical approaches can be traced to the writings of authors in the early part of the twentieth century or before.

Formalism, which acquired prominence in English and American criticism in the middle part of the twentieth century, actually began in the early part of the century in Moscow and Petrograd (St. Petersburg). The word *formalism* was initially a pejorative term because formalists focused on patterns and devices in a work of literature and ignored the subject matter. Soon, however, formalism's logical appeal took hold, and formalism was advocated by Victor Shklovsky, Boris Eichenbaum, and Roman Jakobson in the 1920s. Although many literary theorists since Aristotle have stressed the importance of structure, the roots of structuralist criticism can be traced more directly to the Russian formalists and to the French anthropologist Claude Levi-Strauss (1908–   ), who held that all cultural phenomena have an underlying structural system. Deconstruction both reacts against the tenets of structuralism and builds on the theories of German philosophers Friedrich Nietzsche (1844–1900) and Martin Heidegger (1889–1976), who questioned the validity and verifiability of "truth," "knowledge," and other basic philosophical concepts.

Social criticism (feminism, Marxism, cultural studies, New Historicism, queer theory, postcolonialism, and American multiculturalism) also had precursors in earlier writing. For example, Mary Wollstonecraft's *A Vindication of the Rights of Woman* (1792) was an early forerunner of feminism. Virginia Woolf's *A Room of One's Own* (1929) anticipated feminist criticism by addressing the effects on women of the patriarchal Western society and identifying deeply entrenched attitudes of male-oriented society that hindered women in the pursuit of their creative possibilities. Similarly, Marxist criticism is based on the writings of Karl Marx and Friedrich Engels; they borrowed their key term *ideology* from French philosophers of the late eighteenth century who used it to label the study of how sense perceptions develop into concepts. The term *Marxism* itself was used in the same period to mean a rigidly held set of political ideas. Marx and Engels adapted and changed the terms, investing them with new meaning that built on meanings already present in the culture. New Historicism — an even more recent mode of literary study (beginning in the 1980s) — reacts to formalism, structuralism, and deconstruction, arguing that the historical context is an integral part of a literary work and that the text cannot be considered in isolation.

Personal criticism too has its origins in earlier writing. For instance, the roots of psychoanalytic criticism can be traced to the psychological criticism of the early nineteenth century. Thomas Carlyle (1795–1881) suggested in 1827 that the best criticism of the day was psychological, deriving meaning from a poem by analyzing the mental state and personality structure of the author. Reader-response criticism, an approach begun in the 1960s, focuses on the reader and the reader's process and experience, rather than on the text or the text and its historical context.

Cultural studies, which, broadly construed, includes New Historicism, queer theory, postcolonialism, and American multiculturalism, emphasizes the social and historical context of a work of literature and extends the reach of criticism to popular culture and to any artifact a given culture creates.

GLOSSARY OF LITERARY TERMS

Action What happens in a drama.

Alexandrine Verse with six iambic feet (iambic hexameter), a common form in French poetry but relatively rare in English poetry.

Allegorical figure or **framework** See **Allegory.**

Allegory Story with two parallel and consistent levels of meaning, one literal and one figurative, in which the figurative level offers a moral or political lesson; John Bunyan's *The Pilgrim's Progress* and Nathaniel Hawthorne's "Young Goodman Brown" are examples of moral allegory. An **allegorical figure** has only one meaning (for instance, it may represent good or evil), as opposed to a **symbol,** which may suggest a complex network of meanings. An **allegorical framework** is the system of ideas that conveys the allegory's message.

Alliteration Repetition of consonant sounds (usually the initial sounds) in a series of words, as in Blake's "The Chimney Sweeper": "So your chimneys I sweep, and in soot I sleep." Alliteration may be reinforced by repeated sounds within and at the ends of words.

Allusion Reference, often to literature, history, mythology, or the Bible, that is unacknowledged in the text but that the author expects a reader to recognize. An example of allusion in a title is Charles Baxter's "Gryphon" (a mythical beast).

Ambiguity Device in which authors intentionally evoke a number of possible meanings of a word or grammatical structure by leaving unclear which meaning they intend.

Anapest See **Meter.**

Antagonist Character who is in conflict with or opposition to the protagonist; the villain. Sometimes the antagonist may be a force or situation (war or poverty) rather than a person.

Antihero Modern character who possesses the opposite attributes of a hero. Rather than being dignified and powerful, the antihero tends to be passive and ineffectual. Willy Loman, the main character in Arthur Miller's *Death of a Salesman,* is an antihero.

Apostrophe Figure of speech in which an absent character or a personified force or object is addressed directly, as if it were present or could comprehend: "O Rose, thou art sick!"

Archetype Image or symbol that is so common or important that it seems to have universal significance. The psychologist Carl Jung believed that because archetypes are an inherent part of psyches, we recognize them subconsciously when we encounter them and therefore give them a greater meaning than they would otherwise possess. Many archetypes appear in classical myths (for example, a journey to the underworld).

Arena stage Stage on which the actors are surrounded by the audience; also called **theater in the round.**

Aside Brief comment spoken by an actor to the audience (such as, "Here she comes. I'll play a fine trick on her now!") and assumed not to be heard by the other characters.

Assonance Repetition of the same or similar vowel sounds in a series of words: "creep three feet."

Atmosphere Tone or mood of a literary work, often established by the setting and language. Atmosphere is the emotional aura that determines readers' expectations about a work — for example, the sense of doom established at the beginning of Shakespeare's *Macbeth.*

Aubade Poem about morning, usually celebrating the dawn.

Ballad Narrative poem, rooted in an oral tradition, usually arranged in quatrains rhyming *abcb* and containing a refrain.

Ballad stanza See **Stanza.**

Beast fable Short tale, usually including a moral, in which animals assume human characteristics — for example, Aesop's "The Tortoise and the Hare."

Beginning rhyme See **Rhyme.**

Black comedy Comedy that relies on the morbid and absurd. Often black comedies (also called *dark comedies*) are so satiric that they become ironic and tragic; examples are Joseph Heller's novel *Catch 22* and Edward Albee's play *The Sandbox*.

Blank verse Lines of unrhymed iambic pentameter in no particular stanzaic form. Because iambic pentameter resembles the rhythms of ordinary English speech, blank verse is often unobtrusive; for instance, Shakespeare's noble characters usually use it, though they may seem to us at first reading to be speaking in prose. See **Meter.**

Blocking Decisions about how characters move and where they stand on stage in a dramatic production.

Box set Stage setting that gives the audience the illusion of looking into a room.

Cacophony Harsh or unpleasant spoken sound created by clashing consonants such as "The vorpal blade went snicker-snack!" in Lewis Carroll's "Jabberwocky."

Caesura Strong or long pause in the middle of a poetic line, created by punctuation or by the sense of the poem, as in Yeats's "Leda and the Swan": "And Agamemnon dead. Being so caught up. . . ."

Carpe diem "Seize the day"; the philosophy arguing that one should enjoy life today before it passes by, as seen in Herrick's "To the Virgins, to Make Much of Time."

Catastrophe The moment in a tragedy after the climax, when the rising action has ended and the falling action has begun, when the protagonist begins to understand the implications of events that will lead to his or her downfall.

Catharsis Aristotle's term for the emotional reaction or "purgation" that takes place in an audience watching a tragedy.

Character Fictional representation of a person, usually but not necessarily in a psychologically realistic way. E. M. Forster classified characters as **round** (well developed, closely involved in the action and responsive to it) or **flat** (static, stereotypical, or operating as **foils** for the protagonist). Characters can also be classified as **dynamic** (growing and changing in the course of the action) or **static** (remaining unchanged).

Characterization Way in which writers develop their characters and reveal those characters' traits to readers.

Choragos See **Chorus.**

Chorus Group of actors in classical Greek drama who comment in unison on the action and the hero; they are led by the **Choragos.**

Classicism Attitude toward art that values symmetry, clarity, discipline, and objectivity. **Neoclassicism,** practiced in eighteenth-century Europe, appreciated those qualities as found in Greek and Roman art and culture.

Cliché Overused phrase or expression.

Climax Point of greatest tension or importance, where the decisive action of a play or story takes place.

Closed form Type of poetic structure that has a recognizable rhyme scheme, meter, or stanzaic pattern; also called *fixed form*.

Closet drama Play meant to be read instead of performed — for example, Shelley's *Prometheus Unbound*.

Comedy Any literary work, but especially a play, in which events end happily, a character's fortunes are reversed for the better, and a community is drawn more closely together, often by the marriage of one or more protagonists at the end.

Comedy of humours Comedy that focuses on characters whose behavior is controlled by a single characteristic trait, or humour, such as *Volpone* (1606) by Ben Jonson.

Comedy of manners Satiric comedy that achieved great popularity in the nineteenth century. This form focuses on the manners and customs of society and directs its satire against the characters who violate its social conventions and norms. *The Importance of Being Earnest* by Oscar Wilde is a comedy of manners.

Common measure See **Stanza.**

Conceit See **Metaphor.**

Concrete poem Poem whose typographical appearance on the page reinforces its theme, as with George Herbert's "Easter Wings."

Conflict Struggle between opposing forces (protagonist and antagonist) in a work of literature.

Connotation Meaning that a word suggests beyond its literal, dictionary meaning; its emotional associations, judgments, or opinions. Connotations can be positive, neutral, or negative. For example, *family* has a positive connotation when it describes a group of loving relatives; a neutral connotation when it describes a biological category; and a negative connotation when it describes a criminal organization.

Consonance See **Rhyme.**

Convention See **Literary convention.**

Conventional symbol See **Symbol.**

Cosmic irony See **Irony.**

Couplet See **Stanza.**

Crisis Point at which the decisive action of the plot occurs.

Dactyl See **Meter.**

Denotation Dictionary meaning of a word; its explicit, literal meaning.

Denouement See **Resolution.**

Deus ex machina "The god from the machine": any improbable resolution of plot involving the intervention of some force or agent from outside the story.

Dialect Particular regional variety of language, which may differ from the more widely used standard or written language in its pronunciation, grammar, or vocabulary. Eliza Doolittle's cockney dialect in the George Bernard Shaw play *Pygmalion* is an example.

Dialogue Conversation between two or more characters.

Diction Word choice that determines the level of language used in a piece of literature. **Formal diction** is lofty and elaborate (typical of Shakespearean nobility); **informal diction** is idiomatic and relaxed (like the narrative in John Updike's "A&P"). **Jargon** is the specialized diction of a professional or occupational group (such as computer scientists). **Idioms** are the colloquial expressions, including slang, of a particular group or society.

Didactic poetry Poetry whose purpose is to make a point or teach a lesson, particularly common in the eighteenth century.

Double entendre Phrase or word with a deliberate double meaning, one of which is usually sexual.

Double plot See **Plot.**

Drama Literature written to be performed.

Dramatic irony See **Irony.**

Dramatic monologue Type of poem perfected by Robert Browning that consists of a single speaker talking to one or more listeners and often revealing much more about the speaker than he or she seems to intend; Browning's "My Last Duchess" is an example of this form.

Dramatis personae Characters in a play.

Dynamic character See **Character.**

Elegy Poem commemorating someone's death, usually in a reflective or mournful tone, such as A. E. Housman's "To an Athlete Dying Young."

Elision Leaving out an unstressed syllable or vowel, usually in order to keep a regular meter in a line of poetry ("o'er" instead of "over," for example).

End rhyme See **Rhyme.**

End-stopped line Line of poetry that has a full pause at the end, typically indicated by a period or semicolon.

Enjambment See **Run-on line.**

Envoi Three-line conclusion to a sestina that includes all six of the poem's key words, three placed at the ends of lines and three within the lines. See **Sestina.**

Epic Long narrative poem, such as the *Iliad* or the *Aeneid*, recounting the adventures of heroes on whose actions the fate of a nation or race depends. Frequently the gods or other supernatural beings take active interest in the events.

Epigram Short pithy poem or statement — for example, Dorothy Parker's comment on an actress's performance, "She runs the gamut of emotions from A to B."

Epiphany Term first applied to literature by James Joyce to describe a sudden moment of revelation about the deep meaning of something, such as the boy's realization at the end of "Araby."

Euphemism Word consciously chosen for its pleasant **connotations;** often used for subjects such as sex and death, whose frank discussion is somewhat taboo in our society. For example, a euphemism for *to die* is *to pass away*.

Euphony Pleasant spoken sound created by smooth consonants such as "ripple" or "pleasure."

Exposition First stage of a plot, where the author presents the information about characters or setting that a reader or viewer will need to understand the subsequent action.

Expressionism Artistic and literary movement that attempts to portray inner experience. It moves away from realistic portrayals of life and is characterized by violent exaggeration of objective reality and extremes of mood and feeling. In drama, expressionistic stage sets mirror the inner states of the character.

Extended metaphor See **Metaphor.**

Extended simile See **Metaphor.** Also see **Conceit.**

Eye rhyme See **Rhyme.**

Fable Short tale, often involving animals or supernatural beings and stressing plot above character development, whose object is to teach a pragmatic or moral lesson. See **Beast fable.**

Fairy tale See **Folktale.**

Falling action Stage in a play's plot during which the intensity of the climax subsides.

Falling meter Trochaic and dactylic meters, so called because they move from stressed to unstressed syllables. See **Rising meter.**

Fantasy Work of literature that takes place in an unreal world or contains unreal or incredible characters. J. R. R. Tolkien's *The Lord of the Rings* is one example.

Farce Comedy in which stereotypical characters engage in boisterous horseplay and slapstick humor, as in Chekhov's *The Brute*.

Feminine rhyme See **Rhyme.**

Fiction Form of narrative that is primarily imaginative, though its form may resemble that of factual writing like history and biography.

Figures of speech Expressions — such as **hyperbole, metaphor, metonymy, personification, simile, synechdoche,** and **understatement**— that use words to achieve effects beyond ordinary language.

Flashback Variation on chronological order that presents an event or situation that occurred before the time in which the story's action takes place.

Flat character See **Character.**

Foil Minor character whose role is to highlight the main character by presenting a contrast with him or her.

Folktale Contemporary version of an old, even ancient, oral tale that can be traced back centuries through many different cultures. Folktales include fairy tales, myths, and fables.

Foot See **Meter.**

Foreshadowing Presentation early in a story of situations, characters, or objects that seem to have no special importance but in fact are later revealed to have great significance. For example, a casual mention of a character's memory for faces becomes significant when his fate hinges on his recognizing a person from his past.

Form Structure or shape of a literary work; the way a work's parts fit together to form a whole. In poetry, form is described in terms of the presence (or absence) of elements like rhyme, meter, and stanzaic pattern. See **Open form** and **Closed form.**

Formal diction See **Diction.**

Free verse See **Open form.**

Freytag's pyramid Classic dramatic plots include *exposition*, *complication* (the introduction of elements that will lead to conflict and ultimately crisis), *climax*, *catastrophe*, and *resolution*. In his *Technique of the Drama* (1863) Gustav Freytag suggested that this pattern resembles a pyramid, with rising action leading to the climax and giving way to falling action.

Genre Category of literature. Fiction, drama, and poetry are the three major genres; subgenres include the novel, the farce, and the lyric poem.

Haiku Seventeen-syllable, three-line form of Japanese verse that almost always uses concrete imagery and deals with the natural world.

Hamartia Aristotle's term for the "tragic flaw" in characters that eventually causes their downfall in Greek tragedy.

Hermeneutics Traditionally, the use of the Bible to interpret other historical or current events; in current critical theory, the principles and procedures followed to determine the meaning of a text.

Heroic couplet See **Stanza.**

High comedy Term introduced in 1877 by George Meredith to denote comedy that appeals to the intellect, such as Shakespeare's *As You Like It*. See **Low comedy.**

Hubris Tragic flaw of overwhelming pride that exists in the protagonist of a tragedy.

Hyperbole Figurative language that depends on intentional overstatement; Mark Twain often used it to create humor; Jonathan Swift used it for **satire.**

Iamb See **Meter.**

Imagery Words and phrases that describe the concrete experience of the five senses, most often sight. A **pattern of imagery** is a group of related images developed throughout a work. **Synesthesia** is a form of imagery that mixes the experience of the senses (hearing something visual, smelling something audible, and so on): "He smelled the blue fumes of her scent." **Static imagery** freezes the moment to give it the timeless quality of painting or sculpture. **Kinetic imagery** attempts to show motion or change.

Imagism Movement in modern poetry much influenced by **haiku,** stressing terseness and concrete imagery. **Imagists** were a group of early twentieth-century American poets, including Ezra Pound, William Carlos Williams, and Amy Lowell, who focused on visual images and created new rhythms and meters.

Imperfect rhyme See **Rhyme.**

In medias res Latin phrase describing works like Homer's *Iliad* that begin in the middle of the action in order to catch a reader's interest.

Informal diction See **Diction.**

Internal rhyme See **Rhyme.**

Irony Literary device or situation that depends on the existence of at least two separate and contrasting levels of meaning or experience. **Dramatic** or **tragic irony,** such as that found in *Oedipus the King,* depends on the audience's knowing something the protagonist has not yet realized. **Situational irony** exists when what happens is at odds with what the story's situation leads readers to expect will happen, as in Browning's "Porphyria's Lover." **Cosmic irony** (or irony of fate) exists when fate frustrates any effort a character might make to control or reverse his or her destiny. **Verbal irony** occurs when what is said is in contrast with what is meant. Verbal irony can be expressed as **understatement, hyperbole,** or **sarcasm.**

Jargon Specialized language associated with a particular trade or profession.

Kinetic imagery Imagery that attempts to show motion or change. See, for example, William Carlos Williams's "The Great Figure."

Literary canon Group of literary works generally acknowledged by critics and teachers to be the best and most significant to have emerged from our history. Many contemporary teachers and critics have attempted to expand the canon to include works by women and by writers of color.

Literary convention Something whose meaning is so widely understood within a society that authors can expect their audiences to accept and comprehend it unquestioningly — for example, the division of plays into acts or the fact that stepmothers in fairy tales are likely to be wicked.

Literary criticism Descriptions, analyses, interpretations, or evaluations of works of literature by experts in the field.

Literary symbol See **Symbol.**

Low comedy Introduced by George Meredith, it refers to comedy with little or no intellectual appeal. Low comedy is used as comic relief in *Macbeth*. See **High comedy.**

Lyric Form of poetry, usually brief and intense, that expresses a poet's subjective response to the world. In classical times, lyrics were set to music. The romantic poets, particularly Keats, often wrote lyrics about love, death, and nature.

Masculine rhyme See **Rhyme.**

Meditation Lyric poem that focuses on a physical object — for example, Keats's "Ode on a Grecian Urn" — using this object as a vehicle for considering larger issues.

Melodrama Sensational play that appeals shamelessly to the emotions, contains elements of tragedy but ends happily, and often relies on set plots and stock characters.

Metaphor Concise form of comparison equating two things that may at first seem completely dissimilar, often an abstraction and a concrete image — for example, "My love's a fortress." An **extended metaphor** (or **conceit**) is a comparison used throughout a work; in Tillie Olsen's "I Stand Here Ironing," the mother compares her daughter to a dress waiting to be ironed, thus conveying her daughter's passivity and vulnerability. See **Simile.**

Meter Regular pattern of stressed and unstressed syllables, each repeated unit of which is called a **foot:** an **anapest** has three syllables, two unstressed and the third stressed; a **dactyl** has three syllables, the first stressed and the subsequent ones unstressed. An **iamb** has two syllables, unstressed followed by stressed; a **trochee** has a stressed syllable followed by an unstressed one; a **spondee** has two stressed syllables; and a **pyrrhic** has two unstressed syllables. A poem's meter is described in terms of the kind of foot (anapest, for example) and the number of feet found in each line. The number of feet is designated by the Greek prefix for the number, so one foot per line is called *monometer*, two feet is *dimeter*, followed by *trimeter, tetrameter, pentameter, hexameter*, and so on. The most common meter in English is *iambic pentameter*. See also **Rising meter** and **Falling meter.**

Metonymy Figure of speech in which the term for one thing can be applied to another with which it is closely associated — for example, using "defend the flag" to mean "defend the nation."

Mimesis Aristotle's term for the purpose of literature, which he felt was "imitation" of life.

Monologue Extended speech by one character.

Mood Atmosphere created by the elements of a literary work (setting, characterization, imagery, tone, and so on).

Morality play Medieval Christian allegory, in which personified abstractions, such as Selfishness and Pride, struggle for a person's soul.

Motivation Reasons behind a character's behavior that make us accept or believe that character.

Mystery play Medieval play depicting biblical stories.

Myth Anonymous story reflecting the religious and social values of a culture or explaining natural phenomena, often involving gods and heroes.

Narrative The "storytelling" of a piece of fiction; the forward-moving recounting of episode and description. When an event that occurred earlier is told during a later sequence of events, it is called a **flashback;** suggesting earlier in a narration something that will occur later on is called **foreshadowing.**

Narrator Person who tells the story. See **Point of view.**

Naturalism Nineteenth-century movement whose followers believed that life should not be idealized when depicted in literature. Rather, literature should show that human experience is a continual (and for the most part losing) struggle against the natural world. Émile Zola, Jack London, and Stephen Crane are important practitioners of naturalism.

New Comedy Greek comedies of the fourth and third centuries B.C. that followed **Old Comedy.** They were comedies of romance with stock characters and conventional settings. They lacked the satire, abusive language, and bawdiness of Old Comedy.

Novel Fictional narrative, traditionally realistic, relating a series of events or following the history of a character or group of characters through a period of time.

Novella Extended short story, usually concentrated in episode and action (like a short story) but involving greater character development (like a novel); Franz Kafka's "The Metamorphosis" is a novella.

Octave See **Sonnet.**

Ode Relatively long lyric poem, common in antiquity and adapted by the romantic poets, for whom it was a serious poem of formal diction, often addressed to some significant object (such as a nightingale or the west wind) that has stimulated the poet's imagination.

Old Comedy The first comedies, written in Greece in the fifth century B.C., which heavily satirized the religious and social issues of the day. The chief practitioner of Old Comedy was Aristophanes. See **New Comedy.**

Onomatopoeia Word whose sound resembles what it describes: "snap, crackle, pop." Lewis Carroll's "Jabberwocky" uses onomatopoeia.

Open form Form of poetry that makes use of varying line lengths, abandoning stanzaic divisions, breaking lines in unexpected places, and even dispensing with any pretense of formal structure. Sometimes called *free verse* or *vers libre*. See **Form.**

Ottava rima See **Stanza.**

Oxymoron Phrase combining two seemingly incompatible elements: "crashing silence."

Parable Story that teaches a lesson, such as the parable of the prodigal son in the New Testament.

Paradox Seemingly contradictory situation. Adrienne Rich's "A Woman Mourned by Daughters" uses paradox.

Parody Exaggerated imitation of a serious piece of literature for humorous effect. Shakespeare's "My mistress' eyes are nothing like the sun" is a parody of traditional Renaissance love poetry.

Pastoral Literary work, such as Christopher Marlowe's lyric poem "The Passionate Shepherd to His Love," that deals nostalgically and usually unrealistically with a simple, preindustrial rural life; the name comes from the fact that traditionally pastorals feature shepherds.

Pastoral romance Prose tale set in an idealized rural world; popular in Renaissance England.

Pathos Suffering that exists simply to satisfy the sentimental or morbid sensibilities of the audience.

Pattern of imagery See **Imagery.**

Perfect rhyme See **Rhyme.**

Persona Narrator or speaker of a poem or story; in Greek tragedy, a persona was a mask worn by an actor.

Personification A figure of speech that endows inanimate objects or abstract ideas with life or human characteristics: "the river wept."

Petrarchan sonnet See **Sonnet.**

Picaresque Episodic, often satirical work, presenting the life story of a rogue or rascal — for example, Cervantes' *Don Quixote*. The form emerged in sixteenth-century Spain.

Picture-frame stage Stage that looks like a room with a missing fourth wall through which the audience views the play. The **proscenium arch** separates the audience from the play.

Plot Way in which the events of the story are arranged. When there are two stories of more or less equal importance, the work has a **double plot;** when there is more than one story but one string of events is clearly the most significant, the other stories are called **subplots.** Plot in fiction often follows the pattern of action in drama, rising to a **climax** and then falling to a **resolution.**

Poetic rhythm See **Rhythm.**

Point of view Perspective from which a story is told. The storyteller may be a major character in the story or a character who witnesses the story's events (*first-person narrator*) or someone who does not figure in the action at all (*third-person narrator*), in which case he or she may know the actions and internal doings of everyone in the story (*omniscient narrator*) or just know some part of these (*limited omniscient narrator*).

The narrator may be an *observer* or a *participant*. If he or she is untrustworthy (stupid or bad, for instance), the story has an *unreliable narrator;* narrators who are unreliable because they do not understand what they are reporting (children, for instance) are called *naive narrators*. If the perspective on the events is the same as one would get by simply watching the action unfold on stage, the point of view is *dramatic* or *objective*.

Popular fiction Works aimed at a mass audience.

Prologue First part of a play (originally of a Greek tragedy) in which the actor gives the background or explanations that the audience needs to follow the rest of the drama.

Props (short for **properties**) Pictures, furnishings, and so on that decorate the stage for a play.

Proscenium arch Arch that surrounds the opening in a **picture-frame stage;** through this arch the audience views the performances.

Prose poem Open form poem whose long lines appear to be prose set in paragraphs — for example, Carolyn Forché's "The Colonel."

Protagonist Principal character of a drama or a work of fiction; the hero. The *tragic hero* is the noble protagonist in classical Greek drama who falls because of a tragic flaw.

Pyrrhic See **Meter.**

Quatrain See **Stanza.**

Realism Writing that stresses life as it really is. Realism relies on careful description of setting and the trappings of daily life, psychological probability, and the lives of ordinary people. Ibsen's *A Doll House* is an example.

Resolution Also called the **denouement,** this is the final stage in the plot of a drama or work of fiction. Here the action comes to an end, and remaining loose ends are tied up.

Rhyme Repetition of concluding sounds in different words, often intentionally used at the ends of poetic lines. In **masculine rhyme** (also called *rising rhyme*) single syllables correspond. In **feminine rhyme** (also called *double rhyme* or *falling rhyme*) two syllables correspond, the second of which is stressed. In **triple rhyme,** three syllables correspond. **Eye rhyme** occurs when words look as though they should rhyme but are pronounced differently ("cough/ tough"). In **perfect rhyme,** the corresponding vowel and consonant sounds of accented syllables must be preceded by different consonants — for example, the *b* and *h* in "born" and "horn." **Imperfect rhyme,** also called *near rhyme*, *slant rhyme*, or *consonance* occurs when consonants in two words are the same but intervening vowels are different — for example, "pick /pack," "lads/lids." The most common type of rhyme within a poem is **end rhyme,** where the rhyming syllables are placed at the end of a line. **Internal rhyme** consists of rhyming words found within a line of poetry. **Beginning rhyme** occurs in the first syllable or syllables of a line.

Rhyme royal See **Stanza.**

Rhythm Regular recurrence of sounds in a poem. Ordinarily, rhythm is determined by the arrangement of metrical feet in a line, but sometimes *sprung rhythm*, introduced by Gerard Manley Hopkins, is used. In this type of rhythm, the number of strong stresses in a line determines the rhythm, regardless of how many weak stresses there might be.

Rising action Stage in a play's plot during which the action builds in intensity. See **Freytag's pyramid.**

Rising meter Iambic and anapestic meters, so called because they move from unstressed to stressed syllables. See **Falling meter.**

Romance Type of narrative that deals with love and adventure in a nonrealistic way, most popular in the Middle Ages but sometimes used by more modern authors, such as Hawthorne.

Romantic comedy Comedy such as Shakespeare's *Much Ado about Nothing* in which love is the main subject and idealized lovers endure great difficulties to get to the inevitable happy ending.

Romanticism Eighteenth- and nineteenth-century literary movement that valued subjectivity, individuality, the imagination, nature, excess, the exotic, and the mysterious.

Round character See **Character.**

Run-on line Line of poetry that ends with no punctuation or natural pause and consequently runs over into the next line; also called *enjambment*.

Sarcasm Form of irony in which apparent praise is used to convey strong, bitter criticism.

Satire Literary attack on folly or vanity by means of humor; usually intended to improve society.

Scansion Process of determining the meter of a poem by analyzing the strong and weak stresses in a line to find the unit of **meter** (each recurring pattern of stresses) and the number of these units (or **feet**) in each line.

Scrim Curtain that when illuminated from the front appears solid but when lit from the back becomes transparent.

Sentimental comedy Reaction against the **comedy of manners.** This type of comedy relies on sentimental emotion rather than on wit or humor and focuses on the virtues of life.

Sestet See **Sonnet.**

Sestina Poem composed of six six-line stanzas and a three-line conclusion called an **envoi.** Each line ends with one of six key words.

The alternation of these six words in different positions — but always at the ends of lines — in the poem's six stanzas creates a rhythmic verbal pattern that unifies the poem.

Setting Background against which the action of a work takes place: the historical time, locale, season, time of day, weather, and so on.

Shakespearean sonnet See **Sonnet.**

Short-short story Short fictional narrative that is generally under five pages (or fifteen hundred words) in length.

Short story Fictional narrative centered on one climatic event and usually developing only one character in depth; its scope is narrower than that of the **novel,** and it often uses setting and characterization more directly to make its theme clear.

Simile Comparison of two seemingly unlike things using the words *like* or *as:* "My love is like an arrow through my heart." See **Metaphor.**

Situational irony See **Irony.**

Soliloquy Convention of drama in which a character speaks directly to the audience, revealing thoughts and feelings that other characters present on stage are assumed not to hear.

Sonnet Fourteen-line poem, usually a **lyric** in *iambic pentameter* (see **Meter**). It has a strict rhyme scheme in one of two forms: the *Italian,* or **Petrarchan sonnet** (an eight-line **octave** rhymed *abba/abba* with a six-line **sestet** rhymed *cdc/cdc* or a variation) and the *English,* or **Shakespearean sonnet** (three quatrains rhymed *abab/cdcd/efef* with a concluding couplet rhymed gg).

Speaker See **Persona.**

Spenserian stanza See **Stanza.**

Spondee See **Meter.**

Stage directions Words in a play that describe an actor's role apart from the dialogue, dealing with movements, attitudes, and so on.

Stage setting (set) Scenery and props in the production of a play. In *expressionist* stage settings, scenery and props are exaggerated and distorted to reflect the workings of a troubled, even abnormal mind. *Surrealistic* stage settings are designed to mirror the uncontrolled images of dreams or nightmares. See **Staging.**

Staging Overall production of a play in performance: the sets, costumes, lighting, sound, music, and so on.

Stanza Group of lines in a poem that forms a metrical or thematic unit. Each stanza is usually separated from others by a blank space on the page. Some common stanzaic forms are the **couplet** (two lines), **tercet** (three lines), **quatrain** (four lines), **sestet** (six lines), and **octave** (eight lines). The **heroic couplet,** first used by Chaucer and especially popular throughout the eighteenth century, notably in Alexander Pope's poetry, consists of two rhymed lines of iambic pentameter, with a weak pause after the first line and a strong pause after the second. **Terza rima,** a form used by Dante, has a rhyme scheme (*aba, bcb, ded*) that creates an interlocking series of stanzas. The **ballad stanza** alternates lines of eight and six syllables. Typically, only the second and fourth lines rhyme. **Common measure** is a four-line stanzaic pattern closely related to the ballad stanza. It differs in that its rhyme scheme is *abab* rather than *abcb*. **Rhyme royal** is a seven-line stanza (*ababbcc*) set in iambic pentameter. **Ottava rima** is an eight-line stanza (*abababcc*) set in iambic pentameter. The **Spenserian stanza** is a nine-line form (*ababbcbcc*) with the first eight lines in iambic pentameter and the last line in iambic hexameter.

Static character See **Character.**

Static imagery Imagery that freezes a moment to give it the timeless quality of painting or sculpture. Much visual imagery is static.

Stock character Stereotypical character who behaves consistently and whom the audience of a play can recognize and classify instantly: the town drunk, the nerd, and so on.

Stream of consciousness Form of narration controlled not by external events but by the thoughts and subjective impressions of the narrator, commonly found in modern literature, such as the work of Virginia Woolf and James Joyce.

Stress Accent or emphasis, either strong or weak, given to each syllable in a piece of writing, as determined by conventional pronunciation (cărpĕt, not cărpét) and intended emphasis ("going dówn, dówn, dówn tŏ thĕ bóttŏm ŏf thĕ ócĕan"). Strong stresses are marked with a ´ and weak ones with a ˘.

Structure Formal pattern or arrangement of elements to form a whole in a piece of literature.

Style How an author selects and arranges words to express ideas and, ultimately, theme.

Subplot See **Plot.**

Surrealism Literary movement that allows unconventional use of syntax; chronology; juxtaposition; and bizarre, dreamlike images in prose and poetry.

Symbol Person, object, action, or idea whose meaning transcends its literal or denotative sense in a complex way. For instance, if someone wears a rose in a lapel to a dance, the rose may simply be a decoration, but in Blake's "The Sick Rose" it becomes a symbol because it takes on a range of paradoxical and complementary meanings. A symbol is invested with significance beyond what it could carry on its own. **Universal symbols,** such as the grim reaper, may be called **archetypes; conventional symbols,** such as national flags, evoke a general and agreed-upon response from most people. There are also *private symbols,* such as the "gyre" created by Yeats, which the poet himself invested with extraordinary significance.

Synecdoche Figure of speech in which a part of something is used to represent the whole — for example, "hired hand" represents a laborer.

Synesthesia See **Imagery.**

Tale Short story often involving mysterious atmosphere and supernatural or inexplicable events, such as "The Tell-Tale Heart" by Edgar Allan Poe.

Ten-minute play Short play that can be performed in ten minutes or less.

Tercet See **Stanza.**

Terza rima See **Stanza.**

Theater in the round See **Arena stage.**

Theater of the Absurd Type of drama that discards conventions of plot, character, and motivation in order to depict a world in which nothing makes sense. Albee's *The Sandbox* is an example.

Theme Central or dominant idea of a piece of literature, made concrete by the details and emphasis in the work itself.

Thrust stage Stage that juts out into the audience so the action may be viewed from three sides.

Tone Attitude of the speaker or author of a work toward the subject itself or the audience, as determined by the word choice and arrangement of the piece.

Tragedy Literary work, especially a play, that recounts the downfall of an individual. *Greek tragedy* demanded a noble protagonist whose fall could be traced to a *tragic personal flaw*. *Shakespearean tragedy* also treats noble figures, but the reasons for their tragedies may be less clear-cut than in Greek drama. *Domestic* or *modern tragedy* tends to deal with the fates of ordinary people.

Tragic irony See **Irony.**

Tragicomedy Type of Elizabethan and Jacobean drama that uses elements of both tragedy and comedy.

Triple rhyme See **Rhyme.**

Trochee See **Meter.**

Understatement Intentional downplaying of a situation's significance, often for ironic or humorous effect, as in Mark Twain's famous comment on reading his own obituary, "The reports of my death are greatly exaggerated."

Unities Rules that require a dramatic work to be unified in terms of its time, place, and action. *Oedipus the King* illustrates the three unities.

Universal symbol See **Symbol.**

Verbal irony See **Irony.**

Villanelle A nineteen-line poem composed of five tercets and a concluding quatrain; its rhyme scheme is *aba aba aba aba aba abaa*. Two different lines are systematically repeated in the poem: line 1 appears again in lines 6, 12, and 18, and line 3 reappears as lines 9, 15, and 19. Thus, each tercet concludes with an exact (or close) duplication of either line 1 or line 3, and the final quatrain concludes by repeating both line 1 and line 3.

Visual poetry Poetry that focuses as much on the words' appearance on the page as on what the words say, using a combination of media that may include video, photography, and even sound as well as text.

Wagons Sets mounted on wheels, which make rapid changes of scenery possible.

CREDITS

This page constitutes an extension of the copyright page. We have made every effort to trace the ownership of all copyrighted material and to secure permission from copyright holders. In the event of any question arising as to the use of any material, we will be pleased to make the necessary corrections in future printings. Thanks are due to the following authors, publishers, and agents for permission to use the material indicated.

Chapter 1. 6–7: Luisa Valenzuela, "All about Suicide," translated by Helen Lane, from STRANGE THINGS HAPPEN HERE: A SELECTION OF SHORT STORIES. English translation copyright © 1979 by Harcourt Brace & Company. Reprinted by permission of Houghton Mifflin Harcourt Publishing Company. **7–8:** Wole Soyinka, "Telephone Conversation." Copyright © 1962, 1990 by Wole Soyinka. Reprinted with permission by Melanie Jackson Agency, LLC. **13–14:** Ezra Pound, excerpt from Canto LXXVI from The Cantos of Ezra Pound. Copyright 1934, 1937, 1940, 1948, © 1956, 1959, 1962, 1963, 1966, and 1968 by Ezra Pound. Reprinted by permission of New Directions Publishing Corp.

Chapter 2. 19–20: Maya Angelou, "My Arkansas" from AND STILL I RISE. Copyright © 1978 by Maya Angelou. Used by permission of Random House, Inc.

Chapter 9. 171–175: Ernest Hemingway, "Hills Like White Elephants" from THE SHORT STORIES OF ERNEST HEMINGWAY. Copyright 1938 by Ernest Hemingway, renewed © 1966 by Mary Hemingway. Reprinted by permission of Scribner, an imprint of Simon & Schuster Adult Publishing. All rights reserved.

Chapter 10. 177–178: Julia Alvarez, "Snow" from HOW THE GARCIA GIRLS LOST THEIR ACCENTS. Copyright © 1984, 1991 by Julia Alvarez. Published by Plume, an imprint of Penguin Group (USA) and originally in hardcover by Algonquin Books of Chapel Hill. Reprinted by permission of Susan Bergholz Literary Services, New York, NY and Lamy, NM. All rights reserved. **178–180:** Aimee Bender, "Jinx" from WILLFUL CREATURES: STORIES. Copyright © 2005 by Aimee Bender. Used by permission of Doubleday, a division of Random House, Inc. **180:** Jorge Luis Borges, "The Plot" from THE ALEPH AND OTHER STORIES. Copyright © by Jorge Luis Borges. Used by permission of Penguin, a division of Penguin Group (USA) Inc. and The Wylie Agency, LLC. **181:** Dave Eggers, "Accident" from THE GUARDIAN (April 16, 2005). Copyright © 2005 by Dave Eggers. Reprinted with the permission of the author. **183:** Jamaica Kincaid, "Girl" from AT THE BOTTOM OF THE RIVER. Copyright © 1983 by Jamaica Kincaid. Reprinted by permission of Farrar, Straus & Giroux, LLC. **184–187:** Alice Munro, "Prue" from THE MOONS OF JUPITER AND OTHER STORIES. Copyright © 1982 by Alice Munro. Used by permission of Alfred A. Knopf, a division of Random House, Inc. and William Morris Agency LLC on behalf of the Author. **187–190:** ZZ Packer, "Buffalo Soldiers" from GRANTA 97 (Spring 2007). Copyright © 2007 by ZZ Packer. Reprinted with the permission of the author.**190:** Annie Proulx, "55 Miles to the Gas Pump" from CROSS RANGE: WYOMING STORIES. Copyright © 1999 by Dead Line, Ltd. Reprinted with the permission of Scribner, an imprint of Simon & Schuster Adult Publishing Group. All rights reserved. **191–192:** John Updike, "Oliver's Evolution" from LICKS OF LOVE: SHORT STORIES AND A SEQUEL. Copyright © 2000 by John Updike. Used by permission of Alfred A. Knopf, a division of Random House, Inc. **192–193:** David Foster Wallace, "Incarnations of Burned Children" from OBLIVION: STORIES. Copyright © 2004 by David Foster Wallace. Reprinted by permission of Little, Brown & Company.

Chapter 11. 197–200: Alberto Alvaro Ríos, "The Secret Lion" from THE IGUANA KILLER: TWELVE STORIES OF THE HEART. Copyright © 1984 by Alberto Alvaro Ríos. Reprinted with the permission of Confluence Press.

Chapter 12. 224–225: Ben Katchor, "Goner Pillow Company" from METROPOLIS (February 2005). Reprinted with the permission of METROPOLIS. **229–230:** Larry Fondation, "Deportation at Breakfast." Reprinted with the permission of the author. **232–236:** Nadine Gordimer, "Once upon a Time" from JUMP AND OTHER STORIES. Copyright © 1991 by Felix Licensing B.V. Reprinted by permission of Farrar, Straus & Giroux, LLC and Penguin

Books (Canada), a Division of Pearson Canada, Inc. **237–241:** Stephen Dobyns, "Kansas" from EATING NAKED. Originally published in CLACKAMAS LITERARY REVIEW. Copyright © 2000 by Stephen Dobyns. Reprinted by permission of Henry Holt and Company LLC. **243–250:** William Faulkner, "A Rose for Emily" from COLLECTED STORIES OF WILLIAM FAULKNER. Copyright 1930 and renewed © 1958 by William Faulkner. Used by permission of Random House, Inc.

Chapter 13. 258: Art Spiegelman, "Eye Ball" from THE NEW YORKER (September 18, 2006). Copyright © 2006 by Art Spiegelman. Reprinted with the permission of The Wylie Agency, Inc. **259–264:** John Updike, "A&P" from PIGEON FEATHERS AND OTHER STORIES. Copyright © 1962, and renewed 1990 by John Updike. Used by permission of Alfred A. Knopf, a division of Random House, Inc. **271–275:** Zadie Smith, "The Girl with Bangs" from McSweeney's 6 (2001). Copyright © 2001 by Zadie Smith. Reprinted with the permission of A. P. Watt, Ltd. on behalf of Zadie Smith. **277–288:** Charles Baxter, "Gryphon" from THROUGH THE SAFETY NET. Copyright © 1985 by Charles Baxter. Used courtesy Darhansoff Verrill Feldman Literary Agents. **290–302:** Jhumpa Lahiri, "The Third and Final Continent" from INTERPRETER OF MALADIES. Copyright © 1999 by Jhumpa Lahiri. Reprinted by permission of Houghton Mifflin Harcourt Publishing Company. All rights reserved.

Chapter 14. 310–312: Marjane Satrapi, excerpt from PERSEPOLIS. Copyright © 2003 by Marjane Satrapi. Used by permission of Pantheon Books, a division of Random House, Inc. **318–321:** Lan Samantha Chang, "Water Names" from HUNGER: A NOVELLA AND STORIES. Copyright © 1998 by Lan Samantha Chang. Used by permission of W. W. Norton & Company, Inc. **322–330:** Sherman Alexie, "This Is What It Means to Say Phoenix, Arizona" from THE LONE RANGER AND TONTO FISTFIGHT IN HEAVEN. Copyright © 1993, 2005 by Sherman Alexie. Used by permission of Grove/Atlantic, Inc. **332–342:** Ralph Ellison, "Battle Royal" from INVISIBLE MAN. Copyright 1948 by Ralph Ellison. Used by permission of Random House, Inc. **344–350:** Tillie Olsen, "I Stand Here Ironing" from TELL ME A RIDDLE. Copyright © 1961 by Tillie Olsen. Reprinted by permission of The Frances Goldin Literary Agency.

Chapter 15. 364–373: Shaun Tan, excerpt from THE ARRIVAL. Copyright © 2006 by Shaun Tan. Reprinted with the permission of Arthur A. Levine Books, an imprint of Scholastic, Inc. **374–383:** Richard Wright, "Big Black Good Man" from *Eight Men*. Copyright 1940, © 1961 by Richard Wright, renewed © 1989 by Ellen Wright. Reprinted by permission of HarperCollins Publishers. **391–404:** William Faulkner, "Barn Burning" from COLLECTED STORIES OF WILLIAM FAULKNER. Copyright 1950 by Random House, Inc., renewed © 1977 by Jill Faulkner Summers. Used by permission of Random House, Inc. **406–410:** Edwidge Danticat, "New York Day Woman" from KRIK? KRAK! Copyright © 1995 by Edwidge Danticat. Reprinted with the permission of Soho Press. **411–414:** Miranda July, "Birthmark" from NO ONE BELONGS HERE MORE THAN YOU. Copyright © 2007 by Miranda July. Reprinted with the permission of Scribner, a division of Simon & Schuster Adult Publishing Group. All rights reserved.

Chapter 16. 424–433: R. Crumb, "A Hunger Artist" from R. CRUMB'S KAFKA. Copyright © 1993 by R. Crumb. **440–445:** Jonathan Safran Foer, "A Primer for the Punctuation of Heart Disease" from THE NEW YORKER (June 2002). Reprinted with the permission of Jonathan Safran Foer and Aragi, Inc. **447–457:** Flannery O'Connor, "A Good Man Is Hard to Find" from A GOOD MAN IS HARD TO FIND AND OTHER STORIES. Copyright 1953 by Flannery O'Connor and renewed © 1981 by Regina O'Connor. Reprinted by permission of Houghton Mifflin Harcourt Publishing Company. **473–485:** Tim O'Brien, "The Things They Carried" from THE THINGS THEY CARRIED. Copyright © 1990 by Tim O'Brien. Reprinted by permission of Houghton Mifflin Harcourt Publishing Company. All rights reserved.

Chapter 17. 494–498: Alison Bechdel, excerpt from FUN HOME. Copyright © 2006 by Alison Bechdel. Reprinted by permission of Houghton Mifflin Harcourt Publishing Company. All rights reserved. **499–507:** Alice Hoffman, "Saint Helene" from PLOUGHSHARES (Winter 2005–2006). Copyright © 2005 by Alice Hoffman. Reprinted with the permission of Elaine Markson Literary Agency. **509–515:** Shirley Jackson, "The Lottery" from THE LOTTERY AND OTHER STORIES. Copyright 1948, 1949 by Shirley Jackson. Copyright renewed © 1976, 1977 by Laurence Hyman, Barry Hyman, Mrs. Sarah Webster and Mrs. Joanne Schnurer. Reprinted by permission of Farrar, Straus & Giroux, LLC. **517–523:** Alice Walker, "Everyday Use" from IN LOVE AND TROUBLE: STORIES OF BLACK WOMEN. Copyright © 1973 by Alice Walker. Reprinted with the permission of Houghton Mifflin Harcourt Publishing Company. **526–537:** Raymond Carver, "Cathedral" from CATHEDRAL. Copyright © 1983 by Raymond Carver. Used by permission of Alfred A. Knopf, a division of Random House, Inc.

Chapter 18. 556–567: Lynda Barry, "Two Questions" from McSWEENEY'S 13. Used courtesy of Darhansoff Verrill Feldman Literary Agents. **568–574:** Eudora Welty, "A Worn Path" from A CURTAIN OF GREEN AND OTHER STORIES. Copyright 1941 and renewed 1969 by Eudora Welty. Reprinted by permission of Houghton Mifflin Harcourt Publishing Company. **577–588:** David Michael Kaplan, "Doe Season" from COMFORT. First appeared in *The Atlantic Monthly* (1985), and in BEST AMERICAN SHORT STORIES 1986. Copyright © 1985 by David Michael Kaplan. Reprinted with the permission of Brandt & Hochman Literary Agents, Inc. **589–600:** D. H. Lawrence,

"The Rocking-Horse Winner" from THE COMPLETE SHORT STORIES OF D. H. LAWRENCE. Copyright 1933 by The Estate of D. H. Lawrence, renewed 1961 by Angelo Ravagli and C. M. Weekley, Executors of The Estate of Frieda Lawrence. Used by permission of Viking Penguin a division of Penguin Group (USA) Inc. **602–607:** Michael Chabon, "The Little Knife" from A MODEL WORLD. Copyright © 1991 by Michael Chabon. Reprinted by permission of HarperCollins Publishers. **608–611:** Tobias Wolff, "Bullet in the Brain" from THE NIGHT IN QUESTION: STORIES. Copyright © 1996 by Tobias Wolff. Used by permission of Alfred A. Knopf, a division of Random House, Inc. **613:** Robert Huff, "Rainbow" from THE VENTRILOQUIST: NEW AND SELECTED POEMS. Copyright © 1977 by the Rector and Visitors of the University of Virginia. Reprinted with the permission of The University of Virginia Press.

Chapter 19. 617–628: Joyce Carol Oates, "Where Are You Going, Where Have You Been?" from THE WHEEL OF LOVE AND OTHER STORIES. Copyright © 1970 by Ontario Review. Reprinted by permission of John Hawkins & Associates, Inc. **630–633:** Joyce Carol Oates, "When Characters from the Page Are Made Flesh on the Screen" from THE NEW YORK TIMES (March 23, 1986). Copyright © 1986 by The New York Times Company. Reprinted with the permission of Blanche C. Gregory, as agent for the author. **637–640:** Mike Tierce and John Michael Crafton, excerpt from "Connie's Tambourine Man: A New Reading of Arnold Friend" from STUDIES IN SHORT FICTION 22 (1985): 219–224. Copyright © 1985 by Newberry College. Reprinted with permission. **639:** Bob Dylan, excerpt from "Hey, Mr. Tambourine Man." Copyright © 1965; renewed Special Rider Music. All rights reserved. International copyright secured. Reprinted by permission. **639:** Bob Dylan, excerpt from "Like a Rolling Stone." Copyright © 1966; renewed Special Rider Music. All rights reserved. International copyright secured. Reprinted by permission. **640–641:** Bob Dylan, "It's All Over Now, Baby Blue." Copyright © 1965; renewed 1993 Special Rider Music. All rights reserved. International copyright secured. Reprinted by permission. **649:** Bo Diddley, excerpt from "Who Do You Love?" (words and music by Ellas McDaniel).

Chapter 20. 660–662: Chinuna Achebe, "Dead Men's Path" from GIRLS AT WAR AND OTHER STORIES. Copyright © 1972, 1973 by Chinua Achebe. Used by permission of Doubleday, a division of Random House, Inc. and Emma Sweeney Literary Agency, LLC. **662–664:** Margaret Atwood, "Happy Endings" from GOOD BONES AND SIMPLE MURDERS. Copyright © 1983, 1992, 1994 by O.W. Toad Ltd. Used by permission of Doubleday, a division of Random House, Inc. and McClelland & Stewart Ltd. **662–664:** Margaret Atwood, "Happy Endings" from GOOD BONES AND SIMPLE MURDERS. Copyright © 1983, 1992, 1994 by O.W. Toad Ltd. Used by permission of Doubleday, a division of Random House, Inc. and McClelland & Stewart Ltd., The Canadian Publishers. **665–687:** James Baldwin, "Sonny's Blues" © 1957 by James Baldwin was originally published in PARTISAN REVIEW. Copyright renewed. Collected in GOING TO MEET THE MAN, published by Vintage Books. (New York: Dial Press, 1965). Reprinted by arrangement with the James Baldwin Estate. **687–694:** T. Coraghessan Boyle, "Greasy Lake" from GREASY LAKE AND OTHER STORIES. Copyright © 1979, 1981, 1982, 1983, 1984, 1985 by T. Coraghessan Boyle. Used by permission of Viking Penguin, a division of Penguin Group (USA) Inc. **695–700:** Chitra Banerjee Divakaruni, "The Disappearance" from ARRANGED MARRIAGE. Copyright © 1995 by Chitra Banerjee Divakaruni. Used by permission of Doubleday, a division of Random House, Inc. **700–706:** Louise Erdrich, "Sister Godzilla" from A FEAST OF DOVES. Originally published in THE ATLANTIC MONTHLY 287 (February 2001). Copyright © 2001, 2008 by Louise Erdrich. Reprinted with the permission of HarperCollins Publishers. **707–711:** Gabriel García Márquez, "A Very Old Man with Enormous Wings" from LEAF STORM AND OTHER STORIES, translated by Gregory Rabassa. Copyright © 1971 by Gabriel García Márquez. Reprinted by permission of HarperCollins Publishers. **712–719:** Ha Jin, "Saboteur" from THE BRIDEGROOM. Copyright © 2000 by Ha Jin. Used by permission of Pantheon Books, a division of Random House, Inc. **723–729:** Franz Kafka, "A Hunger Artist" from FRANZ KAFKA: THE COMPLETE STORIES, edited by Nahum H. Glazer, translated by Willa and Edwin Muir. Copyright 1946, 1947, 1948, 1949, 1954, © 1958, 1971 by Schocken Books, Inc. Used by permission of Schocken Books, a division of Random House, Inc. **729–733:** Jonathan Lethem, "The Spray" from MEN AND CARTOONS: STORIES. Copyright © 2004 by Jonathan Lathem. Used by permission of Doubleday, a division of Random House, Inc. **733–735:** Naguib Mahfouz, "Half a Day," translated by Denys Johnson, from THE TIME AND THE PLACE AND OTHER STORIES. Copyright © 1991 by American University in Cairo Press. Used by permission of Doubleday, a division of Random House, Inc. **735–745:** Bobbie Ann Mason, "Shiloh" from SHILOH AND OTHER STORIES. Copyright © 1982 by Bobbie Ann Mason. Reprinted with the permission of International Creative Management, Inc. **745–749:** Haruki Murakami, "The Year of Spaghetti" from BLIND WILLOW, SLEEPING WOMAN. Copyright © 2006 by Haruki Murakami. Used by permission of Alfred A. Knopf, a division of Random House, Inc. **749–759:** Flannery O'Connor, "Everything That Rises Must Converge" from EVERYTHING THAT RISES MUST CONVERGE. Copyright © 1964, 1965 by The Estate of Flannery O'Connor. Reprinted by permission of Farrar Straus & Giroux, LLC. **763–769:** Katherine Anne Porter, "The Jilting of Granny Weatherall" from FLOWERING JUDAS AND OTHER STORIES. Copyright 1930 and renewed © 1956 by Katherine Anne Porter. Reprinted by permission of Houghton Mifflin Harcourt Publishing Company. **769–777:** John Steinbeck, "The

Chrysanthemums" from THE LONG VALLEY. Copyright © 1937, renewed 1965 by John Steinbeck. Used by permission of Viking Penguin, a division of Penguin Group (USA) Inc. **777–785:** Amy Tan, "Two Kinds" from THE JOY LUCK CLUB. Copyright © 1989 by Amy Tan. Used by permission of G. P. Putnam's Sons, a division of Penguin Group (USA) Inc. **785–792:** Anne Tyler, "Teenage Wasteland." Originally appeared in SEVENTEEN (November 1983). Copyright © 1983 by Anne Tyler. Reprinted by the permission of Russell & Volkening as agents for the author.

Chapter 21. 794–795: Marianne Moore, "Poetry" from THE COLLECTED POEMS OF MARIANNE MOORE. Copyright 1935 by Marianne Moore, renewed © 1963 by Marianne Moore and T. S. Eliot. Reprinted with the permission of Scribner, an imprint of Simon & Schuster Adult Publishing. All rights reserved. **795–796:** Nikki Giovanni, "Poetry" from THE WOMEN AND THE MEN. Copyright © 1970, 1974, 1975 by Nikki Giovanni. Reprinted by permission of HarperCollins Publishers. **800–801:** Bob Holman, 6 short poems. Copyright © by Bob Holman. Reprinted with the permission of the author. **803:** E. E. Cummings, "1(a" from COMPLETE POEMS 1904–1962, edited by George J. Firmage. Copyright 1940, © 1968, 1991 by the Trustees for the E. E. Cummings Trust. Used by permission of Liveright Publishing Corporation.

Chapter 22. 808–809: "Brother, Can You Spare a Dime?" by E. Y. "Yip" Harburg and Jay Gorney. Copyright 1932 (Renewed) Warner Bros. Inc. Rights for the extended renewal term in the U.S. controlled by Glocca Morra Music (ASCAP) and Gorney Music (ASCAP). All rights administered by Next Decade Entertainment, Inc. All rights reserved. Used by Permission of Alfred Publishing Co., Inc. **810–812:** "Babylon." Words and Music by David Gray. Copyright © 2000 by Chrysalis Music, Ltd. All rights reserved. International copyright secured. Reprinted with permission. **812–813:** Aimee Mann, "Invisible Ink" lyrics. Lyrics and music by Aimee Mann. ASCAP 2006. Reprinted with the permission of Michael Hausman Artist Management. **813:** Hank Williams, "I'm So Lonesome I Could Cry." Copyright 1949 Sony/ATV Songs LLC. All rights administered by Sony/ATV Music Publishing, 8 Music Square West, Nashville, TN 37203. All rights reserved. Used by permission.

Chapter 23. 818–819: Robert Hayden, "Those Winter Sundays" from ANGLE OF ASCENT: NEW AND SELECTED POEMS. Copyright © 1975, 1972, 1970, 1966 by Robert Hayden. Used by permission of Liveright Publishing Corporation. **819–820:** Seamus Heaney, "Digging" from OPENED GROUND: SELECTED POEMS 1966–1996. Copyright © 1998 by Seamus Heaney. Reprinted by permission of Farrar, Straus & Giroux, LLC.

Chapter 24. 838: Emily Dickinson, "I'm nobody! Who are you?" from THE COMPLETE POEMS OF EMILY DICKINSON, edited by Thomas H. Johnson. Copyright 1951, © 1955, 1979, 1983 by the President and Fellows of Harvard College. Reprinted by permission of the publishers and the Trustees of Amherst College. **839–840:** Louise Glück, "Gretel in Darkness" from THE FIRST FOUR BOOKS OF POEMS. Copyright © 1968, 1971, 1972, 1973, 1974, 1975, 1976, 1977, 1978, 1979, 1980, 1995 by Louise Glück. Reprinted by permission of HarperCollins Publishers. **842–843:** Langston Hughes, "Negro" from THE COLLECTED POEMS OF LANGSTON HUGHES, edited by Arnold Rampersad. Copyright © 1994 by The Estate of Langston Hughes. Used by permission of Alfred A. Knopf, a division of Random House, Inc. **845–846:** Leslie Marmon Silko, "Where Mountain Lion Lay Down with Deer" from STORYTELLER. Copyright © 1981 by Leslie Marmon Silko. Reprinted with the permission of The Wylie Agency, Inc. **846–848:** Janice Mirikitani, "Suicide Note" from SHREDDING SILENCE. Copyright © 1987 by Janice Mirikitani. Reprinted by permission of Celestial Arts, an imprint of Ten Speed Press, Berkeley, CA, www.tenspeed.com. **849:** Robert Frost, "Fire and Ice" from THE POETRY OF ROBERT FROST, edited by Edward Connery Lathem. Copyright 1923, © 1969 by Henry Holt and Company, copyright 1944, 1951 by Robert Frost. Reprinted by permission of Henry Holt and Company LLC. **854:** Adam Zagajewski, "Try to Praise the Mutilated World" from WITHOUT END. Copyright © 2002 by Adam Zagajewski. Translation copyright © 2002 by Farrar, Straus & Giroux, LLC. Reprinted by permission of Farrar, Straus & Giroux, LLC. **856:** Sylvia Plath, "Morning Song" from ARIEL. Copyright © 1961, 1963 by Ted Hughes. Reprinted by permission of HarperCollins Publishers and Faber and Faber, Ltd. **858–859:** Deborah Garrison, "Please Fire Me" from A WORKING GIRL CAN'T WIN AND OTHER POEMS. Copyright © 1998 by Deborah Garrison. Used by permission of Random House, Inc. **863–864:** Ariel Dorfman, "Hope" from LAST WALTZ IN SANTIAGO AND OTHER POEMS OF EXILE AND DISAPPEARANCE. Copyright © 2002 by Ariel Dorfman. Reprinted with the permission of The Wylie Agency, Inc. **864–865:** W. H. Auden, "The Unknown Citizen" from W. H. AUDEN: COLLECTED POEMS, edited by Edward Mendelson. Copyright 1940 and renewed © 1968 by W. H. Auden. Used by permission of Random House, Inc. **866–868:** Anne Sexton, "Cinderella" from TRANSFORMATIONS. Copyright © 1971 by Anne Sexton. Reprinted by permission of Houghton Mifflin Harcourt Publishing Company. All rights reserved.

Chapter 25. 875: Sipho Sepamla, "Words, Words, Words." No portion of this text may be reprinted without permission. **878–879:** William Stafford, "For the Grave of Daniel Boone" from STORIES THAT COULD BE TRUE. Copyright © 1977 by William Stafford. Reprinted with the permission of The Estate of William Stafford. **880:** Rhina Espaillat, "Bilingual/Bilingue" from WHERE HORIZONS GO. Copyright © 1998 by Rhina Espillat. Reprinted with the permission of Truman State University Press. **881:** James Wright, "Autumn Begins in Martins Ferry, Ohio" from

COLLECTED POEMS. Copyright © 1971 by James Wright. Reprinted by permission of Wesleyan University Press, www.wesleyan.edu/wespress. **882:** Adrienne Rich, "Living in Sin" from THE FACT OF A DOORFRAME: SELECTED POEMS 1950–2001. Copyright © 2002, 1955 by Adrienne Rich. Used by permission of W. W. Norton & Company, Inc. **883–884:** E. E. Cummings, "in Just-" from COMPLETE POEMS 1904–1962, edited by George J. Firmage. Copyright 1923, 1951, © 1991 by the Trustees for the E. E. Cummings Trust. Used by permission of Liveright Publishing Corporation. **885:** Robert Pinsky, "ABC" from JERSEY RAIN. Copyright © 2000 by Robert Pinsky. Reprinted by permission of Farrar, Straus & Giroux, LLC. **885–886:** Theodore Roethke, "I Knew a Woman" from THE COLLECTED POEMS OF THEODORE ROETHKE. Copyright 1954 by Theodore Roethke. Used by permission of Doubleday, a division of Random House, Inc. **886–887:** Kay Ryan, "Crib" from ELEPHANT ROCKS. Copyright © 1996 by Kay Ryan. Used by permission of Grove/Atlantic, Inc. **888:** Margaret Atwood, "The city planners" from THE CIRCLE GAME. Copyright © 1966, 1998 by Margaret Atwood. Reprinted with the permission of House of Anansi Press, Toronto. **889–891:** Jim Sagel, "Baca Grande" from HISPANICS IN THE UNITED STATES. Reprinted with the permission of Bilingual Press/Editorial Bilingüe, Arizona State University, Tempe, AZ. **892–893:** Mark Halliday, "The Value of Education" from SLATE (June 21, 2000). Reprinted with the permission of the author. **893–894:** Hart Crane, "Royal Palm" from THE COMPLETE POEMS OF HART CRANE, edited by Marc Simon. Copyright 1933, © 1958, 1966 by Liveright Publishing Corporation. Used by permission of Liveright Publishing Corporation. **894–895:** Charles Bukowski, "Dog Fight" from WHAT MATTERS MOST IS HOW WELL YOU WALK THROUGH THE FIRE. Copyright © 1999 by Linda Lee Bukowski. Reprinted with the permission of HarperCollins Publishers. **896:** Gwendolyn Brooks, "We Real Cool" from BLACKS. Copyright © 1991 by Gwendolyn Brooks Blakely. Reprinted by consent of Brooks Permissions. **896–897:** Gwendolyn Brooks, "What Shall I Give My Children?" from "The Womanhood" from ANNIE ALLEN. Copyright 1949 by Gwendolyn Brooks. Reprinted by consent of Brooks Permissions. **899–900:** E. E. Cummings, "anyone lived in a pretty how town" from COMPLETE POEMS 1904–1962, edited by George J. Firmage. Copyright 1940, © 1968, 1991 by the Trustees for the E. E. Cummings Trust. Used by permission of Liveright Publishing Corporation. **901–902:** Emily Dickinson, "My Life had stood—a loaded Gun" from THE COMPLETE POEMS OF EMILY DICKINSON, edited by Thomas H. Johnson. Copyright 1951, © 1955, 1979, 1983 by the President and Fellows of Harvard College. Reprinted by permission of the publishers and the Trustees of Amherst College.

Chapter 26. 904–905: Jane Flanders, "Cloud Painter" from TIMEPIECE. Copyright © 1988 by Jane Flanders. Reprinted by permission of the University of Pittsburgh Press. **906:** William Carlos Williams, "The Red Wheelbarrow" from COLLECTED POEMS: 1909–1939, Volume I. Copyright © 1938 by New Directions Publishing Corporation. Reprinted by permission of New Directions Publishing Corp. **907:** Ezra Pound, "In a Station of the Metro" from PERSONAE. Copyright 1926 by Ezra Pound. Reprinted by permission of New Directions Publishing Corp. **907–908:** Gary Snyder, "Some good things to be said for the Iron Age" from REGARDING WAVE. Copyright © 1970 by Gary Snyder. Reprinted by permission of New Directions Publishing Corp. **908–909:** Suzanne E. Berger, "The Meal" from LEGACIES (Cambridge, Mass.: Alice James Books, 1984). Copyright © 1984 by Suzanne E. Berger. Reprinted with the permission of the author. **909:** William Carlos Williams, "The Great Figure" from COLLECTED POEMS: 1909–1939, Volume I. Copyright 1938 by New Directions Publishing Corporation. Reprinted by permission of New Directions Publishing Corp. **911:** Richard Wilbur, "Sleepless at Crown Point" from THE MIND-READER. Copyright © 1973 and renewed 2001 by Richard Wilbur. Reprinted by permission of Houghton Mifflin Harcourt Publishing Company. **911:** Ted Kooser, "Wild Plums in Blossom" from THE NATIONAL POETRY REVIEW (Summer 2005). Copyright © 2005 by Ted Kooser. Reprinted with the permission of the author. **912:** Bill Coyle, "Spring: The Star Magnolia" from THE GOD OF THIS WORLD TO HIS PROPHET. Copyright © 2006 by Bill Coyle. Reprinted with the permission of Ivan R. Dee, Publisher. **914:** Robert Frost, "Nothing Gold Can Stay" from THE POETRY OF ROBERT FROST, edited by Edward Connery Lathem. Copyright 1923, © 1969 by Henry Holt and Company, copyright 1944 1951 by Robert Frost. Reprinted by permission of Henry Holt and Company LLC. **914–915:** Jean Toomer, "Reapers" from CANE. Copyright 1923 by Boni & Liveright, renewed 1951 by Jean Toomer. Used by permission of Liveright Publishing Corporation. **917:** Kobayashi Issa, ["Not yet having become a Buddha"], translated by R. H. Blyth, from HAIKU. Reprinted by permission of The Hokuseido Press, Tokyo. **918–919:** Billy Collins, "Litany" from NINE HORSES. Copyright © 2002 by Billy Collins. Used by permission of Random House, Inc. **920:** Octavio Paz, "Daybreak" from COLLECTED POEMS 1957–1987. Copyright © 1986 by Octavio Paz and Eliot Weinberger. Reprinted by permission of New Directions Publishing Corp. **920–921:** Octavio Paz, "Nightfall" from COLLECTED POEMS 1957–1987. Copyright © 1986 by Octavio Paz and Eliot Weinberger. Reprinted by permission of New Directions Publishing Corp.

Chapter 27. 924–925: Langston Hughes, "Harlem (2)" from THE COLLECTED POEMS OF LANGSTON HUGHES, edited by Arnold Rampersad. Copyright © 1994 by The Estate of Langston Hughes. Used by permission of Alfred A. Knopf, a division of Random House, Inc. **925–926:** Lawrence Ferlinghetti, "Constantly Risking Absurdity" from A CONEY ISLAND OF THE MIND. Copyright © 1958 by Lawrence Ferlinghetti. Reprinted by permission of New Directions Publishing Corp. **926–927:** Audre Lorde, "Rooming houses are old women" from CHOSEN POEMS: OLD AND NEW. Copyright © 1973, 1970, 1968 by Audre Lorde. Used by permission of W. W. Norton & Company, Inc. **928–929:** N. Scott Momaday, "Simile" from IN THE PRESENCE OF THE SUN: STORIES AND POEMS, 1961–1991 (New York: St. Martin's Press, 1992). Copyright © 1976, 1992 by N. Scott Momaday. Reprinted with the permission of the author. **929:** Sylvia Plath, "Metaphors" from CROSSING THE WATER. Copyright © 1960, 1963 by Ted Hughes. Reprinted by permission of HarperCollins Publishers and Faber and Faber, Ltd. **930:** Richard Wilbur, "Mind" from THINGS OF THIS WORLD. Copyright © 1956 and renewed 1984 by Richard Wilbur. Reprinted by permission of Houghton Mifflin Harcourt Publishing Company. **930–931:** John Updike, "Ex-Basketball Player" from COLLECTED POEMS 1953–1993. Copyright © 1993 by John Updike. Used by permission of Alfred A. Knopf, a division of Random House, Inc. **931:** Randall Jarrell, "The Death of the Ball Turret Gunner" from THE COMPLETE POEMS. Copyright © 1969, renewed 1997 by Mary von S. Jarrell. Reprinted by permission of Farrar, Straus & Giroux, LLC. **932–933:** Marge Piercy, "The secretary chant" from CIRCLES ON THE WATER. Copyright © 1982 by Marge Piercy. Used by permission of Alfred A. Knopf, a division of Random House, Inc. **935:** Martín Espada, "My Father as a Guitar" from A MAYAN ASTRONOMER IN HELL'S KITCHEN. Copyright © 2000 by Martín Espada. Used by permission of the author and W. W. Norton & Company, Inc. **936–938:** Sylvia Plath, "Daddy" from ARIEL. Copyright © 1961, 1963 by Ted Hughes. Reprinted by permission of HarperCollins Publishers and Faber and Faber, Ltd. **939–940:** David Huddle, "Holes Commence Falling" from SUMMER LAKE: NEW AND SELECTED POEMS. Copyright © 1999 by David Huddle. Reprinted with the permission of Louisiana State University Press. **943–944:** Robert Frost, "Out, Out—" from THE POETRY OF ROBERT FROST, edited by Edward Connery Lathem. Copyright 1923, © 1969 by Henry Holt and Company, copyright 1944, 1951 by Robert Frost. Reprinted by permission of Henry Holt and Company LLC. **945:** Donald Hall, "My Son, My Executioner" from OLD AND NEW POEMS. Copyright © 1990 by Donald Hall. Reprinted by permission of Houghton Mifflin Harcourt Publishing Company. All rights reserved. **946:** Margaret Atwood, "You fit into me" from SELECTED POEMS 1965–1975. Copyright © 1976 by Margaret Atwood. Reprinted with the permission of House of Anansi Press, Toronto. **947:** Carmine Starnino, "What My Mother's Hands Smell Like" from CREDO, page 33. Reprinted with the permission of McGill-Queen's University Press. **948:** Sonia Sanchez, "On Passing thru Morgantown, Pa." from HOMEGIRLS AND HANDGRENADES. Copyright © 1984, 2007 by Sonia Sanchez. Reprinted with the permission of White Pine Press, www.whitepine.org. **952–953:** Allen Ginsberg, "A Supermarket in California" from COLLECTED POEMS 1947–1980. Copyright © 1955 by Allen Ginsberg. Reprinted by permission of HarperCollins Publishers.

Chapter 28. 957: Gwendolyn Brooks, "Sadie and Maud" from BLACKS. Copyright © 1991 by Gwendolyn Brooks Blakely. Reprinted by consent of Brooks Permissions. **958:** E. E. Cummings, excerpt from "the moon is hiding" from COMPLETE POEMS 1904–1962, edited by George J. Firmage. Copyright 1923, 1951, © 1991 by the Trustees for the E. E. Cummings Trust. Copyright © 1976 by George James Firmage. Used by permission of Liveright Publishing Corporation. **961–962:** Emily Dickinson, "I like to see it lap the Miles—" from THE COMPLETE POEMS OF EMILY DICKINSON, edited by Thomas H. Johnson. Copyright 1951, © 1955, 1979, 1983 by the President and Fellows of Harvard College. Reprinted by permission of the publishers and the Trustees of Amherst College. **963:** Lenrie Peters, excerpt from "We have come home" from Selected Poems. Copyright © 1967, 1989 by Lenrie Peters. Reprinted by permission of Heinemann Educational. **963:** Mark Strand, excerpt from "Pot Roast" from SELECTED POEMS. Copyright © 1980 by Mark Strand. Used by permission of Alfred A. Knopf, a division of Random House, Inc. **963–964:** Adrienne Rich, "Aunt Jennifer's Tigers" from THE FACT OF A DOORFRAME: SELECTED POEMS 1950–2001. Copyright © 2002, 1951 by Adrienne Rich. Used by permission of W. W. Norton & Company, Inc. **964–965:** Etheridge Knight, "For Malcolm, a Year After" from POEMS FROM PRISON. Copyright © 1968 by Etheridge Knight. Reprinted with the permission of Broadside Press. **967:** N. Scott Momaday, "Comparatives" from IN THE PRESENCE OF THE SUN: STORIES AND POEMS, 1961–1991 (New York: St. Martin's Press, 1992). Copyright © 1976, 1992 by N. Scott Momaday. Reprinted with the permission of the author. **969:** T. S. Eliot, excerpt from "Virginia" from THE COLLECTED POEMS, 1909–1932. Copyright 1936 by Houghton Mifflin Harcourt Publishing Company and renewed © 1964 by T. S. Eliot. Reprinted by permission of Houghton Mifflin Harcourt Publishing Company and Faber & Faber, Ltd. **969:** T. S. Eliot, excerpt from "Virginia" from THE COLLECTED POEMS, 1909–1932. Copyright 1936 by Houghton Mifflin Harcourt Publishing Company and renewed © 1964 by T. S. Eliot. Reprinted by permission of Houghton Mifflin Harcourt Publishing Company and Faber & Faber, Ltd. **969–970:** Ogden Nash, "The Lama." Copyright 1931 by Ogden Nash, renewed. Reprinted by permission of Curtis Brown Ltd. **970:** Richard Wilbur, "In Trackless Woods" from COLLECTED POEMS 1943–2000. Copyright © 2004 by Richard Wilbur. Reprinted with the permission of Houghton Mifflin Harcourt Publishing Company. **972–973:** W. H. Auden, "As I Walked Out One Evening" from W. H. AUDEN: COLLECTED POEMS, edited by Edward Mendelson. Copyright 1940 and renewed © 1968 by W. H. Auden. Used by permission of Random House, Inc. **974:** Galway Kinnell, "Blackberry Eating" from MORTAL ACTS, MORTAL WORDS. Copyright © 1980 by Galway Kinnell. Reprinted by permission of Houghton Mifflin Harcourt Publishing Company. All rights reserved. **974–975:** Lydia Davis, "A Mown Lawn" from SAMUEL JOHNSON IS INDIGNANT. Copyright © 2001 by Lydia Davis. Reprinted by permission of Farrar, Straus & Giroux, LLC. **975:** Kay Ryan, "Lighthouse Keeping" from THE NIAGARA POEMS. Copyright © 2005 by Kay Ryan. Used by permission of Grove/Atlantic, Inc.

Chapter 29. 986: A. E. Stallings, "Explaining an Affinity for Bats" from HAPAX. Copyright © 2006 by A. E. Stallings. Reprinted with the permission of TriQuarterly Books/Northwestern University Press. **986–987:** Sor Juana Ines de la Cruz, "Sonnet I," translated by Rhina P. Espaillat (2007). **988:** Gwendolyn Brooks, "First Fight, Then Fiddle" from BLACKS. Copyright © 1991 by Gwendolyn Brooks Blakely. Reprinted by consent of Brooks Permissions. **989:** Alberto Alvaro Ríos, "Nani" from WHISPERING TO FOOL THE WIND. Copyright © 1982 by Alberto Alvaro Ríos. Reprinted with the permission of the author. **990–991:** Elizabeth Bishop, "Sestina" from THE COMPLETE POEMS 1927–1979. Copyright © 1979, 1983 by Alice Helen Methfessel. Reprinted by permission of Farrar, Straus & Giroux, LLC. **991–992:** Theodore Roethke, "The Waking" from THE COLLECTED POEMS OF THEODORE ROETHKE. Copyright 1953 by Theodore Roethke. Used by permission of Doubleday, a division of Random House, Inc. **992–993:** Mary Jo Salter, "Refrain" from HENRY PURCELL IN JAPAN. Copyright © 1985 by Mary Jo Salter. Used by permission of Alfred A. Knopf, a division of Random House, Inc. **994:** Martín Espada, "Why I Went to College" from A MAYAN ASTRONOMER IS HELL'S KITCHEN. Copyright © 2000 by Martín Espada. Used by permission of the author and W. W. Norton & Company, Inc. **995–996:** Matsuo Bashō, "Four Haiku" from THE PENGUIN BOOK OF JAPANESE VERSE, translated by Geoffrey Bownas and Anthony Thwaite. Translation copyright © 1964, 1998 by Geoffrey Bownas and Anthony Thwaite. Reprinted with the permission of the translators. **996:** Carolyn Kizer, "After Bashō" from YIN: NEW POEMS. Copyright © 1984 by Carolyn Kizer. Reprinted with the permission of BOA Editions, Ltd., www.boaeditions.org. **997–998:** Jack Kerouac, "American Haiku" from AMERICAN HAIKUS. Copyright © 1959 by Jack Kerouac. Reprinted with the permission of Sll/Sterling Lord Literistic. **999–1000:** Carl Sandburg, "Chicago" from CHICAGO POEMS. Copyright 1916 by Holt, Rinehart and Winston, renewed 1944 by Carl Sandburg. Reprinted by permission of Houghton Mifflin Harcourt Publishing Company. **1000–1001:** E. E. Cummings, "the/ sky/ was" from COMPLETE POEMS 1904–1962, edited by George J. Firmage. Copyright 1925, 1953, © 1991 by the Trustees for the E. E. Cummings Trust. Used by permission of Liveright Publishing Corporation. **1003:** William Carlos Williams, "Spring and All" from COLLECTED POEMS: 1909–1939, Volume I. Copyright 1938 by New Directions Publishing Corporation. Reprinted by permission of New Directions Publishing Corp. **1004:** Carolyn Forché, "The Colonel" from THE COUNTRY BETWEEN US. Originally published in WOMEN'S INTERNATIONAL RESOURCE EXCHANGE. Copyright © 1981 by Carolyn Forché. Reprinted by permission of HarperCollins Publishers. **1005:** Tomas Transtömer, "Answers to Letters," translated by Robin Fulton, from THE GREAT ENIGMA: NEW COLLECTED POEMS. Copyright © 2003 by Tomas Transtömer. Reprinted by permission of New Directions Publishing Corp. **1006:** Pat Mora, "Immigrants" from BORDERS. (© 1986 Arte Público Press–University of Houston). Reprinted with the permission of the publisher. **1007:** May Swenson, "Women" [alternate version]. Reprinted with the permission of The Literary Estate of May Swenson. **1009:** Greg Williamson, "Group Photo with Winter Trees" from ERRORS IN THE SCRIPT. Reprinted with permission of The Overlook Press.

Chapter 30. 1013: Robert Frost, "For Once, Then, Something" from THE POETRY OF ROBERT FROST, edited by Edward Connery Lathem. Copyright 1923, © 1969 by Henry Holt and Company, copyright 1944, 1951 by Robert Frost. Reprinted by permission of Henry Holt and Company LLC. **1014:** Emily Dickinson, "Volcanoes be in Sicily" from THE COMPLETE POEMS OF EMILY DICKINSON, edited by Thomas H. Johnson. Copyright 1951, © 1955, 1979, 1983 by the President and Fellows of Harvard College. Reprinted by permission of the publishers and the Trustees of Amherst College. **1015:** Langston Hughes, "Island" from THE COLLECTED POEMS OF LANGSTON HUGHES, edited by Arnold Rampersad. Copyright © 1994 by The Estate of Langston Hughes. Used by permission of Alfred A. Knopf, a division of Random House, Inc. **1020–1022:** Adrienne Rich, "Diving into the Wreck" from THE FACT OF A DOORFRAME: SELECTED POEMS 1950–2001. Copyright © 2002 by Adrienne Rich. Copyright © 1973 by W. W. Norton & Company, Inc. Used by permission of W. W. Norton & Company, Inc. **1024:** Wole Soyinka, "Future Plans" from A SHUTTLE IN THE CRYPT. Copyright © 1972 by Wole Soyinka. Reprinted by permission of Hill & Wang, a division of Farrar, Straus & Giroux, LLC. **1025:** William Meredith, "Dreams of Suicide" from EFFORT AT SPEECH: NEW AND SELECTED POEMS. Copyright © 1997 by William Meredith. Used by permission of the author and TriQuarterly Books/Northwestern University Press. All rights reserved. **1026:** Bill Coyle, "Post-Colonial Studies" from THE GOD OF THIS WORLD TO THIS PROPHET. Copyright © 2006 by Bill Coyle. Reprinted with the permission of Ivan R. Dee, Publisher. **1028:** Countee Cullen, "Yet Do I Marvel" from COLOR. Copyrights held by the Amistad Research Center, Tulane University, administered by Thompson and Thompson, Brooklyn, NY. **1029:** H. D. (Hilda Doolittle), "Helen" from COLLECTED POEMS 1912–1944. Copyright © 1982 by the Estate of Hilda Doolittle. Reprinted by permission of New Directions Publishing Corp. **1030:**

William Butler Yeats, "Leda and the Swan" from THE COLLECTED WORKS OF W. B. YEATS, VOLUME I: THE POEMS, REVISED, edited by Richard J. Finneran. Copyright 1928 by The Macmillan Company, renewed © 1956 by Georgie Yeats. Reprinted with the permission of Scribner, an imprint of Simon & Schuster Adult Publishing Group. All rights reserved. **1031:** Derek Walcott, "Sea Grapes" from COLLECTED POEMS 1948–1984. Copyright © 1986 by Derek Walcott. Reprinted by permission of Farrar, Straus & Giroux, LLC. **1032:** W. H. Auden, "Musée des Beaux Arts" from W. H. AUDEN: COLLECTED POEMS, edited by Edward Mendelson. Copyright 1940 and renewed © 1968 by W. H. Auden. Used by permission of Random House, Inc. **1033–1034:** T. S. Eliot, "Journey of the Magi" from THE COLLECTED POEMS, 1909–1932. Copyright 1936 by Houghton Mifflin Harcourt Publishing Company and renewed © 1964 by T. S. Eliot. Reprinted by permission of Houghton Mifflin Harcourt Publishing Company and Faber & Faber, Ltd.

Chapter 31. 1039: Sharon Olds, "I Go Back to May 1937" from GOLD CELL. Copyright © 1987 by Sharon Olds. Used by permission of Alfred A. Knopf, a division of Random House, Inc. **1039–1040:** Theodore Roethke, "My Papa's Waltz" from THE COLLECTED POEMS OF THEODORE ROETHKE. Copyright 1942 by Hearst Magazines, Inc. Used by permission of Doubleday, a division of Random House, Inc. **1040:** Robert Hayden, "Those Winter Sundays" from ANGLE OF ASCENT: NEW AND SELECTED POEMS. Copyright © 1975, 1972, 1970, 1966 by Robert Hayden. Used by permission of Liveright Publishing Corporation. **1040–41:** Seamus Heaney, "Digging" from OPENED GROUND: SELECTED POEMS 1966–1996. Copyright © 1998 by Seamus Heaney. Reprinted by permission of Farrar, Straus & Giroux, LLC. **1041–1042:** Louis Simpson, "Working Late" from THE OWNER OF THE HOUSE: NEW COLLECTED POEMS, 1940–2001. Copyright © 2003 by Louis Simpson. Reprinted with the permission of BOA Editions Ltd., www.boaeditions.org. **1042:** Edna St. Vincent Millay, "The courage that my mother had" from COLLECTED POEMS (New York: Harper, 1967). Copyright 1923, 1951, 1954, © 1982 by Edna St. Vincent Millay and Norma Millay Ellis. All rights reserved. Reprinted with the permission of Elizabeth Barnett, Literary Executor, The Millay Society. **1042–1043:** Raymond Carver, "Photograph of My Father in His Twenty-Second Year" from FIRES. Copyright © 1983 by Raymond Carver. Reprinted with the permission of The Wylie Agency, Inc. **1043:** Judith Ortiz Cofer, "My Father in the Navy: A Childhood Memory" from REACHING FOR THE MAINLAND & SELECTED NEW POEMS. Reprinted with the permission of Bilingual Press/Editorial Bilingüe, Arizona State University, Tempe. **1045–1046:** Adrienne Rich, "A Woman Mourned by Daughters" from COLLECTED EARLY POEMS: 1950–1970. Copyright © 1993, 1967, 1963 by Adrienne Rich. Used by permission of W. W. Norton & Company, Inc. **1046:** Dylan Thomas, "Do not go gentle into that good night" from THE POEMS OF DYLAN THOMAS. Copyright 1952 by Dylan Thomas. Reprinted with the permission of New Directions Publishing Corp. **1048–1049:** Mary Oliver, "Sleeping in the Forest" from TWELVE MOONS. Originally published in The Ohio Review. Copyright © 1978 by Mary Oliver. Reprinted with the permission of Little, Brown & Company. **1049:** Jaime Sabines, "The Moon" from POEMAS SUELTOS, translated by W. S. Merwin. Reprinted in PIECES OF SHADOW: SELECTED POEMS. Copyright © 1996 by W. S. Merwin. Reprinted with the permission of The Wylie Agency, Inc. **1050–1052:** Robert Frost, "Birches" from THE POETRY OF ROBERT FROST, edited by Edward Connery Lathem. Copyright 1923, © 1969 by Henry Holt and Company, copyright 1944, 1951 by Robert Frost. Reprinted by permission of Henry Holt and Company LLC. **1052:** William Stafford, "Traveling through the Dark" from THE WAY IT IS: NEW & SELECTED POEMS. Copyright © 1962, 1998 by The Estate of William Stafford. Reprinted with the permission of Graywolf Press, Saint Paul, Minnesota. **1052–1053:** Mark Haddon, "Trees" from THE TALKING HORSE AND THE SAD GIRL AND THE VILLAGE UNDER THE SEA. Copyright © 2006 by Mark Haddon. Used by permission of Vintage Books, a division of Random House, Inc. and Picador. **1053:** Carl Sandburg, "The Fog" from CHICAGO POEMS. Copyright 1916 by Holt, Rinehart and Winston, renewed 1944 by Carl Sandburg. Reprinted by permission of Houghton Mifflin Harcourt Publishing Company. **1053:** Joy Harjo, "Morning Song" from A MAP TO THE NEXT WORLD: POEMS AND TALES. Copyright © 2000 by Joy Harjo. Used by permission of W. W. Norton & Company, Inc. **1056:** Edna St. Vincent Millay, "What Lips My Lips Have Kissed" from COLLECTED POEMS (New York: Harper, 1967). Copyright 1923, 1951, 1954, © 1982 by Edna St. Vincent Millay and Norma Millay Ellis. All rights reserved. Reprinted with the permission of Elizabeth Barnett, Literary Executor, The Millay Society. **1056:** Dorothy Parker, "General Review of the Sex Situation" from THE PORTABLE DOROTHY PARKER. Copyright 1926, renewed 1954 by Dorothy Parker. Used by permission of Viking Penguin, a division of Penguin Group (USA) Inc. **1057:** W. H. Auden, "Stop all the clocks, cut off the telephone" from W. H. AUDEN: COLLECTED POEMS, edited by Edward Mendelson. Copyright 1940 and renewed © 1968 by W. H. Auden. Used by permission of Random House, Inc. **1057–1058:** Sandra Cisneros, "In My Little Museum of Erotica" from PLOUGHSHARES (Winter 2004–2005). Copyright © 2004 by Sandra Cisneros. Reprinted with the permission of Susan Bergholz Literary Services, New York, NY and Lamy, NM. All rights reserved. **1058–1059:** George Elliott Clark, "Monologue for Selah Bringing Sleep to Whylah Falls" from WHYLAH FALLS: TENTH ANNIVERSARY EDITION. Copyright © 1990, 2000 by George Elliott Clark. Reprinted with the permission of Raincoast Books, 9050 Shaughnessy Street, Vancouver, BC, Canada, V6P 6E5. **1059:** Alan Shapiro, "A Parting Gift" from TANTALUS IN LOVE. Copyright © 2005 by Alan Shapiro. Reprinted by permission of Houghton Mifflin Harcourt Publishing Company. All rights reserved. **1060:** Tupac Shakur, "Love Is Just Complicated" from THE ROSE THAT GREW FROM CONCRETE. Copyright © 1999 by Tupac Shakur. Reprinted with the permission of International Creative Management, Inc. **1063–1064:** Robert Lowell, "For the Union Dead" from FOR THE UNION DEAD. Copyright © 1959 by Robert Lowell. Copyright renewed 1987 by Harriet Lowell, Caroline Lowell, and Sheridan Lowell. Reprinted by permission of Farrar, Straus & Giroux, LLC. **1065–1066:** Boris Slutsky, "How Did They Kill My Grandmother?" from POST-WAR RUSSIAN POETRY, translated by Elaine Feinstein. Copyright © 1974 by Elaine Feinstein. Reprinted with the permission of Elaine Feinstein. **1066:** Denise Levertov, "What Were They Like?" from POEMS 1960–1967. Copyright © 1966 by Dense Levertov. Reprinted by permission of New Directions Publishing Corp. **1067:** Yusef Komunyakaa, "Facing It" from DIEN CAI DAU. Copyright © 1988 by Yusef Komunyakaa. Reprinted with the permission of Wesleyan University Press. **1067–1068:** Eliza Griswold, "Buying Rations in Kabul" from WIDEAWAKE FIELD. Copyright © 2007 by Eliza Griswold. Reprinted by permission of Farrar, Strauss, & Giroux, LLC. **1069–1070:** Edwin Muir, "Horses" from FIRST POEMS. Copyright © 1960 by Willa Muir. Reprinted with the permission of Faber & Faber, Ltd. **1071–1072:** Wislawa Szymborska, "The End and the Beginning" from MIRACLE FAIR, translated by Joanna Trzeciak. Copyright © 2001 by Joanna Trzeciak. Used by permission of W. W. Norton & Company, Inc.

Chapter 32. 1078: Langston Hughes, "The Negro Speaks of Rivers" from THE COLLECTED POEMS OF LANGSTON HUGHES, edited by Arnold Rampersad. Copyright © 1994 by The Estate of Langston Hughes. Used by permission of Alfred A. Knopf, a division of Random House, Inc. **1078–1079:** Langston Hughes, "Mother to Son" from THE COLLECTED POEMS OF LANGSTON HUGHES, edited by Arnold Rampersad. Copyright © 1994 by The Estate of Langston Hughes. Used by permission of Alfred A. Knopf, a division of Random House, Inc. **1079:** Langston Hughes, "Dream Variations" from THE COLLECTED POEMS OF LANGSTON HUGHES, edited by Arnold Rampersad. Copyright © 1994 by The Estate of Langston Hughes. Used by permission of Alfred A. Knopf, a division of Random House, Inc. **1079–1080:** Langston Hughes, "The Weary Blues" from THE COLLECTED POEMS OF LANGSTON HUGHES, edited by Arnold Rampersad. Copyright © 1994 by The Estate of Langston Hughes. Used by permission of Alfred A. Knopf, a division of Random House, Inc. **1080–1081:** Langston Hughes, "I, Too" from THE COLLECTED POEMS OF LANGSTON HUGHES, edited by Arnold Rampersad. Copyright © 1994 by The Estate of Langston Hughes. Used by permission of Alfred A. Knopf, a division of Random House, Inc. **1081:** Langston Hughes, "Song for a Dark Girl" from THE COLLECTED POEMS OF LANGSTON HUGHES, edited by Arnold Rampersad. Copyright © 1994 by The Estate of Langston Hughes. Used by permission of Alfred A. Knopf, a division of Random House, Inc. **1081–1082:** Langston Hughes, "Ballad of the Landlord" from THE COLLECTED POEMS OF LANGSTON HUGHES, edited by Arnold Rampersad. Copyright © 1994 by The Estate of Langston Hughes. Used by permission of Alfred A. Knopf, a division of Random House, Inc. **1082–1083:** Langston Hughes, "Theme for English B" from THE COLLECTED POEMS OF LANGSTON HUGHES, edited by Arnold Rampersad. Copyright © 1994 by The Estate of Langston Hughes. Used by permission of Alfred A. Knopf, a division of Random House, Inc. **1083–1084:** Langston Hughes, "Dream Boogie" from THE COLLECTED POEMS OF LANGSTON HUGHES, edited by Arnold Rampersad. Copyright © 1994 by The Estate of Langston Hughes. Used by permission of Alfred A. Knopf, a division of Random House, Inc. **1084–1086:** Langston Hughes, "Birmingham Sunday (September 15, 1963)" from THE COLLECTED POEMS OF LANGSTON HUGHES, edited by Arnold Rampersad. Copyright © 1994 by The Estate of Langston Hughes. Used by permission of Alfred A. Knopf, a division of Random House, Inc. **1086:** Langston Hughes, "Old Walt" from THE COLLECTED POEMS OF LANGSTON HUGHES, edited by Arnold Rampersad. Copyright © 1994 by The Estate of Langston Hughes. Used by permission of Alfred A. Knopf, a division of Random House, Inc. **1086:** Langston Hughes, "Genius Child" from THE COLLECTED POEMS OF LANGSTON HUGHES, edited by Arnold Rampersad. Copyright © 1994 by The Estate of Langston Hughes. Used by permission of Alfred A. Knopf, a division of Random House, Inc. **1087:** Langston Hughes, "Lenox Avenue: Midnight" from THE COLLECTED POEMS OF LANGSTON HUGHES, edited by Arnold Rampersad. Copyright © 1994 by The Estate of Langston Hughes. Used by permission of Alfred A. Knopf, a division of Random House, Inc. **1087–1088:** Langston Hughes, "Un-American Investigators" from THE COLLECTED POEMS OF LANGSTON HUGHES, edited by Arnold Rampersad. Copyright © 1994 by The Estate of Langston Hughes. Used by permission of Alfred A. Knopf, a division of Random House, Inc. **1088–1089:** Langston Hughes, "Dinner Guest: Me" from THE COLLECTED POEMS OF LANGSTON HUGHES, edited by Arnold Rampersad. Copyright © 1994 by The Estate of Langston Hughes. Used by permission of Alfred A. Knopf, a division of Random House, Inc. **1089–1091:** Langston Hughes, "Ballad of Booker T." from THE COLLECTED POEMS OF LANGSTON HUGHES, edited by Arnold Rampersad. Copyright © 1994 by The Estate of Langston Hughes. Used by permission of Alfred A. Knopf, a division of Random House, Inc. **1092–1094:** Langston Hughes, excerpt from "The Negro Artist and the Racial Mountain." Copyright 1926, 1935, 1947 by Langston Hughes. Reprinted by permission of Harold Ober Associates Incorporated. **1094–1096:** Langston Hughes, "To Negro Writers." Copyright 1926, 1935, 1947 by Langston Hughes. Reprinted by permission of Harold Ober Associates Incorporated. **1096–1099:** Langston Hughes, excerpt from "My Adventures as a Social Poet." Copyright 1926, 1935, 1947 by Langston Hughes. Reprinted by permission of Harold Ober Associates Incorporated. **1104–1105:** Herman Beavers, excerpt from "Dead Rocks and Sleeping Men: Aurality in the Aesthetic of Langston Hughes" from LANGSTON HUGHES REVIEW 11.1 (Spring 1992). Reprinted with the permission of the Langston Hughes Society. **1109–1110:** George B. Hutchinson, excerpt from Langston Hughes and the "Other' Whitman" from THE CONTINUING PRESENCE OF WALT WHITMAN: THE LIFE AFTER THE LIFE, edited by Robert K. Martin. Copyright © 1992. Reprinted with the permission of University of Iowa Press. **1110:** Langston Hughes, excerpt from "To You" from THE COLLECTED POEMS OF LANGSTON HUGHES, edited by Arnold Rampersad. Copyright © 1994 by The Estate of Langston Hughes. Used by permission of Alfred A. Knopf, a division of Random House, Inc.

Chapter 33. 1117: Kim Addonizio, "Verities" from POETRY (September 2005). Copyright © 2005 by Kim Addonizio. Reprinted with the permission of the author. **1119–1120:** Julia Alvarez, "Papi Working" from THE OTHER SIDE: EL OTRO LADO. Copyright © 1996 by Julia Alvarez. Published by Plume/Penguin, a division of Penguin Group (USA). Reprinted by permission of Susan Bergholz Literary Agency, New York, NY and Lamy, NM. All rights reserved. **1120:** Maya Angelou, "Africa" from OH PRAY MY WINGS ARE GONNA FIT ME WELL. Copyright © 1975 by Maya Angelou. Used by permission of Random House, Inc. **1124:** John Ashbery, "You Would Have Thought" from CAN YOU HEAR, BIRD? Copyright © 1995 by John Ashbery. Reprinted with the permission of Georges Borchardt, Inc. for the author. **1125–1126:** Elizabeth Bishop, "The Fish" from THE COMPLETE POEMS 1927–1979. Copyright © 1979, 1983 by Alice Helen Methfessel. Reprinted by permission of Farrar, Straus & Giroux, LLC. **1126–1127:** Elizabeth Bishop, "One Art" from THE COMPLETE POEMS 1927–1979. Copyright © 1979, 1983 by Alice Helen Methfessel. Reprinted by permission of Farrar, Straus & Giroux, LLC. **1129–1130:** Eavan Boland, "The Emigrant Irish" from OUTSIDE HISTORY: SELECTED POEMS 1980–1990. Copyright © 1987 by Eavan Boland. Used by permission of W. W. Norton & Company, Inc. **1131–1133:** Gwendolyn Brooks, "The *Chicago Defender* Send a Man to Little Rock," "First Fight, Then Fiddle," "Medgar Evers," "Sadie and Maud," and "We Real Cool" from BLACKS. Copyright © 1991 by Gwendolyn Brooks Blakely. Reprinted by consent of Brooks Permissions. **1136:** Lucille Clifton, "praise song" from BLESSING THE BOATS: NEW AND SELECTED POEMS 1988–2000. Copyright © 2000 by Lucille Clifton. Reprinted with the permission of BOA Editions Ltd. **1136–1137:** Judith Ortiz Cofer, "Claims" from REACHING FOR THE MAINLAND & SELECTED NEW POEMS. Reprinted with the permission of Bilingual Press/Editorial Bilingüe, Arizona State University, Tempe, AZ. **1138–1139:** Billy Collins, "Introduction to Poetry" from THE APPLE THAT ASTONISHED PARIS. Copyright © 1988 by Billy Collins. Reprinted with the permission of the University of Arkansas Press. **1140:** E. E. Cummings, "Buffalo Bill's" from COMPLETE POEMS 1904–1962, edited by George J. Firmage. Copyright 1923, 1951, © 1991 by the Trustees for the E. E. Cummings Trust. Used by permission of Liveright Publishing Corporation. **1141:** E. E. Cummings, "next to of course god america i" from COMPLETE POEMS 1904–1962, edited by George J. Firmage. Copyright 1926, 1954, © 1991 by the Trustees for the E. E. Cummings Trust. Used by permission of Liveright Publishing Corporation. **1141:** Emily Dickinson, "After great pain, a formal feeling comes—" from THE COMPLETE POEMS OF EMILY DICKINSON, edited by Thomas H. Johnson. Copyright 1951, © 1955, 1979, 1983 by the President and Fellows of Harvard College. Reprinted by permission of the publishers and the Trustees of Amherst College. **1141–1142:** Emily Dickinson, "Because I Could not stop for Death—" from THE COMPLETE POEMS OF EMILY DICKINSON, edited by Thomas H. Johnson. Copyright 1951, © 1955, 1979, 1983 by the President and Fellows of Harvard College. Reprinted by permission of the publishers and the Trustees of Amherst College. **1142–1143:** Emily Dickinson, "'Heaven'—is what I cannot reach!" from THE COMPLETE POEMS OF EMILY DICKINSON, edited by Thomas H. Johnson. Copyright 1951, © 1955, 1979, 1983 by the President and Fellows of Harvard College. Reprinted by permission of the publishers and the Trustees of Amherst College. **1143:** Emily Dickinson, "I dwell in Possibility" from THE COMPLETE POEMS OF EMILY DICKINSON, edited by Thomas H. Johnson. Copyright 1951, © 1955, 1979, 1983 by the President and Fellows of Harvard College. Reprinted by permission of the publishers and the Trustees of Amherst College. **1143–1144:** Emily Dickinson, "I heard a Fly buzz—when I died—" from THE COMPLETE POEMS OF EMILY DICKINSON, edited by Thomas H. Johnson. Copyright 1951, © 1955, 1979, 1983 by the President and Fellows of Harvard College. Reprinted by permission of the publishers and the Trustees of Amherst College. **1144:** Emily Dickinson, "I never saw a Moor—" from THE COMPLETE POEMS OF EMILY DICKINSON, edited by Thomas H. Johnson. Copyright 1951, © 1955, 1979, 1983 by the President and Fellows of Harvard College. Reprinted by permission of the publishers and the Trustees of Amherst College. **1144:** Emily Dickinson, "I taste a liquor never brewed—" from THE COMPLETE POEMS OF EMILY DICKINSON, edited by Thomas H. Johnson. Copyright 1951, © 1955, 1979, 1983 by the President and Fellows of Harvard College. Reprinted by permission of the publishers and the Trustees of Amherst College. **1145:** Emily Dickinson, "Much Madness is divinest Sense—" from THE COMPLETE POEMS OF EMILY DICKINSON, edited by Thomas H.

Johnson. Copyright 1951, © 1955, 1979, 1983 by the President and Fellows of Harvard College. Reprinted by permission of the publishers and the Trustees of Amherst College. **1145:** Emily Dickinson, "Some keep the Sabbath going to Church—" from THE COMPLETE POEMS OF EMILY DICKINSON, edited by Thomas H. Johnson. Copyright 1951, © 1955, 1979, 1983 by the President and Fellows of Harvard College. Reprinted by permission of the publishers and the Trustees of Amherst College. **1145–1146:** Emily Dickinson, "The Soul selects her own Society" from THE COMPLETE POEMS OF EMILY DICKINSON, edited by Thomas H. Johnson. Copyright 1951, © 1955, 1979, 1983 by the President and Fellows of Harvard College. Reprinted by permission of the publishers and the Trustees of Amherst College. **1146:** Emily Dickinson, "Success is counted sweetest" from THE COMPLETE POEMS OF EMILY DICKINSON, edited by Thomas H. Johnson. Copyright 1951, © 1955, 1979, 1983 by the President and Fellows of Harvard College. Reprinted by permission of the publishers and the Trustees of Amherst College. **1146:** Emily Dickinson, "Tell all the Truth but tell it slant" from THE COMPLETE POEMS OF EMILY DICKINSON, edited by Thomas H. Johnson. Copyright 1951, © 1955, 1979, 1983 by the President and Fellows of Harvard College. Reprinted by permission of the publishers and the Trustees of Amherst College. **1146–1147:** Emily Dickinson, "There is no Frigate like a Book" from THE COMPLETE POEMS OF EMILY DICKINSON, edited by Thomas H. Johnson. Copyright 1951, © 1955, 1979, 1983 by the President and Fellows of Harvard College. Reprinted by permission of the publishers and the Trustees of Amherst College. **1147:** Emily Dickinson, "There's a certain Slant of light" from THE COMPLETE POEMS OF EMILY DICKINSON, edited by Thomas H. Johnson. Copyright 1951, © 1955, 1979, 1983 by the President and Fellows of Harvard College. Reprinted by permission of the publishers and the Trustees of Amherst College. **1147:** Emily Dickinson, "This is my letter to the World" from THE COMPLETE POEMS OF EMILY DICKINSON, edited by Thomas H. Johnson. Copyright 1951, © 1955, 1979, 1983 by the President and Fellows of Harvard College. Reprinted by permission of the publishers and the Trustees of Amherst College. **1151–1155:** T. S. Eliot, "The Love Song of J. Alfred Prufrock" from THE COLLECTED POEMS, 1909–1932. Reprinted by permission of Faber and Faber, Ltd. **1155:** Louise Erdrich, "Indian Boarding School: The Runaways." Copyright © 1984 by Louise Erdrich. Reprinted with the permission of The Wylie Agency, Inc. **1156:** Robert Frost, "Acquainted with the Night" from THE POETRY OF ROBERT FROST, edited by Edward Connery Lathem. Copyright 1928, © 1969 by Henry Holt and Company, copyright © 1956 by Robert Frost. Reprinted by permission of Henry Holt and Company LLC. **1157:** Robert Frost, "Desert Places" from The Poetry of Robert Frost, edited by Edward Connery Lathem. Copyright © 1969 by Henry Holt and Company, copyright 1936 by Robert Frost. Copyright © 1964 by Lesley Frost Ballantine. Reprinted by permission of Henry Holt and Company LLC. **1157:** Robert Frost, "Design" from The Poetry of Robert Frost, edited by Edward Connery Lathem. Copyright © 1969 by Henry Holt and Company, copyright 1936 by Robert Frost. Copyright © 1964 by Lesley Frost Ballantine. Reprinted by permission of Henry Holt and Company LLC. **1158–1159:** Robert Frost, "Mending Wall" from THE POETRY OF ROBERT FROST, edited by Edward Connery Lathem. Copyright 1923, © 1969 by Henry Holt and Company, copyright 1944, 1951 by Robert Frost. Reprinted by permission of Henry Holt and Company LLC. **1159:** Robert Frost, "The Road Not Taken" from THE POETRY OF ROBERT FROST, edited by Edward Connery Lathem. Copyright 1923, © 1969 by Henry Holt and Company, copyright 1944, 1951 by Robert Frost. Reprinted by permission of Henry Holt and Company LLC. **1159–1160:** Robert Frost, "Stopping by Woods on a Snowy Evening" from THE POETRY OF ROBERT FROST, edited by Edward Connery Lathem. Copyright 1923, © 1969 by Henry Holt and Company, copyright 1944, 1951 by Robert Frost. Reprinted by permission of Henry Holt and Company LLC. **1160–1161:** Federico Garcia Lorca, "Arbolé, Arbolé" © Herederos de Federico Garcia Lorca, from Obras Completas (Galaxia/Gutenberg, 1996 edition). Translation copyright © Stephen Spender and J. L. Gili and Herederos de Federico Garcia Lorca. All rights reserved. For information regarding rights and permissions, please contact William Peter Kosmas, 8 Franklin Square, London W14 9UU or lorca@artslaw.co.uk. **1161–1162:** Nikki Giovanni, "Nikki-Rosa" from BLACK FEELING, BLACK TALK, BLACK JUDGMENT. Compilation copyright © 1968, 1970 by Nikki Giovanni. Reprinted by permission of HarperCollins Publishers. **1162–1163:** Thom Gunn, "The Man with Night Sweats" from THE MAN WITH NIGHT SWEATS: POEMS. Copyright © 1992 by Thom Gunn. Reprinted by permission of Farrar, Straus & Giroux, LLC. **1164–1165:** Seamus Heaney, "Mid-Term Break" from OPENED GROUND: SELECTED POEMS 1966–1996. Copyright © 1998 by Seamus Heaney. Reprinted by permission of Farrar, Straus & Giroux, LLC. **1165–1166:** Garret Kaoru Hongo, "And Your Soul Shall Dance" from YELLOW LIGHT. Copyright © 1982 by Garret Kaoru Hongo. Reprinted by permission of Wesleyan University Press. **1166–1167:** Ted Hughes, "Where I Sit Writing My Letter" from FLOWERS AND INSECTS: SOME INSECTS AND A PAIR OF SPIDERS. Copyright © 1986 by Ted Hughes. Used by permission of Alfred A. Knopf, a division of Random House, Inc. and Faber and Faber, Ltd. **1167:** Donald Justice, "Men at Forty" from COLLECTED POEMS. Copyright © 1967 by Donald Justice. Used by permission of Alfred A. Knopf, Inc. **1167–1168:** Mary Karr, "A Blessing from My Sixteen Years' Son" from SINNERS WELCOME: POEMS. Copyright © 2006 by Mary Karr. Reprinted by permission of HarperCollins Publishers. **1173:** Ted Kooser, "Selecting a Reader" from SURE SIGNS: NEW AND SELECTED POEMS. Copyright © 1980 by Ted Kooser. Reprinted with the permission of the University of Pittsburgh Press. **1173–1174:** Philip Larkin, "The Explosion" from HIGH WINDOWS. Copyright © 1974 by Philip Larkin. Reprinted by permission of Farrar, Straus & Giroux, LLC and Faber & Faber, Ltd. **1174–1175:** Li-Young Lee, "The Gift" from ROSE. Copyright ©1986 by Li-Young Lee. Reprinted with the permission of BOA Editions Ltd., www.boaeditions.org. **1175:** Li-Young Lee, "Little Father" from BOOK OF MY NIGHTS. Copyright © 2001 by Li-Young Lee. Reprinted with the permission of BOA Editions, Ltd., www.boaeditions.org. **1176:** Doris Lessing, "Learning Geography, 1945" and "And in 2005" from THE SPECTATOR (March 12, 2005): 55. Copyright © 2005. **1176–1177:** Philip Levine, "The Old Testament" from THE SIMPLE TRUTH: POEMS. Copyright © 1994 by Philip Levine. Used by permission of Alfred A. Knopf, a division of Random House, Inc. **1177–1178:** Thomas Lux, "Eyes Scooped Out and Replaced by Hot Coals" from GOD PARTICLES. Copyright © 2008 by Thomas Lux. Reprinted with the permission of Houghton Mifflin Harcourt Publishing Company. All rights reserved. **1178–1179:** Archibald MacLeish, "Ars Poetica" from COLLECTED POEMS 1917–1982. Copyright © 1985 by The Estate of Archibald MacLeish. Reprinted by permission of Houghton Mifflin Harcourt Publishing Company. All rights reserved. **1180:** James Merrill, "Page from the Koran" from COLLECTED POEMS, edited by J. D. McClatchy and Stephen Yenser. Copyright © 2001 by the Literary Estate of James Merrill at Washington University. Used by permission of Alfred A. Knopf, a division of Random House, Inc. **1180–1181:** W. S. Merwin, "Blueberries after Dark" from THE SHADOW OF SIRIUS. Copyright © 2008 by W. S. Merwin. Reprinted with the permission of Copper Canyon Press, www.coppercanyonpress.org. **1182–1183:** Thylias Moss, "Interpretation of a Poem by Frost" from RAINBOW REMNANTS IN ROCK BOTTOM GHETTO SKY. Copyright © 1991 by Thylias Moss. Reprinted with the permission of Persea Books, Inc., (New York). **1183–1184:** Pablo Neruda, "The United Fruit Co." from NERUDA AND VALLEJO: SELECTED POEMS, translated by Robert Bly. Copyright © 1971 by Robert Bly. Reprinted with the permission of the translator. **1184–1185:** Frank O'Hara, "Ave Maria" from LUNCH POEMS. Copyright © 1964 by Frank O'Hara. Reprinted by permission of City Lights Books. **1185–1186:** Sharon Olds, "The One Girl at the Boys' Party" from THE DEAD AND THE LIVING. Copyright © 1983 by Sharon Olds. Used by permission of Alfred A. Knopf, a division of Random House, Inc. **1186:** Linda Pastan, "Ethics" from WAITING FOR MY LIFE. Copyright © 1981 by Linda Pastan. Used by permission of W. W. Norton & Company, Inc. **1187:** Linda Pastan, "Marks" from THE FIVE STAGES OF GRIEF. Copyright © 1978 by Linda Pastan. Used by permission of W. W. Norton & Company, Inc. **1187:** Marge Piercy, "Barbie doll" from CIRCLES ON THE WATER. Copyright © 1982 by Marge Piercy. Used by permission of Alfred A. Knopf, a division of Random House, Inc. **1189:** Sylvia Plath, "Mirror" from CROSSING THE WATER. Copyright © 1960, 1963 by Ted Hughes. Reprinted by permission of HarperCollins Publishers and Faber and Faber, Ltd. **1190–1191:** Henry Reed, "Naming of Parts" from HENRY REED: COLLECTED POEMS, edited by Jon Stallworthy. Copyright © 1991. Reprinted with the permission of Oxford University Press, Ltd. **1193:** Sonia Sanchez, "right on: white america" from WE A BADDDDD PEOPLE. Reprinted with the permission of Broadside Press. **1197:** Louis Simpson, "American Poetry" from THE OWNER OF THE HOUSE: NEW COLLECTED POEMS. Copyright © 2003 by Louis Simpson. Reprinted with the permission of BOA Editions, Ltd., www.boaeditions.org. **1197–1198:** Stevie Smith, "Not Waving but Drowning" from THE COLLECTED POEMS OF STEVIE SMITH. Copyright © 1972 by Stevie Smith. Reprinted by permission of New Directions Publishing Corp. **1198–1199:** Cathy Song, "Lost Sister" from PICTURE BRIDE. Copyright © 1983 by Cathy Song. Reprinted with the permission of Yale University Press. **1200:** Gary Soto, "Saturday at the Canal" from A FIRE IN MY HANDS, REVISED AND EXPANDED EDITION. Copyright © 1990 by Gary Soto. Reprinted by permission of Houghton Mifflin Harcourt Publishing Company. **1200:** Wole Soyinka, "Hamlet" from A SHUTTLE IN THE CRYPT. Copyright © 1972 by Wole Soyinka. Reprinted by permission of Hill & Wang, a division of Farrar, Straus & Giroux, LLC. **1202:** Wallace Stevens, "The House Was Quiet and the World Was Calm" from THE COLLECTED POEMS OF WALLACE STEVENS. Copyright 1954 by Wallace Stevens and renewed © 1982 by Holly Stevens. Used by permission of Alfred A. Knopf, a division of Random House, Inc. **1202–1203:** Adrienne Su, "The English Canon" from SANCTUARY. Originally from NEW LETTERS 65, no 3 (1999). Reprinted with the permission of the author, New Letters and the Curators of the University of Missouri-Kansas City, and Manic D Press, San Francisco. **1205–1206:** Dylan Thomas, "Fern Hill" from THE POEMS OF DYLAN THOMAS. Copyright 1952 by Dylan Thomas. Reprinted by permission of New Directions Publishing Corp. **1206:** Mona Van Duyn, "Earth Tremors Felt in Missouri" from SELECTED POEMS. Copyright © 2002 by Mona Van Duyn. Used by permission of Alfred A. Knopf, a division of Random House, Inc. **1209:** Richard Wilbur, "The Ride" from NEW AND COLLECTED POEMS. Copyright © 1988 by Richard Wilbur. Reprinted by permission of Houghton Mifflin Harcourt Publishing Company. **1212:** Charles Wright, "October" from THE WORLD OF TEN THOUSAND THINGS: POEMS 1980–1990. Copyright © 1990 by Charles Wright. Reprinted by permission of Farrar Straus & Giroux, LLC. **1213:** William Butler Yeats, "Crazy Jane Talks with the Bishop" from THE COLLECTED WORKS OF W.B. YEATS, VOLUME I: THE POEMS, REVISED, edited by Richard J. Finneran. Copyright 1933 by The Macmillan Company, renewed © 1961 by Bertha Georgie Yeats. Reprinted with the permission of Scribner, an imprint of Simon & Schuster Adult Publishing Group. All rights reserved. **1214:** William Butler Yeats, "Sailing to Byzantium" from

THE COLLECTED WORKS OF W.B. YEATS, VOLUME I: THE POEMS, REVISED, edited by Richard J. Finneran. Copyright 1928 by The Macmillan Company, renewed © 1956 by Georgie Yeats. Reprinted with the permission of Scribner, an imprint of Simon & Schuster Adult Publishing Group. All rights reserved. **1215–1216:** Adam Zagajewski, "Poetry Searches for Radiance" from THE NEW YORKER (December 23 and 30, 2002). Copyright © 2002 by Adam Zagajewski. Reprinted with the permission of the author.

Chapter 35. 1250–1261: Anton Chekhov, "The Brute" from THE BRUTE AND OTHER FARCES, edited by Eric Bentley. Copyright © 1958. Reprinted with the permission of Applause Theatre Books.

Chapter 36. 1265–1266: Wendy Wasserstein, "Workout" from SEVEN ONE-ACT PLAYS. Copyright © 1995 by Wendy Wasserstein. Reprinted with the permission of Dramatists Play Service Inc. **1266–1269:** Joyce Carol Oates, "When I Was a Little Girl and My Mother Didn't Want Me" from ONTARIO REVIEW (1997). Copyright © 1997 by Ontario Review. Reprinted by permission of John Hawkins Associates, Inc.

Chapter 38. 1314–1317: Warren Leight, "Nine Ten" from TAKE TEN II: MORE TEN MINUTE PLAYS. Copyright © 2003 by Warren Leight. Reprinted with the permission of the William Morris Agency for the Author. **1331–1400:** Lorraine Hansberry, "A Raisin in the Sun." Copyright © 1958 by Robert Nemiroff, as an unpublished work. Copyright © 1959, 1966, 1984 by Robert Nemiroff. Used by permission of Random House, Inc. **1402–1454:** Henrik Ibsen, "A Doll House" from THE COMPLETE MAJOR PROSE PLAYS OF HENRIK IBSEN, translated by Rolf Fjelde. Copyright © 1965, 1970, 1978 by Rolf Fjelde. Used by permission of Dutton Signet, a division of Penguin Group (USA) Inc.

Chapter 39. 1470–1474: August Strindberg, "The Stronger," translated by Elizabeth Sprigge. Copyright © 1955 by Elizabeth Sprigge. Reprinted with the permission of Curtis Brown Ltd. **1531–1602:** Arthur Miller, "Death of a Salesman." Copyright 1949, renewed © 1977 by Arthur Miller. Used by permission of Viking Penguin, a division of Penguin Group (USA) Inc. **1605–1714:** William Shakespeare, "Hamlet" from THE RIVERSIDE SHAKESPEARE, SECOND EDITION, edited by G. Blakemore Evans. Copyright © 1997 Heinle/Arts & Sciences, a part of Cengage Learning, Inc. Reprinted by permission, www.cengage.com/permissions.

Chapter 40. 1725–1730: David Ives, "Words, Words, Words" from ALL IN THE TIMING: SIX ONE-ACT COMEDIES. Copyright © 1994 by David Ives. Reprinted with the permission of the author. **1732–1743:** Milcha Sanchez-Scott, "The Cuban Swimmer." Copyright © 1984, 1988 by Milcha Sanchez-Scott. Reprinted by permission of William Morris Agency, Inc. on behalf of the Author. CAUTION: Professionals and amateurs are hereby warned that Long Day's Journey Into Night is subject to a royalty. It is fully protected under the copyright laws of the United States of America and all countries covered by the International Copyright Union (including the Dominion of Canada and the rest of the British Commonwealth), the Bern Convention, the Pan-American Copyright Convention, and the Universal Copyright Convention as well as all countries with which the United States has reciprocal copyright relations. All rights, including professional/amateur stage rights, motion picture, recitation, lecturing, public reading, radio broadcasting, television, video or sound recording, all other forms of mechanical or electronic reproduction, such as CD-ROM, CD-I, information storage and retrieval systems and photocopying, and the rights of translation into foreign languages, are strictly reserved. Particular emphasis is laid upon the matter of readings, permission for which must be secured from the Author's Agent in writing. Inquiries concerning rights should be addressed to William Morris Agency, Inc., 1325 Avenue of the Americas, New York, NY 10019, attn. Eric Lupfer. **1745–1785:** Sophocles, "Oedipus the King," translated by Thomas Gould, from Oedipus the King: A Translation with Commentary. Copyright © 1970. Reprinted by permission of Pearson Education, Upper Saddle River, NJ. **1787–1847:** William Shakespeare, "A Midsummer Night's Dream" from THE RIVERSIDE SHAKESPEARE, SECOND EDITION, edited by G. Blakemore Evans. Copyright © 1997 Heinle/Arts & Sciences, a part of Cengage Learning, Inc. Reprinted by permission, www.cengage.com/permissions.

Chapter 41. 1863–1892: Dudley Fitts and Robert Fitzgerald, "Antigone" from SOPHOCLES, THE OEDIPUS CYCLE: AN ENGLISH VERSION. Copyright 1939 by Harcourt Brace & Company and renewed 1967 by Dudley Fitts and Robert Fitzgerald. Reprinted by permission of the publisher. CAUTION: All rights, including professional, amateur, motion picture, recitation, lecturing, public reading, radio broadcasting, and television are strictly reserved. Inquiries on all rights should be addressed to Houghton Mifflin Harcourt Publishing Company, Permission Department, Orlando, FL 32887–8777. **1894–1900:** Samuel Beckett, "Krapp's Last Tape" from KRAPP'S LAST TAPE AND OTHER DRAMATIC PIECES. Copyright © 1960, 1984 by Samuel Beckett. Used by permission of Grove/Atlantic, Inc. **1902–1954:** August Wilson, "Fences." Copyright © 1986 by August Wilson. Used by permission of Dutton Signet, a division of Penguin Group (USA) Inc.

Chapter 42. 1961–2009: Tennessee Williams, THE GLASS MENAGERIE. Copyright 1945 by The University of the South, renewed © 1973 by Tennessee Williams. Reprinted by permission of Georges Borchardt, Inc. on behalf of the Tennessee Williams Estate. **2010–2012:** Tennessee Williams, author's Production Notes for The Glass Menagerie. Copyright 1945 by The University of the South, renewed © 1973 by Tennessee Williams. Reprinted by permission of Georges Borchardt, Inc. on behalf of the Tennessee Williams Estate. **2013–2016:** Tennessee

Williams, excerpt from TENNESSEE WILLIAMS: MEMOIRS. Copyright © 1975, renewed 2003 by The University of the South. Reprinted with the permission of Georges Borchardt, Inc., on behalf of the Tennessee Williams Estate. **2016–2017:** Jean Evans, interview with Tennessee Williams from NEW YORK PM (1945). No portion of this text may be reprinted without permission of the publisher. **2017–2020:** Thomas L. King, excerpt from "Irony and Distance in The Glass Menagerie" from THEATRE JOURNAL 25.2 (1973): 85–94. Copyright © by The Johns Hopkins University Press. Reprinted with the permission of The Johns Hopkins University Press. **2020–2022:** Nancy Marie Patterson Tischler, excerpt from STUDENT COMPANION TO TENNESSEE WILLIAMS. Copyright © 2000. Reprinted with the permission of Greenwood Publishing Group, Inc., Westport, CT. **2024–2026:** Tom Scanlan, excerpt from "Family, Drama, and American Dreams" from REACTIONS II: TENNESSEE WILLIAMS. Copyright © 1978. Reprinted with the permission of Greenwood Publishing Group, Inc., Westport, CT. **2027–2030:** James Fisher, excerpt from "'The Angels of Fructification': Tennessee Williams, Tony Kushner, and Images of Homosexuality on the American Stage" from THE MISSISSIPPI QUARTERLY 49.1 (Winter 1995): 13–20. Reprinted with permission. **2031–2038:** Tennessee Williams, "Portrait of a Girl in Glass" from THE COLLECTED STORIES OF TENNESSEE WILLIAMS. Copyright 1948 by The University of the South, renewed © 1976 by The University of the South. Reprinted by permission of New Directions Publishing Corp.

Poetry Sampler Insert: PS2: Rita Dove, "Sonnet in Primary Colors" from MOTHER LOVE. Copyright © 1995 by Rita Dove. Used by permission of W. Norton & Company, Inc. **PS3:** Allen Ginsberg, "Cézanne's Ports" from COLLECTED POEMS 1947–1980. Copyright © 1984 by Allen Ginsberg. Reprinted by permission of HarperCollins Publishers. **PS4:** Robert Hayden, "Monet's 'Waterlilies'" from ANGLE OF ASCENT: NEW AND SELECTED POEMS. Copyright © 1975, 1972, 1970, 1966 by Robert Hayden. Used by permission of Liveright Publishing Corporation. **PS5:** Cathy Song, "Girl Powdering Her Neck" from PICTURE BRIDE. Copyright © 1983 by Cathy Song. Reprinted with the permission of Yale University Press. **PS7:** Kevin Young, "The Fun Gallery" from TO REPEL GHOSTS: FIVE SIDES IN B MINOR. Copyright © 2001 by Kevin Young. Reprinted with the permission of Zoland Books, a division of Steerforth Press.

INDEX OF FIRST LINES OF POETRY

INDEX OF AUTHORS AND TITLES

INDEX OF LITERARY TERMS